Contents

Masterpieces of the Enlightenment

part 1 — 308–314

Masterpieces of the Nineteenth Century:
Varieties of Romanticism

MAP: EUROPE, AND EASTERN AMERICA, CA. 1866

Masterpieces of the Nineteenth Century: Realism, Naturalism, Symbolism

MAP: EUROPE, CA. 1870

Masterpieces of the Twentieth Century: Varieties of Modernism

Masterpieces of the Twentieth Century: Contemporary Explorations

MAP: THE WORLD TODAY

Preface to the
Seventh Edition

The Seventh Edition of *The Norton Anthology of World Masterpieces* marks an exciting stage in the development of an anthology whose first appearance, in 1956, brought a fresh approach to the teaching of literature in North American colleges and universities. The readers of that First Edition were encouraged to focus on the literary work as a whole, not small samples; on the broad sweep of the Western tradition, not separate nations; on works treasured by generations of readers—in some cases, over thousands of years; and on the thought-provoking recurrence of themes, artistic forms, and diverse images of human identity. You will find the same indispensable features in this edition, as well as important changes that reflect the evolution both of the anthology and of educational expectations. This Seventh Edition is dedicated anew to exploring the Western tradition—a vital tapestry woven from Homer and Sappho, from Joyce and Akhmatova, from Ovid and Ariosto, from Beckett and Achebe. Throughout these volumes, you will encounter not only the canon of the First Edition (which remains part of the Seventh) but also new writers, women and men, from a variety of countries and cultural backgrounds, writing in a number of languages. You will also encounter more discussions of literature's cultural dimensions, improved translations, a detailed revision of all editorial apparatus, and new contextual aids such as maps, timelines, and pronouncing glossaries for unfamiliar words and names. Whether you are adding a few new selections to a tried and true list or striking out in new directions with different themes and combinations of works, you will find the Seventh Edition an eminently readable and teachable anthology.

Changes in this edition have taken several forms: introducing new authors and works for their intrinsic interest; adding small sections to existing larger pieces in order to fill out a theme or narrative line; choosing an alternate work by the same author when it speaks strongly to current concerns, or grouping several works to highlight features they share.

Most exciting, of course, are the many new selections and the opportunities they bring for different combinations among themselves and with the works you have already been teaching. Roman comedy is now represented by Plautus's *Pseudolus,* a perennial favorite whose farcical effects—the tricks and triumph of the wily servant, the bluster of the braggart soldier, the miserly father who stands in the way of his son's love affair—have been borrowed by generations of playwrights from Shakespeare and Molière to the authors of the twentieth-century Broadway hit *A Funny Thing Happened on the Way to the Forum*. With Lucian's *A True Story,* a marvelously comic narrative of its protagonist's impossible trials and tribulations, we introduce a vein of fantasy. This vein reappears, albeit more elegantly, with the epic parody of Ariosto's *Orlando Furioso*. Wild adventures involving numerous heroes and villains constitute this romantic poem, whose title character ("Orlando gone crazy"), driven mad by frustrated love for a Chinese princess, is a startling variant on the hero of *The Song of Roland*. Fantasy is also evident in *The Thousand and One Nights*, a chain-tale sequence as influential in Europe as in the Arab world for its magical creations and for the all-important character of Shahrazad, the eternal spinner of tales. On a harsher note, there are the medieval fabliaux and the famous adventures of Renard the Fox, whose trial at the court of King Lion and brutal revenge on his enemies is given here. Those of you who have enjoyed teaching the ever-popular *Sir Gawain and the Green Knight* will welcome two other tales from Arthurian legend, Sir Thomas Malory's *Morte Darthur*, which describes the tangled and ultimately fatal relationship of King Arthur, Queen Guinevere, and the noble knight Sir Lancelot, and Marie de France's *Lanval*, which gives an entirely different picture of Lancelot as he leaves Camelot for fairyland.

New to the Renaissance section is Lope de Vega's unusual play *Fuente Ovejuna*, a romantic comedy about consent, set during an actual peasant uprising of 1476 in a small village of Cordoba, Spain, that has disturbing political overtones. The play's happy ending arrives only after the entire village has withstood torture and refused to name the uprising's ringleaders. Also new to that section, Shakespeare's *Othello* explores both the psychological and social drama of the Moor's jealousy and downfall and the way that cultural stereotypes play a role in establishing character from within and from without. New among the nineteenth-century selections, Dorothy Wordsworth's *Grasmere Journals* express the very personal world of the intimate journal, as the keen observation of details gradually reveals both the observer's own personality and those of her companions (including, in this case, her brother, the poet William Wordsworth). Selections of Zuni ritual poetry begin the twentieth-century sections, which also contain a variety of short fiction by Russian, American, Canadian, and Polish writers: Chekhov's famous tale of uncertain love, *The Lady with the Dog*; Faulkner's *The Bear*, printed complete to convey the full scope of its look at the legacy of slavery in the South; Richard Wright's story of adolescent coming-of-age (or just the reverse), *The Man Who Was Almost a Man*; Tadeusz Borowski's terrifying Holocaust story, *Ladies and Gentlemen, to the Gas Chamber*; Flannery O'Connor's chilling tale of multiple murders, *A Good Man Is Hard to Find*; Alice Munro's complex evocation of childhood memories, *Walker Brothers Cowboy*; and Leslie Marmon Silko's retelling of a Native American tale, *Yellow Woman*. Also included are the central chapters of a fascinating combination of fiction, autobiography, and essay: Virginia Woolf's passionate analysis of the woman writer's position in *A Room of One's Own*.

Complete pieces inserted into existing groups include the poignant tales of Abraham and Isaac and of Jacob and Esau in the Old Testament selections (Genesis 22, 25, 27), as well as the glorious love poetry of the Song of Songs; and Matthew 13 (*Why Jesus Teaches in Parables*) in the New Testament. Ovid (in a newly included translation by Allen Mandelbaum) is now represented by eight tales—the most recent additions being Europa and Jove, Ceres and Proserpina, Iphis and Ianthe, Pygmalion, Myrrha and Cinyras,

Venus and Adonis—that together explore different images of love and gender. Catullus and Petrarch appear in more-substantial selections, with three additional poems (and a new translation) by the Roman poet and five additional poems by the Italian. Marie de France is represented by two of her best-known and most poignant *lais, Lanval* and *Laüstic*. Newly appearing stories from Boccaccio include the paradoxical account of the making of a saint *(The First Story of the First Day)* and the influential tale of patient Griselda and her tyrannical husband *(The Tenth Story of the Tenth Day)*; from Chaucer, the bawdy, popular *Wife of Bath's Prologue and Tale*. Many themes from these stories reappear, with special emphasis on the stereotyping of gender roles, in six stories of court and domestic intrigue (five of them new to this edition) from the *Heptameron* of Marguerite de Navarre. Adding to the fantastic twists of Rabelais's narrative *Gargantua and Pantagruel* are a rollicking debate conducted completely in body language and an impossible journey to another world flourishing inside Pantagruel's giant mouth. In the twentieth-century, Rilke's *Archaic Torso of Apollo* is complemented by three more poems of similar intensely physical description: *The Panther, The Swan,* and *Spanish Dancer.*

Among smaller narrative additions are the death of Patroclus in the *Iliad* (Book XVI); Augustine's departure from Carthage for Rome in the *Confessions* (Book V); Ganelon's trial at the end of *The Song of Roland* (especially interesting for its legal arguments and attempt to intimidate the jury); and, in *Paradise Lost,* the preliminary drama of Satan's malevolent entry into paradise, Adam and Eve's innocent conversation, and the angel's warning to Adam (Books 4 and 8).

Previous editions of this anthology have minimized the presence of lyric poetry in translation, recognizing—as so cogently argued in the Note on Translation printed at the end of each volume—that the precise language and music of an original poem will never be identical with its translation. Yet good translations often achieve a poetry of their own and occupy a pivotal position in their own language; read and appreciated for themselves, they simultaneously preserve and pass on important aspects of a major artistic imagination. Sappho, Catullus, Petrarch, Heine, and Baudelaire have had influence far beyond the range of those who could read the original poems. The images and emotions of European Romantic poetry and the abstract vision, liberated verse forms, and linguistic play of Symbolist poetry still echo in twentieth-century literature and will undoubtedly reverberate in that of the twenty-first.

New to this edition, therefore, is a series of poetry clusters representing the best and most influential work of a range of poets in four periods: medieval, Romantic, Symbolist, and Dada-Surrealist. The poems therein may be read for themselves (some have appeared separately in earlier editions) or as part of a significant spectrum of poetic expression. The medieval cluster includes familiar names from the Sixth Edition (Villon, Dante, and the Archpoet) and those less well known to the contemporary audience. Here, men and women from a variety of traditions—Arabic, Judaic, Welsh, Spanish, French, Provençal, Italian, English, German—demonstrate the multifarious vitality of medieval literature. To complement the considerable representation of English Romantic poetry we offer a cluster of continental poetry in translation: Victor Hugo, Giacomo Leopardi, and Heinrich Heine, included in earlier editions, are joined by the Spanish, Russian, French, and German writers Gustavo Adolfo Bécquer, Rosalía de Castro, Anna Petrovna Bunina, Alphonse de Lamartine, Friedrich Hölderlin, and Novalis (Friedrich von Hardenberg). Symbolist poets (or, more precisely, the great nineteenth-century poets Charles Baudelaire, Stéphane Mallarmé, Paul Verlaine, and Arthur Rimbaud, who inspired the Symbolist movement) are presented individually but may also be considered as a set of remarkable precursors of modern literature. Finally, a cluster of Dada-Surrealist poems that range from slashing, rebellious humor to ecstatic celebrations of love introduces the free association and dreamlike structures of this visionary movement with its strong links to modern art and film. Select as you will, whether within a group or by reaching out to writers in the larger anthology; we believe that you will find in each cluster a wealth of fascinating short texts and remarkable access into another period's emotional and intellectual horizons.

How to choose, as you turn from the virtual library before you to the inevitable constraint of available time? In the forty-one complete longer works printed here, and the scores of shorter works, substantial segments, and poems, you have an inexhaustible series of options to fit whatever course pattern you choose. Perhaps you have decided to proceed by theme or genre, in chronological order, or by comparative principle; you have only to select among a variety of works from different countries, languages, and cultural backgrounds. New entries in the Seventh Edition add to your options—and suggest further dimensions—in drama (Plautus's farce, Lope de Vega's romantic comedy), poetry (more individual poets as well as the new groupings), longer prose fiction (Lucian's comic novel, Ariosto's parody of chivalric romance), and shorter fiction from medieval to modern times (from *The Thousand and One Nights* to Flannery O'Connor's *A Good Man Is Hard to Find*). Many of the new inclusions—from any period—involve ethical, social, psychological, and political issues that are of contemporary concern, such as the impact of cultural stereotypes (*Othello* and *A Room of One's Own*) or of mass victimization (*Ladies and Gentlemen, to the Gas Chamber*). In each instance, the editors (who are all practicing teachers) have selected and prepared texts that are significant in their own areas of scholarly expertise, meaningful in the larger context of world literature, and able to delight, captivate, and challenge students.

From the beginning, the editors of *The Norton Anthology of World Masterpieces* have balanced the competing—and, we like to think, complementary—claims of teaching and scholarship, of the specialist's focused expertise and the generalist's broader perspectives. The founding editors set the example that guides their successors. In this edition, we welcome three new successor editors: William G. Thalmann (Ph.D., Yale), Professor of Classics at the University of Southern California; Lee Patterson (Ph.D., Yale), Professor of English at Yale University; and Heather James (Ph.D., University of California, Berkeley), Associate Professor of English at the University of Southern California. Three founding editors have recently assumed Emeritus status: Bernard M. W. Knox, eminent classical scholar and legendary teacher and lecturer; P. M. Pasinetti, who combines the intellectual breadth of the Renaissance scholar with a novelist's creative intuition; and, most notably, Maynard Mack, General Editor and presiding genius of all previous editions, a noted Enlightenment scholar whose wisdom, humanity, and gracefully worn knowledge have brought illumination to both editors and anthology. A fourth founding editor, Rene Wellek, died in 1995. A comparatist best known for his theoretical work and history of criticism, he was committed to the idea of teaching Western literary tradition in a truly international context, to the concept of literary masterpieces, and to the accessibility of these masterpieces for the enthusiastic and careful reader. It seems only appropriate, therefore, to dedicate this Seventh Edition to his memory.

Acknowledgments

Among our many critics, advisers, and friends, the following were of special help in providing suggestions and corrections: Joseph Barbarese (Rutgers University); Carol Clover (University of California, Berkeley); Patrick J. Cook (George Washington University); Janine Gerzanics (University of Southern California); Matthew Giancarlo (Yale University); Kevis Goodman (University of California at Berkeley); Roland Greene (University of Oregon); Dmitri Gutas (Yale University); John H. Hayes (Emory University); Suzanne Keen (Washington and Lee University); Charles S. Kraszewski (King's College); Gregory F. Kuntz; Michelle Latiolais (University of California at Irvine); Sharon L. James (Bryn Mawr College); Ivan Marcus (Yale University); Timothy Martin (Rutgers University, Camden); Fred C. Robinson (Yale University); John Rogers (Yale University); Robert Rothstein (University of Massachusetts); Lawrence Senelick (Boston University); Jack Shreve (Alleghany Community College); Frank Stringfellow (University of Miami); Nancy Vickers (Bryn Mawr College); and Jack Welch (Abilene Christian University).

We would also like to thank the following people who contributed to the planning of the Seventh Edition: Frank M. Acuna (Mount San Antonio Community College); Gene Antonio (DeKalb College); Julie Atkins (Marymount University); Robert Bagg (University of Massachusetts); Sandra C. Barnhill (South Plains College); Ronald Bogue (University of Georgia); Wendy Bashant (Coe College); Scott Boltwood (Emory and Henry College); John C. Bonnell (Macomb County Community College); Phyllis R. Brown (Santa Clara University); Ruth A. Cameron (Eastern Nazarene College); Mark Coleman (SUNY at Potsdam); Rosemary D. Cox (DeKalb College); Fara Darland (Scottsdale Community College); Catherine Callaway Dauterman (College of Notre Dame); William J. DeSaegher (Point Loma Nazarene University); John R. Dunlap (Santa Clara University); S. A. Eisenstein (Los Angeles City College); John H. Esperian (Community College of Southern Nevada); Anne M. Evans (Napa Valley College); Stephen D. Fox (Gallaudet University); Shearle Furnish (West Texas A & M University); C. Herbert Gilliland (United States Naval Academy); Tassie Gwilliam (University of Miami); Boyd Hagy (Marymount University); Mark Halperin (Central Washington University); Charles Heglan (University of South Florida); M. Susan Herdrich (Spokane Community College); Walter Hesford (University of Idaho); Alan Jacobs (Wheaton College); Alison Jasper (California Polytechnic State University); David L. Jeffrey (University of Ottawa); M. S. Johnston (Manhate State University); Martha Kallstrom (Georgia Southern University); Anne Kane-Lavin (Adirondack Community College); Jane M. Kinney (Valdosta State University); Alfred Kolb (Quinsigamond Community College); Alice S. Mandanis (Marymount University); Kay McClellan (South Plains College);

Victoria E. McClure (South Plains College); David McCracken (University of Washington); Patricia R. Menhart (Broward Community College); Robert I. Modica (Pima Community College); Michael W. Murphy (University of Wisconsin at Green Bay); Bradley Nystrom (California State University); Beryl Parker (John Abbot College); Sharon L. Romino (Fairmount State College); Merilyn L. Schiedat (Glendale Community College); Jonna G. Semeiks (Long Island University); Edward A. Shaw (University of Central Florida); Virginia L. Stein (Community College of Allegheny County); James Stokes (University of Wisconsin at Stevens Point); Gerard F. Strasser (Pennsylvania State University); Satya P. Tandon (Mohawk Valley Community College); Jon Thomson (United States Naval Academy); Burt Thorp (University of North Dakota); Robert Weathersby (Dalton College); David Whalen (Hillsdale College); Jack Williams (California State University); Katharine M. Wilson (University of Georgia); and L. Zancu (Millersville University).

Phonetic Equivalents

for use with the Pronouncing Glossaries preceding most
selections in this volume

a as in *cat*
ah as in *father*
ai as in *light*
ay as in *day*
aw as in *raw*
e as in *pet*
ee as in *street*
ehr as in *air*
er as in *bird*
eu as in *lurk*
g as in *good*
i as in *sit*
j as in *joke*
nh a nasal sound (as in French *vin, vẽ*)
o as in *pot*
oh as in *no*
oo as in *boot*
oy as in *toy*
or as in *bore*
ow as in *now*
s as in *mess*
ts as in *ants*
u as in *us*
zh as in *vision*

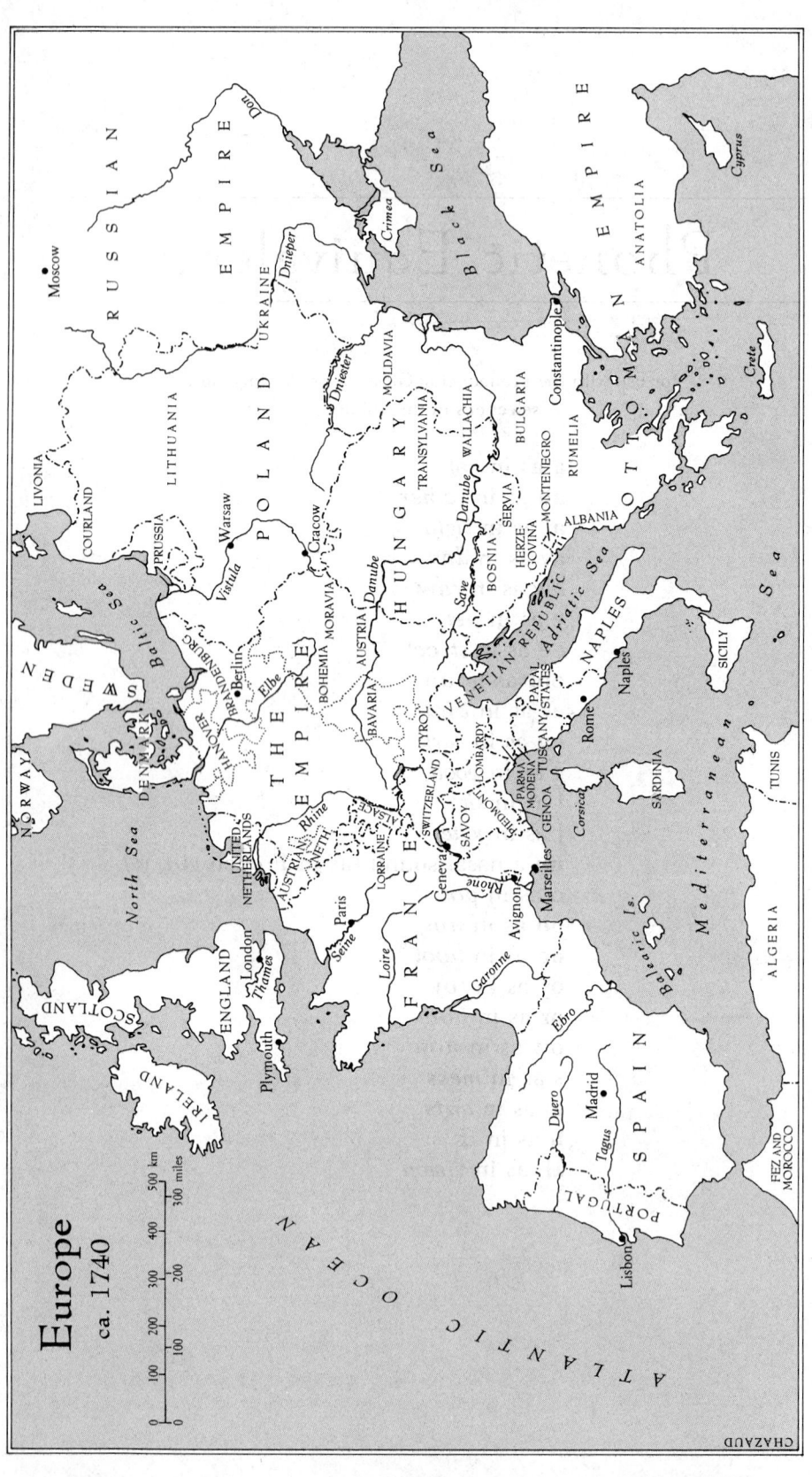

Europe
ca. 1740

CHAZAUD

Masterpieces of the Enlightenment

"I wonder if it is not better to try to correct and moderate men's passions than to try to suppress them altogether." The sentence, from Jean-Baptiste Molière's 1669 preface to his biting comedy about religious hypocrisy, *Tartuffe*, captures something of the anxiety and the optimism of a period for which subsequent generations have found no adequate single designation. "The Neo-Classic Period," "The Age of Reason," "The Enlightenment": such labels suggest, accurately enough, that thinkers between (roughly) 1660 and 1770 emphasized the powers of the mind and turned to the Roman past for models. But these terms do not convey the awareness of limitation expressed in Molière's sentence, an awareness as typical of the historical period to which the sentence belongs as is the expressed aspiration toward correctness and moderation. The effort to correct and moderate the passions might prove less foolhardy than the effort to suppress them, but both endeavors would involve human nature's struggle with itself, a struggle necessarily perpetual. "On life's vast ocean diversely we sail, / Reason the card, but Passion is the gale," Alexander Pope's *Essay on Man* (1733) pointed out. One could hope to steer with reason as guide only by remembering the omnipresence of passion as impetus. Eighteenth-century thinkers analyzed, and eighteenth-century imaginative writers dramatized, intricate interchanges and conflicts between these aspects of our selves.

The drama of reason and passion played itself out in society, the system of association human beings had devised partly to control passion and institutionalize reason. Structured on the basis of a rigid class system, the traditional social order began to face incipient challenges in the eighteenth century as new commerce generated new wealth, whose possessors felt entitled to claim their own share of social power. The threat to established hierarchies extended even to kings. Thomas Hobbes, in *Leviathan* (1651), had argued for the secular origins of the social contract. Kings arise, he said, not by divine ordinance but out of human need; they exist to prevent what would otherwise be a war of all on all. Monarchs still presided over European nations in the eighteenth century, but with less security than before. The English had executed their ruler in 1649; the French would perform another royal decapitation before the end of the eighteenth century. The mortality of kings had become a political fact, a fact implying the conceivable instability of the social order over which kings presided.

A sense of the contingencies of the human condition impinged on many minds in a world where men and women no longer automatically assumed God's benign supervision of human affairs or the primacy of their own Christian obligations. The fierce strife between Protestants and Catholics lapsed into relative quiescence by the end of the seventeenth century, but the Protestant English deposed their king in 1688 because of his marriage to a Catholic princess and their fear of a Catholic dynasty; and in France Louis XIV in 1685 revoked the Edict of Nantes, which had granted religious toleration to Protestants. The overt English struggle of Cavaliers and Puritans ended with the restoration of Charles II to the throne in 1660. Religious differences now became translated into divisions of social class and of political conviction—

1

divisions no less powerful for lacking the claim of supernatural authority. To England, the eighteenth century brought two unsuccessful but bitterly divisive rebellions on behalf of the deposed Stuart succession, as well as the cataclysmic American Revolution. In France, the century ended in revolution. Throughout the eighteenth century, wars erupted over succession to European thrones and over nationalistic claims, although no fighting took place on such a scale as that of the devastating Thirty Years' War (1618–48). On the whole, divisions *within* nations (in France and England) assumed greater importance than those between nations.

Philosophers now turned their attention to defining the possibilities and limitations of the human position in the material universe. "I think, therefore I am," René Descartes pronounced, declaring the mind the source of individual being. But this idea proved less reassuring than it initially seemed. Subsequent philosophers, exploring the concept's implications, realized the possibility of the mind's isolation in its own constructions. Perhaps, Wilhelm Leibniz suggested, no real communication can take place between one consciousness and another. Possibly, according to David Hume, the idea of individual identity itself derives from the mind's efforts to manufacture continuity out of discontinuous memories. Philosophers pointed out the impossibility of knowing for sure even the reality of the external world: the only certainty is that we think it exists. If contemplating the nature of human reason thus led philosophic skeptics to restrict severely the area of what we can know with certainty, other contemplations induced other thinkers to insist on the existence, beyond ourselves, of an entirely rational physical and moral universe. Isaac Newton's demonstrations of the order of natural law greatly encouraged this line of thought. The fullness and complexity of the perceived physical world testified, as many wrote, to the sublime rationality of a divine plan. The Planner, however, did not necessarily supervise the day-to-day operations of His arrangements; He might rather, as a popular analogy had it, resemble the watchmaker who winds the watch and leaves it running.

Deism, evoking a depersonalized deity, insisted on the logicality of the universe and encouraged the separation of ethics from religion. Ethics, too, could be understood as a matter of reason. "He that thinks reasonably must think morally," Samuel Johnson observed, echoing the noble horses Jonathan Swift had imagined in the fourth book of *Gulliver's Travels*. But such statements expressed wish more than perception. Awareness of the passions continued to haunt thinkers yearning for rationality. Swift's Houyhnhnms, creatures of his imagination, might achieve flawless rationality (with accompanying wisdom and benevolence) but actual human beings could only dream of such an ideal, while experiencing—as men and women have always experienced—the confusion of conflicting impulses often at war with the dictates of reason.

Although the social, economic, and political organizations in which the thinkers of this period participated hardly resemble our own, the questions they raised about the human condition have plagued the Western mind ever since. If we no longer locate the solution to all problems in an unattainable ideal of "reason," we too struggle to find the limits of certainty, experience problems of identity and isolation, and recognize the impossibility of altogether controlling internal forces now identified as "the unconscious" rather than "the passions." But we confront such issues largely from the position of isolated individuals. In the late seventeenth and early eighteenth centuries, in England and on the Continent, the sense of obligation to society had far more power than it possesses today. Society provided the standards and the instruments of control that might help to counter the tumult of individual impulse.

SOCIETY

Society, in this period, designates both a powerful idea and an omnipresent fact of experience. Prerevolutionary French society, like English society in the same period, depended on clear hierarchical structures. The literature of both countries issued from a small cultural elite, writing for others of their kind and assuming the rightness of their own knowledge of how people should feel and behave.

For the English and French upper classes, as for the ancient Romans they admired, public life mattered more than private. At one level, the "public" designated the realms of government and diplomacy: occupations allowing and encouraging oratory, frequent travel, negotiation, the exercise of political and economic power. In this sense, the public world belonged entirely to men, who determined the course of government, defined the limits of the important, enforced their sense of the fitness of things. By another definition, "public" might refer to the life of formal social intercourse. In France, such social life took place often in "salons," gatherings to engage in intellectual, as well as frivolous, conversation. Women typically presided over these salons, thus declaring both their intellectual authority and their capacity to combine high thought with high style. Until rather late in the eighteenth century, on the other hand, England allowed women no such commanding position; there, men controlled intellectual and political discourse. The male voice, accordingly, dominated English literature until the development of the novel provided new opportunities for women writers and for the articulation of domestic values.

Both the larger and the more limited public spheres depended on well-defined codes of behavior. The discrepancy between the forms of self-presentation dictated by these codes and the operations such forms might disguise—a specific form of the reason–passion conflict—provides one of the insistent themes of French and English literature in the century beginning around 1660. Molière, examining religious sham; de La Fayette, considering the dilemma of a woman whose sense of propriety wars with her desire; Swift, lashing the English for institutionalized hypocrisy; Pope, calling attention to ambiguities inherent in sexual mores; Voltaire and Johnson, sending naive fictional protagonists to encounter the world's inconsistencies of profession and practice—such writers call attention to the deceptiveness and the possible misuses of social norms, as well as to their necessity. None suggests that the codes themselves are at fault. If people lived up to what they profess, the world would be a better place; ideally, they would modify not their standards of behavior but their tendency to hide behind them.

We in the twentieth century have become accustomed to the notion of the sacredness of the individual, encouraged to believe in the high value of expressiveness, originality, specialness. Eighteenth-century writers, on the other hand, assumed the superior importance of the social group and of shared opinion. "Expressiveness," in their view, should provide an instrument for articulating the will of the community, not the eccentric desires of individuals. The mad astronomer in Johnson's *Rasselas,* who as a result of isolation develops an exaggerated sense of his own power, epitomizes the danger of allowing oneself to believe too readily in the self's specialness. Society implies subordination: not only class hierarchy but individual submission to the good of the group.

French writers of imaginative literature often used domestic situations as ways to examine larger problems. Marriage, an institution at once social and personal, provides a useful image for human relationship as social and emotional fact. The developing eighteenth-century novel, in England and France alike, would assume marriage as the normal goal for men and women; Molière, Racine, and de La Fayette, writing before the turn of the century, examine economic, psychological, moral, and social implications of specific imagined marriages. The sexual alliances of rulers, Racine's subject in *Phaedra,* have literal consequences far beyond the individuals involved. Molière evokes a private family to suggest how professed sentiment can obscure the operations of ambition; de La Fayette depicts intricate social and emotional pressures impinging on men and women of good will. All three understand marriage as social microcosm, a society in miniature, not merely as a structure for fulfillment of personal desire.

In England, writers in genres other than the novel typically focus their attention on a broader panorama. Pope, Swift, and Johnson, like Voltaire satirists of the human scene, consider varied operations of social law and pressure. In *The Rape of the Lock,* Pope uses a card party to epitomize social structures. Swift imagines idealized forms of social institutions ranging from marriage to Parliament, contrasting the ideals with evocations of their actual English counterparts; or he fantasizes the horrifying consequences of venture capitalism in the processing of infants for food. Johnson's and Voltaire's world tourists witness and participate in a vast range of sobering experience. In general, women fill subordinate roles in the harsh social environments evoked by these satiric works. Dr. Johnson praised Shakespeare because he did not make love the only spring of action; other passions, Johnson suggested, more powerfully motivate human activity. As the evoked social scene widens, erotic love plays a less important part and the position of women becomes increasingly insignificant: women's sphere is the home, and home life matters less than does public life. It is perhaps not irrelevant to note that no work in this section (with the horrifying exception of *A Modest Proposal*) describes or evokes children. Only in adulthood do people assume social responsibility; only then do they provide interesting substance for social commentary.

NATURE

Society establishes one locus of reality for eighteenth-century thinkers, although they understand it as a human construct. Nature comprises another assumed measure of the real. The meanings of the word *nature* vary greatly in eighteenth-century usage, but two large senses are most relevant to the works here included: nature as the inherent order of things, including the physical universe, hence evidence of the deity's plan; and nature meaning specifically *human* nature.

Despite their pervasive awareness of natural contingency (vividly dramatized by Voltaire among others, in his account of the disastrous Lisbon earthquake), writers of this period locate their sense of permanence particularly in the idea of nature. Pope's *Essay on Man* comprises one of the most extensive—as well as intensive— examinations of the concept of natural order and its implications. Emphasizing the inadequacy of human reason, the poem insistently reminds the reader of limitation. We cannot hope to grasp the arrangement of the universe, Pope tells us: how can a part comprehend the whole? Human pride in reason only obscures from its possessors the great truths of a universal structure as flawlessly articulated in every detail as the stellar systems Newton and others had revealed. Contemplation of nature can both humble and exalt its practitioner, teaching the insufficiency of human powers in comparison with divine but also reminding human beings that they inhabit a wondrous universe in which all functions precisely as it should.

The notion of a permanent, divinely ordained natural order offers a good deal of comfort to those aware of flaws in actual social arrangements. It embodies an ideal of harmony, of order in variety, which, although it cannot be fully grasped by human intelligence, can yet provide a model for social complexities. It posits a *system,* a structure of relationships that at some theoretical level necessarily makes sense; thus it provides an assumed substructure of rationality for all experience of irrationality. It supplies a means of valuing all appearances of the natural world: every flower, every minnow, has meaning beyond itself, as part of the great pattern. The ardency with which the period's thinkers cling to belief in such a pattern suggests once more a pervasive anxiety about what human reason could not do. Human beings create a vision of something at once sublimely reasonable and beyond reason's grasp to reassure themselves that the limits of the rational need not coincide with the limits of the human.

The permanence of the conceptual natural order corresponds to that of human nature, as conceived in the eighteenth century. Human nature, it was generally believed, remains in all times and places the same. Thus Racine could re-present a fable from Greek tragedy, using classical setting and characters, with complete assurance that his imagining of Phaedra's conflict and suffering would speak to his contemporaries without falsifying the classical original. Despite social divergencies, fundamental aspects of personality do in fact remain constant: all people hope and fear, feel envy and lust, possess the capacity to reason. All suffer loss, all face death. Thinkers of the Enlightenment emphasized these common aspects of humanity far more than they considered cultural divergencies. Readers and writers alike could draw on this conviction about universality. It provided a test of excellence: if an author's imagining of character failed to conform to what eighteenth-century readers understood as human nature, a work might be securely judged inadequate. Conversely, the idea of a constant human nature held out the hope of longevity for writers who successfully evoked it. Moral philosophers could define human obligation and possibility in the conviction that they too wrote for all time; ethical standards would never change. Like the vision of order in the physical universe, the notion of constancy in human nature provided bedrock for an increasingly secularized society.

CONVENTION AND AUTHORITY

Eighteenth-century society, like all societies, operated, and its literary figures wrote, on the basis of established conventions. Manners are social conventions: agreed-on systems of behavior declared appropriate for specific situations. Guides to manners proliferated in the eighteenth century, expressing a widespread sense that commitment to decorum helped preserve society's important standards. Literary conventions—agreed-on systems of verbal behavior—served comparable purposes in another sphere. Like established codes of manners, such conventions declare continuity between present and past.

The literary conventions of the past, like outmoded manners or styles of dress, may strike the twentieth-century reader as antiquated and artificial. A woman who curtseyed in a modern living room, a man who appeared in a wig, would seem to us ridiculous, even insane; but, of course, a young woman in jeans would strike our predecessors as equally perverse. The plaintive lyrics of current country music, like the extravagances of rap, operate within restrictive conventions that affect their hearers as "natural" only because they are familiar. Eighteenth-century writers had at their disposal an established set of conventions for every traditional literary genre. As the repetitive rhythms of the country ballad tell listeners what to expect, these literary conventions provided readers with clues about the kind of experience they could anticipate in a given poem or play.

Underlying all specific conventions was the classical assumption that literature existed to delight and to instruct its readers. The various genres represented in this period embody such belief in literature's dual function. Stage comedy and tragedy, the early novel, satire in prose and verse, didactic poetry, the philosophic tale: each form developed its own set of devices for involving audiences and readers in situations requiring moral choice, as well as for creating pleasure. The insistence in drama on unity of time and place (stage action occupying no more time than its representation, with no change of scene) exemplifies one such set, intended to facilitate in audiences the kind of belief encouraging maximum emotional and moral effect. The elevated diction of the *Essay on Man* ("Mark how it mounts, to Man's imperial race, / From the green myriads in the peopled grass"), like the mannered but less dignified language of *The Rape of the Lock* ("Here thou, great Anna! whom three realms obey, / Dost sometimes counsel take—and sometimes tea"), and the two-dimensional characters of Johnson's and Voltaire's tales: such (to us) unfamiliar aspects of these texts provide signals about authorial intention and about anticipated reader response.

One dominant convention of twentieth-century poetry and prose is something we call "realism." In fiction, verse, and drama, writers often attempt to convey the literal feel of experience, the shape in which events actually occur in the world, the way people really talk. Racine, Pope, Voltaire pursued no such goal. Despite their concern with permanent patterns of thought and feeling, they employed deliberate and obvious forms of artifice as modes of emphasis and of indirection. The rapidity with which de La Fayette summarizes crucial events (as when her heroine's mother reports some thirty years of court history in two or three pages), like the sonorous verse in which Racine's characters reflect on their passions ("I hate my life, abominate my lust; / Longing by death to rescue my good name / And hide my black love from the light of day"), embodies a form of stylization. Artistic transformation of life, the period's writers believed, involves the imposition of formal order on the endless flux of event and feeling. The formalities of this literature constitute part of its meaning: its statement that what experience shows as unstable, art makes stable.

Reliance on convention as a mode of control expressed an aspect of the period's constant effort toward elusive stability. The classical past, for many, provided an emblem of that stability, a standard of permanence. But some felt a problem inherent in the high valuing of the past, a problem dramatized by the so-called quarrel of Ancients and Moderns in England and in France. At stake in this controversy was the value of permanence as against the value of change. Proponents of the Ancients believed that the giants of Greece and Rome had not only established standards applicable to all subsequent accomplishment but provided models of achievement never to be excelled. Homer wrote the first great epics; subsequent endeavors in the same genre could only imitate him. Innovation came when it came by making the old new, as Pope makes a woman's dressing for conquest new by comparing it to the arming of Achilles. Moderns who valued originality for its own sake, who multiplied worthless publications, who claimed significance for what time had not tested thereby testified to their own inadequacies and their foolish pride.

Those proud to be Moderns, on the other hand, held that men (possibly even women) standing on the shoulders of the Ancients could see farther than their predecessors. The new conceivably exceeded in value the old; one might discover flaws even in revered figures of the classic past. Not everything had yet been accomplished; fresh possibilities remained always possible. This view, of course, corresponds to one widely current since the eighteenth century, but it did not triumph easily: many powerful thinkers of the late seventeenth and early eighteenth century adhered to the more conservative position.

Also at issue in this debate was the question of authority. What position should one assume who hoped to write and be read? Did authority reside only in tradition? If so, one must write in classical forms, rely on classical allusions. Until late in the eighteenth century, virtually all important writers attempted to ally themselves with the authority of tradition, declaring themselves part of a community extending through time as well as space. The problems of authority became particularly important in connection with satire, a popular Enlightenment form. Satire involves criticism of vice and folly; Molière, Pope, Swift, Voltaire, Johnson at least on occasion wrote in the satiric mode. To establish the right to criticize fellow men and women, the satirist must establish a rhetorical ascendancy such as the pulpit gives the priest—an ascendancy most readily obtained by at least implicit alliance with literary and moral tradition. The satirist, like the moral philosopher, cannot afford to seem idiosyncratic when prescribing and condemning the behavior of others. The fact that satire flourished so richly in this period suggests another version of the central conflict between reason and passion, the forces of stability and of instability. In its heightened description of the world (people eating babies, young women initiating epic battles over the loss of a lock of hair), satire calls attention to the powerful presence of the irrational, opposing to that presence the clarity of the satirist's own claim to reason and tradition. As it chastises human beings for their eruptions of passion, urging resistance and control, satire reminds its readers of the universality of the irrational as well as of opposition to it. The effort "to correct and moderate men's [and women's] passions," that great theme of the Enlightenment, can equally generate hope or despair: opposed moods richly expressed throughout this period.

FURTHER READING

Useful books on the Enlightenment include, for English background, H. Nicolson, *The Age of Reason: The Eighteenth Century* (1960), and, for an opposed view, D. Greene, *The Age of Exuberance: Backgrounds to Eighteenth-Century English Literature* (1970). For the intellectual and social situation in France, L. Crocker, *An Age of Crisis: Man and World in Eighteenth-Century French Thought* (1959); L. Gossman, *French Society and Culture: Background for Eighteenth-Century Literature* (1972); and A. Adam, *Grandeur and Illusion: French Literature and Society, 1600–1715* (1972). An excellent treatment of the period's literature in England is M. Price, *To the Palace of Wisdom: Studies in Order and Energy from Dryden to Blake* (1964). M. Williamson, *Raising Their Voices, 1650–1750* (1990), discusses women's contributions to the English Enlightenment. A good introduction to the intellectual situation of eighteenth-century England is J. Sambrook, *The Eighteenth Century: The Intellectual and Cultural Context of English Literature, 1700–1789* (1986). For the artistic situation of France, see T. M. Kavanaugh, *Esthetics of the Moment: Literature and Art in the French Enlightenment* (1996).

THE ENLIGHTENMENT

TEXTS	CONTEXTS
	1660 Civil War in England ends with Charles II's ascension to the throne (the "Restoration")
1664 Jean-Baptiste Poquelin Molière, ***Tartuffe***	
1665 François de La Rochefoucauld, *Reflections*	
	1666 Isaac Newton uncovers laws of gravitation • London, already stricken by plague, is destroyed in the Great Fire and subsequently rebuilt in more orderly fashion
1667 Publication of John Milton's *Paradise Lost*	
	1670 The London-based Hudson's Bay Company is incorporated by royal charter to trade in North America
1677 Jean Racine, **Phaedra**	
1678 Marie de la Vergne de La Fayette, ***The Princess of Clèves***	
1690 John Locke, *Essay Concerning Human Understanding*	
1691 Sor Juana Inés de la Cruz, **Reply to Sor Filotea de la Cruz**	
	1694 Bank of England is chartered, forerunner of modern national banks and treasury systems; London stock exchange follows in 1698
	1697 Russian czar Peter the Great visits Western Europe and England, resolves to Westernize Russia
	1707 United Kingdom of Great Britain formed by union of England and Scotland
	1709 Up to 100,000 slaves a year cross the Atlantic, 20,000 to Britain's Caribbean colonies alone
1710 First British copyright law, transferring rights of property in a published work from publisher to author	
1717 Alexander Pope, ***The Rape of the Lock***	
1719 Daniel Defoe publishes *Robinson Crusoe*, often called the first true novel in English	
	1721 J. S. Bach, *The Brandenburg Concertos*
1726 Jonathan Swift, ***Gulliver's Travels***	

Boldface titles indicate works in the anthology.

THE ENLIGHTENMENT

TEXTS	CONTEXTS
1729 Swift, *A Modest Proposal*	
1733–1734 Alexander Pope, *An Essay on Man*	
1751 First edition of French *Encyclopédie*, edited by Denis Diderot	
	1753 British Museum founded
1755 Samuel Johnson publishes the *Dictionary of the English Language,* the first comprehensive English dictionary on historical principles	
	1756–1763 Seven Years' War, involving nine European powers; Britain acquires Canada and Florida, Spain gets Cuba and the Philippines, France wins colonies in India and Africa as well as Guadeloupe and Martinique
1759 François-Marie Arouet de Voltaire, *Candide* • Samuel Johnson, *The History of Rasselas, Prince of Abissinia*	
	1765 James Watt, a Scott, invents the steam engine, first in a series of mechanical innovations ushering in the Industrial Revolution
1771 First publication of *Encyclopedia Britannica* and complete French *Encyclopédie* testify to characteristic "Enlightenment" impulse to organize knowledge	1775–1783 American War of Independence; Declaration of Independence, 1776 • Constitution of the United States, 1787, the year of Mozart's opera *Don Giovanni*
	1789 French Revolution begins; French National Assembly adopts the Declaration of the Rights of Man
1792 Mary Wollstonecraft, *Vindication of the Rights of Woman,* makes feminist case for female equality	
	1799 After successful conquests throughout Europe, Napoleon Bonaparte becomes first consul—in effect, dictator—of France • Ludwig van Beethoven writes first symphony (1799–1800)

JEAN-BAPTISTE POQUELIN MOLIÈRE
1622–1673

Son of a prosperous Paris merchant, Jean-Baptiste Molière (originally named Poquelin) devoted his entire adult life to the creation of stage illusion, as playwright and as actor. At about the age of twenty-five, he joined a company of traveling players established by the Béjart family; with them he toured the provinces for about twelve years. In 1658 the company was ordered to perform for Louis XIV in Paris; a year later, Molière's first great success, *The High-Brow Ladies* (*Les Précieuses ridicules*), was produced. The theatrical company to which he belonged, patronized by the king, became increasingly successful, developing finally (1680) into the Comédie Française. In 1662, Molière married Armande Béjart. He died a few hours after performing in the lead role of his own play *The Imaginary Invalid*.

Molière wrote both broad farce and comedies of character, in which he caricatured some form of vice or folly by embodying it in a single figure. His targets included the miser, the aspiring but vulgar middle class, female would-be intellectuals, the hypochondriac, and in *Tartuffe*, the religious hypocrite.

In *Tartuffe* (1664), as in his other plays, Molière employs classic comic devices of plot and character—here, a foolish, stubborn father blocking the course of young love; an impudent servant commenting on her superiors' actions; a happy ending involving a marriage facilitated by implausible means. He often uses such devices, however, to comment on his own immediate social scene, imagining how universal patterns play themselves out in a specific historical context. *Tartuffe* had contemporary relevance so transparent that the Catholic Church forced the king to ban it, although Molière managed to have it published and produced once more by 1669.

The play's emotional energy derives not from the simple discrepancy of man and mask in Tartuffe ("Is not a face quite different from a mask?" inquires the normative character Cléante, who has no trouble making such distinctions) but from the struggle for erotic, psychic, and economic power in which people employ their masks. One can readily imagine modern equivalents for the stresses and strains within Orgon's family. Orgon, an aging man with grown children, seeks ways to preserve control. His mother, Madame Pernelle, encourages his efforts, thus fostering her illusion that *she* still runs things. Orgon identifies his own interests with those of the hypocritical Tartuffe, toward whom he plays a benevolent role. Because Tartuffe fulsomely hails him as benefactor, Orgon feels utterly powerful in relation to his fawning dependent. When he orders his passive daughter Mariane to marry Tartuffe, he reveals his vision of complete domestic autocracy. Tartuffe's lust, one of those passions forever eluding human mastery, disturbs Orgon's arrangements; in the end, the will of the offstage king orders everything, as though a benevolent god had intervened.

To make Tartuffe a specifically religious hypocrite is an act of inventive daring. Orgon, like his mother, conceals from himself his will to power by verbally subordinating himself to that divinity which Tartuffe too invokes. Although one may easily accept Molière's defense of his intentions (not to mock faith but to attack its misuse), it is not hard to see why the play might trouble religious authorities. Molière suggests how readily religious faith lends itself to misuse, how high-sounding pieties allow men and women to evade self-examination and immediate responsibilities. Tartuffe deceives others by his grandiosities of mortification ("Hang up my hair shirt") and charity; he encourages his victims in their own grandiosities. Orgon can indulge a fantasy of self-subordination (remarking of Tartuffe, "He guides our lives") at the same time that he furthers his more hidden desire for power. Religion offers ready justification for a course manifestly destructive as well as self-seeking.

Cléante, before he meets Tartuffe, claims (accurately) to understand him by his effects on others. Throughout the play, Cléante speaks in the voice of wisdom, counseling moderation, common sense, and self-control, calling attention to folly. More important, he emphasizes how the issues Molière examines in this comedy relate to dominant late seventeenth-century themes:

> Ah, Brother, man's a strangely fashioned creature
> Who seldom is content to follow Nature,
> But recklessly pursues his inclination
> Beyond the narrow bounds of moderation,
> And often, by transgressing Reason's laws,
> Perverts a lofty aim or noble cause.

To follow Nature means to act appropriately to the human situation in the created universe. Humankind occupies a middle position, between beasts and angels; such aspirations as Orgon's desire to control his daughter completely, or his apparent wish to submit himself absolutely to Tartuffe's claim of heavenly wisdom, imply a hope to surpass limitations inherent in the human condition. As Cléante's observations suggest, "to follow Nature," given the rationality of the universe, implies adherence to "Reason's laws." All transgression involves failure to submit to reason's dictates. Molière, with his stylized comic plot, makes that point as insistently as does Racine, who depicts grand passions and cataclysmic effects from them.

Although Cléante understands and can enunciate the principles of proper conduct, his wisdom has no direct effect on the play's action. Although the comedy suggests a social world in which women exist in utter subordination to fathers and husbands, in the plot, two women bring about the clarifications that unmask the villain. The virtuous wife, Elmire, object of Tartuffe's lust, and the articulate servant girl, Dorine, confront the immediate situation with pragmatic inventiveness. Dorine goads others to response; Elmire encourages Tartuffe to play out his sexual fantasies before a hidden audience. Both women have a clear sense of right and wrong, although they express it in less resounding terms than does Cléante. Their concrete insistence on facing what is really going on, cutting through all obfuscation, rescues the men from entanglement in their own abstract formulations.

The women's clarifications, however, do not resolve the comedy's dilemmas. Suddenly the context shifts: economic terms replace erotic ones. It is as though Tartuffe were only playing in his attempt to seduce Elmire; now we get to what really matters: money. For all his claims of disinterestedness, Tartuffe has managed to get control of his dupe's property. Control of property, the action gradually reveals, amounts to power over life itself: prison threatens Orgon, and the prospect of expulsion from their home menaces him and his family alike. Only the convenient and ostentatious artifice of royal intervention rescues the victims and punishes their betrayer.

Comedies conventionally end in the restoration of order, declaring that good inevitably triumphs; rationality renews itself despite the temporary deviations of the foolish and the vicious. At the end of *Tartuffe*, Orgon and his mother have been chastened by revelation of their favorite's depravity, Mariane has been allowed to marry her lover, Tartuffe has been judged, the king's power and justice have reasserted themselves and been acknowledged. In the organization of family and nation (metaphorically a larger family), order reassumes dominion. Yet the arbitrary intervention of the king leaves a disturbing emotional residue. The play has demonstrated that Tartuffe's corrupt will to power (as opposed to Orgon's merely foolish will) can ruthlessly aggrandize itself. Money speaks, in Orgon's society as in ours; possession of wealth implies total control over others. Only a kind of miracle can save Orgon. The miracle occurs, given the benign world of comedy, but the play reminds its readers of the extreme precariousness with which reason finally triumphs, even given the presence of such reasonable people as Cléante and Elmire. Tartuffe's monstrous lust, for women, money, power, genuinely endangers the social structure. *Tartuffe* enforces recognition of the constant threats to rationality, of how much we have at stake in trying to use reason as principle of action.

K. Mantzius, *Molière* (1908), provides a good biographical introduction to Molière. Useful critical studies include J. D. Hubert, *Molière and the Comedy of Intellect*

(1962); L. Gossman, *Men and Masks: A Study of Molière* (1963); Jacques Guichar-naud, ed., *Molière: A Collection of Critical Essays* (1964); and N. Gross, *From Gesture to Idea: Esthetics and Ethics in Molière's Comedy* (1982). An excellent treatment of Molière in his historical context is W. D. Howarth, *Molière: A Playwright and His Audience* (1984). Harold C. Knutson, *The Triumph of Wit* (1988), examines Molière in relation to Shakespeare and Ben Jonson. Martin Turnell, *The Classical Moment: Studies of Corneille, Molière, and Racine* (1975), offers useful insight into French dramatic tradition.

PRONOUNCING GLOSSARY

The following list uses common English syllables and stress accents to provide rough equiv-alents of selected words whose pronunciation may be unfamiliar to the general reader.

Cléante: *clay-ahnt'*	Molière: *moh-lyehr'*
Damis: *dah-meece'*	Orante: *oh-rahnt'*
Dorine: *do-reen'*	Orgon: *or-gohnh'*
Elmire: *el-meer'*	Pernelle: *payr-nel'*
Flipote: *flee-pot'*	Tartuffe: *tahr-tewf'*
Laurent: *lor-awnh'*	Valère: *vah-lehr'*
Loyal: *lwah-yal'*	Vincennes: *vanh-sahnhz*

Tartuffe[1]

Preface

Here is a comedy that has excited a good deal of discussion and that has been under attack for a long time; and the persons who are mocked by it have made it plain that they are more powerful in France than all whom my plays have satirized up to this time. Noblemen, ladies of fashion, cuckolds, and doctors all kindly consented to their presentation, which they themselves seemed to enjoy along with everyone else; but hypocrites do not understand banter: they became angry at once, and found it strange that I was bold enough to represent their actions and to care to describe a profession shared by so many good men. This is a crime for which they cannot forgive me, and they have taken up arms against my comedy in a terrible rage. They were careful not to attack it at the point that had wounded them: they are too crafty for that and too clever to reveal their true character. In keeping with their lofty custom, they have used the cause of God to mask their private interests; and *Tartuffe,* they say, is a play that offends piety: it is filled with abominations from beginning to end, and nowhere is there a line that does not deserve to be burned. Every syllable is wicked, the very gestures are criminal, and the slightest glance, turn of the head, or step from right to left conceals mysteries that they are able to explain to my disadvantage. In vain did I submit the play to the criticism of my friends and the scrutiny of the public: all the corrections I could make, the judgment of the king and queen[2] who saw the play, the approval of great princes and ministers of state who

---

1. Translated by Richard Wilbur. The first version of *Tartuffe* was performed in 1664 and the second in 1667. When a second edition of the third version was printed in June 1669, Molière added his three petitions to Louis XIV; they follow the "Preface."   2. Louis XIV was married to Marie Thérèse of Austria.

honored it with their presence, the opinion of good men who found it worthwhile, all this did not help. They will not let go of their prey, and every day
of the week they have pious zealots abusing me in public and damning me
out of charity.

I would care very little about all they might say except that their devices
make enemies of men whom I respect and gain the support of genuinely
good men, whose faith they know and who, because of the warmth of their
piety, readily accept the impressions that others present to them. And it is
this which forces me to defend myself. Especially to the truly devout do I
wish to vindicate my play, and I beg of them with all my heart not to condemn
it before seeing it, to rid themselves of preconceptions, and not aid the cause
of men dishonored by their actions.

If one takes the trouble to examine my comedy in good faith, he will surely
see that my intentions are innocent throughout, and tend in no way to make
fun of what men revere; that I have presented the subject with all the precautions that its delicacy imposes; and that I have used all the art and skill
that I could to distinguish clearly the character of the hypocrite from that of
the truly devout man. For that purpose I used two whole acts to prepare the
appearance of my scoundrel. Never is there a moment's doubt about his
character; he is known at once from the qualities I have given him; and from
one end of the play to the other, he does not say a word, he does not perform an action which does not depict to the audience the character of a
wicked man, and which does not bring out in sharp relief the character of
the truly good man which I oppose to it.

I know full well that by way of reply, these gentlemen try to insinuate that
it is not the role of the theater to speak of these matters; but with their
permission, I ask them on what do they base this fine doctrine. It is a proposition they advance as no more than a supposition, for which they offer not
a shred of proof; and surely it would not be difficult to show them that
comedy, for the ancients, had its origin in religion and constituted a part of
its ceremonies; that our neighbors, the Spaniards, have hardly a single holiday celebration in which a comedy is not a part; and that even here in
France, it owes its birth to the efforts of a religious brotherhood who still
own the Hôtel de Bourgogne, where the most important mystery plays of our
faith were presented;[3] that you can still find comedies printed in gothic letters under the name of a learned doctor[4] of the Sorbonne; and without going
so far, in our own day the religious dramas of Pierre Corneille[5] have been
performed to the admiration of all France.

If the function of comedy is to correct men's vices, I do not see why any
should be exempt. Such a condition in our society would be much more
dangerous than the thing itself; and we have seen that the theater is admirably suited to provide correction. The most forceful lines of a serious moral
statement are usually less powerful than those of satire; and nothing will
reform most men better than the depiction of their faults. It is a vigorous
blow to vices to expose them to public laughter. Criticism is taken lightly,

3. A reference to the *Confrérie de la Passion et Résurrection de Notre-Seigneur* (Fraternity of the passion
and resurrection of our Savior), founded in 1402. The Hôtel de Bourgogne was a theater in rivalry with
Molière's.   4. Probably Maître Jehán Michel, a medical doctor who wrote mystery plays.   5. Corneille
(1606–1684) and Racine were France's two greatest writers of classic tragedy. The two dramas Molière
doubtlessly had in mind were *Polyeucte* (1643) and *Théodore, vierge et martyre* (1645).

but men will not tolerate satire. They are quite willing to be mean, but they never like to be ridiculed.

I have been attacked for having placed words of piety in the mouth of my impostor. Could I avoid doing so in order to represent properly the character of a hypocrite? It seemed to me sufficient to reveal the criminal motives which make him speak as he does, and I have eliminated all ceremonial phrases, which nonetheless he would not have been found using incorrectly. Yet some say that in the fourth act he sets forth a vicious morality; but is not this a morality which everyone has heard again and again? Does my comedy say anything new here? And is there any fear that ideas so thoroughly detested by everyone can make an impression on men's minds; that I make them dangerous by presenting them in the theater; that they acquire authority from the lips of a scoundrel? There is not the slightest suggestion of any of this; and one must either approve the comedy of *Tartuffe* or condemn all comedies in general.

This has indeed been done in a furious way for some time now, and never was the theater so much abused.[6] I cannot deny that there were Church Fathers who condemned comedy; but neither will it be denied me that there were some who looked on it somewhat more favorably. Thus authority, on which censure is supposed to depend, is destroyed by this disagreement; and the only conclusion that can be drawn from this difference of opinion among men enlightened by the same wisdom is that they viewed comedy in different ways, and that some considered it in its purity, while others regarded it in its corruption and confused it with all those wretched performances which have been rightly called performances of filth.

And in fact, since we should talk about things rather than words, and since most misunderstanding comes from including contrary notions in the same word, we need only to remove the veil of ambiguity and look at comedy in itself to see if it warrants condemnation. It will surely be recognized that as it is nothing more than a clever poem which corrects men's faults by means of agreeable lessons, it cannot be condemned without injustice. And if we listened to the voice of ancient times on this matter, it would tell us that its most famous philosophers have praised comedy—they who professed so austere a wisdom and who ceaselessly denounced the vices of their times. It would tell us that Aristotle spent his evenings at the theater[7] and took the trouble to reduce the art of making comedies to rules. It would tell us that some of its greatest and most honored men took pride in writing comedies themselves;[8] and that others did not disdain to recite them in public; that Greece expressed its admiration for this art by means of handsome prizes and magnificent theaters to honor it; and finally, that in Rome this same art also received extraordinary honors; I do not speak of Rome run riot under the license of the emperors, but of disciplined Rome, governed by the wisdom of the consuls, and in the age of the full vigor of Roman dignity.

I admit that there have been times when comedy became corrupt. And what do men not corrupt every day? There is nothing so innocent that men

6. Molière had in mind Nicole's two attacks on the theater: *Visionnaires* (1666) and *Traité de la Comédie* (1667), as well as the prince de Conti's *Traité de la Comédie* (1666).   7. A reference to Aristotle's *Poetics* (composed between 335 and 322 B.C., the year of his death).   8. Scipio Africanus Minor (ca. 185–129 B.C.), the Roman consul and general responsible for the final destruction of Carthage in 146 B.C., collaborated with Terence (Publius Terentius Afer, ca. 195 or 185–ca. 159 B.C.), a writer of comedies.

cannot turn it to crime; nothing so beneficial that its values cannot be reversed; nothing so good in itself that it cannot be put to bad uses. Medical knowledge benefits mankind and is revered as one of our most wonderful possessions; and yet there was a time when it fell into discredit, and was often used to poison men. Philosophy is a gift of Heaven; it has been given to us to bring us to the knowledge of a God by contemplating the wonders of nature; and yet we know that often it has been turned away from its function and has been used openly in support of impiety. Even the holiest of things are not immune from human corruption, and every day we see scoundrels who use and abuse piety, and wickedly make it serve the greatest of crimes. But this does not prevent one from making the necessary distinctions. We do not confuse in the same false inference the goodness of things that are corrupted with the wickedness of the corrupt. The function of an art is always distinguished from its misuse; and as medicine is not forbidden because it was banned in Rome,[9] nor philosophy because it was publicly condemned in Athens,[1] we should not suppress comedy simply because it has been condemned at certain times. This censure was justified then for reasons which no longer apply today; it was limited to what was then seen; and we should not seize on these limits, apply them more rigidly than is necessary, and include in our condemnation the innocent along with the guilty. The comedy that this censure attacked is in no way the comedy that we want to defend. We must be careful not to confuse the one with the other. There may be two persons whose morals may be completely different. They may have no resemblance to one another except in their names, and it would be a terrible injustice to want to condemn Olympia, who is a good woman, because there is also an Olympia who is lewd. Such procedures would make for great confusion everywhere. Everything under the sun would be condemned; now since this rigor is not applied to the countless instances of abuse we see every day, the same should hold for comedy, and those plays should be approved in which instruction and virtue reign supreme.

I know there are some so delicate that they cannot tolerate a comedy, who say that the most decent are the most dangerous, that the passions they present are all the more moving because they are virtuous, and that men's feelings are stirred by these presentations. I do not see what great crime it is to be affected by the sight of a generous passion; and this utter insensitivity to which they would lead us is indeed a high degree of virtue! I wonder if so great a perfection resides within the strength of human nature, and I wonder if it is not better to try to correct and moderate men's passions than to try to suppress them altogether. I grant that there are places better to visit than the theater; and if we want to condemn every single thing that does not bear directly on God and our salvation, it is right that comedy be included, and I should willingly grant that it be condemned along with everything else. But if we admit, as is in fact true, that the exercise of piety will permit interruptions, and that men need amusement, I maintain that there is none more innocent than comedy. I have dwelled too long on this matter. Let me finish with the words of a great prince on the comedy, *Tartuffe*.[2]

---

9. Pliny the Elder says that the Romans expelled their doctors at the same time that the Greeks did theirs.   1. An allusion to Socrates' condemnation to death.   2. One of Molière's benefactors who liked the play was the prince de Condé; de Condé had *Tartuffe* read to him and also privately performed for him.

Eight days after it had been banned, a play called *Scaramouche the Hermit*[3] was performed before the court; and the king, on his way out, said to this great prince: "I should really like to know why the persons who make so much noise about Molière's comedy do not say a word about *Scaramouche.*" To which the prince replied, "It is because the comedy of *Scaramouche* makes fun of Heaven and religion, which these gentlemen do not care about at all, but that of Molière makes fun of *them*, and that is what they cannot bear."

THE AUTHOR

FIRST PETITION[4]

(*Presented to the King on the Comedy of Tartuffe*)

Sire,

As the duty of comedy is to correct men by amusing them, I believed that in my occupation I could do nothing better than attack the vices of my age by making them ridiculous; and as hypocrisy is undoubtedly one of the most common, most improper, and most dangerous, I thought, Sire, that I would perform a service for all good men of your kingdom if I wrote a comedy which denounced hypocrites and placed in proper view all of the contrived poses of these incredibly virtuous men, all of the concealed villainies of these counterfeit believers who would trap others with a fraudulent piety and a pretended virtue.

I have written this comedy, Sire, with all the care and caution that the delicacy of the subject demands; and so as to maintain all the more properly the admiration and respect due to truly devout men, I have delineated my character as sharply as I could; I have left no room for doubt; I have removed all that might confuse good with evil, and have used for this painting only the specific colors and essential lines that make one instantly recognize a true and brazen hypocrite.

Nevertheless, all my precautions have been to no avail. Others have taken advantage of the delicacy of your feelings on religious matters, and they have been able to deceive you on the only side of your character which lies open to deception: your respect for holy things. By underhanded means, the Tartuffes have skillfully gained Your Majesty's favor, and the models have succeeded in eliminating the copy, no matter how innocent it may have been and no matter what resemblance was found between them.

Although the suppression of this work was a serious blow for me, my misfortune was nonetheless softened by the way in which Your Majesty explained his attitude on the matter; and I believed, Sire, that Your Majesty removed any cause I had for complaint, as you were kind enough to declare

---

3. A troupe of Italian comedians had just performed the licentious farce, in which a hermit dressed as a monk makes love to a married woman, announcing that *questo e per mortificar la carne* ("this is to mortify the flesh").   **4.** The first of the three *petitions* or *placets* to Louis XIV concerning the play. On May 12, 1664, *Tartuffe*—or at least the first three acts roughly as they now stand—was performed at Versailles. A cabal unfavorable to Molière, including the archbishop of Paris, Hardouin de Péréfixe, Queen Mother Anne of Austria, certain influential courtiers, and the Brotherhood or Company of the Holy Sacrament (formed in 1627 to enforce morality), arranged that the play be banned and Molière censured.

that you found nothing in this comedy that you would forbid me to present in public.

Yet, despite this glorious declaration of the greatest and most enlightened king in the world, despite the approval of the Papal Legate[5] and of most of our churchmen, all of whom, at private readings of my work, agreed with the views of Your Majesty, despite all this, a book has appeared by a certain priest[6] which boldly contradicts all of these noble judgments. Your Majesty expressed himself in vain, and the Papal Legate and churchmen gave their opinion to no avail: sight unseen, my comedy is diabolical, and so is my brain; I am a devil garbed in flesh and disguised as a man,[7] a libertine, a disbeliever who deserves a punishment that will set an example. It is not enough that fire expiate my crime in public, for that would be letting me off too easily: the generous piety of this good man will not stop there; he will not allow me to find any mercy in the sight of God; he demands that I be damned, and that will settle the matter.

This book, Sire, was presented to Your Majesty; and I am sure that you see for yourself how unpleasant it is for me to be exposed daily to the insults of these gentlemen, what harm these abuses will do my reputation if they must be tolerated, and finally, how important it is for me to clear myself of these false charges and let the public know that my comedy is nothing more than what they want it to be. I will not ask, Sire, for what I need for the sake of my reputation and the innocence of my work: enlightened kings such as you do not need to be told what is wished of them; like God, they see what we need and know better than we what they should give us. It is enough for me to place my interests in Your Majesty's hands, and I respectfully await whatever you may care to command.

(*August, 1664*)

SECOND PETITION[8]

(*Presented to the King in His Camp Before the City of Lille, in Flanders*)

Sire,

It is bold indeed for me to ask a favor of a great monarch in the midst of his glorious victories; but in my present situation, Sire, where will I find protection anywhere but where I seek it, and to whom can I appeal against the authority of the power[9] that crushes me, if not to the source of power and authority, the just dispenser of absolute law, the sovereign judge and master of all?

My comedy, Sire, has not enjoyed the kindnesses of Your Majesty. All to no avail, I produced it under the title of *The Hypocrite* and disguised the

5. Cardinal Legate Chigi, nephew to Pope Alexander VII, heard a reading of *Tartuffe* at Fontainebleau on August 4, 1664.   6. Pierre Roullé, the curate of St. Barthélémy, who wrote a scathing attack on the play and sent his book to the king.   7. Molière took some of these phrases from Roullé.   8. On August 5, 1667, *Tartuffe* was performed at the Palais-Royal. The opposition—headed by the first president of parliament—brought in the police, and the play was stopped. Since Louis was campaigning in Flanders, friends of Molière brought the second *placet* to Lille. Louis had always been favorable toward the playwright; in August 1665 Molière's company, the *Troupe de Monsieur* (nominally sponsored by Louis's brother Philippe, duc d'Orléans), had become the *Troupe du Roi*.   9. President de Lanvignon, in charge of the Paris police.

principal character as a man of the world; in vain I gave him a little hat, long hair, a wide collar, a sword, and lace clothing,[1] softened the action and carefully eliminated all that I thought might provide even the shadow of grounds for discontent on the part of the famous models of the portrait I wished to present; nothing did any good. The conspiracy of opposition revived even at mere conjecture of what the play would be like. They found a way of persuading those who in all other matters plainly insist that they are not to be deceived. No sooner did my comedy appear than it was struck down by the very power which should impose respect; and all that I could do to save myself from the fury of this tempest was to say that Your Majesty had given me permission to present the play and I did not think it was necessary to ask this permission of others, since only Your Majesty could have refused it.

I have no doubt, Sire, that the men whom I depict in my comedy will employ every means possible to influence Your Majesty, and will use, as they have used already, those truly good men who are all the more easily deceived because they judge of others by themselves.[2] They know how to display all of their aims in the most favorable light; yet, no matter how pious they may seem, it is surely not the interests of God which stir them; they have proven this often enough in the comedies they have allowed to be performed hundreds of times without making the least objection. Those plays attacked only piety and religion, for which they care very little; but this play attacks and makes fun of them, and that is what they cannot bear. They will never forgive me for unmasking their hypocrisy in the eyes of everyone. And I am sure that they will not neglect to tell Your Majesty that people are shocked by my comedy. But the simple truth, Sire, is that all Paris is shocked only by its ban, that the most scrupulous persons have found its presentation worthwhile, and men are astounded that individuals of such known integrity should show so great a deference to people whom everyone should abominate and who are so clearly opposed to the true piety which they profess.

I respectfully await the judgment that Your Majesty will deign to pronounce: but it's certain, Sire, that I need not think of writing comedies if the Tartuffes are triumphant, if they thereby seize the right to persecute me more than ever, and find fault with even the most innocent lines that flow from my pen.

Let your goodness, Sire, give me protection against their envenomed rage, and allow me, at your return from so glorious a campaign, to relieve Your Majesty from the fatigue of his conquests, give him innocent pleasures after such noble accomplishments, and make the monarch laugh who makes all Europe tremble!

(August, 1667)

1. There is evidence that in 1664 Tartuffe played his role dressed in a cassock, thus allying him more directly to the clergy.   2. Molière apparently did not know that de Lanvignon had been affiliated with the Company of the Holy Sacrament for the previous ten years.

THIRD PETITION

(*Presented to the King*)

Sire,

A very honest doctor[3] whose patient I have the honor to be, promises and will legally contract to make me live another thirty years if I can obtain a favor for him from Your Majesty. I told him of his promise that I do not deserve so much, and that I should be glad to help him if he will merely agree not to kill me. This favor, Sire, is a post of canon at your royal chapel of Vincennes, made vacant by death.

May I dare to ask for this favor from Your Majesty on the very day of the glorious resurrection of *Tartuffe*, brought back to life by your goodness? By this first favor I have been reconciled with the devout, and the second will reconcile me with the doctors.[4] Undoubtedly this would be too much grace for me at one time, but perhaps it would not be too much for Your Majesty, and I await your answer to my petition with respectful hope.

(*February, 1669*)

CHARACTERS[5]

MADAME PERNELLE, *Orgon's mother*	VALÈRE, *in love with Mariane*
ORGON, *Elmire's husband*	CLÉANTE, *Orgon's brother-in-law*
ELMIRE, *Orgon's wife*	TARTUFFE, *a hypocrite*
DAMIS, *Orgon's son, Elmire's stepson*	DORINE, *Mariane's lady's-maid*
MARIANE, *Orgon's daughter, Elmire's*	M. LOYAL, *a bailiff*
stepdaughter, in love with Valère	A POLICE OFFICER
	FLIPOTE, *Mme Pernelle's maid*

The SCENE throughout: ORGON's *house in Paris*

Act I

SCENE 1[6]

MADAME PERNELLE *and* FLIPOTE, *her maid*, ELMIRE,
MARIANE, DORINE, DAMIS, CLÉANTE

MADAME PERNELLE   Come, come, Flipote; it's time I left this place.
ELMIRE   I can't keep up, you walk at such a pace.
MADAME PERNELLE   Don't trouble, child; no need to show me out.
It's not your manners I'm concerned about.
ELMIRE   We merely pay you the respect we owe.   5

3. A physician friend, M. de Mauvillain, who helped Molière with some of the medical details of *Le Malade imaginaire*.   4. Doctors are ridiculed to varying degrees in earlier plays of Molière: *Dom Juan, L'Amour médecin*, and *Le Médecin malgré lui*.   5. The name Tartuffe has been traced back to an older word associated with liar or charlatan: *truffer*, "to deceive" or "to cheat." Then there was also the Italian actor Tartufo, physically deformed and truffle shaped. Most of the other names are typical of this genre of court comedy and possess rather elegant connotations of pastoral and *bergerie*. Dorine would be a *demoiselle de compagne* and not a mere maid, that is, a female companion to Mariane of roughly the same social status. This in part accounts for the liberties she takes in conversation with Orgon, Madame Pernelle, and others. Her name is short for Théodorine.   6. In French drama, the scene changes every time a character enters or exits.

But, Mother, why this hurry? Must you go?
MADAME PERNELLE   I must. This house appals me. No one in it
  Will pay attention for a single minute.
  I offer good advice, but you won't hear it.
  Children, I take my leave much vexed in spirit.   10
  You all break in and chatter on and on.
  It's like a madhouse with the keeper gone.
DORINE   If . . .
MADAME PERNELLE
         Girl, you talk too much, and I'm afraid
  You're far too saucy for a lady's-maid.
  You push in everywhere and have your say.   15
DAMIS   But . . .
MADAME PERNELLE
        You, boy, grow more foolish every day.
  To think my grandson should be such a dunce!
  I've said a hundred times, if I've said it once,
  That if you keep the course on which you've started,
  You'll leave your worthy father broken-hearted.   20
MARIANE   I think . . .
MADAME PERNELLE   And you, his sister, seem so pure,
  So shy, so innocent, and so demure.
  But you know what they say about still waters.
  I pity parents with secretive daughters.
ELMIRE   Now, Mother . . .
MADAME PERNELLE   And as for you, child, let me add   25
  That your behavior is extremely bad,
  And a poor example for these children, too.
  Their dear, dead mother did far better than you.
  You're much too free with money, and I'm distressed
  To see you so elaborately dressed.   30
  When it's one's husband that one aims to please,
  One has no need of costly fripperies.
CLÉANTE   Oh, Madam, really . . .
MADAME PERNELLE   You are her brother, Sir,
  And I respect and love you; yet if I were
  My son, this lady's good and pious spouse,   35
  I wouldn't make you welcome in my house.
  You're full of worldly counsels which, I fear,
  Aren't suitable for decent folk to hear.
  I've spoken bluntly, Sir; but it behooves us
  Not to mince words when righteous fervor moves us.   40
DAMIS   Your man Tartuffe is full of holy speeches . . .
MADAME PERNELLE   And practises precisely what he preaches.
  He's a fine man, and should be listened to.
  I will not hear him mocked by fools like you.
DAMIS   Good God! Do you expect me to submit   45
  To the tyranny of that carping hypocrite?
  Must we forgo all joys and satisfactions
  Because that bigot censures all our actions?

DORINE   To hear him talk—and he talks all the time—
   There's nothing one can do that's not a crime.   50
   He rails at everything, your dear Tartuffe.
MADAME PERNELLE   Whatever he reproves deserves reproof.
   He's out to save your souls, and all of you
   Must love him, as my son would have you do.
DAMIS   Ah no, Grandmother, I could never take   55
   To such a rascal, even for my father's sake.
   That's how I feel, and I shall not dissemble.
   His every action makes me seethe and tremble
   With helpless anger, and I have no doubt
   That he and I will shortly have it out.   60
DORINE   Surely it is a shame and a disgrace
   To see this man usurp the master's place—
   To see this beggar who, when first he came,
   Had not a shoe or shoestring to his name
   So far forget himself that he behaves   65
   As if the house were his, and we his slaves.
MADAME PERNELLE   Well, mark my words, your souls would fare far better
   If you obeyed his precepts to the letter.
DORINE   You see him as a saint. I'm far less awed;
   In fact, I see right through him. He's a fraud.   70
MADAME PERNELLE   Nonsense!
DORINE   His man Laurent's the same, or worse;
   I'd not trust either with a penny purse.
MADAME PERNELLE   I can't say what his servant's morals may be;
   His own great goodness I can guarantee.
   You all regard him with distaste and fear   75
   Because he tells you what you're loath to hear,
   Condemns your sins, points out your moral flaws,
   And humbly strives to further Heaven's cause.
DORINE   If sin is all that bothers him, why is it
   He's so upset when folk drop in to visit?   80
   Is Heaven so outraged by a social call
   That he must prophesy against us all?
   I'll tell you what I think: if you ask me,
   He's jealous of my mistress' company.
MADAME PERNELLE   Rubbish!
   [*To* ELMIRE.]
                     He's not alone, child, in complaining   85
   Of all of your promiscuous entertaining.
   Why, the whole neighborhood's upset, I know,
   By all these carriages that come and go,
   With crowds of guests parading in and out
   And noisy servants loitering about.   90
   In all of this, I'm sure there's nothing vicious;
   But why give people cause to be suspicious?
CLÉANTE   They need no cause; they'll talk in any case.
   Madam, this world would be a joyless place
   If, fearing what malicious tongues might say,   95

We locked our doors and turned our friends away.
And even if one did so dreary a thing,
D' you think those tongues would cease their chattering?
One can't fight slander; it's a losing battle;
Let us instead ignore their tittle-tattle.   100
Let's strive to live by conscience' clear decrees,
And let the gossips gossip as they please.
DORINE   If there is talk against us, I know the source:
It's Daphne and her little husband, of course.
Those who have greatest cause for guilt and shame   105
Are quickest to besmirch a neighbor's name.
When there's a chance for libel, they never miss it;
When something can be made to seem illicit
They're off at once to spread the joyous news,
Adding to fact what fantasies they choose.   110
By talking up their neighbor's indiscretions
They seek to camouflage their own transgressions,
Hoping that others' innocent affairs
Will lend a hue of innocence to theirs,
Or that their own black guilt will come to seem   115
Part of a general shady color-scheme.
MADAME PERNELLE   All this is quite irrelevant. I doubt
That anyone's more virtuous and devout
Than dear Orante; and I'm informed that she
Condemns your mode of life most vehemently.   120
DORINE   Oh, yes, she's strict, devout, and has no taint
Of worldliness; in short, she seems a saint.
But it was time which taught her that disguise;
She's thus because she can't be otherwise.
So long as her attractions could enthrall,   125
She flounced and flirted and enjoyed it all,
But now that they're no longer what they were
She quits a world which fast is quitting her,
And wears a veil of virtue to conceal
Her bankrupt beauty and her lost appeal.   130
That's what becomes of old coquettes today:
Distressed when all their lovers fall away,
They see no recourse but to play the prude,
And so confer a style on solitude.
Thereafter, they're severe with everyone,   135
Condemning all our actions, pardoning none,
And claiming to be pure, austere, and zealous
When, if the truth were known, they're merely jealous,
And cannot bear to see another know
The pleasures time has forced them to forgo.   140
MADAME PERNELLE [*Initially to* ELMIRE.]
That sort of talk[7] is what you like to hear;

---

7. In the original, a reference to a collection of novels about chivalry found in *La Bibliothèque bleue* (The blue library), written for children.

Therefore you'd have us all keep still, my dear,
While Madam rattles on the livelong day.
Nevertheless, I mean to have my say.
I tell you that you're blest to have Tartuffe   145
Dwelling, as my son's guest, beneath this roof;
That Heaven has sent him to forestall its wrath
By leading you, once more, to the true path;
That all he reprehends is reprehensible,
And that you'd better heed him, and be sensible.   150
These visits, balls, and parties in which you revel
Are nothing but inventions of the Devil.
One never hears a word that's edifying:
Nothing but chaff and foolishness and lying,
As well as vicious gossip in which one's neighbor   155
Is cut to bits with épée, foil, and saber.
People of sense are driven half-insane
At such affairs, where noise and folly reign
And reputations perish thick and fast.
As a wise preacher said on Sunday last,   160
Parties are Towers of Babylon,[8] because
The guests all babble on with never a pause;
And then he told a story which, I think . . .
[To CLÉANTE.] I heard that laugh, Sir, and I saw that wink!
Go find your silly friends and laugh some more!   165
Enough; I'm going; don't show me to the door.
I leave this household much dismayed and vexed;
I cannot say when I shall see you next.
        [Slapping FLIPOTE.]
Wake up, don't stand there gaping into space!
I'll slap some sense into that stupid face.   170
Move, move, you slut.

SCENE 2

CLÉANTE, DORINE

CLÉANTE   I think I'll stay behind;
    I want no further pieces of her mind.
    How that old lady . . .
DORINE   Oh, what wouldn't she say
    If she could hear you speak of her that way!
    She'd thank you for the *lady*, but I'm sure   5
    She'd find the *old* a little premature.
CLÉANTE   My, what a scene she made, and what a din!
    And how this man Tartuffe has taken her in!
DORINE   Yes, but her son is even worse deceived;
    His folly must be seen to be believed.   10

8. Tower of Babel. Madame Pernelle's malapropism is the cause of Cléante's laughter.

In the late troubles,[9] he played an able part
And served his king with wise and loyal heart,
But he's quite lost his senses since he fell
Beneath Tartuffe's infatuating spell.
He calls him brother, and loves him as his life,   15
Preferring him to mother, child, or wife.
In him and him alone will he confide;
He's made him his confessor and his guide;
He pets and pampers him with love more tender
Than any pretty maiden could engender,   20
Gives him the place of honor when they dine,
Delights to see him gorging like a swine,
Stuffs him with dainties till his guts distend,
And when he belches, cries "God bless you, friend!"
In short, he's mad; he worships him; he dotes;   25
His deeds he marvels at, his words, he quotes,
Thinking each act a miracle, each word
Oracular as those that Moses heard.
Tartuffe, much pleased to find so easy a victim,
Has in a hundred ways beguiled and tricked him,   30
Milked him of money, and with his permission
Established here a sort of Inquisition.
Even Laurent, his lackey, dares to give
Us arrogant advice on how to live;
He sermonizes us in thundering tones   35
And confiscates our ribbons and colognes.
Last week he tore a kerchief into pieces
Because he found it pressed in a *Life of Jesus:*
He said it was a sin to juxtapose
Unholy vanities and holy prose.   40

SCENE 3

ELMIRE, MARIANE, DAMIS, CLÉANTE, DORINE

ELMIRE [*To* CLÉANTE.]   You did well not to follow; she stood in the door
And said *verbatim* all she'd said before.
I saw my husband coming. I think I'd best
Go upstairs now, and take a little rest.
CLÉANTE   I'll wait and greet him here; then I must go.   5
I've really only time to say hello.
DAMIS   Sound him about my sister's wedding, please.
I think Tartuffe's against it, and that he's
Been urging Father to withdraw his blessing.
As you well know, I'd find that most distressing.   10
Unless my sister and Valère can marry,
My hopes to wed *his* sister will miscarry.

9. A series of political disturbances during the minority of Louis XIV. Specifically, these consisted of the
Fronde ("opposition") of the Parlement (1648–49) and the *Fronde* of the Princes (1650–53). Orgon is
depicted as supporting Louis XIV in these outbreaks and their resolution.

And I'm determined . . .

DORINE   He's coming.

SCENE 4

ORGON, CLÉANTE, DORINE

ORGON   Ah, Brother, good-day.

CLÉANTE   Well, welcome back, I'm sorry I can't stay.
   How was the country? Blooming, I trust, and green?

ORGON   Excuse me, Brother; just one moment.
   [*To* DORINE.]   Dorine . . .
   [*To* CLÉANTE.] To put my mind at rest, I always learn   5
   The household news the moment I return.
   [*To* DORINE.] Has all been well, these two days I've been gone?
   How are the family? What's been going on?

DORINE   Your wife, two days ago, had a bad fever,
   And a fierce headache which refused to leave her.   10

ORGON   Ah. And Tartuffe?

DORINE   Tartuffe? Why, he's round and red.
   Bursting with health, and excellently fed.

ORGON   Poor fellow!

DORINE   That night, the mistress was unable
   To take a single bite at the dinner-table.
   Her headache-pains, she said, were simply hellish.   15

ORGON   Ah. And Tartuffe?

DORINE   He ate his meal with relish,
   And zealously devoured in her presence
   A leg of mutton and a brace of pheasants.

ORGON   Poor fellow!

DORINE   Well, the pains continued strong,
   And so she tossed and tossed the whole night long,   20
   Now icy-cold, now burning like a flame.
   We sat beside her bed till morning came.

ORGON   Ah. And Tartuffe?

DORINE   Why, having eaten, he rose
   And sought his room, already in a doze,
   Got into his warm bed, and snored away   25
   In perfect peace until the break of day.

ORGON   Poor fellow!

DORINE   After much ado, we talked her
   Into dispatching someone for the doctor.
   He bled her, and the fever quickly fell.

ORGON   Ah. And Tartuffe?

DORINE   He bore it very well.   30
   To keep his cheerfulness at any cost,
   And make up for the blood Madame had lost,
   He drank, at lunch, four beakers full of port.

ORGON   Poor fellow.

DORINE   Both are doing well, in short.

I'll go and tell Madame that you've expressed   35
Keen sympathy and anxious interest.

SCENE 5

ORGON, CLÉANTE

CLÉANTE   That girl was laughing in your face, and though
  I've no wish to offend you, even so
  I'm bound to say that she had some excuse.
  How can you possibly be such a goose?
  Are you so dazed by this man's hocus-pocus   5
  That all the world, save him, is out of focus?
  You've given him clothing, shelter, food, and care;
  Why must you also . . .
ORGON   Brother, stop right there.
  You do not know the man of whom you speak.
CLÉANTE   I grant you that. But my judgment's not so weak   10
  That I can't tell, by his effect on others . . .
ORGON   Ah, when you meet him, you two will be like brothers!
  There's been no loftier soul since time began.
  He is a man who . . . a man who . . . an excellent man.
  To keep his precepts is to be reborn,   15
  And view this dunghill of a world with scorn.
  Yes, thanks to him I'm a changed man indeed.
  Under his tutelage my soul's been freed
  From earthly loves, and every human tie:
  My mother, children, brother, and wife could die,   20
  And I'd not feel a single moment's pain.
CLÉANTE   That's a fine sentiment, Brother; most humane.
ORGON   Oh, had you seen Tartuffe as I first knew him,
  Your heart, like mine, would have surrendered to him.
  He used to come into our church each day   25
  And humbly kneel nearby, and start to pray.
  He'd draw the eyes of everybody there
  By the deep fervor of his heartfelt prayer;
  He'd sigh and weep, and sometimes with a sound
  Of rapture he would bend and kiss the ground;   30
  And when I rose to go, he'd run before
  To offer me holy-water at the door.
  His serving-man, no less devout than he,
  Informed me of his master's poverty;
  I gave him gifts, but in his humbleness   35
  He'd beg me every time to give him less.
  "Oh, that's too much," he'd cry, "too much by twice!
  I don't deserve it. The half, Sir, would suffice."
  And when I wouldn't take it back, he'd share
  Half of it with the poor, right then and there.   40
  At length, Heaven prompted me to take him in
  To dwell with us, and free our souls from sin.

He guides our lives, and to protect my honor
Stays by my wife, and keeps an eye upon her;
He tells me whom she sees, and all she does,   45
And seems more jealous than I ever was!
And how austere he is! Why, he can detect
A moral sin where you would least suspect;
In smallest trifles, he's extremely strict.
Last week, his conscience was severely pricked   50
Because, while praying, he had caught a flea
And killed it, so he felt, too wrathfully.[1]

CLÉANTE   Good God, man! Have you lost your common sense—
Or is this all some joke at my expense?
How can you stand there and in all sobriety . . .   55

ORGON   Brother, your language savors of impiety.
Too much free-thinking's made your faith unsteady,
And as I've warned you many times already,
'Twill get you into trouble before you're through.

CLÉANTE   So I've been told before by dupes like you: 60
Being blind, you'd have all others blind as well;
The clear-eyed man you call an infidel,
And he who sees through humbug and pretense
Is charged, by you, with want of reverence.
Spare me your warnings, Brother; I have no fear   65
Of speaking out, for you and Heaven to hear,
Against affected zeal and pious knavery.
There's true and false in piety, as in bravery,
And just as those whose courage shines the most
In battle, are the least inclined to boast,   70
So those whose hearts are truly pure and lowly
Don't make a flashy show of being holy.
There's a vast difference, so it seems to me,
Between true piety and hypocrisy:
How do you fail to see it, may I ask?   75
Is not a face quite different from a mask?
Cannot sincerity and cunning art,
Reality and semblance, be told apart?
Are scarecrows just like men, and do you hold
That a false coin is just as good as gold?   80
Ah, Brother, man's a strangely fashioned creature
Who seldom is content to follow Nature,
But recklessly pursues his inclination
Beyond the narrow bounds of moderation,
And often, by transgressing Reason's laws,   85
Perverts a lofty aim or noble cause.
A passing observation, but it applies.

ORGON   I see, dear Brother, that you're profoundly wise;
You harbor all the insight of the age.

1. In the *Golden Legend* (*Legenda sanctorum*), a popular collection of the lives of the saints written in the thirteenth century, it is said of St. Marcarius the Elder (d. 390) that he dwelt naked in the desert for six months, a penance he felt appropriate for having killed a flea.

You are our one clear mind, our only sage,   90
The era's oracle, its Cato[2] too,
And all mankind are fools compared to you.
CLÉANTE   Brother, I don't pretend to be a sage,
Nor have I all the wisdom of the age.
There's just one insight I would dare to claim: 95
I know that true and false are not the same;
And just as there is nothing I more revere
Than a soul whose faith is steadfast and sincere,
Nothing that I more cherish and admire
Than honest zeal and true religious fire,   100
So there is nothing that I find more base
Than specious piety's dishonest face—
Than these bold mountebanks, these histrios
Whose impious mummeries and hollow shows
Exploit our love of Heaven, and make a jest   105
Of all that men think holiest and best;
These calculating souls who offer prayers
Not to their Maker, but as public wares,
And seek to buy respect and reputation
With lifted eyes and sighs of exaltation;   110
These charlatans, I say, whose pilgrim souls
Proceed, by way of Heaven, toward earthly goals,
Who weep and pray and swindle and extort,
Who preach the monkish life, but haunt the court,
Who make their zeal the partner of their vice—   115
Such men are vengeful, sly, and cold as ice,
And when there is an enemy to defame
They cloak their spite in fair religion's name,
Their private spleen and malice being made
To seem a high and virtuous crusade,   120
Until, to mankind's reverent applause,
They crucify their foe in Heaven's cause.
Such knaves are all too common; yet, for the wise,
True piety isn't hard to recognize,
And, happily, these present times provide us   125
With bright examples to instruct and guide us.
Consider Ariston and Périandre;
Look at Oronte, Alcidamas, Clitandre;[3]
Their virtue is acknowledged; who could doubt it?
But you won't hear them beat the drum about it.   130
They're never ostentatious, never vain,
And their religion's moderate and humane;
It's not their way to criticize and chide:
They think censoriousness a mark of pride,
And therefore, letting others preach and rave,   135
They show, by deeds, how Christians should behave.

---

2. Roman statesman (95–46 B.C.) with an enduring reputation for honesty and incorruptibility.
3. Vaguely Greek and Roman names derived from the elegant literature of the day.

They think no evil of their fellow man,
But judge of him as kindly as they can.
They don't intrigue and wangle and conspire;
To lead a good life is their one desire;   140
The sinner wakes no rancorous hate in them;
It is the sin alone which they condemn;
Nor do they try to show a fiercer zeal
For Heaven's cause than Heaven itself could feel.
These men I honor, these men I advocate   145
As models for us all to emulate.
Your man is not their sort at all, I fear:
And, while your praise of him is quite sincere,
I think that you've been dreadfully deluded.

ORGON   Now then, dear Brother, is your speech concluded?   150
CLÉANTE   Why, yes.
ORGON   Your servant, Sir.
       [*He turns to go.*]
CLÉANTE   No, Brother; wait.
There's one more matter. You agreed of late
That young Valère might have your daughter's hand.
ORGON   I did.
CLÉANTE   And set the date, I understand.
ORGON   Quite so.
CLÉANTE   You've now postponed it; is that true?   155
ORGON   No doubt.
CLÉANTE   The match no longer pleases you?
ORGON   Who knows?
CLÉANTE   D'you mean to go back on your word?
ORGON   I won't say that.
CLÉANTE   Has anything occurred
Which might entitle you to break your pledge?
ORGON   Perhaps.
CLÉANTE   Why must you hem, and haw, and hedge?   160
The boy asked me to sound you in this affair . . .
ORGON   It's been a pleasure.
CLÉANTE   But what shall I tell Valère?
ORGON   Whatever you like.
CLÉANTE   But what have you decided?
What are your plans?
ORGON   I plan, Sir, to be guided
By Heaven's will.
CLÉANTE   Come, Brother, don't talk rot.   165
You've given Valère your word; will you keep it, or not?
ORGON   Good day.
CLÉANTE   This looks like poor Valère's undoing;
I'll go and warn him that there's trouble brewing.

Act II

SCENE 1

ORGON, MARIANE

ORGON   Mariane.
MARIANE   Yes, Father?
ORGON   A word with you; come here.
MARIANE   What are you looking for?
ORGON [*Peering into a small closet.*]   Eavesdroppers, dear.
  I'm making sure we shan't be overheard.
  Someone in there could catch our every word.
  Ah, good, we're safe. Now, Mariane, my child,   5
  You're a sweet girl who's tractable and mild,
  Whom I hold dear, and think most highly of.
MARIANE   I'm deeply grateful, Father, for your love.
ORGON   That's well said, Daughter; and you can repay me
  If, in all things, you'll cheerfully obey me.   10
MARIANE   To please you, Sir, is what delights me best.
ORGON   Good, good. Now, what d'you think of Tartuffe, our guest?
MARIANE   I, Sir?
ORGON   Yes. Weigh your answer; think it through.
MARIANE   Oh, dear. I'll say whatever you wish me to.
ORGON   That's wisely said, my Daughter. Say of him, then,   15
  That he's the very worthiest of men,
  And that you're fond of him, and would rejoice
  In being his wife, if that should be my choice.
  Well?
MARIANE   What?
ORGON   What's that?
MARIANE   I . . .
ORGON   Well?
MARIANE   Forgive me, pray.
ORGON   Did you not hear me?
MARIANE   Of *whom*, Sir, must I say   20
  That I am fond of him, and would rejoice
  In being his wife, if that should be your choice?
ORGON   Why, of Tartuffe.
MARIANE   But, Father, that's false, you know.
  Why would you have me say what isn't so?
ORGON   Because I am resolved it shall be true.   25
  That it's my wish should be enough for you.
MARIANE   You can't mean, Father . . .
ORGON   Yes, Tartuffe shall be
  Allied by marriage[4] to this family,

---

4. This assertion is important and more than a mere device in the plot of the day. The second *placet*, or petition, insists that Tartuffe be costumed as a layman, and Orgon's plan for him to marry again asserts Tartuffe's position in the laity. In the 1664 version of the play Tartuffe had been dressed in a cassock, suggesting the priesthood, and Molière was now anxious to avoid any suggestion of this kind.

And he's to be your husband, is that clear?
It's a father's privilege . . .   30

SCENE 2

DORINE, ORGON, MARIANE

ORGON [*To* DORINE.]   What are you doing in here?
  Is curiosity so fierce a passion
  With you, that you must eavesdrop in this fashion?
DORINE There's lately been a rumor going about—
  Based on some hunch or chance remark, no doubt—   5
  That you mean Mariane to wed Tartuffe.
  I've laughed it off, of course, as just a spoof.
ORGON You find it so incredible?
DORINE   Yes, I do.
  I won't accept that story, even from you.
ORGON Well, you'll believe it when the thing is done.   10
DORINE Yes, yes, of course. Go on and have your fun.
ORGON I've never been more serious in my life.
DORINE Ha!
ORGON   Daughter, I mean it; you're to be his wife.
DORINE No, don't believe your father; it's all a hoax.
ORGON See here, young woman . . .
DORINE   Come, Sir, no more jokes;   15
  You can't fool us.
ORGON   How dare you talk that way?
DORINE All right, then: we believe you, sad to say.
  But how a man like you, who looks so wise
  And wears a moustache of such splendid size,
  Can be so foolish as to . . .
ORGON   Silence, please!   20
  My girl, you take too many liberties.
  I'm master here, as you must not forget.
DORINE Do let's discuss this calmly; don't be upset.
  You can't be serious, Sir, about this plan.
  What should that bigot want with Mariane?   25
  Praying and fasting ought to keep him busy.
  And then, in terms of wealth and rank, what is he?
  Why should a man of property like you
  Pick out a beggar son-in-law?
ORGON   That will do.
  Speak of his poverty with reverence.   30
  His is a pure and saintly indigence
  Which far transcends all worldly pride and pelf.
  He lost his fortune, as he says himself,
  Because he cared for Heaven alone, and so
  Was careless of his interests here below.   35
  I mean to get him out of his present straits
  And help him to recover his estates—
  Which, in his part of the world, have no small fame.

Poor though he is, he's a gentleman just the same.
DORINE   Yes, so he tells us; and, Sir, it seems to me   40
Such pride goes very ill with piety.
A man whose spirit spurns this dungy earth
Ought not to brag of lands and noble birth;
Such worldly arrogance will hardly square
With meek devotion and the life of prayer.   45
. . . But this approach, I see, has drawn a blank;
Let's speak, then, of his person, not his rank.
Doesn't it seem to you a trifle grim
To give a girl like her to a man like him?
When two are so ill-suited, can't you see   50
What the sad consequence is bound to be?
A young girl's virtue is imperilled, Sir,
When such a marriage is imposed on her;
For if one's bridegroom isn't to one's taste,
It's hardly an inducement to be chaste,   55
And many a man with horns upon his brow
Has made his wife the thing that she is now.
It's hard to be a faithful wife, in short,
To certain husbands of a certain sort,
And he who gives his daughter to a man she hates   60
Must answer for her sins at Heaven's gates.
Think, Sir, before you play so risky a role.
ORGON   This servant-girl presumes to save my soul!
DORINE   You would do well to ponder what I've said.
ORGON   Daughter, we'll disregard this dunderhead.   65
Just trust your father's judgment. Oh, I'm aware
That I once promised you to young Valère;
But now I hear he gambles, which greatly shocks me;
What's more, I've doubts about his orthodoxy.
His visits to church, I note, are very few.   70
DORINE   Would you have him go at the same hours as you,
And kneel nearby, to be sure of being seen?
ORGON   I can dispense with such remarks, Dorine.
[*To* MARIANE.] Tartuffe, however, is sure of Heaven's blessing.
And that's the only treasure worth possessing.   75
This match will bring you joys beyond all measure;
Your cup will overflow with every pleasure;
You two will interchange your faithful loves
Like two sweet cherubs, or two turtle-doves.
No harsh word shall be heard, no frown be seen,   80
And he shall make you happy as a queen.
DORINE   And she'll make him a cuckold, just wait and see.
ORGON   What language!
DORINE   Oh, he's a man of destiny;
He's *made* for horns, and what the stars demand
Your daughter's virtue surely can't withstand.   85
ORGON   Don't interrupt me further. Why can't you learn
That certain things are none of your concern?

DORINE   It's for your own sake that I interfere.
     [*She repeatedly interrupts* ORGON *just as he is turning to speak to*
     his daughter.]
ORGON   Most kind of you. Now, hold your tongue, d'you hear?
DORINE   If I didn't love you . . .
ORGON   Spare me your affection.   90
DORINE   I'll love you, Sir, in spite of your objection.
ORGON   Blast!
DORINE   I can't bear, Sir, for your honor's sake,
     To let you make this ludicrous mistake.
ORGON   You mean to go on talking?
DORINE   If I didn't protest
     This sinful marriage, my conscience couldn't rest.   95
ORGON   If you don't hold your tongue, you little shrew . . .
DORINE   What, lost your temper? A pious man like you?
ORGON   Yes! Yes! You talk and talk. I'm maddened by it.
     Once and for all, I tell you to be quiet.
DORINE   Well, I'll be quiet. But I'll be thinking hard.   100
ORGON   Think all you like, but you had better guard
     That saucy tongue of yours, or I'll . . .
     [*Turning back to* MARIANE.]   Now, child,
     I've weighed this matter fully.
DORINE [*Aside.*]   It drives me wild
     That I can't speak.
          [ORGON *turns his head, and she is silent.*]
ORGON   Tartuffe is no young dandy,
     But, still, his person . . .
DORINE [*Aside.*]   Is as sweet as candy.   105
ORGON   Is such that, even if you shouldn't care
     For his other merits . . .
          [*He turns and stands facing* DORINE, *arms crossed.*]
DORINE [*Aside.*]   They'll make a lovely pair.
     If I were she, no man would marry me
     Against my inclination, and go scot-free.
     He'd learn, before the wedding-day was over,   110
     How readily a wife can find a lover.
ORGON [*To* DORINE.]   It seems you treat my orders as a joke.
DORINE   Why, what's the matter? 'Twas not to you I spoke.
ORGON   What *were* you doing?
DORINE   Talking to myself, that's all.
ORGON   Ah! [*Aside.*] One more bit of impudence and gall,   115
     And I shall give her a good slap in the face.
          [*He puts himself in position to slap her;* DORINE, *whenever he*
          glances at her, stands immobile and silent.]
     Daughter, you shall accept, and with good grace,
     The husband I've selected . . . Your wedding-day . . .
     [*To* DORINE.] Why don't you talk to yourself?
DORINE   I've nothing to say.
ORGON   Come, just one word.
DORINE   No thank you, Sir. I pass.   120

ORGON   Come, speak; I'm waiting.
DORINE   I'd not be such an ass.
ORGON [*Turning to* MARIANE.]
  In short, dear Daughter, I mean to be obeyed,
  And you must bow to the sound choice I've made.
DORINE [*Moving away.*]   I'd not wed such a monster, even in jest.
        [ORGON *attempts to slap her, but misses.*]
ORGON   Daughter, that maid of yours is a thorough pest;   125
  She makes me sinfully annoyed and nettled.
  I can't speak further; my nerves are too unsettled.
  She's so upset me by her insolent talk,
  I'll calm myself by going for a walk.

                    SCENE 3

                DORINE, MARIANE

DORINE [*Returning.*]   Well, have you lost your tongue, girl? Must I play
  Your part, and say the lines you ought to say?
  Faced with a fate so hideous and absurd,
  Can you not utter one dissenting word?
MARIANE   What good would it do? A father's power is great.   5
DORINE   Resist him now, or it will be too late.
MARIANE   But . . .
DORINE   Tell him one cannot love at a father's whim;
  That you shall marry for yourself, not him;
  That since it's you who are to be the bride,
  It's you, not he, who must be satisfied;   10
  And that if his Tartuffe is so sublime,
  He's free to marry him at any time.
MARIANE   I've bowed so long to Father's strict control,
  I couldn't oppose him now, to save my soul.
DORINE   Come, come, Mariane. Do listen to reason, won't you?   15
  Valère has asked your hand. Do you love him, or don't you?
MARIANE   Oh, how unjust of you! What can you mean
  By asking such a question, dear Dorine?
  You know the depth of my affection for him;
  I've told you a hundred times how I adore him.   20
DORINE   I don't believe in everything I hear;
  Who knows if your professions were sincere?
MARIANE   They were, Dorine, and you do me wrong to doubt it;
  Heaven knows that I've been all too frank about it.
DORINE   You love him, then?
MARIANE   Oh, more than I can express.   25
DORINE   And he, I take it, cares for you no less?
MARIANE   I think so.
DORINE   And you both, with equal fire,
  Burn to be married?
MARIANE   That is our one desire.
DORINE   What of Tartuffe, then? What of your father's plan?
MARIANE   I'll kill myself, if I'm forced to wed that man.   30

DORINE   I hadn't thought of that recourse. How splendid!
  Just die, and all your troubles will be ended!
  A fine solution. Oh, it maddens me
  To hear you talk in that self-pitying key.
MARIANE   Dorine, how harsh you are! It's most unfair.   35
  You have no sympathy for my despair.
DORINE   I've none at all for people who talk drivel
  And, faced with difficulties, whine and snivel.
MARIANE   No doubt I'm timid, but it would be wrong . . .
DORINE   True love requires a heart that's firm and strong.   40
MARIANE   I'm strong in my affection for Valère,
  But coping with my father is his affair.
DORINE   But if your father's brain has grown so cracked
  Over his dear Tartuffe that he can retract
  His blessing, though your wedding-day was named,   45
  It's surely not Valère who's to be blamed.
MARIANE   If I defied my father, as you suggest,
  Would it not seem unmaidenly, at best?
  Shall I defend my love at the expense
  Of brazenness and disobedience?   50
  Shall I parade my heart's desires, and flaunt . . .
DORINE   No, I ask nothing of you. Clearly you want
  To be Madame Tartuffe, and I feel bound
  Not to oppose a wish so very sound.
  What right have I to criticize the match?   55
  Indeed, my dear, the man's a brilliant catch.
  Monsieur Tartuffe! Now, there's a man of weight!
  Yes, yes, Monsieur Tartuffe, I'm bound to state,
  Is quite a person; that's not to be denied;
  'Twill be no little thing to be his bride.   60
  The world already rings with his renown;
  He's a great noble—in his native town;
  His ears are red, he has a pink complexion,
  And all in all, he'll suit you to perfection.
MARIANE   Dear God!
DORINE   Oh, how triumphant you will feel   65
  At having caught a husband so ideal!
MARIANE   Oh, do stop teasing, and use your cleverness
  To get me out of this appalling mess.
  Advise me, and I'll do whatever you say.
DORINE   Ah, no, a dutiful daughter must obey   70
  Her father, even if he weds her to an ape.
  You've a bright future; why struggle to escape?
  Tartuffe will take you back where his family lives,
  To a small town aswarm with relatives—
  Uncles and cousins whom you'll be charmed to meet.   75
  You'll be received at once by the elite,
  Calling upon the bailiff's⁵ wife, no less—

5. A high-ranking official in the judiciary, not simply a sheriff's deputy as today.

Even, perhaps, upon the mayoress,[6]
Who'll sit you down in the *best* kitchen chair.[7]
Then, once a year, you'll dance at the village fair   80
To the drone of bagpipes—two of them, in fact—
And see a puppet-show, or an animal act.[8]
Your husband . . .
MARIANE   Oh, you turn my blood to ice!
Stop torturing me, and give me your advice.
DORINE [*Threatening to go.*]
Your servant, Madam.
MARIANE.   Dorine, I beg of you . . .   85
DORINE   No, you deserve it; this marriage must go through.
MARIANE   Dorine!
DORINE   No.
MARIANE   Not Tartuffe! You know I think him . . .
DORINE   Tartuffe's your cup of tea, and you shall drink him.
MARIANE   I've always told you everything, and relied . . .
DORINE   No. You deserve to be tartuffified.   90
MARIANE   Well, since you mock me and refuse to care,
I'll henceforth seek my solace in despair:
Despair shall be my counsellor and friend,
And help me bring my sorrows to an end.[*She starts to leave.*]
DORINE   There now, come back; my anger has subsided.   95
You do deserve some pity, I've decided.
MARIANE   Dorine, if Father makes me undergo
This dreadful martyrdom, I'll die, I know.
DORINE   Don't fret; it won't be difficult to discover
Some plan of action . . . But here's Valère, your lover.   100

SCENE 4

VALÈRE, MARIANE, DORINE

VALÈRE   Madam, I've just received some wondrous news
Regarding which I'd like to hear your views.
MARIANE   What news?
VALÈRE   You're marrying Tartuffe.
MARIANE   I find
That Father does have such a match in mind.
VALÈRE   Your father, Madam . . .
MARIANE   . . . has just this minute said   5
That it's Tartuffe he wishes me to wed.
VALÈRE   Can he be serious?
MARIANE   Oh, indeed he can;
He's clearly set his heart upon the plan.
VALÈRE   And what position do you propose to take,
Madam?

6. The wife of a tax collector (*élue*), an important official controlling imports, elected by the Estates General.   7. In elegant society of Molière's day, there was a hierarchy of seats, and the use of each was determined by rank. The seats descended from *fauteuils* to *chaises, perroquets, tabourets,* and *pliants.* Thus Mariane would get the lowest seat in the room.   8. In the original, *fagotin,* literally "a monkey dressed up in a man's clothing."

MARIANE Why—I don't know.
VALÈRE   For heaven's sake—   10
  You don't know?
MARIANE   No.
VALÈRE   Well, well!
MARIANE   Advise me, do.
VALÈRE Marry the man. That's my advice to you.
MARIANE That's your advice?
VALÈRE   Yes.
MARIANE   Truly?
VALÈRE   Oh, absolutely.
  You couldn't choose more wisely, more astutely.
MARIANE Thanks for this counsel; I'll follow it, of course.   15
VALÈRE Do, do; I'm sure 'twill cost you no remorse.
MARIANE To give it didn't cause your heart to break.
VALÈRE I gave it, Madam, only for your sake.
MARIANE And it's for your sake that I take it, Sir.
DORINE [Withdrawing to the rear of the stage.]
  Let's see which fool will prove the stubborner.   20
VALÈRE So! I am nothing to you, and it was flat
  Deception when you . . .
MARIANE   Please, enough of that.
  You've told me plainly that I should agree
  To wed the man my father's chosen for me,
  And since you've deigned to counsel me so wisely,   25
  I promise, Sir, to do as you advise me.
VALÈRE Ah, no, 'twas not by me that you were swayed.
  No, your decision was already made;
  Though now, to save appearances, you protest
  That you're betraying me at my behest.   30
MARIANE Just as you say.
VALÈRE   Quite so. And I now see
  That you were never truly in love with me.
MARIANE Alas, you're free to think so if you choose.
VALÈRE I choose to think so, and here's a bit of news:
  You've spurned my hand, but I know where to turn   35
  For kinder treatment, as you shall quickly learn.
MARIANE I'm sure you do. Your noble qualities
  Inspire affection . . .
VALÈRE   Forget my qualities, please.
  They don't inspire you overmuch, I find.
  But there's another lady I have in mind   40
  Whose sweet and generous nature will not scorn
  To compensate me for the loss I've borne.
MARIANE I'm no great loss, and I'm sure that you'll transfer
  Your heart quite painlessly from me to her.
VALÈRE I'll do my best to take it in my stride.   45
  The pain I feel at being cast aside
  Time and forgetfulness may put an end to.
  Or if I can't forget, I shall pretend to.

No self-respecting person is expected
To go on loving once he's been rejected.   50
MARIANE   Now, that's a fine, high-minded sentiment.
VALÈRE   One to which any sane man would assent.
Would you prefer it if I pined away
In hopeless passion till my dying day?
Am I to yield you to a rival's arms   55
And not console myself with other charms?
MARIANE   Go then; console yourself; don't hesitate.
I wish you to; indeed, I cannot wait.
VALÈRE   You wish me to?
MARIANE   Yes.
VALÈRE   That's the final straw.
Madam, farewell. Your wish shall be my law.   60
      [*He starts to leave, and then returns: this repeatedly.*]
MARIANE   Splendid.
VALÈRE [*Coming back again.*]   This breach, remember, is of your making;
It's you who've driven me to the step I'm taking.
MARIANE   Of course.
VALÈRE [*Coming back again.*]   Remember, too, that I am merely
Following your example.
MARIANE   I see that clearly.
VALÈRE   Enough. I'll go and do your bidding, then.   65
MARIANE   Good.
VALÈRE [*Coming back again.*]   You shall never see my face again.
MARIANE   Excellent.
VALÈRE [*Walking to the door, then turning about.*]
                  Yes?
MARIANE   What?
VALÈRE   What's that? What did you say?
MARIANE   Nothing. You're dreaming.
VALÈRE   Ah. Well, I'm on my way.
Farewell, Madame.
      [*He moves slowly away.*]
MARIANE   Farewell.
DORINE [*To* MARIANE.]   If you ask me,
Both of you are as mad as mad can be.   70
Do stop this nonsense, now. I've only let you
Squabble so long to see where it would get you.
Whoa there, Monsieur Valère!
      [*She goes and seizes* VALÈRE *by the arm; he makes a great show of
      resistance.*]
VALÈRE   What's this, Dorine?
DORINE   Come here.
VALÈRE   No, no, my heart's too full of spleen.
Don't hold me back; her wish must be obeyed.   75
DORINE   Stop!
VALÈRE   It's too late now; my decision's made.
DORINE   Oh, pooh!
MARIANE [*Aside.*]   He hates the sight of me, that's plain.

I'll go, and so deliver him from pain.

DORINE [*Leaving* VALÈRE, *running after* MARIANE.]
    And now *you* run away! Come back.

MARIANE   No, no
    Nothing you say will keep me here. Let go!   80

VALÈRE [*Aside.*]   She cannot bear my presence, I perceive.
    To spare her further torment, I shall leave.

DORINE [*Leaving* MARIANE, *running after* VALÈRE.]
    Again! You'll not escape, Sir; don't you try it.
    Come here, you two. Stop fussing and be quiet.
        [*She takes* VALÈRE *by the hand, then* MARIANE, *and draws them together.*]

VALÈRE [*To* DORINE.]   What do you want of me?   85

MARIANE [*To* DORINE.]   What is the point of this?

DORINE   We're going to have a little armistice.
    [*To* VALÈRE.] Now, weren't you silly to get so overheated?

VALÈRE   Didn't you see how badly I was treated?

DORINE [*To* MARIANE.]   Aren't you a simpleton, to have lost your
    head?   90

MARIANE   Didn't you hear the hateful things he said?

DORINE [*To* VALÈRE.]   You're both great fools. Her sole desire, Valère,
    Is to be yours in marriage. To that I'll swear.
    [*To* MARIANE.] He loves you only, and he wants no wife
    But you, Mariane. On that I'll stake my life.   95

MARIANE [*To* VALÈRE.]   Then why you advised me so, I cannot see.

VALÈRE [*To* MARIANE.]   On such a question, why ask advice of *me?*

DORINE   Oh, you're impossible. Give me your hands, you two.
    [*To* VALÈRE.] Yours first.

VALÈRE [*Giving* DORINE *his hand.*]   But why?

DORINE [*To* MARIANE.]   And now a hand from you.   100

MARIANE [*Also giving* DORINE *her hand.*]
    What are you doing?

DORINE   There: a perfect fit.
    You suit each other better than you'll admit.
        [VALÈRE *and* MARIANE *hold hands for some time without looking at each other.*]

VALÈRE [*Turning toward* MARIANE.]
    Ah, come, don't be so haughty. Give a man
    A look of kindness, won't you, Mariane?
        [MARIANE *turns toward* VALÈRE *and smiles.*]

DORINE   I tell you, lovers are completely mad!   105

VALÈRE [*To* MARIANE.]   Now come, confess that you were very bad
    To hurt my feelings as you did just now.
    I have a just complaint, you must allow.

MARIANE   *You* must allow that you were most unpleasant . . .

DORINE   Let's table that discussion for the present;   110
    Your father has a plan which must be stopped.

MARIANE   Advise us, then; what means must we adopt?

DORINE   We'll use all manner of means, and all at once.
    [*To* MARIANE.] Your father's addled; he's acting like a dunce.

Therefore you'd better humor the old fossil.   115
Pretend to yield to him, be sweet and docile,
And then postpone, as often as necessary,
The day on which you have agreed to marry.
You'll thus gain time, and time will turn the trick.
Sometimes, for instance, you'll be taken sick,   120
And that will seem good reason for delay;
Or some bad omen will make you change the day—
You'll dream of muddy water, or you'll pass
A dead man's hearse, or break a looking-glass.
If all else fails, no man can marry you   125
Unless you take his ring and say "I do."
But now, let's separate. If they should find
Us talking here, our plot might be divined.
[*To* VALÈRE.] Go to your friends, and tell them what's occurred,
And have them urge her father to keep his word.   130
Meanwhile, we'll stir her brother into action,
And get Elmire,[9] as well, to join our faction.
Good-bye.
VALÈRE [*To* MARIANE.]   Though each of us will do his best,
It's your true heart on which my hopes shall rest.   135
MARIANE [*To* VALÈRE.]   Regardless of what Father may decide,
None but Valère shall claim me as his bride.
VALÈRE   Oh, how those words content me! Come what will . . .
DORINE   Oh, lovers, lovers! Their tongues are never still.
Be off, now.
VALÈRE [*Turning to go, then turning back.*]
        One last word . . .
DORINE   No time to chat: 140
You leave by this door; and *you* leave by that.
    [DORINE *pushes them, by the shoulders, toward opposing doors.*]

Act III

SCENE 1

DAMIS, DORINE

DAMIS   May lightning strike me even as I speak,
May all men call me cowardly and weak,
If any fear or scruple holds me back
From settling things, at once, with that great quack!
DORINE   Now, don't give way to violent emotion.   5
Your father's merely talked about this notion,
And words and deeds are far from being one.
Much that is talked about is never done.
DAMIS   No, I must stop that scoundrel's machinations;

---

9. Orgon's second wife.

I'll go and tell him off; I'm out of patience.   10
DORINE   Do calm down and be practical. I had rather
  My mistress dealt with him—and with your father.
  She has some influence with Tartuffe, I've noted.
  He hangs upon her words, seems most devoted,
  And may, indeed, be smitten by her charm.   15
  Pray Heaven it's true! 'Twould do our cause no harm.
  She sent for him, just now, to sound him out
  On this affair you're so incensed about;
  She'll find out where he stands, and tell him, too,
  What dreadful strife and trouble will ensue   20
  If he lends countenance to your father's plan.
  I couldn't get in to see him, but his man
  Says that he's almost finished with his prayers.
  Go, now. I'll catch him when he comes downstairs.
DAMIS   I want to hear this conference, and I will.   25
DORINE   No, they must be alone.
DAMIS   Oh, I'll keep still.
DORINE   Not you. I know your temper. You'd start a brawl,
  And shout and stamp your foot and spoil it all.
  Go on.
DAMIS   I won't; I have a perfect right . . .
DORINE   Lord, you're a nuisance! He's coming; get out of sight.   30
  [DAMIS *conceals himself in a closet at the rear of the stage.*]

SCENE 2

TARTUFFE, DORINE

TARTUFFE [*Observing* DORINE, *and calling to his manservant off-stage.*]
  Hang up my hair-shirt, put my scourge in place,
  And pray, Laurent, for Heaven's perpetual grace.
  I'm going to the prison now, to share
  My last few coins with the poor wretches there.
DORINE [*Aside.*]   Dear God, what affectation! What a fake!   5
TARTUFFE   You wished to see me?
DORINE   Yes . . .
TARTUFFE [*Taking a handkerchief from his pocket.*]
                             For mercy's sake,
  Please take this handkerchief, before you speak.
DORINE   What?
TARTUFFE   Cover that bosom,[1] girl. The flesh is weak.
  And unclean thoughts are difficult to control.
  Such sights as that can undermine the soul.   10
DORINE   Your soul, it seems, has very poor defenses,
  And flesh makes quite an impact on your senses.
  It's strange that you're so easily excited;
  My own desires are not so soon ignited,

---

1. The Brotherhood of the Holy Sacrament practiced alms giving to prisoners and kept a careful, censorious check on women's clothing if they deemed it lascivious. Thus Molière's audience would have identified Tartuffe as sympathetic—hypocritically—to the aims of the organization.

And if I saw you naked as a beast, 15
  Not all your hide would tempt me in the least.
TARTUFFE Girl, speak more modestly; unless you do,
  I shall be forced to take my leave of you.
DORINE Oh, no, it's I who must be on my way;
  I've just one little message to convey. 20
  Madame is coming down, and begs you, Sir,
  To wait and have a word or two with her.
TARTUFFE Gladly.
DORINE [*Aside.*]   *That* had a softening effect!
  I think my guess about him was correct.
TARTUFFE Will she be long?
DORINE   No: that's her step I hear. 25
  Ah, here she is, and I shall disappear.

SCENE 3

ELMIRE, TARTUFFE

TARTUFFE May Heaven, whose infinite goodness we adore,
  Preserve your body and soul forevermore,
  And bless your days, and answer thus the plea
  Of one who is its humblest votary.
ELMIRE I thank you for that pious wish. But please, 5
  Do take a chair and let's be more at ease.
        [*They sit down.*]
TARTUFFE I trust that you are once more well and strong?
ELMIRE Oh, yes: the fever didn't last for long.
TARTUFFE My prayers are too unworthy, I am sure,
  To have gained from Heaven this most gracious cure; 10
  But lately, Madam, my every supplication
  Has had for object your recuperation.
ELMIRE You shouldn't have troubled so. I don't deserve it.
TARTUFFE Your health is priceless, Madam, and to preserve it
  I'd gladly give my own, in all sincerity. 15
ELMIRE Sir, you outdo us all in Christian charity.
  You've been most kind. I count myself your debtor.
TARTUFFE 'Twas nothing, Madam. I long to serve you better.
ELMIRE There's a private matter I'm anxious to discuss.
  I'm glad there's no one here to hinder us. 20
TARTUFFE I too am glad; it floods my heart with bliss
  To find myself alone with you like this.
  For just this chance I've prayed with all my power—
  But prayed in vain, until this happy hour.
ELMIRE This won't take long, Sir, and I hope you'll be 25
  Entirely frank and unconstrained with me.
TARTUFFE Indeed, there's nothing I had rather do
  Than bare my inmost heart and soul to you.
  First, let me say that what remarks I've made
  About the constant visits you are paid 30
  Were prompted not by any mean emotion,

But rather by a pure and deep devotion,
A fervent zeal . . .
ELMIRE   No need for explanation.
Your sole concern, I'm sure, was my salvation.
TARTUFFE [*Taking* ELMIRE's *hand and pressing her fingertips.*]
Quite so; and such great fervor do I feel . . .   35
ELMIRE   Ooh! Please! You're pinching!
TARTUFFE   'Twas from excess of zeal.
I never meant to cause you pain, I swear.
I'd rather . . .
     [*He places his hand on* ELMIRE's *knee.*]
ELMIRE   What can your hand be doing there?
TARTUFFE   Feeling your gown: what soft, fine-woven stuff!
ELMIRE   Please, I'm extremely ticklish. That's enough.   40
     [*She draws her chair away;* TARTUFFE *pulls his after her.*]
TARTUFFE [*Fondling the lace collar of her gown.*]
My, my, what lovely lacework on your dress!
The workmanship's miraculous, no less.
I've not seen anything to equal it.
ELMIRE   Yes, quite. But let's talk business for a bit.
They say my husband means to break his word   45
And give his daughter to you, Sir. Had you heard?
TARTUFFE   He did once mention it. But I confess
I dream of quite a different happiness.
It's elsewhere, Madam, that my eyes discern
The promise of that bliss for which I yearn.   50
ELMIRE   I see: you care for nothing here below.
TARTUFFE   Ah, well—my heart's not made of stone, you know.
ELMIRE   All your desires mount heavenward, I'm sure,
In scorn of all that's earthly and impure.
TARTUFFE   A love of heavenly beauty does not preclude   55
A proper love for earthly pulchritude;
Our senses are quite rightly captivated
By perfect works our Maker has created.
Some glory clings to all that Heaven has made;
In you, all Heaven's marvels are displayed.   60
On that fair face, such beauties have been lavished,
The eyes are dazzled and the heart is ravished;
How could I look on you, O flawless creature,
And not adore the Author of all Nature,
Feeling a love both passionate and pure   65
For you, his triumph of self-portraiture?
At first, I trembled lest that love should be
A subtle snare that Hell had laid for me;
I vowed to flee the sight of you, eschewing
A rapture that might prove my soul's undoing;   70
But soon, fair being, I became aware
That my deep passion could be made to square
With rectitude, and with my bounden duty,
I thereupon surrendered to your beauty.

It is, I know, presumptuous on my part   75
To bring you this poor offering of my heart,
And it is not my merit, Heaven knows,
But your compassion on which my hopes repose.
You are my peace, my solace, my salvation;
On you depends my bliss—or desolation;   80
I bide your judgment and, as you think best,
I shall be either miserable or blest.

ELMIRE   Your declaration is most gallant, Sir,
But don't you think it's out of character?
You'd have done better to restrain your passion   85
And think before you spoke in such a fashion.
It ill becomes a pious man like you . . .

TARTUFFE   I may be pious, but I'm human too:
With your celestial charms before his eyes,
A man has not the power to be wise.   90
I know such words sound strangely, coming from me,
But I'm no angel, nor was meant to be,
And if you blame my passion, you must needs
Reproach as well the charms on which it feeds.
Your loveliness I had no sooner seen   95
Than you became my soul's unrivalled queen;
Before your seraph glance, divinely sweet,
My heart's defenses crumbled in defeat,
And nothing fasting, prayer, or tears might do
Could stay my spirit from adoring you.   100
My eyes, my sighs have told you in the past
What now my lips make bold to say at last,
And if, in your great goodness, you will deign
To look upon your slave, and ease his pain,—
If, in compassion for my soul's distress,   105
You'll stoop to comfort my unworthiness,
I'll raise to you, in thanks for that sweet manna,
An endless hymn, an infinite hosanna.
With me, of course, there need be no anxiety,
No fear of scandal or of notoriety.   110
These young court gallants, whom all the ladies fancy,
Are vain in speech, in action rash and chancy;
When they succeed in love, the world soon knows it;
No favor's granted them but they disclose it
And by the looseness of their tongues profane   115
The very altar where their hearts have lain.
Men of my sort, however, love discreetly,
And one may trust our reticence completely.
My keen concern for my good name insures
The absolute security of yours;   120
In short, I offer you, my dear Elmire,
Love without scandal, pleasure without fear.

ELMIRE   I've heard your well-turned speeches to the end,
And what you urge I clearly apprehend.

Aren't you afraid that I may take a notion   125
To tell my husband of your warm devotion,
And that, supposing he were duly told,
His feelings toward you might grow rather cold?

TARTUFFE   I know, dear lady, that your exceeding charity
Will lead your heart to pardon my temerity;   130
That you'll excuse my violent affection
As human weakness, human imperfection;
And that—O fairest!—you will bear in mind
That I'm but flesh and blood, and am not blind.

ELMIRE   Some women might do otherwise, perhaps,   135
But I shall be discreet about your lapse;
I'll tell my husband nothing of what's occurred
If, in return, you'll give your solemn word
To advocate as forcefully as you can
The marriage of Valère and Mariane,   140
Renouncing all desire to dispossess
Another of his rightful happiness,
And . . .

SCENE 4

DAMIS, ELMIRE, TARTUFFE

DAMIS [*Emerging from the closet where he has been hiding.*]
                No! We'll not hush up this vile affair;
I heard it all inside that closet there,
Where Heaven, in order to confound the pride
Of this great rascal, prompted me to hide.
Ah, now I have my long-awaited chance   5
To punish his deceit and arrogance,
And give my father clear and shocking proof
Of the black character of his dear Tartuffe.

ELMIRE   Ah no, Damis; I'll be content if he
Will study to deserve my leniency.   10
I've promised silence—don't make me break my word;
To make a scandal would be too absurd.
Good wives laugh off such trifles, and forget them;
Why should they tell their husbands, and upset them?

DAMIS   You have your reasons for taking such a course,   15
And I have reasons, too, of equal force.
To spare him now would be insanely wrong.
I've swallowed my just wrath for far too long
And watched this insolent bigot bringing strife
And bitterness into our family life.   20
Too long he's meddled in my father's affairs,
Thwarting my marriage-hopes, and poor Valère's.
It's high time that my father was undeceived,
And now I've proof that can't be disbelieved—
Proof that was furnished me by Heaven above.   25
It's too good not to take advantage of.

This is my chance, and I deserve to lose it
If, for one moment, I hesitate to use it.
ELMIRE   Damis . . .
DAMIS   No, I must do what I think right.
Madam, my heart is bursting with delight,   30
And, say whatever you will, I'll not consent
To lose the sweet revenge on which I'm bent.
I'll settle matters without more ado;
And here, most opportunely, is my cue.[2]

SCENE 5

ORGON, DAMIS, TARTUFFE, ELMIRE

DAMIS   Father, I'm glad you've joined us. Let us advise you
Of some fresh news which doubtless will surprise you.
You've just now been repaid with interest
For all your loving-kindness to our guest.
He's proved his warm and grateful feelings toward you;   5
It's with a pair of horns he would reward you.
Yes, I surprised him with your wife, and heard
His whole adulterous offer, every word.
She, with her all too gentle disposition,
Would not have told you of his proposition;   10
But I shall not make terms with brazen lechery,
And feel that not to tell you would be treachery.
ELMIRE   And I hold that one's husband's peace of mind
Should not be spoilt by tattle of this kind.
One's honor doesn't require it: to be proficient   15
In keeping men at bay is quite sufficient.
These are my sentiments, and I wish, Damis,
That you had heeded me and held your peace.

SCENE 6

ORGON, DAMIS, TARTUFFE

ORGON   Can it be true, this dreadful thing I hear?
TARTUFFE   Yes, Brother, I'm a wicked man, I fear:
A wretched sinner, all depraved and twisted,
The greatest villain that has ever existed.
My life's one heap of crimes, which grows each minute;   5
There's naught but foulness and corruption in it;
And I perceive that Heaven, outraged by me,
Has chosen this occasion to mortify me.
Charge me with any deed you wish to name;
I'll not defend myself, but take the blame.   10
Believe what you are told, and drive Tartuffe

2. In the original stage directions, Tartuffe now reads silently from his breviary—in the Roman Catholic Church, the book containing the Divine Office for each day, which those in holy orders are required to recite.

Like some base criminal from beneath your roof;
Yes, drive me hence, and with a parting curse:
I shan't protest, for I deserve far worse.

ORGON [*To* DAMIS.]   Ah, you deceitful boy, how dare you try   15
To stain his purity with so foul a lie?

DAMIS   What! Are you taken in by such a fluff?
Did you not hear . . . ?

ORGON   Enough, you rogue, enough!

TARTUFFE   Ah, Brother, let him speak: you're being unjust.
Believe his story; the boy deserves your trust.   20
Why, after all, should you have faith in me?
How can you know what I might do, or be?
Is it on my good actions that you base
Your favor? Do you trust my pious face?
Ah, no, don't be deceived by hollow shows;   25
I'm far, alas, from being what men suppose;
Though the world takes me for a man of worth,
I'm truly the most worthless man on earth.
[*To* DAMIS] Yes, my dear son, speak out now: call me the chief
Of sinners, a wretch, a murderer, a thief;   30
Load me with all the names men most abhor;
I'll not complain; I've earned them all, and more;
I'll kneel here while you pour them on my head
As a just punishment for the life I've led.

ORGON [*To* TARTUFFE]
This is too much, dear Brother.
[*To* DAMIS.]   Have you no heart?   35

DAMIS   Are you so hoodwinked by this rascal's art . . . ?

ORGON   Be still, you monster.
[*To* TARTUFFE.]   Brother, I pray you, rise.
[*To* DAMIS.] Villain!

DAMIS: But . . .

ORGON   Silence!

DAMIS   Can't you realize . . . ?

ORGON   Just one word more, and I'll tear you limb from limb.

TARTUFFE   In God's name, Brother, don't be harsh with him.   40
I'd rather far be tortured at the stake
Than see him bear one scratch for my poor sake.

ORGON [*To* DAMIS.]   Ingrate!

TARTUFFE   If I must beg you, on bended knee,
To pardon him . . .

ORGON [*Falling to his knees, addressing* TARTUFFE
                         Such goodness cannot be!
[*To* DAMIS.] Now, *there's* true charity!

DAMIS   What, you . . . ?

ORGON   Villain, be still!   45
I know your motives; I know you wish him ill:
Yes, all of you—wife, children, servants, all—
Conspire against him and desire his fall,
Employing every shameful trick you can

To alienate me from this saintly man.   50
Ah, but the more you seek to drive him away,
The more I'll do to keep him. Without delay,
I'll spite this household and confound its pride
By giving him my daughter as his bride.
DAMIS   You're going to force her to accept his hand?   55
ORGON   Yes, and this very night, d'you understand?
I shall defy you all, and make it clear
That I'm the one who gives the orders here.
Come, wretch, kneel down and clasp his blessed feet,
And ask his pardon for your black deceit.   60
DAMIS   I ask that swindler's pardon? Why, I'd rather . . .
ORGON   So! You insult him, and defy your father!
A stick! A stick! [*To* TARTUFFE.] No, no—release me, do.
[*To* DAMIS.] Out of my house this minute! Be off with you,
And never dare set foot in it again.   65
DAMIS   Well, I shall go, but . . .
ORGON   Well, go quickly, then.
I disinherit you; an empty purse
Is all you'll get from me—except my curse!

SCENE 7

ORGON, TARTUFFE

ORGON   How he blasphemed your goodness! What a son!
TARTUFFE   Forgive him, Lord, as I've already done.
[*To* ORGON.] You can't know how it hurts when someone tries
To blacken me in my dear brother's eyes.
ORGON   Ahh!
TARTUFFE   The mere thought of such ingratitude   5
Plunges my soul into so dark a mood . . .
Such horror grips my heart . . . I gasp for breath,
And cannot speak, and feel myself near death.
ORGON [*He runs, in tears, to the door through which he has just driven
      his son.*]
You blackguard! Why did I spare you? Why did I not
Break you in little pieces on the spot?   10
Compose yourself, and don't be hurt, dear friend.
TARTUFFE   These scenes, these dreadful quarrels, have got to end.
I've much upset your household, and I perceive
That the best thing will be for me to leave.
ORGON   What are you saying!
TARTUFFE   They're all against me here;   15
They'd have you think me false and insincere.
ORGON   Ah, what of that? Have I ceased believing in you?
TARTUFFE   Their adverse talk will certainly continue,
And charges which you now repudiate
You may find credible at a later date.   20
ORGON   No, Brother, never.
TARTUFFE   Brother, a wife can sway

Her husband's mind in many a subtle way.
ORGON   No, no.
TARTUFFE   To leave at once is the solution;
   Thus only can I end their persecution.
ORGON   No, no, I'll not allow it; you shall remain.   25
TARTUFFE   Ah, well; 'twill mean much martyrdom and pain,
   But if you wish it . . .
ORGON   Ah!
TARTUFFE   Enough; so be it.
   But one thing must be settled, as I see it.
   For your dear honor, and for our friendship's sake,
   There's one precaution I feel bound to take.   30
   I shall avoid your wife, and keep away . . .
ORGON   No, you shall not, whatever they may say.
   It pleases me to vex them, and for spite
   I'd have them see you with her day and night.
   What's more, I'm going to drive them to despair   35
   By making you my only son and heir;
   This very day, I'll give to you alone
   Clear deed and title to everything I own.
   A dear, good friend and son-in-law-to-be
   Is more than wife, or child, or kin to me.   40
   Will you accept my offer, dearest son?
TARTUFFE   In all things, let the will of Heaven be done.
ORGON   Poor fellow! Come, we'll go draw up the deed.
   Then let them burst with disappointed greed!

Act IV

SCENE 1

CLÉANTE, TARTUFFE

CLÉANTE   Yes, all the town's discussing it, and truly,
   Their comments do not flatter you unduly.
   I'm glad we've met, Sir, and I'll give my view
   Of this sad matter in a word or two.
   As for who's guilty, that I shan't discuss;   5
   Let's say it was Damis who caused the fuss;
   Assuming, then, that you have been ill-used
   By young Damis, and groundlessly accused,
   Ought not a Christian to forgive, and ought
   He not to stifle every vengeful thought?   10
   Should you stand by and watch a father make
   His only son an exile for your sake?
   Again I tell you frankly, be advised:
   The whole town, high and low, is scandalized;
   This quarrel must be mended, and my advice is   15
   Not to push matters to a further crisis.

No, sacrifice your wrath to God above,
And help Damis regain his father's love.
TARTUFFE   Alas, for my part I should take great joy
In doing so. I've nothing against the boy.   20
I pardon all, I harbor no resentment;
To serve him would afford me much contentment.
But Heaven's interest will not have it so:
If he comes back, then I shall have to go.
After his conduct—so extreme, so vicious—   25
Our further intercourse would look suspicious.
God knows what people would think! Why, they'd describe
My goodness to him as a sort of bribe;
They'd say that out of guilt I made pretense
Of loving-kindness and benevolence—   30
That, fearing my accuser's tongue, I strove
To buy his silence with a show of love.
CLÉANTE   Your reasoning is badly warped and stretched,
And these excuses, Sir, are most far-fetched.
Why put yourself in charge of Heaven's cause?   35
Does Heaven need our help to enforce its laws?
Leave vengeance to the Lord, Sir; while we live,
Our duty's not to punish, but forgive;
And what the Lord commands, we should obey
Without regard to what the world may say.   40
What! Shall the fear of being misunderstood
Prevent our doing what is right and good?
No, no: let's simply do what Heaven ordains,
And let no other thoughts perplex our brains.
TARTUFFE   Again, Sir, let me say that I've forgiven   45
Damis, and thus obeyed the laws of Heaven;
But I am not commanded by the Bible
To live with one who smears my name with libel.
CLÉANTE   Were you commanded, Sir, to indulge the whim
Of poor Orgon, and to encourage him   50
In suddenly transferring to your name
A large estate to which you have no claim?
TARTUFFE   'Twould never occur to those who know me best
To think I acted from self-interest.
The treasures of this world I quite despise;   55
Their specious glitter does not charm my eyes;
And if I have resigned myself to taking
The gift which my dear Brother insists on making,
I do so only, as he well understands,
Lest so much wealth fall into wicked hands,   60
Lest those to whom it might descend in time
Turn it to purposes of sin and crime,
And not, as I shall do, make use of it
For Heaven's glory and mankind's benefit.
CLÉANTE   Forget these trumped-up fears. Your argument   65
Is one the rightful heir might well resent;

It *is* a moral burden to inherit
Such wealth, but give Damis a chance to bear it.
And would it not be worse to be accused
Of swindling, than to see that wealth misused?   70
I'm shocked that you allowed Orgon to broach
This matter, and that you feel no self-reproach;
Does true religion teach that lawful heirs
May freely be deprived of what is theirs?
And if the Lord has told you in your heart   75
That you and young Damis must dwell apart,
Would it not be the decent thing to beat
A generous and honorable retreat,
Rather than let the son of the house be sent,
For your convenience, into banishment?   80
Sir, if you wish to prove the honesty
Of your intentions . . .

TARTUFFE   Sir, it is a half past three.
I've certain pious duties to attend to,
And hope my prompt departure won't offend you.

CLÉANTE [*Alone.*]   Damn.

SCENE 2

ELMIRE, MARIANE, CLÉANTE, DORINE

DORINE   Stay, Sir, and help Mariane, for Heaven's sake!
She's suffering so, I fear her heart will break.
Her father's plan to marry her off tonight
Has put the poor child in a desperate plight.
I hear him coming. Let's stand together, now,   5
And see if we can't change his mind, somehow,
About this match we all deplore and fear.

SCENE 3

ORGON, ELMIRE, MARIANE, CLÉANTE, DORINE

ORGON   Hah! Glad to find you all assembled here.
[*To* MARIANE.] This contract, child, contains your happiness,
And what it says I think your heart can guess.

MARIANE [*Falling to her knees.*]
Sir, by that Heaven which sees me here distressed,
And by whatever else can move your breast,   5
Do not employ a father's power, I pray you,
To crush my heart and force it to obey you,
Nor by your harsh commands oppress me so
That I'll begrudge the duty which I owe—
And do not so embitter and enslave me   10
That I shall hate the very life you gave me.
If my sweet hopes must perish, if you refuse
To give me to the one I've dared to choose,
Spare me at least—I beg you, I implore—

The pain of wedding one whom I abhor;   15
And do not, by a heartless use of force,
Drive me to contemplate some desperate course.
ORGON [*Feeling himself touched by her.*]
    Be firm, my soul. No human weakness, now.
MARIANE   I don't resent your love for him. Allow
    Your heart free rein, Sir; give him your property,   20
    And if that's not enough, take mine from me;
    He's welcome to my money; take it, do,
    But don't, I pray, include my person too.
    Spare me, I beg you; and let me end the tale
    Of my sad days behind a convent veil.   25
ORGON   A convent! Hah! When crossed in their amours,
    All lovesick girls have the same thought as yours.
    Get up! The more you loathe the man, and dread him,
    The more ennobling it will be to wed him.
    Marry Tartuffe, and mortify your flesh!   30
    Enough; don't start that whimpering afresh.
DORINE   But why . . . ?
ORGON   Be still, there. Speak when you're spoken to.
    Not one more bit of impudence out of you.
CLÉANTE   If I may offer a word of counsel here . . .
ORGON   Brother, in counselling you have no peer;   35
    All your advice is forceful, sound, and clever;
    I don't propose to follow it, however.
ELMIRE [*To* ORGON.]   I am amazed, and don't know what to say;
    Your blindness simply takes my breath away.
    You are indeed bewitched, to take no warning   40
    From our account of what occurred this morning.
ORGON   Madam, I know a few plain facts, and one
    Is that you're partial to my rascal son;
    Hence, when he sought to make Tartuffe the victim
    Of a base lie, you dared not contradict him.   45
    Ah, but you underplayed your part, my pet;
    You should have looked more angry, more upset.
ELMIRE   When men make overtures, must we reply
    With righteous anger and a battle-cry?
    Must we turn back their amorous advances   50
    With sharp reproaches and with fiery glances?
    Myself, I find such offers merely amusing,
    And make no scenes and fusses in refusing;
    My taste is for good-natured rectitude,
    And I dislike the savage sort of prude   55
    Who guards her virtue with her teeth and claws,
    And tears men's eyes out for the slightest cause:
    The Lord preserve me from such honor as that,
    Which bites and scratches like an alley-cat!
    I've found that a polite and cool rebuff   60
    Discourages a lover quite enough.
ORGON   I know the facts, and I shall not be shaken.

ELMIRE   I marvel at your power to be mistaken.
   Would it, I wonder, carry weight with you
   If I could *show* you that our tale was true?   65
ORGON   Show me?
ELMIRE   Yes.
ORGON   Rot.
ELMIRE   Come, what if I found a way
   To make you see the facts as plain as day?
ORGON   Nonsense.
ELMIRE   Do answer me; don't be absurd.
   I'm not now asking you to trust our word.
   Suppose that from some hiding-place in here   70
   You learned the whole sad truth by eye and ear—
   What would you say of your good friend, after that?
ORGON   Why, I'd say . . . nothing, by Jehoshaphat!
   It can't be true.
ELMIRE   You've been too long deceived,
   I'm quite tired of being disbelieved.   75
   Come now: let's put my statements to the test,
   And you shall see the truth made manifest.
ORGON   I'll take that challenge. Now do your uttermost.
   We'll see how you make good your empty boast.
ELMIRE [*To* DORINE.]   Send him to me.
DORINE   He's crafty; it may be hard   80
   To catch the cunning scoundrel off his guard.
ELMIRE   No, amorous men are gullible. Their conceit
   So blinds them that they're never hard to cheat.
   Have him come down.
   [*To* CLÉANTE *and* MARIANE.] Please leave us, for a bit.

SCENE 4

ELMIRE, ORGON

ELMIRE   Pull up this table, and get under it.
ORGON   What?
ELMIRE   It's essential that you be well-hidden.
ORGON   Why there?
ELMIRE   Oh, Heavens! Just do as you are bidden.
   I have my plans; we'll soon see how they fare.
   Under the table, now; and once you're there,   5
   Take care that you are neither seen nor heard.
ORGON   Well, I'll indulge you, since I gave my word
   To see you through this infantile charade.
ELMIRE   Once it is over, you'll be glad we played.
      [*To her husband, who is now under the table.*]
   I'm going to act quite strangely, now, and you   10
   Must not be shocked at anything I do.
   Whatever I may say, you must excuse
   As part of that deceit I'm forced to use.
   I shall employ sweet speeches in the task

Of making that impostor drop his mask;   15
I'll give encouragement to his bold desires,
And furnish fuel to his amorous fires.
Since it's for your sake, and for his destruction,
That I shall seem to yield to his seduction,
I'll gladly stop whenever you decide   20
That all your doubts are fully satisfied.
I'll count on you, as soon as you have seen
What sort of man he is, to intervene,
And not expose me to his odious lust
One moment longer than you feel you must.   25
Remember: you're to save me from my plight
Whenever . . . He's coming! Hush! Keep out of sight!

SCENE 5

TARTUFFE, ELMIRE, ORGON

TARTUFFE   You wish to have a word with me, I'm told.
ELMIRE   Yes, I've a little secret to unfold.
Before I speak, however, it would be wise
To close that door, and look about for spies.
            [TARTUFFE *goes to the door, closes it, and returns.*]
The very last thing that must happen now   5
Is a repetition of this morning's row.
I've never been so badly caught off guard.
Oh, how I feared for you! You saw how hard
I tried to make that troublesome Damis
Control his dreadful temper, and hold his peace.   10
In my confusion, I didn't have the sense
Simply to contradict his evidence;
But as it happened, that was for the best,
And all has worked out in our interest.
This storm has only bettered your position;   15
My husband doesn't have the least suspicion,
And now, in mockery of those who do,
He bids me be continually with you.
And that is why, quite fearless of reproof,
I now can be alone with my Tartuffe,   20
And why my heart—perhaps too quick to yield—
Feels free to let its passion be revealed.
TARTUFFE   Madam, your words confuse me. Not long ago,
You spoke in quite a different style, you know.
ELMIRE   Ah, Sir, if that refusal made you smart,   25
It's little that you know of woman's heart,
Or what that heart is trying to convey
When it resists in such a feeble way!
Always, at first, our modesty prevents
The frank avowal of tender sentiments: 30
However high the passion which inflames us,
Still, to confess its power somehow shames us.

Thus we reluct, at first, yet in a tone
Which tells you that our heart is overthrown,
That what our lips deny, our pulse confesses,   35
And that, in time, all noes will turn to yesses.
I fear my words are all too frank and free,
And a poor proof of woman's modesty;
But since I'm started, tell me, if you will—
Would I have tried to make Damis be still,   40
Would I have listened, calm and unoffended,
Until your lengthy offer of love was ended,
And been so very mild in my reaction,
Had your sweet words not given me satisfaction?
And when I tried to force you to undo   45
The marriage-plans my husband has in view,
What did my urgent pleading signify
If not that I admired you, and that I
Deplored the thought that someone else might own
Part of a heart I wished for mine alone?   50
TARTUFFE   Madam, no happiness is so complete
As when, from lips we love, come words so sweet;
Their nectar floods my every sense, and drains
In honeyed rivulets through all my veins.
To please you is my joy, my only goal;   55
Your love is the restorer of my soul;
And yet I must beg leave, now, to confess
Some lingering doubts as to my happiness.
Might this not be a trick? Might not the catch
Be that you wish me to break off the match   60
With Mariane, and so have feigned to love me?
I shan't quite trust your fond opinion of me
Until the feelings you've expressed so sweetly
Are demonstrated somewhat more concretely,
And you have shown, by certain kind concessions,   65
That I may put my faith in your professions
ELMIRE [*She coughs, to warn her husband.*]
Why be in such a hurry? Must my heart
Exhaust its bounty at the very start?
To make that sweet admission cost me dear,
But you'll not be content, it would appear,   70
Unless my store of favors is disbursed
To the last farthing, and at the very first.
TARTUFFE   The less we merit, the less we dare to hope,
And with our doubts, mere words can never cope.
We trust no promised bliss till we receive it;   75
Not till a joy is ours can we believe it.
I, who so little merit your esteem,
Can't credit this fulfillment of my dream,
And shan't believe it, Madam, until I savor
Some palpable assurance of your favor.   80
ELMIRE   My, how tyrannical your love can be,

And how it flusters and perplexes me!
How furiously you take one's heart in hand,
And make your every wish a fierce command!
Come, must you hound and harry me to death?   85
Will you not give me time to catch my breath?
Can it be right to press me with such force,
Give me no quarter, show me no remorse,
And take advantage, by your stern insistence,
Of the fond feelings which weaken my resistance?   90
TARTUFFE   Well, if you look with favor upon my love,
Why, then, begrudge me some clear proof thereof?
ELMIRE   But how can I consent without offense
To Heaven, toward which you feel such reverence?
TARTUFFE   If Heaven is all that holds you back, don't worry. 95
I can remove that hindrance in a hurry.
Nothing of that sort need obstruct our path.
ELMIRE   Must one not be afraid of Heaven's wrath?
TARTUFFE   Madam, forget such fears, and be my pupil,
And I shall teach you how to conquer scruple.   100
Some joys, it's true, are wrong in Heaven's eyes;
Yet Heaven is not averse to compromise;
There is a science, lately formulated,
Whereby one's conscience may be liberated,[3]
And any wrongful act you care to mention   105
May be redeemed by purity of intention.
I'll teach you, Madam, the secrets of that science;
Meanwhile, just place on me your full reliance.
Assuage my keen desires, and feel no dread:
The sin, if any, shall be on my head.   110
        [ELMIRE *coughs, this time more loudly.*]
You've a bad cough.
ELMIRE   Yes, yes, It's bad indeed.
TARTUFFE [*Producing a little paper bag.*]
    A bit of licorice may be what you need.
ELMIRE   No, I've a stubborn cold, it seems. I'm sure it
Will take much more than licorice to cure it.
TARTUFFE   How aggravating.
ELMIRE   Oh, more than I can say.   115
TARTUFFE   If you're still troubled, think of things this way:
No one shall know our joys, save us alone,
And there's no evil till the act is known;
It's scandal, Madam, which makes it an offense,
And it's no sin to sin in confidence.   120
ELMIRE [*Having coughed once more.*]
    Well, clearly I must do as you require,
And yield to your importunate desire.
It is apparent, now, that nothing less
Will satisfy you, and so I acquiesce.

---

3. Molière created his own footnote to this line: "It is a scoundrel who speaks."

To go so far is much against my will;   125
I'm vexed that it should come to this; but still,
Since you are so determined on it, since you
Will not allow mere language to convince you,
And since you ask for concrete evidence, I
See nothing for it, now, but to comply.   130
If this is sinful, if I'm wrong to do it,
So much the worse for him who drove me to it.
The fault can surely not be charged to me.
TARTUFFE   Madam, the fault is mine, if fault there be,
And . . .
ELMIRE   Open the door a little, and peek out;   135
I wouldn't want my husband poking about.
TARTUFFE   Why worry about the man? Each day he grows
More gullible; one can lead him by the nose.
To find us here would fill him with delight,
And if he saw the worst, he'd doubt his sight.   140
ELMIRE   Nevertheless, do step out for a minute
Into the hall, and see that no one's in it.

SCENE 6

ORGON, ELMIRE

ORGON [*Coming out from under the table.*]
That man's a perfect monster, I must admit!
I'm simply stunned. I can't get over it.
ELMIRE   What, coming out so soon? How premature!
Get back in hiding, and wait until you're sure.
Stay till the end, and be convinced completely;   5
We mustn't stop till things are proved concretely.
ORGON   Hell never harbored anything so vicious!
ELMIRE   Tut, don't be hasty. Try to be judicious.
Wait, and be certain that there's no mistake.
No jumping to conclusions, for Heaven's sake!   10
[*She places* ORGON *behind her, as* TARTUFFE *re-enters.*]

SCENE 7

TARTUFFE, ELMIRE, ORGON

TARTUFFE [*Not seeing* ORGON.]
Madam, all things have worked out to perfection;
I've given the neighboring rooms a full inspection;
No one's about; and now I may at last . . .
ORGON [*Intercepting him.*]   Hold on, my passionate fellow, not so fast!
I should advise a little more restraint.   5
Well, so you thought you'd fool me, my dear saint!
How soon you wearied of the saintly life—
Wedding my daughter, and coveting my wife!
I've long suspected you, and had a feeling
That soon I'd catch you at your double-dealing.   10

Just now, you've given me evidence galore;
  It's quite enough; I have no wish for more.
ELMIRE [*To* TARTUFFE.]   I'm sorry to have treated you so slyly,
  But circumstances forced me to be wily.
TARTUFFE Brother, you can't think . . .
ORGON   No more talk from you;   15
  Just leave this household, without more ado.
TARTUFFE What I intended . . .
ORGON   That seems fairly clear.
  Spare me your falsehoods and get out of here.
TARTUFFE No, I'm the master, and you're the one to go!
  This house belongs to me, I'll have you know,   20
  And I shall show you that you can't hurt *me*
  By this contemptible conspiracy,
  That those who cross me know not what they do,
  And that I've means to expose and punish you,
  Avenge offended Heaven, and make you grieve   25
  That ever you dared order me to leave.

SCENE 8

ELMIRE, ORGON

ELMIRE What was the point of all that angry chatter?
ORGON Dear God, I'm worried. This is no laughing matter.
ELMIRE How so?
ORGON   I fear I understood his drift.
  I'm much disturbed about that deed of gift.
ELMIRE You gave him . . . ?
ORGON   Yes, it's all been drawn and signed.   5
  But one thing more is weighing on my mind.
ELMIRE What's that?
ORGON   I'll tell you; but first let's see if there's
  A certain strong-box in his room upstairs.

Act V

SCENE 1

ORGON, CLÉANTE

CLÉANTE Where are you going so fast?
ORGON   God knows!
CLÉANTE   Then wait;
  Let's have a conference, and deliberate
  On how this situation's to be met.
ORGON That strong-box has me utterly upset;
  This is the worst of many, many shocks.   5
CLÉANTE Is there some fearful mystery in that box?
ORGON My poor friend Argas brought that box to me

With his own hands, in utmost secrecy;
'Twas on the very morning of his flight.
It's full of papers which, if they came to light,   10
Would ruin him—or such is my impression.
CLÉANTE   Then why did you let it out of your possession?
ORGON   Those papers vexed my conscience, and it seemed best
  To ask the counsel of my pious guest.
  The cunning scoundrel got me to agree   15
  To leave the strong-box in his custody,
  So that, in case of an investigation,
  I could employ a slight equivocation
  And swear I didn't have it, and thereby,
  At no expense to conscience, tell a lie.   20
CLÉANTE   It looks to me as if you're out on a limb.
  Trusting him with that box, and offering him
  That deed of gift, were actions of a kind
  Which scarcely indicate a prudent mind.
  With two such weapons, he has the upper hand,   25
  And since you're vulnerable, as matters stand,
  You erred once more in bringing him to bay.
  You should have acted in some subtler way.
ORGON   Just think of it: behind that fervent face,
  A heart so wicked, and a soul so base!   30
  I took him in, a hungry beggar, and then . . .
  Enough, by God! I'm through with pious men:
  Henceforth I'll hate the whole false brotherhood,
  And persecute them worse than Satan could.
CLÉANTE   Ah, there you go—extravagant as ever!   35
  Why can you not be rational? You never
  Manage to take the middle course, it seems,
  But jump, instead, between absurd extremes.
  You've recognized your recent grave mistake
  In falling victim to a pious fake;   40
  Now, to correct that error, must you embrace
  An even greater error in its place,
  And judge our worthy neighbors as a whole
  By what you've learned of one corrupted soul?
  Come, just because one rascal made you swallow   45
  A show of zeal which turned out to be hollow,
  Shall you conclude that all men are deceivers,
  And that, today, there are no true believers?
  Let atheists make that foolish inference;
  Learn to distinguish virtue from pretense,   50
  Be cautious in bestowing admiration,
  And cultivate a sober moderation.
  Don't humor fraud, but also don't asperse
  True piety; the latter fault is worse,
  And it is best to err, if err one must,   55
  As you have done, upon the side of trust.

SCENE 2

DAMIS, ORGON, CLÉANTE

DAMIS Father, I hear that scoundrel's uttered threats
 Against you; that he pridefully forgets
 How, in his need, he was befriended by you,
 And means to use your gifts to crucify you.
ORGON It's true, my boy. I'm too distressed for tears. 5
DAMIS Leave it to me, Sir; let me trim his ears.
 Faced with such insolence, we must not waver.
 I shall rejoice in doing you the favor
 Of cutting short his life, and your distress.
CLÉANTE What a display of young hotheadedness! 10
 Do learn to moderate your fits of rage.
 In this just kingdom, this enlightened age,
 One does not settle things by violence.

SCENE 3

MADAME PERNELLE, MARIANE, ELMIRE, DORINE, DAMIS, ORGON, CLÉANTE

MADAME PERNELLE I hear strange tales of very strange events.
ORGON Yes, strange events which these two eyes beheld.
 The man's ingratitude is unparalleled.
 I save a wretched pauper from starvation,
 House him, and treat him like a blood relation, 5
 Shower him every day with my largesse,
 Give him my daughter, and all that I possess;
 And meanwhile the unconscionable knave
 Tries to induce my wife to misbehave;
 And not content with such extreme rascality, 10
 Now threatens me with my own liberality,
 And aims, by taking base advantage of
 The gifts I gave him out of Christian love,
 To drive me from my house, a ruined man,
 And make me end a pauper, as he began. 15
DORINE Poor fellow!
MADAME PERNELLE No, my son, I'll never bring
 Myself to think him guilty of such a thing.
ORGON How's that?
MADAME PERNELLE The righteous always were maligned.
ORGON Speak clearly, Mother. Say what's on your mind. 20
MADAME PERNELLE I mean that I can smell a rat, my dear.
 You know how everybody hates him, here.
ORGON That has no bearing on the case at all.
MADAME PERNELLE I told you a hundred times, when you were small,
 That virtue in this world is hated ever; 25
 Malicious men may die, but malice never.
ORGON No doubt that's true, but how does it apply?

MADAME PERNELLE   They've turned you against him by a clever lie.
ORGON   I've told you, I was there and saw it done.
MADAME PERNELLE   Ah, slanderers will stop at nothing, Son.   30
ORGON   Mother, I'll lose my temper . . . For the last time,
  I tell you I was witness to the crime.
MADAME PERNELLE   The tongues of spite are busy night and noon,
  And to their venom no man is immune.
ORGON   You're talking nonsense. Can't you realize   35
  I saw it; saw it; saw it with my eyes?
  Saw, do you understand me? Must I shout it
  Into your ears before you'll cease to doubt it?
MADAME PERNELLE   Appearances can deceive, my son. Dear me,
  We cannot always judge by what we see.   40
ORGON   Drat! Drat!
MADAME PERNELLE   One often interprets things awry;
  Good can seem evil to a suspicious eye.
ORGON   Was I to see his pawing at Elmire
  As an act of charity?
MADAME PERNELLE   Till his guilt is clear,   45
  A man deserves the benefit of the doubt.
  You should have waited, to see how things turned out.
ORGON   Great God in Heaven, what more proof did I need?
  Was I to sit there, watching, until he'd . . .
  You drive me to the brink of impropriety.   50
MADAME PERNELLE   No, no, a man of such surpassing piety
  Could not do such a thing. You cannot shake me.
  I don't believe it, and you shall not make me.
ORGON   You vex me so that, if you weren't my mother,
  I'd say to you . . . some dreadful thing or other.   55
DORINE   It's your turn now, Sir, not to be listened to;
  You'd not trust us, and now she won't trust you.
CLÉANTE   My friends, we're wasting time which should be spent
  In facing up to our predicament.
  I fear that scoundrel's threats weren't made in sport.   60
DAMIS   Do you think he'd have the nerve to go to court?
ELMIRE   I'm sure he won't: they'd find it all too crude
  A case of swindling and ingratitude.
CLÉANTE   Don't be too sure. He won't be at a loss
  To give his claims a high and righteous gloss;   65
  And clever rogues with far less valid cause
  Have trapped their victims in a web of laws.
  I say again that to antagonize
  A man so strongly armed was most unwise.
ORGON   I know it; but the man's appalling cheek   70
  Outraged me so, I couldn't control my pique.
CLÉANTE   I wish to Heaven that we could devise
  Some truce between you, or some compromise.
ELMIRE   If I had known what cards he held, I'd not
  Have roused his anger by my little plot.   75
ORGON [To DORINE, as M. LOYAL enters.]

What is that fellow looking for? Who is he?
Go talk to him—and tell him that I'm busy.

SCENE 4

MONSIEUR LOYAL, MADAME PERNELLE, ORGON, DAMIS, MARIANE, DORINE,
ELMIRE, CLÉANTE

MONSIEUR LOYAL   Good day, dear sister. Kindly let me see
Your master.
DORINE   He's involved with company,
And cannot be disturbed just now, I fear.
MONSIEUR LOYAL   I hate to intrude; but what has brought me here
Will not disturb your master, in any event.   5
Indeed, my news will make him most content.
DORINE   Your name?
MONSIEUR LOYAL   Just say that I bring greetings from
Monsieur Tartuffe, on whose behalf I've come.
DORINE [To ORGON.]   Sir, he's a very gracious man, and bears
A message from Tartuffe, which, he declares,   10
Will make you most content.
CLÉANTE   Upon my word,
I think this man had best be seen, and heard.
ORGON   Perhaps he has some settlement to suggest.
How shall I treat him? What manner would be best?
CLÉANTE   Control your anger, and if he should mention   15
Some fair adjustment, give him your full attention.
MONSIEUR LOYAL   Good health to you, good Sir. May Heaven confound
Your enemies, and may your joys abound.
ORGON [Aside, to CLÉANTE.]   A gentle salutation: it confirms
My guess that he is here to offer terms.   20
MONSIEUR LOYAL   I've always held your family most dear;
I served your father, Sir, for many a year.
ORGON   Sir, I must ask your pardon; to my shame,
I cannot now recall your face or name.
MONSIEUR LOYAL   Loyal's my name; I come from Normandy,   25
And I'm a bailiff, in all modesty.
For forty years, praise God, it's been my boast
To serve with honor in that vital post,
And I am here, Sir, if you will permit
The liberty, to serve you with this writ   30
ORGON   To—what?
MONSIEUR LOYAL   Now, please, Sir, let us have no friction:
It's nothing but an order of eviction.
You are to move your goods and family out
And make way for new occupants, without
Deferment or delay, and give the keys ...   35
ORGON   I? Leave this house?
MONSIEUR LOYAL   Why yes, Sir, if you please.
This house, Sir, from the cellar to the roof,
Belongs now to the good Monsieur Tartuffe,

And he is lord and master of your estate
By virtue of a deed of present date,   40
Drawn in due form, with clearest legal phrasing . . .

DAMIS   Your insolence is utterly amazing!

MONSIEUR LOYAL   Young man, my business here is not with you
  But with your wise and temperate father, who,
  Like every worthy citizen, stands in awe   45
  Of justice, and would never obstruct the law.

ORGON   But . . .

MONSIEUR LOYAL   Not for a million, Sir, would you rebel
  Against authority; I know that well.
  You'll not make trouble, Sir, or interfere
  With the execution of my duties here.   50

DAMIS   Someone may execute a smart tattoo
  On that black jacket[4] of yours, before you're through.

MONSIEUR LOYAL   Sir, bid your son be silent. I'd much regret
  Having to mention such a nasty threat
  Of violence, in writing my report.   55

DORINE [Aside.]   This man Loyal's a most disloyal sort!

MONSIEUR LOYAL   I love all men of upright character,
  And when I agreed to serve these papers, Sir,
  It was your feelings that I had in mind.
  I couldn't bear to see the case assigned   60
  To someone else, who might esteem you less
  And so subject you to unpleasantness.

ORGON   What's more unpleasant than telling a man to leave
  His house and home?

MONSIEUR LOYAL   You'd like a short reprieve?
  If you desire it, Sir, I shall not press you,   65
  But wait until tomorrow to dispossess you.
  Splendid. I'll come and spend the night here, then,
  Most quietly, with half a score of men.
  For form's sake, you might bring me, just before
  You go to bed, the keys to the front door.   70
  My men, I promise, will be on their best
  Behavior, and will not disturb your rest.
  But bright and early, Sir, you must be quick
  And move out all your furniture, every stick:
  The men I've chosen are both young and strong,   75
  And with their help it shouldn't take you long.
  In short, I'll make things pleasant and convenient,
  And since I'm being so extremely lenient,
  Please show me, Sir, a like consideration,
  And give me your entire cooperation.   80

ORGON [Aside.]   I may be all but bankrupt, but I vow
  I'd give a hundred louis, here and now,
  Just for the pleasure of landing one good clout

---

4. In the original, *justaucorps à longues basques,* a close-fitting, long black coat with skirts, the customary
dress of a bailiff.

Right on the end of that complacent snout.
CLÉANTE   Careful; don't make things worse.
DAMIS   My bootsole itches   85
  To give that beggar a good kick in the breeches.
DORINE   Monsieur Loyal, I'd love to hear the whack
  Of a stout stick across your fine broad back.
MONSIEUR LOYAL   Take care: a woman too may go to jail if
  She uses threatening language to a bailiff.   90
CLÉANTE   Enough, enough, Sir. This must not go on.
  Give me that paper, please, and then begone.
MONSIEUR LOYAL   Well, *au revoir*. God give you all good cheer!
ORGON   May God confound you, and him who sent you here!

SCENE 5

ORGON, CLÉANTE, MARIANE, ELMIRE, MADAME PERNELLE, DORINE, DAMIS

ORGON   Now, Mother, was I right or not? This writ
  Should change your notion of Tartuffe a bit.
  Do you perceive his villainy at last?
MADAME PERNELLE   I'm thunderstruck. I'm utterly aghast.
DORINE   Oh, come, be fair. You mustn't take offense   5
  At this new proof of his benevolence.
  He's acting out of selfless love, I know.
  Material things enslave the soul, and so
  He kindly has arranged your liberation
  From all that might endanger your salvation.   10
ORGON   Will you not ever hold your tongue, you dunce?
CLÉANTE   Come, you must take some action, and at once.
ELMIRE   Go tell the world of the low trick he's tried.
  The deed of gift is surely nullified
  By such behavior, and public rage will not   15
  Permit the wretch to carry out his plot.

SCENE 6

VALÈRE, ORGON, CLÉANTE, ELMIRE, MARIANE, MADAME PERNELLE,
DAMIS, DORINE

VALÈRE   Sir, though I hate to bring you more bad news,
  Such is the danger that I cannot choose.
  A friend who is extremely close to me
  And knows my interest in your family
  Has, for my sake, presumed to violate   5
  The secrecy that's due to things of state,
  And sends me word that you are in a plight
  From which your one salvation lies in flight.
  That scoundrel who's imposed upon you so
  Denounced you to the King an hour ago   10
  And, as supporting evidence, displayed
  The strong-box of a certain renegade
  Whose secret papers, so he testified,

You had disloyally agreed to hide.
I don't know just what charges may be pressed,   15
But there's a warrant out for your arrest;
Tartuffe has been instructed, furthermore,
To guide the arresting officer to your door.
CLÉANTE   He's clearly done this to facilitate
His seizure of your house and your estate.   20
ORGON   That man, I must say, is a vicious beast!
VALÈRE   You can't afford to delay, Sir, in the least.
My carriage is outside, to take you hence;
This thousand louis should cover all expense.
Let's lose no time, or you shall be undone;   25
The sole defense, in this case, is to run.
I shall go with you all the way, and place you
In a safe refuge to which they'll never trace you.
ORGON   Alas, dear boy, I wish that I could show you
My gratitude for everything I owe you.   30
But now is not the time; I pray the Lord
That I may live to give you your reward.
Farewell, my dears; be careful . . .
CLÉANTE   Brother, hurry.
We shall take care of things; you needn't worry.

SCENE 7

The OFFICER, TARTUFFE, VALÈRE, ORGON, ELMIRE, MARIANE,
MADAME PERNELLE, DORINE, CLÉANTE, DAMIS

TARTUFFE   Gently, Sir, gently; stay right where you are.
No need for haste; your lodging isn't far.
You're off to prison, by order of the Prince.
ORGON   This is the crowning blow, you wretch; and since
It means my total ruin and defeat,   5
Your villainy is now at last complete.
TARTUFFE   You needn't try to provoke me; it's no use.
Those who serve Heaven must expect abuse.
CLÉANTE   You are indeed most patient, sweet, and blameless.
DORINE   How he exploits the name of Heaven! It's shameless.   10
TARTUFFE   Your taunts and mockeries are all for naught;
To do my duty is my only thought.
MARIANE   Your love of duty is most meritorious,
And what you've done is little short of glorious.
TARTUFFE   All deeds are glorious, Madam, which obey   15
The sovereign prince who sent me here today.
ORGON   I rescued you when you were destitute;
Have you forgotten that, you thankless brute?
TARTUFFE   No, no, I well remember everything;
But my first duty is to serve my King.   20
That obligation is so paramount
That other claims, beside it, do not count;
And for it I would sacrifice my wife,

  My family, my friend, or my own life.
ELMIRE Hypocrite!
DORINE   All that we most revere, he uses 25
  To cloak his plots and camouflage his ruses.
CLÉANTE If it is true that you are animated
  By pure and loyal zeal, as you have stated,
  Why was this zeal not roused until you'd sought
  To make Orgon a cuckold, and been caught? 30
  Why weren't you moved to give your evidence
  Until your outraged host had driven you hence?
  I shan't say that the gift of all his treasure
  Ought to have damped your zeal in any measure;
  But if he is a traitor, as you declare, 35
  How could you condescend to be his heir?
TARTUFFE [*To the* OFFICER.]
  Sir, spare me all this clamor; it's growing shrill.
  Please carry out your orders, if you will.
OFFICER[5] Yes, I've delayed too long, Sir. Thank you kindly.
  You're just the proper person to remind me. 40
  Come, you are off to join the other boarders
  In the King's prison, according to his orders.
TARTUFFE Who? I, Sir?
OFFICER   Yes.
TARTUFFE   To prison? This can't be true!
OFFICER I owe an explanation, but not to you.
  [*To* ORGON.] Sir, all is well; rest easy, and be grateful. 45
  We serve a Prince to whom all sham is hateful,
  A Prince who sees into our inmost hearts,
  And can't be fooled by any trickster's arts.
  His royal soul, though generous and human,
  Views all things with discernment and acumen; 50
  His sovereign reason is not lightly swayed,
  And all his judgments are discreetly weighed.
  He honors righteous men of every kind,
  And yet his zeal for virtue is not blind,
  Nor does his love of piety numb his wits 55
  And make him tolerant of hypocrites.
  'Twas hardly likely that this man could cozen
  A King who's foiled such liars by the dozen.
  With one keen glance, the King perceived the whole
  Perverseness and corruption of his soul, 60
  And thus high Heaven's justice was displayed:
  Betraying you, the rogue stood self-betrayed.
  The King soon recognized Tartuffe as one
  Notorious by another name, who'd done
  So many vicious crimes that one could fill 65
  Ten volumes with them, and be writing still.

---

5. In the original, *un exempt*. He would actually have been a gentleman from the king's personal bodyguard with the rank of lieutenant colonel or "master of the camp."

But to be brief: our sovereign was appalled
By this man's treachery toward you, which he called
The last, worst villainy of a vile career,
And bade me follow the impostor here   70
To see how gross his impudence could be,
And force him to restore your property.
Your private papers, by the King's command,
I hereby seize and give into your hand.
The King, by royal order, invalidates   75
The deed which gave this rascal your estates,
And pardons, furthermore, your grave offense
In harboring an exile's documents.
By these decrees, our Prince rewards you for
Your loyal deeds in the late civil war,[6]   80
And shows how heartfelt is his satisfaction
In recompensing any worthy action,
How much he prizes merit, and how he makes
More of men's virtues than of their mistakes.

DORINE   Heaven be praised!

MADAME PERNELLE.   I breathe again, at last.   85

ELMIRE   We're safe.

MARIANE   I can't believe the danger's past.

ORGON [*To* TARTUFFE.]   Well, traitor, now you see . . .

CLÉANTE   Ah, brother, please
Let's not descend to such indignities.
Leave the poor wretch to his unhappy fate,
And don't say anything to aggravate   90
His present woes; but rather hope that he
Will soon embrace an honest piety,
And mend his ways, and by a true repentance
Move our just King to moderate his sentence.
Meanwhile, go kneel before your sovereign's throne   95
And thank him for the mercies he has shown.

ORGON   Well said: let's go at once and, gladly kneeling,
Express the gratitude which all are feeling.
Then, when that first great duty has been done,
We'll turn with pleasure to a second one,   100
And give Valère, whose love has proven so true,
The wedded happiness which is his due.

6. A reference to Orgon's role in supporting the king during the *Frondes*.

MARIE DE LA VERGNE DE LA FAYETTE
1634–1693

The Princess of Clèves, Marie de La Fayette's masterpiece, is generally agreed to be the first important French novel. Out of the psychological situation of a woman who rejects romantic love, it generates fiction of compelling interest.

The author of this singular work had an unusual career. At the age of twenty-two, Marie de la Vergne married the comte de La Fayette, who thereupon took her to one of his estates in rural Auvergne. The young woman, born in Paris, had always lived in the metropolis, where her mother and her stepfather (her father had died when she was sixteen) frequented intellectual circles on the fringe of the court. Until 1659, de La Fayette remained in the country, bearing and raising two sons; then she returned alone to Paris, where she handled some of her husband's business affairs, became hostess of an important literary salon whose frequenters included Madame de Sévigné and the duc de La Rochefoucauld, and developed friendships with important figures at court. She wrote five novels and *Memoirs of the French Court for the Years 1688 and 1689,* a historical work reporting both such public events as the English revolution that deposed James II and the private affairs of figures more or less directly connected with important happenings. She outlived her husband by thirteen years.

The Princess of Clèves, first published (anonymously) in 1678, won instantaneous popular success. Set in the sixteenth-century French court, it incorporated the names and on occasion the histories of real people; even the prince of Clèves, in this novel the heroine's husband, once actually lived (d. 1564). (In reality he never married.) However, its immediate interest, as well as its lasting appeal, depend not on its historical allusions but on its psychological profundity. At a time when virtually all French fiction took the form of long, fanciful romances, it inaugurated a new novelistic tradition of concern with character and narrative economy.

The single event in *The Princess of Clèves* that most intensely interested de La Fayette's contemporaries involved the heroine's confession to her husband of her interest in another man. The princess acknowledges her attraction to the duke of Nemours not to justify it but to ask for help in combating it. She wishes to remain a faithful wife, although many around her at court happily conduct adulterous love affairs; she yearns to retreat to the country to avoid constant anguishing temptation. Her husband finds this confession as astonishing as de La Fayette's readers did; her would-be lover, who overhears it, is equally amazed. The remarkable action calls attention to the princess's overwhelming desire to keep her integrity as a person, which her desire would destroy. At no time does she deviate significantly from her yearning after virtue.

The novelist provides a psychological history of her heroine's devotion to goodness, reporting the young woman's early relation to her mother and that mother's undeviating insistence on the importance of female chastity and fidelity. When the mother dies, the orphaned daughter incorporates more strongly than ever the doctrines her parent has taught. Her acceptance of such standards appears a form of repression: she feels no erotic passion for her devoted husband, and the narrative provides no reason to expect her to develop capacity for such feeling. When a handsome, brave, courteous, intelligent, kind, and witty aristocrat falls in love with her, when the princess realizes that she now feels that passion she has never experienced, the stage is set for a conventional conflict of love and duty. The novel renders exactly this conflict—but in ways far from conventional.

The Princess of Clèves is not, as it may seem, only a story of female self-abnegation. It is relevant to remember that the princess's lover, for his beloved's sake, gives up his chance to marry the queen of England, a bit of *male* abnegation, and an indication of the female protagonist's emotional power. The heroine suppresses erotic impulse—

or, at any rate, such impulse's expression—but she allows herself gratification compatible with her goodness: the satisfaction of the dominance she achieves by her steady withholding of response. She does not consciously experience her situation as one of mastery; the reader, however, may realize her innocent force.

The twentieth-century reader, like de La Fayette's contemporaries, finds himself or herself caught up in knotty problems of psychological interpretation. Is the princess honorable or needlessly cruel in confessing to her husband? Does she behave like a child or like a mature woman? Does she reject her lover at last out of virtue or (as she herself suggests) from fear of his eventual infidelity? Does she consolidate or yield her power by this rejection? Does she choose happiness or misery in committing herself to celibate widowhood?

The reader's problem of understanding and interpreting the protagonist duplicates the situation of characters within the fiction. In the confined social and political world here depicted, shifting sexual alliances often prefigure movements of power. Royal marriages dictate national policy; royal love affairs may have equally potent effects; the sexual arrangements of those near the throne imply political consequences. Hence the effort to understand people's sexual behavior involves, by extension, matters of public importance. For the princess herself, however, love remains an intensely personal matter, despite her full awareness of how personal meanings can enlarge themselves. The princess thinks about her virtue, her commitments, her feelings. And she thinks about how to protect those feelings from the knowledge of the avid watchers and interpreters who compose her society.

Everyone watches everyone else in the court of Henri II, where "what appears is seldom the truth." For the princess and the duke, looking at one another, in the flesh or in some form of representation, is their most fulfilling erotic activity. The duke steals a miniature of his beloved, who watches him doing so. The princess, alone in her pavilion, gazes at a painted battle scene including a depiction of the duke. Outside her window, the duke, himself unseen, watches her looking at his picture. At the edge of the park, another watcher, sent by the princess's husband, seeks to comprehend the duke's activities. This third watcher represents the social world constantly impinging on individual desire; the duke's watching, like the princess's contemplation of his image, epitomizes desire. Similarly, in a late episode (after the prince's death), the duke watches the princess from a distant window. She in turn watches his window from her own apartment, her erotic imagination aroused by the idea that her lover seeks opportunity merely to look at her. But she can allow herself no satisfaction beyond this attenuated variety. As she says proudly in her final interview with the duke, "You have seen that my feelings did not guide my actions."

The court's obsessive watching generates an atmosphere of tension. Every appearance provides matter for speculation: the colors a nobleman wears in a tournament, a letter falling out of someone's pocket, the degree of splendor with which a lady dresses for a ball. Often watchers make mistakes, which then become part of the dense social texture enveloping everyone. The princess would like to remove herself from the arena of watchers, but proper social behavior demands participation, as object or as subject.

The woman at the novel's center of interest and of power initiates little action. She provides an interesting contrast with Racine's Phaedra, also central to an imaginative work, a woman torn by passion and forever acting to disastrous effect. The princess of Clèves, more passive, only allows herself to be loved. The prince, her husband, feels intense passion for her; she keeps it alive by never reciprocating it; he dies partly of grief over her imagined infidelity. The duke who loves her wins her acknowledged love in return, but she will not marry him after her husband dies: withholding herself, she cannot become vulnerable to the possible diminution of his passion. Her beauty has the greater power over observers because she refuses to bestow it.

The princess's withholding, although she gains power from it, derives from no desire for power. On the contrary, it declares a woman's experience of powerlessness.

Her mother's urging of chastity insists on love's dangers; she explains "how insincere men are, how false and deceitful." In a society where "love was always mixed with politics, and politics with love," where "ambition and gallantry were the sole occupation of the court," the princess's self-protection is only sensible. Although *The Princess of Clèves,* like other works of its period, endorses the principle of controlling passion by reason, it also reveals the costs of such control. And it suggests awareness that actual—as opposed to ideal—social orders reflect the shape of individual passion more clearly than they declare the organizing force of reason.

The array of characters in the opening pages of *The Princess of Clèves* may seem forbidding; it is difficult for modern readers to keep them straight or to remember their connections with one another. In fact, the novel provides necessary information as it goes along, and one need not know historical facts to enjoy the fictional arrangement of them. A preliminary summary of the situation and characters specified in the first section may, however, be helpful. Henri II of France (1519–1559), known as a patron of the arts and as a brave soldier, heads the court. The queen, Catherine de Médicis (1529–1589), has less social and political power than does the king's longtime mistress, Diane de Poitiers, duchess of Valentinois (1499–1566). Also politically important is the woman usually referred to as "Madame," the king's sister, Marguerite (1525–1574). The two dominant factions at court are headed by the duke of Montmorency, constable of France (1492–1567), member of an enormously powerful family, and François de Lorraine, chevalier of Guise (d. 1562). Various marital alliances link the families of these persons with the duchess of Valentinois, to whose patronage all aspire.

The title character, the princess, and her mother are entirely fictional, but they are said to belong to the family of another historical character, the powerful François de Vendôme, vidame of Chartres (1522–1560). Both the prince, whom the protagonist marries, and Jacques de Savoie, duke of Nemours (1531–1585), whom she loves, actually existed.

The most important historical facts to keep in mind are the rivalries between the duchess of Valentinois and the queen and between the Montmorency and Guise families. The court intrigues reported in the novel mainly stem from these oppositions.

The best general introduction to de La Fayette is S. Haig's biographical and critical study, *Madame de Lafayette* (1970). M. Turnell, *The Novel in France* (1950), contains a short treatment of *The Princess of Clèves.* More sophisticated is L. Gregorio, *Order in the Court: History and Society in La Princesse de Clèves* (1986). Important recent studies include Michael Paulson, *A Critical Analysis of de La Fayette's La princesse de Clèves as a Royal Exemplary Novel* (1991), and John Campbell, *Questions of Interpretation in La Princesse de Clèves* (1996).

PRONOUNCING GLOSSARY

The following list uses common English syllables and stress accents to provide rough equivalents of selected words whose pronunciation may be unfamiliar to the general reader.

Châtelart: *sha'-te-lahr*

Chevalier de Guise: *she-vah'-lyay deu geez*

Clèves: *klev*

De La Fayette: *deu lah fai-et'*

Lignerolles: *leen-ye-rohl'*

Nemours: *neu-moor'*

Nevers: *neu-vehr'*

Orléans: *ohr-lay-onh'*

Piennes: *pee-en'*

Poitiers: *pwah-tyay'*

Randan: *rahn-dahnh'*

Savoie: *sah-vwah'*

Tournon: *toor-nohnh'*

Valentinois: *vahl-ahn-ti-nwah'*

Vendôme: *vahn-dohm'*

Vidame of Chartres: *vee-dahm' of shahr'-treu*

The Princess of Clèves[1]

Part I

There never was in France so brilliant a display of magnificence and gallantry as during the last years of the reign of Henri II. This monarch was gallant, handsome, and susceptible; although his love for Diane de Poitiers, Duchess of Valentinois, had lasted twenty years, its ardor had not diminished, as his conduct testified.

He was remarkably skilful in physical exercises, and devoted much attention to them; every day was filled with hunting and tennis, dancing, running at the ring,[2] and sports of that kind. The favorite colors and the initials of Madame de Valentinois were to be seen everywhere, and she herself used to appear dressed as richly as Mademoiselle de la Marck, her granddaughter, who was then about to be married.

The fact that the queen was there, accounted for her presence. This princess, although she had passed her first youth, was still beautiful; she was fond of splendor, magnificence, and pleasure. The king had married her while still Duke of Orléans, in the lifetime of his elder brother, the dauphin, who afterward died at Tournon, mourned as a worthy heir to the position of Francis I, his father.

The queen's ambition made her like to reign. She seemed indifferent to the king's attachment to the Duchess of Valentinois, and never betrayed any jealousy; but she was so skilled a dissembler that it was hard to discover her real feelings, and she was compelled by policy to keep the duchess near her if she wanted to see anything of the king. As for him, he liked the society of women, even of those with whom he was not at all in love. He was with the queen every day at her audience,[3] when all the most attractive lords and ladies were sure to appear.

At no court had there ever been gathered together so many lovely women and brave men. It seemed as if Nature had made an effort to show her highest beauty in the greatest lords and ladies. Madame Elisabeth of France, afterwards queen of Spain, began to show her wonderful intelligence and that unrivalled beauty which was so fatal to her. Mary Stuart, the queen of Scotland, who had just married the dauphin and was called the crown princess, or dauphiness, was faultless in mind and body. She had been brought up at the French court and had acquired all its polish; she was endowed by Nature with so strong a love for the softer graces that in spite of her youth she admired and understood them perfectly. Her mother-in-law, the queen, and Madame, the king's sister, were also fond of poetry, of comedy, and of music. The interest which King Francis I had felt in poetry and letters still prevailed in France and since the king, his son, was devoted to physical exercise, pleasures of all sorts were to be found at the court. But what rendered the court especially fine and majestic was the great number of princes and lords of exceptional merit; those I am about to name were, in their different ways, the ornament and the admiration of their age.

The King of Navarre inspired universal respect by his exalted rank and his

---

1. Translated by Thomas Sergeant Perry.   2. A court game in which men mounted on horseback competed to carry away a suspended metal ring on the point of a lance.   3. A formal gathering.

royal bearing. He excelled in the art of war; but the Duke of Guise had shown himself so strong a rival that he had often laid aside his command to enter the duke's service as a private soldier in the most dangerous battles. This duke had manifested such admirable bravery with such remarkable success that he was an object of envy to every great commander. He had many conspicuous qualities besides his personal courage,—he possessed a vast and profound intelligence, a noble, lofty mind, and equal capacity for war and affairs. His brother, the Cardinal of Lorraine, was born with an unbridled ambition, and had acquired vast learning; this he turned to his profit by using it in defence of Catholicism, which had begun to be attacked. The Chevalier de Guise, afterwards known as the Grand Prior, was loved by all; he was handsome, witty, clever, and his courage was renowned throughout Europe. The short, ill-favored body of the Prince of Condé held a great and haughty soul, and an intelligence that endeared him to even the most beautiful women. The Duke of Nevers, famous for his military prowess and his important services to the state, though somewhat advanced in years was adored by all the court. He had three handsome sons,—the second, known as the Prince of Clèves, was worthy to bear that proud title; he was brave and grand, and was withal endowed with a prudence rare in the young. The Vidame[4] of Chartres, a scion of the old house of Vendôme, a name not despised by princes of the blood, had won equal triumphs in war and gallantry; he was handsome, attractive, brave, hardy, generous; all his good qualities were distinct and striking,—in short, he was the only man fit to be compared, if such comparison be possible, with the Duke of Nemours. This nobleman was a masterpiece of Nature; the least of his fascinations was his extreme beauty; he was the handsomest man in the world. What made him superior to every one else was his unrivalled courage and a charm manifested in his mind, his expression, and his actions, such as no other showed. He possessed a certain playfulness that was equally attractive to men and women; he was unusually skilful in physical exercises; and he dressed in a way that every one tried in vain to imitate; moreover, his bearing was such that all eyes followed him whenever he appeared. There was no lady in the court who would not have been flattered by his attentions; few of those to whom he had devoted himself could boast of having resisted him; and even many in whom he had shown no interest made very clear their affection for him. He was so gentle and courteous that he could not refuse some attentions to those who tried to please him,—hence he had many mistresses; but it was hard to say whom he really loved. He was often to be seen with the dauphiness; her beauty, her gentleness, her desire to please every one, and the especial regard she showed for this prince, made some imagine that he dared to raise his eyes to her. The Guises, whose niece she was, had acquired influence and position by her marriage; they aspired to an equality with the princes of the blood and to a share of the power exercised by the Constable[5] of Montmorency. It was to the constable that the king confided the greater part of the cares of state, while he treated the Duke of Guise and the Marshal of Saint-André as his favorites. But those attached to his person by favor or position could only keep their place by submitting to the Duchess of Valentinois, who,

4. A title that designated the lay representative of a bishop and the commander of the bishop's troops.   5. A title that designated the highest-ranking official of the court.

although no longer young or beautiful, ruled him so despotically that she may be said to have been the mistress of his person and of the state.

The king had always loved the constable, and at the beginning of his reign had summoned him from the exile into which he had been sent by Francis I. The court was divided between the Guises and the constable, who was the favorite of the princes of the blood. Both parties had always struggled for the favor of the Duchess of Valentinois. The Duke of Aumale, brother of the Duke of Guise, had married one of her daughters. The constable aspired to the same alliance, not satisfied with having married his eldest son to Madame Diane, a daughter of the king by a lady of Piedmont who entered a convent after the birth of her child. The promises which Monsieur de Montmorency had made to Mademoiselle de Piennes, one of the queen's maids-of-honor, had proved a serious obstacle to this match; and although the king had removed it with extreme patience and kindness, the constable still felt insecure until he had won over the Duchess of Valentinois and had separated her from the Guises, whose greatness had begun to alarm her. She had delayed in every way in her power the marriage between the dauphin and the Queen of Scotland; this young queen's beauty and intelligence, and the position given to the Guises by this marriage, were very odious to her. She especially detested the Cardinal of Lorraine, who had addressed her in bitter, even contemptuous terms. She saw that he was intriguing with the queen; hence the constable found her ready to join forces with him by bringing about the marriage of Mademoiselle de la Marck, her granddaughter, to Monsieur d'Anville, his second son, who succeeded to his post in the reign of Charles IX. The constable did not expect that Monsieur d'Anville would have any objections to this marriage, as had been the case with Monsieur de Montmorency; but though the reasons were more hidden, the difficulties were no less obstinate. Monsieur d'Anville was desperately in love with the crown princess; and although his passion was hopeless, he could not persuade himself to contract other ties. The Marshal of Saint-André was almost the only courtier who had taken sides with neither faction; he was one of the favorites, but this position he held simply by his own merits. Ever since he had been the dauphin, the king had been attached to this nobleman, and later had made him marshal of France, at an age when men are satisfied with lesser honors. His advance gave him a distinction which he maintained by his personal worth and charm, by a costly table and rich surroundings, and by more splendor than any private individual had yet displayed. The king's generosity warranted this sumptuousness. There was no limit to this monarch's generosity to those he loved. He did not possess every great quality, but he had many, and among them the love of war and a good knowledge of it. This accounted for his many successes; and if we except the battle of St. Quentin, his reign was an unbroken series of victories. He had won the battle of Renty in person, Piedmont had been conquered, the English had been driven from France, and the Emperor Charles V had seen his good fortune desert him before the city of Metz,[6] which he had besieged in vain with all the forces of the Empire and of Spain. Nevertheless, since the defeat of St. Quentin had

6. Henri II had continued the struggle of his father, Francis I, against Charles V, leader of the Holy Roman Empire, for supremacy in Europe and particularly for control in Italy. The battles mentioned here belong to that struggle. The French armies were defeated at Saint-Quentin in 1557. The French drove the English from Calais in 1558. The French captured Metz in 1552.

diminished our hope of conquest, and fortune seemed to favor one king as much as the other, they were gradually led to favor peace.

The Dowager Duchess of Lorraine had begun to lead the way to a cessation of hostilities at the time of the dauphin's marriage, and ever since then there had been secret negotiations. At last Cercamp, in the Province of Artois, was chosen as the place of meeting. The Cardinal of Lorraine, the constable, and the Marshal of Saint-André appeared in behalf of the King of France; the Duke of Alva and the Prince of Orange in behalf of Philip II. The Duke and Duchess of Lorraine were the mediators. The leading articles were the marriage of Madame Elisabeth of France to Don Carlos, Infanta of Spain, and that of Madame, the king's sister, with Monsieur de Savoie.

Meanwhile the king remained on the frontier, and there heard of the death of Mary, queen of England. He sent the Count of Randan to Elizabeth to congratulate her on ascending the throne. She was very glad to receive him, because her rights were so insecure that it was of great service to her to have them acknowledged by the king. The count found her well informed about the interests of France and the capabilities of those who composed the court, but especially familiar with the reputation of the Duke of Nemours. She spoke of this nobleman so often and with such warmth that when Monsieur de Randan returned and recounted his journey to the king, he told him that there was nothing to which Monsieur de Nemours could not aspire, and that she would be capable of marrying him. That very evening the king spoke to this nobleman, and made Monsieur de Randan repeat to him his conversation with Elizabeth, urging him to essay this great fortune. At first Monsieur de Nemours thought that the king was jesting; but when he saw his mistake he said,—

"At any rate, sire, if I undertake a fantastic enterprise under the advice and in behalf of your Majesty, I beg of you to keep it secret until success shall justify me before the public, and to guard me from appearing vain enough to suppose that a queen who has never seen me should wish to marry me from love."

The king promised to speak of the plan to no one but the constable, and agreed that secrecy was essential for its success. Monsieur de Randan advised Monsieur de Nemours to visit England as a simple traveller; but the latter could not make up his mind to do this. He sent Lignerolles, an intelligent young man, one of his favorites, to ascertain the queen's feeling and to try to open the matter. Meanwhile he went to see the Duke of Savoy, who was then at Brussels with the King of Spain. The death of Mary of England[7] raised great obstacles to any treaty of peace; the commission broke up at the end of November, and the king returned to Paris.

At that moment there appeared at court a young lady to whom all eyes were turned, and we may well believe that she was possessed of faultless beauty, since she aroused admiration where all were well accustomed to the sight of handsome women. Of the same family as the Vidame of Chartres, she was one of the greatest heiresses in France. Her father had died young, leaving her under the charge of his wife, Madame de Chartres, whose kindness, virtue, and worth were beyond praise. After her husband's death she had withdrawn from court for many years; during this period she had devoted

---

7. Mary Tudor (1516–1558), "Bloody Mary," wife of Philip II of Spain.

herself to the education of her daughter, not merely cultivating her mind and her beauty, but also seeking to inspire her with the love of virtue and to make her attractive. Most mothers imagine that it is enough never to speak of gallantry to their daughters to guard them from it forever. Madame de Chartres was of a very different opinion; she often drew pictures of love to her daughter, showing her its fascinations, in order to give her a better understanding of its perils. She told her how insincere men are, how false and deceitful; she described the domestic miseries which illicit love-affairs entail, and, on the other hand, pictured to her the peaceful happiness of a virtuous woman's life, as well as the distinction and elevation which virtue gives to a woman of rank and beauty. She taught her, too, how hard it was to preserve this virtue without extreme care, and without that one sure means of securing a wife's happiness, which is to love her husband and to be loved by him.

This heiress was, then, one of the greatest matches in France, and although she was very young, many propositions of marriage had been made to her. Madame de Chartres, who was extremely proud, found almost nothing worthy of her daughter, and the girl being in her sixteenth year, she was anxious to take her to court. The Vidame went to welcome her on her arrival, and was much struck by the marvellous beauty of Mademoiselle de Chartres,—and with good reason: her delicate complexion and her blond hair gave her a unique brilliancy; her features were regular, and her face and person were full of grace and charm.

The day after her arrival she went to match some precious stones at the house of an Italian who dealt in them. He had come from Florence with the queen, and had grown so rich by his business that his house seemed that of some great nobleman rather than of a merchant. The Prince of Clèves happened to come in while she was there; he was so struck by her beauty that he could not conceal his surprise, and Mademoiselle de Chartres could not keep from blushing when she saw his astonishment: she succeeded, however, in regaining her composure without paying any further attention to the prince than civility required for a man of his evident importance. Monsieur de Clèves gazed at her admiringly, wondering who this beauty was whom he did not know. He perceived from her bearing and her suite[8] that she must be a lady of high rank. She was so young that he thought she must be unmarried; but since she had not her mother with her, and the Italian, who did not know her, addressed her as "madame," he was in great doubt, and stared at her with continual surprise. He saw that his glances embarrassed her, unlike most young women, who always take pleasure in seeing the effect of their beauty; it even seemed to him that his presence made her anxious to go away, and in fact she left very soon. Monsieur de Clèves consoled himself for her departure with the hope of finding out who she was, and was much disappointed to learn that no one knew. He was so struck by her beauty and evident modesty that from that moment he conceived for her the greatest love and esteem. That evening he called on Madame, the king's sister.

This princess was held in high esteem on account of her influence with the king, her brother; and this influence was so great that when the king made peace he consented to restore Piedmont to enable her to marry Monsieur de Savoie. Although she had always meant to marry, she had determined to give her hand to none but a sovereign, and had for that reason

---

8. Group of attendants or servants.

refused the King of Navarre when he was Duke of Vendôme, and had always felt an interest in Monsieur de Savoie after seeing him at Nice on the occasion of the interview between Francis I and Pope Paul III.[9] Since she possessed great intelligence and a fine taste, she drew pleasant persons about her, and at certain hours the whole court used to visit her.

Thither Monsieur de Clèves went, as was his habit. He was so full of the wit and beauty of Mademoiselle de Chartres that he could speak of nothing else; he talked freely of his adventure, and set no limit to his praise of the young woman he had seen but did not know. Madame said to him that there was no such person as he described, and that if there were, every one would have known about her. Madame de Dampierre, her lady-in-waiting and a friend of Madame de Chartres, when she heard the conversation moved near the princess and said to her in a low voice that doubtless it was Mademoiselle de Chartres whom Monsieur de Clèves had seen. Madame turned towards him and said that if he would return the next day, she would show him this beauty who had so impressed him. Mademoiselle de Chartres made her appearance the next day. The queen received her with every imaginable attention, and she was greeted with such admiration by every one that she heard around her nothing but praise. This she received with such noble modesty that she seemed not to hear it, or at least not to be affected by it. Then she visited the apartments of Madame, the king's sister. The princess, after praising her beauty, told her the surprise she had given to Monsieur de Clèves. A moment after, that person appeared.

"Come," she said to him, "see if I have not kept my word, and if, when I point out Mademoiselle de Chartres to you, I do not show you the beauty you sought; at any rate, thank me for telling her how much you already admire her."

Monsieur de Clèves was filled with joy to find that this young woman whom he had found so attractive was of a rank proportionate to her beauty. He went up to her and asked her to remember that he had been the first to admire her, and that without knowing her he had felt all the respect and esteem that were her due.

The Chevalier de Guise, his friend, and he left the house together. At first they praised Mademoiselle de Chartres without stint; then they found that they were praising her too much, and both stopped saying what they thought of her: but they were compelled to talk about her on the following days wherever they met. This new beauty was for a long time the general subject of conversation. The queen praised her warmly and showed an extraordinary regard for her; the dauphiness made her one of her favorites, and begged Madame de Chartres to bring her to see her very often; the daughters of the king invited her to all their entertainments,—in short, she was loved and admired by the whole court, except by Madame de Valentinois. It was not that this new beauty gave her any uneasiness,—her long experience had made her sure of the king,—but she so hated the Vidame of Chartres, whom she had desired to ally with herself by the marriage of one of her daughters, while he had joined the queen's party, that she could not look with favor on any one who bore his name and seemed to enjoy his friendship.

The Prince of Clèves fell passionately in love with Mademoiselle de Char-

9. The meeting took place in 1538. The pope helped arrange a ten-year truce between France and the empire.

tres, and was eager to marry her; but he feared lest the pride of Madame de Chartres should prevent her from giving her daughter to a man who was not the eldest of his family. Yet this family was so distinguished, and the Count of Eu, who was the head of the house, had just married a woman so near to royalty, that it was timidity rather than any true reason that inspired the fear of Monsieur de Clèves. He had many rivals; the Chevalier de Guise seemed to him the most formidable, on account of his birth, his ability, and the brilliant position of his family. This prince had fallen in love with Mademoiselle de Chartres the first day he saw her; he had noticed the passion of Monsieur de Clèves just as the latter had noticed his. Though the two men were friends, the separation which resulted from this rivalry gave them no chance to explain themselves, and their friendship cooled without their having courage to come to an understanding. The good fortune of Monsieur de Clèves in being the first to see Mademoiselle de Chartres seemed to him a happy omen, and to promise him some advantage over his rivals; but he foresaw serious obstacles on the part of the Duke of Nevers, his father. This duke was bound to the Duchess of Valentinois by many ties; she was an enemy of the Vidame, and this was reason enough to prevent the Duke of Nevers from consenting that his son should think of that nobleman's niece.

Madame de Chartres, who had already taken such pains to fill her daughter with a love of virtue, did not remit them in this place where they were still so necessary, and bad examples were so frequent. Ambition and gallantry were the sole occupation of the court, busying men and women alike. There were so many interests and so many different intrigues in which women took part that love was always mingled with politics, and politics with love. No one was calm or indifferent; every one sought to rise, to please, to serve, or to injure; no one was weary or idle, every one was taken up with pleasure or intrigue. The ladies had their special interest in the queen, in the crown princess, in the Queen of Navarre, in Madame the king's sister, or in the Duchess of Valentinois, according to their inclinations, their sense of right, or their humor. Those who had passed their first youth and assumed an austere virtue, were devoted to the queen; those who were younger and sought pleasure and gallantry, paid their court to the crown princess. The Queen of Navarre had her favorites; she was young, and had much influence over her husband the king,[1] who was allied with the constable, and hence highly esteemed. Madame the king's sister still preserved some of her beauty, and gathered several ladies about herself. The Duchess of Valentinois was sought by all those whom she deigned to regard; but the women she liked were few, and with the exception of those who enjoyed her intimacy and confidence, and whose disposition bore some likeness to her own, she received only on the days when she assumed to hold a court like the queen.

All these different cliques were separated by rivalry and envy. Then, too, the women who belonged to each one of them were also jealous of one another, either about their chances of advancement, or about their lovers; often their interests were complicated by other pettier, but no less important questions. Hence there was in this court a sort of well-ordered agitation, which rendered it very charming, but also very dangerous, for a young woman. Madame de Chartres saw this peril, and thought only of protecting

1. Antoine de Bourbon (1518–1562), king of Navarre, father of Henri IV of France.

her daughter from it. She besought her, not as a mother, but as a friend, to confide to her all the sweet speeches that might be made to her, and promised her aid in all those matters which so often embarrass the young.

The Chevalier de Guise made his feelings for Mademoiselle de Chartres and his intentions so manifest that every one could see them; yet he well knew the very grave difficulties that stood in his way. He was aware that he was not a desirable match, because his fortune was too small for his rank. He knew, too, that his brothers would disapprove of his marrying, through fear of the loss of position which sometimes befalls great families through the marriage of younger sons. The Cardinal of Lorraine soon proved to him that his fears were well grounded, for he denounced the chevalier's love for Mademoiselle de Chartres very warmly, though he concealed his true reasons. The cardinal nourished a hatred for the Vidame, which was hidden at the time, and only broke out later. He would have preferred to see his brother ally himself with any other family than that of the Vidame, and gave such public expression to his dislike that Madame de Chartres was plainly offended. She took great pains to show that the Cardinal of Lorraine had no cause for fear, and that she herself never contemplated the match. The Vidame adopted the same course, and with a better understanding of the cardinal's objection, because he knew the underlying reason.

The Prince of Clèves had concealed his passion quite as little as had the Chevalier de Guise. The Duke of Nevers was sorry to hear of this attachment, but thought that his son would forget it at a word from him; great was his surprise when he found him determined to marry Mademoiselle de Chartres. He opposed this determination with a warmth so ill concealed that the whole court soon had wind of it, and it came to the knowledge of her mother. She had never doubted that Monsieur de Nevers would regard this match as an advantageous one for his son, and was much surprised that both the house of Clèves and that of Guise dreaded the alliance instead of desiring it. She was so chagrined that she sought to marry her daughter to some one who could raise her above those who fancied themselves superior to her; and after carefully going over the ground, pitched on the prince dauphin, the son of the Duke of Montpensier. He was of the right age to marry, and held the highest position at court. Since Madame de Chartres was a very clever woman, and was aided by the Vidame, who at that time had great influence, while her daughter was in every way a good match, she played her cards so cleverly and successfully that Monsieur de Montpensier appeared to desire the marriage, and it seemed as if nothing could stand in its way.

The Vidame, though aware of Monsieur d'Anville's devotion to the crown princess, still thought that he might make use of the influence which she had over him to induce him to speak well of Mademoiselle de Chartres to the king and to the Prince of Montpensier, whose intimate friend he was. He mentioned this to the princess, who took up the matter eagerly, since it promised advancement to a young woman of whom she had become very fond. This she told the Vidame, assuring him that though she knew she should offend her uncle, the Cardinal of Lorraine, this would be no objection, because she had good grounds for disliking him, since he every day furthered the queen's interests in opposition to her own.

Persons in love are always glad of any excuse for talking about the object of their affection. As soon as the Vidame had gone, the crown princess ordered Châtelart, the favorite of Monsieur d'Anville and the confidant of his love for her, to tell him to be at the queen's reception that evening. Châtelart received this command with great delight. He belonged to a good family of Dauphiné, but his merit and intelligence had raised him to a higher place than his birth warranted. He was received and treated with kindness by all the great lords at the court, and the favor of the family of Montmorency had attached him especially to Monsieur d'Anville. He was handsome and skilled in all physical exercises; he sang agreeably, wrote verses, and had a gallant, ardent nature, which so attracted Monsieur d'Anville that he made him a confidant of his love for the crown princess. The confidence brought him into the society of that lady, and thus began that unhappy passion, which robbed him of his reason and finally cost him his life.

Monsieur d'Anville did not fail to make his appearance that evening in the queen's drawing-room; he was pleased that the dauphiness had chosen him to aid her, and he promised faithfully to obey her commands. But Madame de Valentinois had heard of the contemplated marriage and had laid her plans to thwart it; she had been so successful in arousing the king's opposition that when Monsieur d'Anville spoke of it, he showed his disapproval, and commanded him to apprise the Prince of Montpensier of it. It is easy to imagine the feelings of Madame de Chartres at the failure of a plan she had so much desired, especially when her ill-success gave so great an advantage to her enemies and did so much harm to her daughter.

The crown princess kindly expressed to Mademoiselle de Chartres her regrets at not being able to further her interests. "You see," she said, "I have but very little power; I am so detested by the queen and the Duchess of Valentinois that they or their attendants always oppose everything I desire. Still," she added, "I have always tried to please them, and they hate me only on account of my mother, who used to fill them with uneasiness and jealousy. The king had been in love with her before he loved Madame de Valentinois, and in his early married life, before he had any children, though he loved this duchess, he seemed bent on dissolving that marriage to marry the queen my mother. Madame de Valentinois dreaded the woman he had loved so well, lest her wit and beauty should diminish her own power, and entered into an alliance with the constable, who was also opposed to the king's marrying a sister of the Guises. They won over the late king; and though he hated the Duchess of Valentinois as much as he loved the queen, he joined with them in preventing the king from dissolving his marriage. In order to make this impossible, they arranged my mother's marriage with the King of Scotland, whose first wife had been Madame Magdeleine, the king's sister,—this they did because it was the first thing that offered; though they broke the promises that had been made to the King of England, who was deeply in love with her. In fact, this matter nearly caused a falling out between the two kings. Henry VIII could not be consoled for not marrying my mother; and whenever any other French princess was proposed to him, he used to say that she would never take the place of the one they had taken from him. It is true that my mother was a perfect beauty, and it is remarkable that when she was the widow of a duke of Longueville, three kings should have wanted to marry her. It was her misfortune to be married to the least important of them all, and to be sent to a kingdom where she has found nothing but unhappiness. I am told that I am like her; I dread the same sad fate, and whatever happiness seems to be awaiting me, I doubt if I ever enjoy it."

Mademoiselle de Chartres assured the crown princess that these gloomy presentiments were so fantastic that they could not long disturb her, and that she ought not to doubt that her good fortune would give the lie to her fears.

Henceforth no one dared to think of Mademoiselle de Chartres, through fear of displeasing the king or of not succeeding in winning a young woman who had aspired to a prince of the blood. None of these considerations moved Monsieur de Clèves. The death of his father, the Duke of Nevers, which happened at that time, left him free to follow his own inclinations, and as soon as the period of mourning had passed, he thought of nothing but marrying Mademoiselle de Chartres. He was glad to make his proposal at a time when circumstances had driven away all rivals and when he felt almost sure that she would not refuse him. What dimmed his joy was the fear of not being agreeable to her; and he would have preferred the happiness of pleasing her to the certainty of marrying her when she did not love him.

The Chevalier de Guise had somewhat aroused his jealousy; but since this was inspired more by his rival's merits than by the conduct of Mademoiselle de Chartres, he thought of nothing but ascertaining whether by good fortune she would approve of his designs. He met her only at the queen's rooms or in company, yet he managed to speak to her of his intentions and hopes in the most respectful way; he begged her to let him know how she felt towards him, and told her that his feelings for her were such that he should be forever unhappy if she obeyed her mother only from a sense of duty.

Mademoiselle de Chartres, having a very noble heart, was really grateful to the Prince of Clèves for what he did. This gratitude lent to her answer a certain gentleness, which was quite sufficient to feed the hope of a man as much in love as he was, and he counted on attaining at least a part of what he desired.

Mademoiselle repeated this conversation to her mother, who said that Monsieur de Clèves was of such high birth, possessed so many fine qualities, and seemed so discreet for a man of his age, that if she inclined to marry him she would herself gladly give her consent. Mademoiselle de Chartres replied that she had noticed the same fine qualities, and that she would rather marry him than any one else, but that she had no special love for him.

The next day the prince had his offer formally made to Madame de Chartres; she accepted it, being willing to give her daughter a husband she did not love. The marriage settlement was drawn up, the king was told of it, and the marriage became known to every one.

Monsieur de Clèves was very happy, although not perfectly satisfied; it gave him much pain to see that what Mademoiselle de Chartres felt for him was only esteem and gratitude, and he could not flatter himself that she nourished any warmer feeling; for had she done so, she would have readily shown it in their closer intimacy. Within a few days he complained to her of this.

"Is it possible," he said, "that I may not be happy in my marriage? Yet assuredly I am not happy. You have a sort of kindly feeling for me which cannot satisfy me; you are not impatient, uneasy, or grieved: you are as indifferent to my love as if this were given to your purse, and not to your charms."

"You do wrong to complain," she replied. "I do not know what more you can ask; it seems to me that you have no right to demand anything more."

"It is true," he said, "that you have a certain air with which I should be satisfied if there were anything behind it; but instead of your being restrained by a sense of propriety, it is a sense of propriety which inspires your actions. I do not touch your feelings or your heart; my presence causes you neither pleasure nor pain."

"You cannot doubt," she made answer, "that I am glad to see you, and I blush so often when I do see you that you may be sure that the sight of you affects me."

"I am not deceived by your blushes," he urged; "they come from modesty, and not from any thrill of your heart, and I do not exaggerate their importance."

Mademoiselle de Chartres did not know what to answer; these distinctions were outside of her experience. Monsieur de Clèves saw only too well how far removed she was from feeling for him as he should have liked, when he saw that she had no idea of what that feeling was.

The Chevalier de Guise returned from a journey a few days before the wedding. He had seen so many insurmountable obstacles in the way of his marrying Mademoiselle de Chartres that he knew he had no chance of success; yet he was evidently distressed at seeing her become the wife of another. This grief did not extinguish his passion, and he remained quite as much in love as before. Mademoiselle de Chartres had not been ignorant of his devotion. On his return he let her know that she was the cause of the deep gloom that marked his face; and he had so much merit and charm that it was almost impossible to make him unhappy without regretting it. Hence she was depressed; but this pity went no further, and she told her mother how much pain this prince's love caused her.

Madame de Chartres admired her daughter's frankness, and with good reason, for it could not be fuller or simpler; she regretted, however, that her heart was not touched, especially when she saw that the prince had not affected it any more than the others. Hence she took great pains to attach her to her future husband, and to impress upon her what she owed him for the interest he had taken in her before he knew who she was, and for the proof he had given of his love in choosing her at a time when no one else ventured to think of her.

The marriage ceremony took place at the Louvre,[2] and in the evening the king and queen, with all the court, supped at the house of Madame de Chartres, who received them with great splendor. The Chevalier de Guise did not venture to make himself conspicuous by staying away, but his dejection was evident.

Monsieur de Clèves did not find that Mademoiselle de Chartres had altered her feelings when she changed her name. His position as her husband gave him greater privileges, but no different place in her heart. Though he had married her, he did not cease to be her lover,[3] because there was always left something for him to desire; and though she lived on the best of terms with him, he was not yet perfectly happy. He preserved for her a violent and restless passion, which marred his joy. Jealousy had no part in it, for never had a husband been further from feeling it, or a wife from inspiring it. Yet she was exposed to all the temptations of the court, visiting the queen and the king's sister every day. All the young and fashionable men met her at her

---

2. At this time, a royal residence.   3. I.e., he continued to love her.

own house and at that of her brother-in-law, the Duke of Nevers, whose doors were always open; but she always had an air that inspired respect, and seemed so remote from gallantry that the Marshal of Saint-André, though bold and protected by the king's favor, was touched by her beauty without venturing to show it except by delicate attentions. There were many others who felt as did the marshal; and Madame de Chartres added to her daughter's natural modesty such a keen sense of propriety that she made her seem like a woman to be sighed for in vain.

The Duchess of Lorraine, while trying to bring about peace, had also tried to arrange the marriage of her son, the Duke of Lorraine, and had succeeded; he was to marry Madame Claude of France, the king's second daughter. The wedding had been settled for the month of February.

Meanwhile the Duke of Nemours had remained at Brussels, completely taken up with his plans for England. He was always sending and receiving messengers. His hopes grew from day to day, and at last Lignerolles told him that it was time for him to appear and finish in person what had been so well begun. He received this news with all the satisfaction that an ambitious man can feel at seeing himself raised to a throne simply through his reputation. He had gradually grown so accustomed to the contemplation of this great piece of good fortune that whereas at first he had regarded it as an impossibility, all difficulties had vanished, and he foresaw no obstacles.

He at once despatched to Paris orders for a magnificent outfit, that he might make his appearance in England with a splendor proportionate to his designs, and also hastened to court to be present at the wedding of the Duke of Lorraine. He arrived the day before the formal betrothal, and that same evening went to report to the king the condition of affairs and to receive his advice and commands about his future conduct. Thence he went to pay his respects to the queens. Madame de Clèves was not there, so that she did not see him, and was not even aware of his arrival. She had heard every one speak of this prince as the handsomest and most agreeable man at court, and Madame the Dauphiness had spoken of him so often and in such terms that she felt some curiosity to see him.

Madame de Clèves spent the day of the betrothal at home dressing herself for the ball in the evening at the Louvre. When she made her appearance, her beauty and the splendor of her dress aroused general admiration. The ball opened, and while she was dancing with Monsieur de Guise, there was a certain commotion at the door of the ballroom, as if some one were entering for whom way was being made. Madame de Clèves finished her dance, and while she was looking about for another partner, the king called out to her to take the gentleman who had just arrived. She turned, and saw a man, who she thought must be Monsieur de Nemours, stepping over some seats to reach the place where the dancing was going on. No one ever saw this prince for the first time without amazement; and this evening he was more striking than ever in the rich attire which set off his natural beauty to such great advantage; and it was also hard to see Madame de Clèves for the first time without astonishment.

Monsieur de Nemours was so amazed by her beauty that when he drew near her and bowed to her he could not conceal his wonder and delight. When they began their dance, a murmur of admiration ran through the ballroom. The king and the queens remembered that the pair had never met, and saw how strange it was that they should be dancing together without being acquainted. They summoned them when they had finished the set, and without giving them a chance to speak to any one, asked if each would not like to know who the other was, and whether either had any idea.

"As for me, Madame," said Monsieur de Nemours, "I have no doubts; but since Madame de Clèves has not the same reasons for guessing who I am that I have for recognizing her, I must beg your Majesty to be good enough to tell her my name."

"I fancy," said the dauphiness, "that she knows it as well as you know hers."

"I assure you, Madame," said Madame de Clèves, who seemed a little embarrassed, "that I cannot guess so well as you think."

"You can guess very well," replied the dauphiness, "and you are very kind to Monsieur de Nemours in your unwillingness to acknowledge that you recognize him without ever having seen him before."

The queen interrupted the conversation, that the ball might go on, and Monsieur de Nemours danced with the dauphiness. This lady was a perfect beauty, and had always appeared to be one in the eyes of Monsieur de Nemours before he went to Flanders; but all that evening he admired no one but Madame de Clèves.

The Chevalier de Guise, who never ceased worshipping her, was standing near, and this incident caused him evident pain. He regarded it as a sure sign that fate meant that Monsieur de Nemours should fall in love with Madame de Clèves; and whether it was that he saw something in her face, or that jealousy sharpened his fears, he believed that she had been moved by the sight of this prince, and he could not keep from telling her that Monsieur de Nemours was very fortunate in making her acquaintance in such a gallant and unusual way.

Madame de Clèves went home so full of what had happened at the ball that though it was very late, she went to her mother's room to tell her about it; and she praised Monsieur de Nemours with a certain air that made Madame de Chartres entertain the same suspicion as the Chevalier de Guise.

The next day the wedding took place; Madame de Clèves there saw the Duke of Nemours, and was even more struck by his admirable grace and dignity than before.

On succeeding days she met him at the drawing-room of the dauphiness, saw him playing tennis with the king and riding at the ring, and heard him talk; and she always found him so superior to every one else, and so much outshining all in conversation wherever he might be, by the grace of his person and the charm of his wit, that he soon made a deep impression on her heart.

Then, too, the desire to please made the Duke of Nemours, who was already deeply interested, more charming than ever; and since they met often, and found each other more attractive than any one else at court, they naturally experienced great delight in being together.

The Duchess of Valentinois took part in all the merry-making, and the king showed her all the interest and attention that he had done when first in love with her. Madame de Clèves, who was then of an age at which it is usual to believe that no woman can ever be loved after she is twenty-five years old, regarded with great amazement the king's attachment to this duchess, who was a grandmother and had just married[4] her granddaughter. She often spoke of it to Madame de Chartres. "Is it possible," she asked, "that the king has been in love so long? How could he get interested in a woman much older than himself, and who had been his father's mistress, as well as that of a great many other men, as I have heard?"

"It is true," was the answer, "that neither merit nor fidelity inspired the king's passion, or has kept it alive. And this is something which is scarcely to be excused; for had this woman had youth and beauty as well as rank, had she loved no one else, had she loved the king with untiring constancy, for himself alone, and not solely for his wealth and position, and had she used her power for worthy objects such as the king desired, it would have been easy to admire his great devotion to her. If," Madame de Chartres went on, "I were not afraid that you would say of me what is always said of women of my age, that we like to talk about old times, I would tell you the beginning of the king's love for this duchess; and many things that happened at the court of the late king bear much resemblance to what is now going on."

"So far from accusing you of repeating old stories," said Madame de Clèves, "I regret that you have told me so little about the present, and that you have not taught me the different interests and intrigues of the court. I am so ignorant of them that a few days ago I thought the constable was on the best of terms with the queen."

"You were very far from the truth," replied Madame de Chartres. "The queen hates the constable, and if she ever gets any power he will learn it very quickly. She knows that he has often told the king that of all his children it is only his bastards who look like him."

"I should never have imagined this hatred," interrupted Madame de Clèves, "after seeing the zeal with which the queen wrote to the constable when he was in prison, the joy she manifested at his return, and the familiarity of her address as regards him."

"If you judge from appearances here," replied Madame de Chartres, "you will be often mistaken; what appears is seldom the truth.

"But to return to Madame de Valentinois: you know her name is Diane de Poitiers. She is of illustrious family, being descended from the old dukes of Aquitaine; her grandmother was a natural daughter of Louis XI,—in short, there is no common blood in her veins. Saint-Vallier, her father, was implicated in the affair of the Constable of Bourbon, of which you have heard, was condemned to be beheaded, and was led to the scaffold. His daughter, who was remarkably beautiful, and had already pleased the late king, managed, I don't know how, to save her father's life. His pardon was granted him when he was expecting the mortal stroke; but fear had so possessed him that he did not recover consciousness, but died a few days later. His daughter made her appearance at court as the king's mistress. His journey to Italy and his imprisonment interrupted this passion. When he returned from Spain and Madame Regénte went to meet him at Bayonne, she had with her all her young women, among whom was Mademoiselle de Pisseleu, afterwards Duchess of Estampes. The king fell in love with her, though she was inferior in birth, beauty, and intelligence to Madame de Valentinois: the only advantage she had was that she was younger. I have often heard her say that she

4. Married off.

was born on the day that Diane de Poitiers was married; but that remark was more malicious than truthful, for I am much mistaken if the Duchess of Valentinois did not marry Monsieur de Brézé, grand seneschal of Normandy, at the same time that the king fell in love with Madame d'Estampes. Never was there fiercer hatred than existed between those two women. The Duchess of Valentinois could not forgive Madame d'Estampes for depriving her of the title of the king's mistress. Madame d'Estampes was madly jealous of Madame de Valentinois because the king maintained his relations with her. This king was never rigorously faithful to his mistresses; there was always one who had the title and the honors, but the ladies of what was called the little band shared his attentions. The death of his oldest son, it was supposed by poison, at Tournon, was a great blow to him. He had much less love for his second son, the present king, who was in every way far less to his taste, and whom he even regarded as lacking courage and spirit. He was lamenting this one day to Madame de Valentinois, whereupon she said she would like to make him fall in love with her, that he might become livelier and more agreeable. She succeeded, as you know. This love has lasted more than twenty years, without being dimmed by time or circumstances.

"At first the late king objected to it,—whether because he was still enough in love with Madame de Valentinois to feel jealous, or because he was influenced by Madame d'Estampes, who was in despair when the dauphin became attached to her enemy, is uncertain; however that may be, he viewed this passion with an anger and a disapproval that were apparent every day. His son feared neither his wrath nor his hate; and since nothing could induce him to abate or to conceal his attachment, the king was forced to endure it as best he could. His son's opposition to his wishes estranged him still more, and attached him more closely to the Duke of Orléans, his third son. This prince was handsome, energetic, ambitious, of a somewhat tempestuous nature, which needed to be controlled, but who in time would become a really fine man.

"The elder son's rank as dauphin and the father's preference for the Duke of Orléans inspired a rivalry between them which amounted to hatred. This rivalry had begun in their childhood, and lasted until the death of the latter. When the emperor entered French territory[5] he gave his whole preference to the Duke of Orléans. This so pained the dauphin that when the emperor was at Chantilly he tried to compel the constable to arrest him, without waiting for the king's orders; but the constable refused. Afterward the king blamed him for not following his son's advice; and this had a good deal to do with his leaving the court.

"The division between the two brothers induced the Duchess of Estampes to rely on the Duke of Orléans for protection against the influence which Madame de Valentinois had over the king. In this she succeeded; the duke, without falling in love with her, was as warm in defence of her interests as was the dauphin in defence of those of Madame de Valentinois. Hence there were two cabals in the court such as you can imagine; but the intrigues were not limited to two women's quarrels.

"The emperor, who had maintained his friendship for the Duke of Orléans,

---

5. Despite the enmity between France and the empire, Charles V was allowed to cross France in 1539 on his way to put down a revolt in The Netherlands.

had frequently offered him the duchy of Milan. In the subsequent negotiations about peace, he raised hopes in the breast of the duke that he would give him the seventeen provinces[6] and his daughter's hand. The dauphin, however, desired neither peace nor this marriage. He made use of the constable, whom he had always loved, to convince the king how important it was not to give to his successor a brother so powerful as would be the Duke of Orléans in alliance with the emperor and governing the seventeen provinces. The constable agreed the more heartily with the dauphin's views because he also opposed those of Madame d'Estampes, who was his avowed enemy, and ardently desired that the power of the Duke of Orléans should be increased.

"At that time the dauphin was in command of the king's army in Champagne, and had reduced that of the emperor to such extremities that it would have utterly perished had not the Duchess of Estampes, fearing that too great success would prevent our granting peace and consenting to the marriage, secretly sent word to the enemy to surprise Epernay and Château-Thierry, which were full of supplies. This they did, and thereby saved their whole army.

"This duchess did not long profit by her treason. Soon afterward the Duke of Orléans died at Farmoutier of some contagious disease. He loved one of the most beautiful women of the court, and was beloved by her. I shall not tell you who it was, because her life since that time has been most decorous; and she has tried so hard to have her affection for the prince forgotten that she deserves to have her reputation left untarnished. It so happened that she heard of her husband's death on the same day that she heard of that of Monsieur d'Orléans; consequently she was able to conceal her real grief without an effort.

"The king did not long survive his son's decease,—he died two years later. He urged the dauphin to make use of the services of the Cardinal of Tournon and of the Amiral d'Annebauld, without saying a word about the constable, who at that time was banished to Chantilly. Nevertheless, the first thing the present king did after his father's death was to call the constable back and intrust him with the management of affairs.

"Madame d'Estampes was sent away, and became the victim of all the ill-treatment she might have expected from an all-powerful enemy. The Duchess of Valentinois took full vengeance on this duchess and on all who had displeased her. Her power over the king seemed the greater because it had not appeared while he was dauphin. During the twelve years of his reign she has been in everything absolute mistress. She disposes of places and controls affairs of every sort; she secured the dismissal of the Cardinal of Tournon, of the Chancelier Olivier, and of Villeroy. Those who have endeavored to open the king's eyes to her conduct have been ruined for their pains. The Count of Taix, commander-in-chief of the artillery, who did not like her, could not keep from talking about her love affairs, and especially about one with the Count of Brissac, of whom the king was already very jealous. Yet she managed so well that the Count of Taix was disgraced and deprived of his position; and impossible as it may sound, he was succeeded by the Count of Brissac, whom she afterward made a marshal of France. Still, the king's jealousy became so violent that he could not endure having this marshal

6. The Spanish Netherlands, which included most of modern Belgium and Holland.

remain at court; but though usually jealousy is a hot and violent passion, it is modified and tempered in him by his extreme respect for his mistress, so that the only means he ventured to use to rid himself of his rival was by intrusting to him the government of Piedmont. There he has spent several years; last winter, however, he returned, under the pretext of asking for men and supplies for the army under his command. Possibly the desire of seeing Madame de Valentinois and dread of being forgotten had something to do with this journey. The king received him very coldly. The Guises, who do not like him, did not dare betray their feelings, on account of Madame de Valentinois, so they made use of the Vidame, his open enemy, to prevent his getting any of the things he wanted. It was not hard to injure him. The king hated him, and was made uneasy by his presence; consequently he was obliged to go back without getting any advantage from his journey,—unless, possibly, he had rekindled in the heart of Madame de Valentinois feelings which absence had nearly extinguished. The king has had many other grounds for jealousy, but either he has not known them, or he has not dared to complain.

"I am not sure, my dear," added Madame de Chartres, "that you may not think I have told you more than you cared to hear."

"Not at all," answered Madame de Clèves; "and if I were not afraid of tiring you, I should ask you many more questions."

Monsieur de Nemours' love for Madame de Clèves was at first so violent that he lost all interest in those he had formerly loved, and with whom he had kept up relations during his absence. He not merely did not seek any excuses for deserting them, he would not even listen to their complaints or reply to their reproaches. The dauphiness, for whom he had nourished very warm feelings, was soon forgotten by the side of Madame de Clèves. His impatience for his journey to England began to abate, and he ceased to hasten his preparations for departure. He often visited the crown princess, because Madame de Clèves was frequently in her apartments, and he was not unwilling to give some justification to the widespread suspicions about his feelings for the dauphiness. Madame de Clèves seemed to him so rare a prize that he decided to conceal all signs of his love rather than let it be generally known. He never spoke of it even to his intimate friend the Vidame de Chartres, to whom he usually confided everything. He was so cautious and discreet that no one suspected his love for Madame de Clèves except the Chevalier de Guise; and the lady herself would scarcely have perceived it had not her own interest in him made her watch him very closely, so that she became sure of it.

Madame de Clèves did not find herself so disposed to tell her mother what she thought of this prince's feelings as had been the case with her other lovers; and without definitely deciding on reserve, she yet never spoke of the subject. But Madame de Chartres soon perceived this, as well as her daughter's interest in him. This knowledge gave her distinct pain, for she well understood how dangerous it was for Madame de Clèves to be loved by a man like Monsieur de Nemours, especially when she was already disposed to admire him. An incident that happened a few days later confirmed her suspicions of this liking.

The Marshal of Saint-André, who was always on the look-out for opportunities to display his magnificence, made a pretext of desiring to show his house, which had just been finished, and invited the king to do him the honor of supping there with the queens. The marshal was also glad to be able to show to Madame de Clèves his lavish splendor.

A few days before the one of the supper, the dauphin, whose health was delicate, had been ailing and had seen no one. His wife, the crown princess, had spent the whole day with him, and toward evening, as he felt better, he received all the persons of quality who were in his ante-chamber. The crown princess went to her own apartment, where she found Madame de Clèves and a few other ladies with whom she was most intimate.

Since it was already late, and the crown princess was not dressed, she did not go to the queen, but sent word she could not come; she then had her jewels brought, to decide what she should wear at the Marshal of Saint-André's ball, and to give some, according to a promise she had made, to Madame de Clèves. While they were thus occupied, the Prince of Condé, whose rank gave him free admission everywhere, entered. The crown princess said to him that he doubtless came from her husband, and asked what was going on in his apartments.

"They are having a discussion, Madame, with Monsieur de Nemours," he answered. "He defends the side he has taken so eagerly that he must have a personal interest in it. I fancy he has a mistress who makes him uneasy when she goes to a ball, for he maintains that it makes a lover unhappy to see the woman he loves at such a place."

"What!" said the dauphiness, "Monsieur de Nemours does not want his mistress to go to a ball? I thought husbands might object, but I never supposed that lovers could have such a feeling."

"Monsieur de Nemours," replied the Prince of Condé, "declares that a ball is most distressing to lovers, whether they are loved or not. He says if their love is returned, they have the pain of being loved less for several days; that there is not a woman in the world who is not prevented from thinking of her lover by the demands of her toilet,[7] which entirely engrosses her attention; that women dress for every one as well as for those they love; that when they are at the ball they are anxious to please all who look at them; that when they are proud of their beauty, they feel a pleasure in which the lover plays but a small part. He says, too, that one who sighs in vain suffers even more when he sees his mistress at an entertainment; that the more she is admired by the public, the more one suffers at not being loved, through fear lest her beauty should kindle some love happier than his own; finally, that there is no pain so keen as seeing one's mistress at a ball, except knowing that she is there while absent one's self."

Madame de Clèves, though pretending not to hear what the Prince of Condé was saying, listened attentively. She readily understood her share in the opinion expressed by Monsieur de Nemours, especially when he spoke of his grief at not being at the ball with his mistress, because he was not to be at that given by the Marshal of Saint-André, being ordered by the king to go to meet the Duke of Ferrara.

The crown princess laughed with the Prince of Condé, and expressed her disapproval of the views of Monsieur de Nemours. "There is only one condition, Madame," said the prince, "on which Monsieur de Nemours is willing

7. The process of dressing.

that his mistress should go to a ball, and that is that he himself should give her permission. He said that last year when he gave a ball to your Majesty, he thought that his mistress did him a great favor in coming to it, though she seemed to be there only as one of your suite; that it is always a kindness to a lover to take part in any entertainment that he gives; and that it is also agreeable to a lover to have his mistress see him the host of the whole court and doing the honors fittingly."

"Monsieur de Nemours did well," said the dauphiness, with a smile, "to let his mistress go to that ball; for so many women claimed that position that if they had not come, there would have been scarcely any one there."

As soon as the Prince of Condé had begun to speak of what Monsieur de Nemours thought of the ball, Madame de Clèves was very anxious not to go to that of the Marshal of Saint-André. She readily agreed that it was not fitting for a woman to go to the house of a man who was in love with her, and she was glad to have so good a reason for doing a kindness to Monsieur de Nemours. Nevertheless, she took away the jewels which the crown princess had given her; that evening, however, when she showed them to her mother, she told her that she did not mean to wear them, that the Marshal of Saint-André had made his love for her so manifest that she felt sure he meant to have it thought that she was to have some part in the entertainment he was to give to the king, and that under the pretext of doing honor to the king he would pay her attentions which might perhaps prove embarrassing.

Madame de Chartres argued for some time against her daughter's decision, which she thought singular, but at last yielded, and told her she must pretend to be ill, in order to have a good excuse for not going, because her real reasons would not be approved and should not be suspected. Madame de Clèves gladly consented to stay at home for a few days, in order not to meet Monsieur de Nemours, who left without having the pleasure of knowing that she was not going to the ball.

The duke returned the day after the ball, and heard that she had not been there; but inasmuch as he did not know that his talk with the dauphin had been repeated to her, he was far from thinking that he was fortunate enough to be the cause of her absence.

The next day, when Monsieur de Nemours was calling on the queen and talking with the dauphiness, Madame de Chartres and Madame de Clèves happened to come in and approached this princess. Madame de Clèves was not in full dress, as if she were not very well, though her countenance belied her attire.

"You look so well," said the crown princess, "that I can scarcely believe that you have been ill. I fancy that the Prince of Condé, when he told you what Monsieur de Nemours thought about the ball, convinced you that you would do a kindness to the Marshal of Saint-André by going to his ball, and that that was the reason you stayed away."

Madame de Clèves blushed at the dauphiness's accurate guess which she thus expressed before Monsieur de Nemours.

Madame de Chartres saw at once why her daughter did not go to the ball, and in order to throw Monsieur de Nemours off the track, she at once addressed the dauphiness with an air of sincerity. "I assure you, Madame," she said, "that your Majesty pays an honor to my daughter which she does not deserve. She was really ill; but I am sure that if I had not forbidden it, she would have accompanied you, unfit as she was, to have the pleasure of seeing the wonderful entertainment last evening."

The dauphiness believed what Madame de Chartres said, and Monsieur de Nemours was vexed to see how probable her story was; nevertheless the confusion of Madame de Clèves made him suspect that the dauphiness's conjecture was not without some foundation in fact. At first Madame de Clèves had been annoyed because Monsieur de Nemours had reason to suppose that it was he who had kept her from going to the ball, and then she felt regret that her mother had entirely removed the grounds for this supposition.

Although the attempt to make peace at Cercamp had failed, negotiations still continued, and matters had assumed such a shape that toward the end of February a meeting was held at Câteau-Cambrésis.[8] The same commissioners had assembled there, and the departure of the Marshal of Saint-André freed Monsieur de Nemours from a rival who was more to be dreaded on account of his close observation of all those who approached Madame de Clèves than from any real success of his own.

Madame de Chartres did not wish to let her daughter see that she knew her feeling for this prince, lest she should make her suspicious of the advice she wanted to give her. One day she began to talk about him. She spoke of him in warm terms, but craftily praised his discretion in being unable to fall really in love and in seeking only pleasure, not a serious attachment, in his relations with women. "To be sure," she went on, "he has been suspected of a great passion for the dauphiness; I notice that he visits her very often, and I advise you to avoid talking with him as much as possible, especially in private, because you are on such terms with the crown princess that people would say that you were their confidant, and you know how disagreeable that would be. I think that if the report continues, you would do well to see less of the crown princess, that you may not be connected with love-affairs of that sort."

Madame de Clèves had never heard Monsieur de Nemours and the dauphiness talked about, and was much surprised by what her mother said. She was so sure that she had misunderstood the prince's feelings for her that she changed color. Madame de Chartres noticed this, but company coming in at that moment, Madame de Clèves went home and locked herself up in her room.

It is impossible to express her grief when her mother's words opened her eyes to the interest she took in Monsieur de Nemours; she had never dared to acknowledge it to herself. Then she saw that her feelings for him were what Monsieur de Clèves had so often supplicated, and she felt the mortification of having them for another than a husband who so well deserved them. She felt hurt and embarrassed, fearing that Monsieur de Nemours might have used her as a pretext for seeing the dauphiness; and this thought decided her to tell Madame de Chartres what she had hitherto kept secret.

The next morning she went to her mother to carry out this decision; but Madame de Chartres was a little feverish, and did not care to talk with her. The illness seemed so slight, however, that Madame de Clèves called on the

---

8. Negotiations were beginning toward a peace treaty between France and the empire. The death of Queen Mary of England ended the preliminary meetings that had begun at Cercamp in 1558; the next year they resumed and ended with the treaty of Câteau-Cambrésis.

dauphiness after dinner, and found her in her room with two or three ladies with whom she was on intimate terms.

"We were talking about Monsieur de Nemours," said the queen when she saw her, "and were surprised to see how much he is changed since his return from Brussels; before he went, he had an infinite number of mistresses, and it was a positive disadvantage to him, because he used to be kind both to those who were worthy and to those who were not. Since his return, however, he will have nothing to do with any of them. There has never been such a change. His spirits, moreover, seem to be affected, as he is much less cheerful than usual."

Madame de Clèves made no answer; she thought with a sense of shame that she would have taken all that they said about the change in him for a proof of his passion if she had not been undeceived. She was somewhat vexed with the dauphiness for trying to explain and for expressing surprise at something of which she must know the real reason better than any one else. She could not keep from showing her annoyance, and when the other ladies withdrew, she went up to the crown princess and said in a low voice,—

"Is it for my benefit that you have just spoken, and do you want to hide from me that you are the cause of the altered conduct of Monsieur de Nemours?"

"You are unjust," said the crown princess; "you know that I never keep anything from you. It is true that before he went to Brussels, Monsieur de Nemours meant to have me understand that he did not hate me; but since his return he seems to have forgotten all about it, and I confess that I am a little curious about the reason of this change. I shall probably find it out," she went on, "as the Vidame de Chartres, his intimate friend, is in love with a young woman over whom I have some power, and I shall know from her what has made this change."

The dauphiness spoke with an air that carried conviction to Madame de Clèves, who found herself calmer and happier than she had been before. When she went back to her mother, she found her much worse than when she had left her. She was more feverish, and for some days it seemed as if she were going to be really ill. Madame de Clèves was in great distress, and did not leave her mother's room. Monsieur de Clèves spent nearly all his time there too, both to comfort his wife and to have the pleasure of seeing her: his love had not lessened.

Monsieur de Nemours, who had always been one of his friends, had not neglected him since his return from Brussels. During the illness of Madame de Chartres he found it possible to see Madame de Clèves very often, under pretence of calling on her husband or of stopping to take him to walk. He even sought him at hours when he knew he was not in; then he would say that he would wait for him, and used to stay in the ante-chamber of Madame de Chartres, where were assembled many persons of quality. Madame de Clèves would often look in, and although she was in great anxiety, she seemed no less beautiful to Monsieur de Nemours. He showed her how much he sympathized with her distress, and soon convinced her that it was not with the dauphiness that he was in love.

She could not keep from being embarrassed, and yet delighted to see him; but when he was out of her sight and she remembered that this pleasure was the beginning of an unhappy passion, she felt she almost hated him, so much did the idea of guilty love pain her.

Madame de Chartres rapidly grew worse, and soon her life was despaired of; she heard the doctors' opinion of her danger with a courage proportionate to her virtue and piety. After they had left her, she dismissed all who were present, and sent for Madame de Clèves.

"We have to part, my daughter," she said, holding out her hand; "and the peril in which you are and the need you have of me, double my pain in leaving you. You have an affection for Monsieur de Nemours; I do not ask you to confess it, as I am no longer able to make use of your sincerity in order to guide you. It is long since I perceived this affection, but I have been averse to speaking to you about it, lest you should become aware of it yourself. Now you know it only too well. You are on the edge of a precipice: a great effort, a violent struggle, alone can save you. Think of what you owe your husband, think of what you owe yourself, and remember that you are in danger of losing that reputation which you have acquired and which I have so ardently desired for you. Take strength and courage, my daughter: withdraw from the court; compel your husband to take you away. Do not be afraid of making a difficult decision. Terrible as it may appear at first, it will in the end be pleasanter than the consequences of a love-affair. If any other reasons than virtue and duty can persuade you to what I wish, let me say that if anything is capable of destroying the happiness I hope for in another world, it would be seeing you fall like so many women; but if this misfortune must come to you, I welcome death that I may not see it."

Madame de Clèves' tears fell on her mother's hand, which she held clasped in her own, and Madame de Chartres saw that she was moved. "Good-by, my daughter," she said; "let us put an end to a conversation which moves us both too deeply, and remember, if you can, all I have just said to you."

With these words she turned away and bade her daughter call her women, without hearing or saying more. Madame de Clèves left her mother's room in a state that may be imagined, and Madame de Chartres thought of nothing but preparing herself for death. She lingered two days more, but refused again to see her daughter,—the only person she loved.

Madame de Clèves was in sore distress; her husband never left her side, and as soon as Madame de Chartres had died, he took her into the country, to get her away from a place which continually renewed her grief, which was intense. Although her love and gratitude to her mother counted for a great deal, the need she felt of her support against Monsieur de Nemours made the blow even more painful. She lamented being left to herself when she had her emotions so little under control, and when she so needed some one to pity her and give her strength. Her husband's kindness made her wish more than ever to be always true to him. She showed him more affection and kindliness than she had ever done before, and she wanted him always by her side; for it seemed to her that her attachment to him would prove a defence against Monsieur de Nemours.

This prince went to visit Monsieur de Clèves in the country, and did his best to see Madame de Clèves; but she declined to receive him, knowing that she could not fail to find him charming. Moreover, she resolutely determined to avoid every occasion of meeting him, so far as she was able.

Monsieur de Clèves repaired[9] to Paris to pay his respects at court, promising his wife to return the next day; but he did not return till the day after.

"I expected you all day yesterday," Madame de Clèves said to him when he arrived, "and I ought to find fault with you for not returning when you promised. You know that if I could feel a new sorrow in the state I am in, it would be at the death of Madame de Tournon, of which I heard this morning. I should have been distressed by it even if I had not known her. It is always painful when a young and beautiful woman like her dies after an illness of only two days, and much more so when it is one of the persons I liked best in the world, and who seemed as modest as she was worthy."

"I was sorry not to return yesterday," answered Monsieur de Clèves; "but it was so imperatively necessary that I should console an unhappy man that I could not possibly leave him. As for Madame de Tournon, I advise you not to be too profoundly distressed, if you mourn her as an upright woman who deserved your esteem."

"You surprise me," said Madame de Clèves, "as I have often heard you say that there was no woman at court whom you esteemed more highly."

"That is true," he answered; "but women are incomprehensible, and the more I see of them, the happier I feel that I have married you, and I cannot be sufficiently grateful for my good fortune."

"You think better of me than I deserve," exclaimed Madame de Clèves, with a sigh, "and it is much too soon to think me worthy of you. But tell me, please, what has undeceived you about Madame de Tournon."

"I have long been undeceived in regard to her," he replied, "and have long known that she loved the Count of Sancerre, to whom she held out hopes that she would marry him."

"I can scarcely believe," interrupted Madame de Clèves, "that Madame de Tournon, after the extraordinary reluctance to matrimony which she showed after she became a widow, and after her public assertions that she would never marry again, should have given Sancerre any hopes."

"If she had given them only to him," replied Monsieur de Clèves, "there would be little occasion for surprise; but what is astounding is that she also gave them to Estouteville at the same time, and I will tell you the whole story."

Part II

"You know," Monsieur de Clèves continued, "what good friends Sancerre and I are; yet when, about two years ago, he fell in love with Madame de Tournon, he took great pains to conceal it from me, as well as from every one else, and I was far from suspecting it. Madame de Tournon appeared still inconsolable for her husband's death, and was still living in the most absolute retirement. Sancerre's sister was almost the only person she saw, and it was at her house that the count fell in love with her.

"One evening when there was to be a play at the Louvre, and while they were waiting for the king and Madame de Valentinois in order to begin, word was brought that she was ill and that the king would not come. Every one guessed that the duchess's illness was some quarrel with the king. We knew

9. Went.

how jealous he had been of the Marshal of Brissac during his stay at court; but the marshal had gone back to Piedmont a few days before, and we could not imagine the cause of this falling-out.

"While I was talking about it with Sancerre, Monsieur d'Anville came into the hall and whispered to me that the king was in a state of distress and anger most piteous to see; that when he and Madame de Valentinois were reconciled a few days before, after their quarrels about the Marshal of Brissac, the king had given her a ring and asked her to wear it. While she was dressing for the play, he had noticed its absence, and had asked her the reason. She seemed surprised to miss it, and asked her women for it; but they, unfortunately, perhaps because they had not been put on their guard, said that it was some four or five days since they had seen it.

"'That exactly corresponded with the date of the Marshal of Brissac's departure,' Monsieur d'Anville went on; 'and the king is convinced that she gave him the ring when she bade him good-by. This thought has so aroused all his jealousy, which was by no means wholly extinguished, that, contrary to his usual custom, he flew into a rage and reproached her bitterly. He has gone back to his room in great distress, whether because he thinks that Madame de Valentinois has given away his ring, or because he fears that he has displeased her by his wrath, I do not know.'

"As soon as Monsieur d'Anville had finished, I went up to Sancerre to tell him the news, assuring him that it was a secret that had just been told me, and was to go no farther.

"The next morning I called rather early on my sister-in-law, and found Madame de Tournon there. She did not like Madame de Valentinois, and knew very well that my sister-in-law also had no reason for being fond of her. Sancerre had seen her when he left the play, and had told her about the king's quarrel with the duchess; this she had come to repeat to my sister-in-law, either not knowing or not remembering that it was I who had told her lover.

"When I came in, my sister-in-law said to Madame de Tournon that I could be trusted with what she had just told her, and without waiting for permission she repeated to me word for word everything I had told Sancerre the previous evening. You will understand my surprise. I looked at Madame de Tournon, who seemed embarrassed, and her embarrassment aroused my suspicions. I had mentioned the matter to no one but Sancerre, who had left me after the play, without saying where he was going; but I remembered hearing him praise Madame de Tournon very warmly. All these things opened my eyes, and I soon decided that there was a love-affair between them, and that he had seen her after he left me.

"I was so annoyed to find that he kept the matter secret from me that I said a good many things that made it clear to Madame de Tournon that she had been imprudent; as I handed her to her carriage, I assured her that I envied the happiness of the person who had informed her of the falling-out of the king and Madame de Valentinois.

"At once I went to see Sancerre; I reproached him, and said that I knew of his passion for Madame de Tournon, but I did not say how I had found it out. He felt obliged to make a complete confession. I then told him how it was I had discovered his secret, and he told me all about the affair; he said that inasmuch as he was a younger son, and far from having any claims to such an honor, she was yet determined to marry him. No one could be more surprised than I was. I urged Sancerre to hasten his marriage, and told him that he would be justified in fearing anything from a woman who was so full of craft that she could play so false a part before the public. He said in reply that her grief had been sincere, but that it had yielded before her affection for him, and that she could not suddenly make this great change manifest. He brought up many other things in her defence, which showed me clearly how much in love he was; he assured me that he would persuade her to let me know all about the passion he had for her, since it was she who had let out the secret,—and in fact he compelled her to consent, though with much difficulty, and I was from that time fully admitted to their confidence.

"I have never seen a woman so honorable and agreeable toward her lover; yet I was always pained by her affectation of grief. Sancerre was so much in love, and so well satisfied with the way she treated him, that he was almost afraid to urge their marriage, lest she should think that he was moved thereto by interest rather than passion. Still, he often talked to her about it, and she seemed to have decided to marry him; she even began to leave her retirement and to reappear in the world,—she used to come to my sister-in-law's at the time when part of the court used to be there. Sancerre came very seldom; but those who were there every evening and met her often, found her very charming.

"Shortly after she began to come out again into society, Sancerre imagined that he detected some coolness in her love for him. He spoke to me about it several times without rousing any anxiety in me by his complaints; but when at length he told me that instead of hastening, she seemed to be postponing their marriage, I began to think that he had good grounds for uneasiness. I said that even if Madame de Tournon's passion should lessen after lasting for two years, he ought not to be surprised; that even if it did not lessen, and though it should not be strong enough to persuade her to marry him, he ought not to complain; since their marriage would injure her much in the eyes of the public, not only because he was not a very good match for her, but because it would affect her reputation: hence that all he could reasonably desire was that she should not deceive him and feed him with false hopes. I also said that if she had not the courage to marry him, or if she should confess that she loved some one else, he ought not to be angry or complain, but preserve his esteem and gratitude for her.

" 'I give you the advice,' I said to him, 'which I should take myself; for I am so touched by sincerity that I believe that if my mistress, or my wife, were to confess that any one pleased her, I should be distressed without being angered, and should lay aside the character of lover or husband to advise and sympathize with her.' "

At these words Madame de Clèves blushed, finding a certain likeness to her own condition which surprised her and distressed her for some time.

"Sancerre spoke to Madame de Tournon," Monsieur de Clèves went on, "telling her everything I had advised; but she reassured him with such tact and seemed so pained by his suspicions that she entirely dispelled them. Nevertheless she postponed their marriage until after a long journey which he was about to make; but her conduct was so discreet up to the time of his departure, and she seemed so grieved at parting with him, that I, as well as he, believed that she truly loved him. He went away about three months ago.

During his absence I saw Madame de Tournon very seldom; you have taken up all my time, and I only knew that Sancerre was to return soon.

"The day before yesterday, on my arrival in Paris, I heard that she was dead. I at once sent to his house to find out if they had heard from him, and was told that he had arrived the day before,—the very day of Madame de Tournon's death. I went at once to see him, knowing very well in what a state I should find him; but his agony far exceeded what I had imagined. Never have I seen such deep and tender grief. As soon as he saw me, he embraced me, bursting into tears. 'I shall never see her again,' he said, 'I shall never see her again; she is dead! I was not worthy of her; but I shall soon follow her.'

"After that he was silent; then from time to time he repeated: 'She is dead, and I shall never see her again!' Thereupon he would again burst into tears, and seemed out of his head. He told me he had received but few letters from her while away, but that this did not surprise him, because he well knew her aversion to running any risk in writing letters. He had no doubt that she would have married him on his return; and he looked upon her as the most amiable and faithful woman who had ever lived; he believed that she loved him tenderly, and that he had lost her at the moment when he made sure of winning her forever. These thoughts plunged him into the deepest distress, by which he was wholly overcome, and I confess that I was deeply moved.

"Nevertheless, I was obliged to leave him to go to the king, but I promised to return soon. This I did; but imagine my surprise when I found that he was in an entirely different mood. He was pacing up and down his room with a wild face, and he stopped as if he were beside himself and said: 'Come, come! see the most desperate man in the world; I am ten thousand times unhappier than I was before, and what I have just heard of Madame de Tournon is worse than her death.'

"I thought that his grief had crazed him, for I could imagine nothing more terrible than the death of a loved mistress who returns one's love. I told him that so long as his grief had been within bounds I had understood and sympathized with it; but that I should cease to pity him if he gave way to despair and lost his mind. 'I wish I could lose it, and my life too,' he exclaimed. 'Madame de Tournon was unfaithful to me; and I ascertained her infidelity and treachery the day after I heard of her death, at a time when my soul was filled with the deepest grief and the tenderest love that were ever felt,—at a time when my heart was filled with the thought of her as the most perfect creature that had ever lived, and the most generous to me. I find that I was mistaken in her, and that she does not deserve my tears; nevertheless, I have the same grief from her death as if she had been faithful to me, and I suffer from her infidelity as if she were not dead. Had I known of her changed feeling before she died, I should have been wild with wrath and jealousy, and should have been in some way hardened against the blow of her death; but now I can get no consolation from it or hate her.'

"You may judge of my surprise at what Sancerre told me; I asked him how he found this out. He told me that the moment I had left his room, Estoute-ville, an intimate friend of his, though he knew nothing of his love for Madame de Tournon, had come to see him; that as soon as he had sat down, he burst into tears and said he begged his pardon for not having told him before what he was about to say; that he had come to open his heart to him;

and that he saw before him a man utterly crushed by the death of Madame de Tournon.

" 'That name,' said Sancerre, 'surprised me so that my first impulse was to tell him that I was much more distressed than he; but I was unable to speak a word. He went on and told me that he had been in love with her for six months; that he had always meant to tell me, but she had forbidden it so firmly that he had not dared to disobey her; that almost ever since he fell in love with her she had taken a tender interest in him; that he only visited her secretly; that he had had the pleasure of consoling her for the loss of her husband; and, finally, that he was on the point of marrying her at the time of her death, but that this marriage, which would have been one of love, would have appeared to be one of duty and obedience, because she had won over her father to command this marriage, in order that there should not be any great change in her conduct, which had indicated an unwillingness to contract a second marriage.

" 'While Estouteville was speaking,' Sancerre went on, 'I fully believed him, because what he said seemed likely, and the time he had mentioned as that when he fell in love with Madame de Tournon coincided with that of her altered treatment of me. But a moment after, I thought him a liar, or at least out of his senses, and I was ready to tell him so. I thought, however, I would first make sure; hence I began to question him and to show that I had my doubts. At last I was so persistent in the search of my unhappiness that he asked if I knew Madame de Tournon's handwriting, and placed on my bed four of her letters and her portrait. My brother happened to come in at that moment. Estouteville's face was so stained with tears that he had to go away in order not to be seen in that state; he told me that he would come back that evening to get the things he left. I sent my brother away, pretending that I was not feeling well, being impatient to read the letters, and still hoping to find something which would convince me that Estouteville was mistaken. But, alas, what did I not find! What tenderness, what protestations, what promises to marry him, what letters! She had never written me any like them. So,' he went on, 'I suffer at the same time grief for her death and for her faithlessness,—two misfortunes which have often been compared, but have never been felt at the same time by one person. I confess, to my shame, that I feel much more keenly her death than her change; I cannot find her guilty enough to deserve to die. If she were still alive, I should have the pleasure of reproaching her, of avenging myself by showing her how great was her injustice. But I shall never see her again.' He repeated, 'I shall never see her again,—that is the bitterest blow of all; I would gladly give up my life for hers. What a wish! If she were to return, she would live for Estouteville. How happy I was yesterday!' he exclaimed, 'how happy I was then! I was the most sorely distressed man in the world; but my distress was in the order of nature, and I drew some comfort from the thought that I could never be consoled. To-day all my feelings are false ones; I pay to the pretended love she felt for me the same tribute that I thought due to a real affection. I can neither hate nor love her memory; I am incapable of consolation or of grief. At least,' he said, turning suddenly toward me, 'let me, I beg of you, never see Estouteville again; his very name fills me with horror. I know very well that I have no reason to blame him; it is my own fault for concealing from him my love for Madame de Tournon; if he had known of it, he would perhaps have never cared for her, and she would not have been unfaithful to me. He came to see me to confide his grief; I really pity him. Yes, and with good reason,' he exclaimed; 'he loved Madame de Tournon and was loved by her. He will never see her again; yet I feel that I cannot keep from hating him. Once more, I beg of you never to let me see him again.'

"Thereupon Sancerre burst again into tears, mourning Madame de Tournon, saying to her the tenderest things imaginable; thence he changed to hatred, complaints, reproaches, and denunciations of her conduct. When I saw him in this desperate state I knew that I should need some aid in calming him, so I sent for his brother, whom I had just left with the king. I went out to speak to him in the hall before he came in, and I told him what a state Sancerre was in. We gave orders that he was not to see Estouteville, and spent a good part of the night trying to persuade him to listen to reason. This morning I found him in still deeper distress; his brother is staying with him, and I have returned to you."

"No one could be more surprised than I am," said Madame de Clèves, "for I thought Madame de Tournon incapable of both love and deception."

"Address and dissimulation,"[1] answered Monsieur de Clèves, "could not go further. Notice that when Sancerre thought she had changed toward him, she really had, and had begun to love Estouteville. She told her new lover that he consoled her for her husband's death, and that it was he who was the cause of her returning to society; while it seemed to Sancerre that it was because we had decided that she should no longer appear to be in such deep affliction. She was able to persuade Estouteville to conceal their relations, and to seem obliged to marry him by her father's orders, as if it were the result of her care for her reputation,—and this in order to abandon Sancerre without leaving him ground for complaint. I must go back," continued Monsieur de Clèves, "to see this unhappy man, and I think you had better return to Paris. It is time for you to see company and to begin to receive the number of visits that await you."

Madame de Clèves gave her consent, and they returned the next day. She found herself more tranquil about Monsieur de Nemours than she had been; Madame de Chartres' dying words and her deep grief had for a time dulled her feelings, and she thought they had entirely changed.

The evening of Madame de Clèves' arrival the dauphiness came to see her, and after expressing her sympathy with her affliction, said that in order to drive away her sad thoughts she would tell her everything that had taken place at court during her absence, and narrated many incidents. "But what I most want to tell you," she added, "is that it is certain that Monsieur de Nemours is passionately in love, and that his most intimate friends are not only not in his confidence, but they can't even guess whom it is whom he loves. Yet this love is strong enough to make him neglect, or rather give up, the hope of a crown."

The dauphiness then told Madame de Clèves the whole plan about England. "I heard what I have just told you," she went on, "from Monsieur d'Anville; and he said to me this morning that the king sent last evening for Monsieur de Nemours, after reading some letters from Lignerolles, who is anxious to return, and had written to the king that he was unable to explain

1. Skill and tact.

to the Queen of England Monsieur de Nemours' delay; that she is beginning to be offended; and that although she has given no positive answer, she had said enough to warrant him in starting. The king read this letter to Monsieur de Nemours, who instead of talking seriously, as he had done in the beginning, only laughed and joked about Lignerolles' hopes. He said that the whole of Europe would blame his imprudence if he were to presume to go to England as a claimant for the queen's hand without being assured of success. 'It seems to me too,' he went on, 'that I should not choose the present time for my journey, when the King of Spain is doing his best to marry her.[2] In a love-affair he would not be a very formidable rival; but I think that in a question of marrying, your Majesty would not advise me to try my chances against him.' 'I do advise you so in the present circumstances,' answered the king. 'But you have no occasion to fear him. I know that he has other thoughts, and even if he had not, Queen Mary was too unhappy under the Spanish yoke for one to believe that her sister wishes to assume it, or would let herself be dazzled by the splendor of so many united crowns.' 'If she does not let herself be dazzled by them,' went on Monsieur de Nemours, 'probably she will wish to marry for love; she has loved Lord Courtenay for several years. Queen Mary also loved him, and she would have married him, with the consent of the whole of England, had she not known that the youth and beauty of her sister Elizabeth attracted him more than the desire of reigning. Your Majesty knows that her violent jealousy caused her to throw them both into prison, then to exile Lord Courtenay, and finally decided her to marry the King of Spain. I believe that Elizabeth, now that she is on the throne, will recall this lord and thus choose a man she has loved, who is very attractive, and who has suffered so much for her, rather than another whom she has never seen.' 'I should agree with you,' replied the king, 'if Courtenay were still living; but some days ago I heard that he had died at Padua, where he was living in banishment. I see very well,' he added, as he left Monsieur de Nemours, 'that it will be necessary to celebrate your marriage as we should celebrate the dauphin's, by sending ambassadors to marry the Queen of England by procuration.'

"Monsieur d'Anville and the Vidame, who were present while the king was talking with Monsieur de Nemours, are convinced that it is this great passion which has dissuaded him from this plan. The Vidame, who is more intimate than any one with him, said to Madame de Martigues that the prince is changed beyond recognition; and what amazes him still more is that he never finds him engaged or absent, so that he supposes he never meets the woman he loves; and what is so surprising, is to see Monsieur de Nemours in love with a woman who does not return his passion."

All this story that the dauphiness told her was as poison to Madame de Clèves. It was impossible for her not to feel sure that she was the woman whose name was unknown; and she was overwhelmed with gratitude and tenderness when she learned from one who had the best means of knowing that this prince, who had already aroused her interest, hid his passion from every one, and for love of her gave up his chances of a crown. It is impossible to describe her agitation. If the dauphiness had observed her with any care,

2. At the death of his wife, Mary Tudor, in 1558, Philip II of Spain (1527–1598) considered marrying her sister, Elizabeth of England.

she would at once have seen that the story she had just repeated was by no means without interest to her; but having no suspicion of the truth, she went on without noticing her. "Monsieur d'Anville," she added, "who, as I said, told me all this, thinks that I know more about it than he does, and he has so high an opinion of my charms that he is convinced that I am the only person who can make such a great change in Monsieur de Nemours."

Madame de Clèves was agitated by this last remark of the crown princess, though not in the same way as a few moments before. "I should readily agree with Monsieur d'Anville," she replied, "and it is certainly probable, Madame, that no one but a princess like you could make him indifferent to the Queen of England."

"I should at once acknowledge it," said the dauphiness, "if I knew that was the case, and I should know if it were true. Love-affairs of that sort do not escape the notice of those who inspire them; they are the first to perceive them. Monsieur de Nemours has never paid me any but the most insignificant attentions; but there is nevertheless so great a difference between his way with me and his present conduct that I can assure you I am not the cause of the indifference he shows for the crown of England.

"I forget everything while I am with you," she went on, "and it had slipped my mind that I must go to see Madame Elisabeth.[3] You know that peace is nearly concluded, but what you don't know is that the King of Spain would not agree to a single article except on the condition that he, instead of the prince Don Carlos, his son, should marry this princess. The king had great difficulty in agreeing to this; at last he yielded, and has gone to tell Madame. I fancy she will be inconsolable; it certainly cannot be pleasant to marry a man of the age and temper of the King of Spain, especially for her, who, in all the pride of youth and beauty, expected to marry a young prince for whom she has a fancy, though she has never seen him. I don't know whether the king will find her as docile as he wishes, and he has asked me to go to see her; for he knows that she is fond of me, and imagines that I have some influence over her. I shall then make a very different visit, for I must go to congratulate Madame, the king's sister. Everything is arranged for her marriage with Monsieur de Savoie, and he will be here shortly. Never was a person of the age of that princess so glad to marry. The court will be finer and larger than it has ever been, and in spite of your afflictions you must come and help us show the foreigners that we have some famous beauties here."

Then the dauphiness left Madame de Clèves, and the next day Madame Elisabeth's marriage was known to every one. A few days later the king and the queens called on Madame de Clèves. Monsieur de Nemours, who had awaited her return with extreme impatience, and was very desirous of speaking to her alone, put off his call until every one should have left and it was unlikely that others would come in. His plan was successful, and he arrived just as the latest visitors were taking their departure.

The princess was still lying down;[4] it was warm, and the sight of Monsieur de Nemours gave her face an additional color, which did not lessen her beauty. He sat down opposite her with the timidity and shyness that real

3. Elizabeth of France (1545–1568), daughter of Henri II. Philip indeed married her; although she was "inconsolable" about the idea, she was in fact happy with him. 4. It was common at this period for women to receive visitors in their bedrooms.

passion gives. It was some time before he spoke; Madame de Clèves was equally confused, so that they kept a long silence. At last Monsieur de Nemours took courage, and expressed his sympathy with her grief. Madame de Clèves, who was glad to keep the conversation on this safe topic, spoke for some time about the loss she had experienced; and finally she said that when time should have dimmed the intensity of her grief, it would still leave a deep and lasting impression, and that her whole nature had been changed by it.

"Great afflictions and violent passions," replied Monsieur de Nemours, "do greatly alter people; as for me, I am entirely changed since I returned from Flanders. Many persons have noticed this alteration, and even the dauphiness spoke of it last evening."

"It is true," said Madame de Clèves, "that she has noticed it, and I think I have heard her say something about it."

"I am not sorry, Madame," Monsieur de Nemours continued, "that she perceived it, but I should prefer that she should not be the only one to notice it. There are persons to whom one does not dare to give any other marks of the love one feels for them than those which do not affect them in any but an indirect way; and since one does not dare to show one's love, one would at least desire that they should see that one wishes not to be loved by any one else. One would like to have them know that there is no beauty, of whatever rank, whom one would not regard with indifference, and that there is no crown which one would wish to buy at the price of never seeing them. Women generally judge the love one has for them," he went on, "by the pains one takes to please them and to pursue them; but that is an easy matter, provided they are charming. What is difficult is not to yield to the pleasure of pursuing them—it is to avoid them, from fear of showing to the public or to them one's feelings; and the most distinctive mark of a true attachment is to become entirely different from what one was, to be indifferent to ambition or pleasure after having devoted one's whole life to one or the other."

Madame de Clèves readily understood the reference to her in these words. It seemed to her that she ought to answer them and express her disapproval; it also seemed to her that she ought not to listen to them or show that she took his remarks to herself: she believed that she ought to speak, and also that she ought to say nothing. The remarks of Monsieur de Nemours pleased and offended her equally; she saw in them a confirmation of what the crown princess had made her think,—she found them full of gallantry and respect, but also bold and only too clear. Her interest in the prince caused an agitation which she could not control. The vaguest words of a man one likes produce more emotion than the open declarations of a man one does not like. Hence she sat without saying a word, and Monsieur de Nemours noticed her silence, which would have seemed to him a happy omen, if the arrival of Monsieur de Clèves had not put an end to the talk and to his visit.

The Prince de Clèves had come to tell his wife the latest news about Sancerre; but she had no great curiosity about the rest of that affair. She was so interested in what had just happened that she could hardly hide her inattention. When she was able to think it all over, she perceived that she had been mistaken when she fancied that she had become indifferent to Monsieur de Nemours. His words had made all the impression he could desire, and had thoroughly convinced her of his passion. His actions harmonized too well with his words for her to have any further doubts on the subject. She did not any longer indulge in the hope of not loving him; she merely determined to give him no further sign of it. This was a difficult undertaking,—how difficult she knew already. She was aware that her only chance of success lay in avoiding the prince, and her mourning enabled her to live in retirement; she made it a pretext for not going to places where she might meet him. She was in great dejection; her mother's death appeared to be the cause, and she sought no other.

Monsieur de Nemours was in despair at not seeing her oftener; and knowing that he should not meet her at any assembly or entertainment at which the whole court was present, he could not make up his mind to go to them; he pretended a great interest in hunting, and made up hunting-parties on the days of the queens' assemblies. For a long time a slight indisposition served as a pretext for staying at home, and thus escaping going to places where he knew that Madame de Clèves would not be.

Monsieur de Clèves was ailing at nearly the same time, and Madame de Clèves never left his room during his illness; but when he was better and began to see company, and among others Monsieur de Nemours, who, under the pretext of being still weak, used to spend a good part of every day with him, she determined not to stay there. Nevertheless, she could not make up her mind to leave during his first visits; it was so long since she had seen him that she was anxious to meet him again. He too managed to make her listen to him, by what seemed like general talk; though she understood, from its reference to what he had said in his previous visit to her, that he went hunting to get an opportunity for meditation, and that he stayed away from the assemblies because she was not there.

At last Madame de Clèves put into execution her decision to leave her husband's room when the duke should be there, though she found it a difficult task: Monsieur de Nemours observed that she avoided him, and was much pained.

Monsieur de Clèves did not at first notice his wife's conduct; but at last he saw that she was unwilling to stay in his room when company was present. He spoke to her about it, and she replied that she did not think it quite proper that she should meet every evening all the young men of the court. She begged him to let her lead a more retired life than she had done before, because the presence of her mother, who was renowned for her virtue, had authorized many things impossible for a woman of her age.

Monsieur de Clèves, who was generally kind and pleasant to his wife, was not so on this occasion; he told her he was averse to any change in her conduct. She was tempted to tell him that there was a report that Monsieur de Nemours was in love with her; but she did not feel able to mention his name. She was also ashamed to assign a false reason, and to hide the truth from a man who had so good an opinion of her.

A few days later, the king happened to be with the queen when she was receiving, and the company was talking about horoscopes and predictions. Opinions were divided about the credence that ought to be given to them. The queen was inclined to believe in them; she maintained that after so many predictions had come true, it was impossible to doubt the exactness of this science. Others again held that the small number of lucky hits out of the numerous predictions that were made, proved that they were merely the result of chance.

"In former times," said the king, "I was very curious about the future; but

I was told so much that was false or improbable that I became convinced that we can know nothing certain. A few years ago a famous astrologer came here. Every one went to see him, I as well as the rest, but without saying who I was; and I carried with me Monsieur de Guise and D'Escars, sending them into the room in front of me. Nevertheless the astrologer addressed me first, as if he thought I was their master; perhaps he knew me, although he said something to me which seemed to show that he did not know who I was. He prophesied that I should be killed in a duel; then he told Monsieur de Guise that he would be killed from behind, and D'Escars that he would have his skull broken by a kick from a horse. Monsieur de Guise was almost angry at hearing this,—as if he were accused of running away; D'Escars was no more pleased at learning that he was going to perish by such an unfortunate accident,—so that we all left the astrologer in extreme discontent. I have no idea what will happen to Monsieur de Guise or to D'Escars, but it is very unlikely that I shall be killed in a duel. The King of Spain and I have just made peace; and even if we had not, I doubt if we should resort to a personal combat, and it seems unlikely that I should challenge him, as my father challenged Charles V."

After the king had mentioned the unhappy end which had been foretold him, those who had supported astrology gave up and agreed that it was unworthy of belief. "For my part," said Monsieur de Nemours, "I am the last man in the world to place any confidence in it;" and turning to Madame de Clèves, near whom he was, he said in a low voice: "I was told that I should be made happy by the kindness of the woman for whom I should have the most violent and the most respectful passion. You may judge, Madame, whether I ought to believe in predictions."

The dauphiness, who fancied, from what Monsieur de Nemours had said aloud, that he was mentioning some absurd prophecy that had been made about him, asked him what he was saying to Madame de Clèves. He would have been embarrassed by this question if he had had less presence of mind; but he answered without hesitation: "I was saying, Madame, that it had been predicted about me that I should rise to a lofty position to which I should not even dare to aspire."

"If that is the only prediction that has been made about you," replied the dauphiness, smiling, and thinking of the English scheme, "I do not advise you to denounce astrology; you might find good reasons for supporting it."

Madame de Clèves understood what the crown princess referred to; but she also understood that the happiness of which Monsieur de Nemours spoke was not that of being king of England.

As it was some time since her mother's death, Madame de Clèves had to appear again in society and to resume her visits at court. She met Monsieur de Nemours at the dauphiness's and at her own house, whither he often came with young nobles of his own age, in order not to be talked about; but she never saw him without an agitation which he readily perceived.

In spite of the care she took to escape his glances and to talk less with him than with others, certain things inadvertently escaped her which convinced this prince that she was not indifferent to him. A less observant man than he would not, perhaps, have noticed them; but so many women had been in love with him that it was hard for him not to know when he was loved. He perceived that the Chevalier de Guise was his rival, and that prince knew that Monsieur de Nemours was his. He was the only man at court who would have discovered this truth; his interest had rendered him more clear-sighted than the others. The knowledge they had of each other's feelings so embittered their relations that although there was no open breach, they were opposed in everything. In running at the ring and in all the amusements in which the king took part they were always on different sides, and their rivalry was too intense to be hidden.

The English scheme often recurred to Madame de Clèves, and she felt that Monsieur de Nemours would not be able to withstand the king's advice and Lignerolles' urging. She noticed with pain that this last had not yet re-turned, and she awaited him with impatience. If she had followed his move-ments, she would have learned the condition of that matter; but the same feeling that inspired her curiosity compelled her to conceal it, and she con-tented herself with making inquiries about the beauty, intelligence, and char-acter of Queen Elizabeth. A portrait of her was carried to the palace, and she found Elizabeth more beautiful than was pleasant to her, and she could not refrain from saying that it must flatter her.

"I don't think so," replied the dauphiness, who was present. "Elizabeth has a great reputation as a beauty and as the possessor of a mind far above the common, and I know that all my life she has been held up to me as an example. She ought to be attractive if she is like Anne Boleyn, her mother. Never was there a more amiable woman or one more charming both in appearance and disposition. I have been told that her face was exceptionally vivacious, and that she in no way resembled most English beauties."

"It seems to me," said Madame de Clèves, "that I have heard that she was born in France."

"Those who think so," replied the crown princess, "are in error, and I will tell you her history in a few words. She was born of a good English family. Henry VIII had been in love with her sister and her mother, and it had even been suspected that she was his daughter. She came here with the sister of Henry VII, who married Louis XII. This young and gallant princess found it very hard to leave the court of France after her husband's death; but Anne Boleyn, who shared her mistress's feelings, decided to stay. The late king was in love with her, and she remained as maid of honor to Queen Claude. This queen died, and Madame Marguerite, the king's sister, the Duchess of Alençon, since then Queen of Navarre, whose stories you have seen, added Anne to her suite; it was from her that this queen received her inclination toward the new religion. Then Anne returned to England, where she delighted every one. She had French manners, which please all nations; she sang well, and danced charmingly. She was made a lady in waiting to Queen Catherine of Aragon, and King Henry VIII fell desperately in love with her.

"Cardinal Wolsey, his favorite and prime minister, desired to be made pope; and being dissatisfied with the emperor for not supporting his claims, he resolved to avenge himself by allying the king his master with France. He suggested to Henry VIII that his marriage with the emperor's aunt was null and void, and proposed to him to marry the Duchess of Alençon, whose husband had just died. Anne Boleyn, being an ambitious woman, looked on this divorce as a possible step to the throne. She began to instill into the King of England the principles of Lutheranism, and persuaded the late king to urge at Rome Henry's divorce, in the hope of his marriage with Madame d'Alençon. Cardinal Wolsey contrived to be sent to France on other pretexts to arrange this affair; but his master would not consent to have the proposition made, and sent orders to Calais that this marriage was not to be mentioned.

"On his return from France, Cardinal Wolsey was received with honors equal to those paid to the king himself; never did a favorite display such haughtiness and vanity. He arranged an interview between the two kings, which took place at Boulogne. Francis I offered his hand to Henry VIII, who was unwilling to take it; they treated each other with great splendor, each giving the other clothes like those he himself wore. I remember having heard that those the late king sent to the King of England were of crimson satin trimmed with pearls and diamonds arranged in triangles, the cloak of white velvet embroidered with gold. After spending a few days at Boulogne, they went to Calais. Anne Boleyn was quartered in the house with Henry VIII in the queen's suite, and Francis I made her the same presents and paid her the same honors as if she had been a queen herself. At last, after being in love with her for nine years, Henry married her, without waiting for the annulment of his first marriage, which he had long been asking of Rome. The pope at once excommunicated him; this so enraged Henry that he declared himself the head of the Church, and carried all England into the unhappy change of religion in which you now see it.

"Anne Boleyn did not long enjoy her grandeur, for one day, when she thought her position assured by the death of Catherine of Aragon, she happened to be present with all the court when the Viscount Rochford, her brother, was running at the ring. The king was suddenly overwhelmed by such an access of jealousy that he instantly left the spot, hastened to London, and gave orders for the arrest of the queen, the Viscount Rochford, and many others whom he believed to be the queen's lovers or confidants. Although this jealousy seemed the work of a moment, it had for some time been instigated by the Viscountess Rochford, who could not endure her husband's intimacy with the queen, and represented it to the king as criminal intimacy; consequently he, being already in love with Jane Seymour, thought only of getting rid of Anne Boleyn. In less than three weeks he succeeded in having the queen and her brother brought to trial and beheaded, and he married Jane Seymour. He had afterward several wives, whom he either divorced or put to death, among others Catherine Howard, who had been the confidante of the Viscountess of Rochford, and was beheaded with her. Hence she was punished for the crimes with which she had blackened Anne Boleyn, and Henry VIII, having reached a monstrous size, died."

All the ladies present thanked the dauphiness for teaching them so much about the English court, and among others Madame de Clèves, who could not refrain from asking more questions about Queen Elizabeth.

The dauphiness had miniatures painted of all the beauties of the court to send to the queen her mother. The day when that of Madame de Clèves was receiving the last touches the crown princess came to spend the afternoon with her. Monsieur de Nemours was also there, for he neglected no opportunity of seeing Madame de Clèves, although he never seemed to court her society. She was so beautiful that day that he would surely have fallen in love with her then if he had not done so already; but he did not dare to sit with his eyes fixed on her, while she feared lest he should show too plainly the pleasure he found in looking at her.

The crown princess asked Monsieur de Clèves for a miniature he had of his wife, to compare it with the one that was painting. All who were there expressed their opinion of both, and Madame de Clèves asked the painter to make a little correction in the hair of the old one. The artist took the miniature out of its case, and after working on it, set it down on the table.

For a long time Monsieur de Nemours had been desiring to have a portrait of Madame de Clèves. When he saw this one, though it belonged to her husband, whom he tenderly loved, he could not resist the temptation to steal it; he thought that among the many persons present he should not be suspected.

The dauphiness was seated on the bed, speaking low to Madame de Clèves, who was standing in front of her. One of the curtains was only partly closed, and Madame de Clèves was able to see Monsieur de Nemours, whose back was against the table at the foot of the bed, without turning his head pick up something from this table. She at once guessed that it was her portrait, and she was so embarrassed that the crown princess noticed she was not listening to her, and asked her what she was looking at. At these words Monsieur de Nemours turned round and met Madame de Clèves' eyes fastened on him; he felt sure that she must have seen what he had just done.

Madame de Clèves was greatly embarrassed. Her reason bade her ask for her portrait; but if she asked for it openly, she would announce to every one the prince's feelings for her, and by asking for it privately, she would give him an opportunity to speak to her of his love, so that at last she judged it better to let him keep it,—and she was very glad to be able to grant him a favor without his knowing that she did it of her own choice. Monsieur de Nemours, who observed her embarrassment and guessed its cause, came up to her and said in a low voice: "If you saw what I ventured to do, be good enough, Madame, to let me suppose that you know nothing about it; I do not dare to ask anything more." Then he went away, without waiting for an answer.

The dauphiness, accompanied by all her ladies, went out for a walk. Monsieur de Nemours locked himself up in his own room, being unable to contain his joy at having in his possession a portrait of Madame de Clèves. He felt all the happiness that love can give. He loved the most charming woman of the court, and felt that in spite of herself she loved him; he saw in everything she did the agitation and embarrassment which love evokes in the innocence of early youth.

That evening every one looked carefully for the portrait; when they found the case, no one supposed that it had been stolen, but that it had been dropped somewhere. Monsieur de Clèves was distressed at its loss, and after hunting for it in vain, told his wife, but evidently in jest, that she doubtless had some mysterious lover to whom she had given the portrait, or who had stolen it, for no one but a lover would care for the portrait without the case.

Although these words were not said seriously, they made a deep impression on the mind of Madame de Clèves and filled her with remorse. She thought of the violence of her love for Monsieur de Nemours, and perceived that she could not control either her words or her face. She reflected that Lignerolles had returned, and that the English scheme had no terrors for her; that she had no longer grounds for suspecting the dauphiness; and finally, that, as she was without further defence, her only safety was in flight. Since, however, she knew she could not go away, she saw that she was in a most perilous condition, and ready to fall into what she judged to be the greatest possible misfortune,—namely, betraying to Monsieur de Nemours the interest she felt in him. She recalled everything her mother had said to her on her death-bed, and her advice to try everything rather than enter upon a love-affair. She remembered what her husband had said about her sincerity when he was speaking about Madame de Tournon, and it seemed to her that it was her duty to confess her passion for Monsieur de Nemours. She pondered over this for a long time; then she was astonished that the thought occurred to her: she deemed it madness, and fell back into the agony of indecision.

Part III

When peace was signed,[5] Madame Elisabeth, though with great repugnance, determined to obey her father the king. The Duke of Alva had been deputed to marry her in the name of the Catholic king, and he was expected to arrive shortly. The Duke of Savoy was also expected; he was to marry Madame the king's sister, and the two weddings were to take place at the same time. The king thought of nothing but making these events illustrious by entertainments at which he could display all the brilliancy and splendor of his court. It was suggested that plays and ballets should be sumptuously set upon the stage; but the king thought that too meagre a form of entertainment, and desired something more magnificent. He determined to have a tournament at which the foreigners might enter, and to admit the populace as spectators. All the princes and young noblemen gladly furthered the king's plan, and especially the Duke of Ferrara, Monsieur de Guise, and Monsieur de Nemours, who surpassed all others in exercises of this sort. The king chose them to be, with himself, the four champions of the tournament.

It was announced throughout the whole kingdom that a tournament would be opened in the city of Paris on the fifteenth day of June by His Very Christian Majesty and by the Prince Alphonso of Este Duke of Ferrara, Francis of Lorraine Duke of Guise, and James of Savoy Duke of Nemours, who were ready to meet all comers. The first combat was to be on horseback, with four antagonists, with four assaults with the lance, and one for the ladies; the second combat with swords, either singly or in couples, as should be determined; the third combat on foot, three assaults with the pike, and six with the sword. The champions were to supply the lances, swords, and pikes, from which the assailants might choose their weapons. Any one striking a horse in the attack was to be put out of the ranks. There would be four masters of the camp who should have command, and those of the assailants who should be most successful would receive a prize, of a value to be determined by the judges. All the assailants, French or foreign, were to be obliged to come and touch one or more of the shields hanging by the steps at the end of the lists; there they would find an officer to receive and enroll them according to their rank and the shields they had touched. The assailants were to have a gentleman bring their shields with their arms, to be hung by the steps three days before the beginning of the tournament, otherwise they would not be received without the permission of the champions.

A great field was made ready near the Bastile, extending from the caste of

5. The peace treaty of Câteau-Cambrésis (April 1559).

Tournelles, across the Rue St. Antoine, to the royal mews. On each side scaffolding was raised, with rows of seats and covered boxes and galleries, fine to look upon, and capable of holding a vast number of spectators. All the princes and lords were thinking of nothing but their preparations to make a magnificent appearance, and were busily occupied in working some device into their initials or mottoes that should flatter the woman they loved.

A few days before the Duke of Alva's arrival the king went to play tennis with Monsieur de Nemours, the Chevalier de Guise, and the Vidame of Chartres. The queens went with their suites, and Madame de Clèves among the others, to watch the game. After it was over, and they were leaving the court, Châtelart went up to the dauphiness and told her that he had just found a love-letter that had fallen from Monsieur de Nemours' pocket. The crown princess, who was always curious about everything that concerned that prince, told Châtelart to give it to her; she took it, and followed the queen her mother-in-law, who was going with the king to see the preparations for the tournament. After they had been there some time the king sent for some horses which he had recently bought. Though they had not been broken, he wanted to mount them, and he also had them saddled for the gentlemen with him. The king and Monsieur de Nemours got on the most fiery ones, and they tried to spring at one another. Monsieur de Nemours, fearful of injuring the king, backed his horse suddenly against a post with such violence that he was dismounted. The attendants ran up to him and thought he was seriously injured; Madame de Clèves thought him more hurt than did the others. Her interest in him inspired an agitation which she did not think of concealing; she went up to him with the queens, and her color was so changed that a man less interested than the Chevalier de Guise would have noticed it. He remarked it at once, and gave much more attention to the condition of Madame de Clèves than to that of Monsieur de Nemours. This prince was so stunned by the fall that his head had to be supported by those about him. When he came to himself, the first person he saw was Madame de Clèves; he read on her face all the pity she felt, and his expression showed that he was grateful. He then thanked the queens for their kindness, and apologized for appearing before them in such a state. The king ordered him to go home and lie down.

After Madame had recovered from her fright she began to recall the way she had betrayed it. The Chevalier de Guise did not leave her long to enjoy the hope that no one had observed it. As he gave her his hand to lead her from the field, he said: "I am more to be pitied, Madame, than Monsieur de Nemours. Pardon me if I abandon the profound reserve which I have always shown in regard to you, and if I betray the keen grief I feel at what I have just seen; it is the first time that I have been bold enough to speak to you, and it will be the last. Death, or at any rate an eternal separation, will remove me from a place where I cannot live, now that I have lost the sad consolation of believing that all those who dare to look upon you are as unhappy as I."

Madame de Clèves answered with a few disjointed words, as if she did not understand what the Chevalier de Guise meant. At any other time she would have been offended at his speaking of his feelings for her; but at that moment she thought only of her pain at perceiving that he had detected her own for Monsieur de Nemours. The Chevalier de Guise was so overwhelmed and pained by this discovery that he at once resolved never to think of winning

Madame de Clèves' love; but the abandonment of a design which had seemed
so difficult and glorious required one of equal moment to take its place,
hence he thought of going to take Rhodes,[6]—a plan he had already meditated. When he died, in the flower of his youth, just when he had acquired
a reputation as one of the greatest princes of his century, his only regret was
that he had not been able to carry out that noble project, which seemed on
the point of accomplishment.

Madame de Clèves at once went to the queen, with her mind intent on
what had just happened. Monsieur de Nemours came there soon afterward,
in magnificent attire, as if he had forgotten what had just happened. He
appeared even gayer than usual, and his delight at what he thought he had
seen added to his content. Every one was surprised to see him, and asked
him how he felt, except Madame de Clèves, who remained by the fire-place,
as if she did not see him. The king came out of his room, and observing him
there, called him to ask about his mishap. As Monsieur de Nemours passed
by Madame de Clèves, he said in a low voice: "I have received to-day,
Madame, tokens of your pity, but not those I most deserve." Madame de
Clèves had suspected that the prince had noticed her emotion at his accident, and his words showed her that she was not mistaken. She was deeply
pained to see that she could not control her emotions, and had even made
them manifest to the Chevalier de Guise. It distressed her, too, to perceive
that Monsieur de Nemours had read them; but this distress was tempered
by a certain pleasure.

The dauphiness, who was impatient to know what was in the letter that
Châtelart had given her, went up to Madame de Clèves. "Read this letter,"
she said; "it is addressed to Monsieur de Nemours, and apparently is from
that mistress for whom he has left all the others. If you cannot read it now,
keep it; come to me this evening and give it back to me, and tell me whether
you know the handwriting." With these words the crown princess turned
away from Madame de Clèves, leaving her so astonished and agitated that
she could scarcely move. Her emotion and impatience were so great that she
could not stay longer with the queen, and she went home, though it was
much earlier than her usual hour of leaving. Her hands, in which she held
the letter, trembled; her thoughts were all confused, and she felt an unendurable pain such as she had never known. As soon as she was safe in her
room she opened the letter, and read as follows:—

"I love you too much to let you think that the change you see in me is the
result of my fickleness; I want you to know that the real cause is your infidelity. You are surprised that I say your 'infidelity'; you have concealed it so
craftily, and I have taken such pains to hide from you my knowledge of it,
that you are naturally astonished that I should have detected it. I am myself
surprised that I have been able to keep it from you. Never was there any grief
like mine; I imagined that you felt for me a violent passion. I did not conceal
what I felt for you, and at the time when I let you see it, I learned that you
were deceiving me, that you loved another, and, according to all appearances,
were sacrificing me to a new mistress. I knew it the day of the running at

6. The Turks had recaptured the island of Rhodes from the Christians in 1523. François de Lorraine,
chevalier de Guise, in fact later led an expedition there. He was killed at the battle of Dreux in the religious
wars against the Huguenots in 1563, at the age of twenty-nine.

the ring, and that is why I was not there. I pretended to be ill, in order to conceal my emotion; but I really became so, for my body could not stand the intense agitation. When I began to get better, I pretended to be still suffering, in order to have an excuse for not seeing or writing to you; I wanted time to decide how I should act toward you. Twenty times at least I formed and changed my decision; but at last I judged you unworthy to see my grief, and I determined to hide it from you. I wished to wound your pride by letting you see my love for you fade away. I thought thus to diminish the price of the sacrifice you made of it; I did not wish you to have the pleasure of showing how much I loved you in order to appear more amiable. I resolved to write to you indifferent, dull letters, to suggest to the woman to whom you gave them that you were loved less. I did not wish her to have the pleasure of learning that I knew of her triumph over me, or to add to her triumph by my despair and reproaches. I thought I could not punish you sufficiently by breaking with you, and that I should inflict but a slight pain if I ceased to love you when you had ceased to love me. I thought you must love me, if you were to know the pang of not being loved, which tormented me so sorely. I thought that if anything could rekindle the feelings you had had for me, it was by showing that my own were changed, but to show this by pretending to hide it from you, as if I had not strength to tell you. I decided on this; but how hard it was to do so, and when I saw you, how almost impossible to carry it out! Hundreds of times I was ready to spoil all with my reproaches and tears. The state of my health helped me to conceal my emotion and distress. Afterward I was borne up by the pleasure of dissimulating to you as you dissimulated to me; nevertheless I did myself such violence to tell you and to write to you that I loved you, that you saw sooner than I had intended that I had not meant to let you see that my feelings were altered. You were wounded, and complained to me. I tried to reassure you, but in such an artificial way that you were more convinced than ever that I did not love you. At last I succeeded in what I had meant to do. The capriciousness of your heart made you turn again toward me when you saw me leaving you. I have tasted all the joy of vengeance; it has seemed to me that you loved me better than ever, and I have shown you that I did not love you. I have had reason to believe that you had entirely abandoned her for whom you had left me. I have also had grounds for supposing that you never spoke to her of me. But your return and your desertion have not been able to make good your fickleness; your heart has been divided between me and another; you have deceived me: that is enough to deprive me of the pleasure of being loved by you as I thought I deserved, and to fix me in the resolution that I had formed never to see you again, which so surprises you."

Madame de Clèves read and re-read this letter several times without understanding it; all that she made out was that Monsieur de Nemours did not love her as she had thought, and that he loved other women, whom he deceived as he did her. This was a grievous blow to a woman of her character, who was deeply in love, and had just shown this to a man whom she deemed unworthy, in sight of another whom she maltreated for love of his rival. Never was sorrow more bitter! It seemed to her that what had happened that day gave it a special sting, and that if Monsieur de Nemours had not had reason to suppose that she loved him, she would not care whether he had loved another woman. But she deceived herself; the pang she found so unendur-able was that of jealousy, with all its hideous accompaniments. This letter showed her that Monsieur de Nemours had had a love affair for some time. She thought that it attested the writer's cleverness and worth, and she seemed a woman who deserved to be loved. She appeared to have more courage than herself, and she envied her the strength of character she showed in concealing her feelings from Monsieur de Nemours. The end of the letter showed that the woman thought herself still loved; she imagined that his constant discretion, which had so touched her, was perhaps only the effect of his love for the other, whom he feared to offend. In a word, all her thoughts only fed her grief and despair. How often she thought of herself; how often of her mother's counsels! How bitterly she regretted that she had not withdrawn from the world, in spite of Monsieur de Clèves, or that she had not followed her plan of confessing to him her feeling for Monsieur de Nemours! She judged that she would have done better to tell everything to a husband whose generosity she knew, and who would be interested in keep-ing her secret, than to betray it to a man unworthy of it, who was moved to love of her by no other feeling than pride or vanity. In a word, she deemed every evil that could befall her, every misery to which she might be reduced, insignificant by the side of letting Monsieur de Nemours see that she loved him, and knowing that he loved another woman. Her only consolation was that henceforth she need have no fear of herself, and that she was entirely cured of her love for him.

She gave no thought to the dauphiness's command to come to her that evening; she went to bed and pretended to be indisposed, so that when Mon-sieur de Clèves came back from seeing the king, he was told that she was asleep. But she was far from enjoying the calmness that induces sleep. She spent the night in self-reproach and in reading over the letter.

Madame de Clèves was not the only person whose rest was disturbed by this letter. The Vidame of Chartres, who had lost it, not Monsieur de Nemours, was very uneasy about it. He had spent the evening with Monsieur de Guise, who had given a grand supper to his brother-in-law, the Duke of Ferrara, and all the young men of the court. It so happened that during the supper the conversation turned to bright letters, and the Vidame said he had in his pocket the brightest letter that ever was written. He was asked to show it to them, but he refused. Monsieur de Nemours thereupon declared that he had never had it, and was only boasting. The Vidame replied that he tempted him to commit an indiscretion, but he would not show the letter, though he would read a few passages that would prove that few men ever received one like it. At the same time he felt for the letter, but could not find it; he sought everywhere in vain. They laughed at his discomfiture, but he seemed so uneasy that they soon stopped talking about it. He left before the others, hastening home to see if he had left the missing letter there. While he was still hunting for it, a first *valet de chambre*[7] of the queen came to tell him that the Vicomtesse d'Uzès thought it well to let him know that they were talking at the queen's apartment about a love-letter he had dropped from his pocket while he was playing tennis; that they had repeated a good deal that was in the letter; that the queen had expressed a strong desire to

---

7. A personal manservant.

see it; that she had asked one of her gentlemen-in-waiting for it; but he had answered that he had given it to Châtelart.

The *valet de chambre* said many other things to the Vidame which only added to his distress. He went out at once to see a gentleman who was a great friend of Châtelart; he made him get out of bed, although it was very late, to go and ask for the letter, without telling him who wanted it or who had written it. Châtelart, who was confident that it had been written to Monsieur de Nemours, and that he was in love with the dauphiness, felt sure that he knew who had asked for it. He replied, with malicious joy, that he had handed the letter to the dauphiness. The gentleman brought this answer back to the Vidame of Chartres; it gave him only fresh uneasiness. After long hesitation about what he should do, he decided that Monsieur de Nemours was the only man who could aid him.

The Vidame thereupon went to the house of the duke, and entered his bedroom at about daybreak. The prince was sleeping calmly; what he had seen that day of Madame de Clèves gave him only agreeable thoughts. He was much surprised when he was awakened by the Vidame, and he asked him whether this had been done out of revenge for what he had said at the supper. The Vidame's countenance showed that he had come on some serious matter. "I have come," he said, "to confide to you the most important event of my life. I know very well that you have no cause to be grateful, because I do this at a moment when I need your aid; but I know that I should have sunk in your esteem if without being compelled by necessity I had told you what I am about to say. Some time yesterday I dropped the letter of which I was speaking last evening; it is of extreme importance that no one should know that it was written to me. It has been seen by a number of persons who were at the tennis-court when I dropped it. Now, you were there too, and I beg of you to say that it was you who lost it."

"You must suppose that I am not in love with any woman," answered Monsieur de Nemours, smiling, "to make such a proposition to me, and to imagine that there is no one with whom I might fall out if I let it be thought that I receive letters of that sort."

"I beg you," said the Vidame, "to listen to me seriously. If you have a mistress, as I do not doubt, though I have no idea who she is, it will be easy for you to explain yourself, and I will tell you how to do it. Even if you do not have an explanation with her, your falling-out will last but a few moments; whereas I by this mischance bring dishonor to a woman who has loved me passionately, and is one of the most estimable women in the world; and moreover, from another quarter I bring upon myself an implacable hatred, which will certainly cost me my fortune, and may cost me something more."

"I do not understand what you tell me," replied Monsieur de Nemours; "but you imply that the current rumors about the interest a great princess takes in you are not entirely without foundation."

"They are not," exclaimed the Vidame; "but would to God they were! In that case I should not be in my present trouble. But I must tell you what has happened, to give you an idea of what I have to fear.

"Ever since I have been at court, the queen has always treated me with much distinction and amiability, and I have reason to believe that she has had a kindly feeling for me; yet there was nothing marked about it, and I had never dreamed of other feelings toward me than those of respect. I was even much in love with Madame de Themines; the sight of her is enough to prove that a man can have a great deal of love for her when she loves him,—and she loved me. Nearly two years ago, when the court was at Fontainebleau, I happened to talk with the queen two or three times when very few people were there. It seemed to me that I pleased her, and that she was interested in all that I said. One day especially we were talking about confidence. I said I did not confide wholly in any one; that one always repented absolute unreserve sooner or later; and that I knew a number of things of which I had never spoken to any one. The queen said that she thought better of me for that; that she had not found any one in France who had any reserve; and that this had troubled her greatly, because it had prevented her confiding in any one; that one must have somebody to talk to, especially persons of her rank. The following days she several times resumed the same conversation, and told me many tolerably secret things that were happening. At last it seemed to me that she wanted to test my reserve, and that she wished to intrust me with some of her own secrets. This thought attached me to her; I was flattered by the distinction, and I paid her my court with more assiduity than usual. One evening, when the king and all the ladies had gone out to ride in the forest, she remained at home, because she did not feel well, and I stayed with her. She went down to the edge of the pond and let go of the equerry's hand, to walk more freely. After she had made a few turns, she came near me and bade me follow her. 'I want to speak to you,' she said, 'and you will see from what I wish to say that I am a friend of yours.' Then she stopped and gazed at me intently. 'You are in love,' she went on, 'and because you do not confide in any one, you think that your love is not known; but it is known even to the persons interested. You are watched; it is known where you see your mistress: a plan has been made to surprise you. I do not know who she is, I do not ask you; I only wish to save you from the misfortunes into which you may fall.' Observe, please, the snare the queen set for me, and how difficult it was to escape it. She wanted to find out whether I was in love; and by not asking with whom, and by showing that her sole intention was to aid me, she prevented my thinking that she was speaking to me from curiosity or with premeditation.

"Nevertheless, in the face of all appearances I made out the truth. I was in love with Madame de Themines; but though she loved me, I was not fortunate enough to meet her in any private place where we could be surprised, hence I saw that it was not she whom the queen meant. I knew too that I had a love-affair with a woman less beautiful and less severe than Madame de Themines, and it was not impossible that the place where I used to meet her had been discovered; but since I took but little interest in her, it was easy for me to escape from perils of that sort by ceasing to see her. Hence I decided to confess nothing to the queen, but to assure her that I had long since given up the desire to win the love of such women as might smile on me, because I deemed them unworthy of an honorable man's devotion, and it would take women far above them to fascinate me. 'You are not frank,' replied the queen; 'I know the opposite of what you say. The way in which I speak to you binds you to conceal nothing from me. I want you to be one of my friends,' she went on; 'but when I give you that place, I must know all your ties. Consider whether you care to purchase it at the price of informing me; I give you two days to think it over. But be careful what you say to me at the expiration of that time, and remember that if I find out afterward that you have deceived me, I shall never pardon you so long as I live.' Thereupon the queen left me, without awaiting my reply.

"You may well imagine that I was much impressed by what she had just said. The two days she had given me for consideration did not seem to me too long. I perceived that she wished to know whether I was in love, and hoped that I was not. I saw the importance of the decision I was about to make. My vanity was not a little flattered by a love-affair with a queen, and a queen who was still so charming. To be sure, I love Madame de Themines, and although I was unfaithful to her in a way with that other woman I mentioned, I could not make up my mind to break with her. I also saw the danger to which I exposed myself in deceiving the queen, and how hard it would be to deceive her; yet I could not decide to refuse what fortune offered me, and I determined to risk the consequences of my evil conduct. I broke with that woman with whom my relations might be discovered, and I hoped to conceal those I had with Madame de Themines.

"At the expiration of the two days that the queen had granted me, as I was entering a room where all her ladies were assembled, she said to me aloud, with a seriousness that surprised me,—

" 'Have you thought over that matter of which I spoke to you, and do you know the truth about it?'

" 'Yes, Madame,' I replied, 'and it is as I told your Majesty.'

" 'Come this evening at the hour that I shall write to you, and I will give you the rest of my orders.'

"I made a deep bow, without answering, and did not fail to appear at the hour set. I found her in the gallery with her secretary and some of her ladies. As soon as she saw me, she came up to me and led me to the other end of the gallery.

" 'Well!' she said, 'is it after due reflection that you have nothing to say to me, and does not my treatment of you deserve that you should speak to me frankly?'

" 'It is because I am frank with you, Madame,' I replied, 'that I have nothing to tell you; and I swear to your Majesty, with all the respect I owe you, that I am not in love with any lady of the court.'

" 'I am willing to believe it,' resumed the queen, 'because I wish to; and I wish it because I desire that you should be unreservedly attached to me; and I could not possibly be satisfied with your friendship if you were in love. One may trust those who are, but it is impossible to have confidence in their secrecy. They are too inattentive and have too many distractions; their mistress is their main interest,—and that would not suit the way in which I want you to be attached to me. Remember, it is on account of your oath that you are free that I choose you for the recipient of my confidence. Remember that I wish yours without reserve, that I want you to have no friend, man or woman, except such as shall be agreeable to me, and that you will give up every aim except pleasing me. I shall not let harm come to your fortune,—I shall look after that more zealously than you do; and whatever I do for you, I shall consider myself more than paid if I find that you are to me what I hope. I choose you in order to confide in you all my anxieties, and to help me endure them. You will see that they are not light. To all appearance I suffer no pain from the king's attachment to Madame de Valentinois; but I can scarcely bear it. She controls the king; she is false to him; she despises me; all my people are devoted to her. My daughter-in-law, the crown princess, is vain of her beauty and of her uncle's power, and pays no respect to me. The Constable of Montmorency is master of the king and of the kingdom; he hates me, and has given me tokens of his hatred which I can never forget. The Marshal of Saint-André is an audacious young favorite, who treats me no better than do the others. The full list of my sufferings would arouse your compassion. Hitherto I have not dared to trust any one; I do put confidence in you: act in such a way that I shall not repent of it, and be my sole consolation.'

"The queen's eyes filled with tears as she said these last words, and I was on the point of throwing myself at her feet, so deeply was I moved by the kindness she showed me. Since that day she has had perfect confidence in me; she never takes a step without talking it over with me, and my alliance with her still lasts.

Part IV

"Still, though much taken up by my new intimacy with the queen, I was bound to Madame de Themines by a feeling which I could not overcome. It seemed to me that her love for me was waning; and although if I had been wise I should have taken advantage of this change I saw in her to try to forget her, as it was, my love for her redoubled, and I managed so ill that the queen in time learned something about this attachment. Persons of her nation[8] are always inclined to jealousy, and possibly her feelings toward me were warmer than she herself supposed. But at last the report that I was in love gave her such distress and grief that I very often felt sure that I had wholly lost her favor. I reassured her by my attentions, submissiveness, and by many false oaths; but I could not have long deceived her if Madame de Themines' altered demeanor had not at last set me free in spite of myself. She made me see that she loved me no longer, and I was so sure of this that I felt compelled to cease persecuting her with my attentions. Some time after, she wrote me the letter that I have lost. That told me that she knew about my relations with the other woman I mentioned, and that this was the reason of the change. Since, then, there was no one to divide my attentions, the queen was tolerably satisfied with me; but inasmuch as my feeling for her was not of a sort to render me incapable of another attachment, and it is impossible for a man to control his heart by force of will, I fell in love with Madame de Martigues, in whom I had been much interested before, when she was a Villemontais[9] and maid-of-honor to the dauphiness. I had reason for believing that she did not hate me, and that she was pleased with my discreet conduct, although she did not understand all its reasons. The queen has no suspicions about this affair, but there is another which torments her a great deal. Since Madame de Martigues is always with the crown princess, I go there oftener than usual. The queen has taken it into her head that it is with this princess that I am in love. The dauphiness's rank, which is equal to her

<hr>

8. Italy. 9. I.e., before her marriage: Villemontais was her maiden name.

own, and her advantages of youth and beauty, inspire a jealousy which amounts to madness, and she cannot conceal her hatred of her daughter-in-law. The Cardinal of Lorraine, who seems to me to have been for a long time an aspirant for the queen's good graces, and who sees me occupying a place that he would like to fill, under the pretence of bringing about a reconciliation between her and the crown princess is looking into the causes of their dissension. I do not doubt that he has found out the real cause of the queen's bitterness, and I fancy that he has done me many an evil turn, though without showing his hand. That is the state of affairs now. Judge then what will be the effect of the letter I lost when I was unfortunate enough to put it into my pocket to return it to Madame de Themines. If the queen sees this letter, she will know that I have deceived her, and that at almost the same time when I was false to her on account of Madame de Themines, I was false to Madame de Themines on account of another woman. Judge then what sort of an opinion she will have of me, and whether she will ever believe me again. If she does not see this letter, what shall I say to her? She knows that it has been in the dauphiness's hands; she will think that Chatelart recognized that princess's handwriting, and that the letter is from her; she will imagine that she is perhaps the woman whose jealousy is mentioned,—in a word, there is nothing which she may not think, and there is nothing I may not fear from her thoughts. Add to this that I am sincerely interested in Madame de Martigues, that the crown princess will certainly show her this letter, and that she will believe it was written very recently. So I shall be embroiled both with the woman I love best in the world and with the woman from whom I have most to fear. Consider now whether I am not justified in begging you to say that the letter is yours and in asking you as a favor to try to get it from the dauphiness."

"It is very plain," said Monsieur de Nemours, "that one could hardly be in more serious perplexity than you are; and you must confess that you got into it by your own fault. I have been accused of being a faithless lover and of carrying on several love-affairs at the same time; but I am nothing by the side of you, for I should never have dreamed of doing what you have done. Could you suppose it possible to keep on good terms with Madame de Themines when you formed your alliance with the queen; and did you hope to become intimate with the queen and yet succeed deceiving her? She is an Italian and a queen, and hence suspicious, jealous, and haughty. When your good luck rather than your good conduct got you out of one entanglement, you got into a new one, and imagined that here, amid the whole court, you could love Madame de Martigues without the queen's knowing anything about it. You could not have been too careful to rid her of the mortification of having taken the first steps. She has a violent passion for you. You are too discreet to say so, and I am too discreet to ask any questions; but she loves you, she distrusts you, and the facts justify her."

"Is it for you to overwhelm me with reproaches?" interrupted the Vidame. "Ought not your experience to make you indulgent to my faults? Still, I am willing to confess that I did wrong; but consider, I beg of you, how to get me out of my present complications. It seems to me that you must see the crown princess as soon as she is up, and ask her for the letter as if it were yours."

"I have already told you," replied Monsieur de Nemours, "that this is a somewhat extraordinary request, and one that, the circumstances being what they are, I do not find very easy to grant. Then, too, if the letter was seen to fall from your pocket, how can I convince them that it fell from mine?"

"I thought I had said that they told the dauphiness that it was from yours that it fell."

"What!" said Monsieur de Nemours with some asperity, for he saw at once that this mistake might complicate matters with Madame de Clèves. "So the dauphiness has been told that I dropped this letter?"

"Yes," answered the Vidame; "that is what they told her,—and the mistake arose in this way: there were several of the queen's gentlemen in one of the rooms by the tennis-court where our clothes were hanging, and when we sent for them the letter dropped; these gentlemen took it up and read it aloud. Some thought it was written to you; others, that it was written to me. Chatelart, who took it, and from whom I have just tried to get it, said he had given it to the crown princess as a letter of yours; those who mentioned it to the queen unfortunately said it was mine,—so you can easily do what I wish, and get me out of this terrible complication."

Monsieur de Nemours had always been very fond of the Vidame of Chartres, and his relationship to Madame de Clèves rendered him still dearer. Nevertheless, he could not make up his mind to run the risk of her hearing of this letter as something in which he was concerned. He began to meditate profoundly, and the Vidame, guessing the nature of his thoughts, said: "I really believe you are afraid of falling out with your mistress; and I should be inclined to think that it is about the dauphiness that you are anxious, were it not that your freedom from any jealousy of Monsieur d'Anville forbids the thought. But however that may be, you must not sacrifice your peace of mind to mine, and I will make it possible for you to prove to the woman you love that this letter was written to me, and not to you. Here is a note from Madame d'Amboise; she is a friend of Madame de Themines, and to her she has confided all her feelings about me. In this note she asks me for her friend's letter,—the one I lost. My name is on the note, and its contents prove beyond the possibility of doubt that the letter she asks for is the one that has been picked up. I intrust this note to you, and I am willing that you should show it to your mistress in order to clear yourself. I beg of you not to lose a moment, but to go to the dauphiness this morning."

Monsieur de Nemours gave his promise to the Vidame of Chartres and took Madame d'Amboise's note. But his intention was not to see the crown princess; he thought he had something more urgent to do. He felt sure that she had already spoken about this letter to Madame de Clèves, and he could not endure that a woman he loved so much should have any reason for thinking that he was attached to any other.

He went to her house as soon as he thought she might be awake, and sent up word that he would not ask to have the honor at such an extraordinary hour if it were not on very important business. Madame de Clèves was not yet up; she was much embittered and agitated by the gloomy thoughts that had tormented her all night. She was extremely surprised when she heard that Monsieur de Nemours wanted to see her. Grieved as she was, she did not hesitate to send him word that she was ill, and unable to see him.

He was not pained by this refusal; an act of coolness at a time when she might be jealous was no unfavorable omen. He went to Monsieur de Clèves' apartments and told him that he had just called on his wife; that he was very sorry he could not see her, because he wished to speak to her of a matter of importance in which the Vidame of Chartres was interested. In a few words he told Monsieur de Clèves how serious the matter was, and Monsieur de Clèves took him at once to his wife's room. Nothing but the darkness enabled her to hide her agitation and surprise at seeing Monsieur de Nemours brought into her room by her husband. Monsieur de Clèves said that there was some question about a letter, and the Vidame's interests required her aid; he added that Monsieur de Nemours would tell her what was to be done, and that he should go to the king, who had just sent for him.

Monsieur de Nemours was left alone with Madame de Clèves,—which was exactly what he wanted. "I have come, Madame," he began, "to ask you if the dauphiness has not spoken to you about a letter which Châtelart gave her."

"She said something about it to me," answered Madame de Clèves; "but I don't understand how this letter concerns my uncle, and I am able to assure you that his name is not mentioned in it."

"True, Madame," Monsieur de Nemours went on, "his name is not mentioned; nevertheless, it was written to him, and it is of the utmost importance to him that you should get it out of her hands."

"I fail to understand," said Madame de Clèves, "how it concerns him that this letter should not be seen, and why it should be asked for in his name."

"If you will kindly listen to me," said Monsieur de Nemours, "I will speedily explain the matter to you, and you will soon see that the Vidame is so implicated that I should not have said anything about it even to the Prince of Clèves if I had not needed his assistance in order to have the honor of seeing you."

"I think that all that you might take the trouble to say to me would be useless," replied Madame de Clèves, somewhat tartly; "and it is much better that you should go to the crown princess and tell her frankly your interest in this letter, since it has been said that it belongs to you."

The vexation that Monsieur de Nemours saw in Madame de Clèves gave him the keenest pleasure he had yet known, and fully consoled him for his impatience to explain himself. "I do not know, Madame," he began, "what may have been said to the dauphiness; but this letter does not concern me personally, and it was written to the Vidame."

"That I believe," replied Madame de Clèves; "but the dauphiness has been told the contrary, and it will not seem to her likely that the Vidame's letters should fall out of your pockets. That is why, unless you have some good reason for concealing the truth from her, I advise you to confess it to her."

"I have nothing to confess to her," he went on; "the letter is none of mine, and if there is any one I wish to convince of this, it is not the crown princess. But, Madame, since the Vidame's fate is at stake, permit me to tell you some things which you will find quite worth listening to."

The silence of Madame de Clèves showed that she was willing to listen, and Monsieur de Nemours repeated in as few words as possible what the Vidame had told him. Although this might well have surprised, or at least interested, her, Madame de Clèves listened with such marked indifference that she seemed to doubt it or to find it unworthy of her attention. She maintained this indifference until Monsieur de Nemours mentioned Madame d'Amboise's note to the Vidame of Chartres, which was the proof of all he had just been saying. Since Madame de Clèves knew that she was a friend of Madame de Themines, it seemed to her possible that Monsieur de Nemours had been speaking the truth, and she began to think that possibly the letter in question had not been written to him. This thought suddenly dispelled her indifference. The prince read her the note, which exonerated him completely, and then handed it to her for examination, telling her that perhaps she knew the handwriting; she was compelled to take it and to read the address, and indeed every word, in order to make sure that the letter asked for was the one in her possession. Monsieur de Nemours said everything he could think of to convince her; and since a pleasant truth is readily believed, he succeeded in proving to Madame de Clèves that he had no part whatsoever in the letter.

Then she began to reflect on the Vidame's troubles and danger, to blame his evil conduct, and to desire means to aid him. She was surprised at the queen's behavior; she confessed to Monsieur de Nemours that the letter was in her possession,—in a word, so soon as she thought him innocent, she interested herself at once with the utmost cordiality in the very things that at first left her perfectly indifferent. They agreed that it was not necessary to return the letter to the crown princess, lest she should show it to Madame de Martigues, who knew Madame de Themines' handwriting, and would at once have guessed, from her interest in the Vidame, that the letter had been written to him. They also thought that it was better not to confide to the dauphiness the part concerning her mother-in-law, the queen. Madame de Clèves, under the pretext of her concern for her uncle's affairs, gladly promised to keep every secret that Monsieur de Nemours might intrust to her.

This prince would have talked with her about other things than the Vidame's affairs, and would have taken advantage of this opportunity to speak to her with greater freedom than he had ever done, were it not that word was brought to Madame de Clèves that the dauphiness had sent for her; Monsieur de Nemours consequently was obliged to withdraw. He went to see the Vidame, to tell him that after leaving him he had thought it better to see his niece, Madame de Clèves, than to go straight to the dauphiness. He brought forward many good arguments in support of what he had done and to make success seem probable.

Meanwhile Madame de Clèves dressed in all haste to go to the crown princess. She had scarcely entered the room when the dauphiness called her to her, and said in a low voice,—

"I have been waiting two hours for you, and never had more difficulty in concealing the truth than I have had this morning. The queen has heard about the letter I gave you yesterday, and thinks it was the Vidame of Chartres who dropped it; you know she takes a good deal of interest in him. She wanted to see the letter, and sent to ask Châtelart for it; he told her he had given it to me, and then they came to ask me for it, under the pretext that it was a very bright letter, which the queen was anxious to see. I did not dare say that you had it; I feared she would think that it had been placed in your hands because the Vidame is your uncle, and that there was some understanding between you and me. It has already occurred to me that she did not like his seeing me often; so I said the letter was in the pocket of the clothes I wore yesterday, and that those who had the key of the room in which they were locked had gone out. So give me the letter at once, that I may send it to her; and let me look at it before I send it, to see if I know the handwriting."

Madame de Clèves was even more embarrassed than she had expected. "I don't know, Madame," she answered, "what you will do; for Monsieur de Clèves, to whom I had given it, gave it back to Monsieur de Nemours, who came this morning to get him to ask you to return it to him. Monsieur de Clèves was imprudent enough to say that it was in his possession, and weak enough to yield to Monsieur de Nemours' entreaties and to give it to him."

"You have put me in the greatest possible embarrassment," said the dauphiness, "and you did very wrong to return the letter to Monsieur de Nemours; since I gave it you, you ought not to have returned it without my permission. What can I say to the queen, and what will she think? She will believe, and on good grounds, that this letter concerns me, and that there is something between the Vidame and me. She will never believe that the letter belongs to Monsieur de Nemours."

"I am extremely sorry," answered Madame de Clèves, "for the trouble I have caused,—I see just how great it is; but it is Monsieur de Clèves' fault, not mine."

"It is yours," retorted the dauphiness, "because you gave him the letter. There is not another woman in the world who would confide to her husband everything she knows."

"I acknowledge that I was wrong, Madame," said Madame de Clèves; "but think rather of repairing than of discussing my fault."

"Don't you remember pretty well what was in the letter?" asked the crown princess.

"Yes, Madame," was the reply; "I remember it, for I read it over more than once."

"In that case, you must go at once and write it in a disguised hand. This copy I will send to the queen. She will not show it to any one who has seen the original; and even if she should, I shall always maintain that it was the one that Châtelart gave me, and he will not dare to deny it."

Madame de Clèves agreed to this plan, and all the more readily because she thought she would send for Monsieur de Nemours to let her have the letter again, in order to copy it word for word, and so far as possible imitate the handwriting; in this way she thought the queen could not fail to be deceived. As soon as she got home she told her husband about the dauphiness's embarrassment, and begged him to send for Monsieur de Nemours; this was done, and he came at once. Madame de Clèves repeated to him what she had just told her husband, and asked him for the letter. Monsieur de Nemours replied that he had already given it back to the Vidame de Chartres, who was so glad to see it again and to be out of danger that he had at once sent it to Madame de Themines. Madame de Clèves was in new trouble; but at last, after discussing the matter together, they determined to write the letter from memory. They locked themselves up to work, left word at the door that no one was to be let in, and sent off Monsieur de Nemours' servants. This appearance of mystery and of confidence was far from unpleasant to this prince, and even to Madame de Clèves. The presence of her husband and the thought that she was furthering the Vidame's interests almost calmed her scruples. She felt only the pleasure of seeing Monsieur de Nemours; it was a fuller and purer joy than any she had ever felt, and it inspired her with a liveliness and ease that Monsieur de Nemours had never seen in her, and his love for her was only deepened. Since he had never before had such pleasant moments, his own spirits rose, and when Madame de Clèves wanted to recall the letter and to write, he, instead of aiding her seriously, did nothing but interrupt her with idle jests. Madame de Clèves was quite as merry; so that they had been long shut up together, and twice word had come from the dauphiness urging Madame de Clèves to make haste, before half the letter was written.

Monsieur de Nemours was only too happy to prolong so pleasant a visit, and forgot his friend's interests. Madame de Clèves was amusing herself, and forgot those of her uncle. At last, at four o'clock, the letter was hardly finished, and the handwriting was so unlike that of the original that it was impossible that the queen should not at once detect the truth; and she was not deceived by it. Although they did their best to convince her that the letter was written to Monsieur de Nemours, she remained convinced, not only that it was addressed to the Vidame de Chartres, but that the dauphiness had something to do with it, and that there was some understanding between him and her. This thought so intensified her hatred of this princess that she never forgave her, and persecuted her till she drove her from France.

As for the Vidame of Chartres, he was ruined so far as she was concerned; and whether it was that the Cardinal of Lorraine had already acquired an ascendency over her, or that the affair of this letter, in which she saw that she had been deceived, opened her eyes to the other deceptions of which the Vidame had been guilty, it is certain that he could never bring about a satisfactory reconciliation. Their intimacy was at an end, and she accomplished his ruin afterward at the time of the conspiracy of Amboise,[1] in which he was implicated.

After the letter had been sent to the crown princess, Monsieur de Clèves and Monsieur de Nemours went away. Madame de Clèves was left alone; and as soon as she was deprived of the presence of the man she loved, she seemed to awaken from a dream. She thought with surprise of the difference between her state of mind the previous evening and that she then felt; she pictured the coldness and harshness she had shown to Monsieur de Nemours so long as she had supposed that Madame de Themines' letter had been written to him, and the tranquillity and happiness that had succeeded them when he had proved to her that this letter in no way concerned him. When she recalled that the day before she had reproached herself, as if it were a crime, for having shown an interest that mere compassion had called forth, and that by her harshness she had betrayed a feeling of jealousy,—a certain proof of affection,—she scarcely recognized herself. When she thought further that Monsieur de Nemours saw that she was aware of his love; when he saw that, in spite of this, she treated him with perfect cordiality in her husband's presence,—indeed that she had treated him with more kindness than ever before, that she was the cause of her husband's sending for him, and that they had just passed an afternoon together privately,—she saw that there was an understanding between herself and Monsieur de Nemours; that

---

1. A 1560 conspiracy led by Louis de Bourbon, prince of Condé, and the Huguenot party in an effort to destroy the influence of the Guises over King Francis II. The plot failed.

she was deceiving a husband who deserved to be deceived less than any husband in the world; and she was ashamed to appear so unworthy of esteem even before the eyes of her lover. But what pained her more than all the rest was the memory of the state in which she had passed the night, and the acute grief she had suffered from the thought that Monsieur de Nemours loved another and that she had been deceived.

Up to that time she had not known the stings of mistrust and jealousy; her only thought had been to keep from loving Monsieur de Nemours, and she had not yet begun to fear that he loved another. Although the suspicions that this letter had aroused were wholly removed, they opened her eyes to the danger of being deceived, and gave her impressions of mistrust and jealousy such as she had never felt before. She was astounded that she had never yet thought how improbable it was that a man like Monsieur de Nemours, who had always treated women with such fickleness, should be capable of a sincere and lasting attachment. She thought it almost impossible that she could ever be satisfied with his love. "But if I could be," she asked herself, "what could I do with it? Do I wish it? Could I return it? Do I wish to begin a love-affair? Do I wish to fail in my duty to Monsieur de Clèves? Do I wish to expose myself to the cruel repentance and mortal anguish that are inseparable from love? I am overwhelmed by an affection which carries me away in spite of myself; all my resolutions are vain; I thought yesterday what I think to-day, and I act to-day in direct contradiction to my resolutions of yesterday. I must tear myself away from the society of Monsieur de Nemours; I must go to the country, strange as the trip may seem; and if Monsieur de Clèves persists in opposing it, or in demanding my reasons, perhaps I shall do him and myself the wrong of telling them to him." She held firm to this resolution, and spent the evening at home, instead of going to find out from the dauphiness what had become of the Vidame's pretended letter.

When Monsieur de Clèves came home she told him she wanted to go into the country; that she was not feeling well, and needed a change of air. Monsieur de Clèves, who felt sure from her appearance that there was nothing serious ailed her, at first laughed at the proposed trip, and told her that she forgot the approaching marriages of the princesses and the tournament, and that she would not have time enough to make her preparations for appearing in due splendor alongside the other ladies. Her husband's arguments did not move her; she begged him, when he went to Compiègne with the king, to let her go to Coulommiers,[2]—a country-house they were building at a day's journey from Paris. Monsieur de Clèves gave his consent; so she went off with the intention of not returning at once, and the king left for a short stay at Compiègne.

Monsieur de Nemours felt very bad at not seeing Madame de Clèves again after the pleasant afternoon he had spent with her, which had so fired his hopes. His impatience to meet her once more left him no peace; so that when the king returned to Paris he determined to make a visit to his sister, the Duchess of Mercœur, who lived in the country not far from Coulommiers. He proposed to the Vidame to go with him; the latter gladly consented, to the delight of Monsieur de Nemours, who hoped to make sure of seeing Madame de Clèves by calling in company with the Vidame.

2. About twenty-five miles east of Paris.

Madame de Mercœur was delighted to see them, and at once began to devise plans for their amusement. While they were deer-hunting, Monsieur de Nemours lost his way in the forest; and when he asked what road he should take, he was told that he was near Coulommiers. When he heard this word, "Coulommiers," he at once, without thinking, without forming any plan, dashed off in that direction. He got once more into the forest, and followed such paths as seemed to him to lead to the castle. These paths led to a summer-house, which consisted of a large room with two closets,[3] one opening on a flower-garden separated from the forest by a fence, and the other opening on one of the walks of the park. He entered the summer-house, and was about to stop and admire it, when he saw Monsieur and Madame de Clèves coming along the path, followed by a number of servants. Surprised at seeing Monsieur de Clèves, whom he had left with the king, his first impulse was to hide. He entered the closet near the flower-garden, with the intention of escaping by a door opening into the forest; but when he saw Madame de Clèves and her husband sitting in the summer-house, while their servants stayed in the park, whence they could not reach him without coming by Monsieur and Madame de Clèves, he could not resist the temptation to watch her, or overcome his curiosity to listen to her conversation with her husband, of whom he was more jealous than of any of his rivals.

He heard Monsieur de Clèves say to his wife: "But why don't you wish to return to Paris? What can keep you in the country? For some time you have had a taste for solitude which surprises me and pains me, because it keeps us apart. I find you in even lower spirits than usual, and I am afraid something distresses you."

"I have nothing on my mind," she answered, with some embarrassment; "but the bustle of a court is so great, and our house is always so thronged, that it is impossible for mind and body not to be tired and to need rest."

"Rest," he answered, "is not needed by persons of your age. Neither at home nor at court do you get tired, and I should be rather inclined to fear that you are glad to get away from me."

"If you thought that, you would do me great injustice," she replied, with ever-growing embarrassment; "but I beg of you to leave me here. If you could stay too I should be very glad, provided you would stay alone, and did not care for the throng of people who almost never leave you."

"Ah, Madame," exclaimed Monsieur de Clèves, "your air and your words show me that you have reasons for wishing to be alone which I don't know, and which I beg of you to tell me."

For a long time the prince besought her to tell him the reason, but in vain; and after she had refused in a way that only redoubled his curiosity, she stood for a time silent, with eyes cast down; then, raising her eyes to his, she said suddenly,—

"Don't compel me to confess something which I have often meant to tell you, but had not the strength. Only remember that prudence does not require that a woman of my age, who is mistress of her actions, should remain exposed to the temptations of the court."

"What is it you suggest, Madame?" exclaimed Monsieur de Clèves. "I should not dare to say, for fear of offending you."

3. Small private rooms for reading or meditation.

Madame de Clèves did not answer, and her silence confirming her husband's suspicions, he went on,—

"You are silent, and your silence tells me I am not mistaken."

"Well, sir," she answered, falling on her knees, "I am going to make you a confession such as no woman has ever made to her husband; the innocence of my actions and of my intentions gives me strength to do so. It is true that I have reasons for keeping aloof from the court, and I wish to avoid the perils that sometimes beset women of my age. I have never given the slightest sign of weakness, and I should never fear displaying any, if you would leave me free to withdraw from court, or if Madame de Chartres still lived to guide my actions. Whatever the dangers of the course I take, I pursue it with pleasure, in order to keep myself worthy of you. I beg your pardon a thousand times if my feelings offend you; at any rate I shall never offend you by my actions. Remember that to do what I am now doing requires more friendship and esteem for a husband than any one has ever had. Guide me, take pity on me, love me, if you can."

All the time she was speaking, Monsieur de Clèves sat with his head in his hands; he was really beside himself, and did not once think of lifting his wife up. But when she had finished, and he looked down and saw her, her face wet with tears, and yet so beautiful, he thought he should die of grief. He kissed her, and helped her to her feet.

"Do you, Madame, take pity on me," he said, "for I deserve it; and excuse me if in the first moments of a grief so poignant as mine I do not respond as I should to your appeal. You seem to me worthier of esteem and admiration than any woman that ever lived; but I also regard myself as the unhappiest of men. The first moment that I saw you, I was filled with love of you; neither your indifference to me nor the fact that you are my wife has cooled it: it still lives. I have never been able to make you love me, and I see that you fear you love another. And who, Madame, is the happy man that inspires this fear? Since when has he charmed you? What has he done to please you? What was the road he took to your heart? I found some consolation for not having touched it in the thought that it was beyond any one's reach; but another has succeeded where I have failed. I have all the jealousy of a husband and of a lover; but it is impossible to suffer as a husband after what you have told me. Your noble conduct makes me feel perfectly secure, and even consoles me as a lover. Your confidence and your sincerity are infinitely dear to me; you think well enough of me not to suppose that I shall take any unfair advantage of this confession. You are right, Madame,—I shall not; and I shall not love you less. You make me happy by the greatest proof of fidelity that a woman ever gave her husband; but, Madame, go on and tell me who it is you are trying to avoid."

"I entreat you, do not ask me," she replied; "I have determined not to tell you, and I think that the more prudent course."

"Have no fear, Madame," said Monsieur de Clèves; "I know the world too well to suppose that respect for a husband ever prevents men falling in love with his wife. He ought to hate those who do so, but without complaining; so once more, Madame, I beg of you to tell me what I want to know."

"You would urge me in vain," she answered; "I have strength enough to keep back what I think I ought not to say. My avowal is not the result of

weakness, and it requires more courage to confess this truth than to undertake to hide it."

Monsieur de Nemours lost not a single word of this conversation, and
Madame de Clèves' last remark made him quite as jealous as it made her
husband. He was himself so desperately in love with her that he supposed
every one else was just as much so. It was true in fact that he had many
rivals, but he imagined even more than there were; and he began to wonder
whom Madame de Clèves could mean. He had often believed that she did
not dislike him, and he had formed this opinion from things which now
seemed so slight that he could not imagine he had kindled a love so intense
that it called for this desperate remedy. He was almost beside himself with
excitement, and could not forgive Monsieur de Clèves for not insisting on
knowing the name his wife was hiding.

Monsieur de Clèves, however, was doing his best to find it out, and after
he had entreated her in vain, she said: "It seems to me that you ought to be
satisfied with my sincerity; do not ask me anything more, and do not give me
reason to repent what I have just done. Content yourself with the assurance
I give you that no one of my actions has betrayed my feelings, and that not
a word has ever been said to me at which I could take offence."

"Ah, Madame," Monsieur de Clèves suddenly exclaimed, "I cannot believe
you! I remember your embarrassment the day your portrait was lost. You
gave it away, Madame,—you gave away that portrait which was so dear to
me, and belonged to me so legitimately. You could not hide your feelings; it
is known that you are in love: your virtue has so far preserved you from the
rest."

"Is it possible," the princess burst forth, "that you could suspect any misrepresentation in a confession like mine, which there was no ground for my
making? Believe what I say: I purchase at a high price the confidence that I
ask of you. I beg of you, believe that I did not give away the portrait; it is
true that I saw it taken, but I did not wish to show that I saw it, lest I should
be exposed to hearing things which no one had yet dared to say."

"How then did you see his love?" asked Monsieur de Clèves. "What marks
of love were given to you?"

"Spare me the mortification," was her answer, "of repeating all the details
which I am ashamed to have noticed, and have only convinced me of my
weakness."

"You are right, Madame," he said, "I am unjust. Deny me when I shall ask
such things, but do not be angry if I ask them."

At this moment some of the servants who were without, came to tell Monsieur de Clèves that a gentleman had come with a command from the king
that he should be in Paris that evening. Monsieur de Clèves was obliged to
leave at once, and he could say to his wife nothing except that he begged her
to return the next day, and besought her to believe that though he was sorely
distressed, he felt for her an affection and esteem which ought to satisfy her.

When he had gone, and Madame de Clèves was alone and began to think
of what she had done, she was so amazed that she could scarcely believe it
true. She thought that she had wholly alienated her husband's love and
esteem, and had thrown herself into an abyss from which escape was impossible. She asked herself why she had done this perilous thing, and saw that
she had stumbled into it without intention. The strangeness of such a confession, for which she knew no precedent, showed her all her danger.

But when she began to think that this remedy, violent as it was, was the only one that could protect her against Monsieur de Nemours, she felt that she could not regret it, and that she had not gone too far. She spent the whole night in uncertainty, anxiety, and fear; but at last she grew calm. She felt a vague satisfaction in having given this proof of fidelity to a husband who so well deserved it, who had such affection and esteem for her, and who had just shown these by the way in which he had received her avowal.

Meanwhile Monsieur de Nemours had left the place where he had over-heard a conversation which touched him keenly, and had hastened into the forest. What Madame de Clèves had said about the portrait gave him new life, by showing him that it was he whom she did not hate. He first gave himself up to this joy; but it was not of long duration, for he reflected that the same thing which showed him that he had touched the heart of Madame de Clèves, ought to convince him that he would never receive any token of it, and that it was impossible to gain any influence over a woman who resorted to so strange a remedy. He felt, nevertheless, great pleasure in having brought her to this extremity. He felt a certain pride in making himself loved by a woman so different from all others of her sex,—in a word, he felt a hundred times happier and unhappier. Night came upon him in the forest, and he had great difficulty in finding the way back to Madame de Mercœur's. He reached there at daybreak. He found it very hard to explain what had delayed him, but he made the best excuses he could, and returned to Paris that same day with the Vidame.

Monsieur de Nemours was so full of his passion and so surprised by what he had heard that he committed a very common imprudence,—that of speak-ing in general terms of his own feelings and of describing his own adventures under borrowed names. On his way back he turned the conversation to love: he spoke of the pleasure of being in love with a worthy woman; he mentioned the singular effects of this passion; and, finally, not being able to keep to himself his astonishment at what Madame de Clèves had done, he told the whole story to the Vidame, without naming her and without saying that he had any part in it. But he manifested such warmth and admiration that the Vidame at once suspected that the story concerned the prince himself. He urged him strongly to acknowledge this; he said that he had long known that he nourished a violent passion, and that it was wrong not to trust in a man who had confided to him the secret of his life. Monsieur de Nemours was too much in love to acknowledge his love; he had always hidden it from the Vidame, though he loved him better than any man at court. He answered that one of his friends had told him this adventure, and had made him prom-ise not to speak of it, and he besought him to keep his secret. The Vidame promised not to speak of it; nevertheless, Monsieur de Nemours repented having told him.

Meanwhile, Monsieur de Clèves had gone to the king, his heart sick with a mortal wound. Never had a husband felt warmer love or higher respect for his wife. What he had heard had not lessened his respect, but this had assumed a new form. His most earnest desire was to know who had suc-ceeded in pleasing her. Monsieur de Nemours was the first to occur to him, as the most fascinating man at court, and the Chevalier de Guise and the Marshal of Saint-André as two men who had tried to please her and had paid her much attention; so that he decided it must be one of these three. He reached the Louvre, and the king took him into his study to tell him that he had chosen him to carry Madame to Spain; that he had thought that the prince would discharge this duty better than any one; and that no one would do so much credit to France as Madame de Clèves. Monsieur de Clèves accepted this appointment with due respect, and even looked upon it as something that would remove his wife from court without attracting any attention; but the date of their departure was still too remote to relieve his present embarrassment. He wrote at once to Madame de Clèves to tell her what the king had said, and added that he was very anxious that she should come to Paris. She returned in obedience to his request, and when they met, each found the other in the deepest gloom.

Monsieur de Clèves addressed her in the most honorable terms, and seemed well worthy of the confidence she had placed in him.

"I have no uneasiness about your conduct," he said; "you have more strength and virtue than you think. It is not dread of the future that distresses me; I am only distressed at seeing that you have for another feelings that I have not been able to inspire in you."

"I do not know how to answer you," she said; "I am ready to die with shame when I speak to you. Spare me, I beg of you, these painful conversations. Regulate my conduct; let me see no one,—that is all I ask; but permit me never to speak of a thing which makes me seem so little worthy of you, and which I regard as so unworthy of me."

"You are right, Madame," he answered; "I abuse your gentleness and your confidence. But do you too take some pity on the state into which you have cast me, and remember that whatever you have told me, you conceal from me a name which excites an unendurable curiosity. Still, I do not ask you to gratify it; but I must say that I believe the man I must envy to be the Marshal of Saint-André, the Duke of Nemours, or the Chevalier de Guise."

"I shall not answer," she said, blushing, "and I shall give you no occasion for lessening or strengthening your suspicions; but if you try to find out by watching me, you will surely make me so embarrassed that every one will notice it. In Heaven's name," she went on, "invent some illness, that I may see no one!"

"No, Madame," he replied, "it would soon be found that it was not real; and moreover I want to place my confidence in you alone,—that is the course my heart recommends, and my reason too. In your present mood, by leaving you free, I protect you by a closer guard than I could persuade myself to set about you."

Monsieur de Clèves was right; the confidence he showed in his wife proved a stronger protection against Monsieur de Nemours and inspired her to make austerer resolutions than any form of constraint could have done. She went to the Louvre and visited the dauphiness as usual; but she avoided Monsieur de Nemours with so much care that she took away nearly all his happiness at thinking that she loved him. He saw nothing in her actions which did not prove the contrary. He was almost ready to believe that what he had heard was a dream, so unlikely did it appear. The only thing that assured him that he was not mistaken was the extreme sadness of Madame de Clèves, in spite of all her efforts to conceal it. Possibly kind words and glances would not have so fanned Monsieur de Nemours' love as did this austere conduct.

One evening, when Monsieur and Madame de Clèves were with the queen, some one said that it was reported that the king was going to name another nobleman of the court to accompany Madame to Spain. Monsieur de Clèves fixed his eyes on his wife when the speaker added that it would be either the Chevalier de Guise or the Marshal of Saint-André. He noticed that she showed no agitation at either of these names, or at the mention of their joining the party. This led him to think that it was neither of these that she dreaded to see; and wishing to determine the matter, he went to the room where the king was. After a short absence he returned to his wife and whispered to her that he had just learned that it would be Monsieur de Nemours who would go with them to Spain.

The name of Monsieur de Nemours and the thought of seeing him every day during a long journey, in her husband's presence, so agitated Madame de Clèves that she could not conceal it, and wishing to assign other reasons, she answered,—

"The choice of that gentleman will be very disagreeable for you; he will divide all the honors, and I think you ought to try to have some one else appointed."

"It is not love of glory, Madame," said Monsieur de Clèves, "that makes you dread that Monsieur de Nemours should come with me. Your regret springs from another cause. This regret tells me what another woman would have told by her delight. But do not be alarmed; what I have just told you is not true: I made it up to make sure of a thing which I had only too long inclined to believe." With these words he went away, not wishing by his presence to add to his wife's evident embarrassment.

At that moment Monsieur de Nemours entered, and at once noticed Madame de Clèves' condition. He went up to her, and said in a low voice that he respected her too much to ask what made her so thoughtful. His voice aroused her from her revery; and looking at him, without hearing what he said, full of her own thoughts and fearful that her husband would see him by her side, she said: "In Heaven's name, leave me alone!"

"Alas! Madame," he replied, "I leave you only too much alone. Of what can you complain? I do not dare to speak to you, or even to look at you; I never come near you without trembling. How have I brought such a remark on myself, and why do you make me seem to have something to do with the depression in which I find you?"

Madame de Clèves deeply regretted that she had given Monsieur de Nemours an opportunity to speak to her more frankly than he had ever done. She left him without giving him any answer, and went home in a state of agitation such as she had never known. Her husband soon noticed this; he perceived that she was afraid lest he should speak to her about what had just happened. He followed her into her room and said to her,—

"Do not try to avoid me, Madame; I shall say nothing that could displease you. I beg your pardon for surprising you as I did; I am sufficiently punished by what I learned. Monsieur de Nemours was the man whom I most feared. I see your danger: control yourself for your own sake, and, if possible, for mine. I do not ask this as your husband, but as a man, all of whose happiness you make, and who feels for you a tenderer and stronger love than he whom your heart prefers." Monsieur de Clèves nearly broke down at these last words, which he could hardly utter. His wife was much moved, and bursting into tears, she embraced him with a gentleness and a sorrow that almost brought him to the same condition. They remained for some time perfectly silent, and separated without having strength to utter a word.

The preparations for Madame Elisabeth's marriage were completed, and the Duke of Alva[4] arrived for the ceremony. He was received with all the pomp and formality that the occasion required. The king sent the Prince of Condé, the Cardinals of Lorraine and Guise, the Dukes of Lorraine, Ferrara, Aumale, Bouillon, Guise, and Nemours to meet him. They were accompanied by many gentlemen and a great number of pages wearing their liveries. The king himself received the Duke of Alva at the first door of the Louvre with two hundred gentlemen in waiting, with the constable at their head. As the duke drew near the king, he wished to embrace his knees;[5] but the king prevented him, and made him walk by his side to call on the queen and on Madame Elisabeth, to whom the Duke of Alva brought a magnificent present from his master. He then called on Madame Marguerite, the king's sister, to convey to her the compliments of Monsieur de Savoie, and to assure her that he would arrive in a few days. There were large receptions at the Louvre, to show the Duke of Alva and the Prince of Orange, who accompanied him, the beauties of the court.

Madame de Clèves did not dare to stay away, much as she desired it, through fear of displeasing her husband, who gave her special orders to go. What made him even more determined was the absence of Monsieur de Nemours. He had gone to meet Monsieur de Savoie, and after that prince's arrival he was obliged to be with him almost all the time, to help him in his preparations for the wedding ceremonies; hence Madame de Clèves did not meet him so often as usual, and she was able to enjoy a little peace.

The Vidame of Chartres had not forgotten the talk he had had with Monsieur de Nemours. He had made up his mind that the adventure this prince had told him was his own, and he watched him so closely that perhaps he would have made out the truth, had not the arrival of the Duke of Alva and of Monsieur de Savoie so changed and busied the court that he had no further opportunity. His desire for more information, or, rather, the natural tendency to tell all one knows to the woman one loves, make him mention to Madame de Martigues the extraordinary conduct of the woman who had confessed to her husband the love she felt for another man. He assured her that it was Monsieur de Nemours who had inspired this violent passion, and he besought her to aid him in observing this prince. Madame de Martigues was greatly interested in what the Vidame had told her, and her curiosity about the dauphiness's relations with Monsieur de Nemours made her more anxious than ever to get to the bottom of the affair.

A few days before the one set for the wedding the crown princess gave a supper to her father-in-law the king and the Duchess of Valentinois. Madame de Clèves, who was delayed in dressing, started for the Louvre a little later than usual, and on her way met a gentleman coming from the dauphiness to fetch her. When she entered the room the crown princess called out to her from the bed on which she was lying that she had been waiting for her with the utmost impatience.

"I fancy, Madame," she replied, "that I have no cause to be grateful to you for this impatience; it is doubtless for some other reason that you were eager to see me."

"You are right," said the dauphiness; "but, nevertheless, you ought to be obliged to me, for I am going to tell you something that I am sure you will be very glad to hear."

4. He acted as a stand-in for Philip II at the marriage.   5. An act of homage.

Madame de Clèves knelt down by the side of the bed in such a way that, fortunately for her, her face was in the dark. "You know," said the crown princess, "how anxious we have been to find out the cause of the change in the Duke of Nemours; I think I have found out, and it is something that will surprise you. He is desperately in love with one of the most beautiful women of the court, and the lady returns his love."

These words, which Madame de Clèves could not take to herself, because she thought that no one knew of her love for this prince, gave her a pang that may be easily imagined.

"I see nothing in that," she replied, "which is surprising for a man of his age and appearance."

"But that," resumed the dauphiness, "is not the surprising part; what is amazing is the fact that this woman who loves Monsieur de Nemours has never given him any token of it, and that her fear that she may not always be able to control her passion has caused her to confess it to her husband to persuade him to take her away from court. And it is Monsieur de Nemours himself who is the authority for what I say."

If Madame de Clèves had been grieved at first by thinking that the affair in no way concerned her, these last words of the dauphiness filled her with despair, since they made it sure that it did concern her only too deeply. She could make no reply, but remained with her head resting on the bed while the dauphiness went on talking, too much taken up with what she was saying to notice her embarrassment. When Madame de Clèves had recovered some of her self-control, she answered,—

"This does not sound like a very probable story, and I wonder who told it to you."

"It was Madame de Martigues, who heard it from the Vidame. You know he is her lover; he told it to her as a secret, as he heard it from the Duke of Nemours. It is true that the Duke of Nemours did not mention the lady's name and did not even acknowledge that it was he who was loved; but the Vidame de Chartres has no doubt about that."

As the dauphiness pronounced these last words, some one drew near the bed. Madame de Clèves was turned away so that she could not see who it was; but she knew when the dauphiness exclaimed, with an air of surprise and amusement, "There he is himself, and I am going to ask how much truth there is in it."

Madame de Clèves knew that it must be the Duke of Nemours, and so it was. Without turning toward him, she leaned over to the crown princess and whispered to her to be careful not to say a word about this adventure, that he had told it to the Vidame in confidence, and that this would very possibly set them by the ears. The dauphiness answered laughingly that she was absurdly prudent, and turned toward Monsieur de Nemours. He was arrayed for the evening entertainment, and addressed her with all his usual grace.

"I believe, Madame," he began, "that I can think, without impertinence, that you were talking about me when I came in, that you wanted to ask me something, and that Madame de Clèves objected."

"You are right," replied the dauphiness; "but I shall not be as obliging to her as I usually am. I want to know whether a story I have heard is true, and whether you are the man who is in love with and is loved by a lady of the court who carefully conceals her passion from you and has confessed it to her husband."

Madame de Clèves' agitation and embarrassment cannot be conceived, and she would have welcomed death as an escape from her sufferings; but Monsieur de Nemours was even more embarrassed, if that is possible. This statement from the lips of the dauphiness, who, he had reason to believe, did not hate him, in the presence of Madame de Clèves, whom he loved better than any woman at court, and who also loved him, so overwhelmed him that he could not control his face. The embarrassment into which his blunder had plunged Madame de Clèves, and the thought of the good reason he gave her to hate him, made it impossible for him to answer. The dauphiness, noticing his intense confusion, said to Madame de Clèves: "Look at him, look at him, and see whether this is not his own story!"

Meanwhile Monsieur de Nemours, recovering from his first agitation, and recognizing the importance of escaping from this dangerous complication, suddenly recovered his presence of mind and regained his composure.

"I must acknowledge, Madame," he said, "that no one could be more surprised and distressed than I am by the Vidame de Chartres' treachery in repeating the adventure of one of my friends which I told to him in confidence. I might easily revenge myself," he went on, smiling in a way that almost dispelled the dauphiness's suspicions; "since he has confided to me matters of considerable importance. But I fail to understand why you do me the honor of implicating me in this affair. The Vidame cannot say that it concerns me, because I told him the very opposite. It may do very well to represent me as a man in love; but it will hardly do to represent me as a man who is loved,—which, Madame, is what you do."

Monsieur de Nemours was very glad to say something to the dauphiness which had some connection with his appearance in former times, in order to divert her thoughts. She caught his meaning; but without referring to these last words of his, she continued to harp on his evident confusion.

"I was embarrassed, Madame," he replied, "out of zeal for my friend and from fear of the reproaches he would be justified in making to me for repeating a thing dearer to him than life. Nevertheless, he only told me half, and did not mention the name of the woman he loves. I simply know that he is more in love and more to be pitied than any man in the world."

"Do you find him so worthy of pity," asked the crown princess, "because he is loved?"

"Are you sure that he is?" he answered; "and do you think that a woman who felt a real love would confide it to her husband? This woman, I am sure, knows nothing about love, and has mistaken for it a faint feeling of gratitude for his devotion to her. My friend cannot nourish any hope; but, wretched as he is, he has at least the consolation of having made her fearful of loving him, and he would not change his fate for that of any man in the world."

"Your friend's love is easily satisfied," said the crown princess, "and I begin to think that you can't be talking about yourself; I am inclined to agree with Madame de Clèves, who maintains that there can be no truth in the whole story."

"I don't think there can be," said Madame de Clèves, who had not yet said a word; "and if it were true, how could it become known? It is extremely unlikely that a woman capable of such an extraordinary thing would have the weakness to tell of it. Evidently a husband would not think of doing such a thing, unless he were a husband very unworthy of the confidence that was placed in him."

Monsieur de Nemours, who saw that Madame de Clèves' suspicions had fallen on her husband, was very glad to strengthen them; he knew that he was his strongest rival.

"Jealousy," he replied, "and the desire to find out more than he had been told, may induce a husband to commit a great many indiscretions."

Madame de Clèves was at the end of her strength; and being unable to carry on the conversation further, she was about to say that she did not feel well, when, fortunately for her, the Duchess of Valentinois came in to tell the dauphiness that the king would arrive very soon. The crown princess accordingly went into her room to dress; whereupon Monsieur de Nemours came up to Madame de Clèves as she was about to follow her, and said,—

"Madame, I would give my life to speak to you a moment; but of all the important things I should have to say to you, nothing seems to me more important than to beg you to believe that if I have said anything which might seem to refer to the dauphiness, I have done so for reasons which do not concern her."

Madame de Clèves pretended not to hear him, but moved away without looking at him and joined the suite of the king, who had just come in. There being a great crowd present, her foot caught in her dress, and she made a misstep; she took advantage of this excuse to leave a place where she had no strength to stay longer, and went away pretending that she could not stand.

Monsieur de Clèves went to the Louvre, and being surprised not to see his wife, he was told of the accident that had just happened to her. He left at once, to find out how she was; he found her in bed, and she told him that she was but slightly hurt. When he had been with her for some time he saw that she was exceedingly sad; this surprised him, and he asked her, "What is the matter? You seem to suffer in some other way than that you have told me."

"I could not be in greater distress than I am," she answered. "What use did you make of the extraordinary, I might say foolish, confidence I had in you? Was I not worthy of secrecy on your part? And even if I was unworthy of it, did not your own interest urge it? Was it necessary that your curiosity to know a name which I ought not to tell you, could force you to confide in any one else in order to discover it? Nothing but curiosity could have led you to commit such an imprudence. The consequences have been most disastrous; the story is known, and has just been told to me, without any notion that I was the person most concerned."

"What do you say, Madame?" he replied. "You accuse me of having repeated what passed between us, and you tell me the story is known! I shall not defend myself from the charge of repeating it; you can't believe it, and you must have taken to yourself something said about some other woman."

"Oh, sir," she said, "in the whole world there is not another case like mine; there is not another woman capable of doing what I have done! Chance could not make any one invent it; no one has ever imagined it,—the very thought never entered any one's mind but mine. The dauphiness has just told me the whole story; she heard it from the Vidame of Chartres, and he had it from Monsieur de Nemours."

"Monsieur de Nemours!" exclaimed Monsieur de Clèves, with a gesture expressive of the wildest despair. "What, Monsieur de Nemours knows that you love him and that I know it!"

"You always want to fix on Monsieur de Nemours rather than any one else," she replied; "I told you that I should never say anything about your suspicions. I cannot say whether Monsieur de Nemours knows my share in this affair, or the part you assign to him; but he told it to the Vidame de Chartres, saying that he had it from one of his friends, who did not give the name of the woman. This friend of Monsieur de Nemours must be one of your friends, and you must have told the story to him in an effort to get some information."

"Is there a friend in the world," he exclaimed, "to whom any one would make a confidence of that sort? And would any one try to confirm his suspicions by telling another what one would wish to hide from one's self? Consider rather to whom you have spoken. It is more likely that the secret got out from you than from me. You could not endure your misery alone, and you sought solace in making a confidant of some friend who has played you false."

"Do not torment me further," she burst forth, "and do not be so cruel as to charge me with a fault which you have committed. Could you suspect me of that? And because I was capable of speaking to you, am I capable of speaking of it to any one else?"

His wife's confession had so convinced Monsieur de Clèves of her frankness, and she so warmly denied having mentioned the incident to any one, that Monsieur de Clèves did not know what to think. For his own part, he was sure that he had repeated nothing; it was something nobody could have guessed: it was known, and it must have become known through one of them. But what caused the liveliest grief was the knowledge that this secret was in somebody's hands, and apparently would be soon divulged.

Madame de Clèves' thoughts were nearly the same; she held it equally impossible that her husband should have spoken and should not have spoken. What Monsieur de Nemours had said, that curiosity might make a husband indiscreet, seemed to apply so well to just the state of mind in which Monsieur de Clèves was, that she could not think it was a mere strange coincidence; and this probability compelled her to believe that Monsieur de Clèves had abused her confidence in him. They were both so busy with their thoughts that they for a long time did not speak, and when they broke the silence, it was but to repeat what they had already said very often, and they felt farther apart than they had ever been.

It is easy to picture the way they passed the night. Monsieur de Clèves' constancy had been nearly worn out by his effort to endure the unhappiness of seeing his wife, whom he adored, touched with love for another man. His courage was wellnigh exhausted; he even doubted whether this was an opportunity to make use of it, in a matter in which his pride and honor were so sorely wounded. He no longer knew what to think of his wife; he could not decide what course of action he should urge her to take nor how he should himself act; on all sides he saw nothing but precipices and steep abysses. At last, after long distress and uncertainty, reflecting that he should soon have to go to Spain, he made up his mind to do nothing that should confirm any one's suspicions or knowledge of his unhappy condition. He went to Madame de Clèves and told her that it was not worth while to discuss which of them had betrayed their secret, but that it was very important to prove that the story that had been told was a mere invention in no way referring to her; that it depended on her to convince Monsieur de Nemours and the rest of this; that she had only to treat him with the severity and coldness which she ought to have for a man who made love to her, and that in this way she would soon dispel the notion that she had any interest in him. Hence, he argued, there was no need of her distressing herself about what he might have thought, because if henceforth she should betray no weakness, his opinion would necessarily change; and above all, he urged upon her the necessity of going to the palace and into the world as much as usual.

When he had finished, Monsieur de Clèves left his wife without awaiting her answer. She thought what he had said very reasonable, and her indignation against Monsieur de Nemours made her think it would be very easy to carry it out; but she found it very hard to appear at all the wedding festivities with a calm face and an easy mind. Nevertheless, since she had been selected to carry the train of the dauphiness's dress,—a special honor to her alone of all the princesses,—she could not decline it without exciting much attention and wonder. Hence she resolved to make a great effort to control herself; but the rest of the day she devoted to preparations and to indulging the feelings that harassed her. She shut herself up alone in her room. What most distressed her was to have grounds for complaint against Monsieur de Nemours, with no chance of excusing him. She felt sure that he had told the story to the Vidame,—this he had acknowledged; and she felt sure too, from the way in which he spoke of it, that he knew that she was implicated. What excuse could be found for so great a piece of imprudence, and what had become of the prince's discretion, that had once so touched her? "He was discreet," she said to herself, "so long as he thought himself unhappy; but the mere thought of happiness, vague as it was, put an end to his discretion. He could not imagine that he was loved without wishing it to be known. He has said everything he could say. I have not confessed that it was he whom I loved; he suspected it, and showed his suspicions. If he had been sure of it, he would have done the same thing. I did wrong to think that there ever was a man capable of concealing what flattered his vanity. Yet it is for this man, whom I thought so different from other men, that I find myself in the same plight as other women whom I so little resemble. I have lost the love and esteem of a husband who ought to make me happy; soon every one will look upon me as a woman possessed by a mad and violent passion. The man for whom I feel it is no longer ignorant of it, and it is to escape just these evils that I have imperilled all my peace of mind, and even my life." These sad reflections were followed by a torrent of tears; but whatever the grief by which she felt herself overwhelmed, she knew that she could have endured it if she had been satisfied with Monsieur de Nemours.

This prince's state of mind was no more tranquil. His imprudence in unbosoming himself to the Vidame of Chartres, and the cruel results of this imprudence, caused him great pain. He could not without intense mortification recall Madame de Clèves' agitation and embarrassment. He could not forgive himself for having spoken about that affair in terms which, though courteous in themselves, must have seemed coarse and impolite, since they had implied to Madame de Clèves that he knew that she was the woman who was deeply in love, and with him. All that he could wish was a conversation with her; but he thought this more to be dreaded than desired. "What should I have to say to her?" he exclaimed. "Should I once more undertake to tell her what I have already made too clear to her? Shall I let her see that I know she loves me,—I, who have never dared to tell her that I loved her? Shall I begin by speaking to her openly of my passion, in order to appear like a man emboldened by hope? Can I think merely of going near her, and should I dare to embarrass her by my presence? How could I justify myself? I have no excuse, I am unworthy to appear before Madame de Clèves, and I do not venture to hope that she will ever look at me again. By my own fault, I have given her a better protection against me than any she sought, and sought perhaps in vain. By my imprudence I have lost the happiness and pride of being loved by the most charming and estimable woman in the world. If I had lost this happiness without her suffering, without having inflicted on her a bitter blow, that would be some consolation; and at this moment I feel more keenly the harm I have done her than I did when I was in her presence."

Monsieur de Nemours long tortured himself with these thoughts. The desire to see Madame de Clèves perpetually haunted him, and he began to look about for means of communicating with her. He thought of writing to her; but he considered, after his blunder, and in view of her character, that the best thing he could do would be to show his profound respect, and by silence and evident distress to make it clear that he did not dare to meet her, and to wait until time, chance, or her own interest in him should work in his favor. He resolved also to forbear from reproaching the Vidame of Chartres for his treachery, lest he should confirm his suspicions.

The betrothal of Madame Elisabeth, which was to take place on the morrow, and the wedding, which was to be celebrated on the following day, so occupied the court that Madame de Clèves and Monsieur de Nemours had no difficulty in concealing their grief and annoyance from the public. The dauphiness referred only lightly to their talk with Monsieur de Nemours, and Monsieur de Clèves took pains not to say anything more to his wife about what had happened, so that soon she found herself more at ease than she had supposed possible.

The betrothal was celebrated at the Louvre; and after the banquet and the ball, the whole royal household went to the bishop's palace to pass the night, as was the custom. The next morning the Duke of Alva, who always dressed very simply, put on a coat of cloth of gold, mingled with red, yellow, and black, and all covered with precious stones; on his head he wore a crown. The Prince of Orange, arrayed in equal splendor, came with his servants, and all the Spaniards with theirs, to fetch the Duke of Alva from the Villeroy mansion, where he was staying; and they started, walking four abreast, for the bishop's palace. As soon as they arrived, they went in due order to the church. The king conducted Madame Elisabeth, who also wore a crown; her dress was held by Mesdemoiselles de Montpensier and De Longueville; then came the queen, but not wearing a crown; after her came the dauphiness, the king's sister, Madame de Lorraine, and the Queen of Navarre, with princesses holding their trains. The queens and princesses had all their maids-of-honor magnificently dressed in the same colors that they themselves wore, so that the maids-of-honor could be at once distinguished by the colors of their dresses. They ascended the platform set up in the church, and the wedding ceremony took place. Then they returned to dinner at the bishop's palace, and at about five left for the palace, to be present at the banquet to which the parliament, the sovereign courts,[6] and the city officials had been invited. The king, the queens, the princes, and princesses ate at the marble table in the great hall of the palace, the Duke of Alva being seated near the new Queen of Spain. Below the steps of the marble table, on the king's right hand, was a table for the ambassadors, the archbishops, and the knights of the order,[7] and on the other side a table for the members of parliament.

The Duke of Guise, dressed in a robe of cloth of gold, was the king's major-domo, the Prince of Condé his head butler, the Duke of Nemours his cup-bearer.[8] After the tables were removed, the ball began; it was interrupted by the ballets and by extraordinary shows; then it was renewed, until, after midnight, the king and all the court returned to the Louvre. Though Madame de Clèves was very much depressed, she yet appeared in the eyes of every one, and especially in those of Monsieur de Nemours, incomparably beautiful. He did not dare to speak to her, although the confusion of the ceremony gave him many opportunities; but his demeanor was so dejected, and he showed such fear of approaching her, that she began to deem him less blameworthy, though he had not said a word in excuse of his conduct. His behavior was the same on the succeeding days, and continued to produce the same impression on Madame de Clèves.

At last the day of the tournament came. The queens betook themselves to the galleries and the raised seats set apart for them. The four champions appeared at the end of the lists, with a number of horses and servants, who formed the most magnificent spectacle ever seen in France.

The king's colors were plain black and white, which he always wore for the sake of Madame de Valentinois, who was a widow. The Duke of Ferrara and all his suite wore yellow and red. Monsieur de Guise appeared in pink and white: no one knew why he wore these colors; but it was remembered that they were those of a beautiful woman whom he had loved before she was married, and still loved, though he did not dare to show it. Monsieur de Nemours wore yellow and black,—why, no one knew. Madame de Clèves, however, had no difficulty in guessing: she remembered telling him one day that she liked yellow, and was sorry she was a blonde, because she could never wear that color. He believed that he could appear in it without indiscretion, because since Madame de Clèves never wore it, no one could suspect that it was hers.

Never was there seen greater skill than the four champions displayed. Although the king was the best horseman in the kingdom, it was hard to know to whom to give the palm.[9] Monsieur de Nemours showed a grace in all he did that inclined in his favor women less interested than Madame de Clèves. As soon as she saw him at the end of the lists she felt an unusual emotion, and every time he ran she could scarcely conceal her joy when he escaped without harm.

Toward evening, when all was nearly over, and the company on the point of withdrawing, the evil fate of the country made the king wish to break another lance. He ordered the Count of Montgomery, who was very skilful,

6. Legal courts of appeal. The Parliament of Paris was essentially a judicial body.   7. The Order of the Knights of Malta, a military religious order that had led many battles against the Turks.   8. The positions of butler and cupbearer were honorific designations only for the duration of the ceremonies.   9. An ancient symbol of victory. Here, award the victory.

to enter the lists. The count begged the king to excuse him, and made every apology he could think of; but the king, with some annoyance, sent him word that he insisted upon it. The queen sent a message to the king beseeching him not to run again, saying that he had done so well he ought to be satisfied, and that she entreated him to come to her. He answered that it was for love of her that he was going to run again, and entered the field. She sent Monsieur de Savoie to beg him again to come; but all was in vain. He started, the lances broke, and a splinter from that of the Count of Montgomery struck him in the eye and remained in it. He fell at once to the ground. His equerries and Monsieur de Montgomery, one of the marshals of the field, ran up to him, and were alarmed to see him so severely wounded. The king was not alarmed; he said it was a slight matter, and that he forgave the count. It is easy to conceive the excitement and distress caused by this unhappy accident after a day devoted to merry-making. As soon as the king had been carried to his bed the surgeons examined his wound, which they found very serious. The constable at that moment recalled the prediction made to the king that he should be slaim in single combat, and he had no doubt that the prophecy would come true.

As soon as the King of Spain, who was then in Brussels, heard of this accident, he sent his physician, a man of vast experience; but he thought the king's state desperate.

The court, thus distracted and torn by conflicting interests, was much excited on the eve of this great event; but all dissensions were quieted, and there seemed to be no other cause of anxiety than the king's health. The queens, the princes, and the princesses scarcely left his ante-chamber.

Madame de Clèves, knowing that she was compelled to be there and to meet Monsieur de Nemours, and that she could not hide from her husband the embarrassment that the sight of him would produce; knowing too that the mere presence of this prince would excuse him and overthrow all her plans,—decided to feign illness. The court was too busy to notice her conduct or to make out how much was true and how much feigned in her illness. Her husband alone could know the truth; but she was not sorry to have him know it, so she remained at home, thinking little of the great change that was impending, and perfectly free to indulge in her own reflections. Every one was with the king. Monsieur de Clèves came at certain hours to tell her the news. He treated her as he had always done, except that when they were alone his manner was a little colder and stiffer. He never spoke to her again about what had happened, and she lacked the strength and deemed it unwise to reopen the subject.

Monsieur de Nemours, who had expected to find a few moments to speak to Madame de Clèves, was much surprised and pained not to have even the pleasure of seeing her. The king grew so much worse that on the seventh day his physicians gave him up. He received the news of his approaching death with wonderful firmness, all the more admirable because he died by such an unfortunate accident, in the prime of life, full of happiness, adored by his subjects, and loved by a mistress whom he madly worshipped. The evening before his death he had Madame his sister married with Monsieur de Savoie, very quietly.

It is easy to conceive in what state was Madame de Valentinois. The queen did not permit her to see the king, and sent to her to ask for the king's seals and for the crown jewels, which were in her keeping. The duchess asked if the king was dead; and when they told her no, she said: "Then I have no master, and no one can compel me to return what he intrusted to my hands."

As soon as he had died, at the castle of Tournelles, the Duke of Ferrara, the Duke of Guise, and the Duke of Nemours conducted to the Louvre the queen-dowager, the king, and his wife the queen.[1] Monsieur de Nemours escorted the queen-dowager. Just as they were starting, she drew back a little and told her daughter-in-law she was to go first; but it was easy to see that there was more vexation than politeness in this compliment.

Part V

The Cardinal of Lorraine had acquired complete ascendency over the mind of the queen-dowager; the Vidame de Chartres had completely fallen from her good graces, but his love for Madame de Martigues and his enjoyment of his freedom had prevented him from suffering from this change as much as he might have done. During the ten days of the king's illness the cardinal had had abundant leisure to form his plans and to persuade the queen to take measures in conformity with his projects; hence as soon as the king was dead, the queen ordered the constable to remain at the castle of Tournelles to keep watch by the body of the late king and to take charge of the customary ceremonies. This order kept him aloof from everything, and prevented all action on his part. He sent a messenger to the king of Navarre to summon him in all diligence, in order that they might combine to oppose the promotion that evidently awaited the Guises. The command of the army was given to the Duke of Guise; that of the treasury to the Cardinal of Lorraine; the Duchess of Valentinois was driven from the court; the Cardinal of Tournon, the avowed enemy of the constable, was recalled, as well as the Chancelier Olivier, the open enemy of the Duchess of Valentinois, so that the aspect of the court was completely changed. The Duke of Guise was made equal to the princes of the blood, and allowed to carry the king's mantle at the funeral; he and his brothers were placed high in authority, not merely through the cardinal's influence over the queen, but also because she believed that she could overthrow them if they should offend her, while she would not be able to overthrow the constable, who was supported by the princes of the blood.

After the funeral the constable went to the Louvre, but met with a cold reception from the king. He desired to speak with the king in private; but the king called the Guises and told him in their presence that he advised him to seek retirement, that the treasury and the command of the army were already disposed of, and that whenever he might need his counsels he should summon him. The queen-dowager received him even more coldly than the king; she went so far as to remind him of his insulting remark to the late king about his children not looking like him. The King of Navarre arrived, and was received no better. The Prince of Condé, who was less patient than his brother, complained bitterly, but all in vain; he was exiled from court under the pretext of sending him to Flanders to sign the ratification of the treaty of peace.[2] The King of Navarre was shown a forged letter of the King

1. The new king, Francis II, married to Mary Stuart, who became Mary, queen of Scots, after her husband's death in 1560. *The queen-dowager*: former king's widow, Catherine de Médicis.   2. Again, the Treaty of Câteau-Cambrésis, by which France gave up its claims in Italy.

of Spain which accused him of making attempts on his territory, and he was made to fear for his own possessions, and induced to return to his kingdom. The queen made this easy for him by assigning to him the duty of escorting Madame Elisabeth; she even obliged him to start before her, so that there was no one left at court to oppose the power of the household of Guise.

Although it was most unfortunate for Monsieur de Clèves that he could not escort Madame Elisabeth, he still could not complain, in view of the lofty rank of the man who was preferred; but the deprivation of the dignity was not what pained him, but rather that his wife lost an opportunity of absenting herself from court without exciting comment.

A few days after the king's death it was decided that the court should go to Rheims for the coronation. Madame de Clèves, who had hitherto stayed at home under pretence of illness, begged her husband to excuse her from accompanying the court, and to let her go to Coulommiers to get strength from the change of air. He replied that he would not ask her whether it was care for her health that compelled her to give up the journey, but that he was willing she should not take it. He readily consented to a plan he had already decided on. High as was his opinion of his wife's virtue, he saw very clearly that it was not well for her to be exposed longer to meeting a man she loved.

Monsieur de Nemours soon learned that Madame de Clèves was not to accompany the court. He could not bear to think of leaving without seeing her; and the day before he was to start he called on her as late as he could, in order to find her alone. Fortune favored him, and as he entered the court-yard he met Madame de Nevers and Madame de Martigues coming out. They told him they had left her alone. He went upstairs in a state of agitation that can only be compared with that of Madame de Clèves when his name was announced. Her fear that he would mention his love; her apprehension lest she should give him a favorable answer; the anxiety that this visit would give her husband; the difficulty of repeating or concealing everything that happened,—all crowded on her mind at once, and so embarrassed her that she determined to avoid the thing she desired most in the world. She sent one of her maids to Monsieur de Nemours, who was in the hall, to tell him that she was not feeling well, and much regretted that she could not have the honor of receiving him. It was a grievous blow to him that he could not see Madame de Clèves because she was unwilling to receive him. He was to leave the next day, and there was no chance of his meeting her. He had not spoken to her since their conversation at the crown princess's, and he had reason to believe that his mistake in speaking to the Vidame had shattered all his hopes; consequently, he went away in deep rejection.

As soon as Madame de Clèves had somewhat recovered from the agitation of the prince's threatened visit, all the arguments that had made her decline it vanished from her mind; she even thought she had made a mistake, and if she had dared, and there had still been time, she would have called him back.

Madame de Nevers and Madame de Martigues, after leaving her, went to the crown princess's and found Monsieur de Clèves there. The princess asked them where they had been. They said they had just come from Madame de Clèves', where they had spent the afternoon with a number of persons, and that they had left no one there except Monsieur de Nemours.

These words, which they thought thoroughly insignificant, were quite the opposite for Monsieur de Clèves, although it must have been evident to him that Monsieur de Nemours could easily find opportunities to speak to his wife. Nevertheless, the thought that he was with her alone, and able to speak to her of his love, seemed to him at that moment such a new and unendurable thing that his jealousy flamed out with greater fury than ever. He was not able to stay longer with the dauphiness, but left, not knowing why he did so, or whether he meant to interrupt Monsieur de Nemours. As soon as he got home he looked to see if that gentleman was still there; and when he had the consolation of finding him gone, he rejoiced to think that he could not have stayed long. He fancied that perhaps it was not Monsieur de Nemours of whom he ought to be jealous; and although he did not really doubt it, he tried his best to do so: but so many things pointed in that direction that he could not long enjoy the happiness of uncertainty. He went straight to his wife's room, and after a little talk on indifferent matters, he could not refrain from asking her what she had done and whom she had seen. Observing that she did not mention Monsieur de Nemours, he asked her, trembling with excitement, if those were all she had seen, in order to give her an opportunity to mention him, and thus save him from the pain of thinking she was capable of deception. Since she had not seen him, she said nothing about him; whereupon Monsieur de Clèves, in a tone that betrayed his distress, asked:

"And Monsieur de Nemours, didn't you see him, or have you forgotten him?"

"I did not see him, in point of fact; I was not feeling well, and I sent my regrets by one of my maids."

"Then you were ill for him alone," he went on, "since you received everybody else? Why this difference for him? Why is he not the same to you as all the rest? Why should you dread meeting him? Why do you show him that you make use of the power his passion gives you over him? Would you dare to refuse to see him if you did not know that he is able to distinguish your severity from incivility? Why should you be severe to him? From a person in your position, Madame, everything is a favor except indifference."

"I never thought," answered Madame de Clèves, "that however suspicious you might be of Monsieur de Nemours, you would reproach me for not seeing him."

"I do, however," he went on, "and with good cause. Why do you decline to see him, if he has not said anything to you? But, Madame, he has spoken to you; had his silence been the only sign of his passion, it would have made no such deep impression. You have not been able to tell me the whole truth; you have even repented telling me the little you did, and you have not the strength to go on. I am more unhappy than I supposed,—I am the unhappiest of men. You are my wife, I love you devotedly, and I see you love another man! He is the most fascinating man at court, he sees you every day, he knows that you love him. And I," he exclaimed,—"I could bring myself to believe that you would overcome your passion for him! I must have lost my reason when I imagined such a thing possible."

"I don't know," replied Madame de Clèves, sadly, "whether you were wrong in judging such extraordinary conduct as mine so favorably; I don't feel sure that I was right in thinking that you would do me justice."

"Do not doubt it Madame," said Monsieur de Clèves. "You were mistaken; you expected of me things quite as impossible as what I expected of you. How could you expect me to retain my self-control? Have you forgotten that I loved you madly and that I was your husband? Either case is enough to drive a man wild: what must it be when the two combine? And see what they do! I am torn by wild and uncertain feelings that I cannot control; I find myself no longer worthy of you,—you seem no more worthy of me. I adore you, and I hate you; I offend you, and I beg your pardon; I admire you, and I am ashamed of my admiration,—in a word, I have lost all my calmness, all my reason. I do not know how I have been able to live since you spoke with me at Coulommiers, and since the day when you learned from the dauphiness that your adventure was known. I cannot conjecture how it came out, or what passed between Monsieur de Nemours and you on this subject. You will never tell me, and I don't ask you to tell me; I beg of you only to remember that you have made me the unhappiest man in the world."

With those words Monsieur de Clèves left his wife's room, and went away the next morning without seeing her, although he wrote her a letter full of grief, consideration, and gentleness. She wrote him a touching answer, containing such assurances about her past and future conduct that, since they sprang from the truth and were her real feelings, the letter carried great weight with Monsieur de Clèves and calmed him somewhat. Moreover, since Monsieur de Nemours was also on his way to join the king, her husband had the consolation of knowing that he was separated from Madame de Clèves. Whenever she spoke with her husband, the love he showed her, the uprightness of his treatment of her, her own affection for him, and her sense of duty, made an impression on her heart which effaced all thought of Monsieur de Nemours. But this was only for a time; the remembrance of him soon returned with greater force than ever.

The first days after that prince had left, she scarcely noticed his absence; then it began to appear painful,—for since she began to love him, hardly a day had passed in which she had not either feared or hoped to see him; and it was to her a melancholy thought that chance could no longer make her meet him.

She went to Coulommiers, taking with her copies she had had made of the large pictures with which Madame de Valentinois had adorned her fine house at Anet.[3] All the memorable events of the king's reign were represented in these pictures. Among others was one of the Siege of Metz, with excellent likenesses of the principal officers, among whom was Monsieur de Nemours; and that was perhaps why Madame de Clèves cared for the pictures.

Madame de Martigues, having been unable to accompany the court, promised to spend a few days with her at Coulommiers. The queen's favor, which they both enjoyed, did not make them jealous or hostile; they were good friends, although they did not confide to each other everything. Madame de Clèves knew that Madame de Martigues loved the Vidame, but Madame de Martigues did not know that Madame de Clèves loved Monsieur de Nemours and was loved by him. The fact that she was a niece of the Vidame endeared her to Madame de Martigues; and Madame de Clèves was drawn toward her as a woman who, like herself, was in love, and with her lover's most intimate friend.

3. A château, about forty miles east of Paris, built for her by Henri II.

Madame de Martigues kept her promise, and went to Coulommiers. She found Madame de Clèves leading a most retired life,—indeed, she had sought absolute solitude, spending her evenings in the gardens, unaccompanied by her servants. She used to go into the summer-house where Monsieur de Nemours had overheard her talking with her husband, and enter the closet which opened on the garden. Her women and the servants would stay in the summer-house or in the other closet, coming to her only when they were called. Madame de Martigues had never seen Coulommiers; she was delighted with all the loveliness she found there, and especially with the comfort of this summer-house, in which she and Madame de Clèves spent every evening. Their solitude after dark, in the most beautiful place in the world, made easy prolonged talks between these two young women, who were both in love; and although they did not confide in each other, they delighted in talking together. Madame de Martigues would have been very sorry to leave Coulommiers if she had not been going to meet the Vidame; she went to Chambord, where was the whole court.

The new king was crowned at Rheims by the Cardinal of Lorraine, and the rest of the summer was to be spent at the castle of Chambord, then newly built. The queen manifested great pleasure at seeing Madame de Martigues again; and after giving expression to her joy, she asked after Madame de Clèves and what she was doing in the country. Monsieur de Nemours and Monsieur de Clèves were then with the queen. Madame de Martigues, who had been delighted with Coulommiers, described its beauty, and spoke at great length of the summer-house in the wood and of the pleasant evenings she had passed there with Madame de Clèves. Monsieur de Nemours, who was sufficiently familiar with the place to know what Madame de Martigues was talking about, thought that it might be possible to see Madame de Clèves there without being seen by her. He questioned Madame de Martigues, in order to get further information; and Monsieur de Clèves, who had kept his eyes on him while Madame de Martigues was talking, fancied that he detected his design. The questions that Monsieur de Nemours asked only strengthened his suspicions, so that he felt sure the duke intended to go to see his wife. He was right; this plan so attracted Monsieur de Nemours that after spending the night in devising plans to carry it into execution, the next morning he asked leave of the king to go to Paris on some pretext he had invented.

Monsieur de Clèves had no doubt about his reasons for going away, but he determined to seek information on his wife's conduct, and no longer to remain in cruel uncertainty. He desired to leave at the same time with Monsieur de Nemours, and from some place of concealment to discover what success he might have; but he feared lest their simultaneous absence might attract attention, or that Monsieur de Nemours might get wind of it and adopt other measures; so he determined to rely on one of the gentlemen in his suite, in whose fidelity and intelligence he felt confidence. He told him in what trouble he was, and what Madame de Clèves virtue had been hitherto, and ordered him to follow in Monsieur de Nemours' footsteps, to watch him closely, and to see if he did not go to Coulommiers and enter the garden by night.

This gentleman, who was well suited for the duty, discharged it with the utmost exactness. He followed Monsieur de Nemours to a village half a league from Coulommiers, where the prince stopped, and the gentleman easily guessed that this was to await the approach of night. He did not think it well to wait there too, but passed through the village and made his way into the forest, to a spot which he thought Monsieur de Nemours would have to pass. He was not mistaken; as soon as night had fallen, he heard footsteps, and though it was dark, he easily recognized Monsieur de Nemours. He saw him walk about the garden as if to find out if he could hear some one, and to choose the most convenient spot for entering it. The palings were very high, and there were some beyond to bar the way, so that it was not easy to get in; nevertheless, Monsieur de Nemours succeeded. As soon as he had made his way into the garden, he had no difficulty in making out where Madame de Clèves was, as he saw many lights in the closet. All the windows were open; and creeping along the palings, he approached it with an emotion that can easily be imagined. He hid behind one of the long windows by which one entered the closet, to see what Madame de Clèves was doing. He saw that she was alone; she was so beautiful that he could scarcely control his rapture at the spectacle. It was warm, and her head and shoulders had no other covering than her loosely fastened hair. She was on a couch behind a table, on which were many baskets of ribbons; she was picking some out, and Monsieur de Nemours observed that they were of the same colors that he had worn in the tournament. He saw that she was fastening bows on a very peculiar stick that he had carried for some time and had given to his sister, from whom Madame de Clèves had taken it, without seeming to recognize it as belonging to Monsieur de Nemours. When she had finished her work with a grace and gentleness that reflected on her face the feelings that filled her heart, she took a light and drew near to a large table opposite the picture of the Siege of Metz, in which was the portrait of Monsieur de Nemours; then she sat down and gazed at this portrait with a rapt attention such as love alone could give.

It would be impossible to describe everything that Monsieur de Nemours felt at this moment. To see, in the deep night, in the most beautiful spot in the world, the woman he adored; to see her without her seeing him, busied with things that bore reference to him and to the hidden love she felt for him,—all that is something no other lover ever enjoyed or imagined.

Monsieur de Nemours was so entranced that he stood motionless, contemplating Madame de Clèves, without remembering that every moment was precious. When he had come to his senses again, he thought he ought to wait till she came into the garden before speaking to her; this he reflected would be safer, because then she would be farther from her maids. When, however, he saw that she remained in the closet, he decided to go in there. When he tried to do it, he was overwhelmed with agitation and with the fear of displeasing her. He could not bear the thought of seeing the face, just before so gentle, suddenly darken with anger and surprise.

He thought it madness, not his undertaking to see Madame de Clèves without being seen, but to think of showing himself; he saw everything that he had not before thought of. It seemed to him foolhardy to surprise at midnight a woman to whom he had never spoken of his love. He thought he had no right to assume that she would consent to listen to him, and he knew she would have good grounds for indignation at the danger to which he exposed her from the possible consequences of his acts. All his courage abandoned him, and more than once he was on the point of deciding that he would go back without seeing her. But he was so anxious to speak to her, and so encouraged by what he had seen, that he pushed on a few steps, though in such agitation that his scarf caught on the window and made a noise. Madame de Clèves turned her head; and whether it was that her mind was full of this prince, or that his face was actually in the light, she thought that she recognized him; and without hesitation or turning toward him, she rejoined her maids. She was so agitated that she had to trump up an excuse of not feeling well; and she said it also to attract their attention and thus give Monsieur de Nemours time to beat a retreat. After a little reflection she decided that she had been mistaken, and that the vision of Monsieur de Nemours was a mere illusion. She knew that he had been at Chambord, and she judged it extremely unlikely that he could have undertaken so perilous an enterprise; several times she was on the point of going back into the closet to see if there was any one in the garden. Perhaps she hoped as much as she feared to find Monsieur de Nemours there; but at last reason and prudence prevailed over every other feeling, and she decided that she should do better to stay where she was than to seek any further information. She was long in making up her mind to leave a place near which he might be, and it was almost morning when she returned to the castle.

Monsieur de Nemours stayed in the garden as long as he saw a light. He had not given up all hope of seeing Madame de Clèves again, although he was sure that she had recognized him and had only left in order to avoid him; but when he saw the servants locking the doors, he knew that he had no further chance. He retraced his steps, passing by the place where the friend of Monsieur de Clèves was in waiting. This gentleman followed him to the village, whence he had started in the evening. Monsieur de Nemours determined to spend the whole day there, in order to return to Coulommiers that night, to see if Madame de Clèves would be cruel enough to flee from him, or not to let him look at her. Although he was highly delighted to find that her mind was occupied with him, he was deeply pained to see her so instinctively taking flight.

Never was there a tenderer or intenser love than that which animated this prince. He strolled beneath the willows beside a little brook which ran behind the house in which he was concealed. He kept himself out of sight as much as possible, that no one might know of his presence. He gave himself up to the transports of love, and his heart was so full that he could not keep from shedding a few tears; but these were not of grief, they were tempered with all the sweetness that only love can give.

He recalled all Madame de Clèves' actions since he had fallen in love with her,—the honorable and modest severity with which she had treated him, although she loved him. "For she does indeed love me," he exclaimed; "she loves me,—I cannot doubt it. The most fervent protestations, the greatest favors, are no surer tokens than those I have received; and yet she treats me with the same austerity as if she hated me. I thought time would bring a change, but I can expect nothing more from it; I see her always on her guard against me and against herself. If she did not love me, I should try to please her; but I do please her, she loves me, and hides her love. What then am I to hope,—what change in my fate can I expect. What! the most charming woman in the world loves me, and I cannot enjoy the supreme happiness that comes from the first certainty of being loved, except in the agony of being ill-treated! Show, fair princess," he called aloud, "that you love me; show me that you really feel! If you will only once let me hear from you what your feelings are, I am willing that you should resume for ever the severity with which you overwhelm me. At least look at me with those eyes that I saw gazing at my portrait. Could you look at it with such gentleness, and then flee from me so cruelly? What do you fear? Why do you so dread my love? You love me, and you hide your love to no purpose; you have yourself given me tokens of its unawares. I know my good fortune: let me enjoy it, and cease making me unhappy. Is it possible that Madame de Clèves loves me, and I am still unhappy? How beautiful she was last night! How could I resist my longing to fling myself at her feet? Had I done so, I might have prevented her flight; my respectful bearing would have reassured her. But perhaps she did not recognize me,—I distress myself more than I should; and the sight of a man at such an extraordinary hour frightened her."

These thoughts haunted Monsieur de Nemours all day. He awaited the night with impatience, and when it had come he took once more the road to Coulommiers. The friend of Monsieur de Clèves, having assumed a disguise to avoid being recognized, followed him as he had done the previous evening, and saw him enter the same garden. Then Monsieur de Nemours perceived that Madame de Clèves was unwilling to run the risk of his trying to see her; every entrance was closed. He wandered in every direction to find some light, but his search was vain.

Madame de Clèves, suspecting that Monsieur de Nemours might come back, stayed in her own room; she feared lest strength to flee should be denied her, and she did not wish to risk the possibility of speaking to him in a manner that might contradict her previous conduct. Although Monsieur de Nemours had no hope of seeing her, he could not make up his mind to leave at once a place where she had been so often. He spent the whole night in the garden, finding some slight consolation in at least gazing on the same objects which she saw every day. The sun had risen before he thought of leaving; but at last the fear of being observed compelled him to go.

It was impossible for him to return without seeing Madame de Clèves; hence he went to see Madame de Mercœur, who was then living in her house not far from Coulommiers. She was extremely surprised at her brother's arrival. He invented some specious excuse for his journey, which completely deceived her, and at last managed so cleverly that she herself proposed their calling on Madame de Clèves. This plan they carried out that very day, and Monsieur de Nemours told his sister that he would leave her at Coulommiers to return with all speed to the king. He devised this plan of parting from her at Coulommiers in the hope that she would be the first to leave; in this way he imagined he could not fail to have an opportunity of speaking to Madame de Clèves.

When they reached Coulommiers, they found Madame de Clèves walking in a broad path along the edge of the flower-garden. The sight of Monsieur de Nemours embarrassed her not a little, and made her sure that it was he whom she had seen the previous night. This conviction filled her with anger that he should have been so bold and imprudent. He noticed with pain her evident coldness. The talk ran on insignificant subjects, and yet he succeeded in displaying so much wit and amiability, and so much admiration for Madame de Clèves, that he finally dispelled some of her coolness, in spite of her determination not to be appeased.

When he had got over his first timidity, he expressed great curiosity to see the summer-house in the wood; he described it as the most delightful spot in the world, and with so many details that Madame de Mercœur said he must have often seen it, to be so familiar with all its beauty.

"Still, I do not believe," answered Madame de Clèves, "that Monsieur de Nemours has ever been in it; it has been finished only a very short time."

"It is not long, either, since I was there," he retorted, looking at her; "and I do not know whether I ought not to be very glad that you have forgotten having seen me there."

Madame de Mercœur, who was busy looking at the garden, paid no attention to what her brother was saying. Madame de Clèves, blushing, and casting down her eyes so as not to see Monsieur de Nemours, said:

"I do not remember ever having seen you there, and if you ever have been there, it was without my knowledge."

"It is true, Madame," he said, "that I have been there without your permission, and I have spent there the most blissful and the most wretched moments of my life."

Madame de Clèves knew only too well what he meant; but she made no answer. She was thinking how she should keep Madame de Mercœur from going into the closet which contained the portrait of Monsieur de Nemours: this she did not want her to see. She succeeded so well that the time passed imperceptibly, and Madame de Mercœur spoke of leaving; but when Madame de Clèves noticed that Madame de Mercœur and her brother were not going away together, she saw the impending danger, and was as much embarrassed as she had been in Paris, and she decided on the same course. Her fear lest this visit should only confirm her husband's suspicions helped her to form this decision, and in order to prevent Monsieur de Nemours from being alone with her, she told Madame de Mercœur that she would accompany her to the edge of the forest, and ordered her carriage to follow her. This prince's grief at finding Madame de Clèves as austere as ever was so keen that he turned pale. Madame de Mercœur asked him if he was ill; but he looked at Madame de Clèves without being seen by any one, and let her see that he was suffering from nothing but despair. Nevertheless, he was compelled to let them go without daring to follow them; and after what he had said, he could not go back with his sister. He returned to Paris, and left it the next day.

Monsieur de Clèves' friend had watched him all the while. He also returned to Paris; and when he saw that Monsieur de Nemours had left for Chambord, he took the post in order to get there before him, and to make his report about his expedition. His master was awaiting his return to determine his life's unhappiness.

As soon as Monsieur de Clèves saw him, he read in his expression and his silence that he had brought only bad news. He remained for some time overwhelmed with grief, his head bowed, unable to speak; then he motioned to him to withdraw. "Go," he said; "I see what you have to tell me, but I am not strong enough to hear it."

"I have nothing to report," answered the gentleman, "from which it is possible to form an accurate judgment. It is true that Monsieur de Nemours entered the garden in the woods two nights running, and called at Coulommiers the next day with Madame de Mercœur."

"That is enough," replied Monsieur de Clèves, "that is enough;" and then, again motioning to him to leave, he added, "I have no need of further information."

The gentleman was forced to leave his master plunged in despair. Never, perhaps, has there been more poignant grief, and few men who possessed so much spirit and so affectionate a heart as Monsieur de Clèves have suffered the agony of discovering at the same time a wife's infidelity and the mortification of being deceived by a woman.

Monsieur de Clèves was overwhelmed by this grievous blow. That same night he was seized with a fever of such severity that at once his life was in peril. Word was sent to Madame de Clèves, and she went to him with all speed. He was worse when she reached him, and she noticed something cold and icy in his manner toward her that greatly surprised and pained her. He even seemed to be annoyed at the attention she paid him; but at last she thought this was perhaps a result of his illness.

As soon as Madame de Clèves had arrived at Blois, where the court was at that time, Monsieur de Nemours was filled with joy at knowing that she was in the same place as himself. He tried to see her, and called at the house every day, under pretext of inquiring after Monsieur de Clèves; but it was all in vain. She never left her husband's room, and was very anxious about him. Monsieur de Nemours regretted that she suffered so much; he readily saw how this grief would be likely to rekindle her love for Monsieur de Clèves, and how this affection would prove a dangerous foe to the love she bore in her heart. This feeling depressed him for some time; but the extreme seriousness of Monsieur de Clèves' illness soon gave him new hopes. He saw that Madame de Clèves would soon be free to follow her own wishes, and that in the future he might find lasting happiness. This thought filled him with almost painful rapture, and he banished it from his mind, lest he should be too miserable if his hopes were disappointed.

Meanwhile Monsieur de Clèves was almost given up. One of the last days of his illness, after he had passed a very bad night, he said, toward morning, that he would like to rest. Madame de Clèves alone stayed in his room. It seemed to her that, instead of resting, he was very uneasy; she went up to him and knelt down by his bed, with her face covered with tears. Monsieur de Clèves had made up his mind to say nothing about his grievance against her; but her attentions and her sorrow, which seemed genuine, and which he sometimes regarded as tokens of deceit and treachery, produced such conflicting and painful feelings that he could not repress them.

"You, Madame," he said, "are shedding a great many tears for a death of which you are the cause, and which cannot give you the sorrow which you display. I am no longer able to reproach you," he went on, in a voice weakened by illness and grief, "but I am dying of the cruel suffering you have inflicted on me. Was it necessary that so extraordinary an action as that of speaking to me as you did at Coulommiers should have so little result? Why confide to me your love for Monsieur de Nemours, if your virtue was not strong enough to resist it? I loved you so that I was glad to be deceived,—I confess it to my shame; I have since longed for the false tranquillity of which you robbed me. Why did you not leave me in the calm blindness in which so many husbands are happy? I should perhaps have never known that you loved Monsieur de Nemours. I am dying," he went on; "but bear it in mind that you make me welcome death, and that since you have robbed me of the love and esteem I felt for you, I dread living. What would life be to me, if I had to spend it with a woman I have loved so much and who has so cruelly deceived me, or if I had to live apart from her, after a scene of violence utterly repugnant to my disposition and to the love I bear you? My love for you, Madame, has been far deeper than you know; I have concealed the greater part of it, from fear of tormenting you or of lessening your esteem by a manner unbecoming to a husband; I really deserved your affection. I say it once more: I die without regret, since I could not win this, and now can no longer wish for it. Farewell, Madame. Some day you will mourn a man who had for you a true and lawful love. You will know the misery that overtakes women who fall into these entanglements, and you will learn the difference between being loved as I loved you, and being loved by men who, while protesting their love, seek only the honor of misleading you. But my death will leave you free, and you will be able to make Monsieur de Nemours happy without doing anything criminal. What do I care what may happen when I shall be no more? Must I be weak enough to look upon it?"

Madame de Clèves was so far from imagining that her husband could suspect her that she listened to him without understanding what he was saying, and supposing that he was blaming her interest in Monsieur de Nemours. At last, suddenly grasping his meaning, she exclaimed,—

"I a criminal! The very thought of it never entered my head. The severest virtue could command no different course of conduct than mine, and I have not done one thing of which I should not be glad to have you an eye-witness."

"Should you have been glad," asked Monsieur de Clèves, looking at her somewhat disdainfully, "to have had me for an eye-witness of the nights you spent with Monsieur de Nemours? Ah! Madame, am I speaking of you when I speak of a woman who has spent nights with a man?"

"No," she answered, "no; it is not of me that you are speaking,—I have never passed nights or moments with Monsieur de Nemours; he has never seen me in private; I have never had anything to do with him or listened to him, and I will swear—"

"Say no more," interrupted Monsieur de Clèves; "false oaths or a confession would give me equal pain."

Madame de Clèves could not answer; her tears and her grief choked her. At last, making a great effort, she said: "Look at me, at least; listen to me. If it concerned me alone, I should endure these reproaches; but it is your life that is at stake. Listen to me for your own sake; it is impossible that, with all the truth on my side, I should not convince you of my innocence."

"Would to God that you could convince me!" he exclaimed. "But what can you say to me? Was not Monsieur de Nemours at Coulommiers with his sister, and had he not passed the two previous nights with you in the garden in the forest?"

"If that is my crime," she replied, "I can clear myself easily. I don't ask you to believe me, but believe your servants: ask them if I was in the garden the evening Monsieur de Nemours came to Coulommiers, and if I didn't leave it the evening before, two hours earlier than usual."

She then told him how she had imagined she saw some one in the garden, and confessed that she had thought it was Monsieur de Nemours. She spoke with such earnestness, and the truth, even when improbable, carries such weight, that Monsieur de Clèves was almost convinced of her innocence.

"I do not know," he said, "whether I dare believe you; I am so near death that I do not want to see anything that might make me long to live. Your explanation comes too late; but it will always be a consolation to think that you are worthy of the esteem I have had for you. I beg of you to let me have the additional consolation of knowing that my memory will be dear to you, and that if it had depended on you, you would have had for me the feeling you have had for another."

He wanted to go on; but a sudden faintness made it impossible, and Madame de Clèves summoned the physicians. They found him almost lifeless. Nevertheless he lingered a few days longer, and at last died, having displayed admirable firmness.

Madame de Clèves was almost crazed by the intensity of her grief. The queen at once came to see her, and carried her to a convent, without her knowing whither she was going. Her sisters-in-law brought her to Paris before she was yet able to realize her afflictions. When she began to be strong enough to think about it, and saw what a husband she had lost, and reflected that she was the cause of his death by means of her love for another man, the horror she felt at herself and at Monsieur de Nemours cannot be described.

At first this prince did not venture to pay her any other attentions than such as etiquette required. He knew Madame de Clèves well enough to be sure that anything more marked would displease her; but what he learned later assured him that he would have to maintain this reserve for a long time. One of his equerries told him that Monsieur de Clèves' gentleman,[4] a friend of his, had told him, in his deep regret for the loss of his master, that Monsieur de Nemours' trip to Coulommiers was the cause of his death. Monsieur de Nemours was extremely surprised to hear this; but on thinking it over, he made out a part of the truth, and conjectured what would be the feelings of Madame de Clèves, and how she would detest him if she thought her husband's illness had been due to jealousy. He thought that the best thing would be not to have his name brought to her notice, and he regulated his conduct accordingly, painful as he found it.

The prince went to Paris, and could not refrain from calling on Madame de Clèves to ask how she was. He was informed that she saw no one, and had even given orders that she was not to be told who had inquired after her. Possibly these rigid orders were given solely on account of the prince, and to avoid hearing his name mentioned. But Monsieur de Nemours was too desperately in love to be able to live with absolutely no chance of seeing Madame de Clèves. He resolved to try every means, no matter how difficult, to escape from such an unendurable condition of affairs.

The princess's grief passed all bounds of reason. Her dying husband, —dying for her sake, and filled with such tender love for her,—was never sent from her mind; she continually recalled everything she owed him, and blamed herself for not having loved him,—as if that were a thing that depended on her will. Her sole consolation was the thought that she mourned him as he deserved, and that for the rest of her life she would only do what he would have approved if he had lived.

She had often wondered how he knew that Monsieur de Nemours had

---

4. Attendant. *Equerries:* personal attendants.

come to Coulommiers; she did not suspect that the prince had spoken of it, and it even seemed to her that it was immaterial whether he had said anything about it, so thoroughly rid of her passion did she feel. Nevertheless, she was deeply distressed to think that he was the cause of her husband's death, and she remembered with sorrow the fear that had tormented Monsieur de Clèves on his deathbed lest she should marry him; but all these various sources of grief were lost in that over her husband's death, and the others sank into insignificance.

After many months had passed, she recovered from her violent grief, becoming sad and languid. Madame de Martigues made a visit to Paris, and saw her repeatedly during her stay there. She talked with her about the court and of all that had happened; and although Madame de Clèves seemed to take no interest, Madame de Martigues went on talking in order to divert her. She told her all about the Vidame, Monsieur de Guise, and all the other men of note.

"As for Monsieur de Nemours," she said, "I do not know whether his occupations have taken the place of gallantry, but he is less cheerful than he used to be; he shuns the society of women; he continually runs up to Paris, and I believe is here now."

Monsieur de Nemours' name surprised Madame de Clèves and made her blush; she changed the subject, and Madame de Martigues did not notice her confusion.

The next day, the princess, being anxious to find some occupation suitable for her condition, went to see a man living close by who worked in silk in a peculiar way, with the intention of undertaking something of the sort herself. After looking at what he had to show, her eyes fell on the door of a room in which she thought there were some more, and asked to have it opened. The man replied that he did not have the key, and that it was occupied by a man who came there sometimes to draw the fine houses and gardens to be seen from the windows. "He is the handsomest man in the world," he went on, "and does not seem obliged to support himself by his work. Whenever he comes here, I see him always looking at the houses and gardens, but I have never seen him at work."

Madame de Clèves listened with great attention; what Madame de Martigues had said about Monsieur de Nemours coming some times to Paris, as well as her vision of this handsome man who had taken quarters near her house, made her think of that prince, and suggested that he was trying to see her. This thought produced in her an agitation which she could not understand. She went to the windows to see on what they looked, and saw that it was on her garden and her own apartment; and when she was in her room she saw the same window to which she had been told that the stranger used to come. The conjecture that it was Monsieur de Nemours entirely altered the current of her thoughts; she no longer felt the sad tranquillity which she had begun to enjoy,—she was uneasy and agitated. At last, unable to endure her loneliness, she went out to take the air in a garden in the faubourgs,[5] where she expected to find solitude. At first she supposed no one was there; the place seemed deserted, and she strolled about for some little time.

5. Suburbs.

After passing through a little thicket, she saw at the end of the path, in the most retired part of the garden, a sort of summer-house open on all sides, and she turned in that direction. When she had got near it, she saw a man lying on the benches who seemed sunk in deep thought, and she recognized Monsieur de Nemours. At the sight of him she stopped short; but her servants, who were following her, made some noise that aroused him. Without looking at them, he arose, to avoid their company, and turned into another path, bowing deeply, so that he was unable to see whom he was saluting.

Had Monsieur de Nemours known from whom he was running away, he would have eagerly retraced his steps; but as it was, he followed the path and went out by a sidegate, at which his carriage was waiting. This incident made a deep impression on Madame de Clèves' heart; all her love was suddenly rekindled with its former fervor. She went on and sat down in the place which Monsieur de Nemours had just left, and there she remained, completely overwhelmed. Her mind was full of this prince, more fascinating than any man in the world; loving her long with respect and constancy; giving up everything for her; respecting even her grief; trying to see her, without himself being seen; abandoning the court, where he was a favorite, to look upon the walls behind which she was immured, to come and muse in places where he could not hope to meet her,—in short, a man worthy to be loved for his love alone, and for whom she felt a passion so violent that she would have loved him even if he had not loved her, and one moreover of a lofty nature perfectly in harmony with her own. Duty and virtue could not restrain her emotions; every obstacle vanished; and of all her past she remembered nothing but her love for Monsieur de Nemours and his for her.

All these thoughts were new to the princess; she had been so lost in grief for her husband's death that she had given them no attention. With the sight of Monsieur de Nemours they all recurred to her. But when they came fastest, and she remembered that this same man whom now she thought of as able to marry her was the one she had loved during her husband's lifetime and was the cause of his death; that on his deathbed he had manifested his fear lest she should marry him,—her rigid virtue was so pained by the thought that it seemed to her quite as grievous a crime to marry Monsieur de Nemours as it had been to love him while her husband was living. She gave herself up to these reflections, which were so hostile to her happiness, and confirmed them by many arguments concerning her peace of mind and the evils she foresaw in case she married him. At last, after spending two hours there, she returned home, convinced that she ought to avoid the sight of him as a real obstacle to her duty.

But this conviction, the product of reason and virtue, did not control her heart, which remained attached to Monsieur de Nemours with a violence that reduced her to a most restless and pitiable state. That night was one of the unhappiest she had ever known. In the morning her first thought was to go to see if there was any one at the window which commanded her house; she looked out and saw Monsieur de Nemours. This surprised her, and she drew back so quickly that he felt sure she must have recognized him. This he had long wished might happen, since he had devised this method of seeing her; and when it seemed hopeless, he used to go and meditate in the garden where she had seen him.

Worn out at last by grief and uncertainty, the duke made up his mind to find some way of determining his fate. "Why should I wait?" he asked. "I have long known she loved me; she is free, and duty no longer stands in her way. Why should she force me to see her without being seen by her and with no chance to speak to her? Can love have so absolutely destroyed my reason and my boldness that I am not what I was when in love before? I was bound to respect Madame de Clèves' grief; but I have respected it too long, and I am giving her time to forget the affection she feels for me."

Thereupon he began to devise some way of seeing her. He fancied that there was no good reason for concealing his love from the Vidame of Chartres, and he resolved to speak to him and to confide to him his plans about his niece. The Vidame was then in Paris, like all the rest of the court, who had come to town to make their preparations for accompanying the king, who was to escort the Queen of Spain. Accordingly, Monsieur de Nemours called on the Vidame and frankly told him everything he had kept hidden until then, except Madame de Clèves' feelings, which he did not wish to appear to know.

The Vidame heard him with great pleasure, and answered that, with no knowledge of his feelings, he had often, since Madame de Clèves had become a widow, thought that she was the only woman worthy of him. Monsieur de Nemours besought his aid in getting a chance to address her, in order to find out her intentions.

The Vidame proposed taking him to call on her; but Monsieur de Nemours feared that she would not like this, because she did not yet see any one. They decided that the Vidame should invite her to come and see him on some pretext or other, and that Monsieur de Nemours should enter by a hidden staircase, in order not to be seen. This was carried out according to their plans. Madame de Clèves came; the Vidame went to receive her, and led her into a small room at the end of his apartment. Shortly after, Monsieur de Nemours came in, as if by chance. Madame de Clèves was much surprised to see him; she blushed, and tried to hide her blushes. The Vidame began to talk about unimportant subjects, and then went away, under the pretext of having some orders to give. He asked Madame de Clèves to do the honors in his place, and said he should return in a moment.

It would be impossible to express the feelings of Monsieur de Nemours and Madame de Clèves when they for the first time found themselves alone and free to talk. They remained for a long time without a word; then at last Monsieur de Nemours broke the silence. "Will you, Madame, forgive the Vidame," he said, "for having given me an opportunity to see you and to speak with you, which you have always cruelly denied me?"

"I ought not to forgive him," she replied, "for having forgotten my position and to what he exposes my reputation." As she uttered these words she started to leave; but Monsieur de Nemours delayed her, saying:

"Do not be alarmed, Madame; no one knows that I am here, and there is no danger. Listen to me, Madame,—if not through kindness, at least through love of yourself, and in order to protect yourself against the extravagances to which I shall certainly be led by an uncontrollable passion."

For the first time Madame de Clèves yielded to her tenderness for Monsieur de Nemours, and looking at him with eyes full of gentleness and charm, she said: "But what do you hope from the kindness that you ask of me? You would certainly regret obtaining it, and I should regret granting it. You deserve a happier fate than you have yet had, and can have in the future, unless you seek it elsewhere."

"I, Madame, find such happiness elsewhere! Is there any other happiness than winning your love? Although I have never spoken with you, I cannot think that you are ignorant of my affection, or that you do not know that it is truer and warmer than ever. How much it has been tried by events unknown to you, and how much by your severity!"

"Since you wish me to speak, and I decide it best," answered Madame de Clèves, sitting down, "I will do so, with a frankness that you will not always find in women. I shall not tell you that I have not noticed your attachment to me,—perhaps you could not believe me if I were to say so; I confess, then, not only that I have noticed it, but also just as you wished it to appear."

"And, Madame, if you have seen it," he interrupted, "is it possible that you have not been touched by it; and may I venture to ask if it has made no impression on your heart?"

"You should have judged of that from my conduct," she replied; "but I should be glad to know what you have thought of it."

"I should have to be in a happier condition to dare to tell you," he answered, "and my fate has too little relation with what I should say. All that I can tell you, Madame, is that you would not have confessed to Monsieur de Clèves what you concealed from me, and that you would have concealed from him what you would have let me see."

"How were you able to find out," she asked, blushing, "that I confessed anything to Monsieur de Clèves?"

"I heard it from your own lips, Madame," he replied; "but as an excuse for my boldness in listening to you, consider whether I misused what I had heard, whether my hopes were strengthened by it, whether I became bold enough to speak to you."

He began to tell her how he had heard her conversation with Monsieur de Clèves: but she interrupted him in the middle.

"Say no more," she said; "I now see how you came to know too much: that you did, was very plain to me at the dauphiness's when she had heard the story from those to whom you had told it."

Monsieur de Nemours then explained to her how that had happened.

"Do not apologize," she resumed; "I forgave you a long time ago, before you told me how it occurred. But since you have yourself heard from me what I had meant to keep a secret from you all my life, I confess that you have inspired me with emotions unknown before I saw you, and so unfamiliar to me that they filled me with a surprise which greatly added to the agitation they produced. I confess this with the less shame because I may now do it innocently, and you have seen that my feelings did not guide my actions."

"Do you believe, Madame," exclaimed Monsieur de Nemours, falling on his knees, "that I am not ready to die at your feet with joy and rapture?"

"I only tell you," she answered, smiling, "what you already know only too well."

"Ah! Madame," he said, "what a difference between finding something out by accident, and hearing it from you, and seeing that you wish me to know it."

"It is true," said she, "that I wish you to know it, and that I take pleasure in telling you. I am not certain that I do not tell it more from love of myself than from love of you; for certainly this avowal will have no consequences, and I shall follow the rigid rules that my condition imposes."

"You will not think of such a thing, Madame," replied Monsieur de Nemours; "you are bound by no further duty; you are free; and if I dared, I should even tell you that it depends on you so to act that your duty shall some day oblige you to preserve the feelings that you have for me."

"My duty," she replied, "forbids my ever thinking of any one, and of you last of all, for reasons unknown to you."

"Perhaps they are not, Madame," he pleaded; "but those are no true reasons. I have reason to believe that Monsieur de Clèves thought me happier than I was, and imagined that you approved of mad freaks of mine which my passion suggested without your knowledge."

"Let us not speak of that affair," she said. "I cannot bear the thought of it; it fills me with shame, and its consequences were too painful. It is only too likely that you are the cause of Monsieur de Clèves' death; the suspicions you aroused, your inconsiderate conduct, cost him his life as truly as if you had taken it with your own hands. Think of what I should do if you had come to such extremities and the same unhappy result had followed. I know very well this is not the same thing in the eyes of the world; but in mine there is no difference, for I know it was from you he got his death, and on account of me."

"Oh! Madame," interposed Monsieur de Nemours, "what phantom of duty do you oppose to my happiness? What! Madame, a vain and baseless fancy can prevent your making happy a man you do not hate, when he has conceived the hope of passing his life with you, his fate leading him to love you as the best woman in the world, finding in you every charming trait, incurring not your hatred, and seeing in you everything that best becomes a woman,—for, Madame, there is no other woman who combines what you do. Men who marry their mistresses who love them, tremble from fear lest they should renew their misconduct with others; but nothing of the sort is to be feared in you: you are only to be admired. Can I have foreseen such felicity only to find you raising obstacles? Ah! Madame, you forget that you chose me from other men,—or rather, you did not; you made a mistake, and I have flattered myself."

"You did not flatter yourself," she replied; "the reasons for my acting as I do would not, perhaps, seem to me so strong, had I not chosen you as you suspect,—and that is what makes me foresee unhappiness if I should take an interest in you."

"I have no answer," he said, "when you show me that you fear unhappiness; but I confess that, after all you have been good enough to say to me, I did not expect to be opposed by such a cruel argument." "It is so far from uncomplimentary to you," she answered, "that I shall even find it hard to tell it to you."

"Alas! Madame, what can you fear will flatter me too much after what you have just said to me?"

"I wish still to speak to you as frankly as I began," she explained, "and I want to dispense with all the reserve and formalities that I should respect in a first conversation; but I beg of you to listen to me without interruption.

"I think it but a slight reward for your affection that I should hide from you none of my feelings, but should let you see them exactly as they are.

This probably will be the only time in my life that I shall take the liberty of letting you see them; nevertheless, I cannot confess to you without deep shame that the certainty of not being loved by you as I am, seems to me a horrible misfortune; that if there were not already insurmountable claims of duty, I doubt if I could make up my mind to risk this unhappiness. I know that you are free, as I am, and that we are so situated that the world would probably blame neither of us if we should marry; but do men keep their love in these permanent unions? Ought I to expect a miracle in my case, and can I run the risk of seeing this passion, which would be my only happiness, fade away? Monsieur de Clèves was perhaps the only man in the world capable of keeping his love after marriage. My fate forbade my enjoying this blessing. Perhaps, too, his love only survived because he found none in me. But I should not have the same way of preserving yours; I believe that the obstacles you have met have made you constant; those were enough to make you yearn to conquer them, and my involuntary actions,—things you learned by chance,—gave you enough hope to keep you interested."

"Oh! Madame," replied Monsieur de Nemours, "I can no longer maintain the silence you impose on me; you do me too much injustice, and you let me see how far you are from being prejudiced in my favor."

"I confess," she said, "that I may be moved by my emotions, but they cannot blind me; nothing can prevent my seeing that you are born with every disposition for gallantry, and with all the qualities proper to secure speedy success. You have already been in love several times,—you would be again very often. I should not make you happy; I should see you interested in another as you have been in me: this would inflict on me a mortal blow, and I should never feel sure that I should not be jealous. I have said too much to try to hide from you that you have already made me feel this passion, and that I suffered cruel tortures that evening when the queen gave me that letter from Madame de Themines which was said to be directed to you, and that the impression left on me is that jealousy is the greatest unhappiness in the world.

"Vanity or taste makes all women try to secure you; there are few whom you do not please,—my own experience teaches me that there are few whom you might not please. I should always imagine that you were loved and in love, and I should not be often wrong. Yet in this condition I could only suffer,—I should not dare to complain. One may make reproaches to a lover, but can a woman reproach her husband for ceasing to love her? If I could become hardened to that misfortune, could I become hardened to imagining that I saw Monsieur de Clèves charging you with his death, reproaching me for loving you, and showing the difference between his affection and yours? It is impossible to resist such arguments; I must remain in my present position and in my immovable determination never to leave it."

"But do you think you can, Madame?" exclaimed Monsieur de Nemours. "Do you think that your resolutions can hold out against a man who worships you and is fortunate enough to please you? It is harder than you think, Madame, to resist what pleases us and one who loves us. You have done it by an austere virtue which is almost without a precedent; but this virtue no longer conflicts with your emotions, and these I hope you will follow, in spite of yourself."

"I know that there is nothing harder than what I undertake; I mistrust my own strength, supported by all my arguments. What I think due to the memory of Monsieur de Clèves would be ineffectual, if it were not reinforced by my anxiety for my own peace of mind; and these arguments need to be strengthened by those of duty. But though I mistrust myself, I think I shall never overcome my scruples, and I do not hope to overcome my interest in you. It will make me unhappy, and I shall deny myself the pleasure of seeing you, whatever pain this may cost me. I am in a position which makes that a crime which at any other time would be permissible, and mere etiquette forbids that we should meet."

Monsieur de Nemours flung himself at her feet and gave expression to all the emotion that filled him. He manifested, by his words and tears, the liveliest and tenderest passion that heart ever felt. Madame de Clèves was not unmoved; and looking at Monsieur de Nemours with eyes heavy with tears, she exclaimed,—

"Why must I charge you with the death of Monsieur de Clèves? Why did I not learn to know you when I was free; or why did I not know you before I was married? Why does fate divide us by such an insuperable obstacle?"

"There is no obstacle," pleaded Monsieur de Nemours; "you alone thwart my happiness, you alone impose a law which virtue and reason could not impose."

"It is true," she replied, "that I make a great sacrifice to a duty which exists only in my imagination. Wait to see what time will do. Monsieur de Clèves has but just died, and that fatal event is too recent for me to judge clearly. Meanwhile you have the pleasure of having won the love of a woman who would never have loved had she not seen you; be sure that my feelings for you will never change and will always survive, whatever I do.

"Good by," she said. "This conversation fills me with shame. Repeat it to the Vidame; I give my consent,—nay, I beg of you to do so."

With these words she left the room, Monsieur de Nemours being unable to prevent her. She found the Vidame in the next room. He saw her so agitated that he did not dare to speak to her, and he handed her to her carriage without a word. He went back to Monsieur de Nemours, who was in such a whirl of joy, sadness, surprise, and admiration,—in short, so possessed by all the emotions that spring from a passion full of hope and dread,—that he seemed beside himself. It was long before the Vidame got any clear notion of what they had said; finally, however, he succeeded; and Monsieur de Chartres, without being the least in love, had no less admiration for the virtue, intelligence, and worth of Madame de Clèves than had Monsieur de Nemours himself. They tried to determine the prince's probable chances; and whatever the fears that love might arouse, the prince agreed with the Vidame that it was impossible that Madame de Clèves should persist in her resolutions. Nevertheless, they agreed to follow her orders, from fear lest, if the duke's love for her should become known, she should in some way bind herself, and would not change from fear of its being thought that she had loved him while her husband was living.

Monsieur de Nemours determined to join the king, as he could no longer stay away, and he made up his mind to start without even trying to see Madame de Clèves again. He begged the Vidame to speak to her. He told him a number of things to say to her, and suggested countless arguments with which to overcome her scruples. At last a good part of the night was gone before Monsieur de Nemours thought of leaving to seek repose.

Madame de Clèves was in no condition to find rest; it was for her such a new thing to lay aside the reserve which she had imposed upon herself, to permit a man to tell her that he loved her, to confess that she too was in love, that she did not recognize herself. She was amazed at what she had done, and repented it bitterly; she was also made happy by it,—she was completely upset by love and agitation. She went over once more the arguments in defence of her duty which stood in the way of her happiness; she lamented their strength, and regretted having stated them so strongly to Monsieur de Nemours. Although the thought of marrying him had occurred to her the moment she saw him again in the garden, it had not made so deep an impression on her as had her talk with him; and at moments she could scarcely believe that she would be unhappy if she should marry him. She would have liked to be able to say that she was wrong both in her scruples about the past and in her fears for the future. At other moments reason and duty convinced her of the opposite, and decided her not to marry again or ever to see Monsieur de Nemours; but this resolution was extremely repugnant to her when her heart was so much moved and had so recently seen the joys of love. At last, in order to allay her agitation, she thought it was not necessary for her to do herself the violence of forming a decision,—etiquette left her still much time for making up her mind; but she resolved to abide by her determination to have nothing to do with Monsieur de Nemours meanwhile.

The Vidame came to see her, and pleaded his friend's cause with all possible skill and earnestness; but he could not persuade her to modify her own conduct or that which she had imposed on Monsieur de Nemours. She told him that she did not mean to change her present condition, that she knew it would be hard for her to carry out this intention, but that she hoped she should be strong enough to do so. She showed him how firmly convinced she was that Monsieur de Nemours had caused her husband's death, and that she should do wrong in marrying him; so that the Vidame feared it would not be easy to convince her of the opposite. He did not confide to this prince what he thought, and when he reported his talk with her, he let him enjoy all the hope that reason can awaken in a man who is loved.

The next day they left to join the king. The Vidame, at the request of Monsieur de Nemours, wrote to Madame de Clèves, in order to speak of him; and in a second letter, which soon followed, Monsieur de Nemours added a few lines himself. But Madame de Clèves, who did not wish to infringe her rules, and who feared the perils of correspondence, told the Vidame that she should decline to receive his letters if he continued to write about Monsieur de Nemours; and this she said so earnestly that this prince himself begged his friend never to mention his name.

The court left to escort the Queen of Spain as far as Poitou. Madame de Clèves was left to herself during their absence, and the farther she was removed from Monsieur de Nemours and from anything that could remind her of him, the more she recalled the memory of Monsieur de Clèves, which she was bent on keeping ever present before her. Her reasons for not marrying Monsieur de Nemours seemed strong so far as her duty, and irrefutable so far as her tranquillity, was concerned. The fading of his love after marriage, and all the pangs of jealousy, which she regarded as certain, showed her the misery to which she would expose herself; but she saw too that she had assumed an impossible task in undertaking to resist the most fascinating of men, whom she loved and who loved her, in a matter which offended neither virtue nor propriety. She decided that only separation could give her strength; and this she felt that she needed, not merely to maintain her determination not to marry, but also to protect herself from the sight of Monsieur de Nemours. Hence she resolved to make a long journey during the time that etiquette forced her to spend in retirement. Some large estates that she owned in the Pyrénées seemed to her the best place she could choose. She started a few days before the court returned; and just before leaving, she wrote to the Vidame to beg that no one should inquire after her or write to her.

Monsieur de Nemours was as much afflicted by her absence as another man would have been by the death of the woman he loved. The thought of this long separation from Madame de Clèves was a constant source of suffering, especially after he had tasted the pleasure of meeting her and seeing that she loved him. He could do nothing but grieve, and his grief increased daily. Madame de Clèves, as a result of all her agitation, fell seriously ill after her arrival at her country place, and news of this reached the court. Monsieur de Nemours was inconsolable, and fell into the most unbounded despair. The Vidame had great difficulty in keeping him from letting his love be seen, as well as from following after her to find out how she was. The Vidame's relationship and intimacy served as a pretext for sending constant letters. At last word came that she had passed the turning point of her dangerous illness, but was still so weak that all were very anxious.

This long and near view of death enabled Madame de Clèves to judge mundane matters in a very different spirit from that of health. Her imminent peril taught her indifference to everything, and the length of her illness enforced this upon her. Yet when she had recovered, she found that she had not wholly forgotten Monsieur de Nemours; but she summoned to her aid every argument she could devise against marrying him. The conflict was a stern one; but at last she conquered what was left of this passion, which was already diminished by her reflections during her illness. The thought of death had revived her memory of Monsieur de Clèves; and this, harmonizing with her sense of duty, made a strong impression on her heart. The affections and ties of the world appeared to her as they appear to persons of enlarged views. Her health, which was still delicate, helped her to preserve those feelings; but knowing how circumstances affect the wisest resolutions, she was unwilling to run the risk of seeing her own altered, or of returning to the place where lived the man she had loved. Under the pretext of needing change of air, she withdrew to a religious house, without making known her determination to leave the court.

When Monsieur de Nemours heard of this, he at once saw what a decisive step it was, and feared that he had no more ground for hope. Yet the destruction of his hopes did not prevent his doing his utmost to bring about her return; he made the queen write to her, and even persuaded the Vidame to visit her: but it was all to no purpose. The Vidame saw her; she did not tell him that she had resolved upon this, but he decided that she would never return. At last Monsieur de Nemours went himself, under the pretext of going to the baths.[6] She was much moved and astonished when she heard

6. At a resort or spa where bathing, usually in natural springs, is part of the medical treatment.

that he had come. She sent him a message by one of her trusty companions that she begged him not to be surprised if she was unwilling to run the risk of seeing him again and of having the feelings she felt bound to maintain swept away by his presence; that she wanted him to know that having found her duty and her peace of mind unalterably opposed to her interest in him, everything else in the world seemed so indifferent that she had abandoned it entirely, had given all her thoughts to another life, and had no other feeling left but her desire to have him share the same sentiments.

Monsieur de Nemours thought he should die of grief in the presence of the woman who brought this message. He begged her twenty times to go back to Madame de Clèves, to entreat her to let him see her; but she told him that Madame de Clèves had forbidden her, not only to bring her any message from him, but even to repeat to her what he might say. At last he had to leave, as completely overwhelmed with grief as a man could be who had lost all hopes of ever seeing again a woman whom he loved with the most violent and the most natural passion possible. Yet he did not yield even then; he did everything he could to induce her to alter her decision. At last, when years had passed, time and separation allayed his grief and extinguished his passion. Madame de Clèves led such a life that it was evident she meant never to go into the world again; part of each year she spent in this religious house, and the other part at home, but in retirement, busied with severer tasks than those of the austerest convents. Her life, which was not long, furnished examples of the loftiest virtue.

JEAN RACINE
1639–1699

Jean Racine's capacity to communicate the full intensity of passion in tragedies marked by their formal decorum and their elevated tone gave him immediate and lasting fame among French dramatists. He brings to material adapted from classic texts an immediacy of psychological insight to which twentieth-century audiences readily respond.

Born into the family of a government official in the Valois district, eighty miles from Paris, Racine attended the College de Beauvais. Later (1655–59) he studied in the Jansenist center of Port-Royal. (Jansenism, a strict Catholic movement emphasizing moral self-examination and severely controlled conduct, exercised a profound influence on Racine.) In 1660, encouraged by the poet Jean de la Fontaine, Racine came to Paris, where his early plays failed, driving him to a period of seclusion in Provence. When he returned to Paris in 1663, however, the Court and the nobility patronized him, and he rapidly developed a reputation as a major playwright. In 1677 he left Paris and returned to Port-Royal, an environment appropriate to his increasing interest in religious thought. He married Catherine de Romanet, with whom he had seven children, most of whom became nuns or priests. Remaining in the country, he wrote history, made short trips to Paris, and traveled as historiographer with Louis XIV's campaigns. Buried at Port-Royal, his body was exhumed in 1711 and reburied next to Pascal at the church of St. Étienne-du-Mont in Paris.

Only one of Racine's twelve plays, an early comedy, deviated from the tragic mode. His first tragedies imitated the work of his contemporary Pierre Corneille; later he chose biblical and classical models. *Phaedra* (1677) adapts, with new emphasis, the action of Euripides' *Hippolytus*, making the guilty woman rather than the relatively passive man the protagonist and using the highly charged sexual situation between the two to generate intense psychological drama. To twentieth-century readers, the play's most immediately obvious aspect may be its conventional formalities: long declamatory speeches, stylized exchanges in compressed half lines, the artificiality of conveying such complicated relationships and histories through the action of a single day. Such devices, however—which would have seemed as artificial to seventeenth-century audiences as they do to us, although more familiar—intensify the impact of the central characters' anguish and their desperate attempts to deal with it. If the play's surface is formal, its depths seethe with passion.

Passion, of course, is the subject of *Phaedra*. The conflict between reason and passion that preoccupied many thinkers in the late seventeenth and early eighteenth centuries—that conflict resolved on the side of reason at such great cost for the princess of Clèves—here plays itself out with stark urgency. Passion triumphs, in *Phaedra*, over all principles of control, bringing death to the two central characters and misery to their survivors. As in Greek tragedy, although by rather different means, the reader feels not only the self-destructiveness of the human psyche but the pathos and the heroism of the doomed effort to transcend the limits of the given.

The play opens not with Phaedra herself but with Hippolytus, meditating about his heroic father, Theseus. Like Molière, Racine uses the family as microcosm of larger social orders, but the intense conflicts that throb beneath the surface in many real-life families here undergo no comic transformation. Hippolytus has his own problems, quite apart from Phaedra. Blessed and burdened with a larger-than-life father, he must choose whether to try to imitate that father or to seek other ways of being a man. "I sucked that pride which seems so strange to you / From an Amazonian mother," he tells his friend Theramenes, alluding to the "austere and proud / Persuasions" that have prevented him from feeling interest in any woman. But matters cannot remain so simple. Theseus has distinguished himself in two ways: by heroic womanizing (he leaves a trail of women behind him wherever he goes) and by heroic action, the conquering and destruction of monsters human and inhuman. As the play opens, Hippolytus acknowledges in himself the first incursions of love. No longer can his adolescent defense, his refusal of any resemblance to his father, serve him. When Theseus returns, Hippolytus will beg permission to seek his own heroism:

> Before you'd lived as long as I have done,
> More than one tyrant, monsters more than one
> Had felt your strength of arm, your sword's keen blade . . .
> Let me at long last show my courage.

He wants, he says, even by death to "prove to all the world I was your son." By the time he makes this plea, however, his innocent desire to prove his manhood, to declare his separateness from and worthiness of his father, has been overwhelmed by darker forces.

Phaedra's impulses are less innocent—less "natural," she suggests. In a poignant passage, she imagines Hippolytus and his youthful beloved, Aricia, expressing their love in a natural setting, themselves a part of the natural world. She understands her own sin as an internal revolution of feeling against control; she speaks of desperately seeking her "lost reason" in the entrails of sacrifices she makes to Venus, trying to avert her fate. Never does she excuse herself, never does she believe herself justified in loving the son of the man who kidnapped her into marriage. When Theseus is thought dead, Phaedra declares herself unworthy to rule a nation because she cannot rule herself. Yet such moral awareness fails to help her: knowing her sin, she continues to enact it, at least in feeling. The play evokes the full torment of such experience.

As for powerful Theseus, conqueror of women, defier of the supernatural, ally of Neptune—this kingly figure returns to find himself powerless at home. The son and wife who by social convention exist in utter subordination to him turn into enemies he has no capacity to master. First his wife's nurse tells him that his son has attempted to seduce Phaedra. The rivalry of sons and fathers lies deep: if sons fear they can never equal their fathers, fathers fear that the young necessarily overcome the old. Theseus believes the nurse's bare assertion, unsupported by substantial evidence. He banishes his son and invokes Neptune's power to destroy him. Then Aricia's hints lead him to suspect his wife, who confesses her own emotional sin while already on the verge of self-inflicted death. Theseus remains alone, bereft, his tyrannical impulse now devoid of domestic object. His own passions, too quickly fired—jealous possessiveness of his wife, jealous rivalry with his son—have deprived him of two beings he loved.

The play provides no villains. Phaedra, in some versions of the story a monster of lust, here becomes a woman struggling against her nature, as profoundly committed to standards of control as to the violent feelings that overthrow them. Hippolytus, in the process of self-discovery, at a delicate balance point between youth and maturity, cannot protect himself against the alternations of closely linked love and hate in a woman whose passions, and whose self-awareness, far exceed his. Theseus, in the ignorance of success, fails in comprehension, not understanding himself, his wife, or his son. All three exemplify the pathos and the dignity of the human struggle to be human.

Phaedra dies with the word *purity* on her lips, seeking self-purification in death, the only course now possible to her. Hippolytus dies in the beauty of his youth, deprived of age's suffering and fulfillment. Theseus lives to try once more to rule adequately, perhaps chastened by suffering into greater awareness. The names of the Greek gods survive in this drama: Aphrodite torments Phaedra, Neptune serves Theseus's impetuous will. But the gods now function as projections of human passion: Phaedra's sexual lust, Theseus's lust for power. Phaedra's torment suggests a Christian effort at purification, a Christian ideal of self-denial. The drama, in Racine's handling of the ancient story, projects on a giant screen conflicts all men and women undergo, the surge of feeling warring with the ideal of self-restraint. By concentrating the play of passions within a small family group and a confined space of time, while recalling connections between the characters' feelings and historical events that lie behind them; by giving Theseus and Phaedra heroic dignity and stature; by linking this family with the fate of nations, Racine forces his readers to feel the intensity and the large significance of feelings and happenings that might in other treatments seem merely sordid. He gives his characters timeless reality—speaking to his time, and to ours.

To translate Racine into English involves particularly difficult problems, since the French Alexandrine couplet, composed of twelve-syllable lines, does not adapt naturally to English verse. Richard Wilbur's version uses the common English pentameter, the ten-syllable line, to construct fluent, pointed, and dignified verse. His couplets by their formal elegance remind the reader steadily of the discipline that the play embodies and celebrates.

A useful biography of Racine is G. Brereton, *Jean Racine: A Critical Biography* (1951), which combines biography with literary criticism. Valuable critical insight is provided by O. de Mourgues, *Racine: Or, The Triumph of Relevance* (1967); Richard Parish, *Racine: The Limits of Tragedy* (1993); and P. J. Yarrow, *Racine* (1978). A treatment of French tragic drama that includes extensive and valuable material on Racine is Albert Cook, *French Tragedy: The Power of Enactment* (1981). For an interpretation that includes stage history of Racine's plays, see D. Maskell, *Racine: A Theatrical Reading* (1991). Intended especially for students is Philip Butler, *A Student's Guide to Racine* (1974).

PRONOUNCING GLOSSARY

The following list uses common English syllables and stress accents to provide rough equivalents of selected words whose pronunciation may be unfamiliar to the general reader.

Acheron: *ah'-ker-awn*

Ariadne: *ah-ree-ahd'-ne*

Aricia: *ah-ree'-sha*

Cocytus: *coh-sai'-tuhs*

Euripides: *yoo-rip'-uh-deez*

Hippolytus: *hip-pol'-i-tuhs*

Ismene: *is-mee'-ne*

Medea: *me-dee'-a*

Mycenae: *mai-see'-nee*

Oenone: *ee-noh'-ne*

Panope: *pah'-no-pe*

Pasiphaë: *pa-si'-fa-ee*

Peirithous: *pay-rith'-oo-uhs*

Peloponnesus: *pel-luh-puh-nee'-suhs*

Phaedra: *fee'-drah*

Scythia: *si'-thee-uh*

Taenarus: *ten'-a-ruhs*

Theramenes: *the-ram'-uh-neez*

Theseus: *thee'-see-uhs*

Troezen: *troh'-zen*

Phaedra[1]

CHARACTERS

THESEUS, *son of Aegeus, King of Athens*

PHAEDRA, *wife of Theseus, daughter of Minos and Pasiphaë*

HIPPOLYTUS, *son of Theseus and Antiope, Queen of the Amazons*

ARICIA, *princess of the blood royal of Athens*

THERAMENES, *Hippolytus' tutor*

OENONE, *Phaedra's nurse and confidante*

ISMENE, *Aricia's confidante*

PANOPE, *lady-in-waiting to Phaedra*

GUARDS

The action takes place within and without a palace at Troezen, a town in the Peloponnesus.

Act I

SCENE 1

HIPPOLYTUS, THERAMENES

HIPPOLYTUS   No, dear Theramenes, I've too long delayed
In pleasant Troezen; my decision's made.
I'm off; in my anxiety, I commence
To tax myself with shameful indolence.
My father has been gone six months and more,   5
And yet I do not know what distant shore
Now hides him, or what trials he now may bear.

---

1. Translated by Richard Wilbur.

THERAMENES   You'll go in search of him, my lord? But where?
  Already, to appease your fears, I've plied
  The seas which lie on Corinth's either side;   10
  I've asked for Theseus among tribes who dwell
  Where Acheron[2] goes plunging into Hell;
  Elis I've searched and, from Taenarus[3] bound,
  Reached even that sea where Icarus[4] was drowned.
  In what fresh hope, in what unthought-of places,   15
  Do you set out to find your father's traces?
  Who knows, indeed, if he wants the truth about
  His long, mysterious absence to come out,
  And whether, while we tremble for him, he's
  Not fondling some new conquest at his ease   20
  And planning to deceive her like the rest? . . .
HIPPOLYTUS   Enough, Theramenes. In King Theseus' breast,
  The foolish fires of youth have ceased to burn;
  No tawdry dalliance hinders his return.
  Phaedra need fear no rivals now; the King   25
  Long since, for her sake, ceased philandering.
  I go then, out of duty—and as a way
  To flee a place in which I dare not stay.
THERAMENES   Since when, my lord, have you begun to fear
  This peaceful place your childhood held so dear,   30
  And which I've often known you to prefer
  To Athens' court, with all its pomp and stir?
  What danger or affliction drives you hence?
HIPPOLYTUS   Those happy times are gone. All's altered since
  The Gods dispatched to us across the sea   35
  The child of Minos and Pasiphaë.[5]
THERAMENES   Ah. Then it's Phaedra's presence in this place
  That weighs on you. She'd hardly seen your face
  When, as the King's new consort, she required
  Your banishment, and got what she desired.   40
  But now her hatred for you, once so great,
  Has vanished, or has cooled, at any rate.
  And why, my lord, should you feel threatened by
  A dying woman who desires to die?
  Sick unto death—with what, she will not say,   45
  Weary of life and of the light of day,
  Could Phaedra plot to do you any harm?
HIPPOLYTUS   Her vain hostility gives me no alarm.
  It is, I own, another enemy.
  The young Aricia, from whom I flee,   50
  Last of a line which sought to overthrow

---

2. A river that flows into Hades; across it Charon ferried the dead.   3. A point of land in southern Greece, near Sparta. Elis is a district of Greece on the west coast of the Peloponnesus.   4. Son of Daedalus. Escaping from Crete by means of wings made by his father, Icarus flew so high that the sun melted the wax holding his wings together, and he fell to his death.   5. Phaedra was the daughter of King Minos of Crete and Pasiphaë, sister to Circe. Enamored of a white bull sent by Poseidon, Pasiphaë consequently gave birth to the Minotaur, the Cretan monster later killed by Theseus. Phaedra was thus half-sister to the Minotaur.

Our house.

THERAMENES   What! Will you also be her foe?
That gentle maiden, though of Pallas' line,
Had no part in her brothers' base design.[6]
If she is guiltless, why should you hate her, Sir?   55

HIPPOLYTUS   I would not flee her if I hated her.

THERAMENES   Dare I surmise, then, why you're leaving us?
Are you no longer that Hippolytus
Who spurned love's dictates and refused with scorn
The yoke which Theseus has so often borne?   60
Has Venus, long offended by your pride,
Contrived to see her Theseus justified
By making you confess her power divine
And bow, like other men, before her shrine?
Are you in love, Sir?

HIPPOLYTUS   What do you mean, dear man   65
You who have known me since my life began?
How can you wish that my austere and proud
Persuasions be so basely disvowed?
I sucked that pride which seems so strange to you
From an Amazonian mother,[7] and when I grew   70
To riper years, and knew myself, I thought
My given nature to be nobly wrought.
You then, devoted friend, instructed me
In all my father's brilliant history,
And you recall how glowingly I heard   75
His exploits, how I hung on every word
As you portrayed a sire whose deeds appease
Men's longing for another Hercules—
Those monsters slain, those brigands all undone,
Procrustes, Sciron, Sinis, Cercyon,—   80
The Epidaurian giant's scattered bones,
The Minotaur's foul blood on Cretan stones!
But when you told me of less glorious feats,
His far-flung chain of amorous deceits,
Helen of Sparta[8] kidnapped as a maid;   85
Sad Periboea[9] in Salamis betrayed;
Others, whose very names escape him now,
Too-trusting hearts, deceived by sigh and vow;
Wronged Ariadne,[1] telling the rocks her moan,
Phaedra abducted, though to grace a throne,—   90
You know how, loathing stories of that sort,
I begged you oftentimes to cut them short,
And wished posterity might never hear

6. Theseus killed all fifty sons of Pallas because they threatened his kingdom of Athens. Aricia is Pallas's daughter.   7. Hippolytus's mother was Antiope, sister of Hippolyta, queen of the Amazons.   8. Daughter of Zeus and Leda, later the wife of Menelaus of Sparta (and the cause of the Trojan War). In her girlhood she was abducted by Theseus and Peirithoüs; her brothers rescued her and brought her back home.   9. The mother of Ajax, one of the women Theseus seduced and abandoned.   1. Phaedra's sister, who was abandoned by Theseus on the island of Naxos after she rescued him from the Minotaur.

The worser half of Theseus' great career.
Shall I, in my turn, be subjected so   95
To passion, by the Gods be brought so low—
The more disgraced because I cannot claim
Such honors as redeem King Theseus' name,
And have not, by the blood of monsters, won
The right to trespass as my sire has done?   100
And even if my pride laid down its arms,
Could I surrender to Aricia's charms?
Would not my wayward passions heed the ban
Forbidding her to me, or any man?
The King's no friend to her, and has decreed   105
That she not keep alive her brothers' seed;
Fearing some new shoot from their guilty stem,
He wants her death to be the end of them;
For her, the nuptial torch shall never blaze;
He's doomed her to be single all her days.   110
Shall I take up her cause then, brave his rage,
Set a rebellious pattern for the age,
Commit my youth to love's delirium . . . ?
THERAMENES   Ah, Sir, if love's appointed hour has come,
It's vain to reason; Heaven will not hear.   115
What Theseus bans, he makes you hold more dear.
His hate for her but stirs your flames the more,
And lends new grace to her whom you adore.
Why fear, my lord, a love that's true and chaste?
Of what's so sweet, will you not dare to taste?   120
Shall timid scruples make your blood congeal?
What Hercules once felt, may you not feel?
What hearts has Venus' power failed to sway?
Where would you be, who strive with her today,
If fierce Antiope had not grown tame[2]   125
And loved king Theseus with a virtuous flame?
But come, my lord, why posture and debate?
Admit that you have changed, and that of late
You're seen less often, in your lonely pride,
Racing your chariot by the oceanside,   130
Or deftly using Neptune's[3] art to train
Some charger to obey the curb and rein.
The woods less often echo to our cries.
A secret fire burns in your heavy eyes.
No question of it: you're sick with love, you feel   135
A wasting passion which you would conceal.
Has fair Aricia wakened your desire?
HIPPOLYTUS   I'm off, Theramenes, to find my sire.
THERAMENES   Will you not see the Queen before you go,
My lord?

2. As an Amazon, Antiope was committed to chastity.   3. Or Poseidon, god of the sea, who was also
identified with Hippios, god of horses.

HIPPOLYTUS
        I mean to. You may tell her so.   140
Duty requires it of me. Ah, but here's
Her dear Oenone; what new grief prompts her tears?

SCENE 2

HIPPOLYTUS, OENONE, THERAMENES

OENONE   Alas, my lord, what grief could equal mine?
The Queen has gone into a swift decline.
I nurse her, tend her day and night, but she
Is dying of some nameless malady.
Disorder rules within her heart and head.   5
A restless pain has dragged her from her bed;
She longs to see the light; but in her keen
Distress she is unwilling to be seen. . . .
She's coming.
HIPPOLYTUS   I understand, and I shall go.
My hated face would but increase her woe.   10

SCENE 3

PHAEDRA, OENONE

PHAEDRA   Let's go no farther; stay, Oenone dear.
I'm faint; my strength abandons me, I fear.
My eyes are blinded by the glare of day,
And now I feel my trembling knees give way.
Alas!
      [*She sits.*]
OENONE   O Gods, abate our misery!   5
PHAEDRA   These veils, these baubles, how they burden me!
What meddling hand has twined my hair, and made
Upon my brow so intricate a braid?
All things oppress me, vex me, do me ill.
OENONE   Her wishes war against each other still.   10
'Twas you who, full of self-reproach, just now
Insisted that our hands adorn your brow;
You who called back your strength so that you might
Come forth again and once more see the light.
Yet, seeing it, you all but turn and flee,   15
Hating the light which you came forth to see.
PHAEDRA   Founder of our sad race, bright god of fire,
You whom my mother dared to boast her sire,[4]
Who blush perhaps to see my wretched case,
For the last time, O Sun, I see your face.   20
OENONE   Can't you shake off that morbid wish? Must I
Forever hear you laying plans to die?
What is this pact with death which you have made?

---

4. Helios, the sun god, was the father of Phaedra's mother, Pasiphaë.

PHAEDRA Oh, to be sitting in the woods' deep shade!
  When shall I witness, through a golden wrack   25
  Of dust, a chariot flying down the track?
OENONE What, Madam?
PHAEDRA   Where am I? Madness! What did I say?
  Where have I let my hankering senses stray?
  The Gods have robbed me of my wits. A rush
  Of shame, Oenone, causes me to blush.   30
  I make my guilty torments all too plain.
  My eyes, despite me, fill with tears of pain.
OENONE If you must blush, then blush for your perverse
  Silence, which only makes your sickness worse.
  Spurning our care, and deaf to all we say—   35
  Is it your cruel design to die this way?
  What madness dooms your life in middle course?
  What spell, what poison has dried up its source?
  Three times the night has overrun the skies
  Since sleep last visited your hollow eyes,   40
  And thrice the day has made dim night retreat
  Since you, though starving, have refused to eat.
  What frightful evil does your heart intend?
  What right have you to plot your own life's end?
  You thereby wrong the Gods who authored you;   45
  Betray the spouse to whom your faith is due;
  Betray your children by the selfsame stroke,
  And thrust their necks beneath a heavy yoke.
  Yes, on the day their mother's life is done,
  Proud hopes will stir in someone else's son—   50
  Your foe, the foe of all your lineage, whom
  An Amazon once carried in her womb:
  Hippolytus . . .
PHAEDRA   Gods!
OENONE   My words strike home at last.
PHAEDRA Oh, wretched woman, what was that name which passed
  Your lips?
OENONE   Ah, now you're roused to anger. Good.   55
  That name has made you shudder, as it should.
  Live, then. Let love and duty fire your spirit.
  Live, lest a Scythian's[5] son should disinherit
  Your children, lest he crush the noblest fruit
  Of Greece and of the Gods beneath his boot.   60
  But lose no time; each moment now could cost
  Your life; retrieve the strength that you have lost,
  While still your feeble fires, which sink so low,
  Smoulder and may be fanned into a glow.
PHAEDRA Alas, my guilty flame has burnt too long.   65
OENONE Come, what remorse can flay you so? What wrong
  Can you have done to be so crushed with guilt?

---

5. Scythia, home of the Amazons, was for the Greeks associated with barbarians.

There is no innocent blood your hands have spilt.
PHAEDRA   My hands, thank Heaven, are guiltless, as you say.
  Gods! That my heart were innocent as they!   70
OENONE   What fearful notion can your thoughts have bred
  So that your heart still shrinks from it in dread?
PHAEDRA   I've said enough, Oenone. Spare me the rest.
  I die, to keep that horror unconfessed.
OENONE   Then die, and keep your heartless silence, do;   75
  But someone else must close your eyes for you.
  Although your flickering life has all but fled,
  I shall go down before you to the dead.
  There are a thousand roads that travel there;
  I'll choose the shortest, in my just despair.   80
  O cruel mistress! When have I failed or grieved you?
  Remember: at your birth, these arms received you.
  For you I left my country, children, kin:
  Is this the prize my faithfulness should win?
PHAEDRA   What can you gain by this? Why rant and scold?   85
  You'd shake with terror if the truth were told.
OENONE   Great Gods! What words could match the terror I
  Must daily suffer as I watch you die?
PHAEDRA   When you have learnt my crime, my fate, my shame,
  I'll die no less, but with a guiltier name.   90
OENONE   My lady, by the tears which stain my face,
  And by your trembling knees which I embrace,
  Enlighten me; deliver me from doubt.
PHAEDRA   You've asked it. Rise.
OENONE   I'm listening. Come, speak out.
PHAEDRA   O Gods! What shall I say to her? Where shall I start?   95
OENONE   Speak, speak. Your hesitations wound my heart.
PHAEDRA   Alas, how Venus hates us! As Love's thrall,
  Into what vileness did my mother fall!
OENONE   Dear Queen, forget it; to the end of time
  Let silence shroud the memory of that crime.   100
PHAEDRA   O sister Ariadne! Through love, once more,
  You died abandoned on a barren shore![6]
OENONE   Madame, what's this? What anguish makes you trace
  So bitterly the tale of all your race?
PHAEDRA   And now, since Venus wills it, I must pine   105
  And die, the last of our accursèd line.
OENONE   You are in love?
PHAEDRA   I feel love's raging thirst.
OENONE   For whom?
PHAEDRA   Of all dire things, now hear the worst.
  I love . . . From that dread name I shrink, undone;
  I love . . .
OENONE   Whom?
PHAEDRA   Think of a Scythian woman's son,   110

6. Ariadne died on Naxos after Theseus's desertion of her.

A prince I long ill-used and heaped with blame.
OENONE   Hippolytus? Gods!
PHAEDRA   'Twas you who spoke his name.
OENONE   Just Heaven! All my blood begins to freeze.
O crime, despair, most curst of families!
Why did we voyage to this ill-starred land   115
And set our feet upon its treacherous strand?
PHAEDRA   My ills began far earlier. Scarcely had I
Pledged with Aegeus' son our marriage-tie,
Secure in that sweet joy a bride should know,
When I, in Athens, met my haughty foe.   120
I stared, I blushed, I paled, beholding him;
A sudden turmoil set my mind aswim;
My eyes no longer saw, my lips were dumb;
My body burned, and yet was cold and numb.
I knew myself possessed by Venus, whose   125
Fierce flames torment the quarry she pursues.
I thought to appease her then by constant prayer,
And built for her a temple, decked with care.
I made continual sacrifice, and sought
In entrails[7] for a spirit less distraught—   130
But what could cure a lovesick soul like mine?
In vain my hands burnt incense at her shrine:
Though I invoked the Goddess' name, 'twas he
I worshipped; I saw his image constantly,
And even as I fed the altar's flame   135
Made offering to a god I dared not name.
I shunned him; but—O horror and disgrace!—
My eyes beheld him in his father's face.
At last I knew that I must act, must urge
Myself, despite myself, to be his scourge.   140
To rid me of the foe I loved, I feigned
A harsh stepmother's malice, and obtained
By ceaseless cries my wish that he be sent
From home and father into banishment.
I breathed once more, Oenone; once he was gone,   145
My blameless days could flow more smoothly on.
I hid my grief, was faithful to my spouse,
And reared the offspring of our luckless vows.
Ah, mocking Fate! What use was all my care?
Brought by my spouse himself to Troezen, there   150
I yet again beheld my exiled foe:
My unhealed wound began once more to flow.
Love hides no longer in these veins, at bay:
Great Venus fastens on her helpless prey.
I look with horror on my crime; I hate   155
My life; my passion I abominate.
I hoped by death to keep my honor bright,

---

7. Examining the entrails of an animal sacrifice was a means of prophecy.

And hide so dark a flame from day's pure light;
Yet, yielding to your tearful argument,
I've told you all; of that I'll not repent   160
Provided you do not, as death draws near,
Pour more unjust reproaches in my ear,
Or seek once more in vain to fan a fire
Which flickers and is ready to expire.

SCENE 4

PHAEDRA, OENONE, PANOPE

PANOPE   Madam, there's grievous news which I'd withhold
If I were able; but it must be told.
Death's claimed your lord, who feared no other foe—
Of which great loss you are the last to know.
OENONE   You tell us, Panope . . . ?
PANOPE   That the Queen in vain   5
Prays for her Theseus to return again;
That mariners have come to port, from whom
Hippolytus has learned his father's doom.
PHAEDRA   Gods!
PANOPE   Who'll succeed him, Athens can't agree.
The Prince your son commands much loyalty,   10
My lady; yet, despite their country's laws,[8]
Some make the alien woman's son their cause;
Some plot, they say, to put in Theseus' place
Aricia, the last of Pallas' race.
Of both these threats I thought that you should know.   15
Hippolytus has rigged his ship to go,
And if, in Athens' ferment, he appeared,
The fickle mob might back him, it is feared.
OENONE   Enough. The Queen has heard you. She'll give thought
To these momentous tidings you have brought.   20

SCENE 5

PHAEDRA, OENONE

OENONE   Mistress, I'd ceased to urge you not to die;
I thought to follow you to the grave, since my
Dissuasions had no longer any force:
But this dark news prescribes a change of course.
Your destiny now wears a different face: 5
The King is dead, and you must take his place.
He leaves a son who needs your sheltering wing—
A slave without you; if you live, a king.
Who else will soothe his orphan sorrows, pray?
If you are dead, who'll wipe his tears away?   10

---

8. Athenian law made the son of an Athenian and a non-Greek woman illegitimate. As noted, Hippolytus's mother was an Amazon. It is not clear why Phaedra's children are not similarly classified.

His innocent cries, borne up to Heaven, will make
The Gods, his forebears, curse you for his sake.
Live, then: there's nothing now you're guilty of.
Your love's become like any other love.
With Theseus' death, those bonds exist no more   15
Which made your passion something to abhor.
Hippolytus need no longer cause you fear;
Seeing him now, your conscience can be clear.
Perhaps, convinced that you're his bitter foe,
He means to lead the rebels. Make him know   20
His error; win him over; stay his hand.
He's king, by right, of Troezen's pleasant land;
But as for bright Minerva's[9] citadel,
It is your son's by law, as he knows well.
You should, indeed, join forces, you and he: 25
Aricia is your common enemy.
PHAEDRA   So be it. By your advice I shall be led;
I'll live, if I can come back from the dead,
And if my mother-love still has the power
To rouse my weakened spirits in this hour.   30

Act II

SCENE 1

ARICIA, ISMENE

ARICIA   Hippolytus asks to see me? Can this be?
He seeks me out to take his leave of me?
There's no mistake, Ismene?
ISMENE   Indeed, there's not.
This shows how Theseus' death has changed your lot.
Expect now to receive from every side   5
The homage which, through him, you've been denied.
At last, Aricia rules her destiny;
Soon, at her feet, all Greece shall bend the knee.
ARICIA   This is no doubtful rumor, then? I've shed
The bonds of slavery? My oppressor's dead?   10
ISMENE   The Gods relent, my lady. It is so.
Theseus has joined your brothers' shades below.
ARICIA   And by what mishap did he come to grief?
ISMENE   The tales are many, and they strain belief.
Some say that he, abducting from her home   15
A new beloved, was swallowed by the foam.
It's even thought, as many tongues now tell,
That, faring with Pirithoüs down to Hell,[1]

---

9. The Greek goddess Athene, protector of Athens.   1. Theseus went to Hades with Pentithoüs, king of the Lapiths—with whom he had earlier abducted Helen—to help his friend steal Persephone. Hercules freed Theseus, whom the god Hades had imprisoned, but could not free Pentithoüs, who was later killed.

He walked alive amid the dusky ranks
Of souls, and saw Cocytus'² dismal banks,   20
But found himself a prisoner in that stern
Domain from which no mortal can return.
ARICIA   Shall I believe that, while he still draws breath,
A man can penetrate the realms of death?
What spell could lure him to that fearsome tract?   25
ISMENE   Theseus is dead. You, only, doubt the fact.
All Athens grieves; the news was scarcely known
When Troezen raised Hippolytus to its throne.
Here in this palace, trembling for her son,
Phaedra confers on what must now be done.   30
ARICIA   You think Hippolytus will be more kind
Than Theseus was to me, that he'll unbind
My chains, and show me pity?
ISMENE   Madam, I do.
ARICIA   Isn't the man's cold nature known to you?
What makes you think that, scorning women, he   35
Will yet show pity and respect to me?
He long has shunned us, and as you well know
Haunts just those places where we do not go.
ISMENE   He's called, I know, the most austere of men,
But I have seen him in your presence, when,   40
Intrigued by his repute, I thought to observe
His celebrated pride and cold reserve.
His manner contradicted all I'd heard:
At your first glance, I saw him flushed and stirred.
His eyes, already full of languor, tried   45
To leave your face, but could not turn aside.
He has, though love's a thing he may despise,
If not a lover's tongue, a lover's eyes.
ARICIA   Ismene, how your words delight my ear!
Even if baseless, they are sweet to hear.   50
O you who know me, can you believe of me,
Sad plaything of a ruthless destiny,
Forever fed on tears and bitterness,
That love could touch me, and its dear distress?
Last offspring of that king whom Earth once bore,³   55
I only have escaped the rage of war.
I lost six brothers, young and fresh as May,
In whom the hopes of our great lineage lay:
The sharp sword reaped them all; Earth, soaked and red,
Drank sadly what Erectheus' heirs had shed.   60
You know that, since their death, a harsh decree
Forbids all Greeks to pay their court to me,
Lest, through my progeny, I should revive
My brothers' ashes, and keep their cause alive.

---

2. River in Hades, tributary to Acheron.   3. Erectheus, their ancestor, son of Earth and reared by
Athene.

But you know too with what disdain I bore 65
The ban of our suspicious conqueror.
You know how I, a lifelong enemy
Of love, gave thanks for Theseus' tyranny,
Since he forbade what I was glad to shun.
But then . . . but then I had not seen his son. 70
Not that my eyes alone, charmed by his grace,
Have made me love him for his form or face,
Mere natural gifts for which he seems to care
But little, or of which he's unaware.
I find in him far nobler gifts than these— 75
His father's strengths, without his frailties.
I love, I own, a heart that's never bowed
Beneath Love's yoke, but stayed aloof and proud.
Small glory Phaedra gained from Theseus' sighs!
More proud than she, I spurn the easy prize 80
Of love-words said a thousand times before,
And of a heart that's like an open door.
Ah, but to move a heart that's firm as stone,
To teach it pangs which it has never known,
To bind my baffled captive in a chain 85
Against whose sweet constraint he strives in vain:
There's what excites me in Hippolytus; he's
A harder conquest than was Hercules,
Whose heart, so often vanquished and inflamed,
Less honored those by whom he had been tamed. 90
But, dear Ismene, how rashly I have talked!
My hopes may all too easily be balked,
And I may humbly grieve in future days
Because of that same pride which now I praise.
Of fortune can it be . . . ?

ISMENE   You'll shortly learn; 95
He's coming.

SCENE 2

HIPPOLYTUS, ARICIA, ISMENE

HIPPOLYTUS   Madam, I felt, ere leaving here,
That I should make your altered fortunes clear.
My sire is dead. My fears divined, alas,
By his long absence, what had come to pass.
Death only, ending all his feats and frays, 5
Could hide him from the world so many days.
The Gods have yielded to destroying Fate
Hercules' heir[4] and friend and battle-mate.
Although you hated him, I trust that you
Do not begrudge such praise as was his due. 10
One thought, however, soothes my mortal grief:

---

4. *Heir* in the sense of being, like Hercules, a destroyer of monsters.

I now may offer you a just relief,
Revoking the most cruel of decrees.
Your heart, your hand, bestow them as you please;
For here in Troezen, where I now shall reign,   15
Which was my grandsire Pittheus' domain,
And which with one voice gives its throne to me,
I make you free as I; indeed, more free.
ARICIA   Your goodness stuns me, Sir. By this excess
   Of noble sympathy for my distress,   20
   You leave me, more than you could dream, still yoked
   By those strict laws which you have just revoked.
HIPPOLYTUS   Athens, unsure of who should rule, divides
   'Twixt you and me, and the Queen's son besides.
ARICIA   They speak of *me?*
HIPPOLYTUS   Their laws, I'm well aware,   25
   Would seem to void my claim as Theseus' heir,
   Because an alien bore me. But if my one
   Opponent were my brother, Phaedra's son,
   I would, my lady, have the better cause,
   And would contest those smug and foolish laws.   30
   What checks me is a truer claim, your own;
   I yield, or, rather, give you back, a throne
   And scepter which your sires inherited
   From that great mortal whom the Earth once bred.
   Aegeus,[5] though adopted, took their crown.   35
   Theseus, his son, enlarged the state, cast down
   Her foes, and was the choice of everyone,
   Leaving your brothers in oblivion.
   Now Athens calls you back within her walls.
   Too long she's grieved for these dynastic brawls;   40
   Too long your kinsmen's blood has drenched her earth,
   Rising in steam from fields which gave it birth.
   Troezen is mine, then. The domain of Crete
   Offers to Phaedra's son a rich retreat.
   Athens is yours. I go now to combine   45
   In your cause all your partisans and mine.
ARICIA   These words so daze me that I almost fear
   Some dream, some fancy has deceived my ear.
   Am I awake? This plan which you have wrought—
   What god, what god inspired you with the thought?   50
   How just that, everywhere, men praise your name!
   And how the truth, my lord, exceeds your fame!
   You'll press my claims, against your interest?
   'Twas kind enough that you should not detest
   My house and me, should not be governed by   55
   Old hatreds. . . .
HIPPOLYTUS   Hate you, Princess? No, not I.
   I'm counted rough and proud, but don't assume

---

5. Pandion's son by adoption, and Theseus's father.

That I'm the issue of some monster's womb.
What hate-filled heart, what brute however wild
Could look upon your face and not grow mild?   60
Could I withstand your sweet, beguiling spell?
ARICIA   What's this, my lord?
HIPPOLYTUS   I've said too much. Ah, well.
My reason can't rein in my heart, I see.
Since I have spoken thus impetuously,
I must go on, my lady, and make plain   65
A secret I no longer can contain.
You see before you a most sorry prince,
A signal case of blind conceit. I wince
To think how I, Love's enemy, long disdained
Its bonds, and all whom passion had enchained;   70
How, pitying poor storm-tossed fools, I swore
Ever to view such tempests from the shore;
And now, like common men, for all my pride,
Am lost to reason in a raging tide.
One moment saw my vain defenses fall: 75
My haughty spirit is at last in thrall.
For six months now, ashamed and in despair,
I've borne Love's piercing arrow everywhere;
I've striven with you, and with myself, and though
I shun you, you are everywhere I go;   80
In the deep woods, your image haunts my sight;
The light of day, the shadows of the night,
All things call up your charms before my eyes
And vie to make my rebel heart your prize.
What use to struggle? I am not as before: 85
I seek myself, and find myself no more.
My bow, my javelins and my chariot pall;
What Neptune taught me once, I can't recall;
My idle steeds forget the voice they've known,
And the woods echo to my plaints alone.   90
You blush, perhaps, for so uncouth a love
As you have caused, and which I tell you of.
What a rude offer of my heart I make!
How strange a captive does your beauty take!
Yet that should make my offering seem more rich.   95
Remember, it's an unknown tongue in which
I speak; don't scorn these words, so poorly turned,
Which, but for you, my lips had never learned.

SCENE 3

HIPPOLYTUS, ARICIA, THERAMENES, ISMENE

THERAMENES   My lord: the Queen, they tell me, comes this way.
It's you she seeks.
HIPPOLYTUS   Me?
THERAMENES   Why, I cannot say.

But Phaedra's sent ahead to let you know
That she must speak with you before you go.

HIPPOLYTUS   I, talk with Phaedra? What should we talk about?   5

ARICIA   My lord, you can't refuse to hear her out.
Malignant toward you as the Queen appears,
You owe some pity to her widow's tears.

HIPPOLYTUS   But now you'll leave me! And I shall sail before
I learn my fate from her whom I adore,   10
And in whose hands I leave this heart of mine. . . .

ARICIA   Go, Prince; pursue your generous design.
Make Athens subject to my royal sway.
All of your gifts I gladly take this day.
But that great empire, glorious though it be,   15
Is not the offering most dear to me.

SCENE 4

HIPPOLYTUS, THERAMENES

HIPPOLYTUS   Are we ready, friend? But the Queen's coming: hark.
Go, bid them trim our vessel; we soon embark.
Quick, give the order and return, that you
May free me from a vexing interview.

SCENE 5

PHAEDRA, HIPPOLYTUS, OENONE

PHAEDRA [*To* OENONE, *at stage rear.*]
He's here. Blood rushes to my heart: I'm weak,
And can't recall the words I meant to speak.

OENONE   Think of your son, whose one hope rests with you.

PHAEDRA   My lord, they say you leave us. Before you do,
I've come to join your sorrows and my tears,   5
And tell you also of a mother's fears.
My son now lacks a father; and he will learn
Ere long that death has claimed me in my turn.
A thousand foes already seek to end
His hopes, which you, you only, can defend.   10
Yet I've a guilty fear that I have made
Your ears indifferent to his cries for aid.
I tremble lest you visit on my son
Your righteous wrath at what his mother's done.

HIPPOLYTUS   So base a thought I could not entertain.   15

PHAEDRA   Were you to hate me, I could not complain,
My lord. You've seen me bent on hurting you,
Though what was in my heart you never knew.
I sought your enmity. I would not stand
Your dwelling with me in the selfsame land.   20
I vilified you, and did not feel free
Till oceans separated you and me.
I went so far, indeed, as to proclaim

That none should, in my hearing, speak your name.
Yet if the crime prescribes the culprit's fate,   25
If I must hate you to have earned your hate,
Never did woman more deserve, my lord,
Your pity, or less deserve to be abhorred.
HIPPOLYTUS   It's common, Madam, that a mother spites
The stepson who might claim her children's rights.   30
I know that in a second marriage-bed
Anxiety and mistrust are often bred.
Another woman would have wished me ill
As you have, and perhaps been harsher still.
PHAEDRA   Ah, Prince! The Gods, by whom I swear it, saw   35
Fit to except me from that general law.
By what a different care am I beset!
HIPPOLYTUS   My lady, don't give way to anguish yet.
Your husband still may see the light of day;
Heaven may hear us, and guide his sail this way.   40
Neptune protects him, and that deity
Will never fail to heed my father's plea.
PHAEDRA   No one goes twice among the dead; and since
Theseus has seen those gloomy regions, Prince,
No god will bring him back, hope though you may,   45
Nor greedy Acheron yield up his prey.
But no! He is not dead; he breathes in you.
My husband still seems present to my view.
I see him, speak with him . . . Ah, my lord, I feel
Crazed with a passion which I can't conceal.   50
HIPPOLYTUS   In your strong love, what wondrous power lies!
Theseus, though dead, appears before your eyes.
For love of him your soul is still on fire.
PHAEDRA   Yes, Prince, I burn for him with starved desire,
Though not as he was seen among the shades,   55
The fickle worshiper of a thousand maids,
Intent on cuckolding the King of Hell;
But constant, proud, a little shy as well,
Young, charming, irresistible, much as we
Depict our Gods, or as you look to me.   60
He had your eyes, your voice, your virile grace,
It was your noble blush that tinged his face
When, crossing on the waves, he came to Crete
And made the hearts of Minos' daughters⁶ beat.
Where were you then? Why no Hippolytus   65
Among the flower of Greece he chose for us?
Why were you yet too young to join that band
Of heroes whom he brought to Minos' land?
You would have slain the Cretan monster then,
Despite the endless windings of his den.⁷   70

6. Phaedra and Ariadne.   7. The Minotaur inhabited the heart of a maze. Ariadne provided Theseus
with a ball of thread by which he left a trail behind him and could retrace his steps after killing the monster.

My sister would have armed you with a skein
Of thread, to lead you from that dark domain.
But no: I'd first have thought of that design,
Inspired by love; the plan would have been mine.
It's I who would have helped you solve the maze,   75
My Prince, and taught you all its twisting ways.
What I'd have done to save that charming head!
My love would not have trusted to a thread.
No, Phaedra would have wished to share with you
Your perils, would have wished to lead you through   80
The Labyrinth, and thence have side by side
Returned with you; or else, with you, have died.

HIPPOLYTUS   Gods! What are you saying, Madam? Is Theseus not
Your husband, and my sire? Have you forgot?

PHAEDRA   You think that I forget those things? For shame,   85
My lord. Have I no care for my good name?

HIPPOLYTUS   Forgive me, Madam. I blush to have misread
The innocent intent of what you said.
I'm too abashed to face you; I shall take
My leave. . . .

PHAEDRA   Ah, cruel Prince, 'twas no mistake.   90
You understood; my words were all too plain.
Behold then Phaedra as she is, insane
With love for you. Don't think that I'm content
To be so, that I think it innocent,
Or that by weak compliance I have fed   95
The baneful love that clouds my heart and head.
Poor victim that I am of Heaven's curse,[8]
I loathe myself; you could not hate me worse.
The Gods could tell how in this breast of mine
They lit the flame that's tortured all my line,   100
Those cruel Gods for whom it is but play
To lead a feeble woman's heart astray.
You too could bear me out; remember, do,
How I not only shunned but banished you.
I wanted to be odious in your sight;   105
To balk my love, I sought to earn your spite.
But what was gained by all of that distress?
You hated me the more; I loved no less,
And what you suffered made you still more dear.
I pined, I withered, scorched by many a tear.   110
That what I say is true, your eyes could see
If for a moment they could look at me.
What have I said? Do you suppose I came
To tell, of my free will, this tale of shame?
No, anxious for a son I dared not fail,   115
I came to beg you not to hate him. Frail
Indeed the heart is that's consumed by love!

8. Phaedra feels herself a victim of Venus, the goddess of love; she loves Hippolytus against her will.

Alas, it's only you I've spoken of.
Avenge yourself, now; punish my foul desire.
Come, rid the world, like your heroic sire,   120
Of one more monster; do as he'd have done.
Shall Theseus' widow dare to love his son?
No, such a monster is too vile to spare.
Here is my heart. Your blade must pierce me there.
In haste to expiate its wicked lust,   125
My heart already leaps to meet your thrust.
Strike, then. Or if your hatred and disdain
Refuse me such a blow, so sweet a pain,
If you'll not stain your hand with my abhorred
And tainted blood, lend me at least your sword.   130
Give it to me!
OENONE   Just Gods! What's this, my Queen?
Someone is coming. You must not be seen.
Quick! Flee! You'll be disgraced if you delay.

SCENE 6

HIPPOLYTUS, THERAMENES

THERAMENES Did I see Phaedra vanish, dragged away?
Why do I find you pale and overcome?
Where is your sword, Sir? Why are you stricken dumb?
HIPPOLYTUS Theramenes, I'm staggered. Let's go in haste.
I view myself with horror and distaste.   5
Phaedra . . . but no, great Gods! This thing must not
Be told, but ever buried and forgot.
THERAMENES Sir, if you wish to sail, our ship's prepared.
But Athens' choice already is declared.
Her clans have all conferred; their leaders name   10
Your brother; Phaedra has achieved her aim.
HIPPOLYTUS Phaedra?
THERAMENES   A herald's come at their command
To give the reins of state into her hand.
Her son is king.
HIPPOLYTUS   Gods, what she is you know;
Is it her virtue you've rewarded so?   15
THERAMENES Meanwhile, it's rumored that the King's not dead,
That in Epirus he has shown his head.
But I, who searched that land, know well, my lord . . .
HIPPOLYTUS No, let all clues be weighed, and none ignored.
We'll track this rumor down. Should it appear   20
Too insubstantial to detain us here,
We'll sail, and at whatever cost obtain
Great Athens' crown for one who's fit to reign.

Act III

SCENE 1

PHAEDRA, OENONE

PHAEDRA   Ah, let their honors deck some other brow.
  Why urge me? How can I let them see me now?
  D'you think to soothe my anguished heart with such
  Vain solace? Hide me, rather. I've said too much.
  My frenzied love's burst forth in act and word.   5
  I've spoken what should never have been heard.
  And how he heard me! How, with many a shift,
  The brute pretended not to catch my drift!
  How ardently he longed to turn and go!
  And how his blushes caused my shame to grow!   10
  Why did you come between my death and me?
  Ah, when his sword-point neared my breast, did he
  Turn pale with horror, and snatch back the blade?
  No. I had touched it, and that touch had made
  Him see it as a thing defiled and stained,   15
  By which his pure hand must not be profaned.
OENONE   Dwelling like this on all you're grieved about,
  You feed a flame which best were beaten out.
  Would it not suit King Minos' child to find
  In loftier concerns her peace of mind,   20
  To flee an ingrate whom you love in vain,
  Assume the conduct of the State, and reign?
PHAEDRA   I, reign? You'd trust the State to my control,
  When reason rules no longer in my soul?
  When passion's overthrown me? When, from the weight   25
  Of shame I bear, I almost suffocate?
  When I am dying?
OENONE   Flee him.
PHAEDRA   How could I? How?
OENONE   You once could banish him; can't you shun him now?
PHAEDRA   Too late. He knows what frenzy burns in me.
  I've gone beyond the bounds of modesty.   30
  My conqueror has heard my shame confessed,
  And hope, despite me, has crept into my breast.
  'Twas you who, when my life was near eclipse
  And my last breath was fluttering on my lips,
  Revived me with sweet lies that took me in.   35
  You said that now my love was free of sin.
OENONE   Ah, whether or not your woes are on my head,
  To save you, what would I not have done or said?
  But if an insult ever roused your spleen,
  How can you pardon his disdainful mien?   40
  How stonily, and with what cold conceit
  He saw you all but grovel at his feet!

Oh, but his arrogance was rude and raw!
Why did not Phaedra see the man I saw?
PHAEDRA   This arrogance which irks you may grow less.   45
Bred in the forests, he has their ruggedness,
And, trained in harsh pursuits since he was young,
Has never heard, till now, love's gentle tongue.
No doubt it was surprise which made him mute,
And we do wrong to take him for a brute.   50
OENONE   Remember that an Amazon gave him life.
PHAEDRA   True: yet she learned to love like any wife.
OENONE   He has a savage hate for womankind.
PHAEDRA   No fear of rivals, then, need plague my mind.
Enough. Your counsels now are out of season.   55
Oenone, serve my madness, not my reason.
His heart is armored against love; let's seek
Some point where his defenses may be weak.
Imperial rule was in his thoughts, I feel;
He wanted Athens; that he could not conceal;   60
His vessels' prows already pointed there,
With sails all set and flapping in the air.
Go in my name, then; find this ambitious boy;
Dangle the crown before him like a toy.
His be the sacred diadem; in its stead   65
I ask no honor but to crown his head,
And yield a power I cannot hold. He'll school
My son in princely arts, teach him to rule,
And play for him, perhaps, a father's role.
Both mother and son I yield to his control.   70
Sway him, Oenone, by every wile that's known;
Your words will please him better than my own.
Sigh, groan, harangue him; picture me as dying;
Make use of supplication and of crying;
I'll sanction all you say. Go. I shall find,   75
When you return, what fate I am assigned.

SCENE 2

PHAEDRA, *alone*

PHAEDRA   O you who see to what I have descended,
Implacable Venus, is your vengeance ended?
Your shafts have all struck home; your victory's
Complete; what need for further cruelties?
If you would prove your pitiless force anew,   5
Attack a foe who's more averse to you.
Hippolytus flouts you; braving your divine
Wrath, he has never knelt before your shrine.
His proud ears seem offended by your name.
Take vengeance, Goddess; our causes are the same.   10

Force him to love . . . Oenone! You've returned
So soon? He hates me, then; your words were spurned.

SCENE 3

PHAEDRA, OENONE

OENONE Madam, your hopeless love must be suppressed.
Call back the virtue which you once possessed.
The King, whom all thought dead, will soon be here;
Theseus has landed; Theseus is drawing near.
His people rush to see him, rapturous.   5
I'd just gone out to seek Hippolytus
When a great cry went up on every hand. . . .
PHAEDRA My husband lives, Oenone; I understand.
I have confessed a love he will abhor.
He lives, and I have wronged him. Say no more.   10
OENONE What?
PHAEDRA   I foresaw this, but you changed my course.
Your tears won out over my just remorse.
I might have died this morning, mourned and chaste;
I took your counsels, and I die disgraced.
OENONE You die?
PHAEDRA   Just Heaven! Think what I have done!   15
My husband's coming; with him will be his son.
I'll see the witness of my vile desire
Watch with what countenance I can greet his sire,
My heart still heavy with rejected sighs,
And tears which could not move him in my eyes.   20
Mindful of Theseus' honor, will he conceal
The scandal of my passion, do you feel,
Deceiving both his sire and king? Will he
Contain the horror that he feels for me?
His silence would be vain. What ill I've done   25
I know, Oenone, and I am not one
Of those bold women who, at ease in crime,
Are never seen to blush at any time.
I know my mad deeds, I recall them all.
I think that in this place each vault, each wall   30
Can speak, and that, impatient to accuse,
They wait to give my trusting spouse their news.
I'll die, then; from these horrors I'll be free.
It is so sad a thing to cease to be?
Death is not fearful to a suffering mind.   35
My only fear's the name I leave behind.
For my poor children, what a dire bequest!
Each has the blood of Jove within his breast,
But whatsoever pride of blood they share,
A mother's crime's a heavy thing to bear.   40

I tremble lest—alas, too truly!—they
Be chided for their mother's guilt some day.
I tremble lest, befouled by such a stain,
Neither should dare to lift his head again.

OENONE   I pity both of them; you could not be   45
More justified in your anxiety.
But why expose them to such insult? Why
Witness against yourself? You've but to die,
And folk will say that Phaedra, having strayed
From virtue, flees the husband she betrayed.   50
Hippolytus will rejoice that, cutting short
Your days, you lend his charges your support.
How shall I answer your accuser? He
Will have no trouble in refuting me.
I'll watch him gloating hatefully, and hear   55
Him pour your shame in every listening ear.
Let Heaven's fire consume me ere I do!
But come, speak frankly; is he still dear to you?
How do you see this prince so full of pride?

PHAEDRA   I see a monster, of whom I'm terrified.   60

OENONE   Then why should he triumph, when all can be reversed?
You fear the man. Dare to accuse him first
Of that which he might charge you with today.
What could belie you? The facts all point his way:
The sword which by good chance he left behind,   65
Your past mistrust, your present anguished mind,
His sire long cautioned by your warning voice,
And he sent into exile by your choice.

PHAEDRA   I, charge an innocent man with doing ill?

OENONE   Trust to my zeal. You've only to be still.   70
Like you I tremble, and feel a sharp regret.
I'd sooner face a thousand deaths. And yet
Since, lacking this sad remedy, you'll perish;
Since, above all, it is your life I cherish,
I'll speak to Theseus. He will do no more   75
Than doom his son to exile, as before.
A sire, when he must punish, is still a sire;
A lenient sentence will appease his ire.
But even if guiltless blood must flow, the cost
Were less than if your honor should be lost.   80
That honor is too dear to risk; its cause
Is priceless, and its dictates are your laws.
You must give up, since honor is at stake,
Everything, even virtue, for its sake.
Ah! Here comes Theseus.

PHAEDRA   And Hippolytus, he   85
In whose cold eyes I read the end of me.
Do what you will; I yield myself to you.
In my confusion, I know not what to do.

SCENE 4

THESEUS, HIPPOLYTUS, PHAEDRA, OENONE, THERAMENES

THESEUS Fortune has blessed me after long delay,
  And in your arms, my lady . . .
PHAEDRA   Theseus, stay,
  And don't profane the love those words express.
  I am not worthy of your tenderness.
  You have been wronged. Fortune or bitter fate   5
  Did not, while you were absent, spare your mate.
  Unfit to please you, or to be at your side,
  Henceforth my only thought must be to hide.

SCENE 5

THESEUS, HIPPOLYTUS, THERAMENES

THESEUS Why am I welcomed in this curious vein?
HIPPOLYTUS That, Father, only Phaedra can explain.
  But if my prayers can move you, grant me, Sir,
  Never again to set my eyes on her.
  Allow Hippolytus to say farewell   5
  To any region where your wife may dwell.
THESEUS Then you, my son, would leave me?
HIPPOLYTUS   I never sought her
  When to this land she came, 'twas you who brought her.
  Yes, you, my lord, when last you left us, bore
  Aricia and the Queen to Troezen's shore.   10
  You bade me be their guardian then; but how
  Should any duties here detain me now?
  Too long my youthful skill's been thrown away
  Amidst these woods, upon ignoble prey.
  May I not flee my idle pastimes here   15
  To stain with worthier blood my sword or spear?
  Before you'd lived as long as I have done,
  More than one tyrant, monsters more than one
  Had felt your strength of arm, your sword's keen blade;
  Already, scourging such as sack and raid,   20
  You had made safe the coasts of either sea.
  The traveler lost his fears of banditry,
  And Hercules, to whom your fame was known,
  Welcomed your toils, and rested from his own.
  But I, the unknown son of such a sire,   25
  Lack even the fame my mother's deeds inspire.[9]
  Let me at long last show my courage, and,
  If any monster has escaped your hand,
  Bring back its pelt and lay it at your feet,
  Or let me by a glorious death complete   30
  A life that will defy oblivion

---

9. Hippolytus's mother also performed brave deeds.

And prove to all the world I was your son.
THESEUS   What have I found? What horror fills this place,
  And makes my family flee before my face?
  If my unwished return makes all grow pale,   35
  Why, Heaven, did you free me from my jail?
  I'd one dear friend. He had a hankering
  To steal the consort of Epirus'[1] king.
  I joined his amorous plot, though somewhat loath;
  But outraged Fate brought blindness on us both.   40
  The tyrant caught me, unarmed and by surprise.
  I saw Pirithoüs with my weeping eyes
  Flung by the barbarous king to monsters then,
  Fierce beasts who drink the blood of luckless men.
  Me he confined where never light invades,   45
  In caverns near the empire of the shades.
  After six months, Heaven pitied my mischance.
  Escaping from my guardians' vigilance,
  I cleansed the world of one more fiend, and threw
  To his own beasts the bloody corpse to chew.   50
  But now when, joyful, I return to see
  The dearest whom the Gods have left to me;
  Now, when my spirits, glad once more and light,
  Would feast again upon that cherished sight,
  I'm met with shudders and with frightened faces;   55
  All flee me, all deny me their embraces.
  Touched by the very terror I beget,
  I wish I were Epirus' prisoner yet.
  Speak! Phaedra says that I've been wronged. By whom?
  Why has the culprit not yet met his doom?   60
  Has Greece, so often sheltered by my arm,
  Chosen to shield this criminal from harm?
  You're silent. Is my own son, if you please,
  In some alliance with my enemies?
  I shall go in, and end this maddening doubt.   65
  Both crime and culprit must be rooted out,
  And Phaedra tell why she is so distraught.

SCENE 6

HIPPOLYTUS, THERAMENES

HIPPOLYTUS   How her words chilled me! What was in her thought?
  Will Phaedra, who is still her frenzy's prey,
  Accuse herself, and throw her life away?
  What will the King say? Gods! What love has done
  To poison all this house while he was gone!   5
  And I, who burn for one who bears his curse,
  Am altered in his sight, and for the worse!
  I've dark forebodings; something ill draws near.

---

1. A district in western Greece, on the Ionian Sea.

Yet surely innocence need never fear.
Come, let's consider now how I may best   10
Revive the kindness in my father's breast,
And tell him of a love which he may take
Amiss, but all his power cannot shake.

Act IV

SCENE 1

THESEUS, OENONE

THESEUS   What do I hear? How bold and treacherous
To plot against his father's honor thus!
How sternly you pursue me, Destiny!
Where shall I turn? I know not. Where can I be?
O love and kindness not repaid in kind!   5
Outrageous scheme of a degenerate mind!
To seek his lustful end he had recourse,
Like any blackguard, to the use of force.
I recognize the sword his passion drew—
My gift, bestowed with nobler deeds in view.   10
Why did our ties of blood prove no restraint?
Why too did Phaedra make no prompt complaint?
Was it to spare the culprit?
OENONE   It was rather
That she, in pity, wished to spare his father.
Ashamed because her beauty had begot   15
So foul a passion, and so fierce a plot,
By her own hand, my lord, she sought to die,
And darken thus the pure light of her eye.
I saw her raise her arm; to me you owe
Her life, because I ran and stayed the blow.   20
Now, pitying both her torment and your fears,
I have, against my will, spelled out her tears.
THESEUS   The traitor! Ah, no wonder he turned pale.
When first he sighted me, I saw him quail.
'Twas strange to see no greeting in his face.   25
My heart was frozen by his cold embrace.
But did he, even in Athens, manifest
This guilty love by which he is possessed?
OENONE   The Queen, remember, could not tolerate him.
It was his infamous love which made her hate him.   30
THESEUS   That love, I take it, was rekindled here
In Troezen?
OENONE   I've told you all, my lord. I fear
I've left the Queen too long in mortal grief.
Let me now haste to bring her some relief.

SCENE 2

THESEUS, HIPPOLYTUS

THESEUS   Ah, here he comes. Gods! By that noble mien
    What eye would not be duped, as mine has been!
    Why must the brow of an adulterer
    Be stamped with virtue's sacred character?
    Should there not be clear signs by which one can   5
    Divine the heart of a perfidious man?

HIPPOLYTUS   May I enquire what louring cloud obscures,
    My lord, that royal countenance of yours?
    Dare you entrust the secret to your son?

THESEUS   Dare you appear before me, treacherous one?   10
    Monster, at whom Jove's thunder should be hurled!
    Foul brigand, like those of whom I cleaned the world!
    Now that your vile, unnatural love has led
    You even to attempt your father's bed,
    How dare you show your hated self to me   15
    Here in the precincts of your infamy,
    Rather than seek some unknown land where fame
    Has never brought the tidings of my name?
    Fly, wretch. Don't brave the hate which fills my soul,
    Or tempt a wrath it pains me to control.   20
    I've earned, forevermore, enough disgrace
    By fathering one who'd do a deed so base,
    Without your death upon my hands, to soil
    A noble history of heroic toil.
    Fly, and unless you wish to join the band   25
    Of knaves who've met quick justice at my hand,
    Take care lest by the sun's eye you be found
    Setting an insolent foot upon this ground.
    Now, never to return, be off; take flight;
    Cleanse all my realms of your abhorrent sight.   30
    And you, O Neptune, if by courage I
    Once cleared your shores of murderers, hear my cry.
    Recall that, as reward for that great task,
    You swore to grant the first thing I should ask.
    Pent in a cruel jail for endless hours,   35
    I never called on your immortal powers.
    I've hoarded up the aid you promised me
    Till greater need should justify my plea.
    I make it now. Avenge a father's wrong.
    Seize on this traitor, and let your rage be strong.   40
    Drown in his blood his brazen lust. I'll know
    Your favor by the fury that you show.

HIPPOLYTUS   Phaedra accuses me of lust? I'm weak
    With horror at the thought, and cannot speak;
    By all these sudden blows I'm overcome;   45
    They leave me stupefied, and stricken dumb.

THESEUS   Scoundrel, you thought that Phaedra'd be afraid
   To tell of the depraved assault you made.
   You should have wrested from her hands the hilt
   Of the sharp sword that points now to your guilt;   50
   Or, better, crowned your outrage of my wife
   By robbing her at once of speech and life.
HIPPOLYTUS   In just resentment of so black a lie,
   I might well let the truth be known, but I
   Suppress what comes too near your heart. Approve,   55
   My lord, a silence which bespeaks my love.
   Restrain, as well, your mounting rage and woe:
   Review my life; recall the son you know.
   Great crimes grow out of small ones. If today
   A man first oversteps the bounds, he may   60
   Abuse in time all laws and sanctities;
   For crime, like virtue, ripens by degrees;
   But when has one seen innocence, in a trice,
   So change as to embrace the ways of vice?
   Not in a single day could time transmute   65
   A virtuous man to an incestuous brute.
   I had an Amazon mother, brave and chaste,
   Whose noble blood my life has not debased.
   And when I left her hands, 'twas Pitteus,[2] thought
   Earth's wisest man, by whom my youth was taught.   70
   I shall not vaunt such merits as I've got,
   But if one virtue's fallen to my lot,
   It is, my lord, a fierce antipathy
   To just that vice imputed now to me.
   It is for that Hippolytus is known   75
   In Greece—for virtue cold and hard as stone.
   By harsh austerity I am set apart.
   The daylight is not purer than my heart.
   Yet I, it's charged, consumed by lechery . . .
THESEUS   This very boast betrays your guilt. I see   80
   What all your vaunted coldness signifies:
   Phaedra alone could please your lustful eyes;
   No other woman moved you, or could inspire
   Your scornful heart with innocent desire.
HIPPOLYTUS   No, Father: hear what it's time I told you of;   85
   I have not scorned to feel a blameless love.
   I here confess my only true misdeed:
   I am in love, despite what you decreed.
   Aricia has enslaved me; my heart is won,
   And Pallas' daughter has subdued your son.   90
   I worship her against your orders, Sir,
   Nor could I burn or sigh except for her.
THESEUS   You love her? Gods! But no, I see your game.

2. The most learned man of his age, Theseus's guardian. After marrying Phaedra, Theseus sent Hippolytus
to Pitteus (or Pitheus), who had adopted him as heir to the throne of Troezen.

You play the criminal to clear your name.
HIPPOLYTUS   Six months I've shunned her whom my heart adored.   95
  I came in fear to tell you this, my lord.
  Why must you be so stubbornly mistaken?
  To win your trust, what great oath must be taken?
  By Earth, and Heaven, and all the things that be . . .
THESEUS   A rascal never shrinks from perjury.   100
  Cease now to weary me with sly discourse,
  If your false virtue has but that resource.
HIPPOLYTUS   My virtue may seem false and sly to you,
  But Phaedra has good cause to know it true.
THESEUS   Ah, how your impudence makes my temper boil!   105
HIPPOLYTUS   How long shall I be banished? On what soil?
THESEUS   Were you beyond Alcides' pillars,[3] I
  Would think yet that a rogue was too nearby.
HIPPOLYTUS   Who will befriend me now—a man suspected
  Of such a crime, by such a sire rejected?   110
THESEUS   Go look for friends who think adultery cause
  For accolades, and incest for applause,
  Yes, ingrates, traitors, to law and honor blind,
  Fit to protect a blackguard of your kind.
HIPPOLYTUS   Incest! Adultery! Are these still your themes?   115
  I'll say no more. Yet Phaedra's mother, it seems,
  And, as you know, Sir, all of Phaedra's line
  Knew more about such horrors than did mine.
THESEUS   So! You dare storm and rage before my face?
  I tell you for the last time: leave this place.   120
  Be off, before I'm roused to violence
  And have you, in dishonor, driven hence.

SCENE 3

THESEUS, *alone*

THESEUS   Poor wretch, the path you take will end in blood.
  What Neptune swore by Styx, that darkest flood
  Which frights the Gods themselves, he'll surely do.
  And none escapes when vengeful Gods' pursue.
  I loved you; and in spite of what you've done,   5
  I mourn your coming agonies, my son.
  But you have all too well deserved my curse.
  When was a father ever outraged worse?
  Just Gods, who see this grief which drives me wild,
  How could I father such a wicked child?   10

SCENE 4

PHAEDRA, THESEUS

PHAEDRA   My lord, I hasten to you, full of dread.
  I heard your threatening voice, and what it said.

---

3. The Pillars of Hercules, the two points of land on either side of the Strait of Gibraltar, at the western end of the Mediterranean and thus representing one edge of the known world.

Pray Heaven no deed has followed on your threat.
I beg you, if there is time to save him yet,
To spare your son; spare me the dreadful sound   5
Of blood, your own blood, crying from the ground.
Do not impose on me the endless woe
Of having caused your hand to make it flow.
THESEUS   No, Madam, my blood's not on my hands. But he,
The thankless knave, has not escaped from me.   10
A God's great hand will be his nemesis
And your avenger. Neptune owes me this.
PHAEDRA   Neptune! And will your angry prayers be heard?
THESEUS   What! Are you fearful lest he keep his word?
No, rather join me in my righteous pleas.   15
Recount to me my son's black treacheries;
Stir up my sluggish wrath, that's still too cold.
He has done crimes of which you've not been told:
Enraged at you, he slanders your good name:
Your mouth is full of lies, he dares to claim;   20
He states that heart and soul, his love is pledged
To Aricia.
PHAEDRA   What, my lord!
THESEUS   So he alleged;
But I saw through so obvious a trick.
Let's hope that Neptune's justice will be quick.
I go now to his altars, to implore   25
A prompt fulfillment of the oath he swore.

SCENE 5

PHAEDRA, *alone*

PHAEDRA   He's gone. What news assails my ear? What ill-
Extinguished fire flares in my bosom still?
By what a thunderbolt I am undone!
I'd flown here with one thought, to save his son.
Escaping from Oenone's arms by force,   5
I'd yielded to my torturing remorse.
How far I might have gone, I cannot guess.
Guilt might perhaps have driven me to confess.
Perhaps, had shock not caused my voice to fail,
I might have blurted out my hideous tale.   10
Hippolytus can feel, but not for me!
Aricia has his love, his loyalty!
Gods! When he steeled himself against my sighs
With that forbidding brow, those scornful eyes,
I thought his heart, which love-darts could not strike,   15
Was armed against all womankind alike.
And yet another's made his pride surrender;
Another's made his cruel eyes grow tender.
Perhaps his heart is easy to ensnare.
It's me, alone of women, he cannot bear!   20
Shall I defend a man by whom I'm spurned?

SCENE 6

PHAEDRA, OENONE

PHAEDRA   Oenone dear, do you know what I have learned?
OENONE   No, but in truth I'm quaking still with fear
  Of the wild urge that sent you rushing here:
  I feared some blunder fatally adverse.
PHAEDRA   I had a rival. Who would have thought it, Nurse?   5
OENONE   What?
PHAEDRA   Yes, Hippolytus is in love; it's true.
  That savage creature no one could subdue,
  Who scorned regard, who heard no lovers' pleas,
  That tiger whom I viewed with trembling knees,
  Is tame now, broken by a woman's art: 10
  Aricia's found the way into his heart.
OENONE   Aricia?
PHAEDRA   O pain I never felt before!
  What new, sharp torments have I kept in store!
  All that I've suffered—frenzies, fears, the dire
  Oppression of remorse, my heart on fire,   15
  The merciless rebuff he gave to me—
  All were but foretastes of this agony.
  They love each other! By what magic, then,
  Did they beguile me? Where did they meet, and when?
  You knew. Why did you keep me unaware,   20
  Deceived as to their furtive love-affair?
  Were they much seen together? Were they known
  To haunt the deep woods, so as to be alone?
  Alas, they'd perfect liberty to meet.
  Heaven smiled on hearts so innocent and sweet;   25
  Without remorse, they savored love's delight;
  For them, each dawn arose serene and bright—
  While I, creation's outcast, hid away
  From the Sun's eye, and fled the light of day.
  Death was the only God I dared implore.   30
  I longed for him; I prayed to be no more.
  Quenching my thirst with tears, and fed on gall,
  Yet in my woe too closely watched by all,
  I dared not weep and grieve in fullest measure;
  I sipped in secret at that bitter pleasure;   35
  And often, wearing a serene disguise,
  I kept my pain from welling in my eyes.
OENONE   What will their love avail them? They will never
  Meet again.
PHAEDRA   But they will love forever.
  Even as I speak—ah, deadly thought!—they dare   40
  To mock my crazed desire and my despair.
  Despite this exile which will make them part,
  They swear forever to be joined in heart.
  No, no, their bliss I cannot tolerate,

Oenone. Take pity on my jealous hate.   45
Aricia must die. Her odious house
Must once more feel the anger of my spouse.
Nor can the penalty be light, for her
Misdeeds are darker than her brothers' were.
In my wild jealousy I will plead with him.   50
I'll what? Has my poor reason grown so dim?
I, jealous! And it's with Theseus I would plead!
My husband lives, and still my passions feed
On whom? Toward whom do all my wishes tend?
At every word, my hair stands up on end.   55
The measure of my crimes is now replete.
I foul the air with incest and deceit.
My murderous hands are itching to be stained
With innocent blood, that vengeance be obtained.
Wretch that I am, how can I live, how face   60
That sacred Sun, great elder of my race?
My grandsire was, of all the Gods, most high;
My forebears fill the world, and all the sky.
Where can I hide? For Hades' night I yearn.
No, there my father holds the dreadful urn   65
Entrusted to his hands by Fate, it's said:
There Minos judges all the ashen dead.
Ah, how his shade will tremble with surprise
To see his daughter brought before his eyes—
Forced to confess a throng of sins, to tell   70
Of crimes perhaps unheard of yet in Hell!
What will you say then, Father? As in a dream,
I see you drop the fearful urn;[4] you seem
To ponder some new torment fit for her,
Yourself become your own child's torturer.   75
Forgive me. A cruel God destroys your line;
Behold her hand in these mad deeds of mine.
My heart, alas! not once enjoyed the fruit
Of its dark, shameful crime. In fierce pursuit,
Misfortune dogs me till, with my last breath,   80
My sad life shall, in torments, yield to death.
OENONE   My lady, don't give in to needless terror.
Look freshly at your pardonable error.
You love. But who can conquer Destiny?
Lured by a fatal spell, you were not free.   85
Is that a marvel hitherto unknown?
Has Love entrapped no heart but yours alone?
Weakness is natural to us, is it not?
You are a mortal; accept your mortal lot.
To chafe against our frail estate is vain.   90
Even the Gods who on Olympus reign,

---

4. After his death, Minos of Crete became, along with his brother Rhadamanthus, one of the judges of
souls in the underworld. The urn held the lots determining to what abode in the underworld the souls of
the dead were to be sent.

And with their thunders chasten men for crime,
Have felt illicit passions many a time.
PHAEDRA Ah, what corrupting counsels do I hear?
Wretch! Will you pour such poison in my ear   95
Right to the end? Look how you've ruined me.
You dragged me back to all I sought to flee.
You blinded me to duty; called it no wrong
To see Hippolytus, whom I'd shunned so long.
Ah, meddling creature, why did your sinful tongue   100
Falsely accuse a soul so pure and young?
He'll die, it may be, if the Gods can bear
To grant his maddened father's impious prayer.
No, say no more. Go, monster whom I hate.
Go, let me face at last my own sad fate.   105
May Heaven reward you for your deeds! And may
Your punishment forever give dismay
To all who, like yourself, by servile arts
Nourish the weaknesses of princes' hearts,
Incline them to pursue the baser path,   110
And smooth for them the way to sin and wrath—
Accursèd flatterers, the worst of things
That Heaven's anger can bestow on kings!
OENONE I've given my life to her. Ah, Gods! It hurts
To be thus thanked. Yet I have my just deserts.   115

Act V

SCENE 1

HIPPOLYTUS, ARICIA

ARICIA Come, in this mortal danger, will you not make
Your loving sire aware of his mistake?
If, scorning all my tears, you can consent
To parting and an endless banishment,
Go, leave Aricia in her life alone.   5
But first assure the safety of your own.
Defend your honor against a foul attack,
And force your sire to call his prayers back.
There yet is time. What moves you, if you please,
Not to contest Queen Phaedra's calumnies?   10
Tell Theseus the truth.
HIPPOLYTUS   What more should I
Have told him? How she smirched their marriage-tie?
How could I, by disclosing everything,
Humiliate my father and my king?
It's you alone I've told these horrors to.   15
I've bared my heart but to the Gods and you.
Judge of my love, which forced me to confide

What even from myself I wished to hide.
But, mind you, keep this secret ever sealed.
Forget, if possible, all that I've revealed,   20
And never let those pure lips part to bear
Witness, my lady, to this vile affair.
Let us rely upon the Gods' high laws:
Their honor binds them to defend my cause;
And Phaedra, sooner or later brought to book,   25
Will blush for crimes their justice cannot brook.
To that restraint I ask you to agree.
In all things else, just anger makes me free.
Come, break away from this, your slavish plight;
Dare follow me, dare join me in my flight;   30
Be quit of an accursèd country where
Virtue must breathe a foul and poisoned air.
Under the cover of this turbulence
Which my disfavor brings, slip quickly hence.
I can assure a safe escape for you.   35
Your only guards are of my retinue.
Strong states will champion us; upon our side
Is Sparta; Argos' arms are open wide:
Let's plead then to these friends our righteous case,
Lest Phaedra, profiting by our disgrace,   40
Deny our lineal claims to either throne,
And pledge her son my birthright and your own.
Come, let us seize the moment; we mustn't wait.
What holds you back? You seem to hesitate.
It's zeal for you that moves me to be bold.   45
When I am all on fire, what makes you cold?
Are you afraid to join a banished man?
ARICIA   Alas, my lord, how sweet to share that ban!
   What deep delight, as partner of your lot,
   To live with you, by all the world forgot!   50
   But since no blessèd tie unites us two,
   Can I, in honor, flee this land with you?
   The sternest code, I know, would not deny
   My right to break your father's bonds and fly;
   I'd grieve no loving parents thus; I'm free,   55
   As all are, to escape from tyranny.
   But, Sir, you love me, and my fear of shame . . .
HIPPOLYTUS   Ah, never doubt my care for your good name.
   It is a nobler plan that I propose:
   Flee with your husband from our common foes.   60
   Freed my mischance, since Heaven so commands,
   We need no man's consent to join our hands.
   Not every nuptial needs the torch's light.
   At Troezen's gate, amidst that burial site
   Where stand our princes' ancient sepulchers,   65
   There is a temple feared by perjurers.
   No man there dares to break his faith, on pain

Of instant doom, or swear an oath in vain;
There all deceivers, lest they surely die,
Bridle their tongues and are afraid to lie.   70
There, if you trust me, we will go, and of
Our own accord shall pledge eternal love;
The temple's God will witness to our oath;
We'll pray that he be father to us both.
I shall invoke all deities pure and just.   75
The chaste Diana, Juno[5] the august,
And all the Gods who know my faithfulness
Will guarantee the vows I shall profess.
ARICIA   The king is coming. Go, Prince, make no delay.
To cloak my own departure, I'll briefly stay.   80
Go, go; but leave with me some faithful guide
Who'll lead my timid footsteps to your side.

SCENE 2

THESEUS, ARICIA, ISMENE

THESEUS   O Gods, bring light into my troubled mind;
Show me the truth which I've come here to find.
ARICIA   Make ready for our flight, Ismene dear.

SCENE 3

THESEUS, ARICIA

THESEUS   Your color changes, Madame, and you appear
Confused. Why was Hippolytus here with you?
ARICIA   He came, my lord, to say a last adieu.
THESEUS   Ah, yes. You've tamed his heart, which none could capture.
And taught his stubborn lips to sigh with rapture.   5
ARICIA   I shan't deny the truth, my lord. No, he
Did not inherit your malignity,
Nor treat me as a criminal, in your fashion.
THESEUS   I see. He's sworn, no doubt, eternal passion.
Put no reliance on the vows of such   10
A fickle lover. He's promised others as much.
ARICIA   He, Sir?
THESEUS   You should have taught him not to stray.
How could you share his love in that base way?
ARICIA   How could you let a shameful lie besmear
The stainless honor of his young career?   15
Have you so little knowledge of his heart?
Can't you tell sin and innocence apart?
Must some black cloud bedim your eyes alone
To the bright virtue for which your son is known?
Shall slander ruin him? That were too much to bear.   20
Turn back: repent now of your murderous prayer.

5. The wife of Jupiter and queen of the gods. Diana was goddess of the moon and of chastity.

Fear, my lord, fear lest the stern deities
So hate you as to grant your wrathful pleas.
Our sacrifices anger Heaven at times;
Its gifts are often sent to scourge our crimes.   25
THESEUS   Your words can't cover up that sin of his:
Love's blinded you to what the scoundrel is.
But I've sure proofs on which I may rely:
I have seen tears—yes, tears which could not lie.
ARICIA   Take care, my lord. You have, in many lands,   30
Slain countless monsters with your conquering hands;
But all are not destroyed; there still lives one
Who . . . No, I am sworn to silence by your son.
Knowing his wish to shield your honor, I'd
Afflict him if I further testified.   35
I'll imitate his reticence, and flee
Your presence, lest the truth should burst from me.

SCENE 4

THESEUS, *alone*

THESEUS   What does she mean? These speeches which begin
And then break off—what are they keeping in?
Is this some sham those two have figured out?
Have they conspired to torture me with doubt?
But I myself, despite my stern control—   5
What plaintive voice cries from my inmost soul?
I feel a secret pity, a surge of pain.
Oenone must be questioned once again.
I'll have more light on this. Not all is known.
Guards, go and bring Oenone here, alone.   10

SCENE 5

THESEUS, PANOPE

PANOPE   I don't know what the Queen may contemplate,
My lord, but she is in a frightening state.
Mortal despair is what her looks bespeak;
Death's pallor is already on her cheek.
Oenone, driven from her in disgrace,   5
Has thrown herself into the sea's embrace.
None knows what madness caused the thing she did;
Beneath the waves she lies forever hid.
THESEUS   What do you tell me?
PANOPE   This death has left the Queen
No calmer; her distraction grows more keen.   10
At moments, to allay her dark unrest,
She clasps her children, weeping, to her breast;
Then, with a sudden horror, she will shove
Them both away, and starve her mother-love.
She wanders aimlessly about the floor;   15

Her blank eye does not know us any more.
Thrice she has written; and thrice, before she'd done,
Torn up the letter which she had begun.
We cannot help her. I beg you, Sire, to try.
THESEUS   Oenone's dead? And Phaedra wants to die?   20
O bring me back my son, and let him clear
His name! If he'll but speak, I now will hear.
O Neptune, let your gifts not be conferred
Too swiftly; let my prayers go unheard.
Too much I've trusted what may not be true,   25
Too quickly raised my cruel hands to you.
How I'd despair if what I asked were done!

SCENE 6

THESEUS, THERAMENES

THESEUS   Is it you, Theramenes? Where have you left my son?
You've been his mentor since his tenderest years.
But why do I behold you drenched in tears?
Where's my dear son?
THERAMENES   Too late, Sire, you restore
Your love to him. Hippolytus is no more.   5
THESEUS   Gods!
THERAMENES   I have seen the best of mortals slain,
My lord, and the least guilty, I maintain.
THESEUS   My son is dead? What! Just when I extend
My arms to him, Heaven's haste has caused his end?
What thunderbolt bereaved me? What was his fate?   10
THERAMENES   Scarcely had we emerged from Troezen's gate:
He drove his chariot, and his soldiery
Were ranged about him, mute and grave as he.
Brooding, he headed toward Mycenae. Lax
In his hands, the reins lay on his horses' backs.   15
His haughty chargers, quick once to obey
His voice, and give their noble spirits play,
Now, with hung head and mournful eye, seemed part
Of the sad thoughts that filled their master's heart.
Out of the sea-deeps then a frightful cry   20
Arose, to tear the quiet of the sky,
And a dread voice from far beneath the ground
Replies in groans to that appalling sound.
Our hearts congeal; blood freezes in our veins.
The horses, hearing, bristle up their manes.   25
And now there rises from the sea's calm breast
A liquid mountain with a seething crest.
The wave approaches, breaks, and spews before
Our eyes a raging monster on the shore.
His huge brow's armed with horns; the spray unveils   30
A body covered all with yellow scales;
Half bull he is, half dragon; fiery, bold;

His thrashing tail contorts in fold on fold.
With echoing bellows now he shakes the strand.
The sky, aghast, beholds him; he makes the land   35
Shudder; his foul breath chokes the atmosphere;
The wave which brought him in recoils in fear.
All flee, and in a nearby temple save
Their lives, since it is hopeless to be brave.
Hippolytus alone dares make a stand.   40
He checks his chargers, javelins in hand,
Has at the monster and, with a sure-aimed throw,
Pierces his flank: a great wound starts to flow.
In rage and pain the beast makes one dread spring,
Falls near the horses' feet, still bellowing,   45
Rolls over toward them, with fiery throat takes aim
And covers them with smoke and blood and flame.
Sheer panic takes them; deaf now, they pay no heed
To voice or curb, but bolt in full stampede;
Their master strives to hold them back, in vain.   50
A bloody slaver drips from bit and rein.
It's said that, in that tumult, some caught sight
Of a God who spurred those dusty flanks to flight.
Fear drives them over rocks; the axletree
Screeches and breaks. The intrepid Prince must see   55
His chariot dashed to bits, for all his pains;
He falls at last, entangled in the reins.
Forgive my grief. That cruel sight will be
An everlasting source of tears for me.
I've seen, my lord, the heroic son you bred   60
Dragged by the horses which his hand had fed.
His shouts to them but make their fear more strong.
His body seems but one great wound, ere long.
The plain re-echoes to our cries of woe.
At last, their headlong fury starts to slow: 65
They stop, then, near that graveyard which contains,
In royal tombs, his forebears' cold remains.
I run to him in tears; his guards are led
By the bright trail of noble blood he shed;
The rocks are red with it; the briars bear   70
Their red and dripping trophies of his hair.
I reach him; speak his name; his hand seeks mine;
His eyelids lift a moment, then decline.
"Heaven takes," he says, "my innocent life away.
Protect my sad Aricia, I pray.   75
If ever, friend, my sire is disabused,
And mourns his son who falsely was accused,
Bid him appease my blood and plaintive shade
By dealing gently with that captive maid.
Let him restore . . ." His voice then died away,   80
And in my arms a mangled body lay
Which the God's wrath had claimed, a sorry prize

Which even his father would not recognize.
THESEUS   My son, dear hope whom folly made me kill!
O ruthless Gods, too well you did my will!   85
I'll henceforth be the brokenest of men.
THERAMENES   Upon this scene came shy Aricia then,
Fleeing your wrath, and ready to espouse
Your son before the Gods by holy vows.
She comes, and sees the red and steaming grass;   90
She sees—no sight for loving eyes, alas!—
Hippolytus sprawled there, lacking form or hue.
At first, she won't believe her loss is true.
Not recognizing her beloved, she
Both looks at him and asks where he may be.   95
At last she knows too well what's lying there;
She lifts to the Gods a sad, accusing stare;
Then, moaning, cold, and all but dead, the sweet
Maid drops unconscious at her lover's feet.
Ismene, weeping, kneels and seeks to bring   100
Her back to life—a life of suffering.
And I, my lord, have come, who now detest
This world, to bring a hero's last request,
And so perform the bitter embassy
Which, with his dying breath, he asked of me.   105
But look: his mortal enemy comes this way.

SCENE 7

THESEUS, PHAEDRA, THERAMENES, PANOPE, GUARDS

THESEUS   Well, Madam, my son's no more; you've won the day!
Ah, but what qualms I feel! What doubts torment
My heart, and plead that he was innocent!
But, madam, claim your victim. He is dead.
Enjoy his death, unjust or merited.   5
I'm willing to be evermore deceived.
You've called him guilty; let it be believed.
His death is grief enough for me to bear
Without my further probing this affair,
Which could not bring his dear life back again   10
And might perhaps but aggravate my pain.
No, far from you and Troezen, I shall flee
My dead son's torn and bloody memory.
It will pursue me ever, like a curse:
Would I were banished from the universe!   15
All seems to chide my wicked wrathfulness.
My very fame now adds to my distress.
How shall I hide, who have a name so great?
Even the Gods' high patronage I hate.
I go to mourn this murderous gift of theirs,   20
Nor trouble them again with useless prayers.
Do for me what they might, it could not pay

For what their deadly favor took away.
PHAEDRA   Theseus, my wrongful silence must be ended.
Your guiltless son must be at last defended.   25
He did no ill.
THESEUS   How curst a father am I!
I doomed him, trusting in your heartless lie!
Do you think to be excused for such a crime?
PHAEDRA   Hear me, my lord. I have but little time.
I was the lustful and incestuous one   30
Who dared desire your chaste and loyal son.
Heaven lit a fatal blaze within my breast.
Detestable Oenone did the rest.
She, fearing lest Hippolytus, who knew
Of my vile passion, might make it known to you,   35
Abused my weakness and, by a vicious ruse,
Made haste to be the first one to accuse.
For that she's paid; fleeing my wrath, she found
Too mild a death, and in the waves is drowned.
Much though I wished to die then by the sword,   40
Your son's pure name cried out to be restored.
That my remorse be told, I chose instead
A slower road that leads down to the dead.
I drank, to give my burning veins some peace,
A poison which Medea[6] brought to Greece.   45
Already, to my heart, the venom gives
An alien coldness, so that it scarcely lives;
Already, to my sight, all clouds and fades—
The sky, my spouse, the world my life degrades;
Death dims my eyes, which soiled what they could see,   50
Restoring to the light its purity.
PANOPE   She's dead, my lord!
THESEUS   Would that I could inter
The memory of her black misdeeds with her!
Let's go, since now my error's all too clear,
And mix my poor son's blood with many a tear,   55
Embrace his dear remains, and expiate
The fury of a prayer which now I hate.
To his great worth all honor shall be paid,
And, further to appease his angry shade,
Aricia, despite her brother's offense,   60
Shall be my daughter from this moment hence.

---

6. A sorceress who helped Jason get the Golden Fleece; later, deserted by him, she killed her rival and her own children and burned her palace before fleeing to Athens. According to one legend, she tried to poison Theseus.

SOR JUANA INÉS DE LA CRUZ
1648–1695

One hardly expects to find a spirited defense of women's intellectual rights issuing from the pen of a seventeenth-century Mexican nun, but *Reply to Sor Filotea de la Cruz,* by Sister Juana Inés de la Cruz, is exactly that. In the guise of declaring her humility and her religious subordination, this nun manages to advance claims for her sex more far-reaching and profound than any previously offered.

Born into an upper-class family, Sister Juana in her teens served as lady-in-waiting at the Viceregal court. She soon took the veil, however; her *Reply* suggests a reason in her desire for a safe environment in which to pursue her intellectual interests. Religious vocation did not prevent her from writing in secular forms: lyric poetry and drama. Indeed, she achieved an important literary reputation, later coming to be known throughout the Spanish-speaking world as the "Tenth Muse." Since her religious superiors intermittently rebuked her for her worldly interests, however, she appears to have developed a powerful sense of guilt. It is said that the natural disturbances and disasters—a solar eclipse, storms, and famine—plaguing Mexico City in the 1690s intensified her guilt; in 1694, she reaffirmed her faith, signing the statement in her own blood with the words, "I, Sister Juana Inés de la Cruz, the worst in the world." She died after nursing the sick in an epidemic.

The *Reply* stems directly from Sister Juana's venture into theological polemic. In 1690 she wrote a commentary on a sermon delivered forty years earlier by the Portuguese Jesuit Antonio de Vieira, a sermon in which he disputed with St. Augustine and St. Thomas about the nature of Christ's greatest expression of love at His life's end. Her commentary, in the form of a letter, was published, without her consent, by the bishop of Puebla. The bishop provided the title, *Athenagoric Letter,* or "letter worthy of the wisdom of Athena," but he also prefixed his own letter to Sister Juana, signed with the pseudonym "Filotea de la Cruz." Here he advised the nun to focus her attention and her talents more on religious matters. In her *Reply* (1691), she nominally accepted the bishop's rebuke; the smooth surface of her elegant prose, however, conceals both rage and determination to assert her right—and that of other women—to a fully realized life of the mind.

The artistry of this piece of self-defense demonstrates Sister Juana's powers and thus constitutes part of her justification. Systematically refusing to make any overt claims for herself, she declares her desire to do whatever her associates wish or demand of her. While asserting her own unimportance, she illustrates the range of her knowledge and of her rhetorical skill. The sheer abundance of her biblical allusions and of her quotations from theological texts, for instance, proves that she has mastered a large body of religious material and that she has not sacrificed religious to secular study. Her elaborate protestations of deference, her vocabulary of insignificance, her narrative of subservience: all show the verbal dexterity that enables her to achieve her own rhetorical ends even as she denies her commitment to purely personal goals.

If she acknowledges no self-seeking, she nevertheless declares and demonstrates her ungovernable passion for the life of the mind. She tells of how she joined the convent despite fears that the community "would intrude upon the peaceful silence of my books." "Certain learned persons," however, explained to her that her desire for solitary intellectual experience constituted "temptation." She therefore entered the religious life, believing, she says, "that I was fleeing from myself, but—wretch that I am!—I brought with me my worst enemy, my inclination, which I do not know whether to consider a gift or a punishment from Heaven; for once dimmed and encumbered by the many activities common to Religion, that inclination exploded in me like gunpowder." Although this sentence explicitly labels her intellectual inclinations her worst enemy and suggests that they might be considered divine punishment, the same sentence dramatizes the uncontrollable, explosive force of those inclinations and hints at the negative potential of religious experience, which dims and encumbers the mind. No matter how often Sister Juana admits that her longings amount to a form of "vice," she embodies in her prose the energy and the vividness they generate and makes her audience feel their positive weight.

The autobiographical aspects of Sister Juana's self-defense give it special immediacy for modern readers, who may recognize versions of their own dilemmas in her narrative of difficulties. Of course, girls no longer have to trick their way into learning or plead for permission to dress in boy's clothes to go to a university. But even twentieth-century young women have been known to experience the kind of hostility Sister Juana reports as the response to her remarkable achievement. Yet more recognizable as a frequent form of female anxiety is the nun's concern to proclaim her responsiveness to others, her "tender and affable nature," which causes the other nuns, she says, to hold her "in great affection." She insists that she fills all the responsibilities of a woman as well as displays the kinds of capacity more generally associated with men, and she performs her womanly and her religious duties *first*, reserving her scholarly pursuits for leisure hours.

But of course her larger argument depends on her utter denial that intelligence or a thirst for knowledge should be considered a sex-linked characteristic. She draws on history for evidence of female intellectual power; one may feel the irony of the fact that her list of female worthies requires so much annotation today. The names of these notable women have hardly become household words. Still, these names, these histories, do exist, providing powerful support for Sister Juana's position. Even more forceful is the testimony of her own experience: her account of how, deprived of books, she finds matter for intellectual inquiry everywhere—in the yolk of an egg, the spinning of a top, the reading of the Bible. This is, the reader comes to believe, a woman born to think. If she arouses uneasiness when she implicitly equates herself, as object of persecution, with Christ, she also makes one feel directly the horror of women's official exclusion, in the past, from intellectual pursuits.

Little has been written in English about Sister Juana. A volume in the Twayne series by Gerard Flynn, *Sor Juana Inés de la Cruz* (1971), provides a biographical, critical, and bibliographical introduction. She is also treated in histories of Latin American literature: for example, J. Franco, *An Introduction to Spanish-American Literature* (1969). An important critical work, belatedly translated into English, is Octavio Paz, *Sor Juana; Or, The Traps of Faith* (1988). Other studies include Stephanie Merrini, ed., *Feminist Perspectives on Sor Juana Inés de la Cruz* (1991), and F. Royer, *The Tenth Muse: Sor Juana Inés de la Cruz* (1952).

PRONOUNCING GLOSSARY

The following list uses common English syllables and stress accents to provide rough equivalents of selected words whose pronunciation may be unfamiliar to the general reader.

Albertus Magnus: *ahl-bayr'-tus mahg'-noos*

Arete: *ah-ray'-tee*

Atenagórica: *ah-tay-nah-goh'-ree-kah*

Duquesa of Abeyro: *doo-kay'-zah of ah-bay'-roh*

Machiavelli: *mah-kee-ah-vel'-ee*

señora: *sen-yoh'rah*

sueño: *swayn'-yoh*

Reply to Sor Filotea de la Cruz[1]

My most illustrious *señora*, dear lady. It has not been my will, my poor health, or my justifiable apprehension that for so many days delayed my response.

1. Translated by Margaret Sayers Peden.

How could I write, considering that at my very first step my clumsy pen encountered two obstructions in its path? The first (and, for me, the most uncompromising) is to know how to reply to your most learned, most prudent, most holy, and most loving letter. For I recall that when Saint Thomas, the Angelic Doctor of Scholasticism, was asked about his silence regarding his teacher Albertus Magnus,[2] he replied that he had not spoken because he knew no words worthy of Albertus. With so much greater reason, must not I too be silent? Not, like the Saint, out of humility, but because in reality I know nothing I can say that is worthy of you. The second obstruction is to know how to express my appreciation for a favor as unexpected as extreme, for having my scribblings printed, a gift so immeasurable as to surpass my most ambitious aspiration, my most fervent desire, which even as an entity of reason never entered my thoughts. Yours was a kindness, finally, of such magnitude that words cannot express my gratitude, a kindness exceeding the bounds of appreciation, as great as it was unexpected—which is as Quintilian[3] said: *aspirations engender minor glory; benefices,[4] major.* To such a degree as to impose silence on the receiver.

When the blessedly sterile—that she might miraculously become fecund—Mother of John the Baptist saw in her house such an extraordinary visitor as the Mother of the Word, her reason became clouded and her speech deserted her; and thus, in the place of thanks, she burst out with doubts and questions: *And whence is to me [that the mother of my Lord should come to me?]*[5] And whence cometh such a thing to *me*? And so also it fell to Saul when he found himself the chosen, the anointed, King of Israel: *Am I not a son of Jemini, of the least tribe of Israel, and my kindred the last among all the families of the tribe of Benjamin? Why then hast thou spoken this word to me?*[6] And thus say I, most honorable lady. Why do I receive such favor? By chance, am I other than an humble nun, the lowliest creature of the world, the most unworthy to occupy your attention? "Wherefore then speakest thou so to me?" "And whence is this to me?" Nor to the first obstruction do I have any response other than I am little worthy of your eyes; nor to the second, other than wonder, in the stead of thanks, saying that I am not capable of thanking you for the smallest part of that which I owe you. This is not pretended modesty, lady, but the simplest truth issuing from the depths of my heart, that when the letter which with propriety you called *Atenagórica*[7] reached my hands, in print, I burst into tears of confusion (withal, that tears do not come easily to me) because it seemed to me that your favor was but a remonstrance God made against the wrong I have committed, and that in the same way He corrects others with punishment He wishes to subject me with benefices, with this special favor for which I know myself to be myself to be His debtor, as for an infinitude of others from His boundless kindness. I looked upon this favor as a particular way to shame and confound me, it being the most exquisite means of castigation, that of causing me, by my own intellect, to be the judge who pronounces sentence and who denounces my ingratitude. And thus, when here in my solitude I think on these things, I am wont

---

2. St. Albert the Great (1193?–1280), scholastic philosopher, called the Universal Doctor; he exercised great influence on his student Thomas Aquinas. 3. Marcus Fabius Quintilianus (ca. A.D. 35–100), born in Spain, became a famous Roman orator and wrote on rhetoric. 4. I.e., good works. 5. Luke 1.43. 6. 1 Samuel 9.21. 7. Sister Juana's letter criticizing Father Vieira's sermon was retitled by the bishop *Carta Atenagórica* (Letter worthy of Athena). Athena was the Greek goddess of wisdom.

to say: Blessed art Thou, oh Lord, for Thou hast not chosen to place in the hands of others my judgment, nor yet in mine, but hast reserved that to Thy own, and freed me from myself, and from the necessity to sit in judgment on myself, which judgment, forced from my own intellect, could be no less than condemnation, but Thou hast reserved me to Thy mercy, because Thou lovest me more than I can love myself.

I beg you, lady, to forgive this digression to which I was drawn by the power of truth, and, if I am to confess all the truth, I shall confess that I cast about for some manner by which I might flee the difficulty of a reply, and was sorely tempted to take refuge in silence. But as silence is a negative thing, though it explains a great deal through the very stress of not explaining, we must assign some meaning to it that we may understand what the silence is intended to say, for if not, silence will say nothing, as that is its very office: *to say nothing*. The holy Chosen Vessel, Saint Paul, having been caught up into paradise, and having heard the arcane secrets of God, *heard secret words, which it is not granted to man to utter.*[8] He does not say what he heard; he says that he cannot say it. So that of things one cannot say, it is needful to say at least that they cannot be said, so that it may be understood that not speaking is not the same as having nothing to say, but rather being unable to express the many things there are to say. Saint John says that if all the marvels our Redeemer wrought "were written every one, the world itself, I think, would not be able to contain the books that should be written."[9] And Vieyra[1] says on this point that in this single phrase the Evangelist said more than in all else he wrote; and this same Lusitanian[2] Phoenix speaks well (but when does he not speak well, even when he does not speak well of others?) because in those words Saint John said everything left unsaid and expressed all that was left to be expressed. And thus I, lady, shall respond only that I do not know how to respond; I shall thank you in saying only that I am incapable of thanking you; and I shall say, through the indication of what I leave to silence, that it is only with the confidence of one who is favored and with the protection of one who is honorable that I presume to address your magnificence, and if this be folly, be forgiving of it, for folly may be good fortune, and in this manner I shall provide further occasion for your benignity and you will better shape my intellect.

Because he was halting of speech, Moses thought himself unworthy to speak with Pharaoh, but after he found himself highly favored of God, and thus inspired, he not only spoke with God Almighty but dared ask the impossible: *shew me thy face.*[3] In this same manner, lady, and in view of how you favor me, I no longer see as impossible the obstructions I posed in the beginning: for who was it who had my letter printed unbeknownst to me? Who entitled it, who bore the cost, who honored it, it being so unworthy in itself, and in its author? What will such a person not do, not pardon? What would he fail to do, or fail to pardon? And thus, based on the supposition that I speak under the safe-conduct of your favor, and with the assurance of your benignity, and with the knowledge that like a second Ahasuerus[4] you have

---

8. 2 Corinthians 12.4. 9. John 21.25. 1. Antonio Vieira (1608–1697), author of the sermon that Sister Juana had earlier criticized, was a Portuguese ecclesiastic whose most important work was converting the Indians of Brazil. 2. Roman name for Portugal. 3. Exodus 33.13. 4. King of Persia, who stretched out his gold scepter to his queen, Esther, and said he would grant her whatever she wished (Esther 5.2–3).

offered to me to kiss the top of the golden scepter of your affection as a sign of conceding to me your benevolent license to speak and offer judgments in your exalted presence, I say to you that I have taken to heart your most holy admonition that I apply myself to the study of the Sacred Books, which, though it comes in the guise of counsel, will have for me the authority of a precept, but with the not insignificant consolation that even before your counsel I was disposed to obey your pastoral suggestion as your direction, which may be inferred from the premise and argument of my Letter. For I know well that your most sensible warning is not directed against it, but rather against those worldly matters of which I have written.[5] And thus I had hoped with the Letter to make amends for any lack of application you may (with great reason) have inferred from others of my writings; and, speaking more particularly, I confess to you with all the candor of which you are deserving, and with the truth and clarity which are the natural custom in me, that my not having written often of sacred matters was not caused by disaffection or by want of application, but by the abundant fear and reverence due those Sacred Letters, knowing myself incapable of their comprehension and unworthy of their employment. Always resounding in my ears, with no little horror, I hear God's threat and prohibition to sinners like myself. *Why dost thou declare my justices, and take my covenant in thy mouth?*[6] This question, as well as the knowledge that even learned men are forbidden to read the Canticle of Canticles[7] until they have passed thirty years of age, or even Genesis—the latter for its obscurity; the former in order that the sweetness of those epithalamia not serve as occasion for imprudent youth to transmute their meaning into carnal emotion, as borne out by my exalted Father Saint Jerome,[8] who ordered that these be the last verses to be studied, and for the same reason: *And finally, one may read without peril the Song of Songs, for if it is read one may suffer harm through not understanding those Epithalamia of the spiritual wedding which is expressed in carnal terms.* And Seneca[9] says: *In the early years the faith is dim.* For how then would I have dared take in my unworthy hands these verses, defying gender, age, and, above all, custom? And thus I confess that many times this fear has plucked my pen from my hand and has turned my thoughts back toward the very same reason from which they had wished to be born: which obstacle did not impinge upon profane matters, for a heresy against art is not punished by the Holy Office but by the judicious with derision, and by critics with censure, and censure, *just or unjust, is not to be feared,* as it does not forbid the taking of communion or hearing of mass, and offers me little or no cause for anxiety, because in the opinion of those who defame my art, I have neither the obligation to know nor the aptitude to triumph. If, then, I err, I suffer neither blame nor discredit: I suffer no blame, as I have no obligation; no discredit, as I have no possibility of triumphing—*and no one is obliged to do the impossible.* And, in truth, I have written nothing except when compelled and constrained, and then only to give pleasure to others; not alone without pleasure of my own, but with absolute repugnance, for I

5. Sister Juana had published secular poetry and drama.   6. Psalms 50.16.   7. The Song of Solomon (also called Song of Songs), which employs erotic imagery.   8. Eusebius Sophronius Hieronymus (ca. 342–420), ascetic and scholar, most learned of the Latin Church fathers, a prolific author of treatises and commentaries. Sister Juana belonged to a Jeronymite convent; Jerome had founded the order.   9. Lucius Annaeus Seneca (ca. 3 B.C.–A.D. 63), Roman philosopher and orator.

have never deemed myself one who has any worth in letters or the wit necessity demands of one who would write; and thus my customary response to those who press me, above all in sacred matters, is, what capacity of reason have I? what application? what resources? what rudimentary knowledge of such matters beyond that of the most superficial scholarly degrees? Leave these matters to those who understand them; I wish no quarrel with the Holy Office, for I am ignorant, and I tremble that I may express some proposition that will cause offense or twist the true meaning of some scripture. I do not study to write, even less to teach—which in one like myself were unseemly pride—but only to the end that if I study, I will be ignorant of less. This is my response, and these are my feelings.

I have never written of my own choice, but at the urging of others, to whom with reason I might say, *You have compelled me.*[1] But one truth I shall not deny (first, because it is well-known to all, and second, because although it has not worked in my favor, God has granted me the mercy of loving truth above all else), which is that from the moment I was first illuminated by the light of reason, my inclination toward letters has been so vehement, so overpowering, that not even the admonitions of others—and I have suffered many—nor my own meditations—and they have not been few—have been sufficient to cause me to forswear this natural impulse that God placed in me: the Lord God knows why, and for what purpose. And He knows that I have prayed that He dim the light of my reason, leaving only that which is needed to keep His Law, for there are those who would say that all else is unwanted in a woman, and there are even those who would hold that such knowledge does injury. And my Holy Father knows too that as I have been unable to achieve this (my prayer has not been answered), I have sought to veil the light of my reason—along with my name—and to offer it up only to Him who bestowed it upon me, and He knows that none other was the cause of my entering into Religion, notwithstanding that the spiritual exercises and company of a community were repugnant to the freedom and quiet I desired for my studious endeavors. And later, in that community, the Lord God knows—and, in the world, only the one who must know[2]—how diligently I sought to obscure my name, and how this was not permitted, saying it was temptation: and so it would have been. If it were in my power, lady, to repay you in some part what I owe you, it might be done by telling you this thing which has never before passed my lips, except to be spoken to the one who should hear it. It is my hope that by having opened wide to you the doors of my heart, by having made patent to you its most deeply-hidden secrets, you will deem my confidence not unworthy of the debt I owe to your most august person and to your most uncommon favors.

Continuing the narrations of my inclinations, of which I wish to give you a thorough account, I will tell you that I was not yet three years old when my mother determined to send one of my elder sisters to learn to read at a school for girls we call the *Amigas.* Affection, and mischief, caused me to follow her, and when I observed how she was being taught her lessons I was so inflamed with the desire to know how to read, that deceiving—for so I knew it to be—the mistress, I told her that my mother had meant for me to have lessons too. She did not believe it, as it was little to be believed, but, to

1. 2 Corinthians 12.11.   2. Presumably her confessor, Father Antonio Núñez.

humour me, she acceded. I continued to go there, and she continued to teach me, but now, as experience had disabused her, with all seriousness; and I learned so quickly that before my mother knew of it I could already read, for my teacher had kept it from her in order to reveal the surprise and reap the reward at one and the same time. And I, you may be sure, kept the secret, fearing that I would be whipped for having acted without permission. The woman who taught me, may God bless and keep her, is still alive and can bear witness to all I say. I also remember that in those days, my tastes being those common to that age, I abstained from eating cheese because I had heard that it made one slow of wits, for in me the desire for learning was stronger than the desire for eating—as powerful as that is in children. When later, being six or seven, and having learned how to read and write, along with all the other skills of needlework and household arts that girls learn, it came to my attention that in Mexico City there were Schools, and a University, in which one studied the sciences. The moment I heard this, I began to plague my mother with insistent and importunate pleas: she should dress me in boy's clothing and send me to Mexico City to live with relatives, to study and be tutored at the University. She would not permit it, and she was wise, but I assuaged my disappointment by reading the many and varied books belonging to my grandfather, and there were not enough punishments, nor reprimands, to prevent me from reading: so that when I came to the city many marveled, not so much at my natural wit, as at my memory, and at the amount of learning I had mastered at an age when many have scarcely learned to speak well.

I began to study Latin grammar—in all, I believe, I had no more than twenty lessons—and so intense was my concern that though among women (especially a woman in the flower of her youth) the natural adornment of one's hair is held in such high esteem, I cut off mine to the breadth of some four to six fingers, measuring the place it had reached, and imposing upon myself the condition that if by the time it had again grown to that length I had not learned such and such a thing I had set for myself to learn while my hair was growing, I would again cut it off as punishment for being so slow-witted. And it did happen that my hair grew out and still I had not learned what I had set for myself—because my hair grew quickly and I learned slowly—and in fact I did cut it in punishment for such stupidity: for there seemed to me no cause for a head to be adorned with hair and naked of learning—which was the more desired embellishment. And so I entered the religious order, knowing that life there entailed certain conditions (I refer to superficial, and not fundamental, regards) most repugnant to my nature; but given the total antipathy I felt for marriage, I deemed convent life the least unsuitable and the most honorable I could elect if I were to insure my salvation. Working against that end, first (as, finally, the most important) was the matter of all the trivial aspects of my nature which nourished my pride, such as wishing to live alone, and wishing to have no obligatory occupation that would inhibit the freedom of my studies, nor the sounds of a community that would intrude upon the peaceful silence of my books. These desires caused me to falter some while in my decision, until certain learned persons enlightened me, explaining that they were temptation, and, with divine favor, I overcame them, and took upon myself the state which now so unworthily I hold. I believed that I was fleeing from myself, but—wretch that I am!—I brought with me my worst enemy, my inclination, which I do not know whether to consider a gift or a punishment from Heaven, for once dimmed and encumbered by the many activities common to Religion, that inclination exploded in me like gunpowder, proving how *privation is the source of appetite.*

I turned again (which is badly put, for I never ceased), I continued, then, in my studious endeavour (which for me was respite during those moments not occupied by my duties) of reading and more reading, of study and more study, with no teachers but my books. Thus I learned how difficult it is to study those soulless letters, lacking a human voice or the explication of a teacher. But I suffered this labor happily for my love of learning. Oh, had it only been for love of God, which were proper, how worthwhile it would have been! I strove mightily to elevate these studies, to dedicate them to His service, as the goal to which I aspired was to study Theology—it seeming to me debilitating for a Catholic not to know everything in this life of the Divine Mysteries that can be learned through natural means—and, being a nun and not a layperson, it was seemly that I profess my vows to learning through ecclesiastical channels; and especially, being a daughter of a Saint Jerome and a Saint Paula,[3] it was essential that such erudite parents not be shamed by a witless daughter. This is the argument I proposed to myself, and it seemed to me well-reasoned. It was, however (and this cannot be denied) merely glorification and approbation of my inclination, and enjoyment of it offered as justification. And so I continued, as I have said, directing the course of my studies toward the peak of Sacred Theology, it seeming necessary to me, in order to scale those heights, to climb the steps of the human sciences and arts; for how could one undertake the study of the Queen of Sciences if first one had not come to know her servants?

How, without Logic, could I be apprised of the general and specific way in which the Holy Scripture is written? How, without Rhetoric, could I understand its figures, its tropes, its locutions? How, without Physics,[4] so many innate questions concerning the nature of animals, their sacrifices, wherein exist so many symbols, many already declared, many still to be discovered? How should I know whether Saul's being refreshed by the sound of David's harp was due to the virtue and natural power of Music, or to a transcendent power God wished to place in David? How, without Arithmetic, could one understand the computations of the years, days, months, hours, those mysterious weeks communicated by Gabriel to Daniel,[5] and others for whose understanding one must know the nature, concordance, and properties of numbers? How, without Geometry, could one measure the Holy Ark of the Covenant and the Holy City of Jerusalem, whose mysterious measures are foursquare in their dimensions, as well as the miraculous proportions of all their parts? How, without Architecture, could one know the great Temple of Solomon, of which God Himself was the Author who conceived the disposition and the design, and the Wise King but the overseer who executed it, of which temple there was no foundation without mystery, no column without symbolism, no cornice without allusion, no architrave without sig-

3. A Roman woman (d. 404), converted to Christianity after her daughter's death, who founded a nunnery next to St. Jerome's monastery at Bethlehem and helped Jerome in his studies.   4. I.e., physic, or medicine.   5. While Daniel was praying, Gabriel came to him to interpret, in great chronological detail, a vision Daniel had previously had (Daniel 9.21–27).

nificance; and similarly others of its parts, of which the least fillet was never intended solely for the service and complement of Art, but as symbol of greater things? How, without great knowledge of the laws and parts of which History is comprised, could one understand historical Books? Or those recapitulations in which many times what happened first is seen in the narrated account to have happened later? How, without great learning in Canon and Civil Law, could one understand Legal Books? How, without great erudition, could one apprehend the secular histories of which the Holy Scripture makes mention, such as the many customs of the Gentiles, their many rites, their many ways of speaking? How without the abundant laws and lessons of the Holy Fathers could one understand the obscure lesson of the Prophets? And without being expert in Music, how could one understand the exquisite precision of the musical proportions that grace so many Scriptures, particularly those in which Abraham beseeches God in defense of the Cities,[6] asking whether He would spare the place were there but fifty just men therein; and then Abraham reduced that number to five less than fifty, forty-five, which is a ninth, and is as Mi to Re; then to forty, which is a tone, and is as Re to Mi; from forty to thirty, which is a diatessaron, the interval of the perfect fourth; from thirty to twenty, which is the perfect fifth; and from twenty to ten, which is the octave, the diapason; and as there are no further harmonic proportions, made no further reductions. How might one understand this without Music? And there in the Book of Job, God says to Job: *Shalt thou be able to join together the shining stars the Pleiades, or canst thou stop the turning about of Arcturus? Canst thou bring forth the day star in its time, and make the evening star to rise upon the children of the earth?*[7] Which message, without knowledge of Astrology, would be impossible to apprehend. And not only these noble sciences; there is no applied art that is not mentioned. And, finally, in consideration of the Book that comprises all books, and the Science in which all sciences are embraced, and for whose comprehension all sciences serve, and even after knowing them all (which we now see is not easy, nor even possible), there is one condition that takes precedence over all the rest, which is uninterrupted prayer and purity of life, that one may entreat of God that purgation of spirit and illumination of mind necessary for the understanding of such elevated matters: and if that be lacking, none of the aforesaid will have been of any purpose.

Of the Angelic Doctor Saint Thomas[8] the Church affirms: *When reading the most difficult passages of the Holy Scripture, he joined fast with prayer. And he was wont to say to his companion Brother Reginald that all he knew derived not so much from study or his own labor as from the grace of God.* How then should I—so lacking in virtue and so poorly read—find courage to write? But as I had acquired the rudiments of learning, I continued to study ceaselessly divers subjects, having for none any particular inclination, but for all in general; and having studied some more than others was not owing to preference, but to the chance that more books on certain subjects had fallen into my hands, causing the election of them through no discretion of my own. And as I was not directed by preference, nor, forced by the need to fulfill certain scholarly requirements, constrained by time in the pursuit of

6. Abraham beseeches God to save Sodom for the sake of its just inhabitants (Genesis 18.23–33).   7. Job 38.31–32.   8. Thomas Aquinas (ca. 1225–1274), Dominican theologian, author of *Summa Theologica* (ca. 1266), and for centuries the most important authority on Church doctrine.

any subject, I found myself free to study numerous topics at the same time, or to leave some for others; although in this scheme some order was observed, for some I deigned[9] study and others diversion, and in the latter I found respite from the former. From which it follows that though I have studied many things I know nothing, as some have inhibited the learning of others. I speak specifically of the practical aspect of those arts that allow practice, because it is clear that when the pen moves the compass must lie idle, and while the harp is played the organ is stilled, *et sic de caeteris*.[1] And because much practice is required of one who would acquire facility, none who divides his interest among various exercises may reach perfection. Whereas in the formal and theoretical arts the contrary is true, and I would hope to persuade all with my experience, which is that one need not inhibit the other, but, in fact, each may illuminate and open the way to others, by nature of their variations and their hidden links, which were placed in this universal chain by the wisdom of their Author in such a way that they conform and are joined together with admirable unity and harmony. This is the very chain the ancients believed did issue from the mouth of Jupiter, from which were suspended all things linked one with another, as is demonstrated by the Reverend Father Athanasius Kircher[2] in his curious book, *De Magnate*. All things issue from God, Who is at once the center and the circumference from which and in which all lines begin and end.

I myself can affirm that what I have not understood in an author in one branch of knowledge I may understand in a second in a branch that seems remote from the first. And authors, in their elucidation, may suggest metaphorical examples in other arts: as when logicians say that to prove whether parts are equal, the means is to the extremes as a determined measure to two equidistant bodies; or in stating how the argument of the logician moves, in the manner of a straight line, along the shortest route, while that of the rhetorician moves as a curve, by the longest, but that both finally arrive at the same point. And similarly, as it is when they say that the Exegetes are like an open hand, and the Scholastics like a closed fist.[3] And thus it is no apology, nor do I offer it as such, to say that I have studied many subjects, seeing that each augments the other; but that I have not profited is the fault of my own ineptitude and the inadequacy of my intelligence, not the fault of the variety. But what may be offered as exoneration is that I undertook this great task without benefit of teacher, or fellow students with whom to confer and discuss, having for a master no other than a mute book, and for a colleague, an insentient inkwell; and in the stead of explication and exercise, many obstructions, not merely those of my religious obligations (for it is already known how useful and advantageous is the time employed in them), rather, all the attendant details of living in a community: how I might be reading, and those in the adjoining cell would wish to play their instruments, and sing; how I might be studying, and two servants who had quarreled would select me to judge their dispute; or how I might be writing, and a friend come to visit me, doing me no favor but with the best of will, at which time one must not only accept the inconvenience, but be grateful for the hurt. And such occurrences are the normal state of affairs, for as the

9. Deemed, considered.   1. And so for other things (Latin).   2. German Jesuit scientist (1601?– 1680), author of *Magnes sive de arte magnetica* (The magnet: or, of the magnetic science).   3. The Exegetes emphasized interpretation; the Scholastics, logic.

times I set apart for study are those remaining after the ordinary duties of the community are fulfilled, they are the same moments available to my sisters, in which they may come to interrupt my labor; and only those who have experience of such a community will know how true this is, and how it is only the strength of my vocation that allows me happiness; that, and the great love existing between me and my beloved sisters, for as love is union, it knows no extremes of distance.

With this I confess how interminable has been my labor; and how I am unable to say what I have with envy heard others state—that they have not been plagued by the thirst for knowledge: blessed are they. For me, not the knowing (for still I do not know), merely the desiring to know, has been such torment that I can say, as has my Father Saint Jerome (although not with his accomplishment) . . . *my conscience is witness to what effort I have expended, what difficulties I have suffered, how many times I have despaired, how often I have ceased my labors and turned to them again, driven by the hunger for knowledge; my conscience is witness, and that of those who have lived beside me.* With the exception of the companions and witnesses (for I have been denied even this consolation), I can attest to the truth of these words. And to the fact that even so, my black inclination has been so great that it has conquered all else!

It has been my fortune that, among other benefices,[4] I owe to God a most tender and affable nature, and because of it my sisters (who being good women do not take note of my faults) hold me in great affection, and take pleasure in my company; and knowing this, and moved by the great love I hold for them—having greater reason than they—I enjoy even more *their* company. Thus I was wont in our rare idle moments to visit among them, offering them consolation and entertaining myself in their conversation. I could not help but note, however, that in these times I was neglecting my study, and I made a vow not to enter any cell unless obliged by obedience or charity; for without such a compelling constraint—the constraint of mere intention not being sufficient—my love would be more powerful than my will. I would (knowing well my frailty) make this vow for the period of a few weeks, or a month; and when that time had expired, I would allow myself a brief respite of a day or two before renewing it, using that time not so much for rest (for *not* studying has never been restful for me) as to assure that I not be deemed cold, remote, or ungrateful in the little-deserved affection of my dearest sisters.

In this practice one may recognize the strength of my inclination. I give thanks to God, Who willed that such an ungovernable force be turned toward letters and not to some other vice. From this it may also be inferred how obdurately against the current my poor studies have sailed (more accurately, have foundered). For still to be related is the most arduous of my difficulties—those mentioned until now, either compulsory or fortuitous, being merely tangential—and still unreported the more directly aimed slings and arrows that have acted to impede and prevent the exercise of my study. Who would have doubted, having witnessed such general approbation, that I sailed before the wind across calm seas, amid the laurels of widespread acclaim. But our Lord God knows that it has not been so; He knows how from amongst

4. Benefits or kindnesses.

the blossoms of this very acclaim emerged such a number of aroused vipers, hissing their emulation and their persecution, that one could not count them. But the most noxious, those who most deeply wounded me, have not been those who persecuted me with open loathing and malice, but rather those who in loving me and desiring my well-being (and who are deserving of God's blessing for their good intent) have mortified and tormented me more than those others with their abhorrence. "Such studies are not in conformity with sacred innocence; surely she will be lost; surely she will, by cause of her very perspicacity and acuity, grow heady at such exalted heights." How was I to endure? An uncommon sort of martyrdom in which I was both martyr and executioner. And for my (in me, twice hapless) facility in making verses, even though they be sacred verses, what sorrows have I not suffered? What sorrows not ceased to suffer? Be assured, lady, it is often that I have meditated on how one who distinguishes himself—or one on whom God chooses to confer distinction, for it is only He who may do so—is received as a common enemy, because it seems to some that he usurps the applause they deserve, or that he dams up the admiration to which they aspired, and so they persecute that person.

That politically barbaric law of Athens by which any person who excelled by cause of his natural gifts and virtues was exiled from his Republic in order that he not threaten the public freedom still endures, is still observed in our day, although not for the reasons held by the Athenians. Those reasons have been replaced by another, no less efficient though not as well founded, seeming, rather, a maxim more appropriate to that impious Machiavelli[5]—which is to abhor one who excels, because he deprives others of regard. And thus it happens, and thus it has always happened.

For if not, what was the cause of the rage and loathing the Pharisees[6] directed against Christ, there being so many reasons to love Him? If we behold His presence, what is more to be loved than that Divine beauty? What more powerful to stir one's heart? For if ordinary human beauty holds sway over strength of will, and is able to subdue it with tender and enticing vehemence, what power would Divine beauty exert, with all its prerogatives and sovereign endowments? What might move, what effect, what not move and not effect, such incomprehensible beauty, that beauteous face through which, as through a polished crystal, were diffused the rays of Divinity? What would not be moved by that semblance which beyond incomparable human perfections revealed Divine illuminations? If the visage of Moses, merely from conversation with God, caused men to fear to come near him,[7] how much finer must be the face of God-made-flesh? And among other virtues, what more to be loved than that celestial modesty? That sweetness and kindness disseminating mercy in every movement? That profound humility and gentleness? Those words of eternal life and eternal wisdom? How therefore is it possible that such beauty did not stir their souls, that they did not follow after Him, enamored and enlightened?

The Holy Mother, my Mother Teresa,[8] says that when she beheld the

---

5. Niccolò Machiavelli (1469–1527), Italian statesman whose writings (notably *The Prince*) advocated political unscrupulousness.   6. The Pharisees, members of a strict Jewish sect that emphasized conformity to the law, were according to the New Testament of the Bible prominent in plotting the death of Jesus (Mark 3.6, John 11.47–57).   7. Exodus 34.30.   8. St. Teresa de Ávila (1515–1582), a mystical writer, responsible for a great awakening of religious fervor.

beauty of Christ never again was she inclined toward any human creature, for she saw nothing that was not ugliness compared to such beauty. How was it then that in men it engendered such contrary reactions? For although they were uncouth and vile and had no knowledge or appreciation of His perfections, not even as they might profit from them, how was it they were not moved by the many advantages of such benefices as He performed for them, healing the sick, resurrecting the dead, restoring those possessed of the devil? How was it they did not love Him? But God is witness that it was for these very acts they did not love Him, that they despised Him. As they themselves testified.

They gather together in their council and say: *What do we? for this man doth many miracles.*[9] Can this be cause? If they had said: here is an evil-doer, a transgressor of the law, a rabble-rouser who with deceit stirs up the populace, they would have lied—as they did indeed lie when they spoke these things. But there were more apposite reasons for effecting what they desired, which was to take His life; and to give as reason that he had performed wondrous deeds seems not befitting learned men, for such were the Pharisees. Thus it is that in the heat of passion learned men erupt with such irrelevancies; for we know it as truth that only for this reason was it determined that Christ should die. Oh, men, if men you may be called, being so like to brutes, what is the cause of so cruel a determination? Their only response is that "this man doth many miracles." May God forgive them. Then is performing signal deeds cause enough that one should die? This "he doth many miracles" evokes *the root of Jesse, who standeth for an ensign of the people,*[1] and that *and for a sign which shall be contradicted.*[2] He is a sign? Then He shall die. He excels? Then He shall suffer, for that is the reward for one who excels.

Often on the crest of temples are placed as adornment figures of the winds and of fame, and to defend them from the birds, they are covered with iron barbs; this appears to be in defense, but is in truth obligatory propriety: the figure thus elevated cannot survive without the very barbs that prick it; there on high is found the animosity of the air, on high the ferocity of the elements, on high is unleashed the anger of the thunderbolt, on high stands the target for slings and arrows. Oh unhappy eminence, exposed to such uncounted perils. Oh sign, become the target of envy and the butt of contradiction. Whatever eminence, whether that of dignity, nobility, riches, beauty, or science, must suffer this burden; but the eminence that undergoes the most severe attack is that of reason. First, because it is the most defenseless, for riches and power strike out against those who dare attack them; but not so reason, for while it is the greater it is more modest and long-suffering, and defends itself less. Second, as Gracian[3] stated so eruditely, *favors in man's reason are favors in his nature.*

For no other cause except that the angel is superior in reason is the angel above man; for no other cause does man stand above the beast but by his reason; and thus, as no one wishes to be lower than another, neither does he confess that another is superior in reason, as reason is a consequence of being superior. One will abide, and will confess that another is nobler than

9. John 11.47.   1. Isaiah 11.10.   2. Luke 2.34.   3. Baltasar Gracián (1601–1658), Spanish Jesuit philosopher.

he, that another is richer, more handsome, and even that he is more learned, but that another is richer in reason scarcely any will confess: *Rare is he who will concede genius*. That is why the assault against this virtue works to such profit.

When the soldiers mocked, made entertainment and diversion of our Lord Jesus Christ, they brought Him a worn purple garment and a hollow reed, and a crown of thorns to crown Him King of Fools.[4] But though the reed and the purple were an affront, they did not cause suffering. Why does only the crown give pain? Is it not enough that like the other emblems the crown was a symbol of ridicule and ignominy, as that was its intent? No. Because the sacred head of Christ and His divine intellect were the depository of wisdom, and the world is not satisfied for wisdom to be the object of mere ridicule, it must also be done injury and harm. A head that is a storehouse of wisdom can expect nothing but a crown of thorns. What garland may human wisdom expect when it is known what was bestowed on that divine wisdom? Roman pride crowned the many achievements of their Captains with many crowns: he who defended the city received the civic crown; he who fought his way into the hostile camp received the camp crown; he who scaled the wall, the mural;[5] he who liberated a beseiged city, or any army besieged either in the field or in the enemy camp, received the obsidional, the siege, crown; other feats were crowned with naval, ovation, or triumphal crowns, as described by Pliny and Aulus Gellius.[6] Observing so many and varied crowns, I debated as to which Christ's crown must have been, and determined that it was the siege crown, for (as well you know, lady) that was the most honored crown and was called obsidional after *obsidio*, which means siege; which crown was made not from gold, or silver, but from the leaves and grasses flourishing on the field where the feat was achieved. And as the heroic feat of Christ was to break the siege of the Prince of Darkness, who had laid siege to all the earth, as is told in the Book of Job, quoting Satan: *I have gone round about the earth, and walked through it*,[7] and as St. Peter says: *As a roaring lion, goeth about seeking whom he may devour*.[8] And our Master came and caused him to lift the siege: *Now shall the prince of this world be cast out*.[9] So the soldiers crowned Him not with gold or silver but with the natural fruit of the world, which was the field of battle—and which, after the curse *Thorns also and thistles shall it bring forth to thee*,[1] produced only thorns—and thus it was a most fitting crown for the courageous and wise Conqueror, with which His mother Synagogue crowned Him. And the daughters of Zion, weeping, came out to witness the sorrowful triumph,[2] as they had come rejoicing for the triumph of Solomon,[3] because the triumph of the wise is earned with sorrow and celebrated with weeping, which is the manner of the triumph of wisdom; and as Christ is the King of wisdom, He was the first to wear that crown; and as it was sanctified on His brow, it removed all fear and dread from those who are wise, for they know they need aspire to no other honor.

The Living Word, Life, wished to restore life to Lazarus, who was dead.

---

4. Matthew 27.28–31.   5. Pertaining to walls; the word *crown* is understood.   6. Latin writer (second century A.D.), author of *Noctes Atticae*, valuable for its quotations from lost works. Pliny the Younger (62?–ca. 113) was a Roman orator and statesman and author of well-known letters about Roman life.   7. Job 1.7.   8. 1 Peter 5.8.   9. John 12.31.   1. The curse on Adam and Eve after the Fall (Genesis 3.18).   2. Luke 23.27–28.   3. Song of Solomon 3.11.

His disciples did not know His purpose and they said to Him: *Rabbi, the Jews but now sought to stone thee; and goest thou thither again?* And the Redeemer calmed their fear: *Are there not twelve hours of the day?*[4] It seems they feared because there had been those who wished to stone Him when He rebuked them, calling them thieves and not shepherds of sheep.[5] And thus the disciples feared that if He returned to the same place—for even though rebukes be just, they are often badly received—He would be risking his life. But once having been disabused and having realized that He was setting forth to raise up Lazarus from the dead, what was it that caused Thomas, like Peter in the Garden, to say *Let us also go, that we may die with him?*[6] What say you, Sainted Apostle? The Lord does not go out to die; whence your misgiving? For Christ goes not to rebuke, but to work an act of mercy, and therefore they will do Him no harm. These same Jews could have assured you, for when He reproved those who wished to stone Him, *Many good works I have shewed you from my Father; for which of those works do you stone me?* they replied: *For a good work we stone thee not; but for blasphemy.*[7] And as they say they will not stone Him for doing good works, and now He goes to do a work so great as to raise up Lazarus from the dead, whence your misgiving? Why do you fear? Were it not better to say: let us go to gather the fruits of appreciation for the good work our Master is about to do; to see him lauded and applauded for His benefice; to see men marvel at His miracle. Why speak words seemingly so alien to the circumstance as *Let us also go?* Ah, woe, the Saint feared as a prudent man and spoke as an Apostle. Does Christ not go to work a miracle? Why, what *greater* peril? It is less to be suffered that pride endure rebukes than envy witness miracles. In all the above, most honored lady, I do not wish to say (nor is such folly to be found in me) that I have been persecuted for my wisdom, but merely for my love of wisdom and letters, having achieved neither one nor the other.

At one time even the Prince of the Apostles was very far from wisdom, as is emphasized in that *But Peter followed afar off.*[8] Very distant from the laurels of a learned man is one so little in his judgment that he was *Not knowing what he said.*[9] And being questioned on his mastery of wisdom, he himself was witness that he had not achieved the first measure: *But he denied him, saying: Woman, I know him not.*[1] And what becomes of him? We find that having this reputation of ignorance, he did not enjoy its good fortune, but, rather, the affliction of being taken for wise. And why? There was no other motive but: *This man also was with him*[2] He was fond of wisdom, it filled His heart, He followed after it, He prided himself as a pursuer and lover of wisdom; and although He followed from so *afar off* that He neither understood nor achieved it, His love for it was sufficient that He incur its torments. And there was present that soldier to cause Him distress, and a certain maidservant to cause Him grief. I confess that I find myself very distant from the goals of wisdom, for all that I have desired to follow it, even from *afar off.* But in this I have been brought closer to the fire of persecution, to the crucible of torment, and to such lengths that they have asked that study be forbidden to me.

At one time this was achieved through the offices of a very saintly and

---

4. John 11.8–9. 5. John 10.1–31. 6. John 11.16. 7. John 10.32–33. 8. Luke 22.54.
9. Refers to Peter (Luke 9.33). 1. Luke 22.57. 2. A serving maid says this of Peter, who thereupon denies knowing Jesus (Luke 22.56).

ingenuous Abbess who believed that study was a thing of the Inquisition, who commanded me not to study. I obeyed her (the three some[3] months her power to command endured) in that I did not take up a book; but that I study not at all is not within my power to achieve, and this I could not obey, for though I did not study in books, I studied all the things that God had wrought, reading in them, as in writing and in books, all the workings of the universe. I looked on nothing without reflection; I heard nothing without meditation, even in the most minute and imperfect things; because as there is no creature, however lowly, in which one cannot recognize that *God made me,* there is none that does not astound reason, if properly meditated on. Thus, I reiterate, I saw and admired all things; so that even the very persons with whom I spoke, and the things they said, were cause for a thousand meditations. Whence the variety of genius and wit, being all of a single species? Which the temperaments and hidden qualities that occasioned such variety? If I saw a figure, I was forever combining the proportion of its lines and measuring it with my reason and reducing it to new proportions. Occasionally as I walked along the far wall of one of our dormitories (which is a most capacious room) I observed that though the lines of the two sides were parallel and the ceiling perfectly level, in my sight they were distorted, the lines seeming to incline toward one another, the ceiling seeming lower in the distance than in proximity: from which I inferred that *visual* lines run straight but not parallel, forming a pyramidal figure. I pondered whether this might not be the reason that caused the ancients to question whether the world were spherical. Because, although it so seems, this could be a deception of vision, suggesting concavities where possibly none existed.

This manner of reflection has always been my habit, and is quite beyond my will to control; on the contrary, I am wont to become vexed that my intellect makes me weary; and I believed that it was so with everyone, as well as making verses, until experience taught me otherwise; and it is so strong in me this nature, or custom, that I look at nothing without giving it further examination. Once in my presence two young girls were spinning a top and scarcely had I seen the motion and the figure described, when I began, out of this madness of mine, to meditate on the effortless *motus*[4] of the spherical form, and how the impulse persisted even when free and independent of its cause—for the top continued to dance even at some distance from the child's hand, which was the causal force. And not content with this, I had flour brought and sprinkled about, so that as the top danced one might learn whether these were perfect circles it described with its movement; and I found that they were not, but, rather, spiral lines that lost their circularity as the impetus declined. Other girls sat playing at spillikins[5] (surely the most frivolous game that children play); I walked closer to observe the figures they formed, and seeing that by chance three lay in a triangle, I set to joining one with another, recalling that this was said to be the form of the mysterious ring of Solomon,[6] in which he was able to see the distant splendor and images of the Holy Trinity, by virtue of which the ring worked such prodigies and marvels. And the same shape was said to form David's harp, and that is why Saul was refreshed at its sound; and harps today largely conserve that shape.

---

3. I.e., "the three or so."   4. Motion.   5. Jackstraws, or pick-up sticks.   6. It may, like Solomon's seal, have contained the image of the star of David, composed of triangles.

And what shall I tell you, lady, of the natural secrets I have discovered while cooking? I see that an egg holds together and fries in butter or in oil, but, on the contrary, in syrup shrivels into shreds; observe that to keep sugar in a liquid state one need only add a drop or two of water in which a quince or other bitter fruit has been soaked; observe that the yolk and the white of one egg are so dissimilar that each with sugar produces a result not obtainable with both together. I do not wish to weary you with such inconsequential matters, and make mention of them only to give you full notice of my nature, for I believe they will be occasion for laughter. But, lady, as women, what wisdom may be ours if not the philosophies of the kitchen? Lupercio Leonardo[7] spoke well when he said: how well one may philosophize when preparing dinner. And I often say, when observing these trivial details: had Aristotle prepared victuals, he would have written more. And pursuing the manner of my cogitations, I tell you that this process is so continuous in me that I have no need for books. And on one occasion, when because of a grave upset of the stomach the physicians forbade me to study, I passed thus some days, but then I proposed that it would be less harmful if they allowed me books, because so vigorous and vehement were my cogitations that my spirit was consumed more greatly in a quarter of an hour than in four days' studying books. And thus they were persuaded to allow me to read. And moreover, lady, not even have my dreams been excluded from this ceaseless agitation of my imagination; indeed, in dreams it is wont to work more freely and less encumbered, collating with greater clarity and calm the gleanings of the day, arguing and making verses, of which I could offer you an extended catalogue, as well as of some arguments and inventions that I have better achieved sleeping than awake. I relinquish this subject in order not to tire you, for the above is sufficient to allow your discretion and acuity to penetrate perfectly and perceive my nature, as well as the beginnings, the methods, and the present state of my studies.

Even, lady, were these merits (and I see them celebrated as such in men), they would not have been so in me, for I cannot but study. If they are faults, then, for the same reasons, I believe I have none. Nevertheless, I live always with so little confidence in myself that neither in my study, nor in any other thing, do I trust my judgment; and thus I remit the decision to your sovereign genius, submitting myself to whatever sentence you may bestow, without controversy, without reluctance, for I have wished here only to present you with a simple narration of my inclination toward letters.

I confess, too, that though it is true, as I have stated, that I had no need of books, it is nonetheless also true that they have been no little inspiration, in divine as in human letters. Because I find a Debbora[8] administering the law, both military and political, and governing a people among whom there were many learned men. I find a most wise Queen of Saba,[9] so learned that she dares to challenge with hard questions the wisdom of the greatest of all wise men, without being reprimanded for doing so, but, rather, as a consequence, to judge unbelievers. I see many and illustrious women; some blessed with the gift of prophecy, like Abigail, others of persuasion, like

---

7. Lupercio Leonardo de Argensola (1559–1639), poet, playwright, and historian.   8. Or Deborah, a prophetess who judged the Israelites (Judges 4.4–14).   9. Or Sheba, who tested King Solomon with questions (1 Kings 10.1–3).

Esther; others with pity, like Rehab; others with perseverance, like Anna,[1] the mother of Samuel; and an infinite number of others, with divers gifts and virtues.

If I again turn to the Gentiles, the first I encounter are the Sibyls,[2] those women chosen by God to prophesy the principal mysteries of our Faith, and with learned and elegant verses that surpass admiration. I see adored as a goddess of the sciences a woman like Minerva,[3] the daughter of the first Jupiter and mistress over all the wisdom of Athens. I see a Polla Argentaria, who helped Lucan, her husband, write his epic *Pharsalia*.[4] I see the daughter of the divine Tiresias, more learned than her father. I see a Zenobia, Queen of the Palmyrans, as wise as she was valiant. An Arete, most learned daughter of Aristippus.[5] A Nicostrate,[6] framer of Latin verses and most erudite in Greek. An Aspasia Milesia, who taught philosophy and rhetoric, and who was a teacher of the philosopher Pericles. An Hypatia, who taught astrology, and studied many years in Alexandria. A Leontium, a Greek woman, who questioned the philosopher Theophrastus, and convinced him. A Julia, a Corinna, a Cornelia;[7] and, finally, a great throng of women deserving to be named, some as Greeks, some as muses, some as seers; for all were nothing more than learned women, held, and celebrated—and venerated as well— as such by antiquity. Without mentioning an infinity of other women whose names fill books. For example, I find the Egyptian Catherine,[8] studying and influencing the wisdom of all the wise men of Egypt. I see a Gertrudis[9] studying, writing, and teaching. And not to overlook examples close to home, I see my most holy mother Paula, learned in Hebrew, Greek, and Latin, and most able in interpreting the Scriptures. And what greater praise than, having as her chronicler a Jeronimus Maximus,[1] that Saint scarcely found himself competent for his task, and says, with that weighty deliberation and energetic precision with which he so well expressed himself: "If all the members of my body were tongues, they still would not be sufficient to proclaim the wisdom and virtue of Paula." Similarly praiseworthy was the widow Blesilla; also, the illustrious virgin Eustochium,[2] both daughters of this same saint; especially the second, who, for her knowledge, was called the Prodigy of the World. The Roman Fabiola[3] was most well-versed in the Holy Scripture. Proba Falconia, a Roman woman, wrote elegant centos,[4] containing verses from Virgil, about the mysteries of Our Holy Faith. It is well-known by all that Queen

1. Or Hannah, who after years of childlessness received the answer to her prayers in the birth of Samuel (1 Samuel 1.1–20). Abigail was the wife of a surly husband, Nabal. After Nabal insulted King David, she went to the king with presents and prophesied his future triumphs, thus saving her husband's life (1 Samuel 25.2–35). Esther persuaded her husband, King Ahasuerus, to protect the Jews (Esther 5–9). Rehab, or Rahab, was a harlot who protected two Israelites from the King of Jericho (Joshua 2.1–7).   2. Female prophets of the ancient world.   3. Or Athena, goddess of wisdom.   4. Epic poem on the civil war between Caesar and Pompey, properly called *Bellum Civile* (ca. A.D. 62–65).   5. Greek philosopher (ca. 435–ca. 360 B.C.). Tiresias was a legendary blind Theban seer. His daughter was Manto, known for her skill in divination by fire. Zenobia, the learned widow of Odenathus, declared her independence from Rome and expanded the Middle-Eastern territory under her rule, naming herself Augusta, empress of Rome. She was finally defeated and captured in 272.   6. Or Carmentis, legendary daughter of Pallas, king of Arcadia, and (in legend) inventor of the Roman alphabet.   7. Noted for her devotion to her children's education after her husband's death (second century B.C.); she was the second daughter of Scipio Africanus and wife of Tiberius Sempronius Gracchus. Julia Domna (second century A.D.), wife of the Roman emperor Septimius Severus, known for her learning as Julia the Philosopher. Corinna (ca. 500? B.C.), a lyric poet of Tanagra who wrote for a group of women.   8. St. Catherine (fourth century?), allegedly so wise she could refute fifty philosophers at once.   9. St. Gertrude (d.1302), Benedictine nun and visionary, an important mystic.   1. St. Jerome.   2. Blesilla and Eustochium were daughters of St. Paula and, like her, were taught by St. Jerome.   3. One of Jerome's disciples.   4. Compositions made up of verses from other authors.

Isabel,[5] wife of the tenth Alfonso, wrote about astrology. Many others I do not list, out of the desire not merely to transcribe what others have said (a vice I have always abominated); and many are flourishing today, as witness Christina Alexandra, Queen of Sweden,[6] as learned as she is valiant and magnanimous, and the Most Honorable Ladies, the Duquesa of Abeyro and the Condesa of Villaumbrosa.

The venerable Doctor Arce[7] (by his virtue and learning a worthy teacher of the Scriptures) in his scholarly *Bibliorum* raises this question: *Is it permissible for women to dedicate themselves to the study of the Holy Scriptures, and to their interpretation?* and he offers as negative arguments the opinions of many saints, especially that of the Apostle: *Let women keep silence in the churches; for it is not permitted them to speak,* etc.[8] He later cites other opinions and, from the same Apostle, verses from his letter to Titus: *The aged women in like manner, in holy attire . . . teaching well,*[9] with interpretations by the Holy Fathers. Finally he resolves, with all prudence, that teaching publicly from a University chair, or preaching from the pulpit, is not permissible for women; but that to study, write, and teach privately not only is permissible, but most advantageous and useful. It is evident that this is not to be the case with all women, but with those to whom God may have granted special virtue and prudence, and who may be well advanced in learning, and having the essential talent and requisites for such a sacred calling. This view is indeed just, so much so that not only women, who are held to be so inept, but also men, who merely for being men believe they are wise, should be prohibited from interpreting the Sacred Word if they are not learned and virtuous and of gentle and well-inclined natures; that this is not so has been, I believe, at the root of so much sectarianism and so many heresies. For there are many who study but are ignorant, especially those who are in spirit arrogant, troubled, and proud, so eager for new interpretations of the Word (which itself rejects new interpretations) that merely for the sake of saying what no one else has said they speak a heresy, and even then are not content. Of these the Holy Spirit says: *For wisdom will not enter into a malicious soul.*[1] To such as these more harm results from knowing than from ignorance. A wise man has said: he who does not know Latin is not a complete fool; but he who knows it is well qualified to be.[2] And I would add that a fool may reach perfection (if ignorance may tolerate perfection) by having studied his tittle of philosophy and theology and by having some learning of tongues, by which he may be a fool in many sciences and languages: a great fool cannot be contained solely in his mother tongue.

For such as these, I reiterate, study is harmful, because it is as if to place a sword in the hands of a madman; which, though a most noble instrument for defense, is in his hands his own death and that of many others. So were the Divine Scriptures in the possession of the evil Pelagius and the intractable Arius, of the evil Luther, and the other heresiarchs like our own Doctor (who was neither ours nor a doctor) Cazalla.[3] To these men, wisdom was

5. Of Spain, wife of Alfonso X, Alfonso the Wise (1221–1284). 6. She attracted many scholars and artists to her court (1626–1689). 7. Juan Díaz de Arce (1594–1653), author of theological books. 8. 1 Corinthians 14.34. 9. Titus 2.3–5. 1. Book of Wisdom 1.4 (in the Apocrypha). 2. Alludes to the Spanish proverb "A fool, unless he knows Latin, is never a great fool." 3. Augustino Cazallo (1510–1559), Spanish Protestant executed by the Inquisition for promulgating Lutheran doctrine. Pelagius was a heretical monk (ca. 355–ca. 425) who taught that people do not need divine grace since they have a natural tendency to seek the good. Arius was a Libyan theologian (ca. 256–

harmful, although it is the greatest nourishment and the life of the soul; in the same way that in a stomach of sickly constitution and adulterated complexion, the finer the nourishment it receives, the more arid, fermented, and perverse are the humors it produces; thus these evil men: the more they study, the worse opinions they engender, their reason being obstructed with the very substance meant to nourish it, and they study much and digest little, exceeding the limits of the vessel of their reason. Of which the Apostle says: *For I say, by the grace that is given me, to all that are among you, not to be more wise than it behoveth to be wise, but to be wise unto sobriety, and according as God hath divided to every one the measure of faith.*[4] And in truth, the Apostle did not direct these words to women, but to men; and that *keep silence* is intended not only for women, but for *all* incompetents. If I desire to know as much, or more, than Aristotle or Saint Augustine, and if I have not the aptitude of Saint Augustine or Aristotle, though I study more than either, not only will I not achieve learning, but I will weaken and dull the workings of my feeble reason with the disproportionateness of the goal.

Oh, that each of us—I, being ignorant, the first—should take the measure of our talents before we study, or, more importantly, write, with the covetous ambition to equal and even surpass others, how little spirit we should have for it, and how many errors we should avoid, and how many tortured intellects of which we have experience, we should have had no experience! And I place my own ignorance in the forefront of all these, for if I knew all I should, I would not write. And I protest that I do so only to obey you; and with such apprehension that you owe me more that I have taken up my pen in fear than you would have owed had I presented you more perfect works. But it is well that they go to your correction. Cross them out, tear them up, reprove me, and I shall appreciate that more than all the vain applause others may offer. *That just men shall correct me in mercy, and shall reprove me; but let not the oil of the sinner fatten my head.*[5] And returning again to our Arce, I say that in affirmation of his opinion he cites the words of my father, Saint Jerome: *To Leta, Upon the Education of Her Daughter.* Where he says: *Accustom her tongue, still young, to the sweetness of the Psalms. Even the names through which little by little she will become accustomed to form her phrases should not be chosen by chance, but selected and repeated with care; the prophets must be included, of course, and the apostles, as well, and all the Patriarchs beginning with Adam and down to Matthew and Luke, so that as she practices other things she will be readying her memory for the future. Let your daily task be taken from the flower of the Scriptures.* And if this Saint desired that a young girl scarcely beginning to talk be educated in this fashion, what would he desire for his nuns and his spiritual daughters? These beliefs are illustrated in the examples of the previously mentioned Eustochium and Fabiola, and Marcella, her sister, and Pacatula, and others whom the Saint honors in his epistles, exhorting them to this sacred exercise, as they are recognized in the epistle I cited, *Let your daily task . . .* which is affirmation of and agreement with the *aged women . . . teaching well* of Saint Paul. My illustrious Father's *Let your daily task . . .* makes clear that the teacher of the child is to be Leta herself, the child's mother.

Oh, how much injury might have been avoided in our land if our aged

---

336), founder of the Arian heresy that declared that Christ was neither eternal nor equal with God. Martin Luther (1483–1546), was the German leader of the Protestant Reformation and, from Sister Juana's point of view, another heretic.   **4.** Romans 12.3.   **5.** Psalms 141.5.

women had been learned, as was Leta, and had they known how to instruct as directed by Saint Paul and by my Father, Saint Jerome. And failing this, and because of the considerable idleness to which our poor women have been relegated, if a father desires to provide his daughters with more than ordinary learning, he is forced by necessity, and by the absence of wise elder women, to bring men to teach the skills of reading, writing, counting, the playing of musical instruments, and other accomplishments, from which no little harm results, as is experienced every day in doleful examples of perilous association, because through the immediacy of contact and the intimacy born from the passage of time, what one may never have thought possible is easily accomplished. For which reason many prefer to leave their daughters unpolished and uncultured rather than to expose them to such notorious peril as that of familiarity with men, which quandary could be prevented if there were learned elder women, as Saint Paul wished to see, and if the teaching were handed down from one to another, as is the custom with domestic crafts and all other traditional skills.

For what objection can there be that an older woman, learned in letters and in sacred conversation and customs, have in her charge the education of young girls? This would prevent these girls being lost either for lack of instruction or for hesitating to offer instruction through such dangerous means as male teachers, for even when there is no greater risk of indecency than to seat beside a modest woman (who still may blush when her own father looks directly at her) a strange man who treats her as if he were a member of the household and with the authority of an intimate, the modesty demanded in interchange with men, and in conversation with them, is suf- ficient reason that such an arrangement not be permitted. For I do not find that the custom of men teaching women is without its peril, lest it be in the severe tribunal of the confessional, or from the remote decency of the pulpit, or in the distant learning of books—never in the personal contact of imme- diacy. And the world knows this is true; and, notwithstanding, it is permitted solely from the want of learned elder women. Then is it not detrimental, the lack of such women? This question should be addressed by those who, bound to that *Let women keep silence in the church,* say that it is blasphemy for women to learn and teach, as if it were not the Apostle himself who said: *The aged women . . . teaching well.* As well as the fact that this prohibition touches upon historical fact as reported by Eusebium:[6] which is that in the early Church, women were charged with teaching the doctrine to one another in the temples and the sound of this teaching caused confusion as the Apostles were preaching and this is the reason they were ordered to be silent; and even today, while the homilist is preaching, one does not pray aloud.

Who will argue that for the comprehension of many Scriptures one must be familiar with the history, customs, ceremonies, proverbs, and even the manners of speaking of those times in which they were written, if one is to apprehend the references and allusions of more than a few passages of the Holy Word. *And rend your heart and not your garments.*[7] Is this not a refer- ence to the ceremony in which Hebrews rent their garments as a sign of grief, as did the evil pontiff when he said that Christ had blasphemed? In

6. Probably Eusebius of Caesaria (ca. 263–339?), an early Church historian.   7. Joel 2.13.

many scriptures the Apostle writes of succour for widows; did they not refer to the customs of those times? Does not the example of the valiant woman, *Her husband is honourable in the gates,*[8] allude to the fact that the tribunals of the judges were at the gates of the cities? That *Dare terram Deo,* give of your land to God, did that not mean to make some votive offering? And did they not call the public sinners *hiemantes,* those who endure the winter, because they made their penance in the open air instead of at a town gate as others did? And Christ's plaint to that Pharisee who had neither kissed him nor given him water for his feet,[9] was that not because it was the Jews' usual custom to offer these acts of hospitality? And we find an infinite number of additional instances not only in the Divine Letters, but human, as well, such as *adorate purpuram,* venerate the purple, which meant obey the King; *manumittere eum,* manumit them, alluding to the custom and ceremony of striking the slave with one's hand to signify his freedom. That *intonuit coelum,* heaven thundered, in Virgil, which alludes to the augury of thunder from the west, which was held to be good.[1] Martial's *tu nunquam leporem edisti,*[2] you never ate hare, has not only the wit of ambiguity in its *leporem,*[3] but, as well, the allusion to the reputed propensity of hares [to bless with beauty those who dine on them]. That proverb, *maleam legens, que sunt domi obliviscere,* to sail along the shore of Malia is to forget what one has at home, alludes to the great peril of the promontory of Laconia.[4] That chaste matron's response to the unwanted suit of her pretender: "the hinge-pins shall not be oiled for my sake, nor shall the torches blaze," meaning that she did not want to marry, alluded to the ceremony of anointing the doorways with oils and lighting the nuptial torches in the wedding ceremony, as if now we would say, they shall not prepare the thirteen coins for my dowry, nor shall the priest invoke the blessing. And thus it is with many comments of Virgil and Homer and all the poets and orators. In addition, how many are the difficulties found even in the grammar of the Holy Scripture, such as writing a plural for a singular, or changing from the second to third persons, as in the Psalms, *Let him kiss me with the kiss of his mouth, for thy breasts are better than wine.*[5] Or placing adjectives in the genitive instead of the accusative, as in *Calicem salutaris accipiam,* I will take the chalice of salvation.[6] Or to replace the feminine with the masculine, and, in contrast, to call any sin adultery.

All this demands more investigation than some believe, who strictly as grammarians, or, at most, employing the four principles of applied logic, attempt to interpret the Scriptures while clinging to that *Let the women keep silence in the church,* not knowing how it is to be interpreted. As well as that other verse, *Let the women learn in silence.*[7] For this latter scripture works more to women's favor than their disfavor, as it commands them to learn; and it is only natural that they must maintain silence while they learn. And it is also written, *Hear, oh Israel, and be silent.*[8] Which addresses the entire congregation of men and women, commanding all to silence, because if one is to hear and learn, it is with good reason that he attend and be silent. And

8. Proverbs 31.23.   9. Luke 7.44–45.   1. Sister Juana possibly misremembers *Aeneid* 2.693: "thunder on the left."   2. Marcus Valerius Martialis (ca. 40–ca. 104), Roman epigrammatic poet; "Edisti numquam, Gellia, tu leporem" (*Epigrams* 5.29).   3. This word can also mean charm, grace, attractiveness.   4. The site of ancient Sparta, conquered by Macedonia in the fourth century B.C.   5. Song of Solomon 1.2.   6. Psalms 116.13.   7. 1 Timothy 2.11.   8. Not a biblical quotation.

if it is not so, I would want these interpreters and expositors of Saint Paul to explain to me how they interpret that scripture, *Let the women keep silence in the church*. For either they must understand it to refer to the material church, that is the church of pulpits and cathedras,[9] or to the spiritual, the community of the faithful, which is the Church. If they understand it to be the former, which, in my opinion, is its true interpretation, then we see that if in fact it is not permitted of women to read publicly in church, nor preach, why do they censure those who study privately? And if they understand the latter, and wish that the prohibition of the Apostle be applied transcendentally—that not even in private are women to be permitted to write or study— how are we to view the fact that the Church permitted a Gertrudis, a Santa Teresa, a Saint Birgitta, the Nun of Agreda,[1] and so many others, to write? And if they say to me that these women were saints, they speak the truth; but this poses no obstacle to my argument. First, because Saint Paul's proposition is absolute, and encompasses all women not excepting saints, as Martha and Mary, Marcella, Mary, mother of Jacob, and Salome,[2] all were in their time, and many other zealous women of the early church. But we see, too, that the Church allows women who are not saints to write, for the Nun of Agreda and Sor María de la Antigua[3] are not canonized, yet their writings are circulated. And when Santa Teresa and the others were writing, they were not as yet canonized. In which case, Saint Paul's prohibition was directed solely to the public office of the pulpit, for if the Apostle had forbidden women to write, the Church would not have allowed it. Now I do not make so bold as to teach—which in me would be excessively presumptuous— and as for writing, that requires a greater talent than mine, and serious reflection. As Saint Cyprian[4] says: *The things we write require most conscientious consideration.* I have desired to study that I might be ignorant of less; for (according to Saint Augustine[5]) some things are learned to be enacted and others only to be known: *We learn some things to know them, others, to do them.* Then, where is the offense to be found if even what is licit to women—which is to teach by writing—I do not perform, as I know that I am lacking in means, following the counsel of Quintilian: *Let each person learn not only from the precepts of others, but also let him reap counsel from his own nature.*

If the offense is to be found in the *Atenagórica* letter, was that letter anything other than the simple expression of my feeling, written with the implicit permission of our Holy Mother Church? For if the Church, in her most sacred authority, does not forbid it, why must others do so? That I proffered an opinion contrary to that of de Vieyra was audacious, but, as a Father, was it not audacious that he speak against the three Holy Fathers of the Church? My reason, such as it is, is it not as unfettered as his, as both issue from the same source? Is his opinion to be considered as a revelation, as a principle

9. The cathedra is the throne of the bishop in his church.   1. Maria de Agreda (1602–1635), Spanish Franciscan nun, author of *The Mystic City of God* (1670), a work allegedly divinely inspired. Birgitta, or Bridget (1303–1373), of Sweden.   2. In the King James Bible, Mary, the mother of James (or Jacob), and Salome came to the empty sepulcher to anoint Jesus' body (Mark 16.1). Martha and Mary were sisters. Mary anointed Jesus' feet (John 12.3). Martha was preoccupied with household tasks (Luke 10.40–42). Marcella was one of the women taught by Jerome.   3. Spanish nun (1544–1617).   4. Thascius Caecilius Cyprianus (ca. 200–258), one of the Church fathers, known for his efforts to enforce Church discipline.   5. Aurelius Augustinus (354–430), baptized by St. Ambrose in 387, author of *De Civitate Dei*, a vindication of the Church that long possessed great authority.

of the Holy Faith, that we must accept blindly? Furthermore, I maintained at all times the respect due such a virtuous man, a respect in which his defender was sadly wanting, ignoring the phrase of Titus Lucius:[6] *Respect is companion to the arts*. I did not touch a thread of the robes of the Society of Jesus; nor did I write for other than the consideration of the person who suggested that I write. And, according to Pliny, *how different the condition of one who writes from that of one who merely speaks*. Had I believed the letter was to be published I would not have been so inattentive. If, as the censor says, the letter is heretical, why does he not denounce it? And with that he would be avenged, and I content, for, which is only seemly, I esteem more highly my reputation as a Catholic and obedient daughter of the Holy Mother Church than all the approbation due a learned woman. If the letter is rash, and he does well to criticize it, then laugh, even if with the laugh of the rabbit, for I have not asked that he approve; as I was free to dissent from de Vieyra, so will anyone be free to oppose my opinion.

But how I have strayed, lady. None of this pertains here, nor is it intended for your ears, but as I was discussing my accusers I remembered the words of one that recently have appeared, and, though my intent was to speak in general, my pen, unbidden, slipped, and began to respond in particular. And so, returning to our Arce, he says that he knew in this city two nuns: one in the Convent of the Regina, who had so thoroughly committed the Breviary to memory that with the greatest promptitude and propriety she applied in her conversation its verses, psalms, and maxims of saintly homilies. The other, in the Convent of the Conception, was so accustomed to reading the Epistles of my Father Saint Jerome, and the Locutions of this Saint, that Arce says, *It seemed I was listening to Saint Jerome himself, speaking in Spanish*. And of this latter woman he says that after her death he learned that she had translated these Epistles into the Spanish language. What pity that such talents could not have been employed in major studies with scientific principles. He does not give the name of either, although he offers these women as confirmation of his opinion, which is that not only is it licit, but most useful and essential for women to study the Holy Word, and even more essential for nuns; and that study is the very thing to which your wisdom exhorts me, and in which so many arguments concur.

Then if I turn my eyes to the oft-chastized faculty of making verses—which is in me so natural that I must discipline myself that even this letter not be written in that form—I might cite those lines, *All I wished to express took the form of verse*.[7] And seeing that so many condemn and criticize this ability, I have conscientiously sought to find what harm may be in it, and I have not found it, but, rather, I see verse acclaimed in the mouths of the Sibyls; sanctified in the pens of the Prophets, especially King David, of whom the exalted Expositor my beloved Father[8] says (explicating the measure of his meters): *in the manner of Horace and Pindar, now it hurries along in iambs, now it rings in alcaic, now swells in sapphic, then arrives in broken feet*. The greater part of the Holy Books are in meter, as is the Book of Moses; and those of Job (as Saint Isidore[9] states in his *Etymologiae*) are in heroic verse.

---

6. Better known as Saturantius Apuleius, greatly celebrated in his time (second century A.D.) for eloquence.   7. Ovid's *Tristia* 4.10.25ff.   8. Jerome.   9. Spanish archbishop (ca. 560–636), who helped organize the Church in Spain.

Solomon wrote the Canticle of Canticles in verse; and Jeremias, his *Lamentations*. And so, says Cassiodorus:[1] *All poetic expression had as its source the Holy Scriptures.* For not only does our Catholic Church not disdain verse, it employs verse in its hymns, and recites the lines of Saint Ambrose,[2] Saint Thomas, Saint Isidore, and others. Saint Bonaventure[3] was so taken with verse that he writes scarcely a page where it does not appear. It is readily apparent that Saint Paul had studied verse, for he quotes and translates verses of Aratus: *For in him we live, and move, and are.*[4] And he quotes also that verse of Parmenides: *The Cretians are always liars, evil beasts, slothful bellies.*[5] Saint Gregory Nazianzen[6] argues in elegant verses the questions of matrimony and virginity. And, how should I tire? The Queen of Wisdom, Our Lady, with Her sacred lips, intoned the Canticle of the Magnificat;[7] and having brought forth this example, it would be offensive to add others that were profane, even those of the most serious and learned men, for this alone is more than sufficient confirmation; and even though Hebrew elegance could not be compressed into Latin measure, for which reason, although the sacred translator, more attentive to the importance of the meaning, omitted the verse, the Psalms retain the number and divisions of verses, and what harm is to be found in them? For misuse is not the blame of art, but rather of the evil teacher who perverts the arts, making of them the snare of the devil; and this occurs in all the arts and sciences.

And if the evil is attributed to the fact that a woman employs them, we have seen how many have done so in praiseworthy fashion; what then is the evil in my being a woman? I confess openly my own baseness and meanness; but I judge that no couplet of mine has been deemed indecent. Furthermore, I have never written of my own will, but under the pleas and injunctions of others; to such a degree that the only piece I remember having written for my own pleasure was a little trifle they called *El sueño*.[8] That letter, lady, which you so greatly honored, I wrote more with repugnance than any other emotion; both by reason of the fact that it treated sacred matters, for which (as I have stated) I hold such reverent awe, and because it seems to wish to impugn, a practice for which I have natural aversion; and I believe that had I foreseen the blessed destiny to which it was fated—for like a second Moses I had set it adrift, naked, on the waters of the Nile of silence, where you, a princess, found and cherished it[9]—I believe, I reiterate, that had I known, the very hands of which it was born would have drowned it, out of the fear that these clumsy scribblings from my ignorance appear before the light of your great wisdom; by which one knows the munificence of your kindness, for your goodwill applauds precisely what your reason must wish to reject. For as fate cast it before your doors, so exposed, so orphaned, that it fell to you even to give it a name, I must lament that among other deformities it also bears the blemish of haste; both because of the unrelenting ill-health I suffer, and for the profusion of duties imposed on me by obedience, as well

1. Flavius Magnus Aurelius Cassiodorus (ca. 485–ca.580), Roman monk and author of *Institutiones*, a course of studies for monks. 2. Bishop of Milan (339–397), who had an important share in the conversion of St. Augustine. 3. Franciscan bishop and cardinal (1221–1274), who preached the importance of study. 4. Acts 17.28. 5. Titus 1.12. 6. Gregorius Nazianzenus, bishop of Constantinople and associate of Jerome. The allusion is to the first of his forty moral poems, 732 lines eulogizing virginity. 7. Luke 1.46–55. 8. *The Dream*, one of Sister Juana's best-known poems, which tells of the flight of her soul toward learning. 9. Because Pharaoh had ordered all male Hebrew infants killed, Moses' mother placed him in a basket by the Nile, where he was found and rescued by Pharaoh's daughter (Exodus 2.1–10).

as the want of anyone to guide me in my writing and the need that it all come from my hand, and, finally, because the writing went against my nature and I wished only to keep my promise to one whom I could not disobey, I could not find the time to finish properly, and thus I failed to include whole treatises and many arguments that presented themselves to me, but which I omitted in order to put an end to the writing—many, that had I known the letter was to be printed, I would not have excluded, even if merely to satisfy some objections that have since arisen and which could have been refuted. But I shall not be so ill-mannered as to place such indecent objects before the purity of your eyes, for it is enough that my ignorance be an offense in your sight, without need of entrusting to it the effronteries of others. If they should wing your way (and they are of such little weight that this will happen), then you will command what I am to do; for, if it does not run contrary to your will, my defense shall be not to take up my pen, for I deem that one affront need not occasion another, if one recognizes the error in the very place it lies concealed. As my Father Saint Jerome says, *good discourse seeks not things,* and Saint Ambrose, *it is the nature of a guilty conscience to lie concealed.* Nor do I consider that I have been impugned, for one statute of the Law states: *An accusation will not endure unless nurtured by the person who brought it forth.* What *is* a matter to be weighed is the effort spent in copying the accusation. A strange madness, to expend more effort in denying acclaim than in earning it! I, lady, have chosen not to respond (although others did so without my knowledge); it suffices that I have seen certain treatises, among them one so learned I send it to you so that reading it will compensate in part for the time you squandered on my writing. If, lady, you wish that I act contrary to what I have proposed here for your judgment and opinion, the merest indication of your desire will, as is seemly, countermand my inclination, which, as I have told you, is to be silent, for although Saint John Chrysostom[1] says, *those who slander must be refuted, and those who question, taught,* I know also that Saint Gregory[2] says, *It is no less a victory to tolerate enemies than to overcome them.* And that patience conquers by tolerating and triumphs by suffering. And if among the Roman Gentiles it was the custom when their captains were at the highest peak of glory—when returning triumphant from other nations, robed in purple and wreathed with laurel, crowned-but-conquered kings pulling their carriages in the stead of beasts, accompanied by the spoils of the riches of all the world, the conquering troops adorned with the insignia of their heroic feats, hearing the plaudits of the people who showered them with titles of honor and renown such as Fathers of the Nation, Columns of the Empire, Walls of Rome, Shelter of the Republic, and other glorious names—a soldier went before these captains in this moment of the supreme apogee of glory and human happiness crying out in a loud voice to the conqueror (by his consent and order of the Senate): Behold how you are mortal; behold how you have this or that defect, not excepting the most shameful, as happened in the triumph of Caesar, when the vilest soldiers clamored in his ear: *Beware, Romans, for we bring you the bald adulterer.* Which was done so that in the midst of such honor the conquerers not be swelled up with pride, and that the ballast of

---

1. Syrian prelate (ca. 347–407), known as the greatest orator of the Church, author of many homilies and treatises.   2. Gregory the Great (ca. 540–604), pope from 590, deeply concerned with the reformation of the Church.

these insults act as counterweight to the bellying sails of such approbation, and that the ship of good judgment not founder amidst the winds of acclamation. If this, I say, was the practice among Gentiles, who knew only the light of Natural Law, how much might we Catholics, under the injunction to love our enemies, achieve by tolerating them? And in my own behalf I can attest that calumny has often mortified me, but never harmed me, being that I hold as a great fool one who having occasion to receive credit suffers the difficulty and loses the credit, as it is with those who do not resign themselves to death, but, in the end, die anyway, their resistance not having prevented death, but merely deprived them of the credit of resignation and caused them to die badly when they might have died well. And thus, lady, I believe these experiences do more good than harm, and I hold as greater the jeopardy of applause to human weakness, as we are wont to appropriate praise that is not our own, and must be ever watchful, and carry graven on our hearts those words of the Apostle: *Or what hast thou that thou hast not received? And if thou hast received, why doest thou glory as if thou hadst not received it?*[3] so that these words serve as a shield to fend off the sharp barbs of commendations, which are as spears which when not attributed to God (whose they are), claim our lives and cause us to be thieves of God's honor and usurpers of the talents He bestowed on us and the gifts that He lent to us, for which we must give the most strict accounting. And thus, lady, I fear applause more than calumny, because the latter, with but the simple act of patience becomes gain, while the former requires many acts of reflection and humility and proper recognition so that it not become harm. And I know and recognize that it is by special favor of God that I know this, as it enables me in either instance to act in accord with the words of Saint Augustine: *One must believe neither the friend who praises nor the enemy who detracts.* Although most often I squander God's favor, or vitiate with such defects and imperfections that I spoil what, being His, was good. And thus in what little of mine that has been printed, neither the use of my name, nor even consent for the printing, was given by my own counsel, but by the license of another who lies outside my domain, as was also true with the printing of the *Atenagórica* letter, and only a few *Exercises of the Incarnation* and *Offerings of the Sorrow* were printed for public devotions with my pleasure, but without my name; of which I am sending some few copies that (if you so desire) you may distribute them among our sisters, the nuns of that holy community, as well as in that city. I send but one copy of the *Sorrows* because the others have been exhausted and I could find no other copy. I wrote them long ago, solely for the devotions of my sisters, and later they were spread abroad; and their contents are disproportionate as regards my unworthiness and my ignorance, and they profited that they touched on matters of our exalted Queen; for I cannot explain what it is that inflames the coldest heart when one refers to the Most Holy Mary. It is my only desire, esteemed lady, to remit to you works worthy of your virtue and wisdom; as the poet said: *Though strength may falter, good will must be praised. In this, I believe, the gods will be content.*

If ever I write again, my scribbling will always find its way to the haven of your holy feet and the certainty of your correction, for I have no other jewel with which to pay you, and, in the lament of Seneca, he who has once

---

3. Corinthians 11.4.

bestowed benefices has committed himself to continue; and so you must be repaid out of your own munificence, for only in this way shall I with dignity be freed from debt and avoid that the words of that same Seneca come to pass: *It is contemptible to be surpassed in benefices.*[4] For in his gallantry the generous creditor gives to the poor debtor the means to satisfy his debt. So God gave his gift to a world unable to repay Him: He gave his son that He be offered a recompense worthy of Him.

If, most venerable lady, the tone of this letter may not have seemed right and proper, I ask forgiveness for its homely familiarity, and the less than seemly respect in which by treating you as a nun, one of my sisters, I have lost sight of the remoteness of your most illustrious person; which, had I seen you without your veil, would never have occurred; but you in all your prudence and mercy will supplement or amend the language, and if you find unsuitable the *Vos* of the address I have employed, believing that for the reverence I owe you, Your Reverence seemed little reverent, modify it in whatever manner seems appropriate to your due, for I have not dared exceed the limits of your custom, nor transgress the boundary of your modesty.

And hold me in your grace, and entreat for me divine grace, of which the Lord God grant you large measure, and keep you, as I pray Him, and am needful. From this convent of our Father Saint Jerome in Mexico City, the first day of the month of March of sixteen hundred and ninety-one. Allow me to kiss your hand, your most favored

JUANA INÉS DE LA CRUZ

4. *On Benefits* 5.2.1.

JONATHAN SWIFT
1667–1745

In virtually all his writing, Jonathan Swift displays his gift for making other people uncomfortable. He makes us uneasy by making us aware of our own moral inadequacies, and by his wit, energy, and inventiveness, he actually compels us to enjoy the process of being brought to such awareness.

Born in Dublin to English parents, Swift was educated at Trinity College, Dublin. In 1689, the young man went to England, where he served as secretary to the statesman Sir William Temple. During his residence at Moor Park, Sir William's estate, Swift became friendly with Esther Johnson, daughter of the steward there; he remained on close terms with her for the rest of his life. (His playful, intimate letters to her—he used the name "Stella"—were published in a collection called *Journal to Stella*.) In 1692, Swift received an M.A. from Oxford University; three years later, he took orders, becoming a clergyman in the Anglican Church but continuing in Sir William's employ, although with intermittent stays in Ireland. Early in the eighteenth century, he began his career of political journalism; he also published brilliant satiric works, including *A Tale of a Tub* (1704), of which he is supposed to have said, late in his life, "What a genius I had when I composed that book!" Although he had hoped for church advancement in England, as a reward for his writings in the Tory cause, in 1713 he was instead named dean of St. Patrick's Cathedral, Dublin. He spent the rest of his life in Ireland (save for two brief visits to friends in England) writing passionately on behalf of the oppressed Irish people. In his final years, he was declared mentally incompetent, suffering, presumably, from senility. As he had prophesied in his verses *On the Death of Dr. Swift*, "He gave what little wealth he had / To build a house for fools and mad"; the mental hospital founded by his legacy still exists in Dublin.

For *Gulliver's Travels* (1726) Swift used the travel book, a form hovering between fact and fiction, as his model. Lemuel Gulliver, ship's surgeon, travels into four imagined nations. The first book takes him to Lilliput, where he duly observes the customs and traditions of a race of people six inches high. The narrative of their preoccupations and procedures mocks the pettiness of the English, although Gulliver, himself involved in the intrigues of his tiny hosts, fails to note the resemblance between Lilliput and his native land. His simple patriotism survives through the second book, where Gulliver encounters the giants of Brobdingnag, whose benevolent king, after hearing Gulliver's patriotic account of England, comments, "I cannot but conclude the bulk of your natives, to be the most pernicious race of little odious vermin that nature ever suffered to crawl upon the surface of the earth." The third book is more various, and Gulliver on the whole seems less gullible in his encounters with the ludicrous or dangerous results of abstract speculation divorced from practical concerns (philosophers, for instance, so deep in ratiocination that they have to be attended by "flappers," servants who "flap" them into awareness of immediate actuality), with the ghosts of great men from the past who stress the lies of historians and the moral and physical decline of their descendants, and with the terrifying Struldbrugs, who grow old but live forever in horrible senility.

Book Four, printed here, has always presented problems to critics. More directly than any other imaginative work of its period, it confronts problems inherent in the idealization of reason as sufficient guide to human conduct. It is easy enough to see that Swift has here imagined an absolute separation between the animal and the rational aspects of human nature. As Gulliver gradually and with horror realizes (the reader undergoing a comparable process), the disgusting Yahoos manifest degraded human form and embody characteristics of human beings deprived of all rational capacity. They act on the basis of pure—and ugly—passion: lust, envy, avarice, greed, rage. The Houyhnhnms, the governing class of horses, treat them as beasts, but consider them more ungovernable than other creatures; Gulliver, looking at them, sees a horrifying version of the human, become (by the absence of reason) subhuman.

As for the Houyhnhnms, those noble horses exemplify pure rationality. They lead monotonous, orderly lives, with no need for disagreement (the truth being self-evident to rational creatures) or excitement. Under their influence, Gulliver wants to stay forever in this land without literal or metaphorical salt. After the Houyhnhnms expel him, Gulliver can make no distinction among human beings: he condemns the benevolent Pedro Mendez as a Yahoo, resents his connection with his own wife and children, and spends as much time as possible in his stable. Life with the Houyhnhnms has driven him mad: he cannot adjust to English actuality.

The question is, Why? By one interpretation, Gulliver judges rightly in perceiving his fellow human beings as essentially Yahoos. His Houyhnhnm master concludes, Gulliver says, that humans are "a sort of animals to whose share . . . some small pittance of reason had fallen, whereof we made no other use than by its assistance to aggravate our natural corruptions, and to acquire new ones which nature had not given us." Perhaps he is right. The Houyhnhnms exemplify an ideal to which human beings should aspire, although they can never reach it; to call attention to the monotony of their lives or the failure of their curiosity only reveals the reader's participation in human depravity. Pedro Mendez is a good man, as men go, but the gulf between the best of humans and a Houyhnhnm gapes so hugely that Gulliver sees correctly in detesting all humans. If he implicitly excepts himself, he thus acknowledges the difference his education by Houyhnhnms has made: at least he knows the gulf's existence.

Another view has it that the Houyhnhnms exemplify a way of being utterly irrelevant to humankind, as well as deeply boring. To hate the animal and glorify the rational denies the inextricable mixture of our nature. Gulliver's pride leads him to aspire to an essentially inhuman state; he wishes, sinfully, to exceed ordained natural limits. Moreover, he ignores the Christian virtue of charity, the command to love one's neighbors. Captain Mendez demonstrates that virtue; Gulliver cannot perceive the moral distinction between the generous captain and the bloodthirsty natives who shoot the Englishman with an arrow shortly after he leaves the Houyhnhnms, producing a lasting scar. Gulliver's condemnation of pride in others emphasizes his blindness to his own flaws.

A compromise position might remind us that to declare the Houyhnhnms irrelevant perhaps leaves the reader in rather too comfortable a position, considering Swift's declared intention "to vex the world rather than divert it." Gulliver's Travels, this comment implies, involves serious attack. We can perhaps dismiss the Houyhnhnms as boring (they have virtually nothing to talk about) or heartless (they make no distinctions of parentage; they expel Gulliver despite his ardent desire to remain) because our natures include more than reason and we appropriately value principles of conduct beyond the rational. Gulliver becomes crazy when he returns to England, unable to accept his full human nature and to make necessary distinctions; given the limits of the human condition, men and women must find the way to operate within them. Gulliver fails and, failing, reminds us of necessities to which we must adapt. The Houyhnhnms provide no solution to human problems: their extirpation of passion, their narrow commitment to reason, prove "inhumane." (They are, after all, horses!) Humankind, as Swift suggested in a letter, is only capable of reason, not fully reasonable; perhaps the spontaneous generosity of the Portuguese captain exemplifies the greatest good to which human beings should aspire.

On the other hand, we claim to value reason; Gulliver has seen in pure form an ideal to which we pay lip service. His realization of the terrible discrepancy between ideal and actual has made it impossible for him to function in his own society. It has given him a harsh perspective by which he sees how morally intolerable social arrangements in fact are. The readiness of most people to compromise, given social necessity, shows how far they are from taking seriously the values they profess. Swift calls our attention to the divergences in our own lives between what we say we believe and how we actually behave. The reality of reason exceeds human capacities; Gulliver's Travels reminds us that we live by hypocrisies. The Houyhnhnms thus tell us something about ourselves despite their lack of humanity.

The problems in interpretation that Gulliver's Travels has always generated come partly from the fact that we receive all information about Gulliver's experience from the traveler himself, an untrustworthy source. In reading his narrative, we must assess his understanding—a slippery process, since we lack a point of reference. Gulliver's Travels abounds in allusions to such phenomena as corrupt lawyers and politicians, avaricious doctors, mass slaughter in wars over trivial pretexts—aspects of our experience and of Gulliver's and reminders that this narrative has something to do with us. The necessity of arriving at a coherent judgment of Gulliver and his experiences implicates the reader in the moral problem of how to judge—and perhaps how to change—society.

Such implication of the reader in often uncomfortable processes of judgment typifies an important aspect of satire. A Modest Proposal (1729), Swift's attack on the economic oppression of the Irish by the English, keeps the reader constantly off balance, trying to understand exactly who is being criticized and why. Swift is writing out of his firsthand awareness of the suffering caused by English policies in Ireland. Absentee landlords who never saw the actual situation of their tenants, British politicians who made policy at a distance, presumably did not know that Ireland had become a land of the starving. In Swift's view, however, the Irish people collaborated by their apathy with the oppressors. In A Modest Proposal, he attacks English and Irish alike.

Even more emphatically than Gulliver, the nameless speaker in *A Modest Proposal* proves an undependable guide, tempting us to identify with his tone of rationality and compassion, only to reveal that his plausible economic orientation leads to advocacy of cannibalism. He offers a series of morally sound and economically feasible suggestions for solutions to Ireland's problems, but draws back immediately, declaring them impossible, since no one will put them in practice. The satire indicts the English for inhumanity, the Irish for passivity, and the economically oriented proposer of remedies for moral blindness. But it also reaches out to criticize the reader as representative of all who endure calmly the intolerable actuality in the world (but not, perhaps, where we have to see it ourselves) of our own inhumanity to our fellow human beings. Swift's self-chosen epitaph, on his tomb, may be translated, "Where fierce indignation no longer tears the heart." *A Modest Proposal* exemplifies the lacerating power of that indignation.

A good introduction to Swift's life and character is I. Ehrenpreis, *The Personality of Jonathan Swift* (1958). For a more recent biography see J. McMinn, *Jonathan Swift: A Literary Life* (1991). An interpretation of the writer in his intellectual context is K. Williams, *Jonathan Swift and the Age of Compromise* (1959). E. Zimmerman, *Swift's Narrative Satires: Author and Authority* (1983), provides acute interpretation of the prose satires. Useful and varied collections of essays about Swift include C. Probyn, ed., *Jonathan Swift: The Contemporary Background* (1978); C. Rawson, ed., *The Art of Swift's Satire: A Revised Focus* (1983); C. Rawson, ed., *Swift: A Collection of Critical Essays* (1994); and Harold Bloom, ed., *Jonathan Swift's Gulliver's Travels* (1986). R. A. Greenberg, ed., *Gulliver's Travels* (1970), is annotated and includes critical essays.

PRONOUNCING GLOSSARY

The following list uses common English syllables and stress accents to provide rough equivalents of selected words whose pronunciation may be unfamiliar to the general reader.

Brobdingrag: *brahb'-ding-rag*   Lilliput: *lil-ee-put*

Houyhnhnm: *whin'-im*   Psalmanazar: *sahl-mahn'-ah-zahr*

From Gulliver's Travels[1]

A Letter from Captain Gulliver to His Cousin Sympson[2]

I hope you will be ready to own publicly, whenever you shall be called to it, that by your great and frequent urgency you prevailed on me to publish a very loose and uncorrect account of my travels; with direction to hire some young gentlemen of either University to put them in order, and correct the style, as my Cousin Dampier[3] did by my advice, in his book called *A Voyage round the World*. But I do not remember I gave you power to consent that anything should be omitted, and much less that anything should be inserted: therefore, as to the latter, I do here renounce everything of that kind; particularly a paragraph about her Majesty the late Queen Anne, of most pious and glorious memory; although I did reverence and esteem her more than

---

1. Swift's full title for this work was *Travels into Several Remote Nations of the World. In Four Parts. By Lemuel Gulliver, First a Surgeon, and then a Captain of several Ships.* The text is based on the Dublin edition of Swift's work (1735).   2. In this letter, first published in 1735, Swift complains, among other matters, of the alterations in his original text made by the publisher, Benjamin Motte, in the interest of what he considered political discretion.   3. William Dampier (1652–1715), the explorer, whose account of his circumnavigation of the globe Swift had read.

any of human species. But you, or your interpolator, ought to have considered that as it was not my inclination, so was it not decent to praise any animal of our composition before my master Houyhnhnm; and besides, the fact was altogether false; for to my knowledge, being in England during some part of her Majesty's reign, she did govern by a chief Minister; nay, even by two successively; the first whereof was the Lord of Godolphin, and the second the Lord of Oxford; so that you have made me *say the thing that was not*. Likewise, in the account of the Academy of Projectors, and several passages of my discourse to my master Houyhnhnm, you have either omitted some material circumstances, or minced or changed them in such a manner, that I do hardly know mine own work. When I formerly hinted to you something of this in a letter, you were pleased to answer that you were afraid of giving offense; that people in power were very watchful over the press; and apt not only to interpret, but to punish everything which looked like an *inuendo* (as I think you called it). But pray, how could that which I spoke so many years ago, and at above five thousand leagues distance, in another reign, be applied to any of the Yahoos, who now are said to govern the herd; especially, at a time when I little thought on or feared the unhappiness of living under them. Have not I the most reason to complain, when I see these very Yahoos carried by Houyhnhnms in a vehicle, as if these were brutes, and those the rational creatures? And, indeed, to avoid so monstrous and detestable a sight was one principal motive of my retirement hither.[4]

Thus much I thought proper to tell you in relation to yourself, and to the trust I reposed in you.

I do in the next place complain of my own great want of judgment, in being prevailed upon by the intreaties and false reasonings of you and some others, very much against mine own opinion, to suffer my travels to be published. Pray bring to your mind how often I desired you to consider, when you insisted on the motive of public good, that the Yahoos were a species of animals utterly incapable of amendment by precepts or examples; and so it hath proved; for instead of seeing a full stop put to all abuses and corruptions, at least in this little island, as I had reason to expect, behold, after above six months warning. I cannot learn that my book hath produced one single effect according to mine intentions; I desired you would let me know by a letter, when party and faction were extinguished; judges learned and upright; pleaders honest and modest, with some tincture of common sense; and Smithfield[5] blazing with pyramids of law books; the young nobility's education entirely changed; the physicians banished; the female Yahoos abounding in virtue, honor, truth, and good sense; courts and levees of great ministers thoroughly weeded and swept; wit, merit, and learning rewarded; all disgracers of the press in prose and verse, condemned to eat nothing but their own cotton,[6] and quench their thirst with their own ink. These, and a thousand other reformations, I firmly counted upon by your encouragement; as indeed they were plainly deducible from the precepts delivered in my book. And, it must be owned that seven months were a sufficient time to correct every vice and folly to which Yahoos are subject; if their natures had been capable of the least disposition to virtue or wisdom; yet so far have you been from answering

---

4. To Nottinghamshire in central England.   5. An area of London, used in the sixteenth century for burning heretics, that should now be used (Swift implies) to burn the incentives to litigation.   6. The fiber favored for paper making.

mine expectation in any of your letters, that on the contrary, you are loading our carrier every week with libels, and keys, and reflections, and memoirs, and second parts; wherein I see myself accused of reflecting upon great statesfolk; of degrading human nature (for so they have still the confidence to style it) and of abusing the female sex. I find likewise, that the writers of those bundles are not agreed among themselves; for some of them will not allow me to be author of mine own travels; and others make me author of books to which I am wholly a stranger.

I find likewise that your printer hath been so careless as to confound the times, and mistake the dates of my several voyages and returns; neither assigning the true year, or the true month, or day of the month; and I hear the original manuscript is all destroyed, since the publication of my book. Neither have I any copy left; however, I have sent you some corrections, which you may insert, if ever there should be a second edition; and yet I cannot stand to them, but shall leave that matter to my judicious and candid readers, to adjust it as they please.

I hear some of our sea Yahoos find fault with my sea language, as not proper in many parts, nor now in use. I cannot help it. In my first voyages, while I was young, I was instructed by the oldest mariners, and learned to speak as they did. But I have since found that the sea Yahoos are apt, like the land ones, to become new fangled in their words; which the latter change every year; insomuch, as I remember upon each return to mine own country, their old dialect was so altered, that I could hardly understand the new. And I observe, when any Yahoo comes from London out of curiosity to visit me at mine own house, we neither of us are able to deliver our conceptions in a manner intelligible to the other.

If the censure of Yahoos could any way affect me, I should have great reason to complain that some of them are so bold as to think my book of travels a mere fiction out of mine own brain; and have gone so far as to drop hints that the Houyhnhnms and Yahoos have no more existence than the inhabitants of Utopia.

Indeed I must confess that as to the people of Lilliput, Brobdingrag (for so the word should have been spelled, and not erroneously Brobdingnag) and Laputa, I have never yet heard of any Yahoo so presumptuous as to dispute their being, or the facts I have related concerning them; because the truth immediately strikes every reader with conviction. And, is there less probability in my account of the Houyhnhnms or Yahoos, when it is manifest as to the latter, there are so many thousands even in this city, who only differ from their brother brutes in Houyhnhnmland, because they use a sort of a jabber, and do not go naked. I wrote for their amendment, and not their approbation. The united praise of the whole race would be of less consequence to me, than the neighing of those two degenerate Houyhnhnms I keep in my stable; because, from these, degenerate as they are, I still improve in some virtues, without any mixture of vice.

Do these miserable animals presume to think that I am so far degenerated as to defend my veracity; Yahoo as I am, it is well known through all Houyhnhnmland, that by the instructions and example of my illustrious master, I was able in the compass of two years (although I confess with the utmost difficulty) to remove that infernal habit of lying, shuffling, deceiving, and equivocating, so deeply rooted in the very souls of all my species; especially the Europeans.

I have other complaints to make upon this vexatious occasion; but I forbear troubling myself or you any further. I must freely confess that since my last return, some corruptions of my Yahoo nature have revived in me by conversing with a few of your species, and particularly those of mine own family, by an unavoidable necessity; else I should never have attempted so absurd a project as that of reforming the Yahoo race in this kingdom; but I have now done with all such visionary schemes for ever.

The Publisher to the Reader

The author of these travels, Mr. Lemuel Gulliver, is my ancient and intimate friend; there is likewise some relation between us by the mother's side. About three years ago Mr. Gulliver, growing weary of the concourse of curious people coming to him at his house in Redriff,[7] made a small purchase of land, with a convenient house, near Newark, in Nottinghamshire, his native country; where he now lives retired, yet in good esteem among his neighbors.

Although Mr. Gulliver were born in Nottinghamshire, where his father dwelt, yet I have heard him say his family came from Oxfordshire; to confirm which, I have observed in the churchyard at Banbury, in that county, several tombs and monuments of the Gullivers.

Before he quitted Redriff, he left the custody of the following papers in my hands, with the liberty to dispose of them as I should think fit. I have carefully perused them three times; the style is very plain and simple; and the only fault I find is that the author, after the manner of travelers, is a little too circumstantial. There is an air of truth apparent through the whole; and indeed the author was so distinguished for his veracity, that it became a sort of proverb among his neighbors at Redriff, when anyone affirmed a thing, to say, it was as true as if Mr. Gulliver had spoke it.

By the advice of several worthy persons, to whom, with the author's permission, I communicated these papers, I now venture to send them into the world; hoping they may be, at least for some time, a better entertainment to our young noblemen, than the common scribbles of politics and party.

This volume would have been at least twice as large, if I had not made bold to strike out innumerable passages relating to the winds and tides, as well as to the variations and bearings in the several voyages; together with the minute descriptions of the management of the ship in storms, in the style of sailors; likewise the account of the longitudes and latitudes, wherein I have reason to apprehend that Mr. Gulliver may be a little dissatisfied; but I was resolved to fit the work as much as possible to the general capacity of readers. However, if my own ignorance in sea affairs shall have led me to commit some mistakes, I alone am answerable for them; and if any traveler hath a curiosity to see the whole work at large, as it came from the hand of the author, I will be ready to gratify him.

As for any further particulars relating to the author, the reader will receive satisfaction from the first pages of the book.

RICHARD SYMPSON

7. Rotherhithe, a district in south London then frequented by sailors.

Part IV

A Voyage to the Country of the Houyhnhnms[8]

CHAPTER I

The Author sets out as Captain of a ship. His men conspire against him, confine him a long time to his cabin, set him on shore in an unknown land. He travels up into the country. The Yahoos, a strange sort of animal, described. The Author meets two Houyhnhnms.

I continued at home with my wife and children about five months in a very happy condition, if I could have learned the lesson of knowing when I was well. I left my poor wife big with child, and accepted an advantageous offer made me to be Captain of the *Adventure*, a stout merchantman of 350 tons; for I understood navigation well, and being grown weary of a surgeon's employment at sea, which however I could exercise upon occasion, I took a skillful young man of that calling, one Robert Purefoy, into my ship. We set sail from Portsmouth upon the 7th day of September, 1710; on the 14th we met with Captain Pocock of Bristol, at Tenariff, who was going to the Bay of Campeachy[9] to cut logwood. On the 16th he was parted from us by a storm; I heard since my return that his ship foundered and none escaped, but one cabin boy. He was an honest man and a good sailor, but a little too positive in his own opinions, which was the cause of his destruction, as it hath been of several others. For if he had followed my advice, he might at this time have been safe at home with his family as well as myself.

I had several men died in my ship of calentures,[1] so that I was forced to get recruits out of Barbadoes and the Leeward Islands,[2] where I touched by the direction of the merchants who employed me; which I had soon too much cause to repent, for I found afterwards that most of them had been buccaneers. I had fifty hands on board; and my orders were that I should trade with the Indians in the South Sea, and make what discoveries I could. These rogues whom I had picked up debauched my other men, and they all formed a conspiracy to seize the ship and secure me; which they did one morning, rushing into my cabin, and binding me hand and foot, threatening to throw me overboard, if I offered to stir. I told them I was their prisoner, and would submit. This they made me swear to do, and then unbound me, only fastening one of my legs with a chain near my bed, and placed a sentry at my door with his piece charged, who was commanded to shoot me dead if I attempted my liberty. They sent me down victuals and drink, and took the government of the ship to themselves. Their design was to turn pirates and plunder the Spaniards, which they could not do, till they got more men. But first they resolved to sell the goods in the ship, and then go to Madagascar for recruits, several among them having died since my confinement. They sailed many weeks, and traded with the Indians; but I knew not what course they took, being kept close prisoner in my cabin, and expecting nothing less than to be murdered, as they often threatened me.

8. The word suggests the sound of a horse neighing.   9. Probably Campeche, in southeast Mexico, on the western side of the Yucatán peninsula. Tenariff (now Tenerife) is the largest of the Canary Islands, off northwest Africa in the Atlantic.   1. Tropical fever.   2. The northern group of the Lesser Antilles in the West Indies, extending southeast from Puerto Rico. Barbados is the easternmost of the West Indies.

Upon the 9th day of May, 1711, one James Welch came down to my cabin; and said he had orders from the Captain to set me ashore. I expostulated with him, but in vain; neither would he so much as tell me who their new Captain was. They forced me into the longboat, letting me put on my best suit of clothes, which were as good as new, and a small bundle of linen, but no arms except my hanger;[3] and they were so civil as not to search my pockets, into which I conveyed what money I had, with some other little necessaries. They rowed about a league, and then set me down on a strand. I desired them to tell me what country it was; they all swore, they knew no more than myself, but said that the Captain (as they called him) was resolved, after they had sold the lading, to get rid of me in the first place where they discovered land. They pushed off immediately, advising me to make haste, for fear of being overtaken by the tide, and bade me farewell.

In this desolate condition I advanced forward, and soon got upon firm ground, where I sat down on a bank to rest myself, and consider what I had best to do. When I was a little refreshed, I went up into the country, resolving to deliver myself to the first savages I should meet, and purchase my life from them by some bracelets, glass rings, and other toys, which sailors usually provide themselves with in those voyages, and whereof I had some about me. The land was divided by long rows of trees, not regularly planted, but naturally growing; there was great plenty of grass, and several fields of oats. I walked very circumspectly for fear of being surprised, or suddenly shot with an arrow from behind, or on either side. I fell into a beaten road, where I saw many tracks of human feet, and some of cows, but most of horses. At last I beheld several animals in a field, and one or two of the same kind sitting in trees. Their shape was very singular, and deformed, which a little discomposed me, so that I lay down behind a thicket to observe them better. Some of them coming forward near the place where I lay, gave me an opportunity of distinctly marking their form. Their heads and breasts were covered with a thick hair, some frizzled and others lank; they had beards like goats, and a long ridge of hair down their backs, and the fore parts of their legs and feet; but the rest of their bodies were bare, so that I might see their skins, which were of a brown buff color. They had no tails, nor any hair at all on their buttocks, except about the anus; which, I presume Nature had placed there to defend them as they sat on the ground; for this posture they used, as well as lying down, and often stood on their hind feet. They climbed high trees, as nimbly as a squirrel, for they had strong extended claws before and behind, terminating in sharp points, and hooded.[4] They would often spring, and bound, and leap with prodigious agility. The females were not so large as the males; they had long lank hair on their heads, and only a sort of down on the rest of their bodies, except about the anus, and pudenda. Their dugs hung between their forefeet, and often reached almost to the ground as they walked. The hair of both sexes was of several colors, brown, red, black, and yellow. Upon the whole, I never beheld in all my travels so disagreeable an animal, or one against which I naturally conceived so strong an antipathy. So that thinking I had seen enough, full of contempt and aversion, I got up and pursued the beaten road, hoping it might direct me to the cabin of some Indian: I had not gone far when I met one of these creatures full in my way, and coming up directly to me. The ugly monster, when he saw me, distorted

---

3. A small sword.   4. Concealed, or sheathed by flesh.

several ways every feature of his visage, and stared as at an object he had never seen before; then approaching nearer, lifted up his forepaw, whether out of curiosity or mischief, I could not tell; but I drew my hanger, and gave him a good blow with the flat side of it; for I durst not strike him with the edge, fearing the inhabitants might be provoked against me, if they should come to know that I had killed or maimed any of their cattle. When the beast felt the smart, he drew back, and roared so loud, that a herd of at least forty came flocking about me from the next field, howling and making odious faces; but I ran to the body of a tree, and leaning my back against it, kept them off, by waving my hanger. Several of this cursed brood getting hold of the branches behind, leaped up into the tree, from whence they began to discharge their excrements on my head; however, I escaped pretty well, by sticking close to the stem of the tree, but was almost stifled with the filth, which fell about me on every side.

In the midst of this distress, I observed them all to run away on a sudden as fast as they could; at which I ventured to leave the tree, and pursue the road, wondering what it was that could put them into this fright. But looking on my left hand, I saw a horse walking softly in the field; which my persecutors having sooner discovered, was the cause of their flight. The horse started a little when he came near me, but soon recovering himself, looked full in my face with manifest tokens of wonder; he viewed my hands and feet, walking round me several times. I would have pursued my journey, but he placed himself directly in the way, yet looking with a very mild aspect, never offering the least violence. We stood gazing at each other for some time; at last I took the boldness, to reach my hand towards his neck, with a design to stroke it; using the common style and whistle of jockies when they are going to handle a strange horse. But, this animal seeming to receive my civilities with disdain, shook his head, and bent his brows, softly raising up his left forefoot to remove my hand. Then he neighed three or four times, but in so different a cadence, that I almost began to think he was speaking to himself in some language of his own.

While he and I were thus employed, another horse came up; who applying himself to the first in a very formal manner, they gently struck each other's right hoof before, neighing several times by turns, and varying the sound, which seemed to be almost articulate. They went some paces off, as if it were to confer together, walking side by side, backward and forward, like persons deliberating upon some affair of weight; but often turning their eyes towards me, as it were to watch that I might not escape. I was amazed to see such actions and behavior in brute beasts; and concluded with myself that if the inhabitants of this country were endued with a proportionable degree of reason, they must needs be the wisest people upon earth. This thought gave me so much comfort, that I resolved to go forward until I could discover some house or village, or meet with any of the natives, leaving the two horses to discourse together as they pleased. But the first, who was a dapple grey, observing me to steal off, neighed after me in so expressive a tone that I fancied myself to understand what he meant; whereupon I turned back, and came near him, to expect his farther commands; but concealing my fear as much as I could; for I began to be in some pain, how this adventure might terminate; and the reader will easily believe I did not much like my present situation.

The two horses came up close to me, looking with great earnestness upon my face and hands. The grey steed rubbed my hat all round with his right fore hoof, and discomposed it so much that I was forced to adjust it better, by taking it off, and settling it again; whereat both he and his companion (who was a brown bay) appeared to be much surprised; the latter felt the lappet of my coat, and finding it to hang loose about me, they both looked with new signs of wonder. He stroked my right hand, seeming to admire the softness, and color; but he squeezed it so hard between his hoof and his pastern,[5] that I was forced to roar; after which they both touched me with all possible tenderness. They were under great perplexity about my shoes and stockings, which they felt very often, neighing to each other, and using various gestures, not unlike those of a philosopher, when he would attempt to solve some new and difficult phenomenon.

Upon the whole, the behavior of these animals was so orderly and rational, so acute and judicious, that I at last concluded, they must needs be magicians, who had thus metamorphosed themselves upon some design; and seeing a stranger in the way, were resolved to divert themselves with him; or perhaps were really amazed at the sight of a man so very different in habit, feature, and complexion from those who might probably live in so remote a climate. Upon the strength of this reasoning, I ventured to address them in the following manner: "Gentlemen, if you be conjurers, as I have good cause to believe, you can understand any language; therefore I make bold to let your worships know that I am a poor distressed Englishman, driven by his misfortunes upon your coast; and I entreat one of you, to let me ride upon his back, as if he were a real horse, to some house or village, where I can be relieved. In return of which favor, I will make you a present of this knife and bracelet" (taking them out of my pocket). The two creatures stood silent while I spoke, seeming to listen with great attention; and when I had ended, they neighed frequently towards each other, as if they were engaged in serious conversation. I plainly observed, that their language expressed the passions very well, and the words might with little pains be resolved into an alphabet more easily than the Chinese.

I could frequently distinguish the word *Yahoo,* which was repeated by each of them several times; and although it were impossible for me to conjecture what it meant, yet while the two horses were busy in conversation, I endeavored to practice this word upon my tongue; and as soon as they were silent, I boldly pronounced "Yahoo" in a loud voice, imitating, at the same time, as near as I could, the neighing of a horse; at which they were both visibly surprised, and the grey repeated the same word twice, as if he meant to teach me the right accent, wherein I spoke after him as well as I could, and found myself perceivably to improve every time, although very far from any degree of perfection. Then the bay tried me with a second word, much harder to be pronounced; but reducing it to the English orthography, may be spelt thus *Houyhnhnm.* I did not succeed in this so well as the former, but after two or three farther trials, I had better fortune; and they both appeared amazed at my capacity.

After some farther discourse, which I then conjectured might relate to me, the two friends took their leaves, with the same compliment of striking each

5. The part of a horse's foot between the joint at the rear and the hoof.

other's hoof; and the grey made me signs that I should walk before him; wherein I thought it prudent to comply, till I could find a better director. When I offered to slacken my pace, he would cry, "Hhuun, Hhuun"; I guessed his meaning, and gave him to understand, as well as I could that I was weary, and not able to walk faster; upon which, he would stand a while to let me rest.

CHAPTER II

The Author conducted by a Houyhnhnm to his house. The house described. The Author's reception. The food of the Houyhnhnms. The Author in distress for want of meat is at last relieved. His manner of feeding in that country.

Having traveled about three miles, we came to a long kind of building, made of timber, stuck in the ground, and wattled across; the roof was low, and covered with straw. I now began to be a little comforted, and took out some toys, which travelers usually carry for presents to the savage Indians of America and other parts, in hopes the people of the house would be thereby encouraged to receive me kindly. The horse made me a sign to go in first; it was a large room with a smooth clay floor, and a rack and manger extending the whole length on one side. There were three nags, and two mares, not eating, but some of them sitting down upon their hams, which I very much wondered at; but wondered more to see the rest employed in domestic business; the last seemed but ordinary cattle; however this confirmed my first opinion, that a people who could so far civilize brute animals must needs excel in wisdom all the nations of the world. The grey came in just after, and thereby prevented any ill treatment, which the others might have given me. He neighed to them several times in a style of authority, and received answers.

Beyond this room there were three others, reaching the length of the house, to which you passed through three doors, opposite to each other, in the manner of a vista; we went through the second room towards the third; here the grey walked in first, beckoning me to attend; I waited in the second room, and got ready my presents, for the master and mistress of the house; they were two knives, three bracelets of false pearl, a small looking glass and a bead necklace. The horse neighed three or four times, and I waited to hear some answers in a human voice, but I heard no other returns than in the same dialect, only one or two a little shriller than his. I began to think that this house must belong to some person of great note among them, because there appeared so much ceremony before I could gain admittance. But, that a man of quality should be served all by horses, was beyond my comprehension. I feared my brain was disturbed by my sufferings and misfortunes; I roused myself, and looked about me in the room where I was left alone; this was furnished as the first, only after a more elegant manner. I rubbed my eyes often, but the same objects still occurred. I pinched my arms and sides, to awake myself, hoping I might be in a dream. I then absolutely concluded that all these appearances could be nothing else but necromancy and magic. But I had no time to pursue these reflections; for the grey horse came to the door, and made me a sign to follow him into the third room; where I saw a very comely mare, together with a colt and foal, sitting on their haunches, upon mats of straw, not unartfully made, and perfectly neat and clean.

The mare soon after my entrance, rose from her mat, and coming up close, after having nicely observed my hands and face, gave me a most contemptuous look; then turning to the horse, I heard the word Yahoo often repeated betwixt them; the meaning of which word I could not then comprehend, although it were the first I had learned to pronounce; but I was soon better informed, to my everlasting mortification: for the horse beckoning to me with his head, and repeating the word, "Hhuun, Hhuun," as he did upon the road, which I understood was to attend him, led me out into a kind of court, where was another building at some distance from the house. Here we entered, and I saw three of those detestable creatures, which I first met after my landing, feeding upon roots, and the flesh of some animals, which I afterwards found to be that of asses and dogs, and now and then a cow dead by accident or disease. They were all tied by the neck with strong withes,[6] fastened to a beam; they held their food between the claws of their forefeet, and tore it with their teeth.

The master horse ordered a sorrel nag, one of his servants, to untie the largest of these animals, and take him into a yard. The beast and I were brought close together; and our countenances diligently compared, both by master and servant, who thereupon repeated several times the word "Yahoo." My horror and astonishment are not to be described, when I observed, in this abominable animal, a perfect human figure; the face of it indeed was flat and broad, the nose depressed, the lips large, and the mouth wide; but these differences are common to all savage nations, where the lineaments of the countenance are distorted by the natives suffering their infants to lie groveling on the earth, or by carrying them on their backs, nuzzling with their face against the mother's shoulders. The forefeet of the Yahoo differed from my hands in nothing else but the length of the nails, the coarseness and brownness of the palms, and the hairiness on the backs. There was the same resemblance between our feet, with the same differences, which I knew very well, although the horses did not, because of my shoes and stockings; the same in every part of our bodies, except as to hairiness and color, which I have already described.

The great difficulty that seemed to stick with the two horses was to see the rest of my body so very different from that of a Yahoo, for which I was obliged to my clothes, whereof they had no conception; the sorrel nag offered me a root, which he held (after their manner, as we shall describe in its proper place) between his hoof and pastern; I took it in my hand, and having smelled it, returned it to him again as civilly as I could. He brought out of the Yahoo's kennel a piece of ass's flesh, but it smelled so offensively that I turned from it with loathing; he then threw it to the Yahoo, by whom it was greedily devoured. He afterwards showed me a wisp of hay, and a fetlock[7] full of oats; but I shook my head, to signify that neither of these were food for me. And indeed, I now apprehended that I must absolutely starve, if I did not get to some of my own species; for as to those filthy Yahoos, although there were few greater lovers of mankind, at that time, than myself, yet I confess I never saw any sensitive being so detestable on all accounts; and the more I came near them, the more hateful they grew, while I stayed in that country. This the master horse observed by my behavior, and therefore

6. Fibers braided into rope.   7. The joint at the back of a horse's foot, just above the hoof, in which the Houyhnhnm holds the oats.

sent the Yahoo back to his kennel. He then put his forehoof to his mouth, at which I was much surprised, although he did it with ease, and with a motion that appeared perfectly natural; and made other signs to know what I would eat; but I could not return him such an answer as he was able to apprehend; and if he had understood me, I did not see how it was possible to contrive any way for finding myself nourishment. While we were thus engaged, I observed a cow passing by; whereupon I pointed to her, and expressed a desire to let me go and milk her. This had its effect; for he led me back into the house, and ordered a mare-servant to open a room, where a good store of milk lay in earthen and wooden vessels, after a very orderly and cleanly manner. She gave me a large bowl full, of which I drank very heartily, and found myself well refreshed.

About noon I saw coming towards the house a kind of vehicle, drawn like a sledge by four Yahoos. There was in it an old steed, who seemed to be of quality; he alighted with his hind feet forward, having by accident got a hurt in his left forefoot. He came to dine with our horse, who received him with great civility. They dined in the best room, and had oats boiled in milk for the second course, which the old horse eat warm, but the rest cold. Their mangers were placed circular in the middle of the room, and divided into several partitions, round which they sat on their haunches upon bosses of straw. In the middle was a large rack with angles answering to every partition of the manger. So that each horse and mare eat their own hay, and their own mash of oats and milk, with much decency and regularity. The behavior of the young colt and foal appeared very modest; and that of the master and mistress extremely cheerful and complaisant to their guest. The grey ordered me to stand by him; and much discourse passed between him and his friend concerning me, as I found by the stranger's often looking on me, and the frequent repetition of the word Yahoo.

I happened to wear my gloves; which the master grey observing, seemed perplexed; discovering signs of wonder what I had done to my forefeet; he put his hoof three or four times to them, as if he would signify, that I should reduce them to their former shape, which I presently did, pulling off both my gloves, and putting them into my pocket. This occasioned farther talk, and I saw the company was pleased with my behavior, whereof I soon found the good effects. I was ordered to speak the few words I understood; and while they were at dinner, the master taught me the names for oats, milk, fire, water, and some others which I could readily pronounce after him, having from my youth a great facility in learning languages.

When dinner was done, the master horse took me aside, and by signs and words made me understand the concern he was in that I had nothing to eat. Oats in their tongue are called *hlunnh*. This word I pronounced two or three times; for although I had refused them at first, yet upon second thoughts, I considered that I could contrive to make a kind of bread, which might be sufficient with milk to keep me alive, till I could make my escape to some other country, and to creatures of my own species. The horse immediately ordered a white mare-servant of his family to bring me a good quantity of oats in a sort of wooden tray. These I heated before the fire as well as I could, and rubbed them till the husks came off, which I made a shift to winnow from the grain; I ground and beat them between two stones, then took water, and made them into a paste or cake, which I toasted at the fire, and eat warm with milk. It was at first a very insipid diet, although common enough in many parts of Europe, but grew tolerable by time; and having been often reduced to hard fare in my life, this was not the first experiment I had made how easily nature is satisfied. And I cannot but observe that I never had one hour's sickness, while I staid in this island. It is true, I sometimes made a shift to catch a rabbit, or bird, by springes made of Yahoos' hairs; and I often gathered wholesome herbs, which I boiled, or ate as salads with my bread; and now and then, for a rarity, I made a little butter, and drank the whey. I was at first at a great loss for salt; but custom soon reconciled the want of it; and I am confident that the frequent use of salt among us is an effect of luxury, and was first introduced only as a provocative to drink; except where it is necessary for preserving of flesh in long voyages, or in places remote from great markets. For we observe no animal to be fond of it but man;[8] and as to myself, when I left this country, it was a great while before I could endure the taste of it in anything that I eat.

This is enough to say upon the subject of my diet, wherewith other travelers fill their books, as if the readers were personally concerned whether we fare well or ill. However, it was necessary to mention this matter, lest the world should think it impossible that I could find sustenance for three years in such a country, and among such inhabitants.

When it grew towards evening, the master horse ordered a place for me to lodge in; it was but six yards from the house, and separated from the stable of the Yahoos. Here I got some straw, and covering myself with my own clothes, slept very sound. But I was in a short time better accommodated, as the reader shall know hereafter, when I come to treat more particularly about my way of living.

CHAPTER III

The Author studious to learn the language, the Houyhnhnm his master assists in teaching him. The language described. Several Houyhnhnms of quality come out of curiosity to see the Author. He gives his master a short account of his voyage.

My principal endeavor was to learn the language, which my master (for so I shall henceforth call him) and his children, and every servant of his house were desirous to teach me. For they looked upon it as a prodigy, that a brute animal should discover such marks of a rational creature. I pointed to everything, and enquired the name of it, which I wrote down in my journal book when I was alone, and corrected my bad accent, by desiring those of the family to pronounce it often. In this employment, a sorrel nag, one of the under servants, was very ready to assist me.

In speaking, they pronounce through the nose and throat, and their language approaches nearest to the High Dutch or German, of any I know in Europe; but is much more graceful and significant. The Emperor Charles V made almost the same observation, when he said, that if he were to speak to his horse, it should be in High Dutch.[9]

The curiosity and impatience of my master were so great, that he spent

---

8. Gulliver's error; many animals are very fond of salt.　　9. Charles was reputed to have said he would address God in Spanish, women in Italian, men in French, and his horse in German.

many hours of his leisure to instruct me. He was convinced (as he afterwards told me) that I must be a Yahoo, but my teachableness, civility, and cleanliness astonished him; which were qualities altogether so opposite to those animals. He was most perplexed about my clothes, reasoning sometimes with himself whether they were a part of my body; for I never pulled them off till the family were asleep, and got them on before they waked in the morning. My master was eager to learn from whence I came; how I acquired those appearances of reason, which I discovered in all my actions; and to know my story from my own mouth, which he hoped he should soon do by the great proficiency I made in learning and pronouncing their words and sentences. To help my memory, I formed all I learned into the English alphabet, and writ the words down with the translations. This last, after some time, I ventured to do in my master's presence. It cost me much trouble to explain to him what I was doing; for the inhabitants have not the least idea of books or literature.

In about ten weeks time I was able to understand most of his questions; and in three months could give him some tolerable answers. He was extremely curious to know from what part of the country I came, and how I was taught to imitate a rational creature; because the Yahoos (whom he saw I exactly resembled in my head, hands, and face, that were only visible) with some appearance of cunning, and the strongest disposition to mischief, were observed to be the most unteachable of all brutes. I answered that I came over the sea, from a far place, with many others of my own kind, in a great hollow vessel made of the bodies of trees; that my companions forced me to land on this coast, and then left me to shift for myself. It was with some difficulty, and by the help of many signs, that I brought him to understand me. He replied that I must needs be mistaken, or that I *said the thing which was not.* (For they have no word in their language to express lying or falsehood.) He knew it was impossible that there could be a country beyond the sea, or that a parcel of brutes could move a wooden vessel whither they pleased upon water. He was sure no Houyhnhnm alive could make such a vessel, or would trust Yahoos to manage it.

The word Houyhnhnm, in their tongue, signifies a Horse; and in its etymology, the Perfection of Nature. I told my master that I was at a loss for expression, but would improve as fast as I could; and hoped in a short time I should be able to tell him wonders; he was pleased to direct his own mare, his colt, and foal, and the servants of the family to take all opportunities of instructing me; and every day for two or three hours, he was at the same pains himself; several horses and mares of quality in the neighborhood came often to our house, upon the report spread of a wonderful Yahoo, that could speak like a Houyhnhnm, and seemed in his words and actions to discover some glimmerings of reason. These delighted to converse with me; they put many questions, and received such answers as I was able to return. By all which advantages, I made so great a progress, that in five months from my arrival, I understood whatever was spoke, and could express myself tolerably well.

The Houyhnhnms who came to visit my master, out of a design of seeing and talking with me, could hardly believe me to be a right Yahoo, because my body had a different covering from others of my kind. They were astonished to observe me without the usual hair or skin, except on my head, face, and hands; but I discovered that secret to my master, upon an accident, which happened about a fortnight before.

I have already told the reader, that every night when the family were gone to bed, it was my custom to strip and cover myself with my clothes; it happened one morning early, that my master sent for me, by the sorrel nag, who was his valet; when he came, I was fast asleep, my clothes fallen off on one side, and my shirt above my waist. I awaked at the noise he made, and observed him to deliver his message in some disorder; after which he went to my master, and in a great fright gave him a very confused account of what he had seen; this I presently discovered; for going as soon as I was dressed, to pay my attendance upon his honor, he asked me the meaning of what his servant had reported; that I was not the same thing when I slept as I appeared to be at other times; that his valet assured him, some part of me was white, some yellow, at least not so white, and some brown.

I had hitherto concealed the secret of my dress, in order to distinguish myself as much as possible, from that cursed race of Yahoos; but now I found it in vain to do so any longer. Besides, I considered that my clothes and shoes would soon wear out, which already were in a declining condition, and must be supplied by some contrivance from the hides of Yahoos, or other brutes; whereby the whole secret would be known. I therefore told my master, that in the country from whence I came, those of my kind always covered their bodies with the hairs of certain animals prepared by art, as well for decency, as to avoid inclemencies of air both hot and cold; of which, as to my own person I would give him immediate conviction, if he pleased to command me; only desiring this excuse, if I did not expose those parts that nature taught us to conceal. He said, my discourse was all very strange, but especially the last part; for he could not understand why Nature should teach us to conceal what Nature had given. That neither himself nor family were ashamed of any parts of their bodies; but however I might do as I pleased. Whereupon, I first unbuttoned my coat, and pulled it off. I did the same with my waistcoat; I drew off my shoes, stockings, and breeches. I let my shirt down to my waist, and drew up the bottom, fastening it like a girdle about my middle to hide my nakedness.

My master observed the whole performance with great signs of curiosity and admiration. He took up all my clothes in his pastern, one piece after another, and examined them diligently; he then stroked my body very gently, and looked round me several times; after which he said, it was plain I must be a perfect Yahoo; but that I differed very much from the rest of my species, in the whiteness and smoothness of my skin, my want of hair in several parts of my body, the shape and shortness of my claws behind and before, and my affectation of walking continually on my two hinder feet. He desired to see no more; and gave me leave to put on my clothes again, for I was shuddering with cold.

I expressed my uneasiness at his giving me so often the appellation of Yahoo, an odious animal, for which I had so utter an hatred and contempt. I begged he would forbear applying that word to me, and take the same order in his family, and among his friends whom he suffered to see me. I requested likewise, that the secret of my having a false covering to my body might be known to none but himself, at least as long as my present clothing should last; for as to what the sorrel nag his valet had observed, his honor might command him to conceal it.

All this my master very graciously consented to; and thus the secret was kept till my clothes began to wear out, which I was forced to supply by several contrivances, that shall hereafter be mentioned. In the meantime, he desired I would go on with my utmost diligence to learn their language, because he was more astonished at my capacity for speech and reason, than at the figure of my body, whether it were covered or no; adding that he waited with some impatience to hear the wonders which I promised to tell him.

From thenceforward he doubled the pains he had been at to instruct me; he brought me into all company, and made them treat me with civility, because, as he told them privately, this would put me into good humor, and make me more diverting.

Every day when I waited on him, beside the trouble he was at in teaching, he would ask me several questions concerning myself, which I answered as well as I could; and by those means he had already received some general ideas, although very imperfect. It would be tedious to relate the several steps, by which I advanced to a more regular conversation, but the first account I gave of myself in any order and length was to this purpose:

That, I came from a very far country, as I already had attempted to tell him, with about fifty more of my own species; that we traveled upon the seas, in a great hollow vessel made of wood, and larger than his honor's house. I described the ship to him in the best terms I could; and explained by the help of my handkerchief displayed, how it was driven forward by the wind. That, upon a quarrel among us, I was set on shore on this coast, where I walked forward without knowing whither, till he delivered me from the persecution of those execrable Yahoos. He asked me who made the ship, and how it was possible that the Houyhnhnms of my country would leave it to the management of brutes? My answer was that I durst proceed no farther in my relation, unless he would give me his word and honor that he would not be offended; and then I would tell him the wonders I had so often promised. He agreed; and I went on by assuring him, that the ship was made by creatures like myself, who in all the countries I had traveled, as well as in my own, were the only governing, rational animals; and that upon my arrival hither, I was as much astonished to see the Houyhnhnms act like rational begins, as he or his friends could be in finding some marks of reason in a creature he was pleased to call a Yahoo; to which I owned my resemblance in every part, but could not account for their degenerate and brutal nature. I said farther, that if good fortune ever restored me to my native country, to relate my travels hither, as I resolved to do; everybody would believe that I *said the thing which was not*; that I invented the story out of my own head; and with all possible respect to himself, his family, and friends, and under his promise of not being offended, our countrymen would hardly think it probable, that a Houyhnhnm should be the presiding creature of a nation, and a Yahoo the brute.

CHAPTER IV

The Houyhnhnms' notion of truth and falsehood. The author's discourse disapproved by his master. The author gives a more particular account of himself, and the accidents of his voyages.

My master heard me with great appearances of uneasiness in his countenance; because *doubting* or *not believing* are so little known in this country, that the inhabitants cannot tell how to behave themselves under such circumstances. And I remember in frequent discourses with my master concerning the nature of manhood, in other parts of the world, having occasion to talk of *lying* and *false representation,* it was with much difficulty that he comprehended what I meant; although he had otherwise a most acute judgment. For he argued thus: that the use of speech was to make us understand one another, and to receive information of facts; now if anyone *said the thing which was not,* these ends were defeated; because I cannot properly be said to understand him; and I am so far from receiving information, that he leaves me worse than in ignorance; for I am led to believe a thing *black* when it is *white,* and *short* when it is *long.* And these were all the notions he had concerning that faculty of *lying,* so perfectly well understood, and so universally practiced among human creatures.

To return from this digression; when I asserted that the Yahoos were the only governing animals in my country, which my master said was altogether past his conception, he desired to know, whether we had Houyhnhnms among us, and what was their employment; I told him we had great numbers; that in summer they grazed in the fields, and in winter were kept in houses, with hay and oats, where Yahoo servants were employed to rub their skins smooth, comb their manes, pick their feet, serve them with food, and make their beds. "I understand you well," said my master; "it is now very plain from all you have spoken, that whatever share of reason the Yahoos pretend to, the Houyhnhnms are your masters; I heartily wish our Yahoos would be so tractable." I begged his honor would please to excuse me from proceeding any farther, because I was very certain that the account he expected from me would be highly displeasing. But he insisted in commanding me to let him know the best and the worst; I told him he should be obeyed. I owned that the Houyhnhnms among us, whom we called Horses, were the most generous[1] and comely animal we had; that they excelled in strength and swiftness; and when they belonged to persons of quality, employed in traveling, racing, and drawing chariots, they were treated with much kindness and care, till they fell into diseases, or became foundered in the feet; but then they were sold, and used to all kind of drudgery till they died; after which their skins were stripped and sold for what they were worth, and their bodies left to be devoured by dogs and birds of prey. But the common race of horses had not so good fortune, being kept by farmers and carriers, and other mean people, who put them to greater labor, and fed them worse. I described as well as I could, our way of riding; the shape and use of a bridle, a saddle, a spur, and a whip; of harness and wheels. I added, that we fastened plates of a certain hard substance called iron at the bottom of their feet, to

1. Noble.

preserve their hoofs from being broken by the stony ways on which we often traveled.

My master, after some expressions of great indignation, wondered how we dared to venture upon a Houyhnhnm's back; for he was sure, that the weakest servant in his house would be able to shake off the strongest Yahoo; or by lying down, and rolling upon his back, squeeze the brute to death. I answered that our horses were trained up from three or four years old to the several uses we intended them for; that if any of them proved intolerably vicious, they were employed for carriages; that they were severely beaten while they were young for any mischievous tricks; that the males, designed for the common use of riding or draught, were generally castrated about two years after their birth, to take down their spirits, and make them more tame and gentle; that they were indeed sensible of rewards and punishments; but his honor would please to consider that they had not the least tincture of reason any more than the Yahoos in this country.

It put me to the pains of many circumlocutions to give my master a right idea of what I spoke; for their language doth not abound in variety of words, because their wants and passions are fewer than among us. But it is impossible to express his noble resentment at our savage treatment of the Houyhnhnm race; particularly after I had explained the manner and use of castrating horses among us, to hinder them from propagating their kind, and to render them more servile. He said, if it were possible there could be any country where Yahoos alone were endued with reason, they certainly must be the governing animal, because reason will in time always prevail against brutal strength. But, considering the frame of our bodies, and especially of mine, he thought no creature of equal bulk was so ill-contrived for employing that reason in the common offices of life; whereupon he desired to know whether those among whom I lived resembled me or the Yahoos of his country. I assured him that I was as well shaped as most of my age; but the younger and the females were much more soft and tender, and the skins of the latter generally as white as milk. He said I differed indeed from other Yahoos, being much more cleanly, and not altogether so deformed; but in point of real advantage, he thought I differed for the worse. That my nails were of no use either to my fore or hinder feet; as to my forefeet, he could not properly call them by that name, for he never observed me to walk upon them; that they were too soft to bear the ground; that I generally went with them uncovered, neither was the covering I sometimes wore on them of the same shape, or so strong as that on my feet behind. That I could not walk with any security; for if either of my hinder feet slipped, I must inevitably fall. He then began to find fault with other parts of my body; the flatness of my face, the prominence of my nose, my eyes placed directly in front, so that I could not look on either side without turning my head; that I was not able to feed myself without lifting one of my forefeet to my mouth; and therefore nature had placed those joints to answer that necessity. He knew not what could be the use of those several clefts and divisions in my feet behind; that these were too soft to bear the hardness and sharpness of stones without a covering made from the skin of some other brute; that my whole body wanted a fence against heat and cold, which I was forced to put on and off every day with tediousness and trouble. And lastly, that he observed every animal in his country naturally to abhor the Yahoos, whom the weaker avoided, and the stronger drove from them. So that supposing us to have the gift of reason, he could not see how it were possible to cure that natural antipathy which every creature discovered against us; nor consequently, how we could tame and render them serviceable. However, he would (as he said) debate the matter no farther, because he was more desirous to know my own story, the country where I was born, and the several actions and events of my life before I came hither.

I assured him how extremely desirous I was that he should be satisfied in every point; but I doubted much whether it would be possible for me to explain myself on several subjects whereof his honor could have no conception, because I saw nothing in his country to which I could resemble them. That however, I would do my best, and strive to express myself by similitudes, humbly desiring his assistance when I wanted proper words; which he was pleased to promise me.

I said, my birth was of honest parents, in an island called England, which was remote from this country, as many days journey as the strongest of his honor's servants could travel in the annual course of the sun. That I was bred a surgeon, whose trade it is to cure wounds and hurts in the body, got by accident or violence. That my country was governed by a female man, whom we called a queen.[2] That I left it to get riches, whereby I might maintain myself and family when I should return. That in my last voyage, I was Commander of the ship and had about fifty Yahoos under me, many of which died at sea, and I was forced to supply them by others picked out from several nations. That our ship was twice in danger of being sunk; the first time by a great storm, and the second, by striking against a rock. Here my master interposed, by asking me, how I could persuade strangers out of different countries to venture with me, after the losses I had sustained, and the hazards I had run. I said, they were fellows of desperate fortunes, forced to fly from the places of their birth, on account of their poverty or their crimes. Some were undone by lawsuits; others spent all they had in drinking, whoring, and gaming; others fled for treason; many for murder, theft, poisoning, robbery, perjury, forgery, coining false money; for committing rapes or sodomy; for flying from their colors, or deserting to the enemy; and most of them had broken prison. None of these durst return to their native countries for fear of being hanged, or of starving in a jail; and therefore were under a necessity of seeking livelihood in other places.

During this discourse, my master was pleased often to interrupt me. I had made use of many circumlocutions in describing to him the nature of the several crimes, for which most of our crew had been forced to fly their country. This labor took up several days conversation before he was able to comprehend me. He was wholly at a loss to know what could be the use or necessity of practicing those vices. To clear up which I endeavored to give him some ideas of the desire of power and riches; of the terrible effects of lust, intemperance, malice, and envy. All this I was forced to define and describe by putting of cases, and making suppositions. After which, like one whose imagination was struck with something never seen or heard of before, he would lift up his eyes with amazement and indignation. Power, government, war, law, punishment, and a thousand other things had no terms,

---

2. Queen Anne (1665–1714), the last Stuart ruler.

wherein that language could express them; which made the difficulty almost insuperable to give my master any conception of what I meant; but being of an excellent understanding, much improved by contemplation and converse, he at last arrived at a competent knowledge of what human nature in our parts of the world is capable to perform; and desired I would give him some particular account of that land, which we call Europe, especially, of my own country.

CHAPTER V

The Author, at his master's commands, informs him of the state of England. The causes of war among the princes of Europe. The Author begins to explain the English Constitution.

The reader may please to observe that the following extract of many conversations I had with my master contains a summary of the most material points, which were discoursed at several times for above two years; his honor often desiring fuller satisfaction as I farther improved in the Houyhnhnm tongue. I laid before him, as well as I could, the whole state of Europe; I discoursed of trade and manufactures, of arts and sciences; and the answers I gave to all the questions he made, as they arose upon several subjects, were a fund of conversation not to be exhausted. But I shall here only set down the substance of what passed between us concerning my own country, reducing it into order as well as I can, without any regard to time or other circumstances, while I strictly adhere to truth. My only concern is that I shall hardly be able to do justice to my master's arguments and expressions; which must needs suffer by my want of capacity, as well as by a translation into our barbarous English.

In obedience therefore to his honor's commands, I related to him the Revolution under the Prince of Orange; the long war with France entered into by the said Prince, and renewed by his successor the present queen; wherein the greatest powers of Christendom were engaged, and which still continued. I computed at his request, that about a million of Yahoos might have been killed in the whole progress of it; and perhaps a hundred or more cities taken, and five times as many ships burned or sunk.[3]

He asked me what were the usual causes or motives that made one country to go to war with another. I answered, they were innumerable; but I should only mention a few of the chief. Sometimes the ambition of princes, who never think they have land or people enough to govern; sometimes the corruption of ministers, who engage their master in a war in order to stifle or divert the clamor of the subjects against their evil administration. Difference in opinions hath cost many millions of lives; for instance, whether flesh be bread, or bread be flesh; whether the juice of a certain berry be blood or wine; whether whistling be a vice or a virtue; whether it be better to kiss a post, or throw it into the fire; what is the best color for a coat, whether black, white, red, or grey; and whether it should be long or short, narrow or wide, dirty or clean;[4] with many more. Neither are any wars so furious and bloody,

---

3. Gulliver relates recent English history: the Glorious Revolution of 1688 and the War of the Spanish Succession (1703–13). He greatly exaggerates the casualties in the war.   4. Gulliver refers to the religious controversies of the Reformation and Counter-Reformation: the doctrine of transubstantiation, the use of music in church services, the veneration of the Crucifix, and the wearing of priestly vestments.

or of so long continuance, as those occasioned by difference in opinion, especially if it be in things indifferent.

Sometimes the quarrel between two princes is to decide which of them shall dispossess a third of his dominions, where neither of them pretend to any right. Sometimes one prince quarreleth with another, for fear the other should quarrel with him. Sometimes a war is entered upon, because the enemy is too strong, and sometimes because he is too weak. Sometimes our neighbors want the things which we have, or have the things which we want; and we both fight, till they take ours or give us theirs. It is a very justifiable cause of war to invade a country after the people have been wasted by famine, destroyed by pestilence, or embroiled by factions amongst themselves. It is justifiable to enter into a war against our nearest ally, when one of his towns lies convenient for us, or a territory of land, that would render our dominions round and compact. If a prince send forces into a nation, where the people are poor and ignorant, he may lawfully put half of them to death, and make slaves of the rest, in order to civilize and reduce them from their barbarous way of living. It is a very kingly, honorable, and frequent practice, when one prince desires the assistance of another to secure him against an invasion, that the assistant, when he hath driven out the invader, should seize on the dominions himself, and kill, imprison, or banish the prince he came to relieve. Alliance by blood or marriage is a sufficient cause of war between princes; and the nearer the kindred is, the greater is their disposition to quarrel; poor nations are hungry, and rich nations are proud; and pride and hunger will ever be at variance. For these reasons, the trade of a soldier is held the most honorable of all others: because a soldier is a Yahoo hired to kill in cold blood as many of his own species, who have never offended him, as possibly he can.

There is likewise a kind of beggarly princes in Europe, not able to make war by themselves, who hire out their troops to richer nations for so much a day to each man; of which they keep three fourths to themselves, and it is the best part of their maintenance; such are those in many northern parts of Europe.

"What you have told me," said my master, "upon the subject of war, doth indeed discover most admirably the effects of that reason you pretend to; however, it is happy that the shame is greater than the danger; and that Nature hath left you utterly uncapable of doing much mischief; for your mouths lying flat with your faces, you can hardly bite each other to any purpose, unless by consent. Then, as to the claws upon your feet before and behind, they are so short and tender, that one of our Yahoos would drive a dozen of yours before him. And therefore in recounting the numbers of those who have been killed in battle, I cannot but think that you have *said the thing which is not.*"

I could not forebear shaking my head and smiling a little at his ignorance. And, being no stranger to the art of war, I gave him a description of cannons, culverins, muskets, carabines, pistols, bullets, powder, swords, bayonets, battles, sieges, retreats, attacks, undermines, countermines, bombardments, sea fights; ships sunk with a thousand men; twenty thousand killed on each side; dying groans, limbs flying in the air; smoke, noise, confusion, trampling to death under horses' feet; flight, pursuit, victory; fields strewed with carcasses left for food to dogs, and wolves, and birds of prey; plundering, stripping, ravishing, burning, and destroying. And, to set forth the valor of my own dear countrymen, I assured him that I had seen them blow up a hundred enemies at once in a siege, and as many in a ship; and beheld the dead bodies drop down in pieces from the clouds, to the great diversion of all the spectators.

I was going on to more particulars, when my master commanded me silence. He said, whoever understood the nature of Yahoos might easily believe it possible for so vile an animal, to be capable of every action I had named, if their strength and cunning equaled their malice. But, as my discourse had increased his abhorrence of the whole species, so he found it gave him a disturbance in his mind, to which he was wholly a stranger before. He thought his ears being used to such abominable words, might by degrees admit them with less detestation. That, although he hated the Yahoos of this country, yet he no more blamed them for their odious qualities, than he did a *gnnayh* (a bird of prey) for its cruelty, or a sharp stone for cutting his hoof. But, when a creature pretending to reason could be capable of such enormities, he dreaded lest the corruption of that faculty might be worse than brutality itself. He seemed therefore confident, that instead of reason, we were only possessed of some quality fitted to increase our natural vices; as the reflection from a troubled stream returns the image of an ill-shapen body, not only larger, but more distorted.

He added that he had heard too much upon the subject of war, both in this and some former discourses. There was another point which a little perplexed him at present. I had said that some of our crew left their country on account of being ruined by law: that I had already explained the meaning of the word; but he was at a loss how it should come to pass, that the law which was intended for every man's preservation, should be any man's ruin. Therefore he desired to be farther satisfied what I meant by law, and the dispensers thereof, according to the present practice in my own country; because he thought nature and reason were sufficient guides for a reasonable animal, as we pretended to be, in showing us what we ought to do, and what to avoid.

I assured his honor that law was a science wherein I had not much conversed, further than by employing advocates, in vain, upon some injustices that had been done me. However, I would give him all the satisfaction I was able.

I said there was a society of men among us, bred up from their youth in the art of proving by words multiplied for the purpose, that white is black, and black is white, according as they are paid. To this society all the rest of the people are slaves.

"For example. If my neighbor hath a mind to my cow, he hires a lawyer to prove that he ought to have my cow from me. I must then hire another to defend my right; it being against all rules of law that any man should be allowed to speak for himself. Now in this case, I who am the true owner lie under two great disadvantages. First, my lawyer being practiced almost from his cradle in defending falsehood is quite out of his element when he would be an advocate for justice, which as an office unnatural, he always attempts with great awkwardness, if not with ill-will. The second disadvantage is that my lawyer must proceed with great caution, or else he will be reprimanded by the judges, and abhorred by his breathren, as one who would lessen the practice of the law. And therefore I have but two methods to preserve my cow. The first is to gain over my adversary's lawyer with a double fee; who will then betray his client, by insinuating that he hath justice on his side. The second way is for my lawyer to make my cause appear as unjust as he can; by allowing the cow to belong to my adversary; and this if it be skillfully done, will certainly bespeak the favor of the bench.

"Now, your honor is to know that these judges are persons appointed to decide all controversies of property, as well as for the trial of criminals; and picked out from the most dextrous lawyers who are grown old or lazy; and having been biased all their lives against truth and equity, lie under such a fatal necessity of favoring fraud, perjury, and oppression, that I have known some of them to have refused a large bribe from the side where justice lay, rather than injure the faculty,[5] by doing anything unbecoming their nature or their office.

"It is a maxim among these lawyers, that whatever hath been done before may legally be done again; and therefore they take special care to record all the decisions formerly made against common justice and the general reason of mankind. These, under the name of *precedents*, they produce as authorities to justify the most iniquitous opinions; and the judges never fail of directing accordingly.

"In pleading, they studiously avoid entering into the merits of the cause; but are loud, violent, and tedious in dwelling upon all circumstances which are not to the purpose. For instance, in the case already mentioned, they never desire to know what claim or title my adversary hath to my cow; but whether the said cow were red or black; her horns long or short; whether the field I graze her in be round or square; whether she were milked at home or abroad; what diseases she is subject to, and the like. After which they consult precedents, adjourn the cause, from time to time, and in ten, twenty, or thirty years come to an issue.

"It is likewise to be observed, that this society hath a peculiar cant and jargon of their own, that no other mortal can understand, and wherein all their laws are written, which they take special care to multiply; whereby they have wholly confounded the very essence of truth and falsehood, of right and wrong; so that it will take thirty years to decide whether the field, left me by my ancestors for six generations, belong to me, or to a stranger three hundred miles off.

"In the trial of persons accused for crimes against the state, the method is much more short and commendable: the judge first sends to sound the disposition of those in power; after which he can easily hang or save the criminal, strictly preserving all the forms of law."

Here my master interposing said it was a pity that creatures endowed with such prodigious abilities of mind as these lawyers, by the description I gave of them must certainly be, were not rather encouraged to be instructors of others in wisdom and knowledge. In answer to which, I assured his honor that in all points out of their own trade, they were usually the most ignorant and stupid generation among us, the most despicable in common conversation, avowed enemies to all knowledge and learning; and equally disposed to pervert the general reason of mankind, in every other subject of discourse as in that of their own profession.

5. Profession.

CHAPTER VI

A continuation of the state of England, under Queen Anne. The character of a first minister in the courts of Europe.

My master was yet wholly at a loss to understand what motives could incite this race of lawyers to perplex, disquiet, and weary themselves by engaging in a confederacy of injustice, merely for the sake of injuring their fellow animals; neither could he comprehend what I meant in saying they did it for hire. Whereupon I was at much pains to describe to him the use of money, the materials it was made of, and the value of the metals; that when a Yahoo had got a great store of this precious substance, he was able to purchase whatever he had a mind to; the finest clothing, the noblest houses, great tracts of land, the most costly meats and drinks; and have his choice of the most beautiful females. Therefore since money alone was able to perform all these feats, our Yahoos thought they could never have enough of it to spend or to save, as they found themselves inclined from their natural bent either to profusion or avarice. That the rich man enjoyed the fruit of the poor man's labor, and the latter were a thousand to one in proportion to the former. That the bulk of our people was forced to live miserably, by laboring every day for small wages to make a few live plentifully. I enlarged myself much on these and many other particulars to the same purpose, but his honor was still to seek, for he went upon a supposition that all animals had a title to their share in the productions of the earth; and especially those who presided over the rest. Therefore he desired I would let him know what these costly meats were, and how any of us happened to want[6] them. Whereupon I enumerated as many sorts as came into my head, with the various methods of dressing them, which could not be done without sending vessels by sea to every part of the world, as well for liquors to drink, as for sauces, and innumerable other conveniencies. I assured him, that this whole globe of earth must be at least three times gone round, before one of our better female Yahoos could get her breakfast, or a cup to put it in. He said, "That must needs be a miserable country which cannot furnish food for its own inhabitants." But what he chiefly wondered at, was how such vast tracts of ground as I described, should be wholly without fresh water, and the people put to the necessity of sending over the sea for drink. I replied that England (the dear place of my nativity) was computed to produce three times the quantity of food, more than its inhabitants are able to consume, as well as liquors extracted from grain, or pressed out of the fruit of certain trees, which made excellent drink; and the same proportion in every other convenience of life. But, in order to feed the luxury and intemperance of the males, and the vanity of the females, we sent away the greatest part of our necessary things to other countries, from whence in return we brought the materials of diseases, folly, and vice, to spend among ourselves. Hence it follows of necessity, that vast numbers of our people are compelled to seek their livelihood by begging, robbing, stealing, cheating, pimping, foreswearing, flattering, suborning, forging, gaming, lying, fawning, hectoring, voting, scribbling, star gazing, poisoning, whoring, canting, libeling, freethinking, and the like occu-

6. Lack.

pations; every one of which terms, I was at much pains to make him understand.

That, wine was not imported among us from foreign countries, to supply the want of water or other drinks, but because it was a sort of liquid which made us merry, by putting us out of our senses; diverted all melancholy thoughts, begat wild extravagant imaginations in the brain, raised our hopes, and banished our fears; suspended every office of reason for a time, and deprived us of the use of our limbs, until we fell into a profound sleep; although it must be confessed, that we always awaked sick and dispirited; and that the use of this liquor filled us with diseases, which made our lives uncomfortable and short.

But beside all this, the bulk of our people supported themselves by furnishing the necessities or conveniencies of life to the rich, and to each other. For instance, when I am at home and dressed as I ought to be, I carry on my body the workmanship of an hundred tradesmen; the building and furniture of my house employ as many more; and five times the number to adorn my wife.

I was going on to tell him of another sort of people, who get their livelihood by attending the sick; having upon some occasions informed his honor that many of my crew had died of diseases. But here it was with the utmost difficulty that I brought him to apprehend what I meant. He could easily conceive that a Houyhnhnm grew weak and heavy a few days before his death; or by some accident might hurt a limb. But that nature, who worketh all things to perfection, should suffer any pains to breed in our bodies, he thought impossible; and desired to know the reason of so unaccountable an evil. I told him, we fed on a thousand things which operated contrary to each other; that we eat when we were not hungry, and drank without the provocation of thirst; that we sat whole nights drinking strong liquors without eating a bit, which disposed us to sloth, inflamed our bodies, and precipitated or prevented digestion. That, prostitute female Yahoos acquired a certain malady, which bred rottenness in the bones of those who fell into their embraces; that this and many other diseases were propagated from father to son; so that great numbers come into the world with complicated maladies upon them; that it would be endless to give him a catalogue of all diseases incident to human bodies; for they could not be fewer than five or six hundred, spread over every limb, and joint; in short, every part, external and intestine, having diseases appropriated to each. To remedy which, there was a sort of people bred up among us, in the profession or pretense of curing the sick. And because I had some skill in the faculty, I would in gratitude to his honor let him know the whole mystery and method by which they proceed.

Their fundamental is that all diseases arise from repletion; from whence they conclude, that a great evacuation of the body is necessary, either through the natural passage, or upwards at the mouth. Their next business is, from herbs, minerals, gums, oils, shells, salts, juices, seaweed, excrements, barks of trees, serpents, toads, frogs, spiders, dead men's flesh and bones, birds, beasts and fishes, to form a composition for smell and taste the most abominable, nauseous, and detestable, that they can possibly contrive, which the stomach immediately rejects with loathing, and this they call a vomit. Or else from the same storehouse, with some other poisonous additions, they command us to take in at the orifice above or below (just as the physician then happens to be disposed) a medicine equally annoying and disgustful to the bowels; which relaxing the belly, drives down all before it; and this they call a purge, or a clyster. For nature (as the physicians allege) having intended the superior anterior orifice only for the intromission of solids and liquids, and the inferior posterior for ejection, these artists ingeniously considering that in all diseases nature is forced out of her seat; therefore to replace her in it, the body must be treated in a manner directly contrary, but interchanging the use of each orifice; forcing solids and liquids in at the anus, and making evacuations at the mouth.

But, besides real diseases, we are subject to many that are only imaginary, for which the physicians have invented imaginary cures; these have their several names, and so have the drugs that are proper for them; and with these our female Yahoos are always infested.

One great excellency in this tribe is their skill at prognostics, wherein they seldom fail; their predictions in real diseases, when they rise to any degree of malignity, generally portending death, which is always in their power, when recovery is not, and therefore, upon any unexpected signs of amendment, after they have pronounced their sentence, rather than be accused as false prophets, they know how to approve[7] their sagacity to the world by a seasonable dose.

They are likewise of special use to husbands and wives, who are grown weary of their mates; to eldest sons, to great ministers of state, and often to princes.

I had formerly upon occasion discoursed with my master upon the nature of government in general, and particularly of our own excellent constitution, deservedly the wonder and envy of the whole world. But having here accidentally mentioned a minister of state, he commanded me some time after to inform him what species of Yahoo I particularly meant by that appellation.

I told him that a first or chief minister of state, whom I intended to describe, was a creature wholly exempt from joy and grief, love and hatred, pity and anger; at least makes use of no other passions but a violent desire of wealth, power, and titles; that he applies his words to all uses, except to the indication of his mind; that he never tells a truth, but with an intent that you should take it for a lie; nor a lie, but with a design that you should take it for a truth; that those he speaks worst of behind their backs are in the surest way to preferment; and whenever he begins to praise you to others or to yourself, you are from that day forlorn. The worst mark you can receive is a promise, especially when it is confirmed with an oath; after which every wise man retires, and gives over all hopes.

There are three methods by which a man may rise to be chief minister: the first is by knowing how with prudence to dispose of a wife, a daughter, or a sister; the second, by betraying or undermining his predecessor; and the third is by a furious zeal in public assemblies against the corruptions of the court. But a wise prince would rather choose to employ those who practice the last of these methods; because such zealots prove always the most obsequious and subservient to the will and passions of their master. That, these

7. Prove.

ministers having all employments at their disposal, preserve themselves in power by bribing the majority of a senate or great council; and at last by an expedient called an Act of Indemnity (whereof I described the nature to him) they secure themselves from after-reckonings, and retire from the public, laden with the spoils of the nation.

The palace of a chief minister is a seminary to breed up others in his own trade; the pages, lackies, and porter, by imitating their master, become ministers of state in their several districts, and learn to excel in the three principal ingredients, of insolence, lying, and bribery. Accordingly, they have a subaltern court paid to them by persons of the best rank; and sometimes by the force of dexterity and impudence, arrive through several gradations to be successors to their lord.

He is usually governed by a decayed wench, or favorite footman, who are the tunnels through which all graces are conveyed, and may properly be called, in the last resort, the governors of the kingdom.

One day, my master, having heard me mention the nobility of my country, was pleased to make me a compliment which I could not pretend to deserve: that, he was sure, I must have been born of some noble family, because I far exceeded in shape, color, and cleanliness, all the Yahoos of his nation, although I seemed to fail in strength, and agility, which must be imputed to my different way of living from those other brutes; and besides, I was not only endowed with the faculty of speech, but likewise with some rudiments of reason, to a degree, that with all his acquaintance I passed for a prodigy.

He made me observe, that among the Houyhnhnms, the white, the sorrel, and the iron grey were not so exactly shaped as the bay, the dapple grey, and the black; nor born with equal talents of mind, or a capacity to improve them; and therefore continued always in the condition of servants, without ever aspiring to match out of their own race, which in that country would be reckoned monstrous and unnatural.

I made his honor my most humble acknowledgements for the good opinion he was pleased to conceive of me; but assured him at the same time, that my birth was of the lower sort, having been born of plain, honest parents, who were just able to give me a tolerable education; that, nobility among us was altogether a different thing from the idea he had of it; that, our young noblemen are bred from their childhood in idleness and luxury; that, as soon as years will permit, they consume their vigor, and contract odious diseases among lewd females; and when their fortunes are almost ruined, they marry some woman of mean birth, disagreeable person, and unsound constitution, merely for the sake of money, whom they hate and despise. That, the productions of such marriages are generally scrofulous, rickety or deformed children; by which means the family seldom continues above three generations, unless the wife take care to provide a healthy father among her neighbors, or domestics, in order to improve and continue the breed. That a weak diseased body, a meager countenance, and sallow complexion are the true marks of noble blood; and a healthy robust appearance is so disgraceful in a man of quality, that the world concludes his real father to have been a groom or a coachman. The imperfections of his mind run parallel with those of his body; being a composition of spleen, dullness, ignorance, caprice, sensuality, and pride.

Without the consent of this illustrious body, no law can be enacted, repealed, or altered, and these nobles have likewise the decision of all our possessions without appeal.

CHAPTER VII

The Author's great love of his native country. His master's observations upon the constitution and administration of England, as described by the Author, with parallel cases and comparisons. His master's observations upon human nature.

The reader may be disposed to wonder how I could prevail on myself to give so free a representation of my own species, among a race of mortals who were already too apt to conceive the vilest opinion of humankind, from that entire congruity betwixt me and their Yahoos. But I must freely confess that the many virtues of those excellent quadrupeds placed in opposite view to human corruptions had so far opened my eyes, and enlarged my understanding, that I began to view the actions and passions of man in a very different light; and to think the honor of my own kind not worth managing; which, besides, it was impossible for me to do before a person of so acute a judgment as my master, who daily convinced me of a thousand faults in myself, whereof I had not the least perception before, and which with us would never be numbered even among human infirmities. I had likewise learned from his example an utter detestation of all falsehood or disguise; and truth appeared so amiable to me, that I determined upon sacrificing everything to it.

Let me deal so candidly with the reader as to confess that there was yet a much stronger motive for the freedom I took in my representation of things. I had not been a year in this country, before I contracted such a love and veneration for the inhabitants, that I entered on a firm resolution never to return to humankind, but to pass the rest of my life among these admirable Houyhnhnms in the contemplation and practice of every virtue; where I could have no example or incitement to vice. But it was decreed by fortune, my perpetual enemy, that so great a felicity should not fall to my share. However, it is now some comfort to reflect that in what I said of my countrymen, I extenuated their faults as much as I durst before so strict an examiner; and upon every article, gave as favorable a turn as the matter would bear. For, indeed, who is there alive that will not be swayed by his bias and partiality to the place of his birth?

I have related the substance of several conversations I had with my master, during the greatest part of the time I had the honor to be in his service; but have indeed for brevity sake omitted much more than is here set down.

When I had answered all his questions, and his curiosity seemed to be fully satisfied; he sent for me one morning early, and commanding me to sit down at some distance (an honor which he had never before conferred upon me), he said he had been very seriously considering my whole story, as far as it related both to myself and my country; that, he looked upon us as a sort of animal to whose share, by what accident he could not conjecture, some small pittance of reason had fallen, whereof we made no other use than by its assistance to aggravate our natural corruptions, and to acquire new ones which nature had not given us. That we disarmed ourselves of the few abilities she had bestowed; had been very successful in multiplying our original wants, and seemed to spend our whole lives in vain endeavors to supply them by our own inventions. That, as to myself, it was manifest I had neither the strength or agility of a common Yahoo; that I walked infirmly on my hinder feet; had found out a contrivance to make my claws of no use or defense, and to remove the hair from my chin, which was intended as a shelter from the sun and the weather. Lastly, that I could neither run with speed, nor climb trees like my brethren (as he called them) the Yahoos in this country.

That our institutions of government and law were plainly owing to our gross defects in reason, and by consequence, in virtue; because reason alone is sufficient to govern a rational creature; which was therefore a character we had no pretense to challenge, even from the account I had given of my own people; although he manifestly perceived, that in order to favor them, I had concealed many particulars, and often *said the thing which was not*.

He was the more confirmed in this opinion, because he observed that I agreed in every feature of my body with other Yahoos, except where it was to my real disadvantage in point of strength, speed, and activity, the shortness of my claws, and some other particulars where nature had no part; so, from the representation I had given him of our lives, our manners, and our actions, he found as near a resemblance in the disposition of our minds. He said the Yahoos were known to hate one another more than they did any different species of animals; and the reason usually assigned was the odiousness of their own shapes, which all could see in the rest, but not in themselves. He had therefore begun to think it not unwise in us to cover our bodies, and by that invention, conceal many of our deformities from each other, which would else be hardly supportable. But he now found he had been mistaken; and that the dissentions of those brutes in his country were owing to the same cause with ours, as I had described them. For, if (said he) you throw among five Yahoos as much food as would be sufficient for fifty, they will, instead of eating peaceably, fall together by the ears, each single one impatient to have all to itself; and therefore a servant was usually employed to stand by while they were feeding abroad, and those kept at home were tied at a distance from each other. That, if a cow died of age or accident, before a Houyhnhnm could secure it for his own Yahoos, those in the neighborhood would come in herds to seize it, and then would ensue such a battle as I had described, with terrible wounds made by their claws on both sides, although they seldom were able to kill one another, for want of such convenient instruments of death as we had invented. At other times the like battles have been fought between the Yahoos of several neighborhoods without any visible cause; those of one district watching all opportunities to surprise the next before they are prepared. But if they find their project hath miscarried, they return home, and for want of enemies, engage in what I call a civil war among themselves.

That, in some fields of his country, there are certain shining stones of several colors, whereof the Yahoos are violently fond; and when part of these stones are fixed in the earth, as it sometimes happeneth, they will dig with their claws for whole days to get them out, and carry them away, and hide them by heaps in their kennels; but still looking round with great caution, for fear their comrades should find out their treasure. My master said he could never discover the reason of this unnatural appetite, or how these stones could be of any use to a Yahoo; but now he believed it might proceed from the same principle of avarice, which I had ascribed to mankind. That he had once, by way of experiment, privately removed a heap of these stones from the place where one of his Yahoos had buried it, whereupon, the sordid animal missing his treasure, by his loud lamenting brought the whole herd to the place, there miserably howled, then fell to biting and tearing the rest; began to pine away, would neither eat nor sleep, nor work, till he ordered a servant privately to convey the stones into the same hole, and hide them as before; which when his Yahoo had found, he presently recovered his spirits and good humor; but took care to remove them to a better hiding place; and hath ever since been a very serviceable brute.

My master farther assured me, which I also observed myself; that in the fields where these shining stones abound, the fiercest and most frequent battles are fought, occasioned by perpetual inroads of the neighboring Yahoos.

He said it was common when two Yahoos discovered such a stone in a field, and were contending which of them should be the proprietor, a third would take the advantage, and carry it away from them both; which my master would needs contend to have some resemblance with our suits at law; wherein I thought it for our credit not to undeceive him; since the decision he mentioned was much more equitable than many decrees among us; because the plaintiff and defendant there lost nothing beside the stone they contended for; whereas our courts of equity would never have dismissed the cause while either of them had anything left.

My master continuing his discourse said there was nothing that rendered the Yahoos more odious, than their undistinguished appetite to devour everything that came in their way, whether herbs, roots, berries, corrupted flesh of animals, or all mingled together; and it was peculiar in their temper, that they were fonder of what they could get by rapine or stealth at a greater distance, than much better food provided for them at home. If their prey held out, they would eat till they were ready to burst, after which nature had pointed out to them a certain root that gave them a general evacuation.

There was also another kind of root very juicy, but something rare and difficult to be found, which the Yahoos fought for with much eagerness, and would suck it with great delight; it produced the same effects that wine hath upon us. It would make them sometimes hug, and sometimes tear one another; they would howl and grin, and chatter, and reel, and tumble, and then fall asleep in the mud.

I did indeed observe that the Yahoos were the only animals in this country subject to any diseases; which however, were much fewer than horses have among us, and contracted not by any ill treatment they meet with, but by the nastiness and greediness of that sordid brute. Neither has their language any more than a general appellation for those maladies; which is borrowed from the name of the beast, and called *Hnea Yahoo,* or the Yahoo's Evil; and the cure prescribed is a mixture of their own dung and urine, forcibly put down the Yahoo's throat. This I have since often known to have been taken with success, and do here freely recommend it to my countrymen, for the public good, as an admirable specific against all diseases produced by repletion.

As to learning, government, arts, manufactures, and the like, my master confessed he could find little or no resemblance between the Yahoos of that country and those in ours. For he only meant to observe what parity there was in our natures. He had heard indeed some curious Houyhnhnms observe that in most herds there was a sort of ruling Yahoo (as among us there is generally some leading or principal stag in a park) who was always more deformed in body, and mischievous in disposition, than any of the rest. That this leader had usually a favorite as like himself as he could get, whose employment was to lick his master's feet and posteriors, and drive the female Yahoos to his kennel; for which he was now and then rewarded with a piece of ass's flesh. This favorite is hated by the whole herd; and therefore to protect himself, keeps always near the person of his leader. He usually continues in office till a worse can be found; but the very moment he is discarded, his successor, at the head of all the Yahoos in that district, young and old, male and female, come in a body, and discharge their excrements upon him from head to foot. But how far this might be applicable to our courts and favorites, and ministers of state, my master said I could best determine.

I durst make no return to this malicious insinuation, which debased human understanding below the sagacity of a common hound, who hath judgment enough to distinguish and follow the cry of the ablest dog in the pack, without being ever mistaken.

My master told me there were some qualities remarkable in the Yahoos, which he had not observed me to mention, or at least very slightly, in the accounts I had given him of humankind. He said, those animals, like other brutes, had their females in common; but in this differed, that the she-Yahoo would admit the male while she was pregnant; and that the hes would quarrel and fight with the females as fiercely as with each other. Both which practices were such degrees of infamous brutality, that no other sensitive creature ever arrived at.

Another thing he wondered at in the Yahoos was their strange disposition to nastiness and dirt; whereas there appears to be a natural love of cleanliness in all other animals. As to the two former accusations, I was glad to let them pass without any reply, because I had not a word to offer upon them in defense of my species, which otherwise I certainly had done from my own inclinations. But I could have easily vindicated humankind from the imputation of singularity upon the last article, if there had been any swine in that country (as unluckily for me there were not) which although it may be a sweeter quadruped than a Yahoo, cannot I humbly conceive in justice pretend to more cleanliness; and so his honor himself must have owned, if he had seen their filthy way of feeding, and their custom of wallowing and sleeping in the mud.

My master likewise mentioned another quality, which his servants had discovered in several Yahoos, and to him was wholly unaccountable. He said, a fancy would sometimes take a Yahoo, to retire into a corner, to lie down and howl, and groan, and spurn away all that came near him, although he were young and fat, and wanted neither food nor water; nor did the servants imagine what could possibly ail him. And the only remedy they found was to set him to hard work, after which he would infallibly come to himself. To this I was silent out of partiality to my own kind; yet here I could plainly discover the true seeds of spleen,[8] which only seizeth on the lazy, the luxurious, and the rich; who, if they were forced to undergo the same regimen, I would undertake for the cure.

His Honor had farther observed, that a female Yahoo would often stand behind a bank or a bush, to gaze on the young males passing by, and then appear, and hide, using many antic gestures and grimaces; at which time it was observed, that she had a most offensive smell; and when any of the males advanced, would slowly retire, looking back, and with a counterfeit show of fear, run off into some convenient place where she knew the male would follow her.

At other times, if a female stranger came among them, three or four of her own sex would get about her, and stare and chatter, and grin, and smell her all over; and then turn off with gestures that seemed to express contempt and disdain.

Perhaps my master might refine a little in these speculations, which he had drawn from what he observed himself, or had been told by others; however, I could not reflect without some amazement, and much sorrow, that the rudiments of lewdness, coquetry, censure, and scandal, should have place by instinct in womankind.

I expected every moment that my master would accuse the Yahoos of those unnatural appetites in both sexes, so common among us. But nature it seems hath not been so expert a school-mistress; and these politer pleasures are entirely the productions of art and reason, on our side of the globe.

CHAPTER VIII

The Author relateth several particulars of the Yahoos. The great virtues of the Houyhnhnms. The education and exercises of their youth. Their general assembly.

As I ought to have understood human nature much better than I supposed it possible for my master to do, so it was easy to apply the character he gave of the Yahoos to myself and my countrymen; and I believed I could yet make farther discoveries from my own observation. I therefore often begged his honor to let me go among the herds of Yahoos in the neighborhood; to which he always very graciously consented, being perfectly convinced that the hatred I bore those brutes would never suffer me to be corrupted by them; and his honor ordered one of his servants, a strong sorrel nag, very honest and good-natured, to be my guard; without whose protection I durst not undertake such adventures. For I have already told the reader how much I was pestered by those odious animals upon my first arrival. I afterwards failed very narrowly three or four times of falling into their clutches, when I happened to stray at any distance without my hanger. And I have reason to believe, they had some imagination that I was of their own species, which I often assisted myself, by stripping up my sleeves, and shewing my naked arms and breast in their sight, when my protector was with me; at which times they would approach as near as they durst, and imitate my actions after the manner of monkeys, but ever with great signs of hatred; as a tame jackdaw with cap and stockings is always persecuted by the wild ones, when he happens to be got among them.

8. Hypochondria.

They are prodigiously nimble from their infancy; however, I once caught a young male of three years old, and endeavored by all marks of tenderness to make it quiet; but the little imp fell a squalling, scratching, and biting with such violence, that I was forced to let it go; and it was high time, for a whole troop of old ones came about us at the noise; but finding the cub was safe (for away it ran) and my sorrel nag being by, they durst not venture near us. I observed the young animal's flesh to smell very rank, and the stink was somewhat between a weasel and a fox, but much more disagreeable. I forgot another circumstance (and perhaps I might have the reader's pardon, if it were wholly omitted) that while I held the odious vermin in my hands, it voided its filthy excrements of a yellow liquid substance, all over my clothes; but by good fortune there was a small brook hard by, where I washed myself as clean as I could; although I durst not come into my master's presence until I were sufficiently aired.

By what I could discover, the Yahoos appear to be the most unteachable of all animals, their capacities never reaching higher than to draw or carry burdens. Yet I am of opinion, this defect ariseth chiefly from a perverse, restive disposition. For they are cunning, malicious, treacherous and revengeful. They are strong and hardy, but of a cowardly spirit, and by consequence insolent, abject, and cruel. It is observed that the red-haired of both sexes are more libidinous and mischievous than the rest, whom yet they much exceed in strength and activity.

The Houyhnhnms keep the Yahoos for present use in huts not far from the house; but the rest are sent abroad to certain fields, where they dig up roots, eat several kinds of herbs, and search about for carrion, or sometimes catch weasels and *luhimuhs* (a sort of wild rat) which they greedily devour. Nature hath taught them to dig deep holes with their nails on the side of a rising ground, wherein they lie by themselves; only the kennels of the females are larger, sufficient to hold two or three cubs.

They swim from their infancy like frogs, and are able to continue long under water, where they often take fish, which the females carry home to their young. And upon this occasion, I hope the reader will pardon my relating an odd adventure.

Being one day abroad with my protector the sorrel nag, and the weather exceeding hot, I entreated him to let me bathe in a river that was near. He consented, and I immediately stripped myself stark naked, and went down softly into the stream. It happened that a young female Yahoo standing behind a bank, saw the whole proceeding; and inflamed by desire, as the nag and I conjectured, came running with all speed, and leaped into the water within five yards of the place where I bathed. I was never in my life so terribly frighted; the nag was grazing at some distance, not suspecting any harm; she embraced me after a most fulsome manner; I roared as loud as I could, and the nag came galloping towards me, whereupon she quitted her grasp, with the utmost reluctancy, and leaped upon the opposite bank, where she stood gazing and howling all the time I was putting on my clothes.

This was matter of diversion to my master and his family, as well as of mortification to myself. For now I could no longer deny that I was a real Yahoo, in every limb and feature, since the females had a natural propensity to me as one of their own species; neither was the hair of this brute of a red color (which might have been some excuse for an appetite a little irregular) but black as a sole, and her countenance did not make an appearance altogether so hideous as the rest of the kind; for I think, she could not be above eleven years old.

Having already lived three years in this country, the reader I suppose will expect that I should, like other travelers, give him some account of the manners and customs of its inhabitants, which it was indeed my principal study to learn.

As these noble Houyhnhnms are endowed by Nature with a general disposition to all virtues, and have no conceptions or ideas of what is evil in a rational creature; so their grand maxim is to cultivate reason, and to be wholly governed by it. Neither is reason among them a point problematical as with us, where men can argue with plausibility on both sides of a question; but strikes you with immediate conviction; as it must needs do where it is not mingled, obscured, or discolored by passion and interest. I remember it was with extreme difficulty that I could bring my master to understand the meaning of the word "opinion," or how a point could be disputable; because reason taught us to affirm or deny only where we are certain; and beyond our knowledge we cannot do either. So that controversies, wranglings, disputes, and positiveness in false or dubious propositions are evils unknown among the Houyhnhnms. In the like manner when I used to explain to him our several systems of natural philosophy, he would laugh that a creature pretending to reason should value itself upon the knowledge of other people's conjectures, and in things, where that knowledge, if it were certain, could be of no use. Wherein he agreed entirely with the sentiments of Socrates, as Plato delivers them, which I mention as the highest honor I can do that prince of philosophers. I have often since reflected what destruction such a doctrine would make in the libraries of Europe; and how many paths to fame would be then shut up in the learned world.

Friendship and benevolence are the two principal virtues among the Houyhnhnms; and these not confined to particular objects, but universal to the whole race. For a stranger from the remotest part is equally treated with the nearest neighbor, and wherever he goes, looks upon himself as at home. They preserve decency and civility in the highest degrees, but are altogether ignorant of ceremony. They have no fondness for[9] their colts or foals; but the care they take in educating them proceedeth entirely from the dictates of reason. And I observed my master to show the same affection to his neighbor's issue that he had for his own. They will have it that nature teaches them to love the whole species, and it is reason only that maketh a distinction of persons, where there is a superior degree of virtue.

When the matron Houyhnhnms have produced one of each sex, they no longer accompany with their consorts, except they lose one of their issue by some casualty, which very seldom happens; but in such a case they meet again; or when the like accident befalls a person whose wife is past bearing, some other couple bestows on him one of their own colts, and then go together a second time, until the mother be pregnant. This caution is necessary to prevent the country from being overburdened with numbers. But the race of inferior Houyhnhnms bred up to be servants is not so strictly

9. Attachment to.

limited upon this article; these are allowed to produce three of each sex, to be domestics in the noble families.

In their marriages they are exactly careful to choose such colors as will not make any disagreeable mixture in the breed. Strength is chiefly valued in the male, and comeliness in the female; not upon the account of love, but to preserve the race from degenerating; for, where a female happens to excel in strength, a consort is chosen with regard to comeliness. Courtship, love, presents, jointures, settlements, have no place in their thoughts, or terms whereby to express them in their language. The young couple meet and are joined, merely because it is the determination of their parents and friends; it is what they see done every day; and they look upon it as one of the necessary actions in a reasonable being. But the violation of marriage, or any other unchastity, was never heard of; and the married pair pass their lives with the same friendship and mutual benevolence that they bear to all others of the same species who come in their way, without jealousy, fondness, quarreling, or discontent.

In educating the youth of both sexes, their method is admirable, and highly deserveth our imitation. These are not suffered to taste a grain of oats, except upon certain days, till eighteen years old; nor milk, but very rarely; and in summer they graze two hours in the morning, and as many in the evening, which their parents likewise observe; but the servants are not allowed above half that time; and a great part of the grass is brought home, which they eat at the most convenient hours, when they can be best spared from work.

Temperance, industry, exercise, and cleanliness are the lessons equally enjoined to the young ones of both sexes; and my master thought it monstrous in us to give the females a different kind of education from the males, except in some articles of domestic management; whereby, as he truly observed, one half of our natives were good for nothing but bringing children into the world; and to trust the care of their children to such useless animals, he said was yet a greater instance of brutality.

But the Houyhnhnms train up their youth to strength, speed, and hardiness, by exercising them in running races up and down steep hills, or over hard stony grounds; and when they are all in a sweat, they are ordered to leap over head and ears into a pond or a river. Four times a year the youth of certain districts meet to show their proficiency in running, and leaping, and other feats of strength or agility; where the victor is rewarded with a song made in his or her praise. On this festival the servants drive a herd of Yahoos into the field, laden with hay, and oats, and milk for a repast to the Houyhnhnms; after which these brutes are immediately driven back again, for fear of being noisome to the assembly.

Every fourth year, at the vernal equinox, there is a representative council of the whole nation, which meets in a plain about twenty miles from our house, and continueth about five or six days. Here they inquire into the state and condition of the several districts; whether they abound or be deficient in hay or oats, or cows or Yahoos? And wherever there is any want (which is but seldom) it is immediately supplied by unanimous consent and contribution. Here likewise the regulation of children is settled: as for instance, if a Houyhnhnm hath two males, he changeth one of them with another who hath two females, and when a child hath been lost by any casualty, where the mother is past breeding, it is determined what family in the district shall breed another to supply the loss.

CHAPTER IX

A grand debate at the general assembly of the Houyhnhnms, and how it was determined. The learning of the Houyhnhnms. Their buildings. Their manner of burials. The defectiveness of their language.

One of these grand assemblies was held in my time, about three months before my departure, whither my master went as the representative of our district. In this council was resumed their old debate, and indeed, the only debate that ever happened in their country; whereof my master after his return gave me a very particular account.

The question to be debated was whether the Yahoos should be exterminated from the face of the earth. One of the members for the affirmative offered several arguments of great strength and weight, alleging that, as the Yahoos were the most filthy, noisome, and deformed animal which nature ever produced, so they were the most restive and indocile, mischievous, and malicious; they would privately suck the teats of the Houyhnhnms' cows; kill and devour their cats, trample down their oats and grass, if they were not continually watched; and commit a thousand other extravagancies. He took notice of a general tradition, that Yahoos had not been always in their country, but that many ages ago, two of these brutes appeared together upon a mountain; whether produced by the heat of the sun upon corrupted mud and slime, or from the ooze and froth of the sea, was never known. That these Yahoos engendered, and their brood in a short time grew so numerous as to overrun and infest the whole nation. That the Houyhnhnms to get rid of this evil, made a general hunting, and at last enclosed the whole herd; and destroying the older, every Houyhnhnm kept two young ones in a kennel, and brought them to such a degree of tameness as an animal so savage by nature can be capable of acquiring, using them for draft and carriage. That there seemed to be much truth in this tradition, and that those creatures could not be *ylnhniamshy* (or aborigines of the land) because of the violent hatred the Houyhnhnms as well as all other animals bore them; which although their evil disposition sufficiently deserved, could never have arrived at so high a degree, if they had been aborigines, or else they would have long since been rooted out. That the inhabitants taking a fancy to use the service of the Yahoos, had very imprudently neglected to cultivate the breed of asses, which were a comely animal, easily kept, more tame and orderly, without any offensive smell, strong enough for labor, although they yield to the other in agility of body; and if their braying be no agreeable sound, it is far preferable to the horrible howlings of the Yahoos.

Several others declared their sentiments to the same purpose, when my master proposed an expedient to the assembly, whereof he had indeed borrowed the hint from me. He approved of the tradition, mentioned by the honorable member, who spoke before; and affirmed, that the two Yahoos said to be first seen among them, had been driven thither over the sea; that coming to land, and being forsaken by their companions, they retired to the mountains, and degenerating by degrees, became in process of time much more savage than those of their own species in the country from whence these two originals came. The reason of his assertion was that he had now in his possession a certain wonderful Yahoo (meaning myself) which most of them had heard of, and many of them had seen. He then related to them how he first found me; that my body was all covered with an artificial composure of the skins and hairs of other animals; that I spoke in a language of my own, and had thoroughly learned theirs; that I had related to him the accidents which brought me thither; that when he saw me without my covering, I was an exact Yahoo in every part, only of a whiter color, less hairy and with shorter claws. He added how I had endeavored to persuade him that in my own and other countries the Yahoos acted as the governing, rational animal, and held the Houyhnhnms in servitude; that he observed in me all the qualities of a Yahoo, only a little more civilized by some tincture of reason, which however was in a degree as far inferior to the Houyhnhnm race as the Yahoos of their country were to me; that among other things, I mentioned a custom we had of castrating Houyhnhnms when they were young, in order to render them tame; that the operation was easy and safe; that it was no shame to learn wisdom from brutes, as industry is taught by the ant, and building by the swallow (for so I translate the world *lyhannh*, although it be a much larger fowl). That this invention might be practiced upon the younger Yahoos here, which, besides rendering them tractable and fitter for use, would in an age put an end to the whole species without destroying life. That in the meantime the Houyhnhnms should be exhorted to cultivate the breed of asses, which, as they are in all respects more valuable brutes, so they have this advantage, to be fit for service at five years old, which the others are not till twelve.

This was all my master thought fit to tell me at that time, of what passed in the grand council. But he was pleased to conceal one particular, which related personally to myself, whereof I soon felt the unhappy effect, as the reader will know in its proper place, and from whence I date all the succeeding misfortunes of my life.

The Houyhnhnms have no letters, and consequently, their knowledge is all traditional. But there happening few events of any moment among a people so well united, naturally disposed to every virtue, wholly governed by reason, and cut off from all commerce with other nations, the historical part is easily preserved without burdening their memories. I have already observed that they are subject to no diseases, and therefore can have no need of physicians. However, they have excellent medicines composed of herbs, to cure accidental bruises and cuts in the pastern or frog of the foot by sharp stones, as well as other maims and hurts in the several parts of the body.

They calculate the year by the revolution of the sun and the moon, but use no subdivisions into weeks. They are well enough acquainted with the motions of those two luminaries, and understand the nature of eclipses; and this is the utmost progress of their astronomy.

In poetry they must be allowed to excel all other mortals; wherein the justness of their similes, and the minuteness, as well as exactness of their descriptions, are indeed inimitable. Their verses abound very much in both of these, and usually contain either some exalted notions of friendship and benevolence, or the praises of those who were victors in races and other bodily exercises. Their buildings, although very rude and simple, are not inconvenient, but well contrived to defend them from all injuries of cold and heat. They have a kind of tree, which at forty years old loosens in the root, and falls with the first storm; it grows very straight, and being pointed like stakes with a sharp stone (for the Houyhnhnms know not the use of iron), they stick them erect in the ground about ten inches asunder, and then weave in oat straw, or sometimes wattles, betwixt them. The roof is made after the same manner, and so are the doors.

The Houyhnhnms use the hollow part between the pastern and the hoof of their forefeet as we do our hands, and this with greater dexterity than I could at first imagine. I have seen a white mare of our family thread a needle (which I lent her on purpose) with that joint. They milk their cows, reap their oats, and do all the work which requires hands in the same manner. They have a kind of hard flints, which by grinding against other stones they form into instruments that serve instead of wedges, axes, and hammers. With tools made of these flints, they likewise cut their hay, and reap their oats, which there groweth naturally in several fields; the Yahoos draw home the sheaves in carriages, and the servants tread them in certain covered huts, to get out the grain, which is kept in stores. They make a rude kind of earthen and wooden vessels, and bake the former in the sun.

If they can avoid casualties, they die only of old age, and are buried in the obscurest places that can be found, their friends and relations expressing neither joy nor grief at their departure; nor does the dying person discover the least regret that he is leaving the world, any more than if he were upon returning home from a visit to one of his neighbors; I remember my master having once made an appointment with a friend and his family to come to his house upon some affair of importance; on the day fixed, the mistress and her two children came very late; she made two excuses, first for her husband, who, as she said, happened that very morning to *lhnuwnh*. The word is strongly expressive in their language, but not easily rendered into English; it signifies, *to retire to his first Mother*. Her excuse for not coming sooner was that her husband dying late in the morning, she was a good while consulting her servants about a convenient place where his body should be laid; and I observed she behaved herself at our house, as cheerfully as the rest; she died about three months after.

They live generally to seventy or seventy-five years, very seldom to four-score; some weeks before their death they feel a gradual decay, but without pain. During this time they are much visited by their friends, because they cannot go abroad with their usual ease and satisfaction. However, about ten days before their death, which they seldom fail in computing, they return the visits that have been made by those who are nearest in the neighborhood, being carried in a convenient sledge drawn by Yahoos; which vehicle they use, not only upon this occasion, but when they grow old, upon long journeys, or when they are lamed by any accident. And therefore when the dying Houyhnhnms return those visits, they take a solemn leave of their friends, as if they were going to some remote part of the country, where they designed to pass the rest of their lives.

I know not whether it may be worth observing, that the Houyhnhnms have no word in their language to express anything that is evil, except what they borrow from the deformities or ill qualities of the Yahoos. Thus they denote the folly of a servant, an omission of a child, a stone that cuts their feet, a continuance of foul or unseasonable weather, and the like, by adding to each the epithet of Yahoo. For instance, *hhnm Yahoo, whnaholm Yahoo, ynlhmnd-wihlma Yahoo,* and an ill-contrived house, *ynholmhnmrohlnw Yahoo.*

I could with great pleasure enlarge farther upon the manners and virtues of this excellent people; but intending in a short time to publish a volume by itself expressly upon that subject, I refer the reader thither. And in the meantime, proceed to relate my own sad catastrophe.

CHAPTER X

The Author's economy, and happy life among the Houyhnhnms. His great improvement in virtue, by conversing with them. Their conversations. The Author hath notice given him by his master that he must depart from the country. He falls into a swoon for grief, but submits. He contrives and finishes a canoe, by the help of a fellow servant, and puts to sea at a venture.

I had settled my little economy to my own heart's content. My master had ordered a room to be made for me after their manner, about six yards from the house; the sides and floors of which I plastered with clay, and covered with rush mats of my own contriving; I had beaten hemp, which there grows wild, and made of it a sort of ticking; this I filled with the feathers of several birds I had taken with springes made of Yahoos' hairs, and were excellent food. I had worked two chairs with my knife, the sorrel nag helping me in the grosser and more laborious part. When my clothes were worn to rags, I made myself others with the skins of rabbits, and of a certain beautiful animal about the same size, called *nnuhnoh,* the skin of which is covered with a fine down. Of these I likewise made very tolerable stockings. I soled my shoes with wood which I cut from a tree, and fitted to the upper leather, and when this was worn out, I supplied it with the skins of Yahoos, dried in the sun. I often got honey out of hollow trees, which I mingled with water, or eat it with my bread. No man could more verify the truth of these two maxims, that *Nature is very easily satisfied;* and, that *Necessity is the mother of invention.* I enjoyed perfect health of body, and tranquility of mind; I did not feel the treachery or inconstancy of a friend, nor the inquiries of a secret or open enemy. I had no occasion of bribing, flattering, or pimping to procure the favor of any great man, or of his minion. I wanted no fence against fraud or oppression; here was neither physician to destroy my body, nor lawyer to ruin my fortune; no informer to watch my words and actions, or forge accusations against me for hire; here were no gibers, censurers, backbiters, pickpockets, highwaymen, housebreakers, attorneys, bawds, buffoons, gamesters, politicians, wits, splenetics, tedious talkers, controvertists, ravishers, murderers, robbers, virtuosos; no leaders or followers of party and faction; no encouragers to vice, by seducement or examples; no dungeons, axes, gibbets, whipping posts, or pillories; no cheating shopkeepers or mechanics; no pride, vanity or affectation; no fops, bullies, drunkards, strolling whores, or poxes; no ranting, lewd, expensive wives; no stupid, proud pedants; no importunate, overbearing, quarrelsome, noisy, roaring, empty, conceited, swearing companions; no scoundrels raised from the dust upon the merit of their vices; or nobility thrown into it on account of their virtues; no lords, fiddlers, judges, or dancing masters.

I had the favor of being admitted to several Houyhnhnms, who came to visit or dine with my master; where his honor graciously suffered me to wait in the room, and listen to their discourse. Both he and his company would often descend to ask me questions, and receive my answers. I had also sometimes the honor of attending my master in his visits to others. I never presumed to speak, except in answer to a question; and then I did it with inward regret, because it was a loss of so much time for improving myself; but I was infinitely delighted with the station of an humble auditor in such conversations, where nothing passed but what was useful, expressed in the fewest and most significant words; where (as I have already said) the greatest decency was observed, without the least degree of ceremony; where no person spoke without being pleased himself, and pleasing his companions; where there was no interruption, tediousness, heat, or difference of sentiments. They have a notion, that when people are met together, a short silence doth much improve conversation; this I found to be true; for during those little intermissions of talk, new ideas would arise in their minds, which very much enlivened the discourse. Their subjects are generally on friendship and benevolence; on order and economy; sometimes upon the visible operations of nature, or ancient traditions; upon the bounds and limits of virtue; upon the unerring rules of reason; or upon some determinations, to be taken at the next great assembly; and often upon the various excellencies of poetry. I may add, without vanity, that my presence often gave them sufficient matter for discourse, because it afforded my master an occasion of letting his friends into the history of me and my country, upon which they were all pleased to discant in a manner not very advantageous to human kind; and for that reason I shall not repeat what they said; only I may be allowed to observe that his honor, to my great admiration, appeared to understand the nature of Yahoos much better than myself. He went through all our vices and follies, and discovered many which I had never mentioned to him; by only supposing what qualities a Yahoo of their country, with a small proportion of reason, might be capable of exerting; and concluded, with too much probability, how vile as well as miserable such a creature must be.

I freely confess, that all the little knowledge I have of any value was acquired by the lectures I received from my master, and from hearing the discourses of him and his friends; to which I should be prouder to listen, than to dictate to the greatest and wisest assembly in Europe. I admired the strength, comeliness, and speed of the inhabitants; and such a constellation of virtues in such amiable persons produced in me the highest veneration. At first, indeed, I did not feel that natural awe which the Yahoos and all other animals bear towards them; but it grew upon me by degrees, much sooner than I imagined, and was mingled with a respectful love and gratitude, that they would condescend to distinguish me from the rest of my species.

When I thought of my family, my friends, my countrymen, or human race in general, I considered them as they really were, Yahoos in shape and disposition, perhaps a little more civilized, and qualified with the gift of speech; but making no other use of reason than to improve and mutiply those vices, whereof their brethren in this country had only the share that nature allotted them. When I happened to behold the reflection of my own form in a lake or fountain, I turned away my face in horror and detestation of myself, and could better endure the sight of a common Yahoo than of my own person. By conversing with the Houyhnhnms, and looking upon them with delight,

I fell to imitate their gait and gesture, which is now grown into a habit; and my friends often tell me in a blunt way, that I trot like a horse; which, however, I take for a great compliment; neither shall I disown, that in speaking I am apt to fall into the voice and manner of the Houyhnhnms, and hear myself ridiculed on that account without the least mortification.

In the midst of this happiness, when I looked upon myself to be fully settled for life, my master sent for me one morning a little earlier than his usual hour. I observed by his countenance that he was in some perplexity, and at a loss how to begin what he had to speak. After a short silence, he told me, he did not know how I would take what he was going to say; that, in the last general assembly, when the affair of the Yahoos was entered upon, the representatives had taken offense at his keeping a Yahoo (meaning myself) in his family more like a Houyhnhnm than a brute animal. That he was known frequently to converse with me, as if he could receive some advantage of pleasure in my company; that such a practice was not agreeable to reason or nature, or a thing ever heard of before among them. The assembly did therefore exhort him, either to employ me like the rest of my species, or command me to swim back to the place from whence I came. That the first of these expedients was utterly rejected by all the Houyhnhnms who had ever seen me at his house or their own; for, they alleged, that because I had some rudiments of reason, added to the natural pravity of those animals, it was to be feared, I might be able to seduce them into the woody and mountainous parts of the country, and bring them in troops by night to destroy the Houyhnhnms' cattle, as being naturally of the ravenous kind, and averse from labor.

My master added that he was daily pressed by the Houyhnhnms of the neighborhood to have the assembly's exhortation executed, which he could not put off much longer. He doubted[1] it would be impossible for me to swim to another country; and therefore wished I would contrive some sort of vehicle resembling those I had described to him, that might carry me on the sea; in which work I should have the assistance of his own servants, as well as those of his neighbors. He concluded that for his own part he could have been content to keep me in his service as long as I lived; because he found I had cured myself of some bad habits and dispositions, by endeavoring, as far as my inferior nature was capable, to imitate the Houyhnhnms.

I should here observe to the reader, that a decree of the general assembly in this country is expressed by the word *hnhloayn*, which signifies an exhortation, as near as I can render it; for they have no conception how a rational creature can be compelled, but only advised, or exhorted; because no person can disobey reason without giving up his claim to be a rational creature.

I was struck with the utmost grief and despair at my master's discourse; and being unable to support the agonies I was under, I fell into a swoon at his feet; when I came to myself, he told me that he concluded I had been dead (for these people are subject to no such imbecilities of nature). I answered, in a faint voice, that death would have been too great an happiness; that although I could not blame the assembly's exhortation, or the urgency of his friends; yet in my weak and corrupt judgment, I thought it might consist with reason to have been less rigorous. That I could not swim

---

1. Suspected.

a league, and probably the nearest land to theirs might be distant above an hundred; that many materials, necessary for making a small vessel to carry me off, were wholly wanting in this country, which, however, I would attempt in obedience and gratitude to his honor, although I concluded the thing to be impossible, and therefore looked on myself as already devoted[2] to destruction. That the certain prospect of an unnatural death was the least of my evils; for, supposing I should escape with life by some strange adventure, how could I think with temper[3] of passing my days among Yahoos, and relapsing into my old corruptions, for want of examples to lead and keep me within the paths of virtue. That I knew too well upon what solid reasons all the determinations of the wise Houyhnhnms were founded, not to be shaken by arguments of mine, a miserable Yahoo; and therefore after presenting him with my humble thanks for the offer of his servants' assistance in making a vessel, and desiring a reasonable time for so difficult a work, I told him I would endeavor to preserve a wretched being; and, if ever I returned to England, was not without hopes of being useful to my own species by celebrating the praises of the renowned Houyhnhnms, and proposing their virtues to the imitation of mankind.

My master in a few words made me a very gracious reply, allowed me the space of two months to finish my boat, and ordered the sorrel nag, my fellow servant (for so at this distance I may presume to call him), to follow my instructions, because I told my master that his help would be sufficient, and I knew he had a tenderness for me.

In his company my first business was to go to that part of the coast where my rebellious crew had ordered me to be set on shore. I got upon a height, and looking on every side into the sea, fancied I saw a small island towards the northeast; I took out my pocket glass, and could then clearly distinguish it about five leagues off, as I computed; but it appeared to the sorrel nag to be only a blue cloud; for, as he had no conception of any country besides his own, so he could not be as expert in distinguishing remote objects at sea, as we who so much converse in that element.

After I had discovered this island, I considered no farther; but resolved, it should, if possible, be the first place of my banishment, leaving the consequence to fortune.

I returned home, and consulting with the sorrel nag, we went into a copse at some distance, where I with my knife, and he with a sharp flint fastened very artificially,[4] after their manner, to a wooden handle, cut down several oak wattles about the thickness of a walking staff, and some larger pieces. But I shall not trouble the reader with a particular description of my own mechanics; let it suffice to say, that in six weeks time, with the help of the sorrel nag, who performed the parts that required most labor, I finished a sort of Indian canoe; but much larger, covering it with the skins of Yahoos, well stitched together, with hempen threads of my own making. My sail was likewise composed of the skins of the same animal; but I made use of the youngest I could get, the older being too tough and thick; and I likewise provided myself with four paddles. I laid in a stock of boiled flesh, of rabbits and fowls; and took with me two vessels, one filled with milk, and the other with water.

2. Doomed.   3. Equanimity.   4. Adroitly.

I tried my canoe in a large pond near my master's house, and then corrected in it what was amiss, stopping all the chinks with Yahoo's tallow, till I found it staunch, and able to bear me and my freight. And when it was as complete as I could possibly make it, I had it drawn on a carriage very gently by Yahoos, to the seaside, under the conduct of the sorrel nag and another servant.

When all was ready, and the day came for my departure, I took leave of my master and lady, and the whole family, my eyes flowing with tears and my heart quite sunk with grief. But his honor, out of curiosity, and perhaps (if I may speak it without vanity) partly out of kindness, was determined to see me in my canoe; and got several of his neighboring friends to accompany him. I was forced to wait above an hour for the tide, and then observing the wind very fortunately bearing towards the island to which I intended to steer my course, I took a second leave of my master; but as I was going to prostrate myself to kiss his hoof, he did me the honor to raise it gently to my mouth. I am not ignorant how much I have been censured for mentioning this last particular. Detractors are pleased to think it improbable that so illustrious a person should descend to give so great a mark of distinction to a creature so inferior as I. Neither have I forgot how apt some travelers are to boast of extraordinary favors they have received. But, if these censurers were better acquainted with the noble and courteous disposition of the Houyhnhnms, they would soon change their opinion. I paid my respects to the rest of the Houyhnhnms in his honor's company; then getting into my canoe, I pushed off from shore.

CHAPTER XI

The Author's dangerous voyage. He arrives at New Holland, hoping to settle there. Is wounded with an arrow by one of the natives. Is seized and carried by force into a Portuguese ship. The great civilities of the Captain. The Author arrives at England.

I began this desperate voyage on February 15, 1714/5,[5] at 9 o'clock in the morning. The wind was very favorable; however, I made use at first only of my paddles; but considering I should soon be weary, and that the wind might probably chop about, I ventured to set up my little sail; and thus, with the help of the tide, I went at the rate of a league and a half an hour, as near as I could guess. My master and his friends continued on the shore, till I was almost out of sight; and I often heard the sorrel nag (who always loved me) crying out, *"Hnuy illa nyha maiah Yahoo"* ("Take care of thyself, gentle Yahoo").

My design was, if possible, to discover some small island uninhabited, yet sufficient by my labor to furnish me with necessaries of life, which I would have thought a greater happiness than to be first minister in the politest court of Europe, so horrible was the idea I conceived of returning to live in the society and under the government of Yahoos. For in such a solitude as I desired, I could at least enjoy my own thoughts, and reflect with delight on the virtues of those inimitable Houyhnhnms, without any opportunity of degenerating into the vices and corruptions of my own species.

5. I.e., 1714. The year began on March 25.

The reader may remember what I related when my crew conspired against me, and confined me to my cabin, how I continued there several weeks, without knowing what course we took; and when I was put ashore in the longboat, how the sailors told me with oaths, whether true or false, that they knew not in what part of the world we were. However, I did then believe us to be about 10 degrees southward of the Cape of Good Hope, or about 45 degrees southern latitude, as I gathered from some general words I overheard among them, being I supposed to the southeast in their intended voyage to Madagascar. And although this were but little better than conjecture, yet I resolved to steer my course eastward, hoping to reach the southwest coast of New Holland, and perhaps some such island as I desired, lying westward of it. The wind was full west, and by six in the evening I computed I had gone eastward at least eighteen leagues; when I spied a very small island about half a league off, which I soon reached. It was nothing but a rock with one creek,[6] naturally arched by the force of tempests. Here I put in my canoe, and climbing a part of the rock, I could plainly discover land to the east, extending from south to north. I lay all night in my canoe; and repeating my voyage early in the morning, I arrived in seven hours to the southeast point of New Holland.[7] This confirmed me in the opinion I have long entertained, that the maps and charts place this country at least three degrees more to the east than it really is; which thought I communicated many years ago to my worthy friend Mr. Herman Moll,[8] and gave him my reasons for it, although he hath rather chosen to follow other authors.

I saw no inhabitants in the place where I landed; and being unarmed, I was afraid of venturing far into the country. I found some shellfish on the shore, and eat them raw, not daring to kindle a fire, for fear of being discovered by the natives. I continued three days feeding on oysters and limpets, to save my own provisions; and I fortunately found a brook of excellent water, which gave me great relief.

On the fourth day, venturing out early a little too far, I saw twenty or thirty natives upon a height, not above five hundred yards from me. They were stark naked, men, women, and children round a fire, as I could discover by the smoke. One of them spied me, and gave notice to the rest; five of them advanced towards me, leaving the women and children at the fire. I made what haste I could to the shore, and getting into my canoe, shoved off; the savages observing me retreat, ran after me; and before I could get far enough into the sea, discharged an arrow, which wounded me deeply on the inside of my left knee. (I shall carry the mark to my grave.) I apprehended the arrow might be poisoned; and paddling out of the reach of their darts (being a calm day) I made a shift to suck the wound, and dress it as well as I could.

I was at a loss what to do, for I durst not return to the same landing place, but stood to the north, and was forced to paddle; for the wind, although very gentle, was against me, blowing northwest. As I was looking about for a secure landing place, I saw a sail to the north northeast, which appearing every minute more visible, I was in some doubt whether I should wait for them or no; but at last my detestation of the Yahoo race prevailed; and turning my canoe, I sailed and paddled together to the south, and got into the same creek from whence I set out in the morning, choosing rather to trust

6. A bay.   7. Present-day Republic of South Africa.   8. A famous contemporary mapmaker.

myself among these barbarians than live with European Yahoos. I drew up my canoe as close as I could to the shore, and hid myself behind a stone by the little brook, which, as I have already said, was excellent water.

The ship came within half a league of this creek, and sent out her longboat with vessels to take in fresh water (for the place it seems was very well known), but I did not observe it until the boat was almost on shore; and it was too late to seek another hiding place. The seamen at their landing observed my canoe, and rummaging it all over, easily conjectured that the owner could not be far off. Four of them well armed searched every cranny and lurking hole, till at last they found me flat on my face behind the stone. They gazed a while in admiration at my strange uncouth dress; my coat made of skins, my wooden-soled shoes, and my furred stockings; from whence, however, they concluded I was not a native of the place, who all go naked. One of the seamen in Portuguese bid me rise, and asked who I was. I understood that language very well, and getting upon my feet, said I was a poor Yahoo, banished from the Houyhnhnms, and desired they would please to let me depart. They admired to hear me answer them in their own tongue, and saw by my complexion I must be an European; but were at a loss to know what I meant by Yahoos and Houyhnhnms, and at the same time fell a laughing at my strange tone in speaking, which resembled the neighing of a horse. I trembled all the while betwixt fear and hatred; I again desired leave to depart, and was gently moving to my canoe; but they laid hold on me, desiring to know what country I was of? whence I came? with many other questions. I told them I was born in England, from whence I came about five years ago, and then their country and ours was at peace. I therefore hoped they would not treat me as an enemy, since I meant them no harm, but was a poor Yahoo, seeking some desolate place where to pass the remainder of his unfortunate life.

When they began to talk, I thought I never heard or saw any thing so unnatural; for it appeared to me as monstrous as if a dog or a cow should speak in England, or a Yahoo in Houyhnhnmland. The honest Portuguese were equally amazed at my strange dress, and the odd manner of delivering my words, which however they understood very well. They spoke to me with great humanity, and said they were sure their Captain would carry me *gratis* to Lisbon, from whence I might return to my own country; that two of the seamen would go back to the ship, to inform the Captain of what they had seen, and receive his orders; in the meantime, unless I would give my solemn oath not to fly, they would secure me by force. I thought it best to comply with their proposal. They were very curious to know my story, but I gave them very little satisfaction; and they all conjectured, that my misfortunes had impaired my reason. In two hours the boat, which went laden with vessels of water, returned with the Captain's commands to fetch me on board. I fell on my knees to preserve my liberty; but all was in vain, and the men having tied me with cords, heaved me into the boat, from whence I was taken into the ship, and from thence into the Captain's cabin.

His name was Pedro de Mendez; he was a very courteous and generous person; he entreated me to give some account of myself, and desired to know what I would eat or drink; said I should be used as well as himself, and spoke so many obliging things, that I wondered to find such civilities from a Yahoo. However, I remained silent and sullen; I was ready to faint at the very smell of him and his men. At last I desired something to eat out of my own canoe; but he ordered me a chicken and some excellent wine, and then directed that I should be put to bed in a very clean cabin. I would not undress myself, but lay on the bedclothes; and in half an hour stole out, when I thought the crew was at dinner; and getting to the side of the ship, was going to leap into the sea, and swim for my life, rather than continue among Yahoos. But one of the seamen prevented me, and having informed the Captain, I was chained to my cabin.

After dinner Don Pedro came to me, and desired to know my reason for so desperate an attempt; assured me he only meant to do me all the service he was able; and spoke so very movingly, that at last I descended to treat him like an animal which had some little portion of reason. I gave him a very short relation of my voyage; of the conspiracy against me by my own men; of the country where they set me on shore, and of my five years residence there. All which he looked upon as if it were a dream or a vision; whereat I took great offense; for I had quite forgot the faculty of lying, so peculiar to Yahoos in all countries where they preside, and consequently the disposition of suspecting truth in others of their own species. I asked him whether it were the custom of his country to *say the thing that was not?* I assured him I had almost forgot what he meant by falsehood; and if I had lived a thousand years in Houyhnhnmland, I should never have heard a lie from the meanest servant. That I was altogether indifferent whether he believed me or no; but however, in return for his favors, I would give so much allowance to the corruption of his nature, as to answer any objection he would please to make; and he might easily discover the truth.

The Captain, a wise man, after many endeavors to catch me tripping in some part of my story, at last began to have a better opinion of my veracity. But he added that since I professed so inviolable an attachment to truth, I must give him my word of honor to bear him company in this voyage without attempting anything against my life; or else he would continue me a prisoner till we arrived at Lisbon. I gave him the promise he required; but at the same time protested that I would suffer the greatest hardships rather than return to live among Yahoos.

Our voyage passed without any considerable accident. In gratitude to the Captain I sometimes sat with him at his earnest request, and strove to conceal my antipathy against humankind, although it often broke out; which he suffered to pass without observation. But the greatest part of the day, I confined myself to my cabin, to avoid seeing any of the crew. The Captain had often entreated me to strip myself of my savage dress, and offered to lend me the best suit of clothes he had. This I would not be prevailed on to accept, abhorring to cover myself with anything that had been on the back of a Yahoo. I only desired he would lend me two clean shirts, which having been washed since he wore them, I believed would not so much defile me. These I changed every second day, and washed them myself.

We arrived at Lisbon, Nov. 5, 1715. At our landing, the Captain forced me to cover myself with his cloak, to prevent the rabble from crowding about me. I was conveyed to his own house; and at my earnest request, he led me up to the highest room backwards.[9] I conjured him to conceal from all per-

9. At the rear.

sons what I had told him of the Houyhnhnms; because the least hint of such a story would not only draw numbers of people to see me, but probably put me in danger of being imprisoned, or burned by the Inquisition. The Captain persuaded me to accept a suit of clothes newly made; but I would not suffer the tailor to take my measure; however, Don Pedro being almost of my size, they fitted me well enough. He accoutred me with other necessaries, all new, which I aired for twenty-four hours before I would use them.

The Captain had no wife, nor above three servants, none of which were suffered to attend at meals; and his whole deportment was so obliging, added to very good human understanding, that I really began to tolerate his company. He gained so far upon me, that I ventured to look out of the back window. By degrees I was brought into another room, from whence I peeped into the street, but drew my head back in a fright. In a week's time he seduced me down to the door. I found my terror gradually lessened, but my hatred and contempt seemed to increase. I was at last bold enough to walk the street in his company, but kept my nose well stopped with rue, or sometimes with tobacco.

In ten days, Don Pedro, to whom I had given some account of my domestic affairs, put it upon me as a point of honor and conscience that I ought to return to my native country, and live at home with my wife and children. He told me there was an English ship in the port just ready to sail, and he would furnish me with all things necessary. It would be tedious to repeat his arguments, and my contradictions. He said it was altogether impossible to find such a solitary island as I had desired to live in; but I might command in my own house, and pass my time in a manner as recluse as I pleased.

I complied at last, finding I could not do better. I left Lisbon the 24th day of November, in an English merchantman, but who was the Master I never inquired. Don Pedro accompanied me to the ship, and lent me twenty pounds. He took kind leave of me, and embraced me at parting; which I bore as well as I could. During this last voyage I had no commerce with the Master, or any of his men; but pretending I was sick kept close in my cabin. On the fifth of December, 1715, we cast anchor in the Downs about nine in the morning, and at three in the afternoon I got safe to my house at Redriff.

My wife and family received me with great surprise and joy, because they concluded me certainly dead; but I must freely confess, the sight of them filled me only with hatred, disgust, and contempt; and the more, by reflecting on the near alliance I had to them. For, although since my unfortunate exile from the Houyhnhnm country, I had compelled myself to tolerate the sight of Yahoos, and to converse with Don Pedro de Mendez; yet my memory and imaginations were perpetually filled with the virtues and ideas of those exalted Houyhnhnms. And when I began to consider that by copulating with one of the Yahoo species, I had become a parent of more, it struck me with the utmost shame, confusion, and horror.

As soon as I entered the house, my wife took me in her arms, and kissed me; at which, having not been used to the touch of that odious animal for so many years, I fell in a swoon for almost an hour. At the time I am writing, it is five years since my last return to England; during the first year I could not endure my wife or children in my presence, the very smell of them was intolerable; much less could I suffer them to eat in the same room. To this

278 / Jonathan Swift

hour they dare not presume to touch my bread, or drink out of the same cup; neither was I ever able to let one of them take me by the hand. The first money I laid out was to buy two young stone-horses,[1] which I keep in a good stable, and next to them the groom is my greatest favorite; for I feel my spirits revived by the smell he contracts in the stable. My horses understand me tolerably well; I converse with them at least four hours every day. They are strangers to bridle or saddle; they live in great amity with me, and friendship to each other.

CHAPTER XII

The Author's veracity. His design in publishing this work. His censure of those travelers who swerve from the truth. The Author clears himself from any sinister ends in writing. An objection answered. The method of planting colonies. His native country commended. The right of the crown to those countries described by the Author is justified. The difficulty of conquering them. The Author takes his last leave of the reader; proposeth his manner of living for the future; gives good advice, and concludeth.

Thus, gentle reader, I have given thee a faithful history of my travels for sixteen years, and above seven months; wherein I have not been so studious of ornament as of truth. I could perhaps like others have astonished thee with strange improbable tales; but I rather chose to relate plain matter of fact in the simplest manner and style; because my principal design was to inform, and not to amuse thee.

It is easy for us who travel into remote countries, which are seldom visited by Englishmen or other Europeans, to form descriptions of wonderful animals both at sea and land. Whereas a traveler's chief aim should be to make men wiser and better, and to improve their minds by the bad as well as good example of what they deliver concerning foreign places.

I could heartily wish a law were enacted, that every traveler, before he were permitted to publish his voyages, should be obliged to make oath before the Lord High Chancellor that all he intended to print was absolutely true to the best of his knowledge; for then the world would no longer be deceived as it usually is, while some writers, to make their works pass the better upon the public, impose the grossest falsities on the unwary reader. I have perused several books of travels with great delight in my younger days; but, having since gone over most parts of the globe, and been able to contradict many fabulous accounts from my own observation, it hath given me a great disgust against this part of reading, and some indignation to see the credulity of mankind so impudently abused. Therefore, since my acquaintance were pleased to think my poor endeavors might not be unacceptable to my country; I imposed on myself as a maxim, never to be swerved from, that I would *strictly adhere to truth*; neither indeed can I be ever under the least temptation to vary from it, while I retain in my mind the lectures and example of my noble master, and the other illustrious Houyhnhnms, of whom I had so long the honor to be an humble hearer.

1. Stallions.

——Nec si miserum Fortuna Sinonem
Finxit, vanum etiam, mendacemque improba finget.[2]

I know very well how little reputation is to be got by writings which require neither genius nor learning, nor indeed any other talent, except a good memory, or an exact *Journal*. I know likewise, that writers of travels, like dictionary-makers, are sunk into oblivion by the weight and bulk of those who come last, and therefore lie uppermost. And it is highly probable that such travelers who shall hereafter visit the countries described in this work of mine, may be detecting my errors (if there be any) and adding many new discoveries of their own, jostle me out of vogue, and stand in my place, making the world forget that ever I was an author. This indeed would be too great a mortification if I wrote for fame; but, as my sole intention was the PUBLIC GOOD, I cannot be altogether disappointed. For, who can read the virtues I have mentioned in the glorious Houyhnhnms, without being ashamed of his own vices, when he considers himself as the reasoning, governing animal of his country? I shall say nothing of those remote nations where Yahoos preside; amongst which the least corrupted are the Brobdingnagians, whose wise maxims in morality and government it would be our happiness to observe. But I forbear descanting further, and rather leave the judicious reader to his own remarks and applications.

I am not a little pleased that this work of mine can possibly meet with no censurers; for what objections can be made against a writer who relates only plain facts that happened in such distant countries, where we have not the least interest with respect either to trade or negotiations? I have carefully avoided every fault with which common writers of travels are often too justly charged. Besides, I meddle not the least with any party, but write without passion, prejudice, or ill-will against any man or number of men whatsoever. I write for the noblest end, to inform and instruct mankind, over whom I may, without breach of modesty, pretend to some superiority, from the advantages I received by conversing so long among the most accomplished Houyhnhnms. I write without any view towards profit or praise. I never suffer a word to pass that may look like reflection, or possibly give the least offense even to those who are most ready to take it. So that, I hope, I may with justice pronounce myself an Author perfectly blameless; against whom the tribes of answerers, considerers, observers, reflectors, detecters, remarkers will never be able to find matter for exercising their talents.

I confess it was whispered to me that I was bound in duty as a subject of England, to have given in a memorial to a secretary of state, at my first coming over; because, whatever lands are discovered by a subject, belong to the Crown. But I doubt whether our conquests in the countries I treat of would be as easy as those of Ferdinando Cortez[3] over the naked Americans. The Lilliputians, I think, are hardly worth the charge of a fleet and army to reduce them; and I question whether it might be prudent or safe to attempt the Brobdingnagians; or, whether an English army would be much at their ease with the Flying Island over their heads. The Houyhnhnms, indeed,

2. Fortune has made a derelict of Sinon / but the bitch won't make an empty liar of him, too (Latin; from Virgil's *Aeneid* 2).   3. Hernando Cortés (1485–1547), who destroyed the Aztec Empire.

appear not to be so well prepared for war, a science to which they are perfect strangers, and especially against missive weapons. However, supposing myself to be a minister of state, I could never give my advice for invading them. Their prudence, unanimity, unacquaintedness with fear, and their love of their country would amply supply all defects in the military art. Imagine twenty thousand of them breaking into the midst of an European army, confounding the ranks, overturning the carriages, battering the warriors' faces into mummy, by terrible yerks[4] from their hinder hoofs: for they would well deserve the character given to Augustus, *Recalcitrat undique tutus.*[5] But instead of proposals for conquering that magnanimous nation, I rather wish they were in a capacity or disposition to send a sufficient number of their inhabitants for civilizing Europe; by teaching us the first principles of Honor, Justice, Truth, Temperance, Public Spirit, Fortitude, Chastity, Friendship, Benevolence, and Fidelity. The names of all which Virtues are still retained among us in most languages, and are to be met with in modern as well as ancient authors, which I am able to assert from my own small reading.

But I had another reason which made me less forward to enlarge his majesty's dominions by my discoveries: to say the truth, I had conceived a few scruples with relation to the distributive justice of princes upon those occasions. For instance, a crew of pirates are driven by a storm they know not whither; at length a boy discovers land from the topmast; they go on shore to rob and plunder; they see an harmless people, are entertained with kindness, they give the country a new name, they take formal possession of it for the king, they set up a rotten plank or a stone for a memorial, they murder two or three dozen of the natives, bring away a couple more by force for a sample, return home, and get their pardon. Here commences a new dominion acquired with a title by Divine Right. Ships are sent with the first opportunity; the natives driven out or destroyed, their princes tortured to discover their gold; a free license given to all acts of inhumanity and lust; the earth reeking with the blood of its inhabitants: and this execrable crew of butchers employed in so pious an expedition is a *modern colony* sent to convert and civilize an idolatrous and barbarous people.

But this description, I confess, doth by no means affect the British nation, who may be an example to the whole world for their wisdom, care, and justice in planting colonies; their liberal endowments for the advancement of religion and learning; their choice of devout and able pastors to propagate Christianity; their caution in stocking their provinces with people of sober lives and conversations from this the Mother Kingdom; their strict regard to the distribution of justice, in supplying the civil administration through all their colonies with officers of the greatest abilities, utter strangers to corruption: and to crown all, by sending the most vigilant and virtuous governors, who have no other views than the happiness of the people over whom they preside, and the honor of the king their master.

But, as those countries which I have described do not appear to have any desire of being conquered, and enslaved, murdered, or driven out by colonies, nor abound either in gold, silver, sugar, or tobacco, I did humbly conceive they were by no means proper objects of our zeal, our valor, or our interest.

---

4. Kicks. *Mummy:* pulp.   5. He kicks backward, at every point on his guard (Latin; Horace's *Satires* 2.20).

However, if those whom it may concern, think fit to be of another opinion, I am ready to depose, when I shall be lawfully called, that no European did ever visit these countries before me. I mean, if the inhabitants ought to be believed.

But, as to the formality of taking possession in my sovereign's name, it never came once into my thoughts; and if it had, yet as my affairs then stood, I should perhaps in point of prudence and self-preservation have put it off to a better opportunity.

Having thus answered the only objection that can be raised against me as a traveler, I here take a final leave of my courteous readers, and return to enjoy my own speculations in my little garden at Redriff; to apply those excellent lessons of virtue which I learned among the Houyhnhnms; to instruct the Yahoos of my own family as far as I shall find them docible animals; to behold my figure often in a glass, and thus if possible habituate myself by time to tolerate the sight of a human creature; to lament the brutality of Houyhnhnms in my own country, but always treat their persons with respect, for the sake of my noble master, his family, his friends, and the whole Houyhnhnm race, whom these of ours have the honor to resemble in all their lineaments, however their intellectuals came to degenerate.

I began last week to permit my wife to sit at dinner with me, at the farthest end of a long table; and to answer (but with the utmost brevity) the few questions I ask her. Yet the smell of a Yahoo continuing very offensive, I always keep my nose well stopped with rue, lavender, or tobacco leaves. And although it be hard for a man late in life to remove old habits, I am not altogether out of hopes in some time to suffer a neighbor Yahoo in my company, without the apprehensions I am yet under of his teeth or his claws.

My reconcilement to the Yahoo kind in general might not be so difficult, if they would be content with those vices and follies only which nature hath entitled them to. I am not in the least provoked at the sight of a lawyer, a pickpocket, a colonel, a fool, a lord, a gamester, politician, a whoremonger, a physician, an evidence, a suborner, an attorney, a traitor, or the like: this is all according to the due course of things. But when I behold a lump of deformity, and diseases both in body and mind, smitten with pride, it immediately breaks all the measures of my patience; neither shall I be ever able to comprehend how such an animal and such a vice could tally together. The wise and virtuous Houyhnhnms, who abound in all excellencies that can adorn a rational creature, have no name for this vice in their language, which hath no terms to express anything that is evil, except those whereby they describe the detestable qualities of their Yahoos, among which they were not able to distinguish this of pride, for want of thoroughly understanding human nature, as it showeth itself in other countries, where that animal presides. But I, who had more experience, could plainly observe some rudiments of it among the wild Yahoos.

But the Houyhnhnms, who live under the government of reason, are no more proud of the good qualities they possess, than I should be for not wanting a leg or an arm, which no man in his wits would boast of, although he must be miserable without them. I dwell the longer upon this subject from the desire I have to make the society of an English Yahoo by any means not insupportable; and therefore I here entreat those who have any tincture of this absurd vice, that they will not presume to appear in my sight.

A Modest Proposal[1]

for Preventing the Children of poor People in Ireland, *from being a Burden to their Parents or Country; and for making them beneficial to the Publick.*

Written in the year 1729

It is a melancholy object to those who walk through this great town,[2] or travel in the country, when they see the streets, the roads, and cabin-doors crowded with beggars of the female sex, followed by three, four, or six children, all in rags, and importuning every passenger for an alms. These mothers, instead of being able to work for their honest livelihood, are forced to employ all their time in strolling to beg sustenance for their helpless infants: who, as they grow up, either turn thieves for want of work, or leave their dear native country to fight for the Pretender in Spain, or sell themselves to the Barbadoes.[3]

I think it is agreed by all parties, that this prodigious number of children in the arms, or on the backs, or at the heels of their mothers, and frequently of their fathers, is, in the present deplorable state of the kingdom, a very great additional grievance; and, therefore, whoever could find out a fair, cheap, and easy method of making these children sound and useful members of the commonwealth, would deserve so well of the public, as to have his statue set up for a preserver of the nation.

But my intention is very far from being confined to provide only for the children of professed beggars; it is of a much greater extent, and shall take in the whole number of infants at a certain age, who are born of parents in effect as little able to support them as those who demand our charity in the streets.

As to my own part, having turned my thoughts for many years upon this important subject, and maturely weighed the several schemes of other projectors,[4] I have always found them grossly mistaken in their computation. It is true, a child, just dropped from its dam, may be supported by her milk for a solar year with little other nourishment; at most, not above the value of two shillings, which the mother may certainly get, or the value in scraps, by her lawful occupation of begging; and it is exactly at one year old that I propose to provide for them in such a manner, as, instead of being a charge upon their parents or the parish, or wanting food and raiment for the rest of their lives, they shall, on the contrary, contribute to the feeding, and partly to the clothing, of many thousands.

There is likewise another advantage in my scheme, that it will prevent those voluntary abortions, and that horrid practice of women murdering their bastard children, alas, too frequent among us, sacrificing the poor innocent babes, I doubt more to avoid the expense than the shame, which would move tears and pity in the most savage and inhuman breast.

1. The complete text edited by Herbert Davis.　2. Dublin.　3. At this time a British possession, with a prosperous sugar industry. Workers were needed in the sugar plantations. *The Pretender:* James Edward (1688–1766), son of the Catholic King James II of England, called the "Old Pretender" (in distinction to his son Charles, nine years old at the time of this work, called the "Young Pretender"). Many thought him a legitimate claimant to the throne.　4. Planners.

The number of souls in this kingdom being usually reckoned one million and a half, of these I calculate there may be about two hundred thousand couple whose wives are breeders; from which number I subtract thirty thousand couple, who are able to maintain their own children (although I apprehend there cannot be so many, under the present distresses of the kingdom); but this being granted, there will remain an hundred and seventy thousand breeders. I again subtract fifty thousand for those women who miscarry, or whose children die by accident or disease within the year. There only remain a hundred and twenty thousand children of poor parents annually born. The question therefore is how this number shall be reared and provided for? which, as I have already said, under the present situation of affairs, is utterly impossible by all the methods hitherto proposed. For we can neither employ them in handicraft or agriculture; we neither build houses (I mean in the country) nor cultivate land: they can very seldom pick up a livelihood by stealing until they arrive at six years old, except where they are of towardly parts;[5] although I confess they learn the rudiments much earlier; during which time they can, however, be properly looked upon only as probationers; as I have been informed by a principal gentleman in the county of Cavan, who protested to me, that he never knew above one or two instances under the age of six, even in a part of the kingdom so renowned for the quickest proficiency in that art.

I am assured by our merchants that a boy or a girl before twelve years old is no saleable commodity; and even when they come to this age they will not yield above three pounds or three pounds and half-a-crown at most, on the exchange; which cannot turn to account either to the parents or kingdom, the charge of nutriment and rags having been at least four times that value.

I shall now, therefore, humbly propose my own thoughts, which I hope will not be liable to the least objection.

I have been assured by a very knowing American of my acquaintance in London, that a young healthy child, well nursed, is, at a year old, a most delicious, nourishing, and wholesome food, whether stewed, roasted, baked, or boiled; and I make no doubt that it will equally serve in a fricassee or a ragout.

I do therefore humbly offer it to public consideration, that of the hundred and twenty thousand children already computed, twenty thousand may be reserved for breed, whereof only one-fourth part to be males; which is more than we allow to sheep, black cattle, or swine; and my reason is, that these children are seldom the fruits of marriage, a circumstance not much regarded by our savages, therefore one male will be sufficient to serve four females. That the remaining hundred thousand may, at a year old, be offered in sale to the persons of quality and fortune through the kingdom; always advising the mother to let them suck plentifully in the last month, so as to render them plump and fat for a good table. A child will make two dishes at an entertainment for friends; and when the family dines alone, the fore or hind quarter will make a reasonable dish, and, seasoned with a little pepper or salt, will be very good boiled on the fourth day, especially in winter.

I have reckoned, upon a medium,[6] that a child just born will weigh twelve

5. Particularly talented, unusually gifted.   6. Average.

284 / Jonathan Swift

pounds, and in a solar year, if tolerably nursed, increaseth to twenty-eight pounds.

I grant this food will be somewhat dear,[7] and therefore very proper for landlords, who, as they have already devoured most of the parents, seem to have the best title to the children.

Infants' flesh will be in season throughout the year, but more plentifully in March, and a little before and after: for we are told by a grave author, an eminent French physician,[8] that fish being a prolific diet, there are more children born in Roman Catholic countries about nine months after Lent than at any other season; therefore, reckoning a year after Lent, the markets will be more glutted than usual, because the number of popish infants is at least three to one in this kingdom; and therefore it will have one other collateral advantage, by lessening the number of papists among us.

I have already computed the charge of nursing a beggar's child (in which list I reckon all cottagers, labourers, and four-fifths of the farmers) to be about two shillings per annum,[9] rags included; and I believe no gentleman would repine to give ten shillings for the carcass of a good fat child, which, as I have said, will make four dishes of excellent nutritive meat, when he has only some particular friend, or his own family, to dine with him. Thus the squire will learn to be a good landlord, and grow popular among his tenants; the mother will have eight shillings net profit, and be fit for work till she produces another child.

Those who are more thrifty (as I must confess the times require) may flay the carcass; the skin of which, artificially dressed, will make admirable gloves for ladies, and summer-boots for fine gentlemen.

As to our city of Dublin, shambles[1] may be appointed for this purpose in the most convenient parts of it, and butchers we may be assured will not be wanting; although I rather recommend buying the children alive, and dressing them hot from the knife, as we do roasting pigs.

A very worthy person, a true lover of his country, and whose virtues I highly esteem, was lately pleased, in discoursing on this matter, to offer a refinement upon my scheme. He said, that many gentlemen of this kingdom, having of late destroyed their deer, he conceived that the want of venison might be well supplied by the bodies of young lads and maidens, not exceeding fourteen years of age, nor under twelve; so great a number of both sexes in every country being now ready to starve for want of work and service; and these to be disposed of by their parents, if alive, or otherwise by their nearest relations. But, with due deference to so excellent a friend, and so deserving a patriot, I cannot be altogether in his sentiments; for as to the males, my American acquaintance assured me from frequent experience, that their flesh was generally tough and lean, like that of our schoolboys, by continual exercise, and their taste disagreeable; and to fatten them would not answer the charge. Then as to the females, it would, I think, with humble submission, be a loss to the public, because they soon would become breeders themselves: and besides, it is not improbable that some scrupulous people might be apt to censure such a practice (although indeed very unjustly) as a

7. Expensive. 8. François Rabelais (1494?–1553), French satirist and author of *Gargantua and Pantagruel* (1532–52). 9. Per year. 1. Slaughterhouses.

little bordering upon cruelty; which, I confess hath always been with me the strongest objection against any project, how well soever intended.

But in order to justify my friend, he confessed that this expedient was put into his head by the famous Psalmanazar,[2] a native of the island Formosa, who came from thence to London above twenty years ago; and in conversation told my friend, that in his country, when any young person happened to be put to death, the executioner sold the carcass to persons of quality as a prime dainty; and that in his time the body of a plump girl of fifteen, who was crucified for an attempt to poison the emperor, was sold to his Imperial Majesty's prime minister of state, and other great mandarins of the court, in joints from the gibbet,[3] at four hundred crowns. Neither indeed can I deny, that if the same use were made of several plump young girls in this town, who, without one single groat to their fortunes, cannot stir abroad without a chair,[4] and appear at playhouse and assemblies in foreign fineries which they never will pay for, the kingdom would not be the worse.

Some persons of a desponding spirit are in great concern about the vast number of poor people who are aged, diseased, or maimed; and I have been desired to employ my thoughts what course may be taken to ease the nation of so grievous an encumbrance. But I am not in the least pain upon that matter, because it is very well known, that they are every day dying, and rotting, by cold and famine, and filth and vermin, as fast as can be reasonably expected. And as to the younger labourers, they are now in almost as hopeful a condition: they cannot get work, and consequently pine away for want of nourishment, to a degree, that if at any time they are accidentally hired to common labour, they have not strength to perform it; and thus the country and themselves are happily delivered from the evils to come.

I have too long digressed, and therefore shall return to my subject. I think the advantages by the proposal which I have made are obvious and many, as well as of the highest importance.

For first, as I have already observed, it would greatly lessen the number of papists, with whom we are yearly overrun, being the principal breeders of the nation as well as our most dangerous enemies; and who stay at home on purpose with a design to deliver the kingdom to the Pretender, hoping to take their advantage by the absence of so many good Protestants, who have chosen rather to leave their country than stay at home and pay tithes against their conscience to an idolatrous Episcopal curate.

Secondly, the poorer tenants will have something valuable of their own, which by law may be made liable to distress,[5] and help to pay their landlord's rent; their corn and cattle being already seized, and money a thing unknown.

Thirdly, whereas the maintenance of an hundred thousand children, from two years old and upwards, cannot be computed at less than ten shillings a piece per annum, the nation's stock will be thereby increased fifty thousand pounds per annum; besides the profit of a new dish introduced to the tables of all gentlemen of fortune in the kingdom who have any refinement in taste.

2. George Psalmanazar (1679?–1763), a literary impostor born in southern France who claimed to be a native of Formosa and a recent Christian convert. He published a catechism in an invented language that he called Formosan, as well as a description of Formosa with an introductory autobiography.   3. The post from which the bodies of criminals were hung in chains after execution. *Joints:* portions of a carcass carved up by a butcher.   4. I.e., a sedan chair, an enclosed seat carried on poles by men.   5. The legal seizing of goods to satisfy a debt, particularly for unpaid rent.

And the money will circulate among ourselves, the goods being entirely of our own growth and manufacture.

Fourthly, the constant breeders, besides the gain of eight shillings sterling per annum by the sale of their children, will be rid of the charge of maintaining them after the first year.

Fifthly, this food would likewise bring great custom to taverns; where the vinters will certainly be so prudent as to procure the best receipts[6] for dressing it to perfection, and, consequently, have their houses frequented by all the fine gentlemen, who justly value themselves upon their knowledge in good eating: and a skilful cook, who understands how to oblige his guests, will contrive to make it as expensive as they please.

Sixthly, this would be a great inducement to marriage, which all wise nations have either encouraged by rewards, or enforced by laws and penalties. It would increase the care and tenderness of mothers towards their children, when they were sure of a settlement for life to the poor babes, provided in some sort by the public, to their annual profit instead of expense. We should soon see an honest emulation among the married women, which of them could bring the fattest child to the market. Men would become as fond of their wives during the time of their pregnancy, as they are now of their mares in foal, their cows in calf, or sows when they are ready to farrow; nor offer to beat or kick them (as is too frequent a practice) for fear of a miscarriage.

Many other advantages might be enumerated. For instance, the addition of some thousand carcasses in our exportation of barrelled beef; the propagation of swine's flesh, and improvement in the art of making good bacon, so much wanted among us by the great destruction of pigs, too frequent at our tables, which are no way comparable in taste or magnificence to a well-grown, fat yearling child, which, roasted whole, will make a considerable figure at a Lord Mayor's feast, or any other public entertainment. But this, and many others, I omit, being studious of brevity.

Supposing that one thousand families in this city would be constant customers for infants' flesh, besides others who might have it at merry meetings, particularly weddings and christenings. I compute that Dublin would take off annually about twenty thousand carcasses; and the rest of the kingdom (where probably they will be sold somewhat cheaper) the remaining eighty thousand.

I can think of no one objection that will possibly be raised against this proposal, unless it should be urged, that the number of people will be thereby much lessened in the kingdom. This I freely own, and it was indeed one principal design in offering it to the world. I desire the reader will observe that I calculate my remedy *for this one individual kingdom of Ireland, and for no other that ever was, is, or I think ever can be, upon earth.* Therefore let no man talk to me of other expedients: *of taxing our absentees at five shillings a pound: of using neither clothes nor household-furniture except what is of our own growth and manufacture: of utterly rejecting the materials and instruments that promote foreign luxury: of curing the expensiveness of pride, vanity, idleness, and gaming in our women; of introducing a vein of parsimony, prudence, and temperance: of learning to love our country, wherein we differ even*

6. Recipes.

from Laplanders, and the inhabitants of Topinamboo:[7] of quitting our animosities and factions, nor act any longer like the Jews,[8] who were murdering one another at the very moment their city was taken: of being a little cautious not to sell our country and consciences for nothing: of teaching landlords to have at least one degree of mercy towards their tenants: lastly, of putting a spirit of honesty, industry, and skill into our shopkeepers; who, if a resolution could now be taken to buy only our native goods, would immediately unite to cheat and exact upon us in the price, the measure, and the goodness, nor could ever yet be brought to make one fair proposal of just dealing, though often and earnestly invited to it.[9]

Therefore I repeat, let no man talk to me of these and the like expedients, till he hath at least some glimpse of hope that there will ever be some hearty and sincere attempts to put them in practice.

But, as to myself, having been wearied out for many years with offering vain, idle, visionary thoughts, and at length utterly despairing of success, I fortunately fell upon this proposal; which, as it is wholly new, so it hath something solid and real, of no expense and little trouble, full in our own power, and whereby we can incur no danger in disobliging England. For this kind of commodity will not bear exportation, the flesh being of too tender a consistence to admit a long continuance in salt, although perhaps I could name a country[1] which would be glad to eat up our whole nation without it.

After all, I am not so violently bent upon my own opinion as to reject any offer proposed by wise men which shall be found equally innocent, cheap, easy, and effectual. But before something of that kind shall be advanced in contradiction to my scheme, and offering a better, I desire the author, or authors, will be pleased maturely to consider two points. First, as things now stand, how they will be able to find food and raiment for a hundred thousand useless mouths and backs? And, secondly, there being a round million of creatures in human figure throughout this kingdom, whose whole subsistence put into a common stock would leave them in debt two millions of pounds sterling, adding those who are beggars by profession, to the bulk of farmers, cottagers, and labourers, with the wives and children who are beggars in effect; I desire those politicians who dislike my overture, and may perhaps be so bold as to attempt an answer, that they will first ask the parents of these mortals, whether they would not at this day think it a great happiness to have been sold for food at a year old, in the manner I prescribe, and thereby have avoided such a perpetual scene of misfortunes as they have since gone through, by the oppression of landlords, the impossibility of paying rent without money or trade, the want of common sustenance, with neither house nor clothes to cover them from the inclemencies of weather, and the most inevitable prospect of entailing the like, or greater miseries, upon their breed for ever.

I profess, in the sincerity of my heart, that I have not the least personal interest in endeavouring to promote this necessary work, having no other motive than the public good of my country, by advancing our trade, providing for infants, relieving the poor, and giving some pleasure to the rich. I have

7. In Brazil.   8. Referring to the factionalism under Herod Agrippa II at the time of the destruction of Jerusalem by the Roman emperor Titus.   9. The italicized proposals are Swift's serious suggestions for remedying the situation of Ireland.   1. England.

no children by which I can propose to get a single penny; the youngest being nine years old, and my wife past child-bearing.

ALEXANDER POPE
1688–1744

"If Pope be not a poet, where is poetry to be found?" Samuel Johnson inquired. Transmuting the commonplace, claiming as subject matter everything from the minutiae of social existence to speculation about the nature of universal order, Alexander Pope made unlikely raw material into brilliant poetry.

Born to Roman Catholic parents in the year of the Glorious Revolution that deposed Catholic James II in favor of Protestant William and Mary, Pope lived when repressive legislation against Catholics restricted his financial, educational, professional, and residential possibilities. He could not attend a university or hold public employment; he had to live ten miles outside London. Sickly and undersized (he probably suffered a tubercular infection in infancy), he was educated largely at home. He also educated himself by literary friendships beginning in his youth; throughout his life, he enjoyed close associations with other men and with a few women, in particular his neighbor and intimate friend Martha Blount, to whom he left his estate. Increasingly, he won wealth and reputation by his writing, notably his translations of Homer. Following Candide's course of cultivating his garden, he perfected his grounds and grotto at Twickenham, living in retirement from the city. He died of asthma and edema.

Pope's work ranged through most of the poetic genres of his period. Beginning, as Virgil had done, with pastorals, he later produced *An Essay on Criticism,* versified advice about proper literary and critical procedure, and went on to publish a great philosophic poem, *An Essay on Man,* and to edit Shakespeare's plays. The bulk of his verse, however, was satiric. In *The Dunciad* (1743), he provided a satiric epic for his age, a history of the progress of dullness.

Writing to a woman friend, Pope described *The Rape of the Lock* (1717) as "at once the most a satire, and the most inoffensive, of anything of mine. . . . 'Tis a sort of writing very like tickling." He thus suggests the tonal complexity of a work that conveys serious social criticism through a fanciful and playful fable narrated in verse of surpassing grace and elegance. The joke of the poem, as well as its serious point, derives from the cataclysmic disturbance a young woman makes over her loss of a lock of hair. Pope adapts epic conventions to his narrative of trivia, including even a supernatural species—the sylphs—parodying the functions of the Greek gods. These reminders of the epic, a genre by definition concerned with important matters, emphasize the poet's consciousness of the relative triviality of eighteenth-century high-society preoccupations. The world Belinda inhabits confuses small things with great; "Puffs, powders, patches, Bibles, billet-doux" occupy her dressing table in indiscriminate assembly. Members of this society take their own pleasure more seriously than anything else: "wretches hang that jurymen may dine." Men and women coexist in fascinated tension, tension that, given even slight provocation, explodes in hostilities. Sexual issues govern the conflict: women guard their "honor," the reputation of chastity, more intently than they preserve their physical purity; men seek to violate both. The ideals of good sense and good humor, expressed in the poem by Clarissa, govern no one in action. Instead, both sexes value beauty (which, as Clarissa points out, fades) and accept it as an excuse for emotional self-indulgence (the theme of Umbriel's excursion to the Cave of Spleen). In its accounts of moral and psychological confusion, of hysterical fits and battles, the poem employs the familiar satiric techniques of exaggeration and distortion intended to reveal the truth and to inspire reform.

But *The Rape of the Lock* celebrates as well as criticizes. The delicacy and grace of the verse, the ethereal beauty of the sylphs, recapitulate Belinda's genuine grace and beauty: "If to her share some female errors fall,/Look on her face, and you'll forget 'em all." Belinda's world operates mainly on the basis of style. In its separation of style from moral substance, the society demands criticism; but the beauty it values—elegant conversation, boat trips on the Thames, magnificent women—like the beauty the poet creates, has meaning in itself. When the disputed lock of hair ascends to the constellations, when the poet calls attention to his own preservation of Belinda's beauty and fame, *The Rape of the Lock* reminds us that praise and blame sometimes appropriately attach to the same objects. Its mixture of playfulness and seriousness, of beauty and harshness, mark the poem's unique achievement.

In *An Essay on Man* (1733–34), a very different work, Pope set out to consider, in successive epistles, humanity in relation to the universe, to itself, to society, and to happiness: an enterprise of ambition almost comparable to Milton's in *Paradise Lost*. Indeed, in the first section of the poem Pope alludes specifically to his predecessor, describing the world as a "Garden, tempting with forbidden fruit" and declaring his own intention to "vindicate [Milton had used *justify*] the ways of God to man." Unlike Milton, Pope pursues this goal not through a dramatic fable but by an extended versified meditation on the philosophic issues involved. That meditation, however, generates its own drama.

Pope draws on a number of intellectual traditions to define the human condition in both cosmic and social terms. The breadth of his reference—to Catholic and Protestant theology, to Platonic and Stoic philosophy, to his period's notions of plenitude and natural order—itself reinforces the underlying assumption of universal, unchanging human nature. The poet evokes a timeless vision of humanity in the universe, poised at the middle of the Great Chain of Being that extends from God to the most minute forms of life, with the fullest possible range of being above and below humankind. Complaints that the poem's philosophy is shallow ignore the complexity of its synthesis and the seriousness of its ideas. The resounding assertion that concludes the first epistle, for instance ("One truth is clear, WHATEVER IS, IS RIGHT"), implies no unawareness of human misery or evil. Abundant examples of both have been presented in the text. The point is, rather, that the nature of God's plan—by definition not fully comprehensible to human reason—must allow evil for the sake of larger good. And human beings, to possess free will, must have available to them the choice of evil. Such assumptions belong to the intellectual position called "philosophical optimism"—by no means equivalent to what we usually think of as optimism, the faith that everything will turn out well in the long run. The belief expounded in *An Essay on Man*, on the contrary, allows the possibility that matters may turn out badly for individual men and women but assumes that personal misfortune takes its place in a larger, essentially benign, pattern.

The first epistle of the poem, printed here, progresses through ten logically connected sections. It begins by insisting on the necessary limitation of human judgment: we see only parts, not the whole. Nonetheless, this fact does not imply the imperfection of humankind; it means, rather, that we are adapted to our position in the general order of things. Our ignorance of future events and our hope for eternal life give us the possibility of happiness. The poem then indicts human beings for pride and impiety (we claim more power of judgment and more knowledge than we can have), for the absurdity of assuming themselves the center of the created universe, and for the unreasonableness of complaints against the providential order (we demand, the poet suggests, both the perfection of angels and the physical sensitivities of animals, although increase in our capacities would bring misery). Turning to the nature of the universal order, the argument insists on the gradations of faculties from the lower animals to humankind, then suggests that this order extends farther than we can know: any interference with it would destroy the whole. Even the speculative possibility of such interference suggests the insanity of human pride. Our only proper course is absolute submission to Providence.

This logical sequence structures the *Essay on Man,* but we should not read the poem only as a versified handbook of eighteenth-century philosophy. Here, as in *The Rape of the Lock,* Pope displays his poetic brilliance, converting philosophic argument into a rich emotional and intellectual texture. He draws us into the poem by addressing us directly, reminding us of our own tendencies to presumption, our own inevitable desire to understand the universe as revolving around us. "In Pride, in reas'ning Pride, our error lies": we all share bewilderment at our situation, we all need to interpret it, we all face, every day, our necessary limitations. The poet rapidly shifts tone, sometimes berating his readers, sometimes reminding us (and himself) of his own participation in the universal dilemma, sometimes assuming a godlike perspective and suggesting his superior knowledge. By his changing voice, his changing forms of address, he makes dramatic the futile, yet noble, effort to understand what only the deity can fully comprehend.

At its best, *An Essay on Man* transforms philosophy into emotional experience. It generates drama out of shifting, intersecting perspectives: the lamb licking the hand of its butcher, the Indian looking forward to a Heaven his dog will share, the scientist trying to interpret the physical universe. It also makes the abstract vividly specific and concrete, as when reflection on the necessary limitation of human faculties produces the penetrating image of someone dying "of a rose in aromatic pain." Pope's imagination summons up a vast range of concrete reference, and it does not avoid the disturbing: we are invited to think of the human condition in the universe as comparable to that of the ox, which tills the fields, goes to slaughter, or finds itself worshiped as a god, according to accidents of situation. The fly's "microscopic eye" excels our powers; we resemble weeds more than oaks. Yet the poet, ranging from the conversational ease of his opening lines to the ringing certainties of his conclusion, incorporates perceptions of human inadequacy into assertions of a grand scheme, which he makes not only rational but exciting.

Pope has been the subject of a great deal of writing. Biographies include G. Sherburn, *The Early Career of Alexander Pope* (1934), and M. Mack, *Alexander Pope* (1985). A range of responses is represented in M. Mack and J. A. Winn, eds., *Pope: Recent Essays by Several Hands* (1980); H. Bloom, ed., *Alexander Pope* (1985); and W. Jackson and R. P. Yoder, eds., *Critical Essays on Alexander Pope* (1993). Perceptive critical books include R. A. Brower, *Alexander Pope: The Poetry of Allusion* (1959), and T. R. Edwards, *This Dark Estate: A Reading of Pope* (1963). Other useful studies include D. B. Morris, *The Genius of Sense* (1984); L. Damrosch Jr., *The Imaginative World of Alexander Pope* (1987); and Helen Deutsch, *Resemblance and Disgrace: Alexander Pope and the Deformation of Culture* (1996).

PRONOUNCING GLOSSARY

The following list uses common English syllables and stress accents to provide rough equivalents of selected words whose pronunciation may be unfamiliar to the general reader.

Borgia: *bohr'-jah*

Le Comte de Gabalis: *leu kahmt du gah'-bah-lee*

Rosicrucian: *roh-zee-kru'-shan*

Scylla: *sil'-ah*

The Rape of the Lock[1]

An Heroi-Comical Poem

Nolueram, Belinda, tuos violare capillos;
sed juvat hoc precibus me tribuisse tuis.[2]
—MARTIAL

TO MRS. ARABELLA FERMOR

MADAM,

It will be in vain to deny that I have some regard for this piece, since I dedicate it to you. Yet you may bear me witness, it was intended only to divert a few young ladies, who have good sense and good humor enough to laugh not only at their sex's little unguarded follies, but at their own. But as it was communicated with the air of a secret, it soon found its way into the world. An imperfect copy having been offered to a bookseller, you had the good nature for my sake to consent to the publication of one more correct; this I was forced to, before I had executed half my design, for the machinery was entirely wanting to complete it.

The machinery, Madam, is a term invented by the critics, to signify that part which the deities, angels, or demons are made to act in a poem; for the ancient poets are in one respect like many modern ladies: let an action be never so trivial in itself, they always make it appear of the utmost importance. These machines I determined to raise on a very new and odd foundation, the Rosicrucian[3] doctrine of spirits.

I know how disagreeable it is to make use of hard words before a lady; but 'tis so much the concern of a poet to have his works understood, and particularly by your sex, that you must give me leave to explain two or three difficult terms.

The Rosicrucians are a people I must bring you acquainted with. The best account I know of them is in a French book called *Le Comte de Gabalis*,[4] which both in its title and size is so like a novel, that many of the fair sex have read it for one by mistake. According to these gentlemen, the four elements are inhabited by spirits, which they call Sylphs, Gnomes, Nymphs, and Salamanders. The Gnomes or Demons of earth delight in mischief; but the Sylphs, whose habitation is in the air, are the best-conditioned creatures imaginable. For they say, any mortals may enjoy the most intimate familiarities with these gentle spirits, upon a condition very easy to all true adepts, an inviolate preservation of chastity.

As to the following cantos, all the passages of them are as fabulous as the vision at the beginning, or the transformation at the end; (except the loss of your hair, which I always mention with reverence). The human persons are as fictitious as the airy ones; and the character of Belinda, as it is now managed, resembles you in nothing but in beauty.

---

1. Text and notes by Samuel Holt Monk.   2. "I was unwilling, Belinda, to ravish your locks; but I rejoice to have conceded this to your prayers" (Martial, *Epigrams* XII. lxxxiv. 1–2). Pope substituted his heroine for Martial's Polytimus. The epigraph is intended to suggest that the poem was published at Miss Fermor's request.   3. A system of arcane philosophy introduced into England from Germany in the seventeenth century.   4. By the Abbé de Montfaucon de Villars, published in 1670.

If this poem had as many graces as there are in your person, or in your mind, yet I could never hope it should pass through the world half so uncensured as you have done. But let its fortune be what it will, mine is happy enough, to have given me this occasion of assuring you that I am, with the truest esteem,

MADAM,
Your most obedient, humble servant,

A. POPE

CANTO I

What dire offense from amorous causes springs,
What mighty contests rise from trivial things,
I sing—This verse to Caryll,[5] Muse! is due:
This, even Belinda may vouchsafe to view:
Slight is the subject, but not so the praise,   5
If she inspire, and he approve my lays.
    Say what strange motive, Goddess! could compel
A well-bred lord t' assault a gentle belle?
Oh, say what stranger cause, yet unexplored,
Could make a gentle belle reject a lord?   10
In tasks so bold can little men engage,
And in soft bosoms dwells such mighty rage?
    Sol through white curtains shot a timorous ray,
And oped those eyes that must eclipse the day.
Now lapdogs give themselves the rousing shake,   15
And sleepless lovers just at twelve awake:
Thrice rung the bell, the slipper knocked the ground,
And the pressed watch[6] returned a silver sound.
Belinda still her downy pillow pressed,
Her guardian Sylph prolonged the balmy rest: 20
'Twas he had summoned to her silent bed
The morning dream that hovered o'er her head.
A youth more glittering than a birthnight beau[7]
(That even in slumber caused her cheek to glow)
Seemed to her ear his winning lips to lay,   25
And thus in whispers said, or seemed to say:
    "Fairest of mortals, thou distinguished care
Of thousand bright inhabitants of air!
If e'er one vision touched thy infant thought,
Of all the nurse and all the priest have taught,   30
Of airy elves by moonlight shadows seen,
The silver token, and the circled green,[8]
Or virgins visited by angel powers,
With golden crowns and wreaths of heavenly flowers,
Hear and believe! thy own importance know,   35

5. John Caryll (1666?–1736), a close friend of Pope's who suggested that he write this poem.   6. A watch that chimes the hour and the quarter hour when the stem is pressed down. *Thrice rung the bell:* Belinda thus summons her maid.   7. Courtiers wore especially fine clothes on the sovereign's birthday.   8. According to popular belief, fairies skim off the cream from jugs of milk left standing overnight and leave a coin in payment. *The circled green:* rings of bright green grass, which are common in England even in winter, were held to be due to the round dances of fairies.

Nor bound thy narrow views to things below.
Some secret truths, from learned pride concealed,
To maids alone and children are revealed:
What though no credit doubting wits may give?
The fair and innocent shall still believe.   40
Know, then, unnumbered spirits round thee fly,
The light militia of the lower sky:
These, though unseen, are ever on the wing,
Hang o'er the box,⁹ and hover round the Ring.
Think what an equipage thou hast in air,   45
And view with scorn two pages and a chair.¹
As now your own, our beings were of old,
And once enclosed in woman's beauteous mold
Thence, by a soft transition, we repair
From earthly vehicles to these of air.   50
Think not, when woman's transient breath is fled,
That all her vanities at once are dead:
Succeeding vanities she still regards,
And though she plays no more o'erlooks the cards.
Her joy in gilded chariots, when alive,   55
And love of ombre,² after death survive.
For when the Fair in all their pride expire,
To their first elements³ their souls retire:
The sprites of fiery termagants in flame
Mount up, and take a Salamander's name.⁴   60
Soft yielding minds to water glide away,
And sip, with Nymphs, their elemental tea.⁵
The graver prude sinks downward to a Gnome,
In search of mischief still on earth to roam.
The light coquettes in Sylphs aloft repair,   65
And sport and flutter in the fields of air.
    "Know further yet; whoever fair and chaste
Rejects mankind, is by some Sylph embraced:
For spirits, freed from mortal laws, with ease
Assume what sexes and what shapes they please.   70
What guards the purity of melting maids,
In courtly balls, and midnight masquerades,
Safe from the treacherous friend, the daring spark,
The glance by day, the whisper in the dark,
When kind occasion prompts their warm desires,   75
When music softens, and when dancing fires?
'Tis but their Sylph, the wise Celestials know,
Though Honor is the word with men below.
    "Some nymphs there are, too conscious of their face,
For life predestined to the Gnomes' embrace.   80
These swell their prospects and exalt their pride,

---

9. *Box* in the theater and the fashionable circular drive (*Ring*) in Hyde Park.   1. Sedan chair.   2. The popular card game. See III.27ff. and note.   3. The four elements out of which all things were believed to have been made were fire, water, earth, and air. One or another of these elements was supposed to be predominant in both the physical and psychological makeup of each human being. In this context they are spoken of as "humors."   4. Pope borrowed his supernatural beings from Rosicrucian mythology. Each element was inhabited by a spirit, as the following lines explain. The salamander is a lizardlike animal, in antiquity believed to live in fire.   5. Pronounced *tay.*

When offers are disdained, and love denied:
Then gay ideas[6] crowd the vacant brain,
While peers, and dukes, and all their sweeping train,
And garters, stars, and coronets appear,   85
And in soft sounds, 'your Grace' salutes their ear.
'Tis these that early taint the female soul,
Instruct the eyes of young coquettes to roll,
Teach infant cheeks a bidden blush to know,
And little hearts to flutter at a beau.   90
   "Oft, when the world imagine women stray,
The Sylphs through mystic mazes guide their way,
Through all the giddy circle they pursue,
And old impertinence expel by new.
What tender maid but must a victim fall   95
To one man's treat, but for another's ball?
When Florio speaks what virgin could withstand,
If gentle Damon did not squeeze her hand?
With varying vanities, from every part,
They shift the moving toyshop[7] of their heart;   100
Where wigs with wigs, with sword-knots sword-knots strive,
Beaux banish beaux, and coaches coaches drive.
This erring mortals levity may call;
Oh, blind to truth! the Sylphs contrive it all.
   "Of these am I, who thy protection claim,   105
A watchful sprite, and Ariel is my name.
Late, as I ranged the crystal wilds of air,
In the clear mirror of thy ruling star
I saw, alas! some dread event impend,
Ere to the main this morning sun descend,   110
But Heaven reveals not what, or how, or where:
Warned by thy Sylph, O pious maid, beware!
This to disclose is all thy guardian can:
Beware of all, but most beware of Man!"
   He said; when Shock,[8] who thought she slept too long,   115
Leaped up, and waked his mistress with his tongue.
'Twas then, Belinda, if report say true,
Thy eyes first opened on a billet-doux;
Wounds, charms, and ardors were no sooner read,
But all the vision vanished from thy head.   120
   And now, unveiled, the toilet stands displayed,
Each silver vase in mystic order laid.
First, robed in white, the nymph intent adores,
With head uncovered, the cosmetic powers.
A heavenly image in the glass appears;   125
To that she bends, to that her eyes she rears.
The inferior priestess, at her altar's side,
Trembling begins the sacred rites of Pride.
Unnumbered treasures ope at once, and here
The various offerings of the world appear;   130
From each she nicely culls with curious toil,

6. Images.   7. A shop stocked with baubles and trifles.   8. Belinda's lapdog.

And decks the goddess with the glittering spoil.
This casket India's glowing gems unlocks,
And all Arabia breathes from yonder box.
The tortoise here and elephant unite,   135
Transformed to combs, the speckled and the white.
Here files of pins extend their shining rows,
Puffs, powders, patches, Bibles, billet-doux.
Now awful Beauty puts on all its arms;
The fair each moment rises in her charms,   140
Repairs her smiles, awakens every grace,
And calls forth all the wonders of her face;
Sees by degrees a purer blush arise,
And keener lightnings quicken in her eyes.
The busy Sylphs surround their darling care,   145
These set the head, and those divide the hair,
Some fold the sleeve, whilst others plait the gown;
And Betty's⁹ praised for labors not her own.

CANTO II

    Not with more glories, in the ethereal plain,
The sun first rises o'er the purpled main,
Than, issuing forth, the rival of his beams
Launched on the bosom of the silver Thames.
Fair nymphs and well-dressed youths around her shone,   5
But every eye was fixed on her alone.
On her white breast a sparkling cross she wore,
Which Jews might kiss, and infidels adore.
Her lively looks a sprightly mind disclose,
Quick as her eyes, and as unfixed as those: 10
Favors to none, to all she smiles extends;
Oft she rejects, but never once offends.
Bright as the sun, her eyes the gazers strike,
And, like the sun, they shine on all alike.
Yet graceful ease, and sweetness void of pride,   15
Might hide her faults, if belles had faults to hide:
If to her share some female errors fall,
Look on her face, and you'll forget 'em all.
    This nymph, to the destruction of mankind,
Nourished two locks which graceful hung behind   20
In equal curls, and well conspired to deck
With shining ringlets the smooth ivory neck.
Love in these labyrinths his slaves detains,
And mighty hearts are held in slender chains.
With hairy springes we the birds betray,   25
Slight lines of hair surprise the finny prey,
Fair tresses man's imperial race ensnare,
And beauty draws us with a single hair.
    The adventurous Baron the bright locks admired,
He saw, he wished, and to the prize aspired.   30
Resolved to win, he meditates the way,

9. Belinda's maid, the "inferior priestess" mentioned in line 127.

By force to ravish, or by fraud betray;
For when success a lover's toil attends,
Few ask if fraud or force attained his ends.
    For this, ere Phoebus rose, he had implored   35
Propitious Heaven, and every power adored,
But chiefly Love—to Love an altar built,
Of twelve vast French romances, neatly gilt.
There lay three garters, half a pair of gloves,
And all the trophies of his former loves.   40
With tender billet-doux he lights the pyre,
And breathes three amorous sighs to raise the fire.
Then prostrate falls, and begs with ardent eyes
Soon to obtain, and long possess the prize:
The powers gave ear, and granted half his prayer,   45
The rest the winds dispersed in empty air.
    But now secure the painted vessel glides,
The sunbeams trembling on the floating tides,
While melting music steals upon the sky,
And softened sounds along the waters die.   50
Smooth flow the waves, the zephyrs gently play,
Belinda smiled, and all the world was gay.
All but the Sylph—with careful thoughts oppressed,
The impending woe sat heavy on his breast.
He summons straight his denizens of air;   55
The lucid squadrons round the sails repair:
Soft o'er the shrouds aërial whispers breathe
That seemed but zephyrs to the train beneath.
Some to the sun their insect-wings unfold,
Waft on the breeze, or sink in clouds of gold.   60
Transparent forms too fine for mortal sight,
Their fluid bodies half dissolved in light,
Loose to the wind their airy garments flew,
Thin glittering textures of the filmy dew,
Dipped in the richest tincture of the skies,   65
Where light disports in ever-mingling dyes,
While every beam new transient colors flings,
Colors that change whene'er they wave their wings.
Amid the circle, on the gilded mast,
Superior by the head was Ariel placed;   70
His purple[1] pinions opening to the sun,
He raised his azure wand, and thus begun:
    "Ye Sylphs and Sylphids, to your chief give ear!
Fays, Fairies, Genii, Elves, and Daemons, hear!
Ye know the spheres and various tasks assigned   75
By laws eternal to the aërial kind.
Some in the fields of purest ether play,
And bask and whiten in the blaze of day.
Some guide the course of wandering orbs on high,
Or roll the planets through the boundless sky.   80

---

1. In eighteenth-century poetic diction, the word might mean "blood-red," "purple," or simply (as is likely here) "brightly colored." The word derives from Virgil, *Eclogue* IX.40, *pupureus*.

Some less refined, beneath the moon's pale light
Pursue the stars that shoot athwart the night,
Or suck the mists in grosser air below,
Or dip their pinions in the painted bow,
Or brew fierce tempests on the wintry main,   85
Or o'er the glebe distill the kindly rain.
Others on earth o'er human race preside,
Watch all their ways, and all their actions guide:
Of these the chief the care of nations own,
And guard with arms divine the British Throne.   90
    "Our humbler province is to tend the Fair,
Not a less pleasing, though less glorious care:
To save the powder from too rude a gale,
Nor let the imprisoned essences exhale;
To draw fresh colors from the vernal flowers   95
To steal from rainbows e'er they drop in showers
A brighter wash;[2] to curl their waving hairs,
Assist their blushes, and inspire their airs;
Nay oft, in dreams invention we bestow,
To change a flounce, or add a furbelow.   100
    "This day black omens threat the brightest fair,
That e'er deserved a watchful spirit's care;
Some dire disaster, or by force or slight,
But what, or where, the Fates have wrapped in night:
Whether the nymph shall break Diana's[3] law,   105
Or some frail china jar receive a flaw,
Or stain her honor or her new brocade,
Forget her prayers, or miss a masquerade,
Or lose her heart, or necklace, at a ball;
Or whether Heaven has doomed that Shock must fall.   110
Haste, then, ye spirits! to your charge repair:
The fluttering fan be Zephyretta's care;
The drops[4] to thee, Brillante, we consign;
And, Momentilla, let the watch be thine;
Do thou, Crispissa,[5] tend her favorite Lock;   115
Ariel himself shall be the guard of Shock.
    "To fifty chosen Sylphs, of special note,
We trust the important charge, the petticoat;
Oft have we known that sevenfold fence to fail,
Though stiff with hoops, and armed with ribs of whale.   120
Form a strong line about the silver bound,
And guard the wide circumference around.
    "Whatever spirit, careless of his charge,
His post neglects, or leaves the fair at large,
Shall feel sharp vengeance soon o'ertake his sins, 125
Be stopped in vials, or transfixed with pins,
Or plunged in lakes of bitter washes lie,
Or wedged whole ages in a bodkin's eye;[6]
Gums and pomatums shall his flight restrain,

---

2. Cosmetic lotion.   3. Diana was the goddess of chastity.   4. Diamond earrings.   5. From Latin
crispere, to curl.   6. A blunt needle with a large eye, used for drawing ribbon through eyelets in the
edging of women's garments.

While clogged he beats his silken wings in vain,   130
Or alum styptics with contracting power
Shrink his thin essence like a riveled[7] flower:
Or, as Ixion fixed,[8] the wretch shall feel
The giddy motion of the whirling mill,
In fumes of burning chocolate shall glow,   135
And tremble at the sea that froths below!"
    He spoke; the spirits from the sails descend;
Some, orb in orb, around the nymph extend;
Some thread the mazy ringlets of her hair;
Some hang upon the pendants of her ear: 140
With beating hearts the dire event they wait,
Anxious, and trembling for the birth of Fate.

CANTO III

    Close by those meads, forever crowned with flowers,
Where Thames with pride surveys his rising towers,
There stands a structure of majestic frame,
Which from the neighboring Hampton[9] takes its name.
Here Britain's statesmen oft the fall foredoom   5
Of foreign tyrants and of nymphs at home;
Here thou, great Anna! whom three realms obey,
Dost sometimes counsel take—and sometimes tea.
    Hither the heroes and the nymphs resort,
To taste awhile the pleasures of a court;   10
In various talk the instructive hours they passed,
Who gave the ball, or paid the visit last;
One speaks the glory of the British Queen,
And one describes a charming Indian screen;
A third interprets motions, looks, and eyes;   15
At every word a reputation dies.
Snuff, or the fan, supply each pause of chat,
With singing, laughing, ogling, and all that.
    Meanwhile, declining from the noon of day,
The sun obliquely shoots his burning ray;   20
The hungry judges soon the sentence sign,
And wretches hang that jurymen may dine;
The merchant from the Exchange returns in peace,
And the long labors of the toilet cease.
Belinda now, whom thirst of fame invites,   25
Burns to encounter two adventurous knights,
At ombre[1] singly to decide their doom
And swells her breast with conquests yet to come.
Straight the three bands prepare in arms to join,

---

7. To "rivel" is to "contract into wrinkles and corrugations" (Johnson's *Dictionary*).   8. In the Greek myth Ixion was punished in the underworld by being bound on an ever-turning wheel.   9. Hampton Court, the royal palace, about fifteen miles up the Thames from London.   1. The game that Belinda plays against the baron and another young man is too complicated for complete explication here. Pope has carefully arranged the cards so that Belinda wins. The baron's hand is strong enough to be a threat, but the third player's is of little account. The hand is played exactly according to the rules of ombre, and Pope's description of the cards is equally accurate. Each player holds nine cards (line 30). The "Matadores" (line 33), when spades are trumps, are "Spadillio" (line 49), the ace of spades; "Manillio" (line 51), the two of spades; "Basto" (line 53), the ace of clubs; Belinda holds all three of these.

Each band the number of the sacred nine.   30
Soon as she spreads her hand, the aërial guard
Descend, and sit on each important card:
First Ariel perched upon a Matadore,
Then each according to the rank they bore;
For Sylphs, yet mindful of their ancient race,   35
Are, as when women, wondrous fond of place.
　　Behold, four Kings in majesty revered,
With hoary whiskers and a forky beard;
And four fair Queens whose hands sustain a flower,
The expressive emblem of their softer power;   40
Four Knaves in garbs succinct,² a trusty band,
Caps on their heads, and halberts in their hand;
And parti-colored troops, a shining train,
Draw forth to combat on the velvet plain.
The skillful nymph reviews her force with care;   45
"Let Spades be trumps!' she said, and trumps they were.
　　Now move to war her sable Matadores,
In show like leaders of the swarthy Moors.
Spadillio first, unconquerable lord!
Led off two captive trumps, and swept the board.   50
As many more Manillio forced to yield,
And marched a victor from the verdant field.
Him Basto followed, but his fate more hard
Gained but one trump and one plebeian card.
With his broad saber next, a chief in years,   55
The hoary Majesty of Spades appears,
Puts forth one manly leg, to sight revealed,
The rest his many-colored robe concealed.
The rebel Knave, who dares his prince engage,
Proves the just victim of his royal rage.   60
Even mighty Pam,³ that kings and queens o'erthrew
And mowed down armies in the fights of loo,
Sad chance of war! now destitute of aid,
Falls undistinguished by the victor Spade.
　　Thus far both armies to Belinda yield;   65
Now to the Baron fate inclines the field.
His warlike amazon her host invades,
The imperial consort of the crown of Spades.
The Club's black tyrant first her victim died,
Spite of his haughty mien and barbarous pride.   70
What boots the regal circle on his head,
His giant limbs, in state unwieldy spread?
That long behind he trails his pompous robe,
And of all monarchs only grasps the globe?
　　The Baron now his Diamonds pours apace;   75
The embroidered King who shows but half his face,
And his refulgent Queen, with powers combined
Of broken troops an easy conquest find.
Clubs, Diamonds, Hearts, in wild disorder seen,

2. Girded up.　　3. The knave of clubs, the highest trump in the game of loo.

With throngs promiscuous strew the level green.   80
Thus when dispersed a routed army runs,
Of Asia's troops, and Afric's sable sons,
With like confusion different nations fly,
Of various habit, and of various dye,
The pierced battalions disunited fall   85
In heaps on heaps; one fate o'erwhelms them all.
    The Knave of Diamonds tries his wily arts,
And wins (oh, shameful chance!) the Queen of Hearts.
At this, the blood the virgin's cheek forsook,
A livid paleness spreads o'er all her look;   90
She sees, and trembles at the approaching ill,
Just in the jaws of ruin, and Codille,[4]
And now (as oft in some distempered state)
On one nice trick depends the general fate.
An Ace of Hearts steps forth: the King unseen   95
Lurked in her hand, and mourned his captive Queen.
He springs to vengeance with an eager pace,
And falls like thunder on the prostrate Ace.
The nymph exulting fills with shouts the sky,
The walls, the woods, and long canals reply.   100
    O thoughtless mortals! ever blind to fate,
Too soon dejected, and too soon elate:
Sudden these honors shall be snatched away,
And cursed forever this victorious day.
    For lo! the board with cups and spoons is crowned,   105
The berries crackle, and the mill turns round;[5]
On shining altars of Japan[6] they raise
The silver lamp; the fiery spirits blaze:
From silver spouts the grateful liquors glide,
While China's earth receives the smoking tide.   110
At once they gratify their scent and taste,
And frequent cups prolong the rich repast.
Straight hover round the fair her airy band;
Some, as she sipped, the fuming liquor fanned,
Some o'er her lap their careful plumes displayed,   115
Trembling, and conscious of the rich brocade.
Coffee (which makes the politician wise,
And see through all things with his half-shut eyes)
Sent up in vapors to the Baron's brain
New stratagems, the radiant Lock to gain.   120
Ah, cease, rash youth! desist ere 'tis too late,
Fear the just Gods, and think of Scylla's fate![7]
Changed to a bird, and sent to flit in air,
She dearly pays for Nisus' injured hair!
    But when to mischief mortals bend their will,   125
How soon they find fit instruments of ill!

4. The term applied to losing a hand at cards.   5. That is, coffee is roasted and ground.   6. That is,
small, lacquered tables. The word "altars" suggests the ritualistic character of coffee drinking in Belinda's
world.   7. Scylla, daughter of Nisus, was turned into a sea bird because, for the sake of her love for
Minos of Crete, who was besieging her father's city of Megara, she cut from her father's head the purple
lock on which his safety depended. She is not the Scylla of the "Scylla and Charybdis" episode in the
Odyssey.

Just then, Clarissa drew with tempting grace
A two-edged weapon from her shining case:
So ladies in romance assist their knight,
Present the spear, and arm him for the fight.   130
He takes the gift with reverence, and extends
The little engine on his fingers' ends;
This just behind Belinda's neck he spread,
As o'er the fragrant steams she bends her head.
Swift to the Lock a thousand sprites repair,   135
A thousand wings, by turns, blow back the hair,
And thrice they twitched the diamond in her ear,
Thrice she looked back, and thrice the foe drew near.
Just in that instant, anxious Ariel sought
The close recesses of the virgin's thought;   140
As on the nosegay in her breast reclined,
He watched the ideas rising in her mind,
Sudden he viewed, in spite of all her art,
An earthly lover lurking at her heart.
Amazed, confused, he found his power expired,   145
Resigned to fate, and with a sigh retired.
    The Peer now spreads the glittering forfex[8] wide,
T' enclose the Lock; now joins it, to divide.
Even then, before the fatal engine closed,
A wretched Sylph too fondly interposed;   150
Fate urged the shears, and cut the Sylph in twain
(But airy substance soon unites again):
The meeting points the sacred hair dissever
From the fair head, forever, and forever!
    Then flashed the living lightning from her eyes,   155
And screams of horror rend the affrighted skies.
Not louder shrieks to pitying heaven are cast,
When husbands, or when lapdogs breathe their last;
Or when rich china vessels fallen from high,
In glittering dust and painted fragments lie!   160
"Let wreaths of triumph now my temples twine,"
The victor cried, "the glorious prize is mine!
While fish in streams, or birds delight in air,
Or in a coach and six the British Fair,
As long as Atalantis[9] shall be read,   165
Or the small pillow grace a lady's bed,
While visits shall be paid on solemn days,
When numerous wax-lights in bright order blaze,
While nymphs take treats, or assignations give,
So long my honor, name, and praise shall live!   170
What Time would spare, from Steel receives its date,
And monuments, like men, submit to fate!
Steel could the labor of the Gods destroy,
And strike to dust the imperial towers of Troy;
Steel could the works of mortal pride confound,   175

8. Scissors.   9. Mrs. Manley's New Atalantis (1709) was notorious for its thinly concealed allusions to contemporary scandals.

And hew triumphal arches to the ground.
What wonder then, fair nymph! thy hairs should feel,
The conquering force of unresisted Steel?"

CANTO IV

But anxious cares the pensive nymph oppressed,
And secret passions labored in her breast.
Not youthful kings in battle seized alive,
Not scornful virgins who their charms survive,
Not ardent lovers robbed of all their bliss,   5
Not ancient ladies when refused a kiss,
Not tyrants fierce that unrepenting die,
Not Cynthia when her manteau's¹ pinned awry,
E'er felt such rage, resentment, and despair,
As thou, sad virgin! for thy ravished hair.   10
    For, that sad moment, when the Sylphs withdrew
And Ariel weeping from Belinda flew,
Umbriel,² a dusky, melancholy sprite
As ever sullied the fair face of light,
Down to the central earth, his proper scene,   15
Repaired to search the gloomy Cave of Spleen.³
    Swift on his sooty pinions flits the Gnome,
And in a vapor⁴ reached the dismal dome.
No cheerful breeze this sullen region knows,
The dreaded east is all the wind that blows.   20
Here in a grotto, sheltered close from air,
And screened in shades from day's detested glare,
She sighs forever on her pensive bed,
Pain at her side, and Megrim⁵ at her head.
    Two handmaids wait the throne: alike in place,   25
But differing far in figure and in face.
Here stood Ill-Nature like an ancient maid,
Her wrinkled form in black and white arrayed;
With store of prayers for mornings, nights, and noons,
Her hand is filled; her bosom with lampoons.   30
    There Affectation, with a sickly mien,
Shows in her cheek the roses of eighteen,
Practiced to lisp, and hang the head aside,
Faints into airs, and languishes with pride,
On the rich quilt sinks with becoming woe,   35
Wrapped in a gown, for sickness and for show.
The fair ones feel such maladies as these,
When each new nightdress gives a new disease.
    A constant vapor⁶ o'er the palace flies,
Strange phantoms rising as the mists arise;   40
Dreadful as hermit's dreams in haunted shades,
Or bright as visions of expiring maids.
Now glaring fiends, and snakes on rolling spires,⁷

1. Negligee, or loose robe.   2. The name suggests shade and darkness.   3. Ill humor.   4. Punning
on *vapor* as (1) mist and (2) an excessively emotional (even peevish) state of mind, appropriate to the realm
of "spleen."   5. Headache.   6. Emblematic of "the vapors"—hypochondria, melancholy, peevishness,
often affected by fashionable women.   7. Coils.

Pale specters, gaping tombs, and purple fires;
Now lakes of liquid gold, Elysian scenes,   45
And crystal domes, and angels in machines.[8]
    Unnumbered throngs on every side are seen
Of bodies changed to various forms by Spleen.
Here living teapots stand, one arm held out,
One bent; the handle this, and that the spout: 50
A pipkin[9] there, like Homer's tripod, walks;
Here sighs a jar, and there a goose pie talks;
Men prove with child, as powerful fancy works,
And maids, turned bottles, call aloud for corks.
    Safe passed the Gnome through this fantastic band,   55
A branch of healing spleenwort[1] in his hand.
Then thus addressed the Power: "Hail, wayward Queen!
Who rule the sex to fifty from fifteen:
Parent of vapors and of female wit,
Who give the hysteric or poetic fit,   60
On various tempers act by various ways,
Make some take physic, others scribble plays;
Who cause the proud their visits to delay,
And send the godly in a pet to pray.
A nymph there is that all your power disdains,   65
And thousands more in equal mirth maintains.
But oh! if e'er thy Gnome could spoil a grace,
Or raise a pimple on a beauteous face,
Like citron-waters[2] matrons' cheeks inflame,
Or change complexions at a losing game;   70
If e'er with airy horns[3] I planted heads,
Or rumpled petticoats, or tumbled beds,
Or caused suspicion when no soul was rude,
Or discomposed the headdress of a prude,
Or e'er to costive lapdog gave disease,   75
Which not the tears of brightest eyes could ease,
Hear me, and touch Belinda with chagrin:[4]
That single act gives half the world the spleen."
    The Goddess with a discontented air
Seems to reject him though she grants his prayer.   80
A wondrous bag with both her hands she binds,
Like that where once Ulysses held the winds;[5]
There she collects the force of female lungs,
Sighs, sobs, and passions, and the war of tongues.
A vial next she fills with fainting fears,   85
Soft sorrows, melting griefs, and flowing tears.
The Gnome rejoicing bears her gifts away,

---

8. Mechanical devices used in the theaters for spectacular effects. The fantasies of neurotic women here merge with the sensational stage effects popular with contemporary audiences.   **9.** An earthen pot. In *Iliad* XVIII.434–40, Vulcan furnishes the gods with self-propelling "tripods" (three-legged stools).   **1.** An herb, efficacious against the spleen. Pope alludes to the golden bough that Aeneas and the Cumaean sybil carry with them for protection into the underworld in *Aeneid* VI.   **2.** Brandy flavored with orange or lemon peel.   **3.** The symbol of the cuckold; here "airy," because they exist only in the jealous suspicions of the husband, the victim of the mischievous Umbriel.   **4.** Ill humor.   **5.** Aeolus (later conceived of as god of the winds) gave Ulysses a bag containing all the winds adverse to his voyage home. When his ship was in sight of Ithaca, his companions opened the bag and the storms that ensued drove Ulysses far away (*Odyssey* X.19ff.).

Spreads his black wings, and slowly mounts to day.
    Sunk in Thalestris'[6] arms the nymph he found,
Her eyes dejected and her hair unbound.   90
Full o'er their heads the swelling bag he rent,
And all the Furies issued at the vent.
Belinda burns with more than mortal ire,
And fierce Thalestris fans the rising fire.
"O wretched maid!" she spread her hands, and cried   95
(While Hampton's echoes, "Wretched maid!" replied),
"Was it for this you took such constant care
The bodkin, comb, and essence to prepare?
For this your locks in paper durance bound,
For this with torturing irons wreathed around?   100
For this with fillets strained your tender head,
And bravely bore the double loads of lead?[7]
Gods! shall the ravisher display your hair,
While the fops envy, and the ladies stare!
Honor forbid! at whose unrivaled shrine   105
Ease, pleasure, virtue, all, our sex resign.
Methinks already I your tears survey,
Already hear the horrid things they say,
Already see you a degraded toast,
And all your honor in a whisper lost!   110
How shall I, then, your helpless fame defend?
'Twill then be infamy to seem your friend!
And shall this prize, the inestimable prize,
Exposed through crystal to the gazing eyes,
And heightened by the diamond's circling rays,   115
On that rapacious hand forever blaze?
Sooner shall grass in Hyde Park Circus grow,
And wits take lodgings in the sound of Bow;[8]
Sooner let earth, air, sea, to chaos fall,
Men, monkeys, lapdogs, parrots, perish all!"   120
    She said; then raging to Sir Plume repairs,
And bids her beau demand the precious hairs
(Sir Plume of amber snuffbox justly vain,
And the nice conduct of a clouded cane).
With earnest eyes, and round unthinking face,   125
He first the snuffbox opened, then the case,
And thus broke out—"My Lord, why, what the devil!
Z—ds! damn the lock! 'fore Gad, you must be civil!
Plague on't! 'tis past a jest—nay prithee, pox!
Give her the hair'—he spoke, and rapped his box.   130
    "It grieves me much," replied the Peer again,
"Who speaks so well should ever speak in vain.
But by this Lock, this sacred Lock I swear
(Which never more shall join its parted hair;

6. The name is borrowed from a queen of the Amazons, hence a fierce and warlike woman. Thalestris, according to legend, traveled thirty days in order to have a child by Alexander the Great. Plutarch denies the story.   7. The frame on which the elaborate coiffures of the day were arranged.   8. A person born within sound of the bells of St. Mary-le-Bow in Cheapside is said to be a cockney. No fashionable wit would have so vulgar an address.

Which never more its honors shall renew, 135
Clipped from the lovely head where late it grew),
That while my nostrils draw the vital air,
This hand, which won it, shall forever wear."
He spoke, and speaking, in proud triumph spread
The long-contended honors[9] of her head. 140
    But Umbriel, hateful Gnome, forbears not so;
He breaks the vial whence the sorrows flow.
Then see! the nymph in beauteous grief appears,
Her eyes half languishing, half drowned in tears;
On her heaved bosom hung her drooping head, 145
Which with a sigh she raised, and thus she said:
    "Forever cursed be this detested day,
Which snatched my best, my favorite curl away!
Happy! ah, ten times happy had I been,
If Hampton Court these eyes had never seen! 150
Yet am not I the first mistaken maid,
By love of courts to numerous ills betrayed.
Oh, had I rather unadmired remained
In some lone isle, or distant northern land;
Where the gilt chariot never marks the way, 155
Where none learn ombre, none e'er taste bohea![1]
There kept my charms concealed from mortal eye,
Like roses that in deserts bloom and die.
What moved my mind with youthful lords to roam?
Oh, had I stayed, and said my prayers at home! 160
'Twas this the morning omens seemed to tell,
Thrice from my trembling hand the patch box[2] fell;
The tottering china shook without a wind,
Nay, Poll sat mute, and Shock was most unkind!
A Sylph too warned me of the threats of fate, 165
In mystic visions, now believed too late!
See the poor remnants of these slighted hairs!
My hands shall rend what e'en thy rapine spares.
These in two sable ringlets taught to break,
Once gave new beauties to the snowy neck; 170
The sister lock now sits uncouth, alone,
And in its fellow's fate foresees its own;
Uncurled it hangs, the fatal shears demands,
And tempts once more thy sacrilegious hands.
Oh, hadst thou, cruel! been content to seize 175
Hairs less in sight, or any hairs but these!"

CANTO V

    She said: the pitying audience melt in tears.
But Fate and Jove had stopped the Baron's ears.
In vain Thalestris with reproach assails,
For who can move when fair Belinda fails?

9. Ornaments, hence locks; a Latinism.   1. A costly sort of tea.   2. A box to hold the ornamental patches of court plaster worn on the face by both sexes. Cf. *Spectator* 81.

Not half so fixed the Trojan[3] could remain,   5
While Anna begged and Dido raged in vain.
Then grave Clarissa graceful waved her fan;
Silence ensued, and thus the nymph began:
    "Say why are beauties praised and honored most,
The wise man's passion, and the vain man's toast?   10
Why decked with all that land and sea afford,
Why angels called, and angel-like adored?
Why round our coaches crowd the white-gloved beaux,
Why bows the side box from its inmost rows?
How vain are all these glories, all our pains,   15
Unless good sense preserve what beauty gains;
That men may say when we the front box grace,
'Behold the first in virtue as in face!'
Oh! if to dance all night, and dress all day,
Charmed the smallpox, or chased old age away,   20
Who would not scorn what housewife's cares produce,
Or who would learn one earthly thing of use?
To patch, nay ogle, might become a saint,
Nor could it sure be such a sin to paint.
But since, alas! frail beauty must decay,   25
Curled or uncurled, since locks will turn to gray;
Since painted, or not painted, all shall fade,
And she who scorns a man must die a maid;
What then remains but well our power to use,
And keep good humor still whate'er we lose?   30
And trust me, dear, good humor can prevail
When airs, and flights, and screams, and scolding fail.
Beauties in vain their pretty eyes may roll;
Charms strike the sight, but merit wins the soul."[4]
    So spoke the dame, but no applause ensued;   35
Belinda frowned, Thalestris called her prude.
"To arms, to arms!" the fierce virago cries,
And swift as lightning to the combat flies.
All side in parties, and begin the attack;
Fans clap, silks rustle, and tough whalebones crack;   40
Heroes' and heroines' shouts confusedly rise,
And bass and treble voices strike the skies.
No common weapons in their hands are found,
Like Gods they fight, nor dread a mortal wound.
    So when bold Homer makes the Gods engage,   45
And heavenly breasts with human passions rage;
'Gainst Pallas, Mars; Latona, Hermes arms;
And all Olympus rings with loud alarms:
Jove's thunder roars, heaven trembles all around,
Blue Neptune storms, the bellowing deeps resound: 50
Earth shakes her nodding towers, the ground gives way,
And the pale ghosts start at the flash of day!

3. Aeneas, who forsook Dido at the bidding of the gods, despite her reproaches and the supplications of her sister Anna. Virgil compares him to a steadfast oak that withstands a storm (*Aeneid* IV.437–43).   4. The speech is a close parody of Pope's own translation of the speech of Sarpedon to Glaucus, first published in 1709 and slightly revised in his version of the *Iliad* (XII.371–96).

Triumphant Umbriel on a sconce's height
Clapped his glad wings, and sat to view the fight:
Propped on their bodkin spears, the sprites survey   55
The growing combat, or assist the fray.
　　While through the press enraged Thalestris flies,
And scatters death around from both her eyes,
A beau and witling perished in the throng,
One died in metaphor, and one in song.   60
"O cruel nymph! a living death I bear,"
Cried Dapperwit, and sunk beside his chair.
A mournful glance Sir Fopling upwards cast,
"Those eyes are made so killing"—was his last.
Thus on Maeander's flowery margin lies   65
The expiring swan, and as he sings he dies.
　　When bold Sir Plume had drawn Clarissa down,
Chloe stepped in, and killed him with a frown;
She smiled to see the doughty hero slain,
But, at her smile, the beau revived again.   70
Now Jove suspends his golden scales in air,
Weighs the men's wits against the lady's hair;
The doubtful beam long nods from side to side;
At length the wits mount up, the hairs subside.
　　See, fierce Belinda on the Baron flies,   75
With more than usual lightning in her eyes;
Nor feared the chief the unequal fight to try,
Who sought no more than on his foe to die.
　　But this bold lord with manly strength endued,
She with one finger and a thumb subdued: 80
Just where the breath of life his nostrils drew,
A charge of snuff the wily virgin threw;
The Gnomes direct, to every atom just,
The pungent grains of titillating dust.
Sudden, with starting tears each eye o'erflows,   85
And the high dome re-echoes to his nose.
　　"Now meet thy fate," incensed Belinda cried,
And drew a deadly bodkin⁵ from her side.
(The same, his ancient personage to deck,
Her great-great-grandsire wore about his neck,   90
In three seal rings; which after, melted down,
Formed a vast buckle for his widow's gown:
Her infant grandame's whistle next it grew,
The bells she jingled, and the whistle blew;
Then in a bodkin graced her mother's hairs,   95
Which long she wore, and now Belinda wears.)
　　"Boast not my fall," he cried, "insulting foe!
Thou by some other shalt be laid as low.
Nor think to die dejects my lofty mind:
All that I dread is leaving you behind!   100
Rather than so, ah, let me still survive,
And burn in Cupid's flames—but burn alive."

---

5. An ornamental pin shaped like a dagger, to be worn in the hair.

"Restore the Lock!" she cries; and all around
"Restore the Lock!" the vaulted roofs rebound.
Not fierce Othello in so loud a strain   105
Roared for the handkerchief that caused his pain.[6]
But see how oft ambitious aims are crossed,
And chiefs contend till all the prize is lost!
The lock, obtained with guilt, and kept with pain,
In every place is sought, but sought in vain: 110
With such a prize no mortal must be blessed,
So Heaven decrees! with Heaven who can contest?
    Some thought it mounted to the lunar sphere,
Since all things lost on earth are treasured there.
There heroes' wits are kept in ponderous vases,   115
And beaux' in snuffboxes and tweezer cases.
There broken vows and deathbed alms are found,
And lovers' hearts with ends of riband bound,
The courtier's promises, and sick man's prayers,
The smiles of harlots, and the tears of heirs,   120
Cages for gnats, and chains to yoke a flea,
Dried butterflies, and tomes of casuistry.
    But trust the Muse—she saw it upward rise,
Though marked by none but quick, poetic eyes
(So Rome's great founder[7] to the heavens withdrew,   125
To Proculus alone confessed in view);
A sudden star, it shot through liquid air,
And drew behind a radiant trail of hair.
Not Berenice's[8] locks first rose so bright,
The heavens bespangling with disheveled light.   130
The Sylphs behold it kindling as it flies,
And pleased pursue its progress through the skies.
    This the beau monde shall from the Mall[9] survey,
And hail with music its propitious ray.
This the blest lover shall for Venus take,   135
And send up vows from Rosamonda's Lake.[1]
This Partridge soon shall view in cloudless skies,
When next he looks through Galileo's eyes;[2]
And hence the egregious wizard shall foredoom
The fate of Louis, and the fall of Rome.   140
    Then cease, bright nymph! to mourn thy ravished hair,
Which adds new glory to the shining sphere!
Not all the tresses that fair head can boast,
Shall draw such envy as the Lock you lost.
For, after all the murders of your eye,   145
When, after millions slain, yourself shall die:
When those fair suns shall set, as set they must,
And all those tresses shall be laid in dust,

6. *Othello* III.4.   7. Romulus, the "founder" and first king of Rome, was snatched to heaven in a storm cloud while reviewing his army in the Campus Martius (Livy I.16).   8. Berenice, the wife of Ptolemy III, dedicated a lock of her hair to the gods to ensure her husband's safe return from war. It was turned into a constellation.   9. A walk laid out by Charles II in St. James's Park, a resort for strollers of all sorts.   1. In St. James's Park; associated with unhappy lovers.   2. A telescope. John Partridge was an astrologer whose annually published predictions had been amusingly satirized by Swift and other wits in 1708.

This Lock the Muse shall consecrate to fame,
And 'midst the stars inscribe Belinda's name.   150

An Essay on Man

To Henry St. John, Lord Bolingbroke

EPISTLE I

ARGUMENT OF THE NATURE AND STATE OF MAN, WITH RESPECT TO THE UNI-
VERSE. Of man in the abstract—I. That we can judge only with regard to our
own system, being ignorant of the relations of systems and things, ver. 17,
&c.—II. That man is not to be deemed imperfect, but a being suited to his
place and rank in the creation, agreeable to the general order of things, and
conformable to ends and relations to him unknown, ver. 35, &c.—III. That
it is partly upon his ignorance of future events, and partly upon the hope of
a future state, that all his happiness in the present depends, ver. 77, &c.—
IV. The pride of aiming at more knowledge, and pretending to more perfection, the cause of man's error and misery. The impiety of putting himself in
the place of God, and judging of the fitness or unfitness, perfection or imperfection, justice or injustice of his dispensations, ver. 113, &c.—V. The
absurdity of conceiting himself the final cause of the creation, or expecting
that perfection in the moral world which is not in the natural, ver. 131, &c.—
VI. The unreasonableness of his complaints against Providence, while on the
one hand he demands the perfections of the angels, and on the other the
bodily qualifications of the brutes; though, to possess any of the sensitive
faculties in a higher degree, would render him miserable, ver. 173, &c.—
VII. That throughout the whole visible world, an universal order and gradation in the sensual and mental faculties is observed, which causes a subordination of creature to creature, and of all creatures to man. The
gradations of sense, instinct, thought, reflection, reason: that reason alone
countervails all the other faculties, ver. 207.—VIII. How much further this
order and subordination of living creatures may extend, above and below us;
were any part of which broken, not that part only, but the whole connected
creation must be destroyed, ver. 233—IX. The extravagance, madness, and
pride of such a desire, ver. 259.—X. The consequence of all, the absolute
submission due to Providence, both as to our present and future state, ver.
281, &c., to the end.

Awake, my St. John![1] leave all meaner things
To low ambition, and the pride of Kings.
Let us (since Life can little more supply
Than just to look about us and to die)
Expatiate free o'er all this scene of Man;   5
A mighty maze! but not without a plan;
A Wild, where weeds and flowers promiscuous shoot;
Or Garden, tempting with forbidden fruit.

1. Pope's friend, who had thus far neglected to keep his part of their friendly bargain: Pope was to write
his philosophical speculations in verse; Bolingbroke was to write his in prose.

Together let us beat this ample field,
Try what the open, what the covert yield; 10
The latent tracts, the giddy heights, explore
Of all who blindly creep, or sightless soar;
Eye Nature's walks, shoot Folly as it flies,
And catch the Manners living as they rise;
Laugh where we must, be candid where we can; 15
But vindicate the ways of God to man.[2]

    I. Say first, of God above, or Man below,
What can we reason, but from what we know?
Of Man, what see we but his station here,
From which to reason, or to which refer? 20
Through worlds unnumbered though the God be known,
'Tis ours to trace him only in our own.
He, who through vast immensity can pierce,
See worlds on worlds compose one universe,
Observe how system into system runs, 25
What other planets circle other suns,
What varied Being peoples every star,
May tell why Heaven has made us as we are.
But of this frame the bearings, and the ties,
The strong connections, nice dependencies, 30
Gradations just, has thy pervading soul
Looked through? or can a part contain the whole?
    Is the great chain,[3] that draws all to agree,
And drawn supports, upheld by God, or thee?

    II. Presumptuous Man! the reason wouldst thou find, 35
Why formed so weak, so little, and so blind?
First, if thou canst, the harder reason guess,
Why formed no weaker, blinder, and no less?
Ask of thy mother earth, why oaks are made
Taller or stronger than the weeds they shade? 40
Or ask of yonder argent fields above,
Why Jove's satellites[4] are less than JOVE?
    Of Systems possible, if 'tis confest.
That Wisdom infinite must form the best,
Where all must full[5] or not coherent be, 45
And all that rises, rise in due degree;
Then, in the scale of reasoning life,'tis plain,
There must be, somewhere, such a rank as Man:
And all the question (wrangle e'er so long)
Is only this, if God has placed him wrong? 50
    Respecting Man, whatever wrong we call,
May, must be right, as relative to all.
In human works, though laboured on with pain,

2. Cf. Milton's *Paradise Lost* I.26. Pope's theme is essentially the same as Milton's, and even the opening image of the garden reminds one of the earlier poet's Paradise.   3. A reference to the popular eighteenth-century notion of the Great Chain of Being, in which elements of the universe took their places in a hierarchy ranging from the lowest matter to God.   4. Here pronounced *satéllités*.   5. According to the principle of plenitude, there can be no gaps in the Chain.

A thousand movements scarce one purpose gain;
In God's, one single can its end produce;   55
Yet serves to second too some other use.
So Man, who here seems principal alone,
Perhaps acts second to some sphere unknown,
Touches some wheel, or verges to some goal;
'Tis but a part we see, and not a whole.   60
    When the proud steed shall know why Man restrains
His fiery course, or drives him o'er the plains;
When the dull Ox, why now he breaks the clod,
Is now a victim, and now Egypt's God:
Then shall Man's pride and dullness comprehend   65
His actions', passions', being's use and end;
Why doing, suffering, checked, impelled; and why
This hour a slave, the next a deity.
    Then say not Man's imperfect, Heaven in fault;
Say rather, Man's as perfect as he ought: 70
His knowledge measured to his state and place;
His time a moment, and a point his space.
If to be perfect in a certain sphere,
What matter, soon or late, or here or there?
The blest to-day is as completely so,   75
As who began a thousand years ago.

    III. Heaven from all creatures hides the book of Fate,
All but the page prescribed, their present state:
From brutes what men, from men what spirits know:
Or who could suffer Being here below?   80
The lamb thy riot dooms to bleed to-day,
Had he thy Reason, would he skip and play?
Pleased to the last, he crops the flowery food,
And licks the hand just raised to shed his blood.
Oh blindness to the future! kindly given,   85
That each may fill the circle marked by Heaven:
Who sees with equal eye, as God of all,
A hero perish, or a sparrow fall,
Atoms or systems into ruin hurled,
And now a bubble burst, and now a world.   90
    Hope humbly then; with trembling pinions soar;
Wait the great teacher Death; and God adore.
What future bliss, he gives not thee to know,
But gives that Hope to be thy blessing now.
Hope springs eternal in the human breast: 95
Man never Is, but always To be blest:
The soul, uneasy and confined from home,
Rests and expatiates in a life to come.
    Lo, the poor Indian! whose untutored mind
Sees God in clouds, or hears him in the wind;   100
His soul, proud Science never taught to stray
Far as the solar walk, or milky way;
Yet simple Nature to his hope has given,
Behind the cloud-topt hill, an humbler heaven;

Some safer world in depth of woods embraced, 105
Some happier island in the watery waste,
Where slaves once more their native land behold,
No fiends torment, no Christians thirst for gold.
To Be, contents his natural desire,
He asks no Angel's wing, no Seraph's fire; 110
But thinks, admitted to that equal sky,
His faithful dog shall bear him company.

    IV. Go, wiser thou! and, in thy scale of sense,
Weigh thy Opinion against Providence;
Call imperfection what thou fanciest such, 115
Say, here he gives too little, there too much:
Destroy all Creatures for thy sport or gust,
Yet cry, If Man's unhappy, God's unjust;
If Man alone engross not Heaven's high care,
Alone made perfect here, immortal there: 120
Snatch from his hand the balance and the rod,
Re-judge his justice, be the GOD of GOD.
In Pride, in reasoning Pride, our error lies;
All quit their sphere, and rush into the skies.
Pride still is aiming at the blest abodes, 125
Men would be Angels, Angels would be Gods.
Aspiring to be Gods, if Angels fell,
Aspiring to be Angels, Men rebel:
And who but wishes to invert the laws
Of ORDER, sins against the Eternal Cause. 130

    V. Ask for what end the heavenly bodies shine,
Earth for whose use? Pride answers, "'Tis for mine:
For me kind Nature wakes her genial Power,
Suckles each herb, and spreads out ev'ry flower;
Annual for me, the grape, the rose, renew, 135
The juice nectareous, and the balmy dew;
For me, the mine a thousand treasures brings;
For me, health gushes from a thousand springs;
Seas roll to waft me, suns to light me rise;
My footstool earth, my canopy the skies." 140
    But errs not Nature from this gracious end,
From burning suns when livid deaths descend,
When earthquakes swallow, or when tempests sweep
Towns to one grave, whole nations to the deep?
"No," 'tis replied, "the first Almighty Cause 145
Acts not by partial, but by general laws;
The exceptions few; some change since all began:
And what created perfect?"—Why then Man?
If the great end be human happiness,
Then Nature deviates; and can man do less? 150
As much that end a constant course requires
Of showers and sunshine, as of man's desires;
As much eternal springs and cloudless skies,
As Men forever temperate, calm, and wise.

If plagues or earthquakes break not Heaven's design,   155
Why then a Borgia, or a Catiline?[6]
Who knows but He whose hand the lightning forms,
Who heaves old Ocean, and who wings the storms;
Pours fierce Ambition in a Caesar's mind,
Or turns young Ammon[7] loose to scourge mankind?   160
From pride, from pride, our very reasoning springs;
Account for moral, as for natural things:
Why charge we Heaven in those, in these acquit?
In both, to reason right is to submit.
 Better for Us, perhaps, it might appear,   165
Where there all harmony, all virtue here;
That never air or ocean felt the wind;
That never passion discomposed the mind.
But ALL subsists by elemental strife;
And Passions are the elements of Life.   170
The general ORDER, since the whole began,
Is kept in Nature, and is kept in Man.

 VI. What would this Man? Now upward will he soar,
And little less than Angel, would be more;
Now looking downwards, just as grieved appears   175
To want the strength of bulls, the fur of bears.
Made for his use all creatures if he call,
Say what their use, had he the powers of all?
Nature to these, without profusion, kind,
The proper organs, proper powers assigned;   180
Each seeming want compénsated of course,
Here with degrees of swiftness, there of force;
All in exact proportion to the state;
Nothing to add, and nothing to abate.
Each beast, each insect, happy in its own: 185
Is Heaven unkind to Man, and Man alone?
Shall he alone, whom rational we call,
Be pleased with nothing, if not blessed with all?
 The bliss of Man (could Pride that blessing find)
Is not to act or think beyond mankind;   190
No powers of body or of soul to share,
But what his nature and his state can bear.
Why has not Man a microscopic eye?
For this plain reason, Man is not a Fly.
Say what the use, were finer optics[8] given,   195
T' inspect a mite, not comprehend the heaven?
Or touch, if tremblingly alive all o'er,
To smart and agonize at every pore?
Or quick effluvia[9] darting through the brain,
Die of a rose in aromatic pain?   200
If nature thundered in his opening ears,

6. Roman who conspired against the state in 63 B.C. Cesare Borgia (1476–1507), an Italian prince notorious for his crimes. 7. Alexander the Great, who when he visited the oracle of Zeus Ammon in Egypt was hailed by the priest there as son of the god. 8. Eyes. 9. Stream of minute particles.

And stunned him with the music of the spheres,[1]
How would he wish that Heaven had left him still
The whispering Zephyr, and the purling rill?
Who finds not Providence all good and wise,   205
Alike in what it gives, and what denies?

    VII. Far as Creation's ample range extends,
The scale of sensual, mental powers ascends:
Mark how it mounts, to Man's imperial race,
From the green myriads in the peopled grass: 210
What modes of sight betwixt each wide extreme,
The mole's dim curtain, and the lynx's[2] beam:
Of smell, the headlong lioness between,
And hound sagacious[3] on the tainted green:
Of hearing, from the life that fills the Flood,   215
To that which warbles through the vernal wood:
The spider's touch, how exquisitely fine!
Feels at each thread, and lives along the line:
In the nice bee, what sense so subtly true
From poisonous herbs extracts the healing dew?   220
How Instinct varies in the grovelling swine,
Compared, half-reasoning elephant, with thine!
'Twixt that, and Reason, what a nice barriér,
For ever separate, yet for ever near!
Remembrance and Reflection how allied;   225
What thin partitions Sense from Thought divide:
And Middle natures,[4] how they long to join,
Yet never pass the insuperable line!
Without this just gradation, could they be
Subjected, these to those, or all to thee?   230
The powers of all subdued by thee alone,
Is not thy Reason all these powers in one?

    VIII. See, through this air, this ocean, and this earth,
All matter quick, and bursting into birth.
Above, how high, progressive life may go!   235
Around, how wide! how deep extend below!
Vast chain of Being! which from God began,
Natures ethereal, human, angel, man,
Beast, bird, fish, insect, what no eye can see,
No glass can reach; from Infinite to thee,   240
From thee to Nothing.—On superior powers
Were we to press, inferior might on ours:
Or in the full creation leave a void,
Where, one step broken, the great scale's destroyed:
From Nature's chain whatever link you strike,   245
Tenth or ten thousandth, breaks the chain alike.

---

1. The old notion that the movement of the planets created a "higher" music.   2. According to legend, one of the keenest sighted animals. *Dim curtain:* the mole's poor vision.   3. Here, exceptionally quick of scent.   4. Animals that seem to share the characteristics of several different classes, e.g., the duck-billed platypus.

And, if each system in gradation roll
Alike essential to the amazing Whole,
The least confusion but in one, not all
That system only, but the Whole must fall.   250
Let Earth unbalanced from her orbit fly,
Planets and Suns run lawless through the sky;
Let ruling angels from their spheres be hurled,
Being on Being wrecked, and world on world;
Heaven's whole foundations to their center nod,   255
And Nature tremble to the throne of God.
All this dread ORDER break—for whom? for thee?
Vile worm!—oh Madness! Pride! Impiety!

    IX. What if the foot, ordained the dust to tread,
Or hand, to toil, aspired to be the head?   260
What if the head, the eye, or ear repined
To serve mere engines to the ruling Mind?
Just as absurd for any part to claim
To be another, in this general frame:
Just as absurd, to mourn the tasks or pains,   265
The great directing MIND of ALL ordains.
    All are but parts of one stupendous whole,
Whose body Nature is, and God the soul;
That, changed through all, and yet in all the same;
Great in the earth, as in the ethereal frame;   270
Warms in the sun, refreshes in the breeze,
Glows in the stars, and blossoms in the trees,
Lives through all life, extends through all extent,
Spreads undivided, operates unspent;
Breathes in our soul, informs our mortal part,   275
As full, as perfect, in a hair as heart;
As full, as perfect, in vile Man that mourns,
As the rapt Seraph that adores and burns:
To him no high, no low, no great, no small;
He fills, he bounds, connects, and equals all.   280

    X. Cease then, nor ORDER imperfection name:
Our proper bliss depends on what we blame.
Know thy own point: this kind, this due degree
Of blindness, weakness, Heaven bestows on thee.
Submit.—In this, or any other sphere,   285
Secure to be as blest as thou canst bear:
Safe in the hand of one disposing Power,
Or in the natal, or the mortal hour.
All Nature is but Art, unknown to thee;
All Chance, Direction, which thou canst not see;   290
All Discord, Harmony not understood;
All partial Evil, universal Good:
And, spite of Pride, in erring Reason's spite,
One truth is clear, WHATEVER IS, IS RIGHT.[5]

5. Epistle II deals with "the Nature and State of Man with respect to himself, as an Individual"; Epistle III examines "the Nature and State of Man with respect to Society"; and the last epistle concerns "the Nature and State of Man with Respect to Happiness."

FRANÇOIS-MARIE AROUET DE VOLTAIRE
1694–1778

Voltaire's *Candide* (1759) brings to near perfection the art of black comedy. It subjects its characters to an accumulation of horrors so bizarre that they provoke a bewildered response of laughter as self-protection—even while they demand that the reader pay attention to the serious implications of such extravagance.

Voltaire had prepared himself to write such a work by varied experience—including that of political imprisonment. He was born François-Marie Arouet, son of a minor treasury official in Paris. After attending a Jesuit school, he took up the study of law, which, however, he soon abandoned. In his early twenties (1717–18), he spent eleven months in the Bastille for writing satiric verses about the aristocracy. His incarceration did not dissuade him from a literary career; by 1718 he was using the name *Voltaire* and beginning to acquire literary and social reputation—as well as some wealth (his speculations in the Compagnie des Indes made him rich by 1726). Money, however, did not protect him from spending more time in the Bastille during that year; after his release, he passed three years in exile, mainly in England. From 1734 to 1749, he studied widely, living with Madame du Châtelet on her estate at Cirey. For the next three years he stayed with Frederick the Great of Prussia at his Potsdam court; after that arrangement collapsed, Voltaire bought property in Switzerland and in adjacent France, settling first at his own château, Les Delices, outside Geneva, and later at nearby Ferney, in France. His international reputation as writer and social critic steadily increased; in the year of his death, he returned triumphantly to Paris.

Like his English contemporary Samuel Johnson, Voltaire wrote in many important genres: tragedy, epic, history, philosophy, fiction. His *Philosophical Dictionary* (1764), with its witty and penetrating definitions, typifies his range and acumen and his participation in his period's effort to take control of experience by intellect. While still a young man, Voltaire wrote a *History of Charles XII* of Sweden, a work unusual for its time in its novelistic technique and its assumption that "history" includes the personal lives of powerful individuals and has nothing to do with divine intervention. Before *Candide* he had published another philosophic tale, *Zadig* (1748), following the pattern of Oriental narrative. Like *Candide*, *Zadig* goes through an experiential education; it teaches him inconclusive lessons about life's unforeseeable contingencies.

Candide mocks both the artificial order of fiction (through its ludicrously multiplied recognition scenes and its symmetrical division of the protagonist's travels into three equal parts) and what Voltaire suggests is the equally artificial order posited by philosophic optimists. The view of the universe suggested by Pope's *Essay on Man,* for instance, insists on the rationality of a pattern ungraspable by human reason. *Candide* implicitly argues, however, that it does so only by attending to the abstract and undemonstrable and ignoring the omnipresent pain of immediate experience. Gottfried Leibniz, the German philosopher, provides Voltaire's most specific target in *Candide,* with the complexities of his version of optimism reduced for satiric purposes to the facile formula "Everything is for the best in this best of all possible worlds." The formulation is, of course, unfair to Leibniz, whose philosophic optimism, like Pope's, implies belief in an unknowable universal order—roughly equivalent to Christian Providence—but no lack of awareness about the actual misery and depravity human beings experience.

The exuberance and extravagance of Voltaire's imagination force us to laugh at what we may feel embarrassed to laugh at: the plight of the woman whose buttock has been cut off to make rump steak for her hungry companions, the weeping of two girls whose monkey-lovers have been killed, the situation of six exiled, poverty-stricken kings. Like Swift, Voltaire keeps his readers off balance. Raped, cut to pieces, hanged, stabbed in the belly, the central characters of *Candide* keep coming back to life at opportune moments, as though no disaster could have permanent or ultimately destructive effects. Such reassuring fantasy suggests that we don't need to worry, it is all a joke, an outpouring of fertile fancy designed to ridicule an outmoded philosophic system with no particular relevance to us. On the other hand, historical reality keeps intruding. Those six hungry kings are real, actual figures, actually dispossessed. Candide sees Admiral Byng executed: an admiral who really lived and really died by firing squad for not engaging an enemy with sufficient ferocity. The Lisbon earthquake actually occurred; thirty to forty thousand people lost their lives in it. The extravagances of reality equal those of the storyteller; Voltaire demands that the reader imaginatively confront and somehow come to terms with horrors that surround us still.

The real problem, *Candide* suggests, is not natural or human disaster so much as human complacency. When Candide sees Admiral Byng shot, he comments on the injustice of the execution. "That's perfectly true, came the answer; but in this country it is useful from time to time to kill one admiral in order to encourage the others." Early in the nineteenth century, William Wordsworth wrote, "much it grieved my heart to think / What man has made of man." His tone and perspective differ dramatically from Voltaire's, but his point is the same: human beings use their faculties to increase corruption. Failure to take seriously any human death is a form of moral corruption; failure to acknowledge the intolerability of war, in all its concrete detail of rape and butchery, epitomizes such corruption at its worst.

In a late chapter of *Candide,* the central character, less naive than he once was, inquires about whether people have always massacred one another. Have they, he asks, "always been liars, traitors, ingrates, thieves, weaklings, sneaks, cowards, backbiters, gluttons, drunkards, misers, climbers, killers, calumniators, sensualists, fanatics, hypocrites, and fools?" His interlocutor, Martin, responds that, just as hawks have always devoured pigeons, human beings have always manifested the same vices. This ironic variation on the period's conviction of the universality and continuity of human nature epitomizes Voltaire's sense of outrage, which in some respects parallels Swift's in the fourth part of *Gulliver's Travels.* Swift demonstrates the implications of "reason" considered as an ideal and shows its irrelevance to actual human behavior; Voltaire shows how the claim of a rational universal order avoids the hard problems of living in a world where human beings have become liars, traitors, and so on. His Swiftian catalog of vice and folly expresses the moral insufficiency and perversity of humankind. Martin's cynical assumption that people are naturally corrupt, as hawks naturally eat smaller birds, constitutes another form of avoidance. The assumed inevitability of vice, like belief that all is for the best, justifies passivity. Nothing *can* be done, nothing *should* be done, or nothing *matters* (the view of Lord Pococurante, another figure Candide encounters). So the characters of this fiction, including Candide himself, mainly pursue self-gratification. Even this course they do not follow judiciously: when Candide and Cacambo find themselves in the earthly paradise of Eldorado, "the two happy men resolved to be so no longer," driven by fantasies of improving their condition. Yet, unlike Gulliver, they acquire wisdom at last, learning to withstand "three great evils, boredom, vice, and poverty," by working hard at what comes to hand and avoiding futile theorizing about the nature of the universe.

Although Voltaire's picture of the human condition reveals the same indignation that marks Swift's, he allows at least conditional hope for moderate satisfaction in this life. Candide's beloved Cunégonde loses all her beauty, but she becomes an accomplished pastry cook; Candide possesses a garden he can cultivate. Greed, malice, and lust do not comprise the total possibility for humankind. If Voltaire's tone sometimes expresses outrage, at other times it verges on the playful. When, for example, he mocks the improbabilities of romance by his characters' miraculous resuscitations or parodies the restrictions of classical form by sending Candide and his friends on an epic journey, one can feel his amused awareness of our human need to make order and our human desire to comfort ourselves by fictions. But as he insists that much of the order we claim to perceive itself comprises a comforting fiction, as he uses satire's fierce energies to challenge our complacencies, he reveals once more the underside of the Enlightenment ideal of reason. That we human beings have reason, Voltaire tells us, is no ground on which to flatter ourselves; rightly used, it exposes our insufficiencies.

Biographies and critical studies of Voltaire include R. Aldington, *Voltaire* (1934); G. Brandes, *The Life of Voltaire* (undated); I. O. Wade, *Voltaire and "Candide"* (1959); and T. Besterman, *Voltaire* (1969). A good general introduction is P. E. Richter and Ilona Ricardo, *Voltaire* (1980). A work placing Voltaire in a broad context is F. M. Keener, *The Chain of Becoming* (1983), on Voltaire and his English contemporaries. Two useful works specifically about *Candide* are William Bottiglia, *Voltaire's Candide: Analysis of a Classic* (1964) and Haydn Mason, *Candide: Optimism Demolished* (1992)

PRONOUNCING GLOSSARY

The following list uses common English syllables and stress accents to provide rough equivalents of selected words whose pronunciation may be unfamiliar to the general reader.

Abare: *a-bahr'*

Cacambo: *ka-kahm'-bo*

Candide: *kahn-deed'*

Cunégonde: *kew-nay-gohnd'*

Giroflée: *zhee-roh-flay'*

Issachar: *ee-sah-shahr'*

Pangloss: *pan-glaws'*

Paquette: *pah-ket'*

Pococurante: *poh-koh-ku-rahnt'*

Thunder-Ten-Tronckh: *tun-dayr'–ten–trawnk*

Candide, or Optimism[1]

translated from the German of Doctor Ralph with the additions which were found in the Doctor's pocket when he died at Minden in the Year of Our Lord 1759

CHAPTER 1

How Candide Was Brought up in a Fine Castle and How He Was Driven Therefrom

There lived in Westphalia,[2] in the castle of the Baron of Thunder-Ten-Tronckh, a young man on whom nature had bestowed the perfection of gentle manners. His features admirably expressed his soul; he combined an honest mind with great simplicity of heart; and I think it was for this reason that they called him Candide. The old servants of the house suspected that he was the son of the Baron's sister by a respectable, honest gentleman of the neighborhood, whom she had refused to marry because he could prove only seventy-one quarterings,[3] the rest of his family tree having been lost in the passage of time.

The Baron was one of the most mighty lords of Westphalia, for his castle had a door and windows. His great hall was even hung with a tapestry. The

1. Translated and with notes by Robert M. Adams. 2. A province of western Germany, near Holland and the lower Rhineland. Flat, boggy, and drab, it is noted chiefly for its excellent ham. In a letter to his niece, written during his German expedition of 1750, Voltaire described the "vast, sad, sterile, detestable countryside of Westphalia." 3. Genealogical divisions of one's family-tree. Seventy-one of them is a grotesque number to have, representing something over 2,000 years of uninterrupted nobility.

dogs of his courtyard made up a hunting pack on occasion, with the stable-boys as huntsmen; the village priest was his grand almoner. They all called him "My Lord," and laughed at his stories.

The Baroness, who weighed in the neighborhood of three hundred and fifty pounds, was greatly respected for that reason, and did the honors of the house with a dignity which rendered her even more imposing. Her daughter Cunégonde,[4] aged seventeen, was a ruddy-cheeked girl, fresh, plump, and desirable. The Baron's son seemed in every way worthy of his father. The tutor Pangloss was the oracle of the household, and little Candide listened to his lectures with all the good faith of his age and character.

Pangloss gave instruction in metaphysico-theologico-cosmoloonigology.[5] He proved admirably that there cannot possibly be an effect without a cause and that in this best of all possible worlds the Baron's castle was the best of all castles and his wife the best of all possible Baronesses.

—It is clear, said he, that things cannot be otherwise than they are, for since everything is made to serve an end, everything necessarily serves the best end. Observe: noses were made to support spectacles, hence we have spectacles. Legs, as anyone can plainly see, were made to be breeched, and so we have breeches. Stones were made to be shaped and to build castles with; thus My Lord has a fine castle, for the greatest Baron in the province should have the finest house; and since pigs were made to be eaten, we eat pork all year round.[6] Consequently, those who say everything is well are uttering mere stupidities; they should say everything is for the best.

Candide listened attentively and believed implicitly; for he found Miss Cunégonde exceedingly pretty, though he never had the courage to tell her so. He decided that after the happiness of being born Baron of Thunder-Ten-Tronckh, the second order of happiness was to be Miss Cunégonde; the third was seeing her every day, and the fourth was listening to Master Pangloss, the greatest philosopher in the province and consequently in the entire world.

One day, while Cunégonde was walking near the castle in the little woods that they called a park, she saw Dr. Pangloss in the underbrush; he was giving a lesson in experimental physics to her mother's maid, a very attractive and obedient brunette. As Miss Cunégonde had a natural bent for the sciences, she watched breathlessly the repeated experiments which were going on; she saw clearly the doctor's sufficient reason, observed both cause and effect, and returned to the house in a distracted and pensive frame of mind, yearning for knowledge and dreaming that she might be the sufficient reason of young Candide—who might also be hers.

As she was returning to the castle, she met Candide, and blushed; Candide blushed too. She greeted him in a faltering tone of voice; and Candide talked to her without knowing what he was saying. Next day, as everyone was rising from the dinner table, Cunégonde and Candide found themselves behind a

---

4. Cunégonde gets her odd name from Kunigunda (wife to Emperor Henry II) who walked barefoot and blindfolded on red-hot irons to prove her chastity; Pangloss gets his name from Greek words meaning all-tongue.   5. The "looney" buried in this burlesque word corresponds to a buried *nigaud*—"booby" in the French. Christian Wolff, disciple of Leibniz, invented and popularized the word "cosmology." The catch phrases in the following sentence, echoed by popularizers of Leibniz, make reference to the determinism of his system, its linking of cause with effect, and its optimism.   6. The argument from design supposes that everything in this world exists for a specific reason; Voltaire objects not to the argument as a whole, but to the abuse of it.

screen; Cunégonde dropped her handkerchief, Candide picked it up; she held his hand quite innocently, he kissed her hand quite innocently with remarkable vivacity and emotion; their lips met, their eyes lit up, their knees trembled, their hands wandered. The Baron of Thunder-Ten-Tronckh passed by the screen and, taking note of this cause and this effect, drove Candide out of the castle by kicking him vigorously on the backside. Cunégonde fainted; as soon as she recovered, the Baroness slapped her face; and everything was confusion in the most beautiful and agreeable of all possible castles.

CHAPTER 2

What Happened to Candide Among the Bulgars[7]

Candide, ejected from the earthly paradise, wandered for a long time without knowing where he was going, weeping, raising his eyes to heaven, and gazing back frequently on the most beautiful of castles which contained the most beautiful of Baron's daughters. He slept without eating, in a furrow of a plowed field, while the snow drifted over him; next morning, numb with cold, he dragged himself into the neighboring village, which was called Waldberghoff-trarbk-dikdorff; he was penniless, famished, and exhausted. At the door of a tavern he paused forlornly. Two men dressed in blue[8] took note of him:

—Look, chum, said one of them, there's a likely young fellow of just about the right size.

They approached Candide and invited him very politely to dine with them.

—Gentlemen, Candide replied with charming modesty, I'm honored by your invitation, but I really don't have enough money to pay my share.

—My dear sir, said one of the blues, people of your appearance and your merit don't have to pay; aren't you five feet five inches tall?

—Yes, gentlemen, that is indeed my stature, said he, making a bow.

—Then, sir, you must be seated at once; not only will we pay your bill this time, we will never allow a man like you to be short of money; for men were made only to render one another mutual aid.

—You are quite right, said Candide; it is just as Dr. Pangloss always told me, and I see clearly that everything is for the best.

They beg him to accept a couple of crowns, he takes them, and offers an I.O.U.; they won't hear of it, and all sit down at table together.

—Don't you love dearly . . . ?

—I do indeed, says he, I dearly love Miss Cunégonde.

—No, no, says one of the gentlemen, we are asking if you don't love dearly the King of the Bulgars.

—Not in the least, says he, I never laid eyes on him.

—What's that you say? He's the most charming of kings, and we must drink his health.

—Oh, gladly, gentlemen; and he drinks.

7. Voltaire chose this name to represent the Prussian troops of Frederick the Great because he wanted to make an insinuation of pederasty against both the soldiers and their master. Cf. French *bougre,* English "bugger." 8. The recruiting officers of Frederick the Great, much feared in eighteenth-century Europe, wore blue uniforms. Frederick had a passion for sorting out his soldiers by size; several of his regiments would accept only six-footers.

—That will do, they tell him; you are now the bulwark, the support, the defender, the hero of the Bulgars; your fortune is made and your future assured.

Promptly they slip irons on his legs and lead him to the regiment. There they cause him to right face, left face, present arms, order arms, aim, fire, doubletime, and they give him thirty strokes of the rod. Next day he does the drill a little less awkwardly and gets only twenty strokes; the third day, they give him only ten, and he is regarded by his comrades as a prodigy.

Candide, quite thunderstruck, did not yet understand very clearly how he was a hero. One fine spring morning he took it into his head to go for a walk, stepping straight out as if it were a privilege of the human race, as of animals in general, to use his legs as he chose.[9] He had scarcely covered two leagues when four other heroes, each six feet tall, overtook him, bound him, and threw him into a dungeon. At the court-martial they asked which he preferred, to be flogged thirty-six times by the entire regiment or to receive summarily a dozen bullets in the brain. In vain did he argue that the human will is free and insist that he preferred neither alternative; he had to choose; by virtue of the divine gift called "liberty" he decided to run the gauntlet thirty-six times, and actually endured two floggings. The regiment was composed of two thousand men. That made four thousand strokes, which laid open every muscle and nerve from his nape to his butt. As they were preparing for the third beating, Candide, who could endure no more, begged as a special favor that they would have the goodness to smash his head. His plea was granted; they bandaged his eyes and made him kneel down. The King of the Bulgars, passing by at this moment, was told of the culprit's crime; and as this king had a rare genius, he understood, from everything they told him of Candide, that this was a young metaphysician, extremely ignorant of the ways of the world, so he granted his royal pardon, with a generosity which will be praised in every newspaper in every age. A worthy surgeon cured Candide in three weeks with the ointments described by Dioscorides.[1] He already had a bit of skin back and was able to walk when the King of the Bulgars went to war with the King of the Abares.[2]

CHAPTER 3

How Candide Escaped from the Bulgars, and What Became of Him

Nothing could have been so fine, so brisk, so brilliant, so well-drilled as the two armies. The trumpets, the fifes, the oboes, the drums, and the cannon produced such a harmony as was never heard in hell. First the cannons battered down about six thousand men on each side; then volleys of musket fire removed from the best of worlds about nine or ten thousand rascals who were cluttering up its surface. The bayonet was a sufficient reason for the demise of several thousand others. Total casualties might well amount to

9. This episode was suggested by the experience of a Frenchman named Courtilz, who had deserted from the Prussian army and been bastinadoed for it. Voltaire intervened with Frederick to gain his release. But it also reflects the story that Wolff, Leibniz's disciple, got into trouble with Frederick's father when someone reported that his doctrine denying free will had encouraged several soldiers to desert. "The argument of the grenadier," who was said to have pleaded preestablished harmony to justify his desertion, so infuriated the king that he had Wolff expelled from the country.   1. Dioscorides' treatise on *materia medica*, dating from the first century A.D., was not the most up to date.   2. A tribe of semicivilized Scythians, who might be supposed at war with the Bulgars; allegorically, the Abares are the French, who opposed the Prussians in the Seven Years' War (1756–63). According to the title page of 1761, "Doctor Ralph," the dummy author of *Candide*, himself perished at the battle of Minden (Westphalia) in 1759.

thirty thousand men or so. Candide, who was trembling like a philosopher, hid himself as best he could while this heroic butchery was going on.

Finally, while the two kings in their respective camps celebrated the victory by having *Te Deum*s sung, Candide undertook to do his reasoning of cause and effect somewhere else. Passing by mounds of the dead and dying, he came to a nearby village which had been burnt to the ground. It was an Abare village, which the Bulgars had burned, in strict accordance with the laws of war. Here old men, stunned from beatings, watched the last agonies of their butchered wives, who still clutched their infants to their bleeding breasts; there, disemboweled girls, who had first satisfied the natural needs of various heroes, breathed their last; others, half-scorched in the flames, begged for their death stroke. Scattered brains and severed limbs littered the ground.

Candide fled as fast as he could to another village; this one belonged to the Bulgars, and the heroes of the Abare cause had given it the same treatment. Climbing over ruins and stumbling over corpses, Candide finally made his way out of the war area, carrying a little food in his knapsack and never ceasing to dream of Miss Cunégonde. His supplies gave out when he reached Holland; but having heard that everyone in that country was rich and a Christian, he felt confident of being treated as well as he had been in the castle of the Baron before he was kicked out for the love of Miss Cunégonde.

He asked alms of several grave personages, who all told him that if he continued to beg, he would be shut up in a house of correction and set to hard labor.

Finally he approached a man who had just been talking to a large crowd for an hour on end; the topic was charity. Looking doubtfully at him, the orator demanded:

—What are you doing here? Are you here to serve the good cause?

—There is no effect without a cause, said Candide modestly; all events are linked by the chain of necessity and arranged for the best. I had to be driven away from Miss Cunégonde, I had to run the gauntlet, I have to beg my bread until I can earn it; none of this could have happened otherwise.

—Look here, friend, said the orator, do you think the Pope is Antichrist?[3]

—I haven't considered the matter, said Candide; but whether he is or not, I'm in need of bread.

—You don't deserve any, said the other; away with you, you rascal, you rogue, never come near me as long as you live.

Meanwhile, the orator's wife had put her head out of the window, and, seeing a man who was not sure the Pope was Antichrist, emptied over his head a pot full of——Scandalous! The excesses into which women are led by religious zeal!

A man who had never been baptized, a good Anabaptist[4] named Jacques, saw this cruel and heartless treatment being inflicted on one of his fellow creatures, a featherless biped possessing a soul;[5] he took Candide home with him, washed him off, gave him bread and beer, presented him with two

---

3. Voltaire is satirizing extreme Protestant sects that have sometimes seemed to make hatred of Rome the sum and substance of their creed.   4. Holland, as the home of religious liberty, had offered asylum to the Anabaptists, whose radical views on property and religious discipline had made them unpopular during the sixteenth century. Granted tolerance, they settled down into respectable burghers. Since this behavior confirmed some of Voltaire's major theses, he had a high opinion of contemporary Anabaptists. 5. Plato's famous minimal definition of man, which he corrected by the addition of a soul to distinguish man from a plucked chicken.

florins, and even undertook to give him a job in his Persian-rug factory—for these items are widely manufactured in Holland. Candide, in an ecstasy of gratitude, cried out:

—Master Pangloss was right indeed when he told me everything is for the best in this world; for I am touched by your kindness far more than by the harshness of that black-coated gentleman and his wife.

Next day, while taking a stroll about town, he met a beggar who was covered with pustules, his eyes were sunken, the end of his nose rotted off, his mouth twisted, his teeth black, he had a croaking voice and a hacking cough, and spat a tooth every time he tried to speak.

CHAPTER 4

How Candide Met His Old Philosophy Tutor, Doctor Pangloss, and What Came of It

Candide, more touched by compassion even than by horror, gave this ghastly beggar the two florins that he himself had received from his honest Anabaptist friend Jacques. The phantom stared at him, burst into tears, and fell on his neck. Candide drew back in terror.

—Alas, said one wretch to the other, don't you recognize your dear Pangloss any more?

—What are you saying? You, my dear master! you, in this horrible condition? What misfortune has befallen you? Why are you no longer in the most beautiful of castles? What has happened to Miss Cunégonde, that pearl among young ladies, that masterpiece of Nature?

—I am perishing, said Pangloss.

Candide promptly led him into the Anabaptist's stable, where he gave him a crust of bread, and when he had recovered:—Well, said he, Cunégonde?

—Dead, said the other.

Candide fainted. His friend brought him around with a bit of sour vinegar which happened to be in the stable. Candide opened his eyes.

—Cunégonde, dead! Ah, best of worlds, what's become of you now? But how did she die? It wasn't of grief at seeing me kicked out of her noble father's elegant castle?

—Not at all, said Pangloss; she was disemboweled by the Bulgar soldiers, after having been raped to the absolute limit of human endurance; they smashed the Baron's head when he tried to defend her, cut the Baroness to bits, and treated my poor pupil exactly like his sister. As for the castle, not one stone was left on another, not a shed, not a sheep, not a duck, not a tree; but we had the satisfaction of revenge, for the Abares did exactly the same thing to a nearby barony belonging to a Bulgar nobleman.

At this tale Candide fainted again; but having returned to his senses and said everything appropriate to the occasion, he asked about the cause and effect, the sufficient reason, which had reduced Pangloss to his present pitiful state.

—Alas, said he, it was love; love, the consolation of the human race, the preservative of the universe, the soul of all sensitive beings, love, gentle love.

—Unhappy man, said Candide, I too have had some experience of this love, the sovereign of hearts, the soul of our souls; and it never got me anything but a single kiss and twenty kicks in the rear. How could this lovely cause produce in you such a disgusting effect?

Pangloss replied as follows:—My dear Candide! you knew Paquette, that pretty maidservant to our august Baroness. In her arms I tasted the delights of paradise, which directly caused these torments of hell, from which I am now suffering. She was infected with the disease, and has perhaps died of it. Paquette received this present from an erudite Franciscan, who took the pains to trace it back to its source; for he had it from an elderly countess, who picked it up from a captain of cavalry, who acquired it from a marquise, who caught it from a page, who had received it from a Jesuit, who during his novitiate got it directly from one of the companions of Christopher Columbus. As for me, I shall not give it to anyone, for I am a dying man.

—Oh, Pangloss, cried Candide, that's a very strange genealogy. Isn't the devil at the root of the whole thing?

—Not at all, replied that great man; it's an indispensable part of the best of worlds, a necessary ingredient; if Columbus had not caught, on an American island, this sickness which attacks the source of generation and sometimes prevents generation entirely—which thus strikes at and defeats the greatest end of Nature herself—we should have neither chocolate nor cochineal. It must also be noted that until the present time this malady, like religious controversy, has been wholly confined to the continent of Europe. Turks, Indians, Persians, Chinese, Siamese, and Japanese know nothing of it as yet; but there is a sufficient reason for which they in turn will make its acquaintance in a couple of centuries. Meanwhile, it has made splendid progress among us, especially among those big armies of honest, well-trained mercenaries who decide the destinies of nations. You can be sure that when thirty thousand men fight a pitched battle against the same number of the enemy, there will be about twenty thousand with the pox on either side.

—Remarkable indeed, said Candide, but we must see about curing you.

—And how can I do that, said Pangloss, seeing I don't have a cent to my name? There's not a doctor in the whole world who will let your blood or give you an enema without demanding a fee. If you can't pay yourself, you must find someone to pay for you.

These last words decided Candide; he hastened to implore the help of his charitable Anabaptist, Jacques, and painted such a moving picture of his friend's wretched state that the good man did not hesitate to take in Pangloss and have him cured at his own expense. In the course of the cure, Pangloss lost only an eye and an ear. Since he wrote a fine hand and knew arithmetic, the Anabaptist made him his bookkeeper. At the end of two months, being obliged to go to Lisbon on business, he took his two philosophers on the boat with him. Pangloss still maintained that everything was for the best, but Jacques didn't agree with him.

—It must be, said he, that men have corrupted Nature, for they are not born wolves, yet that is what they become. God gave them neither twenty-four-pound cannon nor bayonets, yet they have manufactured both in order to destroy themselves. Bankruptcies have the same effect, and so does the justice which seizes the goods of bankrupts in order to prevent the creditors from getting them.[6]

—It was all indispensable, replied the one-eyed doctor, since private misfortunes make for public welfare, and therefore the more private misfortunes there are, the better everything is.

6. Voltaire had suffered losses from various bankruptcy proceedings.

While he was reasoning, the air grew dark, the winds blew from all directions, and the vessel was attacked by a horrible tempest within sight of Lisbon harbor.

CHAPTER 5

Tempest, Shipwreck, Earthquake, and What Happened to Doctor Pangloss, Candide, and the Anabaptist, Jacques

Half of the passengers, weakened by the frightful anguish of seasickness and the distress of tossing about on stormy waters, were incapable of noticing their danger. The other half shrieked aloud and fell to their prayers, the sails were ripped to shreds, the masts snapped, the vessel opened at the seams. Everyone worked who could stir, nobody listened for orders or issued them. The Anabaptist was lending a hand in the after part of the ship when a frantic sailor struck him and knocked him to the deck; but just at that moment, the sailor lurched so violently that he fell head first over the side, where he hung, clutching a fragment of the broken mast. The good Jacques ran to his aid, and helped him to climb back on board, but in the process was himself thrown into the sea under the very eyes of the sailor, who allowed him to drown without even glancing at him. Candide rushed to the rail, and saw his benefactor rise for a moment to the surface, then sink forever. He wanted to dive to his rescue; but the philosopher Pangloss prevented him by proving that the bay of Lisbon had been formed expressly for this Anabaptist to drown in. While he was proving the point *a priori*, the vessel opened up and everyone perished except for Pangloss, Candide, and the brutal sailor who had caused the virtuous Anabaptist to drown; this rascal swam easily to shore, while Pangloss and Candide drifted there on a plank.

When they had recovered a bit of energy, they set out for Lisbon; they still had a little money with which they hoped to stave off hunger after escaping the storm.

Scarcely had they set foot in the town, still bewailing the loss of their benefactor, when they felt the earth quake underfoot; the sea was lashed to a froth, burst into the port, and smashed all the vessels lying at anchor there. Whirlwinds of fire and ash swirled through the streets and public squares; houses crumbled, roofs came crashing down on foundations, foundations split; thirty thousand inhabitants of every age and either sex were crushed in the ruins.[7] The sailor whistled through his teeth, and said with an oath:— There'll be something to pick up here.

—What can be the sufficient reason of this phenomenon? asked Pangloss.

—The Last Judgment is here, cried Candide.

But the sailor ran directly into the middle of the ruins, heedless of danger in his eagerness for gain; he found some money, laid violent hands on it, got drunk, and, having slept off his wine, bought the favors of the first street-walker he could find amid the ruins of smashed houses, amid corpses and suffering victims on every hand. Pangloss however tugged at his sleeve.

—My friend, said he, this is not good form at all; your behavior falls short of that required by the universal reason; it's untimely, to say the least.

---

7. The great Lisbon earthquake and fire occurred on November 1, 1755; between thirty and forty thousand deaths resulted.

—Bloody hell, said the other, I'm a sailor, born in Batavia; I've been four times to Japan and stamped four times on the crucifix;[8] get out of here with your universal reason.

Some falling stonework had struck Candide; he lay prostrate in the street, covered with rubble, and calling to Pangloss:—For pity's sake bring me a little wine and oil; I'm dying.

—This earthquake is nothing novel, Pangloss replied; the city of Lima, in South America, underwent much the same sort of tremor, last year; same causes, same effects; there is surely a vein of sulphur under the earth's surface reaching from Lima to Lisbon.

—Nothing is more probable, said Candide; but, for God's sake, a little oil and wine.

—What do you mean, probable? replied the philosopher; I regard the case as proved.

Candide fainted and Pangloss brought him some water from a nearby fountain.

Next day, as they wandered amid the ruins, they found a little food which restored some of their strength. Then they fell to work like the others, bringing relief to those of the inhabitants who had escaped death. Some of the citizens whom they rescued gave them a dinner as good as was possible under the circumstances; it is true that the meal was a melancholy one, and the guests watered their bread with tears; but Pangloss consoled them by proving that things could not possibly be otherwise.

—For, said he, all this is for the best, since if there is a volcano at Lisbon, it cannot be somewhere else, since it is unthinkable that things should not be where they are, since everything is well.

A little man in black, an officer of the Inquisition,[9] who was sitting beside him, politely took up the question, and said:—It would seem that the gentleman does not believe in original sin, since if everything is for the best, man has not fallen and is not liable to eternal punishment.

—I most humbly beg pardon of your excellency, Pangloss answered, even more politely, but the fall of man and the curse of original sin entered necessarily into the best of all possible worlds.

—Then you do not believe in free will? said the officer.

—Your excellency must excuse me, said Pangloss; free will agrees very well with absolute necessity, for it was necessary that we should be free, since a will which is determined . . .

Pangloss was in the middle of his sentence, when the officer nodded significantly to the attendant who was pouring him a glass of port, or Oporto, wine.

---

8. The Japanese, originally receptive to foreign visitors, grew fearful that priests and proselytizers were merely advance agents of empire and expelled both the Portuguese and Spanish early in the seventeenth century. Only the Dutch were allowed to retain a small foothold, under humiliating conditions, of which the notion of stamping on the crucifix is symbolic. It was never what Voltaire suggests here, an actual requirement for entering the country.   9. Specifically, a *familier* or *poursuivant,* an undercover agent with powers of arrest.

CHAPTER 6

How They Made a Fine Auto-da-Fé to Prevent Earthquakes, and How Candide Was Whipped

After the earthquake had wiped out three quarters of Lisbon, the learned men of the land could find no more effective way of averting total destruction than to give the people a fine auto-da-fé;[1] the University of Coimbra had established that the spectacle of several persons being roasted over a slow fire with full ceremonial rites is an infallible specific against earthquakes.

In consequence, the authorities had rounded up a Biscayan convicted of marrying a woman who had stood godmother to his child, and two Portuguese who while eating a chicken had set aside a bit of bacon used for seasoning.[2] After dinner, men came with ropes to tie up Doctor Pangloss and his disciple Candide, one for talking and the other for listening with an air of approval; both were taken separately to a set of remarkably cool apartments, where the glare of the sun is never bothersome; eight days later they were both dressed in *san-benitos* and crowned with paper mitres;[3] Candide's mitre and *san-benito* were decorated with inverted flames and with devils who had neither tails nor claws; but Pangloss's devils had both tails and claws, and his flames stood upright. Wearing these costumes, they marched in a procession, and listened to a very touching sermon, followed by a beautiful concert of plainsong. Candide was flogged in cadence to the music; the Biscayan and the two men who had avoided bacon were burned, and Pangloss was hanged, though hanging is not customary. On the same day there was another earthquake, causing frightful damage.[4]

Candide, stunned, stupefied, despairing, bleeding, trembling, said to himself:—If this is the best of all possible worlds, what are the others like? The flogging is not so bad, I was flogged by the Bulgars. But oh my dear Pangloss, greatest of philosophers, was it necessary for me to watch you being hanged, for no reason that I can see? Oh my dear Anabaptist, best of men, was it necessary that you should be drowned in the port? Oh Miss Cunégonde, pearl of young ladies, was it necessary that you should have your belly slit open?

He was being led away, barely able to stand, lectured, lashed, absolved, and blessed, when an old woman approached and said,—My son, be of good cheer and follow me.

CHAPTER 7

How an Old Woman Took Care of Candide, and How He Regained What He Loved

Candide was of very bad cheer, but he followed the old woman to a shanty; she gave him a jar of ointment to rub himself, left him food and drink; she showed him a tidy little bed; next to it was a suit of clothing.

---

1. Literally, "act of faith," a public ceremony of repentance and humiliation. Such an auto-da-fé was actually held in Lisbon, June 20, 1756.   2. The Biscayan's fault lay in marrying someone within the forbidden bounds of relationship, an act of spiritual incest. The men who declined pork or bacon were understood to be crypto-Jews.   3. The cone-shaped paper cap (intended to resemble a bishop's mitre) and flowing yellow cape were customary garb for those pleading before the Inquisition.   4. In fact, the second quake occurred December 21, 1755.

—Eat, drink, sleep, she said; and may Our Lady of Atocha, Our Lord St. Anthony of Padua, and Our Lord St. James of Compostela watch over you. I will be back tomorrow.

Candide, still completely astonished by everything he had seen and suffered, and even more by the old woman's kindness, offered to kiss her hand.

—It's not *my* hand you should be kissing, said she. I'll be back tomorrow; rub yourself with the ointment, eat and sleep.

In spite of his many sufferings, Candide ate and slept. Next day the old woman returned bringing breakfast; she looked at his back and rubbed it herself with another ointment; she came back with lunch; and then she returned in the evening, bringing supper. Next day she repeated the same routine.

—Who are you? Candide asked continually. Who told you to be so kind to me? How can I ever repay you?

The good woman answered not a word; she returned in the evening, and without food.

—Come with me, says she, and don't speak a word.

Taking him by the hand, she walks out into the countryside with him for about a quarter of a mile; they reach an isolated house, quite surrounded by gardens and ditches. The old woman knocks at a little gate, it opens. She takes Candide up a secret stairway to a gilded room furnished with a fine brocaded sofa; there she leaves him, closes the door, disappears. Candide stood as if entranced; his life, which had seemed like a nightmare so far, was now starting to look like a delightful dream.

Soon the old woman returned; on her feeble shoulder leaned a trembling woman, of a splendid figure, glittering in diamonds, and veiled.

—Remove the veil, said the old woman to Candide.

The young man stepped timidly forward, and lifted the veil. What an event! What a surprise! Could it be Miss Cunégonde? Yes, it really was! She herself! His knees give way, speech fails him, he falls at her feet, Cunégonde collapses on the sofa. The old woman plies them with brandy, they return to their senses, they exchange words. At first they could utter only broken phrases, questions and answers at cross purposes, sighs, tears, exclamations. The old woman warned them not to make too much noise, and left them alone.

—Then it's really you, said Candide, you're alive, I've found you again in Portugal. Then you never were raped? You never had your belly ripped open, as the philosopher Pangloss assured me?

—Oh yes, said the lovely Cunégonde, but one doesn't always die of these two accidents.

—But your father and mother were murdered then?

—All too true, said Cunégonde, in tears.

—And your brother?

—Killed too.

—And why are you in Portugal? and how did you know I was here? and by what device did you have me brought to this house?

—I shall tell you everything, the lady replied; but first you must tell me what has happened to you since that first innocent kiss we exchanged and the kicking you got because of it.

Candide obeyed her with profound respect; and though he was overcome, though his voice was weak and hesitant, though he still had twinges of pain from his beating, he described as simply as possible everything that had happened to him since the time of their separation. Cunégonde lifted her eyes to heaven; she wept at the death of the good Anabaptist and at that of Pangloss; after which she told the following story to Candide, who listened to every word while he gazed on her with hungry eyes.

CHAPTER 8

Cunégonde's Story

—I was in my bed and fast asleep when heaven chose to send the Bulgars into our castle of Thunder-Ten-Tronckh. They butchered my father and brother, and hacked my mother to bits. An enormous Bulgar, six feet tall, seeing that I had swooned from horror at the scene, set about raping me; at that I recovered my senses, I screamed and scratched, bit and fought, I tried to tear the eyes out of that big Bulgar—not realizing that everything which had happened in my father's castle was a mere matter of routine. The brute then stabbed me with a knife on my left thigh, where I still bear the scar.

—What a pity! I should very much like to see it, said the simple Candide.

—You shall, said Cunégonde; but shall I go on?

—Please do, said Candide.

So she took up the thread of her tale:—A Bulgar captain appeared, he saw me covered with blood and the soldier too intent to get up. Shocked by the monster's failure to come to attention, the captain killed him on my body. He then had my wound dressed, and took me off to his quarters, as a prisoner of war. I laundered his few shirts and did his cooking; he found me attractive, I confess it, and I won't deny that he was a handsome fellow, with a smooth, white skin; apart from that, however, little wit, little philosophical training; it was evident that he had not been brought up by Doctor Pangloss. After three months, he had lost all his money and grown sick of me; so he sold me to a Jew named Don Issachar, who traded in Holland and Portugal, and who was mad after women. This Jew developed a mighty passion for my person, but he got nowhere with it; I held him off better than I had done with the Bulgar soldier; for though a person of honor may be raped once, her virtue is only strengthened by the experience. In order to keep me hidden, the Jew brought me to his country house, which you see here. Till then I had thought there was nothing on earth so beautiful as the castle of Thunder-Ten-Tronckh; I was now undeceived.

—One day the Grand Inquisitor took notice of me at mass; he ogled me a good deal, and made known that he must talk to me on a matter of secret business. I was taken to his palace; I told him of my rank; he pointed out that it was beneath my dignity to belong to an Israelite. A suggestion was then conveyed to Don Issachar that he should turn me over to My Lord the Inquisitor. Don Issachar, who is court banker and a man of standing, refused out of hand. The inquisitor threatened him with an auto-da-fé. Finally my Jew, fearing for his life, struck a bargain by which the house and I would belong to both of them as joint tenants; the Jew would get Mondays, Wednesdays, and the Sabbath, the inquisitor would get the other days of the week. That has been the arrangement for six months now. There have been quarrels; sometimes it has not been clear whether the night from Saturday to

Sunday belonged to the old or the new dispensation. For my part, I have so far been able to hold both of them off; and that, I think, is why they are both still in love with me.

—Finally, in order to avert further divine punishment by earthquake, and to terrify Don Issachar, My Lord the Inquisitor chose to celebrate an auto-da-fé. He did me the honor of inviting me to attend. I had an excellent seat; the ladies were served with refreshments between the mass and the execution. To tell you the truth, I was horrified to see them burn alive those two Jews and that decent Biscayan who had married his child's godmother; but what was my surprise, my terror, my grief, when I saw, huddled in a *san-benito* and wearing a mitre, someone who looked like Pangloss! I rubbed my eyes, I watched his every move, I saw him hanged; and I fell back in a swoon. Scarcely had I come to my senses again, when I saw you stripped for the lash; that was the peak of my horror, consternation, grief, and despair. I may tell you, by the way, that your skin is even whiter and more delicate than that of my Bulgar captain. Seeing you, then, redoubled the torments which were already overwhelming me. I shrieked aloud, I wanted to call out, 'Let him go, you brutes!' but my voice died within me, and my cries would have been useless. When you had been thoroughly thrashed: 'How can it be,' I asked myself, 'that agreeable Candide and wise Pangloss have come to Lisbon, one to receive a hundred whiplashes, the other to be hanged by order of My Lord the Inquisitor, whose mistress I am? Pangloss must have deceived me cruelly when he told me that all is for the best in this world.'

—Frantic, exhausted, half out of my senses, and ready to die of weakness, I felt as if my mind were choked with the massacre of my father, my mother, my brother, with the arrogance of that ugly Bulgar soldier, with the knife slash he inflicted on me, my slavery, my cookery, my Bulgar captain, my nasty Don Issachar, my abominable inquisitor, with the hanging of Doctor Pangloss, with that great plainsong *miserere* which they sang while they flogged you—and above all, my mind was full of the kiss which I gave you behind the screen, on the day I saw you for the last time. I praised God, who had brought you back to me after so many trials. I asked my old woman to look out for you, and to bring you here as soon as she could. She did just as I asked; I have had the indescribable joy of seeing you again, hearing you and talking with you once more. But you must be frightfully hungry; I am, myself; let us begin with a dinner.

So then and there they sat down to table; and after dinner, they adjourned to that fine brocaded sofa, which has already been mentioned; and there they were when the eminent Don Issachar, one of the masters of the house, appeared. It was the day of the Sabbath; he was arriving to assert his rights and express his tender passion.

CHAPTER 9

What Happened to Cunégonde, Candide, the Grand Inquisitor,
and a Jew

This Issachar was the most choleric Hebrew seen in Israel since the Babylonian captivity.

—What's this, says he, you bitch of a Christian, you're not satisfied with the Grand Inquisitor? Do I have to share you with this rascal, too?

So saying, he drew a long dagger, with which he always went armed, and, supposing his opponent defenceless, flung himself on Candide. But our good Westphalian had received from the old woman, along with his suit of clothes, a fine sword. Out it came, and though his manners were of the gentlest, in short order he laid the Israelite stiff and cold on the floor, at the feet of the lovely Cunégonde.

—Holy Virgin! she cried. What will become of me now? A man killed in my house! If the police find out, we're done for.

—If Pangloss had not been hanged, said Candide, he would give us good advice in this hour of need, for he was a great philosopher. Lacking him, let's ask the old woman.

She was a sensible body, and was just starting to give her opinion of the situation, when another little door opened. It was just one o'clock in the morning, Sunday morning. This day belonged to the inquisitor. In he came, and found the whipped Candide with a sword in his hand, a corpse at his feet, Cunégonde in terror, and an old woman giving them both good advice.

Here now is what passed through Candide's mind in this instant of time; this is how he reasoned:—If this holy man calls for help, he will certainly have me burned, and perhaps Cunégonde as well; he has already had me whipped without mercy; he is my rival; I have already killed once; why hesitate?

It was a quick, clear chain of reasoning; without giving the inquisitor time to recover from his surprise, he ran him through, and laid him beside the Jew.

—Here you've done it again, said Cunégonde; there's no hope for us now. We'll be excommunicated, our last hour has come. How is it that you, who were born so gentle, could kill in two minutes a Jew and a prelate?

—My dear girl, replied Candide, when a man is in love, jealous, and just whipped by the Inquisition, he is no longer himself.

The old woman now spoke up and said:—There are three Andalusian steeds in the stable, with their saddles and bridles; our brave Candide must get them ready: my lady has some gold coin and diamonds; let's take to horse at once, though I can only ride on one buttock; we will go to Cadiz. The weather is as fine as can be, and it is pleasant to travel in the cool of the evening.

Promptly, Candide saddled the three horses. Cunégonde, the old woman, and he covered thirty miles without a stop. While they were fleeing, the Holy Brotherhood[5] came to investigate the house; they buried the inquisitor in a fine church, and threw Issachar on the dunghill.

Candide, Cunégonde, and the old woman were already in the little town of Avacena, in the middle of the Sierra Morena; and there, as they sat in a country inn, they had this conversation.

---

5. A semireligious order with police powers, very active in eighteenth-century Spain.

CHAPTER 10

In Deep Distress, Candide, Cunégonde, and the Old Woman
Reach Cadiz; They Put to Sea

—Who then could have robbed me of my gold and diamonds? said Cunégonde, in tears. How shall we live? what shall we do? where shall I find other inquisitors and Jews to give me some more?

—Ah, said the old woman, I strongly suspect that reverend Franciscan friar who shared the inn with us yesterday at Badajoz. God save me from judging him unfairly! But he came into our room twice, and he left long before us.

—Alas, said Candide, the good Pangloss often proved to me that the fruits of the earth are a common heritage of all, to which each man has equal right. On these principles, the Franciscan should at least have left us enough to finish our journey. You have nothing at all, my dear Cunégonde?

—Not a maravedi, said she.

—What to do? said Candide.

—We'll sell one of the horses, said the old woman; I'll ride on the croup behind my mistress, though only on one buttock, and so we will get to Cadiz.

There was in the same inn a Benedictine prior; he bought the horse cheap. Candide, Cunégonde, and the old woman passed through Lucena, Chillas, and Lebrixa, and finally reached Cadiz. There a fleet was being fitted out and an army assembled, to reason with the Jesuit fathers in Paraguay, who were accused of fomenting among their flock a revolt against the kings of Spain and Portugal near the town of St. Sacrement.[6] Candide, having served in the Bulgar army, performed the Bulgar manual of arms before the general of the little army with such grace, swiftness, dexterity, fire, and agility, that they gave him a company of infantry to command. So here he is, a captain; and off he sails with Miss Cunégonde, the old woman, two valets, and the two Andalusian steeds which had belonged to My Lord the Grand Inquisitor of Portugal.

Throughout the crossing, they spent a great deal of time reasoning about the philosophy of poor Pangloss.

—We are destined, in the end, for another universe, said Candide; no doubt that is the one where everything is well. For in this one, it must be admitted, there is some reason to grieve over our physical and moral state.

—I love you with all my heart, said Cunégonde; but my soul is still harrowed by thoughts of what I have seen and suffered.

—All will be well, replied Candide; the sea of this new world is already better than those of Europe, calmer and with steadier winds. Surely it is the New World which is the best of all possible worlds.

—God grant it, said Cunégonde; but I have been so horribly unhappy in the world so far, that my heart is almost dead to hope.

—You pity yourselves, the old woman told them; but you have had no such misfortunes as mine.

6. Actually, Colonia del Sacramento. Voltaire took great interest in the Jesuit role in Paraguay, which he has much oversimplified and largely misrepresented here in the interests of his satire. In 1750 they did, however, offer armed resistance to an agreement made between Spain and Portugal. They were subdued and expelled in 1769.

Cunégonde nearly broke out laughing; she found the old woman comic in pretending to be more unhappy than she.

—Ah, you poor old thing, said she, unless you've been raped by two Bulgars, been stabbed twice in the belly, seen two of your castles destroyed, witnessed the murder of two of your mothers and two of your fathers, and watched two of your lovers being whipped in an auto-da-fé, I do not see how you can have had it worse than me. Besides, I was born a baroness, with seventy-two quarterings, and I have worked in a scullery.

—My lady, replied the old woman, you do not know my birth and rank; and if I showed you my rear end, you would not talk as you do, you might even speak with less assurance.

These words inspired great curiosity in Candide and Cunégonde, which the old woman satisfied with this story.

CHAPTER 11

The Old Woman's Story

—My eyes were not always bloodshot and red-rimmed, my nose did not always touch my chin, and I was not born a servant. I am in fact the daughter of Pope Urban the Tenth and the Princess of Palestrina.[7] Till the age of fourteen, I lived in a palace so splendid that all the castles of all your German barons would not have served it as a stable; a single one of my dresses was worth more than all the assembled magnificence of Westphalia. I grew in beauty, in charm, in talent, surrounded by pleasures, dignities, and glowing visions of the future. Already I was inspiring the young men to love; my breast was formed—and what a breast! white, firm, with the shape of the Venus de Medici; and what eyes! what lashes, what black brows! What fire flashed from my glances and outshone the glitter of the stars, as the local poets used to tell me! The women who helped me dress and undress fell into ecstasies, whether they looked at me from in front or behind; and all the men wanted to be in their place.

—I was engaged to the ruling prince of Massa-Carrara; and what a prince he was! as handsome as I, softness and charm compounded, brilliantly witty, and madly in love with me. I loved him in return as one loves for the first time, with a devotion approaching idolatry. The wedding preparations had been made, with a splendor and magnificence never heard of before; nothing but celebrations, masks, and comic operas, uninterruptedly; and all Italy composed in my honor sonnets of which not one was even passable. I had almost attained the very peak of bliss, when an old marquise who had been the mistress of my prince invited him to her house for a cup of chocolate. He died in less than two hours, amid horrifying convulsions. But that was only a trifle. My mother, in complete despair (though less afflicted than I), wished to escape for a while the oppressive atmosphere of grief. She owned a handsome property near Gaeta.[8] We embarked on a papal galley gilded like the altar of St. Peter's in Rome. Suddenly a pirate ship from Salé swept down and boarded us. Our soldiers defended themselves as papal troops usually

7. Voltaire left behind a comment on this passage, a note first published in 1829: "Note the extreme discretion of the author; hitherto there has never been a pope named Urban X; he avoided attributing a bastard to a known pope. What circumspection! what an exquisite conscience!"   8. About halfway between Rome and Naples.

do; falling on their knees and throwing down their arms, they begged of the corsair absolution *in articulo mortis.*[9]

—They were promptly stripped as naked as monkeys, and so was my mother, and so were our maids of honor, and so was I too. It's a very remarkable thing, the energy these gentlemen put into stripping people. But what surprised me even more was that they stuck their fingers in a place where we women usually admit only a syringe. This ceremony seemed a bit odd to me, as foreign usages always do when one hasn't traveled. They only wanted to see if we didn't have some diamonds hidden there; and I soon learned that it's a custom of long standing among the genteel folk who swarm the seas. I learned that my lords the very religious knights of Malta never overlook this ceremony when they capture Turks, whether male or female; it's one of those international laws which have never been questioned.

—I won't try to explain how painful it is for a young princess to be carried off into slavery in Morocco with her mother. You can imagine everything we had to suffer on the pirate ship. My mother was still very beautiful; our maids of honor, our mere chambermaids, were more charming than anything one could find in all Africa. As for myself, I was ravishing, I was loveliness and grace supreme, and I was a virgin. I did not remain so for long; the flower which had been kept for the handsome prince of Massa-Carrara was plucked by the corsair captain; he was an abominable negro, who thought he was doing me a great favor. My Lady the Princess of Palestrina and I must have been strong indeed to bear what we did during our journey to Morocco. But on with my story; these are such common matters that they are not worth describing.

—Morocco was knee deep in blood when we arrived. Of the fifty sons of the emperor Muley-Ismael,[1] each had his faction, which produced in effect fifty civil wars, of blacks against blacks, of blacks against browns, halfbreeds against halfbreeds; throughout the length and breadth of the empire, nothing but one continual carnage.

—Scarcely had we stepped ashore, when some negroes of a faction hostile to my captor arrived to take charge of his plunder. After the diamonds and gold, we women were the most prized possessions. I was now witness of a struggle such as you never see in the temperate climate of Europe. Northern people don't have hot blood; they don't feel the absolute fury for women which is common in Africa. Europeans seem to have milk in their veins; it is vitriol or liquid fire which pulses through these people around Mount Atlas. The fight for possession of us raged with the fury of the lions, tigers, and poisonous vipers of that land. A Moor snatched my mother by the right arm, the first mate held her by the left; a Moorish soldier grabbed one leg, one of our pirates the other. In a moment's time almost all our girls were being dragged four different ways. My captain held me behind him while with his scimitar he killed everyone who braved his fury. At last I saw all our Italian women, including my mother, torn to pieces, cut to bits, murdered by the monsters who were fighting over them. My captive companions, their captors, soldiers, sailors, blacks, browns, whites, mulattoes, and at last my captain, all were killed, and I remained half dead on a mountain of corpses.

9. Literally, when at the point of death. Absolution from a corsair in the act of murdering one is of very dubious validity.   1. Having reigned for more than fifty years, a potent and ruthless sultan of Morocco, he died in 1727 and left his kingdom in much the condition described.

Similar scenes were occurring, as is well known, for more than three hundred leagues around, without anyone skimping on the five prayers a day decreed by Mohammed.

—With great pain, I untangled myself from this vast heap of bleeding bodies, and dragged myself under a great orange tree by a neighboring brook, where I collapsed, from terror, exhaustion, horror, despair, and hunger. Shortly, my weary mind surrendered to a sleep which was more of a swoon than a rest. I was in this state of weakness and languor, between life and death, when I felt myself touched by something which moved over my body. Opening my eyes, I saw a white man, rather attractive, who was groaning and saying under his breath: 'O *che sciagura d'essere senza coglioni!'*[2]

CHAPTER 12

The Old Woman's Story Continued

—Amazed and delighted to hear my native tongue, and no less surprised by what this man was saying, I told him that there were worse evils than those he was complaining of. In a few words, I described to him the horrors I had undergone, and then fainted again. He carried me to a nearby house, put me to bed, gave me something to eat, served me, flattered me, comforted me, told me he had never seen anyone so lovely, and added that he had never before regretted so much the loss of what nobody could give him back.

'I was born at Naples,' he told me, 'where they caponize two or three thousand children every year; some die of it, others acquire a voice more beautiful than any woman's, still others go on to become governors of kingdoms.[3] The operation was a great success with me, and I became court musician to the Princess of Palestrina . . . '

'Of my mother,' I exclaimed.

'Of your mother,' cried he, bursting into tears; 'then you must be the princess whom I raised till she was six, and who already gave promise of becoming as beautiful as you are now!'

'I am that very princess; my mother lies dead, not a hundred yards from here, buried under a pile of corpses.'

—I told him my adventures, he told me his: that he had been sent by a Christian power to the King of Morocco, to conclude a treaty granting him gunpowder, cannon, and ships with which to liquidate the traders of the other Christian powers.

'My mission is concluded,' said this honest eunuch; 'I shall take ship at Ceuta and bring you back to Italy. *Ma che sciagura d'essere senza coglioni!'*

—I thanked him with tears of gratitude, and instead of returning me to Italy, he took me to Algiers and sold me to the dey of that country. Hardly had the sale taken place, when that plague which has made the rounds of Africa, Asia, and Europe broke out in full fury at Algiers. You have seen earthquakes; but tell me, young lady, have you ever had the plague?

—Never, replied the baroness.

—If you had had it, said the old woman, you would agree that it is far worse than an earthquake. It is very frequent in Africa, and I had it. Imagine,

---

2. "Oh what a misfortune to have no testicles!"   **3.** The castrato Farinelli (1705–1782), originally a singer, came to exercise considerable political influence on the kings of Spain, Philip V and Ferdinand VI.

if you will, the situation of a pope's daughter, fifteen years old, who in three months' time had experienced poverty, slavery, had been raped almost every day, had seen her mother quartered, had suffered from famine and war, and who now was dying of pestilence in Algiers. As a matter of fact, I did not die; but the eunuch and the dey and nearly the entire seraglio of Algiers perished.

—When the first horrors of this ghastly plague had passed, the slaves of the dey were sold. A merchant bought me and took me to Tunis; there he sold me to another merchant, who resold me at Tripoli; from Tripoli I was sold to Alexandria, from Alexandria resold to Smyrna, from Smyrna to Constantinople. I ended by belonging to an aga of janizaries, who was shortly ordered to defend Azov against the besieging Russians.[4]

—The aga, who was a gallant soldier, took his whole seraglio with him, and established us in a little fort amid the Maeotian marshes,[5] guarded by two black eunuchs and twenty soldiers. Our side killed a prodigious number of Russians, but they paid us back nicely. Azov was put to fire and sword without respect for age or sex; only our little fort continued to resist, and the enemy determined to starve us out. The twenty janizaries had sworn never to surrender. Reduced to the last extremities of hunger, they were forced to eat our two eunuchs, lest they violate their oaths. After several more days, they decided to eat the women too.

—We had an imam,[6] very pious and sympathetic, who delivered an excellent sermon, persuading them not to kill us altogether.

'Just cut off a single rumpsteak from each of these ladies,' he said, 'and you'll have a fine meal. Then if you should need another, you can come back in a few days and have as much again; heaven will bless your charitable action, and you will be saved.'

—His eloquence was splendid, and he persuaded them. We underwent this horrible operation. The imam treated us all with the ointment that they use on newly circumcised children. We were at the point of death.

—Scarcely had the janizaries finished the meal for which we furnished the materials, when the Russians appeared in flat-bottomed boats; not a janizary escaped. The Russians paid no attention to the state we were in; but there are French physicians everywhere, and one of them, who knew his trade, took care of us. He cured us, and I shall remember all my life that when my wounds were healed, he made me a proposition. For the rest, he counselled us simply to have patience, assuring us that the same thing had happened in several other sieges, and that it was according to the laws of war.

—As soon as my companions could walk, we were herded off to Moscow. In the division of booty, I fell to a boyar who made me work in his garden, and gave me twenty whiplashes a day; but when he was broken on the wheel after about two years, with thirty other boyars, over some little court intrigue,[7] I seized the occasion; I ran away; I crossed all Russia; I was for a long time a chambermaid in Riga, then at Rostock, Vismara, Leipzig, Cassel, Utrecht, Leyden, The Hague, Rotterdam; I grew old in misery and shame,

---

4. Azov, near the mouth of the Don, was besieged by the Russians under Peter the Great in 1695–96. *Janizaries:* an elite corps of the Ottoman armies.   5. The Roman name of the so-called Sea of Azov, a shallow swampy lake near the town.   6. In effect, a chaplain.   7. Voltaire had in mind an ineffectual conspiracy against Peter the Great known as the "revolt of the streltsy" or musketeers, which took place in 1698. Though easily put down, it provoked from the emperor a massive and atrocious program of reprisals.

having only half a backside and remembering always that I was the daughter of a Pope; a hundred times I wanted to kill myself, but always I loved life more. This ridiculous weakness is perhaps one of our worst instincts; is anything more stupid than choosing to carry a burden that really one wants to cast on the ground? to hold existence in horror, and yet to cling to it? to fondle the serpent which devours us till it has eaten out our heart?

—In the countries through which I have been forced to wander, in the taverns where I have had to work, I have seen a vast number of people who hated their existence; but I never saw more than a dozen who deliberately put an end to their own misery: three negroes, four Englishmen, four Genevans, and a German professor named Robeck.[8] My last post was as servant to the Jew Don Issachar; he attached me to your service, my lovely one; and I attached myself to your destiny, till I have become more concerned with your fate than with my own. I would not even have mentioned my own misfortunes, if you had not irked me a bit, and if it weren't the custom, on shipboard, to pass the time with stories. In a word, my lady, I have had some experience of the world, I know it; why not try this diversion? Ask every passenger on this ship to tell you his story, and if you find a single one who has not often cursed the day of his birth, who has not often told himself that he is the most miserable of men, then you may throw me overboard head first.

CHAPTER 13

How Candide Was Forced to Leave the Lovely Cunégonde and the Old Woman

Having heard out the old woman's story, the lovely Cunégonde paid her the respects which were appropriate to a person of her rank and merit. She took up the wager as well, and got all the passengers, one after another, to tell her their adventures. She and Candide had to agree that the old woman had been right.

—It's certainly too bad, said Candide, that the wise Pangloss was hanged, contrary to the custom of autos-da-fé; he would have admirable things to say of the physical evil and moral evil which cover land and sea, and I might feel within me the impulse to dare to raise several polite objections.

As the passengers recited their stories, the boat made steady progress, and presently landed at Buenos Aires. Cunégonde, Captain Candide, and the old woman went to call on the governor, Don Fernando d'Ibaraa y Figueroa y Mascarenes y Lampourdos y Souza. This nobleman had the pride appropriate to a man with so many names. He addressed everyone with the most aristocratic disdain, pointing his nose so loftily, raising his voice so mercilessly, lording it so splendidly, and assuming so arrogant a pose, that everyone who met him wanted to kick him. He loved women to the point of fury; and Cunégonde seemed to him the most beautiful creature he had ever seen. The first thing he did was to ask directly if she were the captain's wife. His manner of asking this question disturbed Candide; he did not dare say she was his wife, because in fact she was not; he did not dare say she was his

8. Johann Robeck (1672–1739) published a treatise advocating suicide and showed his conviction by drowning himself at the age of sixty-seven.

sister, because she wasn't that either; and though this polite lie was once common enough among the ancients,[9] and sometimes serves moderns very well, he was too pure of heart to tell a lie.

—Miss Cunégonde, said he, is betrothed to me, and we humbly beg your excellency to perform the ceremony for us.

Don Fernando d'Ibaraa y Figueroa y Mascarenes y Lampourdos y Souza twirled his moustache, smiled sardonically, and ordered Captain Candide to go drill his company. Candide obeyed. Left alone with My Lady Cunégonde, the governor declared his passion, and protested that he would marry her tomorrow, in church or in any other manner, as it pleased her charming self. Cunégonde asked for a quarter-hour to collect herself, consult the old woman, and make up her mind.

The old woman said to Cunégonde:—My lady, you have seventy-two quarterings and not one penny; if you wish, you may be the wife of the greatest lord in South America, who has a really handsome moustache; are you going to insist on your absolute fidelity? You have already been raped by the Bulgars; a Jew and an inquisitor have enjoyed your favors; miseries entitle one to privileges. I assure you that in your position I would make no scruple of marrying My Lord the Governor, and making the fortune of Captain Candide.

While the old woman was talking with all the prudence of age and experience, there came into the harbor a small ship bearing an alcalde and some alguazils.[1] This is what had happened.

As the old woman had very shrewdly guessed, it was a long-sleeved Franciscan who stole Cunégonde's gold and jewels in the town of Badajoz, when she and Candide were in flight. The monk tried to sell some of the gems to a jeweler, who recognized them as belonging to the Grand Inquisitor. Before he was hanged, the Franciscan confessed that he had stolen them, indicating who his victims were and where they were going. The flight of Cunégonde and Candide was already known. They were traced to Cadiz, and a vessel was hastily dispatched in pursuit of them. This vessel was now in the port of Buenos Aires. The rumor spread that an alcalde was aboard, in pursuit of the murderers of My Lord the Grand Inquisitor. The shrewd old woman saw at once what was to be done.

—You cannot escape, she told Cunégonde, and you have nothing to fear. You are not the one who killed my lord, and, besides, the governor, who is in love with you, won't let you be mistreated. Sit tight.

And then she ran straight to Candide:—Get out of town, she said, or you'll be burned within the hour.

There was not a moment to lose; but how to leave Cunégonde, and where to go?

CHAPTER 14

How Candide and Cacambo Were Received by the Jesuits of Paraguay

Candide had brought from Cadiz a valet of the type one often finds in the provinces of Spain and in the colonies. He was one quarter Spanish, son of

---

9. Voltaire has in mind Abraham's adventures with Sarah (Genesis 12) and Isaac's with Rebecca (Genesis 26).   1. Police officers.

a halfbreed in the Tucuman;[2] he had been choirboy, sacristan, sailor, monk, merchant, soldier, and lackey. His name was Cacambo, and he was very fond of his master because his master was a very good man. In hot haste he saddled the two Andalusian steeds.

—Hurry, master, do as the old woman says; let's get going and leave this town without a backward look.

Candide wept:—O my beloved Cunégonde! must I leave you now, just when the governor is about to marry us! Cunégonde, brought from so far, what will ever become of you?

—She'll become what she can, said Cacambo; women can always find something to do with themselves; God sees to it; let's get going.

—Where are you taking me? where are we going? what will we do without Cunégonde? said Candide.

—By Saint James of Compostela, said Cacambo, you were going to make war against the Jesuits, now we'll go make war for them. I know the roads pretty well, I'll bring you to their country, they will be delighted to have a captain who knows the Bulgar drill; you'll make a prodigious fortune. If you don't get your rights in one world, you will find them in another. And isn't it pleasant to see new things and do new things?

—Then you've already been in Paraguay? said Candide.

—Indeed I have, replied Cacambo; I was cook in the College of the Assumption, and I know the government of Los Padres[3] as I know the streets of Cadiz. It's an admirable thing, this government. The kingdom is more than three hundred leagues across; it is divided into thirty provinces. Los Padres own everything in it, and the people nothing; it's a masterpiece of reason and justice. I myself know nothing so wonderful as Los Padres, who in this hemisphere make war on the kings of Spain and Portugal, but in Europe hear their confessions; who kill Spaniards here, and in Madrid send them to heaven; that really tickles me; let's get moving, you're going to be the happiest of men. Won't Los Padres be delighted when they learn they have a captain who knows the Bulgar drill!

As soon as they reached the first barricade, Cacambo told the frontier guard that a captain wished to speak with My Lord the Commander. A Paraguayan officer ran to inform headquarters by laying the news at the feet of the commander. Candide and Cacambo were first disarmed and deprived of their Andalusian horses. They were then placed between two files of soldiers; the commander was at the end, his three-cornered hat on his head, his cassock drawn up, a sword at his side, and a pike in his hand. He nods, and twenty-four soldiers surround the newcomers. A sergeant then informs them that they must wait, that the commander cannot talk to them, since the reverend father provincial has forbidden all Spaniards from speaking, except in his presence, and from remaining more than three hours in the country.

—And where is the reverend father provincial? says Cacambo.

—He is reviewing his troops after having said mass, the sergeant replies, and you'll only be able to kiss his spurs in three hours.

—But, says Cacambo, my master the captain, who, like me, is dying from hunger, is not Spanish at all, he is German; can't we have some breakfast while waiting for his reverence?

2. A province of Argentina, to the northwest of Buenos Aires.   3. The Jesuit fathers.

The sergeant promptly went off to report this speech to the commander.

—God be praised, said this worthy; since he is German, I can talk to him; bring him into my bower.

Candide was immediately led into a leafy nook surrounded by a handsome colonnade of green and gold marble and trellises amid which sported parrots, birds of paradise,[4] hummingbirds, guinea fowl, and all the rarest species of birds. An excellent breakfast was prepared in golden vessels; and while the Paraguayans ate corn out of wooden bowls in the open fields under the glare of the sun, the reverend father commander entered into his bower.

He was a very handsome young man, with an open face, rather blonde in coloring, with ruddy complexion, arched eyebrows, liquid eyes, pink ears, bright red lips, and an air of pride, but a pride somehow different from that of a Spaniard or a Jesuit. Their confiscated weapons were restored to Candide and Cacambo, as well as their Andalusian horses; Cacambo fed them oats alongside the bower, always keeping an eye on them for fear of an ambush.

First Candide kissed the hem of the commander's cassock, then they sat down at the table.

—So you are German? said the Jesuit, speaking in that language.

—Yes, your reverence, said Candide.

As they spoke these words, both men looked at one another with great surprise, and another emotion which they could not control.

—From what part of Germany do you come? said the Jesuit.

—From the nasty province of Westphalia, said Candide; I was born in the castle of Thunder-Ten-Tronckh.

—Merciful heavens! cries the commander. Is it possible?

—What a miracle! exclaims Candide.

—Can it be you? asks the commander.

—It's impossible, says Candide.

They both fall back in their chairs, they embrace, they shed streams of tears.

—What, can it be you, reverend father! you, the brother of the lovely Cunégonde! you, who were killed by the Bulgars! you, the son of My Lord the Baron! you, a Jesuit in Paraguay! It's a mad world, indeed it is. Oh, Pangloss! Pangloss! how happy you would be, if you hadn't been hanged.

The commander dismissed his negro slaves and the Paraguayans who served his drink in crystal goblets. He thanked God and Saint Ignatius a thousand times, he clasped Candide in his arms, their faces were bathed in tears.

—You would be even more astonished, even more delighted, even more beside yourself, said Candide, if I told you that My Lady Cunégonde, your sister, who you thought was disemboweled, is enjoying good health.

—Where?

—Not far from here, in the house of the governor of Buenos Aires; and to think that I came to make war on you!

Each word they spoke in this long conversation added another miracle.

4. In this passage and several later ones, Voltaire uses in conjunction two words, both of which mean hummingbird. The French system of classifying hummingbirds, based on the work of the celebrated Buffon, distinguishes *oiseaux-mouches* with straight bills from *colibris* with curved bills. This distinction is wholly fallacious. Hummingbirds have all manner of shaped bills, and the division of species must be made on other grounds entirely. At the expense of ornithological accuracy, I have therefore introduced birds of paradise to get the requisite sense of glitter and sheen.

Their souls danced on their tongues, hung eagerly at their ears, glittered in their eyes. As they were Germans, they sat a long time at table, waiting for the reverend father provincial; and the commander spoke in these terms to his dear Candide.

CHAPTER 15

How Candide Killed the Brother of His Dear Cunégonde

—All my life long I shall remember the horrible day when I saw my father and mother murdered and my sister raped. When the Bulgars left, that adorable sister of mine was nowhere to be found; so they loaded a cart with my mother, my father, myself, two serving girls, and three little murdered boys, to carry us all off for burial in a Jesuit chapel some two leagues from our ancestral castle. A Jesuit sprinkled us with holy water; it was horribly salty, and a few drops got into my eyes; the father noticed that my lid made a little tremor; putting his hand on my heart, he felt it beat; I was rescued, and at the end of three weeks was as good as new. You know, my dear Candide, that I was a very pretty boy; I became even more so; the reverend father Croust,[5] superior of the abbey, conceived a most tender friendship for me; he accepted me as a novice, and shortly after, I was sent to Rome. The Father General had need of a resupply of young German Jesuits. The rulers of Paraguay accept as few Spanish Jesuits as they can; they prefer foreigners, whom they think they can control better. I was judged fit, by the Father General, to labor in this vineyard. So we set off, a Pole, a Tyrolean, and myself. Upon our arrival, I was honored with the posts of subdeacon and lieutenant; today I am a colonel and a priest. We are giving a vigorous reception to the King of Spain's men; I assure you they will be excommunicated as well as trounced on the battlefield. Providence has sent you to help us. But is it really true that my dear sister, Cunégonde, is in the neighborhood, with the governor of Buenos Aires?

Candide reassured him with a solemn oath that nothing could be more true. Their tears began to flow again.

The baron could not weary of embracing Candide; he called him his brother, his savior.

—Ah, my dear Candide, said he, maybe together we will be able to enter the town as conquerors, and be united with my sister Cunégonde.

—That is all I desire, said Candide; I was expecting to marry her, and I still hope to.

—You insolent dog, replied the baron, you would have the effrontery to marry my sister, who has seventy-two quarterings! It's a piece of presumption for you even to mention such a crazy project in my presence.

Candide, terrified by this speech, answered:—Most reverend father, all the quarterings in the world don't affect this case; I have rescued your sister out of the arms of a Jew and an inquisitor; she has many obligations to me, she wants to marry me. Master Pangloss always taught me that men are equal; and I shall certainly marry her.

—We'll see about that, you scoundrel, said the Jesuit baron of Thunder-Ten-Tronckh; and so saying, he gave him a blow across the face with the flat

5. A Jesuit rector at Colmar with whom Voltaire had quarreled in 1754.

of his sword. Candide immediately drew his own sword and thrust it up to the hilt in the baron's belly; but as he drew it forth all dripping, he began to weep.

—Alas, dear God! said he, I have killed my old master, my friend, my brother-in-law; I am the best man in the world, and here are three men I've killed already, and two of the three were priests.

Cacambo, who was standing guard at the entry of the bower, came running.

—We can do nothing but sell our lives dearly, said his master; someone will certainly come; we must die fighting.

Cacambo, who had been in similar scrapes before, did not lose his head; he took the Jesuit's cassock, which the commander had been wearing, and put it on Candide; he stuck the dead man's square hat on Candide's head, and forced him onto horseback. Everything was done in the wink of an eye.

—Let's ride, master; everyone will take you for a Jesuit on his way to deliver orders; and we will have passed the frontier before anyone can come after us.

Even as he was pronouncing these words, he charged off, crying in Spanish:—Way, make way for the reverend father colonel!

CHAPTER 16

What Happened to the Two Travelers with Two Girls,
Two Monkeys, and the Savages Named Biglugs

Candide and his valet were over the frontier before anyone in the camp knew of the death of the German Jesuit. Foresighted Cacambo had taken care to fill his satchel with bread, chocolate, ham, fruit, and several bottles of wine. They pushed their Andalusian horses forward into unknown country, where there were no roads. Finally a broad prairie divided by several streams opened before them. Our two travelers turned their horses loose to graze; Cacambo suggested that they eat too, and promptly set the example. But Candide said:—How can you expect me to eat ham when I have killed the son of My Lord the Baron, and am now condemned never to see the lovely Cunégonde for the rest of my life? Why should I drag out my miserable days, since I must exist far from her in the depths of despair and remorse? And what will the *Journal de Trévoux*[6] say of all this?

Though he talked this way, he did not neglect the food. Night fell. The two wanderers heard a few weak cries which seemed to be voiced by women. They could not tell whether the cries expressed grief or joy; but they leaped at once to their feet, with that uneasy suspicion which one always feels in an unknown country. The outcry arose from two girls, completely naked, who were running swiftly along the edge of the meadow, pursued by two monkeys who snapped at their buttocks. Candide was moved to pity; he had learned marksmanship with the Bulgars, and could have knocked a nut off a bush without touching the leaves. He raised his Spanish rifle, fired twice, and killed the two monkeys.

—God be praised, my dear Cacambo! I've saved these two poor creatures from great danger. Though I committed a sin in killing an inquisitor and a

6. A newspaper published by the Jesuit order, founded in 1701 and consistently hostile to Voltaire.

Jesuit, I've redeemed myself by saving the lives of two girls. Perhaps they are two ladies of rank, and this good deed may gain us special advantages in the country.

He had more to say, but his mouth shut suddenly when he saw the girls embracing the monkeys tenderly, weeping over their bodies, and filling the air with lamentations.

—I wasn't looking for quite so much generosity of spirit, said he to Cacambo; the latter replied:—You've really fixed things this time, master; you've killed the two lovers of these young ladies.

—Their lovers! Impossible! You must be joking, Cacambo; how can I believe you?

—My dear master, Cacambo replied, you're always astonished by every-thing. Why do you think it so strange that in some countries monkeys suc-ceed in obtaining the good graces of women? They are one quarter human, just as I am one quarter Spanish.

—Alas, Candide replied, I do remember now hearing Master Pangloss say that such things used to happen, and that from these mixtures there arose pans, fauns, and satyrs, and that these creatures had appeared to various grand figures of antiquity; but I took all that for fables.

—You should be convinced now, said Cacambo; it's true, and you see how people make mistakes who haven't received a measure of education. But what I fear is that these girls may get us into real trouble.

These sensible reflections led Candide to leave the field and to hide in a wood. There he dined with Cacambo; and there both of them, having duly cursed the inquisitor of Portugal, the governor of Buenos Aires, and the baron, went to sleep on a bed of moss. When they woke up, they found themselves unable to move; the reason was that during the night the Biglugs,[7] natives of the country, to whom the girls had complained of them, had tied them down with cords of bark. They were surrounded by fifty naked Biglugs, armed with arrows, clubs, and stone axes. Some were boiling a caldron of water, others were preparing spits, and all cried out:—It's a Jesuit, a Jesuit! We'll be revenged and have a good meal; let's eat some Jesuit, eat some Jesuit!

—I told you, my dear master, said Cacambo sadly, I said those two girls would play us a dirty trick.

Candide, noting the caldron and spits, cried out:—We are surely going to be roasted or boiled. Ah, what would Master Pangloss say if he could see these men in a state of nature? All is for the best, I agree; but I must say it seems hard to have lost Miss Cunégonde and to be stuck on a spit by the Biglugs.

Cacambo did not lose his head.

—Don't give up hope, said he to the disconsolate Candide; I understand a little of the jargon these people speak, and I'm going to talk to them.

—Don't forget to remind them, said Candide, of the frightful inhumanity of eating their fellow men, and that Christian ethics forbid it.

—Gentlemen, said Cacambo, you have a mind to eat a Jesuit today? An excellent idea; nothing is more proper than to treat one's enemies so. Indeed, the law of nature teaches us to kill our neighbor, and that's how men behave

7. Voltaire's name is "Oreillons" from Spanish "Orejones," a name mentioned in Garcilaso de Vega's *His-toria General del Perú* (1609), on which Voltaire drew for many of the details in his picture of South America.

the whole world over. Though we Europeans don't exercise our right to eat our neighbors, the reason is simply that we find it easy to get a good meal elsewhere; but you don't have our resources, and we certainly agree that it's better to eat your enemies than to let the crows and vultures have the fruit of your victory. But, gentlemen, you wouldn't want to eat your friends. You think you will be spitting a Jesuit, and it's your defender, the enemy of your enemies, whom you will be roasting. For my part, I was born in your country; the gentleman whom you see is my master, and far from being a Jesuit, he has just killed a Jesuit, the robe he is wearing was stripped from him; that's why you have taken a dislike to him. To prove that I am telling the truth, take his robe and bring it to the nearest frontier of the kingdom of Los Padres; find out for yourselves if my master didn't kill a Jesuit officer. It won't take long; if you find that I have lied, you can still eat us. But if I've told the truth, you know too well the principles of public justice, customs, and laws, not to spare our lives.

The Biglugs found this discourse perfectly reasonable; they appointed chiefs to go posthaste and find out the truth; the two messengers performed their task like men of sense, and quickly returned bringing good news. The Biglugs untied their two prisoners, treated them with great politeness, offered them girls, gave them refreshments, and led them back to the border of their state, crying joyously:—He isn't a Jesuit, he isn't a Jesuit!

Candide could not weary of exclaiming over his preservation.

—What a people! he said. What men! what customs! If I had not had the good luck to run a sword through the body of Miss Cunégonde's brother, I would have been eaten on the spot! But, after all, it seems that uncorrupted nature is good, since these folk, instead of eating me, showed me a thousand kindnesses as soon as they knew I was not a Jesuit.

CHAPTER 17

Arrival of Candide and His Servant at the Country of Eldorado, and That They Saw There

When they were out of the land of the Biglugs, Cacambo said to Candide:
—You see that this hemisphere is no better than the other; take my advice, and let's get back to Europe as soon as possible.

—How to get back, asked Candide, and where to go? If I go to my own land, the Bulgars and Abares are murdering everyone in sight; if I go to Portugal, they'll burn me alive; if we stay here, we risk being skewered any day. But how can I ever leave that part of the world where Miss Cunégonde lives?

—Let's go toward Cayenne, said Cacambo, we shall find some Frenchmen there, for they go all over the world; they can help us; perhaps God will take pity on us.

To get to Cayenne was not easy; they knew more or less which way to go, but mountains, rivers, cliffs, robbers, and savages obstructed the way everywhere. Their horses died of weariness; their food was eaten; they subsisted for one whole month on wild fruits, and at last they found themselves by a little river fringed with coconut trees, which gave them both life and hope.

Cacambo, who was as full of good advice as the old woman, said to Candide:—We can go no further, we've walked ourselves out; I see an abandoned canoe on the bank, let's fill it with coconuts, get into the boat, and float with the current; a river always leads to some inhabited spot or other. If we don't find anything pleasant, at least we may find something new.

—Let's go, said Candide, and let Providence be our guide.

They floated some leagues between banks sometimes flowery, sometimes sandy, now steep, now level. The river widened steadily; finally it disappeared into a chasm of frightful rocks that rose high into the heavens. The two travelers had the audacity to float with the current into this chasm. The river, narrowly confined, drove them onward with horrible speed and a fearful roar. After twenty-four hours, they saw daylight once more; but their canoe was smashed on the snags. They had to drag themselves from rock to rock for an entire league; at last they emerged to an immense horizon, ringed with remote mountains. The countryside was tended for pleasure as well as profit; everywhere the useful was joined to the agreeable. The roads were covered, or rather decorated, with elegantly shaped carriages made of a glittering material, carrying men and women of singular beauty, and drawn by great red sheep which were faster than the finest horses of Andalusia, Tetuan, and Mequinez.

—Here now, said Candide, is a country that's better than Westphalia.

Along with Cacambo, he climbed out of the river at the first village he could see. Some children of the town, dressed in rags of gold brocade, were playing quoits at the village gate; our two men from the other world paused to watch them; their quoits were rather large, yellow, red, and green, and they glittered with a singular luster. On a whim, the travelers picked up several; they were of gold, emeralds, and rubies, and the least of them would have been the greatest ornament of the Great Mogul's throne.

—Surely, said Cacambo, these quoit players are the children of the king of the country.

The village schoolmaster appeared at that moment, to call them back to school.

—And there, said Candide, is the tutor of the royal household.

The little rascals quickly gave up their game, leaving on the ground their quoits and playthings. Candide picked them up, ran to the schoolmaster, and presented them to him humbly, giving him to understand by sign language that their royal highnesses had forgotten their gold and jewels. With a smile, the schoolmaster tossed them to the ground, glanced quickly but with great surprise at Candide's face, and went his way.

The travelers did not fail to pick up the gold, rubies, and emeralds.

—Where in the world are we? cried Candide. The children of this land must be well trained, since they are taught contempt for gold and jewels.

Cacambo was as much surprised as Candide. At last they came to the finest house of the village; it was built like a European palace. A crowd of people surrounded the door, and even more were in the entry; delightful music was heard, and a delicious aroma of cooking filled the air. Cacambo went up to the door, listened, and reported that they were talking Peruvian; that was his native language, for every reader must know that Cacambo was born in Tucuman, in a village where they talk that language exclusively.

—I'll act as interpreter, he told Candide; it's an hotel, let's go in.

Promptly two boys and two girls of the staff, dressed in cloth of gold, and wearing ribbons in their hair, invited them to sit at the host's table. The meal consisted of four soups, each one garnished with a brace of parakeets, a boiled condor which weighed two hundred pounds, two roast monkeys of an excellent flavor, three hundred birds of paradise in one dish and six hundred hummingbirds in another, exquisite stews, delicious pastries, the whole thing served up in plates of what looked like rock crystal. The boys and girls of the staff poured them various beverages made from sugar cane.

The diners were for the most part merchants and travelers, all extremely polite, who questioned Cacambo with the most discreet circumspection, and answered his questions very directly.

When the meal was over, Cacambo as well as Candide supposed he could settle his bill handsomely by tossing onto the table two of those big pieces of gold which they had picked up; but the host and hostess burst out laughing, and for a long time nearly split their sides. Finally they subsided.

—Gentlemen, said the host, we see clearly that you're foreigners; we don't meet many of you here. Please excuse our laughing when you offered us in payment a couple of pebbles from the roadside. No doubt you don't have any of our local currency, but you don't need it to eat here. All the hotels established for the promotion of commerce are maintained by the state. You have had meager entertainment here, for we are only a poor town; but everywhere else you will be given the sort of welcome you deserve.

Cacambo translated for Candide all the host's explanations, and Candide listened to them with the same admiration and astonishment that his friend Cacambo showed in reporting them.

—What is this country, then, said they to one another, unknown to the rest of the world, and where nature itself is so different from our own? This probably is the country where everything is for the best; for it's absolutely necessary that such a country should exist somewhere. And whatever Master Pangloss said of the matter, I have often had occasion to notice that things went badly in Westphalia.

CHAPTER 18

What They Saw in the Land of Eldorado

Cacambo revealed his curiosity to the host, and the host told him:—I am an ignorant man and content to remain so; but we have here an old man, retired from the court, who is the most knowing person in the kingdom, and the most talkative.

Thereupon he brought Cacambo to the old man's house. Candide now played second fiddle, and acted as servant to his own valet. They entered an austere little house, for the door was merely of silver and the paneling of the rooms was only gold, though so tastefully wrought that the finest paneling would not surpass it. If the truth must be told, the lobby was only decorated with rubies and emeralds; but the patterns in which they were arranged atoned for the extreme simplicity.

The old man received the two strangers on a sofa stuffed with bird-of-paradise feathers, and offered them several drinks in diamond carafes; then he satisfied their curiosity in these terms.

—I am a hundred and seventy-two years old, and I heard from my late father, who was liveryman to the king, about the astonishing revolutions in Peru which he had seen. Our land here was formerly part of the kingdom of the Incas, who rashly left it in order to conquer another part of the world, and who were ultimately destroyed by the Spaniards. The wisest princes of their house were those who had never left their native valley; they decreed, with the consent of the nation, that henceforth no inhabitant of our little kingdom should ever leave it; and this rule is what has preserved our innocence and our happiness. The Spaniards heard vague rumors about this land, they called it El Dorado;[8] and an English knight named Raleigh even came somewhere close to it about a hundred years ago; but as we are surrounded by unscalable mountains and precipices, we have managed so far to remain hidden from the rapacity of the European nations, who have an inconceivable rage for the pebbles and mud of our land, and who, in order to get some, would butcher us all to the last man.

The conversation was a long one; it turned on the form of the government, the national customs, on women, public shows, the arts. At last Candide, whose taste always ran to metaphysics, told Cacambo to ask if the country had any religion.

The old man grew a bit red.

—How's that? he said. Can you have any doubt of it? Do you suppose we are altogether thankless scoundrels?

Cacambo asked meekly what was the religion of Eldorado. The old man flushed again.

—Can there be two religions? he asked. I suppose our religion is the same as everyone's, we worship God from morning to evening.

—Then you worship a single deity? said Cacambo, who acted throughout as interpreter of the questions of Candide.

—It's obvious, said the old man, that there aren't two or three or four of them. I must say the people of your world ask very remarkable questions.

Candide could not weary of putting questions to this good old man; he wanted to know how the people of Eldorado prayed to God.

—We don't pray to him at all, said the good and respectable sage; we have nothing to ask him for, since everything we need has already been granted; we thank God continually.

Candide was interested in seeing the priests; he had Cacambo ask where they were. The old gentleman smiled.

—My friends, said he, we are all priests; the king and all the heads of household sing formal psalms of thanksgiving every morning, and five or six thousand voices accompany them.

—What! you have no monks to teach, argue, govern, intrigue, and burn at the stake everyone who disagrees with them?

—We should have to be mad, said the old man; here we are all of the same mind, and we don't understand what you're up to with your monks.

Candide was overjoyed at all these speeches, and said to himself:—This is very different from Westphalia and the castle of My Lord the Baron; if our friend Pangloss had seen Eldorado, he wouldn't have called the castle of Thunder-Ten-Tronckh the finest thing on earth; to know the world one must travel.

After this long conversation, the old gentleman ordered a carriage with six

8. The myth of this land of gold somewhere in Central or South America had been widespread since the sixteenth century. *The Discovery of Guiana,* published in 1595, described Sir Walter Ralegh's infatuation with the myth of Eldorado and served to spread the story still further.

sheep made ready, and gave the two travelers twelve of his servants for their journey to the court.

—Excuse me, said he, if old age deprives me of the honor of accompanying you. The king will receive you after a style which will not altogether displease you, and you will doubtless make allowance for the customs of the country if there are any you do not like.

Candide and Cacambo climbed into the coach; the six sheep flew like the wind, and in less than four hours they reached the king's palace at the edge of the capital. The entryway was two hundred and twenty feet high and a hundred wide; it is impossible to describe all the materials of which it was made. But you can imagine how much finer it was than those pebbles and sand which we call gold and jewels.

Twenty beautiful girls of the guard detail welcomed Candide and Cacambo as they stepped from the carriage, took them to the baths, and dressed them in robes woven of hummingbird feathers; then the high officials of the crown, both male and female, led them to the royal chamber between two long lines, each of a thousand musicians, as is customary. As they approached the throne room, Cacambo asked an officer what was the proper method of greeting his majesty: if one fell to one's knees or on one's belly; if one put one's hands on one's head or on one's rear; if one licked up the dust of the earth—in a word, what was the proper form?[9]

—The ceremony, said the officer, is to embrace the king and kiss him on both cheeks.

Candide and Cacambo fell on the neck of his majesty, who received them with all the dignity imaginable, and asked them politely to dine.

In the interim, they were taken about to see the city, the public buildings rising to the clouds, the public markets and arcades, the fountains of pure water and of rose water, those of sugar cane liquors which flowed perpetually in the great plazas paved with a sort of stone which gave off odors of gilly-flower and rose petals. Candide asked to see the supreme court and the hall of parliament; they told him there was no such thing, that lawsuits were unknown. He asked if there were prisons, and was told there were not. What surprised him more, and gave him most pleasure, was the palace of sciences, in which he saw a gallery two thousand paces long, entirely filled with mathematical and physical in struments.

Having passed the whole afternoon seeing only a thousandth part of the city, they returned to the king's palace. Candide sat down to dinner with his majesty, his own valet Cacambo, and several ladies. Never was better food served, and never did a host preside more jovially than his majesty. Cacambo explained the king's witty sayings to Candide, and even when translated they still seemed witty. Of all the things which astonished Candide, this was not, in his eyes, the least astonishing.

They passed a month in this refuge. Candide never tired of saying to Cacambo:—It's true, my friend, I'll say it again, the castle where I was born does not compare with the land where we now are; but Miss Cunégonde is not here, and you doubtless have a mistress somewhere in Europe. If we stay here, we shall be just like everybody else, whereas if we go back to our own

9. Candide's questions are probably derived from those of Gulliver on a similar occasion, in the third part of *Gulliver's Travels*.

world, taking with us just a dozen sheep loaded with Eldorado pebbles, we shall be richer than all the kings put together, we shall have no more inquisitors to fear, and we shall easily be able to retake Miss Cunégonde.

This harangue pleased Cacambo; wandering is such pleasure, it gives a man such prestige at home to be able to talk of what he has seen abroad, that the two happy men resolved to be so no longer, but to take their leave of his majesty.

—You are making a foolish mistake, the king told them; I know very well that my kingdom is nothing much; but when you are pretty comfortable somewhere, you had better stay there. Of course I have no right to keep strangers against their will, that sort of tyranny is not in keeping with our laws or our customs; all men are free; depart when you will, but the way out is very difficult. You cannot possibly go up the river by which you miraculously came; it runs too swiftly through its underground caves. The mountains which surround my land are ten thousand feet high, and steep as walls; each one is more than ten leagues across; the only way down is over precipices. But since you really must go, I shall order my engineers to make a machine which can carry you conveniently. When we take you over the mountains, nobody will be able to go with you, for my subjects have sworn never to leave their refuge, and they are too sensible to break their vows. Other than that, ask of me what you please.

—We only request of your majesty, Cacambo said, a few sheep loaded with provisions, some pebbles, and some of the mud of your country.

The king laughed.

—I simply can't understand, said he, the passion you Europeans have for our yellow mud; but take all you want, and much good may it do you.

He promptly gave orders to his technicians to make a machine for lifting these two extraordinary men out of his kingdom. Three thousand good physicists worked at the problem; the machine was ready in two weeks' time, and cost no more than twenty million pounds sterling, in the money of the country. Cacambo and Candide were placed in the machine; there were two great sheep, saddled and bridled to serve them as steeds when they had cleared the mountains, twenty pack sheep with provisions, thirty which carried presents consisting of the rarities of the country, and fifty loaded with gold, jewels, and diamonds. The king bade tender farewell to the two vagabonds.

It made a fine spectacle, their departure, and the ingenious way in which they were hoisted with their sheep up to the top of the mountains. The technicians bade them good-bye after bringing them to safety, and Candide had now no other desire and no other object than to go and present his sheep to Miss Cunégonde.

—We have, said he, enough to pay off the governor of Buenos Aires—if, indeed, a price can be placed on Miss Cunégonde. Let us go to Cayenne, take ship there, and then see what kingdom we can find to buy up.

CHAPTER 19

What Happened to Them at Surinam, and How Candide
Got to Know Martin

The first day was pleasant enough for our travelers. They were encouraged by the idea of possessing more treasures than Asia, Europe, and Africa could bring together. Candide, in transports, carved the name of Cunégonde on the trees. On the second day two of their sheep bogged down in a swamp and were lost with their loads; two other sheep died of fatigue a few days later; seven or eight others starved to death in a desert; still others fell, a little after, from precipices. Finally, after a hundred days' march, they had only two sheep left. Candide told Cacambo:—My friend, you see how the riches of this world are fleeting; the only solid things are virtue and the joy of seeing Miss Cunégonde again.

—I agree, said Cacambo, but we still have two sheep, laden with more treasure than the king of Spain will ever have; and I see in the distance a town which I suspect is Surinam; it belongs to the Dutch. We are at the end of our trials and on the threshold of our happiness.

As they drew near the town, they discovered a negro stretched on the ground with only half his clothes left, that is, a pair of blue drawers; the poor fellow was also missing his left leg and his right hand.

—Good Lord, said Candide in Dutch, what are you doing in that horrible condition, my friend?

—I am waiting for my master, Mr. Vanderdendur,[1] the famous merchant, answered the negro.

—Is Mr. Vanderdendur, Candide asked, the man who treated you this way?

—Yes, sir, said the negro, that's how things are around here. Twice a year we get a pair of linen drawers to wear. If we catch a finger in the sugar mill where we work, they cut off our hand; if we try to run away, they cut off our leg: I have undergone both these experiences. This is the price of the sugar you eat in Europe. And yet, when my mother sold me for ten Patagonian crowns on the coast of Guinea, she said to me: 'My dear child, bless our witch doctors, reverence them always, they will make your life happy; you have the honor of being a slave to our white masters, and in this way you are making the fortune of your father and mother.' Alas! I don't know if I made their fortunes, but they certainly did not make mine. The dogs, monkeys, and parrots are a thousand times less unhappy than we are. The Dutch witch doctors who converted me tell me every Sunday that we are all sons of Adam, black and white alike. I am no genealogist; but if these preachers are right, we must all be remote cousins; and you must admit no one could treat his own flesh and blood in a more horrible fashion.

—Oh Pangloss! cried Candide, you had no notion of these abominations! I'm through, I must give up your optimism after all.

—What's optimism? said Cacambo.

—Alas, said Candide, it is a mania for saying things are well when one is in hell.

And he shed bitter tears as he looked at this negro, and he was still weeping as he entered Surinam.

The first thing they asked was if there was not some vessel in port which could be sent to Buenos Aires. The man they asked was a Spanish merchant who undertook to make an honest bargain with them. They arranged to meet

---

1. A name perhaps intended to suggest VanDuren, a Dutch bookseller with whom Voltaire had quarreled. In particular, the incident of gradually raising one's price recalls VanDuren, to whom Voltaire had successively offered 1,000, 1,500, 2,000, and 3,000 florins for the return of the manuscript of Frederick the Great's *Anti-Machiavel*.

in a café; Candide and the faithful Cacambo, with their two sheep, went there to meet with him.

Candide, who always said exactly what was in his heart, told the Spaniard of his adventures, and confessed that he wanted to recapture Miss Cunégonde.

—I shall take good care *not* to send you to Buenos Aires, said the merchant; I should be hanged, and so would you. The lovely Cunégonde is his lordship's favorite mistress.

This was a thunderstroke for Candide; he wept for a long time; finally he drew Cacambo aside.

—Here, my friend, said he, is what you must do. Each one of us has in his pockets five or six millions' worth of diamonds; you are cleverer than I; go get Miss Cunégonde in Buenos Aires. If the governor makes a fuss, give him a million; if that doesn't convince him, give him two millions; you never killed an inquisitor, nobody will suspect you. I'll fit out another boat and go wait for you in Venice. That is a free country, where one need have no fear either of Bulgars or Abares or Jews or inquisitors.

Cacambo approved of this wise decision. He was in despair at leaving a good master who had become a bosom friend; but the pleasure of serving him overcame the grief of leaving him. They embraced, and shed a few tears; Candide urged him not to forget the good old woman. Cacambo departed that very same day; he was a very good fellow, that Cacambo.

Candide remained for some time in Surinam, waiting for another merchant to take him to Italy, along with the two sheep which were left him. He hired servants and bought everything necessary for the long voyage; finally Mr. Vanderdendur, master of a big ship, came calling.

—How much will you charge, Candide asked this man, to take me to Venice—myself, my servants, my luggage, and those two sheep over there?

The merchant set a price of ten thousand piastres; Candide did not blink an eye.

—Oh, ho, said the prudent Vanderdendur to himself, this stranger pays out ten thousand piastres at once, he must be pretty well fixed.

Then, returning a moment later, he made known that he could not set sail under twenty thousand.

—All right, you shall have them, said Candide.

—Whew, said the merchant softly to himself, this man gives twenty thousand piastres as easily as ten.

He came back again to say he could not go to Venice for less than thirty thousand piastres.

—All right, thirty then, said Candide.

—Ah ha, said the Dutch merchant, again speaking to himself; so thirty thousand piastres mean nothing to this man; no doubt the two sheep are loaded with immense treasures; let's say no more; we'll pick up the thirty thousand piastres first, and then we'll see.

Candide sold two little diamonds, the least of which was worth more than all the money demanded by the merchant. He paid him in advance. The two sheep were taken aboard. Candide followed in a little boat, to board the vessel at its anchorage. The merchant bides his time, sets sail, and makes his escape with a favoring wind. Candide, aghast and stupefied, soon loses him from view.

—Alas, he cries, now there is a trick worthy of the old world!

He returns to shore sunk in misery; for he had lost riches enough to make the fortunes of twenty monarchs.

Now he rushes to the house of the Dutch magistrate, and, being a bit disturbed, he knocks loudly at the door; goes in, tells the story of what happened, and shouts a bit louder than is customary. The judge begins by fining him ten thousand piastres for making such a racket; then he listens patiently to the story, promises to look into the matter as soon as the merchant comes back, and charges another ten thousand piastres as the costs of the hearing.

This legal proceeding completed the despair of Candide. In fact he had experienced miseries a thousand times more painful, but the coldness of the judge, and that of the merchant who had robbed him, roused his bile and plunged him into a black melancholy. The malice of men rose up before his spirit in all its ugliness, and his mind dwelt only on gloomy thoughts. Finally, when a French vessel was ready to leave for Bordeaux, since he had no more diamond-laden sheep to transport, he took a cabin at a fair price, and made it known in the town that he would pay passage and keep, plus two thousand piastres, to any honest man who wanted to make the journey with him, on condition that this man must be the most disgusted with his own condition and the most unhappy man in the province.

This drew such a crowd of applicants as a fleet could not have held. Candide wanted to choose among the leading candidates, so he picked out about twenty who seemed companionable enough, and of whom each pretended to be more miserable than all the others. He brought them together at his inn and gave them a dinner, on condition that each would swear to tell truthfully his entire history. He would select as his companion the most truly miserable and rightly discontented man, and among the others he would distribute various gifts.

The meeting lasted till four in the morning. Candide, as he listened to all the stories, remembered what the old woman had told him on the trip to Buenos Aires, and of the wager she had made, that there was nobody on the boat who had not undergone great misfortunes. At every story that was told him, he thought of Pangloss.

—That Pangloss, he said, would be hard put to prove his system. I wish he was here. Certainly if everything goes well, it is in Eldorado and not in the rest of the world.

At last he decided in favor of a poor scholar who had worked ten years for the booksellers of Amsterdam. He decided that there was no trade in the world with which one should be more disgusted.

This scholar, who was in fact a good man, had been robbed by his wife, beaten by his son, and deserted by his daughter, who had got herself abducted by a Portuguese. He had just been fired from the little job on which he existed; and the preachers of Surinam were persecuting him because they took him for a Socinian.[2] The others, it is true, were at least as unhappy as he, but Candide hoped the scholar would prove more amusing on the voyage. All his rivals declared that Candide was doing them a great injustice, but he pacified them with a hundred piastres apiece.

---

2. A follower of Faustus and Laelius Socinus, sixteenth-century Polish theologians, who proposed a form of "rational" Christianity which exalted the rational conscience and minimized such mysteries as the trinity. The Socinians, by a special irony, were vigorous optimists.

CHAPTER 20

What Happened to Candide and Martin at Sea

The old scholar, whose name was Martin, now set sail with Candide for Bordeaux. Both men had seen and suffered much; and even if the vessel had been sailing from Surinam to Japan via the Cape of Good Hope, they would have been able to keep themselves amused with instances of moral evil and physical evil during the entire trip.

However, Candide had one great advantage over Martin, that he still hoped to see Miss Cunégonde again, and Martin had nothing to hope for; besides, he had gold and diamonds, and though he had lost a hundred big red sheep loaded with the greatest treasures of the earth, though he had always at his heart a memory of the Dutch merchant's villainy, yet, when he thought of the wealth that remained in his hands, and when he talked of Cunégonde, especially just after a good dinner, he still inclined to the system of Pangloss.

—But what about you, Monsieur Martin, he asked the scholar, what do you think of all that? What is your idea of moral evil and physical evil?

—Sir, answered Martin, those priests accused me of being a Socinian, but the truth is that I am a Manichee.[3]

—You're joking, said Candide; there aren't any more Manichees in the world.

—There's me, said Martin; I don't know what to do about it, but I can't think otherwise.

—You must be possessed of the devil, said Candide.

—He's mixed up with so many things of this world, said Martin, that he may be in me as well as elsewhere; but I assure you, as I survey this globe, or globule, I think that God has abandoned it to some evil spirit—all of it except Eldorado. I have scarcely seen one town which did not wish to destroy its neighboring town, no family which did not wish to exterminate some other family. Everywhere the weak loathe the powerful, before whom they cringe, and the powerful treat them like brute cattle, to be sold for their meat and fleece. A million regimented assassins roam Europe from one end to the other, plying the trades of murder and robbery in an organized way for a living, because there is no more honest form of work for them; and in the cities which seem to enjoy peace and where the arts are flourishing, men are devoured by more envy, cares, and anxieties than a whole town experiences when it's under siege. Private griefs are worse even than public trials. In a word, I have seen so much and suffered so much, that I am a Manichee.

—Still there is some good, said Candide.

—That may be, said Martin, but I don't know it.

In the middle of this discussion, the rumble of cannon was heard. From minute to minute the noise grew louder. Everyone reached for his spyglass. At a distance of some three miles they saw two vessels fighting; the wind brought both of them so close to the French vessel that they had a pleasantly comfortable seat to watch the fight. Presently one of the vessels caught the

---

3. Mani, a Persian sage and philosopher of the third century A.D., taught (probably under the influence of traditions stemming from Zoroaster and the worshipers of the sun god Mithra) that the earth is a field of dispute between two almost equal powers, one of light and one of darkness, both of which must be propitiated.

other with a broadside so low and so square as to send it to the bottom. Candide and Martin saw clearly a hundred men on the deck of the sinking ship; they all raised their hands to heaven, uttering fearful shrieks; and in a moment everything was swallowed up.

—Well, said Martin, that is how men treat one another.

—It is true, said Candide, there's something devilish in this business.

As they chatted, he noticed something of a striking red color floating near the sunken vessel. They sent out a boat to investigate; it was one of his sheep. Candide was more joyful to recover this one sheep than he had been afflicted to lose a hundred of them, all loaded with big Eldorado diamonds.

The French captain soon learned that the captain of the victorious vessel was Spanish and that of the sunken vessel was a Dutch pirate. It was the same man who had robbed Candide. The enormous riches which this rascal had stolen were sunk beside him in the sea, and nothing was saved but a single sheep.

—You see, said Candide to Martin, crime is punished sometimes; this scoundrel of a Dutch merchant has met the fate he deserved.

—Yes, said Martin; but did the passengers aboard his ship have to perish too? God punished the scoundrel, and the devil drowned the others.

Meanwhile the French and Spanish vessels continued on their journey, and Candide continued his talks with Martin. They disputed for fifteen days in a row, and at the end of that time were just as much in agreement as at the beginning. But at least they were talking, they exchanged their ideas, they consoled one another. Candide caressed his sheep.

—Since I have found you again, said he, I may well rediscover Miss Cunégonde.

CHAPTER 21

Candide and Martin Approach the Coast of France: They Reason Together

At last the coast of France came in view.

—Have you ever been in France, Monsieur Martin? asked Candide.

—Yes, said Martin, I have visited several provinces. There are some where half the inhabitants are crazy, others where they are too sly, still others where they are quite gentle and stupid, some where they venture on wit; in all of them the principal occupation is love-making, the second is slander, and the third stupid talk.

—But, Monsieur Martin, were you ever in Paris?

—Yes, I've been in Paris; it contains specimens of all these types; it is a chaos, a mob, in which everyone is seeking pleasure and where hardly anyone finds it, at least from what I have seen. I did not live there for long; as I arrived, I was robbed of everything I possessed by thieves at the fair of St. Germain; I myself was taken for a thief, and spent eight days in jail, after which I took a proofreader's job to earn enough money to return on foot to Holland. I knew the writing gang, the intriguing gang, the gang with fits and convulsions.[4] They say there are some very civilized people in that town; I'd like to think so.

4. The Jansenists, a sect of strict Catholics, became notorious for spiritual ecstasies. Their public displays reached a height during the 1720s, and Voltaire described them in Le Siècle de Louis XIV (chap. 37), as well as in the article "Convulsions" in the Philosophical Dictionary.

—I myself have no desire to visit France, said Candide; you no doubt realize that when one has spent a month in Eldorado, there is nothing else on earth one wants to see, except Miss Cunégonde. I am going to wait for her at Venice; we will cross France simply to get to Italy; wouldn't you like to come with me?

—Gladly, said Martin; they say Venice is good only for the Venetian nobles, but that on the other hand they treat foreigners very well when they have plenty of money. I don't have any; you do, so I'll follow you anywhere.

—By the way, said Candide, do you believe the earth was originally all ocean, as they assure us in that big book belonging to the ship's captain?[5]

—I don't believe that stuff, said Martin, nor any of the dreams which people have been peddling for some time now.

—But why, then, was this world formed at all? asked Candide.

—To drive us mad, answered Martin.

—Aren't you astonished, Candide went on, at the love which those two girls showed for the monkeys in the land of the Biglugs that I told you about?

—Not at all, said Martin, I see nothing strange in these sentiments; I have seen so many extraordinary things that nothing seems extraordinary any more.

—Do you believe, asked Candide, that men have always massacred one another as they do today? That they have always been liars, traitors, ingrates, thieves, weaklings, sneaks, cowards, backbiters, gluttons, drunkards, misers, climbers, killers, calumniators, sensualists, fanatics, hypocrites, and fools?

—Do you believe, said Martin, that hawks have always eaten pigeons when they could get them?

—Of course, said Candide.

—Well, said Martin, if hawks have always had the same character, why do you suppose that men have changed?

—Oh, said Candide, there's a great deal of difference, because freedom of the will . . .

As they were disputing in this manner, they reached Bordeaux.

CHAPTER 22

What Happened in France to Candide and Martin

Candide paused in Bordeaux only long enough to sell a couple of Dorado pebbles and to fit himself out with a fine two-seater carriage, for he could no longer do without his philosopher Martin; only he was very unhappy to part with his sheep, which he left to the academy of science in Bordeaux. They proposed, as the theme of that year's prize contest, the discovery of why the wool of the sheep was red; and the prize was awarded to a northern scholar[6] who demonstrated by A plus B minus C divided by Z that the sheep ought to be red and die of sheep rot.

But all the travelers with whom Candide talked in the roadside inns told him:—We are going to Paris.

This general consensus finally inspired in him too a desire to see the capital; it was not much out of his road to Venice.

5. The Bible: Genesis 1.   6. Maupertuis Le Lapon, philosopher and mathematician, whom Voltaire had accused of trying to adduce mathematical proofs of the existence of God.

He entered through the Faubourg Saint-Marceau,[7] and thought he was in the meanest village of Westphalia.

Scarcely was Candide in his hotel, when he came down with a mild illness caused by exhaustion. As he was wearing an enormous diamond ring, and people had noticed among his luggage a tremendously heavy safe, he soon found at his bedside two doctors whom he had not called, several intimate friends who never left him alone, and two pious ladies who helped to warm his broth. Martin said:—I remember that I too was ill on my first trip to Paris; I was very poor; and as I had neither friends, pious ladies, nor doctors, I got well.

However, as a result of medicines and bleedings, Candide's illness became serious. A resident of the neighborhood came to ask him politely to fill out a ticket, to be delivered to the porter of the other world.[8] Candide wanted nothing to do with it. The pious ladies assured him it was a new fashion; Candide replied that he wasn't a man of fashion. Martin wanted to throw the resident out the window. The cleric swore that without the ticket they wouldn't bury Candide. Martin swore that he would bury the cleric if he continued to be a nuisance. The quarrel grew heated; Martin took him by the shoulders and threw him bodily out the door; all of which caused a great scandal, from which developed a legal case.

Candide got better; and during his convalescence he had very good company in to dine. They played cards for money; and Candide was quite surprised that none of the aces were ever dealt to him, and Martin was not surprised at all.

Among those who did the honors of the town for Candide there was a little abbé from Perigord, one of those busy fellows, always bright, always useful, assured, obsequious, and obliging, who waylay passing strangers, tell them the scandal of the town, and offer them pleasures at any price they want to pay. This fellow first took Candide and Martin to the theatre. A new tragedy was being played. Candide found himself seated next to a group of wits. That did not keep him from shedding a few tears in the course of some perfectly played scenes. One of the commentators beside him remarked during the intermission:—You are quite mistaken to weep, this actress is very bad indeed; the actor who plays with her is even worse; and the play is even worse than the actors in it. The author knows not a word of Arabic, though the action takes place in Arabia; and besides, he is a man who doesn't believe in innate ideas. Tomorrow I will show you twenty pamphlets written against him.

—Tell me, sir, said Candide to the abbé, how many plays are there for performance in France?

—Five or six thousand, replied the other.

—That's a lot, said Candide; how many of them are any good?

—Fifteen or sixteen, was the answer.

—That's a lot, said Martin.

---

7. A district on the left bank, notably grubby in the eighteenth century. "As I entered [Paris] through the Faubourg Saint-Marceau, I saw nothing but dirty stinking little streets, ugly black houses, a general air of squalor and poverty, beggars, carters, menders of clothes, sellers of herb-drinks and old hats." Jean-Jacques Rousseau, *Confessions*, Book IV.   8. In the middle of the eighteenth century, it became customary to require persons who were grievously ill to sign *billets de confession*, without which they could not be given absolution, admitted to the last sacraments, or buried in consecrated ground.

Candide was very pleased with an actress who took the part of Queen Elizabeth in a rather dull tragedy[9] that still gets played from time to time.

—I like this actress very much, he said to Martin, she bears a slight resemblance to Miss Cunégonde; I should like to meet her.

The abbé from Perigord offered to introduce him. Candide, raised in Germany, asked what was the protocol, how one behaved in France with queens of England.

—You must distinguish, said the abbé; in the provinces, you take them to an inn; at Paris they are respected while still attractive, and thrown on the dunghill when they are dead.[1]

—Queens on the dunghill! said Candide.

—Yes indeed, said Martin, the abbé is right; I was in Paris when Miss Monime herself[2] passed, as they say, from this life to the other; she was refused what these folk call 'the honors of burial,' that is, the right to rot with all the beggars of the district in a dirty cemetery; she was buried all alone by her troupe at the corner of the Rue de Bourgogne; this must have been very disagreeable to her, for she had a noble character.

—That was extremely rude, said Candide.

—What do you expect? said Martin; that is how these folk are. Imagine all the contradictions, all the incompatibilities you can, and you will see them in the government, the courts, the churches, and the plays of this crazy nation.

—Is it true that they are always laughing in Paris? asked Candide.

—Yes, said the abbé, but with a kind of rage too; when people complain of things, they do so amid explosions of laughter; they even laugh as they perform the most detestable actions.

—Who was that fat swine, said Candide, who spoke so nastily about the play over which I was weeping, and the actors who gave me so much pleasure?

—He is a living illness, answered the abbé, who makes a business of slandering all the plays and books; he hates the successful ones, as eunuchs hate successful lovers; he's one of those literary snakes who live on filth and venom; he's a folliculator . . .

—What's this word *folliculator?* asked Candide.

—It's a folio filler, said the abbé, a Fréron.[3]

It was after this fashion that Candide, Martin, and the abbé from Perigord chatted on the stairway as they watched the crowd leaving the theatre.

—Although I'm in a great hurry to see Miss Cunégonde again, said Candide, I would very much like to dine with Miss Clairon,[4] for she seemed to me admirable.

The abbé was not the man to approach Miss Clairon, who saw only good company.

---

9. *Le Comte d'Essex* by Thomas Corneille.   1. Voltaire engaged in a long and vigorous campaign against the rule that actors and actresses could not be buried in consecrated ground. The superstition probably arose from a feeling that by assuming false identities they drained their own souls.   2. Adrienne Lecouvreur (1690–1730), so called because she made her debut as Monime in Racine's *Mithridate*. Voltaire had assisted at her secret midnight funeral and wrote an indignant poem about it.   3. A successful and popular journalist, who had attacked several of Voltaire's plays, including *Tancrède*.   4. Actually Claire Leris (1723–1803). She had played the lead role in *Tancrède* and was for many years a leading figure on the Paris stage.

—She has an engagement tonight, he said; but I shall have the honor of introducing you to a lady of quality, and there you will get to know Paris as if you had lived here for years.

Candide, who was curious by nature, allowed himself to be brought to the lady's house, in the depths of the Faubourg St.-Honoré; they were playing faro;[5] twelve melancholy punters held in their hands a little sheaf of cards, blank summaries of their bad luck. Silence reigned supreme, the punters were pallid, the banker uneasy; and the lady of the house, seated beside the pitiless banker, watched with the eyes of a lynx for the various illegal redoublings and bets at long odds which the players tried to signal by folding the corners of their cards; she had them unfolded with a determination which was severe but polite, and concealed her anger lest she lose her customers. The lady caused herself to be known as the Marquise of Parolignac.[6] Her daughter, fifteen years old, sat among the punters and tipped off her mother with a wink to the sharp practices of these unhappy players when they tried to recoup their losses. The abbé from Perigord, Candide, and Martin came in; nobody arose or greeted them or looked at them; all were lost in the study of their cards.

—My Lady the Baroness of Thunder-Ten-Tronckh was more civil, thought Candide.

However, the abbé whispered in the ear of the marquise, who, half rising, honored Candide with a gracious smile and Martin with a truly noble nod; she gave a seat and dealt a hand of cards to Candide, who lost fifty thousand francs in two turns; after which they had a very merry supper. Everyone was amazed that Candide was not upset over his losses; the lackeys, talking together in their usual lackey language, said:—He must be some English milord.

The supper was like most Parisian suppers: first silence, then an indistinguishable rush of words; then jokes, mostly insipid, false news, bad logic, a little politics, a great deal of malice. They even talked of new books.

—Have you seen the new novel by Dr. Gauchat, the theologian?[7] asked the abbé from Perigord.

—Oh yes, answered one of the guests; but I couldn't finish it. We have a horde of impudent scribblers nowadays, but all of them put together don't match the impudence of this Gauchat, this doctor of theology. I have been so struck by the enormous number of detestable books which are swamping us that I have taken up punting at faro.

—And the Collected Essays of Archdeacon T————[8] asked the abbé, what do you think of them?

—Ah, said Madame de Parolignac, what a frightful bore he is! He takes such pains to tell you what everyone knows; he discourses so learnedly on matters which aren't worth a casual remark! He plunders, and not even wittily, the wit of other people! He spoils what he plunders, he's disgusting! But

5. A game of cards, about which it is necessary to know only that a number of punters play against a banker or dealer. The pack is dealt out two cards at a time, and each player may bet on any card as much as he pleases. The sharp practices of the punters consist essentially of tricks for increasing their winnings without corresponding risks. 6. A *paroli* is an illegal redoubling of one's bet; her name therefore implies a title grounded in cardsharping. 7. He had written against Voltaire, and Voltaire suspected him (wrongly) of having written the novel *L'Oracle des nouveaux philosophes*. 8. His name was Trublet, and he had said, among other disagreeable things, that Voltaire's epic poem, the *Henriade*, made him yawn and that Voltaire's genius was "the perfection of mediocrity."

he'll never disgust me again; a couple of pages of the archdeacon have been enough for me.

There was at table a man of learning and taste, who supported the marquise on this point. They talked next of tragedies; the lady asked why there were tragedies which played well enough but which were wholly unreadable. The man of taste explained very clearly how a play could have a certain interest and yet little merit otherwise; he showed succinctly that it was not enough to conduct a couple of intrigues, such as one can find in any novel, and which never fail to excite the spectator's interest; but that one must be new without being grotesque, frequently touch the sublime but never depart from the natural; that one must know the human heart and give it words; that one must be a great poet without allowing any character in the play to sound like a poet; and that one must know the language perfectly, speak it purely, and maintain a continual harmony without ever sacrificing sense to mere sound.

—Whoever, he added, does not observe all these rules may write one or two tragedies which succeed in the theatre, but he will never be ranked among the good writers; there are very few good tragedies; some are idylls in well-written, well-rhymed dialogue, others are political arguments which put the audience to sleep, or revolting pompousities; still others are the fantasies of enthusiasts, barbarous in style, incoherent in logic, full of long speeches to the gods because the author does not know how to address men, full of false maxims and emphatic commonplaces.

Candide listened attentively to this speech and conceived a high opinion of the speaker; and as the marquise had placed him by her side, he turned to ask her who was this man who spoke so well.

—He is a scholar, said the lady, who never plays cards and whom the abbé sometimes brings to my house for supper; he knows all about tragedies and books, and has himself written a tragedy that was hissed from the stage and a book, the only copy of which ever seen outside his publisher's office was dedicated to me.

—What a great man, said Candide, he's Pangloss all over.

Then, turning to him, he said:—Sir, you doubtless think everything is for the best in the physical as well as the moral universe, and that nothing could be otherwise than as it is?

—Not at all, sir, replied the scholar, I believe nothing of the sort. I find that everything goes wrong in our world; that nobody knows his place in society or his duty, what he's doing or what he ought to be doing, and that outside of mealtimes, which are cheerful and congenial enough, all the rest of the day is spent in useless quarrels, as of Jansenists against Molinists,[9] parliament-men against churchmen, literary men against literary men, courtiers against courtiers, financiers against the plebs, wives against husbands, relatives against relatives—it's one unending warfare.

Candide answered:—I have seen worse; but a wise man, who has since had the misfortune to be hanged, taught me that everything was marvelously well arranged. Troubles are just the shadows in a beautiful picture.

9. The Jansenists (from Corneille Jansen, 1585–1638) were a relatively strict party of religious reform; the Molinists (from Luis Molina) were the party of the Jesuits. Their central issue of controversy was the relative importance of divine grace and human will to the salvation of man.

—Your hanged philosopher was joking, said Martin; the shadows are horrible ugly blots.

—It is human beings who make the blots, said Candide, and they can't do otherwise.

—Then it isn't their fault, said Martin.

Most of the faro players, who understood this sort of talk not at all, kept on drinking; Martin disputed with the scholar, and Candide told part of his story to the lady of the house.

After supper, the marquise brought Candide into her room and sat him down on a divan.

—Well, she said to him, are you still madly in love with Miss Cunégonde of Thunder-Ten-Tronckh?

—Yes, ma'am, replied Candide. The marquise turned upon him a tender smile.

—You answer like a young man of Westphalia, said she; a Frenchman would have told me: 'It is true that I have been in love with Miss Cunégonde; but since seeing you, madame, I fear that I love her no longer.'

—Alas, ma'am, said Candide, I will answer any way you want.

—Your passion for her, said the marquise, began when you picked up her handkerchief; I prefer that you should pick up my garter.

—Gladly, said Candide, and picked it up.

—But I also want you to put it back on, said the lady; and Candide put it on again.

—Look you now, said the lady, you are a foreigner; my Paris lovers I sometimes cause to languish for two weeks or so, but to you I surrender the very first night, because we must render the honors of the country to a young man from Westphalia.

The beauty, who had seen two enormous diamonds on the two hands of her young friend, praised them so sincerely that from the fingers of Candide they passed over to the fingers of the marquise.

As he returned home with his Perigord abbé, Candide felt some remorse at having been unfaithful to Miss Cunégonde; the abbé sympathized with his grief; he had only a small share in the fifty thousand francs which Candide lost at cards, and in the proceeds of the two diamonds which had been half-given, half-extorted. His scheme was to profit, as much as he could, from the advantage of knowing Candide. He spoke at length of Cunégonde, and Candide told him that he would beg forgiveness for his beloved for his infidelity when he met her at Venice.

The Perigordian overflowed with politeness and unction, taking a tender interest in everything Candide said, everything he did, and everything he wanted to do.

—Well, sir, said he, so you have an assignation at Venice?

—Yes indeed, sir, I do, said Candide; it is absolutely imperative that I go there to find Miss Cunégonde.

And then, carried away by the pleasure of talking about his love, he recounted, as he often did, a part of his adventures with that illustrious lady of Westphalia.

—I suppose, said the abbé, that Miss Cunégonde has a fine wit and writes charming letters.

—I never received a single letter from her, said Candide; for, as you can imagine, after being driven out of the castle for love of her, I couldn't write; shortly I learned that she was dead; then I rediscovered her; then I lost her again, and I have now sent, to a place more than twenty-five hundred leagues from here, a special agent whose return I am expecting.

The abbé listened carefully, and looked a bit dreamy. He soon took his leave of the two strangers, after embracing them tenderly. Next day Candide, when he woke up, received a letter, to the following effect:

—Dear sir, my very dear lover, I have been lying sick in this town for a week, I have just learned that you are here. I would fly to your arms if I could move. I heard that you had passed through Bordeaux; that was where I left the faithful Cacambo and the old woman, who are soon to follow me here. The governor of Buenos Aires took everything, but left me your heart. Come; your presence will either return me to life or cause me to die of joy.

This charming letter, coming so unexpectedly, filled Candide with inexpressible delight, while the illness of his dear Cunégonde covered him with grief. Torn between these two feelings, he took gold and diamonds, and had himself brought, with Martin, to the hotel where Miss Cunégonde was lodging. Trembling with emotion, he enters the room; his heart thumps, his voice breaks. He tries to open the curtains of the bed, he asks to have some lights.

—Absolutely forbidden, says the serving girl; light will be the death of her. And abruptly she pulls shut the curtain.

—My dear Cunégonde, says Candide in tears, how are you feeling? If you can't see me, won't you at least speak to me?

—She can't talk, says the servant.

But then she draws forth from the bed a plump hand, over which Candide weeps a long time, and which he fills with diamonds, meanwhile leaving a bag of gold on the chair.

Amid his transports, there arrives a bailiff followed by the abbé from Perigord and a strong-arm squad.

—These here are the suspicious foreigners? says the officer; and he has them seized and orders his bullies to drag them off to jail.

—They don't treat visitors like this in Eldorado, says Candide.

—I am more a Manichee than ever, says Martin.

—But, please sir, where are you taking us? says Candide.

—To the lowest hole in the dungeons, says the bailiff.

Martin, having regained his self-possession, decided that the lady who pretended to be Cunégonde was a cheat, the abbé from Perigord was another cheat who had imposed on Candide's innocence, and the bailiff still another cheat, of whom it would be easy to get rid.

Rather than submit to the forms of justice, Candide, enlightened by Martin's advice and eager for his own part to see the real Cunégonde again, offered the bailiff three little diamonds worth about three thousand pistoles apiece.

—Ah, my dear sir! cried the man with the ivory staff, even if you have committed every crime imaginable, you are the most honest man in the world. Three diamonds! each one worth three thousand pistoles! My dear sir! I would gladly die for you, rather than take you to jail. All foreigners get arrested here; but let me manage it; I have a brother at Dieppe in Normandy; I'll take you to him; and if you have a bit of a diamond to give him, he'll take care of you, just like me.

—And why do they arrest all foreigners? asked Candide.

The abbé from Perigord spoke up and said:—It's because a beggar from Atrebatum[1] listened to some stupidities; that made him commit a parricide, not like the one of May, 1610, but like the one of December, 1594, much on the order of several other crimes committed in other years and other months by other beggars who had listened to stupidities.

The bailiff then explained what it was all about.[2]

—Foh! what beasts! cried Candide. What! monstrous behavior of this sort from a people who sing and dance? As soon as I can, let me get out of this country, where the monkeys provoke the tigers. In my own country I've lived with bears; only in Eldorado are there proper men. In the name of God, sir bailiff, get me to Venice where I can wait for Miss Cunégonde.

—I can only get you to Lower Normandy, said the guardsman.

He had the irons removed at once, said there had been a mistake, dismissed his gang, and took Candide and Martin to Dieppe, where he left them with his brother. There was a little Dutch ship at anchor. The Norman, changed by three more diamonds into the most helpful of men, put Candide and his people aboard the vessel, which was bound for Portsmouth in England. It wasn't on the way to Venice, but Candide felt like a man just let out of hell; and he hoped to get back on the road to Venice at the first possible occasion.

CHAPTER 23

Candide and Martin Pass the Shores of England;
What They See There

—Ah, Pangloss! Pangloss! Ah, Martin! Martin! Ah, my darling Cunégonde! What is this world of ours? sighed Candide on the Dutch vessel.

—Something crazy, something abominable, Martin replied.

—You have been in England; are people as crazy there as in France?

—It's a different sort of crazy, said Martin. You know that these two nations have been at war over a few acres of snow near Canada, and that they are spending on this fine struggle more than Canada itself is worth.[3] As for telling you if there are more people in one country or the other who need a strait jacket, that is a judgment too fine for my understanding; I know only that the people we are going to visit are eaten up with melancholy.

As they chatted thus, the vessel touched at Portsmouth. A multitude of people covered the shore, watching closely a rather bulky man who was kneeling, his eyes blindfolded, on the deck of a man-of-war. Four soldiers, stationed directly in front of this man, fired three bullets apiece into his brain, as peaceably as you would want; and the whole assemblage went home, in great satisfaction.[4]

---

1. The Latin name for the district of Artois, from which came Robert-François Damiens, who tried to stab Louis XV in 1757. The assassination failed, like that of Châtel, who tried to kill Henri IV in 1594, but unlike that of Ravaillac, who succeeded in killing him in 1610.   2. The point, in fact, is not too clear since arresting foreigners is an indirect way at best to guard against homegrown fanatics, and the position of the abbé from Perigord in the whole transaction remains confused. Has he called in the officer just to get rid of Candide? If so, why is he sardonic about the very suspicions he is trying to foster? Candide's reaction is to the notion that Frenchmen should be capable of political assassination at all; it seems excessive.   3. The wars of the French and English over Canada dragged intermittently through the eighteenth century till the peace of Paris sealed England's conquest (1763). Voltaire thought the French should concentrate on developing Louisiana, where the Jesuit influence was less marked.   4. Candide has witnessed the execution of Admiral John Byng, defeated off Minorca by the French fleet under Galisonnière and executed by firing squad on March 14, 1757. Voltaire had intervened to avert the execution.

—What's all this about? asked Candide. What devil is everywhere at work?
He asked who was that big man who had just been killed with so much ceremony.

—It was an admiral, they told him.

—And why kill this admiral?

—The reason, they told him, is that he didn't kill enough people; he gave battle to a French admiral, and it was found that he didn't get close enough to him.

—But, said Candide, the French admiral was just as far from the English admiral as the English admiral was from the French admiral.

—That's perfectly true, came the answer; but in this country it is useful from time to time to kill one admiral in order to encourage the others.

Candide was so stunned and shocked at what he saw and heard, that he would not even set foot ashore; he arranged with the Dutch merchant (without even caring if he was robbed, as at Surinam) to be taken forthwith to Venice.

The merchant was ready in two days; they coasted along France, they passed within sight of Lisbon, and Candide quivered. They entered the straits, crossed the Mediterranean, and finally landed at Venice.

—God be praised, said Candide, embracing Martin; here I shall recover the lovely Cunégonde. I trust Cacambo as I would myself. All is well, all goes well, all goes as well as possible.

CHAPTER 24
About Paquette and Brother Giroflée

As soon as he was in Venice, he had a search made for Cacambo in all the inns, all the cafés, all the stews—and found no trace of him. Every day he sent to investigate the vessels and coastal traders; no news of Cacambo.

—How's this? said he to Martin. I have had time to go from Surinam to Bordeaux, from Bordeaux to Paris, from Paris to Dieppe, from Dieppe to Portsmouth, to skirt Portugal and Spain, cross the Mediterranean, and spend several months at Venice—and the lovely Cunégonde has not come yet! In her place, I have met only that impersonator and that abbé from Perigord. Cunégonde is dead, without a doubt; and nothing remains for me too but death. Oh, it would have been better to stay in the earthly paradise of Eldorado than to return to this accursed Europe. How right you are, my dear Martin; all is but illusion and disaster.

He fell into a black melancholy, and refused to attend the fashionable operas or take part in the other diversions of the carnival season; not a single lady tempted him in the slightest. Martin told him:—You're a real simpleton if you think a half-breed valet with five or six millions in his pockets will go to the end of the world to get your mistress and bring her to Venice for you. If he finds her, he'll take her for himself; if he doesn't, he'll take another. I advise you to forget about your servant Cacambo and your mistress Cunégonde.

Martin was not very comforting. Candide's melancholy increased, and Martin never wearied of showing him that there is little virtue and little happiness on this earth, except perhaps in Eldorado, where nobody can go.

While they were discussing this important matter and still waiting for

Cunégonde, Candide noticed in St. Mark's Square a young Theatine[5] monk who had given his arm to a girl. The Theatine seemed fresh, plump, and flourishing; his eyes were bright, his manner cocky, his glance brilliant, his step proud. The girl was very pretty, and singing aloud; she glanced lovingly at her Theatine, and from time to time pinched his plump cheeks.

—At least you must admit, said Candide to Martin, that these people are happy. Until now I have not found in the whole inhabited earth, except Eldorado, anything but miserable people. But this girl and this monk, I'd be willing to bet, are very happy creatures.

—I'll bet they aren't, said Martin.

—We have only to ask them to dinner, said Candide, and we'll find out if I'm wrong.

Promptly he approached them, made his compliments, and invited them to his inn for a meal of macaroni, Lombardy partridges, and caviar, washed down with wine from Montepulciano, Cyprus, and Samos, and some Lacrima Christi. The girl blushed but the Theatine accepted gladly, and the girl followed him, watching Candide with an expression of surprise and confusion, darkened by several tears. Scarcely had she entered the room when she said to Candide:—What, can it be that Master Candide no longer knows Paquette?

At these words Candide, who had not yet looked carefully at her because he was preoccupied with Cunégonde, said to her:—Ah, my poor child! so you are the one who put Doctor Pangloss in the fine fix where I last saw him.

—Alas, sir, I was the one, said Paquette; I see you know all about it. I heard of the horrible misfortunes which befell the whole household of My Lady the Baroness and the lovely Cunégonde. I swear to you that my own fate has been just as unhappy. I was perfectly innocent when you knew me. A Franciscan, who was my confessor, easily seduced me. The consequences were frightful; shortly after My Lord the Baron had driven you out with great kicks on the backside, I too was forced to leave the castle. If a famous doctor had not taken pity on me, I would have died. Out of gratitude, I became for some time the mistress of this doctor. His wife, who was jealous to the point of frenzy, beat me mercilessly every day; she was a gorgon. The doctor was the ugliest of men, and I the most miserable creature on earth, being continually beaten for a man I did not love. You will understand, sir, how dangerous it is for a nagging woman to be married to a doctor. This man, enraged by his wife's ways, one day gave her as a cold cure a medicine so potent that in two hours' time she died amid horrible convulsions. Her relatives brought suit against the bereaved husband; he fled the country, and I was put in prison. My innocence would never have saved me if I had not been rather pretty. The judge set me free on condition that he should become the doctor's successor. I was shortly replaced in this post by another girl, dismissed without any payment, and obliged to continue this abominable trade which you men find so pleasant and which for us is nothing but a bottomless pit of misery. I went to ply the trade in Venice. Ah, my dear sir, if you could imagine what it is like to have to caress indiscriminately an old merchant, a lawyer, a monk, a gondolier, an abbé; to be subjected to every sort of insult and outrage; to be reduced, time and again, to borrowing a skirt in order to go

5. A Catholic order founded in 1524 by Cardinal Cajetan and G. P. Caraffa, later Pope Paul IV.

have it lifted by some disgusting man; to be robbed by this fellow of what one has gained from that; to be shaken down by the police, and to have before one only the prospect of a hideous old age, a hospital, and a dunghill, you will conclude that I am one of the most miserable creatures in the world.

Thus Paquette poured forth her heart to the good Candide in a hotel room, while Martin sat listening nearby. At last he said to Candide:—You see, I've already won half my bet.

Brother Giroflée[6] had remained in the dining room, and was having a drink before dinner.

—But how's this? said Candide to Paquette. You looked so happy, so joyous, when I met you; you were singing, you caressed the Theatine with such a natural air of delight; you seemed to me just as happy as you now say you are miserable.

—Ah, sir, replied Paquette, that's another one of the miseries of this business; yesterday I was robbed and beaten by an officer, and today I have to seem in good humor in order to please a monk.

Candide wanted no more; he conceded that Martin was right. They sat down to table with Paquette and the Theatine; the meal was amusing enough, and when it was over, the company spoke out among themselves with some frankness.

—Father, said Candide to the monk, you seem to me a man whom all the world might envy; the flower of health glows in your cheek, your features radiate pleasure; you have a pretty girl for your diversion, and you seem very happy with your life as a Theatine.

—Upon my word, sir, said Brother Giroflée, I wish that all the Theatines were at the bottom of the sea. A hundred times I have been tempted to set fire to my convent, and go turn Turk. My parents forced me, when I was fifteen years old, to put on this detestable robe, so they could leave more money to a cursed older brother of mine, may God confound him! Jealousy, faction, and fury spring up, by natural law, within the walls of convents. It is true, I have preached a few bad sermons which earned me a little money, half of which the prior stole from me; the remainder serves to keep me in girls. But when I have to go back to the monastery at night, I'm ready to smash my head against the walls of my cell; and all my fellow monks are in the same fix.

Martin turned to Candide and said with his customary coolness:

—Well, haven't I won the whole bet?

Candide gave two thousand piastres to Paquette and a thousand to Brother Giroflée.

—I assure you, said he, that with that they will be happy.

—I don't believe so, said Martin; your piastres may make them even more unhappy than they were before.

—That may be, said Candide; but one thing comforts me, I note that people often turn up whom one never expected to see again; it may well be that, having rediscovered my red sheep and Paquette, I will also rediscover Cunégonde.

—I hope, said Martin, that she will some day make you happy; but I very much doubt it.

---

6. His name means "carnation" and Paquette means "daisy."

—You're a hard man, said Candide.

—I've lived, said Martin.

—But look at these gondoliers, said Candide; aren't they always singing?

—You don't see them at home, said Martin, with their wives and squalling children. The doge has his troubles, the gondoliers theirs. It's true that on the whole one is better off as a gondolier than as a doge; but the difference is so slight, I don't suppose it's worth the trouble of discussing.

—There's a lot of talk here, said Candide, of this Senator Pococurante,[7] who has a fine palace on the Brenta and is hospitable to foreigners. They say he is a man who has never known a moment's grief.

—I'd like to see such a rare specimen, said Martin.

Candide promptly sent to Lord Pococurante, asking permission to call on him tomorrow.

CHAPTER 25

Visit to Lord Pococurante, Venetian Nobleman

Candide and Martin took a gondola on the Brenta, and soon reached the palace of the noble Pococurante. The gardens were large and filled with beautiful marble statues; the palace was handsomely designed. The master of the house, sixty years old and very rich, received his two inquisitive visitors perfectly politely, but with very little warmth; Candide was disconcerted and Martin not at all displeased.

First two pretty and neatly dressed girls served chocolate, which they whipped to a froth. Candide could not forbear praising their beauty, their grace, their skill.

—They are pretty good creatures, said Pococurante; I sometimes have them into my bed, for I'm tired of the ladies of the town, with their stupid tricks, quarrels, jealousies, fits of ill humor and petty pride, and all the sonnets one has to make or order for them; but, after all, these two girls are starting to bore me too.

After lunch, Candide strolled through a long gallery, and was amazed at the beauty of the pictures. He asked who was the painter of the two finest.

—They are by Raphael, said the senator; I bought them for a lot of money, out of vanity, some years ago; people say they're the finest in Italy, but they don't please me at all; the colors have all turned brown, the figures aren't well modeled and don't stand out enough, the draperies bear no resemblance to real cloth. In a word, whatever people may say, I don't find in them a real imitation of nature. I like a picture only when I can see in it a touch of nature itself, and there are none of this sort. I have many paintings, but I no longer look at them.

As they waited for dinner, Pococurante ordered a concerto performed. Candide found the music delightful.

—That noise? said Pococurante. It may amuse you for half an hour, but if it goes on any longer, it tires everybody though no one dares to admit it. Music today is only the art of performing difficult pieces, and what is merely difficult cannot please for long. Perhaps I should prefer the opera, if they had not found ways to make it revolting and monstrous. Anyone who likes

---

7. His name means "small care."

bad tragedies set to music is welcome to them; in these performances the scenes serve only to introduce, inappropriately, two or three ridiculous songs designed to show off the actress's sound box. Anyone who wants to, or who can, is welcome to swoon with pleasure at the sight of a castrate wriggling through the role of Caesar or Cato, and strutting awkwardly about the stage. For my part, I have long since given up these paltry trifles which are called the glory of modern Italy, and for which monarchs pay such ruinous prices.

Candide argued a bit, but timidly; Martin was entirely of a mind with the senator.

They sat down to dinner, and after an excellent meal adjourned to the library. Candide, seeing a copy of Homer in a splendid binding, complimented the noble lord on his good taste.

—That is an author, said he, who was the special delight of great Pangloss, the best philosopher in all Germany.

—He's no special delight of mine, said Pococurante coldly. I was once made to believe that I took pleasure in reading him; but that constant recital of fights which are all alike, those gods who are always interfering but never decisively, that Helen who is the cause of the war and then scarcely takes any part in the story, that Troy which is always under siege and never taken— all that bores me to tears. I have sometimes asked scholars if reading it bored them as much as it bores me; everyone who answered frankly told me the book dropped from his hands like lead, but that they had to have it in their libraries as a monument of antiquity, like those old rusty coins which can't be used in real trade.

Your Excellence doesn't hold the same opinion of Virgil? said Candide.

—I concede, said Pococurante, that the second, fourth, and sixth books of his *Aeneid* are fine; but as for his pious Aeneas, and strong Cloanthes, and faithful Achates, and little Ascanius, and that imbecile King Latinus, and middle-class Amata, and insipid Lavinia, I don't suppose there was ever anything so cold and unpleasant. I prefer Tasso and those sleepwalkers' stories of Ariosto.

—Dare I ask, sir, said Candide, if you don't get great enjoyment from reading Horace?

—There are some maxims there, said Pococurante, from which a man of the world can profit, and which, because they are formed into vigorous couplets, are more easily remembered; but I care very little for his trip to Brindisi, his description of a bad dinner, or his account of a quibblers' squabble between some fellow Pupilus, whose words he says *were full of pus,* and another whose words *were full of vinegar.*[8] I feel nothing but extreme disgust at his verses against old women and witches; and I can't see what's so great in his telling his friend Maecenas that if he is raised by him to the ranks of lyric poets, he will strike the stars with his lofty forehead. Fools admire everything in a well-known author. I read only for my own pleasure; I like only what is in my style.

Candide, who had been trained never to judge for himself, was much astonished by what he heard; and Martin found Pococurante's way of thinking quite rational.

8. *Satires* I.vii; Pococurante, with gentlemanly negligence, has corrupted Rupilius to Pupilus. Horace's poems against witches are *Epodes* V, VIII, XII; the one about striking the stars with his lofty forehead is *Odes* I.i.

—Oh, here is a copy of Cicero, said Candide. Now this great man I suppose you're never tired of reading.

—I never read him at all, replied the Venetian. What do I care whether he pleaded for Rabirius or Cluentius? As a judge, I have my hands full of lawsuits. I might like his philosophical works better, but when I saw that he had doubts about everything, I concluded that I knew as much as he did, and that I needed no help to be ignorant.

—Ah, here are eighty volumes of collected papers from a scientific academy, cried Martin; maybe there is something good in them.

—There would be indeed, said Pococurante, if one of these silly authors had merely discovered a new way of making pins; but in all those volumes there is nothing but empty systems, not a single useful discovery.

—What a lot of stage plays I see over there, said Candide, some in Italian, some in Spanish and French.

—Yes, said the senator, three thousand of them, and not three dozen good ones. As for those collections of sermons, which all together are not worth a page of Seneca, and all these heavy volumes of theology, you may be sure I never open them, nor does anybody else.

Martin noticed some shelves full of English books.

—I suppose, said he, that a republican must delight in most of these books written in the land of liberty.

—Yes, replied Pococurante, it's a fine thing to write as you think; it is mankind's privilege. In all our Italy, people write only what they do not think; men who inhabit the land of the Caesars and Antonines dare not have an idea without the permission of a Dominican. I would rejoice in the freedom that breathes through English genius, if partisan passions did not corrupt all that is good in that precious freedom.

Candide, noting a Milton, asked if he did not consider this author a great man.

—Who? said Pococurante. That barbarian who made a long commentary on the first chapter of Genesis in ten books of crabbed verse?[9] That clumsy imitator of the Greeks, who disfigures creation itself, and while Moses represents the eternal being as creating the world with a word, has the messiah take a big compass out of a heavenly cupboard in order to design his work? You expect me to admire the man who spoiled Tasso's hell and devil? who disguises Lucifer now as a toad, now as a pigmy? who makes him rehash the same arguments a hundred times over? who makes him argue theology? and who, taking seriously Ariosto's comic story of the invention of firearms, has the devils shooting off cannon in heaven? Neither I nor anyone else in Italy has been able to enjoy these gloomy extravagances. The marriage of Sin and Death, and the monster that Sin gives birth to, will nauseate any man whose taste is at all refined; and his long description of a hospital is good only for a gravedigger. This obscure, extravagant, and disgusting poem was despised at its birth; I treat it today as it was treated in its own country by its contemporaries. Anyhow, I say what I think, and care very little whether other people agree with me.

Candide was a little cast down by this speech; he respected Homer, and had a little affection for Milton.

9. The first edition of *Paradise Lost* had ten books, which Milton later expanded to twelve.

—Alas, he said under his breath to Martin, I'm afraid this man will have a supreme contempt for our German poets.

—No harm in that, said Martin.

—Oh what a superior man, said Candide, still speaking softly, what a great genius this Pococurante must be! Nothing can please him.

Having thus looked over all the books, they went down into the garden. Candide praised its many beauties.

—I know nothing in such bad taste, said the master of the house; we have nothing but trifles here; tomorrow I am going to have one set out on a nobler design.

When the two visitors had taken leave of his excellency:—Well now, said Candide to Martin, you must agree that this was the happiest of all men, for he is superior to everything he possesses.

—Don't you see, said Martin, that he is disgusted with everything he possesses? Plato said, a long time ago, that the best stomachs are not those which refuse all food.

—But, said Candide, isn't there pleasure in criticizing everything, in seeing faults where other people think they see beauties?

—That is to say, Martin replied, that there's pleasure in having no pleasure?

—Oh well, said Candide, then I am the only happy man . . . or will be, when I see Miss Cunégonde again.

—It's always a good thing to have hope, said Martin.

But the days and the weeks slipped past; Cacambo did not come back, and Candide was so buried in his grief, that he did not even notice that Paquette and Brother Giroflée had neglected to come and thank him.

CHAPTER 26

About a Supper that Candide and Martin Had with Six Strangers, and Who They Were

One evening when Candide, accompanied by Martin, was about to sit down for dinner with the strangers staying in his hotel, a man with a soot-colored face came up behind him, took him by the arm, and said:—Be ready to leave with us, don't miss out.

He turned and saw Cacambo. Only the sight of Cunégonde could have astonished and pleased him more. He nearly went mad with joy. He embraced his dear friend.

—Cunégonde is here, no doubt? Where is she? Bring me to her, let me die of joy in her presence.

—Cunégonde is not here at all, said Cacambo, she is at Constantinople.

—Good Heavens, at Constantinople! but if she were in China, I must fly there, let's go.

—We will leave after supper, said Cacambo; I can tell you no more; I am a slave, my owner is looking for me, I must go wait on him at table; mum's the word; eat your supper and be prepared.

Candide, torn between joy and grief, delighted to have seen his faithful agent again, astonished to find him a slave, full of the idea of recovering his mistress, his heart in a turmoil, his mind in a whirl, sat down to eat with Martin, who was watching all these events coolly, and with six strangers who had come to pass the carnival season at Venice.

Cacambo, who was pouring wine for one of the strangers, leaned respectfully over his master at the end of the meal, and said to him:—Sire, Your Majesty may leave when he pleases, the vessel is ready.

Having said these words, he exited. The diners looked at one another in silent amazement, when another servant, approaching his master, said to him:—Sire, Your Majesty's litter is at Padua, and the bark awaits you.

The master nodded, and the servant vanished. All the diners looked at one another again, and the general amazement redoubled. A third servant, approaching a third stranger, said to him:—Sire, take my word for it, Your Majesty must stay here no longer; I shall get everything ready.

Then he too disappeared.

Candide and Martin had no doubt, now, that it was a carnival masquerade. A fourth servant spoke to a fourth master:—Your Majesty will leave when he pleases—and went out like the others. A fifth followed suit. But the sixth servant spoke differently to the sixth stranger, who sat next to Candide. He said:—My word, sire, they'll give no more credit to Your Majesty, nor to me either; we could very well spend the night in the lockup, you and I. I've got to look out for myself, so good-bye to you.

When all the servants had left, the six strangers, Candide, and Martin remained under a pall of silence. Finally Candide broke it.

—Gentlemen, said he, here's a funny kind of joke. Why are you all royalty? I assure you that Martin and I aren't.

Cacambo's master spoke up gravely then, and said in Italian:—This is no joke, my name is Achmet the Third.[1] I was grand sultan for several years; then, as I had dethroned my brother, my nephew dethroned me. My viziers had their throats cut; I was allowed to end my days in the old seraglio. My nephew, the Grand Sultan Mahmoud, sometimes lets me travel for my health; and I have come to spend the carnival season at Venice.

A young man who sat next to Achmet spoke after him, and said:—My name is Ivan; I was once emperor of all the Russias.[2] I was dethroned while still in my cradle; my father and mother were locked up, and I was raised in prison; I sometimes have permission to travel, though always under guard, and I have come to spend the carnival season at Venice.

The third said:—I am Charles Edward, king of England;[3] my father yielded me his rights to the kingdom, and I fought to uphold them; but they tore out the hearts of eight hundred of my partisans, and flung them in their faces. I have been in prison; now I am going to Rome, to visit the king, my father, dethroned like me and my grandfather; and I have come to pass the carnival season at Venice.

The fourth king then spoke up, and said:—I am a king of the Poles;[4] the luck of war has deprived me of my hereditary estates; my father suffered the same losses; I submit to Providence like Sultan Achmet, Emperor Ivan, and King Charles Edward, to whom I hope heaven grants long lives; and I have come to pass the carnival season at Venice.

The fifth said:—I too am a king of the Poles;[5] I lost my kingdom twice,

1. Ottoman ruler (1673–1736); he was deposed in 1730.   2. Ivan VI reigned from his birth in 1740 until 1756, then was confined in the Schlusselberg, and executed in 1764.   3. This is the Young Pretender (1720–1788), known to his supporters as Bonnie Prince Charlie. The defeat so theatrically described took place at Culloden, April 16, 1746.   4. Augustus III (1696–1763), Elector of Saxony and King of Poland, dethroned by Frederick the Great in 1756.   5. Stanislas Leczinski (1677–1766), father-in-law of Louis XV, who abdicated the throne of Poland in 1736, was made Duke of Lorraine and in that capacity befriended Voltaire.

but Providence gave me another state, in which I have been able to do more good than all the Sarmatian kings ever managed to do on the banks of the Vistula. I too have submitted to Providence, and I have come to pass the carnival season at Venice.

It remained for the sixth monarch to speak.

—Gentlemen, said he, I am no such great lord as you, but I have in fact been a king like any other. I am Theodore; I was elected king of Corsica.[6] People used to call me *Your Majesty,* and now they barely call me *Sir;* I used to coin currency, and now I don't have a cent; I used to have two secretaries of state, and now I scarcely have a valet; I have sat on a throne, and for a long time in London I was in jail, on the straw; and I may well be treated the same way here, though I have come, like your majesties, to pass the carnival season at Venice.

The five other kings listened to his story with noble compassion. Each one of them gave twenty sequins to King Theodore, so that he might buy a suit and some shirts; Candide gave him a diamond worth two thousand sequins.

—Who in the world, said the five kings, is this private citizen who is in a position to give a hundred times as much as any of us, and who actually gives it?[7]

Just as they were rising from dinner, there arrived at the same establishment four most serene highnesses, who had also lost their kingdoms through the luck of war, and who came to spend the rest of the carnival season at Venice. But Candide never bothered even to look at these newcomers because he was only concerned to go find his dear Cunégonde at Constantinople.

CHAPTER 27

Candide's Trip to Constantinople

Faithful Cacambo had already arranged with the Turkish captain who was returning Sultan Achmet to Constantinople to make room for Candide and Martin on board. Both men boarded ship after prostrating themselves before his miserable highness. On the way, Candide said to Martin:—Six dethroned kings that we had dinner with! and yet among those six there was one on whom I had to bestow charity! Perhaps there are other princes even more unfortunate. I myself have only lost a hundred sheep, and now I am flying to the arms of Cunégonde. My dear Martin, once again Pangloss is proved right, all is for the best.

—I hope so, said Martin.

—But, said Candide, that was a most unlikely experience we had at Ven-

6. Theodore von Neuhof (1690–1756), an authentic Westphalian, an adventurer and a soldier of fortune, who in 1736 was (for about eight months) the elected king of Corsica. He spent time in an Amsterdam as well as a London debtor's prison.   7. A late correction of Voltaire's makes this passage read:
—Who is this man who is in a position to give a hundred times as much as any of us, and who actually gives it? Are you a king too, sir?
—No, gentlemen, and I have no desire to be.
But this reading, though Voltaire's on good authority, produces a conflict with Candide's previous remark:—
Why are you all royalty? I assure you that Martin and I aren't.
Thus, it has seemed better for literary reasons to follow an earlier reading. Voltaire was very conscious of his situation as a man richer than many princes; in 1758 he had money on loan to no fewer than three highnesses, Charles Eugene, Duke of Wurtemburg; Charles Theodore, Elector Palatine; and the Duke of Saxe-Gotha.

ice. Nobody ever saw, or heard tell of, six dethroned kings eating together at an inn.

—It is no more extraordinary, said Martin, than most of the things that have happened to us. Kings are frequently dethroned; and as for the honor we had from dining with them, that's a trifle which doesn't deserve our notice.[8]

Scarcely was Candide on board than he fell on the neck of his former servant, his friend Cacambo.

—Well! said he, what is Cunégonde doing? Is she still a marvel of beauty? Does she still love me? How is her health? No doubt you have bought her a palace at Constantinople.

—My dear master, answered Cacambo, Cunégonde is washing dishes on the shores of the Propontis, in the house of a prince who has very few dishes to wash; she is a slave in the house of a onetime king named Ragotski,[9] to whom the Great Turk allows three crowns a day in his exile; but, what is worse than all this, she has lost all her beauty and become horribly ugly.

—Ah, beautiful or ugly, said Candide, I am an honest man, and my duty is to love her forever. But how can she be reduced to this wretched state with the five or six millions that you had?

—All right, said Cacambo, didn't I have to give two millions to Señor don Fernando d'Ibaraa y Figueroa y Mascarenes y Lampourdos y Souza, governor of Buenos Aires, for his permission to carry off Miss Cunégonde? And didn't a pirate cleverly strip us of the rest? And didn't this pirate carry us off to Cape Matapan, to Melos, Nicaria, Samos, Petra, to the Dardanelles, Marmora, Scutari? Cunégonde and the old woman are working for the prince I told you about, and I am the slave of the dethroned sultan.

—What a lot of fearful calamities linked one to the other, said Candide. But after all, I still have a few diamonds, I shall easily deliver Cunégonde. What a pity that she's become so ugly!

Then, turning toward Martin, he asked:—Who in your opinion is more to be pitied, the Emperor Achmet, the Emperor Ivan, King Charles Edward, or myself?

—I have no idea, said Martin; I would have to enter your hearts in order to tell.

—Ah, said Candide, if Pangloss were here, he would know and he would tell us.

—I can't imagine, said Martin, what scales your Pangloss would use to weigh out the miseries of men and value their griefs. All I will venture is that the earth holds millions of men who deserve our pity a hundred times more than King Charles Edward, Emperor Ivan, or Sultan Achmet.

—You may well be right, said Candide.

In a few days they arrived at the Black Sea canal. Candide began by repurchasing Cacambo at an exorbitant price; then, without losing an instant, he flung himself and his companions into a galley to go search out Cunégonde on the shores of Propontis, however ugly she might be.

There were in the chain gang two convicts who bent clumsily to the oar,

---

8. Another late change adds the following question:—*What does it matter whom you dine with as long as you fare well at table?* I have omitted it, again on literary grounds.　　9. Francis Leopold Rakoczy (1676–1735), who was briefly king of Transylvania in the early eighteenth century. After 1720 he was interned in Turkey.

and on whose bare shoulders the Levantine[1] captain delivered from time to time a few lashes with a bullwhip. Candide naturally noticed them more than the other galley slaves, and out of pity came closer to them. Certain features of their disfigured faces seemed to him to bear a slight resemblance to Pangloss and to that wretched Jesuit, that baron, that brother of Miss Cunégonde. The notion stirred and saddened him. He looked at them more closely.

—To tell you the truth, he said to Cacambo, if I hadn't seen Master Pangloss hanged, and if I hadn't been so miserable as to murder the baron, I should think they were rowing in this very galley.

At the names of 'baron' and 'Pangloss' the two convicts gave a great cry, sat still on their bench, and dropped their oars. The Levantine captain came running, and the bullwhip lashes redoubled.

—Stop, stop, captain, cried Candide. I'll give you as much money as you want.

—What, can it be Candide? cried one of the convicts.

—What, can it be Candide? cried the other.

—Is this a dream? said Candide. Am I awake or asleep? Am I in this galley? Is that My Lord the Baron, whom I killed? Is that Master Pangloss, whom I saw hanged?

—It is indeed, they replied.

—What, is that the great philosopher? said Martin.

—Now, sir, Mr. Levantine Captain, said Candide, how much money do you want for the ransom of My Lord Thunder-Ten-Tronckh, one of the first barons of the empire, and Master Pangloss, the deepest metaphysician in all Germany?

—Dog of a Christian, replied the Levantine captain, since these two dogs of Christian convicts are barons and metaphysicians, which is no doubt a great honor in their country, you will give me fifty thousand sequins for them.

—You shall have them, sir, take me back to Constantinople and you shall be paid on the spot. Or no, take me to Miss Cunégonde.

The Levantine captain, at Candide's first word, had turned his bow toward the town, and he had them rowed there as swiftly as a bird cleaves the air.

A hundred times Candide embraced the baron and Pangloss.

—And how does it happen I didn't kill you, my dear baron? and my dear Pangloss, how can you be alive after being hanged? and why are you both rowing in the galleys of Turkey?

—Is it really true that my dear sister is in this country? asked the baron.

—Yes, answered Cacambo.

—And do I really see again my dear Candide? cried Pangloss.

Candide introduced Martin and Cacambo. They all embraced; they all talked at once. The galley flew, already they were back in port. A Jew was called, and Candide sold him for fifty thousand sequins a diamond worth a hundred thousand, while he protested by Abraham that he could not possibly give more for it. Candide immediately ransomed the baron and Pangloss. The latter threw himself at the feet of his liberator, and bathed them with tears; the former thanked him with a nod, and promised to repay this bit of money at the first opportunity.

1. From the eastern Mediterranean.

—But is it really possible that my sister is in Turkey? said he.

—Nothing is more possible, replied Cacambo, since she is a dishwasher in the house of a prince of Transylvania.

At once two more Jews were called; Candide sold some more diamonds; and they all departed in another galley to the rescue of Cunégonde.

CHAPTER 28

What Happened to Candide, Cunégonde, Pangloss, Martin, &c.

—Let me beg your pardon once more, said Candide to the baron, pardon me, reverend father, for having run you through the body with my sword.

—Don't mention it, replied the baron. I was a little too hasty myself, I confess it; but since you want to know the misfortune which brought me to the galleys, I'll tell you. After being cured of my wound by the brother who was apothecary to the college, I was attacked and abducted by a Spanish raiding party; they jailed me in Buenos Aires at the time when my sister had just left. I asked to be sent to Rome, to the father general. Instead, I was named to serve as almoner in Constantinople, under the French ambassador. I had not been a week on this job when I chanced one evening on a very handsome young ichoglan.[2] The evening was hot; the young man wanted to take a swim; I seized the occasion, and went with him. I did not know that it is a capital offense for a Christian to be found naked with a young Moslem. A cadi sentenced me to receive a hundred blows with a cane on the soles of my feet, and then to be sent to the galleys. I don't suppose there was ever such a horrible miscarriage of justice. But I would like to know why my sister is in the kitchen of a Transylvanian king exiled among Turks.

—But how about you, my dear Pangloss, said Candide; how is it possible that we have met again?

—It is true, said Pangloss, that you saw me hanged; in the normal course of things, I should have been burned, but you recall that a cloudburst occurred just as they were about to roast me. So much rain fell that they despaired of lighting the fire; thus I was hanged, for lack of anything better to do with me. A surgeon bought my body, carried me off to his house, and dissected me. First he made a cross-shaped incision in me, from the navel to the clavicle. No one could have been worse hanged than I was. In fact, the executioner of the high ceremonials of the Holy Inquisition, who was a subdeacon, burned people marvelously well, but he was not in the way of hanging them. The rope was wet, and tightened badly; it caught on a knot; in short, I was still breathing. The cross-shaped incision made me scream so loudly that the surgeon fell over backwards; he thought he was dissecting the devil, fled in an agony of fear, and fell downstairs in his flight. His wife ran in, at the noise, from a nearby room; she found me stretched out on the table with my cross-shaped incision, was even more frightened than her husband, fled, and fell over him. When they had recovered a little, I heard her say to him: 'My dear, what were you thinking of, trying to dissect a heretic? Don't you know those people are always possessed of the devil? I'm going to get the priest and have him exorcised.' At these words, I shuddered, and

2. A page to the sultan.

collected my last remaining energies to cry: 'Have mercy on me!' At last the Portuguese barber[3] took courage; he sewed me up again; his wife even nursed me; in two weeks I was up and about. The barber found me a job and made me lackey to a Knight of Malta who was going to Venice; and when this master could no longer pay me, I took service under a Venetian merchant, whom I followed to Constantinople.

—One day it occurred to me to enter a mosque; no one was there but an old imam and a very attractive young worshipper who was saying her prayers. Her bosom was completely bare; and between her two breasts she had a lovely bouquet of tulips, roses, anemones, buttercups, hyacinths, and primroses. She dropped her bouquet, I picked it up, and returned it to her with the most respectful attentions. I was so long getting it back in place that the imam grew angry, and, seeing that I was a Christian, he called the guard. They took me before the cadi, who sentenced me to receive a hundred blows with a cane on the soles of my feet, and then to be sent to the galleys. I was chained to the same galley and precisely the same bench as My Lord the Baron. There were in this galley four young fellows from Marseilles, five Neapolitan priests, and two Corfu monks, who assured us that these things happen every day. My Lord the Baron asserted that he had suffered a greater injustice than I; I, on the other hand, proposed that it was much more permissible to replace a bouquet in a bosom than to be found naked with an ichoglan. We were arguing the point continually, and getting twenty lashes a day with the bullwhip, when the chain of events within this universe brought you to our galley, and you ransomed us.

—Well, my dear Pangloss, Candide said to him, now that you have been hanged, dissected, beaten to a pulp, and sentenced to the galleys, do you still think everything is for the best in this world?

—I am still of my first opinion, replied Pangloss; for after all I am a philosopher, and it would not be right for me to recant since Leibniz could not possibly be wrong, and besides pre-established harmony is the finest notion in the world, like the plenum and subtle matter.[4]

CHAPTER 29

How Candide Found Cunégonde and the Old Woman Again

While Candide, the baron, Pangloss, Martin, and Cacambo were telling one another their stories, while they were disputing over the contingent or non-contingent events of this universe, while they were arguing over effects and causes, over moral evil and physical evil, over liberty and necessity, and over the consolations available to one in a Turkish galley, they arrived at the shores of Propontis and the house of the prince of Transylvania. The first sight to meet their eyes was Cunégonde and the old woman, who were hanging out towels on lines to dry.

The baron paled at what he saw. The tender lover Candide, seeing his

3. The two callings of barber and surgeon, since they both involved sharp instruments, were interchangeable in the early days of medicine.   4. Rigorous determinism requires that there be no empty spaces in the universe, so wherever it seems empty, one posits the existence of the "plenum." "Subtle matter" describes the soul, the mind, and all spiritual agencies—which can, therefore, be supposed subject to the influence and control of the great world machine, which is, of course, visibly material. Both are concepts needed to round out the system of optimistic determinism.

lovely Cunégonde with her skin weathered, her eyes bloodshot, her breasts fallen, her cheeks seamed, her arms red and scaly, recoiled three steps in horror, and then advanced only out of politeness. She embraced Candide and her brother; everyone embraced the old woman; Candide ransomed them both.

There was a little farm in the neighborhood; the old woman suggested that Candide occupy it until some better fate should befall the group. Cunégonde did not know she was ugly, no one had told her; she reminded Candide of his promises in so firm a tone that the good Candide did not dare to refuse her. So he went to tell the baron that he was going to marry his sister.

—Never will I endure, said the baron, such baseness on her part, such insolence on yours; this shame at least I will not put up with; why, my sister's children would not be able to enter the Chapters in Germany.[5] No, my sister will never marry anyone but a baron of the empire.

Cunégonde threw herself at his feet, and bathed them with her tears; he was inflexible.

—You absolute idiot, Candide told him, I rescued you from the galleys, I paid your ransom, I paid your sister's; she was washing dishes, she is ugly, I am good enough to make her my wife, and you still presume to oppose it! If I followed my impulses, I would kill you all over again.

—You may kill me again, said the baron, but you will not marry my sister while I am alive.

CHAPTER 30
Conclusion

At heart, Candide had no real wish to marry Cunégonde; but the baron's extreme impertinence decided him in favor of the marriage, and Cunégonde was so eager for it that he could not back out. He consulted Pangloss, Martin, and the faithful Cacambo. Pangloss drew up a fine treatise, in which he proved that the baron had no right over his sister and that she could, according to all the laws of the empire, marry Candide morganatically.[6] Martin said they should throw the baron into the sea. Cacambo thought they should send him back to the Levantine captain to finish his time in the galleys, and then send him to the father general in Rome by the first vessel. This seemed the best idea; the old woman approved, and nothing was said to his sister; the plan was executed, at modest expense, and they had the double pleasure of snaring a Jesuit and punishing the pride of a German baron.

It is quite natural to suppose that after so many misfortunes, Candide, married to his mistress, and living with the philosopher Pangloss, the philosopher Martin, the prudent Cacambo, and the old woman—having, besides, brought back so many diamonds from the land of the ancient Incas—must have led the most agreeable life in the world. But he was so cheated by the Jews[7] that nothing was left but his little farm; his wife, growing every day more ugly, became sour-tempered and insupportable; the old woman was ailing and even more ill-humored than Cunégonde. Cacambo,

5. Knightly assemblies.   6. A morganatic marriage confers no rights on the partner of lower rank or on the offspring.   7. Voltaire's anti-Semitism, derived from various unhappy experiences with Jewish financiers, is not the most attractive aspect of his personality.

who worked in the garden and went into Constantinople to sell vegetables, was worn out with toil, and cursed his fate. Pangloss was in despair at being unable to shine in some German university. As for Martin, he was firmly persuaded that things are just as bad wherever you are; he endured in patience. Candide, Martin, and Pangloss sometimes argued over metaphysics and morals. Before the windows of the farmhouse they often watched the passage of boats bearing effendis, pashas, and cadis into exile on Lemnos, Mytilene, and Erzeroum; they saw other cadis, other pashas, other effendis coming, to take the place of the exiles and to be exiled in their turn. They saw various heads, neatly impaled, to be set up at the Sublime Porte.[8] These sights gave fresh impetus to their discussions; and when they were not arguing, the boredom was so fierce that one day the old woman ventured to say:— I should like to know which is worse, being raped a hundred times by negro pirates, having a buttock cut off, running the gauntlet in the Bulgar army, being flogged and hanged in an auto-da-fé, being dissected and rowing in the galleys—experiencing, in a word, all the miseries through which we have passed—or else just sitting here and doing nothing?

—It's a hard question, said Candide.

These words gave rise to new reflections, and Martin in particular concluded that man was bound to live either in convulsions of misery or in the lethargy of boredom. Candide did not agree, but expressed no positive opinion. Pangloss asserted that he had always suffered horribly; but having once declared that everything was marvelously well, he continued to repeat the opinion and didn't believe a word of it.

One thing served to confirm Martin in his detestable opinions, to make Candide hesitate more than ever, and to embarrass Pangloss. It was the arrival one day at their farm of Paquette and Brother Giroflée, who were in the last stages of misery. They had quickly run through their three thousand piastres, had split up, made up, quarreled, been jailed, escaped, and finally Brother Giroflée had turned Turk. Paquette continued to ply her trade everywhere, and no longer made any money at it.

—I told you, said Martin to Candide, that your gifts would soon be squandered and would only render them more unhappy. You have spent millions of piastres, you and Cacambo, and you are no more happy than Brother Giroflée and Paquette.

—Ah ha, said Pangloss to Paquette, so destiny has brought you back in our midst, my poor girl! Do you realize you cost me the end of my nose, one eye, and an ear? And look at you now! eh! what a world it is, after all!

This new adventure caused them to philosophize more than ever.

There was in the neighborhood a very famous dervish, who was said to be the best philosopher in Turkey; they went to ask his advice. Pangloss was spokesman, and he said:—Master, we have come to ask you to tell us why such a strange animal as man was created.

—What are you getting into? answered the dervish. Is it any of your business?

—But, reverend father, said Candide, there's a horrible lot of evil on the face of the earth.

---

8. The gate of the sultan's palace is often used by extension to describe his government as a whole. But it was in fact a real gate where the heads of traitors and public enemies were gruesomely exposed.

—What does it matter, said the dervish, whether there's good or evil? When his highness sends a ship to Egypt, does he worry whether the mice on board are comfortable or not?

—What shall we do then? asked Pangloss.

—Hold your tongue, said the dervish.

—I had hoped, said Pangloss, to reason a while with you concerning effects and causes, the best of possible worlds, the origin of evil, the nature of the soul, and pre-established harmony.

At these words, the dervish slammed the door in their faces.

During this interview, word was spreading that at Constantinople they had just strangled two viziers of the divan,[9] as well as the mufti, and impaled several of their friends. This catastrophe made a great and general sensation for several hours. Pangloss, Candide, and Martin, as they returned to their little farm, passed a good old man who was enjoying the cool of the day at his doorstep under a grove of orange trees. Pangloss, who was as inquisitive as he was explanatory, asked the name of the mufti who had been strangled.

—I know nothing of it, said the good man, and I have never cared to know the name of a single mufti or vizier. I am completely ignorant of the episode you are discussing. I presume that in general those who meddle in public business sometimes perish miserably, and that they deserve their fate; but I never listen to the news from Constantinople; I am satisfied with sending the fruits of my garden to be sold there.

Having spoken these words, he asked the strangers into his house; his two daughters and two sons offered them various sherbets which they had made themselves, Turkish cream flavored with candied citron, orange, lemon, lime, pineapple, pistachio, and mocha coffee uncontaminated by the inferior coffee of Batavia and the East Indies. After which the two daughters of this good Moslem perfumed the beards of Candide, Pangloss, and Martin.

—You must possess, Candide said to the Turk, an enormous and splendid property?

I have only twenty acres, replied the Turk; I cultivate them with my children, and the work keeps us from three great evils, boredom, vice, and poverty.

Candide, as he walked back to his farm, meditated deeply over the words of the Turk. He said to Pangloss and Martin:—This good old man seems to have found himself a fate preferable to that of the six kings with whom we had the honor of dining.

—Great place, said Pangloss, is very perilous in the judgment of all the philosophers; for, after all, Eglon, king of the Moabites, was murdered by Ehud; Absalom was hung up by the hair and pierced with three darts; King Nadab, son of Jeroboam, was killed by Baasha; King Elah by Zimri; Ahaziah by Jehu; Athaliah by Jehoiada; and Kings Jehoiakim, Jeconiah, and Zedekiah were enslaved. You know how death came to Croesus, Astyages, Darius, Dionysius of Syracuse, Pyrrhus, Perseus, Hannibal, Jugurtha, Ariovistus, Caesar, Pompey, Nero, Otho, Vitellius, Domitian, Richard II of England, Edward II, Henry VI, Richard III, Mary Stuart, Charles I, the three Henrys of France, and the Emperor Henry IV? You know . . .

—I know also, said Candide, that we must cultivate our garden.

9. Intimate advisers of the sultan.

—You are perfectly right, said Pangloss; for when man was put into the garden of Eden, he was put there *ut operaretur eum,* so that he should work it; this proves that man was not born to take his ease.

—Let's work without speculating, said Martin; it's the only way of rendering life bearable.

The whole little group entered into this laudable scheme; each one began to exercise his talents. The little plot yielded fine crops. Cunégonde was, to tell the truth, remarkably ugly; but she became an excellent pastry cook. Paquette took up embroidery; the old woman did the laundry. Everyone, down even to Brother Giroflée, did something useful; he became a very adequate carpenter, and even an honest man; and Pangloss sometimes used to say to Candide:—All events are linked together in the best of possible worlds; for, after all, if you had not been driven from a fine castle by being kicked in the backside for love of Miss Cunégonde, if you hadn't been sent before the Inquisition, if you hadn't traveled across America on foot, if you hadn't given a good sword thrust to the baron, if you hadn't lost all your sheep from the good land of Eldorado, you wouldn't be sitting here eating candied citron and pistachios.

—That is very well put, said Candide, but we must cultivate our garden.

SAMUEL JOHNSON
1709–1784

In *The History of Rasselas, Prince of Abissinia* (1759), his longest philosophic tale, Samuel Johnson offers a dignified but moving account of the futility of human endeavor. The narrative, written hastily and allegedly published to defray his mother's funeral expenses, distills the melancholy reflections of a fifty-year-old man whose observations and experience alike convince him that human happiness depends mainly on the preservation of illusion.

Son of a Lichfield bookseller, Johnson received his early education at Lichfield Grammar School. In 1728 he entered Pembroke College Oxford, but poverty forced him to leave without a degree three years later. An attempt at teaching, and later a brief period as schoolmaster, proved unsuccessful; in 1737 he went to London and began to earn a living by writing for the *Gentleman's Magazine.* He had married, in 1735, a widow much older than he; her death, in 1752, left him desolate.

Before long Johnson became distinguished as conversationalist and as writer, known particularly for *The Rambler* (a periodical published from 1750 to 1752; Johnson himself wrote all but 4½ of its 208 numbers) and the *Dictionary of the English Language* (1755), an almost incredible achievement for one man. In 1762, he was granted a royal pension of three hundred pounds a year; in 1775, his old university conferred upon him the degree of Doctor in Civil Laws. Meanwhile, he had formed a close attachment to the Scotsman James Boswell, thirty-one years younger than he, of whom he saw much in London and with whom he traveled through the highlands and islands of Scotland. (Subsequently, Boswell wrote a life of Johnson.) His second intimate relationship was with Henry Thrale, a London brewer, and his wife, Hester, a woman of strong literary interests. With them Johnson made his only trip abroad, to Paris. A group of other distinguished men joined him in founding The Literary Club (1764), which met regularly for conversation. By the time of Johnson's death in 1784, he was unquestionably the most famous literary figure in England.

Johnson wrote poetic adaptations of the classics; original verse in Latin and in English; a travel book; fiction; a tragic drama; literary criticism; philosophic, satiric, and meditative essays; biography; and a dictionary. He edited Shakespeare's plays, with a preface that defined the playwright's place for the mid-eighteenth-century consciousness and that still speaks eloquently to us today. His final work, *Lives of the Poets* (1779–81), biographical and critical introductions to fifty-two English poets, exemplified at its best his gift for forceful judgment and discrimination. Sometimes he was wrong, by our standards: he disapproved, for example, of Milton's *Lycidas*. More often, he provided definitive statements about poetic careers and accomplishments.

Rasselas, published almost simultaneously with Voltaire's *Candide,* was immediately compared to the French work; Johnson himself found the resemblance striking. Both books employ the fictional device of a naive protagonist whose travels educate him in the evils of the world. In tone and in implication, though, the two fictions differ greatly. Voltaire's satiric intensity and violence much exceed Johnson's; on the other hand, Candide, after far worse disasters than Rasselas faces, arrives at a more specific course of hopeful action than his English counterpart can discover.

Although Johnson was born eleven years after Voltaire, his point of view derives from an earlier era. The context in which Rasselas learns the futility of human endeavor is that of Christian humanism, the intellectual position that focuses attention on human beings and their moral responsibilities within the context of Christian belief. When the princess, having seen the catacombs, concludes, "To me, . . . the choice of life is become less important; I hope hereafter to think only on the choice of eternity," she reveals the book's underlying assumptions. Human beings, because of their humanity, struggle to attain goals which, won, prove less than satisfactory. They live in illusion, governing themselves by hopes and fears disproportionate to actuality. The reality that should focus their attention, the afterlife of reward and punishment, seldom concerns them; they dwell resolutely in the irrelevant. They lack not only adequate reason, but sufficiently active faith.

Unlike Voltaire's Pangloss, Johnson's characters do not rely on universalizing interpretations. They do not worry about whether theirs is the best or the worst of all possible worlds; their blinkered vision directs itself to personal and immediate concerns. Rasselas and his sister, trying to make their own "choice of life," seeking models of fulfillment and happiness, repeatedly find the inadequacy of human effort. Even more important, they discover what a chapter title calls "the dangerous prevalence [meaning dominance] of imagination": the degree to which reason proves subject to desire, as individuals, seeing only what they want to see, beguile themselves into temporary satisfaction. The story ends with the "Conclusion, In Which Nothing Is Concluded"; the travelers, still not free of hopeful fantasy, return to Abyssinia. They have not encountered great natural disasters, striking instances of human malice or lust, or large-scale carnage; but neither have they found much ground for expecting earthly happiness. The satirist's tone, Voltaire's tone, by its very vehemence suggests belief that human beings, once aware of their own corruption, might at least minimally improve. Johnson's elevated, dignified, ponderous utterance, on the other hand, rings with the authority of conviction. The world he describes seems in no way subject to change.

This is not to say, however, that *Rasselas* makes its readers feel hopeless. The vigor and authority of the narrative voice carry comfort, conveying a sense of the possibility of knowledge and understanding. Rasselas and Nekayah, voices rather than developed characters, achieve no dazzling insight as a result of their efforts to understand the choices open to them. Never differentiated in personality, they serve mainly as mouthpieces for positions Johnson wishes to represent. Nonetheless, as instruments of communication they suggest a way of finding at least conditional value in this world. The fable that contains them implies the importance, the educational potential, of *experience,* exemplified by the travel and the purposeful investigations the characters undertake, and of *talk*. Rasselas and his sister learn not only by looking but by discussing. They talk with their mentor, Imlac, the voice of wisdom within the narrative—wisdom that has been derived from its possessor's previous experience, a fact reinforcing the stress on the moral significance of what the travelers see and do. But Rasselas and Nekayah also talk with one another, discovering the meaning of what they have seen by a process of mutual assessment, of sharing and of questioning. If all faith in the possibility of ultimate earthly satisfaction proves illusory, what the travelers take for granted—their companionship—yet continues to sustain them. The human community contains the saving possibility of communal reassurance; the verbal sharing of experience intensifies its value. And the effort to say precisely what one knows is a self-sufficiently valuable enterprise, an enterprise corroborating the importance of Johnson's writing of the tale: for that, too, is an effort at *saying*.

So *Rasselas*, although somber in its assessments, does not imply despair. Reminding its readers as well as its characters of the vital "choice of eternity," it reiterates Johnson's typical insistence on human life as a condition offering much to endure, little to enjoy. But it also suggests the nature and the importance of the little enjoyment and insight possible to human beings; and it implicitly invites readers to take their own lives seriously, to understand and value the moral possibilities of all experience, and to share the restrained, ambiguous excitement of seeing things as they are.

J. Boswell, *The Life of Samuel Johnson* (1791), remains a brilliant account of its subject. The definitive modern biography is W. J. Bate, *Samuel Johnson* (1977). Bate's earlier, shorter book, *The Achievement of Samuel Johnson* (1955), provides an excellent introduction. J. T. Boulton, ed., *Johnson, The Critical Heritage,* (1977), assembles critical statements from the eighteenth century onward. More recent essays are collected in P. J. Korshin, ed., *Johnson after Two Hundred Years,* (1986); H. Bloom, ed., *Dr. Samuel Johnson and James Boswell* (1985); and Prem Nath, ed., *Fresh Reflections on Samuel Johnson* (1987).

PRONOUNCING GLOSSARY

The following list uses common English syllables and stress accents to provide rough equivalents of selected words whose pronunciation may be unfamiliar to the general reader.

Nekayah: *ne-ky'-yah*   Rasselas: *ra-se-las*

Pekuah: *pek-'yoo-ah*

From The History of Rasselas, Prince of Abissinia[1]

CHAPTER 1

Description of a Palace in a Valley

Ye who listen with credulity to the whispers of fancy, and persue with eagerness the phantoms of hope; who expect that age will perform the promises of youth, and that the deficiencies of the present day will be supplied by the morrow; attend to the history of Rasselas prince of Abissinia.

Rasselas was the fourth son of the mighty emperour, in whose dominions the Father of Waters[2] begins his course; whose bounty pours down the streams of plenty, and scatters over half the world the harvests of Egypt.

---

1. The text is that of the sixth edition (London, 1783), the last version published in Johnson's lifetime.
2. The Nile.

According to the custom which has descended from age to age among the monarchs of the torrid zone, Rasselas was confined in a private palace, with the other sons and daughters of Abissinian royalty, till the order of succession should call him to the throne.

The place, which the wisdom or policy of antiquity had destined for the residence of the Abissinian princes, was a spacious valley in the kingdom of Amhara, surrounded on every side by mountains, of which the summits overhang the middle part. The only passage, by which it could be entered, was a cavern that passed under a rock, of which it has long been disputed whether it was the work of nature or of human industry. The outlet of the cavern was concealed by a thick wood, and the mouth which opened into the valley was closed with gates of iron, forged by the artificers of ancient days, so massy that no man could without the help of engines open or shut them.

From the mountains on every side, rivulets descended that filled all the valley with verdure and fertility, and formed a lake in the middle inhabited by fish of every species, and frequented by every fowl whom nature has taught to dip the wing in water. This lake discharged its superfluities by a stream which entered a dark cleft of the mountain on the northern side, and fell with dreadful noise from precipice to precipice till it was heard no more.

The sides of the mountains were covered with trees, the banks of the brooks were diversified with flowers; every blast shook spices from the rocks, and every month dropped fruits upon the ground. All animals that bite the grass, or browse the shrub, whether wild or tame, wandered in this extensive circuit, secured from beasts of prey by the mountains which confined them. On one part were flocks and herds feeding in the pastures, on another all the beasts of chase frisking in the lawns; the sprightly kid was bounding on the rocks, the subtle[3] monkey frolicking in the trees, and the solemn elephant reposing in the shade. All the diversities of the world were brought together, the blessings of nature were collected, and its evils extracted and excluded.

The valley, wide and fruitful, supplied its inhabitants with the necessaries of life, and all delights and superfluities were added at the annual visit which the emperour paid his children, when the iron gate was opened to the sound of musick; and during eight days every one that resided in the valley was required to propose whatever might contribute to make seclusion pleasant, to fill up the vacancies of attention, and lessen the tediousness of time. Every desire was immediately granted. All the artificers of pleasure were called to gladden the festivity; the musicians exerted the power of harmony, and the dancers shewed their activity before the princes, in hope that they should pass their lives in this blissful captivity, to which these only were admitted whose performance was thought able to add novelty to luxury. Such was the appearance of security and delight which this retirement afforded, that they, to whom it was new, always desired that it might be perpetual; and as those, on whom the iron gate had once closed, were never suffered[4] to return, the effect of longer experience could not be known. Thus every year produced new schemes of delight, and new competitors for imprisonment.

The palace stood on an eminence raised about thirty paces above the surface of the lake. It was divided into many squares or courts, built with greater or less magnificence, according to the rank of those for whom they

3. Cunning.   4. Permitted.

were designed. The roofs were turned into arches of massy stone joined by a cement that grew harder by time, and the building stood from century to century deriding the solstitial rains and equinoctial hurricanes, without need of reparation.

This house, which was so large as to be fully known to none but some ancient officers who successively inherited the secrets of the place, was built as if suspicion herself had dictated the plan. To every room there was an open and secret passage, every square had a communication with the rest, either from the upper stories by private galleries, or by subterranean passages from the lower apartments. Many of the columns had unsuspected cavities, in which a long race of monarchs had reposited their treasures. They then closed up the opening with marble, which was never to be removed but in the utmost exigencies of the kingdom; and recorded their accumulations in a book which was itself concealed in a tower not entered but by the emperour, attended by the prince who stood next in succession.

CHAPTER 2

The Discontent of Rasselas in the Happy Valley

Here the sons and daughters of Abissinia lived only to know the soft vicissitudes[5] of pleasure and repose, attended by all that were skilful to delight, and gratified with whatever the senses can enjoy. They wandered in gardens of fragrance, and slept in the fortresses of security. Every art was practised to make them pleased with their own condition. The sages who instructed them, told them of nothing but the miseries of publick life, and described all beyond the mountains as regions of calamity, where discord was always raging, and where man preyed upon man.

To heighten their opinion of their own felicity, they were daily entertained with songs, the subject of which was the *happy valley*. Their appetites were excited by frequent enumerations of different enjoyments, and revelry and merriment was the business of every hour from the dawn of morning to the close of even.

These methods were generally successful; few of the princes had ever wished to enlarge their bounds, but passed their lives in full conviction that they had all within their reach that art or nature could bestow, and pitied those whom fate had excluded from this seat of tranquillity, as the sport of chance and the slaves of misery.

Thus they rose in the morning and lay down at night, pleased with each other and with themselves, all but Rasselas, who in the twenty-sixth year of his age, began to withdraw himself from their pastimes and assemblies, and to delight in solitary walks and silent meditation. He often sat before tables covered with luxury, and forgot to taste the dainties that were placed before him: he rose abruptly in the midst of the song, and hastily retired beyond the sound of musick. His attendants observed the change and endeavoured to renew his love of pleasure: he neglected their officiousness,[6] repulsed their invitations, and spent day after day on the banks of rivulets sheltered with trees, where he sometimes listened to the birds in the branches, sometimes observed the fish playing in the stream, and anon cast his eyes upon the

5. Alternations.   6. Helpfulness.

pastures and mountains filled with animals, of which some were biting the herbage, and some sleeping among the bushes.

This singularity of his humour made him much observed. One of the Sages, in whose conversation he had formerly delighted, followed him secretly, in hope of discovering the cause of his disquiet. Rasselas, who knew not that any one was near him, having for some time fixed his eyes upon the goats that were brousing among the rocks, began to compare their condition with his own.

"What," said he, "makes the difference between man and all the rest of the animal creation? Every beast that strays beside me has the same corporal necessities with myself; he is hungry and crops the grass, he is thirsty and drinks the stream, his thirst and hunger are appeased, he is satisfied and sleeps; he rises again and is hungry, he is again fed and is at rest. I am hungry and thirsty like him, but when thirst and hunger cease I am not at rest; I am, like him, pained with want, but am not, like him, satisfied with fulness. The intermediate hours are tedious and gloomy; I long again to be hungry that I may again quicken my attention. The birds peck the berries or the corn, and fly away to the groves where they sit in seeming happiness on the branches, and waste their lives in tuning one unvaried series of sounds. I likewise can call the lutanist and the singer, but the sounds that pleased me yesterday weary me to-day, and will grow yet more wearisome tomorrow. I can discover within me no power of perception which is not glutted with its proper pleasure, yet I do not feel myself delighted. Man surely has some latent sense for which this place affords no gratification, or he has some desires distinct from sense which must be satisfied before he can be happy."

After this he lifted up his head, and seeing the moon rising, walked towards the palace. As he passed through the fields, and saw the animals around him, "Ye, said he, are happy, and need not envy me that walk thus among you, burdened with myself; nor do I, ye gentle beings, envy your felicity; for it is not the felicity of man. I have many distresses from which ye are free; I fear pain when I do not feel it; I sometimes shrink at evils recollected, and sometimes start at evils anticipated: surely the equity of providence has balanced peculiar sufferings with peculiar enjoyments."

With observations like these the prince amused himself as he returned, uttering them with a plaintive voice, yet with a look that discovered[7] him to feel some complacence in his own perspicacity, and to receive some solace of the miseries of life, from consciousness of the delicacy with which he felt, and the eloquence with which he bewailed them. He mingled cheerfully in the diversions of the evening, and all rejoiced to find that his heart was lightened.

[Rasselas remains dissatisfied in the Happy Valley and attempts to escape by means of wings; the wings, however, drop their inventor in the lake.]

CHAPTER 7

The Prince Finds a Man of Learning

The prince was not much afflicted by this disaster, having suffered himself to hope for a happier event, only because he had no other means of escape

7. Revealed.

in view. He still persisted in his design to leave the happy valley by the first opportunity.

His imagination was now at a stand; he had no prospect of entering into the world; and, notwithstanding all his endeavours to support himself, discontent by degrees preyed upon him, and he began again to lose his thoughts in sadness, when the rainy season, which in these countries is periodical, made it inconvenient to wander in the woods.

The rain continued longer and with more violence than had been ever known: the clouds broke on the surrounding mountains, and the torrents streamed into the plain on every side, till the cavern was too narrow to discharge the water. The lake overflowed its banks, and all the level of the valley was covered with the inundation. The eminence, on which the palace was built, and some other spots of rising ground, were all that the eye could now discover. The herds and flocks left the pastures, and both the wild beasts and the tame retreated to the mountains.

This inundation confined all the princes to domestick amusements, and the attention of Rasselas was particularly seized by a poem, which Imlac rehearsed upon the various conditions of humanity. He commanded the poet to attend him in his apartment, and recite his verses a second time; then entering into familiar talk, he thought himself happy in having found a man who knew the world so well, and could so skilfully paint the scenes of life. He asked a thousand questions about things, to which, though common to all other mortals, his confinement from childhood had kept him a stranger. The poet pitied his ignorance, and loved his curiosity, and entertained him from day to day with novelty and instruction, so that the prince regretted the necessity of sleep, and longed till the morning should renew his pleasure.

As they were sitting together, the prince commanded Imlac to relate his history, and to tell by what accident he was forced, or by what motive induced, to close his life in the happy valley. As he was going to begin his narrative, Rasselas was called to a concert, and obliged to restrain his curiosity till the evening.

CHAPTER 8

The History of Imlac

The close of the day is, in the regions of the torrid zone, the only season of diversion and entertainment, and it was therefore midnight before the musick ceased, and the princesses retired. Rasselas then called for his companion, and required him to begin the story of his life.

"Sir, said Imlac, my history will not be long: the life that is devoted to knowledge passes silently away, and is very little diversified by events. To talk in publick, to think in solitude, to read and to hear, to inquire, and answer inquiries, is the business of a scholar. He wanders about the world without pomp or terrour, and is neither known nor valued but by men like himself.

"I was born in the kingdom of Goiama, at no great distance from the fountain[8] of the Nile. My father was a wealthy merchant, who traded between the inland countries of Africk and the ports of the Red Sea. He was

8. Source.

honest, frugal, and diligent, but of mean[9] sentiments, and narrow comprehension: he desired only to be rich, and to conceal his riches, lest he should be spoiled[1] by the governours of the province."

"Surely, said the prince, my father must be negligent of his charge, if any man in his dominions dares take that which belongs to another. Does he not know that kings are accountable for injustice permitted as well as done? If I were emperour, not the meanest[2] of my subjects should be oppressed with impunity. My blood boils when I am told that a merchant durst not enjoy his honest gains for fear of losing them by the rapacity of power. Name the governour who robbed the people, that I may declare his crimes to the emperour."

"Sir, said Imlac, your ardour is the natural effect of virtue animated by youth: the time will come when you will acquit your father, and perhaps hear with less impatience of the governour. Oppression is, in the Abissinian dominions, neither frequent nor tolerated; but no form of government has been yet discovered, by which cruelty can be wholly prevented. Subordination supposes power on one part, and subjection on the other; and if power be in the hands of men, it will sometimes be abused. The vigilance of the supreme magistrate may do much, but much will still remain undone. He can never know all the crimes that are committed, and can seldom punish all that he knows.

"This, said the prince, I do not understand, but I had rather hear thee than dispute. Continue thy narration."

"My father, proceeded Imlac, originally intended that I should have no other education, than such as might qualify me for commerce; and discovering in me great strength of memory, and quickness of apprehension, often declared his hope that I should be some time the richest man in Abissinia."

"Why, said the prince, did thy father desire the increase of his wealth, when it was already greater than he durst discover or enjoy? I am unwilling to doubt thy veracity, yet inconsistencies cannot both be true."

"Inconsistencies, answered Imlac, cannot both be right, but, imputed to man, they may both be true. Yet diversity is not inconsistency. My father might expect a time of greater security. However, some desire is necessary to keep life in motion, and he, whose real wants are supplied, must admit those of fancy."

"This, said the prince, I can in some measure conceive. I repent that I interrupted thee."

"With this hope, proceeded Imlac, he sent me to school; but when I had once found the delight of knowledge, and felt the pleasure of intelligence and the pride of invention, I began silently to despise riches, and determined to disappoint the purpose of my father, whose grossness of conception raised my pity. I was twenty years old before his tenderness would expose me to the fatigue of travel, in which time I had been instructed, by successive masters, in all the literature of my native country. As every hour taught me something new, I lived in a continual course of gratifications; but, as I advanced towards manhood, I lost much of the reverence with which I had been used to look on my instructors; because, when the lesson was ended. I did not find them wiser or better than common men.

9. Ignoble, small-minded.   1. Plundered.   2. Lowliest.

"At length my father resolved to initiate me in commerce, and opening one of his subterranean treasuries, counted out ten thousand pieces of gold. This, young man, said he, is the stock with which you must negociate.[3] I began with less than the fifth part, and you see how diligence and parsimony have increased it. This is your own to waste or to improve. If you squander it by negligence or caprice, you must wait for my death before you will be rich: if, in four years, you double your stock, we will thenceforward let subordination cease, and live together as friends and partners; for he shall always be equal with me, who is equally skilled in the art of growing rich.

"We laid our money upon camels, concealed in bales of cheap goods, and travelled to the shore of the Red Sea. When I cast my eye on the expanse of waters, my heart bounded like that of a prisoner escaped. I felt an unextinguishable curiosity kindle in my mind, and resolved to snatch this opportunity of seeing the manners of other nations, and of learning sciences[4] unknown in Abissinia.

"I remembered that my father had obliged me to the improvement of my stock, not by a promise which I ought not to violate, but by a penalty which I was at liberty to incur; and therefore determined to gratify my predominant desire, and by drinking at the fountains of knowledge, to quench the thirst of curiosity.

"As I was supposed to trade without connexion with my father, it was easy for me to become acquainted with the master of a ship, and procure a passage to some other country. I had no motives of choice to regulate my voyage; it was sufficient for me that, wherever I wandered, I should see a country which I had not seen before. I therefore entered a ship bound for Surat,[5] having left a letter for my father declaring my intention."

CHAPTER 9
The History of Imlac Continued

"When I first entered upon the world of waters, and lost sight of land, I looked round about me with pleasing terrour, and thinking my soul enlarged by the boundless prospect, imagined that I could gaze round for ever without satiety; but, in a short time, I grew weary of looking on barren uniformity, where I could only see again what I had already seen. I then descended into the ship, and doubted for a while whether all my future pleasures would not end like this, in disgust and disappointment. Yet, surely, said I, the ocean and the land are very different; the only variety of water is rest and motion, but the earth has mountains and vallies, deserts and cities: it is inhabited by men of different customs and contrary opinions; and I may hope to find variety in life, though I should miss it in nature.

"With this thought I quieted my mind and amused myself during the voyage, sometimes by learning from the sailors the art of navigation, which I have never practised, and sometimes by forming schemes for my conduct in different situations, in not one of which I have been ever placed.

"I was almost weary of my naval amusements when we landed safely at Surat. I secured my money, and purchasing some commodities for show, joined myself to a caravan that was passing into the inland country. My

3. Do business.   4. Forms of knowledge.   5. An Indian port.

companions, for some reason or other, conjecturing that I was rich, and, by my inquiries and admiration,[6] finding that I was ignorant, considered me as a novice whom they had a right to cheat, and who was to learn at the usual expence the art of fraud. They exposed me to the theft of servants, and the exaction of officers, and saw me plundered upon false pretences, without any advantage to themselves, but that of rejoicing in the superiority of their own knowledge."

"Stop a moment, said the prince. Is there such depravity in man, as that he should injure another without benefit to himself? I can easily conceive that all are pleased with superiority; but your ignorance was merely accidental, which being neither your crime nor your folly, could afford them no reason to applaud themselves; and the knowledge which they had, and which you wanted,[7] they might as effectually have shewn by warning, as betraying you."

"Pride, said Imlac, is seldom delicate, it will please itself with very mean advantages; and envy feels not its own happiness, but when it may be compared with the misery of others. They were my enemies, because they grieved to think me rich; and my oppressors, because they delighted to find me weak."

"Proceed, said the prince: I doubt not of the facts which you relate, but imagine that you impute them to mistaken motives."

"In this company, said Imlac, I arrived at Agra, the capital of Indostan, the city in which the great Mogul commonly resides. I applied myself to the language of the country, and in a few months was able to converse with the learned men; some of whom I found morose and reserved, and others easy and communicative; some were unwilling to teach another what they had with difficulty learned themselves; and some shewed that the end of their studies was to gain the dignity of instructing.

"To the tutor of the young princes I recommended myself so much, that I was presented to the emperour as a man of uncommon knowledge. The emperour asked me many questions concerning my country and my travels; and though I cannot now recollect any thing that he uttered above the power of a common man, he dismissed me astonished at his wisdom, and enamoured of his goodness.

"My credit was now so high, that the merchants, with whom I had travelled, applied to me for recommendations to the ladies of the Court. I was surprised at their confidence of solicitation, and gently reproached them with their practices on the road. They heard me with cold indifference, and shewed no tokens of shame or sorrow.

"They then urged their request with the offer of a bribe; but what I would not do for kindness, I would not do for money; and refused them, not because they had injured me, but because I would not enable them to injure others; for I knew they would have made use of my credit to cheat those who should buy their wares.

"Having resided at Agra till there was no more to be learned, I travelled into Persia, where I saw many remains of ancient magnificence, and observed many new accommodations[8] of life. The Persians are a nation eminently social, and their assemblies afforded me daily opportunities of remarking[9]

---

6. Astonishment.   7. Lacked.   8. Comforts, conveniences.   9. Noting.

characters and manners, and of tracing human nature through all its variations.

"From Persia I passed into Arabia, where I saw a nation at once pastoral and warlike; who live without any settled habitation; whose only wealth is their flocks and herds; and who have yet carried on, through all ages, an hereditary war with all mankind, though they neither covet nor envy their possessions."

CHAPTER 10

Imlac's History Continued. A Dissertation upon Poetry.

"Wherever I went, I found that poetry was considered as the highest learning, and regarded with a veneration somewhat approaching to that which man would pay to the Angelick Nature. And yet it fills me with wonder, that, in almost all countries, the most ancient poets are considered as the best: whether it be that every other kind of knowledge is an acquisition gradually attained, and poetry is a gift conferred at once; or that the first poetry of every nation surprised them as a novelty, and retained the credit by consent which it received by accident at first: or whether, as the province of poetry is to describe Nature and Passion, which are always the same, the first writers took possession of the most striking objects for description, and the most probable occurrences for fiction, and left nothing to those that followed them, but transcription of the same events, and new combinations of the same images. Whatever be the reason, it is commonly observed that the early writers are in possession of nature, and their followers of art: that the first excel in strength and invention, and the latter in elegance and refinement.

"I was desirous to add my name to this illustrious fraternity. I read all the poets of Persia and Arabia, and was able to repeat by memory the volumes that are suspended in the mosque of Mecca.[1] But I soon found that no man was ever great by imitation. My desire of excellence impelled me to transfer my attention to nature and to life. Nature was to be my subject, and men to be my auditors: I could never describe what I had not seen: I could not hope to move those with delight or terrour, whose interests and opinions I did not understand.

"Being now resolved to be a poet, I saw every thing with a new purpose; my sphere of attention was suddenly magnified: no kind of knowledge was to be overlooked. I ranged mountains and deserts for images and resemblances, and pictured upon my mind every tree of the forest and flower of the valley. I observed with equal care the crags of the rock and the pinnacles of the palace. Sometimes I wandered along the mazes of the rivulet, and sometimes watched the changes of the summer clouds. To a poet nothing can be useless. Whatever is beautiful, and whatever is dreadful, must be familiar to his imagination: he must be conversant with all that is awfully[2] vast or elegantly little. The plants of the garden, the animals of the wood, the minerals of the earth, and meteors of the sky, must all concur to store his mind with inexhaustible variety: for every idea is useful for the enforcement or decoration of moral or religious truth; and he, who knows most, will have most power of diversifying his scenes, and of gratifying his reader with remote allusions and unexpected instruction.

---

1. Because they have won prizes.   2. Impressively.

"All the appearances of nature I was therefore careful to study, and every country which I have surveyed has contributed something to my poetical powers."

"In so wide a survey, said the prince, you must surely have left much unobserved. I have lived, till now, within the circuit of these mountains, and yet cannot walk abroad without the sight of something which I had never beheld before, or never heeded."

"The business of a poet, said Imlac, is to examine, not the individual, but the species; to remark general properties and large appearances; he does not number the streaks of the tulip, or describe the different shades in the verdure of the forest. He is to exhibit in his portraits of nature such prominent and striking features, as recall the original to every mind; and must neglect the minuter discriminations, which one may have remarked, and another have neglected, for those characteristicks which are alike obvious to vigilance and carelessness.

"But the knowledge of nature is only half the task of a poet; he must be acquainted likewise with all the modes of life. His character requires that he estimate the happiness and misery of every condition; observe the power of all the passions in all their combinations, and trace the changes of the human mind as they are modified by various institutions and accidental influences of climate or custom, from the sprightliness of infancy to the despondence of decrepitude. He must divest himself of the prejudices of his age or country; he must consider right and wrong in their abstracted and invariable state; he must disregard present laws and opinions, and rise to general and transcendental truths, which will always be the same: he must therefore content himself with the slow progress of his name; contemn the applause of his own time, and commit his claims to the justice of posterity. He must write as the interpreter of nature, and the legislator of mankind, and consider himself as presiding over the thoughts and manners of future generations; as a being superior to time and place.

"His labour is not yet at an end: he must know many languages and many sciences; and, that his style may be worthy of his thoughts, must, by incessant practice, familiarize to himself every delicacy of speech, and grace of harmony."

CHAPTER 11

Imlac's Narrative Continued, A Hint on Pilgrimage

Imlac now felt the enthusiastic fit,[3] and was proceeding to aggrandize his own profession, when the prince cried out, "Enough! Thou hast convinced me, that no human being can ever be a poet. Proceed with thy narration."

"To be a poet, said Imlac, is indeed very difficult." "So difficult, returned the prince, that I will at present hear no more of his labours. Tell me whither you went when you had seen Persia."

"From Persia, said the poet, I travelled through Syria, and for three years resided in Palestine, where I conversed with great numbers of the northern and western nations of Europe; the nations which are now in possession of all power and all knowledge; whose armies are irresistible, and whose fleets command the remotest parts of the globe. When I compared these men with

---

3. I.e., a fit of extravagant emotion.

the natives of our own kingdom, and those that surround us, they appeared almost another order of beings. In their countries it is difficult to wish for any thing that may not be obtained: a thousand arts, of which we never heard, are continually labouring for their convenience and pleasure; and whatever their own climate has denied them is supplied by their commerce."

"By what means, said the prince, are the Europeans thus powerful, or why, since they can so easily visit Asia and Africa for trade or conquest, cannot the Asiaticks and Africans invade their coasts, plant colonies in their ports, and give laws to their natural princes? The same wind that carries them back would bring us thither."

"They are more powerful, Sir, than we, answered Imlac, because they are wiser; knowledge will always predominate over ignorance, as man governs the other animals. But why their knowledge is more than ours, I know not what reason can be given, but the unsearchable will of the Supreme Being."

"When, said the prince with a sigh, shall I be able to visit Palestine, and mingle with this mighty confluence of nations? Till that happy moment shall arrive, let me fill up the time with such representations as thou canst give me. I am not ignorant of the motive that assembles such numbers in that place, and cannot but consider it as the centre of wisdom and piety, to which the best and wisest men of every land must be continually resorting."

"There are some nations, said Imlac, that send few visitants to Palestine; for many numerous and learned sects in Europe concur to censure pilgrimage as superstitious, or deride it as ridiculous."

"You know, said the prince, how little my life has made me acquainted with diversity of opinions; it will be too long to hear the arguments on both sides; you, that have considered them, tell me the result."

"Pilgrimage, said Imlac, like many other acts of piety, may be reasonable or superstitious according to the principles upon which it is performed. Long journeys in search of truth are not commanded. Truth, such as is necessary to the regulation of life, is always found where it is honestly sought. Change of place is no natural cause of the increase of piety, for it inevitably produces dissipation of mind.[4] Yet, since men go every day to view the fields where great actions have been performed, and return with stronger impressions of the event, curiosity of the same kind may naturally dispose us to view that country whence our religion had its beginning; and I believe no man surveys those awful[5] scenes without some confirmation of holy resolutions. That the Supreme Being may be more easily propitiated in one place than in another, is the dream of idle superstition; but that some places may operate upon our own minds in an uncommon manner, is an opinion which hourly experience will justify. He who supposes that his vices may be more successfully combated in Palestine, will, perhaps, find himself mistaken, yet he may go thither without folly: he who thinks they will be more freely pardoned, dishonours at once his reason and religion."

"These, said the prince, are European distinctions. I will consider them another time. What have you found to be the effect of knowledge? Are those nations happier than we?"

"There is so much infelicity, said the poet, in the world, that scarce any man has leisure from his own distresses to estimate the comparative happiness of others. Knowledge is certainly one of the means of pleasure, as is

4. Scattering of attention.   5. Awe-inspiring.

confessed by the natural desire which every mind feels of increasing its ideas. Ignorance is mere privation, by which nothing can be produced: it is a vacuity in which the soul sits motionless and torpid for want of attraction; and, without knowing why, we always rejoice when we learn, and grieve when we forget. I am therefore inclined to conclude, that if nothing counteracts the natural consequence of learning, we grow more happy as our minds take a wider range.

"In enumerating the particular comforts of life we shall find many advantages on the side of the Europeans. They cure wounds and diseases with which we languish and perish. We suffer inclemencies of weather which they can obviate. They have engines[6] for the dispatch of many laborious works, which we must perform by manual industry. There is such communication between distant places, that one friend can hardly be said to be absent from another. Their policy removes all publick inconveniencies: they have roads cut through their mountains, and bridges laid upon their rivers. And, if we descend to the privacies of life, their habitations are more commodious, and their possessions are more secure."

"They are surely happy, said the prince, who have all these conveniencies, of which I envy none so much as the facility with which separated friends interchange their thoughts."

"The Europeans, answered Imlac, are less unhappy than we, but they are not happy. Human life is every where a state in which much is to be endured, and little to be enjoyed."

[With the help of Imlac, Rasselas, joined by his sister Nekayah, tunnels to freedom. In Cairo, with the world before them, they begin to "review it at leisure."]

CHAPTER 18

The Prince Finds a Wise and Happy Man

As he [Rasselas] was one day walking in the street, he saw a spacious building which all were, by the open doors, invited to enter: he followed the stream of people, and found it a hall or school of declamation, in which professors read lectures to their auditory. He fixed his eye upon a sage raised above the rest, who discoursed with great energy on the government of the passions. His look was venerable, his action graceful, his pronunciation clear, and his diction elegant. He shewed, with great strength of sentiment, and variety of illustration, that human nature is degraded and debased, when the lower faculties predominate over the higher; that when fancy, the parent of passion, usurps the dominion of the mind, nothing ensues but the natural effect of unlawful government, perturbation and confusion; that she betrays the fortresses of the intellect to rebels, and excites her children to sedition against reason their lawful sovereign. He compared reason to the sun, of which the light is constant, uniform, and lasting: and fancy to a meteor, of bright but transitory lustre, irregular in its motion, and delusive in its direction.

He then communicated the various precepts given from time to time for

6. Machines.

the conquest of passion, and displayed the happiness of those who had obtained the important victory, after which man is no longer the slave of fear, nor the fool of hope; is no more emaciated by envy, inflamed by anger, emasculated by tenderness, or depressed by grief; but walks on calmly through the tumults or privacies of life, as the sun pursues alike his course through the calm or the stormy sky.

He enumerated many examples of heroes immoveable by pain or pleasure, who looked with indifference on those modes or accidents to which the vulgar[7] give the names of good and evil. He exhorted his hearers to lay aside their prejudices, and arm themselves against the shafts of malice or misfortune, by invulnerable patience; concluding, that this state only was happiness, and that this happiness was in every one's power.

Rasselas listened to him with the veneration due to the instructions of a superior being, and, waiting for him at the door, humbly implored the liberty of visiting so great a master of true wisdom. The lecturer hesitated a moment, when Rasselas put a purse of gold into his hand, which he received with a mixture of joy and wonder.

"I have found, said the prince, at his return to Imlac, a man who can teach all that is necessary to be known, who, from the unshaken throne of rational fortitude, looks down on the scenes of life changing beneath him. He speaks, and attention watches his lips. He reasons, and conviction closes his periods.[8] This man shall be my future guide: I will learn his doctrines, and imitate his life."

"Be not too hasty, said Imlac, to trust, or to admire, the teachers of morality: they discourse like angels, but they live like men."

Rasselas, who could not conceive how any man could reason so forcibly without feeling the cogency of his own arguments, paid his visit in a few days, and was denied admission. He had now learned the power of money, and made his way by a piece of gold to the inner apartment, where he found the philosopher in a room half darkened, with his eyes misty, and his face pale. "Sir, said he, you are come at a time when all human friendship is useless; what I suffer cannot be remedied, what I have lost cannot be supplied. My daughter, my only daughter, from whose tenderness I expected all the comforts of my age, died last night of a fever. My views, my purposes, my hopes are at an end: I am now a lonely being disunited from society."

"Sir, said the prince, mortality is an event by which a wise man can never be surprised; we know that death is always near, and it should therefore always be expected." "Young man, answered the philosopher, you speak like one that has never felt the pangs of separation." "Have you then forgot the precepts, said Rasselas, which you so powerfully enforced? Has wisdom no strength to arm the heart against calamity? Consider, that external things are naturally variable, but truth and reason are always the same." "What comfort, said the mourner, can truth and reason afford me? of what effect are they now, but to tell me, that my daughter will not be restored?"

The prince, whose humanity would not suffer him to insult misery with reproof, went away convinced of the emptiness of rhetorical sound, and the inefficacy of polished periods and studied sentences.

7. Common people.　8. Sentences.

[After various unsuccessful efforts to find examples of happiness, Rasselas and his sister decided to divide the enterprise between them. He will investigate the splendor of courts; she will look into the satisfactions of humbler life.]

CHAPTER 24

The Prince Examines the Happiness of High Stations

Rasselas applauded the design, and appeared next day with a splendid retinue at the court of the Bassa.[9] He was soon distinguished for his magnificence, and admitted as a prince whose curiosity had brought him from distant countries, to an intimacy with the great officers, and frequent conversation with the Bassa himself.

He was at first inclined to believe, that the man must be pleased with his own condition, whom all approached with reverence, and heard with obedience, and who had the power to extend his edicts to a whole kingdom. "There can be no pleasure, said he, equal to that of feeling at once the joy of thousands all made happy by wise administration. Yet, since, by the law of subordination, this sublime delight can be in one nation but the lot of one, it is surely reasonable to think, that there is some satisfaction more popular and accessible, and that millions can hardly be subjected to the will of a single man, only to fill his particular breast with incommunicable content."

These thoughts were often in his mind, and he found no solution of the difficulty. But as presents and civilities gained him more familiarity, he found that almost every man who stood high in employment hated all the rest, and was hated by them, and that their lives were a continual succession of plots and detections, stratagems and escapes, faction and treachery. Many of those, who surrounded the Bassa, were sent only to watch and report his conduct; every tongue was muttering censure, and every eye was searching for a fault.

At last the letters of revocation arrived, the Bassa was carried in chains to Constantinople, and his name was mentioned no more.

"What are we now to think of the prerogatives of power, said Rasselas to his sister; is it without any efficacy to good? or, is the subordinate degree only dangerous, and the supreme safe and glorious? Is the Sultan the only happy man in his dominions? or, is the Sultan himself subject to the torments of suspicion, and the dread of enemies?"

In a short time the second Bassa was deposed. The Sultan, that had advanced him, was murdered by the Janisaries,[1] and his successor had other views and different favourites.

CHAPTER 25

The Princess Pursues Her Inquiry with More Diligence than Success

The princess, in the mean time, insinuated herself into many families; for there are few doors, through which liberality, joined with good humour, cannot find its way. The daughters of many houses were airy[2] and cheerful, but

---

9. A high official in Egypt. 1. Turkish guards. 2. Lively.

Nekayah had been too long accustomed to the conversation of Imlac and her brother to be much pleased with childish levity and prattle which had no meaning. She found their thoughts narrow, their wishes low, and their merriment often artificial. Their pleasures, poor as they were, could not be preserved pure, but were embittered by petty competitions and worthless emulation. They were always jealous of the beauty of each other; of a quality to which solicitude can add nothing, and from which detraction can take nothing away. Many were in love with triflers like themselves, and many fancied that they were in love when in truth they were only idle. Their affection was [seldom] fixed on sense or virtue, and therefore seldom ended but in vexation. Their grief, however, like their joy, was transient; every thing floated in their mind unconnected with the past or future, so that one desire easily gave way to another, as a second stone cast into the water effaces and confounds the circles of the first.

With these girls she played as with inoffensive animals, and found them proud of her countenance,[3] and weary of her company.

But her purpose was to examine more deeply, and her affability easily persuaded the hearts that were swelling with sorrow to discharge their secrets in her ear: and those whom hope flattered, or prosperity delighted, often courted her to partake their pleasures.

The princess and her brother commonly met in the evening in a private summer-house on the bank of the Nile, and related to each other the occurrences of the day. As they were sitting together, the princess cast her eyes upon the river that flowed before her. "Answer, said she, great father of waters, thou that rollest thy floods through eighty nations, to the invocations of the daughter of thy native king. Tell me if thou waterest, through all thy course, a single habitation from which thou dost not hear the murmurs of complaint?"

"You are then, said Rasselas, not more successful in private houses than I have been in courts." "I have, since the last partition of our provinces, said the princess, enabled myself to enter familiarly into many families, where there was the fairest shew of prosperity and peace, and know not one house that is not haunted by some fury that destroys their quiet.

"I did not seek ease among the poor, because I concluded that there it could not be found. But I saw many poor, whom I had supposed to live in affluence. Poverty has, in large cities, very different appearances: it is often concealed in splendour, and often in extravagance. It is the care of a very great part of mankind to conceal their indigence from the rest: they support themselves by temporary expedients, and every day is lost in contriving for the morrow.

"This, however, was an evil, which, though frequent, I saw with less pain, because I could relieve it. Yet some have refused my bounties; more offended with my quickness to detect their wants, than pleased with my readiness to succour them: and others, whose exigencies compelled them to admit my kindness, have never been able to forgive their benefactress. Many, however, have been sincerely grateful, without the ostentation of gratitude, or the hope of other favours."

3. Favor.

CHAPTER 26

The Princess Continues Her Remarks on Private Life

Nekayah perceiving her brother's attention fixed, proceeded in her narrative.

"In families, where there is or is not poverty, there is commonly discord: if a kingdom be, as Imlac tells us, a great family, a family likewise is a little kingdom, torn with factions, and exposed to revolutions. An unpracticed observer expects the love of parents and children to be constant and equal; but this kindness seldom continues beyond the years of infancy: in a short time the children become rivals to their parents. Benefits are allayed by reproaches, and gratitude debased by envy.

"Parents and children seldom act in concert: each child endeavours to appropriate the esteem or fondness of the parents, and the parents, with yet less temptation, betray each other to their children; thus some place their confidence in the father, and some in the mother, and by degrees, the house is filled with artifices and feuds.

"The opinions of children and parents, of the young and the old, are naturally opposite, by the contrary effects of hope and despondence, of expectation and experience, without crime or folly on either side. The colours of life in youth and age appear different, as the face of nature in spring and winter. And how can children credit the assertions of parents, which their own eyes show them to be false?

"Few parents act in such a manner as much to enforce their maxims by the credit of their lives. The old man trusts wholly to slow contrivance and gradual progression: the youth expects to force his way by genius, vigour, and precipitance. The old man pays regard to riches, and the youth reverences virtue. The old man deifies prudence: the youth commits himself to magnanimity and chance. The young man, who intends no ill, believes that none is intended, and therefore acts with openness and candour:[4] but his father, having suffered the injuries of fraud, is impelled to suspect, and too often allured to practise it. Age looks with anger on the temerity of youth, and youth with contempt on the scrupulosity of age. Thus parents and children, for the greatest part, live on to love less and less: and, if those whom nature has thus closely united are the torments of each other, where shall we look for tenderness and consolation?"

"Surely, said the prince, you must have been unfortunate in your choice of acquaintance: I am unwilling to believe, that the most tender of all relations is thus impeded in its effects by natural necessity."

"Domestick discord, answered she, is not inevitably and fatally necessary; but yet it is not easily avoided. We seldom see that a whole family is virtuous: the good and evil cannot well agree; and the evil can yet less agree with one another: even the virtuous fall sometimes to variance, when their virtues are of different kinds, and tending to extremes. In general, those parents have most reverence who most deserve it: for he that lives well cannot be despised.

"Many other evils infest private life. Some are the slaves of servants whom

4. Generosity.

they have trusted with their affairs. Some are kept in continual anxiety to the caprice of rich relations, whom they cannot please, and dare not offend. Some husbands are imperious, and some wives perverse: and, as it is always more easy to do evil than good, though the wisdom or virtue of one can very rarely make many happy, the folly or vice of one may often make many miserable."

"If such be the general effect of marriage, said the prince, I shall, for the future, think it dangerous to connect my interest with that of another, lest I should be unhappy by my partner's fault."

"I have met, said the princess, with many who live single for that reason; but I never found that their prudence ought to raise envy. They dream away their time without friendship, without fondness, and are driven to rid themselves of the day, for which they have no use, by childish amusements, or vicious delights. They act as beings under the constant sense of some known inferiority, that fills their minds with rancour, and their tongues with censure. They are peevish at home, and malevolent abroad; and, as the outlaws of human nature, make it their business and their pleasure to disturb that society which debars them from its privileges. To live without feeling or exciting sympathy, to be fortunate without adding to the felicity of others, or afflicted with out tasting the balm of pity, is a state more gloomy than solitude: it is not retreat, but exclusion from mankind. Marriage has many pains, but celibacy has no pleasures."

"What then is to be done? said Rasselas; the more we inquire, the less we can resolve. Surely he is most likely to please himself that has no other inclination to regard."

CHAPTER 27

Disquisition Upon Greatness

The conversation had a short pause. The prince, having considered his sister's observations, told her, that she had surveyed life with prejudice, and supposed misery where she did not find it. "Your narrative, says he, throws yet a darker gloom upon the prospects of futurity: the predictions of Imlac were but faint sketches of the evils painted by Nekayah. I have been lately convinced that quiet is not the daughter of grandeur, or of power: that her presence is not to be bought by wealth, nor enforced by conquest. It is evident, that as any man acts in a wider compass, he must be more exposed to opposition from enmity or miscarriage from chance; whoever has many to please or to govern, must use the ministry of many agents, some of whom will be wicked, and some ignorant; by some he will be misled, and by others betrayed. If he gratifies one he will offend another: those that are not favoured will think themselves injured; and, since favours can be conferred but upon few, the greater number will be always discontented."

"The discontent, said the princess, which is thus unreasonable, I hope that I shall always have spirit to despise, and you, power to repress."

"Discontent, answered Rasselas, will not always be without reason under the most just and vigilant administration of publick affairs. None, however attentive, can always discover that merit which indigence or faction may happen to obscure; and none, however powerful, can always reward it. Yet, he that sees inferiour desert[5] advanced above him, will naturally impute that preference to partiality or caprice; and, indeed, it can scarcely be hoped that any man, however magnanimous by nature, or exalted by condition, will be able to persist for ever in the fixed and inexorable justice of distribution: he will sometimes indulge his own affections, and sometimes those of his favourites; he will permit some to please him who can never serve him; he will discover in those whom he loves, qualities which in reality they do not possess; and to those, from whom he receives pleasure, he will in his turn endeavour to give it. Thus will recommendations sometimes prevail which were purchased by money, or by the more destructive bribery of flattery and servility.

"He that has much to do will do something wrong, and of that wrong must suffer the consequences; and, if it were possible that he should always act rightly, yet when such numbers are to judge of his conduct, the bad will censure and obstruct him by malevolence, and the good sometimes by mistake.

"The highest stations cannot therefore hope to be the abodes of happiness, which I would willingly believe to have fled from thrones and palaces to seats[6] of humble privacy and placid obscurity. For what can hinder the satisfaction, or intercept the expectations, of him whose abilities are adequate to his employments, who sees with his own eyes the whole circuit of his influence, who chooses by his own knowledge all whom he trusts, and whom none are tempted to deceive by hope or fear? Surely he has nothing to do but to love and to be loved, to be virtuous and to be happy."

"Whether perfect happiness would be procured by perfect goodness, said Nekayah, this world will never afford an opportunity of deciding. But this, at least, may be maintained, that we do not always find visible happiness in proportion to visible virtue. All natural, and almost all political evils, are incident alike to the bad and good: they are confounded in the misery of a famine, and not much distinguished in the fury of a faction; they sink together in a tempest, and are driven together from their country by invaders. All that virtue can afford is quietness of conscience, a steady prospect of a happier state; this may enable us to endure calamity with patience; but remember that patience must suppose pain."

CHAPTER 28

Rasselas and Nekayah Continue Their Conversation

"Dear princess, said Rasselas, you fall into the common errours of exaggeratory declamation, by producing, in a familiar disquisition, examples of national calamities, and scenes of extensive misery, which are found in books rather than in the world, and which, as they are horrid, are ordained to be rare. Let us not imagine evils which we do not feel, nor injure life by misrepresentations. I cannot bear that querulous eloquence which threatens every city with a siege like that of Jerusalem,[7] that makes famine attend on every flight of locusts, and suspends pestilence on the wing of every blast that issues from the south.

5. Merit, worth.   6. Residences.   7. The siege of A.D. 70, after which Titus captured and destroyed the city.

"On necessary and inevitable evils, which overwhelm kingdoms at once, all disputation is vain: when they happen they must be endured. But it is evident, that these bursts of universal distress are more dreaded than felt; thousands and ten thousands flourish in youth, and wither in age, without the knowledge of any other than domestick evils, and share the same plea- sures and vexations, whether their kings are mild or cruel, whether the armies of their country pursue their enemies, or retreat before them. While courts are disturbed with intestine[8] competitions, and ambassadors are negociating in foreign countries, the smith still plies his anvil, and the husbandman drives his plow forward; the necessaries of life are required and obtained; and the successive business of the seasons continues to make its wonted revolutions.

"Let us cease to consider what, perhaps, may never happen, and what, when it shall happen, will laugh at human speculation. We will not endeav- our to modify the motions of the elements, or to fix the destiny of kingdoms. It is our business to consider what beings like us may perform; each labouring for his own happiness, by promoting within his circle, however narrow, the happiness of others.

"Marriage is evidently the dictate of nature; men and women are made to be companions of each other, and therefore I cannot be persuaded but that marriage is one of the means of happiness."

"I know not, said the princess, whether marriage be more than one of the innumerable modes of human misery. When I see and reckon the various forms of connubial infelicity, the unexpected causes of lasting discord, the diversities of temper, the oppositions of opinion, the rude collisions of con- trary desire where both are urged by violent impulses, the obstinate contests of disagreeable virtues, where both are supported by consciousness of good intention, I am sometimes disposed to think with the severer casuists of most nations, that marriage is rather permitted than approved, and that none, but by the instigation of a passion too much indulged, entangle themselves with indissoluble compacts."

"You seem to forget, replied Rasselas, that you have, even now, represented celibacy as less happy than marriage. Both conditions may be bad, but they cannot both be worst. Thus it happens when wrong opinions are entertained, that they mutually destroy each other, and leave the mind open to truth."

"I did not expect, answered the princess, to hear that imputed to falsehood which is the consequence only of frailty. To the mind, as to the eye, it is difficult to compare with exactness objects vast in their extent, and various in their parts. Where we see or conceive the whole at once, we readily note the discriminations, and decide the preference: but of two systems, of which neither can be surveyed by any human being in its full compass of magnitude and multiplicity of complication, where is the wonder, that judging of the whole by parts, I am alternately affected by one and the other as either presses on my memory or fancy? We differ from ourselves just as we differ from each other, when we see only part of the question, as in the multifarious relations of politicks and morality; but when we perceive the whole at once, as in numerical computations, all agree in one judgment, and none ever varies his opinion."

"Let us not add, said the prince, to the other evils of life, the bitterness of controversy, nor endeavour to vie with each other in subtleties of argument.

8. Internal.

We are employed in a search, of which both are equally to enjoy the success, or suffer by the miscarriage. It is therefore fit that we assist each other. You surely conclude too hastily from the infelicity of marriage against its institution: will not the misery of life prove equally that life cannot be the gift of heaven? The world must be peopled by marriage, or peopled without it."

"How the world is to be peopled, returned Nekayah, is not my care, and needs not be yours. I see no danger that the present generation should omit to leave successors behind them: we are not now inquiring for the world, but for ourselves."

CHAPTER 29

The Debate of Marriage Continued

"The good of the whole, says Rasselas, is the same with the good of all its parts. If marriage be best for mankind it must be evidently best for individuals, or a permanent and necessary duty must be the cause of evil, and some must be inevitably sacrificed to the convenience of others. In the estimate which you have made of the two states, it appears that the incommodities of a single life are, in a great measure, necessary and certain, but those of the conjugal state accidental and avoidable.

"I cannot forbear to flatter myself, that prudence and benevolence will make marriage happy. The general folly of mankind is the cause of general complaint. What can be expected but disappointment and repentance from a choice made in the immaturity of youth, in the ardour of desire, without judgment, without foresight, without inquiry after conformity of opinions, similarity of manners, rectitude of judgment, or purity of sentiment.

"Such is the common process of marriage. A youth or maiden meeting by chance, or brought together by artifice, exchange glances, reciprocate civilities, go home, and dream of one another. Having little to divert attention, or diversify thought, they find themselves uneasy when they are apart, and therefore conclude that they shall be happy together. They marry, and discover what nothing but voluntary blindness before had concealed; they wear out life in altercations, and charge nature with cruelty.

"From those early marriages proceeds likewise the rivalry of parents and children: the son is eager to enjoy the world before the father is willing to forsake it, and there is hardly room at once for two generations. The daughter begins to bloom before the mother can be content to fade, and neither can forbear to wish for the absence of the other.

"Surely all these evils may be avoided by that deliberation and delay which prudence prescribes to irrevocable choice. In the variety and jollity of youthful pleasures life may be well enough supported without the help of a partner. Longer time will increase experience, and wider views will allow better opportunities of inquiry and selection: one advantage, at least, will be certain; the parents will be visibly older than their children."

"What reason cannot collect, said Nekayah, and what experiment has not yet taught, can be known only from the report of others. I have been told that late marriages are not eminently happy. This is a question too important to be neglected, and I have often proposed it to those, whose accuracy of remark, and comprehensiveness of knowledge, made their suffrages[9] worthy

9. Opinions.

of regard. They have generally determined, that it is dangerous for a man and woman to suspend their fate upon each other, at a time when opinions are fixed, and habits are established; when friendships have been contracted on both sides, when life has been planned into method, and the mind has long enjoyed the contemplation of its own prospects.

"It is scarcely possible that two travelling through the world under the conduct of chance, should have been both directed to the same path, and it will not often happen that either will quit the track which custom has made pleasing. When the desultory levity of youth has settled into regularity, it is soon succeeded by pride ashamed to yield, or obstinacy delighting to contend. And even though mutual esteem produces mutual desire to please, time itself, as it modifies unchangeably the external mien, determines likewise the direction of the passions, and gives an inflexible rigidity to the manners. Long customs are not easily broken: he that attempts to change the course of his own life, very often labours in vain; and how shall we do that for others, which we are seldom able to do for ourselves?"

"But surely, interposed the prince, you suppose the chief motive of choice forgotten or neglected. Whenever I shall seek a wife, it shall be my first question, whether she be willing to be led by reason?"

"Thus it is, said Nekayah, that philosophers are deceived. There are a thousand familiar disputes which reason never can decide; questions that elude investigation, and make logick ridiculous; cases where something must be done, and where little can be said. Consider the state of mankind, and inquire how few can be supposed to act upon any occasions, whether small or great, with all the reasons of action present to their minds. Wretched would be the pair above all names of wretchedness, who should be doomed to adjust by reason, every morning, all the minute detail of a domestick day.

"Those who marry at an advanced age, will probably escape the encroachments of their children; but, in diminution of this advantage, they will be likely to leave them, ignorant and helpless, to a guardian's mercy: or, if that should not happen, they must at least go out of the world before they see those whom they love best either wise or great.

"From their children, if they have less to fear, they have less also to hope, and they lose, without equivalent, the joys of early love, and the convenience of uniting with manners pliant, and minds susceptible of new impressions, which might wear away their dissimilitudes by long cohabitation, as soft bodies, by continual attrition, conform their surfaces to each other.

"I believe it will be found that those who marry late are best pleased with their children, and those who marry early with their partners."

"The union of these two affections, said Rasselas, would produce all that could be wished. Perhaps there is a time when marriage might unite them, a time neither too early for the father, nor too late for the husband."

"Every hour, answered the princess, confirms my prejudice in favour of the position so often uttered by the mouth of Imlac, 'That nature sets her gifts on the right hand and on the left.' Those conditions, which flatter hope and attract desire, are so constituted, that, as we approach one, we recede from another. There are goods so opposed that we cannot seize both but, by too much prudence, may pass between them at too great a distance to reach either. This is often the fate of long consideration; he does nothing who endeavours to do more than is allowed to humanity. Flatter not yourself with contrarieties of pleasure. Of the blessings set before you make your choice, and be content. No man can taste the fruits of autumn while he is delighting his scent with the flowers of the spring: no man can, at the same time, fill his cup from the source and from the mouth of the Nile."

[They decide to visit the pyramids, as monuments of the past. Nekayah's attendant, Pekuah, is frightened and remains behind.]

CHAPTER 31

They Enter the Pyramid

Pekuah descended to the tents, and the rest entered the pyramid: they passed through the galleries, surveyed the vaults of marble, and examined the chest in which the body of the founder is supposed to have been reposited. They then sat down in one of the most spacious chambers to rest a while before they attempted to return.

"We have now, said Imlac, gratified our minds with an exact view of the greatest work of man, except the wall of China.

"Of the wall it is very easy to assign the motive. It secured a wealthy and timorous nation from the incursions of Barbarians, whose unskilfulness in arts made it easier for them to supply their wants by rapine than by industry, and who from time to time poured in upon the habitations of peaceful commerce, as vultures descend upon domestick fowl. Their celerity and fierceness made the wall necessary, and their ignorance made it efficacious.

"But for the pyramids no reason has ever been given adequate to the cost and labour of the work. The narrowness of the chambers proves that it could afford no retreat from enemies, and treasures might have been reposited at far less expence with equal security. It seems to have been erected only in compliance with that hunger of imagination which preys incessantly upon life, and must be always appeased by some employment. Those who have already all that they can enjoy, must enlarge their desires. He that has built for use, till use is supplied, must begin to build for vanity, and extend his plan to the utmost power of human performance, that he may not be soon reduced to form another wish.

"I consider this mighty structure as a monument of the insufficiency of human enjoyments. A king, whose power is unlimited, and whose treasures surmount all real and imaginary wants, is compelled to solace, by the erection of a pyramid, the satiety of dominion and tastelessness of pleasures, and to amuse the tediousness of declining life, by seeing thousands labouring without end, and one stone, for no purpose, laid upon another. Whoever thou art, that, not content with a moderate condition, imaginest happiness in royal magnificence, and dreamest that command or riches can feed the appetite of novelty with perpetual gratifications, survey the pyramids, and confess thy folly!"

[Pekuah is kidnapped by an Arab, but eventually returns to her friends.]

CHAPTER 34

The History of a Man of Learning

They returned to Cairo, and were so well pleased at finding themselves together, that none of them went much abroad. The prince began to love learning, and one day declared to Imlac, that he intended to devote himself to science,[1] and pass the rest of his days in literary solitude.

"Before you make your final choice, answered Imlac, you ought to examine its hazards, and converse with some of those who are grown old in the company of themselves. I have just left the observatory of one of the most learned astronomers in the world, who has spent forty years in unwearied attention to the motions and appearances of the celestial bodies, and has drawn out his soul in endless calculations. He admits a few friends once a month to hear his deductions and enjoy his discoveries. I was introduced as a man of knowledge worthy of his notice. Men of various ideas, and fluent conversation, are commonly welcome to those whose thoughts have been long fixed upon a single point, and who find the images of other things stealing away. I delighted him with my remarks; he smiled at the narrative of my travels, and was glad to forget the constellations, and descend for a moment into the lower world.

"On the next day of vacation I renewed my visit, and was so fortunate as to please him again. He relaxed from that time the severity of his rule, and permitted me to enter at my own choice. I found him always busy, and always glad to be relieved. As each knew much which the other was desirous of learning, we exchanged our notions with great delight. I perceived that I had every day more of his confidence, and always found new cause of admiration in the profundity of his mind. His comprehension is vast, his memory capacious and retentive, his discourse is methodical, and his expression clear.

"His integrity and benevolence are equal to his learning. His deepest researches and most favourite studies are willingly interrupted for any opportunity of doing good by his counsel or his riches. To his closest retreat, at his most busy moments, all are admitted that want his assistance: "For though I exclude idleness and pleasure, I will never, says he, bar my doors against charity. To man is permitted the contemplation of the skies, but the practice of virtue is commanded.""

"Surely, said the princess, this man is happy."

"I visited him, said Imlac, with more and more frequency, and was every time more enamoured of his conversation: he was sublime without haughtiness, courteous without formality, and communicative without ostentation. I was at first, great princess, of your opinion, thought him the happiest of mankind, and often congratulated him on the blessing that he enjoyed. He seemed to hear nothing with indifference but the praises of his condition, to which he always returned a general answer, and diverted the conversation to some other topick."

"Amidst this willingness to be pleased, and labour to please, I had quickly reason to imagine that some painful sentiment pressed upon his mind. He often looked up earnestly towards the sun, and let his voice fall in the midst of his discourse. He would sometimes when we were alone, gaze upon me in silence with the air of a man who longed to speak what he was yet resolved to suppress. He would often send for me with vehement injunctions of haste, though, when I came to him, he had nothing extraordinary to say. And sometimes, when I was leaving him, would call me back, pause a few moments, and then dismiss me.

1. Knowledge.

CHAPTER 40

The Astronomer Discovers the Cause of His Uneasiness

"At last the time came when the secret burst his reserve. We were sitting together last night in the turret of his house, watching the emersion[2] of a satellite of Jupiter. A sudden tempest clouded the sky, and disappointed our observation. We sat a while silent in the dark, and then he addressed himself to me in these words; "Imlac, I have long considered thy friendship as the greatest blessing of my life. Integrity without knowledge is weak and useless, and knowledge without integrity is dangerous and dreadful. I have found in thee all the qualities requisite for trust, benevolence, experience, and forti-tude. I have long discharged an office which I must soon quit at the call of nature, and shall rejoice in the hour of imbecility and pain to devolve it upon thee."

"I thought myself honoured by this testimony, and protested, that whatever could conduce to his happiness would add likewise to mine."

"Hear Imlac, what thou wilt not without difficulty credit. I have possessed for five years the regulation of weather, and the distribution of the seasons: the sun has listened to my dictates, and passed from tropick to tropick by my direction; the clouds, at my call, have poured their waters, and the Nile has overflowed at my command; I have restrained the rage of the dogstar, and mitigated the fervours of the crab.[3] The winds alone, of all the elemental powers, have hitherto refused my authority, and multitudes have perished by equinoctial tempests, which I found myself unable to prohibit or restrain. I have administered this great office with exact justice, and made to the different nations of the earth an impartial dividend of rain and sunshine. What must have been the misery of half the globe, if I had limited the clouds to particular regions, or confined the sun to either side of the equator?"

CHAPTER 41

The Opinion of the Astronomer is Explained and Justified

"I suppose he discovered in me, through the obscurity of the room, some tokens of amazement and doubt, for, after a short pause, he proceeded thus:"

"Not to be easily credited will neither surprise nor offend me; for I am, probably, the first of human beings to whom this trust has been imparted. Nor do I know whether to deem this distinction a reward or punishment; since I have possessed it I have been far less happy than before, and nothing but the consciousness of good intention could have enabled me to support the weariness of unremitted vigilance."

"How long, Sir, said I, has this great office been in your hands?"

"About ten years ago, said he, my daily observations of the changes of the sky led me to consider, whether, if I had the power of the seasons, I could confer greater plenty upon the inhabitants of the earth. This contemplation

---

2. Reappearance (after having been obscured, e.g., by clouds).   3. The constellation Cancer, associated with the summer solstice. *The dogstar:* Sirius, which rises in late summer and was supposed to cause insanity.

fastened on my mind, and I sat days and nights in imaginary dominion, pouring upon this country and that the showers of fertility, and seconding every fall of rain with a due proportion of sunshine. I had yet only the will to do good, and did not imagine that I should ever have the power.

"One day, as I was looking on the fields withering with heat, I felt in my mind a sudden wish that I could send rain on the southern mountains, and raise the Nile to an inundation. In the hurry of my imagination I commanded rain to fall, and by comparing the time of my command, with that of the inundation, I found that the clouds had listened to my lips."

"Might not some other cause, said I, produce this concurrence? the Nile does not always rise on the same day."

"Do not believe, said he with impatience, that such objections could escape me: I reasoned long against my own conviction, and laboured against truth with the utmost obstinacy. I sometimes suspected myself of madness, and should not have dared to impart this secret but to a man like you, capable of distinguishing the wonderful from the impossible, and the incredible from the false."

"Why, Sir, said I, do you call that incredible, which you know, or think you know, to be true?"

"Because, said he, I cannot prove it by any external evidence; and I know too well the laws of demonstration to think that my conviction ought to influence another, who cannot, like me, be conscious of its force. I, therefore, shall not attempt to gain credit by disputation. It is sufficient that I feel this power, that I have long possessed, and every day exerted it. But the life of man is short, the infirmities of age increase upon me, and the time will soon come, when the regulator of the year must mingle with the dust. The care of appointing a successor has long disturbed me; the night and the day have been spent in comparisons of all the characters which have come to my knowledge, and I have yet found none so worthy as thyself.

CHAPTER 42

The Astronomer Leaves Imlac His Directions

"Hear, therefore, what I shall impart with attention, such as the welfare of a world requires. If the task of a king be considered as difficult, who has the care only of a few millions, to whom he cannot do much good or harm, what must be the anxiety of him, on whom depends the action of the elements, and the great gifts of light and heat!—Hear me therefore with attention.

"I have diligently considered the position of the earth and sun, and formed innumerable schemes in which I changed their situation. I have sometimes turned aside the axis of the earth, and sometimes varied the ecliptick of the sun: but I have found it impossible to make a disposition by which the world may be advantaged; what one region gains, another loses by any imaginable alteration, even without considering the distant parts of the solar system with which we are unacquainted. Do not therefore, in thy administration of the year, indulge thy pride by innovation; do not please thyself with thinking that thou canst make thyself renowned to all future ages, by disordering the seasons. The memory of mischief is no desirable fame. Much less will it become thee to let kindness or interest[4] prevail. Never rob other countries of rain to pour it on thine own. For us the Nile is sufficient."

"I promised, that when I possessed the power, I would use it with inflexible integrity; and he dismissed me, pressing my hand." "My heart, said he, will be now at rest, and my benevolence will no more destroy my quiet; I have found a man of wisdom and virtue, to whom I can cheerfully bequeath the inheritance of the sun."

The prince heard this narration with very serious regard; but the princess smiled, and Pekuah convulsed herself with laughter. "Ladies, said Imlac, to mock the heaviest of human afflictions is neither charitable nor wise. Few can attain this man's knowledge, and few practise his virtues; but all may suffer his calamity. Of the uncertainties of our present state, the most dreadful and alarming is the uncertain continuance of reason."

The princess was recollected, and the favourite was abashed. Rasselas, more deeply affected, inquired of Imlac, whether he thought such maladies of the mind frequent, and how they were contracted?

CHAPTER 43

The Dangerous Prevalence of Imagination

"Disorders of intellect, answered Imlac, happen much more often than superficial observers will easily believe. Perhaps, if we speak with rigorous exactness, no human mind is in its right state. There is no man whose imagination does not sometimes predominate over his reason, who can regulate his attention wholly by his will, and whose ideas will come and go at his command. No man will be found in whose mind airy notions do not sometimes tyrannize, and force him to hope or fear beyond the limits of sober probability. All power of fancy over reason is a degree of insanity; but while this power is such as we can control and repress, it is not visible to others, nor considered as any depravation of the mental faculties: it is not pronounced madness but when it comes ungovernable, and apparently[5] influences speech or action.

"To indulge the power of fiction, and send imagination out upon the wing, is often the sport of those who delight too much in silent speculation. When we are alone we are not always busy; the labour of excogitation is too violent to last long; the ardour of inquiry will sometimes give way to idleness or satiety. He who has nothing external that can divert him, must find pleasure in his own thoughts, and must conceive himself what he is not; for who is pleased with what he is? He then expatiates in boundless futurity, and culls from all imaginable conditions that which for the present moment he should most desire, amuses his desires with impossible enjoyments, and confers upon his pride unattainable dominion. The mind dances from scene to scene, unites all pleasures in all combinations, and riots in delights, which nature and fortune, with all their bounty, cannot bestow.

"In time, some particular train of ideas fixes the attention, all other intellectual gratifications are rejected, the mind, in weariness or leisure, recurs constantly to the favourite conception, and feasts on the luscious falsehood,

4. Self-interest.   5. Obviously. *Comes:* becomes.

whenever she is offended with the bitterness of truth. By degrees the reign of fancy is confirmed; she grows first imperious, and in time despotick. The fictions begin to operate as realities, false opinions fasten upon the mind, and life passes in dreams of rapture or of anguish.

"This, Sir, is one of the dangers of solitude, which the hermit has confessed not always to promote goodness, and the astronomer's misery has proved to be not always propitious to wisdom."

"I will no more, said the favourite, imagine myself the queen of Abissinia. I have often spent the hours, which the princess gave to my own disposal, in adjusting ceremonies and regulating the court; I have repressed the pride of the powerful, and granted the petitions of the poor; I have built new palaces in more happy situations, planted groves upon the tops of mountains, and have exulted in the beneficence of royalty, till, when the princess entered, I had almost forgotten to bow down before her."

"And I, said the princess, will not allow myself any more to play the shepherdess in my waking dreams. I have often soothed my thoughts with the quiet and innocence of pastoral employments, till I have in my chamber heard the winds whistle, and the sheep bleat: sometimes freed the lamb entangled in the thicket, and sometimes with my crook encountered the wolf. I have a dress like that of the village maids, which I put on to help my imagination, and a pipe on which I play softly, and suppose myself followed by my flocks."

"I will confess, said the prince, an indulgence of fantastick delight more dangerous than yours. I have frequently endeavoured to image the possibility of a perfect government, by which all wrong should be restrained, all vice reformed, and all the subjects preserved in tranquillity and innocence. This thought produced innumerable schemes of reformation, and dictated many useful regulations and salutary edicts. This has been the sport, and sometimes the labour, of my solitude; and I start, when I think with how little anguish I once supposed the death of my father and my brothers."

"Such, says Imlac, are the effects of visionary schemes: when we first form them we know them to be absurd, but familiarize them by degrees, and in time lose sight of their folly."

CHAPTER 44

They Discourse with an Old Man

The evening was now far past, and they rose to return home. As they walked along the bank of the Nile, delighted with the beams of the moon quivering on the water, they saw at a small distance an old man, whom the prince had often heard in the assembly of the sages. "Yonder, said he, is one whose years have calmed his passions, but not clouded his reason: let us close the disquisitions of the night, by inquiring what are his sentiments of his own state, that we may know whether youth alone is to struggle with vexation, and whether any better hope remains for the latter part of life."

Here the sage approached and saluted them. They invited him to join their walk, and prattled a while, as acquaintances that had unexpectedly met one another. The old man was cheerful and talkative, and the way seemed short in his company. He was pleased to find himself not disregarded, accompanied them to their house, and, at the prince's request, entered with them. They placed him in the seat of honour, and set wine and conserves before him.

"Sir, said the princess, an evening walk must give to a man of learning, like you, pleasures which ignorance and youth can hardly conceive. You know the qualities and the causes of all that you behold, the laws by which the river flows, the periods in which the planets perform their revolutions. Every thing must supply you with contemplation, and renew the consciousness of your own dignity."

"Lady, answered he, let the gay and the vigorous expect pleasure in their excursions, it is enough that age can obtain ease. To me the world has lost its novelty: I look round, and see what I remember to have seen in happier days. I rest against a tree, and consider, that in the same shade I once disputed upon the annual overflow of the Nile with a friend who is now silent in the grave. I cast my eyes upwards, fix them on the changing moon, and think with pain on the vicissitudes of life. I have ceased to take much delight in physical truth; for what have I to do with those things which I am soon to leave?"

"You may at least recreate yourself, said Imlac, with the recollection of an honourable and useful life, and enjoy the praise which all agree to give you."

"Praise, said the sage, with a sigh, is to an old man an empty sound. I have neither mother to be delighted with the reputation of her son, nor wife to partake the honours of her husband. I have outlived my friends and my rivals. Nothing is now of much importance; for I cannot extend my interest beyond myself. Youth is delighted with applause, because it is considered as the earnest of some future good, and because the prospect of life is far extended: but to me, who am now declining to decrepitude, there is little to be feared from the malevolence of men, and yet less to be hoped from their affection or esteem. Something they may yet take away, but they can give me nothing. Riches would now be useless, and high employment would be pain. My retrospect of life recalls to my view many opportunities of good neglected, much time squandered upon trifles, and more lost in idleness and vacancy.[6] I leave many great designs unattempted, and many great attempts unfinished. My mind is burdened with no heavy crime, and therefore I compose myself to tranquillity; endeavour to abstract my thoughts from hopes and cares, which, though reason knows them to be vain, still try to keep their old possession of the heart; expect, with serene humility, that hour which nature cannot long delay; and hope to possess, in a better state, that happiness which here I could not find, and that virtue which here I have not attained."

He rose and went away, leaving his audience not much elated with the hope of long life. The prince consoled himself with remarking, that it was not reasonable to be disappointed by this account; for age had never been considered as the season of felicity, and if it was possible to be easy in decline and weakness, it was likely that the days of vigour and alacrity might be happy: that the noon of life might be bright, if the evening could be calm.

The princess suspected that age was querulous and malignant, and delighted to repress the expectations of those who had newly entered the

6. Inactivity.

world. She had seen the possessors of estates look with envy on their heirs, and known many who enjoyed pleasure no longer than they can confine it to themselves.

Pekuah conjectured, that the man was older than he appeared, and was willing to impute his complaints to delirious dejection; or else supposed that he had been unfortunate, and was therefore discontented: "For nothing, said she, is more common, than to call our own condition the condition of life."

Imlac, who had no desire to see them depressed, smiled at the comforts which they could so readily procure to themselves, and remembered, that at the same age, he was equally confident of unmingled prosperity, and equally fertile of consolatory expedients. He forbore to force upon them unwelcome knowledge, which time itself would too soon impress. The princess and her lady retired; the madness of the astronomer hung upon their minds, and they desired Imlac to enter upon his office, and delay next morning the rising of the sun.

CHAPTER 45

The Princess and Pekuah Visit the Astronomer

The princess and Pekuah having talked in private of Imlac's astronomer, thought his character at once so amiable and so strange, that they could not be satisfied without a nearer knowledge; and Imlac was requested to find the means of bringing them together.

This was somewhat difficult; the philosopher had never received any visits from women, though he lived in a city that had in it many Europeans who followed the manners of their own countries, and many from other parts of the world, that lived there with European liberty. The ladies would not be refused, and several schemes were proposed for the accomplishment of their design. It was proposed to introduce them as strangers in distress, to whom the sage was always accessible; but, after some deliberation, it appeared, that by this artifice, no acquaintance could be formed, for their conversation would be short, and they could not decently importune him often. "This, said Rasselas, is true; but I have yet a stronger objection against the misrepresentation of your state. I have always considered it as treason against the great republic of human nature, to make any man's virtues the means of deceiving him, whether on great or little occasions. All imposture weakens confidence, and chills benevolence. When the sage finds that you are not what you seemed, he will feel the resentment natural to a man who, conscious of great abilities, discovers that he has been tricked by understandings meaner than his own, and, perhaps, the distrust, which he can never afterwards wholly lay aside, may stop the voice of counsel, and close the hand of charity; and where will you find the power of restoring his benefactions to mankind, or his peace to himself?"

To this no reply was attempted, and Imlac began to hope that their curiosity would subside; but, next day, Pekuah told him, she had now found an honest pretence for a visit to the astronomer, for she would solicit permission to continue under him the studies in which she had been initiated by the Arab, and the princess might go with her either as a fellow-student, or because a woman could not decently come alone. "I am afraid, said Imlac, that he will be soon weary of your company: men advanced far in knowledge do not love to repeat the elements of their art, and I am not certain that even of the elements, as he will deliver them connected with inferences, and mingled with reflections, you are a very capable auditress." "That, said Pekuah, must be my care: I ask of you only to take me thither. My knowledge is, perhaps, more than you imagine it, and, by concurring always with his opinions, I shall make him think it greater than it is."

The astronomer, in pursuance of this resolution, was told, that a foreign lady, travelling in search of knowledge, had heard of his reputation, and was desirous to become his scholar. The uncommonness of the proposal raised at once his surprise and curiosity, and when, after a short deliberation, he consented to admit her, he could not stay without impatience till the next day.

The ladies dressed themselves magnificently, and were attended by Imlac to the astronomer, who was pleased to see himself approached with respect by persons of so splendid an appearance. In the exchange of the first civilities he was timorous and bashful; but when the talk became regular, he recollected his powers, and justified the character[7] which Imlac had given. Inquiring of Pekuah, what could have turned her inclination towards astronomy? he received from her a history of her adventure at the pyramid, and of the time passed in the Arab's island. She told her tale with ease and elegance, and her conversation took possession of his heart. The discourse was then turned to astronomy: Pekuah displayed what she knew: he looked upon her as a prodigy of genius, and entreated her not to desist from a study which she had so happily begun.

They came again and again, and were every time more welcome than before. The sage endeavoured to amuse them, that they might prolong their visits, for he found his thoughts grow brighter in their company; the clouds of solicitude vanished by degrees, as he forced himself to entertain them, and he grieved when he was left at their departure to his old employment of regulating the seasons.

The princess and her favourite had now watched his lips for several months, and could not catch a single word from which they could judge whether he continued, or not, in the opinion of his preternatural commission. They often contrived to bring him to an open declaration; but he easily eluded all their attacks, and on which side soever they pressed him, escaped from them to some other topick.

As their familiarity increased, they invited him often to the house of Imlac, where they distinguished him by extraordinary respect. He began gradually to delight in sublunary pleasures. He came early, and departed late; laboured to recommend himself by assiduity and compliance; excited their curiosity after new arts, that they might still want his assistance; and when they made any excursion of pleasure or inquiry, entreated to attend them.

By long experience of his integrity and wisdom, the prince and his sister were convinced that he might be trusted without danger; and lest he should draw any false hopes from the civilities which he received, discovered to him their condition, with the motives of their journey; and required his opinion on the choice of life.

"Of the various conditions which the world spreads before you, which you

7. Characterization.

shall prefer, said the sage, I am not able to instruct you. I can only tell that I have chosen wrong. I have passed my time in study without experience; in the attainment of sciences which can, for the most part, be but remotely useful to mankind. I have purchased knowledge at the expence of all the common comforts of life: I have missed the endearing elegance of female friendship, and the happy commerce of domestick tenderness. If I have obtained any prerogatives above other students, they have been accompanied with fear, disquiet, and scrupulosity; but even of these prerogatives, whatever they were, I have, since my thoughts have been diversified by more inter-course with the world, begun to question the reality. When I have been for a few days lost in pleasing dissipation,[8] I am always tempted to think that my inquiries have ended in errour, and that I have suffered much, and suf-fered it in vain."

Imlac was delighted to find that the sage's understanding was breaking through its mists, and resolved to detain him from the planets till he should forget his task of ruling them, and reason should recover its original influ-ence.

From this time the astronomer was received into familiar friendship, and partook of all their projects and pleasures: his respect kept him attentive, and the activity of Rasselas did not leave much time unengaged. Something was always to be done; the day was spent in making observations which furnished talk for the evening, and the evening was closed with a scheme for the morrow.

The sage confessed to Imlac, that since he had mingled in the gay tumults of life, and divided his hours by a succession of amusements, he found the conviction of his authority over the skies fade gradually from his mind, and began to trust less to an opinion which he never could prove to others, and which he now found subject to variation, from causes in which reason had no part. "If I am accidentally left alone for a few hours, said he, my inveterate persuasion rushes upon my soul, and my thoughts are chained down by some irresistible violence; but they are soon disentangled by the prince's conver-sation, and instantaneously released at the entrance of Pekuah. I am like a man habitually afraid of spectres, who is set at ease by a lamp, and wonders at the dread which harassed him in the dark; yet, if his lamp be extinguished, feels again the terrours which he knows that when it is light he shall feel no more. But I am sometimes afraid lest I indulge my quiet by criminal negli-gence, and voluntarily forget the great charge with which I am intrusted. If I favour myself in a known errour, or am determined by my own ease in a doubtful question of this importance, how dreadful is my crime!"

"No disease of the imagination, answered Imlac, is so difficult of cure, as that which is complicated with the dread of guilt: fancy and conscience then act interchangeably upon us, and so often shift their places, that the illusions of one are not distinguished from the dictates of the other. If fancy presents images not moral or religious, the mind drives them away when they give it pain, but when melancholick notions take the form of duty, they lay hold on the faculties without opposition, because we are afraid to exclude or banish them. For this reason the superstitious are often melancholy, and the mel-ancholy almost always superstitious.

8. Frivolity.

"But do not let the suggestions of timidity overpower your better reason: the danger of neglect can be but as the probability of the obligation, which when you consider it with freedom, you find very little, and that little growing every day less. Open your heart to the influence of the light, which, from time to time, breaks in upon you: when scruples importune you, which you in your lucid moments know to be vain, do not stand to parley, but fly to business or to Pekuah, and keep this thought always prevalent, that you are only one atom of the mass of humanity, and have neither such virtue nor vice, as that you should be singled out for supernatural favours or afflictions."

CHAPTER 46

The Prince Enters, and Brings a New Topick

"All this, said the astronomer, I have often thought, but my reason has been so long subjugated by an uncontrollable and overwhelming idea, that it durst not confide in its own decisions. I now see how fatally I betrayed my quiet, by suffering chimeras to prey upon me in secret; but melancholy shrinks from communication, and I never found a man before, to whom I could impart my troubles, though I had been certain of relief. I rejoice to find my own sentiments confirmed by yours, who are not easily deceived, and can have no motive or purpose to deceive. I hope that time and variety will dissipate the gloom that has so long surrounded me, and the latter part of my days will be spent in peace."

"Your learning and virtue, said Imlac, may justly give you hopes."

Rasselas then entered with the princess and Pekuah, and inquired, whether they had contrived any new diversion for the next day? "Such, said Nekayah, is the state of life, that none are happy but by the anticipation of change: the change itself is nothing; when we have made it, the next wish is to change again. The world is not yet exhausted; let me see something to-morrow which I never saw before."

[They visit the catacombs, "ancient repositories in which the bodies of the earliest generations were lodged."]

CHAPTER 47

Imlac discourses on the Nature of the Soul

"What reason, said the prince, can be given why the Egyptians should thus expensively preserve those carcases which some nations consume with fire, others lay to mingle with the earth, and all agree to remove from their sight, as soon as decent rites can be performed?"

"The original[9] of ancient customs, said Imlac, is commonly unknown; for the practice often continues when the cause has ceased; and concerning superstitious ceremonies it is vain to conjecture; for what reason did not dictate, reason cannot explain. I have long believed that the practice of embalming arose only from tenderness to the remains of relations or friends, and to this opinion I am more inclined, because it seems impossible that this care should have been general: had all the dead been embalmed, their repos-

9. Origin.

itories must in time have been more spacious than the dwellings of the living. I suppose only the rich or honourable were secured from corruption, and the rest left to the course of nature.

"But it is commonly supposed that the Egyptians believed the soul to live as long as the body continued undissolved, and therefore tried this method of eluding death."

"Could the wise Egyptians, said Nekayah, think so grossly of the soul? If the soul could once survive its separation, what could it afterwards receive or suffer from the body?"

"The Egyptians would doubtless think erroneously, said the astronomer, in the darkness of heathenism, and the first dawn of philosophy. The nature of the soul is still disputed amidst all our opportunities of clearer knowledge: some yet say, that it may be material, who, nevertheless, believe it to be immortal."

"Some, answered Imlac, have indeed said that the soul is material, but I can scarcely believe that any man has thought it, who knew how to think; for all the conclusions of reason enforce the immateriality of mind, and all the notices of sense and investigations of science concur to prove the unconsciousness of matter.

"It was never supposed that cogitation is inherent in matter, or that every particle is a thinking being. Yet, if any part of matter be devoid of thought, what part can we suppose to think? Matter can differ from matter only in form, density, bulk, motion, and direction of motion. To which of these, however varied or combined, can consciousness be annexed? To be round or square, to be solid or fluid, to be great or little, to be moved slowly or swiftly one way or another, are modes of material existence, all equally alien from the nature of cogitation. If matter be once without thought, it can only be made to think by some new modification, but all the modifications which it can admit are equally unconnected with cogitative powers."

"But the materialists, said the astronomer, urge that matter may have qualities with which we are unacquainted."

"He who will determine, returned Imlac, against that which he knows, because there may be something which he knows not; he that can set hypothetical possibility against acknowledged certainty, is not to be admitted among reasonable beings. All that we know of matter is, that matter is inert, senseless, and lifeless; and if this conviction cannot be opposed but by referring us to something that we know not, we have all the evidence that human intellect can admit. If that which is known may be over-ruled by that which is unknown, no being, not omniscient, can arrive at certainty."

"Yet let us not, said the astronomer, too arrogantly limit the Creator's power."

"It is no limitation of omnipotence, replied the poet, to suppose that one thing is not consistent with another, that the same proposition cannot be at once true and false, that the same number cannot be even and odd, that cogitation cannot be conferred on that which is created incapable of cogitation."

"I know not, said Nekayah, any great use of this question. Does that immateriality, which, in my opinion, you have sufficiently proved, necessarily include eternal duration?"

"Of immateriality, said Imlac, our ideas are negative, and therefore obscure. Immateriality seems to imply a natural power of perpetual duration as a consequence of exemption from all causes of decay: whatever perishes is destroyed by the solution of its contexture, and separation of its parts; nor can we conceive how that which has no parts, and therefore admits no solution, can be naturally corrupted or impaired."

"I know not, said Rasselas, how to conceive any thing without extension; what is extended must have parts, and you allow, that whatever has parts may be destroyed."

"Consider your own conceptions, replied Imlac, and the difficulty will be less. You will find substance without extension. An ideal form is no less real than material bulk: yet an ideal form has no extension. It is no less certain, when you think on a pyramid, that your mind possesses the idea of a pyramid, than that the pyramid itself is standing. What space does the idea of a pyramid occupy more than the idea of a grain of corn? or how can either idea suffer laceration? As is the effect such is the cause; as thought, such is the power that thinks; a power impassive and indiscernible."[1]

"But the Being, said Nekayah, whom I fear to name, the Being which made the soul, can destroy it."

"He, surely, can destroy it, answered Imlac, since, however unperishable, it receives from a superiour nature its power of duration. That it will not perish by any inherent cause of decay, or principle of corruption, may be shewn by philosophy; but philosophy can tell no more. That it will not be annihilated by him that made it, we must humbly learn from higher authority."

The whole assembly stood awhile silent and collected. "Let us return, said Rasselas, from this scene of mortality. How gloomy would be these mansions of the dead to him who did not know that he should never die; that what now acts shall continue its agency, and what now thinks shall think on for ever. Those that lie here stretched before us, the wise and the powerful of ancient times, warn us to remember the shortness of our present state: they were, perhaps snatched away while they were busy like us in the choice of life."

"To me, said the princess, the choice of life is become less important; I hope hereafter to think only on the choice of eternity."

They then hastened out of the caverns, and, under the protection of their guard, returned to Cairo.

CHAPTER 48

The Conclusion, in which Nothing is Concluded

It was now the time of the inundation of the Nile: a few days after their visit to the catacombs, the river began to rise.

They were confined to their house. The whole region being under water gave them no invitation to any excursions, and, being well supplied with materials for talk, they diverted themselves with comparisons of the different forms of life which they had observed, and with various schemes of happiness, which each of them had formed.

Pekuah was never so much charmed with any place as the convent of St.

1. Indivisible.

Anthony, where the Arab restored her to the princess, and wished only to fill it with pious maidens, and to be made prioress of the order: she was weary of expectation and disgust, and would gladly be fixed in some unvariable state.

The princess thought, that of all sublunary things, knowledge was the best: She desired first to learn all sciences, and then purposed to found a college of learned women, in which she would preside, that, by conversing with the old, and educating the young, she might divide her time between the acquisition and communication of wisdom, and raise up for the next age models of prudence, and patterns of piety.

The prince desired a little kingdom, in which he might administer justice in his own person, and see all the parts of government with his own eyes, but he could never fix the limits of his dominion, and was always adding to the number of his subjects.

Imlac and the astronomer were contented to be driven along the stream of life, without directing their course to any particular port.

Of these wishes that they had formed they well knew that none could be obtained. They deliberated awhile what was to be done, and resolved, when the inundation should cease, to return to Abissinia.

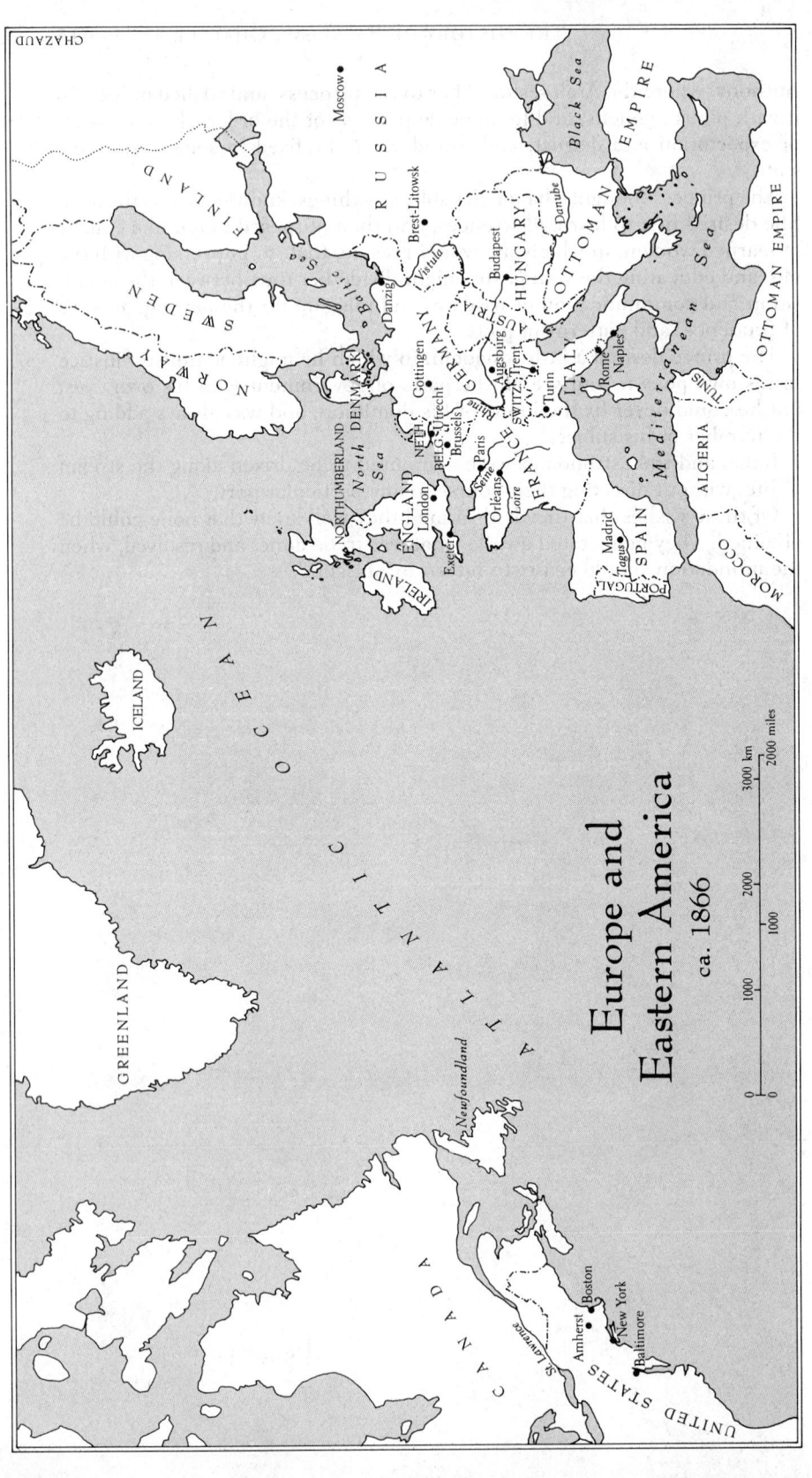

Europe and
Eastern America
ca. 1866

Masterpieces of the Nineteenth Century: Varieties of Romanticism

"Bliss was it in that dawn to be alive, / But to be young was very heaven." William Wordsworth alludes here to his experience, at the age of seventeen, of the French Revolution. The possibility of referring to a national cataclysm in such terms suggests the remarkable shift in sensibility, in dominant assumptions, in intellectual preoccupations, that occurred late in the eighteenth century. We call the evidence of that shift "Romanticism"—a designation so grandly inclusive as to defy definition. If our terms for the late seventeenth and early eighteenth centuries ("Enlightenment," "Age of Reason") emphasize one aspect of the prevailing intellectual culture to the exclusion of others equally important, the label *Romanticism* refers to so many cultural manifestations that one can hardly pin it down. In general, it implies new emphases on imagination, on feeling, on the value of the primitive and untrammeled, and particularly a narrowing of outlook from the universal to the particular, from humankind or "man" (the subject of Pope's *Essay*) to nation or ethnic group, and from the stability of community to the "fulfillment" of the individual. Such shifts have important political and philosophic as well as literary implications.

In the writings of individuals, one finds lines of continuity between the late and early parts of the eighteenth century; but when it comes to generalizations, all the important truths appear to have reversed themselves. In the middle of the century, reason was the guide to certainty; at the century's end, *feeling* tested authenticity. Earlier, tradition still anchored experience; now, the ideal of joyous liberation implied rejection of traditional authority. Wisdom had long associated itself with maturity, even with old age; by the 1790s, William Blake hinted at the child's superior insight, and Wordsworth openly claimed for the infant holy wisdom inevitably lost in the process of aging. Johnson had valued experience as a vital path to knowledge; at the beginning of the nineteenth century, innocence—in its nature evanescent—provided a more generally treasured resource.

Cause and effect, in such massive shifts of perspective, can never be ascertained. The French Revolution derived from new ideas about the sacredness of the individual; it also helped generate such ideas. Without trying to distinguish causes from effects—indeed, with a strong suspicion that the period's striking phenomena constitute simultaneous causes and effects—one can specify a number of ways that the world appeared to change, as the eighteenth century approached the nineteenth, as well as ways that these changes both solidified themselves and evoked challenges later in the nineteenth century.

NEW AND OLD

The embattled farmers of Concord, Massachusetts, fired the shot heard round the world in 1775; fourteen years later, the Bastille fell. Both the American and the French revolutions developed out of strong convictions about the innate rights of individual human beings—in other words, Protestantism in political form. Those who developed revolutionary theory glimpsed new human possibility. The hope of salvation lay in the overturning of established institutions. Swift, in *Gulliver's Travels*, had made a clear distinction between institutions as ideal constructions of human reason and their corruption in practice. Lawyers might be a money-grubbing, hypocritical lot; but the idea of law, of a social structure designed to ensure the provision of justice, has its own inherent power. The theory of revolution implied radical assault on virtually all social institutions. Fundamental hierarchies of government, notions of sovereignty and of aristocracy, inherited systems of distinction—all fell. Old conventions, once emblems of social and of literary stability, now exemplified the dead hand of the past. Only a few years before, the old, the inherited, and the traditional embodied truth, its power attested by its survival. But the revolutionaries felt themselves to be originators; the newness of what they proposed gave it the almost religious authority suggested by Wordsworth's allusions to "bliss" and "heaven."

The blessed state evoked by the new political thinkers embodied a sense of infinite possibility. Pope had written, in *Essay on Man*, "The bliss of Man (could Pride that blessing find) / Is not to act or think beyond mankind." By the century's end, people were doing their best to "think beyond mankind"—or, at any rate, beyond what had been considered normal limitations. Evidence of this abounds, in revolutionary sermons preached from pulpits even in England, in writings by such flamboyant defenders of human rights as Thomas Paine, in the development, even, of a political theory about women's social position. Mary Wollstonecraft was not the first to note the oppression of women; a century before her, Mary Astell had suggested the need for broader female education, and outcries on the subject emerged sporadically even earlier in the seventeenth century. But Wollstonecraft's *Vindication of the Rights of Woman* (1792) offered the first detailed argument that the ideal of fulfilled human possibility for men and for women demanded political acknowledgment of women's equality.

The very existence of such a work (which achieved a second edition in the year of its first publication) testifies to the atmosphere of political expectancy in which men and women could rethink "self-evident" principles. Replacing the ideal of hierarchy (what Dr. Johnson reverenced as "subordination"), for example, was the revolutionary notion of human brotherhood. Liberty, equality, and fraternity, the French proclaimed; the new American nation celebrated essentially the same ideals. In practice, though, *fraternity* turned out to involve the citizens specifically of France, or of the new United States. The emphasis on individual uniqueness extended itself to national uniqueness. In America particularly, ideas of national character and of national destiny developed almost talismanic force. Although peace generally prevailed among nations in the early nineteenth century, the developing distinctions dividing one country imaginatively from another foretold future danger.

New ideas with massive practical consequences included more than the political. In 1776, Adam Smith published *The Wealth of Nations,* a theory of laissez-faire economics presaging the enormous importance of money in subsequent history. Matters of exchange and acquisition, Smith argued, could be left to regulate themselves—a doctrine behind which still lurked unobtrusively the confidence, expressed in market terms, that Pope had expressed in religious ones: "All Chance, Direction, which thou canst not see, / All Discord, Harmony, not understood." As manufacturing and trade developed increasing financial vitality, however, their importance as financial resources in fact heightened discord, through growing nationalism. Early in the century, at the end of "Windsor Forest" (1713), Pope had recognized in Britain's trade a form of power. A century later, the acceleration of this power would have astonished Pope. No longer did agriculture provide England's central economic resource. New forms of manufacture provided new substance for trade, generated new fortunes, produced a new social class—a "middle class" with the influence of wealth and without the inherited system of responsibilities, restrictions, and decorums that had helped control aristocratic possessors of wealth in preceding generations. Aristocrats had used their money, on the whole, to enlarge and beautify their estates. The new money-holders developed new ideas about what money might do. Reinvested, it could support innovation in manufacture and trade. It could educate the children of the uneducated; it could buy them (as it had been doing for a century) husbands and wives from the aristocracy; it could help obviate ancient class distinctions. England's increasing economic ascendancy in the nineteenth century derived not only from new money but from the development of men willing and able to employ money ingeniously as power.

The enlarged possibilities of manufacture testified to practical applications of scientific research, another area of activity in which the new overwhelmingly replaced the old. In England and America especially, inventions multiplied: the steam engine, the spinning jenny, the cotton gin. Increasingly often, and in increasing numbers, men and women left their native rural environments to congregate in cities, where opportunities for relatively unskilled workers abounded—and where more and more people lived in congestion, poverty, and misery.

More vividly, perhaps, than ever before in history, the world was changing—was becoming, in fact, the world we ourselves assume, in which *mankind* as an ideal wanes, nations define themselves in psychic and military opposition to one another, money constitutes immediate power, science serves manufacture and hence commerce. From the beginning of these crucial changes, certain thinkers and writers realized the destructive possibilities inherent in every form of "progress." Blake, for example, glimpsed London's economic brutality and human wastefulness; his "revolutionary" impulses expressed themselves partly in resistance to the consequences of the new. That is to say, the new gave way to the newer, as it had not previously done on such a scale. No longer did the impulse to conserve past values express itself with the authority and power that Swift and Johnson had brought to the theme. As M. H. Abrams has written, "the Romantic period was eminently an age obsessed with the fact of violent change." Such change might provide ground for fear; it also supplied the substance for hope.

INDIVIDUALISM

Immanuel Kant (1724–1804), a German philosopher whose work influenced virtually all philosophers after him, questioned the power of reason to provide the most significant forms of knowledge—knowledge of the ultimately real. Feeling, on the other hand, might offer a guide. The individual will must engage itself in ethical struggle to locate and experience the good. Such followers of Kant as Johann Fichte (1762–1814) more clearly suggested an identification between will and what we call ego. The idea of the self took on ever greater importance, for philosophers and for poets, for political thinkers, autobiographers, and novelists.

To locate authority in the self rather than in society implies yet another radical break with the assumptions of the previous period. The idea of the self's importance is so familiar to us that it may be difficult to imagine the startling implications of the new focus. "I know the feelings of my heart, and I know men," Jean-Jacques Rousseau writes, at the beginning of his *Confessions.* "I am not made like any of those I have seen; I venture to believe that I am not made like any of those who are in existence." Samuel Johnson would have felt certain that a man who could write such words must be mad, like the astronomer in *Rasselas* who believes himself to control the weather. Yet faith in the absolute uniqueness of every consciousness became increasingly prevalent. Rousseau's significance for his period derives partly from the fact that his stress on the feelings of his heart and on his own specialness aroused recognition in his audience. No longer did the universality of human nature supply comfort to individuals; now they might seek reassurance instead in their uniqueness. It was the ultimate development of protestantism—to everyone his or her own church.

Not only could individuals now see themselves as unique but they could also understand themselves as *good*. In its earlier forms, Christianity had emphasized the fallen nature of the human soul. Every self, according to this view, contains the potential for violence and destructiveness. One must rely on God's grace for salvation, which cannot depend on human worth. At the secular level, human beings need institutions to provide the controls that save us from anarchy—from the evil latent in ourselves. Rousseau and his successors articulated the opposite position, stressing the essential goodness of human nature and the corresponding danger of institutional restraint. Repressiveness now became the fearful enemy, uniformity the menace. We may recognize the fear of external control today in the slogans of those celebrating the importance of "individual rights," and we still hear the older faith in institutions in the proponents of "law and order."

The new emphasis on the individual opened new possibilities for writers of poetry and prose alike. Even the grotesque and deviant became interesting. Victor Hugo could explore the psychology of Satan, for example: the angel cast out of heaven and falling through the abyss, undergoing a process of increasing horror, enduring the going out of light, but remaining defiant throughout his long ordeal. Unlike John Milton, who directed attention to cosmic drama on a large scale, Hugo concentrates his focus to create an impression of poignance as well as nightmare. In Russia, Alexander Pushkin investigated the psychology (as well as the social arrangements) of a group of people concerned only with money, generating a quite different sense of horror.

As these instances will suggest, stress on the individual implied revaluation of inner as opposed to outer experience. Previously, life in the public arena had been assumed to test human capacities and to provide meaningful forms of experience. After Rousseau, however, psychic experience could provide the proper measure of an individual's emotional capacity. To place value *there* opened the possibility of taking women as seriously as men, children as seriously as adults, "savages" as seriously as civilized beings. Indeed, women, children, and "primitive" peoples were often thought to exceed cultivated adult males in their capacity both to feel and to express their feelings spontaneously—although the social subordination of such groups continued unchanged.

Even before Rousseau, the novel of sensibility in England and on the Continent revealed interest in highly developed emotional responsiveness. Johann Wolfgang von Goethe's *The Sorrows of Young Werther* (1774) made its author famous and inspired a cult of introverted, melancholy young people. In England, Henry Mackenzie's *The Man of Feeling* (1771) associated intense emotion with benevolent action. By the latter part of the century, the Gothic novel had become an important form—a novelistic mode, often practiced by women, that typically placed a young woman at the center of the action. The heroines of such novels confront a kind of experience (usually involving at least apparent supernatural elements) for which their social training, that important resource of earlier heroines, provided no help; instead, quick intuitions and subtle feelings ensure their triumph over apparently insurmountable obstacles with no loss of feminine delicacy.

Given the view of feeling's centrality that replaced the earlier stress on passion's fruitful tension with reason, a broader spectrum of feeling drew literary attention. From its beginnings (*The Princess of Clèves* is an early example), the novel had tended to emphasize (usually in decorous terms) love between the sexes. Now romantic love became a central subject of poetry and drama as well. More-surprising kinds of emotion also attracted notice. William Blake imagined a chimney sweep's emotional relation to the idea of heaven; Samuel Taylor Coleridge and Percy Bysshe Shelley made poetry of dejection; Alfred, Lord Tennyson, at the midpoint of the nineteenth century, wove his anxieties about the revelations of recent scientific inquiry into the texture of an elegiac poem. Rosalía de Castro wrote of the death of her child; Giacomo Leopardi could produce a lyric called *To Himself*, exploring his personal relation to large ideas; Friedrich Hölderlin, in Germany, like Wordsworth and Coleridge in England, used the making of poetry as a subject for thought and feeling alike. As these examples indicate, painful as well as pleasurable emotion interested readers and writers. The poet, Wordsworth said, is a man speaking to men; poetry originates in recollected emotion and recapitulates lost feeling. Lyric, not epic, typifies poetry for Wordsworth, who understands his genre as a form of emotional communication.

Wordsworth's definition ignores the fact that women, too (including his own sister, Dorothy), wrote poetry. Emily Brontë, Christina Rossetti, Rosalía de Castro, Anna Petrovna Bunina, Emily Dickinson—such women writing in different countries evoked intense passion in verse. In the Romantic novel, too, women excelled in the rendering of powerful feeling. The Brontë sisters, like George Eliot after them in England, like the equally passionate George Sand in France, wrote under male pseudonyms but established distinctively female visions of the struggle not only for love but also for freedom and power within a context of social restriction. Mary Shelley (daughter of Mary Wollstonecraft and wife of the poet Shelley) in her eloquent fable of creativity, *Frankenstein* (1818), epitomizes the peculiar intensity of much women's writing in this period.

As the nineteenth century wore on, hope for a new terrestrial Eden faded. The efflorescence of commerce and the innovations of science turned out to have negative as well as positive consequences. As the novels of Charles Dickens and William Thackeray insist, the new middle class frequently became the repository of moral mediocrity. The autocracy of money had effects more brutal than those of inherited privilege. Science, once the emblem of progress, began to generate theological confusion. Charles Darwin's *Origin of Species* (1859) stated clearly humanity's mean rather than transcendent origins: animal and plant species had evolved over the centuries, adapting themselves to their environment through the process of natural selection. Fossils found in rocks provided supporting evidence for this theory—an assertion troubling to many Christians because it contradicted the biblical account of creation. Eight years after Darwin's revolutionary work, Karl Marx published *Das Kapital,* with its dialectical theory of history and its vision of capitalism's eventual decay and of the working class inevitably triumphant. In the United States civil war raged from 1860 to 1865, its central issue states' rights, a topic that, of course, implicated the morality of slavery—that by-product of agricultural capitalism. Neither the making of money nor the effort to fathom natural law seemed merely reassuring.

In the face of history's threats—the menace of Marx's prophecy and of Darwin's biology, the chaos of civil war—to insist on the importance of private experience offered tentative security, a standing place, a temporary source of authority. The voices of blacks and, in increasing numbers, of women could now be heard: placing high value on the personal implied respecting all persons. The American Civil War made African Americans for the first time truly visible to the society that both contained and denied them. Slave narratives—sometimes wholly or partly fictionized, sometimes entirely authentic renditions of often horrifying experience—provided useful propaganda for the abolitionist cause, the ideology opposed to the institution of slavery. They also opened a new emotional universe. In their typical emphasis, for instance, on the salvationary force of reading and writing (for most slaves officially forbidden knowledge), these narratives illuminated a new area of the taken-for-granted, thus extending the enterprise of Romantic poetry.

The capacity for revelatory illumination belonged, according to the dominant nineteenth-century view, to imagination, a mysterious and virtually sacred power of individual consciousness. When Johnson, in *Rasselas,* suggested that all predominance of imagination over reason constituted a degree of insanity, he intended, to put it crudely, an antithesis of true and false. Imagination, the faculty of generating images, had no necessary anchor in the communal, historical experience that tested truth. For Wordsworth and Coleridge and those who came after them, imagination was a visionary and unifying force (a new incarnation of the seventeenth century's inner light or candle of the Lord) through which the gifted person discovered and communicated new truth. (Johnson, of course, would have denied the possibility of "new" truth.) As Coleridge wrote,

> from the soul itself must issue forth
> A light, a glory, a fair luminous cloud
> Enveloping the Earth.

Imagination derived from the soul, the aspect of human being that links the human with the eternal. Through it, men and women can transcend earthly limitations, can express high aspiration, can escape, and help one another escape, the dreariness of mortality without necessarily positing a life beyond the present one.

A corollary of the high value attached to creative imagination was a new concern with originality. The notion of "the genius," the man or woman so gifted as to operate by principles unknown to ordinary mortals, developed only in the late eighteenth century. Previously, a person *had* rather than *was* a genius: the term designated a particular tendency or gift (a genius for cooking, say) rather than a human being with vast creative power. Now the genius was revered for his or her extraordinary difference from others, idealized as a being set apart; and the literary or artistic products of genius, it could be assumed, would correspondingly differ from everything previously produced. Yet the writers of this movement also recorded their anxiety about the claim of specialness implicit in the idea of genius. Goethe's *Faust*, a rewriting of an old legend, emphasizes the danger inherent in the desire to do what no one had ever done, to be what no one had ever been.

Despite all reservations, though, newness now became as never before a measure of value. The language, the themes, the forms of the preceding century would no longer suffice. In the early eighteenth century, literary figures wishing to congratulate themselves and their contemporaries would compare their artistic situation to that of Rome under the benevolent patronage of Augustus Caesar. A hundred years later, the note of self-congratulation would express itself in the claim of an unprecedented situation, unprecedented kinds of accomplishment. John Keats in a letter characterized Wordsworth as representing "the egotistical sublime." Such sublimity—authority and grandeur emanating from a unique self still in touch with something beyond itself—was the nineteenth century's special achievement.

NATURE

Nature and nature's laws, the rationally ordered universe, provided the foundation for much early eighteenth-century thought. In the nineteenth century, nature's importance possibly increased—but *nature* now meant something new. *Wuthering Heights* (1847) creates a setting of windswept moors for its romantic lovers—both environment and metaphor of their love. Wordsworth could value a host of daffodils, or fog-enveloped hills, or an icy lake. Lamartine appealed to the landscape to embody the characteristics of his lost love. The physical reality of the natural world, in its varied abundance, became a matter of absorbing interest for poets and novelists. Nature provided an alternative to the human, a possibility for imaginative as well as literal escape. Its imagery—flowers, clouds, ocean—became the common poetic stock. Workers still hastened from the country to the city, because the city housed possibilities of wealth; yet educated men and women increasingly declared their nostalgia for rural or sylvan landscapes embodying peace and beauty.

Nature, in the nineteenth-century mind, however, did not consist only in physical details. It also implied a totality, an enveloping whole greater than the sum of its parts, a vast unifying spirit. Wordsworth evokes

> a sense sublime
> Of something far more deeply interfused,
> Whose dwelling is the light of setting suns,
> And the round ocean and the living air,

> And the blue sky, and in the mind of man:
> A motion and a spirit, that impels
> All thinking things, all objects of all thought,
> And rolls through all things.

Coleridge and Shelley, Bécquer and de Castro, hint similar visions, vague yet comforting. The unifying whole, as Wordsworth's language suggests, depends less on rational system than on emotional association. Human beings link themselves with the infinite by what Wordsworth elsewhere terms "wise passiveness," the capacity to submit to feeling and be led by it to transcendence. Natural detail, too, acquires value by evoking and symbolizing emotion. Nature belongs to the realm of the nonrational, the superrational. It can be linked, as it is for Anna Petrovna Bunina, with a sense of misery and pain, or it can evoke, as it does for Dorothy Wordsworth, possibilities of utter joy and transcendence.

The idea of the natural can also imply the uncivilized, or precivilized. Philosophers have differed dramatically in their hypotheses about what humankind was like in its "natural" state. Thomas Hobbes, in the seventeenth century, argued that the natural human condition was one of conflict. Society developed to curb the violent impulses human beings would manifest without its restraint. The prevailing nineteenth-century view, on the other hand, made civilization the agent of corruption. Rousseau expounded the crippling effect of institutions. The child raised with the greatest possible freedom, he maintained, would develop in more admirable ways than one subjected to system. By the second half of the eighteenth century, a French novelist could contrast the decadent life of Europe unfavorably with existence on an unspoiled island (Bernardin de Saint-Pierre, *Paul and Virginia,* 1788); Thomas Chatterton, before committing suicide in 1770 at the age of eighteen, wrote poems rich in nostalgia for a more primitive stage of social development that he tried to pass off as medieval works; the forged Ossian poems (1760–63) of James Macpherson, purportedly ancient texts, attracted a large and enthusiastic audience. New interest manifested itself in ballads, poetic survivals of the primitive; Romantic poets imitated the form. The interest in a simpler past, a simpler life, continued throughout the nineteenth century: in Victorian England, Tennyson recast Arthurian legend in modern verse; the Pre-Raphaelites evoked the medieval in visual and verbal arts.

The revolutionary fervor of the late eighteenth century had generated a vision of infinite human possibility, political and personal. The escapist implications of the increasing emphasis on nature, the primitive, the uncomplicated past, suggest, however, a sense of alienation. Blake, Wordsworth, Shelley, all wrote poems of social protest. "Society" would not help the individual work out his or her salvation; on the contrary, it embodied forces opposed to individual development. Indeed, the word *society* had come to embody the impulses that desecrated nature and oppressed the poor in the interests of industry and "progress." Melancholy marked the Romantic hero (Lord Byron in his poetic self-manifestations; Heathcliff in fiction, for example) and tinged nineteenth-century poetry and fiction. The satiric spirit—that spirit of social reform—was in abeyance. Hope lay in the individual's separation from, not participation in, society. In the woods and mountains, one might feel free.

The Waste Land (1922), T. S. Eliot's twentieth-century epic, contains the line "In the mountains, there you feel free," a line given complex ironic overtones by its context. Its occurrence, however, may remind us how powerfully ideas that came into currency in the late eighteenth and early nineteenth centuries survive into our own time. The world of the Romantic period specifically prefigures our own, despite all the differences dividing the two cultures. We have developed more fully important Romantic tendencies: stress on the sacredness of the individual, suspicion of social institutions, belief in expressed feeling as the sign of authenticity, nostalgia for simpler ways of being, faith in genius, valuing of originality and imagination, an ambivalent relation to science. Although Wordsworth and Dickinson and Melville employ vocabularies and use references partly strange to us, they speak directly to the preoccupations of our time. By attending closely to them, we may learn more about ourselves: not only in the common humanity that we share with all our predecessors but in our special historical situation as both direct heirs of nineteenth-century assumptions and rebels against them. Chronology provides little guide to the Romantic period. Jean-Jacques Rousseau, the first writer included in this section, died before Gustavo Bécquer was born. The Romantic movement, as subsequent critics have defined it, extends from the late eighteenth to the late nineteenth century, but it is overlapped throughout by other sets of literary and philosophic assumptions.

FURTHER READING

Useful introductions to the Romantic period include L. Furst, *Romanticism in Perspective: A Comparative Study of Aspects of the Romantic Movements in England, France, and Germany* (1979); R. F. Gleckner and G. E. Enscoe, eds., *Romanticism: Points of View* (1962), a collection of essays by various contributors; Charles Larmore, *The Romantic Legacy* (1996); and M. Cranston, *The Romantic Movement* (1994). On French Romanticism, see P. T. Comeau, *Diehards and Innovators: The French Romantic Struggle, 1800–1830* (1988); on Germany, T. Ziolkowski, *German Romanticism and Its Institutions* (1990); on English and American developments, B. Taylor, R. Bain, and M. H. Abrams, *The Cast of Consciousness: Concepts of the Mind in British and American Romanticism* (1987); on the English and German situation, C. Jacobs, *Uncontainable Romanticism* (1989).

VARIETIES OF ROMANTICISM

TEXTS	CONTEXTS
1781–1788 Jean-Jacques Rousseau, *Confessions*	1781 Immanuel Kant, *Critique of Pure Reason*
	1787 Wolfgang Amadeus Mozart's *Don Giovanni* is first performed
	1789 The National Assembly in France issues its charter, *Declaration of the Rights of Man*
1794 William Blake, *Songs of Innocence and of Experience*	
1798 William Wordsworth and Samuel Taylor Coleridge, *Lyrical Ballads* • Dorothy Wordsworth begins her journals	
1800 Novalis, *Hymns to the Night*	
	1801 United Kingdom of Great Britain (England and Scotland) and Ireland established
1802 Coleridge, *Dejection: An Ode*	
	1803 President Thomas Jefferson purchases French "Louisiana"
	1804 Napoleon crowned emperor of France
1806 First published lyrics by Anna Petrovna Bunina	
1808 Johann Wolfgang von Goethe, *Faust, Part I* (*Part II*, 1832)	
1812–1870 Charles Dickens, English novelist	
	1815 Battle of Waterloo, ending Napoleon's career
1816 Coleridge, *Kubla Khan* • John Keats, *On First Looking into Chapman's Homer*	
1818–1820 Lyrics by Percy Bysshe Shelley and John Keats	
1820 Alphonse de Lamartine, *Poetic Meditations*, his first collection of poems	
1824 Giacomo Leopardi, *Canzoni,* his first collection of poems	
1827 Heinrich Heine, *Book of Songs*	
1828 Victor Hugo, *Odes and Ballads*	
	1831 First preparation of chloroform inaugurates a new medical era
1834 Alexander Sergeyevich Pushkin, *The Queen of Spades*	

Boldface titles indicate works in the anthology.

VARIETIES OF ROMANTICISM

TEXTS	CONTEXTS
	1837 Victoria crowned queen of the United Kingdom • Electric telegraph patented
1842 Alfred, Lord Tennyson, *Ulysses*	
1845 Frederick Douglass, *Narrative of the Life of Frederick Douglass, An American Slave*	
1847 Charlotte Brontë, *Jane Eyre* • Emily Brontë, *Wuthering Heights*	
	1848 Karl Marx and Friedrich Engels, *Communist Manifesto* • Revolutions in France, Italy, Austria, Prague • Gold discovered in California
1850 Alfred, Lord Tennyson, *In Memoriam A. H. H.*	
1842–1855 Robert Browning writes poems, including *"Childe Roland to the Dark Tower Came"*	
	1854 Electric lightbulb invented
1855 Walt Whitman, *Song of Myself*	
	1859 Charles Darwin's *Origin of Species*, presenting his theory of evolution
	1861 Serfs emancipated in Russia • Beginning of American Civil War
	1863 Emancipation Proclamation frees slaves in the Confederate States of America
	1864 Louis Pasteur, who formulated germ theory of infection, invents pasteurization
	1865 American Civil War ends • President Abraham Lincoln assassinated • Thirteenth amendment emancipates all slaves in the United States
	1867 Karl Marx, *Capital*
	1874 First Impressionist Exhibition, Paris
	1876 Alexander Graham Bell invents the telephone
1884 Rosalía de Castro, *Beside the River Sar*	
1890 Emily Dickinson, *Poems,* published posthumously	
1891 Herman Melville leaves manuscript of *Billy Budd, Sailor* at his death; not published until 1924	
	1894 X rays discovered by Bavarian physicist Wilhelm Röntgen

JEAN-JACQUES ROUSSEAU
1712–1778

It would be difficult to overstate the historical importance of Jean-Jacques Rousseau's *Confessions* (composed between 1765 and 1770, published 1781–88), which inaugurated a new form of autobiography and suggested new ways of thinking about the self and its relation to other selves. Even for readers two centuries after its first publication, the book's sheer audacity compels attention, demanding that we rethink easy assumptions about important and trivial, right and wrong.

The facts of Rousseau's life are not altogether clear, partly because the *Confessions*, despite its claim of absolute truthfulness, sometimes appears more concerned to create a self-justifying story than to confine itself strictly to actuality. The son of a Geneva watchmaker, Rousseau left home in his teens and lived for some time with Françoise-Louise de Warens, his protector and eventually his mistress, the "mamma" of the *Confessions*. He worked at many occupations, from secretary to government official (under the king of Sardinia). In Paris, where he settled in 1745, he lived with Thérèse le Vasseur; he claims she bore him five children, all consigned to an orphanage, but the claim has never been substantiated (or, for that matter, disproved). At various times his controversial writing forced Rousseau to leave France, usually for Switzerland; in 1766 he went to England as the guest of the philosopher David Hume. He was allowed to return to Paris in 1770 only on condition that he write nothing against the government or the Church.

Rousseau's social ideas, elaborated in his didactic novels *Julie: or, the New Eloise* (1761) and *Émile* (1762) as well as in his autobiographical writings and political treatises (for example, *The Social Contract*, 1762), stirred much contemporary discussion. He believed in the destructiveness of institutions, the gradual corruption of humankind throughout history, the importance of nature and of feeling in individual development and consequently in society. As he writes in *Émile*, "I hate books; they only teach us to talk about things we know nothing about." He proposes to teach children by immersing them first in the natural, then in the human world, preventing the corruption of their bodies and their feelings. For a time he was a music teacher, and he published several works on music, including a dictionary, and composed a comic opera called *The Village Soothsayer* (1752).

The *Confessions* presents its subject as a man (and boy) striving always to express natural impulses and recurrently frustrated by society's demands and assumptions. The central figure described here rather resembles Candide in his naiveté and good feeling. Experience chastens him less than it does Candide, however, although he reports many psychic hard knocks. For Voltaire's didactic purposes, his character's experience was more important than his personality; for Rousseau, his own nature has much more significance than anything that happens to him. His account of that nature becomes ever more complicated as the *Confessions* continue and the writer concerns himself increasingly with the problem of his relation to society at large. His sense of alienation alternates with wistful longing for inclusion as he delineates the dilemmas of the extraordinary individual in a world full of people primarily concerned to accrete wealth and power.

To read even a few pages of the work reveals how completely Rousseau exemplifies several of his period's dominant values. He describes himself as a being of powerful passions but confused ideas, he makes feeling the guide of conduct, he glorifies imagination and romantic love, he believes the common people morally superior to the upper classes. The emphasis on imagination and passion for him seems not a matter of ideology but of experience: life presents itself to him in this way. The fact emphasizes the degree to which the movement we call Romanticism involved genuine revision. Everything looked different in the late eighteenth century, everything demanded categories changed from those previously accepted without question. The new way of looking at the world that characterizes the Romantic movement, inasmuch as it implies valuing the inner life of emotion and fancy for its own sake (not for the sake of any insight it might provide), always includes the danger of narcissism, a kind of concentration on the self that shuts out awareness of the reality and integrity of others. Rousseau, in the *Confessions,* vividly expresses the narcissistic side of Romanticism.

Implicit in Rousseau's ways of understanding himself and his life are new moral assumptions as well. Honesty of a particular kind becomes the highest value; however disreputable his behavior, Rousseau can feel comfortable about it because he reports it accurately. What Johnson or Pope would see as self-indulgence, care exclusively for one's own pleasure, seems acceptable to Rousseau because of the minute, exacting attention devoted to it. The autobiographer examines each nuance of his own happiness, as if to know it fully constituted moral achievement. To take the self this seriously as subject—not in relation to a progress of education or of salvation, merely in its moment-to-moment being—implies belief in self-knowledge (knowledge of feeling, thought, action) as a high moral achievement. This is not the slowly achieved, arduous discipline recommended by Socrates but a somewhat more indulgent form of self-contemplation. To connect it, as Rousseau does, with morality conveys the view that self-absorption without self-judgment provides valuable and sufficient insight.

In his presentation of self, Rousseau contrasts vividly with his great predecessor, Montaigne. Rousseau insists on his uniqueness: "I am not made like any of those I have seen; I venture to believe that I am not made like any of those who are in existence." He presents himself for the reader's contemplation as a remarkable phenomenon. Montaigne, on the other hand, reminds us constantly of what author and reader (and humankind in general) have in common. "Not only does the wind of accidents stir me according to its blowing, but I am also stirred and troubled by the instability of my attitude; and he who examines himself closely will seldom find himself twice in the same state." The movement within the sentence from *I* to the universalizing *he* characterizes a more outward-looking mode.

It must be said, however, that the intensity of Rousseau's self-concentration makes his subject compelling for others as well. However distasteful one might find his obsessive focus, it is difficult to stop reading. The writer hints—makes us believe— that he will reveal all secrets about himself; and learning such secrets, despite Rousseau's insistence on his own uniqueness, tells us of human weakness, inconsistency, power, scope—tells us, therefore, something of ourselves.

F. C. Green, *Jean-Jacques Rousseau: A Critical Study of His Life and Writings* (1955), provides biography and criticism. Thomas McFarland, *Romanticism and the Heritage of Rousseau* (1995), examines the relation of Rousseau's assumptions to those of the Romantic movement. A thorough evaluation of Rousseau's achievement is L. G. Crocker, *Jean-Jacques Rousseau: A New Interpretative Analysis of His Works* (1973). More directly focused on the *Confessions* is H. Williams, *Rousseau and Romantic Autobiography* (1983). More recent studies include T. M. Kavanagh, *Writing the Truth: Authority and Desire in the Works of Rousseau* (1987); M. Morgenstern, *Rousseau and the Politics of Ambiguity* (1996); and C. Kelly, *Rousseau's Exemplary Life: The Confessions as Political Philosophy* (1987). A collection of essays by various authors is H. Bloom, ed., *Jean-Jacques Rousseau* (1988).

PRONOUNCING GLOSSARY

The following list uses common English syllables and stress accents to provide rough equivalents of selected words whose pronunciation may be unfamiliar to the general reader.

de Vulson: *deu vyewl-sohnh'* Jean-Jacques Rousseau: *zhahnh-zhahk*
de Warens: *deu vah-rahnh'* *roo-soh'*

Lausanne: *loh-zahn'*   Saône: *sohn*
Montaigne: *mohn-ten'*   Turin: *tyew-ranh'*
Nyon: *nee-yohnh'*   Vaud: *voh*
St. Marceau: *sanh mahr-soh'*   Vévay: *vay-vay'*

From Confessions

Part I

BOOK I

[*The Years 1712–1719*]

I am commencing an undertaking, hitherto without precedent, and which
will never find an imitator. I desire to set before my fellows the likeness of a
man in all the truth of nature, and that man myself.

Myself alone! I know the feelings of my heart, and I know men. I am not
made like any of those I have seen; I venture to believe that I am not made
like any of those who are in existence. If I am not better, at least I am
different. Whether Nature has acted rightly or wrongly in destroying the
mould in which she cast me, can only be decided after I have been read.

Let the trumpet of the Day of Judgment sound when it will, I will present
myself before the Sovereign Judge with this book in my hand. I will say boldly:
"This is what I have done, what I have thought, what I was. I have told the
good and the bad with equal frankness. I have neither omitted anything bad,
nor interpolated anything good. If I have occasionally made use of some
immaterial embellishments, this has only been in order to fill a gap caused
by lack of memory. I may have assumed the truth of that which I knew might
have been true, never of that which I knew to be false. I have shown myself
as I was: mean and contemptible, good, high-minded and sublime, according
as I was one or the other. I have unveiled my inmost self even as Thou hast
seen it, O Eternal Being. Gather round me the countless host of my fellow-
men; let them hear my confessions, lament for my unworthiness, and blush
for my imperfections. Then let each of them in turn reveal, with the same
frankness, the secrets of his heart at the foot of the Throne, and say, if he
dare, '*I was better than that man!*' " * * *

I felt before I thought: this is the common lot of humanity. I experienced
it more than others. I do not know what I did until I was five or six years old.
I do not know how I learned to read; I only remember my earliest reading,
and the effect it had upon me; from that time I date my uninterrupted self-
consciousness. My mother had left some romances behind her, which my
father and I began to read after supper. At first it was only a question of
practising me in reading by the aid of amusing books; but soon the interest
became so lively, that we used to read in turns without stopping, and spent
whole nights in this occupation. We were unable to leave off until the volume
was finished. Sometimes, my father, hearing the swallows begin to twitter in
the early morning, would say, quite ashamed, "Let us go to bed; I am more
of a child than yourself."

In a short time I acquired, by this dangerous method, not only extreme facility in reading and understanding what I read, but a knowledge of the passions that was unique in a child of my age. I had no idea of things in themselves, although all the feelings of actual life were already known to me. I had conceived nothing, but felt everything. These confused emotions which I felt one after the other, certainly did not warp the reasoning powers which I did not as yet possess; but they shaped them in me of a peculiar stamp, and gave me odd and romantic notions of human life, of which experience and reflection have never been able wholly to cure me. * * *

How could I become wicked, when I had nothing but examples of gentleness before my eyes, and none around me but the best people in the world? My father, my aunt, my nurse, my relations, our friends, our neighbours, all who surrounded me, did not, it is true, obey me, but they loved me; and I loved them in return. My wishes were so little excited and so little opposed, that it did not occur to me to have any. I can swear that, until I served under a master, I never knew what a fancy was. Except during the time I spent in reading or writing in my father's company, or when my nurse took me for a walk, I was always with my aunt, sitting or standing by her side, watching her at her embroidery or listening to her singing; and I was content. Her cheerfulness, her gentleness and her pleasant face have stamped so deep and lively an impression on my mind that I can still see her manner, look, and attitude; I remember her affectionate language: I could describe what clothes she wore and how her head was dressed, not forgetting the two little curls of black hair on her temples, which she wore in accordance with the fashion of the time.

I am convinced that it is to her I owe the taste, or rather passion, for music, which only became fully developed in me a long time afterwards. She knew a prodigious number of tunes and songs which she used to sing in a very thin, gentle voice. This excellent woman's cheerfulness of soul banished dreaminess and melancholy from herself and all around her. The attraction which her singing possessed for me was so great, that not only have several of her songs always remained in my memory, but even now, when I have lost her, and as I grow older, many of them, totally forgotten since the days of my childhood, return to my mind with inexpressible charm. Would anyone believe that I, an old dotard, eaten up by cares and troubles, sometimes find myself weeping like a child, when I mumble one of those little airs in a voice already broken and trembling?

* * * I have spent my life in idle longing, without saying a word, in the presence of those whom I loved most. Too bashful to declare my taste, I at least satisfied it in situations which had reference to it and kept up the idea of it. To lie at the feet of an imperious mistress, to obey her commands, to ask her forgiveness—this was for me a sweet enjoyment; and, the more my lively imagination heated my blood, the more I presented the appearance of a bashful lover. It may be easily imagined that this manner of making love does not lead to very speedy results, and is not very dangerous to the virtue of those who are its object. For this reason I have rarely possessed, but have none the less enjoyed myself in my own way—that is to say, in imagination. Thus it has happened that my senses, in harmony with my timid disposition

and my romantic spirit, have kept my sentiments pure and my morals blame-less, owing to the very tastes which, combined with a little more impudence, might have plunged me into the most brutal sensuality. * * *

I am a man of very strong passions, and, while I am stirred by them, nothing can equal my impetuosity; I forget all discretion, all feelings of respect, fear and decency; I am cynical, impudent, violent and fearless; no feeling of shame keeps me back, no danger frightens me; with the exception of the single object which occupies my thoughts, the universe is nothing to me. But all this lasts only for a moment, and the following moment plunges me into complete annihilation. In my calmer moments I am indolence and timidity itself; everything frightens and discourages me; a fly, buzzing past, alarms me; a word which I have to say, a gesture which I have to make, terrifies my idleness; fear and shame overpower me to such an extent that I would gladly hide myself from the sight of my fellow-creatures. If I have to act, I do not know what to do; if I have to speak, I do not know what to say; if anyone looks at me, I am put out of countenance. When I am strongly moved I sometimes know how to find the right words, but in ordinary con-versation I can find absolutely nothing, and my condition is unbearable for the simple reason that I am obliged to speak.

Add to this, that none of my prevailing tastes centre in things that can be bought. I want nothing but unadulterated pleasures, and money poisons all. For instance, I am fond of the pleasures of the table; but, as I cannot endure either the constraint of good society or the drunkenness of the tavern, I can only enjoy them with a friend; alone, I cannot do so, for my imagination then occupies itself with other things, and eating affords me no pleasure. If my heated blood longs for women, my excited heart longs still more for affection. Women who could be bought for money would lose for me all their charms; I even doubt whether it would be in me to make use of them. I find it the same with all pleasures within my reach; unless they cost me nothing, I find them insipid. I only love those enjoyments which belong to no one but the first man who knows how to enjoy them.

* * * I worship freedom; I abhor restraint, trouble, dependence. As long as the money in my purse lasts, it assures my independence; it relieves me of the trouble of finding expedients to replenish it, a necessity which always inspired me with dread; but the fear of seeing it exhausted makes me hoard it carefully. The money which a man possesses is the instrument of freedom; that which we eagerly pursue is the instrument of slavery. Therefore I hold fast to that which I have, and desire nothing.

My disinterestedness is, therefore, nothing but idleness; the pleasure of possession is not worth the trouble of acquisition. In like manner, my extravagance is nothing but idleness; when the opportunity of spending agreeably presents itself, it cannot be too profitably employed. Money tempts me less than things, because between money and the possession of the desired object there is always an intermediary, whereas between the thing itself and the enjoyment of it there is none. If I see the thing, it tempts me; if I only see the means of gaining possession of it, it does not. For this reason I have committed thefts, and even now I sometimes pilfer trifles which tempt me, and which I prefer to take rather than to ask for; but neither when a child nor a grown-up man do I ever remember to have robbed anyone of a farthing, except on one occasion, fifteen years ago, when I stole seven *livres* ten *sous*.

*   *   *

BOOK II

[The Years 1728–1731]

* * * I have drawn the great moral lesson, perhaps the only one of any practical value, to avoid those situations of life which bring our duties into conflict with our interests, and which show us our own advantage in the misfortunes of others; for it is certain that, in such situations, however sincere our love of virtue, we must, sooner or later, inevitably grow weak without perceiving it, and become unjust and wicked in act, without having ceased to be just and good in our hearts.

This principle, deeply imprinted on the bottom of my heart, which, although somewhat late, in practice guided my whole conduct, is one of those which have caused me to appear a very strange and foolish creature in the eyes of the world, and, above all, amongst my acquaintances. I have been reproached with wanting to pose as an original, and different from others. In reality, I have never troubled about acting like other people or differently from them. I sincerely desired to do what was right. I withdrew, as far as it lay in my power, from situations which opposed my interests to those of others, and might, consequently, inspire me with a secret, though involuntary, desire of injuring them.

* * * I loved too sincerely, too completely, I venture to say, to be able to be happy easily. Never have passions been at once more lively and purer than mine; never has love been tenderer, truer, more disinterested. I would have sacrificed my happiness a thousand times for that of the person whom I loved; her reputation was dearer to me than my life, and I would never have wished to endanger her repose for a single moment for all the pleasures of enjoyment. This feeling has made me employ such carefulness, such secrecy, and such precaution in my undertakings, that none of them have ever been successful. My want of success with women has always been caused by my excessive love for them.

*   *   *

BOOK III

[The Years 1731–1732]

* * * I only felt the full strength of my attachment when I no longer saw her.[1] When I saw her, I was only content; but, during her absence, my restlessness became painful. The need of living with her caused me outbreaks of tenderness which often ended in tears. I shall never forget how, on the day of a great festival, while she was at vespers, I went for a walk outside the town, my heart full of her image and a burning desire to spend my life with her. I had sense enough to see that at present this was impossible, and that

---

1. Rousseau refers here to Françoise-Louise de Warens, whom he also calls "mamma."

the happiness which I enjoyed so deeply could only be short. This gave to my reflections a tinge of melancholy, about which, however, there was nothing gloomy, and which was tempered by flattering hopes. The sound of the bells, which always singularly affects me, the song of the birds, the beauty of the daylight, the enchanting landscape, the scattered country dwellings in which my fancy placed our common home—all these produced upon me an impression so vivid, tender, melancholy and touching, that I saw myself transported, as it were, in ecstasy, into that happy time and place, wherein my heart, possessing all the happiness it could desire, tasted it with inexpressible rapture, without even a thought of sensual pleasure. I never remember to have plunged into the future with greater force and illusion than on that occasion; and what has struck me most in the recollection of this dream after it had been realised, is that I have found things again exactly as I had imagined them. If ever the dream of a man awake resembled a prophetic vision, it was assuredly that dream of mine. I was only deceived in the imaginary duration; for the days, the years, and our whole life were spent in serene and undisturbed tranquillity, whereas in reality it lasted only for a moment. Alas! my most lasting happiness belongs to a dream, the fulfilment of which was almost immediately followed by the awakening. * * *

Two things, almost incompatible, are united in me in a manner which I am unable to understand: a very ardent temperament, lively and tumultuous passions, and, at the same time, slowly developed and confused ideas, which never present themselves until it is too late. One might say that my heart and my mind do not belong to the same person. Feeling takes possession of my soul more rapidly than a flash of lightning; but, instead of illuminating, inflames and dazzles me. I feel everything and see nothing. I am carried away by my passions, but stupid; in order to think, I must be cool. The astonishing thing is that, notwithstanding, I exhibit tolerably sound judgment, penetration, even finesse, if I am not hurried; with sufficient leisure I can compose excellent impromptus; but I have never said or done anything worthy of notice on the spur of the moment. I could carry on a very clever conversation through the post, as the Spaniards are said to carry on a game of chess. When I read of that Duke of Savoy, who turned round on his journey, in order to cry, "At your throat, Parisian huckster," I said, "There you have myself!"

This sluggishness of thought, combined with such liveliness of feeling, not only enters into my conversation, but I feel it even when alone and at work. My ideas arrange themselves in my head with almost incredible difficulty; they circulate in it with uncertain sound, and ferment till they excite and heat me, and make my heart beat fast; and, in the midst of this excitement, I see nothing clearly and am unable to write a single word—I am obliged to wait. Imperceptibly this great agitation subsides, the confusion clears up, everything takes its proper place, but slowly, and only after a period of long and confused agitation.

* * *

BOOK IV

[*The Years 1731–1732*]

* * * I returned, not to Nyon, but to Lausanne.[2] I wanted to sate myself with the sight of this beautiful lake, which is there seen in its greatest extent. Few of the secret motives which have determined me to act have been more rational. Things seen at a distance are rarely powerful enough to make me act. The uncertainty of the future has always made me look upon plans, which need considerable time to carry them out, as decoys for fools. I indulge in hopes like others, provided it costs me nothing to support them; but if they require continued attention, I have done with it. The least trifling pleasure which is within my reach tempts me more than the joys of Paradise. However, I make an exception of the pleasure which is followed by pain; this has no temptation for me, because I love only pure enjoyments, and these a man never has when he knows that he is preparing for himself repentance and regret. * * *

Why is it that, having found so many good people in my youth, I find so few in my later years? Is their race extinct? No; but the class in which I am obliged to look for them now, is no longer the same as that in which I found them. Among the people, where great passions only speak at intervals, the sentiments of nature make themselves more frequently heard; in the higher ranks they are absolutely stifled, and, under the mask of sentiment, it is only interest or vanity that speaks.

* * * Whenever I approach the Canton[3] of Vaud, I am conscious of an impression in which the remembrance of Madame de Warens, who was born there, of my father who lived there, of Mademoiselle de Vulson who enjoyed the first fruits of my youthful love, of several pleasure trips which I made there when a child and, I believe, some other exciting cause, more mysterious and more powerful than all this, is combined. When the burning desire of this happy and peaceful life, which flees from me and for which I was born, inflames my imagination, it is always the Canton of Vaud, near the lake, in the midst of enchanting scenery, to which it draws me. I feel that I must have an orchard on the shore of this lake and no other, that I must have a loyal friend, a loving wife, a cow, and a little boat. I shall never enjoy perfect happiness on earth until I have all that. I laugh at the simplicity with which I have several times visited this country merely in search of this imaginary happiness. I was always surprised to find its inhabitants, especially the women, of quite a different character from that which I expected. How contradictory it appeared to me! The country and its inhabitants have never seemed to me made for each other.

During this journey to Vévay,[4] walking along the beautiful shore, I abandoned myself to the sweetest melancholy. My heart eagerly flung itself into a thousand innocent raptures; I was filled with emotion, I sighed and wept like a child. How often have I stopped to weep to my heart's content, and, sitting on a large stone, amused myself with looking at my tears falling into the water! * * *

---

2. In southwest Switzerland, the capital of Vaud, which is situated between the Lake of Geneva, the Jura mountains, and the Bernese Alps.   3. Roughly equivalent to a state.   4. Resort town in Vaud, on the Lake of Geneva.

How greatly did the entrance into Paris belie the idea I had formed of it! The external decorations of Turin,[5] the beauty of its streets, the symmetry and regularity of the houses, had made me look for something quite different in Paris. I had imagined to myself a city of most imposing aspect, as beautiful as it was large, where nothing was to be seen but splendid streets and palaces of gold and marble. Entering by the suburb of St. Marceau, I saw nothing but dirty and stinking little streets, ugly black houses, a general air of slovenliness and poverty, beggars, carters, menders of old clothes, criers of decoctions and old hats. All this, from the outset, struck me so forcibly, that all the real magnificence I have since seen in Paris has been unable to destroy this first impression, and I have always retained a secret dislike against residence in this capital. I may say that the whole time, during which I afterwards lived there, was employed solely in trying to find means to enable me to live away from it.

Such is the fruit of a too lively imagination, which exaggerates beyond human exaggeration, and is always ready to see more than it has been told to expect. I had heard Paris so much praised, that I had represented it to myself as the ancient Babylon,[6] where, if I had ever visited it, I should, perhaps, have found as much to take off from the picture which I had drawn of it. The same thing happened to me at the Opera, whither I hastened to go the day after my arrival. The same thing happened to me later at Versailles;[7] and again, when I saw the sea for the first time; and the same thing will always happen to me, when I see anything which has been too loudly announced; for it is impossible for men, and difficult for Nature herself, to surpass the exuberance of my imagination.

* * * The sight of the country, a succession of pleasant views, the open air, a good appetite, the sound health which walking gives me, the free life of the inns, the absence of all that makes me conscious of my dependent position, of all that reminds me of my condition—all this sets my soul free, gives me greater boldness of thought, throws me, so to speak, into the immensity of things, so that I can combine, select, and appropriate them at pleasure, without fear or restraint. I dispose of Nature in its entirety as its lord and master; my heart, roaming from object to object, mingles and identifies itself with those which soothe it, wraps itself up in charming fancies, and is intoxicated with delicious sensations. If, in order to render them permanent, I amuse myself by describing them by myself, what vigorous outlines, what fresh colouring, what power of expression I give them!

* * * At night I lay in the open air, and, stretched on the ground or on a bench, slept as calmly as upon a bed of roses. I remember, especially, that I spent a delightful night outside the city, on a road which ran by the side of the Rhône or Saône,[8] I do not remember which. Raised gardens, with terraces, bordered the other side of the road. It had been very hot during the day; the evening was delightful; the dew moistened the parched grass; the night was calm, without a breath of wind; the air was fresh, without being cold; the sun, having gone down, had left in the sky red vapours, the reflection of which cast a rose-red tint upon the water; the trees on the terraces were full of nightingales answering one another. I walked on in a kind of

5. City in northwest Italy.　6. City in ancient Mesopotamia, noted for extreme luxury.　7. Town southwest of Paris containing the splendid palace built for Louis XIV.　8. French rivers that join courses at Lyons.

ecstasy, abandoning my heart and senses to the enjoyment of all, only regretting, with a sigh, that I was obliged to enjoy it alone. Absorbed in my delightful reverie, I continued my walk late into the night, without noticing that I was tired. At last, I noticed it. I threw myself with a feeling of delight upon the shelf of a sort of niche or false door let into a terrace wall; the canopy of my bed was formed by the tops of trees; a nightingale was perched just over my head, and lulled me to sleep with his song; my slumbers were sweet, my awaking was still sweeter. * * *

In relating my journeys, as in making them, I do not know how to stop. My heart beat with joy when I drew near to my dear mamma, but I walked no faster. I like to walk at my ease, and to stop when I like. A wandering life is what I want. To walk through a beautiful country in fine weather, without being obliged to hurry, and with a pleasant prospect at the end, is of all kinds of life the one most suited to my taste. My idea of a beautiful country is already known. No flat country, however beautiful, has ever seemed so to my eyes. I must have mountain torrents, rocks, firs, dark forests, mountains, steep roads to climb or descend, precipices at my side to frighten me.

* * *

BOOK V

[The Years 1732–1736]

* * * It is sometimes said that the sword wears out the scabbard. That is my history. My passions have made me live, and my passions have killed me. What passions? will be asked. Trifles, the most childish things in the world, which, however, excited me as much as if the possession of Helen or the throne of the universe had been at stake. In the first place—women. When I possessed one, my senses were calm; my heart, never. The needs of love devoured me in the midst of enjoyment; I had a tender mother, a dear friend; but I needed a mistress. I imagined one in her place; I represented her to myself in a thousand forms, in order to deceive myself. If I had thought that I held mamma in my arms when I embraced her, these embraces would have been no less lively, but all my desires would have been extinguished; I should have sobbed from affection, but I should never have felt any enjoyment. Enjoyment! Does this ever fall to the lot of man? If I had ever, a single time in my life, tasted all the delights of love in their fulness, I do not believe that my frail existence could have endured it; I should have died on the spot.

Thus I was burning with love, without an object; and it is this state, perhaps, that is most exhausting. I was restless, tormented by the hopeless condition of poor mamma's affairs, and her imprudent conduct, which were bound to ruin her completely at no distant date. My cruel imagination, which always anticipates misfortunes, exhibited this particular one to me continually, in all its extent and in all its results. I already saw myself compelled by want to separate from her to whom I had devoted my life, and without whom I could not enjoy it. Thus my soul was ever in a state of agitation; I was devoured alternately by desires and fears.

* * *

BOOK VI

[*The Year 1736*]

* * * At this period commences the brief happiness of my life; here approach the peaceful, but rapid moments which have given me the right to say, *I have lived*. Precious and regretted moments! Begin again for me your delightful course; and, if it be possible, pass more slowly in succession through my memory, than you did in your fugitive reality. What can I do, to prolong, as I should like, this touching and simple narrative, to repeat the same things over and over again, without wearying my readers by such repetition, any more than I was wearied of them myself, when I recommenced the life again and again? If all this consisted of facts, actions, and words, I could describe, and in a manner, give an idea of them; but how is it possible to describe what was neither said nor done, nor even thought, but enjoyed and felt, without being able to assign any other reason for my happiness than this simple feeling? I got up at sunrise, and was happy; I walked, and was happy; I saw mamma, and was happy; I left her, and was happy; I roamed the forests and hills, I wandered in the valleys, I read, I did nothing, I worked in the garden, I picked the fruit, I helped in the work of the house, and happiness followed me everywhere—happiness, which could not be referred to any definite object, but dwelt entirely within myself, and which never left me for a single instant. * * *

I should much like to know, whether the same childish ideas ever enter the hearts of other men as sometimes enter mine. In the midst of my studies, in the course of a life as blameless as a man could have led, the fear of hell still frequently troubled me. I asked myself: "In what state am I? If I were to die this moment, should I be damned?" According to my Jansenists,[9] there was no doubt about the matter; but, according to my conscience, I thought differently. Always fearful, and a prey to cruel uncertainty, I had recourse to the most laughable expedients to escape from it, for which I would unhesitatingly have anyone locked up as a madman if I saw him doing as I did. One day, while musing upon this melancholy subject, I mechanically amused myself by throwing stones against the trunks of trees with my usual good aim, that is to say, without hardly hitting one. While engaged in this useful exercise, it occurred to me to draw a prognostic from it to calm my anxiety. I said to myself: "I will throw this stone at the tree opposite; if I hit it, I am saved; if I miss it, I am damned." While speaking, I threw my stone with a trembling hand and a terrible palpitation of the heart, but with so successful an aim that it hit the tree right in the middle, which, to tell the truth, was no very difficult feat, for I had been careful to choose a tree with a thick trunk close at hand. From that time I have never had any doubt about my salvation! When I recall this characteristic incident, I do not know whether to laugh or cry at myself. You great men, who are most certainly laughing, may congratulate yourselves; but do not mock my wretchedness, for I swear to you that I feel it deeply. * * *

9. A sect of strict Catholics, named for Cornelis Jansen (1585–1638). Voltaire mentions them in *Candide*, chaps. 21 and 22.

JOHANN WOLFGANG VON GOETHE
1749–1832

Recasting the ancient legend of Faust, Johann Wolfgang von Goethe created a powerful symbol of the Romantic imagination in all its aspiration and anxiety. Faust
himself, central character of the epic drama, emerges as a Romantic hero, ever testing
the limits of possibility. Yet to achieve his ends he must make a contract with the
Devil: as if to say that giving full scope to imagination necessarily partakes of sin.

Goethe's *Faust* (Part I, 1808; Part II, 1832) constituted the crowning masterpiece
of a life rich in achievement. Goethe exemplifies the nineteenth-century meaning of
genius. Accomplished as poet, dramatist, novelist, and autobiographer, he also practiced law, served as a diplomat, and pursued scientific research. He had a happy
childhood in Frankfurt, after which he studied law at Leipzig and then at Strasbourg,
where in 1770–71 he met Gottfried Herder, leader of a new literary movement called
the Sturm und Drang (Storm and Stress) movement. Participants in this movement
emphasized the importance of revolt against established standards; they interested
Goethe in such newly discovered forms as the folk song and in the literary vitality of
Shakespeare, as opposed to more formally constricted writers.

During the brief period when he practiced law, after an unhappy love affair, Goethe
wrote *The Sorrows of Young Werther* (1774), a novel of immense influence in establishing the image of the introspective, self-pitying, melancholy Romantic hero. In
1775 he accepted an invitation to the court of Charles Augustus, duke of Saxe-
Weimar. He remained in Weimar for the rest of his life, for ten years serving the duke
as chief minister. A trip to Italy from 1786 to 1788 aroused his interest in classic
sources. He wrote dramas based on classic texts, most notably *Iphigenia* (1787); novels (for example, *Elective Affinities*, 1809) that pointed the way to the psychological
novel; lyric poetry; and an important autobiography, *Poetry and Truth* (1811–33). He
also did significant work in botany and physiology. Increasingly famous, he became
in his own lifetime a legendary figure; all Europe flocked to Weimar to visit him.

The legend of Dr. Faustus (the real Johannes Faustus, a scholar, lived from 1480
to 1540), in most versions a seeker after forbidden knowledge, had attracted other
writers before Goethe. The most important previous literary embodiment of the tale
was Christopher Marlowe's *Doctor Faustus* (ca. 1588), a drama ending in its protagonist's damnation as a result of his search for illegitimate power through learning.
Goethe's Faust meets no such fate. Pursuing not knowledge but experience, he
embodies the ideal of limitless aspiration in all its glamour and danger. His contract
with Mephistopheles provides that he will die at the moment he declares himself
satisfied, content to rest in the present; he stakes his life and his salvation on his
capacity ever to yearn for something beyond.

In Part I of Goethe's play, the protagonist's vision of the impossible locates itself
specifically in the figure of Margaret (in German, *Margarete* or its diminutive,
Gretchen), the simple, innocent girl whom he possesses physically but with whom he
can never attain total union. In a speech epitomizing Romantic attitudes toward
nature and toward emotion (especially the emotion of romantic love), Faust responds
to his beloved's question "Do you believe in God?"

> Does not the heaven vault above?
> Is the earth not firmly based down here?
> And do not, friendly,
> Eternal stars arise?
> Do we not look into each other's eyes,
> And all in you is surging
> To your head and heart,

And weaves in timeless mystery,
Unseeable, yet seen, around you?
Then let it fill your heart entirely,
And when your rapture in this feeling is complete,
Call it then as you will,
Call it bliss! heart! love! God!
I do not have a name
For this. Feeling is all.

The notion of *bliss*, for Pope associated with respect for limitation, for Wordsworth connected with revolutionary vision, here designates an unnameable feeling, derived from experience of nature and of romantic love, possibly identical with God, but valued partly for its very vagueness.

Modern readers may feel that Faust bullies Margaret, allowing her no reality except as instrument for his desires. In a poignant moment early in the play, interrupting Faust's rhapsody about her "meekness" and "humility," Margaret suggests, "If you should think of me one moment only . . ." Faust seems incapable of any such awareness, too busy inventing his loved one to see her as she is. He dramatically represents the "egotistical sublime," with a kind of imaginative grandeur inseparable from his utter absorption in the wonder of his own being, his own experience.

Yet the action of Part I turns on Faust's development of just that consciousness of another's reality that seemed impossible for him, and Margaret is the agent of his development. In the great final scene—Margaret in prison, intermittently mad, condemned to death for murdering her illegitimate child by Faust—the woman again appeals to the man to think about her, to *know* her: "Do you know, my love, *whom* you are setting free?" Her anguish, his responsibility for it, force themselves on Faust. He wishes he had never been born: his lust for experience has resulted in this terrible culpability, this agonizing loss. At the final moment of separation, with Margaret's spiritual redemption proclaimed from above, Faust implicitly acknowledges the full reality of the woman he has lost and thus, even though he departs with Mephistopheles, distinguishes himself from his Satanic mentor. Mephistopheles in his nature cannot grasp a reality utterly apart from his own; he can recognize only what belongs to him. Faust, at least fleetingly, realizes the otherness of the woman and the value of what he has lost.

Mephistopheles, at the outset witty and powerful in his own imagination, gradually reveals his limitations. In the *Prologue in Heaven*, the Devil seems energetic, perceptive, enterprising, fearless: as the Lord says, a "joker," apparently more playful than malign. His bargain with the Lord turns on his belief in the essentially "beastly" nature of humankind: like Gulliver's Houyhnhnm master, he emphasizes the human misuse of reason. Although the scene is modeled on the interchange between God and Satan in the Book of Job, it differs significantly in that the Lord gives an explicit reason for allowing the Tempter to function. "Man errs as long as he will," He says, but He adds that Mephistopheles's value is in prodding humanity into action. The introductory scene thus suggests that Mephistopheles will function as an agent of salvation rather than damnation. The Devil's subsequent exchanges with Faust, in Mephistopheles's mind predicated on his own superior knowledge and comprehension, gradually make one realize that the man in significant respects knows more than does the Devil. Mephistopheles, for example, can understand Faust's desire for Margaret only in sexual terms. His witty cynicism seems more and more inadequate to the actual situation. By the end of Part I, Faust's suffering has enlarged him; but from the beginning, his capacity for sympathy marks his potential superiority to the Devil.

The *Walpurgis Night* section, with the *Walpurgis Night's Dream*, marks a stage in Faust's education and an extreme moment in the play's dramatic structure. Goethe here allows himself to indulge in unrestrained fantasy—grotesque, obscene, comic, with an explosion of satiric energy in the dream. The shifting tone and reference of these passages embody ways in which the diabolic might be thought to operate in human terms. While Margaret suffers the consequences of her sin, Faust experiences the ambiguous freedom of the imagination, always at the edge of horror.

The pattern of Faust's moral development in Part I prepares the reader for a non-tragic denouement to the drama as a whole. In Part II, which he worked on for some thirty years, completing it only the year before his death, Goethe moves from the individual to the social. Faust marries Helen of Troy, who gives birth to Euphorion, symbol of new humanity. He turns soldier to save a kingdom; he reclaims land from the sea; finally he rests contented in a vision of happy community generated by the industry of humankind. Mephistopheles thinks this his moment of victory: now Faust has declared himself satisfied. But since his satisfaction depends still on aspiration, on a dream of the future, the angels rescue him at last and take him to heaven.

One cannot read *Faust* with twentieth-century expectations of what a play should be like. This is above all *poetic* drama, to be read with pleasure in the richness of its language, the fertility and daring of its imagination. Although its cast of characters natural and supernatural and its sequence of supernaturally generated events are far from "realistic," it addresses problems still very much with us. How can individual ambition and desire be reconciled with responsibility to others? Does a powerful imagination—an artist's, say, or a scientist's—justify its possessor in ignoring social obligations? Goethe investigates such perplexing issues in symbolic terms, drawing his readers into personal involvement by playing on their emotions even as he questions the proper functions and limitations of commitment to desire—that form of emotional energy that leads to the greatest human achievements, but involves the constant danger of debilitating narcissism.

E. Ludwig, *Goethe, The History of a Man, 1749–1832* (1928), is a solid biography. A biography that also contextualizes Goethe is N. Boyle, *Goethe: The Poet and the Age* (1991). Also useful are V. Lange, ed., *Goethe: A Collection of Critical Essays* (1960); and the essays contained in the critical edition of W. Arndt and C. Hamlin, eds., *Faust* (1976). See also H. Hatfield, *Goethe: A Critical Introduction* (1963); M. Bidney, *Blake and Goethe* (1988); and specifically for *Faust*, L. Dieckmann, *Goethe's Faust: A Critical Reading* (1972). A study relating Goethe's play to other versions of the Faust legend is A. Hoelzel, *The Paradoxical Quest: A Study of Faustian Vicissitudes* (1988). A varied group of essays appears in Reinhold Grimm and Jost Hermand, eds., *Our Faust? Roots and Ramifications of a Modern German Myth* (1987).

PRONOUNCING GLOSSARY

The following list uses common English syllables and stress accents to provide rough equivalents of selected words whose pronunciation may be unfamiliar to the general reader.

Altmayer: *ahlt'-maier*

Auerbach: *aw'-er-bahk*

Elend: *ay'-lend*

encheirisis naturae: *en-kai-ray'-sis nah-tu'-rai*

Euphorion: *oy-foh'-ree-on*

Faust: *fowst*

Goethe: *gur'te*

Leipzig: *laip'-zig*

Proktophantasmist: *prohk-toh-fan-tas'-mist*

Schierke: *sheer'ke*

Sturm und Drang: *shturm unt drahng*

Te Deum: *tay day'-um*

Wagner: *vahg'-ner*

Walpurgis: *vahl-poor'-gis*

Werther: *vayr'-ter*

Zenien: *tsay'-nee-en*

Faust[1]

Prologue in Heaven[2]

[*The* LORD, *the* HEAVENLY HOSTS. *Later,* MEPHISTOPHELES.[3] *The three* ARCHANGELS *step forward.*]

RAPHAEL   The sun intones, in ancient tourney
With brother spheres, a rival air;
And his predestinated journey,
He closes with a thundrous blare.
His sight, as none can comprehend it,   5
Gives strength to angels; the array
Of works, unfathomably splendid,
Is glorious as on the first day.

GABRIEL   Unfathomably swiftly speeded,
Earth's pomp revolves in whirling flight,   10
As Eden's brightness is succeeded
By deep and dread-inspiring night;
In mighty torrents foams the ocean
Against the rocks with roaring song—
In ever-speeding spheric motion,   15
Both rock and sea are swept along.

MICHAEL   And rival tempests roar and ravage
From sea to land, from land to sea,
And, raging, form a chain of savage,
Deeply destructive energy.   20
There flames a flashing devastation
To clear the thunder's crashing way;
Yet, Lord, thy herald's admiration
Is for the mildness of thy day.

THE THREE   The sight, as none can comprehend it,   25
Gives strength to angels; thy array
Of works, unfathomably splendid
Is glorious as on the first day.

MEPHISTOPHELES   Since you, oh Lord, have once again drawn near,
And ask how we have been, and are so genial,   30
And since you used to like to see me here,
You see me, too, as if I were a menial.
I cannot speak as nobly as your staff,
Though by this circle here I shall be spurned:
My pathos would be sure to make you laugh,   35
Were laughing not a habit you've unlearned.
Of suns and worlds I know nothing to say;
I only see how men live in dismay.
The small god of the world will never change his ways
And is as whimsical—as on the first of days.   40
His life might be a bit more fun,

---

1. Translated by Walter Kaufmann.   **2.** The scene is patterned on Job 1.6–12 and 2.1–6.   **3.** The origin of the name remains debatable. It may come from Hebrew, Persian, or Greek, with such meanings as "destroyer-liar," "no friend of Faust," and "no friend of light."

Had you not given him that spark of heaven's sun;
He calls it reason and employs it, resolute
To be more brutish than is any brute.
He seems to me, if you don't mind, Your Grace,   45
Like a cicada of the long-legged race,
That always flies, and, flying, springs,
And in the grass the same old ditty sings;
If only it were grass he could repose in!
There is no trash he will not poke his nose in.   50
THE LORD Can you not speak but to abuse?
Do you come only to accuse?
Does nothing on the earth seem to you right?
MEPHISTOPHELES No, Lord. I find it still a rather sorry sight.
Man moves me to compassion, so wretched is his plight.   55
I have no wish to cause him further woe.
THE LORD Do you know Faust?
MEPHISTOPHELES   The doctor?[4]
THE LORD   Aye, my servant.
MEPHISTOPHELES   Lo!
He serves you[5] most peculiarly, I think.
Not earthly are the poor fool's meat and drink.
His spirit's ferment drives him far,   60
And he half knows how foolish is his quest:
From heaven he demands the fairest star,
And from the earth all joys that he thinks best;
And all that's near and all that's far
Cannot soothe the upheaval in his breast.   65
THE LORD Though now he serves me but confusedly,
I shall soon lead him where the vapor clears.
The gardener knows, however small the tree,
That bloom and fruit adorn its later years.
MEPHISTOPHELES What will you bet? You'll lose him yet to me, 70
If you will graciously connive
That I may lead him carefully.
THE LORD As long as he may be alive,
So long you shall not be prevented.
Man errs as long as he will strive.   75
MEPHISTOPHELES Be thanked for that; I've never been contented
To waste my time upon the dead.
I far prefer full cheeks, a youthful curly-head.
When corpses come, I have just left the house—
I feel as does the cat about the mouse.   80
THE LORD Enough—I grant that you may try to clasp him,
Withdraw this spirit from his primal source
And lead him down, if you can grasp him,
Upon your own abysmal course—
And stand abashed when you have to attest: 85

---

4. Of philosophy.   5. In the German text, Mephistopheles shifts from *du* to *ihr*, indicating his lack of respect for God.

A good man in his darkling aspiration
Remembers the right road throughout his quest.
MEPHISTOPHELES   Enough—he will soon reach his station;
  About my bet I have no hesitation,
  And when I win, concede your stake   90
  And let me triumph with a swelling breast:
  Dust he shall eat, and that with zest,
  As my relation does, the famous snake.
THE LORD   Appear quite free on that day, too;
  I never hated those who were like you: 95
  Of all the spirits that negate,
  The knavish jester gives me least to do.
  For man's activity can easily abate,
  He soon prefers uninterrupted rest;
  To give him this companion hence seems best   100
  Who roils and must as Devil help create.
  But you, God's rightful sons, give voice
  To all the beauty in which you rejoice;
  And that which ever works and lives and grows
  Enfold you with fair bonds that love has wrought,   105
  And what in wavering apparition flows
  That fortify with everlasting thought.
      [*The heavens close, the* ARCHANGELS *disperse.*]
MEPHISTOPHELES [*Alone.*]   I like to see the Old Man now and then
  And try to be not too uncivil.
  It's charming in a noble squire when   110
  He speaks humanely with the very Devil.

The First Part of the Tragedy

NIGHT

[*In a high-vaulted, narrow Gothic den,* FAUST, *restless in his arm-chair at the desk.*]
FAUST   I have, alas, studied philosophy,
  Jurisprudence and medicine, too,
  And, worst of all, theology
  With keen endeavor, through and through—
  And here I am, for all my lore,   5
  The wretched fool I was before.
  Called Master of Arts, and Doctor to boot,
  For ten years almost I confute
  And up and down, wherever it goes,
  I drag my students by the nose—   10
  And see that for all our science and art
  We can know nothing. It burns my heart.
  Of course, I am smarter than all the shysters,
  The doctors, and teachers, and scribes, and Christers;
  No scruple nor doubt could make me ill,   15

I am not afraid of the Devil or hell—
But therefore I also lack all delight,
Do not fancy that I know anything right,
Do not fancy that I could teach or assert
What would better mankind or what might convert.   20
I also have neither money nor treasures,
Nor worldly honors or earthly pleasures;
No dog would want to live longer this way!
Hence I have yielded to magic to see
Whether the spirit's mouth and might   25
Would bring some mysteries to light,
That I need not with work and woe
Go on to say what I don't know;
That I might see what secret force
Hides in the world and rules its course.   30
Envisage the creative blazes
Instead of rummaging in phrases.

Full lunar light, that you might stare
The last time now on my despair!
How often I've been waking here   35
At my old desk till you appeared,
And over papers, notes, and books
I caught, my gloomy friend, your looks.
Oh, that up on a mountain height
I could walk in your lovely light   40
And float with spirits round caves and trees,
Weave in your twilight through the leas,
Cast dusty knowledge overboard,
And bathe in dew until restored.

Still this old dungeon, still a mole!   45
Cursed be this moldy walled-in hole
Where heaven's lovely light must pass,
And lose its luster, through stained glass.
Confined with books, and every tome
Is gnawed by worms, covered with dust,   50
And on the walls, up to the dome,
A smoky paper, spots of rust;
Enclosed by tubes and jars that breed
More dust, by instruments and soot,
Ancestral furniture to boot—   55
That is your world! A world indeed!

And need you ask why in your breast
Your cramped heart throbs so anxiously?
Life's every stirring is oppressed
By an unfathomed agony?   60
Instead of living nature which
God made man for with holy breath,

Must[6] stifles you, and every niche
Holds skulls and skeletons and death.

Flee! Out into the open land!   65
And this book full of mystery,
Written in Nostradamus'[7] hand—
Is it not ample company?
Stars' orbits you will know; and bold,
You learn what nature has to teach;   70
Your soul is freed, and you behold
The spirits' words, the spirits' speech.
Though dry reflection might expound
These holy symbols, it is dreary:
You float, oh spirits, all around;   75
Respond to me, if you can hear me.
    [*He opens the book and sees the symbol of the macrocosm.*[8]]
What jubilation bursts out of this sight
Into my senses—now I feel it flowing,
Youthful, a sacred fountain of delight,
Through every nerve, my veins are glowing.   80
Was it a god that made these symbols be
That soothe my feverish unrest,
Filling with joy my anxious breast,
And with mysterious potency
Make nature's hidden powers around me, manifest?   85

Am I a god? Light grows this page—
In these pure lines my eye can see
Creative nature spread in front of me.
But now I grasp the meaning of the sage:
"The realm of spirits is not far away;   90
Your mind is closed, your heart is dead.
Rise, student, bathe without dismay
In heaven's dawn your mortal head."
    [*He contemplates the symbol.*]
All weaves itself into the whole,
Each living in the other's soul.   95
How heaven's powers climb up and descend,
Passing the golden pails from hand to hand!
Bliss-scented, they are winging
Through the sky and earth—their singing
Is ringing through the world.   100

What play! Yet but a play, however vast!
Where, boundless nature, can I hold you fast?
And where you breasts? Wells that sustain

---

6. Mustiness, mold.   7. Latin name of the French astrologer and physician Michel de Notredame (1503–1566). His collection of rhymed prophecies, *The Centuries,* appeared in 1555.   8. The great world (literal trans.); the universe as a whole. It represents the ordered, harmonious universe in its totality.

All life—the heaven and the earth are nursed.
The wilted breast craves you in thirst—   105
You well, you still—and I languish in vain?
> [*In disgust, he turns some pages and beholds the symbol of the earth
> spirit.*⁹]

How different is the power of this sign!
You, spirit of the earth, seem close to mine:
I look and feel my powers growing,
As if I'd drunk new wine I'm glowing,   110
I feel a sudden courage, and should dare
To plunge into the world, to bear
All earthly grief, all earthly joy—compare
With gales my strength, face shipwreck without care.
Now there are clouds above—   115
The moon conceals her light—
The lamp dies down.
It steams. Red light rays dash
About my head—a chill
Blows from the vaulting dome   120
And seizes me.
I feel you near me, spirit I implored.
Reveal yourself!
Oh, how my heart is gored
By never felt urges,   125
And my whole body surges—
My heart is yours; yours, too, am I.
You must. You must. Though I should have to die.
> [*He seizes the book and mysteriously pronounces the symbol of the
> spirit. A reddish flame flashes, and the* SPIRIT *appears in the flame.*]

SPIRIT   Who calls me?
FAUST [*Turning away.*]   Vision of fright!   130
SPIRIT   With all your might you drew me near
You have been sucking at my sphere,
And now—
FAUST   I cannot bear your sight!
SPIRIT   You have implored me to appear,
Make known my voice, reveal my face;   135
Your soul's entreaty won my grace:
Here I am! What abject fear
Grasps you, oh superman! Where is the soul's impassioned
Call? And where the breast that even now had fashioned
A world to bear and nurse within—that trembled thus,   140
Swollen with joy that it resembled us?
Where are you, Faust, whose voice pierced my domain,
Who surged against me with his might and main?
Could it be you who at my breath's slight shiver
Are to the depths of life aquiver,   145

---

9. This figure seems to be a symbol for the energy of terrestrial nature—neither good nor bad, merely powerful.

A miserably writhing worm?
FAUST   Should I, phantom of fire, fly?
   It's I, it's Faust; your peer am I!
SPIRIT   In the floods of life and creative storm
   To and fro I wave.   150
   Weave eternally.
   And birth and grave,
   An eternal sea,
   A changeful strife,
   A glowing life: 155
   At the roaring loom of the ages I plod
   And fashion the life-giving garment of God.
FAUST   You that traverse worlds without end,
   Sedulous spirit, I feel close to you.
SPIRIT   Peer of the spirit that you comprehend   160
   Not mine! [Vanishes.]
FAUST [Collapsing.]   Not yours?
   Whose then?
   I, image of the godhead!
   And not even yours!   165
      [A knock.]
   O death! My famulus[1]—I know it well.
   My fairest happiness destroyed!
   This wealth of visions I enjoyed
   The dreary creeper must dispel!
      [WAGNER enters in a dressing gown and night cap, a light in his
      hand. FAUST turns away in disgust.]
WAGNER   Forgive! I hear your declamation;   170
   Surely, you read a Grecian tragedy?
   I'd profit from some work in this vocation,
   These days it can be used effectively.
   I have been told three times at least
   That a comedian could instruct a priest.   175
FAUST   Yes, when the priest is a comedian for all his Te Deum.[2]
   As happens more often than one would own.
WAGNER   Ah, when one is confined to one's museum
   And sees, the world on holidays alone,
   But from a distance, only on occasion,   180
   How can one guide it by persuasion?
FAUST   What you don't feel, you will not grasp by art,
   Unless it wells out of your soul
   And with sheer pleasure takes control,
   Compelling every listener's heart.   185
   But sit—and sit, and patch and knead,
   Cook a ragout, reheat your hashes,
   Blow at the sparks and try to breed
   A fire out of piles of ashes!
   Children and apes may think it great,   190

1. Assistant to a medieval scholar.   2. A chant of praise to God.

If that should titillate your gum,
But from heart to heart you will never create.
If from your heart it does not come.
WAGNER   Yet much depends on the delivery;
  I still lack much; don't you agree?   195
FAUST   Oh, let him look for honest gain!
  Let him not be a noisy fool!
  All that makes sense you can explain
  Without the tricks of any school.
  If you have anything to say,   200
  Why juggle words for a display?
  Your glittering rhet'ric, subtly disciplined,
  Which for mankind thin paper garlands weaves,
  Is as unwholesome as the foggy wind
  That blows in autumn through the wilted leaves.   205
WAGNER   Oh God, art is forever
  And our life is brief.
  I fear that with my critical endeavor
  My head and heart may come to grief.
  How hard the scholars' means are to array   210
  With which one works up to the source;
  Before we have traversed but half the course,
  We wretched devils pass away.
FAUST   Parchment—is that the sacred fount
  From which you drink to still your thirst forever?   215
  If your refreshment does not mount.
  From your own soul, you gain it never.
WAGNER   Forgive! It does seem so sublime,
  Entering into the spirit of the time
  To see what wise men, who lived long ago, believed,   220
  Till we at last have all the highest aims achieved.
FAUST   Up to the stars—achieved indeed!
  My friend, the times that antecede
  Our own are books safely protected
  By seven seals.[3] What spirit of the time you call,   225
  Is but the scholars' spirit, after all,
  In which times past are now reflected.
  In truth, it often is pathetic,
  And when one sees it, one would run away:
  A garbage pail, perhaps a storage attic,   230
  At best a pompous moralistic play
  With wonderfully edifying quips,
  Most suitable to come from puppets' lips.
WAGNER   And yet the world! Man's heart and spirit! Oh,
  That everybody knew part of the same!   235
FAUST   The things that people claim to know!
  Who dares to call the child by its true name?
  The few that saw something like this and, starry-eyed

3. Revelation 5.1.

But foolishly, with glowing hearts averred
Their feelings and their visions before the common herd   240
Have at all times been burned and crucified.
I beg you, friend, it is deep in the night;
We must break off this interview.
WAGNER   Our conversation was so erudite,
I should have liked to stay awake with you.   245
Yet Easter comes tomorrow; then permit
That I may question you a bit.
Most zealously I've studied matters great and small;
Though I know much, I should like to know all.
        [*Exit.*]
FAUST [*Alone.*]   Hope never seems to leave those who affirm,   250
The shallow minds that stick to must and mold—
They dig with greedy hands for gold
And yet are happy if they find a worm.
Dare such a human voice be sounded
Where I was even now surrounded   255
By spirits' might? And yet I thank you just this once,
You, of all creatures the most wretched dunce.
You tore me from despair that had surpassed
My mind and threatened to destroy my sense.
Alas, the apparition was so vast   260
That I felt dwarfed in impotence.

I, image of the godhead, that began
To dream eternal truth was within reach,
Exulting on the heavens' brilliant beach
As if I had stripped off the mortal man;   265
I, more than cherub, whose unbounded might
Seemed even then to flow through nature's veins,
Shared the creative joys of God's domains—
Presumptuous hope for which I pay in pains:
One word of thunder swept me from my height.   270

I may no longer claim to be your peer:
I had the power to attract you here,
But to retain you lacked the might.
In that moment of bliss, alack,
In which I felt so small, so great,   275
You, cruel one, have pushed me back
Into uncertain human fate.
Who teaches me? What should I shun?
Should I give in to that obsession?
Not our sufferings only, the deeds that we have done   280
Inhibit our life's progression.

Whatever noblest things the mind received,
More and more foreign matter spoils the theme;
And when the good of this world is achieved,
What's better seems an idle dream.   285

That gave us our life, the noblest urges
Are petrified in the earth's vulgar surges.

Where fantasy once rose in glorious flight,
Hopeful and bold to capture the sublime,
It is content now with a narrow site,   290
Since joy on joy crashed on the rocks of time.
Deep in the heart there dwells relentless care
And secretly infects us with despair;
Restless, she sways and poisons peace and joy
She always finds new masks she can employ: 295
She may appear as house and home, as child and wife,
As fire, water, poison, knife—
What does not strike, still makes you quail,
And what you never lose, for that you always wail.

I am not like the gods! That was a painful thrust;   300
I'm like the worm that burrows in the dust,
Who, as he makes of dust his meager meal,
Is crushed and buried by a wanderer's heel.
Is it not dust that stares from every rack
And narrows down this vaulting den?   305
This moths' world full of bric-a-brac
In which I live as in a pen?
Here I should find for what I care?
Should I read in a thousand books, maybe,
That men have always suffered everywhere,   310
Though now and then some man lived happily?—
Why, hollow skull, do you grin like a faun?
Save that your brain, like mine, once in dismay
Searched for light day, but foundered in the heavy dawn
And, craving truth, went wretchedly astray.   315
You instruments, of course, can scorn and tease
With rollers, handles, cogs, and wheels:
I found the gate, you were to be the keys;
Although your webs are subtle, you cannot break the seals.
Mysterious in the light of day,   320
Nature, in veils, will not let us perceive her,
And what she is unwilling to betray,
You cannot wrest from her with thumbscrews, wheel, or lever.
You ancient tools that rest upon the rack,
Unused by me, but used once by my sire,[4]   325
You ancient scroll that slowly has turned black
As my lamp on this desk gave off its smoky fire—

Far better had I squandered all of my wretched share
Than groan under this wretched load and thus address it!
What from your fathers you received as heir,   330
Acquire if you would possess it.

4. Later we find that Faust's father was a doctor of medicine.

What is not used is but a load to bear;
But if today creates it, we can use and bless it.

Yet why does this place over there attract my sight?
Why is that bottle as a magnet to my eyes?   335
Why does the world seem suddenly so bright,
As when in nightly woods one sees the moon arise?
I welcome you, incomparable potion,
Which from your place I fetch now with devotion:
In you I honor human wit and art.   340
You essence from all slumber-bringing flowers,
You extract of all subtly fatal powers,
Bare to your master your enticing heart!
I look upon you, soothed are all my pains,
I seize you now, and all my striving wanes,   345
The spirit's tidal wave now ebbs away.
Slowly I float into the open sea,
The waves beneath me now seem gay and free,
To other shores beckons another day.
A fiery chariot floats on airy pinions   350
Cleaving the ether—tarry and descend!
Uncharted orbits call me, new dominions
Of sheer creation, active without end.
This higher life, joys that no mortal won!
You merit this—but now a worm, despairing?   355
Upon the mild light of the earthly sun
Turn, bold, your back! And with undaunted daring
Tear open the eternal portals
Past which all creatures slink in silent dread.
The time has come to prove by deeds that mortals   360
Have as much dignity as any god,
And not to tremble at that murky cave
Where fantasy condemns itself to dwell
In agony. The passage brave
Whose narrow mouth is lit by all the flames of hell;   365
And take this step with cheerful resolution,
Though it involve the risk of utter dissolution.

Now you come down to me, pure crystal vase,
Emerge again out of your ancient case
Of which for many years I did not think.   370
You glistened at my father's joyous feasts
And cheered the solemn-looking guests,
When you were passed around for all to drink.
The many pictures, glistening in the light,
The drinker's duty rhyming to explain them,[5]   375
To scan your depths and in one draught to drain them,
Bring back to mind many a youthful night.

---

5. Faust here alludes to the drinking of toasts. The maker of a toast often produced impromptu rhymes.

There is no friend now to fulfill this duty,
Nor shall I exercise my wit upon your beauty.
Here is a juice that fast makes drunk and mute;   380
With its brown flood it fills this crystal bowl,
I brewed it and shall drink it whole
And offer this last drink with all my soul
Unto the morning as a festive high salute. [*He puts the bowl to his lips.*]
    [*Chime of bells and choral song.*]
CHOIR OF ANGELS   Christ is arisen.   385
    Hail the meek-spirited
    Whom the ill-merited,
    Creeping, inherited
    Faults held in prison.
FAUST   What deeply humming strokes, what brilliant tone   390
  Draws from my lips the crystal bowl with power?
  Has the time come, deep bells, when you make known
  The Easter holiday's first holy hour?
  Is this already, choirs, the sweet consoling hymn
  That was first sung around his tomb by cherubim,   395
  Confirming the new covenant?
CHOIR OF WOMEN   With myrrh, when bereaved,
    We had adorned him;
    We that believed
    Laid down and mourned him.   400
    Linen we twined
    Round the adored—
    Returning, we cannot find
    Christ, our Lord.
CHOIR OF ANGELS   Christ is arisen.   405
    Blessed be the glorious
    One who victorious
    Over laborious
    Trials has risen.
FAUST   Why would you, heaven's tones, compel   410
  Me gently to rise from my dust?
  Resound where tenderhearted people dwell:
  Although I hear the message, I lack all faith or trust;
  And faith's favorite child is miracle.
  For those far spheres I should not dare to strive,   415
  From which these tidings come to me;
  And yet these chords, which I have known since infancy:
  Call me now, too, back into life.
  Once heaven's love rushed at me as a kiss
  In the grave silence of the Sabbath day,   420
  The rich tones of the bells, it seemed, had much to say,
  And every prayer brought impassioned bliss.
  An unbelievably sweet yearning
  Drove me to roam through wood and lea,
  Crying, and as my eyes were burning,   425
  I felt a new world grow in me.

This song proclaimed the spring feast's free delight, appealing
To the gay games of youth—they plead:
Now memory entices me with childlike feeling
Back from the last, most solemn deed.   430
Sound on, oh hymns of heaven, sweet and mild!
My tears are flowing; earth, take back your child!
CHOIR OF DISCIPLES   Has the o'ervaulted one
     Burst from his prison,
     The living-exalted one   435
     Gloriously risen,
     Is in this joyous birth
     Zest for creation near—
     Oh, on the breast of earth
     We are to suffer here.   440
     He left his own
     Pining in sadness;
     Alas, we bemoan,
     Master, your gladness.
CHOIR OF ANGELS   Christ is arisen   445
     Out of corruption's womb.
     Leave behind prison,
     Fetters and gloom!
     Those who proceed for him,
     Lovingly bleed for him,   450
     Brotherly feed for him,
     Travel and plead for him,
     And to bliss lead for him,
     For you the Master is near,
     For you he is here.   455

BEFORE THE CITY GATE

[*People of all kinds are walking out.*]
SOME APPRENTICES   Why do you go that way?
OTHERS   We are going to Hunter's Lodge today.
THE FIRST   But we would rather go to the mill.
AN APPRENTICE   Go to the River Inn, that's my advice.
ANOTHER   I think, the way there isn't nice.   5
THE OTHERS   Where are you going?
A THIRD ONE   Up the hill.
A FOURTH ONE   Burgdorf would be much better. Let's go there with the
    rest:
   The girls there are stunning, their beer is the best,
   And it's first-class, too, for a fight.
A FIFTH ONE   You are indeed a peppy bird,   10
   Twice spanked, you're itching for the third.
   Let's not, the place is really a fright.
SERVANT GIRL   No, no! I'll go back to the town again.
ANOTHER   We'll find him at the poplars, I'm certain it is true.
THE FIRST   What's that to me? Is it not plain,   15

He'll walk and dance only with you?
He thinks, you are the only one.
And why should I care for your fun?
THE OTHER ONE   He will not be alone. He said,
  Today he'd bring the curly-head.   20
STUDENT   Just see those wenches over there!
  Come, brother, let us help the pair.
  A good strong beer, a smarting pipe,
  And a maid, nicely dressed—that is my type!
CITIZEN'S DAUGHTER   Look there and see those handsome blades!   25
  I think it is a crying shame:
  They could have any girl that meets with their acclaim,
  And chase after these silly maids.
SECOND STUDENT [To the FIRST.]   Don't go so fast; behind us are two more,
  And they are dressed at least as neatly.   30
  I know one girl, she lives next door,
  And she bewitches me completely.
  The way they walk, they seem demure,
  But won't mind company, I'm sure.
THE FIRST   No, brother, I don't like those coy addresses.   35
  Come on, before we lose the wilder prey.
  The hand that wields the broom on Saturday
  Will, comes the Sunday, give the best caresses.
CITIZEN   No, the new mayor is no good, that's what I say.
  Since he's in, he's fresher by the day.   40
  What has he done for our city?
  Things just get worse; it is a pity!
  We must obey, he thinks he's clever,
  And we pay taxes more than ever.
BEGGAR [Sings.]   Good gentlemen and ladies fair,   45
      So red of cheek, so rich in dress,
      Be pleased to look on my despair,
      To see and lighten my distress.
      Let me not grind here, vainly waiting!
      For only those who give are gay,   50
      And when all men are celebrating,
      Then I should have my harvest day.
ANOTHER CITIZEN   On Sun- and holidays, there is no better fun,
  Than chattering of wars and warlike fray,
  When off in Turkey, far away,   55
  One people beats the other one.
  We stand at the window, drink a wine that is light,
  Watch the boats glide down the river, see the foam,
  And cheerfully go back at night,
  Grateful that we have peace at home.   60
THIRD CITIZEN   Yes, neighbor, that is nicely said.
  Let them crack skulls, and wound, and maim,
  Let all the world stand on its head;
  But here, at home, all should remain the same.
OLD WOMAN [To the CITIZEN'S DAUGHTERS.]

Ah, how dressed up! So pretty and so young! 65
Who would not stop to stare at you?
Don't be puffed up, I'll hold my tongue.
I know your wish, and how to get it, too.
CITIZEN'S DAUGHTER   Come quickly, Agatha! I take good heed
Not to be seen with witches; it's unwise.— 70
Though on St. Andrew's Night[6] she brought indeed
My future lover right before my eyes.
THE OTHER ONE   She showed me mine, but in a crystal ball
With other soldiers, bold and tall;
I have been looking ever since, 75
But so far haven't found my prince.
SOLDIERS   Castles with lofty
Towers and banners,
Maidens with haughty,
Disdainful manners 80
I want to capture.
Fair is the dare,
Splendid the pay.
And we let trumpets
Do our wooing,
For our pleasures 85
And our undoing.
Life is all storming,
Life is all splendor,
Maidens and castles 90
Have to surrender.
Fair is the dare,
Splendid the pay.
And then the soldiers
March on away. 95
[FAUST and WAGNER.]
FAUST   Released from the ice are river and creek,
Warmed by the spring's fair quickening eye;
The valley is green with hope and joy;
The hoary winter has grown so weak
He has withdrawn to the rugged mountains. 100
From there he sends, but only in flight,
Impotent showers of icy hail
That streak across the greening vale;
But the sun will not suffer the white;
Everywhere stirs what develops and grows, 105
All he would quicken with color that glows;
Flowers are lacking, blue, yellow, and red,
But he takes dressed-up people instead.
Turn around now and look down

6. St. Andrew's Eve, November 29, the traditional time for young girls to consult fortune-tellers about
their future lovers or husbands.

From the heights back to the town.   110
Out of the hollow gloomy gate
Surges and scatters a motley horde.
All seek sunshine. They celebrate
The resurrection of the Lord.
For they themselves are resurrected   115
From lowly houses, musty as stables,
From trades to which they are subjected,
From the pressure of roofs and gables,
From the stifling and narrow alleys,
From the churches' reverent night   120
They have emerged into the light.
Look there! Look, how the crowd now sallies
Gracefully into the gardens and leas,
How on the river, all through the valley,
Frolicsome floating boats one sees,   125
And, overloaded beyond its fill,
This last barge now is swimming away.
From the far pathways of the hill
We can still see how their clothes are gay.
I hear the village uproar rise;   130
Here is the people's paradise,
And great and small shout joyously:
Here I am human, may enjoy humanity.
WAGNER   To take a walk with you, good sir,
Is a great honor and reward,   135
But I myself should never so far err,
For the uncouth I always have abhorred.
This fiddling, bowling, loud delight—
I hate these noises of the throng;
They rage as if plagued by an evil sprite   140
And call it joy and call it song.
        [PEASANTS *under the linden tree. Dance and Song.*]
The shepherd wished to dance and dressed
With ribbons, wreath, and motley vest,
He was a dandy beau.
Around the linden, lass and lad.   145
Were crowding, dancing round like mad.
Hurrah! Hurrah!
Hurrah! Hi-diddle-dee!
Thus went the fiddle bow.

He pressed into the dancing whirl   150
His elbow bumped a pretty girl,
And he stepped on her toe.
The lively wench, she turned and said:
"You seem to be a dunderhead!"
Hurrah! Hurrah!   155
Hurrah! Hi-diddle-dee!
Don't treat a poor girl so.

The circle whirled in dancing flight,
Now they danced left, now they danced right,
The skirts flow high and low.   160
Their cheeks were flushed and they grew warm
And rested, panting, arm in arm.
Hurrah! Hurrah!
Hurrah! Hi-diddle-dee!
With waists and elbows so.   165

Please do not make so free with me!
For many fool their bride-to-be
And lie, as you well know.
And yet he coaxed the girl aside,
And from the linden, far and wide: 170
Hurrah! Hurrah!
Hurrah! Hi-diddle-dee!
Clamor and fiddle bow.

OLD PEASANT   Dear doctor, it is good of you
That you don't spurn us on this day   175
But find into this swarming throng,
Though a great scholar, still your way.
So please accept the finest mug;
With a good drink it has been filled,
I offer it and wish aloud: 180
Not only may your thirst be stilled;
As many drops as it conveys
Ought to be added to your days.

FAUST   I take the bumper and I, too,
Thank and wish health to all of you.   185
[*The people gather around in a circle.*]

OLD PEASANT   Indeed, it is most kind of you
That you appear this happy day;
When evil days came in the past,
You always helped in every way.
And many stand here, still alive,   190
Whom your good father toiled to wrest
From the hot fever's burning rage
When he prevailed over the pest.[7]
And you, a young man at that time,
Made to the sick your daily round.   195
While many corpses were brought out,
You always emerged safe and sound,
And took these trials in your stride:
The Helper helped the helper here.

ALL   Health to the man so often tried!   200
May he yet help for many a year!

FAUST   Bow down before Him, all of you,
Who teaches help and sends help, too. [*He walks on with* WAGNER.]

---

7. Pestilence or plague.

WAGNER   Oh, what a feeling you must have, great man,
　　When crowds revere you like a mighty lord.　　　　　　　　205
　　Oh, blessed are all those who can
　　Employ their gifts for such reward.
　　The father shows you to his son,
　　They ask what gives and come and run,
　　The fiddle stops, the dance is done.　　　　　　　　　　210
　　You walk, they stand in rows to see,
　　Into the air their caps will fly—
　　A little more, and they would bend their knee
　　As if the Holy Host[8] went by.
FAUST   Now just a few more steps uphill to the big stone,　　215
　　From our wandering we can rest up there.
　　I often sat there, thoughtful and alone,
　　And vexed myself with fasting and with prayer.
　　In hope still rich, with faith still blessed,
　　I thought entreaties, tears, and sighs　　　　　　　　　220
　　Would force the Master of the Skies
　　To put an end to the long pest.
　　The crowd's applause now sounds like caustic fun.
　　I only wish you could read in my heart
　　How little father and son　　　　　　　　　　　　　225
　　Deserve such fame for their poor art.
　　My father was obscure, if quite genteel,
　　And pondered over nature and every sacred sphere
　　In his own cranky way, though quite sincere,
　　With ardent, though with wayward, zeal.　　　　　　　230
　　And with proficient devotees,
　　In his black kitchen he would fuse
　　After unending recipes,
　　Locked in, the most contrary brews.
　　They made red lions, a bold wooer came,　　　　　　　235
　　In tepid baths was mated to a lily;
　　And then the pair was vexed with a wide-open flame
　　From one bride chamber to another, willy-nilly.
　　And when the queen appeared, all pied,
　　Within the glass after a spell,　　　　　　　　　　240
　　The medicine was there, and though the patients died,
　　Nobody questioned: who got well?[9]
　　And thus we raged fanatically
　　In these same mountains, in this valley,
　　With hellish juice worse than the pest.　　　　　　　245
　　Though thousands died from poison that I myself would give,
　　Yes, though they perished, I must live
　　To hear the shameless killers blessed.
WAGNER   I cannot see why you are grieved.
　　What more can honest people do　　　　　　　　　　250

8. The Eucharist, the consecrated bread and wine of the Sacrament.　9. This confusing sequence evokes a kind of medicine closely allied to magic and inappropriate to the needs of the ill people seeking help.

Than be conscientious and pursue
With diligence the art that they received?
If you respect your father as a youth,
You'll learn from him what you desire;
If as a man you add your share of truth   255
To ancient lore, your son can go still higher.
FAUST Oh, happy who still hopes to rise
Out of this sea of errors and false views!
What one does *not* know, one could utilize,
And what one knows one cannot use.   260
But let the beauty offered by this hour
Not be destroyed by our spleen!
See how, touched by the sunset's parting power,
The huts are glowing in the green.
The sun moves on, the day has had its round;   265
He hastens on, new life greets his salute.
Oh,[1] that no wings lift me above the ground
To strive and strive in his pursuit!
In the eternal evening light
The quiet world would lie below   270
With every valley tranquil, on fire every height,
The silver stream to golden rivers flow.
Nor could the mountain with its savage guise
And all its gorges check my godlike ways;
Already ocean with its glistening bays   275
Spreads out before astonished eyes.
At last the god sinks down, I seem forsaken;
But I feel new unrest awaken
And hurry hence to drink his deathless light,
The day before me, and behind me night,   280
The billows under me, and over me the sky.
A lovely dream, while he makes his escape.
The spirit's wings will not change our shape:
Our body grows no wings and cannot fly.
Yet it is innate in our race   285
That our feelings surge in us and long
When over us, lost in the azure space
The lark trills out her glorious song;
When over crags where fir trees quake
In icy winds, the eagle soars,   290
And over plains and over lakes
The crane returns to homeward shores.
WAGNER I, too, have spells of eccentricity,
But such unrest has never come to me.
One soon grows sick of forest, field, and brook,   295
And I shall never envy birds their wings.
Far greater are the joys the spirit brings—
From page to page, from book to book.

1. Alas.

Thus winter nights grow fair and warm the soul;
Yes, blissful life suffuses every limb,   300
And when one opens up an ancient parchment scroll,
The very heavens will descend on him.
FAUST   You are aware of only one unrest;
Oh, never learn to know the other!
Two souls, alas, are dwelling in my breast,   305
And one is striving to forsake its brother.
Unto the world in grossly loving zest,
With clinging tendrils, one adheres;
The other rises forcibly in quest
Of rarefied ancestral spheres.   310
If there be spirits in the air
That hold their sway between the earth and sky,
Descend out of the golden vapors there
And sweep me into iridescent life.
Oh, came a magic cloak into my hands   315
To carry me to distant lands,
I should not trade it for the choicest gown,
Nor for the cloak and garments of the crown.
WAGNER   Do not invoke the well-known throng that flow
Through mists above and spread out in the haze,   320
Concocting danger in a thousand ways
For man wherever he may go.
From the far north the spirits' deadly fangs
Bear down on you with arrow-pointed tongues;
And from the east they come with withering pangs   325
And nourish themselves from your lungs.
The midday sends out of the desert those
Who pile heat upon heat upon your crown,
While evening brings the throng that spells repose—
And then lets you, and fields and meadows, drown.   330
They gladly listen, but are skilled in harm,
Gladly obey, because they like deceit;
As if from heaven sent, they please and charm,
Whispering like angels when they cheat.
But let us go! The air has cooled, the world   335
Turned gray, mists are unfurled.
When evening comes one values home,
Why do you stand amazed? What holds your eyes?
What in the twilight merits such surprise?
FAUST   See that black dog through grain and stubble roam?   340
WAGNER   I noticed him way back, but cared not in the least.
FAUST   Look well! For what would *you* take this strange beast?
WAGNER   Why, for a poodle fretting doggedly
As it pursues the tracks left by its master.
FAUST   It spirals all around us, as you see,   345
And it approaches, fast and faster.
And if I do not err, a fiery eddy
Whirls after it and marks the trail.

WAGNER   I see the poodle, as I said already;
   As for the rest, your eyesight seems to fail.   350
FAUST   It seems to me that he winds magic snares
   Around our feet, a bond of future dangers.
WAGNER   He jumps around, unsure, and our presence scares
   The dog who seeks his master, and finds instead two strangers.
FAUST   The spiral narrows, he is near!   355
WAGNER   You see, a dog and not a ghost is here.
   He growls, lies on his belly, thus he waits,
   He wags his tail: all canine traits.
FAUST   Come here and walk along with us!
WAGNER   He's poodlishly ridiculous.   360
   You stand and rest, and he waits, too;
   You speak to him, and he would climb on you;
   Lose something, he will bring it back again,
   Jump in the lake to get your cane.
FAUST   You seem quite right, I find, for all his skill,   365
   No trace of any spirit: all is drill.
WAGNER   By dogs that are expertly trained
   The wisest man is entertained.
   He quite deserves your favor: it is prudent
   To cultivate the students' noble student.   370
     [*They pass through the City Gate.*]

STUDY

FAUST [*Entering with the poodle.*]   The fields and meadows I have fled
   As night enshrouds them and the lakes;
   With apprehensive, holy dread
   The better soul in us awakes.
   Wild passions have succumbed to sleep,   5
   All vehement exertions bow;
   The love of man stirs in us deep,
   The love of God is stirring now.

Be quiet, poodle! Stop running around!
Why do you snuffle at the sill like that?   10
Lie down behind the stove—not on the ground:
Take my best cushion for a mat.
As you amused us on our way
With running and jumping and did your best,
Let me look after you and say: 15
Be quiet, please, and be my guest.

   When in our narrow den
   The friendly lamp glows on the shelf,
   Then light pervades our breast again
   And fills the heart that knows itself.   20
   Reason again begins to speak,
   Hope blooms again with ancient force,
   One longs for life and one would seek
   Its rivers and, alas, its source.

Stop snarling poodle! For the sacred strain   25
To which my soul is now submitting
Beastly sounds are hardly fitting.
We are accustomed to see *men* disdain
What they don't grasp;
When it gives trouble, they profane   30
Even the beautiful and the good.
Do dogs, too, snarl at what's not understood?

    Even now, however, though I tried my best,
    Contentment flows no longer through my breast.
    Why does the river rest so soon, and dry up, and   35
    Leave us to languish in the sand?
    How well I know frustration!
    This want, however, we can overwhelm:
    We turn to the supernatural realm,
    We long for the light of revelation   40
    Which is nowhere more magnificent
    Than in our New Testament.
    I would for once like to determine—
    Because I am sincerely perplexed—
    How the sacred original text[2]   45
    Could be translated into my beloved German.

        [*He opens a tome and begins.*]
It says: "In the beginning was the *Word*."[3]
Already I am stopped. It seems absurd.
The *Word* does not deserve the highest prize,
I must translate it otherwise   50
If I am well inspired and not blind.
It says: In the beginning was the *Mind.*
Ponder that first line, wait and see,
Lest you should write too hastily.
Is mind the all-creating source?   55
It ought to say: In the beginning there was *Force.*
Yet something warns me as I grasp the pen,
That my translation must be changed again.
The spirit helps me. Now it is exact.
I write: In the beginning was the *Act.*   60

If I am to share my room with you,
Poodle, stop moaning so!
And stop your bellow,
For such a noisy, whiny fellow
I do not like to have around.   65
One of us, black hound,
Will have to give ground.
With reluctance I change my mind:
The door is open, you are not confined.
But what must I see!   70
Can that happen naturally?

2. I.e., the Greek. 3. John 1.1.

Is it a shadow? Am I open-eyed?
How grows my poodle long and wide!
He reaches up like rising fog—
This is no longer the shape of a dog!   75
Oh, what a specter I brought home!
A hippopotamus of foam,
With fiery eyes; how his teeth shine!
You are as good as mine:
For such a semi-hellish brow   80
The Key of Solomon⁴ will do.

SPIRITS [*In the corridor.*]   One has been caught inside.
    Do not follow him! Abide!
    As a fox in a snare,
    Hell's old lynx is caught in there.   85
    But give heed!
    Float up high, float down low,
    To and fro,
    And he tries, and he is freed.
    Can you avail him?   90
    Then do not fail him!
    For you must not forget,
    We are in his debt.

FAUST   Countering the beast, I might well
First use the fourfold spell: 95

    Salamander shall broil,
    Undene shall grieve,
    Sylphe shall leave,
    Kobold⁵ shall toil.

Whoever ignores   100
The elements' cores,
Their energy
And quality,
Cannot command
In the spirits' land.   105

    Disappear flashing,
    Salamander!
    Flow together, splashing,
    Undene!
    Glow in meteoric beauty,   110
    Sylphe!
    Do your domestic duty,
    Incubus! Incubus!
    Step forward and finish thus.

None of the four   115
Is this beast's core.
It lies quite calmly there and beams;

---

4. The *Clavicula Salomonis*, a standard work used by magicians for conjuring; in many medieval legends, Solomon was noted as a great magician.   5. A spirit of the earth. *Salamander:* spirit of fire. *Undene:* or undine, spirit of water. *Sylphe:* or sylph, spirit of air.

I have not hurt it yet, it seems.
Now listen well
To a stronger spell.   120

    If you should be
    Hell's progeny,
    Then see this symbol
    Before which tremble
    The cohorts of Hell!   125

Already it bristles and starts to swell.

    Spirit of shame,
    Can you read the name
    Of the Uncreated,
    Defying expression,   130
    With whom the heavens are sated,
    Who was pierced in transgression?

Behind the stove it swells
As an elephant under my spells;
It fills the whole room and quakes,   135
It would turn into mist and fleet.
Stop now before the ceiling breaks!
Lie down at your master's feet!

    You see, I do not threaten in vain:
    With holy flames I cause you pain.   140
    Do not require
    The threefold glowing fire![6]
    Do not require
    My art in its full measure!

MEPHISTOPHELES [*Steps forward from behind the stove, dressed as a traveling scholar, while the mist clears away.*]
    Why all the noise? Good sir, what is your pleasure?   145
FAUST   Then this was our poodle's core!
    Simply a traveling scholar? The *casus*[7] makes me laugh.
MEPHISTOPHELES   Profound respects to you and to your lore:
    You made me sweat with all your chaff.
FAUST   What is your name?
MEPHISTOPHELES   This question seems minute   150
    For one who thinks the word so beggarly,
    Who holds what seems in disrepute,
    And craves only reality.[8]
FAUST   Your real being no less than your fame
    Is often shown, sirs, by your name,   155
    Which is not hard to analyze
    When one calls you the Liar, Destroyer, God of Flies.[9]
    Enough, who are you then?

---

6. Perhaps the Trinity or a triangle with divergent rays.   7. Occurrence.   8. Mephistopheles refers to Faust's substitution of *Act* for *Word* in the passage from John (see line 60).   9. An almost literal translation of the name of the Philistine deity Beelzebub.

MEPHISTOPHELES   Part of that force which would
     Do evil evermore, and yet creates the good.
FAUST   What is it that this puzzle indicates?   160
MEPHISTOPHELES   I am the spirit that negates.
     And rightly so, for all that comes to be
     Deserves to perish wretchedly;
     'Twere better nothing would begin.
     Thus everything that your terms, sin,   165
     Destruction, evil represent—
     That is my proper element.
FAUST   You call yourself a part, yet whole make your debut?
MEPHISTOPHELES   The modest truth I speak to you.
     While man, this tiny world of fools, is droll   170
     Enough to think himself a whole,
     I am part of the part that once was everything,
     Part of the darkness which gave birth to light,
     That haughty light which envies mother night
     Her ancient rank and place and would be king—   175
     Yet it does not succeed: however it contend,
     It sticks to bodies in the end.
     It streams from bodies, it lends bodies beauty,
     A body won't let it progress;
     So it will not take long, I guess,   180
     And with the bodies it will perish, too.
FAUST   I understand your noble duty:
     Too weak for great destruction, you
     Attempt it on a minor scale.
MEPHISTOPHELES   And I admit it is of slight avail.   185
     What stands opposed to our Nought,
     The some, your wretched world—for aught
     That I have so far undertaken,
     It stands unruffled and unshaken:
     With billows, fires, storms, commotion,   190
     Calm, after all, remain both land and ocean.
     And that accursed lot, the brood of beasts and men,
     One cannot hurt them anyhow.
     How many have I buried now!
     Yet always fresh new blood will circulate again.   195
     Thus it goes on—I could rage in despair!
     From water, earth, and even air,
     A thousand seeds have ever grown
     In warmth and cold and drought and mire!
     If I had not reserved myself the fire,   200
     I should have nothing of my own.
FAUST   And thus, I see, you would resist
     The ever-live creative power
     By clenching your cold devil's fist
     Resentfully—in vain you glower.   205
     Try something new and unrelated,
     Oh you peculiar son of chaos!

MEPHISTOPHELES   Perchance your reasoning might sway us—
  The next few times we may debate it.
  But for the present, may I go?   210
FAUST   I cannot see why you inquire.
  Now that we met, you ought to know
  That you may call as you desire.
  Here is the window, here the door,
  A chimney there, if that's preferred.   215
MEPHISTOPHELES   I cannot leave you that way, I deplore:
  By a small obstacle I am deterred:
  The witch's foot on your threshold, see—
FAUST   The pentagram[1] distresses you?
  Then, son of hell, explain to me: 220
  How could you enter here without ado?
  And how was such a spirit cheated?
MEPHISTOPHELES   Behold it well: It is not quite completed;
  One angle—that which points outside—
  Is open just a little bit.   225
FAUST: That was indeed a lucky hit.
  I caught you and you must abide.
  How wonderful, and yet how queer!
MEPHISTOPHELES   The poodle never noticed, when he first jumped in
      here,
  But now it is a different case;   230
  The Devil cannot leave this place.
FAUST   The window's there. Are you in awe?
MEPHISTOPHELES   The devils and the demons have a law:
  Where they slipped in, they always must withdraw.
  The first time we are free, the second time constrained.   235
FAUST   For hell, too, laws have been ordained?
  Superb! Then one should surely make a pact,
  And one of you might enter my employ.
MEPHISTOPHELES   What we would promise you, you would enjoy,
  And none of it we would subtract.   240
  But that we should not hurry so,
  And we shall talk about it soon;
  For now I ask the single boon
  That you permit me now to go.
FAUST   For just a moment stay with me   245
  And let me have some happy news.
MEPHISTOPHELES   Not now. I'll come back presently,
  Then you may ask me what you choose.
FAUST   You were not caught by my device
  When you were snared like this tonight.   250
  Who holds the Devil, hold him tight!
  He can't expect to catch him twice.
MEPHISTOPHELES   If you prefer it, I shall stay
  With you, and I shall not depart,

---

1. A magic five-pointed star designed to keep away evil spirits.

Upon condition that I may 255
Amuse you with some samples of my art.
FAUST   Go right ahead, you are quite free—
Provided it is nice to see.
MEPHISTOPHELES   Right in this hour you will obtain
More for your senses than you gain 260
In a whole year's monotony.
What tender spirits now will sing,
The lovely pictures that they bring
Are not mere magic for the eye:
They will delight your sense of smell, 265
Be pleasing to your taste as well,
Excite your touch, and give you joy.
No preparation needs my art,
We are together, let us start.
SPIRITS   Vanish, you darkling 270
   Arches above him.
   Friendlier beaming,
   Sky should be gleaming
   Down upon us.
   Ah, that the darkling 275
   Clouds had departed!
   Stars now are sparkling,
   More tenderhearted
   Suns shine on us.
   Spirits aerial, 280
   Fair and ethereal,
   Wavering and bending,
   Sail by like swallows.
   Yearning unending
   Sees them and follows, 285
   Garments are flowing,
   Ribbons are blowing,
   Covering the glowing
   Land and the bower
   Where, in the hedges, 290
   Thinking and dreaming,
   Lovers make pledges.
   Bower on bower.
   Tendrils are streaming;
   Heavy grapes shower 295
   Their sweet excesses
   Into the presses;
   In streams are flowing
   Wines that are glowing,
   Foam, effervescent, 300
   Through iridescent
   Gems; they are storming
   Down from the mountains;
   Lakes they are forming,

Beautiful fountains   305
Where hills are ending,
Birds are descending,
Drink and fly onward,
Fly ever sunward,
Fly from the highlands   310
Toward the ocean
Where brilliant islands
Sway in soft motion.
Jubilant choirs
Soothe all desires,   315
And are entrancing
Those who are dancing
Like whirling satyrs,
But the throng scatters.
Some now are scaling   320
Over the mountains,
Others are sailing
Toward the fountains,
Others are soaring,
All life adoring,   325
All crave the far-off
Love-spending star of
Rapturous bliss.

MEPHISTOPHELES   He sleeps. I thank you, airy, tender throng.
    You made him slumber with your song.   330
    A splendid concert. I appreciate this.
    You are not yet the man to hold the Devil fast.
    Go, dazzle him with dream shapes, sweet and vast,
    Plunge him into an ocean of untruth.
    But now, to break the threshold's spell at last,   335
    I have to get a rat's sharp tooth.
    I need no conjuring today,
    One's rustling over there and will come right away.
    The lord of rats, the lord of mice,
    Of flies and frogs, bedbugs and lice,   340
    Bids you to dare now to appear
    To gnaw upon this threshold here,
    Where he is dabbing it with oil.
    Ah, there you come. Begin your toil.
    The point that stopped me like a magic hedge   345
    Is way up front, right on the edge.
    Just one more bite, and that will do.
    Now, Faustus, sleep and dream, till I come back to you.

FAUST [*Awakening.*]   Betrayed again? Fooled by a scheme?
    Should spirits' wealth so suddenly decay   350
    That I behold the Devil in a dream,
    And that a poodle jumps away?

STUDY

[FAUST, MEPHISTOPHELES.]

FAUST   A knock? Come in! Who comes to plague me now?
MEPHISTOPHELES   It's I.
FAUST   Come in!
MEPHISTOPHELES   You have to say it thrice.
FAUST   Come in, then.
MEPHISTOPHELES   Now you're nice.
   We should get along well, I vow.
   To chase your spleen away, allow   5
   That I appear a noble squire:[2]
   Look at my red and gold attire,
   A little cloak of silk brocade,
   The rooster's feather in my hat,
   And the long, nicely pointed blade—   10
   And now it is my counsel that
   You, too, should be like this arrayed;
   Then you would feel released and free,
   And you would find what life can be.
FAUST   I shall not cease to feel in all attires,   15
   The pains of our narrow earthly day.
   I am too old to be content to play,
   Too young to be without desire.
   What wonders could the world reveal?
   You must renounce! You ought to yield!   20
   That is the never-ending drone
   Which we must, our life long, hear,
   Which, hoarsely, all our hours intone
   And grind into our weary ears.
   Frightened I waken to the dismal dawn,   25
   Wish I had tears to drown the sun
   And check the day that soon will scorn
   My every wish—fulfill not one.
   If I but think of any pleasure,
   Bright critic day is sure to chide it,   30
   And if my heart creates itself a treasure,
   A thousand mocking masks deride it.
   When night descends at last, I shall recline
   But anxiously upon my bed;
   Though all is still, no rest is mine   35
   As dreams enmesh my mind in dread.
   The god that dwells within my heart
   Can stir my depths, I cannot hide—
   Rules all my powers with relentless art,
   But cannot move the world outside;   40
   And thus existence is for me a weight,
   Death is desirable, and life I hate.

2. In the popular plays based on the Faust legend, the Devil often appeared as a monk when the play catered to a Protestant audience and as a noble squire when the audience was predominantly Catholic.

MEPHISTOPHELES   And yet when death approaches, the welcome is not
    great.
FAUST   Oh, blessed whom, as victory advances,
    He lends the blood-drenched laurel's grace,   45
    Who, after wildly whirling dances,
    Receives him in a girl's embrace!
    Oh, that before the lofty spirit's power
    I might have fallen to the ground, unsouled!
MEPHISTOPHELES   And yet someone, in that same nightly hour   50
    Refused to drain a certain bowl.
FAUST   You seem to eavesdrop quite proficiently.
MEPHISTOPHELES   Omniscient I am not, but there is much I see.
FAUST   As in that terrifying reeling
    I heard the sweet familiar chimes   55
    That duped the traces of my childhood feeling
    With echoes of more joyous times,
    I now curse all that would enamor
    The human soul with lures and lies,
    Enticing it with flattering glamour   60
    To live on in this cave of sighs.
    Cursed above all our high esteem,
    The spirit's smug self-confidence,
    Cursed be illusion, fraud, and dream
    That flatter our guileless sense!   65
    Cursed be the pleasing make-believe
    Of fame and long posthumous life!
    Cursed be possessions that deceive,
    As slave and plough, and child and wife!
    Cursed, too, be Mammon[3] when with treasures   70
    He spurs us on to daring feats,
    Or lures us into slothful pleasures
    With sumptuous cushions and smooth sheets!
    A curse on wine that mocks our thirst!
    A curse on love's last consummations!   75
    A curse on hope! Faith, too, be cursed!
    And cursed above all else be patience!
CHOIR OF SPIRITS [*Invisible.*]   Alas!
        You have shattered
        The beautiful world   80
        With brazen fist;
        It falls, it is scattered—
        By a demigod destroyed.
        We are trailing
        The ruins into the void   85
        And wailing
        Over beauty undone
        And ended.

---

3. The Aramaic word for "riches," used in the New Testament of the Bible. Medieval writers interpreted the word as a proper noun, the name of the Devil, as representing covetousness or avarice.

Earth's mighty son,
More splendid   90
Rebuild it, you that are strong,
Build it again within!
And begin
A new life, a new way,
Lucid and gay,   95
And play
New songs.

MEPHISTOPHELES   These are the small
    Ones of my thralls.
    Hear how precociously they plead   100
    For pleasure and deed!
    To worldly strife
    From your lonely life
    Which dries up sap and sense,
    They would lure you hence.   105

Stop playing with your melancholy
That, like a vulture, ravages your breast;
The worst of company still cures this folly,
For you are human with the rest.
Yet that is surely not to say   110
That you should join the herd you hate.
I'm not one of the great,
But if you want to make your way
Through the world with me united,
I should surely be delighted   115
To be yours, as of now,
Your companion, if you allow;
And if you like the way I behave,
I shall be your servant, or your slave.

FAUST   And in return, what do you hope to take?   120

MEPHISTOPHELES   There's so much time—so why insist?

FAUST   No, no! The Devil is an egoist
    And would not just for heaven's sake
    Turn into a philanthropist.
    Make your conditions very clear;   125
    Where such a servant lives, danger is near.

MEPHISTOPHELES   *Here* you shall be the master, I be bond,
    And at your nod I'll work incessantly;
    But when we meet again *beyond,*
    Then you shall do the same for me.   130

FAUST   Of the beyond I have no thought;
    When you reduce this world to nought,
    The other one may have its turn.
    My joys come from this earth, and there,
    That sun has burnt on my despair: 135
    Once I have left those, I don't care:
    What happens is of no concern.

I do not even wish to hear
Whether beyond they hate and love,
And whether in that other sphere   140
One realm's below and one above.
MEPHISTOPHELES   So minded, dare it cheerfully.
Commit yourself and you shall see
My arts with joy. I'll give you more
Than any man has seen before.   145
FAUST   What would you, wretched Devil, offer?
Was ever a man's spirit in its noble striving
Grasped by your like, devilish scoffer?
But have you food that is not satisfying,
Red gold that rolls off without rest,   150
Quicksilver-like, over your skin—
A game in which no man can win—
A girl who, lying at my breast,
Ogles already to entice my neighbor,
And honor—that perhaps seems best—   155
Though like a comet it will turn to vapor?
Show me fruit that, before we pluck them, rot,
And trees whose foliage every day makes new!
MEPHISTOPHELES   Such a commission scares me not,
With such things I can wait on you.   160
But, worthy friend, the time comes when we would
Recline in peace and feast on something good.
FAUST   If ever I recline, calmed, on a bed of sloth,
You may destroy me then and there.
If ever flattering you should wile me   165
That in myself I find delight,
If with enjoyment you beguile me,
Then break on me, eternal night!
This bet I offer.
MEPHISTOPHELES I accept it.
FAUST   Right.
If to the moment I should say: 170
Abide, you are so fair—
Put me in fetters on that day,
I *wish* to perish then, I swear.
Then let the death bell ever toll,
Your service done, you shall be free,   175
The clock may stop, the hand may fall,
As time comes to an end for me.
MEPHISTOPHELES   Consider it, for we shall not forget it.
FAUST   That is a right you need not waive.
I did not boast, and I shall not regret it.   180
As I grow stagnant I shall be a slave,
Whether or not to anyone indebted.
MEPHISTOPHELES   At the doctor's banquet[4] tonight I shall do

4. The dinner given by a successful candidate for a Ph.D. degree.

My duties as a servant without fail.
But for life's sake, or death's—just one detail: 185
Could you give me a line or two?
FAUST   You pedant need it black on white?
Are man and a man's word indeed new to your sight?
Is not my spoken word sufficient warrant
When it commits my life eternally?   190
Does not the world rush on in every torrent,
And a mere promise should hold me?
Yet this illusion our heart inherits,
And who would want to shirk his debt?
Blessed who counts loyalty among his merits.   195
No sacrifice will he regret.
And yet a parchment, signed and sealed, is an abhorrent
Specter that haunts us, and it makes us fret.
The word dies when we seize the pen,
And wax and leather lord it then.   200
What, evil spirit, do you ask?
Paper or parchment, stone or brass?
Should I use chisel, style, or quill?
It is completely up to you.
MEPHISTOPHELES   Why get so hot and overdo   205
Your rhetoric? Why must you shrill?
Use any sheet, it is the same;
And with a drop of blood you sign your name.
FAUST   If you are sure you like this game,
Let it be done to humor you.   210
MEPHISTOPHELES   Blood is a very special juice.
FAUST   You need not fear that someday I retract.
That all my striving I unloose
Is the whole purpose of the pact.
Oh, I was puffed up all too boldly,   215
At your rank only is my place.
The lofty spirit spurned me coldly,
And nature hides from me her face.
Torn is the subtle thread of thought,
I loathe the knowledge I once sought.   220
In sensuality's abysmal land
Let our passions drink their fill!
In magic veils, not pierced by skill,
Let every wonder be at hand!
Plunge into time's whirl that dazes my sense,   225
Into the torrent of events!
And let enjoyment, distress,
Annoyance and success
Succeed each other as best they can;
For restless activity proves a man.   230
MEPHISTOPHELES   You are not bound by goal or measure.
If you would nibble everything
Or snatch up something on the wing,

You're welcome to what gives you pleasure.
But help yourself and don't be coy!   235
FAUST   Do you not hear, I have no thought of joy!
    The reeling whirl I seek, the most painful excess,
    Enamored hate and quickening distress.
    Cured from the craving to know all, my mind
    Shall not henceforth be closed to any pain,   240
    And what is portioned out to all mankind,
    I shall enjoy deep in my self, contain
    Within my spirit summit and abyss,
    Pile on my breast their agony and bliss,
    And thus let my own self grow into theirs, unfettered,   245
    Till as they are, at last I, too, am shattered.
MEPHISTOPHELES   Believe me who for many a thousand year
    Has chewed this cud and never rested,
    That from the cradle to the bier
    The ancient leaven cannot be digested.   250
    Trust one like me, this whole array
    Is for a God—there's no contender:
    He dwells in his eternal splendor,
    To darkness we had to surrender,
    And you need night as well as day.   255
FAUST   And yet it is my will.
MEPHISTOPHELES   It does sound bold.
    But I'm afraid, though you are clever,
    Time is too brief, though art's forever.
    Perhaps you're willing to be told.
    Why don't you find yourself a poet,   260
    And let the gentleman ransack his dreams:
    And when he finds a noble trait, let him bestow it
    Upon your worthy head in reams and reams:
    The lion's daring,
    The swiftness of the hind,   265
    The northerner's forbearing
    And the Italian's fiery mind,
    Let him resolve the mystery
    How craft can be combined with magnanimity,
    Or how a passion-crazed young man   270
    Might fall in love after a plan.
    If there were such a man, I'd like to meet him,
    As Mr. Microcosm I would greet him.
FAUST   Alas, what am I, if I can
    Not reach for mankind's crown which merely mocks   275
    Our senses' craving like a star?
MEPHISTOPHELES   You're in the end—just what you are!
    Put wigs on with a million locks
    And put your foot on ell-high socks,
    You still remain just what you are.   280
FAUST   I feel, I gathered up and piled up high
    In vain the treasures of the human mind:
    When I sit down at last, I cannot find

New strength within—it is all dry.
My stature has not grown a whit,   285
No closer to the Infinite.
MEPHISTOPHELES   Well, my good sir, to put it crudely,
You see matters just as they lie;
We have to look at them more shrewdly,
Or all life's pleasures pass us by.   290
Your hands and feet—indeed that's trite—
And head and seat are yours alone;
Yet all in which I find delight,
Should they be less my own?
Suppose I buy myself six steeds: 295
I buy their strength; while I recline
I dash along at whirlwind speeds,
For their two dozen legs are mine.
Come on! Let your reflections rest
And plunge into the world with zest!   300
I say, the man that speculates
Is like a beast that in the sand,
Led by an evil spirit, round and round gyrates,
And all about lies gorgeous pasture land.
FAUST   How shall we set about it?
MEPHISTOPHELES   Simply leave.   305
What torture room is this? What site of grief?
Is this the noble life of prudence—
You bore yourself and bore your students?
Oh, let your neighbor, Mr. Paunch, live so!
Why work hard threshing straw, when it annoys?   310
The best that you could ever know
You may not tell the little boys.
Right now I hear one in the aisle.
FAUST   I simply cannot face the lad.
MEPHISTOPHELES   The poor chap waited quite a while,   315
I do not want him to leave sad.
Give me your cap and gown. Not bad! [*He dresses himself up.*]
This mask ought to look exquisite!
Now you can leave things to my wit.
Some fifteen minutes should be all I need;   320
Meanwhile get ready for our trip, and speed!
        [*Exit* FAUST.]
MEPHISTOPHELES [*In* FAUST's *long robe.*]
Have but contempt for reason and for science,
Man's noblest force spurn with defiance,
Subscribe to magic and illusion,
The Lord of Lies aids your confusion,   325
And, pact or no, I hold you tight.—
The spirit which he has received from fate
Sweeps ever onward with unbridled might,
Its hasty striving is so great
It leaps over the earth's delights.   330
Through life I'll drag him at a rate,

Through shallow triviality,
That he shall writhe and suffocate;
And his insatiability,
With greedy lips, shall see the choicest plate   335
And ask in vain for all that he would cherish—
And were he not the Devil's mate
And had not signed, he still must perish.
　　　　[A STUDENT *enters.*]
STUDENT　I have arrived quite recently
　And come, full of humility,   340
　To meet that giant intellect
　Whom all refer to with respect.
MEPHISTOPHELES　This is a charming pleasantry.
　A man as others are, you see.—
　Have you already called elsewhere?   345
STUDENT　I pray you, take me in your care.
　I am, believe me, quite sincere,
　Have some odd cash and lots of cheer;
　My mother scarcely let me go,
　But there is much I hope to know.   350
MEPHISTOPHELES　This is just the place for you to stay.
STUDENT　To be frank, I should like to run away.
　I cannot say I like these walls,
　These gloomy rooms and somber halls.
　It seems so narrow, and I see   355
　No patch of green, no single tree;
　And in the auditorium
　My hearing, sight, and thought grow numb.
MEPHISTOPHELES　That is a question of mere habit.
　The child, offered the mother's breast,   360
　Will not in the beginning grab it;
　But soon it clings to it with zest.
　And thus at wisdom's copious breasts
　You'll drink each day with greater zest.
STUDENT　I'll hang around her neck, enraptured;   365
　But tell me first: how is she captured?
MEPHISTOPHELES　Before we get into my views—
　What Department do you choose?
STUDENT　I should like to be erudite,
　And from the earth to heaven's height   370
　Know every law and every action:
　Nature and science is what I need.
MEPHISTOPHELES　That is the way; you just proceed
　And scrupulously shun distraction.
STUDENT　Body and soul, I am a devotee;   375
　Though, naturally, everybody prays
　For some free time and liberty
　On pleasant summer holidays.
MEPHISTOPHELES　Use well your time, so swiftly it runs on!
　Be orderly, and time is won!   380

My friend, I shall be pedagogic,
And say you ought to start with Logic.
For thus your mind is trained and braced,
In Spanish boots it will be laced,
That on the road of thought maybe   385
It henceforth creep more thoughtfully,
And does not crisscross here and there,
Will-o'-the-wisping through the air.
Days will be spent to let you know
That what you once did at one blow,   390
Like eating and drinking so easy and free,
Can only be done with One, Two, Three.
Yet the web of thought has no such creases
And is more like a weaver's masterpieces:
One step, a thousand threads arise,   395
Hither and thither shoots each shuttle,
The threads flow on, unseen and subtle,
Each blow effects a thousand ties.
The philosopher comes with analysis
And proves it had to be like this: 400
The first was so, the second so,
And hence the third and fourth was so,
And were not the first and the second here,
Then the third and fourth could never appear.
That is what all the students believe,   405
But they have never learned to weave.
Who would study and describe the living, starts
By driving the spirit out of the parts:
In the palm of his hand he holds all the sections,
Lacks nothing, except the spirit's connections.   410
Encheirisis naturae[5] the chemists baptize it,
Mock themselves and don't realize it.
STUDENT   I did not quite get everything.
MEPHISTOPHELES   That will improve with studying:
   You will reduce things by and by   415
   And also learn to classify.
STUDENT   I feel so dazed by all you said
   As if a mill went around in my head.
MEPHISTOPHELES   Then, without further circumvention,
   Give metaphysics your attention.   420
   There seek profoundly to attain
   What does not fit the human brain;
   Whether you do or do not understand,
   An impressive word is always at hand.
   But now during your first half-year,   425
   Keep above all our order here.
   Five hours a day, you understand,

---

5. The natural process by which substances are united into a living organism—a name for an action no one understands.

And when the bell peals, be on hand.
Before you come, you must prepare,
Read every paragraph with care,   430
Lest you, forbid, should overlook
That all he says is in the book.
But write down everything, engrossed
As if you took dictation from the Holy Ghost.
STUDENT   Don't say that twice—I understood: 435
   I see how useful it's to write,
   For what we possess black on white
   We can take home and keep for good.
MEPHISTOPHELES   But choose a field of concentration!
STUDENT   I have no hankering for jurisprudence.   440
MEPHISTOPHELES   For that I cannot blame the students,
   I know this science is a blight.
   The laws and statutes of a nation
   Are an inherited disease,
   From generation unto generation   445
   And place to place they drag on by degrees.
   Wisdom becomes nonsense; kindness, oppression:
   To be a grandson is a curse.
   The right that is innate in us
   Is not discussed by the profession.   450
STUDENT   My scorn is heightened by your speech.
   Happy the man that you would teach!
   I almost think theology would pay.
MEPHISTOPHELES   I should not wish to lead you astray.
   When it comes to this discipline,   455
   The way is hard to find, wrong roads abound,
   And lots of hidden poison lies around
   Which one can scarcely tell from medicine.
   Here, too, it would be best you heard
   One only and staked all upon your master's word.   460
   Yes, stick to words at any rate;
   There never was a surer gate
   Into the temple, Certainty.
STUDENT   Yet some idea there must be.
MEPHISTOPHELES   All right. But do not plague yourself too
      anxiously;   465
   For just where no ideas are
   The proper word is never far.
   With words a dispute can be won,
   With words a system can be spun,
   In words one can believe unshaken,   470
   And from a word no tittle can be taken.
STUDENT   Forgive, I hold you up with many questions,
   But there is one more thing I'd like to see.
   Regarding medicine, maybe,
   You have some powerful suggestions?   475
   Three years go by so very fast,
   And, God, the field is all too vast.

If but a little hint is shown,
One can attempt to find one's way.
MEPHISTOPHELES [*Aside.*]   I'm sick of this pedantic tone.   480
The Devil now again I'll play.
[*Aloud.*] The spirit of medicine is easy to know:
Through the macro- and microcosm you breeze,
And in the end you let it go
As God may please.   485
In vain you roam about to study science,
For each learns only what he can;
Who places on the moment his reliance,
He is the proper man.
You are quite handsome, have good sense,   490
And no doubt, you have courage, too,
And if you have self-confidence,
Then others will confide in you.
And give the women special care;
Their everlasting sighs and groans   495
In thousand tones
Are cured at *one* point everywhere.
And if you seem halfway discreet,
They will be lying at your feet.
First your degree inspires trust,   500
As if your art had scarcely any peers;
Right at the start, remove her clothes and touch her bust,
Things for which others wait for years and years.
Learn well the little pulse to squeeze,
And with a knowing, fiery glance you seize   505
Her freely round her slender waist
To see how tightly she is laced.
STUDENT   That looks much better, sir. For one sees how and where.
MEPHISTOPHELES   Gray, my dear friend, is every theory,
And green alone life's golden tree.   510
STUDENT   All this seems like a dream, I swear.
Could I impose on you sometime again
And drink more words of wisdom then?
MEPHISTOPHELES   What I can give you, you shall get.
STUDENT   Alas, I cannot go quite yet: 515
My album I must give to you;
Please, sir, show me this favor, too.
MEPHISTOPHELES   All right. [*He writes and returns it.*]
STUDENT [*Reads.*]   Eritis sicut Deus, scientes bonum et malum.[6] [*Closes
the book reverently and takes his leave.*]
MEPHISTOPHELES   Follow the ancient text and my relation, the
snake;   520
Your very likeness to God will yet make you quiver and quake.
[FAUST *enters.*]
FAUST   Where are we heading now?
MEPHISTOPHELES   Wherever you may please.

6. A slight alteration of the serpent's words to Eve in Genesis: "Ye shall be as God, knowing good and evil"
(Latin).

We'll see the small world, then the larger one.
You will reap profit and have fun
As you sweep through this course with ease.   525
FAUST With my long beard I hardly may
  Live in this free and easy way.
  The whole endeavor seems so futile;
  I always felt the world was strange and brutal.
  With others, I feel small and harassed,   530
  And I shall always be embarrassed.
MEPHISTOPHELES Good friend, you will become less sensitive:
  Self-confidence will teach you how to live.
FAUST How shall we get away from here?
  Where are your carriage, groom and steed?   535
MEPHISTOPHELES I rather travel through the air:
  We spread this cloak—that's all we need
  But on this somewhat daring flight,
  Be sure to keep your luggage light.
  A little fiery air, which I plan to prepare,   540
  Will raise us swiftly off the earth;
  Without ballast we'll go up fast—
  Congratulations, friend, on your rebirth!

AUERBACH'S KELLER IN LEIPZIG

[Jolly fellows' drinking bout.]
FROSCH Will no one drink and no one laugh?
  I'll teach you not to look so wry.
  Today you look like sodden chaff
  And usually blaze to the sky
BRANDER It's all your fault; you make me sick: 5
  No joke, and not a single dirty trick.
FROSCH *[Pours a glass of wine over* BRANDER's *head.]*
  There you have both.
BRANDER   You filthy pig!
FROSCH You said I shouldn't be a prig.
SIEBEL Let those who fight, stop or get out!
  With all your lungs sing chorus, swill, and shout!   10
  Come! Holla-ho!
ALTMAYER   Now this is where I quit.
  Get me some cotton or my ears will split.
SIEBEL When the vault echoes and the place
  Is quaking, then you can enjoy a bass.
FROSCH Quite right! Throw out who fusses because he is lampooned! 15
  A! tara lara da!
ALTMAYER A! tara lara da!
FROSCH The throats seem to be tuned.
    [Sings.] Dear Holy Roman Empire,
    What holds you still together?   20
BRANDER A nasty song! It reeks of politics!
  A wretched song! Thank God in daily prayer,

That the old Empire isn't your affair!
At least I think it is much to be grateful for
That I'm not Emperor nor Chancellor.   25
And yet we, too, need someone to respect—
I say, a Pope let us elect.
You know the part that elevates
And thereby proves the man who rates.
FROSCH [*Sings.*]   Oh, Dame Nightingale, arise!   30
    Bring my sweet love ten thousand sighs!
SIEBEL   No sighs for your sweet love! I will not have such mush.
FROSCH   A sigh and kiss for her! You cannot make me blush.
    [*Sings.*] Ope the latch in silent night!
    Ope the latch, your love invite!   35
    Shut the latch, there is the dawn!
SIEBEL   Go, sing and sing and sing, pay compliments and fawn!
    The time will come when I shall laugh:
    She led me by the nose, and you are the next calf.
    Her lover should be some mischievous gnome!   40
    He'd meet her at a crossroads and make light,
    And an old billy goat that's racing home
    From Blocksberg could still bleat to her "Good night!"
    A decent lad of real flesh and blood
    Is far too good to be her stud.   45
    I'll stand no sighs, you silly ass,
    But throw rocks through her window glass.
BRANDER [*Pounding on the table.*]
    Look here! Look here! Listen to me!
    My friends, confess I know what's right;
    There are lovers here, and you'll agree   50
    That it's only civility
    That I should try to honor them tonight.
    Watch out! This song's the latest fashion.
    And join in the refrain with passion!
    [*Sings.*] A cellar once contained a rat   55
        That couldn't have been uncouther,
        Lived on grease and butter and grew fat—
        Just like old Doctor Luther.[7]
        The cook put poison in his food,
        Then he felt cramped and just as stewed,   60
        As if love gnawed his vitals.
CHORUS [*Jubilant.*]   As if love gnawed his vitals.
BRANDER   He dashed around, he dashed outdoors,
        Sought puddles and swilled rain,
        He clawed and scratched up walls and floors,   65
        But his frenzy was in vain;
        He jumped up in a frightful huff,
        But soon the poor beast had enough,
        As if love gnawed his vitals.

---

7. Martin Luther (1483–1546), German leader of the Protestant Reformation, hence an object of distaste
for Catholics.

CHORUS   As if love gnawed his vitals.   70
BRANDER   At last he rushed in open day
    Into the kitchen, crazed with fear,
    Dropped near the stove and writhed and lay,
    And puffed out his career.
    The poisoner only laughed: I hope   75
    He's at the end now of his rope,
    As if love gnawed his vitals.
CHORUS   As if love gnawed his vitals.
SIEBEL   How pleased these stupid chaps are! That's,
    I think, indeed a proper art   80
    To put out poison for poor rats.
BRANDER   I see, you'd like to take their part.
ALTMAYER   Potbelly with his shiny top!
    His ill luck makes him mild and tame.
    He sees the bloated rat go flop—   85
    And sees himself: they look the same.
        [FAUST and MEPHISTOPHELES enter.]
MEPHISTOPHELES   Above all else, it seems to me,
    You need some jolly company
    To see life can be fun—to say the least:
    The people here make every day a feast.   90
    With little wit and boisterous noise,
    They dance and circle in their narrow trails
    Like kittens playing with their tails.
    When hangovers don't vex these boys,
    And while their credit's holding out,   95
    They have no cares and drink and shout.
BRANDER   Those two are travelers, I swear.
    I tell it right off by the way they stare.
    They have been here at most an hour.
FROSCH   No doubt about it. Leipzig is a flower,   100
    It is a little Paris and educates its people.
SIEBEL   What may they be? Who knows the truth?
FROSCH   Leave it to me! A drink that interposes—
    And I'll pull like a baby tooth
    The worms they hide, out of these fellows' noses.   105
    They seem to be of noble ancestry,
    For they look proud and act disdainfully.
BRANDER   They are mere quacks and born in squalor.
ALTMAYER   Maybe.
FROSCH   Watch out! We shall commence.
MEPHISTOPHELES [To FAUST.]   The Devil people never sense,   110
    Though he may hold them by the collar.
FAUST   Good evening, gentlemen.
SIEBEL   Thank you, to you the same.
    [Softly, looking at MEPHISTOPHELES from the side.]
    Look at his foot. Why is it lame?[8]

8. By tradition, the Devil had a cloven foot, split like a sheep's hoof.

MEPHISTOPHELES   We'll join you, if you grant the liberty.
 The drinks they have are poor, their wine not very mellow,   115
 So we'll enjoy your company.
ALTMAYER   You seem a most fastidious fellow.
FROSCH   Did you leave Rippach rather late and walk?
 And did you first have dinner with Master Jackass there?
MEPHISTOPHELES   Tonight we had no time to spare.   120
 Last time, however, we had quite a talk.
 He had a lot to say of his relations
 And asked us to send each his warmest salutations. [*He bows to* FROSCH.]
ALTMAYER [*Softly.*]   You got it! He's all right.
SIEBEL   A pretty repartee!
FROSCH   I'll get him yet. Just wait and see.   125
MEPHISTOPHELES   Just now we heard, if I'm not wrong,
 Some voices singing without fault.
 Indeed this seems a place for song;
 No doubt, it echoes from the vault.
FROSCH   Are you perchance a virtuoso?   130
MEPHISTOPHELES   Oh no, the will is great, the power only so-so.
ALTMAYER   Give us a song!
MEPHISTOPHELES   As many as you please.
SIEBEL   But let us have a brand-new strain!
MEPHISTOPHELES   We have just recently returned from Spain,
 The beauteous land of wine and melodies.   135
  [*Sings.*] A king lived long ago
  Who had a giant flea—
FROSCH   Hear, hear! A flea! That's what I call a jest.
 A flea's a mighty pretty guest.
MEPHISTOPHELES [*Sings.*]   A king lived long ago   140
  Who had a giant flea,
  He loved him just as though
  He were his son and heir.
  He sent his tailor a note
  And offered the tailor riches   145
  If he would measure a coat
  And also take measure for breeches.
BRANDER   Be sure to tell the tailor, if he twinkles,
 That he must take fastidious measure;
 He'll lose his head, not just the treasure,   150
 If in the breeches there are wrinkles.
MEPHISTOPHELES   He was in silk arrayed,
  In velvet he was dressed,
  Had ribbons and brocade,
  A cross upon his chest   155
  A fancy star, great fame—
  A minister, in short;
  And all his kin became
  Lords at the royal court.
  The other lords grew lean   160
  And suffered with their wives,

The royal maid and the queen
Were all but eaten alive,
But weren't allowed to swat them
And could not even scratch,   165
While we can swat and blot them
And kill the ones we catch.

CHORUS [*Jubilant.*]   While we can swat and blot them
And kill the ones we catch.

FROSCH   Bravo! Bravo! That was a treat!   170
SIEBEL   That is the end all fleas should meet.
BRANDER   Point your fingers and catch 'em fine!
ALTMAYER   Long live our freedom! And long live wine!
MEPHISTOPHELES   When freedom is the toast, my own voice I should
   add,
Were your forsaken wines only not quite so bad.⁹   175
SIEBEL   You better mind your language, lad.
MEPHISTOPHELES   I only fear the landlord might protest,
   Else I should give each honored guest
   From our cellar a good glass.
SIEBEL   Let's go! The landlord is an ass.   180
FROSCH   If you provide good drinks, you shall be eulogized;
   But let your samples be good-sized.
   When I'm to judge, I'm telling him,
   I want my snout full to the brim.
ALTMAYER [*Softly.*]   They're from the Rhineland, I presume.   185
MEPHISTOPHELES   Bring me a gimlet.
BRANDER   What could that be for?
   You couldn't have the casks in the next room?
ALTMAYER   The landlord keeps his tools right there behind the door.
MEPHISTOPHELES [*Takes the gimlet. To* FROSCH.]
   What would you like? Something that's cool?
FROSCH   What do you mean? You got a lot of booze?   190
MEPHISTOPHELES   I let each have what he may choose.
ALTMAYER [*To* FROSCH.]   Oho! You lick your chops and start to drool.
FROSCH   If it is up to me, I'll have a Rhenish brand:
   There's nothing that competes with our fatherland.
MEPHISTOPHELES [*Boring a hole near the edge of the table where* FROSCH
   sits.]   Now let us have some wax to make a cork that sticks.   195
ALTMAYER   Oh, is it merely parlor tricks?
MEPHISTOPHELES [*To* BRANDER.]   And you?
BRANDER   I want a good champagne—
   Heady; I do not like it plain.
      [MEPHISTOPHELES *bores; meanwhile someone else has made the wax
      stoppers and plugged the holes.*]
BRANDER   Not all that's foreign can be banned,
   For what is far is often fine.   200
   A Frenchman is a thing no German man can stand,
   And yet we like to drink their wine.

---

9. Cursed.

SIEBEL [*As* MEPHISTOPHELES *approaches his place.*]
  I must confess, I think the dry tastes bad,
  The sweet alone is exquisite.
MEPHISTOPHELES [*Boring.*] Tokay[1] will flow for you, my lad.   205
ALTMAYER I think, you might as well admit,
  Good gentlemen, that these are simply jests.
MEPHISTOPHELES Tut, tut! With such distinguished guests
  That would be quite a lot to dare.
  So don't be modest, and declare   210
  What kind of wine you would prefer.
ALTMAYER I like them all, so I don't care.
    [*After all the holes have been bored and plugged.*]
MEPHISTOPHELES [*With strange gestures.*] The grape the vine adorns,
  The billy goat sports horns;
  The wine is juicy, vines are wood,   215
  The wooden table gives wine as good,
  Profound insight! Now you perceive
  A miracle; only believe!
  Now pull the stoppers and have fun!
ALL [*As they pull out the stoppers and the wine each asked for flows into his
  glass.*] A gorgeous well for everyone!   220
MEPHISTOPHELES Be very careful lest it overrun!
    [*They drink several times.*]
ALL [*Sing.*] We feel gigantically well,
  Just like five hundred sows.
MEPHISTOPHELES Look there how well men are when they are free.
FAUST I should like to get out of here.   225
MEPHISTOPHELES First watch how their bestiality
  Will in full splendor soon appear.
SIEBEL [*Drinks carelessly and spills his wine on the floor where it turns into
  a flame.*] Help! Fire! Help! Hell blew a vent!
MEPHISTOPHELES [*Conjuring the flame.*] Be quiet, friendly element!
  [*To the fellow.*] For this time it was only a drop of purgatory.   230
SIEBEL You'll pay for it, and you can save your story!
  What do you think we are, my friend?
FROSCH Don't dare do that a second time, you hear!
ALTMAYER Just let him leave in silence; that is what I say, gents!
SIEBEL You have the brazen impudence   235
  To do your hocus-pocus here?
MEPHISTOPHELES Be still, old barrel!
SIEBEL   Broomstick, you!
  Will you insult us? Mind your prose!
BRANDER Just wait and see, there will be blows.
ALTMAYER [*Pulls a stopper out of the table and fire leaps at him.*]
  I burn! I burn!
SIEBEL   It's magic, as I said.   240
  He is an outlaw. Strike him dead!
    [*They draw their knives and advance on* MEPHISTOPHELES.]

---

1. A sweet Hungarian wine.

MEPHISTOPHELES [*With solemn gestures.*]
    False images prepare
    Mirages in the air.
    Be here and there!
        [*They stand amazed and stare at each other.*]
ALTMAYER   Where am I? What a gorgeous land!   245
FROSCH   And vineyards! Am I mad?
SIEBEL   And grapes right by my hand!
BRANDER   See in the leaves that purple shape?
    I never saw that big a grape!
        [*Grabs* SIEBEL's *nose. They all do it to each other and raise their
        knives.*]
MEPHISTOPHELES   [*As above.*] Fall from their eyes, illusion's band!
    Remember how the Devil joked.   250
        [*He disappears with* FAUST, *the revelers separate.*]
SIEBEL   What's that?
ALTMAYER   Hah?
FROSCH   Your nose I stroked?
BRANDER   [*To* SIEBEL.] And yours is in my hand!
ALTMAYER   The shock is more than I can bear.
    I think I'll faint. Get me a chair!
FROSCH   What was all this? Who understands?   255
SIEBEL   Where is the scoundrel? I'm so sore,
    If I could only get my hands—
ALTMAYER   I saw him whiz right through the cellar door,
    Riding a flying barrel. Zounds,
    The fright weighs on me like a thousand pounds.   260
[*Turning toward the table.*]   Do you suppose the wine still flows?
SIEBEL   That was a fraud! You're asinine!
FROSCH   I surely thought that I drank wine.
BRANDER   But what about the grapes, I say.
ALTMAYER   Who says there are no miracles today!   265

WITCH'S KITCHEN

[*On a low stove, a large caldron stands over the fire. In the steam
that rises from it, one can see several shapes. A longtailed* FEMALE
MONKEY *sits near the caldron, skims it, and sees to it that it does not
overflow. The* MALE MONKEY *with the little ones sits next to her and
warms himself. Walls and ceiling are decorated with the queerest
implements of witchcraft.* FAUST *and* MEPHISTOPHELES *enter.*]
FAUST   How I detest this crazy sorcery!
    I should get well, you promise me,
    In this mad frenzy of a mess?
    Do I need the advice of hag fakirs?
    And should this quackish sordidness   5
    Reduce my age by thirty years?
    I'm lost if that's all you could find.
    My hope is drowned in sudden qualm.
    Has neither nature nor some noble mind

Invented or contrived a wholesome balm?   10

MEPHISTOPHELES   My friend, that was nice oratory!

  Indeed, to make you young there is one way that's apter;

  But, I regret, that is another story

  And forms quite an amazing chapter.

FAUST   I want to know it.

MEPHISTOPHELES   All right, you need no sorcery   15

  And no physician and no dough.

  Just go into the fields and see

  What fun it is to dig and hoe;

  Live simply and keep all your thoughts

  On a few simple objects glued;   20

  Restrict yourself and eat the plainest food;

  Live with the beasts, a beast: it is no thievery

  To dress the fields you work, with your own dung.

  That is the surest remedy:

  At eighty, you would still be young.   25

FAUST   I am not used to that and can't, I am afraid,

  Start now to work with hoe and spade.

  For me a narrow life like that's too small.

MEPHISTOPHELES   We need the witch then after all.

FAUST   Why just the hag with all her grime!   30

  Could you not brew it—with *your* head!

MEPHISTOPHELES   A splendid way to waste my time!

  A thousand bridges I could build instead.[2]

  Science is not enough, nor art;

  In this work patience plays a part.   35

  A quiet spirit plods and plods at length;

  Nothing but time can give the brew its strength.

  With all the things that go into it,

  It's sickening just to *see* them do it.

  The Devil taught them, true enough   40

  But he himself can't make the stuff.

     [*He sees the* ANIMALS.]

  Just see how delicate they look!

  This is the maid, and that the cook.

  [*To the* ANIMALS.] It seems the lady isn't home?

ANIMALS   She went to roam   45

    Away from home,

    Right through the chimney in the dome.

MEPHISTOPHELES   And how long will she walk the street?

ANIMALS   As long as we warm our feet.

MEPHISTOPHELES [*To* FAUST.]   How do you like this dainty pair?   50

FAUST   They are inane beyond comparison.

MEPHISTOPHELES   A conversation like this one

  Is just the sort of thing for which I care.

  [*To the* ANIMALS.] Now tell me, you accursed group,

  Why do you stir that steaming mess?   55

2. According to folk legend, the Devil built bridges at the request of human beings. As a reward, he caught either the first or the thirteenth soul to cross each new bridge.

ANIMALS   We cook a watery beggars' soup.

MEPHISTOPHELES   You should do a brisk business.

MALE MONKEY [*Approaches* MEPHISTOPHELES *and fawns.*]
    Oh please throw the dice
    And lose, and be nice
    And let me get wealthy!   60
    We are in the ditch,
    And if I were rich,
    Then I might be healthy.

MEPHISTOPHELES   How happy every monkey thinks he'd be,
  If he could play the lottery.   65
    [*Meanwhile the monkey youngsters have been playing with a large
    ball, and now they roll it forward.*]

MALE MONKEY   The world and ball
    Both rise and fall
    And roll and wallow;
    It sounds like glass,
    It bursts, alas,   70
    The inside's hollow.
    Here it is light,
    There still more bright,
    Life's mine to swallow!
    Dear son, I say,   75
    Please keep away!
    You'll die first.
    It's made of clay
    It will burst.

MEPHISTOPHELES   The sieve there, chief—?   80

MALE MONKEY [*Gets it down.*]   If you were a thief,
    I'd be wise to you.
    [*He runs to the* FEMALE MONKEY *and lets her see through it.*]
    Look through, be brief!
    You know the thief,
    But may not say *who*?   85

MEPHISTOPHELES [*Approaching the fire.*]   And here this pot?

BOTH BIG MONKEYS   The half-witted sot!
    Does not know the pot,
    Does not know the kettle!

MEPHISTOPHELES   You impolite beast!   90

MALE MONKEY   Take this brush at least
    And sit down and settle!
    [*He makes* MEPHISTOPHELES *sit down.*]

FAUST [*Who has been standing before a mirror all this time, now stepping
close to it, now back.*] What blissful image is revealed
  To me behind this magic glass!
  Lend me your swiftest pinions, love, that I might pass   95
  From here to her transfigured field!
  When I don't stay right on this spot, but, pining,
  Dare to step forward and go near
  Mists cloud her shape and let it disappear.

The fairest image of a woman! 100
Indeed, could woman be so fair?
Or is this body which I see reclining
Heaven's quintessence from another sphere?
Is so much beauty found on earth?
MEPHISTOPHELES   Well, if a god works hard for six whole days, my
    friend, 105
And then says bravo in the end,
It ought to have a little worth.
For now, stare to your heart's content!
I could track down for you just such a sweet—
What bliss it would be to get her consent, 110
To marry her and be replete.
    [FAUST *gazes into the mirror all the time.* MEPHISTOPHELES, *stretch-*
    ing in the armchair and playing with the brush, goes on speaking.]
I sit here like the king upon his throne:
The scepter I hold here, I lack the crown alone.
ANIMALS [*Who have so far moved around in quaint confusion, bring a crown*
    to MEPHISTOPHELES, *clamoring loudly.*]   Oh, please be so good.
    With sweat and with blood 115
    This crown here to lime!
    [*They handle the crown clumsily and break it into two pieces with*
    which they jump around.]
    It's done, let it be!
    We chatter and see,
    We listen and rhyme—
FAUST [*At the mirror.*]   Alas, I think I'll lose my wits. 120
MEPHISTOPHELES [*Pointing toward the* ANIMALS.]
    I fear that my head, too, begins to reel.
ANIMALS   And if we score hits
    And everything fits,
    It's thoughts that we feel.
FAUST [*As above.*]   My heart and soul are catching fire. 125
    Please let us go away from here!
MEPHISTOPHELES [*In the same position as above.*]
    The one thing one has to admire
    Is that their poetry is quite sincere.
    [*The caldron which the* FEMALE MONKEY *has neglected begins to*
    run over, and a huge flame blazes up through the chimney. The
    WITCH *scoots down through the flame with a dreadful clamor.*]
WITCH   Ow! Ow! Ow! Ow!
You damned old beast! You cursed old sow! 130
You leave the kettle and singe the frau.
You cursed old beast! [*Sees* FAUST *and* MEPHISTOPHELES.]
    What goes on here?
    Why are you here?
    Who are you two? 135
    Who sneaked inside?
    Come, fiery tide!
    Their bones be fried!

[*She plunges the skimming spoon into the caldron and spatters flames at* FAUST, MEPHISTOPHELES, *and the* ANIMALS. *The* ANIMALS *whine.*]

MEPHISTOPHELES [*Reversing the brush he holds in his hand, and striking into the glasses and pots.*]

    In two! In two!
    There lies the brew.   140
    There lies the glass.
    A joke, my lass,
    The beat, you ass,
    For melodies from you.

[*As the* WITCH *retreats in wrath and horror.*]

You know me now? You skeleton! You shrew!   145
You know your master and your lord?
What holds me? I could strike at you
And shatter you and your foul monkey horde.
Does not the scarlet coat reveal His Grace?
Do you not know the rooster's feather, ma'am?   150
Did I perchance conceal my face?
Or must I tell you who I am?

WITCH   Forgive the uncouth greeting, though
  You have no cloven feet, you know.
  And your two ravens, where are they?   155

MEPHISTOPHELES   For just this once you may get by,
  For it has been some time, I don't deny,
  Since I have come your way,
  And culture which licks out at every stew
  Extends now to the Devil, too: 160
  Gone is the Nordic phantom that former ages saw;
  You see no horns, no tail or claw.
  And as regards the foot with which I can't dispense,
  That does not look the least bit suave;
  Like other young men nowadays, I hence   165
  Prefer to pad my calves.

WITCH [*Dancing.*]   I'll lose my wits, I'll lose my brain
  Since Squire Satan has come back again.

MEPHISTOPHELES   That name is out, hag! Is that plain?

WITCH   But why? It never gave you pain!   170

MEPHISTOPHELES   It's dated, called a fable; men are clever,
  But they are just as badly off as ever:
  The Evil One is gone, the evil ones remain.
  You call me baron, hag, and you look out:
  I am a cavalier with cavalierly charms,   175
  And my nobility don't dare to doubt!
  Look here and you will see my coat of arms!

[*He makes an indecent gesture.*]

WITCH [*Laughs immoderately.*]   Ha! Ha! That is your manner, sir!
  You are a jester as you always were.

MEPHISTOPHELES [*To* FAUST.]   My friend, mark this, but don't repeat
    it: 180

This is the way a witch likes to be treated.

WITCH   Now tell me why you came in here.

MEPHISTOPHELES   A good glass of the famous juice, my dear!
But I must have the oldest kind:
Its strength increases with each year.   185

WITCH   I got a bottle on this shelf
From which I like to nip myself;
By now it doesn't even stink.
I'll give you some, it has the power.
[*Softly.*] But if, quite unprepared, this man should have a drink,   190
He could, as you know well, not live another hour.

MEPHISTOPHELES   He is a friend of mine, and he will take it well
The best you have is not too good for him.
Now draw your circle, say your spell,
And fill a bumper to the brim.   195

> [*The* WITCH *draws a circle with curious gestures and puts quaint
> objects into it, while the glasses begin to tinkle, the caldrons begin
> to resound and they make music. In the end, she gets a big book and
> puts the* MONKEYS *into the circle, and they serve her as a desk and
> have to hold a torch for her. She motions* FAUST *to step up.*]

FAUST [*To* MEPHISTOPHELES.]   No, tell me why these crazy antics?
The mad ado, the gestures that are frantic,
The most insipid cheat—this stuff
I've known and hated long enough.

MEPHISTOPHELES   Relax! It's fun—a little play;   200
Don't be so serious, so sedate!
Such hocus-pocus is a doctor's way,
Of making sure the juice will operate.

> [*He makes* FAUST *step into the circle.*]

WITCH [*Begins to recite from the book with great emphasis.*]
This you must know!
From one make ten,   205
And two let go,
Take three again,
Then you'll be rich.
The four you fix.
From five and six,   210
Thus says the witch,
Make seven and eight,
That does the trick;
And nine is one,
And ten is none.   215
That is the witch's arithmetic.

FAUST   It seems to me the old hag runs a fever.

MEPHISTOPHELES   You'll hear much more before we leave her.
I know, it sounds like that for many pages.
I lost much time on this accursed affliction   220
Because a perfect contradiction
Intrigues not only fools but also sages.
This art is old and new, forsooth:

It was the custom in all ages
To spread illusion and not truth   225
With Three in One and One in Three.[3]
They teach it twittering like birds;
With fools there is no intervening.
Men usually believe, if only they hear words,
That there must also be some sort of meaning.   230
WITCH [*Continues.*]   The lofty prize
    Of science lies
    Concealed today as ever.
    Who has no thought,
    To him it's brought   235
    To own without endeavor.
FAUST   What nonsense does she put before us?
My head aches from her stupidness.
It seems as if I heard a chorus
Of many thousand fools, no less.   240
MEPHISTOPHELES   Excellent sybil, that is quite enough!
Now pour the drink—just put the stuff
Into this bowl here. Fill it, sybil, pour;
My friend is safe from any injuries:
He has a number of degrees   245
And has had many drinks before.
    [*The* WITCH *pours the drink into a bowl with many ceremonies; as*
    FAUST *puts it to his lips, a small flame spurts up.*]
MEPHISTOPHELES   What is the matter? Hold it level!
Drink fast and it will warm you up.
You are familiar with the Devil,
And shudder at a fiery cup?   250
    [*The* WITCH *breaks the circle.* FAUST *steps out.*]
MEPHISTOPHELES   Come on! Let's go! You must not rest.
WITCH   And may this gulp give great delight!
MEPHISTOPHELES [*To the* WITCH.]   If there is anything that you request,
Just let me know the next Walpurgis Night.[4]
WITCH   Here is a song; just sing it now and then,   255
And you will feel a queer effect indeed.
MEPHISTOPHELES [*To* FAUST.]   Come quickly now before you tire,
And let me lead while you perspire
So that the force can work out through your skin.
I'll teach you later on to value noble leisure,   260
And soon you will perceive the most delightful pleasure,
As Cupid starts to stir and dance like jumping jinn.[5]
FAUST   One last look at the mirror where I stood!
So beauteous was that woman's form!
MEPHISTOPHELES   No! No! The paragon of womanhood   265
You shall soon see alive and warm.
[*Softly.*] You'll soon find with this potion's aid,
Helen of Troy in every maid.

---

3. The Christian doctrine of the Trinity.   4. May Day Eve (April 30), when witches are supposed to
assemble on the Brocken, a peak in the Harz Mountains, which are in central Germany.   5. A supernatural being that can take human or animal form.

STREET

[FAUST. MARGARET *passing by.*]

FAUST   Fair lady, may I be so free
  To offer my arm and company?
MARGARET   I'm neither a lady nor am I fair,
  And can go home without your care.
     [*She frees herself and exits.*]
FAUST   By heaven, this young girl is fair!   5
  Her like I don't know anywhere.
  She is so virtuous and pure,
  But somewhat pert and not demure.
  The glow of her cheeks and her lips so red
  I shall not forget until I am dead.   10
  Her downcast eyes, shy and yet smart,
  Are stamped forever on my heart;
  Her curtness and her brevity
  Was sheer enchanting ecstasy!
     [MEPHISTOPHELES *enters.*]
FAUST   Get me that girl, and don't ask why!   15
MEPHISTOPHELES   Which one?
FAUST   She only just went by.
MEPHISTOPHELES   That one! She saw her priest just now,
  And he pronounced her free of sin.
  I stood right there and listened in.
  She's so completely blemishless   20
  That there was nothing to confess.
  Over her I don't have any power.
FAUST   She is well past her fourteenth year.
MEPHISTOPHELES   Look at the gay Lothario[6] here!
  He would like to have every flower,   25
  And thinks each prize or pretty trick
  Just waits around for him to pick;
  But sometimes that just doesn't go.
FAUST   My Very Reverend Holy Joe,
  Leave me in peace with law and right!   30
  I tell you, if you don't comply,
  And this sweet young blood doesn't lie
  Between my arms this very night,
  At midnight we'll have parted ways.
MEPHISTOPHELES   Think of the limits of my might.   35
  I need at least some fourteen days
  To find a handy evening.
FAUST   If I had peace for seven hours,
  I should not need the Devil's powers
  To seduce such a little thing.   40
MEPHISTOPHELES   You speak just like a Frenchman. Wait
  I beg you, and don't be annoyed:
  What have you got when it's enjoyed?

---

6. The seducer in Nicholas Rowe's play *The Fair Penitent* (1703); hence, figuratively, any seducer. The German reads *Hans Liederlich,* meaning a profligate, since *liederlich* means "careless" or "dissolute."

The fun is not nearly so great
As when you bit by bit imbibe it,   45
And first resort to playful folly
To knead and to prepare your dolly,
The way some Gallic tales describe it.
FAUST   I've appetite without all that.
MEPHISTOPHELES   Now without jokes or tit-for-tat: 50
    I tell you, with this fair young child
    We simply can't be fast or wild.
    We'd waste our time storming and running;
    We have to have recourse to cunning.
FAUST   Get something from the angel's nest!   55
    Or lead me to her place of rest!
    Get me a kerchief from her breast,
    A garter from my darling's knee.
MEPHISTOPHELES   Just so you see, it touches me
    And I would soothe your agony,   60
    Let us not linger here and thus delay:
    I'll take you to her room today.
FAUST   And shall I see her? Have her?
MEPHISTOPHELES   No.
    To one of her neighbors she has to go.
    But meanwhile you may at your leisure   65
    Relish the hopes of future pleasure,
    Till you are sated with her atmosphere.
FAUST   Can we go now?
MEPHISTOPHELES   It's early yet, I fear.
FAUST   Get me a present for the dear!
    [Exit.]
MEPHISTOPHELES   A present right away? Good! He will be a hit.   70
    There's many a nice place I know
    With treasures buried long ago;
    I better look around a bit.
        [Exit.]

                          EVENING

    [A small neat room.]
MARGARET [Braiding and binding her hair.]
    I should give much if I could say
    Who was that gentleman today.
    He looked quite gallant, certainly,
    And is of noble family;
    That much even his forehead told—   5
    How else could he have been so bold?
        [Exit. Enter MEPHISTOPHELES, FAUST.]
MEPHISTOPHELES   Come in, but very quietly!
FAUST [After a short silence.]   I beg you, leave and let me be!
MEPHISTOPHELES [Sniffing around.]   She's neater than a lot of girls I see.
    [Exit.]

FAUST [*Looking up and around.*]   Sweet light of dusk, guest from above   10
   That fills this shrine, be welcome you!
   Seize now my heart, sweet agony of love
   That languishes and feeds on hope's clear dew!
   What sense of calm embraces me,
   Of order and complete content!   15
   What bounty in this poverty!
   And in this prison, ah, what ravishment!
      [*He throws himself into the leather armchair by the bed.*]
   Welcome me now, as former ages rested
   Within your open arms in grief and joy!
   How often was this fathers' throne contested   20
   By eager children, prized by girl and boy!
   And here, perhaps, her full cheeks flushed with bliss,
   My darling, grateful for a Christmas toy,
   Pressed on her grandsire's withered hand a kiss.
   I feel your spirit, lovely maid,   25
   Of ordered bounty breathing here
   Which, motherly, comes daily to your aid
   To teach you how a rug is best on tables laid
   And how the sand should on the floor appear.[7]
   Oh godlike hand, to you it's given   30
   To make a cottage, a kingdom of heaven.
   And here!
      [*He lifts a bed curtain.*]
         What raptured shudder makes me stir?
   How I should love to be immured
   Where in light dreams nature matured
   The angel that's innate in her,   35
   Here lay the child, developed slowly,
   Her tender breast with warm life fraught,
   And here, through weaving pure and holy,
   The image of the gods was wrought.

   And you! Alas, what brought you here?   40
   I feel so deeply moved, so queer!
   What do you seek? Why is your heart so sore?
   Poor Faust! I do not know you any more.

   Do magic smells surround me here?
   Immediate pleasure was my bent,   45
   But now—in dreams of love I'm all but spent.
   Are we mere puppets of the atmosphere?

   If she returned this instant from her call,
   How for your mean transgression you would pay!
   The haughty lad would be so small,   50
   Lie at her feet and melt away.
MEPHISTOPHELES [*Entering.*]   Let's go! I see her in the lane!

---

7. Floors were sprinkled with sand after cleaning.

FAUST   Away! I'll never come again.
MEPHISTOPHELES   Here is a fairly decent case,
   I picked it up some other place.   55
   Just leave it in the chest up there.
   She'll go out of her mind, I swear;
   For I put things in it, good sir,
   To win a better one than her.
   But child is child and play is play.   60
FAUST   I don't know—should I?
MEPHISTOPHELES   Why delay?
   You do not hope to save your jewel?
   Or I'll give your lust this advice:
   Don't waste fair daytime like this twice,
   Nor my exertions: it is cruel.   65
   It is not simple greed, I hope!
   I scratch my head, I fret and mope—
       [*He puts the case into the chest and locks it again.*]
   Away! Let's go!—
   It's just to make the child fulfill
   Your heart's desire and your will;   70
   And you stand and frown
   As if you had to lecture in cap and gown—
   As if in gray there stood in front of you
   Physics and Metaphysics, too.
   Away!
       [*Exeunt.*]
MARGARET [*With a lamp.*]   It seems so close, so sultry now, 75
       [*She opens the window.*]
   And yet outside it's not so warm.
   I feel so strange, I don't know how—
   I wish my mother would come home.
   A shudder grips my body, I feel chilly—
   How fearful I am and how silly!   80
       [*She begins to sing as she undresses.*]
   In Thule[8] there was a king,
   Faithful unto the grave,
   To whom his mistress, dying,
   A golden goblet gave.

   Nothing he held more dear.   85
   At every meal he used it;
   His eyes would fill with tears
   As often as he mused it.

   And when he came to dying,
   The towns in his realm he told.   90
   Naught to his heir denying,
   Except the goblet of gold.

---

8. The fabled *ultima Thule* of Latin literature—those distant lands just beyond the reach of every explorer. Goethe wrote the ballad in 1774; it was published in 1782 and set to music by several composers.

He dined at evenfall
With all his chivalry
In the ancestral hall   95
In the castle by the sea.

The old man rose at last
And drank life's sunset glow.
And the sacred goblet he cast
Into the flood below.   100

He saw it plunging, drinking.
And sinking into the sea;
His eyes were also sinking,
And nevermore drank he.

　　[*She opens the chest to put away her clothes and sees the case.*]
How did this lovely case get in my chest?   105
I locked it after I got dressed.
It certainly seems strange. And what might be in there?
It might be a security
Left for a loan in Mother's care.
There is a ribbon with a key;   110
I think I'll open it and see.
What is that? God in heaven! There—
I never saw such fine array!
These jewels! Why a lord's lady could wear
These on the highest holiday.   115
How would this necklace look on me?
Who owns all this? It is so fine.

　　[*She adorns herself and steps before the mirror.*]
If those earrings were only mine!
One looks quite different right away.
What good is beauty, even youth?   120
All that may be quite good and fair,
But does it get you anywhere?
Their praise is half pity, you can be sure.
For gold contend,
On gold depend   125
All things. Woe to us poor!

PROMENADE

　　[FAUST *walking up and down, lost in thought.* MEPHISTOPHELES
　　enters.]
MEPHISTOPHELES　By the pangs of despised love! By the elements of hell!
　　I wish I knew something worse to curse by it as well!
FAUST　What ails you? Steady now, keep level!
　　I never saw a face like yours today.
MEPHISTOPHELES　I'd wish the Devil took me straightaway,   5
　　If I myself were not a devil.
FAUST　Has something in your head gone bad?
　　It sure becomes you raving like one mad.

MEPHISTOPHELES   Just think, the jewels got for Margaret—
  A dirty priest took the whole set.   10
  The mother gets to see the stuff
  And starts to shudder, sure enough:
  She has a nose to smell things out—
  In prayerbooks she keeps her snout—
  A whiff of anything makes plain   15
  Whether it's holy or profane.
  She sniffed the jewelry like a rat
  And knew no blessings came with that.
  My child, she cried, ill-gotten wealth
  Will soil your soul and spoil your health.   20
  We'll give it to the Mother of the Lord
  And later get a heavenly reward.
  Poor Margaret went into a pout;
  She thought: a gift horse![9] and, no doubt,
  Who[1] brought it here so carefully   25
  Could not be godless, certainly.
  The mother called a priest at once,
  He saw the gems and was no dunce;
  He drooled and then said: Without question,
  Your instinct is quite genuine,   30
  Who overcomes himself will win.
  The Church has a superb digestion,
  Whole countries she has gobbled up,
  But never is too full to sup;
  The Church alone has the good health   35
  For stomaching ill-gotten wealth.
FAUST   Why, everybody does: a Jew
  And any king can do it, too.
MEPHISTOPHELES   So he picked up a clasp, necklace, and rings,
  Like toadstools or some worthless things,   40
  And did not thank them more nor less
  Than as if it were nuts or some such mess,
  And he promised them plenty after they died—
  And they were duly edified.
FAUST   And Gretchen?[2]
MEPHISTOPHELES   She, of course, feels blue,   45
  She sits and doesn't know what to do,
  Thinks day and night of every gem—
  Still more of him who furnished them.
FAUST   My darling's grief distresses me.
  Go, get her some new jewelry.   50
  The first one was a trifling loss.
MEPHISTOPHELES   Oh sure, it's child's play for you, boss.
FAUST   Just fix it all to suit my will;
  Try on the neighbor, too, your skill.

9. Like the wooden horse in which Greek soldiers entered Troy to capture it; an emblem of treachery.   1. Whoever.   2. Diminutive of the German *Margarete*. She is given this name through much of the play.

Don't, Devil, act like sluggish paste! 55
Get some new jewels and make haste!
MEPHISTOPHELES   Yes, gracious lord, it is a pleasure.
     [FAUST *exits.*]
MEPHISTOPHELES   A fool in love just doesn't care
And, just to sweeten darling's leisure,
He'd make sun, moon, and stars into thin air. 60
     [*Exit.*]

THE NEIGHBOR'S HOUSE

MARTHA [*Alone.*]   May God forgive my husband! He
Was certainly not good to me.
He went into the world to roam
And left me on the straw at home.
God knows that I have never crossed him, 5
And loved him dearly; yet I lost him.
[*She cries.*] Perhaps—the thought kills me—he died!—
If it were only certified!
     [MARGARET *enters.*]
MARGARET   Dame Martha!
MARTHA   Gretchen, what could it be?
MARGARET   My legs feel faint, though not with pain: 10
I found another case, again
Right in my press,³ of ebony,
With things more precious all around
Than was the first case that I found.
MARTHA   You must not show them to your mother, 15
She'd tell the priest as with the other.
MARGARET   Oh look at it! Oh see! Please do!
MARTHA [*Adorns her.*]   You lucky, lucky creature, you!
MARGARET   Unfortunately, it's not meet
To wear them in the church or street. 20
MARTHA   Just come here often to see me,
Put on the jewels secretly,
Walk up and down an hour before the mirror here,
And we shall have a good time, dear.
Then chances come, perhaps a holiday, 25
When we can bit by bit, gem after gem display,
A necklace first, than a pearl in your ear;
Your mother—we can fool her, or she may never hear.
MARGARET   Who brought the cases and has not appeared?
It certainly seems very weird. 30
     [*A knock.*]
Oh God, my mother—is it her?
MARTHA [*Peeping through the curtain.*]   It is a stranger—come in, sir!
     [MEPHISTOPHELES *enters.*]
MEPHISTOPHELES   I'll come right in and be so free,

---

3. A type of cupboard in which pressed linens were stored.

If the ladies will grant me the liberty.
    [*Steps back respectfully as he sees* MARGARET.]
To Martha Schwerdtlein I wished to speak.   35
MARTHA   It's I. What does your honor seek?
MEPHISTOPHELES [*Softly to her.*]   I know you now, that satisfies me,
  You have very elegant company;
  Forgive my intrusion; I shall come back soon—
  If you don't mind, this afternoon.   40
MARTHA [*Loud.*]   Oh goodness gracious! Did you hear?
  He thinks you are a lady, dear!
MARGARET   I'm nothing but a poor young maid;
  You are much too kind, I am afraid;
  The gems and jewels are not my own.   45
MEPHISTOPHELES   It is not the jewelry alone!
  Your noble eyes—indeed, it is your whole way!
  How glad I am that I may stay!
MARTHA   What is your errand? Please, good sir—
MEPHISTOPHELES   I wish I had better news for her!   50
  And don't get cross with your poor guest:
  Your husband is dead and sends his best.
MARTHA   Is dead? The faithful heart! Oh dear!
  My husband is dead! I shall faint right here.
MARGARET   Oh my dear woman! Don't despair!   55
MEPHISTOPHELES   Let me relate the sad affair.
MARGARET   I should sooner never be a bride:
  The grief would kill me if he died.
MEPHISTOPHELES   Joy needs woe, woe requires joy.
MARTHA   Tell me of the end of my sweet boy.   60
MEPHISTOPHELES   In Padua, in Italy,
  He is buried in St. Anthony
  In ground that has been duly blessed
  For such cool, everlasting rest.
MARTHA   Surely, there is something more you bring.   65
MEPHISTOPHELES   One solemn and sincere request:
  For his poor soul they should three hundred masses sing.
  That's all, my purse is empty, though not of course my breast.
MARTHA   What? Not a gem? No work of art?
  I am sure, deep in his bag the poorest wanderer   70
  Keeps some remembrance that gives pleasure,
  And sooner starves than yields this treasure.
MEPHISTOPHELES   Madam, don't doubt it breaks my heart.
  And you may rest assured, he was no squanderer.
  He knew his errors well, and he repented,   75
  Though his ill fortune was the thing he most lamented.
MARGARET   That men are so unfortunate and poor!
  I'll say some Requiems, and for his soul I'll pray.
MEPHISTOPHELES   You would deserve a marriage right away,
  For you are charming, I am sure.   80
MARGARET   Oh no! I must wait to be wed.
MEPHISTOPHELES   If not a husband, have a lover instead.

It is one of heaven's greatest charms
To hold such a sweetheart in one's arms.
MARGARET   That is not the custom around here.   85
MEPHISTOPHELES   Custom or not, it's done, my dear.
MARTHA   Please tell me more!
MEPHISTOPHELES   I stood beside the bed he died on;
It was superior to manure,
Of rotted straw, and yet he died a Christian, pure,
And found that there was more on his unsettled score.   90
"I'm hateful," he cried; "wicked was my life,
As I forsook my trade and also left my wife.
To think of it now makes me die.
If only she forgave me even so!"
MARTHA [*Weeping.*]   The darling! I forgave him long ago.   95
MEPHISTOPHELES   "And yet, God knows, she was far worse than I."
MARTHA   He lied—alas, lied at the brink of death!
MEPHISTOPHELES   Surely, he made up things with dying breath,
If ever I saw death before.
"To pass the time, I could not look around," he said;   100
"First she got children, then they needed bread—
When I say bread, I mean much more—
And she never gave peace for me to eat my share."
MARTHA   Did he forget my love, my faithfulness and care
And how I slaved both day and night?   105
MEPHISTOPHELES   Oh no, he thought of that with all his might;
He said: "When we left Malta for another trip,
I prayed for wife and children fervently,
So heaven showed good grace to me.
And our boat soon caught a Turkish ship   110
That had the mighty sultan's gold on it.
Then fortitude got its reward,
And I myself was given, as was fit,
My share of the great sultan's hoard."
MARTHA   Oh how? Oh where? Might it be buried now?   115
MEPHISTOPHELES   The winds have scattered it, and who knows how?
A pretty girl in Naples, sweet and slim,
Cared for him when he was without a friend
And did so many deeds of love for him
That he could feel it till his blessed end.   120
MARTHA   The rogue! He robbed children and wife!
No misery, no lack of bread
Could keep him from his shameful life!
MEPHISTOPHELES   You see! For that he now is dead.
If I were in your place, I'd pause   125
To mourn him for a year, as meet,
And meanwhile I would try to find another sweet.
MARTHA   Oh God, the way my first one was
I'll hardly find another to be mine!
How could there be a little fool that's fonder?   130
Only he liked so very much to wander,

And foreign women, and foreign wine,
And that damned shooting of the dice.
MEPHISTOPHELES   Well, well! It could have been quite nice,
Had he been willing to ignore   135
As many faults in you, or more.
On such terms, I myself would woo
And willingly change rings with you.
MARTHA   The gentleman is pleased to jest.
MEPHISTOPHELES [*Aside.*]   I better get away from here;   140
She'd keep the Devil to his word, I fear.
[*To* GRETCHEN.] And how is your heart? Still at rest?
MARGARET   What do you mean, good sir?
MEPHISTOPHELES [*Aside.*]   You good, innocent child!
[*Aloud.*] Good-by, fair ladies!
MARGARET   Good-by.
MARTHA   Oh, not so fast and wild!   145
I'd like to have it certified
That my sweetheart was buried, and when and where he died.
I always hate to see things done obliquely
And want to read his death in our weekly.
MEPHISTOPHELES   Yes, lady, what is testified by two   150
Is everywhere known to be true;
And I happen to have a splendid mate
Whom I'll take along to the magistrate.
I'll bring him here.
MARTHA   Indeed, please do!
MEPHISTOPHELES   And will this maiden be here, too?   155
A gallant lad! Has traveled much with me
And shows young ladies all courtesy.
MARGARET   I would have to blush before him, poor thing.[4]
MEPHISTOPHELES   Not even before a king!
MARTHA   Behind the house, in my garden, then,   160
Tonight we shall expect the gentlemen.

STREET

[FAUST. MEPHISTOPHELES.]
FAUST   How is it? Well? Can it be soon?
MEPHISTOPHELES   Oh bravo! Now you are on fire?
Soon Gretchen will still your desire.
At Martha's you may see her later this afternoon:
That woman seems expressly made   5
To ply the pimps' and gypsies' trade.
FAUST   Oh good!
MEPHISTOPHELES   But something's wanted from us, too.
FAUST   One good turn makes another due.
MEPHISTOPHELES   We merely have to go and testify   10
That the remains of her dear husband lie

4. Referring to herself, not to Faust.

In Padua where Anthony once sat.
FAUST   Now we shall have to go there. Now that was smart of you!
MEPHISTOPHELES   Sancta simplicitas![5] Who ever thought of that?
Just testify, and hang whether it's true!   15
FAUST   If you know nothing better, this plan has fallen through.
MEPHISTOPHELES   Oh, holy man! You are no less!
Is this the first time in your life that you
Have testified what is not true?
Of God and all the world, and every single part,   20
Of man and all that stirs inside his head and heart
You gave your definitions with power and finesse.
With brazen cheek and haughty breath.
And if you stop to think, I guess,
You know as much of that, you must confess,   25
As you know now of Mr. Schwerdtlein's death.
FAUST   You are and you remain a sophist and a liar.
MEPHISTOPHELES   Yes, if one's knowledge were not just a little higher.
Tomorrow, won't you, pure as air,
Deceive poor Gretchen and declare   30
Your soul's profoundest love, and swear?
FAUST   With all my heart.
MEPHISTOPHELES   Good and fair!
Then faithfulness and love eternal
And the super-almighty urge supernal—
Will that come from your heart as well?   35
FAUST   Leave off! It will.—When, lost in feeling,
For this urge, for this surge
I seek a name, find none, and, reeling
All through the world with all my senses gasping,
At all the noblest words I'm grasping   40
And call this blaze in which I flame,
Infinite, eternal eternally—
Is that a game or devilish jugglery?
MEPHISTOPHELES   I am still right.
FAUST   Listen to me,
I beg of you, and don't wear out my lung: 45
Whoever would be right and only has a tongue,
Always will be.
Come on! I'm sick of prating, spare your voice,
For you are right because I have no choice.

GARDEN

[MARGARET *on* FAUST's *arm,* MARTHA *with* MEPHISTOPHELES, *walking up and down.*]
MARGARET   I feel it well, good sir, you're only kind to me:
You condescend—and you abash.
It is the traveler's courtesy

---

5. Holy simplicity (Latin).

To put up graciously with trash.
I know too well, my poor talk never can   5
Give pleasure to a traveled gentleman.
FAUST   One glance from you, one word gives far more pleasure
Than all the wisdom of this world. [*He kisses her hand.*]
MARGARET   Don't incommode yourself! How could you kiss it? You?
It is so ugly, is so rough.   10
But all the things that I have had to do!
For Mother I can't do enough.
        [*They pass.*]
MARTHA   And you, sir, travel all the time, you say?
MEPHISTOPHELES   Alas, our trade and duty keeps us going!
Though when one leaves the tears may well be flowing,   15
One never is allowed to stay.
MARTHA   While it may do in younger years
To sweep around the world, feel free and suave,
There is the time when old age nears,
And then to creep alone, a bachelor, to one's grave.   20
That's something everybody fears.
MEPHISTOPHELES   With dread I see it far away.
MARTHA   Then, my dear sir, consider while you may.
        [*They pass.*]
MARGARET   Yes, out of sight is out of mind.
You are polite, you can't deny,   25
And often you have friends and find
That they are cleverer than I.
FAUST   Oh dearest, trust me, what's called clever on this earth
Is often vain and rash rather than clever.
MARGARET   What?
FAUST   Oh, that the innocent and simple never   30
Appreciate themselves and their own worth!
That meekness and humility, supreme
Among the gifts of loving, lavish nature—
MARGARET   If you should think of me one moment only,
I shall have time enough to think of you and dream.   35
FAUST   Are you so often lonely?
MARGARET   Yes; while our household is quite small,
You see, I have to do it all.
We have no maid, so I must cook, and sweep, and knit.
And sew, and run early and late;   40
And mother is in all of it
So accurate!
Not that it's necessary; our need is not so great.
We could afford much more than many another:
My father left a tidy sum to mother,   45
A house and garden near the city gate.
But now my days are rather plain:
A soldier is my brother,
My little sister dead.
Sore was, while she was living, the troubled life I led;   50

But I would gladly go through all of it again:
   She was so dear to me.
FAUST   An angel, if like you.
MARGARET   I brought her up, and she adored me, too.
   She was born only after father's death;
   Mother seemed near her dying breath,   55
   As stricken as she then would lie,
   Though she got well again quite slowly, by and by.
   She was so sickly and so slight,
   She could not nurse the little mite;
   So I would tend her all alone,   60
   With milk and water; she became my own.
   Upon my arms and in my lap
   She first grew friendly, tumbled, and grew up.
FAUST   You must have felt the purest happiness.
MARGARET   But also many hours of distress.   65
   The baby's cradle stood at night
   Beside my bed, and if she stirred I'd wake,
   I slept so light.
   Now I would have to feed her, now I'd take
   Her into my bed, now I'd rise   70
   And dandling pace the room to calm the baby's cries.
   And I would wash before the sun would rise,
   Fret in the market and over the kitchen flame,
   Tomorrow as today, always the same.
   One's spirits, sir, are not always the best,   75
   But one can relish meals and relish rest.
       [They pass.]
MARTHA   Poor woman has indeed a wretched fate:
   A bachelor is not easy to convert.
MEPHISTOPHELES   For one like you the job is not too great;
   You might convince me if you are alert.   80
MARTHA   Be frank, dear sir, so far you have not found?
   Has not your heart in some way yet been bound?
MEPHISTOPHELES   A hearth one owns and a good wife, we're told,
   Are worth as much as pearls and gold.
MARTHA   I mean, have you not ever had a passion?   85
MEPHISTOPHELES   I always was received in the most friendly fashion.
MARTHA   Would say: weren't you ever in earnest in your breast?
MEPHISTOPHELES   With women one should never presume to speak in
   jest.
MARTHA   Oh, you don't understand.
MEPHISTOPHELES   I'm sorry I'm so blind!
   But I do understand—that you are very kind.   90
       [They pass.]
FAUST   Oh little angel, you did recognize
   Me as I came into the garden?
MARGARET   Did you not notice? I cast down my eyes.
FAUST   My liberty you're then prepared to pardon?
   What insolence presumed to say   95

As you left church the other day?
MARGARET   I was upset, I did not know such daring
  And no one could have spoken ill of me.
  I thought that something in my bearing
  Must have seemed shameless and unmaidenly.   100
  He seemed to have the sudden feeling
  That this wench could be had without much dealing.
  Let me confess, I didn't know that there
  Were other feelings stirring in me, and they grew;
  But I was angry with myself, I swear,   105
  That I could not get angrier with you.
FAUST   Sweet darling!
MARGARET   Let me do this! [*She plucks a daisy and pulls out the*
  petals one by one.]
FAUST   A nosegay? Or what shall it be?
MARGARET
  No, it is just a game.
FAUST   What?
MARGARET   Go, you will laugh at me. [*She pulls out petals*
  and murmurs.]
FAUST
  What do you murmur?
MARGARET [*Half aloud.*]   He loves me—loves me not.
FAUST   You gentle countenance of heaven!   110
MARGARET [*Continues.*]   Loves me—not—loves me—not—
  [*Tearing out the last leaf, in utter joy.*]
  He loves me.
FAUST   Yes, my child. Let this sweet flower's word
  Be as a god's word to you. He loves you.
  Do you know what this means? He loves you. [*He takes both her hands.*]
MARGARET   My skin creeps.   115
FAUST   Oh, shudder not! But let this glance,
  And let this clasp of hands tell you
  What is unspeakable:
  To yield oneself entirely and feel
  A rapture which must be eternal.   120
  Eternal! For its end would be despair.
  No, no end! No end!
       [MARGARET *clasps his hands, frees herself, and runs away. He stands*
       for a moment, lost in thought; then he follows her.]
MARTHA [*Entering.*]   The night draws near.
MEPHISTOPHELES   Yes, and we want to go.
MARTHA   I should ask you to tarry even so,
  But this place simply is too bad: 125
  It is as if nobody had
  Work or labor
  Except to spy all day long on his neighbor,
  And one gets talked about, whatever life one leads.
  And our couple?
MEPHISTOPHELES   Up that path I heard them whirr—   130

Frolicking butterflies.
MARTHA   He is taking to her.
MEPHISTOPHELES   And she to him. That's how the world proceeds.

A GARDEN BOWER

[MARGARET *leaps into it, hides behind the door, puts the tip of one finger to her lips, and peeks through the crack.*]
MARGARET   He comes.
FAUST [*Entering.*]   Oh rogue, you're teasing me.
Now I see. [*He kisses her.*]
MARGARET [*Seizing him and returning the kiss.*]
Dearest man! I love you from my heart.
        [MEPHISTOPHELES *knocks.*]
FAUST [*Stamping his foot.*]
Who's there?
MEPHISTOPHELES   A friend.
FAUST   A beast!
MEPHISTOPHELES   The time has come to part.
MARTHA [*Entering.*]
Yes, it is late, good sir.
FAUST   May I not take you home?   5
MARGARET   My mother would—Farewell!
FAUST   Must I leave then?
Farewell.
MARTHA   Adieu.
MARGARET   Come soon again!
        [FAUST *and* MEPHISTOPHELES *exeunt.*]
MARGARET   Dear God, the things he thought and said!
How much goes on in a man's head!
Abashed, I merely acquiesce   10
And cannot answer, except Yes!
I am a poor, dumb child and cannot see
What such a man could find in me.
        [*Exit.*]

·   WOOD AND CAVE

FAUST [*Alone.*]   Exalted spirit, all you gave me, all
That I have asked. And it was not in vain
That amid flames you turned your face toward me.
You gave me royal nature as my own dominion,
Strength to experience her, enjoy her. Not   5
The cold amazement of a visit only
You granted me, but let me penetrate
Into her heart as into a close friend's.
You lead the hosts of all that is alive
Before my eyes, teach me to know my brothers   10
In quiet bushes and in air and water.
And when the storm roars in the wood and creaks,
The giant fir tree, falling, hits and smashes

The neighbor branches and the neighbor trunks,
And from its hollow thud the mountain thunders,   15
Then you lead me to this safe cave and show
Me to myself, and all the most profound
And secret wonders of my breast are opened.
And when before my eyes the pure moon rises
And passes soothingly, there float to me   20
From rocky cliffs and out of dewy bushes
The silver shapes of a forgotten age,
And soften meditation's somber joy.
Alas, that man is granted nothing perfect
I now experience. With this happiness   25
Which brings me close and closer to the gods,
You gave me the companion whom I can
Forego no more, though with cold impudence
He makes me small in my own eyes and changes
Your gifts to nothing with a few words' breath.   30
He kindles in my breast a savage fire
And keeps me thirsting after that fair image.
Thus I reel from desire to enjoyment,
And in enjoyment languish for desire.

MEPHISTOPHELES [*Enters.*]   Have you not led this life quite long
    enough?   35
  How can it keep amusing you?
  It may be well for once to try such stuff
  But then one turns to something new.

FAUST   I wish that you had more to do
  And would not come to pester me.   40

MEPHISTOPHELES   All right. I gladly say adieu—
  You should not say that seriously.
  A chap like you, unpleasant, mad, and cross,
  Would hardly be a serious loss.
  All day long one can work and slave away.   45
  And what he likes and what might cause dismay,
  It simply isn't possible to say.

FAUST   That is indeed the proper tone!
  He wants my thanks for being such a pest.

MEPHISTOPHELES   If I had left you wretch alone,   50
  Would you then live with greater zest?
  Was it not I that helped you to disown,
  And partly cured, your feverish unrest
  Yes, but[6] for me, the earthly zone
  Would long be minus one poor guest.   55
  And now, why must you sit like an old owl
  In caves and rocky clefts, and scowl?
  From soggy moss and dripping stones you lap your food
  Just like a toad, and sit and brood.
  A fair, sweet way to pass the time!   60

6. Were it not.

    Still steeped in your doctoral slime!

FAUST   How this sojourn in the wilderness
    Renews my vital force, you cannot guess.
    And if you apprehended this,
    You would be Devil enough, to envy me my bliss.   65

MEPHISTOPHELES   A supernatural delight!
    To lie on mountains in the dew and night,
    Embracing earth and sky in raptured reeling,
    To swell into a god—in one's own feeling—
    To probe earth's marrow with vague divination,   70
    Sense in your breast the whole work of creation,
    With haughty strength enjoy, I know not what,
    Then overflow into all things with love so hot,
    Gone is all earthly inhibition,
    And then the noble intuition— [*With a gesture.*]   75
    Of—need I say of what emission?

FAUST   Shame!

MEPHISTOPHELES   That does not meet with your acclaim;
    You have the right to cry indignant: shame!
    One may not tell chaste ears what, beyond doubt,
    The chastest heart could never do without.   80
    And, once for all, I don't grudge you the pleasure
    Of little self-deceptions at your leisure;
    But it can't last indefinitely.
    Already you are spent again,
    And soon you will be rent again,   85
    By madness and anxiety.
    Enough of that. Your darling is distraught,
    Sits inside, glum and in despair,
    She can't put you out of her mind and thought
    And loves you more than she can bear.   90
    At first your raging love was past control,
    As brooks that overflow when filled with melted snow;
    You poured it out into her soul,
    But now your little brook is low.
    Instead of posing in the wood,   95
    It seems to me it might be good
    If for her love our noble lord
    Gave the poor monkey some reward.
    Time seems to her intolerably long;
    She stands at her window and sees the clouds in the sky   100
    Drift over the city wall and go by.
    Were I a little bird! thus goes her song
    For days and half the night long.
    Once she may be cheerful, most of the time sad,
    Once she has spent her tears,   105
    Then she is calm, it appears,
    And always loves you like mad.

FAUST   Serpent! Snake!

MEPHISTOPHELES [*Aside.*]   If only I catch the rake!

FAUST   Damnable fiend! Get yourself hence,   110
　　And do not name the beautiful maid!
　　Let not the lust for her sweet limbs invade
　　And ravish once again my frenzied sense!
MEPHISTOPHELES   What do you mean? She thinks you've run away:
　　And it is half-true, I must say.   115
FAUST   I am near her, however far I be,
　　She'll never be forgotten and ignored;
　　Indeed, I am consumed with jealousy
　　That her lips touch the body of the Lord.[7]
MEPHISTOPHELES   I'm jealous of my friend when she exposes   120
　　The pair of twins that feed among the roses.[8]
FAUST   Begone, pander!
MEPHISTOPHELES   Fine! Your wrath amuses me.
　　The God who fashioned man and maid
　　Was quick to recognize the noblest trade,   125
　　And procured opportunity.
　　Go on! It is a woeful pain!
　　You're to embrace your love again,
　　Not sink into the tomb.
FAUST   What are the joys of heaven in her arms?   130
　　Let me embrace her, feel her charms—
　　Do I not always sense her doom?
　　Am I not fugitive? without a home?
　　Inhuman, without aim or rest,
　　As, like the cataract, from rock to rock I foam,   135
　　Raging with passion, toward the abyss?
　　And nearby, she—with childlike blunt desires
　　Inside her cottage on the Alpine leas,
　　And everything that she requires
　　Was in her own small world at ease.   140
　　And I, whom the gods hate and mock,
　　Was not satisfied
　　That I seized the rock
　　And smashed the mountainside.
　　Her—her peace I had to undermine.   145
　　You, hell, desired this sacrifice upon your shrine.
　　Help, Devil, shorten this time of dread.
　　What must be done, come let it be.
　　Let then her fate come shattering on my head,
　　And let her perish now with me.   150
MEPHISTOPHELES   How now it boils again and how you shout.
　　Go in and comfort her, you dunce.
　　Where such a little head sees no way out,
　　He thinks the end must come at once.
　　Long live who holds out undeterred!   155
　　At other times you have the Devil's airs.

7. When the bread of Communion miraculously turns to the body of Christ.   8. Cf. Song of Solomon
4.5: "Thy two breasts are like two young roes that are twins, which feed among the lilies."

In all the world there's nothing more absurd
Than is a Devil who despairs.

GRETCHEN'S ROOM

GRETCHEN [*At the spinning wheel, alone.*]
My peace is gone,
My heart is sore;
I find it never
And nevermore.

Where him I not have   5
There is my grave.
This world is all
Turned into gall.

And my poor head
Is quite insane,   10
And my poor mind
Is rent with pain.

My peace is gone,
My heart is sore;
I find it never   15
And nevermore.

For him only I look
From my window seat,
For him only I go
Out into the street.   20

His lofty gait,
His noble guise,
The smile of his mouth,
The force of his eyes,

And his words' flow—   25
Enchanting bliss—
The touch of his hand,
And, oh, his kiss.

My peace is gone,
My heart is sore;   30
I find it never
And nevermore.

My bosom surges
For him alone,
Oh that I could clasp him   35
And hold him so,

And kiss him
To my heart's content,
Till in his kisses
I were spent.   40

MARTHA'S GARDEN

[MARGARET. FAUST.]

MARGARET Promise me, Heinrich.[9]

FAUST   Whatever I can.

MARGARET How is it with your religion, please admit—
  You certainly are a very good man,
  But I believe you don't think much of it.

FAUST Leave that, my child. I love you, do not fear   5
  And would give all for those whom I hold dear,
  Would not rob anyone of church or creed.

MARGARET That is not enough, it is faith we need.

FAUST Do we?

MARGARET   Oh that I had some influence!
  You don't respect the holy sacraments.   10

FAUST I do respect them.

MARGARET   But without desire.
  The mass and confession you do not require.
  Do you believe in God?

FAUST   My darling who may say
  I believe in God?
  Ask priests and sages, their reply   15
  Looks like sneers that mock and prod
  The one who asked the question.

MARGARET   Then you deny him there?

FAUST Do not mistake me, you who are so fair.
  Him—who may name?
  And who proclaim: 20
  I believe in him?
  Who may feel,
  Who dare reveal
  In words: I believe him not?
  The All-Embracing,   25
  The All-Sustaining,
  Does he not embrace and sustain
  You, me, himself?
  Does not the heaven vault above?
  Is the earth not firmly based down here?   30
  And do not, friendly,
  Eternal stars rise?
  Do we not look into each other's eyes,
  And all in you is surging
  To your head and heart,   35
  And weaves in timeless mystery,
  Unseeable, yet seen, around you?
  Then let it fill your heart entirely,
  And when your rapture in this feeling is complete,
  Call it then as you will,   40

9. Faust. In the legend, Faust's name was generally Johann (John). Goethe changed it to Heinrich (Henry).

Call it bliss! heart! love! God!
I do not have a name
For this. Feeling is all;
Names are but sound and smoke
Befogging heaven's blazes.   45
MARGARET   Those are very fair and noble phrases;
  The priest says something, too, like what you spoke—
  Only his words are not quite so—
FAUST   Wherever you go,
  All hearts under the heavenly day   50
  Say it, each in its own way;
  Why not I in mine?
MARGARET   When one listens to you, one might incline
  To let it pass—but I can't agree,
  For you have no Christianity.   55
FAUST   Dear child!
MARGARET   It has long been a grief to me
  To see you in such company.
FAUST   Why?
MARGARET   The man that goes around with you
  Seems hateful to me through and through: 60
  In all my life there's not a thing
  That gave my heart as sharp a sting
  As his repulsive eyes.
FAUST   Sweet doll, don't fear him anywise.
MARGARET   His presence makes me feel quite ill.   65
  I bear all other men good will;
  But just as to see you I languish,
  This man fills me with secret anguish;
  He seems a knave one should not trust.
  May God forgive me if I am unjust.   70
FAUST   There must be queer birds, too, you know.
MARGARET   But why live with them even so?
  Whenever he comes in,
  He always wears a mocking grin
  And looks half threatening: 75
  One sees, he has no sympathy for anything;
  It is written on his very face
  That he thinks love is a disgrace.
  In your arm I feel good and free,
  Warm and abandoned as can be;   80
  Alas, my heart and feelings are choked when he comes, too.
FAUST   Oh, you foreboding angel, you.
MARGARET   It makes my heart so sore
  That, when he only comes our way,
  I feel I do not love you any more;   85
  And where he is, I cannot pray.
  It eats into my heart. Oh you,
  Dear Heinrich, must feel that way, too.
FAUST   That is just your antipathy.

MARGARET   I must go.
FAUST   Will there never be   90
  At your sweet bosom one hour of rest
  When soul touches on soul and breast on breast?
MARGARET   Had I my own room when I sleep,
  I should not bolt the door tonight;
  But Mother's slumber is not deep,   95
  And if she found us thus—oh fright,
  Right then and there I should drop dead.
FAUST   My angel, if that's what you dread,
  Here is a bottle. Merely shake
  Three drops into her cup,   100
  And she won't easily wake up.
MARGARET   What should I not do for your sake?
  It will not harm her if one tries it?
FAUST   Dear, if it would, would I advise it?
MARGARET   When I but look at you, I thrill,   105
  I don't know why, my dear, to do your will;
  I have already done so much for you
  That hardly anything seems left to do.
      [*Exit. Enter* MEPHISTOPHELES.]
MEPHISTOPHELES   The monkey! Is she gone?
FAUST   You spied?
MEPHISTOPHELES   Are you surprised?
  I listened and I understood   110
  Our learned doctor just was catechized.
  I hope that it may do you good.
  The girls are quite concerned to be apprised
  If one is pious and obeys tradition.
  If yes, they trust they can rely on his submission.   115
FAUST   You monster will not see nor own
  That this sweet soul, in loyalty,
  Full of her own creed
  Which alone,
  She trusts, can bring salvation, lives in agony   120
  To think her lover lost, however she may plead.
MEPHISTOPHELES   You supersensual, sensual wooer,
  A maiden leads you by the nose.
FAUST   You freak of filth and fire! Evildoer!
MEPHISTOPHELES   And what a knowledge of physiognomy she shows.   125
  She feels, she knows not what, whenever I'm about;
  She finds a hidden meaning in my eyes:
  I am a demon, beyond doubt,
  Perhaps the Devil, that is her surmise.
  Well, tonight—?
FAUST   What's that to you?   130
MEPHISTOPHELES   I have my pleasure in it, too.

AT THE WELL

[GRETCHEN *and* LIESCHEN *with jugs.*]
LIESCHEN   Of Barbara you haven't heard?
GRETCHEN   I rarely see people—no, not a word.
LIESCHEN   Well, Sibyl just told me in front of the school:
   That girl has at last been made a fool.
   That comes from having airs.
GRETCHEN   How so?
LIESCHEN   It stinks!   5
   She is feeding two when she eats and drinks.
GRETCHEN   Oh!
LIESCHEN   At last she has got what was coming to her.
   She stuck to that fellow like a burr.
   That was some prancing,   10
   In the village, and dancing,
   She was always the first in line;
   And he flirted with her over pastries and wine;
   And she thought that she looked divine—
   But had no honor, no thought of her name,   15
   And took his presents without any shame.
   The way they slobbered and carried on;
   But now the little flower is gone.
GRETCHEN   Poor thing!
LIESCHEN   That you don't say!
   When girls like us would be spinning away,   20
   And mother kept us at home every night,
   She was with her lover in sweet delight
   On the bench by the door, in dark alleys they were,
   And the time was never too long for her.
   Now let her crouch and let her bend down   25
   And do penance in a sinner's gown!
GRETCHEN   He will surely take her to be his wife.
LIESCHEN   He would be a fool! A handsome boy
   Will elsewhere find more air and joy.
   He's already gone.
GRETCHEN   That is not fair!   30
LIESCHEN   And if she gets him, let her beware:
   Her veil the boys will throw to the floor,
   And we shall strew chaff in front of her door.[1]
   [*Exit.*]
GRETCHEN [*Going home.*]   How I once used to scold along
   When some poor woman had done wrong.   35
   How for another person's shame
   I found not words enough of blame.
   How black it seemed—I made it blacker still,
   And yet not black enough to suit my will.
   I blessed myself, would boast and grin—   40

---

1. In Germany this treatment was reserved for young women who had sexual relations before marriage.

And now myself am caught in sin.
Yet—everything that brought me here,
God, was so good, oh, was so dear.

CITY WALL

[*In a niche in the wall, an image of the Mater Dolorosa.*[2] *Ewers with flowers in front of it.*]

GRETCHEN [*Puts fresh flowers into the ewers.*]
Incline,
Mother of pain,
Your face in grace to my despair.

A sword in your heart,
With pain rent apart,   5
Up to your son's dread death you stare.

On the Father your eyes,
You send up sighs
For your and your son's despair.

Who knows   10
My woes—
Despair in every bone!

How my heart is full of anguish,
How I tremble, how I languish,
Know but you, and you alone.   15

Wherever I may go,
What woe, what woe, what woe
Is in my bosom aching!

Scarcely alone am I,
I cry, I cry, I cry;   20
My heart in me is breaking.

The pots in front of my window
I watered with tears as the dew,
When early in the morning
I broke these flowers for you.   25

When bright into my room
The sun his first rays shed,
I sat in utter gloom
Already on my bed.

Help! Rescue me from shame and death!   30
Incline,
Mother of pain,
Your face in grace to my despair.

___

2. Sorrowful mother (Latin; literal trans.); i.e., the Virgin Mary.

NIGHT

[*Street in front of* GRETCHEN's *door.*]
VALENTINE [*Soldier,* GRETCHEN's *brother.*]
   When I would sit at a drinking bout
   Where all had much to brag about,
   And many fellows raised their voice
   To praise the maidens of their choice,
   Glass after glass was drained with toasting,   5
   I listened smugly to their boasting,
   My elbow propped up on the table,
   And sneered at fable after fable.
   I'd stroke my beard and smile and say,
   Holding my bumper in my hand: 10
   Each may be nice in her own way,
   But is there one in the whole land
   Like sister Gretchen to outdo her,
   Hear, hear! Clink! Clink! it went around;
   And some would cry: It's true, yes sir,   15
   There is no other girl like her!
   The braggarts sat without a sound.
   And *now*—I could tear out my hair
   And dash my brain out in despair!
   His nose turned up, a scamp can face me,   20
   With taunts and sneers he can disgrace me;
   And I should I sit, like one in debt,
   Each chance remark should make me sweat!
   I'd like to grab them all and maul them,
   But liars I could never call them.   25

   What's coming there? What sneaks in view?
   If I mistake not, there are two.
   If it is he, I'll spare him not,
   He shall not living leave this spot.
       [FAUST *and* MEPHISTOPHELES *enter.*]
FAUST   How from the window of that sacristy   30
   The light of the eternal lamp is glimmering,
   And weak and weaker sideward shimmering,
   As night engulfs it like the sea.
   My heart feels like this nightly street.
MEPHISTOPHELES   And I feel like a cat in heat,   35
   That creeps around a fire escape
   Pressing against the wall its shape.
   I feel quite virtuous, I confess,
   A little thievish lust, a little rammishness.
   Thus I feel spooking through each vein   40
   The wonderful Walpurgis Night.
   In two days it will come again,
   And waking then is pure delight.
FAUST   And will the treasure that gleams over there
   Rise in the meantime up into the air?   45

MEPHISTOPHELES   Quite soon you may enjoy the pleasure
   Of taking from the pot the treasure.
   The other day I took a squint
   And saw fine lion dollars in't.
FAUST   Not any jewelry, not a ring   50
   To adorn my beloved girl?
MEPHISTOPHELES   I did see something like a string,
   Or something like it, made of pearl.
FAUST   Oh, that is fine, for it's unpleasant
   To visit her without a present.   55
MEPHISTOPHELES   It should not cause you such distress
   When you have gratis such success.
   Now that the sky gleams with its starry throng,
   Prepare to hear a work of art:
   I shall sing her a moral song   60
   To take no chance we fool her heart.
   [*Sings to the cither.*[3]]
       It's scarcely day,
       Oh, Katie, say,
       Why do you stay
       Before your lover's door?   65
       Leave now, leave now!
       For in you'll go
       A maid, I know,
       Come out a maid no more.

       You ought to shun   70
       That kind of fun;
       Once it is done,
       Good night, you poor, poor thing.
       For your own sake
       You should not make   75
       Love to a rake
       Unless you have the ring.[4]
VALENTINE [*Comes forward.*]   Whom would you lure? God's element!
   Rat-catching piper! Oh, perdition!
   The Devil take your instrument!   80
   The Devil then take the musician!
MEPHISTOPHELES   The cither is all smashed. It is beyond repair.
VALENTINE   Now let's try splitting skulls. Beware!
MEPHISTOPHELES [*To* FAUST.]   Don't withdraw, doctor! Quick, don't
    tarry!
   Stick close to me, I'll lead the way.   85
   Unsheathe your toothpick, don't delay;
   Thrust out at him, and I shall parry.
VALENTINE   Then parry that!
MEPHISTOPHELES   Of course.
VALENTINE   And that.
MEPHISTOPHELES   All right.

---

3. Or zither, a stringed instrument.   4. Lines 63–78 are adapted by Goethe from Shakespeare's *Hamlet*
4.5.

VALENTINE   I think the Devil must be in this fight.
    What could that be? My hand is getting lame.   90
MEPHISTOPHELES [*To* FAUST.]   Thrust home!
VALENTINE [*Falls.*]   Oh God!
MEPHISTOPHELES   The rogue is tame.
    Now hurry hence, for we must disappear:
    A murderous clamor rises instantly,
    And while the police does not trouble me,   95
    The blood ban is a thing I fear.
MARTHA [*At a window.*]   Come out! Come out!
GRETCHEN [*At a window.*]   Quick! Bring a light.
MARTHA [*As above.*]   They swear and scuffle, yell and fight.
PEOPLE   There is one dead already, see.   100
MARTHA [*Coming out.*]   The murderers—where did they run?
GRETCHEN [*Coming out.*]   Who lies there?
PEOPLE   Your own mother's son.
GRETCHEN   Almighty God! What misery!
VALENTINE   I'm dying. That is quickly said,
    And still more quickly done.   105
    Why do you women wail in dread?
    Come here, listen to me.
        [*All gather around him.*]
    My Gretchen, you are still quite green,
    Not nearly smart enough or keen,
    You do not do things right.   110
    In confidence, I should say more:
    Since after all you are a whore,
    Be one with all your might.
GRETCHEN   My brother! God! What frightful shame!
VALENTINE   Leave the Lord God out of this game.   115
    What has been done, alas, is done,
    And as it must, it now will run.
    You started secretly with one,
    Soon more will come to join the fun,
    And once a dozen lays you down,   120
    You might as well invite the town.

    When shame is born and first appears,
    It is an underhand delight,
    And one drags the veil of night
    Over her head and ears;   125
    One is tempted to put her away.
    But as she grows, she gets more bold,
    Walks naked even in the day,
    Though hardly fairer to behold.
    The more repulsive grows her sight,   130
    The more she seeks day's brilliant light.

    The time I even now discern
    When honest citizens will turn,
    Harlot, away from you and freeze
    As from a corpse that breeds disease.   135

Your heart will flinch, your heart will falter
When they will look you in the face.
You'll wear no gold, you'll wear no lace,
Nor in the church come near the altar.
You will no longer show your skill   140
At dances, donning bow and frill,
But in dark corners on the side
With beggars and cripples you'll seek to hide;
And even if God should at last forgive,
Be cursed as long as you may live!   145
MARTHA   Ask God to show your own soul grace.
    Don't make it with blasphemies still more base.
VALENTINE   That I could lay my hands on you,
    You shriveled, pimping bugaboo,
    Then, I hope, I might truly win   150
    Forgiveness for my every sin.
GRETCHEN   My brother! This is agony!
VALENTINE   I tell you, do not bawl at me.
    When you threw honor overboard,
    You pierced my heart more than the sword.   155
    Now I shall cross death's sleeping span
    To God, a soldier and an honest man.
        [*Dies.*]

CATHEDRAL

[*Service, Organ, and Singing.* GRETCHEN *among many people.* EVIL
    SPIRIT *behind* GRETCHEN.]
EVIL SPIRIT   How different you felt, Gretchen,
    When in innocence
    You came before this altar;
    And from the well-worn little book
    You prattled prayers,   5
    Half childish games,
    Half God in your heart!
    Gretchen!
    Where are your thoughts?
    And in your heart   10
    What misdeed?
    Do you pray for your mother's soul that went
    Because of you from sleep to lasting, lasting pain?
    Upon your threshold, whose blood?
    And underneath your heart,   15
    Does it not stir and swell,
    Frightened and frightening you
    With its foreboding presence?
GRETCHEN   Oh! Oh!
    That I were rid of all the thoughts   20
    Which waver in me to and fro
    Against me!

CHOIR *Dies irae, dies illa*
      Solvet saeclum in favilla.[5]
      [*Sound of the organ.*]

EVIL SPIRIT Wrath grips you.   25
  The great trumpet sounds.
  The graves are quaking.
  And your heart,
  Resurrected
  From ashen calm   30
  To flaming tortures,
  Flares up.

GRETCHEN Would I were far!
  I feel as if the organ had
  Taken my breath,   35
  As if the song
  Dissolved my heart!

CHOIR *Judex ergo cum sedebit,*
      Quidquid latet adparebit,
      Nil inultum remanebit.[6]   40

GRETCHEN I feel so close.
  The stony pillars
  Imprison me.
  The vault above
  Presses on me.—Air!   45

EVIL SPIRIT Hide yourself. Sin and shame
  Do not stay hidden.
  Air? Light?
  Woe unto you!

CHOIR *Quid sum miser tunc dicturus?*   50
      Quem patronum rogaturus?
      Cum vix justus sit securus.[7]

EVIL SPIRIT The transfigured turn
  Their countenance from you.
  To hold out their hands to you   55
  Makes the pure shudder.
  Woe!

CHOIR *Quid sum miser tunc dicturus?*

GRETCHEN Neighbor! Your smelling salts! [*She faints.*]

WALPURGIS NIGHT

[*Harz Mountains. Region of Schierke and Elend.* FAUST *and* MEPHI-
STOPHELES.]

MEPHISTOPHELES How would you like a broomstick now to fly?
  I wish I had a billy goat that's tough.
  For on this road we still have to climb high.

---

5. Day of wrath, that day that dissolves the world into ashes (Latin). The choir sings a famous thirteenth-century hymn by Thomas Celano.   6. When the judge shall be seated, what is hidden shall appear, nothing shall remain unavenged (Latin).   7. What shall I say in my wretchedness? To whom shall I appeal when scarcely the righteous man is safe (Latin).

FAUST   As long as I feel fresh, and while my legs are spry,
   This knotted staff seems good enough.   5
   Why should we shun each stumbling block?
   To creep first through the valleys' lovely maze,
   And then to scale this wall of rock
   From which the torrent foams in silver haze—
   There is the zest that spices our ways.   10
   Around the birches weaves the spring,
   Even the fir tree feels its spell:
   Should it not stir in our limbs as well?
MEPHISTOPHELES   Of all that I don't feel a thing.
   In me the winter is still brisk,   15
   I wish my path were graced with frost and snow.
   How wretchedly the moon's imperfect disk
   Arises now with its red, tardy glow,
   And is so dim that one could bump one's head
   At every step against a rock or tree!   20
   Let's use a will-o'-the-wisp[8] instead!
   I see one there that burns quite merrily.
   Hello there! Would you come and join us, friend?
   Why blaze away to no good end?
   Please be so kind and show us up the hill!   25
WILL-O'-THE-WISP   I hope my deep respect will help me force
   My generally flighty will;
   For zigzag is the rule in our course.
MEPHISTOPHELES   Hear! Hear! It's man you like to imitate!
   Now, in the Devil's name, go straight—   30
   Or I shall blow your flickering life span out.
WILL-O'-THE-WISP   You are the master of the house, no doubt,
   And I shall try to serve you nicely.
   But don't forget, the mountain is magic-mad today,
   And if Will-o'-the-wisp must guide you on your way,   35
   You must not take things too precisely.
FAUST, MEPHISTOPHELES, AND WILL-O'-THE-WISP [*In alternating song.*]
   In the sphere of dream and spell
   We have entered now indeed.
   Have some pride and guide us well
   That we get ahead with speed   40
   In the vast deserted spaces!

   See the trees behind the trees,
   See how swiftly they change places,
   And the cliffs that bow with ease,
   Craggy noses, long and short,   45
   How they snore and how they snort!

   Through the stones and through the leas
   Tumble brooks of every sort.

8. *Ignis fatuus*, a wavering light formed by marsh gas. In German folklore thought to lead travelers to their destruction.

Is it splash or melodies?
Is it love that wails and prays,   50
Voices of those heavenly days?
What we hope and what we love!
Echoes and dim memories
Of forgotten times come back.

Oo-hoo! Shoo-hoo! Thus they squawk,   55
Screech owl, plover, and the hawk;
Did they all stay up above?
Are those salamanders crawling?
Bellies bloated, long legs sprawling!
And the roots, as serpents, coil   60
From the rocks through sandy soil,
With their eerie bonds would scare us,
Block our path and then ensnare us;
Hungry as a starving leech,
Their strong polyp's tendrils reach   65
For the wanderer. And in swarms
Mice of myriad hues and forms
Storm through moss and heath and lea.
And a host of fireflies
Throng about and improvise   70
The most maddening company.

Tell me: do we now stand still,
Or do we go up the hill?
Everything now seems to mill,
Rocks and trees and faces blend,   75
Will-o'-the-wisps grow and extend
And inflate themselves at will.
MEPHISTOPHELES   Grip my coat and hold on tight!
  Here is such a central height
  Where one sees, and it amazes,   80
  In the mountain, Mammon's blazes.[9]
FAUST   How queer glimmers a dawnlike sheen
  Faintly beneath this precipice,
  And plays into the dark ravine
  Of the near bottomless abyss.   85
  Here mists arise, there vapors spread,
  And here it gleams deep in the mountain,
  Then creeps along, a tender thread,
  And gushes up, a glistening fountain.

  Here it is winding in a tangle,   90
  With myriad veins the gorges blaze,
  And here in this congested angle
  A single stream shines through the haze.

9. Mammon is imagined as leading a group of fallen angels in digging out gold and gems from the ground of hell, presumably for Satan's palace, as described in Milton's *Paradise Lost* I.678ff.

There sparks are flying at our right,
As plentiful as golden sand. 95
But look! In its entire height
The rock becomes a firebrand.
MEPHISTOPHELES   Sir Mammon never spares the light
To hold the feast in proper fashion.
How lucky that you saw this sight! 100
I hear the guests approach in wanton passion.
FAUST   The tempests lash the air and rave,
And with gigantic blows they hit my shoulders.
MEPHISTOPHELES   You have to clutch the ribs of those big hoary boulders,
Or they will hurtle you to that abysmal grave. 105
A fog blinds the night with its hood.
Do you hear the crashes in the wood?
Frightened, the owls are scattered.
Hear how the pillars
Of ever green castles are shattered. 110
Quaking and breaking of branches!
The trunks' overpowering groaning!
The roots' creaking and moaning!
In a frightfully tangled fall
They crash over each other, one and all, 115
And through the ruin-covered abysses
The frenzied air howls and hisses.
Do you hear voices up high?
In the distance and nearby?
The whole mountain is afire 120
With a furious magic choir.
WITCHES' CHORUS   The witches ride to Blocksberg's top,
The stubble is yellow, and green the crop.
They gather on the mountainside,
Sir Urian[1] comes to preside. 125
We are riding over crag and brink,
The witches fart, the billy goats stink.
VOICE   Old Baubo[2] comes alone right now,
She is riding on a mother sow.
CHORUS   Give honor to whom honor's due! 130
Dame Baubo, lead our retinue!
A real swine and mother, too,
The witches' crew will follow you.
VOICE   Which way did you come?
VOICE   By the Ilsenstone.
I peeped at the owl who was roosting alone. 135
Did she ever make eyes!
VOICE   Oh, go to hell!
Why ride so pell-mell?
VOICE   See how she has flayed me!
The wounds she made me!

---

1. A name for the Devil.   2. In Greek mythology, the nurse of Demeter, noted for her obscenity and bestiality.

WITCHES' CHORUS   The way is wide, the way is long;   140
    Just see the frantic pushing throng!
    The broomstick pokes, the pitchfork thrusts
    The infant chokes, the mother bursts.
WIZARDS' HALF CHORUS   Slow as the snail's is our pace,
    The women are ahead and race;   145
    When it goes to the Devil's place,
    By a thousand steps they win the race.
OTHER HALF   If that is so, we do not mind it:
    With a thousand steps the women find it;
    But though they rush, we do not care: 150
    With one big jump the men get there.
VOICE [*Above.*]   Come on, come on from Rocky Lake!
VOICES [*From below.*]   We'd like to join you and partake.
  We wash, but though we are quite clean,
  We're barren as we've always been.   155
BOTH CHORUSES   The wind is hushed, the star takes flight,
    The dreary moon conceals her light.
    As it whirls by, the wizards' choir
    Scatters a myriad sparks of fire.
VOICE [*From below.*]   Halt, please! Halt, ho!   160
VOICE [*From above.*]   Who calls out of the cleft below?
VOICE [*Below.*]   Take me along! Take me along!
  I've been climbing for three hundred years,
  And yet the peak I cannot find.
  But I would like to join my kind.   165
BOTH CHORUSES   The stick and broom can make you float,
    So can pitchfork and billy goat;
    Who cannot rise today to soar,
    That man is doomed for evermore.
HALF-WITCH [*Below.*]   I move and move and try and try;   170
  How did the others get so high?
  At home I'm restless through and through,
  And now shall miss my chance here, too.
WITCHES' CHORUS   The salve gives courage to the witch,
    For sails we use a rag and switch,   175
    A tub's a ship, if you know how;
    If you would ever fly, fly now!
BOTH CHORUSES   We near the peak, we fly around,
    Now sweep down low over the ground,
    And cover up the heath's vast regions   180
    With witches' swarms and wizards' legions.
    [*They alight.*]
MEPHISTOPHELES   They throng and push, they rush and clatter.
  They hiss and whirl, they pull and chatter.
  It glistens, sparks, and stinks and flares;
  Those are indeed the witches' airs!   185
  Stay close to me, or we'll be solitaires!
  Where are you?
FAUST [*Far away.*]   Here.
MEPHISTOPHELES   So far? Almost a loss!

Then I must show them who is boss.
Back! Squire Nick is coming! Back, sweet rabble! Slump!
Here, Doctor, take a hold! And now in one big jump   190
Let's leave behind this noisy crowd;
Even for me it's much too loud.
On that side is a light with quite a special flare,
Let's penetrate the bushes' shroud;
Come, come! Now let us slink in there!   195

FAUST   Spirit of Contradiction! Go on! I'll follow him.
   I must say, it's exceptionally bright
   To wander to the Blocksberg in the Walpurgis Night,
   To isolate ourselves to follow out some whim.

MEPHISTOPHELES   You see that multicolored flare?   200
   A cheerful club is meeting there:
   In small groups one is not alone.

FAUST   I'd rather be up there: around that stone
   The fires blaze, they have begun;
   The crowds throng to the Evil One   205
   Where many riddles must be solved.

MEPHISTOPHELES   But many new ones are evolved.
   Leave the great world, let it run riot,
   And let us stay where it is quiet.
   It's something that has long been done,   210
   To fashion little worlds within the bigger one.
   I see young witches there, completely nude,
   And old ones who are veiled as shrewdly.
   Just for my sake, don't treat them rudely;
   It's little effort and great fun!   215
   There are some instruments that grind and grit.
   Damnable noise! One must get used to it.
   Come on! Come on! Please do not fret!
   I'll lead the way and take you to this place,
   And you will be quite grateful yet!   220
   What do you say? There isn't enough space?
   Just look! You barely see the other end.
   A hundred fires in a row, my friend!
   They dance, they chat, they cook, they drink, they court;
   Now you just tell me where there's better sport!   225

FAUST   When you will introduce us at this revel,
   Will you appear a sorcerer or devil?

MEPHISTOPHELES   I generally travel, without showing my station,
   But on a gala day one shows one's decoration.
   I have no garter[3] I could show,   230
   But here the cloven foot is honored, as you know.
   Do you perceive that snail? It comes, though it seems stiff;
   For with its eager, groping face
   It knows me with a single whiff.
   Though I'd conceal myself, they'd know me in this place.   235

---

3. I.e., he has no decoration of nobility, such as the Order of the Garter.

Come on! From flame to flame we'll make our tour,
I am the go-between, and you the wooer.
    [*To some who sit around dying embers.*]
Old gentlemen, why tarry outside? Enter!
I'd praise you if I found you in the center,
Engulfed by youthful waves and foam;   240
You are alone enough when you are home.
GENERAL   Who ever thought nations were true,
Though you have served them with your hands and tongue;
For people will, as women do,
Reserve their greatest favors for the young.   245
STATESMAN   Now they are far from what is sage;
The old ones should be kept in awe;
For, truly, when our word was law,
Then was indeed the golden age.
PARVENU   We, too, had surely ample wits,   250
And often did things that we shouldn't;
But now things are reversed and go to bits,
Just when we changed our mind and wished they wouldn't.
AUTHOR   Today, who even looks at any book
That makes some sense and is mature?   255
And our younger generation—look,
You never saw one that was so cocksure.
MEPHISTOPHELES [*Who suddenly appears very old.*]
I think the Judgment Day must soon draw nigh,
For this is the last time I can attend this shrine;
And as my little cask runs dry,   260
The world is certain to decline.
HUCKSTER-WITCH   Please, gentlemen, don't pass like that!
Don't miss this opportunity!
Look at my goods attentively:
There is a lot to marvel at.   265
And my shop has a special charm—
You will not find its peer on earth:
All that I sell has once done harm
To man and world and what has worth.
There is no dagger here which has not gored;   270
No golden cup from which, to end a youthful life,
A fatal poison was not poured;
No gems that did not help to win another's wife;
No sword but broke the peace with sly attack,
By stabbing, for example, a rival in the back.   275
MEPHISTOPHELES   Dear cousin, that's no good in times like these!
What's done is done; what's done is trite.
You better switch to novelties,
For novelties alone excite.
FAUST   I must not lose my head, I swear;   280
For this is what I call a fair.
MEPHISTOPHELES   This eddy whirls to get above,
And you are shoved, though you may think you shove.

FAUST And who is that?

MEPHISTOPHELES   That little madam?
    That's Lilith.[4]

FAUST   Lilith?

MEPHISTOPHELES   The first wife of Adam.   285
    Watch out and shun her captivating tresses:
    She likes to use her never-equaled hair
    To lure a youth into her luscious lair,
    And he won't lightly leave her lewd caresses.

FAUST There two sit, one is young, one old;   290
    They certainly have jumped and trolled!

MEPHISTOPHELES   They did not come here for a rest.
    There is another dance. Come, let us do our best.

FAUST [*Dancing with the young one.*]
    A pretty dream once came to me
    In which I saw an apple tree;   295
    Two pretty apples gleamed on it,
    They lured me, and I climbed a bit.

THE FAIR ONE   You find the little apples nice
    Since first they grew in Paradise.
    And I am happy telling you   300
    That they grow in my garden, too.

MEPHISTOPHELES [*With the old one.*]
    A wanton dream once came to me
    In which I saw a cloven tree.
    It had the most tremendous hole;
    Though it was big, it pleased my soul.   305

THE OLD ONE   I greet you with profound delight,
    My gentle, cloven-footed knight!
    Provide the proper grafting-twig,
    If you don't mind the hole so big.

PROKTOPHANTASMIST[5]   Damnable folk! How dare you make such fuss!   310
    Have we not often proved to you
    That tales of walking ghosts cannot be true?
    And now you dance just like the rest of us!

THE FAIR ONE [*Dancing.*]   What does he want at our fair?

FAUST [*Dancing.*]   Oh, he! You find him everywhere.   315
    What others dance, he must assess;
    No step has really occurred, unless
    His chatter has been duly said.
    And what annoys him most, is when we get ahead.
    If you would turn in circles, in endless repetition,   320
    As he does all the time in his old mill,
    Perhaps he would not take it ill,
    Especially if you would first get his permission.

---

4. According to rabbinical legend, Adam's first wife; the *female* mentioned in Genesis 1.27: "So God created man in his own image, in the image of God created he him; male and female created he them." After Eve was created, Lilith became a ghost who seduced men and inflicted evil on children.   5. A German coinage meaning "Rump-ghostler." The figure caricatures Friedrich Nicolai (1733–1811), who opposed modern movements in German thought and literature and had parodied Goethe's *The Sorrows of Young Werther* (1774).

PROKTOPHANTASMIST   You still are there! Oh no! That's without precedent.
   Please go! Have we not brought enlightenment?   325
   By our rules these devils are not daunted;
   We are so smart, but Tegel[6] is still haunted.
   To sweep illusion out, my energies were spent,
   But things never get clean; that's without precedent.
THE FAIR ONE   Why don't you stop annoying us and quit!   330
PROKTOPHANTASMIST   I tell you spirits to your face,
   The spirit's despotism's a disgrace:
   My spirit can't make rules for it.
      [*The dancing goes on.*]
   Today there's nothing I can do;
   But traveling is always fun,   335
   And I still hope, before my final step is done,
   I'll ban the devils, and the poets, too.
MEPHISTOPHELES   He'll sit down in a puddle and unbend:
   That is how his condition is improved;
   For when the leeches prosper on his fat rear end,[7]   340
   The spirits and his spirit are removed.
      [*To* FAUST, *who has left the dance.*]
   Why did you let that pretty woman go
   Who sang so nicely while you danced?
FAUST   She sang, and suddenly there pranced
   Out of her mouth a little mouse, all red.   345
MEPHISTOPHELES   That is a trifle and no cause for dread!
   Who cares? At least it was not gray.
   Why bother on this glorious lovers' day?
FAUST   Then I saw—
MEPHISTOPHELES   What?
FAUST   Mephisto, do you see
   That pale, beautiful child, alone there on the heather?   350
   She moves slowly but steadily,
   She seems to walk with her feet chained together.
   I must confess that she, forbid,
   Looks much as my good Gretchen did.
MEPHISTOPHELES   That does nobody good; leave it alone!   355
   It is a magic image, a lifeless apparition.
   Encounters are fraught with perdition;
   Its icy stare turns human blood to stone
   In truth, it almost petrifies;
   You know the story of Medusa's[8] eyes.   360
FAUST   Those are the eyes of one that's dead I see,
   No loving hand closed them to rest.
   That is the breast that Gretchen offered me,
   And that is the sweet body I possessed.
MEPHISTOPHELES   That is just sorcery; you're easily deceived!   365
   All think she is their sweetheart and are grieved.

---

6. A town near Berlin, where ghosts had been reported.   7. Nicolai claimed that he had been bothered
by ghosts but had repelled them by applying leeches to his rump.   8. The Gorgon with hair of serpents
whose glance turned people to stone.

FAUST What rapture! Oh, what agony!
  I cannot leave her, cannot flee.
  How strange, a narrow ruby band should deck,
  The sole adornment, her sweet neck,   370
  No wider than a knife's thin blade.
MEPHISTOPHELES I see it, too; it is quite so.
  Her head under her arm she can parade,
  Since Perseus lopped it off, you know.—
  Illusion holds you captive still.   375
  Come, let us climb that little hill,
  The Prater's⁹ not so full of glee;
  And if they're not bewitching me,
  There is a theatre I see.
  What will it be?
SERVIBILIS   They'll resume instantly.   380
  We'll have the seventh play, a brand-new hit;
  We do not think, so many are exacting.
  An amateur has written it,
  And amateurs do all the acting.
  Forgive, good sirs, if now I leave you;   385
  It amateurs me to draw up the curtain.
MEPHISTOPHELES When it's on Blocksberg I perceive you,
  I'm glad; for that's where you belong for certain.

WALPURGIS NIGHT'S DREAM OR THE GOLDEN WEDDING OF OBERON AND TITANIA

*Intermezzo*¹

STAGE MANAGER This time we can keep quite still,
    Mieding's² progeny;
    Misty vale and hoary hill,
    That's our scenery.
HERALD To make a golden wedding day   5
    Takes fifty years to the letter;
    But when their quarrels pass away,
    That gold I like much better.
OBERON If you spirits can be seen,
    Show yourselves tonight;   10
    Fairy king and fairy queen
    Now will reunite.
PUCK³ Puck is coming, turns about,
    And drags his feet to dance;
    Hundreds come behind and shout   15
    And join with him and prance.
ARIEL⁴ Ariel stirs up a song,
    A heavenly pure air;
    Many gargoyles come along,

9. A famous park in Vienna.   1. Brief interlude. Oberon and Titania are king and queen of the fairies.   2. Johann Martin Mieding (d. 1782), a master carpenter and scene builder in the Weimar theater.   3. A mischievous spirit.   4. A helpful sprite.

And many who are fair. 20

OBERON You would get along, dear couple?
Learn from us the art;
If you want to keep love supple,
You only have to part.

TITANIA He is sulky, sullen she, 25
Grab them, upon my soul;
Take her to the Southern Sea,
And him up to the pole.

ORCHESTRA TUTTI [*Fortissimo.*] Snout of Fly, Mosquito Nose,
With family additions, 30
Frog O'Leaves and Crick't O'Grass,
Those are the musicians.

SOLO Now the bagpipe's joining in,
A soap bubble it blows;
Hear the snicker-snacking din 35
Come through his blunted nose.

SPIRIT IN PROCESS OF FORMATION Spider feet, belly of toad,
And little wings, he'll grow 'em;
There is no animal like that,
But it's a little poem. 40

A LITTLE COUPLE Mighty leaps and nimble feet,
Through honey scent up high;
While you bounce enough, my sweet,
Still you cannot fly.

INQUISITIVE TRAVELER Is that not mummery right there? 45
Can that be what I see?
Oberon who is so fair
Amid this company!

ORTHODOX No claws or tail or satyr's fleece!
And yet you cannot cavil: 50
Just like the gods of ancient Greece,
He, too, must be a devil.

NORDIC ARTIST What I do in the local clime,
Are sketches of this tourney;
But I prepare, while it is time, 55
For my Italian journey.

PURIST Bad luck brought me to these regions:
They could not be much louder;
And in the bawdy witches' legions
Two only have used powder. 60

YOUNG WITCH White powder, just like dresses, serves
Old hags who are out of luck;
I want to show my luscious curves,
Ride naked on my buck.

MATRON Our manners, dear, are far too neat 65
To argue and to scold;
I only hope that young and sweet,
Just as you are, you mold.

CONDUCTOR Snout of Fly, Mosquito Nose,

Leave off the naked sweet; 70
Frog O'Leaves and Crick't O'Grass
Get back into the beat!

WEATHERCOCK [*To one side.*]   The most exquisite company!
Each girl should be a bride;
The bachelors, grooms; for one can see 75
How well they are allied.

WEATHERCOCK [*To the other side.*]   The earth should open up and gape
To swallow this young revel,
Or I will make a swift escape
To hell to see the Devil. 80

XENIEN[5]   We appear as insects here,
Each with a little stinger,
That we may fittingly revere
Satan, our sire and singer.

HENNINGS[6]   Look at their thronging legions play, 85
Naïve, with little art;
The next thing they will dare to say
Is that they're good at heart.

MUSAGET[7]   To dwell among the witches' folk
Seems quite a lot of fun; 90
They are the ones I should invoke,
Not Muses, as I've done.

CI-DEVANT GENIUS OF THE AGE[8]   Choose your friends well and you
will zoom,
Join in and do not pass us!
Blocksberg has almost as much room 95
As Germany's Parnassus.[9]

INQUISITIVE TRAVELER   Say, who is that haughty man
Who walks as if he sits?
He sniffs and snuffles as best he can:
"He smells out Jesuits." 100

CRANE   I like to fish where it is clear,
Also in muddy brew;
That's why the pious man is here
To mix with devils, too.

CHILD OF THE WORLD   The pious need no fancy prop, 105
All vehicles seem sound:
Even up here on Blocksberg's top
Conventicles abound.

DANCERS   It seems, another choir succeeds,
I hear the drums resuming. 110
"That dull sound comes out of the reeds,
It is the bitterns' booming."

BALLET MASTER   How each picks up his legs and toddles,

5. Literally, polemical verses written by Goethe and Friedrich von Schiller (1739–1805). The characters here are versions of Goethe himself.   6. August Adolf von Hennings (1746–1826), publisher of a journal called *Genius of the Age* that had attacked Schiller.   7. The title of a collection of Hennings's poetry.   8. I.e., "Former Genius of the Age"; probably alludes to the journal's change of title in 1800 to *Genius of the 19th Century.*   9. A mountain sacred to Apollo and the Muses; hence figuratively the locale of poetic excellence.

And comes by hook or crook!
The stooped one jumps, the plump one waddles: 115
They don't know how they look!

FIDDLER   They hate each other, wretched rabble,
And each would kill the choir;
They're harmonized by bagpipe babble,
As beasts by Orpheus' lyre.[1]   120

DOGMATIST   I am undaunted and resist
Both skeptic and critique;
The Devil simply must exist,
Else *what* would he be? Speak!

IDEALIST   Imagination is in me   125
Today far too despotic;
If I am everything I see,
Then I must be idiotic.

REALIST   The spirits' element is vexing,
I wish it weren't there;   130
I never saw what's so perplexing,
It drives me to despair.

SUPERNATURALIST   I am delighted by this whir,
And glad that they persist;
For from the devils I infer,   135
Good spirits, too, exist.

SKEPTIC   They follow little flames about,
And think they're near the treasure;
Devil alliterates with doubt
So I am here with pleasure.   140

CONDUCTOR   Snout of Fly, Mosquito Nose,
Damnable amateurs!
Frog O'Leaves and Crick't O'Grass
You are musicians, sirs!

ADEPTS   Sansouci,[2] that is the name   145
Of our whole caboodle;
Walking meets with ill acclaim,
So we move on our noodle.

NE'ER-DO-WELLS   We used to be good hangers-on
And sponged good wine and meat;   150
We danced till our shoes were gone,
And now walk on bare feet.

WILL-O'-THE-WISPS   We come out of the swamps where we
Were born without a penny;
But now we join the revelry,   155
As elegant as any.

SHOOTING STAR   I shot down from starry height
With brilliant, fiery charm;
But I lie in the grass tonight:
Who'll proffer me his arm?   160

---

1. In Greek mythology, Orpheus's music was said to have the power to quiet wild animals.   2. Without care or unhappiness (French).

MASSIVE MOB All around, give way! Give way!
    Trample down the grass!
    Spirits come, and sometimes they
    Form a heavy mass.
PUCK Please don't walk like elephants, 165
    And do not be so rough;
    Let no one be as plump as Puck,
    For he is plump enough.
ARIEL If nature gave with lavish grace,
    Or Spirit, wings and will, 170
    Follow in my airy trace
    Up to the roses' hill!
ORCHESTRA [*Pianissimo.*] Floating clouds and wreaths of fog
    Dawn has quickly banished;
    Breeze in leaves, wind in the bog, 175
    And everything has vanished.

DISMAL DAY

[*Field.* FAUST. MEPHISTOPHELES.]

FAUST In misery! Despairing! Long lost wretchedly on the earth, and
now imprisoned! As a felon locked up in a dungeon with horrible
torments, the fair ill-fated creature! It's come to that! To that!—
Treacherous, despicable Spirit—and that you have kept from me!—
Keep standing there, stand! Roll your devilish eyes wrathfully 5
in your face! Stand and defy me with your intolerable presence!
Imprisoned! In irreparable misery! Handed over to evil spirits and
judging, unfeeling mankind! And meanwhile you soothe me with
insipid diversions; hide her growing grief from me, and let her perish
helplessly! 10
MEPHISTOPHELES She's not the first one.
FAUST Dog! Abominable monster!—Change him, oh infinite spirit!
Change back this worm into his dogshape, as he used to amuse
himself in the night when he trotted along before me, rolled in front
of the feet of the harmless wanderer and, when he stumbled, clung 15
to his shoulders. Change him again to his favorite form that he may
crawl on his belly in the sand before me and I may trample on him
with my feet, the caitiff!—Not the first one!—Grief! Grief! past what
a human soul can grasp, that more than one creature has sunk into
the depth of this misery, that the first one did not enough for 20
the guilt of all the others, writhing in the agony of death before the
eyes of the everforgiving one! The misery of this one woman surges
through my heart and marrow, and you grin imperturbed over the
fate of thousands!
MEPHISTOPHELES Now we're once again at our wit's end where your 25
human minds snap. Why do you seek fellowship with us if you can't
go through with it? You would fly, but get dizzy? Did we impose on
you, or you on us?
FAUST Don't bare your greedy teeth at me like that! It sickens me!—
Great, magnificent spirit that deigned to appear to me, that know 30

my heart and soul—why forge me to this monster who gorges himself
on harm, and on corruption—feasts.

MEPHISTOPHELES   Have you finished?

FAUST   Save her! or woe unto you! The most hideous curse upon you
for millenniums!   35

MEPHISTOPHELES   I cannot loosen the avenger's bonds, nor open his
bolts.—Save her!—Who was it that plunged her into ruin? I or you?
[FAUST *looks around furiously.*] Are you reaching for thunder? Well
that it was not given to you wretched mortals! Shattering those who
answer innocently, is the tyrant's way of easing his embarrassment.   40

FAUST   Take me there! She shall be freed!

MEPHISTOPHELES   And the dangers you risk? Know that blood-guilt
from your hand still lies on the town. Over the slain man's site avenging spirits hover, waiting for the returning murderer.

FAUST   That, too, from you? A world's murder and death upon you,   45
monster! Guide me to her, I say, and free her!

MEPHISTOPHELES   I shall guide you; hear what I can do. Do I have all
the power in the heaven and on the earth? I shall make the jailer's
senses foggy, and you may get the keys and lead her out with human
hands. I shall stand guard, magic horses shall be prepared, and   50
I shall carry you away. That I can do.

FAUST   Up and away!

NIGHT, OPEN FIELD

[FAUST *and* MEPHISTOPHELES, *storming along on black horses.*]

FAUST   What are they weaving around the Ravenstone?

MEPHISTOPHELES   I do not know what they do and brew.

FAUST   Floating to, floating fro, bowing and bending.

MEPHISTOPHELES   A witches' guild.

FAUST   They strew and dedicate.   5

MEPHISTOPHELES   Go by! Go by!

DUNGEON

FAUST [*With a bunch of keys and a lamp before a small iron gate.*]
A long unwonted shudder grips,
Mankind's entire grief grips me.
She's here, behind this wall that drips,
And all her crime was a fond fantasy.
You hesitate to go in?   5
You dread to see her again?
On! Your wavering waves on death's decree. [*He seizes the lock.*]
    [*Song from within.*]

GRETCHEN   My mother, the whore,
Who has murdered me—
My father, the rogue,   10
Who has eaten me—
My little sister alone
Picked up every bone,
In a cool place she put them away;

Into a fair bird I now have grown;   15
    Fly away, fly away!
FAUST [*Unlocking.*]   She does not dream how her lover at the door
   Hears the clanking chains and the rustling straw. [*Enters.*]
MARGARET [*Hiding on her pallet.*]   Oh! Oh! They come. Death's bitterness!
FAUST [*Softly.*]   Still! Still! I come to set you free.   20
MARGARET [*Groveling toward his feet.*]   If you are human, pity my distress.
FAUST   You'll awaken the guards. Speak quietly.
      [*He seizes the chains to unlock them.*]
MARGARET [*On her knees.*]   Who, hangman, could give
   You over me this might?
   You come for me in the middle of the night.   25
   Have pity on me, let me live!
   Is it not time when the morning chimes have rung?
      [*She gets up.*]
   I am still so young, so very young.
   And must already die.
   I was beautiful, too, and that was why.   30
   Near was the friend, now he is away.
   Torn lies the wreath, the flowers decay.
   Do not grip me so brutally. What shall I do?
   Spare me. What have I done to you?
   Let me not in vain implore.   35
   After all, I have never seen you before.
FAUST   After such grief, can I live any more?
MARGARET   Now I am entirely in your might.
   Only let me nurse the baby again.
   I fondled it all through the night;   40
   They took it from me to give me pain,
   And now they say I put it away.
   And I shall never again be gay.
   They sing songs about me. The people are wicked.
   An ancient fairy tale ends that way,   45
   Who made them pick it?
FAUST [*Casts himself down.*]   One loving you lies at your feet
   To end your bondage. Listen, sweet!
MARGARET [*Casts herself down beside him.*]
   Ah, let us kneel, send to the saints our prayers!
   See, underneath these stairs,   50
   Underneath the sill
   There seethes hell.
   The Devil
   Makes a thundering noise
   With his angry revel.   55
FAUST [*Loud.*]   Gretchen! Gretchen!
MARGARET [*Attentively.*]   That was my lover's voice!
      [*She jumps up. The chains drop off.*]
   Where is he? I heard him call. I am free.
   No one shall hinder me.
   To his neck I shall fly,   60

On his bosom lie.
He called Gretchen. He stood on the sill.
Amid the wailing and howling of hell,
Through the angry and devilish jeers
The sweet and loving tone touched my ears. 65
FAUST   It is I.
MARGARET   It is you. Oh, do say it again. [*She seizes him.*]
It is he. It is he. Where, then, is all my pain?
Where the fear of the dungeon? the chain?
It is you. Come to save me. 70
I am saved!
Now I see the road again, too,
Where, for the first time, I laid eyes on you—
And the garden and the gate
Where I and Martha stand and wait. 75
FAUST [*Striving away.*]   Come on! Come on!
MARGARET   O Stay!
Because I am so happy where you are staying. [*Caresses him.*]
FAUST   Do not delay.
If you keep on delaying, 80
We shall have to pay dearly therefor.
MARGARET   What? You cannot kiss any more?
My friend, you were not gone longer than this—
And forgot how to kiss?
Why, at your neck, do I feel such dread, 85
When once from your eyes and from what you said
A whole heaven surged down to fill me,
And you would kiss me as if you wanted to kill me?
Kiss me!
Else I'll kiss you. [*She embraces him.*] 90
Oh, grief! Your lips are cold,
Are mute.
Where
Is your loving air?
Who took it from me? [*She turns away from him.*] 95
FAUST   Come, follow me, dearest, and be bold!
I shall caress you a thousandfold;
Only follow me! That is all I plead.
MARGARET [*Turning toward him.*]   And is it you? Is it you indeed?
FAUST   It is I. Come along! 100
MARGARET   You take off the chain,
And take me into your lap again.
How is it that you do not shrink from me?—
Do you know at all, my friend, whom you make free?
FAUST   Come! Come! Soon dawns the light of day. 105
MARGARET   I've put my mother away,
I've drowned my child, don't you see?
Was it not given to you and to me?
You, too—it is you! Could it merely seem?
Give me your hand! It is no dream. 110

Your dear hand!—But alas, it is wet.
Wipe it off! There is yet
Blood on this one.
Oh God! What have you done!
Sheathe your sword; 115
I am begging you.
FAUST   Let the past be forever past—oh Lord,
You will kill me, too.
MARGARET   Oh no, you must outlive us!
I'll describe the graves you should give us. 120
Care for them and sorrow
Tomorrow:
Give the best place to my mother,
And next to her lay my brother;
Me, a little aside, 125
Only don't make the space too wide!
And the little one at my right breast.
Nobody else will lie by my side.—
Oh, to lie with you and to hide
In your arms, what happiness! 130
Now it is more than I can do;
I feel, I must force myself on you,
And you, it seems, push back my caress;
And yet it is you, and look so pure, so devout.
FAUST   If you feel, it is I, come out! 135
MARGARET   Out where?
FAUST   Into the open.
MARGARET   If the grave is there,
If death awaits us, then come!
From here to the bed of eternal rest, 140
And not a step beyond—no!
You are leaving now? Oh, Heinrich, that I could go!
FAUST   You can! If only you would! Open stands the door.
MARGARET   I may not go; for me there is no hope any more.
What good to flee? They lie in wait for me. 145
To have to go begging is misery,
And to have a bad conscience, too.
It is misery to stray far and forsaken,
And, anyhow, I would be taken.
FAUST   I shall stay with you. 150
MARGARET   Quick! Quick! I pray.
Save your poor child.
On! Follow the way
Along the brook,
Over the bridge, 155
Into the wood,
To the left where the planks stick
Out of the pond.
Seize it—oh, quick!
It wants to rise, 160

It is still struggling.
Save! Save!
FAUST   Can you not see,
It takes *one* step, and you are free.
MARGARET   If only we were past the hill!   165
My mother sits there on a stone,
My scalp is creeping with dread!
My mother sits there on a stone
And wags and wags her head;
She becks not, she nods not, her head is heavy and sore,   170
She has slept so long, she awakes no more.
She slept that we might embrace.
Those were the days of grace.
FAUST   In vain is my pleading, in vain what I say;
What can I do but bear you away?   175
MARGARET   Leave me! No, I shall suffer no force!
Do not grip me so murderously!
After all, I did everything else you asked.
FAUST   The day dawns. Dearest! Dearest!
MARGARET   Day. Yes, day is coming. The last day breaks;   180
It was to be my wedding day.
Tell no one that you have already been with Gretchen.
My veil! Oh pain!
It just happened that way.
We shall meet again,   185
But not dance that day.
The crowd is pushing, no word is spoken.
The alleys below
And the streets overflow.
The bell is tolling, the wand is broken.   190
How they tie and grab me, now one delivers
Me to the block and gives the sign,
And for every neck quivers
The blade that quivers for mine.
Mute lies the world as a grave.   195
FAUST   That I had never been born!
MEPHISTOPHELES [*Appears outside.*]   Up! Or you are lost.
Prating and waiting and pointless wavering.
My horses are quavering,
Over the sky creeps the dawn.   200
MARGARET   What did the darkness spawn?
He! He! Send him away!
What does he want in this holy place?
He wants me!
FAUST   You shall live.
MARGARET   Judgment of God! I give   205
Myself to you.
MEPHISTOPHELES [*To* FAUST.]   Come! Come! I shall abandon you with
her.
MARGARET   Thine I am, father. Save me!

You angels, hosts of heaven, stir,
Encamp about me, be my guard.   210
Heinrich! I quail at thee.
MEPHISTOPHELES   She is judged.
VOICE [*From above.*]   Is saved.
MEPHISTOPHELES [*To* FAUST.]   Hither to me! [*Disappears with*
FAUST.]
VOICE [*From within, fading away.*]   Heinrich! Heinrich!

WILLIAM BLAKE
1757–1827

Few works so ostentatiously "simple" as William Blake's *Songs of Innocence and of
Experience* (1794) can ever have aroused such critical perplexity. Employing uncomplicated vocabulary and, often, variants of traditional ballad structure; describing the
experience usually of naive subjects; supplying no obvious intellectual substance,
these short lyrics have long fascinated and baffled their readers.

With no formal education, Blake, son of a London hosier, was at the age of fourteen
apprenticed to the engraver James Basire. He developed both as painter and as
engraver, partly influenced by the painter Henry Fuseli and the sculptor John Flax-
man, both his friends, but remaining always highly individual in style and technique.
An acknowledged mystic, he saw visions from the age of four: trees filled with angels,
God looking at him through the window. His highly personal view of a world penetrated by the divine helped to form both his visual and his verbal art. In 1800, Blake
moved from London to Felpham, where the poet William Hayley was his patron. He
returned to London in 1803 and remained there for the rest of his life, married but
childless, engaged in writing, printing, and engraving.

Blake felt a close relation between the visual and the verbal; he illustrated the works
of many poets, notably Milton and Dante. His first book, *Poetical Sketches* (1783),
was conventionally published, but he produced all of his subsequent books himself,
combining pictorial engravings with lettering, striking off only a few copies of each
work by hand. Gradually, in increasingly long poems, he developed an elaborate private mythology, with important figures appearing in one work after another. His major
mythic poems include *The Marriage of Heaven and Hell* (1793), *America* (1793), *The
Book of Los* (1795), *Milton* (1804), *Jerusalem* (1804), and *The Four Zoas* (which he
never completed).

As his short poem *Mock On, Mock On, Voltaire, Rousseau* testifies, Blake was
bitterly opposed to what he thought the destructive and repressive rationalism of the
eighteenth century. Voltaire and Rousseau might have been surprised to find themselves thus associated; they belong together, in Blake's view, because both implicitly
oppose not only orthodox Christianity but the more private variety of revealed religion
so vital to Blake himself. Although, like his contemporaries, Blake idealizes imagination and emotion and believes in the sacredness of the individual, he entirely avoids
the "egotistical sublime," neither speaking directly of himself in his poetry, as Wordsworth did, nor, like Goethe, creating self-absorbed characters. In his short lyrics he
adopts many different voices; the difficulties of interpretation stem partly from this
fact. He insistently deals with metaphysical questions about our place in the universe
and with social questions about the nature of human responsibility.

In *Songs of Innocence,* the speaker is often a child: asking questions of a lamb, meditating on his own blackness, describing the experience of a chimney sweep. Ostensibly these children in their innocence feel no anger or bitterness at the realities of the world in which they find themselves. The "little black boy" ensures himself a future when the "little English boy" will resemble him and love him; the child addressing the lamb evokes a realm of pure delight; the chimney sweep comforts himself with conventional morality and with a companion's dream. When an adult observer watches children, as in *Holy Thursday,* he too sees a benign arrangement, in which children are "flowers of London town," supervised by "agèd men, wise guardians of the poor." In the *Introduction* to the volume, the adult speaker receives empowering advice from a child, who instructs him to write. Everything is for the best in this best of all possible worlds.

But not quite. Disturbing undertones reverberate through even the most "innocent" of these songs. Innocence is, after all, by definition a state automatically lost through experience and never possible to regain. If the children evoked by the text still possess their innocence, the adult reader does not. *The Little Black Boy* suggests the kind of ambiguity evoked by the conjunction between innocent speaker and experienced reader. The poem opens with a situation that the speaker does not entirely understand—but one likely to be painfully familiar to the reader. "White as an angel is the English child: / But I am black as if bereaved of light": the child's similes indicate how completely he has incorporated the value judgments of his society, in which white suggests everything good and black means deficiency and deprivation. In this context, the mother's teaching, a comforting myth, becomes comprehensible as a way of dealing with her child's bewilderment and anxiety about his difference. At the end of the poem, the boy extends his mother's story into a prophetic vision in which black means protective power ("I'll shade him from the heat till he can bear / To lean in joy upon our father's knee"), and difference disappears into likeness, hostility into love. The vision evokes an ideal situation located in an imagined afterlife; it has only an antithetical connection to present actuality. Its emphatic divergence from real social conditions creates the subterranean disturbance characteristic of Blake's lyrics, the disturbance that calls attention to the serious social criticism implicit even in lyrics that may appear sweet to the point of blandness.

For all Blake's dislike of the earlier eighteenth century, he shares with his forebears one important assumption: his poetry, too, instructs as well as pleases. The innocent chimney sweep evokes parental death and betrayal, horrifying working conditions (soot and nakedness, darkness and shaved heads), and compensatory dreams. He never complains, but when he ends with the tag "So if all do their duty, they need not fear harm," it generates moral shock. The discrepancy between the child's purity and his brutal exploitation indicts the society that allows such things. Innocence may be its own protection, these poems suggest, but that fact does not obviate social guilt.

If the *Songs of Innocence,* for all their atmosphere of brightness, cheer, and peace, convey outrage at the ways that social institutions harm those they should protect, the *Songs of Experience* more directly evoke a world worn, constricted, burdened with misery created by human beings. Now a new version of *The Chimney Sweeper* openly states what the earlier poem suggested:

> "And because I am happy, & dance & sing,
> They think they have done me no injury,
> And are gone to praise God & his Priest & King,
> Who make up a heaven of our misery."

The child understands the protective self-blinding of adults.

London in its sixteen lines sums up many of the collection's implications. Like most of the *Songs of Experience, London* presents an adult speaker, a wanderer through the city, who finds wherever he goes, in every face, "Marks of weakness, marks of woe." The city is the repository of suffering: men and infants and chimney sweepers cry; soldiers sigh; harlots curse. All are victims of corrupt institutions: blackening

Church, bloody palace. Marriage and death interpenetrate; the curses of illness and corruption pass through the generations. The speaker reports only what he sees and hears, without commentary. He evokes a society in dreadful decay, and he conveys his despairing rage at a situation he cannot remedy.

Blake's lyrics, in their mixture of the visionary and the observational, strike notes far different from those of satire. Like the visionary observations of Swift and Voltaire, though, they insist on the connection between literature and life. Literature has transformative capacity, but it works with the raw material of actual experience. And its visions have the power to insist on the necessity of change.

Blake has provided material for an enormous outpouring of critical work. Particularly useful for the student are the collections of critical essays, N. Frye, ed., *Blake* (1966), and H. Adams, ed., *Critical Essays on William Blake* (1991). Valuable longer studies include M. Schorer, *William Blake: The Politics of Vision* (1946); H. Adams, *William Blake: A Reading of the Shorter Poems* (1963); E. D. Hirsch, *Innocence and Experience* (1969); D. G. Gilham, *William Blake* (1973); and S. Gardner, *Blake's Innocence and Experience Retraced* (1986). H. Bloom, ed., *William Blake* (1985), provides a useful compendium of criticism; N. Hilton, ed., *Essential Articles for the Study of William Blake* (1986), is more wide ranging. A valuable general study is E. Larrissy, *William Blake* (1985).

Songs of Innocence and of Experience

SHEWING THE TWO CONTRARY STATES OF THE HUMAN SOUL

Songs of Innocence[1]

Introduction

Piping down the valleys wild
Piping songs of pleasant glee
On a cloud I saw a child,
And he laughing said to me,

"Pipe a song about a Lamb";   5
So I piped with merry chear;
"Piper pipe that song again"—
So I piped, he wept to hear.

"Drop thy pipe thy happy pipe
Sing thy songs of happy chear";   10
So I sung the same again
While he wept with joy to hear.

"Piper sit thee down and write
In a book that all may read"—
So he vanished from my sight.   15
And I plucked a hollow reed,

And I made a rural pen,
And I stained the water clear,

---

1. The text for all of Blake's works is edited by David V. Erdman and Harold Bloom. *Songs of Innocence* (1789) was later combined with *Songs of Experience* (1794), and the poems were etched and accompanied by Blake's illustrations, the process accomplished by copper engravings stamped on paper, then colored by hand.

And I wrote my happy songs
Every child may joy to hear.   20

The Lamb

Little Lamb, who made thee?
  Dost thou know who made thee?
Gave thee life & bid thee feed,
By the stream & o'er the mead;
Gave thee clothing of delight,   5
Softest clothing wooly bright;
Gave thee such a tender voice,
Making all the vales rejoice!
  Little Lamb who made thee?
  Dost thou know who made thee?   10

Little Lamb I'll tell thee,
  Little Lamb I'll tell thee!
He is callèd by thy name,
For he calls himself a Lamb:
He is meek & he is mild,   15
He became a little child:
I a child & thou a lamb,
We are callèd by his name.[1]
  Little Lamb God bless thee.
  Little Lamb God bless thee.   20

The Little Black Boy

My mother bore me in the southern wild,
And I am black, but O! my soul is white;
White as an angel is the English child:
But I am black as if bereaved of light.

My mother taught me underneath a tree,   5
And sitting down before the heat of day,
She took me on her lap and kissèd me,
And pointing to the east, began to say:

"Look on the rising sun: there God does live,
And gives his light, and gives his heat away;   10
And flowers and trees and beasts and men receive
Comfort in morning, joy in the noon day.

"And we are put on earth a little space,
That we may learn to bear the beams of love,
And these black bodies and this sun-burnt face   15
Is but a cloud, and like a shady grove.

---

1. Christians use the name of Christ to designate themselves.

"For when our souls have learned the heat to bear,
The cloud will vanish; we shall hear his voice,
Saying: 'Come out from the grove, my love & care,
And round my golden tent like lambs rejoice.' "   20

Thus did my mother say, and kissèd me;
And thus I say to little English boy:
When I from black and he from white cloud free,
And round the tent of God like lambs we joy,

I'll shade him from the heat till he can bear   25
To lean in joy upon our father's knee;
And then I'll stand and stroke his silver hair,
And be like him, and he will then love me.

Holy Thursday[1]

'Twas on a Holy Thursday, their innocent faces clean,
The children walking two & two, in red & blue & green,[2]
Grey headed beadles[3] walked before with wands as white as snow,
Till into the high dome of Paul's they like Thames' waters flow.

O what a multitude they seemed, these flowers of London town!   5
Seated in companies they sit with radiance all their own.
The hum of multitudes was there, but multitudes of lambs,
Thousands of little boys & girls raising their innocent hands.

Now like a mighty wind they raise to heaven the voice of song,
Or like harmonious thunderings the seats of heaven among.   10
Beneath them sit the agèd men, wise guardians[4] of the poor;
Then cherish pity, lest you drive an angel from your door.[5]

The Chimney Sweeper

When my mother died I was very young,
And my father sold me[1] while yet my tongue
Could scarcely cry " 'weep![2] 'weep! 'weep! 'weep!"
So your chimneys I sweep & in soot I sleep.

There's little Tom Dacre, who cried when his head   5
That curled like a lamb's back, was shaved, so I said,

---

1. Ascension Day, forty days after Easter, when children from charity schools were marched to St. Paul's Cathedral.   2. Each school had its own distinctive uniform.   3. Ushers and minor functionaries, whose job was to maintain order.   4. The governors of the charity schools.   5. See Hebrews 13.2: "Be not forgetful to entertain strangers: for thereby some have entertained angels unawares."   1. It was common practice in Blake's day for fathers to sell, or indenture, their children to become chimney sweeps. The average age at which such children began working was six or seven; they were generally employed for seven years, until they were too big to ascend the chimneys.   2. The child's lisping effort to say "sweep," as he walks the streets looking for work.

And what shoulder, & what art,
Could twist the sinews of thy heart?   10
And when thy heart began to beat,
What dread hand? & what dread feet?

What the hammer? what the chain?
In what furnace was thy brain?
What the anvil? what dread grasp   15
Dare its deadly terrors clasp?

When the stars threw down their spears,
And watered heaven with their tears,
Did he smile his work to see?
Did he who made the Lamb make thee?   20

Tyger! Tyger! burning bright
In the forests of the night,
What immortal hand or eye
Dare frame thy fearful symmetry?

The Sick Rose

O Rose, thou art sick.
The invisible worm
That flies in the night
In the howling storm

Has found out thy bed   5
Of crimson joy,
And his dark secret love
Does thy life destroy.

London

I wander thro' each chartered¹ street,
Near where the chartered Thames does flow,
And mark in every face I meet
Marks of weakness, marks of woe.

In every cry of every Man,   5
In every Infant's cry of fear,
In every voice, in every ban,
The mind-forged manacles I hear:

How the Chimney-sweeper's cry
Every blackening Church appalls;²   10

1. Hired (literally). Blake implies that the streets and the river are controlled by commercial interests.   2. Makes white (literally), punning also on *appall* (to dismay) and *pall* (the cloth covering a corpse or bier).

And the hapless Soldier's sigh
Runs in blood down Palace walls.

But most thro' midnight streets I hear
How the youthful Harlot's curse
Blasts the new-born Infant's tear,[3]   15
And blights with plagues the Marriage hearse.

The Chimney Sweeper

A little black thing among the snow
Crying " 'weep, 'weep," in notes of woe!
"Where are thy father & mother? say?"
"They are both gone up to the church to pray.

"Because I was happy upon the heath,   5
And smiled among the winter's snow;
They clothèd me in the clothes of death,
And taught me to sing the notes of woe.

"And because I am happy, & dance & sing,
They think they have done me no injury,   10
And are gone to praise God & his Priest & King,
Who make up a heaven of our misery."

Mock On, Mock On, Voltaire, Rousseau

Mock on, Mock on, Voltaire, Rousseau;
Mock on, Mock on, 'tis all in vain.
You throw the sand against the wind,
And the wind blows it back again.

And every sand becomes a Gem   5
Reflected in the beams divine;
Blown back, they blind the mocking Eye,
But still in Israel's paths they shine.

The Atoms of Democritus[1]
And Newton's Particles of light[2]   10
Are sands upon the Red sea shore,
Where Israel's tents do shine so bright.

And Did Those Feet

And did those feet[1] in ancient time
Walk upon England's mountains green?

3. The harlot infects the parents with venereal disease, and thus the infant is inflicted with neonatal blindness.   1. Greek philosopher (460?–362? B.C.), who advanced a theory that all things are merely patterns of atoms.   2. Sir Isaac Newton's (1642–1727) corpuscular theory of light. For Blake, both men were condemned as materialists.   1. A reference to an ancient legend that Jesus came to England with Joseph of Arimathea.

And was the holy Lamb of God
On England's pleasant pastures seen?

And did the Countenance Divine   5
Shine forth upon our clouded hills?
And was Jerusalem builded here,
Among those dark Satanic Mills?[2]

Bring me my Bow of burning gold:
Bring me my Arrows of desire: 10
Bring me my Spear: O clouds unfold!
Bring me my Chariot of fire!

I will not cease from Mental Fight,
Nor shall my Sword sleep in my hand,
Till we have built Jerusalem   15
In England's green & pleasant Land.

2. Possibly industrial England, but *mills* also meant for Blake eighteenth-century arid, mechanistic philosophy.

WILLIAM WORDSWORTH
1770–1850

William Wordsworth both proclaimed and embodied the *newness* of the Romantic movement. In his preface to the second edition of *Lyrical Ballads* (1800), a collection of poems by him and his friend Samuel Taylor Coleridge, he announced the advent of a poetic revolution. Like other revolutionaries, Wordsworth and Coleridge created their identities by rebelling against and travestying their predecessors. Now no longer would poets write in "dead" forms; now they had discovered a "new" direction, "new" subject matter; now poetry could at last serve as an important form of human communication. Reading Wordsworth's poems with the excitement of that revolution long past, we can still feel the power of his desire to communicate. The human heart is his subject; he writes, in particular, of growth and of memory and of the perplexities inherent in the human condition.

Born at Cockermouth, Cumberland, to the family of an attorney, Wordsworth attended St. John's College, Cambridge, from 1787 to 1791. The next year, early in the French Revolution, he spent in France, where he met Annette Vallon and had a daughter by her. In 1795, Wordsworth met Coleridge; two years later, Wordsworth and his sister, Dorothy, moved to Alfoxden, near Coleridge's home in Nether Stowey, in the county of Somerset. There the two men conceived the idea of collaboration; in 1798, the first edition of their *Lyrical Ballads* appeared, anonymously. The next year, Wordsworth and his sister settled in the Lake District of northwest England. In 1802, the poet married Mary Hutchinson, with whom he had five children. He received the sinecure of stamp distributor in 1813 and in 1843 succeeded Robert Southey as England's poet laureate, having long since abandoned the political radicalism of his youth.

Wordsworth wrote little prose, except for the famous preface of 1800 and another preface in 1815; his accomplishment was almost entirely poetic. His early work employed conventional eighteenth-century techniques, but *Lyrical Ballads* marked a new direction: an effort to employ simple language and to reveal the high significance of simple themes, the transcendent importance of the everyday. Between 1798 and 1805 he composed his nineteenth-century version of an epic, *The Prelude*, an account of the development of a poet's mind—his own. His subsequent work included odes, sonnets, and many poems written to mark specific occasions.

It would be difficult to overestimate the extent of Wordsworth's historical and poetic importance. In *The Prelude*, not published until 1850, he not only made powerful poetry out of his own experience but also specified a way of valuing experience:

> There are in our existence spots of time,
> That with distinct pre-eminence retain
> A renovating virtue, whence, depressed
> By false opinion and contentious thought,
> Or aught of heavier or more deadly weight,
> In trivial occupations, and the round
> Of ordinary intercourse, our minds
> Are nourished and invisibly repaired;
> A virtue, by which pleasure is enhanced,
> That penetrates, enables us to mount
> When high, more high, and lifts us up when fallen.

To take seriously the moment, this passage suggests, enables us to resist the dulling force of everyday life ("trivial occupations") and provides the means of personal salvation.

Wordsworth often uses religious language (a religious reference is hinted in the idea of being lifted up when fallen) to insist on the importance of his doctrine. He inaugurated an attempt—lasting far into the century—to establish and sustain a secular religion to substitute for Christian faith. The attempt was, even for Wordsworth, only intermittently successful. *The Prelude* records experiences of persuasive visionary intensity, as when the poet speaks of seeing a shepherd in the distance:

> Or him have I descried in distant sky,
> A solitary object and sublime,
> Above all height! like an aerial cross
> Stationed alone upon a spiry rock
> Of the Chartreuse, for worship.

But such "spots of time" exist in isolation; it is difficult to maintain a saving faith on their basis.

The two long poems printed here treat the problem of discovering and sustaining faith. *Lines Composed a Few Miles Above Tintern Abbey*, first published in *Lyrical Ballads*, and *Ode on Intimations of Immortality*, published in 1807 but written between 1802 and 1806, share a preoccupation with loss and with the saving power of memory. Both speak of personal experience, although the ode, a more formal poem, also generalizes to a hypothetical "we." Both insist that nature—the external world experienced through the senses and the containing pattern assumed beyond that world—offers the possibility of wisdom to combat the pain inherent in human growth.

But it would be a mistake to assume that the poems exist to promulgate a doctrine of natural salvation, although some readers have considered their "pantheism" (the belief that God pervades every part of His created universe) their most important aspect. Both poems evoke an intellectual and emotional process, not a conclusion; they sketch dramas of human development.

In *Tintern Abbey*, the speaker conveys his relief at returning to a sylvan scene that has been important to him in memory. His recollections of this natural beauty, he says, have helped sustain him in the confusion and weariness of city life; he thinks they may also have encouraged him toward goodness and serenity. But this second suggestion, that memories of nature have a moral effect, is only hypothetical, qualified in the text by such words and phrases as "I trust" and "perhaps." Indeed, the poem's next section opens with explicit statement that this may "Be but a vain belief." True or false, though, the belief comforts the speaker, who then recalls his more direct relation with nature in the past, when "The sounding cataract / Haunted me like a passion." He hopes, but cannot quite be sure, that his present awareness of "the still, sad music of humanity" and of the great "presence" that infuses nature compensates for what he has sacrificed in losing the immediacy of youthful experience.

The last section of *Tintern Abbey* emphasizes still more that the speaker is struggling with depression over his sense of loss; he observes that the presence of his "dearest Friend," his sister, would protect his "genial spirits" from decay even without his faith in what he has learned. That sister now becomes the focus for his thoughts about nature; he imagines her growth as like his own, but perfected, and her power of memory as able to contain not only the beauties of the landscape but his presence as part of that landscape. The poem thus resolves itself with emphasis on a human relationship, between the man and his sister, as well as on the importance of nature. Its emotional power derives partly from its evocation of the *need* to believe in nature as a form of salvation and of the process of development through which that need manifests itself.

At about the same time that he wrote the *Ode on Intimations of Immortality,* Wordsworth composed his sonnet *The World Is Too Much with Us*:

> . . . we lay waste our powers
> Little we see in Nature that is ours;
> . . . we are out of tune.

Despite the rhapsodic tone that dominates the ode, it too reveals itself as a hard-won act of faith, an effort to combat the view of the present world conveyed in the sonnet.

The ode opens with insistence on loss: "The things which I have seen I now can see no more." The speaker feels grief; he tries to deny it, because it seems at odds with the harmony and joy of the natural world. Yet the effort fails: even natural beauty speaks to him of what he no longer possesses. Stanzas V through VIII emphasize the association of infancy with natural communion and the inevitable deprivation attending growth. In stanza IX, the speaker attempts to value what still remains to him: it's all he has, he's grateful for it. In the concluding stanzas, however, he arrives at a new revelation: now nature acquires value not as a form of unmixed ecstasy, but in connection with the experience of human suffering:

> Though nothing can bring back the hour
> Of splendour in the grass, of glory in the flower;
> We will grieve not, rather find
> Strength in what remains behind; . . .
> In the soothing thoughts that spring
> Out of human suffering . . .

It is "the human heart by which we live" that finally enables the poet to experience the wonder of a flower, now become the source of "Thoughts that do often lie too deep for tears."

The view that the processes of maturing involve giving up a kind of wisdom accessible only to children belongs particularly to the Romantic period, but most people at least occasionally feel that in growing up they have left behind something they would rather keep. Wordsworth's poetic expression of the effort to come to terms with such feelings may remind his readers of barely noticed aspects of their own experience.

G. M. Harper, *Wordsworth* (1916–1929), remains the standard biography. A more recent biographical study is S. C. Gill, *William Wordsworth* (1989). Other important works (critical in emphasis) include R. D. Havens, *The Mind of a Poet* (1950); G. Hartman, *Wordsworth's Poetry* (1964); Thomas McFarland, *William Wordsworth:*

Intensity and Achievement (1992); and J. H. Alexander, *Reading Wordsworth* (1987). A useful collection of critical essays is G. Gilpin, ed., *Critical Essays on William Wordsworth* (1990). Valuable contextualization is provided by P. Fletcher and J. Murphy, eds., *Wordworth in Context* (1992).

PRONOUNCING GLOSSARY

The following list uses common English syllables and stress accents to provide rough equivalents of selected words whose pronunciation may be unfamiliar to the general reader.

Proteus: *proh'-tee-us*   Triton: *try'-tun*

Lines Composed a Few Miles Above Tintern Abbey

On Revisiting the Banks of the Wye During a Tour, July 13, 1798

Five years have past; five summers, with the length
Of five long winters! and again I hear
These waters, rolling from their mountain-springs
With a soft inland murmur.—Once again
Do I behold these steep and lofty cliffs,   5
That on a wild secluded scene impress
Thoughts of more deep seclusion; and connect
The landscape with the quiet of the sky.
The day is come when I again repose
Here, under this dark sycamore, and view   10
These plots of cottage-ground, these orchard-tufts,
Which at this season, with their unripe fruits,
Are clad in one green hue, and lose themselves
'Mid groves and copses. Once again I see
These hedge-rows, hardly hedge-rows, little lines   15
Of sportive wood run wild: these pastoral farms,
Green to the very door; and wreaths of smoke
Sent up, in silence, from among the trees!
With some uncertain notice, as might seem
Of vagrant dwellers in the houseless woods,   20
Or of some Hermit's cave, where by his fire
The Hermit sits alone.

               These beauteous forms,
Through a long absence, have not been to me
As is a landscape to a blind man's eye:
But oft, in lonely rooms, and 'mid the din   25
Of towns and cities, I have owed to them,
In hours of weariness, sensations sweet,
Felt in the blood, and felt along the heart;
And passing even into my purer mind,
With tranquil restoration:—feelings too   30
Of unremembered pleasure: such, perhaps,
As have no slight or trivial influence
On that best portion of a good man's life,
His little, nameless, unremembered, acts
Of kindness and of love. Nor less, I trust,   35

To them I may have owed another gift,
Of aspect more sublime; that blessèd mood,
In which the burthen of the mystery,
In which the heavy and the weary weight
Of all this unintelligible world,   40
Is lightened:—that serene and blessèd mood,
In which the affections gently lead us on,—
Until, the breath of this corporeal frame
And even the motion of our human blood
Almost suspended, we are laid asleep   45
In body, and become a living soul:
While with an eye made quiet by the power
Of harmony, and the deep power of joy,
We see into the life of things.

                            If this
Be but a vain belief, yet, oh! how oft—   50
In darkness and amid the many shapes
Of joyless daylight; when the fretful stir
Unprofitable, and the fever of the world,
Have hung upon the beatings of my heart—
How oft, in spirit, have I turned to thee,   55
O sylvan Wye! thou wanderer thro' the woods,
How often has my spirit turned to thee!

    And now, with gleams of half-extinguished thought,
With many recognitions dim and faint,
And somewhat of a sad perplexity,   60
The picture of the mind revives again:
While here I stand, not only with the sense
Of present pleasure, but with pleasing thoughts
That in this moment there is life and food
For future years. And so I dare to hope,   65
Though changed, no doubt, from what I was when first
I came among these hills; when like a roe
I bounded o'er the mountains, by the sides
Of the deep rivers, and the lonely streams,
Wherever nature led: more like a man   70
Flying from something that he dreads, than one
Who sought the thing he loved. For nature then
(The coarser pleasures of my boyish days,
And their glad animal movements all gone by)
To me was all in all.—I cannot paint   75
What then I was. The sounding cataract
Haunted me like a passion: the tall rock,
The mountain, and the deep and gloomy wood,
Their colours and their forms, were then to me
An appetite; a feeling and a love,   80
That had no need of a remoter charm,
By thought supplied, nor any interest
Unborrowed from the eye.—That time is past,
And all its aching joys are now no more,
And all its dizzy raptures. Not for this   85

Faint I, nor mourn nor murmur; other gifts
Have followed; for such loss, I would believe,
Abundant recompense. For I have learned
To look on nature, not as in the hour
Of thoughtless youth; but hearing oftentimes   90
The still, sad music of humanity,
Nor harsh nor grating, though of ample power
To chasten and subdue. And I have felt
A presence that disturbs me with the joy
Of elevated thoughts; a sense sublime   95
Of something far more deeply interfused,
Whose dwelling is the light of setting suns,
And the round ocean and the living air,
And the blue sky, and in the mind of man:
A motion and a spirit, that impels   100
All thinking things, all objects of all thought,
And rolls through all things. Therefore am I still
A lover of the meadows and the woods,
And mountains; and of all that we behold
From this green earth; of all the mighty world   105
Of eye, and ear,—both what they half create,
And what perceive; well pleased to recognise
In nature and the language of the sense,
The anchor of my purest thoughts, the nurse,
The guide, the guardian of my heart, and soul   110
Of all my moral being.

                  Nor perchance,
If I were not thus taught, should I the more
Suffer my genial[1] spirits to decay:
For thou art with me here upon the banks
Of this fair river; thou my dearest Friend,   115
My dear, dear Friend; and in thy voice I catch
The language of my former heart, and read
My former pleasures in the shooting lights
Of thy wild eyes. Oh! yet a little while
May I behold in thee what I was once,   120
My dear, dear Sister! and this prayer I make,
Knowing that Nature never did betray
The heart that loved her; 'tis her privilege,
Through all the years of this our life, to lead
From joy to joy: for she can so inform   125
The mind that is within us, so impress
With quietness and beauty, and so feed
With lofty thoughts, that neither evil tongues,
Rash judgments, nor the sneers of selfish men,
Nor greetings where no kindness is, nor all   130
The dreary intercourse of daily life,
Shall e'er prevail against us, or disturb
Our cheerful faith, that all which we behold
Is full of blessings. Therefore let the moon

---

1. Generative, creative.

Shine on thee in thy solitary walk; 135
And let the misty mountain-winds be free
To blow against thee: and, in after years,
When these wild ecstasies shall be matured
Into a sober pleasure; when thy mind
Shall be a mansion for all lovely forms, 140
Thy memory be as a dwelling-place
For all sweet sounds and harmonies; oh! then,
If solitude, or fear, or pain, or grief
Should be thy portion, with what healing thoughts
Of tender joy wilt thou remember me, 145
And these my exhortations! Nor, perchance—
If I should be where I no more can hear
Thy voice, nor catch from thy wild eyes these gleams
Of past existence—wilt thou then forget
That on the banks of this delightful stream 150
We stood together; and that I, so long
A worshipper of Nature, hither came
Unwearied in that service; rather say
With warmer love—oh! with far deeper zeal
Of holier love. Nor wilt thou then forget 155
That after many wanderings, many years
Of absence, these steep woods and lofty cliffs,
And this green pastoral landscape, were to me
More dear, both for themselves and for thy sake!

Ode on Intimations of Immortality

From Recollections of Early Childhood

> The Child is father of the Man;
> And I could wish my days to be
> Bound each to each by natural piety.

I

There was a time when meadow, grove, and stream,
The earth, and every common sight,
    To me did seem
    Apparelled in celestial light,
The glory and the freshness of a dream. 5
It is not now as it hath been of yore;—
    Turn wheresoe'er I may,
      By night or day,
The things which I have seen I now can see no more.

II

    The Rainbow comes and goes, 10
    And lovely is the Rose;
    The Moon doth with delight
Look round her when the heavens are bare,

Waters on a starry night
Are beautiful and fair;   15
The sunshine is a glorious birth;
But yet I know, where'er I go,
That there hath past away a glory from the earth.

III

Now, while the birds thus sing a joyous song,
   And while the young lambs bound   20
     As to the tabor's sound,
To me alone there came a thought of grief:
A timely utterance gave that thought relief,
   And I again am strong:
The cataracts blow their trumpets from the steep;   25
No more shall grief of mine the season wrong;
I hear the Echoes through the mountains throng,
The Winds come to me from the fields of sleep,
   And all the earth is gay;
     Land and sea   30
  Give themselves up to jollity,
   And with the heart of May
Doth every Beast keep holiday;—
   Thou Child of Joy,
Shout round me, let me hear thy shouts, thou happy   35
  Shepherd-boy!

IV

Ye blessèd Creatures, I have heard the call
   Ye to each other make; I see
The heavens laugh with you in your jubilee;
   My heart is at your festival,   40
    My head hath its coronal,
The fulness of your bliss, I feel—I feel it all.
   Oh evil day! if I were sullen
   While Earth herself is adorning,
    This sweet May-morning,   45
   And the Children are culling
    On every side,
   In a thousand valleys far and wide,
   Fresh flowers; while the sun shines warm,
And the Babe leaps up on his Mother's arm:—   50
   I hear, I hear, with joy I hear!
   —But there's a Tree, of many, one,
A single Field which I have looked upon,
Both of them speak of something that is gone:
   The Pansy at my feet   55
   Doth the same tale repeat:
Whither is fled the visionary gleam?
Where is it now, the glory and the dream?

V

Our birth is but a sleep and a forgetting:
The Soul that rises with us, our life's Star,   60
    Hath had elsewhere its setting,
      And cometh from afar:
    Not in entire forgetfulness,
    And not in utter nakedness,
But trailing clouds of glory do we come   65
    From God, who is our home:
Heaven lies about us in our infancy!
Shades of the prison-house begin to close
    Upon the growing Boy,
But He beholds the light, and whence it flows,   70
    He sees it in his joy;
The Youth, who daily farther from the east
    Must travel, still is Nature's Priest,
    And by the vision splendid
    Is on his way attended;   75
At length the Man perceives it die away,
And fade into the light of common day.

VI

Earth fills her lap with pleasures of her own;
Yearnings she hath in her own natural kind,
And, even with something of a Mother's mind,   80
    And no unworthy aim,
    The homely Nurse doth all she can
To make her Foster-child, her Inmate, Man,
    Forget the glories he hath known,
And that imperial palace whence he came.   85

VII

Behold the Child among his new-born blisses,
A six years' Darling of a pigmy size!
See, where 'mid work of his own hand he lies,
Fretted by sallies of his mother's kisses,
With light upon him from his father's eyes!   90
See, at his feet, some little plan or chart,
Some fragment from his dream of human life,
Shaped by himself with newly-learnèd art;
    A wedding or a festival,
    A mourning or a funeral;   95
    And this hath now his heart,
    And unto this he frames his song:
    Then will he fit his tongue
To dialogues of business, love, or strife;
    But it will not be long   100
    Ere this be thrown aside,
    And with new joy and pride

The little Actor cons another part;
Filling from time to time his "humorous stage"
With all the Persons, down to palsied Age, 105
That Life brings with her in her equipage;
    As if his whole vocation
    Were endless imitation.

VIII

Thou, whose exterior semblance doth belie
    Thy Soul's immensity; 110
Thou best Philosopher, who yet dost keep
Thy heritage, thou Eye among the blind,
That, deaf and silent, read'st the eternal deep,
Haunted for ever by the eternal mind,—
    Mighty Prophet! Seer blest! 115
    On whom those truths do rest,
Which we are toiling all our lives to find,
In darkness lost, the darkness of the grave;
Thou, over whom thy Immortality
Broods like the Day, a Master o'er a Slave, 120
A Presence which is not to be put by;
    [To whom the grave
Is but a lonely bed without the sense or sight
    Of day or the warm light,
A place of thought where we in waiting lie;]¹ 125
Thou little Child, yet glorious in the might
Of heaven-born freedom on thy being's height,
Why with such earnest pains dost thou provoke
The years to bring the inevitable yoke,
Thus blindly with thy blessedness at strife? 130
Full soon thy Soul shall have her earthly freight,
And custom lie upon thee with a weight,
Heavy as frost, and deep almost as life!

IX

    O joy! that in our embers
    Is something that doth live, 135
    That nature yet remembers
    What was so fugitive!
The thought of our past years in me doth breed
Perpetual benediction: not indeed
For that which is most worthy to be blest; 140
Delight and liberty, the simple creed
Of Childhood, whether busy or at rest,
With new-fledged hope still fluttering in his breast—
    Not for these I raise
    The song of thanks and praise; 145
    But for those obstinate questionings

---

1. The lines within brackets were included in the *Ode* in the 1807 and 1815 editions of Wordsworth's poems but were omitted in the 1820 and subsequent editions, as a result of Coleridge's severe censure of them.

Of sense and outward things,
   Fallings from us, vanishings;
   Blank misgivings of a Creature
Moving about in worlds not realized,   150
High instincts before which our mortal Nature
Did tremble like a guilty Thing surprised:
     But for those first affections,
     Those shadowy recollections,
   Which, be they what they may,   155
Are yet the fountain-light of all our day,
Are yet a master-light of all our seeing;
  Uphold us, cherish, and have power to make
Our noisy years seem moments in the being
Of the eternal Silence: truths that wake,   160
       To perish never;
Which neither listlessness, nor mad endeavour,
      Nor Man nor Boy,
Nor all that is at enmity with joy,
Can utterly abolish or destroy!   165
   Hence in a season of calm weather
    Though inland far we be,
Our Souls have sight of that immortal sea
    Which brought us hither,
   Can in a moment travel thither,   170
And see the Children sport upon the shore,
And hear the mighty waters rolling evermore.

X

Then sing, ye Birds, sing, sing a joyous song!
    And let the young Lambs bound
    As to the tabor's sound!   175
We in thought will join your throng,
    Ye that pipe and ye that play,
    Ye that through your hearts to-day
    Feel the gladness of the May!
What though the radiance which was once so bright   180
Be now for ever taken from my sight,
  Though nothing can bring back the hour
Of splendour in the grass, of glory in the flower;
    We will grieve not, rather find
    Strength in what remains behind;   185
    In the primal sympathy
    Which having been must ever be;
    In the soothing thoughts that spring
    Out of human suffering;
    In the faith that looks through death,   190
In years that bring the philosophic mind.

XI

And O, ye Fountains, Meadows, Hills, and Groves,
Forebode not any severing of our loves!

Yet in my heart of hearts I feel your might;
I only have relinquished one delight   195
To live beneath your more habitual sway.
I love the Brooks which down their channels fret,
Even more than when I tripped lightly as they;
The innocent brightness of a new-born Day
        Is lovely yet;   200
The Clouds that gather round the setting sun
Do take a sober colouring from an eye
That hath kept watch o'er man's mortality;
Another race hath been, and other palms are won.
Thanks to the human heart by which we live,   205
Thanks to its tenderness, its joys, and fears,
To me the meanest flower that blows can give
Thoughts that do often lie too deep for tears.

Composed upon Westminster Bridge,
September 3, 1802

Earth has not anything to show more fair:
Dull would he be of soul who could pass by
A sight so touching in its majesty;
This City now doth, like a garment, wear
The beauty of the morning; silent, bare,   5
Ships, towers, domes, theatres, and temples lie
Open unto the fields, and to the sky;
All bright and glittering in the smokeless air.
Never did sun more beautifully steep
In his first splendour, valley, rock, or hill;   10
Ne'er saw I, never felt, a calm so deep!
The river glideth at his own sweet will:
Dear God! the very houses seem asleep;
And all that mighty heart is lying still!

The World Is Too Much with Us

The world is too much with us; late and soon,
Getting and spending, we lay waste our powers:
Little we see in Nature that is ours;
We have given our hearts away, a sordid boon![1]
This Sea that bares her bosom to the moon,   5
The winds that will be howling at all hours,
And are up-gathered now like sleeping flowers;
For this, for everything, we are out of tune;
It moves us not.—Great God! I'd rather be

---

1. Gift. *Sordid:* refers to the act of giving the heart away.

A Pagan suckled in a creed outworn;   10
So might I, standing on this pleasant lea,
Have glimpses that would make me less forlorn;
Have sight of Proteus[2] rising from the sea;
Or hear old Triton[3] blow his wreathèd horn.

2. An old man of the sea who, in the *Odyssey*, could assume a variety of shapes.   3. A sea deity, usually represented as blowing on a conch shell.

DOROTHY WORDSWORTH
1771–1855

The era inaugurated by Jean-Jacques Rousseau encouraged self-reflection and the development of a highly articulated language of feeling. Among the writers about themselves who flourished during the period of Romanticism, Dorothy Wordsworth occupies a unique position. Her voluminous journals include relatively little open discussion of her personal feelings. Instead, she perfects a technique of indirect self-revelation through intense concentration on details of the world outside her.

In her youth, Dorothy Wordsworth was separated from her four brothers after the death of their mother when Dorothy was seven years old. In 1795, however, her brother William was lent a house in Dorset, where she joined him, acting as home-maker. From that time on, she lived with William, even after he married in 1802. Like William, she became close to Samuel Taylor Coleridge, and she accompanied the two men to Germany in 1798–99. As the journals reveal, she led a quiet domestic life. After a serious illness in 1829, she was an invalid for the rest of her life.

The Grasmere Journals, from which the selections printed here are taken, record the texture of Dorothy's daily existence with William at Dove Cottage, Grasmere, in the English Lake District. The two of them had moved there in 1799, taking pleasure in the first home they had owned. They lived close to Grasmere Lake, in a landscape of hills, mountains, woods, and water of striking beauty, through which they walked almost every day. They also created a garden, transplanting plants from the wild. William wrote poems; Dorothy copied them out for him. She made bread and pies, sewed, read aloud and to herself. She enjoyed her association with their neighbors, as well as the more intense friendship with Coleridge and with the Hutchinson sisters—Mary, whom William married, and Sara, with whom Coleridge, already married and the father of two sons, fell disastrously in love. The journals report these facts in considerable detail.

But they do far more. Wordsworth responded to what she saw with the eye of a poet. She noted the precise aspects of flowers; the names of birds; and the look of the clouds on a summer day, of the fleece on sheep, of the moon in its varying appearances. Seldom does she write in any detail directly of her own emotions. The characteristic sequence of the *Journals* printed here includes only one moment of sharp, open self-revelation: "I shall be beloved—I want no more." Unlike Rousseau, Wordsworth does not appear to consider herself remarkable. But she uses the minute particulars of what she sees as an indirect means of expressing feeling, and the *Journals* convey an emotional life of subtle complexity. Thus she describes crows flying: "We watched the crows at a little distance from us become white as silver as they flew in the sunshine, and when they went still further they looked like shapes of water passing over the green fields." The precision of the observation and the brilliance of the image ("shapes of water") express the passion of the watcher, for whom powerful meaning inheres in the natural world.

Consciously, Dorothy wrote her journals, as she did so much else, for the sake of her brother. William read them and used them as data for his poetry. Dorothy writes of daffodils that they "tossed and reeled and danced and seemed as if they verily laughed with the wind." William, two years later, describes "a jocund company" of daffodils in *I Wandered Lonely as a Cloud*:

> Ten thousand saw I at a glance,
> Tossing their heads in sprightly dance.

Dorothy had provided him with raw material. But the power of her writing does not depend on her brother's conversion of it to verse. In its own right, it expresses a subtle and compelling sensibility.

The *Journals* make no ostentatious claim of profundity, but they evoke a consistent vision of unity between inanimate and animate nature, including humankind. One of Wordsworth's characteristic rhetorical devices is the sentence composed largely of miscellaneous nouns, their conjunction evoking a sense of pattern created by the observer but also inherent in the universe. For example: "Lasses spreading dung, a dog's barking now and then, cocks crowing, birds twittering, the snow in patches at the top of the highest hills, yellow palms, purple and green twigs on the birches, ashes with their glittering spikes quite bare." Utterly unpretentious, the lucid prose brings the world alive.

Little effort has been made here to annotate the names of local people and places in the anthologized selections. They have scanty importance for a modern reader, except through what Wordsworth has made of them.

The source of the text is Dorothy Wordsworth, *The Grasmere Journals*, ed. Pamela Woolf (1991).

Recent biographies of Dorothy Wordsworth include R. Gittings and J. Manton, *Dorothy Wordsworth* (1985), and E. Gunn, *A Passion for the Particular: Dorothy Wordsworth: A Portrait* (1981). A useful study placing Dorothy and William Wordsworth in political and intellectual context is A. M. Ellis, *Rebels and Conservatives: Dorothy and William Wordsworth and Their Circle* (1967).

PRONOUNCING GLOSSARY

The following list uses common English syllables and stress accents to provide rough equivalents of selected words whose pronunciation may be unfamiliar to the general reader.

Eusemere: *yooz'-meer*   Loughrigg: *luf'-rig*

Grasmere: *gras'-meer*   Wytheburn: *waith'-burn*

From The Grasmere Journals

[This selection from the *Journals* begins in mid-April 1802.]

Wednesday 14th

William did not rise till dinner time. I walked with Mrs. C. I was ill out of spirits—disheartened. Wm and I took a long walk in the rain.

Thursday 15th

It was a threatening misty morning—but mild. We set off after dinner from Eusemere—Mrs. Clarkson went a short way with us but turned back. The wind was furious and we thought we must have returned. We first rested in the large boat-house, then under a furze bush opposite Mr. Clarkson's, saw the plough going in the field. The wind seized our breath; the lake was rough. There was a boat by itself floating in the middle of the bay below Water Millock—We rested again in the Water Millock lane. The hawthorns are black and green, the birches here and there greenish but there is yet more of purple to be seen on the twigs. We got over into a field to avoid some cows—people working, a few primroses by the roadside, woodsorrel flowers, the anemone, scentless violets, strawberries, and that starry yellow flower which Mrs. C calls pile wort.[1] When we were in the woods beyond Gowbarrow park we saw a few daffodils close to the water side, we fancied that the lake had floated the seeds ashore and that the little colony had so sprung up—But as we went along there were more and yet more and at last under the boughs of the trees, we saw that there was a long belt of them along the shore, about the breadth of a country turnpike road. I never saw daffodils so beautiful; they grew among the mossy stones about and about them, some rested their heads upon these stones as on a pillow for weariness and the rest tossed and reeled and danced and seemed as if they verily laughed with the wind that blew upon them over the lake, they looked so gay, ever glancing, ever changing. This wind blew directly over the lake to them. There was here and there a little knot and a few stragglers a few yards higher up but they were so few as not to disturb the simplicity and unity and life of that one busy highway—We rested again and again. The bays were stormy and we heard the waves at different distances and in the middle of the water like the sea—Rain came on, we were wet when we reached Luffs' but we called in. Luckily all was chearless and gloomy so we faced the storm—we *must* have been wet if we had waited—put on dry clothes at Dobson's. I was very kindly treated by a young woman, the landlady looked sour but it is her way. She gave us a goodish supper, excellent ham and potatoes. We paid 7/2 when we came away. William was sitting by a bright fire when I came downstairs. He soon made his way to the library piled up in a corner of the window. He brought out a volume of Enfield's Speaker, another miscellany, and an odd volume of Congreve's[3] plays. We had a glass of warm rum and water—we enjoyed ourselves and wished for Mary.[4] It rained and blew when we went to bed. N.B. deer in Gowbarrow park like to skeletons.

Friday 16th April (Good Friday)

When I undrew my curtains in the morning, I was much affected by the beauty of the prospect and the change. The sun shone, the wind had passed away, the hills looked chearful. The river was very bright as it flowed into the lake. The church rises up behind a little knot of rocks, the steeple not so high as an ordinary three story house. Bees, in a row in the garden under the wall. After Wm had shaved we set forward. The valley is at first broken by little rocky woody knolls that make retiring places, fairy valleys in the vale, the river winds along under these hills travelling not in a bustle but not slowly

1. I.e., the lesser celandine.   2. Seven shillings, approximately twenty-eight dollars. In a subsequent note, Wordsworth wrote that they had paid one shilling more than they should have,   3. William Congreve (1670–1729), Restoration dramatist, best known for his witty comedies. *Speaker: The Speaker, or, Miscellaneous Pieces Selected from the Best English Writers, and Disposed Under Proper Heads, for the Improvement of Youth in Reading and Speaking* (1778), compiled by William Enfield.   4. Mary Hutchinson (1770–1859), whom William later married.

to the lake. We saw a fisherman in the flat meadow on the other side of the water; he came towards us and threw his line over the two-arched bridge. It is a bridge of a heavy construction, almost bending inwards in the middle, but it is grey and there is a look of ancientry in the architecture of it that pleased me. As we go on the vale opens out more into one vale with somewhat of a cradle bed. Cottages with groups of trees on the side of the hills. We passed a pair of twin children two years old—and sate on the next bridge which we crossed, a single arch, we rested again upon the turf and looked at the same bridge—we observed arches in the water occasioned by the large stones sending it down in two streams—a sheep came plunging through the river, stumbled up the bank and passed close to us, it had been frightened by an insignificant little dog on the other side, its fleece dropped a glittering shower under its belly—primroses by the roadside, pile wort that shone like stars of gold in the sun, violets, strawberries, retired and half buried among the grass. When we came to the foot of Brothers' Water I left William sitting on the bridge and went along the path on the right side of the lake through the wood—I was delighted with what I saw—the water under the boughs of the bare old trees, the simplicity of the mountains and the exquisite beauty of the path. There was one grey cottage. I repeated "The Glowworm"[5] as I walked along—I hung over the gate, and thought I could have stayed for ever. When I returned I found William writing a poem descriptive of the sights and sounds we saw and heard. There was the gentle flowing of the stream, the glittering lively lake, green fields without a living creature to be seen on them, behind us, a flat pasture with forty-two cattle feeding, to our left the road leading to the hamlet, no smoke there, the sun shone on the bare roofs. The people were at work ploughing, harrowing and sowing— lasses spreading dung, a dog's barking now and then, cocks crowing, birds twittering, the snow in patches at the top of the highest hills, yellow palms, purple and green twigs on the birches, ashes[6] with their glittering spikes quite bare. The hawthorn a bright green with black stems under, the oak and the moss of the oak glossy. We then went on, passed two sisters at work, *they first passed us,* one with two pitch forks in her hand. The other had a spade. We had some talk with them. They laughed aloud after we were gone, per- haps half in wantonness, half boldness. William finished his poem before we got to the foot of Kirkstone. There were hundreds of cattle in the vale. There we ate our dinner. The walk up Kirkstone was very interesting. The becks[7] among the rocks were all alive—Wm showed me the little mossy streamlet which he had before loved when he saw its bright green track in the snow. The view above Ambleside, very beautiful. There we sate and looked down on the green vale. We watched the crows at a little distance from us become white as silver as they flew in the sunshine, and when they went still further they looked like shapes of water passing over the green fields. The whitening of Ambleside Church is a great deduction from the beauty of it seen from this point. We called at the Luffs', the Boddingtons there, did not go in and went round by the fields. I pulled off, my stockings intending to wade the beck but I was obliged to put them on and we climbed over the wall at the bridge. The post[8] passed us. No letters! Rydale Lake was in its own evening

---

5. *Among All Lovely Things My Love Had Been.*   6. I.e., ash trees.   7. Creeks, small streams.
8. Mailman.

brightness, the islands and points distinct. Jane Ashburner came up to us when we were sitting upon the wall—we rode in her cart to Tom Dawson's—all well. The garden looked pretty in the half moonlight half daylight. As we went up the vale of Brothers' Water more and more cattle feeding, one hundred of them.

Saturday 17th

A mild warm rain. We sate in the garden all the morning. William dug a little. I transplanted a honey suckle. The lake was still, the sheep on the island reflected in the water, like the grey deer we saw in Gowbarrow park. We walked after tea by moonlight. I had been in bed in the afternoon and William had slept in his chair. We walked towards Rydale first then backwards and forwards below Mr. Olliff's. The village was beautiful in the moonlight—Helm Crag we observed very distinct. The dead hedge round Benson's field bound together at the top by an interlacing of ash sticks which made a chain of silver when we faced the moon—a letter from C, and also from S. H.[9] I saw a robin chacing a scarlet butterfly this morning.

Sunday 18th

I lay in bed late. Again a mild grey morning with rising vapours we sate in the orchard—William wrote the poem on the robin and the butterfly. I went to drink tea at Luff's but as we did not dine till six o'clock it was late. It was mist and small[1] rain all the way but very pleasant. William met me at Rydale—Aggy[2] accompanied me thither. We sate up late. He met me with the conclusion of the poem of the robin.[3] I read it to him in bed. We left out some lines.

Monday 19th

A mild rain, very warm. Wm worked in the garden, I made pies and bread. After dinner the mist cleared away and sun shone. William walked to Luff's. I was not very well and went to bed. Wm came home pale and tired. I could not rest when I got to bed.

Tuesday 20th

A beautiful morning, the sun shone—William wrote a conclusion to the poem of the butterfly, "I've watch'd you now a full half-hour." I was quite out of spirits and went into the orchard—When I came in he had finished the poem. We sate in the orchard after dinner, it was a beautiful afternoon. The sun shone upon the level fields and they grew greener beneath the eye—houses, village all chearful, people at work. We sate in the orchard and repeated "The Glowworm" and other poems. Just when William came to a well or a trough which there is in Lord Darlington's Park he began to write that poem of the glow-worm, not being able to ride[4] upon the long trot—

---

9. Sara Hutchinson, sister of Mary. C: Samuel Taylor Coleridge (1772–1834), the Wordsworths' fellow poet and close friend.   1. Light.   2. Agnes Fisher, a friend.   3. *The Redbreast and the Butterfly.*   4. A mistake for "write." William could write only when the horse was walking.

interrupted in going through the Town of Staindrop. Finished it about two miles and a half beyond Staindrop—he did not feel the jogging of the horse while he was writing but when he had done he felt the effect of it and his fingers were cold with his gloves. His horse fell with him on the other side of St. Helen's, Auckland.—So much for "The Glowworm": It was written coming from Middleham on Monday, April 12th, 1802. On Tuesday 20th when we were sitting after tea Coleridge came to the door. I started Wm with my voice—C came up palish but I afterwards found he looked well. William was not well and I was in low spirits.

Wednesday 21st

William and I sauntered a little in the garden. Coleridge came to us and repeated the verses he wrote to Sara—I was affected with them and was on the whole, not being well, in miserable spirits. The sunshine—the green fields and the fair sky made me sadder; even the little happy sporting lambs seemed but sorrowful to me. The pile wort spread out on the grass a thousand shining stars, the primroses were there and the remains of a few daffodils. The well which we cleaned out last night is still but a little muddy pond, though full of water. I went to bed after dinner, could not sleep, went to bed again. Read Ferguson's life[5] and a poem or two—fell asleep for five minutes and awoke better. We got tea. Sate comfortably in the evening. I went to bed early.

Thursday 22nd

A fine mild morning—we walked into Easedale. The sun shone. Coleridge talked of his plan of sowing the laburnum in the woods—The waters were high for there had been a great quantity of rain in the night. I was tired and sate under the shade of a holly tree that grows upon a rock—I sate there and looked down the stream. I then went to the single holly behind that single rock in the field and sate upon the grass till they came from the waterfall. I saw them there and heard Wm flinging stones into the river whose roaring was loud even where I was. When they returned William was repeating the poem "I have thoughts that are fed by the Sun."[6] It had been called to his mind by the dying away of the stunning of the waterfall when he came behind a stone. When we had got into the vale a heavy rain came on. We saw a family of little children sheltering themselves under a wall before the rain came on, they sate in a row making a canopy for each other of their clothes. The servant lass was planting potatoes near them. Coleridge changed his clothes—we were all wet—Wilkinson[7] came in while we were at dinner. Coleridge and I after dinner drank black currants and water.

Friday 23rd April 1802

It being a beautiful morning we set off at eleven o'clock intending to stay out of doors all the morning. We went towards Rydale and before we got to

---

5. David Irving, *Poetical Works of Robert Fergusson with the Life of the Author* (1800).   6. A poem that William had recently written; he never published it.   7. Probably the Reverend Joseph Wilkinson (1764–1831).

Tom Dawson's we determined to go under Nab Scar.[8] Thither we went. The sun shone and we were lazy. Coleridge pitched upon several places to sit down upon but we could not be all of one mind respecting sun and shade so we pushed on to the foot of the scar. It was very grand when we looked up, very stony, here and there a budding tree. William observed that the umbrella yew tree that breasts the wind had lost its character as a tree and had become something like to solid wood. Coleridge and I pushed on before. We left William sitting on the stones feasting with silence—and C and I sate down upon a rock seat—a couch it might be under the bower of William's eglantine, Andrew's broom.[9] He was below us and we could see him—he came to us and repeated his poems while we sate beside him upon the ground. He had made himself a seat in the crumbly ground. After we had lingered long looking into the vales—Ambleside vale with the copses, the village under the hill and the green fields—Rydale with a lake all alive and glittering yet but little stirred by breezes, and our own dear Grasmere first making a little round lake of nature's own with never a house never a green field—but the copses and the bare hills, enclosing it and the river flowing out of it. Above rose the Coniston Fells in their own shape and colour—not man's hills but all for themselves, the sky and the clouds and a few wild creatures. C went to search for something new. We saw him climbing up towards a rock, he called us and we found him in a bower, the sweetest that was ever seen—the rock on one side is very high and all covered with ivy which hung loosely about and bore bunches of brown berries. On the other side it was higher than my head. We looked down upon the Ambleside vale that seemed to wind away from us, the village *lying* under the hill. The fir tree island was reflected beautifully—we now first saw that the trees are planted in rows. About this bower there is mountain ash, common ash, yew tree, ivy, holly, hawthorn, mosses and flowers, and a carpet of moss—Above at the top of the rock there is another spot—it is scarce a bower, a little parlour, one not *enclosed* by walls but shaped out for a resting place by the rocks and the ground rising about it. It had a sweet moss carpet—We resolved to go and plant flowers in both these places tomorrow. We wished for Mary and Sara. Dined late. After dinner Wm and I worked in the garden. C read. A letter from Sara.

Saturday 24th

A very wet day. William called me out to see a waterfall behind the barberry tree—We walked in the evening to Rydale—Coleridge and I lingered behind—C stopped up the little runner[1] by the road side to make a lake. We all stood to look at Glowworm Rock—a primrose that grew there and just looked out on the road from its own sheltered bower. The clouds moved as William observed in one regular body like a multitude in motion, a sky all clouds over, not one cloud. On our return it broke a little out and we saw

8. Rock or crag (obsolete). Nab Scar was a large local crag.   9. Allusion to two of William's poems from 1800. In *The Waterfall and the Eglantine*, an eglantine grows too close to a waterfall and is swept away in the wintertime. In *The Oak and the Broom*, narrated by the shepherd Andrew, an oak is struck by lightning in a storm while the smaller, carefree broom plant survives.   1. Rivulet.

here and there a star. One appeared but for a moment in a lake—pale blue sky.

Sunday 25th April

After breakfast we set off with Coleridge towards Keswick. Wilkinson overtook us near the Potters' and interrupted our discourse. C got into a gig with Mr. Beck,[2] and drove away from us. A shower came on but it was soon over— we spent the morning in the orchard. Read the Prothalamium[3] of Spenser— walked backwards and forwards. Mr. Simpson[4] drank tea with us. I was not well before tea. Mr. S sent us some quills by Molly Ashburner and his brother's book.[5] The Luffs called at the door.

Monday 26th

I copied Wm's poems for Coleridge. Letters from Peggy[6] and Mary H—wrote to Peggy and Coleridge. A terrible rain and wind all day. Went to bed at twelve o'clock.

Tuesday 27th

A fine morning. Mrs. Luff called. I walked with her to the boat-house— William met me at the top of the hill with his fishing-rod in his hand. I turned with him and we sate on the hill looking to Rydale. I left him intending to join him but he came home, and said his line would not stand the pulling— he had had several bites. He sate in the orchard, I made bread. Miss Simpson called. I walked with her to Goans. When I came back I found that he and John Fisher had cleaned out the well—John had sodden[7] about the bee-stand. In the evening Wm began to write "The Tinker."[8] We had a letter and verses from Coleridge.

Wednesday 28th April

A fine sunny but coldish morning. I copied the Prioress's tale.[9] Wm was in the orchard—I went to him—he worked away at his poem, though he was ill and tired—I happened to say that when I was a child I would not have pulled a strawberry blossom. I left him and wrote out the Manciple's Tale.[1] At dinner-time he came in with the poem of "Children gathering flowers"[2]— but it was not quite finished and it kept him long off his dinner. It is now done, he is working at "The Tinker," he promised me he would get his tea and do no more but I have got mine an hour and a quarter and he has scarcely begun his. I am not quite well—We have let the bright sun go down without walking—now a heavy shower comes on and I guess we shall not walk at all—I wrote a few lines to Coleridge. Then we walked backwards and for-

2. Probably James Beck, a local gentleman.   3. A poem celebrating an aristocratic marriage (1596), by Edmund Spenser (1522–1599).   4. Probably Bartholomew Simpson, an old man at this time.   5. *Science Revived, or The Vision of Alfred. A Poem in Eight Books* (1802), by the Reverend Joseph Simpson.   6. Once a servant of the Wordsworths; her last name is unknown.   7. Laid sod.   8. Unpublished.   9. William had translated Geoffrey Chaucer's tale into modern English.   1. Another of Chaucer's *Canterbury Tales* that William had translated.   2. Later published as *Foresight*.

wards between our house and Olliff's. We talked about T Hutchinson and
Bell Addison.[3] William left me sitting on a stone. When we came in we
corrected the Chaucers but I could not finish them tonight, went to bed.

Thursday 29th

A beautiful morning. The sun shone and all was pleasant. We sent off our
parcel to Coleridge by the waggon. Mr. Simpson heard the cuckow today.
Before we went out, after I had written down "The Tinker" which William
finished this morning, Luff called. He was very lame, limped into the
kitchen—he came on a little pony. We then went to Johns Grove, sate a
while at first. Afterwards William lay, and I lay in the trench under the
fence—he with his eyes shut and listening to the waterfalls and the birds.
There was no one waterfall above another—it was a sound of waters in the
air—the voice of the air. William heard me breathing and rustling now and
then but we both lay still, and unseen by one another—he thought that it
would be as sweet thus to lie so in the grave, to hear the *peaceful* sounds of
the earth and just to know that one's dear friends were near. The lake was
still; there was a boat out. Silver how reflected with delicate purple and
yellowish hues as I have seen spar[4]—Lambs on the island and running races
together by the half dozen in the round field near us. The copses green*ish*,
hawthorn green.—Came home to dinner then went to Mr. Simpson. We
rested a long time under a wall. Sheep and lambs were in the field—cottages
smoking. As I lay down on the grass, I observed the glittering silver line on
the ridges of the backs of the sheep, owing to their situation respecting the
sun—which made them look beautiful but with something of strangeness,
like animals of another kind—as if belonging to a more splendid world. Met
old Mr. S at the door—Mrs. S poorly—I got mullens and pansies—I was sick
and ill[5] and obliged to come home soon. We went to bed immediately—I
slept up stairs. The air coldish where it was felt somewhat frosty.

Friday April 30th

We came into the orchard directly after breakfast, and sate there. The lake
was calm—the sky cloudy. We saw two fishermen by the lake side. William
began to write the poem of the Celandine.[6] I wrote to Mary H—sitting on
the fur gown. Walked backwards and forwards with William—he repeated
his poem to me—then he got to work again and would not give over[7]—he
had not finished his dinner till five o'clock. After dinner we took up the fur
gowns into The Hollins[8] above. We found a sweet seat and thither we will
often go. We spread the gown, put on each a cloak and there we lay—William
fell asleep—he had a bad head ache owing to his having been disturbed the
night before with reading C's letter which Fletcher had brought to the door—
I did not sleep but I lay with half shut eyes, looking at the prospect as in a
vision almost I was so resigned to it—Loughrigg Fell was the most distant
hill, then came the lake slipping in between the copses and above the copse

3. Isabella Addison (1784–1807), who married the Hutchinsons' cousin John Monkhouse. Tom Hutchinson (1773–1849), brother of Sara and Mary.   4. A crystalline mineral that shines in the sun.
5. Nauseated and generally did not feel well. *Mulleins:* plants of the snapdragon family.   6. *To the
Lesser Celandine.*   7. Stop.   8. A wood full of holly trees near the Wordsworths' house.

the round swelling field, nearer to me a wild intermixture of rocks, trees, and slacks[9] of grassy ground.—When we turned the corner of our little shelter we saw the church and the whole vale. It is a blessed place. The birds were about us on all sides—skobbys,[1] robins, bullfinches. Crows now and then flew over our heads as we were warned by the sound of the beating of the air above. We stayed till the light of day was going and the little birds had begun to settle their singing—But there was a thrush not far off that seemed to sing louder and clearer than the thrushes had sung when it was quite day. We came in at eight o'clock, got tea. Wrote to Coleridge, and I wrote to Mrs. Clarkson[2] part of a letter. We went to bed at twenty minutes past eleven with prayers that Wm might sleep well.

Saturday May 1st

Rose not till half past eight—a heavenly morning—as soon as breakfast was over we went into the garden and sowed the scarlet beans about the house. It was a clear sky, a heavenly morning. I sowed the flowers. William helped me. We then went and sate in the orchard till dinnertime, it was very hot. William wrote "The Celandine." We planned a shed, for the sun was too much for us. After dinner we went again to our old resting place in the Hollins under the rock. We first lay under a holly where we saw nothing but the holly tree and a budding elm mossed with[3] and the sky above our heads. But that holly tree had a beauty about it more than its own, knowing as we did where we were. When the sun had got low enough we went to the rock shade—Oh the overwhelming beauty of the vale below—greener than green. Two ravens flew high high in the sky and the sun shone upon their bellys and their wings long after there was none of his light to be seen but a little space on the top of Loughrigg Fell. We went down to tea at eight o'clock—had lost the poem[4] and returned after tea. The landscape was fading, sheep and lambs quiet among the rocks. We walked towards King's[5] and backwards and forwards. The sky was perfectly cloudless. N.B. is it often so? three solitary stars in the middle of the blue vault, one or two on the points of the high hills. Wm wrote "The Celandine" second part tonight. Heard the cuckow today this first of May.

Sunday 2nd May

Again a heavenly morning—Letter from Coleridge.

4 May 1802 to 16 January 1803

Tuesday May 4th

William had slept pretty well and though he went to bed nervous and jaded in the extreme he rose refreshed. I wrote "The Leech Gatherer"[6] for him

---

9. Hollows, dips in the ground.   1. Or scobbies, a north country name for chaffinches, which are small birds.   2. Catherine Clarkson (1772–1856), a close neighbor and friend.   3. A word has apparently been left out here.   4. Not the one William had been writing in the morning but the idea for a second poem on the celandine: *Pleasures newly found are sweet.* The idea returned to him in the evening.   5. Thomas King (1772–1831), who had a house in Grasmere, not far away.   6. Later published as *Resolution and Independence. Wrote:* i.e., wrote out, copied.

which he had begun the night before and of which he wrote several stanzas in bed this Monday morning. It was very hot, we called at Mr. Simpson's door as we passed but did not go in. We rested several times by the way, read and repeated "The Leech gatherer." We were almost melted before we were at the top of the hill. We saw Coleridge on the Wytheburn side of the water, he crossed the beck to us. Mr. Simpson was fishing there. William and I ate a luncheon, then went on towards the waterfall. It is a glorious wild solitude under that lofty purple crag. It stood upright by itself. Its own self and its shadow below, one mass—all else was sunshine. We went on further. A bird at the top of the crags was flying round and round and looked in thinness and transparency, shape and motion, like a moth. We climbed the hill but looked in vain for a shade except at the foot of the great waterfall, and there we did not like to stay on account of the loose stones above our heads. We came down and rested upon a moss covered rock, rising out of the bed of the river. There we lay, ate our dinner and stayed there till about four o'clock or later—Wm and C repeated and read verses. I drank a little brandy and water and was in heaven. The stags horn[7] is very beautiful and fresh springing upon the fells. Mountain ashes, green. We drank tea at a farm house. The woman had not a pleasant countenance, but was civil enough. She had a pretty boy a year old whom she suckled. We parted from Coleridge at Sara's Crag after having looked at the letters which C carved in the morning. I kissed them all. Wm deepened the T with C's penknife.[8] We sate afterwards on the wall, seeing the sun go down and the reflections in the still water. C looked well and parted from us chearfully, hopping up upon the side stones. On the Rays we met a woman with two little girls, one in her arms, the other about four years old walking by her side, a pretty little thing, but half starved. She had on a pair of slippers that had belonged to some gentleman's child, down at the heels, but it was not easy to keep them on—but, poor thing! young as she was, she walked carefully with them. Alas too young for such cares and such travels—The mother when we accosted her told us that her husband had left her and gone off with another woman and how she "*pursued*" them. Then her fury kindled and her eyes rolled about. She changed again to tears. She was a Cockermouth woman—thirty years of age a child at Cockermouth when I was—I was moved and gave her a shilling, I believe 6d[9] more than I ought to have given. We had the crescent moon with the "auld moon in her arms"[1]—We rested often:—always upon the bridges. Reached home at about ten o'clock. The Lloyds had been here in our absence. We went soon to bed. I repeated verses to William while he was in bed—he was soothed and I left him. "This is the Spot"[2] over and over again.

Wednesday 5th May 1802

A very fine morning rather cooler than yesterday. We planted three-fourths of the bower. I made bread—we sate in the orchard. The thrush sang all day

7. A type of moss.   8. Coleridge had carved their initials in the rock. The *T* that William deepened is Coleridge's middle initial.   9. A sixpence or half a shilling; perhaps roughly equivalent to two dollars now.   1. *The Ballad of Sir Patrick Spens.*   2. Lines that William had written two years earlier; he published them only in part.

as he always sings. I wrote to the Hutchinsons and to Coleridge, packed off *Thalaba*.[3] William had kept off work till near bedtime when we returned from our walk—then he began again and went to bed very nervous—we walked in the twilight and walked till night came on—the moon had the old moon in her arms but not so plain to be seen as the night before. When we went to bed it was a boat without the circle.[4] I read "The Lover's Complaint"[5] to Wm in bed and left him composed.

6th May Thursday 1802

A sweet morning. We have put the finishing stroke to our bower and here we are sitting in the orchard. It is one o'clock. We are sitting upon a seat under the wall which I found my brother building up when I came to him with his apple—he had intended that it should have been done before I came. It is a nice cool shady spot. The small birds are singing—Lambs bleating, cuckow calling—The thrush sings by fits, Thomas Ashburner's axe is going quietly (without passion) in the orchard—Hens are cackling, flies humming, the women talking together at their doors—Plumb and pear trees are in blossom, apple trees greenish—the opposite woods green, the crows are cawing. We have heard ravens. The ash trees are in blossom, birds flying all about us. The stitchwort is coming out, there is one budding lychnis.[6] The primroses are passing their prime. Celandine, violets and wood sorrel for ever more—little geranium and pansies on the wall. We walked in the evening to Tail End to enquire about hurdles[7] for the orchard shed and about Mr. Luff's flower—The flower dead—no hurdles. I went to look at the falling wood—Wm also, when he had been at Benson's went with me. They have left a good many small oak trees but we dare not hope that they are all to remain. The ladies are come to Mr. Gell's cottage; we saw them as we went and their light when we returned. When we came in we found a magazine and review and a letter from Coleridge with verses to Hartley[8] and Sara H. We read the review etc. The moon was a perfect boat, a silver boat, when we were out in the evening. The birch tree is all over green in *small* leaf. More light and elegant than when it is full out. It bent to the breezes as if for the love of its own delightful motions. Sloe thorns and hawthorns in the hedges.

Friday 7th May

William had slept uncommonly well so, feeling himself strong, he fell to work at "The Leech Gatherer"—he wrote hard at it till dinner time, then he gave over tired to death—he had finished the poem. I was making Derwent's frocks.[9] After dinner we sate in the orchard. It was a thick hazy dull air. The thrush sang almost continually—the little birds were more than usually busy with their voices. The sparrows are now full fledged. The nest is so full that they lie upon one another, they sit quietly in their nest with closed mouths.

---

3. Robert Southey, *Thalaba the Destroyer* (1801), an epic poem in twelve books.   4. I.e., the moon appeared thus.   5. By Shakespeare.   6. Cuckoo flower or ragged robin. *Stitchwort:* stellaria, a flower with large white blossoms; it was supposed to alleviate stitches, or pains in the side.   7. Withes and stakes for enclosures.   8. Coleridge's son. The poem is *Do you ask what the birds say?*   9. Garments for Coleridge's infant son.

I walked to Rydale after tea, which we drank by the kitchen fire. The evening very dull—a terrible kind of threatening brightness at sunset above Easedale. The sloe thorn beautiful in the hedges, and in the wild spots higher up among the hawthorns. No letters. William met me—he had been digging in my absence and cleaning the well. We walked up beyond Lewthwaites. A very dull sky, coolish crescent moon now and then. I had a letter brought me from Mrs. Clarkson. While we were walking in the orchard I observed the sorrel leaves opening at about nine o'clock—William went to bed tired with thinking about a poem.

Saturday Morning May 8th 1802

We sowed the scarlet beans in the orchard. I read *Henry V*[1] there—William lay on his back on the seat. "Wept, For names, sounds paths delights and duties lost"—Taken from a poem upon Cowley's wish to retire to the plantations, read in the review.[2] I finished Derwent's frocks—after dinner William added a step to the orchard steps.

Sunday Morning May 9th 1802

The air considerably colder today but the sun shone all day—William worked at "The Leech Gatherer" almost incessantly from morning till tea-time. I copied "The Leech-Gatherer" and other poems for Coleridge—I was oppressed and sick at heart for he wearied himself to death. After tea he wrote two stanzas in the manner of Thomson's *Castle of Indolence*[3]—and was tired out. Bad news of Coleridge.

Monday May 10th

A fine clear morning but coldish—William is still at work though it is past ten o'clock—he will be tired out I am sure—My heart fails in me—he worked a little at odd things, but after dinner he gave over—an affecting letter from Mary H. We sate in the orchard before dinner. Old Joyce spent the day. I wrote to Mary H. Mrs. Jameson and Miss Simpson called just when William was going to bed at eight o'clock. I wrote to Coleridge, sent off reviews and poems, went to bed at twelve o'clock. William did not sleep till three o'clock.

Tuesday May 11th

A cool air. William finished the stanzas[4] about C and himself—he did not go out today. Miss. Simpson came in to tea which was lucky enough for it interrupted his labours. I walked with her to Rydale—the evening cool—the moon only now and then to be seen—the lake purple as we went—primroses still in abundance. William did not meet me, he completely finished his poems. I finished Derwent's frocks. We went to bed at twelve o'clock. Wm pretty well he looked very well, he complains that he gets cold in his chest.

1. By Shakespeare.   2. From an anonymous poem, published in the March 1802 *Monthly Review*, that imagines the seventeenth-century poet Abraham Cowley on an American plantation.   3. A poem in Spenserian stanzas (1748) by the Scottish poet James Thomson (1700–1748).   4. William wrote them the manner of *The Castle of Indolence*.

Wednesday 12th

A sunshiny but coldish morning—we walked into Easedale and returned by George Rownson's and the lane. We brought home heckberry blossom, crab blossom—the anemone nemorosa—marsh marygold—speedwell, that beautiful blue one the colour of the blue-stone or glass used in jewellery, with its beautiful pearl-like chives—anemones are in abundance and still the dear dear primroses violets in beds, pansies in abundance, and the little celandine. I pulled a branch of the taller celandine. Butterflies of all colours—I often see some small ones of a pale purple lilac or emperor's eye colour[5] something of the colour of that large geranium which grows by the lake side. Wm observed the beauty of Geordy Green's house. We see it from our orchard. Wm pulled ivy with beautiful berries—I put it over the chimney piece—sate in the orchard the hour before dinner, coldish. We have now dined. My head aches—William is sleeping in the window. In the evening we were sitting at the table, writing, when we were rouzed by Coleridge's voice below—he had walked, looked palish but was not much tired. We sate up till one o'clock all together. Then William went to bed and I sate with C in the sitting room (where he slept) till quarter past two o'clock. Wrote to MH.

13th May Thursday 1802

The day was very cold, with snow showers. Coleridge had intended going in the morning to Keswick but the cold and showers hindered him. We went with him after tea as far as the plantations by the roadside descending to Wytheburn—he did not look very well when we parted from him.—We sate an hour at Mr. Simpson's.

Friday May 14th 1802

A very cold morning—hail and snow showers all day. We went to Brothers' Wood, intending to get plants and to go along the shore of the lake to the foot. We did go a part of the way, but there was no pleasure in stepping along that difficult sauntering road in this ungenial weather. We turned again and walked backwards and forwards in Brothers' Wood. William teased himself with seeking an epithet for the cuckow. I sate a while upon my last summer's seat, the mossy stone—William's unemployed beside me, and the space between where Coleridge has so often lain. The oak trees are just putting forth yellow knots of leaves. The ashes with their flowers passing away and leaves coming out. The blue hyacinth is not quite full blown—gowans[6] are coming out—marsh marygolds in full glory—the little star plant a star without a flower. We took home a great load of gowans and planted them in the cold about the orchard. After dinner I worked[7] bread then came and mended stockings beside William. He fell asleep. After tea I walked to Rydale for letters. It was a strange night. The hills were covered over with a slight covering of hail or snow, just so as to give them a hoary winter look with the black rocks—The woods looked miserable, the coppices green as grass which looked quite unnatural and they seemed half shrivelled up as if

5. I.e., the color of the purple emperor butterfly.   6. Daisylike field flowers.   7. Kneaded.

they shrunk from the air. O thought I! what a beautiful thing God has made winter to be by stripping the trees and letting us see their shapes and forms. What a freedom does it seem to give to the storms! There were several new flowers out but I had no pleasure in looking at them—I walked as fast as I could back again with my letter from S. H. which I skimmed over at Tommy Fleming's. Met Wm at the top of White Moss. We walked a little beyond Olliff's—near ten when we came in. Wm and Molly had dug the ground and planted potatoes in my absence. We wrote to Coleridge—sent off a letter to Annette,[8] bread and frocks to the C's—Went to bed at half past eleven, William very nervous—after he was in bed haunted with altering "The Rainbow."[9]

Saturday Morning [15th]

It is now quarter past ten and he is not up. Miss Simpson called when I was in bed—I have been in the garden. It looks fresh and neat in spite of the frost. Molly tells me they had thick ice on a jug at their door last night.

Saturday 15th

A very cold and cheerless morning. I sate mending stockings all the morning. I read in Shakespeare. William lay very late because he slept till last night. It snowed this morning just like Christmas. We had a melancholy letter from Coleridge just at bed-time—. It distressed me very much and I resolved upon going to Keswick[1] the next day.

[The following is written on the blotting-paper opposite this date:]

S T Coleridge
Dorothy Wordsworth   William Wordsworth
Mary Hutchinson   Sara Hutchinson
William   Coleridge   Mary
Dorothy   Sara
16th May
1802
John Wordsworth[2]

Sunday 16th

William was at work all the morning. I did not go to Keswick. A sunny cold frosty day a snow-shower at night. We were a good while in the orchard in the morning.

Monday 17th May

William was not well—he went with me to Wytheburn Water. He left me in a post chaise. Hail showers, snow and cold attacked me. The people were

8. Annette Vallon (1766–1841), a Frenchwoman from Blois, who had borne William an illegitimate daughter after his visit to France in 1791–92.   9. Probably *My heart leaps up*, composed March 26, 1802.   1. Where Coleridge lived.   2. Dorothy and William's brother (1772–1805).

graving peats[3] under Nadel Fell.—A lark and thrush singing near Coleridge's house—Barcrofts[4] there. A letter from MH.

Tuesday 18th May

Terribly cold. Coleridge not well. Froude called, Wilkinsons called, I not well. C and I walked in the evening in the Garden warmer in the evening wrote to M and S.[5]

Wednesday 19th May 1802

A grey morning—not quite so cold. C and I set off at half past nine o'clock. Met William, near the six mile stone. We sate down by the road side, and then went to Wytheburn Water. Longed to be at the island, sate in the sun, Coleridge's bowels bad, mine also. We drank tea at John Stanley's—the evening cold and clear, a glorious light on Skiddaw. I was tired—brought a cloak down from Mr. Simpsons. Packed up books for Coleridge then got supper and went to bed.

Thursday 20th May

A frosty clear morning. I lay in bed late—William got to work. I was somewhat tired. We sate in the orchard sheltered all the morning. In the evening there was a fine rain. We received a letter from Coleridge, telling us that he wished us not to go to Keswick.

Friday 21st May

A very warm gentle morning—a little rain. Wm wrote two sonnets on Buonaparte after I had read Milton's sonnets to him. In the evening he went with Mr. Simpson with Borwick's boat to gather ling[6] in Bainriggs. I planted about the well—was much heated and I think I caught cold.

Saturday 22nd May

A very hot morning, a hot wind as if coming from a sand desert. We met Coleridge, he was sitting under Sara's rock when we reached him—he turned with us—we sate a long time under the wall of a sheep-fold, had some interesting melancholy talk about his private affairs. We drank tea at a farm house. The woman was very kind. There was a woman with three children travelling from Workington to Manchester. The woman served them liberally. Afterwards she said that she never suffered any to go away without a trifle "sec as we have." The woman at whose house we drank tea the last time was rich and senseless—she said "she never served any but their own poor"—C came home with us. We sate some time in the orchard. Then they came in to supper—mutton chops and potatoes. Letters from S & MH.

---

3. Carving peat moss for use as fuel.   4. The Barcroft family lived in Keswick.   5. Mary and Sara Hutchinson.   6. Heather.

Sunday [23rd]

I sate with C in the orchard all the morning. William was very nervous. I was ill in the afternoon, took laudanum. We walked in Bainriggs after tea, saw the juniper—umbrella shaped.—C went to S & M Points,[7] joined us on White Moss.

Monday 24th May 1802

A very hot morning. We were ready to go off with Coleridge, but foolishly sauntered and Miss Taylor and Miss Stanley called. William and Coleridge and I went afterwards to the top of the Rays. I was ill and left them, lay down at Mrs. Simpsons. I had sent off a letter to Mary by C. I wrote again and to C, then went to bed. William slept not till five o'clock.

Tuesday 25th

Very hot—I went to bed after dinner—We walked in the evening. Papers and short note from C—again no sleep for Wm.

Wednesday 26th

I was very unwell—went to bed again after dinner. We walked a long time backwards and forwards between Johns Grove and the lane upon the turf—a beautiful night, not cloudless, it has never been so since May day.

Thursday 27th

I was in bed all day—very ill. William wrote to Rd, Cʳ. and Cook.[8] Wm went after tea into the orchard. I slept in his bed—he slept downstairs. He slept better than before.

Friday 28th

I was much better than yesterday, though poorly. Wm tired himself with hammering at a passage. I was out of spirits. After dinner he was better and I grew better. We sate in the orchard. The sky cloudy, the air sweet and cool. The young bullfinches in their party coloured[9] raiment bustle about among the blossoms and poize themselves like wire dancers or tumblers, shaking the twigs and dashing off the blossoms. There is yet one primrose in the orchard—the stitchwort is fading—the wild columbines are coming into beauty—the vetches are in abundance blossoming and seeding. That pretty little waxy looking dial-like yellow flower, the speedwell, and some others whose names I do not yet know. The wild columbines are coming into beauty—some of the gowans fading. In the garden we have lilies and many other flowers. The scarlet beans are up in crowds. It is now between eight and nine o'clock. It has rained sweetly for two hours and a half—the air is

7. Rocks that they had named for Mary and Sara Hutchinson.   8. Their brothers Richard (the eldest, 1768–1816), a lawyer, and Christopher (1774–1846), a clergyman. Richard Cooke was Richard Wordsworth's legal associate.   9. Or particolored; showing different colors.

very mild. The heckberry blossoms are dropping off fast, almost gone—barberries are in beauty—snowballs coming forward—May roses blossoming.

Saturday 29th

I was much better. I made bread and a wee rhubarb tart and batter pudding for William. We sate in the orchard after dinner William finished his poem on Going for Mary. I wrote it out—I wrote to Mary H, having received a letter from her in the evening. A sweet day. We nailed up the honeysuckles, and hoed the scarlet beans.

Sunday 30th May 1802

I wrote to Mrs. Clarkson. It was a clear but cold day. The Simpsons called in the evening. I had been obliged to go to bed before tea and was unwell all day. Gooseberries a present from Peggy Hodgson. I wrote to my Aunt Cookson.

Monday 31st

I was much better. We sate out all the day. Mary Jameson dined. I wrote out the poem on "Our Departure" which he seemed to have finished. In the evening Miss Simpson brought us a letter from MH and a complimentary and critical letter to W from John Wilson of Glasgow post paid.[1] I went a little way with Miss S. My tooth broke today. They will soon be gone. Let that pass. I shall be beloved—I want no more.

Tuesday [1st]

A very sweet day, but a sad want of rain. We went into the orchard before dinner after I had written to MH. Then on to Mr. Olliff's intakes—we found some torn birds' nests. The columbine was growing upon the rocks, here and there a solitary plant—sheltered and shaded by the tufts and bowers of trees. It is a graceful slender creature, a female seeking retirement and growing freest and most graceful where it is most alone. I observed that the more shaded plants were always the tallest—a short note and gooseberries from Coleridge.

Wednesday 2nd June 1802

In the morning we observed that the scarlet beans were drooping in the leaves in great numbers owing, we guess to an insect. We sate a while in the orchard—then we went to the old carpenter's about the hurdles. Yesterday an old man called, a grey-headed man, above seventy years of age; he said he had been a soldier, that his wife and children had died in Jamaica. He had a beggar's wallet over his shoulders, a coat of shreds and patches altogether of a drab colour—he was tall and though his body was bent he had the look of one used to have been upright. I talked a while to him, and then

---

1. It was customary for the recipients of letters to pay the postage.

gave him a piece of cold bacon and a penny—said he "You're a fine woman!" I could not help smiling. I suppose he meant "You're a kind woman!" Afterwards a woman called travelling to Glasgow. After dinner William was very unwell. We went into Frank's field, crawled up the little glen and planned a seat, then went to Mr. Olliff's Hollins and sate there—found a beautiful shell-like purple fungus in Frank's field. After tea we walked to Butterlip How and backwards and forwards there. All the young oak tree leaves are dry as powder. A cold south wind portending rain. After we came in we sate in deep silence at the window—I on a chair and William with his hand on my shoulder. We were deep in silence and love, a blessed hour. We drew to the fire before bed-time and ate some broth for our suppers. I ought to have said that on Tuesday evening, namely June 1st, we walked upon the turf near John's Grove. It was a lovely night. The clouds of the western sky reflected a saffron light upon the upper end of the lake—all was still—We went to look at Rydale. There was an alpine fire-like red upon the tops of the mountains. This was gone when we came in view of the lake. But we saw the lake in a new and most beautiful point of view between two little rocks, and behind a small ridge that had concealed it from us.—This White Moss a place made for all kinds of beautiful works of art and nature, woods and valleys, fairy valleys and fairy tairns,[2] miniature mountains, alps above alps. Little John Dawson[3] came past us from the woods with a huge stick over his shoulder.

Thursday 3rd June 1802

A very fine rain. I lay in bed till ten o'clock. William much better than yesterday—We walked into Easedale, sheltered in a cow-house. Came home wet—the cuckow sang and we watched the little birds as we sate at the door of the cow-house—the oak copses are brown as in autumn, with the late frosts—scattered over with green trees, birches or hazels—the ashes are coming into full leaf—some of them injured. We came home quite wet. We have been reading the Life and some of the writings of poor Logan[4] since dinner. "And everlasting Longings for the lost." It is an affecting line. There are many affecting lines and passages in his poems. William is now sleeping—with the window open, lying on the window seat. The thrush is singing. There are I do believe a thousand buds on the honeysuckle tree, all small and far from blowing[5] save one that is retired behind the twigs close to the wall and as snug as a bird's nest. John's rose tree is very beautiful blended with the honeysuckle.

On Tuesday evening when we were among the rocks we saw in the woods what seemed to be a man, resting or looking about him. He had a piece of wood near him. William was on before me when we returned, and as I was going up to him, I found that this supposed man was John Dawson. I spoke to him and I suppose he thought I asked him what my brother had said to him before, for he replied, "*William* asks me how my head is"—Poor fellow!—he says it is worse and worse and he walks as if he were afraid of putting his body in motion.

---

2. Or tarns, pools. 3. A three-year-old child. 4. John Logan (1748–1788), a poet whose life William and Dorothy read in *The Works of the British Poets with Prefaces, Biographical and Critical* (1795), ed. Robert Anderson. 5. Blossoming.

Yesterday morning William walked as far as the Swan with Aggy Fisher. She was going to attend upon Goan's dying infant. She said "There are many heavier crosses than the death of an infant," and went on "There was a woman in this vale who buried four grown-up children in one year, and I have heard her say when many years were gone by that she had more pleasure in thinking of these four than of her living children, for as children get up and have families of their own their duty to their parents *'wears out and weakens.'* She could trip lightly by the graves of those who died when they were young—with a light step, as she went to church on a Sunday."

Thursday June 3rd

We walked while dinner was getting ready up into Mr. King's Hollins. I was weak and made my way down alone, for Wm took a difficult way. After dinner we walked upon the turf path—a showery afternoon. A very affecting letter came from MH while I was sitting in the window reading Milton's "Pense-roso"[6] to William. I answered this letter before I went to bed.

Friday June 4th

It was a very sweet morning, there had been much rain in the night. William had slept miserably—but knowing this I lay in bed while he got some sleep but was much disordered, he shaved himself then we went into the orchard— dined late. In the evening we walked on our favorite path. Then we came in and sate in the orchard. The evening was dark and warm—a tranquil night—I left William in the orchard. I read "Mother Hubbard's Tale"[7] before I went to bed.

Saturday 5th

A fine showery morning. I made both pies and bread, but we first walked into Easedale, and sate under the oak trees upon the mossy stones. There were one or two slight showers. The gowans were flourishing along the banks of the stream. The strawberry flower (geum)[8] hanging over the brook—all things soft and green.—In the afternoon William sate in the orchard. I went there, was tired and fell asleep. Mr. Simpson drank tea, Mrs. Smith called with her daughter. We walked late in the evening upon our path. We began the letter to John Wilson.

Sunday 6th June 1802

A showery morning. We were writing the letter to John Wilson when Ellen came—Molly at Goan's child's funeral. After dinner I walked into John Fisher's intake with Ellen. She brought us letters from Coleridge, Mrs. Clark- son and Sara Hutchinson. William went out in the evening and sate in the orchard, it was a showery day. In the evening there was one of the heaviest showers I ever remember.

---

6. *Il Penseroso* (1645), by John Milton.   7. *Prosopopoeia: or Mother Hubbard's Tale*, by Edmund Spenser (1591).   8. A small rosaceous plant.

Monday June 7th

I wrote to Mary H. this morning, sent the C Indolence poem. Copied the letter to John Wilson, and wrote to my brother Richard and Mrs. Coleridge. In the evening I walked with Ellen to Butterlip How and to George Mackareth's for the horse—it was a very sweet evening—there was the cuckow and the little birds—the copses still injured, but the trees in general looked most soft and beautiful in tufts. William was walking when we came in—he had slept miserably for two nights past so we all went to bed soon. I went with Ellen in the morning to Rydale Falls. Letters from Annette, Mary H and Cook.

Tuesday June 8th

Ellen and I rode to Windermere. We had a fine sunny day, neither hot nor cold. I mounted the horse at the quarry—we had no difficulties or delays but at the gates. I was enchanted with some of the views. From the High Ray the view is very delightful, rich and festive, water and wood, houses, groves, hedgerows, green fields, and mountains—white houses large and small—We passed two or three nice looking statesmen's houses. Mr. Curwen's shrubberies looked pitiful enough under the native trees. We put up our horses, ate our dinner by the water-side and walked up to the station. Then we went to the island, walked round it, and crossed the lake with our horse in the ferry. The shrubs have been cut away in some parts of the island. I observed to the boatman that I did not think it improved—he replied—"We think it is for one could hardly see the house before." It seems to me to be, however, no better than it was. They have made no natural glades, it is merely a lawn with a few miserable young trees standing as if they were half starved. There are no sheep no cattle upon these lawns. It is neither one thing or another—neither *natural* nor wholly cultivated and artificial which it was before, and that great house! Mercy upon us! If it *could* be concealed it would be well for all who are pained to see the pleasantest of earthly spots deformed by man. But it *cannot* be covered. Even the tallest of our old oak trees would not reach to the top of it. When we went into the boat there were two men standing at the landing place. One seemed to be about sixty, a man with a jolly red face—he looked as if he might have lived many years in Mr. Curwen's house. He wore a blue jacket and trowsers, as the people who live close by Windermere particularly at the places of chief resort in affectation, I suppose. He looked significantly at our boatman just as we were rowing off and said "Thomas mind you take off the directions off that cask. You know what I mean. It will serve as a blind for them, *you* know. It was a blind business both for you and the coachman and me and all of us. Mind you take off the directions—A wink's as good as a nod with some folks"—and then he turned round looking at his companion with such an air of self-satisfaction and deep insight into unknown things!—I could hardly help laughing outright at him. The laburnums blossom freely at the island and in the shrubberies on the shore—they are blighted everywhere else. Roses of various sorts were out. The brooms were in full glory everywhere, "veins of gold"[9] among the copses. The hawthorns in the valley fading away—beautiful

9. From William's poem *To Joanna* (1800).

upon the hills. We reached home at three o'clock. After tea William went out and walked and wrote that poem,[1]

"The sun has long been set" etc.—

He first went up to G Mackareths with the horse. Afterwards he walked on our own path and wrote the lines, he called me into the orchard and there repeated them to me—he then stayed there till eleven o'clock.

Wednesday June 9th

Wm slept ill. A soaking all-day rain. We should have gone to Mr. Simpson's to tea but we walked up after tea. Lloyds called. The hawthorns on the mountain sides like orchards in blossom. Brought rhubarb down. It rained hard. Ambleside Fair. I wrote to Christopher and MH.

Thursday June 10th

I wrote to Mrs. Clarkson and Luff—went with Ellen to Rydale. Coleridge came in with a sack-full of books etc. and a branch of mountain ash. He had been attacked by a cow—he came over by Grisdale—a furious wind. Mr. Simpson drank tea. William very poorly—we went to bed latish. I slept in sitting room.

Friday June 11th

A wet day. William had slept very ill. Wm and C walked out—I went to bed after dinner not well. I was tired with making beds cooking etc.—Molly being very ill.

Saturday June 12th

A rainy morning. C set off before dinner. We went with him to the Rays but it rained so we went no further—sheltered under a wall—He would be sadly wet for a furious shower came on just when we parted.—We got no dinner, but gooseberry pie to our tea. I baked both pies and bread, and walked with William first on our own path but it was too wet there, next over the rocks to the road, and backward and forward, and last of all up to Mr. King's. Miss Simpson and Robert had called. Letters from Sara and Annette.

Sunday June 13th

A fine morning. Sunshiny and bright, but with rainy clouds. William had slept better—but not well—he has been altering the poem to Mary this morning, he is now washing his feet. I wrote out poems for our journey and I wrote a letter to my Uncle Cookson. Mr. Simpson came when we were in the orchard in the morning and brought us a beautiful drawing which he had done. In the evening we walked first on our own path. There we walked a good while—It was a silent night. The stars were out by ones and twos but no cuckow, no little birds, the air was not warm, and we have observed that

---

1. The poem was published in 1807, with the first line as its title.

since Tuesday 8th when William wrote, "The sun has long been set," that we have had no birds singing after the evening is fairly set in. We walked to our new view of Rydale, but it put on a sullen face. There was an owl hooting in Bainriggs. Its first halloo was so like a human shout that I was surprized when it made its second call, tremulous and lengthened out, to find that the shout had come from an owl. The full moon (not quite full) was among a company of steady island clouds, and the sky bluer about it than the natural sky blue. William observed that the full moon above a dark fir grove is a fine image of the descent of a superior being. There was a shower which drove us into John's grove before we had quitted our favorite path—we walked upon John's path before we went to view Rydale. We went to bed immediately on our return home.

Monday June 14th

I was very unwell—went to bed before I drank my tea—was sick and afterwards almost asleep when Wm brought me a letter from Mary which he read to me sitting by the bed-side—Wm wrote to Mary and Sara about "The Leech Gatherer." I wrote to both of them in one and to Annette, to Coleridge also. I was better after tea.—I walked with Wm—when I had put up my parcel on our own path—we were driven away by the horses that go on the commons. Then we went to look at Rydale, walked a little in the fir grove, went again to the top of the hill and came home—a mild and sweet night—Wm stayed behind me. I threw him the cloak out of the window, the moon overcast, he sate a few minutes in the orchard, came in sleepy, and hurried to bed—I carried him his bread and butter.

Tuesday 15th

A sweet grey mild morning the birds sing soft and low—William has not slept all night. It wants only ten minutes of ten and he is in bed yet. After William rose we went and sate in the orchard till dinner time. We walked a long time in the evening upon our favorite path—the owls hooted, the night-hawk sang to itself incessantly, but there were no little birds, no thrushes. I left William writing a few lines about the night-hawk and other images of the evening, and went to seek for letters—none were come.—We walked backwards and forwards a little, after I returned to William, and then up as far as Mr. King's. Came in. There was a basket of lettuces, a letter from MH about the delay of mine and telling of one she had sent by the other post, one from Wade and one from Sara to C—William did not read them—MH growing fat.

Wednesday 16th

We walked towards Rydale for letters—met Frank Baty with the expected one from Mary. We went up into Rydale woods and read it there, we sate near an old wall which fenced a hazel grove, which Wm said was exactly like the filbert grove at Middleham. It is a beautiful spot, a sloping or rather steep piece of ground, with hazels growing "tall and erect,"[2] in clumps at distances almost seeming regular as if they had been planted. We returned to dinner.

2. From William's poem *Nutting* (1800).

I wrote to Mary after dinner while Wm sate in the orchard. Old Mr. Simpson drank tea with us. When Mr. S was gone I read my letter to William, speaking to Mary about having a cat. I spoke of the little birds keeping us company— and William told me that that very morning a bird had perched upon his leg—he had been lying very still and had watched this little creature, it had come under the bench where he was sitting and then flew up to his leg, he thoughtlessly stirred himself to look further at it and it flew onto the apple tree above him. It was a little young creature, that had just left its nest, equally unacquainted with man and unaccustomed to struggle against storms and winds. While it was upon the apple tree the wind blew about the stiff boughs and the bird seemed bemazed and not strong enough to strive with it. The swallows come to the sitting-room window as if wishing to build but I am afraid they will not have courage for it, but I believe they will build at my room window. They twitter and make a bustle and a little chearful song hanging against the panes of glass, with their soft white bellies close to the glass, and their forked fish-like tails. They swim round and round and again they come.—It was a sweet evening. We first walked to the top of the hill to look at Rydale and then to Butterlip How—I do not now see the brownness that was in the coppices. The lower hawthorn blossoms passed away, those on the hills are a faint white. The wild guelder rose is coming out, and the wild roses. I have seen no honeysuckles yet except our own one nestling and a tree of the yellow kind at Mrs. Townley's the day I went with Ellen to Windermere. Foxgloves are now frequent, the first I saw was that day with Ellen, and the first ripe strawberries—a letter from Coleridge. I read the first Canto of *The Fairy Queen*[3] to William. William went to bed immediately.

Thursday 17th

William had slept well. I took castor oil and lay in bed till twelve o'clock. William injured himself with working a little.—When I got up we sate in the orchard, a sweet mild day. Miss Hudson called. I went with her to the top of the hill. When I came home I found William at work, attempting to alter a stanza in the poem on our going for Mary which I convinced him did not need altering—We sate in the house after dinner. In the evening walked on our favorite path, a short letter from Coleridge. William added a little to the ode[4] he is writing.

Friday June 18th

When we were sitting after breakfast, William about to shave, Luff came in. It was a sweet morning. He had rode over the fells—he brought news about Lord Lowther's intention to pay all debts[5] etc. and a letter from Mr. Clarkson. He saw our garden, was astonished at the scarlet beans etc. When he was gone he wrote to Coleridge, MH, and my brother Richard about the affair. Wm determined to go to Eusemere on Monday. In the afternoon we walked to Rydale with our letters, found no letters there. A sweet evening, I had a

---

3. *The Faerie Queene* (1590, 1596), by Edmund Spenser. 4. *Ode: Intimations of Immortality*, completed in 1804. 5. Sir James Lowther, earl of Lonsdale (1736–1802), had owed forty-five hundred pounds to the Wordsworths' father for legal services. A lawsuit to recover the money had been unsuccessful. When his cousin Sir William Lowther (1757–1844) succeeded him, he agreed to pay his predecessor's debts. The Wordsworths received eighty-five hundred pounds (including interest) in 1804.

woful headache and was ill in stomach from agitation of mind—went to bed at nine o'clock but did not sleep till late.

Saturday 19th

The swallows were very busy under my window this morning—I slept pretty well, but William has got no sleep. It is after eleven and he is still in bed— a fine morning—Coleridge when he was last here, told us that for many years there being no Quaker meeting held at Keswick, a single old Quaker woman used to go regularly alone every Sunday, to attend the meeting-house and there used to sit and perform her worship, alone, in that beautiful place among those fir-trees, in that spacious vale, under the great mountain Skid-daw!!! Poor old Willy—we never pass by his grave close to the churchyard gate without thinking of him and having his figure brought back to our minds. He formerly was an ostler at Hawkshead, having spent a little estate. In his old age he was boarded or as they say *let* by the parish. A boy of the house that hired him was riding one morning pretty briskly beside John Fisher's, "Hallo! has aught particular happened," said John to the boy "Nay naught at aw nobbut auld Willy's dead." He was going to order the passing bell to be told.[6]—On Thursday morning Miss Hudson of Workington called. She said "O! I love flowers! I sow flowers in the parks several miles from home and my mother and I visit them and watch them how they grow." This may show that botanists may be often deceived when they find rare flowers growing far from houses. This was a very ordinary young woman, such as in any town in the north of England one may find a score. I sate up a while after William— he then called me down to him. (I was writing to Mary H.) I read Churchill's *Rosciad*[7] returned again to my writing and did not go to bed till he called to me. The shutters were closed, but I heard the birds singing. There was our own thrush shouting with an impatient shout—so it sounded to me. The morning was still, the twittering of the little birds was very gloomy. The owls had hooted a quarter of an hour before. Now the cocks were crowing. It was near daylight. I put out my candle and went to bed. In a little time I thought I heard William snoring, so I composed myself to sleep—Charles Lloyd called—"Smiling at my sweet Brother."[8]

Sunday 20th

He had slept better than I could have expected but he was far from well all day; we were in the orchard a great part of the morning. After tea we walked upon our own path for a long time. We talked sweetly together about the disposal of our riches. We lay upon the sloping turf. Earth and sky were so lovely that they melted our very hearts. The sky to the north was of a chas-tened yet rich yellow fading into pale blue and streaked and scattered over with steady islands of purple melting away into shades of pink. It made my heart almost feel like a vision to me. We afterwards took our cloaks and sate in the orchard. Mr. and Miss Simpson called. We told them of our expected good fortune. We were astonished and somewhat hurt to see how coldly Mr. Simpson received it—Miss S seemed very glad. We went into the house when they left us, and Wm went to bed. I sate up about an hour, he then called me to talk to him—he could not fall asleep. I wrote to Montagu.

6. Tolled.　　7. *The Rosciad* (1761), a satiric poem by Charles Churchill.　　8. Quotation unidentified.

SAMUEL TAYLOR COLERIDGE
1772–1834

For Samuel Taylor Coleridge, the mystery of the imagination provided the most compelling and perplexing of subjects. In prose and in verse, by reasoned discussion and by poetic symbol making, he explored the subject, affirming imagination's virtually divine status as a creative power and suggesting his own emotional dependence on it.

Son of an English clergyman, Coleridge attended Jesus College, Cambridge, from 1791 to 1793. In 1795, he married Sara Fricker; the same year he met Wordsworth and began the fruitful collaboration leading to *Lyrical Ballads*. In 1810, his period of greatest poetic creativity already over, he separated from his wife; subsequently, he became increasingly addicted to opium. Known for his brilliant conversation, he spent much time talking and lecturing as well as writing.

The most intellectual of the English Romantics, Coleridge, after an early trip to Germany, was strongly influenced by the German Idealist philosophers, notably Immanuel Kant and Johann Fichte. His best-known critical work, *Biographia Literaria* (1817), in which he develops most fully and explicitly his theory of imagination, contains many borrowings from German sources. His output of poetry was relatively small. In some of his most important poems (such as *The Rime of the Ancient Mariner*), he tries to incorporate the supernatural into essentially psychological narrative. He was also much interested in the native English ballad tradition, which on occasion influenced his choice of stanzaic form and meter.

Like other Romantic poets, Coleridge was fascinated by the aeolian harp (it figures in the first stanza of *Dejection: An Ode*), an instrument that makes music without human intervention, by the action of wind on its strings. *Kubla Khan*, a poem recording (according to Coleridge's prefatory note) what the writer remembered of a dream stimulated by opium, makes up a kind of poetic equivalent for the aeolian harp: a work for which its author disclaims conscious responsibility. It simply came to his mind, he says, to be broken off when he was interrupted by a person from Porlock. The poem, therefore, makes no claim to rational coherence, but it has always invited exegesis. Evoking a lush and splendid setting, it yet contains ominous suggestions: the ruler who presides over the magnificence of landscape ("deep romantic chasm," river, caves, incense-bearing trees) and building, hears "Ancestral voices prophesying war." The theme of mingled beauty and danger intensifies as the poem focuses on the figure of a singer, a "damsel with a dulcimer," whose power the poem's speaker wishes to "revive" within himself. Then he could re-create the vision of Kubla Khan's domain, and people would respond to him with "holy dread," recognizing his association with the magic, the sacred, the dangerous, the unpredictable and uncontrollable power of imagination. Thus the singer becomes an image for the poet, and we are reminded that the uncannily evocative scene of the poem's opening section itself issues from the poetic imagination, which creates for its possessor and for his readers a new version of reality, closer to the heart's desire than our workaday world, but not without danger—including the danger of becoming lost in it.

In *Dejection: An Ode*, Coleridge concerns himself with the same theme in more extended personal terms. Paradoxically, this poem—mourning his loss of creative imagination—demonstrates the active presence of that quality whose absence it deplores, as it creates out of the dullness of depression a rich emotional and psychological texture. Like Wordsworth's *Ode on Intimations of Immortality*, *Dejection* confronts the speaker's sense of diminishing power. He has lost the "joy" that he considers associated with the spontaneity of youth. More emphatically than Wordsworth, Coleridge attributes even the beauty of nature to the human imagination:

O Lady! we receive but what we give,
And in our life alone does Nature live: . . .
    Ah! from the soul itself must issue forth
A light, a glory, a fair luminous cloud
    Enveloping the Earth—

One cannot hope for inspiration from nature, cannot expect to receive from without that reassurance and pleasure whose sources are within. As the poem develops, it demonstrates the operation of imagination on the external world by hearing meaning—meaning related to human action and suffering—in the sound of wind and storm. The imaginative activity provides its own solace; although the speaker never ceases to assert his dejection, he, like Wordsworth, is enabled finally to displace his vision of joy, harmony, and peace onto the figure of a woman who will embody all that he now feels impossible for himself.

In its emphasis on the "shaping spirit of Imagination," that presiding power of Romantic poetry, *Dejection* makes a strong statement of Coleridge's central concern. By its capacity to evoke emotional complexity—longing for what is lost, resentment at its passing, struggle to repossess what is mourned—and to demonstrate the patterns in which the mind deals with its own problems, it exemplifies the subtlety and the force of his poetic achievement.

There are two important recent biographies: R. Holmes, *Coleridge: Early Visions* (1989), the first part of a projected two-part biography; and R. Ashton, *The Life of Samuel Taylor Coleridge: A Critical Biography* (1996). J. L. Lowes, *The Road to Xanadu* (1927), provides a fascinating study of the sources of *Kubla Khan*. For criticism, see also J. Cornwell, *Coleridge* (1973); J. Beer, *Coleridge's Poetic Intelligence* (1975); G. Davidson, *Coleridge's Career* (1990); and D. Suttana, ed., *New Approaches to Coleridge: Biographical and Critical Essays* (1981). Useful works that treat Coleridge in conjunction with Wordsworth are G. W. Ruoff, *Wordsworth and Coleridge* (1989), and P. Magnuson, *Coleridge and Wordsworth* (1988).

PRONOUNCING GLOSSARY

The following list uses common English syllables and stress accents to provide rough equivalents of selected words whose pronunciation may be unfamiliar to the general reader.

Aeolian: *ee-oh'-lee-an*   Xanadu: *zan'-a-doo*
Purchas: *pur'-chus*

Kubla Khan

Or, a Vision in a Dream. A Fragment

The following fragment is here published at the request of a poet of great and deserved celebrity [Lord Byron], and, as far as the Author's own opinions are concerned, rather as a psychological curiosity, than on the ground of any supposed *poetic* merits.

In the summer of the year 1797, the Author, then in ill health, had retired to a lonely farm-house between Porlock and Linton, on the Exmoor confines of Somerset and Devonshire.[1] In consequence of a slight indisposition, an anodyne had been prescribed, from the effects of which he fell asleep in his

1. A high moorland shared by the two southwestern counties in England.

chair at the moment that he was reading the following sentence, or words of the same substance, in "Purchas's Pilgrimage":[2] "Here the Khan Kubla commanded a palace to be built, and a stately garden thereunto. And thus ten miles of fertile ground were inclosed with a wall." The Author continued for about three hours in a profound sleep, at least of the external senses, during which time he has the most vivid confidence, that he could not have composed less than from two to three hundred lines; if that indeed can be called composition in which all the images rose up before him as *things*, with a parallel production of the correspondent expressions, without any sensation or consciousness of effort.[3] On awaking he appeared to himself to have a distinct recollection of the whole, and taking his pen, ink, and paper, instantly and eagerly wrote down the lines that are here preserved. At this moment he was unfortunately called out by a person on business from Porlock, and detained by him above an hour, and on his return to his room, found, to his no small surprise and mortification, that though he still retained some vague and dim recollection of the general purport of the vision, yet, with the exception of some eight or ten scattered lines and images, all the rest had passed away like the images on the surface of a stream into which a stone has been cast, but, alas! without the after restoration of the latter!

> Then all the charm
> Is broken—all that phantom-world so fair
> Vanishes, and a thousand circlets spread,
> And each mis-shape[s] the other. Stay awhile,
> Poor youth! who scarcely dar'st lift up thine eyes—
> The stream will soon renew its smoothness, soon
> The visions will return! And lo, he stays,
> And soon the fragments dim of lovely forms
> Come trembling back, unite, and now once more
> The pool becomes a mirror.[4]

Yet from the still surviving recollections in his mind, the Author has frequently purposed to finish for himself what had been originally, as it were, given to him. Σαμερον αδιον ασω:[5] but the to-morrow is yet to come. . . .

> In Xanadu did Kubla Khan[6]
> A stately pleasure-dome decree:
> Where Alph,[7] the sacred river, ran
> Through caverns measureless to man
>   Down to a sunless sea.   5
> So twice five miles of fertile ground
> With walls and towers were girdled round:

2. Samuel Purchas (1575?–1626) published *Purchas his Pilgrimage, or Relations of the World and the Religions observed in all Ages* in 1613. The passage in Purchas is slightly different: "In Xamdu did Cublai Can build a stately Palace, encompassing sixteene miles of plaine ground with a wall, wherein are fertile meddowes, pleasant Springs, delightfull Streames, and all sorts of beasts of chase and game, and in the middest thereof a sumptuous house of pleasure, which may be removed from place to place" (book 4, chap. 13).   3. Coleridge's statement that he dreamed the poem and wrote down what he could later remember verbatim has been queried, most recently by medical opinion. The belief that opium produces special dreams, or even any dreams at all, seems to lack confirmation.   4. From Coleridge's poem *The Picture; or, the Lover's Resolution*, lines 91–100.   5. From Theocritus's *Idylls* 1.145: "I'll sing a sweeter song tomorrow" (Greek).   6. Mongol emperor (1215?–1294), visited by Marco Polo.   7. J. L. Lowes, in *The Road to Xanadu* (1927), thinks that Coleridge may have had in mind the river Alpheus—linked with the Nile—mentioned by Virgil.

And there were gardens bright with sinuous rills,
Where blossomed many an incense-bearing tree;
And here were forests ancient as the hills,   10
Enfolding sunny spots of greenery.

But oh! that deep romantic chasm which slanted
Down the green hill athwart a cedarn cover!
A savage place! as holy and enchanted
As e'er beneath a waning moon was haunted   15
By woman wailing for her demon-lover!
And from this chasm, with ceaseless turmoil seething,
As if this earth in fast thick pants were breathing,
A mighty fountain momently was forced:
Amid whose swift half-intermitted burst   20
Huge fragments vaulted like rebounding hail,
Or chaffy grain beneath the thresher's flail:
And 'mid these dancing rocks at once and ever
It flung up momently the sacred river.
Five miles meandering with a mazy motion   25
Through wood and dale the sacred river ran,
Then reached the caverns measureless to man,
And sank in tumult to a lifeless ocean:
And 'mid this tumult Kubla heard from far
Ancestral voices prophesying war!   30
    The shadow of the dome of pleasure
        Floated midway on the waves;
    Where was heard the mingled measure
        From the fountain and the caves.
It was a miracle of rare device,   35
A sunny pleasure-dome with caves of ice!
    A damsel with a dulcimer
    In a vision once I saw:
    It was an Abyssinian maid,
    And on her dulcimer she played,   40
    Singing of Mount Abora.[8]
    Could I revive within me
    Her symphony and song,
    To such a deep delight 'twould win me,
That with music loud and long,   45
I would build that dome in air,
That sunny dome! those caves of ice!
And all who heard should see them there,
And all should cry, Beware! Beware!
His flashing eyes, his floating hair!   50
Weave a circle round him thrice,
And close your eyes with holy dread,
For he on honey-dew hath fed,
And drunk the milk of Paradise.

---

8. Lowes argues that this may have been "Mt. Amara," mentioned by Milton in *Paradise Lost* (4.28), or Amhara in Samuel Johnson's *Rasselas*.

Dejection: An Ode

Late, late yestreen I saw the new Moon,
With the old Moon in her arms;
And I fear, I fear, my Master dear!
We shall have a deadly storm.
                    Ballad of Sir Patrick Spence

I

Well! If the Bard was weather-wise, who made
    The grand old ballad of Sir Patrick Spence,
    This night, so tranquil now, will not go hence
Unroused by winds, that ply a busier trade
Than those which mould yon cloud in lazy flakes,   5
Or the dull sobbing draft, that moans and rakes
Upon the strings of this Aeolian lute,[1]
        Which better far were mute.
    For lo! the New-moon winter-bright!
    And overspread with phantom light,   10
    (With swimming phantom light o'erspread
    But rimmed and circled by a silver thread)
I see the old Moon in her lap, foretelling
    The coming-on of rain and squally blast.
And oh! that even now the gust were swelling,   15
    And the slant night-shower driving loud and fast!
Those sounds which oft have raised me, whilst they awed,
        And sent my soul abroad,
Might now perhaps their wonted impulse give,
Might startle this dull pain, and make it move and live!   20

II

A grief without a pang, void, dark, and drear,
    A stifled, drowsy, unimpassioned grief,
    Which finds no natural outlet, no relief,
        In word, or sigh, or tear—
O Lady! in this wan and heartless mood,   25
To other thoughts by yonder throstle[2] woo'd,
    All this long eve, so balmy and serene,
Have I been gazing on the western sky,
    And its peculiar tint of yellow green:
And still I gaze—and with how blank an eye!   30
And those thin clouds above, in flakes and bars,
That give away their motion to the stars;
Those stars, that glide behind them or between,
Now sparkling, now bedimmed, but always seen:
Yon crescent Moon, as fixed as if it grew   35
In its own cloudless, starless lake of blue;
I see them all so excellently fair,
I see, not feel, how beautiful they are!

1. A frame fitted with strings or wires that produce musical tones when the wind hits them. Named after Aeolus, god of the winds.   2. The song thrush.

III

My genial spirits³ fail;
   And what can these avail   40
To lift the smothering weight from off my breast?
     It were a vain endeavour,
     Though I should gaze forever
On that green light that lingers in the west:
I may not hope from outward forms to win   45
The passion and the life, whose fountains are within.

IV

O Lady! we receive but what we give,
And in our life alone does Nature live:
Ours is her wedding garment, ours her shroud!
   And would we aught behold of higher worth,   50
Than that inanimate cold world allowed
To the poor loveless ever-anxious crowd,
   Ah! from the soul itself must issue forth
A light, a glory, a fair luminous cloud
     Enveloping the Earth—   55
And from the soul itself must there be sent
   A sweet and potent voice, of its own birth,
Of all sweet sounds the life and element!

V

O pure of heart! thou need'st not ask of me
What this strong music in the soul may be!   60
What, and wherein it doth exist,
This light, this glory, this fair luminous mist,
This beautiful and beauty-making power.
   Joy, virtuous Lady! Joy that ne'er was given,
Save to the pure, and in their purest hour,   65
Life, and Life's effluence, cloud at once and shower,
Joy, Lady! is the spirit and the power,
Which wedding Nature to us gives in dower
   A new Earth and new Heaven,
Undreamt of by the sensual and the proud—   70
Joy is the sweet voice, Joy the luminous cloud—
     We in ourselves rejoice!
And thence flows all that charms or ear or sight,
   All melodies the echoes of that voice,
All colours a suffusion from that light.   75

VI

There was a time when, though my path was rough,
   This joy within me dallied with distress,
   And all misfortunes were but as the stuff

---

3. Generative spirits; creativity. This poem was written soon after Wordsworth had composed the first four
stanzas of the *Ode on Intimations of Immortality*, and the themes are similar.

Whence Fancy made me dreams of happiness:
For hope grew round me, like the twining vine,   80
And fruits, and foliage, not my own, seemed mine.
But now afflictions bow me down to earth:
Nor care I that they rob me of my mirth;
    But oh! each visitation[4]
Suspends what nature gave me at my birth,   85
    My shaping spirit of Imagination.[5]
For not to think of what I needs must feel,
    But to be still and patient, all I can;
And haply by abstruse research to steal
    From my own nature all the natural man—   90
    This was my sole resource, my only plan:
Till that which suits a part infects the whole,
And now is almost grown the habit of my soul.

VII

Hence, viper thoughts, that coil around my mind,
    Reality's dark dream!   95
I turn from you, and listen to the wind,
    Which long has raved unnoticed. What a scream
Of agony by torture lengthened out
That lute sent forth! Thou Wind that rav'st without,
    Bare crag, or mountain-tairn,[6] or blasted tree,   100
Or pine-grove whither woodman never clomb,
Or lonely house, long held the witches' home,
    Methinks were fitter instruments for thee,
Mad Lutanist![7] who in this month of showers,
Of dark-brown gardens, and of peeping flowers,   105
Mak'st Devils' yule[8] with worse than wintry song,
The blossoms, buds, and timorous leaves among.
    Thou Actor, perfect in all tragic sounds!
Thou mighty Poet, e'en to frenzy bold!
    What tell'st thou now about?   110
    'Tis of the rushing of an host in rout,
    With groans, of trampled men, with smarting wounds—
At once they groan with pain, and shudder with the cold!
But hush! there is a pause of deepest silence!
    And all that noise, as of a rushing crowd,   115
With groans, and tremulous shudderings—all is over—
    It tells another tale,[9] with sounds less deep and loud!
    A tale of less affright,
    And tempered with delight,
As Otway's self[1] had framed the tender lay,—   120
    'Tis of a little child

---

4. Of the *misfortunes* (line 78) and *afflictions* (line 82).   5. Coleridge made much of the distinction between *Fancy* (line 79) and *Imagination*. Fancy makes pleasant combinations of images; Imagination is a higher faculty of the mind that combines images in such a way that they create a higher reality, a poetic "truth" more valid than that which is perceived by the ordinary senses.   6. Or tarn; small mountain lake.   7. The storm wind in line 99.   8. Originally, a heathen feast.   9. The story of Wordsworth's *Lucy Gray*.   1. Originally, "William's," referring to Wordsworth. *As*: as if. Thomas Otway (1652–1685), a tragic dramatist, admired for his mastery of pathos.

Upon a lonesome wild,
Not far from home, but she hath lost her way:
And now moans low in bitter grief and fear,
And now screams loud, and hopes to make her mother hear.   125

VIII

'Tis midnight, but small thoughts have I of sleep.
Full seldom may my friend such vigils keep!
Visit her, gentle Sleep! with wings of healing,
  And may this storm be but a mountain birth,
May all the stars hang bright above her dwelling,   130
  Silent as though they watched the sleeping Earth!
    With light heart may she rise,
    Gay fancy, cheerful eyes,
  Joy lift her spirit, joy attune her voice;
To her may all things live, from pole to pole,   135
Their life the eddying of her living soul!
    O simple spirit, guided from above,
  Dear Lady! friend devoutest of my choice,
  Thus mayest thou ever, evermore rejoice.

PERCY BYSSHE SHELLEY
1792–1822

A longing for alternatives to things as they are dominates much of Shelley's poetry. Whether he writes of his own dejection, of the energizing force of the west wind, or of the political situation of England, he writes often from conviction that matters could and should be better.

Son of a country squire in Sussex, Shelley led a privileged early life, attending Eton and Oxford. He was, however, expelled from Oxford after a single year, for writing a work called *The Necessity of Atheism*: already he had begun to defy convention. He dramatized his defiance yet more forcefully in 1814, when, after three years of marriage (and two children) with Harriet Westbrook, he eloped with Mary Wollstonecraft Godwin, daughter of two advanced social thinkers. Harriet committed suicide; the lovers married and had several children. Shelley was on friendly terms with other important Romantic writers; in Italy, where he moved in 1818, he associated closely with Byron. He was drowned while sailing off the Italian coast.

Productive as a poet, Shelley mastered tones ranging from the satiric to the prophetic. His most important works include *Prometheus Unbound* (1820), a philosophic-visionary-revolutionary expansion of a classical theme; *Epipsychidon* (1821), a defense of free love; and the elegy *Adonais* (1821), for the death of Keats. He also wrote a verse play having to do with the incest of a father and daughter, *The Cenci* (1819).

At the end of his essay *A Defence of Poetry*, posthumously published in 1840, Shelley insists on poetry's necessary connection with the future. Poets, he says, are "the mirrors of the gigantic shadows which futurity casts upon the present . . . : the influence which is moved not but moves. Poets are the unacknowledged legislators of the World." His own lyrics corroborate such grandiose claims by insistently establishing images of the possible. The sonnet *England in 1819,* for example, after twelve lines of nouns and noun clauses about the political and social horrors of the current English situation, concludes that all these phenomena "Are graves from which a glorious Phantom may / Burst, to illumine our tempestuous day." The possibility—never the certainty—of good coming from evil always exists.

Like Coleridge, Shelley writes about his own dejection, interspersing penetrating images of natural beauty with detailed presentation of his painful psychic state. In the poem called *Stanzas Written in Dejection,* the speaker dreams of death as a kind of mild fulfillment, a reabsorption into nature. The ending of the poem, however, has less dismal implications. Finally, the speaker compares himself with the dying day as a presence in memory. Men do not love him, but would regret his passing; the day, which he has enjoyed, will linger "like joy in Memory." The comparison, which at first appears to sustain the mood of self-pity, also transcends that self-perpetuating emotion: it reminds the speaker of the capacity for enjoyment that he retains even in his bleakest mood. While he fancies his own easeful death, he still takes pleasure in the scene around him; that pleasure remains a lasting element in memory.

Ode to the West Wind makes a particularly emphatic statement of the good-from-evil theme. Images of violence and sinister power ("Thou, from whose unseen presence the leaves dead / Are driven, like ghosts from an enchanter fleeing") dominate the early part of the poem. The third section creates an atmosphere of luxurious beauty but ends with the depths of the sea growing suddenly "grey with fear" at the wind's advent. In the next section, however, the speaker places himself in relation with the natural force he has described, begging to be lifted, to "share /. The impulse of thy strength." Finally, in imagination, the poet becomes the "lyre" (in effect, Coleridge's aeolian harp) of the wind, now revealed as a force of inspiration and change, which enables him to function as "The trumpet of a prophecy!" *Defence of Poetry* describes poets as "the trumpets which sing to battle"; in *Ode to the West Wind,* Shelley suggests that they acquire such inspirational capacity by imaginative union with nature and, particularly, as in the west wind blowing away the remnants of the past year, with the forces of regeneration and reform.

E. Blunden, *Shelley: A Life Story* (1946), provides a useful biography. A critically oriented biography is P. Hodgart, *A Preface to Shelley* (1985). For criticism, see C. Baker, *Shelley's Major Poetry: The Fabric of a Vision* (1948); E. Wasserman, *Shelley* (1971); R. Holmes, *Shelley: The Pursuit* (1974); J. Hall, *The Transforming Image: A Study of Shelley's Major Poetry* (1980); S. M. Sperry, *Shelley's Major Verse* (1989); and M. O'Neill, *The Human Mind's Imaginings* (1989).

PRONOUNCING GLOSSARY

The following list uses common English syllables and stress accents to provide rough equivalents of selected words whose pronunciation may be unfamiliar to the general reader.

Baiæ: *by'-ee*　　　　　　　　Mænad: *mee'-nad*

Stanzas Written in Dejection— December 1818, Near Naples

The Sun is warm, the sky is clear,
The waves are dancing fast and bright,
Blue isles and snowy mountains wear
The purple noon's transparent might,

The breath of the moist earth is light   5
Around its unexpanded buds;
Like many a voice of one delight,
The winds, the birds, the Ocean-floods,
The City's voice, itself is soft like Solitude's.

I see the Deep's untrampled floor   10
With green and purple seaweeds strown;
I see the waves upon the shore
Like light dissolved in star-showers, thrown;
I sit upon the sands alone;
The lightning of the noontide Ocean   15
Is flashing round me, and a tone
Arises from its measured motion,
How sweet! did any heart now share in my emotion.

Alas, I have nor hope nor health
Nor peace within nor calm around,   20
Nor that content surpassing wealth
The sage in meditation found,
And walked with inward glory crowned;
Nor fame nor power nor love nor leisure—
Others I see whom these surround,   25
Smiling they live and call life pleasure:
To me that cup has been dealt in another measure.

Yet now despair itself is mild,
Even as the winds and waters are;
I could lie down like a tired child   30
And weep away the life of care
Which I have borne and yet must bear
Till Death like Sleep might steal on me,
And I might feel in the warm air
My cheek grow cold, and hear the Sea   35
Breathe o'er my dying brain its last monotony.

Some might lament that I were cold,
As I, when this sweet day is gone,
Which my lost heart, too soon grown old,
Insults with this untimely moan—   40
They might lament,—for I am one
Whom men love not, and yet regret;
Unlike this day, which, when the Sun
Shall on its stainless glory set,
Will linger though enjoyed, like joy in Memory yet.   45

England in 1819

An old, mad, blind, despised, and dying King;[1]
Princes,[2] the dregs of their dull race, who flow

1. George III (1738–1820).   2. The king's sons, including the prince regent, whose dissolute behavior gave rise to public scandals.

Through public scorn,—mud from a muddy spring;
Rulers who neither see nor feel nor know,
But leechlike to their fainting country cling   5
Till they drop, blind in blood, without a blow.
A people starved and stabbed in th' untilled field;
An army, whom liberticide and prey
Makes as a two-edged sword to all who wield;
Golden and sanguine[3] laws which tempt and slay;   10
Religion Christless, Godless—a book sealed;
A senate, Time's worst statute,[4] unrepealed—
Are graves from which a glorious Phantom may
Burst, to illumine our tempestuous day.

Ode to the West Wind

I

O wild West Wind, thou breath of Autumn's being,
Thou, from whose unseen presence the leaves dead
Are driven, like ghosts from an enchanter fleeing,

Yellow, and black, and pale, and hectic red,
Pestilence-stricken multitudes: O Thou,   5
Who chariotest to their dark wintry bed

The winged seeds, where they lie cold and low,
Each like a corpse within its grave, until
Thine azure sister of the Spring shall blow

Her clarion o'er the dreaming earth, and fill   10
(Driving sweet buds like flocks to feed in air)
With living hues and odours plain and hill:

Wild Spirit, which art moving everywhere;
Destroyer and Preserver; hear, O hear!

II

Thou on whose stream,'mid the steep sky's commotion,   15
Loose clouds like Earth's decaying leaves are shed,
Shook from the tangled boughs of Heaven and Ocean,

Angels of rain and lightning; there are spread
On the blue surface of thine aery surge,
Like the bright hair uplifted from the head   20

Of some fierce Mænad,[1] even from the dim verge
Of the horizon to the zenith's height,
The locks of the approaching storm. Thou Dirge

Of the dying year, to which this closing night
Will be the dome of a vast sepulchre,   25
Vaulted with all thy congregated might

3. Bloody, causing bloodshed. *Golden:* bought. The laws favor the rich and powerful.   4. The law by
which the civil liberties of Roman Catholics and dissenters from the state religion (Anglicanism) were
restricted.   1. Ecstatic female worshiper of Bacchus, Greek god of wine.

Of vapors, from whose solid atmosphere
Black rain and fire and hail will burst: O hear!

III

Thou who didst waken from his summer dreams
The blue Mediterranean, where he lay,   30
Lulled by the coil of his crystalline streams,

Beside a pumice isle in Baiæ's bay,[2]
And saw in sleep old palaces and towers
Quivering within the wave's intenser day,

All overgrown with azure moss and flowers   35
So sweet, the sense faints picturing them! Thou
For whose path the Atlantic's level powers

Cleave themselves into chasms, while far below
The sea-blooms and the oozy woods which wear
The sapless foliage of the ocean, know   40

Thy voice, and suddenly grow grey with fear,
And tremble and despoil themselves: O hear!

IV

If I were a dead leaf thou mightest bear;
If I were a swift cloud to fly with thee;
A wave to pant beneath thy power, and share   45

The impulse of thy strength, only less free
Than thou, O Uncontrollable! If even
I were as in my boyhood, and could be

The comrade of thy wanderings over Heaven,
As then, when to outstrip thy skiey speed   50
Scarce seemed a vision; I would ne'er have striven

As thus with thee in prayer in my sore need.
Oh! lift me as a wave, a leaf, a cloud!
I fall upon the thorns of life! I bleed!

A heavy weight of hours has chained and bowed   55
One too like thee: tameless, and swift, and proud.

V

Make me thy lyre,[3] even as the forest is:
What if my leaves are falling like its own!
The tumult of thy mighty harmonies

Will take from both a deep, autumnal tone,   60
Sweet though in sadness. Be thou, Spirit fierce,
My spirit! Be thou me, impetuous one!

2. West of Naples; the Roman emperors built villas there.   3. Ancient harp. The allusion is also to the aeolian harp, an instrument played by the wind and a frequent image for the poet played by inspiration.

Drive my dead thoughts over the universe
Like withered leaves to quicken a new birth!
And, by the incantation of this verse,   65

Scatter, as from an unextinguished hearth
Ashes and sparks, my words among mankind!
Be through my lips to unawakened Earth

The trumpet of a prophecy! O Wind,
If Winter comes, can Spring be far behind?   70

A Defence of Poetry

[Conclusion]

* * * Poetry is the record of the best and happiest moments of the happiest
and best minds. We are aware of evanescent visitations of thought and feeling sometimes associated with place or person, sometimes regarding our own
mind alone, and always arising unforeseen and departing unbidden, but elevating and delightful beyond all expression: so that even in the desire and
the regret they leave, there cannot but be pleasure, participating as it does
in the nature of its object. It is as it were the interpenetration of a diviner
nature through our own; but its footsteps are like those of a wind over a sea,
which the coming calm erases, and whose traces remain only as on the wrinkled sand which paves it. These and corresponding conditions of being are
experienced principally by those of the most delicate sensibility and the most
enlarged imagination; and the state of mind produced by them is at war with
every base desire. The enthusiasm of virtue, love, patriotism, and friendship
is essentially linked with these emotions, and whilst they last, self appears
as what it is, an atom to a Universe. Poets are not only subject to these
experiences as spirits of the most refined organization, but they can colour
all that they combine with the evanescent hues of this ethereal world; a word,
or a trait in the representation of a scene or a passion, will touch the
enchanted chord, and reanimate, in those who have ever experienced these
emotions, the sleeping, the cold, the buried image of the past. Poetry thus
makes immortal all that is best and most beautiful in the world; it arrests
the vanishing apparitions which haunt the interlunations of life, and veiling
them or[1] in language or in form sends them forth among mankind, bearing
sweet news of kindred joy to those with whom their sisters abide—abide,
because there is no portal of expression from the caverns of the spirit which
they inhabit into the universe of things. Poetry redeems from decay the visitations of the divinity in man.

                                    *   *   *

The first part of these remarks has related to Poetry in its elements and
principles; and it has been shown, as well as the narrow limits assigned them
would permit, that what is called poetry, in a restricted sense, has a common
source with all other forms of order and of beauty according to which the

---

1. Either. *Interlunations:* dark periods between the old and new moon.

materials of human life are susceptible of being arranged, and which is poetry in an universal sense.

The second part[2] will have for its object an application of these principles to the present state of the cultivation of Poetry, and a defence of the attempt to idealize the modern forms of manners and opinion, and compel them into a subordination to the imaginative and creative faculty. For the literature of England, an energetic development of which has ever preceded or accompanied a great and free development of the national will, has arisen as it were from a new birth. In spite of the low-thoughted envy which would undervalue contemporary merit, our own will be a memorable age in intellectual achievements, and we live among such philosophers and poets as surpass beyond comparison any who have appeared since the last national struggle for civil and religious liberty.[3] The most unfailing herald, companion, and follower of the awakening of a great people to work a beneficial change in opinion or institution, is Poetry. At such periods there is an accumulation of the power of communicating and receiving intense and impassioned conceptions respecting man and nature. The persons in whom this power resides, may often, as far as regards many portions of their nature, have little apparent correspondence with that spirit of good of which they are the ministers. But even whilst they deny and abjure, they are yet compelled to serve, the Power which is seated upon the throne of their own soul. It is impossible to read the compositions of the most celebrated writers of the present day without being startled with the electric life which burns within their words. They measure the circumference and sound the depths of human nature with a comprehensive and all-penetrating spirit, and they are themselves perhaps the most sincerely astonished at its manifestations, for it is less their spirit than the spirit of the age. Poets are the hierophants[4] of an unapprehended inspiration, the mirrors of the gigantic shadows which futurity casts upon the present, the words which express what they understand not; the trumpets which sing to battle, and feel not what they inspire: the influence which is moved not, but moves. Poets are the unacknowledged legislators of the World.

2. The second part was never written.   3. The English Civil War. The great poet of that age was Milton.   4. Interpreters, as priests who interpret sacred mysteries.

JOHN KEATS
1795–1821

A poet "half in love with easeful Death," to quote a line from his *Ode to a Nightingale*, John Keats expressed with compelling intensity the Romantic longing for the unattainable, a concept that he defined in ways very different from Goethe's. In a series of brilliant lyrics, he explored subtle links between the passion for absolute beauty, which provides an imagined alternative to the everyday world's sordidness and disappointment, and the desire to melt into extinction, another form of that alternative.

At the age of sixteen, Keats was apprenticed to a druggist and surgeon; in 1816, he was licensed as an apothecary—but almost immediately abandoned medicine for poetry. Son of a hostler (a groom for horses) at a London inn, he had earlier attended school at Enfield, where he manifested an interest in literature encouraged by his friend Charles Cowden Clarke, the headmaster's son. Through Leigh Hunt, a leading political radical, poet, and critic, whose literary circle he joined in 1816, Keats came to know Shelley, William Hazlitt, and Charles Lamb, important members of the Romantic movement. He had a brief love affair with Fanny Brawne, to whom he became engaged in 1819; the next year he went to Italy, seeking a cure for his tuberculosis, only to die in Rome.

Although his first book, *Poems* (1817), met with some critical success, the long mythological poem *Endymion,* which he published a year later, became an object of attack by conservative literary reviews (*Blackwood's* and the *Quarterly*). Shelley, in his elegy for Keats (*Adonais,* 1821), encouraged the myth that the harsh reviews caused the poet's death. In fact, Keats lived long enough to publish his most important volume—written scarcely five years after he first tried his hand at poetry—*Lamia, Isabella, The Eve of St. Agnes, and Other Poems* (1820), which won critical applause and contained most of the poems for which he is remembered today.

Some of Keats's greatest works return to a form popular in the eighteenth century: the ode addressed to an abstraction (for example, melancholy) or another nonhuman object (for example, a nightingale or an urn). Although the basic literary device seems highly artificial, Keats uses it powerfully to express his characteristic sense of beauty so intensely experienced that it almost corresponds to pain.

> My heart aches, and a drowsy numbness pains
> My sense, as though of hemlock I had drunk . . .
> 'Tis not through envy of thy happy lot,
> But being too happy in thy happiness. . . .

Ode on Melancholy, in its sharp contrast to Coleridge's and Shelley's poems on dejection as well as to seventeenth- and eighteenth-century evocations of melancholy, illustrates particularly well Keats's special exemplification of the Romantic sensibility. In the first stanza, the speaker explicitly rejects traditional concomitants of melancholy—yew, the death-moth, the owl—because such associations suggest a kind of passivity or inertia that might "drown the wakeful anguish of the soul," interfering with the immediate and intense experience of melancholy that he actively seeks. Instead, he advocates trying to live as completely as possible in the immediacy of emotion. Melancholy, he continues, dwells with beauty and joy and pleasure, all in their nature evanescent. To fully feel the wonder of beauty or happiness implies awareness that it will soon vanish. Only those capable of active participation in their own positive emotions can hope to know melancholy; paradoxically, the result of energetic commitment to the life of feeling is the utter submission to melancholy's power: one can hope to "be among her cloudy trophies hung."

Prose summary of such an argument risks sounding ridiculous or incomprehensible, for Keats's emotional logic inheres in the imagery and the music of his poems, which exert their own compelling force. Without any previous belief in the desirability of melancholy as an emotion, the reader, absorbed into a rich sequence of images, feels swept into an experience comparable to that which the poem endorses. The ode generates its own sense of beauty and of melancholy and of the close relation between the two. Its brilliantly evocative specificity of physical reference always suggests more than is directly said, more than paraphrase can encompass:

> Aye, in the very temple of Delight
> Veiled Melancholy has her sovereign shrine,
> Though seen of none save him whose strenuous tongue
> Can burst Joy's grape against his palate fine . . .

Everyone can recall the sensuous pleasure of a grape releasing its juice into the mouth, but it would be difficult to elucidate the full implications of the "strenuous tongue" or of "Joy's grape." Keat's great poetic gift manifests itself most unmistakably in his extraordinary power of suggestion—not only in the odes, but in the ballad-imitation, *La Belle Dame sans Merci*, with its haunting, half-told story, and in the understated sonnets, asserting the speaker's feeling but always hinting more emotion than they directly affirm.

A first-rate critical biography is A. Ward, *John Keats: The Making of a Poet* (1963). Also useful are W. J. Bate, *John Keats* (1963); S. Coote, *John Keats: A Life* (1995); T. Hilton, *Keats and His World* (1971); C. T. Watts, *A Preface to Keats* (1985); J. Barnard, *John Keats* (1987); H. Bloom, ed., *The Odes of Keats* (1987), a collection of essays; and H. De Almeida, *Critical Essays on John Keats* (1990).

PRONOUNCING GLOSSARY

The following list uses common English syllables and stress accents to provide rough equivalents of selected words whose pronounciation may be unfamiliar to the general reader.

Arcady: *ahr'-kah-dee* Lethe: *lee'-thee*

Darien: *day'-ree-en* Proserpine: *pro'-ser-pain*

Hippocrene: *hip'-oh-kreen* Provençal: *proh-vahn-sahl'*

La Belle Dame sans Merci: *lah bel dahm* Tempe: *tem'-pee*
  sahnh mayr-see'

On First Looking into Chapman's Homer[1]

Much have I traveled in the realms of gold,
  And many goodly states and kingdoms seen;
  Round many western islands have I been
Which bards in fealty to Apollo[2] hold.
Oft of one wide expanse had I been told   5
  That deep-browed Homer ruled as his demesne;[3]
  Yet did I never breathe its pure serene
Till I heard Chapman speak out loud and bold:
Then felt I like some watcher of the skies
  When a new planet swims into his ken;   10
Or like stout Cortez[4] when with eagle eyes
  He stared at the Pacific—and all his men
Looked at each other with a wild surmise—
  Silent, upon a peak in Darien.

Bright Star

Bright star, would I were steadfast as thou art—
  Not in lone splendor hung aloft the night,

---

1. Keat's friend and former teacher Charles Cowden Clarke had introduced Keats to George Chapman's translations of the *Iliad* (1611) and the *Odyssey* (1616) the night before this poem was written.   2. God of poetic inspiration.   3. Realm, kingdom.   4. In fact, Vasco Núñez de Balboa (c. 1475–1519), Spanish conquistador, not Hernando Cortés (1485–1547), another Spaniard, was the European explorer who first saw the Pacific from Darien, Panama.

And watching, with eternal lids apart,
    Like nature's patient, sleepless Eremite,[1]
The moving waters at their priestlike task   5
    Of pure ablution round earth's human shores,
Or gazing on the new soft fallen mask
    Of snow upon the mountains and the moors—
No—yet still steadfast, still unchangeable,
    Pillowed upon my fair love's ripening breast,   10
To feel forever its soft fall and swell,
    Awake forever in a sweet unrest,
Still, still to hear her tender-taken breath,
And so live ever—or else swoon to death.

La Belle Dame sans Merci[1]

I

O what can ail thee, knight at arms,
    Alone and palely loitering?
The sedge has withered from the lake
    And no birds sing!

II

O what can ail thee, knight at arms,   5
    So haggard, and so woebegone?
The squirrel's granary is full
    And the harvest's done.

III

I see a lily on thy brow
    With anguish moist and fever dew,   10
And on thy cheeks a fading rose
    Fast withereth too.

IV

I met a lady in the meads,[2]
    Full beautiful, a faery's child,
Her hair was long, her foot was light   15
    And her eyes were wild.

V

I made a garland for her head,
    And bracelets too, and fragrant zone;[3]

1. Hermit.   1. The beautiful lady without pity (French); from a medieval poem by Alain Chartier.
2. Meadows. Here the knight answers the question asked in lines 5–6.   3. Girdle.

She looked at me as she did love
    And made sweet moan.   20

VI

I set her on my pacing steed
    And nothing else saw all day long,
For sidelong would she bend and sing
    A faery's song.

VII

She found me roots of relish sweet,   25
    And honey wild, and manna[4] dew,
And sure in language strange she said
    "I love thee true."

VIII

She took me to her elfin grot[5]
    And there she wept and sighed full sore,[6]   30
And there I shut her wild wild eyes
    With kisses four.

IX

And there she lullèd me asleep,
    And there I dreamed, ah woe betide!
The latest[7] dream I ever dreamt   35
    On the cold hill's side.

X

I saw pale kings, and princes too,
    Pale warriors, death-pale were they all;
They cried, "La belle dame sans merci
    Thee hath in thrall!"[8]   40

XI

I saw their starved lips in the gloam[9]
    With horrid warning gapèd wide,
And I awoke, and found me here
    On the cold hill's side.

XII

And this is why I sojourn here,   45
    Alone and palely loitering;
Though the sedge withered from the lake
    And no birds sing.

4. The supernatural substance with which God fed the children of Israel in the wilderness (Exodus 16 and Joshua 5.12).   5. Cavern.   6. With great grief.   7. Last.   8. Bondage.   9. Twilight.

Ode on a Grecian Urn

I

Thou still unravished bride of quietness,
  Thou foster-child of silence and slow time,
Sylvan historian, who canst thus express
  A flowery tale more sweetly than our rhyme:
What leaf-fringed legend haunts about thy shape   5
  Of deities or mortals, or of both,
    In Tempe or the dales of Arcady?[1]
  What men or gods are these? What maidens loth?
What mad pursuit? What struggle to escape?
    What pipes and timbrels? What wild ecstasy?   10

II

Heard melodies are sweet, but those unheard
  Are sweeter; therefore, ye soft pipes, play on;
Not to the sensual ear, but, more endeared,
  Pipe to the spirit ditties of no tone:
Fair youth, beneath the trees, thou canst not leave   15
  Thy song, nor ever can those trees be bare;
    Bold lover, never, never canst thou kiss,
Though winning near the goal—yet, do not grieve;
    She cannot fade, though thou hast not thy bliss,
  For ever wilt thou love, and she be fair!   20

III

Ah, happy, happy boughs! that cannot shed
  Your leaves, nor ever bid the Spring adieu;
And, happy melodist, unwearièd,
  For ever piping songs for ever new;
More happy love! more happy, happy love!   25
  For ever warm and still to be enjoyed,
    For ever panting, and for ever young;
All breathing human passion far above,
    That leaves a heart high-sorrowful and cloyed,
    A burning forehead, and a parching tongue.   30

IV

Who are these coming to the sacrifice?
  To what green altar, O mysterious priest,
Lead'st thou that heifer lowing at the skies,
  And all her silken flanks with garlands drest?
What little town by river or sea shore,   35
  Or mountain-built with peaceful citadel,
    Is emptied of this folk, this pious morn?
And, little town, thy streets for evermore

---

1. A mountainous region in the Peloponnese, traditionally regarded as the place of ideal rustic, bucolic contentment. *Tempe:* a valley in Thessaly between Mount Olympus and Mount Ossa.

Will silent be; and not a soul to tell
    Why thou art desolate, can e'er return.   40

V

O Attic shape! Fair attitude! with brede[2]
Of marble men and maidens overwrought,
With forest branches and the trodden weed;
    Thou, silent form, dost tease us out of thought
As doth eternity: Cold Pastoral!   45
    When old age shall this generation waste,
        Thou shalt remain, in midst of other woe
Than ours, a friend to man, to whom thou say'st,
    "Beauty is truth, truth beauty,"—that is all
        Ye know on earth, and all ye need to know.   50

Ode to a Nightingale

I

My heart aches, and a drowsy numbness pains
    My sense, as though of hemlock I had drunk,
Or emptied some dull opiate to the drains
    One minute past, and Lethe-wards[1] had sunk:
'Tis not through envy of thy happy lot,   5
    But being too happy in thy happiness,
        That thou, light-winged Dryad[2] of the trees,
            In some melodious plot
Of beechen green, and shadows numberless,
    Singest of summer in full-throated ease.   10

II

O for a draught of vintage! that hath been
    Cooled a long age in the deep-delvèd earth,
Tasting of Flora[3] and the country green,
    Dance, and Provençal[4] song, and sunburnt mirth!
O for a beaker full of the warm South!   15
    Full of the true, the blushful Hippocrene,[5]
        With beaded bubbles winking at the brim,
            And purple-stainèd mouth;
That I might drink, and leave the world unseen,
    And with thee fade away into the forest dim: 20

III

Fade far away, dissolve, and quite forget
    What thou among the leaves hast never known,
The weariness, the fever, and the fret

2. Pattern. *Attic:* classical (literally, Athenian). 1. I.e., toward Lethe, the river of forgetfulness in Greek mythology. 2. Wood nymph. 3. The goddess of flowers and spring; here, flowers. 4. From Provence, the district in France associated with the troubadours. 5. The fountain on Mount Helicon, in Greece, sacred to the muse of poetry.

Here, where men sit and hear each other groan;
Where palsy shakes a few, sad, last gray hairs,   25
   Where youth grows pale, and spectre-thin, and dies;
    Where but to think is to be full of sorrow
      And leaden-eyed despairs;
   Where beauty cannot keep her lustrous eyes,
    Or new love pine at them beyond tomorrow.   30

IV

Away! away! for I will fly to thee,
   Not charioted by Bacchus and his pards,⁶
But on the viewless wings of Poesy,
   Though the dull brain perplexes and retards:
Already with thee! tender is the night,   35
   And haply⁷ the Queen-Moon is on her throne,
    Clustered around by all her starry Fays;⁸
      But here there is no light,
   Save what from heaven is with the breezes blown
    Through verdurous glooms and winding mossy ways.   40

V

I cannot see what flowers are at my feet,
   Nor what soft incense hangs upon the boughs,
But, in embalmèd darkness, guess each sweet
   Wherewith the seasonable month endows
The grass, the thicket, and the fruit-tree wild;   45
   White hawthorn, and the pastoral eglantine;
    Fast-fading violets covered up in leaves;
      And mid-May's eldest child,
   The coming musk-rose, full of dewy wine,
    The murmurous haunt of flies on summer eves.   50

VI

Darkling⁹ I listen; and for many a time
   I have been half in love with easeful Death,
Called him soft names in many a musèd rhyme,
   To take into the air my quiet breath;
Now more than ever seems it rich to die,   55
   To cease upon the midnight with no pain,
    While thou art pouring forth thy soul abroad
      In such an ecstasy!
Still wouldst thou sing, and I have ears in vain—
   To thy high requiem become a sod.¹   60

VII

Thou wast not born for death, immortal Bird!
   No hungry generations tread thee down;
The voice I hear this passing night was heard

---

6. Leopards. Bacchus (Dionysus) was traditionally supposed to be accompanied by leopards, lions, goats, and so on.   7. Perhaps.   8. Fairies.   9. In the dark.   1. I.e., like dirt, unable to hear.

In ancient days by emperor and clown:
Perhaps the self-same song that found a path   65
    Through the sad heart of Ruth, when, sick for home,
        She stood in tears amid the alien corn;[2]
            The same that ofttimes hath
    Charmed magic casements, opening on the foam
        Of perilous seas, in faery lands forlorn.   70

VIII

Forlorn! the very word is like a bell
    To toll me back from thee to my sole self!
Adieu! the fancy cannot cheat so well
    As she is famed to do, deceiving elf.
Adieu! adieu! thy plaintive anthem fades   75
    Past the near meadows, over the still stream,
        Up the hill-side; and now 'tis buried deep
            In the next valley-glades:
    Was it a vision, or a waking dream?
        Fled is that music:—do I wake or sleep?   80

Ode on Melancholy

I

No, no, go not to Lethe,[1] neither twist
    Wolfsbane, tight-rooted, for its poisonous wine;
Nor suffer thy pale forehead to be kissed
    By nightshade, ruby grape of Proserpine;[2]
Make not your rosary of yew-berries,[3]   5
    Nor let the beetle, nor the death-moth[4] be
        Your mournful Psyche,[5] nor the downy owl
A partner in your sorrow's mysteries;
    For shade to shade will come too drowsily,
        And drown the wakeful anguish of the soul.   10

II

But when the melancholy fit shall fall
    Sudden from heaven like a weeping cloud,
That fosters the droop-headed flowers all,
    And hides the green hill in an April shroud;
Then glut thy sorrow on a morning rose,   15
    Or on the rainbow of the salt sand-wave,
        Or on the wealth of globèd peonies;
Or if thy mistress some rich anger shows,
    Imprison her soft hand, and let her rave,
        And feed deep, deep upon her peerless eyes.   20

---

2. See the Book of Ruth. After her Ephrathite husband died, she returned to his native land with her mother-in-law.   **1.** The river of forgetfulness in Hades.   **2.** Wife of Pluto, queen of the underworld.   **3.** Wolfsbane, nightshade, and yew berries are all poisonous.   **4.** The death's-head moth has markings that resemble a skull. The scarab beetle, depicted in Egyptian tombs, was an emblem of death.   **5.** The soul, portrayed by the Greeks as a butterfly.

III

She[6] dwells with Beauty—Beauty that must die;
    And Joy, whose hand is ever at his lips
Bidding adieu; and aching Pleasure nigh,
    Turning to Poison while the bee-mouth sips:
Aye, in the very temple of Delight   25
    Veiled Melancholy has her sovereign shrine,
        Though seen of none save him whose strenuous tongue
Can burst Joy's grape against his palate fine;
His soul shall taste the sadness of her might,
    And be among her cloudy trophies hung.[7]   30

To Autumn

I

Season of mists and mellow fruitfulness,
    Close bosom-friend of the maturing sun;
Conspiring with him how to load and bless
    With fruit the vines that round the thatch-eaves run;
To bend with apples the mossed cottage-trees,   5
    And fill all fruit with ripeness to the core;
        To swell the gourd, and plump the hazel shells
With a sweet kernel; to set budding more,
    And still more, later flowers for the bees,
    Until they think warm days will never cease,   10
        For Summer has o'er-brimmed their clammy cells.

II

Who hath not seen thee oft amid thy store?
    Sometimes whoever seeks abroad may find
Thee sitting careless on a granary floor,
    Thy hair soft-lifted by the winnowing wind;   15
Or on a half-reaped furrow sound asleep,
    Drowsed with the fume of poppies, while thy hook
        Spares the next swath and all its twinèd flowers:
And sometimes like a gleaner thou dost keep
    Steady thy laden head across a brook;   20
    Or by a cyder-press, with patient look,
        Thou watchest the last oozings hours by hours.

III

Where are the songs of Spring? Ay, where are they?
    Think not of them, thou hast thy music too,—
While barrèd clouds bloom the soft-dying day,   25
    And touch the stubble-plains with rosy hue;
Then in a wailful choir the small gnats mourn

---

6. Melancholy.   7. The Greeks placed war trophies in their temples to commemorate victories.

Among the river sallows,[8] borne aloft
Or sinking as the light wind lives or dies;
And full-grown lambs loud bleat from hilly bourn;   30
Hedge-crickets sing; and now with treble soft
The red-breast whistles from a garden-croft;
And gathering swallows twitter in the skies.

8. Willows.

CONTINENTAL ROMANTIC LYRICS: A SELECTION

This group of poems from four European countries exemplifies both the scope and the consistency of the Romantic imagination. Like their English counterparts, the writers represented here concern themselves with time, death, nature, and love and with the connections among these vast subjects. They express emotions ranging from extreme depression to exhilaration. As one can see even in translation, these poets explore a broad spectrum of metrical possibilities. Although they write mainly in the first person, they consistently meditate, explicitly or implicitly, the links between the self and the world—both the natural world and that composed of other people (including, in Heinrich Heine's *Silesian Weavers,* the political realm). In their insistence on feeling's importance and complexity, its capacity to guide the individual toward profound insight, they reveal why it is that Romantic poetry continues to communicate directly with readers living long after the era of its writing.

This poetry characteristically reveals a spiritual dimension even when its ostensible concerns appear relatively trivial. Thus Rosalía de Castro, feeling the heat of a summer day, finds herself aware of "the anguish of the soul," and Friedrich Hölderlin, also contemplating a summer scene, perceives the water into which swans dip their heads as "holy." Often, though, the poets directly confront metaphysical issues. Like Wordsworth, they may feel themselves united with the natural universe (see, for example, Gustavo Adolfo Bécquer's *Nameless Spirit*). But they also explore the emotional reverberations of Christianity. The German poet known as Novalis (born Friedrich von Hardenberg) unites his preoccupation with time and his sense of loss with his Christian convictions, imagining Jesus not only as the type of perfection but as the representative of vanished serenity and nobility of spirit. Victor Hugo, employing the lyric impulse to illuminate a narrative plot, evokes the almost inconceivable emotional experience of Satan falling from heaven to hell. Whether writing openly or covertly of religious feeling, Romantic poets consciously and often triumphantly stretch the limits of the expressible.

Particularly striking in this group of selections, as in the entire body of Romantic lyrics, is the complex symbolic use made of material from the natural world. Anna Petrovna Bunina, for instance, an early nineteenth-century Russian poet, begins *From the Seashore* with a scene of calm natural beauty—quiet sea, shining sky, birds in their nests. The poem then mutates into an equally peaceful domestic scene, only to return to a new figuration of the sea, invoked now as a prospective grave. The shift calls attention to the way that human beings attach meanings to nature in accord with mutable psychic conditions.

The French poet Alphonse de Lamartine, in his long lyric, *The Lake,* explores the assignment of meaning to nature yet more fully, using his memory of an idyllic summer evening in a boat with his beloved to reflect on the ineluctable passing of time. Now the woman he loves is dying. In the earlier time, she spoke to him about the need to live intensely, given the flight of the moments, using the boat trip as a metaphor:

"We have no port, time itself has no shore;
It glides by, and we pass away."

Now, the speaker can only hope that the beauty of the lake and its surroundings will survive as a symbol of their love, possessing a kind of permanence that human beings cannot attain.

Yet more mysterious are the allusions to nature in Heine's lyrics, which rely on subtle suggestion rather than overt statement. Writing, for instance, of a pine tree in the north that dreams during the winter of a faraway palm tree, he evokes the omnipresence of human longing without ever mentioning the human. "Death is like the long cool night," he writes in another poem, without explaining, but his allusion to young nightingales singing in the trees captures a sense of death as beautiful, remote, and haunting.

These lyricists value the inexpressibility of powerful feeling. At the same time, they set themselves the impossible task of communicating precisely what defies expression. The sheer musicality of their verse helps to convey emotion, as they create powerful (and often untranslatable) verbal melodies through the rhythms of their stanzaic forms and the varied movement of their lines. By strategies of indirection, they often succeed in persuading their readers that lyric verse can after all convey the kinds of feeling that most of us lock within ourselves. The poems collected here investigate experience both commonplace and extraordinary; interrogate the universe; but most important, explore and imagine the depths of human emotion.

Because chronological differences have little significance across national boundaries, the selections are arranged in alphabetical order by author.

GUSTAVO ADOLFO BÉCQUER
1836–1870

Although his major literary reputation developed only after his death, Gustavo Adolfo Bécquer (*goo-stah'-voh ah-dol'-foh beh-hay'*), a pseudonym for Gustavo Adolfo Domínguez Bastida, is now generally considered the most important of the Spanish Romantic poets. Born in Seville, he was orphaned at the age of nine. He made his living—supporting a wife and two sons—by various means (government official, translator, journalist), but he always thought of himself as a writer, producing not only poetry but prose fiction and nonfiction. His early death resulted from tuberculosis.

Bécquer's poetry often attempts to express the ineffable, to convey his sense of spiritual exhilaration in the natural world. But the poet relies most often on simple, direct diction, in an attempt to familiarize grand ideas.

The selections printed here were translated by Bruce Phenix, who attempts both to offer as literal a rendition as possible of Bécquer's meaning and to convey the rhythm and movement of the Spanish text. The poems here included come from *Rimas*, a collection of Bécquer's verse in which individual poems are assigned only numbers, not titles. First lines have been used as titles in this anthology.

Although Bécquer has been the subject of much literary analysis in Spanish, little has been written about him in English. One useful study is E. L. King, *Gustavo Adolfo Bécquer: From Painter to Poet* (1953).

[I Know a Strange, Gigantic Hymn]

I know a strange, gigantic hymn
that heralds a dawn in the night of the soul,

and these pages are cadences of this hymn
that the air carries abroad in the shadows.

    I should like to write it, subduing   5
the rebel against man, impoverished language,
in words that were at the same time
sighs and laughs, colours and notes.

    But in vain is the struggle; for there is no cipher
capable of containing it, and scarcely, oh beautiful one!   10
holding your hands in mine,
could I sing it, by ear, to you alone.

[Nameless Spirit]

    Nameless spirit,
indefinable essence,
I live with the formless
life of idea.

    I swim in the void,   5
I quiver in the bonfire of the sun,
I palpitate among the shadows
and I float with the mists.

    I am the gold braid
of the distant star;   10
I am the lukewarm, serene light
of the high moon.

    I am the burning cloud
that undulates in the west:
I am the luminous wake   15
of the wandering star.

    I am snow on the peaks,
I am fire on the sands,
a blue wave on the seas,
and foam on the shores.   20

    I am a note in the lute,
perfume in the violet,
a fleeting flame in the tombs,
and ivy in the ruins.

    I deafen in the torrent,   25
and I hiss in the lightning,
and I blind in the flash,
and I roar in the storm.

I laugh in the hills,
I whisper in the tall grass,   30
I sigh in the pure wave,
and I weep in the dead leaf.

I undulate with the atoms
of the smoke that rises,
and slowly goes up to the sky   35
in an immense spiral.

I, on the gilded threads
that the insects hang,
swing between the trees
in the fiery noonday heat.   40

I run after the nymphs
who in the cool stream
of the crystalline brook
frolic naked.

I, in forests of corals   45
carpeted by white pearls,
pursue in the ocean
the swift naiads.

I, in the hollow caverns
where the sun never penetrates,   50
mingling with the gnomes
observe their riches.

I look for the now obliterated
traces of the centuries,
and I know of those empires   55
of which not even the name is left.

I follow in rapid giddiness
the worlds that revolve,
and my pupil[1] embraces
the whole of creation.   60

I know of those regions
both where no noise reaches,
and where formless stars
wait for the breath of life.

I am the bridge that crosses   65
over the abyss,
I am the unknown ladder
that joins Heaven to the Earth.

1. Eye.

I am the invisible
ring that fastens   70
the world of form
to the world of idea.

I, in short, am that spirit,
unfamiliar essence,
mysterious perfume,   75
of which the poet is the vessel.

ANNA PETROVNA BUNINA
1774–1829

One of the first woman poets to be published in Russia, Anna Petrovna Bunina
(*ah'-na pet-rohv'-na boo-nee'-na*) insisted, in the face of her parents' disapproval, on
pursuing a literary career and on developing her intellectual capacities. She had inherited a small amount of money, which made it possible for her initially to hire tutors
and to spend her time writing, demonstrating a gift for lyric verse that drew on details
of the natural world as a means for expressing personal feeling. After she began
publishing poetry (in 1806), she acquired literary supporters who tried to ease her
financial and physical circumstances when she developed cancer in 1815. She died
of the disease.

In the poem printed here, Bunina begins with a deceptively calm natural scene,
lovingly evoking the appearance and mood of the sea just after sunset. The poem
gradually builds intensity as it turns to the experience of human misery, ending with
an appeal to the sea to abandon its calm to better respond to the speaker's mood.
Like many other Romantic lyrics, the poem draws on the idea of harmony between
humanity and nature—but only to declare the insufficiency of nature to the personal
anguish in which "Poison flows / In my veins."

Pamela Perkins translated this selection.

Nothing has yet been written in English about Bunina.

From the Seashore

The bright sea
Flowed from the sky,
In quiet the waves
Lap along the shore,
Brief ripples   5
Faintly tremble.

The sun's gone down,
There is no moon,
In the scarlet glow
The west is shining,   10
Birds in their nests,
Flocks in the tree-crests.

Everything suddenly fell silent,
Everything in its place.
In the room it is quiet,   15
There is no rustle;
The children are nestled
Modestly in the corners.

Lina touched
The strings of the harp;   20
The golden harp
Gave voice;
Sounds in harmony
Sing with Lina.

In a rose flame   25
The hearth gives light;
The bright fire
Leaps along the coals;
The smoke dark-silver
Curls in a column.   30

The fierce flame
scorches the soul;
The heart languishes,
Everything has withered;
Poison flows   35
In my veins.

Tears ran dry
In troubled eyes,
Sighs stopped
The chest from heaving,   40
Speech dies down
On cold lips.

Sea, start to churn!
Be a grave for me!
Golden harp,   45
Strike like thunder!
Fire, flow,
Warm this poor woman!

ROSALÍA DE CASTRO
1837–1885

An illegitimate child of a priest, who, of course, could not recognize her, the Spanish
writer Rosalía de Castro (*roh-za-lee'-a day kahs'-troh*) frequently expresses in her verse

a sense of despair that may, critics have speculated, derive from the ambiguities of her birth. She began writing poetry as a child and published her first volume at the age of twenty. A year later, she married, subsequently giving birth to seven children. She died of cancer.

Beside the River Sar (1884), from which the selections printed here come, was the last volume published in de Castro's lifetime. Predominantly melancholy in tone, the poems express spiritual questioning, sorrow, and intense responsiveness to the environment. They are characteristically modest in tone (note, for example, *As I Composed This Little Book*). At times they reveal the author's intimate reactions to her own experience, as in *Mild Was the Air,* a lyric about the death of one of her infant children.

These poems were translated by S. Griswold Morley.

De Castro is the subject of a volume in the Twayne series: K. Kulp-Hill, *Rosalía de Castro* (1977).

[As I Composed This Little Book]

As I composed this little book, I thought:
Although my songs may never bring me fame,
    Simple they are and brief,
And may achieve, perhaps, my longed-for aim.
For they can be sure-fixed in memory   5
As are the prayers and rituals of belief,
Fervent though short, we learned in infancy.
Those we do not forget, in spite of grief
And time and distance and the destroying flame
Of passion. That is why my songs are brief   10
And simple,—though they may not bring me fame.

[Mild Was the Air]

    Mild was the air
    And still the day;
    The rain fell gently
    With never a stay.
    I hushed my sobs   5
    And softly wept;—
    My child was dying
    As he slept.
He left this world, and peace was in his heart;
I watched his going, and mine was torn apart!   10

    Throw earth upon the unburied body . . . earth!
Before corruption fastens on his flesh!
Be calm; the grave is covered now. Quite soon
Up from the newly broken clods the grass
Will push; it will be green and fresh.   15

    What are you seeking, you of the roving glance
And cloudy thought, prowling about that tomb?

With what is there to dust returning, fret
Not yourself. He'll not offend you more
Or love you more, who rests within that room.   20

    Oh, never, never more! Can it be true
That all is ended now forever? No,
Surely immensity can have no end,
Eternity can never cease to flow.

    You have left me forever; but my soul   25
Yearns with the eagerness of love to greet
My darling. You will come, or I shall go,
    Whither we twain can meet.

    Within my body something of you remains
      That cannot die,   30
And God, because He is just and because He is good,
      Will never try
To take it from me. Somewhere—on earth, in Heaven,
Beyond all sounded space—you will find me,
I shall find you. For certainly I know   35
Immensity can never have an end,
Eternity can never cease to flow.

    But . . . he is gone, gone never to return!
Ay, that is true. To man, guest of a day
In this our world, nothing eternal is.   40
Within its circle he is born and lives and dies,
As every creature is born and lives and dies;
    It is the earthly way.

[A Glowworm Scatters Flashes]

    A glowworm scatters flashes through the moss;
A star gleams in its high remote domain.
Abyss above, and in the depths abyss:
What things come to an end and what remain?
    Man's thought—we call it science!—peers and pries   5
Into the soundless dark. But it is vain:
When all is done, we still are ignorant
Of what things reach an end, and what remain.

    Kneeling before an image rudely carved,
I sink my spirit in the Infinite,   10
And—is it impious?—I vacillate
And tremble, questioning Heaven and Hell of it.

    My Deity, shattered in a thousand bits,
Has fallen to chasms where I cannot see.

I rush to seek Him, and my groping meets   15
A solitary vast vacuity.

When lo! from their lofty marble niches,
Angels gazed down in sorrow; and in my ears
Murmured a gentle voice: "Unhappy soul,
        Take hope; pour out thy tears   20
Before the feet of the Most High;
But well remember this: No insolent cry
        To Heaven makes its way
From one whose heart adores material things,
Who makes an idol out of Adam's clay."   25

[The Feet of Spring Are on the Stair]

        The feet of Spring are on the stair;
Her breath is sweet and warm and rare;
Beneath the soil in amorous heat
Seeds are astir with restless beat,
And atoms drifting in the air,   5
Afloat and silent, pair by pair,
        Kiss as they meet.

        Youth's blood is eager, youth's heart is hot,
Its courage leaps, its bold mad thought
Believes that man—oh, dreams of youth!—   10
Is, like the gods, immortal. What
If dreams are lies? This much is truth:
Unblest are they who dreamless draw their breath,
And fortunate who in a dream find death.

        How swift the passage of each thing   15
        In our sad world!
By a wild giant, quivering
        Our lives are whirled!
Yesterday bud, today a rose,
And then the sun-scorched blossom goes   20
        As Summer masters Spring.

[Candescent[1] Lies the Air]

        Candescent lies the air.
A fox explores the unfrequented road.
        The brook which cleanly flowed
As crystal, turns now noisome, where
        A pine, motionless, misses   5
        The breeze and its inconstant kisses.

---

1. Glowing or dazzling as from great heat.

A stifling silence quells the countryside.
    Only the insect's drone,
    Persistent, shrilling
Over the breathless landscape, filling   10
The shadows moist and wide,
Like a low death-rattle, makes a monotone.

In summer, to the fighter worn and dull,
    The midmost hour of day
    Is best called night.   15
    Then more than ever weigh
Upon him the unconquerable might
Of matter, and the anguish of the soul.

Return, return, ye chill wild nights of winter,
Our well-tried friends of a not distant time!   20
Give us again your nipping frost and rime,
To cool the blood inflamed by sorry summer,
Insufferable with its flaming rays—
Yes, sorry! though it bring the fruited wheat!

[The Ailing Woman Felt Her Forces Ebb]

The ailing woman felt her forces ebb
With summer, and knew her time was imminent.
    "In autumn I shall die,"
She thought, half-melancholy, half-content,
"And I shall feel the leaves, that will be dead   5
Like me, drop on the grave in which I lie."

Not even Death would do her so much pleasure.
    Cruel to her he too,
In winter spared her life, and when anew
The earth was being born in blossoming,   10
Slew her by inches to the joyous hymns
    Of fair and merry spring!

HEINRICH HEINE
1797–1856

Born in Germany, of Jewish parents, Heinrich Heine is most famous as a lyric poet, although he also composed drama, narrative poetry, political commentary, and literary criticism. As *The Silesian Weavers* suggests, he had strong revolutionary sympathies, which drew him to Paris in 1831. There he died, after a prolonged illness.

Simple diction and frequent reliance on the metrical patterns of traditional ballads characterize many of Heine's lyrics, which have frequently been set to music. Naive though the lyrics often seem, they have dark undertones. When Heine openly confronts political actualities, one ground for his despair becomes apparent: he sees

German society as divided between the uncaring and tyrannical rich and the profoundly oppressed poor, and he finds the structure of social inequity intolerable.

Hal Draper translated the selections printed here.

Biographies of Heine include Philip Kossoff, *Valiant Heart* (1983). Valuable critical studies are Jeffrey L. Sammons, *Heinrich Heine, the Elusive Poet* (1969) and Ursula Franklin, *Exiles and Ironists* (1988).

PRONOUNCING GLOSSARY

The following list uses common English syllables and stress accents to provide rough equivalents of selected words whose pronunciation may be unfamiliar to the general reader.

Heinrich Heine: *hain'-rik hai'-ne*   Silesian: *sai-lee'-zhahn*

[A Pine Is Standing Lonely]

A pine is standing lonely
In the North on a bare plateau.
He sleeps; a bright white blanket
Enshrouds him in ice and snow.

He's dreaming of a palm tree   5
Far away in the Eastern land
Lonely and silently mourning
On a sunburnt rocky strand.

[A Young Man Loves a Maiden]

A young man loves a maiden
Who chooses another instead;
This other loves still another
And these two haply wed.

The maiden out of anger   5
Marries, with no regard,
The first good man she runs into—
The young lad takes it hard.

It is so old a story,
Yet somehow always new;   10
And he that has just lived it,
It breaks his heart in two.

[Ah, Death Is Like the Long Cool Night]

Ah, death is like the long cool night,
And life is like the sultry day.
Dusk falls now; I grow sleepy;
The day makes me tired of light.

Over my bed there's a tree that gleams—   5
Young nightingales are singing there,
Of love, love only, singing—
I hear it even in dreams.

The Silesian Weavers[1]

In somber eyes no tears of grieving;
Grinding their teeth, they sit at their weaving;
"O Germany, at your shroud we sit,
We're weaving a threefold curse in it—
    We're weaving, we're weaving!   5

"A curse on the god we prayed to, kneeling
With cold in our bones, with hunger reeling;
We waited and hoped, in vain persevered,
He scorned us and duped us, mocked and jeered—
    We're weaving, we're weaving!   10

"A curse on the king[2] of the rich man's nation
Who hardens his heart at our supplication,
Who wrings the last penny out of our hides
And lets us be shot like dogs besides—
    We're weaving, we're weaving!   15

"A curse on this false fatherland, teeming
With nothing but shame and dirty scheming,
Where every flower is crushed in a day,
Where worms are regaled on rot and decay—
    We're weaving, we're weaving!   20

"The shuttle flies, the loom creaks loud,
Night and day we weave your shroud—
Old Germany, at your shroud we sit,
We're weaving a threefold curse in it,
    We're weaving, we're weaving!"   25

1. Silesia was a province of the kingdom of Prussia in northeast Germany. This poem was occasioned by
violent uprisings of weavers protesting intolerable working conditions during June 1844.   2. Friedrich
Wilhelm IV (1795–1861). Heine's poem is prophetic: in 1848 the king, though not deposed, was forced
by revolution to grant a constitution to Prussia.

FRIEDRICH HÖLDERLIN
1770–1843

Important partly for his capacity to combine classical and Romantic sensibility, the
German poet Friedrich Hölderlin (*freed'-rick hul'der-lin*) wrote his considerable body
of lyric verse early in his life, before becoming incurably schizophrenic at the age of

thirty-six. He had prepared himself for the ministry but decided that he was unsuited for such a vocation and found work—not very successfully—as a tutor. In his lyrics, which have become celebrated only in the twentieth century, he records and evokes intensities of personal feeling, with particular emphasis, as the selections printed here reveal, on what it means for human beings to live in time.

The poems are translated by Christopher Middleton, who successfully evokes Hölderlin's range of tones and meters.

A valuable biographical and critical study is L. S. Salzberger, *Hölderlin* (1952). Also useful is E. L. Stahl, *Hölderlin's Symbolism* (1945).

The Half of Life

With yellow pears the country,
Brimming with wild roses,
Hangs into the lake,
You gracious swans,
And drunk with kisses   5
Your heads you dip
Into the holy lucid water.

Where, ah where shall I find,
When winter comes, the flowers,
And where the sunshine   10
And shadows of the earth?
Walls stand
Speechless and cold, in the wind
The weathervanes clatter.

Hyperion's[1] Song of Fate

You walk up there in the light
  On floors like velvet, blissful spirits.
    Shining winds divine
      Touch you lightly
        As a harper touches holy   5
          Strings with her fingers.

Fateless as babes asleep
  They breathe, the celestials.
    Chastely kept
      In a simple bud,   10
        For them the spirit
          Flowers eternal,
            And in bliss their eyes
              Gaze in eternal
                Calm clarity.   15

1. In Greek mythology, a Titan, father of Aurora, goddess of dawn.

But to us it is given
To find no resting place,
We faint, we fall,
Suffering, human,
Blindly from one   20
To the next moment
Like water flung
From rock to rock down
Long years into uncertainty.

Brevity

Why make it so short? Have you lost your old liking
For song? Why, in days of hope, when young,
    You sang and sang,
        There scarce was an end of it.

My song is short as my luck was. Who'd go   5
    Gaily swimming at sundown? It's gone, earth's cold,
        And the annoying nightbird
            Flits, close, blocking your vision.

To the Fates

Grant me a single summer, you lords of all,
    A single autumn, for the fullgrown song,
        So that, with such sweet playing sated,
            Then my heart may die more willing.

The soul, in life robbed of its godly right,   5
    Rests not, even in Orcus[1] down below;
        Yet should I once achieve my heart's
            First holy concern, the poem,

Welcome then, O stillness of the shadow world!
    Even if down I go without my   10
        Music, I shall be satisfied; once
            Like gods I shall have lived, more I need not.

---

1. Hades.

VICTOR HUGO
1802–1885

Celebrated as poet, dramatist, and novelist, Victor Hugo was a towering figure in his generation of French literary figures. He wrote in virtually every available genre and explored an enormous range of subject and feeling, helping throughout to articulate the principles of Romanticism. His various political allegiances determined some of his actions: for twenty years he exiled himself to the island of Guernsey (a possession of the British Crown), believing his life in danger after President Louis Napoleon seized power. Always, though, he devoted himself to writing. *Et nox facta est*, printed here, is the first section of the epic *The End of Satan* and depicts the fallen angel's defiant plunge from heaven. Hugo's portrait of Satan demonstrates both psychological acuity and powerful identification with the figure of a rebel. The poem makes one feel both the terror and the ugliness of Satan's nay-saying and the splendor of his refusal.

The translator is Mary Ann Caws, who has evoked the dignity and the intensity of Hugo's verse.

A. Maurois, *Victor Hugo and His World* (1966), trans. O. Bernard, provides a useful introduction. S. Guerlac, *The Impersonal Sublime* (1990), and the collection of critical essays edited by H. Bloom, *Victor Hugo* (1988), are also valuable.

PRONOUNCING GLOSSARY

The following list uses common English syllables and stress accents to provide rough equivalents of selected words whose pronunciation may be unfamiliar to the general reader.

Victor Hugo: *vik-tor' ew-goh'*

Et nox facta est[1]

I

He[2] had been falling in the abyss some four thousand years.

Never had he yet managed to grasp a peak,
Nor lift even once his towering forehead.
He sank deeper in the dark and the mist, aghast,
Alone, and behind him, in the eternal nights,   5
His wing feathers fell more slowly still.
He fell dumbfounded, grim, and silent,
Sad, his mouth open and his feet towards the heavens,
The horror of the chasm imprinted on his livid face.
He cried: "Death!" his fists stretched out in the empty dark.   10
Later this word was man and was named Cain.[3]

He was falling. A rock struck his hand quite suddenly;
He held on to it, as a dead man holds on to his tomb,
And stopped. Someone, from on high, cried out to him: "Fall!

1. Written as part of *The End of Satan*, an epic poem never completed. The Latin title (And there was night) contrasts with the biblical "And there was light" (Genesis 1.3). 2. Satan, formerly the rebellious Archangel Lucifer, thrown out of heaven by God (Revelation 12.7–9 and Isaiah 14.12). 3. The first murderer, son of Adam and brother of Abel, the victim (Genesis 4.1–15).

The suns will go out around you, accursed!"   15
And the voice was lost in the immensity of horror.
And pale, he looked toward the eternal dawn.
The suns were far off, but shone still.
Satan raised his head and spoke, his arms in the air:
"You lie!" This word was later the soul of Judas.[4]   20

Like the gods of bronze erect upon their pilasters,
He waited a thousand years, eyes fixed upon the stars.
The suns were far off, but were still shining.
The thunder then rumbled in the skies unhearing, cold.
Satan laughed, and spat towards the thunder.   25
Filled by the visionary shadow, the immensity
Shivered. This spitting out was later Barabbas.[5]

A passing breath made him fall lower still.

II

The fall of the damned one began once again.—Terrible,
Somber, and pierced with holes luminous as a sieve,   30
The sky full of suns withdrew, brightness
Trembled, and in the night the great fallen one,
Naked, sinister, and pulled by the weight of his crime,
Fell, and his head wedging the abyss apart.
Lower! Lower, and still lower! Everything presently   35
Fled from him; no obstacle to seize in passing,
No mountain, no crumbling rock, no stone,
Nothing, shadow! and from fright he closed his eyes.

And when they opened, three suns only
Shone, and shadow had eaten away the firmament.   40
All the other suns had perished.

III

A rock

Emerged from blackest mist like some arm approaching.
He grasped it, and his feet touched summits.

Then the dreadful being called Never
Dreamed. His forehead sank between his guilty hands.   45
The three suns, far off, like three great eyes,
Watched him, and he watched them not.
Space resembled our earthly plains,
At evening, when the horizon sinking, retreating,
Blackens under the white eyes of the ghostly twilight.   50
Long rays entwined the feet of the great exile.
Behind him his shadow filled the infinite.
The peaks of chaos mingled in themselves.
In an instant he felt some horrendous growth of wings;
He felt himself become a monster, and that the angel in him   55

4. Judas Iscariot, the apostle who betrayed Jesus (Matthew 26.47–50, 27.3–5). 5. The condemned
criminal who was freed instead of Jesus (Mark 15.6–15).

Was dying, and the rebel then knew regret.
He felt his shoulder, so bright before,
Quiver in the hideous cold of membraned wing,
And folding his arms with his head lifted high,
This bandit, as if grown greater through affront,   60
Alone in these depths that only ruin inhabits,
Looked steadily at the shadow's cave.
The noiseless darkness grew in the nothingness.
Obscure opacity closed off the gaping sky;
And making beyond the last promontory   65
A triple crack in the black pane,
The three suns mingled their three lights.
You would have thought them three wheels of a chariot of fire,
Broken after some battle in the high firmament.
Like prows, the mountains from the mist emerged.   70
"So," cried Satan, "so be it! still I can see!
He shall have the blue sky, the black sky is mine.
Does he think I will come weeping to his door?
I hate him. Three suns suffice. What do I care?
I hate the day, the blueness, fragrance and the light."   75

Suddenly he shivered; there remained only one.

IV

The abyss was fading. Nothing kept its shape.
Darkness seemed to swell its giant wave.
Something nameless and submerged, something
That is no longer, takes its leave, falls silent;   80
And no one could have said, in this deep horror,
If this frightful remnant of a mystery or a world,
Like the vague mist where the dream takes flight,
Was called shipwreck or was called night;
And the archangel felt himself become a phantom.   85
He shouted: "Hell!" This word later made Sodom.[6]

And the voice repeated slowly on his forehead:
"Accursed! all about you the stars will go dark."

And already the sun was only a star.

V

And all disappeared slowly under a veil.   90
Then the archangel quaked; Satan learned to shiver.
Toward the star trembling livid on the horizon
He hurled himself, leaping from peak to peak.
Then, although with horror at the wings of a beast,
Although it was the clothing of emprisonment,   95
Like a bird going from bush to bush,
Horrendous he took his flight from mount to mount,
And this convict began running in his cell.

6. Biblical city, with Gomorrah a symbol of corruption and decadence. Both were destroyed by God (Genesis 18.20–19.28).

He ran, he flew, he shouted: "Star of gold! Brother!⁷
Wait for me! I'm running! Don't go out yet!   100
Don't leave me alone!"

                        Thus the monster
Crossed the first lakes of the dead immensity,
Former chaos, emptied and already stagnant,
And into the lugubrious depths he plunged.

Now the star was only a spark.   105

He went down further in universal shadow,
Sank further, cast himself wallowing in the night,
Climbed the filthy mountains, their damp gleaming front,
Whose base is unsteady in the cesspool deeps,
And trembling stared before him.

                                    The spark   110
Was only a red dot in the depth of the dark abyss.

                                VI

As between two battlements the archer leans
On the wall, when twilight has reached his keep,
Wild he leaned from the mountain top,
And upon the star, hoping to arouse its flame,   115
He started to blow as upon some ember.
And anguish caused his fierce nostrils to swell.
The breath rushing from his chest
Is now upon earth and called hurricane.

With his breath a great noise stirred the shadow, an ocean   120
No being dwells in and no fires illumine.
The mountains found nearby took their flight,
The monstrous chaos full of fright arose
And began to shriek: Jehovah Jehovah!
The infinite opened, rent apart like a cloth,   125
But nothing moved in the lugubrious star;
And the damned one, crying: "Don't go out yet! I'll go on!
I'll get there!" resumed again his desperate flight.
And the glaciers mingled with the nights resembling them
Turned on their backs like frightened beasts,   130
And the black tornadoes and the hideous chasms
Bent in terror, while above them,
Flying toward the star like some arrow to the goal,
There passed, wild and haggard, this terrible supplicant.

And ever since it has seen this frightening flight,   135
This bitter abyss, aghast like a fleeing man
Retains forever the horror and the craze,
So monstrous was it to see, in the shadow immense,
Opening his atrocious wing far from the heavens,
This bat flying from his eternal prison!   140

---

7. Lucifer means "Light Bearer."

VII

He flew for ten thousand years.

For ten thousand years,
Stretching forth his livid neck and his frenzied hands,
He flew without finding a peak on which to rest.
The star seemed sometimes to fade and to go out,   145
And the horror of the tomb caused the angel to shiver;
Then a pale brightness, vague, strange, uncertain,
Reappeared: and in joy, he cried: "Onward!"
Around him hovered the north wind birds.
He was flying. The infinite never ceases to start again.   150
His flight circled immense in that sea.
The night watched his horrible talons fleeing.
As a cloud feels its whirlwinds fall,
He felt his strength crumble in the chasm.
The winter murmured: tremble! and the shadow said: suffer!   155

Finally he perceived a black peak far off
Which a fearsome reflection in the shadow inflamed.
Satan, like a swimmer in his effort supreme,
Stretched out his wing, with claws and bald, and specter-pale,
Panting, broken, tired, and smoking with sweat,   160
He sank down on the edge of the abrupt descent.[8]

VIII

There was the sun dying in the abyss.
The star, in the deepest fog had no air to revive it,
Grew cold, dim, and was slowly destroyed.
Its sinister round was seen in the night;   165
And in this somber silence its fiery ulcers were seen
Subsiding under a leprosy of dark.
Coal of a world put out! torch blown out by God!
Its crevices still showed a trace of fire,
As if the soul could be seen through holes in the skull.   170
At the center there quivered and flickered a flame
Now and then licking the outermost edge,
And from each crater flashes came
Shivering like flaming swords,
And fading noiselessly as dreams.   175
The star was almost black. The archangel was tired
Beyond voice or breath, a pity to see.
And the star in death throes under his savage glance,
Was dying, doing battle. With its somber apertures
Into the cold darkness it spewed now and again   180
Burning streams, crimson lumps, and smoking hills,
Rocks foaming with initial brightness:
As if this giant of life and light
Engulfed by the mist where all is fading,
Had refused to die without insulting the night   185
And spitting its lava in the shadow's face.

8. Literally, escarpment, the steep wall before a fortification or cliff.

About it time and space and number,
Form, and noise expired, making
The forbidding and black oneness of void.
Then the specter Nothing[9] raised its head from the abyss.   190

Suddenly, from the heart of the star, a jet of sulphur
Sharp, clamorous like one dying in delirium,
Burst sudden, shining, splendid with surprise,
And lighting from far a thousand deathly forms,
Massive, pierced to the shadow's depths   195
The monstrous porches of endless deep.
Night and immensity formed
Their angels. Satan, wild and out of breath,
His vision dazzled and full of this flashing,
Beat with his wing, opened his hands and then shivered   200
And cried: "Despair! see it growing pale!"

The archangel understood, as does the mast in its sinking,
That he was the drowned man of the shadows' flood;
He furled once more his wing with its granite nails,
And wrung his hands. And the star went out.   205

IX

Now, near the skies, at chasm's edge where nothing changes,
One feather escaped from the archangel's wing
Remained and quivered, pure and white.
The angel on whose forehead the dazzling dawn is born
Saw and grasped it, observing the sublime sky: 210
"Lord, must it too fall into the abyss?"
God turned about, absorbed in being and in Life,
And said "Do not discard what has not fallen."[1]

                    *   *   *

Black caves of the past, porches of time passed
With no date and no radiance, somber, unmeasured,   215
Cycles previous to man, chaos, heavens,
World terrible and rich in prodigious beings,
Oh fearful fog where the preadamites
Appeared, standing in limitless shadow.
Who could fathom you, oh chasms, oh unknown times.   220
The thinker barefoot like the poor,
Through respect for the One unseen, the sage,
Digs in the depths of origin and age,
Fathoms and seeks beyond the colossi,[2] further
Than the facts witnessed by the present sky,   225
Reaches with pale visage suspected things,
And finds, lifting the darkness of years

---

9. Satan.   1. In the second part of *The End of Satan*—*Satan's Feather*—the feather is brought to life by a divine glance and becomes the female spirit Liberty. She wins God's permission to plunge into hell in an attempt to redeem her father (part 3), and in part 4 the repentant Archangel is released and re-created as Lucifer.   2. Giants of preadamic time.

And the layers of days, worlds, voids,
Gigantic centuries dead beneath giants of centuries.
And thus the wise man dreams in the deep of the night   230
His face illumined by glints of the abyss.

ALPHONSE DE LAMARTINE
1790–1869

Celebrated among the French Romantics for his "poetry of the soul," lyric meditations that united passion, philosophy, and religious humanism, Alphonse de Lamartine was also a novelist and statesman who served in various diplomatic and elected positions before retiring in disgust at Louis Napoleon's coup d'état in 1851. His father was an aristocrat who had narrowly escaped the guillotine in the French Revolution; he himself had early royalist sympathies but became a liberal and a prominent opposition figure in the revolution of 1848, even holding a top position in the short-lived provisional government.

Poetry, Lamartine said, echoes our deepest intuitions and intelligence: it is a sincere expression of the whole human being. He boasted that he had "brought poetry down from Parnassus" and taught it to express human emotions. Much of his own poetry draws on personal life, and *The Lake,* whose lyrical passion inspired a generation of French romantics, recalls a brief but intense love affair between the poet and a young married woman, Julie Charles. Meeting one summer when both were at a health resort on Lake Bourget in the French Alps, they separated over the winter but promised to meet again the next year. When the poet returned to the lake, however, Julie was already dying and he found himself alone. *The Lake* is Lamartine's elegy to his lost love, a melodious complaint that moves from the intimate situation of two lovers to a meditation on nature and time.

Andrea Moorhead's remarkably faithful translation suggests Lamartine's lyrical yet philosophical voice.

The standard biography of Lamartine is H. R. Whitehouse, *The Life of Lamartine* (1918; reprinted 1969). M. E. Birkett, *Lamartine and the Poetics of Landscape* (1982), examines the poet's transformation of landscape to convey human thoughts and emotions.

PRONOUNCING GLOSSARY

The following list uses common English syllables and stress accents to provide rough equivalents of selected words whose pronunciation may be unfamiliar to the general reader.

Bourget: *boor-zhay'*   Lamartine: *lah-mahr-teen'*

The Lake

And thus, forever driven towards new shores,
Swept into eternal night without return,
Will we never, for even one day, drop anchor
     On time's vast ocean?

O lake! Only a year has now gone by,[1]   5
And to these dear waves she would have seen again,
Look! I'm returning alone to rest on the very rock
   Where you last saw her rest!

Then as now, you rumbled under these great rocks;
Then as now, you broke against their torn flanks;   10
The wind hurling the foam from your waves
   Onto her adored feet.

One evening, you recall? We drifted in silence;
Far off on the water and under the stars hearing
Only the rhythmic sound of oars striking   15
   Your melodious waves.

Suddenly strains unknown on earth
Echoed from the enchanted shore;
The water paid heed, and the voice so dear
   To me spoke these words: 20

"O time, suspend your flight! and you, blessed hours,
   Suspend your swift passage.
Allow us to savor the fleeting delights
   Of our most happy days!

So many wretched people beseech you: 25
   Flow, flow quickly for them;
Take away the cares devouring them;
   Overlook the happy.

But I ask in vain for just a few more moments,
   Time escaping me flees;   30
While I beg the night: 'Slow down,' already
   It fades into the dawn.

Then let us love, let us love! And the fleeting hours
   Let us hasten to enjoy.
We have no port, time itself has no shore;   35
   It glides by, and we pass away."

Jealous time, will these moments of such intoxication,
Love flooding us with overwhelming bliss,
Fly past us with the same speed
   As dark and painful days?   40

What! will we not keep at least the trace of them?
What! They are gone forever? Totally lost?
This time that gave them and is obliterating them,
   Will it never return them to us?

---

1. They met in October 1816; it is now August 1817.

Eternity, nothingness, past, somber abysses,   45
What are you doing with the days you swallow up?
Speak: will you ever give back the sublime bliss
    You stole from us?

O lake! silent rocks! shaded grottoes! dark forest!
You whom time can spare or even rejuvenate,   50
Preserve, noble nature, preserve from this night
    At least the memory!

May it live in your peace, may it be in your storms,
Beautiful lake, and in the light of your glad slopes,
And in these tall dark firs and in these savage rocks,   55
    Overhanging your waves.

May it be in the trembling zephyr passing by,
In the endless sounds that carry from shore to shore
In the silver faced star[2] that whitens your surface
    With its softened brilliance.   60

May the moaning wind and sighing reed,
May the delicate scent of your fragrant breeze,
May everything that we hear and see and breathe,
    Awaken the memory of—their love!

---

2. The moon.

GIACOMO LEOPARDI
1798–1837

The product of a rigid upbringing by aristocratic parents, the Italian Giacomo Leopardi (*jah'-koh-moh lay-oh-pahr'-dee*) grew to adulthood plagued by many ailments, a hunchback close to blindness. But his intellectual powers were highly developed, and he soon developed a fine reputation as scholar, poet, and translator. His poetry characteristically expresses a poignant sensitivity to the beauty and promise of everyday life, as well as despair at its inevitable destruction with the passage of time. Only the poetic imagination, which allows Leopardi to grasp and transcend his own mortality, offers an escape: "And sweet to me the foundering in this sea [of eternity]," he writes in *The Infinite*.

Ottavio M. Casale translated the selections printed here, skillfully conveying the rhythms of Leopardi's free verse.

The best biography of Leopardi is I. Origo, *Leopardi: A Biography* (1935). For critical insight, see the commentary in O. M. Casale, *A Leopardi Reader* (1981); J. P. Barricelli, *Giacomi Leopardi* (1986); and D. Bini, *A Fragrance from the Desert: Poetry and Philosophy in Giacomo Leopardi* (1983).

The Infinite

This lonely hill has always been so dear
To me, and dear the hedge which hides away
The reaches of the sky. But sitting here
And wondering, I fashion in my mind
The endless spaces far beyond, the more   5
Than human silences, and deepest peace;
So that the heart is on the edge of fear.
And when I hear the wind come blowing through
The trees, I pit its voice against that boundless
Silence and summon up eternity,   10
And the dead seasons, and the present one,
Alive with all its sound. And thus it is
In this immensity my thought is drowned:
And sweet to me the foundering in this sea.

To Himself

Now you may rest forever,
My tired heart. The last illusion is dead
That I believed eternal. Dead. I can
So clearly see—not only hope is gone
But the desire to be deceived as well.   5
Rest, rest forever.
You have beaten long enough. Nothing is worth
Your smallest motion, nor the earth your sighs.
This life is bitterness
And vacuum, nothing else. The world is mud.   10
From now on calm yourself.
Despair for the last time. The only gift
Fate gave our kind was death. Henceforth, heap scorn
Upon yourself, Nature, the ugly force
That, hidden, orders universal ruin,   15
And the boundless emptiness of everything.

To Sylvia

Sylvia. Do you remember still
The moments of your mortal lifetime here,
When such a loveliness
Shone in the elusive laughter of your eyes,
And you, contemplative and gay, climbed toward   5
The summit of your youth?

The tranquil chambers held,
The paths re-echoed, your perpetual song,

When at your woman's tasks
You sat, content to concentrate upon   10
The future beckoning within your mind.
It was the fragrant May,
And thus you passed your time.

   I often used to leave
The dear, belabored pages which consumed   15
So much of me and of my youth, and from
Ancestral balconies
Would lean to hear the music of your voice,
Your fingers humming through
The intricacies of the weaving work.   20
And I would gaze upon
The blue surrounding sky,
The paths and gardens golden in the sun,
And there the far-off sea, and here the mountain.
No human tongue can tell   25
What I felt then within my brimming heart.

   What tendernesses then,
What hopes, what hearts were ours, O Sylvia mine!
How large a thing seemed life, and destiny!
When I recall those bright anticipations,   30
Bitterness invades,
And I turn once again to mourn my lot.
O Nature, Nature, why
Do you not keep the promises you gave?
Why trick the children so?   35

   Before the winter struck the summer grass,
You died, my gentle girl,
Besieged by hidden illness and possessed.
You never saw the flowering of your years.
Your heart was never melted by the praise   40
Of your dark hair, your shy,
Enamoured eyes. Nor did you with your friends
Conspire on holidays to talk of love.

   The expectation failed
As soon for me, and fate denied my youth.   45
Ah how gone by, gone by,
You dear companion of my dawning time,
The hope that I lament!
Is this the world we knew? And these the joys
The love, the labors, happenings we shared?   50
And this the destiny
Of human beings? My poor one, when
The truth rose up, you fell,
And from afar you pointed me the way
To coldest death and the stark sepulchre.   55

The Village Saturday

The sun is falling as the peasant girl
Returns from the open fields,
Bearing a swathe of grass and in her hand
Her customary bunch of violets
And roses which will grace   5
Her hair and breast the coming holiday.
And, spinning, the old woman sits upon
The steps among her neighbors,
Their faces turned against the dying light;
And she tells tales of her green days, when she   10
Adorned her body for the holidays
And, slenderly robust,
Would dance the night away
Among the companions of her lovely prime.
The very air seems now to deepen, the sky   15
Turns darker blue. Down from the hills and roofs
Returning shadows fall
At the whitening of the moon.

Now bells declare the time
Is near, the festive day,   20
The hour of heart's renewal.
The shouting lads invade
The village square in troops,
Leaping now here, now there,
Making such happy chatter.   25
Meanwhile the whistling laborer comes back
To take his meager meal
And ruminate about his day of rest.

And then, when every other lamp is out
And other sounds are stilled—   30
Listen—a pounding hammer and a saw:
It is the carpenter,
Awake and hurrying by lanternlight
Inside his shuttered shop
To end his task before the morning breaks.   35

Of all the seven days this is the one
Most cherished, full of joy and expectation.
The passing hours will bring tomorrow soon,
And tedium and sadness,
When each shall turn inside   40
His mind to his habitual travail.

O playful little boy,
Your flowering time is like a day of grace,

So brightly blue,
Anticipating the great feast of life.   45
My child, enjoy the season.
I will not tell you more; but if the day
Seems slow in coming, do not grieve too much.

NOVALIS (FRIEDRICH VON HARDENBERG)
1772–1801

Born into a family of the German nobility, Friedrich von Hardenberg assumed the pseudonym Novalis on the basis of his family's earlier use of the name "de Novali." He studied first law, then mining, and ended his career as a mine inspector at a saltworks. His achievement as poet and philosopher, however, despite his short life (he died of tuberculosis), powerfully influenced later Romantic thought. *Hymns to the Night*, from which the selection printed here is taken, expressed his grief over the death, also from tuberculosis, of the young girl to whom he had been engaged. In the hymns, Novalis insists that death provides the entrance into a higher life, and he anticipates his eventual union with his fiancée and with the universe as a whole.

The translator is Charles E. Passage, who attempts to convey Novalis's characteristic combination of mystical and sentimental feeling.

Useful studies of Novalis include F. Hiebal, *Novalis: German Poet, European Thinker, Christian Mystic* (1954), and B. Haywood, *Novalis, The Veil of Imagery: A Study of the Poetic Works of Friedrich von Hardenberg, 1772–1801* (1959).

PRONOUNCING GLOSSARY

The following list uses common English syllables and stress accents to provide rough equivalents of selected words whose pronunciation may be unfamiliar to the general reader.

Friedrich von Hardenberg: *freed'-rick*   Novalis: *noh-vahl'-is*

   fon hahr'-den-berg

Yearning for Death

Down now into the dark earth's womb,
From Light's domain away!
Wild rage of grief and pangs of gloom
Mark glad departure's day.
In narrow barque[1] we swiftly ply   5
To land along the shores of sky.

---
1. Boat.

Praised be the everlasting Night,
Praised be eternal slumber!
Day's heat has withered us, and blight
Of sorrows without number.   10
For alien lands we no more yearn,
To our Father's house we would return.

In this world what can us betide
Our love and constancy?
When old things have been put aside   15
What use can new things be?
O! lonely stands and all undone
Whoever loves the times foregone.

The times foregone, when in bright dance
High spirits flamed, and when   20
The Father's hand and countenance
Were still in mankind's ken,
And nobly, simply, many bore
The lofty image that he bore.

The times foregone, when full-bloom-blowing   25
Primaeval races throve,
And children toward God's kingdom going
For death and torment strove;
And when, though life and pleasure spoke,
Yet many hearts, for loving, broke.   30

Those times, when God himself revealed
Himself with youthful ardor,
And with love's strength his sweet life sealed
In young death as a martyr,
Refusing not the smart and pain,   35
That it might be our dearer gain.

We see them now, with anxious yearning,
Shrouded in dark of night;
In temporal life our hot thirst's burning
Will not be slaked outright;   40
Unto our homeland we must go
That we that holy time may know.

What holds up our return? To rest
Our loved ones are long laid.
At their graves closes our lives' quest,   45
Sad are we and afraid.
There is no more for us to seek,
The heart is sated, the world is bleak.

A mystic shudder, sweet, unbounded,
Now courses through our marrow;   50
Methinks from the far distance sounded

An echo of our sorrow.
Perhaps our loved ones likewise longing
Have wafted us this sigh of longing.

Down to the sweet bride[2] come away,   55
To Jesus whom we love!
Good cheer! The evening dawn shows gray
On them who grieve and love.
Dream bursts our bonds and sinks us free
To our Father's arms eternally.   60

2. Jesus, as the bride of humankind.

ALEXANDER SERGEYEVICH PUSHKIN
1799–1837

In his best-known story, *The Queen of Spades,* Alexander Pushkin combines familiar elements of Romantic fiction—the penniless young woman; the ambitious, passionate young man; the decayed beauty; the ghost—in a tale with intense ironic overtones, a tale later a favorite of the great Russian novelist Fyodor Dostoevsky. Pushkin's own life story sounds like a Romantic novel. Born into an aristocratic Russian family, neglected by his parents, he early began an extensive amatory and poetic career, publishing his first poem at the age of fifteen and becoming notorious about the same time for his many erotic involvements. At eighteen he graduated from a distinguished boarding school and accepted appointment in the Foreign Service; six years later, the various instances of his defiance of authority resulted in expulsion from the service and confinement, under police surveillance, on a paternal estate. After the death of Tsar Alexander I and the abortive military uprising that followed (an uprising involving several of Pushkin's friends, five of whom were subsequently hanged), Pushkin—by then a well-known poet—was befriended (1826) by the new tsar, Nicholas. He moved back to Moscow, then to Petersburg, leading a moneyed and relatively carefree life. In 1831, however, he married a nineteen-year-old woman, whose apparently flirtatious behavior embittered his subsequent life. He died after a duel with his wife's putative lover.

Producing short lyrics, narrative poems, a great novel in verse (*Eugene Onegin*), lyrical drama (notably *Boris Gudonov*), versified folk tales, and prose fiction, Pushkin established himself as one of Russia's greatest writers. His interest in his nation's past, his tendency to challenge authority, his fascination with the character and situation of strong individuals: such obsessive concerns link his work with that of his Romantic contemporaries elsewhere in Europe. Goethe, Byron, and early nineteenth-century French novelists had a marked influence on him. He retained also, however, the kind of clarity, discipline, and ironic distance more often associated with the literature of the preceding century.

The treatment of love and sexuality in *The Queen of Spades* exemplifies the complexity of Pushkin's approach. First of all we hear the story of the "Muscovite Venus," the beautiful young gambler who pays her debts by learning the secret of three infallible cards. Then we encounter a young woman suffering in her dependent position and longing for a "deliverer." Hermann, the immediate object of Lisaveta's dreams, has his own sexual fantasies: himself a young man, he imagines becoming the lover of the eighty-seven-year-old countess. At this point, if not before, the reader begins to realize that something's wrong here: this is not the kind of romantic tale we're used to. Describing Hermann's first glimpse of Lisaveta, Pushkin writes, "Hermann saw a small, fresh face and a pair of dark eyes. That moment decided his fate." A Romantic cliché—except that the young man sees Lisaveta not as an object of devotion but as a means to an end. He sends her a love letter, copied word for word from a German novel. His rapidly developing passion focuses on financial, not erotic, gain.

Lisaveta's character remains somewhat more ambiguous. The narrator invokes sympathy for her plight, at the mercy of a tyrannical employer who makes endless irrational demands and who never pays her. Her situation prohibits her from enjoying the kinds of amorous gratification other young women can expect. We can understand, therefore, why her dreams should concentrate specifically on a deliverer. Like Hermann, although far less unscrupulous, she may indulge in intrigues as a means to an end—in her case, not money but liberty.

The Queen of Spades contains no completely attractive characters. If Lisaveta's victimization arouses compassion, her lack of moral force or determination may also provoke irritation. Hermann's will to succeed, on the other hand, makes him a potential hero; but his obsession with money and his mean-spirited expediency alienate most readers. The countess, old and approaching death, uses the power of her money and rank with utter disregard for the needs or feelings of others. Even such a minor figure as the countess's grandson, Tomsky, playing with Lisaveta's feelings, going through his ritualized flirtation with Princess Polina, seems thoroughly contaminated by the values of the world he inhabits.

Indeed, those values provide the central subject of this tale. Pushkin employs conventions of the kind of ghost story common in folk tales to convey serious criticism of a social structure corrupted by universal concentration on money. Gambling provides not only the chief male activity but also the central metaphor of the story. Everyone is out for what he or she can get. The countess, whose days at the card table are past, uses her money to buy subservience; Lisaveta is willing to risk her reputation, maybe even her chastity, for the possibility of escaping servitude; Hermann frightens someone to death in an effort to make his fortune; Tomsky plays elaborate social games of advance and retreat, trying to get his princess. The queen of spades is a conventional symbol of death; the kind of death most important in Pushkin's story is not literal—not the countess's demise—but figurative: it is the spiritual death suffered by the other characters, over whose world the countess/queen of spades metaphorically presides.

The "Conclusion" of The Queen of Spades, a deadpan summary of the characters' future careers, epitomizes the story's central concerns. Hermann's madness dramatizes the financial obsession he has displayed from the beginning; Lisaveta's marriage, to an anonymous "very agreeable young man" with a good position "somewhere," emphasizes the degree to which she has always wished for marriage as rescue, not as attachment to a particular beloved other. In her married state, Lisaveta, ironically, "is bringing up a poor relative," recapitulating the structure of exploitation from which she herself suffered. Tomsky, relatively unimportant to the plot line, supplies the subject for the story's concluding sentence: his promotion and his "good" marriage remind us that everyone in the society here described seeks personal advantage at all costs. Hermann has simply paid the cost in the most dramatic way.

Henri Troyat, Pushkin (1971), is an excellent biography. For biography and criticism, the student might also consult Walter Arndt, Pushkin Threefold: Narrative, Lyric, Polemic and Ribald Verse (1972); John Bayley, Pushkin: A Comparative Commentary (1971); P. Debreczeny, The Other Pushkin: A Study of Alexander Pushkin's

Prose (1983); John Oliver Killens, *Great Black Russian* (1989); and D. M. Bethea, ed., *Pushkin Today* (1993), an ambitious collection of essays. A useful biography is Stephanie Sandler, *Distant Pleasures* (1989).

PRONOUNCING GLOSSARY

The following list uses common English syllables and stress accents to provide rough equivalents of selected words whose pronunciation may be unfamiliar to the general reader.

Chekalinsky: *che-kah-leen'-skee*

Eletskaya: *ye-lyet'-skah-yuh*

Fedotovna: *fye-daw'-tuv-nuh*

Ilyitch: *il-yeech'*

Lisaveta Ivanovna: *lyee-zah-vye'-tuh*
ee-vah'-nuv-nuh

Richelieu: *ree'-she-lyeuh*

St-Germain: *sanh-zher-manh'*

The Queen of Spades[1]

CHAPTER ONE

> *And on rainy days*
> *They gathered*
> *Often;*
> *Their stakes—God help them!—*
> *Wavered from fifty*
> *To a hundred,*
> *And they won*
> *And marked up their winnings*
> *With chalk.*
> *Thus on rainy days*
> *Were they*
> *Busy.*[2]

There was a card party one day in the rooms of Narumov, an officer of the Horse Guards. The long winter evening slipped by unnoticed; it was five o'clock in the morning before the assembly sat down to supper. Those who had won ate with a big appetite; the others sat distractedly before their empty plates. But champagne was brought in, the conversation became more lively, and everyone took a part in it.

"And how did you get on, Surin?" asked the host.

"As usual, I lost. I must confess, I have no luck: I never vary my stake, never get heated, never lose my head, and yet I always lose!"

"And weren't you tempted even once to back[3] on a series . . . ? Your strength of mind astonishes me."

"What about Hermann then," said one of the guests, pointing at the young Engineer.[4] "He's never held a card in his hand, never doubled a single stake in his life, and yet he sits up until five in the morning watching us play."

"The game fascinates me," said Hermann, "but I am not in the position to sacrifice the essentials of life in the hope of acquiring the luxuries."

1. Translated by Gillon R. Aitken.   2. Like most of the chapter epigraphs, this was presumably written by Pushkin himself.   3. Bet.   4. A member of the Corps of Engineers, concerned with fortifications.

"Hermann's a German: he's cautious—that's all," Tomsky observed. "But if there's one person I can't understand, it's my grandmother, the Countess Anna Fedotovna."

"How? Why?" the guests inquired noisily.

"I can't understand why it is," Tomsky continued, "that my grandmother doesn't gamble."

"But what's so astonishing about an old lady of eighty not gambling?" asked Narumov.

"Then you don't know . . . ?"

"No, indeed; I know nothing."

"Oh well, listen then:

"You must know that about sixty years ago my grandmother went to Paris, where she made something of a hit. People used to chase after her to catch a glimpse of *la vénus moscovite*; Richelieu[5] paid court to her, and my grandmother vouches that he almost shot himself on account of her cruelty. At that time ladies used to play faro.[6] On one occasion at the Court, my grandmother lost a very great deal of money on credit to the Duke of Orleans. Returning home, she removed the patches[7] from her face, took off her hooped petticoat, announced her loss to my grandfather and ordered him to pay back the money. My late grandfather, as far as I can remember, was a sort of lackey to my grandmother. He feared her like fire; on hearing of such a disgraceful loss, however, he completely lost his temper; he produced his accounts, showed her that she had spent half a million francs in six months, pointed out that neither their Moscow nor their Saratov estates were in Paris, and refused point-blank to pay the debt. My grandmother gave him a box on the ear and went off to sleep on her own as an indication of her displeasure. In the hope that this domestic infliction would have had some effect on him, she sent for her husband the next day; she found him unshakeable. For the first time in her life she approached him with argument and explanation, thinking that she could bring him to reason by pointing out that there are debts and debts, that there is a big difference between a Prince and a coach-maker. But my grandfather remained adamant, and flatly refused to discuss the subject any further. My grandmother did not know what to do. A little while before, she had become acquainted with a very remarkable man. You have heard of Count St-Germain,[8] about whom so many marvellous stories are related. You know that he held himself out to be the Wandering Jew, and the inventor of the elixir of life, the philosopher's stone and so forth. Some ridiculed him as a charlatan and in his memoirs Casanova declares that he was a spy. However, St-Germain, in spite of the mystery which surrounded him, was a person of venerable appearance and much in demand in society. My grandmother is still quite infatuated with him and becomes quite angry if anyone speaks of him with disrespect. My grandmother knew that he had large sums of money at his disposal. She decided to have recourse to him, and wrote asking him to visit her without delay. The eccentric old man at

---

5. Louis-François-Arnand de Vignerod du Plessis, duc de Richelieu (1696–1788), French aristocrat renowned throughout the eighteenth century for both his military and his sexual exploits. *La vénus moscovite*: the Venus of Moscow (French). Venus was the goddess of love.   6. A card game much used for gambling.   7. I.e., beauty patches, artificial "beauty marks" made of black silk or court plaster and worn on the face or neck.   8. Celebrated adventurer (ca. 1710–1784?) who frequented the French, German, and Russian courts.

once called on her and found her in a state of terrible grief. She depicted her husband's barbarity in the blackest light, and ended by saying that she pinned all her hopes on his friendship and kindness.

"St-Germain reflected. 'I could let you have this sum,' he said, 'but I know that you would not be at peace while in my debt, and I have no wish to bring fresh troubles upon your head. There is another solution—you can win back the money."

" 'But, my dear Count," my grandmother replied, 'I tell you—we have no money at all.'

" 'In this case money is not essential,' St-Germain replied. 'Be good enough to hear me out."

"And at this point he revealed to her the secret for which any one of us here would give a very great deal . . ."

The young gamblers listened with still great attention. Tomsky lit his pipe, drew on it and continued:

"That same evening my grandmother went to Versailles, *au jeu de la Reine.*[9] The Duke of Orleans kept the bank; inventing some small tale, my grandmother lightly excused herself for not having brought her debt, and began to play against him. She chose three cards and played them one after the other: all three won and my grandmother recouped herself completely."

"Pure luck!" said one of the guests.

"A fairy-tale," observed Hermann.

"Perhaps the cards were marked!" said a third.

"I don't think so," Tomsky replied gravely.

"What!" cried Narumov. "You have a grandmother who can guess three cards in succession, and you haven't yet contrived to learn her secret."

"No, not much hope of that!" replied Tomsky. "She had four sons, including my father; all four were desperate gamblers, and yet she did not reveal her secret to a single one of them, although it would have been a good thing if she had told them—told me, even. But this is what I heard from my uncle, Count Ivan Ilyitch, and he gave me his word for its truth. The late Chaplitsky—the same who died a pauper after squandering millions—in his youth once lost nearly 300,000 roubles—to Zoritch, if I remember rightly. He was in despair. My grandmother, who was most strict in her attitude towards the extravagances of young men, for some reason took pity on Chaplitsky. She told him the three cards on condition that he played them in order; and at the same time she exacted his solemn promise that he would never play again as long as he lived. Chaplitsky appeared before his victor; they sat down to play. On the first card Chaplitsky staked 50,000 roubles and won straight off; he doubled his stake, redoubled—and won back more than he had lost. . . .

"But it's time to go to bed; it's already a quarter to six."

Indeed, the day was already beginning to break. The young men drained their glasses and dispersed.

9. To the queen's game (French).

CHAPTER TWO

"Il paraît que monsieur est décidément pour les suivantes."
"Que voulez-vous, madame? Elles sont plus fraîches."
FASHIONABLE CONVERSATION

The old Countess * * *[1] was seated before the looking-glass in her dressing-room. Three lady's maids stood by her. One held a jar of rouge, another a box of hairpins, and the third a tall bonnet with flame-coloured ribbons. The Countess no longer had the slightest pretensions to beauty, which had long since faded from her face, but she still preserved all the habits of her youth, paid strict regard to the fashions of the seventies, and devoted to her dress the same time and attention as she had done sixty years before. At an embroidery frame by the window sat a young lady, her ward.

"Good morning, *grand'maman!*" said a young officer as he entered the room. *"Bonjour, mademoiselle Lise. Grand'maman,*[2] I have a request to make of you."

"What is it, Paul?"

"I want you to let me introduce one of my friends to you, and to allow me to bring him to the ball on Friday."

"Bring him straight to the ball and introduce him to me there. Were you at * * *'s yesterday?"

"Of course. It was very gay; we danced until five in the morning. How charming Eletskaya was!"

"But, my dear, what's charming about her? Isn't she like her grandmother, the Princess Darya Petrovna . . . ? By the way, I dare say she's grown very old now, the Princess Darya Petrovna?"

"What do you mean, 'grown old'?" asked Tomsky thoughtlessly. "She's been dead for seven years."

The young lady raised her head and made a sign to the young man. He remembered then that the death of any of her contemporaries was kept secret from the old Countess, and he bit his lip. But the Countess heard the news, previously unknown to her, with the greatest indifference.

"Dead!" she said. "And I didn't know it. We were maids of honour together, and when we were presented, the Empress . . ."

And for the hundredth time the Countess related the anecdote to her grandson.

"Come, Paul," she said when she had finished her story, "help me to stand up. Lisanka, where's my snuff-box?"

And with her three maids the Countess went behind a screen to complete her dress. Tomsky was left alone with the young lady.

"Whom do you wish to introduce?" Lisaveta Ivanovna asked softly.

"Narumov. Do you know him?"

"No. Is he a soldier or a civilian?"

"A soldier."

"An Engineer?"

"No, he's in the Cavalry. What made you think he was an Engineer?"

1. Asterisks in this selection are the author's and are intended to suggest that the proper name of an actual person has been omitted. The epigram can be translated as: "It appears that the gentleman is decidedly in favor of servant girls." "What would you have me do, Madam? They are fresher [than upper-class women]" (French).   2. Russian aristocrats often spoke French. Lisaveta is here called by the French name Lise, and Pavel, Paul.

The young lady smiled but made no reply.

"Paul!" cried the Countess from behind the screen. "Bring along a new novel with you some time, will you, only please not one of those modern ones."

"What do you mean, *grand'maman?*"

"I mean not the sort of novel in which the hero strangles either of his parents or in which someone is drowned.[3] I have a great horror of drowned people."

"Such novels don't exist nowadays. Wouldn't you like a Russian one?"

"Are there such things? Send me one, my dear, please send me one."

"Will you excuse me now, *grand'maman*, I'm in a hurry. Good-bye, Lisaveta Ivanovna. What made you think that Narumov was in the Engineers?"

And Tomsky left the dressing-room.

Lisaveta Ivanovna was left on her own; she put aside her work and began to look out of the window. Presently a young officer appeared from behind the corner house on the other side of the street. A flush spread over her cheeks; she took up her work again and lowered her head over the frame. At this moment, the Countess returned, fully dressed.

"Order the carriage, Lisanka," she said, "and we'll go for a drive."

Lisanka got up from behind her frame and began to put away her work.

"What's the matter with you, my child? Are you deaf?" shouted the Countess. "Order the carriage this minute."

"I'll do so at once," the young lady replied softly and hastened into the ante-room.

A servant entered the room and handed the Countess some books from the Prince Pavel Alexandrovitch.

"Good, thank him," said the Countess. "Lisanka, Lisanka, where are you running to?"

"To get dressed."

"Plenty of time for that, my dear. Sit down. Open the first volume and read to me."

The young lady took up the book and read a few lines.

"Louder!" said the Countess. "What's the matter with you, my child? Have you lost your voice, or what . . . ? Wait . . . move that footstool up to me . . . nearer . . . that's right!"

Lisaveta Ivanovna read a further two pages. The Countess yawned.

"Put the book down," she said; "what rubbish! Have it returned to Prince Pavel with my thanks. . . . But where is the carriage?"

"The carriage is ready," said Lisaveta Ivanovna, looking out into the street.

"Then why aren't you dressed?" asked the Countess. "I'm always having to wait for you—it's intolerable, my dear!"

Lisa ran up to her room. Not two minutes elapsed before the Countess began to ring with all her might. The three lady's maids came running in through one door and the valet through another.

"Why don't you come when you're called?" the Countess asked them. "Tell Lisaveta Ivanovna that I'm waiting for her."

Lisaveta Ivanovna entered the room wearing her hat and cloak.

---

3. Novels of the sort the countess does not wish to read were typical of the then current decadent movement in French literature.

"At last, my child!" said the Countess. "But what clothes you're wearing . . . ! Whom are you hoping to catch? What's the weather like? It seems windy."

"There's not a breath of wind, your Ladyship," replied the valet.

"You never know what you're talking about! Open that small window. There; as I thought: windy and bitterly cold. Unharness the horses. Lisaveta, we're not going out—there was no need to dress up like that."

"And this is my life," thought Lisaveta Ivanovna.

And indeed Lisaveta Ivanovna was a most unfortunate creature. As Dante says: "You shall learn the salt taste of another's bread, and the hard path up and down his stairs";[4] and who better to know the bitterness of dependence than the poor ward of a well-born old lady? The Countess * * * was far from being wicked, but she had the capriciousness of a woman who has been spoiled by the world, and the miserliness and cold-hearted egotism of all old people who have done with loving and whose thoughts lie with the past. She took part in all the vanities of the *haut-monde*;[5] she dragged herself to balls, where she sat in a corner, rouged and dressed in old-fashioned style, like some misshapen but essential ornament of the ball-room; on arrival, the guests would approach her with low bows, as if in accordance with an established rite, but after that, they would pay no further attention to her. She received the whole town at her house, and although no longer able to recognise the faces of her guests, she observed the strictest etiquette. Her numerous servants, grown fat and grey in her hall and servants' room, did exactly as they pleased, vying with one another in stealing from the dying old lady. Lisaveta Ivanovna was the household martyr. She poured out the tea, and was reprimanded for putting in too much sugar; she read novels aloud, and was held guilty of all the faults of the authors; she accompanied the Countess on her walks, and was made responsible for the state of the weather and the pavement. There was a salary attached to her position, but it was never paid; meanwhile, it was demanded of her to be dressed like everybody else—that is, like the very few who could afford to dress well. In society she played the most pitiable role. Everybody knew her, but nobody took any notice of her; at balls she danced only when there was a partner short, and ladies only took her arm when they needed to go to the dressing-room to make some adjustment to their dress. She was proud and felt her position keenly, and looked around her in impatient expectation of a deliverer; but the young men, calculating in their flightiness, did not honour her with their attention, despite the fact that Lisaveta Ivanovna was a hundred times prettier than the cold, arrogant but more eligible young ladies on whom they danced attendance. Many a time did she creep softly away from the bright but wearisome drawing-room to go and cry in her own poor room, where stood a papered screen, a chest of drawers, a small looking-glass and a painted bedstead, and where a tallow candle burned dimly in its copper candle-stick.

One day—two days after the evening described at the beginning of this story, and about a week previous to the events just recorded—Lisaveta Ivanovna was sitting at her embroidery frame by the window, when, happening to glance out into the street, she saw a young Engineer, standing motionless

4. *Paradiso* 17.59. 5. High society (French).

with his eyes fixed upon her window. She lowered her head and continued with her work; five minutes later she looked out again—the young officer was still standing in the same place. Not being in the habit of flirting with passing officers, she ceased to look out of the window, and sewed for about two hours without raising her head. Dinner was announced. She got up and began to put away her frame, and, glancing casually out into the street, she saw the officer again. She was considerably puzzled by this. After dinner, she approached the window with a feeling of some disquiet, but the officer was no longer outside, and she thought no more of him.

Two days later, while preparing to enter the carriage with the Countess, she saw him again. He was standing just by the front-door, his face concealed by a beaver collar; his dark eyes shone from beneath his cap. Without knowing why, Lisaveta Ivanovna felt afraid, and an unaccountable trembling came over her as she sat down in the carriage.

On her return home, she hastened to the window—the officer was standing in the same place as before, his eyes fixed upon her; she drew back, tormented by curiosity and agitated by a feeling that was quite new to her.

Since then, not a day had passed without the young man appearing at the customary hour beneath the windows of their house. A sort of mute acquaintance grew up between them. At work in her seat, she used to feel him approaching, and would raise her head to look at him—for longer and longer each day. The young man seemed to be grateful to her for this: she saw, with the sharp eye of youth, how a sudden flush would spread across his pale cheeks on each occasion that their glances met. After a week she smiled at him. . . .

When Tomsky asked leave of the Countess to introduce one of his friends to her; the poor girl's heart beat fast. But on learning that Narumov was in the Horse Guards, and not in the Engineers, she was sorry that, by an indiscreet question, she had betrayed her secret to the light-hearted Tomsky.

Hermann was the son of a Russianised German, from whom he had inherited a small amount of money. Being firmly convinced of the necessity of ensuring his independence, Hermann did not draw on the income that this yielded, but lived on his pay, forbidding himself the slightest extravagance. Moreover, he was secretive and ambitious, and his companions rarely had occasion to laugh at his excessive thrift. He had strong passions and a fiery imagination, but his tenacity of spirit saved him from the usual errors of youth. Thus, for example, although at heart a gambler, he never took a card in his hand, for he reckoned that his position did not allow him (as he put it) "to sacrifice the essentials of life in the hope of acquiring the luxuries"—and meanwhile, he would sit up at the card table for whole nights at a time, and follow the different turns of the game with feverish anxiety.

The story of the three cards had made a strong impression on his imagination, and he could think of nothing else all night.

"What if the old Countess should reveal her secret to me?" he thought the following evening as he wandered through the streets of Petersburg. "What if she should tell me the names of those three winning cards? Why not try my luck . . . ? Become introduced to her, try to win her favour, perhaps become her lover . . . ? But all that demands time, and she's eighty-seven; she might die in a week, in two days . . . ! And the story itself . . . ? Can one really believe it . . . ? No! Economy, moderation and industry; these are my three winning cards, these will treble my capital, increase it sevenfold, and earn for me ease and independence!"

Reasoning thus, he found himself in one of the principal streets of Petersburg, before a house of old-fashioned architecture. The street was crowded with vehicles; one after another, carriages rolled up to the lighted entrance. From them there emerged, now the shapely little foot of some beautiful young woman, now a rattling jack-boot, now the striped stocking and elegant shoe of a diplomat. Furs and capes flitted past the majestic hall-porter. Hermann stopped.

"Whose house is this?" he asked the watchman at the corner.

"The Countess * * *'s," the watchman replied.

Hermann started. His imagination was again fired by the amazing story of the three cards. He began to walk around near the house, thinking of its owner and her mysterious faculty. It was late when he returned to his humble rooms; for a long time he could not sleep; and when at last he did drop off, cards, a green table,[6] heaps of banknotes and piles of golden coins appeared to him in his dreams. He played one card after the other, doubled his stake decisively, won unceasingly, and raked in the golden coins and stuffed his pockets with the banknotes. Waking up late, he sighed at the loss of his imaginary fortune, again went out to wander about the town and again found himself outside the house of the Countess * * *. Some unknown power seemed to have attracted him to it. He stopped and began to look at the windows. At one he saw a head with long black hair, probably bent down over a book or a piece of work. The head was raised. Hermann saw a small, fresh face and a pair of dark eyes. That moment decided his fate.

CHAPTER THREE

*Vous m'écrivez, mon ange, des lettres de
quatre pages plus vite que je ne puis
les lire.*[7]
CORRESPONDENCE

Scarcely had Lisaveta Ivanovna taken off her hat and cloak when the Countess sent for her and again ordered her to have the horses harnessed. They went out to take their seats in the carriage. At the same moment as the old lady was being helped through the carriage doors by two footmen, Lisaveta Ivanovna saw her Engineer standing close by the wheel; he seized her hand; before she could recover from her fright, the young man had disappeared—leaving a letter in her hand. She hid it in her glove and throughout the whole of the drive neither heard nor saw a thing. As was her custom when riding in her carriage, the Countess kept up a ceaseless flow of questions: "Who was it who met us just now? What's this bridge called? What's written on that signboard?" This time Lisaveta Ivanovna's answers were so vague and inappropriate that the Countess became angry.

"What's the matter with you, my child? Are you in a trance or something? Don't you hear me or understand what I'm saying . . . ? Heaven be thanked that I'm still sane enough to speak clearly."

6. Tables on which gambling took place were typically covered with green baize.   7. My angel, you write me four-page-long letters faster than I can read them (French).

Lisaveta Ivanovna did not listen to her. On returning home, she ran up to her room and drew the letter out of her glove; it was unsealed. Lisaveta Ivanovna read it through. The letter contained a confession of love; it was tender, respectful and taken word for word from a German novel. But Lisaveta Ivanovna had no knowledge of German and was most pleased by it.

Nevertheless, the letter made her feel extremely uneasy. For the first time in her life she was entering into a secret and confidential relationship with a young man. His audacity shocked her. She reproached herself for her imprudent behaviour, and did not know what to do. Should she stop sitting at the window and by a show of indifference cool off the young man's desire for further acquaintance? Should she send the letter back to him? Or answer it with cold-hearted finality? There was nobody to whom she could turn for advice: she had no friend or preceptress. Lisaveta Ivanovna resolved to answer the letter.

She sat down at her small writing-table, took a pen and some paper, and lost herself in thought. Several times she began her letter—and then tore it up; her manner of expression seemed to her to be either too condescending or too heartless. At last she succeeded in writing a few lines that satisfied her:

> I am sure that your intentions are honourable, and that you did not wish to offend me by your rash behaviour, but our acquaintance must not begin in this way. I return your letter to you and hope that in the future I shall have no cause to complain of undeserved disrespect.

The next day, as soon as she saw Hermann approach, Lisaveta Ivanovna rose from behind her frame, went into the ante-room, opened a small window, and threw her letter into the street, trusting to the agility of the young officer to pick it up. Hermann ran forward, took hold of the letter and went into a confectioner's shop. Breaking the seal of the envelope, he found his own letter and Lisaveta Ivanovna's answer. It was as he had expected, and he returned home, deeply preoccupied with his intrigue.

Three days afterwards, a bright-eyed young girl brought Lisaveta Ivanovna a letter from a milliner's shop. Lisaveta Ivanovna opened it uneasily, envisaging a demand for money, but she suddenly recognised Hermann's handwriting.

"You have made a mistake, my dear," she said; "this letter is not for me."

"Oh, but it is!" the girl answered cheekily and without concealing a sly smile. "Read it."

Lisaveta Ivanovna ran her eyes over the note. Hermann demanded a meeting.

"It cannot be," said Lisaveta Ivanovna, frightened at the haste of his demand and the way in which it was made: "this is certainly not for me."

And she tore the letter up into tiny pieces.

"If the letter wasn't for you, why did you tear it up?" asked the girl. "I would have returned it to the person who sent it."

"Please, my dear," Lisaveta Ivanovna said, flushing at the remark, "don't bring me any more letters in the future. And tell the person who sent you that he should be ashamed of . . ."

But Hermann was not put off. By some means or other, he sent a letter to Lisaveta Ivanovna every day. The letters were no longer translated from the German. Hermann wrote them inspired by passion, and used a language true to his character; these letters were the expression of his obsessive desires and the disorder of his unfettered imagination. Lisaveta Ivanovna no longer thought of returning them to him: she revelled in them, began to answer them, and with each day, her replies became longer and more tender. Finally, she threw out of the window the following letter:

> This evening there is a ball at the * * * Embassy. The Countess will be there. We will stay until about two o'clock. Here is your chance to see me alone. As soon as the Countess has left the house, the servants will probably go to their quarters—with the exception of the hall-porter, who normally goes out to his closet anyway. Come at half-past eleven. Walk straight upstairs. If you meet anybody in the ante-room, ask whether the Countess is at home. You will be told 'No'—and there will be nothing you can do but go away. But it is unlikely that you will meet anybody. The lady's maids sit by themselves, all in the one room. On leaving the hall, turn to the left and walk straight on until you come to the Countess' bedroom. In the bedroom, behind a screen, you will see two small doors: the one on the right leads into the study, which the Countess never goes into; the one on the left leads into a corridor and thence to a narrow winding staircase: this staircase leads to my bedroom.

Hermann quivered like a tiger as he awaited the appointed hour. He was already outside the Countess' house at ten o'clock. The weather was terrible; the wind howled, and a wet snow fell in large flakes upon the deserted streets, where the lamps shone dimly. Occasionally a passing cab-driver leaned forward over his scrawny nag, on the look-out for a late passenger. Feeling neither wind nor snow, Hermann waited, dressed only in his frock-coat. At last the Countess' carriage was brought round. Hermann saw two footmen carry out in their arms the bent old lady, wrapped in a sable fur, and immediately following her, the figure of Lisaveta Ivanovna, clad in a light cloak, and with her head adorned with fresh flowers. The doors were slammed and the carriage rolled heavily away along the soft snow. The hall-porter closed the front door. The windows became dark. Hermann began to walk about near the deserted house; he went up to a lamp and looked at his watch; it was twenty minutes past eleven. He remained beneath the lamp; his eyes fixed upon the hands of his watch, waiting for the remaining minutes to pass. At exactly half-past eleven, Hermann ascended the steps of the Countess' house and reached the brightly-lit porch. The hall-porter was not there. Hermann ran up the stairs, opened the door into the ante-room and saw a servant asleep by the lamp in a soiled antique armchair. With a light, firm tread Hermann stepped past him. The drawing-room and reception-room were in darkness, but the lamp in the ante-room sent through a feeble light. Hermann passed through into the bedroom. Before an icon-case, filled with old-fashioned images,[8] glowed a gold sanctuary lamp. Faded brocade armchairs and dull gilt divans with soft cushions were ranged in sad symmetry around the room, the walls of which were hung with Chinese silk. Two portraits, painted in Paris by Madame Lebrun,[9] were hung from one of the walls. One

8. I.e., religious images.   9. Marie-Louise-Élisabeth Vigée-Lebrun (1755–1842), French portrait painter, particularly of the aristocracy and royalty.

of these featured a plump, red-faced man of about forty, in a light-green uniform and with a star pinned to his breast; the other—a beautiful young woman with an aquiline nose and powdered hair, brushed back at the temples and adorned with a rose. In the corners of the room stood porcelain shepherdesses, table clocks from the workshop of the celebrated Leroy, little boxes, roulettes,¹ fans and the various lady's playthings which had been popular at the end of the last century, when the Montgolfiers' balloon and Mesmer's magnetism² were invented. Hermann went behind the screen, where stood a small iron bedstead; on the right was the door leading to the study; on the left the one which led to the corridor. Hermann opened the latter, and saw the narrow, winding staircase which led to the poor ward's room. . . . But he turned back and stepped into the dark study.

The time passed slowly. Everything was quiet. The clock in the drawing-room struck twelve; one by one the clocks in all the other rooms sounded the same hour, and then all was quiet again. Hermann stood leaning against the cold stove. He was calm; his heart beat evenly, like that of a man who has decided upon some dangerous but necessary action. One o'clock sounded; two o'clock; he heard the distant rattle of the carriage. He was seized by an involuntary agitation. The carriage drew near and stopped. He heard the sound of the carriage-steps being let down. The house suddenly came alive. Servants ran here and there, voices echoed through the house and the rooms were lit. Three old maid-servants hastened into the bedroom, followed by the Countess, who, tired to death, lowered herself into a Voltairean armchair.³ Hermann peeped through a crack. Lisaveta Ivanovna went past him. Hermann heard her hurried steps as she went up the narrow staircase. In his heart there echoed something like the voice of conscience, but it grew silent, and his heart once more turned to stone.

The Countess began to undress before the looking-glass. Her rose-bedecked cap was unfastened; her powdered wig was removed from her grey, closely-cropped hair. Pins fell in showers around her. Her yellow dress, embroidered with silver, fell at her swollen feet. Hermann witnessed all the loathsome mysteries of her dress; at last the Countess stood in her dressing-gown and night-cap; in this attire, more suitable to her age, she seemed less hideous and revolting.

Like most old people, the Countess suffered from insomnia. Having undressed, she sat down by the window in the Voltairean armchair and dismissed her maidservants. The candles were carried out; once again the room was lit by a single sanctuary lamp. Looking quite yellow, the Countess sat rocking to and fro in her chair, her flabby lips moving. Her dim eyes reflected a complete absence of thought and, looking at her, one would have thought that the awful old woman's rocking came not of her own volition, but by the action of some hidden galvanism.

Suddenly, an indescribable change came over her death-like face. Her lips ceased to move, her eyes came to life: before the Countess stood an unknown man.

1. Little balls; or possibly portable devices for playing the gambling game of roulette. Julien Leroy (1686–1759), famous French clockmaker.   2. Franz Anton Mesmer (1734–1815) argued that a person can transmit personal force to others in the form of "animal magnetism." Joseph-Michel (1740–1810) and Jacques-Étienne (1745–1799) Montgolfier, French brothers, helped develop the hot-air balloon and conducted the first untethered flights.   3. A large armchair with a high back.

"Don't be alarmed, for God's sake, don't be alarmed," he said in a clear, low voice. "I have no intention of harming you; I have come to beseech a favour of you."

The old woman looked at him in silence, as if she had not heard him. Hermann imagined that she was deaf, and bending right down over her ear, he repeated what he had said. The old woman kept silent as before.

"You can ensure the happiness of my life," Hermann continued, "and it will cost you nothing: I know that you can guess three cards in succession. . . ."

Hermann stopped. The Countess appeared to understand what was demanded of her; she seemed to be seeking words for her reply.

"It was a joke," she said at last. "I swear to you, it was a joke."

"There's no joking about it," Hermann retorted angrily. "Remember Chaplitsky whom you helped to win."

The Countess was visibly disconcerted, and her features expressed strong emotion; but she quickly resumed her former impassivity.

"Can you name these three winning cards?" Hermann continued.

The Countess was silent. Hermann went on:

"For whom do you keep your secret? For your grandsons? They are rich and they can do without it; they don't know the value of money. Your three cards will not help a spendthrift. He who cannot keep his paternal inheritance will die in want, even if he has the devil at his side. I am not a spendthrift; I know the value of money. Your three cards will not be lost on me. Come . . . !"

He stopped and awaited her answer with trepidation. The Countess was silent. Hermann fell upon his knees.

"If your heart has ever known the feeling of love," he said, "if you remember its ecstasies, if you ever smiled at the wailing of your new-born son, if ever any human feeling has run through your breast, I entreat you by the feelings of a wife, a lover, a mother, by everything that is sacred in life, not to deny my request! Reveal your secret to me! What is it to you . . . ? Perhaps it is bound up with some dreadful sin, with the loss of eternal bliss, with some contract made with the devil . . . Consider: you are old; you have not long to live—I am prepared to take your sins on my own soul. Only reveal to me your secret. Realise that the happiness of a man is in your hands, that not only I, but my children, my grandchildren, my great-grandchildren will bless your memory and will revere it as something sacred. . . ."

The old woman answered not a word.

Hermann stood up.

"You old witch!" he said, clenching his teeth. "I'll force you to answer. . . ."

With these words he drew a pistol from his pocket. At the sight of the pistol, the Countess, for the second time, exhibited signs of strong emotion. She shook her head and raising her hand as though to shield herself from the shot, she rolled over on her back and remained motionless.

"Stop this childish behaviour now," Hermann said, taking her hand. "I ask you for the last time: will you name your three cards or won't you?"

The Countess made no reply. Hermann saw that she was dead.

CHAPTER FOUR

7 Mai 18* *
Homme sans moeurs et sans religion![4]
CORRESPONDENCE

Still in her ball dress, Lisaveta Ivanovna sat in her room, lost in thought. On her arrival home, she had quickly dismissed the sleepy maid who had reluctantly offered her services, had said that she would undress herself, and with a tremulous heart had gone up to her room, expecting to find Hermann there and yet hoping not to find him. Her first glance assured her of his absence and she thanked her fate for the obstacle that had prevented their meeting. She sat down, without undressing, and began to recall all the circumstances which had lured her so far in so short a time. It was not three weeks since she had first seen the young man from the window—and yet she was already in correspondence with him, and already he had managed to persuade her to grant him a nocturnal meeting! She knew his name only because some of his letters had been signed; she had never spoken to him, nor heard his voice, nor heard anything about him . . . until that very evening. Strange thing! That very evening, Tomsky, vexed with the Princess Polina * * * for not flirting with him as she usually did, had wished to revenge himself by a show of indifference: he had therefore summoned Lisaveta Ivanovna and together they had danced an endless mazurka. All the time they were dancing, he had teased her about her partiality to officers of the Engineers, had assured her that he knew far more than she would have supposed possible, and indeed, some of his jests were so successfully aimed that on several occasions Lisaveta Ivanovna had thought that her secret was known to him.

"From whom have you discovered all this?" she asked, laughing.

"From a friend of the person whom you know so well," Tomsky answered; "from a most remarkable man!"

"Who is this remarkable man?"

"He is called Hermann."

Lisaveta made no reply, but her hands and feet turned quite numb.

"This Hermann," Tomsky continued, "is a truly romantic figure: he has the profile of a Napoleon, and the soul of a Mephistopheles. I should think that he has at least three crimes on his conscience. . . . How pale you have turned. . . . !"

"I have a headache. . . . What did this Hermann—or whatever his name is—tell you?"

"Hermann is most displeased with his friend: he says that he would act quite differently in his place . . . I even think that Hermann himself has designs on you; at any rate he listens to the exclamations of his enamoured friend with anything but indifference."

"But where has he seen me?"

"At church, perhaps; on a walk—God only knows! Perhaps in your room, whilst you were asleep: he's quite capable of it . . ."

Three ladies approaching him with the question: *"oublie ou regret?"*[5] inter-

---

4. A man without morals and without religion! (French).   5. The ladies cut in, offering the man a choice: *oublie* (forgetting) or *regret*. He does not know which lady is which. He chooses correctly the one with whom he wants to dance.

rupted the conversation which had become so agonisingly interesting to Lisaveta Ivanovna.

The lady chosen by Tomsky was the Princess Polina * * * herself. She succeeded in clearing up the misunderstanding between them during the many turns and movements of the dance, after which he conducted her to her chair. Tomsky returned to his own place. He no longer had any thoughts for Hermann or Lisaveta Ivanovna, who desperately wanted to renew her interrupted conversation; but the mazurka came to an end and shortly afterwards the old Countess left.

Tomsky's words were nothing but ball-room chatter, but they made a deep impression upon the mind of the young dreamer. The portrait, sketched by Tomsky, resembled the image she herself had formed of Hermann, and thanks to the latest romantic novels, Hermann's quite commonplace face took on attributes that both frightened and captivated her imagination. Now she sat, her uncovered arms crossed, her head, still adorned with flowers, bent over her bare shoulders. . . . Suddenly the door opened, and Hermann entered. She shuddered.

"Where have you been?" she asked in a frightened whisper.

"In the old Countess' bedroom," Hermann answered: "I have just left it. The Countess is dead."

"Good God! What are you saying?"

"And it seems," Hermann continued, "that I am the cause of her death."

Lisaveta Ivanovna looked at him, and the words of Tomsky echoed in her mind: "he has at least three crimes on his conscience"! Hermann sat down beside her on the window sill and told her everything.

Lisaveta Ivanovna listened to him with horror. So those passionate letters, those ardent demands, the whole impertinent and obstinate pursuit—all that was not love! Money—that was what his soul craved for! It was not she who could satisfy his desire and make him happy! The poor ward had been nothing but the unknowing assistant of a brigand, of the murderer of her aged benefactress! . . . She wept bitterly, in an agony of belated repentance. Hermann looked at her in silence; his heart was also tormented; but neither the tears of the poor girl nor the astounding charm of her grief disturbed his hardened soul. He felt no remorse at the thought of the dead old lady. He felt dismay for only one thing: the irretrievable loss of the secret upon which he had relied for enrichment.

"You are a monster!" Lisaveta Ivanovna said at last.

"I did not wish for her death," Hermann answered. "My pistol wasn't loaded."

They were silent.

The day began to break. Lisaveta Ivanovna extinguished the flickering candle. A pale light lit up her room. She wiped her tear-stained eyes and raised them to Hermann: he sat by the window, his arms folded and with a grim frown on his face. In this position he bore an astonishing resemblance to a portrait of Napoleon. Even Lisaveta Ivanovna was struck by the likeness.

"How am I going to get you out of the house?" Lisaveta Ivanovna said at last. "I had thought of leading you along the secret staircase, but that would mean going past the Countess' bedroom, and I am afraid."

"Tell me how to find this secret staircase; I'll go on my own."

Lisaveta Ivanovna stood up, took a key from her chest of drawers, handed it to Hermann, and gave him detailed instructions. Hermann pressed her cold, unresponsive hand, kissed her bowed head and left.

He descended the winding staircase and once more entered the Countess' bedroom. The dead old lady sat as if turned to stone; her face expressed a deep calm. Hermann stopped before her and gazed at her for a long time, as if wishing to assure himself of the dreadful truth; finally, he went into the study, felt for the door behind the silk wall hangings, and, agitated by strange feelings, he began to descend the dark staircase.

"Along this very staircase," he thought, "perhaps at this same hour sixty years ago, in an embroidered coat, his hair dressed *à l'oiseau royal*,[6] his three-cornered hat pressed to his heart, there may have crept into this very bedroom a young and happy man now long since turned to dust in his grave—and to-day the aged heart of his mistress ceased to beat."

At the bottom of the staircase Hermann found a door, which he opened with the key Lisaveta Ivanovna had given him, and he found himself in a corridor which led into the street.

CHAPTER FIVE

That evening there appeared before me
the figure of the late Baroness von V* *.
She was all in white and she said to me:
"How are you, Mr. Councillor!"
                                        SWEDENBORG[7]

Three days after the fateful night, at nine o'clock in the morning, Hermann set out for the * * * monastery, where a funeral service for the dead Countess was going to be held. Although unrepentant, he could not altogether silence the voice of conscience, which kept on repeating: "You are the murderer of the old woman!" Having little true religious belief, he was extremely superstitious. He believed that the dead Countess could exercise a harmful influence on his life, and he had therefore resolved to be present at the funeral, in order to ask her forgiveness.

The church was full. Hermann could scarcely make his way through the crowd of people. The coffin stood on a rich catafalque beneath a velvet canopy. Within it lay the dead woman, her arms folded upon her chest, and dressed in a white satin robe, with a lace cap on her head. Around her stood the members of her household: servants in black coats, with armorial ribbons upon their shoulders and candles in their hands; the relatives—children, grandchildren, great-grandchildren—in deep mourning. Nobody cried; tears would have been *une affectation*. The Countess was so old that her death could have surprised nobody, and her relatives had long considered her as having outlived herself. A young bishop pronounced the funeral sermon. In simple, moving words, he described the peaceful end of the righteous woman, who for many years had been in quiet and touching preparation for a Christian end. "The angel of death found her," the speaker said, "waiting for the midnight bridegroom, vigilant in godly meditation." The service was completed with sad decorum. The relatives were the first to take leave of the

6. In the style of the royal bird (French, literal trans.); an antiquated and elaborate hairstyle.
7. Emmanuel Swedenborg (1688–1772), Swedish theologian, believed that he had several experiences of divine revelation, some involving appearances to him of the dead.

body. Then the numerous guests went up to pay final homage to her who had so long participated in their frivolous amusements. They were followed by all the members of the Countess' household, the last of whom was an old housekeeper of the same age as the Countess. She was supported by two young girls who led her up to the coffin. She had not the strength to bow down to the ground—and merely shed a few tears as she kissed the cold hand of her mistress. After that, Hermann decided to approach the coffin. He knelt down and for several minutes lay on the cold floor, which was strewn with fir branches; at last he got up, as pale as the dead woman herself; he went up the steps of the catafalque and bent his head over the body of the Countess. . . . At that very moment it seemed to him that the dead woman gave him a mocking glance, and winked at him. Hermann, hurriedly stepping back, missed his footing, and crashed on his back against the ground. He was helped to his feet. At the same moment, Lisaveta Ivanovna was carried out in a faint to the porch of the church. These events disturbed the solemnity of the gloomy ceremony for a few moments. A subdued murmur rose among the congregation, and a tall, thin chamberlain, a near relative of the dead woman, whispered in the ear of an Englishman standing by him that the young officer was the Countess' illegitimate son, to which the Englishman replied coldly: "Oh?"

For the whole of that day Hermann was exceedingly troubled. He went to a secluded inn for dinner and, contrary to his usual custom and in the hope of silencing his inward agitation, he drank heavily. But the wine fired his imagination still more. Returning home, he threw himself on to his bed without undressing, and fell into a heavy sleep.

It was already night when he awoke: the moon lit up his room. He glanced at his watch; it was a quarter to three. He found he could not go back to sleep; he sat down on his bed and thought about the funeral of the old Countess.

At that moment somebody in the street glanced in at his window, and immediately went away again. Hermann paid no attention to the incident. A minute or so later, he heard the door into the front room being opened. Hermann imagined that it was his orderly, drunk as usual, returning from some nocturnal outing. But he heard unfamiliar footsteps and the soft shuffling of slippers. The door opened: a woman in a white dress entered. Hermann mistook her for his old wet-nurse and wondered what could have brought her out at that time of the night. But the woman in white glided across the room and suddenly appeared before him—and Hermann recognised the Countess!

"I have come to you against my will," she said in a firm voice, "but I have been ordered to fulfill your request. Three, seven, ace, played in that order, will win for you, but only on condition that you play not more than one card in twenty-four hours, and that you never play again for the rest of your life. I'll forgive you my death if you marry my ward, Lisaveta Ivanovna. . . . "

With these words, she turned round quietly, walked towards the door and disappeared, her slippers shuffling. Herman heard the door in the hall bang, and again saw somebody look in at him through the window.

For a long time Hermann could not collect his senses. He went out into the next room. His orderly was lying asleep on the floor; Hermann could scarcely wake him. The orderly was, as usual, drunk, and it was impossible to get any sense out of him. The door into the hall was locked. Hermann returned to his room, lit a candle, and recorded the details of his vision.

CHAPTER SIX

"Attendez!"[8]
"How dare you say to me: 'Attendez'?"
"Your Excellency, I said: 'Attendez, sir'!"

Two fixed ideas can no more exist in one mind than, in the physical sense, two bodies can occupy one and the same place. "Three, seven, ace" soon eclipsed from Hermann's mind the form of the dead old lady. "Three, seven, ace" never left his thoughts, were constantly on his lips. At the sight of a young girl, he would say: "How shapely she is! Just like the three of hearts." When asked the time, he would reply: "About seven." Every pot-bellied man he saw reminded him of an ace. "Three, seven, ace," assuming all possible shapes, persecuted him in his sleep: the three bloomed before him in the shape of some luxuriant flower, the seven took on the appearance of a Gothic gateway, the ace—of an enormous spider. To the exclusion of all others, one thought alone occupied his mind—making use of the secret which had cost him so much. He began to think of retirement and of travel. He wanted to try his luck in the public gaming-houses of Paris. Chance spared him the trouble.

There was in Moscow a society of rich gamblers, presided over by the celebrated Chekalinsky, a man whose whole life had been spent at the card-table, and who had amassed millions long ago, accepting his winnings in the form of promissory notes and paying his losses with ready money. His long experience had earned him the confidence of his companions, and his open house, his famous cook and his friendliness and gaiety had won him great public respect. He arrived in Petersburg. The younger generation flocked to his house, forgetting balls for cards, and preferring the enticements of faro to the fascinations of courtship. Narumov took Hermann to meet him.

They passed through a succession of magnificent rooms, full of polite and attentive waiters. Several generals and privy councillors were playing whist; young men, sprawled out on brocade divans, were eating ices and smoking their pipes. In the drawing-room, seated at the head of a long table, around which were crowded about twenty players, the host kept bank. He was a most respectable-looking man of about sixty; his head was covered with silvery grey hair, and his full, fresh face expressed good nature; his eyes, enlivened by a perpetual smile, shone brightly. Narumov introduced Hermann to him. Chekalinsky shook his hand warmly, requested him not to stand on ceremony, and went on dealing.

The game lasted a long time. More than thirty cards lay on the table. Chekalinsky paused after each round in order to give the players time to arrange their cards, wrote down their losses, listened politely to their demands, and more politely still allowed them to retract any stake accidentally left on the table. At last the game finished. Chekalinsky shuffled the cards and prepared to deal again.

8. Wait! (French). Attendants at the gaming table called *Attendez* to indicate the end of the period to place bets.

"Allow me to place a stake," Hermann said, stretching out his hand from behind a fat gentleman who was punting[9] there.

Chekalinsky smiled and nodded silently, as a sign of his consent. Narumov laughingly congratulated Hermann on forswearing a longstanding principle and wished him a lucky beginning.

"I've staked," Hermann said, as he chalked up the amount, which was very considerable, on the back of his card.

"How much is it?" asked the banker, screwing up his eyes. "Forgive me, but I can't make it out."

"47,000 roubles," Hermann replied.

At these words every head in the room turned, and all eyes were fixed on Hermann.

"He's gone out of his mind!" Narumov thought.

"Allow me to observe to you," Chekalinsky said with his invariable smile, "that your stake is extremely high: nobody here has ever put more than 275 roubles on any single card."

"What of it?" retorted Hermann. "Do you take me or not?"

Chekalinsky, bowing, humbly accepted the stake.

"However, I would like to say," he said, "that, being judged worthy of the confidence of my friends, I can only bank against ready money. For my own part, of course, I am sure that your word is enough, but for the sake of the order of the game and of the accounts, I must ask you to place your money on the card."

Hermann drew a banknote from his pocket and handed it to Chekalinsky who, giving it a cursory glance, put it on Hermann's card.

He began to deal. On the right a nine turned up, on the left a three.[1]

"The three wins," said Hermann, showing his card.

A murmur arose among the players. Chekalinsky frowned, but instantly the smile returned to his face.

"Do you wish to take the money now?" he asked Hermann.

"If you would be so kind."

Chekalinsky drew a number of banknotes from his pocket and settled up immediately. Hermann took up his money and left the table. Narumov was too astounded even to think. Hermann drank a glass of lemonade and went home.

The next evening he again appeared at Chekalinsky's. The host was dealing. Hermann walked up to the table; the players already there immediately gave way to him. Chekalinsky bowed graciously.

Hermann waited for the next deal, took a card and placed on it his 47,000 roubles together with the winnings of the previous evening.

Chekalinsky began to deal. A knave turned up on the right, a seven on the left.

Hermann showed his seven.

There was a general cry of surprise, and Chekalinsky was clearly disconcerted. He counted out 94,000 roubles and handed them to Hermann, who pocketed them coolly and immediately withdrew.

The following evening Hermann again appeared at the table. Everyone

9. Betting against the dealer.   1. Bets in faro are made on the positions of cards. A player selects a card and places it facedown in front of him or her; if the card turns up on the dealer's left, the player wins; if on the right, the dealer wins.

was expecting him; the generals and privy councillors abandoned their whist in order to watch such unusual play. The young officers jumped up from their divans; all the waiters gathered in the drawing-room. Hermann was surrounded by a crowd of people. The other players held back their cards, impatient to see how Hermann would get on. Hermann stood at the table and prepared to play alone against the pale but still smiling Chekalinsky. Each unsealed a pack of cards. Chekalinsky shuffled. Hermann drew and placed his card, covering it with a heap of banknotes. It was like a duel. A deep silence reigned all around.

His hands shaking, Chekalinsky began to deal. On the right lay a queen, on the left an ace.

"The ace wins," said Hermann and showed his card.

"Your queen has lost," Chekalinsky said kindly.

Hermann started: indeed, instead of an ace, before him lay the queen of spades. He could not believe his eyes, could not understand how he could have slipped up.

At that moment it seemed to him that the queen of spades winked at him and smiled. He was struck by an unusual likeness . . .

"The old woman!" he shouted in terror.

Chekalinsky gathered up his winnings. Hermann stood motionless. When he left the table, people began to converse noisily.

"Famously punted!" the players said.

Chekalinsky shuffled the cards afresh; play went on as usual.

CONCLUSION

Hermann went mad. He is now installed in Room 17 at the Obukhov Hospital; he answers no questions, but merely mutters with unusual rapidity: "Three, seven, ace! Three, seven, queen!"

Lisaveta Ivanovna has married a very agreeable young man, who has a good position in the service somewhere; he is the son of the former steward of the old Countess. Lisaveta Ivanovna is bringing up a poor relative.

Tomsky has been promoted to the rank of Captain, and is going to marry Princess Polina.

ALFRED, LORD TENNYSON
1809–1892

Tennyson's poetry expresses a conflict—characteristic of his historical period but also of human experience generally—between the tendency to despair and the desire to hope. Hope locates itself, for Tennyson, in the human capacity to struggle toward future goals and, on occasion, in religious faith. Mortality causes despair: the death of others, the inevitable sense of increasing weakness as one ages, the scientific discovery that whole species have disappeared in the world's history. It is Tennyson's ability to remind us of both contradictory emotions, and of the degree to which they inevitably coexist and alternate, that makes his poetry compelling.

The poet's pervasive melancholy came partly from experience. Son of an Anglican clergyman, he spent four unhappy years in school before his father consented to allow him to be tutored at home. He attended Trinity College, Cambridge, where, with his friend Arthur Hallam, he belonged to an undergraduate society called The Apostles, whose members discussed contemporary social, religious, scientific, and literary issues. The friendship with Hallam retained its intensity after his undergraduate years; by 1830, Hallam had become engaged to Tennyson's sister. Three years later, however, at the age of twenty-two, Hallam died suddenly in Vienna. The loss acutely affected Tennyson, who during the next seventeen years gradually composed the long elegiac poem *In Memoriam A. H. H.* to record the profound emotional and intellectual effects on him of his friend's death.

In 1836, Tennyson became engaged to Emily Sellwood, but largely because of financial difficulties, he did not marry her until 1850, the year in which, after the publication of *In Memoriam*, he was made poet laureate. Five years earlier, he had received a pension. He lived quietly for the rest of his life, increasingly famous; in 1884, he was created first Baron Tennyson.

Tennyson's earliest independent collections of poems (1830 and 1833; he had published a collaborative volume with his brother in 1827) were the target of fierce critical attack, another cause for melancholy. He published nothing more until 1842, when a collection called simply *Poems* met great critical success. Subsequently revered as a kind of national spokesman, Tennyson won popularity particularly with *The Princess* (1847, revised 1855), *Maud* (1855), and *The Idylls of the King* (1859, 1885), a retelling of the legends of King Arthur.

In *Ulysses* (1842), Tennyson, imagining the situation of the Greek hero after his return to domestic peace, evokes the excitement and moral grandeur of the human capacity for aspiration.

> that which we are, we are;
> One equal temper of heroic hearts,
> Made weak by time and fate, but strong in will
> To strive, to seek, to find, and not to yield.

In another meditation on classic themes, *Tithonus* (published in 1860, written in 1833), he puts the other side of the case. "The woods decay, the woods decay and fall," the poem begins; its imagined speaker, a man who has been granted immortality at his own request, wishes to return the gift. "Why should a man desire in any way / To vary from the kindly race of men?" Ulysses insists on the specialness of his sort of man; Tithonus knows the burden of specialness. In conjunction, the two poems call attention to the fact that neither the Enlightenment nor the early Romantic view of experience seems entirely adequate to this poet. Tithonus's desire to share the common fate of humankind throbs with melancholy; he feels that fate as doom, although he equally experiences his exemption from it as doom. Ulysses' condescension to his prudent son ("Most blameless is he. . . . / He works his work, I mine") underlines the sense of desperation in his insistent striving. No alternative form of action or commitment satisfies the imagination.

In Memoriam, Tennyson's most ambitious work, suggests reasons for the poet's inability to imagine fulfillment. The problem is not merely temperament, but the effect on his consciousness of intellectual and social actuality as well as the loss and the possibility of loss made palpable to him by Hallam's death.

> Are God and Nature then at strife,
> That Nature lends such evil dreams?
> So careful of the type she seems,
> So careless of the single life.

That stanza comes from number 55 of the 125 linked poems that make up the whole. The next in the series begins,

> "So careful of the type?" but no, . . .
>   She [Nature] cries, "A thousand types are gone;
> I care for nothing, all shall go."

Reality offers not the slightest assurance of survival; contemporary scientists, studying fossils, had revealed the extinction of entire species. "Man, [Nature's] last work, who seemed so fair, / Such splendid purpose in his eyes"—with a Ulysses' capacity for fine imaginings—even man, humankind in general, may face extinction (a possibility that today looks ever more compelling). The poem concludes with the faintest possible religious hope:

> O life as futile, then, as frail!
>   O for thy voice to soothe and bless!
>   What hope of answer, or redress?
> Behind the veil, behind the veil.

By the end of the entire sequence, the poet has arrived at a more affirmative vision; he claims to have discovered God through his own pain and through the processes of feeling, which he asserts as more revelatory than those of logic. Indeed, *In Memoriam* persuasively evokes the slow reconciliation of mourning, giving its readers vicarious experience of the despair, the false starts, the inconsistencies of grief. The poem's power, however, derives not only from its record of personal emotional experience but from its demonstration, its embodiment, of how the intellectual and the emotional intertwine. The private loss of a friend assimilates itself to a more general loss of faith and certainty characteristic of the Victorian period. The determination to strive, to seek, to find, and not to yield generated scientific discovery, industrial and mercantile development. As early as 1850, though, such achievements threatened established social and theological orders. Tennyson re-creates for us what such threats felt like to those actually experiencing them. He writes an elegy not only for Arthur Hallam but for the larger losses of his moment in history.

For useful biography, see L. Ormond, *Alfred Tennyson: A Literary Life* (1993). Important criticism includes J. Buckley, *Tennyson: The Growth of a Poet* (1961); C. Ricks, *Tennyson* (1972); M. Shaw, *Alfred, Lord Tennyson* (1988); H. F. Tucker, *Tennyson and the Doom of Romanticism* (1988); and H. Tucker, ed., *Critical Essays on Alfred, Lord Tennyson* (1993). A valuable general guide is F. B. Pinion, *Tennyson Companion: Life and Works* (1984).

PRONOUNCING GLOSSARY

The following list uses common English syllables and stress accents to provide rough equivalents of selected words whose pronunciation may be unfamiliar to the general reader.

Aeonian: *ay-ohn'-ee-an*   Hyades: *hai'-u-deez*

Arcady: *ahr'-kah-dee*   Telemachus: *tel-em'-u-kus*

Argive: *ahr-gaive*   Tithonus: *ti-thoh'-nus*

Ulysses

> It little profits that an idle king,
> By this still hearth, among these barren crags,
> Matched with an agèd wife, I mete and dole
> Unequal laws unto a savage race,
> That hoard, and sleep, and feed, and know not me.   5

I cannot rest from travel; I will drink
Life to the lees. All times I have enjoyed
Greatly, have suffered greatly, both with those
That loved me, and alone; on shore, and when
Through scudding drifts the rainy Hyades[1]   10
Vexed the dim sea. I am become a name;
For always roaming with a hungry heart
Much have I seen and known,—cities of men
And manners, climates, councils, governments,
Myself not least, but honored of them all,—   15
And drunk delight of battle with my peers,
Far on the ringing plains of windy Troy.
I am a part of all that I have met;
Yet all experience is an arch wherethrough
Gleams that untravelled world whose margin fades   20
Forever and forever when I move.
How dull it is to pause, to make an end,
To rust unburnished, not to shine in use!
As though to breathe were life! Life piled on life
Were all too little, and of one to me   25
Little remains; but every hour is saved
From that eternal silence, something more,
A bringer of new things; and vile it were
For some three suns to store and hoard myself,
And this gray spirit yearning in desire   30
To follow knowledge like a sinking star,
Beyond the utmost bound of human thought.
    This is my son, mine own Telemachus,
To whom I leave the scepter and the isle[2]—
Well-loved of me, discerning to fulfill   35
This labor, by slow prudence to make mild
A rugged people, and through soft degrees
Subdue them to the useful and the good.
Most blameless is he, centered in the sphere
Of common duties, decent not to fail   40
In offices of tenderness, and pay
Meet adoration to my household gods,
When I am gone. He works his work, I mine.
    There lies the port; the vessel puffs her sail;
There gloom the dark, broad seas. My mariners,   45
Souls that have toiled, and wrought, and thought with me—
That ever with a frolic welcome took
The thunder and the sunshine, and opposed
Free hearts, free foreheads—you and I are old;
Old age hath yet his honor and his toil;   50
Death closes all. But something ere the end,
Some work of noble note, may yet be done,
Not unbecoming men that strove with gods.
The lights begin to twinkle from the rocks;
The long day wanes; the slow moon climbs; the deep   55

1. A cluster of seven stars in the constellation of Taurus. The ancients supposed that when Hyades rose
with the sun, rainy weather would follow.   2. Ithaca.

Moans round with many voices. Come, my friends,
'Tis not too late to seek a newer world.
Push off, and sitting well in order smite
The sounding furrows; for my purpose holds
To sail beyond the sunset, and the baths   60
Of all the western stars, until I die.
It may be that the gulfs will wash us down;
It may be we shall touch the Happy Isles,[3]
And see the great Achilles,[4] whom we knew.
Though much is taken, much abides; and though   65
We are not now that strength which in old days
Moved earth and heaven, that which we are, we are;
One equal temper of heroic hearts,
Made weak by time and fate, but strong in will
To strive, to seek, to find, and not to yield.   70

Tithonus[1]

The woods decay, the woods decay and fall,
The vapors weep their burthen to the ground,
Man comes and tills the field and lies beneath,
And after many a summer dies the swan.
Me only cruel immortality[2]   5
Consumes; I wither slowly in thine arms,
Here at the quiet limit of the world,
A white-haired shadow roaming like a dream
The ever-silent spaces of the East,
Far-folded mists, and gleaming halls of morn.   10
    Alas! for this gray shadow, once a man—
So glorious in his beauty and thy choice,
Who madest him thy chosen, that he seemed
To his great heart none other than a God!
I asked thee, "Give me immortality."   15
Then didst thou grant mine asking with a smile,
Like wealthy men who care not how they give.
But thy strong Hours[3] indignant worked their wills,
And beat me down and marred and wasted me,
And though they could not end me, left me maimed   20
To dwell in presence of immortal youth,
Immortal age beside immortal youth,
And all I was in ashes. Can thy love,
Thy beauty, make amends, though even now,
Close over us, the silver star,[4] thy guide,   25
Shines in those tremulous eyes that fill with tears
To hear me? Let me go; take back thy gift.

3. In Greek myth, the abode of the warriors after death.   4. Comrade-in-arms of Ulysses at Troy.   1. A prince of Troy loved by Aurora, goddess of dawn, in whose palace he is depicted as living.   2. From Zeus, Aurora obtained for Tithonus the gift of immortality but not of eternal youth.   3. Or Horae, goddesses of the seasons and of growth and decay.   4. The morning star that precedes the dawn.

Why should a man desire in any way
To vary from the kindly race of men,
Or pass beyond the goal of ordinance   30
Where all should pause, as is most meet[5] for all?
    A soft air fans the cloud apart; there comes
A glimpse of that dark world where I was born.
Once more the old mysterious glimmer steals
From thy pure brows, and from thy shoulders pure,   35
And bosom beating with a heart renewed.
Thy cheek begins to redden through the gloom,
Thy sweet eyes brighten slowly close to mine,
Ere yet they blind the stars, and the wild team[6]
Which love thee, yearning for thy yoke, arise,   40
And shake the darkness from their loosened manes,
And beat the twilight into flakes of fire.
    Lo! ever thus thou growest beautiful
In silence, then before thine answer given
Departest, and thy tears are on my cheek.   45
    Why wilt thou ever scare me with thy tears,
And make me tremble lest a saying learnt,
In days far-off, on that dark earth, be true?
"The Gods themselves cannot recall their gifts."
    Ay me! ay me! with what another heart   50
In days far-off, and with what other eyes
I used to watch—if I be he that watched—
The lucid outline forming round thee; saw
The dim curls kindle into sunny rings;
Changed with thy mystic change, and felt my blood   55
Glow with the glow that slowly crimsoned all
Thy presence and thy portals, while I lay,
Mouth, forehead, eyelids, growing dewy-warm
With kisses balmier than half-opening buds
Of April, and could hear the lips that kissed   60
Whispering I knew not what of wild and sweet,
Like that strange song I heard Apollo[7] sing,
While Ilion like a mist rose into towers.[8]
    Yet hold me not forever in thine East;
How can my nature longer mix with thine?   65
Coldly thy rosy shadows bathe me, cold
Are all thy lights, and cold my wrinkled feet
Upon thy glimmering thresholds, when the steam
Floats up from those dim fields about the homes
Of happy men that have the power to die,   70
And grassy barrows[9] of the happier dead.
Release me, and restore me to the ground.
Thou seest all things, thou wilt see my grave;
Thou wilt renew thy beauty morn by morn,
I earth in earth forget these empty courts,   75
And thee returning on thy silver wheels.

---

5. Suitable.   6. Of supernatural horses; they draw Aurora's chariot into the sky at dawn.   7. God of
music and patron of Troy.   8. According to legend, the walls of Troy (Ilion) were raised by the sound of
Apollo's song.   9. Burial mounds.

From *In Memoriam A. H. H.*

Obit. MDCCCXXXIII

[Prologue]

Strong Son of God, immortal Love,[1]
    Whom we, that have not seen thy face,
    By faith, and faith alone, embrace,
Believing where we cannot prove;

Thine are these orbs of light and shade;[2]   5
    Thou madest Life in man and brute;
    Thou madest Death; and lo, thy foot
Is on the skull which thou hast made.[3]

Thou wilt not leave us in the dust:
    Thou madest man, he knows not why,   10
    He thinks he was not made to die;
And thou hast made him: thou art just.

Thou seemest human and divine,
    The highest, holiest manhood, thou.
    Our wills are ours, we know not how;   15
Our wills are ours, to make them thine.

Our little systems have their day;
    They have their day and cease to be;[4]
    They are but broken lights of thee,[5]
And thou, O Lord, art more than they.   20

We have but faith: we cannot know,
    For knowledge is of things we see;
    And yet we trust it comes from thee,
A beam in darkness: let it grow.

Let knowledge grow from more to more,   25
    But more of reverence in us dwell;
    That mind and soul, according well,
May make one music as before,

But vaster. We are fools and slight;
    We mock thee when we do not fear: 30
    But help thy foolish ones to bear;
Help thy vain worlds to bear thy light.

---

1. 1 John 4.8: "He that loveth not knoweth not God; for God is love." 1 John 4.15: "Whosoever shall confess that Jesus is the Son of God, God dwelleth in him, and he in God."   2. I.e., the Earth and the planets, part of each of which is sunlit, the rest in shadow.   3. I.e., Jesus crushes Death underfoot, a common motif in painting and sculpture.   4. Transient theological and philosophical systems, contrasted with the enduring systems of the stars.   5. Refracted, as by a prism.

Forgive what seemed my sin in me,
   What seemed my worth since I began;
   For merit lives from man to man,   35
And not from man, O Lord, to thee.

Forgive my grief for one removed,
   Thy creature, whom I found so fair.
   I trust he lives in thee, and there
I find him worthier to be loved.   40

Forgive these wild and wandering cries,
   Confusions of a wasted[6] youth;
   Forgive them where they fail in truth,
And in thy wisdom make me wise.

1

I held it truth, with him[7] who sings
   To one clear harp in divers[8] tones,
   That men may rise on stepping-stones
Of their dead selves to higher things.

But who shall so forecast the years   5
   And find in loss a gain to match?
   Or reach a hand through time to catch
The far-off interest of tears?

Let Love clasp Grief lest both be drowned,
   Let darkness keep her raven gloss.   10
   Ah, sweeter to be drunk with loss,
To dance with Death, to beat the ground,

Than that the victor Hours[9] should scorn
   The long result of love, and boast,
   "Behold the man that loved and lost,   15
But all he was is overworn."[1]

2

Old yew,[2] which graspest at the stones
   That name the underlying dead,
   Thy fibers net the dreamless head,
Thy roots are wrapped about the bones.

6. Laid waste (by Hallam's loss).   7. Goethe, who in the second part of *Faust* and elsewhere voices his
conception of spiritual progress through the outgrowing of one's former selves.   8. Various.   9. Or
Horae, goddesses of the seasons and of growth and decay.   1. Worn out, exhausted.   2. Evergreen
capable of reaching great age. It is often planted in graveyards as a symbol of immortality.

The seasons bring the flower again,   5
    And bring the firstling[3] to the flock;
    And in the dusk of thee the clock
Beats out the little lives of men.

O, not for thee the glow, the bloom,
    Who changest not in any gale,   10
    Nor branding summer suns avail
To touch thy thousand years of gloom;

And gazing on thee, sullen tree,
    Sick for thy stubborn hardihood,
    I seem to fail from out my blood   15
And grow incorporate into thee.

3

O Sorrow, cruel fellowship,
    O Priestess in the vaults of Death,
    O sweet and bitter in a breath,
What whispers from thy lying lip?

"The stars," she whispers, "blindly run;   5
    A web is woven across the sky;
    From out waste places comes a cry,
And murmurs from the dying sun;

"And all the phantom, Nature, stands—
    With all the music in her tone,   10
    A hollow echo of my own,—
A hollow form with empty hands."

And shall I take a thing so blind,
    Embrace her as my natural good;
    Or crush her, like a vice of blood,   15
Upon the threshold of the mind?

      *   *   *

5

I sometimes hold it half a sin
    To put in words the grief I feel;
    For words, like Nature, half reveal
And half conceal the Soul within.

3. Firstborn.

But, for the unquiet heart and brain,　　　　　　　　5
　　A use in measured language lies;
　　The sad mechanic exercise,
Like dull narcotics, numbing pain.

In words, like weeds,[4] I'll wrap me o'er,
　　Like coarsest clothes against the cold;　　　　　10
　　But that large grief which these enfold
Is given in outline and no more.

*　　*　　*

7

Dark house,[5] by which once more I stand
　　Here in the long unlovely street,
　　Doors, where my heart was used to beat
So quickly, waiting for a hand,

A hand that can be clasped no more—　　　　　　5
　　Behold me, for I cannot sleep,
　　And like a guilty thing I creep
At earliest morning to the door.

He is not here; but far away
　　The noise of life begins again,　　　　　　　　10
　　And ghastly through the drizzling rain
On the bald street breaks the blank day.

*　　*　　*

10

I hear the noise about thy keel;[6]
　　I hear the bell struck in the night;
　　I see the cabin-window bright;
I see the sailor at the wheel.

Thou bring'st the sailor to his wife,　　　　　　5
　　And traveled men from foreign lands;
　　And letters unto trembling hands;
And, thy dark freight, a vanished life.

So bring him; we have idle dreams;
　　This look of quiet flatters thus　　　　　　　10
　　Our home-bred fancies. O, to us,
The fools of habit, sweeter seems

---

4. Garments (with allusion to mourning garments).　　**5.** The Hallam family residence.　　**6.** Of the ship bringing Hallam's body back from Vienna.

To rest beneath the clover sod,
   That takes the sunshine and the rains,
   Or where the kneeling hamlet drains   15
The chalice of the grapes of God;[7]

Than if with thee the roaring wells
   Should gulf him fathom-deep in brine,
   And hands so often clasped in mine,
Should toss with tangle[8] and with shells.   20

11

Calm is the morn without a sound,
   Calm as to suit a calmer grief,
   And only through the faded leaf
The chestnut pattering to the ground;[9]

Calm and deep peace on this high wold,[1]   5
   And on these dews that drench the furze,
   And all the silvery gossamers
That twinkle into green and gold;

Calm and still light on yon great plain
   That sweeps with all its autumn bowers,   10
   And crowded farms and lessening towers,
To mingle with the bounding main;

Calm and deep peace in this wide air,
   These leaves that redden to the fall,
   And in my heart, if calm at all,   15
If any calm, a calm despair;

Calm on the seas, and silver sleep,
   And waves that sway themselves in rest,
   And dead calm in that noble breast
Which heaves but with the heaving deep.   20

                    *   *   *

15

Tonight the winds begin to rise
   And roar from yonder dropping day;
   The last red leaf is whirled away,
The rooks[2] are blown about the skies;

---

7. This stanza mentions alternate modes of burial: in the churchyard or under the chancel where worshipers kneel for the Sacrament.   8. Seaweed.   9. The time is September, when Hallam's body is still en route.   1. Open uplands; i.e., Tennyson is at his home in Somersby, Lincolnshire.   2. European crowlike birds.

The forest cracked, the waters curled, 5
   The cattle huddled on the lea;[3]
   And wildly dashed on tower and tree
The sunbeam strikes along the world:

And but for fancies, which aver
   That all thy motions gently pass 10
   Athwart a plane of molten glass,
I scarce could brook the strain and stir

That makes the barren branches loud;
   And but for fear it is not so,
   The wild unrest that lives in woe 15
Would dote and pore on yonder cloud[4]

That rises upward always higher,
   And onward drags a laboring breast,
   And topples round the dreary west,
A looming bastion fringed with fire. 20

16

What words are these have fall'n from me?
   Can calm despair and wild unrest
   Be tenants of a single breast,
Or Sorrow such a changeling be?

Or doth she only seem to take 5
   The touch of change in calm or storm,
   But knows no more of transient form
In her deep self, than some dead lake

That holds the shadow of a lark
   Hung in the shadow of a heaven? 10
   Or has the shock, so harshly given,
Confused me like the unhappy bark[5]

That strikes by night a craggy shelf,
   And staggers blindly ere she sink?
   And stunned me from my power to think 15
And all my knowledge of myself;

And made me that delirious man
   Whose fancy fuses old and new,
   And flashes into false and true,
And mingles all without a plan? 20

*   *   *

3. Pasture.   4. In the midst of a gathering storm, the poet's imagination soothes him with the fancy that Hallam's ship moves gently toward England on a glass-calm sea. Only a fear that this fancy may delude him (and Hallam's crossing be really in danger) prevents the stormy unrest within him from romantically luxuriating in the stormy sunset all around him.   5. Ship.

19

The Danube to the Severn[6] gave
   The darkened heart that beat no more;
   They laid him by the pleasant shore,
And in the hearing of the wave.[7]

There twice a day the Severn fills;   5
   The salt sea-water passes by,
   And hushes half the babbling Wye,[8]
And makes a silence in the hills.

The Wye is hushed nor moved along,
   And hushed my deepest grief of all,   10
   When filled with tears that cannot fall,
I brim with sorrow drowning song.

The tide flows down, the wave again
   Is vocal in its wooded walls;
   My deeper anguish also falls,   15
And I can speak a little then.

*   *   *

21

I sing to him that rests below,
   And, since the grasses round me wave,
   I take the grasses of the grave,
And make them pipes[9] whereon to blow.

The traveler hears me now and then,   5
   And sometimes harshly will he speak:
   "This fellow would make weakness weak,
And melt the waxen hearts of men."

Another answers: "Let him be,
   He loves to make parade of pain,   10
   That with his piping he may gain
The praise that comes to constancy."

A third is wroth:[1] "Is this an hour
   For private sorrow's barren song,
   When more and more the people throng   15
The chairs and thrones of civil power?

---

6. The church at Clevedon, Somerset, where Hallam was buried, is on the Severn. Vienna, where he died, is on the Danube.   7. Tennyson was not present at the funeral and did not learn until years later that Hallam had been buried in the church, not in the graveyard by the river.   8. The tides reach far up the Bristol Channel into the Severn and the Wye, its tributary.   9. Alluding to the pipes of mourning shepherds in pastoral elegy, the genre to which *In Memoriam* in part belongs.   1. Very angry.

"A time to sicken and to swoon,
    When Science reaches forth her arms
    To feel from world to world, and charms
Her secret from the latest moon?"[2]   20

Behold, ye speak an idle thing;
    Ye never knew the sacred dust.
    I do but sing because I must,
And pipe but as the linnets sing;

And one is glad; her note is gay,   25
    For now her little ones have ranged;
    And one is sad; her note is changed,
Because her brood is stolen away.

22

The path by which we twain did go,
    Which led by tracts that pleased us well,
    Through four sweet years arose and fell,
From flower to flower, from snow to snow;

And we with singing cheered the way,   5
    And, crowned with all the season lent,
    From April on to April went,
And glad at heart from May to May.

But where the path we walked began
    To slant the fifth autumnal slope,   10
    As we descended following Hope,
There sat the Shadow feared of man;

Who broke our fair companionship,
    And spread his mantle dark and cold,
    And wrapt thee formless in the fold,   15
And dulled the murmur on thy lip,

And bore thee where I could not see
    Nor follow, though I walk in haste,
    And think that somewhere in the waste[3]
The Shadow sits and waits for me.   20

---

2. From 1846 to 1848, astronomers discovered the planet Neptune and one of its moons, some of the satellites of Uranus, and the eighth moon of Saturn.   3. Wasteland.

23

Now, sometimes in my sorrow shut,
    Or breaking into song by fits,
    Alone, alone, to where he sits,
The Shadow cloaked from head to foot,

Who keeps the keys of all the creeds,   5
    I wander, often falling lame,
    And looking back to whence I came,
Or on to where the pathway leads;

And cry, How changed from where it ran
    Through lands where not a leaf was dumb,   10
    But all the lavish hills would hum
The murmur of a happy Pan;[4]

When each by turns was guide to each,
    And Fancy light from Fancy caught,
    And Thought leapt out to wed with Thought   15
Ere Thought could wed itself with Speech;

And all we met was fair and good,
    And all was good that Time could bring,
    And all the secret of the Spring
Moved in the chambers of the blood;   20

And many an old philosophy
    On Argive heights divinely sang,
    And round us all the thicket rang
To many a flute of Arcady.[5]

                    *   *   *

27

I envy not in any moods
    The captive void of noble rage,
    The linnet born within the cage,
That never knew the summer woods;

I envy not the beast that takes   5
    His license in the field of time,
    Unfettered by the sense of crime,
To whom a conscience never wakes;

---

4. God of flocks and shepherds, and hence of pastoral poetry.   **5.** I.e., they were like shepherds on the hills of Greece when what is now "old philosophy" was brand new or on the plains of Arcady (home of pastoral poetry) when pastoral poetry was young.

    Nor, what may count itself as blest,
        The heart that never plighted troth[6]   10
        But stagnates in the weeds of sloth;
    Nor any want-begotten rest.[7]

    I hold it true, whate'er befall;
        I feel it, when I sorrow most;
        'Tis better to have loved and lost   15
    Than never to have loved at all.

28

The time draws near the birth of Christ.
    The moon is hid, the night is still;
    The Christmas bells from hill to hill
Answer each other in the mist.

Four voices of four hamlets round,   5
    From far and near, on mead and moor,
    Swell out and fail, as if a door
Were shut between me and the sound;

Each voice four changes on the wind,
    That now dilate, and now decrease,   10
    Peace and goodwill, goodwill and peace,
Peace and goodwill, to all mankind.

This year I slept and woke with pain,
    I almost wished no more to wake,
    And that my hold on life would break   15
Before I heard those bells again;

But they my troubled spirit rule,
    For they controlled me when a boy;
    They bring me sorrow touched with joy,
The merry, merry bells of Yule.   20

        *   *   *

50

Be near me when my light is low,
    When the blood creeps, and the nerves prick
    And tingle; and the heart is sick,
And all the wheels of being slow.

---

6. Became engaged to be married.   7. I.e., any rest that comes from a lack or deficiency—specifically, from a failure to be fully human, a state that would entail vulnerability.

Be near me when the sensuous frame 5
 Is racked with pangs that conquer trust;
 And Time, a maniac scattering dust,[8]
And Life, a Fury slinging flame.[9]

Be near me when my faith is dry,
 And men the flies of latter spring, 10
 That lay their eggs, and sting and sing
And weave their petty cells and die.

Be near me when I fade away,
 To point the term of human strife,
 And on the low dark verge of life 15
The twilight of eternal day.

*   *   *

54

O, yet we trust that somehow good
 Will be the final goal of ill,
 To pangs of nature, sins of will,
Defects of doubt, and taints of blood;

That nothing walks with aimless feet; 5
 That not one life shall be destroyed,
 Or cast as rubbish to the void,
When God hath made the pile complete;

That not a worm is cloven in vain;
 That not a moth with vain desire 10
 Is shriveled in a fruitless fire,
Or but subserves another's gain.

Behold, we know not anything;
 I can but trust that good shall fall
 At last—far off—at last, to all, 15
And every winter change to spring.

So runs my dream; but what am I?
 An infant crying in the night;
 An infant crying for the light,
And with no language but a cry. 20

---

8. I.e., the dust from which life comes and to which it returns.   9. The Furies, avenging deities of Greek myth, carry torches.

55

The wish, that of the living whole
    No life may fail beyond the grave,
    Derives it not from what we have
The likest God within the soul?

Are God and Nature then at strife,   5
    That Nature lends such evil dreams?
    So careful of the type[1] she seems,
So careless of the single life,[2]

That I, considering everywhere
    Her secret meaning in her deeds   10
    And finding that of fifty seeds
She often brings but one to bear,

I falter where I firmly trod,
    And falling with my weight of cares
    Upon the great world's altar-stairs   15
That slope through darkness up to God,

I stretch lame hands of faith, and grope,
    And gather dust and chaff, and call
    To what I feel is Lord of all,
And faintly trust the larger hope.   20

56

"So careful of the type?" but no.
    From scarpèd[3] cliff and quarried stone
    She cries, "A thousand types are gone;[4]
I care for nothing, all shall go.

"Thou makest thine appeal to me: 5
    I bring to life, I bring to death;
    The spirit does but mean the breath:
I know no more." And he, shall he,

Man, her last work, who seemed so fair,
    Such splendid purpose in his eyes,   10
    Who rolled the psalm to wintry skies,
Who built him fanes[5] of fruitless prayer,

1. Species.   2. The significance of nature's prodigality and destructiveness was widely debated during Tennyson's lifetime.   3. Shorn away vertically to expose the rock strata of different ages.   4. That whole species had disappeared, not merely individuals, had become evident from Charles Lyell's researchers, published in his *Principles of Geology* (1830–33) and *Elements of Geology* (1838).   5. Temples.

Who trusted God was love indeed
  And love Creation's final law—
  Though Nature, red in tooth and claw   15
With ravin,[6] shrieked against his creed—

Who loved, who suffered countless ills,
  Who battled for the True, the Just,
  Be blown about the desert dust,
Or sealed within the iron hills?   20

No more? A monster then, a dream,
  A discord. Dragons of the prime,[7]
  That tear each other in their slime,
Were mellow music matched with him.

O life as futile, then, as frail!   25
  O for thy[8] voice to soothe and bless!
  What hope of answer, or redress?
Behind the veil,[9] behind the veil.

*   *   *

78

Again at Christmas did we weave
  The holly round the Christmas hearth;
  The silent snow possessed the earth,
And calmly fell our Christmas-eve:

The yule-clog[1] sparkled keen with frost,   5
  No wing of wind the region swept,
  But over all things brooding slept
The quiet sense of something lost.

As in the winters left behind,
  Again our ancient games had place,   10
  The mimic picture's[2] breathing grace,
And dance and song and hoodman-blind.[3]

Who showed a token of distress?
  No single tear, no mark of pain:
  O sorrow, then can sorrow wane?   15
O grief, can grief be changed to less?

O last regret, regret can die!
  No—mixed with all this mystic frame,
  Her deep relations are the same,
But with long use her tears are dry.   20

*   *   *

6. Prey.   7. Prehistoric creatures.   8. Hallam's.   9. Death.   1. Yule log.   2. The game may
be charades.   3. Blindman's buff.

95

By night we lingered on the lawn,
  For underfoot the herb was dry;
  And genial warmth; and o'er the sky
The silvery haze of summer drawn;

And calm that let the tapers burn   5
  Unwavering; not a cricket chirred;
  The brook alone far-off was heard,
And on the board the fluttering urn.[4]

And bats went round in fragrant skies,
  And wheeled or lit the filmy shapes   10
  That haunt the dusk, with ermine capes
And woolly breasts and beaded eyes;

While now we sang old songs that pealed
  From knoll to knoll, where, couched at ease,
  The white kine[5] glimmered, and the trees   15
Laid their dark arms about the field.

But when those others, one by one,
  Withdrew themselves from me and night,
  And in the house light after light
Went out, and I was all alone,   20

A hunger seized my heart; I read
  Of that glad year which once had been,
  In those fall'n leaves which kept their green,
The noble letters of the dead.

And strangely on the silence broke   25
  The silent-speaking words, and strange
  Was love's dumb cry defying change
To test his worth; and strangely spoke

The faith, the vigor, bold to dwell
  On doubts that drive the coward back,   30
  And keen through wordy snares to track
Suggestion to her inmost cell.

So word by word, and line by line,
  The dead man touched me from the past,
  And all at once it seemed at last   35
The living soul was flashed on mine,

And mine in this was wound, and whirled
  About empyreal[6] heights of thought,

---

4. Boiling tea urn. *Board:* table.   **5.** Cattle.   **6.** Sublime.

And came on that which is, and caught
   The deep pulsations of the world,   40

Æonian[7] music measuring out
   The steps of Time—the shocks of Chance—
   The blows of Death. At length my trance
Was canceled, stricken through with doubt.

Vague words! but ah, how hard to frame   45
   In matter-molded forms of speech,
   Or even for intellect to reach
Through memory that which I became;

Till now the doubtful dusk revealed
   The knolls once more where, couched at ease,   50
   The white kine glimmered, and the trees
Laid their dark arms about the field;

And sucked from out the distant gloom
   A breeze began to tremble o'er
   The large leaves of the sycamore,   55
And fluctuate all the still perfume,

And gathering freshlier overhead,
   Rocked the full-foliaged elms, and swung
   The heavy-folded rose, and flung
The lilies to and fro, and said,   60

"The dawn, the dawn," and died away;
   And East and West, without a breath,
   Mixt their dim lights, like life and death,
To broaden into boundless day.

          *   *   *

106

Ring out, wild bells, to the wild sky,
   The flying cloud, the frosty light:
   The year is dying in the night;
Ring out, wild bells, and let him die.

Ring out the old, ring in the new,   5
   Ring, happy bells, across the snow:
   The year is going, let him go;
Ring out the false, ring in the true.

     out the grief that saps the mind,
     or those that here we see no more;   10
     ing out the feud of rich and poor,
     ig in redress to all mankind.

Ring out a slowly dying cause,
    And ancient forms of party strife;
    Ring in the nobler modes of life,   15
With sweeter manners, purer laws.

Ring out the want, the care, the sin,
    The faithless coldness of the times;
    Ring out, ring out my mournful rhymes,
But ring the fuller minstrel in.   20

Ring out false pride in place and blood,
    The civic slander and the spite;
    Ring in the love of truth and right,
Ring in the common love of good.

Ring out old shapes of foul disease;   25
    Ring out the narrowing lust of gold;
    Ring out the thousand wars of old,
Ring in the thousand years of peace.[8]

Ring in the valiant man and free,
    The larger heart, the kindlier hand;   30
    Ring out the darkness of the land,
Ring in the Christ that is to be.

           *   *   *

118

Contèmplate all this work of Time,
    The giant laboring in his youth;
    Nor dream of human love and truth,
As dying Nature's earth and lime;[9]

But trust that those we call the dead   5
    Are breathers of an ampler day
    For ever nobler ends. They say,
The solid earth whereon we tread

In tracts of fluent heat began,
    And grew to seeming-random forms,   10
    The seeming prey of cyclic storms,
Till at the last arose the man;

Who throve and branched from clime to clime,
    The herald of a higher race,

8. The poet has in mind Revelation 20, where it is said that Satan will be bound in chains for a thou-
years, during which time the martyrs will be "priest of God and of Christ, and shall reig
him."   9. The products of the decay of flesh and bone.

And of himself in higher place,   15
If so he type[1] this work of time

Within himself, from more to more;
   Or, crowned with attributes of woe
   Like glories, move his course, and show
That life is not as idle ore,   20

But iron dug from central gloom,
   And heated hot with burning fears,
   And dipped in baths of hissing tears,
And battered with the shocks of doom

To shape and use. Arise and fly   25
   The reeling Faun, the sensual feast;
   Move upward, working out the beast,
And let the ape and tiger die.

          * * *

124

That which we dare invoke to bless;
   Our dearest faith; our ghastliest doubt;
   He, They, One, All;[2] within, without;
The Power in darkness whom we guess,—

I found Him not in world or sun,   5
   Or eagle's wing, or insect's eye,
   Nor through the questions men may try,
The petty cobwebs we have spun.

If e'er when faith had fallen asleep,
   I heard a voice, "believe no more,"   10
   And heard an ever-breaking shore
That tumbled in the Godless deep,

A warmth within the breast would melt
   The freezing reason's colder part,
   And like a man in wrath the heart   15
Stood up and answered, "I have felt."

No, like a child in doubt and fear:
   But that blind clamor made me wise;
   Then was I as a child that cries,
But, crying, knows his father near;   20

And what I am beheld again
   What is, and no man understands;
   And out of darkness came the hands
That reach through nature, molding men.

1. Copy, emulate.   2. Christ, as part of the Trinity, seen as three elements and as indivisible.

[Epilogue]³

*   *   *

Today the grave is bright for me,
  For them⁴ the light of life increased,
  Who stay to share the morning feast,
Who rest tonight beside the sea.

Let all my genial spirits advance   5
  To meet and greet a whiter⁵ sun;
  My drooping memory will not shun
The foaming grape⁶ of eastern France.

It circles round, and fancy plays,
  And hearts are warmed and faces bloom,   10
  As drinking health to bride and groom
We wish them store of happy days.

Nor count me all to blame if I
  Conjecture of a stiller guest,
  Perchance, perchance, among the rest,   15
And, though in silence, wishing joy.

But they must go, the time draws on,
  And those white-favored⁷ horses wait;
  They rise, but linger; it is late;
Farewell, we kiss, and they are gone.   20

A shade falls on us like the dark
  From little cloudlets on the grass,
  But sweeps away as out we pass
To range the woods, to roam the park,

Discussing how their courtship grew,   25
  And talk of others that are wed,
  And how she looked, and what he said,
And back we come at fall of dew.

Again the feast, the speech, the glee,
  The shade of passing thought, the wealth   30
  Of words and wit, the double health,
The crowning cup, the three-times-three,⁸

---

3. The Epilogue celebrates the wedding of Tennyson's sister Cecilia to his friend Edmund Lushington (October 10, 1842) and brings the poem of mourning full circle to its conclusion in a marriage and in the prospect of a new birth.   4. The new husband and wife.   5. More joyous and hopeful because of the marriage.   6. Champagne.   7. Wearing white ribbons for the wedding.   8. Rousing cheers.

And last the dance;—till I retire.
    Dumb is that tower[9] which spake so loud,
    And high in heaven the streaming cloud,   35
And on the downs a rising fire:

And rise, O moon, from yonder down,
    Till over down and over dale
    All night the shining vapor sail
And pass the silent-lighted town,   40

The white-faced halls, the glancing rills,
    And catch at every mountain head,
    And o'er the friths[1] that branch and spread
Their sleeping silver through the hills;

And touch with shade the bridal doors,   45
    With tender gloom the roof, the wall;
    And breaking let the splendor fall
To spangle all the happy shores

By which they rest, and ocean sounds,
    And, star and system rolling past,   50
    A soul shall draw from out the vast
And strike his being into bounds,

And, moved through life of lower phase,
    Result in man, be born and think,
    And act and love, a closer link   55
Betwixt us and the crowning race

Of those that, eye to eye, shall look
    On knowledge; under whose command
    Is Earth and Earth's, and in their hand
Is Nature like an open book;   60

No longer half-akin to brute,
    For all we thought and loved and did,
    And hoped, and suffered, is but seed
Of what in them is flower and fruit;

Whereof the man that with me trod   65
    This planet was a noble type
    Appearing ere the times were ripe,
That friend of mine who lives in God,

That God, which ever lives and loves,
    One God, one law, one element,   70
    And one far-off divine event,
To which the whole creation moves.

---

9. The church tower where wedding bells recently rang.   1. Narrow bays of the sea.

ROBERT BROWNING
1812–1889

The pleasure of reading Robert Browning's dramatic monologues—the poems for which he is best known—involves the delight of encountering a vividly realized personality but is also, often, the kind of enjoyment one gets from detective fiction. An imaginary speaker utters words designed to generate a specific effect; from these words, typically, one can deduce a story never actually told. The poet allows us the enjoyment of figuring out what has really happened as well as more familiar poetic pleasures.

Browning was the son of a bank clerk who later became a prosperous banker. After attending the University of London, he traveled on the Continent. Back in England, he became friendly with other important Victorian literary figures: Charles Dickens, Thomas Carlyle, and Leigh Hunt, for example. His romance with the semi-invalid Elizabeth Barrett, also a poet, eventuated in marriage in 1846; the two lived mainly in Italy for the remaining fifteen years of her life. Although Browning returned to England after his wife's death, he made frequent visits to the Continent and died in Venice.

Browning wrote verse plays and introspective Shelleyan lyrics, but his most popular poems have always been the dramatic monologues, originally included in such volumes as *Bells and Pomegranates* (1841–46), *Men and Women* (1855), and *Dramatis Personae* (1864). His most ambitious work was *The Ring and the Book* (1868–69), a linked series of blank verse dramatic monologues based on a Renaissance murder trial. In this long poem, in the course of which several people report the same events from very different points of view, Browning most clearly concentrates on the problem implicit in all his monologues, that of perspective. The nature of a story depends on who tells it: Browning's verse insistently reminds us of this fact.

My Last Duchess (1842), probably Browning's best-known and most popular monologue, in fifty-six lines exemplifies the characteristic technique. The speaker, a duke, prefers his wife's portrait to her corporeal existence, having put an end to her life because he found her gaiety and spiritual generosity offensive to his aristocratic pride. He explains his attitude to an envoy with whom he is negotiating for a new bride, with no awareness that his story reflects badly on himself. The pleasure of reading the poem derives largely from experiencing simultaneous communications: the story the duke thinks he tells, of offended dignity, and the story he really tells, of narcissistic self-indulgence.

The Bishop Orders His Tomb at Saint Praxed's Church (1845) invites more complicated responses to the personality it evokes. The imagined sixteenth-century bishop reveals his lack of real allegiance to the Church he nominally serves. He has violated his vows of celibacy, having had at least one mistress and several children. He feels powerful competitive impulses, as well as rage and envy, toward his predecessor as bishop. Even on his deathbed, he remains utterly absorbed in the things of this world: the lump of lapis lazuli he has buried, the splendor of the marble he imagines for his tomb. The mass itself exists in his memory and imagination only as a sensuous experience:

> And then how I shall lie through centuries,
> And hear the blessed mutter of the mass,
> And see God made and eaten all day long,
> And feel the steady candle-flame, and taste
> Good strong thick stupefying incense-smoke!

If one wished to summarize this bishop in abstract terms, one might allude to "the corruption of the Church." Indeed, he exemplifies such corruption in many different ways, by what he fails to say as well as by what he says. "And thence ye may perceive the world's a dream": occasionally such tag lines erupt in his speech, but his lack of real religious feeling is all too apparent. He imagines himself lying in his tomb in his church through eternity; he does not think of an afterlife in heaven—or, for that matter, in hell, perhaps his more likely destination. Browning, however, implicitly insists on the difference between people and abstractions. To sum up this bishop in terms of ecclesiastical corruption would leave out the fact of his enormous vitality, a vitality that informs the entire poem. The dramatic monologue makes the bishop's feeling come alive, makes the reader sympathetically understand his reluctance to leave behind beauty he has valued all his life.

Browning uses the superficially remote situation he has evoked to reiterate the great Romantic theme—we have encountered it most vividly in Wordsworth and in Keats—of the poignance and the inevitability of loss. Instead of considering the problem of loss in autobiographical terms, he enters imaginatively into the experience of an invented character.

> She, men would have to be your mother once,
> Old Gandolf envied me, so fair she was!
> What's done is done, and she is dead beside,
> Dead long ago, and I am Bishop since,
> And as she died so must we die ourselves.

The dying man's emotions recapitulate a feeling we have all had: the sadness of memory, even memory of happy experiences (in this case, love of a woman and triumph over an enemy), when it tells us of what is irretrievably gone. The bishop holds on still to what he knows he must lose. His speech, as Browning captures it, expresses in its rhythms and its idiom the enduring vigor of his personality, even on the edge of death.

> Ah, ye hope
> To revel down my villas while I gasp
> Bricked o'er with beggar's mouldy travertine
> Which Gandolf from his tomb-top chuckles at!

This is not a man who has given up: he insists on the preoccupations of his life as he faces his death. The poem, demanding no judgment of the bishop, suggests, rather, the inadequacy of judgment as a reaction to the multiplicity of any single human being.

Browning's greatest gift as a poet is his capacity to convey an energetic sense of pleasure in the reality of experience. "Grow old along with me, / The best is yet to be," urges a character in one of his poems. But he also recognizes the cost of such intense living as that the bishop enjoys, since all human existence involves loss. The tonal complexity of *The Bishop Orders His Tomb* suggests the kind of richness typical of the Victorian period, with its faith and hope in the possibilities of human accomplishment mingled with doubt about what it all means in the end.

"*Childe Roland to the Dark Tower Came*" (1855), on the other hand, supplies little faith or hope. A nightmare vision that lends itself to no ready rational explanation, the poem narrates, in the first person, the experience of a quester who understands neither the purpose nor the meaning of his quest. (Nor can the reader deduce purpose or meaning.) The speaker finds himself in a landscape of despair; he remembers the failures of those who have preceded him. Increasingly conscious of loss and failure, he yet finally blows on his horn a call of challenge, not knowing what he challenges or why. The affirmation implicit in that final challenge promises no cheerful outcome. It constitutes a kind of existential defiance of impossibility. The poem's peculiar appeal for twentieth-century readers depends on its acknowledgment of the kind of dark consciousness that can afflict anyone. Browning here explains nothing away. Indeed, he explains nothing at all.

A useful biography of Browning is C. Ryals, *The Life of Robert Browning: A Critical Biography* (1993). W. C. De Vane, *A Browning Handbook* (1935), provides indispensable guidance. Valuable criticism includes I. Jack, *Browning's Major Poetry* (1973); L. Erickson, *Robert Browning: His Poetry and His Audiences* (1984); J. Woolford, *Browning, the Revisionary* (1988); and H. Bloom, ed., *Robert Browning* (1985), a collection of essays.

684 / Robert Browning

PRONOUNCING GLOSSARY

The following list uses common English syllables and stress accents to provide rough equivalents of selected words whose pronunciation may be unfamiliar to the general reader.

Apollyon: *a-pol'-yon*

Elucescebat: *ay-loo-say-say'-but*

Frascati: *frah-skah'-tee*

Tophet: *toh'-fet*

My Last Duchess

Ferrara

That's my last Duchess painted on the wall,
Looking as if she were alive. I call
That piece a wonder, now: Frà Pandolf's hands
Worked busily a day, and there she stands.
Will't please you sit and look at her? I said   5
'Frà Pandolf' by design, for never read
Strangers like you that pictured countenance,
The depth and passion of its earnest glance,
But to myself they turned (since none puts by
The curtain I have drawn for you, but I)   10
And seemed as they would ask me, if they durst,
How such a glance came there; so, not the first
Are you to turn and ask thus. Sir, 'twas not
Her husband's presence only, called that spot
Of joy into the Duchess' cheek: perhaps   15
Frà Pandolf chanced to say 'Her mantle laps
Over my lady's wrist too much,' or 'Paint
Must never hope to reproduce the faint
Half-flush that dies along her throat:' such stuff
Was courtesy, she thought, and cause enough   20
For calling up that spot of joy. She had
A heart—how shall I say?—too soon made glad,
Too easily impressed; she liked whate'er
She looked on, and her looks went everywhere.
Sir, 'twas all one! My favour at her breast,   25
The dropping of the daylight in the West,
The bough of cherries some officious fool
Broke in the orchard for her, the white mule
She rode with round the terrace—all and each
Would draw from her alike the approving speech,   30
Or blush, at least. She thanked men,—good! but thanked
Somehow—I know not how—as if she ranked
My gift of a nine-hundred-years-old name
With anybody's gift. Who'd stoop to blame
This sort of trifling? Even had you skill   35
In speech—(which I have not)—to make your will
Quite clear to such an one, and say, 'Just this
Or that in you disgusts me; here you miss,
Or there exceed the mark'—and if she let
Herself be lessoned so, nor plainly set   40

Her wits to yours, forsooth, and make excuse,
—E'en then would be some stooping; and I choose
Never to stoop. Oh sir, she smiled, no doubt,
Whene'er I passed her; but who passed without
Much the same smile? This grew; I gave commands;   45
Then all smiles stopped together. There she stands
As if alive. Will't please you rise? We'll meet
The company below, then. I repeat,
The Count your master's known munificence
Is ample warrant that no just pretence   50
Of mine for dowry will be disallowed;
Though his fair daughter's self, as I avowed
At starting, is my object. Nay, we'll go
Together down, sir. Notice Neptune, though,
Taming a sea-horse, thought a rarity,   55
Which Clause of Innsbruck cast in bronze for me!

The Bishop Orders His Tomb at Saint Praxed's Church[1]

Rome, 15—

Vanity, saith the preacher, vanity![2]
Draw round my bed: is Anselm keeping back?
Nephews—sons mine . . . ah God, I know not! Well—
She, men would have to be your mother once,
Old Gandolf[3] envied me, so fair she was!   5
What's done is done, and she is dead beside,
Dead long ago, and I am Bishop since,
And as she died so must we die ourselves,
And thence ye may perceive the world's a dream.
Life, how and what is it? As here I lie   10
In this state-chamber, dying by degrees,
Hours and long hours in the dead night, I ask
"Do I live, am I dead?" Peace, peace seems all.
Saint Praxed's ever was the church for peace;
And so, about this tomb of mine. I fought   15
With tooth and nail to save my niche, ye know:
—Old Gandolf cozened me, despite my care;
Shrewd was that snatch from out the corner south
He graced his carrion with, God curse the same!
Yet still my niche is not so cramped but thence   20
One sees the pulpit o' the epistle-side,[4]
And somewhat of the choir, those silent seats,
And up into the aery dome where live
The angels, and a sunbeam's sure to lurk:
And I shall fill my slab of basalt there,   25
And 'neath my tabernacle[5] take my rest,
With those nine columns round me, two and two,

1. The bishop, his tomb, and the character Gandolf are all fictional. Saint Praxed's church, seen by Browning in 1844, is named after a second-century Roman virgin. 2. Ecclesiastes 1.2. 3. The bishop's predecessor. 4. I.e., the right side as the congregation faces the altar, from which during the service some portion of St. Paul's Epistles is read. 5. Here, the canopy over his tomb.

The odd one at my feet where Anselm stands:
Peach-blossom marble all, the rare, the ripe
As fresh-poured red wine of a mighty pulse.   30
—Old Gandolf with his paltry onion-stone,[6]
Put me where I may look at him! True peach,
Rosy and flawless: how I earned the prize!
Draw close: that conflagration of my church
—What then? So much was saved if aught were missed!   35
My sons, ye would not be my death? Go dig
The white-grape vineyard where the oil-press stood,
Drop water gently till the surface sink,
And if ye find . . . Ah God, I know not, I! . . .
Bedded in store of rotten fig-leaves soft,   40
And corded up in a tight olive-frail,[7]
Some lump, ah God, of lapis lazuli,[8]
Big as a Jew's head cut off at the nape,
Blue as a vein o'er the Madonna's breast . . .
Sons, all have I bequeathed you, villas, all,   45
That brave Frascati[9] villa with its bath,
So, let the blue lump poise between my knees,
Like God the Father's globe on both his hands
Ye worship in the Jesu Church[1] so gay,
For Gandolf shall not choose but see and burst!   50
Swift as a weaver's shuttle[2] fleet our years:
Man goeth to the grave, and where is he?
Did I say basalt for my slab, sons? Black—
'Twas ever antique-black[3] I meant! How else
Shall ye contrast my frieze to come beneath?   55
The bas-relief in bronze ye promised me,
Those Pans and Nymphs ye wot[4] of, and perchance
Some tripod, thyrsus,[5] with a vase or so,
The Saviour at his sermon on the mount,
Saint Praxed in a glory, and one Pan   60
Ready to twitch the Nymph's last garment off,
And Moses with the tables[6] . . . but I know
Ye mark me not! What do they whisper thee,
Child of my bowels, Anselm? Ah, ye hope
To revel down my villas while I gasp   65
Bricked o'er with beggar's mouldy travertine[7]
Which Gandolf from his tomb-top chuckles at!
Nay, boys, ye love me—all of jasper,[8] then!
'Tis jasper ye stand pledged to, lest I grieve.
My bath must needs be left behind, alas!   70
One block, pure green as a pistachio-nut,
There's plenty jasper somewhere in the world—
And have I not Saint Praxed's ear to pray
Horses for ye, and brown Greek manuscripts,
And mistresses with great smooth marbly limbs?   75

6. A lesser grade of green marble.   7. Basket made of rushes, for figs, raisins, olives, and so on.   8. A
bright blue semiprecious stone.   9. A wealthy Roman suburb.   1. The principal Jesuit church in
Rome.   2. Job 7.6.   3. A grade of good marble.   4. Know. Pans and nymphs were Greek nature
deities.   5. A staff tipped with a pinecone, associated with the Greek god Bacchus.   6. The stone
tablets on which the Ten Commandments were inscribed.   7. A cheap, flaky Italian building
stone.   8. Reddish quartz.

—That's if ye carve my epitaph aright,
Choice Latin, picked phrase, Tully's[9] every word,
No gaudy ware like Gandolf's second line—
Tully, my masters? Ulpian[1] serves his need!
And then how I shall lie through centuries,   80
And hear the blessed mutter of the mass,
And see God made and eaten[2] all day long,
And feel the steady candle-flame, and taste
Good strong thick stupefying incense-smoke!
For as I lie here, hours of the dead night,   85
Dying in state and by such slow degrees,
I fold my arms as if they clasped a crook,[3]
And stretch my feet forth straight as stone can point,
And let the bedclothes, for a mortcloth,[4] drop
Into great laps and folds of sculptor's-work: 90
And as yon tapers dwindle, and strange thoughts
Grow, with a certain humming in my ears,
About the life before I lived this life,
And this life too, popes, cardinals, and priests,
Saint Praxed at his[5] sermon on the mount,   95
Your tall pale mother with her talking eyes,
And new-found agate urns as fresh as day,
And marble's language, Latin pure, discreet,
—Aha, *Elucescebat*[6] quoth our friend?
No Tully, said I, Ulpian at the best!   100
Evil and brief hath been my pilgrimage.
All lapis, all, sons! Else I give the Pope
My villas! Will ye ever eat my heart?
Ever your eyes were as a lizard's quick,
They glitter like your mother's for my soul,   105
Or ye would heighten my impoverished frieze,
Piece out its starved design, and fill my vase
With grapes, and add a vizor and a Term,[7]
And to the tripod ye would tie a lynx
That in his struggle throws the thyrsus down,   110
To comfort me on my entablature
Whereon I am to lie till I must ask
'Do I live, am I dead?' There, leave me, there!
For ye have stabbed me with ingratitude
To death—ye wish it—God, ye wish it! Stone—   115
Gritstone,[8] a-crumble! Clammy squares which sweat
As if the corpse they keep were oozing through—
And no more lapis to delight the world!
Well go! I bless ye. Fewer tapers there,
But in a row: and, going, turn your backs   120
—Ay, like departing altar-ministrants,
And leave me in my church, the church for peace,

9. Marcus Tullius Cicero (106–43 B.C.), Roman writer and master of Latin prose style. 1. Ulpianus Domitius (A.D. 170–228), lawyer, secretary to Emperor Alexander Severus, writer of nonclassical Latin. 2. A reference to the Sacrament of Communion. 3. The bishop's crosier. 4. Funeral pall or winding sheet. 5. Roger Cruik interprets the drowsy bishop as conflating the two allusions of lines 59–60, to Christ's Sermon on the Mount and to the (female) St. Prassede. 6. "He was illustrious," or "famous." In classical Latin the word would be *elucebat*. *Elucescebat* is an example of the less elegant Latin associated with Ulpian's era. 7. A pillar bearing a statue or a bust. *Vizor:* a masked figure. 8. Sandstone, a cheap substitute for marble.

That I may watch at leisure if he leers—
Old Gandolf, at me, from his onion-stone,
As still he envied me, so fair she was!   125

"Childe Roland to the Dark Tower Came"

(*See Edgar's Song in* Lear)[1]

I

My first thought was, he lied in every word,
   That hoary cripple, with malicious eye
   Askance to watch the working of his lie
On mine, and mouth scarce able to afford
Suppression of the glee, that pursed and scored   5
   Its edge, at one more victim gained thereby.

II

What else should he be set for, with his staff?
   What, save to waylay with his lies, ensnare
   All travellers who might find him posted there,
And ask the road? I guessed what skull-like laugh   10
Would break, what crutch 'gin[2] write my epitaph
   For pastime in the dusty thoroughfare,

III

If at his counsel I should turn aside
   Into that ominous tract which, all agree,
   Hides the Dark Tower. Yet acquiescingly   15
I did turn as he pointed: neither pride
Nor hope rekindling at the end descried,
   So much as gladness that some end might be.

IV

For, what with my whole world-wide wandering,
   What with my search drawn out through years, my hope 20
   Dwindled into a ghost not fit to cope
With that obstreperous joy success would bring,—
I hardly tried now to rebuke the spring
   My heart made, finding failure in its scope.

V

As when a sick man very near to death   25
   Seems dead indeed, and feels begin and end
   The tears and takes the farewell of each friend,
And hears one bid the other go, draw breath
Freelier outside, ("since all is o'er," he saith,
   "And the blow fallen no grieving can amend");   30

---

1. Shakespeare's *King Lear* 3.4.173.   2. Begin to.

VI

While some discuss if near the other graves
    Be room enough for this, and when a day
    Suits best for carrying the corpse away,
With care about the banners, scarves and staves:
And still the man hears all, and only craves   35
    He may not shame such tender love and stay.

VII

Thus, I had so long suffered in this quest,
    Heard failure prophesied so oft, been writ
    So many times among "The Band"—to wit,
The knights who to the Dark Tower's search addressed   40
Their steps—that just to fail as they, seemed best,
    And all the doubt was now—should I be fit?

VIII

So, quiet as despair, I turned from him,
    That hateful cripple, out of his highway
    Into the path he pointed. All the day   45
Had been a dreary one at best, and dim
Was settling to its close, yet shot one grim
    Red leer to see the plain catch its estray.[3]

IX

For mark! no sooner was I fairly found
    Pledged to the plain, after a pace or two,   50
    Than, pausing to throw backward a last view
O'er the safe road,'twas gone; grey plain all round:
Nothing but plain to the horizon's bound.
    I might go on; nought else remained to do.

X

So, on I went. I think I never saw   55
    Such starved ignoble nature; nothing throve:
    For flowers—as well expect a cedar grove!
But cockle, spurge, according to their law
Might propagate their kind, with none to awe,
    You'd think; a burr had been a treasure-trove.   60

XI

No! penury, inertness and grimace,
    In some strange sort, were the land's portion. "See
    Or shut your eyes," said Nature peevishly,
"It nothing skills: I cannot help my case:
'Tis the Last Judgment's fire must cure this place,   65
    Calcine its clods and set my prisoners free."

---

3. In law, a stray and unclaimed domestic animal.

XII

If there pushed any ragged thistle-stalk
　　Above its mates, the head was chopped; the bents[4]
　　Were jealous else. What made those holes and rents
In the dock's[5] harsh swarth leaves, bruised as to baulk　　70
All hope of greenness? 'tis a brute must walk
　　Pashing their life out, with a brute's intents.

XIII

As for the grass, it grew as scant as hair
　　In leprosy; thin dry blades pricked the mud
　　Which underneath looked kneaded up with blood.　　75
One stiff blind horse, his every bone a-stare,
Stood stupefied, however he came there:
　　Thrust out past service from the devil's stud!

XIV

Alive? he might be dead for aught I know,
　　With that red gaunt and colloped[6] neck a-strain,　　80
　　And shut eyes underneath the rusty mane;
Seldom went such grotesqueness with such woe;
I never saw a brute I hated so;
　　He must be wicked to deserve such pain.

XV

I shut my eyes and turned them on my heart.　　85
　　As a man calls for wine before he fights,
　　I asked one draught of earlier, happier sights,
Ere fitly I could hope to play my part.
Think first, fight afterwards—the soldier's art:
　　One taste of the old time sets all to rights.　　90

XVI

Not it! I fancied Cuthbert's reddening face
　　Beneath its garniture of curly gold,
　　Dear fellow, till I almost felt him fold
An arm in mine to fix me to the place,
That way he used. Alas, one night's disgrace!　　95
　　Out went my heart's new fire and left it cold.

XVII

Giles then, the soul of honour—there he stands
　　Frank as ten years ago when knighted first.
　　What honest men should dare (he said) he durst.
Good—but the scene shifts—faugh! what hangman-hands　　100
Pin to his breast a parchment?[7] his own bands
　　Read it. Poor traitor, spit upon and curst!

---

4. Coarse grasses.　5. Any of several coarse weeds of the buckwheat family.　6. Ridged.　7. Containing an account of the crime for which he is condemned.

XVIII

Better this present than a past like that;
   Back therefore to my darkening path again!
   No sound, no sight as far as eye could strain.   105
Will the night send a howlet[8] or a bat?
I asked: when something on the dismal flat
   Came to arrest my thoughts and change their train.

XIX

A sudden little river crossed my path
   As unexpected as a serpent comes.   110
   No sluggish tide congenial to the glooms;
This, as it frothed by, might have been a bath
For the fiend's glowing hoof—to see the wrath
   Of its black eddy bespate[9] with flakes and spumes.

XX

So petty yet so spiteful! All along,   115
   Low scrubby alders kneeled down over it;
   Drenched willows flung them headlong in a fit
Of mute despair, a suicidal throng:
The river which had done them all the wrong,
   Whate'er that was, rolled by, deterred no whit.   120

XXI

Which, while I forded,—good saints, how I feared
   To set my foot upon a dead man's cheek,
   Each step, or feel the spear I thrust to seek
For hollows, tangled in his hair or beard!
—It may have been a water-rat I speared,   125
   But, ugh! it sounded like a baby's shriek.

XXII

Glad was I when I reached the other bank.
   Now for a better country. Vain presage!
   Who were the strugglers, what war did they wage,
Whose savage trample thus could pad the dank   130
Soil to a plash? Toads in a poisoned tank,
   Or wild cats in a red-hot iron cage—

XXIII

The fight must so have seemed in that fell[1] cirque.
   What penned them there, with all the plain to choose?
   No foot-print leading to the horrid mews,   135
None out of it. Mad brewage set to work
Their brains, no doubt, like galley-slaves the Turk
   Pits for his pastime, Christians against Jews.

8. Owl.   9. Spattered.   1. Cruel, terrible.

XXIV

And more than that—a furlong on—why, there!
   What bad use was that engine for, that wheel,   140
   Or brake, not wheel—that harrow fit to reel
Men's bodies out like silk? with all the air
Of Tophet's[2] tool, on earth left unaware,
   Or brought to sharpen its rusty teeth of steel.

XXV

Then came a bit of stubbed ground, once a wood,   145
   Next a marsh, it would seem, and now mere earth
   Desperate and done with; (so a fool finds mirth,
Makes a thing and then mars it, till his mood
Changes and off he goes!) within a rood[3]—
   Bog, clay and rubble, sand and stark black dearth.   150

XXVI

Now blotches rankling, coloured gray and grim,
   Now patches where some leanness of the soul's
   Broke into moss or substances like boils;
Then came some palsied oak, a cleft in him
Like a distorted mouth that splits its rim   155
   Gaping at death, and dies while it recoils.

XXVII

And just as far as ever from the end!
   Nought in the distance but the evening, nought
   To point my footstep further! At the thought,
A great black bird. Apollyon's[4] bosom-friend,   160
Sailed past, nor beat his wide wing dragon-penned[5]
   That brushed my cap—perchance the guide I sought.

XXVIII

For, looking up, aware I somehow grew,
   'Spite of the dusk, the plain had given place
   All round to mountains—with such name to grace   165
Mere ugly heights and heaps now stolen in view
How thus they had surprised me,—solve it, you![6]
   How to get from them was no clearer case.

XXIX

Yet half I seemed to recognize some trick
   Of mischief happened to me, God knows when—   170
   In a bad dream perhaps. Here ended, then,
Progress this way. When, in the very nick

---

2. Hell (Hebrew).   3. Quarter acre (forty square rods).   4. "The angel of the bottomless pit" (Revelation 9.11).   5. Dragon-winged.   6. The speaker addresses an imaginary listener—or the reader of the poem.

Of giving up, one time more, came a click
  As when a trap shuts—you're inside the den!

XXX

Burningly it came on me all at once,   175
  This was the place! those two hills on the right,
  Crouched like two bulls locked horn in horn in fight;
While to the left, a tall scalped mountain . . . Dunce,
Dotard, a-dozing at the very nonce,[7]
  After a life spent training for the sight!   180

XXXI

What in the midst lay but the Tower itself?
  The round squat turret, blind as the fool's heart,
  Built of brown stone, without a counterpart
In the whole world. The tempest's mocking elf
Points[8] to the shipman thus the unseen shelf   185
  He strikes on, only when the timbers start.

XXXII

Not see? because of night perhaps?—why, day
  Came back again for that! before it left,
  The dying sunset kindled through a cleft:
The hills, like giants at a hunting, lay,   190
Chin upon hand, to see the game at bay,—
  "Now stab and end the creature—to the heft!"

XXXIII

Not hear? when noise was everywhere! it tolled
  Increasing like a bell. Names in my ears
  Of all the lost adventurers my peers,—   195
How such a one was strong, and such was bold,
And such was fortunate, yet each of old
  Lost, lost! one moment knelled the woe of years.

XXXIV

There they stood, ranged along the hill-sides, met
  To view the last of me, a living frame   200
  For one more picture! in a sheet of flame
I saw them and I knew them all. And yet
Dauntless the slug-horn[9] to my lips I set,
  And blew. *"Childe Roland to the Dark Tower came."*

7. Occasion.   8. Points out.   9. Trumpet; the word was apparently invented by the poet Thomas Chatterton (1752–1770).

FREDERICK DOUGLASS
1818?–1895

The *Narrative of the Life of Frederick Douglass, An American Slave* (1845) powerfully details the struggle for identity of a black man who, in the mid-nineteenth century, came to realize his own exclusion from the American myth of liberty and justice for all. His autobiographical record epitomizes the experience of many pre–Civil War slaves, but in its narrative skill it also suggests how the writer's effort to achieve selfhood and freedom partakes of a more nearly universal pattern, incident to men and women of whatever color.

Virtually everything that is known of Douglass's early life comes from the *Narrative* itself, which ends half a century before his death. The book became an immediate best-seller but also a subject of controversy when accusations of fraud (promptly refuted) were made against it by a man who claimed to have known Douglass as a slave and to know him incapable of writing such a book. Because the autobiography's publication endangered its author, who might have been returned to slavery, Douglass subsequently went to Great Britain for two years of highly successful lecture appearances. At the end of 1846, two Englishwomen purchased his freedom from his old master, Hugh Auld, and Douglass returned to the United States in March 1847. He then began a journalistic career, writing and publishing a series of newspapers and making himself a leader of his people who continued to locate and to proclaim the injustices to which blacks were subject. Late in his life, he held a number of diplomatic posts, including minister resident and consul general to the Republic of Haiti and chargé d'affaires for Santo Domingo. He died in Washington, D.C., and was buried in Rochester, New York.

Douglass gradually enlarged and elaborated his *Narrative,* which exists in three subsequent versions: *My Bondage and My Freedom* (1855) and two different editions of *Life and Times of Frederick Douglass* (1881, 1892). The earliest, shortest form has the greatest narrative integrity and clarity. For literary as well as historical reasons (its status as an important document in the abolitionist crusade), it merits reprinting. It belongs to a genre familiar in its time: thousands of slave narratives were published in America—and in many cases translated into European languages—between the end of the eighteenth century and the beginning of the American Civil War. They won a large, enthusiastic readership; by making the horrors of slavery emotionally immediate, they intensified abolitionist sentiment. From the first publication of Douglass's work, it was acknowledged as unusually forceful by virtue of its rhetorical control and its narrative skill.

Douglass casts his autobiography as an account of self-discovery. The contrast between the openings of the *Narrative* and of Rousseau's *Confessions* is instructive. Rousseau begins by proclaiming that he differs importantly from everyone else in his unique and early established personality and character. Douglass, on the other hand, starts by reporting what he does *not* know of himself. He must guess his own age, he doesn't know his birthday, he has only rumor to tell him his father's identity. Although he knows his mother, he spends virtually no time with her; she comes to him and leaves him in the dark. Most children develop their sense of who they are by precisely the clues missing in Douglass's experience: age, parentage, such ritual occasions as birthdays. Douglass has only a generic identity: slave. Like other slave children, he wears nothing but a shirt—not the trousers that would symbolize his maleness, not shoes to protect his feet, nothing to differentiate him from others of his kind. Like the other children, he eats cornmeal mush from a trough on the floor, thus, as he notes, treated like a pig and reduced to animality. Everything in Douglass's experience denies his individuality and declares his lack of particularized identity.

The narrative constructed by a man who has finally, arduously, discovered his selfhood recapitulates the process of that discovery: a process with language at its heart.

The book ends with its author claiming his name: "I subscribe myself, FREDERICK DOUGLASS." The name itself is a triumph, not his father's or his mother's but the freshly bestowed name of his freedom. The author has won with difficulty the power to subscribe himself, to sign his name, for it involves the capacity to read and write as well as the claim to a name. Each step of the winning—learning to read, learning to write, acquiring a name—involves painful self-testing, but the *word* proves for Douglass literally a means to salvation.

Douglass believes his arrival in Baltimore, to serve the Aulds, a sign of Providential intervention: in Baltimore he learns to read. Mrs. Auld, wife of his master, begins to teach the boy the alphabet; her husband warns her to desist. Reading, he says, "would forever unfit him to be a slave." Douglass comments: "It was a new and special revelation, explaining dark and mysterious things, with which my youthful understanding had struggled, but struggled in vain." The word *revelation* has almost religious force: the child's vision of reading as the key to freedom saves his soul. From this point on in his story—and he is only about eight years old at the time—words lead Douglass to succeeding revelations. He defies all efforts to shut him up "in mental darkness." From little white street urchins he acquires the sustaining "bread of knowledge." At the age of twelve or thereabouts, he reads a book called *The Columbian Orator,* which contains forceful antislavery arguments, and is thus enabled for the first time to utter his thoughts. Without the authority of the written word, the contact through it with other minds, he could not know how to articulate what he thinks, could hardly know what it is he thinks. He puzzles over the word *abolitionist,* hearing but not understanding it. When he figures out its meaning, he has passed another milestone. A slave's thoughts must be free, this account suggests, before he can hope for meaningful freedom of body; and freedom of thought comes only through knowledge of the word.

We know that the writer successfully achieves freedom, but he makes gripping drama out of the gradual reporting of how he does so. First he must painfully learn to write, another step toward taking possession of language. For his first, agonizingly abortive attempt at escape, he writes passes for himself and his friends, briefly preempting the glory of being his own master. Subjected subsequently to more brutalized conditions, he sustains himself by making an imaginary speech, in what he remembers as elaborate literary language, to the fleet of ships he sees on Chesapeake Bay, images of freedom. He defies his brutal overseer, claims his manhood, teaches fellow slaves to read; finally, as though by magic, he escapes. (He withholds details of the escape to protect others; the effect of this suppression on the narrative is to suggest that the escape occurs almost as the inevitable, natural culmination of the process of self-discovery.) A friendly white man gives him a new name. And finally Douglass discovers his own voice and his own words: the *Narrative* concludes with his assuming the role of orator on behalf of his people.

Despite its emphasis on the power of language, the autobiography reminds us also that language cannot express everything. Rousseau exhaustively explores his own feelings; Douglass recurrently comments on the inexpressibility of his deepest feelings. At the end of Chapter I, Frederick, a small child, watches his aunt whipped until she is covered with blood. "It was a most terrible spectacle. I wish I could commit to paper the feelings with which I beheld it." His feelings exceed the possibility of verbal representation. Other episodes of comparable brutality elicit the same response: the narrator feels more than he can say. The reader is recurrently reminded that the horrible reality to which Douglass's words refer is in fact a reality beyond words.

Douglass's development of identity, his ultimate subscription of his new name as the sign of his self, leads to no claim of uniqueness. On the contrary, the identity he claims is partly *communal*. "Sincerely and earnestly hoping that this little book may do something toward throwing light on the American slave system, and hastening the glad day of deliverance to the millions of my brethren in bonds—faithfully relying upon the power of truth, love, and justice, for success in my humble efforts—and solemnly pledging my self anew to the sacred cause,—I subscribe myself, FREDERICK DOUGLASS." The "little book" exists not to establish Douglass's difference but to declare his unity. Now he possesses his own name, his own differentiating clothes, his own wife, his own self-defined occupation; but as much as when he was a half-naked child gobbling mush with the others, he feels part of a group. His love for fellow slaves, a recurrent theme of his story, provides the foundation for his identity—not, like Rousseau, emotionally isolated, but part of a sustaining community.

His language, both in the final paragraph just quoted and elsewhere, suggests that he partakes also of an even wider community. He evokes "truth" and "justice," proclaimed ideals of the American nation. He quotes John Greenleaf Whittier, "the slaves' poet," to express feelings he finds it hard to state for himself. Everywhere his prose rings with biblical rhythms and allusions. Frederick Douglass is not only a slave, not only an ex-slave; he is a literary man, an American, a Christian, claiming, relying on, and valuing these larger forms of communion as well as his union with his race— and implicitly demanding that others who call themselves Americans or Christians acknowledge his participation with them and accept the responsibility such acknowledgment implies.

An illuminating biography of Douglass, which elaborates on the information of the *Narrative*, is N. Huggins, *Slave and Citizen: The Life of Frederick Douglass* (1980). A biography placing Douglass in the context of the nineteenth-century antislavery movement is W. S. McFeely, *Frederick Douglass* (1991). For critical approaches, see W. E. Martin, *The Mind of Frederick Douglass* (1984); W. B. Rogers, *"We Are All Together Now": Frederick Douglass, William Lloyd Garrison, and the Prophetic Tradition* (1995); and W. L. Andrews, ed., *Critical Essays on Frederick Douglass* (1991).

Narrative of the Life of Frederick Douglass, An American Slave[1]

CHAPTER I

I was born in Tuckahoe, near Hillsborough, and about twelve miles from Easton, in Talbot county, Maryland. I have no accurate knowledge of my age, never having seen any authentic record containing it. By far the larger part of the slaves know as little of their ages as horses know of theirs, and it is the wish of most masters within my knowledge to keep their slaves thus ignorant. I do not remember to have ever met a slave who could tell of his birthday. They seldom come nearer to it than planting-time, harvest-time, cherry-time, spring-time, or fall-time. A want of information concerning my own was a source of unhappiness to me even during childhood. The white children could tell their ages. I could not tell why I ought to be deprived of the same privilege. I was not allowed to make any inquiries of my master concerning it. He deemed all such inquiries on the part of a slave improper and impertinent, and evidence of a restless spirit. The nearest estimate I can give makes me now between twenty-seven and twenty-eight years of age. I come to this, from hearing my master say, some time during 1835, I was about seventeen years old.

My mother was named Harriet Bailey. She was the daughter of Isaac and Betsey Bailey, both colored, and quite dark. My mother was of a darker complexion than either my grandmother or grandfather.

---

1. The text, printed in its entirety, is that of the first American edition, published by the Massachusetts Anti-Slavery Society in Boston in 1845.

My father was a white man. He was admitted to be such by all I ever heard speak of my parentage. The opinion was also whispered that my master was my father; but of the correctness of this opinion, I know nothing; the means of knowing was withheld from me. My mother and I were separated when I was but an infant—before I knew her as my mother. It is a common custom, in the part of Maryland from which I ran away, to part children from their mothers at a very early age. Frequently, before the child has reached its twelfth month, its mother is taken from it, and hired out on some farm a considerable distance off, and the child is placed under the care of an old woman, too old for field labor. For what this separation is done, I do not know, unless it be to hinder the development of the child's affection toward its mother, and to blunt and destroy the natural affection of the mother for the child. This is the inevitable result.

I never saw my mother, to know her as such, more than four or five times in my life; and each of those times was very short in duration, and at night. She was hired by a Mr. Stewart, who lived about twelve miles from my home. She made her journeys to see me in the night, travelling the whole distance on foot, after the performance of her day's work. She was a field hand, and a whipping is the penalty of not being in the field at sunrise, unless a slave has special permission from his or her master to the contrary—a permission which they seldom get, and one that gives to him that gives it the proud name of being a kind master. I do not recollect of ever seeing my mother by the light of day. She was with me in the night. She would lie down with me, and get me to sleep, but long before I waked she was gone. Very little communication ever took place between us. Death soon ended what little we could have while she lived, and with it her hardships and suffering. She died when I was about seven years old, on one of my master's farms, near Lee's Mill. I was not allowed to be present during her illness, at her death, or burial. She was gone long before I knew anything about it. Never having enjoyed, to any considerable extent, her soothing presence, her tender and watchful care, I received the tidings of her death with much the same emotions I should have probably felt at the death of a stranger.

Called thus suddenly away, she left me without the slightest intimation of who my father was. The whisper that my master was my father, may or may not be true; and, true or false, it is of but little consequence to my purpose whilst the fact remains, in all its glaring odiousness, that slaveholders have ordained, and by law established, that the children of slave women shall in all cases follow the condition of their mothers; and this is done too obviously to administer to their own lusts, and make a gratification of their wicked desires profitable as well as pleasurable; for by this cunning arrangement, the slaveholder, in cases not a few, sustains to his slaves the double relation of master and father.

I know of such cases; and it is worthy of remark that such slaves invariably suffer greater hardships, and have more to contend with, than others. They are, in the first place, a constant offence to their mistress. She is ever disposed to find fault with them; they can seldom do any thing to please her; she is never better pleased than when she sees them under the lash, especially when she suspects her husband of showing to his mulatto children favors which he withholds from his black slaves. The master is frequently compelled to sell this class of his slaves, out of deference to the feelings of his white wife; and, cruel as the deed may strike any one to be, for a man to sell his own children to human flesh-mongers, it is often the dictate of humanity for him to do so; for, unless he does this, he must not only whip them himself, but must stand by and see one white son tie up his brother, of but few shades darker complexion than himself, and ply the gory lash to his naked back; and if he lisp one word of disapproval, it is set down to his parental partiality, and only makes a bad matter worse, both for himself and the slave whom he would protect and defend.

Every year brings with it multitudes of this class of slaves. It was doubtless in consequence of a knowledge of this fact, that one great statesman of the south predicted the downfall of slavery by the inevitable laws of population. Whether this prophecy is ever fulfilled or not, it is nevertheless plain that a very different-looking class of people are springing up at the south, and are now held in slavery, from those originally brought to this country from Africa; and if their increase will do no other good, it will do away the force of the argument, that God cursed Ham,[2] and therefore American slavery is right. If the lineal descendants of Ham are alone to be scripturally enslaved, it is certain that slavery at the south must soon become unscriptural; for thousands are ushered into the world, annually, who, like myself, owe their existence to white fathers, and those fathers most frequently their own masters.

I have had two masters. My first master's name was Anthony. I do not remember his first name. He was generally called Captain Anthony—a title which, I presume, he acquired by sailing a craft on the Chesapeake Bay. He was not considered a rich slaveholder. He owned two or three farms, and about thirty slaves. His farms and slaves were under the care of an overseer. The overseer's name was Plummer. Mr. Plummer was a miserable drunkard, a profane swearer, and a savage monster. He always went armed with a cowskin and a heavy cudgel. I have known him to cut and slash the women's heads so horribly, that even master would be enraged at his cruelty, and would threaten to whip him if he did not mind himself. Master, however, was not a humane slaveholder. It required extraordinary barbarity on the part of an overseer to affect him. He was a cruel man, hardened by a long life of slaveholding. He would at times seem to take great pleasure in whipping a slave. I have often been awakened at the dawn of day by the most heart-rending shrieks of an own aunt of mine, whom he used to tie up to a joist, and whip upon her naked back till she was literally covered with blood. No words, no tears, no prayers, from his gory victim, seemed to move his iron heart from its bloody purpose. The louder she screamed, the harder he whipped; and where the blood ran fastest, there he whipped longest. He would whip her to make her scream, and whip her to make her hush; and not until overcome by fatigue, would he cease to swing the blood-clotted cowskin. I remember the first time I ever witnessed this horrible exhibition. I was quite a child, but I well remember it. I never shall forget it whilst I remember any thing. It was the first of a long series of such outrages, of which I was doomed to be a witness and a participant. It struck me with awful force. It was the blood-stained gate, the entrance to the hell of slavery, through which I was about to pass. It was a most terrible spectacle. I wish I could commit to paper the feelings with which I beheld it.

2. It was thought that Noah cursed his second son, Ham, for mocking him; that black skin resulted from the curse; and that all black people descended from Ham. In fact, according to Genesis 9.20–27 and 10.6–14, Noah cursed not Ham but Ham's son Canaan, while Ham's son Cush was black.

This occurrence took place very soon after I went to live with my old master, and under the following circumstances. Aunt Hester went out one night,—where or for what I do not know,—and happened to be absent when my master desired her presence. He had ordered her not to go out evenings, and warned her that she must never let him catch her in company with a young man, who was paying attention to her, belonging to Colonel Lloyd. The young man's name was Ned Roberts, generally called Lloyd's Ned. Why master was so careful of her, may be safely left to conjecture. She was a woman of noble form, and of graceful proportions, having very few equals, and fewer superiors, in personal appearance, among the colored or white women of our neighborhood.

Aunt Hester had not only disobeyed his orders in going out, but had been found in company with Lloyd's Ned; which circumstance, I found, from what he said while whipping her, was the chief offence. Had he been a man of pure morals himself, he might have been thought interested in protecting the innocence of my aunt; but those who knew him will not suspect him of any such virtue. Before he commenced whipping Aunt Hester, he took her into the kitchen, and stripped her from neck to waist, leaving her neck, shoulders, and back, entirely naked. He then told her to cross her hands, calling her at the same time a d———d b———h. After crossing her hands, he tied them with a strong rope, and led her to a stool under a large hook in the joist, put in for the purpose. He made her get upon the stool, and tied her hands to the hook. She now stood fair for his infernal purpose. Her arms were stretched up at their full length, so that she stood upon the ends of her toes. He then said to her, "Now, you d———d b———h, I'll learn you how to disobey my orders!" and after rolling up his sleeves, he commenced to lay on the heavy cowskin, and soon the warm, red blood (amid heart-rending shrieks from her, and horrid oaths from him) came dripping to the floor. I was so terrified and horror-stricken at the sight, that I hid myself in a closet, and dared not venture out till long after the bloody transaction was over. I expected it would be my turn next. It was all new to me. I had never seen any thing like it before. I had always lived with my grandmother on the outskirts of the plantation, where she was put to raise the children of the younger women. I had therefore been, until now, out of the way of the bloody scenes that often occurred on the plantation.

CHAPTER II

My master's family consisted of two sons, Andrew and Richard; one daughter, Lucretia, and her husband, Captain Thomas Auld. They lived in one house, upon the home plantation of Colonel Edward Lloyd. My master was Colonel Lloyd's clerk and superintendent. He was what might be called the overseer of the overseers. I spent two years of childhood on this plantation in my old master's family. It was here that I witnessed the bloody transaction recorded in the first chapter; and as I received my first impressions of slavery on this plantation, I will give some description of it, and of slavery as it there existed. The plantation is about twelve miles north of Easton, in Talbot county, and is situated on the border of Miles River. The principal products raised upon it were tobacco, corn, and wheat. These were raised in great abundance; so that, with the products of this and the other farms belonging to him, he was able to keep in almost constant employment a large sloop, in carrying them to market at Baltimore. This sloop was named *Sally Lloyd*, in honor of one of the colonel's daughters. My master's son-in-law, Captain Auld, was master of the vessel; she was otherwise manned by the colonel's own slaves. Their names were Peter, Isaac, Rich, and Jake. These were esteemed very highly by the other slaves, and looked upon as the privileged ones of the plantation; for it was no small affair, in the eyes of the slaves, to be allowed to see Baltimore.

Colonel Lloyd kept from three to four hundred slaves on his home plantation, and owned a large number more on the neighboring farms belonging to him. The names of the farms nearest to the home plantation were Wye Town and New Design. "Wye Town" was under the overseership of a man named Noah Willis. New Design was under the overseership of a Mr. Townsend. The overseers of these, and all the rest of the farms, numbering over twenty, received advice and direction from the managers of the home plantation. This was the great business place. It was the seat of government for the whole twenty farms. All disputes among the overseers were settled here. If a slave was convicted of any high misdemeanor, became unmanageable, or evinced a determination to run away, he was brought immediately here, severely whipped, put on board the sloop, carried to Baltimore, and sold to Austin Woolfolk, or some other slave-trader, as a warning to the slaves remaining.

Here, too, the slaves of all the other farms received their monthly allowance of food, and their yearly clothing. The men and women slaves received, as their monthly allowance of food, eight pounds of pork, or its equivalent in fish, and one bushel of corn meal. Their yearly clothing consisted of two coarse linen shirts, one pair of linen trousers, like the shirts, one jacket, one pair of trousers for winter, made of coarse negro cloth, one pair of stockings, and one pair of shoes; the whole of which could not have cost more than seven dollars. The allowance of the slave children was given to their mothers, or the old women having the care of them. The children unable to work in the field had neither shoes, stockings, jackets, nor trousers, given to them; their clothing consisted of two coarse linen shirts per year. When these failed them, they went naked until the next allowance-day. Children from seven to ten years old, of both sexes, almost naked, might be seen at all seasons of the year.

There were no beds given the slaves, unless one coarse blanket be considered such, and none but the men and women had these. This, however, is not considered a very great privation. They find less difficulty from the want of beds, than from the want of time to sleep; for when their day's work in the field is done, the most of them having their washing, mending, and cooking to do, and having few or none of the ordinary facilities for doing either of these, very many of their sleeping hours are consumed in preparing for the field the coming day; and when this is done, old and young, male and female, married and single, drop down side by side, on one common bed,— the cold, damp floor,—each covering himself or herself with their miserable blankets; and here they sleep till they are summoned to the field by the driver's horn. At the sound of this, all must rise, and be off to the field. There must be no halting; every one must be at his or her post; and woe betides them who hear not this morning summons to the field; for if they are not awakened by the sense of hearing, they are by the sense of feeling: no age nor sex finds any favor. Mr. Severe, the overseer, used to stand by the door of the quarter, armed with a large hickory stick and heavy cowskin, ready to whip any one who was so unfortunate as not to hear, or, from any other cause, was prevented from being ready to start for the field at the sound of the horn.

Mr. Severe was rightly named: he was a cruel man. I have seen him whip a woman, causing the blood to run half an hour at the time; and this, too, in the midst of her crying children, pleading for their mother's release. He seemed to take pleasure in manifesting his fiendish barbarity. Added to his cruelty, he was a profane swearer. It was enough to chill the blood and stiffen the hair of an ordinary man to hear him talk. Scarce a sentence escaped him but that was commenced or concluded by some horrid oath. The field was the place to witness his cruelty and profanity. His presence made it both the field of blood and of blasphemy. From the rising till the going down of the sun, he was cursing, raving, cutting, and slashing among the slaves of the field, in the most frightful manner. His career was short. He died very soon after I went to Colonel Lloyd's; and he died as he lived, uttering, with his dying groans, bitter curses and horrid oaths. His death was regarded by the slaves as the result of a merciful providence.

Mr. Severe's place was filled by a Mr. Hopkins. He was a very different man. He was less cruel, less profane, and made less noise, than Mr. Severe. His course was characterized by no extraordinary demonstrations of cruelty. He whipped, but seemed to take no pleasure in it. He was called by the slaves a good overseer.

The home plantation of Colonel Lloyd wore the appearance of a country village. All the mechanical operations for all the farms were performed here. The shoemaking and mending, the blacksmithing, cartwrighting, coopering, weaving, and grain-grinding, were all performed by the slaves on the home plantation. The whole place wore a business-like aspect very unlike the neighboring farms. The number of houses, too, conspired to give it advantage over the neighboring farms. It was called by the slaves the *Great House Farm*. Few privileges were esteemed higher, by the slaves of the out-farms, than that of being selected to do errands at the Great House Farm. It was associated in their minds with greatness. A representative could not be prouder of his election to a seat in the American Congress, than a slave on one of the out-farms would be of his election to do errands at the Great House Farm. They regarded it as evidence of great confidence reposed in them by their overseers; and it was on this account, as well as a constant desire to be out of the field from under the driver's lash, that they esteemed it a high privilege, one worth careful living for. He was called the smartest and most trusty fellow, who had this honor conferred upon him the most frequently. The competitors for this office sought as diligently to please their overseers, as the office-seekers in the political parties seek to please and deceive the people. The same traits of character might be seen in Colonel Lloyd's slaves, as are seen in the slaves of the political parties.

The slaves selected to go to the Great House Farm, for the monthly allowance for themselves and their fellow-slaves, were peculiarly enthusiastic. While on their way, they would make the dense old woods, for miles around, reverberate with their wild songs, revealing at once the highest joy and the deepest sadness. They would compose and sing as they went along, consulting neither time nor tune. The thought that came up, came out—if not in the word, in the sound;—and as frequently in the one as in the other. They would sometimes sing the most pathetic sentiment in the most rapturous tone, and the most rapturous sentiment in the most pathetic tone. Into all of their songs they would manage to weave something of the Great House Farm. Especially would they do this, when leaving home. They would then sing most exultingly the following words:—

> "I am going away to the Great House Farm!
> O, yea! O, yea! O!"

This they would sing, as a chorus, to words which to many would seem unmeaning jargon, but which, nevertheless, were full of meaning to themselves. I have sometimes thought that the mere hearing of those songs would do more to impress some minds with the horrible character of slavery, than the reading of whole volumes of philosophy on the subject could do.

I did not, when a slave, understand the deep meaning of those rude and apparently incoherent songs. I was myself within the circle; so that I neither saw nor heard as those without might see and hear. They told a tale of woe which was then altogether beyond my feeble comprehension; they were tones loud, long, and deep; they breathed the prayer and complaint of souls boiling over with the bitterest anguish. Every tone was a testimony against slavery, and a prayer to God for deliverance from chains. The hearing of those wild notes always depressed my spirit, and filled me with ineffable sadness. I have frequently found myself in tears while hearing them. The mere recurrence to those songs, even now, afflicts me; and while I am writing these lines, an expression of feeling has already found its way down my cheek. To those songs I trace my first glimmering conception of the dehumanizing character of slavery. I can never get rid of that conception. Those songs still follow me, to deepen my hatred of slavery, and quicken my sympathies for my brethren in bonds. If any one wishes to be impressed with the soul-killing effects of slavery, let him go to Colonel Lloyd's plantation, and, on allowance-day, place himself in the deep pine woods, and there let him, in silence, analyze the sounds that shall pass through the chambers of his soul,—and if he is not thus impressed, it will only be because "there is no flesh in his obdurate heart."

I have often been utterly astonished, since I came to the north, to find persons who could speak of the singing, among slaves, as evidence of their contentment and happiness. It is impossible to conceive of a greater mistake. Slaves sing most when they are most unhappy. The songs of the slave represent the sorrows of his heart; and he is relieved by them, only as an aching heart is relieved by its tears. At least, such is my experience. I have often sung to drown my sorrow, but seldom to express my happiness. Crying for joy, and singing for joy, were alike uncommon to me while in the jaws of slavery. The singing of a man cast away upon a desolate island might be as appropriately considered as evidence of contentment and happiness, as the singing of a slave; the songs of the one and of the other are prompted by the same emotion.

CHAPTER III

Colonel Lloyd kept a large and finely cultivated garden, which afforded almost constant employment for four men, besides the chief gardener, (Mr.

M'Durmond). This garden was probably the greatest attraction of the place. During the summer months, people came from far and near—from Baltimore, Easton, and Annapolis—to see it. It abounded in fruits of almost every description, from the hardy apple of the north to the delicate orange of the south. This garden was not the least source of trouble on the plantation. Its excellent fruit was quite a temptation to the hungry swarms of boys, as well as the older slaves, belonging to the colonel, few of whom had the virtue or the vice to resist it. Scarcely a day passed, during the summer, but that some slave had to take the lash for stealing fruit. The colonel had to resort to all kinds of stratagems to keep his slaves out of the garden. The last and most successful one was that of tarring his fence all around; after which, if a slave was caught with tar upon his person, it was deemed sufficient proof that he had either been into the garden, or had tried to get in. In either case, he was severely whipped by the chief gardener. This plan worked well; the slaves became as fearful of tar as of the lash. They seemed to realize the impossibility of touching *tar* without being defiled.[3]

The colonel also kept a splendid riding equipage. His stable and carriage-house presented the appearance of some of our large city livery establishments. His horses were of the finest form and noblest blood. His carriage-house contained three splendid coaches, three or four gigs, besides dearborns and barouches[4] of the most fashionable style.

This establishment was under the care of two slaves—old Barney and young Barney—father and son. To attend to this establishment was their sole work. But it was by no means an easy employment; for in nothing was Colonel Lloyd more particular than in the management of his horses. The slightest inattention to these was unpardonable, and was visited upon those, under whose care they were placed, with the severest punishment; no excuse could shield them, if the colonel only suspected any want of attention to his horses—a supposition which he frequently indulged, and one which, of course, made the office of old and young Barney a very trying one. They never knew when they were safe from punishment. They were frequently whipped when least deserving, and escaped whipping when most deserving it. Every thing depended upon the looks of the horses, and the state of Colonel Lloyd's own mind when his horses were brought to him for use. If a horse did not move fast enough, or hold his head high enough, it was owing to some fault of his keepers. It was painful to stand near the stable-door, and hear the various complaints against the keepers when a horse was taken out for use. "This horse has not had proper attention. He has not been sufficiently rubbed and curried, or he has not been properly fed; his food was too wet or too dry; he got it too soon or too late; he was too hot or too cold; he had too much hay, and not enough of grain; or he had too much grain, and not enough of hay; instead of old Barney's attending to the horse, he had very improperly left it to his son." To all these complaints, no matter how unjust, the slave must answer never a word. Colonel Lloyd could not brook any contradiction from a slave. When he spoke, a slave must stand, listen, and tremble; and such was literally the case. I have seen Colonel Lloyd make old Barney, a man between fifty and sixty years of age, uncover his bald head, kneel down upon the cold, damp ground, and receive upon his naked and

3. Compare the proverb "He who touches pitch shall be defiled."   4. Light four-wheeled carriages (*dearborns*) and carriages with a front seat for the driver and two facing back seats for couples (*barouches*).

toil-worn shoulders more than thirty lashes at the time. Colonel Lloyd had three sons—Edward, Murray, and Daniel,—and three sons-in-law, Mr. Winder, Mr. Nicholson, and Mr. Lowndes. All of these lived at the Great House Farm, and enjoyed the luxury of whipping the servants when they pleased, from old Barney down to William Wilkes, the coach-driver. I have seen Winder make one of the house-servants stand off from him a suitable distance to be touched with the end of his whip, and at every stroke raise great ridges upon his back.

To describe the wealth of Colonel Lloyd would be almost equal to describing the riches of Job.[5] He kept from ten to fifteen house-servants. He was said to own a thousand slaves, and I think this estimate quite within the truth. Colonel Lloyd owned so many that he did not know them when he saw them; nor did all the slaves of the out-farms know him. It is reported of him, that, while riding along the road one day, he met a colored man, and addressed him in the usual manner of speaking to colored people on the public highways of the south: "Well, boy, whom do you belong to?" "To Colonel Lloyd," replied the slave. "Well, does the colonel treat you well?" "No, sir," was the ready reply. "What, does he work you too hard?" "Yes, sir." "Well, don't he give you enough to eat?" "Yes, sir, he gives me enough, such as it is."

The colonel, after ascertaining where the slave belonged, rode on; the man also went on about his business, not dreaming that he had been conversing with his master. He thought, said, and heard nothing more of the matter, until two or three weeks afterwards. The poor man was then informed by his overseer that, for having found fault with his master, he was now to be sold to a Georgia trader. He was immediately chained and handcuffed; and thus, without a moment's warning, he was snatched away, and forever sundered, from his family and friends, by a hand more unrelenting than death. This is the penalty of telling the truth, of telling the simple truth, in answer to a series of plain questions.

It is partly in consequence of such facts, that slaves, when inquired of as to their condition and the character of their masters, almost universally say they are contented, and that their masters are kind. The slaveholders have been known to send in spies among their slaves, to ascertain their views and feelings in regard to their condition. The frequency of this has had the effect to establish among the slaves the maxim, that a still tongue makes a wise head. They suppress the truth rather than take the consequences of telling it, and in so doing prove themselves a part of the human family. If they have any thing to say of their masters, it is generally in their masters' favor, especially when speaking to an untried man. I have been frequently asked, when a slave, if I had a kind master, and do not remember ever to have given a negative answer; nor did I, in pursuing this course, consider myself as uttering what was absolutely false; for I always measured the kindness of my master by the standard of kindness set up among slaveholders around us. Moreover, slaves are like other people, and imbibe prejudices quite common to others. They think their own better than that of others. Many, under the influence of this prejudice, think their own masters are better than the mas-

5. Job 1.3: "His substance also was seven thousand sheep, and three thousand camels, and five hundred yoke of oxen, and five hundred she asses, and a very great household; so that this man was the greatest of all the men of the east."

ters of other slaves; and this, too, in some cases, when the very reverse is true. Indeed, it is not uncommon for slaves even to fall out and quarrel among themselves about the relative goodness of their masters, each contending for the superior goodness of his own over that of the others. At the very same time, they mutually execrate their masters when viewed separately. It was so on our plantation. When Colonel Lloyd's slaves met the slaves of Jacob Jepson, they seldom parted without a quarrel about their masters; Colonel Lloyd's slaves contending that he was the richest, and Mr. Jepson's slaves that he was the smartest, and most of a man. Colonel Lloyd's slaves would boast his ability to buy and sell Jacob Jepson. Mr. Jepson's slaves would boast his ability to whip Colonel Lloyd. These quarrels would almost always end in a fight between the parties, and those that whipped were supposed to have gained the point at issue. They seemed to think that the greatness of their masters was transferable to themselves. It was considered as being bad enough to be a slave; but to be a poor man's slave was deemed a disgrace indeed!

CHAPTER IV

Mr. Hopkins remained but a short time in the office of overseer. Why his career was so short, I do not know, but suppose he lacked the necessary severity to suit Colonel Lloyd. Mr. Hopkins was succeeded by Mr. Austin Gore, a man possessing, in an eminent degree, all those traits of character indispensable to what is called a first-rate overseer. Mr. Gore had served Colonel Lloyd, in the capacity of overseer, upon one of the out-farms, and had shown himself worthy of the high station of overseer upon the home or Great House Farm.

Mr. Gore was proud, ambitious, and persevering. He was artful, cruel, and obdurate. He was just the man for such a place, and it was just the place for such a man. It afforded scope for the full exercise of all his powers, and he seemed to be perfectly at home in it. He was one of those who could torture the slightest look, word, or gesture, on the part of the slave, into impudence, and would treat it accordingly. There must be no answering back to him; no explanation was allowed a slave, showing himself to have been wrongfully accused. Mr. Gore acted fully up to the maxim laid down by slaveholders,— "It is better that a dozen slaves suffer under the lash, than that the overseer should be convicted, in the presence of the slaves, of having been at fault." No matter how innocent a slave might be—it availed him nothing, when accused by Mr. Gore of any misdemeanor. To be accused was to be convicted, and to be convicted was to be punished; the one always following the other with immutable certainty. To escape punishment was to escape accusation; and few slaves had the fortune to do either, under the overseership of Mr. Gore. He was just proud enough to demand the most debasing homage of the slave, and quite servile enough to crouch, himself, at the feet of the master. He was ambitious enough to be contented with nothing short of the highest rank of overseers, and persevering enough to reach the height of his ambition. He was cruel enough to inflict the severest punishment, artful enough to descend to the lowest trickery, and obdurate enough to be insensible to the voice of a reproving conscience. He was, of all the overseers, the most dreaded by the slaves. His presence was painful; his eye flashed confusion; and seldom was his sharp, shrill voice heard, without producing horror and trembling in their ranks.

Mr. Gore was a grave man, and, though a young man, he indulged in no jokes, said no funny words, seldom smiled. His words were in perfect keeping with his looks, and his looks were in perfect keeping with his words. Overseers will sometimes indulge in a witty word, even with the slaves; not so with Mr. Gore. He spoke but to command, and commanded but to be obeyed; he dealt sparingly with his words, and bountifully with his whip, never using the former where the latter would answer as well. When he whipped, he seemed to do so from a sense of duty, and feared no consequences. He did nothing reluctantly, no matter how disagreeable; always at his post, never inconsistent. He never promised but to fulfil. He was, in a word, a man of the most inflexible firmness and stone-like coolness.

His savage barbarity was equalled only by the consummate coolness with which he committed the grossest and most savage deeds upon the slaves under his charge. Mr. Gore once undertook to whip one of Colonel Lloyd's slaves, by the name of Demby. He had given Demby but few stripes, when, to get rid of the scourging, he ran and plunged himself into a creek, and stood there at the depth of his shoulders, refusing to come out. Mr. Gore told him that he would give him three calls, and that, if he did not come out at the third call, he would shoot him. The first call was given. Demby made no response, but stood his ground. The second and third calls were given with the same result. Mr. Gore then, without consultation or deliberation with any one, not even giving Demby an additional call, raised his musket to his face, taking deadly aim at his standing victim, and in an instant poor Demby was no more. His mangled body sank out of sight, and blood and brains marked the water where he had stood.

A thrill of horror flashed through every soul upon the plantation, excepting Mr. Gore. He alone seemed cool and collected. He was asked by Colonel Lloyd and my old master, why he resorted to this extraordinary expedient. His reply was, (as well as I can remember,) that Demby had become unmanageable. He was setting a dangerous example to the other slaves,—one which, if suffered to pass without some such demonstration on his part, would finally lead to the total subversion of all rule and order upon the plantation. He argued that if one slave refused to be corrected, and escaped with his life, the other slaves would soon copy the example; the result of which would be, the freedom of the slaves, and the enslavement of the whites. Mr. Gore's defence was satisfactory. He was continued in his station as overseer upon the home plantation. His fame as an overseer went abroad. His horrid crime was not even submitted to judicial investigation. It was committed in the presence of slaves, and they of course could neither institute a suit, nor testify against him; and thus the guilty perpetrator of one of the bloodiest and most foul murders goes unwhipped of justice, and uncensured by the community in which he lives. Mr. Gore lived in St. Michael's, Talbot county, Maryland, when I left there; and if he is still alive, he very probably lives there now; and if so, he is now, as he was then, as highly esteemed and as much respected as though his guilty soul had not been stained with his brother's blood.

I speak advisedly when I say this,—that killing a slave, or any colored person, in Talbot county, Maryland, is not treated as a crime, either by the courts or the community. Mr. Thomas Lanman, of St. Michael's, killed two slaves, one of whom he killed with a hatchet, by knocking his brains out. He used to boast of the commission of the awful and bloody deed. I have heard him do so laughingly, saying, among other things, that he was the only bene-factor of his country in the company, and that when others would do as much as he had done, we should be relieved of "the d———d niggers."

The wife of Mr. Giles Hicks, living but a short distance from where I used to live, murdered my wife's cousin, a young girl between fifteen and sixteen years of age, mangling her person in the most horrible manner, breaking her nose and breastbone with a stick, so that the poor girl expired in a few hours afterward. She was immediately buried, but had not been in her untimely grave but a few hours before she was taken up and examined by the coroner, who decided that she had come to her death by severe beating. The offence for which this girl was thus murdered was this:—She had been set that night to mind Mrs. Hicks's baby, and during the night she fell asleep, and the baby cried. She, having lost her rest for several nights previous, did not hear the crying. They were both in the room with Mrs. Hicks. Mrs. Hicks, finding the girl slow to move, jumped from her bed, seized an oak stick of wood by the fireplace, and with it broke the girl's nose and breastbone, and thus ended her life. I will not say that this most horrid murder produced no sensation in the community. It did produce sensation, but not enough to bring the murderess to punishment. There was a warrant issued for her arrest, but it was never served. Thus she escaped not only punishment, but even the pain of being arraigned before a court for her horrid crime.

Whilst I am detailing bloody deeds which took place during my stay on Colonel Lloyd's plantation, I will briefly narrate another, which occurred about the same time as the murder of Demby by Mr. Gore.

Colonel Lloyd's slaves were in the habit of spending a part of their nights and Sundays in fishing for oysters, and in this way made up the deficiency of their scanty allowance. An old man belonging to Colonel Lloyd, while thus engaged, happened to get beyond the limits of Colonel Lloyd's, and on the premises of Mr. Beal Bondly. At this trespass, Mr. Bondly took offence, and with his musket came down to the shore, and blew its deadly contents into the poor old man.

Mr. Bondly came over to see Colonel Lloyd the next day, whether to pay him for his property, or to justify himself in what he had done, I know not. At any rate, this whole fiendish transaction was soon hushed up. There was very little said about it at all, and nothing done. It was a common saying, even among little white boys, that it was worth a half-cent to kill a "nigger," and a half-cent to bury one.

CHAPTER V

As to my own treatment while I lived on Colonel Lloyd's plantation, it was very similar to that of the other slave children. I was not old enough to work in the field, and there being little else than field work to do, I had a great deal of leisure time. The most I had to do was to drive up the cows at evening, keep the fowls out of the garden, keep the front yard clean, and run off errands for my old master's daughter, Mrs. Lucretia Auld. The most of my leisure time I spent in helping Master Daniel Lloyd in finding his birds, after he had shot them. My connection with Master Daniel was of some advantage to me. He became quite attached to me, and was a sort of protector of me. He would not allow the older boys to impose upon me, and would divide his cakes with me.

I was seldom whipped by my old master, and suffered little from any thing else than hunger and cold. I suffered much from hunger, but much more from cold. In hottest summer and coldest winter, I was kept almost naked—no shoes, no stockings, no jacket, no trousers, nothing on but a coarse tow linen shirt, reaching only to my knees. I had no bed. I must have perished with cold, but that, the coldest nights, I used to steal a bag which was used for carrying corn to the mill. I would crawl into this bag, and there sleep on the cold, damp, clay floor, with my head in and feet out. My feet had been so cracked with the frost, that the pen with which I am writing might be laid in the gashes.

We were not regularly allowanced. Our food was coarse corn meal boiled. This was called *mush*. It was put into a large wooden tray or trough, and set down upon the ground. The children were then called, like so many pigs, and like so many pigs they would come and devour the mush; some with oystershells, others with pieces of shingle, some with naked hands, and none with spoons. He that ate fastest got most; he that was strongest secured the best place; and few left the trough satisfied.

I was probably between seven and eight years old when I left Colonel Lloyd's plantation. I left it with joy. I shall never forget the ecstasy with which I received the intelligence that my old master (Anthony) had determined to let me go to Baltimore, to live with Mr. Hugh Auld, brother to my old master's son-in-law, Captain Thomas Auld. I received this information about three days before my departure. They were three of the happiest days I ever enjoyed. I spent the most part of all these three days in the creek, washing off the plantation scurf, and preparing myself for my departure.

The pride of appearance which this would indicate was not my own. I spent the time in washing, not so much because I wished to, but because Mrs. Lucretia had told me I must get all the dead skin off my feet and knees before I could go to Baltimore; for the people in Baltimore were very cleanly, and would laugh at me if I looked dirty. Besides, she was going to give me a pair of trousers, which I should not put on unless I got all the dirt off me. The thought of owning a pair of trousers was great indeed! It was almost a sufficient motive, not only to make me take off what would be called by pig-drovers the mange, but the skin itself. I went at it in good earnest, working for the first time with the hope of reward.

The ties that ordinarily bind children to their homes were all suspended in my case. I found no severe trial in my departure. My home was charmless; it was not home to me; on parting from it, I could not feel that I was leaving any thing which I could have enjoyed by staying. My mother was dead, my grandmother lived far off, so that I seldom saw her. I had two sisters and one brother, that lived in the same house with me; but the early separation of us from our mother had well nigh blotted the fact of our relationship from our memories. I looked for home elsewhere, and was confident of finding none which I should relish less than the one which I was leaving. If, however, I found in my new home hardship, hunger, whipping, and nakedness, I had the consolation that I should not have escaped any one of them by staying.

Having already had more than a taste of them in the house of my old master, and having endured them there, I very naturally inferred my ability to endure them elsewhere, and especially at Baltimore; for I had something of the feeling about Baltimore that is expressed in the proverb, that "being hanged in England is preferable to dying a natural death in Ireland." I had the strongest desire to see Baltimore. Cousin Tom, though not fluent in speech, had inspired me with that desire by his eloquent description of the place. I could never point out any thing at the Great House, no matter how beautiful or powerful, but that he had seen something at Baltimore far exceeding, both in beauty and strength, the object which I pointed out to him. Even the Great House itself, with all its pictures, was far inferior to many buildings in Baltimore. So strong was my desire, that I thought a gratification of it would fully compensate for whatever loss of comforts I should sustain by the exchange. I left without a regret, and with the highest hopes of future happiness.

We sailed out of Miles River for Baltimore on a Saturday morning. I remember only the day of the week, for at that time I had no knowledge of the days of the month, nor the months of the year. On setting sail, I walked aft, and gave to Colonel Lloyd's plantation what I hoped would be the last look. I then placed myself in the bows of the sloop, and there spent the remainder of the day in looking ahead, interesting myself in what was in the distance rather than in things near by or behind.

In the afternoon of that day, we reached Annapolis, the capital of the State. We stopped but a few moments, so that I had no time to go on shore. It was the first large town that I had ever seen, and though it would look small compared with some of our New England factory villages, I thought it a wonderful place for its size—more imposing even than the Great House Farm!

We arrived at Baltimore early on Sunday morning, landing at Smith's Wharf, not far from Bowley's Wharf. We had on board the sloop a large flock of sheep; and after aiding in driving them to the slaughterhouse of Mr. Curtis on Louden Slater's Hill, I was conducted by Rich, one of the hands belonging on board of the sloop, to my new home in Alliciana Street, near Mr. Gardner's ship-yard, on Fells Point.

Mr. and Mrs. Auld were both at home, and met me at the door with their little son Thomas, to take care of whom I had been given. And here I saw what I had never seen before; it was a white face beaming with the most kindly emotions; it was the face of my new mistress, Sophia Auld. I wish I could describe the rapture that flashed through my soul as I beheld it. It was a new and strange sight to me, brightening up my pathway with the light of happiness. Little Thomas was told, there was his Freddy,—and I was told to take care of little Thomas; and thus I entered upon the duties of my new home with the most cheering prospect ahead.

I look upon my departure from Colonel Lloyd's plantation as one of the most interesting events of my life. It is possible, and even quite probable, that but for the mere circumstance of being removed from that plantation to Baltimore, I should have to-day, instead of being here seated by my own table, in the enjoyment of freedom and the happiness of home, writing this Narrative, been confined in the galling chains of slavery. Going to live at Baltimore laid the foundation, and opened the gateway, to all my subsequent prosperity. I have ever regarded it as the first plain manifestation of that kind providence which has ever since attended me, and marked my life with so many favors. I regarded the selection of myself as being somewhat remarkable. There were a number of slave children that might have been sent from the plantation to Baltimore. There were those younger, those older, and those of the same age. I was chosen from among them all, and was the first, last, and only choice.

I may be deemed superstitious, and even egotistical, in regarding this event as a special interposition of divine Providence in my favor. But I should be false to the earliest sentiments of my soul, if I suppressed the opinion. I prefer to be true to myself, even at the hazard of incurring the ridicule of others, rather than to be false, and incur my own abhorrence. From my earliest recollection, I date the entertainment of a deep conviction that slavery would not always be able to hold me within its foul embrace; and in the darkest hours of my career in slavery, this living word of faith and spirit of hope departed not from me, but remained like ministering angels to cheer me through the gloom. This good spirit was from God, and to him I offer thanksgiving and praise.

CHAPTER VI

My new mistress proved to be all she appeared when I first met her at the door,—a woman of the kindest heart and finest feelings. She had never had a slave under her control previously to myself, and prior to her marriage she had been dependent upon her own industry for a living. She was by trade a weaver; and by constant application to her business, she had been in a good degree preserved from the blighting and dehumanizing effects of slavery. I was utterly astonished at her goodness. I scarcely knew how to behave towards her. She was entirely unlike any other white woman I had ever seen. I could not approach her as I was accustomed to approach other white ladies. My early instruction was all out of place. The crouching servility, usually so acceptable a quality in a slave, did not answer when manifested toward her. Her favor was not gained by it; she seemed to be disturbed by it. She did not deem it impudent or unmannerly for a slave to look her in the face. The meanest slave was put fully at ease in her presence, and none left without feeling better for having seen her. Her face was made of heavenly smiles, and her voice of tranquil music.

But, alas! this kind heart had but a short time to remain such. The fatal poison of irresponsible power was already in her hands, and soon commenced its infernal work. That cheerful eye, under the influence of slavery, soon became red with rage; that voice, made all of sweet accord, changed to one of harsh and horrid discord; and that angelic face gave place to that of a demon.

Very soon after I went to live with Mr. and Mrs. Auld, she very kindly commenced to teach me the A, B, C. After I had learned this, she assisted me in learning to spell words of three or four letters. Just at this point of my progress, Mr. Auld found out what was going on, and at once forbade Mrs. Auld to instruct me further, telling her, among other things, that it was unlawful, as well as unsafe, to teach a slave to read. To use his own words, further, he said, "If you give a nigger an inch, he will take an ell. A nigger should know nothing but to obey his master—to do as he is told to do. Learning would *spoil* the best nigger in the world. Now," said he, "if you teach that nigger (speaking of myself) how to read, there would be no keeping him. It would forever unfit him to be a slave. He would at once become unmanageable, and of no value to his master. As to himself, it could do him no good, but a great deal of harm. It would make him discontented and unhappy." These words sank deep into my heart, stirred up sentiments within that lay slumbering, and called into existence an entirely new train of thought. It was a new and special revelation, explaining dark and mysterious things, with which my youthful understanding had struggled, but struggled in vain. I now understood what had been to me a most perplexing difficulty— to wit, the white man's power to enslave the black man. It was a grand achievement, and I prized it highly. From that moment, I understood the pathway from slavery to freedom. It was just what I wanted, and I got it at a time when I the least expected it. Whilst I was saddened by the thought of losing the aid of my kind mistress, I was gladdened by the invaluable instruction which, by the merest accident, I had gained from my master. Though conscious of the difficulty of learning without a teacher, I set out with high hope, and a fixed purpose, at whatever cost of trouble, to learn how to read. The very decided manner with which he spoke, and strove to impress his wife with the evil consequences of giving me instruction, served to convince me that he was deeply sensible of the truths he was uttering. It gave me the best assurance that I might rely with the utmost confidence on the results which, he said, would flow from teaching me to read. What he most dreaded, that I most desired. What he most loved, that I most hated. That which to him was a great evil, to be carefully shunned, was to me a great good, to be diligently sought; and the argument which he so warmly urged, against my learning to read, only served to inspire me with a desire and determination to learn. In learning to read, I owe almost as much to the bitter opposition of my master, as to the kindly aid of my mistress. I acknowledge the benefit of both.

I had resided but a short time in Baltimore before I observed a marked difference, in the treatment of slaves, from that which I had witnessed in the country. A city slave is almost a freeman, compared with a slave on the plantation. He is much better fed and clothed, and enjoys privileges altogether unknown to the slave on the plantation. There is a vestige of decency, a sense of shame, that does much to curb and check those outbreaks of atrocious cruelty so commonly enacted upon the plantation. He is a desperate slaveholder, who will shock the humanity of his nonslaveholding neighbors with the cries of his lacerated slave. Few are willing to incur the odium attaching to the reputation of being a cruel master; and above all things, they would not be known as not giving a slave enough to eat. Every city slaveholder is anxious to have it known of him, that he feeds his slaves well; and it is due to them to say, that most of them do give their slaves enough to eat. There are, however, some painful exceptions to this rule. Directly opposite to us, on Philpot Street, lived Mr. Thomas Hamilton. He owned two slaves. Their names were Henrietta and Mary. Henrietta was about twenty-two years of age, Mary was about fourteen; and of all the mangled and emaciated creatures I ever looked upon, these two were the most so. His heart must be harder than stone, that could look upon these unmoved. The head, neck, and shoulders of Mary were literally cut to pieces. I have frequently felt her head, and found it nearly covered with festering sores, caused by the lash of her cruel mistress. I do not know that her master ever whipped her, but I have been an eye-witness to the cruelty of Mrs. Hamilton. I used to be in Mr. Hamilton's house nearly every day. Mrs. Hamilton used to sit in a large chair in the middle of the room, with a heavy cowskin always by her side, and scarce an hour passed during the day but was marked by the blood of one of these slaves. The girls seldom passed her without her saying, "Move faster, you *black gip!*"[6] at the same time giving them a blow with the cowskin over the head or shoulders, often drawing the blood. She would then say, "Take that, you *black gip!*"—continuing, "If you don't move faster, I'll move you!" Added to the cruel lashings to which these slaves were subjected, they were kept nearly half-starved. They seldom knew what it was to eat a full meal. I have seen Mary contending with the pigs for the offal thrown into the street. So much was Mary kicked and cut to pieces, that she was oftener called *"pecked"* than by her name.

CHAPTER VII

I lived in Master Hugh's family about seven years. During this time, I succeeded in learning to read and write. In accomplishing this, I was compelled to resort to various stratagems. I had no regular teacher. My mistress, who had kindly commenced to instruct me, had, in compliance with the advice and direction of her husband, not only ceased to instruct, but had set her face against my being instructed by any one else. It is due, however, to my mistress to say of her, that she did not adopt this course of treatment immediately. She at first lacked the depravity indispensable to shutting me up in mental darkness. It was at least necessary for her to have some training in the exercise of irresponsible power, to make her equal to the task of treating me as though I were a brute.

My mistress was, as I have said, a kind and tender-hearted woman; and in the simplicity of her soul she commenced, when I first went to live with her, to treat me as she supposed one human being ought to treat another. In entering upon the duties of a slaveholder, she did not seem to perceive that I sustained to her the relation of a mere chattel, and that for her to treat me as a human being was not only wrong, but dangerously so. Slavery proved as injurious to her as it did to me. When I went there, she was a pious, warm, and tender-hearted woman. There was no sorrow or suffering for which she had not a tear. She had bread for the hungry, clothes for the naked, and comfort for every mourner that came within her reach. Slavery soon proved its ability to divest her of these heavenly qualities. Under its influence, the tender heart became stone, and the lamblike disposition gave way to one of tiger-like fierceness. The first step in her downward course was in her ceasing to instruct me. She now commenced to practise her husband's precepts. She finally became even more violent in her opposition than her husband himself. She was not satisfied with simply doing as well as he had commanded; she seemed anxious to do better. Nothing seemed to make her more angry than to see me with a newspaper. She seemed to think that here lay the danger.

6. Cheat, swindler.

I have had her rush at me with a face made all up of fury, and snatch from me a newspaper, in a manner that fully revealed her apprehension. She was an apt woman; and a little experience soon demonstrated, to her satisfaction, that education and slavery were incompatible with each other.

From this time I was most narrowly watched. If I was in a separate room any considerable length of time, I was sure to be suspected of having a book, and was at once called to give an account of myself. All this, however, was too late. The first step had been taken. Mistress, in teaching me the alphabet, had given me the *inch*, and no precaution could prevent me from taking the *ell*.

The plan which I adopted, and the one by which I was most successful, was that of making friends of all the little white boys whom I met in the street. As many of these as I could, I converted into teachers. With their kindly aid, obtained at different times and in different places, I finally succeeded in learning to read. When I was sent of errands, I always took my book with me, and by going one part of my errand quickly, I found time to get a lesson before my return. I used also to carry bread with me, enough of which was always in the house, and to which I was always welcome; for I was much better off in this regard than many of the poor white children in our neighborhood. This bread I used to bestow upon the hungry little urchins, who, in return, would give me that more valuable bread of knowledge. I am strongly tempted to give the names of two or three of those little boys, as a testimonial of the gratitude and affection I bear them; but prudence forbids;—not that it would injure me, but it might embarrass them; for it is almost an unpardonable offence to teach slaves to read in this Christian country. It is enough to say of the dear little fellows, that they lived on Philpot Street, very near Durgin and Bailey's ship-yard. I used to talk this matter of slavery over with them. I would sometimes say to them, I wished I could be as free as they would be when they got to be men. "You will be free as soon as you are twenty-one, *but I am a slave for life!* Have not I as good a right to be free as you have?" These words used to trouble them; they would express for me the liveliest sympathy, and console me with the hope that something would occur by which I might be free.

I was now about twelve years old, and the thought of being *a slave for life* began to bear heavily upon my heart. Just about this time, I got hold of a book entitled "The Columbian Orator."[7] Every opportunity I got, I used to read this book. Among much of other interesting matter, I found in it a dialogue between a master and his slave. The slave was represented as having run away from his master three times. The dialogue represented the conversation which took place between them, when the slave was retaken the third time. In this dialogue, the whole argument in behalf of slavery was brought forward by the master, all of which was disposed of by the slave. The slave was made to say some very smart as well as impressive things in reply to his master—things which had the desired though unexpected effect; for the conversation resulted in the voluntary emancipation of the slave on the part of the master.

In the same book, I met with one of Sheridan's[8] mighty speeches on and

7. Caleb Bingham, *The Columbian Orator: Containing a Variety of Original and Selected Pieces: Together with Rules, Calculated to Improve Youth and Others others in the Ornamental and Useful Art of Eloquence* (1807). 8. Thomas Sheridan (1719–1788), lecturer and writer on elocution.

in behalf of Catholic emancipation. These were choice documents to me. I read them over and over again with unabated interest. They gave tongue to interesting thoughts of my own soul, which had frequently flashed through my mind, and died away for want of utterance. The moral which I gained from the dialogue was the power of truth over the conscience of even a slaveholder. What I got from Sheridan was a bold denunciation of slavery, and a powerful vindication of human rights. The reading of these documents enabled me to utter my thoughts, and to meet the arguments brought forward to sustain slavery; but while they relieved me of one difficulty, they brought on another even more painful than the one of which I was relieved. The more I read, the more I was led to abhor and detest my enslavers. I could regard them in no other light than a band of successful robbers, who had left their homes, and gone to Africa, and stolen us from our homes, and in a strange land reduced us to slavery. I loathed them as being the meanest as well as the most wicked of men. As I read and contemplated the subject, behold! that very discontentment which Master Hugh had predicted would follow my learning to read had already come, to torment and sting my soul to unutterable anguish. As I writhed under it, I would at times feel that learning to read had been a curse rather than a blessing. It had given me a view of my wretched condition, without the remedy. It opened my eyes to the horrible pit, but to no ladder upon which to get out. In moments of agony, I envied my fellow-slaves for their stupidity. I have often wished myself a beast. I preferred the condition of the meanest reptile to my own. Any thing, no matter what, to get rid of thinking! It was this everlasting thinking of my condition that tormented me. There was no getting rid of it. It was pressed upon me by every object within sight or hearing, animate or inanimate. The silver trump of freedom had roused my soul to eternal wakefulness. Freedom now appeared, to disappear no more forever. It was heard in every sound, and seen in every thing. It was ever present to torment me with a sense of my wretched condition. I saw nothing without seeing it, I heard nothing without hearing it, and felt nothing without feeling it. It looked from every star, it smiled in every calm, breathed in every wind, and moved in every storm.

I often found myself regretting my own existence, and wishing myself dead; and but for the hope of being free, I have no doubt but that I should have killed myself, or done something for which I should have been killed. While in this state of mind, I was eager to hear any one speak of slavery. I was a ready listener. Every little while, I could hear something about the abolition-ists. It was some time before I found what the word meant. It was always used in such connections as to make it an interesting word to me. If a slave ran away and succeeded in getting clear, or if a slave killed his master, set fire to a barn, or did any thing very wrong in the mind of a slaveholder, it was spoken of as the fruit of *abolition*. Hearing the word in this connection very often, I set about learning what it meant. The dictionary afforded me little or no help. I found it was "the act of abolishing;" but then I did not know what was to be abolished. Here I was perplexed. I did not dare to ask any one about its meaning, for I was satisfied that it was something they wanted me to know very little about. After a patient waiting, I got one of our city papers, containing an account of the number of petitions from the north, praying for the abolition of slavery in the District of Columbia, and of the slave trade between the States. From this time I understood the words *abolition* and *abolitionist,* and always drew near when that word was spoken, expecting to hear something of importance to myself and fellow-slaves. The light broke in upon me by degrees. I went one day down on the wharf of Mr. Waters; and seeing two Irishmen unloading a scow of stone, I went, unasked, and helped them. When we had finished, one of them came to me and asked me if I were a slave. I told him I was. He asked, "Are ye a slave for life?" I told him that I was. The good Irishman seemed to be deeply affected by the statement. He said to the other that it was a pity so fine a little fellow as myself should be a slave for life. He said it was a shame to hold me. They both advised me to run away to the north; that I should find friends there, and that I should be free. I pretended not to be interested in what they said, and treated them as if I did not understand them; for I feared they might be treacherous. White men have been known to encourage slaves to escape, and then, to get the reward, catch them and return them to their masters. I was afraid that these seemingly good men might use me so; but I nevertheless remembered their advice, and from that time I resolved to run away. I looked forward to a time at which it would be safe for me to escape. I was too young to think of doing so immediately; besides, I wished to learn how to write, as I might have occasion to write my own pass. I consoled myself with the hope that I should one day find a good chance. Meanwhile, I would learn to write.

The idea as to how I might learn to write was suggested to me by being in Durgin and Bailey's ship-yard, and frequently seeing the ship carpenters, after hewing, and getting a piece of timber ready for use, write on the timber the name of that part of the ship for which it was intended. When a piece of timber was intended for the larboard side, it would be marked thus—"L." When a piece was for the starboard side, it would be marked thus—"S." A piece for the larboard forward, would be marked thus—"L.F." When a piece was for starboard side forward, it would be marked thus—"S.F." For larboard aft, it would be marked thus—"L.A." For starboard aft, it would be marked thus—"S.A." I soon learned the names of these letters, and for what they were intended when placed upon a piece of timber in the ship-yard. I immediately commenced copying them, and in a short time was able to make the four letters named. After that, when I met with any boy who I knew could write, I would tell him I could write as well as he. The next word would be, "I don't believe you. Let me see you try it." I would then make the letters which I had been so fortunate as to learn, and ask him to beat that. In this way I got a good many lessons in writing, which it is quite possible I should never have gotten in any other way. During this time, my copy-book was the board fence, brick wall, and pavement; my pen and ink was a lump of chalk. With these, I learned mainly how to write. I then commenced and continued copying the Italics in Webster's Spelling Book, until I could make them all without looking on the book. By this time, my little Master Thomas had gone to school, and learned how to write, and had written over a number of copy-books. These had been brought home, and shown to some of our near neighbors, and then laid aside. My mistress used to go to class meeting at the Wilk Street meetinghouse every Monday afternoon, and leave me to take care of the house. When left thus, I used to spend the time in writing in the spaces left in Master Thomas's copy-book, copying what he had written. I continued to do this until I could write a hand very similar to that of Master Thomas. Thus, after a long, tedious effort for years, I finally succeeded in learning how to write.

CHAPTER VIII

In a very short time after I went to live at Baltimore, my old master's youngest son Richard died; and in about three years and six months after his death, my old master, Captain Anthony, died, leaving only his son, Andrew, and daughter, Lucretia, to share his estate. He died while on a visit to see his daughter at Hillsborough. Cut off thus unexpectedly, he left no will as to the disposal of his property. It was therefore necessary to have a valuation of the property, that it might be equally divided between Mrs. Lucretia and Master Andrew. I was immediately sent for, to be valued with the other property. Here again my feelings rose up in detestation of slavery. I had now a new conception of my degraded condition. Prior to this, I had become, if not insensible to my lot, at least partly so. I left Baltimore with a young heart overborne with sadness, and a soul full of apprehension. I took passage with Captain Rowe, in the schooner *Wild Cat*, and, after a sail of about twenty-four hours, I found myself near the place of my birth. I had now been absent from it almost, if not quite, five years. I, however, remembered the place very well. I was only about five years old when I left it, to go and live with my old master on Colonel Lloyd's plantation; so that I was now between ten and eleven years old.

We were all ranked together at the valuation. Men and women, old and young, married and single, were ranked with horses, sheep, and swine. There were horses and men, cattle and women, pigs and children, all holding the same rank in the scale of being, and all were subjected to the same narrow examination. Silvery-headed age and sprightly youth, maids and matrons, had to undergo the same indelicate inspection. At this moment, I saw more clearly than ever the brutalizing effects of slavery upon both slave and slaveholder.

After the valuation, then came the division. I have no language to express the high excitement and deep anxiety which were felt among us poor slaves during this time. Our fate for life was now to be decided. We had no more voice in that decision than the brutes among whom we were ranked. A single word from the white men was enough—against all our wishes, prayers, and entreaties—to sunder forever the dearest friends, dearest kindred, and strongest ties known to human beings. In addition to the pain of separation, there was the horrid dread of falling into the hands of Master Andrew. He was known to us all as being a most cruel wretch,—a common drunkard, who had, by his reckless mismanagement and profligate dissipation, already wasted a large portion of his father's property. We all felt that we might as well be sold at once to the Georgia traders, as to pass into his hands; for we knew that that would be our inevitable condition,—a condition held by us all in the utmost horror and dread.

I suffered more anxiety than most of my fellow-slaves. I had known what it was to be kindly treated; they had known nothing of the kind. They had seen little or nothing of the world. They were in very deed men and women of sorrow, and acquainted with grief.[9] Their backs had been made familiar

---

9. In Isaiah 53.3, the Lord's servant is described as "a man of sorrows, and acquainted with grief."

with the bloody lash, so that they had become callous; mine was yet tender; for while at Baltimore I got few whippings, and few slaves could boast of a kinder master and mistress than myself; and the thought of passing out of their hands into those of Master Andrew—a man who, but a few days before, to give me a sample of his bloody disposition, took my little brother by the throat, threw him on the ground, and with the heel of his boot stamped upon his head till the blood gushed from his nose and ears—was well calculated to make me anxious as to my fate. After he had committed this savage outrage upon my brother, he turned to me, and said that was the way he meant to serve me one of these days,—meaning, I suppose, when I came into his possession.

Thanks to a kind Providence, I fell to the portion of Mrs. Lucretia, and was sent immediately back to Baltimore, to live again in the family of Master Hugh. Their joy at my return equalled their sorrow at my departure. It was a glad day to me. I had escaped a [fate] worse than lion's jaws. I was absent from Baltimore, for the purpose of valuation and division, just about one month, and it seemed to have been six.

Very soon after my return to Baltimore, my mistress, Lucretia, died, leaving her husband and one child, Amanda; and in a very short time after her death, Master Andrew died. Now all the property of my old master, slaves included, was in the hands of strangers,—strangers who had had nothing to do with accumulating it. Not a slave was left free. All remained slaves, from the youngest to the oldest. If any one thing in my experience, more than another, served to deepen my conviction of the infernal character of slavery, and to fill me with unutterable loathing of slaveholders, it was their base ingratitude to my poor old grandmother. She had served my old master faithfully from youth to old age. She had been the source of all his wealth; she had peopled his plantation with slaves; she had become a great grandmother in his service. She had rocked him in infancy, attended him in childhood, served him through life, and at his death wiped from his icy brow the cold death-sweat, and closed his eyes forever. She was nevertheless left a slave—a slave for life—a slave in the hands of strangers; and in their hands she saw her children, her grandchildren, and her great-grandchildren, divided, like so many sheep, without being gratified with the small privilege of a single word, as to their or her own destiny. And, to cap the climax of their base ingratitude and fiendish barbarity, my grandmother, who was now very old, having outlived my old master and all his children, having seen the beginning and end of all of them, and her present owners finding she was of but little value, her frame already racked with the pains of old age, and complete helplessness fast stealing over her once active limbs, they took her to the woods, built her a little hut, put up a little mud-chimney, and then made her welcome to the privilege of supporting herself there in perfect loneliness; thus virtually turning her out to die! If my poor old grandmother now lives, she lives to suffer in utter loneliness; she lives to remember and mourn over the loss of children, the loss of grandchildren, and the loss of great-grandchildren. They are, in the language of the slave's poet, Whittier,—

> "Gone, gone, sold and gone
> To the rice swamp dank and lone,
> Where the slave-whip ceaseless swings,
> Where the noisome insect stings,

> Where the fever-demon strews
> Poison with the falling dews,
> Where the sickly sunbeams glare
> Through the hot and misty air:—
> Gone, gone, sold and gone
> To the rice swamp dank and lone,
> From Virginia hills and waters—
> Woe is me, my stolen daughters!"[1]

The hearth is desolate. The children, the unconscious children, who once sang and danced in her presence, are gone. She gropes her way, in the darkness of age, for a drink of water. Instead of the voices of her children, she hears by day the moans of the dove, and by night the screams of the hideous owl. All is gloom. The grave is at the door. And now, when weighed down by the pains and aches of old age, when the head inclines to the feet, when the beginning and ending of human existence meet, and helpless infancy and painful old age combine together—at this time, this most needful time, the time for the exercise of that tenderness and affection which children only can exercise towards a declining parent—my poor old grandmother, the devoted mother of twelve children, is left all alone, in yonder little hut, before a few dim embers. She stands—she sits—she staggers—she falls—she groans—she dies—and there are none of her children or grandchildren present, to wipe from her wrinkled brow the cold sweat of death, or to place beneath the sod her fallen remains. Will not a righteous God visit[2] for these things?

In about two years after the death of Mrs. Lucretia, Master Thomas married his second wife. Her name was Rowena Hamilton. She was the eldest daughter of Mr. William Hamilton. Master now lived in St. Michael's. Not long after his marriage, a misunderstanding took place between himself and Master Hugh; and as a means of punishing his brother, he took me from him to live with himself at St. Michael's. Here I underwent another most painful separation. It, however, was not so severe as the one I dreaded at the division of property; for, during this interval, a great change had taken place in Master Hugh and his once kind and affectionate wife. The influence of brandy upon him, and of slavery upon her, had effected a disastrous change in the characters of both; so that, as far as they were concerned, I thought I had little to lose by the change. But it was not to them that I was attached. It was to those little Baltimore boys that I felt the strongest attachment. I had received many good lessons from them, and was still receiving them, and the thought of leaving them was painful indeed. I was leaving, too, without the hope of ever being allowed to return. Master Thomas had said he would never let me return again. The barrier betwixt himself and brother he considered impassable.

I then had to regret that I did not at least make the attempt to carry out my resolution to run away; for the chances of success are tenfold greater from the city than from the country.

I sailed from Baltimore for St. Michael's in the sloop *Amanda,* Captain

---

1. John Greenleaf Whittier, American poet (1807–1892), wrote a large group of antislavery poems. This one is *The Farewell of a Virginia Slave Mother to her Daughters Sold into Southern Bondage.*   2. I.e., visit vengeance. Compare Exodus 32.34: "Nevertheless, in the day when I visit their sin upon them."

Edward Dodson. On my passage, I paid particular attention to the direction which the steamboats took to go to Philadelphia. I found, instead of going down, on reaching North Point they went up the bay, in a north-easterly direction. I deemed this knowledge of the utmost importance. My determination to run away was again revived. I resolved to wait only so long as the offering of a favorable opportunity. When that came, I was determined to be off.

CHAPTER IX

I have now reached a period of my life when I can give dates. I left Baltimore, and went to live with Master Thomas Auld, at St. Michael's, in March, 1832. It was now more than seven years since I lived with him in the family of my old master, on Colonel Lloyd's plantation. We of course were now almost entire strangers to each other. He was to me a new master, and I to him a new slave. I was ignorant of his temper and disposition; he was equally so of mine. A very short time, however, brought us into full acquaintance with each other. I was made acquainted with his wife not less than with himself. They were well matched, being equally mean and cruel. I was now, for the first time during a space of more than seven years, made to feel the painful gnawings of hunger—a something which I had not experienced before since I left Colonel Lloyd's plantation. It went hard enough with me then, when I could look back to no period at which I had enjoyed a sufficiency. It was tenfold harder after living in Master Hugh's family, where I had always had enough to eat, and of that which was good. I have said Master Thomas was a mean man. He was so. Not to give a slave enough to eat, is regarded as the most aggravated development of meanness even among slaveholders. The rule is, no matter how coarse the food, only let there be enough of it. This is the theory; and in the part of Maryland from which I came, it is the general practice,—though there are many exceptions. Master Thomas gave us enough of neither coarse nor fine food. There were four of us slaves in the kitchen—my sister Eliza, my aunt Priscilla, Henny, and myself; and we were allowed less than a half of a bushel of corn-meal per week, and very little else, either in the shape of meat or vegetables. It was not enough for us to subsist upon. We were therefore reduced to the wretched necessity of living at the expense of our neighbors. This we did by begging and stealing, whichever came handy in the time of need, the one being considered as legitimate as the other. A great many times have we poor creatures been nearly perishing with hunger, when food in abundance lay mouldering in the safe and smoke-house, and our pious mistress was aware of the fact; and yet that mistress and her husband would kneel every morning, and pray that God would bless them in basket and store!

Bad as all slaveholders are, we seldom meet one destitute of every element of character commanding respect. My master was one of this rare sort. I do not know of one single noble act ever performed by him. The leading trait in his character was meanness; and if there were any other element in his nature, it was made subject to this. He was mean; and, like most other mean men, he lacked the ability to conceal his meanness. Captain Auld was not born a slaveholder. He had been a poor man, master only of a Bay craft. He came into possession of all his slaves by marriage; and of all men, adopted slaveholders are the worst. He was cruel, but cowardly. He commanded without firmness. In the enforcement of his rules, he was at times rigid, and at times lax. At times, he spoke to his slaves with the firmness of Napoleon and the fury of a demon; at other times, he might well be mistaken for an inquirer who had lost his way. He did nothing of himself. He might have passed for a lion, but for his ears.[3] In all things noble which he attempted, his own meanness shone most conspicuous. His airs, words, and actions, were the airs, words, and actions of born slaveholders, and, being assumed, were awkward enough. He was not even a good imitator. He possessed all the disposition to deceive, but wanted the power. Having no resources within himself, he was compelled to be the copyist of many, and being such, he was forever the victim of inconsistency; and of consequence he was an object of contempt, and was held as such even by his slaves. The luxury of having slaves of his own to wait upon him was something new and unprepared for. He was a slaveholder without the ability to hold slaves. He found himself incapable of managing his slaves either by force, fear, or fraud. We seldom called him "master;" we generally called him "Captain Auld," and were hardly disposed to title him at all. I doubt not that our conduct had much to do with making him appear awkward, and of consequence fretful. Our want of reverence for him must have perplexed him greatly. He wished to have us call him master, but lacked the firmness necessary to command us to do so. His wife used to insist upon our calling him so, but to no purpose. In August, 1832, my master attended a Methodist camp-meeting held in the Bay-side, Talbot county, and there experienced religion. I indulged a faint hope that his conversion would lead him to emancipate his slaves, and that, if he did not do this, it would, at any rate, make him more kind and humane. I was disappointed in both these respects. It neither made him to be humane to his slaves, nor to emancipate them. If it had any effect on his character, it made him more cruel and hateful in all his ways; for I believe him to have been a much worse man after his conversion than before. Prior to his conversion, he relied upon his own depravity to shield and sustain him in his savage barbarity; but after his conversion, he found religious sanction and support for his slaveholding cruelty. He made the greatest pretensions to piety. His house was the house of prayer. He prayed morning, noon, and night. He very soon distinguished himself among his brethren, and was soon made a class-leader and exhorter. His activity in revivals was great, and he proved himself an instrument in the hands of the church in converting many souls. His house was the preachers' home. They used to take great pleasure in coming there to put up; for while he starved us, he stuffed them. We have had three or four preachers there at a time. The names of those who used to come most frequently while I lived there, were Mr. Storks, Mr. Ewery, Mr. Humphry, and Mr. Hickey. I have also seen Mr. George Cookman at our house. We slaves loved Mr. Cookman. We believed him to be a good man. We thought him instrumental in getting Mr. Samuel Harrison, a very rich slaveholder, to emancipate his slaves; and by some means got the impression that he was laboring to effect the emancipation of all the slaves. When he was at our house, we were sure to be called in to prayers. When the others were there, we were sometimes

3. A variation on Aesop's fable of the ass in the lion's skin, in which the fox says, "I should have been frightened too, if I had heard you bray."

called in and sometimes not. Mr. Cookman took more notice of us than either of the other ministers. He could not come among us without betraying his sympathy for us, and, stupid as we were, we had the sagacity to see it.

While I lived with my master in St. Michael's, there was a white young man, a Mr. Wilson, who proposed to keep a Sabbath school for the instruction of such slaves as might be disposed to learn to read the New Testament. We met but three times, when Mr. West and Mr. Fairbanks, both class-leaders, with many others, came upon us with sticks and other missiles, drove us off, and forbade us to meet again. Thus ended our little Sabbath school in the pious town of St. Michael's.

I have said my master found religious sanction for his cruelty. As an example, I will state one of many facts going to prove the charge. I have seen him tie up a lame young woman, and whip her with a heavy cowskin upon her naked shoulders, causing the warm red blood to drip; and, in justification of the bloody deed, he would quote this passage of Scripture—"He that knoweth his master's will, and doeth it not, shall be beaten with many stripes."[4]

Master would keep this lacerated young woman tied up in this horrid situation four or five hours at a time. I have known him to tie her up early in the morning, and whip her before breakfast; leave her, go to his store, return to dinner, and whip her again, cutting her in the places already made raw with his cruel lash. The secret of master's cruelty toward "Henny" is found in the fact of her being almost helpless. When quite a child, she fell into the fire, and burned herself horribly. Her hands were so burnt that she never got the use of them. She could do very little but bear heavy burdens. She was to master a bill of expense; and as he was a mean man, she was a constant offence to him. He seemed desirous of getting the poor girl out of existence. He gave her away once to his sister; but, being a poor gift, she was not disposed to keep her. Finally, my benevolent master, to use his own words, "set her adrift to take care of herself." Here was a recently-converted man, holding on upon the mother, and at the same time turning out her helpless child, to starve and die! Master Thomas was one of the many pious slaveholders who hold slaves for the very charitable purpose of taking care of them.

My master and myself had quite a number of differences. He found me unsuitable to his purpose. My city life, he said, had had a very pernicious effect upon me. It had almost ruined me for every good purpose, and fitted me for every thing which was bad. One of my greatest faults was that of letting his horse run away, and go down to his father-in-law's farm, which was about five miles from St. Michael's. I would then have to go after it. My reason for this kind of carelessness, or carefulness, was, that I could always get something to eat when I went there. Master William Hamilton, my master's father-in-law, always gave his slaves enough to eat. I never left there hungry, no matter how great the need of my speedy return. Master Thomas at length said he would stand it no longer. I had lived with him nine months, during which time he had given me a number of severe whippings, all to no good purpose. He resolved to put me out, as he said, to be broken; and, for this purpose, he let me for one year to a man named Edward Covey. Mr. Covey was a poor man, a farm-renter. He rented the place upon which he

4. Luke 12.47.

lived, as also the hands with which he tilled it. Mr. Covey had acquired a very high reputation for breaking young slaves, and this reputation was of immense value to him. It enabled him to get his farm tilled with much less expense to himself than he could have had it done without such a reputation. Some slaveholders thought it not much loss to allow Mr. Covey to have their slaves one year, for the sake of the training to which they were subjected, without any other compensation. He could hire young help with great ease, in consequence of this reputation. Added to the natural good qualities of Mr. Covey, he was a professor of religion—a pious soul—a member and a class-leader in the Methodist church. All of this added weight to his reputation as a "nigger-breaker." I was aware of all the facts, having been made acquainted with them by a young man who had lived there. I nevertheless made the change gladly; for I was sure of getting enough to eat, which is not the smallest consideration to a hungry man.

CHAPTER X

I left Master Thomas's house, and went to live with Mr. Covey, on the 1st of January, 1833. I was now, for the first time in my life, a field hand. In my new employment, I found myself even more awkward than a country boy appeared to be in a large city. I had been at my new home but one week before Mr. Covey gave me a very severe whipping, cutting my back, causing the blood to run, and raising ridges on my flesh as large as my little finger. The details of this affair are as follows: Mr. Covey sent me, very early in the morning of one of our coldest days in the month of January, to the woods, to get a load of wood. He gave me a team of unbroken oxen. He told me which was the in-hand ox, and which the off-hand ox. He then tied the end of a large rope around the horns of the in-hand ox, and gave me the other end of it, and told me, if the oxen started to run, that I must hold on upon the rope. I had never driven oxen before, and of course I was very awkward. I, however, succeeded in getting to the edge of the woods with little difficulty; but I had got a very few rods into the woods, when the oxen took fright, and started full tilt, carrying the cart against trees, and over stumps, in the most frightful manner. I expected every moment that my brains would be dashed out against the trees. After running thus for a considerable distance, they finally upset the cart, dashing it with great force against a tree, and threw themselves into a dense thicket. How I escaped death, I do not know. There I was, entirely alone, in a thick wood, in a place new to me. My cart was upset and shattered, my oxen were entangled among the young trees, and there was none to help me. After a long spell of effort, I succeeded in getting my cart righted, my oxen disentangled, and again yoked to the cart. I now proceeded with my team to the place where I had, the day before, been chopping wood, and loaded my cart pretty heavily, thinking in this way to tame my oxen. I then proceeded on my way home. I had now consumed one half of the day. I got out of the woods safely, and now felt out of danger. I stopped my oxen to open the woods gate; and just as I did so, before I could get hold of my ox-rope, the oxen again started, rushed through the gate, catching it between the wheel and the body of the cart, tearing it to pieces, and coming within a few inches of crushing me against the gate-post. Thus twice, in one short day, I escaped death by the merest chance. On my return, I told Mr. Covey what had happened, and how it happened. He ordered me to return to the woods again immediately. I did so, and he followed on after me. Just as I got into the woods, he came up and told me to stop my cart, and that he would teach me how to trifle away my time, and break gates. He then went to a large gum-tree, and with his axe cut three large switches, and, after trimming them up neatly with his pocket-knife, he ordered me to take off my clothes. I made him no answer, but stood with my clothes on. He repeated his order. I still made him no answer, nor did I move to strip myself. Upon this he rushed at me with the fierceness of a tiger, tore off my clothes, and lashed me till he had worn out his switches, cutting me so savagely as to leave the marks visible for a long time after. This whipping was the first of a number just like it, and for similar offences.

I lived with Mr. Covey one year. During the first six months, of that year, scarce a week passed without his whipping me. I was seldom free from a sore back. My awkwardness was almost always his excuse for whipping me. We were worked fully up to the point of endurance. Long before day we were up, our horses fed, and by the first approach of day we were off to the field with our hoes and ploughing teams. Mr. Covey gave us enough to eat, but scarce time to eat it. We were often less than five minutes taking our meals. We were often in the field from the first approach of day till its last lingering ray had left us; and at saving-fodder time, midnight often caught us in the field binding blades.[5]

Covey would be out with us. The way he used to stand it was this. He would spend the most of his afternoons in bed. He would then come out fresh in the evening, ready to urge us on with his words, example, and frequently with the whip. Mr. Covey was one of the few slaveholders who could and did work with his hands. He was a hard-working man. He knew by himself just what a man or a boy could do. There was no deceiving him. His work went on in his absence almost as well as in his presence; and he had the faculty of making us feel that he was ever present with us. This he did by surprising us. He seldom approached the spot where we were at work openly, if he could do it secretly. He always aimed at taking us by surprise. Such was his cunning, that we used to call him, among ourselves, "the snake." When we were at work in the cornfield, he would sometimes crawl on his hands and knees to avoid detection, and all at once he would rise nearly in our midst, and scream out, "Ha, ha! Come, come! Dash on, dash on!" This being his mode of attack, it was never safe to stop a single minute. His comings were like a thief in the night. He appeared to us as being ever at hand. He was under every tree, behind every stump, in every bush, and at every window, on the plantation. He would sometimes mount his horse, as if bound to St. Michael's, a distance of seven miles, and in half an hour afterwards you would see him coiled up in the corner of the wood-fence, watching every motion of the slaves. He would, for this purpose, leave his horse tied up in the woods. Again, he would sometimes walk up to us, and give us orders as though he was upon the point of starting on a long journey, turn his back upon us, and make as though he was going to the house to get ready; and, before he would get half way thither, he would turn short and crawl into a fence-corner, or behind some tree, and there watch us till the going down of the sun.

Mr. Covey's *forte* consisted in his power to deceive. His life was devoted

5. Gathering cut grain into bundles or sheaves.

to planning and perpetrating the grossest deceptions. Every thing he possessed in the shape of learning or religion, he made conform to his disposition to deceive. He seemed to think himself equal to deceiving the Almighty. He would make a short prayer in the morning, and a long prayer at night; and, strange as it may seem, few men would at times appear more devotional than he. The exercises of his family devotions were always commenced with singing; and, as he was a very poor singer himself, the duty of raising the hymn generally came upon me. He would read his hymn, and nod at me to commence. I would at times do so; at others, I would not. My noncompliance would almost always produce much confusion. To show himself independent of me, he would start and stagger through with his hymn in the most discordant manner. In this state of mind, he prayed with more than ordinary spirit. Poor man! such was his disposition, and success at deceiving, I do verily believe that he sometimes deceived himself into the solemn belief, that he was a sincere worshipper of the most high God; and this, too, at a time when he may be said to have been guilty of compelling his woman slave to commit the sin of adultery. The facts in the case are these: Mr. Covey was a poor man; he was just commencing in life; he was only able to buy one slave; and, shocking as is the fact, he bought her, as he said, for a *breeder*. This woman was named Caroline. Mr. Covey bought her from Mr. Thomas Lowe, about six miles from St. Michael's. She was a large, able-bodied woman, about twenty years old. She had already given birth to one child, which proved her to be just what he wanted. After buying her, he hired a married man of Mr. Samuel Harrison, to live with him one year; and him he used to fasten up with her every night! The result was, that, at the end of the year, the miserable woman gave birth to twins. At this result Mr. Covey seemed to be highly pleased, both with the man and the wretched woman. Such was his joy, and that of his wife, that nothing they could do for Caroline during her confinement was too good, or too hard, to be done. The children were regarded as being quite an addition to his wealth.

If at any one time of my life more than another, I was made to drink the bitterest dregs of slavery, that time was during the first six months of my stay with Mr. Covey. We were worked in all weathers. It was never too hot or too cold; it could never rain, blow, hail, or snow, too hard for us to work in the field. Work, work, work, was scarcely more the order of the day than of the night. The longest days were too short for him, and the shortest nights too long for him. I was somewhat unmanageable when I first went there, but a few months of this discipline tamed me. Mr. Covey succeeded in breaking me. I was broken in body, soul, and spirit. My natural elasticity was crushed, my intellect languished, the disposition to read departed, the cheerful spark that lingered about my eye died; the dark night of slavery closed in upon me; and behold a man transformed into a brute!

Sunday was my only leisure time. I spent this in a sort of beast-like stupor, between sleep and wake, under some large tree. At times I would rise up, a flash of energetic freedom would dart through my soul, accompanied with a faint beam of hope, that flickered for a moment, and then vanished. I sank down again, mourning over my wretched condition. I was sometimes prompted to take my life, and that of Covey, but was prevented by a combination of hope and fear. My sufferings on this plantation seem now like a dream rather than a stern reality.

Our house stood within a few rods of the Chesapeake Bay, whose broad bosom was ever white with sails from every quarter of the habitable globe. Those beautiful vessels, robed in purest white, so delightful to the eye of freemen, were to me so many shrouded ghosts, to terrify and torment me with thoughts of my wretched condition. I have often, in the deep stillness of a summer's Sabbath, stood all alone upon the lofty banks of that noble bay, and traced, with saddened heart and tearful eye, the countless number of sails moving off to the mighty ocean. The sight of these always affected me powerfully. My thoughts would compel utterance; and there, with no audience but the Almighty, I would pour out my soul's complaint, in my rude way, with an apostrophe[6] to the moving multitude of ships:—

"You are loosed from your moorings, and are free; I am fast in my chains, and am a slave! You move merrily before the gentle gale, and I sadly before the bloody whip! You are freedom's swift-winged angels, that fly round the world; I am confined in bands of iron! O that I were free! O, that I were on one of your gallant decks, and under your protecting wing! Alas! betwixt me and you, the turbid waters roll. Go on, go on. O that I could also go! Could I but swim! If I could fly! O, why was I born a man, of whom to make a brute! The glad ship is gone; she hides in the dim distance. I am left in the hottest hell of unending slavery. O God, save me! God, deliver me! Let me be free! Is there any God? Why am I a slave? I will run away. I will not stand it. Get caught, or get clear, I'll try it. I had as well die with ague as the fever. I have only one life to lose. I had as well be killed running as die standing. Only think of it; one hundred miles straight north, and I am free! Try it? Yes! God helping me, I will. It cannot be that I shall live and die a slave. I will take to the water. This very bay shall bear me into freedom. The steam boats steered in a north-east course from North Point. I will do the same; and when I get to the head of the bay, I will turn my canoe adrift, and walk straight through Delaware into Pennsylvania. When I get there, I shall not be required to have a pass; I can travel without being disturbed. Let but the first opportunity offer, and, come what will, I am off. Meanwhile, I will try to bear up under the yoke. I am not the only slave in the world. Why should I fret? I can bear as much as any of them. Besides, I am but a boy, and all boys are bound to some one. It may be that my misery in slavery will only increase my happiness when I get free. There is a better day coming."

Thus I used to think, and thus I used to speak to myself; goaded almost to madness at one moment, and at the next reconciling myself to my wretched lot.

I have already intimated that my condition was much worse, during the first six months of my stay at Mr. Covey's, than in the last six. The circumstances leading to the change in Mr. Covey's course toward me form an epoch in my humble history. You have seen how a man was made a slave; you shall see how a slave was made a man. On one of the hottest days of the month of August, 1833, Bill Smith, William Hughes, a slave named Eli, and myself, were engaged in fanning wheat.[7] Hughes was clearing the fanned wheat from before the fan, Eli was turning, Smith was feeding, and I was carrying wheat to the fan. The work was simple, requiring strength rather than intellect; yet, to one entirely unused to such work, it came very hard.

6. An exclamatory form of address.   7. Separating the grain from the chaff.

About three o'clock of that day, I broke down; my strength failed me; I was seized with a violent aching of the head, attended with extreme dizziness; I trembled in every limb. Finding what was coming, I nerved myself up, feeling it would never do to stop work. I stood as long as I could stagger to the hopper with grain. When I could stand no longer, I fell, and felt as if held down by an immense weight. The fan of course stopped; every one had his own work to do; and no one could do the work of the other, and have his own go on at the same time.

Mr. Covey was at the house, about one hundred yards from the treading-yard where we were fanning. On hearing the fan stop, he left immediately, and came to the spot where we were. He hastily inquired what the matter was. Bill answered that I was sick, and there was no one to bring wheat to the fan. I had by this time crawled away under the side of the post and rail-fence by which the yard was enclosed, hoping to find relief by getting out of the sun. He then asked where I was. He was told by one of the hands. He came to the spot, and, after looking at me awhile, asked me what was the matter. I told him as well as I could, for I scarce had strength to speak. He then gave me a savage kick in the side, and told me to get up. I tried to do so, but fell back in the attempt. He gave me another kick, and again told me to rise. I again tried, and succeeded in gaining my feet; but, stooping to get the tub with which I was feeding the fan, I again staggered and fell. While down in this situation, Mr. Covey took up the hickory slat with which Hughes had been striking off the half-bushel measure, and with it gave me a heavy blow upon the head, making a large wound, and the blood ran freely; and with this again told me to get up. I made no effort to comply, having now made up my mind to let him do his worst. In a short time after receiving this blow, my head grew better. Mr. Covey had now left me to my fate. At this moment I resolved, for the first time, to go to my master, enter a complaint, and ask his protection. In order to [do] this, I must that afternoon walk seven miles; and this, under the circumstances, was truly a severe undertaking. I was exceedingly feeble; made so as much by the kicks and blows which I received, as by the severe fit of sickness to which I had been subjected. I, however, watched my chance, while Covey was looking in an opposite direction, and started for St. Michael's. I succeeded in getting a considerable distance on my way to the woods, when Covey discovered me, and called after me to come back, threatening what he would do if I did not come. I disregarded both his calls and his threats, and made my way to the woods as fast as my feeble state would allow; and thinking I might be overhauled by him if I kept the road, I walked through the woods, keeping far enough from the road to avoid detection, and near enough to prevent losing my way. I had not gone far before my little strength again failed me. I could go no farther. I fell down, and lay for a considerable time. The blood was yet oozing from the wound on my head. For a time I thought I should bleed to death; and think now that I should have done so, but that the blood so matted my hair as to stop the wound. After lying there about three quarters of an hour, I nerved myself up again, and started on my way, through bogs and briers, barefooted and bareheaded, tearing my feet sometimes at nearly every step; and after a journey of about seven miles, occupying some five hours to perform it, I arrived at master's store. I then presented an appearance enough to affect any but a heart of iron. From the crown of my head to my feet, I was covered with blood. My hair was all clotted with dust and blood; my shirt was stiff with blood. My legs and feet were torn in sundry places with briers and thorns, and were also covered with blood. I suppose I looked like a man who had escaped a den of wild beasts, and barely escaped them. In this state I appeared before my master, humbly entreating him to interpose his authority for my protection. I told him all the circumstances as well as I could, and it seemed, as I spoke, at times to affect him. He would then walk the floor, and seek to justify Covey by saying he expected I deserved it. He asked me what I wanted. I told him, to let me get a new home; that as sure as I lived with Mr. Covey again, I should live with but to die with him; that Covey would surely kill me; he was in a fair way for it. Master Thomas ridiculed the idea that there was any danger of Mr. Covey's killing me, and said that he knew Mr. Covey; that he was a good man, and that he could not think of taking me from him; that, should he do so, he would lose the whole year's wages; that I belonged to Mr. Covey for one year, and that I must go back to him, come what might; and that I must not trouble him with any more stories, or that he would himself *get hold of me*. After threatening me thus, he gave me a very large dose of salts, telling me that I might remain in St. Michael's that night, (it being quite late) but that I must be off back to Mr. Covey's early in the morning; and that if I did not, he would *get hold of me*, which meant that he would whip me. I remained all night, and, according to his orders, I started off to Covey's in the morning, (Saturday morning), wearied in body and broken in spirit. I got no supper that night, or breakfast that morning. I reached Covey's about nine o'clock; and just as I was getting over the fence that divided Mrs. Kemp's fields from ours, out ran Covey with his cowskin, to give me another whipping. Before he could reach me, I succeeded in getting to the cornfield; and as the corn was very high, it afforded me the means of hiding. He seemed very angry, and searched for me a long time. My behavior was altogether unaccountable. He finally gave up the chase, thinking, I suppose, that I must come home for something to eat; he would give himself no further trouble in looking for me. I spent that day mostly in the woods, having the alternative before me,—to go home and be whipped to death, or stay in the woods and be starved to death. That night, I fell in with Sandy Jenkins, a slave with whom I was somewhat acquainted. Sandy had a free wife who lived about four miles from Mr. Covey's; and it being Saturday, he was on his way to see her. I told him my circumstances, and he very kindly invited me to go home with him. I went home with him, and talked this whole matter over, and got his advice as to what course it was best for me to pursue. I found Sandy an old adviser. He told me, with great solemnity, I must go back to Covey; but that before I went, I must go with him into another part of the woods, where there was a certain *root*, which, if I would take some of it with me, carrying it *always on my right side*, would render it impossible for Mr. Covey, or any other white man, to whip me. He said he had carried it for years; and since he had done so, he had never received a blow, and never expected to while he carried it. I at first rejected the idea, that the simple carrying of a root in my pocket would have any such effect as he had said, and was not disposed to take it; but Sandy impressed the necessity with much earnestness, telling me it could do no harm, if it did no good. To please him, I at length took the root, and, according to his direction, carried it upon my right side. This was Sunday morning.

I immediately started for home; and upon entering the yard gate, out came Mr. Covey on his way to meeting. He spoke to me very kindly, bade me drive the pigs from a lot near by, and passed on towards the church. Now, this singular conduct of Mr. Covey really made me begin to think that there was something in the *root* which Sandy had given me; and had it been on any other day than Sunday, I could have attributed the conduct to no other cause than the influence of that root; and as it was, I was half inclined to think the *root* to be something more than I at first had taken it to be. All went well till Monday morning. On this morning, the virtue of the *root* was fully tested. Long before daylight, I was called to go and rub, curry, and feed, the horses. I obeyed, and was glad to obey. But whilst thus engaged, whilst in the act of throwing down some blades from the loft, Mr. Covey entered the stable with a long rope; and just as I was half out of the loft, he caught hold of my legs, and was about tying me. As soon as I found what he was up to, I gave a sudden spring, and as I did so, he holding to my legs, I was brought sprawling on the stable floor. Mr. Covey seemed now to think he had me, and could do what he pleased; but at this moment—from whence came the spirit I don't know—I resolved to fight; and, suiting my action to the resolution, I seized Covey hard by the throat; and as I did so, I rose. He held on to me, and I to him. My resistance was so entirely unexpected, that Covey seemed taken all aback. He trembled like a leaf. This gave me assurance, and I held him uneasy, causing the blood to run where I touched him with the ends of my fingers. Mr. Covey soon called out to Hughes for help. Hughes came, and, while Covey held me, attempted to tie my right hand. While he was in the act of doing so, I watched my chance, and gave him a heavy kick close under the ribs. This kick fairly sickened Hughes, so that he left me in the hands of Mr. Covey. This kick had the effect of not only weakening Hughes, but Covey also. When he saw Hughes bending over with pain, his courage quailed. He asked me if I meant to persist in my resistance. I told him I did, come what might; that he had used me like a brute for six months, and that I was determined to be used so no longer. With that, he strove to drag me to a stick that was lying just out of the stable door. He meant to knock me down. But just as he was leaning over to get the stick, I seized him with both hands by his collar, and brought him by a sudden snatch to the ground. By this time, Bill came. Covey called upon him for assistance. Bill wanted to know what he could do. Covey said, "Take hold of him, take hold of him!" Bill said his master hired him out to work, and not to help to whip me; so he left Covey and myself to fight our own battle out. We were at it for nearly two hours. Covey at length let me go, puffing and blowing at a great rate, saying that if I had not resisted, he would not have whipped me half so much. The truth was, that he had not whipped me at all. I considered him as getting entirely the worst end of the bargain; for he had drawn no blood from me, but I had from him. The whole six months afterwards, that I spent with Mr. Covey, he never laid the weight of his finger upon me in anger. He would occasionally say, he didn't want to get hold of me again. "No," thought I, "you need not; for you will come off worse than you did before."

This battle with Mr. Covey was the turning-point in my career as a slave. It rekindled the few expiring embers of freedom, and revived within me a sense of my own manhood. It recalled the departed self-confidence, and inspired me again with a determination to be free. The gratification afforded by the triumph was a full compensation for whatever else might follow, even death itself. He only can understand the deep satisfaction which I experienced, who has himself repelled by force the bloody arm of slavery. I felt as I never felt before. It was a glorious resurrection, from the tomb of slavery, to the heaven of freedom. My long-crushed spirit rose, cowardice departed, bold defiance took its place; and I now resolved that, however long I might remain a slave in form, the day had passed forever when I could be a slave in fact. I did not hesitate to let it be known of me, that the white man who expected to succeed in whipping, must also succeed in killing me.

From this time I was never again what might be called fairly whipped, though I remained a slave four years afterwards. I had several fights, but was never whipped.

It was for a long time a matter of surprise to me why Mr. Covey did not immediately have me taken by the constable to the whipping-post, and there regularly whipped for the crime of raising my hand against a white man in defence of myself. And the only explanation I can now think of does not entirely satisfy me; but such as it is, I will give it. Mr. Covey enjoyed the most unbounded reputation for being a first-rate overseer and negro-breaker. It was of considerable importance to him. That reputation was at stake; and had he sent me—a boy about sixteen years old—to the public whipping-post, his reputation would have been lost; so, to save his reputation, he suffered me to go unpunished.

My term of actual service to Mr. Edward Covey ended on Christmas day, 1833. The days between Christmas and New Year's day are allowed as holidays; and, accordingly, we were not required to perform any labor, more than to feed and take care of the stock. This time we regarded as our own, by the grace of our masters; and we therefore used or abused it nearly as we pleased. Those of us who had families at a distance, were generally allowed to spend the whole six days in their society. This time, however, was spent in various ways. The staid, sober, thinking and industrious ones of our number would employ themselves in making corn-brooms, mats, horse-collars, and baskets; and another class of us would spend the time in hunting opossums, hares, and coons. But by far the larger part engaged in such sports and merriments as playing ball, wrestling, running foot-races, fiddling, dancing, and drinking whisky; and this latter mode of spending the time was by far the most agreeable to the feelings of our masters. A slave who would work during the holidays was considered by our masters as scarcely deserving them. He was regarded as one who rejected the favor of his master. It was deemed a disgrace not to get drunk at Christmas; and he was regarded as lazy indeed, who had not provided himself with the necessary means, during the year, to get whisky enough to last him through Christmas.

From what I know of the effect of these holidays upon the slave, I believe them to be among the most effective means in the hands of the slaveholder in keeping down the spirit of insurrection. Were the slaveholders at once to abandon this practice, I have not the slightest doubt it would lead to an immediate insurrection among the slaves. These holidays serve as conductors, or safety-valves, to carry off the rebellious spirit of enslaved humanity. But for these, the slave would be forced up to the wildest desperation; and woe betide the slaveholder, the day he ventures to remove or hinder the operation of those conductors! I warn him that, in such an event, a spirit will go forth in their midst, more to be dreaded than the most appalling earthquake.

The holidays are part and parcel of the gross fraud, wrong, and inhumanity of slavery. They are professedly a custom established by the benevolence of the slaveholders; but I undertake to say, it is the result of selfishness, and one of the grossest frauds committed upon the down-trodden slave. They do not give the slaves this time because they would not like to have their work during its continuance, but because they know it would be unsafe to deprive them of it. This will be seen by the fact, that the slaveholders like to have their slaves spend those days just in such a manner as to make them as glad of their ending as of their beginning. Their object seems to be, to disgust their slaves with freedom, by plunging them into the lowest depths of dissipation. For instance, the slaveholders not only like to see the slave drink of his own accord, but will adopt various plans to make him drunk. One plan is, to make bets on their slaves, as to who can drink the most whisky without getting drunk; and in this way they succeed in getting whole multitudes to drink to excess. Thus, when the slave asks for virtuous freedom, the cunning slaveholder, knowing his ignorance, cheats him with a dose of vicious dissipation, artfully labelled with the name of liberty. The most of us used to drink it down, and the result was just what might be supposed: many of us were led to think that there was little to choose between liberty and slavery. We felt, and very properly too, that we had almost as well be slaves to man as to rum. So, when the holidays ended, we staggered up from the filth of our wallowing, took a long breath, and marched to the field,—feeling, upon the whole, rather glad to go, from what our master had deceived us into a belief was freedom, back to the arms of slavery.

I have said that this mode of treatment is a part of the whole system of fraud and inhumanity of slavery. It is so. The mode here adopted to disgust the slave with freedom, by allowing him to see only the abuse of it, is carried out in other things. For instance, a slave loves molasses; he steals some. His master, in many cases, goes off to town, and buys a large quantity; he returns, takes his whip, and commands the slave to eat the molasses, until the poor fellow is made sick at the very mention of it. The same mode is sometimes adopted to make the slaves refrain from asking for more food than their regular allowance. A slave runs through his allowance, and applies for more. His master is enraged at him; but, not willing to send him off without food, gives him more than is necessary, and compels him to eat it within a given time. Then, if he complains that he cannot eat it, he is said to be satisfied neither full nor fasting, and is whipped for being hard to please! I have an abundance of such illustrations of the same principle, drawn from my own observation, but think the cases I have cited sufficient. The practice is a very common one.

On the first of January, 1834, I left Mr. Covey, and went to live with Mr. William Freeland, who lived about three miles from St. Michael's. I soon found Mr. Freeland a very different man from Mr. Covey. Though not rich, he was what would be called an educated southern gentleman. Mr. Covey, as I have shown, was a well-trained negro-breaker and slave-driver. The former (slaveholder though he was) seemed to possess some regard for honor, some reverence for justice, and some respect for humanity. The latter seemed totally insensible to all such sentiments. Mr. Freeland had many of the faults peculiar to slaveholders, such as being very passionate and fretful; but I must do him the justice to say, that he was exceedingly free from those degrading vices to which Mr. Covey was constantly addicted. The one was open and frank, and we always knew where to find him. The other was a most artful deceiver, and could be understood only by such as were skilful enough to detect his cunningly-devised frauds. Another advantage I gained in my new master was, he made no pretensions to, or profession of, religion; and this, in my opinion, was truly a great advantage. I assert most unhesitatingly, that the religion of the south is a mere covering for the most horrid crimes,—a justifier of the most appalling barbarity,—a sanctifier of the most hateful frauds,—and a dark shelter under which the darkest, foulest, grossest, and most infernal deeds of slaveholders find the strongest protection. Were I to be again reduced to the chains of slavery, next to that enslavement, I should regard being the slave of a religious master the greatest calamity that could befall me. For of all slaveholders with whom I have ever met, religious slaveholders are the worst. I have ever found them the meanest and basest, the most cruel and cowardly, of all others. It was my unhappy lot not only to belong to a religious slaveholder, but to live in a community of such religionists. Very near Mr. Freeland lived the Rev. Daniel Weeden, and in the same neighborhood lived the Rev. Rigby Hopkins. These were members and ministers in the Reformed Methodist Church. Mr. Weeden owned, among others, a woman slave, whose name I have forgotten. This woman's back, for weeks, was kept literally raw, made so by the lash of this merciless, *religious* wretch. He used to hire hands. His maxim was, Behave well or behave ill, it is the duty of a master occasionally to whip a slave, to remind him of his master's authority. Such was his theory, and such his practice.

Mr. Hopkins was even worse than Mr. Weeden. His chief boast was his ability to manage slaves. The peculiar feature of his government was that of whipping slaves in advance of deserving it. He always managed to have one or more of his slaves to whip every Monday morning. He did this to alarm their fears, and strike terror into those who escaped. His plan was to whip for the smallest offences, to prevent the commission of large ones. Mr. Hopkins could always find some excuse for whipping a slave. It would astonish one, unaccustomed to a slaveholding life, to see with what wonderful ease a slaveholder can find things, of which to make occasion to whip a slave. A mere look, word, or motion,—a mistake, accident, or want of power,—are all matters for which a slave may be whipped at any time. Does a slave look dissatisfied? It is said, he has the devil in him, and it must be whipped out. Does he speak loudly when spoken to by his master? Then he is getting high-minded, and should be taken down a button-hole lower. Does he forget to pull off his hat at the approach of a white person? Then he is wanting in reverence, and should be whipped for it. Does he ever venture to vindicate his conduct, when censured for it? Then he is guilty of impudence,—one of the greatest crimes of which a slave can be guilty. Does he ever venture to suggest a different mode of doing things from that pointed out by his master? He is indeed presumptuous, and getting above himself; and nothing less than a flogging will do for him. Does he, while ploughing, break a plough,—or, while hoeing, break a hoe? It is owing to his carelessness, and for it a slave must always be whipped. Mr. Hopkins could always find something of this sort to justify the use of the lash, and he seldom failed to embrace such opportunities. There was not a man in the whole county, with whom the slaves who had the getting their own home, would not prefer to live, rather than with this Rev. Mr. Hopkins. And yet there was not a man any where round, who made higher professions of religion, or was more active in revivals,—more attentive to the class, love-feast, prayer and preaching meetings, or more devotional in his family,—that prayed earlier, later, louder, and longer,—than this same reverend slave-driver, Rigby Hopkins.

But to return to Mr. Freeland, and to my experience while in his employment. He, like Mr. Covey, gave us enough to eat; but, unlike Mr. Covey, he also gave us sufficient time to take our meals. He worked us hard, but always between sunrise and sunset. He required a good deal of work to be done, but gave us good tools with which to work. His farm was large, but he employed hands enough to work it, and with ease, compared with many of his neighbors. My treatment, while in his employment, was heavenly, compared with what I experienced at the hands of Mr. Edward Covey.

Mr. Freeland was himself the owner of but two slaves. Their names were Henry Harris and John Harris. The rest of his hands he hired. These consisted of myself, Sandy Jenkins,[8] and Handy Caldwell. Henry and John were quite intelligent, and in a very little while after I went there, I succeeded in creating in them a strong desire to learn how to read. This desire soon sprang up in the others also. They very soon mustered up some old spelling-books, and nothing would do but that I must keep a Sabbath school. I agreed to do so, and accordingly devoted my Sundays to teaching these my loved fellow-slaves how to read. Neither of them knew his letters when I went there. Some of the slaves of the neighboring farms found what was going on, and also availed themselves of this little opportunity to learn to read. It was understood, among all who came, that there must be as little display about it as possible. It was necessary to keep our religious masters at St. Michael's unacquainted with the fact, that, instead of spending the Sabbath in wrestling, boxing, and drinking whiskey, we were trying to learn how to read the will of God; for they had much rather see us engaged in those degrading sports, than to see us behaving like intellectual, moral, and accountable beings. My blood boils as I think of the bloody manner in which Messrs. Wright Fairbanks and Garrison West, both class-leaders, in connection with many others, rushed in upon us with sticks and stones, and broke up our virtuous little Sabbath school, at St. Michael's—all calling themselves Christians! humble followers of the Lord Jesus Christ! But I am again digressing.

I held my Sabbath school at the house of a free colored man, whose name I deem it imprudent to mention; for should it be known, it might embarrass him greatly, though the crime of holding the school was committed ten years ago. I had at one time over forty scholars, and those of the right sort, ardently desiring to learn. They were of all ages, though mostly men and women. I look back to those Sundays with an amount of pleasure not to be expressed. They were great days to my soul. The work of instructing my dear fellow-slaves was the sweetest engagement with which I was ever blessed. We loved each other, and to leave them at the close of the Sabbath was a severe cross

8. This is the same man who gave me the roots to prevent my being whipped by Mr. Covey. He was "a clever soul." We used frequently to talk about the fight with Covey, and as often as we did so, he would claim my success as the result of the roots which he gave me. This superstition is very common among the more ignorant slaves. A slave seldom dies but that his death is attributed to trickery [Douglass's note].

indeed. When I think that those precious souls are to-day shut up in the prison-house of slavery, my feelings overcome me, and I am almost ready to ask, "Does a righteous God govern the universe? and for what does he hold the thunders in his right hand, if not to smite the oppressor, and deliver the spoiled out of the hand of the spoiler?" These dear souls came not to Sabbath school because it was popular to do so, nor did I teach them because it was reputable to be thus engaged. Every moment they spent in that school, they were liable to be taken up, and given thirty-nine lashes. They came because they wished to learn. Their minds had been starved by their cruel masters. They had been shut up in mental darkness. I taught them, because it was the delight of my soul to be doing something that looked like bettering the condition of my race. I kept up my school nearly the whole year I lived with Mr. Freeland; and, beside my Sabbath school, I devoted three evenings in the week, during the winter, to teaching the slaves at home. And I have the happiness to know, that several of those who came to Sabbath school learned how to read; and that one, at least, is now free through my agency.

The year passed off smoothly. It seemed only about half as long as the year which preceded it. I went through it without receiving a single blow. I will give Mr. Freeland the credit of being the best master I ever had, *till I became my own master.* For the ease with which I passed the year, I was, however, somewhat indebted to the society of my fellow-slaves. They were noble souls; they not only possessed loving hearts, but brave ones. We were linked and interlinked with each other. I loved them with a love stronger than any thing I have experienced since. It is sometimes said that we slaves do not love and confide in each other. In answer to this assertion, I can say, I never loved any or confided in any people more than my fellow-slaves, and especially those with whom I lived at Mr. Freeland's. I believe we would have died for each other. We never undertook to do any thing, of any importance, without a mutual consultation. We never moved separately. We were one; and as much so by our tempers and dispositions, as by the mutual hardships to which we were necessarily subjected by our condition as slaves.

At the close of the year 1834, Mr. Freeland again hired me of my master, for the year 1835. But, by this time, I began to want to live *upon free land* as well as *with Freeland;* and I was no longer content, therefore, to live with him or any other slaveholder. I began, with the commencement of the year, to prepare myself for a final struggle, which should decide my fate one way or the other. My tendency was upward. I was fast approaching manhood, and year after year had passed, and I was still a slave. These thoughts roused me—I must do something. I therefore resolved that 1835 should not pass without witnessing an attempt, on my part, to secure my liberty. But I was not willing to cherish this determination alone. My fellow-slaves were dear to me. I was anxious to have them participate with me in this, my life-giving determination. I therefore, though with great prudence, commenced early to ascertain their views and feelings in regard to their condition, and to imbue their minds with thoughts of freedom. I bent myself to devising ways and means for our escape, and meanwhile strove, on all fitting occasions, to impress them with the gross fraud and inhumanity of slavery. I went first to Henry, next to John, then to the others. I found, in them all, warm hearts and noble spirits. They were ready to hear, and ready to act when a feasible plan should be proposed. This was what I wanted. I talked to them of our want of manhood, if we submitted to our enslavement without at least one noble effort to be free. We met often, and consulted frequently, and told our hopes and fears, recounted the difficulties, real and imagined, which we should be called on to meet. At times we were almost disposed to give up, and try to content ourselves with our wretched lot; at others, we were firm and unbending in our determination to go. Whenever we suggested any plan, there was shrinking—the odds were fearful. Our path was beset with the greatest obstacles; and if we succeeded in gaining the end of it, our right to be free was yet questionable—we were yet liable to be returned to bondage. We could see no spot, this side of the ocean, where we could be free. We knew nothing about Canada. Our knowledge of the north did not extend farther than New York; and to go there, and be forever harassed with the frightful liability of being returned to slavery—with the certainty of being treated tenfold worse than before—the thought was truly a horrible one, and one which it was not easy to overcome. The case sometimes stood thus: At every gate through which we were to pass, we saw a watchman—at every ferry a guard—on every bridge a sentinel—and in every wood a patrol. We were hemmed in upon every side. Here were the difficulties, real or imagined—the good to be sought, and the evil to be shunned. On the one hand, there stood slavery, a stern reality, glaring frightfully upon us,—its robes already crimsoned with the blood of millions, and even now feasting itself greedily upon our own flesh. On the other hand, away back in the dim distance, under the flickering light of the north star, behind some craggy hill or snow-covered mountain, stood a doubtful freedom—half frozen—beckoning us to come and share its hospitality. This in itself was sometimes enough to stagger us; but when we permitted ourselves to survey the road, we were frequently appalled. Upon either side we saw grim death, assuming the most horrid shapes. Now it was starvation, causing us to eat our own flesh;—now we were contending with the waves, and were drowned;—now we were overtaken, and torn to pieces by the fangs of the terrible bloodhound. We were stung by scorpions, chased by wild beasts, bitten by snakes, and finally, after having nearly reached the desired spot,—after swimming rivers, encountering wild beasts, sleeping in the woods, suffering hunger and nakedness,—we were overtaken by our pursuers, and, in our resistance, we were shot dead upon the spot! I say, this picture sometimes appalled us, and made us

"rather bear those ills we had,
Than fly to others, that we knew not of."[9]

In coming to a fixed determination to run away, we did more than Patrick Henry,[1] when he resolved upon liberty or death. With us it was a doubtful liberty at most, and almost certain death if we failed. For my part, I should prefer death to hopeless bondage.

Sandy, one of our number, gave up the notion, but still encouraged us. Our company then consisted of Henry Harris, John Harris, Henry Bailey, Charles Roberts, and myself. Henry Bailey was my uncle, and belonged to

---

9. Shakespeare's *Hamlet* 3.1.81–82: "rather bear those ills we have,/Than fly to others, that we know not of." 1. American statesman and orator (1736–1799) whose most famous utterance was "Give me liberty or give me death."

my master. Charles married my aunt: he belonged to my master's father-in-law, Mr. William Hamilton.

The plan we finally concluded upon was, to get a large canoe belonging to Mr. Hamilton, and upon the Saturday night previous to Easter holidays, paddle directly up the Chesapeake Bay. On our arrival at the head of the bay, a distance of seventy or eighty miles from where we lived, it was our purpose to turn our canoe adrift, and follow the guidance of the north star till we got beyond the limits of Maryland. Our reason for taking the water route was, that we were less liable to be suspected as runaways; we hoped to be regarded as fishermen; whereas, if we should take the land route, we should be subjected to interruptions of almost every kind. Any one having a white face, and being so disposed, could stop us, and subject us to examination.

The week before our intended start, I wrote several protections, one for each of us. As well as I can remember, they were in the following words, to wit:—

"This is to certify that I, the undersigned, have given the bearer, my servant, full liberty to go to Baltimore, and spend the Easter holidays. Written with mine own hand, &c., 1835.

"WILLIAM HAMILTON,
"Near St. Michael's, in Talbot county, Maryland."

We were not going to Baltimore; but, in going up the bay, we went toward Baltimore, and these protections were only intended to protect us while on the bay.

As the time drew near for our departure, our anxiety became more and more intense. It was truly a matter of life and death with us. The strength of our determination was about to be fully tested. At this time, I was very active in explaining every difficulty, removing every doubt, dispelling every fear, and inspiring all with the firmness indispensable to success in our undertaking; assuring them that half was gained the instant we made the move; we had talked long enough; we were now ready to move; if not now, we never should be; and if we did not intend to move now, we had as well fold our arms, sit down, and acknowledge ourselves fit only to be slaves. This, none of us were prepared to acknowledge. Every man stood firm; and at our last meeting, we pledged ourselves afresh, in the most solemn manner, that, at the time appointed, we would certainly start in pursuit of freedom. This was in the middle of the week, at the end of which we were to be off. We went, as usual, to our several fields of labor, but with bosoms highly agitated with thoughts of our truly hazardous undertaking. We tried to conceal our feelings as much as possible; and I think we succeeded very well.

After a painful waiting, the Saturday morning, whose night was to witness our departure, came. I hailed it with joy, bring what of sadness it might. Friday night was a sleepless one for me. I was, by common consent, at the head of the whole affair. The responsibility of success or failure lay heavily upon me. The glory of the one, and the confusion of the other, were alike mine. The first two hours of that morning were such as I never experienced before, and hope never to again. Early in the morning, we went, as usual, to the field. We were spreading manure; and all at once, while thus engaged, I was overwhelmed with an indescribable feeling, in the fulness of which I turned to Sandy, who was near by, and said, "We are betrayed!" "Well," said he, "that thought has this moment struck me." We said no more. I was never more certain of any thing.

The horn was blown as usual, and we went up from the field to the house for breakfast. I went for the form, more than for want of any thing to eat that morning. Just as I got to the house, in looking out at the lane gate, I saw four white men, with two colored men. The white men were on horseback, and the colored ones were walking behind, as if tied. I watched them a few moments till they got up to our lane gate. Here they halted, and tied the colored men to the gate-post. I was not yet certain as to what the matter was. In a few moments, in rode Mr. Hamilton, with a speed betokening great excitement. He came to the door, and inquired if Master William was in. He was told he was at the barn. Mr. Hamilton, without dismounting, rode up to the barn with extraordinary speed. In a few moments, he and Mr. Freeland returned to the house. By this time, the three constables rode up, and in great haste dismounted, tied their horses, and met Master William and Mr. Hamilton returning from the barn; and after talking awhile, they all walked up to the kitchen door. There was no one in the kitchen but myself and John. Henry and Sandy were up at the barn. Mr. Freeland put his head in at the door, and called me by name, saying, there were some gentlemen at the door who wished to see me. I stepped to the door, and inquired what they wanted. They at once seized me, and, without giving me any satisfaction, tied me—lashing my hands closely together. I insisted upon knowing what the matter was. They at length said, that they had learned I had been in a "scrape," and that I was to be examined before my master; and if their information proved false, I should not be hurt.

In a few moments, they succeeded in tying John. They then turned to Henry, who had by this time returned, and commanded him to cross his hands. "I won't!" said Henry, in a firm tone, indicating his readiness to meet the consequences of his refusal. "Won't you?" said Tom Graham, the constable. "No, I won't!" said Henry, in a still stronger tone. With this, two of the constables pulled out their shining pistols, and swore, by their Creator, that they would make him cross his hands or kill him. Each cocked his pistol, and, with fingers on the trigger, walked up to Henry, saying, at the same time, if he did not cross his hands, they would blow his damned heart out. "Shoot me, shoot me!" said Henry; "you can't kill me but once. Shoot, shoot,—and be damned! *I won't be tied!*" This he said in a tone of loud defiance; and at the same time, with a motion as quick as lightning, he with one single stroke dashed the pistols from the hand of each constable. As he did this, all hands fell upon him, and, after beating him some time, they finally overpowered him, and got him tied.

During the scuffle, I managed, I know not how, to get my pass out, and, without being discovered, put it into the fire. We were all now tied; and just as we were to leave for Easton jail, Betsy Freeland, mother of William Freeland, came to the door with her hands full of biscuits, and divided them between Henry and John. She then delivered herself of a speech, to the following effect:—addressing herself to me, she said, "*You devil! You yellow devil!* it was you that put it into the heads of Henry and John to run away. But for you, you long-legged mulatto devil! Henry nor John would never have thought of such a thing." I made no reply, and was immediately hurried off towards St. Michael's. Just a moment previous to the scuffle with Henry, Mr. Hamilton suggested the propriety of making a search for the protections which he had understood Frederick had written for himself and the rest. But, just at the moment he was about carrying his proposal into effect, his aid was needed in helping to tie Henry; and the excitement attending the scuffle caused them either to forget, or to deem it unsafe, under the circumstances, to search. So we were not yet convicted of the intention to run away.

When we got about half way to St. Michael's, while the constables having us in charge were looking ahead, Henry inquired of me what he should do with his pass. I told him to eat it with his biscuit, and own nothing; and we passed the word around, *"Own nothing"*; and *"Own nothing!"* said we all. Our confidence in each other was unshaken. We were resolved to succeed or fail together, after the calamity had befallen us as much as before. We were now prepared for any thing. We were to be dragged that morning fifteen miles behind horses, and then to be placed in the Easton jail. When we reached St. Michael's, we underwent a sort of examination. We all denied that we ever intended to run away. We did this more to bring out the evidence against us, than from any hope of getting clear of being sold; for, as I have said, we were ready for that. The fact was, we cared but little where we went, so we went together. Our greatest concern was about separation. We dreaded that more than any thing this side of death. We found the evidence against us to be the testimony of one person; our master would not tell who it was; but we came to a unanimous decision among ourselves as to who their informant was. We were sent off to the jail at Easton. When we got there, we were delivered up to the sheriff, Mr. Joseph Graham, and by him placed in jail. Henry, John, and myself, were placed in one room together—Charles, and Henry Bailey, in another. Their object in separating us was to hinder concert.

We had been in jail scarcely twenty minutes, when a swarm of slave traders, and agents for slave traders, flocked into jail to look at us, and to ascertain if we were for sale. Such a set of beings I never saw before! I felt myself surrounded by so many fiends from perdition. A band of pirates never looked more like their father, the devil. They laughed and grinned over us, saying, "Ah, my boys! we have got you, haven't we?" And after taunting us in various ways, they one by one went into an examination of us, with intent to ascertain our value. They would impudently ask us if we would not like to have them for our masters. We would make them no answer, and leave them to find out as best they could. Then they would curse and swear at us, telling us that they could take the devil out of us in a very little while, if we were only in their hands.

While in jail, we found ourselves in much more comfortable quarters than we expected when we went there. We did not get much to eat, nor that which was very good; but we had a good clean room, from the windows of which we could see what was going on in the street, which was very much better than though we had been placed in one of the dark, damp cells. Upon the whole, we got along very well, so far as the jail and its keeper were concerned. Immediately after the holidays were over, contrary to all our expectations, Mr. Hamilton and Mr. Freeland came up to Easton, and took Charles, the two Henrys, and John, out of jail, and carried them home, leaving me alone. I regarded this separation as a final one. It caused me more pain than any thing else in the whole transaction. I was ready for any thing rather than separation. I supposed that they had consulted together, and had decided that, as I was the whole cause of the intention of the others to run away, it was hard to make the innocent suffer with the guilty; and that they had, therefore, concluded to take the others home, and sell me, as a warning to the others that remained. It is due to the noble Henry to say, he seemed almost as reluctant at leaving the prison as at leaving home to come to the prison. But we knew we should, in all probability, be separated, if we were sold; and since he was in their hands, he concluded to go peaceably home.

I was now left to my fate. I was all alone, and within the walls of a stone prison. But a few days before, and I was full of hope. I expected to have been safe in a land of freedom; but now I was covered with gloom, sunk down to the utmost despair. I thought the possibility of freedom was gone. I was kept in this way about one week, at the end of which, Captain Auld, my master, to my surprise and utter astonishment, came up, and took me out, with the intention of sending me, with a gentleman of his acquaintance, into Alabama. But, from some cause or other, he did not send me to Alabama, but concluded to send me back to Baltimore, to live again with his brother Hugh, and to learn a trade.

Thus, after an absence of three years and one month, I was once more permitted to return to my old home at Baltimore. My master sent me away, because there existed against me a very great prejudice in the community, and he feared I might be killed.

In a few weeks after I went to Baltimore, Master Hugh hired me to Mr. William Gardner, an extensive ship-builder, on Fell's Point. I was put there to learn how to calk. It, however, proved a very unfavorable place for the accomplishment of this object. Mr. Gardner was engaged that spring in building two large man-of-war brigs, professedly for the Mexican government. The vessels were to be launched in the July of that year, and in failure thereof, Mr. Gardner was to lose a considerable sum; so that when I entered, all was hurry. There was no time to learn any thing. Every man had to do that which he knew how to do. In entering the shipyard, my orders from Mr. Gardner were, to do whatever the carpenters commanded me to do. This was placing me at the beck and call of about seventy-five men. I was to regard all these as masters. Their word was to be my law. My situation was a most trying one. At times I needed a dozen pair of hands. I was called a dozen ways in the space of a single minute. Three or four voices would strike my ear at the same moment. It was—"Fred., come help me to cant this timber here."—"Fred., come carry this timber yonder."—"Fred., bring that roller here."—"Fred., go get a fresh can of water."—"Fred., come help saw off the end of this timber."—"Fred., go quick, and get the crowbar."—"Fred., hold on the end of this fall."—"Fred., go to the blacksmith's shop, and get a new punch."—"Hurra,[2] Fred.! run and bring me a cold chisel."—"I say, Fred., bear a hand, and get up a fire as quick as lightning under that steam-box."—"Halloo, nigger! come, turn this grindstone."—"Come, come! move, move! and bowse[3] this timber forward."—"I say, darky, blast your eyes, why don't you heat up some pitch?"—"Halloo! halloo! halloo!" (Three voices at the same time.) "Come here!—Go there!—Hold on where you are! Damn you, if you move, I'll knock your brains out!"

2. Hurry.   3. Lift or haul (usually with the help of block and tackle).

This was my school for eight months, and I might have remained there longer, but for a most horrid fight I had with four of the white apprentices, in which my left eye was nearly knocked out, and I was horribly mangled in other respects. The facts in the case were these: Until a very little while after I went there, white and black ship-carpenters worked side by side, and no one seemed to see any impropriety in it. All hands seemed to be very well satisfied. Many of the black carpenters were freemen. Things seemed to be going on very well. All at once, the white carpenters knocked off, and said they would not work with free colored workmen. Their reason for this, as alleged, was, that if free colored carpenters were encouraged, they would soon take the trade into their own hands, and poor white men would be thrown out of employment. They therefore felt called upon at once to put a stop to it. And, taking advantage of Mr. Gardner's necessities, they broke off, swearing they would work no longer, unless he would discharge his black carpenters. Now, though this did not extend to me in form, it did reach me in fact. My fellow-apprentices very soon began to feel it degrading to them to work with me. They began to put on airs, and talk about the "niggers" taking the country, saying we all ought to be killed; and, being encouraged by the journeymen, they commenced making my condition as hard as they could, by hectoring me around, and sometimes striking me. I, of course, kept the vow I made after the fight with Mr. Covey, and struck back again, regardless of consequences; and while I kept them from combining, I succeeded very well; for I could whip the whole of them, taking them separately. They, however, at length combined, and came upon me, armed with sticks, stones, and heavy handspikes. One came in front with a half brick. There was one at each side of me, and one behind me. While I was attending to those in front, and on either side, the one behind ran up with the handspike, and struck me a heavy blow upon the head. It stunned me. I fell, and with this they all ran upon me, and fell to beating me with their fists. I let them lay on for a while, gathering strength. In an instant, I gave a sudden surge, and rose to my hands and knees. Just as I did that, one of their number gave me, with his heavy boot, a powerful kick in the left eye. My eyeball seemed to have burst. When they saw my eye closed, and badly swollen, they left me. With this I seized the handspike, and for a time pursued them. But here the carpenters interfered, and I thought I might as well give it up. It was impossible to stand my hand against so many. All this took place in sight of not less than fifty white ship-carpenters, and not one interposed a friendly word; but some cried, "Kill the damned nigger! Kill him! kill him! He struck a white person." I found my only chance for life was in flight. I succeeded in getting away without an additional blow, and barely so; for to strike a white man is death by Lynch law,—and that was the law in Mr. Gardner's ship-yard; nor is there much of any other out of Mr. Gardner's ship-yard.

I went directly home, and told the story of my wrongs to Master Hugh; and I am happy to say of him, irreligious as he was, his conduct was heavenly, compared with that of his brother Thomas under similar circumstances. He listened attentively to my narration of the circumstances leading to the savage outrage, and gave many proofs of his strong indignation of it. The heart of my once overkind mistress was again melted into pity. My puffed-out eye and blood-covered face moved her to tears. She took a chair by me, washed the blood from my face, and, with a mother's tenderness, bound up my head, covering the wounded eye with a lean piece of fresh beef. It was almost compensation for my suffering to witness, once more, a manifestation of kindness from this, my once affectionate old mistress. Master Hugh was very much enraged. He gave expression to his feelings by pouring out curses upon the heads of those who did the deed. As soon as I got a little the better of my bruises, he took me with him to Esquire Watson's, on Bond Street, to see what could be done about the matter. Mr. Watson inquired who saw the assault committed. Master Hugh told him it was done in Mr. Gardner's ship-yard, at midday, where there were a large company of men at work. "As to that," he said, "the deed was done, and there was no question as to who did it." His answer was, he could do nothing in the case, unless some white man would come forward and testify. He could issue no warrant on my word. If I had been killed in the presence of a thousand colored people, their testimony combined would have been insufficient to have arrested one of the murderers. Master Hugh, for once, was compelled to say this state of things was too bad. Of course, it was impossible to get any white man to volunteer his testimony in my behalf, and against the white young men. Even those who may have sympathized with me were not prepared to do this. It required a degree of courage unknown to them to do so; for just at that time, the slightest manifestation of humanity toward a colored person was denounced as abolitionism, and that name subjected its bearer to frightful liabilities. The watchwords of the bloody-minded in that region, and in those days, were, "Damn the abolitionists!" and "Damn the niggers!" There was nothing done, and probably nothing would have been done if I had been killed. Such was, and such remains, the state of things in the Christian city of Baltimore.

Master Hugh, finding he could get no redress, refused to let me go back again to Mr. Gardner. He kept me himself, and his wife dressed my wound till I was again restored to health. He then took me into the ship-yard of which he was foreman, in the employment of Mr. Walter Price. There I was immediately set to calking, and very soon learned the art of using my mallet and irons. In the course of one year from the time I left Mr. Gardner's, I was able to command the highest wages given to the most experienced calkers. I was now of some importance to my master. I was bringing him from six to seven dollars per week. I sometimes brought him nine dollars per week: my wages were a dollar and a half a day. After learning how to calk, I sought my own employment, made my own contracts, and collected the money which I earned. My pathway became much more smooth than before; my condition was now much more comfortable. When I could get no calking to do, I did nothing. During these leisure times, those old notions about freedom would steal over me again. When in Mr. Gardner's employment, I was kept in such a perpetual whirl of excitement, I could think of nothing, scarcely, but my life; and in thinking of my life, I almost forgot my liberty. I have observed this in my experience of slavery,—that whenever my condition was improved, instead of its increasing my contentment, it only increased my desire to be free, and set me to thinking of plans to gain my freedom. I have found that, to make a contented slave, it is necessary to make a thoughtless one. It is necessary to darken his moral and mental vision, and, as far as possible, to annihilate the power of reason. He must be made to feel that slavery is right; and he can be brought to that only when he ceases to be a man.

I was now getting, as I have said, one dollar and fifty cents per day. I contracted for it; I earned it; it was paid to me; it was rightfully my own; yet, upon each returning Saturday night, I was compelled to deliver every cent of that money to Master Hugh. And why? Not because he earned it,—not because he had any hand in earning it,—not because I owed it to him,—nor because he possessed the slightest shadow of a right to it; but solely because he had the power to compel me to give it up. The right of the grim-visaged pirate upon the high seas is exactly the same.

CHAPTER XI

I now come to that part of my life during which I planned, and finally succeeded in making, my escape from slavery. But before narrating any of the peculiar circumstances, I deem it proper to make known my intention not to state all the facts connected with the transaction. My reasons for pursuing this course may be understood from the following: First, were I to give a minute statement of all the facts, it is not only possible, but quite probable, that others would thereby be involved in the most embarrassing difficulties. Secondly, such a statement would most undoubtedly induce greater vigilance on the part of slaveholders than has existed heretofore among them; which would, of course, be the means of guarding a door whereby some dear brother bondman might escape his galling chains. I deeply regret the necessity that impels me to suppress any thing of impor- tance connected with my experience in slavery. It would afford me great pleasure indeed, as well as materially add to the interest of my narrative, were I at liberty to gratify a curiosity, which I know exists in the minds of many, by an accurate statement of all the facts pertaining to my most for- tunate escape. But I must deprive myself of this pleasure, and the curious of the gratification which such a statement would afford. I would allow myself to suffer under the greatest imputations which evil-minded men might suggest, rather than exculpate myself, and thereby run the hazard of closing the slightest avenue by which a brother slave might clear himself of the chains and fetters of slavery.

I have never approved of the very public manner in which some of our western friends have conducted what they call the *underground railroad*,[4] but which, I think, by their open declarations, has been made most emphat- ically the *upperground railroad*. I honor those good men and women for their noble daring, and applaud them for willingly subjecting themselves to bloody persecution, by openly avowing their participation in the escape of slaves. I, however, can see very little good resulting from such a course, either to themselves or the slaves escaping; while, upon the other hand, I see and feel assured that those open declarations are a positive evil to the slaves remain- ing, who are seeking to escape. They do nothing towards enlightening the slave, whilst they do much towards enlightening the master. They stimulate him to greater watchfulness, and enhance his power to capture his slave. We owe something to the slaves south of the line[5] as well as to those north of it; and in aiding the latter on their way to freedom, we should be careful to do nothing which would be likely to hinder the former from escaping from slav-

---

4. A system set up by opponents of slavery to help fugitive slaves from the South escape to free states and to Canada.   5. The Mason-Dixon line, the boundary between Pennsylvania and Maryland and between slave and free states.

ery. I would keep the merciless slaveholder profoundly ignorant of the means of flight adopted by the slave. I would leave him to imagine himself surrounded by myriads of invisible tormentors, ever ready to snatch from his infernal grasp his trembling prey. Let him be left to feel his way in the dark; let darkness commensurate with his crime hover over him; and let him feel that at every step he takes, in pursuit of the flying bondman, he is running the frightful risk of having his hot brains dashed out by an invisible agency. Let us render the tyrant no aid; let us not hold the light by which he can trace the footprints of our flying brother. But enough of this. I will now proceed to the statement of those facts, connected with my escape, for which I am alone responsible, and for which no one can be made to suffer but myself.

In the early part of the year 1838, I became quite restless. I could see no reason why I should, at the end of each week, pour the reward of my toil into the purse of my master. When I carried to him my weekly wages, he would, after counting the money, look me in the face with a robber-like fierceness, and ask, "Is this all?" He was satisfied with nothing less than the last cent. He would, however, when I made him six dollars, sometimes give me six cents, to encourage me. It had the opposite effect. I regarded it as a sort of admission of my right to the whole. The fact that he gave me any part of my wages was proof, to my mind, that he believed me entitled to the whole of them. I always felt worse for having received any thing; for I feared that the giving me a few cents would ease his conscience, and make him feel himself to be a pretty honorable sort of robber. My discontent grew upon me. I was ever on the look-out for means of escape; and, finding no direct means, I determined to try to hire my time, with a view of getting money with which to make my escape. In the spring of 1838, when Master Thomas came to Baltimore to purchase his spring goods, I got an opportunity, and applied to him to allow me to hire my time. He unhesitatingly refused my request, and told me this was another stratagem by which to escape. He told me I could go nowhere but that he could get me; and that, in the event of my running away, he should spare no pains in his efforts to catch me. He exhorted me to content myself, and be obedient. He told me, if I would be happy, I must lay out no plans for the future. He said, if I behaved myself properly, he would take care of me. Indeed, he advised me to complete thoughtlessness of the future, and taught me to depend solely upon him for happiness. He seemed to see fully the pressing necessity of setting aside my intellectual nature, in order to [insure] contentment in slavery. But in spite of him, and even in spite of myself, I continued to think, and to think about the injustice of my enslavement, and the means of escape.

About two months after this, I applied to Master Hugh for the privilege of hiring my time. He was not acquainted with the fact that I had applied to Master Thomas, and had been refused. He too, at first, seemed disposed to refuse; but, after some reflection, he granted me the privilege, and proposed the following terms: I was to be allowed all my time, make all contracts with those for whom I worked, and find my own employment; and, in return for this liberty, I was to pay him three dollars at the end of each week; find myself in calking tools, and in board and clothing. My board was two dollars and a half per week. This, with the wear and tear of clothing and calking tools, made my regular expenses about six dollars per week. This amount I was compelled to make up, or relinquish the privilege of hiring my time. Rain or shine, work or no work, at the end of each week the money must be forthcoming, or I must give up my privilege. This arrangement, it will be perceived, was decidedly in my master's favor. It relieved him of all need of looking after me. His money was sure. He received all the benefits of slave-holding without its evils; while I endured all the evils of a slave, and suffered all the care and anxiety of a freeman. I found it a hard bargain. But, hard as it was, I thought it better than the old mode of getting along. It was a step towards freedom to be allowed to bear the responsibilities of a freeman, and I was determined to hold on upon it. I bent myself to the work of making money. I was ready to work at night as well as day, and by the most untiring perseverance and industry, I made enough to meet my expenses, and lay up a little money every week. I went on thus from May till August. Master Hugh then refused to allow me to hire my time longer. The ground for his refusal was a failure on my part, one Saturday night, to pay him for my week's time. This failure was occasioned by my attending a camp meeting about ten miles from Baltimore. During the week, I had entered into an engagement with a number of young friends to start from Baltimore to the camp ground early Saturday evening; and being detained by my employer, I was unable to get down to Master Hugh's without disappointing the company. I knew that Master Hugh was in no special need of the money that night. I therefore decided to go to camp meeting, and upon my return pay him the three dol-lars. I staid at the camp meeting one day longer than I intended when I left. But as soon as I returned, I called upon him to pay him what he considered his due. I found him very angry; he could scarce restrain his wrath. He said he had a great mind to give me a severe whipping. He wished to know how I dared go out of the city without asking his permission. I told him I hired my time, and while I paid him the price which he asked for it, I did not know that I was bound to ask him when and where I should go. This reply troubled him; and, after reflecting a few moments, he turned to me, and said I should hire my time no longer; that the next thing he should know of, I would be running away. Upon the same plea, he told me to bring my tools and clothing home forthwith. I did so; but instead of seeking work, as I had been accus-tomed to do previously to hiring my time, I spent the whole week without the performance of a single stroke of work. I did this in retaliation. Saturday night, he called upon me as usual for my week's wages. I told him I had no wages; I had done no work that week. Here we were upon the point of coming to blows. He raved, and swore his determination to get hold of me. I did not allow myself a single word; but was resolved, if he laid the weight of his hand upon me, it should be blow for blow. He did not strike me, but told me that he would find me in constant employment in future. I thought the matter over during the next day, Sunday, and finally resolved upon the third day of September, as the day upon which I would make a second attempt to secure my freedom. I now had three weeks during which to prepare for my journey. Early on Monday morning, before Master Hugh had time to make any engagement for me, I went out and got employment of Mr. Butler, at his ship-yard near the draw-bridge, upon what is called the City Block, thus making it unnecessary for him to seek employment for me. At the end of the week, I brought him between eight and nine dollars. He seemed very well pleased, and asked me why I did not do the same the week before. He little knew what my plans were. My object in working steadily was to remove any suspicion he might entertain of my intent to run away; and in this I succeeded admirably. I suppose he thought I was never better satisfied with my condition than at the very time during which I was planning my escape. The second week passed, and again I carried him my full wages; and so well pleased was he, that he gave me twenty-five cents, (quite a large sum for a slaveholder to give a slave,) and bade me to make a good use of it. I told him I would.

Things went on without very smoothly indeed, but within there was trouble. It is impossible for me to describe my feelings as the time of my contemplated start drew near. I had a number of warm-hearted friends in Baltimore,—friends that I loved almost as I did my life,—and the thought of being separated from them forever was painful beyond expression. It is my opinion that thousands would escape from slavery, who now remain, but for the strong cords of affection that bind them to their friends. The thought of leaving my friends was decidedly the most painful thought with which I had to contend. The love of them was my tender point, and shook my decision more than all things else. Besides the pain of separation, the dread and apprehension of a failure exceeded what I had experienced at my first attempt. The appalling defeat I then sustained returned to torment me. I felt assured that, if I failed in this attempt, my case would be a hopeless one— it would seal my fate as a slave forever. I could not hope to get off with any thing less than the severest punishment, and being placed beyond the means of escape. It required no very vivid imagination to depict the most frightful scenes through which I should have to pass, in case I failed. The wretchedness of slavery, and the blessedness of freedom, were perpetually before me. It was life and death with me. But I remained firm, and, according to my resolution, on the third day of September, 1838, I left my chains, and succeeded in reaching New York without the slightest interruption of any kind. How I did so,—what means I adopted,—what direction I travelled, and by what mode of conveyance,—I must leave unexplained, for the reasons before mentioned.

I have been frequently asked how I felt when I found myself in a free State. I have never been able to answer the question with any satisfaction to myself. It was a moment of the highest excitement I ever experienced. I suppose I felt as one may imagine the unarmed mariner to feel when he is rescued by a friendly man-of-war from the pursuit of a pirate. In writing to a dear friend, immediately after my arrival at New York, I said I felt like one who had escaped a den of hungry lions. This state of mind, however, very soon subsided; and I was again seized with a feeling of great insecurity and loneliness. I was yet liable to be taken back, and subjected to all the tortures of slavery. This in itself was enough to damp the ardor of my enthusiasm. But the loneliness overcame me. There I was in the midst of thousands, and yet a perfect stranger; without home and without friends, in the midst of thousands of my own brethren—children of a common Father, and yet I dared not to unfold to any one of them my sad condition. I was afraid to speak to any one for fear of speaking to the wrong one, and thereby falling into the hands of money-loving kidnappers, whose business it was to lie in wait for the panting fugitive, as the ferocious beasts of the forest lie in wait for their prey. The motto which I adopted when I started from slavery was this—"Trust no man!" I saw in every white man an enemy, and in almost every colored man cause for distrust. It was a most painful situation; and, to understand it, one must needs experience it, or imagine himself in similar circumstances. Let him be a fugitive slave in a strange land—a land given up to be the hunting-ground for slaveholders—whose inhabitants are legalized kidnappers—where he is every moment subjected to the terrible liability of being seized upon by his fellow-men, as the hideous crocodile seizes upon his prey!—I say, let him place himself in my situation—without home or friends—without money or credit—wanting shelter, and no one to give it—wanting bread, and no money to buy it,—and at the same time let him feel that he is pursued by merciless men-hunters, and in total darkness as to what to do, where to go, or where to stay,—perfectly helpless both as to the means of defence and means of escape,—in the midst of plenty, yet suffering the terrible gnawings of hunger,—in the midst of houses, yet having no home,—among fellow-men, yet feeling as if in the midst of wild beasts, whose greediness to swallow up the trembling and half-famished fugitive is only equalled by that with which the monsters of the deep swallow up the helpless fish upon which they subsist,—I say, let him be placed in this most trying situation,—the situation in which I was placed,—then, and not till then, will he fully appreciate the hardships of, and know how to sympathize with, the toil-worn and whip-scarred fugitive slave.

Thank Heaven, I remained but a short time in this distressed situation. I was relieved from it by the humane hand of Mr. DAVID RUGGLES,[6] whose vigilance, kindness, and perseverance, I shall never forget. I am glad of an opportunity to express, as far as words can, the love and gratitude I bear him. Mr. Ruggles is now afflicted with blindness, and is himself in need of the same kind offices which he was once so forward in the performance of toward others. I had been in New York but a few days, when Mr. Ruggles sought me out, and very kindly took me to his boarding-house at the corner of Church and Lespenard Streets. Mr. Ruggles was then very deeply engaged in the memorable *Darg* case, as well as attending to a number of other fugitive slaves, devising ways and means for their successful escape; and, though watched and hemmed in on almost every side, he seemed to be more than a match for his enemies. Very soon after I went to Mr. Ruggles, he wished to know of me where I wanted to go; as he deemed it unsafe for me to remain in New York. I told him I was a calker, and should like to go where I could get work. I thought of going to Canada; but he decided against it, and in favor of my going to New Bedford, thinking I should be able to get work there at my trade. At this time, Anna,[7] my intended wife, came on; for I wrote to her immediately after my arrival at New York, (notwithstanding my homeless, houseless, and helpless condition,) informing her of my successful flight, and wishing her to come on forthwith. In a few days after her arrival, Mr. Ruggles called in the Rev. J. W. C. Pennington, who, in the presence of Mr. Ruggles, Mrs. Michaels, and two or three others, performed the marriage ceremony, and gave us a certificate, of which the following is an exact copy:—

6. A black abolitionist (1810–1849), at this time living in New York, who helped many slaves to escape.   7. She was free [Douglass's note].

"THIS may certify, that I joined together in holy matrimony Frederick Johnson[8] and Anna Murray, as man and wife, in the presence of Mr. David Ruggles and Mrs. Michaels.

"JAMES W. C. PENNINGTON.
"*New York, Sept.* 15, 1838."

Upon receiving this certificate, and a five-dollar bill from Mr. Ruggles, I shouldered one part of our baggage, and Anna took up the other, and we set out forthwith to take passage on board of the steamboat John W. Richmond for Newport, on our way to New Bedford. Mr. Ruggles gave me a letter to a Mr. Shaw in Newport, and told me, in case my money did not serve me to New Bedford, to stop in Newport and obtain further assistance; but upon our arrival at Newport, we were so anxious to get to a place of safety, that, notwithstanding we lacked the necessary money to pay our fare, we decided to take seats in the stage, and promise to pay when we got to New Bedford. We were encouraged to do this by two excellent gentlemen, residents of New Bedford, whose names I afterward ascertained to be Joseph Ricketson and William C. Taber. They seemed at once to understand our circumstances, and gave us such assurance of their friendliness as put us fully at ease in their presence. It was good indeed to meet with such friends, at such a time. Upon reaching New Bedford, we were directed to the house of Mr. Nathan Johnson, by whom we were kindly received, and hospitably provided for. Both Mr. and Mrs. Johnson took a deep and lively interest in our welfare. They proved themselves quite worthy of the name of abolitionists. When the stage-driver found us unable to pay our fare, he held on upon our baggage as security for the debt. I had but to mention the fact to Mr. Johnson, and he forthwith advanced the money.

We now began to feel a degree of safety, and to prepare ourselves for the duties and responsibilities of a life of freedom. On the morning after our arrival at New Bedford, while at the breakfast-table, the question arose as to what name I should be called by. The name given me by my mother was, "Frederick Augustus Washington Bailey." I, however, had dispensed with the two middle names long before I left Maryland so that I was generally known by the name of "Frederick Bailey." I started from Baltimore bearing the name of "Stanley." When I got to New York, I again changed my name to "Frederick Johnson," and thought that would be the last change. But when I got to New Bedford, I found it necessary again to change my name. The reason of this necessity was, that there were so many Johnsons in New Bedford, it was already quite difficult to distinguish between them. I gave Mr. Johnson the privilege of choosing me a name, but told him he must not take from me the name of "Frederick." I must hold on to that, to preserve a sense of my identity. Mr. Johnson had just been reading the "Lady of the Lake,"[9] and at once suggested that my name be "Douglass." From that time until now I have been called "Frederick Douglass;" and as I am more widely known by that name than by either of the others, I shall continue to use it as my own.

I was quite disappointed at the general appearance of things in New Bedford. The impression which I had received respecting the character and condition of the people of the north, I found to be singularly erroneous. I had

8. I had changed my name from Frederick *Bailey* to that of *Johnson* [Douglass's note].   9. A narrative poem by Sir Walter Scott (1810) about the fortunes of the Douglas clan in Scotland.

very strangely supposed, while in slavery, that few of the comforts, and scarcely any of the luxuries, of life were enjoyed at the north, compared with what were enjoyed by the slaveholders of the south. I probably came to this conclusion from the fact that northern people owned no slaves. I supposed that they were about upon a level with the non-slaveholding population of the south. I knew *they* were exceedingly poor, and I had been accustomed to regard their poverty as the necessary consequence of their being non-slaveholders. I had somehow imbibed the opinion that, in the absence of slaves, there could be no wealth, and very little refinement. And upon coming to the north, I expected to meet with a rough, hard-handed, and uncultivated population, living in the most Spartan-like simplicity, knowing nothing of the ease, luxury, pomp, and grandeur of southern slaveholders. Such being my conjectures, any one acquainted with the appearance of New Bedford may very readily infer how palpably I must have seen my mistake.

In the afternoon of the day when I reached New Bedford, I visited the wharves, to take a view of the shipping. Here I found myself surrounded with the strongest proofs of wealth. Lying at the wharves, and riding in the stream, I saw many ships of the finest model, in the best order, and of the largest size. Upon the right and left, I was walled in by granite warehouses of the widest dimensions, stowed to their utmost capacity with the necessaries and comforts of life. Added to this, almost every body seemed to be at work, but noiselessly so, compared with what I had been accustomed to in Baltimore. There were no loud songs heard from those engaged in loading and unloading ships. I heard no deep oaths or horrid curses on the laborer. I saw no whipping of men; but all seemed to go smoothly on. Every man appeared to understand his work, and went at it with a sober, yet cheerful earnestness, which betokened the deep interest which he felt in what he was doing, as well as a sense of his own dignity as a man. To me this looked exceedingly strange. From the wharves I strolled around and over the town, gazing with wonder and admiration at the splendid churches, beautiful dwellings, and finely-cultivated gardens; evincing an amount of wealth, comfort, taste, and refinement, such as I had never seen in any part of slaveholding Maryland.

Every thing looked clean, new, and beautiful. I saw few or no dilapidated houses, with poverty-stricken inmates; no half-naked children and bare-footed women, such as I had been accustomed to see in Hillsborough, Easton, St. Michael's, and Baltimore. The people looked more able, stronger, healthier, and happier, than those of Maryland. I was for once made glad by a view of extreme wealth, without being saddened by seeing extreme poverty. But the most astonishing as well as the most interesting thing to me was the condition of the colored people, a great many of whom, like myself, had escaped thither as a refuge from the hunters of men. I found many, who had not been seven years out of their chains, living in finer houses, and evidently enjoying more of the comforts of life, than the average of slave-holders in Maryland. I will venture to assert that my friend Mr. Nathan Johnson (of whom I can say with a grateful heart, "I was hungry, and he gave me meat; I was thirsty, and he gave me drink; I was a stranger, and he took me in")[1] lived in a neater house; dined at a better table; took, paid for, and read, more

1. Matthew 25.35: "For I was an hungered, and ye gave me meat: I was thirsty, and ye gave me drink: I was a stranger, and ye took me in."

newspapers; better understood the moral, religious, and political character of the nation,—than nine tenths of the slaveholders in Talbot county Maryland. Yet Mr. Johnson was a working man. His hands were hardened by toil, and not his alone, but those also of Mrs. Johnson. I found the colored people much more spirited than I had supposed they would be. I found among them a determination to protect each other from the blood-thirsty kidnapper, at all hazards. Soon after my arrival, I was told of a circumstance which illustrated their spirit. A colored man and a fugitive slave were on unfriendly terms. The former was heard to threaten the latter with informing his master of his whereabouts. Straightway a meeting was called among the colored people, under the stereotyped notice, "Business of importance!" The betrayer was invited to attend. The people came at the appointed hour, and organized the meeting by appointing a very religious old gentleman as president, who, I believe, made a prayer, after which he addressed the meeting as follows: *"Friends, we have got him here, and I would recommend that you young men just take him outside the door, and kill him!"* With this, a number of them bolted at him; but they were intercepted by some more timid than themselves, and the betrayer escaped their vengeance, and has not been seen in New Bedford since. I believe there have been no more such threats, and should there be hereafter, I doubt not that death would be the consequence.

I found employment, the third day after my arrival, in stowing a sloop with a load of oil. It was new, dirty, and hard work for me; but I went at it with a glad heart and a willing hand. I was now my own master. It was a happy moment, the rapture of which can be understood only by those who have been slaves. It was the first work, the reward of which was to be entirely my own. There was no Master Hugh standing ready, the moment I earned the money, to rob me of it. I worked that day with a pleasure I had never before experienced. I was at work for myself and newly-married wife. It was to me the starting-point of a new existence. When I got through with that job, I went in pursuit of a job of calking; but such was the strength of prejudice against color, among the white calkers, that they refused to work with me, and of course I could get no employment.[2] Finding my trade of no immediate benefit, I threw off my calking habiliments, and prepared myself to do any kind of work I could get to do. Mr. Johnson kindly let me have his woodhorse and saw, and I very soon found myself a plenty of work. There was no work too hard—none too dirty. I was ready to saw wood, shovel coal, carry the hod, sweep the chimney, or roll oil casks,—all of which I did for nearly three years in New Bedford, before I became known to the anti-slavery world.

In about four months after I went to New Bedford there came a young man to me, and inquired if I did not wish to take the "Liberator."[3] I told him I did; but, just having made my escape from slavery, I remarked that I was unable to pay for it then. I, however, finally became a subscriber to it. The paper came, and I read it from week to week with such feelings as it would be quite idle for me to attempt to describe. The paper became my meat and my drink. My soul was set all on fire. Its sympathy for my brethren in bonds— its scathing denunciations of slaveholders—its faithful exposures of slavery— and its powerful attacks upon the upholders of the institution—sent a thrill of joy through my soul, such as I had never felt before!

2. I am told that colored persons can now get employment at calking in New Bedford—a result of anti-slavery effort [Douglass's note].   3. William Lloyd Garrison's antislavery newspaper, which began publication in 1831.

I had not long been a reader of the "Liberator," before I got a pretty correct idea of the principles, measures and spirit of the anti-slavery reform. I took right hold of the cause. I could do but little; but what I could, I did with a joyful heart, and never felt happier than when in an anti-slavery meeting. I seldom had much to say at the meetings, because what I wanted to say was said so much better by others. But, while attending an anti-slavery convention at Nantucket, on the 11th of August, 1841, I felt strongly moved to speak, and was at the same time much urged to do so by Mr. William C. Coffin, a gentleman who had heard me speak in the colored people's meeting at New Bedford. It was a severe cross, and I took it up reluctantly. The truth was, I felt myself a slave, and the idea of speaking to white people weighed me down. I spoke but a few moments, when I felt a degree of freedom, and said what I desired with considerable ease. From that time until now, I have been engaged in pleading the cause of my brethren—with what success, and with what devotion, I leave those acquainted with my labors to decide.

APPENDIX

I find, since reading over the foregoing Narrative, that I have, in several instances, spoken in such a tone and manner, respecting religion, as may possibly lead those unacquainted with my religious views to suppose me an opponent of all religion. To remove the liability of such misapprehension, I deem it proper to append the following brief explanation. What I have said respecting and against religion, I mean strictly to apply to the *slaveholding religion* of this land, and with no possible reference to Christianity proper; for, between the Christianity of this land, and the Christianity of Christ, I recognize the widest possible difference—so wide, that to receive the one as good, pure, and holy, is of necessity to reject the other as bad, corrupt, and wicked. To be the friend of the one, is of necessity to be the enemy of the other. I love the pure, peaceable, and impartial Christianity of Christ: I therefore hate the corrupt, slaveholding, women-whipping, cradle-plundering, partial and hypocritical Christianity of this land. Indeed, I can see no reason, but the most deceitful one, for calling the religion of this land Christianity. I look upon it as the climax of all misnomers, the boldest of all frauds, and the grossest of all libels. Never was there a clearer case of "stealing the livery of the court of heaven to serve the devil in." I am filled with unutterable loathing when I contemplate the religious pomp and show, together with the horrible inconsistencies, which every where surround me. We have men-stealers for ministers, women-whippers for missionaries, and cradle-plunderers for church members. The man who wields the blood-clotted cowskin during the week fills the pulpit on Sunday, and claims to be a minister of the meek and lowly Jesus. The man who robs me of my earnings at the end of each week meets me as a class-leader on Sunday morning, to show me the way of life, and the path of salvation. He who sells my sister, for purposes of prostitution, stands forth as the pious advocate of purity. He who proclaims it a religious duty to read the Bible denies me the right of learning to read the name of the God who made me. He who is the religious advocate of marriage robs whole millions of its sacred influence, and leaves them to the ravages of wholesale pollution. The warm defender of the sacredness of the family relation is the same that scatters whole families,—sundering husbands and wives, parents and children, sisters and brothers,—

leaving the hut vacant, and the hearth desolate. We see the thief preaching against theft, and the adulterer against adultery. We have men sold to build churches, women sold to support the gospel, and babes sold to purchase Bibles for the *poor heathen! all for the glory of God and the good of souls!* The slave auctioneer's bell and the church-going bell chime in with each other, and the bitter cries of the heart-broken slave are drowned in the religious shouts of his pious master. Revivals of religion and revivals in the slave-trade go hand in hand together. The slave prison and the church stand near each other. The clanking of fetters and the rattling of chains in the prison, and the pious psalm and solemn prayer in the church, may be heard at the same time. The dealers in the bodies and souls of men erect their stand in the presence of the pulpit, and they mutually help each other. The dealer gives his blood-stained gold to support the pulpit, and the pulpit, in return, covers his infernal business with the garb of Christianity. Here we have religion and robbery the allies of each other—devils dressed in angels' robes, and hell presenting the semblance of paradise.

> "Just God! and these are they,
>   Who minister at thine altar, God of right!
> Men who their hands, with prayer and blessing, lay
>   On Israel's ark of light.
>
> "What! preach, and kidnap men?
>   Give thanks, and rob thy own afflicted poor?
> Talk of thy glorious liberty, and then
>   Bolt hard the captive's door?
>
> "What! servants of thy own
>   Merciful Son, who came to seek and save
> The homeless and the outcast, fettering down
>   The tasked and plundered slave!
>
> "Pilate and Herod friends!
>   Chief priests and rulers, as of old, combine!
> Just God and holy! is that church which lends
>   Strength to the spoiler thine?"

The Christianity of America is a Christianity, of whose votaries it may be as truly said, as it was of the ancient scribes and Pharisees, "They bind heavy burdens, and grievous to be borne, and lay them on men's shoulders, but they themselves will not move them with one of their fingers. All their works they do for to be seen of men.—— They love the uppermost rooms at feasts, and the chief seats in the synagogues, ... and to be called of men, Rabbi, Rabbi.—— But woe unto you, scribes and Pharisees, hypocrites! for ye neither go in yourselves, neither suffer ye them that are entering to go in. Ye devour widows' houses, and for a pretence make long prayers; therefore ye shall receive the greater damnation. Ye compass sea and land to make one proselyte, and when he is made, ye make him twofold more the child of hell than yourselves.—— Woe unto you, scribes and Pharisees, hypocrites! for ye pay tithe of mint, and anise, and cumin, and have omitted the weightier matters of the law, judgment, mercy, and faith; these ought ye to have done, and not to leave the other undone. Ye blind guides! which strain at a gnat, and swallow a camel. Woe unto you, scribes and Pharisees, hypocrites! for ye make clean the outside of the cup and of the platter; but within, they are full of extortion and excess.—— Woe unto you, scribes and Pharisees, hypocrites! for ye are like unto whited sepulchres, which indeed appear beautiful outward, but are within full of dead men's bones, and of all uncleanness. Even so ye also outwardly appear righteous unto men, but within ye are full of hypocrisy and iniquity."[4]

Dark and terrible as is this picture, I hold it to be strictly true of the overwhelming mass of professed Christians in America. They strain at a gnat, and swallow a camel. Could any thing be more true of our churches? They would be shocked at the proposition of fellowshipping a *sheep*-stealer; and at the same time they hug to their communion a *man*-stealer, and brand me with being an infidel, if I find fault with them for it. They attend with Pharisaical strictness to the outward forms of religion, and at the same time neglect the weightier matters of the law, judgment, mercy, and faith. They are always ready to sacrifice, but seldom to show mercy. They are they who are represented as professing to love God whom they have not seen, whilst they hate their brother whom they have seen. They love the heathen on the other side of the globe. They can pray for him, pay money to have the Bible put into his hand, and missionaries to instruct him; while they despise and totally neglect the heathen at their own doors.

Such is, very briefly, my view of the religion of this land; and to avoid any misunderstanding, growing out of the use of general terms, I mean, by the religion of this land, that which is revealed in the words, deeds, and actions, of those bodies, north and south, calling themselves Christian churches, and yet in union with slaveholders. It is against religion, as presented by these bodies, that I have felt it my duty to testify.

I conclude these remarks by copying the following portrait of the religion of the south, (which is, by communion and fellowship, the religion of the north) which I soberly affirm is "true to the life," and without caricature or the slightest exaggeration. It is said to have been drawn, several years before the present anti-slavery agitation began, by a northern Methodist preacher, who, while residing at the south, had an opportunity to see slaveholding morals, manners, and piety, with his own eyes. "Shall I not visit for these things? saith the Lord. Shall not my soul be avenged on such a nation as this?"[5]

"A Parody.

"Come, saints and sinners, hear me tell
How pious priests whip Jack and Nell,
And women buy and children sell,
And preach all sinners down to hell,
    And sing of heavenly union.

"They'll bleat and baa, dona[6] like goats,
Gorge down black sheep, and strain at motes,
Array their backs in fine black coats,
Then seize their negroes by their throats,
    And choke, for heavenly union.

---

4. Matthew 23.   5. Jeremiah 5.9.   6. Believed to be a printer's error in the original edition for "go on" or "go n-a-a-ah."

"They'll church you if you sip a dram,
And damn you if you steal a lamb;
Yet rob old Tony, Doll, and Sam,
Of human rights, and bread and ham;
    Kidnapper's heavenly union.

"They'll loudly talk of Christ's reward,
And bind his image with a cord,
And scold, and swing the lash abhorred,
And sell their brother in the Lord
    To handcuffed heavenly union.

"They'll read and sing a sacred song,
And make a prayer both loud and long,
And teach the right and do the wrong,
Hailing the brother, sister throng,
    With words of heavenly union.

"We wonder how such saints can sing,
Or praise the Lord upon the wing,
Who roar, and scold, and whip, and sting,
And to their slaves and mammon cling,
    In guilty conscience union.

"They'll raise tobacco, corn, and rye,
And drive, and thieve, and cheat, and lie,
And lay up treasures in the sky,
By making switch and cowskin fly,
    In hope of heavenly union.

"They'll crack old Tony on the skull,
And preach and roar like Bashan bull,
Or braying ass, of mischief full,
Then seize old Jacob by the wool,
    And pull for heavenly union.

"A roaring, ranting, sleek man-thief,
Who lived on mutton, veal, and beef,
Yet never would afford relief
To needy, sable sons of grief,
    Was big with heavenly union.

" 'Love not the world,' the preacher said,
And winked his eye, and shook his head;
He seized on Tom, and Dick, and Ned,
Cut short their meat, and clothes, and bread,
    Yet still loved heavenly union.

"Another preacher whining spoke
Of One whose heart for sinners broke:
He tied old Nanny to an oak,
And drew the blood at every stroke,
    And prayed for heavenly union.

"Two others oped their iron jaws,
And waved their children-stealing paws;
There sat their children in gewgaws;
By stinting negroes' backs and maws,
    They kept up heavenly union.

"All good from Jack another takes,
And entertains their flirts and rakes,
Who dress as sleek as glossy snakes,
And cram their mouths with sweetened cakes;
    And this goes down for union."

  Sincerely and earnestly hoping that this little book may do something toward throwing light on the American slave system, and hastening the glad day of deliverance to the millions of my brethren in bonds—faithfully relying upon the power of truth, love, and justice, for success in my humble efforts—and solemnly pledging my self anew to the sacred cause,—I subscribe myself,
                                              FREDERICK DOUGLASS.

Lynn, Mass., April 28, 1845.

WALT WHITMAN
1819–1892

As insistently as Rousseau, but with a far richer sense of the nature and the importance of his social context, Walt Whitman in his poetry makes himself the center of the universe. He brings to his emphatic self-presentation a detailed, partly ironic, partly celebratory sense of what it means to be an American; his poetry suggests something of what life in the United States must have felt like in the middle of the nineteenth century.

  Born on Long Island, Whitman in his childhood moved with his family to Brooklyn. He was christened Walter, but shortened his first name to distinguish himself from his father. As a young man, he worked as schoolteacher, builder, bookstore owner, journalist, and poet, before moving to Washington to work as a government clerk. There he also served as a volunteer nurse, helping to care for the Civil War wounded. In 1873 he settled in Camden, New Jersey, where he remained for the rest of his life.

  Whitman began writing in his youth, producing a good deal of bad poetry and a novel, a fictionalized temperance tract. He first published *Leaves of Grass* in 1855, after having become an admirer of Emerson and a Jeffersonian Democrat; he continued enlarging and revising the book for the rest of his life. In 1865, he published *Drum Taps,* poems derived from his Civil War experiences; in 1871, *Democratic Vistas,* a collection of political and philosophical essays.

  Whitman's shifting diction—familiar, even slangy, to formal and rhetorical—makes possible a large range of tones in *Song of Myself.* In a single section (21), for example, these two sequences occur in close conjunction:

        I chant the chant of dilation or pride,
        We have had ducking and deprecating about enough,
        I show that size is only development.

> Smile O voluptuous cool-breathed earth!
> Earth of the slumbering and liquid trees!
> Earth of departed sunset—earth of the mountains misty-topt!
> Earth of the vitreous pour of the full moon just tinged with blue!

The first three-line passage, after its formal opening, falls into a pattern like that of colloquial speech. "About enough" belongs to an informal vocabulary; the final line, turning on the word *only,* makes the kind of joke one might make in conversation. ("Size doesn't matter, really, it only comes from growing.") The speaker's claim that he does not endorse conventional judgments, by which bigger is better, and his slightly mocking tone declare his independence and his willingness not to take himself with undue seriousness. Only a few lines later, when he turns to the "voluptuous cool-breathed earth," he sounds like a different person, entirely serious, almost grandiose, about his personal perceptions. Now his rhapsodic tone unites him with the Romantic poets, though his vocabulary still insists on his individuality. The conjunction of "voluptuous" with "cool-breathed," the use of "vitreous" (glasslike) to modify "pour" used as a noun, the idea of "liquid trees": such choices demand the reader's close attention to figure out exactly what the poem is saying, and they emphasize a fresh way of seeing, a precise attention to the look of things. But they also sound like poetry, in a sense familiar to readers of earlier nineteenth-century works—unlike the lines quoted just before, which resemble colloquial prose.

The range of tones here exemplified helps to communicate an important theme of Whitman's poem: the tension and exchange between desire for individuality and for community. *Narrative of the Life of Frederick Douglass* directly and without apparent conflict expresses a sense of community as part of a sense of personal identity. *Song of Myself,* on the other hand, alternates between assertions of specialness and of identification with others.

> I am of old and young, of the foolish as much as the wise, . . .
> One of the Nation of many nations, the smallest the same and the largest the
>   same,
> A Southerner soon as a Northerner, a planter nonchalant and hospitable down
>   by the Oconee I live, . . .
> At home on Kanadian snow-shoes or up in the bush, or with fishermen off
>   Newfoundland,
> At home in the fleet of ice-boats, sailing with the rest and tacking.

Declaring his union not, like Wordsworth, with the natural universe, but with the society of his compatriots, Whitman identifies himself with the enormous variety he perceives and celebrates in his country. But his poem opens "I celebrate myself, and sing myself, / And what I assume you shall assume," insisting on his uniqueness and dominance. Toward the end, these two lines occur: "I too am not a bit tamed, I too am untranslatable, / I sound my barbaric yawp over the roofs of the world." One hears the note of defiant specialness: another characteristic aspect of *Song of Myself.* The poem's power derives partly from its capacity to embody both feelings, the feeling of uniqueness and the sense of shared humanity, feelings that most people experience, sometimes in confusing conjunction. Like his Romantic predecessors, Whitman values emotion, every kind of emotion, for its own sake. He suggests the irrelevance of the notion of contradiction to any understanding of inner life. In the realm of emotion, everything coexists. *Song of Myself* attempts to include all of it.

The poetic daring of *Song of Myself* expresses itself not only in choice of subject matter but in poetic technique. Whitman's lines are unrhymed and avoid the blank verse that had been the norm, instead establishing a new sort of rhythm—one that proved of crucial importance to twentieth-century American poets, who adapted it to their own purposes. Not metrical in any familiar sense, the verse establishes its own hypnotic rhythms, evoking an individual speaking voice, an individual idiom. It even risks the prosaic in its insistence that poetry implies, above all, personal perception and personal voice: "everything" can be included in technique as well as in material.

Out of the Cradle Endlessly Rocking, another of Whitman's best-known pre–Civil War poems, develops a child's imaginative relation with nature in a way that Wordsworth might have approved. A man hears a bird song that evokes for him a past experience—just as, at the beginning of *Remembrance of Things Past,* Proust's narrator finds his childhood returning to his memory at the taste of a madeleine. Reduced to tears by the song and the memory, the speaker, "chanter of pains and joys, uniter of here and hereafter," records and explores his youthful revelation of lyric power, achieved by identification with the bird mourning the loss of its mate.

> Now in a moment I know what I am for, I awake,
> And already a thousand singers, a thousand songs, clearer, louder, and more
>   sorrowful than yours,
> A thousand warbling echoes have started to life within me, never to die.

The poem concludes with the adult speaker meditating on the nature of his creative force in terms recalling Keats's in *Ode to a Nightingale.* Whitman, too, muses about the attraction of death, feels the demonic and the beautiful united in the song that inspires him. His own songs merge in his imagination with the "strong and delicious word" spoken by the sea, another aspect of nature, and one traditionally associated with death (as well as with birth). In poetry marked, like *Song of Myself,* by his powerfully individual rhythm and meter, Whitman reminds us once more of a great Romantic theme: the mystery of creativity.

G. W. Allen, *The Solitary Singer: A Critical Biography of Walt Whitman* (1959), provides both biography and criticism. An important recent study is D. S. Reynolds, *Walt Whitman's America: A Cultural Biography* (1995). M. Hindus, ed., *Walt Whitman: The Critical Heritage* (1971), contains nineteenth-and twentieth-century essays; J. E. Miller Jr., *A Critical Guide to Leaves of Grass* (1957), is helpful. Also valuable are R. Chase, *Walt Whitman Reconsidered* (1955); M. J. Killingsworth, *Whitman's Poetry of the Body* (1989); B. Erkkila, *Whitman the Political Poet* (1989); M. W. Thomas, *The Lunar Light of Whitman's Poetry* (1987); and J. E. Miller, *Leaves of Grass: America's Lyric-Epic of Self and Democracy* (1992). A general guide is G. W. Allen, *The New Walt Whitman Handbook* (1986).

From Song of Myself[1]

1

I celebrate myself, and sing myself,
And what I assume you shall assume,
For every atom belonging to me as good belongs to you.

I loafe and invite my soul,
I lean and loafe at my ease observing a spear of summer grass.   5

My tongue, every atom of my blood, formed from this soil, this air,
Born here of parents born here from parents the same, and their parents
    the same,
I, now thirty-seven years old in perfect health begin,
Hoping to cease not till death.

---

1. First published in 1855. This text is from the 1891–92 edition of *Leaves of Grass,* the so-called Deathbed Edition.

Creeds and schools in abeyance,   10
Retiring back a while suffced at what they are, but never forgotten,
I harbor for good or bad, I permit to speak at every hazard,
Nature without check with original energy.

* * *

4

Trippers and askers surround me,
People I meet, the effect upon me of my early life or the ward and city I
    live in, or the nation,
The latest dates, discoveries, inventions, societies, authors old and new,
My dinner, dress, associates, looks, compliments, dues,
The real or fancied indifference of some man or woman I love,   5
The sickness of one of my folks or of myself, or ill-doing or loss or lack
    of money, or depressions or exaltations,
Battles, the horrors of fratricidal war, the fever of doubtful news, the
    fitful events;
These come to me days and nights and go from me again,
But they are not the Me myself.

Apart from the pulling and hauling stands what I am,   10
Stands amused, complacent, compassionating, idle, unitary,
Looks down, is erect, or bends an arm on an impalpable certain rest,
Looking with side-curved head curious what will come next,
Both in and out of the game and watching and wondering at it.

Backward I see in my own days where I sweated through fog with
    linguists and contenders,   15
I have no mockings or arguments, I witness and wait.

* * *

7

Has any one supposed it lucky to be born?
I hasten to inform him or her it is just as lucky to die, and I know it.

I pass death with the dying and birth with the new-washed babe, and am
    not contained between my hat and boots,
And peruse manifold objects, no two alike and every one good,
The earth good and the stars good, and their adjuncts all good.   5

I am not an earth nor an adjunct of an earth,
I am the mate and companion of people, all just as immortal and
    fathomless as myself,
(They do not know how immortal, but I know.)

Every kind for itself and its own, for me mine male and female,
For me those that have been boys and that love women,   10
For me the man that is proud and feels how it stings to be slighted,
For me the sweet-heart and the old maid, for me mothers and the
    mothers of mothers,
For me lips that have smiled, eyes that have shed tears,
For me children and the begetters of children.

Undrape! you are not guilty to me, nor stale nor discarded,   15
I see through the broadcloth and gingham whether or no,
And am around, tenacious, acquisitive, tireless, and cannot be shaken
    away.

*   *   *

16

I am of old and young, of the foolish as much as the wise,
Regardless of others, ever regardful of others,
Maternal as well as paternal, a child as well as a man,
Stuffed with the stuff that is coarse and stuffed with the stuff that is fine,
One of the Nation of many nations, the smallest the same and the
    largest the same,   5
A Southerner soon as a Northerner, a planter nonchalant and hospitable
    down by the Oconee[2] I live,
A Yankee bound my own was ready for trade, my joints the limberest joints
    on earth and the sternest joints on earth,
A Kentuckian walking the vale of the Elkhorn in my deer-skin leggings,
    a Louisianian or Georgian,
A boatman over lakes or bays or along coasts, a Hoosier, Badger,
    Buckeye;
At home on Kanadian snow-shoes or up in the bush, or with fishermen off
    Newfoundland,   10
At home in the fleet of ice-boats, sailing with the rest and tacking,
At home on the hills of Vermont or in the woods of Maine, or the
    Texan ranch,
Comrade of Californians, comrade of free North-Westerners, (loving their
    big proportions,)
Comrade of raftsmen and coalmen, comrade of all who shake hands
    and welcome to drink and meat,
A learner with the simplest, a teacher of the thoughtfullest,   15
A novice beginning yet experient of myriads of seasons,
Of every hue and caste am I, of every rank and religion,
A farmer, mechanic, artist, gentleman, sailor, quaker,
Prisoner, fancy-man, rowdy, lawyer, physician, priest.

I resist any thing better than my own diversity,   20
Breathe the air but leave plenty after me,
And am not stuck up, and am in my place.

(The moth and the fish-eggs are in their place,
The bright suns I see and the dark suns I cannot see are in their place,
The palpable is in its place and the impalpable is in its place.)   25

*   *   *

---

2. River in Georgia.

21

I am the poet of the Body and I am the poet of the Soul,
The pleasures of heaven are with me and the pains of hell are with me,
The first I graft and increase upon myself, the latter I translate into a
    new tongue.

I am the poet of the woman the same as the man,
And I say it is as great to be a woman as to be a man,   5
And I say there is nothing greater than the mother of men.

I chant the chant of dilation or pride,
We have had ducking and deprecating about enough,
I show that size is only development.

Have you outstript the rest? are you the President?   10
It is a trifle, they will more than arrive there every one, and still pass on.

I am he that walks with the tender and growing night,
I call to the earth and sea half-held by the night.

Press close bare-bosomed night—press close magnetic nourishing night!
Night of south winds—night of the large few stars!   15
Still nodding night—mad naked summer night.

Smile O voluptuous cool-breathed earth!
Earth of the slumbering and liquid trees!
Earth of departed sunset—earth of the mountains misty-topt!
Earth of the vitreous pour of the full moon just tinged with blue!   20
Earth of shine and dark mottling the tide of the river!
Earth of the limpid gray of clouds brighter and clearer for my sake!
Far-swooping elbowed earth—rich apple-blossomed earth!
Smile, for your lover comes.

Prodigal, you have given me love—therefore I to you give love!   25
O unspeakable passionate love.

              *   *   *

24

Walt Whitman, a kosmos, of Manhattan the son,
Turbulent, fleshy, sensual, eating, drinking and breeding,
No sentimentalist, no stander above men and women or apart from them,
No more modest than immodest.

Unscrew the locks from the doors!   5
Unscrew the doors themselves from their jambs!

Whoever degrades another degrades me,
And whatever is done or said returns at last to me.

Through me the afflatus surging and surging, through me the current and
    index.

I speak the pass-word primeval, I give the sign of democracy,   10
By God! I will accept nothing which all cannot have their counterpart
    of on the same terms.

              *   *   *

32

I think I could turn and live with animals, they are so placid and self-
    contained,
I stand and look at them long and long.

They do not sweat and whine about their condition,
They do not lie awake in the dark and weep for their sins,
They do not make me sick discussing their duty to God,   5
Not one is dissatisfied, not one is demented with the mania of owning
    things,
Not one kneels to another, nor to his kind that lived thousands of years
    ago,
Not one is respectable or unhappy over the whole earth.

So they show their relations to me and I accept them,
They bring me tokens of myself, they evince them plainly in their
    possession.   10

I wonder where they get those tokens,
Did I pass that way huge times ago and negligently drop them?

Myself moving forward then and now and forever,
Gathering and showing more always and with velocity,
Infinite and omnigenous,[3] and the like of these among them,   15
Not too exclusive toward the reachers of my remembrancers,
Picking out here one that I love, and now go with him on brotherly terms.

A gigantic beauty of a stallion, fresh and responsive to my caresses,
Head high in the forehead, wide between the ears,
Limbs glossy and supple, tail dusting the ground,   20
Eyes full of sparkling wickedness, ears finely cut, flexibly moving.

His nostrils dilate as my heels embrace him,
His well-built limbs tremble with pleasure as we race around and return.

I but use you a minute, then I resign you, stallion,
Why do I need your paces when I myself out-gallop them?   25
Even as I stand or sit passing faster than you.

*   *   *

46

I know I have the best of time and space, and was never measured and
    never will be measured.

I tramp a perpetual journey, (come listen all!)
My signs are a rain-proof coat, good shoes, and a staff cut from the woods,
No friend of mine takes his ease in my chair,
I have no chair, no church, no philosophy,   5
I lead no man to a dinner-table, library, exchange,
But each man and each woman of you I lead upon a knoll,
My left hand hooking you round the waist,
My right hand pointing to landscapes of continents and the public road.

---

3. Belonging to all races.

Not I, not any one else can travel that road for you,   10
You must travel it for yourself.

It is not far, it is within reach,
Perhaps you have been on it since you were born and did not know,
Perhaps it is everywhere on water and on land.

Shoulder your duds dear son, and I will mine, and let us hasten forth,   15
Wonderful cities and free nations we shall fetch as we go.

* * *

51

The past and present wilt—I have filled them, emptied them,
And proceed to fill my next fold of the future.

Listener up there! what have you to confide to me?
Look in my face while I snuff the sidle of evening,[4]
(Talk honestly, no one else hears you, and I stay only a minute longer.)   5

Do I contradict myself?
Very well then I contradict myself,
(I am large, I contain multitudes.)

I concentrate toward them that are nigh, I wait on the door-slab.

Who has done his day's work? who will soonest be through with his
    supper?   10
Who wishes to walk with me?

Will you speak before I am gone? will you prove already too late?

52

The spotted hawk swoops by and accuses me, he complains of my gab and
    my loitering.

I too am not a bit tamed, I too am untranslatable,
I sound my barbaric yawp over the roofs of the world.

The last scud of day holds back for me,
It flings my likeness after the rest and true as any on the shadowed
    wilds,   5
It coaxes me to the vapor and the dusk.

I depart as air, I shake my white locks at the runaway sun,
I effuse my flesh in eddies, and drift it in lacy jags.

I bequeath myself to the dirt to grow from the grass I love,
If you want me again look for me under your boot-soles.   10

You will hardly know who I am or what I mean,
But I shall be good health to you nevertheless,
And filter and fibre your blood.

---

4. I.e., smell the fragrance of the slowly descending evening.

Failing to fetch me at first keep encouraged,
Missing me one place search another,   15
I stop somewhere waiting for you.

Out of the Cradle Endlessly Rocking

Out of the cradle endlessly rocking,
Out of the mocking-bird's throat, the musical shuttle,
Out of the Ninth-month[1] midnight,
Over the sterile sands and the fields beyond, where the child leaving
      his bed wandered alone, bareheaded, barefoot,
Down from the showered halo,   5
Up from the mystic play of shadows twining and twisting as if they
      were alive,
Out from the patches of briers and blackberries,
From the memories of the bird that chanted to me,
From your memories sad brother, from the fitful risings and fallings I
      heard,
From under that yellow half-moon late-risen and swollen as if with
      tears,   10
From those beginning notes of yearning and love there in the mist,
From the thousand responses of my heart never to cease,
From the myriad thence-aroused words,
From the word stronger and more delicious than any,
From such as now they start the scene revisiting,   15
As a flock, twittering, rising, or overhead passing,
Borne hither, ere all eludes me, hurriedly,
A man, yet by these tears a little boy again,
Throwing myself on the sand, confronting the waves,
I, chanter of pains and joys, uniter of here and hereafter,   20
Taking all hints to use them, but swiftly leaping beyond them,
A reminiscence sing.

Once Paumanok,[2]
When the lilac-scent was in the air and Fifth-month[3] grass was growing,
Up this seashore in some briers,   25
Two feathered guests from Alabama, two together,
And their nest, and four light-green eggs spotted with brown,
And every day the he-bird to and fro near at hand,
And every day the she-bird crouched on her nest, silent, with bright eyes,
And every day I, a curious boy, never too close, never disturbing them,   30
Cautiously peering, absorbing, translating.

Shine! shine! shine!
Pour down your warmth, great sun!
While we bask, we two together.

Two together!   35
Winds blow south, or winds blow north,
Day come white, or night come black,

1. September, in Quaker usage.   2. Pronounced *paw-mah'-nok*. The Native American name for Long
Island, where Whitman grew up.   3. May.

Home, or rivers and mountains from home,
Singing all time, minding no time,
While we two keep together. 40

Till of a sudden,
Maybe killed, unknown to her mate,
One forenoon the she-bird crouched not on the nest,
Nor returned that afternoon, nor the next,
Nor ever appeared again. 45

And thenceforward all summer in the sound of the sea,
And at night under the full of the moon in calmer weather,
Over the hoarse surging of the sea,
Or flitting from brier to brier by day,
I saw, I heard at intervals the remaining one, the he-bird, 50
The solitary guest from Alabama.

Blow! blow! blow!
Blow up sea-winds along Paumanok's shore;
I wait and I wait till you blow my mate to me.

Yes, when the stars glistened, 55
All night long on the prong of a moss-scalloped stake,
Down almost amid the slapping waves,
Sat the lone singer wonderful causing tears.

He called on his mate,
He poured forth the meanings which I of all men know. 60

Yes my brother I know,
The rest might not, but I have treasured every note,
For more than once dimly down to the beach gliding,
Silent, avoiding the moonbeams, blending myself with the shadows,
Recalling now the obscure shapes, the echoes, the sounds and sights
    after their sorts, 65
The white arms out in the breakers tirelessly tossing,
I, with bare feet, a child, the wind wafting my hair,
Listened long and long.

Listened to keep, to sing, now translating the notes,
Following you my brother. 70

Soothe! soothe! soothe!
Close on its wave soothes the wave behind,
And again another behind embracing and lapping, every one close,
But my love soothes not me, not me.

Low hangs the moon, it rose late, 75
It is lagging—O I think it is heavy with love, with love.

O madly the sea pushes upon the land,
With love, with love.

O night! do I not see my love fluttering out among the breakers?
What is that little black thing I see there in the white? 80

Loud! loud! loud!
Loud I call to you, my love!

High and clear I shoot my voice over the waves,
Surely you must know who is here, is here,
You must know who I am, my love.   85

Low-hanging moon!
What is that dusky spot in your brown yellow?
O it is the shape, the shape of my mate!
O moon do not keep her from me any longer.

Land! land! O land!   90
Whichever way I turn, O I think you could give me my mate back again
        if you only would,
For I am almost sure I see her dimly whichever way I look.

O rising stars!
Perhaps the one I want so much will rise, will rise with some of you.

O throat! O trembling throat!   95
Sound clearer through the atmosphere!
Pierce the woods, the earth,
Somewhere listening to catch you must be the one I want.

Shake out carols!
Solitary here, the night's carols!   100
Carols of lonesome love! death's carols!
Carols under that lagging, yellow, waning moon!
O under that moon where she droops almost down into the sea!
O reckless despairing carols.

But soft! sink low!   105
Soft! let me just murmur,
And do you wait a moment you husky-noised sea,
For somewhere I believe I heard my mate responding to me,
So faint, I must be still, be still to listen,
But not altogether still, for then she might not come immediately to me.   110

Hither my love!
Here I am! here!
With this just-sustained note I announce myself to you,
This gentle call is for you my love, for you.

Do not be decoyed elsewhere,   115
That is the whistle of the wind, it is not my voice,
That is the fluttering, the fluttering of the spray,
Those are the shadows of leaves.

O darkness! O in vain!
O I am very sick and sorrowful.   120

O brown halo in the sky near the moon, drooping upon the sea!
O troubled reflection in the sea!

O throat! O throbbing heart!
And I singing uselessly, uselessly all the night.

O past! O happy life! O songs of joy!   125
In the air, in the woods, over fields,
Loved! loved! loved! loved! loved!

But my mate no more, no more with me!
We two together no more.

The aria sinking,   130
All else continuing, the stars shining,
The winds blowing, the notes of the bird continuous echoing,
With angry moans the fierce old mother incessantly moaning,
On the sands of Paumanok's shore gray and rustling,
The yellow half-moon enlarged, sagging down, drooping, the face of
    the sea almost touching,   135
The boy ecstatic, with his bare feet the waves, with his hair the atmo-
    sphere dallying,
The love in the heart long pent, now loose, now at last tumultuously
    bursting,
The aria's meaning, the ears, the soul, swiftly depositing,
The strange tears down the cheeks coursing,
The colloquy there, the trio, each uttering,   140
The undertone, the savage old mother incessantly crying,
To the boy's soul's questions sullenly timing, some drowned secret hissing,
To the outsetting bard.

Demon or bird! (said the boy's soul,)
Is it indeed toward your mate you sing? or is it really to me?   145
For I, that was a child, my tongue's use sleeping, now I have heard you,
Now in a moment I know what I am for, I awake,
And already a thousand singers, a thousand songs, clearer, louder and
    more sorrowful than yours,
A thousand warbling echoes have started to life within me, never to die.

O you singer solitary, singing by yourself, projecting me,   150
O solitary me listening, never more shall I cease perpetuating you,
Never more shall I escape, never more the reverberations,
Never more the cries of unsatisfied love be absent from me,
Never again leave me to be the peaceful child I was before what there
    in the night,
By the sea under the yellow and sagging moon,   155
The messenger there aroused, the fire, the sweet hell within,
The unknown want, the destiny of me.

O give me the clue! (it lurks in the night here somewhere,)
O if I am to have so much, let me have more!

A word then, (for I will conquer it,)   160
The word final, superior to all,
Subtle, sent up—what is it?—I listen;
Are you whispering it, and have been all the time, you sea-waves?
Is that it from your liquid rims and wet sands?

Whereto answering, the sea,   165
Delaying not, hurrying not,
Whispered me through the night, and very plainly before daybreak,
Lisped to me the low and delicious word death,
And again death, death, death, death,
Hissing melodious, neither like the bird nor like my aroused child's
    heart,   170

But edging near as privately for me rustling at my feet,
Creeping thence steadily up to my ears and laving me softly all over.
Death, death, death, death, death.

Which I do not forget,
But fuse the song of my dusky demon and brother,   175
That he sang to me in the moonlight on Paumanok's gray beach,
With the thousand responsive songs at random,
My own songs awaked from that hour,
And with them the key, the word up from the waves,
The word of the sweetest song and all songs,   180
That strong and delicious word which, creeping to my feet,
(Or like some old crone rocking the cradle, swathed in sweet garments,
     bending aside,)
The sea whispered me.

HERMAN MELVILLE
1819–1891

Herman Melville's *Billy Budd, Sailor* has always absorbed and puzzled its readers. Its story appears to deal with the eternal struggle of good and evil as manifested in mortal affairs, but critics disagree about who or what the author considered "good." It has something to say about the nature of justice and of the individual's relation to society—but what? Commentators have asserted that the book affirms Melville's final serene acceptance of life as it is but also that it documents his ironic defiance. We don't know whether Melville had completed the work before he died, or what he intended its title to be. The challenging experience of becoming implicated in the novel's dilemmas, of confronting its perplexing characters, of trying to follow its moral logic, may lead to no firm conclusions, but it can hardly fail to generate imaginative excitement.

Melville's father died when the boy was thirteen, leaving the family in near poverty. This fact helps to account for young Melville's varied moneymaking enterprises. He taught school, kept a store, and clerked in a bank; at the age of twenty, he for the first time shipped out as a sailor. Subsequent ventures at sea included several whaling expeditions. On one of these, he jumped ship in the South Pacific, living for a month on an island in the Marquesas; on another whaling trip, he participated in a mutiny. In 1847, Melville married Elizabeth Shaw. The couple settled in Pittsfield, Massachusetts, where Melville spent his time writing. He attempted in vain to get an appointment to a foreign consulate as a means of support; his lecture tours, also intended to make money, were unsuccessful. Finally, with his wife and four children, he moved to New York City, where in 1867 he obtained a position at the Custom House, which he held for the next eighteen years.

Melville's first novels, including *Typee* (1846) and *Omoo* (1847), seafaring adventure stories based on his own experience, won popular success. His masterpiece, *Moby-Dick* (1851), however, puzzled readers by its allegorical obscurity, its apparent shapelessness, and its highly elaborate language. Melville thought it his best work and felt disappointed and somewhat embittered by its critical failure. Although he continued writing and publishing short stories, novels, and poems, none of his later work achieved popularity.

Billy Budd, Sailor existed only in a heavily revised and at some points barely comprehensible manuscript at the time of the novelist's death. It was printed for the first time, in an imperfect version (*Billy Budd, Foretopman*), in a 1924 edition of Melville's works. In 1948, Frederick Barron Freeman re-edited the novel as *Billy Budd*; his text was supplemented in 1956 by emendations from the manuscript by Elizabeth Treeman. In 1962, *Billy Budd, Sailor,* source of the text printed here, was produced by Harrison Hayford and Merton M. Sealts Jr., who returned to the original manuscript, distinguished Elizabeth Melville's handwriting in it from her husband's, and generated a version substantially different from its predecessors. Although the nature of Melville's intention must remain finally impossible to ascertain, this careful effort to recapture what the novelist actually wrote at least has clear authority for every editorial choice.

The issues raised by the French Revolution, so vivid a part of literary consciousness at the beginning of the nineteenth century, once more provide a novelistic theme at the century's end—but with a new perspective. The events reported in *Billy Budd, Sailor* are said to occur in 1797. The narrator speaks of "those invading waters of novel opinion social, political, and otherwise, which carried away as in a torrent no few minds in those days." His metaphor suggests disapproval of the "novel opinion" that so greatly excited the early Romantics. Captain Vere, an important character whose name associates him with truth ("verity"), utterly resists the "invading waters." The only direct evidence, within the novel, of the actual effects of revolution is the reported mutinies, of which the narrator also appears to disapprove. Such evidence suggests a negative view of the French Revolution in its moral and political effects.

On the other hand, the narrator provides evidence of abundant cause for mutiny, particularly in the brutal practice of impressment, by which men were removed forcibly from nonnaval ships (or from their hometown streets, or their farms) and pressed into navy service, with no legal or practical recourse. When Billy Budd says good-bye to his ship, *Rights-of-Man,* he intends no irony, but others hear irony, as well they may: the concept of human rights is violated in every instance of impressment. Captain Vere's absolute devotion to legality and rule, his lack of openness to new possibility, arguably amount to extreme rigidity, even, possibly, to insanity. The narrator's wariness about "invading waters" may, like Billy's good-bye, be heard as ironic.

The conflicting claims of this series of statements, all supportable, need not be resolved; the important point is that by the end of the nineteenth century, everything that seemed true and exciting at the beginning had been called into question—not refuted, only made dubious. One can readily multiply examples from *Billy Budd, Sailor.* Billy, powerfully associated with images of innocence, resembles a child; a baby, even; a friendly dog; a big horse; Adam before the Fall. A hundred years earlier, Blake had suggested the perceptive power of the innocent, the child who points out that the emperor wears no clothes (or that chimney sweepers must rely on dreams and a black child on his mother's wishful stories to compensate for social injustice). Billy's innocence, on the other hand, has ambiguous implications. What does it mean to be an unfallen man in a fallen world? Billy can neither acquire from experience nor learn from others the knowledge that might make him capable of self-protective suspicion. His utter helplessness indicts his society but also raises troubling questions about the desirability of innocence.

Of course, one might argue that we in the twentieth century, "cynical" in the same sense as the old Dansker in the novel, are suspicious of such figures as Billy and Captain Vere in ways that our forebears would not be. Perhaps so; yet virtually all the questions suggested in the last two paragraphs appear more or less directly in the novelistic text. The narrator reflects about troubling aspects of Billy's innocence; the surgeon raises the possibility that Captain Vere is "unhinged." At many points, the narrative's symbolic language calls insistent attention to itself. It too, however, typically leaves one poised between interpretive alternatives. Here, for instance, is the description of Billy's hanging. "At the same moment it chanced that the vapory fleece hanging low in the East was shot through with a soft glory as of the fleece of the Lamb of God seen in mystical vision, and simultaneously therewith, watched by the wedged mass of upturned faces, Billy ascended; and, ascending, took the full rose of dawn." Are we to take seriously the implicit identification of Billy with Christ? Billy has willingly taken guilt upon himself, has forgiven his condemner, dies in his innocence, and "ascends." On the other hand, he ascends not to heaven but to the yardarm, not in resurrection but in death. Is this a form of transcendence? Or is it irony again, at the expense of those who comfort themselves for social injustice by religious sentimentality?

Possibilities for interpretation depend, the novel tells us, on who formulates the story and who receives it. The book's subtitle, "An Inside Narrative," proves as ambiguous as everything else about it. This account, it suggests, will tell what really happened, as opposed to the newspaper report quoted late in the narrative that makes Billy into a suspicious foreigner who nefariously stabs the noble English Claggart. The storyteller returns intermittently to his insistence that he deals with facts; hence he draws back from the climactic scene between Billy and Captain Vere. Because no one else was present, the narrator can only speculate; in this instance, we will never know what really happened. The dialogue between the purser and the surgeon about the physical peculiarities of the hanging exemplifies the universal difficulty of interpretation. The storyteller is only one more interpreter, with his own biases. Educating us in mistrust by the nature of his story, he leaves us no certainties. The last word on Billy is presented in the sailor's ballad at the end, in which Billy's execution becomes a matter of pathos, not of moral speculation. Perhaps this story does not after all involve the conflict of good and evil; maybe it only provides a record of social contingency. This final possibility explains events as adequately—and as inadequately—as any other hypothesis.

In its questioning of the Romantic verities, revolution and innocence, as in its possibly ironic use of nature ("a soft glory as of the fleece of the Lamb of God"), Melville's novel reminds us how much can happen in a century. It may also remind us how insistently the nineteenth century foretells the twentieth. We are accustomed to feeling that we never get enough dependable information to make accurate judgments in matters of morality; we often distrust, if we think about it, the reliability of the "news" we are lavishly offered. *Billy Budd, Sailor* evokes a world that feels in many troubling respects like our own.

N. Arvin's *Herman Melville* (1950) is an excellent biographical study. Also valuable is D. K. Kirby, *Herman Melville* (1993). Important critical works include L. Thompson, *Melville's Quarrel with God* (1952); W. Berthoff, *The Example of Melville* (1962); and H. Parker, *Reading Billy Budd* (1990). Useful collections of critical essays include R. A. Lee, ed., *Herman Melville: Reassessments* (1984), and R. Milder, ed., *Critical Essays on Melville's Billy Budd, Sailor* (1989). A general guide is J. Bryant, ed., *A Companion to Melville Studies* (1986).

PRONOUNCING GLOSSARY

The following list uses common English syllables and stress accents to provide rough equivalents of selected words whose pronunciation may be unfamiliar to the general reader.

Aldebaran: *al-deb'-ar-an*

Anacharsis: *an-u-kahr'-sis*

Ananias: *a-nu-nai'-us*

Athée: *ah-tay'*

Bucephalus: *boo-sef'-u-lus*

Chiron: *kai'-ron*

Erebus: *ay-ray'-bus*

Hesperides: *hes-payr'-i-deez*

Montaigne: *mohn-ten'-yu*

Murat: *myoo-rah'*

Tecumseh: *tay-kum'-se*

Trafalgar: *trah-fahl'-gar*

Billy Budd, Sailor[1]

(An Inside Narrative)

1

In the time before steamships, or then more frequently than now, a stroller along the docks of any considerable seaport would occasionally have his attention arrested by a group of bronzed mariners, man-of-war's men or merchant sailors in holiday attire, ashore on liberty. In certain instances they would flank, or like a bodyguard quite surround, some superior figure of their own class, moving along with them like Aldebaran[2] among the lesser lights of his constellation. That signal object was the 'Handsome Sailor' of the less prosaic time alike of the military and merchant navies. With no perceptible trace of the vainglorious about him, rather with the offhand unaffectedness of natural regality, he seemed to accept the spontaneous homage of his shipmates.

A somewhat remarkable instance recurs to me. In Liverpool, now half a century ago, I saw under the shadow of the great dingy street-wall of Prince's Dock (an obstruction long since removed) a common sailor so intensely black that he must needs have been a native African of the unadulterate blood of Ham[3]—a symmetric figure much above the average height. The two ends of a gay silk handkerchief thrown loose about the neck danced upon the displayed ebony of his chest, in his ears were big hoops of gold, and a Highland bonnet with a tartan band set off his shapely head. It was a hot noon in July; and his face, lustrous with perspiration, beamed with barbaric good humor. In jovial sallies right and left, his white teeth flashing into view, he rollicked along, the center of a company of his shipmates. These were made up of such an assortment of tribes and complexions as would have well fitted them to be marched up by Anacharsis Cloots[4] before the bar of the first French Assembly as Representatives of the Human Race. At each spontaneous tribute rendered by the wayfarers to this black pagod[5] of a fellow—the tribute of a pause and stare, and less frequently an exclamation—the motley retinue showed that they took that sort of pride in the evoker of it which the Assyrian priests doubtless showed for their grand sculptured Bull when the faithful prostrated themselves.

To return. If in some cases a bit of a nautical Murat[6] in setting forth his person ashore, the Handsome Sailor of the period in question evinced nothing of the dandified Billy-be-Dam, an amusing character all but extinct now, but occasionally to be encountered, and in a form yet more amusing than the original, at the tiller of the boats on the tempestuous Erie Canal or, more likely, vaporing in the groggeries[7] along the towpath. Invariably a proficient in his perilous calling, he was also more or less of a mighty boxer or wrestler.

1. Edited by Harrison Hayford and Merton M. Sealts Jr.   2. A star of the first magnitude in the constellation of Taurus, the Bull, frequently used in navigation.   3. It was thought that Noah cursed his second son, Ham, for mocking him; that black skin resulted from the curse; and that all black people descended from Ham. In fact, according to Genesis 9.20–27 and 10.6–14, Noah cursed not Ham but Ham's son Canaan, while Ham's son Cush was black.   4. Jean-Baptiste du Val-de-Grâce, baron de Cloots, or Clootz (1755–1794), assembled a crowd of assorted nationalities and introduced them at the French National Assembly during the Revolution; he was popularly called "Anacharsis."   5. Meaning not only a pagoda but "an image of a deity, an idol" (Oxford English Dictionary).   6. Joachim Murat (1767–1815), marshal of France and king of Naples, Napoleon's brother-in-law, famous as a dandy.   7. Taverns. Vaporing: boasting or blustering.

It was strength and beauty. Tales of his prowess were recited. Ashore he was the champion; afloat the spokesman; on every suitable occasion always foremost. Close-reefing topsails in a gale, there he was, astride the weather yardarm-end, foot in the Flemish horse[8] as stirrup, both hands tugging at the earing as at a bridle, in very much the attitude of young Alexander curbing the fiery Bucephalus.[9] A superb figure, tossed up as by the horns of Taurus against the thunderous sky, cheerily hallooing to the strenuous file along the spar.

The moral nature was seldom out of keeping with the physical make. Indeed, except as toned by the former, the comeliness and power, always attractive in masculine conjunction, hardly could have drawn the sort of honest homage the Handsome Sailor in some examples received from his less gifted associates.

Such a cynosure, at least in aspect, and something such too in nature, though with important variations made apparent as the story proceeds, was welkin-eyed[1] Billy Budd—or Baby Budd, as more familiarly, under circumstances hereafter to be given, he at last came to be called—aged twenty-one, a foretopman[2] of the British fleet toward the close of the last decade of the eighteenth century. It was not very long prior to the time of the narration that follows that he had entered the King's service, having been impressed on the Narrow Seas from a homeward-bound English merchantman into a seventy-four[3] outward bound, H.M.S. *Bellipotent;* which ship, as was not unusual in those hurried days, having been obliged to put to sea short of her proper complement of men. Plump upon Billy at first sight in the gangway the boarding officer, Lieutenant Ratcliffe, pounced, even before the merchantman's crew was formally mustered on the quarter-deck for his deliberate inspection. And him only he elected. For whether it was because the other men when ranged before him showed to ill advantage after Billy, or whether he had some scruples in view of the merchantman's being rather short-handed, however it might be, the officer contented himself with his first spontaneous choice. To the surprise of the ship's company, though much to the lieutenant's satisfaction, Billy made no demur. But, indeed, any demur would have been as idle as the protest of a goldfinch popped into a cage.

Noting this uncomplaining acquiescence, all but cheerful, one might say, the shipmaster turned a surprised glance of silent reproach at the sailor. The shipmaster was one of those worthy mortals found in every vocation, even the humbler ones—the sort of person whom everybody agrees in calling 'a respectable man.' And—nor so strange to report as it may appear to be— though a ploughman of the troubled waters, lifelong contending with the intractable elements, there was nothing this honest soul at heart loved better than simple peace and quiet. For the rest, he was fifty or thereabouts, a little inclined to corpulence, a prepossessing face, unwhiskered, and of an agreeable color—a rather full face, humanely intelligent in expression. On a fair day with a fair wind and all going well, a certain musical chime in his voice

---

8. A hazardous activity: sailors go out on a yardarm (a spar supporting a sail) by means of foot ropes, one of which is called the *Flemish horse.* 9. Alexander the Great's warhorse. 1. Blue-eyed (*welkin:* sky). 2. Junior to a maintopman like Jack Chase, to whom the book is dedicated. 3. A third-rate ship of the line, equivalent to a light cruiser today. The designation refers to the number of guns the ship carried. *Narrow Seas:* the English Channel and the waters between England and Ireland.

seemed to be the veritable unobstructed outcome of the innermost man. He had much prudence, much conscientiousness, and there were occasions when these virtues were the cause of overmuch disquietude in him. On a passage, so long as his craft was in any proximity to land, no sleep for Captain Graveling. He took to heart those serious responsibilities not so heavily borne by some shipmasters.

Now while Billy Budd was down in the forecastle getting his kit together, the *Bellipotent's* lieutenant, burly and bluff, nowise disconcerted by Captain Graveling's omitting to proffer the customary hospitalities on an occasion so unwelcome to him, an omission simply caused by preoccupation of thought, unceremoniously invited himself into the cabin, and also to a flask from the spirit locker, a receptacle which his experienced eye instantly discovered. In fact he was one of those sea dogs in whom all the hardship and peril of naval life in the great prolonged wars of his time never impaired the natural instinct for sensuous enjoyment. His duty he always faithfully did; but duty is sometimes a dry obligation, and he was for irrigating its aridity, whensoever possible, with a fertilizing decoction of strong waters. For the cabin's proprietor there was nothing left but to play the part of the enforced host with whatever grace and alacrity were practicable. As necessary adjuncts to the flask, he silently placed tumbler and water jug before the irrepressible guest. But excusing himself from partaking just then, he dismally watched the unembarrassed officer deliberately diluting his grog[4] a little, then tossing it off in three swallows, pushing the empty tumbler away, yet not so far as to be beyond easy reach, at the same time settling himself in his seat and smacking his lips with high satisfaction, looking straight at the host.

These proceedings over, the master broke the silence; and there lurked a rueful reproach in the tone of his voice: 'Lieutenant, you are going to take my best man from me, the jewel of 'em.'

'Yes, I know,' rejoined the other, immediately drawing back the tumbler preliminary to a replenishing. 'Yes, I know. Sorry.'

'Beg pardon, but you don't understand, Lieutenant. See here, now. Before I shipped that young fellow, my forecastle was a rat-pit of quarrels. It was black times, I tell you, aboard the *Rights* here. I was worried to that degree my pipe had no comfort for me. But Billy came; and it was like a Catholic priest striking peace in an Irish shindy.[5] Not that he preached to them or said or did anything in particular; but a virtue went out of him, sugaring the sour ones. They took to him like hornets to treacle; all but the buffer[6] of the gang, the big shaggy chap with the fire-red whiskers. He indeed, out of envy, perhaps, of the newcomer, and thinking such a "sweet and pleasant fellow," as he mockingly designated him to the others, could hardly have the spirit of a gamecock, must needs bestir himself in trying to get up an ugly row with him. Billy forebore with him and reasoned with him in a pleasant way—he is something like myself, Lieutenant, to whom aught like a quarrel is hateful—but nothing served. So, in the second dogwatch[7] one day, the Red Whiskers in presence of the others, under pretense of showing Billy just whence a sirloin steak was cut—for the fellow had once been a butcher—insultingly gave him a dig under the ribs. Quick as lightning Billy let fly his arm. I dare say he never meant to do quite so much as he did, but anyhow

4. A mixture of rum and water. 5. Free-for-all fight. 6. Big fellow. 7. From 6:00 to 8:00 P.M.

he gave the burly fool a terrible drubbing. It took about half a minute, I should think. And lord bless you, the lubber was astonished at the celerity. And will you believe it, Lieutenant, the Red Whiskers now really loves Billy— loves him, or is the biggest hypocrite that ever I heard of. But they all love him. Some of 'em do his washing, darn his old trousers for him; the carpenter is at odd times making a pretty little chest of drawers for him. Anybody will do anything for Billy Budd; and it's the happy family here. But now, Lieutenant, if that young fellow goes—I know how it will be aboard the *Rights*. Not again very soon shall I, coming up from dinner, lean over the capstan smoking a quiet pipe—no, not very soon again, I think. Ay, Lieutenant, you are going to take away the jewel of 'em; you are going to take away my peacemaker!' And with that the good soul had really some ado in checking a rising sob.

'Well,' said the lieutenant, who had listened with amused interest to all this and now was waxing merry with his tipple: 'well, blessed are the peacemakers, especially the fighting peacemakers. And such are the seventy-four beauties some of which you see poking their noses out of the portholes of yonder warship lying to for me,' pointing through the cabin window at the *Bellipotent*. 'But courage! Don't look so downhearted, man. Why, I pledge you in advance the royal approbation. Rest assured that His Majesty will be delighted to know that in a time when his hardtack is not sought for by sailors with such avidity as should be, a time also when some shipmasters privily resent the borrowing from them a tar[8] or two for the service; His Majesty, I say, will be delighted to learn that *one* shipmaster at least cheerfully surrenders to the King the flower of his flock, a sailor who with equal loyalty makes no dissent.—But where's my beauty? Ah,' looking through the cabin's open door, 'here he comes; and, by Jove, lugging along his chest—Apollo with his portmanteau!—My man,' stepping out to him, 'you can't take that big box aboard a warship. The boxes there are mostly shot boxes. Put your duds in a bag, lad. Boot and saddle for the cavalryman, bag and hammock for the man-of-war's man.'

The transfer from chest to bag was made. And, after seeing his man into the cutter and then following him down, the lieutenant pushed off from the *Rights-of-Man*. That was the merchant ship's name, though by her master and crew abbreviated in sailor fashion into the *Rights*. The hardheaded Dundee owner was a staunch admirer of Thomas Paine,[9] whose book in rejoinder to Burke's arraignment of the French Revolution had then been published for some time and had gone everywhere. In christening his vessel after the title of Paine's volume the man of Dundee was something like his contemporary ship-owner, Stephen Girard[1] of Philadelphia, whose sympathies, alike with his native land and its liberal philosophers, he evinced by naming his ships after Voltaire, Diderot, and so forth.

But now, when the boat swept under the merchantman's stern, and officer and oarsmen were noting—some bitterly and others with a grin—the name emblazoned there; just then it was that the new recruit jumped up from the bow where the coxswain had directed him to sit, and waving hat to his silent

8. Sailor.   9. American Revolutionary patriot (1737–1809), born in England, published *The Rights of Man* in 1791 as a response to Edmund Burke's *Reflections on the Revolution in France* (1790). Dundee is a seaport in Scotland.   1. Merchant, banker, and philanthropist (1750–1831), a native of France who emigrated at the age of twenty-seven.

shipmates sorrowfully looking over at him from the taffrail, bade the lads a genial good-bye. Then, making a salutation as to the ship herself, 'And good-bye to you too, old *Rights-of-Man.*'

'Down, sir!' roared the lieutenant, instantly assuming all the rigor of his rank, though with difficulty repressing a smile.

To be sure, Billy's action was a terrible breach of naval decorum. But in that decorum he had never been instructed; in consideration of which the lieutenant would hardly have been so energetic in reproof but for the concluding farewell to the ship. This he rather took as meant to convey a covert sally on the new recruit's part, a sly slur at impressment in general, and that of himself in especial. And yet, more likely, if satire it was in effect, it was hardly so by intention, for Billy, though happily endowed with the gaiety of high health, youth, and a free heart, was yet by no means of a satirical turn. The will to it and the sinister dexterity were alike wanting. To deal in double meanings and insinuations of any sort was quite foreign to his nature.

As to his enforced enlistment, that he seemed to take pretty much as he was wont to take any vicissitude of weather. Like the animals, though no philosopher, he was, without knowing it, practically a fatalist. And it may be that he rather liked this adventurous turn in his affairs, which promised an opening into novel scenes and martial excitements.

Aboard the *Bellipotent* our merchant sailor was forthwith rated as an able seaman and assigned to the starboard watch of the foretop. He was soon at home in the service, not at all disliked for his unpretentious good looks and a sort of genial happy-go-lucky air. No merrier man in his mess: in marked contrast to certain other individuals included like himself among the impressed portion of the ship's company; for these when not actively employed were sometimes, and more particularly in the last dogwatch when the drawing near of twilight induced revery, apt to fall into a saddish mood which in some partook of sullenness. But they were not so young as our foretopman, and no few of them must have known a hearth of some sort, others may have had wives and children left, too probably, in uncertain circumstances, and hardly any but must have had acknowledged kith and kin, while for Billy, as will shortly be seen, his entire family was practically invested in himself.

2

Though our new-made foretopman was well received in the top and on the gun decks, hardly here was he that cynosure he had previously been among those minor ship's companies of the merchant marine, with which companies only had he hitherto consorted.

He was young; and despite his all but fully developed frame, in aspect looked even younger than he really was, owing to a lingering adolescent expression in the as yet smooth face all but feminine in purity of natural complexion but where, thanks to his seagoing, the lily was quite suppressed and the rose had some ado visibly to flush through the tan.

To one essentially such a novice in the complexities of factitious life, the abrupt transition from his former and simpler sphere to the ampler and more knowing world of a great warship; this might well have abashed him had there been any conceit or vanity in his composition. Among her miscellaneous multitude, the *Bellipotent* mustered several individuals who however inferior in grade were of no common natural stamp, sailors more signally susceptive of that air which continuous martial discipline and repeated presence in battle can in some degree impart even to the average man. As the Handsome Sailor, Billy Budd's position aboard the seventy-four was something analogous to that of a rustic beauty transplanted from the provinces and brought into competition with the highborn dames of the court. But this change of circumstances he scarce noted. As little did he observe that something about him provoked an ambiguous smile in one or two harder faces among the bluejackets. Nor less unaware was he of the peculiar favorable effect his person and demeanor had upon the more intelligent gentlemen of the quarter-deck. Nor could this well have been otherwise. Cast in a mold peculiar to the finest physical examples of those Englishmen in whom the Saxon strain would seem not at all to partake of any Norman or other admixture, he showed in face that humane look of reposeful good nature which the Greek sculptor in some instances gave to his heroic strong man, Hercules. But this again was subtly modified by another and pervasive quality. The ear, small and shapely, the arch of the foot, the curve in mouth and nostril, even the indurated hand dyed to the orange-tawny of the toucan's bill, a hand telling alike of the halyards and tar bucket; but, above all, something in the mobile expression, and every chance attitude and movement, something suggestive of a mother eminently favored by Love and the Graces; all this strangely indicated a lineage in direct contradiction to his lot. The mysteriousness here became less mysterious through a matter of fact elicited when Billy at the capstan was being formally mustered into the service. Asked by the officer, a small, brisk little gentleman as it chanced, among other questions, his place of birth, he replied, 'Please, sir, I don't know.'

'Don't know where you were born? Who was your father?'

'God knows, sir.'

Struck by the straightforward simplicity of these replies, the officer next asked, 'Do you know anything about your beginning?'

'No, sir. But I have heard that I was found in a pretty silk-lined basket hanging one morning from the knocker of a good man's door in Bristol.'

'*Found*, say you? Well,' throwing back his head and looking up and down the new recruit; 'well, it turns out to have been a pretty good find. Hope they'll find some more like you, my man; the fleet sadly needs them.'

Yes, Billy Budd was a foundling, a presumable by-blow, and, evidently, no ignoble one. Noble descent was as evident in him as in a blood horse.

For the rest, with little or no sharpness of faculty or any trace of the wisdom of the serpent, nor yet quite a dove, he possessed that kind and degree of intelligence going along with the unconventional rectitude of a sound human creature, one to whom not yet has been proffered the questionable apple of knowledge. He was illiterate; he could not read, but he could sing, and like the illiterate nightingale was sometimes the composer of his own song.

Of self-consciousness he seemed to have little or none, or about as much as we may reasonably impute to a dog of Saint Bernard's breed.

Habitually living with the elements and knowing little more of the land than as a beach, or, rather, that portion of the terraqueous globe providentially set apart for dance-houses, doxies, and tapsters, in short what sailors call a 'fiddler's green,'[2] his simple nature remained unsophisticated by those moral obliquities which are not in every case incompatible with that manufacturable thing known as respectability. But are sailors, frequenters of fiddler's greens, without vices? No; but less often than with landsmen do their vices, so called, partake of crookedness of heart, seeming less to proceed from viciousness than exuberance of vitality after long constraint: frank manifestations in accordance with natural law. By his original constitution aided by the co-operating influences of his lot, Billy in many respects was little more than a sort of upright barbarian, much such perhaps as Adam presumably might have been ere the urbane Serpent wriggled himself into his company.

And here be it submitted that apparently going to corroborate the doctrine of man's Fall, a doctrine now popularly ignored, it is observable that where certain virtues pristine and unadulterate peculiarly characterize anybody in the external uniform of civilization, they will upon scrutiny seem not to be derived from custom or convention, but rather to be out of keeping with these, as if indeed exceptionally transmitted from a period prior to Cain's city[3] and citified man. The character marked by such qualities has to an unvitiated taste an untampered-with flavor like that of berries, while the man thoroughly civilized, even in a fair specimen of the breed, has to the same moral palate a questionable smack as of a compounded wine. To any stray inheritor of these primitive qualities found, like Caspar Hauser,[4] wandering dazed in any Christian capital of our time, the good-natured poet's famous invocation, near two thousand years ago, of the good rustic out of his latitude in the Rome of the Caesars, still appropriately holds:

> Honest and poor, faithful in word and thought,
> What hath thee, Fabian, to the city brought?[5]

Though our Handsome Sailor had as much of masculine beauty as one can expect anywhere to see; nevertheless, like the beautiful woman in one of Hawthorne's minor tales,[6] there was just one thing amiss in him. No visible blemish indeed, as with the lady; no, but an occasional liability to a vocal defect. Though in the hour of elemental uproar or peril he was everything that a sailor should be, yet under sudden provocation of strong heart-feeling his voice, otherwise singularly musical, as if expressive of the harmony within, was apt to develop an organic hesitancy, in fact more or less of a stutter or even worse. In this particular Billy was a striking instance that the arch interferer, the envious marplot of Eden, still has more or less to do with every human consignment to this planet of Earth. In every case, one way or another he is sure to slip in his little card, as much as to remind us—I too have a hand here.

The avowal of such an imperfection in the Handsome Sailor should be evidence not alone that he is not presented as a conventional hero, but also that the story in which he is the main figure is no romance.

---

2. A sailor's utopia.   3. I.e., in the time of the Garden of Eden. Cain "builded a city" in Genesis 4.16–17.   4. A German foundling (1812?–1833) who claimed to have been brought up in a primitive wilderness.   5. Martial's *Epigrams* 1.4.1–2, from Cowley's translation in the Bohn edition.   6. *The Birthmark*, in which the *blemish* is on the lady's cheek.

3

At the time of Billy Budd's arbitrary enlistment into the *Bellipotent* that ship was on her way to join the Mediterranean fleet. No long time elapsed before the junction was effected. As one of that fleet the seventy-four participated in its movements, though at times on account of her superior sailing qualities, in the absence of frigates, dispatched on separate duty as a scout and at times on less temporary service. But with all this the story has little concernment, restricted as it is to the inner life of one particular ship and the career of an individual sailor.

It was the summer of 1797. In the April of that year had occurred the commotion at Spithead followed in May by a second and yet more serious outbreak in the fleet at the Nore. The latter is known, and without exaggeration in the epithet, as 'the Great Mutiny.' It was indeed a demonstration more menacing to England than the contemporary manifestoes and conquering and proselyting armies of the French Directory.[7] To the British Empire the Nore Mutiny was what a strike in the fire brigade would be to London threatened by general arson. In a crisis when the kingdom might well have anticipated the famous signal that some years later published along the naval line of battle what it was that upon occasion England expected of Englishmen;[8] *that* was the time when at the mastheads of the three-deckers and seventy-fours moored in her own roadstead—a fleet the right arm of a Power then all but the sole free conservative one of the Old World—the bluejackets, to be numbered by thousands, ran up with huzzas the British colors with the union and cross[9] wiped out; by that cancellation transmuting the flag of founded law and freedom defined, into the enemy's red meteor of unbridled and unbounded revolt. Reasonable discontent growing out of practical grievances in the fleet had been ignited into irrational combustion as by live cinders blown across the Channel from France in flames.

The event converted into irony for a time those spirited strains of Dibdin[1]—as a song-writer no mean auxiliary to the English government at that European conjuncture—strains celebrating, among other things, the patriotic devotion of the British tar: 'And as for my life,'tis the King's!'

Such an episode in the Island's grand naval story her naval historians naturally abridge, one of them (William James)[2] candidly acknowledging that fain would he pass it over did not 'impartiality forbid fastidiousness.' And yet his mention is less a narration than a reference, having to do hardly at all with details. Nor are these readily to be found in the libraries. Like some other events in every age befalling states everywhere, including America, the Great Mutiny was of such character that national pride along with views of policy would fain shade it off into the historical background. Such events cannot be ignored, but there is a considerate way of historically treating them. If a well-constituted individual refrains from blazoning aught amiss or calamitous in his family, a nation in the like circumstance may without reproach be equally discreet.

7. The five directors who governed France from 1795 to 1799, during the Revolution.   8. "England expects every man to do his duty!": Lord Nelson, before the battle at Trafalgar, October 21, 1805.   9. The British Union Jack, or national flag, carries the crosses of St. Andrew, St. George, and St. Patrick, patron saints of Scotland, England, and Ireland.   1. Charles Dibdin (1745–1814), English dramatist, chiefly remembered for his sea chanteys. The ballad quoted is "Poor Jack."   2. *The Naval History of Great Britain* (1860). Melville mistakenly wrote "G. P. R. James."

Though after parleyings between government and the ringleaders, and concessions by the former as to some glaring abuses, the first uprising—that at Spithead—with difficulty was put down, or matters for the time pacified; yet at the Nore the unforeseen renewal of insurrection on a yet larger scale, and emphasized in the conferences that ensued by demands deemed by the authorities not only inadmissible but aggressively insolent, indicated—if the Red Flag did not sufficiently do so—what was the spirit animating the men. Final suppression, however, there was; but only made possible perhaps by the unswerving loyalty of the marine corps and a voluntary resumption of loyalty among influential sections of the crews.

To some extent the Nore Mutiny may be regarded as analogous to the distempering irruption of contagious fever in a frame constitutionally sound, and which anon throws it off.

At all events, of these thousands of mutineers were some of the tars who not so very long afterwards—whether wholly prompted thereto by patriotism, or pugnacious instinct, or by both—helped to win a coronet for Nelson at the Nile, and the naval crown of crowns for him at Trafalgar.[3] To the mutineers, those battles and especially Trafalgar were a plenary absolution and a grand one. For all that goes to make up scenic naval display and heroic magnificence in arms, those battles, especially Trafalgar, stand unmatched in human annals.

4

In this matter of writing, resolve as one may to keep to the main road, some bypaths have an enticement not readily to be withstood. I am going to err into such a bypath. If the reader will keep me company I shall be glad. At the least, we can promise ourselves that pleasure which is wickedly said to be in sinning, for a literary sin the divergence will be.

Very likely it is no new remark that the inventions of our time have at last brought about a change in sea warfare in degree corresponding to the revolution in all warfare effected by the original introduction from China into Europe of gunpowder. The first European firearm, a clumsy contrivance, was, as is well known, scouted[4] by no few of the knights as a base implement, good enough peradventure for weavers too craven to stand up crossing steel with steel in frank fight. But as ashore knightly valor, though shorn of its blazonry, did not cease with the knights, neither on the sea—though nowadays in encounters there a certain kind of displayed gallantry be fallen out of date as hardly applicable under changed circumstances—did the nobler qualities of such naval magnates as Don John of Austria, Doria, Van Tromp, Jean Bart, the long line of British admirals, and the American Decaturs of 1812 become obsolete with their wooden walls.[5]

Nevertheless, to anybody who can hold the Present at its worth without

---

3. Nelson was made a baronet for his victory over the French at Aboukir in 1798; his 1805 victory at Trafalgar is considered one of the greatest in naval history.   4. Scoffed at.   5. A reference to the wooden ships made obsolete by ironclads. Don Juan of Austria (1547–1578) commanded a fleet against the Turks at Lepanto in 1571, the last major sea battle in which oared ships predominated. Andrea Doria (1468–1560) liberated Genoa from the French. Maarten Van Tromp (1596–1653), Dutch admiral, fought successfully against the English. Jean Bart (1651?–1702), a French captain, battled the Dutch. Stephen Decatur (1779–1820) won victories over the Barbary Coast pirates at Tripoli and over the British in the War of 1812.

being inappreciative of the Past, it may be forgiven, if to such an one the solitary old hulk at Portsmouth, Nelson's *Victory,* seems to float there, not alone as the decaying monument of a fame incorruptible, but also as a poetic reproach, softened by its picturesqueness, to the *Monitors*[6] and yet mightier hulls of the European ironclads. And this not altogether because such craft are unsightly, unavoidably lacking the symmetry and grand lines of the old battleships, but equally for other reasons.

There are some, perhaps, who while not altogether inaccessible to that poetic reproach just alluded to, may yet on behalf of the new order be disposed to parry it; and this to the extent of iconoclasm, if need be. For example, prompted by the sight of the star inserted in the *Victory*'s quarter-deck designating the spot where the Great Sailor fell, these martial utilitarians may suggest considerations implying that Nelson's ornate publication of his person in battle was not only unnecessary, but not military, nay, savored of foolhardiness and vanity. They may add, too, that at Trafalgar it was in effect nothing less than a challenge to death; and death came; and that but for his bravado the victorious admiral might possibly have survived the battle, and so, instead of having his sagacious dying injunctions overruled by his immediate successor in command, he himself when the contest was decided might have brought his shattered fleet to anchor, a proceeding which might have averted the deplorable loss of life by shipwreck in the elemental tempest that followed the martial one.

Well, should we set aside the more than disputable point whether for various reasons it was possible to anchor the fleet, then plausibly enough the Benthamites[7] of war may urge the above. But the *might-have-been* is but boggy ground to build on. And, certainly, in foresight as to the larger issue of an encounter, and anxious preparations for it—buoying the deadly way and mapping it out, as at Copenhagen[8]—few commanders have been so painstakingly circumspect as this same reckless declarer of his person in fight.

Personal prudence, even when dictated by quite other than selfish considerations, surely is no special virtue in a military man; while an excessive love of glory, impassioning a less burning impulse, the honest sense of duty, is the first. If the name *Wellington* is not so much of a trumpet to the blood as the simpler name *Nelson,* the reason for this may perhaps be inferred from the above. Alfred in his funeral ode on the victory of Waterloo ventures not to call him the greatest soldier of all time, though in the same ode he invokes Nelson as 'the greatest sailor since our world began.'[9]

At Trafalgar Nelson on the brink of opening the fight sat down and wrote his last brief will and testament. If under the presentiment of the most magnificent of all victories to be crowned by his own glorious death, a sort of priestly motive led him to dress his person in the jewelled vouchers of his own shining deeds; if thus to have adorned himself for the altar and the sacrifice were indeed vainglory, then affectation and fustian is each more

---

6. The *Monitor* was an ironclad launched in 1862 to fight the Confederate *Virginia* (formerly the frigate *Merrimack*) in a battle effectively ending the era of wooden ships.   7. Utilitarian thinkers and followers of Jeremy Bentham (1748–1832), who believed in the greatest good for the greatest number.   8. Where Nelson's careful planning defeated the Danish on April 2, 1801.   9. The quotation comes from Tennyson's *Ode on the Death of the Duke of Wellington* (1852) 6.7.

heroic line in the great epics and dramas, since in such lines the poet but embodies in verse those exaltations of sentiment that a nature like Nelson, the opportunity being given, vitalizes into acts.

5

Yes, the outbreak at the Nore was put down. But not every grievance was redressed. If the contractors, for example, were no longer permitted to ply some practices peculiar to their tribe everywhere, such as providing shoddy cloth, rations not sound, or false in the measure; not the less impressment, for one thing, went on. By custom sanctioned for centuries, and judicially maintained by a Lord Chancellor as late as Mansfield,[1] that mode of manning the fleet, a mode now fallen into a sort of abeyance but never formally renounced, it was not practicable to give up in those years. Its abrogation would have crippled the indispensable fleet, one wholly under canvas, no steam power, its innumerable sails and thousands of cannon, everything in short, worked by muscle alone; a fleet the more insatiate in demand for men, because then multiplying its ships of all grades against contingencies present and to come of the convulsed Continent.

Discontent foreran the Two Mutinies, and more or less it lurkingly survived them. Hence it was not unreasonable to apprehend some return of trouble sporadic or general. One instance of such apprehensions: In the same year with this story, Nelson, then Rear Admiral Sir Horatio, being with the fleet off the Spanish coast, was directed by the admiral in command to shift his pennant from the *Captain* to the *Theseus;* and for this reason: that the latter ship having newly arrived on the station from home, where it had taken part in the Great Mutiny, danger was apprehended from the temper of the men; and it was thought that an officer like Nelson was the one, not indeed to terrorize the crew into base subjection, but to win them, by force of his mere presence and heroic personality, back to an allegiance if not as enthusiastic as his own yet as true.

So it was that for a time, on more than one quarter-deck, anxiety did exist. At sea, precautionary vigilance was strained against relapse. At short notice an engagement might come on. When it did, the lieutenants assigned to batteries felt it incumbent on them, in some instances, to stand with drawn swords behind the men working the guns.

6

But on board the seventy-four in which Billy now swung his hammock, very little in the manner of the men and nothing obvious in the demeanor of the officers would have suggested to an ordinary observer that the Great Mutiny was a recent event. In their general bearing and conduct the commissioned officers of a warship naturally take their tone from the commander, that is if he have that ascendancy of character that ought to be his.

Captain the Honorable Edward Fairfax Vere, to give his full title, was a bachelor of forty or thereabouts, a sailor of distinction even in a time prolific of renowned seamen. Though allied to the higher nobility, his advancement had not been altogether owing to influences connected with that circum-

1. William Murray, Baron Mansfield (1705–1793), lord chief justice of Great Britain from 1756 to 1788.

stance. He had seen much service, been in various engagements, always acquitting himself as an officer mindful of the welfare of his men, but never tolerating an infraction of discipline; thoroughly versed in the science of his profession, and intrepid to the verge of temerity, though never injudiciously so. For his gallantry in the West Indian waters as flag lietutenant under Rodney in that admiral's crowning victory over De Grasse,[2] he was made a post captain.

Ashore, in the garb of a civilian, scarce anyone would have taken him for a sailor, more especially that he never garnished unprofessional talk with nautical terms, and grave in his bearing, evinced little appreciation of mere humor. It was not out of keeping with these traits that on a passage when nothing demanded his paramount action, he was the most undemonstrative of men. Any landsman observing this gentleman not conspicuous by his stature and wearing no pronounced insignia, emerging from his cabin to the open deck, and noting the silent deference of the officers retiring to leeward, might have taken him for the King's guest, a civilian aboard the King's ship, some highly honorable discreet envoy on his way to an important post. But in fact this unobtrusiveness of demeanor may have proceeded from a certain unaffected modesty of manhood sometimes accompanying a resolute nature, a modesty evinced at all times not calling for pronounced action, which shown in any rank of life suggests a virtue aristocratic in kind. As with some others engaged in various departments of the world's more heroic activities, Captain Vere though practical enough upon occasion would at times betray a certain dreaminess of mood. Standing alone on the weather side of the quarter-deck, one hand holding by the rigging, he would absently gaze off at the blank sea. At the presentation to him then of some minor matter interrupting the current of his thoughts, he would show more or less irascibility; but instantly he would control it.

In the navy he was popularly known by the appellation 'Starry Vere.' How such a designation happened to fall upon one who whatever his sterling qualities was without any brilliant ones, was in this wise: A favorite kinsman, Lord Denton, a freehearted fellow, had been the first to meet and congratulate him upon his return to England from his West Indian cruise; and but the day previous turning over a copy of Andrew Marvell's[3] poems had lighted, not for the first time, however, upon the lines entitled 'Appleton House,' the name of one of the seats of their common ancestor, a hero in the German wars of the seventeenth century, in which poem occur the lines:

> This 'tis to have been from the first
> In a domestic heaven nursed,
> Under the discipline severe
> Of Fairfax and the starry Vere.

And so, upon embracing his cousin fresh from Rodney's great victory wherein he had played so gallant a part, brimming over with just family pride in the sailor of their house, he exuberantly exclaimed, 'Give ye joy, Ed; give ye joy, my starry Vere!' This got currency, and the novel prefix serving in familiar parlance readily to distinguish the *Bellipotent*'s captain from another Vere

---

2. The British admiral George Brydges, Baron Rodney (1719–1792), defeated the French admiral de Grasse off Dominica, in the Leeward Islands, in 1782.   3. English lyric poet (1621–1678).

his senior, a distant relative, an officer of like rank in the navy, it remained permanently attached to the surname.

7

In view of the part that the commander of the *Bellipotent* plays in scenes shortly to follow, it may be well to fill out that sketch of him outlined in the previous chapter.

Aside from his qualities as a sea officer Captain Vere was an exceptional character. Unlike no few of England's renowned sailors, long and arduous service with signal devotion to it had not resulted in absorbing and *salting* the entire man. He had a marked leaning toward everything intellectual. He loved books, never going to sea without a newly replenished library, compact but of the best. The isolated leisure, in some cases so wearisome, falling at intervals to commanders even during a war cruise, never was tedious to Captain Vere. With nothing of that literary taste which less heeds the thing conveyed than the vehicle, his bias was toward those books to which every serious mind of superior order occupying any active post of authority in the world naturally inclines: books treating of actual men and events no matter of what era—history, biography, and unconventional writers like Montaigne,[4] who, free from cant and convention, honestly and in the spirit of common sense philosophize upon realities. In this line of reading he found confirmation of his own more reserved thoughts—confirmation which he had vainly sought in social converse, so that as touching most fundamental topics, there had got to be established in him some positive convictions which he forefelt would abide in him essentially unmodified so long as his intelligent part remained unimpaired. In view of the troubled period in which his lot was cast, this was well for him. His settled convictions were as a dike against those invading waters of novel opinion social, political, and otherwise, which carried away as in a torrent no few minds in those days, minds by nature not inferior to his own. While other members of that aristocracy to which by birth he belonged were incensed at the innovators mainly because their theories were inimical to the privileged classes, Captain Vere disinterestedly opposed them not alone because they seemed to him insusceptible of embodiment in lasting institutions, but at war with the peace of the world and the true welfare of mankind.

With minds less stored than his and less earnest, some officers of his rank, with whom at times he would necessarily consort, found him lacking in the companionable quality, a dry and bookish gentleman, as they deemed. Upon any chance withdrawal from their company one would be apt to say to another something like this: 'Vere is a noble fellow, Starry Vere. 'Spite the gazettes,[5] Sir Horatio' (meaning him who became Lord Nelson) 'is at bottom scarce a better seaman or fighter. But between you and me now, don't you think there is a queer streak of the pedantic running through him? Yes, like the King's yarn in a coil of navy rope?'[6]

Some apparent ground there was for this sort of confidential criticism; since not only did the captain's discourse never fall into the jocosely familiar,

---

4. Michel Eyquem de Montaigne (1533–1592), French essayist.   5. Official gazettes that printed accounts of naval careers and honors.   6. A thread was worked into hempen cable to mark it as belonging to the Royal Navy.

but in illustrating of any point touching the stirring personages and events of the time he would be as apt to cite some historic character or incident of antiquity as he would be to cite from the moderns. He seemed unmindful of the circumstance that to his bluff company such remote allusions, however pertinent they might really be, were altogether alien to men whose reading was mainly confined to the journals. But considerateness in such matters is not easy to natures constituted like Captain Vere's. Their honesty prescribes to them directness, sometimes far-reaching like that of a migratory fowl that in its flight never heeds when it crosses a frontier.

8

The lieutenants and other commissioned gentlemen forming Captain Vere's staff it is not necessary here to particularize, nor needs it to make any mention of any of the warrant officers. But among the petty officers[7] was one who, having much to do with the story, may as well be forthwith introduced. His portrait I essay, but shall never hit it. This was John Claggart, the master-at-arms. But that sea title may to landsmen seem somewhat equivocal. Originally, doubtless, that petty officer's function was the instruction of the men in the use of arms, sword or cutlass. But very long ago, owing to the advance in gunnery making hand-to-hand encounters less frequent and giving to niter and sulphur the pre-eminence over steel, that function ceased; the master-at-arms of a great warship becoming a sort of chief of police charged among other matters with the duty of preserving order on the populous lower gun decks.

Claggart was a man about five-and-thirty, somewhat spare and tall, yet of no ill figure upon the whole. His hand was too small and shapely to have been accustomed to hard toil. The face was a notable one, the features all except the chin cleanly cut as those on a Greek medallion; yet the chin, beardless as Tecumseh's,[8] had something of strange protuberant broadness in its make that recalled the prints of the Reverend Dr Titus Oates,[9] the historic deponent with the clerical drawl in the time of Charles II and the fraud of the alleged Popish Plot. It served Claggart in his office that his eye could cast a tutoring glance. His brow was of the sort phrenologically associated with more than average intellect; silken jet curls partly clustering over it, making a foil to the pallor below, a pallor tinged with a faint shade of amber akin to the hue of time-tinted marbles of old. This complexion, singularly contrasting with the red or deeply bronzed visages of the sailors, and in part the result of his official seclusion from the sunlight, though it was not exactly displeasing, nevertheless seemed to hint of something defective or abnormal in the constitution and blood. But his general aspect and manner were so suggestive of an education and career incongruous with his naval function that when not actively engaged in it he looked like a man of high quality, social and moral, who for reasons of his own was keeping incog.[1] Nothing was known of his former life. It might be that he was an Englishman; and yet there lurked a bit of accent in his speech suggesting that possibly he

7. Enlisted men corresponding in rank to noncommissioned officers in the army. *Warrant officers*: ranked above petty and just below commissioned officers. 8. Shawnee chief (1768?–1813) who attempted to unite the American Indians against the United States. 9. In 1678 Oates (1649–1705) invented a plot accusing Jesuits of planning to assassinate Charles II, burn London, and slaughter English Protestants. 1. Incognito, unrecognized.

was not such by birth, but through naturalization in early childhood. Among certain grizzled sea gossips of the gun decks and forecastle went a rumor perdue[2] that the master-at-arms was a *chevalier*[3] who had volunteered into the King's navy by way of compounding for some mysterious swindle whereof he had been arraigned at the King's Bench.[4] The fact that nobody could substantiate this report was, of course, nothing against its secret currency. Such a rumor once started on the gun decks in reference to almost anyone below the rank of a commissioned officer would, during the period assigned to this narrative, have seemed not altogether wanting in credibility to the tarry old wiseacres of a man-of-war crew. And indeed a man of Claggart's accomplishments, without prior nautical experience entering the navy at mature life, as he did, and necessarily allotted at the start to the lowest grade in it; a man too who never made allusion to his previous life ashore; these were circumstances which in the dearth of exact knowledge as to his true antecedents opened to the invidious a vague field for unfavorable surmise.

But the sailors' dogwatch gossip concerning him derived a vague plausibility from the fact that now for some period the British navy could so little afford to be squeamish in the matter of keeping up the muster rolls, that not only were press gangs notoriously abroad both afloat and ashore, but there was little or no secret about another matter, namely, that the London police were at liberty to capture any able-bodied suspect, any questionable fellow at large, and summarily ship him to the dockyard or fleet. Furthermore, even among voluntary enlistments there were instances where the motive thereto partook neither of patriotic impulse nor yet of a random desire to experience a bit of sea life and martial adventure. Insolvent debtors of minor grade, together with the promiscuous lame ducks of morality, found in the navy a convenient and secure refuge, secure because, once enlisted aboard a King's ship, they were as much in sanctuary as the transgressor of the Middle Ages harboring himself under the shadow of the altar. Such sanctioned irregularities, which for obvious reasons the government would hardly think to parade at the time and which consequently, and as affecting the least influential class of mankind, have all but dropped into oblivion, lend color[5] to something for the truth whereof I do not vouch, and hence have some scruple in stating; something I remember having seen in print though the book I cannot recall; but the same thing was personally communicated to me now more than forty years ago by an old pensioner in a cocked hat with whom I had a most interesting talk on the terrace at Greenwich, a Baltimore Negro, a Trafalgar man.[6] It was to this effect: In the case of a warship short of hands whose speedy sailing was imperative, the deficient quota, in lack of any other way of making it good, would be eked out by drafts culled direct from the jails. For reasons previously suggested it would not perhaps be easy at the present day directly to prove or disprove the allegation. But allowed as a verity, how significant would it be of England's straits at the time confronted by those wars which like a flight of harpies rose shrieking from the din and dust of the fallen Bastille.[7] That era appears measurably clear to us who look back at it, and but read of it. But to the grandfathers of us graybeards, the more

2. Surreptitious.   3. A man of high rank.   4. Formerly the supreme court of common law in Great Britain.   5. Appearance of truth.   6. A veteran of the Battle of Trafalgar. *Greenwich*: a hospital near London, a home for retired personnel.   7. The fall of the Bastille (July 14, 1789) signaled the beginning of the French Revolution.

thoughtful of them, the genius of it presented an aspect like that of Camoëns' Spirit of the Cape,[8] an eclipsing menace mysterious and prodigious. Not America was exempt from apprehension. At the height of Napoleon's unexampled conquests, there were Americans who had fought at Bunker Hill who looked forward to the possibility that the Atlantic might prove no barrier against the ultimate schemes of this French portentous upstart from the revolutionary chaos who seemed in act of fulfilling judgment prefigured in the Apocalypse.

But the less credence was to be given to the gun-deck talk touching Claggart, seeing that no man holding his office in a man-of-war can ever hope to be popular with the crew. Besides, in derogatory comments upon anyone against whom they have a grudge, or for any reason or no reason mislike, sailors are much like landsmen: they are apt to exaggerate or romance it.

About as much was really known to the *Bellipotent*'s tars of the master-at-arms' career before entering the service as an astronomer knows about a comet's travels prior to its first observable appearance in the sky. The verdict of the sea quidnuncs[9] has been cited only by way of showing what sort of moral impression the man made upon rude uncultivated natures whose conceptions of human wickedness were necessarily of the narrowest, limited to ideas of vulgar rascality—a thief among the swinging hammocks during a night watch, or the man-brokers and land-sharks of the seaports.

It was no gossip, however, but fact that though, as before hinted, Claggart upon his entrance into the navy was, as a novice, assigned to the least honorable section of a man-of-war's crew, embracing the drudgery, he did not long remain there. The superior capacity he immediately evinced, his constitutional sobriety, an ingratiating deference to superiors, together with a peculiar ferreting genius manifested on a singular occasion; all this, capped by a certain austere patriotism, abruptly advanced him to the position of master-at-arms.

Of this maritime chief of police the ship's corporals, so called, were the immediate subordinates, and compliant ones; and this, as is to be noted in some business departments ashore, almost to a degree inconsistent with entire moral volition. His place put various converging wires of underground influence under the chief's control, capable when astutely worked through his understrappers of operating to the mysterious discomfort, if nothing worse, of any of the sea commonalty.

9

Life in the foretop well agreed with Billy Budd. There, when not actually engaged on the yards yet higher aloft, the topmen, who as such had been picked out for youth and activity, constituted an aerial club lounging at ease against the smaller stun'sails[1] rolled up into cushions, spinning yarns like the lazy gods, and frequently amused with what was going on in the busy world of the decks below. No wonder then that a young fellow of Billy's disposition was well content in such society. Giving no cause of offense to anybody, he was always alert at a call. So in the merchant service it had been

8. The Portuguese poet Luiz Vaz de Camoëns (1524–1580) describes in his epic poem, the *Lusiads*, a monster named Adamastor who attempts to destroy Vasco da Gama and his crew.　9. What now (Latin, literal trans.); a busybody.　1. Studding sails (small auxiliaries to the mainsails).

with him. But now such a punctiliousness in duty was shown that his top-mates would sometimes good-naturedly laugh at him for it. This heightened alacrity had its cause, namely, the impression made upon him by the first formal gangway-punishment he had ever witnessed, which befell the day following his impressment. It had been incurred by a little fellow, young, a novice afterguardsman absent from his assigned post when the ship was being put about; a dereliction resulting in a rather serious hitch to that maneuver, one demanding instantaneous promptitude in letting go and making fast. When Billy saw the culprit's naked back under the scourge, grid-ironed with red welts and worse, when he marked the dire expression in the liberated man's face as with his woolen shirt flung over him by the executioner he rushed forward from the spot to bury himself in the crowd, Billy was horrified. He resolved that never through remissness would he make himself liable to such a visitation or do or omit aught that might merit even verbal reproof. What then was his surprise and concern when ultimately he found himself getting into petty trouble occasionally about such matters as the stowage of his bag or something amiss in his hammock, matters under the police oversight of the ship's corporals of the lower decks, and which brought down on him a vague threat from one of them.

So heedful in all things as he was, how could this be? He could not understand it, and it more than vexed him. When he spoke to his young topmates about it they were either lightly incredulous or found something comical in his unconcealed anxiety. 'Is it your bag, Billy?' said one. 'Well, sew yourself up in it, bully boy, and then you'll be sure to know if anybody meddles with it.'

Now there was a veteran aboard who because his years began to disqualify him for more active work had been recently assigned duty as mainmastman in his watch, looking to the gear belayed[2] at the rail roundabout that great spar near the deck. At off-times the foretopman had picked up some acquaintance with him, and now in his trouble it occurred to him that he might be the sort of person to go to for wise counsel. He was an old Dansker[3] long anglicized in the service, of few words, many wrinkles, and some honorable scars. His wizened face, time-tinted and weather-stained to the complexion of an antique parchment, was here and there peppered blue by the chance explosion of a gun cartridge in action.

He was an *Agamemnon* man, some two years prior to the time of this story having served under Nelson when still captain in that ship immortal in naval memory, which dismantled and in part broken up to her bare ribs is seen a grand skeleton in Haden's etching.[4] As one of a boarding party from the *Agamemnon* he had received a cut slantwise along one temple and cheek leaving a long pale scar like a streak of dawn's light falling athwart the dark visage. It was on account of that scar and the affair in which it was known that he had received it, as well as from his blue-peppered complexion, that the Dansker went among the *Bellipotent*'s crew by the name of 'Board-Her-in-the-Smoke.'

Now the first time that his small weasel eyes happened to light on Billy Budd, a certain grim internal merriment set all his ancient wrinkles into antic

2. Stowed.   3. Dane.   4. *Breaking up of the Agamemnon*, the masterpiece of Sir Francis Seymour Haden (1818–1910).

play. Was it that his eccentric unsentimental old sapience, primitive in its kind, saw or thought it saw something which in contrast with the warship's environment looked oddly incongruous in the Handsome Sailor? But after slyly studying him at intervals, the old Merlin's[5] equivocal merriment was modified; for now when the twain would meet, it would start in his face a quizzing[6] sort of look, but it would be but momentary and sometimes replaced by an expression of speculative query as to what might eventually befall a nature like that, dropped into a world not without some mantraps and against whose subtleties simple courage lacking experience and address,[7] and without any touch of defensive ugliness, is of little avail; and where such innocence as man is capable of does yet in a moral emergency not always sharpen the faculties or enlighten the will.

However it was, the Dansker in his ascetic way rather took to Billy. Nor was this only because of a certain philosophic interest in such a character. There was another cause. While the old man's eccentricities, sometimes bordering on the ursine, repelled the juniors, Billy, undeterred thereby, revering him as a salt hero, would make advances, never passing the old *Agamemnon* man without a salutation marked by that respect which is seldom lost on the aged, however crabbed at times or whatever their station in life.

There was a vein of dry humor, or what not, in the mastman; and, whether in freak of patriarchal irony touching Billy's youth and athletic frame, or for some other and more recondite reason, from the first in addressing him he always substituted *Baby* for Billy, the Dansker in fact being the originator of the name by which the foretopman eventually became known aboard ship.

Well then, in his mysterious little difficulty going in quest of the wrinkled one, Billy found him off duty in a dogwatch ruminating by himself, seated on a shot box of the upper gun deck, now and then surveying with a somewhat cynical regard certain of the more swaggering promenaders there. Billy recounted his trouble, again wondering how it all happened. The salt seer attentively listened, accompanying the foretopman's recital with queer twitchings of his wrinkles and problematical little sparkles of his small ferret eyes. Making an end of his story, the foretopman asked, 'And now, Dansker, do tell me what you think of it.'

The old man, shoving up the front of his tarpaulin and deliberately rubbing the long slant scar at the point where it entered the thin hair, laconically said, 'Baby Budd, *Jemmy Legs*[8] (meaning the master-at-arms) 'is down on you.'

'*Jemmy Legs!*' ejaculated Billy, his welkin eyes expanding.

'What for? Why, he calls me "the sweet and pleasant young fellow," they tell me.'

'Does he so?' grinned the grizzled one; then said, 'Ay, Baby lad, a sweet voice has Jemmy Legs.'

'No, not always. But to me he has. I seldom pass him but there comes a pleasant word.'

'And that's because he's down upon you, Baby Budd.'

Such reiteration, along with the manner of it, incomprehensible to a nov-

5. King Arthur's court magician.   6. Mocking.   7. Skill and tact in handling situations.   8. A disparaging nickname for the master-at-arms, still used in the American navy.

ice, disturbed Billy almost as much as the mystery for which he had sought explanation. Something less unpleasingly oracular he tried to extract; but the old sea Chiron,[9] thinking perhaps that for the nonce he had sufficiently instructed his young Achilles, pursed his lips, gathered all his wrinkles together, and would commit himself to nothing further.

Years, and those experiences which befall certain shrewder men subordinated lifelong to the will of superiors, all this had developed in the Dansker the pithy guarded cynicism that was his leading characteristic.

10

The next day an incident served to confirm Billy Budd in his incredulity as to the Dansker's strange summing up of the case submitted. The ship at noon, going large before the wind, was rolling on her course, and he below at dinner and engaged in some sportful talk with the members of his mess, chanced in a sudden lurch to spill the entire contents of his soup pan upon the new-scrubbed deck. Claggart, the master-at-arms, official rattan[1] in hand, happened to be passing along the battery in a bay of which the mess was lodged, and the greasy liquid streamed just across his path. Stepping over it, he was proceeding on his way without comment, since the matter was nothing to take notice of under the circumstances, when he happened to observe who it was that had done the spilling. His countenance changed. Pausing, he was about to ejaculate something hasty at the sailor, but checked himself, and pointing down to the streaming soup, playfully tapped him from behind with his rattan, saying in a low musical voice peculiar to him at times, 'Handsomely done, my lad! And handsome is as handsome did it, too!' And with that passed on. Not noted by Billy as not coming within his view was the involuntary smile, or rather grimace, that accompanied Claggart's equivocal words. Aridly it drew down the thin corners of his shapely mouth. But everybody taking his remark as meant for humorous, and at which therefore as coming from a superior they were bound to laugh 'with counterfeited glee,'[2] acted accordingly; and Billy, tickled, it may be, by the allusion to his being the Handsome Sailor, merrily joined in; then addressing his messmates exclaimed, 'There now, who says that Jemmy Legs is down on me!'

'And who said he was, Beauty?' demanded one Donald with some surprise. Whereat the foretopman looked a little foolish, recalling that it was only one person, Board-Her-in-the-Smoke, who had suggested what to him was the smoky idea that his master-at-arms was in any peculiar way hostile to him. Meantime that functionary, resuming his path, must have momentarily worn some expression less guarded than that of the bitter smile, usurping the face from the heart—some distorting expression perhaps, for a drummer-boy heedlessly frolicking along from the opposite direction and chancing to come into light collision with his person was strangely disconcerted by his aspect. Nor was the impression lessened when the official, impetuously giving him a sharp cut with the rattan, vehemently exclaimed, 'Look where you go!'

9. A Centaur, half man and half horse, skilled in healing and the wisest of his species; he taught the Greek heroes Achilles, Hercules, and Aesculapius. 1. Swagger stick, light whip. 2. Oliver Goldsmith (1730–1774), *The Deserted Village*, line 201, alluding to the response of students to a severe schoolmaster.

11

What was the matter with the master-at-arms? And, be the matter what it might, how could it have direct relation to Billy Budd, with whom prior to the affair of the spilled soup he had never come into any special contact official or otherwise? What indeed could the trouble have to do with one so little inclined to give offense as the merchantship's 'peacemaker,' even him who in Claggart's own phrase was 'the sweet and pleasant young fellow'? Yes, why should Jemmy Legs, to borrow the Dansker's expression, be 'down' on the Handsome Sailor? But, at heart and not for nothing, as the late chance encounter may indicate to the discerning, down on him, secretly down on him, he assuredly was.

Now to invent something touching the more private career of Claggart, something involving Billy Budd, of which something the latter should be wholly ignorant, some romantic incident implying that Claggart's knowledge of the young bluejacket began at some period anterior to catching sight of him on board the seventy-four—all this, not so difficult to do, might avail in a way more or less interesting to account for whatever of enigma may appear to lurk in the case. But in fact there was nothing of the sort. And yet the cause necessarily to be assumed as the sole one assignable is in its very realism as much charged with that prime element of Radcliffian romance, the mysterious, as any that the ingenuity of the author of *The Mysteries of Udolpho*[3] would devise. For what can more partake of the mysterious than an antipathy spontaneous and profound such as is evoked in certain exceptional mortals by the mere aspect of some other mortal, however harmless he may be, if not called forth by this very harmlessness itself?

Now there can exist no irritating juxtaposition of dissimilar personalities comparable to that which is possible aboard a great warship fully manned and at sea. There, every day among all ranks, almost every man comes into more or less of contact with almost every other man. Wholly there to avoid even the sight of an aggravating object one must needs give it Jonah's toss[4] or jump overboard himself. Imagine how all this might eventually operate on some peculiar human creature the direct reverse of a saint!

But for the adequate comprehending of Claggart by a normal nature these hints are insufficient. To pass from a normal nature to him one must cross 'the deadly space between.' And this is best done by indirection.

Long ago an honest scholar, my senior, said to me in reference to one who like himself is now no more, a man so unimpeachably respectable that against him nothing was ever openly said though among the few something was whispered, 'Yes, X——is a nut not to be cracked by the tap of a lady's fan. You are aware that I am the adherent of no organized religion, much less of any philosophy built into a system. Well, for all that, I think that to try and get into X——, enter his labyrinth and get out again, without a clue derived from some source other than what is known as "knowledge of the world"—that were hardly possible, at least for me.'

'Why,' said I, 'X——, however singular a study to some, is yet human, and

3. An immensely popular Gothic novel by Ann Radcliffe (1764–1823).   4. Jonah 1.15: "So they took up Jonah, and cast him forth into the sea." A nautical expression when an unlucky object or person is put overboard.

knowledge of the world assuredly implies the knowledge of human nature, and in most of its varieties.'

'Yes, but a superficial knowledge of it, serving ordinary purposes. But for anything deeper, I am not certain whether to know the world and to know human nature be not two distinct branches of knowledge, which while they may co-exist in the same heart, yet either may exist with little or nothing of the other. Nay, in an average man of the world, his constant rubbing with it blunts that finer spiritual insight indispensable to the understanding of the essential in certain exceptional characters, whether evil ones or good. In a matter of some importance I have seen a girl wind an old lawyer about her little finger. Nor was it the dotage of senile love. Nothing of the sort. But he knew law better than he knew the girl's heart. Coke and Blackstone[5] hardly shed so much light into obscure spiritual places as the Hebrew prophets. And who were they? Mostly recluses.'

At the time, my inexperience was such that I did not quite see the drift of all this. It may be that I see it now. And, indeed, if that lexicon which is based on Holy Writ were any longer popular, one might with less difficulty define and denominate certain phenomenal men. As it is, one must turn to some authority not liable to the charge of being tinctured with the biblical element.

In a list of definitions included in the authentic translation of Plato, a list attributed to him, occurs this: 'Natural Depravity: a depravity according to nature,' a definition which, though savoring of Calvinism,[6] by no means involves Calvin's dogma as to total mankind. Evidently its intent makes it applicable but to individuals. Not many are the examples of this depravity which the gallows and jail supply. At any rate, for notable instances, since these have no vulgar alloy of the brute in them, but invariably are dominated by intellectuality, one must go elsewhere. Civilization, especially if of the austerer sort, is auspicious to it. It folds itself in the mantle of respectability. It has certain negative virtues serving as silent auxiliaries. It never allows wine to get within its guard. It is not going too far to say that it is without vices or small sins. There is a phenomenal pride in it that excludes them. It is never mercenary or avaricious. In short, the depravity here meant partakes nothing of the sordid or sensual. It is serious, but free from acerbity. Though no flatterer of mankind it never speaks ill of it.

But the thing which in eminent instances signalizes so exceptional a nature is this: Though the man's even temper and discreet bearing would seem to intimate a mind peculiarly subject to the law of reason, not the less in heart he would seem to riot in complete exemption from that law, having apparently little to do with reason further than to employ it as an ambidexter[7] implement for effecting the irrational. That is to say: Toward the accomplishment of an aim which in wantonness of atrocity would seem to partake of the insane, he will direct a cool judgment sagacious and sound. These men are madmen, and of the most dangerous sort, for their lunacy is not continuous, but occasional, evoked by some special object; it is protectively secretive, which is as much as to say it is self-contained, so that when, moreover, most active it is to the average mind not distinguishable from sanity, and for

---

5. Sir Edward Coke (1552–1634) and Sir William Blackstone (1723–1780), noted British jurists and writers on the law.   6. The religious system founded by John Calvin (1509–1564), which emphasizes predestination.   7. Two-handed.

the reason above suggested: that whatever its aims may be—and the aim is never declared—the method and the outward proceeding are always perfectly rational.

Now something such an one was Claggart, in whom was the mania of an evil nature, not engendered by vicious training or corrupting books or licentious living, but born with him and innate, in short 'a depravity according to nature.'

Dark sayings are these, some will say. But why? Is it because they somewhat savor of Holy Writ in its phrase 'mystery of iniquity'?[8] If they do, such savor was far enough from being intended, for little will it commend these pages to many a reader of today.

The point of the present story turning on the hidden nature of the master-at-arms has necessitated this chapter. With an added hint or two in connection with the incident at the mess, the resumed narrative must be left to vindicate, as it may, its own credibility.

12

That Claggart's figure was not amiss, and his face, save the chin, well molded, has already been said. Of these favorable points he seemed not insensible, for he was not only neat but careful in his dress. But the form of Billy Budd was heroic; and if his face was without the intellectual look of the pallid Claggart's, not the less was it lit, like his, from within, though from a different source. The bonfire in his heart made luminous the rose-tan in his cheek.

In view of the marked contrast between the persons of the twain, it is more than probable that when the master-at-arms in the scene last given applied to the sailor the proverb 'Handsome is as handsome does,' he there let escape an ironic inkling, not caught by the young sailors who heard it, as to what it was that had first moved him against Billy, namely, his significant personal beauty.

Now envy and antipathy, passions irreconcilable in reason, nevertheless in fact may spring conjoined like Chang and Eng[9] in one birth. Is Envy then such a monster? Well, though many an arraigned mortal has in hopes of mitigated penalty pleaded guilty to horrible actions, did ever anybody seriously confess to envy? Something there is in it universally felt to be more shameful than even felonious crime. And not only does everybody disown it, but the better sort are inclined to incredulity when it is in earnest imputed to an intelligent man. But since its lodgment is in the heart not the brain, no degree of intellect supplies a guarantee against it. But Claggart's was no vulgar form of the passion. Nor, as directed toward Billy Budd, did it partake of that streak of apprehensive jealousy that marred Saul's visage perturbedly brooding on the comely young David.[1] Claggart's envy struck deeper. If askance he eyed the good looks, cheery health, and frank enjoyment of young life in Billy Budd, it was because these went along with a nature that, as Claggart magnetically felt, had in its simplicity never willed malice or experienced the reactionary bite of that serpent. To him, the spirit lodged within Billy, and looking out from his welkin eyes as from windows, that ineffability

8. 2 Thessalonians 2.7.   9. Famous Siamese twins (1811–1874) who toured the United States.
1. David's comeliness and Saul's jealousy are described in 1 Samuel 16.18, 18.8ff.

it was which made the dimple in his dyed cheek, suppled his joints, and dancing in his yellow curls made him pre-eminently the Handsome Sailor. One person excepted, the master-at-arms was perhaps the only man in the ship intellectually capable of adequately appreciating the moral phenomenon presented in Billy Budd. And the insight but intensified his passion, which assuming various secret forms within him, at times assumed that of cynic disdain, disdain of innocence—to be nothing more than innocent! Yet in an aesthetic way he saw the charm of it, the courageous free-and-easy temper of it, and fain would have shared it, but he despaired of it.

With no power to annul the elemental evil in him, though readily enough he could hide it; apprehending the good, but powerless to be it; a nature like Claggart's, surcharged with energy as such natures almost invariably are, what recourse is left to it but to recoil upon itself and, like the scorpion for which the Creator alone is responsible, act out to the end the part allotted it.

13

Passion, and passion in its profoundest, is not a thing demanding a palatial stage whereon to play its part. Down among the groundlings,[2] among the beggars and rakers of the garbage, profound passion is enacted. And the circumstances that provoke it, however trivial or mean, are no measure of its power. In the present instance the stage is a scrubbed gun deck, and one of the external provocations a man-of-war's man's spilled soup.

Now when the master-at-arms noticed whence came that greasy fluid streaming before his feet, he must have taken it—to some extent wilfully, perhaps—not for the mere accident it assuredly was, but for the sly escape of a spontaneous feeling on Billy's part more or less answering to the antipathy on his own. In effect a foolish demonstration, he must have thought, and very harmless, like the futile kick of a heifer, which yet were the heifer a shod stallion would not be so harmless. Even so was it that into the gall of Claggart's envy he infused the vitriol of his contempt. But the incident confirmed to him certain telltale reports purveyed to his ear by 'Squeak,' one of his more cunning corporals, a grizzled little man, so nicknamed by the sailors on account of his squeaky voice and sharp visage ferreting about the dark corners of the lower decks after interlopers, satirically suggesting to them the idea of a rat in a cellar.

From his chief's employing him as an implicit tool in laying little traps for the worriment of the foretopman—for it was from the master-at-arms that the petty persecutions heretofore adverted to had proceeded—the corporal, having naturally enough concluded that his master could have no love for the sailor, made it his business, faithful understrapper that he was, to foment the ill blood by perverting to his chief certain innocent frolics of the good-natured foretopman, besides inventing for his mouth sundry contumelious epithets he claimed to have overheard him let fall. The master-at-arms never suspected the veracity of these reports, more especially as to the epithets, for he well knew how secretly unpopular may become a master-at-arms, at least a master-at-arms of those days, zealous in his function, and how the

2. The part of the audience that stood on the ground in an Elizabethan theater; the poorest spectators.

bluejackets shoot at him in private their raillery and wit; the nickname by which he goes among them (Jemmy Legs) implying under the form of merriment their cherished disrespect and dislike. But in view of the greediness of hate for pabulum[3] it hardly needed a purveyor to feed Claggart's passion.

An uncommon prudence is habitual with the subtler depravity, for it has everything to hide. And in case of an injury but suspected, its secretiveness voluntarily cuts it off from enlightenment or disillusion; and, not unreluctantly, action is taken upon surmise as upon certainty. And the retaliation is apt to be in monstrous disproportion to the supposed offense; for when in anybody was revenge in its exactions aught else but an inordinate usurer? But how with Claggart's conscience? For though consciences are unlike as foreheads, every intelligence, not excluding the scriptural devils who 'believe and tremble,'[4] has one. But Claggart's conscience being but the lawyer to his will, made ogres of trifles, probably arguing that the motive imputed to Billy in spilling the soup just when he did, together with the epithets alleged, these, if nothing more, made a strong case against him; nay, justified animosity into a sort of retributive righteousness. The Pharisee is the Guy Fawkes[5] prowling in the hid chambers underlying some natures like Claggart's. And they can really form no conception of an unreciprocated malice. Probably the master-at-arms' clandestine persecution of Billy was started to try the temper of the man; but it had not developed any quality in him that enmity could make official use of or even pervert into plausible self-justification; so that the occurrence at the mess, petty if it were, was a welcome one to that peculiar conscience assigned to be the private mentor of Claggart; and, for the rest, not improbably it put him upon new experiments.

14

Not many days after the last incident narrated, something befell Billy Budd that more graveled him than aught that had previously occurred.

It was a warm night for the latitude; and the foretopman, whose watch at the time was properly below, was dozing on the uppermost deck whither he had ascended from his hot hammock, one of hundreds suspended so closely wedged together over a lower gun deck that there was little or no swing to them. He lay as in the shadow of a hillside, stretched under the lee of the booms, a piled ridge of spare spars amidships between foremast and mainmast among which the ship's largest boat, the launch, was stowed. Alongside of three other slumberers from below, he lay near that end of the booms which approaches the foremast; his station aloft on duty as a foretopman being just over the deckstation of the forecastlemen, entitling him according to usage to make himself more or less at home in that neighborhood.

Presently he was stirred into semiconsciousness by somebody, who must have previously sounded the sleep of the others, touching his shoulder, and then, as the foretopman raised his head, breathing into his ear in a quick whisper, 'Slip into the lee forechains, Billy; there is something in the wind. Don't speak. Quick, I will meet you there,' and disappearing.

---

3. Sustenance.   4. James 2.19: "The devils also believe, and tremble."   5. Instigator of the Gunpowder Plot, the plan to blow up the Houses of Parliament and King James I on November 5, 1605. *Pharisee*: follower of a Jewish sect known for its strict observance of the Torah; hence anyone extremely rigid and dogmatic.

Now Billy, like sundry other essentially good-natured ones, had some of the weaknesses inseparable from essential good nature; and among these was a reluctance, almost an incapacity of plumply[6] saying *no* to an abrupt proposition not obviously absurd on the face of it, nor obviously unfriendly, nor iniquitous. And being of warm blood, he had not the phlegm[7] tacitly to negative any proposition by unresponsive inaction. Like his sense of fear, his apprehension as to aught outside of the honest and natural was seldom very quick. Besides, upon the present occasion, the drowse from his sleep still hung upon him.

However it was, he mechanically rose and, sleepily wondering what could be in the wind, betook himself to the designated place, a narrow platform, one of six, outside of the high bulwarks and screened by the great deadeyes and multiple columned lanyards of the shrouds and backstays; and, in a great warship of that time, of dimensions commensurate to the hull's magnitude; a tarry balcony in short, overhanging the sea, and so secluded that one mariner of the *Bellipotent*, a Nonconformist[8] old tar of a serious turn, made it even in daytime his private oratory.[9]

In this retired nook the stranger soon joined Billy Budd. There was no moon as yet; a haze obscured the starlight. He could not distinctly see the stranger's face. Yet from something in the outline and carriage, Billy took him, and correctly, for one of the afterguard.

'Hist! Billy,' said the man, in the same quick cautionary whisper as before. 'You were impressed, weren't you? Well, so was I'; and he paused, as to mark the effect. But Billy, not knowing exactly what to make of this, said nothing. Then the other: 'We are not the only impressed ones, Billy. There's a gang of us.—Couldn't you—help—at a pinch?'

'What do you mean?' demanded Billy, here thoroughly shaking off his drowse.

'Hist, hist!' the hurried whisper now growing husky. 'See here,' and the man held up two small objects faintly twinkling in the night-light; 'see, they are yours, Billy, if you'll only—'

But Billy broke in, and in his resentful eagerness to deliver himself his vocal infirmity somewhat intruded. 'D—d—damme, I don't know what you are d—d—driving at, or what you mean, but you had better g—g—go where you belong!' For the moment the fellow, as confounded, did not stir; and Billy, springing to his feet, said, 'If you d—don't start, I'll t—t—toss you back over the r—rail!' There was no mistaking this, and the mysterious emissary decamped, disappearing in the direction of the mainmast in the shadow of the booms.

'Hallo, what's the matter?' here came growling from a forecastleman awakened from his deck-doze by Billy's raised voice. And as the foretopman reappeared and was recognized by him: 'Ah, Beauty, is it you? Well, something must have been the matter, for you st—st—stuttered.'

'Oh,' rejoined Billy, now mastering the impediment, 'I found an afterguardsman in our part of the ship here, and I bid him be off where he belongs.'

'And is that all you did about it, Foretopman?' gruffly demanded another,

6. Bluntly.   7. Sluggishness, apathy.   8. A Protestant dissenter from the Church of England.   9. A small chapel, especially for private prayer.

an irascible old fellow of brick-colored visage and hair who was known to his associate forecastlemen as 'Red Pepper.' 'Such sneaks I should like to marry to the gunner's daughter!'—by that expression meaning that he would like to subject them to disciplinary castigation over a gun.

However, Billy's rendering of the matter satisfactorily accounted to these inquirers for the brief commotion, since of all the sections of a ship's company the forecastlemen, veterans for the most part and bigoted in their sea prejudices, are the most jealous in resenting territorial encroachments, especially on the part of any of the afterguard, of whom they have but a sorry opinion—chiefly landsmen, never going aloft except to reef or furl the mainsail, and in no wise competent to handle a marlinspike or turn in a deadeye, say.

15

This incident sorely puzzled Billy Budd. It was an entirely new experience, the first time in his life that he had ever been personally approached in underhand intriguing fashion. Prior to this encounter he had known nothing of the afterguardsman, the two men being stationed wide apart, one forward and aloft during his watch, the other on deck and aft.

What could it mean? And could they really be guineas,[1] those two glittering objects the interloper had held up to his (Billy's) eyes? Where could the fellow get guineas? Why, even spare buttons are not so plentiful at sea. The more he turned the matter over, the more he was nonplussed, and made uneasy and discomfited. In his disgustful recoil from an overture which, though he but ill comprehended, he instinctively knew must involve evil of some sort, Billy Budd was like a young horse fresh from the pasture suddenly inhaling a vile whiff from some chemical factory, and by repeated snortings trying to get it out of his nostrils and lungs. This frame of mind barred all desire of holding further parley with the fellow, even were it but for the purpose of gaining some enlightenment as to his design in approaching him. And yet he was not without natural curiosity to see how such a visitor in the dark would look in broad day.

He espied him the following afternoon in his first dogwatch below, one of the smokers on that forward part of the upper gun deck allotted to the pipe. He recognized him by his general cut and build more than by his round freckled face and glassy eyes of pale blue, veiled with lashes all but white. And yet Billy was a bit uncertain whether indeed it were he—yonder chap about his own age chatting and laughing in freehearted way, leaning against a gun; a genial young fellow enough to look at, and something of a rattlebrain, to all appearance. Rather chubby too for a sailor, even an afterguardsman. In short, the last man in the world, one would think, to be overburdened with thoughts, especially those perilous thoughts that must needs belong to a conspirator in any serious project, or even to the underling of such a conspirator.

Although Billy was not aware of it, the fellow, with a sidelong watchful glance, had perceived Billy first, and then noting that Billy was looking at him, thereupon nodded a familiar sort of friendly recognition as to an old

1. English gold coins, not minted after 1813, worth twenty-one shillings (approximately eighty-four dollars).

acquaintance, without interrupting the talk he was engaged in with the group of smokers. A day or two afterwards, chancing in the evening promenade on a gun deck to pass Billy, he offered a flying word of good-fellowship, as it were, which by its unexpectedness, and equivocalness under the circumstances, so embarrassed Billy that he knew not how to respond to it, and let it go unnoticed.

Billy was now left more at a loss than before. The ineffectual speculations into which he was led were so disturbingly alien to him that he did his best to smother them. It never entered his mind that here was a matter which, from its extreme questionableness, it was his duty as a loyal bluejacket to report in the proper quarter. And, probably, had such a step been suggested to him, he would have been deterred from taking it by the thought, one of novice magnanimity, that it would savor overmuch of the dirty work of a telltale. He kept the thing to himself. Yet upon one occasion he could not forebear a little disburdening himself to the old Dansker, tempted thereto perhaps by the influence of a balmy night when the ship lay becalmed; the twain, silent for the most part, sitting together on deck, their heads propped against the bulwarks. But it was only a partial and anonymous account that Billy gave, the unfounded scruples above referred to preventing full disclosure to anybody. Upon hearing Billy's version, the sage Dansker seemed to divine more than he was told; and after a little meditation, during which his wrinkles were pursed as into a point, quite effacing for the time that quizzing expression his face sometimes wore: 'Didn't I say so, Baby Budd?'

'Say what?' demanded Billy.

'Why, *Jemmy Legs* is *down* on you.'

'And what,' rejoined Billy in amazement, 'has *Jemmy Legs* to do with that cracked afterguardsman?'

'Ho, it was an afterguardsman, then. A cat's-paw,[2] a cat's-paw!' And with that exclamation, whether it had reference to a light puff of air just then coming over the calm sea, or a subtler relation to the afterguardsman, there is no telling, the old Merlin gave a twisting wrench with his black teeth at his plug of tobacco, vouchsafing no reply to Billy's impetuous question, though now repeated, for it was his wont to relapse into grim silence when interrogated in skeptical sort as to any of his sententious oracles, not always very clear ones, rather partaking of that obscurity which invests most Delphic[3] deliverances from any quarter.

Long experience had very likely brought this old man to that bitter prudence which never interferes in aught and never gives advice.

16

Yes, despite the Dansker's pithy insistence as to the master-at-arms being at the bottom of these strange experiences of Billy on board the *Bellipotent,* the young sailor was ready to ascribe them to almost anybody but the man who, to use Billy's own expression, 'always had a pleasant word for him.' This is to be wondered at. Yet not so much to be wondered at. In certain matters, some sailors even in mature life remain unsophisticated enough. But a young

---

2. Either a light wind perceived by its impressions on the sea or a seaman employed to entice volunteers.   3. Literally, issuing from the ancient Greek oracle of Apollo at Delphi, which made ambiguous prophecies; hence, obscure in meaning, ambiguous.

seafarer of the disposition of our athletic foretopman is much of a child-man. And yet a child's utter innocence is but its blank ignorance, and the innocence more or less wanes as intelligence waxes. But in Billy Budd intelligence, such as it was, had advanced while yet his simple-mindedness remained for the most part unaffected. Experience is a teacher indeed; yet did Billy's years make his experience small. Besides, he had none of that intuitive knowledge of the bad which in natures not good or incompletely so foreruns experience, and therefore may pertain, as in some instances it too clearly does pertain, even to youth.

And what could Billy know of man except of man as a mere sailor? And the old-fashioned sailor, the veritable man before the mast, the sailor from boyhood up, he, though indeed of the same species as a landsman, is in some respects singularly distinct from him. The sailor is frankness, the landsman is finesse. Life is not a game with the sailor, demanding the long head—no intricate game of chess where few moves are made in straightforwardness and ends are attained by indirection, an oblique, tedious, barren game hardly worth that poor candle burnt out in playing it.

Yes, as a class, sailors are in character a juvenile race. Even their deviations are marked by juvenility, this more especially holding true with the sailors of Billy's time. Then too, certain things which apply to all sailors do more pointedly operate here and there upon the junior one. Every sailor, too, is accustomed to obey orders without debating them; his life afloat is externally ruled for him; he is not brought into that promiscuous[4] commerce with mankind where unobstructed free agency on equal terms—equal superficially, at least—soon teaches one that unless upon occasion he exercise a distrust keen in proportion to the fairness of the appearance, some foul turn may be served him. A ruled undemonstrative distrustfulness is so habitual, not with businessmen so much as with men who know their kind in less shallow relations than business, namely, certain men of the world, that they come at last to employ it all but unconsciously; and some of them would very likely feel real surprise at being charged with it as one of their general characteristics.

17

But after the little matter at the mess Billy Budd no more found himself in strange trouble at times about his hammock or his clothes bag or what not. As to that smile that occasionally sunned him, and the pleasant passing word, these were, if not more frequent, yet if anything more pronounced than before.

But for all that, there were certain other demonstrations now. When Claggart's unobserved glance happened to light on belted Billy rolling along the upper gun deck in the leisure of the second dogwatch, exchanging passing broadsides of fun with other young promenaders in the crowd, that glance would follow the cheerful sea Hyperion[5] with a settled meditative and melancholy expression, his eyes strangely suffused with incipient feverish tears. Then would Claggart look like the man of sorrows.[6] Yes, and sometimes the

---

4. Indiscriminate.   5. In Greek mythology, the Titan god who came to be identified with Apollo, god of youth and beauty.   6. In Isaiah 53.3, the Lord's servant is described as "despised and rejected of men; a man of sorrows, and acquainted with grief."

melancholy expression would have in it a touch of soft yearning, as if Claggart could even have loved Billy but for fate and ban. But this was an evanescence, and quickly repented of, as it were, by an immitigable look, pinching and shriveling the visage into the momentary semblance of a wrinkled walnut. But sometimes catching sight in advance of the foretopman coming in his direction, he would, upon their nearing, step aside a little to let him pass, dwelling upon Billy for the moment with the glittering dental satire of a Guise.[7] But upon any abrupt unforeseen encounter a red light would flash forth from his eye like a spark from an anvil in a dusk smithy. That quick, fierce light was a strange one, darted from orbs which in repose were of a color nearest approaching a deeper violet, the softest of shades.

Though some of these caprices of the pit[8] could not but be observed by their object, yet were they beyond the construing of such a nature. And the thews of Billy were hardly compatible with that sort of sensitive spiritual organization which in some cases instinctively conveys to ignorant innocence an admonition of the proximity of the malign. He thought the master-at-arms acted in a manner rather queer at times. That was all. But the occasional frank air and pleasant word went for what they purported to be, the young sailor never having heard as yet of the 'too fair-spoken man.'

Had the foretopman been conscious of having done or said anything to provoke the ill will of the official, it would have been different with him, and his sight might have been purged if not sharpened. As it was, innocence was his blinder.

So was it with him in yet another matter. Two minor officers, the armorer and captain of the hold, with whom he had never exchanged a word, his position in the ship not bringing him into contact with them, these men now for the first began to cast upon Billy, when they chanced to encounter him, that peculiar glance which evidences that the man from whom it comes has been some way tampered with, and to the prejudice of him upon whom the glance lights. Never did it occur to Billy as a thing to be noted or a thing suspicious, though he well knew the fact, that the armorer and captain of the hold, with the ship's yeoman, apothecary, and others of that grade, were by naval usage messmates of the master-at-arms, men with ears convenient to his confidential tongue.

But the general popularity that came from our Handsome Sailor's manly forwardness upon occasion and irresistible good nature, indicating no mental superiority tending to excite an invidious feeling, this good will on the part of most of his shipmates made him the less to concern himself about such mute aspects toward him as those whereto allusion has just been made, aspects he could not so fathom as to infer their whole import.

As to the afterguardsman, though Billy for reasons already given necessarily saw little of him, yet when the two did happen to meet, invariably came the fellow's offhand cheerful recognition, sometimes accompanied by a passing pleasant word or two. Whatever that equivocal young person's original design may really have been, or the design of which he might have been the deputy, certain it was from his manner upon these occasions that he had wholly dropped it.

7. Henri de Guise (1550–1588), a famed conspirator who could smile throughout his villainy.   8. Of hell.

It was as if his precocity of crookedness (and every vulgar villain is pre-cocious) had for once deceived him, and the man he had sought to entrap as a simpleton had through his very simplicity ignominiously baffled him.

But shrewd ones may opine that it was hardly possible for Billy to refrain from going up to the afterguardsman and bluntly demanding to know his purpose in the initial interview so abruptly closed in the forechains. Shrewd ones may also think it but natural in Billy to set about sounding some of the other impressed men of the ship in order to discover what basis, if any, there was for the emissary's obscure suggestions as to plotting disaffection aboard. Yes, shrewd ones may so think. But something more, or rather something else than mere shrewdness is perhaps needful for the due understanding of such a character as Billy Budd's.

As to Claggart, the monomania in the man—if that indeed it were—as involuntarily disclosed by starts in the manifestations detailed, yet in general covered over by his self-contained and rational demeanor; this, like a sub-terranean fire, was eating its way deeper and deeper in him. Something deci-sive must come of it.

18

After the mysterious interview in the forechains, the one so abruptly ended there by Billy, nothing especially germane to the story occurred until the events now about to be narrated.

Elsewhere it has been said that in the lack of frigates (of course better sailers than line-of-battle ships) in the English squadron up the Straits at that period, the *Bellipotent* 74 was occasionally employed not only as an available substitute for a scout, but at times on detached service of more important kind. This was not alone because of her sailing qualities, not com-mon in a ship of her rate,[9] but quite as much, probably, that the character of her commander, it was thought, specially adapted him for any duty where under unforeseen difficulties a prompt initiative might have to be taken in some matter demanding knowledge and ability in addition to those qualities implied in good seamanship. It was on an expedition of the latter sort, a somewhat distant one, and when the *Bellipotent* was almost at her furthest remove from the fleet, that in the latter part of an afternoon watch she unexpectedly came in sight of a ship of the enemy. It proved to be a frigate. The latter, perceiving through the glass that the weight of men and metal would be heavily against her, invoking her light heels crowded sail to get away. After a chase urged almost against hope and lasting until about the middle of the first dogwatch, she signally succeeded in effecting her escape.

Not long after the pursuit had been given up, and ere the excitement incident thereto had altogether waned away, the master-at-arms, ascending from his cavernous sphere, made his appearance cap in hand by the main-mast respectfully waiting the notice of Captain Vere, then solitary walking the weather side of the quarter-deck, doubtless somewhat chafed at the fail-ure of the pursuit. The spot where Claggart stood was the place allotted to men of lesser grades seeking some more particular interview either with the officer of the deck or the captain himself. But from the latter it was not often

9. Classification.

that a sailor or petty officer of those days would seek a hearing; only some exceptional cause would, according to established custom, have warranted that.

Presently, just as the commander, absorbed in his reflections, was on the point of turning aft in his promenade, he became sensible of Claggart's presence, and saw the doffed cap held in deferential expectancy. Here be it said that Captain Vere's personal knowledge of his petty officer had only begun at the time of the ship's last sailing from home, Claggart then for the first, in transfer from a ship detained for repairs, supplying on board the *Bellipotent* the place of a previous master-at-arms disabled and ashore.

No sooner did the commander observe who it was that now deferentially stood awaiting his notice than a peculiar expression came over him. It was not unlike that which uncontrollably will flit across the countenance of one at unawares encountering a person who, though known to him indeed, has hardly been long enough known for thorough knowledge, but something in whose aspect nevertheless now for the first provokes a vaguely repellent distaste. But coming to a stand and resuming much of his wonted official manner, save that a sort of impatience lurked in the intonation of the opening word, he said, 'Well? What is it, Master-at-arms?'

With the air of a subordinate grieved at the necessity of being a messenger of ill tidings, and while conscientiously determined to be frank yet equally resolved upon shunning overstatement, Claggart at this invitation, or rather summons to disburden, spoke up. What he said, conveyed in the language of no uneducated man, was to the effect following, if not altogether in these words, namely, that during the chase and preparations for the possible encounter he had seen enough to convince him that at least one sailor aboard was a dangerous character in a ship mustering some who not only had taken a guilty part in the late serious troubles, but others also who, like the man in question, had entered His Majesty's service under another form than enlistment.

At this point Captain Vere with some impatience interrupted him: 'Be direct, man; say *impressed men.*'

Claggart made a gesture of subservience, and proceeded. Quite lately he (Claggart) had begun to suspect that on the gun decks some sort of movement prompted by the sailor in question was covertly going on, but he had not thought himself warranted in reporting the suspicion so long as it remained indistinct. But from what he had that afternoon observed in the man referred to, the suspicion of something clandestine going on had advanced to a point less removed from certainty. He deeply felt, he added, the serious responsibility assumed in making a report involving such possible consequences to the individual mainly concerned, besides tending to augment those natural anxieties which every naval commander must feel in view of extraordinary outbreaks so recent as those which, he sorrowfully said it, it needed not to name.

Now at the first broaching of the matter Captain Vere, taken by surprise, could not wholly dissemble his disquietude. But as Claggart went on, the former's aspect changed into restiveness under something in the testifier's manner in giving his testimony. However, he refrained from interrupting him. And Claggart, continuing, concluded with this: 'God forbid, your honor, that the *Bellipotent*'s should be the experience of the—'

'Never mind that!' here peremptorily broke in the superior, his face altering with anger, instinctively divining the ship that the other was about to name, one in which the Nore Mutiny had assumed a singularly tragical character that for a time jeopardized the life of its commander. Under the circumstances he was indignant at the purposed allusion. When the commissioned officers themselves were on all occasions very heedful how they referred to the recent events in the fleet, for a petty officer unnecessarily to allude to them in the presence of his captain, this struck him as a most immodest presumption. Besides, to his quick sense of self-respect it even looked under the circumstances something like an attempt to alarm him. Nor at first was he without some surprise that one who so far as he had hitherto come under his notice had shown considerable tact in his function should in this particular evince such lack of it.

But these thoughts and kindred dubious ones flitting across his mind were suddenly replaced by an intuitional surmise which, though as yet obscure in form, served practically to affect his reception of the ill tidings. Certain it is that, long versed in everything pertaining to the complicated gun-deck life, which like every other form of life has its secret mines and dubious side, the side popularly disclaimed, Captain Vere did not permit himself to be unduly disturbed by the general tenor of his subordinate's report.

Furthermore, if in view of recent events prompt action should be taken at the first palpable sign of recurring insubordination, for all that, not judicious would it be, he thought, to keep the idea of lingering disaffection alive by undue forwardness in crediting an informer, even if his own subordinate and charged among other things with police surveillance of the crew. This feeling would not perhaps have so prevailed with him were it not that upon a prior occasion the patriotic zeal officially evinced by Claggart had somewhat irritated him as appearing rather supersensible and strained. Furthermore something even in the official's self-possessed and somewhat ostentatious manner in making his specifications strangely reminded him of a bandsman,[1] a perjurious witness in a capital case before a courtmartial ashore of which when a lieutenant he (Captain Vere) had been a member.

Now the peremptory check given to Claggart in the matter of the arrested allusion was quickly followed up by this: 'You say that there is at least one dangerous man aboard. Name him.'

'William Budd, a foretopman, your honor.'

'William Budd!' repeated Captain Vere with unfeigned astonishment. 'And mean you the man that Lieutenant Ratcliffe took from the merchantman not very long ago, the young fellow who seems to be so popular with the men—Billy the Handsome Sailor, as they call him?'

'The same, your honor; but for all his youth and good looks, a deep one. Not for nothing does he insinuate himself into the good will of his shipmates, since at the least they will at a pinch say—all hands will—a good word for him, and at all hazards. Did Lieutenant Ratcliffe happen to tell your honor of that adroit fling of Budd's, jumping up in the cutter's bow under the merchantman's stern when he was being taken off? It is even masked by that sort of good-humored air that at heart he resents his impressment. You have but noted his fair cheek. A mantrap may be under the ruddy-tipped daisies.'

1. Crewman charged with the task of stitching bands of canvas into sails to strengthen them.

Now the Handsome Sailor as a signal figure among the crew had naturally enough attracted the captain's attention from the first. Though in general not very demonstrative to his officers, he had congratulated Lieutenant Ratcliffe upon his good fortune in lighting on such a fine specimen of the *genus homo*, who in the nude might have posed for a statue of a young Adam before the Fall. As to Billy's adieu to the ship *Rights-of-Man*, which the boarding lieutenant had indeed reported to him, but, in a deferential way, more as a good story than aught else, Captain Vere, though mistakenly understanding it as a satiric sally, had but thought so much the better of the impressed man for it; as a military sailor, admiring the spirit that could take an arbitrary enlistment so merrily and sensibly. The foretopman's conduct, too, so far as it had fallen under the captain's notice, had confirmed the first happy augury, while the new recruit's qualities as a 'sailor-man' seemed to be such that he had thought of recommending him to the executive officer for promotion to a place that would more frequently bring him under his own observation, namely, the captaincy of the mizzentop, replacing there in the starboard watch a man not so young whom partly for that reason he deemed less fitted for the post. Be it parenthesized here that since the mizzentopmen have not to handle such breadths of heavy canvas as the lower sails on the mainmast and foremast, a young man if of the right stuff not only seems best adapted to duty there, but in fact is generally selected for the captaincy of that top, and the company under him are light hands and often but striplings. In sum, Captain Vere had from the beginning deemed Billy Budd to be what in the naval parlance of the time was called a 'King's bargain': that is to say, for His Britannic Majesty's navy a capital investment at small outlay or none at all.

After a brief pause, during which the reminiscences above mentioned passed vividly through his mind and he weighed the import of Claggart's last suggestion conveyed in the phrase 'mantrap under the daisies,' and the more he weighed it the less reliance he felt in the informer's good faith, suddenly he turned upon him and in a low voice demanded: 'Do you come to me, Master-at-arms, with so foggy a tale? As to Budd, cite me an act or spoken word of his confirmatory of what you in general charge against him. Stay,' drawing nearer to him; 'heed what you speak. Just now, and in a case like this, there is a yardarm-end for the false witness.'

'Ah, your honor!' sighed Claggart, mildly shaking his shapely head as in sad deprecation of such unmerited severity of tone. Then, bridling—erecting himself as in virtuous self-assertion—he circumstantially alleged certain words and acts which collectively, if credited, led to presumptions morally inculpating Budd. And for some of these averments, he added, substantiating proof was not far.

With gray eyes impatient and distrustful essaying to fathom to the bottom Claggart's calm violet ones, Captain Vere again heard him out; then for the moment stood ruminating. The mood he evinced, Claggart—himself for the time liberated from the other's scrutiny—steadily regarded with a look difficult to render: a look curious of the operation of his tactics, a look such as might have been that of the spokesman of the envious children of Jacob deceptively imposing upon the troubled patriarch the blood-dyed coat of young Joseph.[2]

---

2. Genesis 37.1–32: "And they took Joseph's coat, and killed a kid of the goats, and dipped the coat in the blood; and they sent the coat of many colours, and they brought it to their father; and said, This have we found: know now whether it be thy son's coat or no."

Though something exceptional in the moral quality of Captain Vere made him, in earnest encounter with a fellow man, a veritable touchstone of that man's essential nature, yet now as to Claggart and what was really going on in him his feeling partook less of intuitional conviction than of strong suspicion clogged by strange dubieties. The perplexity he evinced proceeded less from aught touching the man informed against—as Claggart doubtless opined—than from considerations how best to act in regard to the informer. At first, indeed, he was naturally for summoning that substantiation of his allegations which Claggart said was at hand. But such a proceeding would result in the matter at once getting abroad, which in the present stage of it, he thought, might undesirably affect the ship's company. If Claggart was a false witness—that closed the affair. And therefore, before trying the accusation, he would first practically test the accuser; and he thought this could be done in a quiet, undemonstrative way.

The measure he determined upon involved a shifting of the scene, a transfer to a place less exposed to observation than the broad quarter-deck. For although the few gunroom officers there at the time had, in due observance of naval etiquette, withdrawn to leeward the moment Captain Vere had begun his promenade on the deck's weather side; and though during the colloquy with Claggart they of course ventured not to diminish the distance; and though throughout the interview Captain Vere's voice was far from him, and Claggart's silvery and low; and the wind in the cordage and the wash of the sea helped the more to put them beyond earshot; nevertheless, the interview's continuance already had attracted observation from some topmen aloft and other sailors in the waist or further forward.

Having determined upon his measures, Captain Vere forthwith took action. Abruptly turning to Claggart, he asked, 'Master-at-arms, is it now Budd's watch aloft?'

'No, your honor.'

Whereupon, 'Mr Wilkes!' summoning the nearest midshipman. 'Tell Albert to come to me.' Albert was the captain's hammock-boy, a sort of sea valet in whose discretion and fidelity his master had much confidence. The lad appeared.

'You know Budd, the foretopman?'

'I do, sir.'

'Go find him. It is his watch off. Manage to tell him out of earshot that he is wanted aft. Contrive it that he speaks to nobody. Keep him in talk yourself. And not till you get well aft here, not till then let him know that the place where he is wanted is my cabin. You understand. Go.—Master-at-arms, show yourself on the decks below, and when you think it time for Albert to be coming with his man, stand by quietly to follow the sailor in.'

19

Now when the foretopman found himself in the cabin, closeted there, as it were, with the captain and Claggart, he was surprised enough. But it was a surprise unaccompanied by apprehension or distrust. To an immature nature essentially honest and humane, forewarning intimations of subtler danger from one's kind come tardily if at all. The only thing that took shape in the young sailor's mind was this: Yes, the captain, I have always thought, looks kindly upon me. Wonder if he's going to make me his coxswain. I should like that. And may be now he is going to ask the master-at-arms about me.'

'Shut the door there, sentry,' said the commander; 'stand without, and let nobody come in.—Now, Master-at-arms, tell this man to his face what you told of him to me,' and stood prepared to scrutinize the mutually confronting visages.

With the measured step and calm collected air of an asylum physician approaching in the public hall some patient beginning to show indications of a coming paroxysm, Claggart deliberately advanced within short range of Billy and, mesmerically looking him in the eye, briefly recapitulated the accusation.

Not at first did Billy take it in. When he did, the rose-tan of his cheek looked struck as by white leprosy. He stood like one impaled and gagged. Meanwhile the accuser's eyes, removing not as yet from the blue dilated ones, underwent a phenomenal change, their wonted rich violet color blurring into a muddy purple. Those lights of human intelligence, losing human expression, were gelidly protruding like the alien eyes of certain uncatalogued creatures of the deep. The first mesmeristic glance was one of serpent fascination; the last was as the paralyzing lurch of the torpedo fish.

'Speak, man!' said Captain Vere to the transfixed one, struck by his aspect even more than by Claggart's. 'Speak! Defend yourself!' Which appeal caused but a strange dumb gesturing and gurgling in Billy; amazement at such an accusation so suddenly sprung on inexperienced nonage; this, and, it may be, horror of the accuser's eyes, serving to bring out his lurking defect and in this instance for the time intensifying it into a convulsed tongue-tie; while the intent head and entire form straining forward in an agony of ineffectual eagerness to obey the injunction to speak and defend himself, gave an expression to the face like that of a condemned vestal priestess in the moment of being buried alive, and in the first struggle against suffocation.[3]

Though at the time Captain Vere was quite ignorant of Billy's liability to vocal impediment, he now immediately divined it, since vividly Billy's aspect recalled to him that of a bright young schoolmate of his whom he had once seen struck by much the same startling impotence in the act of eagerly rising in the class to be foremost in response to a testing question put to it by the master. Going close up to the young sailor, and laying a soothing hand on his shoulder, he said, 'There is no hurry, my boy. Take your time, take your time.' Contrary to the effect intended, these words so fatherly in tone, doubtless touching Billy's heart to the quick, prompted yet more violent efforts at utterance—efforts soon ending for the time in confirming the paralysis, and bringing to his face an expression which was as a crucifixion to behold. The next instant, quick as the flame from a discharged cannon at night, his right arm shot out, and Claggart dropped to the deck. Whether intentionally or but owing to the young athlete's superior height, the blow had taken effect full upon the forehead, so shapely and intellectual-looking a feature in the master-at-arms; so that the body fell over lengthwise, like a heavy plank tilted from erectness. A gasp or two, and he lay motionless.

'Fated boy,' breathed Captain Vere in tone so low as to be almost a whisper, 'what have you done! But here, help me.'

3. Vestal virgins in Rome were buried alive if they violated their vows.

The twain raised the felled one from the loins up into a sitting position. The spare form flexibly acquiesced, but inertly. It was like handling a dead snake. They lowered it back. Regaining erectness, Captain Vere with one hand covering his face stood to all appearance as impassive as the object at his feet. Was he absorbed in taking in all the bearings of the event and what was best not only now at once to be done, but also in the sequel? Slowly he uncovered his face; and the effect was as if the moon emerging from eclipse should reappear with quite another aspect than that which had gone into hiding. The father in him, manifested towards Billy thus far in the scene, was replaced by the military disciplinarian. In his official tone he bade the foretopman retire to a stateroom aft (pointing it out), and there remain till thence summoned. This order Billy in silence mechanically obeyed. Then going to the cabin door where it opened on the quarter-deck, Captain Vere said to the sentry without, 'Tell somebody to send Albert here.' When the lad appeared, his master so contrived it that he should not catch sight of the prone one. 'Albert,' he said to him, 'tell the surgeon I wish to see him. You need not come back till called.'

When the surgeon entered—a self-poised character of that grave sense and experience that hardly anything could take him aback—Captain Vere advanced to meet him, thus unconsciously intercepting his view of Claggart, and interrupting the other's wonted ceremonious salutation, said, 'Nay. Tell me how it is with yonder man,' directing his attention to the prostrate one.

The surgeon looked, and for all his self-command somewhat started at the abrupt revelation. On Claggart's always pallid complexion, thick black blood was now oozing from nostril and ear. To the gazer's professional eye it was unmistakably no living man that he saw.

'Is it so, then?' said Captain Vere, intently watching him. 'I thought it. But verify it.' Whereupon the customary tests confirmed the surgeon's first glance, who now, looking up in unfeigned concern, cast a look of intense inquisitiveness upon his superior. But Captain Vere, with one hand to his brow, was standing motionless. Suddenly, catching the surgeon's arm convulsively, he exclaimed, pointing down to the body, 'It is the divine judgment on Ananias![4] Look!'

Disturbed by the excited manner he had never before observed in the *Bellipotent*'s captain, and as yet wholly ignorant of the affair, the prudent surgeon nevertheless held his peace, only again looking an earnest interrogatory as to what it was that had resulted in such a tragedy.

But Captain Vere was now again motionless, standing absorbed in thought. Again starting, he vehemently exclaimed, 'Struck dead by an angel of God! Yet the angel must hang!'

At these passionate interjections, mere incoherences to the listener as yet unapprised of the antecedents, the surgeon was profoundly discomposed. But now, as recollecting himself, Captain Vere in less passionate tone briefly related the circumstances leading up to the event. 'But come, we must dispatch,' he added. 'Help me to remove him' (meaning the body) 'to yonder compartment,' designating one opposite that where the foretopman remained immured. Anew disturbed by a request that, as implying a desire for

---

4. Acts 5.3–5: "Peter said, Ananias . . . thou hast not lied unto men, but unto God. And Ananias hearing these words fell down, and gave up the ghost."

secrecy, seemed unaccountably strange to him, there was nothing for the subordinate to do but comply.

'Go now,' said Captain Vere with something of his wonted manner. 'Go now. I presently shall call a drumhead court.[5] Tell the lieutenants what has happened, and tell Mr Mordant' (meaning the captain of marines), 'and charge them to keep the matter to themselves.'

20

Full of disquietude and misgiving, the surgeon left the cabin. Was Captain Vere suddenly affected in his mind, or was it but a transient excitement, brought about by so strange and extraordinary a tragedy? As to the drumhead court, it struck the surgeon as impolitic, if nothing more. The thing to do, he thought, was to place Billy Budd in confinement, and in a way dictated by usage, and postpone further action in so extraordinary a case to such time as they should rejoin the squadron, and then refer it to the admiral. He recalled the unwonted agitation of Captain Vere and his excited exclamations, so at variance with his normal manner. Was he unhinged?

But assuming that he is, it is not so susceptible of proof. What then can the surgeon do? No more trying situation is conceivable than that of an officer subordinate under a captain whom he suspects to be not mad, indeed, but yet not quite unaffected in his intellects. To argue his order to him would be insolence. To resist him would be mutiny.

In obedience to Captain Vere, he communicated what had happened to the lieutenants and captain of marines, saying nothing as to the captain's state. They fully shared his own surprise and concern. Like him too, they seemed to think that such a matter should be referred to the admiral.

21

Who in the rainbow can draw the line where the violet tint ends and the orange tint begins? Distinctly we see the difference of the colors, but where exactly does the one first blendingly enter into the other? So with sanity and insanity. In pronounced cases there is no question about them. But in some supposed cases, in various degrees supposedly less pronounced, to draw the exact line of demarcation few will undertake, though for a fee becoming considerate some professional experts will. There is nothing nameable but that some men will, or undertake to, do it for pay.

Whether Captain Vere, as the surgeon professionally and privately surmised, was really the sudden victim of any degree of aberration, every one must determine for himself by such light as this narrative may afford.

That the unhappy event which has been narrated could not have happened at a worse juncture was but too true. For it was close on the heel of the suppressed insurrections, an aftertime very critical to naval authority, demanding from every English sea commander two qualities not readily interfusable—prudence and rigor. Moreover, there was something crucial in the case.

In the jugglery of circumstances preceding and attending the event on

---

5. A court-martial, originally held around an upturned drum, to try offences committed during military operations.

board the *Bellipotent,* and in the light of that martial code whereby it was formally to be judged, innocence and guilt personified in Claggart and Budd in effect changed places. In a legal view the apparent victim of the tragedy was he who had sought to victimize a man blameless; and the indisputable deed of the latter, navally regarded, constituted the most heinous of military crimes. Yet more. The essential right and wrong involved in the matter, the clearer that might be, so much the worse for the responsibility of a loyal sea commander, inasmuch as he was not authorized to determine the matter on that primitive basis.

Small wonder then that the *Bellipotent*'s captain, though in general a man of rapid decision, felt that circumspectness not less than promptitude was necessary. Until he could decide upon his course, and in each detail; and not only so, but until the concluding measure was upon the point of being enacted, he deemed it advisable, in view of all the circumstances, to guard as much as possible against publicity. Here he may or may not have erred. Certain it is, however, that subsequently in the confidential talk of more than one or two gun rooms and cabins he was not a little criticized by some officers, a fact imputed by his friends and vehemently by his cousin Jack Denton to professional jealousy of Starry Vere. Some imaginative ground for invidious comment there was. The maintenance of secrecy in the matter, the confining all knowledge of it for a time to the place where the homicide occurred, the quarter-deck cabin; in these particulars lurked some resemblance to the policy adopted in those tragedies of the palace which have occurred more than once in the capital founded by Peter the Barbarian.[6]

The case indeed was such that fain would the *Bellipotent*'s captain have deferred taking any action whatever respecting it further than to keep the foretopman a close prisoner till the ship rejoined the squadron and then submitting the matter to the judgment of his admiral.

But a true military officer is in one particular like a true monk. Not with more of self-abnegation will the latter keep his vows of monastic obedience than the former his vows of allegiance to martial duty.

Feeling that unless quick action was taken on it, the deed of the foretopman, so soon as it should be known on the gun decks, would tend to awaken any slumbering embers of the Nore among the crew, a sense of the urgency of the case overruled in Captain Vere every other consideration. But though a conscientious disciplinarian, he was no lover of authority for mere authority's sake. Very far was he from embracing opportunities for monopolizing to himself the perils of moral responsibility, none at least that could properly be referred to an official superior or shared with him by his official equals or even subordinates. So thinking, he was glad it would not be at variance with usage to turn the matter over to a summary court of his own officers, reserving to himself, as the one on whom the ultimate accountability would rest, the right of maintaining a supervision of it, or formally or informally interposing at need. Accordingly a drum-head court was summarily convened, he electing the individuals composing it: the first lieutenant, the captain of marines, and the sailing master.

In associating an officer of marines with the sea lieutenant and the sailing master in a case having to do with a sailor, the commander perhaps deviated

6. St. Petersburg, founded by Peter the Great (1672–1725) in 1703.

from general custom. He was prompted thereto by the circumstance that he took that soldier to be a judicious person, thoughtful, and not altogether incapable of grappling with a difficult case unprecedented in his prior experience. Yet even as to him he was not without some latent misgiving, for withal he was an extremely good-natured man, an enjoyer of his dinner, a sound sleeper, and inclined to obesity—a man who though he would always maintain his manhood in battle might not prove altogether reliable in a moral dilemma involving aught of the tragic. As to the first lieutenant and the sailing master, Captain Vere could not but be aware that though honest natures, of approved gallantry upon occasion, their intelligence was mostly confined to the matter of active seamanship and the fighting demands of their profession.

The court was held in the same cabin where the unfortunate affair had taken place. This cabin, the commander's, embraced the entire area under the poop deck. Aft, and on either side, was a small stateroom, the one now temporarily a jail and the other a dead-house, and a yet smaller compartment, leaving a space between expanding forward into a goodly oblong of length coinciding with the ship's beam. A skylight of moderate dimension was overhead, and at each end of the oblong space were two sashed porthole windows easily convertible back into embrasures for short carronades.[7]

All being quickly in readiness, Billy Budd was arraigned, Captain Vere necessarily appearing as the sole witness in the case, and as such temporarily sinking his rank, though singularly maintaining it in a matter apparently trivial, namely, that he testified from the ship's weather side, with that object having caused the court to sit on the lee side. Concisely he narrated all that had led up to the catastrophe, omitting nothing in Claggart's accusation and deposing as to the manner in which the prisoner had received it. At this testimony the three officers glanced with no little surprise at Billy Budd, the last man they would have suspected either of the mutinous design alleged by Claggart or the undeniable deed he himself had done. The first lietuenant, taking judicial primacy and turning toward the prisoner, said, 'Captain Vere has spoken. Is it or is it not as Captain Vere says?'

In response came syllables not so much impeded in the utterance as might have been anticipated. They were these: 'Captain Vere tells the truth. It is just as Captain Vere says, but it is not as the master-at-arms said. I have eaten the King's bread and I am true to the King.'

'I believe you, my man,' said the witness, his voice indicating a suppressed emotion not otherwise betrayed.

'God will bless you for that, your honor!' not without stammering said Billy, and all but broke down. But immediately he was recalled to self-control by another question, to which with the same emotional difficulty of utterance he said, 'No, there was no malice between us. I never bore malice against the master-at-arms. I am sorry that he is dead. I did not mean to kill him. Could I have used my tongue I would not have struck him. But he foully lied to my face and in presence of my captain, and I had to say something, and I could only say it with a blow, God help me!'

In the impulsive aboveboard manner of the frank one the court saw confirmed all that was implied in words that just previously had perplexed them,

7. Large pieces of artillery.

coming as they did from the testifier to the tragedy and promptly following Billy's impassioned disclaimer of mutinous intent—Captain Vere's words, 'I believe you, my man.'

Next it was asked of him whether he knew of or suspected aught savoring of incipient trouble (meaning mutiny, though the explicit term was avoided) going on in any section of the ship's company.

The reply lingered. This was naturally imputed by the court to the same vocal embarrassment which had retarded or obstructed previous answers. But in main it was otherwise here, the question immediately recalling to Billy's mind the interview with the afterguardsman in the forechains. But an innate repugnance to playing a part at all approaching that of an informer against one's own shipmates—the same erring sense of uninstructed honor which had stood in the way of his reporting the matter at the time, though as a loyal man-of-war's man it was incumbent on him, and failure so to do, if charged against him and proven, would have subjected him to the heaviest of penalties; this, with the blind feeling now his that nothing really was being hatched, prevailed with him. When the answer came it was a negative.

'One question more,' said the officer of marines, now first speaking and with a troubled earnestness. 'You tell us that what the master-at-arms said against you was a lie. Now why should he have so lied, so maliciously lied, since you declare there was no malice between you?'

At that question, unintentionally touching on a spiritual sphere wholly obscure to Billy's thoughts, he was nonplussed, evincing a confusion indeed that some observers, such as can readily be imagined, would have construed into involuntary evidence of hidden guilt. Nevertheless, he strove some way to answer, but all at once relinquished the vain endeavor, at the same time turning an appealing glance towards Captain Vere as deeming him his best helper and friend. Captain Vere, who had been seated for a time, rose to his feet, addressing the interrogator. 'The question you put to him comes naturally enough. But how can he rightly answer it?—or anybody else, unless indeed it be he who lies within there,' designating the compartment where lay the corpse. 'But the prone one there will not rise to our summons. In effect, though, as it seems to me, the point you make is hardly material. Quite aside from any conceivable motive actuating the master-at-arms, and irrespective of the provocation to the blow, a martial court must needs in the present case confine its attention to the blow's consequence, which consequence justly is to be deemed not otherwise than as the striker's deed.'

This utterance, the full significance of which it was not at all likely that Billy took in, nevertheless caused him to turn a wistful interrogative look toward the speaker, a look in its dumb expressiveness not unlike that which a dog of generous breed might turn upon his master, seeking in his face some elucidation of a previous gesture ambiguous to the canine intelligence. Nor was the same utterance without marked effect upon the three officers, more especially the soldier. Couched in it seemed to them a meaning unanticipated, involving a prejudgment on the speaker's part. It served to augment a mental disturbance previously evident enough.

The soldier once more spoke, in a tone of suggestive dubiety addressing at once his associates and Captain Vere: 'Nobody is present—none of the ship's company, I mean—who might shed lateral light, if any is to be had, upon what remains mysterious in this matter.'

'That is thoughtfully put,' said Captain Vere; 'I see your drift. Ay, there is a mystery; but, to use a scriptural phrase, it is a "mystery of iniquity," a matter for psychologic theologians to discuss. But what has a military court to do with it? Not to add that for us any possible investigation of it is cut off by the lasting tongue-tie of—him—in yonder,' again designating the mortuary stateroom. 'The prisoner's deed—with that alone we have to do.'

To this, and particularly the closing reiteration, the marine soldier, knowing not how aptly to reply, sadly abstained from saying aught. The first lieutenant, who at the outset had not unnaturally assumed primacy in the court, now overrulingly instructed by a glance from Captain Vere, a glance more effective than words, resumed that primacy. Turning to the prisoner, 'Budd,' he said, and scarce in equable tones, 'Budd, if you have aught further to say for yourself, say it now.'

Upon this the young sailor turned another quick glance toward Captain Vere; then, as taking a hint from that aspect, a hint confirming his own instinct that silence was now best, replied to the lieutenant, 'I have said all, sir.'

The marine—the same who had been the sentinel without the cabin door at the time that the foretopman, followed by the master-at-arms, entered it— he, standing by the sailor throughout these judicial proceedings was now directed to take him back to the after compartment originally assigned to the prisoner and his custodian. As the twain disappeared from view, the three officers, as partially liberated from some inward constraint associated with Billy's mere presence, simultaneously stirred in their seats. They exchanged looks of troubled indecision, yet feeling that decide they must and without long delay. For Captain Vere, he for the time stood—unconsciously with his back toward them, apparently in one of his absent fits—gazing out from a sashed porthole to windward upon the monotonous blank of the twilight sea. But the court's silence continuing, broken only at moments by brief consultations, in low earnest tones, this served to arouse him and energize him. Turning, he to-and-fro paced the cabin athwart; in the returning ascent to windward climbing the slant deck in the ship's lee roll, without knowing it symbolizing thus in his action a mind resolute to surmount difficulties even if against primitive instincts strong as the wind and the sea. Presently he came to a stand before the three. After scanning their faces he stood less as mustering his thoughts for expression than as one inly deliberating how best to put them to well-meaning men not intellectually mature, men with whom it was necessary to demonstrate certain principles that were axioms to himself. Similar impatience as to talking is perhaps one reason that deters some minds from addressing any popular assemblies.

When speak he did, something, both in the substance of what he said and his manner of saying it, showed the influence of unshared studies modifying and tempering the practical training of an active career. This, along with his phraseology, now and then was suggestive of the grounds whereon rested that imputation of a certain pedantry socially alleged against him by certain naval men of wholly practical cast, captains who nevertheless would frankly concede that His Majesty's navy mustered no more efficient officer of their grade than Starry Vere.

What he said was to this effect: 'Hitherto I have been but the witness, little more; and I should hardly think now to take another tone, that of your coadjutor for the time, did I not perceive in you—at the crisis too—a troubled hesitancy, proceeding, I doubt not, from the clash of military duty with moral scruple—scruple vitalized by compassion. For the compassion, how can I otherwise than share it? But, mindful of paramount obligations, I strive against scruples that may tend to enervate decision. Not, gentlemen, that I hide from myself that the case is an exceptional one. Speculatively regarded, it well might be referred to a jury of casuists. But for us here, acting not as casuists or moralists, it is a case practical, and under martial law practically to be dealt with.

'But your scruples: do they move as in a dusk? Challenge them. Make them advance and declare themselves. Come now; do they import something like this: If, mindless of palliating circumstances, we are bound to regard the death of the master-at-arms as the prisoner's deed, then does that deed constitute a capital crime whereof the penalty is a mortal one. But in natural justice is nothing but the prisoner's overt act to be considered? How can we adjudge to summary and shameful death a fellow creature innocent before God, and whom we feel to be so?—Does that state it aright? You sign sad assent. Well, I too feel that, the full force of that. It is Nature. But do these buttons that we wear attest that our allegiance is to Nature? No, to the King. Though the ocean, which is inviolate Nature primeval, though this be the element where we move and have our being as sailors, yet as the King's officers lies our duty in a sphere correspondingly natural? So little is that true, that in receiving our commissions we in the most important regards ceased to be natural free agents. When war is declared are we the commissioned fighters previously consulted? We fight at command. If our judgments approve the war, that is but coincidence. So in other particulars. So now. For suppose condemnation to follow these present proceedings. Would it be so much we ourselves that would condemn as it would be martial law operating through us? For that law and the rigor of it, we are not responsibile. Our vowed responsibility is in this: That however pitilessly that law may operate in any instances, we nevertheless adhere to it and administer it.

'But the exceptional in the matter moves the hearts within you. Even so too is mine moved. But let not warm hearts betray heads that should be cool. Ashore in a criminal case, will an upright judge allow himself off the bench to be waylaid by some tender kinswoman of the accused seeking to touch him with her tearful plea? Well, the heart here, sometimes the feminine in man, is as that piteous woman, and hard though it be, she must here be ruled out.'

He paused, earnestly studying them for a moment; then resumed.

'But something in your aspect seems to urge that it is not solely the heart that moves in you, but also the conscience, the private conscience. But tell me whether or not, occupying the position we do, private conscience should not yield to that imperial one formulated in the code under which alone we officially proceed?'

Here the three men moved in their seats, less convinced than agitated by the course of an argument troubling but the more the spontaneous conflict within.

Perceiving which, the speaker paused for a moment; then abruptly changing his tone, went on.

'To steady us a bit, let us recur to the facts.—In wartime at sea a man-of-war's man strikes his superior in grade, and the blow kills. Apart from its effect the blow itself is, according to the Articles of War, a capital crime. Furthermore—'

'Ay, sir,' emotionally broke in the officer of marines, 'in one sense it was. But surely Budd proposed neither mutiny nor homicide.'

'Surely not, my good man. And before a court less arbitrary and more merciful than a martial one, that plea would largely extenuate. At the Last Assizes[8] it shall acquit. But how here? We proceed under the law of the Mutiny Act.[9] In feature no child can resemble his father more than that Act resembles in spirit the thing from which it derives—War. In His Majesty's service—in this ship, indeed—there are Englishmen forced to fight for the King against their will. Against their conscience, for aught we know. Though as their fellow creatures some of us may appreciate their position, yet as navy officers what reck we of it? Still less recks the enemy. Our impressed men he would fain cut down in the same swath with our volunteers. As regards the enemy's naval conscripts, some of whom may even share our own abhorrence of the regicidal French Directory, it is the same on our side. War looks but to the frontage, the appearance. And the Mutiny Act, War's child, takes after the father. Budd's intent or non-intent is nothing to the purpose.

'But while, put to it by those anxieties in you which I cannot but respect, I only repeat myself—while thus strangely we prolong proceedings that should be summary—the enemy may be sighted and an engagement result. We must do; and one of two things must we do—condemn or let go.'

'Can we not convict and yet mitigate the penalty?' asked the sailing master, here speaking, and falteringly, for the first.

'Gentlemen, were that clearly lawful for us under the circumstances, consider the consequences of such clemency. The people' (meaning the ship's company) 'have native sense; most of them are familiar with our naval usage and tradition; and how would they take it? Even could you explain to them— which our official position forbids—they, long molded by arbitrary discipline, have not that kind of intelligent responsiveness that might qualify them to comprehend and discriminate. No, to the people the foretopman's deed, however it be worded in the announcement, will be plain homicide committed in a flagrant act of mutiny. What penalty for that should follow, they know. But it does not follow. *Why?* they will ruminate. You know what sailors are. Will they not revert to the recent outbreak at the Nore? Ay. They know the well-founded alarm—the panic it struck throughout England. Your clement sentence they would account pusillanimous. They would think that we flinch, that we are afraid of them—afraid of practicing a lawful rigor singularly demanded at this juncture, lest it should provoke new troubles. What shame to us such a conjecture on their part, and how deadly to discipline. You see then, whither, prompted by duty and the law, I steadfastly drive. But I beseech you, my friends, do not take me amiss. I feel as you do for this unfortunate boy. But did he know our hearts, I take him to be of that generous nature that he would feel even for us on whom in this military necessity so heavy a compulsion is laid.'

With that, crossing the deck he resumed his place by the sashed porthole,

8. The highest courts of appeal in Great Britain. Melville refers here to the Last Judgment.   9. First passed in 1689; the act and its successors applied only to the army. The navy followed the King's Regulations and Admiralty Instructions of 1772.

tacitly leaving the three to come to a decision. On the cabin's opposite side the troubled court sat silent. Loyal lieges, plain and practical, though at bottom they dissented from some points Captain Vere had put to them, they were without the faculty, hardly had the inclination, to gainsay one whom they felt to be an earnest man, one too not less their superior in mind than in naval rank. But it is not improbable that even such of his words as were not without influence over them, less came home to them than his closing appeal to their instinct as sea officers: in the forethought he threw out as to the practical consequences to discipline, considering the unconfirmed tone of the fleet at the time, should a man-of-war's man's violent killing at sea of a superior in grade be allowed to pass for aught else than a capital crime demanding prompt infliction of the penalty.

Not unlikely they were brought to something more or less akin to that harassed frame of mind which in the year 1842 actuated the commander of the U.S. brig-of-war *Somers* to resolve, under the so-called Articles of War, Articles modeled upon the English Mutiny Act, to resolve upon the execution at sea of a midshipman and two sailors as mutineers designing the seizure of the brig.[1] Which resolution was carried out though in a time of peace and within not many days' sail of home. An act vindicated by a naval court of inquiry subsequently convened ashore. History, and here cited without comment. True, the circumstances on board the *Somers* were different from those on board the *Bellipotent*. But the urgency felt, well-warranted or otherwise, was much the same.

Says a writer whom few know,[2] 'Forty years after a battle it is easy for a noncombatant to reason about how it ought to have been fought. It is another thing personally and under fire to have to direct the fighting while involved in the obscuring smoke of it. Much so with respect to other emergencies involving considerations both practical and moral, and when it is imperative promptly to act. The greater the fog the more it imperils the steamer, and speed is put on though at the hazard of running somebody down. Little ween the snug card players in the cabin of the responsibilities of the sleepless man on the bridge.'

In brief, Billy Budd was formally convicted and sentenced to be hung at the yardarm in the early morning watch, it being now night. Otherwise, as is customary in such cases, the sentence would forthwith have been carried out. In wartime on the field or in the fleet, a mortal punishment decreed by a drumhead court—on the field sometimes decreed by but a nod from the general—follows without delay on the heel of conviction, without appeal.

22

It was Captain Vere himself who of his own motion communicated the finding of the court to the prisoner, for that purpose going to the compartment where he was in custody and bidding the marine there to withdraw for the time.

Beyond the communication of the sentence, what took place at this interview was never known. But in view of the character of the twain briefly closeted in that stateroom, each radically sharing in the rarer qualities of our

1. Melville's cousin, Guert Gansevoort, was first lieutenant of the *Somers* at the time of a mutiny. The incident may have been in the back of Melville's mind when he wrote *Billy Budd*. 2. Melville himself.

nature—so rare indeed as to be all but incredible to average minds however much cultivated—some conjectures may be ventured.

It would have been in consonance with the spirit of Captain Vere should he on this occasion have concealed nothing from the condemned one— should he indeed have frankly disclosed to him the part he himself had played in bringing about the decision, at the same time revealing his actuating motives. On Billy's side it is not improbable that such a confession would have been received in much the same spirit that prompted it. Not without a sort of joy, indeed, he might have appreciated the brave[3] opinion of him implied in his captain's making such a confidant of him. Nor, as to the sentence itself, could he have been insensible that it was imparted to him as to one not afraid to die. Even more may have been. Captain Vere in end may have developed the passion sometimes latent under an exterior stoical or indifferent. He was old enough to have been Billy's father. The austere dev- otee of military duty, letting himself melt back into what remains primeval in our formalized humanity, may in end have caught Billy to his heart, even as Abraham may have caught young Isaac on the brink of resolutely offering him up in obedience to the exacting behest.[4] But there is no telling the sacrament, seldom if in any case revealed to the gadding world, wherever under circumstances at all akin to those here attempted to be set forth two of great Nature's nobler order embrace. There is privacy at the time, invio- lable to the survivor; and holy oblivion, the sequel to each diviner magna- nimity, providentially covers all at last.

The first to encounter Captain Vere in act of leaving the compartment was the senior lieutenant. The face he beheld, for the moment one expressive of the agony of the strong, was to that officer, though a man of fifty, a startling revelation. That the condemned one suffered less than he who mainly had effected the condemnation was apparently indicated by the former's excla- mation in the scene soon perforce to be touched upon.

23

Of a series of incidents within a brief term rapidly following each other, the adequate narration may take up a term less brief, especially if explanation or comment here and there seem requisite to the better understanding of such incidents. Between the entrance into the cabin of him who never left it alive, and him who when he did leave it left it as one condemned to die; between this and the closeted interview just given, less than an hour and a half had elapsed. It was an interval long enough, however, to awaken spec- ulations among no few of the ship's company as to what it was that could be detaining in the cabin the master-at-arms and the sailor; for a rumor that both of them had been seen to enter it and neither of them had been seen to emerge, this rumor had got abroad upon the gun decks and in the tops, the people of a great warship being in one respect like villagers, taking micro- scopic note of every outward movement or non-movement going on. When therefore, in weather not at all tempestuous, all hands were called in the

3. Fine, superior.   4. Genesis 22.1–18: "God did tempt Abraham, and said . . . Take now thy son, thine only son Isaac, whom thou lovest . . . and offer him . . . for a burnt offering. . . . And Abraham . . . bound Isaac his son, and laid him on the altar upon the wood. And Abraham stretched forth his hand, and took the knife to slay his son. And the angel of the Lord . . . said, Lay not thine hand upon the lad, neither do thou anything unto him: for now I know that thou fearest God. . . . And the angel of the Lord . . . said, . . . I will bless thee . . . because thou hast obeyed my voice."

second dogwatch, a summons under such circumstances not usual in those hours, the crew were not wholly unprepared for some announcement extraordinary, one having connection too with the continued absence of the two men from their wonted haunts.

There was a moderate sea at the time; and the moon, newly risen and near to being at its full, silvered the white spar deck wherever not blotted by the clear-cut shadows horizontally thrown of fixtures and moving men. On either side the quarter-deck the marine guard under arms was drawn up; and Captain Vere, standing in his place surrounded by all the wardroom officers, addressed his men. In so doing, his manner showed neither more nor less than that properly pertaining to his supreme position aboard his own ship. In clear terms and concise he told them what had taken place in the cabin: that the master-at-arms was dead, that he who had killed him had been already tried by a summary court and condemned to death, and that the execution would take place in the early morning watch. The word *mutiny* was not named in what he said. He refrained too from making the occasion an opportunity for any preachment as to the maintenance of discipline, thinking perhaps that under existing circumstances in the navy the consequence of violating discipline shoud be made to speak for itself.

Their captain's announcement was listened to by the throng of standing sailors in a dumbness like that of a seated congregation of believers in hell listening to the clergyman's announcement of his Calvinistic text.

At the close, however, a confused murmur went up. It began to wax. All but instantly, then, at a sign, it was pierced and suppressed by shrill whistles of the boatswain and his mates. The word was given to about ship.

To be prepared for burial Claggart's body was delivered to certain petty officers of his mess. And here, not to clog the sequel with lateral matters, it may be added that at a suitable hour, the master-at-arms was committed to the sea with every funeral honor properly belonging to his naval grade.

In this proceeding as in every public one growing out of the tragedy strict adherence to usage was observed. Nor in any point could it have been at all deviated from, either with respect to Claggart or Billy Budd, without begetting undersirable speculations in the ship's company, sailors, and more particularly men-of-war's men, being of all men the greatest sticklers for usage. For similar cause, all communication between Captain Vere and the condemned one ended with the closeted interview already given, the latter being now surrendered to the ordinary routine preliminary to the end. His transfer under guard from the captain's quarters was effected without unusual precautions—at least no visible ones. If possible, not to let the men so much as surmise that their officers anticipate aught amiss from them is the tacit rule in a military ship. And the more that some sort of trouble should really be apprehended, the more do the officers keep that apprehension to themselves, though not the less unostentatious vigilance may be augmented. In the present instance, the sentry placed over the prisoner had strict orders to let no one have communication with him but the chaplain. And certain unobtrusive measures were taken absolutely to insure this point.

24

In a seventy-four of the old order the deck known as the upper gun deck was the one covered over by the spar deck, which last, though not without its armament, was for the most part exposed to the weather. In general it was at all hours free from hammocks; those of the crew swinging on the lower gun deck and berth deck, the latter being not only a dormitory but also the place for the stowing of the sailors' bags, and on both sides lined with the large chests or movable pantries of the many messes of the men.

On the starboard side of the *Bellipotent*'s upper gun deck, behold Billy Budd under sentry lying prone in irons in one of the bays formed by the regular spacing of the guns comprising the batteries on either side. All these pieces were of the heavier caliber of that period. Mounted on lumbering wooden carriages, they were hampered with cumbersome harness of breeching and strong side-tackles for running them out. Guns and carriages, together with the long rammers and shorter linstocks lodged in loops overhead—all these, as customary, were painted black; and the heavy hempen breechings, tarred to the same tint, wore the like livery of the undertakers. In contrast with the funereal hue of these surroundings, the prone sailor's exterior apparel, white jumper and white duck trousers, each more or less soiled, dimly glimmered in the obscure light of the bay like a patch of discolored snow in early April lingering at some upland cave's black mouth. In effect he is already in his shroud, or the garments that shall serve him in lieu of one. Over him but scarce illuminating him, two battle lanterns swing from two massive beams of the deck above. Fed with the oil supplied by the war contractors (whose gains, honest or otherwise, are in every land an anticipated portion of the harvest of death), with flickering splashes of dirty yellow light they pollute the pale moonshine all but ineffectually struggling in obstructed flecks through the open ports from which the tampioned[5] cannon protrude. Other lanterns at intervals serve but to bring out somewhat the obscurer bays which, like small confessionals or side-chapels in a cathedral, branch from the long dim-vistaed broad aisle between the two batteries of that covered tier.

Such was the deck where now lay the Handsome Sailor. Through the rose-tan of his complexion no pallor could have shown. It would have taken days of sequestration from the winds and the sun to have brought about the effacement of that. But the skeleton in the cheekbone at the point of its angle was just beginning delicately to be defined under the warm-tinted skin. In fervid hearts self-contained, some brief experiences devour our human tissue as secret fire in a ship's hold consumes cotton in the bale.

But now lying between the two guns, as nipped in the vice of fate, Billy's agony, mainly proceeding from a generous young heart's virgin experience of the diabolical incarnate and effective in some men—the tension of that agony was over now. It survived not the something healing in the closeted interview with Captain Vere. Without movement, he lay as in a trance, that adolescent expression previously noted as his taking on something akin to the look of a slumbering child in the cradle when the warm hearthglow of the still chamber at night plays on the dimples that at whiles mysteriously form in the cheek, silently coming and going there. For now and then in the gyved[6] one's trance a serene happy light born of some wandering reminiscence or dream would diffuse itself over his face, and then wane away only anew to return.

5. Plugged with a tampion, which fits into the muzzle of a gun not in use.   6. Shackled, chained.

The chaplain, coming to see him and finding him thus, and perceiving no sign that he was conscious of his presence, attentively regarded him for a space, then slipping aside, withdrew for the time, peradventure feeling that even he, the minister of Christ though receiving his stipend from Mars,[7] had no consolation to proffer which could result in a peace transcending that which he beheld. But in the small hours he came again. And the prisoner, now awake to his surroundings, noticed his approach, and civilly, all but cheerfully, welcomed him. But it was to little purpose that in the interview following, the good man sought to bring Billy Budd to some godly understanding that he must die, and at dawn. True, Billy himself freely referred to his death as a thing close at hand; but it was something in the way that children will refer to death in general, who yet among their other sports will play a funeral with hearse and mourners.

Not that like children Billy was incapable of conceiving what death really is. No, but he was wholly without irrational fear of it, a fear more prevalent in highly civilized communities than those so-called barbarous ones which in all respects stand nearer to unadulterate Nature. And, as elsewhere said, a barbarian Billy radically was—as much so, for all the costume, as his countrymen the British captives, living trophies, made to march in the Roman triumph of Germanicus.[8] Quite as much so as those later barbarians, young men probably, and picked specimens among the earlier British converts to Christianity, at least nominally such, taken to Rome (as today converts from lesser isles of the sea may be taken to London), of whom the Pope at that time, admiring the strangeness of their personal beauty so unlike the Italian stamp, their clear ruddy complexion and curled flaxen locks, exclaimed, 'Angles' (meaning *English,* the modern derivative), 'Angles, do you call them? And is it because they look so like angels?'[9] Had it been later in time, one would think that the Pope had in mind Fra Angelico's seraphs, some of whom, plucking apples in gardens of the Hesperides,[1] have the faint rosebud complexion of the more beautiful English girls.

If in vain the good chaplain sought to impress the young barbarian with ideas of death akin to those conveyed in the skull, dial, and crossbones on old tombstones, equally futile to all appearance were his efforts to bring home to him the thought of salvation and a Savior. Billy listened, but less out of awe or reverence, perhaps, than from a certain natural politeness, doubtless at bottom regarding all that in much the same way that most mariners of his class take any discourse abstract or out of the common tone of the workaday world. And this sailor way of taking clerical discourse is not wholly unlike the way in which the primer of Christianity, full of transcendent miracles, was received long ago on tropic isles by any superior *savage,* so called—a Tahitian, say, of Captain Cook's time or shortly after that time.[2] Out of a natural courtesy he received, but did not appropriate. It was like a gift placed in the palm of an outreached hand upon which the fingers do not close.

But the *Bellipotent*'s chaplain was a discreet man possessing the good

---

7. The god of war. I.e., paid by the navy.   8. Germanicus Caesar (15 B.C.–A.D. 19), granted a triumph in Rome in A.D. 17.   9. Bede's *Ecclesiastical History of the English People* tells this anecdote about Pope Gregory the Great (540?–604).   1. Daughters of Atlas who guarded a tree bearing golden apples on an enchanted island in the western sea. Fra Angelico (1387–1455), the Florentine painter Giovanni da Fiesole.   2. James Cook (1728–1779) was in Tahiti in 1769 and from 1772 to 1775.

sense of a good heart. So he insisted not in his vocation here. At the instance of Captain Vere, a lieutenant had apprised him of pretty much everything as to Billy; and since he felt that innocence was even a better thing than religion wherewith to go to Judgment, he reluctantly withdrew; but in his emotion not without first performing an act strange enough in an Englishman, and under the circumstances yet more so in any regular priest. Stooping over, he kissed on the fair cheek his fellow man, a felon in martial law, one whom though on the confines of death he felt he could never convert to a dogma; nor for all that did he fear for his future.

Marvel not that having been made acquainted with the young sailor's essential innocence the worthy man lifted not a finger to avert the doom of such a martyr to martial discipline. So to do would not only have been as idle as invoking the desert, but would also have been an audacious transgression of the bounds of his function, one as exactly prescribed to him by military law as that of the boatswain or any other naval officer. Bluntly put, a chaplain is the minister of the Prince of Peace serving in the host of the God of War—Mars. As such, he is as incongruous as a musket would be on the altar at Christmas. Why, then, is he there? Because he indirectly subserves the purpose attested by the cannon; because too he lends the sanction of the religion of the meek to that which practically is the abrogation of everything but brute Force.

25

The night so luminous on the spar deck, but otherwise on the cavernous ones below, levels so like the tiered galleries in a coal mine—the luminous night passed away. But like the prophet in the chariot disappearing in heaven and dropping his mantle to Elisha,[3] the withdrawing night transferred its pale robe to the breaking day. A meek, shy light appeared in the East, where stretched a diaphanous fleece of white furrowed vapor. That light slowly waxed. Suddenly *eight bells* was struck aft, responded to by one louder metallic stroke from forward. It was four o'clock in the morning. Instantly the silver whistles were heard summoning all hands to witness punishment. Up through the great hatchways rimmed with racks of heavy shot the watch below came pouring, overspreading with the watch already on deck the space between the mainmast and foremast including that occupied by the capacious launch and the black booms tiered on either side of it, boat and booms making a summit of observation for the powder-boys and younger tars. A different group comprising one watch of topmen leaned over the rail of that sea balcony, no small one in a seventy-four, looking down on the crowd below. Man or boy, none spake but in whisper, and few spake at all. Captain Vere—as before, the central figure among the assembled commissioned officers—stood nigh the break of the poop deck facing forward. Just below him on the quarter-deck the marines in full equipment were drawn up much as at the scene of the promulgated sentence.

At sea in the old time, the execution by halter of a military sailor was generally from the foreyard. In the present instance, for special reasons[4] the

---

3. 2 Kings 2.11–13: "There appeared a chariot of fire, and horses of fire, and parted them both asunder; and Elijah went up by a whirlwind into heaven. And Elisha . . . took up . . . the mantle of Elijah that fell from him."   4. The *special reasons* remain obscure. The text editors suggest that the captain's motives were precautionary; the phrase, an insertion, previously read, "for strategic reasons."

mainyard was assigned. Under an arm of that yard the prisoner was presently brought up, the chaplain attending him. It was noted at the time, and remarked upon afterwards, that in this final scene the good man evinced little or nothing of the perfunctory. Brief speech indeed he had with the condemned one, but the genuine Gospel was less on his tongue than in his aspect and manner towards him. The final preparations personal to the latter being speedily brought to an end by two boatswain's mates, the consummation impended. Billy stood facing aft. At the penultimate moment, his words, his only ones, words wholly unobstructed in the utterance, were these: 'God bless Captain Vere!' Syllables so unanticipated coming from one with the ignominious hemp about his neck—a conventional felon's benediction[5] directed aft towards the quarters of honor; syllables too delivered in the clear melody of a singing bird on the point of launching from the twig—had a phenomenal effect, not unenhanced by the rare personal beauty of the young sailor, spiritualized now through late experiences so poignantly profound.

Without volition, as it were, as if indeed the ship's populace were but the vehicles of some vocal current electric, with one voice from alow and aloft came a resonant sympathetic echo: 'God bless Captain Vere!' And yet at that instant Billy alone must have been in their hearts, even as in their eyes.

At the pronounced words and the spontaneous echo that voluminously rebounded them, Captain Vere, either through stoic self-control or a sort of momentary paralysis induced by emotional shock, stood erectly rigid as a musket in the ship-armorer's rack.

The hull, deliberately recovering from the periodic roll to leeward, was just regaining an even keel when the last signal, a preconcerted dumb one, was given. At the same moment it chanced that the vapory fleece hanging low in the East was shot through with a soft glory as of the fleece of the Lamb of God seen in mystical vision, and simultaneously therewith, watched by the wedged mass of upturned faces, Billy ascended; and, ascending, took the full rose of the dawn.

In the pinioned figure arrived at the yard-end, to the wonder of all no motion was apparent, none save that created by the slow roll of the hull in moderate weather, so majestic in a great ship ponderously cannoned.

26

When some days afterwards, in reference to the singularity just mentioned, the purser, a rather ruddy, rotund person more accurate as an accountant than profound as a philosopher, said at mess to the surgeon, "What testimony to the force lodged in will power," the latter, saturnine, spare, and tall, one in whom a discreet causticity went along with a manner less genial than polite, replied. 'Your pardon, Mr Purser. In a hanging scientifically conducted—and under special orders I myself directed how Budd's was to be effected—any movement following the completed suspension and originating in the body suspended, such movement indicates mechanical spasm in the muscular system. Hence the absence of that is no more attributable to will power, as you call it, than to horsepower—begging your pardon.'

'But this muscular spasm you speak of, is not that in a degree more or less invariable in these cases?'

5. It is a traditional ritual for the condemned man to forgive the official compelled by duty to order his death.

'Assuredly so, Mr Purser.'

'How then, my good sir, do you account for its absence in this instance?'

'Mr Purser, it is clear that your sense of the singularity in this matter equals not mine. You account for it by what you call will power—a term not yet included in the lexicon of science. For me, I do not, with my present knowledge, pretend to account for it at all. Even should we assume the hypothesis that at the first touch of the halyards the action of Budd's heart, intensified by extraordinary emotion at its climax, abruptly stopped—much like a watch when in carelessly winding it up you strain at the finish, thus snapping the chain—even under that hypothesis how account for the phenomenon that followed?'

'You admit, then, that the absence of spasmodic movement was phenomenal.'

'It was phenomenal, Mr Purser, in the sense that it was an appearance the cause of which is not immediately to be assigned.'

'But tell me, my dear sir,' pertinaciously continued the other, 'was the man's death effected by the halter, or was it a species of euthanasia?'[6]

'*Euthanasia*, Mr Purser, is something like your *will power*: I doubt its authenticity as a scientific term—begging your pardon again. It is at once imaginative and metaphysical—in short, Greek.—But,' abruptly changing his tone, 'there is a case in the sick bay that I do not care to leave to my assistants. Beg your pardon, but excuse me.' And rising from the mess he formally withdrew.

27

The silence at the moment of execution and for a moment or two continuing thereafter, a silence but emphasized by the regular wash of the sea against the hull or the flutter of a sail caused by the helmsman's eyes being tempted astray, this emphasized silence was gradually disturbed by a sound not easily to be verbally rendered. Whoever has heard the freshet-wave of a torrent suddenly swelled by pouring showers in tropical mountains, showers not shared by the plain; whoever has heard the first muffled murmur of its sloping advance through precipitous woods may form some conception of the sound now heard. The seeming remoteness of its source was because of its murmurous indistinctness, since it came from close by, even from the men massed on the ship's open deck. Being inarticulate, it was dubious in significance further than it seemed to indicate some capricious revulsion of thought or feeling such as mobs ashore are liable to, in the present instance possibly implying a sullen revocation on the men's part of their involuntary echoing of Billy's benediction. But ere the murmur had time to wax into clamor it was met by a strategic command, the more telling that it came with abrupt unexpectedness: 'Pipe down the starboard watch, Boatswain, and see that they go.'

Shrill as the shriek of the sea hawk, the silver whistles of the boatswain and his mates pierced that ominous low sound, dissipating it; and yielding to the mechanism of discipline the throng was thinned by one-half. For the remainder, most of them were set to temporary employments connected with

6. A quiet and easy death.

trimming the yards and so forth, business readily to be got up to serve occasion by any officer of the deck.

Now each proceeding that follows a mortal sentence pronounced at sea by a drumhead court is characterized by promptitude not perceptibly merging into hurry, though bordering that. The hammock, the one which had been Billy's bed when alive, having already been ballasted with shot and otherwise prepared to serve for his canvas coffin, the last offices of the sea undertakers, the sailmakers' mates, were now speedily completed. When everything was in readiness a second call for all hands, made necessary by the strategic movement before mentioned, was sounded, now to witness burial.

The details of this closing formality it needs not to give. But when the tilted plank let slide its freight into the sea, a second strange human murmur was heard, blended now with another inarticulate sound proceeding from certain larger seafowl who, their attention having been attracted by the peculiar commotion in the water resulting from the heavy sloped dive of the shotted hammock into the sea, flew screaming to the spot. So near the hull did they come, that the stridor or bony creak of their gaunt double-jointed pinions was audible. As the ship under light airs passed on, leaving the burial spot astern, they still kept circling it low down with the moving shadow of their outstretched wings and the croaked requiem of their cries.

Upon sailors as superstitious as those of the age preceding ours, men-of-war's men too who had just beheld the prodigy of repose in the form suspended in air, and now foundering in the deeps; to such mariners the action of the seafowl, though dictated by mere animal greed for prey, was big with no prosaic significance. An uncertain movement began among them, in which some encroachment was made. It was tolerated but for a moment. For suddenly the drum beat to quarters,[7] which familiar sound happening at least twice every day, had upon the present occasion a signal peremptoriness in it. True martial discipline long continued superinduces in average man a sort of impulse whose operation at the official word of command much resembles in its promptitude the effect of an instinct.

The drumbeat dissolved the multitude, distributing most of them along the batteries of the two covered gun decks. There, as wonted, the guns' crew stood by their respective cannon erect and silent. In due course the first officer, sword under arm and standing in his place on the quarter-deck, formally received the successive reports of the sworded lieutenants commanding the sections of batteries below; the last of which reports being made, the summed report he delivered with the customary salute to the commander. All this occupied time, which in the present case was the object in beating to quarters at an hour prior to the customary one. That such variance from usage was authorized by an officer like Captain Vere, a martinet as some deemed him, was evidence of the necessity for unusual action implied in what he deemed to be temporarily the mood of his men. 'With mankind,' he would say, 'forms, measured forms, are everything; and this is the import couched in the story of Orpheus with his lyre spellbinding the wild denizens of the wood.'[8] And this he once applied to the disruption of forms going on across the Channel and the consequences thereof.

7. The signal for the sailors to return to their assigned stations.   8. When Orpheus, in Greek mythology, played his lyre and sang, wild animals were charmed, trees and stones followed him, fish left the water in which they swam, and birds flew about his head.

At this unwonted muster at quarters, all proceeded as at the regular hour. The band on the quarter-deck played a sacred air, after which the chaplain went through the customary morning service. That done, the drum beat the retreat; and toned by music and religious rites subserving the discipline and purposes of war, the men in their wonted orderly manner dispersed to the places allotted them when not at the guns.

And now it was full day. The fleece of low-hanging vapor had vanished, licked up by the sun that late had so glorified it. And the circumambient air in the clearness of its serenity was like smooth white marble in the polished block not yet removed from the marble-dealer's yard.

28

The symmetry of form attainable in pure fiction cannot so readily be achieved in a narration essentially having less to do with fable than with fact. Truth uncompromisingly told will always have its ragged edges; hence the conclusion of such a narration is apt to be less finished than an architectural finial.

How it fared with the Handsome Sailor during the year of the Great Mutiny has been faithfully given. But though properly the story ends with his life, something in way of sequel will not be amiss. Three brief chapters will suffice.

In the general rechristening under the Directory of the craft originally forming the navy of the French monarchy, the St. Louis line-of-battle ship was named the Athée (the Atheist). Such a name, like some other substituted ones in the Revolutionary fleet, while proclaiming the infidel audacity of the ruling power, was yet, though not so intended to be, the aptest name, if one consider it, ever given to a warship; far more so indeed than the Devastation, the Erebus (the Hell), and similar names bestowed upon fighting ships.

On the return passage to the English fleet from the detached cruise during which occurred the events already recorded, the Bellipotent fell in with the Athée. An engagement ensued, during which Captain Vere, in the act of putting his ship alongside the enemy with a view of throwing his boarders across her bulwarks, was hit by a musket ball from a porthole of the enemy's main cabin. More than disabled, he dropped to the deck and was carried below to the same cockpit where some of his men already lay. The senior lieutenant took command. Under him the enemy was finally captured, and though much crippled was by rare good fortune successfully taken into Gibraltar, an English port not very distant from the scene of the fight. There, Captain Vere with the rest of the wounded was put ashore. He lingered for some days, but the end came. Unhappily he was cut off too early for the Nile and Trafalgar. The spirit that 'spite its philosophic austerity may yet have indulged in the most secret of all passions, ambition, never attained to the fulness of fame.

Not long before death, while lying under the influence of that magical drug[9] which, soothing the physical frame, mysteriously operates on the subtler element in man, he was heard to murmur words inexplicable to his attendant: 'Billy Budd, Billy Budd.' That these were not the accents of remorse

9. Opium.

would seem clear from what the attendant said to the *Bellipotent*'s senior officer of marines, who, as the most reluctant to condemn of the members of the drumhead court, too well knew, though here he kept the knowledge to himself, who Billy Budd was.

29

Some few weeks after the execution, among other matters under the head of 'News from the Mediterranean,' there appeared in a naval chronicle of the time, an authorized weekly publication, an account of the affair. It was doubtless for the most part written in good faith, though the medium, partly rumor, through which the facts must have reached the writer served to deflect and in part falsify them. The account was as follows:

'On the tenth of the last month a deplorable occurrence took place on board H.M.S. *Bellipotent*. John Claggart, the ship's master-at-arms, discovering that some sort of plot was incipient among an inferior section of the ship's company, and that the ringleader was one William Budd; he, Claggart, in the act of arraigning the man before the captain, was vindictively stabbed to the heart by the suddenly drawn sheath knife of Budd.

'The deed and the implement employed sufficiently suggest that though mustered into the service under an English name the assassin was no Englishman, but one of those aliens adopting English cognomens whom the present extraordinary necessities of the service have caused to be admitted into it in considerable number.

'The enormity of the crime and the extreme depravity of the criminal appear the greater in view of the character of the victim, a middle-aged man respectable and discreet, belonging to that minor official grade, the petty officers, upon whom, as none know better than the commissioned gentlemen, the efficiency of His Majesty's navy so largely depends. His function was a responsible one, at once onerous and thankless; and his fidelity in it the greater because of his strong patriotic impulse. In this instance as in so many other instances in these days, the character of this unfortunate man signally refutes, if refutation were needed, that peevish saying attributed to the late Dr Johnson, that patriotism is the last refuge of a scoundrel.[1]

'The criminal paid the penalty of his crime. The promptitude of the punishment has proved salutary. Nothing amiss is now apprehended aboard H.M.S. *Bellipotent*.'

The above, appearing in a publication now long ago superannuated and forgotten, is all that hitherto has stood in human record to attest what manner of men respectively were John Claggart and Billy Budd.

30

Everything is for a term venerated in navies. Any tangible object associated with some striking incident of the service is converted into a monument. The spar from which the foretopman was suspended was for some few years kept trace of by the bluejackets. Their knowledges followed it from ship to dockyard and again from dockyard to ship, still pursuing it even

---

1. The saying is quoted in James Boswell's *Life of Samuel Johnson Ll. D.* (1791).

when at last reduced to a mere dockyard boom. To them a chip of it was as a piece of the Cross. Ignorant though they were of the secret facts of the tragedy, and not thinking but that the penalty was somehow unavoidably inflicted from the naval point of view, for all that, they instinctively felt that Billy was a sort of man as incapable of mutiny as of wilful murder. They recalled the fresh young image of the Handsome Sailor, that face never deformed by a sneer or subtler vile freak of the heart within. This impression of him was doubtless deepened by the fact that he was gone, and in a measure mysteriously gone. On the gun decks of the *Bellipotent* the general estimate of his nature and its unconscious simplicity eventually found rude utterance from another foretopman, one of his own watch, gifted, as some sailors are, with an artless *poetic* temperament. The tarry hand made some lines which, after circulating among the shipboard crews for a while, finally got rudely printed at Portsmouth as a ballad. The title given to it was the sailor's.

Billy in the Darbies[2]

Good of the chaplain to enter Lone Bay
And down on his marrowbones here and pray
For the likes just o' me, Billy Budd.—But, look:
Through the port comes the moonshine astray!
It tips the guard's cutlass and silvers this nook;   5
But 'twill die in the dawning of Billy's last day.
A jewel-block[3] they'll make of me tomorrow,
Pendant pearl from the yardarm-end
Like the eardrop I gave to Bristol Molly—
O, 'tis me, not the sentence they'll suspend.   10
Ay, ay, all is up; and I must up too,
Early in the morning, aloft from alow.
On an empty stomach now never it would do.
They'll give me a nibble—bit o' biscuit ere I go.
Sure, a messmate will reach me the last parting cup;   15
But, turning heads away from the hoist and the belay,
Heaven knows who will have the running of me up!
No pipe to those halyards.—But aren't it all sham?
A blur's in my eyes; it is dreaming that I am.
A hatchet to my hawser? All adrift to go?   20
The drum roll to grog, and Billy never know?
But Donald he has promised to stand by the plank;
So I'll shake a friendly hand ere I sink.
But—no! It is dead then I'll be, come to think.
I remember Taff the Welshman when he sank.   25
And his cheek it was like the budding pink.
But me they'll lash in hammock, drop me deep.
Fathoms down, fathoms down, how I'll dream fast asleep.
I feel it stealing now. Sentry, are you there?
Just ease these darbies at the wrist,   30
And roll me over fair!
I am sleepy, and the oozy weeds about me twist.

---

2. Handcuffs or fetters.   3. Carries a studding-sail to the very end of the yard where it is hoisted.

EMILY DICKINSON
1830–1886

Emily Dickinson forces her readers to acknowledge the startling aspects of ordinary life. "Ordinary life" includes the mysterious actuality of death, but it also includes birds and woods and oceans, arguments between people, the weight of depression. In small facts and large, Dickinson perceives enormous meaning.

The poet's life, like her verse, was somewhat mysterious. Born to a prosperous and prominent Amherst, Massachusetts, family (her father, a lawyer, was also treasurer of Amherst College), Dickinson attended Amherst Academy and later, for a year, the Mount Holyoke Female Seminary. Thereafter, however, she remained almost entirely in her father's house, leading the life of a recluse. She had close family attachments and a few close friendships, pursued mainly through correspondence. The most important of these relationships, from a literary point of view, was with the Boston writer and critic Thomas Wentworth Higginson, who eventually published her poems. She had begun writing verse in the late 1850s; in 1862, after seeing an essay of Higginson's in the *Atlantic Monthly,* Dickinson wrote him to ask his opinion of her poems, about three hundred of them in existence by this time. The correspondence thus begun continued to the end of Dickinson's life; Higginson also visited her in Amherst.

At Dickinson's death, 1,775 poems survived; only seven had been published, anonymously. With the help of another friend, Mabel Todd Loomis, Higginson selected poems for a volume, published in 1890, which proved extremely popular. Further selections continued to appear, but not until 1955 did Dickinson's entire body of work reach print.

By 1843, the English poet Elizabeth Barrett Browning had written in verse an exhortation to social reform (*The Cry of the Children*); in 1857, she published a long poem, *Aurora Leigh,* commenting on the oppressed situation of women. Christina Rossetti, born the same year as Dickinson and like her unmarried, in poems like *Goblin Market* (1862) found indirect ways to meditate on female predicaments. Dickinson, on the other hand, seems only peripherally aware of social facts. She alludes to church services, locomotives, female costume; very occasionally (for example, in "My Life had stood—a Loaded Gun—") she refers to the way a woman's life is defined in relation to a man's. More centrally, she finds brilliant and provocative formulations of the emotional import of universal phenomena. We may feel already that death amounts to an incomprehensible and indigestible fact, but we are unlikely to have imagined conversations within a tomb or a personified version of death as carriage driver. By using such images, Dickinson disarmingly suggests a kind of playful innocence. Only gradually does one realize that the naive, childlike perception, devoid of obviously ominous suggestion, conceals a complex, disturbing sense of human self-deception and reluctance to face the truth of experience.

Truth is an important word in Dickinson's poetry. "Tell all the Truth but tell it slant," she advises, pointing out that "The Truth must dazzle gradually / Or every man be blind—." She tells of a man who preaches about " 'Truth' until it proclaimed him a Liar—": truth remains an absolute, both challenging and judging us all. In one of her most haunting poems, she claims the identity of Beauty and Truth (an identity tellingly asserted earlier in Keats's *Ode on a Grecian Urn*) through the fiction of two dead people discussing their profound commitments:

> I died for Beauty—but was scarce
> Adjusted in the Tomb
> When One who died for Truth, was lain
> In an adjoining Room—

Her neighbor asks her why she "failed"; when she explains, he says that beauty and truth "are One":

And so, as Kinsmen, met a Night—
We talked between the Rooms—
Until the Moss had reached our lips—
And covered up—our names—

Until the last two lines, about the moss, the poem appears to evoke a rather cozy vision of death: neighbors amiably conversing from one room to another, as though at a slumber party ("met a Night"), two "Kinsmen" dedicated to noble abstractions and comforted by the companionship of their dedication. Only the word *failed* (meaning "died") disturbs the comfortable atmosphere, by suggesting a view of death as defeat.

The Keats poem that ends by asserting the identity of truth and beauty implies the permanence of both, as embodied in the work of art, the Grecian urn that stimulates the poet's reflections. Dickinson's poem concludes with troubling suggestions of impermanence. Talk of beauty and truth may reassure the talkers, but death necessarily implies forgetfulness: the dead forget and are forgotten, their very identities ("names") lost, their capacity for communication eliminated. Death *is* defeat; the high Romanticism of Keats's ode, on which this poem implicitly comments, blurs that fact. Despite Dickinson's fanciful images and allegories, her poems insist on their own kind of uncompromising realism. They speak of the universal human effort to imagine experience in reassuring terms, but they do not suggest that reality offers much in the way of reassurance: only brief experiences of natural beauty; and even those challenge human constructions. "I started Early—Took my dog—" a poem about visiting the sea begins; but it ends with the sea encountering "the Solid Town— / No One He seemed to know—" and withdrawing.

Dickinson's eccentric punctuation, with dashes as the chief mark of emphasis and interruption, emphasizes the movements of consciousness in her lyrics. In their early publication, the poems were typically given conventional punctuation; only in 1955 did the body of work appear as Dickinson wrote it. The highly personal mode of punctuation emphasizes the fact that this verse contains also a personal and demanding vision.

Emily Dickinson: An Interpretive Biography (1955), by T. H. Johnson, Dickinson's editor, is indispensable. Useful critical sources include C. Blake, ed., *The Recognition of Emily Dickinson* (1964), a collection of criticism since 1890; Albert Gelpi, *Emily Dickinson: The Mind of the Poet* (1966); P. Bennett, *Emily Dickinson: Woman Poet* (1990); S. Juhasz, ed., *Feminist Critics Read Emily Dickinson* (1983), a collection with a specifically feminist orientation; and J. Dobson, *Dickinson and the Strategies of Reticence* (1989). Other critical studies are K. Stocks, *Emily Dickinson and the Modern Consciousness* (1988), and M. N. Smith, *Rowing in Eden: Rereading Emily Dickinson* (1992).

216

Safe in their Alabaster Chambers—
Untouched by Morning
And untouched by Noon—
Sleep the meek members of the Resurrection—
Rafter of satin,
And Roof of stone.   5

Light laughs the breeze
In her Castle above them—
Babbles the Bee in a stolid Ear,

Pipe the Sweet Birds in ignorant cadence—   10
Ah, what sagacity perished here!

258

There's a certain Slant of light,
Winter Afternoons—
That oppresses, like the Heft
Of Cathedral Tunes—

Heavenly Hurt, it gives us—   5
We can find no scar,
But internal difference,
Where the Meanings, are—

None may teach it—Any—
'Tis the Seal Despair—   10
An imperial affliction
Sent us of the Air—

When it comes, the Landscape listens—
Shadows—hold their breath—
When it goes, 'tis like the Distance   15
On the look of Death—

303

The Soul selects her own Society—
Then—shuts the Door—
To her divine Majority—
Present no more—

Unmoved—she notes the Chariots—pausing   5
At her low Gate—
Unmoved—an Emperor be kneeling
Upon her Mat—

I've known her—from an ample nation—
Choose One—   10
Then—close the Valves of her attention—
Like Stone—

328

A Bird came down the Walk—
He did not know I saw—
He bit an Angleworm in halves
And ate the fellow, raw,

And then he drank a Dew 5
From a convenient Grass—
And then hopped sidewise to the Wall
To let a Beetle pass—

He glanced with rapid eyes
That hurried all around— 10
They looked like frightened Beads, I thought—
He stirred his Velvet Head

Like one in danger, Cautious,
I offered him a Crumb
And he unrolled his feathers 15
And rowed him softer home—

Than Oars divide the Ocean,
Too silver for a seam—
Or Butterflies, off Banks of Noon
Leap, plashless as they swim. 20

341

After great pain, a formal feeling comes—
The Nerves sit ceremonious, like Tombs—
The stiff Heart questions was it He, that bore,
And Yesterday, or Centuries before?

The Feet, mechanical, go round— 5
Of Ground, or Air, or Ought[1]—
A Wooden way
Regardless grown,
A Quartz contentment, like a stone—

This is the Hour of Lead— 10
Remembered, if outlived,
As Freezing persons, recollect the Snow—
First—Chill—then Stupor—then the letting go—

435

Much Madness is divinest Sense—
To a discerning Eye—
Much Sense—the starkest Madness—
'Tis the Majority
In this, as All, prevail— 5
Assent—and you are sane—
Demur—you're straightway dangerous—
And handled with a Chain—

1. Zero

449

I died for Beauty—but was scarce
Adjusted in the Tomb
When One who died for Truth, was lain
In an adjoining Room—

He questioned softly "Why I failed"?   5
"For Beauty", I replied—
"And I—for Truth—Themself are One—
We Brethren, are", He said—

And so, as Kinsmen, met a Night—
We talked between the Rooms—   10
Until the Moss had reached our lips—
And covered up—our names—

465

I heard a Fly buzz—when I died—
The Stillness in the Room
Was like the Stillness in the Air—
Between the Heaves of Storm—

The Eyes around—had wrung them dry—   5
And Breaths were gathering firm
For that last Onset—when the King
Be witnessed—in the Room—

I willed my Keepsakes—Signed away
What portion of me be   10
Assignable—and then it was
There interposed a Fly—

With Blue—uncertain stumbling Buzz—
Between the light—and me—
And then the Windows failed—and then   15
I could not see to see—

519

'Twas warm—at first—like Us—
Until there crept upon
A Chill—like frost upon a Glass—
Till all the scene—be gone.

The Forehead copied Stone—   5
The Fingers grew too cold
To ache—and like a Skater's Brook—
The busy eyes—congealed—

It straightened—that was all—
It crowded Cold to Cold   10
It multiplied indifference—
As[1] Pride were all it could—

And even when with Cords—
'Twas lowered, like a Weight—
It made no Signal, nor demurred,   15
But dropped like Adamant.

585

I like to see it lap the Miles—
And lick the Valleys up—
And stop to feed itself at Tanks—
And then—prodigious step

Around a Pile of Mountains—   5
And supercilious peer
In Shanties—by the sides of Roads—
And then a Quarry pare

To fit its Ribs
And crawl between   10
Complaining all the while
In horrid—hooting stanza—
Then chase itself down Hill—

And neigh like Boanerges[1]—
Then—punctual as a Star   15
Stop—docile and omnipotent
At its own stable door—

632

The Brain—is wider than the Sky—
For—put them side by side—
The one the other will contain
With ease—and You—beside—

The Brain is deeper than the sea—   5
For—hold them—Blue to Blue—
The one the other will absorb—
As Sponges—Buckets—do—

---

1. As if.   1. "Sons of thunder," name given by Jesus to the brothers and disciples James and John, presumably because they were thunderous preachers.

The Brain is just the weight of God—
For—Heft them—Pound for Pound— 10
And they will differ—if they do—
As Syllable from Sound—

657

I dwell in Possibility—
A fairer House than Prose—
More numerous of Windows—
Superior—for Doors—

Of Chambers as the Cedars— 5
Impregnable of Eye—
And for an Everlasting Roof
The Gambrels[1] of the Sky—

Of Visitors—the fairest—
For Occupation—This— 10
The spreading wide my narrow Hands
To gather Paradise—

712

Because I could not stop for Death—
He kindly stopped for me—
The Carriage held but just Ourselves—
And Immortality.

We slowly drove—He knew no haste 5
And I had put away
My labor and my leisure too,
For His Civility—

We passed the School, where Children strove
At Recess—in the Ring— 10
We passed the Fields of Gazing Grain—
We passed the Setting Sun—

Or rather—He passed Us—
The Dews drew quivering and chill—
For only Gossamer, my Gown— 15
My Tippet—only Tulle[1]—

We paused before a House that seemed
A Swelling of the Ground—
The Roof was scarcely visible—
The Cornice—in the Ground— 20

1. Slopes, as in the large, arched roofs often seen on barns.   1. Fine, silken netting. *Tippet:* a scarf.

Since then—'tis Centuries—and yet
Feels shorter than the Day
I first surmised the Horses' Heads
Were toward Eternity—

754

My Life had stood—a Loaded Gun—
In Corners—till a Day
The Owner passed—identified—
And carried Me away—

And now We roam in Sovereign Woods—   5
And now We hunt the Doe—
And every time I speak for Him—
The Mountains straight reply—

And do I smile, such cordial light
Upon the Valley glow—   10
It is as a Vesuvian face[1]
Had let its pleasure through—

And when at Night—Our good Day done—
I guard My Master's Head—
'Tis better than the Eider-Duck's   15
Deep Pillow—to have shared—

To foe of His—I'm deadly foe—
None stir the second time—
On whom I lay a Yellow Eye—
Or an emphatic Thumb—   20

Though I than He—may longer live
He longer must—than I—
For I have but the power to kill,
Without—the power to die—

1084

At Half past Three, a single Bird
Unto a silent Sky
Propounded but a single term
Of cautious melody.

At Half past Four, Experiment   5
Had subjugated test
And lo, Her silver Principle
Supplanted all the rest.

1. A face glowing with light like that from an erupting volcano.

At Half past Seven, Element
Nor Implement, be seen—
And Place was where the Presence was
Circumference between.

10

1129

Tell all the Truth but tell it slant—
Success in Circuit lies
Too bright for our infirm Delight
The Truth's superb surprise

As Lightning to the Children eased
With explanation kind
The Truth must dazzle gradually
Or every man be blind—

5

1207

He preached upon "Breadth" till it argued him narrow—
The Broad are too broad to define
And of "Truth" until it proclaimed him a Liar—
The Truth never flaunted a Sign—

Simplicity fled from his counterfeit presence
As Gold the Pyrites[1] would shun—
What confusion would cover the innocent Jesus
To meet so enabled[2] a Man!

5

1564

Pass to thy Rendezvous of Light,
Pangless except for us—
Who slowly ford the Mystery
Which thou hast leaped across!

1593

There came a Wind like a Bugle—
It quivered through the Grass
And a Green Chill upon the Heat
So ominous did pass
We barred the Windows and the Doors

5

---

1. Iron bisulfide, sometimes called fool's gold.   2. Competent.

As from an Emerald Ghost—
The Doom's electric Moccasin[1]
That very instant passed—
On a strange Mob of panting Trees
And Fences fled away   10
And Rivers where the Houses ran
Those looked that lived—that Day—
The Bell within the steeple wild
The flying tidings told—
How much can come   15
And much can go,
And yet abide the World!

---

1. I.e., water moccasin, a poisonous snake.

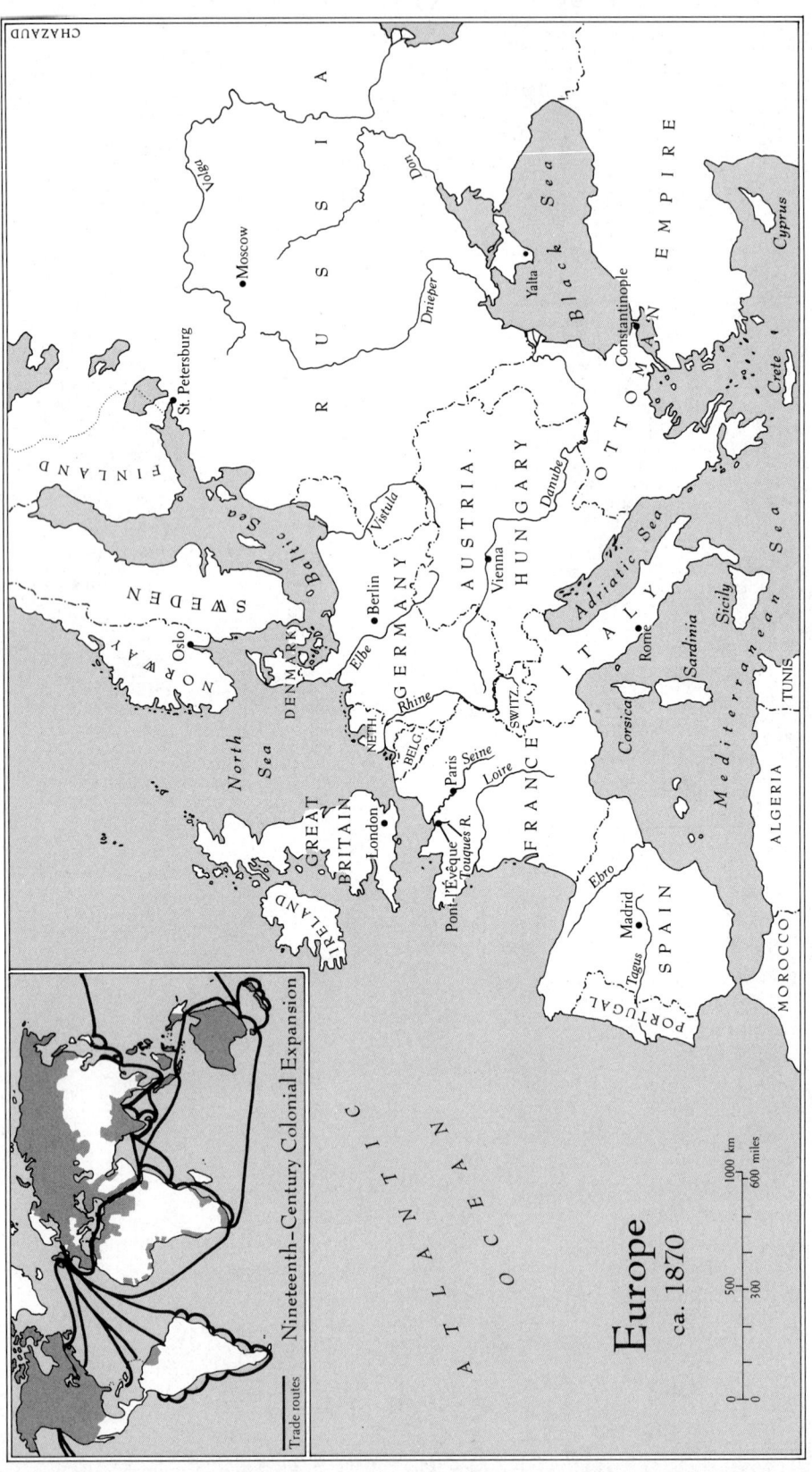

CHAZAUD

Volga

Moscow

Don

Dnieper

Black Sea

Yalta

Constantinople

St. Petersburg

OTTOMAN EMPIRE

Cyprus

FINLAND

RUSSIA

Baltic Sea

SWEDEN

Vistula

AUSTRIA-HUNGARY

Crete

NORWAY

Oslo

DENMARK

Elbe

Berlin

GERMANY

Vienna

Danube

Adriatic Sea

ITALY

Rome

Sardinia

Sicily

Mediterranean Sea

North Sea

Rhine

NETH.

BELG.

SWITZ.

Corsica

TUNIS

ALGERIA

GREAT BRITAIN

London

Paris

Seine

Loire

FRANCE

IRELAND

Pont-l'Évêque

Touques R.

Ebro

MOROCCO

SPAIN

Madrid

Tagus

PORTUGAL

Nineteenth-Century Colonial Expansion

Trade routes

ATLANTIC OCEAN

Europe

ca. 1870

1000 km

600 miles

500

300

0

0

Masterpieces of the Nineteenth Century: Realism, Naturalism, Symbolism

The nineteenth century is (apart from our own) the century of greatest change in the history of Western civilization. The upheavals following the French Revolution broke up the old order of Europe. The Holy Roman Empire and the Papal States were dissolved. Nationalism, nourished by the political and social aspirations of the middle classes, grew by leaps and bounds. Colonial empires were created and vast sections of the globe opened up forcibly to Western trade. "Liberty" became the dominant political slogan of the century, although the various calls for liberty focused on Western society and not on the colonies. In different countries and different decades *liberty* meant different things: here liberation from the rule of the foreigner, there the emancipation of the serf; here the removal of economic restrictions on trade and manufacturing, there the introduction of a constitution, free speech, parliamentary institutions, and agitation for the rights of women. Almost everywhere in Europe, the middle classes established their effective rule, though revolutions in 1830 and 1848 were crushed across Europe and monarchs remained in more or less nominal power. Two large European countries, Germany and Italy, achieved their centuries-old dreams of political unification. The predominance of France, still marked at the beginning of the century, was broken, and England—or rather Great Britain—ruled the seas throughout the century. The smaller European nations, especially in the Balkans, began to emancipate themselves from foreign rule.

These major political changes were caused by, and in their turn caused, great social and economic changes. The Industrial Revolution, which had begun in England in the eighteenth century, spread over the Continent and transformed living conditions radically. The enormous increase in the speed and availability of transportation owing to the development of railroads and steamships and the rapid urbanization following from the establishment of industries changed the whole pattern of human life in most countries and made possible, within a century, an unprecedented increase in population (as much as threefold in most European countries), which was also fostered by the advances of medicine and hygiene. The development of transportation and communication systems brought areas of the world into closer contact and prepared the way for global economic and political systems. The existence of widespread wealth and prosperity is undeniable, although it coexisted with wretched living conditions and other hardships of the early factory workers, many of them women. As the social and political power of the aristocracy declined, the barriers between the social classes diminished appreciably almost everywhere. Middle-class values dominated, and the industrial laborer began to be felt as a political force.

These social and economic changes were closely bound up with shifts in prevailing outlooks and philosophies. Technological innovation is impossible without the discoveries of science. The scientific outlook, hitherto dominant only in a comparatively limited area, spread widely and permeated almost all fields of human thought and endeavor. It raised enormous hopes for the future betterment of our condition on Earth, especially when Darwin's evolutionary theories fortified the earlier, vaguer faith in unlimited progress. "Liberty," "science," "progress," and "evolution" are the concepts that define the mental atmosphere of the nineteenth century in Europe.

But tendencies hostile to these were by no means absent. Feudal or Catholic conservatism succeeded, especially in Austria-Hungary, in Russia, and in much of southern Europe, in preserving old regimes, and the philosophies of a conservative and religious society were reformulated in modern terms. At the same time, in England the very assumptions of the new industrial middle-class society were powerfully attacked by writers such as Carlyle and Ruskin who recommended a return to medieval forms of social cooperation and handicraft. The industrial civilization of the nineteenth century was also opposed by the fierce individualism of many artists and thinkers who were unhappy in the ugly, commercial, and "Philistine" society of the age. The writings of Nietzsche, toward the end of the century, and the whole movement of art for art's sake, which asserted the independence of the artist from society, are the most obvious symptoms of this revolt. The free-enterprise system and the liberalism of the ruling middle classes also early clashed with the rising proletariat; diverse forms of socialism developed, preaching a new collectivism with the stress on equality. Socialism could have Christian or romantic motivations, or it could become "scientific" and revolutionary, as Marx's brand of socialism (a certain stage of which he called "communism") claimed to be.

While up through the eighteenth century religion was, at least in name, a major force in European civilization, in the nineteenth century there was a marked decrease in its influence on both intellectual leaders and ordinary people. Local, intense revivals of religious consciousness, such as the Oxford movement in England, did occur, and the traditional religious institutions were preserved everywhere, but the impact of science on religion was such that many tenets of the old faiths crumbled or were severely weakened. The discoveries of astronomy, geology, evolutionary biology, and archaeology as well as biblical criticism forced, almost everywhere, a restatement of the old creeds. Religion, especially in the Protestant countries, was frequently confined to an inner feeling of religiosity or to a system of morality that preserved the ancient Christian virtues. In Germany during the early nineteenth century, Hegel and his predecessors and followers tried to interpret the world in spiritual terms, outside the bounds of traditional religion. There were many attempts even late in the century to restate this view, but the methods and discoveries of science seemed to invalidate it, and various formulas that took science as their base in building new lay religions of hope in humanity gained popularity. French positivism, English utilitarianism, the evolutionism of Herbert Spencer are some of the best-known examples. Meanwhile, for the first time in history, at least in Europe, profoundly pessimistic and atheistic philosophies arose, of which Schopenhauer's was the most subtle, while extreme materialism was the most widespread. Thus the whole gamut of views of the universe was represented during the century in new and impressive formulations.

The plastic arts did not show a similar vitality. For a long time, in most countries, painting and architecture floundered in a sterile eclecticism—in a bewildering variety of historical masquerades in which the neo-Gothic style was replaced by the neo-Renaissance and that by the neo-Baroque and other decorative revivals of past forms. Only in France did painting (with the Impressionists) find a new style that was genuinely original. In music the highly Romantic art of Richard Wagner attracted the most attention. Wagner's concept of the *Gesamtkunstwerk*—the "total work" combining music, drama, poetry, and spectacle—influenced Symbolist writers and encouraged the tendency to break down distinctions between genres. Otherwise, the individual national schools either continued in their tradition, like Italian opera (Verdi), or founded an idiom of their own, often based on a revival of folklore, as in Russia (Tchaikovsky), Poland (Chopin), Bohemia (Dvořák), and Norway (Grieg).

But literature was the most representative and the most widely influential art of nineteenth-century Europe. It found new forms and methods and expressed the social and intellectual situation of the time most fully and memorably. It was this literature, moreover, that served as a model for many non-Western writers seeking to modernize their own literary traditions on the basis of European masterworks. Nowadays, the cultural assumptions of such literary emulation are criticized by some, and many writers seek to rediscover an earlier, precolonial tradition. The literature of nineteenth-century Europe continues nonetheless to be read and admired in its own right.

REALISM AND NATURALISM

After the great wave of the international Romantic movement had spent its force in the fourth decade of the nineteenth century, European literature moved in the direction of what is usually called *realism*. Realism was not a coherent general movement that established itself unchallenged for a long period of time, as classicism had succeeded in doing during the eighteenth century. Exceptions and reservations there were, but still in retrospect the nineteenth century appears as the period of the great realistic writers: Flaubert in France, Dostoevsky and Tolstoy in Russia, Charles Dickens in England, Henry James in America, Ibsen in Norway.

What is meant by *realism*? The term, in literary use (there is a much older philosophical use), apparently dates back to the Germans at the turn of the century—to Friedrich Schiller and August and Friedrich Schlegel. It cropped up in France as early as 1826 but became a commonly accepted literary and artistic slogan only in the 1850s. When Gustave Courbet's paintings were rejected by the Paris World's Fair of 1855, the artist exhibited them separately as "realist" art and wrote a preface to the exhibit catalog that became an unofficial manifesto for realist art. In the following year, a review called *Réalisme* began publication, and in 1857 a novelist and critic, Champfleury (the pseudonym of Jules-François-Félix Husson), published a volume of critical articles with the title *Le Réalisme*. Since then the word has been bandied about, discussed, analyzed, and abused as all slogans are. It is frequently confused with naturalism, an ancient philosophical term for materialism, epicureanism, or any secularism. As a specifically literary term, it crystallized only in France. In French, as in English, naturalist means, of course, simply student of nature, and the analogy between the writer and the naturalist, specifically the botanist and zoologist, was ready at hand. Émile Zola, in the preface to a new edition of his early novel *Thérèse Raquin* (1866), proclaimed the naturalist creed most boldly. His book, he claims, is "an analytical labor on two living bodies like that of a surgeon on corpses." He proudly counts himself among the group of "naturalist writers."

The program of the groups of writers and critics who used these terms can be easily summarized. The realists wanted a truthful representation in literature of reality—that is, of contemporary life and manners. They thought of their method as inductive, observational, and hence "objective." The personality of the author was to be suppressed or was at least to recede into the background, since reality was to be seen "as it is." The naturalistic program, as formulated by Zola, was substantially the same, except that Zola put greater stress on the analogies to science, considering the procedure of the novelist as identical with that of the experimenting scientist. He also more definitely and exclusively embraced the philosophy of scientific materialism, with its deterministic implications and its stress on heredity and environment, while the older realists were not always so clear in drawing the philosophical consequences. These French theories were anticipated, paralleled, or imitated all over the world of Western literature. In Germany, the movement called Young Germany, with which Heine was associated, had propounded a substantially anti-Romantic realistic program as early as the 1830s, but versions of the French theories definitely triumphed there only in the 1880s. In Russia, as early as the 1840s, the most prominent critic of the time, Vissarion Belinsky, praised the "natural" school of Russian fiction, which described contemporary Russia with fidelity. Italy also, from the late 1870s on, produced an analogous movement, which called itself *verismo*. The English-speaking countries were the last to adopt the critical programs and slogans of the Continent: George Moore and George Gissing brought the French theories to England in the late 1880s, and in the United States William Dean Howells began his campaign for realism in 1886, when he became editor of *Harper's Magazine*. Realistic and naturalistic theories of literature have since been widely accepted, either as the basis of writing or as a standard against which later generations rebel. The once officially promoted doctrine in Russia is called "Socialist Realism," a combination of factual observation and implied socialist message; the novel in the United States is usually considered naturalistic and judged by the standards of nature and truth. Yet twentieth-century novelists in Europe and America have also pushed realism to an extreme in the "literature of fact," in documentary novels, and in often-bewildering series of undifferentiated "objective" perceptions reported by the narrator.

The slogans "realism" and "naturalism" were thus new to the nineteenth century and served as effective formulas directed against the Romantic creed. Truth, contemporaneity, and objectivity were the obvious counterparts of Romantic imagination, of Romantic historicism and its glorification of the past, and of Romantic subjectivity, the exaltation of the ego and the individual. But, of course, the emphasis on truth and objectivity was not really new: these qualities had been demanded by many older, classical theories of imitation, and in the eighteenth century there were great writers such as Denis Diderot who wanted a literal "imitation of life" even on the stage.

The practice of realism, it could be argued, is very old indeed. There are realistic scenes in the *Iliad* and *Odyssey*, and there is plenty of realism in ancient comedy and satire, in medieval stories (fabliaux) like some of Chaucer's and Boccaccio's, in many Elizabethan plays, in the Spanish rogue novels, in the English eighteenth-century novel beginning with Daniel Defoe, and so on almost ad infinitum. But while it would be easy to find in early literature anticipations of almost every single element of modern realism, still the systematic description of contemporary society, with a serious purpose, often even with a tragic tone as well, and with sympathy for heroes drawn from the middle and lower classes, was a real innovation of the nineteenth century.

It is usually rash to explain a literary movement in social and political terms. But the new realistic art surely had something to do with the triumph of the middle classes in France after the July revolution in 1830, and in England after the passage of the Reform Bill in 1832, and with the increasing influence of the middle classes in almost every country. Russia is somewhat of an exception as no large middle class could develop there during the nineteenth century. An absolute feudal regime continued in power and the special character of most of Russian literature must be the result of this distinction, but even in Russia there emerged an "intelligentsia" (the term comes from Russia) that was open to Western ideas and was highly critical of the czarist regime and its official ideology.

But while much nineteenth-century literature reflects the triumph of the middle classes, it would be an error to think of the great realistic writers as spokespeople or mouthpieces of the society they described. Honoré de Balzac was politically a Catholic monarchist who applauded the Bourbon restoration after the fall of Napoleon, but he had an extraordinary imaginative insight into the processes leading to the victory of the middle classes. Flaubert despised the middle-class society of the Third Empire with an intense hatred and the pride of a self-conscious artist. Dickens became increasingly critical of the middle classes and the assumptions of industrial civilization. Dostoevsky, though he took part in a conspiracy against the Russian government early in his life and spent ten years in exile in Siberia, became the propounder of an extremely conservative nationalistic and religious creed that was definitely directed against the revolutionary forces in Russia. Tolstoy, himself a count and a landowner, was violent in his criticism of the czarist regime, especially later in his life, but he cannot be described as friendly to the middle classes, to the aims of the democratic movements in Western Europe, or to the science of the time. Ibsen's political attitude was that of a proud individualist who condemns the "compact majority" and its tyranny. Possibly all art is critical of its society, but in the nineteenth century this criticism became much more explicit, as social and political issues became much more urgent or, at least, were regarded as more urgent by those writing about or within them. To a far greater degree than in earlier centuries, writers felt their isolation from society, viewed the structure and problems of the prevailing order as debatable and reformable, and in spite of all demands for objectivity became, in many cases, social propagandists and reformers in their own right.

The program of realism, while defensible enough as a reaction against Romanticism, raises critical questions that were not answered theoretically by its defenders. What is meant by *truth of representation?* Photographic copying? This seems the implication of many famous pronouncements: "A novel is a mirror walking along the road," said Stendhal (the pseudonym of Marie-Henri Beyle) as early as 1830. But such statements can hardly be taken literally. All art must select and represent; it cannot be and has never been a simple transcript of reality. What such analogies are intended to convey is rather a claim for an all-inclusiveness of subject matter, a protest against the exclusion of themes that before were considered low, sordid, or trivial (like the puddles along the road the mirror walks). Chekhov formulated this protest with the usual parallel between the scientist and the writer: "To a chemist nothing on earth is unclean. A writer must be as objective as a chemist; he must abandon the subjective line: he must know that dung heaps play a very respectable part in a landscape, and that evil passions are as inherent in life as good ones." Thus the truth of realistic art includes the sordid, the low, the disgusting, and the evil; and the implication is that the subject is treated objectively, without interference and falsification by the artist's personality and his own desires.

But in practice, while realistic art succeeded in expanding the themes of art, it could not fulfill the demand for total objectivity. Works of art are written by human beings and inevitably express their personalities and their points of view. As Joseph Conrad admitted, "even the most artful of writers will give himself (and his morality) away in about every third sentence." Objectivity, in the sense that Zola had in mind when he proposed a scientific method in the writing of novels and conceived of the novelist as a sociologist collecting human documents, is impossible in practice. When it has been attempted, it has led only to bad art, to dullness and the display of inert materials, to the confusion between the art of the novel and reporting, documentation. The demand for objectivity can be understood only as a demand for a specific method of narration, in which the author does not interfere explicitly, in his or her own name, and as a rejection of personal themes of introspection and reverie.

The realistic program, while it has made innumerable new subjects available to art, also implies a narrowing of its themes and methods—a condemnation of the fantastic, the historical, the remote, the idealized, the unsullied, the idyllic. Realism professes to present us with a slice of life. But one should recognize that it is an artistic method and convention like any other. Romantic art could, without offending its readers, use coincidences, improbabilities, and even impossibilities that were not, theoretically at least, tolerated in realistic art. Ibsen, for instance, avoided many older conventions of the stage: asides, soliloquies, eavesdropping, sudden unmotivated appearances of new characters, and so on; but his dramas have their own marked conventions, which seem today almost as "unnatural" as those of the Romantics. Realistic theories of literature cannot be upheld in their literal sense; objective and impersonal truth is unobtainable, at least in art, since all art is a making, a creating of a world of symbols that differs radically from the world that we call reality. The value of realism lies in its negation of the conventions of Romanticism, its expansion of the themes of art, and its new demonstration (never forgotten by artists) that literature has to deal also with its time and society and has, at its best, an insight into reality (not only social reality) that is not necessarily identical with that of science. Many of the great writers make us realize the world of their time, evoke an imaginative picture of it that seems truer and will last longer than that of historians and sociologists. But this achievement is owing to their imagination and their art, or craft, two requisites that realistic theory tended to forget or minimize.

When we observe the actual practice of the great realistic writers of the nineteenth century, we notice a sharp contradiction between theory and practice, and an independent evolution of the art of the novel that is obscured for us if we pay too much attention to the theories and slogans of the time, even those that the authors themselves propounded. Flaubert, the high priest of a cult of art for art's sake, the most consistent advocate of absolute objectivity, was actually, at least in a good half of his work, a writer of Romantic fantasies of blood and gold, flesh and jewels. There is some truth in his saying that Madame Bovary is himself, for in the drab story of a provincial adulteress he castigated his own Romanticism and Romantic dreams.

So too with Dostoevsky. Although some of his settings resemble those of the crime novel, he is actually a writer of high tragedy, of a drama of ideas in which ordinary reality is transformed into a symbol of the spiritual world. His technique is closely associated with Balzac's (it is significant that his first publication was a translation of Balzac's *Eugénie Grandet*) and thus with many devices of the sensational melodramatic novel of French Romanticism. Tolstoy's art is more concretely real than that of any of the other great masters mentioned, yet he is, at the same time, the most personal and even literally autobiographical author in the history of the novel—a writer, besides, who knows nothing of detachment toward social and religious problems but frankly preaches his own very personal religion. And if we turn to Ibsen, we find essentially the same situation. Ibsen began as a writer of historical and fantastic dramas and slowly returned to a style that is fundamentally symbolist. All his later plays are organized by symbols, from the duck of *The Wild Duck* (1884) to the white horses in *Rosmersholm* (1886), the burned manuscript in *Hedda Gabler* (1890), and the tower in *The Master Builder* (1892). Even Zola, the propounder of the most scientific theory, was in practice a novelist who used the most extreme devices of melodrama and Symbolism. In *Germinal* (1885), his novel of mining, the mine is the central symbol, alive as an animal, heaving, breathing. It would be an odd reader who could find literal truth in the final catastrophe of the cave-in or even in such naturalistic scenes as a dance where the beer oozes from the nostrils of the drinkers.

One could assert, in short, that all the great realists were at bottom Romanticists, but it is probably wiser to conclude that they were simply artists who created worlds of imagination and knew (at least instinctively) that in art one can say something about reality only through symbols. The attempts at documentary art, at mere reporting and transcribing, are today forgotten.

SYMBOLISM

The later nineteenth century cannot, however, be considered simply an age of realism and naturalism. Poetry addressed in its own way the same questions of truth and reality. By the middle of the century, it was embarked on an exploration of language that would influence all forms of twentieth-century literature. Where prose fiction and drama faced outward, aiming to mirror the real world, poetry turned its attention to the mirror itself: the words that reflect and represent reality. Preserving the Romantic notion of the poet as seer or visionary, emphasizing a heightened self-consciousness and an inquiry into poetic language, the innovators of nineteenth-century poetry explored both creativity and human identity. They examined the perceiving subject's awareness of perceptions and illustrated this awareness in allusive poetry that played with multiple and shifting perspectives and frequently led to a blurring of boundaries between real and imaginary. Traditional verse forms exploded, and the new forms heralded not only modern free verse, prose poems, and spatial poetry but also the innovative language of novelists such as James Joyce, William Faulkner, Alain Robbe-Grillet, and Marguerite Duras.

The evolution was gradual until the middle of the century. Some poets continued to practice a substantially Romantic art: Tennyson, for instance, and Victor Hugo. In England, the Pre-Raphaelite movement—painters and writers such as J. E. Millais (1829–1896), W. H. Hunt (1827–1910), and D. G. Rossetti (1828–1882)—drew their inspiration from the sensuous detail of Italian medieval art in opposition to the honored Renaissance painter Raphael (1483–1520); they upheld a Romantic, escapist, and antirealist program. In France, a large and diverse group of Parnassian poets stemming from Leconte de Lisle (1818–1894) retained Romantic themes while focusing on a precise and delicate use of detail. The most important writer of this period is Charles Baudelaire (1821–1867), whose poetry and writings on art deeply influenced the course of European poetry. Baudelaire's major collection of poems, *The Flowers of Evil*, was published in the same year that Flaubert was brought to trial for *Madame Bovary* (1857). He inspired a poetic movement that would later be called Symbolism, and he remains today the French poet most widely read outside France.

Symbolism as *symbolic representation* is a philosophical concept, and the use of symbols is not restricted to the nineteenth and twentieth centuries. Using one thing to suggest another, or an image to suggest an idea, is as old as art and language. The Neolithic paintings in the caves at Lascaux, France, are symbolic pictures of the hunt. Medieval Christian literature used a shared set of symbols to signify religious concepts through earthly images: the rose symbolized love, the dove the Holy Spirit, and the serpent Satan. As a literary movement, however, Symbolism is a nineteenth-century French phenomenon with affinities to the visionary writings of eighteenth-century German Romanticism, to the Parnassian cult of artistic form and art for art's sake, and to the poetic theories of Edgar Allan Poe. Confusingly enough, the official Symbolist "movement"—whose manifesto appeared only in 1886—derives from, but does not include, the great midcentury poets Baudelaire, Verlaine, Rimbaud, and Mallarmé. These highly individual writers were never part of any movement. Yet there are elements in common, and the ancestors of Symbolism are often discussed in the same breath as their followers. Symbolist poetry tries to manipulate language in an almost magical way to evoke hidden meanings behind the appearances of this world. A symbol in this sense is an image or cluster of images created to suggest another plane of reality that cannot be expressed in more direct and rational terms. Each poem transforms reality in its own manner, leading the reader to its own version of truth. The aim is to touch a primitive level of being where, for example, in Baudelaire's poem *Correspondences*, the five senses fuse: colors have taste, sights have physical texture, sounds have odors, and so on. (This fusion is called *synesthesia*.) Symbolist poetry may lead to abstract or visionary conclusions, but it is firmly based in images as realistic as a rotting carcass, logs falling on the pavement, and a mangy cat trying to find a comfortable spot in rainy weather (Baudelaire's *A Carcass, Song of Autumn I*, and *Spleen LXXVIII*). It is not, therefore, an escape from natural reality so much as a transformation of it, the creation of a new world reassembled in the mind from pieces of the old.

After Symbolic allusion, the second great theme of Symbolist poetry is language: language as a means of communication and language as the necessary but flawed tool of poetic creation. Like Flaubert seeking *le mot juste* (the exact word), Symbolist poets are haunted by the difficulty of writing: Baudelaire described his exhausted brain as a graveyard, and Stéphane Mallarmé felt paralyzed by "the empty paper whose whiteness defends it." The difficulty for the Symbolists is that their ideal poetic language must be distilled out of ordinary language through a totally controlled arrangement of all possible levels of form. Sound patterns, image clusters, and intertwined systems of logical and psychological associations act to create a complex architecture of inner reference. It is the relationship of words that counts, not just their dictionary definitions; the artist is, in a sense, a technician. The extraordinary self-consciousness of the Symbolist poet soon became an accepted element of the poem itself. Some poems focused on difficulties of communication (a characteristic Romantic theme); others, like Baudelaire's *Windows*, asserted joy in using language to imagine other existences and to sense, in return, their own reality. The Symbolists' acute awareness of the possibilities and limitations of language has influenced both philosophers of language and literary theorists in the twentieth century.

Symbolist writers frequently compared their poetry to music, whose characteristics they tried to reproduce; Paul Verlaine (1844–1896) is especially known for the musicality of his verse. Both poetry and music they felt to be pure arts, in which line and harmony (including calculated dissonance) meant more than separate notes or the definitions of individual words. They saw analogies, too, between their art and painting, where distinctive new methods of depicting reality were being developed in the same period. Symbolist poetry and Impressionist art both represented moves away from the conventional realistic representation of reality; and in the poetic as in the art world, they both outraged the average citizen by their apparent betrayal of common sense.

Baudelaire's most important successors were very different figures: an English teacher, Stéphane Mallarmé (1842–1898); a sometime clerk and French teacher, Paul Verlaine; and the adolescent prodigy Arthur Rimbaud (1854–1891). In a short and violent literary career between the ages of fifteen and twenty, Rimbaud attempted to become a seer or *voyant* through hallucinatory writing expressing the "disorder of all the senses." His rebellion against home and authority, his experiments with drugs and alcohol, his love affair with Verlaine, and his search for a transfigured condition beyond ordinary experience all provide themes for this poetic quest. Ultimately, the poet became disenchanted with the efficacy of his magical or "alchemical" art, and he abruptly stopped writing. He left for Africa, where he spent the last eighteen years of his life trying to make a living. A good deal of Rimbaud's legend comes from this extraordinary example of a great poet who simply did not find what he sought in literature and, therefore, ceased to write. Rimbaud's work and the integrity of his spiritual commitment had enormous influence on later writers, especially the surrealists.

Paul Verlaine, conversely, had an immediate influence on the new generation of French poets for whom his revolutionary verse forms held a fascination almost equaled by the scandalous figure of the poet himself. Verlaine's *Art of Poetry* recommended music, nuance, and ambiguity instead of the conventionally prized intellect, clarity, and force; and his own poetry emphasized emotion and mood rather than philosophy or moral persuasion. He introduced short, impressionistic sketches that establish a mood, usually melancholy alienation, and strengthened that mood by creating a related music of word sounds and rhythm. Unlike previous classical poetry with its regular alexandrines (twelve-syllable lines), Verlaine's poems used shorter, irregular, continuous, and almost conversational lines that echo the rhythms of speech. Although his example directly inspired the free verse of later Symbolist and modern poetry, he himself cherished the musicality achieved by patterns of rhythm and rhyme.

Stéphane Mallarmé was a quiet and somewhat scholarly poet who spent his life in a search for absolute poetry *in language*. Mallarmé loved words and distrusted the sloppiness of everyday speech. He envisaged a special poetic language that would be built out of the precisely planned interaction of ordinary words, in poems that would "give a purer sense to the words of the crowd." Mallarmé's long poem *Dice Thrown*, with its startling arrangement of different type sizes and words scattered to create patterns on the page, heralded concrete poetry and other modern attempts to use the silence of blank space as part of poetry. Toward the end of his life, he considered everything he produced to be a fragment of an ultimate Work that he feared he would never be able to write: a massively interrelated composition of pure poetry whose function would be to assert the dignity of human imagination in the face of universal nothingness. Mallarmé uses Symbolist tactics in that he prefers allusion and suggestion to direct speech, or—a specifically Mallarméan theme—potentiality and absence to a fixed and limited reality. Material objects like a bracelet, a fan, a harp, or a lace curtain, are described so as to evoke other elements in another realm of being. A carved angel's wing gilded by the sun evokes a harp; the harp exists only in the imagination, however, and its implied music is doubly unreal because the source is merely suggested, not represented. This music is even more ambiguous than Keats's "melodies . . . unheard," for it is a musical *silence*.

It is paradoxical that none of these poets—Baudelaire, Mallarmé, Rimbaud, or Verlaine—was a member of the Symbolist movement. Symbolist doctrine as such dates to a manifesto issued in 1886 by a minor poet, Jean Moréas (Yánnis Papadia-mantópoulous, 1856–1910). In many ways the movement is a systematization and popularization of ideas gleaned from Baudelaire, Rimbaud, Mallarmé, and Verlaine; especially influential were Verlaine's essays in 1884 describing Rimbaud, Mallarmé, and Tristan Corbière (1845–1875) as outcast or "accursed poets." A number of young poets (often called "Decadents") were attracted to Symbolist ideas and proclaimed Verlaine their master; their publication and literary reviews flourished around the turn of the century. Symbolism as a movement, however, had less impact than the major poets from whom it sprang; and it was the example of these earlier poets that especially influenced writers such as W. B. Yeats, T. S. Eliot, Marcel Proust, Rainer Maria Rilke, Wallace Stevens, and others around the world for whom Symbolist poetry became the model for contemporary poetry and poetics.

A NOTE ON FRENCH POETRY

English poetry receives its rhythm from the accent or stress in words, and the most common English line is iambic pentameter ("Whatever is begotten, born, and dies"). In contrast, the rhythm of French poetry is based on *quantity*—on the number and pattern of syllables in a line. The most common French line is the twelve-syllable, or alexandrine, verse, usually divided into balanced segments of six or four syllables. Baudelaire's *Correspondances* (given in French on page 1147) is a sonnet written in alexandrines that displays many of the conventions of French poetry.

Syllables are divided to reflect the sound of the line when read aloud; thus every syllable should begin with a consonant whenever possible. ("Na / tu / re . . . con / fu / ses / pa / roles.") In traditional French poetry, the unaccented or mute *e* counts as a syllable and is pronounced when it occurs before a sounded consonant (but not otherwise): thus "Com / *me* / les / prai / ries" (line 10) sound the mute *e* but "La / Na / tu / re est / un / tem / ple où" (line 1) does not. The subtle use of the mute *e* provides rich sonorous effects that are evident only in reading aloud.

French rhymes are categorized as rich, sufficient, or weak and also as masculine or feminine. Weak rhymes have only one accented vowel in common: prair*ies* / infi-n*ies* (the *ee* sound). Sufficient rhymes have two elements in common: en*fants* / triom*phants*. A rich rhyme has three or more elements in common: pil*iers* / famil-*iers* (*i, l,* and the diphthong *ier*). A variety of rhymes is desirable. Feminine rhymes end in the sound of a mute *e: paroles / symboles* or *rose / chose.* All other rhymes are masculine. After the sixteenth century most poets alternated masculine and feminine rhymes. In *Correspondances,* Baudelaire uses the Petrarchan sonnet form (two quatrains, two tercets) with a rhyme scheme alternating masculine and feminine rhymes as follows: *mffm fmmf mfm fmm.* The intricacy of these and other poetic effects makes clear why later poets revered Baudelaire as a master of classical form as well as a visionary.

FURTHER READING

E. Auerbach, *Mimesis: The Representation of Reality in Western Literature* (1953), is a wide-ranging book (from Homer to Proust), with chapters on nineteenth-century realism. G. J. Becker, ed., *Documents of Modern Literary Realism* (1973), surveys the development of modern realism and offers documents and essays from 1835 to 1955. H. Levin, *The Gates of Horn: A Study of Five French Realists* (1963), contains much on realism in general, including Stendhal, Balzac, Flaubert, Zola, and Proust. Linda Nochlin, *Realism* (1971), discusses realism in the visual arts. Marcel Raymond, *From Baudelaire to Surrealism* (1933), is a fundamental study of the evolution of the new poetry. Naomi Schor, *Breaking the Chain: Women, Theory, and French Realist Fiction* (1985), discusses the realist fiction of Flaubert, Zola, Balzac, and others in terms of feminist and psychoanalytic theory. Also helpful is R. Wellek, "The Concept of Realism in Literary Scholarship," in *Concepts of Criticism* (1963). Nicholas Boyle and Martin Swales, eds., *Realism in European Literature: Essays in Honour of J. P. Stern* (1986), is a varied and useful collection that includes a discussion of realism related to modernism and language consciousness. Elise Boulding, *The Underside of History: A View of Women through Time* (1992), arranged by periods and sociological categories, contains much pertinent information about the role of women that is omitted from traditional histories. John Rignall, *Realist Fiction and the Strolling Spectator* (1992), indebted to Nietzsche and Walter Benjamin, analyzes realism's distanced point of view in eight nineteenth-century and three twentieth-century novelists. Laurence M. Porter, *The Crisis of French Symbolism* (1990), situates the poetry of Baudelaire, Mallarmé, Verlaine, and Rimbaud between neoclassicism and the Symbolist school. An influential and still valuable presentation is found in *The Symbolist Movement in Literature* (1980, orig. 1899), by the English Symbolist Arthur Symons. P. Mansell Jones, *The Background of Modern French Poetry* (1951, repr. 1968), describes the influence of Poe, Baudelaire, Mallarmé, and Whitman on modern free verse. Georges Poulet, *Exploding Poetry* (1984), trans. Françoise Meltzer, interprets the poetry of Baudelaire and Rimbaud.

PRONOUNCING GLOSSARY

The following list uses common English syllables and stress accents to provide rough equivalents of selected words whose pronunciation may be unfamiliar to the general reader.

Balzac: *bahl-zak'*

Baudelaire: *boh-d'lair'*

Champfleury: *shom-fler-ee'*

Chekhov: *cheh'-hoff*

Chopin: *sho-panh*

Corbière: *core-bee-air'*

Courbet: *coor-bay'*

Dostoevsky: *dos-toy-eff'-skee*

Dvořák: *dvor'-zhak*

fabliaux: *fah-blee-oh'*

Gesamtkunstwerk: *ge-zamt-koonst'-varck*

Grieg: *greeg*

Mallarmé: *mal-are-may'*

Nietzsche: *neech'-uh*

Réalisme: *ray-al-eezm'*

Rimbaud: *ram-boh'*

Schlegel: *shlay'-gel*

Stendhal: *ston-dall'*

Tchaikovsky: *chai-kof'-skee*

Verlaine: *vehr-len'*

Wagner: *vag'-ner*

Zola: *zoh-lah'*

REALISM, NATURALISM, SYMBOLISM

TEXTS	CONTEXTS
1856 Gustave Flaubert, *Madame Bovary*	
1857 Charles Baudelaire, *The Flowers of Evil*	
	1859 Charles Darwin, *Origin of Species*
	1861 Serfs emancipated in Russia
	1861–1865 Civil War in the United States
1864 Fyodor Dostoevsky, *Notes from Underground*	
1866 Dostoevsky, *Crime and Punishment*	
1866 Émile Zola's preface to his novel *Thérèse Raquin* argues for a "naturalist" style analogous to methods in experimental science	
1869 Leo Tolstoy, *War and Peace*	1869 Suez Canal completed
	1870 Ernest Renan's *Life of Jesus* offers a historical approach to the New Testament
1871 George Eliot (Mary Ann Evans), *Middlemarch*	
1874 Paul Verlaine, *Songs without Words*	1874 Claude Monet's painting *Impression: Rising Sun* launches Impressionism as a style
1876 Stéphane Mallarmé, *The Afternoon of a Faun*	1876 Invention of the telephone
	1884–1885 Berlin Conference agrees on procedures for European acquisition of African territory; by 1914, all Africa except Ethiopia and Liberia succumbs to European rule
1886 Arthur Rimbaud's *Illuminations* • Tolstoy, *The Death of Ivan Ilyich*	1886 Friedrich Nietzsche's *Beyond Good and Evil* proclaims a "life force," a "will to power," and a "superman" who embodies these qualities
	1887 Eiffel Tower built for the 1889 Paris World's Fair • Gottlieb Daimler's internal combustion engine for the automobile
1890 Henrik Ibsen, *Hedda Gabler* • *Poems* of Emily Dickinson (1830–1886) published posthumously	
	1894 X rays discovered
	1894–1906 In the Dreyfus Affair, anti-Semitic sentiment polarizes France
	1898 Radium discovered by Marie and Pierre Curie • Spanish-American War breaks out
1899 Anton Chekhov, *The Lady with the Dog*	
1904 Anton Chekhov, *The Cherry Orchard* performed	

Boldface titles indicate works in the anthology.

GUSTAVE FLAUBERT
1821–1880

Gustave Flaubert is rightly considered the exemplary realist novelist and *Madame Bovary* his masterpiece. He displays the objectivity, the detachment from his characters demanded by the theory, and is a great virtuoso of the art of composition and of style while giving a clear picture of the society of his time. It is likewise a picture in which we can see much of ourselves.

Flaubert was born in Rouen, Normandy, on December 12, 1821, to the chief surgeon of the Hôtel Dieu. He was extremely precocious: by the age of sixteen he was writing stories in the romantic taste, which were published only after his death. In 1840 he went to Paris to study law (he had received his baccalaureate from the local *lycée*), but he failed in his examinations and in 1843 suffered a sudden nervous breakdown that kept him at home. In 1846 he moved to Croisset, just outside Rouen on the Seine, where he made his home for the rest of his life, devoting himself to writing. The same year, in Paris, Flaubert met Louise Colet, a minor writer and socialite, who became his mistress. In 1849–51 he visited the Levant, traveling extensively in Greece, Syria, and Egypt. After his return he settled down to the writing of *Madame Bovary,* which took him five full years and which, despite accusations of immorality, was a great popular success. The remainder of his life was uneventful. He made occasional trips to Paris, and one trip, in 1860, to Tunisia to see the ruins of Carthage in preparation for the writing of his novel *Salammbô* (1862). Three more novels followed: *The Sentimental Education* (1869), *The Temptation of St. Anthony* (1874), and the unfinished *Bouvard and Pecuchet* (1881), as well as *Three Tales* (1877), consisting of *A Simple Heart, The Legend of St. Julian the Hospitaler,* and *Herodias.* Flaubert died in Croisset on May 8, 1880.

Madame Bovary (1856) is deservedly considered the showpiece of French realism. It would be impossible to find a novel, certainly before Flaubert, in which relatively humble persons in a humble setting are treated with such seriousness, restraint, verisimilitude, and imaginative clarity. At first sight, *Madame Bovary* is a solidly documented and clearly visualized account of life in a village of the French province of Normandy sometime in the 1840s. We meet a whole spectrum of social types found in such a time and place: the doctor (actually a "health officer" with a lower degree), a pharmacist, a storekeeper, a notary and his clerk, a tax collector, a woman innkeeper and her stable boy, the priest and his sacristan, a neighboring landowner, and a farmer. We are told the story of a young peasant woman brought up in a convent, who marries a dull man and commits adultery first with a ruthless philanderer and then with a spineless younger man. Overwhelmed by debts concealed from her unsuspecting husband, faced by sudden demands for repayment, disillusioned in love, rebuffed by everybody who might help her, she commits suicide by poisoning herself with arsenic. Nothing seems simpler or more ordinary, and the manner of telling seems completely objective, detached, impersonal. A case is presented that is observed with almost scientific curiosity. The descriptions are obviously accurate, sometimes based on expert knowledge; the clubfoot operation and the effects of arsenic poisoning agree with medical evidence. The setting—the topography of the two villages, the interior of the houses, the inn, the pharmacy, the city of Rouen, the cathedral there, the river landscape, and the particular things and sounds—imprints itself vividly on our memory. Every detail serves its purpose of characterization—from the absurd cap of the schoolboy Charles to the mirror and the crucifix in the deathbed scene; from the sound of Binet's lathe turning out napkin rings to the tap of the stable boy's wooden leg. "The technique of *Madame Bovary* has become the model of all novels" (Albert Thibaudet).

But surely the book could not have kept its grip on modern readers if it were only a superbly accurate description of provincial life in France, as the added subtitle,

Mœurs de province (provincial manners) suggests. The book transcends its time and place if one thinks of Emma Bovary as the type of the unfulfilled dreamer, as the failed and foiled romanticist, as a female Don Quixote, corrupted by sentimental reading, caught in a trap of circumstance, pitiful and to be pitied in her horrible self-inflicted death.

This central theme has, however, remained ambiguous. What attracted and shocked readers was the uncertainty about the author's attitude toward Emma, particularly at the time of publication when readers were accustomed to being told clearly by addresses and comments what they were to think of the actions and morals of the characters of a novel. *Madame Bovary,* at publication, caused a scandal. The *Paris Review,* in which it was published serially, and the author were hauled into court for immorality and blasphemy; and the prosecutor described the book as an incitement to adultery and atheism. In his rebuttal, the defense counsel argued that the novel is rather a highly moral work in which adultery is punished, even excessively. Flaubert was acquitted, but neither the prosecutor nor the defending attorney interpreted the book correctly. It is neither a salacious novel nor a didactic tract. Some parts of the book are frankly satirical (and thus far from purely objective): the gross village priest who cannot even understand the distress of Emma is flanked by the fussy, shallow, pseudoscientific, enlightened, "progressive" pharmacist Homais. Though they argue and quarrel, they are finally reduced to a common level when they eat and snore at the wake next to Emma's corpse. The rightly famous scene of the country fair satirizes and parodies the pompous rhetoric of the officials extolling the glories of agriculture, counterpointing it to the equally platitudinous love talk of Rodolphe and the lowing of the cattle in an amalgam that reduces men and women to a common level of animality. Even Emma is not spared: her sentimental religiosity, her taste for luxury, her financial improvidence are diagnosed as disguised eroticism. She would not have minded if Rodolphe had drawn a pistol against her husband. In her desperate search for escape she asks Léon to steal for her. In the last attempt to get money she is ready to sell herself. She is indifferent to her child, deceitful even in small matters. Her longing for sensual satisfaction becomes, in the scenes with Léon in the hotel at Rouen, frantic and corrupt. The author weighted the scales against her: she married an excessively stupid and insensitive man; she met two callous lovers; she is tricked by a merciless usurer; she is utterly alone at last. When Charles meeting Rodolphe after her death and after he had discovered her infidelities tells him, ineptly, awkwardly, "It was the fault of destiny," the author expressly approves of this statement. The novel conveys a sense of inexorable determinism, of the vanity of dreaming, of the impossibility of escape from one's nature and station. It conveys a sense of despair, of alienation in an incomprehensible universe—but also a hatred for all the stupidity, mediocrity and baseness of people there and everywhere. (Flaubert called them bourgeois, but included the proletarian masses in his contempt.) Emma is pitied because she has, at least, a spark of discontent, the yearning to escape the cage of her existence. But baseness triumphs and the book ends with a sudden change to the present tense: "Homais has just received the Cross of the Legion of Honor."

This sense of the inexorable, the fatal, the inescapable is secured also by the precision and firmness of Flaubert's style and the carefully planned architectonics of his composition. If we mean by style the systematic exploitation of the syntactical and lexical possibilities of a language we must class Flaubert with the great stylists. His keen sense of the exact descriptive epithet, the one right word *(le mot juste)*— even when he uses the most trivial cliché or the most recondite scientific term— coheres with the skillful modulations and rhythms of the sentences; the organization of the paragraphs; and the divisions of the sections, which are grouped around a series of pictorial scenes: the schoolroom, the rustic wedding, the ball, the visit to the priest, the country fair, the ride in the woods, the clubfoot operation, the opera, the cathedral, the cab ride, the deathbed, to mention only the most memorable.

Madame Bovary is constantly cited as an example for the handling of narrative perspective. The story begins in the schoolroom ostensibly told by a schoolfellow (the word *we* is used in the first pages); it shifts then to the narration of an omniscient author and, off and on, narrows to the point of view of Emma. Much is seen only through her eyes, but one cannot say that the author identifies with her or enters her mind sympathetically. He keeps his distance and on occasion conveys his own opinion. He is not averse even to moral judgments: he speaks of Emma's hard-hearted and tightfisted peasant nature (p. 889), he refers to her depravity (p. 1018), and Rodolphe is several times condemned for his brutality and cynicism (pp. 928, 965, 972). In the description of extreme unction (p. 1047) the author pronounces solemnly his forgiveness (which he suggests would be also God's) for her coveting all worldly goods, her greediness "for the warm breeze and scents of love," and even her sensuality and lust. But mostly Flaubert depicts the scenes by simple description or reproduction of speech or imagined silent reflections. Things and people become at times symbolic even in an obtrusive way: the wedding bouquet, the plate of boiled beef, and the apparition of the blind beggar who turns up conveniently at the hour of Emma's death. Much is said about her that she could not have observed herself. The famous saying "Madame Bovary c'est moi" ("I am Madame Bovary") cannot be traced back to an earlier date than 1909, when it is reported on distant hearsay in René Descharmes, *Flaubert before 1857*. There are dozens of passages in the letters during the composition of *Madame Bovary* that express Flaubert's distaste for the "vulgarity of his subject," "the fetid smell of the milieu," and his opinion of Emma Bovary as "a woman of false poetry and false sentiments." Usually he defends his choice of theme as a "prodigious *tour de force*," as "an act of crude willpower," as "a deliberate made-up thing," though we suspect him sometimes of exaggerating his efforts to impress his correspondent in Paris, a facile and prolific novelist and poet, Louise Colet.

Still, the saying "Madame Bovary c'est moi" has been widely quoted and accepted because it contains a kernel of truth. In Emma, Flaubert combats his own vices of daydreaming, romanticism, exoticism, of which he thought he could cure himself by writing this antiromantic book. But the identification with Emma distracts us from noticing Flaubert's deep-seated sympathies with the slow-witted, abused, but honest and loving Charles, who rightly opens and closes the book, and for the other good people: Emma's father, the farmer Rouault, kind and distressed by all he could not foresee; Justin, the pharmacist's apprentice adoring Emma from afar, praying on her grave; the clubfoot stable boy tortured and exploited for a dream of medical reputation; poor neglected Berthe sent to the cotton mill; the old peasant woman at the fair who for fifty-four years of service got a medal worth twenty-five francs; and even the blind beggar with his horrible skin disease. Moreover, there is the admirable Dr. Larivière, who appears fleetingly like an apparition from a saner, loftier world of good sense and professional devotion. Thus it seems unjust of the critic Martin Turnell to say that the novel is "an onslaught on the whole basis of human feeling and on all spiritual and moral values."

In Flaubert's mind, the novel was also an assertion of the redeeming power of art. His long struggle with its composition, which took him more than five years of grinding drudgery: five days in which he had written a single page, five or six pages in a week, twenty-five pages in six weeks, thirteen pages in seven weeks, a whole night spent in hunting for the right adjective; the ruthless pruning to which he subjected his enormous manuscript, eliminating many fine touches, similes, metaphors, and descriptions of elusive mental states (as a study of the manuscripts has shown) were to him a victory of art over reality, a passionate search for Beauty, which he knew to be an illusion. But one wonders whether the conflict of Flaubert's scientific detachment and cruel observation with the intense adoration of beauty, the thirst for calculated purity and structure, for "style" as perfection, can be resolved. He tried to achieve this synthesis in *Madame Bovary*. Watching this struggle between heterogeneous elements, and even opposites, explains some of the fascination of the book.

[*Editor's Note.* An explanation of the plot and the stage business is needed to understand properly the performance in *Madame Bovary* of the opera *Lucia di Lammermoor,* which occurs on pages 984–88 of this text. There are substantial differences between the French version, which Flaubert apparently followed, and the original Italian libretto, which will be more familiar to modern music lovers. The basic story is one of family hatred: Edgar, the owner of the castle of Ravenswood in the Scottish Highlands, has been expelled by Lord Henry Ashton who had killed his father. He is in hiding as an outlaw. He loves and is loved clandestinely by Lucy, Lord Henry's sister. The opera opens with a hunting scene on the grounds of Ravenswood castle where Henry, his forester called Gilbert (Normanno in the Italian), and other followers comb the grounds for traces of a mysterious stranger whom they suspect to be the outcast Edgar. They are joined by Lord Arthur, who is a suitor for Lucy's hand and is favored by her brother, as he can save him from financial ruin. Arthur declares his love for Lucy (no such scene is in the Italian). Lucy in the next scene prepares to meet Edgar in a secluded spot; she gives a purse to Gilbert, whom she believes to be her friend though Gilbert is actually scheming with Lord Henry against her. (The scene is not in the Italian original.) Then Lucy is left alone and sings a cavatina beginning: "Que n'avons-nous des ailes" ("If only we had wings"). Edgar appears then, played by Lagardy, a fictional tenor. He tells of his hatred for Lucy's brother because of the death of his father. He had sworn vengeance but is ready to forget it in his love for her. Edgar has to leave on a mission to France, but in parting the lovers pledge their troth and exchange rings. The stretto contains the words "Une fleur pour ma tombe" ("A flower for my tomb"), "donne une larme à l'exilé" ("give a tear for the exiled one"), phrases alluded to in Flaubert's account.

Charles is so obtuse that he thinks Edgar is torturing Lucy, and Emma has to tell him that he is her lover. Charles protests that he heard him vowing vengeance on her family. He had heard him saying: "J'ai juré vengeance et guerre" ("I have sworn vengeance and war"). Charles has also heard Lord Arthur say, "J'aime Lucie et m'en crois aimé" ("I love Lucie and I believe she loves me") and has seen Lord Arthur going off with her father arm in arm. But Charles obviously takes her brother Henry for her father.

The second act begins with Gilbert telling his master Henry that he slipped Lucy's ring from the sleeping Edgar, had made a copy, and will produce it to convince Lucy of Edgar's faithlessness. Charles mistakes the false ring, which is shown to Lucy, for a love gift sent by Edgar. The business with the rings replaces an analogous deception with forged letters in the Italian libretto. Lucy appears dressed for the wedding with Lord Arthur, unhappily resisting and imploring, reminding Emma of her own wedding day and the contrast with her false joy soon turned to bitterness. Brandishing a sword, Edgar suddenly returns voicing his indignation. There follows a sextet (Lucy, Henry, Edgar, Raimondo the minister, Arthur, Gilbert) that suggests to Emma her desire to flee and to be carried off as Edgar wants to carry off Lucy. But the marriage contract has been signed and Edgar curses her. The third act does not interest Emma any more as Léon has appeared in the interval. She does not care for the scene between Lord Henry and his retainer (called here "servant") Gilbert, who introduces a disguised stranger, Edgar, of course. The duet between Henry Lord Ashton and Edgar reaffirms their mutual hatred. The mad scene follows. Lucy flees the marriage chamber; she has stabbed her husband and gone mad. She dreams of Edgar and dies. The great aria that was considered the climax of coloratura singing was lost on Emma, who is absorbed in Léon.

One must assume that Flaubert had the French libretto in front of him or remembered its wordings and stage business accurately. (He had seen the opera first in Rouen in 1840 and again in Constantinople in November 1850.) A modern reader who knows the Italian libretto from recordings may be puzzled by the discrepancies and ascribe to Flaubert's imagination or confused memory what is actually an accurate description of the French version.]

William Berg and Laurey K. Martin, *Gustave Flaubert* (1997), is a general introduction to Flaubert's life and work. Victor Brombert, *The Novels of Flaubert* (1966), has an excellent chapter on *Madame Bovary*; Raymond D. Giraud, ed., *Flaubert: A Collection of Critical Essays* (1964), and Harold Bloom, ed., *Emma Bovary* (1994), provide a range of short studies. Paul de Man, ed., *Gustave Flaubert: Madame Bovary. Backgrounds and Sources: Essays in Criticism* (1965), will help the reader, as will Alison Fairlie, *Flaubert: Madame Bovary* (1962), a good discussion of problems, structures, people, and values addressed to students. The chapter on *Madame Bovary* in Anthony Thorlby, *Gustave Flaubert and the Art of Realism* (1957), is still to be recommended, as is Margaret Lowe, *Toward the Real Flaubert: A Study of Madame Bovary* (1984).

PRONUNCIATION GLOSSARY

The following list uses common English syllables and stress accents to provide rough equivalents of selected words whose pronunciation may be unfamiliar to the general reader.

Berthe: *behrt*

Binet: *bee-nay'*

Bovary: *boh-vahr-ee'*

Canivet: *cah-nee-vay'*

Flaubert: *floh-bair'*

Guillaumin: *gee-oh-manh'*

Homais: *oh-me'*

huissier: *wee-syay'*

Larivière: *lah-ree-vyehr'*

La Vaubyessard: *lah-vohb-yes-ahr'*

Léon Dupuis: *lay-ohn' dyew-pwee'*

Les Bertaux: *lay behr-toh'*

Lestiboudois: *les-tee-boo-dwah'*

Lheureux: *leu-reu'*

Rodolphe Boulanger de la Huchette:
    ro-dawlf' boo-lawn-zhay'
    deu la ew-shet'

Rouault: *roo-oh'*

Rouen: *roo-awnh'*

Tostes: *tost*

Vinçart: *vanh-sahr'*

Yonville: *yohnh-veel'*

Yvetot: *eev-toh'*

Madame Bovary[1]

Part One

I

We were in study-hall when the headmaster entered, followed by a new boy not yet in school uniform and by the handyman carrying a large desk. Their arrival disturbed the slumbers of some of us, but we all stood up in our places as though rising from our work.

The headmaster motioned us to be seated; then, turning to the teacher:

"Monsieur Roger," he said in an undertone, "here's a pupil I'd like you to keep your eye on. I'm putting him in the last year of the lower school. If he does good work and behaves himself we'll move him up to where he ought to be at his age."

The newcomer, who was hanging back in the corner so that the door half hid him from view, was a country lad of about fifteen, taller than any of us.

---

1. Translated by Francis Steegmuller.

He had his hair cut in bangs like a cantor in a village church, and he had a gentle, timid look. He wasn't broad in the shoulders, but his green jacket with its black buttons seemed tight under the arms; and through the vents of his cuffs we could see red wrists that were clearly unaccustomed to being covered. His yellowish breeches were hiked up by his suspenders, and from them emerged a pair of blue-stockinged legs. He wore heavy shoes, hobnailed and badly shined.

We began to recite our lessons. He listened avidly, as though to a sermon—he didn't dare even cross his legs or lean on his elbows; and at two o'clock, when the bell rang for the next class, the teacher had to tell him to line up with the rest of us.

We always flung our caps on the floor when entering a classroom, to free our hands; we hurled them under the seats from the doorway itself, in such a way that they struck the wall and raised a cloud of dust: that was "how it was done."

But whether he had failed to notice this ritual or hadn't dared join in observance of it, his cap was still in his lap when we'd finished reciting our prayer. It was a headgear of composite order, containing elements of an ordinary hat, a hussar's busby, a lancer's cap, a sealskin cap and a nightcap: one of those wretched things whose mute hideousness suggests unplumbed depths, like an idiot's face. Ovoid and stiffened with whalebone, it began with three convex strips; then followed alternating lozenges of velvet and rabbit's fur, separated by a red band; then came a kind of bag, terminating in a cardboard-lined polygon intricately decorated with braid. From this hung a long, excessively thin cord ending in a kind of tassel of gold netting. The cap was new; its peak was shiny.

"Stand up," said the teacher.

He rose. His cap dropped to the floor. Everyone began to laugh.

He bent over for it. A boy beside him sent it down again with his elbow. Once again he picked it up.

"How about getting rid of your helmet?" suggested the teacher, who was something of a wit.

Another loud laugh from the students confused the poor fellow. He didn't know whether to keep the cap in his hand, drop it on the floor, or put it on his head. He sat down again and placed it in his lap.

"Stand up," repeated the professor, "and tell me your name."

The new boy mumbled a name that was unintelligible.

"Say it again!"

The same jumble of syllables came out, drowned in the jeers of the class.

"Louder!" cried the teacher. "Louder!"

With desperate resolve the new boy opened a mouth that seemed enormous, and as though calling someone he cried at the top of his lungs the word "Charbovari!"

This touched off a roar that rose *crescendo*, punctuated with shrill screams. There was a shrieking, a banging of desks as everyone yelled, "Charbovari! Charbovari!" Then the din broke up into isolated cries that slowly diminished, occasionally starting up again along a line of desks where a stifled laugh would burst out here and there like a half-spent firecracker.

But a shower of penalties gradually restored order; and the teacher, finally grasping the name Charles Bovary after it had been several times spelled out and repeated and he had read it aloud himself, at once commanded the poor devil to sit in the dunce's seat, at the foot of the platform. He began to move toward it, then hesitated.

"What are you looking for?" the teacher demanded.

"My c—" the new boy said timidly, casting an uneasy glance around him.

"Everybody will stay and write five hundred lines!"

Like Neptune's "*Quos ego,*"[2] those words, furiously uttered, cut short the threat of a new storm. "Quiet!" the indignant teacher continued, mopping his forehead with a handkerchief he took from his toque. "As for you," he said to the new boy, "you'll copy out for me twenty times all the tenses of *ridiculus sum.*"[3]

Then, more gently: "You'll find your cap. No one has stolen it."

All was calm again. Heads bent over copybooks, and for the next two hours the new boy's conduct was exemplary, even though an occasional spitball, sent from the nib of a pen, struck him wetly in the face. He wiped himself each time with his hand, and otherwise sat there motionless, his eyes lowered.

That evening, in study period, he took his sleeveguards from his desk, arranged his meager equipment, and carefully ruled his paper. We saw him working conscientiously, looking up every word in the dictionary, taking great pains. It was doubtless thanks to this display of effort that he was not demoted to a lower form. For while he had a fair knowledge of grammatical rules, his translations lacked elegance. He had begun his Latin with his village priest: his thrifty parents had sent him away to school as late as possible.

His father, Monsieur Charles-Denis-Bartholomé Bovary, had been an army surgeon's aide, forced to leave the service about 1812 as a result of involvement in a conscription scandal. He had then turned his personal charms to advantage, picking up a dowry of 60,000 francs brought to him by a knit-goods dealer's daughter who had fallen in love with his appearance. He was a handsome man, much given to bragging and clanking his spurs. His side whiskers merged with his mustache, his fingers were always loaded with rings, his clothes were flashy: he had the look of a bully and the easy cajoling ways of a traveling salesman. Once married, he lived off his wife's money for two or three years. He ate well, rose late, smoked big porcelain pipes, stayed out every night to see a show, spent much of his time in cafés. His father-in-law died and left very little; this made him indignant, and he "went into textiles" and lost some money. Then he retired to the country, with the intention of "making things pay." But he knew as little about crops as he did about calico; and since he rode his horses instead of working them in the fields, drank his cider bottled instead of selling it by the barrel, ate his best poultry, and greased his hunting boots with the fat from his pigs, he soon realized that he had better give up all idea of profit-making.

So for two hundred francs[4] a year he rented, in a village on the border of Normandy and Picardy, a dwelling that was half farm, half gentleman's res-

---

2. An unfinished threat (Latin: "you whom I . . .") delivered by the sea god Neptune to winds that had caused ocean storms without his permission (*Aeneid* 1.135).   3. I am a fool (Latin).   4. It is very difficult to transpose monetary values from 1840 into present-day figures, since relationships between the actual value of the franc, the cost of living, and the relative cost of specific items (e.g., rent and real estate) have undergone fundamental changes. A rough calculation of inflation and exchange rates between the franc and the dollar in 1840 and 1998 gives approximately $45; that would show Mme. Bovary destroyed, at the end of the book, by an $18,000 debt.

idence; and there, surly, eaten by discontent, cursing heaven, envying everyone, he shut himself up at the age of forty-five, disgusted with mankind, he
said, and resolved to live in peace.

His wife had been mad about him at the beginning; in her love she had
tendered him a thousand servilities that had alienated him all the more. Once
sprightly, all outgoing and affectionate, with age she had grown touchy, nagging and nervous, like stale wine turning to vinegar. At first she had suffered
uncomplainingly, watching him chase after every trollop in the village and
having him come back to her at night from any one of twenty disgusting
places surfeited and stinking of drink. Then her pride rebelled. She withdrew
into her shell; and swallowing her rage she bore up stoically until her death.
She was always busy, always doing things. She was constantly running to
lawyers, to the judge, remembering when notes fell due and obtaining renew-
als; and at home she was forever ironing, sewing, washing, keeping an eye
on the hired men, figuring their wages. Monsieur, meanwhile, never lifted a
finger. He sat smoking in the chimney corner and spitting into the ashes,
continually falling into a grumpy doze and waking to utter uncomplimentary
remarks.

When she had a child it had to be placed out with a wet nurse. And then
later, when the little boy was back with its parents, he was pampered like a
prince. His mother stuffed him with jams and jellies; his father let him run
barefoot, and fancied himself a disciple of Rousseau to the point of saying
he'd be quite willing to have the boy go naked like a young animal. To counter
his wife's maternal tendencies he tried to form his son according to a certain
virile ideal of childhood and to harden his constitution by subjecting him to
strict discipline, Spartan-style. He sent him to bed without a fire, taught him
to take great swigs of rum and to ridicule religious processions. But the child
was pacific by nature, and such training had little effect. His mother kept
him tied to her apron-strings: she made him paper cutouts, told him stories,
and conversed with him in endless bitter-sweet monologues full of coaxing
chatter. In the isolation of her life she transferred to her baby all her own
poor frustrated ambitions. She dreamed of glamorous careers: she saw him
tall, handsome, witty, successful—a bridge builder or a judge. She taught
him to read, and even, on an old piano she had, to sing two or three sentimental little songs. But from Monsieur Bovary, who cared little for culture,
all this brought merely the comment that it was "useless." Could they ever
afford to give him an education, to buy him a practice or a business? Besides,
"with enough nerve a man could always get ahead in the world." Madame
Bovary pursed her lips, and the boy ran wild in the village.

He followed the hired men and chased crows, pelting them with clods of
earth until they flew off. He ate the wild blackberries that grew along the
ditches, looked after the turkeys with a long stick, pitched hay, roamed the
woods, played hopscotch in the shelter of the church porch when it rained,
and on important feast-days begged the sexton to let him toll the bells so
that he could hang with his full weight from the heavy rope and feel it sweep
him off his feet as it swung in its arc.

He throve like an oak. His hands grew strong and his complexion ruddy.

When he was twelve, his mother had her way: he began his studies. The
priest was asked to tutor him. But the lessons were so short and irregular
that they served little purpose. They took place at odd hurried moments—

in the sacristy between a baptism and a funeral; or else the priest would send for him after the Angelus, when his parish business was over for the day. They would go up to his bedroom and begin, midges and moths fluttering around the candle. There in the warmth the child would fall asleep; and the old man, too, would soon be dozing and snoring, his hands folded over his stomach and his mouth open. Other times, as Monsieur le curé was returning from a sickbed with the holy oils, he would catch sight of Charles scampering in the fields, and would call him over and lecture him for a few minutes, taking advantage of the occasion to make him conjugate a verb right there, under a tree. Rain would interrupt them, or some passer-by whom they knew. However, he was always satisfied with him, and even said that "the young fellow had a good memory."

Things weren't allowed to stop there. Madame was persistent. Shamed into consent—or, rather, his resistance worn down—Monsieur gave in without further struggle. They waited a year, until the boy had made his First Communion, then six months more; and finally Charles was sent to the lycée in Rouen. His father delivered him himself, toward the end of October, during the fortnight of the Saint-Romain fair.

It would be very difficult today for any of us to say what he was like. There was nothing striking about him: he played during recess, worked in study-hall, paid attention in class, slept soundly in the dormitory, ate heartily in the refectory. His local guardian was a wholesale hardware dealer in the rue Ganterie, who called for him one Sunday a month after early closing, sent him for a walk along the riverfront to look at the boats, then brought him back to school by seven, in time for supper. Every Thursday night Charles wrote a long letter to his mother, using red ink and three seals; then he looked over his history notes, or leafed through an old volume of *Anacharsis*[5] that lay around the study-hall. When his class went for outings he talked with the school servant who accompanied them, a countryman like himself.

By working hard he managed to stay about in the middle of the class; once he even got an honorable mention in natural history. But before he finished upper school his parents took him out of the lycée entirely and sent him to study medicine, confident that he could get his baccalaureate degree anyway by making up the intervening years on his own.

His mother choose a room for him, four flights up overlooking the stream called the Eau-de-Robec,[6] in the house of a dyer she knew. She arranged for his board, got him a table and two chairs, and sent home for an old cherry bed; and to keep her darling warm she bought him a small cast-iron stove and a load of wood. Then after a week she went back to her village, urging him a thousand times over to behave himself now that he was on his own.

The curriculum that he read on the bulletin board staggered him. Courses in anatomy, pathology, pharmacy, chemistry, botany, clinical practice, therapeutics, to say nothing of hygiene and materia medica—names of unfamiliar etymology that were like so many doors leading to solemn shadowy sanctuaries.

---

5. *Voyage du jeune Anacharsis en Grèce* (The voyage of young Anacharsis in Greece; 1788) was a popular account of ancient Greece as seen by a barbarian, by Jean-Jacques Barthélemy (1716–1795).   6. Small river, now covered up, that flows through the poorest neighborhood of Rouen, used as a sewer by the factories that border it, thus suggesting Flaubert's description as *"une ignoble petite Venise"* (squalid little Venice).

He understood absolutely nothing of any of it. He listened in vain: he could not grasp it. Even so, he worked. He filled his notebooks, attended every lecture, never missed hospital rounds. In the performance of his daily task he was like a mill-horse that treads blindfolded in a circle, utterly ignorant of what he is grinding.

To save him money, his mother sent him a roast of veal each week by the stagecoach, and off this he lunched when he came in from the hospital, warming his feet by beating them against the wall. Then he had to hurry off to lectures, to the amphitheatre, to another hospital, crossing the entire city again when he returned. At night, after eating the meager dinner his landlord provided, he climbed back up to his room, back to work. Steam rose from his damp clothes as he sat beside the red-hot stove.

On fine summer evenings, at the hour when the warm streets are empty and servant girls play at shuttlecock in front of the houses, he would open his window and lean out. The stream, which makes this part of Rouen a kind of squalid little Venice, flowed just below, stained yellow, purple or blue between its bridges and railings. Workmen from the dye plants, crouching on the bank, washed their arms in the water. Above him, on poles projecting from attics, skeins of cotton were drying in the open. And beyond the rooftops stretched the sky, vast and pure, with the red sun setting. How good it must be in the country! How cool in the beech grove! And he opened his nostrils wide, longing for a whiff of the fresh and fragrant air, but none was ever wafted to where he was.

He grew thinner and taller, and his face took on a kind of plaintive expression that almost made it interesting.

The fecklessness that was part of his nature soon led him to break all his good resolutions. One day he skipped rounds; the next, a lecture; idleness, he found, was to his taste, and gradually he stayed away entirely.

He began to go to cafés. Soon he was crazy about dominoes. To spend his evenings shut up in a dirty public room, clinking black-dotted pieces of sheep's bone on a marble table, seemed to him a marvelous assertion of his freedom that raised him in his own esteem. It was like an initiation into the world, admission to a realm of forbidden delights; and every time he entered the café the feel of the doorknob in his hand gave him a pleasure that was almost sensual. Now many things pent up within him burst their bonds; he learned verses by heart and sang them at student gatherings, developed an enthusiasm for Béranger,[7] learned to make punch, and knew, at long last, the joys of love.

Thanks to that kind of preparation he failed completely the examination that would have entitled him to practice medicine as an *officier de santé*.[8] And his parents were waiting for him at home that very night to celebrate his success!

He set out on foot; at the outskirts of the village he stopped, sent someone for his mother, and told her all. She forgave him, laying his downfall to the unfairness of the examiners, and steadied him by promising to make all expla-

---

7. Pierre-Jean de Béranger (1780–1857), an extremely popular writer of songs that often exalt the glories of the empire of Napoleon I. **8.** Health officer (French). Instituted during the French Revolution, a kind of second-class medical degree, well below the doctorate. The student was allowed to attend a medical school without having passed the equivalent of the *baccalauréat,* and could practice only in the administrative region in which the diploma had been conferred (Bovary is thus tied down to the vicinity of Rouen) and was not allowed to perform major operations, except in the presence of a full-fledged doctor. This diploma was suppressed in 1892.

nations. (It was five years before Monsieur Bovary learned the truth: by that time it was an old story and he could accept it, especially since he couldn't conceive of his own offspring as being stupid.)

Charles set to work again and crammed ceaselessly, memorizing everything on which he could possibly be questioned. He passed with a fairly good grade. What a wonderful day for his mother! Everyone was asked to dinner.

Where should he practice? At Tostes. In that town there was only one elderly doctor, whose death Madame Bovary had long been waiting for; and the old man hadn't yet breathed his last when Charles moved in across the road as his successor.

But it wasn't enough to have raised her son, sent him into medicine, and discovered Tostes for him to practice in: he had to have a wife. She found him one: a *huissier's*[9] widow in Dieppe, forty-five years old, with twelve hundred francs a year.

Ugly though she was, and thin as a lath, with a face as spotted as a meadow in springtime, Madame Dubuc unquestionably had plenty of suitors to choose from. To gain her ends Madame Bovary had to get rid of all the rivals, and her outwitting of one of them, a butcher whose candidacy was favored by the local clergy, was nothing short of masterly.

Charles had envisaged marriage as the beginning of a better time, thinking that he would have greater freedom and be able to do as he liked with himself and his money. But it was his wife who ruled: in front of company he had to say certain things and not others, he had to eat fish on Friday, dress the way she wanted, obey her when she ordered him to dun nonpaying patients. She opened his mail, watched his every move, and listened through the thinness of the wall when there were women in his office.

She had to have her cup of chocolate every morning: there was no end to the attentions she required. She complained incessantly of her nerves, of pains in her chest, of depressions and faintnesses. The sound of anyone moving about near her made her ill; when people left her she couldn't bear her loneliness; when they came to see her it was, of course, "to watch her die." When Charles came home in the evening she would bring her long thin arms out from under her bedclothes, twine them around his neck, draw him down beside her on the edge of the bed, and launch into the tale of her woes: he was forgetting her, he was in love with someone else! How right people had been, to warn her that he'd make her unhappy! And she always ended by asking him to give her a new tonic and a little more love.

II

One night about eleven o'clock they were awakened by a noise: a horse had stopped just at their door. The maid opened the attic window and parleyed for some time with a man who stood in the street below. He had been sent to fetch the doctor; he had a letter. Nastasie came downstairs, shivering, turned the key in the lock and pushed back the bolts one by one. The man left his horse, followed the maid, and entered the bedroom at her heels. Out of his gray-tasseled woolen cap he drew a letter wrapped in a piece of cloth, and with a careful gesture handed it to Charles, who raised himself on his

9. Bailiff's.

pillow to read it. Nastasie stood close to the bed, holding the light. Madame had modestly turned her back and lay facing the wall.

This letter, sealed with a small blue wax seal, begged Monsieur Bovary to come immediately to a farm called Les Bertaux, to set a broken leg. Now, from Tostes to Les Bertaux is at least fifteen miles, going by way of Longueville and Saint-Victor. It was a pitch-black night. Madame Bovary was fearful lest her husband meet with an accident. So it was decided that the stable hand who had brought the letter should start out ahead, and that Charles should follow three hours later: by that time there would be a moon. A boy would be sent out to meet him, to show him the way to the farm and open the field gates.

About four o'clock in the morning Charles set out for Les Bertaux, wrapped in a heavy coat. He was still drowsy from his warm sleep, and the peaceful trot of his mare lulled him like the rocking of a cradle. Whenever she stopped of her own accord in front of one of those spike-edged holes that farmers dig along the roadside to protect their crops, he would wake up with a start, quickly remember the broken leg, and try to recall all the fractures he had ever seen. The rain had stopped; day was breaking, and on the leafless branches of the apple trees birds were perched motionless, ruffling up their little feathers in the cold morning wind. The countryside stretched flat as far as eye could see; and the tufts of trees clustered around the farmhouses were widely spaced dark purple stains on the vast gray surface that merged at the horizon into the dull tone of the sky. From time to time Charles would open his eyes; and then, his senses dimmed by a return of sleep, he would fall again into a drowsiness in which recent sensations became confused with older memories to give him double visions of himself: as husband and as student—lying in bed as he had been only an hour or so before, and walking through a surgical ward as in the past. In his mind the hot smell of poultices mingled with the fresh smell of the dew; he heard at once the rattle of the curtain rings on hospital beds, and the sound of his wife's breathing as she lay asleep. At Vassonville he saw a little boy sitting in the grass beside a ditch.

"Are you the doctor?" the child asked.

And when Charles answered, he took his wooden shoes in his hands and began to run in front of him.

As they continued on their way, the *officier de santé* gathered from what his guide told him that Monsieur Rouault must be a very well-to-do farmer indeed. He had broken his leg the previous evening, on his way back from celebrating Twelfth Night at the home of a neighbor. His wife had been dead for two years. He had with him only his "demoiselle"—his daughter—who kept house for him.

Now the road was more deeply rutted: they were approaching Les Bertaux. The boy slipped through an opening in a hedge, disappeared, then reappeared ahead, opening a farmyard gate from within. The horse was slipping on the wet grass; Charles had to bend low to escape overhanging branches. Kenneled watchdogs were barking, pulling at their chains. As he passed through the gate of Les Bertaux, his horse took fright and shied wildly.

It was a prosperous-looking farm. Through the open upper-halves of the stable doors great plough-horses could be seen placidly feeding from new racks. Next to the outbuildings stood a big manure pile, and in among the chickens and turkeys pecking at its steaming surface were five or six peacocks—favorite show pieces of *cauchois* farmyards.[1] The sheepfold was long, the barn lofty, its walls as smooth as your hand. In the shed were two large carts and four ploughs complete with whips, horse collars and full trappings, the blue wool pads gray under the fine dust that sifted down from the lofts. The farmyard sloped upwards, planted with symmetrically spaced trees, and from near the pond came the merry sound of a flock of geese.

A young woman wearing a blue merino dress with three flounces came to the door of the house to greet Monsieur Bovary, and she ushered him into the kitchen, where a big open fire was blazing. Around its edges the farm hands' breakfast was bubbling in small pots of assorted sizes. Damp clothes were drying inside the vast chimney-opening. The fire shovel, the tongs, and the nose of the bellows, all of colossal proportions, shone like polished steel; and along the walls hung a lavish array of kitchen utensils, glimmering in the bright light of the fire and in the first rays of the sun that were now beginning to come in through the windowpanes.

Charles went upstairs to see the patient. He found him in bed, sweating under blankets, his nightcap lying where he had flung it. He was a stocky little man of fifty, fair-skinned, blue-eyed, bald in front and wearing earrings. On a chair beside him was a big decanter of brandy: he had been pouring himself drinks to keep up his courage. But as soon as he saw the doctor he dropped his bluster, and instead of cursing as he had been doing for the past twelve hours he began to groan weakly.

The fracture was a simple one, without complications of any kind. Charles couldn't have wished for anything easier. Then he recalled his teachers' bedside manner in accident cases, and proceeded to cheer up his patient with all kinds of facetious remarks—a truly surgical attention, like the oiling of a scalpel. For splints, they sent someone to bring a bundle of laths from the carriage shed. Charles selected one, cut it into lengths and smoothed it down with a piece of broken window glass, while the maidservant tore sheets for bandages and Mademoiselle Emma tried to sew some pads. She was a long time finding her workbox, and her father showed his impatience. She made no reply; but as she sewed she kept pricking her fingers and raising them to her mouth to suck.

Charles was surprised by the whiteness of her fingernails. They were almond shaped, tapering, as polished and shining as Dieppe ivories. Her hands, however, were not pretty—not pale enough, perhaps, a little rough at the knuckles; and they were too long, without softness of line. The finest thing about her was her eyes. They were brown, but seemed black under the long eyelashes; and she had an open gaze that met yours with fearless candor.

When the binding was done, the doctor was invited by Monsieur Rouault himself to "have something" before he left.

Charles went down to the parlor on the ground floor. At the foot of a great canopied bed, its calico hangings printed with a design of people in Turkish dress, there stood a little table on which places had been laid for two, a silver mug beside each plate. From a tall oaken cupboard facing the window came an odor of orris root and damp sheets. In corners stood rows of grain sacks— the overflow from the granary, which was just adjoining, approached by three stone steps. The room's only decoration, hanging from a nail in the center

1. From the Caux area, a large chalky plateau region in Normandy (northern France).

of the flaking green-painted wall, was a black pencil drawing of a head of Minerva framed in gold and inscribed at the bottom in Gothic letters "To my dear Papa."

They spoke about the patient first, and then about the weather, about the bitter cold, about the wolves that roamed the fields at night. Mademoiselle Rouault didn't enjoy country life, especially now, with almost the full responsibility of the farm on her shoulders. The room was chilly, and she shivered as she ate. Charles noticed that her lips were full, and that she had the habit of biting them in moments of silence.

Her neck rose out of the low fold of a white collar. The two black sweeps of her hair, pulled down from a fine center part that followed the curve of her skull, were so sleek that each seemed to be one piece. Covering all but the very tips of her ears, it was gathered at the back into a large chignon, and toward the temples it waved a bit—a detail that the country doctor now observed for the first time in his life. Her skin was rosy over her cheekbones. A pair of shell-rimmed eyeglasses, like a man's, was tucked between two buttons of her bodice.

When Charles came back downstairs after going up to take leave of Monsieur Rouault, he found her standing with her forehead pressed against the windowpane, looking out at the garden, where the beanpoles had been thrown down by the wind. She turned around.

"Are you looking for something?" she asked.

"For my riding crop," he said.

And he began to rummage on the bed, behind doors, under chairs. It had fallen on the floor between the grain bags and the wall. Mademoiselle Emma caught sight of it and reached for it, bending down across the sacks. Charles hurried over politely, and as he, too, stretched out his arm he felt his body in slight contact with the girl's back, bent there beneath him. She stood up, blushing crimson, and glanced at him over her shoulder as she handed him his crop.

Instead of returning to Les Bertaux three days later, as he had promised, he went back the very next day, then twice a week regularly, not to mention unscheduled calls he made from time to time, as though by chance.

Everything went well; the bone knit according to the rules; and after forty-six days, when Monsieur Rouault was seen trying to get around his farmyard by himself, everyone began to think of Monsieur Bovary as a man of great competence. Monsieur Rouault said he wouldn't have been better mended by the biggest doctors of Yvetot or even Rouen.

As for Charles, he didn't ask himself why he enjoyed going to Les Bertaux. Had he thought of it, he would doubtless have attributed his zeal to the seriousness of the case, or perhaps to the fee he hoped to earn. Still, was that really why his visits to the farm formed so charming a contrast to the drabness of the rest of his life? On such days he would rise early, set off at a gallop, urge his horse; and when he was almost there he would dismount to dust his shoes on the grass, and put on his black gloves. He enjoyed the moment of arrival, the feel of the gate as it yielded against his shoulder; he enjoyed the rooster crowing on the wall, the farm boys coming to greet him. He enjoyed the barn and the stables; he enjoyed Monsieur Rouault, who would clap him in the palm of the hand and call him his "savior"; he enjoyed hearing Mademoiselle Emma's little sabots on the newly washed flagstones of the kitchen floor. With their high heels they made her a little taller; and when she walked in them ahead of him their wooden soles kept coming up with a quick, sharp, tapping sound against the leather of her shoes.

She always accompanied him to the foot of the steps outside the door. If his horse hadn't been brought around she would wait there with him. At such moments they had already said good-bye, and stood there silent; the breeze eddied around her, swirling the stray wisps of hair at her neck, or sending her apron strings flying like streamers around her waist. Once she was standing there on a day of thaw, when the bark of the trees in the farmyard was oozing sap and the snow was melting on the roofs. She went inside for her parasol, and opened it. The parasol was of rosy iridescent silk, and the sun pouring through it painted the white skin of her face with flickering patches of light. Beneath it she smiled at the springlike warmth; and drops of water could be heard falling one by one on the taut moiré.

During the first period of Charles's visits to Les Bertaux, Madame Bovary never failed to ask about the patient's progress; and in her double-entry ledger she had given Monsieur Rouault a fine new page to himself. But when she heard that he had a daughter she began to make inquiries; and she learned that Mademoiselle Rouault had had her schooling in a convent, with the Ursuline nuns—had received, as the saying went, a "fine education," in the course of which she had been taught dancing, geography, drawing, needlework and a little piano. Think of that!

"So that's why he brightens up when he goes there! That's why he wears his new waistcoat, even in the rain! Ah! So she's at the bottom of it!"

Instinctively she hated her. At first she relieved her feelings by making insinuations. Charles didn't get them. Then she let fall parenthetical remarks which he left unanswered out of fear of a storm; and finally she was driven to point-blank reproaches which he didn't know how to answer. Why was it that he kept going back to Les Bertaux, now that Monsieur Rouault was completely mended and hadn't even paid his bill? Ah! Because there was *a certain person* there. Somebody who knew how to talk. Somebody who did embroidery. Somebody clever. That's what he enjoyed: he had to have city girls! And she went on:

"Rouault's daughter, a city girl! Don't make me laugh! The grandfather was a shepherd, and there's a cousin who barely escaped sentence for assault and battery. Scarcely good reasons for giving herself airs, for wearing silk dresses to church like a countess! Besides—her father, poor fellow: if it hadn't been for last year's colza crop he'd have been hard put to it to pay his debts."

For the sake of peace, Charles stopped going to Les Bertaux. Heloise had made him swear—his hand on his prayer book—that he would never go back there again: she had accomplished it after much sobbing and kissing, in the midst of a great amorous explosion. He yielded; but the strength of his desire kept protesting against the servility of his behavior, and with a naïve sort of hypocrisy he told himself that this very prohibition against seeing her implicitly allowed him to love her. And then the widow he was married to was skinny; she was long in the tooth; all year round she wore a little black shawl with a corner hanging down between her shoulder blades; her rigid form was always sheathed in dresses that were like scabbards; they were always too short; they showed her ankles, her big shoes, and her shoelaces crisscrossing their way up her gray stockings.

Charles's mother came to see them from time to time; but after a few days she invariably took on her daughter-in-law's sharpness against her son, and like a pair of knives they kept scarifying him with their comments and criticisms. He oughtn't to eat so much! Why always offer a drink to everyone who called? So pigheaded not to wear flannel underwear!

Early in the spring it happened that a notary in Ingouville, custodian of the Widow Dubuc's capital, sailed away one fine day, taking with him all his clients' money. To be sure, Heloise still owned her house in the rue Saint-François in Dieppe, as well as a six-thousand-franc interest in a certain ship; nevertheless, of the great fortune she'd always talked so much about, nothing except a few bits of furniture and some clothes had ever been seen in the household. Now, inevitably, everything came under investigation. The house in Dieppe, it turned out, was mortgaged up to its eaves; what she had placed with the notary, God only knew; and her share in the boat didn't amount to more than three thousand. So she'd been lying—lying all along, the dear, good lady! In his rage the older Monsieur Bovary dashed a chair to pieces on the floor and accused his wife of ruining their son's life by yoking him to such an ancient nag, whose harness was worth even less than her carcass. They came to Tostes. The four of them had it out. There were scenes. The weeping Heloise threw herself into her husband's arms and appealed to him to defend her against his parents. Charles began to take her part. The others flew into a rage and left.

But—"the fatal blow had been struck." A week later she was hanging out washing in her yard when suddenly she began to spit blood; and the next day, while Charles was looking the other way, drawing the window curtain, she gave a cry, then a sigh, and fainted. She was dead! Who would have believed it?

When everything was over at the cemetery, Charles returned to the house. There was no one downstairs, and he went up to the bedroom. One of her dresses was still hanging in the alcove. He stayed there until dark, leaning against the writing desk, his mind full of sad thoughts. Poor thing! She had loved him, after all.

III

One morning Monsieur Rouault came to pay Charles for setting his leg—seventy-five francs in two-franc pieces, with a turkey thrown in for good measure. He had heard of his bereavement, and offered him what consolation he could.

"I know what it is," he said, patting him on the shoulder. "I've been through just what you're going through. When I lost my wife I went out into the fields to be by myself. I lay down under a tree and cried. I talked to God, told him all kinds of crazy things. I wished I were dead, like the maggoty moles I saw hanging on the branches. And when I thought of how other men were holding their wives in their arms at that very moment, I began to pound my stick on the ground. I was almost out of my mind. I couldn't eat: the very thought of going to a café made me sick—you'd never believe it. Well, you know, what with one day gradually nosing out another, and spring coming on top of winter and then fall after the summer—it passed bit by bit, drop by drop. It just went away; it disappeared; I mean it grew less and less—there's always part of it you never get rid of entirely; you always feel something here." And he put his hand on his chest. "But it happens to us all, and you mustn't let yourself go, you mustn't want to die just because other people are dead. You must brace up, Monsieur Bovary: things will get better. Come and see us. My daughter talks about you every once in a while; she says you've probably forgotten her. Spring will soon be here: you and I'll go out after a rabbit—it will take your mind off things."

Charles took his advice. He went back to Les Bertaux; he found it unchanged since yesterday—since five months before, that is. The pear trees were already in flower; and the sight of Monsieur Rouault coming and going normally around the place made everything livelier.

The farmer seemed to think that the doctor's grief-stricken condition called for a special show of consideration, and he urged him to keep his hat on, addressed him in a low voice as though he were ill, and even pretended to be angry that no one had thought to cook him something special and light, like custard or stewed pears. He told him funny stories. Charles found himself laughing, but then the thought of his wife returned to sober him. By the end of the meal he had forgotten her again.

He thought of her less and less as he grew used to living alone. The novelty and pleasure of being independent soon made solitude more bearable. Now he could change his meal hours at will, come and go without explanation, stretch out across the bed if he was particularly tired. So he pampered and coddled himself and accepted all the comforting everyone offered. Besides, he wife's death had helped him quite a bit professionally: for a month or so everyone had kept saying, "Poor young man! What a tragedy!" His reputation grew; more and more patients came. Now he went to Les Bertaux whenever he pleased. He was aware of a feeling of hope—nothing very specific, a vague happiness: he thought himself better-looking when he stood at the mirror to brush his whiskers.

One day he arrived about three o'clock. Everyone was in the fields. He went into the kitchen, and at first didn't see Emma. The shutters were closed; the sun, streaming in between the slats, patterned the floor with long thin stripes that broke off at the corners of the furniture and quivered on the ceiling. On the table, flies were climbing up the sides of glasses that had recently been used, and buzzing as they struggled to keep from drowning in the cider at the bottom. The light coming down the chimney turned the soot on the fireback to velvet and gave a bluish cast to the cold ashes. Between the window and the hearth Emma sat sewing; her shoulders were bare, beaded with little drops of sweat.

Country-style, she offered him something to drink. He refused, she insisted, and finally suggested with a laugh that he take a liqueur with her. She brought a bottle of curaçao from the cupboard, reached to a high shelf for two liqueur glasses, filled one to the brim and poured a few drops in the other. She touched her glass to his and raised it to her mouth. Because it was almost empty she had to bend backwards to be able to drink; and with her head tilted back, her neck and her lips outstretched, she began to laugh at tasting nothing; and then the tip of her tongue came out from between her small teeth and began daintily to lick the bottom of the glass.

She sat down again and resumed her work—she was darning a white cotton stocking. She sewed with her head bowed, and she did not speak: nor did Charles. A draft was coming in under the door and blowing a little dust across the stone floor; he watched it drift, and was aware of a pulsating sound inside his head—that, and the clucking of a laying hen outside in the yard. From time to time Emma cooled her cheeks with the palms of her hands, and then cooled her hands against the iron knobs of the tall andirons.

She complained that the heat had been giving her dizzy spells, and asked whether sea bathing would help; then she began to talk about her convent school and Charles about his lycée: words came to them both. They went upstairs to her room. She showed him her old music exercise books, and the little volumes and the oak-leaf wreaths—the latter now lying abandoned in the bottom of a cupboard—that she had won as prizes. Then she spoke of her mother, and the cemetery, and took him out to the garden to see the bed where she picked flowers the first Friday of every month to put on her grave. But their gardener had no understanding of such things: farm help was so trying! She would love, if only for the winter, to live in the city—though she had to say that it was really in summer, with the days so long, that the country was most boring of all. Depending on what she talked about, her voice was clear, or shrill, or would grow suddenly languorous and trail off almost into a murmur, as though she were speaking to herself. One moment she would be gay and wide-eyed; the next, she would half shut her eyelids and seem to be drowned in boredom, her thoughts miles away.

That evening, on his homeward ride, Charles went over one by one the things she had said, trying to remember her exact words and sense their implications, in an effort to picture what her life had been like before their meeting. But in his thoughts he could never see her any differently from the way she had been when he had seen her the first time, or as she had been just now, when he left her. Then he wondered what would become of her, whether she would marry, and whom. Alas! Monsieur Rouault was very rich, and she . . . so beautiful! But Emma's face appeared constantly before his eyes, and in his ears there was a monotonous throbbing, like the humming of a top: "But why don't *you* get married! Why don't *you* get married!"

That night he didn't sleep, his throat was tight, he was thirsty; he got up to drink from his water jug and opened the window; the sky was covered with stars, a hot wind was blowing, dogs were barking in the distance. He stared out in the direction of Les Bertaux.

After all, he thought, nothing would be lost by trying; and he resolved to ask his question when the occasion presented itself; but each time it did, the fear of not finding the proper words paralyzed his lips.

Actually, Rouault wouldn't have been a bit displeased to have someone take his daughter off his hands. She was of no use to him on the farm. He didn't really hold it against her, being of the opinion that she was too clever to have anything to do with farming—that accursed occupation that had never yet made a man a millionaire. Far from having grown rich at it, the poor fellow was losing money every year: he more than held his own in the market place, where he relished all the tricks of the trade, but no one was less suited than he to the actual growing of crops and the managing of a farm. He never lifted a finger if he could help it, and never spared any expense in matters of daily living: he insisted on good food, a good fire, and a good bed. He liked his cider hard, his leg of mutton rare, his coffee well laced with brandy. He took his meals in the kitchen, alone, facing the fire, at a little table that was brought in to him already set, like on the stage.

So when he noticed that Charles tended to be flushed in his daughter's presence—meaning that one of these days he would ask for her hand—he pondered every aspect of the question well in advance. Charles was a bit namby-pamby, not his dream of a son-in-law; but he was said to be reliable, thrifty, very well educated; and he probably wouldn't haggle too much over the dowry. Moreover, Rouault was soon going to have to sell twenty-two of his acres: he owed considerable to the mason and considerable to the harness maker, and the cider press needed a new shaft. "If he asks me for her," he said to himself, "I won't refuse."

Toward the beginning of October, Charles spent three days at Les Bertaux. The last day had slipped by like the others, with the big step put off from one minute to the next. Rouault was escorting him on the first lap of his homeward journey; they were walking along a sunken road; they were just about to part—the moment had come. Charles gave himself to the corner of the hedge; and finally, when they had passed it: "Monsieur Rouault," he murmured, "there's something I'd like to say to you."

They stopped. Charles fell silent.

"Well, tell me what's on your mind! I know it already anyway!" Rouault said with a gentle laugh.

"Monsieur Rouault . . . Monsieur Rouault . . ." Charles stammered.

"Personally I wouldn't like anything better," continued the farmer. "I imagine the child agrees with me, but we'd better ask her. I'll leave you here now, and go back to the house. If it's 'Yes'—now listen to what I'm saying—you won't have to come in: there are too many people around, and besides she'd be too upset. But to take you off the anxious seat I'll slam a shutter against the wall: you can look back and see, if you lean over the hedge."

And he went off.

Charles tied his horse to a tree. He hastily stationed himself on the path and waited. Half an hour went by; then he counted nineteen minutes by his watch. Suddenly there was a noise against the wall: the shutter had swung back; the catch was still quivering.

The next morning he was at the farm by nine. Emma blushed when he entered, laughing a little in an attempt to be casual. Rouault embraced his future son-in-law. They postponed all talk of financial arrangements: there was plenty of time, since the wedding couldn't decently take place before the end of Charles's mourning—that is, toward the spring of the next year.

It was a winter of waiting. Mademoiselle Rouault busied herself with her trousseau. Part of it was ordered in Rouen, and she made her slips and nightcaps herself, copying fashion drawings that she borrowed. Whenever Charles visited the farm they spoke about preparations for the wedding, discussing which room the dinner should be served in, wondering how many courses to have and what the entrees should be.

Emma herself would have liked to be married at midnight, by torchlight; but Rouault wouldn't listen to the idea. So there was the usual kind of wedding, with forty-three guests, and everybody was sixteen hours at table, and the festivities began all over again the next day and even carried over a little into the days following.

IV

The invited guests arrived early in a variety of vehicles—one-horse shays, two-wheeled charabancs, old gigs without tops, vans with leather curtains; and the young men from the nearest villages came in farm carts, standing one behind the other along the sides and grasping the rails to keep from being thrown, for the horses trotted briskly and the roads were rough. They came from as far as twenty-five miles away, from Goderville, from Normanville, from Cany. All the relations of both families had been asked, old quarrels had been patched up, letters sent to acquaintances long lost sight of.

From time to time the crack of a whip would be heard behind the hedge, then after a moment the gate would open and a cart would roll in; it would come at a gallop as far as the doorstep, then stop with a lurch, and out would pour its passengers, rubbing their knees and stretching their arms. The ladies wore country-style headdresses and city-style gowns, with gold watch chains, tippets (the ends crossed and tucked into their belts), or small colored fichus[2] attached at the back with pins and leaving the neck bare. The boys, attired exactly like their papas, looked ill at ease in their new clothes (and indeed many of them were wearing leather shoes that day for the first time in their lives); and next to them would be some speechless, gangling girl of fourteen or sixteen, probably their cousin or their older sister, flushed and awkward in her white First Communion dress let down for the occasion, her hair sticky with scented pomade, terribly worried lest she dirty her gloves. Since there weren't enough stable hands to unharness all the carriages, the men rolled up their sleeves and went to it themselves. According to their social status, they wore tail coats, frock coats, long jackets or short jackets. The tail coats were worthy garments, each of them a prized family possession taken out of the closet only on great occasions; the frock coats had great flaring skirts that billowed in the wind, cylindrical collars, and pockets as capacious as bags; the long jackets were double-breasted, of coarse wool, and usually worn with a cap of some kind, its peak trimmed with brass; and the short jackets were very short indeed, with two back buttons set close together like a pair of eyes, and stiff tails that looked as though a carpenter had hacked them with his axe out of a single block of wood. A few guests (these, of course, would sit at the foot of the table) wore dress smocks—that is, smocks with turned-down collars, fine pleating at the back, and stitched belts low on the hips.

And the shirts! They bulged like breastplates. Every man was freshly shorn; ears stood out from heads; faces were of a holiday smoothness. Some of the guests from farthest away, who had got up before dawn and had to shave in the dark, had slanting gashes under their noses, or patches of skin the size of a three-franc piece peeled from their jaws. During the journey their wounds had been inflamed by the wind, and as a result red blotches adorned many a big beaming white face.

Since the mayor's office was scarcely more than a mile from the farm, the wedding party went there on foot and came back the same way after the church ceremony. The procession was compact at first, like a bright sash festooning the countryside as it followed the narrow path winding between

2. Triangular scarves. *Tippets:* shoulder capes with hanging ends.

the green grain fields; but soon it lengthened out and broke up into different groups, which lingered to gossip along the way. The fiddler went first, the scroll of his violin gay with ribbons; then came the bridal pair; then their families; then their friends in no particular order; and last of all the children, having a good time pulling the bell-shaped flowers from the oat stalks or playing among themselves out of sight of their elders. Emma's gown was too long, and trailed a little; from time to time she stopped to pull it up; and at such moments she would carefully pick off the coarse grasses and thistle spikes with her gloved fingers, as Charles waited empty-handed beside her. Rouault, in a new silk hat, the cuffs of his black tail coat coming down over his hands as far as his fingertips, had given his arm to the older Madame Bovary. The older Monsieur Bovary, who looked on all these people with contempt, and had come wearing simply a single-breasted overcoat of military cut, was acting the barroom gallant with a blond young peasant girl. She bobbed and blushed, tongue-tied and confused. The other members of the wedding party discussed matters of business, or played tricks behind each other's backs, their spirits already soaring in anticipation of the fun. If they listened, they could hear the steady scraping of the fiddle in the fields. When the fiddler realized that he had left everyone far behind, he stopped for breath, carefully rubbed his bow with rosin to make his strings squeak all the better, and then set off again on his course, raising and lowering the neck of his violin to keep time. The sound of the instrument frightened away all the birds for a long distance ahead.

The table was set up in the carriage shed. On it were four roasts of beef, six fricassees of chicken, a veal casserole, three legs of mutton, and in the center a charming little suckling pig flanked by four *andouilles à l'oseille*— pork sausages flavored with sorrel. At the corners stood decanters of brandy. The sweet cider foamed up around its corks, and before anyone was seated, every glass had been filled to the brim with wine. Great dishes of yellow custard, their smooth surfaces decorated with the newlyweds' initials in candy-dot arabesques, were set trembling whenever the table was given the slightest knock. The pies and cakes had been ordered from a caterer in Yvetot. Since he was just starting up in the district, he had gone to considerable pains; and when dessert time came he himself brought to the table a wedding cake that drew exclamations from all. Its base was a square of blue cardboard representing a temple with porticos and colonnades and adorned on all sides with stucco statuettes standing in niches spangled with gold-paper stars. The second tier was a medieval castle in *gâteau de Savoie,* surrounded by miniature fortifications of angelica, almonds, raisins, and orange sections. And finally, on the topmost layer—which was a green meadow, with rocks, jelly lakes, and boats of hazelnut shells—a little Cupid was swinging in a chocolate swing. The tips of the two uprights, the highest points of the whole, were two real rosebuds.

The banquet went on till nightfall. Those who grew tired of sitting took a stroll in the yard or played a kind of shuffleboard in the barn; then they returned to table. A few, toward the end, fell asleep and snored. But everything came to life again with the coffee: there were songs, displays of strength. The men lifted weights, played the game of passing their heads under their arms while holding one thumb on the table, tried to raise carts to their shoulders. Dirty jokes were in order; the ladies were kissed. In the evening, when it came time to go, the horses, stuffed with oats to the bursting point, could scarcely be forced between the shafts; they kicked and reared, broke their harness, brought curses or laughs from their masters. And all night long, under the light of the moon on the country roads, runaway carts were bouncing along ditches at a gallop, leaping over gravel piles and crashing into banks, with women leaning out trying desperately to seize the reins.

Those who stayed at Les Bertaux spent the night drinking in the kitchen. The children fell asleep on the floor.

The bride had begged her father that she be spared the usual pranks. However, a fishmonger cousin (who had actually brought a pair of soles as a wedding present) was just beginning to spurt water from his mouth through the keyhole when Rouault came along and stopped him, explaining that the importance of his son-in-law's position didn't permit such unseemliness. The cousin complied very grudgingly. In his heart he accused Rouault of being a snob, and he joined a group of four or five other guests, who had happened several times in succession to be given inferior cuts of meat at table and so considered that they, too, had been badly treated. The whole group sat there whispering derogatory things about their host, and in veiled language expressed hopes for his downfall.

The older Madame Bovary hadn't opened her mouth all day. No one had consulted her about her daughter-in-law's bridal dress, or the arrangements for the party: she went up to bed early. Her husband didn't accompany her; instead, he sent to Saint-Victor for cigars and sat up till dawn smoking and drinking kirsch and hot water. This variety of grog was new to his fellow guests, and made him feel that their respect for him rose all the higher.

Charles was far from being a wag. He had been dull throughout the festivities, responding but feebly to the witticisms, puns, *doubles-entendres,* teasings and dubious jokes that everyone had felt obliged to toss at him from the moment they had sat down to the soup.

The next day, however, he seemed a different man. It was he who gave the impression of having lost his virginity overnight: the bride made not the slightest sign that could be taken to betray anything at all. Even the shrewdest were nonplused, and stared at her with the most intense curiosity whenever she came near. But Charles hid nothing. He addressed her as *"ma femme,"* using the intimate *"tu,"*[3] kept asking everyone where she was and looking for her everywhere, and often took her out into the yard, where he could be glimpsed through the trees with his arm around her waist, leaning over her as they walked, his head rumpling the yoke of her bodice.

Two days after the wedding the bridal pair left: because of his patients Charles could stay away no longer. Rouault had them driven to Tostes in his cart, going with them himself as far as Vassonville. There he kissed his daughter a last time, got out, and retraced his way. When he had walked about a hundred yards he stopped; and the sight of the cart disappearing in the distance, its wheels spinning in the dust, made him utter a deep sigh. He remembered his own wedding, his own earlier days, his wife's first pregnancy. He, too, had been very happy, the day he had taken her from her father's house to his own. She had ridden pillion behind him as their horse trotted over the snow, for it had been close to Christmas and the fields were

3. The intimate form of "you" (French). *Ma femme:* my wife (French).

white; she had clutched him with one arm, her basket hooked over the other; the wind was whipping the long lace streamers of her *coiffure cauchoise*[4] so that at times they blew across his mouth; and by turning his head he could see her rosy little face close behind his shoulder, smiling silently at him under the gold buckle of her bonnet. From time to time she would warm her fingers by sliding them inside his coat. How long ago it all was! Their boy would be thirty if he were alive today! Then he looked back again, and there was nothing to be seen on the road. He felt dismal, like a stripped and empty house; and as tender memories and black thoughts mingled in his brain, dulled by the vapors of the feast, he considered for a moment turning his steps toward the church. But he was afraid that the sight of it might make him even sadder, so he went straight home.

Monsieur and Madame Charles reached Tostes about six o'clock. The neighbors came to their windows to see their doctor's new wife.

The elderly maidservant appeared, greeted them, apologized for not having dinner ready, and suggested that Madame, in the meantime, might like to make a tour of inspection of her house.

V

The brick house-front was exactly flush with the street, or rather the road. Behind the door hung a coat with a short cape, a bridle, and a black leather cap; and on the floor in the corner lay a pair of gaiters still caked with mud. To the right was the parlor, which served as both dining and sitting room. A canary yellow wallpaper, set off at the top by a border of pale flowers, rippled everywhere on its loose canvas lining; white calico curtains edged with red braid hung crosswise down the length of the windows; and on the narrow mantelpiece a clock ornamented with a head of Hippocrates stood proudly between two silver-plated candlesticks under oval glass domes. Across the hall was Charles's small consulting room, about eighteen feet wide, with a table, three straight chairs and an office armchair. There was a fir bookcase with six shelves, occupied almost exclusively by a set of the *Dictionary of the Medical Sciences,* its pages uncut but its binding battered by a long succession of owners. Cooking smells seeped through the wall during office hours, and the patients' coughs and confidences were quite audible in the kitchen. In the rear, opening directly into the yard (which contained the stables), was a big ramshackle room with an oven, now serving as woodshed, wine bin and storeroom; it was filled with old junk, empty barrels, broken tools, and a quantity of other objects all dusty and nondescript.

The long narrow garden ran back between two clay walls covered with espaliered apricot trees to the thorn hedge that marked it off from the fields. In the middle was a slate sundial on a stone pedestal. Four beds of scrawny rose bushes were arranged symmetrically around a square plot given over to vegetables. At the far end, under some spruces, a plaster priest stood reading his breviary.

Emma went up to the bedrooms. The first was empty; in the second, the conjugal chamber, a mahogany bed stood in an alcove hung with red draperies. A box made of seashells adorned the chest of drawers; and on the desk

4. Cauchois headdress.

near the window, standing in a decanter and tied with white satin ribbon, was a bouquet of orange blossoms—a bride's bouquet: the *other* bride's bouquet! She stared at it. Charles noticed, picked it up, and took it to the attic; and as her boxes and bags were brought up and placed around her, she sat in an armchair and thought of her own bridal bouquet, which was packed in one of those very boxes, wondering what would be done with it if she were to die.

She spent the first few days planning changes in the house. She took the domes off the candlesticks, had the parlor repapered, the stairs painted, and seats made to go around the sundial in the garden. She even made inquiries as to the best way of installing a fountain and a fish pond. And her husband, knowing that she liked to go for drives, bought a secondhand two-wheeled buggy. With new lamps and quilted leather mudguards it looked almost like a tilbury.

He was happy now, without a care in the world. A meal alone with her, a stroll along the highway in the evening, the way she touched her hand to her hair, the sight of her straw hat hanging from a window hasp, and many other things in which it had never occurred to him to look for pleasure—such now formed the steady current of his happiness. In bed in the morning, his head beside hers on the pillow, he would watch the sunlight on the downy gold of her cheeks, half covered by the scalloped tabs of her nightcap. Seen from so close, her eyes appeared larger than life, especially when she opened and shut her eyelids several times on awakening: black when looked at in shadow, dark blue in bright light, they seemed to contain layer upon layer of color, thicker and cloudier beneath, lighter and more transparent toward the lustrous surface. As his own eyes plunged into those depths, he saw himself reflected there in miniature down to his shoulders—his foulard on his head, his nightshirt open. After he had dressed she would go to the window and watch him leave for his rounds; she would lean out between two pots of geraniums, her elbows on the sill, her dressing gown loose around her. In the street, Charles would strap on his spurs at the mounting block; and she would continue to talk to him from above, blowing down to him some bit of flower or leaf she had bitten off in her teeth. It would flutter down hesitantly, weaving semicircles in the air like a bird, and before reaching the ground it would catch in the tangled mane of the old white mare standing motionless at the door. From the saddle Charles would send her a kiss; she would respond with a wave; then she would close the window, and he was off. And on the endless dusty ribbon of the highway, on sunken roads vaulted over by branches, on paths between stands of grain that rose to his knees—the sun on his shoulders and the morning air in his nostrils, his heart full of the night's bliss, his spirit at peace and his flesh content—he would ride on his way ruminating his happiness, like someone who keeps savoring, hours later, the fragrance of the truffles he has eaten for dinner.

Up until now, had there ever been a happy time in his life? His years at the lycée, where he had lived shut in behind high walls, lonely among richer, cleverer schoolmates who laughed at his country accent and made fun of his clothes and whose mothers brought them cookies in their muffs on visiting days? Or later, when he was studying medicine and hadn't enough in his purse to go dancing with some little working girl who might have become his mistress? After that he had lived fourteen months with the widow, whose feet in bed had been like icicles. But now he possessed, and for always, this pretty wife whom he so loved. The universe, for him, went not beyond the silken circuit of her petticoat; and he would reproach himself for not showing her his love, and yearn to be back with her. He would gallop home, rush upstairs, his heart pounding. Emma would be at her dressing table; he would creep up silently behind her and kiss her; she would cry out in surprise.

He couldn't keep from constantly touching her comb, her rings, everything she wore; sometimes he gave her great full-lipped kisses on the cheek, or a whole series of tiny kisses up her bare arm, from her fingertips to her shoulder; and half amused, half annoyed, she would push him away as one does an importunate child.

Before her marriage she had thought that she had love within her grasp; but since the happiness which she had expected this love to bring her hadn't come, she supposed she must have been mistaken. And Emma tried to imagine just what was meant, in life, by the words "bliss," "passion," and "rapture"—words that had seemed so beautiful to her in books.

VI

She had read *Paul and Virginia*,[5] and had dreamed of the bamboo cabin, of the Negro Domingo and the dog Fidèle; and especially she dreamed that she, too, had a sweet little brother for a devoted friend, and that he climbed trees as tall as church steeples to pluck her their crimson fruit, and came running barefoot over the sand to bring her a bird's nest.

When she was thirteen, her father took her to the city to enter her as a boarder in the convent. They stayed at a hotel near Saint-Gervais, where their supper plates were decorated with scenes from the life of Mademoiselle de La Vallière.[6] The explanatory captions, slashed here and there by knife scratches, were all in praise of piety, the sensibilities of the heart, and the splendors of the court.

Far from being unhappy in the convent, at first, she enjoyed the company of the nuns: it was fun when they took her to the chapel, down a long corridor from the refectory. She rarely played during recess, and she was very quick at catechism: it was always Mademoiselle Rouault who answered Monsieur le vicaire's hardest questions. As she continued to live uninterruptedly in the insipid atmosphere of the classrooms, among the white-faced women with their brass crucifixes dangling from their rosaries, she gently succumbed to the mystical languor induced by the perfumes of the altar, the coolness of the holy-water fonts, the gleaming of the candles. Instead of following the Mass she kept her prayer book open at the holy pictures with their sky-blue borders; and she loved the Good Shepherd, the Sacred Heart pierced by sharp arrows, and poor Jesus stumbling and falling under his cross. To mortify herself she tried to go a whole day without eating. She looked for some vow that she might accomplish.

5. A 1784 story of the sentimental tragic love of two young people on the tropical island of Île de France (today, Mauritius). It was the most popular work of Bernardin de Saint-Pierre (1737–1814). 6. One of Louis XIV's mistresses, whose mythologized character is familiar to all readers of Alexandre Dumas's *Le Vicomte de Bragelonne* (a sequel to *The Three Musketeers*).

When she went to confession she invented small sins in order to linger on her knees there in the darkness, her hands joined, her face at the grille, the priest whispering just above her. The metaphors constantly used in sermons—"betrothed," "spouse," "heavenly lover," "mystical marriage"— excited her in a thrilling new way.

Every evening before prayers a piece of religious writing was read aloud in study hall. During the week it would be some digest of Biblical history or the Abbé Frayssinous's lectures; on Sunday it was always a passage from the *Génie du Christianisme*,[7] offered as entertainment. How intently she listened, the first times, to the ringing lamentations of that romantic melancholy, echoed and reechoed by all the voices of earth and heaven! Had her childhood been spent in cramped quarters behind some city shop, she might have been open to the lyric appeal of nature—which usually reaches us only by way of literary interpretations. But she knew too much about country life: she was well acquainted with lowing herds, with dairy maids and ploughs. From such familiar, peaceful aspects, she turned to the picturesque. She loved the sea for its storms alone, cared for vegetation only when it grew here and there among ruins. She had to extract a kind of personal advantage from things; and she rejected as useless everything that promised no immediate gratification—for her temperament was more sentimental than artistic, and what she was looking for was emotions, not scenery.

At the convent there was an old spinster who came for a week every month to look after the linen. As a member of an ancient noble family ruined by the Revolution she was a protégée of the archdiocese; and she ate at the nuns' table in the refectory and always stayed for a chat with them before returning upstairs to her work. The girls often slipped out of study-hall to pay her a visit. She had a repertoire of eighteenth-century love songs, and sang them in a low voice as she sewed. She told stories, kept the girls abreast of the news, did errands for them in the city, and to the older ones would surreptitiously lend one of the novels she always carried in her apron pocket—novels of which the good spinster herself was accustomed to devour long chapters in the intervals of her task. They were invariably about love affairs, lovers, mistresses, harassed ladies swooning in remote pavilions. Couriers were killed at every relay, horses ridden to death on every page; there were gloomy forests, broken hearts, vows, sobs, tears and kisses, skiffs in the moonlight, nightingales in thickets; the noblemen were all brave as lions, gentle as lambs, incredibly virtuous, always beautifully dressed, and wept copiously on every occasion. For six months, when she was fifteen, Emma begrimed her hands with this dust from old lending libraries. Later, reading Walter Scott, she became infatuated with everything historical and dreamed about oaken chests and guardrooms and troubadours. She would have liked to live in some old manor, like those long-waisted chatelaines who spent their days leaning out of fretted Gothic casements, elbow on parapet and chin in hand, watching a white-plumed knight come galloping out of the distance on a black horse. At that time she worshiped Mary Queen of

---

7. An enormously influential book (1802), by François-René de Chateaubriand, celebrating the truths and beauties of Roman Catholicism, just before Napoleon's concordat with Rome. Denis de Frayssinous (1765–1841) was a popular preacher who wrote *Défense du Christianisme* (1825). Under Louis XVIII (restored to the throne after the fall of Napoleon I) he became a bishop and minister of ecclesiastical affairs.

Scots, and venerated women illustrious or ill-starred. In her mind Joan of Arc, Héloise, Agnès Sorel, La Belle Ferronière and Clémence Isaure[8] stood out like comets on the shadowy immensity of history; and here and there (though less clearly outlined than the others against the dim background, and quite unrelated among themselves) were visible also St. Louis and his oak, the dying Bayard, certain atrocities of Louis XI, bits of the Massacre of St. Bartholomew, the plumed crest of Henri IV, and, always, the memory of the hotel plates glorifying Louis XIV.[9]

The sentimental songs she sang in music class were all about little angels with golden wings, madonnas, lagoons, gondoliers—mawkish compositions that allowed her to glimpse, through the silliness of the words and the indiscretions of the music, the alluring, phantasmagoric realm of genuine feeling. Some of her schoolmates brought to the convent the keepsake albums they had received as New Year's gifts. They had to hide them—it was very exciting; they could be read only at night, in the dormitory. Careful not to harm the lovely satin bindings, Emma stared bedazzled at the names of the unknown authors—counts or viscounts, most of them—who had written their signatures under their contributions.

She quivered as she blew back the tissue paper from each engraving: it would curl up into the air, then sink gently down against the page. Behind a balcony railing a young man in a short cloak clasped in his arms a girl in a white dress, a chatelaine bag fastened to her belt; or there were portraits of unidentified aristocratic English beauties with blond curls, staring out at you with their wide light-colored eyes from under great straw hats. Some were shown lolling in carriages, gliding through parks; their greyhound ran ahead, and two little grooms in white knee breeches drove the trotting horses. Others, dreaming on sofas, an opened letter lying beside them, gazed at the moon through a window that was half open, half draped with a black curtain. Coy maidens with tears on their cheeks kissed turtledoves through the bars of Gothic bird cages; or, smiling, their cheeks practically touching their own shoulders, they pulled the petals from daisies with pointed fingers that curved up at the ends like Eastern slippers. Then there were sultans with long pipes swooning under arbors in the arms of dancing girls; there were Giaours,[1] Turkish sabres, fezzes. And invariably there were blotchy, pale landscapes of fantastic countries: pines and palms growing together, tigers on the right, a lion on the left, Tartar minarets on the horizon. Roman ruins in the foreground, a few kneeling camels—all of it set in a very neat and orderly virgin forest, with a great perpendicular sunbeam quivering in the water; and standing out on the water's surface—scratched in white on the steel-gray background—a few widely spaced floating swans.

The bracket lamp above Emma's head shone down on those pictures of

---

8. A half-fictional lady from Toulouse (fourteenth century), popularized in a novel by Florian as an incarnation of the mystical poetry of the troubadours. Héloise, famous for her love affair with the philosopher Abelard (1101–1164). Agnès Sorel (1422–1450), a mistress of Charles VII, rumored to have been poisoned by the future Louis XI. La Belle Ferronière (d. 1540), one of François I's mistresses, wife of the lawyer Le Ferron, who is said to have contracted syphilis for the mere satisfaction of passing it on to the king.
9. Massacre of the Protestants ordered by Catherine de Medici in the night of August 23, 1572. St. Louis (1215–1270), king of France as Louis IX, led the seventh and eighth crusades and was canonized in 1297. According to tradition, he dispensed justice under an oak tree at Vincennes (near Paris). *Bayard*: Seigneur de Pierre du Terrail (1473–1542), one of the most famous French captains, distinguished himself by feats of bravery during the wars of François I. When dying, he chided the connétable de Bourbon for his treason in a famous speech. Louis XI (b. 1421; ruled 1461–83), ruthlessly suppressed the rebellious noblemen.
1. Romantic heroes of the outcast desperado type.

every corner of the world as she turned them over one by one in the silence of the dormitory, the only sound, coming from the distance, that of some belated cab on the boulevards.

When her mother died, she wept profusely for several days. She had a memorial picture made for herself from the dead woman's hair; and in a letter filled with sorrowful reflections on life that she sent to Les Bertaux, she begged to be buried, when her time came, in the same grave. Her father thought she must be ill, and went to see her. Emma was privately pleased to feel that she had so very quickly attained this ideal of ethereal languor, inaccessible to mediocre spirits. So she let herself meander along Lamartinian[2] paths, listening to the throbbing of harps on lakes, to all the songs of dying swans, to the falling of every leaf, to the flight of pure virgins ascending to heaven, and to the voice of the Eternal speaking in the valleys. Gradually these things began to bore her, but she refused to admit it and continued as before, first out of habit, then out of vanity; until one day she discovered with surprise that the whole mood had evaporated, leaving her heart as free of melancholy as her brow was free of wrinkles.

The good nuns, who had been taking her vocation quite for granted, were greatly surprised to find that Mademoiselle Rouault was apparently slipping out of their control. And indeed they had so deluged her with prayers, retreats, novenas and sermons, preached so constantly the respect due the saints and the martyrs, and given her so much good advice about modest behavior and the saving of her soul, that she reacted like a horse too tightly reined: she balked, and the bit fell from her teeth. In her enthusiasms she had always looked for something tangible: she had loved the church for its flowers, music for its romantic words, literature for its power to stir the passions; and she rebelled before the mysteries of faith just as she grew ever more restive under discipline, which was antipathetic to her nature. When her father took her out of school no one was sorry to see her go. The Mother Superior, indeed, remarked that she had lately been displaying a certain lack of reverence toward the community.

Back at home, Emma at first enjoyed giving orders to the servants, then grew sick of country life and longed to be back in the convent. By the time Charles first appeared at Les Bertaux she thought that she was cured of illusions—that she had nothing more to learn, and no great emotions to look forward to.

But in her eagerness for a change, or perhaps overstimulated by this man's presence, she easily persuaded herself that love, that marvelous thing which had hitherto been like a great rosy-plumaged bird soaring in the splendors of poetic skies, was at last within her grasp. And now she could not bring herself to believe that the uneventful life she was leading was the happiness of which she had dreamed.

VII

She reflected occasionally that these were, nevertheless, the most beautiful days of her life—the honeymoon days, as people called them. To be sure, their sweetness would be best enjoyed far off, in one of those lands

---

2. Alphonse de Lamartine (1790–1869), French Romantic poet, whose *Méditations poétiques* (1820) resounds with amorous and religious melancholy.

with exciting names where the first weeks of marriage can be savored so much more deliciously and languidly! The post chaise with its blue silk curtains would have climbed slowly up the mountain roads, and the postilion's song would have reechoed among the cliffs, mingling with the tinkling of goat bells and the dull roar of waterfalls. They would have breathed the fragrance of lemon trees at sunset by the shore of some bay; and at night, alone on the terrace of a villa, their fingers intertwined, they would have gazed at the stars and planned their lives. It seemed to her that certain portions of the earth must produce happiness—as though it were a plant native only to those soils and doomed to languish elsewhere. Why couldn't she be leaning over the balcony of some Swiss chalet? Or nursing her melancholy in a cottage in Scotland, with a husband clad in a long black velvet coat and wearing soft leather shoes, a high-crowned hat and fancy cuffs?

She might have been glad to confide all these things to someone. But how speak about so elusive a malaise, one that keeps changing its shape like the clouds and its direction like the winds? She could find no words; and hence neither occasion nor courage came to hand.

Still, if Charles had made the slightest effort, if he had had the slightest inkling, if his glance had a single time divined her thought, it seemed to her that her heart would have been relieved of its fullness as quickly and easily as a tree drops its ripe fruit at the touch of a hand. But even as they were brought closer together by the details of daily life, she was separated from him by a growing sense of inward detachment.

Charles's conversation was flat as a sidewalk, a place of passage for the ideas of everyman; they wore drab everyday clothes, and they inspired neither laughter nor dreams. When he had lived in Rouen, he said, he had never had any interest in going to the theatre to see the Parisian company that was acting there. He couldn't swim or fence or fire a pistol; one day he couldn't tell her the meaning of a riding term she had come upon in a novel.

Wasn't it a man's role, though, to know everything? Shouldn't he be expert at all kinds of things, able to initiate you into the intensities of passion, the refinements of life, all the mysteries? *This* man could teach you nothing; he knew nothing, he wished for nothing. He took it for granted that she was content; and she resented his settled calm, his serene dullness, the very happiness she herself brought him.

She drew occasionally; and Charles enjoyed nothing more than standing beside her watching her bent over her sketchbook, half shutting his eyes the better to see her work, or rolling her bread-crumb erasers between his thumb and finger. As for the piano, the faster her fingers flew the more he marveled. She played with dash, swooping up and down the keyboard without a break. The strings of the old instrument jangled as she pounded, and when the window was open it could be heard to the end of the village. The *huissier*'s clerk often stopped to listen as he passed on the road—bareheaded, shuffling along in slippers, holding in his hand the notice he was about to post.

Moreover, Emma knew how to run her house. She let Charles's patients know how much they owed him, writing them nicely phrased letters that didn't sound like bills. When a neighbor came to Sunday dinner she always managed to think up some attractive dish. She would arrange greengages in a pyramid on a bed of vine leaves; she served her jellies not in their jars but neatly turned out on a plate; she spoke of buying finger bowls for dessert. All this redounded greatly to Bovary's credit.

He came to esteem himself the higher for having such a wife. He had two of her pencil sketches framed in wide frames, and hung them proudly in the parlor, at the end of long green cords. Citizens returning from Mass saw him standing on his doorstep, wearing a splendid pair of carpet slippers.

He came home from his rounds late—ten o'clock, sometimes midnight. He was hungry at that hour, and since the servant had gone to bed it was Emma who served him. He would take off his coat to be more comfortable at table, tell her every person he had seen, every village he had been to, every prescription he had written; and he would complacently eat what was left of the stew, pare his cheese, munch an apple, pour himself the last drop of wine. Then he would go up to bed, fall asleep the minute he was stretched on his back, and begin to snore.

He had so long been used to wearing cotton nightcaps that he couldn't get his foulard to stay on his head, and in the morning his hair was all over his face and white with down—the strings of his pillowcase often came undone during the night. He always wore heavy boots, with deep creases slanting from instep to ankle and the rest of the uppers so stiff that they seemed to be made of wood. He said that they were "plenty good enough for the country."

His mother approved his thriftiness. As in the past, she came to visit him whenever there was a particularly violent crisis in her own home; and yet she seemed to be prejudiced against her new daughter-in-law. She considered her "too grand in her tastes for the kind of people they were": the younger Bovarys ran through wood, sugar and candles at the rate of some great establishment; and the amount of charcoal they used would have done the cooking for twenty-five. She rearranged Emma's linen in the closets and taught her to check on the butcher when he delivered the meat. Emma listened to these lectures; Madame Bovary did not stint herself; and all day there would be a tremulous-lipped exchange of *"ma fille"* and *"ma mère,"*[3] each of the ladies uttering the sugary words in a voice that quivered with rage.

In Madame Dubuc's day the older woman had known herself to be the favorite; but now Charles's love for Emma seemed to her a desertion, an invasion of her own right; and she looked on sadly at Charles's happiness, like a ruined man staring through a window at revelers in a house that was once his own. Using the device of "Do you remember?" she reminded him of everything she had suffered and sacrificed for his sake; and contrasting all this with Emma's careless ways she pointed out how wrong he was to adore his wife to the exclusion of herself.

Charles didn't know what to answer. He respected his mother, and his love for his wife was boundless; he considered the former's opinions infallible, and yet Emma seemed to him perfect. After the older Madame Bovary's departure he made a fainthearted attempt to repeat one or two of the milder things he had heard her say, using her own phraseology; but with a word or two Emma convinced him he was wrong, and sent him back to his patients.

3. My mother (French). *Ma fille:* my daughter (French).

Throughout all this, following formulas she believed efficacious, she kept trying to experience love. Under the moonlight in the garden she would recite to Charles all the amorous verses she knew by heart, and sing him soulful sighing songs; but it all left her as unruffled as before, and Charles, too, seemed as little lovesick, as little stirred, as ever.

Having thus failed to produce the slightest spark of love in herself, and since she was incapable of understanding what she didn't experience, or of recognizing anything that wasn't expressed in conventional terms, she reached the conclusion that Charles's desire for her was nothing very extraordinary. His transports had become regularized; he embraced her only at certain times. This had now become a habit like any other—like a dessert that could be counted on to end a monotonous meal.

A gamekeeper whom Monsieur had cured of pneumonia made Madame a present of a little Italian greyhound bitch, and she took her with her whenever she went for a stroll: she did this every now and then, for the sake of a moment's solitude, a momentary relief from the everlasting sight of the back garden and the dusty road.

She would walk to the avenue of beeches at Banneville, near the abandoned pavilion at the corner of the wall along the fields. Rushes grow in the ditch there, tall and sharp edged among the grass.

Once arrived she would look around her, to see whether anything had changed since the last time she had come. The foxgloves and the wallflowers were where they had been; clumps of nettles were still growing around the stones; patches of lichen still clung along the three windows, whose perennially closed shutters were rotting away from their rusty iron bars. Her thoughts would be vague at first, straying like her dog, who would be running in circles, barking at yellow butterflies, chasing field mice, nibbling poppies at the edge of a wheatfield. Then her ideas would gradually focus; and sitting on the grass, jabbing it with little pokes of her parasol, Emma would ask herself again and again: "Why—*why*—did I ever marry?"

She wondered whether some different set of circumstances might not have resulted in her meeting some different man; and she tried to picture those imaginary circumstances, the life they would have brought her, the unknown other husband. However she imagined him, he wasn't a bit like Charles. He might have been handsome, witty, distinguished, magnetic—the kind of man her convent schoolmates had doubtless married. What kind of lives were they leading now? Cities, busy streets, buzzing theatres, brilliant balls—such surroundings afforded them unlimited opportunities for deep emotions and exciting sensations. But *her* life was as cold as an attic facing north; and boredom, like a silent spider, was weaving its web in the shadows, in every corner of her heart. She remembered Prize Days, when she had gone up onto the stage to receive her little wreaths. She had been charming, with her braids, her white dress, her prunella-cloth slippers. Gentlemen had leaned over, when she was back in her seat, and paid her compliments; the courtyard had been full of carriages; guests called good-bye to her as they rolled away; the music teacher with his violin case bowed to her as he passed. How far away it all was! How far!

She would call Djali,[4] take her between her knees, stroke her long delicate

---

4. The name of the little she-goat in Hugo's *Notre Dame de Paris*.

head. "Kiss your mistress," she would say, "you happy, carefree thing." The slender Djali would yawn slowly, as a dog does; and the melancholy look in her eyes would touch Emma, and she would liken her to herself, talking to her aloud as though comforting someone in distress.

Sometimes squalls blew up, winds that suddenly swept in from the sea over the plateau of the *pays de Caux*[5] and filled the countryside with fresh, salt-smelling air. The whistling wind would flatten the reeds and rustle the trembling beech leaves, while the tops of the trees swayed and murmured. Emma would pull her shawl close about her shoulders and get up.

Under the double row of trees a green light filtered down through the leaves onto the velvety moss that crunched softly beneath her feet. The sun was setting; the sky showed red between the branches; and the identical trunks of the straight line of trees were like a row of brown columns against a golden backdrop; a terror would seize her, she would call Djali and walk quickly back to Tostes along the highway. There she would sink into an armchair, and sit silent all evening.

Then, late in September, something exceptional happened: she was invited to La Vaubyessard, home of the marquis d'Andervilliers.

The marquis had been a member of the cabinet under the Restoration; and now, hoping to reenter political life, he was paving the way for his candidature to the Chamber of Deputies. He made generous distributions of firewood among the poor in the winter, and in sessions of the departmental council he was always eloquent in demanding better roads for his district. During the hot weather he had had a mouth abscess, which Charles had relieved—miraculously, it seemed—by a timely nick of the scalpel. His steward, sent to Tostes to pay the bill for the operation, reported that evening that he had seen some superb cherries in the doctor's little garden. The cherry trees at La Vaubyessard weren't doing well; Monsieur le marquis asked Charles for a few grafts, made a point of going to thank him personally, saw Emma, and noticed that she had a pretty figure and didn't curtsy like a peasant. So at the château it was decided that the doctor and his young wife could be invited without any transgression of the limits of condescension, and at the same time could be counted on to behave with decorum among their betters.

One Wednesday at three in the afternoon, therefore, Monsieur and Madame Bovary set out in their buggy for La Vaubyessard, a large trunk tied on behind and a hatbox in front. Charles had another box between his legs.

They arrived at nightfall, just as lanterns were being lit in the grounds to illuminate the driveway.

VIII

The château, a modern building in the Italian style, with two projecting wings and three entrances along the front, stretched across the far end of a vast expanse of turf where cows grazed in the open spaces between groups of tall trees. Tufts of shrubbery—rhododendrons, syringas and snowballs—made a variegated border along the curving line of the graveled drive. A stream flowed under a bridge; through the evening haze the thatched farm

---

5. Caux country (French; see n. 1, p. 858).

buildings could be seen scattered over a meadow shut in by two gently rising wooded ridges; and at the rear, in among thick plantings of trees, were the two parallel lines of the coach houses and the stables—remains of the original, ancient château that had been torn down.

Charles's buggy drew up before the middle door; servants appeared, then the marquis, who gave the doctor's wife his arm and led her into the entrance hall.

This had a marble floor and a high ceiling; footsteps and voices echoed as in a church. From the far side rose a straight staircase; and to the left a gallery giving on the garden led to the billiard room: the sound of clicking ivory balls could be heard ahead. As she passed through on her way to the drawing room Emma noticed the men around the table: dignified-looking, with cravats reaching up to their chins and decorations on their chests, they smiled silently as they made their shots. On the dark wall-paneling hung great gilded frames, inscribed at the base with names in black letters. "Jean-Antoine d'Andervilliers d' Yverbonville, comte de la Vaubyessard and baron de la Fresnaye, killed at the battle of Coutras,[6] October 20, 1587." Or: "Jean-Antoine-Henry-Guy d'Andervilliers de la Vaubyessard, admiral of the fleet and knight of the order of St. Michael, wounded in the battle of La Hogue, May 29, 1692, died at La Vaubyessard January 23, 1693." The rest were barely visible, for the lamplight was directed down on the green felt of the tables, and much of the room was in shadow. This darkened the row of pictures: only the crackle of their varnish caught an occasional broken gleam, and here and there some detail of painting lighter than the rest stood out from one of the dim, gold-framed rectangles: a pale forehead, two staring eyes, powdered wigs cascading onto red-coated shoulders, a garter buckle high up on a fleshy calf.

The marquis opened the drawing-room door, and one of the ladies rose. It was the marquise, and she came over to Emma, greeted her, drew her down beside her on a settee and talked to her as easily as though they were old acquaintances. She was a woman of forty or so, with fine shoulders, a hooked nose and a drawling voice; on her auburn hair she was wearing a simple bit of lace, the points falling down behind. Close beside her sat a blond young woman in a high-backed chair; and around the fireplace gentlemen with flowers in their buttonholes were chatting with the ladies.

Dinner was served at seven. The men, more numerous than the ladies, were put at a table in the entrance hall; the ladies sat down in the dining room, with the marquis and the marquise.

Here the air was warm and fragrant; the scent of flowers and fine linen mingled with the odor of cooked meats and truffles. Candle flames cast long gleams on rounded silver dish-covers; the clouded facets of the cut glass shone palely; there was a row of bouquets all down the table; and on the wide bordered plates the napkins stood like bishops' mitres, each with an oval-shaped roll between its folds. Red lobster claws protruded from platters; oversized fruit was piled up on moss in openwork baskets; quail were served in their plumage; steam rose from open dishes; and the platters of carved meat were brought round by the maître d'hotel himself, grave as a judge in

6. In the Gironde; the battle was won by Henri de Navarre against the duc de Joyeuse.

silk stockings, knee breeches, white neckcloth and jabot. He reached them down between the guests, and with a flick of his spoon transferred to each plate the piece desired. Atop the high copper-banded porcelain stove the statue of a woman swathed to the chin in drapery stared down motionless at the company.

Madame Bovary was surprised to notice that several of the ladies had failed to put their gloves in their wineglasses.[7]

At the head of the table, alone among ladies, was an old man. His napkin was tied around his neck like a child's, and he sat hunched over his heaped plate, gravy dribbling from his mouth. The underlids of his eyes hung down and showed red inside, and he wore his hair in a little pigtail wound with black ribbon. This was the marquis's father-in-law, the old duc de Laverdière, favorite of the duc d'Artois in the days of the marquis de Conflans's hunting parties at Le Vaudreuil: he was said to have been Marie-Antoinette's lover between Monsieur de Coigny and Monsieur de Lauzun. He had led a wild, dissipated life, filled with duels, wagers and abductions; he had gone through his money and been the terror of his family. Now, muttering unintelligibly, he pointed his finger at one dish after another, and a servant standing behind his chair shouted their names in his ear. Emma's eyes kept coming back to this pendulous-lipped old man as though he were someone extraordinary, someone august. He had lived at court! He had slept with a queen!

Iced champagne was served, and the feel of the cold wine in her mouth gave Emma a shiver that ran over her from head to toe. She had never seen pomegranates or eaten pineapple. Even the powdered sugar seemed to her whiter and finer than elsewhere.

Then the ladies went up to their rooms to dress for the ball.

Emma devoted herself to her toilette with the meticulous care of an actress the night of her debut. She did her hair as the hairdresser advised, and slipped into her gauzy *barège*[8] gown, which had been laid out for her on the bed.

Charles's trousers were too tight at the waist. And then, "The shoe straps will interfere with my dancing," he said.

"You? Dance?" Emma cried.

"Of course!"

"But you're crazy! Everybody would laugh. You mustn't. It's not suitable for a doctor, anyway," she added.

Charles said no more. He walked up and down waiting for Emma to be ready.

He saw her from behind in a mirror, between two sconces. Her dark eyes seemed darker than ever. Her hair, drawn down smoothly on both sides and slightly fluffed out over the ears, shone with a blue luster; in her chignon a rose quivered on its flexible stem, with artificial dewdrops at the leaf-tips. Her gown was pale saffron, trimmed with three bunches of pompon roses and green sprays.

Charles came up to kiss her on the shoulder. "Don't!" she cried. "You're rumpling me."

7. The ladies in the provinces, unlike their Paris counterparts, did not drink wine at public dinner parties and signified their intention by putting their gloves in their wineglasses. The fact that they fail to do so suggests to Emma the high degree of sophistication of the company.   8. A filmy fabric.

The strains of a violin floated up the stairs; a horn joined in. As Emma went down she had to restrain herself from running.

The quadrilles[9] had begun. More and more guests were arriving; there was something of a crush. Emma stayed near the door on a settee.

When the music stopped, the dance floor was left to the men, who stood there talking in groups, and to the liveried servants, who crossed it with their heavy trays. Along the line of seated women there was a flutter of painted fans; smiles were half hidden behind bouquets; gold-stoppered scent bottles twisted and turned in white-gloved hands, the tight silk binding the wrists and showing the form of the nails. There was a froth of lace around décolletages, a flashing of diamonds at throats; bracelets dangling medals and coins tinkled on bare arms. Hair was sleek and shining in front, twisted and knotted behind; and every coiffure had its wreath or bunch or sprig—of forget-me-nots, jasmine, pomegranate blossoms, wheat-sprays, cornflowers. The dowagers, sitting calm and formidable, wore red headdresses like turbans.

Emma's heart pounded a bit as her partner led her out by the fingertips and she waited in line for the starting signal on the violin. But her nervousness soon wore off, and swaying and nodding in time with the orchestra, she glided forward. She responded with a smile to the violinist's flourishes as he continued to play solo when the other instruments stopped; at such moments the chink of gold pieces came clearly from the gaming tables in the next room; then everything was in full swing again: the cornet blared, once again feet tramped in rhythm, skirts ballooned and brushed together, hands joined and separated; eyes lowered one moment looked intently into yours the next.

Scattered among the dancers or talking in doorways were a number of men—a dozen or so, aged from twenty-five to forty—who were clearly distinguishable from the rest by a certain look of overbreeding common to them all despite differences of age, dress, or feature.

Their coats were better cut and seemed to be of finer cloth; their hair, brought forward in ringlets over the temples, seemed to glisten with more expensive pomades. Their complexion bespoke wealth: they had the pale, very white skin that goes so well with the diaphanous tints of porcelain, the luster of satin, the patina of old wood, and is kept flawless by simple, exquisite fare. These men moved their heads unconstrainedly above low cravats; their long side whiskers drooped onto turned-down collars; they wiped their lips with handkerchiefs that were deliciously scented and monogrammed with huge initials. Those who were beginning to age preserved a youthful look, while the faces of the young had a touch of ripeness. There was an air of indifference about them, a calm produced by the gratification of every passion; and though their manners were suave, one could sense beneath them that special brutality which comes from the habit of breaking down half-hearted resistances that keep one fit and tickle ones vanity—the handling of blooded horses, the pursuit of loose women.

A few steps from Emma a blue-coated gentleman was deep in Italy with a pale young woman in pearls. They were gushing about the massiveness of the piers in St. Peter's, about Tivoli, Vesuvius, Castellamare and the Cascine,[1] the roses in Genoa, the Colosseum by moonlight. And the conver-

---

9. A square dance with four couples, fashionable in the nineteenth century.   1. A park near Florence. Castellamare is a port south of Naples.

sation heard with her other ear was full of words she didn't understand: it was coming from a circle that had formed around a very young man who only the week before had "beaten Miss Arabella and Romulus" and seemed to have won two thousand louis d'or by jumping a certain ditch in England. One of the speakers was complaining that his racers were putting on weight, another that misprints had made the name of his horse unrecognizable in the newspapers.

The air in the ballroom had grown heavy; the lamps were beginning to dim; a number of the men disappeared in the direction of the billiard room. A servant climbed on a chair and broke two panes in a window; at the sound of the smash Madame Bovary turned her head and saw peasants peering in from the garden, their faces pressed against the glass. She thought of Les Bertaux: she saw the farm, the muddy pond, her father in a smock under the apple trees; and she saw herself as she had been there, skimming cream with her finger from the milk jars in the dairy. But amid the splendors of this night her past life, hitherto so vividly present, was vanishing utterly; indeed she was beginning almost to doubt that she had lived it. She was here: and around the brilliant ball was a shadow that veiled all else. She was eating a maraschino ice, at that precise moment, from a gilded silver scallop-shell that she was holding in her left hand; the spoon was between her teeth, her eyes were half shut.

A lady near her dropped her fan just as a gentleman was passing. "Would you be good enough to pick up my fan, Monsieur?" she asked him. "It's there behind the sofa."

The gentleman bowed, and as he stretched out his arm Emma saw the lady toss something into his hat, something white, folded in the shape of a triangle. The gentleman recovered the fan and handed it to the lady respectfully; she thanked him with a nod and began to sniff at her bouquet.

For supper there was an array of Spanish wines and Rhine wines, bisque soup and cream of almond soup. Trafalgar pudding, and platters of all kinds of cold meat in trembling aspic; and after it the carriages began gradually to leave. Drawing back a corner of a muslin curtain, Emma could see their lamps slipping away into the darkness. The settees emptied; some of the card players stayed on; the musicians cooled the tips of their fingers on their tongues; Charles was half asleep, propped up against a door.

At three in the morning the closing cotillion began. Emma had never waltzed. Everyone else was waltzing, including Mademoiselle d'Andervilliers and the marquise; by this time only the hosts and the house guests remained, about a dozen in all. One of the waltzers, whom everyone called simply "Vicomte," and whose very low-cut waistcoat seemed to be molded on his torso, came up to Madame Bovary and for the second time asked her to be his partner. He would lead her, he urged; she'd do very well.

They started out slowly, then quickened their step. They whirled: or, rather, everything—lamps, furniture, walls, floor—whirled around them, like a disc on a spindle. As they passed close to a door the hem of Emma's gown caught on her partner's trousers, and for a moment their legs were all but intertwined; he looked down at her, she up at him; a paralyzing numbness came over her, and she stopped. Then they resumed; and spinning more quickly the vicomte swept her off until they were alone at the very end of the gallery; there, out of breath, she almost fell, and for an instant leaned her head against his chest. Then, still circling, but more slowly, he returned her to her seat. She sank back with her head against the wall, and put her hand over her eyes.

When she opened them, a lady was sitting on a low stool in the middle of the salon, three waltzers on their knees before her. The lady chose the vicomte, and the violin struck up again.

Everyone watched them as they went round and round. She held her body rigid, her head inclined; he maintained the same posture as before, very erect, elbow curved, chin forward. This time he had a partner worthy of him! They danced on and on, long after all the others had dropped out exhausted.

Hosts and guests chatted a few minutes longer; and then, bidding each other good night, or rather good morning, they all went up to bed.

Charles dragged himself up the stairs by the handrail; his legs, he said, were "ready to drop off." He had spent five solid hours on his feet by the card tables watching people play whist, unable to make head or tail of it. So he gave a great sigh of relief when he pulled his shoes off at last.

Emma slipped a shawl over her shoulders, opened the window and leaned out.

The night was very dark. A few drops of rain were falling. She breathed the moist wind, so cooling to her eyeballs. The music was still throbbing in her ears, and she forced herself to stay awake in order to prolong the illusion of this luxurious life she would so soon have to be leaving.

The sky began to lighten. Her glance lingered on the windows of the various rooms as she tried to imagine which of them were occupied by the people she had seen the night before. She longed to know all about their lives, to penetrate into them, to be part of them.

But she was shivering with cold. She undressed and crept into bed beside the sleeping Charles.

Everyone came downstairs for breakfast. The meal lasted ten minutes; to the doctor's surprise, no liqueurs were served. Mademoiselle d'Andervilliers gathered up the remains of the brioches in a basket to feed the swans in the lake; and everyone went for a stroll in the greenhouse, where strange hairy plants were displayed on pyramidal stands, and hanging jars that looked like nests crawling with snakes dripped long, dangling, intertwined green tendrils. From the orangery at the end of the greenhouse a roofed passage led to the outbuildings. To please the young woman the marquis took her to see the stables. Above the basket-shaped racks were porcelain name plates with the horses' names in black letters. Each horse moved restlessly in his stall at the approach of the visitors and the coaxing, clicking sounds they made with their tongues. The boards of the harness-room floor shone like the parquet floor of a drawing room. The carriage harness hung in the middle, on two revolving posts; and the bits, whips, stirrups and curbs were on a line of hooks along the wall.

Charles, meanwhile, had gone to ask a groom to harness his buggy. It was brought around to the front door, and when all the bundles were stowed away, the Bovarys said their thank-yous to the marquis and the marquise and set out for home.

Emma sat silent, watching the turning wheels. Charles drove perched on the edge of the seat, arms wide apart; and the little horse went along at an ambling trot between the overwide shafts. The slack reins slapped against his rump and grew wet with lather; and the case tied on behind thumped heavily and regularly against the body of the buggy.

They were climbing one of the rises near Thibourville when just ahead of them, coming from the opposite direction, there appeared a group of riders, who passed by laughing and smoking cigars. Emma thought she recognized the vicomte; she turned and stared; but all she saw was the bobbing heads of trotting or galloping riders silhouetted against the sky.

Half a mile further along they had to stop: the breeching broke, and Charles mended it with rope. As he was checking his harness he saw something on the ground between the horse's feet, and he picked up a cigar case trimmed with green silk and bearing a crest in the center like a carriage door.

"A couple of cigars in it, too," he said. "I'll smoke them after dinner."

"You've taken up smoking?" Emma demanded.

"Once in a while, when I get the chance."

He put his find in his pocket and gave the pony a flick of the whip.

When they reached home dinner was far from ready. Madame lost her temper. Nastasie talked back.

"It's too much!" Emma cried. "I've had enough of your insolence!" And she gave her notice on the spot.

For dinner there was onion soup and veal with sorrel. Charles, sitting opposite Emma, rubbed his hands with satisfaction: "How good to be home!"

They could hear Nastasie weeping. Charles had an affection for the poor thing. She had kept him company on many an idle evening during his widowerhood. She had been his first patient, his first acquaintance in the village.

"Are you really letting her go?" he finally asked.

"Yes—what's to stop me?"

Then they warmed themselves in the kitchen while their room was made ready. Charles proceeded to smoke. He curled and pursed his lips around the cigar, spat every other minute, shrank back from every puff.

"You're going to make yourself sick," she said scornfully.

He put down his cigar and rushed to the pump for a drink of cold water. Emma snatched the cigar case and quickly flung it to the back of the closet.

The next day was endless. She walked in her garden, up and down the same paths over and over again, stopping to look at the flower beds, the fruit trees, the plaster priest, staring with a kind of amazement at all these things from her past life, things once so familiar. How remote the ball already was! What was it that made tonight seem so very far removed from the day before yesterday? Her visit to La Vaubyessard had opened a breach in her life, like one of those great crevasses that a storm can tear across the face of a mountain in the course of a single night. But there was nothing to do about it. She put her beautiful ball costume reverently away in a drawer—even to her satin slippers, whose soles were yellow from the slippery wax of the dance floor. Her heart was like them: contact with luxury had left an indelible mark on it.

The memory of the ball would not leave her. Every Wednesday she told herself as she woke: "Ah! One week ago . . . two weeks ago . . . three weeks ago, I was there!" Little by little the faces grew confused in her mind; she forgot the tune of the quadrille, the liveries and the splendid rooms became blurred. Some of the details departed—but the yearning remained.

IX

Often when Charles was out she went to the closet and took the green silk cigar case from among the piles of linen where she kept it.

She would look at it, open it, even sniff its lining, fragrant with verbena and tobacco. Whose was it? The vicomte's. A present from his mistress, perhaps. It had been embroidered on some rosewood frame, a charming little piece of furniture kept hidden from prying eyes, over which a pensive girl had bent for hours and hours, her soft curls brushing its surface. Love had breathed through the mesh of the canvas; every stroke of the needle had recorded a hope or a memory; and all these intertwined silken threads bespoke one constant, silent passion. And then one morning the vicomte had taken it away with him. What words had they exchanged as he stood leaning his elbow on one of those elaborate mantelpieces decked with vases of flowers and rococo clocks? She was in Tostes. Whereas he now, was in Paris— in Paris! What was it like, Paris? The very name had such a vastness about it! She repeated it to herself under her breath with a thrill of pleasure; it sounded in her ears like the great bell of a cathedral; it blazed before her eyes everywhere, glamorous even on the labels of her jars of pomade.

At night when the fishmongers passed below her window in their carts, singing *La Marjolaine,* she would awaken; and listening to the sound of the iron-rimmed wheels on the pavement, and then the quick change in the sound as they reached the unpaved road at the end of the village, she would tell herself: "They'll be there tomorrow!"

And she followed them in thought, up and down hills, through villages, along the highway by the light of the stars. Then, somewhere along the way, her dream always petered out.

She bought a map of Paris, and with her fingertip she went for walks. She followed the boulevards, stopping at every corner, between the lines indicating the streets, in front of the white squares that were the houses. Then, closing her tired eyes, she would have a shadowy vision of gas lamps flickering in the wind and carriage steps clattering open in front of theatres.

She subscribed to a women's magazine called *La Corbeille,* and to *Le Sylphe des salons.* She devoured every word of every account of a first night, a horse race, a soirée; she was fascinated by the debut of every new singer, the opening of every new shop. She knew the latest fashions, the addresses of the best tailors, the proper days to go to the Bois[2] and the opera. She pored over the interior decorating details in the novels of Eugène Sue; she read Balzac and George Sand,[3] seeking in their pages vicarious satisfactions for her own desires. She brought her book with her even to meals, and turned the leaves while Charles ate and talked to her. Her readings always brought the vicomte back to her mind: she continually found similarities between him and the fictitious characters. But the circle whose center he was gradually widened; and the halo she had given him spread beyond his image, gilding other dreams.

Paris, city vaster than the ocean, glittered before Emma's eyes in a rosy light. But the teeming life of the tumultuous place was divided into com-

2. Horse races at the Bois de Boulogne.   3. Pseudonym of Aurore Dudevant (1804–1876), prolific woman novelist. Sue (1804–1857), a popular novelist, was extremely successful at that period, both as a writer and as a fashionable dandy.

partments, separated into distinct scenes. Emma was aware of only two or three, which shut out the sight of the others and stood for all of mankind. In drawing rooms with mirrored walls and gleaming floors, around oval tables covered with gold-fringed velvet, moved the world of the ambassadors. It was full of trailing gowns, deep secrets, and unbearable tensions concealed beneath smiles. Then came the circle of the duchesses: here everyone was pale and lay in bed till four; the women—poor darlings!—wore English lace on their petticoat hems; and the men, their true worth unsuspected under their frivolous exteriors, rode horses to death for the fun of it, spent their summers at Baden-Baden,[4] and eventually, when they were about forty, married heiresses. After midnight, the gay, motley world of writers and actresses congregated at candlelit suppers in the private rooms of restaurants. They were profligate as kings, full of idealistic ambitions and fantastic frenzies. They lived on a higher plane than other people, somewhere sublime between heaven and earth, up among the storm clouds. As for the rest of the world, it was in some indeterminate pale beyond the pale; it could scarcely be said to exist. Indeed the closer to her things were, the further away from them her thoughts turned. Everything immediately surrounding her—boring countryside, inane petty bourgeois, the mediocrity of daily life—seemed to her the exception rather than the rule. She had been caught in it all by some accident: out beyond, there stretched as far as eye could see the immense territory of rapture and passions. In her longing she made no difference between the pleasures of luxury and the joys of the heart, between elegant living and sensitive feeling. Didn't love, like Indian plants, require rich soils, special temperatures? Sighs in the moonlight, long embraces, hands bathed in lovers' tears—all the fevers of the flesh and the languors of love—were inseparable from the balconies of great idle-houred castles, from a silk-curtained, thick-carpeted, beflowered boudoir with its bed on a dais, from the sparkle of precious stones and the swank of liveries.

The hired boy at the relay post across the road, who came in every morning to rub down the mare, walked through the hall in his heavy wooden shoes; his smock was in holes, his feet were innocent of stockings. Such was the groom in knee breeches she had to content herself with! When his work was done he left for the day: Charles stabled his horse himself when he returned from his rounds—took off the saddle and attached the halter; and the maid brought a truss of straw and tossed it as best she could into the manger.

To replace Nastasie (who finally departed from Tostes in a torrent of tears) Emma hired a sweet-faced orphan girl of fourteen. She forbade her to wear a cotton nightcap during the day, taught her to address her superiors in the third person, to hand a glass of water on a tray, to knock on doors before entering, and to iron, to starch, to help her dress—tried to turn her into a lady's maid. The girl obeyed without a murmur because she was afraid of losing her place; and since Madame usually left the key in the sideboard, Félicité took a little sugar upstairs with her every night, and ate it by herself in bed after saying her prayers.

Afternoons she sometimes crossed the road for a chat with the postilions while Madame was up in her room.

There Emma wore a shawl-collared dressing gown, open very low over a

4. A fashionable German spa with hot mineral-water springs.

pleated dicky with three gold buttons. Her belt was a cord with large tassels, and her little garnet-colored slippers had rosettes of wide ribbons at the instep. Though she had no one to write to, she had bought herself a blotter, a writing case, a pen and envelopes; she would dust off her whatnot, look at herself in the mirror, take up a book, and then begin to daydream and let it fall to her lap.

She longed to travel; she longed to go back and live in the convent. She wanted to die. And she wanted to live in Paris.

Charles jogged back and forth across the countryside under snow and rain. He ate omelettes at farmhouse tables, thrust his arm into damp beds, had his face spattered with jets of warm blood at bleedings; he listened to death rattles, examined the contents of basins, handled a lot of soiled underclothing. But every night he came home to a blazing fire, a well-set table, a comfortable chair, and a dainty, prettily dressed wife smelling so sweet that he never quite knew where the scent came from, and half wondered whether it wasn't her skin that was perfuming her slip.

She delighted him by countless little niceties: a new way of making sconces out of paper to catch the wax under candles, a flounce that she changed on her dress, or the fancy name of some very plain dish that the maid hadn't got right but that Charles enjoyed eating every bit of. In Rouen she saw ladies with charms dangling from their watch fobs; she bought some charms. She took a fancy to a pair of large blue glass vases for her mantelpiece, and a little later to an ivory workbox with a silver-gilt thimble. The less Charles understood these refinements, the more alluring he found them. They added something to the pleasure of his senses and the charm of his home. They were like a trickle of golden dust along the petty pathway of his life.

His health was good, his appearance hearty; his reputation was secure. The country people liked him because he gave himself no airs. He always fondled the children and never went to a café; moreover, his morals inspired confidence. He was especially successful in treating catarrhs and chest ailments. Actually, Charles had such a dread of killing his patients that he seldom prescribed anything but sedatives—once in a while an emetic or a foot bath or leeches. Not that surgery held any terrors for him: when he bled a patient he bled him hard, like a horse; and he was famous for his iron grip as a tooth puller.

Eventually, "to keep himself up to date," he took out a subscription to the *La Ruche médicale*, a new publication whose prospectus had been sent him. He read a little in it after his dinner, but the heat of the room plus digestion resulted in his falling asleep at the end of five minutes; and he sat there under the lamp with his chin in his hands and his hair falling forward like a mane. Emma looked at him and shrugged her shoulders. Why didn't she at least have for a husband one of those silent, dedicated men who spend their nights immersed in books and who by the time they're sixty and rheumatic have acquired a row of decorations to wear on their ill-fitting black coats? She would have liked the name Bovary—her name—to be famous, on display in all the bookshops, constantly mentioned in the newspapers, known all over France. But Charles had no ambition! A doctor from Yvetot with whom he had recently held a consultation had humiliated him right at the sickbed, in front of the assembled relatives. When Charles told her the story that evening, Emma burst out furiously against the other doctor. Charles was so moved that he shed a tear and kissed her on the forehead. But it was shame that had exasperated her: she wanted to strike him. She went into the hall, opened the window and took a breath of fresh air to calm herself.

"It's pathetic!" she whispered to herself, despair in her heart. "What a booby!"

And indeed he got on her nerves more and more. As he grew older he grew coarser: at the end of a meal he whittled the cork of the wine bottle with his dessert knife and cleaned his teeth with his tongue; he made a gulping noise every time he took a mouthful of soup; and as he put on weight his eyes, small to begin with, seemed to be pushed toward his temples by the puffing of his cheeks.

Emma sometimes tucked the red edge of his sweater up under his vest, or straightened his tie, or threw away a pair of faded old gloves he was about to put on; and it was never, as he believed, for his sake that she did it, but for her own, out of exasperated vanity. And sometimes she told him about things she had read—a passage in a novel or a new play, some high-life anecdote recounted in a gossip column, for Charles was a presence, at least, an ear that was always open, a sure source of approval. She confided many a secret to her dog, after all! She could almost have opened her heart to the logs in the fireplace and the pendulum of the clock.

Deep down, all the while, she was waiting for something to happen. Like a sailor in distress, she kept casting desperate glances over the solitary waste of her life, seeking some white sail in the distant mists of the horizon. She had no idea by what wind it would reach her, toward what shore it would bear her, or what kind of craft it would be—tiny boat or towering vessel, laden with heartbreaks or filled to the gunwales with rapture. But every morning when she awoke she hoped that today would be the day; she listened for every sound, gave sudden starts, was surprised when nothing happened; and then, sadder with each succeeding sunset, she longed for tomorrow.

Spring came again. She found it hard to breathe, the first warm days, when the pear trees were bursting into bloom.

From early in July she began to count on her fingers how many weeks there were till October, thinking that the marquis d'Andervilliers might give another ball at La Vaubyessard. But September passed without letters or visitors.

After the pain of this disappointment had gone, her heart stood empty once more; and then the series of identical days began all over again.

So from now on they were going to continue one after the other like this, always the same, innumerable, bringing nothing! Other people's lives, drab though they might be, held at least the possibility of an event. One unexpected happening often set in motion a whole chain of change: the entire setting of one's life could be transformed. But to her nothing happened. It was God's will. The future was a pitch-black tunnel ending in a locked door.

She gave up her music: why should she play? Who was there to listen? There wasn't a chance of her ever giving a concert in a short-sleeved velvet gown, skimming butterfly fingers over the ivory keys of a grand piano, feeling the public's ecstatic murmur flow around her like a breeze—so why go through the tedium of practicing? She left her drawing books and her embroidery in a closet. What was the use of anything? What was the use? She loathed sewing.

"I've read everything there is to read," she told herself.

And so she sat—holding the fire tongs in the fire till they glowed red, or watching the falling of the rain.

How depressed she was on Sundays, when the churchbell tolled for vespers! With a dull awareness she listened to the cracked sound as it rang out again and again. Sometimes a cat walking slowly along one of the roofs outside her window arched its back against the pale rays of the sun. The wind blew trails of dust on the highway. Far off somewhere a dog was howling. And the bell would keep on giving its regular, monotonous peals that died away over the countryside.

People came out of church. Women with their wooden shoes polished, peasant men in new smocks, little children skipping bareheaded in front of them—all moved toward home. And until dark five or six men, always the same ones, stayed playing their shuffleboard game before the main entrance of the inn.

The winter was a cold one. Every morning the windowpanes were frosted over, and the whitish light that came through—as though filtered through ground glass—sometimes didn't vary all day. By four o'clock it was time to light the lamps.

On sunny days she went out into the garden. The dew had garnished the cabbages with silvery lace, and joined head to head with long shining filaments. There was no sound of birds, everything seemed to be sleeping—the espaliered trees under their straw, the vine like a great sick snake under the wall coping, where she could see many-legged wood lice crawling as she came near. In among the spruces near the hedge the priest in a tricorn reading his breviary had lost his right foot, and the scaling of the plaster in the frost had left a white scurf on his face.

Then she would return upstairs, close her door, poke the coals; and languid in the heat of the fire she would feel boredom descend again, heavier than before. She would have liked to go down for a chat with the maid, but self-respect held her back.

Every day at the same time the schoolmaster in his black silk skullcap opened the shutters of his house; every day at the same time the village policeman passed, his sword buckled around his smock. Morning and evening the post horses crossed the road in threes to drink at the pond. Now and again the bell of a café door would tinkle as it opened; and when there was a wind she could hear the little copper basins that formed the barber's shop-sign creaking on their two rods. His window display consisted of an old fashion plate on one of the panes, and a wax bust of a woman with yellow hair. The barber, too, was accustomed to bewail the waste of his talents, his ruined career; and dreaming of a shop in a large city—in Rouen, perhaps, on the river front, or near the theatre—he paced back and forth all day between the mayor's office and the church, gloomily waiting for customers. When Madame Bovary raised her eyes she always saw him there with his cap over one ear, and his short work jacket, like a sentry on duty.

In the afternoon, sometimes, a man's face appeared outside the parlor windows, a swarthy face with black side whiskers and a slow, wide, gentle smile that showed very white teeth. Then would come the strain of a waltz; and in a miniature drawing room on top of the hurdy-gurdy a set of tiny dancers would begin to revolve. Women in pink turbans, Tyrolians in jackets, monkeys in black tailcoats, gentlemen in knee breeches—they all spun around among the armchairs, sofas and tables, and were reflected in bits of mirror glass joined together at the edges by strips of gold paper. As he turned his crank the man would glance to his right, to his left, and toward the windows. Now and then he would let out a spurt of brown saliva against the curb and raise his knee to lift the instrument and ease the heavy shoulder strap; and the music, now doleful and dragging, now merry and quick, came out of the box through a pink taffeta curtain under a fancy brasswork grill. The tunes it played were tunes that were being heard in other places—in theatres, in drawing rooms, under the lighted chandeliers of ballrooms: echoes from the world that reached Emma this way. Sarabands ran on endlessly in her head; and her thoughts, like dancing girls on some flowery carpet, leapt with the notes from dream to dream, from sorrow to sorrow. Then, when the man had caught in his cap the coin she threw him, he would pull down an old blue wool cover, hoist his organ onto his back, and move heavily off. She always watched him till he disappeared.

But it was above all at mealtime that she could bear it no longer—in that small ground-floor room with its smoking stove, its squeaking door, its sweating walls and its damp floor tiles. All the bitterness of life seemed to be served up to her on her plate; and the steam rising from the boiled meat brought gusts of revulsion from the depths of her soul. Charles was a slow eater; she would nibble a few hazelnuts, or lean on her elbow and draw lines on the oilcloth with the point of her table knife.

Now she let everything in the house go, and the older Madame Bovary was amazed by the change she found when she came to spend part of Lent in Tostes. Emma, once so careful and dainty, now went whole days without putting on a dress; she wore gray cotton stockings, lit the house with cheap tallow candles. She kept saying that they had to be careful, since they weren't rich; and she always went on to add that she was very contented, very happy, that she liked Tostes very much; and she made other surprising statements that shut up her mother-in-law. However, she seemed no more inclined than ever to follow her advice. Once, indeed, when Madame Bovary took it into her head to suggest that employers should keep an eye on their servants' religious life, Emma replied with such a terrible look and such a freezing smile that the dear woman henceforth kept her fingers out of things.

Emma was becoming capricious, hard to please. She would order special dishes for herself and then not touch them; one day she would drink nothing but fresh milk; the next, cups of tea by the dozen. Often she refused absolutely to go out; then she would feel stifled, open the windows, change to a light dress. She would give the maid a tongue-lashing and then turn around and give her presents, or time off to visit the neighbors, just as occasionally she would give a beggar all the silver she had in her purse, though she was anything but tenderhearted or sympathetic to other people's troubles. (In this she was like most sons and daughters of country folk: their souls always keep some of the horniness of their fathers' hands.)

Toward the end of February, Monsieur Rouault celebrated the anniversary of his recovery by bringing his son-in-law a magnificent turkey, and he stayed on at Tostes for three days. Charles was out most of the time with his patients, and it was Emma who kept her father company. He smoked in her bedroom, spit on the andirons, talked about crops, calves, cows, chickens and the village council; when he finally left and she had shut the door behind him, her feeling of relief surprised even herself. But then she no longer hid her scorn for anything or anyone; and she was beginning now and then to express peculiar opinions, condemning what everyone else approved and approving things that were perverse or immoral—a way of talking that made her husband stare at her wide-eyed.

Would this wretchedness last forever? Was there no way out? And yet she was every bit as good as all the other women, who lived in contentment! She had seen duchesses at La Vaubyessard who were dumpier and more common than she, and she cursed God for his injustice. She leaned her head against the wall and wept. She thought, with envy of riotous living, of nights spent at masked balls, of shameless revels and all the mysterious raptures they must bring in their train.

She grew pale and developed palpitations. Charles gave her valerian drops and camphor baths. Everything he tried seemed to exacerbate her the more.

Some days she chattered endlessly, almost feverishly; and such a period of overexcitement would suddenly be followed by a torpor in which she neither spoke nor moved. At such times she would revive herself with eau de Cologne, pouring a bottle of it over her arms.

Since she continually complained about Tostes, Charles supposed that the cause of her illness must have something to do with the town's situation; and struck by this idea he thought seriously of settling somewhere else.

As soon as she knew this she began to drink vinegar to lose weight, acquired a little dry cough, and lost her appetite completely.

It was a wrench for Charles to leave Tostes, after living there four years and just when he was beginning to be really established. Still, if it had to be—He took her to Rouen, to see one of his old teachers. The diagnosis was that she was suffering from a nervous illness: a change of air was indicated.

After looking here and there, Charles learned that in the district of Neufchâtel there was a good-sized market town named Yonville-l'Abbaye, whose doctor, a Polish refugee, had decamped just the week before. So he wrote to the local pharmacist and inquired about the population, the distance to the nearest doctor, how much his predecessor had earned a year, etc.; and when the answers were satisfactory he decided to move by spring if Emma's health didn't improve.

One day when she was going through a drawer in preparation for moving, something pricked her finger. It was the wire around her bridal bouquet. The orange-blossom buds were yellow with dust, and the silver-edged satin ribbons were frayed. She tossed it into the fire. It blazed up quicker than dry straw. Then it lay like a red bush on the ashes, slowly consuming itself. She watched it burn. The pasteboard berries burst open, the brass wire curled, the braid melted; and the shriveled paper petals hovered along the fireback like black butterflies and finally flew away up the chimney.

When they left Tostes in March, Madame Bovary was pregnant.

Part Two

I

Yonville-l'Abbaye (even the ruins of the ancient Capuchin friary from which it derives its name are no longer there) is a market town twenty miles from Rouen, between the highways to Abbeville and Beauvais in the valley of the Rieule. This is a small tributary of the Andelle: it turns the wheels of three mills before joining the larger stream, and contains some trout that boys like to fish for on Sundays.

Branching off from the highway at La Boissière, the road to Yonville continues level until it climbs the hill at Les Leux; and from there it commands a view of the valley. This is divided by the Rieule into two contrasting bits of countryside: everything to the left is grazing land, everything to the right is ploughed field. The pastures extend along the base of a chain of low hills and merge at the far end with the meadows of Bray; while eastward the plain rises gently and grows steadily wider, flaunting its golden grainfields as far as eye can see. The stream, flowing along the edge of the grass, is a white line dividing the color of the meadows from that of the ploughed earth: the country thus resembles a great spread-out cloak, its green velvet collar edged with silver braid.

On the horizon, beyond Yonville loom the oaks of the Argueil forest and the escarpments of the bluffs of Saint-Jean, the latter streaked from top to bottom with long, irregular lines of red: these are marks left by rain, and their brickish color, standing out so sharply against the gray rock of the hill, comes from the iron content of the many springs in the country just beyond.

This is where Normandy, Picardy and the Ile-de-France come together, a mongrel region where the speech of the natives is as colorless as the landscape is lacking in character. Here they make the worst Neufchâtel cheeses in the entire district; and here farming calls for considerable investment: great quantities of manure are needed to fertilize the friable, sandy, stony soil.

Up until 1835 no road was kept open to Yonville, but about that time the cross-cut was made that links the Abbeville and Amiens highways and is sometimes used by carters traveling from Rouen to Flanders. Nevertheless, despite its "new avenues for trade," Yonville-l'Abbaye has stood still. Instead of adopting improved methods of farming, the natives stick to their pastures, worn-out though they are; and the lazy town, spurning the farmland, has continued its spontaneous growth in the direction of the river. The sight of it from a distance, stretched out along the bank, brings to mind a cowherd taking a noonday nap beside the stream.

At the foot of the hill the road crosses the Rieule on a bridge, and then, becoming an avenue planted with young aspens, leads in a straight line to the first outlying houses. These are surrounded by hedges, and their yards are full of scattered outbuildings—cider presses, carriage houses and distilling sheds standing here and there under thick trees with ladders and poles leaning against their trunks and scythes hooked over their branches. The thatched roofs hide the top third or so of the low windows like fur caps pulled down over eyes, and each windowpane, thick and convex, has a bull's-eye in its center like the bottom of a bottle. Some of the plastered house walls with their diagonal black timbers are the background for scraggly espaliered pear trees; and the house doors have little swinging gates to keep out the baby chicks, who come to the sill to peck at brown-bread crumbs soaked in cider. Gradually the yards become narrower, houses are closer together, the hedges disappear; occasionally a fern broom put out to dry is seen hanging from a window; there is a blacksmith shop, a cart-maker's with two or three new carts outside half blocking the roadway. Then comes a white house behind an iron fence, its circular lawn adorned by a cupid holding finger to lips. Two cast-iron urns stand at either end of the entrance terrace; brass plates gleam brightly at the door: this is the notary's house, the finest in town.

The church is across the street, twenty yards further on, at the corner of the main square. The little graveyard surrounding it, enclosed by an elbow-high wall, is so full of graves that the old tombstones, lying flat on the ground, form a continuous pavement divided into rectangular blocks by the grass that pushes up between. The church was remodeled during the last years of the reign of Charles X.[5] The wooden vaulting is beginning to rot at the top: black cavities are appearing here and there in the blue paint. Above the door, in the place usually occupied by an organ, is a gallery for the men, reached by a spiral staircase that echoes loudly under the tread of wooden shoes.

Daylight, coming through the windows of plain glass, falls obliquely on the pews; and here and there on the wall from which they jut out at right angles is tacked a bit of straw matting, with the name of the pew holder in large letters below. Beyond, where the nave narrows, stands the confessional, and opposite it a statuette of the Virgin: she is dressed in a satin gown and a tulle veil spangled with silver stars, and her cheeks are daubed red like some idol from the Sandwich Islands.[6] A painting by a copyist, inscribed "Holy Family: Presented by the Minister of the Interior," hangs over the main altar; and there, flanked by four candlesticks, it closes the vista. The cheap fir choir stalls have never been painted.

The market—that is, a tile roof supported by about twenty pillars—takes up approximately half the main square of Yonville. The town hall, designed, as everyone will tell you, "by a Paris architect," is a kind of Greek temple forming one corner of the square, next door to the pharmacy. Its lower story has three Ionic columns; above is a row of arched windows; and the culminating pediment is filled with a figure of the Gallic cock, one of its claws resting on the Constitution[7] and the other holding the scales of justice.

But what catches the eye the most is across the square from the Lion d'Or hotel: Monsieur Homais' pharmacy! Especially at night, when his lamp is lit, and the red and green glass jars decorating his window cast the glow of their two colors far out across the roadway! Peering through it, as through the glare of Bengal lights,[8] one can catch a glimpse, at that hour, of the dim figure of the pharmacist himself, bent over his desk. The entire façade of his establishment is plastered from top to bottom with inscriptions—in running script, in round hand, in block capitals: "Vichy, Seltzer and Barèges Waters;

5. The last Bourbon king (1757–1836), son of Louis XV. He was expelled by the July Revolution (1830). 6. Old name for Hawaii, after John Montagu, fourth earl of Sandwich (1718–1792), who served as first lord of admiralty when the islands were discovered. 7. The *Charte constitutiouelle de la France*, basis of the French constitution after the revolution, bestowed in 1814 by Louis XVIII and revised in 1830, after the downfall of Charles X. 8. Blue flares used in signaling.

Depurative Fruit Essences; Raspail's Remedy; Arabian Racahout; Darcet's Pastilles; Regnauk's Ointment; Bandages, Baths, Laxative Chocolates, etc." And the shop sign, as wide as the shop itself, proclaims in gold letters: "Homais Pharmacy." At the rear of the shop, behind the great scales fastened to the counter, the word "Laboratory" is inscribed above a glass door; and this door itself, halfway up, bears once again the name "Homais," in gold letters on a black ground.

That is as much as there is to see in Yonville. The street (the only street), long as a rifle shot and lined with a few shops, abruptly ceases to be a street at a turn of the road. If you leave it on the right and follow the base of the bluffs of Saint-Jean, you soon reach the cemetery.

This was enlarged the year of the cholera—one wall was torn down and three adjoining acres were added; but all this new portion is almost uninhabited, and new graves continue as in the past to be dug in the crowded area near the gate. The caretaker, who is also gravedigger and sexton at the church (thus profiting doubly from the parish corpses), has taken advantage of the empty land to plant potatoes. Nevertheless, his little field grows smaller every year, and when there is an epidemic he doesn't know whether to rejoice in the deaths or lament the space taken by the new graves.

"You are feeding on the dead, Lestiboudois!" Monsieur le curé told him, one day.

The somber words gave him pause, and for a time he desisted; but today he continues to plant his tubers, coolly telling everyone that they come up by themselves.

Since the events which we are about to relate, absolutely nothing has changed in Yonville. To this day the tin tricolor still turns atop the church tower; the two calico streamers outside the dry-goods shop still blow in the wind; the spongy foetuses in the pharmacy window continue to disintegrate in their cloudy alcohol; and over the main entrance of the hotel the old golden lion, much discolored by the rains, stares down like a curly-headed poodle on passers-by.

The evening the Bovarys were expected at Yonville, Madame Lefrançois, the widow who owned this hotel, was so frantically busy with her saucepans that large beads of sweat stood out on her face. Tomorrow was market-day, and she had to get everything ready in advance—cut the meat, clean the chickens, make soup, roast and grind the coffee. In addition, she had tonight's dinner to get for her regular boarders and for the new doctor and his wife and their maid. Bursts of laughter came from the billiard room; in the small dining room three millers were calling for brandy; logs were blazing, charcoal was crackling, and on the long table in the kitchen, in among the quarters of raw mutton, stood high piles of plates that shook with the chopping of the spinach on the chopping-block. From the yard came the squawking of the chickens that the kitchen maid was chasing with murderous intent.

Warming his back at the fire was a man in green leather slippers, wearing a velvet skullcap with a gold tassel. His face, slightly pitted by smallpox, expressed nothing, but self-satisfaction, and he seemed as contented with life as the goldfinch in a wicker cage hanging above his head. This was the pharmacist.

"Artémise!" cried the mistress of the inn. "Chop some kindling, fill the decanters, bring some brandy—hurry up! Lord! If I only knew what dessert to offer these people you're waiting for! Listen to their moving-men starting up that racket in the billiard room again! They've left their van in the driveway, too: the Hirondelle will probably crash into it. Call 'Polyte and tell him to put it in the shed! Would you believe it, Monsieur Homais—since this morning they've played at least fifteen games and drunk eight pots of cider! But they're going to ruin my table," she said, staring over at them across the room, her skimming spoon in her hand.

"That wouldn't be much of a loss," replied Monsieur Homais. "You'd buy another one."

"Another billiard table!" cried the widow.

"But this one's falling apart, Madame Lefrançois! I tell you again; it's shortsighted of you not to invest in a new one! Very shortsighted! Players today want narrow pockets and heavy cues, you know. They don't play billiards the way they used to. Everything's changed. We must keep up with the times! Just look at Tellier . . ."

The hostess flushed with anger.

"Say what you like," the pharmacist went on, "his billiard table is nicer than yours. And if a patriotic tournament were to be got up, for Polish independence or Lyons flood relief . . ."[9]

"We're not afraid of fly-by-nights like Tellier," the hostess interrupted, shrugging her heavy shoulders. "Don't worry, Monsieur Homais. As long as the Lion d'Or exists we'll keep our customers. We're a well-established house. But the Café Français . . . One of these mornings you'll find it sealed up, with a nice big notice on the window blinds. A new billiard table?" she went on, talking as though to herself. "But this one's so handy to stack the washing on! And in the hunting season it's slept as many as six! . . . But what's keeping that slowpoke Hivert?"

"You'll wait till he arrives, to give your gentlemen their dinner?" the pharmacist asked.

"Wait? And what about Monsieur Binet? You'll see him come in on the stroke of six: he's the most punctual man in the world. He always has to sit at the same place in the little room: he'd die rather than eat his dinner anywhere else. And finicky! So particular about his cider! Not like Monsieur Léon! Monsieur Léon sometimes doesn't come in till seven, or even halfpast, and half the time he doesn't even know what he's eating. What a nice young man! So polite! So soft-spoken!"

"Ah, Madame! There's a great difference, you know, between someone who's been properly brought up and a tax collector who got his only schooling in the army."

The clock struck six. Binet entered.

He was clad in a blue frock coat that hung straight down all around his skinny body; and the raised peak of his leather cap, its earflaps pulled up and fastened at the top, displayed a bald, squashed-looking forehead, deformed by long pressure of a helmet. He was wearing a coarse wool vest, a crinoline collar, gray trousers, and—as he did in every season—well-shined shoes that bulged in two parallel lines over the rising of his two big toes. Not

---

9. The allusion dates the action of the novel as taking place in 1840; during the winter of 1840, the Rhône overflowed with catastrophic results. At the same time, Louis Philippe was under steady attack for his failure to offer sufficient assistance to the victims of the repression that followed the insurrection of Warsaw (1831).

a hair was out of place in the blond chin whisker outlining his jaw: it was like the edging of a flower bed around his long, dreary face with its small eyes and hooked nose. He was a clever card player, a good hunter, and wrote a fine hand. His hobby was making napkin rings on his own lathe: jealous as an artist and stingy as a bourgeois, he cluttered up his house with his handiwork.

He headed for the small room, but the three millers had to be got out before he would go in. While his table was being set he stood next to the stove without saying a word; then he closed the door and took off his cap as usual.

"He won't wear out his tongue with civilities," the pharmacist remarked, as soon as he was alone with the hostess.

"He never talks a bit more than that," she answered. "Last week I had two cloth salesmen here—two of the funniest fellows you ever listened to. They told me stories that made me laugh till I cried. Would you believe it? He sat there like a clam—didn't open his mouth."

"No imagination," pronounced the pharmacist. "Not a hint of a spark! No manners whatever!"

"And yet they say he has something to him," objected the hostess.

"Something to him?" cried Monsieur Homais. "That man? Something to him? Still, in his own line I suppose he may have," he conceded.

And he went on: "Ah! A business man with vast connections, a lawyer, a doctor, a pharmacist—I can understand it if they get so engrossed in their affairs that they become eccentric, even surly: history is full of such examples. But at least they have important affairs to be engrossed in! Take me, for instance: how often I've turned my desk upside down looking for my pen to write some labels, only to find I'd stuck it behind my ear!"

Meanwhile Madame Lefrançois had approached the door to see whether the Hirondelle wasn't in sight, and she started as a black-clad man that moment entered the kitchen. In the last faint light of dusk it was just possible to make out his florid face and athletic figure.

"What can I offer you, Monsieur le curé?" she asked, reaching down a brass candlestick from a row that stood all ready and complete with candles on the mantelpiece. "A drop of cassis? A glass of wine?"

The priest very politely declined. He had come to fetch his umbrella, he said: he had left it at the convent in Ernemont the other day, and had supposed the Hirondelle would have delivered it by now. He asked Madame Lefrançois to have it brought to him at the rectory during the evening, and then left for the church, where the bell was tolling the Angelus.

When the sound of his footsteps in the square had died away, the pharmacist declared that in his opinion the priest's behavior had been most improper. His refusal to take a glass of something was the most revolting kind of hypocrisy: all priests were secret tipplers, he said, and they were all doing their best to bring back the days of the tithe.

The hostess said some words in the curé's defense. "Besides," she went on, "he could take on four like you. Last year he helped our men get in the straw: he carried as many as six bundles at a time—that shows you how strong he is."

"Bravo!" cried the pharmacist. "Go ahead! Keep sending your daughters to confession to strapping fellows like that! But if I were the government I'd have every priest bled once a month. Yes, a fine generous phlebotomy every month, Madame, in the interests of morals and decency."

"That's enough, Monsieur Homais! You've no respect for religion!"

"On the contrary, I'm a very religious man, in my own way, far more so than all these people with their mummeries and their tricks. I worship God, I assure you! I believe in a Supreme Being, a Creator. Whoever he is—and what difference does it make?—he put us here on earth to fulfill our duties as citizens and parents. But I don't have to go into church and kiss silver platters and hand over my money to fatten up a lot of rascals that eat better than you and I! To him, one can do full honor in a forest, a field—or merely by gazing up at the ethereal vault, like the ancients. My God is the God of Socrates, of Franklin, of Voltaire, of Béranger! My credo is the credo of Rousseau![1] I adhere to the immortal principles of '89! I have no use for the kind of God who goes walking in his garden with a stick, sends his friends to live in the bellies of whales, gives up the ghost with a groan and then comes back to life three days later! Those things aren't only absurd in themselves, Madame—they're completely opposed to all physical laws. It goes to prove, by the way, that priests have always wallowed in squalid ignorance and have wanted nothing better than to drag the entire world down to their own level."

As he ended, he glanced about in search of an audience: for a moment, during his outburst, he had had the illusion that he was addressing the village council. But the mistress of the inn was no longer listening to him: her ears had caught a distant sound of wheels. There was the rattle of a coach, the pounding of loose horseshoes on the road; and the Hirondelle drew up before the door at last.

It was a yellow box-shaped affair mounted on two large wheels that came up as high as the top, blocking the passengers' view and spattering their shoulders. When the carriage was closed the tiny panes of its narrow windows rattled in their frames, and there were mud stains here and there on the ancient coating of dust that even heavy rainstorms never washed off completely. It was drawn by three horses, one ahead and two abreast. Its under side bumped against the ground on down grades.

A number of the local inhabitants made their appearance in the square, and all speaking at once they asked for news, for explanations of the delay, for their packages. Hivert didn't know whom to answer first. It was he who attended to things in the city for the Yonvillians. He shopped for them, brought back rolls of leather for the shoemaker, scrap iron for the blacksmith, a keg of herrings for Madame Lefrançois his employer, ladies' bonnets from the milliner, wigs from the hairdresser; and all along the road on the way back he distributed his packages, standing up on his seat and hurling them over the farmyard fences with a shout as his horses kept galloping ahead.

An accident had delayed him: Madame Bovary's greyhound had run away—disappeared across the fields. They had whistled for her a good fifteen minutes. Hivert had even turned his coach around and gone back over the road for more than a mile, expecting to come upon her any minute; but they'd

---

1. Rousseau's declaration (1762) of faith in God, a religion of his heart, coupled with a criticism of revealed religion. It is included in book 4 of his pedagogic treatise *Émile* but was frequently reprinted as an independent pamphlet.

had to go on without her. Emma had wept and made a scene, blaming it all on Charles. Monsieur Lheureux, the Yonville dry-goods dealer, who was also in the carriage, had tried to comfort her by citing numerous examples of lost dogs' recognizing their masters many years later. There was a famous one, he said, that had returned to Paris all the way from Constantinople. Another had traveled one hundred twenty-five miles in a straight line, swimming four rivers. And his own father had had a poodle who after being gone for twelve years had suddenly jumped up on his back one night in the street, as he was on his way to a friend's house for dinner.

II

Emma stepped out first, followed by Félicité, Monsieur Lheureux, and a wet nurse; and Charles had to be shaken awake in his corner, where he had dozed off as soon as darkness had fallen.

Homais introduced himself: he paid his compliments to Madame and spoke politely to Monsieur, said he was delighted to have been of service to them, and cordially added that he had taken the liberty of inviting himself to share their dinner, his wife being for the moment out of town.

In the kitchen, Madame Bovary crossed to the fireplace. Reaching halfway down her skirt, she grasped it with the tips of two of her fingers, raised it to her ankles, and stretched out a black-shod foot toward the flame, over the leg of mutton that was turning on the spit. She was standing in the full light of the fire, and by its harsh glare one could see the weave of her dress, the pores of her white skin, even her eyelids when she briefly shut her eyes. Now and again she was flooded by a great flow of red, as a gust of wind blew into the fire from the half-open kitchen door.

From the other side of the fireplace a fair-haired young man was silently watching her.

This was Monsieur Léon Dupuis, the second of the Lion d'Or's regular diners, clerk to Maître Guillaumin the notary. Finding Yonville very dull, he dined as late as possible, in the hope that some traveler might turn up at the inn with whom he could have an evening's conversation. On days where there was no work to detain him at the office, he had no way of filling the interval, and ended up arriving on time and enduring a tête-à-tête with Binet straight through from soup to cheese. So it was with pleasure that he accepted the hostess' suggestion that he dine with the new arrivals, and they all went into the large dining room, where their four places had been set: Madame Lefran-çois was making an occasion of it.

Homais asked permission to keep his cap on; he had a dread of head colds. Then, turning to his neighbor: "Madame is a bit tired, I presume? Our old Hirondelle does such a frightful lot of bumping and shaking!"

"It does," Emma answered. "But I always love traveling anyway. I enjoy a change of scene."

The clerk sighed. "It's so boring to be always stuck in the same place!"

"If you were like me," said Charles, "always having to be on horseback . . . "

"But there's nothing more charming than riding, I think," said the clerk, addressing Madame Bovary. "If you have the opportunity, of course."

"As a matter of fact," said the apothecary, "the practice of medicine isn't particularly arduous in this part of the world. The condition of our roads makes it possible to use a gig, and, generally speaking, payment is good—the farmers are well off. Aside from the usual cases of enteritis, bronchitis, liver complaint, etc., our roster of illnesses includes an occasional intermittent fever at harvest time, but on the whole very little that's serious except for a good deal of scrofula, probably the result of the deplorable hygienic conditions in our countryside. Ah! You'll have to fight many a prejudice, Monsieur Bovary; every day your scientific efforts will be thwarted by the peasant's stubborn adherence to his old ways. Plenty of our people still have recourse to novenas and relics and the priest, instead of doing the natural thing and coming to the doctor or the pharmacist. To tell the truth, however, the climate isn't at all bad: we even have a few nonagenarians. The thermometer—this I can tell you from personal observation—goes down in winter to four degrees, and in the hottest season touches twenty-five or thirty degrees Centigrade at the most—that is, twenty-four degrees Réaumur at a maximum, or, in other words, fifty-four degrees Fahrenheit, to use the English scale—not more! You see, we're sheltered from the north winds by the Argueil forest on the one side and from the west winds by the bluffs of Saint-Jean on the other. However, this warmth, which because of the dampness given off by the river and the number of cattle in the pastures, which themselves exhale, as you know, a great deal of ammonia, that is nitrogen, hydrogen, and oxygen (no, just nitrogen and hydrogen), and which, sucking up the humus from the soil, mixing all these different emanations together—making a package of them, so to speak—and combining also with the electricity in the atmosphere when there is any, could in the long run result in noxious miasmas, as in tropical countries; this warmth, I was saying, is actually moderated from the direction from which it comes, or rather the direction from which it could come, namely, from the south, by southeast winds, which being of course cool themselves as a result of crossing the Seine sometimes burst on us all of a sudden like arctic air from Russia!"

"Are there some nice walks in the neighborhood, at least?" Madame Bovary asked, speaking to the young man.

"Oh, hardly any," he answered. "There's one place, called the Pasture, on top of the bluffs at the edge of the woods. I go there Sundays sometimes with a book and watch the sunset."

"There's nothing I love as much as sunsets," she said. "But my favorite place for them is the seashore."

"Oh, I adore the sea," said Monsieur Léon.

"Don't you have the feeling," asked Madame Bovary, "that something happens to free your spirit in the presence of all that vastness? It raises up my soul to look at it, somehow. It makes me think of the infinite, and all kinds of wonderful things."

"Mountain scenery does the same," said Léon. "A cousin of mine traveled in Switzerland last year, and he told me that no one who hasn't been there can imagine the poetry and charm of the lakes and waterfalls and the majesty of the glaciers. You can look across the rivers there and see pine trees so high you can't believe your eyes. They build their chalets right on the edge of precipices. If you look down you can see whole valleys a thousand feet below you through openings in the clouds. Think what it must do to you to see things like that! I'd fall on my knees, I think. I'd want to pray. I can well understand the famous composer who used to play the piano in such places, to get inspiration."

"Are you a musician?" she asked.

"No, but I love music," he answered.

"Ah, don't listen to him, Madame Bovary," interrupted Homais, leaning across his plate. "He's just being modest. What about the other day, my friend? You were singing _L'Ange gardien_[2] in your room—it was delightful. I heard you from the laboratory; you rendered it like a real actor."

Léon lived at the pharmacist's, in a small third-floor room looking out on the square. He blushed at his landlord's compliment. But the latter had already turned back to the doctor and was briefing him on the leading citizens of Yonville. He told stories about them and gave vital statistics. No one knew for sure how well off the notary was; and then there was the Tuvache family, all of them hard to get on with.

Emma went on: "What is your favorite kind of music?"

"Oh, German music. It's the most inspiring."

"Do you know Italian opera?"

"Not yet—but I'll hear some next year when I go to Paris to finish law school."

"As I was just telling your husband," the pharmacist said, "speaking of our poor runaway friend Yanoda, thanks to his extravagance you're going to enjoy one of the most comfortable houses in Yonville. What's especially convenient about it for a doctor is that it has a door opening on the lane, so that people can come and go without being seen. Besides, it has everything a house-keeper needs: laundry, kitchen and pantry, sitting room, fruit closet, etc. Yanoda didn't care how he spent his money! He built an arbor alongside the river at the foot of the garden, just to drink beer in during the summer! If Madame likes gardening, she'll be able to . . ."

"My wife never gardens," said Charles. "She's been advised to take exercise, but even so she'd much rather stay in her room and read."

"So would I," said Léon. "What's more delightful than an evening beside the fire with a nice bright lamp and a book, listening to the wind beating against the windows . . . ?"

"How true!" she said, her great dark eyes fixed widely on him.

"I'm absolutely removed from the world at such times," he said. "The hours go by without my knowing it. Sitting there I'm wandering in countries I can see every detail of—I'm playing a role in the story I'm reading. I actually feel I'm the characters—I live and breathe with them."

"I know!" she said. "I feel the same!"

"Have you ever had the experience," Léon went on, "of running across in a book some vague idea you've had, some image that you realize has been lurking all the time in the back of your mind and now seems to express absolutely your most subtle feelings?"

"Indeed I have," she answered.

"That's why I'm especially fond of poetry," he said. "I find it much more affecting than prose. It's much more apt to make me cry."

"Still, it's tiresome in the long run," Emma replied. "Nowadays I'm crazy about a different kind of thing—stories full of suspense, stories that frighten you. I hate to read about low-class heroes and their down-to-earth concerns, the sort of thing the real world's full of."

---

2. The guardian angel (French). A sentimental romance written by Mme. Pauline Duchambre, author of several such songs that appeared in the keepsakes.

"You're quite right," the clerk approved. "Writing like that doesn't move you: it seems to me to miss the whole true aim of art. Noble characters and pure affections and happy scenes are very comforting things. They're a refuge from life's disillusionments. As for me, they're my *only* means of relief, living here as I do, cut off from the world. Yonville has so little to offer!"

"It's like Tostes, I suppose," Emma said. "That's why I always subscribed to a lending library."

"If Madame would do me the honor of using it," said the pharmacist, who had heard her last words, "I can offer her a library composed of the best authors—Voltaire, Rousseau, Delille,[3] Walter Scott, the *Echo des Feuilletons*. I subscribe to a number of periodicals, too. The *Fanal de Rouen*[4] comes every day: as a matter of fact I happen to be its local correspondent for Buchy, Forges, Neufchâtel, Yonville and all this vicinity."

They had been at table two hours and a half. Artémise was a wretched waitress: she dragged her cloth slippers over the tile floor, brought plates one by one, forgot everything, paid no attention to what was told her, and constantly left the door of the billiard room ajar so that the latch kept banging against the wall.

As he talked, Léon had unconsciously rested his foot on one of the rungs of Madame Bovary's chair. She was wearing a little blue silk scarf that held her pleated batiste collar stiff as a ruff; and as she moved her head the lower part of her face buried itself in the folds or gently rose out of them. Sitting thus side by side while Charles and the pharmacist chatted, they entered into one of those vague conversations in which every new subject that comes up proves to be one more aspect of a core of shared feelings. The names of plays running in Paris, the titles of novels, new dance tunes, the inaccessible great world, Tostes where she had just come from, Yonville where they both were now—all this they went into and talked about until dinner was over.

When coffee was brought in, Félicité went off to prepare the bedroom in the new house, and soon they all got up from the table. Madame Lefrançois was asleep beside her smoldering fire, and the stable-boy, lantern in hand, was waiting to light Monsieur and Madame Bovary home. There were wisps of straw in his red hair, and his left leg was lame. He took Monsieur le curé's umbrella in his other hand, and the company set out.

The town was asleep. The pillars of the market cast long shadows, and the pallor of the road in the moonlight gave the effect of a summer night.

But the doctor's house was only fifty yards from the inn, and almost at once it was time to say good night and they went their separate ways.

The moment she stepped inside the entrance hall Emma felt the chill from the plaster walls fall on her shoulders, like the touch of a damp cloth. The walls were new and the wooden stairs creaked. Upstairs in the bedroom a whitish light came through the uncurtained windows. She could glimpse the tops of trees, and, beyond them, meadows half drowned in the mist that rose up in the moonlight along the river. In the middle of the room was a heap of bureau drawers, bottles, metal and wooden curtain rods; mattresses lying on chairs, basins strewn over the floor—everything had been left there in disorder by the two moving-men.

3. Jacques Delille (1738–1813), who wrote idyllic descriptive poems; *Les Jardins* (1782) is best known.
4. The *Rouen Beacon* (a fictitious newspaper).

It was the fourth time that she had gone to bed in a strange place. The first was the day she entered the convent, the second the day she arrived in Tostes, the third at La Vaubyessard, and now the fourth: each time it had been like the opening of a new phase of her life. She refused to believe that things could be the same in different places; and since what had gone before was so bad, what was to come must certainly be better.

III

The next morning she was barely up when she saw the clerk in the square. She was in her dressing gown. He caught sight of her and bowed. She responded with a brief nod and closed the window.

Léon waited all day for six o'clock to come, but when he entered the inn he found only Monsieur Binet, already at table.

The dinner of the previous evening had been a notable event for him: never before had he spoken for two consecutive hours with a "lady." How did it happen that he had been able to tell her so many things, in words that previously he wouldn't have thought of? He was ordinarily timid, with a reticence that was part modesty, part dissimulation. In Yonville he was thought to have very gentlemanly manners. He listened respectfully to his elders, and seemed not to get excited about politics—a remarkable trait in a young man. Besides, he was talented. He painted in water colors, could read the key of G, and when he didn't play cards after dinner he often took up a book. Monsieur Homais esteemed him because he was educated; Madame Homais liked him because he was helpful: he often spent some time with her children in the garden. They were brats, the Homais children, always dirty, wretchedly brought up, sluggish like their mother. Besides the maid, they were looked after by the pharmacist's apprentice, Justin, a distant cousin of Monsieur Homais, who had been taken in out of charity and was exploited as a servant.

The apothecary proved the best of neighbors. He advised Madame Bovary about tradesmen, had his cider dealer make a special delivery, tasted the brew himself, and saw to it that the barrel was properly installed in the cellar. He told her how to buy butter most advantageously, and made an arrangement for her with Lestiboudois the sacristan, who in addition to his ecclesiastical and funerary functions tended the principal gardens in Yonville by the hour or by the year, depending on the owners' preference.

It wasn't mere kindness that prompted the pharmacist to such obsequious cordiality: there was a scheme behind it.

He had violated the law of 19th Ventôse, Year XI,[5] Article I, which forbids anyone not holding a diploma to practice medicine; and in consequence had been denounced by anonymous informants and summoned to Rouen to the private chambers of the royal prosecutor. The magistrate had received him standing, clad in his robe of office banded at the shoulders with ermine and wearing his high official toque. It was in the morning, before the opening of court. Homais could hear the heavy tread of policemen in the corridor, and in the distance what sounded like heavy locks snapping shut. His ears rang

---

5. The government of the French Republic established a new calendar. The new year began on September 22, 1792; thus the year is 1803. *Ventôse:* windy (French); the sixth month of the new calendar (from February 19 to March 20), making the date March 9.

so that he thought he was going to have a stroke; he had a vision of underground dungeons, his family in tears, his pharmacy sold, all his glass jars scattered among strangers; and when the interview was over he had to go to a café and drink a rum and soda to steady his nerves.

Gradually the memory of this warning faded, and he continued as before to give innocuous consultations in his back room. But his relations with the mayor were not good; he had competitors who would rejoice in his ruin: he had to watch his step. By being polite to Monsieur Bovary he could win his gratitude and insure his looking the other way should he notice anything. So every morning Homais brought him "the paper," and often left the pharmacy in the afternoon to call on him for a moment's conversation.

Charles was in a gloomy state: he had no patients. He sat silent for hours on end, took naps in his consulting room, or watched his wife as she sewed. To keep occupied he acted as handyman around the house, even attempting to paint the attic with what the painters had left behind. But he was worried about money. He had spent so much for repairs at Tostes, for dresses for Madame, for the move, that the entire dowry and three thousand écus besides had been swallowed up in two years. Besides, so many things had been broken or lost between Tostes and Yonville! The plaster priest was one of them: a particularly violent bump had thrown it out of the van, and it had been smashed into a thousand pieces on the cobblestones of Quincampoix.

He had another, happier concern—his wife's pregnancy. As her term drew near she became ever dearer to him. Another bond of the flesh was being forged between them, one which gave him an all-pervasive feeling that their union was now closer. The indolence of her gait, the gentle sway of her uncorseted body, her tired way of sitting in a chair, all filled him with uncontrollable happiness: he would go up to her and kiss her, stroke her face, call her "little mother," try to dance with her; and half laughing, half weeping, he would think of a thousand playful endearments to shower her with. The idea of having begotten a child enchanted him. Now he had everything he could ever hope for. He had been granted all that human life had to offer, and he was serenely ready to enjoy it.

Emma's first reaction to her condition was one of great surprise; and then she was eager to be delivered and know what it was like to be a mother. But since she couldn't spend the money she would have liked and buy embroidered baby bonnets and a boat-shaped cradle with pink silk curtains, she resentfully gave up her own ideas about the layette and ordered the whole thing from a seamstress in the village without indicating any preferences or discussing any details. Thus she had none of the pleasure she might have had in the preparations that whet the appetite of mother love; and this perhaps did something to blunt her affection from the beginning. But Charles spoke of the baby every time they sat down to a meal, and gradually she became accustomed to the idea.

She wanted a son. He would be strong and dark; she would call him Georges; and this idea of having a male child was like a promise of compensation for all her past frustrations. A man is free, at least—free to range the passions and the world, to surmount obstacles, to taste the rarest pleasures. Whereas a woman is continually thwarted. Inert, compliant, she has to struggle against her physical weakness and legal subjection. Her will, like the veil tied to her hat, quivers with every breeze: there is always a desire that entices, always a convention that restrains.

The baby was born one Sunday morning, about six o'clock, as the sun was rising.

"It's a girl!" cried Charles.

She turned her head away and fainted.

Almost immediately Madame Homais rushed in and kissed her, followed by Madame Lefrançois of the Lion d'Or. The pharmacist, a man of discretion, confined himself to a few provisional words of congratulations, spoken through the half-open door. He asked to see the child and pronounced it well formed.

During her convalescence she gave a great deal of thought to a name for her daughter. First she went over all she could think of that had Italian endings—Clara, Louisa, Amanda, Atala; she was tempted by Galsuinde, too, and even more by Isolde and Léocadie. Charles wanted the child named for its mother; Emma was opposed. They went through the almanac from end to end and asked everyone for suggestions.

"Monsieur Léon," said the pharmacist, "told me the other day he's surprised you haven't decided on Madeleine: it's so very fashionable just now."

But the older Madame Bovary protested loudly against a name so associated with sin. Monsieur Homais' predilection was for names that recalled great men, illustrious deeds or noble thoughts: such had been his guiding principle in baptising his own four children. Napoléon stood for fame, Franklin for liberty; Irma was perhaps a concession to romanticism; but Athalie[6] was a tribute to the most immortal masterpiece of the French stage. For—mind you!—his philosophical convictions didn't interfere with his artistic appreciation: in him, the thinker didn't stifle the man of feeling; he was a man of discrimination, quite capable of differentiating between imagination and fanaticism. In the tragedy in question, for example, he condemned the ideas but admired the style, abhorred the conception but praised all the details, found the characters impossible but their speeches marvelous. When he read the famous passages he was carried away, but the thought that the clergy made use of it all for their own purposes distressed him immensely; and so troubling was his confusion of feelings that he would have liked to place a wreath on Racine's brow with his own hands and then have a good long argument with him.

In the end, Emma remembered hearing the marquise at Vaubyessard address a young woman as Berthe, and that promptly became the chosen name. Since Monsieur Rouault was unable to come, Monsieur Homais was asked to be godfather. As presents he brought several items from his pharmaceutical stock, namely, six boxes of jujubes, a full jar of racahout, three packages of marshmallow paste, and six sticks of sugar candy that he found in a cupboard and threw in for good measure. The evening of the ceremony there was a large dinner party. The priest was present: words became rather heated, and with the liqueurs Monsieur Homais broke into Béranger's *Le Dieu des bonnes gens.*[7] Monsieur Léon sang a barcarolle, and the older Madame Bovary (who was godmother) a Napoleonic ballad. Finally the older Monsieur Bovary insisted that the baby be brought down, and proceeded to baptize it with a glass of champagne, pouring the wine over its head. This mockery of the first sacrament brought indignant words from the Abbé Bour-

---

6. A tragedy by Jean Racine, written in 1691 for the pupils of Saint-Cyr. Racine had abandoned the regular stage after a spiritual crisis and wrote two sacred tragedies, *Esther* and *Athalie,* for the young girls of Saint-Cyr.   7. The god of good people; a deistic song by Béranger (see n. 7, p. 855).

nisien; the older Monsieur Bovary replied with a quotation from *La Guerre des dieux;*[8] and the priest started to leave. The ladies implored him to stay; Homais intervened; and after considerable persuasion the abbé sat down again in his chair and calmly took up his saucer and his half-finished demitasse.

The older Monsieur Bovary stayed on for a month at Yonville, dazzling the inhabitants with a magnificent silver-braided policeman's cap that he wore mornings when he smoked his pipe in the square. He was used to drinking large quantities of brandy, and often sent the maid to the Lion d'Or to buy a bottle, which was charged to his son's account; and to perfume his foulards he used up his daughter-in-law's entire supply of eau de Cologne.

Emma didn't in the least dislike his company. He had seen the world: he spoke of Berlin, of Vienna, of Strasbourg, of his years as an army officer, of the mistresses he had had, of the official banquets he had attended. Then he would become gallant; and sometimes, on the stairs or in the garden, he would even seize hold of her waist and cry, "Better watch out, Charles!" The older Madame Bovary was alarmed for her son's happiness, and began to urge her husband to take her home, lest in the long run he corrupt the young woman's mind. Possibly her fears went further: Monsieur Bovary was a man to whom nothing was sacred.

One day Emma suddenly felt that she had to see her little daughter, who had been put out to nurse with the cabinetmaker's wife; and without looking at the almanac to see whether the six weeks of the Virgin[9] had elapsed, she made her way toward the house occupied by Rollet, at the end of the village at the foot of the hills, between the main road and the meadows.

It was noon: the houses had their shutters closed, and under the harsh light of the blue sky the ridges of the glittering slate roofs seemed to be shooting sparks. A sultry wind was blowing. Emma felt weak as she walked; the stones of the footpath hurt her feet, and she wondered whether she shouldn't return home or stop in somewhere to rest.

At that moment Monsieur Léon emerged from a nearby door, a sheaf of papers under his arm. He advanced to greet her and stood in the shade in front of Lheureux's store, under the gray awning.

Madame Bovary said that she was on her way to see her child but was beginning to feel tired.

"If . . ." Léon began, and then dared go no further.

"Have you an appointment somewhere?" she asked him.

And when he replied that he hadn't she asked him to accompany her. By evening the news of this had spread throughout Yonville, and Madame Tuvache, the wife of the mayor, said in her maid's presence that Madame Bovary was risking her reputation.

To reach the wet-nurse's house they had to turn left at the end of the village street, as though going to the cemetery, and follow a narrow path that led them past cottages and yards between privet hedges. These were in bloom; and blooming, too, were veronicas and wild roses and nettles and the wild blackberries that thrust out their slender sprays from the thickets. Through holes in the hedges they could see, in the farmyards, a pig on a

---

8. The war of the gods; a satirical poem by Evarite-Désiré Deforge (later vicomte de Parny; 1753–1814) published in 1799. It ridicules the Christian religion.   9. Originally the six weeks that separate Christmas from Purification (February 2); in those days, the normal period of confinement for a woman after childbirth.

manure pile or cows in wooden collars rubbing their horns against tree trunks. The two of them walked on slowly side by side, she leaning on his arm and he shortening his step to match hers; in front of them hovered a swarm of flies, buzzing in the warm air.

They recognized the house by an old walnut tree that shaded it. It was low, roofed with brown tiles, and from the attic window hung a string of onions. Brushwood propped up against a thorn hedge formed a fence around a bit of garden given over to lettuce, a few plants of lavender, and sweet peas trained on poles. A trickle of dirty water ran off into the grass, and all around were odds and ends of rags, knitted stockings, a red calico wrapper, a large coarsely woven sheet spread out on the hedge. At the sound of the gate the wet nurse appeared, carrying an infant at her breast. With her other hand she was pulling along a frail, unhappy-looking little boy, his face covered with scrofulous sores—the son of a Rouen knit-goods dealer whom his parents were too busy in their shop to bother with.

"Come in," she said. "Your little girl's asleep inside."

The ground-floor bedroom—the only bedroom in the house—had a wide uncurtained bed standing against its rear wall; the window wall (one pane was mended with a bit of wrapping paper) was taken up by the kneading trough. In the corner behind the door was a raised slab for washing, and under it stood a row of heavy boots with shiny hobnails and a bottle of oil with a feather in its mouth. A Mathieu Laensberg almanac[1] lay on the dusty mantelpiece among gun flints, candle ends and bits of tinder. And as a final bit of clutter there was a figure of Fame blowing her trumpets—a picture probably cut out of a perfume advertisement and now fastened to the wall with six shoe tacks.

Emma's baby was asleep in a wicker cradle on the floor, and she took it up in its little blanket and began to sing softly to it and rock it in her arms.

Léon walked around the room: it seemed to him a strange sight, this elegant lady in her nankeen gown here among all this squalor. Madame Bovary blushed; he turned away, fearing that his glance might have been indiscreet; and she put the baby back in its cradle—it had just thrown up over the collar of her dress. The wet nurse quickly wiped off the mess, assuring her it wouldn't show.

"It isn't the first time, you know," she said. "I do nothing but wipe up after her all day long. Would you mind leaving word with Camus the grocer to let me pick up a little soap when I need it? That would be the easiest for you—I wouldn't have to trouble you."

"I will, I will," said Emma. "Good-bye, Madame Rollet."

And she left the house, wiping her feet on the doorsill.

The wet nurse walked with her as far as the gate, talking about how hard it was to have to get up during the night.

"I'm so worn out sometimes I fall asleep in my chair. So couldn't you at least let me have just a pound of ground coffee? It would last me a month; I'd drink it with milk in the morning."

After undergoing a deluge of thanks, Madame Bovary moved on; and then when she had gone a little way down the path there was the sound of sabots and she turned around: it was the wet nurse again.

"What is it now?"

1. A farmer's almanac, begun in 1635 by Laensberg, frequently found in farms and country houses.

And the peasant woman drew her aside behind an elm and began to talk to her about her husband. He "had only his trade and the six francs a year the captain gave him, so . . ."

"Come to the point!" said Emma brusquely.

"Well, what I mean is," the wet nurse said, sighing after every word, "I'm afraid he wouldn't like it, seeing me sitting there drinking coffee by myself; you know how men are, they . . ."

"But you'll both have coffee!" Emma cried. "I just told you I'd give you some! Leave me alone!"

"Ah, Madame, you see he's had terrible cramps in his chest ever since he was wounded, and he says cider makes him feel worse, and . . ."

"Won't you please let me go?"

"So," she went on, making a curtsy, "if it isn't too much to ask"—she curtsied again—"if you would"—and she gave a beseeching glance—"just a little jug of brandy," she finally got out, "and I'll rub your little girl's feet with it—they're as tender as your tongue."

When she was finally rid of the wet nurse, Emma once again took Monsieur Léon's arm. She walked rapidly for a little while; then she slowed, and her glance fell on the shoulder of the young man she was with. His brown hair, smooth and neatly combed, touched the black velvet collar of his frock coat. She noticed that his fingernails were longer than those of most other inhabitants of Yonville. The clerk spent a great deal of time caring for them: he kept a special penknife in his desk for the purpose.

They returned to Yonville along the river. The summer weather had reduced its flow and left uncovered the river walls and water steps of the gardens along its bank. It ran silently, swift and cold-looking; long fine grasses bent with the current, like masses of loose green hair streaming in its limpid depths. Here and there on the tip of a reed or on a water-lily pad a spidery-legged insect was poised or crawling. Sunbeams pierced the little blue air bubbles that kept forming and breaking on the ripples; branchless old willows mirrored their gray bark in the water; in the distance the meadows seemed empty all around them. It was dinner time on the farms, and as they walked the young woman and her companion heard only the rhythm of their own steps on the earth of the path, the words they themselves were uttering, and the whisper of Emma's dress as it rustled around her.

The garden walls, their copings bristling with broken bits of bottles, were as warm as the glass of a greenhouse. Wallflowers had taken root between the bricks; and as she passed, the edge of Madame Bovary's open parasol crumbled some of their faded flowers into yellow dust; or an overhanging branch of honeysuckle or clematis would catch in the fringe and cling for a moment to the silk.

They talked about a company of Spanish dancers scheduled soon to appear at the theatre in Rouen.

"Are you going?" she asked.

"If I can," he answered.

Had they nothing more to say to each other? Their eyes, certainly, were full of more meaningful talk; and as they made themselves utter banalities they sensed the same languor invading them both: it was like a murmur of the soul, deep and continuous, more clearly audible than the sound of their words. Surprised by a sweetness that was new to them, it didn't occur to them to tell each other how they felt or to wonder why. Future joys are like tropic shores: out into the immensity that lies before them they waft their native softness, a fragrant breeze that drugs the traveler into drowsiness and makes him careless of what awaits him on the horizon beyond his view.

In one spot the ground was boggy from the trampling of cattle, and they had to walk on large green stones that had been laid in the mud. She kept stopping to see where to place her foot; and teetering on an unsteady stone, her arms lifted, her body bent, a hesitant look in her eye, she laughed, fearing lest she fall into the puddles.

When they reached her garden, Madame Bovary pushed open the little gate, ran up the steps and disappeared.

Léon returned to his office. His employer was out; he glanced at the piles of papers, sharpened a quill pen, and then—took up his hat and went out again.

He climbed to the Pasture, on the hilltop at the edge of the Argueil forest, and there he stretched out on the ground under the firs and looked up at the sky through his fingers.

"God!" he said to himself. "What a boring existence!"

He felt that he was much to be pitied for having to live in this village, with Homais for a friend and Maître Guillaumin for a master. The latter, completely taken up with business, wore gold-framed spectacles, red side whiskers and a white tie; fine feelings were a closed book to him, though the stiff British manner he affected had impressed the clerk at first. As for Madame Homais, she was the best wife in Normandy, placid as a sheep and devoted to her children, her father, her mother and her cousins; she wept at others' misfortunes, let everything in the house go, and hated corsets. But she was so slow-moving, so boring to listen to, so common-looking and limited in conversation, that it never occurred to him—though she was thirty and he twenty, and they slept in adjoining rooms and he spoke to her every day— that anyone could look on her as a woman, that she had any attributes of her sex except the dress she wore.

Who was there besides? Binet, a few shopkeepers, two or three tavern keepers, the priest, and lastly, Monsieur Tuvache, the mayor, and his two sons—a comfortably-off, surly, dull-witted trio who farmed their own land, ate huge meals with never a guest, faithful churchgoers for all that, and utterly insufferable in company.

But against the background of all these human faces, Emma's stood out— isolated from them and yet further removed than they, for he sensed that some abyss separated him from her.

At first he had gone to her house several times with the pharmacist. Charles had not seemed too eager to have him; and Léon felt helpless, torn as he was between fear of being indiscreet and desire for an intimacy that he considered all but impossible.

IV

With the coming of cold weather Emma moved out of her bedroom into the parlor, a long low-ceilinged room where a chunky branch of coral stood on the mantelpiece in front of the mirror. Sitting in her armchair beside the window, she could watch the villagers go by on the sidewalk.

Twice a day Léon went from his office to the Lion d'Or. Emma could hear him coming in the distance; she would lean forward as she listened, and the young man would slip past on the other side of the window curtain, always dressed the same, never turning his head. At twilight, when she had put down her embroidery and was sitting there with her chin in her left hand, she often started at the sudden appearance of this gliding shadow. She would jump up, order the maid to set the table.

Monsieur Homais often called during dinner. Tasseled cap in hand, he would tiptoe in so as to disturb no one, and he always gave the same greeting: "Good evening, everybody!" Then, sitting down at the table between them, he would ask the doctor for news of his patients, and Charles would ask him what the chances were of being paid. Then they would talk about what was "in the paper." By this time of day Homais knew it almost by heart, and he would repeat it *in toto*, complete with editorials and the news of each and every disaster that had occurred in France and abroad. When these topics ran dry he never failed to comment on the dishes he saw being served. Sometimes, half rising, he would even considerately point out to Madame the tenderest piece of meat; or, turning to the maid, he would advise her on the preparation of her stews and the use of seasoning from a health point of view: he was quite dazzling on the subject of aromas, osmazomes, juices and gelatines. Indeed, Homais had more recipes in his head than there were bottles in his pharmacy, and he excelled at making all kinds of jellies, vinegars and cordials. He was acquainted with all the latest fuel-saving stoves, and with the arts of preserving cheeses and treating spoiled wine.

At eight o'clock Justin always called for him: it was time to shut the pharmacy. Monsieur Homais would give him a quizzical glance, especially if Félicité were in the room, for he had noticed that his pupil was partial to the doctor's house. "My young man's beginning to get ideas," he would say. "Something tells me he's after your maid!"

And there was worse: despite all rebukes, the boy persisted in his habit of listening to conversations. On Sundays, for instance, Madame Homais would summon him to the parlor to take away the children, who had fallen asleep in armchairs, dragging down the loose calico slip covers, and there was no way of getting him to leave the room.

These soirées at the pharmacist's were not very well attended, for his slanderous tongue and his political opinions had alienated one respectable person after another. The clerk was invariably present. At the sound of the doorbell he would run down to greet Madame Bovary, take her shawl, and stow away under the desk in the pharmacy the overshoes she wore when it snowed.

First they would play a few rounds of *trente-et-un*; then Monsieur Homais would play *écarté*[2] with Emma, Léon standing behind her and giving advice. With his hands on the back of her chair, he would look down and see the teeth of her comb piercing her chignon. Each time she threw down a card the right side of her dress gave an upward twist, and he could follow the gradually paling shadow cast down her neck by the knot of her hair, until it

---

2. A card game similar to euchre, in which players win tricks by playing a higher card in the suit. *Trente-et-un:* "Thirty-one" (French), also called "Red and Black": a French gambling game in which cards are dealt in two categories (red and black) until a total of thirty-one or more points is reached; players bet on the winning color.

was lost in a darker shadow. Then her dress would drop down on both sides of her chair, swelling out in full folds and spreading to the floor. Sometimes Léon would feel himself touching it with the sole of his shoe, and he would quickly move away, as though he had been treading on someone.

When they finished their cards, the apothecary and the doctor played dominoes; and Emma would move to another chair, lean her elbows on the table and leaf through *L'Illustration,* or take up the fashion magazine she usually brought with her. Léon would sit beside her, and together they would look at the pictures and wait for each other before turning a page. Often she would ask him to read a poem aloud, and Léon would recite it in a languid voice that he carefully let die away at the love passages. But the noise of the dominoes annoyed him: Monsieur Homais was an expert, easily outplaying Charles. When the score reached three hundred the two of them would stretch out before the fireplace and quickly fall asleep. The fire smoldered, the teapot was empty; Léon continued to read, and Emma listened, absent-mindedly turning the lampshade, its gauzy surface painted with pierrots in carriages and tightrope dancers balancing with their poles. Léon would stop, indicating with a gesture his sleeping audience; and then they would talk in low voices, their conversation seeming the sweeter for not being overheard.

Thus a kind of intimacy grew up between them, a continual exchange of books and ballads. Monsieur Bovary was not jealous; he found it all quite natural.

For his birthday he received a splendid phrenological head, all marked over with numerals down to the thorax and painted blue. This was an offering from the clerk. He was attentive in many other ways, too, even doing errands for Charles in Rouen. When a new novel launched a craze for exotic plants, Léon bought some for Madame, holding them on his knees in the Hirondelle and pricking his fingers on their spikes.

Emma had a railed shelf installed in her window to hold her flowerpots. The clerk, too, had his hanging garden, and they could look out and see each other tending their blossoms.

There was one person in the village who spent even more time at his window than they: from morning till night on Sunday, and every afternoon in good weather, the lean profile of Monsieur Binet could be seen in a dormer bent over his lathe, its monotonous drone audible as far as the Lion d'Or.

One evening when he returned home Léon found in his room a velvet and wool coverlet, with foliage designs on a pale ground. He showed it to Madame Homais, Monsieur Homais, Justin, the children, and the cook, and spoke about it to his employer. Everybody wanted to see it: why should the doctor's wife give presents to the clerk? The whole thing seemed suspicious, and everyone was sure that they must be having an affair.

By speaking incessantly about Emma's charms and intelligence, Léon gave plenty of grounds for the belief. Binet turned on him one day with a snarl: "What's it to me? She doesn't let *me* hang around her!"

He was in agony trying to think of a way of "declaring himself" to her. He was constantly torn between the fear of offending her and shame at his own cowardice; he shed tears of despair and frustrated desire. Every so often he resolved to take energetic action: he wrote letters, only to tear them up; he gave himself time limits, only to extend them. More than once he started out intending to dare all; but in Emma's presence he quickly lost his courage, and if Charles happened to appear at such a moment and invited him to get into the buggy and go with him to see a patient living somewhere nearby, he would accept at once, bow to Madame and drive off. Her husband, after all, was part of herself, was he not?

As for Emma, she never tried to find out whether she was in love with him. Love, to her, was something that comes suddenly, like a blinding flash of lightning—a heaven-sent storm hurled into life, uprooting it, sweeping every will before it like a leaf, engulfing all feelings. It never occurred to her that if the drainpipes of a house are clogged, the rain may collect in pools on the roof; and she suspected no danger until suddenly she discovered a crack in the wall.

V

It was a snowy Sunday afternoon in February.

All of them—Monsieur and Madame Bovary, Homais and Monsieur Léon—had gone to see a new flax mill that was being built in the valley, a mile or so from Yonville. The apothecary had taken Napoléon and Athalie along to give them some exercise, and Justin accompanied them, carrying a supply of umbrellas over his shoulder.

Nothing, however, could have been less interesting than this point of interest. A long rectangular building pierced with innumerable little windows stood in the midst of a large tract of bare land, with a few already rusty gear wheels lying here and there among piles of sand and gravel. It was still unfinished, and the sky could be seen between the rafters. Attached to the ridgepole at the peak of one of the gables was a bouquet of straw and wheat, tied with red, white and blue ribbons that flapped in the wind.

Homais was holding forth. He expatiated to them all on how important the mill was going to be, estimated the strength of the floors and the thickness of the walls, and keenly regretted not owning a carpenter's rule, such as Monsieur Binet possessed for his personal use.

Emma, who had taken his arm, was leaning slightly against his shoulder and looking up at the far-off disc of the sun that was suffusing the mist with its pale brilliance; then she turned her head, and saw—Charles. His cap was pulled down over his eyes; and the quivering of his thick lips in the cold gave him a stupid look. Even his back, his placid back, was irritating to look at: all his dullness was written right there, on his coat.

As she was looking at him, deriving a kind of perverse enjoyment from her very irritation, Léon moved a step closer. White in the cold, his face was more languorous and appealing than ever; a bit of his bare skin showed through a gap in his shirt collar; she could see the tip of one of his ears below a lock of his hair; and his large blue eyes, lifted toward the clouds, seemed to Emma more limpid and lovely than mountain lakes mirroring the sky.

"Stop that!" the apothecary suddenly cried.

And he rushed over to his son, who had just jumped into a heap of lime to whiten his shoes. To his father's scoldings Napoléon replied with howls; Justin scraped off the shoes with a bit of plaster; but a knife was needed, and Charles offered his.

"Ah!" she cried to herself. "He carries a knife around with him, like a peasant!"

The cold was beginning to pinch, and they turned back toward Yonville.

That evening Madame Bovary did not attend her neighbor's soirée; and when Charles had gone and she felt herself alone, the comparison returned to her mind almost with the sharpness of an actual sensation, and with the increased perspective conferred on things by memory. Watching the brightly burning fire from her bed, she saw once again, as at the scene itself, Léon standing there, leaning with one hand on his slender, flexing cane and with the other holding Athalie, who was placidly sucking a piece of ice. She found him charming; she could not take her mind off him; she remembered how he had looked on other occasions, things he had said, the sound of his voice, everything about him; and she kept saying to herself, protruding her lips as though for a kiss: "Charming, charming! . . . Isn't he in love? Who could it be?" she asked herself. "Why—he's in love with me!"

All the evidence burst on her at once; her heart leapt up. The flames in the fireplace cast a merry, flickering light on the ceilings; she lay on her back and stretched out her arms.

Then began the eternal lament: "Oh, if only fate had willed it so! Why didn't it? What stood in the way?"

When Charles came in at midnight she pretended to wake up. He made some noise as he undressed, and she complained of migraine; then she casually asked what had happened during the evening.

"Monsieur Léon went up to his room early," said Charles.

She couldn't help smiling, and she fell asleep filled with new happiness.

At nightfall the next day she had a visit from Monsieur Lheureux, the proprietor of the local dry-goods store. He was a clever man, this tradesman.

Born a Gascon, but long settled in Normandy, he combined his southern volubility with the cunning of his adopted region. His fat, flabby, clean-shaven face looked as though it had been dyed with a faint tincture of licorice, and his white hair emphasized the piercing boldness of his small black eyes. What he had been in earlier life was a mystery to all: peddler, some said; and others, banker in Routot. What was certain was that he could do in his head intricate feats of calculation that startled Binet himself. Polite to the point of obsequiousness, he was continually in a semi-bent position, like someone making a bow or extending an invitation.

He left his hat with its black mourning band at the door, placed a green case on the table, and began by complaining, with many civilities, at not having been honored up till now with Madame's patronage. A poor shop like his could scarcely be expected to attract so elegant a lady: he emphasized the adjective. But she had only to give him an order and he would undertake to supply anything she wanted, whether accessories, lingerie, hosiery and other knit goods, or notions, for he went to the city four times a month regularly. He was in constant touch with the biggest firms. She could mention his name at the Trois Frères, at the Barbe d'Or or at the Grand Sauvage: everyone in those places knew all about him. Today he would just like to show Madame a few articles he happened to have with him, thanks to a lucky buy; out of his box he took half a dozen embroidered collars.

Madame Bovary looked them over.

"I don't need anything," she said.

Then Monsieur Lheureux daintily held out for her inspection three Algerian scarves, some packages of English needles, a pair of straw slippers, and finally four coconut-shell egg cups, carved in an openwork design by convicts. Then, both hands on the table, leaning forward, his neck outstretched, he watched Emma open-mouthed, following her gaze as it wandered uncertainly over the merchandise. From time to time, as though to brush off a bit of dust, he gave a flick of a fingernail to the silk of the scarves, lying there unfolded to their full length; and they quivered and rustled under his touch, their gold sequins gleaming like little stars in the greenish light of the dusk.

"How much are they?"

"They're absurdly cheap," he said. "Besides, there's no hurry. Pay whenever you like—we're not Jews!"

She meditated a few moments, then finally told Monsieur Lheureux once more that she didn't want to buy.

"That's quite all right," he answered impassively. "You and I will do business some other time. I've always known how to get along with the ladies—except my wife."

Emma smiled.

"I just want you to know," he said, dropping his facetious tone and assuming an air of candor, "that I'm not worried about the money. In fact, I could let you have some if you needed it."

Emma made a gesture of surprise.

"Ah," he said quickly, in a low voice. "I wouldn't have to go far to find it, believe me!"

Then he turned the conversation to the subject of Monsieur Tellier, proprietor of the Café Français, whom Monsieur Bovary was treating.

"What's his trouble, anyway? He's got a cough that shakes the house. I'm afraid he may soon need a wooden overcoat more than a flannel undershirt! He was a wild one in his younger days! The kind that doesn't know even the meaning of self-control, Madame! He literally burned his insides out with brandy! Still, it's hard to see an old friend go."

And as he tied up his box he talked on about the doctor's patients.

"It must be the weather," he said, scowling at the windowpanes, "that's causing all this illness. I don't feel right myself: one of these days I'll have to come and talk to Monsieur about a pain I have in my back. Well—au revoir, Madame Bovary; at your service, any time."

And he shut the door softly behind him.

Emma had her dinner brought to her in her bedroom on a tray, and ate it beside the fire. She lingered over her food: everything tasted good.

"How sensible I was!" she told herself, as she thought of the scarves.

She heard footsteps on the stairs: it was Léon. She jumped up and snatched the topmost dish towel from a pile she had left for hemming on the chest of drawers. She looked very busy when he came in.

Conversation languished: Madame Bovary kept letting his remarks drop unanswered, and he seemed very ill at ease. He sat in a low chair beside the fire, toying with her ivory needlecase; she continued to sew, occasionally creasing the cloth together with her fingernail. She said nothing, and he, too, was quiet, captivated by her silence as he would have been by her words.

"Poor fellow!" she was thinking.

"What does she dislike about me?" he was wondering.

Finally Léon said that he would be going to Rouen some day soon on office business.

"Your subscription at the music library has run out," he said. "Shall I renew it?"

"No," she answered.

"Why not?"

"Because . . ."

And pursing her lips she slowly drew out a new length of gray thread.

Her sewing irritated Léon: the cloth seemed to be roughening the tips of her fingers. A compliment occurred to him, but he hadn't the courage to utter it.

"You're giving it up?"

"What?" she asked quickly. "Oh, my music? Heavens, yes! Haven't I got my house and my husband to look after—a thousand things—all kinds of duties that come first?"

She looked at the clock. Charles was late. She pretended to be worried. "He's such a good man," she said, two or three times.

The clerk was fond of Monsieur Bovary, but he was unpleasantly surprised to hear her speak so affectionately of him. Nevertheless he continued the praises she had begun, and assured her that he heard them from everyone, especially the pharmacist.

"Ah, Monsieur Homais is a fine man," said Emma.

"He certainly is," said the clerk.

He began to speak of Madame Homais, whose sloppy appearance usually made them laugh.

"What of it?" Emma interrupted. "A good wife and mother doesn't worry about her clothes."

And once again she fell silent.

It was the same the following days: her talk, her manner, everything changed. She immersed herself in household tasks, went regularly to church, and was stricter with the maid.

She took Berthe away from the wet nurse. Félicité brought her in when there was company, and Madame Bovary undressed her to show off her little legs and arms. She adored children, she said: they were her consolation, her joy, her delight; and she accompanied her caresses with gushings that would have reminded anyone except the Yonvillians of Esmeralda's mother in *Notre-Dame de Paris*.[3]

Nowadays when Charles came in, he found his slippers set out to warm by the fire. Now his vests were never without linings, his shirts never without buttons; it was a pleasure to see the piles of cotton nightcaps stacked so neatly in the closet. She no longer frowned at the idea of taking a walk in the garden; she agreed to all his suggestions without trying to understand his reasons. And when Léon saw him beside the fire in the evening, his face flushed from dinner, his hands folded over his stomach, his feet on the andirons, his eyes moist with happiness, the baby crawling on the carpet, and this slender woman leaning over the back of his armchair to kiss him on the forehead—"I must be mad," he told himself. "How can I ever hope to come near her?"

She seemed so virtuous and inaccessible that he lost all hope, even the faintest.

---

3. A historical novel (1831) by Victor Hugo, in which the mother of Agnes, a girl abducted by gypsies who takes the name Esmeralda, worships a shoe of her stolen child.

But by thus renouncing her, he transformed her into an extraordinary being. She was divested in his eyes of the earthly attributes that held no promise for him; and in his heart she rose higher and higher, withdrawing further from him in a magnificent, soaring apotheosis. His feeling for her was so pure that it did not interfere with his daily life—it was one of those feelings that are cherished because of their very rarity: the distress caused by their loss would be greater than the happiness given by their possession.

Emma grew thinner: her face became paler, more emaciated. With her smooth black hair, her large eyes, her straight nose, her birdlike movements, her new habit of silence, she seemed all but out of contact with life, bearing on her brow the vague mark of a sublime fate. She was so melancholy and so subdued, so sweet and yet so withdrawn, that in her presence he felt transfixed by a glacial spell—just as in a church the fragrance of flowers and the cold given off by marble will sometimes set us shivering. Even other men were not immune to this seduction. The pharmacist put it this way:

"She's got class! She'd hold her own in Le Havre or Dieppe!"

The village housewives admired her for her thrift; Charles's patients for her politeness; the poor for her charity.

And all this time she was torn by wild desires, by rage, by hatred. The trim folds of her dress hid a heart in turmoil, and her reticent lips told nothing of the storm. She was in love with Léon, and she sought the solitude that allowed her to revel undisturbed in his image. The sight of his person spoiled the voluptuousness of her musings. She trembled at the sound of his foot-steps; then, with him before her, the agitation subsided, and she was left with nothing but a vast bewilderment that turned gradually into sadness.

Léon did not know, when he left her house in despair, that she went immediately to the window and watched him disappear down the street. She worried over his every move, watched every expression that crossed his face; she concocted an elaborate story to have a pretext for visiting his room. The pharmacist's wife seemed to her blessed to sleep under the same roof; and her thoughts came continually to rest on that house, like the pigeons from the Lion d'Or that alighted there to soak their pink feet and white wings in the eaves-trough. But the more aware Emma became of her love the more she repressed it in an effort to conceal it and weaken it. She would have been glad had Léon guessed; and she kept imagining accidents and disasters that would open his eyes. It was indolence, probably, or fear, that held her back, and a feeling of shame. She had kept him at too great a distance, she decided: now it was too late; the occasion was lost. Besides, the pride and pleasure she derived from thinking of herself as "virtuous" and from wearing an air of resignation as she looked at herself in the mirror consoled her a little for the sacrifice she thought she was making.

Her carnal desires, her cravings for money, and the fits of depression engendered by her love gradually merged into a single torment; and instead of trying to put it out of her mind she cherished it, spurring herself on to suffer, never missing an opportunity to do so. A dish poorly served or a door left ajar grated on her nerves; she sighed thinking of the velvet gowns she didn't own, the happiness that eluded her, her unattainable dreams, her entire cramped existence.

What exasperated her was Charles's total unawareness of her ordeal. His conviction that he was making her happy she took as a stupid insult: such self-righteousness could only mean that he didn't appreciate her. For whose sake, after all, was she being virtuous? Wasn't he the obstacle to every kind of happiness, the cause of all her wretchedness, the sharp-pointed prong of this many-stranded belt that bound her on all sides?

So he became the sole object of her resentment. Her attempts to conquer this feeling served only to strengthen it, for their failure gave her additional cause for despair and deepened her estrangement from her husband. She had moments of revulsion against her own meekness. She reacted to the drabness of her home by indulging in daydreams of luxury, and to matrimonial caresses by adulterous desires. She wished that Charles would beat her: then she would feel more justified in hating him and betraying him out of revenge. Sometimes she was surprised by the horrible possibilities that she imagined; and yet she had to keep smiling, hear herself say time and again that she was happy, pretend to be so, let everyone believe it!

Still, there were times when she could scarcely stomach the hypocrisy. She would be seized with a longing to run off with Léon, escape to some far-off place where they could begin life anew; but at such moments she would shudder, feeling herself at the brink of a terrifying precipice.

"What's the use—he doesn't love me any more," she would decide. What was to become of her? What help could she hope for? What comfort? What relief?

Such a crisis always left her shattered, gasping, prostrate, sobbing to herself, tears streaming down her face.

"Why in the world don't you tell Monsieur?" the maid would ask her, finding her thus distraught.

"It's nerves," Emma would answer. "Don't mention it to him. It would only upset him."

"Ah, yes," Félicité said, one day. "You're just like the daughter of old Guérin, the fisherman at Le Pollet.[4] I knew her at Dieppe before I came to you. She used to be so sad, so terribly sad, that when she stood in her door she made you think of a funeral pall hanging there. It seems it was some kind of a fog in her head that ailed her. The doctors couldn't do anything for her, or the priest either. When it came over her worst, she'd go off by herself along the beach, and sometimes the customs officer would find her stretched out flat on her face on the pebbles and crying, when he made his rounds. It passed off after she was married, they say."

"With me," said Emma, "it was after I married that it began."

VI

One evening when the window was open and she had been sitting beside it watching Lestiboudois the sacristan trim the boxwood, she suddenly heard the tolling of the Angelus.

It was the beginning of April, primrose time, when soft breezes blow over newly spaded flower beds, and gardens, like women, seem to be primping themselves for the gaieties of summer. Through the slats of the arbor, and all around beyond, she could see the stream flowing through the meadows, winding its vagabond course amid the grass. The evening mist was rising

---

4. Suburb of Dieppe, where the fishermen live.

among the bare poplars, blurring their outlines with a tinge of purple that was paler and more transparent than the sheerest gauze caught on their branches. In the distance cattle were moving: neither their steps nor their lowing could be heard, and the steadily sounding church bell sent its peaceful lament into the evening air.

As the ringing continued, the young woman's thoughts began to stray among old memories of girlhood and the convent. She remembered the tall altar candlesticks that soared above the vases full of flowers and the columned tabernacle. She wished she could be again what she once had been, one in the long line of white-veiled girls, black specked here and there by the stiff cowls of the nuns bowed over their *prie-dieus*. Sundays at Mass when she raised her head she used to see the gentle features of the Virgin among the bluish clouds of rising incense. The memory filled her with emotion: she felt limp and passive, like a bit of bird's-down whirling in a storm; and automatically she turned her steps toward the church, ready for any devotion that would enable her to humble her heart and lose herself entirely.

In the square she met Lestiboudois on his way back: in order not to lose pay by cutting his workday short, he preferred to interrupt his gardening and then go back to it, with the result that he rang the Angelus when it suited him. Besides, early ringing served to remind the village boys that it was time for catechism.

Some of them were already there, playing marbles on the slabs in the cemetery. Others, astride the wall, were swinging their legs, their wooden shoes breaking off the tall nettles that grew between the wall itself and the nearest graves. This was the only spot that was green: all the rest was stones, always covered with a fine dust despite the sacristan's sweeping.

Other boys had taken off their sabots and were running about on the stones as though the cemetery were a smooth floor made specially for them. Their shouts could be heard above the dying sounds of the bell; the heavy rope that hung down from the top of the bell tower and trailed on the ground was swaying ever more slowly. Swallows flew past, twittering as they sliced the air with their swift flight, and disappeared into their yellow nests under the eave-tiles. At the far end of the church a lamp was burning—a wick in a hanging glass, whose light seemed from a distance like a whitish spot dancing on the oil. A long shaft of sunlight cutting across the nave deepened the darkness in the side aisles and corners.

"Where is the priest?" Madame Bovary asked a boy who was happily trying to wrench the turnstile loose from its socket.

"He'll be here," he answered.

Just then the door of the rectory creaked open and the abbé Bournisien appeared. The boys fled helter-skelter into the church.

"Won't they ever behave?" he muttered to himself. "No respect for anything." He picked up a tattered catechism that he had almost stepped on. Then he saw Madame Bovary. "Excuse me," he said. "I didn't place you for a minute."

He stuffed the catechism into his pocket and stood swinging the heavy sacristy key between two fingers.

The setting sun was full in his face; and the black cloth of his cassock, shiny at the elbows and frayed at the hem, seemed paler in its glow. Grease spots and snuff stains ran parallel to the row of little buttons on his broad chest; they were thickest below his neckband, which held back the heavy folds of his red skin; this was sprinkled with yellow splotches, half hidden by the bristles of his graying beard. He had just had his dinner, and was breathing heavily.

"How are you?" he went on.

"Poorly," said Emma. "Not well at all."

"Neither am I," the priest answered. "These first hot days take it out of you terribly, don't they? But what can we do? We're born to suffer, as St. Paul says. What does your husband think is the trouble?"

"My husband!" she said, with a scornful gesture.

The country priest looked surprised. "He must have prescribed something for you, hasn't he?"

"Ah!" said Emma. "It isn't earthly remedies that I need."

But the priest kept looking away, into the church, where the boys were kneeling side by side, each shoving his neighbor with his shoulder and all of them falling down like ninepins.

"Could you tell me . . ." she began.

"Just wait, Riboudet!" he shouted furiously. "I'll box your ears when I get hold of you!"

Then, turning to Emma: "That's the son of Boudet the carpenter; his parents don't bother with him, they let him do as he likes. He'd learn fast if he wanted to: he's very bright. Sometimes as a joke I call him Riboudet—you know, from the name of the hill near Maromme; sometimes I say 'mon Riboudet'—Mont Riboudet! Ha! Ha! The other day I told my little joke to the bishop. He laughed. He was good enough to laugh. And Monsieur Bovary—how is he?"

She seemed not to hear him, and he went on: "Always on the move, probably? He and I are certainly the two busiest people in the parish. He takes care of the bodies," he added, with a heavy laugh, "and I look after the souls."

She fastened her imploring eyes upon him. "Yes," she said. "You must be called on to relieve all kinds of suffering."

"Believe me, I am, Madame Bovary! This very morning I had to go to Bas-Diauville for a cow that had the colic: the peasants thought it was a spell. All their cows, for some reason . . . Excuse me, Madame! Longuemarre! Boudet! Drat you both! Will you cut it out?"

And he rushed into the church.

By now the boys were crowding around the high lectern, climbing up on the cantor's bench and opening the missal; and others, moving stealthily, were about to invade the confessional. But the priest was suddenly upon them, slapping them right and left; seizing them by the coat collar, he lifted them off the ground and then set them on their knees on the stone floor of the choir, pushing them down hard as though he were trying to plant them there.

"Well!" he said, returning to Emma. And then, as he opened his large calico handkerchief, holding a corner of it between his teeth: "As we were saying, farmers have plenty of troubles."

"Other people, too," she answered.

"Of course! Workingmen in the cities, for instance . . ."

"I wasn't thinking of them . . ."

"Ah, but I assure you I've known mothers of families, good women, true saints, who didn't even have a crust of bread."

"I was thinking of women who have bread, Monsieur le curé," Emma said, the corners of her mouth twisting as she spoke, "but who lack . . ."

"Firewood for the winter," the priest anticipated.

"Ah, never mind . . ."

"What do you mean, never mind? It seems to me that to be warm and well fed . . ."

"Oh, my God!" Emma whispered to herself. "My God!"

"Are you feeling ill?" he asked. He looked concerned, and advanced a step. "Something must have disagreed with you. You'd better go home, Madame Bovary, and drink a cup of tea; that will pick you up. Or a glass of water with a little brown sugar."

"What for?"

She looked as though she were emerging from a dream.

"You were holding your hand to your forehead. I thought you must be feeling faint." Then: "But weren't you asking me a question? What was it? I can't recall . . ."

"I? Oh, no, nothing . . . nothing," Emma said.

And her wandering glance came slowly to rest on the old man in his cassock. For a few moments they looked at each other without speaking.

"Well, Madame Bovary," he said, finally, "you'll excuse me, but duty calls. I have to look after my youngsters. First Communion will be here soon: it will be on us before we know it. Time's so short I always keep them an extra hour on Wednesdays after Ascension. Poor things! We can't begin too soon to steer their young souls in the Lord's path—indeed it's what he Himself tells us to do, through the mouth of His divine Son. Keep well, Madame; remember me kindly to your husband!"

And he entered the church, genuflecting just inside the door.

Emma watched him as he disappeared between the double line of pews, treading heavily, his head slightly bent to one side, his half-open hands held with palms outward.

Then she turned stiffly, like a statue on a pivot, and set out for home. Behind her she heard the booming voice of the priest and the lighter voices of the boys.

"Are you a Christian?"

"Yes, I am a Christian."

"What is a Christian?"

"A Christian is one who, after being baptized . . . baptized . . . baptized . . . "

She climbed her stairs holding tight to the rail, and once in her room she sank heavily into a chair.

The whitish light coming through the windowpanes was slowly fading and ebbing away. The various pieces of furniture seemed to be fixed more firmly in their places, lost in shadow as in an ocean of darkness. The fire was out, the clock kept up its tick-tock; and Emma vaguely marveled that all these things should be so quiet while she herself was in such turmoil. Then little Berthe was in front of her, tottering in her knitted shoes between the window and the sewing table, trying to reach her mother and catch hold of the ends of her apron strings.

"Let me alone!" Emma cried, pushing her away.

But a few moments later the little girl was back, this time coming closer. Leaning her arms on her mother's knees she looked up at her with her big blue eyes, and a thread of clear saliva dripped from her lip onto the silk of the apron.

"Let me alone!" Emma cried again, very much annoyed.

The expression on her face frightened the child, who began to scream.

"Won't you let me alone!" she cried, thrusting her off with her elbow.

Berthe fell just at the foot of the chest of drawers, cutting her cheek on one of its brasses. She began to bleed. Madame Bovary rushed to pick her up, broke the bell-rope, called loudly for the maid; and words of self-reproach were on her lips when Charles appeared. It was dinner time; he had just come in.

"Look what's happened, darling," she said, in an even voice. "The baby fell down and hurt herself playing."

Charles reassured her: it was nothing serious, he said, and he went for some adhesive plaster.

Madame Bovary didn't go downstairs for dinner that evening: she insisted on staying alone with her child. As she watched her lying there asleep, her anxiety, such as it was, gradually wore off; and she thought of herself as having been silly and good-hearted indeed to let herself be upset over so small a matter. Berthe had stopped sobbing; and now the cotton coverlet rose and fell imperceptibly with her regular breathing. A few large tears had gathered in the corners of her half-closed eyelids; through the lashes could be seen the pupils, pale and sunken-looking; the adhesive stuck on her cheek pulled the skin to one side.

"It's a strange thing," Emma thought, "what an ugly child she is."

At eleven o'clock, when Charles came back from the pharmacy, where he had gone after dinner to take back the plaster that was left, he found his wife on her feet beside the cradle.

"Really, believe me—it will be all right," he said, kissing her on the forehead. "Don't worry about it, darling: you'll make yourself ill."

He had stayed out a long time. He had not seemed unduly upset, but even so Monsieur Homais had done his best to cheer him up, "raise his morale." The conversation had then turned on the various dangers that beset children because of the absentmindedness of servants. Madame Homais could speak from experience, bearing as she did to this day on her chest the marks of a panful of burning coals that a cook had dropped inside her pinafore when she was small. No wonder the Homais' went out of their way to be careful with their children! In their house knives were never sharpened, floors never waxed. There were iron grills at the windows and heavy bars across the fireplaces. Though taught to be self-reliant, the Homais children couldn't move a step without someone in attendance; at the slightest sign of a cold their father stuffed them with cough syrups, and well past their fourth birthdays they were all mercilessly made to wear padded caps. This, it must be said, was a pet idea of Madame Homais': her husband was secretly worried about it, fearing lest the intellectual organs suffer as a result of such pressure; and he sometimes went so far as to say:

"Do you want to turn them into Caribs or Botocudos?"[5]

5. Two South American peoples.

Charles, meanwhile, had tried several times to end the conversation. "I'd like to have a word with you," he whispered in the clerk's ear; and Léon walked downstairs ahead of him.

"Can he be suspecting something?" he wondered. His heart pounded, and he imagined a thousand contingencies.

Charles, after closing the door behind them, asked him to inquire in Rouen as to the price of a good daguerreotype: he was thinking of paying a delicate tribute to his wife by giving her a sentimental surprise—a portrait of himself in his black tail coat. But he wanted to know, first, "what he was letting himself in for." Such inquiries would be no trouble for Monsieur Léon, since he went to the city almost every week.

What was the purpose of these visits? Homais suspected that there was a story there, an intrigue of some kind. But he was mistaken: Léon was not carrying on any amourette. These days his spirits were lower than ever: Madame Lefrançois could tell it from the amount of food he left on his plate. To find out more about it she questioned the tax collector; but Binet rebuffed her, saying that he "wasn't in the pay of the police."

Nevertheless his table companion struck him as exceedingly odd. Léon often lay back in his chair, stretched out his arms and complained vaguely about life.

"That's because you have no hobbies," said the tax collector.

"What would you advise?"

"If I were you I'd buy myself a lathe!"

"But I wouldn't know how to use it," the clerk answered.

"That's so, you wouldn't," said Binet. And he stroked his chin with an air of mingled scorn and satisfaction.

Léon was tired of loving without having anything to show for it, and he was beginning to feel the depression that comes from leading a monotonous life without any guiding interest or buoyant hope. He was so sick of Yonville and the Yonvillians that the sight of certain people and certain buildings irritated him beyond endurance: the pharmacist, worthy soul that he was, he found utterly unbearable. Still, though he longed for a new position, the prospect of change frightened him.

But now timidity gave way to impatience, and Paris beckoned from afar, with the fanfare of its masked balls, the laughter of its grisettes. Since he would have to finish his law studies there sooner or later, why shouldn't he go now? What was preventing him? And he began to make imaginary plans, sketch out his new existence. He furnished a dream apartment. He would lead an artist's life—take guitar lessons, wear a dressing gown, a Basque beret, blue velvet slippers! And in his mind's eye he particularly admired his overmantel arrangement: a pair of crossed fencing foils, with a skull and the guitar hanging above.

The difficulty lay in obtaining his mother's consent; still, there could scarcely be a more reasonable request. Even his employer was urging him to think of another office, where he could widen his experience. Taking a middle course, therefore, Léon looked for a place as second clerk in Rouen, found nothing, and finally wrote his mother a long detailed letter in which he set forth his reasons for moving to Paris at once. She consented.

He didn't hurry. Every day for a month Hivert transported for him, from Yonville to Rouen and from Rouen to Yonville, trunks, valises and bundles; and after Léon had had his wardrobe restocked and his three armchairs

reupholstered and had bought a whole new supply of foulard handkerchiefs—after he had made more preparations than for a trip around the
world—he kept putting off his departure from week to week, until he
received a second letter from his mother urging him to be on his way, since
he wanted to pass his examination before the summer vacation.

When the moment came for farewells, Madame Homais wept and Justin
sobbed. Homais hid his emotion as a strong man should, and insisted on
carrying his friend's overcoat as far as the notary's. Maître Guillaumin was
to drive Léon to Rouen in his carriage.

There was just time to say good-bye to Monsieur Bovary. When Léon
reached the top of the stairs he was so breathless that he stood still for a
moment. As he entered the room Madame Bovary rose quickly to her feet.

"Here I am again," said Léon.

"I knew you'd come!"

She bit her lip, and the blood rushed under her skin, reddening it from
the roots of her hair to the edge of her collar. She remained standing, leaning
against the wall paneling.

"Monsieur isn't here?" he said.

"He's out."

He repeated: "He's out."

There was a silence. They looked at each other; and their thoughts clung
together in their common anguish like two throbbing hearts.

"I'd love to kiss Berthe," said Léon.

Emma went down a few steps and called Félicité.

He glanced quickly around him, taking in the walls, the tables, the fireplace, as though to record them forever down to their last detail and carry
them away in his memory.

Then she was back, and the maid brought in Berthe, who was swinging a
pinwheel upside down on a string.

Léon kissed her several times on the neck. "Good-bye, sweetheart! Good-
bye!" And he handed her back to her mother.

"You may take her," Emma said to the maid.

They were left alone.

Madame Bovary had turned her back, her face pressed to a windowpane. Léon was holding his cap in his hand and kept brushing it against his
thigh.

"It's going to rain," said Emma.

"I have a coat," he answered.

"Ah!"

She half turned to him, her face lowered. The light seemed to glide down
her forehead to her arching brows as on a marble statue; and there was no
way of knowing what she was gazing at on the horizon or what her deepest
thoughts might be.

"Good-bye, then," he said, sighing deeply.

She raised her head with an abrupt movement.

"Yes, good-bye—you must be on your way."

They both stepped forward: he held out his hand; she hesitated.

"A handshake, then—English style," she said, with a forced laugh, putting
her hand in his.

Léon felt her moist palm in his grasp, and into it seemed to flow the very
essence of his being.

Then he released it; their eyes met again; and he was off.

As he crossed the roofed market he stopped behind a pillar to stare for a last time at the white house with its four green shutters. He thought he saw a shadowy form at the bedroom window; then the curtain, released from its hook as though of its own accord, swung slowly for a moment in long slanting folds and sprang fully out to hang straight and motionless as a plaster wall. Léon set off at a run.

Ahead he saw his employer's gig in the road, and beside it a man in an apron holding the horse. Homais and Maître Guillaumin were talking together, waiting for him.

The apothecary embraced him, tears in his eyes. "Here's your overcoat, my boy: wrap up warm! Look after yourself! Take it easy!"

"Come, Léon—jump in!" said the notary.

Homais leaned over the mudguard, and in a voice broken by sobs gulped the sad, familiar words of parting: *"Bon voyage!"*

"Bon soir!" replied Maître Guillaumin. "Anchors aweigh!"

They rolled off, and Homais went home.

Madame Bovary had opened her window that gave on to the garden, and was watching the clouds.

They were gathering in the west, in the direction of Rouen, twisting rapidly in black swirls; out from behind them shot great sun rays, like the golden arrows of a hanging trophy; and the rest of the sky was empty, white as porcelain. Then came a gust of wind; the poplars swayed; and suddenly the rain was pattering on the green leaves. But soon the sun came out again; chickens cackled; sparrows fluttered their wings in the wet bushes; and rivulets flowing along the gravel carried away the pink flowers of an acacia.

"Ah, by now he must be far away!" she thought.

Monsieur Homais dropped in as usual at half-past six, during dinner.

"Well," he said, sitting down, "so we've sent our young man on his way, have we?"

"I guess so," said the doctor. And then, turning in his chair: "What's new at your house?"

"Nothing much. Just that my wife wasn't quite herself this afternoon. You know how women are—anything upsets them, mine especially. We've no right to complain: their nervous system is much more impressionable than ours."

"Poor Léon!" said Charles. "How will he get along in Paris, do you think? Will he get used to it?"

Madame Bovary sighed.

"Never fear!" said the pharmacist, making a clicking noise with his tongue. "Think of the gay parties in restaurants, the masked balls! The champagne! Everything will go at a merry pace, I assure you!"

"I don't think he'll do anything wrong," Bovary objected.

"Nor do I," Monsieur Homais said quickly, "but he'll have to go along with the others if he doesn't want to be taken for a Jesuit. You have no idea of the life those bohemians lead in the Latin Quarter with their actresses! You know, students are very highly thought of in Paris. If they have even the slightest social grace they're admitted to the very best circles. They're even fallen in love with sometimes by ladies of the Faubourg Saint-Germain.[6] Some of them make very good marriages."

"But," said the doctor, "I'm afraid that in the city he may . . ."

"You're right," interrupted the apothecary. "It's the reverse of the medal. In the city you've got to keep your hand in your watch pocket every minute. Suppose you're sitting in a park. Some fellow comes up to you—well dressed, perhaps even wearing a decoration—somebody you could take for a diplomat. He addresses you, you talk, he ingratiates himself—offers you a pinch of snuff or picks up your hat for you. Then you get friendlier; he takes you to a café, invites you to visit him in the country, introduces you to all kinds of people over your drinks—and three-quarters of the time it's only to get his hands on your purse or lead you into evil ways."

"That's true," said Charles, "but I was thinking chiefly of diseases—typhoid fever, for example: students from the country are susceptible to it."

Emma shuddered.

"Because of the change of diet," agreed the pharmacist, "and the way it upsets the entire system. And don't forget the Paris water! The dishes they serve in restaurants—all those spicy foods—they overheat the blood: don't let anybody tell you they're worth a good stew. I've always said there's nothing like home cooking: it's better for the health. That was why when I was studying pharmacy in Rouen I went to board in a boarding house: I ate where my teachers ate."

And he continued to expound his general opinions and personal preferences until Justin came to fetch him to make an eggnog for a customer.

"Not a moment's peace!" he cried. "It's grind, grind, grind! I can't leave the shop for a minute. I'm like a plough-horse—sweating blood every second. It's a heavy yoke, my friends!"

And when he was at the door: "By the way," he said, "have you heard the news?"

"What news?"

"It is very likely," Homais announced, raising his eyebrows and looking excessively solemn, "that the annual Agricultural Show of the department of the Seine-Inférieure will be held this year at—Yonville-l'Abbaye. There is, at least, a rumor to that effect. The paper referred to it this morning. An event of the very greatest importance for our district! But we'll talk about it later. I can see, thank you. Justin has the lantern."

VII

The next day was a funereal one for Emma. Everything appeared to her as though shrouded in vague, hovering blackness; and grief swirled into her soul, moaning softly like the winter wind in a deserted castle. She was prey to the brooding brought on by irrevocable partings, to the weariness that follows every consummation, to the pain caused by the breaking off of a confirmed habit or the brusque stopping of a prolonged vibration.

It was like the days following her return from La Vaubyessard, when the dance tunes had kept whirling in her head: she was sunk in the same mournful melancholy, the same torpid despair. Léon seemed taller, handsomer, more charming and less distinct: though he had gone, he had not left her; he was there, and the walls of her house seemed to retain his shadow. She

6. The aristocratic quarter of Paris.

kept staring at the rug he had walked on, the empty chairs he had sat in. The stream at the foot of her garden flowed on as usual, rippling past the slippery bank. They had often strolled there, listening to this same murmur of the water over the moss-covered stones. How they had enjoyed the sun! And the shade, too, afternoons by themselves in the garden! He had read aloud to her, bareheaded on a rustic bench, the cool wind from the meadows ruffling the pages of his book and the nasturtiums on the arbor. . . . And now he was gone, the one bright spot in her life, her one possible hope of happiness! Why hadn't she grasped that good fortune when it had offered itself? And when it had first threatened to slip away—why hadn't she seized it with both hands, implored it on her knees? She cursed herself for not having surrendered to her love for Léon: she thirsted for his lips. She was seized with a longing to run after him, to fling herself into his arms, to cry, "Take me! I'm yours!" But the difficulties of such an enterprise discouraged her in advance; and her longings, increased by regret, became all the more violent.

Thereafter, the image she had of Léon became the center of her distress: it glowed more brightly than a travelers' fire left burning on the snow of a Russian steppe. She ran up to it, crouched beside it, stirred it carefully when it was on the verge of extinction, grasped at everything within reach that might bring it back to life. Distant memories and present-day events, experiences actual and imagined, her starved sensuality, her plans for happiness, blown down like dead branches in the wind, her barren "virtue," the collapse of her hopes, the litter of her domestic life—all these she gathered up and used as fuel for her misery.

Nevertheless the flames did die down—whether exhausted from lack of supplies or choked by excessive feeding. Little by little, love was quenched by absence; regret was smothered by routine; and the fiery glow that had reddened her pale sky grew gray and gradually vanished. In this growing inner twilight she even mistook her recoil from her husband for an aspiration toward her lover, the searing waves of hatred for a rekindling of love. But the storm kept raging, her passion burned itself to ashes, no help was forthcoming, no new sun rose on the horizon. Night closed in completely around her, and she was left alone in a horrible void of piercing cold.

Then the bad days of Tostes began all over again. She considered herself far more unhappy now than she had been then, for now she had experienced grief, and she knew that it would never end.

A woman who had assumed such a burden of sacrifice was certainly entitled to indulge herself a little. She bought herself a Gothic *prie-dieu,* and in a month spent fourteen francs on lemons to blanch her fingernails; she wrote to Rouen for a blue cashmere dress; and at Lheureux's she chose the finest of his scarves. She wound it around her waist over her dressing gown, and thus arrayed she closed the shutters and stretched out on her sofa with a book.

She kept changing her way of wearing her hair: she tried it *à la chinoise,*[7] in soft curls, in braids; she tried parting it on one side and turning it under, like a man's.

She decided to learn Italian: she bought dictionaries, a grammar, a supply of paper. She went in for serious reading—history and philosophy. Some-

7. Chinese fashion (French).

times at night Charles would wake up with a start, thinking that someone had come to fetch him to a sickbed. "I'm coming," he would mutter, and it would be the sound of the match that Emma was striking to light her lamp. But her books were like her many pieces of needlepoint: barely begun, they were tossed into the cupboard; she started them, abandoned them, discarded them in favor of new ones.

She had spells in which she would have gone to extremes with very little urging. One day she insisted, Charles to the contrary, that she could drink half a water glass of brandy; and when Charles was foolish enough to dare her, she downed every drop of it.

For all her "flightiness"—that was the Yonville ladies' word for it—Emma did not have a happy look. The corners of her mouth were usually marked with those stiff, pinched lines so often found on the faces of old maids and failures. She was pale, white as a sheet all over; the skin of her nose was drawn down toward the nostrils, and she had a way of staring vacantly at whoever she was talking with. When she discovered two or three gray hairs at her temples she began to talk about growing old.

She often had dizzy spells. One day she even spat blood; and when Charles hovered over her and showed his concern she shrugged. "What of it?" she said.

Charles shut himself in his consulting room, and sitting in his office arm-chair under the phrenological head he put his elbows on the table and wept.

He wrote his mother asking her to come, and they had long conversations on the subject of Emma.

What course to follow? What could be done, since she refused all treatment?

"Do you know what your wife needs?" said the older Madame Bovary. "She needs to be put to work—hard, manual work. If she had to earn her living like so many other people, she wouldn't have those vapors—they come from all those ideas she stuffs her head with, and the idle life she leads."

"She keeps busy, though," Charles said.

"Busy at what? Reading novels and all kinds of bad books—anti-religious books that quote Voltaire and ridicule the priests. It's a dangerous business, son: anyone who lacks respect for religion comes to a bad end."

So it was decided to prevent Emma from reading novels. The project presented certain difficulties, but the old lady undertook to carry it out: on her way through Rouen she would personally call on the proprietor of the lending library and tell him that Emma was canceling her subscription. If he nevertheless persisted in spreading his poison, they would certainly have the right to report him to the police.

Farewells between mother-in-law and daughter-in-law were curt. During the three weeks they had been together they hadn't exchanged four words apart from the formal greetings and absolute essentials called for at mealtime and bedtime.

The older Madame Bovary left on a Wednesday—market day at Yonville.

From early morning, one side of the square was taken up with a row of carts—all tipped up on end, with their shafts in the air, stretching along the house fronts from the church to the hotel. On the other side were canvas booths for the sale of cotton goods, woolen blankets and stockings, horse halters, and rolls of blue ribbon whose ends fluttered in the wind. Heavy hardware was spread out on the ground between pyramids of eggs and cheese baskets bristling with sticky straw; and close by the harvesting machines were the flat poultry boxes, with clucking hens sticking their necks out between the slats. The crowd always filled the same corner, unwilling to move on: sometimes it seemed on the point of pushing through the glass of the pharmacy window. On Wednesdays the shop was never empty, and everyone elbowed his way in, less to buy pharmaceutical products than to consult the pharmacist, so celebrated was Monsieur Homais' reputation in the villages round about. His hearty self-confidence bewitched the country folk: to them he was a greater doctor than all the doctors.

Emma was leaning out her window (she often did this: in the provinces windows take the place of boulevards and theaters) watching the crowd of yokels, when she caught sight of a gentleman in a green velvet frock coat. His dressy yellow gloves contrasted with his heavy gaiters, and he was approaching the doctor's house. Behind him was a peasant who followed along with lowered head and decidedly pensive expression.

"May I see Monsieur?" he asked Justin, who was chatting in the doorway with Félicité. And assuming that he was one of the house servants, he added: "Give him my name—Monsieur Rodolphe Boulanger de la Huchette."

The new arrival had added the "de" and the "La Huchette" to his name not out of vanity as a landowner but rather to indicate more clearly who he was. La Huchette was an estate near Yonville, and he had recently bought the château and its two dependent farms. The latter he worked himself—not too seriously. He kept a bachelor establishment and was rumored to have "a private income of at least fifteen thousand francs a year."

Charles came into the parlor, and Monsieur Boulanger introduced his man, who wanted to be bled because "he felt prickly all over." There was no arguing with him: he said it would "clear him out."

So Bovary told the maid to bring a bandage, and a basin that he asked Justin to hold. The peasant turned pale at once. "There's nothing to be afraid of," Charles told him.

"I'm all right," the man said. "Go ahead."

He held out his sturdy arm with an air of bravado. At the prick of the scalpel the blood spurted out and spattered against the mirror.

"Hold the basin closer!" Charles cried.

"Look at that!" said the peasant. "Just like a fountain! I've got real red blood: that's a good sign, isn't it?"

"Sometimes," remarked the *officier de santé*, "they don't feel anything at first, and then they keel over—especially the husky ones, like this one here."

At those words the peasant dropped the scalpel case, which he had been twisting in his fingers. The back of the chair creaked under the heavy impact of his shoulders, and his hat fell to the floor.

"Just what I thought," said Bovary, pressing the vein with his finger.

The basin began to shake in Justin's hands; his knees wobbled and he turned pale.

"Where's my wife?" Charles cried, and he called her loudly. She came rushing down the stairs.

"Vinegar!" he cried. "We've got a pair of them, damn it!"

In his excitement he had trouble applying the compress.

"It's nothing," said Monsieur Boulanger, quite calmly; and he lifted Justin in his arms and propped him up on the table with his back against the wall.

Madame Bovary set about loosening Justin's cravat. There was a knot in the strings that fastened his shirt, and when she had undone it she rubbed his boyish neck lightly for a few minutes; then she moistened her batiste handkerchief in vinegar and patted his forehead with it, blowing gently on it as she did so.

The teamster revived; but Justin remained in his faint, the pupils of his eyes sunk into the whites like blue flowers in milk.

"We'd better not let him see this," said Charles.

Madame Bovary took away the basin. As she bent down to put it under the table, her dress—a long-waisted, full-skirted yellow summer dress with four flounces—belled out around her on the tile floor of the parlor; and as she put out her arms to steady herself the material billowed and settled, revealing the lines of her body. Then she brought in a pitcher of water, and was dissolving sugar in it when the pharmacist arrived. The maid had gone after him in the midst of the fracas, and when he found his apprentice with his eyes open he breathed a sigh of relief. Then he stalked back and forth in front of him, staring him up and down.

"Idiot!" he said. "Idiot, with a capital I! A terrible thing, a little bloodletting, isn't it! A fine fearless fellow, too. Just look at him! And yet I've seen him go up a tree after nuts like a squirrel—up to the dizziest heights, *Messieurs et Madame!* Say something, can't you? Tell us how good you are! You'll certainly make a fine pharmacist! Don't you know that some day you may be called on to give important evidence in court? The judges may need your expert opinion. You'll have to keep calm at such times, and know what to say! You'll have to show them you're a man, or else be called a fool!"

Justin made no answer, and the apothecary went on:

"Who asked you to come here anyway? You're always bothering Monsieur and Madame! You know perfectly well I always need you Wednesdays! There are twenty people in the shop right now—I left everything out of consideration for you! Go on! Get back there! Keep an eye on things till I come!"

When Justin had put himself to rights and gone, they talked a little about fainting spells. Madame Bovary had never had one.

"That's unusual for a lady," said Monsieur Boulanger. "But there are men who are extraordinarily susceptible, you know. I've seen a second at a duel lose consciousness at the mere sound of the loading of the pistols."

"I don't mind the sight of other people's blood a bit," said the pharmacist. "But the very idea of shedding my own would be enough to turn my stomach if I thought about it too much."

Meanwhile Monsieur Boulanger sent away his man, urging him to stop worrying now that he'd got what he wanted.

"His whim has afforded me the privilege of making your acquaintance," he said; and as he spoke the words he looked at Emma.

Then he put three francs on the corner of the table, bowed casually, and left.

He was soon on the other side of the river (it was the way back to La Huchette); and Emma saw him crossing the meadow under the poplars, occasionally slowing his pace as though he were pondering something.

"She's very nice," he was saying to himself, "very nice, that wife of the doctor's! Lovely teeth, black eyes, a dainty foot—she's like a real Parisian. Where the devil does she come from? How did such a clodhopper ever get hold of her?"

Monsieur Rodolphe Boulanger was thirty-four. He was brutal and shrewd. He was something of a connoisseur: there had been many women in his life. This one seemed pretty, so the thought of her and her husband stayed with him.

"I have an idea he's stupid. I'll bet she's tired of him. His fingernails are dirty and he hasn't shaved in three days. He trots off to see his patients and leaves her home to darn his socks. How bored she must be! Dying to live in town, to dance the polka every night! Poor little thing! She's gasping for love like a carp on a kitchen table gasping for water. A compliment or two and she'd adore me, I'm positive. She'd be sweet! But—how would I get rid of her later?"

And the thought of the troubles inevitable in such an affair brought to his mind by contrast his present mistress, an actress he kept in Rouen. He found he could not evoke her image without a feeling of satiety, and after a time he said to himself:

"Ah, Madame Bovary is much prettier—and what's more, much fresher. Virginie's certainly growing too fat. She's getting on my nerves with all her enthusiasms. And her mania for shrimps . . . !"

The countryside was deserted, and the only sounds were the regular swish of the tall grass against his gaiters and the chirping of crickets hidden in the distant oats. He thought of Emma in the parlor, dressed as he had seen her, and he undressed her.

"I'll have her!" he said aloud, bringing his stick down on a clod of earth in front of him.

And he immediately began to consider the question of strategy.

"Where could we meet? How could we arrange it? The brat would always be around, and the maid, and the neighbors, and the husband—there'd be a lot of headaches. Bah! It would all take too much time."

Then he began all over again:

"Those eyes really bore into you, though! And that pale complexion . . . God! How I love pale women. . . ."

By the time he had reached the top of the hill his mind was made up.

"The only thing to do now is keep my eyes open for opportunities. I'll call on them occasionally and send them presents—game and chickens. I'll have myself bled, if I have to. We'll get to be friends. I'll invite them to the house. . . . And . . . Oh, yes"—it came to him—"we'll soon be having the show. She'll be there. I'll see her. We'll get started. The approach direct: that's the best."

VIII

The great day arrived at last.

The morning of the Agricultural Show all the Yonvillians were standing on their doorsteps discussing the preparations. The pediment of the town hall had been looped with ivy; a marquee had been set up for the banquet in one of the meadows; and in the middle of the square, in front of the church, stood an antiquated fieldpiece that was to be fired as a signal announcing the arrival of the prefect and the proclamation of the prize winners. The Buchy national guard (Yonville had none) had come to join forces with the fire brigade, commanded by Binet. Today he wore a collar even higher than usual; and his bust, tightly encased in his tunic, was so stiff and inflexible that all his animal fluids seemed to be concentrated in his legs, which rose and fell with the music in rhythmic jerks. Since the tax collector and the colonel were rivals, each showed off his talents by drilling his men separately. First the red epaulettes would march up and down, and then the black breastplates. And then it would begin all over again: there was no end to it. Never had there been such a display of pomp! A number of citizens had washed their housefronts the day before; tricolor flags were hanging from half-open windows; all the cafés were full; and in the perfect weather the headdresses of the women seemed whiter than snow, their gold crosses glittered in the bright sun, and their multicolored neckcloths relieved the somber monotony of the men's frock coats and blue smocks. As the farm women dismounted from their horses they undid the big pins that had held their skirts tucked up away from splashing. The men's concern was for their hats: to protect them they had covered them with large pocket handkerchiefs, holding the corners between their teeth as they rode.

The crowd converged on the main street from both ends of the village, from the paths between the houses, from the lanes, and from the houses themselves; knockers could be heard falling against doors as housewives in cotton gloves emerged to watch the festivities. Particularly admired were the two large illumination frames laden with colored glass lamps that flanked the official grandstand; and against the four columns of the town hall stood four poles, each with a little banner bearing a legend in gold letters on a greenish ground. One said "Commerce," another "Agriculture," the third "Industry," and the fourth "Fine Arts."

But the jubilation brightening all faces seemed to cast a gloom over Madame Lefrançois, the hotel-keeper. She was standing on her kitchen steps muttering to herself:

"It's a crime—a crime, that canvas shack! Do they really think the prefect will enjoy eating his dinner in a tent, like a circus performer? They pretend the whole thing's for the good of this village—so why bring a third-class cook over from Neufchâtel? And who's it all for, anyway? A lot of cowherds and riffraff."

The apothecary came by. He was wearing a black tail coat, yellow nankeen trousers, reverse-calf shoes, and—most exceptionally—a hat: a stiff, low-crowned hat.

"Good morning!" he said. "Forgive me for being in such a hurry."

And as the buxom widow asked him where he was going:

"I imagine it must seem funny to you, doesn't it? Considering that most of the time I can't be pried loose from my laboratory any more than the old man's rat from his cheese."

"What cheese is that?" asked the landlady.

"Oh, nothing, nothing," said Homais. "I was merely referring to the fact, Madame Lefrançois, that I usually stay at home, like a recluse. But today things are different. I must absolutely . . ."

"You don't mean you're going *there?*" she said with a scornful look.

"Of course I'm going there," the apothecary replied, surprised. "Don't you know I'm on the advisory committee?"

Madame Lefrançois looked at him for a moment or two and then answered with a smile:

"That's all right, then. But what have you got to do with farming? Do you know anything about it?"

"Certainly I know something about it, being a pharmacist! A pharmacist is a chemist, Madame Lefrançois; and since the aim of chemistry is to discover the laws governing the reciprocal and molecular action of all natural bodies, it follows that agriculture falls within its domain! Take the composition of manures, the fermentation of liquids, the analysis of gasses, the effects of noxious effluvia—what's all that, I ask you, if it isn't chemistry in the strictest sense of the word?"

The landlady made no reply. Homais went on:

"Do you think that to be an agronomist you must till the soil or fatten chickens with your own hands? No: you have to study the composition of various substances—geological strata, atmospheric phenomena, the properties of the various soils, minerals, types of water, the density of different bodies, their capillary attraction. And a hundred other things. You have to be thoroughly versed in all the principles of hygiene—that's an absolute prerequisite if you're going to serve in a supervisory or consultant capacity in anything relating to the construction of farm buildings, the feeding of livestock, the preparation of meals for hired men. And then you've got to know botany, Madame Lefrançois: be able to tell one plant from another— you know what I mean? Which ones are benign and which ones are poisonous, which ones are unproductive and which ones are nutritive; whether it's a good thing to pull them out here and resow them there, propagate some and destroy others. In short, you've got to keep abreast of science by reading pamphlets and publications; you've got to be always on the alert, always on the lookout for possible improvements. . . ."

All this time the landlady never took her eyes off the door of the Café Français. The pharmacist continued:

"Would to God our farmers were chemists, or at least that they listened more carefully to what science has to say. I myself recently wrote a rather considerable little treatise—a monograph of over seventy-two pages, entitled: *Cider: Its Manufacture and Its Effects; Followed by Certain New Observations on This Subject.* I sent it to the Agronomical Society of Rouen, and it even brought me the honor of being admitted to membership in that body—Agricultural Section, Pomology Division. Now if this work of mine had been made available to the public . . ."

The apothecary broke off: Madame Lefrançois' attention was obviously elsewhere.

"Just look at them," she said. "How can they patronize such a filthy place?"

And with shrugs that stretched her sweater tight over her bosom, she pointed with both hands to her competitor's café, out of which came the sound of singing.

"Anyway, it won't be there much longer," she said. "Just a few days more, and then—*finis.*"

Homais drew back in amazement, and she came down her three steps and put her lips to his ear:

"What! Haven't you heard? They're padlocking it this week. It's Lheureux who's forcing the sale; all those notes Tellier signed were murder."

"What an unutterable catastrophe!" The apothecary always had the proper expression ready, whatever the occasion.

The landlady proceeded to tell him the story, which she had from Théodore, Maître Guillaumin's servant; and although she detested Tellier she had nothing but harsh words for Lheureux. He was a wheedler, a cringer.

"Look—there he is now, in the market," she said. "He's greeting Madame Bovary. She's wearing a green hat. In fact, she's on Monsieur Boulanger's arm."

"Madame Bovary!" cried Homais. "I must go and pay her my respects. She might like to have a seat in the enclosure, under the portico."

And ignoring Madame Lefrançois' attempts to detain him with further details, he hurried off, smiling and with springy step, bestowing innumerable salutations right and left, and taking up a good deal of room with his long black coat tails that streamed in the wind behind him.

Rodolphe had seen him coming and had quickened his pace; but Madame Bovary was out of breath, and he slowed and smiled at her. "I was trying to avoid that bore," he said savagely. "You know, the apothecary."

She nudged him with her elbow.

"What does that mean?" he wondered, glancing at her out of the corner of his eye as they moved on.

Her face, seen in profile, was so calm that it gave him no hint. It stood out against the light, framed in the oval of her bonnet, whose pale ribbons were like streaming reeds. Her eyes with their long curving lashes looked straight ahead: they were fully open, but seemed a little narrowed because of the blood that was pulsing gently under the fine skin of her cheekbones. The rosy flesh between her nostrils was all but transparent in the light. She was inclining her head to one side, and the pearly tips of her white teeth showed between her lips.

"Is she laughing at me?" Rodolphe wondered.

But Emma's nudge had been no more than a warning, for Monsieur Lheureux was walking along beside them, now and then addressing them as though to begin conversation.

"What a marvelous day! Everybody's out! The wind is from the east."

Neither Madame Bovary nor Rodolphe made any reply, though at their slightest movement he edged up to them saying, "Beg your pardon?" and touching his hat.

When they were in front of the blacksmith's, instead of following the road as far as the gate Rodolphe turned abruptly into a side path, drawing Madame Bovary with him.

"Good-bye, Monsieur Lheureux!" he called out. "We'll be seeing you!"

"You certainly got rid of him!" she said, laughing.

"Why should we put up with intruders?" he said. "Today I'm lucky enough to be with you, so . . ."

Emma blushed. He left his sentence unfinished, and talked instead about the fine weather and how pleasant it was to be walking on the grass. A few late daisies were blooming around them.

"They're pretty, aren't they?" he said. "If any of the village girls are in love they can come here for their oracles." And he added: "Maybe I should pick one. What do you think?"

"Are you in love?" she asked, coughing a little.

"Ah, ah! Who knows?" answered Rodolphe.

The meadow was beginning to fill up, and housewives laden with big umbrellas, picnic baskets and babies were bumping into everyone. It was constantly necessary to turn aside, out of the way of long lines of girls—servants from farms, wearing blue stockings, low-heeled shoes and silver rings and smelling of the dairy when they came close. They walked holding hands, forming chains the whole length of the meadow, from the row of aspens to the banquet tent. It was time for the judging, and one after another the farmers were filing into a kind of hippodrome marked off by a long rope hung on stakes.

Here stood the livestock, noses to the rope, rumps of all shapes and sizes forming a ragged line. Lethargic pigs were nuzzling the earth with their snouts; calves were lowing and sheep bleating; cows with their legs folded under them lay on the grass, slowly chewing their cud and blinking their heavy eyelids under the midges buzzing around them. Bare-armed teamsters were holding rearing stallions by the halter: these were neighing loudly in the direction of the mares, who stood there quietly, necks outstretched and manes drooping, as their foals rested in their shadow or came now and again to suck. Above the long undulating line of these massed bodies a white mane would occasionally surge up like a wave in the wind, or a pair of sharp horns would stick out, or men's heads would bob up as they ran. Quite apart, outside the arena, a hundred yards off, was a big black bull with a strap harness and an iron ring through its nose, motionless as a brazen image. A ragged little boy held it by a rope.

Meanwhile a group of gentlemen were solemnly advancing between the two rows, inspecting each animal and then conferring in an undertone. One, who seemed the most important, was writing details in a notebook as he walked. This was the chairman of the jury, Monsieur Derozerays de la Panville. As soon as he recognized Rodolphe he quickly stepped forward and addressed him with a cordial smile: "What's this, Monsieur Boulanger? You've deserted us?"

Rodolphe assured him that he was coming directly. But when the chairman had passed:

"I'll certainly *not* be going," he said to Emma. "I like your company better than his."

And though he kept making fun of the show, Rodolphe displayed his blue pass to the guard so that they could walk about unmolested, and he even stopped from time to time in front of some particularly fine exhibit. It was never anything that Madame Bovary cared about: he noticed this, and began to make jokes about the Yonville ladies and the way they dressed; then he apologized for the carelessness of his own costume. This was a mixture of the casual and the refined—the kind of thing that both fascinates and exasperates the common herd, hinting as it does at an eccentric way of life, indulgence in wild passions and "artistic" affections, and a contempt for social conventions. His batiste shirt (it had pleated cuffs) puffed out from the opening of his gray twill vest at each gust of wind; and his broad-striped trousers ended at nankeen shoes trimmed with patent leather so shiny that the grass was reflected in it. He tramped unconcernedly through horse dung, one thumb in his vest pocket, his straw hat tilted over one ear.

"Anyway," he said, "when you live in the country . . ."

"Any trouble you take is wasted," said Emma.

"Completely," replied Rodolphe. "Think of it: there isn't a single person here today capable of appreciating the cut of a coat."

And they talked about the mediocrity of provincial life, so suffocating, so fatal to all noble dreams.

"So," said Rodolphe, "I just get more and more engulfed in gloom as time goes on. . . ."

"You do!" she cried, in surprise. "I thought of you as being very jolly."

"Of course—that's the impression I give: I've learned to wear a mask of mockery when I'm with other people. But many's the time I've passed a cemetery in the moonlight and asked myself if I wouldn't be better off lying there with the rest. . . ."

"Oh! And what about your friends?" she asked. "Have you no thought for them?"

"My friends? What friends? Have I any? Who cares anything about me?"

And he accompanied those last words with a kind of desperate whistle.

But they had to draw apart to make way for a tall tower of chairs borne by a man coming up behind them. He was so excessively laden that the only parts of him visible were the tips of his wooden shoes and his two outstretched hands. It was Lestiboudois, the gravedigger, who was renting out church seats to the crowd. He was highly inventive where his own interests were concerned, and had thought up this way of profiting from the show. It was a good idea: everyone was hailing him at once. The villagers were hot; they clamored for the straw-seated chairs that gave off a smell of incense, and they leaned back with a certain veneration against the heavy slats stained with candle wax.

Then once again Madame Bovary took Rodolphe's arm, and he went on as though talking to himself:

"Yes, so many things have passed me by! I've always been so alone! Ah! If I'd had a purpose in life, if I'd met anyone with true affection, if I'd found somebody who . . . Oh! Then I wouldn't have spared any effort; I'd have surmounted every obstacle, let nothing stand in my way . . . !"

"It seems to me, though," said Emma, "that you're scarcely to be pitied."

"Oh? You think that?" said Rodolphe.

"Yes," she answered, "because after all you're free"—she hesitated—"rich . . . "

"Don't make fun of me," he begged.

And she was swearing that she was doing nothing of the kind, when a cannon shot resounded and everyone began to hurry toward the village.

It was a false alarm: the prefect wasn't even in sight, and the members of the jury were in a quandary, not knowing whether to begin the proceedings or wait a while longer.

Finally at the far end of the square appeared a big hired landau drawn by two skinny horses who were being furiously whipped on by a white-hatted coachman. Binet had just time to shout, "Fall in!" and the colonel to echo him; there was a rush for the stacked rifles; and in the confusion some of the men forgot to button their collars. But the official coach-and-pair seemed to sense the difficulty, and the emaciated beasts, dawdling on their chain, drew up at a slow trot in front of the portico of the town hall just at the moment when the national guard and the fire brigade were deploying into line to the beating of the drums.

"Mark time!" cried Binet.

"Halt!" cried the colonel. "Left, turn!"

And after a present-arms during which the rattle of the metal bands as they slid down the stocks and barrels sounded like a copper cauldron rolling down a flight of stairs, all the rifles were lowered.

Then there emerged from the carriage a gentleman clad in a short, silver-embroidered coat, his forehead high and bald, the back of his head tufted, his complexion wan and his expression remarkably benign. His eyes, very large and heavy-lidded, half shut as he peered at the multitude; and at the same time he lifted his sharp nose and curved his sunken mouth into a smile. He recognized the mayor by his sash, and explained that the prefect had been unable to come. He himself was a prefectural councilor, and he added a few words of apology. Tuvache replied with compliments, the emissary declared himself unworthy of them; and the two officials stood there face to face, their foreheads almost touching, all about them the members of the jury, the village council, the local elite, the national guard and the crowd. Holding his little black three-cornered hat against his chest, the prefectural councilor reiterated his greetings; and Tuvache, bent like a bow, returned his smiles, stammered, clutched uncertainly for words, protested his devotion to the monarchy and his awareness of the honor that was being bestowed on Yonville.

Hippolyte, the stable-boy at the hotel, came to take the horses from the coachman; and limping on his clubfoot he led them through the gateway of the Lion d'Or, where a crowd of peasants gathered to stare at the carriage. There was a roll of the drums, the howitzer thundered, and the gentlemen filed up and took their seats on the platform in red plush armchairs loaned by Madame Tuvache.

All in this group looked alike. Their flabby, fair-skinned, slightly suntanned faces were the color of new cider, and their bushy side whiskers stuck out over high, stiff collars that were held in place by white cravats tied in wide bows. Every vest was of velvet, with a shawl collar; every watch had an oval carnelian seal at the end of a long ribbon; and every one of the gentlemen sat with his hands planted on his thighs, his legs carefully apart, the hard-finished broadcloth of his trousers shining more brightly than the leather of his heavy shoes.

The invited ladies were seated to the rear, under the portico between the columns, while the ordinary citizens faced the platform, either standing, or sitting on chairs. Lestiboudois had retransported to this new location all those that he had previously taken to the meadow; now he kept bringing still more from the church; and he was crowding the place so with his chair-rental business that it was almost impossible for anyone to reach the few steps leading to the platform.

"In my opinion," said Monsieur Lheureux, addressing the pharmacist, who was passing by on his way to take his seat, "they should have set up a pair of Venetian flagstaffs: trimmed with something rich and not too showy they'd have made a very pretty sight."

"Certainly," said Homais. "But what can you expect? The mayor took everything into his own hands. He hasn't much taste, poor Tuvache: in fact, he's completely devoid of what is known as the artistic sense."

Meanwhile Rodolphe, with Madame Bovary, had gone up to the second floor of the town hall, into the "council chamber": it was quite empty—a perfect place, he said, from which to have a comfortable view of the ceremonies. He took three of the stools that stood around the oval table under the king's bust and moved them over to one of the windows; and there they sat down close together.

There was a certain agitation on the platform—prolonged whisperings and consultations. Finally the prefectural councilor rose to his feet. It had become known that he was called Lieuvain, and his name was repeated from one to another in the crowd. He made sure that his sheets of paper were in proper order, peered at them closely, and began:

"Gentlemen: I should like, with your permission (before speaking to you about the object of today's meeting—and this sentiment, I am sure, will be shared by all of you), I should like, with your permission, to pay tribute to the national administration, to the government, to the monarch, gentlemen, to our sovereign, to the beloved king to whom no branch of public or private prosperity is indifferent, and who, with so firm and yet so wise a hand, guides the chariot of state amidst the constant perils of a stormy sea, maintaining at the same time public respect for peace as well as for war—for industry, for commerce, for agriculture, for the fine arts."

"I ought to move a little further back," said Rodolphe.

"Why?" said Emma.

But at that moment the councilor's voice rose to an extraordinary pitch. He was declaiming:

"Gone forever, gentlemen, are the days when civil discord drenched our streets with blood; when the landlord, the businessman, nay, the worker, sank at night into a peaceful slumber trembling lest they be brutally awakened by the sound of inflammatory tocsins; when the most subversive principles were audaciously undermining the foundations . . ."

"It's just that I might be caught sight of from below," said Rodolphe. "If I were, I'd have to spend the next two weeks apologizing; and what with my bad reputation . . ."

"Oh! You're slandering yourself," said Emma.

"No, no, my reputation's execrable, I assure you."

"But, gentlemen," continued the councilor, "if I dismiss those depressing evocations and turn my eyes to the present situation of our cherished fatherland, what do I see before me? Commerce and the arts are thriving everywhere; everywhere new channels of communication, like so many new arteries in the body politic, are multiplying contacts between its various parts; our great manufacturing centers have resumed their activity; religion, its foundations strengthened, appeals to every heart; shipping fills our ports; confidence returns; at long last, France breathes again!"

"Moreover, from the point of view of society it's probably deserved," Rodolphe said.

"What do you mean?" she asked.

"Do you really not know," he said, "that there exist souls that are ceaselessly in torment? That are driven now to dreams, now to action, driven from the purest passions to the most orgiastic pleasures? No wonder we fling ourselves into all kinds of fantasies and follies!"

She stared at him as if he were a traveler from mythical lands. "We poor women," she said, "don't have even that escape."

"A poor escape," he said, "since it doesn't bring happiness."

"But do we ever find happiness?" she asked.

"Yes, it comes along one day," he answered.

"And the point has not been lost on you," the councilor was saying. "Not on you, farmers and workers in the fields! Not on you, champions of progress and morality! The point has not been lost on you, I say, that the storms of political strife are truly more to be dreaded than the disorders of the elements!"

"Yes, it comes along one day," Rodolphe repeated. "All of a sudden, just when we've given up hope. Then new horizons open before us: it's like a voice crying, 'Look! It's here!' We feel the need to pour out our hearts to a given person, to surrender, to sacrifice everything. In such a meeting no words are necessary: each senses the other's thoughts. Each is the answer to the other's dreams." He kept staring at her. "There it is, the treasure so long sought for—there before us: it gleams, it sparkles. But still we doubt; we daren't believe; we stand there dazzled, as though we'd come from darkness into light."

As he ended, Rodolphe enhanced his words with pantomime. He passed his hand over his face, like someone dazed; then he let it fall on Emma's hand. She withdrew hers. The councilor read on:

"And who is there who would wonder at such a statement, gentlemen? Only one so blind, so sunk (I use the word advisedly), so sunk in the prejudices of another age as to persist in his misconceptions concerning the spirit of our farming population. Where, I ask you, is there to be found greater patriotism than in rural areas, greater devotion to the common weal, greater —in one word—intelligence? And by intelligence, gentlemen, I do not mean that superficial intelligence that is a futile ornament of idle minds, but rather that profound and moderate intelligence that applies itself above all to useful ends, contributing in this manner to the good of all, to public improvement and the upholding of the state—that intelligence that is the fruit of respect for law and the performance of duty!"

"Ah, there they go again!" said Rodolphe. "Duty, duty, always duty—I'm sick of that word. Listen to them! They're a bunch of doddering old morons and bigoted old church mice with foot warmers and rosaries, always squeaking, 'Duty! Duty!' at us. I have my own idea of duty. Our duty is to feel what is great and love what is beautiful—not to accept all the social conventions and the infamies they impose on us."

"Still . . . still . . ." objected Madame Bovary.

"No! Why preach against the passions? Aren't they the only beautiful thing in this world, the source of heroism, enthusiasm, poetry, music, the arts, everything?"

"But still," said Emma, "we have to be guided a little by society's opinions; we have to follow its standards of morality."

"Ah! But there are two moralities," he replied. "The petty one, the conventional one, the one invented by man, the one that keeps changing and screaming its head off—that one's noisy and vulgar, like that crowd of fools you see out there. But the other one, the eternal one . . . Ah! This one's all around us and above us, like the landscape that surrounds us and the blue sky that gives us light."

Monsieur Lieuvain had just wiped his mouth with his pocket handkerchief. He resumed:

"Why should I presume, gentlemen, to prove to you who are here today the usefulness of agriculture? Who is it that supplies our needs, who is it that provisions us, if not the farmer? The farmer, gentlemen, sowing with laborious hand the fertile furrows of our countryside, brings forth the wheat which, having been ground and reduced to powder by means of ingenious machinery, emerges in the form of flour, and from thence, transported to our cities, is presently delivered to the baker, who fashions from it a food for the poor man as well as for the rich. Is it not the farmer, once again, who fattens his plentiful flocks in the pastures to provide us with our clothing? For how would we be clothed, for how would we be nourished, without agriculture? Indeed, gentlemen—is there need to seek so far afield for examples? Who among you has not often given thought to the immense benefit we derive from that modest creature—adornment of our kitchen yards— which provides at one and the same time a downy pillow for our beds, its succulent meat for our tables, and eggs? But I should never end, had I to enumerate one after another the different products which properly cultivated soil lavishes on its children like a generous mother. Here, the grape; there, the cider apple; yonder, the colza;[8] elsewhere, a thousand kinds of cheese. And flax, gentlemen, do not forget flax!—an area in which within the past few years there has been considerable development, and one to which I particularly call your attention."

There was no need for him to "call their attention": every mouth in the crowd was open, as though to drink in his words. Tuvache, sitting beside him, listened wide-eyed; Monsieur Derozerays' lids now and again gently shut; and further along the pharmacist, holding his son Napoléon between his knees, cupped his hand to his ear lest he miss a single syllable. The other members of the jury kept slowly nodding their chins against their vests to express their approval. The fire brigade, at the foot of the platform, leaned on their bayonets; and Binet stood motionless, elbow bent, the tip of his sword in the air. He could hear, perhaps, but he certainly could not see, for the visor of his helmet had fallen forward onto his nose. His lieutenant, who was Monsieur Tuvache's younger son, had gone him one better: the helmet he was wearing was far too big for him and kept teetering on his head and showing a corner of the calico nightcap he had on under it. He was smiling from beneath his headgear as sweetly as a baby; and his small pale face, dripping with sweat, wore an expression of enjoyment, exhaustion and drowsiness.

The square was packed solidly with people as far as the houses. Spectators were leaning out of every window and standing on every doorstep; and Justin, in front of the pharmacy show window, seemed nailed to the spot in contemplation of the spectacle. Despite the crowd's silence, Monsieur Lieuvain's voice didn't carry too well in the open air. What came was fragmentary bits of sentences interrupted here and there by the scraping of chairs; then all at once from behind there would resound the prolonged lowing of an ox, and lambs bleated to one another on the street corners. For the cowherds and shepherds had driven their animals in that close, and from time to time a cow would bellow as her tongue tore off some bit of foliage hanging down over her muzzle.

Rodolphe had come close to Emma and was speaking rapidly in a low voice:

8. A plant yielding rapeseed or canola oil, used in cooking.

"Don't you think it's disgusting, the way they conspire to ruin everything? Is there a single sentiment that society doesn't condemn? The noblest instincts, the purest sympathies are persecuted and dragged in the mud; and if two poor souls do find one another, everything is organized to keep them apart. They'll try, just the same; they'll beat their wings, they'll call to each other. Oh! Never fear! Sooner or later, in six months or ten years, they'll come together and love one another, because they can't go against fate and because they were born for each other."

He was leaning forward with his arms crossed on his knees, and lifting his face to Emma's he looked at her fixedly from very near. In his eyes she could see tiny golden lines radiating out all around his black pupils, and she could even smell the perfume of the pomade that lent a gloss to his hair. Then a languor came over her; she remembered the vicomte who had waltzed with her at La Vaubyessard and whose beard had given off this same odor of vanilla and lemon; and automatically she half closed her eyes to breathe it more deeply. But as she did this, sitting up straight in her chair, she saw in the distance, on the farthest horizon, the old stagecoach, the Hirondelle, slowly descending the hill of Les Leux, trailing a long plume of dust behind it. It was in this yellow carriage that Léon had so often returned to her; and that was the road he had taken when he had left forever. For a moment she thought she saw him across the square, at his window; then everything became confused, and clouds passed before her eyes; it seemed to her that she was still whirling in the waltz, under the blaze of the chandeliers, in the vicomte's arms, and that Léon was not far off, that he was coming. . . . And yet all the while she was smelling the perfume of Rodolphe's hair beside her. The sweetness of this sensation permeated her earlier desires, and like grains of sand in the wind these whirled about in the subtle fragrance that was filling her soul. She opened her nostrils wide to breathe in the freshness of the ivy festooning the capitals outside the window. She took off her gloves and wiped her hands; then she fanned herself with her handkerchief, hearing above the beating of the pulse in her temples the murmur of the crowd and the councilor's voice as he intoned his periods.

"Persist!" he was saying. "Perservere! Follow neither the beaten tracks of routine nor the rash counsels of reckless empiricism. Apply yourselves above all to the improvement of the soil, to rich fertilizers, to the development of fine breeds—equine, bovine, ovine and porcine. May this exhibition be for you a peaceful arena where the winner, as he leaves, will stretch out his hand to the loser and fraternize with him, wishing him better luck another time! And you, venerable servants, humblest members of the household, whose painful labors have by no government up until today been given the slightest consideration: present yourselves now, and receive the reward of your silent heroism! And rest assured that the state henceforth has its eyes upon you, that it encourages you, that it protects you, that it will honor your just demands, and lighten, to the best of its ability, the burden of your painful sacrifices!"

Monsieur Lieuvain sat down.

Monsieur Derozerays stood up, and began another speech. His was perhaps not quite so flowery as the councilor's; but it had the advantage of being characterized by a more positive style—by a more specialized knowledge, that is, and more pertinent arguments. There was less praise of the government, and more mention of religion and agriculture. He showed the relation between the two and how they had always worked together for the good of civilization. Rodolphe was talking to Madame Bovary about dreams, forebodings, magnetism. Going back to the cradle of human society, the orator depicted the savage ages when men lived off acorns in the depths of the forest. Then they had cast off their animal skins, garbed themselves in cloth, dug the ground and planted the vine. Was this an advance? Didn't this discovery entail more disadvantages than benefits? That was the problem Monsieur Derozerays set himself. From magnetism Rodolphe gradually moved on to affinities; and as the chairman cited Cincinnatus and his plough, Diocletian planting his cabbages[9] and the Chinese emperors celebrating the New Year by sowing seed, the young man was explaining to the young woman that these irresistible attractions had their roots in some earlier existence.

"Take us, for example," he said. "Why should we have met? How did it happen? It can only be that something in our particular inclinations made us come closer and closer across the distance that separated us, the way two rivers flow together."

He took her hand, and this time she did not withdraw it.

"First prize for all-round farming!" cried the chairman.

"Just this morning, for example, when I came to your house . . ."

"To Monsieur Bizet, of Quincampoix."

"Did I have any idea that I'd be coming with you to the show?"

"Seventy francs!"

"A hundred times I was on the point of leaving, and yet I followed you and stayed with you . . ."

"For the best manures."

" . . . as I'd stay with you tonight, tomorrow, every day, all my life!"

"To Monsieur Caron, of Argueil, a gold medal!"

"Never have I been so utterly charmed by anyone . . ."

"To Monsieur Bain, of Givry-Saint-Martin!"

" . . . so that I'll carry the memory of you with me. . . ."

"For a merino ram . . ."

"Whereas you'll forget me: I'll vanish like a shadow."

"To Monsieur Belot, of Notre-Dame . . ."

"No, though! Tell me it isn't so! Tell me I'll have a place in your thoughts, in your life!"

"Hogs: a tie! To Messieurs Lehérissé and Cullembourg, sixty francs!"

Rodolphe squeezed her hand, and he felt it all warm and trembling in his, like a captive dove that longs to fly away; but then, whether in an effort to free it, or in response to his pressure, she moved her fingers.

"Oh! Thank God! You don't repulse me! How sweet, how kind! I'm yours: you know that now! Let me see you! Let me look at you!"

A gust of wind coming in the windows ruffled the cloth on the table; and down in the square all the tall headdresses of the peasant women rose up like fluttering white butterfly wings.

"Use of oil cakes!" continued the chairman.

He was going faster now.

9. Diocletian (A.D. 245–313), Roman emperor from 284 to 305. He resigned in 305 and retired to Salonae (now Split) in Dalmatia, to cultivate his garden. Cincinnatus was a Roman consul (460 B.C.) who was supposedly called to his office while found plowing.

"Flemish fertilizer . . . flax-raising . . . drainage, long-term leases . . . domestic service!"

Rodolphe had stopped speaking. They were staring at each other. As their desire rose to a peak their dry lips quivered; and, languidly, of their own accord, their fingers intertwined.

"Catherine-Nicaise-Elizabeth Leroux, of Sassetot-la-Guerrière, for fifty-four years of service on the same farm, a silver medal, value twenty-five francs!"

"Where is Catherine Leroux?" repeated the councilor.

There was no sign of her, but there was the sound of whispering voices:

"Go ahead!"

"No!"

"To the left!"

"Don't be scared!"

"Stupid old thing!"

"Is she there or isn't she?" cried Tuvache.

"Yes! Here she is!"

"Then send her up!"

Everyone watched her as she climbed to the platform: a frightened-looking little old woman who seemed to have shriveled inside her shabby clothes. On her feet were heavy wooden clogs, and she wore a long blue apron. Her thin face, framed in a simple coif, was more wrinkled than a withered russet, and out of the sleeves of her red blouse hung her large, gnarled hands. Years of barn dust, washing soda and wool grease had left them so crusted and rough and hard that they looked dirty despite all the clear water they'd been rinsed in; and from long habit of service they hung half open, as though offering their own humble testimony to the hardships they had endured. A kind of monklike rigidity gave a certain dignity to her face, but her pale stare was softened by no hint of sadness or human kindness. Living among animals, she had taken on their muteness and placidity. This was the first time she had ever been in the midst of so great a crowd; and inwardly terrified by the flags and the drums, by the gentlemen in tail coats and by the decoration worn by the councilor, she stood still, uncertain whether to move ahead or to turn and run, comprehending neither the urgings of the crowd nor the smiles of the jury. Thus did half a century of servitude stand before these beaming bourgeois.

"Step forward, venerable Catherine-Nicaise-Elizabeth Leroux!" cried the councilor, who had taken the list of prize winners from the chairman.

Looking at the sheet of paper and at the old woman in turn, he kept urging her forward like a father: "Come right here, come ahead!"

"Are you deaf?" cried Tuvache, jumping up from his chair.

And he proceeded to shout into her ear: "Fifty-four years of service! A silver medal! Twenty-five francs! For you!"

She took the medal and stared at it. Then a beatific smile spread over her face, and as she left the platform those nearby could hear her mumble: "I'll give it to our priest and he'll say some Masses for me."

"Such fanaticism!" hissed the pharmacist, bending toward the notary.

The ceremonies were ended; the crowd dispersed; and now that the speeches had been read everyone resumed his rank and everything reverted to normal. Masters bullied their servants, the servants beat their cows and their sheep, and the cows and the sheep—indolent in their triumph—moved slowly back to their sheds, their horns decked with the green wreaths that were their trophies.

Meanwhile the national guard had gone up to the second floor of the town hall: brioches were impaled on their bayonets, and their drummer bore a basketful of bottles. Madame Bovary took Rodolphe's arm; he escorted her home; they said good-bye at her door; and then he went for a stroll in the meadow until it was time for the banquet.

The feast was long, noisy, clumsily served: the guests were so crowded that they could scarcely move their elbows; and the narrow planks that were used for benches threatened to snap under their weight. They ate enormously, each piling his plate high to get full value for his assessment. Sweat poured off every forehead; and over the table, between the hanging lamps, hovered a whitish vapor, like a river mist on an autumn morning. Rodolphe, his back against the cloth side of the tent, was thinking so much about Emma that he was aware of nothing going on around him. Out on the grass behind him servants were stacking dirty plates; his tablemates spoke to him and he didn't answer; someone kept filling his glass, and his mind was filled with stillness despite the growing noise. He was thinking of the things she had said and of the shape of her lips; her face shone out from the plaques on the shakos as from so many magic mirrors; the folds of her dress hung down the walls; and days of lovemaking stretched endlessly ahead in the vistas of the future.

He saw her again that evening, during the fireworks, but she was with her husband and Madame Homais and the pharmacist. The latter was very worried about stray rockets, and constantly left the others to give Binet a word of advice.

Through overprecaution, the fireworks, which had been delivered in care of Monsieur Tuvache, had been stored in his cellar, with the result that the damp powder could scarcely be got to light; and the culminating number, which was to have depicted a dragon swallowing its own tail, was a complete fiasco. Now and then some pathetic little Roman candle would go off and bring a roar from the gaping crowd—a roar amidst which could be heard the screams of women, fair game for ticklers in the darkness. Emma nestled silently against Charles's shoulder, raising her head to follow the bright trail of the rockets in the black sky. Rodolphe watched her in the glow of the colored lamps.

Gradually these went out, the stars gleamed; then came a few drops of rain, and she tied a scarf over her hair.

Just then the councilor's landau drove out of the hotel yard. The drunken coachman chose that moment to collapse; and high above the hood, between the two lamps, everyone could see the mass of his body swaying right and left with the pitching of the springs.

"There ought to be strong measures taken against drunkenness," said the apothecary. "If I had my way, there'd be a special bulletin board put up on the door of the town hall, and every week there'd be a list posted of all who had intoxicated themselves with alcoholic liquors during that period. Such a thing would be very valuable statistically, a public record that might . . . Excuse me!"

And once again he hurried off toward the captain.

The latter was homeward bound. He was looking forward to rejoining his lathe.

"It might not do any harm," said Homais, "to send one of your men, or go yourself, to . . ."

"Get away and leave me alone," replied the tax collector. "Everything's taken care of."

"You can all stop worrying," the apothecary announced when he was back with his friends. "Monsieur Binet guarantees that all necessary measures have been taken. Not a spark has fallen. The pumps are full. We can safely retire to our beds."

"I can certainly do with some sleep," said Madame Homais, with a vast yawn. "Never mind—we had a wonderfully beautiful day for the show."

Rodolphe echoed her words in a low voice, his eyes soft: "Yes, it was: wonderfully beautiful."

They exchanged good-byes and went their respective ways.

Two days later, in the *Fanal de Rouen*, there was a great article about the Agricultural Show. Homais had written it in a burst of inspiration the very next day.

"Why these festoons, these flowers, these garlands? Whither was it bound, this crowd rushing like the billows of a raging sea under a torrential tropic sun that poured its torrid rays upon our fertile meadows?"

Then he went on to speak of the condition of the peasants. The government was doing something, certainly, but not enough. "Be bold!" he cried, addressing the administration. "A thousand reforms are indispensable: let us accomplish them." Then, describing the arrival of the councilor, he didn't forget "the warlike air of our militia," or "our sprightliest village maidens," or the bald-headed old men, veritable patriarchs, "some of whom, survivors of our immortal phalanxes, felt their hearts throb once again to the manly sound of the drums." His own name came quite early in his listing of the members of the jury, and he even reminded his readers in a footnote that Monsieur Homais, the pharmacist, had sent a monograph concerning cider to the Agricultural Society. When he came to the distribution of the prizes, he depicted the joy of the winners in dithyrambic terms. Father embraced son, brother embraced brother, husband embraced wife. More than one worthy rustic proudly displayed his humble medal to the assemblage; and, returning home to his helpmeet, doubtless wept tears of joy as he hung it on the modest wall of his cot.

"About six o'clock the leading participants in the festivities forgathered at a banquet in the pasture belonging to Monsieur Liégeard. The utmost cordiality reigned throughout. A number of toasts were proposed. By Monsieur Lieuvain: 'To the king!' By Monsieur Tuvache: 'To the prefect!' By Monsieur Derozerays: 'To agriculture!' By Monsieur Homais: 'To those twin sisters, industry and the fine arts!' By Monsieur Leplichey: 'To progress!' After nightfall a brilliant display of fireworks all at once illumined the heavens. It was a veritable kaleidoscope, a true stageset for an opera, and for a moment our modest village imagined itself transported into the midst of an Arabian Nights dream.

"We may mention that no untoward incidents arose to disturb this family gathering."

And he added:

"Only the clergy was conspicuous by its absence. Doubtless a totally different idea of progress obtains in the sacristies. Suit yourselves, *messieurs de Loyola!*"[1]

IX

Six weeks went by without further visit from Rodolphe. Then one evening he came.

The day after the show he had admonished himself: "I mustn't go back right away. That would be a mistake." And at the end of the week he had left for a hunting trip.

After his hunting was over he thought he had waited too long. But then: "If she loved me from the first, she must be impatient to see me again," he reasoned. "And this means she must love me all the more by now. So—back to the attack!"

And when he saw Emma turn pale as he entered the parlor he knew he was right.

She was alone. Daylight was fading. The muslin sash curtains deepened the twilight; and the gilt barometer had just caught a ray of sun and was blazing in the mirror between the lacy edges of the coral.

Rodolphe remained standing, and Emma scarcely replied to his first conventionally polite phrases.

"I've been having all kinds of things happen," he said. "I was ill."

"Anything serious?" she cried.

"Well, not really," he said, sitting beside her on a stool. "It was just that I didn't want to come here again."

"Why?"

"Can't you guess?"

He stared at her—this time so intently that she blushed and lowered her head.

"Emma . . ." he said.

"Monsieur!" she exclaimed, drawing away a little.

"Ah, you can see for yourself," he said, in a resigned voice, "that I was right not to want to come here again. Your name—my heart's full of it—I spoke it without meaning to, and you stopped me. 'Madame Bovary'! Everyone calls you that, and it's not your name at all. It's somebody else's. Somebody else's," he said a second time; and he buried his face in his hands. "I think of you every minute! The thought of you drives me crazy! Forgive me—I won't stay with you. I'll go away—far away—so far that you'll never hear of me again. But today . . . I don't know what power it was that made me come. We can't fight against fate. There's no resisting when an angel smiles. Once something lovely and charming and adorable has wound itself around your heart. . . ."

It was the first time that Emma had had such things said to her; and her pride, like someone relaxing in a steam bath, stretched luxuriously in the warmth of his words.

"No," he continued. "I didn't come, these past few weeks. I haven't seen

1. Ignatius of Loyola (1491–1556), a Spaniard, founded the order of the Jesuits in 1534. The Jesuits were expelled from France in 1762.

you. But everything close to you I've looked at and looked at. At night—night after night—I got up and came here and stared at your house—the roof shining in the moonlight, the trees in the garden swaying at your window, and a little lamp, just a gleam, shining through the windowpanes in the dark. Ah! You little knew that a poor wretch was standing there, so near you and yet so far. . . ."

She turned to him with a sob. "How kind you are . . . !"

"I'm not kind! I love you, that's all! You must know it. Tell me you do: one word! Just one word!"

And Rodolphe was sliding imperceptibly from the stool to his knees when there was a sound of sabots in the kitchen and he saw that the door of the room was ajar.

"You'd be doing me a favor," he said, resuming his position on the stool, "if you'd gratify a whim I have."

The whim was to be taken through her house: he wanted to see it. Madame Bovary saw nothing out of the way in the request, and they were both just rising to their feet when Charles appeared.

"Bonjour, docteur," Rodolphe greeted him.

Flattered to be so addressed, the *officier de santé* was profusely obsequious, and Rodolphe profited from those few moments to regain some of his composure.

"Madame was talking to me about her health," he began, "and . . ."

Charles interrupted him. He was very worried indeed; his wife was having difficulty breathing again. Rodolphe asked whether horseback riding might not be good for her.

"Certainly it would! Just the thing! An excellent suggestion, darling! You ought to follow it."

She pointed out that she had no horse; Monsieur Rodolphe offered her one of his; she declined; he did not insist; and finally, to explain the purpose of his visit, he told Charles that his teamster, the man who had been bled, was still having dizzy spells.

"I'll stop by and see him," said Bovary.

"No, no, I'll send him to you. We'll come here; that will be easier for you."

"Very good; thank you."

As soon as they were alone:

"Why don't you accept Monsieur Boulanger's suggestions? He's being so gracious."

She pouted, made one excuse after another, and finally said that "it might look strange."

"A lot I care about that!" said Charles, turning on his heel. "Health comes first! You're wrong!"

"But how do you expect me to ride a horse if I have no habit?"

"You must order one," he replied.

It was the riding habit that decided her.

When it was ready, Charles wrote to Monsieur Boulanger that his wife was at his disposition, and that they thanked him in advance for his kindness.

The next day at noon Rodolphe presented himself at Charles's door with two riding horses. One of them had pink pompons decorating its ears and bore a lady's buckskin saddle.

Rodolphe had put on a pair of high soft boots, telling himself that she had probably never seen anything like them; and Emma was indeed charmed with his appearance when he came up to the landing in his velvet frock coat and white tricot riding breeches. She was ready and waiting for him.

Justin ran out of the pharmacy to take a look at her, and the apothecary himself left his work for a few moments. He gave Monsieur Boulanger several bits of advice:

"Accidents happen so quickly! Take care! Your horses may be more spirited than you know!"

She heard a sound above her head: it was Félicité drumming on the windowpanes to amuse little Berthe. The child blew her a kiss, and Emma made a sign with her riding crop in answer.

"Have a good ride!" cried Monsieur Homais. "Be careful! That's the main thing! Careful!"

And he waved his newspaper after them as he watched them ride away.

As soon as it felt soft ground, Emma's horse broke into a gallop. Rodolphe galloped at her side. Now and again they exchanged a word. With her head slightly lowered, her hand raised and her right arm outstretched, she let herself go to the rhythmic rocking motion.

At the foot of the hill Rodolphe gave his horse its head: both horses leapt forward as one, and then at the top they as suddenly stopped, and Emma's large blue veil settled and hung still.

It was early October. There was a mist over the countryside. Wisps of vapor lay along the horizon, following the contours of the hills, and elsewhere they were drifting and rising and evaporating. Now and then as the clouds shifted, a ray of sun would light up the roofs of Yonville in the distance, with its riverside gardens, its yards and its church steeple. Emma half closed her eyes trying to pick out her house, and never had the wretched village she lived in looked so very small. From the height on which they were standing the whole valley was like an immense pale lake, dissolving into thin air: clumps of trees stood out here and there like dark rocks, and the tall lines of poplars piercing the fog were like its leafy banks, swaying in the wind.

To one side, over the turf between the firs, the light was dim and the air mild. The reddish earth, the color of snuff, deadened the sound of the hoofs; and the horses kicked fir cones before them as they walked.

For a time Rodolphe and Emma continued to follow the edge of the wood. Now and then she turned her head away to avoid his eyes, and at such moments she saw only the regularly spaced trunks of the firs, almost dizzying in their unbroken succession. The horses were blowing, and the leather creaked in the saddles.

Then they turned into the forest, and at that moment the sun came out.

"God's watching over us," said Rodolphe.

"You think so?" she said.

"Let's go on!" he said.

He clicked his tongue, and both horses broke into a trot.

Tall ferns growing along the path kept catching in Emma's stirrup, and Rodolphe bent over as he rode and pulled them out. At other times he came close to her to push aside overhanging branches, and she felt his knee brush against her leg. Now the sky was blue, and the leaves were still. There were clearings full of heather in bloom, and the sheets of purple alternated with the multicolored tangle of the trees, gray, fawn and gold. Often a faint rustling and fluttering of wings would come from under the bushes; or there would be the cry, at once raucous and sweet, of crows flying off among the oaks.

They dismounted. Rodolphe tethered the horses. She walked ahead of him on the moss between the cart tracks.

But the long skirt of her habit impeded her, even though she held it up by the end; and Rodolphe, walking behind her, kept staring at her sheer white stocking that showed between the black broadcloth and the black shoe as though it were a bit of her naked flesh.

She stopped.

"I'm tired," she said.

"Just a little further," he said. "Come along, try."

Then a hundred yards further on she stopped again; and the veil that slanted down from her man's hat to below her waist covered her face with a translucent blue film, as though she were swimming under limpid water.

"Where are we going?"

He didn't answer. She was breathing quickly. Rodolphe looked this way and that, biting his mustache.

They came to a larger open space, one that had recently been cleared of saplings. They sat down on a log, and Rodolphe spoke to her of his love.

He was careful not to frighten her, at first, by saying anything overbold: he was calm, serious, melancholy.

She listened to him with lowered head, stirring the wood chips on the ground with the toe of her shoe.

But when he said, "Our lives are bound up together now, aren't they?" she answered, "No—you know they can't be."

She rose to leave. He grasped her wrist. She stood still and gave him a long look, her eyes moist and tender. Then she said hastily:

"Please—let's not talk about it any more. Where are the horses? Let's go back."

A movement of angry displeasure escaped him.

"Where are the horses?" she asked again. "Where are the horses?"

Then, smiling a strange smile, staring fixedly, his teeth clenched, he advanced toward her with arms outstretched. She drew back trembling.

"You're frightening me!" she stammered. "What are you doing? Take me back!"

His expression changed. "Since you insist," he said.

And abruptly he was once more considerate, tender, timid. She took his arm and they turned back.

"What was the matter?" he asked. "What came over you? I don't understand. You must have some mistaken idea. I have you in my heart like a Madonna on a pedestal—in an exalted place, secure, immaculate. But I need you if I'm to go on living! I need your eyes, your voice, your thoughts. I beseech you: be my friend, my sister, my angel!"

And he reached out his arm and put it around her waist. She made a halfhearted effort to free herself, but he kept it there, holding her as they walked.

Now they were so close to the horses that they heard them munching leaves.

"Just a little longer," begged Rodolphe. "Let's not go yet. Wait."

He drew her further on, to the edge of a little pond whose surface was green with duck weed and where faded water lilies lay still among the rushes. At the sound of their steps in the grass, frogs leaped to hiding.

"It's wrong of me," she said. "Wrong. I must be out of my mind to listen to you."

"Why? Emma! Emma!"

"Oh! Rodolphe!" The syllables came out slowly, and she pressed against his shoulder.

The broadcloth of her habit clung to the velvet of his coat. She leaned back her head, her white throat swelled in a sigh, and, her resistance gone, weeping, hiding her face, with a long shudder she gave herself to him.

Evening shadows were falling, and the level rays of the sun streamed through the branches and dazzled her eyes. Here and there, all about her, among the leaves and on the ground, were shimmering patches of light, as though hummingbirds winging by had scattered their feathers. All was silent; a soft sweetness seemed to be seeping from the trees; she felt her heart beating again, and her blood flowing in her flesh like a river of milk. Then from far off, beyond the woods in distant hills, she heard a vague, long, drawn-out cry—a sound that lingered; and she listened silently as it mingled like a strain of music with the last vibrations of her quivering nerves. Rodolphe, a cigar between his teeth, was mending a broken bridle with his penknife.

They returned to Yonville by the same route. In the mud they saw, side by side, the hoof prints left there by their own two horses; they saw the same bushes, the same stones in the grass. Nothing around them had changed: and yet to her something had happened that was more momentous than if mountains had moved. Rodolphe reached over, now and then, and raised her hand to his lips.

She was charming on horseback—erect and slender, her knee bent against the animal's mane, her face flushed a little by the air in the red glow of evening.

As she entered the village she made her horse prance on the stone pavement, and people stared at her from their windows.

Her husband, at dinner, found that she looked well; but she seemed not to hear him when he asked about her ride; and she leaned her elbow on the table beside her plate, between the two lighted candles.

"Emma!" he said.

"What?"

"Well, I called on Monsieur Alexandre this afternoon. He bought a filly a few years ago and she's still in fine shape, just a little broken in the knees; I'm sure I could get her for a hundred écus. . . ."

And he went on:

"I thought you might like to have her, so I reserved her. . . . I bought her. . . . Did I do right? Tell me."

She nodded her head in assent. Then, a quarter of an hour later:

"Are you going out tonight?" she asked.

"Yes, why?"

"Oh, nothing—nothing, dear."

And as soon as she was rid of Charles she went upstairs and shut herself in her room.

At first it was as though she were in a daze: she saw the trees, the paths, the ditches, Rodolphe; once again she felt his arms tighten around her as the leaves were all a-tremble and the reeds whistled in the wind.

Then she caught sight of herself in the mirror, and was amazed by the way she looked. Never had her eyes been so enormous, so dark, so deep: her whole being was transfigured by some subtle emanation.

"I have a lover! I have a lover!" she kept repeating to herself, reveling in the thought as though she were beginning a second puberty. At last she was going to know the joys of love, the fever of the happiness she had despaired of. She was entering a marvelous realm where all would be passion, ecstasy, rapture: she was in the midst of an endless blue expanse, scaling the glittering heights of passion; everyday life had receded, and lay far below, in the shadows between those peaks.

She remembered the heroines of novels she had read, and the lyrical legion of those adulterous women began to sing in her memory with sisterly voices that enchanted her. Now she saw herself as one of those *amoureuses* whom she had so envied: she was becoming, in reality, one of that gallery of fictional figures; the long dream of her youth was coming true. She was full of a delicious sense of vengeance. How she had suffered! But now her hour of triumph had come; and love, so long repressed, was gushing forth in joyful effervescence. She savored it without remorse, without anxiety, without distress.

The next day brought a new delight. They exchanged vows. She told him her sorrows. Rodolphe interrupted her with kisses; and she begged him, gazing at him with half-shut eyes, to say her name again and tell her once more that he loved her. They were in the forest, like the day before, this time in a hut used by sabot-makers. The walls were of straw, and the roof was so low that they could not stand erect. They sat side by side on a bed of dry leaves.

From that day on they wrote each other regularly every night. Emma took her letter out into the garden and slipped it into a crack in the terrace wall beside the river; Rodolphe came, took it, and left one for her—one that was always, she complained, too short.

One morning when Charles had gone out before sunrise she was seized with a longing to see Rodolphe at once. She could go quickly to La Huchette, stay there an hour, and be back in Yonville before anyone was up. The thought made her pant with desire, and soon she was halfway across the meadow, walking fast and not looking back.

Day was just breaking. From far off Emma recognized her lover's farm, with its two swallow-tailed weathervanes silhouetted in black against the pale twilight.

Beyond the farmyard was a building that could only be the château. She entered it as though the walls opened of themselves at her approach. A long straight staircase led to an upper hall. Emma turned the latch of a door, and there at the far end of a room she saw a man asleep. It was Rodolphe. She uttered a cry.

"It's you!" he cried. "You, here! How did you come? Ah! Your dress is wet!"

"I love you!" was her answer; and she flung her arms around his neck.

She had dared and won; and from then on, each time that Charles went out early she quickly dressed and stole down the river stairs.

If the cow plank had been raised she had to follow the garden walls that bordered the stream; the bank was slippery, and to keep from falling she would clutch at tufts of faded wallflowers. Then she would strike out across the plowed fields, sinking in, stumbling, her light shoes getting continually stuck in the soft soil. The scarf she had tied over her head fluttered in the wind as she crossed the meadows; she was afraid of the oxen, and would begin to run; and she would arrive breathless, rosy cheeked, everything about her smelling of sap and verdure and fresh air. Rodolphe would still be asleep. She was like a spring morning entering his room.

The yellow curtains masking the windows let through a soft, dull golden light. Emma would grope her way, squinting, dewdrops clinging to her hair like a halo of topazes around her face. And Rodolphe would laugh and draw her to him and strain her to his heart.

Afterwards she would explore the room, opening drawers, combing her hair with his comb, looking at herself in his shaving mirror. Often she took the stem of his pipe in her teeth—a large pipe that he kept on his night table, beside the lemons and lumps of sugar that were there with his water jug.

It always took them a good quarter of an hour to say good-bye. Emma invariably wept: she wished that she never had to leave him. Some irresistible force kept driving her time and again to his side, until one day when she arrived unexpectedly he frowned as though displeased.

"What's wrong?" she cried. "Are you ill? Tell me!"

After some urging, he declared gravely that her visits were becoming fool-hardy and that she was risking her reputation.

X

As time went on she came to share Rodolphe's fears. Love had intoxicated her at first, and she had had no thought beyond it. But now that life was inconceivable without it she was terrified lest she be deprived of any portion of this love, or even that it be in any way interfered with. Each time she returned from one of her visits she cast uneasy glances about her, peering at every figure moving on the horizon, at every dormer in the village from which she might be seen. Her ears picked up the sound of every footstep, every voice, every plow; and she would stand still, paler and more trembling than the leaves of the swaying poplars overhead.

One morning on her way back she suddenly thought she saw a rifle pointing at her. It was slanting out over the edge of a small barrel half hidden in the grass beside a ditch. She felt faint with fright, but continued to walk ahead, and a man emerged from the barrel like a jack-in-the-box. He wore gaiters buckled up to his knees, and his cap was pulled down over his eyes; his lips were trembling with cold and his nose was red. It was Captain Binet, out after wild duck.

"You should have called!" he cried. "When you see a gun you must always give warning."

That reproach was actually the tax collector's attempt to cover up the fright that Emma had given *him*. There was a police ordinance prohibiting duck shooting except from boats, and for all his respect for the law, Monsieur Binet was in the process of committing a violation. He had been expecting the game warden to appear any minute. But fear had added spice to his enjoyment, and in the solitude of his barrel he had been congratulating himself on his luck and his deviltry.

At the sight of Emma he felt relieved of a great weight, and he opened conversation:

"Chilly, isn't it! Really nippy!"

Emma made no answer.

"You're certainly out bright and early," he went on.

"Yes," she stammered. "I've been to see my baby at the nurse's."

"Ah, I see! As for me, I've been right here where I am now ever since daybreak, but it's such dirty weather that unless you have the bird at the very end of your gun . . ."

"Good-bye, Monsieur Binet," she interrupted, turning away.

"Good-bye, Madame," he answered dryly.

And he went back into his barrel.

Emma regretted having taken such brusque leave of the tax collector. Whatever surmises he made would certainly be to her discredit. What she had said about the wet nurse was the worst possible story she could have invented: everyone in Yonville knew perfectly well that little Berthe had been back with her parents for a year. Besides, no one lived out in that direction; that particular path led only to La Huchette. Binet must certainly have guessed where she was coming from: he wouldn't keep his mouth shut, either; he would gossip, unquestionably. All day she racked her brains, trying to dream up all possible lies; and she brooded incessantly about that fool with his game bag.

After dinner Charles, seeing that she looked worried about something, had the idea of distracting her from whatever it was by taking her to call on the pharmacist; and the first person she saw in the pharmacy was, once again, the tax collector! He was standing at the counter in the glow of the red jar, saying, "Give me a half-ounce of vitriol."

"Justin," called the pharmacist, "bring the sulphuric acid."

Then, to Emma, who was about to go up to Madame Homais' quarters:

"No, don't bother to climb the stairs: she'll be coming down directly. Warm yourself at the stove while you wait. Excuse me . . . *Bonjour, docteur.*" (The pharmacist greatly enjoyed uttering the word *docteur,* as though by applying it to someone else he caused some of the glory it held for him to be reflected on himself.) "But be careful not to knock over the mortars," he called to Justin. "No, no! Go get some of the chairs from the little room! You know perfectly well we never move the parlor armchairs."

And Homais was just bustling out from behind the counter to put his armchair back where it belonged when Binet asked him for a half-ounce of sugar acid.

"Sugar acid?" said the pharmacist scornfully. "I don't know what that is. I never heard of it. You want oxalic acid, perhaps? Oxalic is what you mean, isn't it?"

Binet explained that he needed a corrosive: he wanted to make some metal polish to clean the rust off parts of his hunting gear. Emma stood rigid.

"Yes, the weather is certainly unpropitious," said the pharmacist, "what with all this dampness."

"Still," said the tax collector slyly, "there are people who don't mind it."

She was choking.

"Now give me . . ."

"He'll never go!" she thought.

" . . . a half-ounce of rosin and turpentine, four ounces of beeswax, and an ounce and a half of boneblack to clean the patent leather on my outfit."

As the apothecary began cutting the wax, Madame Homais appeared with Irma in her arms, Napoléon beside her and Athalie bringing up the rear. She sat down on the plush-covered bench by the window, while the boy took a stool and his elder sister kept close to the jujube jar, near her dear papa. The latter was pouring things into funnels, corking bottles, gluing labels and wrapping parcels. Everyone watched him in silence: the only sound was an occasional clink of weights in the scales, and a few low-voiced words of advice from the pharmacist to his apprentice.

"How is your little girl?" Madame Homais suddenly asked.

"Quiet!" cried her husband, who was jotting figures on a scratch-pad.

"Why didn't you bring her?" she went on, in an undertone.

"Sh! Sh!" said Emma, pointing to the apothecary.

But Binet, absorbed in checking the pharmacist's arithmetic, seemed to have heard nothing. Then at last he left. Emma gave a deep sigh of relief.

"How heavily you're breathing!" said Madame Homais.

"Don't you find it rather warm?" she answered.

The next day, therefore, Emma and Rodolphe discussed the best way of arranging their meetings. Emma was for bribing her maid with a present, but it would be better if they could find some other, safer place in Yonville. Rodolphe promised to look for one.

From then on, three or four times a week throughout the winter, he came to the garden in the dark of the night. Emma had removed the key from the gate, letting Charles think it was lost.

To announce himself, Rodolphe threw a handful of gravel against the shutters. She always started up; but sometimes she had to wait, for Charles loved to chat beside the fire, and went on and on. She would grow wild with impatience: if she could have accomplished it with a look, she would have flung him out a window. Finally she would begin to get ready for bed, and then she would take up a book and sit quietly reading, as though absorbed. Charles, in bed by this time, would call her.

"Come, Emma," he would say. "It's time."

"Yes, I'm coming," she would answer.

But the candles shone in his eyes, and he would turn to the wall and fall asleep. Then she slipped out, holding her breath, smiling, palpitating, half undressed.

Rodolphe would enfold her in the large full cape he wore and, with his arm around her waist, lead her without a word to the foot of the garden.

It was in the arbor that they spent their time together, on the same dilapidated rustic bench from which Léon used to stare at her so amorously on summer evenings. She scarcely thought of him now.

The stars glittered through the bare branches of the jasmine. Behind them they heard the flowing of the river, and now and again the crackle of dry reeds on the bank. Here and there in the darkness loomed patches of deeper shadow; and sometimes these would suddenly seem to shudder, rear up and then curve downward, like huge black waves threatening to engulf them. In the cold of the night they clasped each other the more tightly, the sighs that came from their lips seemed deeper, their half-seen eyes looked larger; and amidst the silence their soft-spoken words had a crystalline ring that echoed and reechoed in their hearts.

If the night was rainy they sought shelter in the consulting room, between the shed and the stable. She would light a kitchen lamp that she kept hidden behind the books. Rodolphe made himself at home here, as though the place belonged to him. The sight of the bookcase and the desk—indeed the whole room—aroused his hilarity: he couldn't keep from joking about Charles in a way that made Emma uncomfortable. She would have liked him to be more serious—or even more dramatic sometimes, like the night she thought she heard the sound of approaching footsteps in the lane.

"Someone's coming," she whispered.

He blew out the light.

"Have you got your pistols?"

"What for?"

"Why—to defend yourself," said Emma.

"You mean against your husband? That poor . . . ?"

And Rodolphe ended his sentence with a gesture that meant that he could annihilate Charles with a flick of his finger.

This display of fearlessness dazzled her, even though she sensed in it a crudity and bland vulgarity that shocked her.

Rodolphe thought a good deal about that episode of the pistols. If she had spoken in earnest, it was absurd of her, he thought, really an odious thing, for he had no cause to hate poor Charles. He was by no means "devoured by jealousy," as the saying went: and indeed, in this connection, Emma had made him a tremendous vow that he, for his part, thought in rather poor taste.

Besides, she was becoming frightfully sentimental. They had had to exchange miniatures and cut handfuls of each other's hair; and now she was asking for a ring—a real wedding band, as a sign of eternal union. She often talked to him about the "bells of evening," or the "voices of nature"; and then she would go on about her mother and his. Rodolphe's mother had been dead for twenty years, but Emma kept consoling him in the kind of affected language one uses to a bereaved child; and sometimes she would even look at the moon and say to him, "Somewhere up there I'm sure they're both looking down at us and approving of our love."

But she was so pretty! He couldn't remember ever having had so unspoiled a mistress. The purity of her love was something entirely new to him. It was a change from his usual loose habits, and it both flattered his pride and inflamed his senses. Emma's continual raptures, which his bourgeois common sense despised, seemed to him in his heart of hearts charming, since it was he who inspired them.

As time went on he stopped making any effort, secure in the knowledge that he was loved; and imperceptibly his manner changed. No longer did he speak to her, as before, in words so sweet that they made her weep; nor were there any more of those fervid embraces that frenzied her. Their great love, in which she lived completely immersed, seemed to be ebbing away, like the water of a river that was sinking into its own bed; and she saw the mud at the bottom. She refused to believe it; she redoubled her caresses; and Rodolphe hid his indifference less and less.

She didn't know whether she regretted having yielded to him or whether she didn't rather long to love him more dearly. Her humiliating feeling of weakness was turning into resentment: but this melted away in the heat of his embraces. It was not an attachment; it was a kind of permanent seduction. She was in his bondage. It almost frightened her.

Nevertheless, from the outside everything looked more serene than ever, Rodolphe having succeeded in conducting the affair as he pleased; and at the end of six months, when spring came, they were like a married couple peacefully tending to a domestic flame.

It was the time of the year when Monsieur Rouault always sent his turkey, in commemoration of his mended leg. As usual, the present was accompanied by a letter. Emma cut the string tying it to the basket, and read the following:

Dear Children:

I hope these lines find you well and that this one will be up to the others: it seems to me a little tenderer, if I may say so, and meatier. But next time I'll send you a cock for a change, unless you'd rather stick to gobblers, and please send me back the basket along with the last two. I had an accident with the cart shed, one night a heavy wind blew the roof off into the trees. Crops haven't been too good either. I can't tell when I'll come to see you. It's so hard for me to leave the place now that I'm alone.

Here there was a space between the lines, as though the old man had put down his pen to think a while.

As for me, I'm all right, except for a cold I caught the other day at the fair in Yvetot, where I went to hire a shepherd, having got rid of the one I had because he was too particular about his food. All these good-for-nothings give you more trouble than they're worth. This one was disrespectful besides.

I heard from a peddler who stopped in your town to have a tooth drawn that Bovary keeps busy. It doesn't surprise me, and he showed me his tooth; we took a cup of coffee together. I asked if he'd seen you, Emma, he said no, but he'd seen two horses in the stable from which I assume that business is prospering. I'm glad of it, dear children, may the good Lord send you every possible happiness.

It grieves me that I've never seen my beloved granddaughter Berthe Bovary. I've planted a tree of September plums for her under the window of your room and I won't let anybody touch it except to make some jam for her later that I'll keep in the cupboard for her when she comes.

Good-bye, dear children. I kiss you on both cheeks, all three of you.

I am, with all good wishes,
Your loving father,
Théodore Rouault

She sat for a few minutes with the sheet of coarse paper in her hand. The letter was thick with spelling mistakes, and Emma brooded on the affectionate thought that cackled through them like a hen half hidden in a thorn hedge. Her father had dried his writing with ash from the fireplace, for a bit of gray dust drifted out of the letter onto her dress, and she could almost see the old man bending down toward the hearth to take up the tongs. How long it was since she had sat there beside him, on the fireseat, burning the end of a stick in the flame of the crackling furze! She remembered summer evenings, full of sunshine. The foals would whinny when anyone came near, and gallop and gallop to their hearts' content. There had been a beehive under her window, and sometimes the bees, wheeling in the light, would strike against the panes like bouncing golden balls. How happy she had been in those days! How free! How full of hope! How rich in illusions! There were no illusions left now! She had had to part with some each time she had ventured on a new path, in each of her successive conditions—as virgin, as wife, as mistress; all along the course of her life she had been losing them, like a traveler leaving a bit of his fortune in every inn along the road.

But what was making her so unhappy? Where was the extraordinary disaster that had wrought havoc with her life? And she lifted her head and looked about her, as though trying to discover the cause of her suffering.

An April sunbeam was dancing on the china in the whatnot; the fire was burning; she felt the rug soft beneath her slippers; the day was cloudless, the air mild, and she could hear her child shouting with laughter.

The little girl was rolling on the lawn, in the cut grass that Lestiboudois was raking. She was lying on her stomach on a pile that he had got together; Félicité was holding her by the skirt; the gardener was working nearby, and whenever he came close she leaned over toward him, waving her arms in the air.

"Bring her in to me!" her mother cried. And she rushed over and kissed her. "How I love you, darling! How I love you!"

Then, noticing that the tips of the child's ears were a little dirty, she quickly rang for hot water; and she washed her, changed her underclothes, stockings, and shoes, asked a thousand questions about how she felt, as though she were just back from a trip, and finally, giving her more and more kisses, and weeping a little, she handed her back to the maid, who stood gaping at this overflow of affection.

That night Rodolphe found her more reserved than usual.

"It will pass," he thought. "It's some whim."

And on three successive evenings he didn't appear for their rendezvous. When he finally came she was cold, almost disdainful.

"Ah! You'll get nowhere playing that game . . . !" And he pretended not to notice her melancholy sighs or the handkerchief she kept bringing out.

Then Emma's repentance knew no bounds.

She even wondered why she detested Charles, and whether it mightn't be better to try to love him. But there was so little about him to which her resurgent feeling could attach itself that she was at a loss as to how to put her noble resolution into effect. And then one day the apothecary provided the desired opportunity.

XI

Homais had lately read an article extolling a new method of curing clubfoot; and since he was on the side of progress he conceived the patriotic idea that Yonville, to keep abreast of the times, should have its own operation for talipes, as he learnedly called the deformity.

"After all," he said to Emma, "what's the risk? Look." And he enumerated on his fingers the advantages that would accrue from the attempt. "Almost sure success, relief and improved appearance for the patient, and for the surgeon a rapid rise to fame. Why shouldn't your husband fix up poor Hippolyte, at the Lion d'Or? The boy would unquestionably talk about his cure to every traveler at the inn, and then"—here Homais lowered his voice and cast a glance about him—"what is there to keep me from sending a little piece about it to the paper? Ah! An article gets around—people talk about it—a thing like that really snowballs. Who can tell? Who can tell?"

He was right: Bovary might very well succeed. Emma had never had any reason to think that he wasn't skillful in his work; and what satisfaction *she* would derive from persuading him to take a step that would increase his fame and fortune! Something more solid than love to lean on would be only too welcome.

Egged on by her and by the apothecary, Charles consented. He sent to Rouen for Doctor Duval's treatise; and every night, his head in his hands, he buried himself in its pages.

He studied talipes in its various forms—equinus, varus and valgus: in other words, the varying malformations of the foot downwards, inwards, or outwards, sometimes scientifically called *strephocatopodia, strephendopodia* and *strephexopodia;* and he studied *strephypopodia* and *strephanopodia*—downward or upward torsion. And meanwhile Monsieur Homais tried to persuade the stable boy to agree to be operated on. He used every possible argument.

"You'll scarcely feel it—there'll be the very slightest pain if any. It's just a prick, like the tiniest bloodletting. Not nearly as bad as cutting out certain kinds of corns."

Hippolyte rolled his eyes stupidly as he thought it over.

"Besides," the pharmacist went on, "it's not for my sake that I'm urging you, but for yours—out of pure humanity. I'd like to see you rid of that ugly limp, my boy, and that swaying in the lumbar region that must interfere seriously with your work, whatever you say."

Then Homais painted a picture of how much more lively and nimble he would feel, and even intimated that he'd be much more successful with women. The stable boy grinned sheepishly at that. Then Homais played on his vanity:

"Are you a man or aren't you? Think what it would have been like if you'd had to serve in the army and go into combat! Ah, Hippolyte!"

And Homais moved off, declaring that such stubbornness, such blindness in refusing the benefits of science were beyond his understanding.

In the end the poor wretch yielded, unable to stand up against what was a veritable conspiracy. Binet, who never meddled in other people's affairs, Madame Lefrançois, Artémise, the neighbors, even the mayor, Monsieur Tuvache—everybody urged him, lectured him, shamed him; but what finally decided him was that it wouldn't cost him anything. Bovary even offered to supply the apparatus that would be used after the operation. Emma had thought up that bit of generosity, and Charles had agreed, inwardly marveling at what an angel his wife was.

Guided by the pharmacist's advice, he finally succeeded on the third try in having the cabinetmaker and the locksmith construct a sort of box weighing about eight pounds—a complicated mass of iron, wood, tin, leather, screws and nuts.

Meanwhile, in order to know which of Hippolyte's tendons had to be cut, he first had to find out what variety of clubfoot his was.

The foot made almost a straight line with the leg, and at the same time was twisted inward, so that it was an equinus with certain characteristics of a varus, or else a varus with strong equinus features. But with his equinus—which actually was as wide across as an equine hoof, with rough skin, stringy tendons, oversized toes, and black nails that were like the nails of a horseshoe—the taliped[2] ran about fleet as a deer from morning to night. He was constantly to be seen in the square, hopping about among the carts, thrusting his clubfoot ahead of him. Actually, the affected leg seemed to be stronger than the other. From its long years of service it had taken on moral qualities, as it were—qualities of patience and energy; and whenever Hippolyte was given a particularly heavy task to do, it was that leg that he threw his weight on.

Since it was an equinus, the Achilles tendon would have to be cut, and then later, perhaps, the anterior tibial muscle, to take care of the varus. Charles didn't dare risk two operations at once, and indeed he was trembling already lest he interfere with some important part of the foot he knew nothing about.

Neither Ambroise Paré, applying an immediate ligature to an artery for the first time since Celsus had done it fifteen centuries before; nor Dupuytren cutting open an abscess through a thick layer of the brain; nor Gensoul, when he performed the first removal of an upper maxillary—none of them, certainly, felt such a beating of the heart, such a quivering of the hand, such a tenseness of the mind, as Monsieur Bovary when he approached Hippolyte with his tenotomy knife. On a table nearby, just as in a hospital, lay a pile of lint, waxed thread, and a quantity of bandages—a veritable pyramid of bandages, the apothecary's entire stock. It was Monsieur Homais who had been making these preparations ever since early morning, as much to dazzle the multitude as to inflate his self-importance. Charles pierced the skin: there was a sharp snap. The tendon was cut; the operation was over. Hippolyte couldn't stop marveling: he bent over Bovary's hands and covered them with kisses.

"Don't get excited," said the apothecary. "You'll have plenty of occasion to express your gratitude to your benefactor."

And he went out to announce the result to five or six sensation seekers who were waiting in the yard expecting Hippolyte to make his appearance walking normally. Then Charles strapped his patient into the apparatus and went home, where Emma was anxiously awaiting him at the door. She flung her arms around his neck; they sat down at table; he ate heartily, and even asked for a cup of coffee with his dessert—a bit of intemperance he ordinarily allowed himself only on Sunday when there was company.

Their evening together was charming: they spoke of their future, the improvement they expected in their fortunes, changes they would make in their house. He saw himself a man of renown and riches, adored by his wife; and she felt herself pleasantly revived by this new sensation—this noble, wholesome experience of returning at least some of poor Charles's love. For a moment the thought of Rodolphe crossed her mind; but then her eyes swung back to Charles, and she noticed with surprise that his teeth weren't bad at all.

2. A person with clubfoot, or talipes.

They were in bed when Monsieur Homais suddenly entered their room: he had brushed aside the cook's attempts to announce him, and was holding a newly written sheet of paper. It was the publicity article he had prepared for the *Fanal de Rouen:* he had brought it for them to read.

"You read it to us," said Bovary.

He began:

" 'Despite the network of prejudices that still extends across part of the face of Europe, our country districts are beginning to see the light. Just this Tuesday our small community of Yonville was the scene of a surgical experiment that was also an act of pure philanthropy. Monsieur Bovary, one of our most distinguished practitioners . . .' "

"That's going too far! Too far!" cried Charles, choked with emotion.

"Not at all! Certainly not! '. . . performed an operation on a clubfoot. . . .' I didn't use the scientific term—in a newspaper, you know . . . not everybody would understand; the masses have to be . . ."

"You're right," said Bovary. "Go ahead."

"Where was I?" said the pharmacist. "Oh, yes. 'Monsieur Bovary, one of our most distinguished practitioners, performed an operation on a clubfoot. The patient was one Hippolyte Tautain, stable boy for the past twenty-five years at the Lion d'Or hotel, owned by Madame Lefrançois, on the Place d'Armes. The novelty of the enterprise and the interest felt in the patient had attracted such a large throng of our local citizenry that there was a veritable crush outside the establishment. The operation went off like magic, and only a few drops of blood appeared on the skin, as though to announce that the rebellious tendon had finally surrendered to the surgeon's art. The patient, strange though it may seem (we report this fact *de visu*), experienced not the slightest pain. Up to the moment of the present writing, his condition is entirely satisfactory. Everything gives us reason to expect that his convalescence will be rapid. Who knows? At the next village festival we may well see our good friend Hippolyte tripping Bacchic measures amidst a chorus of joyous companions, thus demonstrating to all, by his high spirits and his capers, the completeness of his cure. All honor to our generous men of science! All honor to those tireless benefactors who go without sleep to work for the improvement or the relief of mankind! All honor to them! Now indeed we can proclaim that the blind shall see, the deaf shall hear and the lame shall walk! But what fanaticism promised in times past to the elect, science is now achieving for all men! We shall keep our readers informed concerning the subsequent stages of this remarkable cure.' "

But all that eloquence did not alter the course of events. Five days later Madame Lefrançois rushed into the doctor's house frightened out of her wits, crying: "Help! He's dying! It's driving me mad!"

Charles made a dash for the Lion d'Or; and the pharmacist, catching sight of him as he rushed bareheaded across the square, hurriedly left his pharmacy. He, too, arrived at the hotel breathless, flushed and worried. "What has happened," he inquired of the numerous people climbing the stairs, "to our interesting taliped."

The taliped was writhing—writhing in frightful convulsions, so severe that the apparatus locked around his leg was beating against the wall, threatening to demolish it.

Taking every precaution not to disturb the position of the leg, Charles and Monsieur Homais removed the box—and a terrible sight met their eyes. The foot was completely formless, so immensely swollen that the skin seemed ready to burst; and the entire surface was covered with black and blue spots caused by the much-vaunted apparatus. Hippolyte had been complaining of pain for some time, but no one had paid any attention; now it was clear that he hadn't entirely imagined it, and he was allowed to keep his foot out of the box for several hours. But hardly had the swelling subsided a little than the two experts decided that the treatment should be resumed; and they screwed the apparatus on more tightly than before, to hasten results. Finally, three days later, when Hippolyte could bear it no longer, they removed the box again and were amazed by what they saw. A livid tumescence now extended up the leg, and a dark liquid was oozing from a number of blood blisters. Things were taking a serious turn. Hippolyte had no courage left; and Madame Lefrançois moved him into the small room, just off the kitchen, so that he might at least have some distraction.

But the tax collector, who took his dinner there every evening, complained bitterly of such company, so Hippolyte was moved again, this time into the billiard room.

He lay there, groaning under his heavy blankets, pale, unshaven, hollow eyed, turning and twisting his sweaty head on the dirty, fly-covered pillow. Madame Bovary came to see him. She brought him linen for his poultices, comforted him, tried to cheer him. He had no lack of company, especially on market days, when the peasants crowded around him, playing billiards, dueling with the cues, smoking, drinking, singing, shouting.

"How're you getting along?" they would say, giving him a poke in the shoulder. "You don't look too good. But it's your own fault. You should have . . ." And they would give their advice, telling him about people who had all been cured by methods quite different from the one that had been used on him. Then they would add, by way of comfort: "You fuss too much! Why don't you get up, instead of having everybody wait on you? Well, never mind, old boy—you certainly stink!"

And indeed the gangrene was climbing higher and higher. Bovary was sick about it. He kept coming in every hour, every few minutes. Hippolyte would look at him with terror-filled eyes, and sob and stammer:

"When will I be cured? Help me! Help me! Oh, God, it's terrible!"

And each time the doctor could only go away again, advising him to eat lightly.

"Don't listen to him," Madame Lefrançois would say, when Bovary had left. "They've made you suffer enough already. You'll lose still more of your strength. Here, swallow this!"

And she would give him some tasty soup, or a slice from a leg of mutton, or a bit of bacon, and now and again a little glass of brandy that he hardly dared drink.

The abbé Bournisien, learning that he was getting worse, came to the hotel and asked to see him. He began by condoling with him on his suffering— declaring, however, that he should rejoice in it, since it was the Lord's will, and lose no time taking advantage of this occasion to become reconciled with heaven.

"You've been a little neglectful of your religious duties," he pointed out in a paternal tone. "I've seldom seen you at Mass. How many years is it since you've been to Communion? It's understandable that your work and other distractions should have made you careless about your eternal salvation. But now is the time to think about it. Don't give way to despair: I've known grievous sinners who implored God's mercy when they were about to appear before Him—I know you haven't reached that point yet—and who certainly made better deaths as a result. Be an example to us, as they were! What's to prevent you from saying a Hail Mary and an Our Father every night and morning just as a precaution? Do it! Do it for me, to oblige me! It doesn't amount to much. Will you promise?"

The poor devil promised. The priest came again the following days. He chatted with the hotel keeper, told stories, made jokes and puns that were over Hippolyte's head. Then, at the first possible opening, he would return to religious matters, his face taking on an appropriate expression as he did so.

His zeal seemed to have some effect, for soon the taliped expressed a wish to make a pilgrimage to Bon-Secours if he was cured—to which the abbé replied that he could see nothing against it: two precautions were better than one. What—as he put it—was the risk?

The apothecary railed against what he called the priest's "maneuvers": they were interfering, he claimed, with Hippolyte's convalescence; and he kept saying to Madame Lefrançois, "Leave him alone! Leave him alone! You're confusing him with all your mysticism!"

But the lady wouldn't listen to him. He was "to blame for everything." And on a nail in the wall at the head of the sickbed she defiantly hung a brimming holy-water font with a sprig of boxwood in it.

However, religion seemed to be of no greater help than surgery, and the gangrenous process continued to extend inexorably upward toward the groin. In vain did they change medications and poultices: each day the muscles rotted a little more, and finally Charles replied with an affirmative nod when Madame Lefrançois asked him whether as a last resort she couldn't call in Monsieur Canivet, a celebrated surgeon in Neufchâtel.

This fellow practitioner, a fifty-year-old M.D. of considerable standing and equal self-assurance, laughed with unconcealed scorn when he saw Hippolyte's leg, by now gangrenous to the knee. Then, after declaring flatly that he would have to amputate, he visited the pharmacist and inveighed against the jackasses capable of reducing an unfortunate man to such a plight. He grasped Monsieur Homais by one of his coat buttons and shook him, shouting:

"New-fangled ideas from Paris! It's like strabismus and chloroform and lithotrity—the government ought to forbid such tomfoolery! But everybody wants to be smart nowadays, and they stuff you full of remedies without caring about the consequences! We don't pretend to be so clever, here in the country. We're not such know-it-alls, such la-di-das! We're practitioners, healers! It doesn't occur to us to operate on somebody who's perfectly well! Straighten a clubfoot! Who ever heard of straightening a clubfoot? It's like wanting to iron out a hunchback!"

Those words were a whiplash to Homais, but he hid his discomfiture under an obsequious smile: it was important to humor Canivet, whose prescriptions were sometimes brought into the pharmacy by Yonvillians, and so he made no defense of Bovary and expressed no opinion; he cast principles to the winds, and sacrificed his dignity to the weightier interests of his business.

It was quite an event in the village, that mid-thigh amputation by Doctor

Canivet! All the citizens rose early that morning; and the Grande-Rue, thronged though it was, had something sinister about it, as though it were execution day. At the grocer's, Hippolyte's case was discussed from every angle; none of the stores did any business; and Madame Tuvache, the mayor's wife, didn't budge from her window, so eager was she not to miss the surgeon's arrival.

He drove up in his gig, holding the reins himself. Over the years the right-hand spring had given way under the weight of his corpulence, so that the carriage sagged a little to one side as it rolled along. Beside him, on the higher half of the seat cushion, could be seen a huge red leather case, its three brass clasps gleaming magisterially.

The doctor drew up in the hotel yard with a flourish and called loudly for someone to unharness his mare; and then he went to the stable to see whether she was really being given oats as he had ordered. His first concern, whenever he arrived at a patient's, was always for his mare and his gig. "That Canivet—he's a character!" people said of him; and they thought the more of him for his unshakable self-assurance. The universe might have perished to the last man, and he wouldn't have altered his habits a jot.

Homais made his appearance.

"I'm counting on you," said the doctor. "Are we ready? Let's go!"

But the apothecary blushingly confessed that he was too sensitive to be present at such an operation.

"When you just stand there watching," he said, "your imagination begins to play tricks on you, you know. And I'm of such a nervous temperament anyway that . . ."

"Bah!" interrupted Canivet. "You look more like the apoplectic type to me. It doesn't surprise me, either: you pharmacists are always cooped up in your kitchens—it can't help undermining your constitutions in the long run. Look at me: I'm up every day at four, shave in cold water every season of the year; I'm never chilly, never wear flannel underwear, never catch cold—I'm sound as a bell. I eat well one day, badly the next, however it comes. I take it philosophically. That's why I'm not a bit squeamish, like you. And that's why it's all the same to me whether I carve up a Christian or any old chicken they put in front of me. It's all a question of habit."

Thereupon, with no consideration whatever for Hippolyte, who was sweating with pain and terror under his bedclothes in the billiard room, the two gentlemen proceeded there in the kitchen to engage in a conversation in which the apothecary likened the coolness of a surgeon to that of a general. The comparison pleased Canivet, who expatiated on the demands made by his profession. He looked on it as a kind of sacred charge, even though dishonored nowadays by the activities of the *officiers de santé*. Then, finally giving thought to his patient, he inspected the bandages Homais had brought—the same ones he had furnished the day of the earlier operation— and asked for someone to hold the leg for him while he worked. Lestiboudois was sent for, and Canivet rolled up his sleeves and went into the billiard room. The apothecary stayed outside with Artémise and the landlady, both of the latter whiter than their aprons and all three of them with their ears to the door.

Bovary, meanwhile, didn't dare show himself outside his house. He sat downstairs in the parlor beside the empty fireplace, his chin on his chest, his hands folded, his eyes set. What a misfortune! he was thinking. What a disappointment! Certainly he had taken all conceivable precautions. Fate had played a hand in it. Be that as it may, if Hippolyte were later to die it would be he who would have murdered him. And then—how was he to answer the questions his patients were sure to ask him? What reason could he give for his failure? Perhaps he *had* made some mistake? He sought for what it might be, and failed to find it. The greatest surgeons made mistakes, didn't they? That was something no one would ever believe. Everyone would laugh at him, talk about him. The news would spread to Forges, to Neufchâtel, to Rouen—everywhere! Who knew—other doctors might write letters and articles attacking him! There would be a controversy: he would have to send replies to the newspapers. Hippolyte himself might sue him. He saw himself dishonored, ruined, lost! And his imagination, engendering countless fears, was tossed about like an empty barrel carried out to sea and bobbing on the waves.

Emma, sitting opposite, was watching him. She was not participating in his humiliation. She was experiencing a humiliation of a different sort: the humiliation of having imagined that such a man might be worth something—as though she hadn't twenty times already had full proof of his mediocrity.

Charles began to stride up and down the room. The floor creaked under his heavy boots.

"Sit down!" she said. "You're getting on my nerves!"

He sat down.

How in the world had she managed (she who was so intelligent) to commit yet another blunder? What deplorable mania was it that had made her wreck her life by constant self-sacrifice? She recalled all her desires for luxury, all her spiritual privations, the sordid details of marriage and housekeeping, her dreams mired like wounded swallows, everything she had ever craved for, everything she had denied herself, all the things she might have had. And for whose sake had she given up so much?

The silence that hung over the village was suddenly rent by a scream. Bovary went deathly pale. For an instant her brows contracted in a nervous frown; then she resumed her brooding. It was for him that she had done it— for this creature here, this man who understood nothing, who felt nothing. He was sitting quite calmly, utterly oblivious of the fact that the ridicule henceforth inseparable from his name would disgrace her as well. And she had tried to love him! She had wept tears of repentance at having given herself to another!

"I wonder—could it perhaps have been a valgus?"[3] The question came abruptly from the musing Charles.

At the sudden impact of those words, crashing into her mind like a leaden bullet into a silver dish, Emma felt herself shudder; and she raised her head, straining to understand what he had meant by them. They looked at each other in silence, almost wonderstruck, each of them, to see that the other was there, so far apart had their thoughts carried them. Charles stared at her with the clouded gaze of a drunken man; motionless in his chair, he was listening to the screams that continued to come from the hotel. One followed after another; each was a long, drawn-out succession of tones, and they were

---

3. A twisting of the first toe above or below the other toes.

interspersed with short, shrill shrieks; it was all like the howling of some animal being butchered far away. Emma bit her pale lips; and twisting and turning in her fingers a sliver she had broken off the coral, she stared fixedly at Charles with blazing eyes that were like twin fiery arrows. Everything, everything about him exasperated her now—his face, his clothes, what he didn't say, his entire person, his very existence. She repented her virtue of days past as though it had been a crime; and what virtue she had left now crumbled under the furious assault of her pride. Adultery was triumphant; and she reveled in the prospect of its sordid ironies. The thought of her lover made her reel with desire; heart and soul she flung herself into her longing, borne toward him on waves of new rapture; and Charles seemed to her as detached from her life, as irrevocably gone, as impossible and done for, as though he were a dying man, gasping his last before her eyes.

There was a sound of footsteps on the sidewalk. Charles looked through the lowered blind: in the hot sun near the market Doctor Canivet was mopping his forehead with his handkerchief. Behind him was Homais, carrying a large red box, and they were both heading for the pharmacy.

Flooded with sudden tenderness and despondency, Charles turned to his wife. "Kiss me!" he cried. "Kiss me, darling!"

"Don't touch me!" she flared, scarlet with fury.

"What . . . what is it?" he stammered, bewildered. "What's wrong? You're not yourself! You know how I love you! I need you!"

"Stop!" she cried in a terrible voice.

And rushing from the room she slammed the door so violently that the barometer was flung from the wall and broke to pieces on the floor.

Charles sank into his chair, crushed, wondering what her trouble was, fearing some nervous illness, weeping, and vaguely aware that the air about him was heavy with something baleful and incomprehensible.

When Rodolphe came to the garden that night he found his mistress waiting for him on the lowest step of the river stairs. They fell into each other's arms: and all their accumulated resentments melted like snow in the heat of this embrace.

XII

Once again their love was at high tide.

Now Emma would often take it into her head to write him during the day. Through her window she would signal to Justin, and he would whip off his apron and fly to La Huchette. And when Rodolphe arrived in response to her summons, it was to hear that she was miserable, that her husband was odious, that her life was a torment.

"Can I do anything about it?" he snapped at her one day.

"Ah, if you only would . . ."

She was sitting at his feet staring at nothing, her head between his knees, her hair streaming.

"What could I do?" Rodolphe demanded.

She sighed. "We could go live somewhere else, away from here. . . ."

"You're really crazy!" he said, laughing. "You know it's impossible!"

She tried to pursue the subject, but he pretended not to understand, and spoke of other things.

He saw no reason why there should be all this to-do about so simple a thing as lovemaking.

But for her there was a reason: there was a motive force that gave an additional impetus to her passion. Every day her love for Rodolphe was fanned by her aversion for her husband. The more completely she surrendered to the one, the more intensely she loathed the other: never did Charles seem to her so repulsive, so thick-fingered, so heavy-witted, so common, as when she was alone with him after her meetings with Rodolphe. Acting, at such times, the role of wife, of virtuous woman, she thought feverishly of her lover—of his black hair curling over his tanned forehead, of his body so powerful and yet so elegant, of the cool judgment that went hand in hand with his fiery passion. It was for him that she filed her fingernails with the care of the most exquisite artist, that she kept massaging her skin with cold cream, scenting her handkerchiefs with patchouli. She decked herself with bracelets, rings and necklaces. Whenever he was expected she filled her two big blue glass vases with roses; both her room and herself were made ready for him, as though she were a courtesan awaiting a prince. Félicité was perpetually bleaching lingerie: all day long she was in the kitchen, and Justin often sat there with her, watching her work.

His elbows on the ironing board, he would stare hungrily at all the feminine garments strewn about him—the dimity petticoats, the fichus, the collars, the drawstring pantaloons enormously wide at the waist and narrowing below.

"What is this for?" the boy would ask, touching a crinoline lining or a set of fastenings.

"Don't tell me you've never seen anything!" Félicité would laugh. "As if your Madame Homais didn't wear these same things!"

"Oh, Madame Homais . . ." And he would wonder aloud: "Is she a lady, like Madame?"

But Félicité was getting tired of having him hang around her. She was six years his elder, and Théodore, Maître Guillaumin's servant, was beginning to court her.

"Leave me alone!" she would say, reaching for her starch pot. "Go pound your almonds. You're always fussing around the women. You're a nasty little boy: better wait till you get some hair on your face for that sort of thing."

"Don't be cross. I'll do her shoes for you."

And he would go over to the doorsill and reach for Emma's shoes, all caked with the mud she had brought in from her meetings. It would fall away powdery under his fingers, and he would watch the particles float gently upward in a shaft of sun.

"You act as though you're afraid of spoiling them!" the cook would jeer. She herself wasn't so careful when she cleaned them, for Madame always gave them to her as soon as they looked the least bit worn.

Emma had countless pairs in her wardrobe, and discarded them on the slightest pretext. Charles never said a word.

Nor did he protest at paying three hundred francs for a wooden leg that she felt should be given to Hippolyte. It was cork trimmed and had spring joints—a complicated mechanism hidden under a black trouser leg that ended in a patent-leather shoe. But Hippolyte didn't dare use such a beautiful leg every day, and he begged Madame Bovary to get him another that would be more suitable. Naturally Charles paid for the new one as well.

The stable boy gradually resumed his work. He went about the village as before; and whenever Charles heard the sharp tap of his stick on the cobblestones in the distance, he quickly changed his direction.

It was Monsieur Lheureux, the shopkeeper, who had taken charge of the order. It gave him an opportunity to see a good deal of Emma. He chatted with her about the latest novelties from Paris, about a thousand feminine trifles; he was more than obliging, and never pressed for payment. Emma let herself slide into this easy way of gratifying all her whims. When she decided she wanted to give Rodolphe a handsome riding crop she had seen in an umbrella shop in Rouen, she told Lheureux to get it for her, and he set it on her table a week later.

The next day, however, he appeared with his bill—two hundred and seventy francs, not to mention the centimes. Emma didn't know what to do: all the desk drawers were empty, they owed Lestiboudois two weeks' pay and the maid six months' wages, there were a number of other bills, and Bovary was waiting impatiently for a remittance from Monsieur Derozerays, who usually settled with him once a year, toward the end of June.

She was able to put Lheureux off for a time, but eventually he lost patience: he was hard pressed, he said, his capital was tied up, and if she couldn't give him something on account he'd be forced to take back all the items she had chosen.

"All right, take them!" she said.

"I didn't really mean that," he answered. "Except perhaps for the riding crop. I guess I'll have to ask Monsieur for it back."

"No! No!" she cried.

"Ah ha!" Lheureux thought. "I've got you!"

And feeling sure that he had ferreted out her secret, he left her. "We'll see," he murmured to himself, with his customary little whistle. "We'll see!"

She was wondering how to extricate herself when the cook came in and put a little cylindrical parcel on the mantel. "From Monsieur Derozerays," she said. Emma seized it and opened it. It contained fifteen napoleons—full payment. She heard Charles on the stairs, and she flung the gold pieces into one of her drawers and took the key.

Three days later Lheureux came again.

"I have a suggestion," he said. "If instead of paying the amount we agreed on you'd like to take . . ."

"Here!" she said, and she handed him fourteen napoleons.

The shopkeeper was taken aback. To hide his disappointment he overflowed with apologies and offers of service, all of which Emma declined. When he had left she stood a few moments with her hand in her apron, fingering the two five-franc pieces he had given her in change. She resolved to economize, so that eventually she could pay Charles back. . . .

"Bah!" she said to herself. "He'll never give it a thought."

Besides the riding crop with the silver-gilt knob, Rodolphe had been given a signet ring with the motto *"Amor nel cor"*; also a scarf to use as a muffler, and a cigar case very like the vicomte's that Charles had picked up on the road and Emma still kept.

But he found her presents humiliating, and on several occasions refused them. She was insistent, however, and he gave in, grumbling to himself that she was high-handed and interfering.

Then she had such crazy notions.

"When the bell strikes midnight," she would command him, "think of me." And if he confessed that he hadn't done so, there were strings of reproaches, always ending with the eternal:

"Do you love me?"

"Of course I love you!"

"Very much?"

"Of course."

"You've never loved anybody else, have you?"

That made him laugh: "Do you think you deflowered me?"

When Emma burst into tears he tried to comfort her, protesting his love and saying things to make her smile.

"It's because I love you," she would interrupt. "I love you so much that I can't do without you—you know that, don't you? Sometimes I want so much to see you that it tears me to pieces. 'Where is he?' I wonder. 'Maybe he's with other women. They're smiling at him, he's going up close to them. . . .' Tell me it isn't true! Tell me you don't like any of them! Some of them are prettier than I am, but none of them can love you the way I do. I'm your slave and your concubine! You're my king, my idol! You're good! You're beautiful! You're wise! You're strong!"

He had had such things said to him so many times that none of them had any freshness for him. Emma was like all his other mistresses; and as the charm of novelty gradually slipped from her like a piece of her clothing, he saw revealed in all its nakedness the eternal monotony of passion, which always assumes the same forms and always speaks the same language. He had no perception—this man of such vast experience—of the dissimilarity of feeling that might underlie similarities of expression. Since he had heard those same words uttered by loose women or prostitutes, he had little belief in their sincerity when he heard them now: the more flowery a person's speech, he thought, the more suspect the feelings, or lack of feelings, it concealed. Whereas the truth is that fullness of soul can sometimes overflow in utter vapidity of language, for none of us can ever express the exact measure of his needs or his thoughts or his sorrows; and human speech is like a cracked kettle on which we tap crude rhythms for bears to dance to, while we long to make music that will melt the stars.

But with the superior acumen of those who keep aloof in any relationship, Rodolphe discovered that the affair offered still further possibilities of sensual gratification. He abandoned every last shred of restraint and consideration. He made her into something compliant, something corrupt. Hers was an infatuation to the point of idiocy; the intensity of her admiration for him was matched by the intensity of her own voluptuous feelings; she was in a blissful torpor, a drunkenness in which her very soul lay drowned and shriveled, like the duke of Clarence in his butt of malmsey.[4]

This constant indulgence had its effect on her daily behavior. Her glance

---

4. The duke of Clarence was the younger brother of King Edward IV of England and the elder brother of Richard, duke of Gloucester. He was condemned to death for treason and, according to rumor, drowned in a butt of malmsey (a sweet aromatic wine) in February 1478. See Shakespeare's *Richard III* 1.4.155.

grew bolder, her language freer; she went so far as to be seen smoking a cigarette in public, in Rodolphe's company—"as though," people said, "to show her contempt for propriety." Even those who had given her the benefit of the doubt stopped doing so when they saw her step out of the Hirondelle one day wearing a tight-fitting vest, like a man's. The elder Madame Bovary, who had taken refuge with her son following a particularly unpleasant scene with her husband, was as scandalized as any of the Yonville matrons. There were many other things that she disliked, too: first of all, Charles hadn't followed her advice about the ban on novels; and then she disapproved of "the way the house was run." She took the liberty of saying how she felt, and there were quarrels—one, especially, about Félicité.

Going down the hall the previous night the elder Madame Bovary had surprised her with a man—a man of about forty, with dark chin whiskers, who had slipped out through the kitchen when he had heard her coming. When she reported this, Emma burst out laughing; the older woman lost her temper, declaring that unless one cared nothing for morals oneself, one was bound to keep an eye on the morals of one's servants.

"What kind of social circles do *you* frequent?" Emma retorted, with such an impertinent stare that her mother-in-law asked her whether in taking her servant's part it wasn't really herself that she was defending.

"Get out!" the young woman cried, springing from her chair.

"Emma! Mother!" cried Charles, trying to stop the argument. But in their rage they both rushed from the room.

"What manners!" Emma sneered when he came to her. And she stamped with fury: "What a peasant!"

He hurried to his mother and found her close to hysterics. "Such insolence! She's irresponsible! Maybe worse!"

And she declared she would leave the house at once unless her daughter-in-law came to her and apologized. So Charles sought out his wife again and begged her to give in. He implored her on his knees. "Oh, all right, I'll do it," she said finally.

She held out her hand to her mother-in-law with the dignity of a marquise: "*Excusez-moi, Madame.*" And then in her own room she flung herself flat on the bed and wept like a child, her head buried in the pillow.

She and Rodolphe had agreed that in case of an emergency she would fasten a piece of white paper to the blind, so that if he happened to be in Yonville he could go immediately into the lane behind the house. Emma hung out the signal; after waiting three-quarters of an hour she suddenly saw Rodolphe at the corner of the market. She was tempted to open the window and call to him; as she hesitated he disappeared. She sank back hopelessly in her chair.

But after a short time she thought she heard someone on the sidewalk: it must be he. She went downstairs and across the yard. He was outside the gate. She flung herself into his arms.

"Be careful!" he warned.

"Ah, if you knew what I've been through," she breathed.

And she proceeded to tell him everything—hurriedly, disjointedly, exaggerating some facts and inventing others, and putting in so many parentheses that he lost the thread of her story.

"Come, angel, be brave! Cheer up! Be patient!"

"But I've been patient for four years! I've suffered for four years! A love like ours is something to boast of! I'm on the rack, with those people! I can't stand it any longer! Rescue me, for God's sake!"

She clung to him. Her tear-filled eyes were flashing like undersea fires; her breast rose and fell in quick gasps; never had he found her so desirable. He lost his head. "What must we do?" he said. "What do you want me to do?"

"Oh! Take me away!" she cried. "I implore you: take me away!"

And she crushed her lips to his, as though to catch the consent she hadn't dared hope for—the consent that was now breathed out in a kiss.

"But . . ." Rodolphe began.

"What is it?"

"What about your little girl?"

She pondered a few moments; then: "We'll take her with us—it's the only way."

"What a woman!" he thought as he watched her move off. She had quickly slipped back into the garden: someone was calling her.

The elder Madame Bovary was astonished, the next few days, by her daughter-in-law's transformation. Emma was docility itself, deferential to the point of asking her for a recipe for pickles.

Was it her way of covering her tracks more thoroughly? Or was it a kind of voluptuous stoicism—a deliberate, deeper savoring of the bitterness of everything she was about to abandon? Scarcely the latter, for she noticed nothing around her: she was living as though immersed in advance in her future happiness. With Rodolphe she talked of nothing else. She would lean on his shoulder, and murmur:

"Think of what it will be like when we're in the stagecoach! Can you imagine it? Is it possible? The moment I feel the carriage moving, I think I'll have the sensation we're going up in a balloon, sailing up into the clouds. I'm counting the days. Are you?"

Never had Madame Bovary been as beautiful as now. She had that indefinable beauty that comes from happiness, enthusiasm, success—a beauty that is nothing more or less than a harmony of temperament and circumstances. Her desires, her sorrows, her experience of sensuality, her evergreen illusions, had developed her step by step, like a flower nourished by manure and by the rain, by the wind and the sun; and she was finally blooming in the fullness of her nature. Her eyelids seemed strangely perfect when she half closed them in a long amorous glance; and each of her deep sighs dilated her fine nostrils and raised the fleshy corners of her lips, lightly shadowed by dark down. Some artist skilled in corruption seemed to have designed the knot of her hair: it lay on her neck coiled in a heavy mass, twisted carelessly and always a little differently, for every day it was loosened by embraces. Her voice now took on softer inflections; her body, too; something subtle and penetrating emanated from the very folds of her dress, from the very arch of her foot. Charles found her exquisite and utterly irresistible, as in the first days of their marriage.

When he returned home in the middle of the night he dared not wake her. The porcelain night-light cast a trembling circular glow on the ceiling; and the drawn curtains of the cradle made it look like a tiny white hut swelling out in the darkness beside the bed. Charles looked at both sleepers. He thought he could hear the light breathing of his child. She would be growing rapidly now; every season would bring a change. Already he saw her coming home from school at the end of the day, laughing, her blouse spotted with ink, her basket on her arm. Then they would have to send her away to boarding school: that would cost a good deal—how would they manage? He thought and thought about it. He had the idea of renting a little farm on the outskirts, one that he could supervise himself mornings, as he rode out to see his patients. He would put the profits aside, in the savings bank; later he would buy securities of some kind. Besides, his practice would grow: he was counting on it, for he wanted Berthe to have a good education; he wanted her to be accomplished, to take piano lessions. Ah! How pretty she would be later, at fifteen! She would look just like her mother; and like her, in the summer, she would wear a great straw hat: from a distance they'd be taken for sisters. He pictured her sewing at night beside them in the lamplight; she would embroider slippers for him, and look after the house; she would fill their lives with her sweetness and her gaiety. And then he would think about her marriage. They would find her some fine young man with a good position, who would make her happy. And her happiness would last for ever and ever.

Emma wasn't asleep at such times. She was only pretending to be; and as Charles gradually sank into slumber beside her she lay awake dreaming different dreams.

A team of four horses, galloping every day for a week, had been whirling her and Rodolphe toward a new land from which they would never return. On and on the carriage bore them, and they sat there, arms entwined, saying not a word. Often from a mountaintop they would espy some splendid city, with domes, bridges, ships, forests of lemon trees, and white marble cathedrals whose pointed steeples were crowned with storks' nests. Here the horses slowed, picking their way over the great paving-stones, and the ground was strewn with bouquets of flowers tossed at them by women laced in red bodices. The ringing of bells and the braying of mules mingled with the murmur of guitars and the sound of gushing fountains; pyramids of fruit piled at the foot of pale statues were cooled by the flying spray, and the statues themselves seemed to smile through the streaming water. And then one night they arrived in a fishing village, where brown nets were drying in the wind along the cliff and the line of cottages. Here they stopped: this would be their dwelling place. They would live in a low flat-roofed house in the shade of a palm tree, on a bay beside the sea. They would ride in gondolas, swing in hammocks; and their lives would be easy and ample like the silk clothes they wore, warm like the soft nights that enveloped them, starry like the skies they gazed upon. Nothing specific stood out against the vast background of the future that she thus evoked: the days were all of them splendid, and as alike as the waves of the sea; and the whole thing hovered on the horizon, infinite, harmonious, blue and sparkling in the sun. But then the baby would cough in the cradle, or Bovary would give a snore louder than the rest, and Emma wouldn't fall asleep till morning, when dawn was whitening the windowpanes and Justin was already opening the shutters of the pharmacy.

She had sent for Monsieur Lheureux and told him she would be needing a cloak: "A long cloak with a deep collar and a lining."

"You're going on a trip?" he asked.

"No! But . . . Anyway, I can count on you to get it, can't I? Soon?"

He bowed.

"I'll want a trunk, too. Not too heavy, roomy."

"I know the kind you mean. About three feet by a foot and a half, the sort they're making now."

"And an overnight bag."

"A little too much smoke not to mean fire," Lheureux said to himself.

"And here," said Madame Bovary, unfastening her watch from her belt. "Take this: you can pay for the things out of what you get for it."

But the shopkeeper protested. She was wrong to suggest such a thing, he said; they were well acquainted; he trusted her completely. She mustn't be childish. But she insisted that he take at least the chain, and Lheureux had put it in his pocket and was on his way out when she called him back.

"Hold the luggage for me," she said. "As for the cloak"—she pretended to ponder the question—"don't bring that to me, either. But give me the address of the shop and tell them to have it ready for me when I come."

They were to elope the following month. She would leave Yonville as though to go shopping in Rouen. Rodolphe was to arrange for their reservations and their passports, and would write to Paris to make sure that they would have the coach to themselves as far as Marseilles; and there they would buy a barouche and continue straight on toward Genoa. She would send her things to Lheureux's, whence they would be loaded directly onto the Hirondelle, thus arousing no one's suspicions. In all these plans there was never a mention of little Berthe. Rodolphe avoided speaking of her: perhaps Emma had forgotten her.

He said he needed two weeks more, to wind up some affairs; then, at the end of the first of them, he said he would need an additional two; then he said he was sick; then he went on a trip somewhere. The month of August passed. Finally they decided they would leave without fail on the fourth of September, a Monday.

The Saturday night before that Monday, Rodolphe arrived earlier than usual.

"Is everything ready?" she asked him.

"Yes."

They strolled around the flower beds and sat on the terrace wall.

"You seem sad," said Emma.

"No, why?"

But he kept looking at her strangely—with unusual softness and tenderness.

"Is it because you're going away?" she asked. "Leaving everything that's dear to you, everything that makes up your life? I understand that. . . . But I have nothing—nothing in the world. You're my everything. And I'll be yours. I'll be your family, your country; I'll look after you, I'll love you."

"How sweet you are!" he cried, clasping her in his arms.

"Am I really?" she laughed, melting with pleasure. "Do you love me? Swear that you do?"

"Do I love you! Do I! I adore you, darling!"

The moon, a deep red disc, was rising straight out of the earth beyond the meadows. They could see it climb swiftly between the poplar branches that partially screened it like a torn black curtain; and finally, dazzlingly white, it shone high above them in the empty sky illumined by its light. Now, moving more slowly, it poured onto a stretch of the river a great brightness that flashed like a million stars; and this silvery gleam seemed to be writhing in its depths like a headless serpent covered with luminous scales. It looked, too, like a monstrous many-branched candlestick dripping with molten diamonds. The night spread softly around them; patches of shadow hung in the leaves of the trees. Emma, her eyes half closed, drank in the cool breeze with deep sighs. Lost in their revery, they said not a word. Full and silent as the flowing river, languid as the perfume of the syringas, the sweetness they had known in earlier days once again surged up in their hearts, casting on their memories longer and more melancholy shadows than those of the motionless willows on the grass. Now and again some prowling night animal, hedgehog or weasel, disturbed the leaves; or they heard the sound of a ripe peach as it dropped to the ground.

"What a lovely night!" said Rodolphe.

"We'll have many more," Emma answered.

And as though speaking to herself:

"Yes, it will be good to be traveling. . . . But why should I feel sad? Is it fear of the unknown, or the effect of leaving everything I'm used to? No—it's from too much happiness. How weak of me! Forgive me!"

"There's still time," he cried. "Think carefully—you might be sorry!"

"Never!" she answered impetuously.

And moving close to him:

"What harm can come to me? There's not a desert, not a precipice, not an ocean, that I wouldn't cross with you. Living together will be like an embrace that's tighter and more perfect every day. There'll be nothing to bother us, no cares—nothing in our way. We'll be alone, entirely to ourselves, for ever and ever. Say something, darling! Answer me!"

At regular intervals he answered, "Yes . . . yes . . ." Her fingers were in his hair, and through the great tears that were welling from her eyes she kept repeating his name in a childish voice:

"Rodolphe! Rodolphe! Sweet little Rodolphe!"

Midnight struck.

"Midnight!" she said. "Now it's tomorrow! One more day!"

He stood up to go; and as though his movement were the signal for their flight, Emma suddenly brightened.

"You have the passports?"

"Yes."

"You haven't forgotten anything?"

"No."

"You're sure?"

"Absolutely."

"And you'll be waiting for me at the Hotel de Provence at noon?"

He nodded.

"Till tomorrow, then," said Emma, giving him a last caress.

And she watched him go.

He did not turn around. She ran after him, and leaning out over the water among the bushes:

"Till tomorrow!" she cried.

Already he was on the other side of the river, walking quickly across the meadow.

After several minutes Rodolphe stopped; and when he saw her in her white dress gradually vanishing into the shadows like a wraith, his heart began to pound so violently that he leaned against a tree to keep from falling.

"God, what a fool I am!" he muttered with an obscene curse. "But she certainly made a pretty mistress!"

Emma's beauty and all the joys of their love rushed back into his mind; and for a moment he softened. But then he turned against her.

"After all," he cried, gesticulating and talking aloud to himself to strengthen his resolution, "I can't spend the rest of my life abroad! I can't be saddled with a child! All that trouble! All that expense! No! No! Absolutely not! It would be too stupid!"

XIII

As soon as he reached home Rodolphe sat down at his desk, under the stag's-head trophy that hung on the wall. But when he took up his pen he couldn't think of what to write, and he leaned on his elbows and pondered. Emma seemed to have receded into a far-off past, as though the resolution he had just made had put a great distance between them.

In order to recapture some feeling of her he went to the wardrobe at the head of his bed and took out an old Rheims cookie box that was his storage place for letters from women. Out of it came a smell of damp dust and withered roses. The first thing his eye fell on was a handkerchief spotted with faint stains. It was one of Emma's: she had had a nosebleed one day when they were out together—he hadn't remembered it till now. Then he took up something that had been knocking against the sides of the box: it was the miniature she had given him; she looked much too fussily dressed, he thought, and her ogling expression was preposterous. He kept staring at the artist's handiwork in an attempt to evoke the model as he remembered her, and this gradually resulted in Emma's features becoming confused in his memory, as though the real face and the painted face had been rubbing against each other and wearing each other away. Finally he read some of her letters. They were as brief, as technical, as urgent as business letters, filled chiefly with details pertaining to their trip. He wanted to reread the longer ones, the earlier ones; they were further down in the box, and to get at them he had to disarrange everything else. He found himself mechanically going through the pile of letters and other things, turning up a heterogeneous assortment—bouquets, a garter, a black mask, pins, locks of hair. So many locks of hair! Brunette and blond: some of them, catching in the metal hinges of the box, had broken off as he opened it.

He rummaged among his souvenirs, lingering on the differences of hand-writing and style in the letters—as marked as the differences of spelling. There were affectionate letters, jolly letters, facetious letters, melancholy letters; there were some that begged for love and others that begged for money. Now and then a word brought back a face, a gesture, the sound of a voice; certain letters brought back nothing at all.

All those women, thronging into his memory, got in each other's way; none of them stood out above the rest, leveled down as they all were by the measure of his love. He took up handfuls of the various letters and for some minutes amused himself by letting them stream from one hand to another. In the end he lost interest in the game and put the box back into the wardrobe. "What a lot of nonsense!" he said to himself.

This accurately summed up his opinion, for his companions in pleasure, like children playing in a schoolyard, had so trampled his heart that nothing green could grow there; indeed they were more casual than children—they hadn't even scribbled their names on the walls.

"Come now," he said to himself. "Get busy."

He began to write:

"You must be courageous, Emma: the last thing I want to do is ruin your life. . . ."

"That's absolutely true, after all," he assured himself "I'm acting in her interest; I'm only being honest."

"Have you given really serious thought to your decision? Do you realize into what abyss I was about to hurl you, poor darling? You don't, I'm sure. You were going ahead blind and confident, full of faith in happiness, in the future. . . . Ah! Poor wretched, insane creatures that we are!"

Here Rodolphe paused, looking for some good excuse.

"I could tell her that I've lost all my money. . . . No—that wouldn't stop her anyway: I'd have to go through the whole thing again later. Is there any way of making such women come to their senses?"

He thought for a while, then added:

"I'll never forget you—believe me—and I'll always feel the deepest devotion to you. But some day sooner or later our passion would have cooled—inevitably—it's the way with everything human. We would have had moments of weariness. Who knows—I might even have had the dreadful anguish of witnessing your remorse—and of sharing in it, since it would have been I who caused it. The very thought of the grief in store for you is a torture to me, Emma! Forget me! Why was it ordained that we should meet? Why were you so beautiful? Is the fault mine? In God's name, no! No! Fate alone is to blame—nothing and no one but fate!"

"That's always an effective word," he remarked to himself.

"Ah! Had you been a shallow-hearted creature like so many others, I could very well have gone ahead and let things happen as they might—purely for what was in it for myself—in that case without danger to you. But that marvelous intensity of feelings you have—such a delight for those who know you, such a source of anguish for yourself!—kept you—adorable woman that you are—from realizing the falsity of the position the future held for us. At first I, too, gave it no thought—I was lying in the shade of that ideal happiness we dreamed of as under a poison tree, without thought for the consequences."

"Maybe she'll think I'm giving her up out of stinginess. . . . What's it to me if she does! Let her. . . . And let's get it over with!"

"The world is cruel, Emma. It would have pursued us everywhere. You'd have been subjected to indiscreet questions—calumny—scorn—even insult, perhaps. You—insulted! Oh, my darling! And I would have been the cause of it—I, who wanted to put you on a throne—I, who shall carry away the thought of you like a talisman! Yes—away—for I am punishing myself for the harm I have done you—I am going into exile! Where? How can I tell?

My poor mad brain can give no answer. Adieu, Emma! Continue to be as good as you have always been! Never forget the unfortunate man who lost you! Teach your child my name: tell her to include me in her prayers."

The flames of the two candles were flickering. Rodolphe got up to close the window; and then, back at his desk:

"That's all, I guess," he said to himself. "Oh—just this little bit more, to keep her from coming after me":

"I shall be far away when you read these unhappy lines; I dare not linger—the temptation to see you again is all but irresistible! This is no moment for weakness! I shall come back; and perhaps one day we'll be able to speak of our love with detachment, as a thing of the past. Adieu!"

And he appended one more, last adieu, this time written as two words—"A Dieu!": it seemed to him in excellent taste.

"How shall I sign it?" he wondered. " 'Devotedly'? No . . . 'Your friend'? Yes—that's it."

"Your friend."

He read over his letter and thought it was good.

"Poor little thing!" he thought, suddenly sentimental. "She'll think me as unfeeling as a stone. There ought to be a few tears on it, but weeping's beyond me—what can I do?" He poured some water in a glass, wet a finger, and holding it high above the page shook off a large drop. It made a pale blot on the ink. Then, looking around for something to seal the letter with, his eye fell on the signet ring with the motto "Amor nel cor." "Scarcely appropriate under the circumstances, but what the . . ."

Whereupon he smoked three pipes and went to bed.

When he got up the next day (about two in the afternoon—he slept late) Rodolphe had some apricots picked and arranged in a basket. At the bottom, hidden under some vine leaves, he put the letter; and he ordered Girard, his plough-boy, to deliver it carefully to Madame Bovary. This was his usual way of corresponding with her, sending her fruit or game according to the season.

"If she asks you anything about me," he said, "tell her I've left for a trip. Be sure to give the basket to her personally. Get going, now, and do it right!"

Girard put on his new smock, tied his handkerchief over the apricots, and plodding along in his great hobnailed boots, he set out tranquilly for Yonville.

When he reached Madame Bovary's he found her helping Félicité stack linen on the kitchen table.

"Here," said the plough-boy. "My master sent you this."

A feeling of dread came over her, and as she fumbled in her pocket for some change she stared at the peasant with haggard eyes; he in turn looked at her in bewilderment, failing to understand why anyone should be so upset by such a present. Finally he left. Félicité stayed where she was. The suspense was too great for Emma: she ran into the other room as though for the purpose of carrying in the apricots, dumped them out of the basket, tore away the leaves, found the letter and opened it; and as though she were fleeing from a fire she ran panic-stricken up the stairs toward her room.

Charles had come in: she caught sight of him; he spoke to her; whatever he said, she didn't hear it; and she hurried on up the second flight of stairs, breathless, distracted, reeling, clutching the horrible piece of paper that rattled in her hand like a sheet of tin. At the third-floor landing she stopped outside the closed attic door.

She tried to calm herself: only then did she think of the letter. She must finish it—she didn't dare. Besides, where could she read it? How? She'd be seen.

"I'll be all right in here," she thought; and she pushed open the door and went in.

There the roof slates were throwing down a heat that was all but unbearable; it pressed on her so that she could scarcely breathe. She dragged herself over to the dormer, whose shutters were closed; she pulled back the bolt, and the dazzling sunlight poured in.

Out beyond the rooftops, the open countryside stretched as far as eye could see. Below her the village square was empty; the stone sidewalk glittered; the weathervanes on the houses stood motionless. From the lower floor of a house at the corner came a whirring noise with strident changes of tone: Binet was at his lathe.

Leaning against the window frame she read the letter through, now and then giving an angry sneer. But the more she tried to concentrate, the more confused her thoughts became. She saw Rodolphe, heard his voice, clasped him in her arms; and a series of irregular palpitations, thudding in her breast like great blows from a battering ram, came faster and faster. She cast her eyes about her, longing for the earth to open up. Why not end it all? What was holding her back? She was free to act. And she moved forward. "Do it! Do it!" she ordered herself, peering down at the pavement.

The rays of bright light reflected directly up to her from below were pulling the weight of her body toward the abyss. The surface of the village square seemed to be sliding dizzily up the wall of her house; the floor she was standing on seemed to be tipped up on end, like a pitching ship. Now she was at the very edge, almost hanging out, a great emptiness all around her. The blue of the sky was flooding her; her head felt hollow and filled with the rushing of the wind: all she had to do now was to surrender, yield to the onrush. And the lathe kept whirring, like an angry voice calling her.

But then she heard another voice: "Where are you?" It was Charles.

She listened.

"Where are you? Come down!"

The thought that she had just escaped death almost made her faint from terror; she closed her eyes; then she gave a start as she felt the touch of a hand on her sleeve. It was Félicité.

"Monsieur is waiting, Madame. The soup is on the table."

And she had to go down—had to sit through a meal!

She did her best to eat. Each mouthful choked her. She unfolded her napkin as though to inspect the darns, and began really seriously to devote her attention to it and count the stitches. Suddenly the thought of the letter came back to her. Had she lost it? Where would she lay hands on it? But in her exhaustion of mind she could invent no excuse for leaving the table. Besides, she didn't dare: she was terrified of Charles; he knew everything—she was sure he must! And oddly enough he chose that moment to say:

"I gather we shan't be seeing Monsieur Rodolphe for some time."

She started: "Who told you so?"

"Who told me?" he said, surprised by her abrupt tone. "Girard—I saw him a few minutes ago at the door of the Café Français. He's left for a trip, or he's about to leave."

A sob escaped her.

"What's so surprising about it? He's always going off on pleasure trips. Why shouldn't he? When you're a bachelor and well off . . . Besides, he knows how to give himself a good time, our friend. He's a real playboy. Monsieur Langlois once told me . . ."

He decorously broke off as the maid came in.

Félicité gathered up the apricots that lay scattered over the sideboard and put them back into the basket. Unaware that his wife had turned scarlet, Charles asked for them, took one, and bit into it.

"Oh, perfect!" he said. "Try one."

He held the basket out toward her, and she gently pushed it away.

"Smell them: such fragrance!" he said, moving it back and forth before her.

"I'm stifling in here!" she cried, leaping to her feet. But she forced herself to conquer her spasm. "It's nothing," she said. "Nothing. Just nerves. Sit down; eat your fruit."

Her great dread was lest he question her, insist on doing something for her, never leave her to herself.

Charles had obediently sat down and was spitting apricot pits into his hand and transferring them to his plate.

Suddenly a blue tilbury crossed the square at a smart trot. Emma gave a cry, fell abruptly backwards and lay on the floor.

Rodolphe had decided, after a good deal of thought, to leave for Rouen. Since the Yonville road was the only route from La Huchette to Buchy, he had to pass through the village; and Emma had recognized him in the glow of his carriage lights as they flashed in the gathering dusk like a streak of lightning.

The commotion at the Bovarys' brought the pharmacist running. The table had been knocked over and all the plates were on the floor; gravy, meat, knives, the salt cellar and the cruet stand littered the room; Charles was calling for help; Berthe was frightened and in tears; and Félicité with trembling hands was unlacing Madame, whose entire body was racked with convulsions.

"I'll run to my laboratory and get a little aromatic vinegar," said the apothecary.

And when he had returned and held the flacon under her nostrils and she opened her eyes:

"I knew it," he said. "This stuff would resuscitate a corpse."

"Speak to us!" cried Charles. "Say something! Can you hear me? It's Charles—Charles, who loves you. Do you recognize me? See—here's your little girl—kiss her, darling."

The child stretched out her arms toward her mother, trying to clasp them around her neck. But Emma turned her head away. "No, no," she said brokenly. "Leave me alone."

She fainted again, and they carried her to her bed.

She lay there on her back, mouth open, eyes closed, hands flat beside her, motionless, white as a wax statue. Two rivulets of tears trickled slowly from her eyes onto the pillow.

Charles stood at the foot of the bed. At his side the pharmacist was observing the thoughtful silence appropriate to life's solemn occasions. Then:

"I think she'll be all right," he said. "The paroxysm seems to be over."

"Yes, she's resting a little now," Charles answered, watching her sleep. "Poor thing! Poor thing! It's a real relapse."

Then Homais asked for details, and Charles told him how she had been stricken suddenly while eating apricots.

"Extraordinary!" said the pharmacist. "Still, the apricots may very well have caused the syncope. Some natures react so strongly to certain odors! It would be an interesting subject to study, in both its pathological and its physiological aspects. The priests are well aware of the importance of this phenomenon—they've always made use of aromatics in their ceremonies. They employ them deliberately, to deaden the understanding and induce ecstatic states—women lend themselves to it easily, they're so much more delicate than the rest of us. Cases are recorded of women fainting from the smell of burnt horn, fresh bread . . ."

"Take care not to wake her!" Bovary warned softly.

"And it's not only humans who are subject to such anomalies," continued the apothecary. "Animals are, too. You are certainly not ignorant of the intensely aphrodisiac effect produced by *nepeta cataria,* vulgarly called catnip, on the feline species; and to mention another example—one whose authenticity I myself can vouch for—Bridoux, one of my old schoolmates, now in business in the Rue Malpalu, has a dog which has convulsions if you show it a snuffbox. Bridoux sometimes makes him perform for his friends, at his suburban residence in Bois-Guillaume. Would you believe that a simple sternutative could work such havoc in the organism of a quadruped? It's extremely curious, don't you find?"

"Yes," said Charles, who wasn't listening.

"This is but another illustration," said the pharmacist, smiling with an air of benign self-satisfaction, "of the innumerable irregularities of the nervous system. As far as Madame is concerned, I confess she has always seemed to me a genuine sensitive. For that reason, my good friend, I advise you not to use any of those so-called remedies which attack the temperament under the guise of attacking the symptoms. No—no futile medication. Just a regimen. Sedatives, emollients, dulcifiers. And then, don't you think it would be a good thing to rouse her imagination—something striking?"

"How? What?"

"Ah, that's the problem. That is indeed the problem. 'That is the question,' " he quoted in English, "as I read in the paper recently."

Just then Emma, waking from her sleep, cried: "The letter? Where is the letter?"

They thought her delirious, and from midnight on she was: there could be no doubt that it was brain fever.

For forty-three days Charles did not leave her side. He neglected all his patients; he never lay down; he was constantly feeling her pulse, applying mustard plasters and cold compresses. He sent Justin to Neufchâtel for ice; the ice melted on the way; he sent him back. He called in Doctor Canivet for consultation; he had Doctor Larivière, his old teacher, come from Rouen; he was desperate. What frightened him most was Emma's degree of prostration: she didn't speak, she gave no sign of comprehending or even hearing anything that was said to her; and she seemed to be in no pain. It was as though her body and her soul together had sought rest after all their tribulations. Toward the middle of October she could sit up in bed, propped against pillows. Charles wept when he saw her eat her first slice of bread and jam. Her strength returned; she left her bed for a few hours each afternoon; and one day when she felt better than usual he got her to take his arm and try a walk in the garden. The gravel on the paths was almost hidden under dead leaves; she walked slowly, dragging her slippers; and leaning on Charles's shoulder she smiled continuously.

They made their way to the far end, near the terrace. She drew herself up slowly and held her hand above her eyes: she stared into the distance, the far distance; but on the horizon there were only great grass fires, smoking on the hills.

"You'll tire yourself, darling," said Bovary.

And guiding her gently, trying to induce her to enter the arbor:

"Sit on this bench: you'll be comfortable."

"Oh no! Not there! Not there!" she said in a faltering voice.

Immediately she felt dizzy; and beginning that night there was another onset of her illness. This time it was less clearly identifiable, more complex. Now her heart would pain her, now her chest, now her head, now her limbs. She had vomiting spells, which Charles feared were the first symptoms of cancer.

And as though that were not enough, the poor fellow had money worries!

XIV

To begin with, he didn't know how to make good to Monsieur Homais for all the medicaments that had come from the pharmacy: as a doctor he might have been excused from paying for them, but the obligation embarrassed him. Then, what with the cook acting as mistress, the household expenses were getting to be alarming; there was a deluge of bills; the tradespeople were grumbling; Monsieur Lheureux, especially, was harassing him. The dry-goods dealer, taking advantage of the circumstances to pad his bill, had chosen a moment at the very height of Emma's illness to deliver the cloak, the overnight bag, two trunks instead of one, and a number of other things as well. Charles protested that he had no use for them, but the shopkeeper arrogantly retorted that all those items had been ordered and that he wouldn't take them back. Besides, he said, it would be upsetting to Madame in her convalescence. Monsieur should think it over. In short, he was determined to stand on his rights and carry the matter to court rather than give in. A little later Charles ordered that everything be sent back to the shop; but Félicité forgot; and he had other things on his mind and didn't think of them. Monsieur Lheureux brought the matter up again, and by alternating threats and moans got Charles to sign a six-months' promissory note. No sooner had he signed than he had a bold idea: he would try to borrow a thousand francs from Monsieur Lheureux. So he awkwardly asked whether there was any chance of this, explaining that it would be for one year and at any rate of interest Lheureux might specify. Lheureux ran to his shop, brought back the money, and dictated another promissory note, whereby Bovary promised to pay to his order, the first of the following September, the sum of 1,070 francs. Together with the 180 already stipulated, that came to just 1,250. In this way, loaning at the rate of six percent, plus his commission and at least one-third mark-up on the goods, the whole thing would bring him in a clear 130 francs' profit in twelve months; and he hoped that it wouldn't stop there, that the notes wouldn't be met but renewed, and that his poor little capital, after benefiting from the doctor's care like a patient in a sanatorium, would eventually come back to him considerably plumper, fat enough to burst the bag.

Everything Lheureux touched was successful at this moment. His had been the winning bid for the cider-supply contract at the Neufchâtel public hospital; Maître Guillaumin was promising him some shares in the peatery at Grumesnil; and he was thinking of setting up a new coach service between Argueil and Rouen: such a thing would quickly spell the end of the old rattletrap at the Lion d'Or, and being faster and cheaper and carrying a bigger pay load would give him a monopoly of the Yonville trade.

Charles wondered more than once how he was going to be able to pay back so large a sum the following year; and racking his brains he imagined various expedients, such as applying to his father or selling off something. But his father would turn a deaf ear, and he himself owned nothing that could be sold. The difficulties he foresaw were so formidable that he quickly banished the disagreeable subject from his mind. He reproached himself for having let it distract him from Emma—as though his every thought were her property and he were filching something from her if he took his mind off her for a second.

It was a severe winter. Madame's convalescence was slow. On fine days they pushed her armchair to the window—the one overlooking the square, for she had taken an aversion to the garden, and the blind on that side was always down. She asked that her horse be sold: things that had once given her pleasure she now disliked. She seemed to have no thought for anything beyond her own health. She ate her tiny meals in bed, rang for the maid to ask about her tisanes or just to chat. All this while the snow on the roof of the market filled the room with its monotonous white reflection; then came a spell of rain. And every day Emma looked forward, with a kind of anxious expectation, to the same, unfailingly recurring, trivial events, little though they mattered to her. The greatest of these was the nightly arrival of the Hirondelle, when Madame Lefrançois shouted, other voices replied, and Hippolyte's stable lamp, as he looked for luggage under the hood, shone out like a star in the darkness. At noon Charles always returned from his rounds; after lunch he went out again; then she took a cup of bouillon; and toward five, at the close of day, children passed the house on their way home from school, dragging their wooden shoes along the sidewalk, and invariably, one after the other, hitting their rulers against the shutter hooks.

About this time Monsieur Bournisien usually stopped in. He would ask after her health, give her news, and exhort her to prayer in an affectionate, informal way that wasn't without its charm. Just the sight of his cassock she found comforting.

One day at the height of her sickness, when she thought she was dying, she had asked for Communion; and as her room was made ready for the sacrament—the chest of drawers cleared of its medicine bottles and transformed into an altar, the floor strewn with dahlia blossoms by Félicité—Emma felt something powerful pass over her that rid her of all pain, all perception, all feeling. Her flesh had been relieved of its burdens, even the burden of thought; another life was beginning; it seemed to her that her spirit, ascending to God, was about to find annihilation in this love, like burning incense dissolving in smoke. The sheets of her bed were sprinkled with holy water; the priest drew the white host from the sacred pyx; and she was all but swooning with celestial bliss as she advanced her lips to receive the body of the Saviour. The curtains of her alcove swelled out softly around her like clouds; and the beams of the two wax tapers burning on the chest of drawers seemed to her like dazzling emanations of divine light. Then she let her head fall back: through the vastnesses of space seemed to come the music of seraphic harps; and on a golden throne in an azure sky she thought she saw God the Father in all His glory, surrounded by the saints bearing branches of green palm; He was gesturing majestically, and obedient angels with flaming wings were descending to the earth to bear her to Him in their arms.

This splendid vision, the most beautiful of all possible dreams, stayed in her memory—not eclipsing all else as at the time it occurred, but no less intensely sweet; and she kept straining to recapture the original sensation. Her soul, aching with pride, was at last finding rest in Christian humility; and luxuriating in her own weakness she turned her eyes inward and watched the destruction of her will, which was to open wide the way for an onrush of grace. She was filled with wonderment at the discovery that there was a bliss greater than mere happiness—a love different from and transcending all others—a love without break and without end, a love that increased throughout eternity! Among the illusions born of her hope she glimpsed a realm of purity in which she aspired to dwell: it hovered above the earth, merging with the sky. She conceived the idea of becoming a saint. She bought rosaries and festooned herself with holy medals; she wished she had an emerald-studded reliquary within reach at her bed's head, to kiss every night.

The priest was enchanted by her change of heart, though he was of the opinion that her faith might by its very fervor come to border on heresy and even on extravagance. But not being versed in these matters once they went beyond a certain point, he wrote Monsieur Boulard, the bishop's bookseller, and asked him to send him "something particularly good for a lady who had a very fine mind." As casually as though he were shipping trinkets to savages, the bookseller made up a heterogeneous package of everything just then current in the religious book trade—little question-and-answer manuals, pamphlets couched in the contemptuous language made popular by Monsieur de Maistre,[5] so-called novels in pink bindings and sugary style concocted by romantic-minded seminarists or reformed blue-stockings. There were titles such as *Think It Over Carefully; The Man of the World at the Feet of Mary, by Monsieur de——, recipient of several decorations; The Errors of Voltaire, for the use of the young;* etc.

Madame Bovary wasn't yet sufficiently recovered in mind to apply herself seriously to anything; and besides, she plunged into all this literature far too precipitately. The regulations governing worship annoyed her; she disliked the arrogance of the polemical writings because of their relentless attacks

5. A major theorist (1753–1821) of Catholic conservatism. His books, *Du Pape* (1819) and *Soirées de Saint-Petersbourg* (1821), defended the power of the pope and the sovereign king and argued that the reign of evil on Earth has to be curbed by authority.

on people she had never heard of; and the secular stories flavored with religion seemed to her written out of such ignorance of the world that she was
unwittingly led away from the very truths she was longing to have confirmed.
Nevertheless she persisted; and when the volume fell from her hands she
was convinced that hers was the most exquisite Catholic melancholy that
had ever entered an ethereal soul.

As for the memory of Rodolphe, she had buried it in the depths of her
heart; and there it remained, as solemn and motionless as the mummy of a
pharaoh in an underground chamber. Her great love that lay thus embalmed
gave off a fragrance that permeated everything, adding a touch of tenderness
to the immaculate atmosphere in which she longed to live. When she knelt
at her Gothic *prie-dieu* she addressed the Lord in the same ardent words she
had formerly murmured to her lover in the ecstasies of adultery. It was her
way of praying for faith; but heaven showered no joy upon her, and she would
rise, her limbs aching, with a vague feeling that it was all a vast fraud. This
quest she considered meritorious in itself; and in the pride of her piety Emma
likened herself to those great ladies of yore whose fame she had dreamed of
while gazing at a portrait of La Vallière: how majestically they had trailed
the gorgeous trains of their long gowns, as they withdrew into seclusion to
shed at the feet of Christ all the tears of their life-wounded hearts!

Now she became wildly charitable. She sewed clothes for the poor, sent
firewood to women in childbed; and one day Charles came home to find
three tramps sitting at the kitchen table eating soup. She sent for her daughter—during her illness Charles had left the child with the nurse—and she
determined to teach her to read. Berthe wept and wept, but she never lost
her temper with her. It was a deliberately adopted attitude of resignation, of
indulgence toward all. She used a lofty term whenever she could:

"Is your stomach-ache all gone, my angel?" she would say to her daughter.

The elder Madame Bovary found nothing to reproach her for in all this,
except perhaps her mania for knitting undershirts for orphans instead of
mending her own dish towels. Harassed by the incessant quarrels in her own
home, the old lady enjoyed the peaceful atmosphere of this house; and she
prolonged her visit through Easter to escape the jibes of her husband, whose
invariable habit it was to order pork sausage on Good Friday.

In addition to the company of her mother-in-law, whom she found a
steadying influence because of her unswerving principles and solemn
demeanor, Emma nearly every day had other visits—from Madame Langlois,
Madame Caron, Madame Dubreuil, Madame Tuvache, and, regularly from
two to five, from Madame Homais, who—good soul that she was—had
always refused to believe any of the gossip that was spread about her neighbor. The Homais children visited her, too; Justin brought them. He came
with them up into her bedroom and stood quietly near the door, never saying
a word. Often while he was there Madame Bovary would start to dress, oblivious of him. She would begin by taking out her comb and tossing her head;
and the first time he saw her mass of black hair fall in ringlets to her knees,
it was for the boy like the sudden opening of a door upon something marvelous and new, something whose splendor frightened him.

Emma never noticed his silent eagerness or his timidity. She knew only
that love had disappeared from her life: she had no suspicion that it was
pulsating there so close to her, beneath that coarse shirt, in that adolescent

heart so open to the emanations of her beauty. Moreover, her detachment from everything had become so complete, her language was so sweet and the look in her eye so haughty, her behavior was so mercurial, that there was no longer any way of telling where selfishness and corruption ended and charity and virtue began. One night, for instance, she lost her temper with her servant, who was asking permission to go out and stammering some pretended reason. Then:

"So you love him, do you?" Emma suddenly demanded.

And without waiting for the blushing Félicité to answer, she added, resignedly:

"All right—run along! Enjoy yourself!"

When the weather turned mild she had the garden completely dug up and relandscaped. Bovary objected a little, but he was glad to see her finally caring about things, and she gave more and more evidence of this as her strength returned. She forbade the house to Madame Rollet the nurse, who during her convalescence had formed the habit of coming too often to the kitchen with her own two babes and her little boarder, the latter more ravenous than a cannibal. She cut down on visits from the Homais', discouraged all her other callers, and even went less regularly to church, thus eliciting the apothecary's approval.

"I was afraid you'd been taken in by the mumbo-jumbo," he said amicably.

The abbé Bournisien still came every day, after catechism class. He preferred to sit outdoors in the fresh air—in the "grove," as he called the arbor. This was the hour of Charles's return. Both men would be hot; Félicité would bring them sweet cider, and they would raise their glasses and drink to Madame's complete recovery.

Binet was often there: just below, that is—beside the terrace wall, fishing for crayfish. Bovary would invite him to join them for a drink; he prided himself on being an expert uncorker of cider jugs.

"First," he would say—glancing at his companions complacently and then giving an equally smug look at the landscape—"first you must hold the bottle upright on the table, like this. Then you cut the strings. And then you pry up the cork, a little at a time, gently, gently—the way they open seltzer water in restaurants."

But during this demonstration the cork would often pop out and the cider would splash one or another of them in the face; and the curé never failed to laugh his thick laugh and make his joke:

"Its excellence is certainly *striking!*"

He was a good-hearted fellow—there was no denying it—and he even expressed no objection one day when the pharmacist advised Charles to give Madame a treat and take her to the opera in Rouen, to hear the famous tenor, Lagardy. Homais was surprised at his silence, and asked him how he felt about it; and the priest declared that he considered music less dangerous to morals than literature.

The pharmacist sprang to the defense of letters. The theater, he claimed, served to expose prejudice: it taught virtue under the guise of entertainment:

"*Castigat ridendo mores,*[6] Monsieur Bournisien! Take most of Voltaire's

---

6. "It [comedy] reproves the manners, through laughter" (Latin); a slogan for comedy invented by the poet Jean de Santeuil (1630–1697) and given to the harlequin Dominique to put on the curtain of his theater.

tragedies, for example: it's clever the way he's stuck them full of philosophical remarks—they're a complete education in morals and diplomacy for the people."

"I saw a play once, called the *Gamin de Paris*,"[7] said Binet. "There's an old general in it that's absolutely first-class. A rich fellow seduces a working girl and the general slaps him down and at the end . . ."

"Of course," Homais went on, "there's bad literature just as there's bad pharmaceutics. But to make a blanket condemnation of the greatest of the fine arts seems to be a yokelism, a medievalism worthy of that abominable age when they imprisoned Galileo."[8]

"I know perfectly well," objected the priest, "that there are good writers who write good things. Still, the fact alone that people of different sexes are brought together in a glamorous auditorium that's the last word in worldly luxury—and then the heathenish disguises, the painted faces, the footlights, the effeminate voices—it all can't help encouraging a certain licentiousness and inducing evil thoughts and impure temptations. Such, at least, is the opinion of all the church fathers. After all," he added, suddenly assuming an unctuous tone and rolling himself a pinch of snuff, "if the church condemns play-going she has good reason for doing so: we must submit to her decrees."

"Why," demanded the apothecary, "does she excommunicate actors? They used to take part openly in ecclesiastical ceremonies, you know. Yes, they used to act right in the middle of the choir—put on farcical plays called mysteries. These often violated the laws of decency, I may say."

The priest's only answer was a groan, and the pharmacist persisted:

"It's the same in the Bible. There's more than one spicy bit in that book, you know—some pret-ty dar-ing things!"

And as Monsieur Bournisien made a gesture of annoyance:

"Ah! You'll agree that it's no book to give a young person! I'd be sorry if my daughter Athalie . . ."

"But *we* don't recommend the reading of the Bible!" cried the abbé impatiently. "It's the Protestants!"

"It makes no difference," said Homais. "I'm astonished that in this day and age—an age of enlightenment—anyone should persist in forbidding a form of intellectual diversion that's harmless, morally uplifting, and sometimes—isn't it true, Doctor?—even good for the health."

"I guess so." Charles made his answer in a vacant tone—perhaps because he shared Homais' opinion and didn't want to offend the priest, or perhaps because he had no opinion.

The conversation seemed to be at an end, when the pharmacist saw fit to make one last dig.

"I've known priests," he said, "who made a practice of going out in civilian clothes and watching leg shows."

"Come now," said the priest.

"Oh yes, I've known some!"

And once again separating his syllables by way of significant emphasis, Homais repeated:

"I—have—known—some!"

7. A comedy by Bayard and Vanderbusch performed in 1836 in Paris.   8. Galileo Galilei (1564–1642), astronomer who was confined to his house in Arcetri (near Florence) after his book propounding the view that the Earth circled around the sun was condemned by the Inquisition (in 1633).

"Well, then, they did wrong," said Bournisien with truly Christian patience.

"I should think so! And that wasn't all they were up to, either!" exclaimed the apothecary.

"Monsieur!" The priest jumped to his feet and glared so fiercely that the pharmacist was intimidated.

"All I mean," he said, much more mildly, "is that tolerance is the surest means of bringing souls into the church."

"Quite true, quite true," the curé conceded, sitting down again.

He left a moment or two later, however, and Homais said to the doctor:

"Quite a squabble! How did you like the way I got the better of him? Pretty good, eh? Anyway—follow my advice and take Madame to the opera, if only to give a priest a black eye for once in your life. If I could find a substitute I'd come with you. Don't lose any time getting tickets: Lagardy's giving only one performance—he's scheduled for an English tour at staggering fees. From what they say, he must be quite a lad. He's filthy with money. Everywhere he goes he takes along three mistresses and a cook. All those great artists burn their candles at both ends: they have to lead a wild kind of life—it stimulates their imagination. But they die in the poorhouse, because they haven't the sense to save money when they're young. Well, *bon appétit: à demain!"*

The idea of the opera took rapid root in Bovary's mind. He lost no time suggesting it to his wife. She shook her head, pleading fatigue, trouble and expense; but for once Charles didn't give in, so convinced was he that she would benefit from the excursion. He saw no reason for them not to go: his mother had sent him three hundred francs they had given up hope of getting, their debts of the moment were nothing tremendous, and Lheureux's notes weren't due for so long that there was no use thinking about them. Fancying that Emma was refusing out of consideration for him, Charles insisted the more strongly, and finally she gave in. The next day, at eight in the morning, they bundled themselves into the Hirondelle.

The apothecary, who had nothing in the world to keep him in Yonville, but who was firmly convinced that he couldn't absent himself even briefly, gave a sigh as he watched their departure.

"Bon voyage!" he called to them. "Some people have all the luck!"

And to Emma, who was wearing a blue silk dress with four rows of flounces:

"You're pretty as a picture! You'll be the belle of Rouen!"

The coach took them to the Hotel de la Croix-Rouge in the Place Beauvoisine. It was one of those inns such as you find on the edge of every provincial city, with large stables and small bedrooms, and chickens scratching for oats in the coach yard under muddy gigs belonging to traveling salesmen—comfortable, old-fashioned stopovers, with worm-eaten wooden balconies that creak in the wind on winter nights, constantly full of people, bustle and victuals, their blackened tabletops sticky with spilled coffee-and-brandies, their thick windowpanes yellowed by flies, their napkins spotted blue by cheap red wine. They always seem a little rustic, like farmhands in Sunday clothes; on the street side they have a café, and in back—on the country side—a vegetable garden. Charles went at once to buy tickets. He got the stage boxes mixed up with the top balconies, and the rest of the boxes with the orchestra; he asked for explanations, didn't understand them, was sent from the box office to the manager, came back to the hotel, went back to the box office again. All in all, between the theater and the outer boulevard he covered the entire length of the city several times over.

Madame bought herself a hat, gloves and a bouquet. Monsieur was nervous about missing the beginning; and without stopping for as much as a cup of bouillon they arrived at the theater before the doors were even open.

XV

There was a crowd waiting outside, lined up behind railings on both sides of the entrance. At the adjoining street corners huge posters in fancy lettering announced: "*Lucie de Lammermoor*[9] . . . Lagardy . . . Opéra . . . etc." It was a fine evening; everyone was hot: many a set of curls was drenched in sweat, and handkerchiefs were out, mopping red brows; now and again a soft breeze blowing from the river gently stirred the edges of the canvas awnings over café doors. But just a short distance away there was a coolness, provided by an icy draft smelling of tallow, leather and oil—the effluvia of the Rue des Charettes, with its great, gloomy, barrel-filled warehouses.

Fearing lest they appear ridiculous, Emma insisted that they stroll a bit along the river front before going in; and Bovary, by way of precaution, kept the tickets in his hand and his hand in his trousers pocket, pressed reassuringly against his stomach.

Her heart began to pound as they entered the foyer. A smile of satisfaction rose involuntarily to her lips at seeing the crowd hurry off to the right down the corridor, while she climbed the stairs leading to the first tier. She took pleasure, like a child, in pushing open the wide upholstered doors with one finger; she filled her lungs with the dusty smell of the corridors; and seated in her box she drew herself up with all the airs of a duchess.

The theater began to fill; opera glasses came out of cases; and subscribers exchanged greetings as they glimpsed one another across the house. The arts, for them, were a relaxation from the worries of buying and selling; that was why they had come; but it was quite impossible for them to forget business even here, and their conversation was about cotton, spirits and indigo. The old men looked blank and placid: with their gray-white hair and gray-white skin they were like silver medals that had been tarnished by lead fumes. The young beaux strutted in the orchestra: the openings of their waistcoats were bright with pink or apple-green cravats; and Madame Bovary looked admiringly down at them as they leaned with tightly yellow-gloved hands on their gold-knobbed walking sticks.

Meanwhile the candles were lighted on the music stands and the chandelier came down from the ceiling, the sparkle of its crystals filling the house with sudden gaiety; then the musicians filed in and there was a long cacophony of booming cellos, scraping violins, blaring horns, and piping flutes and flageolets. Then three heavy blows came from the stage; there was a roll of kettledrums and a series of chords from the brasses; and the curtain rose on an outdoor scene.

It was a crossroad in a forest, on the right a spring shaded by an oak. A

9. An opera by Gaetano Donizetti (1797–1848), first performed in Naples in 1835 (in Paris in 1837), based on Walter Scott's novel *The Bride of Lammermoor* (1819). See "Editor's Note," pp. 849–50.

group of country folk and nobles, all with tartans over their shoulders, sang a hunting chorus; then a captain strode in and inveighed against an evil spirit, raising both arms to heaven; another character joined him; they both walked off, and the huntsmen repeated their chorus.

She was back in the books she had read as a girl—deep in Walter Scott. She imagined she could hear the sound of Scottish pipes echoing through the mist across the heather. Her recollection of the novel made it easy for her to grasp the libretto; and she followed the plot line by line, elusive, half-forgotten memories drifting into her thoughts only to be dispelled by the onrush of the music. She let herself be lulled by the melodies, feeling herself vibrate to the very fiber of her being, as though the bows of the violins were playing on her nerve strings. She couldn't take in enough of the costumes, the sets, the characters, the painted trees that shook at the slightest footstep, the velvet bonnets, the cloaks, the swords—all those fanciful things that fluttered on waves of music as though in another world. Then a young woman came forward, tossing a purse to a squire in green. She was left along on the stage, and there came the sound of a flute, like the ripple of a spring or the warbling of a bird. Lucie, looking solemn, began her cavatina in G major: she uttered love laments, begged for wings. And at the moment Emma, too, longed that she might leave life behind and take wing in an embrace. Suddenly Edgar Lagardy came on stage.

He was pale to the point of splendor, with that marmoreal majesty sometimes found among the passionate races of the south. His stalwart figure was clad in a tight brown doublet; a small chased dagger swung at his left hip; and he rolled his eyes about him languorously and flashed his white teeth. People said that a Polish princess had heard him sing one night on the beach at Biarritz, where he was a boat boy, and had fallen in love with him; she had beggared herself for him, and he had left her for other women. This reputation as a ladies' man had done no disservice to his professional career. Shrewd ham actor that he was, he always saw to it that his publicity should include a poetic phrase or two about the charm of his personality and the sensibility of his soul. A fine voice, utter self-possession, more temperament than intelligence, more bombast than feeling—such were the principal attributes of this magnificent charlatan. There was a touch of the hairdresser about him, and a touch of the toreador.

He had the audience in transports from the first. He clasped Lucie in his arms, left her, returned to her, seemed in despair: he would shout with rage, then let his voice expire, plaintive and infinitely sweet; and the notes that poured from his bare throat were full of sobs and kisses. Emma strained forward to watch him, her fingernails scratching the plush of her box. Her heart drank its full of the melodious laments that hung suspended in the air against the sound of the double bases like the cries of shipwrecked sailors against the tumult of a storm. Here was the same ecstasy, the same anguish that had brought her to the brink of death. The soprano's voice seemed but the echo of her own soul, and this illusion that held her under its spell a part of her own life. But no one on earth had ever loved her with so great a love. That last moonlight night, when they had told each other, "Till tomorrow! Till tomorrow!" *he* had not wept as Edgar was weeping now. The house was bursting with applause. The whole stretto was repeated: the lover sang about the flowers on their graves, about vows and exile and fate and hope; and when their voices rose in the final farewell, Emma herself uttered a sharp cry that was drowned in the blast of the final chords.

"What's that lord doing, mistreating her like that?" Charles asked.

"No, no," she answered. "That's her lover."

"But he's swearing vengeance on her family, whereas the other one—the one that came on a while ago—said 'I love Lucie and I think she loves me!' Besides, he walked off arm in arm with her father. That is her father, isn't it, the ugly little one with the cock feather in his hat?"

Despite Emma's explanations, Charles got everything mixed up beginning with the duet in recitative in which Gilbert explains his abominable machinations to his master Ashton. The false engagement ring serving to trick Lucie he took to be a love token sent by Edgar. In fact he couldn't follow the story at all, he said, because of the music: it interfered so with the words.

"What difference does it make?" said Emma. "Be quiet!"

"But I like to know what's going on," he persisted, leaning over her shoulder. "You know I do."

"Be quiet! Be quiet!" she whispered impatiently.

Lucie came on, half borne up by her women; there was a wreath of orange blossoms in her hair, and she was paler than the white satin of her gown. Emma thought of her own wedding day: she saw herself walking toward the church along the little path amid the wheatfields. Why in heaven's name hadn't she resisted and entreated, like Lucie? But no—she had been lighthearted, unaware of the abyss she was rushing toward. Ah! If only in the freshness of her beauty, before defiling herself in marriage, before the disillusionments of adultery, she could have found some great and noble heart to be her life's foundation! Then virtue and affection, sensual joys and duty would all have been one; and she would never have fallen from her high felicity. But that kind of happiness was doubtless a lie, invented to make one despair of any love. Now she well knew the true paltriness of the passions that art painted so large. So she did her best to think of the opera in a different light: she resolved to regard this image of her own griefs as a vivid fantasy, an enjoyable spectacle and nothing more; and she was actually smiling to herself in scornful pity when from behind the velvet curtains at the back of the stage there appeared a man in a black cloak.

A single gesture sent his broad-brimmed Spanish hat to the ground; and the orchestra and the singers abruptly broke into the sextet. Edgar, flashing fury, dominated all the others with his high, clear voice. Ashton flung him his homicidal challenge in solemn tones; Lucie uttered her shrill lament; Arthur sang his asides in middle register; and the chaplain's baritone boomed like an organ while the women, echoing his words, repeated them in delicious chorus. All the characters now formed a single line across the stage; all were gesticulating at once; and rage, vengeance, jealousy, terror, pity and amazement poured simultaneously from their open mouths. The outraged lover brandished his naked sword; his lace collar rose and fell with the heaving of his chest; and he strode up and down, clanking the silver-gilt spurs on his soft, flaring boots. His love, she thought, must be inexhaustible, since he could pour it out in such great quantities on the crowd. Her resolution not to be taken in by the display of false sentiment was swept away by the impact of the singer's eloquence; the fiction that he was embodying drew her to his real life, and she tried to imagine what it was like—that glamorous, fabulous, marvelous life that she, too, might have lived had chance so willed it. They might have met! They might have loved! With him she might have traveled over all the kingdoms of Europe, from capital to capital, sharing his hardships and his triumphs, gathering up the flowers his admirers threw, embroidering his costumes with her own hands; and every night behind the gilded lattice of her box she might have sat open-mouthed, breathing in the outpourings of that divine creature who would be singing for her alone: he would have gazed at her from the stage as he played his role. A mad idea seized her: he was gazing at her now! She was sure of it! She longed to rush into his arms and seek refuge in his strength as in the very incarnation of love; she longed to cry: "Ravish me! Carry me off! Away from here! All my passion and all my dreams are yours—yours alone!"

The curtain fell.

The smell of gas mingled with human exhalations, and the air seemed the more stifling for being stirred up by fans. Emma tried to get out, but there was a crush in the corridors, and she sank back onto a chair, oppressed by palpitations. Charles, fearful lest she fall into a faint, hurried to the bar for a glass of orgeat.

He had a hard time getting back to the box: he held the glass in both hands because his elbows were being jarred at every other step, but even so he spilled three-quarters of it over the shoulders of a Rouen lady in short sleeves, who began to scream like a peacock, as though she were being murdered, when she felt the cold liquid trickling down her spine. While she took her handkerchief to the spots on her beautiful cerise taffeta gown, her mill-owner husband gave poor clumsy Charles a piece of his mind, angrily muttering the words "damages," "cost," and "replacement." Finally Charles made his way to his wife.

"I thought I'd never get out of there," he gasped. "Such a crowd! Such a crowd!"

And he added:

"Guess who I ran into: Monsieur Léon!"

"Léon?"

"Absolutely. He'll be coming along to pay you his respects."

As he uttered the words the former Yonville clerk entered the box.

He held out his hand with aristocratic casualness; and Madame Bovary automatically extended hers—yielding, no doubt, to the attraction of a stronger will. She hadn't touched it since that spring evening when the rain was falling on the new green leaves—the evening they had said farewell as they stood beside the window. But quickly reminding herself of the social requirements of the situation, she roused herself with an effort from her memories and began to stammer hurried phrases:

"Ah, good evening! You here? How amazing . . . !"

"Quiet!" cried a voice from the orchestra, for the third act was beginning.

"So you're living in Rouen?"

"Yes."

"Since when?"

"Sh! Sh!"

People were turning around at them indignantly, and they fell silent.

But from that moment on Emma no longer listened to the music. The chorus of guests, the scene between Ashton and his attendant, the great duet in D major—for her it all took place at a distance, as though the instruments had lost their sound and the characters had moved away. She recalled the card games at the pharmacist's and the walk to the wet nurse's, their readings under the arbor, the tête-à-têtes beside the fire—the whole poor story of their love, so quiet and so long, so discreet, so tender, and yet discarded from her memory. Why was he returning like this? What combination of events was bringing him back into her life? He sat behind her, leaning a shoulder against the wall of the box; and from time to time she quivered as she felt his warm breath on her hair.

"Are you enjoying this?" he asked, leaning over so close that the tip of his mustache brushed against her cheek.

"Heavens no," she said carelessly, "not particularly."

And he suggested that they leave the theater and go somewhere for an ice.

"Oh, not yet! Let's stay!" said Bovary. "Her hair's down: it looks as though it's going to be tragic."

But the mad scene interested Emma not at all: the soprano, she felt, was overdoing her role.

"She's shrieking too loud," she said, turning toward Charles, who was drinking it in.

"Yes . . . perhaps . . . a little," he replied, torn between the fullness of his enjoyment and the respect he had for his wife's opinions.

"It's so hot. . . ." sighed Léon.

"It is. . . . Unbearable."

"Are you uncomfortable?" asked Bovary.

"Yes, I'm stifling; let's go."

Monsieur Léon carefully laid her long lace shawl over her shoulders, and the three of them walked to the river front and sat down on the outdoor terrace of a café. First they spoke of her sickness, Emma interrupting Charles now and then lest, as she said, he bore Monsieur Léon; and Monsieur Léon told them he had just come to Rouen to spend two years in a large office to familiarize himself with the kind of business carried on in Normandy, which was different from anything he had learned about in Paris. Then he asked about Berthe, the Homais', and Madame Lefrançois; and since they had no more to say to each other in front of Charles the conversation soon died.

People coming from the theater strolled by on the sidewalk, humming or bawling at the top of their voices: *"O bel ange, ma Lucie!"* Léon began to show off his musical knowledge. He had heard Tamburini, Rubini, Persiani, Grisi;[1] and in comparison with them, Lagardy, for all the noise he made, was nothing.

"Still," interrupted Charles, who was eating his rum sherbet a tiny bit at a time, "they say he's wonderful in the last act. I was sorry to leave before the end: I was beginning to like it."

"Don't worry," said the clerk, "he'll be giving another performance soon."

But Charles said they were leaving the next day.

"Unless," he said, turning to his wife, "you'd like to stay on by yourself, sweetheart?"

And changing his tune to suit this unexpected opportunity, the young man

1. Antonio Tamburini (1800–1876); Gian-Battista Rubini (1794–1854); Fanny Tacchinardi Persiani, who was the first Lucia (1812–1867); and Giulia Grisi (1811–1869) were all famous bel-canto singers who appeared in Paris in the operas of Rossini and Donizetti.

sang the praises of Lagardy in the final scenes. He was superb, sublime! Charles insisted:

"You can come home Sunday. Yes, make up your mind to do it. You'd be wrong not to, if you think there's the slightest chance it might do you some good."

Meanwhile the tables around them were emptying; a waiter came and stood discreetly nearby; Charles took the hint and drew out his purse; the clerk put a restraining hand on his arm, paid the bill, and noisily threw down a couple of silver coins for the waiter.

"I'm really embarrassed," murmured Bovary, "at the money that you . . ."

The younger man shrugged him off in a friendly way and took up his hat:

"So it's agreed?" he said. "Tomorrow at six?"

Charles repeated that he couldn't stay away that much longer, but that there was nothing to prevent Emma . . .

"Oh," she murmured, smiling a peculiar smile, "I really don't know whether . . ."

"Well, think it over," said Charles. "Sleep on it and we'll decide in the morning."

Then, to Léon, who was walking with them:

"Now that you're back in our part of the world I hope you'll drop in now and then and let us give you dinner?"

The clerk said that he certainly would, especially since he'd soon be going to Yonville anyway on a business matter. They said good night at the corner of the Passage Saint-Herbland as the cathedral clock was striking half past eleven.

Part Three

I

Busy though he had been with his law studies, Monsieur Léon had nevertheless found time to frequent the Chaumière, and in that cabaret he had done very well for himself with the grisettes, who considered him "distinguished-looking." He was the best-behaved student imaginable; his hair was neither too long nor too short, he didn't spend his entire quarter's allowance the day he got it, and he kept on good terms with his professors. As for excesses, he had been too timorous as well as too squeamish to go in for them.

Often, when he sat reading in his room, or under the lindens of the Luxembourg[2] in the evening, he let his law book fall to the ground, and the memory of Emma came back to him. But gradually his feeling for her faded, and other sensual appetites supplanted it. Even so, it persisted in the background, for Léon never gave up all hope: it was as though a vague promise kept dangling before him in the future, like a golden fruit hanging from some exotic tree.

Then, seeing her again after three years, his passion revived. This time, he

2. The gardens of the Palace of Luxembourg (built between 1615 and 1620 for Marie de Medici); they are open to the public and much frequented by students, as they are near the Sorbonne.

decided he must make up his mind to possess her. Much of his shyness had worn off as a result of the gay company he had kept, and he had returned to the provinces filled with contempt for the local ladies, so different from the trim-shod creatures of the boulevards. Before an elegant Parisienne in the salon of some famous, rich, bemedaled physician, the poor clerk would doubtless have trembled like a child; but here on the Rouen river front, in the presence of this wife of an *officier de santé*, he felt at ease, sure in advance that she would be dazzled. Self-confidence depends on surroundings: the same person talks quite differently in the drawing room and in the garret, and a rich woman's virtue is protected by her banknotes quite as effectively as by any cuirass worn under a corset.

After taking leave of Monsieur and Madame Bovary the previous night, Léon had followed them at a distance in the street; and when he saw them turn into the Croix-Rouge, he retraced his steps and spent the rest of the night working out a plan of action.

The next afternoon about five, pale faced, with a tightness in his throat and with the blind resolution of the panic-stricken, he walked into the inn kitchen.

"Monsieur isn't here," a servant told him.

He took that to be a good omen, and went upstairs.

She received him calmly, and even apologized for having forgotten to mention where they were staying.

"Oh, I guessed!" said Léon.

"How?"

He pretended that he had been led to her by pure chance, a kind of instinct. That made her smile; and, ashamed of his blunder, he quickly told her that he had spent the morning looking for her all over the city, in one hotel after another.

"So you decided to stay?" he asked.

"Yes," she said, "and I was wrong. One can't afford to be self-indulgent if one has a thousand things to attend to."

"Oh, I can imagine . . ."

"No, you can't! You're not a woman."

But men had their troubles, too; and so the conversation got under way, with philosophical reflections. Emma expatiated on the vanity of earthly attachments and on the eternal isolation of every human heart. Either to impress her, or naturally taking on the color of her melancholy, the young man declared that he had found his studies prodigiously frustrating. The technicalities of law irritated him, he was tempted by other careers, and in her letters his mother never stopped pestering him. Indeed, as they talked on they both became more specific in their complaints, and less reserved in their confidences. Occasionally they shrank from giving full expression to their thought, and groped for phrases that would convey it obliquely. But she never disclosed having had another passion, and he said nothing about having forgotten her.

Perhaps he no longer remembered the suppers following fancy-dress balls, with the girls costumed as stevedores; and doubtless she didn't recall those early-morning meetings when she had run through the fields to her lover's château. The sounds of the city reached them only faintly, and the room seemed small, designed with them in mind, to make their solitude the closer. Emma, in a dimity dressing gown, leaned her chignon against the back of the old armchair; the yellow wallpaper was like a gold ground behind her; and her bare head was reflected in the mirror, with the white line of her center part and the tips of her ears peeping out from under the sweeps of her hair.

"But forgive me," she said. "I shouldn't bore you with all my complaints!"

"How can you say that!" he said reproachfully.

"Ah!" she said, lifting her lovely tear-bright eyes to the ceiling. "If you knew all the dreams I've dreamed!"

"It's the same with me! Oh, I had a terrible time! Very often I dropped everything and went out and wandered along the quays, trying to forget my thoughts in the noise of the crowd. But I could never drive out the obsession that haunted me. In the window of a print shop on the boulevard there's an Italian engraving showing one of the Muses. She's draped in a tunic and looking at the moon—her hair's streaming down, with forget-me-nots in it. Something made me go back there over and over again: I used to stand in front of that window for hours on end."

Then, in a trembling voice:

"She looked like you a little."

Madame Bovary averted her face lest he see the smile that she couldn't suppress.

"I kept writing you letters," he said, "and then tearing them up."

She made no answer. He went on:

"I used to imagine we'd meet by chance. I kept thinking I saw you on street corners, and I even ran after cabs sometimes, if I saw a shawl or a veil at the window that looked like yours. . . ."

She seemed determined to let him speak without interruption. Arms crossed and head lowered, she stared at the rosettes on her slippers, now and again moving her toes a little under the satin.

Finally she gave a sigh. "The worst thing of all, it seems to me, is to go on leading a futile life the way I do. If our unhappiness were of use to someone, we could find consolation in the thought of sacrifice!"

He launched into a eulogy of virtue, duty, silent renunciation: he, too, he said, had a fantastic need for selfless dedication that he was unable to satisfy.

"What I should love to do," she said, "would be to join an order of nursing Sisters."

"Alas!" he answered. "No such sacred missions are open to men. I can't think of any calling . . . except maybe becoming a doctor. . . ."

She gave a slight shrug and interrupted him, expressing regret that her illness had not been fatal. What a pity! By now she would be past all suffering. Léon at once chimed in with a longing for "the peace of the grave." One night he had even written out his will, asking to be buried in the beautiful velvet-striped coverlet she had given him.

That was how they would have liked to be: what they were doing was to dream up ideals and then refashion their past lives to match them. Speech is a rolling-machine that always stretches the feelings it expresses!

But:

"Why?" she asked him, at his made-up tale about the coverlet.

"Why?" He hesitated. "Because—I was terribly in love with you."

And congratulating himself on having got over the hurdle, Léon watched her face out of the corner of his eye.

It was like the sky when a gust of wind sweeps away the clouds. The mass of sad thoughts that had darkened her blue eyes seemed to lift: her whole face was radiant.

He waited. Finally she answered:

"I always thought so."

They went over, then, the tiny happenings of that far-off time, whose joys and sorrows had been evoked by a single word. He spoke of the clematis bower, of the dresses she had worn, of the furniture in her room—of everything in the house.

"And our poor cactuses—what's become of them?"

"The cold killed them last winter."

"I've thought about them so often, would you believe it? I've pictured them the way they used to look on summer mornings, with the sun on the blinds and your bare arms in among the flowers."

"Poor boy," she said, holding out her hand.

Léon lost no time pressing it to his lips. Then, after taking a deep breath:

"You were a strange, mysterious, captivating force in my life in those days. There was one time, for example, when I came to call on you . . . But you probably don't remember."

"Yes, I do. Go on."

"You were downstairs in the hall, ready to go out, standing on the bottom step. I even remember your hat—it had little blue flowers on it. And without your asking me at all I went with you. I couldn't help it. I felt more and more foolish every minute, though, and I kept on walking near you. I didn't dare really follow you, and yet I couldn't bear to go away. When you went into a shop I stayed in the street, watching you through the window take off your gloves and count the change on the counter. Then you rang Madame Tuvache's bell; you went in; and I stood there like an idiot in front of the big heavy door even after it had closed behind you."

As she listened to him, Madame Bovary marveled at how old she was: all those reemerging details made her life seem vaster, as though she had endless emotional experiences to look back on. Her voice low, her eyes half closed, she kept saying:

"Yes, I remember! I remember! I remember . . . !"

They heard eight o'clock strike from several belfries near the Place Beauvoisine, a section of Rouen full of boarding schools, churches and great deserted mansions. They were no longer speaking; but as they looked at one another they felt a throbbing in their heads: it was as though their very glances had set off a physical vibration. Now they had clasped hands; and in the sweetness of their ecstasy everything merged—the past, the future, their memories and their dreams. Night was darkening the walls of the room: still gleaming in the dimness were the garish colors of four prints showing four scenes from *La Tour de Nesle*,[3] with captions below in Spanish and French. Through the sash window they could see a patch of dark sky between peaked roofs.

She rose to light two candles on the chest of drawers, and then sat down again.

"Well . . . ?" said Léon.

---

3. The Nesle Tower (French); a melodrama by Alexandre Dumas the elder (1803–1870) and Gaillardet (1832) in which Marie de Bourgogne, famous for her crimes, is the main heroine.

"Well . . . ?" she echoed.

And as he wondered how to resume the interrupted conversation, she asked:

"Why has no one ever said such things to me before?"

The clerk assured her warmly that idealistic natures were rarely understood. But he had loved her the moment he saw her, and despair filled him whenever he thought of the happiness that might have been theirs. Had fortune been kind, had they met earlier, they would long since have been united indissolubly.

"I've thought about that, sometimes," she said.

"What a dream!" murmured Léon.

And then, gently fingering the blue border of her long white belt:

"What's to prevent us from beginning all over again, now?"

"No, no," she said. "I'm too old . . . you're too young . . . forget me! You'll find other women to love you . . . and to love."

"Not as I do you!" he cried.

"What a child you are! Come, let's be sensible. I want us to be."

And she explained why they couldn't be lovers, why they must continue to be friends—like brother and sister—as in the past.

Did she mean those things she was saying? Doubtless Emma herself couldn't tell, engrossed as she was by the charm of seduction and the need to defend herself. Looking fondly at the young man, she gently repulsed the timid caresses his trembling hands essayed.

"Ah! Forgive me!" he said, drawing back.

And Emma was seized by a vague terror in the face of this timidity, a greater danger for her than Rodolphe's boldness when he had advanced with outstretched arms. Never had any man seemed to her so handsome. There was an exquisite candor about him. His long, fine, curving eyelashes were lowered; the smooth skin of his cheek was flushing with desire for her—so she thought; and she felt an all but invincible longing to touch it with her lips. She leaned away toward the clock, as though to see the time.

"Heavens!" she said. "How late! How we've been chattering!"

He understood, and rose to go.

"I forgot all about the opera! And poor Bovary left me here on purpose to see it! It was all arranged that I was to go with Monsieur and Madame Lormeaux, of the Rue Grand-Pont!"

It was her last chance, too, for she was leaving the next day.

"Really?" said Léon.

"Yes."

"But I must see you again," he said. "I had something to tell you. . . ."

"What?"

"Something . . . something serious, important. No—really: you mustn't go, you mustn't. If you knew . . . Listen . . . You haven't understood me, then? You haven't guessed . . ."

"On the contrary, you have a very clear way of putting things," said Emma.

"Ah! Now you're laughing at me! Please don't! Have pity on me: let me see you again. Once—just once."

"Well . . ."

She paused; then, as though changing her mind:

"Not here, certainly!"

"Wherever you like."

"Will you . . ."

She seemed to ponder; and then, tersely:

"Tomorrow at eleven in the cathedral."

"I'll be there!" he cried. He seized her hands, but she pulled them away.

They were standing close together, he behind and she with lowered head, and he bent over and kissed her long and lingeringly on the nape of the neck.

"You're crazy, crazy!" she cried between short bursts of laughter as he kissed her again and again.

Then, leaning his head over her shoulder, he seemed to be imploring her eyes to say yes, but the gaze he received was icy and aloof.

Léon stepped back; in the doorway he paused, and tremblingly whispered: "Till tomorrow."

Her only reply was a nod, and like a bird she vanished into the adjoining room.

That night Emma wrote the clerk an endless letter canceling their appointment: everything was over between them, and for the sake of their own happiness they must never meet again. But when she finished the letter she didn't know what to do with it—she hadn't Léon's address.

"I'll give it to him myself," she thought, "when he comes."

Léon, the next morning—humming a tune on his balcony beside his open window—polished his pumps himself, going over them again and again. He donned a pair of white trousers, fine socks, and a green tail coat; he doused his handkerchief with all the perfumes he possessed, had his hair curled, then uncurled it again to make it look more elegantly natural.

"Still too early!" he thought: he was looking at the barber's cuckoo clock, and it pointed to nine.

He read an old fashion magazine, went out, smoked a cigar, walked a few blocks. Finally he decided it was time to go, and set off briskly toward the Parvis Notre-Dame.

It was a fine summer morning. Silver gleamed in jewelers' windows, and the sunlight slanting onto the cathedral flashed on the cut surface of the gray stone; a flock of birds was swirling in the blue sky around the trefoiled turrets; the square, echoing with cries, smelled of the flowers that edged its pavement—roses, jasmine, carnations, narcissus and tuberoses interspersed with well-watered plants of catnip and chickweed. The fountain gurgled in the center; and under great umbrellas, among piles of cantaloupes, bare headed flower women were twisting paper around bunches of violets.

The young man chose one. It was the first time he had bought flowers for a woman; and his chest swelled with pride as he inhaled their fragrance, as though this homage that he intended for another were being paid, instead, to him.

But he was afraid of being seen, and resolutely entered the church.

The verger was just then standing in the left doorway, under the figure of the dancing Salomé. He was in full regalia, with plumed hat, rapier and staff, more majestic than a cardinal, shining like a pyx.

He advanced toward Léon, and with the smiling, bland benignity of a priest questioning a child, he said:

"Monsieur is from out of town, perhaps? Monsieur would like to visit the church?"

"No," said Léon.

He walked down one of the side aisles and up the other, then stood outside and looked over the square; there was no sign of Emma, and he reentered the church and strolled as far as the choir.

The nave was mirrored in the holy-water fonts, with the lower portions of the ogives and some of the stained glass; the reflection of the painted windows broke off at the marble rim only to continue beyond, on the pavement, like a many-colored carpet. Brilliant daylight streamed into the church in three enormous shafts through the three open portals. Now and again a sacristan moved across the far end, dipping before the altar in the half-sidewise genuflection practiced by hurried worshipers. The crystal chandeliers hung motionless. A silver lamp was burning in the choir; and from the side chapels and shadowy corners of the church came an occasional sound like a sigh, and the noise of a metal gate clanging shut and echoing under the lofty vaults.

Léon walked meditatively, keeping near the walls. Never had life seemed so good. Any minute now she would appear, charming, all aquiver, turning around to see whether anyone was looking—with her flounced dress, her gold eyeglass, her dainty shoes, all kinds of feminine elegances he had never had a taste of, and all the ineffable allurement of virtue on the point of yielding. The church was like a gigantic boudoir, suffused by her image: the vaults curved dimly down to breathe in the avowal of her love; the windows were ablaze to cast their splendor on her face; and even the incense burners were lighted, to welcome her like an angel amid clouds of perfume.

But still she didn't come. He took a chair and his eyes rested on a blue stained-glass window showing boatmen carrying baskets. He stared at it fixedly, counting the scales on the fish and the buttonholes in the doublets, his thoughts meanwhile roving in search of Emma.

The verger, standing to one side, was raging inwardly at this person who was taking it upon himself to admire the cathedral on his own. He was behaving monstrously, he considered: he was stealing from him, really—almost committing sacrilege.

Then there was a rustle of silk on the stone pavement, the edge of a hat under a hooded cape. . . . It was she! Léon jumped up and ran to meet her.

She was pale. She walked quickly.

"Read this!" she said, holding out a sheet of paper. "Oh, no!"

And abruptly she drew back her hand and turned into the chapel of the Virgin, where she knelt down against a chair and began to pray.

The young man was irritated by this sanctimonious bit of whimsy; then he felt a certain charm at seeing her, in the midst of a love meeting, plunged into devotions like an Andalusian *marquesa*; but he soon grew impatient, for there seemed to be no end to it.

Emma was praying, or rather forcing herself to pray, in the hope that heaven might miraculously send her strength of will; and to draw down divine aid she filled her eyes with the splendors of the tabernacle, she breathed the fragrance of the sweet-rockets, white and lush in their tall vases, and she listened intently to the silence of the church, which only increased the tumult of her heart.

She rose, and they were about to leave when the verger came swiftly over:

"Madame is perhaps from out of town? Madame would like to visit the church?"

"Oh, no!" the clerk cried.

"Why not?" she retorted.

Her desperate attempt to steady her virtue made her clutch at the Virgin, at the sculptures, at the tombs, at anything that came to hand.

Insisting that they must "begin at the beginning," the verger led them outside the entrance door to the edge of the square, and there pointed with his staff to a large circle of black stones in the pavement, devoid of carving or inscription:

"That," he said majestically, "is the circumference of the great Amboise bell. It weighed forty thousand pounds. It was without equal in all Europe. The workman who cast it died of joy. . . ."

"Let's get away from here," said Léon.

The guide moved on; and back in the chapel of the Virgin he extended his arms in a showman's gesture that took in everything, and addressed them more proudly than a gentleman farmer displaying his fruit trees:

"This plain stone marks the resting place of Pierre de Brézé, lord of La Varenne and Brissac, grand marshal of Poitou and governor of Normandy, killed at the battle of Montlhéry, July 16, 1465."

Léon bit his lips in a fury of impatience.

"And on the right the nobleman in full armor on a rearing horse is his grandson Louis de Brézé, lord of Braval and Montchauvet, comte de Maulevrier, baron de Mauny, royal chamberlain, knight of the order and likewise governor of Normandy, who died July 23, 1531, a Sunday, as it says on the inscription; and below, the man about to descend into the tomb represents the same person exactly. Human mortality has never been more perfectly represented."

Madame Bovary raised her eyeglass. Léon stood still and stared at her, no longer even trying to utter a word or make the slightest move, so discouraged was he by this combination of patter and indifference.

The guide droned on:

"Near him, there, that kneeling weeping woman is his wife, Diane de Poitiers, comtesse de Brézé, duchesse de Valentinois, born 1499, died 1566; and on the left, holding a child, the Holy Virgin. Now face this way: those are the tombs of the Amboises. They were both cardinals and archbishops of Rouen. That one was one of King Louis XII's ministers. He was a great benefactor of the cathedral. In his will he left 30,000 *écus d'or* for the poor."

And immediately, without interrupting his stream of talk, he pushed them into a chapel cluttered with railings, some of which he moved aside to reveal a blockish object that looked like a roughly carved statue.

"This," he said with a deep sigh, "once formed part of the decoration of the tomb of Richard Coeur-de-Lion,[4] king of England and duke of Normandy. It was the Calvinists, Monsieur, who reduced it to the condition in which you see it now. Out of pure malice they buried it in the earth, under Monseigneur's episcopal throne. That door, there, by the way, is the one he uses—Monseigneur, I mean—to reach his residence. Now we'll move on to the gargoyle windows."

But Léon hastily took a silver piece from his pocket and grasped Emma's

---

4. Richard the Lion-Hearted (b. 1157), who was king of England from 1189 to 1199; he died at the siege of the castle of Châlus.

arm. The verger was taken aback, mystified by such premature munificence: the visitor still had so much to see! He called after him:

"Monsieur! The steeple! The steeple!"[5]

"No, thanks," said Léon.

"Monsieur is wrong! It's going to be four hundred forty feet high, only nine feet lower than the Great Pyramid of Egypt. It's entirely of cast iron, it . . . "

Léon fled, for it seemed to him that his love, after being reduced to stone-like immobility in the church for nearly two hours, was now going to vanish like smoke up that truncated pipe, that elongated cage, that fretwork chimney, or what you will, that perches so precariously and grotesquely atop the cathedral like the wild invention of a crazy metalworker.

"But where are we going?" she asked.

Making no answer, he continued swiftly on, and Madame Bovary was already dipping a finger in the holy water when behind them they heard a sound of heavy panting regularly punctuated by the tapping of a staff. Léon turned around.

"Monsieur!"

"What?"

It was the verger, holding about twenty thick paperbound volumes against his stomach. They were "books about the cathedral."

"Fool!" muttered Léon, hurrying out of the church.

An urchin was playing in the square:

"Go get me a cab!"

The youngster vanished like a shot up the Rue des Quatre-Vents, and for a few minutes they were left alone, face to face and a little constrained.

"Oh, Léon! Really—I don't know whether I should . . . !"

She simpered. Then, in a serious tone:

"It's very improper, you know."

"What's improper about it?" retorted the clerk. "Everybody does it in Paris!"

It was an irresistible and clinching argument.

But there was no sign of a cab. Léon was terrified lest she retreat into the church. Finally the cab appeared.

"Drive past the north door, at least!" cried the verger, from the entrance. "Take a look at the Resurrection, the Last Judgment, Paradise, King David, and the souls of the damned in the flames of hell!"

"Where does Monsieur wish to go?" asked the driver.

"Anywhere!" said Léon, pushing Emma into the carriage.

And the lumbering contraption rolled away.

It went down the Rue Grand-Pont, crossed the Place des Arts, the Quai Napoléon and the Pont Neuf, and stopped in front of the statue of Pierre Corneille.

"Keep going!" called a voice from within.

It started off again, and gathering speed on the downgrade beyond the Carrefour Lafayette it came galloping up to the railway station.

"No! Straight on!" cried the same voice.

Rattling out through the station gates, the cab soon turned into the Boul-

5. Added to the cathedral of Rouen, which was built in the Gothic style in stages from the thirteenth century to the early sixteenth, it is a high cast-iron spire (485 feet), generally considered a tasteless disfigurement. Construction was begun in 1824 but not finished until 1876.

evard, where it proceeded at a gentle trot between the double row of tall
elms. The coachman wiped his brow, stowed his leather hat between his
legs, and veered the cab off beyond the side lanes to the grass strip along the
river front.

It continued along the river on the cobbled towing path for a long time in
the direction of Oyssel, leaving the islands behind.

But suddenly it rushed off through Quatre-Mares, Sotteville, the Grande-
Chaussée, the Rue d'Elbeuf, and made its third stop—this time at the Jardin
des Plantes.

"Drive on!" cried the voice, more furiously.

And abruptly starting off again it went through Saint-Sever, along the Quai
des Curandiers and the Quai aux Meules, recrossed the bridge, crossed the
Place du Champ-de-Mars and continued on behind the garden of the hospital, where old men in black jackets were strolling in the sun on a terrace
green with ivy. It went up the Boulevard Bouvreuil, along the Boulevard
Cauchoise, and traversed Mont-Riboudet as far as the hill at Deville.

There it turned back; and from then on it wandered at random, without
apparent goal. It was seen at Saint-Pol, at Lescure, at Mont-Gargan, at
Rouge-Mare and the Place du Gaillardbois; in the rue Maladrerie, the Rue
Dinanderie, and in front of one church after another—Saint-Romain, Saint-
Vivien, Saint-Maclou, Saint-Nicaise; in front of the customs house, at the
Basse Vieille-Tour, at Trois-Pipes, and at the Cimetière Monumental. From
his seat the coachman now and again cast a desperate glance at a café. He
couldn't conceive what locomotive frenzy was making these people persist
in refusing to stop. He tried a few times, only to hear immediate angry exclamation from behind. So he lashed the more furiously at his two sweating
nags, and paid no attention whatever to bumps in the road; he hooked into
things right and left; he was past caring—demoralized, and almost weeping
from thirst, fatigue, and despair.

Along the river front amidst the trucks and the barrels, along the streets
from the shelter of the guard posts, the bourgeois stared wide-eyed at this
spectacle unheard of in the provinces—a carriage with drawn shades that
kept appearing and reappearing, sealed tighter than a tomb and tossing like
a ship.

At a certain moment in the early afternoon, when the sun was blazing
down most fiercely on the old silver-plated lamps, a bare hand appeared from
under the little yellow cloth curtains and threw out some torn scraps of
paper. The wind caught them and scattered them, and they alighted at a
distance, like white butterflies, on a field of flowering red clover.

Then, about six o'clock, the carriage stopped in a side street near the Place
Beauvoisine. A woman alighted from it and walked off, her veil down, without
a backward glance.

II

When she reached the hotel, Madame Bovary was surprised to see no sign
of the stagecoach. Hivert had waited for her fifty-three minutes, and then
driven off.

Nothing really obliged her to go, even though she had said that she would
be back that evening. But Charles would be waiting for her: and in advance

her heart was filled with that craven submissiveness with which many women both redeem their adultery and punish themselves for it.

She quickly packed her bag, paid her bill, and hired a gig in the yard. She told the driver to hurry, and kept urging him on and asking him the time and how many miles they had gone. They caught up with the Hirondelle on the outskirts of Quincampoix.

She shut her eyes almost before she was seated in her corner, and opened them at the outskirts of the village: ahead she saw Félicité standing watch outside the blacksmith's. Hivert pulled up the horses, and the cook, standing on tiptoe to address her through the window, said with an air of mystery:

"Madame, you must go straight to Monsieur Homais'. It's something urgent."

The village was silent as usual. Little pink mounds were steaming in the gutters: it was jelly-making time, and everyone in Yonville was putting up the year's supply the same day. The mound in front of the pharmacy was by far the largest and most impressive, and quite properly so: a laboratory must always be superior to home kitchens; a universal demand must always overshadow mere individual tastes!

She went in. The big armchair was overturned, and—what was more shocking—the *Fanal de Rouen* itself had been left lying on the floor between the two pestles. She pushed open the hall door, and in the middle of the kitchen—amid earthenware jars full of stemmed currants, grated sugar, lump sugar, scales on the table and pans on the fire—she found all the Homais, big and little, swathed to the chin in aprons and wielding forks. Justin was standing there hanging his head, and the pharmacist was shouting:

"Who told you to go get it in the Capharnaum?"

"What is it?" Emma asked. "What's the matter?"

"What's the matter?" replied the apothecary. "We're making jelly. It's on the fire. It threatens to boil over. I call for another pan. And this good-for-nothing, out of sheer laziness, goes and takes—goes into my laboratory and takes off the hook—the key to the Capharnaum!"

Such was the apothecary's name for a small room under the eaves, filled with pharmaceutical utensils and supplies. He often spent long hours there alone, labeling, decanting, repackaging. He considered it not a mere storeroom, but a veritable sanctuary, birthplace of all kinds of pills, boluses, tisanes, lotions and potions concocted by himself and destined to spread his renown throughout the countryside. Not another soul ever set foot in it: so fiercely did he respect the place that he even swept it out himself. If the pharmacy, open to all comers, was the arena where he paraded in all his glory, the Capharnaum was the hideaway where he rapturously pursued his favorite occupations in selfish seclusion. No wonder Justin's carelessness seemed to him a monstrous bit of irreverence. His face was redder than the currants as he continued his tirade:

"Yes, the key to the Capharnaum! The key that guards the acids and the caustic alkalis! And to calmly go and take one of the spare pans! A pan with a lid! One I may never use! Every detail is important in an art as precise as ours! Distinctions must be preserved! Pharmaceutical implements mustn't be used for near-domestic tasks! It's like carving a chicken with a scalpel, as though a judge were to . . ."

"Stop exciting yourself!" Madame Homais kept saying.

And Athalie pulled at his frock coat and cried: "Papa! Papa!"

"No! Leave me alone!" ordered the apothecary. "Leave me alone! God! I might as well be a grocer, I swear! Go ahead—go right ahead—*don't* respect anything! Smash! Crash! Let the leeches loose! Burn the marshmallow! Make pickles in the medicine jars! Slash up the bandages!"

"But you had something to . . ." said Emma.

"One moment, Madame!—Do you know the risk you were running? Didn't you notice anything in the corner, on the left, on the third shelf? Open your mouth! Say something!"

"I . . . don't . . . know . . ." stammered the boy.

"Ah! You don't know! Well, *I* know! You saw a bottle, a blue glass bottle sealed with yellow wax, with white powder in it, and that I myself marked *Dangerous!*? Do you know what's in that bottle? Arsenic! And you go meddling with that! You take a pan that's standing right beside it!"

"Right beside it!" cried Madame Homais, clasping her hands. "Arsenic! You might have poisoned us all!"

And the children began to scream, as though they were already prey to the most frightful gastric pains.

"Or you might have poisoned a patient!" the apothecary persisted. "Do you want me to be hauled into court as a common criminal? Do you want to see me dragged to the scaffold? Don't you know how very careful I am about handling anything, no matter how many million times I may have done it before? Sometimes I'm terrified at the thought of my responsibilities! The government positively hounds us! The legal restrictions are absurd—a veritable sword of Damocles hanging over our heads!"

Emma had given up any attempt to ask what was wanted of her, and the pharmacist breathlessly continued:

"That's your way of being grateful for all the kindness you've been shown! That's how you repay me for the father's care I've showered on you! Where would you be if it weren't for me? What would you be doing? Who gives you your food and your lodging, and training, and clothing—everything you need to become a respectable member of society someday? But to achieve that you've got to bend your back to the oar—get some calluses on your hands, as the saying goes. *Fabricando fit faber, age quod agis.*"[6]

His rage had sent him into Latin: he would have spouted Chinese or Greenlandic had he been able to, for he was in the throes of one of those crises in which the soul lays bare its every last corner, just as the ocean, in the travail of storm, splits open to display everything from the seaweed on its shores to the sand of its deepest bottom.

And he went on:

"I'm beginning to repent bitterly that I ever took you into my charge! I'd have done far better to leave you as I found you—let you wallow in the misery and filth you were born in! You'll never be fit to do anything except look after the cows! You haven't the makings of a scientist! You're scarcely capable of sticking on a label! And you live here at my expense, gorging yourself like a priest, like a pig in clover!"

Emma turned to Madame Homais:

---

6. The artisan becomes proficient through practice; practice what you are supposed to do (Latin).

"I was told to come . . ."

"I know," the lady said, wringing her hands, "but how can I possibly tell you . . . ? It's a calamity . . ."

She left her words unfinished. The apothecary was thundering on:

"Empty it out! Scour it! Take it back! Be quick about it!"

And as he shook Justin by the collar of his overall a book fell out of one of the pockets.

The boy bent down for it, but Homais was quicker, and he picked up the book and stared at it open-mouthed.

"*Conjugal . . . Love!*" he cried, placing a deliberate pause between the two words. "Ah! Very good! *Very good!* Charming, in fact! And with illustrations . . . Really! This goes beyond everything!"

Madame Homais stepped forward as though to look.

"No! Don't touch it!"

The children clamored to see the pictures.

"Leave the room!" he said imperiously.

They left.

First he strode up and down, holding the volume open, rolling his eyes, choking, puffing, apoplectic. Then he walked straight up to his apprentice and stood in front of him, arms folded.

"So you're going in for *all* the vices, are you, you little wretch? Watch out, you're on the downward path! Did it ever occur to you that this wicked book might fall into my children's hands? It might be just the spark that . . . It might sully the purity of Athalie! It might corrupt Napoléon! Physically, he's a man already! Are you sure, at least, that they haven't read it? Can you swear to me . . ."

"Really, Monsieur," said Emma. "Did you have something to tell me?"

"So I did, Madame. . . . Your father-in-law is dead!"

It was true: the elder Bovary had died two days before, very suddenly, from an apoplectic stroke, as he was leaving the table; and Charles, overanxious to spare Emma's sensibilities, had asked Monsieur Homais to acquaint her tactfully with the horrible news.

The pharmacist had devoted much thought to the wording of his announcement. He had rounded it and polished it and given it cadence. It was a masterpiece of discretion and transition, of subtlety and shading. But anger had swept away rhetoric.

Emma, seeing that it was useless to ask for details, left the pharmacy, for Monsieur Homais had resumed his vituperations. He was quieting down, however, and now was grumbling in a fatherly way as he fanned himself with his cap:

"It's not that I disapprove entirely of the book. The author was a doctor. It deals with certain scientific aspects that it does a man no harm to know about—aspects, if I may say so, that a man *has* to know about. But later, later! Wait till you're a man yourself, at least; wait till your character's formed."

The sound of the knocker told the expectant Charles that Emma had arrived, and he came toward her with open arms. There were tears in his voice:

"Ah! *Ma chère amie* . . ."

And he bent down gently to kiss her. But at the touch of his lips the memory of Léon gripped her, and she passed her hand over her face and shuddered.

Nevertheless she answered him. "Yes," she said. "I know . . . I know . . ."

He showed her the letter in which his mother told what had happened, without any sentimental hypocrisy. Her only regret was that her husband had not received the succor of the church: he had died not at home, but at Doudeville, in the street, just outside a café, after a patriotic banquet with some ex-army officers.

Emma handed back the letter. At dinner she pretended a little for the sake of good manners to have no appetite, but when Charles urged her, she proceeded to eat heartily, while he sat opposite her motionless, weighed down by grief.

Now and again he lifted his head and gave her a long, stricken look.

"I wish I could have seen him again!" he sighed.

She made no answer. And finally, when she knew that she must say something:

"How old was your father?"

"Fifty-eight."

"Ah!"

And that was all.

A little later:

"My poor mother!" he said. "What's to become of her now?"

She conveyed with a gesture that she had no idea.

Seeing her so silent, Charles supposed that she, too, was affected, and he forced himself to say no more lest he exacerbate her sorrow, which he found touching. But for a moment he roused himself from his own.

"Did you have a good time yesterday?" he asked.

"Yes."

When the tablecloth was removed, Bovary did not get up, nor did Emma; and as she continued to look at him the monotony of the sight gradually banished all compassion from her heart. He seemed to her insignificant, weak, a nonentity—contemptible in every way. How could she rid herself of him? What an endless evening! She felt torpid, drugged, as though from opium fumes.

From the entry came the sharp tap of a stick on the wooden floor. It was Hippolyte, bringing Madame's bags. To set them down, he swung his wooden leg around in an awkward quarter-circle.

"Charles doesn't even think about him anymore," she remarked to herself as she watched the poor devil, his mop of red hair dripping sweat.

Bovary fumbled in his purse for a coin; and, apparently unaware of the humiliation implicit in the very presence of the man who was standing there, like a living reproach for his incurable ineptitude:

"Oh, you have a pretty bouquet!" he said, noticing Léon's violets on the mantelpiece.

"Yes," she said carelessly. "I bought it just before I left—from a beggar woman."

Charles took up the violets, held their coolness against his tear-reddened eyes, and gently sniffed them. She quickly took them from his hand, and went to put them in a glass of water.

The following day the older Madame Bovary arrived. She and her son did a good deal of weeping. Emma, pleading household duties, kept out of the way. The day after that, they had to consult about mourning, and the three of them sat down together, the ladies with their workboxes, under the arbor on the river bank.

Charles thought about his father, and was surprised to feel so much affection for one whom up till then he had thought he loved but little. The older Madame Bovary thought of her husband. The worst of her times with him seemed desirable now. Everything was submerged in grief, so intensely did she miss the life she was used to; and from time to time as she plied her needle a great tear rolled down her nose and hung there for a moment before dropping. Emma was thinking that scarcely forty-eight hours before they had been together, shut away from the world, in ecstasy, devouring each other with their eyes. She tried to recapture the tiniest details of that vanished day. But the presence of her mother-in-law and her husband interfered. She wished she could hear nothing, see nothing: she wanted merely to be left alone to evoke her love, which depite her best efforts was becoming blurred under the impact of external impressions.

She was ripping the lining of a dress, and scraps of the material lay scattered around her; the older Madame Bovary, never raising her eyes, kept squeaking away with her scissors; and Charles, in his cloth slippers and the old brown frock coat that he used as a dressing gown, kept his hand in his pockets and said no more than the others. Near them, Berthe, in a little white apron, was scraping the gravel of the path with her shovel.

Suddenly they saw Monsieur Lheureux, the dry-goods dealer, push open the gate.

He had come to offer his services "on this very sad occasion." Emma answered that she thought she could do without them. But the shopkeeper did not concede defeat.

"If you'll excuse me," he said, "I'd like to speak to you privately."

And in a low voice:

"It's about that little matter . . . you know what I'm referring to?"

Charles blushed to the roots of his hair.

"Oh, yes . . . of course."

And in his embarrassment he turned to his wife:

"Darling would you take care of . . . ?"

She seemed to understand, for she rose; and Charles said to his mother:

"It's nothing—just some household detail, I imagine."

He didn't want her to learn about the promissory note: he dreaded her comments.

As soon as Emma was alone with Monsieur Lheureux he began to congratulate her rather bluntly on coming into money, and then spoke of indifferent matters—fruit trees, the harvest, and his own health, which was always the same, "so-so, could be worse." He worked like a galley slave, he informed her, and even so, despite what people said about him, he didn't make enough to buy butter for his bread.

Emma let him talk. She had been so prodigiously bored these last two days!

"And you're entirely well again?" he went on. "Your husband was in quite a state, I can tell you! He's a fine fellow, even if we did have a little trouble."

"What trouble?" she asked, for Charles had told her nothing about the dispute over the various items.

"But you know perfectly well!" said Lheureux. "About the little things you wanted—the trunks."

He had pushed his hat forward over his eyes, and with his hands behind his back, smiling, and whistling to himself under his breath, he was staring straight at her in a way she found intolerable. Did he suspect something? She waited in a panic of apprehension. But finally he said:

"We made it up, and I came today to propose another arrangement."

What he proposed was the renewal of the note signed by Bovary. Monsieur should of course do as he pleased: he shouldn't worry, especially now that he was going to have so many other things on his mind.

"He'd really do best to turn it over to somebody else—you, for example. With a power of attorney everything would be very simple, and then you and I could attend to our little affairs together."

She didn't understand. He let the matter drop, and turned the conversation back to dry goods: Madame really couldn't not order something from him. He'd send her a piece of black barège—twelve meters, enough to make a dress.

"The one you have there is all right for the house, but you need another for going out. I saw that the minute I came in. I've got an eye like a Yankee!"

He didn't send the material: he brought it. Then he came again to do the measuring, and again and again on other pretexts, each time putting himself out to be agreeable and helpful—making himself her liegeman, as Homais might have put it—and always slipping in a few words of advice about the power of attorney. He didn't mention the promissory note. It didn't occur to her to think of it: early in her convalescence Charles had, in fact, said something to her about it, but her mind had been so agitated that she had forgotten. Moreover she was careful never to bring up anything about money matters. This surprised her mother-in-law, who attributed her new attitude to the religious sentiments she had acquired during her illness.

But as soon as the older woman left, Emma lost no time in impressing Bovary with her practical good sense. It was up to them, she said, to make inquiries, check on mortgages, see if there were grounds for liquidating the property by auction or otherwise. She used technical terms at random, and impressive words like "order," "the future" and "foresight," and she continually exaggerated the complications attendant on inheritance. Then one day she showed him the draft of a general authorization to "manage and administer his affairs, negotiate all loans, sign and endorse all promissory notes, pay all sums," etc. She had profited from Lheureux's lessons.

Charles naïvely asked her where the document came from.

"From Maître Guillaumin."

And with the greatest coolness imaginable she added:

"I haven't too much confidence in him. You hear such dreadful things about notaries! Perhaps we ought to consult . . . We don't know anyone except . . . We don't know anyone, really."

"Unless Léon . . ." said Charles, who was thinking hard.

But it was difficult to make things clear by letter. So she offered to make the trip. He thanked her but said she mustn't. She insisted. Each outdid the other in consideration. Finally, imitating the pert disobedience of a child, she cried:

"I will, too, go! I will!"

"How good you are!" he said, kissing her on the forehead.

The next morning she set out in the Hirondelle for Rouen to consult Monsieur Léon, and she stayed there three days.

III

They were three full, exquisite, glorious days, a real honeymoon.

They stayed at the Hotel de Boulogne on the river front, living there behind drawn shutters and locked doors; their room was strewn with flowers, and iced fruit drinks were brought up to them all day long.

At dusk they hired a covered boat and went to dine on one of the islands.

From the shipyards came the thumping of caulking irons against hulls. Wisps of tar smoke curled up from among the trees, and on the river floated great oily patches, the color of Florentine bronze, undulating unevenly in the purple glow of the sun.

They drifted downstream amidst anchored craft whose long slanting cables grazed the top of their boat.

The sounds of the city gradually receded—the rattle of wagons, the tumult of voices, the barking of dogs on the decks of ships. As they touched the shore of their island she loosened the silk ribbon of her hat.

They sat in the low-ceilinged room of a restaurant with black fishnets hanging at its door, and ate fried smelts, cream and cherries. Then they stretched out on the grass in an out-of-the-way corner and lay in each other's arms under the poplars: they wished they might live forever, like two Robinson Crusoes, in this little spot that seemed to them in their bliss the most magnificent on earth. It wasn't the first time in their lives that they had seen trees, blue sky and lawn, or heard the flowing of water or the rustle of the breeze in the branches, but never before, certainly, had they looked on it all with such wonder: it was as though nature had not existed before, or had only begun to be beautiful with the slaking of their desires.

At nightfall they returned to the city. The boat followed the shoreline of the islands, and they crouched deep in its shadow, not saying a word. The square-tipped oars clicked in the iron oarlocks: it sounded, in the silence, like the beat of a metronome, and the rope trailing behind kept up its gentle splashing in the water.

One night the moon shone out, and of course they rhapsodized about how melancholy and poetical it was. She even sang a little:

> One night—dost thou remember?—
> We were sailing . . .[7]

Her sweet, small voice died away over the river: borne off on the breeze were the trills that Léon heard flit past him like the fluttering of wings.

She was sitting opposite him, leaning against the wall of the little cabin, the moonlight streaming in on her through an open shutter. In her black dress, its folds spreading out around her like a fan, she looked taller, slimmer. Her head was raised, her hands were clasped, her eyes turned heavenward. One moment she would be hidden by the shadow of some willows; the next, she would suddenly reemerge in the light of the moon like an apparition.

---

7. The beginning of Alphonse de Lamartine's *The Lake* (see p. 873).

Léon, sitting on the bottom beside her, picked up a bright red ribbon.

The boatman looked at it.

"Oh," he said, "that's probably from a party I took out the other day. They were a jolly lot, all right, the men *and* the girls: they brought along food and champagne and music—the whole works. There was one of them, especially—a big, good-looking fellow with a little mustache—he was a riot. They all kept after him. 'Come on, tell us a story, Adolphe'—or Dodolphe, or some name like that."

She shuddered.

"Don't you feel well?" asked Léon, moving closer to her.

"Oh, it's nothing. Just a chill."

"He was another one who never had to worry about where his women would come from," the old boatman added softly, as a compliment to his present passenger.

Then he spit on his hands and took up his oars.

But finally they had to part. Their farewells were sad. He was to write her in care of Madame Rollet; and she gave him such detailed instructions about using a double envelope that he marveled greatly at her shrewdness in love matters.

"So I have your word for it that everything's in order?" she said, as they kissed for the last time.

"Absolutely—But why the devil," he wondered, as he walked home alone through the streets, "is she so set on having that power of attorney?"

IV

Before long, Léon began to give himself superior airs around the office. He kept aloof from his colleagues and totally neglected his work. He waited for Emma's letters, and read them over and over. He wrote to her. He evoked her image with all the strength of his passion and his memories. Far from being lessened by absence, his longing to see her again increased, until finally one Saturday morning he took the road to Yonville.

When he looked down on the valley from the top of the hill and saw the church steeple with its tin flag turning in the wind, he was filled with an exquisite pleasure: smug satisfaction and selfish sentimentality were mingled in it—it was the feeling that a millionaire must experience on revisiting his boyhood village.

He prowled around her house. A light was burning in the kitchen. He watched for her shadow behind the curtains. Not a soul was to be seen.

Madame Lefrançois uttered loud cries at the sight of him, and said that he was "taller and thinner." Artémise, on the other hand, found that he had grown "heavier and darker."

He took his dinner in the small dining room, just as in the old days, but alone, without the tax collector: for Binet, sick of waiting for the Hirondelle, had permanently changed his mealtime to an hour earlier, and now dined on the stroke of five. Even so he never missed a chance to grumble that "the rusty old clock was slow."

Finally Léon got up his courage and knocked on the doctor's door. Madame was in her room: it was a quarter of an hour before she came down. Monsieur seemed delighted to see him again, but didn't stir from the house all evening or all the next day.

Only late Sunday evening did he see her alone, in the lane behind the garden—in the lane, just like Rodolphe. It was during a thunderstorm, and they talked under an umbrella, with lightning flashing around them.

The thought of parting was unbearable.

"I'd rather die!" said Emma.

She clung convulsively to his arm and wept:

"Adieu! Adieu! When will I see you again?"

They separated, then turned back for a last embrace; and it was at that moment that she promised him to find, soon, no matter how, some way in which they would be able to see each other alone and regularly, at least once a week. Emma had no doubt about succeeding. She looked forward to the future with confidence: the inheritance money would shortly be coming in.

On the strength of it she bought, for her bedroom, a pair of wide-striped yellow curtains that Monsieur Lheureux extolled as a bargain. She said she wished she could have a carpet; and Lheureux, assuring her that she wasn't "reaching for the moon," promised very obligingly to find her one. By now she didn't know how she could get along without him. She sent for him twenty times a day, and he always promptly left whatever he was doing and came, without a word of protest. Nor was it clear to anyone why Madame Rollet lunched at her house every day, and even visited with her privately.

It was about this time—the beginning of winter—that she became intensely musical.

One evening while Charles was listening she started the same piece over again four times, each time expressing annoyance with herself. Charles was unaware of anything wrong. "Bravo!" he cried. "Very good! Why stop? Keep going."

"No, I'm playing abominably. My fingers are rusty."

The next day he asked her to "play him something else."

"Very well, if you like."

Charles had to admit that she seemed a little out of practice. She fumbled, struck wrong notes, and finally broke off abruptly:

"That's enough of that! I should take some lessons, but . . ."

She bit her lips and added: "Twenty francs an hour—it's too expensive."

"Yes, it certainly is . . . a little . . ." said Charles, with a silly giggle. "But it seems to me you ought to be able to find somebody for less. There are plenty of musicians without big names who are better than the celebrities."

"Try and find some," said Emma.

When he came in the next day he gave her a sly look, and finally came out with: "You certainly have a way sometimes of thinking you know better than anybody else. I was at Barfeuchères today and Madame Liégeard told me that her three girls—the three at school at the Miséricorde—take lessons at two and a half francs an hour, and from a marvelous teacher!"

She shrugged, and from then on left her instrument unopened.

But whenever she walked by it she would sigh (if Bovary happened to be there): "Ah, my poor piano!"

And she always made a point of telling visitors that she had given up her music and now couldn't possibly go on with it again, for imperative reasons. Everybody pitied her. What a shame! She had so much talent! People even spoke to Bovary about it. They made him feel ashamed, especially the pharmacist.

"You're making a mistake! Natural faculties must never be let lie fallow!

Besides, my friend, look at it this way: by encouraging Madame to take lessons now, you'll save money later on your daughter's lessons. In my opinion, mothers should teach their children themselves. It's an idea of Rousseau's—maybe a little new, still, but bound to prevail eventually, I'm sure, like mother's breast-feeding and vaccination."

So Charles brought up the question of the piano again. Emma answered tartly that they'd better sell it. Poor old piano! It had so often been a source of pride for him, that to see it go would be like watching Emma commit partial suicide.

"If you really want to go ahead with it," he said, "I suppose a lesson now and then wouldn't ruin us."

"But lessons aren't worth taking," she said, "unless they're taken regularly."

That was how she obtained her husband's permission to go to the city once a week to meet her lover. By the end of the first month everyone found that her playing had improved considerably.

V

And so, every Thursday, she rose and dressed without a sound, lest she wake Charles, who would have remarked on her getting ready too early. Then she paced up and down, stood at the windows, looked out at the square. The first light of morning was stealing into the pillared market place; and on the pharmacist's house, its shutters still drawn, the pale tints of dawn were picking out the capital letters of the shop sign.

When the clock said quarter past seven she made her way to the Lion d'Or and was let in by the yawning Artémise. The servant paid her the attention of digging out the smoldering coals from under the ashes, and then left her to herself in the kitchen. From time to time she walked out into the yard. Hivert would be harnessing the horses. He went about it very deliberately, listening as he did so to Madame Lefrançois, who had stuck her head, nightcap and all, out of a window and was briefing him on his errands in a way that anyone else would have found bewildering. Emma tapped her foot on the cobbles.

Finally, when he had downed his bowl of soup, put on his overcoat, lighted his pipe and picked up his whip, he unhurriedly climbed onto the seat.

The Hirondelle set off at a gentle trot, and for the first mile or two kept stopping here and there to take on passengers who stood watching for it along the road, outside their gates. Those who had booked seats the day before kept the coach waiting: some, even, were still in their beds, and Hivert would call, shout, curse, and finally get down from his seat and pound on the doors. The wind whistled in through the cracked blinds.

Gradually the four benches filled up, the coach rattled along, row upon row of apple trees flashed by; and the road, lined on each side by a ditch of yellow water, stretched on and on, narrowing toward the horizon.

Emma knew every inch of it: she knew that after a certain meadow came a road sign, then an elm, a barn, or a road-mender's cabin; sometimes she even shut her eyes, trying to give herself a surprise. But she always knew just how much farther there was to go.

Finally the brick houses crowded closer together, the road rang under the wheels, and now the Hirondelle moved smoothly between gardens: through iron fences were glimpses of statues, artificial mounds crowned by arbors, clipped yews, a swing. Then, all at once, the city came into view.

Sloping downward like an amphitheatre, drowned in mist, it sprawled out shapelessly beyond its bridges. Then open fields swept upward again in a monotonous curve, merging at the top with the uncertain line of the pale sky. Thus seen from above, the whole landscape had the static quality of a painting: ships at anchor were crowded into one corner, the river traced its curve along the foot of the green hills, and on the water the oblong-shaped islands looked like great black fish stopped in their course. From the factory chimneys poured endless trails of brown smoke, their tips continually dissolving in the wind. The roar of foundries mingled with the clear peal of chimes that came from the churches looming in the fog. The leafless trees along the boulevards were like purple thickets in amongst the houses; and the roofs, all of them shiny with rain, gleamed with particular brilliance in the upper reaches of the town. Now and again a gust of wind blew the clouds toward the hill of Sainte-Catherine, like aerial waves breaking soundlessly against a cliff.

A kind of intoxication was wafted up to her from those closely packed lives, and her heart swelled as though the 120,000 souls palpitating below had sent up to her as a collective offering the breath of all the passions she supposed them to be feeling. In the face of the vastness her love grew larger, and was filled with a turmoil that echoed the vague ascending hum. All this love she, in turn, poured out—onto the squares, onto the tree-lined avenues, onto the streets; and to her the old Norman city was like some fabulous capital, a Babylon into which she was making her entry. She leaned far out the window and filled her lungs with air; the three horses galloped on, there was a grinding of stones in the mud beneath the wheels; the coach swayed; Hivert shouted warningly ahead to the wagons he was about to overtake, and businessmen leaving their suburban villas in Bois-Guillaume descended the hill at a respectable pace in their little family carriages.

There was a stop at the city gate: Emma took off her overshoes, changed her gloves, arranged her shawl, and twenty paces farther on she left the Hirondelle.

The city was coming to life. Clerks in caps were polishing shop windows, and women with baskets on their hips stood on street corners uttering loud, regular cries. She walked on, her eyes lowered, keeping close to the house walls and smiling happily under her lowered black veil.

For fear of being seen, she usually didn't take the shortest way. She would plunge into a maze of dark alleys, and emerge, hot and perspiring, close to the fountain at the lower end of the Rue Nationale. This is the part of town near the theater, full of bars and prostitutes. Often a van rumbled by, laden with shaky stage sets. Aproned waiters were sanding the pavement between the tubs of green bushes. There was a smell of absinthe, cigars and oysters.

Then she turned a corner. She recognized him from afar by the way his curly hair hung down below his hat.

He walked ahead on the sidewalk. She followed him to the hotel; he went upstairs, opened the door of the room, went in—What an embrace!

Then, after kisses, came a flood of words. They spoke of the troubles of the week, of their forebodings, their worries about letters; but now they could forget everything, and they looked into each other's eyes, laughing with delight and exchanging loving names.

The bed was a large mahogany one in the form of a boat. Red silk curtains hung from the ceiling and were looped back very low beside the flaring headboard, and there was nothing so lovely in the world as her dark hair and white skin against the deep crimson when she brought her bare arms together in a gesture of modesty, hiding her face in her hands.

The warm room, with its discreet carpet, its pretty knickknacks and its tranquil light, seemed designed for the intimacies of passion. The arrow-tipped curtain rods, the brass ornaments on the furniture and the big knobs on the andirons—all gleamed at once if the sun shone in. Between the candlesticks on the mantelpiece was a pair of those great pink shells that sound like the ocean when you hold them to your ear.

How they loved that sweet, cheerful room, for all its slightly faded splendor! Each piece of furniture was always waiting for them in its place, and sometimes the hairpins she had forgotten the Thursday before were still there, under the pedestal of the clock. They lunched beside the fire, on a little table inlaid with rosewood. Emma carved, murmuring all kinds of endearments as she put the pieces on his plate; and she gave a loud, wanton laugh when the champagne foamed over the fine edge of the glass onto the rings on her fingers. They were so completely lost in their possession of each other that they thought of themselves as being in their own home, destined to live there for the rest of their days, eternal young husband and eternal young wife. They said "our room," "our carpet," "our chairs"; she even said "our slippers," meaning a pair that Léon had given her to gratify a whim. They were of pink satin, trimmed with swansdown. When she sat in his lap her legs swung in the air, not reaching the floor, and the dainty slippers, open all around except at the tip, hung precariously from her bare toes.

He was savoring for the first time the ineffable subtleties of feminine refinement. Never had he encountered this grace of language, this quiet taste in dress, these relaxed, dovelike postures. He marveled at the sublimity of her soul and at the lace on her petticoat. Besides—wasn't she a "lady," and married besides? Everything, in short, that a mistress should be?

With her ever-changing moods, by turns brooding and gay, chattering and silent, fiery and casual, she aroused in him a thousand desires, awakening instincts or memories. She was the *amoureuse* of all the novels, the heroine of all the plays, the vague "she" of all the poetry books. Her shoulders were amber toned, like the bathing odalisques he had seen in pictures; she was long waisted like the feudal chatelaines; she resembled Musset's *"pâle femme de Barcelone,"*[8] too: but at all times she was less woman than angel!

Often, as he looked at her, it seemed to him that his soul, leaving him in quest of her, flowed like a wave around the outline of her head, and then was drawn down into the whiteness of her breast.

He would kneel on the floor before her, and with his elbows on her knees gaze at her smilingly, his face lifted.

She would bend toward him and murmur, as though choking with rapture:

"Don't move! Don't say a word! Just look at me! There's something so sweet in your eyes, something that does me so much good!"

She called him "child": "Do you love me, child?"

---

8. Pale woman of Barcelona (French). Alfred de Musset (1810–1857) frequently incarnates, for Flaubert, the type of stilted romantic sensibility he despises.

She never heard his answer, so fast did his lips always rise to meet her mouth.

On the clock there was a little bronze cupid, simpering and curving its arms under a gilded wreath. They often laughed at it, but when it came time to part, everything grew serious.

Motionless, face to face, they would say, over and over:

"Till Thursday! Till Thursday!"

Then she would abruptly take his face between her hands, quickly kiss him on the forehead, cry, "Adieu!" and run out into the hall.

She always went to a hairdresser in the Rue de la Comédie and had her hair brushed and put in order. Darkness would be falling; in the shops they would be lighting the gas.

She could hear the bell in the theater summoning the actors to the performance, and across the street she would see white-faced men and shabbily dressed women going in through the stage door.

It was hot in this little place with its too-low ceiling and its stove humming in the midst of wigs and pomades. The smell of the curling irons and the touch of the soft hands at work on her head soon made her drowsy, and she dozed off a little in her dressing gown. Often, as he arranged her hair, the coiffeur would ask her to buy tickets for a masked ball.

Then she was off. She retraced her way through the streets, reached the Croix-Rouge, retrieved the overshoes that she had hidden there that morning under a bench, and squeezed herself in among the impatient passengers. To spare the horses, the men got out at the foot of the hill, leaving Emma alone in the coach.

At each bend of the road more and more of the city lights came into view, making a layer of luminous mist that hung over the mass of the houses. Emma would kneel on the cushions and look back, letting her eyes wander over the brilliance. Sobs would burst from her, she would call Léon's name, and send him sweet words, and kisses that were lost in the wind.

On this hill road was a wretched beggar, who wandered with his stick in the midst of the traffic. His clothes were a mass of rags, and his face was hidden under a battered old felt hat that was turned down all around like a basin; when he took this off, it was to reveal two gaping, bloody sockets in place of eyelids. The flesh continually shredded off in red gobbets, and from it oozed a liquid matter, hardening into greenish scabs that reached down to his nose. His black nostrils sniffled convulsively. Whenever he began to talk, he leaned his head far back and gave an idiot laugh; and at such times his bluish eyeballs, rolling round and round, pushed up against the edges of the live wound.

As he walked beside the coaches he sang a little song:

> A clear day's warmth will often move
> A lass to stay in dreams of love . . .

And the rest of it was all about the birds, the sun, and the leaves on the trees.

Sometimes he would loom up all at once from behind Emma, bareheaded. She would draw back with a cry. Hivert always joked with him, urging him to hire a booth at the Saint-Romain fair, or laughingly asking after the health of his sweetheart.

Often while the coach was moving slowly up the hill his hat would suddenly come through the window, and he would be there, clinging with his other hand to the footboard, between the spattering wheels. His voice, at the outset a mere wail, would grow shrill. It would linger in the darkness like a plaintive cry of distress; and through the jingle of the horse bells, the rustle of the trees and the rumble of the empty coach, there was something eerie about it that gave Emma a shudder of horror. The sound spiraled down into the very depths of her soul, like a whirlwind in an abyss, and swept her off into the reaches of a boundless melancholy. But Hivert would become aware that his vehicle was weighed down on one side, and would strike out savagely at the blind man with his whip. The stinging lash would cut into his wounds, and he would drop off into the mud with a shriek.

One by one the Hirondelle's passengers would fall asleep, some with their mouths open, others with their chins on their chests, leaning on their neighbor's shoulder or with an arm in the strap, all the while rocking steadily with the motion of the coach; and the gleam of the lamp, swaying outside above the rumps of the shaft horses and shining in through the chocolate-colored calico curtains, cast blood-red shadows on all those motionless travelers. Emma, numb with sadness, would shiver under her coat; her feet would grow colder and colder, and she felt like death.

Charles would be at the house, waiting: the Hirondelle was always late on Thursdays. Then at last Madame would arrive! She would scarcely take time to kiss her little girl. Dinner wasn't ready—no matter! She forgave the cook: Félicité seemed to have everything her own way, these days.

Often her husband would notice her pallor, and ask whether she were ill.

"No," Emma would say.

"But you're acting so strangely tonight!"

"Oh, it's nothing! It's nothing!"

Some Thursdays she went up to her room almost the minute she came in. Justin would be there and would busy himself silently, cleverer at helping her than an experienced ladies' maid. He would arrange matches, candlesticks, a book, lay out her dressing jacket, open her bed.

"Very good," she would tell him. "Now run along."

For he would be standing there, his hands at his sides and his eyes staring, as though a sudden revery had tied him to the spot with a thousand strands.

The next day was always an ordeal, and the days that followed were even more unbearable, so impatient was she to recover her happiness. It was a fierce desire that was kept aflame by the vividness of her memories, and on the seventh day burst forth freely under Léon's caresses. His transports took the form of overflowing wonderment and gratitude. Emma enjoyed this passion in a way that was both deliberate and intense, keeping it alive by every amorous device at her command, and fearing all the while that someday it would come to an end.

Often she would say to him, sweetly and sadly:

"Ah! Sooner or later you'll leave me! You'll marry! You'll be like all the others."

"What others?"

"Why, men—all men."

And, languidly pushing him away, she would add: "You're faithless, every one of you!"

One day when they were having a philosophical discussion about earthly disillusionments, she went so far as to say (whether testing his jealousy, or yielding to an irresistible need to confide) that in the past, before him, she had loved someone else. "Not like you!" she quickly added; and she swore by her daughter that "nothing had happened."

The young man believed her, but nevertheless asked her what kind of man "he" had been.

"He was a sea captain," she told him.

Did she say that, perhaps, to forestall his making any inquiries, and at the same time to exalt herself by making the supposed victim of her charms sound like an imperious kind of man accustomed to having his way?

This impressed upon the clerk the mediocrity of his own status: he longed to have epaulettes, decorations and titles. Such things must be to her liking, he suspected, judging by her spendthrift ways.

There were a number of her wildest ideas, however, that Emma never said a word about, such as her craving to be driven to Rouen in a blue tilbury drawn by an English horse, with a groom in turned-down boots on the seat. It was Justin who had inspired her with this particular fancy, by begging her to take him into her service as footman; and though being deprived of it didn't prevent her from enjoying each weekly arrival in the city, it certainly added to the bitterness of each return to Yonville.

Often, when they spoke of Paris, she would murmur:

"Ah! How happy we'd be, living there!"

"Aren't we happy here?" the young man would softly ask, passing his hand over her hair.

"Of course we are! I'm being foolish. Kiss me!"

With her husband she was more charming than ever; she made him pistachio creams and played waltzes for him after dinner. He considered himself the luckiest of mortals, and Emma had no fear of discovery—until suddenly, one evening:

"It is Mademoiselle Lempereur you take lessons from, isn't it?"

"Yes."

"Well, I just saw her," said Charles, "at Madame Liégeard's. I talked to her about you: she doesn't know you."

It was like a thunderbolt. But she answered in a natural tone.

"Oh, she must have forgotten my name."

"Or else maybe there's more than one Mademoiselle Lempereur in Rouen who teaches piano."

"Maybe so."

Then, quickly:

"Besides, it just occurs to me: I have her receipts. Look!"

And she went to the secretary, rummaged in all the drawers, mixed up all the papers, and finally grew so rattled that Charles begged her not to go to so much trouble for a few wretched receipts.

"Oh, I'll find them," she said.

And indeed, the following Friday, while Charles was putting on one of his shoes in the dark dressing room where his clothes were kept, he felt a piece of paper between the sole and his sock, and pulled it out and read:

"Three months' lessons, plus supplies. Sixty-five francs. Paid. Félicité Lempereur, *Professeur de musique.*"

"How the devil did this get in my shoe?"

"It probably fell down from the old bill file on the shelf."

From that moment on, she piled lie upon lie, using them as veils to conceal her love.

Lying became a need, a mania, a positive joy—to such a point that if she said that she had walked down the right-hand side of a street the day before, it meant that she had gone down the left.

One morning just after she had gone, rather lightly clad as usual, there was a sudden snowfall; and Charles, looking out the window at the weather, saw Monsieur Bournisien setting out for Rouen in Monsieur Tuvache's buggy. So he ran down with a heavy shawl and asked the priest to give it to Madame as soon as he got to the Croix-Rouge. The moment he reached the inn, Bournisien asked where the wife of the Yonville doctor was. The hotel keeper replied that she spent very little time there. That evening, therefore, finding Madame Bovary in the Hirondelle, the curé told her of the *contretemps:* he seemed to attach little importance to it, however, for he launched into praise of a preacher, the sensation at the cathedral, adored by all the ladies.

Still, though he hadn't asked for explanations, others, in the future, might be less discreet. So she thought it practical to take a room each time at the Croix-Rouge, in order that her fellow villagers might see her there and have no suspicion.

One day, however, Monsieur Lheureux ran into her as she was leaving the Hotel de Boulogne on Léon's arm. She was frightened, thinking that he might talk. He was too smart for that.

But three days later he came into her room, closed the door, and said:

"I'd like some money."

She declared that she had none to give him. Lheureux began to moan, and reminded her of how many times he'd gone out of his way to oblige her.

And indeed, of the two notes signed by Charles, Emma had so far paid off only one. As for the second, the shopkeeper had agreed at her request to replace it with two others, which themselves had been renewed for a very long term. Then he drew out of his pocket a list of goods still unpaid for: the curtains, the carpet, upholstery material for armchairs, several dresses and various toilet articles, totaling about two thousand francs.

She hung her head.

"You may not have any cash," he said, "but you do have some property."

And he mentioned a wretched, tumbledown cottage situated at Barneville, near Aumale, which didn't bring in very much. It had once been part of a small farm that the elder Bovary had sold: Lheureux knew everything, down to the acreage and the neighbors' names.

"If I were you I'd get rid of it," he said. "You'd still have a balance after paying me."

She brought up the difficulty of finding a buyer; he was encouraging about the possibility of locating one. But: "What would I have to do to be able to sell?" she asked.

"Haven't you power of attorney?" he countered.

The words came to her like a breath of fresh air.

"Leave your bill with me," said Emma.

"Oh, it's not worth bothering about," replied Lheureux.

He came again the following week, very proud of having unearthed, after a lot of trouble, a certain Monsieur Langlois, who had been eying the property for a long time without ever mentioning the price he was willing to pay.

"The price doesn't matter!" she cried.

On the contrary, he said: they should take their time, sound Langlois out. The affair was worth the bother of a trip, and since she couldn't make it he offered to go himself and talk things over with Langlois on the spot. On his return he announced that the buyer offered 4,000 francs.

Emma beamed at the news.

"Frankly," he said, "it's a good price."

Half the amount was paid her at once, and when she said that now she'd settle his bill, he told her:

"Honestly, it hurts me to see you hand over every bit of all that money right away."

She stared at the banknotes and had a vision of the countless love-meetings those 2,000 francs represented. "What?" she stammered. "What do you mean?"

"Oh," he said, with a jovial laugh, "there's more than one way of making out a bill. Don't you think I know how it is with married couples?"

And he stared at her, running his fingernails up and down two long sheets of paper he had in his hand. After a long moment he opened his billfold and spread out on the table four more promissory notes, each for a thousand francs.

"Sign these," he said, "and keep all the money."

She gave a choked cry.

"But if I give you the balance," Monsieur Lheureux answered, "don't you see that I'm doing you a service?"

And taking up a pen he wrote at the bottom of the bill: "Received from Madame Bovary the sum of 4,000 francs."

"What's there to worry you? In six months you'll have the rest of the money due on your cottage, and I'll make the last note payable after that date."

She was getting a little mixed up in her arithmetic, and she felt a ringing in her ears as though gold pieces were bursting out of their bags and dropping to the floor all about her. Finally Lheureux explained that he had a friend named Vinçart, a Rouen banker, who would discount these four new notes, following which he himself would pay Madame the balance of what was really owed.

But instead of 2,000 francs, he brought her only 1,800; for his friend Vinçart (as was "only right") had deducted 200, representing commission and discount.

Then he casually asked for a receipt.

"You know . . . in business . . . sometimes . . . And put down the date, please, the date."

A host of things that she could do with the money stretched out before Emma in perspective. She had enough sense to put 3,000 francs aside, and with them she paid, as they came due, the first three notes; but the fourth, as luck would have it, arrived at the house on a Thursday; and Charles, stunned, patiently awaited his wife's return to have it explained to him.

Ah! If she hadn't told him anything about that note it was because she hadn't wanted to bother him with household worries; she sat in his lap, caressed him, cooed at him, and gave a long list of all the indispensables she had bought on credit.

"You'll have to admit," she said, "that considering how many things there were, the bill's not too high."

Charles, at his wits' end, soon had recourse to the inevitable Lheureux, who promised to straighten everything out if Monsieur would sign two more notes, one of them for 700 francs, payable in three months. Charles wrote a pathetic letter to his mother, asking for help. Instead of sending an answer, she came herself; and when Emma asked him if he'd got anything out of her:

"Yes," he answered. "But she insists on seeing the bill."

So early the next morning Emma rushed to Monsieur Lheureux and begged him to make out a different note, for not more than 1,000 francs, for if she were to show the one for 4,000 she would have to say that she had paid off two-thirds of it, and consequently reveal the sale of the cottage. That transaction had been handled very cleverly by the shopkeeper, and never did leak out until later.

Despite the low price of each article, the elder Madame Bovary naturally found such expenditure excessive.

"Couldn't you get along without a carpet? Why re-cover the armchairs? In my day every house had exactly one armchair, for elderly persons—at least, that's the way it was at my mother's, and she was a respectable woman, I assure you. Everybody can't be rich! No amount of money will last if you throw it out the window. It would make me blush to pamper myself the way you do—and I'm an old woman and need looking after. . . . Who's ever seen so much finery? What, silk for linings at two francs when you can find jaconet for half a franc and even less that does perfectly well?"

Emma, stretched out on the settee, answered with the greatest calm:

"That's enough, Madame, that's enough."

Her mother-in-law continued to sermonize, prophesying that they'd end in the poorhouse. Besides, it was all Bovary's fault, she said. At least, though, he'd promised her he'd cancel the power of attorney.

"What!"

"Yes, he's given me his word," said the lady.

Emma opened the window and called Charles in, and the poor fellow had to confess the promise his mother had extracted from him.

Emma disappeared, then quickly returned, majestically holding out to her a large sheet of paper.

"I thank you," said the old woman.

And she threw the power of attorney into the fire.

Emma burst out laughing and didn't stop: her laughter was loud and strident—it was an attack of hysterics.

"Ah, my God!" cried Charles. "You're overdoing things, too! You've no right to come here and make scenes."

His mother shrugged her shoulders and said that "it was all put on."

But Charles, rebellious for the first time in his life, took his wife's part, and the older Madame Bovary said she wanted to go. She departed the next day, and on the doorstep, as he was trying to make her change her mind, she answered:

"No! No! You love her more than you do me, and you're right; that's as it should be. There's nothing I can do about it. You'll see, though . . . . Take care of yourself . . . I can promise you it will be a long time before I come back here to 'make scenes,' as you put it."

Nevertheless Charles was very hangdog with Emma, and she didn't hide her resentment at having been distrusted. He had to entreat her many times before she would consent to accept power of attorney again, and he even went with her to Maître Guillaumin to have a new one drawn up, identical with the first.

"I well understand your doing this," said the notary. "A man of science can't be expected to burden himself with the practical details of existence."

Charles felt soothed by those oily words: they flattered his weakness, making it look like preoccupation with lofty things.

What exultation there was the next Thursday in their room at the hotel, with Léon! She laughed, cried, sang, danced, sent for water ices, insisted on smoking cigarettes. He found her wild, but adorable, superb.

He had no idea what it was that was driving her more and more to fling herself into a reckless pursuit of pleasure. She grew irritable, greedy, voluptuous; and she walked boldly with him in the street—unafraid, she said, of compromising herself. There were times, though, when Emma trembled at the sudden thought of meeting Rodolphe, for she suspected that even though they had parted forever, he still retained some of his power over her.

One night she didn't return to Yonville at all. Charles lost his head, and little Berthe, unwilling to go to bed without *maman*, sobbed as though her heart would break. Justin had gone off down the road to look for her. Monsieur Homais actually stepped out of his pharmacy.

Finally, at eleven o'clock, unable to stand it any longer, Charles harnessed his buggy, jumped in, whipped the horse on, and reached the Croix-Rouge at two in the morning. No sign of her. It occurred to him that Léon might have seen her: but where did he live? Luckily, Charles remembered the address of his employer, and he hastened there.

The sky was beginning to lighten. He made out some escutcheons over a door, and knocked. Without opening, someone shouted the information he wanted, together with a good deal of abuse about people who disturb other people at night.

The house the clerk lived in boasted neither bell nor knocker nor doorman. Charles pounded with his fists on the shutters, but just then a policeman came along: this frightened him, and he slunk away.

"I'm crazy," he told himself. "The Lormeaux' probably kept her to dinner."

But the Lormeaux' no longer lived in Rouen.

"She must have stayed to look after Madame Dubreuil. Oh, no—Madame Dubreuil died ten months ago. So where can she be?"

He had an idea. In a café he asked for the directory and looked up Mademoiselle Lempereur: 74 Rue de la Renelle-des-Maroquiniers was her address.

Just as he turned into that street, Emma herself appeared at the other end. It would be wrong to say that he embraced her: he flung himself on her, crying:

"What kept you, yesterday?"

"I was ill."

"Ill? How? Where?"

She passed her hand over her forehead:

"At Mademoiselle Lempereur's."

"I knew it! I was on my way there."

"Well, there's no use going there now. She's just gone out. But after this don't get so excited. I won't feel free to do a thing if I know that the slightest delay upsets you like this."

It was a kind of permit that she was giving herself—a permit to feel completely unhampered in her escapades. And she proceeded to make free and frequent use of it. Whenever she felt like seeing Léon, she would go off, using any excuse that came to mind; and since he wouldn't be expecting her that day, she would call for him at his office.

It was all very joyous, the first few times. But before long he stopped hiding the truth from her: his employer was complaining loudly of these incursions.

"Bah!" she said. "Come along."

And he slipped out.

She demanded that he dress entirely in black and grow a little pointed beard, to make himself look like the portraits of Louis XIII.[9] She asked to see his rooms, and found them very so-so; he reddened at that, but she didn't notice, and advised him to buy curtains like hers. When he objected to the expense:

"Ah! So you pinch your pennies!" she said, laughing.

Each time, Léon had to tell her everything he had done since their last rendezvous. She asked for a poem, a poem for herself, a love piece written in her honor: he could never find a rhyme for the second line, and ended up copying a sonnet from a keepsake.

He did that less out of vanity than out of a desire to please her. He never disputed any of her ideas; he fell in with all her tastes: he was becoming her mistress, far more than she was his. Her sweet words and her kisses swept away his soul. Her depravity was so deep and so dissembled as to be almost intangible: where could she have learned it?

VI

On his trips to see her he had often taken dinner at the pharmacist's, and he felt obliged out of politeness to invite him in return.

"With pleasure!" Homais answered. "A change will do me good: my life here is such a rut. We'll see a show and eat in a restaurant and really go out on the town."

"Out on the town!" Madame Homais' exclamation was affectionate: she was alarmed by the vague perils he was girding himself to meet.

"Why shouldn't I? Don't you think I ruin my health enough, exposing myself to all those drug fumes? That's women for you! They're jealous of Science, and yet they're up in arms at the mention of even the most legitimate distraction. Never mind, I'll be there. One of these days I'll turn up in Rouen, and we'll turn the town upside down."

In the past, the apothecary would have been careful to avoid such an expression; but now he was going in for a daredevil, Parisian kind of language that he considered very à la mode, and like his neighbor Madame Bovary he asked the clerk many searching questions about life in the big city. He even

9. French king (1601–1643), who ruled 1610–43; the father of Louis XIV.

talked slang in order to show off in front of the "bourgeois," using such terms as *turne, bazar, chicard, chicanard,* the English "Breda Street" for Rue de Bréda and *je me la casse* for *je m'en vais.*[1]

So one Thursday Emma was surprised to find, in the kitchen of the Lion d'Or, none other than Monsieur Homais in traveling garb—that is, wrapped in an old cape that no one had ever seen on him before, with a suitcase in one hand and in the other the foot warmer from his shop. He hadn't breathed a word about his trip to anyone, fearing lest the public be made nervous by his absence.

The idea of revisiting the scenes of his youth apparently excited him, for he didn't stop talking all the way. The wheels had barely stopped turning when he leapt from the coach in search of Léon; and despite the clerk's struggles he dragged him off to lunch at the Café de Normandie. Here Monsieur Homais made a majestic entrance: he kept his hat on, considering it highly provincial to uncover in a public place.

Emma waited for Léon three-quarters of an hour, then rushed to his office. She was at a loss as to what could have happened: in her mind she heaped him with reproaches for his indifference and herself for her weakness; all afternoon she stood with her forehead glued to the windowpanes of their room.

At two o'clock Léon and Homais were still facing each other across their table. The big dining room was emptying; the stovepipe, designed to resemble a palm tree, spread out in a circle of gilded fronds on the white ceiling; and near them, just inside the window, in full sun, a little fountain gurgled into a marble basin, where among watercress and asparagus three sluggish lobsters stretched their claws toward a heap of quail.

Homais was in heaven. He found the *luxe* even more intoxicating than the fine food and drink; still, the Pommard went to his head a little; and when the rum omelet made its appearance he advanced certain immoral theories concerning women. What particularly captivated him was the quality of *chic.* He adored an elegant *toilette* in a handsome *décor,* and as for physical qualities, he wasn't averse to a "plump little morsel."

Léon desperately watched the clock. The apothecary kept drinking, eating, talking.

"You must feel quite deprived, here in Rouen," he suddenly remarked. "But then, your lady-love doesn't live *too* far away."

And as Léon blushed:

"Come, be frank! You won't deny, will you, that in Yonville . . ."

The young man began to stammer.

" . . . at the Bovarys', you did quite some courting of . . ."

"Of whom?"

"Of the maid!"

Homais wasn't joking. But Léon's vanity got the better of his discretion, and despite himself he protested indignantly. Besides, he said, he liked only brunettes.

"I approve your preference," said the pharmacist. "They have more temperament."

And putting his mouth close to his friend's ear, he enumerated the sure

---

1. I'm leaving. *Turne:* sweet. *Bazar:* fabulous. *Chicard:* "in." *Chicanard:* con artist. *Je me la casse:* I'm breaking (out).

signs of temperament in a woman. He even launched into an ethnographical digression: German women were moody, French women licentious, Italian women passionate.

"What about Negro women?" demanded the clerk.

"Much favored by artists," said Homais. "Waiter—two demitasses!"

"Shall we go?" said Léon finally, his patience at an end.

"*Yes,*" said Homais, in English.

But before leaving he insisted on seeing the manager, and offered him his congratulations.

Léon, in the hope of being left alone, now pleaded a business appointment.

"Ah! I'll go with you!" said Homais.

And as he accompanied him through the streets he talked about his wife, about his children, about their future, about his pharmacy, told him in what a rundown state he had found it and to what a peak of perfection he had brought it.

When they reached the Hotel de Boulogne, Léon brusquely took leave of him, ran upstairs and found his mistress close to hysterics.

The mention of the pharmacist's name put her into a rage. He pleaded his case persuasively: it wasn't his fault—surely she knew Monsieur Homais. Could she think for a moment that he preferred his company? But she turned away; he caught hold of her, and winding his arms around her waist he sank to his knees, languorous, passionate, imploring.

She stood there, solemn, almost terrible, transfixing him with her great blazing eyes. Then tears came to cloud them, she lowered her reddened eyelids, held out her hands, and Léon was just pressing them to his lips when a servant knocked and said that someone was asking for Monsieur.

"You'll come back?" she said.

"Yes."

"When?"

"Right away."

"How do you like my little trick?" said the pharmacist, when Léon appeared. "I wanted to help you get away from your company: you gave me the impression you didn't expect to enjoy it. Let's go to Bridoux's and have a glass of cordial."

Léon insisted that he had to return to his office. The apothecary made facetious remarks about legal papers and legal flummery.

"Forget about Cujas and Barthole[2] for a bit, for heaven's sake. Who's to stop you? Be a sport. Let's go to Bridoux's. You'll see his dog: it's very interesting."

And when the clerk stubbornly held out:

"I'll come, too. I'll read a newspaper while I wait, or look through a law book."

Overcome by Emma's anger, Monsieur Homais' chatter, and perhaps by the heavy lunch, Léon stood undecided, as though under the pharmacist's spell.

"Let's go to Bridoux's!" the latter kept repeating. "It's only a step from here—Rue Malpalu."

2. Or Bartole (1313–1357), an Italian jurist in Bologna. Jacques Cujas (1552–1590), a famous jurist who interpreted Roman law in contemporary terms.

Out of cowardice or stupidity, or perhaps yielding to that indefinable impulse that leads us to do the things we most deplore, he let himself be carried off to Bridoux's. They found him in his little yard, superintending three workmen who were pantingly turning the great wheel of a Seltzer-water machine. Homais offered them several bits of advice and embraced Bridoux; they had their cordial. Twenty times Léon started to leave, but the pharmacist caught him by the arm, saying:

"Just a minute! I'm coming. We'll go to the *Fanal de Rouen* and say hello to everybody. I'll introduce you to Thomassin."

He got rid of him, however, and flew to the hotel. Emma was gone.

She had just left in a fury. She hated him. His failure to keep their appointment seemed to her an insult, and she sought additional reasons for seeing no more of him. He was unheroic, weak, commonplace, spineless as a woman, and stingy and timorous to boot.

Gradually, growing calmer, she came to see that she had been unjust to him. But casting aspersions on those we love always does something to loosen our ties. We shouldn't maltreat our idols: the gilt comes off on our hands.

From then on, matters extraneous to their love occupied a greater place in their talk. The letters that Emma sent him were all about flowers, poetry, the moon and the stars: she resorted to these naïve expedients as her passion weakened, trying to keep it alive by artificial means. She continually promised herself that the next rendezvous would carry her to the peak of bliss; but when it was over she had to admit that she had felt nothing extraordinary. Each disappointment quickly gave way to new hope; each time, Emma returned to him more feverish, more avid. She could hardly wait to undress: she pulled so savagely at her corset string that it hissed around her hips like a gliding snake. Then she would tiptoe barefoot to see once again that the door was locked, and in a single movement let fall all her clothes; and, pale, silent, solemn, she would fling herself against his body with a long shudder.

There was something mad, though, something strange and sinister, about that cold, sweating forehead, about those stammering lips, those wildly staring eyes, the clasp of those arms—something that seemed to Léon to be creeping between them, subtly, as though to tear them apart.

He didn't dare question her; but realizing how experienced she was, he told himself that she must have known the utmost extremes of suffering and pleasure. What had once charmed him he now found a little frightening. Then, too, he rebelled against the way his personality was increasingly being submerged: he resented her perpetual triumph over him. He even did his best to stop loving her; then at the sound of her footsteps he would feel his will desert him, like a drunkard at the sight of strong liquor.

She made a point, it is true, of showering him with all kinds of attentions—everything from fine foods to coquetries of dress and languorous glances. She brought roses from Yonville in her bosom and tossed them at him; she worried over his health, gave him advice about how to conduct himself; and one day, to bind him the closer, hoping that heaven itself might take a hand in things, she slipped over his head a medal of the Blessed Virgin. Like a virtuous mother, she inquired about his associates:

"Don't see them," she would say. "Don't go out. Just think about us: love me!"

She wished she could keep an eye on him continually, and it occurred to her to have him followed on the street. There was a kind of tramp near the hotel who always accosted travelers and who would certainly be willing to . . . But her pride rebelled.

"What if he does betray me? Do I care?"

One day when they had said farewell earlier than usual, she caught sight of the walls of her convent as she was walking back alone down the boulevard, and she sank onto a bench in the shade of the elms. How peaceful those days had been! How she had longed for that ineffable emotion of love that she had tried to imagine from her books!

The first months of her marriage, her rides in the forest, the vicomte she had waltzed with, Lagardy singing—all passed again before her eyes. And Léon suddenly seemed as far removed as the others.

"I do love him, though!" she told herself.

No matter: she wasn't happy, and never had been. Why was life so unsatisfactory? Why did everything she leaned on crumble instantly to dust? But why, if somewhere there existed a strong and handsome being—a man of valor, sublime in passion and refinement, with a poet's heart and an angel's shape, a man like a lyre with strings of bronze, intoning elegiac epithalamiums to the heavens—why mightn't she have the luck to meet him? Ah, fine chance! Besides, nothing was worth looking for: everything was a lie! Every smile concealed a yawn of boredom; every joy, a curse; every pleasure, its own surfeit; and the sweetest kisses left on one's lips but a vain longing for fuller delight.

Through the air came a hoarse, prolonged metallic groan, and then the clock of the convent struck four. Only four! And it seemed to her that she had been there on that bench since eternity. But an infinity of passions can be compressed into a minute, like a crowd into a little space. Emma's passions were the sole concern of her life: for money she had no more thought than an archduchess.

One day, however, she was visited by an ill-kempt individual, red faced and bald, who said he had been sent by Monsieur Vinçart of Rouen. He pulled out the pins fastening the side pocket of his long green frock coat, stuck them in his sleeve, and politely handed her a document.

It was a note for 500 francs, signed by her, which Lheureux, despite all his promises, had endorsed over to Vinçart.

She sent her maid for Lheureux. He couldn't come.

The stranger had remained standing, dissimulating under his thick blond eyebrows the inquisitive glances that he cast left and right. "What answer am I to give Monsieur Vinçart?" he asked, with an innocent air.

"Well," said Emma, "tell him . . . that I haven't got . . . I'll have it next week. . . . He should wait . . . yes, I'll have it next week."

Whereupon the fellow went off without a word.

But the next day, at noon, she received a protest of nonpayment; and the sight of the official document, bearing the words "Maître Hareng, *huissier* at Buchy" several times in large letters, gave her such a fright that she hurried to the dry-goods merchant.

She found him in his shop tying up a parcel.

"At your service!" he said. "What can I do for you?"

He didn't interrupt his task: his clerk, a slightly hunchbacked girl of thirteen or so, who also did his cooking, was helping him.

Finally he clattered across the shop in his wooden shoes, climbed up ahead of Madame to the second floor, and showed her into a small office. Here on a large fir desk lay several ledgers, fastened down by a padlocked metal bar that stretched across them. A safe could be glimpsed against the wall, under some lengths of calico—a safe of such size that it certainly contained something besides cash and promissory notes. And indeed Monsieur Lheureux did some pawnbroking: it was here that he kept Madame Bovary's gold chain, along with some earrings that had belonged to poor Tellier. The latter had finally had to sell the Café Français, and had since bought a little grocery business in Quincampoix, where he was dying of his catarrh, his face yellower than the tallow candles he sold.

Lheureux sat down in his broad, rush-bottomed armchair.

"What's new?" he asked her.

"Look!"

And she showed him the document.

"Well, what can I do about it?"

She flew into a rage, reminding him that he had promised not to endorse her notes. He admitted it.

"But my hand was forced: my creditors had a knife at my throat."

"And what's going to happen now?" she asked.

"Oh, it's very simple: a court warrant, then execution; there's no way out."

Emma had to restrain herself from hitting him. She asked quietly whether there wasn't some way of appeasing Monsieur Vinçart.

"Ha! Appease Vinçart! You don't know him: he's fiercer than an Arab."

But Monsieur Lheureux *had* to do something about it!

"Now listen!" he said. "It seems to me I've been pretty nice to you so far."

And opening one of his ledgers:

"Look!"

He moved his finger up the page:

"Let's see . . . let's see . . . August 3,200 francs . . . June 17, 150 . . . March 23, 46. In April . . ."

He stopped, as though afraid of making a blunder.

"I won't even mention the notes your husband signed, one for seven hundred francs, another for three hundred. And as for your payments on account, and the interest, there's no end to it. It's a mess. I won't have anything more to do with it."

She wept; she even called him her "dear Monsieur Lheureux." But he kept laying the blame on "that scoundrelly Vinçart." Besides, he himself didn't have a centime: no one was paying him at the moment; his creditors were tearing the clothes from his back; a poor shopkeeper like himself couldn't advance money.

Emma stopped speaking; and Monsieur Lheureux, nibbling the quill of his pen, seemed disturbed by her silence.

"Of course," he said, "if I were to have something come in one of these days I might . . ."

"After all," she said, "as soon as the balance on Barneville . . ."

"What's that?"

And when he heard that Langlois hadn't yet paid he seemed very surprised. Then, in an oily voice:

"And our terms will be . . . ?"

"Oh, anything you say!"

Then he shut his eyes to help himself think, wrote down a few figures, and assuring her that he was making things hard for himself, taking a great risk, "bleeding himself white," he made out four notes for 250 francs each, payable a month apart.

"Let's hope that Vinçart's willing to listen to me! Anyway, you have my word: I don't say one thing and mean another; I'm open and aboveboard."

Afterwards he casually showed her a few items, not one of which, in his opinion, was worthy of Madame.

"When I think of dress goods like this selling at seven sous a meter and guaranteed dye-fast! Everybody believes it, too! And they don't get undeceived. I can assure you." The admission that he swindled others was meant as clinching proof of his frankness with herself.

Then he called her back and showed her several yards of point lace that he had come upon recently "in a vendue."

"Isn't it splendid?" he said. "It's being used a good deal now for antimacassars: it's the last word."

And quicker than a juggler he wrapped up the lace and handed it to Emma.

"At least," she said, "let me know how much it . . ."

"Oh, we'll talk about that later," he answered, turning abruptly away.

That very evening she made Bovary write his mother and ask her to send the balance of his inheritance at once. Her mother-in-law replied that there was nothing to send: the estate was settled, and in addition to Barneville they could count on a yearly income of 600 francs, which she would forward punctually.

So Madame sent bills to two or three patients, and before long she was sending them to many more, so successful did the expedient prove. She was always careful to add, in a postscript: "Don't speak of this to my husband—you know how proud he is. With regrets. Your humble servant." There were a few complaints, but she intercepted them.

To raise money she began to sell her old gloves, her old hats, all kinds of household odds and ends. She drove a hard bargain: her peasant blood stood her in good stead. And on her trips to the city she combed the curiosity shops for knickknacks, telling herself that Monsieur Lheureux, if no one else, would take them off her hands. She brought ostrich feathers, Chinese porcelains, old chests; she borrowed from Félicité, from Madame Lefrançois, from the landlady of the Croix-Rouge, from anyone and everyone. With part of the money she finally got from Barneville, she paid off two notes, the rest—1,500 francs—dribbled away. She signed new notes—always new notes.

Occasionally she tried to add up some figures, but the totals were so enormous that she couldn't believe them. Then she'd begin all over again, quickly become confused, and push it all aside and forget it.

The house was a gloomy place these days. Tradesmen called, and left with angry faces. Handkerchiefs lay strewn about on the stoves; and Madame Homais was shocked to see little Berthe with holes in her stockings. If Charles ventured some timid remark, Emma retorted savagely that *she* certainly wasn't to blame.

Why these fits of rage? He laid it all to her old nervous illness; and, penitent at having mistaken her infirmities for faults, he cursed his selfishness and longed to run up to her and take her in his arms.

"Oh, no!" he told himself. "I'd only annoy her."

And he did nothing.

After dinner he would walk alone in the garden. Then, with little Berthe in his lap and his medical journal open, he would try to teach the child to read. But she had never been given the slightest schooling, and after a few moments her eyes would grow round and sad, and the tears would come. He would comfort her: he filled the watering can to help her make rivulets in the paths, or broke privet branches that she could plant as trees in the flower beds. None of this harmed the garden, particularly—it was so choked with high grass anyway: they owed so many days' pay to Lestiboudois! Then the little girl would feel chilly and ask for her mother.

"Call Félicité," Charles would tell her. "You know *maman* doesn't like to be disturbed."

It was the onset of autumn, and already the leaves were falling—like two years before, when she had been so ill. When would there be an end to all this? And he would walk up and down, his hands behind his back.

Madame was in her room. No one else was admitted. She stayed there all day long in a torpor, not bothering to dress, now and again burning incense that she had bought at an Algerian shop in Rouen. She couldn't stand having Charles lying like a log at her side all night, and her repeated complaints finally drove him to sleep in the attic. She would read till morning—lurid novels full of orgies and bloodshed.

Sometimes, in sudden terror, she screamed; but when Charles ran in she dismissed him:

"Oh, get out."

At other times, seared by that hidden fire which her adultery kept feeding, consumed with longing, feverish with desire, she would open her window, inhale the cold air, let the heavy mass of her hair stream out in the wind: as she gazed at the stars she wished she were loved by a prince. Thoughts of Léon filled her. At such moments she would have given anything for a single one of their trysts—the trysts that sated her lust.

Those were her gala days. She was determined that they be glorious; and when he couldn't pay for everything himself she freely made up the difference. This happened almost every time. He tried to convince her that they would be just as well off elsewhere, in a more modest hotel, but she always objected.

One day she opened her bag, produced six little silver-gilt spoons—they had been her father's wedding present—and asked him to run out and pawn them for her. Léon obeyed, though he disliked the errand: he was afraid it might compromise him.

Thinking it over later, he came to the conclusion that his mistress was certainly beginning to act strangely: maybe the people who were urging him to break with her weren't so mistaken after all.

For indeed someone had sent his mother a long anonymous letter, warning her that he was "ruining himself with a married woman"; and the lady, having visions of the perennial bogey of respectable families—that ill-defined, baleful female, that siren, that fantastic monster forever lurking in the abysses of love—wrote to Maître Bocage, his employer. This gentleman's handling of the matter was flawless. He talked to the young man for three-quarters of an hour, trying to unseal his eyes and warn him of the precipice ahead. Sooner or later, such an affair would harm his career. He begged him to break it off—and if he couldn't make the sacrifice for his own sake, then he should at least do it for his—namely, for the sake of Maître Bocage.

In the end Léon had promised never to see Emma again; and he reproached himself for not having kept his word, especially considering all the trouble and reproaches she still probably held in store for him—not to mention the jokes his fellow clerks cracked every morning around the stove. Besides, he was about to be promoted to head clerk: this was the time to turn over a new leaf. So he gave up playing the flute and said good-bye to exalted sentiments and romantic dreams. There isn't a bourgeois alive who in the ferment of his youth, if only for a day or for a minute, hasn't thought himself capable of boundless passions and noble exploits. The sorriest little woman-chaser has dreamed of Oriental queens; in a corner of every notary's heart lie the moldy remains of a poet.

These days it only bored him when Emma suddenly burst out sobbing on his breast: like people who can stand only a certain amount of music, he was drowsy and apathetic amidst the shrillness of her love; his heart had grown deaf to its subtler overtones.

By now they knew each other too well: no longer did they experience, in their mutual possession, that wonder that multiplies the joy a hundredfold. She was as surfeited with him as he was tired of her. Adultery, Emma was discovering, could be as banal as marriage.

But what way out was there? She felt humiliated by the degradation of such pleasures; but to no avail: she continued to cling to them, out of habit or out of depravity; and every day she pursued them more desperately, destroying all possible happiness by her excessive demands. She blamed Léon for her disappointed hopes, as though he had betrayed her; and she even longed for a catastrophe that would bring about their separation, since she hadn't the courage to bring it about herself.

Still, she continued to write him loving letters, faithful to the idea that a woman must always write her lover.

But as her pen flew over the paper she was aware of the presence of another man, a phantom embodying her most ardent memories, the most beautiful things she had read and her strongest desires. In the end he became so real and accessible that she tingled with excitement, unable though she was to picture him clearly, so hidden was he, godlike, under his manifold attributes. He dwelt in that enchanted realm where silken ladders swing from balconies moon-bright and flower-scented. She felt him near her: he was coming—coming to ravish her entirely in a kiss. And the next moment she would drop back to earth, shattered; for these rapturous love-dreams drained her more than the greatest orgies.

She lived these days in a state of constant and total exhaustion. She was continually receiving writs—official documents that she barely looked at. She wished she were dead, or in a state of continual sleep.

The Thursday night of the mi-carême—the mid-Lenten festivities—she didn't return to Yonville, but went to a masked ball. She wore velvet knee breeches and red stockings and a peruke, and a cocked hat over one ear. She danced all night to the wild sound of trombones; she was the center of an admiring throng; and morning found her under the portico of the theatre with five or six maskers dressed as stevedores and sailors—friends of Léon's, who were wondering where they might have something to eat.

The nearby cafés were all full. On the river front they found a nondescript restaurant whose owner showed them up to a little room on the fifth floor.

The men whispered in a corner, doubtless consulting about the expense. A clerk, two medical students and a shop assistant: what company she was keeping! As for the women, Emma was quickly aware from their voices that most of them must be of the lowest class. That frightened her, and she drew back her chair and lowered her eyes.

The others began to eat. She did not. Her forehead was afire, her eyelids were smarting, her skin was icy cold. In her head she still felt the quaking of the dance floor under the rhythmic tread of a thousand feet. The smell of punch and cigar smoke made her dizzy. She fainted, and they carried her to the window.

Day was beginning to break, and in the pale sky toward Sainte-Catherine a large streak of red was widening. The leaden river shivered in the wind; the bridges were empty; the street lamps were going out.

Gradually she revived, and somehow she thought of Berthe, asleep out there beyond the horizon, in Félicité's room. But a wagon laden with long strips of iron went by, and the impact of its metallic clang shook the house walls.

Abruptly, she left the place. She took off her costume, told Léon she had to go home, and at last was alone in the Hotel de Boulogne. She loathed everything, including herself. She longed to fly away like a bird, to recapture her youth somewhere far away in the immaculate reaches of space.

She went out, followed the boulevard, crossed the Place Cauchoise and walked through the outskirts of the city to an open street overlooking gardens. She walked swiftly; the fresh air calmed her; and gradually the faces of the crowd, the maskers, the quadrilles, the blazing lights, the supper, and those women she had found herself with all disappeared like mist blown off by the wind. Then she returned to the Croix-Rouge and flung herself down on her bed in the little third-floor room with the prints of the Tour de Nesle. At four that afternoon Hivert woke her.

When she arrived home Félicité showed her a gray sheet of paper stuck behind the clock.

"By virtue of an instrument," she read, "duly setting forth the terms of a judgment to be enforced . . ."

What judgment? The previous day, she found, another paper had arrived; she hadn't seen it; and now she was dumbfounded to read these words:

"To Madame Bovary: You are hereby commanded by order of the king, the law and the courts . . ."

Then, skipping several lines, she saw:

"Within twenty-four hours." What was this? "Pay the total amount of 8,000 francs." And lower down: "There to be subjected to all due processes of law, and notably to execution of distraint upon furniture and effects."

What was to be done? In twenty-four hours: tomorrow! Lheureux, she thought, was probably trying to frighten her again. Suddenly she saw through all his schemes; the reason for his amiability burst upon her. What reassured her was the very enormity of the amount.

Nonetheless, as a result of buying and never paying, borrowing, signing notes and then renewing those same notes, which grew larger and larger each time they came due, she had gradually built up a capital for Monsieur Lheureux that he was impatient to lay his hands on to use in his speculations.

She called on him, assuming a nonchalant air.

"You know what's happened? It's a joke, I suppose?"

"No."

"What do you mean?"

He slowly turned his head away and folded his arms.

"Did you think, my dear lady," he said, "that I was going to go on to the end of time being your supplier and banker just for the love of God? I have to get back what I laid out: let's be fair!"

She was indignant about the size of the amount claimed.

"What can I do about it? The court upheld it. There's a judgment. You were notified. Besides, I have nothing to do with it—it's Vinçart."

"Couldn't you . . . ?"

"Absolutely nothing."

"But . . . still . . . let's talk it over."

And she stammered incoherently that she had known nothing about it, that the whole thing had come as a surprise. . . .

"Whose fault is that?" said Lheureux, with an ironic bow. "I work like a slave, and you go out enjoying yourself."

"Ah! No preaching!"

"It never did anybody any harm," he retorted.

She was craven: she pled with him, she even put her pretty slender white hand on his knee.

"None of that! Are you trying to seduce me, or what?"

"You're contemptible!" she cried.

"Oh! Oh! How you go on!" he said, laughing.

"I'll let everybody know what you're like. I'll tell my husband. . . ."

"Will you? I have something to *show* your husband!"

And out of his safe Lheureux took the receipt for 1,800 francs that she had given him for the note discounted by Vinçart.

"Do you think," he said, "that he won't see through your little swindle, the poor dear man?"

She crumpled, as though hit over the head with a club. He paced back and forth between the window and the desk, saying over and over:

"I'll show it to him! I'll show it to him!"

Then he came close to her and said softly:

"It's no fun, I know; but nobody's ever died of it, after all, and since it's the only way you have left of paying me back my money . . ."

"But where can I find some?" cried Emma, wringing her hands.

"Ah! Bah! A woman like you, with plenty of friends!"

And he transfixed her with a stare so knowing and so terrible that she shuddered to the depths of her being.

"I promise you!" she said. "I'll sign . . ."

"I have enough of your signatures!"

"I'll sell more . . ."

"Face it!" he said, shrugging his shoulders. "You've got nothing left."

And he called through a peephole that communicated with the shop:

"Annette! Don't forget the three cuttings of No. 14."

The servant entered; Emma took the hint, and asked how much money would be required to stop all proceedings.

"It's too late!"

"But if I brought you a few thousand francs—a quarter of the amount, a third, almost all?"

"No—there's no use!"

He pushed her gently toward the stairs.

"I implore you, Monsieur Lheureux—just a few days more!"

She was sobbing.

"Ah! Tears! Very good!"

"You'll drive me to do something desperate!"

"A lot I care!" he said, closing the door behind her.

VII

She was stoical, the next day, when Maître Hareng, the *huissier*, arrived with two witnesses to take inventory of the goods and chattels to be sold.

They began with Bovary's consulting room, and didn't include the phrenological head, which was considered a "professional instrument"; but in the kitchen they counted the plates and the pans, the chairs and the candlesticks, and in the bedroom all the knickknacks on the whatnot. They inspected her dresses, the linen, the *cabinet de toilette:* and her very being, down to its most hidden and intimate details, was laid open, like a dissected corpse, to the stares of those three men.

Maître Hareng, bottomed up in a close-fitting black tail coat, with a white cravat, his shoe straps very tight, kept repeating:

"*Vous permettez,*[3] Madame? *Vous permettez?*"

And frequently he exclaimed:

"Charming! Very pretty!"

Then he would resume his writing, dipping his pen in the inkhorn he held in his left hand.

When they had finished with the various rooms they went up to the attic.

She kept a desk there, where Rodolphe's letters were locked away. They made her open it.

"Ah! Personal papers!" said Maître Hareng, with a discreet smile. "*Mais permettez!* I have to make sure there's nothing else in the box."

And he held the envelopes upside down, very gently, as though expecting them to disgorge gold pieces. She was put into a fury by the sight of that great red hand, with its soft, sluglike fingers, touching those pages that had caused her so many heartthrobs.

They left at last. Félicité came back: she had sent her out to watch for Bovary and keep him away. They quickly installed the watchman in the attic, and he promised to stay there.

Charles, she thought during the evening, looked careworn. She scrutinized him with an agonized stare, reading accusations in the drawn lines of his face. Then, as her eyes roved over the mantelpiece, gay with Chinese fans, over the full curtains, the armchairs, all the things that had tempered the bitterness of her life, she was overcome with remorse, or rather with immense regret; and this, far from eclipsing her passion, only exasperated it. Charles placidly stirred the fire, lounging in his chair.

At one moment the watchman—bored, no doubt, in his hiding place—made a slight noise.

---

3. Permit me (French).

"Is somebody walking around up there?" said Charles.

"No!" she answered. "It's a dormer that's been left open, blowing in the wind."

The next day, Sunday, she left for Rouen, determined to call on every banker she had heard of. Most of them were away in the country or traveling. She persisted, however, and those whom she succeeded in seeing she asked for money, insisting that she must have it, swearing to repay. Some of them laughed in her face; they all refused.

At two o'clock she hurried to Léon's and knocked on his door. No one came to open. Finally he appeared.

"What brings you here?"

"Are you sorry to see me?"

"No . . . but . . ."

And he confessed that his landlord didn't like the tenants to entertain "women."

"I've got to talk to you," she said.

He reached for his key. She stopped him:

"Oh, no—let's go to our place."

And they went to their room in the Hotel de Boulogne.

There she drank a large glass of water. She was very pale.

"Léon," she said to him, "you have to do something for me."

And clutching both his hands tightly in hers, she shook them and said:

"Listen! I've got to have eight thousand francs!"

"But you're out of your mind!"

"Not yet!"

And in a rush she told him all about the execution. She was in desperate straits: Charles had been kept in total ignorance, her mother-in-law hated her, her father could do nothing. He—Léon—must save her. He must go out at once and find her the money that she absolutely had to have.

"How in the world do you expect me . . . ?"

"Don't just stand there, like a spineless fool!"

"You're making things out to be worse than they are," he said stupidly. "You could probably quiet your man with three thousand francs."

All the more reason for trying to do something: it wasn't conceivable that three thousand francs couldn't be found. Besides, Léon's signature could go on the notes instead of hers.

"Go ahead! Try! I've got to have it! Hurry! Oh, try! Try! Then I'll show you how I love you!"

He went out. In an hour he was back.

"I've seen three people," he told her, solemn-faced. "Nothing doing."

They sat face to face across the fire, still and silent. Emma kept shrugging her shoulders, tapping her foot. Then he heard her say, low-voiced:

"If I were in your place I'd know where to find the money!"

"You would? Where?"

"In your office!"

She stared at him.

There was a demonic desperation burning in her eyes, and she narrowed them in a look of lascivious provocation: the young man felt himself giving way before the mute will of this woman who was urging him to crime. He took fright; and to avoid hearing anything further he clapped his hand to his forehead.

"Morel should be back tonight!" he cried. "He won't refuse me, I hope!" (Morel was one of his friends, the son of a wealthy businessman.) "I'll bring it to you tomorrow," he promised.

Emma didn't appear to welcome this hope of relief as joyfully as he had thought. Did she suspect his lie? He blushed as he added:

"But if I'm not back by three, don't wait for me any longer, darling. Now I have to go out. Forgive me! Good-bye!"

He pressed her hand, but it lay inert in his: Emma was drained of all feeling.

Four o'clock struck; and she got up to go back to Yonville, automatic in her obedience to the force of habit.

The day was fine—one of those clear, sharp March days with the sun brilliant in a cloudless sky. Contented-looking Rouennais were strolling in their Sunday best. As she came to the Place du Parvis, vespers in the cathedral had just ended: crowds were pouring out through the three portals, like a river through the three arches of a bridge; and in their midst, immovable as a rock, stood the verger.

She remembered how tremulous she had been, how full of hope, the day she had entered that lofty nave: how it had stretched away before her, on and on—and yet not as infinite as her love! And she kept walking, weeping under her veil, dazed, tottering, almost in a faint.

"Watch out!" The cry came from within a porte-cochère that was swinging open; she stopped, and out came a black horse, prancing between the shafts of a tilbury. A gentleman in sables was holding the reins. Who was he? She knew him. . . . The carriage leapt forward and was gone.

The vicomte! It was the vicomte! She turned to stare: the street was empty. And the encounter left her so crushed, so immeasurably sad, that she leaned against a wall to keep from falling.

Then she thought that she might be mistaken. How could she tell? She had no way of knowing. Everything—everything within her, everything without—was abandoning her. She felt lost, rolling dizzily down into some dark abyss; and she was almost glad, when she reached the Croix-Rouge, to see good old Monsieur Homais. He was watching a case of pharmaceutical supplies being loaded onto the Hirondelle, and in his hand he carried a present for his wife—six *cheminots* wrapped in a foulard handkerchief.

Madame Homais was particularly fond of those heavy turban-shaped rolls, which the Rouennais eat in Lent with salted butter—a last relic of Gothic fare, going back perhaps to the times of the Crusades. The lusty Normans of those days gorged themselves on *cheminots,* picturing them as the heads of Saracens, to be devoured by the light of yellow torches along with flacons of spiced wine and giant slabs of meat. Like those ancients, the apothecary's wife crunched them heroically, despite her wretched teeth; and every time Monsieur Homais made a trip to the city he faithfully brought some back to her, buying them always at the best baker's, in the Rue Massacre.

"Delighted to see you!" he said, offering Emma a hand to help her into the Hirondelle.

Then he put the *cheminots* in the baggage net and sat there hatless, his arms folded, in a pose that was pensive and Napoleonic.

But when the blind beggar made his appearance as usual at the foot of the hill, he exclaimed in indignation:

"I cannot understand why the authorities continue to tolerate such dishonest occupations! All these unfortunates should be put away—and put to work! Progress moves at a snail's pace, no doubt about it: we're still wallowing in the midst of barbarism!"

The blind man held out his hat, and it swung to and fro at the window like a loose piece of upholstery.

"That," pronounced the pharmacist, "is a scrofulous disease."

And though he had often seen the poor devil before, he pretended now to be looking at him for the first time, and he murmured the words "cornea," "opaque cornea," "sclerotic," "facies." Then, in a paternal tone:

"Have you had that frightful affliction long, my friend? You'd do well to follow a diet, instead of getting drunk in cafés."

He urged him to take only good wine and good beer, and to eat good roast meat. The blind man kept singing his song: actually, he seemed fairly close to idiocy. Finally Monsieur Homais took out his purse:

"Here—here's a sou: change it for me and keep half of it for yourself. And don't forget my suggestions—you'll find they help."

Hivert presumed to express certain doubts about their efficacy. But the apothecary swore that he could cure the fellow himself, with an antiphlogistic[4] salve of his own invention, and he gave him his address:

"Monsieur Homais, near the market—ask anyone."

"Come now," said Hivert. "Show the gentleman you're grateful by doing your act."

The blind man squatted on his haunches and threw back his head, and rolling his greenish eyes and sticking out his tongue he rubbed his stomach with both hands, meanwhile uttering a kind of muffled howl, like a famished dog. Emma, shuddering with disgust, flung him a five-franc piece over her shoulder. It was all the money she had in the world: there was something grand, she thought, in thus throwing it away.

The coach was again in motion, when suddenly Monsieur Homais leaned out the window.

"Nothing farinaceous!" he shouted. "No dairy products! Wear woolens next to your skin! Fumigate the diseased areas with the smoke of juniper berries!"

The sight of all the familiar things they passed gradually took Emma's mind off her misery. She was oppressed, crushed with fatigue, and she reached home numb and spiritless, almost asleep.

"Let come what may!" she told herself.

Besides—who knew? Something extraordinary might happen any moment. Lheureux himself might die.

She was awakened the next morning at nine by the sound of voices in the square. People were crowding around the market to read a large notice posted on one of the pillars, and she saw Justin climb on a guard post and deface the notice. Just then the village policeman seized him by the collar. Monsieur Homais came out of his pharmacy, and Madame Lefrançois seemed to be holding forth in the midst of the crowd.

"Madame! Madame!" cried Félicité, rushing in. "It's an outrage!"

And the poor girl, much agitated, showed her a yellow paper she had just

---

4. Anti-inflammatory.

torn off the front door. Emma read in a glance that all the contents of her house were subject to sale.

They looked at each other in silence. There were no secrets between mistress and maid. Finally Félicité murmured:

"If I were you, Madame, I'd go see Maître Guillaumin."

"Do you think so?"

"You know all about the Guillaumins from their manservant," the question meant; "does the master mention me, sometimes?"

"Yes, go ahead: it's worth trying."

She put on her black dress and her bonnet with jade beads; and to keep from being seen (there was still quite a crowd in the square) she avoided the village and took the river path.

She was breathless when she reached the notary's gate. The sky was dark; it was snowing a little.

At the sound of her ring Théodore, in a red vest, emerged from the front door; and he opened the gate for her with an air of familiarity, as though she were someone he knew well, and showed her into the dining room.

A large porcelain stove was purring; the niche above it was filled with a cactus plant; and against the oak-grained wallpaper hung Steuben's "Esmeralda" and Schopin's "Potiphar,"[5] both in black wood frames. The table set for breakfast, the two silver dish warmers, the crystal doorknobs, the parquet floor and the furniture—all gleamed with a meticulous English spotlessness; in the corners of each of the windows were panes of colored glass.

"This," thought Emma, "is the kind of dining room I should have."

The notary came in. He was wearing a dressing gown with palm designs, which he clutched about him with his left hand; and with his right he doffed and then quickly replaced his brown velvet skullcap. This he wore rakishly tilted to the right, and out from under it emerged the ends of three strands of fair hair that were combed up from the back and drawn carefully over his bald cranium.

After offering her a chair he sat down to his breakfast, apologizing profusely for his discourtesy.

"Monsieur," she said, "I want to ask you . . ."

"What, Madame? I'm listening."

She told him of her predicament.

It was no news to Maître Guillaumin: he was secretly associated with the dry-goods merchant, who could always be counted on to supply him with capital for the mortgage loans he arranged for his clients.

Thus he knew—far better than she—the long story of the notes, small at first, carrying the names of various endorsers, made out for long terms and continually renewed; he knew how the shopkeeper had gradually accumulated the various protests of nonpayment, and how he had finally had his friend Vinçart institute the necessary legal proceedings in his name, wishing to avoid acquiring a reputation for bloodthirstiness among his fellow villagers.

She interspersed her story with recriminations against Lheureux, and to

5. The official of the court of Egypt who was Joseph's master; the wife of Potiphar tried to seduce him. The painting represents the seduction scene. Karl Steuben (1877–1856), a German history painter. Esmeralda is the gypsy girl in Hugo's *Notre Dame de Paris*. A painting titled *Esmeralda et Quasimodo* was exhibited in 1839. Schopin was the brother of the composer Chopin.

these the notary returned occasional, empty answers. He ate his chop and drank his tea; his chin kept rubbing against his sky-blue cravat, whose two diamond stickpins were linked by a fine gold chain; and he smiled a strange, sugary, ambiguous smile. Then he noticed that her feet were wet.

"Move closer to the stove! Put them up—higher—against the porcelain."

She was afraid of dirtying it, but his retort was gallant:

"Pretty things never do any harm."

Then she tried to appeal to his emotions: growing emotional herself, she told him about her cramped household budget, her harassments, her needs. He was very sympathetic—an elegant woman like herself!—and without interrupting his meal he gradually turned so that he faced her and his knee brushed against her shoe, whose sole was beginning to curl a little as it steamed in the heat of the stove.

But when she asked him for 3,000 francs he tightened his lips and said that he was very sorry not to have had charge of her capital in the past, for there were a hundred easy ways in which even a lady could invest her money profitably. The Grumesnil peatery, building lots in Le Havre—such speculations were excellent, almost risk-proof; and he let her consume herself with rage at the thought of the fantastic sums she could certainly have made.

"How come," he asked her, "that you never called on me?"

"I really don't know," she said.

"Why didn't you? Did I seem so very frightening to you? But I'm the one who has cause for complaint: we barely know each other! I feel very warmly toward you, though; you realize that now, I hope?"

He reached out his hand, took hers, pressed it to his lips in a greedy kiss, and then kept it on his knee; and he gently fondled her fingers, murmuring a thousand compliments.

His monotonous voice rustled on like a running brook; his eyes were gleaming through the glitter of his glasses; and his hands crept up inside Emma's sleeve and stroked her arm. She felt a panting breath on her cheek. This man was more than she could stand.

She leapt to her feet.

"Monsieur! I'm waiting!"

"What for?" cried the notary, suddenly extremely pale.

"The money."

"But . . ."

Then, yielding to an irresistible surge of desire:

"Yes! Yes!"

He dragged himself toward her on his knees, careless of his dressing gown.

"Please! Don't go! I love you!"

He seized her by the waist.

A flood of crimson rushed to Madame Bovary's face. She shrank back, and with a terrible look she cried:

"It's shameless of you to take advantage of my distress! I'm to be pitied, but I'm not for sale!"

And she walked out.

The notary sat there dumbfounded, his eyes fixed on his beautiful embroidered slippers. They were a gift from a mistress, and the sight of them gradually comforted him. Anyway, he told himself, such an affair would have involved too many risks.

"What a contemptible, lowdown cad!" she said to herself, as she fled tremulously under the aspens lining the road. Disappointment at having failed made her all the more indignant at the insult offered her honor: it seemed to her that Providence was hounding her relentlessly. She was filled with pride at the way she had acted: never before had she esteemed herself so highly; never had she felt such contempt for everyone else. She was at war with the world, and the thought transported her. She longed to lash out at all men, to spit in their faces, grind them all to dust; and she hurried straight on, pale, trembling, furious, scanning the empty horizon with weeping eyes, almost gloating in the hatred that was choking her.

When she caught sight of her house she felt suddenly paralyzed. She couldn't go on, and yet she had to: what escape was there?

Félicité was waiting for her at the door.

"Well?"

"No," said Emma.

And for a quarter of an hour they discussed who in Yonville might be willing to help her. But every time Félicité mentioned someone, Emma answered:

"Out of the question! They'd refuse!"

"And Monsieur will soon be home!"

"I know. . . . Go away and leave me alone."

She had tried everything. Now there was nothing more to be done; so when Charles appeared there would be only one thing to tell him:

"Don't stay here! The very rug you're walking on isn't ours. Not a piece of all this furniture belongs to you—not a pin, not a wisp of straw; and I'm the one who has ruined you!"

Then he would utter a great sob, and then weep floods of tears; and in the end, once the shock was over, he would forgive her.

"Yes," she muttered, through clenched teeth, *"he'll* forgive *me*—the man I wouldn't forgive for setting eyes on me if he offered me a million. . . . Never! Never!"

This thought of Bovary in a position to be condescending put her beside herself. But whether she confessed or not, he would inevitably—sooner or later, today or tomorrow—learn of the disaster; so she could only look forward to that horrible scene and to being subjected to the weight of his magnanimity. Suddenly she felt an urge to try Lheureux once more: but what was the use? Or to write to her father: but it was too late. And perhaps she was regretting, now, not having yielded to the notary, when she heard a horse's trot in the lane. It was Charles: he was opening the gate, his face more ashen than the plaster on the wall. Rushing downstairs, she slipped quickly out into the square; and the mayor's wife, who was chatting in front of the church with Lestiboudois, saw her enter the house of the tax collector.

Madame Tuvache ran to tell Madame Caron. The two ladies climbed up to the latter's attic; and there, hidden behind some laundry that was hanging up to dry, they stood so that they could easily see into Binet's.

He was alone in his garret, busily copying, in wood, one of those ivory ornaments that beggar description, a conglomeration of half-moons and of spheres carved one inside the other, the whole thing standing erect like an obelisk and perfectly useless. He was just beginning on the last section: the end was in sight! In the chiaroscuro of his workshop the golden sawdust flew from his lathe like a spray of sparks under the hooves of a galloping horse; the two wheels spun and whirred; Binet was smiling, chin down and nostrils wide: he looked absorbed, in one of those states of utter bliss such as men seem to find only in humble activities, which divert the mind with easy challenges and gratify it with the most utter and complete success.

"Ah! There she is!" said Madame Tuvache.

But the sound of the lathe made it impossible to know what she was saying.

Finally the two ladies thought they heard the word "francs," and Madame Tuvache whispered:

"She's asking him for a postponement of her taxes."

"Looks like it," said the other.

They saw her pacing up and down the room, looking at the shelves along the wall laden with napkin rings, candlesticks and finials, while Binet contentedly stroked his beard.

"Would she be coming to order something from him?" suggested Madame Tuvache.

"But he never sells anything!" the other reminded her.

The tax collector seemed to be listening, staring as though he didn't understand. She continued to talk, her manner gentle and supplicating. She came close to him; her breast was heaving; now they seemed not to be speaking.

"Is she making advances to him?" said Madame Tuvache.

Binet had gone red to the roots of his hair. She grasped his hands.

"Ah! Just look at that . . . !"

And she must have been suggesting something abominable, for the tax collector—and he was a man of courage: he had fought at Bautzen and Lützen, and taken part in the French campaign,[6] and even been proposed for the Legion of Honor—suddenly recoiled as though he had seen a snake.

"Madame!" he cried. "You must be dreaming!"

"Women like that should be horsewhipped," said Madame Tuvache.

"Where has she gone to?" said Madame Caron.

For even as he was speaking she had vanished. Then they saw her darting down the Grande Rue and turning to the right, as though to reach the cemetery, and they didn't know what to make of it.

"Madame Rollet!" she cried, when she reached the wet nurse's. "I can't breathe! Unlace me!"

She fell sobbing onto the bed. Madame Rollet covered her with a petticoat and stood beside her. Then, when she didn't speak, the peasant woman moved away, took up her wheel and began spinning flax.

"Don't do that!" she murmured: she thought it was Binet's lathe.

"What's the matter with her?" wondered the nurse. "Why did she come here?"

She had come because a kind of terror had sent her—a terror that made her flee her home. Lying on her back, motionless, her eyes vacant, she saw things only in a blur, though she focused her attention on them with idiotic persistence. She stared at the flaking plaster on the wall, at two half-burned

---

6. The battles in France before the Allies captured Paris and forced the abdication of Napoleon and his banishment to Elba in 1814. Bautzen, in Saxony, was the scene of an 1813 battle in which Napoleon defeated the Prussians and Russians. Lützen, in Saxony, was the scene of another victory by Napoleon.

sticks smoking end to end in the fireplace, at a large spider crawling overhead in a crack in the rafter. Gradually she collected her thoughts. She remembered . . . one day with Léon . . . Oh, how far away it was . . . ! The sun was shining on the river, and the air was full of the scent of clematis. . . . Then, swept along in her memories as in a raging torrent, she quickly recalled the previous day.

"What time is it?" she asked.

Madame Rollet went out, held up the fingers of her right hand against the brightest part of the sky, and came slowly back, saying:

"Almost three."

"Ah! Thank you! Thank you!"

For he would be coming. There could be no question about it: by now he had found the money. But probably he would go to her house, having no idea that she was here; and she ordered the nurse to run and fetch him.

"Hurry!"

"I'm on my way, dear lady! I'm on my way!"

She marveled, now, at not having thought of him in the first place: yesterday he had given his word; he wouldn't fail her; and already she saw herself at Lheureux's, laying the three banknotes on his desk. Then she'd have to invent some story that would satisfy Bovary. What would it be?

But the nurse was a long time returning. Still, since there was no clock in the cottage, Emma feared that she might be exaggerating the duration of her absence, and she walked slowly around and around the garden, and down the path by the hedge and quickly back, hoping that the nurse might have returned some other way. Finally, weary of waiting, a prey to suspicions that she resolutely put out of her mind, no longer sure whether she had been there a hundred years or a minute, she sat down in a corner and closed her eyes and put her hands to her ears. The gate squeaked: she leapt up. Before she could speak Madame Rollet said:

"He's not there!"

"What?"

"No, he's not! And Monsieur's crying. He keeps calling your name. Everybody's looking for you."

Emma made no answer. She was gasping and staring wildly about her; the peasant woman, frightened by the expression on her face, instinctively shrank back, thinking her crazed. All at once she clapped her hand to her forehead and gave a cry, for into her mind had come the memory of Rodolphe, like a great lightning-flash in a black night. He was so kind, so sensitive, so generous! And if he should hesitate to help her she'd know how to persuade him: one glance from her eyes would remind him of their lost love. So she set out for La Huchette, unaware that now she was eager to yield to the very thing that had made her so indignant only a short while ago, and totally unconscious that she was prostituting herself.

VIII

As she walked she wondered: "What am I going to say? What shall I tell him first?" Drawing nearer, she recognized the thickets, the trees, the furze on the hill, the château in the distance. She was reliving the sensations of her first love, and at the memory her poor anguished heart swelled tenderly.

A warm wind was blowing in her face; melting snow dripped from the leaf buds onto the grass.

She entered, as she always had, by the little park gate, and then came to the main courtyard, planted around with a double row of thick-crowned lindens, their long branches rustling and swaying. All the dogs in the kennel barked, but though their outcry echoed and reechoed, no one came.

She climbed the wide, straight, wooden-banistered stairs that led up to the hall with its paving of dusty flagstones. A row of doors opened onto it, as in a monastery or an inn. His room was at the far end, the last on the left. When her fingers touched the latch her strength suddenly left her: she was afraid that he would not be there—she almost wished that he wouldn't be, and yet he was her only hope, her last chance of salvation. For a minute she collected her thoughts; then, steeling her courage to the present necessity, she entered.

He was smoking a pipe before the fire, his feet against the mantelpiece.

"Oh, it's you!" he said, rising quickly.

"Yes, here I am. . . . Rodolphe, I want . . . I need some advice. . . ."

Despite her best efforts she couldn't go on.

"You haven't changed—you're as charming as ever!"

"Oh, my charms!" she answered bitterly. "They can't amount to much, since you scorned them."

He launched into apology, justifying his conduct in terms that were vague but the best he could muster.

She let herself be taken in—not so much by what he said, as by the sound of his voice and the very sight of him; and she pretended to believe—or perhaps she actually did believe—the reason he gave for their break. It was a secret, he said, involving the honor—the life, even—of a third person.

She looked at him sadly. "Whatever it was," she said, "I suffered a great deal."

He answered philosophically:

"That's how life is!"

"Has it been kind to you, at least," asked Emma, "since we parted?"

"Oh, neither kind nor unkind, particularly."

"Perhaps it would have been better had we stayed together."

"Yes . . . perhaps!"

"Do you really think so?" she said, coming closer.

And she sighed:

"Oh, Rodolphe! If you knew! I loved you very much!"

She took his hand; and for a few moments their fingers were intertwined—like that first day, at the Agricultural Show! Pride made him struggle against giving in to his feelings. But she leaned heavily against him, and said:

"How did you ever think that I could live without you? Happiness is a habit that's hard to break! I was desperate! I thought I'd die! I'll tell you all about it. And you . . . you stayed away from me . . . !"

It was true: for the past three years he had carefully avoided her, out of the natural cowardice that characterizes the stronger sex; and now Emma went on, twisting and turning her head in coaxing little movements that were loving and catlike.

"You have other women—admit it. Oh, I sympathize with them: I don't blame them. You seduced them, the way you seduced me. You're a man! You have everything to make us love you. But you and I'll begin all over again, won't we? We'll love each other! Look—I'm laughing, I'm happy! Speak to me!"

And indeed she was ravishing to see, with a tear trembling in her eye like a raindrop in a blue flower-cup after a storm.

He drew her onto his lap, and with the back of his hand caressed her sleek hair: in the twilight a last sunbeam was gleaming on it like a golden arrow. She lowered her head, and soon he was kissing her on the eyelids, very gently, just brushing them with his lips.

"But you've been crying!" he said. "Why?"

She burst into sobs: Rodolphe thought it was from the violence of her love; when she didn't answer him he interpreted her silence as the ultimate refuge of her womanly modesty, and exclaimed:

"Ah! Forgive me! You're the only one I really care about! I've been stupid and heartless! I love you—I'll always love you. . . . What is it? Tell me!"

He was on his knees.

"Well, then . . . I'm ruined, Rodolphe! You've got to lend me three thousand francs!"

"But . . . but . . . ?" he said, slowly rising, a worried expression coming over his face.

"You know," she went on quickly, "my husband gave his money to a notary to invest, and the notary absconded. We've borrowed, patients haven't paid. . . . The estate isn't settled yet: we'll be getting something later. But today— just for three thousand francs—they're going to sell us out: now, this very instant. I counted on your friendship. I came to you."

"Ah," thought Rodolphe, suddenly pale. "So that's why she came!"

And after a moment he said, calmly:

"I haven't got it, dear lady."

He wasn't lying. If he had had it he would probably have given it to her, unpleasant though it usually is to make such generous gifts: of all the icy blasts that blow on love, a request for money is the most chilling and havoc wreaking.

For a long moment she stared at him. Then:

"You haven't got it!"

She said it again, several times:

"You haven't got it! I might have spared myself this final humiliation. You never loved me! You're no better than the rest!"

She was giving herself away; she no longer knew what she was saying.

Rodolphe broke in, assuring her that he was "hard up" himself.

"Ah, I pity you!" said Emma. "How I pity you!"

And as her eyes fell on a damascened rifle that glittered in a trophy on the wall:

"When you're as poor as all that you don't put silver on the stock of your gun! You don't buy things with tortoiseshell inlay!" she went on, pointing to the Boulle clock. "Or silver-gilt whistles for your whip!"—she touched them—"or charms for your watch chain! Oh, he has everything! Even a liqueur case in his bedroom! You pamper yourself, you live well, you have a château, farms, woods; you hunt, you make trips to Paris. . . . Why, even things like this," she cried, snatching up his cuff links from the mantelpiece, "the tiniest trifles, you can raise money on . . . ! Oh, I don't want them! Keep them."

And she hurled the two buttons so violently that their gold chain snapped as they struck the wall.

"But I—I'd have given you everything, I'd have sold everything, worked my fingers to the bone, begged in the streets, just for a smile from you, for a look, just to hear you say 'Thank you.' And you sit there calmly in your chair, as though you hadn't made me suffer enough already! If it hadn't been for you I could have been happy! What made you do it? Was it a bet? You loved me, though: you used to say so. . . . And you said so again just now. Ah, you'd have done better to throw me out! My hands are still hot from your kisses; and right there on the rug you swore on your knees that you'd love me forever. You made me believe it: for two years you led me on in a wonderful, marvelous dream. . . . Our plans for going away—you remember? Oh! That letter you wrote me! It tore my heart in two! And now when I come back to him—and find him rich and happy and free—to implore him for help that anybody would give me—come in distress, bringing him all my love—he refuses me, because it would cost him three thousand francs!"

"I haven't got it," answered Rodolphe, with that perfect calm that resigned anger employs as a shield.

She walked out. The walls were quaking, the ceiling was threatening to crush her; and she went back down the long avenue of trees, stumbling against piles of dead leaves that were scattering in the wind. At last she reached the ditch before the gate: she broke her nails on the latch, so frantically did she open it. Then, a hundred yards farther on, out of breath, ready to drop, she paused. She turned: and once again she saw the impassive château, with its park, its gardens, its three courtyards, its many-windowed façade.

She stood there in a daze. Only the pulsing of her veins told her that she was alive: she thought she heard it outside herself, like some deafening music filling the countryside. The earth beneath her feet was as yielding as water, and the furrows seemed to her like immense, dark, breaking waves. All the memories and thoughts in her mind poured out at once, like a thousand fireworks. She saw her father, Lheureux's office, their room in Rouen, another landscape. Madness began to take hold of her; she was frightened, but managed to control herself—without, however, emerging from her confusion, for the cause of her horrible state—the question of money—had faded from her mind. It was only her love that was making her suffer, and she felt her soul leave her at the thought—just as a wounded man, as he lies dying, feels his life flowing out with his blood through the gaping hole.

Night was falling; crows flew overhead.

It suddenly seemed to her that fiery particles were bursting in the air, like bullets exploding as they fell, and spinning and spinning and finally melting in the snow among the tree branches. In the center of each of them appeared Rodolphe's face. They multiplied; they came together; they penetrated her; everything vanished. She recognized the lights of houses, shining far off in the mist.

Suddenly her plight loomed before her, like an abyss. She panted as though her lungs would burst. Then, with a heroic resolve that made her almost happy, she ran down the hill and across the cow plank, ran down the river path and the lane, crossed the square, and came to the pharmacy.

It was empty. She was about to go in, when it occurred to her that the sound of the bell might bring someone; and slipping through the side gate, holding her breath, feeling her way along the walls, she came to the kitchen door. A lighted tallow candle was standing on the stove, and Justin, in shirt-sleeves, was just leaving the room carrying a dish.

"Ah, they're at dinner," she said to herself. "Better wait."

Justin returned to the kitchen. She tapped on the window. He came out.

"The key! The one for upstairs, where the . . ."

"What?"

And he stared at her, astounded by the pallor of her face, which stood out white against the blackness of the night. She seemed to him extraordinarily beautiful, majestic as an apparition from another world; without understanding what she wanted, he had a foreboding of something terrible.

But she went on quickly, in a low voice, a voice that was gentle and melting:

"I want it! Give it to me."

The wall was thin, and they could hear the clinking of forks on plates in the dining room.

She pretended she had to kill some rats that were keeping her awake nights.

"I must go ask Monsieur."

"No! Stay here!"

Then, with a casual air:

"There's no use bothering him: I'll tell him later. Come along, give me a light."

She passed into the hall off which opened the laboratory door. There against the wall hung a key marked "capharnaum."

"Justin!" called the apothecary impatiently.

"Let's go up!"

He followed her.

The key turned in the lock, and she went straight to the third shelf—so well did her memory serve her as guide—seized the blue jar, tore out the cork, plunged in her hand, withdrew it full of white powder, and ate greedily.

"Stop!" he cried, flinging himself on her.

"Be quiet! Someone might come. . . ."

He was frantic, wanted to call out.

"Don't say a word about it: all the blame would fall on your master!"

Then she went home, suddenly at peace—almost as serene as though she had done her duty.

When Charles reached home, overwhelmed by the news of the execution, Emma had just left. He called her name, wept, fainted away, but she didn't come back. Where could she be? He sent Félicité to the pharmacist's, to the mayor's, to the dry-goods shop, to the Lion d'Or—everywhere; and whenever his anguish about her momentarily subsided he saw his reputation ruined, all their money gone, Berthe's future wrecked! What was the cause of it all . . . ? Not a word! He waited until six that evening. Finally, unable to bear it any longer, and imagining that she must have gone to Rouen, he went out to the highway, followed it for a mile or so, met no one, waited a while, and returned.

She was back.

"What happened? . . . Why? . . . Tell me!"

She sat down at her desk and wrote a letter, sealed it slowly, and added the date and the hour. Then she said in a solemn tone:

"Read it tomorrow. Till then, please don't ask me a single question—not one!"

"But . . ."

"Oh, leave me alone!"

And she stretched out on her bed.

An acrid taste in her mouth woke her. She caught sight of Charles and reclosed her eyes.

She observed herself with interest, to see whether there was any pain. No—nothing yet. She heard the ticking of the clock, the sound of the fire, and Charles breathing, standing there beside her bed.

"Dying doesn't amount to much!" she thought. "I'll fall asleep, and everything will be over."

She swallowed a mouthful of water and turned to the wall.

There was still that dreadful taste of ink.

"I'm thirsty! I'm so thirsty!" she whispered.

"What's wrong with you, anyway?" said Charles, handing her a glass.

"Nothing! Open the window . . . I'm choking!"

She was seized by an attack of nausea so sudden that she scarcely had time to snatch her handkerchief from under the pillow.

"Get rid of it!" she said quickly. "Throw it out!"

He questioned her, but she made no answer. She lay very still, fearing that the slightest disturbance would make her vomit. Now she felt an icy coldness creeping up from her feet toward her heart.

"Ah! It's beginning!" she murmured.

"What did you say?"

She twisted her head from side to side in a gentle movement expressive of anguish, and kept opening her jaws as though she had something very heavy on her tongue. At eight o'clock the vomiting resumed.

Charles noticed that there was a gritty white deposit on the bottom of the basin, clinging to the porcelain.

"That's extraordinary! That's peculiar!" he kept saying.

"No!" she said loudly. "You're mistaken."

Very gently, almost caressingly, he passed his hand over her stomach. She gave a sharp scream. He drew back in fright.

She began to moan, softly at first. Her shoulders heaved in a great shudder, and she grew whiter than the sheet her clenched fingers were digging into. Her irregular pulse was almost imperceptible now.

Beads of sweat stood out on her face, which had turned blue and rigid, as though from the breath of some metallic vapor. Her teeth chattered, her dilated eyes stared about her vaguely, and her sole answer to questions was a shake of her head; two or three times she even smiled. Gradually her groans grew louder. A muffled scream escaped her; she pretended that she was feeling better and that she'd soon be getting up. But she was seized with convulsions.

"God!" she cried. "It's horrible!"

He flung himself on his knees beside her bed.

"Speak to me! What did you eat? Answer, for heaven's sake!"

And in his eyes she read a love such as she had never known.

"There . . . over there . . ." she said in a faltering voice.

He darted to the secretary, broke open the seal and read aloud: "No one is to blame . . ." He stopped, passed his hand over his eyes, read it again.

"What . . . ! Help! Help!"

He could only repeat the word: "Poisoned! Poisoned!" Félicité ran to Homais, who spoke loudly as he crossed the square; Madame Lefrançois heard him at the Lion d'Or, other citizens left their beds to tell their neighbors, and all night long the village was awake.

Distracted, stammering, close to collapse, Charles walked in circles around the room. He stumbled against the furniture, tore his hair: never had the pharmacist dreamed there could be so frightful a sight.

He went back to his own house and wrote letters to Monsieur Canivet and Doctor Larivière. He couldn't concentrate, had to begin them over fifteen times. Hippolyte left for Neufchâtel, and Justin spurred Bovary's horse so hard that he left it on the hill at Bois-Guillaume, foundered and all but done for.

Charles tried to consult his medical dictionary: he couldn't see; the lines danced before his eyes.

"Don't lose your head!" said the apothecary. "It's just a question of administering some powerful antidote. What poison is it?"

Charles showed him the letter. It was arsenic.

"Well then!" said Homais. "We must make an analysis."

For he knew that an analysis always had to be made in cases of poisoning.

Charles, who hadn't understood, answered with a groan:

"Do it! Do it! Save her . . . !"

And returning to her side, he sank down on the carpet and leaned his head on the edge of her bed, sobbing.

"Don't cry!" she said. "I shan't be tormenting you much longer."

"Why did you do it? What made you?"

"It was the only thing," she answered.

"Weren't you happy? Am I to blame? But I did everything I could . . . !"

"Yes . . . I know . . . You're good, you're different. . . ."

She slowly passed her hand through his hair. The sweetness of her touch was more than his grief could bear. He felt his entire being give way to despair at the thought of having to lose her just when she was showing him more love than ever in the past; and he could think of nothing to do—he knew nothing, dared nothing: the need for immediate action took away the last of his presence of mind.

Emma was thinking that now she was through with all the betrayals, the infamies, the countless fierce desires that had racked her. She hated no one, now; a twilight confusion was falling over her thoughts, and of all the world's sounds she heard only the intermittent lament of this poor man beside her, gentle and indistinct, like the last echo of an ever-fainter symphony.

"Bring me my little girl," she said, raising herself on her elbow.

"You're not feeling worse, are you?" Charles asked.

"No! No!"

Berthe was carried in by the maid. Her bare feet peeped out from beneath her long nightdress; she looked serious, still half dreaming. She stared in surprise to see the room in such disorder, and she blinked her eyes, dazzled by the candles that were standing here and there on the furniture. They probably reminded her of other mornings—New Year's day or mi-carême,[7] when she was wakened early in just this same way by candlelight and carried to her mother's bed to be given a shoeful of presents; for she asked:

"Where is it, *maman?*"

And when no one answered:

"I don't see my little shoe!"

Félicité held her over the bed, but she kept looking toward the fireplace.

"Did nurse take it away?" she asked.

At the word "nurse," which brought back her adulteries and her calamities, Madame Bovary averted her head, as though another, stronger, poison had risen to her mouth and filled her with revulsion.

"Oh, how big your eyes are, *maman!*" cried Berthe, whom the maid had put on the bed. "How pale you are! You're sweating . . . !"

Her mother looked at her.

"I'm afraid!" cried the little girl, shrinking back.

Emma took her hand to kiss it; she struggled.

"Enough! Take her away!" cried Charles, sobbing at the foot of the bed.

The symptoms momentarily stopped; she seemed calmer; and at each insignificant word she said, each time she breathed a little more easily, his hope gained ground. When Canivet finally arrived he threw himself in his arms, weeping.

"Ah! You've come! Thank you! You're kind! But she's doing better. Here: look at her!"

His colleague was not at all of this opinion. There was no use—as he himself put it—"beating around the bush," and he prescribed an emetic, to empty the stomach completely.

Soon she was vomiting blood. Her lips pressed together more tightly. Her limbs were contorted, her body was covered with brown blotches, her pulse quivered under the doctor's fingers like a taut thread, like a harp string about to snap.

Then she began to scream, horribly. She cursed the poison, railed against it, begged it to be quick; and with her stiffened arms she pushed away everything that Charles, in greater agony than herself, tried to make her drink. He was standing, his handkerchief to his mouth, moaning, weeping, choked by sobs and shaking all over; Félicité rushed about the room; Homais, motionless, kept sighing heavily; and Monsieur Canivet, for all his air of self-assurance, began to manifest some uneasiness:

"What the devil . . . ! But she's purged, and since the cause is removed . . . "

"The effect should subside," said Homais. "It's self-evident."

"Do something to save her!" cried Bovary.

Paying no attention to the pharmacist, who was venturing the hypothesis that "this paroxysm may mark the beginning of improvement," Canivet was about to give her theriaca when there came the crack of a whip, all the windows rattled, and a post chaise drawn at breakneck speed by three mud-

---

7. Mid-Lent.

covered horses flashed around the corner of the marketplace. It was Doctor Larivière.

The sudden appearance of a god wouldn't have caused greater excitement. Bovary raised both hands, Canivet broke off his preparations, and Homais doffed his cap well before the doctor entered.

He belonged to that great surgical school created by Bichat[8]—that generation, now vanished, of philosopher-practitioners, who cherished their art with fanatical love and applied it with enthusiasm and sagacity. Everyone in his hospital trembled when he was angry; and his students so revered him that the moment they set up for themselves they imitated him as much as they could. There was scarcely a town in the district where one of them couldn't be found, wearing a long merino overcoat and a full black tail coat, exactly like his. Doctor Larivière's unbuttoned cuffs partly covered his fleshy hands—extraordinary hands, always ungloved, as though to be the readier to grapple with suffering. Disdainful of decorations, titles and academies, hospitable, generous, a father to the poor, practicing Christian virtues although an unbeliever, he might have been thought of as a saint if he hadn't been feared as a devil because of the keenness of his mind. His scalpel-sharp glance cut deep into your soul, exposing any lie buried under excuses and reticences. His manner was majestic and genial, conscious as he was of his great gifts and his wealth and the forty years of hard work and blameless living he had behind him.

While he was still in the doorway he frowned, catching sight of Emma's cadaverous face as she lay on her back, her mouth open. Then, seeming to listen to Canivet, he passed his forefinger back and forth beneath his nostrils, repeating:

"Yes, yes."

But his shoulders lifted in a slow shrug. Bovary noticed it; their eyes met. The sight of a grieving face was no novelty to the doctor, yet he couldn't keep a tear from dropping onto his shirt front.

He asked Canivet to step into the next room. Charles followed him.

"She's very low, isn't she? How about poultices? What else? Can't you think of something? You've saved so many lives!"

Charles put his arms around him, sagged against his chest, and looked at him anxiously and beseechingly.

"Come, my poor boy, be brave! There's nothing to be done."

And Doctor Larivière turned away.

"You're leaving?"

"I'll be back."

He pretended he had something to say to the coachman, and went out with Canivet, who was no more eager than he to watch Emma die.

The pharmacist joined them in the square. He was temperamentally incapable of staying away from celebrities, and he begged Monsieur Larivière to do him the signal honor of being his guest at lunch.

Someone was quickly sent to the Lion d'Or for pigeons, the butcher was stripped of all his chops, Tuvache supplied cream and Lestiboudois eggs. The apothecary himself helped with the preparations, while Madame Homais pulled at her wrapper strings and said:

---

8. Marie-Françoise-Xavier Bichat (1771–1802), author of an *Anatomie générale* (1801).

"I hope you'll forgive us, Monsieur. In this wretched village, if we don't have a full day's warning . . ."

"The stemmed glasses!!!" whispered Homais.

"If we lived in the city we'd at least have stuffed pigs' feet to fall back on."

"Don't talk so much . . . ! Sit down, Doctor!"

After the first few mouthfuls he considered it appropriate to supply a few details concerning the catastrophe.

"First we had a sensation of siccity in the pharynx, then intolerable pain in the epigastrium, superpurgation, coma."

"How did she poison herself?"

"I have no idea, Doctor, and I can't even imagine where she managed to procure that arsenous oxide."

Justin, who was just then carrying in a pile of plates, was seized with a fit of trembling.

"What's the matter with you?" asked the pharmacist.

At the question the young man dropped everything with a great crash.

"Imbecile!" cried Homais. "Clumsy lout! Damned idiot!"

Then, quickly regaining his self-control:

"I wanted to try an analysis, Doctor, and, *primo*, I carefully inserted into a tube . . ."

"It would have been better," said the surgeon, "if you'd inserted your fingers into her throat."

Canivet said nothing, having just a few minutes before been given, in private, a severe rebuke concerning his emetic. Today he was as meek as he had been arrogant and verbose the day he had operated on Hippolyte: his face was fixed in a continual, approving smile.

Homais blossomed in his role of proud host, and the thought of Bovary's distress added something to his pleasure as he selfishly contrasted their lots. Moreover, the doctor's presence excited him. He displayed all his erudition, dragging in, pell-mell, mention of cantharides, the upas, the manchineel, the bite of the adder.

"I've even read about people being poisoned, Doctor—positively struck down—by blood sausages that had been subjected to excessive fumigation! At least, so it says in a very fine report, written by one of our leading pharmaceutical lights, one of our masters, the illustrious Cadet de Gassicourt!"[9]

Madame Homais reappeared, bearing one of those rickety contraptions that are heated with alcohol, for Homais insisted on brewing his coffee at table—having, needless to say, previously done his own roasting, his own grinding and his own blending.

"*Saccharum*, Doctor?" he said, passing the sugar.

Then he called in all his children, eager to have the surgeon's opinion on their constitutions.

Finally, when Monsieur Larivière was about to leave, Madame Homais asked him to advise her about her husband. His "blood was getting thicker" because of his habit of falling asleep every evening after dinner.

"Oh, he's not thick-*blooded!*"

And smiling a little at his joke, which passed unnoticed, the doctor opened

9. The pharmacist of Emperor Napoleon I who had considerable trouble under the Restoration because of his liberal ideas.

the door. But the pharmacy was thronged, and he had a hard time getting rid of Monsieur Tuvache, who was afraid that his wife would get pneumonia because of her habit of spitting into the fire; then Monsieur Binet complained of often feeling ravenous; Madame Caron had prickling sensations; Lheureux suffered from dizzy spells; Lestiboudois was rheumatic; and Madame Lefrançois had heartburn. Finally the three horses bore him away, and the general verdict was that he had been far from obliging.

Then the attention of the public was distracted by the appearance of Monsieur Bournisien, crossing the market with the holy oils.

Homais paid his debt to his principles by likening priests to ravens: both are attracted by the odor of the dead. Actually, he had a more personal reason for disliking the sight of a priest: a cassock made him think of a shroud, and his execration of the one owed something to his fear of the other.

Nevertheless, not flinching in the face of what he called his "mission," he returned to the Bovary house along with Canivet, whom Monsieur Larivière had urged to stay on to the end. But for his wife's protests, the pharmacist would have taken his two sons along, to inure them to life's great moments, to provide them with a lesson, an example, a momentous spectacle that they would remember later.

The bedroom, as they entered, was mournful and solemn. On the sewing table, now covered with a white napkin, were five or six small wads of cotton in a silver dish, and nearby a large crucifix between two lighted candelabra. Emma lay with her chin sunk on her breast, her eyelids unnaturally wide apart; and her poor hands picked at the sheets in the ghastly and poignant way of the dying, who seem impatient to cover themselves with their shrouds. Pale as a statue, his eyes red as coals, but no longer weeping, Charles stood facing her at the foot of the bed; the priest, on one knee, mumbled under his breath.

She slowly turned her face, and seemed overjoyed at suddenly seeing the purple stole—doubtless recognizing in this interval of extraordinary peace, the lost ecstasy of her first mystical flights and the first visions of eternal bliss.

The priest stood up and took the crucifix; she stretched out her head like someone thirsting; and pressing her lips to the body of the God-Man, she imprinted on it, with every ounce of her failing strength, the most passionate love-kiss she had ever given. Then he recited the *Misereatur* and the *Indulgentiam,* dipped his right thumb in the oil, and began the unctions. First he anointed her eyes, once so covetous of all earthly luxuries; then her nostrils, so gluttonous of caressing breezes and amorous scents; then her mouth, so prompt to lie, so defiant in pride, so loud in lust; then her hands, that had thrilled to voluptuous contacts; and finally the soles of her feet, once so swift when she had hastened to slake her desires, and now never to walk again.

The curé wiped his fingers, threw the oil-soaked bits of cotton into the fire, and returned to the dying woman, sitting beside her and telling her that now she must unite her sufferings with Christ's and throw herself on the divine mercy.

As he ended his exhortations he tried to have her grasp a blessed candle, symbol of the celestial glories soon to surround her. Emma was too weak, and couldn't close her fingers: but for Monsieur Bournisien the candle would have fallen to the floor.

Yet she was no longer so pale, and her face was serene, as though the sacrament had cured her.

The priest didn't fail to point this out: he even explained to Bovary that the Lord sometimes prolonged people's lives when He judged it expedient for their salvation; and Charles remembered another day, when, similarly close to death, she had received communion.

"Perhaps there's hope after all," he thought.

And indeed, she looked all about her, slowly, like someone waking from a dream; then, in a distinct voice, she asked for her mirror, and she remained bowed over it for some time, until great tears flowed from her eyes. Then she threw back her head with a sigh, and sank onto the pillow.

At once her breast began to heave rapidly. Her tongue hung at full length from her mouth; her rolling eyes grew dim like the globes of two lamps about to go out; and one might have thought her dead already but for the terrifying, ever-faster movement of her ribs, which were shaken by furious gasps, as though her soul were straining violently to break its fetters. Félicité knelt before the crucifix, and even the pharmacist flexed his knees a little. Monsieur Canivet stared vaguely out into the square. Bournisien had resumed his praying, his face bowed over the edge of the bed and his long black cassock trailing out behind him into the room. Charles was on the other side, on his knees, his arms stretched out toward Emma. He had taken her hands, and was pressing them, shuddering at every beat of her heart, as at the tremors of a falling ruin. As the death-rattle grew louder, the priest speeded his prayers: they mingled with Bovary's stifled sobs, and at moments everything seemed drowned by the monotonous flow of Latin syllables that sounded like the tolling of a bell.

Suddenly from out on the sidewalk came a noise of heavy wooden shoes and the scraping of a stick, and a voice rose up, a raucous voice singing:

> A clear day's warmth will often move
> A lass to stray in dreams of love.

Emma sat up like a galvanized corpse, her hair streaming, her eyes fixed and gaping.

> To gather up the stalks of wheat
> The swinging scythe keeps laying by,
> Nanette goes stooping in the heat
> Along the furrows where they lie.

"The blind man!" she cried.

Emma began to laugh—a horrible, frantic, desperate laugh—fancying that she saw the beggar's hideous face, a figure of terror looming up in the darkness of eternity.

> The wind blew very hard that day
> And snatched her petticoat away!

A spasm flung her down on the mattress. Everyone drew close. She had ceased to exist.

IX

Anyone's death always releases something like an aura of stupefaction, so difficult is it to grasp this irruption of nothingness and to believe that it has actually taken place. But when Charles realized how still she was, he threw himself on her, crying:

"*Adieu! Adieu!*"

Homais and Canivet led him from the room.

"Control yourself!"

"Let me stay!" he said, struggling. "I'll be reasonable; I won't do anything I shouldn't. But I want to be near her—she's my wife!"

And he wept.

"Weep, weep," said the pharmacist. "Let yourself go: you'll feel the better for it."

Helpless as a child, Charles let himself be taken downstairs to the parlor. Monsieur Homais soon went home.

In the square he was accosted by the blind beggar. Lured by the hope of the antiphlogistic salve, he had dragged himself all the way to Yonville, and now was asking every passer-by where the apothecary lived.

"Good Lord! As though I didn't have other things on my mind! Too bad! Come back later."

He hurried into the pharmacy.

He had to write two letters, prepare a sedative for Bovary, and invent a plausible lie that would cover up the suicide for an article in the *Fanal* and for the crowd that was awaiting him in order to learn the news. When all the Yonvillians had heard his story about the arsenic that Emma had mistaken for sugar while making a custard, Homais returned once more to Bovary.

He found him alone (Canivet had just left), sitting in the armchair beside the window, staring vacantly at the parlor floor.

"Now," said the pharmacist, "what you've got to do is decide on a time for the ceremony."

"Why? What ceremony?"

Then, in a frightened stammer:

"Oh no! I don't have to, do I? I want to keep her!"

To hide his embarrassment Homais took a carafe from the whatnot and began to water the geraniums.

"Ah, thank you!" said Charles. "You're so good!"

He broke off, choked by the flood of memories the pharmacist's action evoked.

To distract him, Homais thought it well to talk about horticulture: plants, he ventured, had to be kept moist. Charles nodded in agreement.

"Anyway, we'll soon be having fine spring weather."

"Ah!" said Bovary.

Not knowing what to say next, the apothecary twitched the sash curtain.

"Ah—there's Monsieur Tuvache going by."

Charles repeated mechanically:

"Monsieur Tuvache going by."

Homais didn't dare broach the subject of funeral arrangements again: it was the priest who eventually made Charles see reason.

He locked himself in his consulting room, took a pen, and after sobbing a while he wrote:

"I want her buried in her bridal dress, with white shoes and a wreath and her hair spread over her shoulders. Three coffins—one oak, one mahogany, one lead. No one has to say anything to me: I'll have the strength to go through with it. Cover her with a large piece of green velvet. I want this done. Do it."

The priest and the pharmacist were much taken aback by Bovary's romantic ideas. Homais expostulated:

"The velvet seems to be supererogatory. Not to mention the expense . . ."

"Is it any concern of yours?" cried Charles. "Leave me alone! You didn't love her! Go away!"

The priest took him by the arm and walked him around the garden, discoursing on the vanity of earthly things. God is all-great, all-good; we must submit to His decrees without complaint; more than that, we must be grateful.

Charles burst into a stream of blasphemy.

"I detest your God!"

"The spirit of rebellion is still in you," sighed the priest.

Bovary had strode away from him and was pacing up and down beside the wall of espaliered fruit trees, grinding his teeth and looking curses at heaven: but not even a leaf stirred in answer.

A fine rain was falling. Charles's shirt was open, and soon he began to shiver. He went back into the house and sat in the kitchen.

At six o'clock there was a clanking in the square. It was the Hirondelle arriving, and he stood with his head against the windowpanes, watching all the passengers get out, one after the other. Félicité put down a mattress for him in the parlor, and he threw himself on it and fell asleep.

Rationalist though he was, Monsieur Homais respected the dead. So, bearing no grudge against poor Charles, he returned that night to watch beside the body. He brought three books with him, and a writing pad for making notes.

He found Monsieur Bournisien already there. Two tall candles were burning at the head of the bed, which had been moved out of the alcove.

The apothecary, oppressed by the silence, soon made a few elegiac remarks concerning "this hapless young woman"; and the priest replied that now there was nothing left to do but pray for her.

"Still," said Homais, "it's one thing or the other: either she died in a state of grace (as the church puts it), and therefore had no need of our prayers; or else she died unrepentant (I believe that is the ecclesiastical term) and in that case . . ."

Bournisien interrupted him, replying testily that prayer was called for nonetheless.

"But," objected the pharmacist, "since God knows all our needs, what purpose can be served by prayer?"

"What?" said the priest. "Prayer? Aren't you a Christian, then?"

"I beg your pardon!" said Homais. "I admire Christianity. It freed the slaves, for one thing; it introduced into the world a moral code that . . ."

"That's not the point! All the texts . . ."

"Oh! Oh! The texts! Look in any history book: everybody knows they were falsified by the Jesuits."

Charles came in, walked up to the bed and slowly parted the curtains.

Emma's head was turned toward her right shoulder. The corner of her open mouth was like a black hole in the lower part of her face; her two thumbs were bent inward toward the palms of her hands; a kind of white dust powdered her lashes; and the outline of her eyes was beginning to disappear in a viscous pallor, as though spiders had been spinning cobwebs over her face. From her breasts to her knees the sheet sagged, rising again at her toes; and it seemed to Charles that some infinite mass, some enormous weight, was pressing on her.

The church clock struck two. The flowing river murmured deeply in the darkness at the foot of the terrace. Now and again Monsieur Bournisien blew his nose loudly, and Homais' pen was scratching on his paper.

"Go back to bed, my friend," he said. "Stop torturing yourself."

When Charles had gone, the pharmacist and the curé resumed their arguments.

"Read Voltaire!" said the one. "Read Holbach! Read the Encyclopedia!"[1]

"Read the *Letters of Some Portuguese Jews!*" said the other. "Read the *Proof of Christianity,*[2] by ex-magistrate Nicolas!"

They grew excited and flushed; both spoke at once, neither listening to the other; Bournisien was shocked by such audacity; Homais marveled at such stupidity; and they were on the point of exchanging insults when Charles suddenly reappeared. He couldn't keep away: it was as though a spell kept drawing him upstairs.

He stood at the foot of the bed to see her better, absorbed in contemplation so intense that he no longer felt any pain.

He recalled stories about catalepsy and the miracles of magnetism; and he told himself that by straining his will to the utmost he might resuscitate her. Once he even leaned over toward her and cried very softly "Emma! Emma!" The force of his breath blew the flickering candle flames against the wall.

At daybreak the older Madame Bovary arrived, and as Charles embraced her he had another fit of weeping. Like the pharmacist, she ventured a few remarks about the funeral expenses, but he flew into such a rage that she said no more, and he sent her straight to the city to buy what was needed.

Charles spent all afternoon alone. Berthe had been taken to Madame Homais'; Félicité stayed upstairs in the bedroom with Madame Lefrançois.

That evening, people called. He rose and shook hands with them, unable to speak; each then took a seat alongside the others, gradually forming a wide semicircle in front of the fireplace. Eyes lowered and legs crossed, they dangled their feet, sighing deeply from time to time. Everyone was bored beyond measure, but no one was willing to be the first to leave.

When Homais returned at nine o'clock (during the past two days he had seemed to spend all his time crossing the square) he brought with him a supply of camphor, benzoin and aromatic herbs. He also had a vase full of chlorine water, to "drive out the miasmas." At that moment the maid, Madame Lefrançois and the older Madame Bovary were clustered around Emma, putting the finishing touches to her toilette: they drew down the long, stiff veil, covering her even to her satin shoes.

1. Paul-Henri Dietrich, baron d'Holbach (1723–1789), friend and disciple of Diderot and one of the most outspoken opponents of religion in the French Enlightenment. The *Encyclopedia,* a dictionary of the sciences, arts, and letters, edited by Diderot and d'Alembert (1751–72), is the intellectual monument of the French Enlightenment, a fountainhead of later secular and agnostic thought.   2. One of the many books defending Roman Catholicism by Jean-Jacques-Auguste Nicolas (1807–1888). *Letters of Some Portuguese Jews* (1769) refers to a book by Abbé Antoine Guéné directed against Voltaire.

Félicité sobbed:

"Ah! Poor mistress! Poor mistress!"

"Look at her," said the hotel keeper, with a sigh. "How pretty she still is! You'd swear she'd be getting up any minute."

Then they bent over to put on her wreath.

They had to lift her head a little, and as they did so a black liquid poured out of her mouth like vomit.

"Heavens! Watch out for her dress!" cried Madame Lefrançois. "Help us, won't you?" she said to the pharmacist. "You wouldn't be afraid, would you?"

"I, afraid?" he answered, shrugging his shoulders. "Take it from me: I saw plenty of things like this at the hospital, when I was studying pharmacy. We used to make punch in the dissecting room while we worked. Death holds no terrors for a philosopher. In fact, as I often say, I intend to leave my body to the hospitals, so that it can eventually be of service to science."

When the curé arrived he asked how Monsieur was; and at the apothecary's reply he said:

"Of course: he still hasn't got over the shock."

Homais went on to congratulate him on not being exposed, like other men, to the risk of losing a beloved wife; and there followed a discussion on the celibacy of the clergy.

"After all," said the pharmacist, "it's against nature for a man to do without women. We've all heard of crimes . . ."

"But drat it all!" cried the priest. "How would you expect anyone who was married to be able to keep the secrets of the confessional, for example?"

Homais attacked confession. Bournisien defended it: he dilated on the acts of restitution it was constantly responsible for, told stories about thieves suddenly turning honest. Soldiers, approaching the tribunal of repentance, had felt the scales drop from their eyes. There was a minister at Fribourg . . .

His fellow watcher had fallen asleep. Bournisien found it somewhat hard to breathe, the air of the room was so heavy, and he opened a window. This woke the pharmacist.

"Here," the priest said. "Take a pinch of snuff. Do—it clears the head."

There was a continual barking somewhere in the distance.

"Do you hear a dog howling?" said the pharmacist.

"People say that they scent the dead," answered the priest. "It's like bees: they leave the hive when someone dies."

Homais didn't challenge those superstitions, for once again he had fallen asleep.

Monsieur Bournisien, more resistant, continued for some time to move his lips in a murmur, then his chin sank gradually lower, his thick black book slipped from his hand, and he began to snore.

They sat opposite one another, stomachs out, faces swollen, both of them scowling—united, after so much dissension, in the same human weakness; and they stirred no more than the corpse that was like another sleeper beside them.

Charles's coming didn't wake them. This was the last time. He had come to bid her farewell.

The aromatic herbs were still smoking, and at the window their swirls of bluish vapor mingled with the mist that was blowing in.

There were a few stars. The night was mild.

Great drops of wax were falling onto the bedsheets from the candles. Charles watched them burn, tiring his eyes in the gleam of their yellow flames.

The watered satin of her dress was shimmering with the whiteness of moonbeams. Emma was invisible under it; and it seemed to him as though she were spreading out beyond herself, melting confusedly into the surroundings—the silence, the night, the passing wind, the damp fragrance that rose from the earth.

Then, suddenly, he saw her in the garden at Tostes, on the seat, against the thorn hedge—or in Rouen, in the street—or on the doorstep of their house, in the farmyard at Les Bertaux. Once again he heard the laughter of the merry lads dancing under the apple trees; the wedding chamber was full of the perfume of her hair, and her dress rustled in his arms with a sound of flying sparks. And now she was wearing that very dress!

He stood there a long time thus recalling all his past happiness—her poses, her gestures, the sound of her voice. Wave of despair followed upon wave, endlessly, like the waters of an overflowing tide.

A terrible curiosity came over him: slowly, with the tips of his fingers, his heart pounding, he lifted her veil. He gave a scream of horror that woke the sleepers. They took him downstairs to the parlor.

Then Félicité came up, to say that he was asking for a lock of her hair.

"Cut some!" answered the apothecary.

She didn't dare, and he stepped forward himself, scissors in hand. He trembled so violently that he nicked the skin on the temples in several places. Finally, steeling himself, Homais slashed blindly two or three times, leaving white marks in the beautiful black tresses.

The pharmacist and the curé resumed their respective occupations—not without dozing off now and again and reproaching each other for doing so each time they awoke. Then Monsieur Bournisien would sprinkle the room with holy water and Homais would pour a little chlorine water on the floor.

Félicité had thought to leave a bottle of brandy for them on the chest of drawers, along with a cheese and a big brioche. Finally, about four in the morning, the apothecary could hold out no longer.

"I confess," he sighed, "that I'd gladly partake of some nourishment."

The priest didn't have to be asked twice. He went out, said his Mass, came back; and they proceeded to eat and clink their glasses, chuckling a little without knowing why, prey to that indefinable gaiety that often succeeds periods of gloom. With the last drink of brandy the priest slapped the pharmacist on the back:

"We'll be good friends yet!" he said.

Downstairs in the hall they met the workmen arriving, and for two hours Charles had to suffer the torture of the sound of the hammer on the planks. Then they brought her down in her oaken coffin, which they fitted inside the two others. The outermost was too wide, and they had to stuff the space between with wool from a mattress. Finally, when the three lids had been planed, nailed on and soldered, the bier was exposed at the door. The house was thrown open, and the Yonvillians began to flock in.

Monsieur Rouault arrived. He fell in a faint in the square at the sight of the black cloth.

X

The pharmacist's letter hadn't reached him until thirty-six hours after the event; and to spare his feelings Monsieur Homais had worded it in such a way that it was impossible for him to know what to think.

On reading it he fell to the ground, as though stricken by apoplexy. Then he gathered that she was *not* dead. But she might be . . . He put on his smock and his hat, fastened a spur to his boot, and set off at a gallop; and during the entire length of his breathless ride he was frantic with anguish. At one point he had to stop and dismount: he couldn't see, he heard voices, he thought he was losing his mind.

At daybreak he caught sight of three black hens asleep in a tree, and he shuddered, terrified by the omen. He promised the Holy Virgin three chasubles for the church, and vowed to walk barefoot from the cemetery at Les Bertaux to the chapel at Vassonville.

He rode into Maromme, shouting ahead to the people at the inn, burst open the gate with his shoulder, dashed up to the oats bag, poured a bottle of sweet cider into the manger; then he remounted his nag, and it was off again, striking sparks from all four shoes.

He kept telling himself that she would certainly live: the doctors would find a remedy—there was no question. He reminded himself of all the miraculous recoveries people had told him of.

Then he had a vision of her dead. She was there, before him stretched on her back in the middle of the road. He pulled at the reins, and the hallucination vanished.

At Quincampoix he drank three coffees in a row to fortify himself.

It occurred to him that they might have put the wrong name on the letter. He rummaged for it in his pocket, felt it there, but didn't dare open it.

He even began to imagine that it might be a practical joke, an attempt to get even with him for something, or a wag's idea of a prank. Besides—if she was dead, he'd know it! But no—the countryside was as always: the sky was blue, the trees were swaying; a flock of sheep crossed the road. He caught sight of the village; people saw him racing by, hunched over his horse, beating it furiously, its saddle girths dripping blood.

Then, when he had regained consciousness, he fell weeping into Bovary's arms:

"My daughter! Emma! My baby! Tell me . . ."

Charles answered, sobbing:

"I don't know, I don't know! It's a curse . . ."

The apothecary drew them apart.

"There's no use going into the horrible details. I'll tell Monsieur all about it later. People are coming. Have some dignity, for heaven's sake! Take it like a philosopher!"

Poor Charles made an effort, and repeated several times:

"Yes! . . . Be brave!"

"All right, then, I'll be brave, God damn it to hell!" the old man cried. "I'll stay with her to the end."

The bell was tolling. Everything was ready. It was time to set out.

Sitting side by side in one of the choir stalls, they watched the three cantors continually crossing back and forth in front of them, intoning. The serpent[3] player blew with all his might. Monsieur Bournisien, in full regalia, sang in a shrill voice: he bowed to the tabernacle, raised his hands, stretched out his arms, Lestiboudois moved about the church with his verger's staff; near the lectern stood the coffin, between four rows of candles. Charles had to restrain himself from getting up and putting them out.

He did his best, however, to work himself up into a religious frame of mind, to seize on the hope of a future life in which he would see her again. He tried to imagine that she had gone on a trip—far off—a long time ago. But when he remembered that she was right there, in the coffin, and that everything was over, and that now she was going to be buried, he was filled with a rage that was fierce and black and desperate. At moments he thought he was beyond feeling; and he relished this ebbing of grief, cursing himself in the same breath for a scoundrel.

A sharp, regular noise, like the tapping of a metal-tipped walking stick, was heard on the stone floor. It came from the far end of the church and stopped abruptly in the side aisle. A man in a coarse brown jacket sank painfully to his knees. It was Hippolyte, the stable boy at the Lion d'Or. He had put on his new leg.

One of the cantors came through the nave, taking up the collection, and one after another the heavy coins clattered onto the silver plate.

"Get it over with! I can't stand much more of this!" cried Bovary, angrily throwing him a five-franc piece.

The cantor thanked him with a ceremonious bow.

The singing and the kneeling and the rising went on and on. He remembered that once, early in their marriage, they had attended Mass together, and that they had sat on the other side, at the right, against the wall. The bell began to toll again. There was a great scraping of chairs. The pallbearers slipped their three poles under the bier, and everyone left the church.

At that moment Justin appeared in the doorway of the pharmacy and abruptly retreated, white-faced and trembling.

People stood at their windows to watch the procession. Charles, at the head, held himself very straight. He put on a brave front and nodded to those who came out from the lanes and the doorways to join the crowd.

The six men, three on each side, walked with short steps, panting a little. The priests, the cantors and the two choirboys recited the *De profundis*; and their voices carried over the fields, rising and falling in waves. Sometimes they disappeared from view at a twist of the path; but the great silver cross was always visible, high up among the trees.

At the rear were the women, in their black cloaks with turned-down hoods; each of them carried a thick lighted candle; and Charles felt himself overcome amidst this endless succession of prayers and lights, these cloying odors of wax and cassocks. A cool breeze was blowing, the rye and the colza were sprouting green; dewdrops shimmered on the thorn hedges along the road. All kinds of joyous sounds filled the air—the rattle of a jolting cart in distant ruts, the repeated crowing of a cock, the thudding of a colt as it bolted off under the apple trees. The pure sky was dappled with rosy clouds; wisps of bluish smoke trailed down over the thatched cottages, their roofs abloom with iris. Charles recognized each farmyard as he passed. He remembered

---

3. A woodwind instrument no longer in use.

leaving them on mornings like this after making sick calls, on his way back home to where she was.

The black pall, embroidered with white tears, flapped up now and again, exposing the coffin beneath. The tired pallbearers were slowing down, and the bier moved forward in a series of jerks, like a boat pitching at every wave.

They reached the cemetery.

The pallbearers continued on to where the grave had been dug in the turf.

Everyone stood around it; and as the priest spoke, the reddish earth, heaped up on the edges, kept sliding down at the corners, noiselessly and continuously.

Then, when the four ropes were in position, the coffin was pushed onto them. He watched it go down. It went down and down.

Finally there was a thud, and the ropes creaked as they came back up. Then Bournisien took the shovel that Lestiboudois held out to him. With his left hand—all the while sprinkling holy water with his right—he vigorously pushed in a large spadeful of earth; and the stones striking the wood of the coffin made that awesome sound that seems to us like the very voice of eternity.

The priest passed his sprinkler to the person beside him. It was Homais. He shook it gravely, then handed it to Charles, who sank on his knees in the pile of earth and threw it into the grave in handfuls, crying, *"Adieu!"* He blew her kisses, and dragged himself toward the grave as though to be swallowed up in it with her.

They led him away, and he soon grew calmer—vaguely relieved, perhaps, like everyone else, that it was all over.

On the way back Monsieur Rouault calmly lit his pipe—a gesture that Homais silently condemned as improper. He noticed, too, that Monsieur Binet had stayed away, that Tuvache had "sneaked off" after the Mass, and that Théodore, the notary's servant, was wearing a blue coat—"as if he couldn't find a black coat, since it's the custom, for heaven's sake!" And he went from group to group communicating his sentiments. Everyone was deploring Emma's death, especially Lheureux, who hadn't failed to attend the funeral.

"Poor little lady! How terrible for her husband!"

"If it hadn't been for me, let me tell you," the apothecary assured him, "he would have tried to do away with himself!"

"Such a good woman! To think that just last Saturday I saw her in my shop!"

"I didn't have the leisure," said Homais, "to prepare a little speech. I'd have liked to say a few words at the grave."

Back home, Charles took off his funeral clothes and Monsieur Rouault got back into his blue smock. It was a new one: all the way from Les Bertaux he had kept wiping his eyes with the sleeve, and the dye had come off on his face, which was still dusty and tear-streaked.

The older Madame Bovary was with them. All three were silent. Finally the old man sighed:

"You remember, my friend, I came to Tostes once, when you had just lost your first wife. That time I tried to comfort you. I could think of something to say; but now . . ."

Then, his chest heaving in a long groan:

"Ah! Everything's over for me! I've seen my wife go . . . then my son . . . and now today my daughter!"

He insisted on leaving immediately for Les Bertaux, saying that he couldn't sleep in that house. He even refused to see his granddaughter.

"No! No! It would be too hard on me. . . . But give her a big kiss for me! Good-bye! . . . You're a good man! And—I'll never forget this!" he said, slapping his thigh. "Don't worry—you'll always get your turkey."

But when he reached the top of the hill he turned around as he had turned around once before, after parting from her on the road to Saint-Victor. The windows of the village were all ablaze in the slanting rays of the sun that was setting beyond the meadow. He shaded his eyes with his hand; and on the horizon he made out a walled enclosure where trees stood in dark clumps here and there among white stones; then he continued on his way at a gentle trot, for his nag was limping.

Weary though they were, Charles and his mother sat up very late that night talking. They spoke of days gone by and of the future: she would come and live in Yonville, she would keep house for him; never again would they be apart. She was astute and ingratiating with him, rejoicing inwardly at the thought of recapturing his affection, which had eluded her for so many years. Midnight struck. The village was silent as usual; and Charles lay awake, thinking ceaselessly of *her*.

Rodolphe, who had spent all day roaming the woods to keep his mind off things, was peacefully asleep in his château; and Léon was sleeping, too, in the distant city.

But there was someone else—someone who was not asleep at that late hour.

On the grave among the firs knelt a young boy, weeping and sobbing in the darkness, his heart overflowing with an immense grief that was tender as the moon and unfathomable as night. Suddenly the gate creaked. It was Lestiboudois, come to fetch his spade, which he had forgotten a while before. He recognized Justin clambering over the wall: at last he knew who was stealing his potatoes!

XI

The next day Charles sent for Berthe. She asked for *maman*: she was away on a trip, she was told, and would bring her back some toys. She mentioned her again several times, then gradually forgot her. Charles found the little girl's cheerfulness depressing. The pharmacist's consolations, too, were an ordeal.

Before long the question of money came up again. Monsieur Lheureux egged on his friend Vinçart as before, and Charles signed notes for enormous sums: he refused absolutely to consider selling the slightest bit of furniture that had belonged to her. His mother fumed; he flew into an even greater rage. He was a completely changed man. She packed up and left.

Then everyone began to snatch what he could. Mademoiselle Lempereur demanded her fees for six months' lessons. Emma had never taken a single one, despite the receipted bills that she had shown Bovary: the two ladies had concocted this device between them. The lending-library proprietor demanded three years' subscription fees. Madame Rollet demanded postage fees for twenty or so letters, and when Charles asked for an explanation she was tactful enough to answer.

"Oh, I don't know anything about them—some personal matters."

Each debt he paid, Charles thought was the last. Then more came—a continual stream.

He dunned patients for back bills, but they showed him the letters his wife had sent and he had to apologize.

Félicité now wore Madame's dresses. Not all, for he had kept a few and used to shut himself up in her dressing room and look at them. The maid was just about her size, and often when Charles caught sight of her from behind he thought it was Emma, and cried out:

"Oh! Don't go! Don't go!"

But at Pentecost she left Yonville without warning, eloping with Théodore and stealing everything that was left of the wardrobe.

It was about this time that "Madame veuve Dupuis" had the honor of announcing to him the "marriage of M. Léon Dupuis, her son, notary at Yvetot, and Mlle. Léocadie Leboeuf, of Bondeville." Charles's letter of congratulation contained the sentence: "How happy this would have made my poor wife!"

One day, wandering aimlessly about the house, he went up to the attic; and through the sole of his slipper he felt a wad of thin paper. He opened it. "You must be courageous, Emma," he read. "The last thing I want to do is ruin your life." It was Rodolphe's letter. It had fallen to the floor in among some boxes and had remained there, and now the draught from the dormer had blown it toward the door. Charles stood there motionless and open-mouthed—in the very spot where Emma, desperate and even paler than he was now, had longed to die. Finally he discovered a small "R" at the bottom of the second page. Who was it? He remembered Rodolphe's attentiveness, his sudden disappearance, and his air of constraint the two or three times they had met since. But the respectful tone of the letter deceived him.

"Perhaps they loved each other platonically," he told himself.

In any case, Charles wasn't one to go to the root of things: he closed his eyes to the evidence, and his hesitant jealousy was drowned in the immensity of his grief.

Everyone must have adored her, he thought. Every man who saw her must certainly have coveted her. This made her the lovelier in his mind; and he conceived a furious desire for her that never stopped; it fed the flames of his despair, and it grew stronger and stronger because now it could never be satisfied.

To please her, as though she were still alive, he adopted her tastes, her ideas: he bought himself patent leather shoes, took to wearing white cravats. He waxed his mustache, and signed—just as she had—more promissory notes. She was corrupting him from beyond the grave.

He was forced to sell the silver piece by piece, then he sold the parlor furniture. But though all the other rooms grew bare, the bedroom—her bedroom—remained as before. Charles went there every day after dinner. He pushed the round table up to the fire, pulled her armchair close to it. He sat opposite. A tallow candle burned in one of the gilded sconces. Berthe, at his side, colored pictures.

It pained him, poor fellow, to see her so shabbily dressed, with her shoes unlaced and the armholes of her smock torn and gaping to below her waist—for the cleaning woman completely neglected her. But she was so sweet and gentle, and she bent her little head so gracefully, letting her fair hair fall against her rosy cheek, that he was flooded with infinite pleasure—an enjoyment that was mixed with bitterness, like an inferior wine tasting of resin. He mended her toys, made puppets for her out of cardboard, sewed up the torn stomachs of her dolls. But the sight of the sewing box, or a bit of loose ribbon, or even a pin caught in a crack in the table, would send him brooding; and then he looked so gloomy that she, too, grew sad.

No one came to see them now, for Justin had run off to Rouen, where he found work as a grocery clerk, and the apothecary's children saw less and less of Berthe. Monsieur Homais was not eager to prolong the intimacy, considering the difference in their social status.

The blind man, whom his salve had not cured, had resumed his beat on the hill at Bois-Guillaume, where he told everyone about the pharmacist's failure—to such a point that Homais, whenever he went to the city, hid behind the Hirondelle's curtains to avoid meeting him face to face. He hated him. He must get rid of him at all costs, he decided, for the sake of his own reputation; and he launched an underhand campaign against him in which he revealed his deep cunning and his criminal vanity. During the next six months paragraphs like the following would appear in the *Fanal de Rouen*:

> Anyone who has ever wended his way toward the fertile fields of Picardy cannot help but have noticed, on the hill at Bois-Guillaume, an unfortunate afflicted with a horrible facial deformity. He pesters travelers, persecutes them, levies a veritable tax upon them. Are we back in the monstrous days of the Middle Ages, when vagabonds were permitted to display, in our public squares, the leprous ulcers and scrofulous sores they brought back from the Crusades?

Or:

> Despite the laws against vagrancy, the approaches to our large cities continue to be infested by bands of beggars. There are some who operate single-handed; and these, perhaps, are not the least dangerous of the lot. What are our Municipal Authorities waiting for?

Sometimes Homais invented ancedotes:

> Yesterday, on the hill at Bois-Guillaume, a skittish horse . . .

And there would follow the story of an accident caused by the blind man.

This went on until the beggar was locked up. But he was released. He took up where he had left off. So did Homais. It was a fight to the finish. Homais was victorious: his enemy was committed to an asylum for the rest of his days.

This success emboldened him; and from then on whenever a dog was run over in the district, or a barn set on fire, or a woman beaten, Homais hastened to publicize the event, inspired always by love of progress and hatred of the clergy. He instituted comparisons between public and religious schools, to the detriment of the latter; he referred to Saint Bartholomew's Eve apropos of every hundred-franc subsidy the government granted the church; he denounced abuses, he flashed the rapier of satire. Such, at least, was the way he put it. In short, Homais was "undermining the foundations": he was becoming a dangerous man.

He found the narrow limitations of journalism stifling, however, and soon he felt the need to produce a book, a "work." So he composed his *General Statistics Concerning the Canton of Yonville, Followed by Climatological Observations*; and statistics led him into philosophy. He dealt with burning issues: the social problem, raising the moral standards of the poor, pisciculture,[4] rubber, railroads, etc. In the end, he felt it a disgrace to be a bourgeois. He affected bohemian ways, he even smoked! He bought two rococo statuettes, very *chic*, to decorate his parlor.

Not that he gave up pharmacy. Far from it! He kept up with all the latest discoveries. He followed every stage in the great development of chocolates. He was the first to introduce into the department of the Seine-Inférieure those two great chocolate health foods, Cho-ca and Revalentia. He became an enthusiastic partisan of Pulvermacher electric health belts; he wore one himself, and at night when he took off his flannel undershirt Madame Homais never failed to be dazzled by the golden spiral that almost hid him from view, and her passion redoubled for this man she saw before her swaddled like a Scythian and splendid as a Magian priest.

He had brilliant ideas for Emma's tombstone. First he suggested a broken column with a drapery; then a pyramid, then a Temple of Vesta, a kind of rotunda, or perhaps a romantic pile of ruins. One element was constant in all his plans—a weeping willow, which he considered the obligatory symbol of grief.

Charles and he made a trip to Rouen together to look at tombstones at a burial specialist's, accompanied by an artist named Vaufrilard, a friend of Bridoux's, who never stopped making puns. Finally, after examining a hundred designs, getting an estimate, and making a second trip to Rouen, Charles decided in favor of a mausoleum whose two principal sides were to be adorned with "a spirit bearing an extinguished torch."

As for the inscription, Homais could think of nothing as eloquent as *Sta viator*. He couldn't get beyond it, rack his brains as he might: he kept repeating *"Sta viator"* to himself over and over again. Finally he had an inspiration— *amabilem conjugem calcas;*[5] and this was adopted.

The strange thing was that Bovary, even though he thought of Emma continually, was forgetting her; and he felt desperate realizing that her image was fading from his memory, struggle as he might to keep it alive. Each night, however, he dreamed of her. It was always the same dream: he approached her, but just when he was about to embrace her she fell into decay in his arms.

The first week, he went to church every evening. Monsieur Bournisien called on him two or three times, then left him alone. The fact is that the priest was becoming decidedly less tolerant—sinking into real fanaticism, as Homais put it. He thundered against the spirit of the modern age, and regularly once a fortnight included in his sermon an account of the last agony of Voltaire—who died eating his own excrement, as everyone knows.

Despite Bovary's frugality, he was quite unable to pay off his old debts.

4. Fish breeding.   5. You are treading on a beloved spouse (Latin). Based on the Latin inscription placed over the spot where the valorous Bavarian field marshal Baron Franz von Mercy died in the Second Battle of Nördlingen (1645): *Sta viator, heroem calcas* (Halt, traveler, you are treading on a hero).

Lheureux refused to renew a single note. Execution was imminent. He had recourse to his mother, who agreed to let him mortgage her house; but she seized the occasion to write him many harsh things about Emma, and in return for her sacrifice she demanded a shawl that had escaped Félicité's depredations. Charles refused to let her have it, and they quarreled.

She made the first overtures toward a reconciliation by offering to take the little girl to live with her: the child could help her in the house. Charles consented. But when the time came for her to leave he couldn't face it, and there was a new break between mother and son, this time irrevocable.

As his bonds with others weakened, his love for his child grew ever stronger. She worried him, however, for occasionally she coughed and had red patches on her cheekbones.

Across the square, in constant view, thriving and jovial, was the family of the pharmacist. He had every reason to be satisfied with his lot. Napoléon helped him in the laboratory, Athalie embroidered him a smoking cap, Irma cut paper circles to cover the jelly jars, and Franklin could recite the multiplication table without stumbling. Homais was the happiest of fathers, the luckiest of men.

Not quite, though! He was eaten with a secret ambition: he wanted the cross of the Legion of Honor. He had plenty of qualifications:

"*First:* during the cholera epidemic, was conspicuous for devotion above and beyond the call of professional duty. *Second:* have published at my own expense various works of public usefulness, such as . . ." (And he cited his treatise on *Cider: Its Manufacture and Its Effects;* also, some observations on the woolly aphis that he had sent to the Academy; his volume of statistics, and even his pharmacist's thesis.) "Not to mention that I am a member of several learned societies." (He belonged to only one.)

"And even suppose," he said with a caper, "that the only thing I had to my credit was my perfect record as a volunteer fireman!"

Homais proceeded to ingratiate himself with the powers that be; he secretly rendered great services to Monsieur le Préfet during an electoral campaign. In short he sold himself; he prostituted himself. He went so far as to address a petition to the sovereign in which he begged him to "do him justice": he called him "our good king" and compared him to Henri IV.

Every morning the apothecary rushed to the newspaper, hoping to find the news of his nomination, but it didn't come. Finally, in his impatience, he had a star-shaped grass plot designed for his garden, to represent the decoration, with two little tufts of greenery as the ribbon. He would walk around it, his arms folded, pondering on governmental stupidity and human ingratitude.

Out of respect, or to prolong the almost sensual pleasure he took in his investigations, Charles had not yet opened the secret compartment of the rosewood desk that Emma had always used. At last, one day, he sat down at it, turned the key and pressed the spring. All Léon's letters were there. No possible doubt, this time! He devoured every last one of them. Then he rummaged in every corner, every piece of furniture, every drawer, looked for hiding places in the walls: he was sobbing, screaming with rage, beside himself, stark mad. He came upon a box, kicked it open. Rodolphe's picture jumped out at him, and all the love letters spilled out with it.

Everyone was amazed at the depth of his depression. He no longer went out, had no visitors, refused even to call on his patients. Everyone said that he "locked himself up to get drunk."

Now and again someone more curious than the rest would peer over the garden hedge and would be startled at the sight of him, wild-eyed, long-bearded, clad in sordid rags, walking and weeping aloud.

Summer evenings he would take his daughter with him and go to the cemetery. They always came back after dark, when the only light in the square was in Binet's dormer.

Still, he was unable to savor his grief to the full, since he had no one with whom he could share it. From time to time he called on Madame Lefrançois, for the sole purpose of talking about "her." But the innkeeper listened to him with only one ear, having her troubles just as he had his: Monsieur Lheureux had finally established his transportation service, *Les Favorites du commerce,* and Hivert, who enjoyed a considerable reputation for his dependability as doer of errands, was demanding an increase in wages and threatening to go to work for her competitor.

One day, at the market in Argueuil, where he had gone to sell his horse—his last asset—he met Rodolphe.

Both men turned pale when they caught sight of each other, Rodolphe, who had merely sent his card with a message of condolence, began by stammering a few excuses; then he grew bolder, and even had the cheek (it was a very hot August day) to invite him to take a bottle of beer in a café.

Sitting opposite him, his elbows on the table, he chewed his cigar as he talked; and Charles was lost in revery as he looked into the face that she had loved. In it, he felt, he was seeing something of her. It was a revelation. He would have liked to be that man.

Rodolphe talked farming, livestock, fertilizers—making use of banalities to stop up all the gaps through which any compromising reference might creep in. Charles wasn't listening. Rodolphe became aware of this; and in the play of expression on Charles's face he could read the sequence of his thoughts. Gradually it grew crimson; Charles's nostrils fluttered, his lips quivered; at one point, filled with somber fury, he stared fixedly at Rodolphe, who in his fright stopped speaking. But almost at once the other man's features reassumed their habitual expression of mournful weariness.

"I don't hold it against you," he said.

Rodolphe sat speechless. And Charles, his head in his hands, repeated, in a dull voice, with all the resignation of a grief that can never be assuaged:

"No, I don't hold it against you, any more."

And he added a bit of rhetoric, the only such utterance that had ever escaped him:

"No one is to blame. It was decreed by fate."

Rodolphe, who had been the instrument of that fate, thought him very meek indeed for a man in his situation—comical, even, and a little contemptible.

The next day Charles sat down on the bench in the arbor. Rays of light came through the trellis, grape leaves traced their shadow on the gravel, the jasmine was fragrant under the blue sky, bettles buzzed about the flowering lilies. A vaporous flood of love-memories swelled in his sorrowing heart, and he was overcome with emotion, like an adolescent.

At seven o'clock little Berthe, who hadn't seen him all afternoon, came to call him to dinner.

She found him with his head leaning back against the wall, his eyes closed, his mouth open; and there was a long lock of black hair in his hands.

"Papa! Come along!" she said.

She thought that he was playing, and gave him a little push. He fell to the ground. He was dead.

Thirty-six hours later Monsieur Canivet arrived, summoned by the apothecary. He performed an autopsy, but found nothing.

When everything was sold, there remained twelve francs and fifteen centimes—enough to pay Mademoiselle Bovary's coach fare to her grandmother's. The old lady died the same year; and since Monsieur Rouault was now paralyzed, it was an aunt who took charge of her. She is poor, and sends her to work for her living in a cotton mill.

Since Bovary's death, three doctors have succeeded one another in Yonville, and not one of them has gained a foothold, so rapidly and so utterly has Homais routed them. The devil himself doesn't have a greater following than the pharmacist: the authorities treat him considerately, and public opinion is on his side.

He has just been awarded the cross of the Legion of Honor.

FYODOR DOSTOEVSKY
1821–1881

Fyodor Dostoevsky has been a central figure in the formation of the modern sensibility. His works are fundamental to the Western tradition of the novel and a strong influence on modern literature in China and Japan. Dostoevsky formulated in fictional terms, in dramatic and even sensational scenes, some of the central predicaments of our time: the choices between God and atheism, good and evil, freedom and tyranny; the recognition of the limits and even of the fall of humanity against the belief in progress, revolution, and utopia. Most important, he captured unforgettably the enormous contradictions of which our common human nature is capable and by which it is torn.

Fyodor Mikhailovich Dostoevsky was born in Moscow on October 30, 1821. His father was a staff doctor at the Hospital for the Poor. Later he acquired an estate and serfs. In 1839 he was killed by one of his peasants in a quarrel. Dostoevsky was sent to the Military Engineering Academy in St. Petersburg, from which he graduated in 1843. He became a civil servant, a draftsman in the St. Petersburg Engineering Corps, but soon resigned because he feared that he would be transferred to the provinces when his writing was discovered. His first novel, *Poor People* (1846), proved a great success with the critics; his second, *The Double* (1846), which followed immediately, was a failure.

Subsequently, Dostoevsky became involved in the Petrashevsky circle, a secret society of antigovernment and socialist tendencies. He was arrested on April 23, 1849, and condemned to be shot. On December 22 he was led to public execution, but he was reprieved at the last moment and sent to penal servitude in Siberia (near Omsk), where he worked for four years in a stockade, wearing fetters, completely cut off from communications with Russia. On his release in February 1854, he was assigned as a common soldier to Semipalatinsk, a small town near the Mongolian frontier. There he received several promotions (eventually becoming an ensign); his rank of nobility, forfeited by his sentence, was restored; and he married the widow of a customs official. In July 1859, Dostoevsky was permitted to return to Russia and, finally, in December 1859, to St. Petersburg—after ten years of his life had been spent in Siberia.

In the last year of his exile, Dostoevsky had resumed writing; and in 1861, shortly after his return, he founded a review, *Time* (*Vremya*). This was suppressed in 1863, though Dostoevsky had changed his political opinions and was now strongly nationalistic and conservative in outlook. He made his first trip to France and England in 1862 and traveled in Europe again in 1863 and 1865, to follow a young woman friend, Apollinaria Suslova, and to indulge in gambling. After his wife's death in 1864 and another unsuccessful journalistic venture, *The Epoch* (*Epokha*, 1864–65), Dostoevsky was for a time almost crushed by gambling debts, emotional entanglements, and frequent epileptic seizures. He barely managed to return from Germany in 1865. In the winter of 1866 he wrote *Crime and Punishment* and, before he had finished it, dictated a shorter novel, *The Gambler,* to meet a deadline. He married his secretary, Anna Grigoryevna Snitkina, early in 1867 and left Russia with her to avoid his creditors. For years they wandered through Germany, Italy, and Switzerland, frequently in abject poverty. Their first child died. In 1871, when the initial chapters of *The Possessed* proved a popular success, Dostoevsky returned to St. Petersburg. He was the editor of a weekly, *The Citizen* (*Grazhdanin*), for a short time and then published a periodical written by himself, *The Diary of a Writer* (1876–81), which won great acclaim. His last novel, *The Brothers Karamazov* (1880), was an immense success, and honors and some prosperity came to him at last. At a Pushkin anniversary celebrated in Moscow in 1880 he gave the main speech. But soon after his return to St. Petersburg he died, on January 28, 1881, not yet sixty years old.

Dostoevsky, like every great writer, can be approached in different ways and read on different levels. We can try to understand him as a religious philosopher, a political commentator, a psychologist, and a novelist; and if we know much about his fascinating and varied life, we might also interpret his works as biographical.

The biographical interpretation is the one that has been pushed furthest. The lurid crimes of Dostoevsky's characters (such as the rape of a young girl) have been ascribed to him, and all his novels have been studied as if they constituted a great personal confession. Dostoevsky certainly did draw from his experiences in his books, as every writer does: he several times described the feelings of a man facing a firing squad as he himself faced it on December 22, 1849, only to be reprieved at the last moment. His writings also reflect his years in Siberia: four years working in a loghouse, in chains, as he describes it in an oddly impersonal book, *Memoirs from the House of the Dead* (1862), and six more years as a common soldier on the borders of Mongolia, in a small, remote provincial town. Similarly, he used the experience of his disease (epilepsy), ascribing great spiritual significance to the ecstatic rapture preceding the actual seizure. He assigned his disease to both his most angelic "good" man, the "Idiot" Prince Myshkin, and his most diabolical, inhuman figure, the cold-blooded unsexed murderer of the old Karamazov, the flunky Smerdyakov. Dostoevsky also used something of his experiences in Germany, where in the 1860s he succumbed to a passion for gambling, which he overcame only much later, during his second marriage. The short novel *The Gambler* (1866) gives an especially vivid account of this life and its moods.

There are other autobiographical elements in Dostoevsky's works, but it seems a gross misunderstanding of his methods and the procedures of art in general to conclude from his writings (as Thomas Mann has done) that he was a "saint and criminal" in one. Dostoevsky, after all, was an extremely hard worker who wrote and rewrote some twenty volumes. He was a novelist who employed the methods of the French sensational novel; he was constantly on the lookout for the most striking occurrences—the most shocking crimes and the most horrible disasters and scandals—because only in such fictional situations could he exalt his characters to their highest pitch, bringing out the clash of ideas and temperaments, revealing the deepest layers of their souls. But these fictions cannot be taken as literal transcriptions of reality and actual experience.

Whole books have been written to explain Dostoevsky's religious philosophy and conception of human nature. The Russian philosopher Berdyayev concludes his excellent study by saying, "So great is the value of Dostoevsky that to have produced him is by itself sufficient justification for the existence of the Russian people in the world." But there is no need for such extravagance. Dostoevsky's philosophy of religion is rather a personal version of extreme mystical Christianity and assumes flesh and blood only in the context of the novels. Reduced to the bare bones of abstract propositions, it amounts to saying that humanity is fallen but is free to choose between evil and Christ. And choosing Christ means taking on oneself the burden of humanity in love and pity, since "everybody is guilty for all and before all." Hence in Dostoevsky there is tremendous stress on personal freedom of choice; and his affirmation of the worth of every individual is combined, paradoxically, with an equal insistence on the substantial identity of all human beings, their equality before God, the bond of love that unites them.

Dostoevsky also develops a philosophy of history, with practical political implications, based on this point of view. According to him, the West is in complete decay; only Russia has preserved Christianity in its original form. The West is either Catholic (and Catholicism is condemned by Dostoevsky as an attempt to force salvation by magic and authority) or bourgeois, and hence materialistic and fallen away from Christ, or socialist, and socialism is to Dostoevsky identical with atheism, as it dreams of a utopia in which human beings would not be free to choose even at the expense of suffering. Dostoevsky—who himself had belonged to a revolutionary group and come into contact with Russian revolutionaries abroad—had an extraordinary insight into the mentality of the Russian underground. In *The Possessed* (1871–72) he gives a lurid satiric picture of these would-be saviors of Russia and humankind. But although he was afraid of the revolution, Dostoevsky himself hoped and prophesied that Russia would save Europe from the dangers of communism, as Russia alone was the uncorrupted Christian land. Put in terms of political propositions (as Dostoevsky himself preaches them in his journal, *The Diary of a Writer*, 1876–81), what he propounds is a conservative Russian nationalism with messianic hopes for Russian Christianity.

When translated into abstractions, Dostoevsky's psychology is as unimpressive as his political theory. It is merely a derivative of theories propounded by German writers about the unconscious, the role of dreams, the ambivalence of human feelings. What makes it electric in the novels is his ability to dramatize it in scenes of sudden revelation, in characters who in today's terminology would be called split personalities, in people twisted by isolation, lust, humiliation, and resentment. The dreams of Raskolnikov may be interpreted according to Freudian psychology; but to the reader without any knowledge of science they are comprehensible in their place in the novel and function as warnings and anticipations.

Dostoevsky was first of all an artist—a novelist who succeeded in using his ideas (many old and venerable, many new and fantastic) and psychological insights for the writing of stories of absorbing interest. As an artist, Dostoevsky treated the novel like a drama, constructing it in large, vivid scenes that end with a scandal or a crime or some act of violence, filling it with unforgettable "stagelike" figures torn by great passions and swayed by great ideas. Then he set this world in an environment of St. Petersburg slums or of towns, monasteries, and country houses, all so vividly realized that we forget how the setting, the figures, and the ideas blend together into one cosmos of the imagination only remotely and obliquely related to any reality of nineteenth-century Russia. We take part in a great drama of pride and humility, good and evil, in a huge allegory of humanity's search for God and itself. We understand and share in this world because it is not merely Russia in the nineteenth century, where people could hardly have talked and behaved as Dostoevsky's people do, but a myth of humanity, universalized as all art is.

Notes from Underground (1864) precedes the four great novels: *Crime and Punishment* (1866), *The Idiot* (1868), *The Possessed,* and *The Brothers Karamazov* (1880). The *Notes* can be viewed as a prologue, an important introduction to the cycle of the four great novels, an anticipation of the mature Dostoevsky's method and thought. Though it cannot compare in dramatic power and scope with these, the story has its own peculiar and original artistry. It is made up of two parts, at first glance seemingly independent: the monologue of the Underground man and the confession that he makes about himself, called *Apropos of Wet Snow.* The monologue, though it includes no action, is dramatic—a long address to an imaginary hostile reader, whom the Underground man ridicules, defies, jeers at, but also flatters. The confession is an autobiographical reminiscence of the Underground man. It describes events that occurred long before the delivery of the monologue, but it functions as a confirmation in concrete terms of the self-portrait drawn in the monologue and as an explanation of the isolation of the hero.

The narrative of the confession is a comic variation on the old theme of the rescue of a fallen woman from vice, a seesaw series of humiliations permitting Dostoevsky to display all the cruelty of his probing psychology. The hero, out of spite and craving for human company, forces himself into the company of former schoolfellows and is shamefully humiliated by them. He reasserts his ego (as he cannot revenge himself on them) in the company of a humble prostitute by impressing her with florid and moving speeches, which he knows to be insincere, about her horrible future. Ironically, he converts her, but when she comes to him and surprises him in a degrading scene with his servant, he humiliates her again. When, even then, she understands and forgives and thus shows her moral superiority, he crowns his spite by deliberately misunderstanding her and forcing money on her. She is the moral victor, and the Underground man returns to his hideout to jeer at humanity. It is hard not to feel that we are shown a tortured and twisted soul almost too despicable to elicit our compassion.

Still it would be a complete misunderstanding of Dostoevsky's story to take the philosophy expounded jeeringly in the long monologue of the first part merely as the irrational railings of a sick personality. The Underground man, though abject and spiteful, represents not only a specific Russian type of the time—the intellectual divorced from the soil and his nation—but also modern humanity, even Everyman, and strangely enough, even the author, who through the mouth of this despicable character, as through a mask, expresses his boldest and most intimate convictions. In spite of all the exaggerated pathos, wild paradox, and jeering irony used by the speaker, his self-criticism and his criticism of society and history must be taken seriously and interpreted patiently if we are to extract the meaning accepted by Dostoevsky.

The Underground man is also the hyperconscious man who examines himself as if in a mirror and sees himself with pitiless candor. His very self-consciousness cripples his will and poisons his feelings. He cannot escape from his ego; he knows that he has acted badly toward the woman, but at the same time he cannot help acting as he does. He knows that he is alone, that there is no bridge from him to humanity, that the world is hostile to him, and that he is humiliated by everyone he meets. But though he resents the humiliation, he cannot help courting it, provoking it, and even enjoying it in his perverse manner. He understands (and knows from his own experience) that something within us all enjoys evil and destruction.

His self-criticism widens, then, into a criticism of the assumptions of modern civilization, of nineteenth-century optimism about human nature and progress, of utilitarianism, and of all kinds of utopias. It is possible to identify specific allusions to a contemporary novel by a radical socialist and revolutionary, Chernyshevsky, titled *What Is to Be Done?* (1863), but we do not need to know the exact target of Dostoevsky's satire to recognize what he attacks: the view that human nature is good, that we generally seek our enlightened self-interest, that science propounds immutable truths, and that a paradise on Earth will be just around the corner once society is reformed along scientific lines. In a series of vivid symbols these assumptions are represented, parodied, exposed. Science says that "twice two makes four" but the Underground man laughs that "twice two makes five is sometimes a very charming thing too." Science means to him (and to Dostoevsky) the victory of the doctrine of fatality, of iron necessity, of determinism, and thus finally of death. Humanity would become an "organ stop," a "piano key," if deterministic science were valid.

Equally disastrous are the implications of the social philosophy of liberalism and of socialism (which Dostoevsky considers its necessary consequence). In this view, we need only follow our enlightened self-interest, need only be rational, and we will become noble and good and the Earth will be a place of prosperity and peace. But the Underground man knows that this conception of human nature is entirely false. What if humankind does not follow, and never will follow, its own enlightened self-interest, is consciously and purposely irrational, even bloodthirsty and evil? History seems to the Underground man to speak a clear language: "civilization has made mankind if not more bloodthirsty, at least more vilely, more loathsomely bloodthirsty." Humanity wills the irrational and evil because it does not want to become an organ stop, a piano key, because it wants to be left with the freedom to choose between good and evil. This freedom of choice, even at the expense of chaos and destruction, is what makes us human.

Actually, we love something other than our own well-being and happiness, love even suffering and pain, because we are human and not animals inhabiting some great organized rational "ant heap." The ant heap, the hen house, the block of tenements, and finally the Crystal Palace (then the newest wonder of architecture, a great hall of iron and glass erected for the Universal Exhibition in London) are the images used by the Underground man to represent his hated utopia. The heroine of *What Is to Be Done?* had dreamed of a building made of cast iron and glass and placed in the middle of a beautiful garden where there would be eternal spring and summer, eternal joy. Dostoevsky had recognized there the utopian dream of Charles Fourier, the French socialist whom he had admired in his youth and whose ideals he had come to hate with a fierce revulsion. But we must realize that the Underground man, and Dostoevsky, despise this "ant heap," this perfectly organized society of automatons, in the name of something higher, in the name of freedom. Dostoevsky does not believe that humanity can achieve freedom and happiness at the same time; happiness can be bought only at the expense of freedom, and all utopian schemes seem to him devices to lure us into the yoke of slavery. This freedom is, of course, not political freedom but freedom of choice, indeterminism, even caprice and willfulness, in the paradoxical formulation of the Underground man.

There are hints at a positive solution only in the one chapter (Part I, Chapter X) that was mutilated by the censor. A letter by Dostoevsky to his brother about the "swine of a censor who let through the passages where I jeered at everything and blasphemed ostensibly" refers to the fact that he "suppressed everything where I drew the conclusion that faith in Christ is needed." In Part I, Chapter XI, of the present text (and Dostoevsky never restored the suppressed passages) the Underground man says merely, "I am lying because I know myself that it is not underground that is better, but something different, quite different, for which I am thirsting, but which I cannot find!" This "something . . . quite different" all the other writings of Dostoevsky show to be the voluntary following of the Christian savior even at the expense of suffering and pain.

In a paradoxical form, through the mouth of one of his vilest characters, Dostoevsky reveals in the story his view of humanity and history—of the evil in human nature and of the blood and tragedy in history—and his criticism of the optimistic, utilitarian, utopian, progressive view of humanity that was spreading to Russia from the West during the nineteenth century and that found its most devoted adherents in the Russian revolutionaries. Preoccupied with criticism, Dostoevsky does not here suggest any positive remedy. But if we understand the *Notes,* we can understand how Raskolnikov, the murderer out of intellect in *Crime and Punishment,* can find salvation at last and how Dmitri, the guilty-guiltless parricide of *The Brothers Karamazov,* can sing his hymn to joy in the Siberian mines. We can even understand the legend of the Grand Inquisitor told by Ivan Karamazov, in which we meet the same criticism of a utopia (this time that of Catholicism) and the same exaltation of human freedom even at the price of suffering.

Monroe C. Beardsley, "Dostoevsky's Metaphor of the 'Underground,'" *Journal of the History of Ideas* 3 (June 1942), is a subtle interpretation of the central metaphor of the *Notes.* Joseph Frank, "Nihilism and *Notes from Underground,*" *Sewanee Review,* 69 (1961), interprets the *Notes* in the context of the history of the times. Robert L. Jackson, *The Underground Man in Russian Literature* (1981), traces the impact of the *Notes* on Russian literature. Konstantin Mochulsky, *Dostoevsky: Life and Work* (1967), is the best general work translated from Russian, the work of an emigré in Paris. René Wellek, ed., *Dostoevsky: A Collection of Critical Essays* (1962), contains an essay by the editor on the history of Dostoevsky criticism. Alba della Fazia Amoia, *Feodor Dostoevsky* (1993), is a general introduction to Dostoevsky's work, aimed at a student audience. Joseph Frank, *Dostoevsky* (1976–95), is an impressive, though still-unfinished, biographical study in four volumes. Frank's *Through the Russian Prism* (1990) includes review essays that examine various approaches to Dostoevsky. Louis Breger, *Dostoevsky: The Author as Psychoanalyst* (1989), takes a psychoanalytic approach in analyzing levels of meaning in Dostoevsky's work as a new sensibility that anticipates the modern novel; he includes a chapter on *Notes.* Malcolm V. Jones, *Dostoyevsky after Bakhtin: Readings in Dostoyevsky's Fantastic Realism* (1990), examines Dostoevsky's "higher realism" in various perspectives and includes a chapter on *Notes.* Nina Pelikan Straus, *Dostoevsky and the Woman Question: Rereadings at the End of a Century* (1994), examines the presence of women and Dostoevsky's construction of the feminine.

PRONOUNCING GLOSSARY

The following list uses common English syllables and stress accents to provide rough equivalents of selected words whose pronunciation may be unfamiliar to the general reader.

Anton Antonych: *ahn-tawn' ahn-taw'-nich*

Apollon: *ah-pah-lawn'*

Ferfichkin: *fehr-feech'-keen*

Fyodor Dostoevsky: *fyo'dor dos-toy-eff'-skee*

Karamazov: *kuh-rah-mah'-zuf*

Kolya: *kawl'-yuh*

Podkharzhevsky: *put-khar-zhef'-skee*

Simonov: *see'-muh-nuf*

Trudolyubov: *troo-dah-lyoo'-buf*

Zverkov: *zvyehr-kof'*

Notes from Underground[1]

I

Underground[2]

I

I am a sick man. . . . [3] I am a spiteful man. I am a most unpleasant man. I think my liver is diseased. Then again, I don't know a thing about my illness; I'm not even sure what hurts. I'm not being treated and never have been, though I respect both medicine and doctors. Besides, I'm extremely superstitious—well at least enough to respect medicine. (I'm sufficiently educated not to be superstitious; but I am, anyway.) No, gentlemen, it's out of spite that I don't wish to be treated. Now then, that's something you probably won't understand. Well, I do. Of course, I won't really be able to explain to you precisely who will be hurt by my spite in this case; I know perfectly well that I can't possibly "get even" with doctors by refusing their treatment; I know better than anyone that all this is going to hurt me alone, and no one else. Even so, if I refuse to be treated, it's out of spite. My liver hurts? Good, let it hurt even more!

I've been living this way for some time—about twenty years. I'm forty now. I used to be in the civil service. But no more. I was a nasty official. I was rude and took pleasure in it. After all, since I didn't accept bribes, at least I had to reward myself in some way. (That's a poor joke, but I won't cross it out. I wrote it thinking that it would be very witty; but now, having realized that I merely wanted to show off disgracefully, I'll make a point of not crossing it out!) When petitioners used to approach my desk for information, I'd gnash my teeth and feel unending pleasure if I succeeded in causing someone distress. I almost always succeeded. For the most part they were all timid people: naturally, since they were petitioners. But among the dandies there was a certain officer whom I particularly couldn't bear. He simply refused to be humble, and he clanged his saber in a loathsome manner. I waged war with him over that saber for about a year and a half. At last I prevailed. He stopped clanging. All this, however, happened a long time ago, during my youth. But do you know, gentlemen, what the main component of my spite really was? Why, the whole point, the most disgusting thing, was the fact that I was shamefully aware at every moment, even at the moment of my greatest bitterness, that not only was I not a spiteful man, I was not even an embittered one, and that I was merely scaring sparrows to no effect and consoling myself by doing so. I was foaming at the mouth—but just bring me some trinket to play with, just serve me a nice cup of tea with sugar, and I'd probably have calmed down. My heart might even have been touched,

1. Translated by Michael Katz.   2. Both the author of these notes and the *Notes* themselves are fictitious, of course. Nevertheless, people like the author of these notes not only may, but actually must exist in our society, considering the general circumstances under which our society was formed. I wanted to bring before the public with more prominence than usual one of the characters of the recent past. He's a representative of the current generation. In the excerpt entitled "Underground" this person introduces himself and his views, and, as it were, wants to explain the reasons why he appeared and why he had to appear in our midst. The following excerpt [*Apropos of Wet Snow*] contains the actual "notes" of this person about several events in his life [Author's note].   3. The ellipses are the author's and do not indicate omissions from this text.

although I'd probably have gnashed my teeth out of shame and then suffered from insomnia for several months afterward. That's just my usual way.

I was lying about myself just now when I said that I was a nasty official. I lied out of spite. I was merely having some fun at the expense of both the petitioners and that officer, but I could never really become spiteful. At all times I was aware of a great many elements in me that were just the opposite of that. I felt how they swarmed inside me, these contradictory elements. I knew that they had been swarming inside me my whole life and were begging to be let out; but I wouldn't let them out, I wouldn't, I deliberately wouldn't let them out. They tormented me to the point of shame; they drove me to convulsions and—and finally I got fed up with them, oh how fed up! Perhaps it seems to you, gentlemen, that I'm repenting about something, that I'm asking your forgiveness for something? I'm sure that's how it seems to you. . . . But really, I can assure you, I don't care if that's how it seems. . . .

Not only couldn't I become spiteful, I couldn't become anything at all: neither spiteful nor good, neither a scoundrel nor an honest man, neither a hero nor an insect. Now I live out my days in my corner, taunting myself with the spiteful and entirely useless consolation that an intelligent man cannot seriously become anything and that only a fool can become something. Yes, sir, an intelligent man in the nineteenth century must be, is morally obliged to be, principally a characterless creature; a man possessing character, a man of action, is fundamentally a limited creature. That's my conviction at the age of forty. I'm forty now; and, after all, forty is an entire lifetime; why it's extreme old age. It's rude to live past forty, it's indecent, immoral! Who lives more than forty years? Answer sincerely, honestly. I'll tell you who: only fools and rascals. I'll tell those old men that right to their faces, all those venerable old men, all those silver-haired and sweet-smelling old men! I'll say it to the whole world right to its face! I have a right to say it because I myself will live to sixty. I'll make it to seventy! Even to eighty! . . . Wait! Let me catch my breath. . . .

You probably think, gentlemen, that I want to amuse you. You're wrong about that, too. I'm not at all the cheerful fellow I seem to be, or that I may seem to be; however, if you're irritated by all this talk (and I can already sense that you are irritated), and if you decide to ask me just who I really am, then I'll tell you: I'm a collegiate assessor. I worked in order to have something to eat (but only for that reason); and last year, when a distant relative of mine left me six thousand rubles in his will, I retired immediately and settled down in this corner. I used to live in this corner before, but now I've settled down in it. My room is nasty, squalid, on the outskirts of town. My servant is an old peasant woman, spiteful out of stupidity; besides, she has a foul smell. I'm told that the Petersburg climate is becoming bad for my health, and that it's very expensive to live in Petersburg with my meager resources. I know all that; I know it better than all those wise and experienced advisers and admonishers. But I shall remain in Petersburg; I shall not leave Petersburg! I shall not leave here because . . . Oh, what difference does it really make whether I leave Petersburg or not?

Now, then, what can a decent man talk about with the greatest pleasure? Answer: about himself.

Well, then, I too will talk about myself.

II

Now I would like to tell you, gentlemen, whether or not you want to hear it, why it is that I couldn't even become an insect. I'll tell you solemnly that I wished to become an insect many times. But not even that wish was granted. I swear to you, gentlemen, that being overly conscious is a disease, a genuine, full-fledged disease. Ordinary human consciousness would be more than sufficient for everyday human needs—that is, even half or a quarter of the amount of consciousness that's available to a cultured man in our unfortunate nineteenth century, especially to one who has the particular misfortune of living in St. Petersburg, the most abstract and premeditated city in the whole world.[4] (Cities can be either premeditated or unpremeditated.) It would have been entirely sufficient, for example, to have the consciousness with which all so-called spontaneous people and men of action are endowed. I'll bet that you think I'm writing all this to show off, to make fun of these men of action, that I'm clanging my saber just like that officer did to show off in bad taste. But, gentlemen, who could possibly be proud of his illnesses and want to show them off?

But what am I saying? Everyone does that; people do take pride in their illnesses, and I, perhaps, more than anyone else. Let's not argue; my objection is absurd. Nevertheless, I remain firmly convinced that not only is being overly conscious a disease, but so is being conscious at all. I insist on it. But let's leave that alone for a moment. Tell me this: why was it, as if on purpose, at the very moment, indeed, at the precise moment that I was most capable of becoming conscious of the subtleties of everything that was "beautiful and sublime,"[5] as we used to say at one time, that I didn't become conscious, and instead did such unseemly things, things that . . . well, in short, probably everyone does, but it seemed as if they occurred to me deliberately at the precise moment when I was most conscious that they shouldn't be done at all? The more conscious I was of what was good, of everything "beautiful and sublime," the more deeply I sank into the morass and the more capable I was of becoming entirely bogged down in it. But the main thing is that all this didn't seem to be occurring accidentally; rather, it was as if it all had to be so. It was as if this were my most normal condition, not an illness or an affliction at all, so that finally I even lost the desire to struggle against it. It ended when I almost came to believe (perhaps I really did believe) that this might really have been my normal condition. But at first, in the beginning, what agonies I suffered during that struggle! I didn't believe that others were experiencing the same thing; therefore, I kept it a secret about myself all my life. I was ashamed (perhaps I still am even now); I reached the point where I felt some secret, abnormal, despicable little pleasure in returning home to my little corner on some disgusting Petersburg night, acutely aware that once again I'd committed some revolting act that day, that what had been done could not be undone, and I used to gnaw and gnaw at myself inwardly, secretly, nagging away, consuming myself until finally the bitterness turned

4. Petersburg was conceived as an imposing city; plans called for regular streets, broad avenues, and spacious squares.   5. This phrase originated in Edmund Burke's (1729–1797) *Philosophical Inquiry into the Origin of Our Ideas of the Sublime and Beautiful* (1756) and was repeated in Immanuel Kant's (1724–1804) *Observations on the Feeling of the Beautiful and the Sublime* (1756). It became a cliché in the writings of Russian critics during the 1830s.

into some kind of shameful, accursed sweetness and at last into genuine, earnest pleasure! Yes, into pleasure, real pleasure! I absolutely mean that. . . . That's why I first began to speak out, because I want to know for certain whether other people share this same pleasure. Let me explain: the pleasure resulted precisely from the overly acute consciousness of one's own humiliation; from the feeling that one had reached the limit; that it was disgusting, but couldn't be otherwise; you had no other choice—you could never become a different person; and that even if there were still time and faith enough for you to change into something else, most likely you wouldn't even want to change, and if you did, you wouldn't have done anything, perhaps because there really was nothing for you to change into. But the main thing and the final point is that all of this was taking place according to normal and fundamental laws of overly acute consciousness and of the inertia which results directly from these laws; consequently, not only couldn't one change, one simply couldn't do anything at all. Hence it follows, for example, as a result of this overly acute consciousness, that one is absolutely right in being a scoundrel, as if this were some consolation to the scoundrel. But enough of this. . . . Oh, my, I've gone on rather a long time, but have I really explained anything? How can I explain this pleasure? But I will explain it! I shall see it through to the end! That's why I've taken up my pen. . . .

For example, I'm terribly proud. I'm as mistrustful and as sensitive as a hunchback or a dwarf; but, in truth, I've experienced some moments when, if someone had slapped my face, I might even have been grateful for it. I'm being serious. I probably would have been able to derive a peculiar sort of pleasure from it—the pleasure of despair, naturally, but the most intense pleasures occur in despair, especially when you're very acutely aware of the hopelessness of your own predicament. As for a slap in the face—why, here the consciousness of being beaten to a pulp would overwhelm you. The main thing is, no matter how I try, it still turns out that I'm always the first to be blamed for everything and, what's even worse, I'm always the innocent victim, so to speak, according to the laws of nature. Therefore, in the first place, I'm guilty inasmuch as I'm smarter than everyone around me. (I've always considered myself smarter than everyone around me, and sometimes, believe me, I've been ashamed of it. At the least, all my life I've looked away and never could look people straight in the eye.) Finally, I'm to blame because even if there were any magnanimity in me, it would only have caused more suffering as a result of my being aware of its utter uselessness. After all, I probably wouldn't have been able to make use of that magnanimity: neither to forgive, as the offender, perhaps, had slapped me in accordance with the laws of nature, and there's no way to forgive the laws of nature; nor to forget, because even if there were any laws of nature, it's offensive nonetheless. Finally, even if I wanted to be entirely unmagnanimous, and had wanted to take revenge on the offender, I couldn't be revenged on anyone for anything because, most likely, I would never have decided to do anything, even if I could have. Why not? I'd like to say a few words about that separately.

III

Let's consider people who know how to take revenge and how to stand up for themselves in general. How, for example, do they do it? Let's suppose that they're seized by an impulse to take revenge—then for a while nothing else remains in their entire being except for that impulse. Such an individual simply rushes toward his goal like an enraged bull with lowered horns; only a wall can stop him. (By the way, when actually faced with a wall such individuals, that is, spontaneous people and men of action, genuinely give up. For them a wall doesn't constitute the evasion that it does for those of us who think and consequently do nothing; it's not an excuse to turn aside from the path, a pretext in which a person like me usually doesn't believe, but one for which he's always extremely grateful. No, they give up in all sincerity. For them the wall possesses some kind of soothing, morally decisive and definitive meaning, perhaps even something mystical . . . But more about the wall later.) Well, then, I consider such a spontaneous individual to be a genuine, normal person, just as tender mother nature wished to see him when she lovingly gave birth to him on earth. I'm green with envy at such a man. He's stupid, I won't argue with you about that; but perhaps a normal man is supposed to be stupid—how do we know? Perhaps it's even very beautiful. And I'm all the more convinced of the suspicion, so to speak, that if, for example, one were to take the antithesis of a normal man—that is, a man of overly acute consciousness, who emerged, of course, not from the bosom of nature, but from a laboratory test tube (this is almost mysticism, gentlemen, but I suspect that it's the case), then this test tube man some-times gives up so completely in the face of his antithesis that he himself, with his overly acute consciousness, honestly considers himself not as a per-son, but a mouse. It may be an acutely conscious mouse, but a mouse none-theless, while the other one is a person and consequently, . . . and so on and so forth. But the main thing is that he, he himself, considers himself to be a mouse; nobody asks him to do so, and that's the important point. Now let's take a look at this mouse in action. Let's assume, for instance, that it feels offended (it almost always feels offended), and that it also wishes to be revenged. It may even contain more accumulated malice than *l'homme de la nature et de la vérité*.[6] The mean, nasty, little desire to pay the offender back with evil may indeed rankle in it even more despicably than in *l'homme de la nature et de la vérité*, because *l'homme de la nature et de la vérité*, with his innate stupidity, considers his revenge nothing more than justice, pure and simple; but the mouse, as a result of its overly acute consciousness, rejects the idea of justice. Finally, we come to the act itself, to the very act of revenge. In addition to its original nastiness, the mouse has already managed to pile up all sorts of other nastiness around itself in the form of hesitations and doubts; so many unresolved questions have emerged from that one single question, that some kind of fatal blow is concocted unwillingly, some kind of stinking mess consisting of doubts, anxieties and, finally, spittle showered upon it by the spontaneous men of action who stand by solemnly as judges and arbiters, roaring with laughter until their sides split. Of course, the only thing left to do is dismiss it with a wave of its paw and a smile of assumed contempt which it doesn't even believe in, and creep ignominiously back into its mousehole. There, in its disgusting, stinking underground, our offended, crushed, and ridiculed mouse immediately plunges into cold, malicious, and,

6. The man of nature and truth (French). The basic idea is borrowed from Jean-Jacques Rousseau's *Con-fessions* (1782–89), namely, that human beings in a state of nature are honest and direct and that they are corrupted only by civilization.

above all, everlasting spitefulness. For forty years on end it will recall its insult down to the last, most shameful detail; and each time it will add more shameful details of its own, spitefully teasing and irritating itself with its own fantasy. It will become ashamed of that fantasy, but it will still remember it, rehearse it again and again, fabricating all sorts of incredible stories about itself under the pretext that they too could have happened; it won't forgive a thing. Perhaps it will even begin to take revenge, but only in little bits and pieces, in trivial ways, from behind the stove, incognito, not believing in its right to be revenged, nor in the success of its own revenge, and knowing in advance that from all its attempts to take revenge, it will suffer a hundred times more than the object of its vengeance, who might not even feel a thing. On its deathbed it will recall everything all over again, with interest compounded over all those years and. . . . But it's precisely in that cold, abominable state of half-despair and half-belief, in that conscious burial of itself alive in the underground for forty years because of its pain, in that powerfully created, yet partly dubious hopelessness of its own predicament, in all that venom of unfulfilled desire turned inward, in all that fever of vacillation, of resolutions adopted once and for all and followed a moment later by repentance—herein precisely lies the essence of that strange enjoyment I was talking about earlier. It's so subtle, sometimes so difficult to analyze, that even slightly limited people, or those who simply have strong nerves, won't understand anything about it. "Perhaps," you'll add with a smirk, "even those who've never received a slap in the face won't understand," and by so doing you'll be hinting to me ever so politely that perhaps during my life I too have received such a slap in the face and that therefore I'm speaking as an expert. I'll bet that's what you're thinking. Well, rest assured, gentlemen, I've never received such a slap, although it's really all the same to me what you think about it. Perhaps I may even regret the fact that I've given so few slaps during my lifetime. But that's enough, not another word about this subject which you find so extremely interesting.

I'll proceed calmly about people with strong nerves who don't understand certain refinements of pleasure. For example, although under particular circumstances these gentlemen may bellow like bulls as loudly as possible, and although, let's suppose, this behavior bestows on them the greatest honor, yet, as I've already said, when confronted with impossibility, they submit immediately. Impossibility—does that mean a stone wall? What kind of stone wall? Why, of course, the laws of nature, the conclusions of natural science and mathematics. As soon as they prove to you, for example, that it's from a monkey you're descended,[7] there's no reason to make faces; just accept it as it is. As soon as they prove to you that in truth one drop of your own fat is dearer to you than the lives of one hundred thousand of your fellow creatures and that this will finally put an end to all the so-called virtues, obligations, and other such similar ravings and prejudices, just accept that too; there's nothing more to do, since two times two is a fact of mathematics. Just you try to object.

"For goodness sake," they'll shout at you, "it's impossible to protest: it's two times two makes four! Nature doesn't ask for your opinion; it doesn't

<hr/>

7. A reference to the theory of evolution by natural selection developed by Charles Darwin (1809–1882). A book on the subject was translated into Russian in 1864.

care about your desires or whether you like or dislike its laws. You're obliged to accept it as it is, and consequently, all its conclusions. A wall, you see, is a wall . . . etc. etc." Good Lord, what do I care about the laws of nature and arithmetic when for some reason I dislike all these laws and I dislike the fact that two times two makes four? Of course, I won't break through that wall with my head if I really don't have the strength to do so, nor will I reconcile myself to it just because I'm faced with such a stone wall and lack the strength.

As though such a stone wall actually offered some consolation and contained some real word of conciliation, for the sole reason that it means two times two makes four. Oh, absurdity of absurdities! How much better it is to understand it all, to be aware of everything, all the impossibilities and stone walls; not to be reconciled with any of those impossibilities or stone walls if it so disgusts you; to reach, by using the most inevitable logical combinations, the most revolting conclusions on the eternal theme that you are somehow or other to blame even for that stone wall, even though it's absolutely clear once again that you're in no way to blame, and, as a result of all this, while silently and impotently gnashing your teeth, you sink voluptuously into inertia, musing on the fact that, as it turns out, there's no one to be angry with; that an object cannot be found, and perhaps never will be; that there's been a substitution, some sleight of hand, a bit of cheating, and that it's all a mess—you can't tell who's who or what's what; but in spite of all these uncertainties and sleights-of-hand, it hurts you just the same, and the more you don't know, the more it hurts!

IV

"Ha, ha, ha! Why, you'll be finding enjoyment in a toothache next!" you cry out with a laugh.

"Well, what of it? There is some enjoyment even in a toothache," I reply. I've had a toothache for a whole month; I know what's what. In this instance, of course, people don't rage in silence; they moan. But these moans are insincere; they're malicious, and malice is the whole point. These moans express the sufferer's enjoyment; if he didn't enjoy it, he would never have begun to moan. This is a good example, gentlemen, and I'll develop it. In the first place, these moans express all the aimlessness of the pain which consciousness finds so humiliating, the whole system of natural laws about which you really don't give a damn, but as a result of which you're suffering nonetheless, while nature isn't. They express the consciousness that while there's no real enemy to be identified, the pain exists nonetheless; the awareness that, in spite of all possible Wagenheims,[8] you're still a complete slave to your teeth; that if someone so wishes, your teeth will stop aching, but that if he doesn't so wish, they'll go on aching for three more months; and finally, that if you still disagree and protest, all there's left to do for consolation is flagellate yourself or beat your fist against the wall as hard as you can, and absolutely nothing else. Well, then, it's these bloody insults, these jeers coming from nowhere, that finally generate enjoyment that can sometimes reach the highest degree of voluptuousness. I beseech you, gentlemen, to listen to

8. The *General Address Book of St. Petersburg* listed eight dentists named Wagenheim; contemporary readers would have recognized the name from signs throughout the city.

the moans of an educated man of the nineteenth century who's suffering from a toothache, especially on the second or third day of his distress, when he begins to moan in a very different way than he did on the first day, that is, not simply because his tooth aches; not the way some coarse peasant moans, but as a man affected by progress and European civilization, a man "who's renounced both the soil and the common people," as they say nowadays. His moans become somehow nasty, despicably spiteful, and they go on for days and nights. Yet he himself knows that his moans do him no good; he knows better than anyone else that he's merely irritating himself and others in vain; he knows that the audience for whom he's trying so hard, and his whole family, have now begun to listen to him with loathing; they don't believe him for a second, and they realize full well that he could moan in a different, much simpler way, without all the flourishes and affectation, and that he's only indulging himself out of spite and malice. Well, it's precisely in this awareness and shame that the voluptuousness resides. "It seems I'm disturbing you, tearing at your heart, preventing anyone in the house from getting any sleep. Well, then, you won't sleep; you too must be aware at all times that I have a toothache. I'm no longer the hero I wanted to pass for earlier, but simply a nasty little man, a rogue. So be it! I'm delighted that you've seen through me. Does it make you feel bad to hear my wretched little moans? Well, then, feel bad. Now let me add an even nastier flourish. . . ." You still don't understand, gentlemen? No, it's clear that one has to develop further and become even more conscious in order to understand all the nuances of this voluptuousness! Are you laughing? I'm delighted. Of course my jokes are in bad taste, gentlemen; they're uneven, contradictory, and lacking in self-assurance. But that's because I have no respect for myself. Can a man possessing consciousness ever really respect himself?

V

Well, and is it possible, is it really possible for a man to respect himself if he even presumes to find enjoyment in the feeling of his own humiliation? I'm not saying this out of any feigned repentance. In general I could never bear to say: "I'm sorry, Daddy, and I won't do it again," not because I was incapable of saying it, but, on the contrary, perhaps precisely because I was all too capable, and how! As if on purpose it would happen that I'd get myself into some sort of mess for which I was not to blame in any way whatsoever. That was the most repulsive part of it. What's more, I'd feel touched deep in my soul; I'd repent and shed tears, deceiving even myself of course, though not feigning in the least. It seemed that my heart was somehow playing dirty tricks on me. . . . Here one couldn't even blame the laws of nature, although it was these very laws that continually hurt me during my entire life. It's disgusting to recall all this, and it was disgusting even then. Of course, a moment or so later I would realize in anger that it was all lies, lies, revolting, made-up lies, that is, all that repentance, all that tenderness, all those vows to mend my ways. But you'll ask why I mauled and tortured myself in that way? The answer is because it was so very boring to sit idly by with my arms folded; so I'd get into trouble. That's the way it was. Observe yourselves better, gentlemen; then you'll understand that it's true. I used to think up adventures for myself, inventing a life so that at least I could live. How many times did it happen, well, let's say, for example, that I took offense, deliberately, for no reason at all? All the while I knew there was no reason for it; I put on airs nonetheless, and would take it so far that finally I really did feel offended. I've been drawn into such silly tricks all my life, so that finally I lost control over myself. Another time, even twice, I tried hard to fall in love. I even suffered, gentlemen, I can assure you. In the depths of my soul I really didn't believe that I was suffering; there was a stir of mockery, but suffer I did, and in a genuine, normal way at that; I was jealous, I was beside myself with anger. . . . And all as a result of boredom, gentlemen, sheer boredom; I was overcome by inertia. You see, the direct, legitimate, immediate result of consciousness is inertia, that is, the conscious sitting idly by with one's arms folded. I've referred to this before. I repeat, I repeat emphatically: all spontaneous men and men of action are so active precisely because they're stupid and limited. How can one explain this? Here's how: as a result of their limitations they mistake immediate and secondary causes for primary ones, and thus they're convinced more quickly and easily than other people that they've located an indisputable basis for action, and this puts them at ease; that's the main point. For, in order to begin to act, one must first be absolutely at ease, with no lingering doubts whatsoever. Well, how can I, for example, ever feel at ease? Where are the primary causes I can rely upon, where's the foundation? Where shall I find it? I exercise myself in thinking, and consequently, with me every primary cause drags in another, an even more primary one, and so on to infinity. This is precisely the essence of all consciousness and thought. And here again, it must be the laws of nature. What's the final result? Why, the very same thing. Remember: I was talking about revenge before. (You probably didn't follow.) I said: a man takes revenge because he finds justice in it. That means, he's found a primary cause, a foundation: namely, justice. Therefore, he's completely at ease, and, as a result, he takes revenge peacefully and successfully, convinced that he's performing an honest and just deed. But I don't see any justice here at all, nor do I find any virtue in it whatever; consequently, if I begin to take revenge, it's only out of spite. Of course, spite could overcome everything, all my doubts, and therefore could successfully serve instead of a primary cause precisely because it's not a cause at all. But what do I do if I don't even feel spite (that's where I began before)? After all, as a result of those damned laws of consciousness, my spite is subject to chemical disintegration. You look—and the object vanishes, the arguments evaporate, a guilty party can't be identified, the offense ceases to be one and becomes a matter of fate, something like a toothache for which no one's to blame, and, as a consequence, there remains only the same recourse: that is, to bash the wall even harder. So you throw up your hands because you haven't found a primary cause. Just try to let yourself be carried away blindly by your feelings, without reflection, without a primary cause, suppressing consciousness even for a moment; hate or love, anything, just in order not to sit idly by with your arms folded. The day after tomorrow at the very latest, you'll begin to despise yourself for having deceived yourself knowingly. The result: a soap bubble and inertia. Oh, gentlemen, perhaps I consider myself to be an intelligent man simply because for my whole life I haven't been able to begin or finish anything. All right, suppose I am a babbler, a harmless, annoying babbler, like the rest of us. But then what is to be done[9] if the direct and single vocation of every intelligent man consists in babbling, that is, in deliberately talking in endless circles?

VI

Oh, if only I did nothing simply as a result of laziness. Lord, how I'd respect myself then. I'd respect myself precisely because at least I'd be capable of being lazy; at least I'd possess one more or less positive trait of which I could be certain. Question: who am I? Answer: a sluggard. Why, it would have been very pleasant to hear that said about oneself. It would mean that I'd been positively identified; it would mean that there was something to be said about me. "A sluggard!" Why, that's a calling and a vocation, a whole career! Don't joke, it's true. Then, by rights I'd be a member of the very best club and would occupy myself exclusively by being able to respect myself continually. I knew a gentleman who prided himself all his life on being a connoisseur of Lafite.[1] He considered it his positive virtue and never doubted himself. He died not merely with a clean conscience, but with a triumphant one, and he was absolutely correct. I should have chosen a career for myself too: I would have been a sluggard and a glutton, not an ordinary one, but one who, for example, sympathized with everything beautiful and sublime. How do you like that? I've dreamt about it for a long time. The "beautiful and sublime" have been a real pain in the neck during my forty years, but then it's been *my* forty years, whereas then—oh, then it would have been otherwise! I would've found myself a suitable activity at once—namely, drinking to everything beautiful and sublime. I would have seized upon every opportunity first to shed a tear into my glass and then drink to everything beautiful and sublime. Then I would have turned everything into the beautiful and sublime; I would have sought out the beautiful and sublime in the nastiest, most indisputable trash. I would have become as tearful as a wet sponge. An artist, for example, has painted a portrait of Ge.[2] At once I drink to the artist who painted that portrait of Ge because I love everything beautiful and sublime. An author has written the words, "Just as you please,"[3] at once I drink to "Just as you please," because I love everything "beautiful and sublime." I'd demand respect for myself in doing this, I'd persecute anyone who didn't pay me any respect. I'd live peacefully and die triumphantly—why, it's charming, perfectly charming! And what a belly I'd have grown by then, what a triple chin I'd have acquired, what a red nose I'd have developed—so that just looking at me any passerby would have said, "Now that's a real plus! That's something really positive!" Say what you like, gentlemen, it's extremely pleasant to hear such comments in our negative age.

9. An oblique reference to the controversial novel by Nikolai Chernyshevsky (1828–1889) titled *What Is to Be Done?* (1863). *Notes from Underground* is in part Dostoevsky's polemical response to it.   1. A variety of red wine from Médoc in France.   2. N. N. Ge (1831–1894), Russian artist, whose painting *The Last Supper* was displayed in Petersburg during the spring of 1863 and provoked considerable controversy.   3. An attack on the writer M. E. Saltykov-Shchedrin, who published a sympathetic review of Ge's painting titled *Just As You Please*.

VII

But these are all golden dreams. Oh, tell me who was first to announce, first to proclaim that man does nasty things simply because he doesn't know his own true interest; and that if he were to be enlightened, if his eyes were to be opened to his true, normal interests, he would stop doing nasty things at once and would immediately become good and noble, because, being so enlightened and understanding his real advantage, he would realize that his own advantage really did lie in the good; and that it's well known that there's not a single man capable of acting knowingly against his own interest; consequently, he would, so to speak, begin to do good out of necessity. Oh, the child! Oh, the pure, innocent babe! Well, in the first place, when was it during all these millennia, that man has ever acted only in his own self interest? What does one do with the millions of facts bearing witness to the one fact that people knowingly, that is, possessing full knowledge of their own true interests, have relegated them to the background and have rushed down a different path, that of risk and chance, compelled by no one and nothing, but merely as if they didn't want to follow the beaten track, and so they stubbornly, willfully forged another way, a difficult and absurd one, searching for it almost in the darkness? Why, then, this means that stubbornness and willfulness were really more pleasing to them than any kind of advantage. . . . Advantage! What is advantage? Will you take it upon yourself to define with absolute precision what constitutes man's advantage? And what if it turns out that man's advantage sometimes not only may, but even must in certain circumstances, consist precisely in his desiring something harmful to himself instead of something advantageous? And if this is so, if this can ever occur, then the whole theory falls to pieces. What do you think, can such a thing happen? You're laughing; laugh, gentlemen, but answer me: have man's advantages ever been calculated with absolute certainty? Aren't there some which don't fit, can't be made to fit into any classification? Why, as far as I know, you gentlemen have derived your list of human advantages from averages of statistical data and from scientific-economic formulas. But your advantages are prosperity, wealth, freedom, peace, and so on and so forth; so that a man who, for example, expressly and knowingly acts in opposition to this whole list, would be, in your opinion, and in mine, too, of course, either an obscurantist or a complete madman, wouldn't he? But now here's what's astonishing: why is it that when all these statisticians, sages, and lovers of humanity enumerate man's advantages, they invariably leave one out? They don't even take it into consideration in the form in which it should be considered, although the entire calculation depends upon it. There would be no great harm in considering it, this advantage, and adding it to the list. But the whole point is that this particular advantage doesn't fit into any classification and can't be found on any list. I have a friend, for instance. . . . But gentlemen! Why, he's your friend, too! In fact, he's everyone's friend! When he's preparing to do something, this gentleman straight away explains to you eloquently and clearly just how he must act according to the laws of nature and truth. And that's not all: with excitement and passion he'll tell you all about genuine, normal human interests; with scorn he'll reproach the shortsighted fools who understand neither their own advantage nor the real meaning of virtue; and then—exactly a quarter of an hour later, without any sudden outside cause, but precisely because of something internal that's stronger than all his interests—he does a complete about-face; that is, he does something which clearly contradicts what he's been saying: it goes against the laws of reason and his own advantage, in a word, against everything. . . . I warn you that my friend is a collective personage; therefore it's rather difficult to blame only him. That's just it, gentlemen; in fact, isn't there something dearer to every man than his own best advantage, or (so as not to violate the rules of logic) isn't there one more advantageous advantage (exactly the one omitted, the one we mentioned before), which is more important and more advantageous than all others and, on behalf of which, a man will, if necessary, go against all laws, that is, against reason, honor, peace, and prosperity—in a word, against all those splendid and useful things, merely in order to attain this fundamental, most advantageous advantage which is dearer to him than everything else?

"Well, it's advantage all the same," you say, interrupting me. Be so kind as to allow me to explain further; besides, the point is not my pun, but the fact that this advantage is remarkable precisely because it destroys all our classifications and constantly demolishes all systems devised by lovers of humanity for the happiness of mankind. In a word, it interferes with everything. But, before I name this advantage, I want to compromise myself personally; therefore I boldly declare that all these splendid systems, all these theories to explain to mankind its real, normal interests so that, by necessarily striving to achieve them, it would immediately become good and noble—are, for the time being, in my opinion, nothing more than logical exercises! Yes, sir, logical exercises! Why, even to maintain a theory of mankind's regeneration through a system of its own advantages, why, in my opinion, that's almost the same as . . . well, claiming, for instance, following Buckle,[4] that man has become kinder as a result of civilization; consequently, he's becoming less bloodthirsty and less inclined to war. Why, logically it all even seems to follow. But man is so partial to systems and abstract conclusions that he's ready to distort the truth intentionally, ready to deny everything that he himself has ever seen and heard, merely in order to justify his own logic. That's why I take this example, because it's such a glaring one. Just look around: rivers of blood are being spilt, and in the most cheerful way, as if it were champagne. Take this entire nineteenth century of ours during which even Buckle lived. Take Napoleon—both the great and the present one.[5] Take North America—that eternal union.[6] Take, finally, that ridiculous Schleswig-Holstein[7]. . . . What is it that civilization makes kinder in us? Civilization merely promotes a wider variety of sensations in man and . . . absolutely nothing else. And through the development of this variety man may even reach the point where he takes pleasure in spilling blood. Why, that's even happened to him already. Haven't you noticed that the most refined bloodshedders are almost always the most civilized gentlemen to whom all these Attila the Huns and Stenka Razins[8] are scarcely fit to hold a

---

4. In his *History of Civilization in England* (1857–61), Henry Thomas Buckle (1821–1862) argued that the development of civilization necessarily leads to the cessation of war. Russia had recently been involved in fierce fighting in the Crimea (1853–56).   5. The French emperors Napoleon I (1769–1821) and his nephew Napoleon III (1808–1873), both of whom engaged in numerous wars, though on vastly different scales.   6. The United States was in the middle of its Civil War (1861–65).   7. The German duchies of Schleswig and Holstein, held by Denmark since 1773, were reunited with Prussia after a brief war in 1864.   8. Cossack leader (d. 1671) who organized a peasant rebellion in Russia. Attila (406?–453 A.D.), king of the Huns, who conducted devastating wars against the Roman emperors.

candle; and if they're not as conspicuous as Attila and Stenka Razin, it's precisely because they're too common and have become too familiar to us. At least if man hasn't become more bloodthirsty as a result of civilization, surely he's become bloodthirsty in a nastier, more repulsive way than before. Previously man saw justice in bloodshed and exterminated whomever he wished with a clear conscience; whereas now, though we consider bloodshed to be abominable, we nevertheless engage in this abomination even more than before. Which is worse? Decide for yourselves. They say that Cleopatra (forgive an example from Roman history) loved to stick gold pins into the breasts of her slave girls and take pleasure in their screams and writhing. You'll say that this took place, relatively speaking, in barbaric times; that these are barbaric times too, because (also comparatively speaking), gold pins are used even now; that even now, although man has learned on occasion to see more clearly than in barbaric times, *he's still far from having learned* how to act in accordance with the dictates of reason and science. Nevertheless, you're still absolutely convinced that he will learn how to do so, as soon as he gets rid of some bad, old habits and as soon as common sense and science have completely re-educated human nature and have turned it in the proper direction. You're convinced that then man will voluntarily stop committing blunders, and that he will, so to speak, never willingly set his own will in opposition to his own normal interests. More than that: then, you say, science itself will teach man (though, in my opinion, that's already a luxury) that in fact he possesses neither a will nor any whim of his own, that he never did, and that he himself is nothing more than a kind of piano key or an organ stop;[9] that, moreover, there still exist laws of nature, so that everything he's done has been not in accordance with his own desire, but in and of itself, according to the laws of nature. Consequently, we need only discover these laws of nature, and man will no longer have to answer for his own actions and will find it extremely easy to live. All human actions, it goes without saying, will then be tabulated according to these laws, mathematically, like tables of logarithms up to 108,000, and will be entered on a schedule; or even better, certain edifying works will be published, like our contemporary encyclopedic dictionaries, in which everything will be accurately calculated and specified so that there'll be no more actions or adventures left on earth.

At that time, it's still you speaking, new economic relations will be established, all ready-made, also calculated with mathematical precision, so that all possible questions will disappear in a single instant, simply because all possible answers will have been provided. Then the crystal palace[1] will be built. And then . . . Well, in a word, those will be our halcyon days. Of course, there's no way to guarantee (now this is me talking) that it won't be, for instance, terribly boring then (because there won't be anything left to do, once everything has been calculated according to tables); on the other hand, everything will be extremely rational. Of course, what don't people think up out of boredom! Why, even gold pins get stuck into other people out of boredom, but that wouldn't matter. What's really bad (this is me talking

9. A reference to the last discourse of the French philosopher Denis Diderot (1713–1784) in the *Conversation of D'Alembert and Diderot* (1769). 1. An allusion to the crystal palace described in Vera Pavlovna's fourth dream in Chernyshevsky's *What Is to Be Done?* and to the actual building designed by Sir Joseph Paxton, erected for the Great Exhibition in London in 1851 and at that time admired as the newest wonder of architecture; Dostoevsky described it in *Winter Notes on Summer Impressions* (1863).

again) is that for all I know, people might even be grateful for those gold pins. For man is stupid, phenomenally stupid. That is, although he's not really stupid at all, he's really so ungrateful that it's hard to find another being quite like him. Why, I, for example, wouldn't be surprised in the least, if, suddenly, for no reason at all, in the midst of this future, universal rationalism, some gentleman with an offensive, rather, a retrograde and derisive expression on his face were to stand up, put his hands on his hips, and declare to us all: "How about it, gentlemen, what if we knock over all this rationalism with one swift kick for the sole purpose of sending all these logarithms to hell, so that once again we can live according to our own stupid will!" But that wouldn't matter either; what's so annoying is that he would undoubtedly find some followers; such is the way man is made. And all because of the most foolish reason, which, it seems, is hardly worth mentioning: namely, that man, always and everywhere, whoever he is, has preferred to act as he wished, and not at all as reason and advantage have dictated; one might even desire something opposed to one's own advantage, and sometimes (this is now my idea) one *positively must do so*. One's very own free, unfettered desire, one's own whim, no matter how wild, one's own fantasy, even though sometimes roused to the point of madness—all this constitutes precisely that previously omitted, most advantageous advantage which isn't included under any classification and because of which all systems and theories are constantly smashed to smithereens. Where did these sages ever get the idea that man needs any normal, virtuous desire? How did they ever imagine that man needs any kind of rational, advantageous desire? Man needs only one thing—his own *independent* desire, whatever that independence might cost and wherever it might lead. And as far as desire goes, the devil only knows. . . .

VIII

"Ha, ha, ha! But in reality even this desire, if I may say so, doesn't exist!" you interrupt me with a laugh. "Why science has already managed to dissect man so now we know that desire and so-called free choice are nothing more than . . . "

Wait, gentlemen, I myself wanted to begin like that. I must confess that even I got frightened. I was just about to declare that the devil only knows what desire depends on and perhaps we should be grateful for that, but then I remembered about science and I . . . stopped short. But now you've gone and brought it up. Well, after all, what if someday they really do discover the formula for all our desires and whims, that is, the thing that governs them, precise laws that produce them, how exactly they're applied, where they lead in each and every case, and so on and so forth, that is, the genuine mathematical formula—why, then all at once man might stop desiring, yes, indeed, he probably would. Who would want to desire according to some table? And that's not all: he would immediately be transformed from a person into an organ stop or something of that sort; because what is man without desire, without will, and without wishes if not a stop in an organ pipe? What do you think? Let's consider the probabilities—can this really happen or not?

"Hmmm . . . ," you decide, "our desires are mistaken for the most part

because of an erroneous view of our own advantage. Consequently, we sometimes desire pure rubbish because, in our own stupidity, we consider it the
easiest way to achieve some previously assumed advantage. Well, and when
all this has been analyzed, calculated on paper (that's entirely possible, since
it's repugnant and senseless to assume in advance that man will never come
to understand the laws of nature) then, of course, all so-called desires will
no longer exist. For if someday desires are completely reconciled with reason,
we'll follow reason instead of desire simply because it would be impossible,
for example, while retaining one's reason, to *desire* rubbish, and thus knowingly oppose one's reason, and desire something harmful to oneself. . . . And,
since all desires and reasons can really be tabulated, since someday the laws
of our so-called free choice are sure to be discovered, then, all joking aside,
it may be possible to establish something like a table, so that we could actually desire according to it. If, for example, someday they calculate and demonstrate to me that I made a rude gesture because I couldn't possibly refrain
from it, that I had to make precisely that gesture, well, in that case, what
sort of *free choice* would there be, especially if I'm a learned man and have
completed a course of study somewhere? Why, then I'd be able to calculate
in advance my entire life for the next thirty years; in a word, if such a table
were to be drawn up, there'd be nothing left for us to do; we'd simply have
to accept it. In general, we should be repeating endlessly to ourselves that
at such a time and in such circumstances nature certainly won't ask our
opinion; that we must accept it as is, and not as we fantasize it, and that if
we really aspire to prepare a table, a schedule, and, well . . . well, even a
laboratory test tube, there's nothing to be done—one must even accept the
test tube! If not, it'll be accepted even without you. . . ."

Yes, but that's just where I hit a snag! Gentlemen, you'll excuse me for
all this philosophizing; it's a result of my forty years in the underground!
Allow me to fantasize. Don't you see: reason is a fine thing, gentlemen,
there's no doubt about it, but it's only reason, and it satisfies only man's
rational faculty, whereas desire is a manifestation of all life, that is, of all
human life, which includes both reason, as well as all of life's itches and
scratches. And although in this manifestation life often turns out to be fairly
worthless, it's life all the same, and not merely the extraction of square roots.
Why, take me, for instance; I quite naturally want to live in order to satisfy
all my faculties of life, not merely my rational faculty, that is, some one-
twentieth of all my faculties. What does reason know? Reason knows only
what it's managed to learn. (Some things it may never learn; while this offers
no comfort, why not admit it openly?) But human nature acts as a whole,
with all that it contains, consciously and unconsciously; and although it may
tell lies, it's still alive. I suspect, gentlemen, that you're looking at me with
compassion; you repeat that an enlightened and cultured man, in a word,
man as he will be in the future, cannot knowingly desire something disad-
vantageous to himself, and that this is pure mathematics. I agree with you:
it really is mathematics. But I repeat for the one-hundredth time, there is
one case, only one, when a man may intentionally, consciously desire even
something harmful to himself, something stupid, even very stupid, namely:
in order *to have the right* to desire something even very stupid and not be
bound by an obligation to desire only what's smart. After all, this very stupid
thing, one's own whim, gentlemen, may in fact be the most advantageous

thing on earth for people like me, especially in certain cases. In particular, it may be more advantageous than any other advantage, even in a case where it causes obvious harm and contradicts the most sensible conclusions of reason about advantage—because in any case it preserves for us what's most important and precious, that is, our personality and our individuality. There are some people who maintain that in fact this is more precious to man than anything else; of course, desire can, if it so chooses, coincide with reason, especially if it doesn't abuse this option, and chooses to coincide in moderation; this is useful and sometimes even commendable. But very often, even most of the time, desire absolutely and stubbornly disagrees with reason and ... and ... and, do you know, sometimes this is also useful and even very commendable? Let's assume, gentlemen, that man isn't stupid. (And really, this can't possibly be said about him at all, if only because if he's stupid, then who on earth is smart?) But even if he's not stupid, he is, nevertheless, monstrously ungrateful. Phenomenally ungrateful. I even believe that the best definition of man is this: a creature who walks on two legs and is ungrateful. But that's still not all; that's still not his main defect. His main defect is his perpetual misbehavior, perpetual from the time of the Great Flood to the Schleswig-Holstein period of human destiny. Misbehavior, and consequently, imprudence; for it's long been known that imprudence results from nothing else but misbehavior. Just cast a glance at the history of mankind; well, what do you see? Is it majestic? Well, perhaps it's majestic; why, the Colossus of Rhodes,[2] for example—that alone is worth something! Not without reason did Mr Anaevsky[3] report that some people consider it to be the product of human hands, while others maintain that it was created by nature itself. Is it colorful? Well, perhaps it's also colorful; just consider the dress uniforms, both military and civilian, of all nations at all times—why, that alone is worth something, and if you include everyday uniforms, it'll make your eyes bulge; not one historian will be able to sort it all out. Is it monotonous? Well, perhaps it's monotonous, too: men fight and fight; now they're fighting; they fought first and they fought last—you'll agree that it's really much too monotonous. In short, anything can be said about world history, anything that might occur to the most disordered imagination. There's only one thing that can't possibly be said about it—that it's rational. You'll choke on the word. Yet here's just the sort of thing you'll encounter all the time: why, in life you're constantly running up against people who are so well-behaved and so rational, such wise men and lovers of humanity who set themselves the lifelong goal of behaving as morally and rationally as possible, so to speak, to be a beacon for their nearest and dearest, simply in order to prove that it's really possible to live one's life in a moral and rational way. And so what? It's a well-known fact that many of these lovers of humanity, sooner or later, by the end of their lives, have betrayed themselves: they've pulled off some caper, sometimes even quite an indecent one. Now I ask you: what can one expect from man as a creature endowed with such strange qualities? Why, shower him with all sorts of earthly blessings, submerge him in happiness over his head so that only little bubbles appear on the surface of this happiness, as if on water, give him such economic prosperity that he'll

2. A large bronze statue of the sun god, Helios, built between 292 and 280 B.C. in the harbor of Rhodes (an island in the Aegean Sea) and considered one of the Seven Wonders of the Ancient World. 3. A. E. Anaevsky was a critic whose articles were frequently ridiculed in literary polemics of the period.

have absolutely nothing left to do except sleep, eat gingerbread, and worry about the continuation of world history—even then, out of pure ingratitude, sheer perversity, he'll commit some repulsive act. He'll even risk losing his gingerbread, and will intentionally desire the most wicked rubbish, the most uneconomical absurdity, simply in order to inject his own pernicious fantastic element into all this positive rationality. He wants to hold onto those most fantastic dreams, his own indecent stupidity solely for the purpose of assuring himself (as if it were necessary) that men are still men and not piano keys, and that even if the laws of nature play upon them with their own hands, they're still threatened by being overplayed until they won't possibly desire anything more than a schedule. But that's not all: even if man really turned out to be a piano key, even if this could be demonstrated to him by natural science and pure mathematics, even then he still won't become reasonable; he'll intentionally do something to the contrary, simply out of ingratitude, merely to have his own way. If he lacks the means, he'll cause destruction and chaos, he'll devise all kinds of suffering and have his own way! He'll leash a curse upon the world; and, since man alone can do so (it's his privilege and the thing that most distinguishes him from other animals), perhaps only through this curse will he achieve his goal, that is, become really convinced that he's a man and not a piano key! If you say that one can also calculate all this according to a table, this chaos and darkness, these curses, so that the mere possibility of calculating it all in advance would stop everything and that reason alone would prevail—in that case man would go insane deliberately in order not to have reason, but to have his own way! I believe this, I vouch for it, because, after all, the whole of man's work seems to consist only in proving to himself constantly that he's a man and not an organ stop! Even if he has to lose his own skin, he'll prove it; even if he has to become a troglodyte, he'll prove it. And after that, how can one not sin, how can one not praise the fact that all this hasn't yet come to pass and that desire still depends on the devil knows what . . . ?

You'll shout at me (if you still choose to favor me with your shouts) that no one's really depriving me of my will; that they're merely attempting to arrange things so that my will, by its own free choice, will coincide with my normal interests, with the laws of nature, and with arithmetic.

But gentlemen, what sort of free choice will there be when it comes down to tables and arithmetic, when all that's left is two times two makes four? Two times two makes four even without my will. Is that what you call free choice?

IX

Gentlemen, I'm joking of course, and I myself know that it's not a very good joke; but, after all, you can't take everything as a joke. Perhaps I'm gnashing my teeth while I joke. I'm tormented by questions, gentlemen; answer them for me. Now, for example, you want to cure man of his old habits and improve his will according to the demands of science and common sense. But how do you know not only whether it's possible, but even if it's *necessary* to remake him in this way? Why do you conclude that human desire *must* undoubtedly be improved? In short, how do you know that such improvement will really be to man's advantage? And, to be perfectly frank, why are you so *absolutely* convinced that not to oppose man's real, normal advantage guaranteed by the conclusions of reason and arithmetic is really always to man's advantage and constitutes a law for all humanity? After all, this is still only an assumption of yours. Let's suppose that it's a law of logic, but perhaps not a law of humanity. Perhaps, gentlemen, you're wondering if I'm insane? Allow me to explain. I agree that man is primarily a creative animal, destined to strive consciously toward a goal and to engage in the art of engineering, that, is, externally and incessantly building new roads for himself *wherever they lead*. But sometimes he may want to swerve aside precisely because he's *compelled* to build these roads, and perhaps also because, no matter how stupid the spontaneous man of action may generally be, nevertheless it sometimes occurs to him that the road, as it turns out, almost always leads *somewhere or other*, and that the main thing isn't so much where it goes, but the fact that it does, and that the well-behaved child, disregarding the art of engineering, shouldn't yield to pernicious idleness which, as is well known, constitutes the mother of all vices. Man loves to create and build roads; that's indisputable. But why is he also so passionately fond of destruction and chaos? Now, then, tell me. But I myself want to say a few words about this separately. Perhaps the reason that he's so fond of destruction and chaos (after all, it's indisputable that he sometimes really loves it, and that's a fact) is that he himself has an instinctive fear of achieving his goal and completing the project under construction? How do you know if perhaps he loves his building only from afar, but not from close up; perhaps he only likes building it, but not living in it, leaving it afterward *aux animaux domestiques*,[4] such as ants or sheep, or so on and so forth. Now ants have altogether different tastes. They have one astonishing structure of a similar type, forever indestructible—the anthill.

The worthy ants began with the anthill, and most likely, they will end with the anthill, which does great credit to their perseverance and steadfastness. But man is a frivolous and unseemly creature and perhaps, like a chess player, he loves only the process of achieving his goal, and not the goal itself. And, who knows (one can't vouch for it), perhaps the only goal on earth toward which mankind is striving consists merely in this incessant process of achieving or to put it another way, in life itself, and not particularly in the goal which, of course, must always be none other than two times two makes four, that is, a formula; after all, two times two makes four is no longer life, gentlemen, but the beginning of death. At least man has always been somewhat afraid of this two times two makes four, and I'm afraid of it now, too. Let's suppose that the only thing man does is search for this two times two makes four; he sails across oceans, sacrifices his own life in the quest; but to seek it out and find it—really and truly, he's very frightened. After all, he feels that as soon as he finds it, there'll be nothing left to search for. Workers, after finishing work, at least receive their wages, go off to a tavern, and then wind up at a police station—now that's a full week's occupation. But where will man go? At any rate a certain awkwardness can be observed each time he approaches the achievement of similar goals. He loves the process, but he's not so fond of the achievement, and that, of course is terribly amusing. In short, man is made in a comical way; obviously there's some sort of catch

4. To domestic animals (French).

in all this. But two times two makes four is an insufferable thing, nevertheless. Two times two makes four—why, in my opinion, it's mere insolence. Two times two makes four stands there brazenly with its hands on its hips, blocking your path and spitting at you. I agree that two times two makes four is a splendid thing; but if we're going to lavish praise, then two times two makes five is sometimes also a very charming little thing.

And why are you so firmly, so triumphantly convinced that only the normal and positive—in short, only well-being is advantageous to man? Doesn't reason ever make mistakes about advantage? After all, perhaps man likes something other than well-being? Perhaps he loves suffering just as much? Perhaps suffering is just as advantageous to him as well-being? Man sometimes loves suffering terribly, to the point of passion, and that's a fact. There's no reason to study world history on this point; if indeed you're a man and have lived at all, just ask yourself. As far as my own personal opinion is concerned, to love only well-being is somehow even indecent. Whether good or bad, it's sometimes also very pleasant to demolish something. After all, I'm not standing up for suffering here, nor for well-being, either. I'm standing up for . . . my own whim and for its being guaranteed to me whenever necessary. For instance, suffering is not permitted in vaudevilles,[5] that I know. It's also inconceivable in the crystal palace; suffering is doubt and negation. What sort of crystal palace would it be if any doubt were allowed? Yet, I'm convinced that man will never renounce real suffering, that is, destruction and chaos. After all, suffering is the sole cause of consciousness. Although I stated earlier that in my opinion consciousness is man's greatest misfortune, still I know that man loves it and would not exchange it for any other sort of satisfaction. Consciousness, for example, is infinitely higher than two times two. Of course, after two times two, there's nothing left, not merely nothing to do, but nothing to learn. Then the only thing possible will be to plug up your five senses and plunge into contemplation. Well, even if you reach the same result with consciousness, that is, having nothing left to do, at least you'll be able to flog yourself from time to time, and that will liven things up a bit. Although it may be reactionary, it's still better than nothing.

X[6]

You believe in the crystal palace, eternally indestructible, that is, one at which you can never stick out your tongue furtively nor make a rude gesture, even with your fist hidden away. Well, perhaps I'm so afraid of this building precisely because it's made of crystal and it's eternally indestructible, and because it won't be possible to stick one's tongue out even furtively.

Don't you see: if it were a chicken coop instead of a palace, and if it should rain, then perhaps I could crawl into it so as not to get drenched; but I would still not mistake a chicken coop for a palace out of gratitude, just because it sheltered me from the rain. You're laughing, you're even saying that in this case there's no difference between a chicken coop and a mansion. Yes, I reply, if the only reason for living is to keep from getting drenched.

But what if I've taken it into my head that this is not the only reason for

5. A dramatic genre, popular on the Russian stage, consisting of scenes from contemporary life acted with a satirical twist, often in racy dialogue.   6. This chapter was badly mutilated by the censor, as Dostoevsky makes clear in the letter to his brother Mikhail, dated March 26, 1864 (see p. 1067).

living, and, that if one is to live at all, one might as well live in a mansion? Such is my wish, my desire. You'll expunge it from me only when you've changed my desires. Well, then, change them, tempt me with something else, give me some other ideal. In the meantime, I still won't mistake a chicken coop for a palace. But let's say that the crystal palace is a hoax, that according to the laws of nature it shouldn't exist, and that I've invented it only out of my own stupidity, as a result of certain antiquated, irrational habits of my generation. But what do I care if it doesn't exist? What difference does it make if it exists only in my own desires, or, to be more precise, if it exists as long as my desires exist? Perhaps you're laughing again? Laugh, if you wish; I'll resist all your laughter and I still won't say I'm satiated if I'm really hungry; I know all the same that I won't accept a compromise, an infinitely recurring zero, just because it exists according to the laws of nature and it *really* does exist. I won't accept as the crown of my desires a large building with tenements for poor tenants to be rented for a thousand years and, just in case, with the name of the dentist Wagenheim on the sign. Destroy my desires, eradicate my ideals, show me something better and I'll follow you. You may say, perhaps, that it's not worth getting involved; but, in that case, I'll say the same thing in reply. We're having a serious discussion; if you don't grant me your attention, I won't grovel for it. I still have my underground.

And, as long as I'm still alive and feel desire—may my arm wither away before it contributes even one little brick to that building! Never mind that I myself have just rejected the crystal palace for the sole reason that it won't be possible to tease it by sticking out one's tongue at it. I didn't say that because I'm so fond of sticking out my tongue. Perhaps the only reason I got angry is that among all your buildings there's still not a single one where you don't feel compelled to stick out your tongue. On the contrary, I'd let my tongue be cut off out of sheer gratitude, if only things could be so arranged that I'd no longer want to stick it out. What do I care if things can't be so arranged and if I must settle for some tenements? Why was I made with such desires? Can it be that I was made this way only in order to reach the conclusion that my entire way of being is merely a fraud? Can this be the whole purpose? I don't believe it.

By the way, do you know what? I'm convinced that we underground men should be kept in check. Although capable of sitting around quietly in the underground for some forty years, once he emerges into the light of day and bursts into speech, he talks on and on and on. . . .

XI

The final result, gentlemen, is that it's better to do nothing! Conscious inertia is better! And so, long live the underground! Even though I said that I envy the normal man to the point of exasperation, I still wouldn't want to be him under the circumstances in which I see him (although I still won't keep from envying him. No, no, in any case the underground is more advantageous!) At least there one can . . . Hey, but I'm lying once again! I'm lying because I know myself as surely as two times two, that it isn't really the underground that's better, but something different, altogether different, something that I long for, but I'll never be able to find! To hell with the underground! Why, here's what would be better: if I myself were to believe even a fraction of everything I've written. I swear to you, gentlemen, that I don't believe one word, not one little word of all that I've scribbled. That is, I do believe it, perhaps, but at the very same time, I don't know why, I feel and suspect that I'm lying like a trooper.

"Then why did you write all this?" you ask me.

"What if I'd shut you up in the underground for forty years with nothing to do and then came back forty years later to see what had become of you? Can a man really be left alone for forty years with nothing to do?"

"Isn't it disgraceful, isn't it humiliating!" you might say, shaking your head in contempt. "You long for life, but you try to solve life's problems by means of a logical tangle. How importunate, how insolent your outbursts, and how frightened you are at the same time! You talk rubbish, but you're constantly afraid of them and make apologies. You maintain that you fear nothing, but at the same time you try to ingratiate yourself with us. You assure us that you're gnashing your teeth, yet at the same time you try to be witty and amuse us. You know that your witticisms are not very clever, but apparently you're pleased by their literary merit. Perhaps you really have suffered, but you don't even respect your own suffering. There's some truth in you, too, but no chastity; out of the pettiest vanity you bring your truth out into the open, into the marketplace, and you shame it. . . . You really want to say something, but you conceal your final word out of fear because you lack the resolve to utter it; you have only cowardly impudence. You boast about your consciousness, but you merely vacillate, because even though your mind is working, your heart has been blackened by depravity, and without a pure heart, there can be no full, genuine consciousness. And how importunate you are; how you force yourself upon others; you behave in such an affected manner. Lies, lies, lies!"

Of course, it was I who just invented all these words for you. That, too, comes from the underground. For forty years in a row I've been listening to all your words through a crack. I've invented them myself, since that's all that's occurred to me. It's no wonder that I've learned it all by heart and that it's taken on such a literary form. . . .

But can you really be so gullible as to imagine that I'll print all this and give it to you to read? And here's another problem I have: why do I keep calling you "gentlemen"? Why do I address you as if you really were my readers? Confessions such as the one I plan to set forth here aren't published and given to other people to read. Anyway, I don't possess sufficient fortitude, nor do I consider it necessary to do so. But don't you see, a certain notion has come into my mind, and I wish to realize it at any cost. Here's the point.

Every man has within his own reminiscences certain things he doesn't reveal to anyone, except, perhaps, to his friends. There are also some that he won't reveal even to his friends, only to himself perhaps, and even then, in secret. Finally, there are some which a man is afraid to reveal even to himself; every decent man has accumulated a fair number of such things. In fact, it can even be said that the more decent the man, the more of these things he's accumulated. Anyway, only recently I myself decided to recall some of my earlier adventures; up to now I've always avoided them, even with a certain anxiety. But having decided not only to recall them, but even to write them down, now is when I wish to try an experiment: is it possible to be absolutely honest even with one's own self and not to fear the whole truth? Incidentally, I'll mention that Heine maintains that faithful autobiographies are almost impossible, and that a man is sure to lie about himself.[7] In Heine's opinion, Rousseau, for example, undoubtedly told untruths about himself in his confession and even lied intentionally, out of vanity. I'm convinced that Heine is correct; I understand perfectly well that sometimes it's possible out of vanity alone to impute all sorts of crimes to oneself, and I can even understand what sort of vanity that might be. But Heine was making judgments about a person who confessed to the public. I, however, am writing for myself alone and declare once and for all that if I write as if I were addressing readers, that's only for show, because it's easier for me to write that way. It's a form, simply a form; I shall never have any readers. I've already stated that. . . . I don't want to be restricted in any way by editing my notes. I won't attempt to introduce any order or system. I'll write down whatever comes to mind.

Well, now, for example, someone might seize upon my words and ask me, if you really aren't counting on any readers, why do you make such compacts with yourself, and on paper no less; that is, if you're not going to introduce any order or system, if you're going to write down whatever comes to mind, etc., etc.? Why do you go on explaining? Why do you keep apologizing?

"Well, imagine that," I reply.

This, by the way, contains an entire psychology. Perhaps it's just that I'm a coward. Or perhaps it's that I imagine an audience before me on purpose, so that I behave more decently when I'm writing things down. There may be a thousand reasons.

But here's something else: why is it that I want to write? If it's not for the public, then why can't I simply recall it all in my own mind and not commit it to paper?

Quite so; but somehow it appears more dignified on paper. There's something more impressive about it; I'll be a better judge of myself; the style will be improved. Besides, perhaps I'll actually experience some relief from the process of writing it all down. Today, for example, I'm particularly oppressed by one very old memory from my distant past. It came to me vividly several days ago and since then it's stayed with me, like an annoying musical motif that doesn't want to leave you alone. And yet you must get rid of it. I have hundreds of such memories; but at times a single one emerges from those hundreds and oppresses me. For some reason I believe that if I write it down I can get rid of it. Why not try?

Lastly, I'm bored, and I never do anything. Writing things down actually seems like work. They say that work makes a man become good and honest. Well, at least there's a chance.

It's snowing today, an almost wet, yellow, dull snow. It was snowing yesterday too, a few days ago as well. I think it was apropos of the wet snow that I recalled this episode and now it doesn't want to leave me alone. And so, let it be a tale apropos of wet snow.

---

7. A reference to the work *On Germany* (1853–54) by the German poet Heinrich Heine (1797–1856), in which on the very first page Heine speaks of Rousseau as lying and inventing disgraceful incidents about himself for his *Confessions*.

II

Apropos of Wet Snow

When from the darkness of delusion
I saved your fallen soul
With ardent words of conviction,
And, full of profound torment,
Wringing your hands, you cursed
The vice that had ensnared you;
When, punishing by recollection
Your forgetful conscience,
You told me the tale
Of all that had happened before,
And, suddenly, covering your face,
Full of shame and horror,
You tearfully resolved,
Indignant, shaken . . .
Etc., etc., etc.
From the poetry of N. A. Nekrasov[8]

I

At that time I was only twenty-four years old. Even then my life was gloomy, disordered, and solitary to the point of savagery. I didn't associate with anyone; I even avoided talking, and I retreated further and further into my corner. At work in the office I even tried not to look at anyone; I was aware not only that my colleagues considered me eccentric, but that they always seemed to regard me with a kind of loathing. Sometimes I wondered why it was that no one else thinks that others regard him with loathing. One of our office-workers had a repulsive pock-marked face which even appeared somewhat villainous. It seemed to me that with such a disreputable face I'd never have dared look at anyone. Another man had a uniform so worn that there was a foul smell emanating from him. Yet, neither of these two gentlemen was embarrassed—neither because of his clothes, nor his face, nor in any moral way. Neither one imagined that other people regarded him with loathing; and if either had so imagined, it wouldn't have mattered at all, as long as their supervisor chose not to view him that way. It's perfectly clear to me now, because of my unlimited vanity and the great demands I accordingly made on myself, that I frequently regarded myself with a furious dissatisfaction verging on loathing; as a result, I intentionally ascribed my own view to everyone else. For example, I despised my own face; I considered it hideous, and I even suspected that there was something repulsive in its expression. Therefore, every time I arrived at work, I took pains to behave as independently as possible, so that I couldn't be suspected of any malice, and I tried to assume as noble an expression as possible. "It may not be a handsome face," I thought, "but let it be noble, expressive, and above all, extremely *intelligent*." But I was agonizingly certain that my face couldn't possibly express all these virtues. Worst of all, I considered it positively stupid. I'd have been reconciled if it had looked intelligent. In fact, I'd even

8. A famous Russian poet and editor of radical sympathies (1821–1878). The poem quoted dates from 1845 and is without title. It ends with the lines "And enter my house bold and free / To become its full mistress!"

have agreed to have it appear repulsive, on the condition that at the same time people would find my face terribly intelligent.

Of course, I hated all my fellow office-workers from the first to the last and despised every one of them; yet, at the same time it was as if I were afraid of them. Sometimes it happened that I would even regard them as superior to me. At this time these changes would suddenly occur: first I would despise them, then I would regard them as superior to me. A cultured and decent man cannot be vain without making unlimited demands on himself and without hating himself, at times to the point of contempt. But, whether hating them or regarding them as superior, I almost always lowered my eyes when meeting anyone. I even conducted experiments: could I endure someone's gaze? I'd always be the first to lower my eyes. This infuriated me to the point of madness. I slavishly worshipped the conventional in everything external. I embraced the common practice and feared any eccentricity with all my soul. But how could I sustain it? I was morbidly refined, as befits any cultured man of our time. All others resembled one another as sheep in a flock. Perhaps I was the only one in the whole office who constantly thought of himself as a coward and a slave; and I thought so precisely because I was so cultured. But not only did I think so, it actually was so: I was a coward and a slave. I say this without any embarrassment. Every decent man of our time is and must be a coward and a slave. This is his normal condition. I'm deeply convinced of it. This is how he's made and what he's meant to be. And not only at the present time, as the result of some accidental circumstance, but in general at all times, a decent man must be a coward and a slave. This is a law of nature for all decent men on earth. If one of them should happen to be brave about something or other, we shouldn't be comforted or distracted: he'll still lose his nerve about something else. That's the single and eternal way out. Only asses and their mongrels are brave, and even then, only until they come up against a wall. It's not worthwhile paying them any attention because they really don't mean anything at all.

There was one more circumstance tormenting me at that time: no one was like me, and I wasn't like anyone else. "I'm alone," I mused, "and they are *everyone*"; and I sank deep into thought.

From all this it's clear that I was still just a boy.

The exact opposite would also occur. Sometimes I would find it repulsive to go to the office: it reached the point where I would often return home from work ill. Then suddenly, for no good reason at all, a flash of skepticism and indifference would set in (everything came to me in flashes); I would laugh at my own intolerance and fastidiousness, and reproach myself for my *romanticism*. Sometimes I didn't even want to talk to anyone; at other times it reached a point where I not only started talking, but I even thought about striking up a friendship with others. All my fastidiousness would suddenly disappear for no good reason at all. Who knows? Perhaps I never really had any, and it was all affected, borrowed from books. I still haven't answered this question, even up to now. And once I really did become friends with others; I began to visit their houses, play préférance,[9] drink vodka, talk about promotions. . . . But allow me to digress.

We Russians, generally speaking, have never had any of those stupid, tran-

---

9. A card game for three players.

scendent German romantics, or even worse, French romantics, on whom nothing produces any effect whatever: the earth might tremble beneath them, all of France might perish on the barricades, but they remain the same, not even changing for decency's sake; they go on singing their transcendent songs, so to speak, to their dying day, because they're such fools. We here on Russian soil have no fools. It's a well-known fact; that's precisely what distinguishes us from foreigners. Consequently, transcendent natures cannot be found among us in their pure form. That's the result of our "positive" publicists and critics of that period, who hunted for the Kostanzhouglo and the Uncle Pyotr Ivanoviches,[1] foolishly mistaking them for our ideal and slandering our own romantics, considering them to be the same kind of transcendents as one finds in Germany or France. On the contrary, the characteristics of our romantics are absolutely and directly opposed to the transcendent Europeans; not one of those European standards can apply here. (Allow me to use the word "romantic"—it's an old-fashioned little word, well-respected and deserving, familiar to everyone.) The characteristics of our romantics are to understand everything, *to see everything, often to see it much more clearly than our most positive minds*; not to be reconciled with anyone or anything, but, at the same time, not to balk at anything; to circumvent everything, to yield on every point, to treat everyone diplomatically; never to lose sight of some useful, practical goal (an apartment at government expense, a nice pension, a decoration)—to keep an eye on that goal through all his excesses and his volumes of lyrical verse, and, at the same time, to preserve intact the "beautiful and sublime" to the end of their lives; and, incidentally, to preserve themselves as well, wrapped up in cotton like precious jewelry, if only, for example, for the sake of that same "beautiful and sublime." Our romantic has a very broad nature and is the biggest rogue of all, I can assure you of that . . . even by my own experience. Of course, all this is true if the romantic is smart. But what am I saying? A romantic is always smart; I merely wanted to observe that although we've had some romantic fools, they really don't count at all, simply because while still in their prime they would degenerate completely into Germans, and, in order to preserve their precious jewels more comfortably, they'd settle over there, either in Weimar or in the Black Forest. For instance, I genuinely despised my official position and refrained from throwing it over merely out of necessity, because I myself sat there working and received good money for doing it. And, as a result, please note, I still refrained from throwing it over. Our romantic would sooner lose his mind (which, by the way, very rarely occurs) than give it up, if he didn't have another job in mind; nor is he ever kicked out, unless he's hauled off to the insane asylum as the "King of Spain,"[2] and only if he's gone completely mad. Then again, it's really only the weaklings and towheads who go mad in our country. An enormous number of romantics later rise to significant rank. What extraordinary versatility! And what a capacity for the most contradictory sensations! I used to be consoled by these thoughts back then, and still am even nowadays. That's why there are so

1. A character in Ivan Goncharov's novel *A Common Story* (1847); a high bureaucrat, a factory owner who teaches lessons of sobriety and good sense to the romantic hero, Alexander Aduyev. Konstanzhouglo is the ideal efficient landowner in the second part of Nikolai Gogol's novel *Dead Souls* (1852).   2. An allusion to the hero of Gogol's short story *Diary of a Madman* (1835). Poprishchin, a low-ranking civil servant, sees his aspirations crushed by the enormous bureaucracy. He ends by going insane and imagining himself to be king of Spain.

many "broad natures" among us, people who never lose their ideals, no matter how low they fall; even though they never lift a finger for the sake of their ideals, even though they're outrageous villains and thieves, nevertheless they respect their original ideals to the point of tears and are extremely honest men at heart. Yes, only among us Russians can the most outrageous scoundrel be absolutely, even sublimely honest at heart, while at the same time never ceasing to be a scoundrel. I repeat, nearly always do our romantics turn out to be very efficient rascals (I use the word "rascal" affectionately); they suddenly manifest such a sense of reality and positive knowledge that their astonished superiors and the general public can only click their tongues at them in amazement.

Their versatility is really astounding; God only knows what it will turn into, how it will develop under subsequent conditions, and what it holds for us in the future. The material is not all that bad! I'm not saying this out of some ridiculous patriotism or jingoism. However, I'm sure that once again you think I'm joking. But who knows? Perhaps it's quite the contrary, that is, you're convinced that this is what I really think. In any case, gentlemen, I'll consider that both of these opinions constitute an honor and a particular pleasure. And do forgive me for this digression.

Naturally, I didn't sustain any friendships with my colleagues, and soon I severed all relations after quarreling with them; and, because of my youthful inexperience at the same time, I even stopped greeting them, as if I'd cut them off entirely. That, however, happened to me only once. On the whole, I was always alone.

At home I spent most of my time reading. I tried to stifle all that was constantly seething within me with external sensations. And of all external sensations available, only reading was possible for me. Of course, reading helped a great deal—it agitated, delighted, and tormented me. But at times it was terribly boring. I still longed to be active; and suddenly I sank into dark, subterranean, loathsome depravity—more precisely, petty vice. My nasty little passions were sharp and painful as a result of my constant, morbid irritability. I experienced hysterical fits accompanied by tears and convulsions. Besides reading, I had nowhere else to go—that is, there was nothing to respect in my surroundings, nothing to attract me. In addition, I was overwhelmed by depression; I possessed a hysterical craving for contradictions and contrasts; and, as a result, I plunged into depravity. I haven't said all this to justify myself. . . . But, no, I'm lying. I did want to justify myself. It's for myself, gentlemen, that I include this little observation. I don't want to lie. I've given my word.

I indulged in depravity all alone, at night, furtively, timidly, sordidly, with a feeling of shame that never left me even in my most loathsome moments and drove me at such times to the point of profanity. Even then I was carrying around the underground in my soul. I was terribly afraid of being seen, met, recognized. I visited all sorts of dismal places.

Once, passing by some wretched little tavern late at night, I saw through a lighted window some gentlemen fighting with billiard cues; one of them was thrown out the window. At some other time I would have been disgusted; but just then I was overcome by such a mood that I envied the gentleman who'd been tossed out; I envied him so much that I even walked into the tavern and entered the billiard room. "Perhaps," I thought, "I'll get into a fight, and they'll throw me out the window, too."

I wasn't drunk, but what could I do—after all, depression can drive a man to this kind of hysteria. But nothing came of it. It turned out that I was incapable of being tossed out the window; I left without getting into a fight.

As soon as I set foot inside, some officer put me in my place.

I was standing next to the billiard table inadvertently blocking his way as he wanted to get by; he took hold of me by the shoulders and without a word of warning or explanation, moved me from where I was standing to another place, and he went past as if he hadn't even noticed me. I could have forgiven even a beating, but I could never forgive his moving me out of the way and entirely failing to notice me.

The devil knows what I would have given for a genuine, ordinary quarrel, a decent one, a more *literary* one, so to speak. But I'd been treated as if I were a fly. The officer was about six feet tall, while I'm small and scrawny. The quarrel, however, was in my hands; all I had to do was protest, and of course they would've thrown me out the window. But I reconsidered and preferred . . . to withdraw resentfully.

I left the tavern confused and upset and went straight home; the next night I continued my petty vice more timidly, more furtively, more gloomily than before, as if I had tears in my eyes—but I continued nonetheless. Don't conclude, however, that I retreated from that officer as a result of any cowardice; I've never been a coward at heart, although I've constantly acted like one in deed, but—wait before you laugh—I can explain this. I can explain anything, you may rest assured.

Oh, if only this officer had been the kind who'd have agreed to fight a duel! But no, he was precisely one of those types (alas, long gone) who preferred to act with their billiard cues or, like Gogol's Lieutenant Pirogov,[3] by appealing to the authorities. They didn't fight duels; in any case, they'd have considered fighting a duel with someone like me, a lowly civilian, to be indecent. In general, they considered duels to be somehow inconceivable, free-thinking, French, while they themselves, especially if they happened to be six feet tall, offended other people rather frequently.

In this case I retreated not out of any cowardice, but because of my unlimited vanity. I wasn't afraid of his height, nor did I think I'd receive a painful beating and get thrown out the window. In fact, I'd have had sufficient physical courage; it was moral fortitude I lacked. I was afraid that everyone present—from the insolent billiard marker to the foul-smelling, pimply little clerks with greasy collars who used to hang about—wouldn't understand and would laugh when I started to protest and speak to them in literary Russian. Because, to this very day, it's still impossible for us to speak about a point of honor, that is, not about honor itself, but a point of honor (*point d'honneur*), except in literary language. One can't even refer to a "point of honor" in everyday language. I was fully convinced (a sense of reality, in spite of all my romanticism!) that they would all simply split their sides laughing, and that the officer, instead of giving me a simple beating, that is, an inoffensive one, would certainly apply his knee to my back and drive me around the billiard table; only then perhaps would he have the mercy to throw me out the window. Naturally, this wretched story of mine couldn't possibly end with this alone. Afterward I used to meet this officer frequently on the street and I

---

3. One of two main characters in Gogol's short story *Nevsky Prospect* (1835). A shallow and self-satisfied officer, he mistakes the wife of a German artisan for a woman of easy virtue and receives a sound thrashing. He decides to lodge an official complaint but, after consuming a cream-filled pastry, thinks better of it.

observed him very carefully. I don't know whether he ever recognized me. Probably not; I reached that conclusion from various observations. As for me, I stared at him with malice and hatred, and continued to do so for several years! My malice increased and became stronger over time. At first I began to make discreet inquiries about him. This was difficult for me to do, since I had so few acquaintances. But once, as I was following him at a distance as though tied to him, someone called to him on the street: that's how I learned his name. Another time I followed him back to his own apartment and for a ten-kopeck piece learned from the doorman where and how he lived, on what floor, with whom, etc.—in a word, all that could be learned from a doorman. One morning, although I never engaged in literary activities, it suddenly occurred to me to draft a description of this officer as a kind of exposé, a caricature, in the form of a tale. I wrote it with great pleasure. I exposed him; I even slandered him. At first I altered his name only slightly, so that it could be easily recognized; but then, upon careful reflection, I changed it. Then I sent the tale off to *Notes of the Fatherland*.[4] But such exposés were no longer in fashion, and they didn't publish my tale. I was very annoyed by that. At times I simply choked on my spite. Finally, I resolved to challenge my opponent to a duel. I composed a beautiful, charming letter to him, imploring him to apologize to me; in case he refused, I hinted rather strongly at a duel. The letter was composed in such a way that if that officer had possessed even the smallest understanding of the "beautiful and sublime," he would have come running, thrown his arms around me, and offered his friendship. That would have been splendid! We would have led such a wonderful life! Such a life! He would have shielded me with his rank; I would have ennobled him with my culture, and, well, with my ideas. Who knows what might have come of it! Imagine it, two years had already passed since he'd insulted me; my challenge was the most ridiculous anachronism, in spite of all the cleverness of my letter in explaining and disguising that fact. But, thank God (to this day I thank the Almighty with tears in my eyes), I didn't send that letter. A shiver runs up and down my spine when I think what might have happened if I had. Then suddenly . . . suddenly, I got my revenge in the simplest manner, a stroke of genius! A brilliant idea suddenly occurred to me. Sometimes on holidays I used to stroll along Nevsky Prospect at about four o'clock in the afternoon, usually on the sunny side. That is, I didn't really stroll; rather, I experienced innumerable torments, humiliations, and bilious attacks. But that's undoubtedly just what I needed. I darted in and out like a fish among the strollers, constantly stepping aside before generals, cavalry officers, hussars, and young ladies. At those moments I used to experience painful spasms in my heart and a burning sensation in my back merely at the thought of my dismal apparel as well as the wretchedness and vulgarity of my darting little figure. This was sheer torture, uninterrupted and unbearable humiliation at the thought, which soon became an incessant and immediate sensation, that I was a fly in the eyes of society, a disgusting, obscene fly—smarter than the rest, more cultured, even nobler—all that goes without saying, but a fly, nonetheless, who incessantly steps aside, insulted and injured by everyone. For what reason did I inflict this torment on myself? Why did I stroll along Nevsky Prospect? I don't know. But something simply *drew* me there at every opportunity.

4. A radical literary and political journal published in Petersburg from 1839 to 1867.

Then I began to experience surges of that pleasure about which I've already spoken in the first chapter. After the incident with the officer I was drawn there even more strongly; I used to encounter him along Nevsky most often, and it was there that I could admire him. He would also go there, mostly on holidays. He, too, would give way before generals and individuals of superior rank; he, too, would spin like a top among them. But he would simply trample people like me, or even those slightly superior; he would walk directly toward them, as if there were empty space ahead of him; and under no circumstance would he ever step aside. I revelled in my malice as I observed him, and . . . bitterly stepped aside before him every time. I was tortured by the fact that even on the street I found it impossible to stand on an equal footing with him. "Why is it you're always first to step aside?" I badgered myself in insane hysteria, at times waking up at three in the morning. "Why always you and not he? After all, there's no law about it; it isn't written down anywhere. Let it be equal, as it usually is when people of breeding meet: he steps aside halfway and you halfway, and you pass by showing each other mutual respect." But that was never the case, and I continued to step aside, while he didn't even notice that I was yielding to him. Then a most astounding idea suddenly dawned on me. "What if," I thought, "what if I were to meet him and . . . not step aside? Deliberately not step aside, even if it meant bumping into him: how would that be?" This bold idea gradually took such a hold that it afforded me no peace. I dreamt about it incessantly, horribly, and even went to Nevsky more frequently so that I could imagine more clearly how I would do it. I was in ecstasy. The scheme was becoming more and more possible and even probable to me. "Of course, I wouldn't really collide with him," I thought, already feeling more generous toward him in my joy, "but I simply won't turn aside. I'll bump into him, not very painfully, but just so, shoulder to shoulder, as much as decency allows. I'll bump into him the same amount as he bumps into me." At last I made up my mind completely. But the preparations took a very long time. First, in order to look as presentable as possible during the execution of my scheme, I had to worry about my clothes. "In any case, what if, for example, it should occasion a public scandal? (And the public there was *superflu:*[5] a countess, Princess D., and the entire literary world.) It was essential to be well-dressed; that inspires respect and in a certain sense will place us immediately on an equal footing in the eyes of high society." With that goal in mind I requested my salary in advance, and I purchased a pair of black gloves and a decent hat at Churkin's store. Black gloves seemed to me more dignified, more *bon ton*[6] than the lemon-colored ones I'd considered at first. "That would be too glaring, as if the person wanted to be noticed"; so I didn't buy the lemon-colored ones. I'd already procured a fine shirt with white bone cufflinks; but my overcoat constituted a major obstacle. In and of itself it was not too bad at all; it kept me warm; but it was quilted and had a raccoon collar, the epitome of bad taste. At all costs I had to replace the collar with a beaver one, just like on an officer's coat. For this purpose I began to frequent the Shopping Arcade; and, after several attempts, I turned up some cheap German beaver. Although these German beavers wear out very quickly and soon begin to look shabby, at first, when they're brand new, they look very fine indeed; after all, I only needed it for a single occasion. I asked the price: it was still expensive.

5. Excessively refined (French). 6. In good taste (French).

After considerable reflection I resolved to sell my raccoon collar. I decided to request a loan for the remaining amount—a rather significant sum for me—from Anton Antonych Setochkin, my office chief, a modest man, but a serious and solid one, who never lent money to anyone, but to whom, upon entering the civil service, I'd once been specially recommended by an important person who'd secured the position for me. I suffered terribly. It seemed monstrous and shameful to ask Anton Antonych for money. I didn't sleep for two or three nights in a row; in general I wasn't getting much sleep those days, and I always had a fever. I would have either a vague sinking feeling in my heart, or else my heart would suddenly begin to thump, thump, thump! . . . At first Anton Antonych was surprised, then he frowned, thought it over, and finally gave me the loan, after securing from me a note authorizing him to deduct the sum from my salary two weeks later. In this way everything was finally ready; the splendid beaver reigned in place of the mangy raccoon, and I gradually began to get down to business. It was impossible to set about it all at once, in a foolhardy way; one had to proceed in this matter very carefully, step by step. But I confess that after many attempts I was ready to despair: we didn't bump into each other, no matter what! No matter how I prepared, no matter how determined I was—it seems that we're just about to bump, when I look up—and once again I've stepped aside while he's gone by without even noticing me. I even used to pray as I approached him that God would grant me determination. One time I'd fully resolved to do it, but the result was that I merely stumbled and fell at his feet because, at the very last moment, only a few inches away from him, I lost my nerve. He stepped over me very calmly, and I bounced to one side like a rubber ball. That night I lay ill with a fever once again and was delirious. Then, everything suddenly ended in the best possible way. The night before I decided once and for all not to go through with my pernicious scheme and to give it all up without success; with that in mind I went to Nevsky Prospect for one last time simply in order to see how I'd abandon the whole thing. Suddenly, three paces away from my enemy, I made up my mind unexpectedly; I closed my eyes and— we bumped into each other forcefully, shoulder to shoulder! I didn't yield an inch and walked by him on a completely equal footing! He didn't even turn around to look at me and pretended that he hadn't even noticed; but he was merely pretending, I'm convinced of that. To this very day I'm convinced of that! Naturally, I got the worst of it; he was stronger, but that wasn't the point. The point was that I'd achieved my goal, I'd maintained my dignity, I hadn't yielded one step, and I'd publicly placed myself on an equal social footing with him. I returned home feeling completely avenged for everything. I was ecstatic. I rejoiced and sang Italian arias. Of course, I won't describe what happened to me three days later; if you've read the first part entitled "Underground," you can guess for yourself. The officer was later transferred somewhere else; I haven't seen him for some fourteen years. I wonder what he's doing nowadays, that dear friend of mine! Whom is he trampling underfoot?

II

But when this phase of my nice, little dissipation ended I felt terribly nauseated. Remorse set in; I tried to drive it away because it was too disgusting. Little by little, however, I got used to that, too. I got used to it all; that is, it wasn't that I got used to it, rather, I somehow voluntarily consented to endure it. But I had a way out that reconciled everything—to escape into "all that was beautiful and sublime," in my dreams, of course. I was a terrible dreamer; I dreamt for three months in a row, tucked away in my little corner. And well you may believe that in those moments I was not at all like the gentlemen who, in his faint-hearted anxiety, had sewn a German beaver onto the collar of his old overcoat. I suddenly became a hero. If my six-foot-tall lieutenant had come to see me then, I'd never have admitted him. I couldn't even conceive of him at that time. It's hard to describe now what my dreams consisted of then, and how I could've been so satisfied with them, but I was. Besides, even now I can take pride in them at certain times. My dreams were particularly sweet and vivid after my little debauchery; they were filled with remorse and tears, curses and ecstasy. There were moments of such positive intoxication, such happiness, that I felt not even the slightest trace of mockery within me, really and truly. It was all faith, hope and love. That's just it: at the time I believed blindly that by some kind of miracle, some external circumstance, everything would suddenly open up and expand; a vista of appropriate activity would suddenly appear—beneficent, beautiful, and most of all, *ready-made* (what precisely, I never knew, but, most of all, it had to be ready-made), and that I would suddenly step forth into God's world, almost riding on a white horse and wearing a laurel wreath. I couldn't conceive of a secondary role; and that's precisely why in reality I very quietly took on the lowest one. Either a hero or dirt—there was no middle ground. That was my ruin because in the dirt I consoled myself knowing that at other times I was a hero, and that the hero covered himself with dirt; that is to say, an ordinary man would be ashamed to wallow in filth, but a hero is too noble to become defiled; consequently, he can wallow. It's remarkable that these surges of everything "beautiful and sublime" occurred even during my petty depravity, and precisely when I'd sunk to the lowest depths. They occurred in separate spurts, as if to remind me of themselves; however, they failed to banish my depravity by their appearance. On the contrary, they seemed to add spice to it by means of contrast; they came in just the right amount to serve as a tasty sauce. This sauce consisted of contradictions, suffering, and agonizing internal analysis; all of these torments and trifles lent a certain piquancy, even some meaning to my depravity—in a word, they completely fulfilled the function of a tasty sauce. Nor was all this even lacking in a measure of profundity. Besides, I would never have consented to the simple, tasteless, spontaneous little debauchery of an ordinary clerk and have endured all that filth! How could it have attracted me then and lured me into the street late at night? No, sir, I had a noble loophole for everything. . . .

   But how much love, oh Lord, how much love I experienced at times in those dreams of mine, in those "escapes into everything beautiful and sublime." Even though it was fantastic love, even though it was never directed at anything human, there was still so much love that afterward, in reality, I no longer felt any impulse to direct it: that would have been an unnecessary luxury. However, everything always ended in a most satisfactory way by a lazy and intoxicating transition into art, that is, into beautiful forms of being, ready-made, largely borrowed from poets and novelists, and adapted to serve every possible need. For instance, I would triumph over everyone; naturally,

everyone else grovelled in the dust and was voluntarily impelled to acknowledge my superiority, while I would forgive them all for everything. Or else,
being a famous poet and chamberlain, I would fall in love; I'd receive an
enormous fortune and would immediately sacrifice it all for the benefit of
humanity, at the same time confessing before all peoples my own infamies,
which, needless to say, were not simple infamies, but contained a great
amount of "the beautiful and sublime," something in the style of Manfred.[7]
Everyone would weep and kiss me (otherwise what idiots they would have
been), while I went about barefoot and hungry preaching new ideas and
defeating all the reactionaries of Austerlitz.[8] Then a march would be played,
a general amnesty declared, and the Pope would agree to leave Rome and
go to Brazil;[9] a ball would be hosted for all of Italy at the Villa Borghese on
the shores of Lake Como,[1] since Lake Como would have been moved to
Rome for this very occasion; then there would be a scene in the bushes, etc.,
etc.—as if you didn't know. You'll say that it's tasteless and repugnant to
drag all this out into the open after all the raptures and tears to which I've
confessed. But why is it so repugnant? Do you really think I'm ashamed of
all this or that it's any more stupid than anything in your own lives, gentlemen? Besides, you can rest assured that some of it was not at all badly
composed. . . . Not everything occurred on the shores of Lake Como. But
you're right; in fact, it is tasteless and repugnant. And the most repugnant
thing of all is that now I've begun to justify myself before you. And even
more repugnant is that now I've made that observation. But enough, otherwise there'll be no end to it: each thing will be more repugnant than the
last. . . .

I was never able to dream for more than three months in a row, and I
began to feel an irresistible urge to plunge into society. To me plunging into
society meant paying a visit to my office chief, Anton Antonych Setochkin.
He's the only lasting acquaintance I've made during my lifetime; I too now
marvel at this circumstance. But even then I would visit him only when my
dreams had reached such a degree of happiness that it was absolutely essential for me to embrace people and all humanity at once; for that reason I
needed to have at least one person on hand who actually existed. However,
one could only call upon Anton Antonych on Tuesdays (his receiving day);
consequently, I always had to adjust the urge to embrace all humanity so
that it occurred on Tuesday. This Anton Antonych lived near Five Corners,[2]
on the fourth floor, in four small, low-ceilinged rooms, each smaller than
the last, all very frugal and yellowish in appearance. He lived with his two
daughters and an aunt who used to serve tea. The daughters, one thirteen,
the other fourteen, had little snub noses. I was very embarrassed by them
because they used to whisper all the time and giggle to each other. The host
usually sat in his study on a leather couch in front of a table together with
some gray-haired guest, a civil servant either from our office or another one.

7. The romantic hero of Byron's poetic tragedy *Manfred* (1817), a lonely, defiant figure whose past conceals
some mysterious crime.   8. The site of Napoleon's great victory in December 1805 over the combined
armies of the Russian czar Alexander I and the Austrian emperor Francis II.   9. Napoleon announced
his annexation of the Papal States to France in 1809 and was promptly excommunicated by Pope Pius VII.
The pope was imprisoned and forced to sign a new concordat, but in 1814 he returned to Rome in triumph.   1. Located in the foothills of the Italian Alps in Lombardy. Villa Borghese was the elegant
summer palace built by Scipione Cardinal Borghese outside the Porta del Popolo in Rome.   2. A well-
known landmark in Petersburg.

I never saw more than two or three guests there, and they were always the same ones. They talked about excise taxes, debates in the Senate, salaries, promotions, His Excellency and how to please him, and so on and so forth. I had the patience to sit there like a fool next to these people for four hours or so; I listened without daring to say a word to them or even knowing what to talk about. I sat there in a stupor; several times I broke into a sweat; I felt numbed by paralysis; but it was good and useful. Upon returning home I would postpone for some time my desire to embrace all humanity.

I had one other sort of acquaintance, however, named Simonov, a former schoolmate of mine. In fact, I had a number of schoolmates in Petersburg, but I didn't associate with them, and I'd even stopped greeting them along the street. I might even have transferred into a different department at the office so as not to be with them and to cut myself off from my hated child-hood once and for all. Curses on that school and those horrible years of penal servitude. In short, I broke with my schoolmates as soon as I was released. There remained only two or three people whom I would greet upon encountering them. One was Simonov, who hadn't distinguished himself in school in any way; he was even-tempered and quiet, but I detected in him a certain independence of character, even honesty. I don't even think that he was all that limited. At one time he and I experienced some rather bright moments, but they didn't last very long and somehow were suddenly clouded over. Evidently he was burdened by these recollections, and seemed in con-stant fear that I would lapse into that former mode. I suspect that he found me repulsive, but not being absolutely sure, I used to visit him nonetheless.

So once, on a Thursday, unable to endure my solitude, and knowing that on that day Anton Antonych's door was locked, I remembered Simonov. As I climbed the stairs to his apartment on the fourth floor, I was thinking how burdensome this man found my presence and that my going to see him was rather useless. But since it always turned out, as if on purpose, that such reflections would impel me to put myself even further into an ambiguous situation, I went right in. It had been almost a year since I'd last seen Simonov.

III

I found two more of my former schoolmates there with him. Apparently they were discussing some important matter. None of them paid any atten-tion to me when I entered, which was strange since I hadn't seen them for several years. Evidently they considered me some sort of ordinary house fly. They hadn't even treated me like that when we were in school together, although they'd all hated me. Of course, I understood that they must despise me now for my failure in the service and for the fact that I'd sunk so low, was badly dressed, and so on, which, in their eyes, constituted proof of my ineptitude and insignificance. But I still hadn't expected such a degree of contempt. Simonov was even surprised by my visits. All this disconcerted me; I sat down in some distress and began to listen to what they were saying.

The discussion was serious, even heated, and concerned a farewell dinner which these gentlemen wanted to organize jointly as early as the following day for their friend Zverkov, an army officer who was heading for a distant province. Monsieur Zverkov had also been my schoolmate all along. I'd begun to hate him especially in the upper grades. In the lower grades he was merely an attractive, lively lad whom everyone liked. However, I'd hated him in the lower grades, too, precisely because he was such an attractive, lively lad. He was perpetually a poor student and had gotten worse as time went on; he managed to graduate, however, because he had influential connections. During his last year at school he'd come into an inheritance of some two hundred serfs, and, since almost all the rest of us were poor, he'd even begun to brag. He was an extremely uncouth fellow, but a nice lad nonetheless, even when he was bragging. In spite of our superficial, fantastic, and high-flown notions of honor and pride, all of us, except for a very few, would fawn upon Zverkov, the more so the more he bragged. They didn't fawn for any advantage; they fawned simply because he was a man endowed by nature with gifts. Moreover, we'd somehow come to regard Zverkov as a cunning fellow and an expert on good manners. This latter point particularly infuriated me. I hated the shrill, self-confident tone of his voice, his adoration for his own witticisms, which were terribly stupid in spite of his bold tongue; I hated his handsome, stupid face (for which, however, I'd gladly have exchanged my own intelligent one), and the impudent bearing typical of officers during the 1840s. I hated the way he talked about his future successes with women. (He'd decided not to get involved with them yet, since he still hadn't received his officer's epaulettes; he awaited those epaulettes impatiently.) And he talked about all the duels he'd have to fight. I remember how once, although I was usually very taciturn, I suddenly clashed with Zverkov when, during our free time, he was discussing future exploits with his friends; getting a bit carried away with the game like a little puppy playing in the sun, he suddenly declared that not a single girl in his village would escape his attention—that it was his *droit de seigneur*,[3] and that if the peasants even dared protest, he'd have them all flogged, those bearded rascals; and he'd double their quit-rent.[4] Our louts applauded, but I attacked him—not out of any pity for the poor girls or their fathers, but simply because everyone else was applauding such a little insect. I got the better of him that time, but Zverkov, although stupid, was also cheerful and impudent. Therefore he laughed it off to such an extent that, in fact, I really didn't get the better of him. The laugh remained on his side. Later he got the better of me several times, but without malice, just so, in jest, in passing, in fun. I was filled with spite and hatred, but I didn't respond. After graduation he took a few steps toward me; I didn't object strongly because I found it flattering; but soon we came to a natural parting of the ways. Afterward I heard about his barrack-room successes as a lieutenant and about his *binges*. Then there were other rumors—about his *successes* in the service. He no longer bowed to me on the street; I suspected that he was afraid to compromise himself by acknowledging such an insignificant person as myself. I also saw him in the theater once, in the third tier, already sporting an officer's gold braids. He was fawning and grovelling before the daughters of some aged general. In those three years he'd let himself go, although he was still as handsome and agile as before; he sagged somehow and had begun to put on weight; it was clear that by the age of thirty he'd be totally flabby. So it was for this Zverkov, who was finally ready

3. Lord's privilege (French); the feudal lord's right to spend the first night with the bride of a newly married serf.   4. The annual sum paid in cash or produce by serfs to landowners for the right to farm their land in feudal Russia, as opposed to the *corvée*, a certain amount of labor owed.

to depart, that our schoolmates were organizing a farewell dinner. They'd kept up during these three years, although I'm sure that inwardly they didn't consider themselves on an equal footing with him.

One of Simonov's two guests was Ferfichkin, a Russified German, a short man with a face like a monkey, a fool who made fun of everybody, my bitterest enemy from the lower grades—a despicable, impudent show-off who affected the most ticklish sense of ambition, although, of course, he was a coward at heart. He was one of Zverkov's admirers and played up to him for his own reasons, frequently borrowing money from him. Simonov's other guest, Trudolyubov, was insignificant, a military man, tall, with a cold demeanor, rather honest, who worshipped success of any kind and was capable of talking only about promotions. He was a distant relative of Zverkov's, and that, silly to say, lent him some importance among us. He'd always regarded me as a nonentity; he treated me not altogether politely, but tolerably.

"Well, if each of us contributes seven rubles," said Trudolyubov, "with three of us that makes twenty-one altogether—we can have a good dinner. Of course, Zverkov won't have to pay."

"Naturally," Simonov agreed, "since we're inviting him."

"Do you really think," Ferfichkin broke in arrogantly and excitedly, just like an insolent lackey bragging about his master-the-general's medals, "do you really think Zverkov will let us pay for everything? He'll accept out of decency, but then he'll order *half a dozen bottles* on his own."

"What will the four of us do with half a dozen bottles?" asked Trudolyubov, only taking note of the number.

"So then, three of us plus Zverkov makes four, twenty-one rubles, in the Hôtel de Paris, tomorrow at five o'clock," concluded Simonov definitively, since he'd been chosen to make the arrangements.

"Why only twenty-one?" I asked in trepidation, even, apparently, somewhat offended. "If you count me in, you'll have twenty-eight rubles instead of twenty-one."

It seemed to me that to include myself so suddenly and unexpectedly would appear as quite a splendid gesture and that they'd all be smitten at once and regard me with respect.

"Do you really want to come, too?" Simonov inquired with displeasure, managing somehow to avoid looking at me. He knew me inside out.

It was infuriating that he knew me inside out.

"And why not? After all, I was his schoolmate, too, and I must admit that I even feel a bit offended that you've left me out," I continued, just about to boil over again.

"And how were we supposed to find you?" Ferfichkin interjected rudely.

"You never got along very well with Zverkov," added Trudolyubov frowning. But I'd already latched on and wouldn't let go.

"I think no one has a right to judge that," I objected in a trembling voice, as if God knows what had happened. "Perhaps that's precisely why I want to take part now, since we didn't get along so well before."

"Well, who can figure you out . . . such lofty sentiments . . . ," Trudolyubov said with an ironic smile.

"We'll put your name down," Simonov decided, turning to me. "Tomorrow at five o'clock at the Hôtel de Paris. Don't make any mistakes."

"What about the money?" Ferfichkin started to say in an undertone to Simonov while nodding at me, but he broke off because Simonov looked embarrassed.

"That'll do," Trudolyubov said getting up. "If he really wants to come so much, let him."

"But this is our own circle of friends," Ferfichkin grumbled, also picking up his hat. "It's not an official gathering. Perhaps we really don't want you at all. . . ."

They left. Ferfichkin didn't even say goodbye to me as he went out; Trudolyubov barely nodded without looking at me. Simonov, with whom I was left alone, was irritated and perplexed, and he regarded me in a strange way. He neither sat down nor invited me to.

"Hmmm . . . yes . . . , so, tomorrow. Will you contribute your share of the money now? I'm asking just to know for sure," he muttered in embarrassment.

I flared up; but in doing so, I remembered that I'd owed Simonov fifteen rubles for a very long time, which debt, moreover, I'd forgotten, but had also never repaid.

"You must agree, Simonov, that I couldn't have known when I came here . . . oh, what a nuisance, but I've forgotten. . . ."

He broke off and began to pace around the room in even greater irritation. As he paced, he began to walk on his heels and stomp more loudly.

"I'm not detaining you, am I?" I asked after a few moments of silence.

"Oh, no!" he replied with a start. "That is, in fact, yes. You see, I still have to stop by at . . . It's not very far from here . . . ," he added in an apologetic way with some embarrassment.

"Oh, good heavens! Why didn't you say so?" I exclaimed, seizing my cap; moreover I did so with a surprisingly familiar air, coming from God knows where.

"But it's really not far . . . only a few steps away . . . ," Simonov repeated, accompanying me into the hallway with a bustling air which didn't suit him well at all. "So, then, tomorrow at five o'clock sharp!" he shouted to me on the stairs. He was very pleased that I was leaving. However, I was furious.

"What possessed me, what on earth possessed me to interfere?" I gnashed my teeth as I walked along the street. "And for such a scoundrel, a pig like Zverkov! Naturally, I shouldn't go. Of course, to hell with them. Am I bound to go, or what? Tomorrow I'll inform Simonov by post. . . ."

But the real reason I was so furious was that I was sure I'd go. I'd go on purpose. The more tactless, the more indecent it was for me to go, the more certain I'd be to do it.

There was even a definite impediment to my going: I didn't have any money. All I had was nine rubles. But of those, I had to hand over seven the next day to my servant Apollon for his monthly wages; he lived in and received seven rubles for his meals.

Considering Apollon's character it was impossible not to pay him. But more about that rascal, that plague of mine, later.

In any case, I knew that I wouldn't pay him his wages and that I'd definitely go.

That night I had the most hideous dreams. No wonder: all evening I was burdened with recollections of my years of penal servitude at school and I couldn't get rid of them. I'd been sent off to that school by distant relatives on whom I was dependent and about whom I've heard nothing since. They dispatched me, a lonely boy, crushed by their reproaches, already introspective, taciturn, and regarding everything around him savagely. My schoolmates received me with spiteful and pitiless jibes because I wasn't like any of them. But I couldn't tolerate their jibes; I couldn't possibly get along with them as easily as they got along with each other. I hated them all at once and took refuge from everyone in fearful, wounded and excessive pride. Their crudeness irritated me. Cynically they mocked my face and my awkward build; yet, what stupid faces they all had! Facial expressions at our school somehow degenerated and became particularly stupid. Many attractive lads had come to us, but in a few years they too were repulsive to look at. When I was only sixteen I wondered about them gloomily; even then I was astounded by the pettiness of their thoughts and the stupidity of their studies, games and conversations. They failed to understand essential things and took no interest in important, weighty subjects, so that I couldn't help considering them beneath me. It wasn't my wounded vanity that drove me to it; and, for God's sake, don't repeat any of those nauseating and hackneyed clichés, such as, "I was merely a dreamer, whereas they already understood life." They didn't understand a thing, not one thing about life, and I swear, that's what annoyed me most about them. On the contrary, they accepted the most obvious, glaring reality in a fantastically stupid way, and even then they'd begun to worship nothing but success. Everything that was just, but oppressed and humiliated, they ridiculed hard-heartedly and shamelessly. They mistook rank for intelligence; at the age of sixteen they were already talking about occupying comfortable little niches. Of course, much of this was due to their stupidity and the poor examples that had constantly surrounded them in their childhood and youth. They were monstrously depraved. Naturally, even this was more superficial, more affected cynicism; of course, their youth and a certain freshness shone through their depravity; but even this freshness was unattractive and manifested itself in a kind of rakishness. I hated them terribly, although, perhaps, I was even worse than they were. They returned the feeling and didn't conceal their loathing for me. But I no longer wanted their affection; on the contrary, I constantly longed for their humiliation. In order to avoid their jibes, I began to study as hard as I could on purpose and made my way to the top of the class. That impressed them. In addition, they all began to realize that I'd read certain books which they could never read and that I understood certain things (not included in our special course) about which they'd never even heard. They regarded this with savagery and sarcasm, but they submitted morally, all the more since even the teachers paid me some attention on this account. Their jibes ceased, but their hostility remained, and relations between us became cold and strained. In the end I myself couldn't stand it: as the years went by, my need for people, for friends, increased. I made several attempts to get closer to some of them; but these attempts always turned out to be unnatural and ended of their own accord. Once I even had a friend of sorts. But I was already a despot at heart; I wanted to exercise unlimited power over his soul; I wanted to instill in him contempt for his surroundings; and I demanded from him a disdainful and definitive break with those surroundings. I frightened him with my passionate friendship, and I reduced him to tears and convulsions. He was a naive and giving soul, but as soon as he'd surrendered himself to me totally, I began to despise him and reject him immediately—as if I only needed to achieve a victory over him, merely to subjugate him. But I was unable to conquer them all; my one friend was not at all like them, but rather a rare exception. The first thing I did upon leaving school was abandon the special job in the civil service for which I'd been trained, in order to sever all ties, break with my past, cover it over with dust. . . . The devil only knows why, after all that, I'd dragged myself over to see this Simonov! . . .

Early the next morning I roused myself from bed, jumped up in anxiety, just as if everything was about to start happening all at once. But I believed that some radical change in my life was imminent and was sure to occur that very day. Perhaps because I wasn't used to it, but all my life, at any external event, albeit a trivial one, it always seemed that some sort of radical change would occur. I went off to work as usual, but returned home two hours earlier in order to prepare. The most important thing, I thought, was not to arrive there first, or else they'd all think I was too eager. But there were thousands of most important things, and they all reduced me to the point of impotence. I polished my boots once again with my own hands. Apollon wouldn't polish them twice in one day for anything in the world; he considered it indecent. So I polished them myself, after stealing the brushes from the hallway so that he wouldn't notice and then despise me for it afterward. Next I carefully examined my clothes and found that everything was old, shabby, and worn out. I'd become too slovenly. My uniform was in better shape, but I couldn't go to dinner in a uniform. Worst of all, there was an enormous yellow stain on the knee of my trousers. I had an inkling that the spot alone would rob me of nine-tenths of my dignity. I also knew that it was unseemly for me to think that. "But this isn't the time for thinking. Reality is now looming," I thought, and my heart sank. I also knew perfectly well at that time, that I was monstrously exaggerating all these facts. But what could be done? I was no longer able to control myself, and was shaking with fever. In despair I imagined how haughtily and coldly that "scoundrel" Zverkov would greet me; with what dull and totally relentless contempt that dullard Trudolyubov would regard me; how nastily and impudently that insect Ferfichkin would giggle at me in order to win Zverkov's approval; how well Simonov would understand all this and how he'd despise me for my wretched vanity and cowardice; and worst of all, how petty all this would be, not *literary*, but commonplace. Of course, it would have been better not to go at all. But that was no longer possible; once I began to feel drawn to something, I plunged right in, head first. I'd have reproached myself for the rest of my life: "So, you retreated, you retreated before reality, you retreated!" On the contrary, I desperately wanted to prove to all this "rabble" that I really wasn't the coward I imagined myself to be. But that's not all: in the strongest paroxysm of cowardly fever I dreamt of gaining the upper hand, of conquering them, of carrying them away, compelling them to love me—if only "for the nobility of my thought and my indisputable wit." They would abandon Zverkov; he'd sit by in silence and embarassment, and I'd crush him. Afterward, perhaps, I'd be reconciled with Zverkov and drink to our *friendship*, but what was most spiteful and insulting for me was that I knew even then, I knew completely and for sure, that I didn't need any of this at all; that in fact I really didn't want to crush them, conquer them, or attract them, and that if I could have ever achieved all that, I'd be the first to say that it wasn't worth a damn. Oh, how I prayed to God that this day would pass quickly! With inexpressible anxiety I approached the window, opened the transom,[5] and peered out into the murky mist of the thickly falling wet snow. . . .

At last my worthless old wall clock sputtered out five o'clock. I grabbed my hat, and, trying not to look at Apollon—who'd been waiting since early morning to receive his wages, but didn't want to be the first one to mention it out of pride—I slipped out the door past him and intentionally hired a smart cab with my last half-ruble in order to arrive at the Hôtel de Paris in style.

IV

I knew since the day before that I'd be the first one to arrive. But it was no longer a question of who was first.

Not only was no one else there, but I even had difficulty finding our room. The table hadn't even been set. What did it all mean? After many inquiries I finally learned from the waiters that dinner had been ordered for closer to six o'clock, instead of five. This was also confirmed in the buffet. It was too embarrassing to ask any more questions. It was still only twenty-five minutes past five. If they'd changed the time, they should have let me know; that's what the city mail was for. They shouldn't have subjected me to such "shame" in my own eyes and . . . and, at least not in front of the waiters. I sat down. A waiter began to set the table. I felt even more ashamed in his presence. Toward six o'clock candles were brought into the room in addition to the lighted lamps already there, yet it hadn't occurred to the waiters to bring them in as soon as I'd arrived. In the next room two gloomy customers, angry-looking and silent, were dining at separate tables. In one of the distant rooms there was a great deal of noise, even shouting. One could hear the laughter of a whole crowd of people, including nasty little squeals in French—there were ladies present at that dinner. In short, it was disgusting. Rarely had I passed a more unpleasant hour, so that when they all arrived together precisely at six o'clock, I was initially overjoyed to see them, as if they were my liberators, and I almost forgot that I was supposed to appear offended.

Zverkov, obviously the leader, entered ahead of the rest. Both he and they were laughing; but, upon seeing me, Zverkov drew himself up, approached me unhurriedly, bowed slightly from the waist almost coquettishly, and extended his hand politely, but not too, with a kind of careful civility, almost as if he were a general both offering his hand, but also guarding against something. I'd imagined, on the contrary, that as soon as he entered he'd burst into his former, shrill laughter with occasional squeals, and that he'd immediately launch into his stale jokes and witticisms. I'd been preparing for them since the previous evening; but in no way did I expect such condescension, such courtesy characteristic of a general. Could it be that he now considered himself so immeasurably superior to me in all respects? If he'd merely wanted to offend me by this superior attitude, it wouldn't have been so bad, I thought; I'd manage to pay him back somehow. But what if, without any desire to offend, the notion had crept into his dumb sheep's

5. A small hinged pane in the window of a Russian house, used for ventilation especially during the winter when the main part of the window is sealed.

brain that he really was immeasurably superior to me and that he could only treat me in a patronizing way? From this possibility alone I began to gasp for air.

"Have you been waiting long?" Trudolyubov asked.

"I arrived at five o'clock sharp, just as I was told yesterday," I answered loudly and with irritation presaging an imminent explosion.

"Didn't you let him know that we changed the time?" Trudolyubov asked, turning to Simonov.

"No, I didn't. I forgot," he replied, but without any regret; then, not even apologizing to me, he went off to order the hors d'oeuvres.

"So you've been here for a whole hour, you poor fellow!" Zverkov cried sarcastically, because according to his notions, this must really have been terribly amusing. That scoundrel Ferfichkin chimed in after him with nasty, ringing laughter that sounded like a dog's yapping. My situation seemed very amusing and awkward to him, too.

"It's not the least bit funny!" I shouted at Ferfichkin, getting more and more irritated. "The others are to blame, not me. They neglected to inform me. It's, it's, it's . . . simply preposterous."

"It's not only preposterous, it's more than that," muttered Trudolyubov, naively interceding on my behalf. "You're being too kind. It's pure rudeness. Of course, it wasn't intentional. And how could Simonov have . . . hmm!"

"If a trick like that had been played on me," said Ferfichkin, "I'd . . ." "Oh, you'd have ordered yourself something to eat," interrupted Zverkov, "or simply asked to have dinner served without waiting for the rest of us."

"You'll agree that I could've done that without asking anyone's permission," I snapped. "If I did wait, it was only because . . ."

"Let's be seated, gentlemen," cried Simonov upon entering. "Everything's ready. I can vouch for the champagne; it's excellently chilled. . . . Moreover, I didn't know where your apartment was, so how could I find you?" he said turning to me suddenly, but once again not looking directly at me. Obviously he was holding something against me. I suspect he got to thinking after what had happened yesterday.

Everyone sat down; I did, too. The table was round. Trudolyubov sat on my left, Simonov, on my right. Zverkov sat across; Ferfichkin, next to him, between Trudolyubov and him.

"Tell-l-l me now, are you . . . in a government department?" Zverkov continued to attend to me. Seeing that I was embarrassed, he imagined in earnest that he had to be nice to me, encouraging me to speak. "Does he want me to throw a bottle at his head, or what?" I thought in a rage. Unaccustomed as I was to all this, I was unnaturally quick to take offense.

"In such and such an office," I replied abruptly, looking at my plate.

"And . . . is it p-p-profitable? Tell-l-l me, what ma-a-de you decide to leave your previous position?"

"What ma-a-a-de me leave my previous position was simply that I wanted to," I dragged my words out three times longer than he did, hardly able to control myself. Ferfichkin snorted. Simonov looked at me ironically; Trudolyubov stopped eating and began to stare at me with curiosity.

Zverkov was jarred, but didn't want to show it.

"Well-l, and how is the support?"

"What support?"

"I mean, the s-salary?"

"Why are you cross-examining me?"

However, I told him right away what my salary was. I blushed terribly.

"That's not very much," Zverkov observed pompously.

"No, sir, it's not enough to dine in café-restaurants!" added Ferfichkin insolently.

"In my opinion, it's really very little," Trudolyubov observed in earnest.

"And how thin you've grown, how you've changed . . . since . . . ," Zverkov added, with a touch of venom now, and with a kind of impudent sympathy, examining me and my apparel.

"Stop embarrassing him," Ferfichkin cried with a giggle.

"My dear sir, I'll have you know that I'm not embarrassed," I broke in at last. "Listen! I'm dining in this 'café-restaurant' at my own expense, my own, not anyone else's; note that, Monsieur Ferfichkin."

"Wha-at? And who isn't dining at his own expense? You seem to be . . ." Ferfichkin seized hold of my words, turned as red as a lobster, and looked me straight in the eye with fury.

"Just so-o," I replied, feeling that I'd gone a bit too far, "and I suggest that it would be much better if we engaged in more intelligent conversation."

"It seems that you're determined to display your intelligence."

"Don't worry, that would be quite unnecessary here."

"What's all this cackling, my dear sir? Huh? Have you taken leave of your senses in that *duh*-partment of yours?"

"Enough, gentlemen, enough," cried Zverkov authoritatively.

"How stupid this is!" muttered Simonov.

"Really, it is stupid. We're gathered here in a congenial group to have a farewell dinner for our good friend, while you're still settling old scores," Trudolyubov said, rudely addressing only me. "You forced yourself upon us yesterday; don't disturb the general harmony now. . . ."

"Enough, enough," cried Zverkov. "Stop it, gentlemen, this'll never do. Let me tell you instead how I very nearly got married a few days ago . . ."

There followed some scandalous, libelous anecdote about how this gentleman very nearly got married a few days ago. There wasn't one word about marriage, however; instead, generals, colonels, and even gentlemen of the bed chamber figured prominently in the story, while Zverkov played the leading role among them all. Approving laughter followed; Ferfichkin even squealed.

Everyone had abandoned me by now, and I sat there completely crushed and humiliated.

"Good Lord, what kind of company is this for me?" I wondered. "And what a fool I've made of myself in front of them all! But I let Ferfichkin go too far. These numbskulls think they're doing me an honor by allowing me to sit with them at their table, when they don't understand that it's I who's done them the honor, and not the reverse. 'How thin I've grown! What clothes!' Oh, these damned trousers! Zverkov's already noticed the yellow spot on my knee. . . . What's the use? Right now, this very moment, I should stand up, take my hat, and simply leave without saying a single word. . . . Out of contempt! And tomorrow—I'll even be ready for a duel. Scoundrels! It's not the seven rubles I care about. But they may think that . . . To hell with it! I don't care about the seven rubles. I'm leaving at once! . . ."

Of course, I stayed.

In my misery I drank Lafite and sherry by the glassful. Being unaccustomed to it, I got drunk very quickly; the more intoxicated I became, the greater my annoyance. Suddenly I felt like offending them all in the most impudent manner—and then I'd leave. To seize the moment and show them all who I really was—let them say: even though he's ridiculous, he's clever . . . and . . . and . . . in short, to hell with them!

I surveyed them all arrogantly with my dazed eyes. But they seemed to have forgotten all about me. *They* were noisy, boisterous and merry. Zverkov kept on talking. I began to listen. He was talking about some magnificent lady whom he'd finally driven to make a declaration of love. (Of course, he was lying like a trooper.) He said that he'd been assisted in this matter particularly by a certain princeling, the hussar Kolya, who possessed some three thousand serfs.

"And yet, this same Kolya who has three thousand serfs hasn't even come to see you off," I said, breaking into the conversation suddenly. For a moment silence fell.

"You're drunk already," Trudolyubov said, finally deigning to notice me, and glancing contemptuously in my direction. Zverkov examined me in silence as if I were an insect. I lowered my eyes. Simonov quickly began to pour champagne.

Trudolyubov raised his glass, followed by everyone but me.

"To your health and to a good journey!" he cried to Zverkov. "To old times, gentlemen, and to our future, hurrah!"

Everyone drank up and pressed around to exchange kisses with Zverkov. I didn't budge; my full glass stood before me untouched.

"Aren't you going to drink?" Trudolyubov roared at me, having lost his patience and turning to me menacingly.

"I wish to make my own speech, all by myself . . . and then I'll drink, Mr. Trudolyubov."

"Nasty shrew!" Simonov muttered.

I sat up in my chair, feverishly seized hold of my glass, and prepared for something extraordinary, although I didn't know quite what I'd say.

"*Silence!*" cried Ferfichkin. "And now for some real intelligence!" Zverkov waited very gravely, aware of what was coming.

"Mr. Lieutenant Zverkov," I began, "you must know that I detest phrases, phrasemongers, and corsetted waists. . . . That's the first point; the second will follow."

Everyone stirred uncomfortably.

"The second point: I hate obscene stories and the men who tell them.[6] I especially hate the men who tell them!"

"The third point: I love truth, sincerity and honesty," I continued almost automatically, because I was beginning to become numb with horror, not knowing how I could be speaking this way. . . . "I love thought, Monsieur Zverkov. I love genuine comradery, on an equal footing, but not . . . hmmm . . . I love . . . But, after all, why not? I too will drink to your health, Monsieur Zverkov. Seduce those Circassian[7] maidens, shoot the enemies of the fatherland, and . . . and . . . To your health, Monsieur Zverkov!"

---

6. A phrase borrowed from the inveterate liar Nozdryov, one of the provincial landowners in the first volume of Gogol's *Dead Souls* (1842).   7. A Muslim people inhabiting a region in the northern Caucasus.

Zverkov rose from his chair, bowed, and said: "I'm most grateful."

He was terribly offended and had even turned pale.

"To hell with him," Trudolyubov roared, banging his fist down on the table.

"No, sir, people should be whacked in the face for saying such things!" squealed Ferfichkin.

"We ought to throw him out!" muttered Simonov.

"Not a word, gentlemen, not a move!" Zverkov cried triumphantly, putting a stop to this universal indignation. "I'm grateful to you all, but I can show him myself how much I value his words."

"Mr. Ferfichkin, tomorrow you'll give me satisfaction for the words you've just uttered!" I said loudly, turning to Ferfichkin with dignity.

"Do you mean a duel? Very well," he replied, but I must have looked so ridiculous as I issued my challenge, it must have seemed so out of keeping with my entire appearance, that everyone, including Ferfichkin, collapsed into laughter.

"Yes, of course, throw him out! Why, he's quite drunk already," Trudolyubov declared in disgust.

"I shall never forgive myself for letting him join us," Simonov muttered again.

"Now's the time to throw a bottle at the lot of them," I thought. So I grabbed a bottle and . . . poured myself another full glass.

" . . . No, it's better to sit it out to the very end!" I went on thinking. "You'd be glad, gentlemen, if I left. But nothing doing! I'll stay here deliberately and keep on drinking to the very end, as a sign that I accord you no importance whatsoever. I'll sit here and drink because this is a tavern, and I've paid good money to get in. I'll sit here and drink because I consider you to be so many pawns, nonexistent pawns. I'll sit here and drink . . . and sing too, if I want to, yes, sir, I'll sing because I have the right to . . . sing . . . hmm."

But I didn't sing. I just tried not to look at any of them; I assumed the most carefree poses and waited impatiently until they would be the first to speak to me. But, alas, they did not. How much, how very much I longed to be reconciled with them at that moment! The clock struck eight, then nine. They moved from the table to the sofa. Zverkov sprawled on the couch, placing one foot on the round table. They brought the wine over, too. He really had ordered three bottles at his own expense. Naturally, he didn't invite me to join them. Everyone surrounded him on the sofa. They listened to him almost with reverence. It was obvious they liked him. "What for? What for?" I wondered to myself. From time to time they were moved to drunken ecstasy and exchanged kisses. They talked about the Caucasus, the nature of true passion, card games, profitable positions in the service; they talked about the income of a certain hussar Podkharzhevsky, whom none of them knew personally, and they rejoiced that his income was so large; they talked about the unusual beauty and charm of Princess D., whom none of them had ever seen; finally, they arrived at the question of Shakespeare's immortality.

I smiled contemptuously and paced up and down the other side of the room, directly behind the sofa, along the wall from the table to the stove and back again. I wanted to show them with all my might that I could get along without them; meanwhile, I deliberately stomped my boots, thumping my heels. But all this was in vain. *They* paid me no attention. I had the forbearance to pace like that, right in front of them, from eight o'clock until eleven, in the very same place, from the table to the stove and from the stove back to the table. "I'm pacing just as I please, and no one can stop me." A waiter who came into the room paused several times to look at me; my head was spinning from all those turns; there were moments when it seemed that I was delirious. During those three hours I broke out in a sweat three times and then dried out. At times I was pierced to the heart with a most profound, venomous thought: ten years would pass, twenty, forty; and still, even after forty years, I'd remember with loathing and humiliation these filthiest, most absurd, and horrendous moments of my entire life. It was impossible to humiliate myself more shamelessly or more willingly, and I fully understood that, fully; nevertheless, I continued to pace from the table to the stove and back again. "Oh, if you only knew what thoughts and feelings I'm capable of, and how cultured I really am!" I thought at moments, mentally addressing the sofa where my enemies were seated. But my enemies behaved as if I weren't even in the room. Once, and only once, they turned to me, precisely when Zverkov started in about Shakespeare, and I suddenly burst into contemptuous laughter. I snorted so affectedly and repulsively that they broke off their conversation immediately and stared at me in silence for about two minutes, in earnest, without laughing, as I paced up and down, from the table to the stove, while *I paid not the slightest bit of attention to them*. But nothing came of it; they didn't speak to me. A few moments later they abandoned me again. The clock struck eleven.

"Gentlemen," exclaimed Zverkov, getting up from the sofa, "Now let's all go *to that place*."[8]

"Of course, of course!" the others replied.

I turned abruptly to Zverkov. I was so exhausted, so broken, that I'd have slit my own throat to be done with all this! I was feverish; my hair, which had been soaked through with sweat, had dried and now stuck to my forehead and temples.

"Zverkov, I ask your forgiveness," I said harshly and decisively. "Ferfichkin, yours too, and everyone's, everyone's. I've insulted you all!" "Aha! So a duel isn't really your sort of thing!" hissed Ferfichkin venomously.

His remark was like a painful stab to my heart.

"No, I'm not afraid of a duel, Ferfichkin! I'm ready to fight with you tomorrow, even after we're reconciled. I even insist upon it, and you can't refuse me. I want to prove that I'm not afraid of a duel. You'll shoot first, and I'll fire into the air."

"He's amusing himself," Simonov observed.

"He's simply taken leave of his senses!" Trudolyubov added.

"Allow us to pass; why are you blocking our way? . . . Well, what is it you want?" Zverkov asked contemptuously. They were all flushed, their eyes glazed. They'd drunk a great deal.

"I ask for your friendship, Zverkov, I've insulted you, but . . . ."

"Insulted me? You? In-sul-ted me? My dear sir, I want you to know that never, under any circumstances, could you possibly insult *me*!"

"And that's enough from you. Out of the way!" Trudolyubov added. "Let's go."

"Olympia is mine, gentlemen, that's agreed!" cried Zverkov.

"We won't argue, we won't," they replied, laughing.

I stood there as if spat on. The party left the room noisily, and Trudolyubov struck up a stupid song. Simonov remained behind for a brief moment to tip the waiters. All of a sudden I went up to him.

"Simonov! Give me six rubles," I said decisively and desperately.

He looked at me in extreme amazement with his dulled eyes. He was drunk, too.

"Are you really going *to that place* with us?"

"Yes!"

"I have no money!" he snapped; then he laughed contemptuously and headed out of the room.

I grabbed hold of his overcoat. It was a nightmare.

"Simonov! I know that you have some money. Why do you refuse me? Am I really such a scoundrel? Beware of refusing me: if you only knew, if you only knew why I'm asking. Everything depends on it, my entire future, all my plans. . . ."

Simonov took out the money and almost threw it at me.

"Take it, if you have no shame!" he said mercilessly, then ran out to catch up with the others.

I remained behind for a minute. The disorder, the leftovers, a broken glass on the floor, spilled wine, cigarette butts, drunkenness and delirium in my head, agonizing torment in my heart; and finally, a waiter who'd seen and heard everything and who was now looking at me with curiosity.

"To that place!" I cried. "Either they'll all fall on their knees, embracing me, begging for my friendship, or . . . or else, I'll give Zverkov a slap in the face."

V

"So here it is, here it is at last, a confrontation with reality," I muttered, rushing headlong down the stairs. "This is no longer the Pope leaving Rome and going to Brazil; this is no ball on the shores of Lake Como!"

"You're a scoundrel," the thought flashed through my mind, "if you laugh at that now."

"So what!" I cried in reply. "Everything is lost now, anyway!"

There was no sign of them, but it didn't matter. I knew where they were going.

At the entrance stood a solitary, late-night cabby in a coarse peasant coat powdered with wet, seemingly warm snow that was still falling. It was steamy and stuffy outside. The little shaggy piebald nag was also dusted with snow and was coughing; I remember that very well. I headed for the rough-hewn sledge; but as soon as I raised one foot to get in, the recollection of how Simonov had just given me six rubles hit me with such force that I tumbled into the sledge like a sack.

"No! There's a lot I have to do to make up for that!" I cried. "But make up for it I will or else I'll perish on the spot this very night. Let's go!" We set off. There was an entire whirlwind spinning around inside my head.

"They won't fall on their knees to beg for my friendship. That's a mirage, an indecent mirage, disgusting, romantic, and fantastic; it's just like the ball on the shores of Lake Como. Consequently, I *must* give Zverkov a slap in the face! I am obligated to do it. And so, it's all decided; I'm rushing there to give him a slap in the face."

"Hurry up!"

The cabby tugged at the reins.

"As soon as I go in, I'll slap him. Should I say a few words first before I slap him in the face? No! I'll simply go in and slap him. They'll all be sitting there in the drawing room; he'll be on the sofa with Olympia. That damned Olympia! She once ridiculed my face and refused me. I'll drag Olympia around by the hair and Zverkov by the ears. No, better grab one ear and lead him around the room like that. Perhaps they'll begin to beat me, and then they'll throw me out. That's even likely. So what? I'll still have slapped him first; the initiative will be mine. According to the laws of honor, that's all that matters. He'll be branded, and nothing can wipe away that slap except a duel.[9] He'll have to fight. So just let them beat me now! Let them, the ingrates! Trudolyubov will hit me hardest, he's so strong. Ferfichkin will sneak up alongside and will undoubtedly grab my hair, I'm sure he will. But let them, let them. That's why I've come. At last these blockheads will be forced to grasp the tragedy in all this! As they drag me to the door, I'll tell them that they really aren't even worth the tip of my little finger!"

"Hurry up, driver, hurry up!" I shouted to the cabby.

He was rather startled and cracked his whip. I'd shouted very savagely.

"We'll fight at daybreak, and that's settled. I'm through with the department. Ferfichkin recently said duh-partment, instead of department. But where will I get pistols? What nonsense! I'll take my salary in advance and buy them. And powder? Bullets? That's what the second will attend to. And how will I manage to do all this by daybreak? And where will I find a second? I have no acquaintances. . . ."

"Nonsense!" I shouted, whipping myself up into even more of a frenzy, "Nonsense!"

"The first person I meet on the street will have to act as my second, just as he would pull a drowning man from the water. The most extraordinary possibilities have to be allowed for. Even if tomorrow I were to ask the director himself to act as my second, he too would have to agree merely out of a sense of chivalry, and he would keep it a secret! Anton Antonych . . ."

The fact of the matter was that at that very moment I was more clearly and vividly aware than anyone else on earth of the disgusting absurdity of my intentions and the whole opposite side of the coin, but . . .

"Hurry up, driver, hurry, you rascal, hurry up!"

"Hey, sir!" that son of the earth replied.

A sudden chill came over me.

"Wouldn't it be better . . . wouldn't it be better . . . to go straight home right now? Oh, my God! Why, why did I invite myself to that dinner yesterday? But no, it's impossible. And my pacing for three hours from the table to the stove? No, they, and no one else will have to pay me back for that pacing! They must wipe out that disgrace!"

"Hurry up!"

"What if they turn me over to the police? They wouldn't dare! They'd be afraid of a scandal. And what if Zverkov refuses the duel out of contempt? That's even likely; but I'll show them. . . . I'll rush to the posting station when he's supposed to leave tomorrow; I'll grab hold of his leg, tear off his overcoat just as he's about to climb into the carriage. I'll fasten my teeth on his arm and bite him. 'Look, everyone, see what a desperate man can be driven to!'

9. Duels as a means of resolving points of honor were officially discouraged but still fairly common.

Let him hit me on the head while others hit me from behind. I'll shout to the whole crowd, 'Behold, here's a young puppy who's going off to charm Circassian maidens with my spit on his face!' "

"Naturally, it'll all be over after that. The department will banish me from the face of the earth. They'll arrest me, try me, drive me out of the service, send me to prison; ship me off to Siberia for resettlement. Never mind! Fifteen years later when they let me out of jail, a beggar in rags, I'll drag myself off to see him. I'll find him in some provincial town. He'll be married and happy. He'll have a grown daughter. . . . I'll say, 'Look, you monster, look at my sunken cheeks and my rags. I've lost everything—career, happiness, art, science, a *beloved woman*—all because of you. Here are the pistols. I came here to load my pistol, and . . . and I forgive you.' Then I'll fire into the air, and he'll never hear another word from me again. . . ."

I was actually about to cry, even though I knew for a fact at that very moment that all this was straight out of Silvio and Lermontov's *Masquerade*.[1] Suddenly I felt terribly ashamed, so ashamed that I stopped the horse, climbed out of the sledge, and stood there amidst the snow in the middle of the street. The driver looked at me in amazement and sighed.

What was I to do? I couldn't go there—that was absurd; and I couldn't drop the whole thing, because then it would seem like . . . Oh, Lord! How could I drop it? After such insults!

"No!" I cried, throwing myself back into the sledge. "It's predestined; it's fate! Drive on, hurry up, *to that place!*"

In my impatience, I struck the driver on the neck with my fist.

"What's the matter with you? Why are you hitting me?" cried the poor little peasant, whipping his nag so that she began to kick up her hind legs.

Wet snow was falling in big flakes; I unbuttoned my coat, not caring about the snow. I forgot about everything else because now, having finally resolved on the slap, *I felt with horror that it was imminent* and that *nothing on earth could possibly stop it.* Lonely street lamps shone gloomily in the snowy mist like torches at a funeral. Snow got in under my overcoat, my jacket, and my necktie, and melted there. I didn't button up; after all, everything was lost, anyway. At last we arrived. I jumped out, almost beside myself, ran up the stairs, and began to pound at the door with my hands and feet. My legs, especially my knees, felt terribly weak. The door opened rather quickly; it was as if they knew I was coming. (In fact, Simonov had warned them that there might be someone else, since at this place one had to give notice and in general take precautions. It was one of those "fashionable shops" of the period that have now been eliminated by the police. During the day it really was a shop; but in the evening men with recommendations were able to visit as guests.) I walked rapidly through the darkened shop into a familiar drawing-room where there was only one small lit candle, and I stopped in dismay: there was no one there.

"Where are they?" I asked.

Naturally, by now they'd all dispersed. . . .

Before me stood a person with a stupid smile, the madam herself, who knew me slightly. In a moment a door opened, and another person came in. Without paying much attention to anything, I walked around the room,

---

1. A drama by Mikhail Lermontov (1835) about romantic conventions of love and honor. Silvio is the protagonist of Alexander Pushkin's short story *The Shot* (1830), about a man dedicated to revenge. Both works conclude with bizarre twists.

and, apparently, was talking to myself. It was as if I'd been delivered from death, and I felt it joyously in my whole being. I'd have given him the slap, certainly, I'd certainly have given him the slap. But now they weren't here and . . . everything had vanished, everything had changed! . . . I looked around. I still couldn't take it all in. I glanced up mechanically at the girl who'd come in: before me there flashed a fresh, young, slightly pale face with straight dark brows and a serious, seemingly astonished look. I liked that immediately; I would have hated her if she'd been smiling. I began to look at her more carefully, as though with some effort: I'd still not managed to collect my thoughts. There was something simple and kind in her face, but somehow it was strangely serious. I was sure that she was at a disadvantage as a result, and that none of those fools had even noticed her. She couldn't be called a beauty, however, even though she was tall, strong, and well built. She was dressed very simply. Something despicable took hold of me; I went up to her. . . .

I happened to glance into a mirror. My overwrought face appeared extremely repulsive: it was pale, spiteful and mean; and my hair was dishevelled. "It doesn't matter. I'm glad," I thought. "In fact, I'm even delighted that I'll seem so repulsive to her; that pleases me. . . ."

VI

Somewhere behind a partition a clock was wheezing as if under some strong pressure, as though someone were strangling it. After this unnaturally prolonged wheezing there followed a thin, nasty, somehow unexpectedly hurried chime, as if someone had suddenly leapt forward. It struck two. I recovered, although I really hadn't been asleep, only lying there half-conscious.

It was almost totally dark in the narrow, cramped, low-ceilinged room, which was crammed with an enormous wardrobe and cluttered with cartons, rags, and all sorts of old clothes. The candle burning on the table at one end of the room flickered faintly from time to time, and almost went out completely. In a few moments total darkness would set in.

It didn't take long for me to come to my senses; all at once, without any effort, everything returned to me, as though it had been lying in ambush ready to pounce on me again. Even in my unconscious state some point had constantly remained in my memory, never to be forgotten, around which my sleepy visions had gloomily revolved. But it was a strange thing: everything that had happened to me that day now seemed, upon awakening, to have occurred in the distant past, as if I'd long since left it all behind.

My mind was in a daze. It was as though something were hanging over me, provoking, agitating, and disturbing me. Misery and bile were welling inside me, seeking an outlet. Suddenly I noticed beside me two wide-open eyes, examining me curiously and persistently. The gaze was coldly detached, sullen, as if belonging to a total stranger. I found it oppressive.

A dismal thought was conceived in my brain and spread throughout my whole body like a nasty sensation, such as one feels upon entering a damp, mouldy underground cellar. It was somehow unnatural that only now these two eyes had decided to examine me. I also recalled that during the course of the last two hours I hadn't said one word to this creature, and that I had considered it quite unnecessary; that had even given me pleasure for some reason. Now I'd suddenly realized starkly how absurd, how revolting as a spider, was the idea of debauchery, which, without love, crudely and shamelessly begins precisely at the point where genuine love is consummated. We looked at each other in this way for some time, but she didn't lower her gaze before mine, nor did she alter her stare, so that finally, for some reason, I felt very uneasy.

"What's your name?" I asked abruptly, to put an end to it quickly.

"Liza," she replied, almost in a whisper, but somehow in a very unfriendly way; and she turned her eyes away.

I remained silent.

"The weather today . . . snow . . . foul!" I observed, almost to myself, drearily placing one arm behind my head and staring at the ceiling.

She didn't answer. The whole thing was obscene.

"Are you from around here?" I asked her a moment later, almost angrily, turning my head slightly toward her.

"No."

"Where are you from?"

"Riga," she answered unwillingly.

"German?"

"No, Russian."

"Have you been here long?"

"Where?"

"In this house."

"Two weeks." She spoke more and more curtly. The candle had gone out completely; I could no longer see her face.

"Are your mother and father still living?"

"Yes . . . no . . . they are."

"Where are they?"

"There . . . in Riga."

"Who are they?"

"Just . . ."

"Just what? What do they do?"

"Tradespeople."

"Have you always lived with them?"

"Yes."

"How old are you?"

"Twenty."

"Why did you leave them?"

"Just because . . ."

That "just because" meant: leave me alone, it makes me sick. We fell silent.

Only God knows why, but I didn't leave. I too started to feel sick and more depressed. Images of the previous day began to come to mind all on their own, without my willing it, in a disordered way. I suddenly recalled a scene that I'd witnessed on the street that morning as I was anxiously hurrying to work. "Today some people were carrying a coffin and nearly dropped it," I suddenly said aloud, having no desire whatever to begin a conversation, but just so, almost accidentally.

"A coffin?"

"Yes, in the Haymarket; they were carrying it up from an underground cellar."

"From a cellar?"

"Not a cellar, but from a basement . . . well, you know . . . from downstairs . . . from a house of ill repute . . . There was such filth all around. . . . Eggshells, garbage . . . it smelled foul . . . it was disgusting."

Silence.

"A nasty day to be buried!" I began again to break the silence.

"Why nasty?"

"Snow, slush . . ." (I yawned.)

"It doesn't matter," she said suddenly after a brief silence.

"No, it's foul. . . ." (I yawned again.) "The grave diggers must have been cursing because they were getting wet out there in the snow. And there must have been water in the grave."

"Why water in the grave?" she asked with some curiosity, but she spoke even more rudely and curtly than before. Something suddenly began to goad me on.

"Naturally, water on the bottom, six inches or so. You can't ever dig a dry grave at Volkovo cemetery."

"Why not?"

"What do you mean, why not? The place is waterlogged. It's all swamp. So they bury them right in the water. I've seen it myself . . . many times. . . ."

(I'd never seen it, and I'd never been to Volkovo cemetery, but I'd heard about it from other people.)

"Doesn't it matter to you if you die?"

"Why should I die?" she replied, as though defending herself.

"Well, someday you'll die; you'll die just like that woman did this morning. She was a . . . she was also a young girl . . . she died of consumption."

"The wench should have died in the hospital. . . ." (She knows all about it, I thought, and she even said "wench" instead of "girl.")

"She owed money to her madam," I retorted, more and more goaded on by the argument. "She worked right up to the end, even though she had consumption. The cabbies standing around were chatting with the soldiers, telling them all about it. Her former acquaintances, most likely. They were all laughing. They were planning to drink to her memory at the tavern." (I invented a great deal of this.)

Silence, deep silence. She didn't even stir.

"Do you think it would be better to die in a hospital?"

"Isn't it just the same? . . . Besides, why should I die?" she added irritably.

"If not now, then later?"

"Well, then later . . ."

"That's what you think! Now you're young and pretty and fresh—that's your value. But after a year of this life, you won't be like that any more; you'll fade."

"In a year?"

"In any case, after a year your price will be lower," I continued, gloating. "You'll move out of here into a worse place, into some other house. And a year later, into a third, each worse and worse, and seven years from now you'll end up in a cellar on the Haymarket. Even that won't be so bad. The real trouble will come when you get some disease, let's say a weakness in the chest . . . or you catch cold or something. In this kind of life it's no laughing matter to get sick. It takes hold of you and may never let go. And so, you die."

"Well, then, I'll die," she answered now quite angrily and stirred quickly.

"That'll be a pity."

"For what?"

"A pity to lose a life."

Silence.

"Did you have a sweetheart? Huh?"

"What's it to you?"

"Oh, I'm not interrogating you. What do I care? Why are you angry? Of course, you may have had your own troubles. What's it to me? Just the same, I'm sorry."

"For whom?"

"I'm sorry for you."

"No need . . . ," she whispered barely audibly and stirred once again.

That provoked me at once. What! I was being so gentle with her, while she . . .

"Well, and what do you think? Are you on the right path then?"

"I don't think anything."

"That's just the trouble—you don't think. Wake up, while there's still time. And there is time. You're still young and pretty; you could fall in love, get married, be happy.[2] . . ."

"Not all married women are happy," she snapped in her former, rude manner.

"Not all, of course, but it's still better than this. A lot better. You can even live without happiness as long as there's love. Even in sorrow life can be good; it's good to be alive, no matter how you live. But what's there besides . . . stench? Phew!"

I turned away in disgust; I was no longer coldly philosophizing. I began to feel what I was saying and grew excited. I'd been longing to expound these cherished *little ideas* that I'd been nurturing in my corner. Something had suddenly caught fire in me, some kind of goal had "manifested itself" before me.

"Pay no attention to the fact that I'm here. I'm no model for you. I may be even worse than you are. Moreover, I was drunk when I came here." I hastened nonetheless to justify myself. "Besides, a man is no example to a woman. It's a different thing altogether; even though I degrade and defile myself, I'm still no one's slave; if I want to leave, I just get up and go. I shake it all off and I'm a different man. But you must realize right from the start that you're a slave. Yes, a slave! You give away everything, all your freedom. Later, if you want to break this chain, you won't be able to; it'll bind you ever more tightly. That's the kind of evil chain it is. I know. I won't say anything else; you might not even understand me. But tell me this, aren't you already in debt to your madam? There, you see!" I added, even though she hadn't answered, but had merely remained silent; but she was listening with all her might. "There's your chain! You'll never buy yourself out. That's the way it's done. It's just like selling your soul to the devil. . . .

---

2. A popular theme treated by Gogol, Chernyshevsky, and Nekrasov, among others. Typically, an innocent and idealistic young man attempts to rehabilitate a prostitute or "fallen" woman.

"And besides . . . I may be just as unfortunate, how do you know, and I may be wallowing in mud on purpose, also out of misery. After all, people drink out of misery. Well, I came here out of misery. Now, tell me, what's so good about this place? Here you and I were . . . intimate . . . just a little while ago, and all that time we didn't say one word to each other; afterward you began to examine me like a wild creature, and I did the same. Is that the way people love? Is that how one person is supposed to encounter another? It's a disgrace, that's what it is!"

"Yes!" she agreed with me sharply and hastily. The haste of her answer surprised even me. It meant that perhaps the very same idea was flitting through her head while she'd been examining me earlier. It meant that she too was capable of some thought. . . . "Devil take it; this is odd, this *kinship*," I thought, almost rubbing my hands together. "Surely I can handle such a young soul."

It was the sport that attracted me most of all.

She turned her face closer to mine, and in the darkness it seemed that she propped her head up on her arm. Perhaps she was examining me. I felt sorry that I couldn't see her eyes. I heard her breathing deeply.

"Why did you come here?" I began with some authority.

"Just so . . ."

"But think how nice it would be living in your father's house! There you'd be warm and free; you'd have a nest of your own."

"And what if it's worse than that?"

"I must establish the right tone," flashed through my mind. "I won't get far with sentimentality."

However, that merely flashed through my mind. I swear that she really did interest me. Besides, I was somewhat exhausted and provoked. After all, artifice goes along so easily with feeling.

"Who can say?" I hastened to reply. "All sorts of things can happen. Why, I was sure that someone had wronged you and was more to blame than you are. After all, I know nothing of your life story, but a girl like you doesn't wind up in this sort of place on her own accord. . . ."

"What kind of a girl am I?" she whispered hardly audibly; but I heard it.

"What the hell! Now I'm flattering her. That's disgusting! But, perhaps it's a good thing. . . ." She remained silent.

"You see, Liza, I'll tell you about myself. If I'd had a family when I was growing up, I wouldn't be the person I am now. I think about this often. After all, no matter how bad it is in your own family—it's still your own father and mother, and not enemies or strangers. Even if they show you their love only once a year, you still know that you're at home. I grew up without a family; that must be why I turned out the way I did—so unfeeling."

I waited again.

"She might not understand," I thought. "Besides, it's absurd—all this moralizing."

"If I were a father and had a daughter, I think that I'd have loved her more than my sons, really," I began indirectly, talking about something else in order to distract her. I confess that I was blushing.

"Why's that?"

Ah, so she's listening!

"Just because. I don't know why, Liza. You see, I knew a father who was a stern, strict man, but he would kneel before his daughter and kiss her hands and feet; he couldn't get enough of her, really. She'd go dancing at a party, and he'd stand in one spot for five hours, never taking his eyes off her. He was crazy about her; I can understand that. At night she'd be tired and fall asleep, but he'd wake up, go in to kiss her, and make the sign of the cross over her while she slept. He used to wear a dirty old jacket and was stingy with everyone else, but would spend his last kopeck on her, buying her expensive presents; it afforded him great joy if she liked his presents. A father always loves his daughters more than their mother does. Some girls have a very nice time living at home. I think that I wouldn't even have let my daughter get married."

"Why not?" she asked with a barely perceptible smile.

"I'd be jealous, so help me God. Why, how could she kiss someone else? How could she love a stranger more than her own father? It's even painful to think about it. Of course, it's all nonsense; naturally, everyone finally comes to his senses. But I think that before I'd let her marry, I'd have tortured myself with worry. I'd have found fault with all her suitors. Nevertheless, I'd have ended up by allowing her to marry whomever she loved. After all, the one she loves always seems the worst of all to the father. That's how it is. That causes a lot of trouble in many families."

"Some are glad to sell their daughters, rather than let them marry honorably," she said suddenly.

Aha, so that's it!

"That happens, Liza, in those wretched families where there's neither God nor love," I retorted heatedly. "And where there's no love, there's also no good sense. There are such families, it's true, but I'm not talking about them. Obviously, from the way you talk, you didn't see much kindness in your own family. You must be very unfortunate. Hmm . . . But all this results primarily from poverty."

"And is it any better among the gentry? Honest folk live decently even in poverty."

"Hmmm . . . Yes. Perhaps. There's something else, Liza. Man only likes to count his troubles; he doesn't calculate his happiness. If he figured as he should, he'd see that everyone gets his share. So, let's say that all goes well in a particular family; it enjoys God's blessing, the husband turns out to be a good man, he loves you, cherishes you, and never leaves you. Life is good in that family. Sometimes, even though there's a measure of sorrow, life's still good. Where isn't there sorrow? If you choose to get married, *you'll find out for yourself.* Consider even the first years of a marriage to the one you love: what happiness, what pure bliss there can be sometimes! Almost without exception. At first even quarrels with your husband turn out well. For some women, the more they love their husbands, the more they pick fights with them. It's true; I once knew a woman like that. 'That's how it is,' she'd say. 'I love you very much and I'm tormenting you out of love, so that you'll feel it.' Did you know that one can torment a person intentionally out of love? It's mostly women who do that. Then she thinks to herself, 'I'll love him so much afterward, I'll be so affectionate, it's no sin to torment him a little now.' At home everyone would rejoice over you, and it would be so pleasant, cheerful, serene, and honorable. . . . Some other women are very jealous. If her husband goes away, I knew one like that, she can't stand it;

she jumps up at night and goes off on the sly to see. Is he there? Is he in that house? Is he with that one? Now that's bad. Even she herself knows that it's bad; her heart sinks and she suffers because she really loves him. It's all out of love. And how nice it is to make up after a quarrel, to admit one's guilt or forgive him! How nice it is for both of them, how good they both feel at once, just as if they'd met again, married again, and begun their love all over again. No one, no one at all has to know what goes on between a husband and wife, if they love each other. However their quarrel ends, they should never call in either one of their mothers to act as judge or to hear complaints about the other one. They must act as their own judges. Love is God's mystery and should be hidden from other people's eyes, no matter what happens. This makes it holier, much better. They respect each other more, and a great deal is based on this respect. And, if there's been love, if they got married out of love, why should love disappear? Can't it be sustained? It rarely happens that it can't be sustained. If the husband turns out to be a kind and honest man, how can the love disappear? The first phase of married love will pass, that's true, but it's followed by an even better kind of love. Souls are joined together and all their concerns are managed in common; there'll be no secrets from one another. When children arrive, each and every stage, even a very difficult one, will seem happy, as long as there's both love and courage. Even work is cheerful; even when you deny yourself bread for your children's sake, you're still happy. After all, they'll love you for it afterward; you're really saving for your own future. Your children will grow up, and you'll feel that you're a model for them, a support. Even after you die, they'll carry your thoughts and feelings all during their life. They'll take on your image and likeness, since they received it from you. Consequently, it's a great obligation. How can a mother and father keep from growing closer? They say it's difficult to raise children. Who says that? It's heavenly joy! Do you love little children, Liza? I love them dearly. You know—a rosy little boy, suckling at your breast; what husband's heart could turn against his wife seeing her sitting there holding his child? The chubby, rosy little baby sprawls and snuggles; his little hands and feet are plump; his little nails are clean and tiny, so tiny it's even funny to see them; his little eyes look as if he already understood everything. As he suckles, he tugs at your breast playfully with his little hand. When the father approaches, the child lets go of the breast, bends way back, looks at his father, and laughs—as if God only knows how funny it is—and then takes to suckling again. Afterward, when he starts cutting teeth, he'll sometimes bite his mother's breast; looking at her sideways his little eyes seem to say, 'See, I bit you!' Isn't this pure bliss—the three of them, husband, wife, and child, all together? You can forgive a great deal for such moments. No, Liza, I think you must first learn how to live by yourself, and only afterward blame others."

"It's by means of images," I thought to myself, "just such images that I can get to you," although I was speaking with considerable feeling, I swear it; and all at once I blushed. "And what if she suddenly bursts out laughing— where will I hide then?" That thought drove me into a rage. By the end of my speech I'd really become excited, and now my pride was suffering somehow. The silence lasted for a while. I even considered shaking her.

"Somehow you . . ." she began suddenly and then stopped.

But I understood everything already: something was trembling in her voice now, not shrill, rude or unyielding as before, but something soft and timid, so timid that I suddenly was rather ashamed to watch her and felt guilty.

"What?" I asked with tender curiosity.

"Well, you . . ."

"What?"

"You somehow . . . it sounds just like a book," she said, and once again something which was noticeably sarcastic was suddenly heard in her voice.

Her remark wounded me dreadfully. That's not what I'd expected.

Yet, I didn't understand that she was intentionally disguising her feelings with sarcasm; that was usually the last resort of people who are timid and chaste of heart, whose souls have been coarsely and impudently invaded; and who, until the last moment, refuse to yield out of pride and are afraid to express their own feelings to you. I should've guessed it from the timidity with which on several occasions she tried to be sarcastic, until she finally managed to express it. But I hadn't guessed, and a malicious impulse took hold of me.

"Just you wait," I thought.

VII

"That's enough, Liza. What do books have to do with it, when this disgusts me as an outsider? And not only as an outsider. All this has awakened in my heart . . . Can it be, can it really be that you don't find it repulsive here? No, clearly habit means a great deal. The devil only knows what habit can do to a person. But do you seriously think that you'll never grow old, that you'll always be pretty, and that they'll keep you on here forever and ever? I'm not even talking about the filth. . . . Besides, I want to say this about your present life: even though you're still young, good-looking, nice, with soul and feelings, do you know, that when I came to a little while ago, I was immediately disgusted to be here with you! Why, a man has to be drunk to wind up here. But if you were in a different place, living as nice people do, I might not only chase after you, I might actually fall in love with you. I'd rejoice at a look from you, let alone a word; I'd wait for you at the gate and kneel down before you; I'd think of you as my betrothed and even consider that an honor. I wouldn't dare have any impure thoughts about you. But here, I know that I need only whistle, and you, whether you want to or not, will come to me, and that I don't have to do your bidding, whereas you have to do mine. The lowliest peasant may hire himself out as a laborer, but he doesn't make a complete slave of himself; he knows that it's only for a limited term. But what's your term? Just think about it. What are you giving up here? What are you enslaving? Why, you're enslaving your soul, something you don't really own, together with your body! You're giving away your love to be defiled by any drunkard! Love! After all, that's all there is! It's a precious jewel, a maiden's treasure, that's what it is! Why, to earn that love a man might be ready to offer up his own soul, to face death. But what's your love worth now? You've been bought, all of you; and why should anyone strive for your love, when you offer everything even without it? Why, there's no greater insult for a girl, don't you understand? Now, I've heard that they console you foolish girls, they allow you to see your own lovers here. But that's merely child's play, deception, making fun of you, while you believe it. And do you

really think he loves you, that lover of yours? I don't believe it. How can he,
if he knows that you can be called away from him at any moment? He'd have
to be depraved after all that. Does he possess even one drop of respect for
you? What do you have in common with him? He's laughing at you and
stealing from you at the same time—so much for his love. It's not too bad,
as long as he doesn't beat you. But perhaps he does. Go on, ask him, if you
have such a lover, whether he'll ever marry you. Why, he'll burst out laughing
right in your face, if he doesn't spit at you or smack you. He himself may be
worth no more than a few lousy kopecks. And for what, do you think, did
you ruin your whole life here? For the coffee they give you to drink, or for
the plentiful supply of food? Why do you think they feed you so well? Another
girl, an honest one, would choke on every bite, because she'd know why she
was being fed so well. You're in debt here, you'll be in debt, and will remain
so until the end, until such time comes as the customers begin to spurn you.
And that time will come very soon; don't count on your youth. Why, here
youth flies by like a stagecoach. They'll kick you out. And they'll not merely
kick you out, but for a long time before that they'll pester you, reproach you,
and abuse you—as if you hadn't ruined your health for the madam, hadn't
given up your youth and your soul for her in vain, but rather, as if you'd
ruined her, ravaged her, and robbed her. And don't expect any support. Your
friends will also attack you to curry her favor, because they're all in bondage
here and have long since lost both conscience and pity. They've become
despicable, and there's nothing on earth more despicable, more repulsive, or
more insulting than their abuse. You'll lose everything here, everything, without exception—your health, youth, beauty, and hope—and at the age of
twenty-two you'll look as if you were thirty-five, and even that won't be too
awful if you're not ill. Thank God for that. Why, you probably think that
you're not even working, that it's all play! But there's no harder work or more
onerous task than this one in the whole world and there never has been. I'd
think that one's heart alone would be worn out by crying. Yet you dare not
utter one word, not one syllable; when they drive you out, you leave as if you
were the guilty one. You'll move to another place, then to a third, then somewhere else, and finally you'll wind up in the Haymarket. And there they'll
start beating you for no good reason at all; it's a local custom; the clients
there don't know how to be nice without beating you. You don't think it's so
disgusting there? Maybe you should go and have a look sometime, and see
it with your own eyes. Once, at New Year's, I saw a woman in a doorway.
Her own kind had pushed her outside as a joke, to freeze her for a little while
because she was wailing too much; they shut the door behind her. At nine
o'clock in the morning she was already dead drunk, dishevelled, half-naked,
and all beaten up. Her face was powdered, but her eyes were bruised; blood
was streaming from her nose and mouth; a certain cabby had just fixed her
up. She was sitting on a stone step, holding a piece of salted fish in her hand;
she was howling, wailing something about her 'fate,' and slapping the fish
against the stone step. Cabbies and drunken soldiers had gathered around
the steps and were taunting her. Don't you think you'll wind up the same
way? I wouldn't want to believe it myself, but how do you know, perhaps
eight or ten years ago this same girl, the one with the salted fish, arrived here
from somewhere or other, all fresh like a little cherub, innocent, and pure;
she knew no evil and blushed at every word. Perhaps she was just like you—

proud, easily offended, unlike all the rest; she looked like a queen and knew that total happiness awaited the man who would love her and whom she would also love. Do you see how it all ended? What if at the very moment she was slapping the fish against that filthy step, dead drunk and dishevelled, what if, even at that very moment she'd recalled her earlier, chaste years in her father's house when she was still going to school, and when her neighbor's son used to wait for her along the path and assure her that he'd love her all his life and devote himself entirely to her, and when they vowed to love one another forever and get married as soon as they grew up! No, Liza, you'd be lucky, very lucky, if you died quickly from consumption somewhere in a corner, in a cellar, like that other girl. In a hospital, you say? All right— they'll take you off, but what if the madam still requires your services? Consumption is quite a disease—it's not like dying from a fever. A person continues to hope right up until the last minute and declares that he's in good health. He consoles himself. Now that's useful for your madam. Don't worry, that's the way it is. You've sold your soul; besides, you owe her money—that means you don't dare say a thing. And while you're dying, they'll all abandon you, turn away from you—because there's nothing left to get from you. They'll even reproach you for taking up space for no good reason and for taking so long to die. You won't even be able to ask for something to drink, without their hurling abuse at you: 'When will you croak, you old bitch? You keep on moaning and don't let us get any sleep—and you drive our customers away.' That's for sure; I've overheard such words myself. And as you're breathing your last, they'll shove you into the filthiest corner of the cellar— into darkness and dampness; lying there alone, what will you think about then? After you die, some stranger will lay you out hurriedly, grumbling all the while, impatiently—no one will bless you, no one will sigh over you; they'll merely want to get rid of you as quickly as possible. They'll buy you a wooden trough and carry you out as they did that poor woman I saw today; then they'll go off to a tavern and drink to your memory. There'll be slush, filth, and wet snow in your grave—why bother for the likes of you? 'Let her down, Vanyukha; after all, it's her fate to go down with her legs up, that's the sort of girl she was. Pull up on that rope, you rascal!' 'It's okay like that.' 'How's it okay? See, it's lying on its side. Was she a human being or not? Oh, never mind, cover it up.' They won't want to spend much time arguing over you. They'll cover your coffin quickly with wet, blue clay and then go off to the tavern. . . . That'll be the end of your memory on earth; for other women, children will visit their graves, fathers, husbands—but for you—no tears, no sighs; no remembrances. No one, absolutely no one in the whole world, will ever come to visit you; your name will disappear from the face of the earth, just as if you'd never been born and had never existed. Mud and filth, no matter how you pound on the lid of your coffin at night when other corpses arise: 'Let me out, kind people, let me live on earth for a little while! I lived, but I didn't really see life; my life went down the drain; they drank it away in a tavern at the Haymarket; let me out, kind people, let me live in the world once again!' "

I was so carried away by my own pathos that I began to feel a lump forming in my throat, and . . . I suddenly stopped, rose up in fright, and, leaning over apprehensively, I began to listen carefully as my own heart pounded. There was cause for dismay.

For a while I felt that I'd turned her soul inside out and had broken her heart; the more I became convinced of this, the more I strived to reach my goal as quickly and forcefully as possible. It was the sport, the sport that attracted me; but it wasn't only the sport. . . .

I knew that I was speaking clumsily, artificially, even bookishly; in short, I didn't know how to speak except "like a book." But that didn't bother me, for I knew, I had a premonition, that I would be understood and that this bookishness itself might even help things along. But now, having achieved this effect, I suddenly lost all my nerve. No, never, never before had I witnessed such despair! She was lying there, her face pressed deep into a pillow she was clutching with her hands. Her heart was bursting. Her young body was shuddering as if she were having convulsions. Suppressed sobs shook her breast, tore her apart, and suddenly burst forth in cries and moans. Then she pressed her face even deeper into the pillow: she didn't want anyone, not one living soul, to hear her anguish and her tears. She bit the pillow; she bit her hand until it bled (I noticed that afterward); or else, thrusting her fingers into her dishevelled hair, she became rigid with the strain, holding her breath and clenching her teeth. I was about to say something, to ask her to calm down; but I felt that I didn't dare. Suddenly, all in a kind of chill, almost in a panic, I groped hurriedly to get out of there as quickly as possible. It was dark: no matter how I tried, I couldn't end it quickly. Suddenly I felt a box of matches and a candlestick with a whole unused candle. As soon as the room was lit up, Liza started suddenly, sat up, and looked at me almost senselessly, with a distorted face and a half-crazy smile. I sat down next to her and took her hands; she came to and threw herself at me, wanting to embrace me, yet not daring to. Then she quietly lowered her head before me.

"Liza, my friend, I shouldn't have . . . you must forgive me," I began, but she squeezed my hands so tightly in her fingers that I realized I was saying the wrong thing and stopped.

"Here's my address, Liza. Come to see me."

"I will," she whispered resolutely, still not lifting her head.

"I'm going now, good-bye . . . until we meet again."

I stood up; she did, too, and suddenly blushed all over, shuddered, seized a shawl lying on a chair, threw it over her shoulders, and wrapped herself up to her chin. After doing this, she smiled again somewhat painfully, blushed, and looked at me strangely. I felt awful. I hastened to leave, to get away.

"Wait," she said suddenly as we were standing in the hallway near the door, and she stopped me by putting her hand on my overcoat. She quickly put the candle down and ran off; obviously she'd remembered something or wanted to show me something. As she left she was blushing all over, her eyes were gleaming, and a smile had appeared on her lips—what on earth did it all mean? I waited against my own will; she returned a moment later with a glance that seemed to beg forgiveness for something. All in all it was no longer the same face or the same glance as before—sullen, distrustful, obstinate. Now her glance was imploring, soft, and, at the same time, trusting, affectionate, and timid. That's how children look at people whom they love very much, or when they're asking for something. Her eyes were light hazel, lovely, full of life, as capable of expressing love as brooding hatred.

Without any explanation, as if I were some kind of higher being who was supposed to know everything, she held a piece of paper out toward me. At that moment her whole face was shining with a most naive, almost childlike triumph. I unfolded the paper. It was a letter to her from some medical student containing a high-flown, flowery, but very respectful declaration of love. I don't remember the exact words now, but I can well recall the genuine emotion that can't be feigned shining through that high style. When I'd finished reading the letter, I met her ardent, curious, and childishly impatient gaze. She'd fixed her eyes on my face and was waiting eagerly to see what I'd say. In a few words, hurriedly, but with some joy and pride, she explained that she'd once been at a dance somewhere, in a private house, at the home of some "very, very good people, *family people*, where they *knew nothing*, nothing at all," because she'd arrived at this place only recently and was just . . . well, she hadn't quite decided whether she'd stay here and she'd certainly leave as soon as she'd paid off her debt. . . . Well, and this student was there; he danced with her all evening and talked to her. It turned out he was from Riga; he'd known her as a child, they'd played together, but that had been a long time ago; he was acquainted with her parents—but he knew nothing, absolutely nothing *about this place* and he didn't even suspect it! And so, the very next day, after the dance, (only some three days ago), he'd sent her this letter through the friend with whom she'd gone to the party . . . and . . . well, that's the whole story."

She lowered her sparkling eyes somewhat bashfully after she finished speaking.

The poor little thing, she'd saved this student's letter as a treasure and had run to fetch this one treasure of hers, not wanting me to leave without knowing that she too was the object of sincere, honest love, and that someone exists who had spoken to her respectfully. Probably that letter was fated to lie in her box without results. But that didn't matter; I'm sure that she'll guard it as a treasure her whole life, as her pride and vindication; and now, at a moment like this, she remembered it and brought it out to exult naively before me, to raise herself in my eyes, so that I could see it for myself and could also think well of her. I didn't say a thing; I shook her hand and left. I really wanted to get away. . . . I walked all the way home in spite of the fact that wet snow was still falling in large flakes. I was exhausted, oppressed, and perplexed. But the truth was already glimmering behind that perplexity. The ugly truth!

VIII

It was some time, however, before I agreed to acknowledge that truth. I awoke the next morning after a few hours of deep, leaden sleep. Instantly recalling the events of the previous day, even I was astonished at my *sentimentality* with Liza last night, at all of yesterday's "horror and pity." "Why, it's an attack of old woman's nervous hysteria, phew!" I decided. "And why on earth did I force my address on her? What if she comes? Then again, let her come, it doesn't make any difference. . . ." But *obviously* that was not the main, most important matter: I had to make haste and rescue at all costs my reputation in the eyes of Zverkov and Simonov. That was my main task. I even forgot all about Liza in the concerns of that morning.

First of all I had to repay last night's debt to Simonov immediately. I resolved on desperate means: I would borrow the sum of fifteen rubles from Anton Antonych. As luck would have it, he was in a splendid mood that morning and gave me the money at once, at my first request. I was so delighted that I signed a promissory note with a somewhat dashing air, and told him *casually* that on the previous evening "I'd been living it up with some friends at the Hôtel de Paris. We were holding a farewell dinner for a comrade, one might even say, a childhood friend, and, you know—he's a great carouser, very spoiled—well, naturally; he comes from a good family, has considerable wealth and a brilliant career; he's witty and charming, and has affairs with certain ladies, you understand. We drank up an extra 'half-dozen bottles' and . . ." There was nothing to it; I said all this very easily, casually, and complacently.

Upon arriving home I wrote to Simonov at once.

To this very day I recall with admiration the truly gentlemanly, good-natured, candid tone of my letter. Cleverly and nobly, and, above all, without unnecessary words, I blamed myself for everything. I justified myself, "if only I could be allowed to justify myself," by saying that, being so totally unaccustomed to wine, I'd gotten drunk with the first glass, which (supposedly) I'd consumed even before their arrival, as I waited for them in the Hôtel de Paris between the hours of five and six o'clock. In particular, I begged for Simonov's pardon; I asked him to convey my apology to all the others, especially to Zverkov, whom, "I recall, as if in a dream," it seems, I'd insulted. I added that I'd have called upon each of them, but was suffering from a bad headache, and, worst of all, I was ashamed. I was particularly satisfied by the "certain lightness," almost casualness (though, still very proper), unexpectedly reflected in my style; better than all possible arguments, it conveyed to them at once that I regarded "all of last night's unpleasantness" in a rather detached way, and that I was not at all, not in the least struck down on the spot as you, gentlemen, probably suspect. On the contrary, I regard this all serenely, as any self-respecting gentleman would. The true story, as they say, is no reproach to an honest young man.

"Why, there's even a hint of aristocratic playfulness in it," I thought admiringly as I reread my note. "And it's all because I'm such a cultured and educated man! Others in my place wouldn't know how to extricate themselves, but I've gotten out of it, and I'm having a good time once again, all because I'm an 'educated and cultured man of our time.' It may even be true that the whole thing occurred as a result of that wine yesterday. Hmmm . . . well, no, it wasn't really the wine. And I didn't have anything to drink between five and six o'clock when I was waiting for them. I lied to Simonov; it was a bold-faced lie—yet I'm not ashamed of it even now. . . ."

But, to hell with it, anyway! The main thing is, I got out of it.

I put six rubles in the letter, sealed it up, and asked Apollon to take it to Simonov. When he heard that there was money in it, Apollon became more respectful and agreed to deliver it. Toward evening I went out for a stroll. My head was still aching and spinning from the events of the day before. But as evening approached and twilight deepened, my impressions changed and became more confused, as did my thoughts. Something hadn't yet died within me, deep within my heart and conscience; it didn't want to die, and it expressed itself as burning anguish. I jostled my way along the more populous, commercial streets, along Meshchanskaya, Sadovaya, near the Yusupov Garden. I particularly liked to stroll along these streets at twilight, just as they became most crowded with all sorts of pedestrians, merchants, and tradesmen, with faces preoccupied to the point of hostility, on their way home from a hard day's work. It was precisely the cheap bustle that I liked, the crass prosaic quality. But this time all that street bustle irritated me even more. I couldn't get a hold of myself or puzzle out what was wrong. Something was rising, rising up in my soul continually, painfully, and didn't want to settle down. I returned home completely distraught. It was just as if some crime were weighing on my soul.

I was constantly tormented by the thought that Liza might come to see me. It was strange, but from all of yesterday's recollections, the one of her tormented me most, somehow separately from all the others. I'd managed to forget the rest by evening, to shrug everything off, and I still remained completely satisfied with my letter to Simonov. But in regard to Liza, I was not at all satisfied. It was as though I were tormented by her alone. "What if she comes?" I thought continually. "Well, so what? It doesn't matter. Let her come. Hmm. The only unpleasant thing is that she'll see, for instance, how I live. Yesterday I appeared before her such a . . . hero . . . but now, hmm! Besides, it's revolting that I've sunk so low. The squalor of my apartment. And I dared go to dinner last night wearing such clothes! And that oilcloth sofa of mine with its stuffing hanging out! And my dressing gown that doesn't quite cover me! What rags! . . . She'll see it all—and she'll see Apollon. That swine will surely insult her. He'll pick on her, just to be rude to me. Of course, I'll be frightened, as usual. I'll begin to fawn before her, wrap myself up in my dressing gown. I'll start to smile and tell lies. Ugh, the indecency! And that's not even the worst part! There's something even more important, nastier, meaner! Yes, meaner! Once again, I'll put on that dishonest, deceitful mask! . . ."

When I reached this thought, I simply flared up.

"Why deceitful? How deceitful? Yesterday I spoke sincerely. I recall that there was genuine feeling in me, too. I was trying no less than to arouse noble feelings in her . . . and if she wept, that's a good thing; it will have a beneficial effect. . . ."

But I still couldn't calm down.

All that evening, even after I returned home, even after nine o'clock, when by my calculations Liza could no longer have come, her image continued to haunt me, and, what's most important, she always appeared in one and the same form. Of all that had occurred yesterday, it was one moment in particular which stood out most vividly: that was when I lit up the room with a match and saw her pale, distorted face with its tormented gaze. What a pitiful, unnatural, distorted smile she'd had at that moment! But little did I know then that even fifteen years later I'd still picture Liza to myself with that same pitiful, distorted, and unnecessary smile which she'd had at that moment.

The next day I was once again prepared to dismiss all this business as nonsense, as the result of overstimulated nerves; but most of all, as exaggeration. I was well aware of this weakness of mine and sometimes was even afraid of it; "I exaggerate everything, that's my problem," I kept repeating to myself hour after hour. And yet, "yet, Liza may still come, all the same"; that was the refrain which concluded my reflections. I was so distressed that I sometimes became furious. "She'll come! She'll definitely come!" If not today, then tomorrow, she'll seek me out! That's just like the damned romanticism of all these *pure hearts*! Oh, the squalor, the stupidity, the narrowness of these "filthy, sentimental souls!" How could all this not be understood, how on earth could it not be understood? . . ." But at this point I would stop myself, even in the midst of great confusion.

"And how few, how very few words were needed," I thought in passing, "how little idyllic sentiment (what's more, the sentiment was artificial, bookish, composed) was necessary to turn a whole human soul according to my wishes at once. That's innocence for you! That's virgin soil!"

At times the thought occurred that I might go to her myself "to tell her everything," and to beg her not to come to me. But at this thought such venom arose in me that it seemed I'd have crushed that "damned" Liza if she'd suddenly turned up next to me. I'd have insulted her, spat at her, struck her, and chased her away!

One day passed, however, then a second, and a third; she still hadn't come, and I began to calm down. I felt particularly reassured and relaxed after nine o'clock in the evening, and even began to daydream sweetly at times. For instance, I'd save Liza, precisely because she'd come to me, and I'd talk to her. . . . I'd develop her mind, educate her. At last I'd notice that she loved me, loved me passionately. I'd pretend I didn't understand. (For that matter, I didn't know why I'd pretend; most likely just for the effect.) At last, all embarrassed, beautiful, trembling, and sobbing, she'd throw herself at my feet and declare that I was her saviour and she loved me more than anything in the world. I'd be surprised, but . . . "Liza," I'd say, "Do you really think that I haven't noticed your love? I've seen everything. I guessed, but dared not be first to make a claim on your heart because I had such influence over you, and because I was afraid you might deliberately force yourself to respond to my love out of gratitude, that you might forcibly evoke within yourself a feeling that didn't really exist. No, I didn't want that because it would be . . . despotism. . . . It would be indelicate (well, in short, here I launched on some European, George Sandian,[3] inexplicably lofty subtleties . . .). But now, now—you're mine, you're my creation, you're pure and lovely, you're my beautiful wife."

> And enter my house bold and free
> To become its full mistress![4]

"Then we'd begin to live happily together, travel abroad, etc., etc." In short, it began to seem crude even to me, and I ended it all by sticking my tongue out at myself.

"Besides, they won't let her out of there, the 'bitch,' " I thought. "After all, it seems unlikely that they'd release them for strolls, especially in the evening (for some reason I was convinced that she had to report there every evening, precisely at seven o'clock). Moreover, she said that she'd yet to become completely enslaved there, and that she still had certain rights; that means, hmm. Devil take it, she'll come, she's bound to come!"

It was a good thing I was distracted at the time by Apollon's rudeness. He

---

3. George Sand was the pseudonym of the French woman novelist Aurore Dudevant (1804–1876), famous also as a promoter of feminism. 4. The last lines of the poem by Nekrasov used as the epigraph of Part II of this story (see p. 1091).

made me lose all patience. He was the bane of my existence, a punishment inflicted on me by Providence. We'd been squabbling constantly for several years now and I hated him. My God, how I hated him! I think that I never hated anyone in my whole life as much as I hated him, especially at those times. He was an elderly, dignified man who worked part-time as a tailor. But for some unknown reason he despised me, even beyond all measure, and looked down upon me intolerably. However, he looked down on everyone. You need only glance at that flaxen, slicked-down hair, at that single lock brushed over his forehead and greased with vegetable oil, at his strong mouth, always drawn up in the shape of the letter V,[5] and you felt that you were standing before a creature who never doubted himself. He was a pedant of the highest order, the greatest one I'd ever met on earth; in addition he possessed a sense of self-esteem appropriate perhaps only to Alexander the Great, King of Macedonia. He was in love with every one of his buttons, every one of his fingernails—absolutely in love, and he looked it! He treated me quite despotically, spoke to me exceedingly little, and, if he happened to look at me, cast a steady, majestically self-assured, and constantly mocking glance that sometimes infuriated me. He carried out his tasks as if he were doing me the greatest of favors. Moreover, he did almost nothing at all for me; nor did he assume that he was obliged to do anything. There could be no doubt that he considered me the greatest fool on earth, and, that if he "kept me on," it was only because he could receive his wages from me every month. He agreed to "do nothing" for seven rubles a month. I'll be forgiven many of my sins because of him. Sometimes my hatred reached such a point that his gait alone would throw me into convulsions. But the most repulsive thing about him was his lisping. His tongue was a bit larger than normal or something of the sort; as a result, he constantly lisped and hissed. Apparently, he was terribly proud of it, imagining that it endowed him with enormous dignity. He spoke slowly, in measured tones, with his hands behind his back and his eyes fixed on the ground. It particularly infuriated me when he used to read the Psalter to himself behind his partition. I endured many battles on account of it. He was terribly fond of reading during the evening in a slow, even singsong voice, as if chanting over the dead. It's curious, but that's how he ended up: now he hires himself out to recite the Psalter over the dead; in addition, he exterminates rats and makes shoe polish. But at that time I couldn't get rid of him; it was as if he were chemically linked to my own existence. Besides, he'd never have agreed to leave for anything. It was impossible for me to live in a furnished room: my own apartment was my private residence, my shell, my case, where I hid from all humanity. Apollon, the devil only knows why, seemed to belong to this apartment, and for seven long years I couldn't get rid of him.

It was impossible, for example, to delay paying him his wages for even two or three days. He'd make such a fuss that I wouldn't know where to hide. But in those days I was so embittered by everyone that I decided, heaven knows why or for what reason, to *punish* Apollon by not paying him his wages for two whole weeks. I'd been planning to do this for some time now, about two years, simply in order to teach him that he had no right to put on such airs around me, and that if I chose to, I could always withhold his wages. I

---

5. The last letter of the old Russian alphabet, triangular in shape.

resolved to say nothing to him about it and even remain silent on purpose, to conquer his pride and force him to be the first one to mention it. Then I would pull all seven rubles out of a drawer and show him that I actually had the money and had intentionally set it aside, but that "I didn't want to, didn't want to, simply didn't want to pay him his wages, and that I didn't want to simply because *that's what I wanted*," because such was "my will as his master," because he was disrespectful and because he was rude. But, if he were to ask respectfully, then I might relent and pay him; if not, he might have to wait another two weeks, or three, or even a whole month. . . .

But, no matter how angry I was, he still won. I couldn't even hold out for four days. He began as he always did, because there had already been several such cases (and, let me add, I knew all this beforehand; I knew his vile tactics by heart), to wit: he would begin by fixing an extremely severe gaze on me. He would keep it up for several minutes in a row, especially when meeting me or accompanying me outside of the house. If, for example, I held out and pretended not to notice these stares, then he, maintaining his silence as before, would proceed to further tortures. Suddenly, for no reason at all, he'd enter my room quietly and slowly, while I was pacing or reading; he'd stop at the door, place one hand behind his back, thrust one foot forward, and fix his gaze on me, no longer merely severe, but now utterly contemptuous. If I were suddenly to ask him what he wanted, he wouldn't answer at all. He'd continue to stare at me reproachfully for several more seconds; then, compressing his lips in a particular way and assuming a very meaningful air, he'd turn slowly on the spot and slowly withdraw to his own room. Two hours later he'd emerge again and suddenly appear before me in the same way. It's happened sometimes that in my fury I hadn't even asked what he wanted, but simply raised my head sharply and imperiously, and begun to stare reproachfully back at him. We would stare at each other thus for some two minutes or more; at last he'd turn slowly and self-importantly, and withdraw for another few hours.

If all this failed to bring me back to my senses and I continued to rebel, he'd suddenly begin to sigh while staring at me. He'd sigh heavily and deeply, as if trying to measure with each sigh the depth of my moral decline. Naturally, it would end with his complete victory: I'd rage and shout, but I was always forced to do just as he wished on the main point of dispute.

This time his usual maneuvers of "severe stares" had scarcely begun when I lost my temper at once and lashed out at him in a rage. I was irritated enough even without that.

"Wait!" I shouted in a frenzy, as he was slowly and silently turning with one hand behind his back, about to withdraw to his own room. "Wait! Come back, come back, I tell you!" I must have bellowed so unnaturally that he turned around and even began to scrutinize me with a certain amazement. He continued, however, not to utter one word, and that was what infuriated me most of all.

"How dare you come in here without asking permission and stare at me? Answer me!"

But after regarding me serenely for half a minute, he started to turn around again.

"Wait!" I roared, rushing up to him. "Don't move! There! Now answer me: why do you come in here to stare?"

"If you've got any orders for me now, it's my job to do 'em," he replied after another pause, lisping softly and deliberately, raising his eyebrows, and calmly shifting his head from one side to the other—what's more, he did all this with horrifying composure.

"That's not it! That's not what I'm asking you about, you executioner!" I shouted, shaking with rage. "I'll tell you myself, you executioner, why you came in here. You know that I haven't paid you your wages, but you're so proud that you don't want to bow down and ask me for them. That's why you came in here to punish me and torment me with your stupid stares, and you don't even sus-s-pect, you torturer, how stupid it all is, how stupid, stupid, stupid, stupid!"

He would have turned around silently once again, but I grabbed hold of him.

"Listen," I shouted to him. "Here's the money, you see! Here it is! (I pulled it out of a drawer.) All seven rubles. But you won't get it, you won't until you come to me respectfully, with your head bowed, to ask my forgiveness. Do you hear?"

"That can't be!" he replied with some kind of unnatural self-confidence.

"It will be!" I shrieked. "I give you my word of honor, it will be!"

"I have nothing to ask your forgiveness for," he said as if he hadn't even noticed my shrieks, "because it was you who called me an 'executioner,' and I can always go lodge a complaint against you at the police station."

"Go! Lodge a complaint!" I roared. "Go at once, this minute, this very second! You're still an executioner! Executioner! Executioner!" But he only looked at me, then turned and, no longer heeding my shouts, calmly withdrew to his own room without looking back.

"If it hadn't been for Liza, none of this would have happened!" I thought to myself. Then, after waiting a minute, pompously and solemnly, but with my heart pounding heavily and forcefully, I went in to see him behind the screen.

"Apollon!" I said softly and deliberately, though gasping for breath, "go at once, without delay to fetch the police supervisor!"

He'd already seated himself at his table, put on his eyeglasses, and picked up something to sew. But, upon hearing my order, he suddenly snorted with laughter.

"At once! Go this very moment! Go, go, or you can't imagine what will happen to you!"

"You're really not in your right mind," he replied, not even lifting his head, lisping just as slowly, and continuing to thread his needle. "Who's ever heard of a man being sent to fetch a policeman against himself? And as for trying to frighten me, you're only wasting your time, because nothing will happen to me."

"Go," I screeched, seizing him by the shoulder. I felt that I might strike him at any moment.

I never even heard the door from the hallway suddenly open at that very moment, quietly and slowly, and that someone walked in, stopped, and began to examine us in bewilderment. I glanced up, almost died from shame, and ran back into my own room. There, clutching my hair with both hands, I leaned my head against the wall and froze in that position.

Two minutes later I heard Apollon's deliberate footsteps.

"There's *some woman* asking for you," he said, staring at me with particular severity; then he stood aside and let her in—it was Liza. He didn't want to leave, and he scrutinized us mockingly.

"Get out, get out!" I commanded him all flustered. At that moment my clock strained, wheezed, and struck seven.

IX

And enter my house bold and free,
To become its full mistress!
From the same poem.[6]

I stood before her, crushed, humiliated, abominably ashamed; I think I was smiling as I tried with all my might to wrap myself up in my tattered, quilted dressing gown—exactly as I'd imagined this scene the other day during a fit of depression. Apollon, after standing over us for a few minutes, left, but that didn't make things any easier for me. Worst of all was that she suddenly became embarrassed too, more than I'd ever expected. At the sight of me, of course.

"Sit down," I said mechanically and moved a chair up to the table for her, while I sat on the sofa. She immediately and obediently sat down, staring at me wide-eyed, and, obviously, expecting something from me at once. This naive expectation infuriated me, but I restrained myself.

She should have tried not to notice anything, as if everything were just as it should be, but she . . . And I vaguely felt that she'd have to pay dearly *for everything*.

"You've found me in an awkward situation, Liza," I began, stammering and realizing that this was precisely the wrong way to begin.

"No, no, don't imagine anything!" I cried, seeing that she'd suddenly blushed. "I'm not ashamed of my poverty. . . . On the contrary, I regard it with pride. I'm poor, but noble. . . . One can be poor and noble," I muttered. "But . . . would you like some tea?"

"No . . . ," she started to say.

"Wait!"

I jumped up and ran to Apollon. I had to get away somehow.

"Apollon," I whispered in feverish haste, tossing down the seven rubles which had been in my fist the whole time, "here are your wages. There, you see, I've given them to you. But now you must rescue me: bring us some tea and a dozen rusks from the tavern at once. If you don't go, you'll make me a very miserable man. You have no idea who this woman is. . . . This means— everything! You may think she's . . . But you've no idea at all who this woman really is!"

Apollon, who'd already sat down to work and had put his glasses on again, at first glanced sideways in silence at the money without abandoning his needle; then, paying no attention to me and making no reply, he continued to fuss with the needle he was still trying to thread. I waited there for about three minutes standing before him with my arms folded *à la Napoleon*.[7] My

6. I.e., from the poem quoted on pp. 1091 and 1130.   7. In the style of Napoleon.

temples were soaked in sweat. I was pale, I felt that myself. But, thank God, he must have taken pity just looking at me. After finishing with the thread, he stood up slowly from his place, slowly pushed back his chair, slowly took off his glasses, slowly counted the money and finally, after inquiring over his shoulder whether he should get a whole pot, slowly walked out of the room. As I was returning to Liza, it occurred to me: shouldn't I run away just as I was, in my shabby dressing gown, no matter where, and let come what may.

I sat down again. She looked at me uneasily. We sat in silence for several minutes.

"I'll kill him." I shouted suddenly, striking the table so hard with my fist that ink splashed out of the inkwell.

"Oh, what are you saying?" she exclaimed, startled.

"I'll kill him, I'll kill him!" I shrieked, striking the table in an absolute frenzy, but understanding full well at the same time how stupid it was to be in such a frenzy.

"You don't understand, Liza, what this executioner is doing to me. He's my executioner. . . . He's just gone out for some rusks; he . . ."

And suddenly I burst into tears. It was a nervous attack. I felt so ashamed amidst my sobs, but I couldn't help it. She got frightened.

"What's the matter? What's wrong with you?" she cried, fussing around me.

"Water, give me some water, over there!" I muttered in a faint voice, realizing full well, however, that I could've done both without the water and without the faint voice. But I was *putting on an act*, as it's called, in order to maintain decorum, although my nervous attack was genuine.

She gave me some water while looking at me like a lost soul. At that very moment Apollon brought in the tea. It suddenly seemed that this ordinary and prosaic tea was horribly inappropriate and trivial after everything that had happened, and I blushed. Liza stared at Apollon with considerable alarm. He left without looking at us.

"Liza, do you despise me?" I asked, looking her straight in the eye, trembling with impatience to find out what she thought.

She was embarrassed and didn't know what to say.

"Have some tea," I said angrily. I was angry at myself, but she was the one who'd have to pay, naturally. A terrible anger against her suddenly welled up in my heart; I think I could've killed her. To take revenge I swore inwardly not to say one more word to her during the rest of her visit. "She's the cause of it all," I thought.

Our silence continued for about five minutes. The tea stood on the table; we didn't touch it. It reached the point of my not wanting to drink on purpose, to make it even more difficult for her; it would be awkward for her to begin alone. Several times she glanced at me in sad perplexity. I stubbornly remained silent. I was the main sufferer, of course, because I was fully aware of the despicable meanness of my own spiteful stupidity; yet, at the same time, I couldn't restrain myself.

"I want to . . . get away from . . . that place . . . once and for all," she began just to break the silence somehow; but, poor girl, that was just the thing she shouldn't have said at that moment, stupid enough as it was to such a person as me, stupid as I was. My own heart even ached with pity for her tactlessness and unnecessary straightforwardness. But something hideous immediately suppressed all my pity; it provoked me even further. Let the whole world go to hell. Another five minutes passed.

"Have I disturbed you?" she began timidly, barely audibly, and started to get up.

But as soon as I saw this first glimpse of injured dignity, I began to shake with rage and immediately exploded.

"Why did you come here? Tell me why, please," I began, gasping and neglecting the logical order of my words. I wanted to say it all at once, without pausing for breath; I didn't even worry about how to begin.

"Why did you come here? Answer me! Answer!" I cried, hardly aware of what I was saying. "I'll tell you, my dear woman, why you came here. You came here because I spoke some *words of pity* to you that time. Now you've softened, and want to hear more 'words of pity.' Well, you should know that I was laughing at you then. And I'm laughing at you now. Why are you trembling? Yes, I was laughing at you! I'd been insulted, just prior to that, at dinner, by those men who arrived just before me that evening. I came intending to thrash one of them, the officer; but I didn't succeed; I couldn't find him; I had to avenge my insult on someone, to get my own back; you turned up and I took my anger out at you, and I laughed at you. I'd been humiliated, and I wanted to humiliate someone else; I'd been treated like a rag, and I wanted to exert some power. . . . That's what it was; you thought that I'd come there on purpose to save you, right? Is that what you thought? Is that it?"

I knew that she might get confused and might not grasp all the details, but I also knew that she'd understand the essence of it very well. That's just what happened. She turned white as a sheet; she wanted to say something. Her lips were painfully twisted, but she collapsed onto a chair just as if she'd been struck down with an ax. Subsequently she listened to me with her mouth gaping, her eyes wide open, shaking with awful fear. It was the cynicism, the cynicism of my words that crushed her. . . .

"To save you!" I continued, jumping up from my chair and rushing up and down the room in front of her, "to save you from what? Why, I may be even worse than you are. When I recited that sermon to you, why didn't you throw it back in my face? You should have said to me, 'Why did you come here? To preach morality or what?' Power, it was the power I needed then, I craved the sport, I wanted to reduce you to tears, humiliation, hysteria—that's what I needed then! But I couldn't have endured it myself, because I'm such a wretch. I got scared. The devil only knows why I foolishly gave you my address. Afterward, even before I got home, I cursed you like nothing on earth on account of that address. I hated you already because I'd lied to you then, because it was all playing with words, dreaming in my own mind. But, do you know what I really want now? For you to get lost, that's what! I need some peace. Why, I'd sell the whole world for a kopeck if people would only stop bothering me. Should the world go to hell, or should I go without my tea? I say, let the world go to hell as long as I can always have my tea. Did you know that or not? And I know perfectly well that I'm a scoundrel, a bastard, an egotist, and a sluggard. I've been shaking from fear for the last three days wondering whether you'd ever come. Do you know what disturbed me most of all these last three days? The fact that I'd appeared to you then as such a hero, and that now you'd suddenly see me in this torn dressing gown, dilapidated and revolting. I said before that I wasn't ashamed of my poverty; well, you should know that I am ashamed, I'm ashamed of it more than anything, more afraid of it than anything, more than if I were a thief, because I'm so vain; it's as if the skin's been stripped away from my body so that even wafts of air cause pain. By now surely even you've guessed that I'll never forgive you for having come upon me in this dressing gown as I was attacking Apollon like a vicious dog. Your saviour, your former hero, behaving like a mangy, shaggy mongrel, attacking his own lackey, while that lackey stood there laughing at me! Nor will I ever forgive you for those tears which, like an embarrassed old woman, I couldn't hold back before you. And I'll never forgive *you* for all that I'm confessing now. Yes—you, you alone must pay for everything because you turned up like this, because I'm a scoundrel, because I'm the nastiest, most ridiculous, pettiest, stupidest, most envious worm of all those living on earth who're no better than me in any way, but who, the devil knows why, never get embarrassed, while all my life I have to endure insults from every louse—that's my fate. What do I care that you don't understand any of this? What do I care, what do I care about you and whether or not you perish there? Why, don't you realize how much I'll hate you now after having said all this with your being here listening to me? After all, a man can only talk like this once in his whole life, and then only in hysteria! . . . What more do you want? Why, after all this, are you still hanging around here tormenting me? Why don't you leave?"

But at this point a very strange thing suddenly occurred.

I'd become so accustomed to inventing and imagining everything according to books, and picturing everything on earth to myself just as I'd conceived of it in my dreams, that at first I couldn't even comprehend the meaning of this strange occurrence. But here's what happened: Liza, insulted and crushed by me, understood much more than I'd imagined. She understood out of all this what a woman always understands first of all, if she sincerely loves—namely, that I myself was unhappy.

The frightened and insulted expression on her face was replaced at first by grieved amazement. When I began to call myself a scoundrel and a bastard, and my tears had begun to flow (I'd pronounced this whole tirade in tears), her whole face was convulsed by a spasm. She wanted to get up and stop me; when I'd finished, she paid no attention to my shouting, "Why are you here? Why don't you leave?" She only noticed that it must have been very painful for me to utter all this. Besides, she was so defenseless, the poor girl. She considered herself immeasurably beneath me. How could she get angry or take offense? Suddenly she jumped up from the chair with a kind of uncontrollable impulse, and yearning toward me, but being too timid and not daring to stir from her place, she extended her arms in my direction. . . . At this moment my heart leapt inside me, too. Then suddenly she threw herself at me, put her arms around my neck, and burst into tears. I, too, couldn't restrain myself and sobbed as I'd never done before.

"They won't let me . . . I can't be . . . good!"[8] I barely managed to say; then I went over to the sofa, fell upon it face down, and sobbed in genuine hys-

8. This epithet *dobryi* ("good") must be read in combination with that in the second sentence of the work, where the hero describes himself as *zloi*—not only "spiteful" but also "evil."

terics for a quarter of an hour. She knelt down, embraced me, and remained motionless in that position.

But the trouble was that my hysterics had to end sometime. And so (after all, I'm writing the whole loathsome truth), lying there on the sofa and pressing my face firmly into that nasty leather cushion of mine, I began to sense gradually, distantly, involuntarily, but irresistibly, that it would be awkward for me to raise my head and look Liza straight in the eye. What was I ashamed of? I don't know, but I was ashamed. It also occurred to my overwrought brain that now our roles were completely reversed; now she was the heroine, and I was the same sort of humiliated and oppressed creature she'd been in front of me that evening—only four days ago. . . . And all this came to me during those few minutes as I lay face down on the sofa!

My God! Was it possible that I envied her?

I don't know; to this very day I still can't decide. But then, of course, I was even less able to understand it. After all, I couldn't live without exercising power and tyrannizing over another person. . . . But . . . but, then, you really can't explain a thing by reason; consequently, it's useless to try.

However, I regained control of myself and raised my head; I had to sooner or later. . . . And so, I'm convinced to this day that it was precisely because I felt too ashamed to look at her, that another feeling was suddenly kindled and burst into flame in my heart—the feeling of domination and possession. My eyes gleamed with passion; I pressed her hands tightly. How I hated her and felt drawn to her simultaneously! One feeling intensified the other. It was almost like revenge! . . . At first there was a look of something resembling bewilderment, or even fear, on her face, but only for a brief moment. She embraced me warmly and rapturously.

X

A quarter of an hour later I was rushing back and forth across the room in furious impatience, constantly approaching the screen to peer at Liza through the crack. She was sitting on the floor, her head leaning against the bed, and she must have been crying. But she didn't leave, and that's what irritated me. By this time she knew absolutely everything. I'd insulted her once and for all, but . . . there's nothing more to be said. She guessed that my outburst of passion was merely revenge, a new humiliation for her, and that to my former, almost aimless, hatred there was added now a *personal*, *envious* hatred of her. . . . However, I don't think that she understood all this explicitly; on the other hand, she fully understood that I was a despicable man, and, most important, that I was incapable of loving her.

I know that I'll be told this is incredible—that it's impossible to be as spiteful and stupid as I am; you may even add that it was impossible not to return, or at least to appreciate, this love. But why is this so incredible? In the first place, I could no longer love because, I repeat, for me love meant tyrannizing and demonstrating my moral superiority. All my life I could never even conceive of any other kind of love, and I've now reached the point that I sometimes think that love consists precisely in a voluntary gift by the beloved person of the right to tyrannize over him. Even in my underground dreams I couldn't conceive of love in any way other than a struggle. It always began with hatred and ended with moral subjugation; afterward, I could never imagine what to do with the subjugated object. And what's so incredible about that, since I'd previously managed to corrupt myself morally; I'd already become unaccustomed to "real life," and only a short while ago had taken it into my head to reproach her and shame her for having come to hear "words of pity" from me. But I never could've guessed that she'd come not to hear words of pity at all, but to love me, because it's in that kind of love that a woman finds her resurrection, all her salvation from whatever kind of ruin, and her rebirth, as it can't appear in any other form. However, I didn't hate her so much as I rushed around the room and peered through the crack behind the screen. I merely found it unbearably painful that she was still there. I wanted her to disappear. I longed for "peace and quiet"; I wanted to remain alone in my underground. "Real life" oppressed me—so unfamiliar was it—that I even found it hard to breathe.

But several minutes passed, and she still didn't stir, as if she were oblivious. I was shameless enough to tap gently on the screen to remind her. . . . She started suddenly, jumped up, and hurried to find her shawl, hat, and coat, as if she wanted to escape from me. . . . Two minutes later she slowly emerged from behind the screen and looked at me sadly. I smiled spitefully; it was forced, however, for *appearance's sake only*; and I turned away from her look.

"Good-bye," she said, going toward the door.

Suddenly I ran up to her, grabbed her hand, opened it, put something in . . . and closed it again. Then I turned away at once and bolted to the other corner, so that at least I wouldn't be able to see. . . .

I was just about to lie—to write that I'd done all this accidentally, without knowing what I was doing, in complete confusion, out of foolishness. But I don't want to lie; therefore I'll say straight out, that I opened her hand and placed something in it . . . out of spite. It occurred to me to do this while I was rushing back and forth across the room and she was sitting there behind the screen. But here's what I can say for sure: although I did this cruel thing deliberately, it was not from my heart, but from my stupid head. This cruelty of mine was so artificial, cerebral, intentionally invented, *bookish*, that I couldn't stand it myself even for one minute—at first I bolted to the corner so as not to see, and then, out of shame and in despair, I rushed out after Liza. I opened the door into the hallway and listened. "Liza! Liza!" I called down the stairs, but timidly, in a soft voice.

There was no answer; I thought I could hear her footsteps at the bottom of the stairs.

"Liza!" I cried more loudly.

No answer. But at that moment I heard down below the sound of the tight outer glass door opening heavily with a creak and then closing again tightly. The sound rose up the stairs.

She'd gone. I returned to my room deep in thought. I felt horribly oppressed.

I stood by the table near the chair where she'd been sitting and stared senselessly into space. A minute or so passed, then I suddenly started: right before me on the chair I saw . . . in a word, I saw the crumpled blue five-ruble note, the very one I'd thrust into her hand a few moments before. It was the same one; it couldn't be any other; I had none other in my apartment. So she'd managed to toss it down on the table when I'd bolted to the other corner.

So what? I might have expected her to do that. Might have expected it?

No. I was such an egotist, in fact, I so lacked respect for other people, that I couldn't even conceive that she'd ever do that. I couldn't stand it. A moment later, like a madman, I hurried to get dressed. I threw on whatever I happened to find, and rushed headlong after her. She couldn't have gone more than two hundred paces when I ran out on the street.

It was quiet; it was snowing heavily, and the snow was falling almost perpendicularly, blanketing the sidewalk and the deserted street. There were no passers-by; no sound could be heard. The street lights were flickering dismally and vainly. I ran about two hundred paces to the crossroads and stopped.

"Where did she go? And why am I running after her? Why? To fall down before her, sob with remorse, kiss her feet, and beg her forgiveness! That's just what I wanted. My heart was being torn apart; never, never will I recall that moment with indifference. But—why?" I wondered. "Won't I grow to hate her, perhaps as soon as tomorrow, precisely because I'm kissing her feet today? Will I ever be able to make her happy? Haven't I found out once again today, for the hundredth time, what I'm really worth? Won't I torment her?"

I stood in the snow, peering into the murky mist, and thought about all this.

"And wouldn't it be better, wouldn't it," I fantasized once I was home again, stifling the stabbing pain in my heart with such fantasies, "wouldn't it be better if she were to carry away the insult with her forever? Such an insult— after all, is purification; it's the most caustic and painful form of consciousness. Tomorrow I would have defiled her soul and wearied her heart. But now that insult will never die within her; no matter how abominable the filth that awaits her, that insult will elevate and purify her . . . by hatred . . . hmm . . . perhaps by forgiveness as well. But will that make it any easier for her?"

And now, in fact, I'll pose an idle question of my own. Which is better: cheap happiness or sublime suffering? Well, come on, which is better?

These were my thoughts as I sat home that evening, barely alive with the anguish in my soul. I'd never before endured so much suffering and remorse; but could there exist even the slightest doubt that when I went rushing out of my apartment, I'd turn back again after going only halfway? I never met Liza afterward, and I never heard anything more about her. I'll also add that for a long time I remained satisfied with my theory about the use of insults and hatred, in spite of the fact that I myself almost fell ill from anguish at the time.

Even now, after so many years, all this comes back to me as *very unpleasant*. A great deal that comes back to me now is very unpleasant, but . . . perhaps I should end these *Notes* here? I think that I made a mistake in beginning to write them. At least, I was ashamed all the time I was writing this *tale*: consequently, it's not really literature, but corrective punishment. After all, to tell you long stories about how, for example, I ruined my life through moral decay in my corner, by the lack of appropriate surroundings, by isolation from any living beings, and by futile malice in the underground— so help me God, that's not very interesting. A novel needs a hero, whereas here all the traits of an anti-hero have been assembled *deliberately*; but the most important thing is that all this produces an extremely unpleasant impression because we've all become estranged from life, we're all cripples, every one of us, more or less. We've become so estranged that at times we feel some kind of revulsion for genuine "real life," and therefore we can't bear to be reminded of it. Why, we've reached a point where we almost regard "real life" as hard work, as a job, and we've all agreed in private that it's really better in books. And why do we sometimes fuss, indulge in whims, and make demands? We don't know ourselves. It'd be even worse if all our whimsical desires were fulfilled. Go on, try it. Give us, for example, a little more independence; untie the hands of any one of us, broaden our sphere of activity, relax the controls, and . . . I can assure you, we'll immediately ask to have the controls reinstated. I know that you may get angry at me for saying this, you may shout and stamp your feet: "Speak for yourself," you'll say, "and for your own miseries in the underground, but don't you dare say 'all of us.'" If you'll allow me, gentlemen; after all, I'm not trying to justify myself by saying *all of us*. What concerns me in particular, is that in my life I've only taken to an extreme that which you haven't even dared to take halfway; what's more, you've mistaken your cowardice for good sense; and, in so deceiving yourself, you've consoled yourself. So, in fact, I may even be "more alive" than you are. Just take a closer look! Why, we don't even know where this "real life" lives nowadays, what it really is, and what it's called. Leave us alone without books and we'll get confused and lose our way at once—we won't know what to join, what to hold on to, what to love or what to hate, what to respect or what to despise. We're even oppressed by being men—men with real bodies and blood of *our very own*. We're ashamed of it; we consider it a disgrace and we strive to become some kind of impossible "general-human-beings." We're stillborn; for some time now we haven't been conceived by living fathers; we like it more and more. We're developing a taste for it. Soon we'll conceive of a way to be born from ideas. But enough; I don't want to write any more "from Underground. . . ."

However, the "notes" of this paradoxalist don't end here. He couldn't resist and kept on writing. But it also seems to us that we might as well stop here.

CHARLES BAUDELAIRE
1821–1867

Few writers have had such impact on succeeding generations as Charles Baudelaire, called both the "first modern poet" and the "father of modern criticism." Nor is his reputation confined to the West, for Baudelaire is the most widely read French poet around the globe. Yet for a long time Baudelaire's literary image was dominated by his reputation as a scandalous writer whose blatant eroticism and open fascination with evil outraged all right-thinking people. Both he and Flaubert were brought to trial in 1857 for "offenses against public and religious morals"—Flaubert for *Madame Bovary* and Baudelaire for his just-published book of poetry *Les Fleurs du Mal* (The flowers of evil). Some of this reputation is justified; the poet did intend to shock, and he displayed in painfully vivid scenes his own spiritual and sensual torment. Haunted by a religiously framed vision of human nature as fallen and corrupt, he lucidly analyzed his own weaknesses as well as the hypocrisy and sins he found in society. Lust, hatred, laziness, a disabling self-awareness that ironized all emotions, a horror of death and decay, and finally an apathy that swallowed up all other vices—all contrasted bitterly with the poet's dreams of a lost Eden, an ideal harmony of being. Perfection existed only in the distance: in scenes of erotic love, faraway voyages, or artistic beauty created often out of ugliness and crude reality. Baudelaire's ability to present realistic detail inside larger symbolic horizons, his constant use of imagery and suggestion, his consummate craftsmanship and the intense musicality of his verse made him a precursor of Symbolism and, in the words of T. S. Eliot, "the greatest exemplar in *modern* poetry in any language."

Baudelaire was born in Paris on April 9, 1821. His father died when the poet was six, and his widowed mother married Captain (later General) Jacques Aupick the following year. In 1832 the family moved to Lyons, and young Charles was placed in boarding school; in 1836 Aupick and his family were reassigned to Paris. Throughout his life Baudelaire remained greatly attached to his mother and detested his disciplinarian stepfather. He was a rebellious and difficult youth whom his parents sent on a long voyage to the Indies in 1841 to remove him from bad influences; but he cut short the trip at Reunion Island and insisted on returning home after ten months. Baudelaire's unconventional behavior and extravagant lifestyle continued to worry his family, especially after he turned twenty-one and received his father's inheritance. In 1844, they obtained a court order to supervise his finances, and from then on the poet subsisted on allowances paid by a notary.

In contrast to the Romantics with their love of nature and pastoral scenes, Baudelaire was a city poet fascinated by the variety and excitement of modern urban life. Living in Paris, he collaborated with other writers; published poems, translations, and criticism in different journals; and in 1842 began a lifelong liaison with Jeanne Duval, the "black Venus" of many poems. When he read Edgar Allan Poe for the first time, he was struck by the similarity of their ideas: by Poe's dedication to beauty, his fascination with bizarre images and death, and above all his emphasis on craftsmanship and perfectly controlled art. The French poet recognized in Poe "not only subjects I had dreamed of, but SENTENCES that I had thought and he had written twenty years earlier." Baudelaire's translations of Poe, collected in five volumes published from 1856 to 1865, were immensely popular and introduced the American writer to a broad European audience.

Public scandal greeted the appearance in 1857 of Baudelaire's major work, *The Flowers of Evil*. French authorities, already annoyed at Flaubert's acquittal, seized the book immediately. Less than two months later, the poet and his publisher were condemned to pay a fine and to delete six poems. A second edition with more poems appeared in 1861, and new lyrics were added to later printings. By now the poet was also well known as a critic. He championed the modern art of his time, interpreting and upholding the spirit of modernity in the art criticism of his 1845, 1846, and 1859 *Salons*; in remarkable studies of the painters Eugène Delacroix and Constantin Guys; and in a spirited defense of the German composer Richard Wagner. His literary criticism, although it included studies of *Madame Bovary*, Victor Hugo, and Théophile Gautier, was in general limited to brief journal reviews. Baudelaire started publishing prose poetry at the beginning of the 1860s, experimenting with a form that was almost unknown in France and in which he hoped to achieve "the miracle of a poetic prose, musical without rhythm or rhyme, able . . . to adapt itself to the soul's lyric movements, to the undulations of reverie, to the sudden starts of consciousness." A slim book of twenty prose poems appeared in 1862; the complete *Little Poems in Prose* (also called *Paris Spleen*) would contain fifty poems in all. Baudelaire's health was precarious during these years. In 1862, he had what was apparently a minor stroke, which he called a "warning" and described with characteristically vivid imagery: "I felt pass over me a draft of wind from imbecility's wing." Four years later, in Belgium, he was stricken with aphasia and hemiplegia; unable to speak, he was brought back to Paris where he died on August 31, 1867.

His audience was never far from Baudelaire's mind. He wished to shock, to startle, to make the reader rethink cherished ideas and values. In the prefatory poem to *The Flowers of Evil, To the Reader*, Baudelaire ends a catalog of human vices by insisting that both he and the reader are caught in a common guilt: "You—hypocrite Reader—my double—my brother!" The poet's insistent theme of *ennui* (pathological boredom or apathy) occurs here at the beginning of the book: it is the melancholy inertia that keeps human beings from acting either for good or for evil, placing them outside the realm of choice, much as Dante relegated to Limbo those who were unwilling to take a moral stand. (In Catholic theology, such spiritual inertia is termed *acedia*.) This *spleen*, as it is also called (from the part of the body governing a splenetic or bilious humor), appears throughout *The Flowers of Evil* as an insidious, debilitating force. In *To the Reader* Baudelaire argues that the devil's most terrifying weapon against humankind is not the litany of sins so colorfully described, but rather his ability to diminish the possibility of action: to evaporate—like a chemist in a laboratory—the precious metal of human will.

The Voyage, placed by Baudelaire at the end of the collection, describes the opposite of inertia: an active search for goals always out of reach. Written in a consciously Byronic tone and intended, according to the poet, to upset current faith in human progress, *The Voyage* describes "progress" as a series of temporary advances that end in disappointment and disgust. These smaller achievements—discovering new lands, inventing new luxuries, gaining fame and fortune, seeking ecstasy in sadism and sensuality—are all bound to deceive because they are merely symbols of a larger unending voyage: the quest for the infinite. Since human beings contain an "inner [spiritual] infinite" they cannot be satisfied with any limits and must constantly travel toward the unknown and the new. The "country" of earthly experience is not adequate for travelers impelled by an inner fire; their voyage ends, therefore, with a final plunge—for answers—into the unfathomable obscurity of death. The last line, "In the depths of the Unknown, we'll discover the New!" became a famous rallying cry for generations who sought new insights by exploring such unmapped frontiers.

Baudelaire alternates between acid melancholy and glimpses of happiness. Not all voyages are unhappy; one of his rare contented and even tender poems is the lyrical *Invitation to the Voyage*, a lover's invitation to an exotic land of peace, beauty, and sensuous harmony. The voyage is imaginary, of course, implying two forms of escape from reality: an escape out of real time into a primeval accord of the senses, and an escape into another artistic vision—the glowing interiors painted by such Dutch masters as Jan Vermeer. A similar but more cynical voyage of escape occurs in *Her Hair*. Here the poet, abandoning himself to passion, buries his face in the dark tide of his mistress's hair as if to submerge himself in the dark ocean of dream. This escape is available only on a temporary basis, however; the woman remains his "oasis" only so long as he adorns her hair with jewels. In both poems, and probably in Baudelaire's poetry in general, we must admit that women do not exist as separate personalities even if there are specific historical figures behind the poems. They are foils for poetic inspiration, conventional images of beauty, coldness, vision, or vice given one or another form. The woman in *A Carcass* exists only as an appropriate listener in a poem that mocks Petrarchan ideals of feminine beauty. Even if male subjectivity governs the descriptions, men are absent, in a different way; they exist only generically, as brothers (or doubles) of the poet himself. What emerges is that Baudelaire is even more clamped in his own solitude, registering repeatedly a personal experience from which he builds an amazingly complex imaginative universe.

Baudelaire was convinced that "every good poet has always been a realist," and he himself was a master of realistic details used for effects that go beyond conventional or photographic realism. The rhythmic thump of firewood being delivered is repeated throughout *Song of Autumn I*, where it coordinates ascending images of death. Imagery in *A Carcass* is more brutal. Even if the contrast between the language of courtly love ("star of my eyes") and crude and obscene descriptions no longer shocks in quite the same way, there remains the striking feat of imagination in which Baudelaire superimposes a swarming, vibrating new life onto the blurred outlines of a decaying animal carcass. The poem's ostensible theme is familiar—*carpe diem*, "seize the day" or "think of the future and love me now," since only a poet can preserve beauty—but one has only to compare Yeats's poem *When You Are Old* to recognize the harshness of this address to the beloved. The mixture of tones is more subtle in the *Spleen* poems, celebrated for their evocation of gray misery. Here Baudelaire inserts mundane items like bats, spiders, old-fashioned clothes, uncorked perfume bottles, and noisy rainspouts. Such down-to-earth details give substance to concurrent mythical or allegorical scenes. A chill revelation of mortality emerges from the sequence of thoroughly practical references to water in *Spleen LXXVIII*, beginning with the rain and fog in the city and including a cat twisting and turning uncomfortably on clammy tiles, the whine of a rainspout, the wheeze of wet wood and a damp clock pendulum, and finally a deck of cards left by an old woman who died of dropsy. If the sequence is interesting as a tour de force of linked images, it also serves cumulatively to evoke an atmosphere of lethargy and decay climaxing in a tiny, altogether unrealistic final scene in which two face cards talk sinisterly of their past loves.

Similar themes are to be found in the prose poems (published as *Little Poems in Prose* or *Paris Spleen*), although with a more openly autobiographical tone and a more homely setting. This prose must also find its own way to be musical "without rhyme." Stanzas become paragraphs; rhythm is created through variations in sentence length, syntax, and sound patterns, and the juxtaposition of scenes and tones. Rhythm is undeniably present, however changed: it is audible in the triple cadence ending *Windows* (helping him "to live, to feel that I am, and what I am") or in the contrasting dialogue leading up to the soul's explosion at the end of *Anywhere out of the World*.

The realism that is often buried in the lyrics of *The Flowers of Evil* appears on the surface in the prose poems. Baudelaire reviews an irritating day in *One O'Clock in the Morning*, recasts the topics of *The Voyage* as an imaginary dialogue in *Anywhere out of the World*, and ponders his solitude and the nature of creative genius in *Crowds* and *Windows*. In *Windows*, after having deduced the life story of an old woman seen across the roofs, he ends by saying that her story is only a "legend"—or, at least, that he does not care whether it is true so long as it provides a point of departure for his own imagination. Correspondingly, the poet relishes crowds because, moving among so many people, he is able to imagine himself in their place: "to be himself or someone else, as he chooses." In each case the artist is visibly alone, experiencing either the melancholy of *spleen* or the joy of an artistic imagination that creates and populates its own world. In verse or in prose, the alternation between dream and reality continues.

Baudelaire is a complex and ironic poet, an inheritor of that Romantic irony that wishes to embrace all the opposites of human existence: good and evil, love and hate, self and other, dream and reality. His is a universe of relationships, of echoes and correspondences. His best-known poem, in fact, is the sonnet *Correspondences*. This poem describes a vision of the mystic unity of all nature, which is demonstrated by the reciprocity of our five senses (*synesthesia*). Nature, says the poet, is a system of perpetual analogies in which one thing always corresponds to another—physical objects to each other (colonnades in a temple, for example, to trees in the forest), spiritual reality to physical reality, and the five senses (taste, smell, touch, sight, and hearing) among themselves—to produce such combinations as "bitter green," a "soft look," or "a harsh sound." Human beings are not usually aware of the "universal analogy"—the forest of the first stanza watches us without our knowing it—but it is the role of the poet to act as seer and guide, urging us toward a state of awareness in which both mind and senses fuse in another dimension. *Correspondences* is no vaguely intuitive poem, however. Even though it describes a state of ecstatic awareness, it works through the stages of a logical argument. The thesis is set out in the first stanza, explained in the second, and illustrated with cumulative examples in the third and fourth. Baudelaire's yearning for mystic harmony does not make him neglect either a base in reality or a rigorous application of intellect. His fusion of idealist vision, realistic detail, and artistic discipline made him the most influential poet of the nineteenth century and the first poet of the modern age.

The selections printed here, from a range of Baudelaire's most influential lyric and prose poems, are translated by different modern poets. While remaining faithful to the original text, each translation necessarily stresses different aspects (for example, images, meter and rhyme, word order, tone, a particular set of associations when more than one is possible) to create a genuine English poem. The footnotes occasionally point out elements that are especially significant in the French text.

Lois Boe Hyslop, *Charles Baudelaire Revisited* (1992), is a useful introductory survey. F. W. Leakey, *Baudelaire, Les Fleurs du Mal* (1992), is a short guide to the poet's major work. Enid Starkie, *Baudelaire* (1953), is the fullest biography in English. Henri Peyre, ed., *Baudelaire: A Collection of Critical Essays* (1962), contains eleven essays on *The Flowers of Evil,* with selections by major writers. Harold Bloom, ed., *Charles Baudelaire* (1987), presents ten contemporary critics on Baudelaire's themes, literary and artistic criticism, selected texts, and relation to Poe. Patricia Clements, *Baudelaire and the English Tradition* (1985), is a penetrating analysis of Baudelaire's influence on English literature from Swinburne to T. S. Eliot; it includes comparisons and contrasts with late Symbolist tradition. Edward Kaplan, *Baudelaire's Prose Poems* (1990), studies the prose poems as a many-sided but coherent ensemble of "fables of modern life." Baudelaire's criticism of literature and art are discussed in Rosemary Lloyd, *Baudelaire's Literary Criticism* (1981) and David Carrier, *High Art: Charles Baudelaire and the Origins of Modernist Painting* (1996). Lloyd's *Selected Letters of Charles Baudelaire: The Conquest of Solitude* (1986) contains personal and literary letters. Laurence M. Porter, *The Crisis of French Symbolism* (1990), has an interesting chapter on Baudelaire's relation to his imagined audience.

PRONOUNCING GLOSSARY

The following list uses common English syllables and stress accents to provide rough equivalents of selected words whose pronunciation may be unfamiliar to the general reader.

Baudelaire: *boh-d'lair'*	Pylades: *pill'-ah-deez*
ennui: *on-wee'*	Venustre: *ven-yew'-struh*

THE FLOWERS OF EVIL

To the Reader[1]

Infatuation, sadism, lust, avarice
possess our souls and drain the body's force;
we spoonfeed our adorable remorse,
like whores or beggars nourishing their lice.

Our sins are mulish, our confessions lies;   5
we play to the grandstand with our promises,
we pray for tears to wash our filthiness,
importantly pissing hogwash through our styes.

---

1. Translated by Robert Lowell. The translation pays primary attention to the insistent rhythm of the original poetic language and keeps the *abba* rhyme scheme.

The devil, watching by our sickbeds, hissed
old smut and folk-songs to our soul, until   10
the soft and precious metal of our will
boiled off in vapor for this scientist.

Each day his flattery[2] makes us eat a toad,
and each step forward is a step to hell,
unmoved, though previous corpses and their smell   15
asphyxiate our progress on this road.

Like the poor lush who cannot satisfy,
we try to force our sex with counterfeits,
die drooling on the deliquescent tits,
mouthing the rotten orange we suck dry.   20

Gangs of demons are boozing in our brain—
ranked, swarming, like a million warrior-ants,[3]
they drown and choke the cistern of our wants;
each time we breathe, we tear our lungs with pain.

If poison, arson, sex, narcotics, knives   25
have not yet ruined us and stitched their quick,
loud patterns on the canvas of our lives,
it is because our souls are still too sick.[4]

Among the vermin, jackals, panthers, lice,
gorillas and tarantulas that suck   30
and snatch and scratch and defecate and fuck
in the disorderly circus of our vice,

there's one more ugly and abortive birth.
It makes no gestures, never beats its breast,
yet it would murder for a moment's rest,[5]   35
and willingly annihilate the earth.

It's BOREDOM. Tears have glued its eyes together.
You know it well, my Reader. This obscene
beast chain-smokes yawning for the guillotine—
you—hypocrite Reader—my double—my brother!   40

Correspondences[1]

Nature is a temple whose living colonnades
Breathe forth a mystic speech in fitful sighs;
Man wanders among symbols in those glades
Where all things watch him with familiar eyes.

2. The Devil is literally described as a puppet master controlling our strings.   3. Literally, intestinal worms.   4. Literally, not bold enough.   5. Literally, swallow the world in a yawn.   1. Translated by Richard Wilbur. The translation keeps the intricate melody of the sonnet's original rhyme scheme.

Like dwindling echoes gathered far away   5
Into a deep and thronging unison
Huge as the night or as the light of day,
All scents and sounds and colors meet as one.

Perfumes there are as sweet as the oboe's sound,
Green as the prairies, fresh as a child's caress,[2]   10
—And there are others, rich, corrupt, profound[3]

And of an infinite pervasiveness,
Like myrrh, or musk, or amber,[4] that excite
The ecstasies of sense, the soul's delight.

Correspondances

La Nature est un temple où de vivants piliers
Laissent parfois sortir de confuses paroles;
L'homme y passe à travers des forêts de symboles
Qui l'observent avec des regards familiers.

Comme de longs échos qui de loin se confondent   5
Dans une ténébreuse et profonde unité,
Vaste comme la nuit et comme la clarté,
Les parfums, les couleurs et les sons se répondent.

Il est des parfums frais comme des chairs d'enfants,
Doux comme les hautbois, verts comme les prairies,   10
—Et d'autres, corrompus, riches et triomphants,

Ayant l'expansion des choses infinies,
Comme l'ambre, le musc, le benjoin et l'encens,
Qui chantent les transports de l'esprit et des sens.

Her Hair[1]

O fleece, that down the neck waves to the nape!
O curls! O perfume nonchalant and rare!
O ecstasy! To fill this alcove[2] shape
With memories that in these tresses sleep,
I would shake them like pennons in the air!   5

Languorous Asia, burning Africa,
And a far world, defunct almost, absent,
Within your aromatic forest stay!

2. Literally, flesh.   3. Literally, triumphant.   4. Or ambergris, a substance secreted by whales.
Ambergris and musk (a secretion of the male musk deer) are used in making perfume.   1. Translated by
Doreen Bell. The translation emulates the French original's challenging *abaab* rhyme pattern.
2. Bedroom.

As other souls on music drift away,
Mine, o my love! still floats upon your scent.   10

I shall go there where, full of sap, both tree
And man swoon in the heat of southern climes;
Strong tresses, be the swell that carries me!
I dream upon your sea of ebony
Of dazzling sails, of oarsmen, masts and flames: 15

A sun-drenched and reverberating port,
Where I imbibe color and sound and scent;
Where vessels, gliding through the gold and moire,
Open their vast arms as they leave the shore
To clasp the pure and shimmering firmament.   20

I'll plunge my head, enamored of its pleasure,
In this black ocean where the other hides;
My subtle spirit then will know a measure
Of fertile idleness and fragrant leisure,
Lulled by the infinite rhythm of its tides!   25

Pavilion, of blue-shadowed tresses spun,
You give me back the azure from afar;
And where the twisted locks are fringed with down
Lurk mingled odors I grow drunk upon
Of oil of coconut, of musk and tar.   30

A long time! always! my hand in your hair
Will sow the stars of sapphire, pearl, ruby,
That you be never deaf to my desire,
My oasis and gourd whence I aspire
To drink deep of the wine of memory!³   35

A Carcass¹

Remember, my love, the item you saw
  That beautiful morning in June:
By a bend in the path a carcass reclined
  On a bed sown with pebbles and stones;

Her legs were spread out like a lecherous whore,   5
  Sweating out poisonous fumes,
Who opened in slick invitational style
  Her stinking and festering womb.

---

3. The last two lines are a question: "Are you not . . . ?"   1. Translated by James McGowan with special attention to imagery. The alternation of long and short lines in English emulates the French meter's rhythmic swing between twelve-syllable and eight-syllable lines in an *abab* rhyme scheme.

The sun on this rottenness focused its rays
    To cook the cadaver till done,   10
And render to Nature a hundredfold gift
    Of all she'd united in one.

And the sky cast an eye on this marvelous meat
    As over the flowers in bloom.
The stench was so wretched that there on the grass   15
    You nearly collapsed in a swoon.

The flies buzzed and droned on these bowels of filth
    Where an army of maggots arose,
Which flowed like a liquid and thickening stream
    On the animate rags of her clothes.[2]   20

And it rose and it fell, and pulsed like a wave,
    Rushing and bubbling with health.
One could say that this carcass, blown with vague breath,
    Lived in increasing itself.

And this whole teeming world made a musical sound   25
    Like babbling brooks and the breeze,
Or the grain that a man with a winnowing-fan
    Turns with a rhythmical ease.

The shapes wore away as if only a dream
    Like a sketch that is left on the page   30
Which the artist forgot and can only complete
    On the canvas, with memory's aid.

From back in the rocks, a pitiful bitch
    Eyed us with angry distaste,
Awaiting the moment to snatch from the bones   35
    The morsel she'd dropped in her haste.

—And you, in your turn, will be rotten as this:
    Horrible, filthy, undone,
Oh sun of my nature and star of my eyes,
    My passion, my angel[3] in one!   40

Yes, such will you be, oh regent of grace,
    After the rites have been read,
Under the weeds, under blossoming grass
    As you molder with bones of the dead.

Ah then, oh my beauty, explain to the worms   45
    Who cherish your body so fine,

2. By extension. The torn flesh is described as "living rags."   3. Series of conventional Petrarchan images that idealize the beloved.

That I am the keeper for corpses of love
Of the form, and the essence divine![4]

Invitation to the Voyage[1]

My child, my sister, dream
How sweet all things would seem
Were we in that kind land to live together,
    And there love slow and long,
    There love and die among   5
Those scenes that image you, that sumptuous weather.
    Drowned suns that glimmer there
    Through cloud-disheveled air
Move me with such a mystery as appears
    Within those other skies   10
    Of your treacherous eyes
When I behold them shining through their tears.

There, there is nothing else but grace and measure,
Richness, quietness, and pleasure.

    Furniture that wears   15
    The lustre of the years
Softly would glow within our glowing chamber,
    Flowers of rarest bloom
    Proffering their perfume
Mixed with the vague fragrances of amber;   20
    Gold ceilings would there be,
    Mirrors deep as the sea,
The walls all in an Eastern splendor hung—
    Nothing but should address
    The soul's loneliness,   25
Speaking her sweet and secret native tongue.

There, there is nothing else but grace and measure,
Richness, quietness, and pleasure.

    See, sheltered from the swells
    There in the still canals   30
Those drowsy ships that dream of sailing forth;
    It is to satisfy
    Your least desire, they ply
Hither through all the waters of the earth.
    The sun at close of day   35
    Clothes the fields of hay,
Then the canals, at last the town entire

---

4. "Any form created by man is immortal. For form is independent of matter . . ." (from Baudelaire's journal *My Heart Laid Bare* 80).   1. Translated by Richard Wilbur. The translation maintains both the rhyme scheme and the rocking motion of the original meter, which follows an unusual pattern of two five-syllable lines followed by one seven-syllable line, and a seven-syllable couplet as refrain.

In hyacinth and gold:
  Slowly the land is rolled
Sleepward under a sea of gentle fire.   40

There, there is nothing else but grace and measure,
Richness, quietness, and pleasure.

Song of Autumn I[1]

Soon we shall plunge into the chilly fogs;
Farewell, swift light! our summers are too short!
I hear already the mournful fall of logs
Re-echoing from the pavement of the court.

All of winter will gather in my soul: 5
Hate, anger, horror, chills, the hard forced work;
And, like the sun in his hell by the north pole,
My heart will be only a red and frozen block.

I shudder, hearing every log that falls;
No scaffold could be built with hollower sounds.   10
My spirit is like a tower whose crumbling walls
The tireless battering-ram brings to the ground.

It seems to me, lulled by monotonous shocks,
As if they were hastily nailing a coffin today.
For whom?—Yesterday was summer. Now autumn knocks.   15
That mysterious sound is like someone's going away.

Spleen LXXVIII[1]

Old Pluvius,[2] month of rains, in peevish mood
Pours from his urn chill winter's sodden gloom
On corpses fading in the near graveyard,
On foggy suburbs pours life's tedium.

My cat seeks out a litter on the stones,   5
Her mangy body turning without rest.
An ancient poet's soul in monotones
Whines in the rain-spouts like a chilblained ghost.

A great bell mourns, a wet log wrapped in smoke
Sings in falsetto to the wheezing clock,   10
While from a rankly perfumed deck of cards

1. Translated by C. F. MacIntyre to follow the original rhyme pattern.   1. Translated by Kenneth O. Hanson, with emphasis on the imagery. The French original uses identical *abab* rhymes in the two quatrains and shifts to *ccd, eed* in the tercets.   2. The rainy time (Latin, literal trans.); a period extending from January 20 to February 18 as the fifth month of the French Revolutionary calendar.

(A dropsical old crone's fatal bequest)
The Queen of Spades, the dapper Jack of Hearts
Speak darkly of dead loves, how they were lost.

Spleen LXXIX[1]

I have more memories than if I had lived a thousand years.

Even a bureau crammed with souvenirs,
Old bills, love letters, photographs, receipts,
Court depositions, locks of hair in plaits,
Hides fewer secrets than my brain could yield.   5
It's like a tomb, a corpse-filled Potter's Field,[2]
A pyramid where the dead lie down by scores.
I am a graveyard that the moon abhors:
Like guilty qualms, the worms burrow and nest
Thickly in bodies that I loved the best.   10
I'm a stale boudoir where old-fashioned clothes
Lie scattered among wilted fern and rose,
Where only the Boucher girls[3] in pale pastels
Can breathe the uncorked scents and faded smells.

Nothing can equal those days for endlessness   15
When in the winter's blizzardy caress
Indifference expanding to Ennui[4]
Takes on the feel of Immortality.
O living matter, henceforth you're no more
Than a cold stone encompassed by vague fear   20
And by the desert, and the mist and sun;
An ancient Sphinx ignored by everyone,
Left off the map, whose bitter irony
Is to sing as the sun sets in that dry sea.[5]

Spleen LXXXI[1]

When the low heavy sky weighs like a lid
Upon the spirit aching for the light
And all the wide horizon's line is hid
By a black day sadder than any night;

When the changed earth is but a dungeon dank   5
Where batlike Hope goes blindly fluttering

1. Translated by Anthony Hecht. The translation follows the original rhymed couplets, except for one technical impossibility: Baudelaire's repetition (in a poem about monotony) of an identical rhyme for eight lines (lines 11–18, the sound of long *a*).   2. A general term describing the common cemetery for those buried at public expense.   3. François Boucher (1703–1770), court painter for Louis XV of France, drew many pictures of young women clothed and nude.   4. Melancholy, paralyzing boredom.   5. Baudelaire combines two references to ancient Egypt, the Sphinx and the legendary statue of Memnon at Thebes, which was supposed to sing at sunset.   1. Translated by Sir John Squire in accord with the original rhyme scheme.

And, striking wall and roof and mouldered plank,
Bruises his tender head and timid wing;

When like grim prison bars stretch down the thin,
Straight, rigid pillars of the endless rain,   10
And the dumb throngs of infamous spiders spin
Their meshes in the caverns of the brain,

Suddenly, bells leap forth into the air,
Hurling a hideous uproar to the sky
As 'twere a band of homeless spirits who fare   15
Through the strange heavens, wailing stubbornly.

And hearses, without drum or instrument,
File slowly through my soul; crushed, sorrowful,
Weeps Hope, and Grief, fierce and omnipotent,
Plants his black banner on my drooping skull.   20

The Voyage¹

To Maxime du Camp ²

I

The child, in love with prints and maps,
Holds the whole world in his vast appetite.
How large the earth is under the lamplight!
But in the eyes of memory, how the world is cramped!

We set out one morning, brain afire,   5
Hearts fat with rancor and bitter desires,
Moving along to the rhythm of wind and waves,
Lull the inner infinite on the finite of seas:

Some are glad, glad to leave a degraded home;
Others, happy to shake off the horror of their hearts,   10
Still others, astrologers drowned in the eyes of woman—
Oh the perfumes of Circe,³ the power and the pig!—

To escape conversion to the Beast, get drunk
On space and light and the flames of skies;
The tongue of the sun and the ice that bites   15
Slowly erase the mark of the Kiss.

But the true voyagers are those who leave
Only to be going; hearts nimble as balloons,

1. Translated by Charles Henri Ford. The French poem is written in the traditional twelve-syllable (alexandrine) line with an *abab* rhyme scheme. 2. A wry dedication to the progress-oriented author of *Modern Songs* (1855), which began "I was born a traveler." 3. In Homer's *Odyssey*, an island sorceress who changed visitors into beasts. Odysseus's men were transformed into pigs.

They never diverge from luck's black sun,
And with or without reason, cry, Let's be gone!   20

Desire to them is nothing but clouds,
They dream, as a draftee dreams of the cannon,
Of vast sensualities, changing, unknown,
Whose name the spirit has never pronounced!

II

We imitate—horrible!—the top and ball   25
In their waltz and bounce; even in sleep
We're turned and tormented by Curiosity,
Who, like a mad Angel, lashes the stars.

Peculiar fortune that changes its goal,
And being nowhere, is anywhere at all!   30
And Man, who is never untwisted from hope,
Scrambling like a madman to get some rest!

The soul's a three-master seeking Icaria;[4]
A voice on deck calls: "Wake up there!"
A voice from the mast-head, vehement, wild: 35
"Love . . . fame . . . happiness!" We're on the rocks!

Every island that the lookout hails
Becomes the Eldorado[5] foretold by Fortune;
Then Imagination embarks on its orgy
But runs aground in the brightness of morning.   40

Poor little lover of visionary fields!
Should he be put in irons, dumped in the sea,
This drunken sailor, discoverer of Americas,
Mirage that makes the gulf more bitter?

So the old vagabond, shuffling in mud,   45
Dreams, nose hoisted, of a shining paradise,
His charmed eye lighting on Capua's[6] coast
At every candle aglow in a hovel.

III

Astounding voyagers! what noble stories
We read in your eyes, deeper than seas;   50
Show us those caskets, filled with rich memories,
Marvelous jewels, hewn from stars and aether.

Yes, we would travel, without sail or steam!
Gladden a little our jail's desolation,

---

4. Greek island in the Aegean Sea, named after the mythological Icarus, who, escaping from prison on wings made by his father, Daedalus, plunged into nearby waters and drowned when they gave way. His name was associated with utopian flights, as in Etienne Cabet's novel about a utopian community, *Voyage to Icaria* (1840). *Three-master*: a ship.   5. Fabled country of gold and abundance.   6. City on the Volturno River in southern Italy, famous for its luxury and sensuality.

Sail over our minds, stretched like a canvas,   55
All your memories, framed with gold horizons.

Tell us, what have you seen?

IV

                "We have seen stars
And tides; we have seen sands, too,
And, despite shocks and unforeseen disasters,
We were often bored, just as we are here.   60

The glory of sun on a violet sea,
The glory of cities in the setting sun,
Kindled our hearts with torment and longing
To plunge into the sky's magnetic reflections.

Neither the rich cities nor sublime landscapes,   65
Ever possessed that mysterious attraction
Of Change and Chance having fun with the clouds.
And always Desire kept us anxious!

—Enjoyment adds force to Appetite!
Desire, old tree nurtured by pleasure,   70
Although your dear bark thicken and harden,
Your branches throb to hold the sun closer!

Great tree, will you outgrow the cypress?
Still we have gathered carefully
Some sketches for your hungry album,   75
Brothers, for whom all things from far away

Are precious! We've bowed down to idols;
To thrones encrusted with luminous rocks;
To figured palaces whose magic pomp
Would ruin your bankers with a ruinous dream;   80

To costumes that intoxicate the eye,
To women whose teeth and nails are dyed,
To clever jugglers, fondled by the snake."[7]

V

And then, and what more?

VI

              "O childish minds!

Not to forget the principal thing,   85
We saw everywhere, without looking for it,

---

7. Snake charmers. The images in this stanza evoke India.

From top to toe of the deadly scale,
The tedious drama of undying sin:

Woman, low slave, vain and stupid,
Without laughter self-loving, and without disgust,   90
Man, greedy despot, lewd, hard and covetous,
Slave of the slave, rivulet in the sewer;

The hangman exulting, the martyr sobbing;
Festivals that season and perfume the blood;[8]
The poison of power unnerving the tyrant,   95
The masses in love with the brutalizing whip;

Many religions, very like our own,
All climbing to heaven; and Holiness,
Like a delicate wallower in a feather bed,
Seeking sensation from hair shirts and nails.   100

Jabbering humanity, drunk with its genius,
As crazy now as it was in the past,
Crying to God in its raging agony:
'O master, fellow creature, I curse thee forever!'

And then the least stupid, brave lovers of Lunacy,   105
Fleeing the gross herd that Destiny pens in,
Finding release in the vast dreams of opium!
—Such is the story, the whole world over."

VII

Bitter knowledge that traveling brings!
The globe, monotonous and small, today,   110
Yesterday, tomorrow, always, throws us our image:
An oasis of horror in a desert of boredom!

Should we go? Or stay? If you can stay, stay;
But go if you must. Some run, some hide
To outwit Time, the enemy so vigilant and   115
Baleful. And many, alas, must run forever

Like the wandering Jew[9] and the twelve apostles,
Who could not escape his relentless net[1]
By ship or by wheel; while others knew how
To destroy him without leaving home.   120

8. Literally, Festivals seasoned and perfumed by blood.   9. According to medieval legend, a Jew who mocked Christ on his way to the cross and was condemned to wander unceasingly until Judgment Day.   1. These three stanzas describe Time (ultimately Death) as a Roman gladiator, the *retiarius*, who used a net to trap his opponent.

When finally he places his foot on our spine,
May we be able to hope and cry, Forward!
As in days gone by when we left for China,
Eyes fixed on the distance, hair in the wind,

With heart as light as a young libertine's   125
We'll embark on the sea of deepening shadows.
Do you hear those mournful, enchanting voices[2]
That sing: "Come this way, if you would taste

The perfumed Lotus. Here you may pick
Miraculous fruits for which the heart hungers.   130
Come and drink deep of this strange,
Soft afternoon that never ends?"

Knowing his voice, we visualize the phantom—
It is our Pylades there, his arms outstretched.
While she whose knees we used to kiss cries out,   135
"For strength of heart, swim back to your Electra!"[3]

VIII

O Death, old captain, it is time! weigh anchor!
This country confounds us; hoist sail and away!
If the sky and sea are black as ink,
Our hearts, as you know them, burst with blinding rays. 140

Pour us your poison, that last consoling draft!
For we long, so the fire burns in the brain,
To sound the abyss, Hell or Heaven, what matter?
In the depths of the Unknown, we'll discover the New!

PARIS SPLEEN[1]

One O'Clock in the Morning

At last! I am alone! Nothing can be heard but the rumbling of a few belated and weary cabs. For a few hours at least silence will be ours, if not sleep. At last! The tyranny of the human face has disappeared, and now there will be no one but myself to make me suffer.

At last! I am allowed to relax in a bath of darkness! First a double turn of the key in the lock. This turn of the key will, it seems to me, increase my solitude and strengthen the barricades that, for the moment, separate me from the world.

Horrible life! Horrible city! Let us glance back over the events of the day:

---

2. The voices of the dead, luring the sailor to the Lotus-land of ease and forgetfulness.   3. In Greek mythology, Orestes and Pylades were close friends ready to sacrifice their lives for each other. Electra was Orestes' faithful sister, who saved him from the Furies.   1. Translated by Louis Varèse.

saw several writers, one of them asking me if you could go to Russia by land
(he thought Russia was an island, I suppose); disagreed liberally with the
editor of a review who to all my objections kept saying: "Here we are on the
side of respectability," implying that all the other periodicals were run by
rascals; bowed to twenty or more persons of whom fifteen were unknown to
me; distributed hand shakes in about the same proportion without having
first taken the precaution of buying gloves; to kill time during a shower,
dropped in on a dancer who asked me to design her a costume of *Venustre*;[2]
went to pay court to a theatrical director who in dismissing me said: "Perhaps
you would do well to see Z. . . . ; he is the dullest, stupidest and most celebrated of our authors; with him you might get somewhere. Consult him and
then we'll see": boasted (why?) of several ugly things I never did, and cravenly
denied some other misdeeds that I had accomplished with the greatest
delight; offense of fanfaronnade,[3] crime against human dignity; refused a
slight favor to a friend and gave a written recommendation to a perfect rogue;
Lord! let's hope that's all!

Dissatisfied with everything, dissatisfied with myself, I long to redeem
myself and to restore my pride in the silence and solitude of the night. Souls
of those whom I have loved, souls of those whom I have sung, strengthen
me, sustain me, keep me from the vanities of the world and its contaminating
fumes; and You, dear God! grant me grace to produce a few beautiful verses
to prove to myself that I am not the lowest of men, that I am not inferior to
those whom I despise.

Crowds

It is not given to every man to take a bath of multitude; enjoying a crowd
is an art; and only he can relish a debauch of vitality at the expense of the
human species, on whom, in his cradle, a fairy has bestowed the love of
masks and masquerading, the hate of home, and the passion for roaming.

Multitude, solitude: identical terms, and interchangeable by the active and
fertile poet. The man who is unable to people his solitude is equally unable
to be alone in a bustling crowd.

The poet enjoys the incomparable privilege of being able to be himself or
someone else, as he chooses. Like those wandering souls who go looking for
a body, he enters as he likes into each man's personality. For him alone
everything is vacant; and if certain places seem closed to him, it is only
because in his eyes they are not worth visiting.

The solitary and thoughtful stroller finds a singular intoxication in this
universal communion. The man who loves to lose himself in a crowd enjoys
feverish delights that the egoist locked up in himself as in a box, and the
slothful man like a mollusk in his shell, will be eternally deprived of. He
adopts as his own all the occupations, all the joys and all the sorrows that
chance offers.

What men call love is a very small, restricted, feeble thing compared with
this ineffable orgy, this divine prostitution of the soul giving itself entire, all

2. Venus. Baudelaire ironically reproduces the dancer's mispronunciation.   3. Boasting.

its poetry and all its charity, to the unexpected as it comes along, to the stranger as he passes.

It is a good thing sometimes to teach the fortunate of this world, if only to humble for an instant their foolish pride, that there are higher joys than theirs, finer and more uncircumscribed. The founders of colonies, shepherds of peoples, missionary priests exiled to the ends of the earth, doubtlessly know something of this mysterious drunkenness; and in the midst of the vast family created by their genius, they must often laugh at those who pity them because of their troubled fortunes and chaste lives.

Windows

Looking from outside into an open window one never sees as much as when one looks through a closed window. There is nothing more profound, more mysterious, more pregnant, more insidious, more dazzling than a window lighted by a single candle. What one can see out in the sunlight is always less interesting than what goes on behind a windowpane. In that black or luminous square life lives, life dreams, life suffers.

Across the ocean of roofs I can see a middle-aged woman, her face already lined, who is forever bending over something and who never goes out. Out of her face, her dress, and her gestures, out of practically nothing at all, I have made up this woman's story, or rather legend, and sometimes I tell it to myself and weep.

If it had been an old man I could have made up his just as well.

And I go to bed proud to have lived and to have suffered in some one besides myself.

Perhaps you will say "Are you sure that your story is the real one?" But what does it matter what reality is outside myself, so long as it has helped me to live, to feel that I am, and what I am?

Anywhere out of the World[1]

Life is a hospital where every patient is obsessed by the desire of changing beds. One would like to suffer opposite the stove, another is sure he would get well beside the window.

It always seems to me that I should be happy anywhere but where I am, and this question of moving is one that I am eternally discussing with my soul.

"Tell me, my soul, poor chilly soul, how would you like to live in Lisbon? It must be warm there, and you would be as blissful as a lizard in the sun. It is a city by the sea; they say that it is built of marble, and that its inhabitants have such a horror of the vegetable kingdom that they tear up all the tress.

---

1. The title (given in English by Baudelaire) is based on a line from Thomas Hood's poem *Bridge of Sighs*: "Anywhere, anywhere—out of the world." Baudelaire probably found the reference in Poe's *Poetic Principle*.

You see it is a country after my own heart; a country entirely made of mineral and light, and with liquid to reflect them."

My soul does not reply.

"Since you are so fond of being motionless and watching the pageantry of movement, would you like to live in the beatific land of Holland? Perhaps you could enjoy yourself in that country which you have so long admired in paintings on museum walls. What do you say to Rotterdam,[2] you who love forests of masts, and ships that are moored on the doorsteps of houses?"

My soul remains silent.

"Perhaps you would like Batavia[3] better? There, moreover, we should find the wit of Europe wedded to the beauty of the tropics."

Not a word. Can my soul be dead?

"Have you sunk into so deep a stupor that you are happy only in your unhappiness? If that is the case, let us fly to countries that are the counterfeits of Death. I know just the place for us, poor soul. We will pack up our trunks for Torneo.[4] We will go still farther, to the farthest end of the Baltic Sea; still farther from life if possible; we will settle at the Pole. There the sun only obliquely grazes the earth, and the slow alternations of daylight and night abolish variety and increase that other half of nothingness, monotony. There we can take deep baths of darkness, while sometimes for our entertainment, the Aurora Borealis will shoot up its rose-red sheafs like the reflections of the fireworks of hell!"

At last my soul explores! "Anywhere! Just so it is out of the world!"

---

2. Large Dutch seaport.   3. Former name of Djakarta, capital of the Dutch East Indies and now the capital city of Indonesia.   4. A city in Finland.

STÉPHANE MALLARMÉ
1842–1898

Of all the Symbolist writers, Mallarmé (*mal-are-may*) is the most compulsive visionary. He uses ordinary words and concrete images, but only as raw material for a wholly imaginary creation. Like Rimbaud, he seeks a way out of sordid reality through the liberating power of the imagination, but unlike the younger poet, he did not turn his back on literature even though his lofty poetic ideals made it increasingly difficult for him to put words on paper. Mallarmé works to purify language; he avoids the direct approach because obliquely he can say more. Thus he suggests, rather than names; keeps several levels of meaning alive at the same time; complicates his syntax and sometimes even misleads us to prolong the pleasure of final discovery. Although Mallarmé's poems are immediately accessible on the level of visual imagery, they also offer the pleasure of a chess game for those who like to pursue intricate structures of thought. He constitutes another example of the poet adventuring on the frontiers of thought; by the second half of the twentieth century, Mallarmé's multileveled patterns of allusion and abstract theories of poetic language had found followers among not only poets but also philosophers of language.

Étienne (called Stéphane) Mallarmé was born in Paris on March 18, 1842, into a settled bourgeois family. His father was deputy clerk in the Registry, and ancestors on both sides of the family had been minor government bureaucrats as far back as the French Revolution. Mallarmé's mother died when he was five, and his sister in

1857: the pain of their loss recurs in images of his later poetry. After graduating from boarding school in 1860, he worked for two years in his grandfather's office before deciding to become a teacher of English. In 1863 he received a teaching position in the southeastern provincial town of Tournon and moved there with his new wife, a young German woman named Maria Gerhard. Their daughter, Geneviève, was born in 1864. A son, Anatole, was born in 1871 and died in 1879.

Mallarmé began publishing poems and articles in 1862, although his output was always meager and he did not produce a collection in book form until 1887. Much of his work was published separately in various journals. His first important group of poems was published in 1866 in the new literary magazine *Contemporary Parnassus,* and his translations of Edgar Allan Poe appeared in 1872. Mallarmé was eager to move to Paris, the capital of the arts, but as a young teacher in the state educational system he was dependent on governmental assignments. Sent in 1886 to Besançon and in 1867 to Avignon, he was finally able to move to Paris in 1871, and there he taught at the Lycée Fontanes. Mallarmé was not a particularly good language teacher, had little aptitude for drills and discipline, and was often a figure of fun for his students. On the other hand, he was an important and charismatic figure for the young writers, artists, and musicians who heard him talk about the nature of poetry at the "Tuesdays," gatherings held every Tuesday evening from 1880 until shortly before his death. Mallarmé's influence was widespread. In 1876 Edouard Manet illustrated Mallarmé's *L'Après-midi d'un faune* (The afternoon of a faun), and in 1894 Claude Debussy composed his musical *Prélude,* which was inspired by the same text. Verlaine included Mallarmé in his account of the new poets, *The Accursed Poets,* and after Verlaine's death Mallarmé was elected "Prince of Poets" by his colleagues in 1896. Upon his retirement from teaching in 1894, Mallarmé lectured on poetry and experimented with different kinds of poetic form, including the typographical arrangements of *Dice Thrown* (1897) that foreshadowed modern concrete poetry. For years, he had worked on the notion of a universal "Book," a complicated text that would be performed and not merely read. Yet he himself finally felt that his vision had outstripped technical possibilities; and when he died on September 9, 1898, the work remained incomplete.

The creative process itself is the central topic of Mallarmé's poetry, whether in the earlier autobiographical poems or in later impersonal scenes from which the narrator is excluded. Mallarmé's particular symbolism builds on allusion and suggestion to evoke a virtual reality, a richer dimension he prefers to ordinary limited realism. The poet is understandably haunted by the difficulty of writing. He describes himself as a grave digger digging his thoughts out of the "cold and niggard soil" of his brain or as paralyzed by the blank whiteness of the paper on which he must write. Escaping into art, he wishes in one poem to imitate the spare perfection of painted Chinese porcelain. Even such a banal object as a fan, fluttering open and then lying closed against a bracelet, can evoke the desired realm of absolute beauty. Oddly enough, a common characteristic of Mallarmé's evocations of beauty, and one that distinguishes them from scenes in Baudelaire, Rimbaud, and Verlaine, is his emphasis on absence. An early poem, *Saint,* illustrates the way the poet plays with a sense of loss or absence while using concrete details to create a series of vivid—though intangible—images.

The saint of the poem (according to a previous title, Saint Cecilia, the patron saint of music), is seen at—perhaps represented on—the window of a cabinet where musical instruments are kept. The cabinet's cedar-wood viol, which no longer gleams with gold as it did when formerly played with accompanying flute and mandolin, and the old book lying open at the Magnificat, together establish the idea of a real, historical music that is now stilled or absent. The poem's single sentence is divided into two contrasting scenes; in the last two stanzas, the saint plays an imaginary harp that suggests an ideal or soundless music. She, the "Musician of silences," has her finger poised on the shape of a golden harp implied by the outstretched wing of a sculptured angel, a "plumage instrumental" that receives from the evening sun all the gilding that was lost to the real instrument of the first stanza. By the end of the poem, the ideal music suggested by the saint's gesture is more present to the reader than the "real" music at the beginning.

The ideal music of this and other poems is created by refining and manipulating ordinary language: purifying "the language of the horde," as Mallarmé says in *The Tomb of Edgar Poe*. This "tomb" or epitaph poem was written for a Baltimore memorial ceremony at which a monument to Poe was erected. Mallarmé describes the American poet as a Saint George confronting the dragon of mediocrity and slander (that is, critics who accused him of writing only drunken fantasies). Another allegory of the alienated poet, *The Virginal, Vibrant, and Beautiful Dawn,* is built around the image of a swan who—refusing to sing about life, warmth, and mundane reality—is finally frozen into the dazzling glacier of his ideal dreams. The sonnet emphasizes images of whiteness, arrested movement, sterility, and chill; the French text intensifies this bleakness by reiterating a shrill *ee* sound throughout all fourteen lines and piling up negative linguistic forms. Mallarmé's artist is a technician, coordinating different relationships among words to invent his "purer" poetic language

Mallarmé's best-known poem, the source of Claude Debussy's orchestral *Prélude* in 1894 and Nijinsky's ballet in 1912, is *The Afternoon of a Faun*. Here the familiar themes of artistic creation, dream, and loss—the doomed attempt to capture perfect form in mere words—underly the warm and sensuous picture of a woodland satyr recounting his erotic pursuit of two nymphs. Was it a dream, he wonders, that he caught the two water nymphs—one passionate, one naive—only to lose them on the brink of possession? The poem is framed by the faun's desire first to "perpetuate" these nymphs in memory and finally to follow them back into dream. It is famous for its vivid and sensual descriptions, for its intricate imagery, and for the extraordinary musicality of its classical verse (the French alexandrine, or twelve-syllable line). Turning to his pipes and to drunken dreams to celebrate a perfect union he could not hold, the faun illustrates once more Mallarmé's theme of poetic creation, describing an ideal beauty that is absent and a sensuously intuited love that remains perpetually not just out of reach but in fact a figment of the imagination.

Frederic St. Aubyn, *Stéphane Mallarmé* (1989), provides a brief biography and thematically arranged discussions of Mallarmé's work. Harold Bloom, ed., *Stéphane Mallarmé* (1987), collects thirteen challenging essays on Mallarmé's work and its implications for poetic practice. Hans-Jost Frey, *Studies in Poetic Discourse* (1996), trans. William Whobrey, offers perceptive essays on Mallarmé, Baudelaire, Rimbaud, and Hölderlin.

The Afternoon of a Faun[1]

Eclogue[2]

THE FAUN

These nymphs that I would perpetuate:
so clear
And light, their carnation,[3] that it floats in the air
Heavy with leafy slumbers.

Did I love a dream?
My doubt, night's ancient hoard, pursues its theme
In branching labyrinths, which, being still   5
The veritable woods themselves, alas, reveal

---

1. All poems translated by Henry Weinfield. In Greek mythology, a faun was a woodland satyr with goatlike hooves and horns.   2. A pastoral poem, usually in dialogue form, originating in Greek poetry. Here, italics indicate the divisions of the faun's internal dialogue.   3. A rosy flesh pink.

My triumph as the ideal fault of roses.
Consider . . .

        if the women of your glosses
Are phantoms of your fabulous[4] desires!
Faun, the illusion flees from the cold, blue eyes   10
Of the chaster nymph like a fountain gushing tears;
But the other, all in sighs, you say, compares
To a hot wind through the fleece that blows at noon?
No! through the motionless and weary swoon
Of stifling heat that suffocates the morning,   15
Save from my flute, no waters murmuring
In harmony flow out into the groves;
And the only wind on the horizon no ripple moves,
Exhaled from my twin pipes and swift to drain
The melody in arid drifts of rain,   20
Is the visible, serene and fictive air
Of inspiration rising as if in prayer.

RELATE, Sicilian shores,[5] whose tranquil fens
My vanity disturbs as do the suns,
Silent beneath the brilliant flowers of flame: 25
"That cutting hollow reeds my art would tame,
I saw far off, against the glaucous gold
Of foliage twined to where the springs run cold,
An animal whiteness languorously swaying;
To the slow prelude that the pipes were playing,   30
This flight of swans—no! naiads[6]—rose in a shower
Of spray . . ."

        Day burns inert in the tawny hour
And excess of hymen is escaped away—
Without a sign, from one who pined for the primal A:[7]
And so, beneath a flood of antique light,   35
As innocent as are the lilies white,
To my first ardors I awake alone.

Besides sweet nothings by their lips made known,
Kisses that only mark their perfidy,
My chest reveals an unsolved mystery . . .   40
The toothmarks of some strange, majestic creature:
Enough! Arcana such as these disclose their nature
Only through vast twin reeds played to the skies,
That, turning to music all that clouds the eyes,
Dream, in a long solo, that we amused   45
The beauty all around us by confused
Equations[8] with our credulous melody;
And dream that the song can make love soar so high

---

4. Fabled; i.e., both marvelous and narrated.   5. An invocation to the surrounding countryside, which recalls the openings of classical poems like the *Iliad* and the *Aeneid*.   6. Water nymphs.   7. The musical note A. In the French text it is *la* (from the do-re-mi scale), which is also the feminine article "the." *Hymen*: marriage or sexual union.   8. Playing his reed pipes, the faun creates a musical line that is equated with the nymphs' silhouette as he remembers it behind closed eyes.

That, purged of all ordinary fantasies
Of back or breast—incessant shapes that rise   50
In blindness—it distills sonorities
From every empty and monotonous line.[9]

Then, instrument of flights;[1] Syrinx malign,
At lakes where you attend me, bloom once more!
Long shall my discourse from the echoing shore   55
Depict those goddesses: by masquerades,[2]
I'll strip the veils that sanctify their shades;
And when I've sucked the brightness out of grapes,
To quell the flood of sorrow that escapes,
I'll lift the empty cluster to the sky,   60
Avidly drunk till evening has drawn nigh,
And blow in laughter through the luminous skins.

Let us inflate our MEMORIES, O nymphs.
"Piercing the reeds, my darting eyes transfix,
Plunged in the cooling waves, immortal necks,   65
And cries of fury echo through the air;
Splendid cascades of tresses disappear
In shimmering jewels. Pursuing them, I find
There, at my feet, two sleepers intertwined,
Bruised in the languor of duality,   70
Their arms about each other heedlessly.
I bear them, still entangled, to a height
Where frivolous shadow never mocks the light
And dying roses yield the sun their scent,
That with the day our passions might be spent."   75
I adore you, wrath of virgins—fierce delight
Of the sacred burden's writhing naked flight
From the fiery lightning of my lips that flash
With the secret terror of the thirsting flesh:
From the cruel one's feet to the heart of the shy,   80
Whom innocence abandons suddenly,
Watered in frenzied or less woeful tears.
"Gay with the conquest of those traitorous fears,
I sinned when I divided the dishevelled
Tuft of kisses that the gods had ravelled.   85
For hardly had I hidden an ardent moan
Deep in the joyous recesses of one
(Holding by a finger, that her swanlike pallor
From her sister's passion might be tinged with color,
The little one, unblushingly demure,   90
When from my arms, loosened[3] by death obscure,
This prey, ungrateful to the end, breaks free,
Spurning the sobs that still transported me."

Others will lead me on to happiness,
Their tresses knotted round my horns, I guess.   95

---

9. Lines 51 and 52 are one line in the French text. 1. In Greek mythology, a nymph who fled from the god Pan and was changed into a reed, from which flutes, or panpipes, are made. 2. Literally, idolatrous pictures (of the nymphs). 3. I.e., his arms were momentarily weakened.

You know, my passion, that, crimson with ripe seeds,
Pomegranates burst in a murmur of bees,
And that our blood, seized by each passing form,
Flows toward desire's everlasting swarm.
In the time when the forest turns ashen and gold   100
And the summer's demise in the leaves is extolled,
Etna![4] when Venus visits her retreat,
Treading your lava with innocent feet,
Though a sad sleep thunders and the flame burns cold,
I hold the queen!
                          Sure punishment[5] . . .

                                          No, but the soul,   105
Weighed down by the body, wordless, struck dumb,
To noon's proud silence must at last succumb:
And so, let me sleep, oblivious of sin,
Stretched out on the thirsty sand, drinking in
The bountiful rays of the wine-growing star!   110

Couple, farewell; I'll see the shade that now you are.

The Tomb[1] of Edgar Poe

As to Himself at last eternity changes him
The Poet reawakens with a naked sword
His century appalled at never having heard
That in this voice triumphant death had sung its hymn.

They, like a writhing hydra, hearing seraphim[2]   5
Bestow a purer sense on the language of the horde,
Loudly proclaimed that the magic potion[3] had been poured
From the dregs of some dishonored mixture of foul slime.

From the war between earth and heaven, what grief!
If understanding cannot sculpt a bas-relief   10
To ornament the dazzling tomb of Poe:

Calm block here fallen from obscure disaster,[4]
Let this granite at least mark the boundaries evermore
To the dark flights of Blasphemy[5] hurled to the future.

---

4. A volcano in Sicily.   5. The faun imagines swift punishment when in his heightened desire he fantasizes seizing Venus, the goddess of love.   1. A *tomb* is also a funeral poem. The poem was written for a memorial ceremony honoring Edgar Allan Poe (1809–1849) in Baltimore, Maryland, and was first published in the 1877 memorial volume.   2. The Angel: the above said Poet [Mallarmé's note]. Mallarmé explained this in English to the memorial organizers. *Hydra*: a mythical many-headed serpent; here compared with those who slandered Poe when he was alive.   3. In plain prose: Charged him with always being drunk [Mallarmé's note]. Critics accused Poe of finding inspiration in drunken fantasies.   4. The memorial marker (*Calm block*) is seen as a meteorite fallen from a dark or negative star (*disaster*); a play on words: *aster* is Greek for "star."   5. Blasphemy: against poets, such as the charge of Poe being drunk [Mallarmé's note]. *Boundaries*: literally, the milestone along French roads, intended here to limit the batlike flights of slander.

Saint[1]

At the window frame concealing
The viol old and destitute
Whose gilded sandalwood, now peeling,
Once shone with mandolin or flute,

Is the Saint, pale, unfolding   5
The old, worn missal,[2] a divine
Magnificat[3] in rivers flowing
Once at vespers and compline:[4]

At the glass of this monstrance,[5] vessel
Touched by a harp that took its shape   10
From the evening flight of an Angel
For the delicate fingertip

Which, without the old, worn missal
Or sandalwood, she balances
On the plumage instrumental,   15
Musician of silences.

[The Virginal, Vibrant, and Beautiful Dawn]

II

The virginal, vibrant, and beautiful dawn,
Will a beat of its drunken wing[1] not suffice
To rend this hard lake haunted beneath the ice
By the transparent glacier of flights never flown?

A swan of former times remembers it's the one   5
Magnificent but hopelessly struggling to resist
For never having sung of a land in which to exist
When the boredom of the sterile winter has shone.

Though its quivering neck will shake free of the agonies
Inflicted on the bird by the space it denies,   10
The horror of the earth will remain where it lies.

Phantom whose pure brightness assigns it this domain,
It stiffens in the cold dream of disdain
That clothes the useless exile of the Swan.[2]

---

1. The original title was "Saint Cecilia Playing on the Wing of an Angel."   2. Literally, an old book, probably containing the music for the old instruments. Cecilia is the patron saint of music.   3. A hymn of praise to God.   4. Evening church services. *Once:* formerly.   5. An altar receptacle to hold the Host, with a small glass window in front.   1. A wild, impulsive gesture; also, an astonishing extended rhyme with *is freed* in French: *d'aile ivre / délivre.*   2. The word *swan* rhymes with *sign* in French (*cygne / signe*), and the capitalized Swan may be read as a symbol of the writer's futile quest for the absolute Sign.

PAUL VERLAINE
1844–1896

The musicality of his verse, his impressionistic yet intimate scenes, and the complex melancholy of his poetic voice serve to distinguish Paul Verlaine among the three great Symbolist poets after Baudelaire. If the abstract Mallarmé and the flamboyant Rimbaud are better known to modern readers, it is Verlaine whose asymmetrical lines and fleeting images influenced the next generation of poets and helped shape twentieth-century free verse. Verlaine's love for the nuance that captures several dimensions of experience and his rejection of fixed categories as a kind of lesser vision are evoked in the mysterious figure of Pierrot, the mournful clown who stands slightly apart from society and recognizes his own alienation. It was an alienation Verlaine knew; he scandalized society by his irregular life and affair with Arthur Rimbaud, and by the time of his death he was both "Prince of Poets" and a symbol of decadence.

Paul-Marie Verlaine was born at Metz, France, in a well-to-do army family that indulged their only son. When Verlaine was seven, his father resigned his commission and the family moved to Paris, where he was educated, frequented the circles of the classically oriented Parnassian poets, and attended law school for a year before deciding to devote himself to poetry. Earning a living in a series of clerical positions, he published his first collection, *Saturnian Poems* (under the sign of Saturn, supposedly signaling a morbid imagination) in 1866; three years later, *Fêtes galantes* (Gallant feasts; elegant pastoral festivities) appeared. Verlaine at this time was already having problems with alcoholism and showing signs of the sudden rages that punctuated his later life; several times, he went so far as to attack his mother. In 1870, under pressure from his family and perhaps hoping to settle down, he married Mathilde Mauté, a devout Catholic and sister of a friend. Anticipations of peace and happiness dominate the poems of *The Good Song*, written shortly before his marriage and published the same year. The next year, however, he met Arthur Rimbaud, and relations with his wife deteriorated sharply; Mathilde left Verlaine in 1872 when he would not break with Rimbaud, and the couple was divorced in 1874. The two poets spent much of the following year in London, but their tempestuous relationship ended in Belgium in July 1873 when Verlaine shot Rimbaud after a quarrel and was imprisoned for two years. Poems from this period were published in 1874 as *Songs without Words,* a paradoxical title that recalls the poet's advice in his *Art of Poetry:* "You must have music first of all." (In fact, Verlaine's poetry has often been set to music.) While in prison, he turned for solace to his childhood Catholicism and wrote poems (later published in *Wisdom,* 1880) that evoke his pain, remorse, and renewed hope of salvation. Emerging from prison in 1875, Verlaine attempted to renew his relationship with Rimbaud but was rebuffed. The famous affair had ended, and with Rimbaud in Africa, Verlaine's only further connection was to edit the *Illuminations* in 1886 and a posthumous collection in 1895.

Verlaine's religious conversion in 1873 did not herald a life of peace and contemplation. After teaching French for a while in England, he returned to Paris and attempted unsuccessfully to regain his job with the city. He also tried farming with a former student, Lucien Létinois. After Létinois's death from typhoid fever, Verlaine moved in with his mother but was again imprisoned for violence. He moved to Paris in 1885, where he lived in poverty and ill health. His continued alcoholism was taking its toll, and he spent much of his life in hospitals until his death in 1896. During the last ten years, however, his literary reputation was on the rise. The next generation of poets in France and England looked to him as a master, admiring both his poetry and his anticonformist ways. Critical studies were written about him; he wrote prolifically, lectured in England, and was hailed as their leader by a new group of self-styled "Decadent" poets in France. In August 1894, Verlaine was elected "Prince of Poets" by his colleagues.

His later poetry is quite different from his early, ambivalent style: it stresses relig-ious themes and a voice of absolute conviction. Some continuity is visible: previous images of the poet's vulnerability before life (*Autumn Song*) become the more reas-suring image of a worshiper's humility before God; the sensuality and dissonances of earlier poems are later used as examples of evil in the poet's battle against sin. On several occasions, Verlaine even parodies his former style. For many readers, however, the volumes of poetry and prose after *Yesteryear and Yesterday* (*Jadis et Naguère*; 1884) are less compelling precisely because they turn to more assertive, explicit, and often conventional forms of expression. Gone is the taste for nuance and ambiguity, the irony and self-conscious pathos, the half-tones and the lilt of asymmetrical rhythms that seem peculiarly Verlaine and without which—as he says in *The Art of Poetry*—everything else is merely literary convention, or "literature."

The five poems printed here come from five different collections published from 1866 to 1884. *Autumn Song*, one of seven "Mournful Landscapes" in the *Saturnian Poems*, captures a moment of experience while displaying Verlaine's intense musi-cality in its short rhymed lines and gently rocking melody. (In the French, the indented lines have three syllables, the others four.) Dead leaves proclaim the end of the year, and the speaker—already disheartened by the melodious cry of the autumn wind—weeps quietly over the passage of time in his own life. In this acute evocation of a state of mind, the melancholy speaker is equated with a dead leaf blown helplessly on the wind (compare Shelley's *Ode to the West Wind*).

Another imaginary landscape, this time a painted one, appears in *Moonlight*, a poem from *Fêtes galantes* that evokes the dreamlike scenes in which the eighteenth-century French artist Antoine Watteau (1684–1721) portrayed aristocratic men and women playing at being romantic shepherds and shepherdesses. *Moonlight* is truly a poem of nuances and masks, of paradoxical images and elusive identity. The moon's half-light illuminates uncertain characters who dance dejectedly inside their fanciful costumes, sing in a sad minor key about love and good luck, and cannot believe in their own happiness; in this painted world, their song itself is part of the moonlight, and the whole scene an image of the addressee's (perhaps Verlaine's) soul. Moonlight reappears in *The White Moonglow* (from *The Good Song*), one of the poems Verlaine gave his fiancée before their marriage. This "exquisite hour" celebrates a moment of intimacy between the two lovers walking at night; it is a swift, delicate sketch in which the human figures never actually appear. Instead, there are overheard voices, frag-mentary or reflected images, and refracted moonlight.

Verlaine is not all moonlight and fading voices, however. In *Wooden Horses*, he depicts a busy merry-go-round in an amusement park peopled by pickpockets and by workers eager to make love on their day off. This time the music is harshly rhythmic, an insistent tempo that is echoed and reinforced by the poem's repetitions: the wooden horses gallop on and on, their riders drunk with dizziness in what begins to seem like a mindless pursuit of passion. Evening comes with velvet elegance in the last stanza, but here it is only a background for amorous couples pairing off to the beat of the drums. All four poems evoke a particular moment of experience, a fleeting subjective impression that is built out of a few telling details and associated rhythm patterns. Such, in fact, is the recommendation of Verlaine's *Art of Poetry*, published in *Yesteryear and Yesterday*. This poem, which became the unofficial manifesto of the new Symbolist school, not only reflects Verlaine's own preferences in 1874 but also outlines a program of antitraditional poetic strategies. No more four-square rhythm; no more fixed images with clear outlines and colors; no wit, eloquence, or rhyme for its own sake; in short, none of the traditional poetic techniques intended to create beautiful and lasting images in explicit, rational verse. Instead, Verlaine proclaimed the joys of the *vers impair*, the "uneven" line whose odd number of syllables creates a floating effect. (*The Art of Poetry* uses a nine-syllable line.) Words are slightly inex-act, perhaps containing suggestive overtones. Composite images express a state of mind; nuances invite a blurring of boundaries and release the imagination; and above all, music and emotion are the poet's guide until words become "soluble" and poetry a natural experience. Verlaine's opposition of "poetry" and "literature," and the example of his own poems, became a model for the young Symbolist poets—among them Jules Laforgue, much admired by the early T. S. Eliot—and helped shape European lyric tradition for many years.

Joanna Richardson, *Verlaine* (1971), is a useful biography. Stefan Zweig, *Paul Verlaine* (1913), trans. O. F. Theis (1980), discusses the poet and his work.

PRONOUNCING GLOSSARY

The following list uses common English syllables and stress accents to provide rough equivalents of selected names whose pronunciation may be unfamiliar to the general reader.

Bois de la Cambre: *bwah-deu-lah-cawm'-br*   Verlaine: *vehr-len'*

Autumn Song[1]

With long sobs
the violin-throbs
  of autumn wound
my heart with languorous
and monotonous   5
  sound.

Choking and pale
when I mind the tale
  the hours keep,
my memory strays   10
down other days
  and I weep;

and I let me go
where ill winds blow,
  now here, now there,   15
harried and sped,
even as a dead
  leaf, anywhere.

Moonlight[1]

Your soul is like a painter's landscape[2] where
charming masks in shepherd mummeries
are playing lutes[3] and dancing with an air
of being sad in their fantastic guise.

---

1. All poems translated by C. F. MacIntyre. The poem is one of the "Mournful Landscapes" in *Saturnian Poems* (1866).   **1.** From *Fêtes galantes* (1869).   **2.** A reference to Antoine Watteau's (1684–1721) dreamlike paintings in which elegant men and women, costumed as shepherds and shepherdesses, play at being pastoral lovers.   **3.** Arab musical instrument associated with serenades that was fashionable in the eighteenth century.

Even while they sing, all in a minor key,   5
of love triumphant and life's careless boon,
they seem in doubt of their felicity,
their song melts in the calm light of the moon,

the lovely melancholy light that sets
the little birds to dreaming in the tree   10
and among the statues makes the jets
of slender fountains sob with ecstasy.

[The White Moonglow][1]

The white moonglow
shines on the trees;
from each bough
a voice flees
as the leaves move . . .   5

Oh, my love.

The pond reflects,
a mirror deep,
the black silhouette
of the willow tree   10
where the wind weeps . . .

Oh, reverie.

Now a tender
and vast appeasement
seems to descend   15
from the firmament
with the irised star[2] . . .

Ah, exquisite hour.

Wooden Horses[1]

By Saint-Gille
let's away,
my light-footed bay.
                    V. Hugo[2]

Turn, good wooden horses, round
a hundred turns, a thousand turns.

1. From *The Good Song* (1870).   2. The multiple reflections of the moonlight.   1. From *Songs without Words* (1874).   2. French poet (1802–1885). Saint-Gilles is a suburb of Brussels, Belgium, with a public fairground.

Forever turn till the axles burn,
turn, turn, to the oboes' sound.

The big soldier and the fattest maid   5
ride your backs as if in their chamber,
because their masters have also made
an outing today in the Bois de la Cambre.³

Turn, turn, horses of their hearts,
while all around your whirling there   10
are the clever sharpers⁴ at their art;
turn to the cornet's bragging blare.

It's as much fun as getting dead
drunk, to ride in this silly ring!
Good for the belly, bad for the head,   15
a plenty good and a plenty bad thing.

Turn, turn, no need today
of any spurs to make you bound,
galloping around and round,
turn, turn, without hope of hay.   20

And hurry, horses of their love,
already night is falling here
and the pigeon flies to join the dove,
far from madame, far from the fair.

Turn! Turn! Slow evening comes,   25
in velvet, buttoned up with stars.
Away the lovers go, in pairs.
Turn to the beat of the joyous drums.

The Art of Poetry¹

You must have music first of all,
and for that a rhythm uneven² is best,
vague in the air and soluble,
with nothing heavy and nothing at rest.

You must not scorn to do some wrong   5
in choosing the words to fill your lines:
nothing more dear than the tipsy song
where the Undefined and Exact combine.

3. An elegant park south of Brussels.　4. Literally, pickpockets.　1. From *Yesteryear and Yesterday* (1884), written in 1874.　2. The *vers impair* (line with an uneven number of syllables), which gives traditional French readers a sense of "nothing at rest." This poem uses a nine-syllable line and—as here— often illustrates its points.

It is the veiled and lovely eye,
the full noon quivering with light;   10
it is, in the cool of an autumn sky,
the blue confusion of stars at night!

Never the Color, always the Shade,
always the nuance is supreme!
Only by shade is the trothal made   15
between flute and horn, of dream with dream!

Epigram's an assassin! Keep
away from him, fierce Wit, and vicious
laughter that makes the Azure[3] weep,
and from all that garlic of vulgar dishes!   20

Take Eloquence and wring his neck!
You would do well, by force and care,
wisely to hold Rhyme in check,
or she's off—if you don't watch—God knows where!

Oh, who will tell the wrongs of Rhyme?   25
What crazy negro or deaf child
made this trinket for a dime,
sounding hollow and false when filed?

Let there be music, again and forever!
Let your verse be a quick-wing'd thing and light—   30
such as one feels when a new love's fervor
to other skies wings the soul in flight.

Happy-go-lucky, let your lines
disheveled run where the dawn winds lure,
smelling of wild mint, smelling of thyme . . .   35
and all the rest is literature.

3. The sky's unbroken azure was, for many Symbolists, an image of absolute poetry as opposed to vulgarity.

ARTHUR RIMBAUD
1854–1891

In a dazzlingly brief literary career, which he abandoned at the age of twenty, Arthur Rimbaud (*ram-boh'*) put his indelible stamp on the visionary and experimental aspects of modern poetry. Taking literally the ancient (and Romantic) notion of the poet as prophet, he determined to make himself a seer, or *voyant*, by whatever violent means were necessary. His writing reveals the mixture of idealism, hope, and faith in his own genius that led him to believe in the possibility of a self-produced apocalypse. It also recounts a futile search for love that permeates his poetic quest; a stormy relationship with the older poet Paul Verlaine; and finally, the bitterness and sense of defeat that drove him to abandon his former life and become a fortune-hunter in Africa. Rimbaud was an especially strong model for the Surrealists and for others in twentieth-century literature who saw in him an example of complete dedication to a poetic ideal that surpassed mere written words: he exemplified a revolutionary reimagining of human experience that would open vistas, explode harmful patterns of thought, and thus bring about a better future. Despite—or perhaps because of— Rimbaud's admission of defeat, he became a mythic figure whose brilliant poems and prose were markers on the way of a career that, in the words of one admirer, passed like a lightning bolt through French literature.

Jean-Nicholas-Arthur Rimbaud was born on October 20, 1854, in Charleville, a town in northeastern France. Rimbaud's father abandoned the family when Arthur was seven, and his embittered mother raised her children in a repressive and disciplinarian atmosphere. In 1870, Rimbaud made the first of his flights from home and spent ten days in jail as a vagrant. Yet he proved to be an unusually gifted student and was encouraged in his literary tastes and endeavors by a sympathetic teacher who introduced him to current poetry. It was this teacher, Georges Izambard, to whom Rimbaud wrote of his poetic ambitions and his desire to make himself a seer by the systematic "derangement of all the senses." In 1871, the poet Paul Verlaine (to whom Rimbaud had sent some of his work) invited Rimbaud to Paris. It was the beginning of a stormy two-year relationship in Paris, London, and Brussels that ended in 1873 when Verlaine shot Rimbaud through the wrist and was sentenced to two years' imprisonment. In that year, at the age of nineteen, Rimbaud decided to give up writing and seek his fortune in commerce. He found his way to many parts of Europe, to Cyprus, to Java, and to Aden, where he worked for an exporting firm, later moving to Harar in Abyssinia. As an independent trader he went on expeditions in Abyssinia and engaged in gun running; despite rumor, it does not appear that he trafficked in slaves. Falling ill with a cancerous tumor on one knee and unable to find adequate treatment, Rimbaud returned to France with a gangrenous leg in May 1891. His leg was amputated at a Marseilles hospital, and he died six months later on November 10, 1891.

In a short and violent literary career—he wrote all his poetry between the ages of fifteen and twenty—Rimbaud combines an aggressive, cynical realism and attempts to transform both self and surroundings into a magically perfect whole. The visionary image sequences of his first major poem (a symbolic voyage titled *The Drunken Boat*), the agonized and mocking autobiographical prose of *A Season in Hell*, and finally the transfigured scenes from real life called *Illuminations* together represent stages in this endeavor to discover—or create—a state of natural innocence and harmony. For a while, Rimbaud believed that he could manipulate language to create the vision of an ideal world. "I have strung ropes from steeple to steeple; garlands from window to window; golden chains from star to star, and I dance."

The Drunken Boat, written when the poet was still sixteen and had never seen the sea, uses the traditional literary theme of the voyage to express his rebellion against guides and restraints. Speaking as a boat let loose on the high seas, the narrator describes a gradually intensifying series of encounters with a total reality—at once beautiful and terrifying—that goes beyond his individual power to sustain. Yet the concluding section is not a resolution of the original need for flight: Rimbaud's boat cannot accept the world of proud commercial shipping or of prison ships, and dreams of the childhood world of a solitary paper boat set adrift in a small pool. The poem ends in a clearer restatement of its original alienation and in an attitude that many have interpreted as prefiguring Rimbaud's eventual departure from Europe and his rejection of poetry.

Rimbaud's attempt to become a *voyant*, to transform his everyday reality by means of the re-creating power of poetry, is both summarized and mocked in the bitter autobiographical prose poem *A Season in Hell*. In an atmosphere of perpetual crisis, alternating between agonized idealism and cynical disbelief, he reviews his quest for perfect truth and love and vividly describes his effort to reach the unknown by pure hallucination. "I saw very plainly a mosque in place of a factory, a school of drummers composed of angels . . . a drawing room at the bottom of the lake . . . I became a fabulous opera." At the end of *A Season in Hell* he tells us that he has rejected these earlier illusions and embraced earth and rugged reality. Yet he never wrote poetry to celebrate his newly rediscovered realism (and may well have completed the *Illuminations* after that point), so that he remains best known for the passion and beauty of his apocalyptic vision.

The *Illuminations* offer a series of transformations that leave only traces of their varied points of departure: bridges in London, plowed fields, a park statue, dawn. They parade illusions and free association, and they cut short logical sequences to develop an almost musical organization of themes and images. Almost all are prose poems, intricately organized in complex rhythmic and visual patterns. Some echo autobiographical themes, but the scenes and allusions are transformed. *Bridges* recalls the London where Rimbaud lived for a time, but it is an impressionistic memory that transforms the real scene. *Barbarian* may echo a previous sea voyage and drug use, but the poem transcends the question of any single source in reality. Set outside normal time and space, "Long after the days and the seasons, and the creatures and the countries," it enacts a withdrawal that moves gradually from echoes of the real world to an elemental core of tenderness and beauty, completely inside the world of imagination.

Clearly the reader cannot approach *Barbarian* as if it were by Lamartine—or even by Baudelaire. Rimbaud's vision has leaped beyond the picturing of actual scenes and beyond the rational core that so often supports even a visionary poem. Instead, he cuts short all explanations and simply presents the vision for itself. *Barbarian* is not, however, merely an impressionistic, unstructured collection of words. It is carefully organized according to an almost musical development of themes and pattern of oppositions: red and white (raw meat and arctic flowers, embers and frost, fire and diamonds, flames and drift ice), heat and cold, subterranean volcanoes and starry sky. On a more fundamental level, it is a world that swings between the real and the ideal, from echoes of a former reality to an ideal world where there are ultimately no complete images, only "forms, sweats, eyes" that will be part of a new creation heralded by a feminine voice reaching into the very heart of this fiery, icy vortex. *Barbarian* ends on a note of openness and ambiguity, as the cyclical opposition of reality and imagination seem about to recommence with "The banner." The poem may foreshadow the future Symbolist doctrines: it disassembles scenes from recognizable reality to assemble a new transcendent vision, and it employs to this end a subtly nonrational language that emulates the patterns of music. Yet Rimbaud is even more closely associated with twentieth-century poetry and with those writers—including the Surrealists—who found in the explosion of poetic form a complete and often violent engagement of the self.

Frederic St. Aubyn, *Arthur Rimbaud* (1988), is a useful biography that also treats Rimbaud's work. Wallace Fowlie, *Rimbaud* (1966), discusses the *Illuminations* and the myth of childhood in Rimbaud. Harold Bloom, ed., *Arthur Rimbaud* (1988), collects eleven essays on various aspects of Rimbaud's work. Georges Poulet, *Exploding Poetry* (1984), trans. Françoise Meltzer, examines poetic worldviews in Baudelaire and Rimbaud.

The Drunken Boat[1]

As I descended black, impassive Rivers,
I sensed that haulers[2] were no longer guiding me:
Screaming Redskins took them for their targets,
Nailed nude to colored stakes: barbaric trees.

I was indifferent to all my crews;   5
I carried English cottons, Flemish wheat.
When the disturbing din of haulers ceased,
The Rivers let me ramble where I willed.

Through the furious ripping of the sea's mad tides,
Last winter, deafer than an infant's mind,   10
I ran! And drifting, green Peninsulas
Did not know roar more gleefully unkind.

A tempest blessed my vigils on the sea.
Lighter than a cork I danced on the waves,
Those endless rollers, as they say, of graves:[3]   15
Ten nights beyond a lantern's[4] silly eye!

Sweeter than sourest apple-flesh to children,
Green water seeped into my pine-wood hull
And washed away blue wine[5] stains, vomitings,
Scattering rudder, anchor, man's lost rule.   20

And then I, trembling, plunged into the Poem
Of the Sea,[6] infused with stars, milk-white,
Devouring azure greens; where remnants, pale
And gnawed, of pensive corpses fell from light;

Where, staining suddenly the blueness, delirium.   25
The slow rhythms of the pulsing glow of day,
Stronger than alcohol and vaster than our lyres,
The bitter reds of love ferment the way!

I know skies splitting into light, whirled spouts
Of water, surfs, and currents: I know the night,   30
The dawn exalted like a flock of doves, pure wing,
And I have seen what men imagine they have seen.

I saw the low sun stained with mystic horrors,
Lighting long, curdled clouds of violet,

1. Translated by Stephen Stepanchev.   2. The image is of a commercial barge being towed along a canal.   3. Victor Hugo's *Oceano nox* (Night on the ocean; Latin) describes the sea as a graveyard in which sailors' corpses roll eternally.   4. Port beacons.   5. A cheap, ordinary, bitter wine.   6. A play on words. *Poem* suggests "creation" (Greek *poiein*, "making"); *Sea*, the source or "mother" of life, sounds the same as "mother" in French (*mer* / *mère*).

Like actors in a very ancient play,   35
Waves rolling distant thrills like lattice[7] light!

I dreamed of green night, stirred by dazzling snows,
Of kisses rising to the sea's eyes, slowly,
The sap-like coursing of surprising currents,
And singing phosphors,[8] flaring blue and gold!   40

I followed, for whole months, a surge like herds
Of insane cattle in assault on the reefs,
Unhopeful that three Marys,[9] come on luminous feet,
Could force a muzzle on the panting seas!

Yes, I struck incredible Floridas[1]   45
That mingled flowers and the eyes of panthers
In skins of men! And rainbows bridled green
Herds beneath the horizon of the seas.

I saw the ferment of enormous marshes, weirs
Where a whole Leviathan[2] lies rotting in the weeds!   50
Collapse of waters within calms at sea,
And distances in cataract toward chasms!

Glaciers, silver suns, pearl waves, and skies like coals,
Hideous wrecks at the bottom of brown gulfs
Where giant serpents eaten by red bugs   55
Drop from twisted trees and shed a black perfume!

I should have liked to show the young those dolphins
In blue waves, those golden fish, those fish that sing.
—Foam like flowers rocked my sleepy drifting,
And, now and then, fine winds supplied me wings.   60

When, feeling like a martyr, I tired of poles and zones,
The sea, whose sobbing made my tossing sweet,
Raised me its dark flowers, deep and yellow whirled,
And, like a woman, I fell on my knees . . .[3]

Peninsula, I tossed upon my shores   65
The quarrels and droppings of clamorous, blond-eyed birds.
I sailed until, across my rotting cords,
Drowned men, spinning backwards, fell asleep! . . .

Now I, a lost boat in the hair of coves,[4]
Hurled by tempest into a birdless air,   70
I, whose drunken carcass neither Monitors
Nor Hansa ships[5] would fish back for men's care;

---

7. Like the ripple of venetian blinds.   8. *Noctiluca*, tiny marine animals.   9. A legend that the three
biblical Marys crossed the sea during a storm to land in Camargue, a region in southern France famous
for its horses and bulls.   1. A name (plural) given to any exotic country.   2. Vast biblical sea monster
(Job 41.1–10).   3. The poet's ellipses; nothing has been omitted.   4. Seaweed.   5. Vessels belonging to the German Hanseatic League of commercial maritime cities. *Monitors*: armored coast guard ships,
after the iron-clad Union warship *Monitor* of the American Civil War.

Free, smoking, rigged with violet fogs,
I, who pierced the red sky like a wall
That carries exquisite mixtures for good poets,   75
Lichens of sun and azure mucus veils;

Who, spotted with electric crescents, ran
Like a mad plank, escorted by seahorses,
When cudgel blows of hot Julys struck down
The sea-blue skies upon wild water spouts;   80

I, who trembled, feeling the moan at fifty leagues
Of rutting Behemoths[6] and thick Maelstroms, I,
Eternal weaver of blue immobilities,
I long for Europe with its ancient quays!

I saw sidereal archipelagoes! and isles   85
Whose delirious skies are open to the voyager:
—Is it in depthless nights you sleep your exile,
A million golden birds, O future Vigor?—

But, truly, I have wept too much! The dawns disturb.
All moons are painful, and all suns break bitterly: 90
Love has swollen me with drunken torpors.
Oh, that my keel might break and spend me in the sea!

Of European waters I desire
Only the black, cold puddle in a scented twilight
Where a child of sorrows squats and sets the sails   95
Of a boat as frail as a butterfly in May.

I can no longer, bathed in languors, O waves,
Cross the wake of cotton-bearers on long trips,
Nor ramble in a pride of flags and flares,
Nor swim beneath the horrible eyes of prison ships.[7]   100

A Season in Hell[1]

Night of Hell

I have swallowed a first-rate draught of poison.—Thrice blessed be the
counsel that came to me!—My entrails are on fire. The violence of the venom
wrings my limbs, deforms me, fells me. I am dying of thirst, I am suffocating,
I cannot cry out. This is hell, the everlasting punishment! Mark how the fire
surges up again! I am burning properly. There you are, demon!

I had caught a glimpse of conversion to righteousness and happiness, salvation. May I describe the vision; the atmosphere of hell does not permit

6. Biblical animal resembling a hippopotamus (Job 40.15–24).   7. Portholes of ships tied at anchor and
used as prisons.   1. Translated by Enid Rhodes Peschel. *Night of Hell* is the second section (after the
preface) of the autobiographical *A Season in Hell*. The first section, *Bad Blood*, describes his solitary childhood and sense of being a member of an "inferior race." It also contrasts an authoritarian and hypocritical
European society with African paganism, which is seen as a freer and more natural existence.

hymns! It consisted of millions of charming creatures, a sweet sacred concert, power and peace, noble ambitions, and goodness knows what else.

Noble ambitions![2]

And yet this is life!—What if damnation is eternal! A man who chooses to mutilate himself is rightly damned, isn't he? I believe that I am in hell, consequently I am there.[3] This is the effect of the catechism. I am the slave of my baptism.[4] Parents, you have caused my affliction and you have caused your own. Poor innocent!—Hell cannot assail pagans.—This is life, nevertheless! Later, the delights of damnation will be deeper. A crime, quickly, that I may sink to nothingness, in accordance with human law.

Be silent, do be silent! . . . There is shame, reproof, in this place: Satan who says that the fire is disgraceful, that my wrath is frightfully foolish.—Enough! . . . The errors that are whispered to me, enchantments, false perfumes, childish melodies.[5]—And to say that I possess truth, that I understand justice: I have a sound and steady judgment, I am prepared for perfection . . . Pride.—The skin of my head is drying up. Pity! Lord, I am terrified. I am thirsty, so thirsty! Ah! childhood, the grass, the rain, the lake upon the stones, *the moonlight when the bell tower was striking twelve*[6] . . . the devil is in the bell tower, at that hour. Mary! Blessed Virgin! . . . —The horror of my stupidity.

Over there, are they not honest-souls, who wish me well? . . . Come . . . I have a pillow over my mouth, they don't hear me, they are phantoms. Besides, no one ever thinks of others. Let no one approach. I reek of burning, that's certain.

The hallucinations are countless. It's exactly what I've always had: no more faith in history, neglect of principles. I shall be silent about this: poets and visionaries would be jealous. I am a thousand times the richest, let us be avaricious like the sea.

Now then! the clock of life has just stopped. I am no longer in the world.—Theology is serious, hell is certainly *below*—and heaven above.—Ecstasy, nightmare, sleep in a nest of flames.

What pranks during my vigilance in the country . . . Satan, Ferdinand,[7] races with the wild seeds . . . Jesus walks on the purplish briers, without bending them . . . Jesus used to walk on the troubled waters.[8] The lantern revealed him to us, a figure standing, pale and with brown tresses, beside a wave of emerald. . . .

I am going to unveil all the mysteries: mysteries religious or natural, death, birth, futurity, antiquity, cosmogony, nothingness, I am a master of phantasmagories.

Listen! . . .

I have all the talents!—There is nobody here and there is somebody: I would not wish to scatter my treasure.—Do you wish for Negro chants, dances of houris?[9] Do you wish me to vanish, to dive in search of the *ring*?[1] Do you? I shall produce gold, cures.

2. Mockery of his childhood idealism and attraction to traditional Catholicism.   3. A parody of French philosopher René Descartes's (1596–1650) phrase "I think, therefore I am," which had become a symbol of well-ordered thought.   4. Since baptism creates the possibility of both heaven and hell.   5. The poetic visions and harmonies that Rimbaud explored with Paul Verlaine.   6. A collection of romanticized childhood memories.   7. Peasant name for the Devil.   8. Jesus' disciples saw him walking on the sea at night (John 6.16–21).   9. Beautiful virgins in the Koranic paradise.   1. At the end of Wagner's opera *Götterdämmerung*, Hagen plunges into the river Rhine to recapture the golden ring of world power.

Rely, then, upon me: faith comforts, guides, heals. All of you, come,—even the little children,[2]—that I may console you, that one may pour out his heart for you,—the marvelous heart!—Poor men, laborers! I do not ask for prayers; with your confidence alone, I shall be happy.

—And let's think of me. This makes me miss the world very little. I have the good fortune not to suffer any longer. My life was nothing but sweet follies, regrettably.

Bah! let's make all the grimaces imaginable.

Decidedly, we are out of the world. No more sound. My sense of touch has disappeared. Ah! my castle, my Saxony,[3] my forest of willows. The evenings, the mornings, the nights, the days . . . Am I weary!

I ought to have my hell for wrath, my hell for pride,—and the hell of the caress; a concert of hells.

I am dying of weariness. This is the tomb, I am going to the worms, horror of horrors! Satan, jester, you wish to undo me, with your spells. I protest. I protest! one jab of the pitchfork, one lick of fire.

Ah! to rise again to life! To cast eyes upon our deformities. And that poison, that kiss a thousand times accursed! My weakness, the cruelty of the world! Dear God, your mercy, hide me, I regard myself too poorly!—I am hidden and I am not.

It is the fire that rises again with the soul condemned to it.

THE ILLUMINATIONS[1]

The Bridges[2]

Crystalline gray skies. A strange pattern of bridges, these straight, those arched, others descending obliquely at angles to the first, and these configurations repeating themselves in the other illuminated circuits of the canal,[3] but all so long and light that the shores, laden with domes, sink and diminish. Some of these bridges are still encumbered with hovels.[4] Others support masts, signals, frail parapets. Minor chords interweave, and flow smoothly; ropes rise from the steep banks. One detects a red jacket, perhaps other costumes and musical instruments. Are these popular tunes, fragments of manorial concerts, remnants of public anthems? The water is gray and blue, ample as an arm of the sea.

A white ray, falling from the summit of the sky, reduces to nothingness this theatrical performance.

2. Parody of Jesus' words "Suffer little children, and forbid them not, to come unto me" (Matthew 19.14).   3. Germanic duchy, part of Rimbaud's visionary memories.   1. Translated by Enid Rhodes Peschel.   2. An impressionistic memory of London.   3. The river Thames as it winds through the city.   4. Houses were once built on London Bridge.

Barbarian

Long after the days and the seasons, and the creatures and the countries,
The banner of bleeding meat[1] on the silk of the seas and of the arctic flowers; (they do not exist.)
Delivered from the old fanfares of heroism—that still attack our heart and our head—far from the former assassins.
—Oh! the banner of bleeding meat on the silk of the seas and of the arctic flowers; (they do not exist.)
Delights!
Blazing coals, raining in squalls of hoarfrost—Delights!—fires in the rain of the wind of diamonds, rain hurled down by the earthly heart eternally carbonized for us—O world!—
(Far from the old retreats and the old flames, that are known, that are felt,)
Blazing coals and froths. Music, veering of whirlpools and collisions of drift ice with the stars.
O Delights, oh world, oh music! And there, the forms, the sweats, the heads of hair and the eyes, floating. And the white tears, boiling—oh delights!—and the feminine voice borne down to the bottom of the volcanoes and the arctic grottoes.
The banner . . .

---

1. Perhaps a description of the Danish flag (a white cross on a red field), which Rimbaud would have seen on a visit to Iceland, then a Danish possession.

LEO TOLSTOY
1828–1910

Count Leo Tolstoy excited the interest of Europe mainly as a public figure: a count owning large estates who decided to give up his wealth and live like a simple Russian peasant–to dress in a blouse, to eat peasant food, and even to plow the fields and make shoes with his own hands. By the time of his death he had become the leader of a religious cult, the propounder of a new religion. It was, in substance, a highly simplified primitive Christianity that he reduced to a few moral commands (such as "Do not resist evil") and from which he drew, with radical consistency, a complete condemnation of modern civilization: the state, courts and law, war, patriotism, marriage, modern art and literature, science and medicine. In debating this Christian anarchism people have tended to forget that Tolstoy established his command of the public ear as a novelist, or they have exaggerated the contrast between the early worldly novelist and the later prophet who repudiated all his early, great novelistic work: *War and Peace*, the enormous epic of the 1812 invasion of Russia, and *Anna Karenina*, the story of an adulterous love, superbly realized in accurately imagined detail.

Tolstoy was born at Yasnaya Polyana, his mother's estate near Tula (about 130 miles south of Moscow), on August 28, 1828. His father was a retired lieutenant colonel; one of his ancestors, the first count, had served Peter the Great as an ambassador. His mother's father was a Russian general-in-chief. Tolstoy lost both parents early in his life and was brought up by aunts. He went to the University of Kazan between 1844 and 1847, drifted along aimlessly for a few years more, and in 1851 became a cadet in the Caucasus. As an artillery officer he saw action in the wars with the mountain tribes and again, in 1854–55, during the Crimean War against the French and English. Tolstoy had written fictional reminiscences of his childhood while he was in the Caucasus; and during the Crimean War he wrote war stories, which established his literary reputation. For some years he lived on his estate, where he founded and himself taught at an extremely "progressive" school for peasant children. He made two trips to western Europe, in 1857 and in 1860–61. In 1862 he married the daughter of a physician, Sonya Bers, with whom he had thirteen children.

In the first years of his married life, between 1863 and 1869, he wrote his enormous novel *War and Peace*. The book made him famous in Russia but was not translated into English until long afterward. Superficially, *War and Peace* is an historical novel about the Napoleonic invasion of Russia in 1812, a huge swarming epic of a nation's resistance to the foreigner. Tolstoy himself interprets history in general as a struggle of anonymous collective forces that are moved by unknown irrational impulses, waves of communal feeling. Heroes, great men and women, are actually not heroes but merely insignificant puppets; the best general is the one who does nothing to prevent the unknown course of Providence. But *War and Peace* is not only an impressive and vivid panorama of historical events but also the profound story—centered in two main characters, Pierre Bezukhov and Prince Andrey Bolkonsky—of a search for meaning in life. Andrey finds meaning in love and forgiveness of his enemies. Pierre, at the end of a long groping struggle, an education by suffering, finds it in an acceptance of ordinary existence, its duties and pleasures, the family, the continuity of the race.

Tolstoy's next long novel, *Anna Karenina* (1875–77), resumes this second thread of *War and Peace*. It is a novel of contemporary manners, a narrative of adultery and suicide. But this vivid story, told with incomparable concrete imagination, is counterpointed and framed by a second story, that of Levin, another seeker after the meaning of life, a figure who represents the author as Pierre did in the earlier book; the work ends with a promise of salvation, with the ideal of a life in which we should "remember God." Thus *Anna Karenina* also anticipates the approaching crisis in Tolstoy's life. When it came, with the sudden revulsion he describes in *A Confession* (1879), he condemned his earlier books and spent the next years in writing pamphlets and tracts expounding his religion.

Only slowly did Tolstoy return to the writing of fiction, now regarded entirely as a means of presenting his creed. The earlier novels seemed to him unclear in their message, overdetailed in their method. Hence Tolstoy tried to simplify his art; he wrote plays with a thesis, stories that are like fables or parables, and one long, rather inferior novel, *The Resurrection* (1899), his most savage satire on Russian and modern institutions.

In 1901 Tolstoy was excommunicated. A disagreement with his wife about the nature of the good life and about financial matters sharpened into a conflict over his last will, which finally led to a complete break: he left home in the company of a doctor friend. He caught cold on the train journey south and died in the house of the stationmaster of Astapovo, on November 20, 1910.

If we look back on Tolstoy's work as a whole, we must recognize its continuity. From the very beginning he was a Rousseauist. As early as 1851, when he was in the Caucasus, his diary announced his intention of founding a new, simplified religion. Even as a young man on his estate he had lived quite simply, like a peasant, except for occasional sprees and debauches. He had been horrified by war from the very beginning, though he admired the heroism of the individual soldier and had remnants of patriotic feeling. All his books concern the same theme, the good life, and they all say that the good life lies outside civilization, near the soil, in simplicity and humility, in love of one's neighbor. Power, the lust for power, luxury are always evil.

Tolstoy's roots as a novelist are part of another, older realistic tradition. He read and knew the English writers of the eighteenth century—and also William Makepeace Thackeray and Anthony Trollope—though he did not care for the recent French writers (he was strong in his disapproval of Gustave Flaubert) except for Guy de Maupassant, who struck him as truthful and useful in his struggle against hypocrisy. Tolstoy's long novels are loosely plotted, though they have large overall designs. They work by little scenes vividly visualized, by an accumulation of exact detail. Each character is drawn by means of repeated emphasis on certain physical traits, like Pierre's shortsightedness and his hairy, clumsy hands, or Princess Marya's luminous eyes, the red patches on her face, and her shuffling gait. This concretely realized surface, however, everywhere recedes into depths: to the depiction of disease, delirium, and death and to glimpses into eternity. In *War and Peace* the blue sky is the recurrent symbol for the metaphysical spirit within us. Tolstoy is so robust, has his feet so firmly on the ground, presents what he sees with such clarity and objectivity, that one can be easily deluded into considering his dominating quality to be physical, sensual, antithetical to Dostoevsky's spirituality. The contrasts between the two greatest Russian novelists are indeed obvious. While Tolstoy's method can be called epic, Dostoevsky's is dramatic; while Tolstoy's view of humanity is Rousseauistic, Dostoevsky stresses the Fall; while Tolstoy rejects history and status, Dostoevsky appeals to the past and desires a hierarchical society, and so on. But these profound differences should not obscure one basic similarity: the deep spirituality of both writers, their rejection of the basic materialism and the conception of truth propounded by modern science and theorists of realism.

The Death of Ivan Ilyich (1886) belongs to the period after Tolstoy's religious conversion when he slowly returned to fiction writing. It represents a happy medium between his early and late manner. Its story and moral are simple and obvious, as always with Tolstoy (in contrast to Dostoevsky). And it expresses what almost all of his works are intended to convey—that humanity is leading the wrong kind of life, that we should return to essentials, to "nature." In *The Death of Ivan Ilyich* Tolstoy combines a savage satire on the futility and hypocrisy of conventional life with a powerful symbolic presentation of isolation in the struggle with death and of hope for a final resurrection. Ivan Ilyich is a Russian judge, an official, but he is also the average man of the prosperous middle classes of his time and ours, and he is also Everyman confronted with disease and dying and death. He is an ordinary person, neither virtuous nor particularly vicious, a "go-getter" in his profession, a "family man," as marriages go, who has children but has drifted apart from his wife. Through his disease, which comes about by a trivial accident in the trivial business of fixing a curtain, Ivan Ilyich is slowly awakened to self-consciousness and a realization of the falsity of his life and ambitions. The isolation that disease imposes on him, the wall of hypocrisy erected around him by his family and his doctors, his suffering and pain, drive him slowly to the recognition of *It*: to a knowledge, not merely theoretical but proved on his pulses, of his own mortality. At first he would like simply to return to his former pleasant and normal life—even in the last days of his illness, knowing he must die, he screams in his agony, "I won't!"—but at the end, struggling in the black sack into which he is being pushed, he sees the light at the bottom. " 'Death is finished,' he said to himself. 'It is no more!' "

The people around him are egotists and hypocrites: his wife, who can remember only how she suffered during his agony; his daughter, who thinks only of the delay in her marriage; his colleagues, who speculate only about the room his death will make for promotions in the court; the doctors, who think only of the name of the disease and not of the patient; all except his shy and frightened son, Vasya, and the servant Gerasim. Because he is young, near to "nature," and free from hypocrisy,

Gerasim is able to make his master more comfortable and even to mention death, while all the others conceal the truth from him. The doctors, especially, are shown as mere specialists, inhuman and selfish. The first doctor is like a judge—like Ivan himself when he sat in court—summing up and cutting off further questions of the patient. The satire at points appears ineffectively harsh in its violence, but it will not seem exceptional to those who know the older Tolstoy's general attitude toward courts, medicine, marriage, and even modern literature. The cult of art is jeered at, in small touches, only incidentally; it belongs, according to Tolstoy, to the falsities of modern civilization, alongside marriage (which merely hides bestial sensuality) and science (which merely hides rapacity and ignorance).

The story is deliberately deprived of any element of suspense, not only by the announcement contained in the title but by the technique of the cutback. We first hear of Ivan Ilyich's death and see the reaction of the widow and friends, and only then listen to the story of his life. The detail, as always in Tolstoy, is superbly concrete and realistic: he does not shy away from the smell of disease, the physical necessity of using a chamber pot, or the sound of screaming. He can employ the creaking of a hassock as a recurrent motif to point out the comedy of hypocrisy played by the widow and her visitor. He can seriously and tragically use the humble image of a black sack or the illusion of the movement of a train.

But all this naturalistic detail serves the one purpose of making us come to realize, as Ivan Ilyich realizes, that not only Caius is mortal but you and I also, and that the life of "civilized" people is a great lie simply because it disguises and ignores its dark background, the metaphysical abyss, the reality of Death. While the presentation of *The Death of Ivan Ilyich* approaches, at moments, the tone of a legend or fable ("Ivan Ilyich's life had been most simple and most ordinary and therefore most terrible"), Tolstoy in this story manages to stay within the concrete situation of his society and to combine the aesthetic method of realism with the universalizing power of symbolic art.

R. F. Christian, *Tolstoy: A Critical Introduction* (1969), is clear, instructive, and informative. E. B. Greenwood, *Tolstoy: The Comprehensive Vision* (1975), is helpful in placing *The Death of Ivan Ilyich* in the perspective of Tolstoy's work as a whole. Some good analysis is found in H. Gifford, ed., *Leo Tolstoy: A Critical Anthology* (1971). Ralph E. Matlaw, *Tolstoy: A Collection of Critical Essays* (1967), and Philip Rahv, *Image and Idea* (1949), both present essays on *The Death of Ivan Ilyich*. Theodore Redpath, *Tolstoy* (1960), provides a brief introduction with good criticism of ideas. Ernest J. Simmons, *Leo Tolstoy* (1946), and A. N. Wilson, *Tolstoy* (1988), are both excellent biographies. Rimvydas Silbajons, *Tolstoy's Aesthetics and His Art* (1991), includes accounts of reactions to the author at home and abroad as well as many substantial quotations.

PRONOUNCING GLOSSARY

The following list uses common English syllables and stress accents to provide rough equivalents of selected words whose pronunciation may be unfamiliar to the general reader.

Fëdor Petrovich: *fyaw'-dur pe-traw'-veech*

Fëdor Vasilievich: *fyaw'-dur vah-seel'-ye-veech*

Gerasim: *gye-rah'-syeem*

Golovin: *guh-lah-veen'*

Ivan Ilyich: *ee-vahn' il-yeech'*

Ivanovich: *ee-vah'-nuh-veech*

Karenina: *kah-re'-nyee-nuh*

The Death of Ivan Ilyich[1]

I

During an interval in the Melvinski trial in the large building of the Law Courts the members and public prosecutor met in Ivan Egorovich Shebek's private room, where the conversation turned on the celebrated Krasovski case. Fëdor Vasilievich warmly maintained that it was not subject to their jurisdiction, Ivan Egorovich maintained the contrary, while Peter Ivanovich, not having entered into the discussion at the start, took no part in it but looked through the *Gazette* which had just been handed in.

"Gentlemen," he said, "Ivan Ilyich has died!"

"You don't say!"

"Here read it yourself," replied Peter Ivanovich, handing Fëdor Vasilievich the paper still damp from the press. Surrounded by a black border were the words: "Praskovya Fëdorovna Golovina, with profound sorrow, informs relatives and friends of the demise of her beloved husband Ivan Ilyich Golovin, Member of the Court of Justice, which occurred on February the 4th of this year 1882. The funeral will take place on Friday at one o'clock in the afternoon."

Ivan Ilyich had been a colleague of the gentlemen present and was liked by them all. He had been ill for some weeks with an illness said to be incurable. His post had been kept open for him, but there had been conjectures that in case of his death Alexeev might receive his appointment, and that either Vinnikov or Shtabel would succeed Alexeev. So on receiving the news of Ivan Ilyich's death the first thought of each of the gentlemen in that private room was of the changes and promotions it might occasion among themselves or their acquaintances.

"I shall be sure to get Shtabel's place or Vinnikov's," thought Fëdor Vasilievich. "I was promised that long ago, and the promotion means an extra eight hundred rubles a year for me besides the allowance."

"Now I must apply for my brother-in-law's transfer from Kaluga," thought Peter Ivanovich. "My wife will be very glad, and then she won't be able to say that I never do anything for her relations."

"I thought he would never leave his bed again," said Peter Ivanovich aloud. "It's very sad."

"But what really was the matter with him?"

"The doctors couldn't say—at least they could, but each of them said something different. When last I saw him I thought he was getting better."

"And I haven't been to see him since the holidays. I always meant to go."

"Had he any property?"

"I think his wife had a little—but something quite trifling."

"We shall have to go to see her, but they live so terribly far away."

"Far away from you, you mean. Everything's far away from your place."

"You see, he never can forgive my living on the other side of the river," said Peter Ivanovich, smiling at Shebek. Then, still talking of the distances between different parts of the city, they returned to the Court.

Besides considerations as to the possible transfers and promotions likely to result from Ivan Ilyich's death, the mere fact of the death of a near

1. Translated by Louise Maude and Aylmer Maude.

acquaintance aroused, as usual, in all who heard of it the complacent feeling that, "it is he who is dead and not I."

Each one thought or felt, "Well, he's dead but I'm alive!" But the more intimate of Ivan Ilyich's acquaintances, his so-called friends, could not help thinking also that they would now have to fulfil the very tiresome demands of propriety by attending the funeral service and paying a visit of condolence to the widow.

Fëdor Vasilievich and Peter Ivanovich had been his nearest acquaintances. Peter Ivanovich had studied law with Ivan Ilyich and had considered himself to be under obligations to him.

Having told his wife at dinner-time of Ivan Ilyich's death, and of his conjecture that it might be possible to get her brother transferred to their circuit, Peter Ivanovich sacrificed his usual nap, put on his evening clothes, and drove to Ivan Ilyich's house.

At the entrance stood a carriage and two cabs. Leaning against the wall in the hall downstairs near the cloak-stand was a coffin-lid covered with cloth of gold, ornamented with gold cord and tassels, that had been polished up with metal powder. Two ladies in black were taking off their fur cloaks. Peter Ivanovich recognized one of them as Ivan Ilyich's sister, but the other was a stranger to him. His colleague Schwartz was just coming downstairs, but on seeing Peter Ivanovich enter he stopped and winked at him, as if to say: "Ivan Ilyich has made a mess of things—not like you and me."

Schwartz's face with his Piccadilly whiskers, and his slim figure in evening dress, had as usual an air of elegant solemnity which contrasted with the playfulness of his character and had a special piquancy here, or so it seemed to Peter Ivanovich.

Peter Ivanovich allowed the ladies to precede him and slowly followed them upstairs. Schwartz did not come down but remained where he was, and Peter Ivanovich understood that he wanted to arrange where they should play bridge that evening. The ladies went upstairs to the widow's room, and Schwartz with seriously compressed lips but a playful look in his eyes, indicated by a twist of his eyebrows the room to the right where the body lay.

Peter Ivanovich, like everyone else on such occasions, entered feeling uncertain what he would have to do. All he knew was that at such times it is always safe to cross oneself. But he was not quite sure whether one should make obeisances while doing so. He therefore adopted a middle course. On entering the room he began crossing himself and made a slight movement resembling a bow. At the same time, as far as the motion of his head and arm allowed, he surveyed the room. Two young men—apparently nephews, one of whom was a high-school pupil—were leaving the room, crossing themselves as they did so. An old woman was standing motionless, and a lady with strangely arched eyebrows was saying something to her in a whisper. A vigorous, resolute Church Reader, in a frock-coat, was reading something in a loud voice with an expression that precluded any contradiction. The butler's assistant, Gerasim, stepping lightly in front of Peter Ivanovich, was strewing something on the floor. Noticing this, Peter Ivanovich was immediately aware of a faint odour of a decomposing body.

The last time he had called on Ivan Ilyich, Peter Ivanovich had seen Gerasim in the study. Ivan Ilyich had been particularly fond of him and he was performing the duty of a sick nurse.

Peter Ivanovich continued to make the sign of the cross slightly inclining his head in an intermediate direction between the coffin, the Reader, and the icons on the table in a corner of the room. Afterwards, when it seemed to him that this movement of his arm in crossing himself had gone on too long, he stopped and began to look at the corpse.

The dead man lay, as dead men always lie, in a specially heavy way, his rigid limbs sunk in the soft cushions of the coffin, with the head forever bowed on the pillow. His yellow waxen brow with bald patches over his sunken temples was thrust up in the way peculiar to the dead, the protruding nose seeming to press on the upper lip. He was much changed and had grown even thinner since Peter Ivanovich had last seen him, but, as is always the case with the dead, his face was handsomer and above all more dignified than when he was alive. The expression on the face said that what was necessary had been accomplished, and accomplished rightly. Besides this there was in that expression a reproach and a warning to the living. This warning seemed to Peter Ivanovich out of place, or at least not applicable to him. He felt a certain discomfort and so he hurriedly crossed himself once more and turned and went out of the door—too hurriedly and too regardless of propriety, as he himself was aware.

Schwartz was waiting for him in the adjoining room with legs spread wide apart and both hands toying with his top-hat behind his back. The mere sight of that playful, well-groomed, and elegant figure refreshed Peter Ivanovich. He felt that Schwartz was above all these happenings and could not surrender to any depressing influences. His very look said that this incident of a church service for Ivan Ilyich could not be a sufficient reason for infringing the order of the session—in other words, that it would certainly not prevent his unwrapping a new pack of cards and shuffling them that evening while a footman placed four fresh candles on the table: in fact, that there was no reason for supposing that this incident would hinder their spending the evening agreeably. Indeed he said this in a whisper as Peter Ivanovich passed him, proposing that they should meet for a game at Fëdor Vasilievich's. But apparently Peter Ivanovich was not destined to play bridge that evening. Praskovya Fëdorovna (a short, fat woman who despite all efforts to the contrary had continued to broaden steadily from her shoulders downwards and who had the same extraordinary arched eyebrows as the lady who had been standing by the coffin), dressed all in black, her head covered with lace, came out of her own room with some other ladies, conducted them to the room where the dead body lay, and said: "The service will begin immediately. Please go in."

Schwartz, making an indefinite bow, stood still, evidently neither accepting nor declining this invitation. Praskovya Fëdorovna recognizing Peter Ivanovich, sighed, went close up to him, took his hand, and said: "I know you were a true friend to Ivan Ilyich . . ." and looked at him awaiting some suitable response. And Peter Ivanovich knew that, just as it had been the right thing to cross himself in that room, so what he had to do here was to press her hand, sigh, and say, "Believe me . . ." So he did all this and as he did it felt that the desired result had been achieved: that both he and she were touched.

"Come with me. I want to speak to you before it begins," said the widow. "Give me your arm."

Peter Ivanovich gave her his arm and they went to the inner rooms, passing Schwartz who winked at Peter Ivanovich compassionately.

"That does for our bridge! Don't object if we find another player. Perhaps you can cut in when you do escape," said his playful look.

Peter Ivanovich sighed still more deeply and despondently, and Praskovya Fëdorovna pressed his arm gratefully. When they reached the drawing-room, upholstered in pink cretonne and lighted by a dim lamp, they sat down at the table—she on a sofa and Peter Ivanovich on a low hassock, the springs of which yielded spasmodically under his weight. Praskovya Fëdorovna had been on the point of warning him to take another seat, but felt that such a warning was out of keeping with her present condition and so changed her mind. As he sat down on the hassock Peter Ivanovich recalled how Ivan Ilyich had arranged this room and had consulted him regarding this pink cretonne with green leaves. The whole room was full of furniture and knick-knacks, and on her way to the sofa the lace of the widow's black shawl caught on the carved edge of the table. Peter Ivanovich rose to detach it, and the springs of the hassock, relieved of his weight, rose also and gave him a push. The widow began detaching her shawl herself, and Peter Ivanovich again sat down, suppressing the rebellious springs of the hassock under him. But the widow had not quite freed herself and Peter Ivanovich got up again, and again the hassock rebelled and even creaked. When this was all over she took out a clean cambric handkerchief and began to weep. The episode with the shawl and the struggle with the hassock had cooled Peter Ivanovich's emotions and he sat there with a sullen look on his face. This awkward situation was interrupted by Sokolov, Ivan Ilyich's butler, who came to report that the plot in the cemetery that Praskovya Fëdorovna had chosen would cost two hundred rubles. She stopped weeping and, looking at Peter Ivanovich with the air of a victim, remarked in French that it was very hard for her. Peter Ivanovich made a silent gesture signifying his full conviction that it must indeed be so.

"Please smoke," she said in a magnanimous yet crushed voice, and turned to discuss with Sokolov the price of the plot for the grave.

Peter Ivanovich while lighting his cigarette heard her inquiring very circumstantially into the prices of different plots in the cemetery and finally decide which she would take. When that was done she gave instructions about engaging the choir. Sokolov then left the room.

"I look after everything myself," she told Peter Ivanovich, shifting the albums that lay on the table; and noticing that the table was endangered by his cigarette-ash, she immediately passed him an ashtray, saying as she did so: "I consider it an affectation to say that my grief prevents my attending to practical affairs. On the contrary, if anything can—I won't say console me, but—distract me, it is seeing to everything concerning him." She again took out her handkerchief as if preparing to cry, but suddenly, as if mastering her feeling, she shook herself and began to speak calmly. "But there is something I want to talk to you about."

Peter Ivanovich bowed, keeping control of the springs of the hassock, which immediately began quivering under him.

"He suffered terribly the last few days."

"Did he?" said Peter Ivanovich.

"Oh, terribly! He screamed unceasingly, not for minutes but for hours.

For the last three days he screamed incessantly. It was unendurable. I cannot understand how I bore it; you could hear him three rooms off. Oh, what I have suffered!"

"Is it possible that he was conscious all that time?" asked Peter Ivanovich.

"Yes," she whispered. "To the last moment. He took leave of us a quarter of an hour before he died, and asked us to take Vasya away."

The thought of the sufferings of this man he had known so intimately, first as a merry little boy, then as a school-mate, and later as a grown-up colleague, suddenly struck Peter Ivanovich with horror, despite an unpleasant consciousness of his own and this woman's dissimulation. He again saw that brow, and that nose pressing down on the lip, and felt afraid for himself.

"Three days of frightful suffering and then death! Why, that might suddenly, at any time, happen to me," he thought, and for a moment felt terrified. But—he did not himself know how—the customary reflection at once occurred to him that this had happened to Ivan Ilyich and not to him, and that it should not and could not happen to him, and that to think that it could would be yielding to depression which he ought not to do, as Schwartz's expression plainly showed. After which reflection Peter Ivanovich felt reassured, and began to ask with interest about the details of Ivan Ilyich's death, as though death was an accident natural to Ivan Ilyich but certainly not to himself.

After many details of the really dreadful physical sufferings Ivan Ilyich had endured (which details he learnt only from the effect those sufferings had produced on Praskovya Fëdorovna's nerves) the widow apparently found it necessary to get to business.

"Oh, Peter Ivanovich, how hard it is! How terribly, terribly hard!" and she again began to weep.

Peter Ivanovich sighed and waited for her to finish blowing her nose. When she had done so he said, "Believe me . . ." and she again began talking and brought out what was evidently her chief concern with him—namely, to question him as to how she could obtain a grant of money from the government on the occasion of her husband's death. She made it appear that she was asking Peter Ivanovich's advice about her pension, but he soon saw that she already knew about that to the minutest detail, more even than he did himself. She knew how much could be got out of the government in consequence of her husband's death, but wanted to find out whether she could possibly extract something more. Peter Ivanovich tried to think of some means of doing so, but after reflecting for a while and, out of propriety, condemning the government for its niggardliness, he said he thought that nothing more could be got. Then she sighed and evidently began to devise means of getting rid of her visitor. Noticing this, he put out his cigarette, rose, pressed her hand, and went out into the anteroom.

In the dining-room where the clock stood that Ivan Ilyich had liked so much and had bought at an antique shop, Peter Ivanovich met a priest and a few acquaintances who had come to attend the service, and he recognized Ivan Ilyich's daughter, a handsome young woman. She was in black and her slim figure appeared slimmer than ever. She had a gloomy, determined, almost angry expression, and bowed to Peter Ivanovich as though he were in some way to blame. Behind her, with the same offended look, stood a wealthy young man, an examining magistrate, whom Peter Ivanovich also knew and who was her fiancé, as he had heard. He bowed mournfully to them and was about to pass into the death-chamber, when from under the stairs appeared the figure of Ivan Ilyich's schoolboy son, who was extremely like this father. He seemed a little Ivan Ilyich, such as Peter Ivanovich remembered when they studied law together. His tear-stained eyes had in them the look that is seen in the eyes of boys of thirteen or fourteen who are not pure-minded.

When he saw Peter Ivanovich he scowled morosely and shamefacedly. Peter Ivanovich nodded to him and entered the death-chamber. The service began: candles, groans, incense, tears, and sobs. Peter Ivanovich stood looking gloomily down at his feet. He did not look once at the dead man, did not yield to any depressing influence, and was one of the first to leave the room. There was no one in the anteroom, but Gerasim darted out of the dead man's room, rummaged with his strong hands among the fur coats to find Peter Ivanovich's and helped him on with it.

"Well, friend Gerasim," said Peter Ivanovich, so as to say something. "It's a sad affair, isn't it?"

"It's God's will. We shall all come to it some day," said Gerasim, displaying his teeth—the even, white teeth of a healthy peasant—and, like a man in the thick of urgent work, he briskly opened the front door, called the coachman, helped Peter Ivanovich into the sledge, and sprang back to the porch as if in readiness for what he had to do next.

Peter Ivanovich found the fresh air particularly pleasant after the smell of incense, the dead body, and carbolic acid.

"Where to, sir?" asked the coachman.

"It's not too late even now. . . . I'll call round on Fëdor Vasilievich."

He accordingly drove there and found them just finishing the first rubber, so that it was quite convenient for him to cut in.

II

Ivan Ilyich's life had been most simple and most ordinary and therefore most terrible.

He had been a member of the Court of Justice, and died at the age of forty-five. His father had been an official who after serving in various ministries and departments in Petersburg had made the sort of career which brings men to positions from which by reason of their long service they cannot be dismissed, though they are obviously unfit to hold any responsible position, and for whom therefore posts are specially created, which though fictitious, carry salaries of from six to ten thousand rubles that are not fictitious, and in receipt of which they live on to a great age.

Such was the Privy Councillor and superfluous member of various superfluous institutions, Ilya Efimovich Golovin.

He had three sons, of whom Ivan Ilyich was the second. The eldest son was following in his father's footsteps only in another department, and was already approaching that stage in the service at which a similar sinecure would be reached. The third son was a failure. He had ruined his prospects in a number of positions and was now serving in the railway department. His father and brothers, and still more their wives, not merely disliked meeting him, but avoided remembering his existence unless compelled to do so. His sister had married Baron Greff, a Petersburg official of her father's type. Ivan Ilyich was *le phénix de la famille*[2] as people said. He was neither as cold and formal as his elder brother nor as wild as the younger, but was a happy mean between them—an intelligent, polished, lively and agreeable man. He had studied with his younger brother at the School of Law, but the latter had failed to complete the course and was expelled when he was in the fifth class. Ivan Ilyich finished the course well. Even when he was at the School of Law he was just what he remained for the rest of his life: a capable, cheerful, good-natured, and sociable man, though strict in the fulfilment of what he considered to be his duty: and he considered his duty to be what was so considered by those in authority. Neither as a boy nor as a man was he a toady, but from early youth was by nature attracted to people of high station as a fly is drawn to the light, assimilating their ways and views of life and establishing friendly relations with them. All the enthusiasms of childhood and youth passed without leaving much trace on him; he succumbed to sensuality, to vanity, and latterly among the highest classes to liberalism, but always within limits which his instinct unfailingly indicated to him as correct.

At school he had done things which had formerly seemed to him very horrid and made him feel disgusted with himself when he did them; but when later on he saw that such actions were done by people of good position and that they did not regard them as wrong, he was able not exactly to regard them as right, but to forget about them entirely or not be at all troubled at remembering them.

Having graduated from the School of Law and qualified for the tenth rank of the civil service, and having received money from his father for his equipment, Ivan Ilyich ordered himself clothes at Scharmer's, the fashionable tailor, hung a medallion inscribed *respice finem*[3] on his watch-chain, took leave of his professor and the prince who was patron of the school, had a farewell dinner with his comrades at Donon's first-class restaurant, and with his new and fashionable portmanteau, linen, clothes, shaving and other toilet appliances, and a travelling rug, all purchased at the best shops, he set off for one of the provinces where, through his father's influence, he had been attached to the governor as an official for special service.

In the province Ivan Ilyich soon arranged as easy and agreeable a position for himself as he had at the School of Law. He performed his official tasks, made his career, and at the same time amused himself pleasantly and decorously. Occasionally he paid official visits to country districts, where he behaved with dignity both to his superiors and inferiors, and performed the duties entrusted to him, which related chiefly to the sectarians,[4] with an exactness and incorruptible honesty of which he could not but feel proud.

In official matters, despite his youth and taste for frivolous gaiety, he was exceedingly reserved, punctilious, and even severe; but in society he was often amusing and witty, and always good-natured, correct in his manner, and *bon enfant*, as the governor and his wife—with whom he was like one of the family—used to say of him.

In the province he had an affair with a lady who made advances to the

---

2. The phoenix of the family (French). The word *phoenix* is used here to mean "rare bird," "prodigy."   3. Regard the end (a Latin motto).   4. The Old Believers, a large group of Russians (about twenty-five million in 1900), members of a sect that originated in a break with the Orthodox Church in the seventeenth century; they were subject to many legal restrictions.

elegant young lawyer, and there was also a milliner; and there were carousals with aides-de-camp who visited the district, and after-supper visits to a certain outlying street of doubtful reputation; and there was too some obsequiousness to his chief and even to his chief's wife, but all this was done with such a tone of good breeding that no hard names could be applied to it. It all came under the heading of the French saying: *"Il faut que jeunesse se passe."*[5] It was all done with clean hands, in clean linen, with French phrases, and above all among people of the best society and consequently with the approval of people of rank.

So Ivan Ilyich served for five years and then came a change in his official life. The new and reformed judicial institutions were introduced, and new men were needed. Ivan Ilyich became such a new man. He was offered the post of Examining Magistrate, and he accepted it though the post was in another province and obliged him to give up the connexions he had formed and to make new ones. His friends met to give him a send-off; they had a group-photograph taken and presented him with a silver cigarette-case, and he set off to his new post.

As examining magistrate Ivan Ilyich was just as *comme il faut* and decorous a man, inspiring general respect and capable of separating his official duties from his private life, as he had been when acting as an official on special service. His duties now as examining magistrate were far more interesting and attractive than before. In his former position it had been pleasant to wear an undress uniform made by Scharmer, and to pass through the crowd of petitioners and officials who were timorously awaiting an audience with the governor, and who envied him as with free and easy gait he went straight into his chief's private room to have a cup of tea and a cigarette with him. But not many people had then been directly dependent on him—only police officials and the sectarians when he went on special missions—and he liked to treat them politely, almost as comrades, as if he were letting them feel that he who had the power to crush them was treating them in this simple, friendly way. There were then but few such people. But now, as an examining magistrate, Ivan Ilyich felt that everyone without exception, even the most important and self-satisfied, was in his power, and that he need only write a few words on a sheet of paper with a certain heading, and this or that important, self-satisfied person would be brought before him in the role of an accused person or a witness, and if he did not choose to allow him to sit down, would have to stand before him and answer his questions. Ivan Ilyich never abused his power; he tried on the contrary to soften its expression, but the consciousness of it and of the possibility of softening its effect, supplied the chief interest and attraction of his office. In his work itself, especially in his examinations, he very soon acquired a method of eliminating all considerations irrelevant to the legal aspect of the case, and reducing even the most complicated case to a form in which it would be presented on paper only in its externals, completely excluding his personal opinion of the matter, while above all observing every prescribed formality. The work was new and Ivan Ilyich was one of the first men to apply the new Code of 1864.[6]

On taking up the post of examining magistrate in a new town, he made

---

5. Youth must have its fling [Translators' note].   6. The emancipation of the serfs in 1861 was followed by a thorough all-round reform of judicial proceedings [Translators' note].

new acquaintances and connexions, placed himself on a new footing, and assumed a somewhat different tone. He took up an attitude of rather dignified aloofness towards the provincial authorities, but picked out the best circle of legal gentlemen and wealthy gentry living in the town and assumed a tone of slight dissatisfaction with the government, of moderate liberalism, and of enlightened citizenship. At the same time, without at all altering the elegance of his toilet, he ceased shaving his chin and allowed his beard to grow as it pleased.

Ivan Ilyich settled down very pleasantly in this new town. The society there, which inclined towards opposition to the governor, was friendly, his salary was larger, and he began to play *vint* [a form of bridge], which he found added not a little to the pleasure of life, for he had a capacity for cards, played good-humouredly, and calculated rapidly and astutely, so that he usually won.

After living there for two years he met his future wife, Praskovya Fëdorovna Mikhel, who was the most attractive, clever, and brilliant girl of the set in which he moved, and among other amusements and relaxations from his labours as examining magistrate, Ivan Ilyich established light and playful relations with her.

While he had been an official on special service he had been accustomed to dance, but now as an examining magistrate it was exceptional for him to do so. If he danced now, he did it as if to show that though he served under the reformed order of things, and had reached the fifth official rank, yet when it came to dancing he could do it better than most people. So at the end of an evening he sometimes danced with Praskovya Fëdorovna, and it was chiefly during these dances that he captivated her. She fell in love with him. Ivan Ilyich had at first no definite intention of marrying, but when the girl fell in love with him he said to himself: "Really, why shouldn't I marry?"

Praskovya Fëdorovna came of a good family, was not bad looking, and had some little property. Ivan Ilyich might have aspired to a more brilliant match, but even this was good. He had his salary, and she, he hoped, would have an equal income. She was well connected, and was a sweet, pretty, and thoroughly correct young woman. To say that Ivan Ilyich married because he fell in love with Praskovya Fëdorovna and found that she sympathized with his views of life would be as incorrect as to say that he married because his social circle approved of the match. He was swayed by both these considerations: the marriage gave him personal satisfaction, and at the same time it was considered the right thing by the most highly placed of his associates.

So Ivan Ilyich got married.

The preparations for marriage and the beginning of married life, with its conjugal caresses, the new furniture, new crockery, and new linen, were very pleasant until his wife became pregnant—so that Ivan Ilyich had begun to think that marriage would not impair the easy, agreeable, gay, and always decorous character of his life, approved of by society and regarded by himself as natural, but would even improve it. But from the first months of his wife's pregnancy, something new, unpleasant, depressing, and unseemly, and from which there was no way of escape, unexpectedly showed itself.

His wife, without any reason—*de gaieté de coeur*[7] as Ivan Ilyich expressed

---

7. From sheer impulsiveness (French).

it to himself—began to disturb the pleasure and propriety of their life. She began to be jealous without any cause, expected him to devote his whole attention to her, found fault with everything, and made coarse and ill-mannered scenes.

At first Ivan Ilyich hoped to escape from the unpleasantness of this state of affairs by the same easy and decorous relation to life that had served him heretofore: he tried to ignore his wife's disagreeable moods, continued to live in his usual easy and pleasant way, invited friends to his house for a game of cards, and also tried going out to his club or spending his evenings with friends. But one day his wife began upbraiding him so vigorously, using such coarse words, and continued to abuse him every time he did not fulfil her demands, so resolutely and with such evident determination not to give way till he submitted—that is, till he stayed at home and was bored just as she was—that he became alarmed. He now realized that matrimony—at any rate with Praskovya Fëdorovna—was not always conducive to the pleasures and amenities of life, but on the contrary often infringed both comfort and propriety, and that he must therefore entrench himself against such infringement. And Ivan Ilyich began to seek for means of doing so. His official duties were the one thing that imposed upon Praskovya Fëdorovna, and by means of his official work and the duties attached to it he began struggling with his wife to secure his own independence.

With the birth of their child, the attempts to feed it and the various failures in doing so, and with the real and imaginary illnesses of mother and child, in which Ivan Ilyich's sympathy was demanded but about which he understood nothing, the need of securing for himself an existence outside his family life became still more imperative.

As his wife grew more irritable and exacting and Ivan Ilyich transferred the centre of gravity of his life more and more to his official work, so did he grow to like his work better and became more ambitious than before.

Very soon, within a year of his wedding, Ivan Ilyich had realized that marriage, though it may add some comforts to life, is in fact a very intricate and difficult affair towards which in order to perform one's duty, that is, to lead a decorous life approved of by society, one must adopt a definite attitude just as towards one's official duties.

And Ivan Ilyich evolved such an attitude towards married life. He only required of it those conveniences—dinner at home, housewife, and bed—which it could give him, and above all that propriety of external forms required by public opinion. For the rest he looked for light-hearted pleasure and propriety, and was very thankful when he found them, but if he met with antagonism and querulousness he at once retired into his separate fenced-off world of official duties, where he found satisfaction.

Ivan Ilyich was esteemed a good official, and after three years was made Assistant Public Prosecutor. His new duties, their importance, the possibility of indicting and imprisoning anyone he chose, the publicity his speeches received, and the success he had in all these things, made his work still more attractive.

More children came. His wife became more and more querulous and ill-tempered, but the attitude Ivan Ilyich had adopted towards his home life rendered him almost impervious to her grumbling.

After seven years' service in that town he was transferred to another province as Public Prosecutor. They moved, but were short of money and his wife did not like the place they moved to. Though the salary was higher the cost of living was greater, besides which two of their children died and family life became still more unpleasant for him.

Praskovya Fëdorovna blamed her husband for every inconvenience they encountered in their new home. Most of the conversations between husband and wife, especially as to the children's education, led to topics which recalled former disputes, and those disputes were apt to flare up again at any moment. There remained only those rare periods of amorousness which still came to them at times but did not last long. These were islets at which they anchored for a while and then again set out upon that ocean of veiled hostility which showed itself in their aloofness from one another. This aloofness might have grieved Ivan Ilyich had he considered that it ought not to exist, but he now regarded the position as normal, and even made it the goal at which he aimed in family life. His aim was to free himself more and more from those unpleasantnesses and to give them a semblance of harmlessness and propriety. He attained this by spending less and less time with his family, and when obliged to be at home he tried to safeguard his position by the presence of outsiders. The chief thing however was that he had his official duties. The whole interest of his life now centered in the official world and that interest absorbed him. The consciousness of his power, being able to ruin anybody he wished to ruin, the importance, even the external dignity of his entry into court, or meetings with his subordinates, his success with superiors and inferiors, and above all his masterly handling of cases, of which he was conscious—all this gave him pleasure and filled his life, together with chats with his colleagues, dinners, and bridge. So that on the whole Ivan Ilyich's life continued to flow as he considered it should do—pleasantly and properly.

So things continued for another seven years. His eldest daughter was already sixteen, another child had died, and only one son was left, a schoolboy and a subject of dissensions. Ivan Ilyich wanted to put him in the School of Law, but to spite him Praskovya Fëdorovna entered him at the High School. The daughter had been educated at home and had turned out well; the boy did not learn badly either.

III

So Ivan Ilyich lived for seventeen years after his marriage. He was already a Public Prosecutor of long standing, and had declined several proposed transfers while awaiting a more desirable post, when an unanticipated and unpleasant occurrence quite upset the peaceful course of his life. He was expecting to be offered the post of presiding judge in a University town, but Hoppe somehow came to the front and obtained the appointment instead. Ivan Ilyich became irritable, reproached Hoppe, and quarrelled both with him and with his immediate superiors—who became colder to him and again passed him over when other appointments were made.

This was in 1880, the hardest year of Ivan Ilyich's life. It was then that it became evident on the one hand that his salary was insufficient for them to live on, and on the other that he had been forgotten, and not only this, but that what was for him the greatest and most cruel injustice appeared to others a quite ordinary occurrence. Even his father did not consider it his duty to help him. Ivan Ilyich felt himself abandoned by everyone, and that they regarded his position with a salary of 3,500 rubles as quite normal and even fortunate. He alone knew that with the consciousness of the injustices done him, with his wife's incessant nagging, and with the debts he had contracted by living beyond his means his position was far from normal.

In order to save money that summer he obtained leave of absence and went with his wife to live in the country at her brother's place.

In the country, without his work, he experienced *ennui* for the first time in his life, and not only *ennui* but intolerable depression, and he decided that it was impossible to go on living like that, and that it was necessary to take energetic measures.

Having passed a sleepless night pacing up and down the veranda, he decided to go to Petersburg and bestir himself, in order to punish those who had failed to appreciate him and to get transferred to another ministry.

Next day, despite many protests from his wife and her brother, he started for Petersburg with the sole object of obtaining a post with a salary of five thousand rubles a year. He was no longer bent on any particular department, or tendency, or kind of activity. All he now wanted was an appointment to another post with a salary of five thousand rubles, either in the administration, in the banks, with the railways, in one of the Empress Marya's Institutions,[8] or even in the customs—but it had to carry with it a salary of five thousand rubles and be in a ministry other than that in which they had failed to appreciate him.

And this quest of Ivan Ilyich's was crowned with remarkable and unexpected success. At Kursk an acquaintance of his, F. I. Ilyin, got into the first-class carriage, sat down beside Ivan Ilyich, and told him of a telegram just received by the governor of Kursk announcing that a change was about to take place in the ministry: Peter Ivanovich was to be superseded by Ivan Semënovich.

The proposed change, apart from its significance for Russia, had a special significance for Ivan Ilyich, because by bringing forward a new man, Peter Petrovich, and consequently his friend Zachar Ivanovich, it was highly favourable for Ivan Ilyich, since Zachar Ivanovich was a friend and colleague of his.

In Moscow his news was confirmed, and on reaching Petersburg Ivan Ilyich found Zachar Ivanovich and received a definite promise of an appointment in his former department of Justice.

A week later he telegraphed to his wife: "Zachar in Miller's place. I shall receive appointment on presentation of report."

Thanks to this change of personnel, Ivan Ilyich had unexpectedly obtained an appointment in his former ministry which placed him two stages above his former colleagues besides giving him five thousand rubles salary and three thousand five hundred rubles for expenses connected with his removal. All his ill humour towards his former enemies and the whole department vanished, and Ivan Ilyich was completely happy.

He returned to the country more cheerful and contented than he had been for a long time. Praskovya Fëdorovna also cheered up and a truce was

8. Reference to the charitable organization founded by the Empress Marya, wife of Paul I, late in the eighteenth century.

arranged between them. Ivan Ilyich told of how he had been fêted by every-body in Petersburg, how all those who had been his enemies were put to shame and now fawned on him, how envious they were of his appointment, and how much everybody in Petersburg had liked him.

Praskovya Fëdorovna listened to all this and appeared to believe it. She did not contradict anything, but only made plans for their life in the town to which they were going. Ivan Ilyich saw with delight that these plans were his plans, that he and his wife agreed, and that, after a stumble, his life was regaining its due and natural character of pleasant lightheartedness and decorum.

Ivan Ilyich had come back for a short time only, for he had to take up his new duties on the 10th of September. Moreover, he needed time to settle into the new place, to move all his belongings from the province, and to buy and order many additional things: in a word, to make such arrangements as he had resolved on, which were almost exactly what Praskovya Fëdorovna too had decided on.

Now that everything had happened so fortunately, and that he and his wife were at one in their aims and moreover saw so little of one another they got on together better than they had done since the first years of marriage. Ivan Ilyich had thought of taking his family away with him at once, but the insistence of his wife's brother and her sister-in-law, who had suddenly become particularly amiable and friendly to him and his family, induced him to depart alone.

So he departed, and the cheerful state of mind induced by his success and by the harmony between his wife and himself, the one intensifying the other, did not leave him. He found a delightful house, just the thing both he and his wife had dreamt of. Spacious, lofty reception rooms in the old style, a convenient and dignified study, rooms for his wife and daughter, a study for his son—it might have been specially built for them. Ivan Ilyich himself superintended the arrangements, chose the wallpapers, supplemented the furniture (preferably with antiques which he considered particularly *comme il faut*), and supervised the upholstering. Everything progressed and progressed and approached the ideal he had set himself: even when things were only half completed they exceeded his expectations. He saw what a refined and elegant character, free from vulgarity, it would all have when it was ready. On falling asleep he pictured to himself how the reception-room would look. Looking at the yet unfinished drawing-room he could see the fireplace, the screen, the what-not, the little chairs dotted here and there, the dishes and plates on the walls, and the bronzes, as they would be when everything was in place. He was pleased by the thought of how his wife and daughter, who shared his taste in this matter, would be impressed by it. They were certainly not expecting as much. He had been particularly successful in finding, and buying cheaply, antiques which gave a particularly aristocratic character to the whole place. But in his letters he intentionally understated everything in order to be able to surprise them. All this so absorbed him that his new duties—though he liked his official work—interested him less than he had expected. Sometimes he even had moments of absent-mindedness during the Court Sessions, and would consider whether he should have straight or curved cornices for his curtains. He was so interested in it all that he often did things himself, rearranging the furniture, or rehanging the curtains. Once when mounting a step-ladder to show the upholsterer, who did not understand, how he wanted the hangings draped, he made a false step and slipped, but being a strong and agile man he clung on and only knocked his side against the knob of the window frame. The bruised place was painful but the pain soon passed, and he felt particularly bright and well just then. He wrote: "I feel fifteen years younger." He thought he would have everything ready by September, but it dragged on till mid-October. But the result was charming not only in his eyes but to everyone who saw it.

In reality it was just what is usually seen in the houses of people of moderate means who want to appear rich, and therefore succeed only in resembling others like themselves: there were damasks, dark wood, plants, rugs, and dull and polished bronzes—all the things people of a certain class have in order to resemble other people of that class. His house was so like the others that it would never have been noticed, but to him it all seemed to be quite exceptional. He was very happy when he met his family at the station and brought them to the newly furnished house all lit up, where a footman in a white tie opened the door into the hall decorated with plants, and when they went on into the drawing room and the study uttering exclamations of delight. He conducted them everywhere, drank in their praises eagerly, and beamed with pleasure. At tea that evening, when Praskovya Fëdorovna among other things asked him about his fall, he laughed, and showed them how he had gone flying and had frightened the upholsterer.

"It's a good thing I'm a bit of an athlete. Another man might have been killed, but I merely knocked myself, just here; it hurts when it's touched, but it's passing off already—it's only a bruise."

So they began living in their new home—in which, as always happens, when they got thoroughly settled in they found they were just one room short—and with the increased income, which as always was just a little (some five hundred rubles) too little, but it was all very nice.

Things went particularly well at first, before everything was finally arranged and while something had still to be done: this thing bought, that thing ordered, another thing moved, and something else adjusted. Though there were some disputes between husband and wife, they were both so well satisfied and had so much to do that it all passed off without any serious quarrels. When nothing was left to arrange it became rather dull and something seemed to be lacking, but they were then making acquaintances, forming habits, and life was growing fuller.

Ivan Ilyich spent his mornings at the law court and came home to dinner, and at first he was generally in a good humour, though he occasionally became irritable just on account of his house. (Every spot on the tablecloth or the upholstery, and every broken window-blind string, irritated him. He had devoted so much trouble to arranging it all that every disturbance of it distressed him.) But on the whole his life ran its course as he believed life should do: easily, pleasantly, and decorously.

He got up at nine, drank his coffee, read the paper, and then put on his undress uniform and went to the law courts. There the harness in which he worked had already been stretched to fit him and he donned it without a hitch: petitioners, inquiries at the chancery, the chancery itself, and the sittings public and administrative. In all this the thing was to exclude everything fresh and vital, which always disturbs the regular course of official business, and to admit only official relations with people, and then only on official grounds. A man would come, for instance, wanting some information. Ivan Ilyich, as one in whose sphere the matter did not lie, would have nothing to do with him: but if the man had some business with him in his official capacity, something that could be expressed on officially stamped paper, he would do everything, positively everything he could within the limits of such relations, and in doing so would maintain the semblance of friendly human relations, that is, would observe the courtesies of life. As soon as the official relations ended, so did everything else. Ivan Ilyich possessed this capacity to separate his real life from the official side of affairs and not mix the two, in the highest degree, and by long practice and natural aptitude had brought it to such a pitch that sometimes, in the manner of a virtuoso, he would even allow himself to let the human and official relations mingle. He let himself do this just because he felt that he could at any time he chose resume the strictly official attitude again and drop the human relation. And he did it all easily, pleasantly, correctly, and even artistically. In the intervals between the sessions he smoked, drank tea, chatted a little about politics, a little about general topics, a little about cards, but most of all about official appointments. Tired, but with the feelings of a virtuoso—one of the first violins who has played his part in an orchestra with precision—he would return home to find that his wife and daughter had been out paying calls, or had a visitor, and that his son had been to school, had done his homework with his tutor, and was duly learning what is taught at High Schools. Everything was as it should be. After dinner, if they had no visitors, Ivan Ilyich sometimes read a book that was being much discussed at the time, and in the evening settled down to work, that is, read official papers, compared the depositions of witnesses, and noted paragraphs of the Code applying to them. This was neither dull nor amusing. It was dull when he might have been playing bridge, but if no bridge was available it was at any rate better than doing nothing or sitting with his wife. Ivan Ilyich's chief pleasure was giving little dinners to which he invited men and women of good social position, and just as his drawing-room resembled all other drawing-rooms so did his enjoyable little parties resemble all other such parties.

Once they even gave a dance. Ivan Ilyich enjoyed it and everything went off well, except that it led to a violent quarrel with his wife about the cakes and sweets. Praskovya Fëdorovna had made her own plans, but Ivan Ilyich insisted on getting everything from an expensive confectioner and ordered too many cakes, and the quarrel occurred because some of those cakes were left over and the confectioner's bill came to forty-five rubles. It was a great and disagreeable quarrel. Praskovya Fëdorovna called him "a fool and an imbecile," and he clutched at his head and made angry allusions to divorce.

But the dance itself had been enjoyable. The best people were there, and Ivan Ilyich had danced with Princess Trufonova, a sister of the distinguished founder of the Society "Bear my Burden."

The pleasures connected with his work were pleasures of ambition; his social pleasures were those of vanity; but Ivan Ilyich's greatest pleasure was playing bridge. He acknowledged that whatever disagreeable incident happened in his life, the pleasure that beamed like a ray of light above everything else was to sit down to bridge with good players, not noisy partners, and of course to four-handed bridge (with five players it was annoying to have to stand out, though one pretended not to mind), to play a clever and serious game (when the cards allowed it) and then to have supper and drink a glass of wine. After a game of bridge, especially if he had won a little (to win a large sum was unpleasant), Ivan Ilyich went to bed in specially good humour.

So they lived. They formed a circle of acquaintances among the best people and were visited by people of importance and by young folk. In their views as to their acquaintances, husband, wife, and daughter were entirely agreed, and tacitly and unanimously kept at arm's length and shook off the various shabby friends and relations who, with much show of affection, gushed into the drawing-room with its Japanese plates on the walls. Soon these shabby friends ceased to obtrude themselves and only the best people remained in the Golovins' set.

Young men made up to Lisa, and Petrishchev, an examining magistrate and Dmitri Ivanovich Petrischchev's son and sole heir, began to be so attentive to her that Ivan Ilyich had already spoken to Praskovya Fëdorovna about it, and considered whether they should not arrange a party for them, or get up some private theatricals.

So they lived, and all went well, without change, and life flowed pleasantly.

IV

They were all in good health. It could not be called ill health if Ivan Ilyich sometimes said that he had a queer taste in his mouth and felt some discomfort in his left side.

But this discomfort increased and, though not exactly painful, grew into a sense of pressure in his side accompanied by ill humour. And his irritability became worse and worse and began to mar the agreeable, easy, and correct life that had established itself in the Golovin family. Quarrels between husband and wife became more and more frequent, and soon the ease and amenity disappeared and even the decorum was barely maintained. Scenes again became frequent, and very few of those islets remained on which husband and wife could meet without an explosion. Praskovya Fëdorovna now had good reason to say that her husband's temper was trying. With characteristic exaggeration she said he had always had a dreadful temper, and that it had needed all her good nature to put up with it for twenty years. It was true that now the quarrels were started by him. His bursts of temper always came just before dinner, often just as he began to eat his soup. Sometimes he noticed that a plate or dish was chipped, or the food was not right, or his son put his elbow on the table, or his daughter's hair was not done as he liked it, and for all this he blamed Praskovya Fëdorovna. At first she retorted and said disagreeable things to him, but once or twice he fell into such a rage at the beginning of dinner that she realized it was due to some physical derangement brought on by taking food, and so she restrained herself and did not answer, but only hurried to get the dinner over. She regarded this self-restraint as highly praiseworthy. Having come to the conclusion that her husband had a dreadful temper and made her life miserable, she began to feel sorry for herself, and the more she pitied herself the more she hated her husband. She began to wish he would die; yet she did not want him to die because then his salary would cease. And this irritated her against him still more. She considered herself dreadfully unhappy just because not even his death could save her, and though she concealed her exasperation, that hidden exasperation of hers increased his irritation also.

After one scene in which Ivan Ilyich had been particularly unfair and after which he had said in explanation that he certainly was irritable but that it was due to his not being well, she said that if he was ill it should be attended to, and insisted on his going to see a celebrated doctor.

He went. Everything took place as he had expected and as it always does. There was the usual waiting and the important air assumed by the doctor, with which he was so familiar (resembling that which he himself assumed in court), and the sounding and listening, and the questions which called for answers that were foregone conclusions and were evidently unnecessary, and the look of importance which implied that "if only you put yourself in our hands we will arrange everything—we know indubitably how it has to be done, always in the same way for everybody alike." It was all just as it was in the law courts. The doctor put on just the same air towards him as he himself put on towards an accused person.

The doctor said that so-and-so indicated that there was so-and-so inside the patient, but if the investigation of so-and-so did not confirm this, then he must assume that and that. If he assumed that and that, then . . . and so on. To Ivan Ilyich only one question was important: was his case serious or not? But the doctor ignored that inappropriate question. From his point of view it was not the one under consideration, the real question was to decide between a floating kidney, chronic catarrh, or appendicitis. It was not a question of Ivan Ilyich's life or death, but one between a floating kidney and appendicitis. And that question the doctor solved brilliantly, as it seemed to Ivan Ilyich, in favour of the appendix, with the reservation that should an examination of the urine give fresh indications the matter would be reconsidered. All this was just what Ivan Ilyich had himself brilliantly accomplished a thousand times in dealing with men on trial. The doctor summed up just as brilliantly, looking over his spectacles triumphantly and even gaily at the accused. From the doctor's summing up Ivan Ilyich concluded that things were bad, but that for the doctor, and perhaps for everybody else, it was a matter of indifference, though for him it was bad. And this conclusion struck him painfully, arousing in him a great feeling of pity for himself and of bitterness towards the doctor's indifference to a matter of such importance.

He said nothing of this, but rose, placed the doctor's fee on the table, and remarked with a sigh: "We sick people probably often put inappropriate questions. But tell me, in general, is this complaint dangerous or not? . . ."

The doctor looked at him sternly over his spectacles with one eye, as if to say: "Prisoner, if you will not keep to the questions put to you, I shall be obliged to have you removed from the court."

"I have already told you what I consider necessary and proper. The analysis may show something more." And the doctor bowed.

Ivan Ilyich went out slowly, seated himself disconsolately in his sledge, and drove home. All the way home he was going over what the doctor had said, trying to translate those complicated, obscure, scientific phrases into plain language and find in them an answer to the question: "Is my condition bad? Is it very bad? Or is there as yet nothing much wrong?" And it seemed to him that the meaning of what the doctor had said was it was very bad.

Everything in the streets seemed depressing. The cabmen, the houses, the passers-by, and the shops, were dismal. His ache, this dull gnawing ache that never ceased for a moment, seemed to have acquired a new and more serious significance from the doctor's dubious remarks. Ivan Ilyich now watched it with a new and oppressive feeling.

He reached home and began to tell his wife about it. She listened, but in the middle of his account his daughter came in with her hat on, ready to go out with her mother. She sat down reluctantly to listen to this tedious story, but could not stand it long, and her mother too did not hear him to the end.

"Well, I am very glad," she said. "Mind now to take your medicine regularly. Give me the prescription and I'll send Gerasim to the chemist's." And she went to get ready to go out.

While she was in the room Ivan Ilyich had hardly taken time to breathe, but he sighed deeply when she left it.

"Well," he thought, "perhaps it isn't so bad after all."

He began taking his medicine and following the doctor's directions, which had been altered after the examination of the urine. But then it happened that there was a contradiction between the indications drawn from the examination of the urine and the symptoms that showed themselves. It turned out that what was happening differed from what the doctor had told him, and that he had either forgotten, or blundered, or hidden something from him. He could not, however, be blamed for that, and Ivan Ilyich still obeyed his orders implicitly and at first derived some comfort from doing so.

From the time of his visit to the doctor, Ivan Ilyich's chief occupation was the exact fulfilment of the doctor's instructions regarding hygiene and the taking of medicine, and the observation of his pain and his excretions. His chief interests came to be people's ailments and people's health. When sickness, deaths, or recoveries were mentioned in his presence, especially when the illness resembled his own, he listened with agitation which he tried to hide, asked questions, and applied what he heard to his own case.

The pain did not grow less, but Ivan Ilyich made efforts to force himself to think that he was better. And he could do this so long as nothing agitated him. But as soon as he had any unpleasantness with his wife, any lack of success in his official work, or held bad cards at bridge, he was at once acutely sensible of his disease. He had formerly borne such mischances, hoping soon to adjust what was wrong, to master it and attain success, or make a grand slam. But now every mischance upset him and plunged him into despair. He would say to himself. "There now, just as I was beginning to get better and the medicine had begun to take effect, comes this accursed misfortune, or unpleasantness . . ." And he was furious with the mishap, or with the people who were causing the unpleasantness and killing him, for he felt that this fury was killing him but could not restrain it. One would have thought that it should have been clear to him that this exasperation with circumstances and people aggravated his illness, and that he ought therefore to ignore unpleasant occurrences. But he drew the very opposite conclusion: he said that he needed peace, and he watched for everything that might disturb it and became irritable at the slightest infringement of it. His condition was rendered worse by the fact that he read medical books and consulted doctors. The progress of his disease was so gradual that he could deceive himself when comparing one day with another—the difference was so slight. But when he consulted the doctors it seemed to him that he was getting worse, and even very rapidly. Yet despite this he was continually consulting them.

That month he went to see another celebrity, who told him almost the same as the first had done but put his questions rather differently, and the interview with this celebrity only increased Ivan Ilyich's doubts and fears. A friend of a friend of his, a very good doctor, diagnosed his illness again quite differently from the others, and though he predicted recovery, his questions and suppositions bewildered Ivan Ilyich still more and increased his doubts. A homeopathist diagnosed the disease in yet another way, and prescribed medicine which Ivan Ilyich took secretly for a week. But after a week, not feeling any improvement and having lost confidence both in the former doctor's treatment and in this one's, he became still more despondent. One day a lady acquaintance mentioned a cure effected by a wonder-working icon. Ivan Ilyich caught himself listening attentively and beginning to believe that it had occurred. This incident alarmed him. "Has my mind really weakened to such an extent?" he asked himself. "Nonsense! It's all rubbish. I mustn't give way to nervous fears but having chosen a doctor must keep strictly to his treatment. That is what I will do. Now it's all settled. I won't think about it, but will follow the treatment seriously till summer, and then we shall see. From now there must be no more of this wavering!" This was easy to say but impossible to carry out. The pain in his side oppressed him and seemed to grow worse and more incessant, while the taste in his mouth grew stranger and stranger. It seemed to him that his breath had a disgusting smell, and he was conscious of a loss of appetite and strength. There was no deceiving himself: something terrible, new, and more important than anything before in his life, was taking place within him of which he alone was aware. Those about him did not understand or would not understand it, but thought everything in the world was going on as usual. That tormented Ivan Ilyich more than anything. He saw that his household, especially his wife and daughter who were in a perfect whirl of visiting, did not understand anything of it and were annoyed that he was so depressed and so exacting, as if he were to blame for it. Though they tried to disguise it he saw that he was an obstacle in their path, and that his wife had adopted a definite line in regard to his illness and kept to it regardless of anything he said or did. Her attitude was this: "You know," she would say to her friends, "Ivan Ilyich can't do as other people do, and keep to the treatment prescribed for him. One day he'll take his drops and keep strictly to his diet and go to bed in good time, but the next day unless I watch him he'll suddenly forget his medicine, eat sturgeon—which is forbidden—and sit up playing cards till one o'clock in the morning."

"Oh, come, when was that?" Ivan Ilyich would ask in vexation. "Only once at Peter Ivanovich's."

"And yesterday with Shebek."

"Well, even if I hadn't stayed up, this pain would have kept me awake."

"Be that as it may you'll never get well like that, but will always make us wretched."

Praskovya Fedorovna's attitude to Ivan Ilyich's illness, as she expressed it both to others and to him, was that it was his own fault and was another of the annoyances he caused her. Ivan Ilyich felt that this opinion escaped her involuntarily—but that did not make it easier for him.

At the law courts too, Ivan Ilyich noticed, or thought he noticed, a strange attitude towards himself. It sometimes seemed to him that people were watching him inquisitively as a man whose place might soon be vacant. Then again, his friends would suddenly begin to chaff him in a friendly way about his low spirits, as if the awful, horrible, and unheard-of thing that was going on within him, incessantly gnawing at him and irresistibly drawing him away, was a very agreeable subject for jests. Schwartz in particular irritated him by his jocularity, vivacity, and *savoir-faire*, which reminded him of what he himself had been ten years ago.

Friends came to make up a set and they sat down to cards. They dealt, bending the new cards to soften them, and he sorted the diamonds in his hand and found he had seven. His partner said "No trumps" and supported him with two diamonds. What more could be wished for? It ought to be jolly and lively. They would make a grand slam. But suddenly Ivan Ilyich was conscious of that gnawing pain, that taste in his mouth, and it seemed ridiculous that in such circumstances he should be pleased to make a grand slam.

He looked at his partner Mikhail Mikhaylovich, who rapped the table with his strong hand and instead of snatching up the tricks pushed the cards courteously and indulgently towards Ivan Ilyich that he might have the pleasure of gathering them up without the trouble of stretching out his hand for them. "Does he think I am too weak to stretch out my arm?" thought Ivan Ilyich, and forgetting what he was doing he over-trumped his partner, missing the grand slam by three tricks. And what was most awful of all was that he saw how upset Mikhail Mikhaylovich was about it but did not himself care. And it was dreadful to realize why he did not care.

They all saw that he was suffering, and said: "We can stop if you are tired. Take a rest." Lie down? No, he was not at all tired, and he finished the rubber. All were gloomy and silent. Ivan Ilyich felt that he had diffused this gloom over them and could not dispel it. They had supper and went away, and Ivan Ilyich was left alone with the consciousness that his life was poisoned and was poisoning the lives of others, and that this poison did not weaken but penetrated more and more deeply into his whole being.

With this consciousness, and with physical pain besides the terror, he must go to bed, often to lie awake the greater part of the night. Next morning he had to get up again, dress, go to the law courts, speak, and write; or if he did not go out, spend at home those twenty-four hours a day each of which was a torture. And he had to live thus all alone on the brink of an abyss, with no one who understood or pitied him.

V

So one month passed and then another. Just before the New Year his brother-in-law came to town and stayed at their house. Ivan Ilyich was at the law courts and Praskovya Fëdorovna had gone shopping. When Ivan Ilyich came home and entered his study he found his brother-in-law there—a healthy, florid man—unpacking his portmanteau himself. He raised his head on hearing Ivan Ilyich's footsteps and looked up at him for a moment without a word. That stare told Ivan everything. His brother-in-law opened his mouth to utter an exclamation of surprise but checked himself, and that action confirmed it all.

"I have changed, eh?"

"Yes, there is a change."

And after that, try as he would to get his brother-in-law to return to the subject of his looks, the latter would say nothing about it. Praskovya Fëdorovna came home and her brother went out to her. Ivan Ilyich locked the door and began to examine himself in the glass, first full face, then in profile. He took up a portrait of himself taken with his wife, and compared it with what he saw in the glass. The change in him was immense. Then he bared his arms to the elbow, looked at them, drew the sleeves down again, sat down on an ottoman, and grew blacker than night.

"No, no, this won't do!" he said to himself, and jumped up, went to the table, took up some law papers and began to read them, but could not continue. He unlocked the door and went into the reception-room. The door leading to the drawing-room was shut. He approached it on tiptoe and listened.

"No, you are exaggerating!" Praskovya Fëdorovna was saying.

"Exaggerating! Don't you see it? Why, he's a dead man! Look at his eyes— there's no light in them. But what is it that is wrong with him?"

"No one knows. Nikolaevich [that was another doctor] said something, but I don't know what. And Leshchetitsky [this was the celebrated specialist] said quite the contrary . . ."

Ivan Ilyich walked away, went to his own room, lay down and began musing: "The kidney, a floating kidney." He recalled all the doctors had told him of how it detached itself and swayed about. And by an effort of imagination he tried to catch that kidney and arrest it and support it. So little was needed for this, it seemed to him. "No, I'll go to see Peter Ivanovich again." [That was the friend whose friend was a doctor.] He rang, ordered the carriage, and got ready to go.

"Where are you going, *Jean?*" asked his wife, with a specially sad and exceptionally kind look.

This exceptionally kind look irritated him. He looked morosely at her.

"I must go to see Peter Ivanovich."

He went to see Peter Ivanovich, and together they went to see his friend, the doctor. He was in, and Ivan Ilyich had a long talk with him.

Reviewing the anatomical and physiological details of what in the doctor's opinion was going on inside him, he understood it all.

There was something, a small thing, in the vermiform appendix. It might all come right. Only stimulate the energy of one organ and check the activity of another, then absorption would take place and everything would come right. He got home rather late for dinner, ate his dinner, and conversed cheerfully, but could not for a long time bring himself to go back to work in his room. At last, however, he went to his study and did what was necessary, but the consciousness that he had put something aside—an important, intimate matter which he would revert to when his work was done—never left him. When he had finished his work he remembered that this intimate matter was the thought of his vermiform appendix. But he did not give himself up to it, and went to the drawing-room for tea. There were callers there, including the examining magistrate who was a desirable match for his daughter, and they were conversing, playing the piano, and singing. Ivan Ilyich, as Praskovya Fëdorovna remarked, spent that evening more cheerfully than usual, but he never for a moment forgot that he had postponed the important matter of the appendix. At eleven o'clock he said good-night and went to his bedroom. Since his illness he had slept alone in a small room next to his study. He undressed and took up a novel by Zola,[9] but instead of reading it he fell into thought, and in his imagination that desired improvement in the vermiform appendix occurred. There was the absorption and evacuation and the reestablishment of normal activity. "Yes, that's it!" he said to himself. one need only assist nature, that's all." He remembered his medicine, rose, took it, and lay down on his back watching for the beneficent action of the medicine and for it to lessen the pain. "I need only take it regularly and avoid all injurious influences. I am already feeling better, much better." He began touching his side: it was not painful to the touch. "There, I really don't feel it. It's much better already." He put out the light and turned on his side. . . . "The appendix is getting better, absorption is occurring." Suddenly he felt the old, familiar, dull, gnawing pain, stubborn and serious. There was the same familiar loathsome taste in his mouth. His heart sank and he felt dazed. "My God! My God!" he muttered. "Again, again! And it will never cease." And suddenly the matter presented itself in a quite different aspect. "Vermiform appendix! Kidney!" he said to himself. "It's not a question of appendix or kidney, but of life and . . . death. Yes, life was there and now it is going, going and I cannot stop it. Yes. Why deceive myself? Isn't it obvious to everyone but me that I'm dying, and that it's only a question of weeks, days . . . it may happen this moment. There was light and now there is darkness. I was here and now I'm going there! Where?" A chill came over him, his breathing ceased, and he felt only the throbbing of his heart.

"When I am not, what will there be? There will be nothing. Then where shall I be when I am no more? Can this be dying? No, I don't want to!" He jumped up and tried to light the candle, felt for it with trembling hands, dropped candle and candlestick on the floor, and fell back on his pillow.

"What's the use? It makes no difference," he said to himself, staring with wide-open eyes into the darkness. "Death. Yes, death. And none of them know or wish to know it, and they have no pity for me. Now they are playing." (He heard through the door the distant sound of a song and its accompaniment.) "It's all the same to them, but they will die too! Fools! I first, and they later, but it will be the same for them. And now they are merry . . . the beasts!"

Anger choked him and he was agonizingly, unbearably miserable. "It is impossible that all men have been doomed to suffer this awful horror!" He raised himself.

"Something must be wrong. I must calm myself—must think it all over from the beginning." And he again began thinking. "Yes, the beginning of my illness: I knocked my side, but I was still quite well that day and the next. It hurt a little, then rather more. I saw the doctors, then followed despondency and anguish, more doctors, and I drew nearer to the abyss. My strength grew less and I kept coming nearer and nearer, and now I have wasted away and there is no light in my eyes. I think of the appendix—but this is death! I think of mending the appendix, and all the while here is death! Can it really be death!" Again terror seized him and he gasped for breath. He leant down

---

9. Émile Zola (1840–1902), French novelist, author of the *Rougon-Macquart* novels (*Nana, Germinal,* and so on). Tolstoy condemned Zola for his naturalistic theories and considered his novels crude and gross.

and began feeling for the matches, pressing with his elbow on the stand beside the bed. It was in his way and hurt him, he grew furious with it, pressed on it still harder, and upset it. Breathless and in despair he fell on his back, expecting death to come immediately.

Meanwhile the visitors were leaving. Praskovya Fëdorovna was seeing them off. She heard something fall and came in.

"What has happened?"

"Nothing. I knocked it over accidentally."

She went out and returned with a candle. He lay there panting heavily, like a man who has run a thousand yards, and stared upwards at her with a fixed look.

"What is it, *Jean?*"

"No . . . o . . . thing. I upset it." ("Why speak of it? She won't understand," he thought.)

And in truth she did not understand. She picked up the stand, lit his candle, and hurried away to see another visitor off. When she came back he still lay on his back, looking upwards.

"What is it? Do you feel worse?"

"Yes."

She shook her head and sat down.

"Do you know, *Jean,* I think we must ask Leshchetitsky to come and see you here."

This meant calling in the famous specialist, regardless of expense. He smiled malignantly and said "No." She remained a little longer and then went up to him and kissed his forehead.

While she was kissing him he hated her from the bottom of his soul and with difficulty refrained from pushing her away.

"Good-night. Please God you'll sleep."

"Yes."

VI

Ivan Ilyich saw that he was dying, and he was in continual despair.

In the depth of his heart he knew he was dying, but not only was he not accustomed to the thought, he simply did not and could not grasp it.

The syllogism he had learned from Kiesewetter's *Logic:*[1] "Caius is a man, men are mortal, therefore Caius is mortal," had always seemed to him correct as applied to Caius, but certainly not as applied to himself. That Caius—man in the abstract—was mortal, was perfectly correct, but he was not Caius, not an abstract man, but a creature quite, quite separate from all others. He had been little Vanya, with a mamma and a papa, with Mitya and Volodya, with the toys, a coachman and a nurse, afterwards with Katenka and with all the joys, griefs, and delights of childhood, boyhood, and youth. What did Caius know of the smell of that striped leather ball Vanya had been so fond of? Had Caius kissed his mother's hand like that, and did the silk of her dress rustle so for Caius? Had he rioted like that at school when the pastry was bad? Had Caius been in love like that? Could Caius preside at a session as he did? "Caius really was mortal, and it was right for him to die; but for me,

1. Karl Kiesewetter (1766–1819) was a German popularizer of Kant's philosophy. His *Outline of Logic According to Kantian Principles* (1796) was widely used in Russian adaptations as a schoolbook.

little Vanya, Ivan Ilyich, with all my thoughts and emotions, it's altogether a different matter. It cannot be that I ought to die. That would be too terrible."

Such was his feeling.

"If I had to die like Caius I should have known it was so. An inner voice would have told me so, but there was nothing of the sort in me and I and all my friends felt that our case was quite different from that of Caius. And now here it is!" he said to himself. "It can't be. It's impossible! But here it is. How is this? How is one to understand it?"

He could not understand it, and tried to drive this false, incorrect, morbid thought away and to replace it by other proper and healthy thoughts. But that thought, and not the thought only but the reality itself, seemed to come and confront him.

And to replace that thought he called up a succession of others, hoping to find in them some support. He tried to get back into the former current of thoughts that had once screened the thought of death from him. But strange to say, all that had formerly shut off, hidden, and destroyed, his consciousness of death, no longer had that effect. Ivan Ilyich now spent most of his time in attempting to re-establish that old current. He would say to himself: "I will take up my duties again—after all I used to live by them." And banishing all doubts he would go to the law courts, enter into conversation with his colleagues, and sit carelessly as was his wont, scanning the crowd with a thoughtful look and leaning both his emaciated arms on the arms of his oak chair; bending over as usual to a colleague and drawing his papers nearer he would interchange whispers with him, and then suddenly raising his eyes and sitting erect would pronounce certain words and open the proceedings. But suddenly in the midst of those proceedings the pain in his side, regardless of the stage the proceedings had reached, would begin its own gnawing work. Ivan Ilyich would turn his attention to it and try to drive the thought of it away, but without success. It would come and stand before him and look at him, and he would be petrified and the light would die out of his eyes, and he would again begin asking himself whether It alone was true. And his colleagues and subordinates would see with surprise and distress that he, the brilliant and subtle judge, was becoming confused and making mistakes. He would shake himself, try to pull himself together, manage somehow to bring the sitting to a close, and return home with the sorrowful consciousness that his judicial labours could not as formerly hide from him what he wanted them to hide, and could not deliver him from It. And what was worst of all was that It drew his attention to itself not in order to make him take some action but only that he should look at It, look it straight in the face: look at it without doing anything, suffer inexpressibly.

And to save himself from this condition Ivan Ilyich looked for consolations—new screens—and new screens were found and for a while seemed to save him, but then they immediately fell to pieces or rather became transparent, as It penetrated them and nothing could veil It.

In these latter days he would go into the drawing-room he had arranged—that drawing-room where he had fallen and for the sake of which (how bitterly ridiculous it seemed) he had sacrificed his life—for he knew that his illness originated with that knock. He would enter and see that something had scratched the polished table. He would look for the cause of this and find that it was the bronze ornamentation of an album, that had got bent.

He would take up the expensive album which he had lovingly arranged, and feel vexed with his daughter and her friends for their untidiness—for the album was torn here and there and some of the photographs turned upside down. He would put it carefully in order and bend the ornamentation back into position. Then it would occur to him to place all those things in another corner of the room, near the plants. He would call the footman, but his daughter or wife would contradict him, and he would dispute and grow angry. But that was all right, for then he did not think about *It*. *It* was invisible.

But then, when he was moving something himself, his wife would say: "Let the servants do it. You will hurt yourself again." And suddenly *It* would flash through the screen and he would see it. It was just a flash, and he hoped it would disappear, but he would involuntarily pay attention to his side. "It sits there as before, gnawing just the same!" And he could no longer forget *It*, but could distinctly see it looking at him from behind the flowers. "What is it all for?"

"It really is so! I lost my life over that curtain as I might have done when storming a fort. Is that possible? How terrible and how stupid. It can't be true! It can't, but it is."

He would go to his study, lie down, and again be alone with *It*: face to face with *It*. And nothing could be done with *It* except to look at it and shudder.

VII

How it happened it is impossible to say because it came about step by step, unnoticed, but in the third month of Ivan Ilyich's illness, his wife, his daughter, his son, his acquaintances, the doctors, the servants, and above all he himself, were aware that the whole interest he had for other people was whether he would soon vacate his place, and at last release the living from the discomfort caused by his presence and be himself released from his sufferings.

He slept less and less. He was given opium and hypodermic injections of morphine, but this did not relieve him. The dull depression he experienced in a somnolent condition at first gave him a little relief, but only as something new; afterwards it became as distressing as the pain itself or even more so.

Special foods were prepared for him by the doctors' orders, but all those foods became increasingly distasteful and disgusting to him.

For his excretions also special arrangements had to be made, and this was a torment to him every time—a torment from the uncleanliness, the unseemliness, and the smell, and from knowing that another person had to take part in it.

But just through this most unpleasant matter, Ivan Ilyich obtained comfort. Gerasim, the butler's young assistant, always came in to carry the things out. Gerasim was a clean, fresh peasant lad, grown stout on town food and always cheerful and bright. At first the sight of him, in his clean Russian peasant costume, engaged on that disgusting task embarrassed Ivan Ilyich.

Once when he got up from the commode too weak to draw up his trousers, he dropped into a soft armchair and looked with horror at his bare, enfeebled thighs with the muscles so sharply marked on them.

Gerasim with a firm light tread, his heavy boots emitting a pleasant smell of tar and fresh winter air, came in wearing a clean Hessian apron, the sleeves of his print shirt tucked up over his strong bare young arms; and refraining from looking at his sick master out of consideration for his feelings, and restraining the joy of life that beamed from his face, he went up to the commode.

"Gerasim!" said Ivan Ilyich in a weak voice.

Gerasim started, evidently afraid he might have committed some blunder, and with a rapid movement turned his fresh, kind, simple young face which just showed the first downy sign of a beard.

"Yes, sir?"

"That must be very unpleasant for you. You must forgive me. I am helpless."

"Oh, why, sir," and Gerasim's eyes beamed and he showed his glistening white teeth, "what's a little trouble? It's a case of illness with you, sir."

And his deft strong hands did their accustomed task, and he went out of the room stepping lightly. Five minutes later he as lightly returned.

Ivan Ilyich was still sitting in the same position in the armchair.

"Gerasim," he said when the latter had replaced the freshly-washed utensil. "Please come here and help me." Gerasim went up to him. "Lift me up. It is hard for me to get up, and I have sent Dmitri away."

Gerasim went up to him, grasped his master with his strong arms deftly but gently, in the same way that he stepped—lifted him, supported him with one hand, and with the other drew up his trousers and would have set him down again, but Ivan Ilyich asked to be led to the sofa. Gerasim, without an effort and without apparent pressure, led him, almost lifting him, to the sofa and placed him on it.

"Thank you. How easily and well you do it all!"

Gerasim smiled again and turned to leave the room. But Ivan Ilyich felt his presence such a comfort that he did not want to let him go.

"One thing more, please move up that chair. No, the other one—under my feet. It is easier for me when my feet are raised."

Gerasim brought the chair, set it down gently in place, and raised Ivan Ilyich's legs on to it. It seemed to Ivan Ilyich that he felt better while Gerasim was holding up his legs.

"It's better when my legs are higher," he said. "Place that cushion under them."

Gerasim did so. He again lifted the legs and placed them, and again Ivan Ilyich felt better while Gerasim held his legs. When he set them down Ivan Ilyich fancied he felt worse.

"Gerasim," he said. "Are you busy now?"

"Not at all, sir," said Gerasim, who had learnt from the townsfolk how to speak to gentlefolk.

"What have you still to do?"

"What have I to do? I've done everything except chopping the logs for tomorrow."

"Then hold my legs up a bit higher, can you?"

"Of course I can. Why not?" And Gerasim raised his master's legs higher and Ivan Ilyich thought that in that position he did not feel any pain at all.

"And how about the logs?"

"Don't trouble about that, sir. There's plenty of time."

Ivan Ilyich told Gerasim to sit down and hold his legs, and began to talk to him. And strange to say it seemed to him that he felt better while Gerasim held his legs up.

After that Ivan Ilyich would sometimes call Gerasim and get him to hold his legs on his shoulders, and he liked talking to him. Gerasim did it all easily, willingly, simply, and with a good nature that touched Ivan Ilyich. Health, strength, and vitality in other people were offensive to him, but Gerasim's strength and vitality did not mortify but soothed him.

What tormented Ivan Ilyich most was the deception, the lie, which for some reason they all accepted, that he was not dying but was simply ill, and that he only need keep quiet and undergo a treatment and then something very good would result. He however knew that do what they would nothing would come of it, only still more agonizing suffering and death. This deception tortured him—their not wishing to admit what they all knew and what he knew, but wanting to lie to him concerning his terrible condition, and wishing and forcing him to participate in that lie. Those lies—lies enacted over him on the eve of his death and destined to degrade this awful, solemn act to the level of their visitings, their curtains, their sturgeon for dinner— were a terrible agony for Ivan Ilyich. And strangely enough, many times when they were going through their antics over him he had been within a hair-breadth of calling out to them: "Stop lying! You know and I know that I am dying. Then at least stop lying about it!" But he had never had the spirit to do it. The awful, terrible act of his dying was, he could see, reduced by those about him to the level of a casual, unpleasant, and almost indecorous inci- dent (as if someone entered a drawing-room diffusing an unpleasant odour) and this was done by that very decorum which he had served all his life long. He saw that no one felt for him, because no one even wished to grasp his position. Only Gerasim recognized and pitied him. And so Ivan Ilyich felt at ease only with him. He felt comforted when Gerasim supported his legs (sometimes all night long) and refused to go to bed, saying: "Don't you worry, Ivan Ilyich. I'll get sleep enough later on," or when he suddenly became familiar and exclaimed: "If you weren't sick it would be another matter, but as it is, why should I grudge a little trouble?" Gerasim alone did not lie; everything showed that he alone understood the facts of the case and did not consider it necessary to disguise them, but simply felt sorry for his ema- ciated and enfeebled master. Once when Ivan Ilyich was sending him away he even said straight out: "We shall all of us die, so why should I grudge a little trouble?"—expressing the fact that he did not think his work burden- some, because he was doing it for a dying man and hoped someone would do the same for him when his time came.

Apart from this lying, or because of it, what most tormented Ivan Ilyich was that no one pitied him as he wished to be pitied. At certain moments after prolonged suffering he wished most of all (though he would have been ashamed to confess it) for someone to pity him as a sick child is pitied. He longed to be petted and comforted. He knew he was an important function- ary, that he had a beard turning grey, and that therefore what he longed for was impossible, but still he longed for it. And in Gerasim's attitude towards him there was something akin to what he wished for, and so that attitude comforted him. Ivan Ilyich wanted to weep, wanted to be petted and cried over, and then his colleague Shebek would come, and instead of weeping and being petted, Ivan Ilyich would assume a serious, severe, and profound air, and by force of habit would express his opinion on a decision of the Court of Appeal and would stubbornly insist on that view. This falsity around him and within him did more than anything else to poison his last days.

VIII

It was morning. He knew it was morning because Gerasim had gone, and Peter the footman had come and put out the candles, drawn back one of the curtains, and begun quietly to tidy up. Whether it was morning or evening, Friday or Sunday, made no difference, it was all just the same: the gnawing, unmitigated, agonizing pain, never ceasing for an instant, the consciousness of life inexorably waning but not yet extinguished, the approach of that ever dreaded and hateful Death which was the only reality, and always the same falsity. What were days, weeks, hours, in such a case?

"Will you have some tea, sir?"

"He wants things to be regular, and wishes the gentlefolk to drink tea in the morning," thought Ivan Ilyich, and only said "No."

"Wouldn't you like to move onto the sofa, sir?"

"He wants to tidy up the room, and I'm in the way. I am uncleanliness and disorder," he thought, and said only:

"No, leave me alone."

The man went on bustling about. Ivan Ilyich stretched out his hand. Peter came up, ready to help.

"What is it, sir?"

"My watch."

Peter took the watch which was close at hand and gave it to his master.

"Half-past eight. Are they up?"

"No sir, except Vladimir Ivanich" (the son) "who has gone to school. Praskovya Fëdorovna ordered me to wake her if you asked for her. Shall I do so?"

"No, there's no need to." "Perhaps I'd better have some tea," he thought, and added aloud: "Yes, bring me some tea."

Peter went to the door, but Ivan Ilyich dreaded being left alone. "How can I keep him here? Oh yes, my medicine." "Peter, give me my medicine." "Why not? Perhaps it may still do me some good." He took a spoonful and swallowed it. "No, it won't help. It's all tomfoolery, all deception," he decided as soon as he became aware of the familiar, sickly, hopeless taste. "No, I can't believe in it any longer. But the pain, why this pain? If it would only cease just for a moment!" And he moaned. Peter turned towards him. "It's all right. Go and fetch me some tea."

Peter went out. Left alone Ivan Ilyich groaned not so much with pain, terrible though that was, as from mental anguish. Always and forever the same, always these endless days and nights. If only it would come quicker! If only *what* would come quicker? Death, darkness? . . . No, no! Anything rather than death!

When Peter returned with the tea on a tray, Ivan Ilyich stared at him for a time in perplexity, not realizing who and what he was. Peter was disconcerted by that look and his embarrassment brought Ivan Ilyich to himself.

"Oh, tea! All right, put it down. Only help me to wash and put on a clean shirt."

And Ivan Ilyich began to wash. With pauses for rest, he washed his hands and then his face, cleaned his teeth, brushed his hair, and looked in the glass. He was terrified by what he saw, especially by the limp way in which his hair clung to his pallid forehead.

While his shirt was being changed he knew that he would be still more frightened at the sight of his body, so he avoided looking at it. Finally he was ready. He drew on a dressing-gown, wrapped himself in a plaid, and sat down in the armchair to take his tea. For a moment he felt refreshed, but as soon as he began to drink the tea he was again aware of the same taste, and the pain also returned. He finished it with an effort, and then lay down stretching out his legs, and dismissed Peter.

Always the same. Now a spark of hope flashes up, then a sea of despair rages, and always pain; always pain, always despair, and always the same. When alone he had a dreadful and distressing desire to call someone, but he knew beforehand that with others present it would be still worse. "Another dose of morphine—to lose consciousness. I will tell him, the doctor, that he must think of something else. It's impossible, impossible, to go on like this."

An hour and another pass like that. But now there is a ring at the door bell. Perhaps it's the doctor? It is. He comes in fresh, hearty, plump, and cheerful, with that look on his face that seems to say: "There now, you're in a panic about something, but we'll arrange it all for you directly!" The doctor knows this expression is out of place here, but he has put it on once for all and can't take it off—like a man who has put on a frock-coat in the morning to pay a round of calls.

The doctor rubs his hands vigorously and reassuringly.

"Brr! How cold it is! There's such a sharp frost; just let me warm myself!" he says, as if it were only a matter of waiting till he was warm, and then he would put everything right.

"Well now, how are you?"

Ivan Ilyich feels that the doctor would like to say: "Well, how are our affairs?" but that even he feels that this would not do, and says instead: "What sort of a night have you had?"

Ivan Ilyich looks at him as much as to say: "Are you really never ashamed of lying?" But the doctor does not wish to understand this question, and Ivan Ilyich says: "Just as terrible as ever. The pain never leaves me and never subsides. If only something . . ."

"Yes, you sick people are always like that. . . . There, now I think I'm warm enough. Even Praskovya Fëdorovna, who is so particular, could find no fault with my temperature. Well, now I can say good-morning," and the doctor presses his patient's hand.

Then, dropping his former playfulness, he begins with a most serious face to examine the patient, feeling his pulse and taking his temperature, and then begins the sounding and auscultation.

Ivan Ilyich knows quite well and definitely that all this is nonsense and pure deception, but when the doctor, getting down on his knee, leans over him, putting his ear first higher then lower, and performs various gymnastic movements over him with a significant expression on his face, Ivan Ilyich submits to it all as he used to submit to the speeches of the lawyers, though he knew very well that they were all lying and why they were lying.

The doctor, kneeling on the sofa, is still sounding him when Praskovya

Fëdorovna's silk dress rustles at the door and she is heard scolding Peter for not having let her know of the doctor's arrival.

She comes in, kisses her husband, and at once proceeds to prove that she has been up a long time already, and only owing to a misunderstanding failed to be there when the doctor arrived.

Ivan Ilyich looks at her, scans her all over, sets against her the whiteness and plumpness and cleanness of her hands and neck, the gloss of her hair, and the sparkle of her vivacious eyes. He hates her with his whole soul. And the thrill of hatred he feels for her makes him suffer from her touch.

Her attitude towards him and his disease is still the same. Just as the doctor had adopted a certain relation to his patient which he could not abandon, so had she formed one towards him—that he was not doing something he ought to do and was himself to blame, and that she reproached him lovingly for this—and she could not now change that attitude.

"You see he doesn't listen to me and doesn't take his medicine at the proper time. And above all he lies in a position that is no doubt bad for him—with his legs up."

She described how he made Gerasim hold his legs up.

The doctor smiled with a contemptuous affability that said: "What's to be done? These sick people do have foolish fancies of that kind, but we must forgive them."

When the examination was over the doctor looked at his watch, and then Praskovya Fëdorovna announced to Ivan Ilyich that it was of course as he pleased, but she had sent to-day for a celebrated specialist who would examine him and have a consultation with Michael Danilovich (their regular doctor).

"Please don't raise any objections. I am doing this for my own sake," she said ironically, letting it be felt that she was doing it all for his sake and only said this to leave him no right to refuse. He remained silent, knitting his brows. He felt that he was so surrounded and involved in a mesh of falsity that it was hard to unravel anything.

Everything she did for him was entirely for her own sake, and she told him she was doing for herself what she actually was doing for herself, as if that was so incredible that he must understand the opposite.

At half-past eleven the celebrated specialist arrived. Again the sounding began and the significant conversations in his presence and in other rooms, about the kidneys and the appendix, and the questions and answers, with such an air of importance that again, instead of the real question of life and death which now alone confronted him, the question arose of the kidney and the appendix which were not behaving as they ought to and would now be attacked by Michael Danilovich and the specialist and forced to amend their ways.

The celebrated specialist took leave of him with a serious though not hopeless look, and in reply to the timid question in Ivan Ilyich, with eyes glistening with fear and hope, put to him as to whether there was a chance of recovery, said that he could not vouch for it but there was a possibility. The look of hope with which Ivan Ilyich watched the doctor out was so pathetic that Praskovya Fëdorovna, seeing it, even wept as she left the room to hand the doctor his fee.

The gleam of hope kindled by the doctor's encouragement did not last long. The same room, the same pictures, curtains, wallpaper, medicine bottles, were all there, and the same aching suffering body, and Ivan Ilyich began to moan. They gave him a subcutaneous injection and he sank into oblivion.

It was twilight when he came to. They brought him his dinner and he swallowed some beef tea with difficulty, and then everything was the same again and night was coming on.

After dinner, at seven o'clock, Praskovya Fëdorovna came into the room in evening dress, her full bosom pushed up by her corset, and with traces of powder on her face. She had reminded him in the morning that they were going to the theatre. Sarah Bernhardt[2] was visiting the town and they had a box, which he had insisted on their taking. Now he had forgotten about it and her toilet offended him, but he concealed his vexation when he remembered that he had himself insisted on their securing a box and going because it would be an instructive and aesthetic pleasure for the children.

Praskovya Fëdorovna came in, self-satisfied but yet with a rather guilty air. She sat down and asked how he was, but, as he saw, only for the sake of asking and not in order to learn about it, knowing that there was nothing to learn—and then went on to what she really wanted to say: that she would not on any account have gone but that the box had been taken and Helen and their daughter were going, as well as Petrishchev (the examining magistrate, their daughter's fiancé) and that it was out of the question to let them go alone; but that she would have much preferred to sit with him for a while; and he must be sure to follow the doctor's orders while she was away.

"Oh, and Fëdor Petrovich" (the fiancé) "would like to come in. May he? And Lisa?"

"All right."

Their daughter came in in full evening dress, her fresh young flesh exposed (making a show of that very flesh which in his own case caused so much suffering), strong, healthy, evidently in love, and impatient with illness, suffering, and death, because they interfered with her happiness.

Fëdor Petrovich came in too, in evening dress, his hair curled à la Capoul, a tight stiff collar round his long sinewy neck, an enormous white shirt-front and narrow black trousers tightly stretched over his strong thighs. He had one white glove tightly drawn on, and was holding his opera hat in his hand.

Following him the schoolboy crept in unnoticed, in a new uniform, poor little fellow, and wearing gloves. Terribly dark shadows showed under his eyes, the meaning of which Ivan Ilyich knew well.

His son had always seemed pathetic to him, and now it was dreadful to see the boy's frightened look of pity. It seemed to Ivan Ilyich that Vasya was the only one besides Gerasim who understood and pitied him.

They all sat down and again asked how he was. A silence followed. Lisa asked her mother about the opera-glasses, and there was an altercation between mother and daughter as to who had taken them and where they had been put. This occasioned some unpleasantness.

Fëdor Petrovich inquired of Ivan Ilyich whether he had ever seen Sarah

---

2. Stage name of Rosine Bernard (1844–1923), famed for romantic and tragic roles.

Bernhardt. Ivan Ilyich did not at first catch the question, but then replied: "No, have you seen her before?"

"Yes, in *Adrienne Lecouvreur.*"[3]

Praskovya Fëdorovna mentioned some rôles in which Sarah Bernhardt was particularly good. Her daughter disagreed. Conversation sprang up as to the elegance and realism of her acting—the sort of conversation that is always repeated and is always the same.

In the midst of the conversation Fëdor Petrovich glanced at Ivan Ilyich and became silent. The others also looked at him and grew silent. Ivan Ilyich was staring with glittering eyes straight before him, evidently indignant with them. This had to be rectified, but it was impossible to do so. The silence had to be broken, but for a time no one dared to break it and they all became afraid that the conventional deception would suddenly become obvious and the truth become plain to all. Lisa was the first to pluck up courage and break that silence, but by trying to hide what everybody was feeling, she betrayed it.

"Well, if we are going it's time to start," she said, looking at her watch, a present from her father, and with a faint and significant smile at Fëdor Petrovich relating to something known only to them. She got up with a rustle of her dress.

They all rose, said good-night, and went away.

When they had gone it seemed to Ivan Ilyich that he felt better; the falsity had gone with them. But the pain remained—that same pain and that same fear that made everything monotonously alike, nothing harder and nothing easier. Everything was worse.

Again minute followed minute and hour followed hour. Everything remained the same and there was no cessation. And the inevitable end of it all became more and more terrible.

"Yes, send Gerasim here," he replied to a question Peter asked.

IX

His wife returned late at night. She came in on tiptoe, but he heard her, opened his eyes, and made haste to close them again. She wished to send Gerasim away and to sit with him herself, but he opened his eyes and said: "No, go away."

"Are you in great pain?"

"Always the same."

"Take some opium."

He agreed and took some. She went away.

Till about three in the morning he was in a state of stupefied misery. It seemed to him that he and his pain were being thrust into a narrow, deep black sack, but though they were pushed further and further in they could not be pushed to the bottom. And this, terrible enough in itself, was accompanied by suffering. He was frightened yet wanted to fall through the sack, he struggled but yet co-operated. And suddenly he broke through, fell, and

3. A play (1849) by the French dramatist Eugène Scribe (1791–1861), in which the heroine was a famous actress of the eighteenth century. Tolstoy considered Scribe, who wrote over four hundred plays, a shoddy, commercial playwright.

regained consciousness. Gerasim was sitting at the foot of the bed dozing quietly and patiently, while he himself lay with his emaciated stockinged legs resting on Gerasim's shoulders; the same shaded candle was there and the same unceasing pain.

"Go away, Gerasim," he whispered.

"It's all right, sir. I'll stay a while."

"No. Go away."

He removed his legs from Gerasim's shoulders, turned sideways onto his arm, and felt sorry for himself. He only waited till Gerasim had gone into the next room and then restrained himself no longer but wept like a child. He wept on account of his helplessness, his terrible loneliness, the cruelty of man, the cruelty of God, and the absence of God.

"Why hast Thou done all this? Why hast Thou brought me here? Why, dost Thou torment me so terribly?"

He did not expect an answer and yet wept because there was no answer and could be none. The pain again grew more acute, but he did not stir and did not call. He said to himself: "Go on! Strike me! But what is it for? What have I done to Thee? What is it for?"

Then he grew quiet and not only ceased weeping but even held his breath and became all attention. It was as though he were listening not to an audible voice but to a voice of his soul, to the current of thoughts arising within him.

"What is it you want?" was the first clear conception capable of expression in words, that he heard.

"What do you want? What do you want?" he repeated to himself.

"What do I want? To live and not to suffer," he answered.

And again he listened with such concentrated attention that even his pain did not distract him.

"To live? How?" asked his inner voice.

"Why, to live as I used to—well and pleasantly."

"As you lived before, well and pleasantly?" the voice repeated.

And in imagination he began to recall the moments of his pleasant life. But strange to say none of those best moments of his pleasant life now seemed at all what they had then seemed—none of them except the first recollections of childhood. There, in childhood, there had been something really pleasant with which it would be possible to live if it could return. But the child who had experienced that happiness existed no longer, it was like a reminiscence of somebody else.

As soon as the period began which had produced the present Ivan Ilyich, all that had then seemed joys now melted before his sight and turned into something trivial and often nasty.

And the further he departed from childhood and the nearer he came to the present the more worthless and doubtful were the joys. This began with the School of Law. A little that was really good was still found there—there was light-heartedness, friendship, and hope. But in the upper classes there had already been fewer of such good moments. Then during the first years of his official career, when he was in the service of the Governor, some pleasant moments again occurred: they were the memories of love for a woman. Then all became confused and there was still less of what was good; later on again there was still less that was good, and the further he went the less there was. His marriage, a mere accident, then the disenchantment that followed it, his wife's bad breath and the sensuality and hypocrisy: then that deadly official life and those preoccupations about money, a year of it, and two, and ten, and twenty, and always the same thing. And the longer it lasted the more deadly it became. "It is as if I had been going downhill while I imagined I was going up. And that is really what it was. I was going up in public opinion, but to the same extent life was ebbing away from me. And now it is all done and there is only death."

"Then what does it mean? Why? It can't be that life is so senseless and horrible. But if it really has been so horrible and senseless, why must I die and die in agony? There is something wrong!"

"Maybe I did not live as I ought to have done," it suddenly occurred to him. "But how could that be, when I did everything properly?" he replied, and immediately dismissed from his mind this, the sole solution of all the riddles of life and death, as something quite impossible.

"Then what do you want now? To live? Live how? Live as you lived in the law courts when the usher proclaimed 'The judge is coming!' The judge is coming, the judge!" he repeated to himself. "Here he is, the judge. But I am not guilty!" he exclaimed angrily. "What is it for?" And he ceased crying, but turning his face to the wall continued to ponder on the same question: Why, and for what purpose, is there all this horror? But however much he pondered he found no answer. And whenever the thought occurred to him, as it often did, that it all resulted from his not having lived as he ought to have done, he at once recalled the correctness of his whole life, and dismissed so strange an idea.

X

Another fortnight passed. Ivan Ilyich now no longer left his sofa. He would not lie in bed but lay on the sofa, facing the wall nearly all the time. He suffered ever the same unceasing agonies and in his loneliness pondered always on the same insoluble question: "What is this? Can it be that it is Death?" And the inner voice answered: "Yes, it is Death."

"Why these sufferings?" And the voice answered, "For no reason—they just are so." Beyond and besides this there was nothing.

From the very beginning of his illness, ever since he had first been to see the doctor, Ivan Ilyich's life had been divided between two contrary and alternating moods: now it was despair and the expectation of this uncomprehended and terrible death, and now hope and an intently interested observation of the functioning of his organs. Now before his eyes there was only a kidney or an intestine that temporarily evaded its duty, and now only that incomprehensible and dreadful death from which it was impossible to escape.

These two states of mind had alternated from the very beginning of his illness, but the further it progressed the more doubtful and fantastic became the conception of the kidney, and the more real the sense of impending death.

He had but to call to mind what he had been three months before and what he was now, to call to mind with what regularity he had been going downhill, for every possibility of hope to be shattered.

Latterly during that loneliness in which he found himself as he lay facing

the back of the sofa, a loneliness in the midst of a populous town and surrounded by numerous acquaintances and relations but that yet could not
have been more complete anywhere—either at the bottom of the sea or under
the earth—during that terrible loneliness Ivan Ilyich had lived only in memories of the past. Pictures of his past rose before him one after another. They
always began with what was nearest in time and then went back to what was
most remote—to his childhood—and rested there. If he thought of the
stewed prunes that had been offered him that day, his mind went back to
the raw shrivelled French plums of his childhood, their peculiar flavour and
the flow of saliva when he sucked their stones, and along with the memory
of that taste came a whole series of memories of those days: his nurse, his
brother, and their toys. "No, I mustn't think of that. . . . It is too painful,"
Ivan Ilyich said to himself, and brought himself back to the present—to the
button on the back of the sofa and the creases in its morocco. "Morocco is
expensive, but it does not wear well: there had been a quarrel about it. It
was a different kind of quarrel and a different kind of morocco that time
when we tore father's portfolio and were punished, and mamma brought us
some tarts. . . ." And again his thoughts dwelt on his childhood, and again it
was painful and he tried to banish them and fix his mind on something else.

Then again together with that chain of memories another series passed
through his mind—of how his illness had progressed and grown worse. There
also the further back he looked the more life there had been. There had been
more of what was good in life and more of life itself. The two merged
together. "Just as the pain went on getting worse and worse, so my life grew
worse and worse," he thought. "There is one bright spot there at the back,
at the beginning of life, and afterwards all becomes blacker and blacker and
proceeds more and more rapidly—in inverse ratio to the square of the distance from death," thought Ivan Ilyich. And the example of a stone falling
downwards with increasing velocity entered his mind. Life, a series of
increasing sufferings, flies further and further towards its end—the most
terrible suffering. "I am flying. . . ." He shuddered, shifted himself, and tried
to resist, but was already aware that resistance was impossible, and again
with eyes weary of gazing but unable to cease seeing what was before them,
he stared at the back of the sofa and waited—awaiting that dreadful fall and
shock and destruction.

"Resistance is impossible!" he said to himself. "If I could only understand
what it is all for! But that too is impossible. An explanation would be possible
if it could be said that I have not lived as I ought to. But it is impossible to
say that," and he remembered all the legality, correctitude, and propriety of
his life. "That at any rate can certainly not be admitted," he thought, and his
lips smiled ironically as if someone could see that smile and be taken in by
it. "There is no explanation! Agony, death. . . . What for?"

XI

Another two weeks went by in this way and during that fortnight an event
occurred that Ivan Ilyich and his wife had desired. Petrishchev formally proposed. It happened in the evening. The next day Praskovya Fëdorovna came
into her husband's room considering how best to inform him of it, but that
very night there had been a fresh change for the worse in his condition. She

found him still lying on the sofa but in a different position. He lay on his back, groaning and staring fixedly straight in front of him.

She began to remind him of his medicines, but he turned his eyes towards her with such a look that she did not finish what she was saying; so great an animosity, to her in particular, did that look express.

"For Christ's sake let me die in peace!" he said.

She would have gone away, but just then their daughter came in and went up to say good morning. He looked at her as he had done at his wife, and in reply to her inquiry about his health said dryly that he would soon free them all of himself. They were both silent and after sitting with him for a while went away.

"Is it our fault?" Lisa said to her mother. "It's as if we were to blame! I am sorry for papa, but why should we be tortured?"

The doctor came at his usual time. Ivan Ilyich answered "Yes" and "No," never taking his angry eyes from him, and at last said: "You know you can do nothing for me, so leave me alone."

"We can ease your sufferings."

"You can't even do that. Let me be."

The doctor went into the drawing-room and told Praskovya Fëdorovna that the case was very serious and that the only resource left was opium to allay her husband's sufferings, which must be terrible.

It was true, as the doctor said, that Ivan Ilyich's physical sufferings were terrible, but worse than the physical sufferings were his mental sufferings which were his chief torture.

His mental sufferings were due to the fact that that night, as he looked at Gerasim's sleepy, good-natured face with its prominent cheek-bones, the question suddenly occurred to him: "What if my whole life has really been wrong?"

It occurred to him that what had appeared perfectly impossible before, namely that he had not spent his life as he should have done, might after all be true. It occurred to him that his scarcely perceptible attempts to struggle against what was considered good by the most highly placed people, those scarcely noticeable impulses which he had immediately suppressed, might have been the real thing, and all the rest false. And his professional duties and the whole arrangement of his life and of his family, and all his social and official interests, might all have been false. He tried to defend all those things to himself and suddenly felt the weakness of what he was defending. There was nothing to defend.

"But if that is so," he said to himself, "and I am leaving this life with the consciousness that I have lost all that was given me and it is impossible to rectify it—what then?"

He lay on his back and began to pass his life in review in quite a new way. In the morning when he saw first his footman, then his wife, then his daughter, and then the doctor, their every word and movement confirmed to him the awful truth that had been revealed to him during the night. In them he saw himself—all that for which he had lived—and saw clearly that it was not real at all, but a terrible and huge deception which had hidden both life and death. This consciousness intensified his physical suffering tenfold. He groaned and tossed about, and pulled at his clothing which choked and stifled him. And he hated them on that account.

He was given a large dose of opium and became unconscious, but at noon his sufferings began again. He drove everybody away and tossed from side to side.

His wife came to him and said:

"*Jean,* my dear, do this for me. It can't do any harm and often helps. Healthy people often do it."

He opened his eyes wide.

"What? Take communion? Why? It's unnecessary! However . . ."

She began to cry.

"Yes, do, my dear. I'll send for our priest. He is such a nice man."

"All right. Very well," he muttered.

When the priest came and heard his confession, Ivan Ilyich was softened and seemed to feel a relief from his doubts and consequently from his sufferings, and for a moment there came a ray of hope. He again began to think of the vermiform appendix and the possibility of correcting it. He received the sacrament with tears in his eyes.

When they laid him down again afterwards he felt a moment's ease, and the hope that he might live awoke in him again. He began to think of the operation that had been suggested to him. "To live! I want to live!" he said to himself.

His wife came in to congratulate him after his communion, and when uttering the usual conventional words she added:

"You feel better, don't you?"

Without looking at her he said "Yes."

Her dress, her figure, the expression of her face, the tone of her voice, all revealed the same thing. "This is wrong, it is not as it should be. All you have lived for and still live for is falsehood and deception, hiding life and death from you." And as soon as he admitted that thought, his hatred and his agonizing physical suffering again sprang up, and with that suffering a consciousness of the unavoidable, approaching end. And to this was added a new sensation of grinding shooting pain and a feeling of suffocation.

The expression of his face when he uttered that "yes" was dreadful. Having uttered it, he looked her straight in the eyes, turned on his face with a rapidity extraordinary in his weak state and shouted:

"Go away! Go away and leave me alone!"

XII

From that moment the screaming began that continued for three days, and was so terrible that one could not hear it through two closed doors without horror. At the moment he answered his wife he realized that he was lost, that there was no return, that the end had come, the very end, and his doubts were still unsolved and remained doubts.

"Oh! Oh! Oh!" he cried in various intonations. He had begun by screaming "I won't!" and continued screaming on the letter "o."

For three whole days, during which time did not exist for him, he struggled in that black sack into which he was being thrust by an invisible, resistless force. He struggled as a man condemned to death struggles in the hands of the executioner, knowing that he cannot save himself. And every moment he felt that despite all his efforts he was drawing nearer and nearer to what terrified him. He felt that his agony was due to his being thrust into that black hole and still more to his not being able to get right into it. He was hindered from getting into it by his conviction that his life had been a good one. That very justification of his life held him fast and prevented his moving forward, and it caused him most torment of all.

Suddenly some force struck him in the chest and side, making it still harder to breathe, and he fell through the hole and there at the bottom was a light. What had happened to him was like the sensation one sometimes experiences in a railway carriage when one thinks one is going backwards while one is really going forwards and suddenly becomes aware of the real direction.

"Yes, it was all not the right thing," he said to himself, "but that's no matter. It can be done. But what *is* the right thing?" he asked himself, and suddenly grew quiet.

This occurred at the end of the third day, two hours before his death. Just then his schoolboy son had crept softly in and gone up to the bedside. The dying man was still screaming desperately and waving his arms. His hand fell on the boy's head, and the boy caught it, pressed it to his lips, and began to cry.

At that very moment Ivan Ilyich fell through and caught sight of the light, and it was revealed to him that though his life had not been what it should have been, this could still be rectified. He asked himself, "What *is* the right thing?" and grew still, listening. Then he felt that someone was kissing his hand. He opened his eyes, looked at his son, and felt sorry for him. His wife came up to him and he glanced at her. She was gazing at him open-mouthed, with undried tears on her nose and cheek and a despairing look on her face. He felt sorry for her too.

"Yes, I am making them wretched," he thought. "They are sorry, but it will be better for them when I die." He wished to say this but had not the strength to utter it. "Besides, why speak? I must act," he thought. With a look at his wife he indicated his son and said: "Take him away . . . sorry for him . . . sorry for you too. . . ." He tried to add, "forgive me," but said "forgo" and waved his hand, knowing that He whose understanding mattered would understand.

And suddenly it grew clear to him that what had been oppressing him and would not leave him was all dropping away at once from two sides, from ten sides, and from all sides. He was sorry for them, he must act so as not to hurt them: release them and free himself from these sufferings. "How good and how simple!" he thought. "And the pain?" he asked himself. "What has become of it? Where are you, pain?"

He turned his attention to it.

"Yes, here it is. Well, what of it? Let the pain be."

"And death . . . where is it?"

He sought his former accustomed fear of death and did not find it. "Where is it? What death?" There was no fear because there was no death.

In place of death there was light.

"So that's what it is!" he suddenly exclaimed aloud. "What joy!"

To him all this happened in a single instant, and the meaning of that instant did not change. For those present his agony continued for another two hours. Something rattled in his throat, his emaciated body twitched, then the gasping and rattle became less and less frequent.

"It is finished!" said someone near him.

He heard these words and repeated them in his soul.

"Death is finished," he said to himself. "It is no more!"

He drew in a breath, stopped in the midst of a sigh, stretched out, and died.

HENRIK IBSEN
1828–1906

Henrik Ibsen was the foremost playwright of his time—treating social themes and ideas and often satirizing the nineteenth-century bourgeoisie—and not only in Norway, his native land. His plays may be viewed historically as the culmination point of the bourgeois drama that has flourished fitfully, in France and Germany particularly, since the eighteenth century, when Diderot advocated and wrote plays about the middle classes, their "conditions" and problems. But they may also be seen as the fountainhead of much twentieth-century drama; in the West the plays of George Bernard Shaw and John Galsworthy, who discuss social problems, and of Maurice Maeterlinck and Anton Chekhov, who learned from the later "symbolist" Ibsen. Ibsen's drama of domestic and political crisis was also immensely popular in China and influenced a generation of modern playwrights.

Ibsen was born at Skien, in Norway, on March 20, 1828. His family had sunk into poverty and finally complete bankruptcy. In 1844, at the age of sixteen, he was sent to Grimstad, another small coastal town, as an apothecary's apprentice. There he lived in almost complete isolation and cut himself off from his family, except for his sister Hedvig. In 1850 he managed to get to Oslo (then Christiania) and to enroll at the university. But he never passed his examinations and in the following year left for Bergen, where he had acquired the position of playwright and assistant stage manager at the newly founded Norwegian Theater. Ibsen supplied the small theater with several historical and romantic plays. In 1857 he was appointed artistic director at the Mollergate Theater in Christiania, and a year later he married Susannah Thoresen. *Love's Comedy* (1862) was his first major success on the stage. Ibsen was then deeply affected by Scandinavianism, the movement for solidarity of the northern nations, and when in 1864 Norway refused to do anything to support Denmark in its war with Prussia and Austria over Schleswig-Holstein, he was so disgusted with his country that he left it for what he thought would be permanent exile. He lived in Rome, in Dresden, in Munich, and in smaller summer resorts, and during this time wrote all his later plays.

After a long period of incubation and experimentation with romantic and historical themes, Ibsen wrote a series of "problem" plays, beginning with *The Pillars of Society* (1877), which in their time created a furor by their fearless criticism of the nineteenth-century social scene: the subjection of women, hypocrisy, hereditary disease, seamy politics, and corrupt journalism. He wrote these plays using naturalistic modes of presentation: ordinary colloquial speech, a simple setting in a drawing room or study, a natural way of introducing or dismissing characters. Ibsen had learned from the "well-made" Parisian play (typified by those of Eugène Scribe) how to confine his action to one climactic situation and how gradually to uncover the past by retrogressive exposition. But he went far beyond it in technical skill and intellectual honesty.

The success of Ibsen's problem plays was international. But we must not forget that he was a Norwegian, the first writer of his small nation (its population at that time was less than two million) to win a reputation outside of Norway. Ibsen more than anyone else widened the scope of world literature beyond the confines of the "great" modern nations, which had entered its community roughly in this order: Italy, Spain, France, England, Germany, Russia. Since the time of Ibsen, other small nations have begun to play their part in the concert of world literature. Paradoxically, however, Ibsen rejected his own land. He had dreamed of becoming a great national poet. Instead, the plays he wrote during his voluntary exile depicted Norwegian society as consisting largely of a stuffy, provincial middle class, redeemed by a few upright, even fiery, individuals of initiative and courage. Only in 1891, when he was sixty-three, did Ibsen return to Christiania for good. He was then famous and widely honored, but lived a very retired life. In 1900 he suffered a stroke that made him a complete invalid for the last years of his life. He died on May 23, 1906.

Ibsen could hardly have survived his time if he had been merely a painter of society, a dialectician of social issues, and a magnificent technician of the theater. True, many of his discussions are now dated. We smile at some of what happens in *A Doll's House* (1879) and *Ghosts* (1881). His stagecraft is not unusual. But Ibsen stays with us because he has more to offer—because he was an artist who managed to create, at his best, works of poetry that, under their mask of sardonic humor, express his dream of humanity reborn by intelligence and self-sacrifice.

Hedda Gabler (1890) surprised and puzzled the large audience all over Europe that Ibsen had won in the 1880s. The play shows nothing of Ibsen's reforming zeal: no general theme emerges that could be used in spreading progressive ideas such as the emancipation of women dramatized in *A Doll's House* (1879), nor is the play an example of Ibsen's peculiar technique of retrospective revelation exhibited in *Rosmersholm* (1886). At first glance it seems mainly a study of a complex, exceptional, and even unique woman. Henry James, reviewing the first English performance, saw it as the picture of "a state of nerves as well as of soul, a state of temper, of health, of chagrin, of despair." Undoubtedly, Hedda is the central figure of the play, but she is no conventional heroine. She behaves atrociously to everyone with whom she comes in contact, and her moral sense is thoroughly defective: she is perverse, egotistical, sadistic, callous, even evil and demonic, truly a *femme fatale*. Still, this impression, while not mistaken, ignores another side of her personality and her situation. The play is, after all, a tragedy (though there are comic touches), and we are to feel pity and terror. Hedda is not simply evil and perverse. We must imagine her as distinguished, well bred, proud, beautiful, and even grand in her defiance of her surroundings and in the final gesture of her suicide. Not for nothing have great actresses excelled in this role. We must pity her as a tortured, tormented creature caught in a web of circumstance, as a victim, in spite of her desperate struggles to dominate and control the fate of those around her.

We are carefully prepared to understand her heritage. She is General Gabler's daughter. Ibsen tells us himself (in a letter to Count Moritz Prozor, dated December 4, 1890) that "I intended to indicate thereby that as a personality she is to be regarded rather as her father's daughter than as her husband's wife." She has inherited an aristocratic view of life. Her father's portrait hangs in her apartment. His pistols tell of the code of honor and the ready escape they offer in a self-inflicted death. Hedda lives in Ibsen's Norway, a stuffy, provincial, middle-class society, and is acutely, even morbidly afraid of scandal. She has, to her own regret, rejected the advances of Eilert, theatrically threatening him with her father's pistol. She envies Thea for the boldness with which she deserted her husband to follow Eilert. She admires Eilert for his escapades, which she romanticizes with the recurrent metaphor of his returning with "vine-leaves in his hair." But she cannot break out of the narrow confines of her society. She is not an emancipated woman.

When she is almost thirty, in reduced circumstances, she accepts a suitable husband, George Tesman. The marriage of convenience turns out to be a ghastly error for which she cannot forgive herself: Tesman is an amiable bore absorbed in his research into the "domestic industries of Brabant in the Middle Ages." His expectations of a professorship in his home town turn out to be uncertain. He has gone into debt, even to his guileless old aunt, in renting an expensive house, and, supreme humiliation for her, Hedda is pregnant by him. The dream of luxury, of becoming a hostess, of keeping thoroughbred horses, is shattered the very first day after their return from the prolonged honeymoon, which for Tesman was also a trip to rummage around in archives. Hedda is deeply stirred by the return of Eilert, her first suitor. She seems vaguely to think of a new relationship, at least, by spoiling his friendship with Thea. She plays with the attentions of Judge Brack. But everything quickly comes to nought: she is trapped in her marriage, unable and unwilling to become unfaithful to her husband; she is deeply disappointed by Eilert's ugly death, saying, "Oh, why does everything I touch become mean and ludicrous? It's like a curse!" She fears the scandal that will follow when her role in Eilert's suicide is discovered and she is called before the police; she can avoid it only by coming under the power of Judge Brack, who is prepared to blackmail her with his knowledge of the circumstances. Her plot to destroy Thea and Eilert's brainchild is frustrated by Thea's having preserved notes and drafts, which Thea eagerly starts to reconstruct with the help of Tesman. Still, while Hedda is in a terrible impasse, her suicide remains a shock, an abrupt, even absurd deed, eliciting the final line from the commonsensical Judge Brack: "But, good God! People don't do such things!" But we must assume that Hedda had pondered suicide long before: the pistol she gave to Eilert implies an unspoken suicide pact. He bungled it; she does it the right way, dying in beauty, shot in the temple and not in the abdomen.

The play is not, however, simply a character study, though Hedda is an extraordinarily complex, contradictory, subtle woman whose portrait, at least on the stage, could not be easily paralleled before Ibsen. It is also an extremely effective, swiftly moving play of action, deftly plotted in its clashes and climaxes. At the end of Act I Hedda seems to have won. The Tesmans, husband and aunt, are put in their place. Thea is lured into making confidences. The scene in Act II in which Hedda appeals to Eilert's pride in his independence and induces him to join in Judge Brack's party is a superb display of Hedda's power and skill. Act II ends with Eilert going off and the two women left alone in their tense though suppressed antagonism. Act III ends with Hedda alone, burning the precious manuscript about the "forces that will shape our civilization and the direction in which that civilization may develop," an obvious contrast to Tesman's research into an irrelevant past. (Ibsen himself always believed in progress, in a utopia he called "the Third Realm.")

The action is compressed into about thirty-six hours and located in a house where only the moving of furniture (the piano into the back room) or the change of light or costumes indicates the passing of time. Tesman is something of a fool. He is totally unaware of Hedda's inner turmoil, he obtusely misunderstands allusions to her pregnancy, he comically encourages the advances of Judge Brack, he complacently settles down to the task of assembling the fragments of Eilert's manuscript, recognizing that "putting other people's papers into order is rather my specialty." Though he seems amiably domestic in his love for his aunts, proud of having won Hedda, ambitious to provide an elegant home for her, his behavior is by no means above reproach. He envies and fears Eilert, gloats over his bad reputation, surreptitiously brings home the lost manuscript, conceals its recovery from Thea; when Hedda tells of its being burned, he is at first shocked, reacting comically with the legal phrase about "appropriating lost property," but is then easily persuaded to accept it when Hedda tells him that she did it for his sake and is completely won over when she reveals her pregnancy. After Eilert's death he feels, however, some guilt and tries to make up by helping in the reconstruction of the manuscript, now that his rival no longer threatens his career. Tesman is given strong speech mannerisms: the frequent use of "what?"—which Hedda, commenting at the end on the progress of the work on the manuscript, imitates sarcastically—and the use of "fancy that." His last inappropriate words, "She's shot herself! Shot herself in the head! Fancy that!" lend a grotesque touch to the tragic end. Aunt Juliana belongs with him: she is a fussy, kindly person, proud of her nephew, awed by his new wife, eager to help with the expected baby, but also easily consoled after the death of her sister: "There's always some poor invalid who needs care and attention."

The other pair, Eilert Loevborg and Thea Elvsted, are sharply contrasted. Thea had the courage to leave her husband; she is devoted to Eilert and seems to have cured him of his addiction to drink but fears that he cannot resist a new temptation. Eilert tells Hedda unkindly that Thea is "silly," and there is some truth to that, inasmuch as she is so easily taken in by Hedda. Her quick settling down to work on the manuscript after Eilert's death suggests some obtuseness, though we must, presumably, excuse it as a theatrical foreshortening.

Judge Brack is a "man of the world," a sensualist who hardly conceals his desire to make Hedda his mistress, by blackmail if necessary, and is dismayed when she escapes his clutches: in his facile philosophy "people usually learn to accept the inevitable."

Eilert, we must assume, is some kind of genius. His book, we have to take on trust, is an important work. We are told that he had squandered an inheritance, had engaged in orgies, and had regaled Hedda with tales of his exploits before she chased him with her pistol. When he comes back to town, ostensibly reformed, dressed conventionally, he immediately starts courting Hedda again. Stung by her contempt for his abstinence, he rushes off to Brack's party, which degenerates into a disgraceful brawl in a brothel. His relapse and the loss of the manuscript destroy his self-esteem and hope for any future. He accepts Hedda's pistol but dies an ignominious, ugly death. We see Eilert mainly reflected in Hedda's imagination as a figure of pagan freedom who, she thinks, has done something noble, beautiful, and courageous in "rising from the feast of life so early." She dies in beauty as she wanted Eilert to die.

This aesthetic suicide must seem to us a supremely futile gesture of revolt. Ibsen always admired the great rebels, the fighters for freedom, but *Hedda Gabler* will appear almost a parodic version of his persistent theme: the individual against society, defying it and escaping it in death.

Yvonne Shafter, *Henrik Ibsen: Life, Work, and Criticism* (1985), is a general work. J. W. McFarlane, ed., *Discussions of Henrik Ibsen* (1962), contains Henry James's "On the Occasion of 'Hedda Gabler.' " Rolf Fjelde, ed., *Ibsen: A Collection of Critical Essays* (1965), has a good essay on *Hedda Gabler*; and James McFarlane, ed., *The Cambridge Companion to Ibsen* (1994), offers sixteen essays on a wide variety of topics. *Ibsen's Heroines* (1985), by Ibsen's friend Lou Andreas-Salomé, has an interesting chapter on Hedda Gabler as an empty soul reaching for greatness. Joan Templeton, *Ibsen's Women* (1997), is an excellent study that includes a chapter on *Hedda Gabler* and a discussion of Ibsen's modernism. Frederick J. Marker and Lise-Lone Marker, *Ibsen's Lively Art: A Performance Study of the Major Plays* (1989), use descriptions of the various performances of *Hedda Gabler* to examine differing interpretations of the main characters.

PRONOUNCING GLOSSARY

The following list uses common English syllables and stress accents to provide rough equivalents of selected words whose pronunciation may be unfamiliar to the general reader.

Eilert Loevborg: *ai'-lert leuhv'-borg*   Rosmersholm: *ross'-merss-holm*

fjord: *fyoord*   Thea Elvsted: *tay'-ah aelf'-sted*

Hedda Gabler[1]

Characters

GEORGE TESMAN, *research graduate in cultural history*	MRS. ELVSTED
	JUDGE BRACK
HEDDA, *his wife*	EILERT LOEVBORG
MISS JULIANA TESMAN, *his aunt*	BERTHA, *a maid*

The action takes place in TESMAN's *villa in the fashionable quarter of town.*

Act I

SCENE—*A large drawing room, handsomely and tastefully furnished; decorated in dark colors. In the rear wall is a broad open doorway, with curtains drawn back to either side. It leads to a smaller room, decorated in the same style as the drawing room. In the right-hand wall of the drawing room, a folding door leads out to the hall. The opposite wall, on the left, contains french windows, also with curtains drawn back on either side. Through the glass we can see part of a verandah, and trees in autumn colors. Downstage stands an oval table, covered by a cloth and surrounded by chairs. Downstage right, against the wall, is a broad stove tiled with dark porcelain; in front of it stand a high-backed armchair, a cushioned footrest, and two footstools. Upstage right, in an alcove, is a corner sofa, with a small, round table. Downstage left, a little away from the wall, is another sofa. Upstage of the french windows, a piano. On either side of the open doorway in the rear wall stand what-nots holding ornaments of terra cotta and majolica. Against the rear wall of the smaller room can be seen a sofa, a table, and a couple of chairs. Above this sofa hangs the portrait of a handsome old man in general's uniform. Above the table a lamp hangs from the ceiling, with a shade of opalescent, milky glass. All round the drawing room bunches of flowers stand in vases and glasses. More bunches lie on the tables. The floors of both rooms are covered with thick carpets. Morning light. The sun shines in through the french windows.*

MISS JULIANA TESMAN, *wearing a hat and carrying a parasol, enters from the hall, followed by* BERTHA, *who is carrying a bunch of flowers wrapped in paper.* MISS TESMAN *is about sixty-five, of pleasant and kindly appearance. She is neatly but simply dressed in grey outdoor clothes.* BERTHA, *the maid, is rather simple and rustic-looking. She is getting on in years.*

MISS TESMAN [*Stops just inside the door, listens, and says in a hushed voice.*] No, bless my soul! They're not up yet.
BERTHA [*Also in hushed tones.*] What did I tell you, miss? The boat didn't get in till midnight. And when they did turn up—Jesus, miss, you should have seen all the things Madam made me unpack before she'd go to bed!
MISS TESMAN Ah, well. Let them have a good lie in. But let's have some nice fresh air waiting for them when they do come down. [*Goes to the french windows and throws them wide open.*]

---

1. Translated by Michael Meyer.

BERTHA [*Bewildered at the table, the bunch of flowers in her hand.*] I'm blessed if there's a square inch left to put anything. I'll have to let it lie here, miss. [*Puts it on the piano.*]

MISS TESMAN Well, Bertha dear, so now you have a new mistress. Heaven knows it nearly broke my heart to have to part with you.

BERTHA [*Snivels.*] What about me, Miss Juju? How do you suppose I felt? After all the happy years I've spent with you and Miss Rena?

MISS TESMAN We must accept it bravely, Bertha. It was the only way. George needs you to take care of him. He could never manage without you. You've looked after him ever since he was a tiny boy.

BERTHA Oh, but Miss Juju, I can't help thinking about Miss Rena, lying there all helpless, poor dear. And that new girl! She'll never learn the proper way to handle an invalid.

MISS TESMAN Oh, I'll manage to train her. I'll do most of the work myself, you know. You needn't worry about my poor sister, Bertha dear.

BERTHA But Miss Juju, there's another thing. I'm frightened Madam may not find me suitable.

MISS TESMAN Oh, nonsense, Bertha. There may be one or two little things to begin with——

BERTHA She's a real lady. Wants everything just so.

MISS TESMAN But of course she does! General Gabler's daughter! Think of what she was accustomed to when the General was alive. You remember how we used to see her out riding with her father? In that long black skirt? With the feather in her hat?

BERTHA Oh, yes, miss. As if I could forget! But, Lord! I never dreamed I'd live to see a match between her and Master Georgie.

MISS TESMAN Neither did I. By the way, Bertha, from now on you must stop calling him Master Georgie. You must say: Dr. Tesman.

BERTHA Yes, Madam said something about that too. Last night—the moment they'd set foot inside the door. Is it true, then, miss?

MISS TESMAN Indeed it is. Just imagine, Bertha, some foreigners have made him a doctor. It happened while they were away. I had no idea till he told me when they got off the boat.

BERTHA Well, I suppose there's no limit to what he won't become. He's that clever. I never thought he'd go in for hospital work, though.

MISS TESMAN No, he's not that kind of doctor. [*Nods impressively.*] In any case, you may soon have to address him by an even grander title.

BERTHA You don't say! What might that be, miss?

MISS TESMAN [*Smiles.*] Ah! If you only knew! [*Moved.*] Dear God, if only poor dear Joachim could rise out of his grave and see what his little son has grown into! [*Looks round.*] But Bertha, why have you done this? Taken the chintz covers off all the furniture!

BERTHA Madam said I was to. Can't stand chintz covers on chairs, she said.

MISS TESMAN But surely they're not going to use this room as a parlor?

BERTHA So I gathered, miss. From what Madam said. He didn't say anything. The Doctor.

[GEORGE TESMAN *comes into the rear room, from the right, humming, with an open, empty travelling bag in his hand. He is about thirty-three, of medium height and youthful appearance, rather plump, with an open, round, contented face, and fair hair and beard. He wears spectacles, and is dressed in comfortable, indoor clothes.*]

MISS TESMAN   Good morning! Good morning, George!

TESMAN [*In open doorway.*]   Auntie Juju! Dear Auntie Juju! [*Comes forward and shakes her hand.*] You've come all the way out here! And so early! What?

MISS TESMAN   Well, I had to make sure you'd settled in comfortably.

TESMAN   But you can't have had a proper night's sleep.

MISS TESMAN   Oh, never mind that.

TESMAN   We were so sorry we couldn't give you a lift. But you saw how it was—Hedda had so much luggage—and she insisted on having it all with her.

MISS TESMAN   Yes, I've never seen so much luggage.

BERTHA [*To* TESMAN.]   Shall I go and ask Madam if there's anything I can lend her a hand with?

TESMAN   Er—thank you, Bertha; no, you needn't bother. She says if she wants you for anything she'll ring.

BERTHA [*Over to right.*]   Oh. Very good.

TESMAN   Oh, Bertha—take this bag, will you?

BERTHA [*Takes it.*]   I'll put it in the attic. [*Goes out into the hall.*]

TESMAN   Just fancy, Auntie Juju, I filled that whole bag with notes for my book. You know, it's really incredible what I've managed to find rooting through those archives. By Jove! Wonderful old things no one even knew existed——

MISS TESMAN   I'm sure you didn't waste a single moment of your honeymoon, George dear.

TESMAN   No, I think I can truthfully claim that. But, Auntie Juju, do take your hat off. Here. Let me untie it for you. What?

MISS TESMAN [*As he does so.*]   Oh dear, oh dear! It's just as if you were still living at home with us.

TESMAN [*Turns the hat in his hand and looks at it.*]   I say! What a splendid new hat!

MISS TESMAN   I bought it for Hedda's sake.

TESMAN   For Hedda's sake? What?

MISS TESMAN   So that Hedda needn't be ashamed of me, in case we ever go for a walk together.

TESMAN [*Pats her cheek.*]   You still think of everything, don't you, Auntie Juju? [*Puts the hat down on a chair by the table.*] Come on, let's sit down here on the sofa. And have a little chat while we wait for Hedda.

[*They sit. She puts her parasol in the corner of the sofa.*]

MISS TESMAN [*Clasps both his hands and looks at him.*]   Oh, George, it's so wonderful to have you back, and be able to see you with my own eyes again! Poor dear Joachim's own son!

TESMAN   What about me! It's wonderful for me to see you again, Auntie Juju. You've been a mother to me. And a father, too.

MISS TESMAN   You'll always keep a soft spot in your heart for your old aunties, won't you, George dear?

TESMAN   I suppose Auntie Rena's no better? What?

MISS TESMAN   Alas, no. I'm afraid she'll never get better, poor dear. She's lying there just as she has for all these years. Please God I may be allowed to keep her for a little longer. If I lost her I don't know what I'd do. Especially now I haven't you to look after.

TESMAN [*Pats her on the back.*]   There, there, there!

MISS TESMAN [*With a sudden change of mood.*]   Oh, but George, fancy you being a married man! And to think it's you who've won Hedda Gabler! The beautiful Hedda Gabler! Fancy! She was always so surrounded by admirers.

TESMAN [*Hums a little and smiles contentedly.*]   Yes, I suppose there are quite a few people in this town who wouldn't mind being in my shoes. What?

MISS TESMAN   And what a honeymoon! Five months! Nearly six.

TESMAN   Well, I've done a lot of work, you know. All those archives to go through. And I've had to read lots of books.

MISS TESMAN   Yes, dear, of course. [*Lowers her voice confidentially.*] But tell me, George—haven't you any—any extra little piece of news to give me?

TESMAN   You mean, arising out of the honeymoon?

MISS TESMAN   Yes.

TESMAN   No, I don't think there's anything I didn't tell you in my letters. My doctorate, of course—but I told you about that last night, didn't I?

MISS TESMAN   Yes, yes, I didn't mean that kind of thing. I was just wondering—are you—are you expecting——?

TESMAN   Expecting what?

MISS TESMAN   Oh, come on, George, I'm your old aunt!

TESMAN   Well actually—yes, I am expecting something.

MISS TESMAN   I knew it!

TESMAN   You'll be happy to hear that before very long I expect to become a professor.

MISS TESMAN   Professor?

TESMAN   I think I may say that the matter has been decided. But, Auntie Juju, you know about this.

MISS TESMAN [*Gives a little laugh.*]   Yes, of course. I'd forgotten. [*Changes her tone.*] But we were talking about your honeymoon. It must have cost a dreadful amount of money, George?

TESMAN   Oh well, you know, that big research grant I got helped a good deal.

MISS TESMAN   But how on earth did you manage to make it do for two?

TESMAN   Well, to tell the truth it was a bit tricky. What?

MISS TESMAN   Especially when one's traveling with a lady. A little bird tells me that makes things very much more expensive.

TESMAN   Well, yes, of course it does make things a little more expensive. But Hedda has to do things in style, Auntie Juju. I mean, she has to. Anything less grand wouldn't have suited her.

MISS TESMAN   No, no, I suppose not. A honeymoon abroad seems to be the vogue nowadays. But tell me, have you had time to look round the house?

TESMAN   You bet. I've been up since the crack of dawn.

MISS TESMAN   Well, what do you think of it?

TESMAN   Splendid. Absolutely splendid. I'm only wondering what we're going to do with those two empty rooms between that little one and Hedda's bedroom.

MISS TESMAN [*Laughs slyly.*]   Ah, George dear, I'm sure you'll manage to find some use for them—in time.

TESMAN   Yes, of course, Auntie Juju, how stupid of me. You're thinking of my books. What?

MISS TESMAN   Yes, yes, dear boy. I was thinking of your books.

TESMAN   You know, I'm so happy for Hedda's sake that we've managed to get this house. Before we became engaged she often used to say this was the only house in town she felt she could really bear to live in. It used to belong to Mrs. Falk—you know, the Prime Minister's widow.

MISS TESMAN   Fancy that! And what a stroke of luck it happened to come into the market. Just as you'd left on your honeymoon.

TESMAN   Yes, Auntie Juju, we've certainly had all the luck with us. What?

MISS TESMAN   But, George dear, the expense! It's going to make a dreadful hole in your pocket, all this.

TESMAN [*A little downcast.*]   Yes, I—I suppose it will, won't it?

MISS TESMAN   Oh, George, really!

TESMAN   How much do you think it'll cost? Roughly, I mean? What?

MISS TESMAN   I can't possibly say till I see the bills.

TESMAN   Well, luckily Judge Brack's managed to get it on very favorable terms. He wrote and told Hedda so.

MISS TESMAN   Don't you worry, George dear. Anyway I've stood security for all the furniture and carpets.

TESMAN   Security? But dear, sweet Auntie Juju, how could you possibly stand security?

MISS TESMAN   I've arranged a mortgage on our annuity.

TESMAN [*Jumps up.*]   What? On your annuity? And—Auntie Rena's?

MISS TESMAN   Yes. Well, I couldn't think of any other way.

TESMAN [*Stands in front of her.*]   Auntie Juju, have you gone completely out of your mind? That annuity's all you and Auntie Rena have.

MISS TESMAN   All right, there's no need to get so excited about it. It's a pure formality, you know. Judge Brack told me so. He was so kind as to arrange it all for me. A pure formality; those were his very words.

TESMAN   I dare say. All the same——

MISS TESMAN   Anyway, you'll have a salary of your own now. And, good heavens, even if we did have to fork out a little—tighten our belts for a week or two—why, we'd be happy to do so for your sake.

TESMAN   Oh, Auntie Juju! Will you never stop sacrificing yourself for me?

MISS TESMAN [*Gets up and puts her hands on his shoulders.*]   What else have I to live for but to smooth your road a little, my dear boy? You've never had any mother or father to turn to. And now at last we've achieved our goal. I won't deny we've had our little difficulties now and then. But now, thank the good Lord, George dear, all your worries are past.

TESMAN   Yes, it's wonderful really how everything's gone just right for me.

MISS TESMAN   Yes! And the enemies who tried to bar your way have been struck down. They have been made to bite the dust. The man who was your most dangerous rival has had the mightiest fall. And now he's lying there in the pit he dug for himself, poor misguided creature.

TESMAN   Have you heard any news of Eilert? Since I went away?

MISS TESMAN   Only that he's said to have published a new book.

TESMAN   What! Eilert Loevborg? You mean—just recently? What?

MISS TESMAN   So they say. I don't imagine it can be of any value, do you? When your new book comes out, that'll be another story. What's it going to be about?

TESMAN   The domestic industries of Brabant[2] in the Middle Ages.

MISS TESMAN   Oh, George! The things you know about!

TESMAN   Mind you, it may be some time before I actually get down to writing it. I've made these very extensive notes, and I've got to file and index them first.

MISS TESMAN   Ah, yes! Making notes; filing and indexing; you've always been wonderful at that. Poor dear Joachim was just the same.

TESMAN   I'm looking forward so much to getting down to that. Especially now I've a home of my own to work in.

MISS TESMAN   And above all, now that you have the girl you set your heart on, George dear.

TESMAN   [Embraces her.]   Oh, yes, Auntie Juju, yes! Hedda's the loveliest thing of all! [Looks towards the doorway.] I think I hear her coming. What?

>   [HEDDA enters the rear room from the left, and comes into the draw-
>   ing room. She is a woman of twenty-nine. Distinguished, aristocratic
>   face and figure. Her complexion is pale and opalescent. Her eyes are
>   steel-grey, with an expression of cold, calm serenity. Her hair is of a
>   handsome auburn color, but is not especially abundant. She is
>   dressed in an elegant, somewhat loose-fitting morning gown.]

MISS TESMAN   [Goes to greet her.]   Good morning, Hedda dear! Good morning!

HEDDA   [Holds out her hand.]   Good morning, dear Miss Tesman. What an early hour to call. So kind of you.

MISS TESMAN   [Seems somewhat embarrassed.]   And has the young bride slept well in her new home?

HEDDA   Oh—thank you, yes. Passably well.

TESMAN   [Laughs.]   Passably. I say, Hedda, that's good! When I jumped out of bed, you were sleeping like a top.

HEDDA   Yes. Fortunately. One has to accustom oneself to anything new, Miss Tesman. It takes time. [Looks left.] Oh, that maid's left the french windows open. This room's flooded with sun.

MISS TESMAN   [Goes towards the windows.]   Oh—let me close them.

HEDDA   No, no, don't do that. Tesman dear, draw the curtains. This light's blinding me.

TESMAN   [At the windows.]   Yes, yes, dear. There, Hedda, now you've got shade and fresh air.

HEDDA   This room needs fresh air. All these flowers—But my dear Miss Tesman, won't you take a seat?

MISS TESMAN   No, really not, thank you. I just wanted to make sure you have everything you need. I must see about getting back home. My poor dear sister will be waiting for me.

---

2. In the Middle Ages, a duchy located in parts of what are now Belgium and the Netherlands.

TESMAN Be sure to give her my love, won't you? Tell her I'll run over and see her later today.

MISS TESMAN Oh yes, I'll tell her that. Oh, George—— [*Fumbles in the pocket of her skirt.*] I almost forgot. I've brought something for you.

TESMAN What's that, Auntie Juju? What?

MISS TESMAN [*Pulls out a flat package wrapped in newspaper and gives it to him.*] Open and see, dear boy.

TESMAN [*Opens the package.*] Good heavens! Auntie Juju, you've kept them! Hedda, this is really very touching. What?

HEDDA [*By the what-nots, on the right.*] What is it, Tesman?

TESMAN My old shoes! My slippers, Hedda!

HEDDA Oh, them. I remember you kept talking about them on our honeymoon.

TESMAN Yes, I missed them dreadfully. [*Goes over to her.*] Here, Hedda, take a look.

HEDDA [*Goes away towards the stove.*] Thanks, I won't bother.

TESMAN [*Follows her.*] Fancy, Hedda, Auntie Rena's embroidered them for me. Despite her being so ill. Oh, you can't imagine what memories they have for me.

HEDDA [*By the table.*] Not for me.

MISS TESMAN No, Hedda's right there, George.

TESMAN Yes, but I thought since she's one of the family now——

HEDDA [*Interrupts.*] Tesman, we really can't go on keeping this maid.

MISS TESMAN Not keep Bertha?

TESMAN What makes you say that, dear? What?

HEDDA [*Points.*] Look at that! She's left her old hat lying on the chair.

TESMAN [*Appalled, drops his slippers on the floor.*] But, Hedda——!

HEDDA Suppose someone came in and saw it?

TESMAN But Hedda—that's Auntie Juju's hat.

HEDDA Oh?

MISS TESMAN [*Picks up the hat.*] Indeed it's mine. And it doesn't happen to be old, Hedda dear.

HEDDA I didn't look at it very closely, Miss Tesman.

MISS TESMAN [*Tying on the hat.*] As a matter of fact, it's the first time I've worn it. As the good Lord is my witness.

TESMAN It's very pretty, too. Really smart.

MISS TESMAN Oh, I'm afraid it's nothing much really. [*Looks round.*] My parasol? Ah, here it is. [*Takes it.*] This is mine, too. [*Murmurs.*] Not Bertha's.

TESMAN A new hat and a new parasol! I say, Hedda, fancy that!

HEDDA Very pretty and charming.

TESMAN Yes, isn't it? What? But Auntie Juju, take a good look at Hedda before you go. Isn't she pretty and charming?

MISS TESMAN Dear boy, there's nothing new in that. Hedda's been a beauty ever since the day she was born. [*Nods and goes right.*]

TESMAN [*Follows her.*] Yes, but have you noticed how strong and healthy she's looking? And how she's filled out since we went away?

MISS TESMAN [*Stops and turns.*] Filled out?

HEDDA [*Walks across the room.*] Oh, can't we forget it?

TESMAN Yes, Auntie Juju—you can't see it so clearly with that dress on. But I've good reason to know——

HEDDA [*By the french windows, impatiently.*]   You haven't good reason to know anything.

TESMAN   It must have been the mountain air up there in the Tyrol—

HEDDA [*Curtly, interrupts him.*]   I'm exactly the same as when I went away.

TESMAN   You keep on saying so. But you're not. I'm right, aren't I, Auntie Juju?

MISS TESMAN [*Has folded her hands and is gazing at her.*]   She's beautiful—beautiful. Hedda is beautiful. [*Goes over to* HEDDA, *takes her head between her hands, draws it down and kisses her hair.*] God bless and keep you, Hedda Tesman. For George's sake.

HEDDA [*Frees herself politely.*]   Oh—let me go, please.

MISS TESMAN [*Quietly, emotionally.*]   I shall come see you both every day.

TESMAN   Yes, Auntie Juju, please do. What?

MISS TESMAN   Good-bye! Good-bye!

> [*She goes out into the hall.* TESMAN *follows her. The door remains open.* TESMAN *is heard sending his love to* AUNT RENA *and thanking* MISS TESMAN *for his slippers. Meanwhile* HEDDA *walks up and down the room raising her arms and clenching her fists as though in desperation. Then she throws aside the curtains from the french windows and stands there, looking out. A few moments later,* TESMAN *returns and closes the door behind him.*]

TESMAN [*Picks up his slippers from the floor.*]   What are you looking at, Hedda?

HEDDA [*Calm and controlled again.*]   Only the leaves. They're so golden. And withered.

TESMAN [*Wraps up the slippers and lays them on the table.*]   Well, we're in September now.

HEDDA [*Restless again.*]   Yes. We're already into September.

TESMAN   Auntie Juju was behaving rather oddly, I thought, didn't you? Almost as though she was in church or something. I wonder what came over her. Any idea?

HEDDA   I hardly know her. Does she often act like that?

TESMAN   Not to the extent she did today.

HEDDA [*Goes away from the french windows.*]   Do you think she was hurt by what I said about the hat?

TESMAN   Oh, I don't think so. A little at first, perhaps——

HEDDA   But what a thing to do, throw her hat down in someone's drawing room. People don't do such things.

TESMAN   I'm sure Auntie Juju doesn't do it very often.

HEDDA   Oh well, I'll make it up with her.

TESMAN   Oh Hedda, would you?

HEDDA   When you see them this afternoon invite her to come out here this evening.

TESMAN   You bet I will! I say, there's another thing which would please her enormously.

HEDDA   Oh?

TESMAN   If you could bring yourself to call her Auntie Juju. For my sake, Hedda? What?

HEDDA   Oh no, really Tesman, you mustn't ask me to do that. I've told you so once before. I'll try to call her Aunt Juliana. That's as far as I'll go.

TESMAN [*After a moment.*]   I say, Hedda, is anything wrong? What?

HEDDA   I'm just looking at my old piano. It doesn't really go with all this.

TESMAN   As soon as I start getting my salary we'll see about changing it.

HEDDA   No, no, don't let's change it. I don't want to part with it. We can move it into that little room and get another one to put in here.

TESMAN [*A little downcast.*]   Yes, we—might do that.

HEDDA [*Picks up the bunch of flowers from the piano.*]   These flowers weren't here when we arrived last night.

TESMAN   I expect Auntie Juju brought them.

HEDDA   Here's a card. [*Takes it out and reads.*] "Will come back later today." Guess who it's from?

TESMAN   No idea. Who? What?

HEDDA   It says: "Mrs. Elvsted."

TESMAN   No, really? Mrs. Elvsted! She used to be Miss Rysing, didn't she?

HEDDA   Yes. She was the one with that irritating hair she was always showing off. I hear she used to be an old flame of yours.

TESMAN [*Laughs.*]   That didn't last long. Anyway, that was before I got to know you, Hedda. By Jove, fancy her being in town!

HEDDA [*Thinks for a moment, then says suddenly.*]   Tell me, Tesman, doesn't he live somewhere up in those parts? You know—Eilert Loevborg?

TESMAN   Yes, that's right. So he does.

[BERTHA *enters from the hall.*]

BERTHA   She's here again, madam. The lady who came and left the flowers. [*Points.*] The ones you're holding.

HEDDA   Oh, is she? Well, show her in.

[BERTHA *opens the door for* MRS. ELVSTED *and goes out.* MRS. ELVSTED *is a delicately built woman with gentle, attractive features. Her eyes are light blue, large, and somewhat prominent, with a frightened, questioning expression. Her hair is extremely fair, almost flaxen, and is exceptionally wavy and abundant. She is two or three years younger than* HEDDA. *She is wearing a dark visiting dress, in good taste but not quite in the latest fashion.*]

HEDDA [*Goes cordially to greet her.*]   Dear Mrs. Elvsted, good morning. How delightful to see you again after all this time.

MRS. ELVSTED [*Nervously, trying to control herself.*]   Yes, it's many years since we met.

TESMAN   And since we met. What?

HEDDA   Thank you for your lovely flowers.

MRS. ELVSTED   Oh, please—I wanted to come yesterday afternoon. But they told me you were away—

TESMAN   You've only just arrived in town, then? What?

MRS. ELVSTED   I got here yesterday, around midday. Oh, I became almost desperate when I heard you weren't here.

HEDDA   Desperate? Why?

TESMAN   My dear Mrs. Rysing—Elvsted—

HEDDA   There's nothing wrong, I hope?

MRS. ELVSTED   Yes, there is. And I don't know anyone else here whom I can turn to.

HEDDA [*Puts the flowers down on the table.*]   Come and sit with me on the sofa—

MRS. ELVSTED Oh, I feel too restless to sit down.

HEDDA You must. Come along, now.

[*She pulls* MRS. ELVSTED *down on to the sofa and sits beside her.*]

TESMAN Well? Tell us, Mrs.—er——

HEDDA Has something happened at home?

MRS. ELVSTED Yes—that is, yes and no. Oh, I do hope you won't misunderstand me——

HEDDA Then you'd better tell us the whole story, Mrs. Elvsted.

TESMAN That's why you've come. What?

MRS. ELVSTED Yes—yes, it is. Well, then—in case you don't already know—Eilert Loevborg is in town.

HEDDA Loevborg here?

TESMAN Eilert back in town? By Jove, Hedda, did you hear that?

HEDDA Yes, of course I heard.

MRS. ELVSTED He's been here a week. A whole week! In this city. Alone. With all those dreadful people——

HEDDA But my dear Mrs. Elvsted, what concern is he of yours?

MRS. ELVSTED [*Gives her a frightened look and says quickly.*] He's been tutoring the children.

HEDDA Your children?

MRS. ELVSTED My husband's. I have none.

HEDDA Oh, you mean your stepchildren.

MRS. ELVSTED Yes.

TESMAN [*Gropingly.*] But was he sufficiently—I don't know how to put it—sufficiently regular in his habits to be suited to such a post? What?

MRS. ELVSTED For the past two to three years he has been living irreproachably.

TESMAN You don't say! By Jove, Hedda, hear that?

HEDDA I hear.

MRS. ELVSTED Quite irreproachably, I assure you. In every respect. All the same—in this big city—with money in his pockets—I'm so dreadfully frightened something may happen to him.

TESMAN But why didn't he stay up there with you and your husband?

MRS. ELVSTED Once his book had come out, he became restless.

TESMAN Oh, yes—Auntie Juju said he's brought out a new book.

MRS. ELVSTED Yes, a big new book about the history of civilization. A kind of general survey. It came out a fortnight ago. Everyone's been buying it and reading it—it's created a tremendous stir——

TESMAN Has it really? It must be something he's dug up, then.

MRS. ELVSTED You mean from the old days?

TESMAN Yes.

MRS. ELVSTED No, he's written it all since he came to live with us.

TESMAN Well, that's splendid news, Hedda. Fancy that!

MRS. ELVSTED Oh, yes! If only he can go on like this!

HEDDA Have you met him since you came here?

MRS. ELVSTED No, not yet, I had such dreadful difficulty finding his address. But this morning I managed to track him down at last.

HEDDA [*Looks searchingly at her.*] I must say I find it a little strange that your husband—hm——

MRS. ELVSTED [*Starts nervously.*] My husband! What do you mean?

HEDDA   That he should send you all the way here on an errand of this kind. I'm surprised he didn't come himself to keep an eye on his friend.

MRS. ELVSTED   Oh, no, no—my husband hasn't the time. Besides, I—er—wanted to do some shopping here.

HEDDA [*With a slight smile.*]   Ah. Well, that's different.

MRS. ELVSTED [*Gets up quickly, restlessly.*]   Please, Mr. Tesman, I beg you—be kind to Eilert Loevborg if he comes here. I'm sure he will. I mean, you used to be such good friends in the old days. And you're both studying the same subject, as far as I can understand. You're in the same field, aren't you?

TESMAN   Well, we used to be, anyway.

MRS. ELVSTED   Yes—so I beg you earnestly, do please, please, keep an eye on him. Oh, Mr. Tesman, do promise me you will.

TESMAN   I shall be only too happy to do so, Mrs. Rysing.

HEDDA   Elvsted.

TESMAN   I'll do everything for Eilert that lies in my power. You can rely on that.

MRS. ELVSTED   Oh, how good and kind you are! [*Presses his hands.*] Thank you, thank you, thank you. [*Frightened.*] My husband's so fond of him, you see.

HEDDA [*Gets up.*]   You'd better send him a note, Tesman. He may not come to you of his own accord.

TESMAN   Yes, that'd probably be the best plan, Hedda. What?

HEDDA   The sooner the better. Why not do it now?

MRS. ELVSTED [*Pleadingly.*]   Oh yes, if only you would!

TESMAN   I'll do it this very moment. Do you have his address, Mrs.—er—Elvsted?

MRS. ELVSTED   Yes. [*Takes a small piece of paper from her pocket and gives it to him.*]

TESMAN   Good, good. Right, well, I'll go inside and—— [*Looks round.*] Where are my slippers? Oh yes, here. [*Picks up the package and is about to go.*]

HEDDA   Try to sound friendly. Make it a nice long letter.

TESMAN   Right, I will.

MRS. ELVSTED   Please don't say anything about my having seen you.

TESMAN   Good heavens no, of course not. What? [*Goes out through the rear room to the right.*]

HEDDA [*Goes over to* MRS. ELVSTED, *smiles, and says softly.*]   Well! Now we've killed two birds with one stone.

MRS. ELVSTED   What do you mean?

HEDDA   Didn't you realize I wanted to get him out of the room?

MRS. ELVSTED   So that he could write the letter?

HEDDA   And so that I could talk to you alone.

MRS. ELVSTED [*Confused.*]   About this?

HEDDA   Yes, about this.

MRS. ELVSTED [*In alarm.*]   But there's nothing more to tell, Mrs. Tesman. Really there isn't.

HEDDA   Oh, yes there is. There's a lot more. I can see that. Come along, let's sit down and have a little chat.

[*She pushes* MRS. ELVSTED *down into the armchair by the stove and seats herself on one of the footstools.*]

MRS. ELVSTED [*Looks anxiously at her watch.*] Really, Mrs. Tesman, I think I ought to be going now.

HEDDA There's no hurry. Well? How are things at home?

MRS. ELVSTED I'd rather not speak about that.

HEDDA But my dear, you can tell me. Good heavens, we were at school together.

MRS. ELVSTED Yes, but you were a year senior to me. Oh, I used to be terribly frightened of you in those days.

HEDDA Frightened of me?

MRS. ELVSTED Yes, terribly frightened. Whenever you met me on the staircase you used to pull my hair.

HEDDA No, did I?

MRS. ELVSTED Yes. And once you said you'd burn it all off.

HEDDA Oh, that was only in fun.

MRS. ELVSTED Yes, but I was so silly in those days. And then afterwards—I mean, we've drifted so far apart. Our backgrounds were so different.

HEDDA Well, now we must try to drift together again. Now listen. When we were at school we used to call each other by our Christian names——

MRS. ELVSTED No, I'm sure you're mistaken.

HEDDA I'm sure I'm not. I remember it quite clearly. Let's tell each other our secrets, as we used to in the old days. [*Moves closer on her footstool.*] There, now. [*Kisses her on the cheek.*] You must call me Hedda.

MRS. ELVSTED [*Squeezes her hands and pats them.*] Oh, you're so kind. I'm not used to people being so nice to me.

HEDDA Now, now, now. And I shall call you Tora, the way I used to.

MRS. ELVSTED My name is Thea.

HEDDA Yes, of course. Of course. I meant Thea. [*Looks at her sympathetically.*] So you're not used to kindness, Thea? In your own home?

MRS. ELVSTED Oh, if only I had a home! But I haven't. I've never had one.

HEDDA [*Looks at her for a moment.*] I thought that was it.

MRS. ELVSTED [*Stares blankly and helplessly.*] Yes—yes—yes.

HEDDA I can't remember exactly now, but didn't you first go to Mr. Elvsted as a housekeeper?

MRS. ELVSTED Governess, actually. But his wife—at the time, I mean— she was an invalid, and had to spend most of her time in bed. So I had to look after the house too.

HEDDA But in the end, you became mistress of the house.

MRS. ELVSTED [*Sadly.*] Yes, I did.

HEDDA Let me see. Roughly how long ago was that?

MRS. ELVSTED When I got married, you mean?

HEDDA Yes.

MRS. ELVSTED About five years.

HEDDA Yes; it must be about that.

MRS. ELVSTED Oh, those five years! Especially that last two or three. Oh, Mrs. Tesman, if you only knew——

HEDDA [*Slaps her hand gently.*] Mrs. Tesman? Oh, Thea!

MRS. ELVSTED I'm sorry, I'll try to remember. Yes—if you had any idea—

HEDDA [*Casually.*] Eilert Loevborg's been up there too, for about three years, hasn't he?

MRS. ELVSTED [*Looks at her uncertainly.*] Eilert Loevborg? Yes, he has.

HEDDA Did you know him before? When you were here?

MRS. ELVSTED   No, not really. That is—I knew him by name, of course.

HEDDA   But up there, he used to visit you?

MRS. ELVSTED   Yes, he used to come and see us every day. To give the children lessons. I found I couldn't do that as well as manage the house.

HEDDA   I'm sure you couldn't. And your husband——? I suppose being a magistrate he has to be away from home a good deal?

MRS. ELVSTED   Yes. You see, Mrs.——you see, Hedda, he has to cover the whole district.

HEDDA [*Leans against the arm of* MRS. ELVSTED's *chair.*]   Poor, pretty little Thea! Now you must tell me the whole story. From beginning to end.

MRS. ELVSTED   Well—what do you want to know?

HEDDA   What kind of a man is your husband, Thea? I mean, as a person. Is he kind to you?

MRS. ELVSTED [*Evasively.*]   I'm sure he does his best to be.

HEDDA   I only wonder if he isn't too old for you. There's more than twenty years between you, isn't there?

MRS. ELVSTED [*Irritably.*]   Yes, there's that too. Oh, there are so many things. We're different in every way. We've nothing in common. Nothing whatever.

HEDDA   But he loves you, surely? In his own way?

MRS. ELVSTED   Oh, I don't know. I think he just finds me useful. And then I don't cost much to keep. I'm cheap.

HEDDA   Now you're being stupid.

MRS. ELVSTED [*Shakes her head.*]   It can't be any different. With him. He doesn't love anyone except himself. And perhaps the children—a little.

HEDDA   He must be fond of Eilert Loevborg, Thea.

MRS. ELVSTED [*Looks at her.*]   Eilert Loevborg? What makes you think that?

HEDDA   Well, if he sends you all the way down here to look for him—— [*Smiles almost imperceptibly.*] Besides, you said so yourself to Tesman.

MRS. ELVSTED [*With a nervous twitch.*]   Did I? Oh yes, I suppose I did. [*Impulsively, but keeping her voice low.*] Well, I might as well tell you the whole story. It's bound to come out sooner or later.

HEDDA   But my dear Thea——?

MRS. ELVSTED   My husband had no idea I was coming here.

HEDDA   What? Your husband didn't know?

MRS. ELVSTED   No, of course not. As a matter of fact, he wasn't even there. He was away at the assizes. Oh, I couldn't stand it any longer, Hedda! I just couldn't. I'd be so dreadfully lonely up there now.

HEDDA   Go on.

MRS. ELVSTED   So I packed a few things. Secretly. And went.

HEDDA   Without telling anyone?

MRS. ELVSTED   Yes. I caught the train and came straight here.

HEDDA   But my dear Thea! How brave of you!

MRS. ELVSTED [*Gets up and walks across the room.*]   Well, what else could I do?

HEDDA   But what do you suppose your husband will say when you get back?

MRS. ELVSTED [*By the table, looks at her.*]   Back there? To him?

HEDDA Yes. Surely——?

MRS. ELVSTED I shall never go back to him.

HEDDA [*Gets up and goes closer.*] You mean you've left your home for good?

MRS. ELVSTED Yes. I didn't see what else I could do.

HEDDA But to do it so openly!

MRS. ELVSTED Oh, it's no use trying to keep a thing like that secret.

HEDDA But what do you suppose people will say?

MRS. ELVSTED They can say what they like. [*Sits sadly, wearily on the sofa.*] I had to do it.

HEDDA [*After a short silence.*] What do you intend to do now? How are you going to live?

MRS. ELVSTED I don't know. I only know that I must live wherever Eilert Loevborg is. If I am to go on living.

HEDDA [*Moves a chair from the table, sits on it near* MRS. ELVSTED *and strokes her hands.*] Tell me, Thea, how did this—friendship between you and Eilert Loevborg begin?

MRS. ELVSTED Oh, it came about gradually. I developed a kind of—power over him.

HEDDA Oh?

MRS. ELVSTED He gave up his old habits. Not because I asked him to. I'd never have dared to do that. I suppose he just noticed I didn't like that kind of thing. So he gave it up.

HEDDA [*Hides a smile.*] So you've made a new man of him. Clever little Thea!

MRS. ELVSTED Yes—anyway, he says I have. And he's made a—sort of— real person of me. Taught me to think—and to understand all kinds of things.

HEDDA Did he give you lessons too?

MRS. ELVSTED Not exactly lessons. But he talked to me. About—oh, you've no idea—so many things! And then he let me work with him. Oh, it was wonderful. I was so happy to be allowed to help him.

HEDDA Did he allow you to help him?

MRS. ELVSTED Yes. Whenever he wrote anything we always—did it together.

HEDDA Like good pals?

MRS. ELVSTED [*Eagerly.*] Pals! Yes—why, Hedda, that's exactly the word he used! Oh, I ought to feel so happy. But I can't. I don't know if it will last.

HEDDA You don't seem very sure of him.

MRS. ELVSTED [*Sadly.*] Something stands between Eilert Loevberg and me. The shadow of another woman.

HEDDA Who can that be?

MRS. ELVSTED I don't know. Someone he used to be friendly with in—in the old days. Someone he's never been able to forget.

HEDDA What has he told you about her?

MRS. ELVSTED Oh, he only mentioned her once, casually.

HEDDA Well! What did he say?

MRS. ELVSTED He said when he left her she tried to shoot him with a pistol.

HEDDA [*Cold, controlled.*] What nonsense. People don't do such things. The kind of people we know.

MRS. ELVSTED No, I think it must have been that red-haired singer he used to——

HEDDA Ah yes, very probably.

MRS. ELVSTED I remember they used to say she always carried a loaded pistol.

HEDDA Well then, it must be her.

MRS. ELVSTED But Hedda, I hear she's come back, and is living here. Oh, I'm so desperate——!

HEDDA [*Glances toward the rear room.*] Ssh! Tesman's coming. [*Gets up and whispers.*] Thea, we mustn't breathe a word about this to anyone.

MRS. ELVSTED [*Jumps up.*] Oh, no, no! Please don't!

[GEORGE TESMAN *appears from the right in the rear room with a letter in his hand, and comes into the drawing room.*]

TESMAN Well, here's my little epistle all signed and sealed.

HEDDA Good. I think Mrs. Elvsted wants to go now. Wait a moment—I'll see you as far as the garden gate.

TESMAN Er—Hedda, do you think Bertha could deal with this?

HEDDA [*Takes the letter.*] I'll give her instructions.

[BERTHA *enters from the hall.*]

BERTHA Judge Brack is here and asks if he may pay his respects to Madam and the Doctor.

HEDDA Yes, ask him to be so good as to come in. And—wait a moment—drop this letter in the post box.

BERTHA [*Takes the letter.*] Very good, madam.

[*She opens the door for* JUDGE BRACK, *and goes out.* JUDGE BRACK *is forty-five; rather short, but well-built, and elastic in his movements. He has a roundish face with an aristocratic profile. His hair, cut short, is still almost black, and is carefully barbered. Eyes lively and humorous. Thick eyebrows. His moustache is also thick, and is trimmed square at the ends. He is wearing outdoor clothes which are elegant but a little too youthful for him. He has a monocle in one eye; now and then he lets it drop.*]

BRACK [*Hat in hand, bows.*] May one presume to call so early?

HEDDA One may presume.

TESMAN [*Shakes his hand.*] You're welcome here any time. Judge Brack—Mrs. Rysing.

[HEDDA *sighs.*]

BRACK [*Bows.*] Ah—charmed——

HEDDA [*Looks at him and laughs.*] What fun to be able to see you by daylight for once, Judge.

BRACK Do I look—different?

HEDDA Yes. A little younger, I think.

BRACK Obliged.

TESMAN Well, what do you think of Hedda? What? Doesn't she look well? Hasn't she filled out——?

HEDDA Oh, do stop it. You ought to be thanking Judge Brack for all the inconvenience he's put himself to——

BRACK Nonsense, it was a pleasure——

HEDDA You're a loyal friend. But my other friend is pining to get away. Au revoir, Judge. I won't be a minute.

[*Mutual salutations.* MRS. ELVSTED *and* HEDDA *go out through the hall.*]

BRACK Well, is your wife satisfied with everything?

TESMAN Yes, we can't thank you enough. That is—we may have to shift one or two things around, she tells me. And we're short of one or two little items we'll have to purchase.

BRACK Oh? Really?

TESMAN But you musn't worry your head about that. Hedda says she'll get what's needed. I say, why don't we sit down? What?

BRACK Thanks, just for a moment. [*Sits at the table.*] There's something I'd like to talk to you about, my dear Tesman.

TESMAN Oh? Ah yes, of course. [*Sits.*] After the feast comes the reckoning. What?

BRACK Oh, never mind about the financial side—there's no hurry about that. Though I could wish we'd arranged things a little less palatially.

TESMAN Good heavens, that'd never have done. Think of Hedda, my dear chap. You know her. I couldn't possibly ask her to live like a suburban housewife.

BRACK No, no—that's just the problem.

TESMAN Anyway, it can't be long now before my nomination[3] comes through.

BRACK Well, you know, these things often take time.

TESMAN Have you heard any more news? What?

BRACK Nothing definite. [*Changing the subject.*] Oh, by the way, I have one piece of news for you.

TESMAN What?

BRACK Your old friend Eilert Loevborg is back in town.

TESMAN I know that already.

BRACK Oh? How did you hear that?

TESMAN She told me. That lady who went out with Hedda.

BRACK I see. What was her name? I didn't catch it.

TESMAN Mrs. Elvsted.

BRACK Oh, the magistrate's wife. Yes, Loevborg's been living up near them, hasn't he?

TESMAN I'm delighted to hear he's become a decent human being again.

BRACK Yes, so they say.

TESMAN I gather he's published a new book, too. What?

BRACK Indeed he has.

TESMAN I hear it's created rather a stir.

BRACK Quite an unusual stir.

TESMAN I say, isn't that splendid news! He's such a gifted chap—and I was afraid he'd gone to the dogs for good.

BRACK Most people thought he had.

TESMAN But I can't think what he'll do now. How on earth will he manage to make ends meet? What?

---

3. For the professorship. Professors at European universities were less numerous and more socially prominent than their contemporary American counterparts.

[*As he speaks his last words,* HEDDA *enters from the hall.*]

HEDDA [*To* BRACK, *laughs slightly scornfully.*]   Tesman is always worrying about making ends meet.

TESMAN   We were talking about poor Eilert Loevborg, Hedda dear.

HEDDA [*Gives him a quick look.*]   Oh, were you? [*Sits in the armchair by the stove and asks casually.*] Is he in trouble?

TESMAN   Well, he must have run through his inheritance long ago by now. And he can't write a new book every year. What? So I'm wondering what's going to become of him.

BRACK   I may be able to enlighten you there.

TESMAN   Oh?

BRACK   You mustn't forget he has relatives who wield a good deal of influence.

TESMAN   Relatives? Oh, they've quite washed their hands of him, I'm afraid.

BRACK   They used to regard him as the hope of the family.

TESMAN   Used to, yes. But he's put an end to that.

HEDDA   Who knows? [*With a little smile.*] I hear the Elvsteds have made a new man of him.

BRACK   And then this book he's just published——

TESMAN   Well, let's hope they find something for him. I've just written him a note. Oh, by the way, Hedda, I asked him to come over and see us this evening.

BRACK   But my dear chap, you're coming to me this evening. My bachelor party.[4] You promised me last night when I met you at the boat.

HEDDA   Had you forgotten, Tesman?

TESMAN   Good heavens, yes, I'd quite forgotten.

BRACK   Anyway, you can be quite sure he won't turn up here.

TESMAN   Why do you think that? What?

BRACK [*A little unwillingly, gets up and rests his hands on the back of his chair.*]   My dear Tesman—and you, too, Mrs. Tesman—there's something I feel you ought to know.

TESMAN   Concerning Eilert?

BRACK   Concerning him and you.

TESMAN   Well, my dear Judge, tell us, please!

BRACK   You must be prepared for your nomination not to come through quite as quickly as you hope and expect.

TESMAN [*Jumps up uneasily.*]   Is anything wrong? What?

BRACK   There's a possibility that the appointment may be decided by competition——

TESMAN   Competition! By Jove, Hedda, fancy that!

HEDDA [*Leans further back in her chair.*]   Ah! How interesting!

TESMAN   But who else——? I say, you don't mean——?

BRACK   Exactly. By competition with Eilert Loevborg.

TESMAN [*Clasps his hands in alarm.*]   No, no, but this is inconceivable! It's absolutely impossible! What?

BRACK   Hm. We may find it'll happen, all the same.

TESMAN   No, but—Judge Brack, they couldn't be so inconsiderate toward me! [*Waves his arms.*] I mean, by Jove, I—I'm a married man! It was on

---

4. A party for men only, whether single or married.

the strength of this that Hedda and I *got* married! We ran up some pretty hefty debts. And borrowed money from Auntie Juju! I mean, good heavens, they practically promised me the appointment. What?

BRACK   Well, well, I'm sure you'll get it. But you'll have to go through a competition.

HEDDA [*Motionless in her armchair.*]   How exciting, Tesman. It'll be a kind of duel, by Jove.

TESMAN   My dear Hedda, how can you take it so lightly?

HEDDA [*As before.*]   I'm not. I can't wait to see who's going to win.

BRACK   In any case, Mrs. Tesman, it's best you should know how things stand. I mean before you commit yourself to these little items I hear you're threatening to purchase.

HEDDA   I can't allow this to alter my plans.

BRACK   Indeed? Well, that's your business. Good-bye. [*To* TESMAN.] I'll come and collect you on the way home from my afternoon walk.

TESMAN   Oh, yes, yes. I'm sorry, I'm all upside down just now.

HEDDA [*Lying in her chair, holds out her hand.*]   Good-bye, Judge. See you this afternoon.

BRACK   Thank you. Good-bye, good-bye.

TESMAN [*Sees him to the door.*]   Good-bye, my dear Judge. You will excuse me, won't you?

[JUDGE BRACK *goes out through the hall.*]

TESMAN [*Pacing up and down.*]   Oh, Hedda! One oughtn't to go plunging off on wild adventures. What?

HEDDA [*Looks at him and smiles.*]   Like you're doing?

TESMAN   Yes. I mean, there's no denying it, it was a pretty big adventure to go off and get married and set up house merely on expectation.

HEDDA   Perhaps you're right.

TESMAN   Well, anyway, we have our home, Hedda. By Jove, yes. The home we dreamed of. And set our hearts on. What?

HEDDA [*Gets up slowly, wearily.*]   You agreed that we should enter society. And keep open house. That was the bargain.

TESMAN   Yes. Good heavens, I was looking forward to it all so much. To seeing you play hostess to a select circle! By Jove! What? Ah, well, for the time being we shall have to make do with each other's company, Hedda. Perhaps have Auntie Juju in now and then. Oh dear, this wasn't at all what you had in mind——

HEDDA   I won't be able to have a liveried footman.[5] For a start.

TESMAN   Oh no, we couldn't possibly afford a footman.

HEDDA   And that thoroughbred horse you promised me——

TESMAN [*Fearfully.*]   Thoroughbred horse!

HEDDA   I mustn't even think of that now.

TESMAN   Heaven forbid!

HEDDA [*Walks across the room.*]   Ah, well. I still have one thing left to amuse myself with.

TESMAN [*Joyfully.*]   Thank goodness for that. What's that, Hedda? What?

HEDDA [*In the open doorway, looks at him with concealed scorn.*]   My pistols, George darling.

TESMAN [*Alarmed.*]   Pistols!

5. A uniformed servant.

HEDDA [*Her eyes cold.*]   General Gabler's pistols.

    [*She goes into the rear room and disappears.*]

TESMAN [*Runs to the doorway and calls after her.*]   For heaven's sake, Hedda dear, don't touch those things. They're dangerous. Hedda—please—for my sake! What?

Act II

SCENE—*The same as in Act I except that the piano has been removed and an elegant little writing table, with a bookcase, stands in its place. By the sofa on the left a smaller table has been placed. Most of the flowers have been removed.* MRS. ELVSTED's *bouquet stands on the larger table, downstage. It is afternoon.*

    HEDDA, *dressed to receive callers, is alone in the room. She is standing by the open french windows, loading a revolver. The pair to it is lying in an open pistol case on the writing table.*

HEDDA [*Looks down into the garden and calls.*]   Good afternoon, Judge.

BRACK [*In the distance, below.*]   Afternoon, Mrs. Tesman.

HEDDA [*Raises the pistol and takes aim.*]   I'm going to shoot you, Judge Brack.

BRACK [*Shouts from below.*]   No, no, no! Don't aim that thing at me!

HEDDA   This'll teach you to enter houses by the back door. [*Fires.*]

BRACK [*Below.*]   Have you gone completely out of your mind?

HEDDA   Oh dear! Did I hit you?

BRACK [*Still outside.*]   Stop playing these silly tricks.

HEDDA   All right, Judge. Come along in.

    [JUDGE BRACK, *dressed for a bachelor party, enters through the french windows. He has a light overcoat on his arm.*]

BRACK   For God's sake! Haven't you stopped fooling around with those things yet? What are you trying to hit?

HEDDA   Oh, I was just shooting at the sky.

BRACK [*Takes the pistol gently from her hand.*]   By your leave, ma'am. [*Looks at it.*] Ah, yes—I know this old friend well. [*Looks around.*] Where's the case? Oh, yes. [*Puts the pistol in the case and closes it.*] That's enough of that little game for today.

HEDDA   Well, what on earth *am* I to do?

BRACK   You haven't had any visitors?

HEDDA [*Closes the french windows.*]   Not one. I suppose the best people are all still in the country.

BRACK   Your husband isn't home yet?

HEDDA [*Locks the pistol case away in a drawer of the writing table.*]   No. The moment he'd finished eating he ran off to his aunties. He wasn't expecting you so early.

BRACK   Ah, why didn't I think of that? How stupid of me.

HEDDA [*Turns her head and looks at him.*]   Why stupid?

BRACK   I'd have come a little sooner.

HEDDA [*Walks across the room.*]   There'd have been no one to receive you. I've been in my room since lunch, dressing.

BRACK   You haven't a tiny crack in the door through which we might have negotiated?

HEDDA You forgot to arrange one.

BRACK Another stupidity.

HEDDA Well, we'll have to sit down here. And wait. Tesman won't be back for some time.

BRACK Sad. Well, I'll be patient.

[HEDDA *sits on the corner of the sofa.* BRACK *puts his coat over the back of the nearest chair and seats himself, keeping his hat in his hand. Short pause. They look at each other.*]

HEDDA Well?

BRACK [*In the same tone of voice.*] Well?

HEDDA I asked first.

BRACK [*Leans forward slightly.*] Yes, well, now we can enjoy a nice, cosy little chat—Mrs. Hedda.

HEDDA [*Leans further back in her chair.*] It seems such ages since we had a talk. I don't count last night or this morning.

BRACK You mean: à deux?[6]

HEDDA Mm—yes. That's roughly what I meant.

BRACK I've been longing so much for you to come home.

HEDDA So have I.

BRACK You? Really, Mrs. Hedda? And I thought you were having such a wonderful honeymoon.

HEDDA Oh, yes. Wonderful!

BRACK But your husband wrote such ecstatic letters.

HEDDA He! Oh, yes! He thinks life has nothing better to offer than rooting around in libraries and copying old pieces of parchment, or whatever it is he does.

BRACK [*A little maliciously.*] Well, that *is* his life. Most of it, anyway.

HEDDA Yes, I know. Well, it's all right for him. But for me! Oh no, my dear Judge. I've been bored to death.

BRACK [*Sympathetically.*] Do you mean that? Seriously?

HEDDA Yes. Can you imagine? Six whole months without ever meeting a single person who was one of us, and to whom I could talk about the kind of things we talk about.

BRACK Yes, I can understand. I'd miss that, too.

HEDDA That wasn't the worst, though.

BRACK What was?

HEDDA Having to spend every minute of one's life with—with the same person.

BRACK [*Nods.*] Yes. What a thought! Morning; noon; and——

HEDDA [*Coldly.*] As I said: every minute of one's life.

BRACK I stand corrected. But dear Tesman is such a clever fellow, I should have thought one ought to be able——

HEDDA Tesman is only interested in one thing, my dear Judge. His special subject.

BRACK True.

HEDDA And people who are only interested in one thing don't make the most amusing company. Not for long, anyway.

BRACK Not even when they happen to be the person one loves?

HEDDA Oh, don't use that sickly, stupid word.

6. Just the two of us.

BRACK [*Starts.*]   But, Mrs. Hedda——!

HEDDA [*Half laughing, half annoyed.*]   You just try it, Judge. Listening to the history of civilization morning, noon and——

BRACK [*Corrects her.*]   Every minute of one's life.

HEDDA   All right. Oh, and those domestic industries of Brabant in the Middle Ages! That really is beyond the limit.

BRACK [*Looks at her searchingly.*]   But, tell me—if you feel like this why on earth did you—? Ha——

HEDDA   Why on earth did I marry George Tesman?

BRACK   If you like to put it that way.

HEDDA   Do you think it so very strange?

BRACK   Yes—and no, Mrs. Hedda.

HEDDA   I'd danced myself tired, Judge. I felt my time was up—— [*Gives a slight shudder.*] No, I mustn't say that. Or even think it.

BRACK   You've no rational cause to think it.

HEDDA   Oh—cause, cause—— [*Looks searchingly at him.*] After all, George Tesman—well, I mean, he's a very respectable man.

BRACK   Very respectable, sound as a rock. No denying that.

HEDDA   And there's nothing exactly ridiculous about him. Is there?

BRACK   Ridiculous? No-o-o, I wouldn't say that.

HEDDA   Mm. He's very clever at collecting material and all that, isn't he? I mean, he may go quite far in time.

BRACK [*Looks at her a little uncertainly.*]   I thought you believed, like everyone else, that he would become a very prominent man.

HEDDA [*Looks tired.*]   Yes, I did. And when he came and begged me on his bended knees to be allowed to love and to cherish me, I didn't see why I shouldn't let him.

BRACK   No, well—if one looks at it like that——

HEDDA   It was more than my other admirers were prepared to do, Judge dear.

BRACK [*Laughs.*]   Well, I can't answer for the others. As far as I myself am concerned, you know I've always had a considerable respect for the institution of marriage. As an institution.

HEDDA [*Lightly.*]   Oh, I've never entertained any hopes of you.

BRACK   All I want is to have a circle of friends whom I can trust, whom I can help with advice or—or by any other means, and into whose houses I may come and go as a—trusted friend.

HEDDA   Of the husband?

BRACK [*Bows.*]   Preferably, to be frank, of the wife. And of the husband too, of course. Yes, you know, this kind of—triangle is a delightful arrangement for all parties concerned.

HEDDA   Yes, I often longed for a third person while I was away. Oh, those hours we spent alone in railway compartments——

BRACK   Fortunately your honeymoon is now over.

HEDDA [*Shakes her head.*]   There's a long way still to go. I've only reached a stop on the line.

BRACK   Why not jump out and stretch your legs a little, Mrs. Hedda?

HEDDA   I'm not the jumping sort.

BRACK   Aren't you?

HEDDA   No. There's always someone around who——

BRACK [*Laughs.*]   Who looks at one's legs?

HEDDA   Yes. Exactly.

BRACK   Well, but surely——

HEDDA [*With a gesture of rejection.*]   I don't like it. I'd rather stay where I am. Sitting in the compartment. *À deux.*

BRACK   But suppose a third person were to step into the compartment?

HEDDA   That would be different.

BRACK   A trusted friend—someone who understood——

HEDDA   And was lively and amusing——

BRACK   And interested in—more subjects than one——

HEDDA [*Sighs audibly.*]   Yes, that'd be a relief.

BRACK [*Hears the front door open and shut.*]   The triangle is completed.

HEDDA [*Half under breath.*]   And the train goes on.

    [GEORGE TESMAN, *in grey walking dress with a soft felt hat, enters from the hall. He has a number of paper-covered books under his arm and in his pockets.*]

TESMAN [*Goes over to the table by the corner sofa.*]   Phew! It's too hot to be lugging all this around. [*Puts the books down.*] I'm positively sweating, Hedda. Why, hullo, hullo! You here already, Judge? What? Bertha didn't tell me.

BRACK [*Gets up.*]   I came in through the garden.

HEDDA   What are all those books you've got there?

TESMAN [*Stands glancing through them.*]   Oh, some new publications dealing with my special subject. I had to buy them.

HEDDA   Your special subject?

BRACK   His special subject, Mrs. Tesman.

    [BRACK *and* HEDDA *exchange a smile.*]

HEDDA   Haven't you collected enough material on your special subject?

TESMAN   My dear Hedda, one can never have too much. One must keep abreast of what other people are writing.

HEDDA   Yes. Of course.

TESMAN [*Rooting among the books.*]   Look—I bought a copy of Eilert Loevborg's new book, too. [*Holds it out to her.*] Perhaps you'd like to have a look at it, Hedda? What?

HEDDA   No, thank you. Er—yes, perhaps I will, later.

TESMAN   I glanced through it on my way home.

BRACK   What's your opinion—as a specialist on the subject?

TESMAN   I'm amazed how sound and balanced it is. He never used to write like that. [*Gathers his books together.*] Well, I must get down to these at once. I can hardly wait to cut the pages.[7] Oh, I've got to change, too. [*To* BRACK.] We don't have to be off just yet, do we? What?

BRACK   Heavens, no. We've plenty of time yet.

TESMAN   Good, I needn't hurry, then. [*Goes with his books, but stops and turns in the doorway.*] Oh, by the way, Hedda, Auntie Juju won't be coming to see you this evening.

HEDDA   Won't she? Oh—the hat, I suppose.

TESMAN   Good heavens, no. How could you think such a thing of Auntie Juju? Fancy——! No, Auntie Rena's very ill.

HEDDA   She always is.

---

7. Books used to be sold with the pages folded but uncut as they came from the printing press; the owner had to cut the pages to read the book.

TESMAN   Yes, but today she's been taken really bad.

HEDDA   Oh, then it's quite understandable that the other one should want to stay with her. Well, I shall have to swallow my disappointment.

TESMAN   You can't imagine how happy Auntie Juju was in spite of everything. At your looking so well after the honeymoon!

HEDDA [*Half beneath her breath, as she rises.*]   Oh, these everlasting aunts!

TESMAN   What?

HEDDA [*Goes over to the french windows.*]   Nothing.

TESMAN   Oh. All right. [*Goes into the rear room and out of sight.*]

BRACK   What was that about the hat?

HEDDA   Oh, something that happened with Miss Tesman this morning. She'd put her hat down on a chair. [*Looks at him and smiles.*] And I pretended to think it was the servant's.

BRACK [*Shakes his head.*]   But my dear Mrs. Hedda, how could you do such a thing? To that poor old lady?

HEDDA [*Nervously, walking across the room.*]   Sometimes a mood like that hits me. And I can't stop myself. [*Throws herself down in the armchair by the stove.*] Oh, I don't know how to explain it.

BRACK [*Behind her chair.*]   You're not really happy. That's the answer.

HEDDA [*Stares ahead of her.*]   Why on earth should I be happy? Can you give me a reason?

BRACK   Yes. For one thing you've got the home you always wanted.

HEDDA [*Looks at him.*]   You really believe that story?

BRACK   You mean it isn't true?

HEDDA   Oh, yes, it's partly true.

BRACK   Well?

HEDDA   It's true I got Tesman to see me home from parties last summer—

BRACK   It was a pity my home lay in another direction.

HEDDA   Yes. Your interests lay in another direction, too.

BRACK [*Laughs.*]   That's naughty of you, Mrs. Hedda. But to return to you and Tesman——

HEDDA   Well, we walked past this house one evening. And poor Tesman was fidgeting in his boots trying to find something to talk about. I felt sorry for the great scholar——

BRACK [*Smiles incredulously.*]   Did you? Hm.

HEDDA   Yes, honestly I did. Well, to help him out of his misery, I happened to say quite frivolously how much I'd love to live in this house.

BRACK   Was that all?

HEDDA   That evening, yes.

BRACK   But—afterwards?

HEDDA   Yes. My little frivolity had its consequences, my dear Judge.

BRACK   Our little frivolities do. Much too often, unfortunately.

HEDDA   Thank you. Well, it was our mutual admiration for the late Prime Minister's house that brought George Tesman and me together on common ground. So we got engaged, and we got married, and we went on our honeymoon, and—Ah well, Judge, I've—made my bed and I must lie in it, I was about to say.

BRACK   How utterly fantastic! And you didn't really care in the least about the house?

HEDDA   God knows I didn't.

BRACK   Yes, but now that we've furnished it so beautifully for you?

HEDDA   Ugh—all the rooms smell of lavender and dried roses. But perhaps Auntie Juju brought that in.

BRACK [*Laughs.*]   More likely the Prime Minister's widow, rest her soul.

HEDDA   Yes, it's got the odor of death about it. It reminds me of the flowers one has worn at a ball—the morning after. [*Clasps her hands behind her neck, leans back in the chair and looks up at him.*] Oh, my dear Judge, you've no idea how hideously bored I'm going to be out here.

BRACK   Couldn't you find some kind of occupation, Mrs. Hedda? Like your husband?

HEDDA   Occupation? That'd interest me?

BRACK   Well—preferably.

HEDDA   God knows what. I've often thought—— [*Breaks off.*] No, that wouldn't work either.

BRACK   Who knows? Tell me about it.

HEDDA   I was thinking—if I could persuade Tesman to go into politics, for example.

BRACK [*Laughs.*]   Tesman! No, honestly, I don't think he's quite cut out to be a politician.

HEDDA   Perhaps not. But if I could persuade him to have a go at it?

BRACK   What satisfaction would that give you? If he turned out to be no good? Why do you want to make him do that?

HEDDA   Because I'm bored. [*After a moment.*] You feel there's absolutely no possibility of Tesman becoming Prime Minister, then?

BRACK   Well, you know, Mrs. Hedda, for one thing he'd have to be pretty well off before he could become that.

HEDDA [*Gets up impatiently.*]   There you are! [*Walks across the room.*] It's this wretched poverty that makes life so hateful. And ludicrous. Well, it is!

BRACK   I don't think that's the real cause.

HEDDA   What is, then?

BRACK   Nothing really exciting has ever happened to you.

HEDDA   Nothing serious, you mean?

BRACK   Call it that if you like. But now perhaps it may.

HEDDA [*Tosses her head.*]   Oh, you're thinking of this competition for that wretched professorship? That's Tesman's affair. I'm not going to waste my time worrying about that.

BRACK   Very well, let's forget about that then. But suppose you were to find yourself faced with what people call—to use the conventional phrase—the most solemn of human responsibilities? [*Smiles.*]   A new responsibility, little Mrs. Hedda.

HEDDA [*Angrily.*]   Be quiet! Nothing like that's going to happen.

BRACK [*Warily.*]   We'll talk about it again in a year's time. If not earlier.

HEDDA [*Curtly.*]   I've no leanings in that direction, Judge. I don't want any—responsibilities.

BRACK   But surely you must feel some inclination to make use of that— natural talent which every woman—

HEDDA [*Over by the french windows.*]   Oh, be quiet, I say! I often think there's only one thing for which I have any natural talent.

BRACK [*Goes closer.*]   And what is that, if I may be so bold as to ask?

HEDDA [*Stands looking out.*] For boring myself to death. Now you know. [*Turns, looks toward the rear room and laughs.*] Talking of boring, here comes the Professor.

BRACK [*Quietly, warningly.*] Now, now, now, Mrs. Hedda!

[GEORGE TESMAN, *in evening dress, with gloves and hat in his hand, enters through the rear room from the right.*]

TESMAN Hedda, hasn't any message come from Eilert? What?

HEDDA No.

TESMAN Ah, then we'll have him here presently. You wait and see.

BRACK You really think he'll come?

TESMAN Yes, I'm almost sure he will. What you were saying about him this morning is just gossip.

BRACK Oh?

TESMAN Yes. Auntie Juju said she didn't believe he'd ever dare to stand in my way again. Fancy that!

BRACK Then everything in the garden's lovely.

TESMAN [*Puts his hat, with his gloves in it, on a chair, right.*] Yes, but you really must let me wait for him as long as possible.

BRACK We've plenty of time. No one'll be turning up at my place before seven or half past.

TESMAN Ah, then we can keep Hedda company a little longer. And see if he turns up. What?

HEDDA [*Picks up* BRACK's *coat and hat and carries them over to the corner sofa.*] And if the worst comes to the worst, Mr. Loevborg can sit here and talk to me.

BRACK [*Offering to take his things from her.*] No, please. What do you mean by "if the worst comes to the worst"?

HEDDA If he doesn't want to go with you and Tesman.

TESMAN [*Looks doubtfully at her.*] I say, Hedda, do you think it'll be all right for him to stay here with you? What? Remember Auntie Juju isn't coming.

HEDDA Yes, but Mrs. Elvsted is. The three of us can have a cup of tea together.

TESMAN Ah, that'll be all right then.

BRACK [*Smiles.*] It's probably the safest solution as far as he's concerned.

HEDDA Why?

BRACK My dear Mrs. Tesman, you always say of my little bachelor parties that they should be attended only by men of the strongest principles.

HEDDA But Mr. Loevborg is a man of principle now. You know what they say about a reformed sinner——

[BERTHA *enters from the hall.*]

BERTHA Madam, there's a gentleman here who wants to see you——

HEDDA Ask him to come in.

TESMAN [*Quietly.*] I'm sure it's him. By Jove. Fancy that!

[EILERT LOEVBORG *enters from the hall. He is slim and lean, of the same age as* TESMAN, *but looks older and somewhat haggard. His hair and beard are of a blackish-brown; his face is long and pale, but with a couple of reddish patches on his cheekbones. He is dressed in an elegant and fairly new black suit, and carries black gloves and a top hat in his hand. He stops just inside the door and bows abruptly. He seems somewhat embarrassed.*]

TESMAN [*Goes over and shakes his hand.*]   My dear Eilert! How grand to see you again after all these years!

EILERT LOEVBORG [*Speaks softly.*]   It was good of you to write, George. [*Goes nearer to* HEDDA.] May I shake hands with you, too, Mrs. Tesman?

HEDDA [*Accepts his hand.*]   Delighted to see you, Mr. Loevborg. [*With a gesture.*] I don't know if you two gentlemen——

LOEVBORG [*Bows slightly.*]   Judge Brack, I believe.

BRACK [*Also with a slight bow.*]   Correct. We—met some years ago——

TESMAN [*Puts his hands on* LOEVBORG's *shoulders.*]   Now you're to treat this house just as though it were your own home, Eilert. Isn't that right, Hedda? I hear you've decided to settle here again? What?

LOEVBORG   Yes, I have.

TESMAN   Quite understandable. Oh, by the bye—I've just bought your new book. Though to tell the truth I haven't found time to read it yet.

LOEVBORG   You needn't bother.

TESMAN   Oh? Why?

LOEVBORG   There's nothing much in it.

TESMAN   By Jove, fancy hearing that from you!

BRACK   But everyone's praising it.

LOEVBORG   That was exactly what I wanted to happen. So I only wrote what I knew everyone would agree with.

BRACK   Very sensible.

TESMAN   Yes, but my dear Eilert——

LOEVBORG   I want to try to re-establish myself. To begin again—from the beginning.

TESMAN [*A little embarrassed.*]   Yes, I—er—suppose you do. What?

LOEVBORG [*Smiles, puts down his hat and takes a package wrapped in paper from his coat pocket.*]   But when this gets published—George Tesman— read it. This is my real book. The one in which I have spoken with my own voice.

TESMAN   Oh, really? What's it about?

LOEVBORG   It's the sequel.

TESMAN   Sequel? To what?

LOEVBORG   To the other book.

TESMAN   The one that's just come out?

LOEVBORG   Yes.

TESMAN   But my dear Eilert, that covers the subject right up to the present day.

LOEVBORG   It does. But this is about the future.

TESMAN   The future! But, I say, we don't know anything about that.

LOEVBORG   No. But there are one or two things that need to be said about it. [*Opens the package.*] Here, have a look.

TESMAN   Surely that's not your handwriting?

LOEVBORG   I dictated it. [*Turns the pages.*] It's in two parts. The first deals with the forces that will shape our civilization. [*Turns further on towards the end.*] And the second indicates the direction in which that civilization may develop.

TESMAN   Amazing! I'd never think of writing about anything like that.

HEDDA [*By the french windows, drumming on the pane.*]   No. You wouldn't.

LOEVBORG [*Puts the pages back into their cover and lays the package on the table.*] I brought it because I thought I might possibly read you a few pages this evening.

TESMAN I say, what a kind idea! Oh, but this evening——? [*Glances at* BRACK.] I'm not quite sure whether——

LOEVBORG Well, some other time, then. There's no hurry.

BRACK The truth is, Mr. Loevborg, I'm giving a little dinner this evening. In Tesman's honor, you know.

LOEVBORG [*Looks round for his hat.*] Oh—then I mustn't——

BRACK No, wait a minute. Won't you do me the honor of joining us?

LOEVBORG [*Curtly, with decision.*] No, I can't. Thank you so much.

BRACK Oh, nonsense. Do—please. There'll only be a few of us. And I can promise you we shall have some good sport, as Mrs. Hed—as Mrs. Tesman puts it.

LOEVBORG I've no doubt. Nevertheless——

BRACK You could bring your manuscript along and read it to Tesman at my place. I could lend you a room.

TESMAN By Jove, Eilert, that's an idea. What?

HEDDA [*Interposes.*] But Tesman, Mr. Loevborg doesn't want to go. I'm sure Mr. Loevborg would much rather sit here and have supper with me.

LOEVBORG [*Looks at her.*] With you, Mrs. Tesman?

HEDDA And Mrs. Elvsted.

LOEVBORG Oh. [*Casually.*] I ran into her this afternoon.

HEDDA Did you? Well, she's coming here this evening. So you really must stay, Mr. Loevborg. Otherwise she'll have no one to see her home.

LOEVBORG That's true. Well—thank you, Mrs. Tesman, I'll stay then.

HEDDA I'll just tell the servant.

[*She goes to the door which leads into the hall, and rings.* BERTHA *enters.* HEDDA *talks softly to her and points towards the rear room.* BERTHA *nods and goes out.*]

TESMAN [*To* LOEVBORG, *as* HEDDA *does this.*] I say, Eilert. This new subject of yours—the—er—future—is that the one you're going to lecture about?

LOEVBORG Yes.

TESMAN They told me down at the bookshop that you're going to hold a series of lectures here during the autumn.

LOEVBORG Yes, I am, I—hope you don't mind, Tesman.

TESMAN Good heavens, no! But——?

LOEVBORG I can quite understand it might queer your pitch a little.

TESMAN [*Dejectedly.*] Oh well, I can't expect you to put them off for my sake.

LOEVBORG I'll wait till your appointment's been announced.

TESMAN You'll wait! But—but—aren't you going to compete with me for the post? What?

LOEVBORG No. I only want to defeat you in the eyes of the world.

TESMAN Good heavens! Then Auntie Juju was right after all! Oh, I knew it, I knew it! Hear that, Hedda? Fancy! Eilert *doesn't* want to stand in our way.

HEDDA [*Curtly.*] Our? Leave me out of it, please.

[*She goes towards the rear room, where* BERTHA *is setting a tray with decanters and glasses on the table.* HEDDA *nods approval, and comes back into the drawing room.* BERTHA *goes out.*]

TESMAN [*While this is happening.*] Judge Brack, what do you think about all this? What?

BRACK Oh, I think honor and victory can be very splendid things——

TESMAN Of course they can. Still——

HEDDA [*Looks at* TESMAN *with a cold smile.*] You look as if you'd been hit by a thunderbolt.

TESMAN Yes, I feel rather like it.

BRACK There was a black cloud looming up, Mrs. Tesman. But it seems to have passed over.

HEDDA [*Points toward the rear room.*] Well, gentlemen, won't you go in and take a glass of cold punch?

BRACK [*Glances at his watch.*] A stirrup cup?[8] Yes, why not?

TESMAN An admirable suggestion, Hedda. Admirable! Oh, I feel so relieved!

HEDDA Won't you have one, too, Mr. Loevborg?

LOEVBORG No, thank you. I'd rather not.

BRACK Great heavens, man, cold punch isn't poison. Take my word for it.

LOEVBORG Not for everyone, perhaps.

HEDDA I'll keep Mr. Loevborg company while you drink.

TESMAN Yes, Hedda dear, would you?

[*He and* BRACK *go into the rear room, sit down, drink punch, smoke cigarettes and talk cheerfully during the following scene.* EILERT LOEVBORG *remains standing by the stove.* HEDDA *goes to the writing table.*]

HEDDA [*Raising her voice slightly.*] I've some photographs I'd like to show you, if you'd care to see them. Tesman and I visited the Tyrol on our way home.

[*She comes back with an album, places it on the table by the sofa and sits in the upstage corner of the sofa.* EILERT LOEVBORG *comes toward her, stops and looks at her. Then he takes a chair and sits down on her left, with his back toward the rear room.*]

HEDDA [*Opens the album.*] You see these mountains, Mr. Loevborg? That's the Ortler group. Tesman has written the name underneath. You see: "The Ortler Group near Meran."[9]

LOEVBORG [*Has not taken his eyes from her; says softly, slowly.*] Hedda— Gabler!

HEDDA [*Gives him a quick glance.*] Ssh!

LOEVBORG [*Repeats softly.*] Hedda Gabler!

HEDDA [*Looks at the album.*] Yes, that used to be my name. When we first knew each other.

LOEVBORG And from now on—for the rest of my life—I must teach myself never to say: Hedda Gabler.

HEDDA [*Still turning the pages.*] Yes, you must. You'd better start getting into practice. The sooner the better.

8. A drink before parting. (Originally, it was taken by riders on horseback just before setting forth.)
9. Or Merano, a city in the Austrian Tyrol, since 1918 in Italy. The scenic features mentioned here and later are tourist attractions. The Ortler Group and the Dolomites are ranges of the Alps. The Ampezzo Valley lies beyond the Dolomites to the east. The Brenner Pass is a major route through the Alps to Austria.

LOEVBORG [*Bitterly.*]   Hedda Gabler married? And to George Tesman?

HEDDA   Yes. Well—that's life.

LOEVBORG   Oh, Hedda, Hedda! How could you throw yourself away like that?

HEDDA [*Looks sharply at him.*]   Stop it.

LOEVBORG   What do you mean?

[TESMAN *comes in and goes toward the sofa.*]

HEDDA [*Hears him coming and says casually.*]   And this, Mr. Loevborg, is the view from the Ampezzo valley. Look at those mountains. [*Glances affectionately up at* TESMAN.] What did you say those curious mountains were called, dear?

TESMAN   Let me have a look. Oh, those are the Dolomites.

HEDDA   Of course. Those are the Dolomites, Mr. Loevborg.

TESMAN   Hedda, I just wanted to ask you, can't we bring some punch in here? A glass for you, anyway. What?

HEDDA   Thank you, yes. And a biscuit[1] or two, perhaps.

TESMAN   You wouldn't like a cigarette?

HEDDA   No.

TESMAN   Right.

[*He goes into the rear room and over to the right.* BRACK *is sitting there, glancing occasionally at* HEDDA *and* LOEVBORG.]

LOEVBORG [*Softly, as before.*]   Answer me, Hedda. How could you do it?

HEDDA [*Apparently absorbed in the album.*]   If you go on calling me Hedda I won't talk to you any more.

LOEVBORG   Mayn't I even when we're alone?

HEDDA   No. You can think it. But you mustn't say it.

LOEVBORG   Oh, I see. Because you love George Tesman.

HEDDA [*Glances at him and smiles.*]   Love? Don't be funny.

LOEVBORG   You don't love him?

HEDDA   I don't intend to be unfaithful to him. That's not what I want.

LOEVBORG   Hedda—just tell me one thing——

HEDDA   Ssh!

[TESMAN *enters from the rear room, carrying a tray.*]

TESMAN   Here we are! Here come the goodies! [*Puts the tray down on the table.*]

HEDDA   Why didn't you ask the servant to bring it in?

TESMAN [*Fills the glasses.*]   I like waiting on you, Hedda.

HEDDA   But you've filled both glasses. Mr. Loevborg doesn't want to drink.

TESMAN   Yes, but Mrs. Elvsted'll be here soon.

HEDDA   Oh yes, that's true. Mrs. Elvsted——

TESMAN   Had you forgotten her? What?

HEDDA   We're so absorbed with these photographs. [*Shows him one.*] You remember this little village?

TESMAN   Oh, that one down by the Brenner Pass. We spent a night there——

HEDDA   Yes, and met all those amusing people.

TESMAN   Oh yes, it was there, wasn't it? By Jove, if only we could have had you with us, Eilert! Ah, well. [*Goes back into the other room and sits down with* BRACK.]

1. Cookie.

LOEVBORG   Tell me one thing, Hedda.

HEDDA   Yes?

LOEVBORG   Didn't you love me either? Not—just a little?

HEDDA   Well now, I wonder? No, I think we were just good pals—Really good pals who could tell each other anything. [*Smiles.*] You certainly poured your heart out to me.

LOEVBORG   You begged me to.

HEDDA   Looking back on it, there was something beautiful and fascinating—and brave—about the way we told each other everything. That secret friendship no one else knew about.

LOEVBORG   Yes, Hedda, yes! Do you remember? How I used to come up to your father's house in the afternoon—and the General sat by the window and read his newspapers—with his back toward us——

HEDDA   And we sat on the sofa in the corner——

LOEVBORG   Always reading the same illustrated magazine——

HEDDA   We hadn't any photograph album.

LOEVBORG   Yes, Hedda. I regarded you as a kind of confessor. Told you things about myself which no one else knew about—then. Those days and nights of drinking and—Oh, Hedda, what power did you have to make me confess such things?

HEDDA   Power? You think I had some power over you?

LOEVBORG   Yes—I don't know how else to explain it. And all those—oblique questions you asked me——

HEDDA   You knew what they meant.

LOEVBORG   But that you could sit there and ask me such questions! So unashamedly——

HEDDA   I thought you said they were oblique.

LOEVBORG   Yes, but you asked them so unashamedly. That you could question me about—about that kind of thing!

HEDDA   You answered willingly enough.

LOEVBORG   Yes—that's what I can't understand—looking back on it. But tell me, Hedda—what you felt for me—wasn't that—love? When you asked me those questions and made me confess my sins to you, wasn't it because you wanted to wash me clean?

HEDDA   No, not exactly.

LOEVBORG   Why did you do it, then?

HEDDA   Do you find it so incredible that a young girl, given the chance to do so without anyone knowing, should want to be allowed a glimpse into a forbidden world of whose existence she is supposed to be ignorant?

LOEVBORG   So that was it?

HEDDA   One reason. One reason—I think.

LOEVBORG   You didn't love me, then. You just wanted—knowledge. But if that was so, why did you break it off?

HEDDA   That was your fault.

LOEVBORG   It was you who put an end to it.

HEDDA   Yes, when I realized that our friendship was threatening to develop into something—something else. Shame on you, Eilert Loevborg! How could you abuse the trust of your dearest friend?

LOEVBORG   [*Clenches his fists.*]   Oh, why didn't you do it? Why didn't you shoot me dead? As you threatened to?

HEDDA   I was afraid. Of the scandal.

LOEVBORG   Yes, Hedda. You're a coward at heart.

HEDDA   A dreadful coward. [*Changes her tone.*] Luckily for you. Well, now you've found consolation with the Elvsteds.

LOEVBORG   I know what Thea's been telling you.

HEDDA   I dare say you told her about us.

LOEVBORG   Not a word. She's too silly to understand that kind of thing.

HEDDA   Silly?

LOEVBORG   She's silly about that kind of thing.

HEDDA   And I am a coward. [*Leans closer to him, without looking him in the eyes, and says quietly.*] But let me tell you something. Something you don't know.

LOEVBORG [*Tensely.*]   Yes?

HEDDA   My failure to shoot you wasn't my worst act of cowardice that evening.

LOEVBORG [*Looks at her for a moment, realizes her meaning and whispers passionately.*]   Oh, Hedda! Hedda Gabler! Now I see what was behind those questions. Yes! It wasn't knowledge you wanted! It was life!

HEDDA [*Flashes a look at him and says quietly.*]   Take care! Don't you delude yourself!

[*It has begun to grow dark.* BERTHA, *from outside, opens the door leading into the hall.*]

HEDDA [*Closes the album with a snap and cries, smiling.*]   Ah, at last! Come in, Thea dear!

[MRS. ELVSTED *enters from the hall, in evening dress. The door is closed behind her.*]

HEDDA [*On the sofa, stretches out her arms toward her.*]   Thea darling, I thought you were never coming!

[MRS. ELVSTED *makes a slight bow to the gentlemen in the rear room as she passes the open doorway, and they to her. Then she goes to the table and holds out her hand to* HEDDA. EILERT LOEVBORG *has risen from his chair. He and* MRS. ELVSTED *nod silently to each other.*]

MRS. ELVSTED   Perhaps I ought to go in and say a few words to your husband?

HEDDA   Oh, there's no need. They're happy by themselves. They'll be going soon.

MRS. ELVSTED   Going?

HEDDA   Yes, they're off on a spree this evening.

MRS. ELVSTED [*Quickly, to* LOEVBORG.]   You're not going with them?

LOEVBORG   No.

HEDDA   Mr. Loevborg is staying here with us.

MRS. ELVSTED [*Takes a chair and is about to sit down beside him.*]   Oh, how nice it is to be here!

HEDDA   No, Thea darling, not there. Come over here and sit beside me. I want to be in the middle.

MRS. ELVSTED   Yes, just as you wish.

[*She goes right of the table and sits on the sofa, on* HEDDA's *right.* LOEVBORG *sits down again in his chair.*]

LOEVBORG [*After a short pause, to* HEDDA.]   Isn't she lovely to look at?

HEDDA [*Strokes her hair gently.*]   Only to look at?

LOEVBORG   Yes. We're just good pals. We trust each other implicitly. We can talk to each other quite unashamedly.

HEDDA   No need to be oblique?

MRS. ELVSTED [*Nestles close to* HEDDA *and says quietly.*]   Oh, Hedda I'm so happy. Imagine—he says I've inspired him!

HEDDA [*Looks at her with a smile.*]   Dear Thea! Does he really?

LOEVBORG   She has the courage of her convictions, Mrs. Tesman.

MRS. ELVSTED   I? Courage?

LOEVBORG   Absolute courage. Where friendship is concerned.

HEDDA   Yes. Courage. Yes. If only one had that——

LOEVBORG   Yes?

HEDDA   One might be able to live. In spite of everything. [*Changes her tone suddenly.*] Well, Thea darling, now you're going to drink a nice glass of cold punch.

MRS. ELVSTED   No, thank you. I never drink anything like that.

HEDDA   Oh. You, Mr. Loevborg?

LOEVBORG   Thank you, I don't either.

MRS. ELVSTED   No, he doesn't, either.

HEDDA [*Looks into his eyes.*]   But if I want you to?

LOEVBORG   That doesn't make any difference.

HEDDA [*Laughs.*]   Have I no power over you at all? Poor me!

LOEVBORG   Not where this is concerned.

HEDDA   Seriously, I think you should. For your own sake.

MRS. ELVSTED   Hedda!

LOEVBORG   Why?

HEDDA   Or perhaps I should say for other people's sake.

LOEVBORG   What do you mean?

HEDDA   People might think you didn't feel absolutely and unashamedly sure of yourself. In your heart of hearts.

MRS. ELVSTED [*Quietly.*]   Oh, Hedda, no!

LOEVBORG   People can think what they like. For the present.

MRS. ELVSTED [*Happily.*]   Yes, that's true.

HEDDA   I saw it so clearly in Judge Brack a few minutes ago.

LOEVBORG   Oh. What did you see?

HEDDA   He smiled so scornfully when he saw you were afraid to go in there and drink with them.

LOEVBORG   Afraid! I wanted to stay here and talk to you.

MRS. ELVSTED   That was only natural, Hedda.

HEDDA   But the Judge wasn't to know that. I saw him wink at Tesman when you showed you didn't dare to join their wretched little party.

LOEVBORG   Didn't dare! Are you saying I didn't dare?

HEDDA   I'm not saying so. But that was what Judge Brack thought.

LOEVBORG   Well, let him.

HEDDA   You're not going, then?

LOEVBORG   I'm staying here with you and Thea.

MRS. ELVSTED   Yes, Hedda, of course he is.

HEDDA [*Smiles, and nods approvingly to* LOEVBORG.]   Firm as a rock! A man of principle! That's how a man should be! [*Turns to* MRS. ELVSTED *and strokes her cheek.*] Didn't I tell you so this morning when you came here in such a panic——

LOEVBORG [*Starts.*]   Panic?

MRS. ELVSTED   [*Frightened.*]   Hedda! But—Hedda!

HEDDA   Well, now you can see for yourself. There's no earthly need for you to get scared to death just because—— [*Stops.*] Well! Let's all three cheer up and enjoy ourselves.

LOEVBORG Mrs. Tesman, would you mind explaining to me what this is all about?

MRS. ELVSTED Oh, my God, my God, Hedda, what are you saying? What are you doing?

HEDDA Keep calm. That horrid Judge has his eye on you.

LOEVBORG Scared to death, were you? For my sake?

MRS. ELVSTED [*Quietly, trembling.*] Oh, Hedda! You've made me so unhappy!

LOEVBORG [*Looks coldly at her for a moment. His face is distorted.*] So that was how much you trusted me.

MRS. ELVSTED Eilert dear, please listen to me——

LOEVBORG [*Takes one of the glasses of punch, raises it and says quietly, hoarsely.*] Skoal, Thea! [*Empties the glass, puts it down and picks up one of the others.*]

MRS. ELVSTED [*Quietly.*] Hedda, Hedda! Why did you want this to happen?

HEDDA I—want it? Are you mad?

LOEVBORG Skoal to you too, Mrs. Tesman. Thanks for telling me the truth. Here's to the truth! [*Empties his glass and refills it.*]

HEDDA [*Puts her hand on his arm.*] Steady. That's enough for now. Don't forget the party.

MRS. ELVSTED No, no, no!

HEDDA Ssh! They're looking at you.

LOEVBORG [*Puts down his glass.*] Thea, tell me the truth——

MRS. ELVSTED Yes!

LOEVBORG Did your husband know you were following me?

MRS. ELVSTED Oh, Hedda!

LOEVBORG Did you and he have an agreement that you should come here and keep an eye on me? Perhaps he gave you the idea? After all, he's a magistrate.[2] I suppose he needed me back in his office. Or did he miss my companionship at the card table?

MRS. ELVSTED [*Quietly, sobbing.*] Eilert, Eilert!

LOEVBORG [*Seizes a glass and is about to fill it.*] Let's drink to him, too.

HEDDA No more now. Remember you're going to read your book to Tesman.

LOEVBORG [*Calm again, puts down his glass.*] That was silly of me, Thea. To take it like that, I mean. Don't be angry with me, my dear. You'll see— yes, and they'll see, too—that though I fell, I—I have raised myself up again. With your help, Thea.

MRS. ELVSTED [*Happily.*] Oh, thank God!

[BRACK *has meanwhile glanced at his watch. He and* TESMAN *get up and come into the drawing room.*]

BRACK [*Takes his hat and overcoat.*] Well, Mrs. Tesman. It's time for us to go.

HEDDA Yes, I suppose it must be.

LOEVBORG [*Gets up.*] Time for me too, Judge.

2. Also translated "sheriff." A civil official with duties associated with the courts.

MRS. ELVSTED [*Quietly, pleadingly.*]   Eilert, please don't!

HEDDA [*Pinches her arm.*]   They can hear you.

MRS. ELVSTED [*Gives a little cry.*]   Oh!

LOEVBORG [*To* BRACK.]   You were kind enough to ask me to join you.

BRACK   Are you coming?

LOEVBORG   If I may.

BRACK   Delighted.

LOEVBORG [*Puts the paper package in his pocket and says to* TESMAN.]   I'd like to show you one or two things before I send it off to the printer.

TESMAN   I say, that'll be fun. Fancy——! Oh, but Hedda, how'll Mrs. Elvsted get home? What?

HEDDA   Oh, we'll manage somehow.

LOEVBORG [*Glances over toward the ladies.*]   Mrs. Elvsted? I shall come back and collect her, naturally. [*Goes closer.*]   About ten o'clock, Mrs. Tesman? Will that suit you?

HEDDA   Yes. That'll suit me admirably.

TESMAN   Good, that's settled. But you mustn't expect me back so early, Hedda.

HEDDA   Stay as long as you c—as long as you like, dear.

MRS. ELVSTED [*Trying to hide her anxiety.*]   Well then, Mr. Loevborg, I'll wait here till you come.

LOEVBORG [*His hat in his hand.*]   Pray do, Mrs. Elvsted.

BRACK   Well, gentlemen, now the party begins. I trust that, in the words of a certain fair lady, we shall enjoy good sport.

HEDDA   What a pity the fair lady can't be there, invisible.

BRACK   Why invisible?

HEDDA   So as to be able to hear some of your uncensored witticisms, your honor.

BRACK [*Laughs.*]   Oh, I shouldn't advise the fair lady to do that.

TESMAN [*Laughs too.*]   I say, Hedda, that's good. By Jove! Fancy that!

BRACK   Well, good night, ladies, good night!

LOEVBORG [*Bows farewell.*]   About ten o'clock, then.

> [BRACK, LOEVBORG *and* TESMAN *go out through the hall. As they do so* BERTHA *enters from the rear room with a lighted lamp. She puts it on the drawing-room table, then goes out the way she came.*]

MRS. ELVSTED [*Has got up and is walking uneasily to and fro.*]   Oh Hedda, Hedda! How is all this going to end?

HEDDA   At ten o'clock, then. He'll be here. I can see him. With a crown of vine-leaves in his hair.[3] Burning and unashamed!

MRS. ELVSTED   Oh, I do hope so!

HEDDA   Can't you see? Then he'll be himself again! He'll be a free man for the rest of his days!

MRS. ELVSTED   Please God you're right.

HEDDA   That's how he'll come! [*Gets up and goes closer.*]   You can doubt him as much as you like. I believe in him! Now we'll see which of us——

MRS. ELVSTED   You're after something, Hedda.

HEDDA   Yes, I am. For once in my life I want to have the power to shape a man's destiny.

---

3. Like Bacchus, the Greek god of wine, and his followers.

MRS. ELVSTED   Haven't you that power already?

HEDDA   No, I haven't. I've never had it.

MRS. ELVSTED   What about your husband?

HEDDA   Him! Oh, if you could only understand how poor I am. And you're allowed to be so rich, so rich! [*Clasps her passionately.*] I think I'll burn your hair off after all!

MRS. ELVSTED   Let me go! Let me go! You frighten me, Hedda!

BERTHA [*In the open doorway.*]   I've laid tea in the dining room, madam.

HEDDA   Good, we're coming.

MRS. ELVSTED   No, no, no! I'd rather go home alone! Now—at once!

HEDDA   Rubbish! First you're going to have some tea, you little idiot. And then—at ten o'clock—Eilert Loevborg will come. With a crown of vine-leaves in his hair!

[*She drags* MRS. ELVSTED *almost forcibly toward the open doorway.*]

Act III

SCENE—*The same. The curtains are drawn across the open doorway, and also across the french windows. The lamp, half turned down, with a shade over it, is burning on the table. In the stove, the door of which is open, a fire has been burning, but it is now almost out.*

MRS. ELVSTED, *wrapped in a large shawl and with her feet resting on a footstool, is sitting near the stove, huddled in the armchair.* HEDDA *is lying asleep on this sofa, fully dressed, with a blanket over her.*

MRS. ELVSTED [*After a pause, suddenly sits up in her chair and listens tensely. Then she sinks wearily back again and sighs.*]   Not back yet! Oh, God! Oh, God! Not back yet!

[BERTHA *tiptoes cautiously in from the hall. She has a letter in her hand.*]

MRS. ELVSTED [*Turns and whispers.*]   What is it? Has someone come?

BERTHA [*Quietly.*]   Yes, a servant's just called with this letter.

MRS. ELVSTED [*Quickly, holding out her hand.*]   A letter! Give it to me!

BERTHA   But it's for the Doctor, madam.

MRS. ELVSTED   Oh. I see.

BERTHA   Miss Tesman's maid brought it. I'll leave it here on the table.

MRS. ELVSTED   Yes, do.

BERTHA [*Puts down the letter.*]   I'd better put the lamp out. It's starting to smoke.

MRS. ELVSTED   Yes, put it out. It'll soon be daylight.

BERTHA [*Puts out the lamp.*]   It's daylight already, madam.

MRS. ELVSTED   Yes. Broad day. And not home yet.

BERTHA   Oh dear, I was afraid this would happen.

MRS. ELVSTED   Were you?

BERTHA   Yes. When I heard that a certain gentleman had returned to town, and saw him go off with them. I've heard all about him.

MRS. ELVSTED   Don't talk so loud. You'll wake your mistress.

BERTHA [*Looks at the sofa and sighs.*]   Yes. Let her go on sleeping, poor dear. Shall I put some more wood on the fire?

MRS. ELVSTED   Thank you, don't bother on my account.

BERTHA   Very good. [*Goes quietly out through the hall.*]

HEDDA [*Wakes as the door closes and looks up.*]   What's that?

MRS. ELVSTED   It was only the maid.

HEDDA [*Looks round.*]   What am I doing here? Oh, now I remember. [*Sits up on the sofa, stretches herself and rubs her eyes.*] What time is it, Thea?

MRS. ELVSTED   It's gone seven.

HEDDA   When did Tesman get back?

MRS. ELVSTED   He's not back yet.

HEDDA   Not home yet?

MRS. ELVSTED [*Gets up.*]   No one's come.

HEDDA   And we sat up waiting for them till four o'clock.

MRS. ELVSTED   God! How I waited for him!

HEDDA [*Yawns and says with her hand in front of her mouth.*]   Oh, dear. We might have saved ourselves the trouble.

MRS. ELVSTED   Did you manage to sleep?

HEDDA   Oh, yes. Quite well, I think. Didn't you get any?

MRS. ELVSTED   Not a wink. I couldn't, Hedda. I just couldn't.

HEDDA [*Gets up and comes over to her.*]   Now, now, now. There's nothing to worry about. I know what's happened.

MRS. ELVSTED   What? Please tell me.

HEDDA   Well, obviously the party went on very late——

MRS. ELVSTED   Oh dear, I suppose it must have. But——

HEDDA   And Tesman didn't want to come home and wake us all up in the middle of the night. [*Laughs.*] Probably wasn't too keen to show his face either, after a spree like that.

MRS. ELVSTED   But where could he have gone?

HEDDA   I should think he's probably slept at his aunts'. They keep his old room for him.

MRS. ELVSTED   No, he can't be with them. A letter came for him just now from Miss Tesman. It's over there.

HEDDA   Oh? [*Looks at the envelope.*]   Yes, it's Auntie Juju's handwriting. Well, he must still be at Judge Brack's, then. And Eilert Loevborg is sitting there, reading to him. With a crown of vine-leaves in his hair.

MRS. ELVSTED   Hedda, you're only saying that. You don't believe it.

HEDDA   Thea, you really are a little fool.

MRS. ELVSTED   Perhaps I am.

HEDDA   You look tired to death.

MRS. ELVSTED   Yes. I am tired to death.

HEDDA   Go to my room and lie down for a little. Do as I say, now; don't argue.

MRS. ELVSTED   No, no. I couldn't possibly sleep.

HEDDA   Of course you can.

MRS. ELVSTED   But your husband'll be home soon. And I must know at once——

HEDDA   I'll tell you when he comes.

MRS. ELVSTED   Promise me, Hedda?

HEDDA   Yes, don't worry. Go and get some sleep.

MRS. ELVSTED   Thank you. All right, I'll try.

[She goes out through the rear room. HEDDA *goes to the french windows and draws the curtains. Broad daylight floods into the room.*

She goes to the writing table, takes a small hand mirror from it and arranges her hair. Then she goes to the door leading into the hall and presses the bell. After a few moments, BERTHA *enters.*]

BERTHA   Did you want anything, madam?

HEDDA   Yes, put some more wood on the fire. I'm freezing.

BERTHA   Bless you, I'll soon have this room warmed up. [*She rakes the embers together and puts a fresh piece of wood on them. Suddenly she stops and listens.*] There's someone at the front door, madam.

HEDDA   Well, go and open it. I'll see to the fire.

BERTHA   It'll burn up in a moment.

[*She goes out through the hall.* HEDDA *kneels on the footstool and puts more wood in the stove. After a few seconds,* GEORGE TESMAN *enters from the hall. He looks tired, and rather worried. He tiptoes toward the open doorway and is about to slip through the curtains.*]

HEDDA [*At the stove, without looking up.*]   Good morning.

TESMAN [*Turns.*]   Hedda! [*Comes nearer.*] Good heavens, are you up already? What?

HEDDA   Yes, I got up very early this morning.

TESMAN   I was sure you'd still be sleeping. Fancy that!

HEDDA   Don't talk so loud. Mrs. Elvsted's asleep in my room.

TESMAN   Mrs. Elvsted? Has she stayed the night here?

HEDDA   Yes. No one came to escort her home.

TESMAN   Oh. No, I suppose not.

HEDDA [*Closes the door of the stove and gets up.*]   Well. Was it fun?

TESMAN   Have you been anxious about me? What?

HEDDA   Not in the least. I asked if you'd had fun.

TESMAN   Oh yes, rather! Well, I thought, for once in a while—The first part was the best; when Eilert read his book to me. We arrived over an hour too early—what about that, eh? By Jove! Brack had a lot of things to see to, so Eilert read to me.

HEDDA [*Sits at the right-hand side of the table.*]   Well? Tell me about it.

TESMAN [*Sits on a footstool by the stove.*]   Honestly, Hedda, you've no idea what a book that's going to be. It's really one of the most remarkable things that's ever been written. By Jove!

HEDDA   Oh, never mind about the book——

TESMAN   I'm going to make a confession to you, Hedda. When he'd finished reading a sort of beastly feeling came over me.

HEDDA   Beastly feeling?

TESMAN   I found myself envying Eilert for being able to write like that. Imagine that, Hedda!

HEDDA   Yes. I can imagine.

TESMAN   What a tragedy that with all those gifts he should be so incorrigible.

HEDDA   You mean he's less afraid of life than most men?

TESMAN   Good heavens, no. He just doesn't know the meaning of the word moderation.

HEDDA   What happened afterwards?

TESMAN   Well, looking back on it I suppose you might almost call it an orgy, Hedda.

HEDDA   Had he vine-leaves in his hair?

TESMAN   Vine-leaves? No, I didn't see any of them. He made a long, rambling oration in honor of the woman who'd inspired him to write this book. Yes, those were the words he used.

HEDDA   Did he name her?

TESMAN   No. But I suppose it must be Mrs. Elvsted. You wait and see!

HEDDA   Where did you leave him?

TESMAN   On the way home. We left in a bunch—the last of us, that is—and Brack came with us to get a little fresh air. Well, then, you see, we agreed we ought to see Eilert home. He'd had a drop too much.

HEDDA   You don't say?

TESMAN   But now comes the funny part, Hedda. Or I should really say the tragic part. Oh, I'm almost ashamed to tell you. For Eilert's sake, I mean—

HEDDA   Why, what happened?

TESMAN   Well, you see, as we were walking toward town I happened to drop behind for a minute. Only for a minute—er—you understand——

HEDDA   Yes, yes——

TESMAN   Well then, when I ran on to catch them up, what do you think I found by the roadside. What?

HEDDA   How on earth should I know?

TESMAN   You mustn't tell anyone, Hedda. What? Promise me that—for Eilert's sake. [Takes a package wrapped in paper from his coat pocket.] Just fancy! I found this.

HEDDA   Isn't this the one he brought here yesterday?

TESMAN   Yes! The whole of that precious, irreplaceable manuscript! And he went and lost it! Didn't even notice! What about that? By Jove! Tragic.

HEDDA   But why didn't you give it back to him?

TESMAN   I didn't dare to, in the state he was in.

HEDDA   Didn't you tell any of the others?

TESMAN   Good heavens, no. I didn't want to do that. For Eilert's sake, you understand.

HEDDA   Then no one else knows you have his manuscript?

TESMAN   No. And no one must be allowed to know.

HEDDA   Didn't it come up in the conversation later?

TESMAN   I didn't get a chance to talk to him any more. As soon as we got into the outskirts of town, he and one or two of the others gave us the slip. Disappeared, by Jove!

HEDDA   Oh? I suppose they took him home.

TESMAN   Yes, I imagine that was the idea. Brack left us, too.

HEDDA   And what have you been up to since then?

TESMAN   Well, I and one or two of the others—awfully jolly chaps, they were—went back to where one of them lived, and had a cup of morning coffee. Morning-after coffee—what? Ah, well. I'll just lie down for a bit and give Eilert time to sleep it off, poor chap, then I'll run over and give this back to him.

HEDDA [Holds out her hand for the package.]   No, don't do that. Not just yet. Let me read it first.

TESMAN   Oh no, really, Hedda dear, honestly, I daren't do that.

HEDDA   Daren't?

TESMAN   No—imagine how desperate he'll be when he wakes up and finds his manuscript's missing. He hasn't any copy, you see. He told me so himself.

HEDDA   Can't a thing like that be rewritten?

TESMAN   Oh no, not possibly, I shouldn't think. I mean, the inspiration, you know——

HEDDA   Oh, yes. I'd forgotten that. [*Casually.*] By the way, there's a letter for you.

TESMAN   Is there? Fancy that!

HEDDA [*Holds it out to him.*]   It came early this morning.

TESMAN   I say, it's from Auntie Juju! What on earth can it be? [*Puts the package on the other footstool, opens the letter, reads it and jumps up.*] Oh, Hedda! She says poor Auntie Rena's dying.

HEDDA   Well, we've been expecting that.

TESMAN   She says if I want to see her I must go quickly. I'll run over at once.

HEDDA [*Hides a smile.*]   Run?

TESMAN   Hedda dear, I suppose you wouldn't like to come with me? What about that, eh?

HEDDA [*Gets up and says wearily and with repulsion.*]   No, no, don't ask me to do anything like that. I can't bear illness or death. I loathe anything ugly.

TESMAN   Yes, yes. Of course. [*In a dither.*] My hat? My overcoat? Oh yes, in the hall. I do hope I won't get there too late, Hedda? What?

HEDDA   You'll be all right if you run.
    [BERTHA *enters from the hall.*]

BERTHA   Judge Brack's outside and wants to know if he can come in.

TESMAN   At this hour? No, I can't possibly receive him now.

HEDDA   I can. [*To* BERTHA.] Ask his honor to come in.
    [BERTHA *goes.*]

HEDDA [*Whispers quickly.*]   The manuscript, Tesman. [*She snatches it from the footstool.*]

TESMAN   Yes, give it to me.

HEDDA   No, I'll look after it for now.
    [*She goes over to the writing table and puts it in the bookcase.* TES-MAN *stands dithering, unable to get his gloves on.* JUDGE BRACK *enters from the hall.*]

HEDDA [*Nods to him.*]   Well, you're an early bird.

BRACK   Yes, aren't I? [*To* TESMAN.] Are you up and about, too?

TESMAN   Yes, I've got to go and see my aunts. Poor Auntie Rena's dying.

BRACK   Oh dear, is she? Then you mustn't let me detain you. At so tragic a——

TESMAN   Yes, I really must run. Good-bye! Good-bye! [*Runs out through the hall.*]

HEDDA [*Goes nearer.*]   You seem to have had excellent sport last night— Judge.

BRACK   Indeed yes, Mrs. Hedda. I haven't even had time to take my clothes off.

HEDDA   *You* haven't either?

BRACK   As you see. What's Tesman told you about last night's escapades?

HEDDA Oh, only some boring story about having gone and drunk coffee somewhere.

BRACK Yes, I've heard about that coffee party. Eilert Loevborg wasn't with them, I gather?

HEDDA No, they took him home first.

BRACK Did Tesman go with him?

HEDDA No, one or two of the others, he said.

BRACK [*Smiles.*] George Tesman is a credulous man, Mrs. Hedda.

HEDDA God knows. But—has something happened?

BRACK Well, yes, I'm afraid it has.

HEDDA I see. Sit down and tell me.

    [*She sits on the left of the table,* BRACK *at the long side of it, near her.*]

HEDDA Well?

BRACK I had a special reason for keeping track of my guests last night. Or perhaps I should say some of my guests.

HEDDA Including Eilert Loevborg?

BRACK I must confess—yes.

HEDDA You're beginning to make me curious.

BRACK Do you know where he and some of my other guests spent the latter half of last night, Mrs. Hedda?

HEDDA Tell me. If it won't shock me.

BRACK Oh, I don't think it'll shock you. They found themselves participating in an exceedingly animated *soirée.*[4]

HEDDA Of a sporting character?

BRACK Of a highly sporting character.

HEDDA Tell me more.

BRACK Loevborg had received an invitation in advance—as had the others. I knew all about that. But he had refused. As you know, he's become a new man.

HEDDA Up at the Elvsteds', yes. But he went?

BRACK Well, you see, Mrs. Hedda, last night at my house, unhappily, the spirit moved him.

HEDDA Yes, I hear he became inspired.

BRACK Somewhat violently inspired. And as a result, I suppose, his thoughts strayed. We men, alas, don't always stick to our principles as firmly as we should.

HEDDA I'm sure you're an exception, Judge Brack. But go on about Loevborg.

BRACK Well, to cut a long story short, he ended up in the establishment of a certain Mademoiselle Danielle.

HEDDA Mademoiselle Danielle?

BRACK She was holding the *soirée.* For a selected circle of friends and admirers.

HEDDA Has she got red hair?

BRACK She has.

HEDDA A singer of some kind?

4. Evening party.

BRACK   Yes—among other accomplishments. She's also a celebrated hunt-
ress—of men, Mrs. Hedda. I'm sure you've heard about her. Eilert
Loevborg used to be one of her most ardent patrons. In his salad days.[5]

HEDDA   And how did all this end?

BRACK   Not entirely amicably, from all accounts. Mademoiselle Danielle
began by receiving him with the utmost tenderness and ended by resorting to her fists.

HEDDA   Against Loevborg?

BRACK   Yes. He accused her, or her friends, of having robbed him. He
claimed his pocketbook had been stolen. Among other things. In short,
he seems to have made a bloodthirsty scene.

HEDDA   And what did this lead to?

BRACK   It led to a general free-for-all, in which both sexes participated.
Fortunately, in the end the police arrived.

HEDDA   The police too?

BRACK   Yes. I'm afraid it may turn out to be rather an expensive joke for
Master Eilert. Crazy fool!

HEDDA   Oh?

BRACK   Apparently he put up a very violent resistance. Hit one of the constables on the ear and tore his uniform. He had to accompany them to
the police station.

HEDDA   Where did you learn all this?

BRACK   From the police.

HEDDA   [To herself.]   So that's what happened. He didn't have a crown of
vine-leaves in his hair.

BRACK   Vine-leaves, Mrs. Hedda?

HEDDA   [In her normal voice again.]   But, tell me, Judge, why do you take
such a close interest in Eilert Loevborg?

BRACK   For one thing it'll hardly be a matter of complete indifference to
me if it's revealed in court that he came there straight from my house.

HEDDA   Will it come to court?

BRACK   Of course. Well, I don't regard that as particularly serious. Still, I
thought it my duty, as a friend of the family, to give you and your husband
a full account of his nocturnal adventures.

HEDDA   Why?

BRACK   Because I've a shrewd suspicion that he's hoping to use you as a
kind of screen.

HEDDA   What makes you think that?

BRACK   Oh, for heaven's sake, Mrs. Hedda, we're not blind. You wait and
see. This Mrs. Elvsted won't be going back to her husband just yet.

HEDDA   Well, if there were anything between those two there are plenty
of other places where they could meet.

BRACK   Not in anyone's home. From now on every respectable house will
once again be closed to Eilert Loevborg.

HEDDA   And mine should be too, you mean?

BRACK   Yes. I confess I should find it more than irksome if this gentleman
were to be granted unrestricted access to this house. If he were super-
fluously to intrude into——

5. Indiscreet youth.

HEDDA   The triangle?

BRACK   Precisely. For me it would be like losing a home.

HEDDA   [*Looks at him and smiles.*]   I see. You want to be the cock of the walk.

BRACK   [*Nods slowly and lowers his voice.*]   Yes, that is my aim. And I shall fight for it with—every weapon at my disposal.

HEDDA   [*As her smile fades.*]   You're a dangerous man, aren't you? When you really want something.

BRACK   You think so?

HEDDA   Yes. I'm beginning to think so. I'm deeply thankful you haven't any kind of hold over me.

BRACK   [*Laughs equivocally.*]   Well, well, Mrs. Hedda—perhaps you're right. If I had, who knows what I might not think up?

HEDDA   Come, Judge Brack. That sounds almost like a threat.

BRACK   [*Gets up.*]   Heaven forbid! In the creation of a triangle—and its continuance—the question of compulsion should never arise.

HEDDA   Exactly what I was thinking.

BRACK   Well, I've said what I came to say. I must be getting back. Good-bye, Mrs. Hedda. [*Goes toward the french windows.*]

HEDDA   [*Gets up.*]   Are you going out through the garden?

BRACK   Yes, it's shorter.

HEDDA   Yes. And it's the back door, isn't it?

BRACK   I've nothing against back doors. They can be quite intriguing—sometimes.

HEDDA   When people fire pistols out of them, for example?

BRACK   [*In the doorway, laughs.*]   Oh, people don't shoot tame cocks.

HEDDA   [*Laughs too.*]   I suppose not. When they've only got one.

[*They nod good-bye, laughing. He goes. She closes the french windows behind him, and stands for a moment, looking out pensively. Then she walks across the room and glances through the curtains in the open doorway. Goes to the writing table, takes* LOEVBORG's *package from the bookcase and is about to leaf through the pages when* BERTHA *is heard remonstrating loudly in the hall.* HEDDA *turns and listens. She hastily puts the package back in the drawer, locks it and puts the key on the inkstand.* EILERT LOEVBORG, *with his overcoat on and his hat in his hand, throws the door open. He looks somewhat confused and excited.*]

LOEVBORG   [*Shouts as he enters.*]   I must come in, I tell you! Let me pass! [*He closes the door, turns, sees* HEDDA, *controls himself immediately and bows.*]

HEDDA   [*At the writing table.*]   Well, Mr. Loevborg, this is rather a late hour to be collecting Thea.

LOEVBORG   And an early hour to call on you. Please forgive me.

HEDDA   How do you know she's still here?

LOEVBORG   They told me at her lodgings that she has been out all night.

HEDDA   [*Goes to the table.*]   Did you notice anything about their behavior when they told you?

LOEVBORG   [*Looks at her, puzzled.*]   Notice anything?

HEDDA   Did they sound as if they thought it—strange?

LOEVBORG   [*Suddenly understands.*]   Oh, I see what you mean. I'm dragging her down with me. No, as a matter of fact I didn't notice anything. I suppose Tesman isn't up yet?

HEDDA No, I don't think so.

LOEVBORG When did he get home?

HEDDA Very late.

LOEVBORG Did he tell you anything?

HEDDA Yes. I gather you had a merry party at Judge Brack's last night.

LOEVBORG He didn't tell you anything else?

HEDDA I don't think so. I was so terribly sleepy——

[MRS. ELVSTED *comes through the curtains in the open doorway.*]

MRS. ELVSTED [*Runs toward him.*] Oh, Eilert! At last!

LOEVBORG Yes—at last. And too late.

MRS. ELVSTED What is too late?

LOEVBORG Everything—now. I'm finished, Thea.

MRS. ELVSTED Oh, no, no! Don't say that!

LOEVBORG You'll say it yourself, when you've heard what I——

MRS. ELVSTED I don't want to hear anything!

HEDDA Perhaps you'd rather speak to her alone? I'd better go.

LOEVBORG No, stay.

MRS. ELVSTED But I don't want to hear anything, I tell you!

LOEVBORG It's not about last night.

MRS. ELVSTED Then what——?

LOEVBORG I want to tell you that from now on we must stop seeing each other.

MRS. ELVSTED Stop seeing each other!

HEDDA [*Involuntarily.*] I knew it!

LOEVBORG I have no further use for you, Thea.

MRS. ELVSTED You can stand there and say that! No further use for me! Surely I can go on helping you? We'll go on working together, won't we?

LOEVBORG I don't intend to do any more work from now on.

MRS. ELVSTED [*Desperately.*] Then what use have I for my life?

LOEVBORG You must try to live as if you had never known me.

MRS. ELVSTED But I can't!

LOEVBORG Try to, Thea. Go back home——

MRS. ELVSTED Never! I want to be wherever you are! I won't let myself be driven away like this! I want to stay here—and be with you when the book comes out.

HEDDA [*Whispers.*] Ah, yes! The book!

LOEVBORG [*Looks at her.*] Our book; Thea's and mine. It belongs to both of us.

MRS. ELVSTED Oh, yes! I feel that, too! And I've a right to be with you when it comes into the world. I want to see people respect and honor you again. And the joy! The joy! I want to share it with you!

LOEVBORG Thea—our book will never come into the world.

HEDDA Ah!

MRS. ELVSTED Not——?

LOEVBORG It cannot. Ever.

MRS. ELVSTED Eilert—what have you done with the manuscript? Where is it?

LOEVBORG Oh, Thea, please don't ask me that!

MRS. ELVSTED   Yes, yes—I must know. I've a right to know. Now!

LOEVBORG   The manuscript. I've torn it up.

MRS. ELVSTED [*Screams.*]   No, no!

HEDDA [*Involuntarily.*]   But that's not——!

LOEVBORG [*Looks at her.*]   Not true, you think?

HEDDA [*Controls herself.*]   Why—yes, of course it is, if you say so. It just sounded so incredible——

LOEVBORG   It's true, nevertheless.

MRS. ELVSTED   Oh, my God, my God, Hedda—he's destroyed his own book!

LOEVBORG   I have destroyed my life. Why not my life's work, too?

MRS. ELVSTED   And you—did this last night?

LOEVBORG   Yes, Thea. I tore it into a thousand pieces. And scattered them out across the fjord.[6] It's good, clean, salt water. Let it carry them away; let them drift in the current and the wind. And in a little while, they will sink. Deeper and deeper. As I shall, Thea.

MRS. ELVSTED   Do you know, Eilert—this book—all my life I shall feel as though you'd killed a little child?

LOEVBORG   You're right. It is like killing a child.

MRS. ELVSTED   But how could you? It was my child, too!

HEDDA [*Almost inaudibly.*]   Oh—the child—!

MRS. ELVSTED [*Breathes heavily.*]   It's all over, then. Well—I'll go now, Hedda.

HEDDA   You're not leaving town?

MRS. ELVSTED   I don't know what I'm going to do. I can't see anything except—darkness.

[*She goes out through the hall.*]

HEDDA [*Waits a moment.*]   Aren't you going to escort her home, Mr. Loevborg?

LOEVBORG   I? Through the streets? Do you want me to let people see her with me?

HEDDA   Of course I don't know what else may have happened last night. But is it so utterly beyond redress?

LOEVBORG   It isn't just last night. It'll go on happening. I know it. But the curse of it is, I don't want to live that kind of life. I don't want to start all that again. She's broken my courage. I can't spit in the eyes of the world any longer.

HEDDA [*As though to herself.*]   That pretty little fool's been trying to shape a man's destiny. [*Looks at him.*] But how could you be so heartless toward her?

LOEVBORG   Don't call me heartless!

HEDDA   To go and destroy the one thing that's made her life worth living? You don't call that heartless?

LOEVBORG   Do you want to know the truth, Hedda?

HEDDA   The truth?

LOEVBORG   Promise me first—give me your word—that you'll never let Thea know about this.

HEDDA   I give you my word.

---

6. Inlet of the sea.

LOEVBORG   Good. Well; what I told her just now was a lie.

HEDDA   About the manuscript?

LOEVBORG   Yes. I didn't tear it up. Or throw it in the fjord.

HEDDA   You didn't? But where is it, then?

LOEVBORG   I destroyed it, all the same. I destroyed it, Hedda!

HEDDA   I don't understand.

LOEVBORG   Thea said that what I had done was like killing a child.

HEDDA   Yes. That's what she said.

LOEVBORG   But to kill a child isn't the worst thing a father can do to it.

HEDDA   What could be worse than that?

LOEVBORG   Hedda—suppose a man came home one morning, after a night of debauchery, and said to the mother of his child: "Look here. I've been wandering round all night. I've been to—such-and-such a place and such-and-such a place. And I had our child with me. I took him to—these places. And I've lost him. Just—lost him. God knows where he is or whose hands he's fallen into."

HEDDA   I see. But when all's said and done, this was only a book——

LOEVBORG   Thea's heart and soul were in that book. It was her whole life.

HEDDA   Yes. I understand.

LOEVBORG   Well, then you must also understand that she and I cannot possibly ever see each other again.

HEDDA   Where will you go?

LOEVBORG   Nowhere. I just want to put an end to it all. As soon as possible.

HEDDA [*Takes a step toward him.*]   Eilert Loevborg, listen to me. Do it—beautifully!

LOEVBORG   Beautifully? [*Smiles.*] With a crown of vine-leaves in my hair? The way you used to dream of me—in the old days?

HEDDA   No. I don't believe in that crown any longer. But—do it beautifully, all the same. Just this once. Good-bye. You must go now. And don't come back.

LOEVBORG   Adieu, madam. Give my love to George Tesman. [*Turns to go.*]

HEDDA   Wait. I want to give you a souvenir to take with you.

[*She goes over to the writing table, opens the drawer and the pistol-case, and comes back to* LOEVBORG *with one of the pistols.*]

LOEVBORG [*Looks at her.*]   This? Is this the souvenir?

HEDDA [*Nods slowly.*]   You recognize it? You looked down its barrel once.

LOEVBORG   You should have used it then.

HEDDA   Here! Use it now!

LOEVBORG [*Puts the pistol in his breast pocket.*]   Thank you.

HEDDA   Do it beautifully, Eilert Loevborg. Only promise me that!

LOEVBORG   Good-bye, Hedda Gabler.

[*He goes out through the hall.* HEDDA *stands by the door for a moment, listening. Then she goes over to the writing table, takes out the package containing the manuscript, glances inside it, pulls some of the pages half out and looks at them. Then she takes it to the armchair by the stove and sits down with the package in her lap. After a moment, she opens the door of the stove; then she opens the packet.*]

HEDDA [*Throws one of the pages into the stove and whispers to herself.*]   I'm burning your child, Thea! You with your beautiful wavy hair! [*She throws a few more pages into the stove.*] The child Eilert Loevborg gave you. [*Throws the rest of the manuscript in.*] I'm burning it! I'm burning your child!

Act IV

SCENE—*The same. It is evening. The drawing room is in darkness. The small room is illuminated by the hanging lamp over the table. The curtains are drawn across the french windows.* HEDDA, *dressed in black, is walking up and down in the darkened room. Then she goes into the small room and crosses to the left. A few chords are heard from the piano. She comes back into the drawing room.*

BERTHA *comes through the small room from the right with a lighted lamp, which she places on the table in front of the corner sofa in the drawing room. Her eyes are red with crying, and she has black ribbons on her cap. She goes quietly out, right.* HEDDA *goes over to the french windows, draws the curtains slightly to one side and looks out into the darkness.*

A few moments later, MISS TESMAN *enters from the hall. She is dressed in mourning, with a black hat and veil.* HEDDA *goes to meet her and holds out her hand.*

MISS TESMAN Well, Hedda, here I am in the weeds of sorrow. My poor sister has ended her struggles at last.

HEDDA I've already heard. Tesman sent me a card.

MISS TESMAN Yes, he promised me he would. But I thought, no, I must go and break the news of death to Hedda myself—here, in the house of life.

HEDDA It's very kind of you.

MISS TESMAN Ah, Rena shouldn't have chosen a time like this to pass away. This is no moment for Hedda's house to be a place of mourning.

HEDDA [*Changing the subject.*] She died peacefully, Miss Tesman?

MISS TESMAN Oh, it was quite beautiful! The end came so calmly. And she was so happy at being able to see George once again. And say goodbye to him. Hasn't he come home yet?

HEDDA No. He wrote that I mustn't expect him too soon. But please sit down.

MISS TESMAN No, thank you, Hedda dear—bless you. I'd like to. But I've so little time. I must dress her and lay her out as well as I can. She shall go to her grave looking really beautiful.

HEDDA Can't I help with anything?

MISS TESMAN Why, you mustn't think of such a thing! Hedda Tesman mustn't let her hands be soiled by contact with death. Or her thoughts. Not at this time.

HEDDA One can't always control one's thoughts.

MISS TESMAN [*Continues.*] Ah, well, that's life. Now we must start to sew poor Rena's shroud. There'll be sewing to be done in this house too before long, I shouldn't wonder. But not for a shroud, praise God.

[GEORGE TESMAN *enters from the hall.*]

HEDDA You've come at last! Thank heavens!

TESMAN   Are you here, Auntie Juju? With Hedda? Fancy that!

MISS TESMAN   I was just on the point of leaving, dear boy. Well, have you done everything you promised me?

TESMAN   No, I'm afraid I forgot half of it. I'll have to run over again tomorrow. My head's in a complete whirl today. I can't collect my thoughts.

MISS TESMAN   But George dear, you mustn't take it like this.

TESMAN   Oh? Well—er—how should I?

MISS TESMAN   You must be happy in your grief. Happy for what's happened. As I am.

TESMAN   Oh, yes, yes. You're thinking of Aunt Rena.

HEDDA   It'll be lonely for you now, Miss Tesman.

MISS TESMAN   For the first few days, yes. But it won't last long, I hope. Poor dear Rena's little room isn't going to stay empty.

TESMAN   Oh? Whom are you going to move in there? What?

MISS TESMAN   Oh, there's always some poor invalid who needs care and attention.

HEDDA   Do you really want another cross like that to bear?

MISS TESMAN   Cross! God forgive you, child. It's been no cross for me.

HEDDA   But now—if a complete stranger comes to live with you——

MISS TESMAN   Oh, one soon makes friends with invalids. And I need so much to have someone to live for. Like you, my dear. Well, I expect there'll soon be work in this house too for an old aunt, praise God!

HEDDA   Oh—please!

TESMAN   By Jove, yes! What a splendid time the three of us could have together if——

HEDDA   If?

TESMAN   [Uneasily.]   Oh, never mind. It'll all work out. Let's hope so—what?

MISS TESMAN   Yes, yes. Well, I'm sure you two would like to be alone. [Smiles.] Perhaps Hedda may have something to tell you, George. Goodbye. I must go home to Rena. [Turns to the door.] Dear God, how strange! Now Rena is with me and with poor dear Joachim.

TESMAN   Fancy that. Yes, Auntie Juju! What?

    [MISS TESMAN goes out through the hall.]

HEDDA   [Follows TESMAN coldly and searchingly with her eyes.]   I really believe this death distresses you more than it does her.

TESMAN   Oh, it isn't just Auntie Rena. It's Eilert I'm so worried about.

HEDDA   [Quickly.]   Is there any news of him?

TESMAN   I ran over to see him this afternoon. I wanted to tell him his manuscript was in safe hands.

HEDDA   Oh? You didn't find him?

TESMAN   No. He wasn't at home. But later I met Mrs. Elvsted and she told me he'd been here early this morning.

HEDDA   Yes, just after you'd left.

TESMAN   It seems he said he'd torn the manuscript up. What?

HEDDA   Yes, he claimed to have done so.

TESMAN   You told him we had it, of course?

HEDDA   No. [Quickly.] Did you tell Mrs. Elvsted?

TESMAN   No, I didn't like to. But you ought to have told him. Think if he should go home and do something desperate! Give me the manuscript, Hedda. I'll run over to him with it right away. Where did you put it?

HEDDA [*Cold and motionless, leaning against the armchair.*] I haven't got it any longer.

TESMAN Haven't got it? What on earth do you mean?

HEDDA I've burned it.

TESMAN [*Starts, terrified.*] Burned it! Burned Eilert's manuscript!

HEDDA Don't shout. The servant will hear you.

TESMAN Burned it! But in heaven's name——! Oh, no, no, no! This is impossible!

HEDDA Well, it's true.

TESMAN But Hedda, do you realize what you've done? That's appropriating lost property! It's against the law! By Jove! You ask Judge Brack and see if I'm not right.

HEDDA You'd be well advised not to talk about it to Judge Brack or anyone else.

TESMAN But how could you go and do such a dreadful thing? What on earth put the idea into your head? What came over you? Answer me! What?

HEDDA [*Represses an almost imperceptible smile.*] I did it for your sake, George.

TESMAN For my sake?

HEDDA When you came home this morning and described how he'd read his book to you——

TESMAN Yes, yes?

HEDDA You admitted you were jealous of him.

TESMAN But, good heavens, I didn't mean it literally!

HEDDA No matter. I couldn't bear the thought that anyone else should push you into the background.

TESMAN [*Torn between doubt and joy.*] Hedda—is this true? But—but—but I never realized you loved me like that! Fancy——

HEDDA Well, I suppose you'd better know. I'm going to have—— [*Breaks off and says violently.*] No, no—you'd better ask your Auntie Juju. She'll tell you.

TESMAN Hedda! I think I understand what you mean. [*Clasps his hands.*] Good heavens, can it really be true! What?

HEDDA Don't shout. The servant will hear you.

TESMAN [*Laughing with joy.*] The servant! I say, that's good! The servant! Why, that's Bertha! I'll run out and tell her at once!

HEDDA [*Clenches her hands in despair.*] Oh, it's destroying me, all this— it's destroying me!

TESMAN I say, Hedda, what's up? What?

HEDDA [*Cold, controlled.*] Oh, it's all so—absurd—George.

TESMAN Absurd? That I'm so happy? But surely——? Ah, well—perhaps I won't say anything to Bertha.

HEDDA No, do. She might as well know too.

TESMAN No, no, I won't tell her yet. But Auntie Juju—I must let her know! And you—you called me George! For the first time! Fancy that! Oh, it'll make Auntie Juju so happy, all this! So very happy!

HEDDA Will she be happy when she hears I've burned Eilert Loevborg's manuscript—for your sake?

TESMAN No, I'd forgotten about that. Of course no one must be allowed to know about the manuscript. But that you're burning with love for me,

Hedda, I must certainly let Auntie Juju know that. I say, I wonder if young wives often feel like that toward their husbands? What?

HEDDA   You might ask Auntie Juju about that too.

TESMAN   I will, as soon as I get the chance. [*Looks uneasy and thoughtful again.*] But I say, you know, that manuscript. Dreadful business. Poor Eilert!

   [MRS. ELVSTED, *dressed as on her first visit, with hat and overcoat, enters from the hall.*]

MRS. ELVSTED [*Greets them hastily and tremulously.*]   Oh, Hedda dear, do please forgive me for coming here again.

HEDDA   Why, Thea, what's happened?

TESMAN   Is it anything to do with Eilert Loevborg? What?

MRS. ELVSTED   Yes—I'm so dreadfully afraid he may have met with an accident.

HEDDA [*Grips her arm.*]   You think so?

TESMAN   But, good heavens, Mrs. Elvsted, what makes you think that?

MRS. ELVSTED   I heard them talking about him at the boarding-house, as I went in. Oh, there are the most terrible rumors being spread about him in town today.

TESMAN   Fancy. Yes, I heard about them too. But I can testify that he went straight home to bed. Fancy that!

HEDDA   Well—what did they say in the boarding-house?

MRS. ELVSTED   Oh, I couldn't find out anything. Either they didn't know, or else—— They stopped talking when they saw me. And I didn't dare to ask.

TESMAN [*Fidgets uneasily.*]   We must hope—we must hope you misheard them, Mrs. Elvsted.

MRS. ELVSTED   No, no, I'm sure it was he they were talking about. I heard them say something about a hospital——

TESMAN   Hospital!

HEDDA   Oh no, surely that's impossible!

MRS. ELVSTED   Oh, I became so afraid. So I went up to his rooms and asked to see him.

HEDDA   Do you think that was wise, Thea?

MRS. ELVSTED   Well, what else could I do? I couldn't bear the uncertainty any longer.

TESMAN   But you didn't manage to find him either? What?

MRS. ELVSTED   No. And they had no idea where he was. They said he hadn't been home since yesterday afternoon.

TESMAN   Since yesterday? Fancy that!

MRS. ELVSTED   I'm sure he must have met with an accident.

TESMAN   Hedda, I wonder if I ought to go into town and make one or two enquiries?

HEDDA   No, no, don't you get mixed up in this.

   [JUDGE BRACK *enters from the hall, hat in hand.* BERTHA, *who has opened the door for him, closes it. He looks serious and greets them silently.*]

TESMAN   Hullo, my dear Judge. Fancy seeing you!

BRACK   I had to come and talk to you.

TESMAN   I can see Auntie Juju's told you the news.

BRACK   Yes, I've heard about that too.

TESMAN   Tragic, isn't it?

BRACK   Well, my dear chap, that depends on how you look at it.

TESMAN [*Looks uncertainly at him.*]   Has something else happened?

BRACK   Yes.

HEDDA   Another tragedy?

BRACK   That also depends on how you look at it, Mrs. Tesman.

MRS. ELVSTED   Oh, it's something to do with Eilert Loevborg!

BRACK [*Looks at her for a moment.*]   How did you guess? Perhaps you've heard already——

MRS. ELVSTED [*Confused.*]   No, no, not at all—I——

TESMAN   For heaven's sake, tell us!

BRACK [*Shrugs his shoulders.*]   Well, I'm afraid they've taken him to the hospital. He's dying.

MRS. ELVSTED [*Screams.*]   Oh God, God!

TESMAN   The hospital! Dying!

HEDDA [*Involuntarily.*]   So quickly!

MRS. ELVSTED [*Weeping.*]   Oh, Hedda! And we parted enemies!

HEDDA [*Whispers.*]   Thea—Thea!

MRS. ELVSTED [*Ignoring her.*]   I must see him! I must see him before he dies!

BRACK   It's no use, Mrs. Elvsted. No one's allowed to see him now.

MRS. ELVSTED   But what's happened to him? You must tell me!

TESMAN   He hasn't tried to do anything to himself? What?

HEDDA   Yes, he has. I'm sure of it.

TESMAN   Hedda, how can you——?

BRACK [*Who has not taken his eyes from her.*]   I'm afraid you've guessed correctly, Mrs. Tesman.

MRS. ELVSTED   How dreadful!

TESMAN   Attempted suicide! Fancy that!

HEDDA   Shot himself!

BRACK   Right again, Mrs. Tesman.

MRS. ELVSTED [*Tries to compose herself.*]   When did this happen, Judge Brack?

BRACK   This afternoon. Between three and four.

TESMAN   But, good heavens—where? What?

BRACK [*A little hesitantly.*]   Where? Why, my dear chap, in his rooms of course.

MRS. ELVSTED   No, that's impossible. I was there soon after six.

BRACK   Well, it must have been somewhere else, then. I don't know exactly. I only know that they found him. He'd shot himself—through the breast.

MRS. ELVSTED   Oh, how horrible! That he should end like that!

HEDDA [*To* BRACK.]   Through the breast, you said?

BRACK   That is what I said.

HEDDA   Not through the head?

BRACK   Through the breast, Mrs. Tesman.

HEDDA   The breast. Yes; yes. That's good, too.

BRACK   Why, Mrs. Tesman?

HEDDA   Oh—no, I didn't mean anything.

TESMAN And the wound's dangerous you say? What?

BRACK Mortal. He's probably already dead.

MRS. ELVSTED Yes, yes—I feel it! It's all over. All over. Oh Hedda——!

TESMAN But, tell me, how did you manage to learn all this?

BRACK [Curtly.] From the police. I spoke to one of them.

HEDDA [Loudly, clearly.] At last! Oh, thank God!

TESMAN [Appalled.] For God's sake, Hedda, what are you saying?

HEDDA I am saying there's beauty in what he has done.

BRACK Mm—Mrs. Tesman——

TESMAN Beauty! Oh, but I say!

MRS. ELVSTED Hedda, how can you talk of beauty in connection with a thing like this?

HEDDA Eilert Loevborg has settled his account with life. He's had the courage to do what—what he had to do.

MRS. ELVSTED No, that's not why it happened. He did it because he was mad.

TESMAN He did it because he was desperate.

HEDDA You're wrong! I know!

MRS. ELVSTED He must have been mad. The same as when he tore up the manuscript.

BRACK [Starts.] Manuscript? Did he tear it up?

MRS. ELVSTED Yes. Last night.

TESMAN [Whispers.] Oh, Hedda, we shall never be able to escape from this.

BRACK Hm. Strange.

TESMAN [Wanders round the room.] To think of Eilert dying like that. And not leaving behind him the thing that would have made his name endure.

MRS. ELVSTED If only it could be pieced together again!

TESMAN Yes, fancy! If only it could! I'd give anything——

MRS. ELVSTED Perhaps it can, Mr. Tesman.

TESMAN What do you mean?

MRS. ELVSTED [Searches in the pocket of her dress.] Look! I kept the notes he dictated it from.

HEDDA [Takes a step nearer.] Ah!

TESMAN You kept them, Mrs. Elvsted! What?

MRS. ELVSTED Yes, here they are. I brought them with me when I left home. They've been in my pocket ever since.

TESMAN Let me have a look.

MRS. ELVSTED [Hands him a wad of small sheets of paper.] They're in a terrible muddle. All mixed up.

TESMAN I say, just fancy if we can sort them out! Perhaps if we work on them together——?

MRS. ELVSTED Oh, yes! Let's try, anyway!

TESMAN We'll manage it. We must! I shall dedicate my life to this.

HEDDA You, George? Your life?

TESMAN Yes—well, all the time I can spare. My book'll have to wait. Hedda, you do understand? What? I owe it to Eilert's memory.

HEDDA Perhaps.

TESMAN Well, my dear Mrs. Elvsted, you and I'll have to pool our brains.

No use crying over spilt milk, what? We must try to approach this matter calmly.

MRS. ELVSTED   Yes, yes, Mr. Tesman. I'll do my best.

TESMAN   Well, come over here and let's start looking at these notes right away. Where shall we sit? Here? No, the other room. You'll excuse us, won't you, Judge? Come along with me, Mrs. Elvsted.

MRS. ELVSTED   Oh, God! If only we can manage to do it!

[TESMAN and MRS. ELVSTED *go into the rear room. He takes off his hat and overcoat. They sit at the table beneath the hanging lamp and absorb themselves in the notes.* HEDDA *walks across to the stove and sits in the armchair. After a moment,* BRACK *goes over to her.*]

HEDDA [*Half aloud.*]   Oh, Judge! This act of Eilert Loevborg's—doesn't it give one a sense of release!

BRACK   Release, Mrs. Hedda? Well, it's a release for him, of course——

HEDDA   Oh, I don't mean him—I mean me! The release of knowing that someone can do something really brave! Something beautiful!

BRACK [*Smiles.*]   Hm—my dear Mrs. Hedda——

HEDDA   Oh, I know what you're going to say. You're a bourgeois at heart too, just like—ah, well!

BRACK [*Looks at her.*]   Eilert Loevborg has meant more to you than you're willing to admit to yourself. Or am I wrong?

HEDDA   I'm not answering questions like that from you. I only know that Eilert Loevborg has had the courage to live according to his own principles. And now, at last, he's done something big! Something beautiful! To have the courage and the will to rise from the feast of life so early!

BRACK   It distresses me deeply, Mrs. Hedda, but I'm afraid I must rob you of that charming illusion.

HEDDA   Illusion?

BRACK   You wouldn't have been allowed to keep it for long, anyway.

HEDDA   What do you mean?

BRACK   He didn't shoot himself on purpose.

HEDDA   Not on purpose?

BRACK   No. It didn't happen quite the way I told you.

HEDDA   Have you been hiding something? What is it?

BRACK   In order to spare poor Mrs. Elvsted's feelings, I permitted myself one or two small—equivocations.

HEDDA   What?

BRACK   To begin with, he is already dead.

HEDDA   He died at the hospital?

BRACK   Yes. Without regaining consciousness.

HEDDA   What else haven't you told us?

BRACK   The incident didn't take place at his lodgings.

HEDDA   Well, that's utterly unimportant.

BRACK   Not utterly. The fact is, you see, that Eilert Loevborg was found shot in Mademoiselle Danielle's boudoir.

HEDDA [*Almost jumps up, but instead sinks back in her chair.*]   That's impossible. He can't have been there today.

BRACK   He was there this afternoon. He went to ask for something he claimed they'd taken from him. Talked some crazy nonsense about a child which had got lost——

HEDDA   Oh! So that was the reason!

BRACK   I thought at first he might have been referring to his manuscript. But I hear he destroyed that himself. So he must have meant his pocket-book—I suppose.

HEDDA   Yes, I suppose so. So they found him there?

BRACK   Yes; there. With a discharged pistol in his breast pocket. The shot had wounded him mortally.

HEDDA   Yes. In the breast.

BRACK   No. In the—hm—stomach. The—lower part——

HEDDA [Looks at him with an expression of repulsion.]   That too! Oh, why does everything I touch become mean and ludicrous? It's like a curse!

BRACK   There's something else, Mrs. Hedda. It's rather disagreeable, too.

HEDDA   What?

BRACK   The pistol he had on him——

HEDDA   Yes? What about it?

BRACK   He must have stolen it.

HEDDA [Jumps up.]   Stolen it! That isn't true! He didn't!

BRACK   It's the only explanation. He must have stolen it. Ssh!

[TESMAN and MRS. ELVSTED have got up from the table in the rear room and come into the drawing room.]

TESMAN [His hands full of papers.]   Hedda, I can't see properly under that lamp. Think!

HEDDA   I am thinking.

TESMAN   Do you think we could possibly use your writing table for a little? What?

HEDDA   Yes, of course. [Quickly.] No, wait! Let me tidy it up first.

TESMAN   Oh, don't you trouble about that. There's plenty of room.

HEDDA   No, no, let me tidy it up first, I say. I'll take this in and put them on the piano. Here.

[She pulls an object, covered with sheets of music, out from under the bookcase, puts some more sheets on top and carries it all into the rear room and away to the left. TESMAN puts his papers on the writing table and moves the lamp over from the corner table. He and MRS. ELVSTED sit down and begin working again. HEDDA comes back.]

HEDDA [Behind MRS. ELVSTED's chair, ruffles her hair gently.]   Well, my pretty Thea! And how is work progressing on Eilert Loevborg's memorial?

MRS. ELVSTED [Looks up at her, dejectedly.]   Oh, it's going to be terribly difficult to get these into any order.

TESMAN   We've got to do it. We must! After all, putting other people's papers into order is rather my specialty, what?

[HEDDA goes over to the stove and sits on one of the footstools. BRACK stands over her, leaning against the armchair.]

HEDDA [Whispers.]   What was that you were saying about the pistol?

BRACK [Softly.]   I said he must have stolen it.

HEDDA   Why do you think that?

BRACK   Because any other explanation is unthinkable, Mrs. Hedda, or ought to be.

HEDDA   I see.

BRACK [Looks at her for a moment.]   Eilert Loevborg was here this morning. Wasn't he?

HEDDA   Yes.

BRACK   Were you alone with him?

EDDA   For a few moments.

BRACK   You didn't leave the room while he was here?

HEDDA   No.

BRACK   Think again. Are you sure you didn't go out for a moment?

HEDDA   Oh—yes, I might have gone into the hall. Just for a few seconds.

BRACK   And where was your pistol-case during this time?

HEDDA   I'd locked it in that——

BRACK   Er—Mrs. Hedda?

HEDDA   It was lying over there on my writing table.

BRACK   Have you looked to see if both the pistols are still there?

HEDDA   No.

BRACK   You needn't bother. I saw the pistol Loevborg had when they found him. I recognized it at once. From yesterday. And other occasions.

HEDDA   Have you got it?

BRACK   No. The police have it.

HEDDA   What will the police do with this pistol?

BRACK   Try to trace the owner.

HEDDA   Do you think they'll succeed?

BRACK [Leans down and whispers.]   No, Hedda Gabler. Not as long as I hold my tongue.

HEDDA [Looks nervously at him.]   And if you don't?

BRACK [Shrugs his shoulders.]   You could always say he'd stolen it.

HEDDA   I'd rather die!

BRACK [Smiles.]   People say that. They never do it.

HEDDA [Not replying.]   And suppose the pistol wasn't stolen? And they trace the owner? What then?

BRACK   There'll be a scandal, Hedda.

HEDDA   A scandal!

BRACK   Yes, a scandal. The thing you're so frightened of. You'll have to appear in court. Together with Mademoiselle Danielle. She'll have to explain how it all happened. Was it an accident, or was it—homicide? Was he about to take the pistol from his pocket to threaten her? And did it go off? Or did she snatch the pistol from his hand, shoot him and then put it back in his pocket? She might quite easily have done it. She's a resourceful lady, is Mademoiselle Danielle.

HEDDA   But I had nothing to do with this repulsive business.

BRACK   No. But you'll have to answer one question. Why did you give Eilert Loevborg this pistol? And what conclusions will people draw when it is proved you did give it to him?

HEDDA [Bows her head.]   That's true. I hadn't thought of that.

BRACK   Well, luckily there's no danger as long as I hold my tongue.

HEDDA [Looks up at him.]   In other words, I'm in your power, Judge. From now on, you've got your hold over me.

BRACK [Whispers, more slowly.]   Hedda, my dearest—believe me—I will not abuse my position.

HEDDA   Nevertheless, I'm in your power. Dependent on your will, and your demands. Not free. Still not free! [Rises passionately.] No. I couldn't bear that. No.

BRACK [*Looks half-derisively at her.*]   Most people resign themselves to the inevitable, sooner or later.

HEDDA [*Returns his gaze.*]   Possibly they do.
[*She goes across to the writing table.*]

HEDDA [*Represses an involuntary smile and says in* TESMAN'*s voice.*]   Well, George. Think you'll be able to manage? What?

TESMAN   Heaven knows, dear. This is going to take months and months.

HEDDA [*In the same tone as before.*]   Fancy that, by Jove! [*Runs her hands gently through* MRS. ELVSTED'*s hair.*] Doesn't it feel strange, Thea? Here you are working away with Tesman just the way you used to work with Eilert Loevborg.

MRS. ELVSTED   Oh—if only I can inspire your husband too!

HEDDA   Oh, it'll come. In time.

TESMAN   Yes—do you know, Hedda, I really think I'm beginning to feel a bit—well—that way. But you go back and talk to Judge Brack.

HEDDA   Can't I be of use to you two in any way?

TESMAN   No, none at all. [*Turns his head.*] You'll have to keep Hedda company from now on, Judge, and see she doesn't get bored. If you don't mind.

BRACK [*Glances at* HEDDA.]   It'll be a pleasure.

HEDDA   Thank you. But I'm tired this evening. I think I'll lie down on the sofa in there for a little while.

TESMAN   Yes, dear—do. What?
[HEDDA *goes into the rear room and draws the curtain behind her. Short pause. Suddenly she begins to play a frenzied dance melody on the piano.*]

MRS. ELVSTED [*Starts up from her chair.*]   Oh, what's that?

TESMAN [*Runs to the doorway.*]   Hedda dear, please! Don't play dance music tonight! Think of Auntie Rena. And Eilert.

HEDDA [*Puts her head out through the curtains.*]   And Auntie Juju. And all the rest of them. From now on I'll be quiet. [*Closes the curtains behind her.*]

TESMAN [*At the writing table.*]   It distresses her to watch us doing this. I say, Mrs. Elvsted, I've an idea. Why don't you move in with Auntie Juju? I'll run over each evening, and we can sit and work there. What?

MRS. ELVSTED   Yes, that might be the best plan.

HEDDA [*From the rear room.*]   I can hear what you're saying, Tesman. But how shall I spend the evenings out here?

TESMAN [*Looking through his papers.*]   Oh, I'm sure Judge Brack'll be kind enough to come over and keep you company. You won't mind my not being here, Judge?

BRACK [*In the armchair, calls gaily.*]   I'll be delighted, Mrs. Tesman. I'll be here every evening. We'll have great fun together, you and I.

HEDDA [*Loud and clear.*]   Yes, that'll suit you, won't it, Judge? The only cock on the dunghill——!
[*A shot is heard from the rear room.* TESMAN, MRS. ELVSTED *and* JUDGE BRACK *start from their chairs.*]

TESMAN   Oh, she's playing with those pistols again.
[*He pulls the curtains aside and runs in.* MRS. ELVSTED *follows him.* HEDDA *is lying dead on the sofa. Confusion and shouting.* BERTHA *enters in alarm from the right.*]

TESMAN [*Screams to* BRACK.]   She's shot herself! Shot herself in the head! By Jove! Fancy that!

BRACK [*Half paralyzed in the armchair.*]   But, good God! People don't do such things!

ANTON CHEKHOV
1860–1904

In plays and stories Anton Chekhov depicts Russia around the turn of the twentieth century with great pity, gentleness, and kindness of heart. More important, with a deep humanity that has outlasted all the problems of his time, he dramatizes universal and almost timeless feelings rather than ideas that date and pass. He differs sharply from the two giants of Russian literature, Dostoevsky and Tolstoy. For one thing, his work is of smaller scope. With the exception of an immature, forgotten novel and a travel book, he wrote only short stories and plays. He belongs, furthermore, to a very different moral and spiritual atmosphere. Chekhov had studied medicine and practiced it for a time. He shared the scientific outlook of his age and had too skeptical a mind to believe in Christianity or in any metaphysical system. He confessed that an intelligent believer was a puzzle to him. His attitude toward his materials and characters is detached, "objective," and his letters to friends insist that a good writer must present both physical details and a character's state of mind without overt interpretation or judgment. He is thus much more in the stream of Western realism than either Tolstoy or Dostoevsky, and the delicate, precise realism of his short stories has served as a model for later writers in Europe, China, and the United States. But extended reading of Chekhov does convey an impression of his view of life. There is implied in his stories a philosophy of kindness and humanity, a love of beauty, a sense of the unexplainable mystery of life, a sense, especially, of the individual's utter loneliness in this universe and among other people. Chekhov's pessimism has nothing of the defiance of the universe or the horror at it that we meet in other writers with similar attitudes; it is somehow merely sad, often pathetic, and yet also comforting and comfortable.

The Russia depicted in Chekhov's stories and plays is of a later period than that presented by Tolstoy and Dostoevsky. It seems to be nearing its end; there is a sense of decadence and frustration that heralds the approach of catastrophe. The aristocracy still keeps up a beautiful front but is losing its fight without much resistance, resignedly. Officialdom is stupid and venal. The Church is backward and narrow minded. The intelligentsia are hopelessly ineffectual, futile, lost in the provinces or absorbed in their egos. The peasants live subject to the lowest degradations of poverty and drink, apparently rather aggravated than improved since the much-heralded emancipation of the serfs in 1861. There seems no hope for society except in a gradual spread of enlightenment, good sense, and hygiene, for Chekhov is skeptical of the revolution and revolutionaries as well as of Tolstoy's followers.

Anton Pavlovich Chekhov was born on January 17, 1860, at Taganrog, a small town on the Sea of Azov. His father was a grocer and haberdasher; his grandfather, a serf who had bought his freedom. Chekhov's father went bankrupt in 1876, and the family moved to Moscow, leaving Anton to finish school in his home town. After his graduation in 1879, he followed his family to Moscow, where he studied medicine. To earn additional money for his family and himself, he started to write humorous sketches and stories for magazines. In 1884 he became a doctor and published his first collection of stories, *Tales of Melpomene*. Over the next several years, two collections of light comic tales brought him success and the opportunity to publish serious literature regularly in Moscow's largest daily newspaper, the *New Times*. In 1884, he also had his first hemorrhage. All the rest of his life he struggled against tuberculosis. His first play, *Ivanov*, was performed in 1887; and by 1889 he had written nine volumes of short stories. The next year, he undertook an arduous journey through Siberia to the island of Sakhalin (north of Japan) and back by boat through the Suez Canal. He saw there the Russian penal settlements and wrote a moving account of his trip in *Sakhalin Island* (1892). In 1898 his play *The Sea Gull* was a great success at the Moscow Art Theater. The next year he moved to Yalta, in the Crimea, and in 1901 married the actress Olga Knipper. He died on July 2, 1904, at Badenweiler in the Black Forest.

Chekhov's stories explore small but significant events in ordinary lives, emphasizing the twists and turns of interpersonal relations rather than (for example) the inexorably advancing plot recommended by Edgar Allan Poe. Whether it is a cabdriver's frustrated attempt to tell his fares about his son's recent death (*Misery*), a widow's final happiness in caring for another woman's child (*The Darling*), a retired clerk's delight in his gooseberry bushes (*Gooseberries*), or the aftermath of a businessman's brief affair at a resort (*The Lady with the Dog*), the author focuses on his characters' inner lives. They meditate on their own actions; observe the beauties of nature; wax philosophical about society or human nature; and most of all, react to the presence of other people. Typically, however, these characters find it hard to communicate with each other and frequently cannot do so at all; isolated in their own private worlds, they rarely make contact with the world of another. Successful or not, these relationships are all-important: they motivate events, illuminate actions, and shape the conclusion, which generally rounds off a stage in the character's life rather than resolving all issues. Chekhov's endings are famously ambiguous, and his conclusions remain—like events in real life—preludes to various possible sequels.

The Lady with the Dog is one of Chekhov's best-known stories. Published in 1899, it tells the story of a love affair sprung up between a man and woman vacationing in Yalta. Both are married, but not to each other, and each expects the affair to be a brief episode; one of many affairs for the banker Dmitri Gurov, and a single experience of romantic love for the dissatisfied Anna Sergeyevna von Diederitz. Anna Sergeyevna, the lady of the title, appears first as a nameless figure known only through local gossip. She is a tourist, walking her dog at a Crimean resort known for brief liaisons. Married young to an unimaginative minor official in a small town, she is bored, has probably read romantic novels, and is willing to risk anything rather than having her entire life pass without an intense experience. Dmitri Gurov, a prosperous Moscow bank official who likes the company of women, decides on a whim to seduce her and soon succeeds.

The physical seduction is strikingly minimized (quite unlike modern fiction); it happens offstage and is merely indicated through subsequent conversation revealing the couple's different reactions. Chekhov shows Gurov thinking about his various former lovers, and Anna Sergeyevna in self-conscious despair at having passed from the role of "lady with the dog" to that of a "fallen woman." He eats watermelon slices while she weeps (in a later scene, he drinks tea). Despite Anna Sergeyevna's remorse, with which Gurov fails to sympathize and in fact is utterly bored, neither is able to forget the other, and the affair resumes a few months after both have returned home. Anna continues to suffer over her position, and Gurov retreats from emotional entanglement into his role as man-about-town; she cannot bear living a double life, but he enjoys the contrast of public and private roles.

The story does not focus solely on the success or failure of a difficult love affair, nonetheless. As the relationship evolves, the protagonists emerge from the near-stereotypes of the beginning to individual personalities possessing a great deal of depth, ambiguity, and—perhaps—openness to change. Gurov's development from a self-satisfied to a self-conscious lover is particularly emphasized; it is his thoughts that we follow as he perceives Anna Sergeyevna first as an object of seduction, later as a woman tragically in love with him, and finally as his true partner. The gulf between the two remains unchanged until he looks in the mirror and realizes his own mortality; suddenly, a feeling of shared vulnerability enables him to reach out to Anna Sergeyevna. Whether or not it enables them to find a satisfactory solution to their dilemma is another question. If the conclusion of the story leaves the lovers' future undecided, it also demonstrates that any sequel we may imagine (and readers usually try to) must take into account both historical possibility and also our idea of what the characters have become.

The plays of Chekhov seem to go furthest in the direction of naturalism, the depiction of a "slice of life," on stage. Compared with Ibsen's plays they seem plotless; they could be described as a succession of little scenes, composed like a mosaic or like the dots or strokes in an Impressionist painting. The characters rarely engage in the usual dialogue; they speak often in little soliloquies, hardly justified by the situation; and they often do not listen to the words of their ostensible partners. They seem alone even in a crowd. Human communication seems difficult and even impossible. There is no clear message, no zeal for social reform; life seems to flow quietly, even sluggishly, until interrupted by some desperate outbreak or even a pistol shot.

Chekhov's last play, *The Cherry Orchard* (written in 1903, first performed at the Moscow Art Theater on January 17, 1904) differs, however, from this pattern in several respects. It has a strongly articulated central theme—the loss of the orchard— and it has a composition that roughly follows the traditional scheme of a well-made play. Arrival and departure from the very same room, the nursery, frame the two other acts: the outdoor idyll of Act II and the dance in Act III. Act III is the turning point of the action: Lopahin appears and announces, somewhat shamefacedly, that he has bought the estate. The orchard was lost from the very beginning—there is no real struggle to prevent its sale—but still the news of Lopahin's purchase is a surprise as he had no intention of buying it but did so only when during the auction sale a rival seemed to have a chance of acquiring it. A leading action runs its course, and many— one may even argue too many—subplots crisscross each other: the shy and awkward love affair of the student Trofimov and the daughter Anya; the love triangle among the three dependents, Yepihodov (the unlucky clerk), Dunyasha (the chambermaid), and Yasha (the conceited and insolent footman). Varya, the practical stepdaughter, has her troubles with Lopahin, and Simeonov-Pishchik is beset by the same financial problems as the owners of the orchard and is rescued by the discovery of some white clay on his estate. The German governess Charlotta drifts around alluding to her obscure origins and past. There are undeveloped references to events preceding the action on stage—the lover in Paris, the drowned boy Grisha—but there is no revelation of the past as in Ibsen, no mystery, no intrigue.

While the events on the stage follow each other naturally, though hardly always in a logical, causal order, a symbolic device is used conspicuously: in Act II after a pause, "suddenly a distant sound is heard, coming from the sky as it were, the sound of a snapping string, mournfully dying away." It occurs again at the very end of the play followed by "the strokes of the ax against a tree far away in the orchard." An attempt is made to explain this sound at its first occurrence as a bucket's fall in a faraway pit or as the cries of a heron or an owl, but the effect is weird and even supernatural; it establishes an ominous mood. Even the orchard carries more than its obvious meaning: it is white, drowned in blossoms when the party arrives in the spring; it is bare and desolate in the autumn when the axes are heard cutting it down. "The old bark on the trees gleams faintly, and the cherry trees seem to be dreaming of things that happened a hundred, two hundred years ago and to be tormented by painful visions," declaims Trofimov, defining his feeling for the orchard as a symbol of repression and serfdom. For Lubov Ranevskaya it is an image of her lost innocence and of the happier past, while Lopahin sees it only as an investment. It seems to draw together the meaning of the play.

But what is this meaning? Can we even decide whether it is a tragedy or a comedy? It has been commonly seen as the tragedy of the downfall of the Russian aristocracy (or more correctly, the landed gentry) victimized by the newly rich, upstart peasantry. One could see the play as depicting the defeat of a group of feckless people at the hand of a ruthless "developer" who destroys nature and natural beauty for profit. Or one could see it as prophesying, through the mouth of the student Trofimov, the approaching end of feudal Russia and the coming happier future. Soviet interpretations and performances leaned that way.

Surely none of these interpretations can withstand inspection in the light of the actual play. They all run counter to Chekhov's professed intentions. He called the play a comedy. In a letter of September 15, 1903, he declared expressly that the play "has not turned out as drama but as comedy, in places even a farce" and a few days later (September 21, 1903) he wrote that "the whole play is gay and frivolous." Chekhov did not like the staging of the play at the Moscow Art Theater and complained of its tearful tone and its slow pace. He objected that "they obstinately call my play a drama in playbill and newspaper advertisements" while he had called it a comedy (April 10, 1904).

No doubt, there are many comical and even farcical characters and scenes in the play. Charlotta with her nut-eating dog, her card tricks, her ventriloquism, her disappearing acts, is a clownish figure. Gayev, the landowner, though "suave and elegant," is a boor, obsessed by his passion for billiards, constantly popping candy into his mouth, telling the waiters in a restaurant about the "decadents" in Paris. Yepihodov, the clerk, carries a revolver and, threatening suicide, asks foolishly whether you have read Buckle (the English historian) and complains of his ill luck: a spider on his chest, a cockroach in his drink. Simeonov-Pishchik empties a whole bottle of pills; eats half a bucket of pickles; quotes Nietzsche supposedly recommending the forging of banknotes; and fat as he is, puffs and prances at the dance ordering the "cavaliers à genoux." Even the serious characters are put into ludicrous predicaments: Trofimov falls down the stairs; Lopahin, coming to announce the purchase of the estate, is almost hit with a stick by Varya (and *was* hit in the original version). Lopahin, teasing his intended Varya, "moos like a cow." The ball, the hunting for the galoshes, and the champagne drinking by Yasha in the last act have all a touch of absurdity. The grand speeches, Gayev's addresses to the bookcase and to nature or Trofimov's about "mankind going forward" and "All Russia is our orchard," are undercut by the contrast between words and character: Gayev is callous and shallow; the "perpetual student," Trofimov never did a stitch of work. He is properly ridiculed and insulted by Lubov for his scant beard and his silly professions of being "above love." One can sympathize with Chekhov's irritation at the pervading gloom imposed by the Moscow production.

Still, we cannot, in spite of the author, completely dismiss the genuine pathos of the central situation and of the central figure, Lubov Ranevskaya. Whatever one may say about her recklessness in financial matters and her guilt in relation to her lover in France, we must feel her deep attachment to the house and the orchard, to the past and her lost innocence, clearly and unhumorously expressed in the first act on her arrival, again and again at the impending sale of the estate, and finally at the parting from her house: "Oh, my orchard—my dear, sweet, beautiful orchard! . . . My life, my youth, my happiness—Good-bye!" That Gayev, before the final parting, seems to have overcome the sense of loss and even looks forward to his job in the bank and that Lubov acknowledges that her "nerves are better" and that "she sleeps well" testifies to the indestructible spirit of brother and sister, but cannot minimize the sense of loss, the pathos of parting, the nostalgia for happier times. Nor is the conception of Lopahin simple. Chekhov emphasized, in a letter to Konstantin Stanislavsky, who was to play the part, that "Lopahin is a decent person in the full sense of the word, and his bearing must be that of a completely dignified and intelligent man." He is not, he says, a profiteering peasant (*kulachok*, October 30, 1903). He admires Lubov and thinks of her with gratitude. He senses the beauty of the poppies in his fields. Even the scene of the abortive encounter with Varya at the end has its quiet pathos in spite of all its awkwardness and the comic touches such as the reference to the broken thermometer. Firs, the eighty-seven-year-old valet, may be grotesque in his deafness and his nostalgia for the good old days of serf-dom, but the very last scene when we see him abandoned in the locked-up house surely ends the play on a note of desolation and even despair.

Chekhov, we must conclude, achieved a highly original and even paradoxical blend of comedy and tragedy, or rather of farce and pathos. Both play and short story present a social picture firmly set in a specific historical time—the dissolution of the landed gentry, the rise of the peasant, the encroachment of the city, newly affluent bour-geoisie and its double standard for women—but they do not propound an obvious social thesis. Chekhov, in his tolerance and tenderness, in his distrust of ideologies and heroics, extends his sympathy to all his characters (with the exception of the crudely ambitious valet Yasha). The glow of his humanity, untrammeled by time and place, keeps *The Cherry Orchard* and *The Lady with the Dog* alive in quite different social and political conditions, as they have the universalizing power of great art.

Donald Rayfield, *The Cherry Orchard: Catastrophe and Comedy* (1994), presents an extended discussion of the play; good chapters are also found in Beverly Hahn, *Chekhov: A Study of the Major Stories and Plays* (1977); Harvey Pitcher, *The Chekhov Play: A New Interpretation* (1973); and Richard Pearce, *Chekhov: A Study of the Four Major Plays* (1983). Francis Fergusson compares Ibsen and Chekhov in "*Ghosts* and *The Cherry Orchard*," in *The Idea of the Theatre* (1949). There is helpful critical analysis in R. L. Jackson, ed., *Chekhov: A Collection of Critical Essays* (1967) and *Reading Chekhov's Text* (1993); in D. Rayfield, *Chekhov: The Evolution of His Art* (1975); and in René Wellek and N. D. Wellek, eds., *Chekhov: New Perspectives* (1984); which includes a sketch of Chekhov criticism in England and America. Lawrence Senelick, *The Chekhov Theatre: A Century of Plays in Performance* (1997), presents a different perspective. Ralph E. Matlaw, ed., *Anton Chekhov's Short Stories* (1979), includes eight valuable essays on aspects of the short stories and selections from Chekhov's letters. Virginia Llewellyn Smith, *Anton Chekhov and the Lady with the Dog* (1973), argues for autobiographical elements in Gurov's portrayal. Nicholas Worrall, *File on Chekhov* (1986), offers an introductory survey with useful cited passages and suggestions for further study. Donald Rayfield, *Anton Chekhov: A Life* (1998), is a revisionary biography that evokes a more complex personality based on newly discovered evidence.

PRONOUNCING GLOSSARY

The following list uses common English syllables and stress accents to provide rough equiv-alents of selected words whose pronunciation may be unfamiliar to the general reader.

Anna Sergeyevna von Diederitz: *ahn'-nuh sehr-gay'-ev-nuh fahn-dee'-duh-reets*

Anton Chekhov: *ahn-tawn' che'-khuf*

Charlotta Ivanovna: *shar-law'-tuh ee-vah'-nuv-nuh*

Dmitri Gurov: *dmee'-tree goo'-ruf*

Firs: *feers*

Leonid Andreyevich Gayev: *lay-ah-neet'-ahn-dray'-uh-veech gah'-yef*

Lubov Andreyevna Ranevskaya: *lyu-bawf' ahn-dray'-uv-nuh rah-nyef'-skah-yuh*

Pyotr Sergeyevich Trofimov: *pyaw'-tr sehr-gay'-eh-veech trah-fee'-muf*

Semyon Yepihodov: *seem-yawn' ye-pee-khaw'-duf*

Simeonov-Pishchik: *see-may-awn'-uf peesh'-cheek*

Yermolay Alexeyevich Lopahin: *yehr-mah-lai' ah-lex-ay'-veech lah-pah'-kheen*

The Lady with the Dog[1]

I

People were telling one another that a newcomer had been seen on the promenade—a lady with a dog. Dmitri Dmitrich Gurov had been a fortnight in Yalta,[2] and was accustomed to its ways, and he, too, had begun to take an interest in fresh arrivals. From his seat in Vernet's outdoor café, he caught sight of a young woman in a toque, passing along the promenade; she was fair and not very tall; after her trotted a white Pomeranian.

Later he encountered her in the municipal park and in the square several times a day. She was always alone, wearing the same toque, and the Pomeranian always trotted at her side. Nobody knew who she was, and people referred to her simply as "the lady with the dog."

"If she's here without her husband, and without any friends," thought Gurov, "it wouldn't be a bad idea to make her acquaintance."

He was not yet forty but had a twelve-year-old daughter and two sons in high school. He had been talked into marrying in his second year at college, and his wife now looked nearly twice as old as he did. She was a tall woman with dark eyebrows, erect, dignified, imposing, and, as she said of herself, a "thinker." She was a great reader, omitted the "hard sign"[3] at the end of words in her letters, and called her husband "Dimitry" instead of Dmitry; and though he secretly considered her shallow, narrow-minded, and dowdy, he stood in awe of her, and disliked being at home. He had first begun deceiving her long ago and he was now constantly unfaithful to her, and this was no doubt why he spoke slightingly of women, to whom he referred as *the lower race*.

He considered that the ample lessons he had received from bitter experience entitled him to call them whatever he liked, but without this "lower race" he could not have existed a single day. He was bored and ill-at-ease in the company of men, with whom he was always cold and reserved, but felt quite at home among women, and knew exactly what to say to them, and how to behave; he could even be silent in their company without feeling the slightest awkwardness. There was an elusive charm in his appearance and disposition which attracted women and caught their sympathies. He knew this and was himself attracted to them by some invisible force.

Repeated and bitter experience had taught him that every fresh intimacy, while at first introducing such pleasant variety into everyday life, and offering itself as a charming, light adventure, inevitably developed, among decent people (especially in Moscow, where they are so irresolute and slow to move), into a problem of excessive complication leading to an intolerably irksome situation. But every time he encountered an attractive woman he forgot all about this experience, the desire for life surged up in him, and everything suddenly seemed simple and amusing.

One evening, then, while he was dining at the restaurant in the park, the lady in the toque came strolling up and took a seat at a neighboring table.

---

1. Translated by Ivy Litvinov.   2. A fashionable seaside resort in the Crimea.   3. Certain progressive intellectuals, anticipating the reform of the Russian alphabet, omitted the hard sign after consonants in writing; here, however, it is an affectation.

Her expression, gait, dress, coiffure, all told him that she was from the upper classes, that she was married, that she was in Yalta for the first time, alone and bored. . . . The accounts of the laxity of morals among visitors to Yalta are greatly exaggerated, and he paid no heed to them, knowing that for the most part they were invented by people who would gladly have transgressed themselves, had they known how to set about it. But when the lady sat down at a neighboring table a few yards away from him, these stories of easy conquests, of excursions to the mountains, came back to him, and the seductive idea of a brisk transitory liaison, an affair with a woman whose very name he did not know, suddenly took possession of his mind.

He snapped his fingers at the Pomeranian and, when it trotted up to him, shook his forefinger at it. The Pomeranian growled. Gurov shook his finger again.

The lady glanced at him and instantly lowered her eyes.

"He doesn't bite," she said, and blushed.

"May I give him a bone?" he asked, and on her nod of consent added in friendly tones: "Have you been long in Yalta?"

"About five days."

"And I am dragging out my second week here."

Neither spoke for a few minutes.

"The days pass quickly, and yet one is so bored here," she said, not looking at him.

"It's the thing to say it's boring here. People never complain of boredom in godforsaken holes like Belyev or Zhizdra, but when they get here it's: 'Oh, the dullness! Oh, the dust!' You'd think they'd come from Granada[4] to say the least."

She laughed. Then they both went on eating in silence, like complete strangers. But after dinner they left the restaurant together, and embarked upon the light, jesting talk of people free and contented, for whom it is all the same where they go, or what they talk about. They strolled along, remarking on the strange light over the sea. The water was a warm, tender purple, the moonlight lay on its surface in a golden strip. They said how close it was, after the hot day. Gurov told her he was from Moscow, that he was really a philologist, but worked in a bank; that he had at one time trained himself to sing in a private opera company, but had given up the idea; that he owned two houses in Moscow. . . . And from her he learned that she had grown up in Petersburg,[5] but had gotten married in the town of S., where she had been living two years, that she would stay another month in Yalta, and that perhaps her husband, who also needed a rest, would join her. She was quite unable to explain whether her husband was a member of the province council, or on the board of the *zemstvo*,[6] and was greatly amused at herself for this. Further, Gurov learned that her name was Anna Sergeyevna.

Back in his own room he thought about her, and felt sure he would meet her the next day. It was inevitable. As he went to bed he reminded himself that only a very short time ago she had been a schoolgirl, like his own daughter, learning her lessons, he remembered how much there was of shyness and constraint in her laughter, in her way of conversing with a stranger—it

---

4. A famous medieval city in Spain, once capital of the Moorish kingdom of Granada and now a tourist center known for its art and architecture. Belyev and Zhizdra are small provincial towns.   5. St. Petersburg, the former capital of Russia: an important port and cultural center.   6. District administration.

was probably the first time in her life that she found herself alone, and in a situation in which men could follow her and watch her, and speak to her, all the time with a secret aim she could not fail to divine. He recalled her slender, delicate neck, her fine gray eyes.

"And yet there's something pathetic about her," he thought to himself as he fell asleep.

II

A week had passed since the beginning of their acquaintance. It was a holiday. Indoors it was stuffy, but the dust rose in clouds out of doors, and people's hats blew off. It was a parching day and Gurov kept going to the outdoor café for fruit drinks and ices to offer Anna Sergeyevna. The heat was overpowering.

In the evening, when the wind had dropped, they walked to the pier to see the steamer come in. There were a great many people strolling about the landing-place; some, bunches of flowers in their hands, were meeting friends. Two peculiarities of the smart Yalta crowd stood out distinctly—the elderly ladies all tried to dress very youthfully, and there seemed to be an inordinate number of generals about.

Owing to the roughness of the sea the steamer arrived late, after the sun had gone down, and it had to maneuver for some time before it could get alongside the pier. Anna Sergeyevna scanned the steamer and passengers through her lorgnette,[7] as if looking for someone she knew, and when she turned to Gurov her eyes were glistening. She talked a great deal, firing off abrupt questions and forgetting immediately what it was she had wanted to know. Then she lost her lorgnette in the crush.

The smart crowd began dispersing, features could no longer be made out, the wind had quite dropped, and Gurov and Anna Sergeyevna stood there as if waiting for someone else to come off the steamer. Anna Sergeyevna had fallen silent, every now and then smelling her flowers, but not looking at Gurov.

"It's turned out a fine evening," he said. "What shall we do? We might go for a drive."

She made no reply.

He looked steadily at her and suddenly took her in his arms and kissed her lips, and the fragrance and dampness of the flowers closed round him, but the next moment he looked behind him in alarm—had anyone seen them?

"Let's go to your room," he murmured.

And they walked off together, very quickly.

Her room was stuffy and smelt of some scent she had bought in the Japanese shop.[8] Gurov looked at her, thinking to himself: "How full of strange encounters life is!" He could remember carefree, good-natured women who were exhilarated by love-making and grateful to him for the happiness he gave them, however short-lived; and there had been others—his wife among them—whose caresses were insincere, affected, hysterical, mixed up with a great deal of quite unnecessary talk, and whose expression seemed to say that all this was not just lovemaking or passion, but something much more

7. Small eyeglasses on a short handle.   8. Probably a tourist shop with imported goods.

significant; then there had been two or three beautiful, cold women, over whose features flitted a predatory expression, betraying a determination to wring from life more than it could give, women no longer in their first youth, capricious, irrational, despotic, brainless, and when Gurov had cooled to these, their beauty aroused in him nothing but repulsion, and the lace trimming on their underclothes reminded him of fish-scales.

But here the timidity and awkwardness of youth and inexperience were still apparent; and there was a feeling of embarrassment in the atmosphere, as if someone had just knocked at the door. Anna Sergeyevna, "the lady with the dog," seemed to regard the affair as something very special, very serious, as if she had become a fallen woman, an attitude he found odd and disconcerting. Her features lengthened and drooped, and her long hair hung mournfully on either side of her face. She assumed a pose of dismal meditation, like a repentant sinner in some classical painting.[9]

"It isn't right," she said. "You will never respect me anymore."

On the table was a watermelon. Gurov cut himself a slice from it and began slowly eating it. At least half an hour passed in silence.

Anna Sergeyevna was very touching, revealing the purity of a decent, naïve woman who had seen very little of life. The solitary candle burning on the table scarcely lit up her face, but it was obvious that her heart was heavy.

"Why should I stop respecting you?" asked Gurov. "You don't know what you're saying."

"May God forgive me!" she exclaimed, and her eyes filled with tears. "It's terrible."

"No need to seek to justify yourself."

"How can I justify myself? I'm a wicked, fallen woman, I despise myself and have not the least thought of self-justification. It isn't my husband I have deceived, it's myself. And not only now, I have been deceiving myself for ever so long. My husband is no doubt an honest, worthy man, but he's a flunky. I don't know what it is he does at his office, but I know he's a flunky. I was only twenty when I married him, and I was devoured by curiosity, I wanted something higher. I told myself that there must be a different kind of life I wanted to live, to live. . . . I was burning with curiosity . . . you'll never understand that, but I swear to God I could no longer control myself, nothing could hold me back, I told my husband I was ill, and I came here. . . . And I started going about like one possessed, like a madwoman . . . and now I have become an ordinary, worthless woman, and everyone has the right to despise me."

Gurov listened to her, bored to death. The naïve accents, the remorse, all was so unexpected, so out of place. But for the tears in her eyes, she might have been jesting or play-acting.

"I don't understand," he said gently. "What is it you want?"

She hid her face against his breast and pressed closer to him.

"Do believe me, I implore you to believe me," she said. "I love all that is honest and pure in life, vice is revolting to me, I don't know what I'm doing. The common people say they are snared by the Devil. And now I can say that I have been snared by the Devil, too."

"Come, come," he murmured.

---

9. A famous painting of Mary Magdalen (see Luke 7.36–50) by the French classical artist Georges de la Tour (1593–1652) shows her seated at a table meditating, her face and long hair illuminated by a candle.

He gazed into her fixed, terrified eyes, kissed her, and soothed her with gentle affectionate words, and gradually she calmed down and regained her cheefulness. Soon they were laughing together again.

When, a little later, they went out, there was not a soul on the promenade, the town and its cypresses looked dead, but the sea was still roaring as it dashed against the beach. A solitary fishing-boat tossed on the waves, its lamp blinking sleepily.

They found a carriage and drove to Oreanda.[1]

"I discovered your name in the hall, just now," said Gurov, "written up on the board. Von Diederitz. Is your husband a German?"

"No. His grandfather was, I think, but he belongs to the Orthodox Church himself."

When they got out of the carriage at Oreanda they sat down on a bench not far from the church, and looked down at the sea, without talking. Yalta could be dimly discerned through the morning mist, and white clouds rested motionless on the summits of the mountains. Not a leaf stirred, the grass-hoppers chirruped, and the monotonous hollow roar of the sea came up to them, speaking of peace, of the eternal sleep lying in wait for us all. The sea had roared like this long before there was any Yalta or Oreanda, it was roaring now, and it would go on roaring, just as indifferently and hollowly, when we had passed away. And it may be that in this continuity, this utter indifference of life and death, lies the secret of our ultimate salvation, of the stream of life on our planet, and of its never-ceasing movement towards perfection.

Side by side with a young woman, who looked so exquisite in the early light, soothed and enchanted by the sight of all this magical beauty—sea, mountains, clouds and the vast expanse of the sky—Gurov told himself that, when you came to think of it, everything in the world is beautiful really, everything but our own thoughts and actions, when we lose sight of the higher aims of life, and of our dignity as human beings.

Someone approached them—a watchman, probably—looked at them and went away. And there was something mysterious and beautiful even in this. The steamer from Feodosia[2] could be seen coming towards the pier, lit up by the dawn, its lamps out.

"There's dew on the grass," said Anna Sergeyevna, breaking the silence.

"Yes. Time to go home."

They went back to the town.

After this they met every day at noon on the promenade, lunching and dining together, going for walks, and admiring the sea. She complained of sleeplessness, of palpitations, asked the same questions over and over again, alternately surrendering to jealousy and the fear that he did not really respect her. And often, when there was nobody in sight in the square or the park, he would draw her to him and kiss her passionately. The utter idleness, these kisses in broad daylight, accompanied by furtive glances and the fear of discovery, the heat, the smell of the sea, and the idle, smart, well-fed people continually crossing their field of vision, seemed to have given him a new lease of life. He told Anna Sergeyevna she was beautiful and seductive, made love to her with impetuous passion, and never left her side, while she was

---

1. A hotel and beach compound near Yalta; the whole area is known as the Ukrainian Riviera.　2. A coastal town seventy miles northeast of Yalta.

always pensive, always trying to force from him the admission that he did not respect her, that he did not love her a bit, and considered her just an ordinary woman. Almost every night they drove out of town, to Oreanda, the waterfall, or some other beauty-spot. And these excursions were invariably a success, each contributing fresh impressions of majestic beauty.

All this time they kept expecting her husband to arrive. But a letter came in which he told his wife that he was having trouble with his eyes, and implored her to come home as soon as possible. Anna Sergeyevna made hasty preparations for leaving.

"It's a good thing I'm going," she said to Gurov. "It's the intervention of fate."

She left Yalta in a carriage, and he went with her as far as the railway station. The drive took nearly a whole day. When she got into the express train, after the second bell had been rung, she said:

"Let me have one more look at you. . . . One last look. That's right."

She did not weep, but was mournful, and seemed ill, the muscles of her cheeks twitching.

"I shall think of you . . . I shall think of you all the time," she said. "God bless you! Think kindly of me. We are parting forever, it must be so, because we ought never to have met. Good-bye—God bless you."

The train steamed rapidly out of the station, its lights soon disappearing, and a minute later even the sound it made was silenced, as if everything were conspiring to bring this sweet oblivion, this madness, to an end as quickly as possible. And Gurov, standing alone on the platform and gazing into the dark distance, listened to the shrilling of the grasshoppers and the humming of the telegraph wires, with a feeling that he had only just awakened. And he told himself that this had been just one more of the many adventures in his life, and that it, too, was over, leaving nothing but a memory. . . . He was moved and sad, and felt a slight remorse. After all, this young woman whom he would never again see had not been really happy with him. He had been friendly and affectionate with her, but in his whole behaviour, in the tones of his voice, in his very caresses, there had been a shade of irony, the insulting indulgence of the fortunate male, who was, moreover, almost twice her age. She had insisted in calling him good, remarkable, high-minded. Evidently he had appeared to her different from his real self, in a word he had involuntarily deceived her. . . .

There was an autumnal feeling in the air, and the evening was chilly.

"It's time for me to be going north, too," thought Gurov, as he walked away from the platform. "High time!"

III

When he got back to Moscow it was beginning to look like winter; the stoves were heated every day, and it was still dark when the children got up to go to school and drank their tea, so that the nurse had to light the lamp for a short time. Frost had set in. When the first snow falls, and one goes for one's first sleigh-ride, it is pleasant to see the white ground, the white roofs; one breathes freely and lightly, and remembers the days of one's youth. The ancient lime-trees and birches, white with hoarfrost, have a good-natured look, they are closer to the heart than cypresses and palms, and beneath their branches one is no longer haunted by the memory of mountains and the sea.

Gurov had always lived in Moscow, and he returned to Moscow on a fine frosty day, and when he put on his fur-lined overcoat and thick gloves, and sauntered down Petrovka Street, and when, on Saturday evening, he heard the church bells ringing, his recent journey and the places he had visited lost their charm for him. He became gradually immersed in Moscow life, reading with avidity three newspapers a day, while declaring he never read Moscow newspapers on principle. Once more he was caught up in a whirl of restaurants, clubs, banquets, and celebrations, once more he glowed with the flattering consciousness that well-known lawyers and actors came to his house, that he played cards in the Medical Club opposite a professor. He could once again eat a whole serving of Moscow Fish Stew served in a pan.

He had believed that in a month's time Anna Sergeyevna would be nothing but a vague memory, and that hereafter, with her wistful smile, she would only occasionally appear to him in dreams, like others before her. But the month was now well over and winter was in full swing, and all was as clear in his memory as if he had parted with Anna Sergeyevna only the day before. And his recollections grew ever more insistent. When the voices of his children at their lessons reached him in his study through the evening stillness, when he heard a song, or the sounds of a music-box in a restaurant, when the wind howled in the chimney, it all came back to him: early morning on the pier, the misty mountains, the steamer from Feodosia, the kisses. He would pace up and down his room for a long time, smiling at his memories, and then memory turned into dreaming, and what had happened mingled in his imagination with what was going to happen. Anna Sergeyevna did not come to him in his dreams, she accompanied him everywhere, like his shadow, following him everywhere he went. When he closed his eyes, she seemed to stand before him in the flesh, still lovelier, younger, tenderer than she had really been, and looking back, he saw himself, too, as better than he had been in Yalta. In the evenings she looked out at him from the bookshelves, the fireplace, the corner, he could hear her breathing, the sweet rustle of her skirts. In the streets he followed women with his eyes, to see if there were any like her. . . .

He began to feel an overwhelming desire to share his memories with someone. But he could not speak of his love at home, and outside his home who was there for him to confide in? Not the tenants living in his house, and certainly not his colleagues at the bank. And what was there to tell? Was it love that he had felt? Had there been anything exquisite, poetic, anything instructive or even amusing about his relations with Anna Sergeyevna? He had to content himself with uttering vague generalizations about love and women, and nobody guessed what he meant, though his wife's dark eyebrows twitched as she said:

"The role of a coxcomb doesn't suit you a bit, Dimitry."

One evening, leaving the Medical Club with one of his card-partners, a government official, he could not refrain from remarking:

"If you only knew what a charming woman I met in Yalta!"

The official got into his sleigh, and just before driving off, turned and called out:

"Dmitry Dmitrich!"

"Yes?"

"You were quite right, you know—the sturgeon was just a *leetle* off."

These words, in themselves so commonplace, for some reason infuriated Gurov, seemed to him humiliating, gross. What savage manners, what people! What wasted evenings, what tedious, empty days! Frantic card-playing, gluttony, drunkenness, perpetual talk always about the same thing. The greater part of one's time and energy went on business that was no use to anyone, and on discussing the same thing over and over again, and there was nothing to show for it all but a stunted, earth-bound existence and a round of trivialities, and there was nowhere to escape to, you might as well be in a madhouse or a convict settlement.

Gurov lay awake all night, raging, and went about the whole of the next day with a headache. He slept badly on the succeeding nights, too, sitting up in bed, thinking, or pacing the floor of his room. He was sick of his children, sick of the bank, felt not the slightest desire to go anywhere or talk about anything.

When the Christmas holidays came, he packed his things, telling his wife he had to go to Petersburg in the interests of a certain young man, and set off for the town of S. To what end? He hardly knew himself. He only knew that he must see Anna Sergeyevna, must speak to her, arrange a meeting, if possible.

He arrived at S. in the morning and engaged the best suite in the hotel, which had a carpet of gray military frieze, and a dusty ink-pot on the table, surmounted by a headless rider, holding his hat in his raised hand. The hall porter told him what he wanted to know: von Diederitz had a house of his own in Staro-Goncharnaya Street. It wasn't far from the hotel, he lived on a grand scale, luxuriously, kept carriage-horses, the whole town knew him. The hall porter pronounced the name "Drideritz."

Gurov strolled over to Staro-Goncharnaya Street and discovered the house. In front of it was a long gray fence with inverted nails hammered into the tops of the palings.

"A fence like that is enough to make anyone want to run away," thought Gurov, looking at the windows of the house and the fence.

He reasoned that since it was a holiday, Anna's husband would probably be at home. In any case it would be tactless to embarrass her by calling at the house. And a note might fall into the hands of the husband, and bring about catastrophe. The best thing would be to wait about on the chance of seeing her. And he walked up and down the street, hovering in the vicinity of the fence, watching for his chance. A beggar entered the gate, only to be attacked by dogs, then, an hour later, the faint, vague sounds of a piano reached his ears. That would be Anna Sergeyevna playing. Suddenly the front door opened and an old woman came out, followed by a familiar white Pomeranian. Gurov tried to call to it, but his heart beat violently, and in his agitation he could not remember its name.

He walked on, hating the gray fence more and more, and now ready to tell himself irately that Anna Sergeyevna had forgotten him, had already, perhaps, found distraction in another—what could be more natural in a young woman who had to look at this accursed fence from morning to night? He went back to his hotel and sat on the sofa in his suite for some time, not knowing what to do, then he ordered dinner, and after dinner, had a long sleep.

"What a foolish, restless business," he thought, waking up and looking towards the dark windowpanes. It was evening by now. "Well, I've had my sleep out. And what am I to do in the night?"

He sat up in bed, covered by the cheap gray quilt, which reminded him of a hospital blanket, and in his vexation he fell to taunting himself.

"You and your lady with a dog . . . there's adventure for you! See what you get for your pains."

On his arrival at the station that morning he had noticed a poster announcing in enormous letters the first performance at the local theatre of *The Geisha*.[3] Remembering this, he got up and made for the theatre.

"It's highly probable that she goes to first nights," he told himself.

The theatre was full. It was a typical provincial theatre, with a mist collecting over the chandeliers, and the crowd in the gallery fidgeting noisily. In the first row of the stalls the local dandies stood waiting for the curtain to go up, their hands clasped behind them. There, in the front seat of the governor's box, sat the governor's daughter, wearing a boa, the governor himself hiding modestly behind the drapes, so that only his hands were visible. The curtain stirred, the orchestra took a long time tuning up their instruments. Gurov's eyes roamed eagerly over the audience as they filed in and occupied their seats.

Anna Sergeyevna came in, too. She seated herself in the third row of the stalls, and when Gurov's glance fell on her, his heart seemed to stop, and he knew in a flash that the whole world contained no one nearer or dearer to him, no one more important to his happiness. This little woman, lost in the provincial crowd, in no way remarkable, holding a silly lorgnette in her hand, now filled his whole life, was his grief, his joy, all that he desired. Lulled by the sounds coming from the wretched orchestra, with its feeble, amateurish violinists, he thought how beautiful she was . . . thought and dreamed. . . .

Anna Sergeyevna was accompanied by a tall, round-shouldered young man with small whiskers, who nodded at every step before taking the seat beside her and seemed to be continually bowing to someone. This must be her husband, whom, in a fit of bitterness, at Yalta, she had called a "flunky." And there really was something of a lackey's servility in his lanky figure, his side-whiskers, and the little bald spot on the top of his head. And he smiled sweetly, and the badge of some scientific society gleaming in his buttonhole was like the number on a footman's livery.

The husband went out to smoke in the first interval, and she was left alone in her seat. Gurov, who had taken a seat in the stalls, went up to her and said in a trembling voice, with a forced smile: "How d'you do?"

She glanced up at him and turned pale, then looked at him again in alarm, unable to believe her eyes, squeezing her fan and lorgnette in one hand, evidently struggling to overcome a feeling of faintness. Neither of them said a word. She sat there, and he stood beside her, disconcerted by her embarrassment, and not daring to sit down. The violins and flutes sang out as they were tuned, and there was a tense sensation in the atmosphere, as if they were being watched from all the boxes. At last she got up and moved rapidly towards one of the exits. He followed her and they wandered aimlessly along

3. An operetta (1896) by the English composer Sidney Jones.

corridors, up and down stairs; figures flashed by in the uniforms of legal officials, high-school teachers and civil servants, all wearing badges; ladies, coats hanging from pegs flashed by; there was a sharp draft, bringing with it an odor of cigarette butts. And Gurov, whose heart was beating violently, thought:

"What on earth are all these people, this orchestra for? . . ."

The next minute he suddenly remembered how, after seeing Anna Sergeyevna off that evening at the station, he had told himself that all was over, and they would never meet again. And how far away the end seemed to be now!

She stopped on a dark narrow staircase over which was a notice bearing the inscription "To the upper circle."[4]

"How you frightened me!" she said, breathing heavily, still pale and half-stunned. "Oh, how you frightened me! I'm almost dead! Why did you come? Oh, why?"

"But, Anna," he said, in low, hasty tones. "But, Anna. . . . Try to understand . . . do try. . . ."

She cast him a glance of fear, entreaty, love, and then gazed at him steadily, as if to fix his features firmly in her memory.

"I've been so unhappy," she continued, taking no notice of his words. "I could think of nothing but you the whole time, I lived on the thoughts of you. I tried to forget—why, oh, why did you come?"

On the landing above them were two schoolboys, smoking and looking down, but Gurov did not care, and, drawing Anna Sergeyevna towards him, began kissing her face, her lips, her hands.

"What are you doing, oh, what are you doing?" she said in horror, drawing back. "We have both gone mad. Go away this very night, this moment. . . . By all that is sacred, I implore you. . . . Somebody is coming."

Someone was ascending the stairs.

"You must go away," went on Anna Sergeyevna in a whisper. "D'you hear me, Dmitry Dmitrich? I'll come to you in Moscow. I have never been happy, I am unhappy now, and I shall never be happy—never! Do not make me suffer still more! I will come to you in Moscow, I swear it! And now we must part! My dear one, my kind one, my darling, we must part."

She pressed his hand and hurried down the stairs, looking back at him continually, and her eyes showed that she was in truth unhappy. Gurov stood where he was for a short time, listening, and when all was quiet, went to look for his coat, and left the theatre.

IV

And Anna Sergeyevna began going to Moscow to see him. Every two or three months she left the town of S., telling her husband that she was going to consult a specialist on female diseases, and her husband believed her and did not believe her. In Moscow she always stayed at the Slavyanski Bazaar,[5] sending a man in a red cap to Gurov the moment she arrived. Gurov went to her, and no one in Moscow knew anything about it.

---

4. The stalls or back rows; a medium-priced area behind the orchestra seats on the main floor.   5. A luxurious hotel in Moscow.

One winter morning he went to see her as usual (the messenger had been to him the evening before, but had not found him at home). His daughter was with him, for her school was on the way and he thought he might as well see her to it.

"It is forty degrees," said Gurov to his daughter, "and yet it is snowing. You see it is only above freezing close to the ground, the temperature in the upper layers of the atmosphere is quite different."

"Why doesn't it ever thunder in winter, Papa?"

He explained this, too. As he was speaking, he kept reminding himself that he was going to a rendezvous and that not a living soul knew about it, or, probably, ever would. He led a double life—one in public, in the sight of all whom it concerned, full of conventional truth and conventional deception, exactly like the lives of his friends and acquaintances, and another which flowed in secret. And, owing to some strange, possibly quite accidental chain of circumstances, everything that was important, interesting, essential, everything about which he was sincere and never deceived himself, everything that composed the kernel of his life, went on in secret, while everything that was false in him, everything that composed the husk in which he hid himself and the truth which was in him—his work at the bank, discussions at the club, his "lower race," his attendance at anniversary celebrations with his wife—was on the surface. He began to judge others by himself, no longer believing what he saw, and always assuming that the real, the only interesting life of every individual goes on as under cover of night, secretly. Every individual existence revolves around mystery, and perhaps that is the chief reason that all cultivated individuals insisted so strongly on the respect due to personal secrets.

After leaving his daughter at the door of her school Gurov set off for the Slavyanski Bazaar. Taking off his overcoat in the lobby, he went upstairs and knocked softly on the door. Anna Sergeyevna, wearing the gray dress he liked most, exhausted by her journey and by suspense, had been expecting him since the evening before. She was pale and looked at him without smiling, but was in his arms almost before he was fairly in the room. Their kiss was lingering, prolonged, as if they had not met for years.

"Well, how are you?" he asked. "Anything new?"

"Wait, I'll tell you in a minute. . . . I can't. . . ."

She could not speak, because she was crying. Turning away, she held her handkerchief to her eyes.

"I'll wait till she's had her cry out," he thought, and sank into a chair.

He rang for tea, and a little later, while he was drinking it, she was still standing there, her face to the window. She wept from emotion, from her bitter consciousness of the sadness of their life; they could only see one another in secret, hiding from people, as if they were thieves. Was not their life a broken one?

"Don't cry," he said.

It was quite obvious to him that this love of theirs would not soon come to an end, and that no one could say when this end would be. Anna Sergeyevna loved him ever more fondly, worshipped him, and there would have been no point in telling her that one day it must end. Indeed, she would not have believed him.

He moved over and took her by the shoulders, intending to fondle her with light words, but suddenly he caught sight of himself in the looking-glass.

His hair was already beginning to turn gray. It struck him as strange that he should have aged so much in the last few years. The shoulders on which his hands lay were warm and quivering. He felt a pity for this life, still so warm and exquisite, but probably soon to fade and droop like his own. Why did she love him so? Women had always believed him different from what he really was, had loved in him not himself but the man their imagination pictured him, a man they had sought for eagerly all their lives. And afterwards when they discovered their mistake, they went on loving him just the same. And not one of them had ever been happy with him. Time had passed, he had met one woman after another, become intimate with each, parted with each, but had never loved. There had been all sorts of things between them, but never love.

And only now, when he was gray-haired, had he fallen in love properly, thoroughly, for the first time in his life.

He and Anna Sergeyevna loved one another as people who are very close and intimate, as husband and wife, as dear friends love one another. It seemed to them that fate had intended them for one another, and they could not understand why she should have a husband, and he a wife. They were like two migrating birds, the male and the female, who had been caught and put into separate cages. They forgave one another all that they were ashamed of in the past and in the present, and felt that this love of theirs had changed them both.

Formerly, in moments of melancholy, he had consoled himself by the first argument that came into his head, but now arguments were nothing to him, he felt profound pity, desired to be sincere, tender.

"Stop crying, my dearest," he said. "You've had your cry, now stop. . . . Now let us have a talk, let us try and think what we are to do."

Then they discussed their situation for a long time, trying to think how they could get rid of the necessity for hiding, deception, living in different towns, being so long without meeting. How were they to shake off these intolerable fetters?

"How? How?" he repeated, clutching his head. "How?"

And it seemed to them that they were within an inch of arriving at a decision, and that then a new, beautiful life would begin. And they both realized that the end was still far, far away, and that the hardest, the most complicated part was only just beginning.

The Cherry Orchard[1]

CHARACTERS

LUBOV ANDREYEVNA RANEVSKAYA, *a landowner*

ANYA, *her seventeen-year-old daughter*

VARYA, *her adopted daughter, twenty-four years old*

LEONID ANDREYEVICH GAYEV, *Mme. Ranevskaya's brother*

YERMOLAY ALEXEYEVICH LOPAHIN, *a merchant*

PYOTR SERGEYEVICH TROFIMOV, *a student*

SIMEONOV-PISHCHIK, *a landowner*

CHARLOTTA IVANOVNA, *a governess*

SEMYON YEPIHODOV, *a clerk*

DUNYASHA, *a maid*

FIRS, *a manservant, aged eighty-seven*

YASHA, *a young valet*

A TRAMP

STATIONMASTER

POST OFFICE CLERK

GUESTS

SERVANTS

The action takes place on MME. RANEVSKAYA's *estate.*

Act I

A room that is still called the nursery. One of the doors leads into ANYA's *room. Dawn, the sun will soon rise. It is May, the cherry trees are in blossom, but it is cold in the orchard; there is a morning frost. The windows are shut. Enter* DUN-YASHA *with a candle, and* LOPAHIN *with a book in his hand.*

LOPAHIN   The train is in, thank God. What time is it?

DUNYASHA   Nearly two. [*Puts out the candle.*] It's light already.

LOPAHIN   How late is the train, anyway? Two hours at least. [*Yawns and stretches.*] I'm a fine one! What a fool I've made of myself! I came here on purpose to meet them at the station, and then I went and overslept. I fell asleep in my chair. How annoying! You might have waked me . . .

DUNYASHA   I thought you'd left. [*Listens.*] I think they're coming!

LOPAHIN [*Listens.*]   No, they've got to get the luggage, and one thing and another . . . [*Pause.*] Lubov Andreyevna spent five years abroad, I don't know what she's like now. . . . She's a fine person—lighthearted, simple. I remember when I was a boy of fifteen, my poor father—he had a shop here in the village then—punched me in the face with his fist and made my nose bleed. We'd come into the yard, I don't know what for, and he'd had a drop too much. Lubov Andreyevna, I remember her as if it were yesterday—she was still young and so slim—led me to the washbasin, in this very room . . . in the nursery. "Don't cry, little peasant," she said, "it'll heal in time for your wedding . . . " [*Pause.*] Little peasant . . . my father was a peasant, it's true, and here I am in a white waistcoat and yellow shoes. A pig in a pastry shop, you might say. It's true I'm rich. I've got a lot of money. . . . But when you look at it closely, I'm a peasant through and through. [*Pages the book.*] Here I've been reading this book

---

1. Translated by Avrahm Yarmolinsky.

and I didn't understand a word of it. . . . I was reading it and fell asleep
. . . [*Pause.*]

DUNYASHA   And the dogs were awake all night, they feel that their masters
are coming.

LOPAHIN   Dunyasha, why are you so—

DUNYASHA   My hands are trembling. I'm going to faint.

LOPAHIN   You're too soft, Dunyasha. You dress like a lady, and look at the
way you do your hair. That's not right. One should remember one's place.
[*Enter* YEPIHODOV *with a bouquet; he wears a jacket and highly
polished boots that squeak badly. He drops the bouquet as he comes
in.*]

YEPIHODOV [*Picking up the bouquet.*]   Here, the gardener sent these, said
you're to put them in the dining room. [*Hands the bouquet to* DUNYASHA.]

LOPAHIN   And bring me some kvass.[2]

DUNYASHA   Yes, sir. [*Exits.*]

YEPIHODOV   There's a frost this morning—three degrees below—and yet
the cherries are all in blossom. I cannot approve of our climate. [*Sighs.*]
I cannot. Our climate does not activate properly. And, Yermolay Alexeyevich, allow me to make a further remark. The other day I bought
myself a pair of boots, and I make bold to assure you, they squeak so
that it is really intolerable. What should I grease them with?

LOPAHIN   Oh, get out! I'm fed up with you.

YEPIHODOV   Every day I meet with misfortune. And I don't complain, I've
got used to it, I even smile.
[DUNYASHA *enters, hands* LOPAHIN *the kvass.*]

YEPIHODOV   I am leaving. [*Stumbles against a chair, which falls over.*]
There! [*Triumphantly, as it were.*] There again, you see what sort of cir-
cumstance, pardon the expression. . . . It is absolutely phenomenal!
[*Exits.*]

DUNYASHA   You know, Yermolay Alexeyevich, I must tell you, Yepihodov
has proposed to me.

LOPAHIN   Ah!

DUNYASHA   I simply don't know . . . he's a quiet man, but sometimes when
he starts talking, you can't make out what he means. He speaks nicely—
and it's touching—but you can't understand it. I sort of like him though,
and he is crazy about me. He's an unlucky man . . . every day something
happens to him. They tease him about it here . . . they call him, Two-
and-Twenty Troubles.

LOPAHIN [*Listening.*]   There! I think they're coming.

DUNYASHA   They *are* coming! What's the matter with me? I feel cold all
over.

LOPAHIN   They really are coming. Let's go and meet them. Will she recognize me? We haven't seen each other for five years.

DUNYASHA [*In a flutter.*]   I'm going to faint this minute. . . . Oh, I'm going
to faint!
[*Two carriages are heard driving up to the house.* LOPAHIN *and* DUN-
YASHA *go out quickly. The stage is left empty. There is a noise in the
adjoining rooms.* FIRS, *who had driven to the station to meet* LUBOV

2. Russian beer, made from rye or barley.

ANDREYEVNA RANEVSKAYA, *crosses the stage hurriedly, leaning on a stick. He is wearing an old-fashioned livery and a tall hat. He mutters to himself indistinctly. The hubbub offstage increases. A* VOICE: *"Come, let's go this way." Enter* LUBOV ANDREYEVNA, ANYA, *and* CHARLOTTA IVANOVNA *with a pet dog on a leash, all in traveling dresses;* VARYA, *wearing a coat and kerchief;* GAYEV, SIMEONOV-PISHCHIK, LOPAHIN, DUNYASHA, *with a bag and an umbrella, servants with luggage. All walk across the room.*]

ANYA   Let's go this way. Do you remember what room this is, Mamma?

MME. RANEVSKAYA [*Joyfully, through her tears.*]   The nursery!

VARYA   How cold it is! My hands are numb. [*To* MME. RANEVSKAYA] Your rooms are just the same as they were, Mamma, the white one and the violet.

MME. RANEVSKAYA   The nursery! My darling, lovely room! I slept here when I was a child . . . [*Cries.*] And here I am, like a child again! [*Kisses her brother and* VARYA, *and then her brother again.*] Varya's just the same as ever, like a nun. And I recognized Dunyasha. [*Kisses* DUNYASHA.]

GAYEV   The train was two hours late. What do you think of that? What a way to manage things!

CHARLOTTA [*To* PISHCHIK.]   My dog eats nuts, too.

PISHCHIK [*In amazement.*]   You don't say!

[*All go out, except* ANYA *and* DUNYASHA.]

DUNYASHA   We've been waiting for you for hours. [*Takes* ANYA's *hat and coat.*]

ANYA   I didn't sleep on the train for four nights and now I'm frozen . . .

DUNYASHA   It was Lent when you left; there was snow and frost, and now . . . My darling! [*Laughs and kisses her.*] I have been waiting for you, my sweet, my darling! But I must tell you something . . . I can't put it off another minute . . .

ANYA [*Listlessly.*]   What now?

DUNYASHA   The clerk, Yepihodov, proposed to me, just after Easter.

ANYA   There you are, at it again . . . [*Straightening her hair.*] I've lost all my hairpins . . . [*She is staggering with exhaustion.*]

DUNYASHA   Really, I don't know what to think. He loves me—he loves me so!

ANYA [*Looking toward the door of her room, tenderly.*]   My own room, my windows, just as though I'd never been away. I'm home! Tomorrow morning I'll get up and run into the orchard. Oh, if I could only get some sleep. I didn't close my eyes during the whole journey—I was so anxious.

DUNYASHA   Pyotr Sergeyevich came the day before yesterday.

ANYA [*Joyfully.*]   Petya!

DUNYASHA   He's asleep in the bathhouse. He has settled there. He said he was afraid of being in the way. [*Looks at her watch.*] I should wake him, but Miss Varya told me not to. "Don't you wake him," she said.

[*Enter* VARYA *with a bunch of keys at her belt.*]

VARYA   Dunyasha, coffee, and be quick. . . . Mamma's asking for coffee.

DUNYASHA   In a minute. [*Exits.*]

VARYA   Well, thank God, you've come. You're home again. [*Fondling* ANYA.] My darling is here again. My pretty one is back.

ANYA   Oh, what I've been through!

VARYA   I can imagine.

ANYA   When we left, it was Holy Week, it was cold then, and all the way Charlotta chattered and did her tricks. Why did you have to saddle me with Charlotta?

VARYA   You couldn't have travelled all alone, darling—at seventeen!

ANYA   We got to Paris, it was cold there, snowing. My French is dreadful. Mamma lived on the fifth floor; I went up there, and found all kinds of Frenchmen, ladies, an old priest with a book. The place was full of tobacco smoke, and so bleak. Suddenly I felt sorry for Mamma, so sorry, I took her head in my arms and hugged her and couldn't let go of her. Afterward Mamma kept fondling me and crying. . . .

VARYA [*Through tears.*]   Don't speak of it . . . don't.

ANYA   She had already sold her villa at Mentone, she had nothing left, nothing. I hadn't a kopeck left either, we had only just enough to get home. And Mamma wouldn't understand! When we had dinner at the stations, she always ordered the most expensive dishes, and tipped the waiters a whole ruble. Charlotta, too. And Yasha kept ordering, too—it was simply awful. You know Yasha's Mamma's footman now, we brought him here with us.

VARYA   Yes, I've seen the blackguard.

ANYA   Well, tell me—have you paid the interest?

VARYA   How could we?

ANYA   Good heavens, good heavens!

VARYA   In August the estate will be put up for sale.

ANYA   My God!

LOPAHIN [*Peeps in at the door and bleats.*]   Meh-h-h. [*Disappears.*]

VARYA [*Through tears.*]   What I couldn't do to him! [*Shakes her fist threateningly.*]

ANYA [*Embracing* VARYA *gently.*]   Varya, has he proposed to you? [VARYA *shakes her head.*] But he loves you. Why don't you come to an understanding? What are you waiting for?

VARYA   Oh, I don't think anything will ever come of it. He's too busy, he has no time for me . . . pays no attention to me. I've washed my hands of him—I can't bear the sight of him. They all talk abut our getting married, they all congratulate me—and all the time there's really nothing to it—it's all like a dream. [*In another tone.*] You have a new brooch—like a bee.

ANYA [*Sadly.*]   Mamma bought it. [*She goes into her own room and speaks gaily like a child.*] And you know, in Paris I went up in a balloon.

VARYA   My darling's home, my pretty one is back. [DUNYASHA *returns with the coffeepot and prepares coffee.* VARYA *stands at the door of* ANYA's *room.*] All day long, darling, as I go about the house, I keep dreaming. If only we could marry you off to a rich man, I should feel at ease. Then I would go into a convent, and afterward to Kiev, to Moscow . . . I would spend my life going from one holy place to another . . . I'd go on and on. . . . What a blessing that would be!

ANYA   The birds are singing in the orchard. What time is it?

VARYA   It must be after two. Time you were asleep, darling. [*Goes into* ANYA's *room.*] What a blessing that would be!

[YASHA *enters with a plaid and a traveling bag, crosses the stage.*]

YASHA [*Finically.*] May I pass this way, please?

DUNYASHA A person could hardly recognize you, Yasha. Your stay abroad has certainly done wonders for you.

YASHA Hm-m . . . and who are you?

DUNYASHA When you went away I was that high—[*Indicating with her hand.*] I'm Dunyasha—Fyodor Kozoyedev's daughter. Don't you remember?

YASHA Hm! What a peach!

> [*He looks round and embraces her. She cries out and drops a saucer. YASHA leaves quickly.*]

VARYA [*In the doorway, in a tone of annoyance.*] What's going on here?

DUNYASHA [*Through tears.*] I've broken a saucer.

VARYA Well, that's good luck.

ANYA [*Coming out of her room.*] We ought to warn Mamma that Petya's here.

VARYA I left orders not to wake him.

ANYA [*Musingly.*] Six years ago father died. A month later brother Grisha was drowned in the river. . . . Such a pretty little boy he was—only seven. It was more than Mamma could bear, so she went away, went away without looking back . . . [*Shudders.*] How well I understand her, if she only knew! [*Pause.*] And Petya Trofimov was Grisha's tutor, he may remind her of it all . . .

> [*Enter* FIRS, *wearing a jacket and a white waistcoat. He goes up to the coffeepot.*]

FIRS [*Anxiously.*] The mistress will have her coffee here. [*Puts on white gloves.*] Is the coffee ready? [*Sternly, to* DUNYASHA.] Here, you! And where's the cream?

DUNYASHA Oh, my God! [*Exits quickly.*]

FIRS [*Fussing over the coffeepot.*] Hah! the addlehead! [*Mutters to himself.*] Home from Paris. And the old master used to go to Paris too . . . by carriage. [*Laughs.*]

VARYA What is it, Firs?

FIRS What is your pleasure, Miss? [*Joyfully.*] My mistress has come home, and I've seen her at last! Now I can die. [*Weeps with joy.*]

> [*Enters* RANEVSKAYA, GAYEV, *and* SIMEONOV-PISHCHIK: *The latter is wearing a tight-waisted, pleated coat of fine cloth, and full trousers.* GAYEV, *as he comes in, goes through the motions of a billiard player with his arms and body.*]

MME. RANEVSKAYA Let's see, how does it go? Yellow ball in the corner! Bank shot in the side pocket!

GAYEV I'll tip it in the corner! There was a time, Sister, when you and I used to sleep in this very room and now I'm fifty-one, strange as it may seem.

LOPAHIN Yes, time flies.

GAYEV Who?

LOPAHIN I say, time flies.

GAYEV It smells of patchouli here.

ANYA I'm going to bed. Good night, Mamma. [*Kisses her mother.*]

MME. RANEVSKAYA My darling child! [*Kisses her hands.*] Are you happy to be home? I can't come to my senses.

ANYA   Good night, Uncle.

GAYEV [*Kissing her face and hands.*]   God bless you, how like your mother you are! [*To his sister.*] At her age, Luba, you were just like her.

    [ANYA *shakes hands with* LOPAHIN *and* PISHCHIK, *then goes out, shutting the door behind her.*]

MME. RANEVSKAYA   She's very tired.

PISHCHIK   Well, it was a long journey.

VARYA [*To* LOPAHIN *and* PISHCHIK.]   How about it, gentlemen? It's past two o'clock—isn't it time for you to go?

MME. RANEVSKAYA [*Laughs.*]   You're just the same as ever, Varya. [*Draws her close and kisses her.*] I'll have my coffee and then we'll all go. [FIRS *puts a small cushion under her feet.*] Thank you, my dear. I've got used to coffee. I drink it day and night. Thanks, my dear old man. [*Kisses him.*]

VARYA   I'd better see if all the luggage has been brought in. [*Exits.*]

MME. RANEVSKAYA   Can it really be I sitting here? [*Laughs.*] I feel like dancing, waving my arms about. [*Covers her face with her hands.*] But maybe I am dreaming! God knows I love my country, I love it tenderly; I couldn't look out of the window in the train, I kept crying so. [*Through tears.*] But I must have my coffee. Thank you, Firs, thank you, dear old man. I'm so happy that you're still alive.

FIRS   Day before yesterday.

GAYEV   He's hard of hearing.

LOPAHIN   I must go soon, I'm leaving for Kharkov about five o'clock. How annoying! I'd like to have a good look at you, talk to you. . . . You're just as splendid as ever.

PISHCHIK [*Breathing heavily.*]   She's even better-looking. . . . Dressed in the latest Paris fashion. . . . Perish my carriage and all its four wheels. . . .

LOPAHIN   Your brother, Leonid Andreyevich, says I'm a vulgarian and an exploiter. But it's all the same to me—let him talk. I only want you to trust me as you used to. I want you to look at me with your touching, wonderful eyes, as you used to. Dear God! My father was a serf of your father's and grandfather's, but you, you yourself, did so much for me once . . . so much . . . that I've forgotten all about that; I love you as though you were my sister—even more.

MME. RANESVSKAYA   I can't sit still, I simply can't. [*Jumps up and walks about in violent agitation.*] This joy is too much for me. . . . Laugh at me, I'm silly! My own darling bookcase! My darling table! [*Kisses it.*]

GAYEV   While you were away, nurse died.

MME. RANEVSKAYA [*Sits down and takes her coffee.*]   Yes, God rest her soul; they wrote me about it.

GAYEV   And Anastasy is dead. Petrushka Kossoy has left me and has gone into town to work for the police inspector. [*Takes a box of sweets out of his pocket and begins to suck one.*]

PISHCHIK   My daughter Dashenka sends her regards.

LOPAHIN   I'd like to tell you something very pleasant—cheering. [*Glancing at his watch.*] I am leaving directly. There isn't much time to talk. But I will put it in a few words. As you know, your cherry orchard is to be sold to pay your debts. The sale is to be on the twenty-second of August; but don't you worry, my dear, you may sleep in peace; there is a way out.

Here is my plan. Give me your attention! Your estate is only fifteen miles from the town; the railway runs close by it; and if the cherry orchard and the land along the riverbank were cut up into lots and these leased for summer cottages, you would have an income of at least 25,000 rubles a year out of it.

GAYEV Excuse me. . . . What nonsense.

MME. RANEVSKAYA I don't quite understand you, Yermolay Alexeyevich.

LOPAHIN You will get an annual rent of at least ten rubles per acre, and if you advertise at once, I'll give you any guarantee you like that you won't have a square foot of ground left by autumn, all the lots will be snapped up. In short, congratulations, you're saved. The location is splendid—by that deep river. . . . Only, of course, the ground must be cleared . . . all the old buildings, for instance, must be torn down, and this house, too, which is useless, and, of course, the old cherry orchard must be cut down.

MME. RANEVSKAYA Cut down? My dear, forgive me, but you don't know what you're talking about. If there's one thing that's interesting—indeed, remarkable—in the whole province, it's precisely our cherry orchard.

LOPAHIN The only remarkable thing about this orchard is that it's a very large one. There's a crop of cherries every other year, and you can't do anything with them; no one buys them.

GAYEV This orchard is even mentioned in the encyclopedia.

LOPAHIN [Glancing at his watch.] If we can't think of a way out, if we don't come to a decision, on the twenty-second of August the cherry orchard and the whole estate will be sold at auction. Make up your minds! There's no other way out—I swear. None, none.

FIRS In the old days, forty or fifty years ago, the cherries were dried, soaked, pickled, and made into jam, and we used to—

GAYEV Keep still, Firs.

FIRS And the dried cherries would be shipped by the cartload. It meant a lot of money! And in those days the dried cherries were soft and juicy, sweet, fragrant. . . . They knew the way to do it, then.

MME. RANEVSKAYA And why don't they do it that way now?

FIRS They've forgotten. Nobody remembers it.

PISHCHIK [To MME. RANEVSKAYA.] What's doing in Paris? Eh? Did you eat frogs there?

MME. RANEVSKAYA I ate crocodiles.

PISHCHIK Just imagine!

LOPAHIN There used to be only landowners and peasants in the country, but now these summer people have appeared on the scene. . . . All the towns, even the small ones, are surrounded by these summer cottages; and in another twenty years, no doubt, the summer population will have grown enormously. Now the summer resident only drinks tea on his porch, but maybe he'll take to working his acre, too, and then your cherry orchard will be a rich, happy, luxuriant place.

GAYEV [Indignantly.] Poppycock!

[Enter VARYA and YASHA.]

VARYA There are two telegrams for you, Mamma dear. [Picks a key from

the bunch at her belt and noisily opens an old-fashioned bookcase.] Here
they are.

MME. RANEVSKAYA They're from Paris. [*Tears them up without reading
them.*] I'm through with Paris.

GAYEV Do you know, Luba, how old this bookcase is? Last week I pulled
out the bottom drawer and there I found the date burnt in it. It was made
exactly a hundred years ago. Think of that! We could celebrate its cen-
tenary. True, it's an inanimate object, but nevertheless, a bookcase . . .

PISHCHIK [*Amazed.*] A hundred years! Just imagine!

GAYEV Yes. [*Tapping it.*] That's something. . . . Dear, honored bookcase,
hail to you who for more than a century have served the glorious ideals
of goodness and justice! Your silent summons to fruitful toil has never
weakened in all those hundred years [*through tears*], sustaining, through
successive generations of our family, courage and faith in a better future,
and fostering in us ideals of goodness and social consciousness. [*Pauses.*]

LOPAHIN Yes . . .

MME. RANEVSKAYA You haven't changed a bit, Leonid.

GAYEV [*Somewhat embarrassed.*] I'll play it off the red in the corner! Tip
it in the side pocket!

LOPAHIN [*Looking at his watch.*] Well, it's time for me to go . . .

YASHA [*Handing pillbox to* MME. RANEVSKAYA.] Perhaps you'll take your
pills now.

PISHCHIK One shouldn't take medicines, dearest lady, they do neither
harm nor good. . . . Give them here, my valued friend. [*Takes the pillbox,
pours the pills into his palm, blows on them, puts them in his mouth, and
washes them down with some kvass.*] There!

MME. RANEVSKAYA [*Frightened.*] You must be mad!

PISHCHIK I've taken all the pills.

LOPAHIN What a glutton!
     [*All laugh.*]

FIRS The gentleman visited us in Easter week, ate half a bucket of pickles,
he did . . . [*Mumbles.*]

MME. RANEVSKAYA What's he saying?

VARYA He's been mumbling like that for the last three years—we're used
to it.

YASHA His declining years!
     [CHARLOTTA IVANOVNA, *very thin, tightly laced, dressed in white, a
     lorgnette at her waist, crosses the stage.*]

LOPAHIN Forgive me, Charlotta Ivanovna, I've not had time to greet you.
[*Tries to kiss her hand.*]

CHARLOTTA [*Pulling away her hand.*] If I let you kiss my hand, you'll be
wanting to kiss my elbow next, and then my shoulder.

LOPAHIN I've no luck today. [*All laugh.*] Charlotta Ivanovna, show us a
trick.

MME. RANEVSKAYA Yes, Charlotta, do a trick for us.

CHARLOTTA I don't see the need. I want to sleep. [*Exits.*]

LOPAHIN In three weeks we'll meet again. [*Kisses* MME. RANEVSKAYA's
hand.*] Good-bye till then. Time's up. [*To* GAYEV.] Bye-bye. [*Kisses* PISH-
CHIK.] Bye-bye. [*Shakes hands with* VARYA, *then with* FIRS *and* YASHA.] I

hate to leave. [*To* MME. RANEVSKAYA.] If you make up your mind about the cottages, let me know; I'll get you a loan of 50,000 rubles.[3] Think it over seriously.

VARYA [*Crossly.*]   Will you never go!

LOPAHIN   I'm going, I'm going. [*Exits.*]

GAYEV   The vulgarian. But, excuse me . . . Varya's going to marry him, he's Varya's fiancé.

VARYA   You talk too much, Uncle.

MME. RANEVSKAYA   Well, Varya, it would make me happy. He's a good man.

PISHCHIK   Yes, one must admit, he's a most estimable man. And my Dashenka . . . she too says that . . . she says . . . lots of things. [*Snores; but wakes up at once.*] All the same, my valued friend, could you oblige me . . . with a loan of 240 rubles? I must pay the interest on the mortgage tomorrow.

VARYA [*Alarmed.*]   We can't, we can't!

MME. RANEVSKAYA   I really haven't any money.

PISHCHIK   It'll turn up. [*Laughs.*] I never lose hope, I thought everything was lost, that I was done for, when lo and behold, the railway ran through my land . . . and I was paid for it. . . . And something else will turn up again, if not today, then tomorrow . . . Dashenka will win two hundred thousand . . . she's got a lottery ticket.

MME. RANEVSKAYA   I've had my coffee, now let's go to bed.

FIRS [*Brushes off* GAYEV; *admonishingly.*]   You've got the wrong trousers on again. What am I to do with you?

VARYA [*Softly.*]   Anya's asleep. [*Gently opens the window.*] The sun's up now, it's not a bit cold. Look, Mamma dear, what wonderful trees. And heavens, what air! The starlings are singing!

GAYEV [*Opens the other window.*]   The orchard is all white. You've not forgotten it? Luba? That's the long alley that runs straight, straight as an arrow; how it shines on moonlight nights, do you remember? You've not forgotten?

MME. RANEVSKAYA [*Looking out of the window into the orchard.*]   Oh, my childhood, my innocent childhood. I used to sleep in this nursery—I used to look out into the orchard, happiness waked with me every morning, the orchard was just the same then . . . nothing has changed. [*Laughs with joy.*] All, all white! Oh, my orchard! After the dark, rainy autumn and the cold winter, you are young again, and full of happiness, the heavenly angels have not left you. . . . If I could free my chest and my shoulders from this rock that weighs on me, if I could only forget the past!

GAYEV   Yes, and the orchard will be sold to pay our debts, strange as it may seem.

MME. RANEVSKAYA   Look! There is our poor mother walking in the orchard . . . all in white . . . [*Laughs with joy.*] It is she!

GAYEV   Where?

VARYA   What are you saying, Mamma dear!

MME. RANEVSKAYA   There's no one there, I just imagined it. To the right,

---

3. The basic unit of currency. One ruble is equal to one hundred kopecks.

where the path turns toward the arbor, there's a little white tree, leaning over, that looks like a woman . . .

[TROFIMOV *enters, wearing a shabby student's uniform and spectacles.*]

MME. RANEVSKAYA   What an amazing orchard! White masses of blossom, the blue sky . . .

TROFIMOV   Lubov Andreyevna! [*She looks round at him.*] I just want to pay my respects to you, then I'll leave at once. [*Kisses her hand ardently.*] I was told to wait until morning, but I hadn't the patience . . .

[MME. RANEVSKAYA *looks at him, perplexed.*]

VARYA [*Through tears.*]   This is Petya Trofimov.

TROFIMOV   Petya Trofimov, formerly your Grisha's tutor. . . . Can I have changed so much?

[MME. RANEVSKAYA *embraces him and weeps quietly.*]

GAYEV [*Embarrassed.*]   Don't, don't, Luba.

VARYA [*Crying.*]   I told you, Petya, to wait until tomorrow.

MME. RANEVSKAYA   My Grisha . . . my little boy . . . Grisha . . . my son.

VARYA   What can one do, Mamma dear, it's God's will.

TROFIMOV [*Softly, through tears.*]   There . . . there.

MME. RANEVSKAYA [*Weeping quietly.*]   My little boy was lost . . . drowned. Why? Why, my friend? [*More quietly.*] Anya's asleep in there, and here I am talking so loudly . . . making all this noise. . . . But tell me, Petya, why do you look so badly? Why have you aged so?

TROFIMOV   A mangy master, a peasant woman in the train called me.

MME. RANEVSKAYA   You were just a boy then, a dear little student, and now your hair's thin—and you're wearing glasses! Is it possible you're still a student? [*Goes toward the door.*]

TROFIMOV   I suppose I'm a perpetual student.

MME. RANEVSKAYA [*Kisses her brother, then* VARYA.]   Now, go to bed. . . . You have aged, too, Leonid.

PISHCHIK [*Follows her.*]   So now we turn in. Oh, my gout! I'm staying the night here . . . Lubov Andreyevna, my angel, tomorrow morning . . . I do need 240 rubles.

GAYEV   He keeps at it.

PISHCHIK   I'll pay it back, dear . . . it's a trifling sum.

MME. RANEVSKAYA   All right, Leonid will give it to you. Give it to him, Leonid.

GAYEV   Me give it to him! That's a good one!

MME. RANEVSKAYA   It can't be helped. Give it to him! He needs it. He'll pay it back.

[MME. RANEVSKAYA, TROFIMOV, PISHCHIK, *and* FIRS *go out;* GAYEV, VARYA, *and* YASHA *remain.*]

GAYEV   Sister hasn't got out of the habit of throwing money around. [*To* YASHA.] Go away, my good fellow, you smell of the barnyard.

YASHA [*With a grin.*]   And you, Leonid Andreyevich, are just the same as ever.

GAYEV   Who? [*To* VARYA.] What did he say?

VARYA [*To* YASHA.]   Your mother's come from the village; she's been sitting in the servants' room since yesterday, waiting to see you.

YASHA   Botheration!

VARYA You should be ashamed of yourself!

YASHA She's all I needed! She could have come tomorrow. [*Exits.*]

VARYA Mamma is just the same as ever; she hasn't changed a bit. If she had her own way, she'd keep nothing for herself.

GAYEV Yes . . . [*Pauses.*] If a great many remedies are offered for some disease, it means it is incurable; I keep thinking and racking my brains; I have many remedies, ever so many, and that really means none. It would be fine if we came in for a legacy; it would be fine if we married off our Anya to a very rich man; or we might go to Yaroslavl and try our luck with our aunt, the Countess. She's very rich, you know . . .

VARYA [*Weeping.*] If only God would help us!

GAYEV Stop bawling. Aunt's very rich, but she doesn't like us. In the first place, Sister married a lawyer who was no nobleman . . . [ANYA *appears in the doorway.*] She married beneath her, and it can't be said that her behavior has been very exemplary. She's good, kind, sweet, and I love her, but no matter what extenuating circumstances you may adduce, there's no denying that she has no morals. You sense it in her least gesture.

VARYA [*In a whisper.*] Anya's in the doorway.

GAYEV Who? [*Pauses.*] It's queer, something got into my right eye—my eyes are going back on me. . . . And on Thursday, when I was in the circuit court—

[*Enter* ANYA.]

VARYA Why aren't you asleep, Anya?

ANYA I can't get to sleep, I just can't.

GAYEV My little pet! [*Kisses* ANYA's *face and hands.*] My child! [*Weeps.*] You are not my niece, you're my angel! You're everything to me. Believe me, believe—

ANYA I believe you, Uncle. Everyone loves you and respects you . . . but, Uncle dear, you must keep still. . . . You must. What were you saying just now about my mother? Your own sister? What made you say that?

GAYEV Yes, yes . . . [*Covers his face with her hand.*] Really, that was awful! Good God! Heaven help me! Just now I made a speech to the bookcase . . . so stupid! And only after I was through, I saw how stupid it was.

VARYA It's true, Uncle dear, you ought to keep still. Just don't talk, that's all.

ANYA If you could only keep still, it would make things easier for you, too.

GAYEV I'll keep still. [*Kisses* ANYA's *and* VARYA's *hands.*] I will. But now about business. On Thursday I was in court; well, there were a number of us there, and we began talking of one thing and another, and this and that, and do you know, I believe it will be possible to raise a loan on a promissory note to pay the interest at the bank.

VARYA If only God would help us!

GAYEV On Tuesday I'll go and see about it again. [*To* VARYA.] Stop bawling. [*To* ANYA.] Your mamma will talk to Lopahin, and he, of course, will not refuse her . . . and as soon as you're rested, you'll go to Yaroslavl to the Countess, your great-aunt. So we'll be working in three directions at once, and the thing is in the bag. We'll pay the interest—I'm sure of it. [*Puts a candy in his mouth.*] I swear on my honor, I swear by anything you like, the estate shan't be sold. [*Excitedly.*] I

swear by my own happiness! Here's my hand on it, you can call me a
swindler and a scoundrel if I let it come to an auction! I swear by my
whole being.

ANYA [*Relieved and quite happy again.*]   How good you are, Uncle, and
how clever! [*Embraces him.*] Now I'm at peace, quite at peace, I'm happy.
[*Enter* FIRS.]

FIRS [*Reproachfully.*]   Leonid Andreyevich, have you no fear of God?
When are you going to bed?

GAYEV   Directly, directly. Go away, Firs, I'll . . . yes, I will undress myself.
Now, children, 'nightie-'nightie. We'll consider details tomorrow, but
now go to sleep. [*Kisses* ANYA *and* VARYA.] I am a man of the eighties;
they have nothing good to say of that period nowadays. Nevertheless, in
the course of my life, I have suffered not a little for my convictions. It's
not for nothing that the peasant loves me; one should know the peasant;
one should know from which—

ANYA   There you go again, Uncle.

VARYA   Uncle dear, be quiet.

FIRS [*Angrily.*]   Leonid Andreyevich!

GAYEV   I'm coming, I'm coming! Go to bed! Double bank shot in the side
pocket! Here goes a clean shot . . .
[*Exits,* FIRS *hobbling after him.*]

ANYA   I am at peace now. I don't want to go to Yaroslavl—I don't like my
great-aunt, but still, I am at peace, thanks to Uncle. [*Sits down.*]

VARYA   We must get some sleep. I'm going now. While you were away,
something unpleasant happened. In the old servants' quarters, there are
only the old people as you know; Yefim, Polya, Yevstigney, and Karp, too.
They began letting all sorts of rascals in to spend the night. . . . I didn't
say anything. Then I heard they'd been spreading a report that I gave
them nothing but dried peas to eat—out of stinginess, you know . . . and
it was all Yevstigney's doing. . . . All right, I thought, if that's how it is, I
thought, just wait. I sent for Yevstigney . . . [*Yawns.*] He comes. . . .
"How's this, Yevstigney?" I say, "You fool . . ." [*Looking at* ANYA.]
Anichka! [*Pauses.*] She's asleep. [*Puts her arm around* ANYA.] Come to
your little bed. . . . Come . . . [*Leads her.*] My darling has fallen asleep.
. . . Come.
[*They go out. Far away beyond the orchard, a shepherd is piping.*
TROFIMOV *crosses the stage and, seeing* VARYA *and* ANYA, *stands still.*]

VARYA   Sh! She's asleep . . . asleep. . . . Come, darling.

ANYA [*Softly, half-asleep.*]   I'm so tired. Those bells . . . Uncle . . . dear. . . .
Mamma and Uncle . . .

VARYA   Come, my precious, come along. [*They go into* ANYA's *room.*]

TROFIMOV [*With emotion.*]   My sunshine, my spring!

Act II

*A meadow. An old, long-abandoned, lopsided little chapel; near it a well, large
slabs, which had apparently once served as tombstones, and an old bench. In the
background the road to the Gayev estate. To one side poplars loom darkly, where
the cherry orchard begins. In the distance a row of telegraph poles, and far off,*

on the horizon, the faint outline of a large city which is seen only in fine, clear weather. The sun will soon be setting. CHARLOTTA, YASHA, *and* DUNYASHA *are seated on the bench.* YEPIHODOV *stands near and plays a guitar. All are pensive.* CHARLOTTA *wears an old peaked cap. She has taken a gun from her shoulder and is straightening the buckle on the strap.*

CHARLOTTA [*Musingly.*]   I haven't a real passport, I don't know how old I am, and I always feel that I am very young. When I was a little girl, my father and mother used to go from fair to fair and give performances, very good ones. And I used to do the *salto mortale*,[4] and all sorts of other tricks. And when papa and mamma died, a German lady adopted me and began to educate me. Very good. I grew up and became a governess. But where I come from and who am I, I don't know. . . . Who were my parents? Perhaps they weren't even married. . . . I don't know . . . [*Takes a cucumber out of her pocket and eats it.*] I don't know a thing. [*Pause.*] One wants so much to talk, and there isn't anyone to talk to. . . . I haven't anybody.
YEPIHODOV [*Plays the guitar and sings.*]   "What care I for the jarring world? What's friend or foe to me? . . ." How agreeable it is to play the mandolin.
DUNYASHA   That's a guitar, not a mandolin. [*Looks in a hand mirror and powders her face.*]
YEPIHODOV   To a madman in love it's a mandolin. [*Sings.*] "Would that the heart were warmed by the fire of mutual love!"
      [YASHA *joins in.*]
CHARLOTTA   How abominably these people sing. Pfui! Like jackals!
DUNYASHA [*To* YASHA.]   How wonderful it must be though to have stayed abroad!
YASHA   Ah, yes, of course, I cannot but agree with you there. [*Yawns and lights a cigar.*]
YEPIHODOV   Naturally. Abroad, everything has long since achieved full perfection.
YASHA   That goes without saying.
YEPIHODOV   I'm a cultivated man, I read all kinds of remarkable books. And yet I can never make out what direction I should take, what is it that I want, properly speaking. Should I live, or should I shoot myself, properly speaking? Nevertheless, I always carry a revolver about me. . . . Here it is . . . [*Shows revolver.*]
CHARLOTTA   I've finished. I'm going. [*Puts the gun over her shoulder.*] You are a very clever man, Yepihodov, and a very terrible one; women must be crazy about you. Br-r-r! [*Starts to go.*] These clever men are all so stupid; there's no one for me to talk to . . . always alone, alone, I haven't a soul . . . and who I am, and why I am, nobody knows. [*Exits unhurriedly.*]
YEPIHODOV   Properly speaking and letting other subjects alone, I must say regarding myself, among other things, that fate treats me mercilessly, like a storm treats a small boat. If I am mistaken, let us say, why then do I wake up this morning, and there on my chest is a spider of enormous dimensions . . . like this . . . [*Indicates with both hands.*] Again, I take up a pitcher of kvass to have a drink, and in it there is something unseemly

4. Somersault (Italian).

to the highest degree, something like a cockroach. [*Pause.*] Have you read Buckle?[5] [*Pause.*] I wish to have a word with you, Avdotya Fyodorovna, if I may trouble you.

DUNYASHA Well, go ahead.

YEPIHODOV I wish to speak with you alone. [*Sighs.*]

DUNYASHA [*Embarrassed.*] Very well. Only first bring me my little cape. You'll find it near the wardrobe. It's rather damp here.

YEPIHODOV Certainly, ma'am; I will fetch it, ma'am. Now I know what to do with my revolver. [*Takes the guitar and goes off playing it.*]

YASHA Two-and-Twenty Troubles! An awful fool, between you and me. [*Yawns.*]

DUNYASHA I hope to God he doesn't shoot himself! [*Pause.*] I've become so nervous, I'm always fretting. I was still a little girl when I was taken into the big house, I am quite unused to the simple life now, and my hands are white, as white as a lady's. I've become so soft, so delicate, so refined, I'm afraid of everything. It's so terrifying; and if you deceive me, Yasha, I don't know what will happen to my nerves. [YASHA *kisses her.*]

YASHA You're a peach! Of course, a girl should never forget herself; and what I dislike more than anything is when a girl don't behave properly.

DUNYASHA I've fallen passionately in love with you; you're educated—you have something to say about everything. [*Pause.*]

YASHA [*Yawns.*] Yes, ma'am. Now the way I look at it, if a girl loves someone, it means she is immoral. [*Pause.*] It's agreeable smoking a cigar in the fresh air. [*Listens.*] Someone's coming this way. . . . It's our madam and the others. [DUNYASHA *embraces him impulsively.*] You go home, as though you'd been to the river to bathe; go to the little path, or else they'll run into you and suspect me of having arranged to meet you here. I can't stand that sort of thing.

DUNYASHA [*Coughing softly.*] Your cigar's made my head ache.

[*Exits.* YASHA *remains standing near the chapel. Enter* MME. RANEVSKAYA, GAYEV, *and* LOPAHIN.]

LOPAHIN You must make up your mind once and for all—there's no time to lose. It's quite a simple question, you know. Do you agree to lease your land for summer cottages or not? Answer in one word, yes or no; only one word!

MME. RANEVSKAYA Who's been smoking such abominable cigars here? [*Sits down.*]

GAYEV Now that the railway line is so near, it's made things very convenient. [*Sits down.*] Here we've been able to have lunch in town. Yellow ball in the side pocket! I feel like going into the house and playing just one game.

MME. RANEVSKAYA You can do that later.

LOPAHIN Only one word! [*Imploringly.*] Do give me an answer!

GAYEV [*Yawning.*] Who?

MME. RANEVSKAYA [*Looks into her purse.*] Yesterday I had a lot of money and now my purse is almost empty. My poor Varya tries to economize by feeding us just milk soup; in the kitchen the old people get nothing but

---

5. Henry Thomas Buckle (1821–1862) wrote a *History of Civilization in England* (1857–61), which was considered daringly materialistic and free thinking.

dried peas to eat, while I squander money thoughtlessly. [*Drops the purse, scattering gold pieces.*] You see, there they go . . . [*Shows vexation.*]

YASHA   Allow me—I'll pick them up. [*Picks up the money.*]

MME. RANEVSKAYA   Be so kind. Yasha. And why did I go to lunch in town? That nasty restaurant, with its music and the tablecloth smelling of soap. . . . Why drink so much, Leonid? Why eat so much? Why talk so much? Today again you talked a lot, and all so inappropriately about the seventies, about the decadents.[6] And to whom? Talking to waiters about decadents!

LOPAHIN   Yes.

GAYEV [*Waving his hand.*]   I'm incorrigible; that's obvious. [*Irritably, to* YASHA.] Why do you keep dancing about in front of me?

YASHA [*Laughs.*]   I can't hear your voice without laughing—

GAYEV   Either he or I—

MME. RANEVSKAYA   Go away, Yasha; run along.

YASHA [*Handing* MME. RANEVSKAYA *her purse.*]   I'm going at once. [*Hardly able to suppress his laughter.*] This minute. [*Exits.*]

LOPAHIN   That rich man, Deriganov, wants to buy your estate. They say he's coming to the auction himself.

MME. RANEVSKAYA   Where did you hear that?

LOPAHIN   That's what they are saying in town.

GAYEV   Our aunt in Yaroslavl has promised to help, but when she will send the money, and how much, no one knows.

LOPAHIN   How much will she send? A hundred thousand? Two hundred?

MME. RANEVSKAYA   Oh, well, ten or fifteen thousand; and we'll have to be grateful for that.

LOPAHIN   Forgive me, but such frivolous people as you are, so queer and unbusinesslike—I never met in my life. One tells you in plain language that your estate is up for sale, and you don't seem to take it in.

MME. RANEVSKAYA   What are we to do? Tell us what to do.

LOPAHIN   I do tell you, every day; every day I say the same thing! You must lease the cherry orchard and the land for summer cottages, you must do it and as soon as possible—right away. The auction is close at hand. Please understand! Once you've decided to have the cottages, you can raise as much money as you like, and you're saved.

MME. RANEVSKAYA   Cottages—summer people—forgive me, but it's all so vulgar.

GAYEV   I agree with you absolutely.

LOPAHIN   I shall either burst into tears or scream or faint! I can't stand it! You've worn me out! [*To* GAYEV.] You're an old woman!

GAYEV   Who?

LOPAHIN   An old woman! [*Gets up to go.*]

MME. RANEVSKAYA [*Alarmed.*]   No, don't go! Please stay, I beg you, my dear. Perhaps we shall think of something.

LOPAHIN   What is there to think of?

MME. RANEVSKAYA   Don't go, I beg you. With you here it's more cheerful anyway. [*Pause.*] I keep expecting something to happen, it's as though the house were going to crash about our ears.

---

6. A group of French poets of the 1880s (Mallarmé is today the most famous) were labeled "decadents" by their enemies and sometimes adopted the name themselves, proud of their refinement and sensitivity.

GAYEV [*In deep thought.*]   Bank shot in the corner. . . . Three cushions in the side pocket. . . .

MME. RANEVSKAYA   We have been great sinners . . .

LOPAHIN   What sins could you have committed?

GAYEV [*Putting a candy in his mouth.*]   They say I've eaten up my fortune in candy! [*Laughs.*]

MME. RANEVSKAYA   Oh, my sins! I've squandered money away recklessly, like a lunatic, and I married a man who made nothing but debts. My husband drank himself to death on champagne, he was a terrific drinker. And then, to my sorrow, I fell in love with another man, and I lived with him. And just then—that was my first punishment—a blow on the head: my little boy was drowned here in the river. And I went abroad, went away forever . . . never to come back, never to see this river again . . . I closed my eyes and ran, out of my mind. . . . But he followed me, pitiless, brutal. I bought a villa near Mentone, because he fell ill there; and for three years, day and night, I knew no peace, no rest. The sick man wore me out, he sucked my soul dry. Then last year, when the villa was sold to pay my debts, I went to Paris, and there he robbed me, abandoned me, took up with another woman, I tried to poison myself—it was stupid, so shameful—and then suddenly I felt drawn back to Russia, back, to my own country, to my little girl. [*Wipes her tears away.*] Lord, Lord! Be merciful, forgive me my sins—don't punish me anymore! [*Takes a telegram out of her pocket.*] This came today from Paris—he begs me to forgive him, implores me to go back . . . [*Tears up the telegram.*] Do I hear music? [*Listens.*]

GAYEV   That's our famous Jewish band, you remember? Four violins, a flute, and a double bass.

MME. RANEVSKAYA   Does it still exist? We ought to send for them some evening and have a party.

LOPAHIN [*Listens.*]   I don't hear anything. [*Hums softly.*] "The Germans for a fee will Frenchify a Russian."[7] [*Laughs.*] I saw a play at the theater yesterday—awfully funny.

MME. RANEVSKAYA   There was probably nothing funny about it. You shouldn't go to see plays, you should look at yourselves more often. How drab your lives are—how full of unnecessary talk.

LOPAHIN   That's true; come to think of it, we do live like fools. [*Pause.*] My pop was a peasant, an idiot; he understood nothing, never taught me anything, all he did was beat me when he was drunk, and always with a stick. Fundamentally, I'm just the same kind of blockhead and idiot. I was never taught anything—I have a terrible handwriting. I write so that I feel ashamed before people, like a pig.

MME. RANEVSKAYA   You should get married, my friend.

LOPAHIN   Yes . . . that's true.

MME. RANEVSKAYA   To our Varya, she's a good girl.

LOPAHIN   Yes.

MME. RANEVSKAYA   She's a girl who comes of simple people, she works all day long; and above all, she loves you. Besides, you've liked her for a long time now.

---

7. Satirical reference to Russian efforts, from the time of Peter the Great (1672–1725), to imitate Western Europe and particularly Parisian culture.

LOPAHIN Well, I've nothing against it. She's a good girl. [*Pause.*]

GAYEV I've been offered a place in the bank—6,000 a year. Have you heard?

MME. RANEVSKAYA You're not up to it. Stay where you are.

[FIRS *enters, carrying an overcoat.*]

FIRS [*To* GAYEV.] Please put this on, sir, it's damp.

GAYEV [*Putting it on.*] I'm fed up with you, brother.

FIRS Never mind. This morning you drove off without saying a word. [*Looks him over.*]

MME. RANEVSKAYA How you've aged, Firs.

FIRS I beg your pardon?

LOPAHIN The lady says you've aged.

FIRS I've lived a long time; they were arranging my wedding and your papa wasn't born yet. [*Laughs.*] When freedom came[8] I was already head footman. I wouldn't consent to be set free then; I stayed on with the master . . . [*Pause.*] I remember they were all very happy, but why they were happy, they didn't know themselves.

LOPAHIN It was fine in the old days! At least there was flogging!

FIRS [*Not hearing.*] Of course. The peasants kept to the masters, the masters kept to the peasants; but now they've all gone their own ways, and there's no making out anything.

GAYEV Be quiet, Firs. I must go to town tomorrow. They've promised to introduce me to a general who might let us have a loan.

LOPAHIN Nothing will come of that. You won't even be able to pay the interest, you can be certain of that.

MME. RANEVSKAYA He's raving, there isn't any general.

[*Enter* TROFIMOV, ANYA, *and* VARYA.]

GAYEV Here come our young people.

ANYA There's Mamma, on the bench.

MME. RANEVSKAYA [*Tenderly.*] Come here, come along, my darlings. [*Embraces* ANYA *and* VARYA.] If you only knew how I love you both! Sit beside me—there, like that. [*All sit down.*]

LOPAHIN Our perpetual student is always with the young ladies.

TROFIMOV That's not any of your business.

LOPAHIN He'll soon be fifty, and he's still a student!

TROFIMOV Stop your silly jokes.

LOPAHIN What are you so cross about, you queer bird?

TROFIMOV Oh, leave me alone.

LOPAHIN [*Laughs.*] Allow me to ask you, what do you think of me?

TROFIMOV What I think of you, Yermolay Alexeyevich, is this: you are a rich man who will soon be a millionaire. Well, just as a beast of prey, which devours everything that comes in its way, is necessary for the process of metabolism to go on, so you, too, are necessary. [*All laugh.*]

VARYA Better tell us something about the planets, Petya.

MME. RANEVSKAYA No, let's go on with yesterday's conversation.

TROFIMOV What was it about?

GAYEV About man's pride.

---

8. Czar (or Tsar) Alexander II (ruled 1855–81) emancipated the serfs in 1861.

TROFIMOV Yesterday we talked a long time, but we came to no conclusion. There is something mystical about man's pride in your sense of the word. Perhaps you're right, from your own point of view. But if you reason simply, without going into subtleties, then what call is there for pride? Is there any sense in it, if man is so poor a thing physiologically, and if, in the great majority of cases, he is coarse, stupid, profoundly unhappy? We should stop admiring ourselves. We should work, and that's all.

GAYEV You die, anyway.

TROFIMOV Who knows? And what does it mean—to die? Perhaps man has a hundred senses, and at his death only the five we know perish, while the other ninety-five remain alive.

MME. RANEVSKAYA How clever you are, Petya!

LOPAHIN [*Ironically.*] Awfully clever!

TROFIMOV Mankind goes forward, developing its powers. Everything that is now unattainable for it will one day come within man's reach and be clear to him; only we must work, helping with all our might those who seek the truth. Here among us in Russia only the very few work as yet. The great majority of the intelligentsia, as far as I can see, seek nothing, do nothing, are totally unfit for work of any kind. They call themselves the intelligentsia, yet they are uncivil to their servants, treat the peasants like animals, are poor students, never read anything serious, do absolutely nothing at all, only talk about science, and have little appreciation of the arts. They are all solemn, have grim faces, they all philosophize and talk of weighty matters. And meanwhile the vast majority of us, ninety-nine out of a hundred, live like savages. At the least provocation— a punch in the jaw, and curses. They eat disgustingly, sleep in filth and stuffiness, bedbugs everywhere, stench and damp and moral slovenliness. And obviously, the only purpose of all our fine talk is to hoodwink ourselves and others. Show me where the public nurseries are that we've heard so much about, and the libraries. We read about them in novels, but in reality they don't exist, there is nothing but dirt, vulgarity, and Asiatic backwardness. I don't like very solemn faces, I'm afraid of them, I'm afraid of serious conversations. We'd do better to keep quiet for a while.

LOPAHIN Do you know, I get up at five o'clock in the morning, and I work from morning till night; and I'm always handling money, my own and other people's, and I see what people around me are really like. You've only to start doing anything to see how few honest, decent people there are. Sometimes when I lie awake at night, I think: "Oh, Lord, thou hast given us immense forests, boundless fields, the widest horizons, and living in their midst, we ourselves ought really to be giants."

MME. RANEVSKAYA Now you want giants! They're only good in fairy tales; otherwise they're frightening.

[YEPIHODOV *crosses the stage at the rear, playing the guitar.*]

MME. RANEVSKAYA [*Pensively.*] There goes Yepihodov.

GAYEV Ladies and gentlemen, the sun has set.

TROFIMOV Yes.

GAYEV [*In a low voice, declaiming as it were.*] Oh, Nature, wondrous Nature, you shine with eternal radiance, beautiful and indifferent! You, whom we call our mother, unite within yourself life and death! You animate and destroy!

VARYA [*Pleadingly.*]   Uncle dear!

ANYA   Uncle, again!

TROFIMOV   You'd better bank the yellow ball in the side pocket.

GAYEV   I'm silent, I'm silent . . .

> [*All sit plunged in thought. Stillness reigns. Only* FIRS's *muttering is audible. Suddenly a distant sound is heard, coming from the sky as it were, the sound of a snapping string, mournfully dying away.*]

MME. RANEVSKAYA   What was that?

LOPAHIN   I don't know. Somewhere far away, in the pits, a bucket's broken loose; but somewhere very far away.

GAYEV   Or it might be some sort of bird, perhaps a heron.

TROFIMOV   Or an owl . . .

MME. RANEVSKAYA [*Shudders.*]   It's weird, somehow. [*Pause.*]

FIRS   Before the calamity the same thing happened—the owl screeched, and the samovar hummed all the time.

GAYEV   Before what calamity?

FIRS   Before the Freedom. [*Pause.*]

MME. RANEVSKAYA   Come, my friends, let's be going. It's getting dark. [*To* ANYA.] You have tears in your eyes. What is it, my little one? [*Embraces her.*]

ANYA   I don't know, Mamma; it's nothing.

TROFIMOV   Somebody's coming.

> [*A* TRAMP *appears, wearing a shabby white cap and an overcoat. He is slightly drunk.*]

TRAMP   Allow me to inquire, will this short cut take me to the station?

GAYEV   It will. Just follow that road.

TRAMP   My heartfelt thanks. [*Coughing.*] The weather is glorious. [*Recites.*] "My brother, my suffering brother. . . . Go down to the Volga!⁹ Whose groans . . . ?" [*To* VARYA.] Mademoiselle, won't you spare 30 kopecks for a hungry Russian?

> [VARYA, *frightened, cries out.*]

LOPAHIN [*Angrily.*]   Even panhandling has its proprieties.

MME. RANEVSKAYA [*Scared.*]   Here, take this. [*Fumbles in her purse.*] I haven't any silver . . . never mind, here's a gold piece.

TRAMP   My heartfelt thanks. [*Exits. Laughter.*]

VARYA [*Frightened.*]   I'm leaving. I'm leaving. . . . Oh, Mamma dearest, at home the servants have nothing to eat, and you gave him a gold piece!

MME. RANEVSKAYA   What are you going to do with me? I'm such a fool. When we get home, I'll give you everything I have. Yermolay Alexeyevich, you'll lend me some more . . .

LOPAHIN   Yes, ma'am.

MME. RANEVSKAYA   Come, ladies and gentlemen, it's time to be going. Oh! Varya, we've settled all about your marriage. Congratulations!

VARYA [*Through tears.*]   Really, Mamma, that's not a joking matter.

LOPAHIN   "Aurelia, get thee to a nunnery, go . . . "

***

9. Lines from poems by Semyon Nadson (1826–1878) and Nikolay Nekrasov (1821–1878).

GAYEV   And do you know, my hands are trembling: I haven't played billiards in a long time.

LOPAHIN   "Aurelia, nymph, in your orisons, remember me!"[1]

MME. RANEVSKAYA   Let's go, it's almost suppertime.

VARYA   He frightened me! My heart's pounding.

LOPAHIN   Let me remind you, ladies and gentlemen, on the twenty-second of August the cherry orchard will be up for sale. Think about that! Think!

[*All except* TROFIMOV *and* ANYA *go out.*]

ANYA [*Laughs.*]   I'm grateful to that tramp, he frightened Varya and so we're alone.

TROFIMOV   Varya's afraid we'll fall in love with each other all of a sudden. She hasn't left us alone for days. Her narrow mind can't grasp that we're above love. To avoid the petty and illusory, everything that prevents us from being free and happy—that is the goal and meaning of our life. Forward! Do not fall behind, friends!

ANYA [*Strikes her hands together.*]   How well you speak! [*Pause.*] It's wonderful here today.

TROFIMOV   Yes, the weather's glorious.

ANYA   What have you done to me, Petya? Why don't I love the cherry orchard as I used to? I loved it so tenderly. It seemed to me there was no spot on earth lovelier than our orchard.

TROFIMOV   All Russia is our orchard. Our land is vast and beautiful, there are many wonderful places in it. [*Pause.*] Think of it, Anya, your grandfather, your great-grandfather and all your ancestors were serf owners, owners of living souls, and aren't human beings looking at you from every tree in the orchard, from every leaf, from every trunk? Don't you hear voices? Oh, it's terrifying! Your orchard is a fearful place, and when you pass through it in the evening or at night, the old bark on the trees gleams faintly, and the cherry trees seem to be dreaming of things that happened a hundred, two hundred years ago and to be tormented by painful visions. What is there to say? We're at least two hundred years behind, we've really achieved nothing yet, we have no definite attitude to the past, we only philosophize, complain of the blues, or drink vodka. It's all so clear: in order to live in the present, we should first redeem our past, finish with it, and we can expiate it only by suffering, only by extraordinary, unceasing labor. Realize that, Anya.

ANYA   The house in which we live has long ceased to be our own, and I will leave it, I give you my word.

TROFIMOV   If you have the keys, fling them into the well and go away. Be free as the wind.

ANYA [*In ecstasy.*]   How well you put that!

TROFIMOV   Believe me, Anya, believe me! I'm not yet thirty, I'm young, I'm still a student—but I've already suffered so much. In winter I'm hungry, sick, harassed, poor as a beggar, and where hasn't Fate driven me? Where haven't I been? And yet always, every moment of the day and

---

1. Lopahin makes comic use of Hamlet's meeting with Ophelia. (Here *Aurelia* conveys the Russian text's distortion of "Ophelia" as "Okhmelia.") Hamlet, seeing her approaching, says: "Nymph, in thy orisons / Be all my sins remembered" (3.1.91–92), and later, suspecting her of spying for her father, sends her off with "Get thee to a nunnery" (3.1.122).

night, my soul is filled with inexplicable premonitions. . . . I have a premonition of happiness, Anya. . . . I see it already!

ANYA [*Pensively.*] The moon is rising.

> [YEPIHODOV *is heard playing the same mournful tune on the guitar.
> The moon rises. Somewhere near the poplars* VARYA *is looking for*
> ANYA *and calling,* "Anya, where are you?"]

TROFIMOV Yes, the moon is rising. [*Pause.*] There it is, happiness, it's
approaching, it's coming nearer and nearer, I can already hear its footsteps. And if we don't see it, if we don't know it, what does it matter?
Others will!

VARYA'S VOICE Anya! Where are you?

TROFIMOV That Varya again! [*Angrily.*] It's revolting!

ANYA Never mind, let's go down to the river. It's lovely there.

TROFIMOV Come on. [*They go.*]

VARYA'S VOICE Anya! Anya!

Act III

*A drawing room separated by an arch from a ballroom. Evening. Chandelier
burning. The Jewish band is heard playing in the anteroom. In the ballroom they
are dancing the* Grand Rond. PISHCHIK *is heard calling,* "Promenade à une
paire!"[2] PISHCHIK *and* CHARLOTTA, TROFIMOV *and* MME. RANEVSKAYA, ANYA *and
the* POST OFFICE CLERK, VARYA *and the* STATIONMASTER, *and others enter the
drawing room in couples.* DUNYASHA *is in the last couple.* VARYA *weeps quietly,
wiping her tears as she dances. All parade through drawing room,* PISHCHIK *calling,* "Grand rond, balancez!"[3] *and* "Les cavaliers à genoux et remerciez vos
dames!"[4] FIRS, *wearing a dress coat, brings in soda water on a tray.* PISHCHIK *and*
TROFIMOV *enter the drawing room.*

PISHCHIK I have high blood pressure; I've already had two strokes. Dancing's hard work for me; but as they say, "If you run with the pack, you
can bark or not, but at least wag your tail." Still, I'm as strong as a horse.
My late lamented father, who would have his joke, God rest his soul,
used to say, talking about our origin, that the ancient line of the
Simeonov-Pishchiks was descended from the very horse that Caligula
had made a senator.[5] [*Sits down.*] But the trouble is, I have no money.
A hungry dog believes in nothing but meat. [*Snores, and wakes up at
once.*] It's the same with me—I can think of nothing but money.

TROFIMOV You know, there *is* something equine about your figure.

PISHCHIK Well, a horse is a fine animal—one can sell a horse.

> [*Sound of billiards being played in an adjoining room.* VARYA *appears
> in the archway.*]

TROFIMOV [*Teasing her.*] Madam Lopahina! Madam Lopahina!

VARYA [*Angrily.*] Mangy master!

TROFIMOV Yes, I am a mangy master and I'm proud of it.

---

2. Promenade with your partner! (French). *Grand Rond:* a ring dance.   3. Make a large circle, get set!
(French).   4. Gentlemen, on your knees and thank your ladies! (French).   5. The mad emperor Caligula (12–41 A.D.) brought his favorite horse into the Roman senate to make it a senator.

VARYA [*Reflecting bitterly.*]   Here we've hired musicians, and what shall we pay them with? [*Exits.*]

TROFIMOV [*To* PISHCHIK.]   If the energy you have spent during your lifetime looking for money to pay interest had gone into something else, in the end you could have turned the world upside down.

PISHCHIK   Nietzsche,[6] the philosopher, the greatest, most famous of men, that colossal intellect, says in his works that it is permissible to forge banknotes.

TROFIMOV   Have you read Nietzsche?

PISHCHIK   Well . . . Dashenka told me. . . . And now I've got to the point where forging banknotes is the only way out for me. . . . The day after tomorrow I have to pay 310 rubles—I already have 130 . . . [*Feels in his pockets. In alarm.*] The money's gone! I've lost my money! [*Through tears.*] Where's my money? [*Joyfully.*] Here it is! Inside the lining . . . I'm all in a sweat . . .

[*Enter* MME. RANEVSKAYA *and* CHARLOTTA.]

MME. RANEVSKAYA [*Hums the "Lezginka."*[7]]   Why isn't Leonid back yet? What is he doing in town? [*To* DUNYASHA.] Dunyasha, offer the musicians tea.

TROFIMOV   The auction hasn't taken place, most likely.

MME. RANEVSKAYA   It's the wrong time to have the band, and the wrong time to give a dance. Well, never mind. [*Sits down and hums softly.*]

CHARLOTTA. [*Hands* PISHCHIK *a pack of cards.*]   Here is a pack of cards. Think of any card you like.

PISHCHIK   I've thought of one.

CHARLOTTA   Shuffle the pack now. That's right. Give it here, my dear Mr. Pishchik. *Eins, zwei, drei!*[8] Now look for it—it's in your side pocket.

PISHCHIK [*Taking the card out of his pocket.*]   The eight of spades! Perfectly right! Just imagine!

CHARLOTTA [*Holding the pack of cards in her hands. To* TROFIMOV.] Quickly, name the top card.

TROFIMOV   Well, let's see—the queen of spades.

CHARLOTTA   Right! [*To* PISHCHIK.] Now name the top card.

PISHCHIK   The ace of hearts.

CHARLOTTA   Right! [*Claps her hands and the pack of cards disappears.*] Ah, what lovely weather it is today! [*A mysterious feminine* VOICE, *which seems to come from under the floor, answers her: "Oh, yes, it's magnificent weather, madam."*] You are my best ideal. [VOICE: "And I find you pleasing too, madam."]

STATIONMASTER [*Applauding.*]   The lady ventriloquist, bravo!

PISHCHIK [*Amazed.*]   Just imagine! Enchanting Charlotta Ivanovna, I'm simply in love with you.

CHARLOTTA   In love? [*Shrugs her shoulders.*] Are you capable of love? *Guter Mensch, aber schlechter Musikant!*[9]

6. Friedrich W. Nietzsche (1844–1900), German philosopher.   7. The music that in the Caucasus mountains accompanies a courtship dance in which the man dances with abandon around the woman, who moves with grace and ease.   8. One, two, three (German).   9. "A good man, but a bad musician" (German), usually quoted in the plural: "*Gute Leute, schlechte Musikanten.*" It comes from *Das Buch le Grand* (1826) by the German poet Heinrich Heine (1799–1856). Here it suggests that Pishchik may be a good man but a bad lover.

TROFIMOV [*Claps* PISHCHIK *on the shoulder.*]   You old horse, you!

CHARLOTTA   Attention please! One more trick! [*Takes a plaid*[1] *from a chair.*] Here is a very good plaid; I want to sell it. [*Shaking it out.*] Does anyone want to buy it?

PISHCHIK [*In amazement.*]   Just imagine!

CHARLOTTA   *Eins, zwei, drei!* [*Raises the plaid quickly, behind it stands* ANYA. *She curtsies, runs to her mother, embraces her, and runs back into the ballroom, amid general enthusiasm.*]

MME. RANEVSKAYA [*Applauds.*]   Bravo! Bravo!

CHARLOTTA   Now again! *Eins, zwei, drei!* [*Lifts the plaid; behind it stands* VARYA, *bowing.*]

PISHCHIK [*In amazement.*]   Just imagine!

[CHARLOTTA *throws the plaid at* PISHCHIK, *curtsies, and runs into the ballroom.*]

PISHCHIK [*Running after her.*]   The rascal! What a woman, what a woman! [*Exits.*]

MME. RANEVSKAYA   And Leonid still isn't here. What is he doing in town so long? I don't understand. It must be all over by now. Either the estate has been sold, or the auction hasn't taken place. Why keep us in suspense so long?

VARYA [*Trying to console her.*]   Uncle's bought it, I feel sure of that.

TROFIMOV [*Mockingly.*]   Oh, yes!

VARYA   Great-aunt sent him an authorization to buy it in her name, and to transfer the debt. She's doing it for Anya's sake. And I'm sure that God will help us, and Uncle will buy it.

MME. RANEVSKAYA   Great-aunt sent fifteen thousand to buy the estate in her name, she doesn't trust us, but that's not even enough to pay the interest. [*Covers her face with her hands.*] Today my fate will be decided, my fate—

TROFIMOV [*Teasing* VARYA.]   Madam Lopahina!

VARYA [*Angrily.*]   Perpetual student! Twice already you've been expelled from the university.

MME. RANEVSKAYA   Why are you so cross, Varya? He's teasing you about Lopahin. Well, what of it? If you want to marry Lopahin, go ahead. He's a good man, and interesting; if you don't want to, don't. Nobody's compelling you, my pet!

VARYA   Frankly, Mamma dear, I take this thing seriously; he's a good man and I like him.

MME. RANEVSKAYA   All right then, marry him. I don't know what you're waiting for.

VARYA   But, Mamma, I can't propose to him myself. For the last two years, everyone's been talking to me about him—talking. But he either keeps silent, or else cracks jokes. I understand; he's growing rich, he's absorbed in business—he has no time for me. If I had money, even a little, say, 100 rubles, I'd throw everything up and go far away—I'd go into a nunnery.

TROFIMOV   What a blessing . . .

VARYA   A student ought to be intelligent. [*Softly, with tears in her voice.*]

1. A small plaid blanket, or lap robe.

How homely you've grown, Petya! How old you look! [*To* MME. RANEV-
SKAYA, *with dry eyes.*] But I can't live without work, Mamma dear; I must
keep busy every minute.

      [*Enter* YASHA.]

YASHA [*Hardly restraining his laughter.*]   Yepihodov has broken a billiard
   cue! [*Exits.*]

VARYA   Why is Yepihodov here? Who allowed him to play billiards? I don't
   understand these people! [*Exits.*]

MME. RANEVSKAYA   Don't tease her, Petya. She's unhappy enough without
   that.

TROFIMOV   She bustles so—and meddles in other people's business. All
   summer long she's given Anya and me no peace. She's afraid of a love
   affair between us. What business is it of hers? Besides, I've given no
   grounds for it, and I'm far from such vulgarity. We are above love.

MME. RANEVSKAYA   And I suppose I'm beneath love? [*Anxiously.*] What
   can be keeping Leonid? If I only knew whether the estate has been sold
   or not. Such a calamity seems so incredible to me that I don't know what
   to think—I feel lost. . . . I could scream. . . . I could do something stupid.
   . . . Save me, Petya, tell me something, talk to me!

TROFIMOV   Whether the estate is sold today or not, isn't it all one? That's
   all done with long ago—there's no turning back, the path is overgrown.
   Calm yourself, my dear. You mustn't deceive yourself. For once in your
   life you must face the truth.

MME. RANEVSKAYA   What truth? You can see the truth, you can tell it from
   falsehood, but I seem to have lost my eyesight, I see nothing. You settle
   every great problem so boldly, but tell me, my dear boy, isn't it because
   you're young, because you don't yet know what one of your problems
   means in terms of suffering? You look ahead fearlessly, but isn't it
   because you don't see and don't expect anything dreadful, because life
   is still hidden from your young eyes? You're bolder, more honest, more
   profound than we are, but think hard, show just a bit of magnanimity,
   spare me. After all, I was born here, my father and mother lived here,
   and my grandfather; I love this house. Without the cherry orchard, my
   life has no meaning for me, and if it really must be sold, then sell me
   with the orchard. [*Embraces* TROFIMOV, *kisses him on the forehead.*] My
   son was drowned here. [*Weeps.*] Pity me, you good, kind fellow!

TROFIMOV   You know, I feel for you with all my heart.

MME. RANEVSKAYA   But that should have been said differently, so differently! [*Takes out her handkerchief—a telegram falls on the floor.*] My
   heart is so heavy today—you can't imagine! The noise here upsets me—
   my inmost being trembles at every sound—I'm shaking all over. But I
   can't go into my own room; I'm afraid to be alone. Don't condemn me,
   Petya. . . . I love you as though you were one of us, I would gladly let you
   marry Anya—I swear I would—only, my dear boy, you must study—you
   must take your degree—you do nothing, you let yourself be tossed by
   Fate from place to place—it's so strange. It's true, isn't it? And you should
   do something about your beard, to make it grow somehow! [*Laughs.*]
   You're so funny!

TROFIMOV [*Picks up the telegram.*]   I've no wish to be a dandy.

MME. RANEVSKAYA   That's a telegram from Paris. I get one every day. One yesterday and one today. That savage is ill again—he's in trouble again. He begs forgiveness, implores me to go to him, and really I ought to go to Paris to be near him. Your face is stern, Petya; but what is there to do, my dear boy? What am I to do? He's ill, he's alone and unhappy, and who is to look after him, who is to keep him from doing the wrong thing, who is to give him his medicine on time? And why hide it or keep still about it—I love him! That's clear. I love him, love him! He's a millstone round my neck, he'll drag me to the bottom, but I love that stone, I can't live without it. [*Presses* TROFIMOV's *hand.*] Don't think badly of me. Petya, and don't say anything, don't say . . .

TROFIMOV [*Through tears.*] Forgive me my frankness in heaven's name; but, you know, he robbed you!

MME. RANEVSKAYA No, no, no, you mustn't say such things! [*Covers her ears.*]

TROFIMOV But he's a scoundrel! You're the only one who doesn't know it. He's a petty scoundrel—a nonentity!

MME. RANEVSKAYA [*Controlling her anger.*] You are twenty-six or twenty-seven years old, but you're still a schoolboy.

TROFIMOV That may be.

MME. RANEVSKAYA You should be a man at your age. You should understand people who love—and ought to be in love yourself. You ought to fall in love! [*Angrily.*] Yes, yes! And it's not purity in you, it's prudishness, you're simply a queer fish, a comical freak!

TROFIMOV [*Horrified.*] What is she saying?

MME. RANEVSKAYA "I am above love!" You're not above love, but simple, as our Firs says, you're an addlehead. At your age not to have a mistress!

TROFIMOV [*Horrified.*] This is frightful! What is she saying! [*Goes rapidly into the ballroom, clutching his head.*] It's frightful—I can't stand it, I won't stay! [*Exits, but returns at once.*] All is over between us! [*Exits into anteroom.*]

MME. RANEVSKAYA [*Shouts after him.*] Petya! Wait! You absurd fellow, I was joking. Petya!

[*Sound of somebody running quickly downstairs and suddenly falling down with a crash.* ANYA *and* VARYA *scream. Sound of laughter a moment later.*]

MME. RANEVSKAYA What's happened?

[ANYA *runs in.*]

ANYA [*Laughing.*] Petya's fallen downstairs! [*Runs out.*]

MME. RANEVSKAYA What a queer bird that Petya is!

[STATIONMASTER, *standing in the middle of the ballroom, recites Alexey Tolstoy's "Magdalene,"*[2] *to which all listen, but after a few lines, the sound of a waltz is heard from the anteroom and the reading breaks off. All dance.* TROFIMOV, ANYA, VARYA *and* MME. RANEVSKAYA *enter from the anteroom.*]

MME. RANEVSKAYA Petya, you pure soul, please forgive me. . . . Let's dance.

[*Dances with* PETYA, ANYA *and* VARYA *dance.* FIRS *enters, puts his*

---

2. Called *The Sinning Woman* in Russian, it begins: "A bustling crowd with happy laughter, / with twanging lutes and clashing cymbals / with flowers and foliage all around / the colonnaded portico." Alexey Tolstoy (1817–1875), popular in his time as a dramatist and poet, was a distant relative of Leo Tolstoy.

stick down by the side door. YASHA *enters from the drawing room and watches the dancers.*]

YASHA   Well, Grandfather?

FIRS   I'm not feeling well. In the old days it was generals, barons, and admirals that were dancing at our balls, and now we have to send for the Post Office Clerk and the Stationmaster, and even they aren't too glad to come. I feel kind of shaky. The old master that's gone, their grandfather, dosed everyone with sealing wax, whatever ailed 'em. I've been taking sealing wax every day for twenty years or more. Perhaps that's what's kept me alive.

YASHA   I'm fed up with you, Grandpop. [*Yawns.*] It's time you croaked.

FIRS   Oh, you addlehead! [*Mumbles.*]

[TROFIMOV *and* MME. RANEVSKAYA *dance from the ballroom into the drawing room.*]

MME. RANEVSKAYA   Merci. I'll sit down a while. [*Sits down.*] I'm tired.
[*Enter* ANYA.]

ANYA [*Excitedly.*]   There was a man in the kitchen just now who said the cherry orchard was sold today.

MME. RANEVSKAYA   Sold to whom?

ANYA   He didn't say. He's gone. [*Dances off with* TROFIMOV.]

YASHA   It was some old man gabbing, a stranger.

FIRS   And Leonid Andreyevich isn't back yet, he hasn't come. And he's wearing his lightweight between-season overcoat; like enough, he'll catch cold. Ah, when they're young they're green.

MME. RANEVSKAYA   This is killing me. Go, Yasha, find out to whom it has been sold.

YASHA   But the old man left long ago. [*Laughs.*]

MME RANEVSKAYA   What are you laughing at? What are you pleased about?

YASHA   That Yepihodov is such a funny one. A funny fellow, Two-and-Twenty Troubles!

MME. RANEVSKAYA   Firs, if the estate is sold, where will you go?

FIRS   I'll go where you tell me.

MME. RANEVSKAYA   Why do you look like that? Are you ill? You ought to go to bed.

FIRS   Yes! [*With a snigger.*] Me go to bed, and who's to hand things round? Who's to see to things? I'm the only one in the whole house.

YASHA [*To* MME. RANEVSKAYA.]   Lubov Andreyevna, allow me to ask a favor of you, be so kind! If you go back to Paris, take me with you, I beg you. It's positively impossible for me to stay here. [*Looking around; sotto voce.*] What's the use of talking? You see for yourself, it's an uncivilized country, the people have no morals, and then the boredom! The food in the kitchen's revolting, and besides there's this Firs wanders about mumbling all sorts of inappropriate words. Take me with you, be so kind!
[*Enter* PISHCHIK.]

PISHCHIK   May I have the pleasure of a waltz with you, charming lady? [MME. RANEVSKAYA *accepts.*] All the same, enchanting lady, you must let me have 180 rubles. . . . You must let me have [*dancing*] just one hundred and eighty rubles. [*They pass into the ballroom.*]

YASHA [*Hums softly.*]   "Oh, wilt thou understand the tumult in my soul?"

[*In the ballroom a figure in a gray top hat and checked trousers is jumping about and waving its arms; shouts: "Bravo, Charlotta Ivanovna!"*]

DUNYASHA [*Stopping to powder her face; to* FIRS.]   The young miss has ordered me to dance. There are so many gentlemen and not enough ladies. But dancing makes me dizzy, my heart begins to beat fast, Firs Nikolayevich. The Post Office Clerk said something to me just now that quite took my breath away.

[*Music stops.*]

FIRS   What did he say?

DUNYASHA   "You're like a flower," he said.

YASHA [*Yawns.*]   What ignorance. [*Exits.*]

DUNYASHA   "Like a flower!" I'm such a delicate girl. I simply adore pretty speeches.

FIRS   You'll come to a bad end.

[*Enter* YEPIHODOV.]

YEPIHODOV [*To* DUNYASHA.]   You have no wish to see me, Avdotya Fyodo-rovna . . . as though I was some sort of insect. [*Sighs.*] Ah, life!

DUNYASHA   What is it you want?

YEPIHODOV   Indubitably you may be right. [*Sighs.*] But of course, if one looks at it from the point of view, if I may be allowed to say so, and apologizing for my frankness, you have completely reduced me to a state of mind. I know my fate. Every day some calamity befalls me, and I grew used to it long ago, so that I look upon my fate with a smile. You gave me your word, and though I—

DUNYASHA   Let's talk about it later, please. But just now leave me alone, I am daydreaming. [*Plays with a fan.*]

YEPIHODOV   A misfortune befalls me every day; and if I may be allowed to say so, I merely smile, I even laugh.

[*Enter* VARYA.]

VARYA [*To* YEPIHODOV.]   Are you still here? What an impertinent fellow you are really! Run along, Dunyasha. [*To* YEPIHODOV.] Either you're play-ing billiards and breaking a cue, or you're wandering about the drawing room as though you were a guest.

YEPIHODOV   You cannot, permit me to remark, penalize me.

VARYA   I'm not penalizing you; I'm just telling you. You merely wander from place to place, and don't do your work. We keep you as a clerk, but heaven knows what for.

YEPIHODOV [*Offended.*]   Whether I work or whether I walk, whether I eat or whether I play billiards, is a matter to be discussed only by persons of understanding and of mature years.

VARYA [*Enraged.*]   You dare say that to me—you dare? You mean to say I've no understanding? Get out of here at once! This minute!

YEPIHODOV [*Scared.*]   I beg you to express yourself delicately.

VARYA [*Beside herself.*]   Clear out this minute! Out with you!

[YEPIHODOV *goes toward the door,* VARYA *following.*]

VARYA   Two-and-Twenty Troubles! Get out—don't let me set eyes on you again!

[*Exit* YEPIHODOV *His voice is heard behind the door*: "I shall lodge a complaint against you!"]

VARYA Oh, you're coming back? [*She seizes the stick left near door by* FIRS.]
Well, come then . . . come . . . I'll show you. . . . Ah, you're coming?
You're coming? . . . Come . . . [*Swings the stick just as* LOPAHIN *enters.*]
LOPAHIN Thank you kindly.
VARYA [*Angrily and mockingly.*] I'm sorry.
LOPAHIN It's nothing. Thank you kindly for your charming reception.
VARYA Don't mention it. [*Walks away, looks back and asks softly.*] I didn't
hurt you, did I?
LOPAHIN Oh, no, not at all. I shall have a large bump, though.
[*Voices from the ballroom* "Lopahin is here! Lopahin!" *Enter*
PISHCHIK.]
PISHCHIK My eyes do see, my ears do hear! [*Kisses* LOPAHIN.] You smell
of cognac, my dear friend. And we've been celebrating here, too.
[*Enter* MME. RANEVSKAYA.]
MME. RANEVSKAYA Is that you, Yermolay Alexeyevich? What kept you so
long? Where's Leonid?
LOPAHIN Leonid Andreyevich arrived with me. He's coming.
MME. RANEVSKAYA Well, what happened? Did the sale take place? Speak!
LOPAHIN [*Embarrassed, fearful of revealing his joy.*] The sale was over at
four o'clock. We missed the train—had to wait till half-past nine. [*Sigh-
ing heavily.*] Ugh. I'm a little dizzy.
[*Enter* GAYEV *In his right hand he holds parcels, with his left he is
wiping away his tears.*]
MME. RANEVSKAYA Well, Leonid? What news? [*Impatiently, through
tears.*] Be quick, for God's sake!
GAYEV [*Not answering, simply waves his hand. Weeping, to* FIRS.] Here,
take these; anchovies, Kerch herrings . . . I haven't eaten all day. What
I've been through! [*The click of billiard balls comes through the open door
of the billiard room and* YASHA's *voice is heard:* "Seven and eighteen!"
GAYEV's *expression changes, he no longer weeps.*] I'm terribly tired. Firs,
help me change. [*Exits, followed by* FIRS.]
PISHCHIK How about the sale? Tell us what happened.
MME. RANEVSKAYA Is the cherry orchard sold?
LOPAHIN Sold.
MME. RANEVSKAYA Who bought it?
LOPAHIN I bought it.
[*Pause,* MME. RANEVSKAYA *is overcome. She would fall to the floor,
were it not for the chair and table near which she stands.* VARYA *takes
the keys from her belt, flings them on the floor in the middle of the
drawing room and goes out.*]
LOPAHIN I bought it. Wait a bit, ladies and gentlemen, please, my head
is swimming, I can't talk. [*Laughs.*] We got to the auction and Deriganov
was there already. Leonid Andreyevich had only 15,000 and straight off
Deriganov bid 30,000 over and above the mortgage. I saw how the land
lay, got into the fight, bid 40,000. He bid 45,000. I bid fifty-five. He kept
adding five thousands, I ten. Well . . . it came to an end. I bid ninety
above the mortgage and the estate was knocked down to me. Now the
cherry orchard's mine! Mine! [*Laughs uproariously.*] Lord! God in
Heaven! The cherry orchard's mine! Tell me that I'm drunk—out of my
mind—that it's all a dream. [*Stamps his feet.*] Don't laugh at me! If my

father and my grandfather could rise from their graves and see all that has happened—how their Yermolay, who used to be flogged, their half-literate Yermolay, who used to run about barefoot in winter, how that very Yermolay has bought the most magnificent estate in the world. I bought the estate where my father and grandfather were slaves, where they weren't even allowed to enter the kitchen. I am asleep—it's only a dream—I only imagine it. . . . It's the fruit of your imagination, wrapped in the darkness of the unknown! [*Picks up the keys, smiling genially.*] She threw down the keys, wants to show she's no longer mistress here. [*Jingles keys.*] Well, no matter. [*The band is warming up.*] Hey, musicians! Strike up! I want to hear you! Come, everybody, and see how Yermolay Lopahin will lay the ax to the cherry orchard and how the trees will fall to the ground. We will build summer cottages there, and our grandsons and great grandsons will see a new life here. Music! Strike up!

> [*The band starts to play.* MME RANEVSKAYA *has sunk into a chair and is weeping bitterly.*]

LOPAHIN [*Reproachfully.*]   Why, why didn't you listen to me? My dear friend, my poor friend, you can't bring it back now. [*Tearfully.*] Oh, if only this were over quickly! Oh, if only our wretched, disordered life were changed!

PISHCHIK [*Takes him by the arm; sotto voce.*]   She's crying. Let's go into the ballroom. Let her be alone. Come. [*Takes his arm and leads him into the ballroom.*]

LOPAHIN   What's the matter? Musicians, play so I can hear you! Let me have things the way I want them. [*Ironically.*] Here comes the new master, the owner of the cherry orchard. [*Accidentally he trips over a little table, almost upsetting the candelabra.*] I can pay for everything. [*Exits with* PISHCHIK.]

> [MME. RANEVSKAYA, *alone, sits huddled up, weeping bitterly. Music plays softly. Enter* ANYA *and* TROFIMOV *quickly.* ANYA *goes to her mother and falls on her knees before her.* TROFIMOV *stands in the doorway.*]

ANYA   Mamma, Mamma, you're crying! Dear, kind, good Mamma, my precious, I love you, I bless you! The cherry orchard is sold, it's gone, that's true, quite true. But don't cry, Mamma, life is still before you, you still have your kind, pure heart. Let us go, let us go away from here, darling. We will plant a new orchard, even more luxuriant than this one. You will see it, you will understand, and like the sun at evening, joy—deep, tranquil joy—will sink into your soul, and you will smile, Mamma. Come, darling, let us go.

Act IV

Scene as in Act I. No window curtains or pictures, only a little furniture, piled up in a corner, as if for sale. A sense of emptiness. Near the outer door and at the back, suitcases, bundles, etc., are piled up. A door open on the left and the voices of VARYA *and* ANYA *are heard.* LOPAHIN *stands waiting.* YASHA *holds a tray with glasses full of champagne.* YEPIHODOV *in the anteroom is tying up a box. Behind the scene a hum of voices: peasants have come to say good-bye. Voice of* GAYEV: "Thanks, brothers, thank you."

YASHA The country folk have come to say good-bye. In my opinion, Yermolay Alexeyevich, they are kindly souls, but there's nothing in their heads.

> [*The hum dies away. Enter* MME. RANEVSKAYA *and* GAYEV: *She is not crying, but is pale, her face twitches and she cannot speak.*]

GAYEV You gave them your purse, Luba. That won't do! That won't do!

MME. RANEVSKAYA I couldn't help it! I couldn't! [*They go out.*]

LOPAHIN [*Calls after them.*] Please, I beg you, have a glass at parting. I didn't think of bringing any champagne from town and at the station I could find only one bottle. Please, won't you? [*Pause.*] What's the matter, ladies and gentlemen, don't you want any? [*Moves away from the door.*] If I'd known, I wouldn't have bought it. Well, then I won't drink any, either. [YASHA *carefully sets the tray down on a chair.*] At least you have a glass, Yasha.

YASHA Here's to the travelers! And good luck to those that stay! [*Drinks.*] This champagne isn't the real stuff, I can assure you.

LOPAHIN Eight rubles a bottle. [*Pause.*] It's devilishly cold here.

YASHA They didn't light the stoves today—it wasn't worth it, since we're leaving. [*Laughs.*]

LOPAHIN Why are you laughing?

YASHA It's just that I'm pleased.

LOPAHIN It's October, yet it's as still and sunny as though it were summer. Good weather for building. [*Looks at his watch, and speaks off.*] Bear in mind, ladies and gentlemen, the train goes in forty-seven minutes, so you ought to start for the station in twenty minutes. Better hurry up!

> [*Enter* TROFIMOV, *wearing an overcoat.*]

TROFIMOV I think it's time to start. The carriages are at the door. The devil only knows what's become of my rubbers; they've disappeared. [*Calling off.*] Anya! My rubbers are gone. I can't find them.

LOPAHIN I've got to go to Kharkov. I'll take the same train you do. I'll spend the winter in Kharkov. I've been hanging round here with you, till I'm worn out with loafing. I can't live without work—I don't know what to do with my hands, they dangle as if they didn't belong to me.

TROFIMOV Well, we'll soon be gone, then you can go on with your useful labors again.

LOPAHIN Have a glass.

TROFIMOV No, I won't.

LOPAHIN So you're going to Moscow now?

TROFIMOV Yes, I'll see them into town, and tomorrow I'll go on to Moscow.

LOPAHIN Well, I'll wager the professors aren't giving any lectures, they're waiting for you to come.

TROFIMOV That's none of your business.

LOPAHIN Just how many years have you been at the university?

TROFIMOV Can't you think of something new? Your joke's stale and flat. [*Looking for his rubbers.*] We'll probably never see each other again, so allow me to give you a piece of advice at parting: don't wave your hands about! Get out of the habit. And another thing: building bungalows, figuring that summer residents will eventually become small farmers, figuring like that is just another form of waving your hands about. . . . Never mind, I love you anyway; you have fine, delicate fingers, like an artist; you have a fine delicate soul.

LOPAHIN [*Embracing him.*] Good-bye, my dear fellow. Thank you for everything. Let me give you some money for the journey, if you need it.

TROFIMOV What for? I don't need it.

LOPAHIN But you haven't any.

TROFIMOV Yes, I have, thank you. I got some money for a translation— here it is in my pocket. [*Anxiously.*] But where are my rubbers?

VARYA [*From the next room.*] Here! Take the nasty things. [*Flings a pair of rubbers onto the stage.*]

TROFIMOV What are you so cross about, Varya? Hm . . . and these are not my rubbers.

LOPAHIN I sowed three thousand acres of poppies in the spring, and now I've made 40,000 on them, clear profit; and when my poppies were in bloom, what a picture it was! So, as I say, I made 40,000; and I am offering you a loan because I can afford it. Why turn up your nose at it? I am a peasant—I speak bluntly.

TROFIMOV Your father was a peasant, mine was a druggist—that proves absolutely nothing whatever. [LOPAHIN *takes out his wallet.*] Don't, put that away! If you were to offer me two hundred thousand, I wouldn't take it. I'm a free man. And everything that all of you, rich and poor alike, value so highly and hold so dear hasn't the slightest power over me. It's like so much fluff floating in the air. I can get on without you, I can pass you by, I'm strong and proud. Mankind is moving toward the highest truth, toward the highest happiness possible on earth, and I am in the front ranks.

LOPAHIN Will you get there?

TROFIMOV I will. [*Pause.*] I will get there, or I will show others the way to get there.

[*The sound of axes chopping down trees is heard in the distance.*]

LOPAHIN Well, good-bye, my dear fellow. It's time to leave. We turn up our noses at one another, but life goes on just the same. When I'm working hard, without resting, my mind is easier, and it seems to me that I, too, know why I exist. But how many people are there in Russia, brother, who exist nobody knows why? Well, it doesn't matter. That's not what makes the wheels go round. They say Leonid Andreyevich has taken a position in the bank, 6,000 rubles a year. Only, of course, he won't stick to it, he's too lazy. . . .

ANYA [*In the doorway.*] Mamma begs you not to start cutting down the cherry trees until she's gone.

TROFIMOV Really, you should have more tact! [*Exits.*]

LOPAHIN Right away—right away! Those men . . . [*Exits.*]

ANYA Has Firs been taken to the hospital?

YASHA I told them this morning. They must have taken him.

ANYA [*To* YEPIHODOV, *who crosses the room.*] Yepihodov, please find out if Firs has been taken to the hospital.

YASHA [*Offended.*] I told Yegor this morning. Why ask a dozen times?

YEPIHODOV The aged Firs, in my definitive opinion, is beyond mending. It's time he was gathered to his fathers. And I can only envy him. [*Puts a suitcase down on a hat box and crushes it.*] There now, of course, I knew it! [*Exits.*]

YASHA [*Mockingly.*] Two-and-Twenty Troubles!

VARYA [*Through the door.*] Has Firs been taken to the hospital?

ANYA Yes.

VARYA Then why wasn't the note for the doctor taken too?

ANYA Oh! Then someone must take it to him. [*Exits.*]

VARYA [*From adjoining room.*] Where's Yasha? Tell him his mother's come and wants to say good-bye.

YASHA [*Waves his hand.*] She tries my patience.

> [DUNYASHA *has been occupied with the luggage. Seeing* YASHA *alone, she goes up to him.*]

DUNYASHA You might just give me one little look, Yasha. You're going away. . . . You're leaving me . . . [*Weeps and throws herself on his neck.*]

YASHA What's there to cry about? [*Drinks champagne.*] In six days I shall be in Paris again. Tomorrow we get into an express train and off we go, that's the last you'll see of us. . . . I can scarcely believe it. *Vive la France!*[3] It don't suit me here, I just can't live here. That's all there is to it. I'm fed up with the ignorance here, I've had enough of it. [*Drinks champagne.*] What's there to cry about? Behave yourself properly, and you'll have no cause to cry.

DUNYASHA [*Powders her face, looking in pocket mirror.*] Do send me a letter from Paris. You know I loved you, Yasha, how I loved you! I'm a delicate creature, Yasha.

YASHA Somebody's coming! [*Busies himself with the luggage; hums softly.*]

> [*Enter* MME. RANEVSKAYA, GAYEV, ANYA, *and* CHARLOTTA.]

GAYEV We ought to be leaving. We haven't much time. [*Looks at* YASHA.] Who smells of herring?

MME. RANEVSKAYA In about ten minutes we should be getting into the carriages. [*Looks around the room.*] Good-bye, dear old home, good-bye, grandfather. Winter will pass, spring will come, you will no longer be here, they will have torn you down. How much these walls have seen! [*Kisses* ANYA *warmly.*] My treasure, how radiant you look! Your eyes are sparkling like diamonds. Are you glad? Very?

ANYA [*Gaily.*] Very glad. A new life is beginning, Mamma.

GAYEV Well, really, everything is all right now. Before the cherry orchard was sold, we all fretted and suffered; but afterward, when the question was settled finally and irrevocably, we all calmed down, and even felt quite cheerful. I'm a bank employee now, a financier. The yellow ball in the side pocket! And anyhow, you are looking better, Luba, there's no doubt of that.

MME. RANEVSKAYA Yes, my nerves are better, that's true. [*She is handed her hat and coat.*] I sleep well. Carry out my things, Yasha. It's time. [*To* ANYA.] We shall soon see each other again, my little girl. I'm going

---

3. Long live France! (French).

to Paris, I'll live there on the money your great-aunt sent us to buy the estate with—long live Auntie! But that money won't last long.

ANYA You'll come back soon, soon, Mamma, won't you? Meanwhile I'll study. I'll pass my high school examination, and then I'll go to work and help you. We'll read all kinds of books together, Mamma, won't we? [*Kisses her mother's hands.*] We'll read in the autumn evenings, we'll read lots of books, and a new wonderful world will open up before us. [*Falls into a revery.*] Mamma, do come back.

MME. RANEVSKAYA I will come back, my precious.

[*Embraces her daughter. Enter* LOPAHIN *and* CHARLOTTA, *who is humming softly.*]

GAYEV Charlotta's happy: she's singing.

CHARLOTTA [*Picks up a bundle and holds it like a baby in swaddling clothes.*] Bye, baby, bye. [*A baby is heard crying:* "Wah! Wah!";] Hush, hush, my pet, my little one. ["Wah! Wah!"] I'm so sorry for you! [*Throws the bundle down.*] You will find me a position, won't you? I can't go on like this.

LOPAHIN We'll find one for you, Charlotta Ivanovna, don't worry.

GAYEV Everyone's leaving us. Varya's going away. We've suddenly become of no use.

CHARLOTTA There's no place for me to live in town, I must go away. [*Hums.*]

[*Enter* PISHCHIK.]

LOPAHIN There's nature's masterpiece!

PISHCHIK [*Gasping.*] Oh . . . let me get my breath . . . I'm in agony. . . . Esteemed friends . . . Give me a drink of water. . . .

GAYEV Wants some money, I suppose. No, thank you . . . I'll keep out of harm's way. [*Exits.*]

PISHCHIK It's a long while since I've been to see you, most charming lady. [*To* LOPAHIN.] So you are here . . . glad to see you, you intellectual giant . . . There . . . [*Gives* LOPAHIN *money.*] Here's 400 rubles, and I still owe you 840.

LOPAHIN [*Shrugging his shoulders in bewilderment.*] I must be dreaming. . . . Where did you get it?

PISHCHIK Wait a minute . . . it's hot. . . . A most extraordinary event! Some Englishmen came to my place and found some sort of white clay on my land . . . [*To* MME. RANEVSKAYA.] And 400 for you . . . most lovely . . . most wonderful . . . [*Hands her the money.*] The rest later. [*Drinks water.*] A young man in the train was telling me just now that a great philosopher recommends jumping off roofs. "Jump!" says he; "that's the long and the short of it!" [*In amazement.*] Just imagine! Some more water!

LOPAHIN What Englishmen?

PISHCHIK I leased them the tract with the clay on it for twenty-four years. . . . And now, forgive me, I can't stay. . . . I must be dashing on. . . . I'm going over to Znoikov . . . to Kardamanov . . . I owe them all money . . . [*Drinks water.*] Good-bye, everybody . . . I'll look in on Thursday . . .

MME. RANEVSKAYA We're just moving into town; and tomorrow I go abroad.

PISHCHIK [*Upset.*] What? Why into town? That's why the furniture is like that . . . and the suitcases. . . . Well, never mind! [*Through tears.*] Never

mind . . . men of colossal intellect, these Englishmen. . . . Never mind
. . . Be happy. God will come to your help. . . . Never mind . . . every-
thing in this world comes to an end. [*Kisses* MME. RANEVSKAYA's *hand.*]
If the rumor reaches you that it's all up with me, remember this old . . .
horse, and say: "Once there lived a certain . . . Simeonov-Pishchik . . .
the kingdom of Heaven be his. . . . " Glorious weather! . . . Yes . . .
[*Exits, in great confusion, but at once returns and says in the doorway.*]
My daughter Dashenka sends her regards. [*Exits.*]

MME. RANEVSKAYA   Now we can go. I leave with two cares weighing on
me. The first is poor old Firs. [*Glancing at her watch.*] We still have
about five minutes.

ANYA   Mamma, Firs has already been taken to the hospital. Yasha sent
him there this morning.

MME. RANEVSKAYA   My other worry is Varya. She's used to getting up early
and working; and now, with no work to do, she is like a fish out of water.
She has grown thin and pale, and keeps crying, poor soul. [*Pause.*] You
know this very well, Yermolay Alexeyevich; I dreamed of seeing her married to you, and it looked as though that's how it would be. [*Whispers to*
ANYA, *who nods to* CHARLOTTA *and both go out.*] She loves you. You find
her attractive. I don't know, I don't know why it is you seem to avoid
each other; I can't understand it.

LOPAHIN   To tell you the truth, I don't understand it myself. It's all a
puzzle. If there's still time, I'm ready now, at once. Let's settle it straight
off, and have done with it! Without you, I feel I'll never be able to
propose.

MME. RANEVSKAYA   That's splendid. After all, it will only take a minute.
I'll call her at once. . . .

LOPAHIN   And luckily, here's champagne, too. [*Looks at the glasses.*]
Empty! Somebody's drunk it all. [*Yasha coughs.*] That's what you might
call guzzling . . .

MME. RANEVSKAYA [*Animatedly.*]   Excellent! We'll go and leave you alone.
Yasha, *allez!*[4] I'll call her. [*At the door.*] Varya, leave everything and come
here. Come! [*Exits with* YASHA.]

LOPAHIN [*Looking at his watch.*]   Yes . . . [*Pause behind the door, smothered laughter and whispering; at last, enter* VARYA.]

VARYA [*Looking over the luggage in leisurely fashion.*]   Strange, I can't find
it . . .

LOPAHIN   What are you looking for?

VARYA   Packed it myself, and I don't remember . . . [*Pause.*]

LOPAHIN   Where are you going now, Varya?

VARYA   I? To the Ragulins'. I've arranged to take charge there—as housekeeper, if you like.

LOPAHIN   At Yashnevo? About fifty miles from here. [*Pause.*] Well, life in
this house is ended!

VARYA [*Examining luggage.*]   Where is it? Perhaps I put it in the chest.
Yes, life in this house is ended. . . . There will be no more of it.

LOPAHIN   And I'm just off to Kharkov—by this next train. I've a lot to do
there. I'm leaving Yepihodov here . . . I've taken him on.

4. Go on! (French).

VARYA   Oh!

LOPAHIN   Last year at this time, it was snowing, if you remember, but now it's sunny and there's no wind. It's cold, though. . . . It must be three below.

VARYA   I didn't look. [*Pause.*] And besides, our thermometer's broken. [*Pause.* VOICE *from the yard:* "Yermolay Alexeyevich!"]

LOPAHIN [*As if he had been waiting for the call.*]   This minute! [*Exits quickly.*]

[VARYA *sits on the floor and sobs quietly, her head on a bundle of clothes. Enter* MME. RANEVSKAYA *cautiously.*]

MME. RANEVSKAYA   Well? [*Pause.*] We must be going.

VARYA [*Wiping her eyes.*]   Yes, it's time, Mamma dear. I'll be able to get to the Ragulins' today, if only we don't miss the train.

MME. RANEVSKAYA [*At the door.*]   Anya, put your things on.

[*Enter* ANYA, GAYEV, CHARLOTTA. GAYEV *wears a heavy overcoat with a hood. Enter servants and coachmen.* YEPIHODOV *bustles about the luggage.*]

MME. RANEVSKAYA   Now we can start on our journey.

ANYA [*Joyfully.*]   On our journey!

GAYEV   My friends, my dear, cherished friends, leaving this house forever, can I be silent? Can I, at leave-taking, refrain from giving utterance to those emotions that now fill my being?

ANYA [*Imploringly.*]   Uncle!

VARYA   Uncle, Uncle dear, don't.

GAYEV [*Forlornly.*]   I'll bank the yellow in the side pocket . . . I'll be silent . . .

[*Enter* TROFIMOV, *then* LOPAHIN.]

TROFIMOV   Well, ladies and gentlemen, it's time to leave.

LOPAHIN   Yepihodov, my coat.

MME. RANEVSKAYA   I'll sit down just a minute. It seems as though I'd never before seen what the walls of this house were like, the ceilings, and now I look at them hungrily, with such tender affection.

GAYEV   I remember when I was six years old sitting on that window sill on Whitsunday,[5] watching my father going to church.

MME. RANEVSKAYA   Has everything been taken?

LOPAHIN   I think so. [*Putting on his overcoat.*] Yepihodov, see that everything's in order.

YEPIHODOV [*In a husky voice.*]   You needn't worry, Yermolay Alexeyevich.

LOPAHIN   What's the matter with your voice?

YEPIHODOV   I just had a drink of water. I must have swallowed something.

YASHA [*Contemptuously.*]   What ignorance!

MME. RANEVSKAYA   When we're gone, not a soul will be left here.

LOPAHIN   Until the spring.

[VARYA *pulls an umbrella out of a bundle, as though about to hit someone with it.* LOPAHIN *pretends to be frightened.*]

VARYA   Come, come, I had no such idea!

TROFIMOV   Ladies and gentlemen, let's get into the carriages—it's time. The train will be in directly.

5. Or Pentecost, a Christian festival occurring on the seventh Sunday after Easter.

VARYA   Petya, there they are, your rubbers, by that trunk. [*Tearfully.*] And what dirty old things, they are!

TROFIMOV [*Puts on rubbers.*]   Let's go, ladies and gentlemen.

GAYEV [*Greatly upset, afraid of breaking down.*]   The train . . . the station. . . . Three cushions in the side pocket, I'll bank this one in the corner . . .

MME. RANEVSKAYA   Let's go.

LOPAHIN   Are we all here? No one in there? [*Locks the side door on the left.*] There are some things stored here, better lock up. Let us go!

ANYA   Good-bye, old house! Good-bye, old life!

TROFIMOV   Hail to you, new life!

[*Exits with* ANYA: VARYA *looks round the room and goes out slowly.* YASHA *and* CHARLOTTA *with her dog go out.*]

LOPAHIN   And so, until the spring. Go along, friends . . . Bye-bye! [*Exits.*]

[MME. RANEVSKAYA *and* GAYEV *remain alone. As though they had been waiting for this, they throw themselves on each other's necks, and break into subdued, restrained sobs, afraid of being overheard.*]

GAYEV [*In despair.*]   My sister! My sister!

MME. RANEVSKAYA   Oh, my orchard—my dear, sweet, beautiful orchard! My life, my youth, my happiness—good-bye! Good-bye!

[*Voice of* ANYA, *gay and summoning:* "Mamma!" *Voice of* TROFIMOV, *gay and excited:* "Halloo!"]

MME. RANEVSKAYA   One last look at the walls, at the windows. . . . Our poor mother loved to walk about this room . . .

GAYEV   My sister, my sister!

[*Voice of* ANYA "Mamma!" *Voice of* TROFIMOV "Halloo!"]

MME. RANEVSKAYA   We're coming.

[*They go out. The stage is empty. The sound of doors being locked, of carriages driving away. Then silence. In the stillness is heard the muffled sound of the ax striking a tree, a mournful, lonely sound.*

Footsteps are heard. FIRS *appears in the doorway on the right. He is dressed as usual in a jacket and white waistcoat and wears slippers. He is ill.*]

FIRS [*Goes to the door, tries the handle.*]   Locked! They've gone . . . [*Sits down on the sofa.*] They've forgotten me. . . . Never mind . . . I'll sit here a bit . . . I'll wager Leonid Andreyevich hasn't put his fur coat on, he's gone off in his light overcoat . . . [*Sighs anxiously.*] I didn't keep an eye on him. . . . Ah, when they're young, they're green . . . [*Mumbles something indistinguishable.*] Life has gone by as if I had never lived. [*Lies down.*] I'll lie down a while . . . There's no strength left in you, old fellow; nothing is left, nothing. Ah, you addlehead!

[*Lies motionless. A distant sound is heard coming from the sky, as it were, the sound of a snapping string mournfully dying away. All is still again, and nothing is heard but the strokes of the ax against a tree far away in the orchard.*]

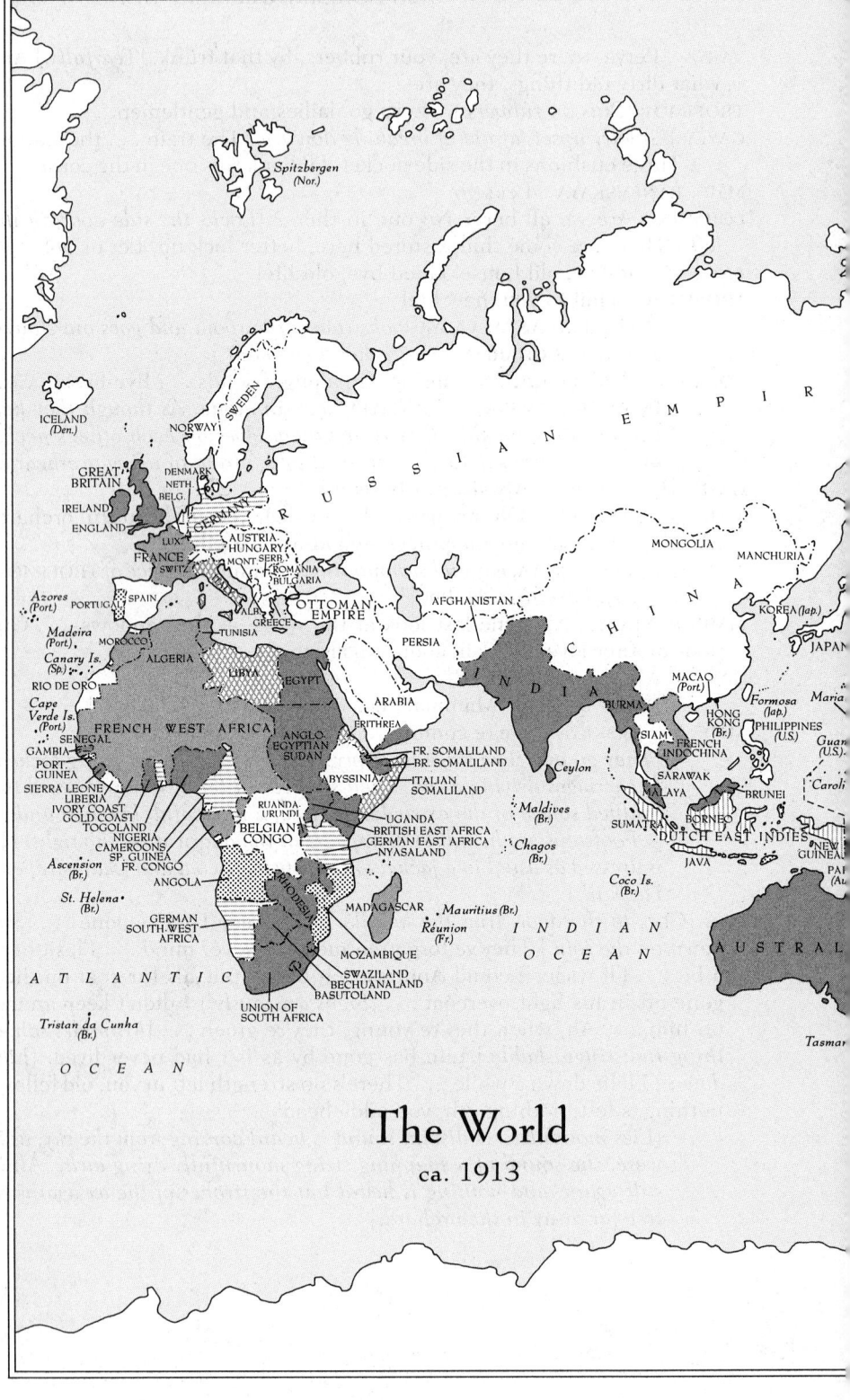

The World

ca. 1913

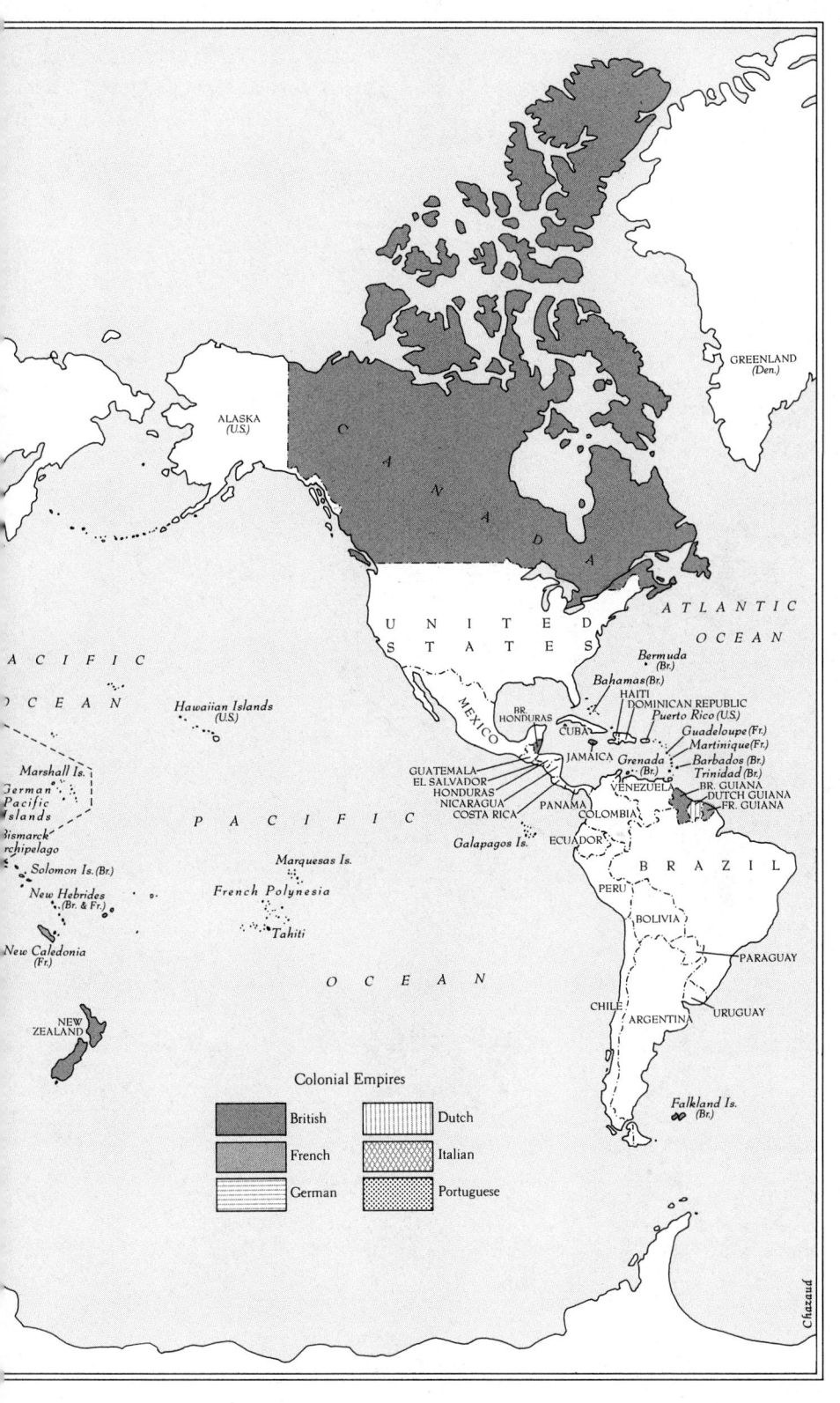

GREENLAND
(Den.)

ALASKA
(U.S.)

C A N A D A

UNITED
STATES

ATLANTIC

OCEAN

PACIFIC

OCEAN

Hawaiian Islands
(U.S.)

Bermuda
(Br.)

Bahamas (Br.)

HAITI
DOMINICAN REPUBLIC
Puerto Rico (U.S.)

MEXICO

BR.
HONDURAS

CUBA

Guadeloupe (Fr.)
Martinique (Fr.)
Barbados (Br.)
Trinidad (Br.)

Marshall Is.

German
Pacific
Islands

Bismarck
Archipelago

Solomon Is. (Br.)

New Hebrides
(Br. & Fr.)

New Caledonia
(Fr.)

JAMAICA   Grenada
(Br.)

GUATEMALA
EL SALVADOR
HONDURAS
NICARAGUA
COSTA RICA

PANAMA

COLOMBIA

PACIFIC

Marquesas Is.

French Polynesia

Tahiti

Galapagos Is.   ECUADOR

VENEZUELA

BR. GUIANA
DUTCH GUIANA
FR. GUIANA

BRAZIL

PERU

BOLIVIA

OCEAN

PARAGUAY

NEW
ZEALAND

CHILE

ARGENTINA

URUGUAY

Colonial Empires

British   Dutch

French   Italian

German   Portuguese

Falkland Is.
(Br.)

Chazaud

Masterpieces of the Twentieth Century: Varieties of Modernism

"Modernism" is central to any discussion of twentieth-century art and literature. It has been called the "tradition of the new," or an attempt to reject old habits of thought while expressing contemporary history in all its chaos, anxiety, technological development, and rapid change. It has also been called the "dehumanization of art," an overly self-conscious style that prizes technical brilliance while ignoring traditional humanistic values. There are many different versions of modernism, for modernism in the broadest sense—as a conscious attempt to exploit new perspectives—permeates artistic expression after the turn of the century. Modernist writers react to the confusion of current history by seeking fresh ways of grasping human experience; they rework conventional modes of expression to create a radically new controlling vision. Their impulse is innovative and oriented toward the future. Whether their style is elaborate or spare, wordy or elliptical, abstract or concrete, they display a highly self-conscious use of language and aim literally to transform the way we see the world.

The twentieth century is not the first age to consider itself modern. Other periods have made a point of being consciously "new," as did the Renaissance ("Rebirth"), the Enlightenment, or the late fifth century B.C. in Athens. Artists and philosophers have always sought better ways of conveying the truth of the world and the human condition. There is, nonetheless, a particular stamp to the twentieth century's idea of modernity. It consists in a remarkable emphasis on *ways of knowing* rather than on objects of knowledge: briefly, on *how* we know *what* we know. This emphasis is accompanied by a criticism of the preceding century's "positivism," seen as an excessive faith in the power of science and rational inquiry to discover unambiguous answers for all problems. Twentieth-century writers point out that positivism's belief in the scientific "rightness" of certain ideas made it blind to its own limits and bias. They suggest that a belief in infallible solutions created only inflexible attitudes, which, transposed into politics, ultimately brought on the bloody conflict of World Wars I and II.

Modern consciousness, however, is inextricably rooted in nineteenth-century culture. The idea of modernity was already a source of public debate and widespread anxiety as the Industrial Revolution transformed social, economic, and political life faster, it seemed, than such changes could peacefully be absorbed. Some saw it as a time of decadence and the loss of stable values. Others saw it more optimistically, as an era in which a progressive Europe would lead the rest of the world to its own pinnacle of achievement (a point of view shared only briefly by the colonized countries). In science, philosophy, social theory, and the arts, the nineteenth century prepared both the evolution and the rebellion of the twentieth.

SCIENTIFIC RATIONALISM

By the end of the nineteenth century, unprecedented developments in science had encouraged people to believe that they would soon master all the secrets of the universe. The Enlightenment notion of the world as a machine—something whose parts could be named and seen to function—came back into favor. Discoveries in different fields seemed to make the universe more rational and hence predictable. In chemistry, there was John Dalton's (1766–1844) atomic theory and Dmitry Mendeleyev's (1834–1907) periodic table of elements; in physics, James Maxwell's (1831–1879) field theory unifying the study of electricity, magnetism, and light. The further development of Newtonian analysis made it possible to study the fixed stars, and spectral analysis showed the essential homogeneity of the universe. Technological applications suggested that these discoveries would serve humanity, not master it. Thermodynamics explained the processes of energy transformation, and locomotives and steamships promised rapid transportation throughout the world. Daguerreotype photography, developed by Louis Daguerre (1789–1851), provided a documentary record. Finally, the history of living nature itself became an object of study when Charles Darwin (1809–1882) examined the evolution of species according to material evidence, without reference to divine laws or purpose.

The enthusiasm for scientific discovery was not confined to scientists. Auguste Comte (1798–1857), a philosopher known as the founder of positivism, held that scientific method constituted a total worldview by which everything would ultimately be explained, including human society. Comte proposed a science of humanity that would analyze and define the laws governing human society (the beginning of sociology). It became evident, however, that the results of "scientific method" depended on the objectivity of the scientist's point of view. Count Gobineau (1816–1882) proposed a "scientific" description of society in which there were three races with innate qualities and in which the white race (predictably, for this white Frenchman) was the superior category. Gobineau's writings laid the groundwork for much "scientific" racism later on. In literature, the historian and critic Hippolyte Taine (1828–1893) proposed a science of culture in which each literary work could be categorized as the combined product of its "race, milieu, and time." The novelist Émile Zola offered as scientific justification for his series on the degeneracy of the Rougon-Macquart family, an *Introduction to the Study of Experimental Medicine* by Dr. Claude Bernard (1813–1878). Nowadays, it is easier to recognize the preexisting bias that flaws these large explanatory systems, and to be cautious of claims of scientific truth, especially in descriptions of human nature.

Social theorists shared with the philosopher Comte the vision of creating a perfect society by understanding social "laws." Utopian socialists such as Charles Fourier (1772–1837), the Comte de Saint-Simon (1760–1825), and the Welsh industrialist Robert Owen (1771–1858) proposed various methods for organizing society and planning its economy. The English philosopher and economist John Stuart Mill (1806–1876) preached the dignity of man, the rights of women, and the possibility of happiness for all. By far the most important and influential theorist was Karl Marx (1819–1883), whose *Communist Manifesto* (1848) and *Capital* (1867) proposed a scientific theory of broad economic forces driving world history. According to Marx the most basic material needs—food, shelter, and the social relationships enabling group survival—provided an economic foundation from which all other aspects of human culture were derived. His vision of modern workers as alienated cogs in the industrial economic machine, no longer owning their own labor, expressed for many the antihuman aspect of modern technological progress. Yet he too believed in the power of rational systems to find answers for social ills; he described the division of modern industrial society into the two competing forces of capital and labor (the proletariat) and proposed the theory of dialectical materialism to explain the processes of history.

REACTIONS TO RATIONALISM

The debate about scientific rationalism was inevitably a debate about knowledge and human values. In the nineteenth century one of the strongest opponents of positivism and its belief in rational solutions was the German philosopher Friedrich Nietzsche (1844–1900). Nietszche focused on the individual, not society, and admired only the *Übermensch,* the superhuman being who refused to be bound by the prevailing social paradigms of nationalism, Christianity, faith in science, loyalty to the state, or bourgeois civilized comfort. Nietzsche's distinction between the Dionysian (instinctual) and the Apollonian (intellectual) forces in human beings, his insistence on the individual's complete freedom (and responsibility) in a world that lacks transcendental law ("God is dead"), and his attack on the unimaginative mediocrity of mass society in the modern industrial world all made him a powerful influence in the early years of the twentieth century. In general, he gave a quasi-philosophical focus to the underlying distrust of rationalist perspectives that was already alive in other parts of the world and had begun to emerge in nineteenth-century Europe in the form of explorations of magic and the occult, theosophy, and the constructed image of an Eastern spirituality complementary to the scientific, soulless West.

The shape and intensity of this debate, as well as its impact on the world at large, were dictated for many years by a historical event that turned the generations of the early twentieth century against everything inherited from the recent past: the Great War, World War I (1914–18). Despite the confident rationalism of the political leaders of "Papa's Europe" (a term of resentment used by many to describe an authoritarian, patriarchal society that claimed to have all the answers), World War I had for the first time involved the whole continent of Europe and the United States in battle and was the first "total war" in which modern weapons spared no one, including civilians. Clearly, something was wrong. A generation of European and American youth was lost in the trenches, and many of the survivors resolved to reexamine the bases of certainty, the structures of knowledge, the systems of belief, and the repositories of authority in a society that had allowed such a war to occur. Their reaction would also be reflected in literature, not only in subject matter but—for many—in a new use of language; in new ways of representing our knowledge of the world; and most especially, in new hesitations about subscribing to any single mode of understanding. They drew on areas beyond the intellect, interrogating modes of human consciousness and feeling in an intellectual attempt to go beyond the self-imposed limitations of previous rationalism.

Several thinkers were particularly important in formulating alternatives to the narrow rationalism of positivist philosophy. The French philosopher Henri Bergson (1859–1941) attacked scientific rationality as artificial and unreal because it froze everything in conceptual space; it ignored the whole dimension of life as it is actually experienced. For Bergson, reality was a fluid, living force *(elán vital)* that could only be apprehended by consciousness. Instead of quantitative and logical inquiry, he proposed intuiting the "immediate data of consciousness" as an alternate, nonscientific means of knowledge. Authors were not slow to perceive the implications of his prescription for representing reality. Marcel Proust, searching to discover his identity through layers of "lost time," or James Joyce, imitating the stream of consciousness in the written flow of words, both reflect a Bergsonian change in the way reality is perceived and represented. Bergson himself received the Nobel Prize in Literature in 1927, both for the creative imagination shown in his own work and for his literary influence.

Sigmund Freud (1856–1939), the founder of psychoanalysis, was another influential figure. Freud's study of subconscious motives and instinctual drives revealed a level of activity that had been largely ignored outside of literature and that was certainly not considered a productive subject for continued "rational" inquiry. His essays and case studies argued that dreams and manias contain their own networks of meaning, and that human beings cannot properly be understood without taking into consideration both the irrational and the rational levels of their existence. All are caught up, he suggested, in the process of mediating the same sexual drives and civilizational repressions that caused neurosis in his own patients.

Many of Freud's theories are questioned today (his assumption that every woman considers herself an incomplete man, for example). Some of his psychoanalytic categories seem too rigid. He rejected divergent views, and he ignored the possibility that his own cultural stereotypes influenced both his theories and his view of patients. Freud's insistence on a fundamental and universally true image of human sexuality has also been explained as a defensive reaction to racial and social discord that included anti-Semitism. To prejudice and alienation, he would oppose a grand unifying image. His chief importance, however, lies elsewhere, in his brilliant and even poetic attempts to clarify patterns of human thought and emotion. He focused attention on the way everyday, "rational" behavior is shaped by unconscious impulses and hidden motivations, and on the way human beings actually create (and modify) their images of self through engaging in dialogue with others. Freud was indebted to the great poets; and he, like Bergson, was honored as a creative artist when he received the Goethe Prize in 1930.

It is probably impossible for any poet, novelist, or playwright after Freud to write without taking into consideration the psychological undercurrents of human behavior—whether or not the author has ever read him. Some post-Freudian writers derive themes and images from the idea of subconscious motivations guiding interpersonal relations and social behavior (Doris Lessing). Others employ a stream of consciousness technique very much like Freud's therapeutic tactic of free association (William Faulkner). Some exploit the aesthetic possibilities of a surface pattern of apparent intentions concealing a contradictory pattern of repressed desires. Still others exploit the technique of an otherwise-empty dialogue that creates its own reality through repetition (Samuel Beckett). Freud can even be cited against his own intentions: the Surrealists, while quoting him, totally reverse his aim by pronouncing madness not an illness to be cured but an insight into a larger reality.

Literature, however, is also a matter of words and not just themes and patterns of consciousness. Different concepts of language have permeated literary expression at different times, and twentieth-century literature is no exception. In the early part of the century, the experimental language used in fiction and poetry shows the influence of psychoanalysis and of Symbolist poetics. Its syntax and imagery emulate Freudian free association, the complex inner patterns favored by nineteenth-century Symbolist poetry, and the artistic effects of Impressionist or Cubist painting. Later works reflect a change in linguistic theory. Nineteenth-century positivism had assumed that language was an accurate tool for direct reference to reality (a view parodied in "The sun is called a sun because it *looks* like a sun"). In contrast, the Swiss linguist Ferdinand de Saussure (1857–1913) and the Austrian philosopher Ludwig Wittgenstein (1889–1951) emphasized that language is tied to society and usage: descriptions are not accurate, for they can never grasp absolute reality or give "real" names. All that language can do, as they see it, is to create socially agreed-on labels ("signifiers" pointing to a "signified"). The sun remains the same gaseous ball whether it is named *sun, soleil,* or *taiyang.* What works in conversation is not the thing itself but the way the label—the word used to describe it—provides a recognizable common ground for different speakers. Language may, therefore, be described as a game played with words: a serious game, since it shapes our vision of reality. Modernist literature shows how words reshape the world we think we know. Thus Wallace Stevens shows how the "moon creeps up / To the bubbling of bassoons," and Gertrude Stein diversifies a carafe into "a kind of glass and a cousin, a spectacle and nothing strange a single hurt color and an arrangement in a system to pointing."

In this perspective, both literature and linguistic systems are seen as *games,* combinations of pieces (words) and rules (grammar, syntax, and other conventions). Writers stressing the gamelike nature of language combine words and word fragments to exhibit the play of relationships, instead of struggling to find the "right word" dear to Flaubert. Game theory can be frustrating in practice. Samuel Beckett's (1906–1989) tongue-tied characters in *Endgame,* or the endlessly chattering narrators of his novels, make brief conversational sense but finally express very little except, perhaps, the absurd inexpressibility of the human condition. At its most extreme, this theory leads to a view of all language as an endless networking of associations: a situation in which real communication is impossible. Reality, instead of becoming more accessible, ultimately disappears inside a web of words.

Yet there are practical conclusions to be drawn from this frustrating prospect. If a work by Borges, Beckett, or Robbe-Grillet persuades us that language determines how we see the world (as well as our own place in it), then we will recognize other shaping uses of language. Not all language games are played by literature. Modern advertising regularly exploits the connections of different communicative worlds. Television commercials race through sets of highly associative words and images to persuade viewers that the sponsor "speaks your language" and is ready to deliver, in that automobile or pair of jeans, the article you really want—wealth, power, cultural identity, or sex appeal. Music videos have established their own recognizable style, using fragmented, kaleidoscopic images (derived from Surrealism) to appeal to the self-consciously fractured vision of today's youth. The idea of human expression as a kind of game has created new techniques for literary criticism, too, and made it possible to identify systems of reference embedded in the written text or alive in oral performance. This emphasis on the shifting play of language has brought new readings of earlier and of modernist works, including those canonical texts that have lasted for centuries precisely because they are not limited to one audience but can make accessible many systems of meaning.

Theories of linguistic play have not been isolated from concurrent developments in the sciences, or from the impact of historical events. Psychology, anthropology, and physics also stressed relationships as they redefined current concepts of human nature and the material world. Gestalt psychology (*Gestalt* is German for "form") after 1912 suggested that the meaning of individual phenomena was to be found not in microscopic analysis of separate pieces but rather in organized wholes. It was the "shape of things" that mattered.

Shapes and the relation of parts were important in structural anthropology, with the anthropologist Claude Lévi-Strauss (b. 1908) describing human society as a system of worldviews, or codes, that could be compared from culture to culture. From his early research on the Nambikwara Indian tribe of Brazil to his later comparisons of primitive with modern cultures, Lévi-Strauss has insisted that anthropological knowledge comes only from an imaginative participation in the codes governing each society (kinship rules, taboos, habits of social interaction, folkloric imagination). Even more influential for modern writers was Jungian psychology—based on the work of Carl Gustav Jung (1875–1961)—which proposed that humanity shared a "collective unconscious," a buried level of universal experience tapped by myth, religion, and art. According to Jung, the common experience of our species was revealed in archetypes (master patterns) like the figures of the hero, seer, or Great Mother, the image of the quest, or the process of death and regeneration. In retrospect, works such as T. S. Eliot's *The Waste Land* may be seen to incorporate archetypal images alluding to a universal level of human experience. In Eliot's case, actual inspiration came from another synthesizing enterprise, James George Frazer's vast masterwork of anthropology *The Golden Bough* (1890–1915), which profoundly influenced the intellectual climate of Europe and America with its demonstration of the striking resemblances among world mythologies and religions.

The social, or "human," sciences were not alone in paying attention to the role played by perception in scientific inquiry. The hard sciences of physics and mathematics were doing the same thing, with results that shocked the general public and intrigued writers and artists. Albert Einstein's theory of relativity (1905) abandoned the concepts of absolute motion and the absolute difference of space and time and, working from pure mathematical logic, proposed that reality should be understood as a four-dimensional continuum (called space-time) that literally could not be expressed either in words or in the old three-dimensional models of Newtonian physics. Since *relativity* implied "relativism" in the popular mind, Einstein's discovery was widely thought to pull the ground out from under any certainty—scientific or religious— about the physical world. Even more disturbing, Werner Heisenberg's uncertainty principle (1927) proclaimed that scientific measurement (in this case, the measurement of electrons) was always a matter of statistical approximation, a "probability function" and not an exact description. Ironically, what was scientifically an increasingly *accurate* perception of the nature of things often seemed just the opposite to the general public. People could no longer find self-evident truths in nature, or go back to basics, when scientists had just shown that the "basic" world of three-dimensional reality was not what it seemed. Many writers, however, and Proust among the earliest, welcomed what they saw as a richer view of experience.

The modern philosophy that coincides with the rise of Modernism is similarly an inquiry into the reliability of appearances. Ever since Plato, Western philosophers have struggled systematically to understand the relationship between appearance and reality. In the twentieth century, such issues are the central concern of the philosophy known as phenomenology (phenomena are literally *things as they appear*) and its offshoot, existentialism. Both approaches investigate the role of perception in establishing reality. The phenomenology proposed by Edmund Husserl (1859–1938) described all consciousness as consciousness *of* something *by* someone and concluded that every object of study should be imagined in "brackets"—not as a thing in itself, but as part of a relationship between perceiver and perceived.

The ethical implications of this view were taken up by the philosophers Martin Heidegger (1889–1976) and Jean-Paul Sartre (1905–1980), who questioned the meaning of existence in a world without preexisting truths, values, or general laws. Heidegger's profoundly somber vision of the "absurd" condition of human beings, "thrown into the world" without any understanding of their fate, influenced many writers and especially the Theater of the Absurd that flourished after World War II, of which Samuel Beckett and Eugène Ionesco (b. 1912) are the best-known writers. Sartre, who was much more of a social activist, derived from the same "absurd" freedom an ideal of human authenticity that consists in choosing our actions at each point, avoiding the bad faith of pretending that others are responsible for our choices, and choosing not just for ourselves but "for all" inasmuch as each choice envisages the creation of a new world. This kind of existentialism, with its appealing image of the lonely tragic hero who acts to benefit society without any hope of reward (Sartre portrayed such a hero as Orestes in *The Flies*, based on Aeschylus's *Oresteia*), had tremendous influence on young writers immediately after World War II. Albert Camus, writing at the same time as Sartre, offers in *The Guest* a good example of existentialism's emphasis on freedom, responsibility, and social "engagement."

Existentialism's popular appeal in the 1940s and 1950s was undoubtedly enhanced by the fact that it was a philosophic attempt to recover clear vision—and a basis for action—in a confused and meaningless world. The notion of philosophical absurdity corresponded to a very real confusion caused by the radical historical changes taking place in the first half of the century. By 1950 there had been two world wars, the second of which was truly global, and a sweeping realignment of geopolitical forces that saw the flourishing of Marxism and the establishment of major Communist states. Almost all the old monarchies had been overthrown, and colonial empires were being dismantled as the emerging nations of Africa and Asia struggled for independence and self-definition. The wielders of authority became the enormous buck-passing bureaucracies of the modern state, multinational corporations, international governmental organizations, and ethnic alliances. Transportation and telecommunications progressed to an extent envisaged only in earlier ages' science fiction and effectively shrank the global community. The rise of the modern industrial state set up new political, cultural, and economic tensions, the most important of which was a widening gulf between the West and "less developed" countries.

These changes in historical conditions had visible effects on literature and art. Cultural parochialism—the belief that there is only one correct view of the world (one's own)—was much harder to maintain when people traveled widely and experienced different ways of life. Racial and ethnic stereotypes were challenged, and traditional ideas of identity and social class were broken down. Romantic heroism and aristocratic rank seemed irrelevant to soldiers who died anonymously in the trenches of World War I or to civilians killed at a distance by bombing raids in both wars. The appropriate symbol for modern, impersonal warfare was the Tomb of the Unknown Soldier; and in literature it was the "common man," not the Romantic hero, whose plight was portrayed. The conventional roles of the sexes came under examination. Western women achieved civil rights they had been denied for centuries: the right to vote (1920 in the United States), the right to have bank accounts and to own and control their own property, the right to be educated equally with men, and the right to enter professions not previously open to them. When women held many jobs previously thought to be masculine ("Rosie the Riveter" was a famous poster in World War II), it was no longer possible to pretend that they were incapable of work outside the home. Indeed, it was clear not only that women were quite capable but that they enjoyed taking responsibility in a variety of careers. The nature of the workplace changed, in addition, as technological advances brought a range of new machines and services. Technology became part of the modern literary consciousness, inspiring both enthusiasm and fear, and initiating all over again the question of human values in a society where so much could be done (and so many controlled) by the use of machines.

A CENTURY OF ISMS

The literary and artistic movements of the twentieth century are part of this evolution; they were shaped by it and helped shape it for others. Many flourished in Europe or America and were exported to other parts of the globe, where they flourished or failed, according to their relevance for local conditions. The twentieth century has been called by some a "century of isms," or of vanguardism, reflecting the fact that so many different groups have tried to find the appropriate artistic response to contemporary history. Expressionism, Dadaism, Surrealism, and Futurism—each worth exploring—are all different ways of expressing the reality of the world. Some appear very unreal at first glance, but all reveal an inner (presumably more important) truth than can be shown by documentary detail alone. Thus expressionists refused the direct representation of reality, or even impressions of it (as in Impressionism), in favor of expressing an inner vision, emotion, or spiritual reality. *The Scream,* a painting by the Norwegian Edvard Munch (1863–1944), evokes a whole realm of spiritual agony, and expressionist writers like the Germans Frank Wedekind (1864–1918) and Gottfried Benn (1886–1956) assert their alienation from an industrial society whose inhumanity repels them. To bring out an underlying psychological distress that "objective" descriptions fail to capture, expressionist writers subordinate conventional (rational) style and let emotion dictate the structure of their works, emphasizing rhythm, disrupted narrative line and broken syntax, and distorted imagery.

Futurism loudly proclaimed its enthusiasm for the dynamic new machine age. F. T. Marinetti (1876–1944) wrote in the first Futurist Manifesto (1908) that "a roaring motor car which seems to run on machine-gun fire is more beautiful than the Winged Victory of Samothrace" (a famous Greek statue). Italian Futurism is still tainted by Marinetti's glorification of terrorism and war, and his delighted description (from the pilot's point of view) of bombs bursting below. Russian Futurism was suppressed, along with other experimental art, by the conservative tastes of the government in the USSR. Nonetheless, the Futurists' experiments in typography, in free association, in rapid shifts and breaks of syntax; their manipulation of sounds and word placement for special effects apart from semantic meaning; their harshness and stark vision; and above all their eagerness to depict the new age, were widely imitated.

Dada-Surrealism is the best known of the "isms," and the only one to have followers today. Dada began in Zurich, Switzerland, in 1916 as a movement of absolute revolt against Papa's Europe, and the word *dada* is a nonsense word that represents the disgust the Dadaists felt for the traditional middle-class values (patriotism, religion, morality, and rationalism) that they blamed for World War I. Dada set out to subvert authority and break all the rules (including those of art), hoping to liberate the creative imagination. Marcel Duchamp (1887–1968) reversed a series of expectations when he named a piece *Why Not Sneeze, Rrose Sélavy?* (1921): it was a small birdcage filled with what looked like sugar lumps but turned out (when you lift the heavy cage) to be carved marble cubes. Tristan Tzara (1896–1963), author of seven Dada manifestoes, attacked the notion of the inspired genius by offering a recipe for the Dada poem: the "poet" was to cut words out of a newspaper, shake them in a paper bag, and pull them out one at a time. Kurt Schwitters created "Merz," pieces of art made from random or found objects. Dada creations were attacks on the mind and emotions; both Dadaists and Surrealists emphasized a "revolution of the mind" that upset ordinary ways of looking at things. Freedom from conventional perspectives, they felt, was a first step in reforming society.

Surrealists especially aimed to bring about a fuller awareness of human experience, including both conscious and unconscious states. In France the Surrealist Manifestoes of 1924 and 1930 proclaimed that Surrealism was a means of expressing "the actual functioning of thought," "the total recuperation of our psychic force by a means that is nothing else than the dizzying descent into ourselves." André Breton, the Surrealist leader, had been a medical intern in a psychiatric clinic during World War I and was interested in Freud's theories of the unconscious. The Surrealists experimented with various means to liberate the unconscious imagination and reach a sublime state they called "the marvelous." Dream-writing, automatic writing (writing rapidly and continuously whatever comes to mind), riddle games, interruption and collage, and chiefly the creation of startling images opened the mind to new possibilities.

The Surrealist image achieves its effect by forcibly yoking two seemingly unrelated elements; it suggests buried connections and possible relationships overlooked by the logical mind. Thus a poem by Paul Eluard, for example, will begin "Earth is blue like an orange, / Never a mistake; words don't lie" and let the reader sort out the connections of shape, color, distance that may allow such a perspective. Readers faced with the absurdity of "like an orange" will reach for whatever pattern of meaning might exist in a vision that just barely seems to offer such connections. And there it is, a tenuous but consistent structural relationship of similarity or difference—in shape, color, size, and distance from the perceiver.

Known for its intensity, playfulness, and openness to change, Surrealism has proved to be the most influential and enduring of all these isms. By the end of the twentieth century, art and literature generally have absorbed the characteristic Surrealist themes of free play, antirationality, and the importance of the unconscious mind, as well as the preferred Surrealist techniques of collage, metamorphosis, and a narrative in which it is hard to distinguish between dream and reality. In this volume, such themes and techniques may be found in the explosive poetic sequences of Aimé Césaire and the magical images of Gabriel García Márquez. As an ironic mark of success, the term *surrealist* has also become a convenient word for unconventional or fantastic works that have no real connection with the movement.

Modernism is the usual term for the change in attitudes and artistic strategy occurring at the beginning of the century. In its broadest sense, modernism embraces all the separate movements just described. Taken more narrowly, it refers to a group of Anglo-American writers (many associated with the Imagists, 1908–17) who favored clear, precise images and common speech and thought of the work as an art object produced by consummate craft rather than as a statement of emotion. James Joyce, Ezra Pound, T. S. Eliot, William Faulkner, and Virginia Woolf are examples of Anglo-American modernism, and of the larger modernism too. Modernism in general is an attempt to construct a new view of the world and of human nature through the self-conscious manipulation of form. Modernists used language in a different way, redefining the world of art much as the philosophers and scientists had redefined the world of their own disciplines. Modernist writers played with shifting and contradictory appearances to suggest the shifting and uncertain nature of reality (Luigi Pirandello); they broke up the logically developing plot typical of the nineteenth-century novel and offered instead unexpected connections or sudden changes of perspective (Woolf); they used interior monologues and free association to express the rhythm of consciousness (Joyce, Woolf); they made much greater use of image clusters, thematic associations, and musical patterning to supply the basic structures of both fiction and poetry (Proust, Wallace Stevens, Eliot); they drew attention to style instead of trying to make it transparent (Eliot, Bertolt Brecht); they blended fantasy with reality while representing real historical or psychological dilemmas (Franz Kafka); they raised age-old questions of human identity in terms of contemporary philosophy and psychology (Proust, Albert Camus). Yet there is another element that unites these figures: their experiments with perspective and language are carried on inside still-traditional concepts of individual psychological depth, and of the artwork as a coherent aesthetic whole. The combination of discontinuous, experimental style with a continuing belief in the wholeness of the human personality and of the artwork carries with it the stamp of what we call the Modernist tradition.

FURTHER READING

The Modern Tradition (1965), Richard Ellmann and Charles Feidelson Jr., eds., is a valuable collection of statements by writers, artists, philosophers, and scientists, arranged by themes. Monique Chefdor, Ricardo Quinones, and Albert Wachtel, eds., *Modernism: Challenges and Perspectives* (1986), offers many valuable essays on international modernism, ranging from definitions to historical practice in art, music, literature, and politics. David Hayman, *Re-Forming the Narrative: Toward a Mechanics of Modernist Fiction* (1987), proposes five tactics that distinguish modernist narrative from earlier fiction; examples include Robbe-Grillet, Kafka, Rilke, Joyce, Beckett, and Borges. Willson Coates and Hayden White, *The Ordeal of Liberal Humanism: An Intellectual History of Western Europe* (1970), is an excellent intellectual history of western Europe after the French Revolution. Harry Levin, "What Was Modernism?" (1962, reprinted in *Refractions*, 1966), is an influential survey of modernist writers as humanists and inheritors of the Enlightenment. Renato Poggioli, *Theory of the Avant-Garde* (1968), locates basic categories of attitudes toward society inside the different arts of the twentieth-century American avant-garde. William S. Rubin, *Dada, Surrealism and Their Heritage* (1968), gives a detailed history of Surrealist art with many superb illustrations. John D. Erickson, *Dada: Performance, Poetry, and Art* (1984), and Herbert S. Gershman, *The Surrealist Revolution in France* (1974), are valuable surveys. Matei Calinescu, *Five Faces of Modernity* (1987), is a subtly argued, informative collection of essays on the aesthetics of modernism, avant-garde, decadence, and kitsch. Morton P. Levitt, *Modernist Survivors: The Contem-*

porary Novel in England, the United States, France, and Latin America (1987), illustrates the impact of literary modernism and the continuity of humanist values. James F. Knapp, *Literary Modernism and the Transformation of Work* (1988), examines work-related themes in English and American modernist literature, and modernism's contradictory attitudes toward a changing economic order. Harry R. Garvin, ed., *Romanticism, Modernism, Postmodernism* (1980), is a useful collection of essays that attempts to define changing views of the artistic imagination and its place in society.

VARIETIES OF MODERNISM

TEXTS	CONTEXTS
	1899–1902 Boer War in South Africa
	1900 Max Planck proposes quantum theory, the first step in the discovery of the atom
1902 Joseph Conrad, *Heart of Darkness*	
1903 Henry James, *The Ambassadors*	1903 Wright brothers invent the powered airplane
1905 Sigmund Freud, *"Dora" (Fragment of an Analysis of a Case of Hysteria)* • F. T. Marinetti, *Futurist Manifesto*	1905 Modern labor movement begins with foundation of International Workers of the World (IWW)
1907 August Strindberg, *The Ghost Sonata*	1907 Japanese immigration to the United States prohibited
1908 Gertrude Stein, *Three Lives*	
	1909 Commercial manufacture of plastic begins
	1910 Mexican Revolution (1910–11) • NAACP founded in United States • Post-Impressionist Exhibition in London
	1912–1913 Balkan wars
1913 Marcel Proust, **Swann's Way**, first volume of *Remembrance of Things Past* (1913–27) • Thomas Mann, **Death in Venice** • D. H. Lawrence, *Sons and Lovers*	
1914 James Joyce, *Dubliners*, which includes **The Dead**	1914–1918 World War I involves Europe, Turkey, and the United States
	1915 Albert Einstein formulates general theory of relativity • First transcontinental phone call, in America
1916 Franz Kafka, **The Metamorphosis** • James Joyce, *A Portrait of the Artist as a Young Man*	
1917 T. S. Eliot, **The Love Song of J. Alfred Prufrock**	1917 Russian Revolution overthrows Romanov Dynasty
1918 Tristan Tzara, **Dada Manifesto**	1918 Women over thirty given vote in Great Britain
	1918–1920 Global influenza epidemic kills millions
	1919 League of Nations formed (U.S. Senate rejects membership, 1920)

Boldface titles indicate works in the anthology.

VARIETIES OF MODERNISM

TEXTS	CONTEXTS
1920 Edith Wharton, *The Age of Innocence*	**1920** Mahatma Gandhi leads India's struggle for independence from Britain
1921 Luigi Pirandello, **Six Characters in Search of an Author**	**1921–1929** Harlem Renaissance, black literary and artistic movement
1922 T. S. Eliot, **The Waste Land** • Paris publication of James Joyce, *Ulysses* (imported copies burned in U.S. Post Office) • Rainer Maria Rilke, *Sonnets to Orpheus*	**1922** Turkey becomes a republic • Irish Free State established • USSR formed • Discovery of Egyptian pharaoh Tutankhamen's tomb
1923 Rainer Maria Rilke, *Duino Elegies*	
1924 Thomas Mann, *The Magic Mountain* • André Breton, *First Surrealist Manifesto*	**1924** Insecticides first used
1926 Franz Kafka, *The Castle* • Paul Eluard, *Capital of Pain*	
1927 Virginia Woolf, *To the Lighthouse*	
1928 William Butler Yeats, *The Tower* • André Breton, *Nadja*	**1928** Sixty-five states sign Kellogg-Briand antiwar pact in Paris • First Five Year Plan in USSR • Penicillin discovered • First scheduled television broadcasts
1929 William Faulkner, *The Sound and the Fury* • Virginia Woolf, **A Room of One's Own**	**1929** Stock market crash heralds beginning of world economic crisis; Great Depression lasts until 1937
1932 Zuni Ritual Poetry published by anthropologist Ruth L. Bunzel	
1933 Federico García Lorca, *Blood Wedding*	**1933** Adolf Hitler given dictatorial powers in Germany • Nazis build first concentration camps
	1934 Stalin begins purges of Communist Party
1937 Wallace Stevens, *The Man with the Blue Guitar*	
1938–40 Bertolt Brecht, **The Good Woman of Setzuan**	
1939 Aimé Césaire, *Notebook of a Return to the Native Land*	**1939** Germany invades Poland and all Europe is drawn into World War II
1940 Richard Wright, *Native Son*	**1941** United States and Japan enter World War II
1942 Albert Camus, *The Stranger* • William Faulkner, **Go Down, Moses**	
1943 T. S. Eliot, **Four Quartets**	
1955 Flannery O'Connor, **A Good Man Is Hard to Find**	
1957 Albert Camus, *Exile and the Kingdom*, which includes **The Guest**	

ZUNI RITUAL POETRY

Although repeatedly invaded since the 1500s and subjected, in turn, to regulation by Spanish, Mexican, and U.S. authority, Oraibi, Taos, Acoma, Zuni, and the other pueblos of the North American Southwest—the continent's oldest towns north of Mexico—have yet to be conquered in the full sense of the term. Bastions of spiritual and social autonomy, the pueblo communities make a profound impression on the nonnative world by the strength of their traditions in an era of change; and of this there can be no more convincing proof than the ceremonial system of Zuni pueblo with its annual cycle of drama, sacrifice, and oratory. Heard at the winter solstice and again, repeatedly, through the phases of the next twelve moons, the spoken word, to the accompaniment of ritual acts, continues to provide the cohesive bond for a growing community of nearly ten thousand people.

Continuously occupied since at least the 1300s, the Zuni territory in western New Mexico has traditionally supported an agricultural economy, dominated by the town, or pueblo, of Zuni itself, surrounded by outlying seasonal farming villages. The raising of livestock became important during the Spanish and Mexican period (1540–1846), but by the mid-twentieth century most Zuni residents had come to rely either on the thriving silversmithing industry or on jobs in off-reservation communities. Farming as a livelihood gradually became insignificant. Yet the agricultural cycle, today, still inspires Zuni ceremonialism.

The often-quoted and deeply admired texts for the Zuni ceremonial round were published just once, in 1932—yet plentifully—by the anthropologist Ruth L. Bunzel under the rubric *Zuni Ritual Poetry*. They comprise one of the two most important bodies of native American oratory on record, exceeded in scope and in quantity only by the Aztec orations preserved in the sixteenth-century Florentine Codex.

As the Zuni orations make clear, the purpose of the ceremonial round is to establish a relationship between "daylight people," or ordinary humans, and the so-called raw people, such as deer, bear, the sun, rainstorms, and corn plants, who consume either raw food or the offerings that the daylight people present to them. In a special category of raw people are the *kokkokwe*, ancestral spirits known in English as kachinas, represented during the ceremonies by masked dancers. Dependent on humans for their nurture, the kachinas and other raw people are given offerings that include the feather-decorated willow shafts called prayer sticks or, in Bunzel's translation, "plume wands." In return the raw people grant "seeds," "breath," "life," "light," and all manner of good fortune. The offerings are sacrificed by depositing, or "planting," them at prescribed locations. Since the Zuni hold that sacrifices were established in the ancient time by the raw people, it is natural enough to find kachinas themselves planting wands during the course of the rituals. In effect these are human sacrifices, with the prayer sticks standing in for the people.

As mentioned, the ceremonial year at Zuni begins with the winter solstice. This major event is followed by a series of winter dances and a calendar of prayer-stick offerings coordinated with the reappearances of the moon. The summer solstice, with its urgent prayers for rain, marks a second ceremonial high point, followed again by the repeating schedule of monthly offerings. Ceremonial activity quickens in the fall with the setting of the date for the great Shalako, a ceremony held shortly before the winter solstice. The selections offered here are from the prayers for three of the annual episodes: the winter solstice observances, the Scalp Dance, and the Shalako.

The winter solstice rites span twenty days, with the solstice itself falling in the middle. This "middle," moreover, is regarded as the center of the entire year. On the first day an announcement is made that prayer sticks will be planted ten days hence. The offerings are not prepared, however, until the ninth day, when the Fire Keeper is appointed. On the tenth day, ideally December 21, the offerings are planted, and the Fire Keeper lights the New Year's fire. With this begins a ten-day "fire taboo," during which no fire may be seen outdoors and no ashes may be removed from any house (the ashes accumulating just as stored crops, one hopes, will accumulate later in the year). When the taboo is lifted the Fire Keeper delivers his prayer, or oration, asking especially for plentiful crops as in the excerpt printed here.

The Scalp Dance, formerly, was performed on the return of a victorious war party to purify any warrior who had taken a scalp and to induct the trophy itself into the company of previously won scalps, regarded as rain makers. The dead in general are a source of contamination, threatening to those who have come into contact with them; but having "attained the place of blessed waters," they also have the power to send rain and, by extension, fruitfulness and good fortune. By the 1970s the Scalp Dance, no longer relevant as an occasional observance, had been brought into the annual round as a fall ritual. In the excerpt from the prayer given here, the scalp is envisioned in its role as rain maker and as an agent of blessing.

The Shalako, the most festive of the ceremonials, attracts an international audience of visitors who arrive at Zuni in time for the grand entrance of the kachinas at the start of eight days of public proceedings. Led by the kachina Sayatasha, the masked party, which includes the troupe of six Shalako (giant kachinas in ten-foot-high bird-like costumes), enters the town and breaks up into small groups, each assigned to a house renovated for the occasion. During the first evening Sayatasha delivers his lengthy "night chant," which includes a house blessing for the benefit of his host. Dances and other rites during the next several days are marked by the presence of the Koyemshi, or clowns, who attend the kachinas and mock them. On the eighth day, with the spectacle finished, the Koyemshi are dismissed from their duties, and the ceremonial year comes to a close.

The ceremonial orations typically request or predict blessings, as can be seen from all the selections presented here. This culminating portion of the "talk" is preceded by a summary of what the speaker has been doing to obtain the desired result, as in the excerpt from the "Shalako House Blessing" (which describes the consecration of the structure and, as a result, the fruitfulness it will one day contain). The avowal of duty is in turn preceded by a statement noting the day or the occasion, making reference to a particular position in the ceremonial year. All three segments—occasion, duty, and result—can be observed in the *Dismissal of the Koyemshi*, presented here in full.

Our selections are from Ruth L. Bunzel, "Zuni Ritual Poetry," *Forty-Seventh Annual Report of the Bureau of American Ethnology* (1932), which includes annotated texts in Zuni and English. Two related works by Bunzel, "Introduction to Zuni Ceremonialism" and "Zuni Katcinas," are in the same volume. Alfonso Ortiz, ed., *Southwest*, vol. 9 of *Handbook of North American Indians* (1979), serves as a guide to the history and culture of Zuni and other pueblos. William M. Clements, *Native American Verbal Art: Texts and Contexts* (1996), includes a discussion of identity and difference in Zuni verbal art and offers an extended bibliography. For recent impressions of Zuni life and Zuni ceremonialism, see Barbara Tedlock, *The Beautiful and the Dangerous* (1992).

PRONOUNCING GLOSSARY

The following list uses common English syllables and stress accents to provide rough equivalents of selected words whose pronunciation may be unfamiliar to the general reader.

Acoma: *ak'-uh-muh/ah'-kuh-muh*   Oraibi: *oh-ai'-bee*
kachinas: *kuh-chee'-nuhz*   Sayatasha: *sah'-yah-tah-shah*
kokkokwe: *koh'-koh-kway*   Shalako: *shah'-lah-koh*
Koyemshi: *koh'-yaym-shee*   Uwanammi: *oo'-wah-nahm-mee*

From A Prayer at the Winter Solstice[1]

* * *

Perhaps if we are lucky
Our earth mother
Will wrap herself in a fourfold robe
Of white meal,
Full of frost flowers;   5
A floor of ice will spread over the world,
The forests,
Because of the cold will lean to one side,
Their arms will break beneath the weight of snow.
When the days are thus   10
The flesh of our earth mother
Will crack with cold.
Then in the spring when she is replete with living waters
Our mothers,
All different kinds of corn   15
In their earth mother
We shall lay to rest.
With their earth mother's living waters
They will be made into new beings;
Into their sun father's daylight   20
They will come out standing;
Yonder to all directions
They will stretch out their hands calling for rain.
Then with their fresh waters
The rain makers[2] will pass us on our roads.   25
Clasping their young ones in their arms
They will rear their children.
Gathering them[3] into our houses,
Following these toward whom our thoughts bend,
With our thoughts following them,   30
Thus we shall always live.

From The Scalp Dance

* * *

Indeed, the enemy,
Though in his life
He was a person given to falsehood,
He has become one to foretell[1]
How the world will be,   5

---

1. All selections translated by Ruth L. Bunzel. Text printed in italics was added by Bunzel.   2. Or
Uwanammi; water spirits who live in all the waters of the earth; cumulus clouds are their houses: mist is
their breath [adapted from Translator's note].   3. The corn at harvest.   1. It is expected that the scalp
will prove an omen of good fortune.

How the days will be.
That during his time,
We may have good days,
Beautiful days,
Hoping for this,   10
We shall keep his days.[2]
Indeed, if we are lucky,
During the enemy's time
Fine rain caressing the earth,
Heavy rain caressing the earth,   15
We shall win.
When the enemy's days are in progress,
The enemy's waters,
We shall win,
His seeds we shall win,   20
His riches we shall win,
His power,
His strong spirit,
His long life,
His old age,   25
In order to win these,
Tirelessly, unwearied,
We shall pass his days.
Now, indeed, the enemy,
Even one who thought himself a man,   30
In a shower of arrows,
In a shower of war clubs,
With bloody head,
The enemy,
Reaching the end of his life,   35
Added to the flesh of our earth mother.

From Shalako

From *Sayatasha's*[1] *Night Chant*

HOUSE BLESSING

*   *   *

Then my father's rain-filled room
I rooted at the north,
I rooted at the west,
I rooted at the south,
I rooted at the east,[2]   5
I rooted above,
Then in the middle of my father's roof,

---

2. I.e., observe the several days' ritual, which is spoken of as the "enemy's time," "enemy's days," or simply "his time."   1. Long Horn; the kachina's mask has a curved horn on the right side.   2. Consecrating the principal room (*rain-filled room*) of the human host (*father*) by stroking each wall with a torch, a whip, or other instrument.

With two plume wands joined together,
I consecrated his roof.
This is well;   10
In order that my father's offspring may increase,
I consecrated the center of his roof.
And then also, the center of my father's floor,
With seeds of all kinds,[3]
I consecrated the center of his floor.   15
This is well;
In order that my father's fourth room[4]
May be bursting with corn,
That even in his doorway,
The shelled corn may be scattered before the door,   20
The beans may be scattered before the door,
That his house may be full of little boys,
And little girls,
And people grown to maturity;
That in his house   25
Children may jostle one another in the doorway,
In order that it may be thus,
I have consecrated the rain-filled room
Of my daylight father,
My daylight mother.   30

*   *   *

DISMISSAL OF THE KOYEMSHI[5]

This many are the days,
My children,
Since with their plume wand they appointed us.
Throughout the winter,
And the summer   5
Anxiously we have awaited our time.
Hither toward the south
We have given our fathers plume wands.[6]
For all our ladder descending children[7]
We have been asking for life.   10
Now we have reached the appointed time.
This night
We have fulfilled the thoughts of our fathers.
Always with one thought
We shall live.   15
My children,
This night
Your children,
Your families,

---

3. Male and female wands joined together (representing fertility) are placed in a decorated box suspended from the ceiling; seeds, in a permanent excavation below the floor. Thus the sixfold blessing encompasses the four directions, the zenith, and the nadir. 4. Innermost room. 5. A troupe of ten clowns appearing in dances throughout the year. Their impersonators, appointed at the winter solstice to serve for twelve months, are here dismissed by their leader, or "father" (who calls them *children*), bringing the Shalako to an end. 6. I.e., raw people (*fathers*) have been given *plume wands* in exchange for benefits conferred on humans. 7. Humans; so called since houses in former times were entered through an opening in the roof.

Happily you will pass on their roads.[8]   20
Happily we shall always live.
Even though we say we have fulfilled their thoughts
No indeed
Anxiously awaiting until we shall again come to our
     appointed time
We shall live henceforth.   25
My children,
Thus I have finished my words for you.
To this end, my children:
May you now go happily to your children.
Asking for life from my fathers   30
Yonder on all sides,
Asking for my fathers' life-giving breath,
Their breath of old age,
And into my warm body,
Drawing their breath,   35
I add to your breath.
To this end, my children
May your roads be fulfilled;
May you grow old;
May you be blessed with life.   40

8. Will meet, will join.

SIGMUND FREUD
1856–1939

Psychoanalysis, for its founder and for those he influenced, was a new cosmology comparable only to the revolutionary discoveries of Nicolaus Copernicus and Charles Darwin. Each changed the way that human beings could think about themselves: Copernicus, by proving the universe did not revolve around Earth; Darwin, by showing that humanity was only one of many evolving biological species; and Sigmund Freud, by offering a model of the unconscious mind and its dependence on drives rooted in sexual desire. Although he was suspicious of philosophers for offering overbroad systems detached from experience, and he always considered himself a scientist, Freud was in fact a system maker whose creative imagination put a personal stamp on everything he wrote. From the early case histories to the later, more speculative, essays on civilization, Freud struggled to understand the nature of human mental activity. Like Proust (to whom he has often been compared), he probed questions of identity, memory, and desire, interrogated personal experience, disclosed his own thought processes, proposed explanations, and constantly reconsidered and revised his ideas. Like fiction writers in general (or at least nineteenth-century fiction writers), Freud imposed a master plot on his scientific inquiries by following a central theme that he tried to bring to a logical conclusion. He himself said that his case histories read like short stories, and he gave the title *The Man Moses, A Historical Novel* to the first draft of *Moses and Monotheism*. The breadth of Freud's appeal may indeed be attributed to the persuasiveness of his prose and to the dramatic power of analytic scenes that are framed in a tight, novel-like structure of plot development and the discovery of answers.

Many of Freud's ideas or terms have entered common usage. The "Freudian slip" (a slip of the tongue that reveals hidden preoccupations), the "Oedipus complex" (a son's rivalry with his father for authority and for his mother's affection), the "Freudian symbol" (an object, especially one linear or curved, that suggests genitalia), the "castration complex," the "death wish," the "repression" of disturbing memories as an unconscious defense mechanism, the "repetition compulsion" that leads people to repeat unpleasant experiences, dreams and "dream work" as the voice of unconscious wishes, free association as a tactic for revealing obsessions, and the multiple forms of narcissism (self-love), all refer to concepts that Freud developed in his work.

Contemporary discussions of personality cannot do without Freud's insights. He did not invent the unconscious, but he focused attention on the strength of its ties to conscious thought. He was the first to interpret dreams as an expression of unconscious impulses. More than that, he described categories by which one could analyze dream structures. Human beings defend themselves from continued contact with painful reality, argued Freud, by transforming the disturbing experience through tactics he called condensation, displacement, representation, symbolization, and a "secondary revision" that retells events in more coherent—and acceptable—form. Interpersonal relationships, he added, were similarly governed by complex buried motivations. Part of the analyst's job was to decipher the underlying pattern suggested by the repressions and revisions of a patient's story. Even in such a controlled medical situation, however, there were two further complications that needed to be taken into account: the "transference" by which a patient sought to make the analyst enact a familiar role in his or her drama, and the "countertransference" that took place when the analyst accepted such a role. In reviewing his first case history (the "Dora" case presented here), Freud asserted that he had not yet sufficiently accounted for his patient's transference. Contemporary critics feel that Freud also never recognized his own countertransference, and the fact that he himself had adopted a role in relating to Dora. Such a situation would not have seemed impossible to Freud, who knew how difficult it was to determine motivation and who was constantly on the lookout for blind spots in theory and practice.

Freud's scientism is colored by a deep respect for art and literature. Writers and artists are cited liberally throughout his work; Goethe, Shakespeare, Dostoevsky, da Vinci, and Michelangelo are used as points of departure for individual studies. He named a fundamental psychoanalytic concept after Sophocles' Oedipus. The creative artist, according to Freud, gives aesthetic form to personal "phantasies" or daydreams, but these fantasies are shared—in one form or another—by every human being. Literature and art display the workings of the mind, even if they do not explicate meanings; Freud planned to reverse the order and to formulate scientific insights accompanied by a "detailed description of mental processes such as we are accustomed to find in the works of imaginative writers." If art and psychoanalysis both reveal mental activity, they also have a similar therapeutic value: psychoanalysis clarifies and cures the individual, and artistic creations—the "mental assets of civilization"—are defenses against destructive impulses that, unchecked, lead straight to barbarism. Paradoxically, modern writers who have learned from Freud (for example, Joyce, Kafka, Beckett, Lessing, and others included in this volume) are less intent on the therapeutic possibilities of art than they are on capturing the unconscious in dream scenes, associative language, and the depiction of complexes or madness. In both instances, nonetheless, the aim is to give a fuller representation of human mental activity by taking into account the role played by unconscious desires.

Sigismund Freud (he later changed the name to Sigmund) was born on May 6, 1856, in the small town of Freiberg in Moravia (now Příbor in the Czech Republic). His father was a small-scale wool merchant, some twenty years older than his third wife, Freud's mother, and the family was relatively poor. In 1860, they moved to

Vienna, a city that Freud claimed to dislike but where he lived for seventy-nine years until forced to flee by the Nazis.

Sigmund was the oldest of his mother's seven children; she doted on him, and the household revolved around this brilliant young son who was expected to achieve great things. He did extremely well in school, graduating from the Gymnasium (academic high school) with impressive grades and beginning his medical studies at the University of Vienna in 1873. Here he had his first serious encounters with anti-Semitism. "I found that I was expected to feel myself inferior and an alien because I was a Jew. I refused absolutely to do the first of these things." Freud later noted that this experience of being considered an outsider, cut off from the "compact majority," taught him to rely on his own judgment and sustained him in later intellectual battles.

In this early period, the young medical student was particularly interested in physiological explanations for human behavior. He studied with the famous physiologist E. W. von Brücke and the brain anatomist Theodor Meynert, receiving his medical degree in 1881. Although he would have preferred a career in research, he prepared for medical practice at the General Hospital so as to be able to support a wife and family. In 1886, he entered private practice as a neurologist and married Martha Bernays after a four-year engagement. Around this time, Freud began to take a greater interest in psychological rather than physiological approaches to brain activity. During the winter of 1885–86 he had studied with the neurologist Jean-Martin Charcot at the Parisian mental hospital of La Salpêtrière. Freud was impressed by Charcot's investigations of hysteria and hypnosis, and he reported on what he had learned when he returned to Vienna. The Viennese medical establishment, however, was shocked by Charcot's ideas (especially the concept of male hysteria). Freud was publicly attacked by his former teacher Meynert and excluded from the laboratories of the General Hospital. In private practice, he continued his work on hysteria, gradually moving from a dependence on medical hypnosis to the use of free association. In 1895 he published (with the Viennese physician Josef Breuer) *Studies on Hysteria*. The book introduced what was called a "cathartic" treatment by which patients would recall, understand, and render harmless painful memories.

Freud felt that hypnosis had only limited value and that its cures were too often temporary; he preferred to explore the broader possibilities of free association. If patients could recall events under hypnosis, he reasoned, they must in fact "know" them at some level of unconscious memory, even if they resisted bringing that material to the surface. Freud's investigation of the selective processes of memory—of what he would call "defense mechanisms" protecting the subject from painful experiences—initiated the study of psychoanalysis proper. He would now describe various defense mechanisms used by individuals to preserve their self-image and sense of well-being. His own self-analysis, undertaken in 1897 after the death of his father, brought forth not only the concept of an Oedipus complex but many other insights into the effects of unconscious processes on conscious behavior and on dreams. *The Interpretation of Dreams*, published in November 1899 (dated 1900), argued that dreams were not random occurrences but had their own coded meaning. Freud included his own "Irma" dream among various examples of the way that dreams censored disturbing material while fulfilling an underlying repressed wish. Interpreting dreams became an important part of his clinical practice and was central to such case histories as *"Dora"* (1905) and *"The Wolfman"* (1918). The influence of unconscious impulses on conscious behavior was also a theme of two other volumes published around the turn of the century: *The Psychopathology of Everyday Life* (1901) and *Jokes and Their Relation to the Unconscious* (1905).

Freud was disappointed at the small response to *The Interpretation of Dreams*, his first major book, and indeed his studies of sexuality attracted far more attention. Contemporary audiences were disconcerted by his clinical descriptions of "normal" and "abnormal" sexual practices, and his recognition of sexual drives in women as well as in men. Even more upsetting was his description of a many-sided or "polymorphously perverse" sexuality in children. Freud was convinced, however, of the causative relation between childhood sexuality, its inevitable channeling and repression, and the adult personality. He continued to explore aspects of human sexuality throughout his work, publishing the controversial *Three Essays on Sexuality* in 1905 and revising and expanding the text through subsequent editions until the sixth and last edition of 1925.

In the last decades of his life, Freud turned to broader speculations and the creation of explanatory structures. With the essay *On Narcissism* (1914), he began to suggest models of the conscious and unconscious mind that included the related concepts of ego, id, super-ego and ego-ideal: very loosely, the ego as rational consciousness; the id as primitive energy ("the dark, inaccessible part of our personality . . . striving to bring about the satisfaction of instinctive needs"); and the super-ego as an internalized ideal image of human behavior, learned from parents and society, that "represents the ethical standards of mankind." An increasingly somber tone accompanied the elaboration of these ideas in *Beyond the Pleasure Principle* (1920), which countered pleasure with a "reality principle" and added the notion of a "death instinct," and in the revised and definitive statement of *The Ego and the Id* (1923). Freud did not content himself with structural models of the individual mind, however, and adapted his theories of mental conflict to larger models of civilization. *Totem and Taboo* (1913), *Group Psychology* (1921), *The Future of an Illusion* (1927), and *Moses and Monotheism* (1938) focused on the relation of individual and group, analyzing particularly the role of religion. Gradually, Freud envisaged an all-encompassing, dialectical scheme in which Eros and Thanatos, the life and death instincts, figured as opposing forces in human beings and in civilization itself. His late study, *Civilization and Its Discontents* (1930), described civilization as a hard-won and not entirely pleasurable prize achieved only through renunciation and control of instinctual desires. The scientific inquiry that began with laboratory studies of cerebral anatomy had emerged in a philosophic essay of grandiose scope and tragic vision. The span of Freud's achievement was noted in the citation for the Goethe Prize awarded that same year: he had "opened access to the driving forces of the soul and thus created the possibility of recognizing the emergence and construction of cultural forms and of curing some of the soul's illnesses."

As the founder of psychoanalysis and a brilliant writer in his own right, Freud was an exceptional innovator whose influence on twentieth-century thought can scarcely be overestimated. He was also a creature of his time, and even those who feel greatly indebted to him recognize the degree to which he shared a traditional nineteenth-century social perspective. Freudian psychology claims universal validity, but its structures are Western and patriarchal: that is, it is based on Western models of a nuclear family, and it is invariably governed by a masculine perspective. The strongest criticism of Freud's theories of sexuality has come, in fact, from those who note in them the subterranean influence of Victorian gender stereotypes. In Freud's day, women had little control over their own lives: fathers, husbands, or male relatives decided what was best for them. Despite his bold recognition of female sexuality, Freud held conventional views of women's social role. One of the more than nine hundred letters he wrote his fianceé during their four-year engagement reveals his personal attitude: "It seems a completely unrealistic notion to send women into the struggle for existence in the same way as men. Am I to think of my delicate sweet girl as a competitor?" Readers may well feel that both aspects emerge in the *"Dora"* case: on the one hand, an intrepid and imaginative researcher pursuing medical truth through all obstacles and, on the other, a man whose analytic attitude toward his patient is shaped by existing cultural attitudes and by what he thinks is "normal" for a young woman her age.

Dora's real name was Ida Bauer. At age eighteen, she was sent to Freud for treatment after her parents had discovered an apparent suicide letter. Her father, who had previously been Freud's patient, hoped that Freud would bring Dora to reason—

which included reconciling her with the "K." family and with Herr K., whom she had accused of propositioning her. Dora was reluctant to undertake the treatment, and she did not welcome Freud's intensifying explanations of what was wrong with her; after eleven weeks she notified him that she would not be coming back. Freud was disappointed not to finish the treatment, especially since his analysis was providing evidence for theories outlined in *The Interpretation of Dreams*. He published his account five years later as a "Fragment of an Analysis of a Case of Hysteria," but this "fragment" continued to occupy his mind and he added footnotes in later editions.

"*Dora*" is the first of Freud's major case histories, and for many years it was a model for students of psychoanalysis. It has also been called a literary masterwork, a short novel told in the first person in which the narrative point of view is as fascinating as the plot and characters. The author's perspective is personal as well as professional, and he is hurt and even a little vindictive when Dora decides to break off the relationship. His preface observes that Dora may be pained to see her case in print, and he reinforces his argument through numerous footnotes that justify and comment personally on his interpretation of events that themselves recall a romantic novel: there are related love stories, misunderstandings and betrayal, and an unhappy heroine whose destiny is the focus of attention. The author arranges the sequence of events "for the sake of presenting the case in a more connected form." He selects some characters for extended description (the father, Herr K.) while dismissing others equally close (the mother) in a few words. Dramatic tension builds as Freud observes and interprets his subject's every move, concluding triumphantly that "he who has eyes to see and ears to hear, becomes convinced that mortals can keep no secret. If their lips are silent, they gossip with their fingertips; betrayal forces its way through every pore." Freud was not unaware of the literary quality of his case histories: he complained mildly that "it still strikes me myself as strange that the case histories I write should read like short stories and that, as one might say, they lack the serious stamp of science." Yet the stamp of science is also evident in "*Dora*": it emerges in the narrator's dedication to discovering the truth of mental processes, in the tightly controlled structure he imposes on his quest and—most obviously—in the clinical detail with which he analyzes evidence. Literature and science come together, finally, in Freud's practice of displaying his own tactical strategy as he goes; with "*Dora*" this laying bare of narrative principles fits both scientific method and modernist literary technique.

In *Dora's Case: Freud-Hysteria-Feminism* (1985), edited by Charles Bernheimer and Claire Kahane, presents twelve major essays on the "*Dora*" case, a two-part introduction, and a biographical note. Peter Gay, *Freud: A Life for Our Time* (1988), is a full, very readable biography by a major cultural historian and Freud scholar. Brief informative biographies are Gerald Levin, *Sigmund Freud* (1975), and Margaret Muckenhoupt, *Sigmund Freud: Explorer of the Unconscious* (1997). Madelon Sprengnether, *The Spectral Mother: Freud, Feminism, and Psychoanalysis* (1990), contains a revisionary discussion of Freud's ambiguous relationship to Dora. Malcolm Bowie, *Freud, Proust and Lacan: Theory as Fiction* (1987), sees the authors as theorists and fiction writers who develop portraits of mental life; chapters on each writer, a chapter comparing Freud and Proust, and a note on translations. Hannah S. Decker, *Freud, Dora and Vienna 1900* (1990), describes the cultural context that influenced both Freud and Dora.

From "Dora"
(Fragment of an Analysis of a Case of Hysteria)[1]

I

The Clinical Picture

In my *Interpretation of Dreams,* published in 1900, I showed that dreams in general can be interpreted, and that after the work of interpretation has been completed they can be replaced by perfectly correctly constructed thoughts which can be assigned a recognizable position in the chain of mental events. I wish to give an example in the following pages of the only practical application of which the art of interpreting dreams seems to admit. I have already mentioned in my book how it was that I came upon the problem of dreams. The problem crossed my path as I was endeavouring to cure psychoneuroses by means of a particular psychotherapeutic method. For, among their other mental experiences, my patients told me their dreams, and these dreams seemed to call for insertion in the long thread of connections which spun itself out between a symptom of the disease and a pathogenic idea. At that time I learnt how to translate the language of dreams into the forms of expression of our own thought-language, which can be understood without further help. And I may add that this knowledge is essential for the psycho-analyst; for the dream is one of the roads along which consciousness can be reached by the psychical material which, on account of the opposition aroused by its content, has been cut off from consciousness and repressed, and has thus become pathogenic. The dream, in short, is one of the *détours by which repression can be evaded*; it is one of the principal means employed by what is known as the indirect method of representation in the mind. The following fragment from the history of the treatment of a hysterical girl is intended to show the way in which the interpretation of dreams plays a part in the work of analysis. It will at the same time give me a first opportunity of publishing at sufficient length to prevent further misunderstanding some of my views upon the psychical processes of hysteria and upon its organic determinants. I need no longer apologize on the score of length, since it is now agreed that the exacting demands which hysteria makes upon physician and investigator can be met only by the most sympathetic spirit of inquiry and not by an attitude of superiority and contempt. For,

> *Nicht Kunst und Wissenschaft allein,*
> *Geduld will bei dem Werke sein!*[2]

If I were to begin by giving a full and consistent case history, it would place the reader in a very different situation from that of the medical observer. The reports of the patient's relatives—in the present case I was given one by the eighteen-year-old girl's father—usually afford a very indistinct picture of the course of the illness. I begin the treatment, indeed, by asking the patient to give me the whole story of his life and illness, but even

1. Translated by Alix and James Strachey. Freud's prefatory remarks have been omitted.   2. "Science is not enough, nor art / In this work patience plays a part" (German). From Goethe's *Faust*, "Witch's Kitchen" 34–35, translated by Walter Kaufmann.

so the information I receive is never enough to let me see my way about the case. This first account may be compared to an unnavigable river whose stream is at one moment choked by masses of rock and at another divided and lost among shallows and sandbanks. I cannot help wondering how it is that the authorities can produce such smooth and precise histories in cases of hysteria. As a matter of fact the patients are incapable of giving such reports about themselves. They can, indeed, give the physician plenty of coherent information about this or that period of their lives; but it is sure to be followed by another period as to which their communications run dry, leaving gaps unfilled, and riddles unanswered; and then again will come yet another period which will remain totally obscure and unilluminated by even a single piece of serviceable information. The connections—even the ostensible ones—are for the most part incoherent, and the sequence of different events is uncertain. Even during the course of their story patients will repeatedly correct a particular or a date, and then perhaps, after wavering for some time, return to their first version. The patients' inability to give an ordered history of their life in so far as it coincides with the history of their illness is not merely characteristic of the neurosis. It also possesses great theoretical significance. For this inability has the following grounds. In the first place, patients consciously and intentionally keep back part of what they ought to tell—things that are perfectly well known to them—because they have not got over their feelings of timidity and shame (or discretion, where what they say concerns other people); this is the share taken by *conscious* disingenuousness. In the second place, part of the anamnestic[3] knowledge, which the patients have at their disposal at other times, disappears while they are actually telling their story, but without their making any deliberate reservations: the share taken by *unconscious* disingenuousness. In the third place, there are invariably true amnesias—gaps in the memory into which not only old recollections but even quite recent ones have fallen—and paramnesias,[4] formed secondarily so as to fill in those gaps.[5] When the events themselves have been kept in mind, the purpose underlying the amnesias can be fulfilled just as surely by destroying a connection, and a connection is most surely broken by altering the chronological order of events. The latter always proves to be the most vulnerable element in the store of memory and the one which is most easily subject to repression. Again, we meet with many recollections that are in what might be described as the first stage of repression, and these we find surrounded with doubts. At a later period the doubts would be replaced by a loss or a falsification of memory.[6]

That this state of affairs should exist in regard to the memories relating to the history of the illness is *a necessary correlate of the symptoms and one which is theoretically requisite*. In the further course of the treatment the patient supplies the facts which, though he had known them all along, had been kept back by him or had not occurred to his mind. The paramnesias prove

3. Recollected, remembered ("anamnesis": calling to memory).   4. "Memories" blended of fantasy and actual experience.   5. Amnesias and paramnesias stand in a complementary relation to each other. When there are large gaps in the memory there will be few mistakes in it. And conversely, paramnesias can at a first glance completely conceal the presence of amnesias [Freud's note].   6. If a patient exhibits doubts in the course of his narrative, an empirical rule teaches us to disregard such expressions of his judgement entirely. If the narrative wavers between two versions, we should incline to regard the first one as correct and the second as a product of repression [Freud's note].

untenable, and the gaps in his memory are filled in. It is only towards the end of the treatment that we have before us an intelligible, consistent, and unbroken case history. Whereas the practical aim of the treatment is to remove all possible symptoms and to replace them by conscious thoughts, we may regard it as a second and theoretical aim to repair all the damages to the patient's memory. These two aims are coincident. When one is reached, so is the other; and the same path leads to them both.

It follows from the nature of the facts which form the material of psycho-analysis that we are obliged to pay as much attention in our case histories to the purely human and social circumstances of our patients as to the somatic data and the symptoms of the disorder. Above all, our interest will be directed towards their family circumstances—and not only, as will be seen later, for the purpose of enquiring into their heredity.

The family circle of the eighteen-year-old girl who is the subject of this paper included, besides herself, her two parents and a brother who was one and a half years her senior. Her father was the dominating figure in this circle, owing to his intelligence and his character as much as to the circum-stances of his life. It was those circumstances which provided the framework for the history of the patient's childhood and illness. At the time at which I began the girl's treatment her father was in his late forties, a man of rather unusual activity and talents, a large manufacturer in very comfortable cir-cumstances. His daughter was most tenderly attached to him, and for that reason her critical powers, which developed early, took all the more offence at many of his actions and peculiarities.

Her affection for him was still further increased by the many severe ill-nesses which he had been through since her sixth year. At that time he he had fallen ill with tuberculosis and the family had consequently moved to a small town in a good climate, situated in one of our southern provinces. There his lung trouble rapidly improved; but, on account of the precautions which were still considered necessary, both parents and children continued for the next ten years or so to reside chiefly in this spot, which I shall call B——. When her father's health was good, he used at times to be away, on visits to his factories. During the hottest part of the summer the family used to move to a health-resort in the hills.

When the girl was about ten years old, her father had to go through a course of treatment in a darkened room on account of a detached retina. As a result of this misfortune his vision was permanently impaired. His gravest illness occurred some two years later. It took the form of a confusional attack, followed by symptoms of paralysis and slight mental disturbances. A friend of his (who plays a part in the story with which we shall be concerned later on) persuaded him, while his condition had scarcely improved, to travel to Vienna with his physician and come to me for advice. I hesitated for some time as to whether I ought not to regard the case as one of tabo-paralysis,[7] but I finally decided upon a diagnosis of a diffuse vascular affection; and since the patient admitted having had a specific infection before his mar-riage, I prescribed an energetic course of anti-luetic[8] treatment, as a result of which all the remaining disturbances passed off. It is no doubt owing to

7. Paralysis resulting from syphilis attacking the spinal cord and sensory nerves.   8. Antisyphilis.

this fortunate intervention of mine that four years later he brought his daughter, who had meanwhile grown unmistakably neurotic, and introduced her to me, and that after another two years he handed her over to me for psychotherapeutic treatment.

I had in the meantime also made the acquaintance in Vienna of a sister of his, who was a little older than himself. She gave clear evidence of a severe form of psychoneurosis without any characteristically hysterical symptoms. After a life which had been weighed down by an unhappy marriage, she died of a marasmus[9] which made rapid advances and the symptoms of which were, as a matter of fact, never fully cleared up. An elder brother of the girl's father, whom I once happened to meet, was a hypochondriacal bachelor.

The sympathies of the girl herself, who, as I have said, became my patient at the age of eighteen, had always been with the father's side of the family, and ever since she had fallen ill she had taken as her model the aunt who has just been mentioned. There could be no doubt, too, that it was from her father's family that she had derived not only her natural gifts and her intellectual precocity but also the predisposition to her illness. I never made her mother's acquaintance. From the accounts given me by the girl and her father I was led to imagine her as an uncultivated woman and above all as a foolish one, who had concentrated all her interests upon domestic affairs, especially since her husband's illness and the estrangement to which it led. She presented the picture, in fact, of what might be called the "housewife's psychosis." She had no understanding of her children's more active interests, and was occupied all day long in cleaning the house with its furniture and utensils and in keeping them clean—to such an extent as to make it almost impossible to use or enjoy them. This condition, traces of which are to be found often enough in normal housewives, inevitably reminds one of forms of obsessional washing and other kinds of obsessional cleanliness. But such women (and this applied to the patient's mother) are entirely without insight into their illness, so that one essential characteristic of an "obsessional neurosis" is lacking. The relations between the girl and her mother had been unfriendly for years. The daughter looked down on her mother and used to criticize her mercilessly, and she had withdrawn completely from her influence.

During the girl's earlier years, her only brother (her elder by a year and a half) had been the model which her ambitions had striven to follow. But in the last few years the relations between the brother and sister had grown more distant. The young man used to try so far as he could to keep out of the family disputes; but when he was obliged to take sides he would support his mother. So that the usual sexual attraction had drawn together the father and daughter on the one side and the mother and son on the other.

The patient, to whom I shall in future give the name of "Dora," had even at the age of eight begun to develop neurotic symptoms. She became subject at that time to chronic dyspnoea[1] with occasional accesses in which the symptom was very much aggravated. The first outset occurred after a short expedition in the mountains and was accordingly put down to over-exertion. In the course of six months, during which she was made to rest and was carefully looked after, this condition gradually passed off. The family doctor

9. A wasting away of the body.   1. Difficult or labored breathing.

seems to have had not a moment's hesitation in diagnosing the disorder as purely nervous and in excluding any organic cause for the dyspnoea; but he evidently considered this diagnosis compatible with the aetiology of over-exertion.

The little girl went through the usual infectious diseases of childhood without suffering any lasting damage. As she herself told me—and her words were intended to convey a deeper meaning—her brother was as a rule the first to start the illness and used to have it very slightly, and she would then follow suit with a severe form of it. When she was about twelve she began to suffer from unilateral headaches in the nature of a migraine, and from attacks of nervous coughing. At first these two symptoms always appeared together, but they became separated later on and ran different courses. The migraine grew rarer, and by the time she was sixteen she had quite got over it. But attacks of *tussis nervosa*,[2] which had no doubt been started by a common catarrh, continued to occur over the whole period. When, at the age of eighteen, she came to me for treatment, she was again coughing in a characteristic manner. The number of these attacks could not be determined; but they lasted from three to five weeks, and on one occasion for several months. The most troublesome symptom during the first half of an attack of this kind, at all events in the last few years, used to be a complete loss of voice. The diagnosis that this was once more a nervous complaint had been established long since; but the various methods of treatment which are usual, including hydrotherapy and the local application of electricity, had produced no result. It was in such circumstances as these that the child had developed into a mature young woman of very independent judgement, who had grown accustomed to laugh at the efforts of doctors, and in the end to renounce their help entirely. Moreover, she had always been against calling in medical advice, though she had no personal objection to her family doctor. Every proposal to consult a new physician aroused her resistance, and it was only her father's authority which induced her to come to me at all.

I first saw her when she was sixteen, in the early summer. She was suffering from a cough and from hoarseness, and even at that time I proposed giving her psychological treatment. My proposal was not adopted, since the attack in question, like the others, passed off spontaneously, though it had lasted unusually long. During the next winter she came and stayed in Vienna with her uncle and his daughters after the death of the aunt of whom she had been so fond. There she fell ill of a feverish disorder which was diagnosed at the time as appendicitis. In the following autumn, since her father's health seemed to justify the step, the family left the health-resort of B—— for good and all. They first moved to the town where her father's factory was situated, and then, scarcely a year later, settled permanently in Vienna.

Dora was by that time in the first bloom of youth—a girl of intelligent and engaging looks. But she was a source of heavy trials for her parents. Low spirits and an alteration in her character had now become the main features of her illness. She was clearly satisfied neither with herself nor with her family; her attitude towards her father was unfriendly, and she was on very bad terms with her mother, who was bent upon drawing her into taking a share in the work of the house. She tried to avoid social intercourse, and

2. Nervous coughing (Latin).

employed herself—so far as she was allowed to by the fatigue and lack of concentration of which she complained—with attending lectures for women and with carrying on more or less serious studies. One day her parents were thrown into a state of great alarm by finding on the girl's writing-desk, or inside it, a letter in which she took leave of them because, as she said, she could no longer endure her life.[3] Her father, indeed, being a man of some perspicacity, guessed that the girl had no serious suicidal intentions. But he was none the less very much shaken; and when one day, after a slight passage of words between him and his daughter, she had a first attack of loss of consciousness[4]—an event which was subsequently covered by an amnesia— it was determined, in spite of her reluctance, that she should come to me for treatment.

No doubt this case history, as I have so far outlined it, does not upon the whole seem worth recording. It is merely a case of *"petite hystérie"* with the commonest of all somatic[5] and mental symptoms: dyspnoea, *tussis nervosa,* aphonia,[6] and possibly migraines, together with depression, hysterical unsociability, and a *taedium vitae*[7] which was probably not entirely genuine. More interesting cases of hysteria have no doubt been published, and they have very often been more carefully described; for nothing will be found in the following pages on the subject of stigmata of cutaneous sensibility, limitation of the visual field, or similar matters. I may venture to remark, however, that all such collections of the strange and wonderful phenomena of hysteria have but slightly advanced our knowledge of a disease which still remains as great a puzzle as ever. What is wanted is precisely an elucidation of the *commonest* cases and of their most frequent and typical symptoms. I should have been very well satisfied if the circumstances had allowed me to give a complete elucidation of this case of *petite hystérie*. And my experiences with other patients leave me in no doubt that my analytic method would have enabled me to do so.

In 1896, shortly after the appearance of my *Studies on Hysteria* (written in conjunction with Dr. J. Breuer, 1895), I asked an eminent fellow-specialist for his opinion on the psychological theory of hysteria put forward in that work. He bluntly replied that he considered it an unjustifiable generalization of conclusions which might hold good for a few cases. Since then I have seen an abundance of cases of hysteria, and I have been occupied with each case for a number of days, weeks, or years. In not a single one of them have I failed to discover the psychological determinants which were postulated in the *Studies*, namely, a psychical trauma, a conflict of affects, and—an additional factor which I brought forward in later publications—a disturbance in the sphere of sexuality. It is of course not to be expected that the patient will come to meet the physician half-way with material which has become

3. As I have already explained, the treatment of the case, and consequently my insight into the complex of events composing it, remained fragmentary. There are therefore many questions to which I have no solution to offer, or in which I can only rely upon hints and conjectures. This affair of the letter came up in the course of one of our sessions, and the girl showed signs of astonishment. "How on earth," she asked, "did they find the letter? It was shut up in my desk." But since she knew that her parents had read this draft of a farewell letter, I conclude that she had herself arranged for it to fall into their hands [Freud's note]. 4. The attack was, I believe, accompanied by convulsions and delirious states. But since this event was not reached by the analysis either, I have no trustworthy recollections on the subject to fall back upon [Freud's note]. 5. Physical, relating to the body. Petite hystérie: minor hysteria (French). 6. Loss of voice. 7. Boredom, fatigue of life (Latin); see Baudelaire's ennui.

pathogenic for the very reason of its efforts to lie concealed; nor must the enquirer rest content with the first "No" that crosses his path.

In Dora's case, thanks to her father's shrewdness which I have remarked upon more than once already, there was no need for me to look about for the points of contact between the circumstances of the patient's life and her illness, at all events in its most recent form. Her father told me that he and his family while they were at B—— had formed an intimate friendship with a married couple who had been settled there for several years. Frau K. had nursed him during his long illness, and had in that way, he said, earned a title to his undying gratitude. Herr[8] K. had always been most kind to Dora. He had gone for walks with her when he was there, and had made her small presents; but no one had thought any harm of that. Dora had taken the greatest care of the K.'s two little children, and been almost a mother to them. When Dora and her father had come to see me two years before in the summer, they had been just on their way to stop with Herr and Frau K., who were spending the summer on one of our lakes in the Alps. Dora was to have spent several weeks at the K.'s, while her father had intended to return home after a few days. During that time Herr K. had been staying there as well. As her father was preparing for his departure the girl had suddenly declared with the greatest determination that she was going with him, and she had in fact put her decision into effect. It was not until some days later that she had thrown any light upon her strange behaviour. She had then told her mother—intending that what she said should be passed on to her father—that Herr K. had had the audacity to make her a proposal while they were on a walk after a trip upon the lake. Herr K. had been called to account by her father and uncle on the next occasion of their meeting, but he had denied in the most emphatic terms having on his side made any advances which could have been open to such a construction. He had then proceeded to throw suspicion upon the girl, saying that he had heard from Frau K. that she took no interest in anything but sexual matters, and that she used to read Mantegazza's *Physiology of Love*[9] and books of that sort in their house on the lake. It was most likely, he had added, that she had been over-excited by such reading and had merely "fancied" the whole scene she had described.

"I have no doubt," continued her father, "that this incident is responsible for Dora's depression and irritability and suicidal ideas. She keeps pressing me to break off relations with Herr K. and more particularly with Frau K., whom she used positively to worship formerly. But that I cannot do. For, to begin with, I myself believe that Dora's tale of the man's immoral suggestions is a phantasy that has forced its way into her mind; and besides, I am bound to Frau K. by ties of honourable friendship and I do not wish to cause her pain. The poor woman is most unhappy with her husband, of whom, by the by, I have no very high opinion. She herself has suffered a great deal with her nerves, and I am her only support. With my state of health I need scarcely assure you that there is nothing wrong in our relations. We are just two poor wretches who give one another what comfort we can by an exchange of

8. Mr. (German). *Frau:* Mrs. (German).   9. Paolo Mantegazza (1831–1910), author of three books on human sexuality. The *Physiology of Love* (1877) is more romantic and less explicit than, e.g., his *Sexual Relations of Mankind.*

friendly sympathy. You know already that I get nothing out of my own wife. But Dora, who inherits my obstinacy, cannot be moved from her hatred of the K.'s. She had her last attack after a conversation in which she had again pressed me to break with them. Please try and bring her to reason."

Her father's words did not always quite tally with this pronouncement; for on other occasions he tried to put the chief blame for Dora's impossible behavior on her mother—whose peculiarities made the house unbearable for every one. But I had resolved from the first to suspend my judgement of the true state of affairs till I had heard the other side as well.

*   *   *

[A brief discussion of trauma theory follows.]

When the first difficulties of the treatment had been overcome, Dora told me of an earlier episode with Herr K., which was even better calculated to act as a sexual trauma. She was fourteen years old at the time. Herr K. had made an arrangement with her and his wife that they should meet him one afternoon at his place of business in the principal square of B—— so as to have a view of a church festival. He persuaded his wife, however, to stay at home, and sent away his clerks, so that he was alone when the girl arrived. When the time for the procession approached, he asked the girl to wait for him at the door which opened on to the staircase leading to the upper story, while he pulled down the outside shutters. He then came back, and, instead of going out by the open door, suddenly clasped the girl to him and pressed a kiss upon her lips. This was surely just the situation to call up a distinct feeling of sexual excitement in a girl of fourteen who had never before been approached. But Dora had at that moment a violent feeling of disgust, tore herself from the man, and hurried past him to the staircase and from there to the street door. She nevertheless continued to meet Herr K. Neither of them ever mentioned the little scene; and according to her account Dora kept it a secret till her confession during the treatment. For some time afterwards, however, she avoided being alone with Herr K. The K.'s had just made plans for an expedition which was to last for some days and on which Dora was to have accompanied them. After the scene of the kiss she refused to join the party, without giving any reason.

In this scene—second in order of mention, but first in order of time—the behaviour of this child of fourteen was already entirely and completely hysterical. I should without question consider a person hysterical in whom an occasion for sexual excitement elicited feelings that were preponderantly or exclusively unpleasurable; and I should do so whether or not the person were capable of producing somatic symptoms. The elucidation of the mechanism of this *reversal of affect* is one of the most important and at the same time one of the most difficult problems in the psychology of the neuroses. In my own judgement I am still some way from having achieved this end; and I may add that within the limits of the present paper I shall be able to bring forward only a part of such knowledge on the subject as I do possess.

In order to particularize Dora's case it is not enough merely to draw attention to the reversal of affect; there has also been a *displacement* of sensation. Instead of the genital sensation which would certainly have been felt by a healthy girl in such circumstances, Dora was overcome by the unpleasurable feeling which is proper to the tract of mucous membrane at the entrance to the alimentary canal—that is by disgust. The stimulation of her lips by the kiss was no doubt of importance in localizing the feeling at that particular place; but I think I can also recognize another factor in operation.[1]

The disgust which Dora felt on that occasion did not become a permanent symptom, and even at the time of the treatment it was only, as it were, potentially present. She was a poor eater and confessed to some disinclination for food. On the other hand, the scene had left another consequence behind it in the shape of a sensory hallucination which occurred from time to time and even made its appearance while she was telling me her story. She declared that she could still feel upon the upper part of her body the pressure of Herr K.'s embrace. In accordance with certain rules of symptom-formation which I have come to know, and at the same time taking into account certain other of the patient's peculiarities, which were otherwise inexplicable,—such as her unwillingness to walk past any man whom she saw engaged in eager or affectionate conversation with a lady—I have formed in my own mind the following reconstruction of the scene. I believe that during the man's passionate embrace she felt not merely his kiss upon her lips but also the pressure of his erect member against her body. This perception was revolting to her; it was dismissed from her memory, repressed, and replaced by the innocent sensation of pressure upon her thorax, which in turn derived an excessive intensity from its repressed source. Once more, therefore, we find a displacement from the lower part of the body to the upper. On the other hand, the compulsive piece of behaviour which I have mentioned was formed as though it were derived from the undistorted recollection of the scene: she did not like walking past any man who she thought was in a state of sexual excitement, because she wanted to avoid seeing for a second time the somatic sign which accompanies it.

It is worth remarking that we have here three symptoms—the disgust, the sensation of pressure on the upper part of the body, and the avoidance of men engaged in affectionate conversation—all of them derived from a single experience, and that it is only by taking into account the interrelation of these three phenomena that we can understand the way in which the formation of the symptoms came about. The disgust is the symptom of repression in the erotogenic oral zone, which, as we shall hear, had been over-indulged in Dora's infancy by the habit of sensual sucking. The pressure of the erect member probably led to an analogous change in the corresponding female organ, the clitoris; and the excitation of this second erotogenic zone was referred by a process of displacement to the simultaneous pressure against the thorax and became fixed there. Her avoidance of men who might possibly be in a state of sexual excitement follows the mechanism of a phobia, its purpose being to safeguard her against any revival of the repressed perception.

In order to show that such a supplement to the story was possible, I questioned the patient very cautiously as to whether she knew anything of the physical signs of excitement in a man's body. Her answer, as touching the present, was "Yes," but, as touching the time of the episode, "I think not."

1. The causes of Dora's disgust at the kiss were certainly not adventitious, for in that case she could not have failed to remember and mention them. I happen to know Herr K., for he was the same person who had visited me with the patient's father, and he was still quite young and of prepossessing appearance [Freud's note].

From the very beginning I took the greatest pains with this patient not to introduce her to any fresh facts in the region of sexual knowledge; and I did this, not from any conscientious motives, but because I was anxious to subject my assumptions to a rigorous test in this case. Accordingly, I did not call a thing by its name until her allusions to it had become so unambiguous that there seemed very slight risk in translating them into direct speech. Her answer was always prompt and frank: she knew about it already. But the question of *where* her knowledge came from was a riddle which her memories were unable to solve. She had forgotten the source of all her information on this subject.

If I may suppose that the scene of the kiss took place in this way, I can arrive at the following derivation for the feelings of disgust.[2] Such feelings seem originally to be a reaction to the smell (and afterwards also to the sight) of excrement. But the genitals can act as a reminder of the excretory functions; and this applies especially to the male member, for that organ performs the function of micturition[3] as well as the sexual function. Indeed, the function of micturition is the earlier known of the two, and the *only* one known during the pre-sexual period. Thus it happens that disgust becomes one of the means of affective expression in the sphere of sexual life. The Early Christian Father's *"inter urinas et faeces nascimur"*[4] clings to sexual life and cannot be detached from it in spite of every effort at idealization. I should like, however, expressly to emphasize my opinion that the problem is not solved by the mere pointing out of this path of association. The fact that this association *can* be called up does not show that it actually *will* be called up. And indeed in normal circumstances it will not be. A knowledge of the paths does not render less necessary a knowledge of the forces which travel along them.

I did not find it easy, however, to direct the patient's attention to her relations with Herr K. She declared that she had done with him. The uppermost layer of all her associations during the sessions, and everything of which she was easily conscious and of which she remembered having been conscious the day before, was always connected with her father. It was quite true that she could not forgive her father for continuing his relations with Herr K. and more particularly with Frau K. But she viewed those relations in a very different light from that in which her father wished them to appear. In her mind there was no doubt that what bound her father to this young and beautiful woman was a common love-affair. Nothing that could help to confirm this view had escaped her perception, which in this connection was pitilessly sharp; *here there were no gaps to be found in her memory.* Their acquaintance with the K.'s had begun before her father's serious illness; but it had not become intimate until the young woman had officially taken on the position of nurse during that illness, while Dora's mother had kept away from the sick-room. During the first summer holidays after his recovery things had happened which must have opened every one's eyes to the true character of this "friendship." The two families had taken a suite of rooms in common at the hotel. One day Frau K. had announced that she could not

2. Here, as in all similar cases, the reader must be prepared to be met not by one but by several causes—by *overdetermination* [Freud's note]. In other words, a single symptom may express or be *determined* by different intertwined causes. 3. Urination. 4. We are born between urine and feces (Latin).

keep the bedroom which she had up till then shared with one of her children. A few days later Dora's father had given up his bedroom, and they had both moved into new rooms—the end rooms, which were only separated by the passage, while the rooms they had given up had not offered any such security against interruption. Later on, whenever she had reproached her father about Frau K., he had been in the habit of saying that he could not understand her hostility and that, on the contrary, his children had every reason for being grateful to Frau K. Her mother, whom she has asked for an explanation of this mysterious remark, had told her that her father had been so unhappy at that time that he had made up his mind to go into the wood and kill himself, and that Frau K., suspecting as much, had gone after him and had persuaded him by her entreaties to preserve his life for the sake of his family. Of course, Dora went on, she herself did not believe this story; no doubt the two of them had been seen together in the wood, and her father had thereupon invented this fairy tale of his suicide so as to account for their rendezvous.[5]

When they had returned to B——, her father had visited Frau K. every day at definite hours, while her husband was at his business. Everybody had talked about it and had questioned her about it pointedly. Herr K. himself had often complained bitterly to her mother, though he had spared her herself any allusions to the subject—which she seemed to attribute to delicacy of feeling on his part. When they had all gone for walks together, her father and Frau K. had always known how to manage things so as to be alone with each other. There could be no doubt that she had taken money from him, for she spent more than she could possibly have afforded out of her own purse or her husband's. Dora added that her father had begun to make handsome presents to Frau K., and in order to make these less conspicuous had at the same time become especially liberal towards her mother and herself. And, while previously Frau K. had been an invalid and had even been obliged to spend months in a sanatorium for nervous disorders because she had been unable to walk, she had now become a healthy and lively woman.

Even after they had left B—— for the manufacturing town, these relations, already of many years' standing, had been continued. From time to time her father used to declare that he could not endure the rawness of the climate, and that he must do something for himself; he would begin to cough and complain, until suddenly he would start off to B——, and from there write the most cheerful letters home. All these illnesses had only been pretexts for seeing his friend again. Then one day it had been decided that they were to move to Vienna and Dora began to suspect a hidden connection. And sure enough, they had scarcely been three weeks in Vienna when she heard that the K.'s had moved there as well. They were in Vienna, so she told me, at that very moment, and she frequently met her father with Frau K. in the street. She also met Herr K. very often, and he always used to turn round and look after her; and once when he had met her out by herself he had followed her for a long way, so as to make sure where she was going and whether she might not have a rendezvous.

On one occasion during the course of the treatment her father again felt

---

5. This is the point of connection with her own pretence at suicide, which may thus be regarded as the expression of a longing for a love of the same kind [Freud's note].

worse, and went off to B—— for several weeks; and the sharp-sighted Dora had soon unearthed the fact that Frau K. had started off to the same place on a visit to her relatives there. It was at this time that Dora's criticisms of her father were the most frequent: he was insincere, he had a strain of falseness in his character, he only thought of his enjoyment, and he had a gift for seeing things in the light which suited him best.

I could not in general dispute Dora's characterization of her father; and there was one particular respect in which it was easy to see that her reproaches were justified. When she was feeling embittered she used to be overcome by the idea that she had been handed over to Herr K. as the price of his tolerating the relations between her father and his wife; and her rage at her father's making such a use of her was visible behind her affection for him. At other times she was quite well aware that she had been guilty of exaggeration in talking like this. The two men had of course never made a formal agreement in which she was treated as an object for barter; her father in particular would have been horrified at any such suggestion. But he was one of those men who know how to evade a dilemma by falsifying their judgement upon one of the conflicting alternatives. If it had been pointed out to him that there might be danger for a growing girl in the constant and unsupervised companionship of a man who had no satisfaction from his own wife, he would have been certain to answer that he could rely upon his daughter, that a man like K. could never be dangerous to her, and that his friend was himself incapable of such intentions, or that Dora was still a child and was treated as a child by K. But as a matter of fact things were in a position in which each of the two men avoided drawing any conclusions from the other's behaviour which would have been awkward for his own plans. It was possible for Herr K. to send Dora flowers every day for a whole year while he was in the neighbourhood, to take every opportunity of giving her valuable presents, and to spend all his spare time in her company, without her parents noticing anything in his behaviour that was characteristic of love-making.

When a patient brings forward a sound and incontestable train of argument during psycho-analytic treatment, the physician is liable to feel a moment's embarrassment, and the patient may take advantage of it by asking: "This is all perfectly correct and true, isn't it? What do you want to change in [it] now that I've told it you?" But it soon becomes evident that the patient is using thoughts of this kind, which the analysis cannot attack, for the purpose of cloaking others which are anxious to escape from criticism and from consciousness. A string of reproaches against other people leads one to suspect the existence of a string of self-reproaches with the same content. All that need be done is to turn back each particular reproach on to the speaker himself. There is something undeniably automatic about this method of defending oneself against a self-reproach by making the same reproach against some one else. A model of it is to be found in the *tu quoque*[6] arguments of children; if one of them is accused of being a liar, he will reply without an instant's hesitation: "You're another." A grown-up person who wanted to throw back abuse would look for some really exposed spot in his

---

6. You too! (Latin).

antagonist and would not lay the chief stress upon the same content being repeated. In paranoia the projection of a reproach on to another person without any alteration in its content and therefore without any consideration for reality becomes manifest as the process of forming delusions.

Dora's reproaches against her father had a "lining" or "backing" of self-reproaches of this kind with a corresponding content in every case, as I shall show in detail. She was right in thinking that her father did not wish to look too closely into Herr K.'s behaviour to his daughter, for fear of being disturbed in his own love-affair with Frau K. But Dora herself had done precisely the same thing. She had made herself an accomplice in the affair, and had dismissed from her mind every sign which tended to show its true character. It was not until after her adventure by the lake that her eyes were opened and that she began to apply such a severe standard to her father. During all the previous years she had given every possible assistance to her father's relations with Frau K. She would never go to see her if she thought her father was there; but, knowing that in that case the children would have been sent out, she would turn her steps in a direction where she would be sure to meet them, and would go for a walk with them. There had been some one in the house who had been anxious at an early stage to open her eyes to the nature of her father's relations with Frau K., and to induce her to take sides against her. This was her last governess, an unmarried woman, no longer young, who was well-read and of advanced views.[7] The teacher and her pupil were for a while upon excellent terms, until suddenly Dora became hostile to her and insisted on her dismissal. So long as the governess had any influence she used it for stirring up feeling against Frau K. She explained to Dora's mother that it was incompatible with her dignity to tolerate such an intimacy between her husband and another woman; and she drew Dora's attention to all the obvious features of their relations. But her efforts were vain. Dora remained devoted to Frau K. and would hear of nothing that might make her think ill of her relations with her father. On the other hand she very easily fathomed the motives by which her governess was actuated. She might be blind in one direction, but she was sharp-sighted enough in the other. She saw that the governess was in love with her father. When he was there, she seemed to be quite another person: at such times she could be amusing and obliging. While the family were living in the manufacturing town and Frau K. was not on the horizon, her hostility was directed against Dora's mother, who was then her more immediate rival. Up to this point Dora bore her no ill-will. She did not become angry until she observed that she herself was a subject of complete indifference to the governess, whose pretended affection for her was really meant for her father. While her father was away from the manufacturing town the governess had no time to spare for her, would not go for walks with her, and took no interest in her studies. No sooner had her father returned from B—— than she was once more ready with every sort of service and assistance. Thereupon Dora dropped her.

The poor woman had thrown a most unwelcome light on a part of Dora's

7. This governess used to read every sort of book on sexual life and similar subjects, and talked to the girl about them, at the same time asking her quite frankly not to mention their conversations to her parents, as one could never tell what line they might take about them. For some time I looked upon this woman as the source of all Dora's secret knowledge, and perhaps I was not entirely wrong in this [Freud's note].

own behaviour. What the governess had from time to time been to Dora, Dora had been to Herr K.'s children. She had been a mother to them, she had taught them, she had gone for walks with them, she had offered them a complete substitute for the slight interest which their own mother showed in them. Herr K. and his wife had often talked of getting a divorce; but it never took place, because Herr K., who was an affectionate father, would not give up either of the two children. A common interest in the children had from the first been a bond between Herr K. and Dora. Her preoccupation with his children was evidently a cloak for something else that Dora was anxious to hide from herself and from other people.

The same inference was to be drawn both from her behaviour towards the children, regarded in the light of the governess's behaviour towards herself, and from her silent acquiescence in her father's relations with Frau K.— namely, that she had all these years been in love with Herr K. When I informed her of this conclusion she did not assent to it. It is true that she at once told me that other people besides (one of her cousins, for instance—a girl who had stopped with them for some time at B——) had said to her: "Why you're simply wild about that man!" But she herself could not be got to recollect any feelings of the kind. Later on, when the quantity of material that had come up had made it difficult for her to persist in her denial, she admitted that she might have been in love with Herr K. at B——, but declared that since the scene by the lake it had all been over. In any case it was quite certain that the reproaches which she made against her father of having been deaf to the most imperative calls of duty and of having seen things in the light which was most convenient from the point of view of his own passions—these reproaches recoiled on her own head.[8]

Her other reproach against her father was that his ill-health was only a pretext and that he exploited it for his own purposes. This reproach, too, concealed a whole section of her own secret history. One day she complained of a professedly new symptom, which consisted of piercing gastric pains. "Whom are you copying now?" I asked her, and found I had hit the mark. The day before she had visited her cousins, the daughters of the aunt who had died. The younger one had become engaged, and this had given occasion to the elder one for falling ill with gastric pains, and she was to be sent off to Semmering.[9] Dora thought it was all just envy on the part of the elder sister; she always got ill when she wanted something, and what she wanted now was to be away from home so as not to have to look on at her sister's happiness.[1] But Dora's own gastric pains proclaimed the fact that she identified herself with her cousin, who, according to her, was a malingerer. Her grounds for this identification were either that she too envied the luckier girl her love, or that she saw her own story reflected in that of the elder sister, who had recently had a love-affair which had ended unhappily. But she had also learned from observing Frau K. what useful things illnesses could become. Herr K. spent part of the year in travelling. Whenever he came back, he used to find his wife in bad health, although, as Dora knew, she had been quite well only the day before. Dora realized that the presence of the husband

8. The question then arises: If Dora loved Herr K., what was the reason for her refusing him in the scene by the lake? Or at any rate, why did her refusal take such a brutal form, as though she were embittered against him? And how could a girl who was in love feel insulted by a proposal which was made in a manner neither tactless nor offensive? [Freud's note]. 9. A fashionable health resort in the mountains near Vienna. 1. An event of everyday occurrence between sisters [Freud's note].

had the effect of making his wife ill, and that she was glad to be ill so as to be able to escape the conjugal duties which she so much detested. At this point in the discussion Dora suddenly brought in an allusion to her own alternations between good and bad health during the first years of her girlhood at B——; and I was thus driven to suspect that her states of health were to be regarded as depending upon something else, in the same way as Frau K.'s. (It is a rule of psycho-analytic technique that an internal connection which is still undisclosed will announce its presence by means of a contiguity—a temporal proximity—of associations; just as in writing, if "a" and "b" are put side by side, it means that the syllable "ab" is to be formed out of them.) Dora had had a very large number of attacks of coughing accompanied by loss of voice. Could it be that the presence or absence of the man she loved had had an influence upon the appearance and disappearance of the symptoms of her illness? If this were so, it must be possible to discover some coincidence or other which would betray the fact. I asked her what the average length of these attacks had been. "From three to six weeks, perhaps." How long had Herr K.'s absences lasted? "Three to six weeks, too," she was obliged to admit. Her illness was therefore a demonstration of her love for K., just as his wife's was a demonstration of her *dislike*. It was only necessary to suppose that her behaviour had been the opposite of Frau K.'s and that she had been ill when he was absent and well when he had come back. And this really seemed to have been so, at least during the first period of the attacks. Later on it no doubt became necessary to obscure the coincidence between her attacks of illness and the absence of the man she secretly loved, lest its regularity should betray her secret. The length of the attacks would then remain as a trace of their original significance.

I remembered that long before, while I was working at Charcot's[2] clinic, I had seen and heard how in cases of hysterical mutism writing operated vicariously in the place of speech. Such patients were able to write more fluently, quicker, and better than others did or than they themselves had done previously. The same thing had happened with Dora. In the first days of her attacks of aphonia "writing had always come specially easy to her." No psychological elucidation was really required for this peculiarity, which was the expression of a physiological substitutive function enforced by necessity; it was noticeable, however, that such an elucidation was easily to be found. Herr K. used to write to her at length while he was travelling and to send her picture post-cards. It used to happen that she alone was informed as to the date of his return, and that his arrival took his wife by surprise. Moreover, that a person will correspond with an absent friend whom he cannot talk to is scarcely less obvious than that if he has lost his voice he will try to make himself understood in writing. Dora's aphonia, then, allowed of the following symbolic interpretation. When the man she loved was away she gave up speaking; speech had lost its value since she could not speak to *him*. On the other hand, writing gained in importance, as being the only means of communication with him in his absence.

Am I now going on to assert that in every instance in which there are periodical attacks of aphonia we are to diagnose the existence of a loved

---

2. Jean-Martin Charcot (1825–1893), French neurologist famous for his research on hysteria and hypnosis. Freud worked at his clinic from 1885 to 1886.

person who is at times away from the patient? Nothing could be further from my intention. The determination of Dora's symptoms is far too specific for it to be possible to expect a frequent recurrence of the same accidental aetiology. But, if so, what is the value of our elucidation of the aphonia in the present case? Have we not merely allowed ourselves to become the victims of a *jeu d'esprit*?[3] I think not. In this connection we must recall the question which has so often been raised, whether the symptoms of hysteria are of psychical or of somatic origin, or whether, if the former is granted, they are necessarily *all* of them psychically determined. Like so many other questions to which we find investigators returning again and again without success, this question is not adequately framed. The alternatives stated in it do not cover the real essence of the matter. As far as I can see, every hysterical symptom involves the participation of *both* sides. It cannot occur without the presence of a certain degree of *somatic compliance* offered by some normal or pathological process in or connected with one of the bodily organs. And it cannot occur more than once—and the capacity for repeating itself is one of the characteristics of a hysterical symptom—unless it has a psychical significance, a *meaning*. The hysterical symptom does not carry this meaning with it, but the meaning is lent to it, soldered to it, as it were; and in every instance the meaning can be a different one, according to the nature of the suppressed thoughts which are struggling for expression. However, there are a number of factors at work which tend to make less arbitrary the relations between the unconscious thoughts and the somatic processes that are at their disposal as a means of expression, and which tend to make those relations approximate to a few typical forms. For therapeutic purposes the most important determinants are those given by the fortuitous psychical material; the clearing-up of the symptoms is achieved by looking for their psychical significance. When everything that can be got rid of by psychoanalysis has been cleared away, we are in a position to form all kinds of conjectures, which probably meet the facts, as regards the somatic basis of the symptoms—a basis which is as a rule constitutional and organic. Thus in Dora's case we shall not content ourselves with a psycho-analytic interpretation of her attacks of coughing and aphonia; but we shall also indicate the organic factor which was the source of the "somatic compliance" that enabled her to express her love for a man who was periodically absent. And if the connection between the symptomatic expression and the unconscious mental content should strike us as being in this case a clever *tour de force*, we shall be relieved to hear that it succeeds in creating the same impression in every other case and in every other instance.

I am prepared to be told at this point that there is no very great advantage in having been taught by psycho-analysis that the clue to the problem of hysteria is to be found not in "a peculiar instability of the molecules of the nerves" or in a liability to "hypnoid states"—but in a "somatic compliance." But in reply to the objection I may remark that this new view has not only to some extent pushed the problem further back, but has also to some extent diminished it. We have no longer to deal with the *whole* problem, but only with the portion of it involving that particular characteristic of hysteria *which differentiates it* from other psychoneuroses. The mental events in all psycho-

3. Play of the mind (French, literal trans.); mental acrobatics.

neuroses proceed for a considerable distance along the same lines before any question arises of the "somatic compliance" which may afford the unconscious mental processes a physical outlet. When this factor is not forthcoming, something other than a hysterical symptom will arise out of the total situation; yet it will still be something of an allied nature, a phobia, perhaps, or an obsession—in short, a psychical symptom.

I now return to the reproach of malingering which Dora brought against her father. It soon became evident that this reproach corresponded to self-reproaches not only concerning her earlier states of ill-health but also concerning the present time. At such points the physician is usually faced by the task of guessing and filling in what the analysis offers him in the shape only of hints and allusions. I was obliged to point out to the patient that her present ill-health was just as much actuated by motives and was just as tendentious as had been Frau K.'s illness, which she had understood so well. There could be no doubt, I said, that she had an aim in view which she hoped to gain by her illness. That aim could be none other than to detach her father from Frau K. She had been unable to achieve this by prayers or arguments; perhaps she hoped to succeed by frightening her father (there was her farewell letter), or by awakening his pity (there were her fainting-fits), or if all this was in vain, at least she would be taking her revenge on him. She knew very well, I went on, how much he was attached to her, and that tears used to come into his eyes whenever he was asked after his daughter's health. I felt quite convinced that she would recover at once if only her father were to tell her that he had sacrificed Frau K. for the sake of her health. But, I added, I hoped he would not let himself be persuaded to do this, for then she would have learned what a powerful weapon she had in her hands, and she would certainly not fail on every future occasion to make use once more of her liability to ill-health. Yet if her father refused to give way to her, I was quite sure she would not let herself be deprived of her illness so easily.

I will pass over the details which showed how entirely correct all of this was, and I will instead add a few general remarks upon the part played in hysteria by the *motives of illness*. A *motive* for being ill is sharply to be distinguished as a concept from a *liability* to being ill—from the material out of which symptoms are formed. The motives have no share in the formation of symptoms, and indeed are not present at the beginning of the illness. They only appear secondarily to it; but it is not until they have appeared that the disease is fully constituted. Their presence can be reckoned upon in every case in which there is real suffering and which is of fairly long standing. A symptom comes into the patient's mental life at first as an unwelcome guest; it has everything against it; and that is why it may vanish so easily, apparently of its own accord, under the influence of time. To begin with there is no use to which it can be put in the domestic economy of the mind; but very often it succeeds in finding one secondarily. Some psychical current or other finds it convenient to make use of it, and in that way the symptom manages to obtain a *secondary function* and remains, as it were, anchored fast in the patient's mental life. And so it happens that any one who tries to make him well is to his astonishment brought up against a powerful resistance, which teaches him that the patient's intention of getting rid of his complaint is not so entirely and completely serious as it seemed. Let us imagine a workman, a bricklayer, let us say, who has fallen off a house and been crippled, and now earns his livelihood by begging at the street-corner. Let us then suppose that a miracle-worker comes along and promises him to make his crooked leg straight and capable of walking. It would be unwise, I think, to look forward to seeing an expression of peculiar bliss upon the man's features. No doubt at the time of the accident he felt he was extremely unlucky, when he realized that he would never be able to do any more work and would have to starve or live upon charity. But since then the very thing which in the first instance threw him out of employment has become his source of income: he lives by his disablement. If that is taken from him he may become totally helpless. He has in the meantime forgotten his trade and lost his habits of industry; he has grown accustomed to idleness, and perhaps to drink as well.

The motives for being ill often begin to be active even in childhood. A little girl in her greed for love does not enjoy having to share the affection of her parents with her brothers and sisters; and she notices that the whole of their affection is lavished on her once more whenever she arouses their anxiety by falling ill. She has now discovered a means of enticing out her parents' love, and will make use of that means as soon as she has the necessary psychical material at her disposal for producing an illness. When such a child has grown up to be a woman she may find all the demands she used to make in her childhood countered owing to her marriage with an inconsiderate husband, who may subjugate her will, mercilessly exploit her capacity for work, and lavish neither his affection nor his money upon her. In that case ill-health will be her one weapon for maintaining her position. It will procure her the care she longs for; it will force her husband to make pecuniary sacrifices for her and to show her consideration, as he would never have done while she was well; and it will compel him to treat her with solicitude if she recovers, for otherwise a relapse will threaten. Her state of ill-health will have every appearance of being objective and involuntary—the very doctor who treats her will bear witness to the fact; and for that reason she will not need to feel any conscious self-reproaches at making such successful use of a means which she had found effective in her years of childhood.

And yet illnesses of this kind *are* the result of intention. They are as a rule levelled at a particular person, and consequently vanish with that person's departure. The crudest and most commonplace views on the character of hysterical disorders—such as are to be heard from uneducated relatives or nurses—are in a certain sense right. It is true that the paralysed and bedridden woman would spring to her feet if a fire were to break out in her room, and that the spoiled wife would forget all her sufferings if her child were to fall dangerously ill or if some catastrophe were to threaten the family circumstances. People who speak of the patients in this way are right except upon a single point: they overlook the psychological distinction between what is conscious and what is unconscious. This may be permissible where children are concerned, but with adults it is no longer possible. That is why all these asseverations that it is "only a question of willing" and all the encouragements and abuse that are addressed to the patient are of no avail. An attempt must first be made by the roundabout methods of analysis to convince the patient herself of the existence in her of an intention to be ill.

It is in combating the motives of illness that the weak point in every kind of therapeutic treatment of hysteria lies. This is quite generally true, and it applies equally to psycho-analysis. Destiny has an easier time of it in this respect: it need not concern itself either with the patient's constitution or with his pathogenic material; it has only to take away a motive for being ill, and the patient is temporarily or perhaps even permanently freed from his illness. How many fewer miraculous cures and spontaneous disappearances of symptoms should we physicians have to register in cases of hysteria, if we were more often given a sight of the human interests which the patient keeps hidden from us! In one case, some stated period of time has elapsed; in a second, consideration for some other person has ceased to operate; in a third, the situation has been fundamentally changed by some external event—and the whole disorder, which up till then had shown the greatest obstinacy, vanishes at a single blow, apparently of its own accord, but really because it has been deprived of its most powerful motive, one of the uses to which it has been put in the patient's life.

Motives that support the patient in being ill are probably to be found in all fully developed cases. But there are some in which the motives are purely internal—such as desire for self-punishment, that is, penitence and remorse. It will be found much easier to solve the therapeutic problem in such cases than in those in which the illness is related to the attainment of some external aim. In Dora's case that aim was clearly to touch her father's heart and to detach him from Frau K.

None of her father's actions seemed to have embittered her so much as his readiness to consider the scene by the lake as a product of her imagination. She was almost beside herself at the idea of its being supposed that she had merely fancied something on that occasion. For a long time I was in perplexity as to what the self-reproach could be which lay behind her passionate repudiation of this explanation of the episode. It was justifiable to suspect that there was something concealed, for a reproach which misses the mark gives no lasting offence. On the other hand, I came to the conclusion that Dora's story must correspond to the facts in every respect. No sooner had she grasped Herr K.'s intention than, without letting him finish what he had to say, she had given him a slap in the face and hurried away. Her behaviour must have seemed as incomprehensible to the man after she had left him as to us, for he must long before have gathered from innumerable small signs that he was secure of the girl's affections. In our discussion of Dora's second dream we shall come upon the solution of this riddle as well as upon the self-reproach which we have hitherto failed to discover.

As she kept on repeating her complaints against her father with a wearisome monotony, and as at the same time her cough continued, I was led to think that this symptom might have some meaning in connection with her father. And apart from this, the explanation of the symptom which I had hitherto obtained was far from fulfilling the requirements which I am accustomed to make of such explanations. According to a rule which I had found confirmed over and over again by experience, though I had not yet ventured to erect it into a general principle, a symptom signifies the representation— the realization—of a phantasy with a sexual content, that is to say, it signifies a sexual situation. It would be better to say that at least *one* of the meanings of a symptom is the representation of a sexual phantasy, but that no such limitation is imposed upon the content of its other meanings. Any one who takes up psycho-analytic work will quickly discover that a symptom has more than one meaning and served to represent several unconscious mental processes simultaneously. And I should like to add that in my estimation a single unconscious mental process or phantasy will scarcely ever suffice for the production of a symptom.

An opportunity very soon occurred for interpreting Dora's nervous cough in this way by means of an imagined sexual situation. She had once again been insisting that Frau K. only loved her father because he was "ein vermögender Mann."[4] Certain details of the way in which she expressed herself (which I pass over here, like most other purely technical parts of the analysis) led me to see that behind this phrase its opposite lay concealed, namely, that her father was "ein unvermögender Mann."[5] This could only be meant in a sexual sense—that her father, as a man, was without means, was impotent. Dora confirmed this interpretation from her conscious language; whereupon I pointed out the contradiction she was involved in if on the one hand she continued to insist that her father's relation with Frau K. was a common love-affair, and on the other hand maintained that her father was impotent, or in other words incapable of carrying on an affair of such a kind. Her answer showed that she had no need to admit the contradiction. She knew very well, she said, that there was more than one way of obtaining sexual gratification. (The source of this piece of knowledge, however, was once more untraceable.) I questioned her further, whether she referred to the use of organs other than the genitals for the purpose of sexual intercourse, and she replied in the affirmative. I could then go on to say that in that case she must be thinking of precisely those parts of the body which in her case were in a state of irritation,—the throat and the oral cavity. To be sure, she would not hear of going so far as this in recognizing her own thoughts; and indeed, if the occurrence of the symptom was to be made possible at all, it was essential that she should not be completely clear on the subject. But the conclusion was inevitable that with her spasmodic cough, which, as is usual, was referred for its exciting stimulus to a tickling in her throat, she pictured to herself a scene of sexual gratification per os[6] between the two people whose love-affair occupied her mind so incessantly. A very short time after she had tacitly accepted this explanation her cough vanished—which fitted in very well with my view; but I do not wish to lay too much stress upon this development, since her cough had so often before disappeared spontaneously.

This short piece of the analysis may perhaps have excited in the medical reader—apart from the scepticism to which he is entitled—feelings of astonishment and horror; and I am prepared at this point to look into these two reactions so as to discover whether they are justifiable. The astonishment is probably caused by my daring to talk about such delicate and unpleasant subjects to a young girl—or, for that matter, to any woman who is sexually active. The horror is aroused, no doubt, by the possibility that an inexperi-

***

4. A man of means (German).   5. A man without means. *Unvermögend* means literally "unable" and is commonly used in the sense of both "not rich" and "impotent."   6. Orally (Latin).

enced girl could know about practices of such a kind and could occupy her imagination with them. I would advise recourse to moderation and reasonableness upon both points. There is no cause for indignation either in the one case or in the other. It is possible for a man to talk to girls and women upon sexual matters of every kind without doing them harm and without bringing suspicion upon himself, so long as, in the first place, he adopts a particular way of doing it, and, in the second place, can make them feel convinced that it is unavoidable. A gynaecologist, after all, under the same conditions, does not hesitate to make them submit to uncovering every possible part of their body. The best way of speaking about such things is to be dry and direct; and that is at the same time the method furthest removed from the prurience with which the same subjects are handled in "society," and to which girls and women alike are so thoroughly accustomed. I call bodily organs and processes by their technical names, and I tell these to the patient if they—the names, I mean—happen to be unknown to her. *J'appelle un chat un chat.*[7] I have certainly heard of some people—doctors and laymen—who are scandalized by a therapeutic method in which conversations of this sort occur, and who appear to envy either me or my patients the titillation which, according to their notions, such a method must afford. But I am too well acquainted with the respectability of these gentry to excite myself over them. I shall avoid the temptation of writing a satire upon them. But there is one thing that I will mention: often, after I have for some time treated a patient who had not at first found it easy to be open about sexual matters, I have had the satisfaction of hearing her exclaim: "Why, after all, your treatment is far more respectable than Mr. X.'s conversation!"

No one can undertake the treatment of a case of hysteria until he is convinced of the impossibility of avoiding the mention of sexual subjects, or unless he is prepared to allow himself to be convinced by experience. The right attitude is: *"pour faire une omelette il faut casser des œufs."*[8] The patients themselves are easy to convince; and there are only too many opportunities of doing so in the course of the treatment. There is no necessity for feeling any compunction at discussing the facts of normal or abnormal sexual life with them. With the exercise of a little caution all that is done is to translate into conscious ideas what was already known in the unconscious; and, after all, the whole effectiveness of the treatment is based upon our knowledge that the affect attached to an unconscious idea operates more strongly and, since it cannot be inhibited, more injuriously than the affect attached to a conscious one. There is never any danger of corrupting an inexperienced girl. For where there is no knowledge of sexual processes even in the unconscious, no hysterical symptom will arise; and where hysteria is found there can no longer be any question of "innocence of mind" in the sense in which parents and educators use the phrase. With children of ten, of twelve, or of fourteen, with boys and girls alike, I have satisfied myself that the truth of this statement can invariably be relied upon.

As regards the second kind of emotional reaction, which is not directed against me this time, but against my patient—supposing that my view of her is correct—and which regards the perverse nature of her phantasies as hor-

---

7. I call a cat a cat (French, literal trans.), i.e., call a spade a spade.   8. You can't make an omelet without breaking eggs (French).

rible, I should like to say emphatically that a medical man has no business to indulge in such passionate condemnation. I may also remark in passing that it seems to me superfluous for a physician who is writing upon the aberrations of the sexual instincts to seize every opportunity of inserting into the text expressions of his personal repugnance at such revolting things. We are faced by a fact; and it is to be hoped that we shall grow accustomed to it, when we have put our own tastes on one side. We must learn to speak without indignation of what we call the sexual perversions—instances in which the sexual function has extended its limits in respect either to the part of the body concerned or to the sexual object chosen. The uncertainty in regard to the boundaries of what is to be called normal sexual life, when we take different races and different epochs into account, should in itself be enough to cool the zealot's ardour. We surely ought not to forget that the perversion which is the most repellent to us, the sensual love of a man for a man, was not only tolerated by a people so far our superiors in cultivation as were the Greeks, but was actually entrusted by them with important social functions. The sexual life of each one of us extends to a slight degree—now in this direction, now in that—beyond the narrow lines imposed as the standard of normality. The perversions are neither bestial nor degenerate in the emotional sense of the word. They are a development of germs all of which are contained in the undifferentiated sexual disposition of the child, and which, by being suppressed or by being diverted to higher, asexual aims—by being "sublimated"—are destined to provide the energy for a great number of our cultural achievements.

* * *

[A discussion follows of the difference between psychoneuroses and perversions, of Dora's thumb sucking, and of the possibility for symptoms to change in meaning.]

Dora's incessant repetition of the same thoughts about her father's relations with Frau K. made it possible to derive still further important material from the analysis.

A train of thought such as this may be described as excessively intense, or better *reinforced*, or "supervalent" in Wernicke's[9] sense. It shows its pathological character in spite of its apparently reasonable content, by the single peculiarity that no amount of conscious and voluntary effort of thought on the patient's part is able to dissipate or remove it. A normal train of thought, however intense it may be, can eventually be disposed of. Dora felt quite rightly that her thoughts about her father required to be judged in a special way. "I can think of nothing else," she complained again and again. "I know my brother says we children have no right to criticize this behaviour of Father's. He declares that we ought not to trouble ourselves about it, and ought even to be glad, perhaps, that he has found a woman he can love, since Mother understands him so little. I can quite see that, and I should like to think the same as my brother, but I can't. I can't forgive him for it."[1]

Now what is one to do in the face of a supervalent thought like this, after one has heard what its conscious grounds are and listened to the ineffectual

9. Carl Wernicke (1848–1905), German neurologist.   1. A supervalent thought of this kind is often the only symptom, beyond deep depression, of a pathological condition which is usually described as "melancholia," but which can be cleared up by psycho-analysis like a hysteria [Freud's note].

protests made against it? Reflection will suggest that *this excessively intense train of thought must owe its reinforcement to the unconscious.* It cannot be resolved by any effort of thought, either because it itself reaches with its root down into unconscious, repressed material, or because another unconscious thought lies concealed behind it. In the latter case, the concealed thought is usually the direct contrary of the supervalent one. Contrary thoughts are always closely connected with each other and are often paired off in such a way that *the one thought is excessively conscious while its counterpart is repressed and unconscious.* This relation between the two thoughts is an effect of the process of repression. For repression is often achieved by means of an excessive reinforcement of the thought contrary to the one which is to be repressed. This process I call *reactive* reinforcement, and the thought which asserts itself with excessive intensity in consciousness and (in the same way as a prejudice) cannot be removed I call a *reactive thought.* The two thoughts then act towards each other much like the two needles of an astatic galvanometer. The reactive thought keeps the objectionable one under repression by means of a certain surplus of intensity; but for that reason it itself is "damped" and proof against conscious efforts of thought. So that the way to deprive the excessively intense thought of its reinforcement is by bringing its repressed contrary into consciousness.

We must also be prepared to meet with instances in which the supervalence of a thought is due not to the presence of one only of these two causes but to a concurrence of both of them. Other complications, too, may arise, but they can easily be fitted into the general scheme.

Let us now apply our theory to the instance provided by Dora's case. We will begin with the first hypothesis, namely, that her preoccupation with her father's relations to Frau K. owed its obsessive character to the fact that its root was unknown to her and lay in the unconscious. It is not difficult to divine the nature of that root from her circumstances and her conduct. Her behaviour obviously went far beyond what would have been appropriate to filial concern. She felt and acted more like a jealous wife—in a way which would have been comprehensible in her mother. By her ultimatum to her father ("either her or me"), by the scenes she used to make, by the suicidal intentions she allowed to transpire—by all this she was clearly putting herself in her mother's place. If we have rightly guessed the nature of the imaginary sexual situation which underlay her cough, in that phantasy she must have been putting herself in Frau K.'s place. She was therefore identifying herself both with the woman her father had once loved and with the woman he loved now. The inference is obvious that her affection for her father was a much stronger one than she knew or than she would have cared to admit: in fact, that she was in love with him.

I have learnt to look upon unconscious love relations like this (which are marked by their abnormal consequences)—between a father and a daughter, or between a mother and a son—as a revival of germs of feeling in infancy. I have shown at length elsewhere at what an early age sexual attraction makes itself felt between parents and children, and I have explained that the legend of Oedipus is probably to be regarded as a poetical rendering of what is typical in these relations. Distinct traces are probably to be found in most people of an early partiality of this kind—on the part of a daughter for her father, or on the part of a son for his mother; but it must be assumed to be more intense from the very first in the case of those children whose constitution marks them down for a neurosis, who develop prematurely and have a craving for love. At this point certain other influences, which need not be discussed here, come into play, and lead to a fixation of this rudimentary feeling of love or to a reinforcement of it; so that it turns into something (either while the child is still young or not until it has reached the age of puberty) which must be put on a par with a sexual inclination and which, like the latter, has the forces of the libido at its command. The external circumstances of our patient were by no means unfavourable to such an assumption. The nature of her disposition had always drawn her towards her father, and his numerous illnesses were bound to have increased her affection for him. In some of these illnesses he would allow no one but her to discharge the lighter duties of nursing. He had been so proud of the early growth of her intelligence that he had made her his confidante while she was still a child. It was really she and not her mother whom Frau K.'s appearance had driven out of more than one position.

When I told Dora that I could not avoid supposing that her affection for her father must at a very early moment have amounted to her being completely in love with him, she of course gave me her usual reply: "I don't remember that." But she immediately went on to tell me something analogous about a seven-year-old girl who was her cousin (on her mother's side) and in whom she often thought she saw a kind of reflection of her own childhood. This little girl had (not for the first time) been the witness of a heated dispute between her parents, and, when Dora happened to come in on a visit soon afterwards, whispered in her ear: "You can't think how I hate that person!" (pointing to her mother), "and when she's dead I shall marry Daddy." I am in the habit of regarding associations such as this, which bring forward something that agrees with the content of an assertion of mine, as a confirmation from the unconscious of what I have said. No other kind of "Yes" can be extracted from the unconscious; there is no such thing at all as an unconscious "No."[2]

For years on end she had given no expression to this passion for her father. On the contrary, she had for a long time been on the closest terms with the woman who had supplanted her with her father, and she had actually, as we know from her self-reproaches, facilitated this woman's relations with her father. Her own love for her father had therefore been recently revived; and, if so, the question arises to what end this had happened. Clearly as a reactive symptom, so as to suppress something else—something, that is, that still exercised power in the unconscious. Considering how things stood, I could not help supposing in the first instance that what was suppressed was her love of Herr K. I could not avoid the assumption that she was still in love with him, but that, for unknown reasons, since the scene by the lake her love had aroused in her violent feelings of opposition, and that the girl had brought forward and reinforced her old affection for her father in order to avoid any further necessity for paying conscious attention to the love which

2. There is another very remarkable and entirely trustworthy form of confirmation from the unconscious, which I had not recognized at the time this was written: namely, an exclamation on the part of the patient of "I didn't think that," or "I didn't think of that." This can be translated point-blank into: "Yes, I was unconscious of that" [Freud's note, added 1923].

she had felt in the first years of her girlhood and which had now become distressing to her. In this way I gained an insight into a conflict which was well calculated to unhinge the girl's mind. On the one hand she was filled with regret at having rejected the man's proposal, and with longing for his company and all the little signs of his affection; while on the other hand these feelings of tenderness and longing were combated by powerful forces, amongst which her pride was one of the most obvious. Thus she had succeeded in persuading herself that she had done with Herr K.—that was the advantage she derived from this typical process of repression; and yet she was obliged to summon up her infantile affection for her father and to exaggerate it, in order to protect herself against the feelings of love which were constantly pressing forward into consciousness. The further fact that she was almost incessantly a prey to the most embittered jealousy seemed to admit of still another determination.[3]

My expectations were by no means disappointed when this explanation of mine was met by Dora with a most emphatic negative. The "No" uttered by a patient after a repressed thought has been presented to his conscious perception for the first time does no more than register the existence of a repression and its severity; it acts, as it were, as a gauge of the repression's strength. If this "No," instead of being regarded as the expression of an impartial judgement (of which, indeed, the patient is incapable), is ignored, and if work is continued, the first evidence soon begins to appear that in such a case "No" signifies the desired "Yes." Dora admitted that she found it impossible to be as angry with Herr K. as he had deserved. She told me that one day she had met Herr K. in the street while she was walking with a cousin of hers who did not know him. The other girl had exclaimed all at once: "Why, Dora, what's wrong with you? You've gone as white as a sheet!" She herself had felt nothing of this change of colour; but I explained to her that the expression of emotion and the play of features obey the unconscious rather than the conscious, and are a means of betraying the former.[4] Another time Dora came to me in the worst of tempers after having been uniformly cheerful for several days. She could give no explanation of this. She felt so contrary today, she said; it was her uncle's birthday, and she could not bring herself to congratulate him, she did not know why. My powers of interpretation were at a low ebb that day; I let her go on talking, and she suddenly recollected that it was Herr K.'s birthday too—a fact which I did not fail to use against her. And it was then no longer hard to explain why the handsome presents she had had on her own birthday a few days before had given her no pleasure. One gift was missing, and that was Herr K.'s, the gift which had plainly once been the most prized of all.

Nevertheless Dora persisted in denying my contention for some time longer, until, towards the end of the analysis, the conclusive proof of its correctness came to light.

I must now turn to consider a further complication to which I should certainly give no space if I were a man of letters engaged upon the creation

---

3. We shall come upon this [in a moment] [Freud's note].   4. Compare the lines: "Ruhing mag ich Euch erscheinen, / Ruhig gehen sehn" [Freud's note]: "Quietly can I watch your coming, / Quietly watch you go" (German). Freud refers to a scene at the beginning of "Ritter Toggenburg," a ballad of love between brother and sister by Friedrich von Schiller (1759–1805) in which the sister hides her emotion from her tearful brother as he departs for the Crusades.

of a mental state like this for a short story, instead of being a medical man engaged upon its dissection. The element to which I must now allude can only serve to obscure and efface the outlines of the fine poetic conflict which we have been able to ascribe to Dora. This element would rightly fall a sacrifice to the censorship of a writer, for he, after all, simplifies and abstracts when he appears in the character of a psychologist. But in the world of reality, which I am trying to depict here, a complication of motives, an accumulation and conjunction of mental activities—in a word, over-determination—is the rule. For behind Dora's supervalent train of thought which was concerned with her father's relations with Frau K. there lay concealed a feeling of jealousy which had that lady as its *object*—a feeling, that is, which could only be based upon an affection on Dora's part for one of her own sex. It has long been known and often been pointed out that at the age of puberty boys and girls show clear signs, even in normal cases, of the existence of an affection for people of their own sex. A romantic and senti-mental friendship with one of her school-friends, accompanied by vows, kisses, promises of eternal correspondence, and all the sensibility of jealousy, is the common precursor of a girl's first serious passion for a man. Thence-forward, in favourable circumstances, the homosexual current of feeling often runs completely dry.

* * *

[Examples follow of Dora's estrangement from her governess and Frau K.]

I then found that the young woman[5] and the scarcely grown girl had lived for years on a footing of the closest intimacy. When Dora stayed with the K.'s she used to share a bedroom with Frau K., and the husband used to be quartered elsewhere. She had been the wife's confidante and adviser in all the difficulties of her married life. There was nothing they had not talked about. Medea[6] had been quite content that Creusa should make friends with her two children; and she certainly did nothing to interfere with the relations between the girl and the children's father. How Dora managed to fall in love with the man about whom her beloved friend had so many bad things to say is an interesting psychological problem. We shall not be far from solving it when we realize that thoughts in the unconscious live very comfortably side by side, and even contraries get on together without disputes—a state of things which persists often enough even in the conscious.

When Dora talked about Frau K., she used to praise her "adorable white body" in accents more appropriate to a lover than to a defeated rival. Another time she told me, more in sorrow than in anger, that she was convinced the presents her father had brought her had been chosen by Frau K., for she recognized her taste. Another time, again, she pointed out that, evidently through the agency of Frau K., she had been given a present of some jew-ellery which was exactly like some that she had seen in Frau K.'s possession and had wished for aloud at the time. Indeed, I can say in general that I never heard her speak a harsh or angry word against the lady, although from the point of view of her supervalent thought she should have regarded her

---

5. Frau K.   6. In Euripides' play *Medea* (431 B.C.), the sorceress Medea takes revenge on her unfaithful husband, Jason, by killing their two children and the king's daughter Creusa, whom Jason had planned to marry after discarding his wife.

as the prime author of her misfortunes. She seemed to behave inconsequently; but her apparent inconsequence was precisely the manifestation of a complicating current of feeling. For how had this woman to whom Dora was so enthusiastically devoted behaved to her? After Dora had brought forward her accusation against Herr K., and her father had written to him and had asked for an explanation, Herr K. had replied in the first instance by protesting sentiments of the highest esteem for her and by proposing that he should come to the manufacturing town to clear up every misunderstanding. A few weeks later, when her father spoke to him at B——, there was no longer any question of esteem. On the contrary, Herr K. spoke of her with disparagement, and produced as his trump card the reflection that no girl who read such books and was interested in such things could have any title to a man's respect. Frau K., therefore, had betrayed her and had calumniated her; for it had only been with her that she had read Mantegazza and discussed forbidden topics. It was a repetition of what had happened with the governess: Frau K. had not loved her for her own sake but on account of her father. Frau K. had sacrificed her without a moment's hesitation so that her relations with her father might not be disturbed. This mortification touched her, perhaps, more nearly and had a greater pathogenic effect than the other one, which she tried to use as a screen for it,—the fact that she had been sacrificed by her father. Did not the obstinacy with which she retained the particular amnesia concerning the sources of her forbidden knowledge point directly to the great emotional importance for her of the accusation against her upon that score, and consequently to her betrayal by her friend?

I believe, therefore, that I am not mistaken in supposing that Dora's supervalent train of thought, which was concerned with her father's relations with Frau K., was designed not only for the purpose of suppressing her love for Herr K., which had once been conscious, but also to conceal her love for Frau K., which was in a deeper sense unconscious. The supervalent train of thought was directly contrary to the latter current of feeling. She told herself incessantly that her father had sacrificed her to this woman, and made noisy demonstrations to show that she grudged her the possession of her father; and in this way she concealed from herself the contrary fact, which was that she grudged her father Frau K.'s love, and had not forgiven the woman she loved for the disillusionment she had been caused by her betrayal. The jealous emotions of a woman were linked in the unconscious with a jealousy such as might have been felt by a man. These masculine or, more properly speaking, *gynaecophilic*[7] currents of feeling are to be regarded as typical of the unconscious erotic life of hysterical girls.

II

The First Dream

Just at a moment when there was a prospect that the material that was coming up for analysis would throw light upon an obscure point in Dora's childhood, she reported that a few nights earlier she had once again had a dream which she had already dreamt in exactly the same way on many pre-

7. Woman-loving.

vious occasions. A periodically recurrent dream was by its very nature particularly well calculated to arouse my curiosity; and in any case it was
justifiable in the interests of the treatment to consider the way in which the
dream worked into the analysis as a whole. I therefore determined to make
an especially careful investigation of it.

Here is the dream as related by Dora: *"A house was on fire.*[8] *My father was
standing beside my bed and woke me up. I dressed quickly. Mother wanted to
stop and save her jewel-case; but Father said: 'I refuse to let myself and my two
children be burnt for the sake of your jewel-case.' We hurried downstairs, and
as soon as I was outside I woke up."*

As the dream was a recurrent one, I naturally asked her when she had first
dreamt it. She told me she did not know. But she remembered having had
the dream three nights in succession at L—— (the place on the lake where
the scene with Herr K. had taken place), and it had now come back again
a few nights earlier, here in Vienna.[9] My expectations from the clearing-up
of the dream were naturally heightened when I heard of its connection with
the events at L——. But I wanted to discover first what had been the exciting
cause of its recent recurrence, and I therefore asked Dora to take the dream
bit by bit and tell me what occurred to her in connection with it. She had
already had some training in dream interpretation from having previously
analysed a few minor specimens.

"Something occurs to me," she said, "but it cannot belong to the dream,
for it is quite recent, whereas I have certainly had the dream before."

"That makes no difference," I replied. "Start away! It will simply turn out
to be the most recent thing that fits in with the dream."

"Very well, then. Father has been having a dispute with Mother in the last
few days, because she locks the dining-room door at night. My brother's
room, you see, has no separate entrance, but can only be reached through
the dining-room. Father does not want my brother to be locked in like that
at night. He says it will not do: something might happen in the night so that
it might be necessary to leave the room."

"And that made you think of the risk of fire?"

"Yes."

"Now, I should like you to pay close attention to the exact words you used.
We may have to come back to them. You said that *'something might happen
in the night so that it might be necessary to leave the room.'*"[1]

But Dora had now discovered the connecting link between the recent
exciting cause of the dream and the original one, for she continued:

"When we arrived at L—— that time, Father and I, he openly said he was
afraid of fire. We arrived in a violent thunderstorm, and saw the small
wooden house without any lightning-conductor. So his anxiety was quite
natural."

What I now had to do was to establish the relation between the events at

8. In answer to an inquiry Dora told me that there had never really been a fire at their house [Freud's
note]. 9. The content of the dream makes it possible to establish that it in fact occurred *for the first
time* at L—— [Freud's note]. 1. I laid stress on these words because they took me aback. They seemed
to have an ambiguous ring about them. Are not certain physical needs referred to in the same words? Now,
in a line of associations ambiguous words (or, as we may call them, "switch-words") act like points at a
junction. If the points are switched across from the position in which they appear to lie in the dream, then
we find ourselves on another set of rails; and along this second track run the thoughts which we are in
search of but which still lie concealed behind the dream [Freud's note].

L—— and the recurrent dreams which she had had there. I therefore said: "Did you have the dream during your first nights at L—— or during your last ones? in other words, before or after the scene in the wood by the lake of which we have heard so much?" (I must explain that I knew that the scene had not occurred on the very first day, and that she had remained at L—— for a few days after it without giving any hint of the incident.)

Her first reply was that she did not know, but after a while she added: "Yes. I think it was after the scene."

So now I knew that the dream was a reaction to that experience. But why had it recurred there three times? I continued my questions: "How long did you stop on at L—— after the scene?"

"Four more nights. On the following day I went away with Father."

"Now I am certain that the dream was an immediate effect of your experience with Herr K. It was at L—— that you dreamed it for the first time, and not before. You have only introduced this uncertainty in your memory so as to obliterate the connection in your mind. But the figures do not quite fit in to my satisfaction yet. If you stayed at L—— for four nights longer, the dream might have occurred four times over. Perhaps this was so?"

She no longer disputed by contention; but instead of answering my question she proceeded:[2] "In the afternoon after our trip on the lake, from which we (Herr K. and I) returned at midday, I had gone to lie down as usual on the sofa in the bedroom to have a short sleep. I suddenly awoke and saw Herr K. standing beside me. . . ."

"In fact, just as you saw your father standing beside your bed in the dream?"

"Yes. I asked him sharply what it was he wanted there. By way of reply he said he was not going to be prevented from coming into his own bedroom when he wanted; besides, there was something he wanted to fetch. This episode put me on my guard, and I asked Frau K. whether there was not a key to the bedroom door. The next morning I locked myself in while I was dressing. That afternoon, when I wanted to lock myself in so as to lie down again on the sofa, the key was gone. I was convinced that Herr K. had removed it."

"Then here we have the theme of locking or not locking a room which appeared in the first association to the dream and also happened to occur in the exciting cause of the recent recurrence of the dream.[3] I wonder whether the phrase 'I dressed quickly' may not also belong to this context?"

"It was then that I made up my mind not to stop on with the K.'s without Father. On the subsequent mornings I could not help feeling afraid that Herr K. would surprise me while I was dressing: so I always dressed very quickly. You see, Father lived at the hotel, and Frau K. used always to go out early so as to go on expeditions with him. But Herr K. did not annoy me again."

"I understand. On the afternoon of the day after the scene in the wood you formed your intention of escaping from his persecution, and during the second, third, and fourth nights you had time to repeat that intention in your

---

2. This was because a fresh piece of material had to emerge from her memory before the question I had put could be answered [Freud's note].   3. I suspected, though I did not as yet say so to Dora, that she had seized upon this element on account of a symbolic meaning which it possessed. "Zimmer" ["room"] in dreams stands very frequently for "Frauenzimmer" [a slightly derogatory word for "woman"; literally, "women's apartments"]. The question whether a woman is "open" or "shut" can naturally not be a matter of indifference. It is well known, too, what sort of "key" effects the opening in such a case [Freud's note].

sleep. (You already knew on the second afternoon—before the dream, therefore—that you would not have the key on the following morning to lock yourself in with while you were dressing; and you could then form the design of dressing as quickly as possible.) But your dream recurred each night, for the very reason that it corresponded to an intention. An intention remains in existence until it has been carried out. You said to yourself, as it were: 'I shall have no rest and I can get no quiet sleep until I am out of this house.' In your account of the dream you turned it the other way and said: 'As *soon as I was outside I woke up.*'"

At this point I shall interrupt my report of the analysis in order to compare this small piece of dream-interpretation with the general statements I have made upon the mechanism of the formation of dreams. I argued in my book, *The Interpretation of Dreams* (1900), that every dream is a wish which is represented as fulfilled, that the representation acts as a disguise if the wish is a repressed one, belonging to the unconscious, and that except in the case of children's dreams only an unconscious wish or one which reaches down into the unconscious has the force necessary for the formation of a dream. I fancy my theory would have been more certain of general acceptance if I had contented myself with maintaining that every dream had a meaning, which could be discovered by means of a certain process of interpretation; and that when the interpretation had been completed the dream could be replaced by thoughts which would fall into place at an easily recognizable point in the waking mental life of the dreamer. I might then have gone on to say that the meaning of a dream turned out to be of as many different sorts as the processes of waking thought; that in one case it would be a fulfilled wish, in another a realized fear, or again a reflection persisting on into sleep, or an intention (as in the instance of Dora's dream), or a piece of creative thought during sleep, and so on. Such a theory would no doubt have proved attractive from its very simplicity, and it might have been supported by a great many examples of dreams that had been satisfactorily interpreted, as for instance by the one which has been analysed in these pages.

But instead of this I formulated a generalization according to which the meaning of dreams is limited to a single form, to the representation of *wishes,* and by so doing I aroused a universal inclination to dissent. I must, however, observe that I did not consider it either my right or my duty to simplify a psychological process so as to make it more acceptable to my readers, when my researches had shown me that it presented a complication which could not be reduced to uniformity until the inquiry had been carried into another field. It is therefore of special importance to me to show that apparent exceptions—such as this dream of Dora's, which has shown itself in the first instance to be the continuation into sleep of an intention formed during the day—nevertheless lend fresh support to the rule which is in dispute.

Much of the dream, however, still remained to be interpreted, and I proceeded with my questions: "What is this about the jewel-case that your mother wanted to save?"

"Mother is very fond of jewellery and had had a lot given her by Father."

"And you?"

"I used to be very fond of jewellery too, once; but I have not worn any since my illness.—Once, four years ago" (a year before the dream), "Father and Mother had a great dispute about a piece of jewellery. Mother wanted to be given a particular thing—pearl drops to wear in her ears. But Father does not like that kind of thing, and he brought her a bracelet instead of the drops. She was furious, and told him that as he had spent so much money on a present she did not like he had better just give it to some one else."

"I dare say you thought to yourself you would accept it with pleasure."

"I don't know.[4] I don't in the least know how Mother comes into the dream; she was not with us at L—— at the time."[5]

"I will explain that to you presently. Does nothing else occur to you in connection with the jewel-case? So far you have only talked about jewellery and have said nothing about a case."

"Yes, Herr K. had made me a present of an expensive jewel-case a little time before."

"Then a return-present would have been very appropriate. Perhaps you do not know that 'jewel-case' is a favourite expression for the same thing that you alluded to not long ago by means of the reticule you were wearing—for the female genitals, I mean."

"I knew you would say that."[6]

"That is to say, you knew that it *was* so.—The meaning of the dream is now becoming even clearer. You said to yourself: 'This man is persecuting me; he wants to force his way into my room. My "jewel-case" is in danger, and if anything happens it will be Father's fault.' For that reason in the dream you chose a situation which expresses the opposite—a danger from which your father is *saving* you. In this part of the dream everything is turned into its opposite; you will soon discover why. As you say, the mystery turns upon your mother. You ask how she comes into the dream? She is, as you know, your former rival in your father's affections. In the incident of the bracelet, you would have been glad to accept what your mother had rejected. Now let us just put 'give' instead of 'accept' and 'withhold' instead of 'reject.' Then it means that you were ready to give your father what your mother withheld from him; and the thing in question was connected with jewellery. Now bring your mind back to the jewel-case which Herr K. gave you. You have there the starting-point for a parallel line of thoughts, in which Herr K. is to be put in the place of your father just as he was in the matter of standing beside your bed. He gave you a jewel-case; so you are to give him your jewel-case. That was why I spoke just now of a 'return-present.' In this line of thoughts your mother must be replaced by Frau K. (You will not deny that she, at any rate, was present at the time.) So you are ready to give Herr K. what his wife withholds from him. That is the thought which has had to be repressed with so much energy, and which has made it necessary for every one of its elements to be turned into its opposite. The dream confirms once more what I had already told you before you dreamt it—that you are summoning up your old love for your father in order to protect yourself against your love for Herr K. But what do all these efforts show? Not only that you are afraid of Herr K., but that you are still more afraid of yourself, and of

4. The regular formula with which she confessed to anything that had been repressed [Freud's note].   5. This remark gave evidence of a complete misunderstanding of the rules of dream-interpretation, though on other occasions Dora was perfectly familiar with them. This fact, coupled with the hesitancy and meagreness of her associations with the jewel-case, showed me that we were here dealing with material which had been very intensely repressed [Freud's note].   6. A very common way of putting aside a piece of knowledge that emerges from the repressed [Freud's note].

the temptation you feel to yield to him. In short, these efforts prove once more how deeply you loved him."[7]

Naturally Dora would not follow me in this part of the interpretation. I myself, however, had been able to arrive at a further step in the interpretation, which seemed to me indispensable both for the anamnesis of the case and for the theory of dreams. I promised to communicate this to Dora at the next session.

The fact was that I could not forget the hint which seemed to be conveyed by the ambiguous words already noticed—*that it might be necessary to leave the room; that an accident might happen in the night.* Added to this was the fact that the elucidation of the dream seemed to me incomplete so long as a particular requirement remained unsatisfied; for, though I do not wish to insist that this requirement is a universal one, I have a predilection for discovering a means of satisfying it. A regularly formed dream stands, as it were, upon two legs, one of which is in contact with the main and current exciting cause, and the other with some momentous event in the years of childhood. The dream sets up a connection between those two factors—the event during childhood and the event of the present day—and it endeavours to re-shape the present on the model of the remote past. For the wish which creates the dream always springs from the period of childhood; and it is continually trying to summon childhood back into reality and to correct the present day by the measure of childhood. I believed that I could already clearly detect those elements of Dora's dream which could be pieced together into an allusion to an event in childhood.

I opened the discussion of the subject with a little experiment, which was, as usual, successful. There happened to be a large match-stand on the table. I asked Dora to look round and see whether she noticed anything special on the table, something that was not there as a rule. She noticed nothing. I then asked her if she knew why children were forbidden to play with matches.

"Yes; on account of the risk of fire. My uncle's children are very fond of playing with matches."

"Not only on that account. They are warned not to 'play with fire,' and a particular belief is associated with the warning."

She knew nothing about it.—"Very well, then; the fear is that if they do they will wet their bed. The antithesis of 'water' and 'fire' must be at the bottom of this. Perhaps it is believed that they will dream of fire and then try and put it out with water. I cannot say exactly. But I notice that the antithesis of water and fire has been extremely useful to you in the dream. Your mother wanted to save the jewel-case so that it should not be *burnt;* while in the dream-thoughts it is a question of the 'jewel-case' not being *wetted.* But fire is not only used as the contrary of water, it also serves directly to represent love (as in the phrase 'to be *consumed* with love'). So that from 'fire' one set of rails runs by way of this symbolic meaning to thoughts of love; while the other set runs by way of the contrary 'water,' and, after sending

---

7. I added: "Moreover, the re-appearance of the dream in the last few days forces me to the conclusion that you consider that the same situation has arisen once again, and that you have decided to give up the treatment—to which, after all, it is only your father who makes you come." The sequel showed how correct my guess had been. At this point my interpretation touches for a moment upon the subject of "transference"—a theme which is of the highest practical and theoretical importance, but into which I shall not have much further opportunity of entering in the present paper [Freud's note].

off a branch line which provides another connection with 'love' (for love also makes things wet), leads in a different direction. And what direction can that be? Think of the expressions you used: that *an accident might happen in the night,* and that *it might be necessary to leave the room.* Surely the allusion must be to a physical need? And if you transpose the accident into childhood what can it be but bed-wetting? But what is usually done to prevent children from wetting their bed? Are they not woken up in the night out of their sleep, *exactly as your father woke you up in the dream?* This, then, must be the actual occurrence which enabled you to substitute your father for Herr K., who really woke you up out of your sleep. I am accordingly driven to conclude that you were addicted to bed-wetting up to a later age than is usual with children. The same must also have been true of your brother; for your father said: '*I refuse to let my two children* go to their destruction. . . . ' Your brother has no other sort of connection with the real situation at the K.'s; he had not gone with you to L——. And now, what have your recollections to say to this?"

"I know nothing about myself," was her reply, "but my brother used to wet his bed up till his sixth or seventh year; and it used sometimes to happen to him in the daytime too."

I was on the point of remarking to her how much easier it is to remember things of that kind about one's brother than about oneself, when she continued the train of recollections which had been revived: "Yes. I used to do it too, for some time, but not until my seventh or eighth year. It must have been serious, because I remember now that the doctor was called in. It lasted till a short time before my nervous asthma."

"And what did the doctor say to it?"

"He explained it as nervous weakness: it would soon pass off, he thought; and he prescribed a tonic."[8]

The interpretation of the dream now seemed to me to be complete.[9] But Dora brought me an addendum to the dream on the very next day. She had forgotten to relate, she said, that each time after waking up she had smelt smoke. Smoke, of course, fitted in well with fire, but it also showed that the dream had a special relation to myself; for when she used to assert that there was nothing concealed behind this or that, I would often say by way of rejoinder: "There can be no smoke without fire!" Dora objected, however, to such a purely personal interpretation, saying that Herr K. and her father were passionate smokers—as I am too, for the matter of that. She herself had smoked during her stay by the lake, and Herr K. had rolled a cigarette for her before he began his unlucky proposal. She thought, too, that she clearly remembered having noticed the smell of smoke on the three occasions of the dream's occurrence at L——, and not for the first time at its recent reappearance. As she would give me no further information, it was left to me to determine how this addendum was to be introduced into the texture of the dream-thoughts. One thing which I had to go upon was the fact that

8. This physician was the only one in whom she showed any confidence, because this episode showed her that he had not penetrated her secret. She felt afraid of any other doctor about whom she had not yet been able to form a judgement, and we can now see that the motive of her fear was the possibility that he might guess her secret [Freud's note]. 9. The essence of the dream might perhaps be translated into words such as these: "The temptation is so strong. Dear Father, protect me again as you used to in my childhood, and prevent my bed from being wetted!" [Freud's note].

the smell of smoke had only come up as an addendum to the dream, and must therefore have had to overcome a particularly strong effort on the part of repression. Accordingly it was probably related to the thoughts which were the most obscurely presented and the most successfully repressed in the dream, to the thoughts, that is, concerned with the temptation to show herself willing to yield to the man. If that were so, the addendum to the dream could scarcely mean anything else than the longing for a kiss, which, with a smoker, would necessarily smell of smoke. But a kiss had passed between Herr K. and Dora some two years further back, and it would certainly have been repeated more than once if she had given way to him. So the thoughts of temptation seemed in this way to have harked back to the earlier scene, and to have revived the memory of the kiss against whose seductive influence the little "thumb-sucker" had defended herself at the time, by the feeling of disgust. Taking into consideration, finally, the indications which seemed to point to there having been a transference on to me—since I am a smoker too—I came to the conclusion that the idea had probably occurred to her one day during a session that she would like to have a kiss from me. This would have been the exciting cause which led her to repeat the warning dream and to form her intention of stopping the treatment. Everything fits together very satisfactorily upon this view; but owing to the characteristics of "transference" its validity is not susceptible of definite proof.

I might at this point hesitate whether I should first consider the light thrown by this dream on the history of the case, or whether I should rather begin by dealing with the objection to my theory of dreams which may be based on it. I shall take the former course.

The significance of enuresis in the early history of neurotics is worth going into thoroughly. For the sake of clearness I will confine myself to remarking that Dora's case of bed-wetting was not the usual one. The disorder was not simply that the habit had persisted beyond what is considered the normal period, but, according to her explicit account, it had begun by disappearing and had then returned at a relatively late age—after her sixth year. Bed-wetting of this kind has, to the best of my knowledge, no more likely cause than masturbation, a habit whose importance in the aetiology of bed-wetting in general is still insufficiently appreciated. In my experience, the children concerned have themselves at one time been very well aware of this connection, and all its psychological consequences follow from it as though they had never forgotten it. Now, at the time when Dora reported the dream, we were engaged upon a line of enquiry which led straight towards an admission that she had masturbated in childhood. A short while before, she had raised the question of why it was that precisely she had fallen ill, and, before I could answer, had put the blame on her father. The justification for this was forthcoming not out of her unconscious thoughts but from her conscious knowledge. It turned out, to my astonishment, that the girl knew what the nature of her father's illness had been. After his return from consulting me she had overheard a conversation in which the name of the disease had been mentioned. At a still earlier period—at the time of the detached retina—an oculist who was called in must have hinted at a luetic aetiology;[1] for the

1. Syphilitic origin.

inquisitive and anxious girl overheard an old aunt of hers saying to her mother: "He was ill before his marriage, you know," and adding something which she could not understand, but which she subsequently connected in her mind with improper subjects.

Her father, then, had fallen ill through leading a loose life, and she assumed that he had handed on his bad health to her by heredity. I was careful not to tell her that, as I have already mentioned, I too was of the opinion that the offspring of luetics were very specially predisposed to severe neuropsychoses. The line of thought in which she brought this accusation against her father was continued in her unconscious material. For several days on end she identified herself with her mother by means of slight symptoms and peculiarities of manner, which gave her an opportunity for some really remarkable achievements in the direction of intolerable behaviour. She then allowed it to transpire that she was thinking of a stay she had made at Franzensbad,[2] which she had visited with her mother—I forget in what year. Her mother was suffering from abdominal pains and from a discharge (a catarrh) which necessitated a cure at Franzensbad. It was Dora's view—and here again she was probably right—that this illness was due to her father, who had thus handed on his venereal disease to her mother. It was quite natural that in drawing this conclusion she should, like the majority of laymen, have confused gonorrhoea and syphilis, as well as what is contagious and what is hereditary. The persistence with which she held to this identification with her mother almost forced me to ask her whether she too was suffering from a venereal disease; and I then learnt that she was afflicted with a catarrh (leucorrhoea)[3] whose beginning, she said, she could not remember.

I then understood that behind the train of thought in which she brought these open accusations against her father there lay concealed as usual a *self-accusation*. I met her half-way by assuring her that in my view the occurrence of leucorrhoea in young girls pointed primarily to masturbation, and I considered that all the other causes which were commonly assigned to that complaint were put in the background by masturbation.[4] I added that she was now on the way to finding an answer to her own question of why it was that precisely she had fallen ill—by confessing that she had masturbated, probably in childhood. Dora denied flatly that she could remember any such thing. But a few days later she did something which I could not help regarding as a further step towards the confession. For on that day she wore at her waist—a thing she never did on any other occasion before or after—a small reticule of a shape which had just come into fashion; and, as she lay on the sofa and talked, she kept playing with it—opening it, putting a finger into it, shutting it again, and so on. I looked on for some time and then explained to her the nature of a "symptomatic act." I give the name of symptomatic acts to those acts which people perform, as we say, automatically, unconsciously, without attending to them, or as if in a moment of distraction. They are actions to which people would like to deny any significance, and which, if questioned about them, they would explain as being indifferent and accidental. Closer observation, however, will show that these actions, about

2. A famous health resort, or "bath," of mineral springs in the northwest Czech Republic, now called Františkovy Lázany.   3. Genital discharge.   4. This is an extreme view which I should no longer maintain today [Freud's note, added 1923].

which consciousness knows nothing or wishes to know nothing, in fact give expression to unconscious thoughts and impulses, and are therefore most valuable and instructive as being manifestations of the unconscious which have been able to come to the surface. There are two sorts of conscious attitudes possible towards these symptomatic acts. If we can ascribe inconspicuous motives to them we recognize their existence; but if no such pretext can be found for conscious use we usually fail altogether to notice that we have performed them. Dora found no difficulty in producing a motive: "Why should I not wear a reticule like this, as it is now the fashion to do?" But a justification of this kind does not dismiss the possibility of the action in question having an unconscious origin. Though on the other hand the existence of such an origin and the meaning attributed to the act cannot be conclusively established. We must content ourselves with recording the fact that such a meaning fits in quite extraordinarily well with the situation as a whole and with the programme laid down by the unconscious.

On some other occasion I will publish a collection of these symptomatic acts as they are to be observed in the healthy and in neurotics. They are sometimes very easy to interpret. Dora's reticule, which came apart at the top in the usual way, was nothing but a representation of the genitals, and her playing with it, her opening it and putting her finger in it, was an entirely unembarrassed yet unmistakable pantomimic announcement of what she would like to do with them—namely, to masturbate. A very entertaining episode of a similar kind occurred to me a short time ago. In the middle of a session the patient—a lady who was no longer young—brought out a small ivory box, ostensibly in order to refresh herself with a sweet. She made some efforts to open it, and then handed it to me so that I might convince myself how hard it was to open. I expressed my suspicion that the box must mean something special, for this was the very first time I had seen it, although its owner had been coming to me for more than a year. To this the lady eagerly replied: "I always have this box about me; I take it with me wherever I go." She did not calm down until I had pointed out to her with a laugh how well her words were adapted to quite another meaning. The box—*Dose*, πυξις[5]—, like the reticule and the jewel-case, was once again only a substitute for the shell of Venus, for the female genitals.

There is a great deal of symbolism of this kind in life, but as a rule we pass it by without heeding it. When I set myself the task of bringing to light what human beings keep hidden within them, not by the compelling power of hypnosis, but by observing what they say and what they show, I thought the task was a harder one than it really is. He that has eyes to see and ears to hear may convince himself that no mortal can keep a secret. If his lips are silent, he chatters with his finger-tips; betrayal oozes out of him at every pore. And thus the task of making conscious the most hidden recesses of the mind is one which it is quite possible to accomplish.

* * *

[Freud continues and comments on the previous material, including its relationship to *dyspnoea* (breathing difficulties) as another symptom of distress.]

---

5. Box, in German and Greek, respectively.

I suspect that we are here concerned with unconscious processes of thought which are twined around a pre-existing structure of organic connections, much as festoons of flowers are twined around a wire; so that on another occasion one might find other lines of thought inserted between the same points of departure and termination. Yet a knowledge of the thought-connections which have been effective in the individual case is of a value which cannot be exaggerated for clearing up the symptoms. It is only because the analysis was prematurely broken off that we have been obliged in Dora's case to resort to framing conjectures and filling in deficiencies. Whatever I have brought forward for filling up the gaps is based upon other cases which have been more thoroughly analysed.

The dream from the analysis of which we have derived this information corresponded, as we have seen, to an intention which Dora carried with her into her sleep. It was therefore repeated each night until the intention had been carried out; and it reappeared years later when an occasion arose for forming an analogous intention. The intention might have been consciously expressed in some such words as these: "I must fly from this house, for I see that my virginity is threatened here; I shall go away with my father, and I shall take precautions not to be surprised while I am dressing in the morning." These thoughts were clearly expressed in the dream; they formed part of a mental current which had achieved consciousness and a dominating position in waking life. Behind them can be discerned obscure traces of a train of thought which formed part of a contrary current and had consequently been suppressed. This other train of thought culminated in the temptation to yield to the man, out of gratitude for the love and tenderness he had shown her during the last few years, and it may perhaps have revived the memory of the only kiss she had so far had from him. But according to the theory which I developed in my *Interpretation of Dreams* such elements as these are not enough for the formation of a dream. On that theory a dream is not an intention represented as having been carried out, but a wish represented as having been fulfilled, and, moreover, in most cases a wish dating from childhood. It is our business now to discover whether this principle may not be contradicted by the present dream.

The dream does in fact contain infantile material, though it is impossible at a first glance to discover any connections between that material and Dora's intention of flying from Herr K.'s house and the temptation of his presence. Why should a recollection have emerged of her bed-wetting when she was a child and of the trouble her father used to take to teach the child clean habits? We may answer this by saying that it was only by the help of the train of thought that it was possible to suppress the other thoughts which were so intensely occupied with the temptation to yield or that it was possible to secure the dominance of the intention which had been formed of combating those other thoughts. The child decided to fly *with* her father; in reality she fled *to* her father because she was afraid of the man who was pursuing her; she summoned up an infantile affection for her father so that it might protect her against her present affection for a stranger. Her father was himself partly responsible for her present danger, for he had handed her over to this strange man in the interests of his own love-affair. And how much better it had been when that same father of hers had loved no one more than her, and had exerted all his strength to save her from the dangers that had then threatened her! The infantile, and now unconscious, wish to put her father in the strange man's place had the potency necessary for the formation of a dream. If there were a past situation similar to a present one, and differing from it only in being concerned with one instead of with the other of the two persons mentioned in the wish, that situation would become the main one in the dream. But there *had* been such a situation. Her father had once stood beside her bed, just as Herr K. had the day before, and had woken her up, with a kiss perhaps, as Herr K. may have meant to do. Thus her intention of flying from the house was not in itself capable of producing a dream; but it became so by being associated with another intention which was founded upon infantile wishes. The wish to replace Herr K. by her father provided the necessary motive power for the dream. Let me recall the interpretation I was led to adopt of Dora's rein-forced train of thought about her father's relations with Frau K. My inter-pretation was that she had at that point summoned up an infantile affection for her father so as to be able to keep her repressed love for Herr K. in its state of repression. This same sudden revulsion in the patient's mental life was reflected in the dream.

* * *

[Freud connects passages from *The Interpretation of Dreams* with Dora's case.]

I add a few remarks which may help towards the synthesis of this dream. The dream-work began on the afternoon of the day after the scene in the wood, after Dora had noticed that she was no longer able to lock the door of her room. She then said to herself: "I am threatened by a serious danger here," and formed her intention of not stopping on in the house alone but of going off with her father. This intention became capable of forming a dream, because it succeeded in finding a continuation in the unconscious. What corresponded to it there was her summoning up her infantile love for her father as a protection against the present temptation. The change which thus took place in her became fixed and brought her into the atti-tude shown by her supervalent train of thought—jealousy of Frau K. on her father's account, as though she herself were in love with him. There was a conflict within her between a temptation to yield to the man's pro-posal and a composite force rebelling against that feeling. This latter force was made up of motives of respectability and good sense, of hostile feel-ings caused by the governess's disclosures (jealousy and wounded pride, as we shall see later), and of a neurotic element, namely, the tendency to a repudiation of sexuality which was already present in her and was based on her childhood history. Her love for her father, which she summoned up to protect her against the temptation, had its origin in this same childhood history.

Her intention of flying to her father, which, as we have seen, reached down into the unconscious, was transformed by the dream into a situation which presented as fulfilled the wish that her father would save her from the danger. In this process it was necessary to put on one side a certain thought which stood in the way; for it was her father himself who had brought her into the danger. The hostile feeling against her father (her desire for revenge), which was here suppressed, was, as we shall discover, one of the motive forces of the second dream.

According to the necessary conditions of dream-formation the imagined situation must be chosen so as to reproduce a situation in infancy. A special triumph is achieved if a recent situation, perhaps even the very situation which is the exciting cause of the dream, can be transformed into an infantile one. This has actually been achieved in the present case, by a purely chance disposition of the material. Just as Herr K. had stood beside her sofa and woken her up, so her father had often done in her childhood. The whole trend of her thoughts could be most aptly symbolized by her substitution of her father for Herr K. in that situation.

* * *

[Freud continues to analyze images of wetness, jewel-case, and locked doors in relation to Dora's dream and her family situation.]

III

The Second Dream

A few weeks after the first dream the second occurred, and when it had been dealt with the analysis was broken off. It cannot be made as completely intelligible as the first, but it afforded a desirable confirmation of an assumption which had become necessary about the patient's mental state, it filled up a gap in her memory, and it made it possible to obtain a deep insight into the origin of another of her symptoms.

Dora described the dream as follows: "*I was walking about in a town which I did not know. I saw streets and squares which were strange to me.*[6] *Then I came into a house where I lived, went to my room, and found a letter from Mother lying there. She wrote saying that as I had left home without my parents' knowledge she had not wished to write to me to say that Father was ill. 'Now he is dead, and if you like*[7] *you can come.' I then went to the station and asked about a hundred times: 'Where is the station?' I always got the same answer: 'Five minutes.' I then saw a thick wood before me which I went into, and there I asked a man whom I met. He said to me: 'Two and a half hours more.'*[8] *He offered to accompany me. But I refused and went alone. I saw the station in front of me and could not reach it. At the same time I had the usual feeling of anxiety that one has in dreams when one cannot move forward. Then I was at home. I must have been travelling in the meantime, but I know nothing about that. I walked into the porter's lodge, and enquired for our flat. The maidservant opened the door to me and replied that Mother and the others were already at the cemetery.*"[9]

It was not without some difficulty that the interpretation of this dream proceeded. In consequence of the peculiar circumstances in which the analysis was broken off—circumstances connected with the content of the

6. To this she subsequently made an important addendum: "*I saw a monument in one of the squares*" [Freud's note].   7. To this came the addendum: "*There was a question-mark after this word, thus: 'like?'*'" [Freud's note].   8. In repeating the dream she said: "*Two hours*" [Freud's note].   9. In the next session Dora brought me two addenda to this: "*I saw myself particularly distinctly going up the stairs,*" and "*After she had answered I went to my room, but not the least sadly, and began reading a big book that lay on my writing-table*" [Freud's note].

dream—the whole of it was not cleared up. And for this reason, too, I am not equally certain at every point of the order in which my conclusions were reached. I will begin by mentioning the subject-matter with which the current analysis was dealing at the time when the dream intervened. For some time Dora herself had been raising a number of questions about the connection between some of her actions and the motives which presumably underlay them. One of these questions was "Why did I say nothing about the scene by the lake for some days after it had happened?" Her second question was: "Why did I then suddenly tell my parents about it?" Moreover, her having felt so deeply injured by Herr K.'s proposal seemed to me in general to need explanation, especially as I was beginning to realize that Herr K. himself had not regarded his proposal to Dora as a mere frivolous attempt at seduction. I looked upon her having told her parents of the episode as an action which she had taken when she was already under the influence of a morbid craving for revenge. A normal girl, I am inclined to think, will deal with a situation of this kind by herself.

I shall present the material produced during the analysis of this dream in the somewhat haphazard order in which it recurs to my mind.

She was wandering about alone in a strange town, and saw streets and squares. Dora assured me that it was certainly not B——, which I had first hit upon, but a town in which she had never been. It was natural to suggest that she might have seen some pictures or photographs and have taken the dream-pictures from them. After this remark of mine came the addendum about the monument in one of the squares and immediately afterwards her recognition of its source. At Christmas she had been sent an album from a German health-resort, containing views of the town; and the very day before the dream she had looked this out to show it to some relatives who were stopping with them. It had been put in a box for keeping pictures in, and she could not lay her hands on it at once. She had therefore said to her mother: *"Where is the box?"*[1] One of the pictures was of a square with a monument in it. The present had been sent to her by a young engineer, with whom she had once had a passing acquaintance in the manufacturing town. The young man had accepted a post in Germany, so as to become sooner self-supporting; and he took every opportunity of reminding Dora of his existence. It was easy to guess that he intended to come forward as a suitor one day, when his position had improved. But that would take time, and it meant waiting.

The wandering about in a strange town was overdetermined. It led back to one of the exciting causes from the day before. A young cousin of Dora's had come to stay with them for the holidays, and Dora had had to show him round Vienna. This cause was, it is true, a matter of complete indifference to her. But her cousin's visit reminded her of her own first brief visit to Dresden. On that occasion she had been a stranger and had wandered about, not failing, of course, to visit the famous picture gallery. Another [male] cousin of hers, who was with them and knew Dresden, had wanted to act as a guide and take her round the gallery. *But she declined and went alone,* and stopped in front of the pictures that appealed to her. She remained *two hours*

---

1. In the dream she said: *"Where is the station?"* The resemblance between the two questions led me to make an inference which I shall go into presently [Freud's note].

in front of the Sistine Madonna, rapt in silent admiration. When I asked her what had pleased her so much about the picture she could find no clear answer to make. At last she said: "The Madonna."

There could be no doubt that these associations really belonged to the material concerned in forming the dream. They included portions which reappeared in the dream unchanged ("she declined and went alone" and "two hours"). I may remark at once that "pictures" was a nodal point in the network of her dream-thoughts (the pictures in the album, the pictures at Dresden). I should also like to single out, with a view to subsequent investigation, the theme of the "Madonna," of the virgin mother. But what was most evident was that in this first part of the dream she was identifying herself with a young man. This young man was wandering about in a strange place, he was striving to reach a goal, but he was being kept back, he needed patience and must wait. If in all this she had been thinking of the engineer, it would have been appropriate for the goal to have been the possession of a woman, of herself. But instead of this it was—a station. Nevertheless, the relation of the question in the dream to the question which had been put in real life allows us to substitute *"box"* for "station."[2] A box and a woman: the notions begin to agree better.

She asked quite a hundred times. . . . This led to another exciting cause of the dream, and this time to one that was less indifferent. On the previous evening they had had company, and afterwards her father had asked her to fetch him the brandy: he could not get to sleep unless he had taken some brandy. She had asked her mother for the key of the sideboard; but the latter had been deep in conversation, and had not answered her, until Dora had exclaimed with the exaggeration of impatience: "I've asked you *a hundred times* already where the key is." As a matter of fact, she had of course only repeated the question about *five times*.[3]

"Where is the *key?*" seems to me to be the masculine counterpart to the question "Where is the *box?*" They are therefore questions referring to—the genitals.

Dora went on to say that during this same family gathering some one had toasted her father and had expressed the hope that he might continue to enjoy the best of health for many years to come, etc. At this a strange quiver passed over her father's tired face, and she had understood what thoughts he was having to keep down. Poor sick man! who could tell what span of life was still to be his?

This brings us to the *contents of the letter* in the dream. Her father was dead, and she had left home by her own choice. In connection with this letter I at once reminded Dora of the farewell letter which she had written to her parents or had at least composed for their benefit. This letter had been intended to give her father a fright, so that he should give up Frau K.; or at any rate to take revenge on him if he could not be induced to do that. We are here concerned with the subject of her death and of her father's death. (Cf. "cemetery" later on in the dream.) Shall we be going astray if we suppose

---

2. *Schachtel*, the word which was used for "box" by Dora in her question, is a depreciatory term for "woman." 3. In the dream the number five occurs in the mention of the period of "five minutes." In my book on the interpretation of dreams I have given several examples of the way in which numbers occurring in the dream-thoughts are treated by dreams. We frequently find them torn out of their true context and inserted into a new one [Freud's note].

that the situation which formed the facade of the dream was a phantasy of revenge directed against her father? The feelings of pity for him which she remembered from the day before would be quite in keeping with this. According to the phantasy she had left home and gone among strangers, and her father's heart had broken with grief and with longing for her. Thus she would be revenged. She understood very clearly what it was that her father needed when he could not get to sleep without a drink of brandy.⁴ We will make a note of Dora's *craving for revenge* as a new element to be taken into account in any subsequent synthesis of her dream-thoughts.

But the contents of the letter must be capable of further determination. What was the source of the words "if you like"? It was at this point that the addendum of there having been a question-mark after the word "like" occurred to Dora, and she then recognized these words as a quotation out of the letter from Frau K. which had contained the invitation to L——, the place by the lake. In that letter there had been a question-mark placed, in a most unusual fashion, in the very middle of a sentence, after the intercalated words "if you would like to come."

So here we were back again at the scene by the lake and at the problems connected with it. I asked Dora to describe the scene to me in detail. At first she produced little that was new. Herr K.'s exordium had been somewhat serious; but she had not let him finish what he had to say. No sooner had she grasped the purport of his words than she had slapped him in the face and hurried away. I enquired what his actual words had been. Dora could only remember one of his pleas: "You know I get nothing out of my wife." In order to avoid meeting him again she had wanted to get back to L—— on foot, by walking round the lake, and *she had asked a man whom she met how far it was.* On his replying that it was *"Two and a half hours,"* she had given up her intention and had after all gone back to the boat, which left soon afterwards. Herr K. had been there too and had come up to her and begged her to forgive him and not to mention the incident. But she had made no reply.—Yes. The *wood* in the dream had been just like the wood by the shore of the lake, the wood in which the scene she had just described once more had taken place. But she had seen precisely the same thick wood the day before, in a picture at the Secessionist⁵ exhibition. In the background of the picture there were *nymphs.*⁶

At this point a certain suspicion of mine became a certainty. The use of *"Bahnhof"*⁷ and *"Friedhof"* to represent the female genitals was striking enough in itself, but it also served to direct my awakened curiosity to the similarity formed *"Vorhof"*⁸—an anatomical term for a particular region of the female genitals. This might have been no more than mistaken ingenuity. But now, with the addition of "nymphs" visible in the background of a "thick

---

4. There can be no doubt that sexual satisfaction is the best soporific, just as sleeplessness is almost always the consequence of lack of satisfaction. Her father could not sleep because he was debarred from sexual intercourse with the woman he loved. (Compare in this connection the phrase discussed just below: "I get nothing out of my wife") [Freud's note].   5. The Vienna Secessionists were a group of recognized *art nouveau* artists—led by painter Gustav Klimt (1862–1918)—who withdrew from established art societies to show their own work.   6. Here for the third time we come upon "picture" (views of towns, the Dresden gallery), but in a much more significant connection. Because of what appears in the picture (the wood, the nymphs), the *"Bild"* ["picture"] is turned into a *"Weibsbild"* [literally, "picture of a woman"—a somewhat derogatory expression for "woman"] [Freud's note].   7. "Station"; literally, "railway-court." *"Friedhof"*: "Cemetery"; literally, "peace-court." Moreover, a "station" is used for purposes of *"Verkehr"* ["traffic," "intercourse," "sexual intercourse"]: this fact determines the psychical coating in a number of cases of railway phobia [Freud's note].   8. Fore court (German, literal trans.); vestibulum.

wood," no further doubts could be entertained. Here was a symbolic geography of sex! "Nymphae," as is known to physicians though not to laymen (and even by the former term is not very commonly used), is the name given to the labia minora, which lie in the background of the "thick wood" of the pubic hair. But any one who employed such technical names as "vestibulum" and "nymphae" must have derived this knowledge from books, and not from popular ones either, but from anatomical text-books or from an encyclopaedia—the common refuge of youth when it is devoured by sexual curiosity. If this interpretation were correct, therefore, there lay concealed behind the first situation in the dream a phantasy of defloration, the phantasy of a man seeking to force an entrance into the female genitals.[9]

I informed Dora of the conclusions I had reached. The impression made upon her must have been forcible, for there immediately appeared a piece of the dream which had been forgotten: *"she went calmly to her room, and began reading a big book that lay on her writing-table."* The emphasis here was upon the two details "calmly" and "big" in connection with "book." I asked whether the book was in encyclopaedia *format,* and she said it was. Now children never read about forbidden subjects in an encyclopaedia *calmly.* They do it in fear and trembling, with an uneasy look over their shoulder to see if some one may not be coming. Parents are very much in the way while reading of this kind is going on. But this uncomfortable situation had been radically improved, thanks to the dream's power of fulfilling wishes. Dora's father was dead, and the others had already gone to the cemetery. She might calmly read whatever she chose. Did not this mean that one of her motives for revenge was a revolt against her parents' constraint? If her father was dead she could read or love as she pleased.

At first she would not remember ever having read anything in an encyclopaedia; but she then admitted that a recollection of an occasion of the kind did occur to her, though it was of an innocent enough nature. At the time when the aunt she was so fond of had been so seriously ill and it had already been settled that Dora was to go to Vienna, a *letter* had come from another uncle, to say that they could not go to Vienna, as a boy of his, a cousin of Dora's therefore, had fallen dangerously ill with appendicitis. Dora had thereupon looked up in the encyclopaedia to see what the symptoms of appendicitis were. From what she had then read she still recollected the characteristic localization of the abdominal pain.

I then remembered that shortly after her aunt's death Dora had had an attack of what had been alleged to be appendicitis. Up till then I had not ventured to count that illness among her hysterical productions. She told me that during the first few days she had had high fever and had felt the pain in her abdomen that she had read about in the encyclopaedia. She had been given cold fomentations but had not been able to bear them. On the second day her period had set in, accompanied by violent pains. (Since her health

9. The phantasy of defloration formed the second component of the situation. The emphasis upon the difficulty of getting forward and the anxiety felt in the dream indicated the stress which the dreamer was so ready to lay upon her virginity—a point alluded to in another place by means of the Sistine Madonna. These sexual thoughts gave an unconscious ground-colouring to the wishes (which were perhaps merely kept secret) concerned with the suitor who was waiting for her in Germany. We have already recognized the phantasy of revenge as the first component of the same situation in the dream. The two components do not coincide completely, but only in part. We shall subsequently come upon the traces of a third and still more important train of thought [Freud's note].

had been bad, the periods had been very irregular.) At that time she used to suffer continually from constipation.

It was not really possible to regard this state as a purely hysterical one. Although hysterical fever does undoubtedly occur, yet it seemed too arbitrary to put down the fever accompanying this questionable illness to hysteria instead of to some organic cause operative at the time. I was on the point of abandoning the track, when she herself helped me along it by producing her last addendum to the dream: *"she saw herself particularly distinctly going up the stairs."*

I naturally required a special determinant for this. Dora objected that she would anyhow have had to go upstairs if she had wanted to get to her flat, which was on an upper floor. It was easy to brush aside this objection (which was probably not very seriously intended) by pointing out that if she had been able to travel in her dream from the unknown town to Vienna without making a railway journey she ought also to have been able to leave out a flight of stairs. She then proceeded to relate that after the appendicitis she had not been able to walk properly and had dragged her right foot. This state of things had continued for a long time, and on that account she had been particularly glad to avoid stairs. Even now her foot sometimes dragged. The doctors whom she had consulted at her father's desire had been very much astonished at this most unusual after-effect of an appendicitis, especially as the abdominal pains had not recurred and did not in any way accompany the dragging of the foot.[1]

Here, then, we have a true hysterical symptom. The fever may have been organically determined—perhaps by one of those very frequent attacks of influenza that are not localized in any particular part of the body. Nevertheless it was now established that the neurosis had seized upon this chance event and made use of it for an utterance of its own. Dora had therefore given herself an illness which she had read up about in the encyclopaedia, and she had punished herself for dipping into its pages. But she was forced to recognize that the punishment could not possibly apply to her reading the innocent article in question. It must have been inflicted as the result of a process of displacement, after another occasion of more guilty reading had become associated with this one; and the guilty occasion must lie concealed in her memory behind the contemporaneous innocent one.[2] It might still be possible, perhaps, to discover the nature of the subjects she had read about on that other occasion.

What, then, was the meaning of this condition, of this attempted simulation of a perityphlitis?[3] The remainder of the disorder, the dragging of one leg, was entirely out of keeping with perityphlitis. It must, no doubt, fit in better with the secret and possibly sexual meaning of the clinical picture; and if it were elucidated might in its turn throw light on the meaning which we were in search of. I looked about for a method of approaching the puzzle.

---

1. We must assume the existence of some somatic connection between the painful abdominal sensations known as "ovarian neuralgia" and locomotor disturbances in the leg on the same side; and we must suppose that in Dora's case the somatic connection had been given an interpretation of a particularly specialized sort, that is to say, that it had been overlaid with and brought into the service of a particular psychological meaning. The reader is referred to my analogous remarks in connection with the analysis of Dora's symptom of coughing and with the relation between catarrh and loss of appetite [Freud's note].   2. This is quite a typical example of the way in which symptoms arise from exciting causes which appear to be entirely unconnected with sexuality [Freud's note].   3. Appendicitis.

Periods of time had been mentioned in the dream; and time is assuredly never a matter of indifference in any biological event. I therefore asked Dora when this attack of appendicitis had taken place; whether it had been before or after the scene by the lake. Every difficulty was resolved at a single blow by her prompt reply: "Nine months later." The period of time is sufficiently characteristic. Her supposed attack of appendicitis had thus enabled the patient with the modest means at her disposal (the pains and the menstrual flow) to realize a phantasy of *childbirth*.[4] Dora was naturally aware of the significance of this period of time, and could not dispute the probability of her having, on the occasion under discussion, read up in the encyclopaedia about pregnancy and childbirth. But what was all this about her dragging her leg? I could now hazard a guess. That is how people walk when they have twisted a foot. So she had made a "false step": which was true indeed if she could give birth to a child nine months after the scene by the lake. But there was still another requirement upon the fulfilment of which I had to insist. I am convinced that a symptom of this kind can only arise where it has an *infantile* prototype. All my experience hitherto has led me to hold firmly to the view that recollections derived from the impressions of later years do not possess sufficient force to enable them to establish themselves as symptoms. I scarcely dared hope that Dora would provide me with the material that I wanted from her childhood, for the fact is that I am not yet in a position to assert the general validity of this rule, much as I should like to be able to do so. But in this case there came an immediate confirmation of it. Yes, said Dora, once when she was a child she had twisted the same foot; she had slipped on one of the steps as she was going *downstairs*. The foot—and it was actually the same one that she afterwards dragged—had swelled up and had to be bandaged and she had had to lie up for some weeks. This had been a short time before the attack of nervous asthma in her eighth year.

The next thing to do was to turn to account our knowledge of the existence of this phantasy: "If it is true that you were delivered of a child nine months after the scene by the lake, and that you are going about to this very day carrying the consequences of your false step with you, then it follows that in your unconscious you must have regretted the upshot of the scene. In your unconscious thoughts, that is to say, you have made an emendation in it. The assumption that underlies your phantasy of childbirth is that on that occasion something took place,[5] that on that occasion you experienced and went through everything that you were in fact obliged to pick up later on from the encyclopaedia. So you see that your love for Herr K. did not come to an end with the scene, but that (as I maintained) it has persisted down to the present day—though it is true that you are unconscious of it."—And Dora disputed the fact no longer.[6]

---

4. I have already indicated that the majority of hysterical symptoms, when they have attained their full pitch of development, represent an imagined situation of sexual life—such as a scene of sexual intercourse, pregnancy, childbirth, confinement, etc. [Freud's note].   5. The phantasy of defloration is thus found to have an application to Herr K., and we begin to see why this part of the dream contained material taken from the scene by the lake—the refusal, two and a half hours, the wood, the invitation to L—— [Freud's note].   6. I may here add a few supplementary interpretations to those that have already been given: The *"Madonna"* was obviously Dora herself; in the first place because of the "adorer" who had sent her the pictures, in the second place because she had won Herr K.'s love chiefly by the motherliness she had shown towards his children, and lastly because she had had a child (just though she was still a girl (this being a direct allusion to the phantasy of childbirth). Moreover, the notion of the "Madonna" is a favourite counter-idea in the mind of girls who feel themselves oppressed by imputations of sexual guilt,—which was the case with Dora [Freud's note].

The labour of elucidating the second dream had so far occupied two hours. At the end of the second session, when I expressed my satisfaction at the result, Dora replied in a depreciatory tone: "Why, has anything so very remarkable come out?" These words prepared me for the advent of fresh revelations.

She opened the third session with these words: "Do you know that I am here for the last time to-day?"—"How can I know, as you have said nothing to me about it?"—"Yes. I made up my mind to put up with it till the New Year.[7] But I shall wait no longer than that to be cured."—"You know that you are free to stop the treatment at any time. But for to-day we will go on with our work. When did you come to this decision?"—"A fortnight ago, I think."—"That sounds just like a maidservant or a governess—a fortnight's warning."—"There was a governess who gave warning with the K.'s, when I was on my visit to them that time at L——, by the lake."—"Really? You have never told me about her. Tell me."

"Well, there was a young girl in the house, who was the children's governess; and she behaved in the most extraordinary way to Herr K. She never said good morning to him, never answered his remarks, never handed him anything at table when he asked for it, and in short treated him like thin air. For that matter he was hardly any politer to her. A day or two before the scene by the lake, the girl took me aside and said she had something to tell me. She then told me that Herr K. had made advances to her at a time when his wife was away for several weeks; he had made violent love to her and had implored her to yield to his entreaties, saying that he got nothing from his wife, and so on."—"Why, those are the very words he used afterwards, when he made his proposal to you and you gave him the slap in his face."—"Yes. She had given way to him, but after a little while he had ceased to care for her, and since then she hated him."—"And this governess had given warning?"—"No. She meant to give warning. She told me that as soon as she felt she was thrown over she had told her parents what had happened. They were respectable people living in Germany somewhere. Her parents said that she must leave the house instantly; and, as she failed to do so, they wrote to her saying that they would have nothing more to do with her, and that she was never to come home again."—"And why had she not gone away?"—"She said she meant to wait a little longer, to see if there might not be some change in Herr K. She could not bear living like that any more, she said, and if she saw no change she should give warning and go away."—"And what became of the girl?"—"I only know that she went away."—"And she did not have a child as a result of the adventure?"—"No."

Here, therefore (and quite in accordance with the rules), was a piece of material information coming to light in the middle of the analysis and helping to solve problems which had previously been raised. I was able to say to Dora: "Now I know your motive for the slap in the face with which you answered Herr K.'s proposal. It was not that you were offended at his suggestions; you were actuated by jealousy and revenge. At the time when the governess was telling you her story you were still able to make use of your gift for putting on one side everything that is not agreeable to your feelings.

7. It was December 31st [Freud's note].

But at the moment when Herr K. used the words 'I get nothing out of my wife'—which were the same words he had used to the governess—fresh emotions were aroused in you and tipped the balance. 'Does he dare,' you said to yourself, 'to treat me like a governess, like a servant?' Wounded pride added to jealousy and to the conscious motives of common sense—it was too much.[8] To prove to you how deeply impressed you were by the governess's story, let me draw your attention to the repeated occasions upon which you have identified yourself with her both in your dream and in your conduct. You told your parents what happened—a fact which we have hitherto been unable to account for—just as the governess wrote and told *her* parents. You give me a fortnight's warning, just like a governess. The letter in the dream which gave you leave to go home is the counterpart of the governess's letter from her parents forbidding her to do so."

"Then why did I not tell my parents at once?"

"How much time did you allow to elapse?"

"The scene took place on the last day of June; I told my mother about it on July 14th."

"Again a fortnight, then—the time characteristic for a person in service. Now I can answer your question. You understood the poor girl very well. She did not want to go away at once, because she still had hopes, because she expected that Herr K.'s affections would return to her again. So that must have been your motive too. You waited for that length of time so as to see whether he would repeat his proposals; if he had, you would have concluded that he was in earnest, and did not mean to play with you as he had done with the governess."

"A few days after I had left he sent me a picture post-card."[9]

"Yes, but when after that nothing more came, you gave free rein to your feelings of revenge. I can even imagine that at that time you were still able to find room for a subsidiary intention, and thought that your accusation might be a means of inducing him to travel to the place where you were living."—"As he actually offered to do at first," Dora threw in.—"In that way your longing for him would have been appeased"—here she nodded assent, a thing which I had not expected—"and he might have made you the amends you desired."

"What amends?"

"The fact is, I am beginning to suspect that you took the affair with Herr K. much more seriously than you have been willing to admit so far. Had not the K.'s often talked of getting a divorce?"

"Yes, certainly. At first she did not want to, on account of the children. And now she wants to, but he no longer does."

"May you not have thought that he wanted to get divorced from his wife so as to marry you? And that now he no longer wants to because he has no one to replace her? It is true that two years ago you were very young. But you told me yourself that your mother was engaged at seventeen and then waited two years for her husband. A daughter usually takes her mother's love-story as her model. So you too wanted to wait for him, and you took it

8. It is not a matter of indifference, perhaps, that Dora may have heard her father make the same complaint about his wife, just as I myself did from his own lips. She was perfectly well aware of its meaning [Freud's note].   9. Here is the point of contact with the engineer, who was concealed behind the figure of Dora herself in the first situation in the dream [Freud's note].

that he was only waiting till you were grown up enough to be his wife. I imagine that this was a perfectly serious plan for the future in your eyes. You have not even got the right to assert that it was out of the question for Herr K. to have had any such intention; you have told me enough about him that points directly towards his having such an intention. Nor does his behaviour at L—— contradict this view. After all, you did not let him finish his speech and do not know what he meant to say to you. Incidentally, the scheme would by no means have been so impracticable. Your father's relations with Frau K.—and it was probably only for this reason that you lent them your support for so long—made it certain that her consent to a divorce could be obtained; and you can get anything you like out of your father. Indeed, if your temptation at L—— had had a different upshot, this would have been the only possible solution for all the parties concerned. And I think that is why you regretted the actual event so deeply and emended it in the phantasy which made its appearance in the shape of the appendicitis. So it must have been a bitter piece of disillusionment for you when the effect of your charges against Herr K. was not that he renewed his proposals but that he replied instead with denials and slanders. You will agree that nothing makes you so angry as having it thought that you merely fancied the scene by the lake. I know now—and this is what you do not want to be reminded of—that you *did* fancy that Herr K.'s proposals were serious, and that he would not leave off until you had married him."

Dora had listened to me without any of her usual contradictions. She seemed to be moved; she said good-bye to me very warmly, with the heartiest wishes for the New Year, and—came no more. Her father, who called on me two or three times afterwards, assured me that she would come back again, and said it was easy to see that she was eager for the treatment to continue. But it must be confessed that Dora's father was never entirely straightforward. He had given his support to the treatment so long as he could hope that I should "talk" Dora out of her belief that there was something more than a friendship between him and Frau K. His interest faded when he observed that it was not my intention to bring about that result. I knew Dora would not come back again. Her breaking off so unexpectedly, just when my hopes of a successful termination of the treatment were at their highest, and her thus bringing those hopes to nothing—this was an unmistakable act of vengeance on her part. Her purpose of self-injury also profited by this action. No one who, like me, conjures up the most evil of those half-tamed demons that inhabit the human breast, and seeks to wrestle with them, can expect to come through the struggle unscathed. Might I perhaps have kept the girl under my treatment if I myself had acted a part, if I had exaggerated the importance to me of her staying on, and had shown a warm personal interest in her—a course which, even after allowing for my position as her physician, would have been tantamount to providing her with a substitute for the affection she longed for? I do not know. Since in every case a portion of the factors that are encountered under the form of resistance remains unknown, I have always avoided acting a part, and have contented myself with practising the humbler arts of psychology. In spite of every theoretical interest and of every endeavour to be of assistance as a physician, I keep the fact in mind that there must be some limits to the extent to which psychological influence may be used, and I respect as one of these limits the patient's own will and understanding.

Nor do I know whether Herr K. would have done any better if it had been revealed to him that the slap Dora gave him by no means signified a final "No" on her part, but that it expressed the jealousy which had lately been roused in her, while her strongest feelings were still on his side. If he had disregarded that first "No," and had continued to press his suit with a passion which left room for no doubts, the result might very well have been a triumph of the girl's affection for him over all her internal difficulties. But I think she might just as well have been merely provoked into satisfying her craving for revenge upon him all the more thoroughly. It is never possible to calculate towards which side the decision will incline in such a conflict of motives: whether towards the removal of the repression or towards its reinforcement. Incapacity for meeting a *real* erotic demand is one of the most essential features of a neurosis. Neurotics are dominated by the opposition between reality and phantasy. If what they long for the most intensely in their phantasies is presented to them in reality, they none the less flee from it; and they abandon themselves to their phantasies the most readily where they need no longer fear to see them realized. Nevertheless, the barrier erected by repression can fall before the onslaught of a violent emotional excitement produced by a real cause; it is possible for a neurosis to be overcome by reality. But we have no general means of calculating through what person or what event such a cure can be effected.

IV

Postscript

It is true that I have introduced this paper as a fragment of an analysis; but the reader will have discovered that it is incomplete to a far greater degree than its title might have led him to expect. It is therefore only proper that I should attempt to give a reason for the omissions—which are by no means accidental.

A number of the results of the analysis have been omitted, because at the time when work was broken off they had either not been established with sufficient certainty or they required further study before any general statement could be made about them. At other points, where it seemed to be permissible, I have indicated the direction along which some particular solution would probably have been found to lie. I have in this paper left entirely out of account the technique, which does not at all follow as a matter of course, but by whose means alone the pure metal of valuable unconscious thoughts can be extracted from the raw material of the patient's associations. This brings with it the disadvantage of the reader being given no opportunity of testing the correctness of my procedure in the course of this exposition of the case. I found it quite impracticable, however, to deal simultaneously with the technique of analysis and with the internal structure of a case of hysteria: I could scarcely have accomplished such a task, and if I had, the result would have been almost unreadable. The technique of analysis demands an entirely separate exposition, which would have to be illustrated by numerous examples chosen from a very great variety of cases and which would not have to take the results obtained in each particular case into account. Nor have I attempted in this paper to substantiate the psychological postulates which will be seen to underlie my descriptions of mental phenomena. A cursory attempt to do so would have effected nothing; an exhaustive one would have been a volume in itself. I can only assure the reader that I approached the study of the phenomena revealed by observation of the psychoneuroses without being pledged to any particular psychological system, and that I then proceeded to adjust my views until they seemed adapted for giving an account of the collection of facts which had been observed. I take no pride in having avoided speculation; the material for my hypotheses was collected by the most extensive and laborious series of observations. The decidedness of my attitude on the subject of the unconscious is perhaps specially likely to cause offence, for I handle unconscious ideas, unconscious trains of thought, and unconscious impulses as though they were no less valid and unimpeachable psychological data than conscious ones. But of this I am certain—that any one who sets out to investigate the same region of phenomena and employs the same method will find himself compelled to take up the same position, however much philosophers may expostulate.

Some of my medical colleagues have looked upon my theory of hysteria as a purely psychological one, and have for that reason pronounced it *ipso facto* incapable of solving a pathological problem. They may perhaps discover from this paper that their objection was based upon their having unjustifiably transferred what is a characteristic of the technique on to the theory itself. It is the therapeutic technique alone that is purely psychological; the theory does not by any means fail to point out that neuroses have an organic basis— though it is true that it does not look for that basis in any pathological anatomical changes, and provisionally substitutes the conception of organic functions for the chemical changes which we should expect to find but which we are at present unable to apprehend. No one, probably, will be inclined to deny the sexual function the character of an organic factor, and it is the sexual function that I look upon as the foundation of hysteria and of the psychoneurosis in general. No theory of sexual life will, I suspect, be able to avoid assuming the existence of some definite sexual substances having an excitant action. Indeed, of all the clinical pictures which we meet with in clinical medicine, it is the phenomena of intoxication and abstinence in connection with the use of certain chronic poisons that most closely resemble the genuine psychoneuroses.

But, once again, in the present paper I have not gone fully into all that might be said today about "somatic compliance," about the infantile germs of perversion, about the erotogenic zones, and about our predisposition towards bisexuality; I have merely drawn attention to the points at which the analysis comes into contact with these organic bases of the symptoms. More than this could not be done with a single case. And I had the same reasons that I have already mentioned for wishing to avoid a cursory discussion of these factors. There is a rich opportunity here for further works, based upon the study of a large number of analyses.

Nevertheless, in publishing this paper, incomplete though it is, I had two objects in view. In the first place, I wished to supplement my book on the interpretation of dreams by showing how an art, which would otherwise be useless, can be turned to account for the discovery of the hidden and repressed parts of mental life. (Incidentally, in the process of analysing the two dreams dealt with in the paper, the technique of dream-interpretation, which is similar to that of psycho-analysis, has come under consideration.) In the second place, I wished to stimulate interest in a whole group of phenomena of which science is still in complete ignorance today because they can only be brought to light by the use of this particular method. No one, I believe, can have had any true conception of the complexity of the psychological events in a case of hysteria—the juxtaposition of the most dissimilar tendencies, the mutual dependence of contrary ideas, the repressions and displacements, and so on. The emphasis laid by Janet[1] upon the *"idée fixe"* which becomes transformed into a symptom amounts to no more than an extremely meagre attempt at schematization. Moreover, it is impossible to avoid the suspicion that, when the ideas attaching to certain excitations are incapable of becoming conscious, those excitations must act upon one another differently, run a different course, and manifest themselves differently from those other excitations which we describe as "normal" and which have ideas attaching to them of which we become conscious. When once things have been made clear up to this point, no obstacle can remain in the way of an understanding of a therapeutic method which removes neurotic symptoms by transforming ideas of the former kind into normal ones.

I was further anxious to show that sexuality does not simply intervene, like a *deus ex machina,* on one single occasion, at some point in the working of the processes which characterize hysteria, but that it provides the motive power for every single symptom, and for every single manifestation of a symptom. The symptoms of the disease are nothing else than *the patient's sexual activity.* A single case can never be capable of proving a theorem so general as this one; but I can only repeat over and over again—for I never find it otherwise—that sexuality is the key to the problem of the psychoneuroses and of the neuroses in general. No one who disdains the key will ever be able to unlock the door. I still await news of the investigations which are to make it possible to contradict this theorem or to limit its scope. What I have hitherto heard against it have been expressions of personal dislike or disbelief. To these it is enough to reply in the words of Charcot: "Ça n'empêche pas d'exister."[2]

Nor is the case of whose history and treatment I have published a fragment in these pages well calculated to put the value of psycho-analytic therapy in its true light. Not only the briefness of the treatment (which hardly lasted three months) but another factor inherent in the nature of the case prevented results being brought about such as are attainable in other instances, where the improvement will be admitted by the patient and his relatives and will approximate more or less closely to a complete recovery. Satisfactory results of this kind are reached when the symptoms are maintained solely by the internal conflict between the impulses concerned with sexuality. In such cases the patient's condition will be seen improving in proportion as he is helped towards a solution of his mental problems by the translation of pathogenic into normal material. The course of events is very different when the symptoms have become enlisted in the service of external motives, as had

1. Pierre Janet (1859–1947), French psychologist and neurologist.   2. That doesn't mean it doesn't exist (French).

happened with Dora during the two preceding years. It is surprising, and might easily be misleading, to find that the patient's condition shows no noticeable alteration even though considerable progress has been made with the work of analysis. But in reality things are not as bad as they seem. It is true that the symptoms do not disappear while the work is proceeding; but they disappear a little while later, when the relations between patient and physician have been dissolved. The postponement of recovery or improvement is really only caused by the physician's own person.

I must go back a little, in order to make the matter intelligible. It may be safely said that during psycho-analytic treatment the formation of new symptoms is invariably stopped. But the productive powers of the neurosis are by no means extinguished; they are occupied in the creation of a special class of mental structures, for the most part unconscious, to which the name of *"transferences"* may be given.

What are transferences? They are new editions or facsimiles of the impulses and phantasies which are aroused and made conscious during the progress of the analysis; but they have this peculiarity, which is characteristic for their species, that they replace some earlier person by the person of the physician. To put it another way: a whole series of psychological experiences are revived, not as belonging to the past, but as applying to the person of the physician at the present moment. Some of these transferences have a content which differs from that of their model in no respect whatever except for the substitution. These then—to keep to the same metaphor—are merely new impressions or reprints. Others are more ingeniously constructed; their content has been subjected to a moderating influence—to *sublimation,* as I call it—and they may even become conscious, by cleverly taking advantage of some real peculiarity in the physician's person or circumstances and attaching themselves to that. These, then, will no longer be new impressions, but revised editions.

If the theory of analytic technique is gone into, it becomes evident that transference is an inevitable necessity. Practical experience, at all events, shows conclusively that there is no means of avoiding it, and that this latest creation of the disease must be combated like all the earlier ones. This happens, however, to be by far the hardest part of the whole task. It is easy to learn how to interpret dreams, to extract from the patient's associations his unconscious thoughts and memories, and to practise similar explanatory arts; for these the patient himself will always provide the text. Transference is the one thing the presence of which has to be detected almost without assistance and with only the slightest clues to go upon, while at the same time the risk of making arbitrary inferences has to be avoided. Nevertheless, transference cannot be evaded, since use is made of it in setting up all the obstacles that make the material inaccessible to treatment, and since it is only after the transference has been resolved that a patient arrives at a sense of conviction of the validity of the connections which have been constructed during the analysis.

Some people may feel inclined to look upon it as a serious objection to a method which is in any case troublesome enough that it itself should multiply the labours of the physician by creating a new species of pathological mental products. They may even be tempted to infer from the existence of transferences that the patient will be injured by analytic treatment. Both these suppositions would be mistaken. The physician's labours are not multiplied by transference; it need make no difference to him whether he has to overcome any particular impulse of the patient's in connection with himself or with some one else. Nor does the treatment force upon the patient, in the shape of transference, any new task which he would not otherwise have performed. It is true that neuroses may be cured in institutions from which psychoanalytic treatment is excluded, that hysteria may be said to be cured not by the method but by the physician, and that there is usually a sort of blind dependence and a permanent bond between a patient and the physician who has removed his symptoms by hypnotic suggestion; but the scientific explanation of all these facts is to be found in the existence of "transferences" such as are regularly directed by patients on to their physicians. Psycho-analytic treatment does not *create* transferences, it merely brings them to light, like so many other hidden psychical factors. The only difference is this—that spontaneously a patient will only call up affectionate and friendly transferences to help towards his recovery; if they cannot be called up, he feels the physician is "antipathetic" to him, and breaks away from him as fast as possible and without having been influenced by him. In psycho-analysis, on the other hand, since the play of motives is different, all the patient's tendencies, including hostile ones, are aroused; they are then turned to account for the purposes of the analysis by being made conscious, and in this way the transference is constantly being destroyed. Transference, which seems ordained to be the greatest obstacle to psycho-analysis, becomes its most powerful ally, if its presence can be detected each time and explained to the patient.

I have been obliged to speak of transference, for it is only by means of this factor that I can elucidate the peculiarities of Dora's analysis. Its great merit, namely, the unusual clarity which makes it seem so suitable as a first introductory publication, is closely bound up with its great defect, which led to its being broken off prematurely. I did not succeed in mastering the transference in good time. Owing to the readiness with which Dora put one part of the pathogenic material at my disposal during the treatment, I neglected the precaution of looking out for the first signs of transference, which was being prepared in connection with another part of the same material—a part of which I was in ignorance. At the beginning it was clear that I was replacing her father in her imagination, which was not unlikely, in view of the difference between our ages. She was even constantly comparing me with him consciously, and kept anxiously trying to make sure whether I was being quite straightforward with her, for her father "always preferred secrecy and roundabout ways." But when the first dream came, in which she gave herself the warning that she had better leave my treatment just as she had formerly left Herr K.'s house, I ought to have listened to the warning myself. "Now," I ought to have said to her, "it is from Herr K. that you have made a transference on to me. Have you noticed anything that leads you to suspect me of evil intentions similar (whether openly or in some sublimated form) to Herr K.'s? Or have you been struck by anything about me or got to know anything about me which has caught your fancy, as happened previously with Herr K.?" Her attention would then have been turned to some detail in our relations, or in my person or circumstances, behind which there lay concealed something analogous but immeasurably more important concerning Herr K. And when this transference had been cleared up, the analysis would have obtained access to new memories, dealing, probably, with actual events. But

I was deaf to this first note of warning, thinking I had ample time before me, since no further stages of transference developed and the material for the analysis had not yet run dry. In this way the transference took me unawares, and, because of the unknown quantity in me which reminded Dora of Herr K., she took her revenge on me as she wanted to take her revenge on him, and deserted me as she believed herself to have been deceived and deserted by him. Thus she *acted out* an essential part of her recollections and phantasies instead of reproducing it in the treatment. What this unknown quantity was I naturally cannot tell. I suspect that it had to do with money, or with jealousy of another patient who had kept up relations with my family after her recovery. When it is possible to work transferences into the analysis at an early stage, the course of the analysis is retarded and obscured, but its existence is better guaranteed against sudden and overwhelming resistances.

In Dora's second dream there are several clear allusions to transference. At the time she was telling me the dream I was still unaware (and did not learn until two days later) that we had only *two hours* more work before us. This was the same length of time which she had spent in front of the Sistine Madonna, and which (by making a correction and putting "two hours" instead of "two and a half hours") she had taken as the length of the walk which she had not made round the lake. The striving and waiting in the dream, which related to the young man in Germany, and had their origin in her waiting till Herr K. could marry her, had been expressed in the transference a few days before. The treatment, she had thought, was too long for her; she would never have the patience to wait so long. And yet in the first few weeks she had had discernment enough to listen without making any such objections when I informed her that her complete recovery would require perhaps a year. Her refusing in the dream to be accompanied, and preferring to go alone, also originated from her visit to the gallery at Dresden, and I was myself to experience them on the appointed day. What they meant was, no doubt: "Men are all so detestable that I would rather not marry. This is my revenge."[3]

If cruel impulses and revengeful motives, which have already been used in the patient's ordinary life for maintaining her symptoms, become transferred on to the physician during treatment, before he has had time to detach them from himself by tracing them back to their sources, then it is not to be wondered at if the patient's condition is unaffected by his therapeutic efforts. For how could the patient take a more effective revenge than by demonstrating upon her own person the helplessness and incapacity of the physician? Nevertheless, I am not inclined to put too low a value on the therapeutic results even of such a fragmentary treatment as Dora's.

It was not until fifteen months after the case was over and this paper composed that I had news of my patient's condition and the effects of my

---

3. The longer the interval of time that separates me from the end of this analysis, the more probable it seems to me that the fault in my technique lay in this omission: I failed to discover in time and to inform the patient that her homosexual (gynaecophilic) love for Frau K. was the strongest unconscious current in her mental life. I ought to have guessed that the main source of her knowledge of sexual matters could have been no one but Frau K.—the very person who later on charged her with being interested in those same subjects. Her knowing all about such things and, at the same time, her always pretending not to know where her knowledge came from was really too remarkable. I ought to have attacked this riddle and looked for the motive of such an extraordinary piece of repression. If I had done this, the second dream would have given me my answer [Freud's note].

treatment. On a date which is not a matter of complete indifference, on the first of April (times and dates, as we know, were never without significance for her), Dora came to see me again: to finish her story and to ask for help once more. One glance at her face, however, was enough to tell me that she was not in earnest over her request. For four or five weeks after stopping the treatment she had been "all in a muddle," as she said. A great improvement had then set in; her attacks had become less frequent and her spirits had risen. In May of that year one of the K.'s two children (it had always been delicate) had died. She took the opportunity of their loss to pay them a visit of condolence, and they received her as though nothing had happened in the last three years. She made it up with them, she took her revenge on them, and she brought her own business to a satisfactory conclusion. To the wife she said: "I know you have an affair with my father"; and the other did not deny it. From the husband she drew an admission of the scene by the lake which he had disputed, and brought the news of her vindication home to her father. Since then she had not resumed her relations with the family.

After this she had gone on quite well till the middle of October, when she had had another attack of aphonia which had lasted for six weeks. I was surprised at this news, and, on my asking her whether there had been any exciting cause, she told me that the attack had followed upon a violent fright. She had seen some one run over by a carriage. Finally she came out with the fact that the accident had occurred to no less a person than Herr K. himself. She had come across him in the street one day; they had met in a place where there was a great deal of traffic; he had stopped in front of her as though in bewilderment, and in his abstraction he had allowed himself to be knocked down by a carriage. She had been able to convince herself, however, that he escaped without serious injury. She still felt some slight emotion if she heard any one speak of her father's affair with Frau K., but otherwise she had no further concern with the matter. She was absorbed in her work, and had no thoughts of marrying.

She went on to tell me that she had come for help on account of a right-sided facial neuralgia, from which she was now suffering day and night. "How long has it been going on?" "Exactly a fortnight."[4] I could not help smiling; for I was able to show her that exactly a fortnight earlier she had read a piece of news that concerned me in the newspaper. (This was in 1902.) And this she confirmed.

Her alleged facial neuralgia was thus a self-punishment—remorse at having once given Herr K. a box on the ear, and at having transferred her feelings of revenge on to me. I do not know what kind of help she wanted from me, but I promised to forgive her for having deprived me of the satisfaction of affording her a far more radical cure for her troubles.

Years have again gone by since her visit. In the meantime the girl has married, and indeed—unless all the signs mislead me—she has married the young man who came into her associations at the beginning of the analysis of the second dream.[5] Just as the first dream represented her turning away from the man she loved to her father—that is to say, her flight from life into

---

4. For the significance of this period of time and its relation to the theme of revenge, see the analysis of the second dream [Freud's note].   5. In the editions of 1909, 1912, and 1921 the following footnote appeared at this point: "This, as I afterwards learnt, was a mistaken notion."

disease—so the second dream announced that she was about to tear herself free from her father and had been reclaimed once more by the realities of life.

WILLIAM BUTLER YEATS
1865–1939

William Butler Yeats is not only the main figure in the Irish literary renaissance but also the twentieth century's greatest poet in the English language. His sensuously evocative descriptions and his fusion of concrete historical examples with an urgent metaphysical vision stir readers around the world. Years after the poet's death, the Nigerian Chinua Achebe borrowed three words from one of his lines as the title of a novel, *Things Fall Apart*—confident that his audience would immediately recognize the source. If the English language has a Symbolist poet, it is once again Yeats for his constant use of allusive imagery and large symbolic structures. Yeats's symbolism is not that of Baudelaire, Mallarmé, or other continental predecessors, however, for the European Symbolists did not share the Irish poet's fascination with occult wisdom and large historical patterns. Yeats adopted a cyclical model of history for which the rise and fall of civilizations are predetermined inside a series of interweaving evolutionary spirals. With this cyclical model, he created a private mythology that allowed him to come to terms with both personal and cultural pain and helped to explain— as symptoms of Western civilization's declining spiral—the plight of contemporary Irish society and the chaos of European culture around World War I. Yeats shares with writers like Rilke and T. S. Eliot the quest for larger meaning in a time of trouble and the use of symbolic language to give verbal form to that quest.

Yeats was born in a Dublin suburb on June 13, 1865, the oldest of four children born to John Butler and Susan Pollexfen Yeats. His father, a cosmopolitan Anglo-Irishman who had turned from law to painting, took over Yeats's education when he found that, at age nine, the boy could not read. J. B. Yeats was a highly argumentative religious skeptic who alternately terrorized his son and awakened his interest in poetry and the visual arts, inspiring at one and the same time both rebellion against scientific rationalism and belief in the higher knowledge of art. His mother's strong ties to her home in County Sligo (where Yeats spent many summers and school holidays) introduced him to the beauties of the Irish countryside and the Irish folklore and supernatural legends that appear throughout his work. Living alternately in Ireland and England for much of his youth, Yeats became part of literary society in both countries and—though an Irish nationalist—was unable to adopt a narrowly patriotic point of view. Even the failed Easter Rebellion of 1916, which he celebrated in *Easter 1916*, and the revolutionary figures who were beloved friends took their place in a larger mythic historical framework. By the end of his life, he had abandoned all practical politics and devoted himself to the reality of personal experience inside a mystic view of history.

For many, it is Yeats's mastery of images that defines his work. From his early use of symbols as private keys, or dramatic metaphors for complex personal emotions, to the immense cosmology of his last work, he continued to create a highly visual poetry whose power derives from the dramatic interweaving of specific images. Symbols such as the Tower, Byzantium, Helen of Troy, the opposition of sun and moon, birds of prey, the blind man, and the fool recur frequently and draw their meaning not from inner connections established inside the poem (as for the French Symbolists) but from an underlying myth based on occult tradition, Irish folklore, history, and Yeats's own personal experience. Symbols as Yeats used them, however, make sense in and among themselves: the "gyre," or spiral unfolding of history, is simultaneously the falcon's spiral flight; and the sphinxlike beast slouching blank-eyed toward Bethlehem in *The Second Coming* is a comprehensible horror capable of many explicit interpretations but resistant to all and, therefore, the more terrifying. Even readers unacquainted with Yeats's mythic system will respond to images precisely expressing a situation or state of mind (for example, golden Byzantium for intellect, art, wisdom— all that "body" cannot supply) and to a visionary organization that proposes shape and context for twentieth-century anxieties.

The nine poems included here cover the range of Yeats's career, which embraced several periods and styles. Yeats had attended art school and planned to be an artist before he turned fully to literature in 1886, and his early works show the influence of the Pre-Raphaelite school in art and literature. Pre-Raphaelitism called for a return to the sensuous representation and concrete particulars found in Italian painting before Raphael (1483–1520), and Pre-Raphaelite poetry evoked a poetic realm of luminous supernatural beauty described in allusive and erotically sensuous detail. Rossetti's *Blessed Damozel,* yearning for her beloved "from the gold bar of heaven," has eyes "deeper than the depth / Of waters stilled at even; / She had three lilies in her hand, / And the stars in her hair were seven." The Pre-Raphaelite fascination with the medieval past (William Morris wrote a *Defense of Guenevere,* King Arthur's adulterous wife) combined with Yeats's own interest in Irish legend, and in 1889 a long poem describing a traveler in fairyland (*The Wanderings of Oisin*) established his reputation and won Morris's praise. The musical, evocative style of Yeats's Pre-Raphaelite period is well shown in *The Lake Isle of Innisfree* (1890), with its hidden "bee-loud glade" where "peace comes dropping slow" and evening, after the "purple glow" of noon, is "full of the linnet's wings." Another poem from the same period, *When You Are Old,* pleads his love for the beautiful actress and Irish nationalist Maud Gonne, whom he met in 1889 and who repeatedly refused to marry him. From the love poems of his youth to his old age, when *The Circus Animals' Desertion* described her as prey to fanaticism and hate, Yeats returned again and again to examine his feelings for this woman, who personified love, beauty, and Irish nationalism along with hope, frustration, and despair.

Yeats's family moved to London in 1887, where he continued an earlier interest in mystical philosophy by taking up theosophy under its Russian interpreter Madame Blavatsky. Madame Blavatsky claimed mystic knowledge from Tibetan monks and preached a doctrine of the Universal Oversoul, individual spiritual evolution through cycles of incarnation, and the world as a conflict of opposites. Yeats was taken with her grandiose cosmology, although he inconveniently wished to test it by experiment and analysis and was ultimately expelled from the society in 1890. He found a more congenial literary model in the works of William Blake, which he coedited in 1893 with F. J. Ellis. Yeats's interest in large mystical systems later waned but never altogether disappeared, and traces may be seen in the introduction that he wrote in 1916 for *Gitanjali,* a collection of poems by the Indian author Rabindranath Tagore.

Several collections of Irish folk and fairy tales and a book describing Irish traditions (*The Celtic Twilight,* 1893) demonstrated a corresponding interest in Irish national identity. In 1896 he had met Lady Gregory, an Irish nationalist who invited him to spend summers at Coole Park, her country house in Galway, and who worked closely with him (and later J. M. Synge) in founding the Irish National Theatre (later the Abbey Theatre). Along with other participants in what was once called the Irish literary renaissance, he aimed to create "a national literature that made Ireland beautiful in the memory . . . freed from provincialism by an exacting criticism." To this end, he wrote *Cathleen ni Houlihan* (1902), a play in which the title character personifies Ireland, which became immensely popular with Irish nationalists. He also established Irish literary societies in Dublin and Ireland, promoted and reviewed Irish books, and lectured and wrote about the need for Irish community. In 1922 he was elected senator of the Irish Free State, serving until 1928.

Gradually, Yeats became embittered by the split between narrow Irish nationalism and the free expression of Irish culture. He was outraged at the attacks on Synge's *Playboy of the Western World* (1907) for its supposed derogatory picture of Irish culture, and he commented scathingly in *Poems Written in Discouragement* (1913, reprinted in *Responsibilities,* 1914) on the inability of the Irish middle class to appreciate art or literature. When he celebrates the abortive Easter uprisings of 1916, it is with a more universal, aesthetic view; "A terrible beauty is born" in the self-sacrifice that leads even a "drunken, vainglorious lout" to be "transformed utterly" by political martyrdom. Except for summers at Coole Park, Yeats in his middle age was spending more time in England than in Ireland. He began his *Autobiographies* in 1914, and wrote symbolic plays intended for small audiences on the model of the Japanese *nō* theater. There is a change in the tone of his works at this time, a new precision and epigrammatic quality that is partly owing to his disappointment with Irish nationalism and partly to the new tastes in poetry promulgated by his friend Ezra Pound and by T. S. Eliot after the example of John Donne and the metaphysical poets.

Yeats's marriage in 1917 to Georgie Hyde-Lees provided him with much-needed stability and also an impetus to work out a larger symbolic scheme. He interpreted his wife's experiments with automatic writing (writing whatever comes to mind, without correction or rational intent) as glimpses into a hidden cosmic order and gradually evolved a total system, which he explained in *A Vision* (1925). The wheel of history takes twenty-six thousand years to turn; and inside that wheel civilizations evolve in roughly two-thousand-year *gyres,* spirals expanding outward until they collapse at the beginning of a new gyre, which will reverse the direction of the old. Human personalities fall into different types within the system, and both gyres and types are related to the different phases of the moon. Yeats's later poems in *The Tower* (1928), *The Winding Stair* (1933), and *Last Poems* (1939) are set in the context of this system. Even when it is not literally present, it suggests an organizing pattern that resolves contraries inside an immense historical perspective. *Leda and the Swan,* on one level an erotic retelling of a mythic rape, also foreshadows the Trojan War—brute force mirroring brute force. In the two poems on the legendary city of Byzantium, Yeats admired an artistic civilization that "could answer all my questions" but that was also only a moment in history. Byzantine art, with its stylized perspectives and mosaics made by arranging tiny colored pieces of stone, was the exact opposite of the Western tendency to imitate nature, and it provided a kind of escape, or healing distance, for the poet. The idea of an inhuman, metallic, abstract beauty separated "out of nature" by art expresses a mystic and Symbolist quest for an invulnerable world distinct from the ravages of time. This world was to be found in an idealized Byzantium, where the poet's body would be transmuted into "such a form as Grecian goldsmiths make / Of hammered gold and gold enamelling / To keep a drowsy Emperor awake; / Or set upon a golden bough to sing / To lords and ladies of Byzantium / Of what is past, or passing, or to come." At the end of *Among School Children,* the sixty-year-old "public man" compensates for the passing of youth by dreaming of pure "Presences" that never fade. Yeats had often adopted the persona of the old man for whom the perspectives of age, idealized beauty, or history were ways to keep human agony at a distance. In *Lapis Lazuli,* the tragic figures of history transcend their roles by the calm "gaiety" with which they accept their fate; the ancient Chinamen carved in the poem's damaged blue stone climb toward a vantage point where they stare detachedly down on the world's tragedies: "Their eyes mid many wrinkles, their eyes, / Their ancient, glittering eyes, are gay."

But the world is still there, its tragedies still take place, and Yeats's poetry is always aware of the physical and emotional roots from which it sprang. Whatever the wished-for distance, his poems are full of passionate feelings, erotic desire and disappointment, delight in sensuous beauty, horror at civil war and anarchy, dismay at degradation and change. By the time of his death on January 28, 1939, Yeats had rejected his Byzantine identity as the golden songbird and sought out "the brutality, the ill breeding, the barbarism of truth." "The Wild Old Wicked Man" replaced earlier druids or ancient Chinamen as spokesman, and in *The Circus Animals' Desertion* Yeats described his former themes as so many circus animals put on display. No matter how much these themes embodied "pure mind," they were based in "a mound of refuse or the sweepings of a street . . . the foul rag-and-bone shop of the heart"— the rose springing from the dunghill. Yeats's poetry, which draws its initial power from the mastery of images and verbal rhythm, continues to resonate in the reader's mind for this attempt to come to terms with reality, to grasp and make sense of human experience in the transfiguring language of art.

Edward Malins presents a brief introduction with biography, illustrations, and maps in *A Preface to Yeats* (1994). Richard Ellmann, *The Identity of Yeats* (1964), is an excellent discussion of Yeats's work as a whole. Norman A. Jeffares has revised his major study, *A New Commentary on the Collected Poems of W. B. Yeats* (1983); a useful reference work is Lester I. Conner, *A Yeats Dictionary: Persons and Places in the Poetry of William Butler Yeats* (1998). Jeffares's *W. B. Yeats: A New Biography* (1989) takes into account new information about the poet. Elizabeth Cullingford, *Gender and History in Yeats's Love Poetry* (1993), examines aesthetic form and cultural perspectives in the love lyrics; Deirdre Toomey, *Yeats and Women* (1997), discusses Yeats's relations with women and the women in his poetry; and Marjorie Elizabeth Howes, *Yeats's Nations: Gender, Class, and Irishness* (1996), stresses political and social views. Essay collections include Harold Bloom, ed., *William Butler Yeats* (1986), and Richard J. Finneran, ed., *Critical Essays on W. B. Yeats* (1986). Essays in Deborah Fleming, ed., *Learning the Trade: Essays on W. B. Yeats and Contemporary Poetry* (1993), discuss Yeats's imprint on various contemporary poets; and contributions to Leonard Orr, ed., *Yeats and Postmodernism* (1991), approach Yeats from different postmodernist perspectives.

PRONOUNCING GLOSSARY

The following list uses common English syllables and stress accents to provide rough equivalents of selected words whose pronunciation may be unfamiliar to the general reader.

Callimachus: *ca-li'-mah-cus*   gyre: *jai-er*

Cuchulain: *coo-hu'-lin*   Quattrocento: *kwah-troh-chen'-toh*

When You Are Old[1]

When you are old and gray and full of sleep,
And nodding by the fire, take down this book,
And slowly read, and dream of the soft look
Your eyes had once, and of their shadows deep;

How many loved your moments of glad grace,   5
And loved your beauty with love false or true,
But one man loved the pilgrim soul in you,
And loved the sorrows of your changing face;

---

1. An adaptation of a love sonnet by the French Renaissance poet Pierre de Ronsard (1524–1585), which begins similarly ("Quand vous serez bien vieille") but ends by asking the beloved to "pluck the roses of life today."

And bending down beside the glowing bars,
Murmur, a little sadly, how Love fled   10
And paced upon the mountains overhead
And hid his face amid a crowd of stars.

Easter 1916[1]

I have met them at close of day
Coming with vivid faces
From counter or desk among grey
Eighteenth-century houses.
I have passed with a nod of the head   5
Or polite meaningless words,
Or have lingered awhile and said
Polite meaningless words,
And thought before I had done
Of a mocking tale or a gibe   10
To please a companion
Around the fire at the club,
Being certain that they and I
But lived where motley is worn:
All changed, changed utterly: 15
A terrible beauty is born.

That woman's[2] days were spent
In ignorant good-will,
Her nights in argument
Until her voice grew shrill.   20
What voice more sweet than hers
When, young and beautiful,
She rode to harriers?
This man had kept a school
And rode our wingèd horse;   25
This other his helper and friend[3]
Was coming into his force;
He might have won fame in the end,
So sensitive his nature seemed,
So daring and sweet his thought.   30
This other man[4] I had dreamed
A drunken, vainglorious lout.
He had done most bitter wrong
To some who are near my heart,
Yet I number him in the song;   35
He, too, has resigned his part

---

1. On Easter Sunday 1916, Irish nationalists began an unsuccessful rebellion against British rule, which lasted throughout the week and ended in the surrender and execution of its leaders. **2.** Constance Gore-Booth (1868–1927), later Countess Markiewicz, an ardent nationalist. **3.** Patrick Pearse (1879–1916) and his friend Thomas MacDonagh (1878–1916), both schoolmasters and leaders of the rebellion and both executed by the British. As a Gaelic poet, Pearse symbolically rode the winged horse of the Muses, Pegasus. **4.** Major John MacBride (1865–1916), who had married and separated from Maud Gonne (1866–1953), Yeats's great love.

In the casual comedy;
He, too, has been changed in his turn,
Transformed utterly:
A terrible beauty is born.   40

Hearts with one purpose alone
Through summer and winter seem
Enchanted to a stone
To trouble the living stream.
The horse that comes from the road,   45
The rider, the birds that range
From cloud to tumbling cloud,
Minute by minute they change;
A shadow of cloud on the stream
Changes minute by minute;   50
A horse-hoof slides on the brim,
And a horse plashes within it;
The long-legged moor-hens dive,
And hens to moor-cocks call;
Minute by minute they live: 55
The stone's in the midst of all.

Too long a sacrifice
Can make a stone of the heart.
O when may it suffice?
That is Heaven's part, our part   60
To murmur name upon name,
As a mother names her child
When sleep at last has come
On limbs that had run wild.
What is it but nightfall?   65
No, no, not night but death;
Was it needless death after all?
For England may keep faith
For all that is done and said.
We know their dream; enough   70
To know they dreamed and are dead;
And what if excess of love
Bewildered them till they died?
I write it out in a verse—
MacDonagh and MacBride   75
And Connolly[5] and Pearse
Now and in time to be,
Wherever green is worn,
Are changed, changed utterly:
A terrible beauty is born.   80

---

5. James Connolly (1870–1916), labor leader and nationalist executed by the British.

The Second Coming[1]

Turning and turning in the widening gyre[2]
The falcon cannot hear the falconer;
Things fall apart; the centre cannot hold;
Mere anarchy is loosed upon the world,
The blood-dimmed tide is loosed, and everywhere   5
The ceremony of innocence is drowned;
The best lack all conviction, while the worst
Are full of passionate intensity.

Surely some revelation is at hand;
Surely the Second Coming is at hand.   10
The Second Coming! Hardly are those words out
When a vast image out of *Spiritus Mundi*[3]
Troubles my sight: somewhere in sands of the desert
A shape with lion body and the head of a man
A gaze blank and pitiless as the sun,   15
Is moving its slow thighs, while all about it
Reel shadows of the indignant desert birds.
The darkness drops again; but now I know
That twenty centuries of stony sleep
Were vexed to nightmare by a rocking cradle,   20
And what rough beast, its hour come round at last,
Slouches towards Bethlehem to be born?

Leda and the Swan[1]

A sudden blow: the great wings beating still
Above the staggering girl, her thighs caressed
By the dark webs, her nape caught in his bill,
He holds her helpless breast upon his breast.

How can those terrified vague fingers push   5
The feathered glory from her loosening thighs?
And how can body, laid in that white rush,
But feel the strange heart beating where it lies?

A shudder in the loins engenders there
The broken wall, the burning roof and tower   10
And Agamemnon dead.[2]

1. The Second Coming of Christ, believed by Christians to herald the end of the world, is transformed here into the prediction of a new birth initiating a new era and terminating the two-thousand-year cycle of Christianity.   2. The cone pattern of the falcon's flight and of historical cycles, in Yeats's vision.   3. World-soul (Latin) or, as *Anima Mundi* in Yeats's *Per Amica Silentia Lunae*, a "great memory" containing archetypal images; recalls C. G. Jung's collective unconscious.   1. Zeus, ruler of the Greek gods, took the form of a swan to rape the mortal Leda; she gave birth to Helen of Troy, whose beauty caused the Trojan War.   2. The ruins of Troy and the death of Agamemnon, the Greek leader, whose sacrifice of his daughter Iphigenia to win the gods' favor caused his wife, Clytemnestra (also a daughter of Leda), to assassinate him on his return.

Being so caught up,
So mastered by the brute blood of the air,
Did she put on his knowledge with his power
Before the indifferent beak could let her drop?

Sailing to Byzantium[1]

1

That is no country for old men. The young
In one another's arms, birds in the trees
—Those dying generations—at their song,
The salmon-falls, the mackerel-crowded seas,
Fish, flesh, or fowl, commend all summer long   5
Whatever is begotten, born, and dies.
Caught in the sensual music all neglect
Monuments of unageing intellect.

2

An aged man is but a paltry thing,
A tattered coat upon a stick, unless   10
Soul clap its hands and sing, and louder sing
For every tatter in its mortal dress,
Nor is there singing school but studying
Monuments of its own magnificence;
And therefore I have sailed the seas and come   15
To the holy city of Byzantium.

3

O sages standing in God's holy fire
As in the gold mosaic of a wall,
Come from the holy fire, perne in a gyre,[2]
And be the singing-masters of my soul.   20
Consume my heart away; sick with desire
And fastened to a dying animal
It knows not what it is; and gather me
Into the artifice of eternity.

4

Once out of nature I shall never take   25
My bodily form from any natural thing,
But such a form as Grecian goldsmiths make
Of hammered gold and gold enamelling
To keep a drowsy Emperor awake;
Or set upon a golden bough to sing   30

1. The ancient name for modern Istanbul, the capital of the Eastern Roman Empire, which represented for Yeats (who had seen Byzantine mosaics in Italy) a highly stylized and perfectly integrated artistic world where "religious, aesthetic, and practical life were one."   2. I.e., come spinning down in a spiral. *Perne:* a spool or bobbin. *Gyre:* the cone pattern of the falcon's flight and of historical cycles, in Yeats's vision.

To lords and ladies of Byzantium
Of what is past, or passing, or to come.

Among School Children

1

I walk through the long schoolroom questioning;
A kind old nun in a white hood replies;
The children learn to cipher and to sing,
To study reading-books and history,
To cut and sew, be neat in everything   5
In the best modern way—the children's eyes
In momentary wonder stare upon
A sixty-year-old smiling public man.[1]

2

I dream of a Ledaean[2] body, bent
Above a sinking fire, a tale that she   10
Told of a harsh reproof, or trivial event
That changed some childish day to tragedy—
Told, and it seemed that our two natures blent
Into a sphere from youthful sympathy,
Or else, to alter Plato's parable,   15
Into the yolk and white of the one shell.[3]

3

And thinking of that fit of grief or rage
I look upon one child or t'other there
And wonder if she stood so at that age—
For even daughters of the swan can share   20
Something of every paddler's heritage—
And had that color upon cheek or hair,
And thereupon my heart is driven wild:
She stands before me as a living child.

4

Her present image floats into the mind—   25
Did Quattrocento finger fashion it
Hollow of cheek[4] as though it drank the wind
And took a mess of shadows for its meat?
And I though never of Ledaean kind
Had pretty plumage once—enough of that,   30
Better to smile on all that smile, and show
There is a comfortable kind of old scarecrow.

1. Yeats was elected senator of the Irish Free State in 1922.   2. Beautiful as Leda or as her daughter
Helen of Troy.   3. In Plato's *Symposium*, Socrates explains love by telling how the gods split human
beings into two halves—like halves of an egg—so that each half seeks its opposite throughout life. Yeats
compares the two parts to the yolk and white of an egg.   4. Italian painters of the fifteenth century (the
Quattrocento), such as Botticelli (1444–1510), were known for their delicate figures.

5

What youthful mother, a shape upon her lap
Honey of generation had betrayed,
And that must sleep, shriek, struggle to escape   35
As recollection or the drug decide,[5]
Would think her son, did she but see that shape
With sixty or more winters on its head,
A compensation for the pang of his birth,
Or the uncertainty of his setting forth?   40

6

Plato thought nature but a spume that plays
Upon a ghostly paradigm of things;
Solider Aristotle played the taws
Upon the bottom of a king of kings;
World-famous golden-thighed Pythagoras[6]   45
Fingered upon a fiddle-stick or strings
What a star sang and careless Muses heard:
Old clothes upon old sticks to scare a bird.

7

Both nuns and mothers worship images,
But those the candles light are not as those   50
That animate a mother's reveries,
But keep a marble or a bronze repose.
And yet they too break hearts—O Presences
That passion, piety, or affection knows,
And that all heavenly glory symbolize—   55
O self-born mockers of man's enterprise;

8

Labor is blossoming or dancing where
The body is not bruised to pleasure soul,
Nor beauty born out of its own despair,
Nor blear-eyed wisdom out of midnight oil.   60
O chestnut tree, great-rooted blossomer,
Are you the leaf, the blossom, or the bole?
O body swayed to music, O brightening glance,
How can we know the dancer from the dance?

Byzantium[1]

The unpurged images of day recede;
The Emperor's drunken soldiery are abed;

5. Yeats's note to this poem recalls the Greek scholar Porphyry (ca. 234–ca. 305), who associates "honey" with "the pleasure arising from copulation" that engenders children; the poet further describes honey as a drug that destroys the child's " 'recollection' of pre-natal freedom."   6. Three Greek philosophers. Plato (427–337 B.C.) believed that nature was only a series of illusionistic reflections or appearances cast by abstract "forms" that were the only true realities. Aristotle (384–322 B.C.), more pragmatic, was Alexander the Great's tutor and spanked him with the "taws" (leather straps). Pythagoras (582–407 B.C.), a demigod to his disciples and thought to have a golden thigh bone, pondered the relationship of music, mathematics, and the stars.   1. The holy city of *Sailing to Byzantium* (p. 1421), seen here as it resists and transforms the blood and mire of human life into its own transcendent world of art.

Night resonance recedes, night-walkers' song
After great cathedral gong;
A starlit or a moonlit dome² disdains   5
All that man is,
All mere complexities,
The fury and the mire of human veins.

Before me floats an image, man or shade,
Shade more than man, more image than a shade;   10
For Hades' bobbin bound in mummy-cloth
May unwind the winding path;³
A mouth that has no moisture and no breath
Breathless mouths may summon;
I hail the superhuman;   15
I call it death-in-life and life-in-death.

Miracle, bird or golden handiwork,
More miracle than bird or handiwork,
Planted on the starlit golden bough,
Can like the cocks of Hades crow,⁴   20
Or, by the moon embittered, scorn aloud
In glory of changeless metal
Common bird or petal
And all complexities of mire or blood.

At midnight on the Emperor's pavement flit   25
Flames that no faggot feeds, nor steel has lit,
Nor storm disturbs, flames begotten of flame,
Where blood-begotten spirits come
And all complexities of fury leave,
Dying into a dance,   30
An agony of trance,
An agony of flame that cannot singe a sleeve.

Astraddle on the dolphin's ⁵ mire and blood,
Spirit after spirit! The smithies break the flood,
The golden smithies of the Emperor!   35
Marbles of the dancing floor
Break bitter furies of complexity,
Those images that yet
Fresh images beget,
That dolphin-torn, that gong-tormented sea.   40

---

2. According to Yeat's system in A Vision (1925), the first "starlit" phase in which the moon does not shine and the fifteenth, opposing phase of the full moon represent complete objectivity (potential being) and complete subjectivity (the achievement of complete beauty). In between these absolute phases lie the evolving "mere complexities" of human life.　3. Unwinding the spool of fate that leads from mortal death to the superhuman. Hades: the realm of the dead in Greek mythology.　4. To mark the transition from death to the dawn of new life.　5. A dolphin rescued the famous singer Arion by carrying him on his back over the sea. Dolphins were associated with Apollo, Greek god of music and prophecy, and in ancient art they are often shown escorting the souls of the dead to the Isles of the Blessed. Here, the dolphin is also flesh and blood, a part of life.

Lapis Lazuli[1]

For Harry Clifton

I have heard that hysterical women say
They are sick of the palette and fiddle-bow,
Of poets that are always gay,
For everybody knows or else should know
That if nothing drastic is done   5
Aeroplane and Zeppelin will come out,
Pitch like King Billy[2] bomb-balls in
Until the town lie beaten flat.

All perform their tragic play,
There struts Hamlet, there is Lear,   10
That's Ophelia, that Cordelia;[3]
Yet they, should the last scene be there,
The great stage curtain about to drop,
If worthy their prominent part in the play,
Do not break up their lines to weep.   15
They know that Hamlet and Lear are gay;
Gaiety transfiguring all that dread.
All men have aimed at, found and lost;
Black out; Heaven blazing into the head:[4]
Tragedy wrought to its uttermost.   20
Though Hamlet rambles and Lear rages,
And all the drop-scenes drop at once
Upon a hundred thousand stages,
It cannot grow by an inch or an ounce.

On their own feet they came, or on shipboard,   25
Camel-back, horse-back, ass-back, mule-back,
Old civilisations put to the sword.
Then they and their wisdom went to rack:
No handiwork of Callimachus[5]
Who handled marble as if it were bronze,   30
Made draperies that seemed to rise
When sea-wind swept the corner, stands;
His long lamp-chimney shaped like the stem
Of a slender palm, stood but a day;
All things fall and are built again,   35
And those that build them again are gay.

---

1. A deep blue semiprecious stone. One of Yeats's letters (to Dorothy Wellesley, July 6, 1935) describes a Chinese carving in lapis lazuli that depicts an ascetic and pupil about to climb a mountain:"Ascetic, pupil, hard stone, eternal theme of the sensual east . . . the east has its solutions always and therefore knows nothing of tragedy."   2. A linkage of past and present. According to an Irish ballad, King William III of England "threw his bomb-balls in" and set fire to the tents of the deposed James II at the Battle of the Boyne in 1690. Also a reference to Kaiser Wilhelm II (King William II) of Germany, who sent zeppelins to bomb London during World War I. *Zeppelin:* a long, cylindrical airship, supported by internal gas chambers.   3. Tragic figures in Shakespeare's plays.   4. The loss of rational consciousness making way for the blaze of inner revelation or "mad" tragic vision. Also suggests the final curtain and an air raid curfew.   5. Athenian sculptor (fifth century B.C.), famous for a gold lamp in the Erechtheum (temple on the Acropolis) and for using drill lines in marble to give the effect of flowing drapery.

Two Chinamen, behind them a third,
Are carved in Lapis Lazuli,
Over them flies a long-legged bird,[6]
A symbol of longevity;   40
The third, doubtless a serving-man,
Carries a musical instrument.

Every discoloration of the stone,
Every accidental crack or dent,
Seems a water-course or an avalanche,   45
Or lofty slope where it still snows
Though doubtless plum or cherry-branch
Sweetens the little half-way house
Those Chinamen climb towards, and I
Delight to imagine them seated there;   50
There, on the mountain and the sky,
On all the tragic scene they stare.
One asks for mournful melodies;
Accomplished fingers begin to play.
Their eyes mid many wrinkles, their eyes,   55
Their ancient, glittering eyes, are gay.

The Circus Animals' Desertion

1

I sought a theme and sought for it in vain,
I sought it daily for six weeks or so.
Maybe at last, being but a broken man,
I must be satisfied with my heart, although
Winter and summer till old age began   5
My circus animals were all on show,
Those stilted boys, that burnished chariot,
Lion and woman[1] and the Lord knows what.

2

What can I but enumerate old themes?
First that sea-rider Oisin led by the nose   10
Through three enchanted islands, allegorical dreams,[2]
Vain gaiety, vain battle, vain repose,
Themes of the embittered heart, or so it seems,
That might adorn old songs or courtly shows;
But what cared I that set him on to ride,   15
I, starved for the bosom of his faery bride?

6. A crane.   1. Yeats enumerates images and themes from his earlier work; here, the sphinx of *The Double Vision of Michael Robartes*.   2. In *The Wanderings of Oisin* (1889), an early poem in which Yeats describes a legendary Irish hero who wandered in fairyland for 150 years.

And then a counter-truth filled out its play,
The Countess Cathleen[3] was the name I gave it;
She, pity-crazed, had given her soul away,
But masterful Heaven had intervened to save it.   20
I thought my dear must her own soul destroy,
So did fanaticism and hate enslave it,
And this brought forth a dream and soon enough
This dream itself had all my thought and love.

And when the Fool and Blind Man stole the bread   25
Cuchulain[4] fought the ungovernable sea;
Heart-mysteries there, and yet when all is said
It was the dream itself enchanted me:
Character isolated by a deed
To engross the present and dominate memory.   30
Players and painted stage took all my love,
And not those things that they were emblems of.

3

Those masterful images because complete
Grew in pure mind, but out of what began?
A mound of refuse or the sweepings of a street,   35
Old kettles, old bottles, and a broken can,
Old iron, old bones, old rags, that raving slut
Who keeps the till. Now that my ladder's gone,
I must lie down where all the ladders start,
In the foul rag-and-bone shop of the heart.   40

3. A play (1892), dedicated to Maud Gonne, in which the countess is saved by heaven after having sold her soul to the Devil in exchange for food for the poor. The figure of Cathleen comes up frequently in Yeats's work and is often taken as a personification of nationalist Ireland.   4. A legendary Irish hero. Yeats is referring to the play *On Baile's Strand* (1904).

LUIGI PIRANDELLO
1867–1936

"Who am I?" and "What is real?" are the persistent and even agonized questions that underlie Luigi Pirandello's novels, short stories, and plays. The term *Pirandellismo* or "Pirandellism"—coined from the author's name—suggests that there are as many truths as there are points of view. Here are already the basic issues of later existential philosophy as seen in writers like Jean-Paul Sartre and Albert Camus: the difficulty of achieving a sense of identity, the impossibility of authentic communication between people, and the overlapping frontiers of appearance and reality. These dilemmas are dramatic crises in self-knowledge and as such are particularly suited for demonstration in the theater. Indeed, Pirandello is best known as an innovative dramatist who revolutionized European stage techniques to break down comfortable illusions of compartmentalized, stable reality. Instead of the late nineteenth century's "well-made play"—with its neatly constructed plot that packaged real life into a conventional beginning, middle, and end, and its consistent characters remaining safely inaccessible on the other side of the footlights—he offers unpredictable plots and characters whose ambiguity puts into question the solidity of identities assumed in everyday life. It is not easy to know the truth, he suggests, or to make oneself known behind the face or "naked mask" that each of us wears in society. Pirandello's theater readily displays its nature as dramatic illusion: plays exist within plays until one is not sure where the "real" play begins or ends, and characters question their own reality and that of the audience. In their manipulation of ambiguous appearances and tragicomic effects, these plays foreshadow the absurdist theater of Samuel Beckett, Eugène Ionesco, and Harold Pinter, the cosmic irony of Antonin Artaud's "theater of cruelty," and the emphasis on spectacle and illusion in works by Jean Genet. Above all, they insist that the most "real" life is that which changes from moment to moment, exhibiting a fluidity that renders difficult and perhaps impossible any single formulation of either character or situation. This fluidity is a cause of existential anguish because it implies perpetual loss; readers may wish to contrast Pirandello's cosmos of uncertain boundaries with the sense of continuity throughout different dimensions of existence that informs, for example, Wole Soyinka's *Death and the King's Horseman*.

Pirandello was born in Girgenti (now Agrigento), Sicily, on June 28, 1867. His father was a sulfur merchant who intended his son to go into business like himself, but Pirandello preferred language and literature. After studying in Palermo and the University of Rome, he traveled to the University of Bonn in 1888, and in 1891 he received a doctorate in romance philology with a thesis on the dialect of his hometown. In 1894, Pirandello made an arranged marriage with the daughter of a rich sulfur merchant. They lived for ten years in Rome, where he wrote poetry and short stories, until the collapse of the sulfur mines destroyed the fortunes of both families, and he was suddenly forced to earn a living. To add to his misfortunes, his wife became insane with a jealous paranoia that lasted until her death in 1918. The author himself died on December 1, 1936.

Pirandello's early work shows a number of different influences. His poetry was indebted to nineteenth-century Italian predecessors like Giosuè Carducci (1835–1907), and in 1896 he translated Goethe's *Roman Elegies*. Soon, however, he turned to short stories or *novelle* under the influence of a narrative style called *verismo* (realism) exemplified in the work of the Sicilian writer Giovanni Verga (1840–1922). Pirandello wrote hundreds of stories of all lengths and—in his clarity, realism, and psychological acuteness (often including a taste for the grotesque)—is recognized as an Italian master of the story much as was Guy de Maupassant in France. Collections include the 1894 *Love without Love* and an anthology in 1922 titled *A Year's Worth of Stories*.

In such stories, and in his early novels, Pirandello begins to develop his characteristic themes: the questioning of appearance and reality, and problems of identity. In *The Outcast* (1901), an irate husband drives his innocent wife out of the house only to take her back when—without his knowing it—the supposed adultery has actually occurred. The hero of Pirandello's best-known novel, *The Late Mattia Pascal,* tries to create a fresh identity for himself and leave behind the old Mattia Pascal. When things become too difficult he returns to his "late" self and begins to write his life story, an early example of the tendency in Pirandello's works to comment on their own composition. The protagonists in these and other works are visibly commonplace, middle-class citizens, neither heroic nor villainous, but prototypes of the twentieth-century antihero who remains aggressively average while taking the center of the stage.

The questions of identity that obsessed Pirandello (he speaks of them as reflecting the "pangs of my spirit") are explored on social, psychological, and metaphysical levels. He was acquainted with the experimental psychology of his day, and learned from works such as Alfred Binet's *Personality Alterations* (1892) about the existence of a subconscious personality beneath our everyday awareness (a theme Pirandello shares with Proust and Freud). Successive layers of personality, conflicts among the various parts, and the simultaneous existence of multiple perspectives shape an identity that is never fixed but always fluid and changing. This identity escapes the grasp of onlookers and subject alike, and expresses a basic incongruity in human existence that challenges the most earnest attempts to create a unified self. The protagonist of a later novel, *One, None, and a Hundred Thousand* (1925–26), finds that what "he" is depends on the viewpoint of a great number of people. Such incongruity can be tragic or comic—or both at once—according to one's attitude, a topic that Pirandello explored in a 1908 essay, *On Humor*, and that is echoed in the double-edged humor of his plays. The "Pirandellian" themes of ambiguous identity, lack of communication, and deceptive appearance reappear in all the genres, however, reaching a particular intensity in his first dramatic success, *It Is So [If You Think So]* (1917), and in the play included here, *Six Characters in Search of an Author*.

Six Characters in Search of an Author and *Henry IV* established Pirandello's stature as a major dramatist. He directed his own company (the Teatro d'Arte di Roma) from 1924 to 1928 and received the Nobel Prize for Literature in 1934. His later plays, featuring fantastic and grotesque elements, did not achieve the wide popularity of their predecessors. In 1936, he published a collection of forty-three plays as *Naked Masks*, a title conceived in 1918 after Luigi Chiarelli's "grotesque theater." Pirandello's characters are "naked" and vulnerable inside the social roles or masks they put on to survive: Henry IV, trapped for life inside a pretense of insanity, or the Father in *Six Characters*, forced to play out a demeaning role in which, he insists, only part of his true nature is revealed. The term *naked mask* also suggests Pirandello's superb manipulation of theatrical ambiguity—the confusion between the actor and the character portrayed—that ultimately prolongs the confusion of appearance and reality, which is one of his chief themes. Pirandello is famous in twentieth-century theater for his use of the play within a play, a technique of embedded dramatic episodes that maintain a life of their own while serving as foil to the overall or governing plot. Dividing lines are sometimes hard to draw when stage dialogue can be taken as referring to either context—a situation that allows for double meanings at the same time that it reiterates the impossibility of real communication.

Six Characters in Search of an Author combines all these elements in an extraordinarily self-reflexive style. At the very beginning, the Stage Hand's interrupted hammering suggests that the audience has chanced on a rehearsal—of still another play by Pirandello—instead of coming to a finished performance; concurrently, Pirandello's stage dialogue pokes fun at his own reputation for obscurity. Just as the Actors are apparently set to rehearse *The Rules of the Game*, six unexpected persons come down the aisle seeking the Producer: they are Characters out of an unwritten novel who demand to be given dramatic existence. The play *Six Characters* is continually in the process of being composed: composed as the interwoven double plot we see on stage, written down in shorthand by the Prompter for the Actors to reproduce, and potentially composed as the Characters' inner drama finally achieves its rightful existence as a work of art. The conflicts between the different levels of the play finally prevent the completion of any but the first work, but it has created a convincing dramatic illusion in the meantime that incorporates the psychological drama of the "six characters" as well as a discussion of the relationship of life and art.

The initial absurdity of the play appears when the six admittedly fictional characters arrive with their claim to be "truer and more real" than the "real" characters they confront. (Of course, to the audience all the actors on stage are equally unreal.) Their greater "truth" is the truth of art with its profound but formally fixed glimpses into human nature. Each Character represents, specifically and in depth, a particular identity created by the author, who later suggested that the Characters should wear masks to distinguish them from the Actors. These masks are not the conventional masks of ancient Greek drama or the Japanese *nō* theater, nor do they function as the ceremonial masks representing spirits in African ritual, masks that temporarily invest the wearer with the spirit's identity and authority. Instead, they are a theatrical device, a symbol and visual reminder of each character's unchanging essence. The

Six Characters are incapable of developing outside their roles and are condemned, in their search for existence, painfully to reenact their essential selves.

Conversely, the fictional characters have a more stable personality than "real" people who are still "nobody," incomplete, open to change and misinterpretation. Characters are "somebody" because their nature has been decided once and for all. Yet there is a further complication to this contrast between real and fictional characters: the Characters have real anxieties in that they want to play their own roles and are disturbed at the prospect of having Actors represent them incorrectly. All human beings, suggests Pirandello, whether fictional or real, are subject to misunderstanding. We even misunderstand ourselves when we think we are the same person in all situations. "We always have the illusion of being the same person for everybody," says the Father, "but it's not true!" When he explains himself as a very human philosopher driven by the Demon of Experiment, his self-image is quite different from the picture held by his vengeful Stepdaughter or the passive Mother who blames him for her expulsion from the house. The Stepdaughter, in turn, appears to love an innocent little sister because she reminds her of an earlier self. It is an entanglement of motives and deceit of mutual understanding that goes beyond the tabloid level of a sordid family scandal and claims a broader scope. Pirandello, in fact, does not intend merely to describe a particular setting or situation; that is the concern of what he calls "historical writers." He belongs to the opposite category of "philosophical writers" whose characters and situations embody "a particular sense of life and acquire from it a universal value."

Six Characters in Search of an Author underwent an interesting evolution to become the play that we see today. First performed in Rome in 1921, where its unsettling plot and characters already scandalized a traditionalist audience, it was reshaped in more radical theatrical form after the remarkable performance produced by Georges Pitoëff in Paris in 1923. Pirandello, who came to Paris somewhat wary of Pitoëff's innovations (he brought on the Characters in a green-lit stage elevator), was soon convinced that the Russian director's stagecraft suggested changes that would enhance the original text. Pitoëff had used his knowledge of technical effects to accentuate the interrelationships of appearance and reality: he extended the stage with several steps leading down into the auditorium (a break in the conventional stage's "fourth wall" that Pirandello was quick to exploit); he underscored the play within a play with rehearsal effects, showing the Stage Hand hammering and the Director arranging suitable props and lighting; he emphasized the division between Characters and Actors by separating groups on stage and dressing the Characters (all except the Little Girl) in black. Pirandello welcomed and expanded on many of these changes. To distinguish even further the Characters from the Actors, he proposed stylized masks as well as black clothes for the former and light-colored summery clothing for the latter. To bring out Madame Pace's grotesque fictionality, he changed her costume from a sober black gown to a garish red silk dress and carrot-colored wool wig. Most striking, however, is the dramatist's development of Pitoëff's steps into a real bridge between the world of the stage and the auditorium, a strategy that allows his Actors (and Characters) to come and go in the "real world" of the audience. Pirandello's revised ending to *Six Characters in Search of an Author* makes a final break with theatrical illusion: with the other characters immobilized on stage, the Stepdaughter races down the steps, through the auditorium, and out into the foyer from which the audience can still hear her distraught laughter.

Pirandello does not hold his audience by uttering grand philosophical truths. There is constant suspense and a process of discovery in *Six Characters*, from the moment that the rehearsal with its complaining Actors and Manager is interrupted and the initial hints of melodrama and family scandal catch our attention in the Stepdaughter's and Mother's complaints. It is a story that could be found in the most sensational papers: an adulterous wife thrust out of her home and supporting herself and her children after her lover's death by sewing, the daughter's turn to prostitution to support the family, the Father's unknowing attempt to seduce his Stepdaughter (interpreted by the latter as the continuation of an old and perverse impulse), and the final drowning and suicide of the two youngest children. Pirandello plays with the sensational aspect of his story by focusing the play on the characters' repeated attempts to portray the seduction scene; Actors and Manager perceive the salable quality of such "human-interest" events and are eager to let the story unfold. The Stepdaughter's protective fondness for her doomed baby sister and her enigmatic reproach to the little Boy ("instead of killing myself, I'd have killed one of those two") hint at the inner plot that is revealed only as the action continues. The interplay of illusion and reality persists to the very end, when the Actors argue about whether the Boy is dead or not, the Producer is terrified as the lights change eerily around the surviving Characters, and the Stepdaughter breaks away from the ending tableau to escape into the audience.

The translation by John Linstrum has been selected on the one hand for its accuracy to the Italian text and its fluent use of contemporary English idiom and on the other for its quality as a performance-oriented script, staged in London in 1979. Readers are encouraged to test the continued liveliness of Pirandello's dialogue by rehearsing their own selection of scenes—or perhaps by relocating them in a contemporary setting. According to director Robert Brustein, whose 1988 production of *Six Characters in Search of an Author* set the action in New York and replaced Madame Pace with a pimp, "Pirandello both encourages and stimulates a pluralism in theater because there can be dozens, hundreds, thousands of productions of *Six Characters*, and every one of them is going to be different."

A good biography and general introduction is found in Susan Bassnett-McGuire, *Pirandello* (1984). Useful introductions are Fiora A. Bassanese, *Understanding Luigi Pirandello* (1997), and Walter Starkie, *Luigi Pirandello, 1867–1936* (1965). Glauco Cambon, ed., *Pirandello: A Collection of Critical Essays* (1967), emphasizes the plays. Richard Sogliuzzo, *Luigi Pirandello, Director* (1982), deals with Pirandello's dramatic theories and practices; it contains a discussion of *Six Characters*. John Louis Di-Gaetani, ed., *A Companion to Pirandello Studies* (1991), is an excellent collection of twenty-seven essays and four appendices on diverse aspects of Pirandello's thought and work; many essays take up *Six Characters*. Luigi Pirandello, *Pirandello's Love Letters to Marta Abba* (1994), ed. and trans. Benito Ortonolani, illuminates the author's personal life in 1925–36 and his plans to reform the Italian theater.

PRONOUNCING GLOSSARY

The following list uses common English syllables and stress accents to provide rough equivalents of selected words whose pronunciation may be unfamiliar to the general reader.

commedia dell'arte: *com-may'-dee-ah del ar'-tay*

Luigi Pirandello: *loo-ee'-jee pee-ran-del'-oh*

Pace: *pah'-chay*

Pitoëff: *pee'-toh-eff*

Six Characters in Search of an Author[1]

A Comedy in the Making

THE CHARACTERS	THE COMPANY
FATHER	THE PRODUCER
MOTHER	THE STAGE STAFF
STEPDAUGHTER	THE ACTORS
SON	
LITTLE BOY	
LITTLE GIRL	
MADAME PACE	

Act One

When the audience enters, the curtain is already up and the stage is just as it would be during the day. There is no set; it is empty, in almost total darkness. This is so that from the beginning the audience will have the feeling of being present, not at a performance of a properly rehearsed play, but at a performance of a play that happens spontaneously. Two small sets of steps, one on the right and one on the left, lead up to the stage from the auditorium. On the stage, the top is off the PROMPTER's *box and is lying next to it. Downstage, there is a small table and a chair with arms for the* PRODUCER: *it is turned with its back to the audience.*

Also downstage there are two small tables, one a little bigger than the other, and several chairs, ready for the rehearsal if needed. There are more chairs scattered on both left and right for the ACTORS *to one side at the back and nearly hidden is a piano.*

When the houselights go down the STAGE HAND *comes on through the back door. He is in blue overalls and carries a tool bag. He brings some pieces of wood on, comes to the front, kneels down and starts to nail them together.*

The STAGE MANAGER *rushes on from the wings.*

STAGE MANAGER   Hey! What are you doing?

STAGE HAND   What do you think I'm doing? I'm banging nails in.

STAGE MANAGER   Now? [*He looks at his watch.*] It's half-past ten already. The Producer will be here in a moment to rehearse.

STAGE HAND   I've got to do my work some time, you know.

STAGE MANAGER   Right—but not now.

STAGE HAND   When?

STAGE MANAGER   When the rehearsal's finished. Come on, get all this out of the way and let me set for the second act of *The Rules of the Game.*[2]
[The STAGE HAND *picks up his tools and wood and goes off, grumbling and muttering. The* ACTORS *of the company come in through*

---

1. Translated by John Linstrum. In the Italian editions, Pirandello notes that he did not divide the play into formal acts or scenes. The translator has marked the divisions for clarity, however, according to the stage directions.   2. *Il giuoco delle parti,* written in 1918. The hero, Leone Gala, pretends to ignore his wife Silia's infidelity until the end, when he takes revenge by tricking her lover Guido Venanzi into taking his place in a fatal duel she had engineered to get rid of her husband.

*the door, men and women, first one then another, then two together
and so on: there will be nine or ten, enough for the parts for the
rehearsal of a play by Pirandello, The Rules of the Game, today's
rehearsal. They come in, say their "Good-mornings" to the* STAGE
MANAGER *and each other. Some go off to the dressing-rooms; others,
among them the* PROMPTER *with the text rolled up under his arm,
scatter about the stage waiting for the* PRODUCER *to start the
rehearsal. Meanwhile, sitting or standing in groups, they chat
together; some smoke, one complains about his part, another one
loudly reads something from "The Stage." It would be as well if the*
ACTORS *and* ACTRESSES *were dressed in colourful clothes, and this
first scene should be improvised naturally and vivaciously. After a
while somebody might sit down at the piano and play a song; the
younger* ACTORS *and* ACTRESSES *start dancing.*]

STAGE MANAGER [*Clapping his hands to call their attention.*]   Come on,
everybody! Quiet please. The Producer's here.
[*The piano and the dancing both stop. The* ACTORS *turn to look out
into the theatre and through the door at the back comes the* PRO-
DUCER; *he walks down the gangway between the seats and, calling
"Good-morning" to the* ACTORS, *climbs up one of the sets of stairs
onto the stage. The* SECRETARY *gives him the post, a few magazines,
a script. The* ACTORS *move to one side of the stage.*]

PRODUCER   Any letters?
SECRETARY   No. That's all the post there is. [*Giving him the script.*]
PRODUCER   Put it in the office. [*Then looking round and turning to the*
STAGE MANAGER.] I can't see a thing here. Let's have some lights please.
STAGE MANAGER   Right. [*Calling.*] Workers please!
[*In a few seconds the side of the stage where the* ACTORS *are standing
is brilliantly lit with white light. The* PROMPTER *has gone into his
box and spread out his script.*]
PRODUCER   Good. [*Clapping hands.*] Well then, let's get started. Anybody
missing?
STAGE MANAGER [*Heavily ironic.*]   Our leading lady.
PRODUCER   Not again! [*Looking at his watch.*] We're ten minutes late
already. Send her a note to come and see me. It might teach her to be
on time for rehearsals. [*Almost before he has finished, the* LEADING
ACTRESS's *voice is heard from the auditorium.*]
LEADING ACTRESS   Morning everybody. Sorry I'm late. [*She is very expen-
sively dressed and is carrying a lap-dog. She comes down the aisle and goes
up on to the stage.*]
PRODUCER   You're determined to keep us waiting, aren't you?
LEADING ACTRESS   I'm sorry. I just couldn't find a taxi anywhere. But you
haven't started yet and I'm not on at the opening anyhow. [*Calling the*
STAGE MANAGER, *she gives him the dog.*] Put him in my dressing-room
for me will you?
PRODUCER   And she's even brought her lap-dog with her! As if we haven't
enough lap-dogs here already. [*Clapping his hands and turning to the*
PROMPTER.] Right then, the second act of *The Rules of the Game.* [*Sits
in his arm-chair.*] Quiet please! Who's on?
[*The* ACTORS *clear from the front of the stage and sit to one side,*

1434 / LUIGI PIRANDELLO

except for three who are ready to start the scene—and the LEADING
ACTRESS. *She has ignored the* PRODUCER *and is sitting at one of the
little tables.*]

PRODUCER   Are you in this scene, then?

LEADING ACTRESS   No—I've just told you.

PRODUCER [*Annoyed.*]   Then get off, for God's sake. [*The* LEADING
ACTRESS *goes and sits with the others. To the* PROMPTER.] Come on then,
let's get going.

PROMPTER [*Reading his script.*]   "The house of Leone Gala. A peculiar
room, both dining-room and study."

PRODUCER [*To the* STAGE MANAGER.]   We'll use the red set.

STAGE MANAGER [*Making a note.*]   The red set—right.

PROMPTER [*Still reading.*]   "The table is laid and there is a desk with books
and papers. Bookcases full of books and china cabinets full of valuable
china. An exit at the back leads to Leone's bedroom. An exit to the left
leads to the kitchen. The main entrance is on the right."

PRODUCER   Right. Listen carefully everybody: there, the main entrance,
there, the kitchen. [*To the* LEADING ACTOR *who plays Socrates.*[3]] Your
entrances and exits will be from there. [*To the* STAGE MANAGER.] We'll
have the French windows there and put the curtains on them.

STAGE MANAGER [*Making a note.*]   Right.

PROMPTER [*Reading.*]   "Scene One. Leone Gala, Guido Venanzi, and
Filippo, who is called Socrates." [*To* PRODUCER.] Have I to read the
directions as well?

PRODUCER   Yes, you have! I've told you a hundred times.

PROMPTER [*Reading.*]   "When the curtain rises, Leone Gala, in a cook's
hat and apron, is beating an egg in a dish with a little wooden spoon.
Filippo is beating another and he is dressed as a cook too. Guido Venanzi
is sitting listening."

LEADING ACTOR   Look, do I really have to wear a cook's hat?

PRODUCER [*Annoyed by the question.*]   I expect so! That's what it says in
the script. [*Pointing to the script.*]

LEADING ACTOR   If you ask me it's ridiculous.

PRODUCER [*Leaping to his feet furiously.*]   Ridiculous? It's ridiculous, is it?
What do you expect me to do if nobody writes good plays any more[4] and
we're reduced to putting on plays by Pirandello? And if you can understand them you must be very clever. He writes them on purpose so
nobody enjoys them, neither actors nor critics nor audience. [*The*
ACTORS *laugh. Then crosses to* LEADING ACTOR *and shouts at him.*] A
cook's hat and you beat eggs. But don't run away with the idea that that's
all you are doing—beating eggs. You must be joking! You have to be
symbolic of the shells of the eggs you are beating. [*The* ACTORS *laugh
again and start making ironical comments to each other.*] Be quiet! Listen
carefully while I explain. [*Turns back to* LEADING ACTOR.] Yes, the shells,
because they are symbolic of the empty form of reason, without its content, blind instinct. You are reason and your wife is instinct: you are

3. Nickname given to Gala's servant, Philip, in *The Rules of the Game*, the play they are rehearsing.   **4.** The producer refers to the realistic, tightly constructed plays (often French) that were internationally popular in the late nineteenth century and a staple of Italian theaters at the beginning of the
twentieth.

playing a game where you have been given parts and in which you are not just yourself but the puppet of yourself.[5] Do you see?

LEADING ACTOR [*Spreading his hands.*]   Me? No.

PRODUCER [*Going back to his chair.*]   Neither do I! Come on, let's get going; you wait till you see the end! You haven't seen anything yet! [*Confidentially.*] By the way, I should turn almost to face the audience if I were you, about three-quarters face. Well, what with the obscure dialogue and the audience not being able to hear you properly in any case, the whole lot'll go to hell. [*Clapping hands again.*] Come on. Let's get going!

PROMPTER   Excuse me, can I put the top back on the prompt-box? There's a bit of a draught.

PRODUCER   Yes, yes, of course. Get on with it.

[*The* STAGE DOORKEEPER, *in a braided cap, has come into the auditorium, and he comes all the way down the aisle to the stage to tell the* PRODUCER *the* SIX CHARACTERS *have come, who, having come in after him, look about them a little puzzled and dismayed. Every effort must be made to create the effect that the* SIX CHARACTERS *are very different from the* ACTORS *of the company. The placings of the two groups, indicated in the directions, once the* CHARACTERS *are on the stage, will help this: so will using different coloured lights. But the most effective idea is to use masks for the* CHARACTERS, *masks specially made of a material that will not go limp with perspiration and light enough not to worry the actors who wear them: they should be made so that the eyes, the nose and the mouth are all free. This is the way to bring out the deep significance of the play. The* CHARACTERS *should not appear as ghosts, but as created realities, timeless creations of the imagination, and so more real and consistent than the changeable realities of the* ACTORS. *The masks are designed to give the impression of figures constructed by art, each one fixed forever in its own fundamental emotion; that is, Remorse for the* FATHER, *Revenge for the* STEPDAUGHTER, *Scorn for the* SON, *Sorrow for the* MOTHER. *Her mask should have wax tears in the corners of the eyes and down the cheeks like the sculptured or painted weeping Madonna in a church. Her dress should be of a plain material, in stiff folds, looking almost as if it were carved and not of an ordinary material you can buy in a shop and have made up by a dressmaker.*

The FATHER *is about fifty: his reddish hair is thinning at the temples, but he is not bald: he has a full moustache that almost covers his young-looking mouth, which often opens in an uncertain and empty smile. He is pale, with a high forehead: he has blue oval eyes, clear and sharp: he is dressed in light trousers and a dark jacket: his voice is sometimes rich, at other times harsh and loud.*

The MOTHER *appears crushed by an intolerable weight of shame and humiliation. She is wearing a thick black veil and is dressed simply in black; when she raises her veil she shows a face like wax, but not suffering, with her eyes turned down humbly.*]

---

5. Leone Gala is a rationalist and an aesthete—the opposite of his impulsive, passionate wife, Silia. By masking his feelings and constantly playing the role of gourmet cook, he chooses his own role and thus becomes his own "puppet."

The STEPDAUGHTER, *who is eighteen years old, is defiant, even insolent. She is very beautiful, dressed in mourning as well, but with striking elegance. She is scornful of the timid, suffering, dejected air of her young brother, a grubby* LITTLE BOY *of fourteen, also dressed in black; she is full of a warm tenderness, on the other hand, for the* LITTLE SISTER (GIRL), *a girl of about four, dressed in white with a black silk sash round her waist.*

The SON *is twenty-two, tall, almost frozen in an air of scorn for the* FATHER *and indifference to the* MOTHER: *he is wearing a mauve overcoat and a long green scarf round his neck.*]

DOORMAN Excuse me, sir.

PRODUCER [*Angrily.*] What the hell is it now?

DOORMAN There are some people here—they say they want to see you, sir.

[*The* PRODUCER *and the* ACTORS *are astonished and turn to look out into the auditorium.*]

PRODUCER But I'm rehearsing! You know perfectly well that no-one's allowed in during rehearsals. [*Turning to face out front.*] Who are you? What do you want?

FATHER [*Coming forward, followed by the others, to the foot of one of the sets of steps.*] We're looking for an author.

PRODUCER [*Angry and astonished.*] An author? Which author?

FATHER Any author will do, sir.

PRODUCER But there isn't an author here because we're not rehearsing a new play.

STEPDAUGHTER [*Excitedly as she rushes up the steps.*] That's better still, better still! We can be your new play.

ACTORS [*Lively comments and laughter from the* ACTORS.] Oh, listen to that, etc.

FATHER [*Going up on the stage after the* STEPDAUGHTER.] Maybe, but if there isn't an author here . . . [*To the* PRODUCER.] Unless you'd like to be . . .

[*Hand in hand, the* MOTHER *and the* LITTLE GIRL, *followed by the* LITTLE BOY, *go up on the stage and wait. The* SON *stays sullenly behind.*]

PRODUCER Is this some kind of joke?

FATHER Now, how can you think that? On the contrary, we are bringing you a story of anguish.

STEPDAUGHTER We might make your fortune for you!

PRODUCER Do me a favour, will you? Go away. We haven't time to waste on idiots.

FATHER [*Hurt but answering gently.*] You know very well, as a man of the theatre, that life is full of all sorts of odd things which have no need at all to pretend to be real because they are actually true.

PRODUCER What the devil are you talking about?

FATHER What I'm saying is that you really must be mad to do things the opposite way round: to create situations that obviously aren't true and try to make them seem to be really happening. But then I suppose that sort of madness is the only reason for your profession.

[*The* ACTORS *are indignant.*]

PRODUCER [*Getting up and glaring at him.*]   Oh, yes? So ours is a profession of madmen, is it?

FATHER   Well, if you try to make something look true when it obviously isn't, especially if you're not forced to do it, but do it for a game . . . Isn't it your job to give life on the stage to imaginary people?

PRODUCER [*Quickly answering him and speaking for the* ACTORS *who are growing more indignant.*]   I should like you to know, sir, that the actor's profession is one of great distinction. Even if nowadays the new writers only give us dull plays to act and puppets to present instead of men, I'd have you know that it is our boast that we have given life, here on this stage, to immortal works.

[*The* ACTORS, *satisfied, agree with and applaud the* PRODUCER].

FATHER [*Cutting in and following hard on his argument.*]   There! You see? Good! You've given life! You've created living beings with more genuine life than people have who breathe and wear clothes! Less real, perhaps, but nearer the truth. We are both saying the same thing.

[*The* ACTORS *look at each other, astonished.*]

PRODUCER   But just a moment! You said before . . .

FATHER   I'm sorry, but I said that before, about acting for fun, because you shouted at us and said you'd no time to waste on idiots, but you must know better than anyone that Nature uses human imagination to lift her work of creation to even higher levels.

PRODUCER   All right then: but where does all this get us?

FATHER   Nowhere. I want to try to show that one can be thrust into life in many ways, in many forms: as a tree or a stone, as water or a butterfly—or as a woman. It might even be as a character in a play.

PRODUCER [*Ironic, pretending to be annoyed.*]   And you, and these other people here, were thrust into life, as you put it, as characters in a play?

FATHER   Exactly! And alive, as you can see.

[*The* PRODUCER *and the* ACTORS *burst into laughter as if at a joke.*]

FATHER   I'm sorry you laugh like that, because we carry in us, as I said before, a story of terrible anguish as you can guess from this woman dressed in black.

[*Saying this, he offers his hand to the* MOTHER *and helps her up the last steps and, holding her still by the hand, leads her with a sense of tragic solemnity across the stage which is suddenly lit by a fantastic light.*

The LITTLE GIRL *and the* (LITTLE) BOY *follow the* MOTHER: *then the* SON *comes up and stands to one side in the background: then the* STEPDAUGHTER *follows and leans against the proscenium arch: the* ACTORS *are astonished at first, but then, full of admiration for the "entrance," they burst into applause—just as if it were a performance specially for them.*]

PRODUCER [*At first astonished and then indignant.*]   My God! Be quiet all of you. [*Turns to the* CHARACTERS.] And you lot get out! Clear off! [*Turns to the* STAGE MANAGER.] Jesus! Get them out of here.

STAGE MANAGER [*Comes forward but stops short as if held back by something strange.*]   Go on out! Get out!

FATHER [*To* PRODUCER.]   Oh no, please, you see, we . . .

PRODUCER [*Shouting.*]   We came here to work, you know.

LEADING ACTOR We really can't be messed about like this.

FATHER [*Resolutely, coming forward.*] I'm astonished! Why don't you believe me? Perhaps you are not used to seeing the characters created by an author spring into life up here on the stage face to face with each other. Perhaps it's because we're not in a script? [*He points to the* PROMPTER's *box.*]

STEPDAUGHTER [*Coming down to the* PRODUCER, *smiling and persuasive.*] Believe me, sir, we really are six of the most fascinating characters. But we've been neglected.

FATHER Yes, that's right, we've been neglected. In the sense that the author who created us, living in his mind, wouldn't or couldn't make us live in a written play for the world of art.[6] And that really is a crime sir, because whoever has the luck to be born a character can laugh even at death. Because a character will never die! A man will die, a writer, the instrument of creation: but what he has created will never die! And to be able to live for ever you don't need to have extraordinary gifts or be able to do miracles. Who was Sancho Panza? Who was Prospero?[7] But they will live for ever because—living seeds—they had the luck to find a fruitful soil, an imagination which knew how to grow them and feed them, so that they will live for ever.

PRODUCER This is all very well! But what do you want here?

FATHER We want to live, sir.

PRODUCER [*Ironically.*] For ever!

FATHER No, no: only for a few moments—in you.

AN ACTOR Listen to that!

LEADING ACTRESS They want to live in us!

YOUNG ACTOR [*Pointing to the* STEPDAUGHTER.] I don't mind . . . so long as I get her.

FATHER Listen, listen: the play is all ready to be put together and if you and your actors would like to, we can work it out now between us.

PRODUCER [*Annoyed.*] But what exactly do you want to do? We don't make up plays like that here! We present comedies and tragedies here.

FATHER That's right, we know that of course. That's why we've come.

PRODUCER And where's the script?

FATHER It's in us, sir. [*The* ACTORS *laugh.*] The play is in us: we are the play and we are impatient to show it to you: the passion inside us is driving us on.

STEPDAUGHTER [*Scornfully, with the tantalising charm of deliberate impudence.*] My passion, if only you knew! My passion for him! [*She points at the* FATHER *and suggests that she is going to embrace him: but stops and bursts into a screeching laugh.*]

FATHER [*With sudden anger.*] You keep out of this for the moment! And stop laughing like that!

STEPDAUGHTER Really? Then with your permission, ladies and gentlemen; even though it's only two months since I became an orphan, just watch how I can sing and dance.

6. In the 1925 preface to *Six Characters*, Pirandello explains that these characters came to him first as characters for a novel that he later abandoned. Haunted by their half-realized personalities, he decided to use the situation in a play.   7. The magician and exiled duke of Milan in Shakespeare's *The Tempest*. Sancho Panza was Don Quixote's servant in Cervantes's novel *Don Quixote* (1605–15).

[*The* ACTORS, *especially the younger, seem strangely attracted to her while she sings and dances and they edge closer and reach out their hands to catch hold of her.*[8] *She eludes them, and when the* ACTORS *applaud her and the* PRODUCER *speaks sharply to her she stays still quite removed from them all.*]

FIRST ACTOR   Very good! etc.

PRODUCER [*Angrily.*]   Be quiet! Do you think this is a nightclub? [*Turns to* FATHER *and asks with some concern.*] Is she a bit mad?

FATHER   Mad? Oh no—it's worse than that.

STEPDAUGHTER [*Suddenly running to the* PRODUCER.]   Yes. It's worse, much worse! Listen please! Let's put this play on at once, because you'll see that at a particular point I—when this darling little girl here— [*Taking the* LITTLE GIRL *by the hand from next to the* MOTHER *and crossing with her to the* PRODUCER.] Isn't she pretty? [*Takes her in her arms.*] Darling! Darling! [*Puts her down again and adds, moved very deeply but almost without wanting to.*] Well, this lovely little girl here, when God suddenly takes her from this poor Mother: and this little idiot here [*Turning to the* LITTLE BOY *and seizing him roughly by the sleeve.*] does the most stupid thing, like the half-wit he is,—then you will see me run away! Yes, you'll see me rush away! But not yet, not yet! Because, after all the intimate things there have been between him and me [*In the direction of the* FATHER, *with a horrible vulgar wink.*] I can't stay with them any longer, to watch the insult to this mother through that supercilious cretin over there. [*Pointing to the* SON.] Look at him! Look at him! Condescending, stand-offish, because he's the legitimate son, him! Full of contempt for me, for the boy and for the little girl: because we are bastards. Do you understand? Bastards. [*Running to the* MOTHER *and embracing her.*] And this poor mother—she—who is the mother of all of us—he doesn't want to recognise her as his own mother—and he looks down on her, he does, as if she were only the mother of the three of us who are bastards—the traitor. [*She says all this quickly, with great excitement, and after having raised her voice on the word "bastards" she speaks quietly, half-spitting the word "traitor."*]

MOTHER [*With deep anguish to the* PRODUCER.]   Sir, in the name of these two little ones, I beg you . . . [*Feels herself grow faint and sways.*] Oh, my God.

FATHER [*Rushing to support her with almost all the* ACTORS *bewildered and concerned.*]   Get a chair someone . . . quick, get a chair for this poor widow.

[*One of the* ACTORS *offers a chair: the others press urgently around. The* MOTHER, *seated now, tries to stop the* FATHER *lifting her veil.*]

ACTORS   Is it real? Has she really fainted? etc.

FATHER   Look at her, everybody, look at her.

MOTHER   No, for God's sake, stop it.

FATHER   Let them look?

MOTHER [*Lifting her hands and covering her face, desperately.*]   Oh, please, I beg you, stop him from doing what he is trying to do; it's hateful.

8. Pirandello uses a contemporary popular song, "Chu-Chin-Chow" from the Ziegfeld Follies of 1917, for the Stepdaughter to display her talents.

PRODUCER [*Overwhelmed, astounded.*]   It's no use, I don't understand this any more. [*To the* FATHER.] Is this woman your wife?

FATHER [*At once.*]   That's right, she is my wife.

PRODUCER   How is she a widow, then, if you're still alive?

[*The* ACTORS *are bewildered too and find relief in a loud laugh.*]

FATHER [*Wounded, with rising resentment.*]   Don't laugh! Please don't laugh like that! That's just the point, that's her own drama. You see, she had another man. Another man who ought to be here.

MOTHER   No, no! [*Crying out.*]

STEPDAUGHTER   Luckily for him he died. Two months ago, as I told you: we are in mourning for him, as you can see.

FATHER   Yes, he's dead: but that's not the reason he isn't here. He isn't here because—well just look at her, please, and you'll understand at once—hers is not a passionate drama of the love of two men, because she was incapable of love, she could feel nothing—except, perhaps a little gratitude (but not to me, to him). She's not a woman; she's a mother. And her drama—and, believe me, it's a powerful one—her drama is focused completely on these four children of the two men she had.

MOTHER   I had them? How dare you say that I had them, as if I wanted them myself? It was him, sir! He forced the other man on me. He made me go away with him!

STEPDAUGHTER [*Leaping up, indignantly.*]   It isn't true!

MOTHER [*Bewildered.*]   How isn't it true?

STEPDAUGHTER   It isn't true, it just isn't true.

MOTHER   What do you know about it?

STEPDAUGHTER   It isn't true. [*To the* PRODUCER.] Don't believe it! Do you know why she said that? She said it because of him, over there. [*Pointing to the* SON.] She tortures herself, she exhausts herself with worry and all because of the indifference of that son of hers. She wants to make him believe that she abandoned him when he was two years old because the Father made her do it.

MOTHER [*Passionately.*]   He did! He made me! God's my witness. [*To the* PRODUCER.] Ask him if it isn't true. [*Pointing to the* FATHER.] Make him tell our son it's true. [*Turning to the* STEPDAUGHTER.] You don't know anything about it.

STEPDAUGHTER   I know that when my father was alive you were always happy and contented. You can't deny it.

MOTHER   No, I can't deny it.

STEPDAUGHTER   He was always full of love and care for you. [*Turning to the* LITTLE BOY *with anger.*] Isn't it true? Admit it. Why don't you say something, you little idiot?

MOTHER   Leave the poor boy alone! Why do you want to make me appear ungrateful? You're my daughter. I don't in the least want to offend your father's memory. I've already told him that it wasn't my fault or even to please myself that I left his house and my son.

FATHER   It's quite true. It was my fault.

LEADING ACTOR [*To other actors.*]   Look at this. What a show!

LEADING ACTRESS   And we're the audience.

YOUNG ACTOR   For a change.

PRODUCER [*Beginning to be very interested.*] Let's listen to them! Quiet! Listen!

> [*He goes down the steps into the auditorium and stands there as if to get an idea of what the scene will look like from the audience's viewpoint.*]

SON [*Without moving, coldly, quietly, ironically.*] Yes, listen to his little scrap of philosophy. He's going to tell you all about the Daemon of Experiment.

FATHER You're a cynical idiot, and I've told you so a hundred times. [*To the* PRODUCER *who is now in the stalls.*] He sneers at me because of this expression I've found to defend myself.

SON Words, words.

FATHER Yes words, words! When we're faced by something we don't understand, by a sense of evil that seems as if it's going to swallow us, don't we all find comfort in a word that tells us nothing but that calms us?

STEPDAUGHTER And dulls your sense of remorse, too. That more than anything.

FATHER Remorse? No, that's not true. It'd take more than words to dull the sense of remorse in me.

STEPDAUGHTER It's taken a little money too, just a little money. The money that he was going to offer as payment, gentlemen.

> [*The* ACTORS *are horrified.*]

SON [*Contemptuously to his stepsister.*] That's a filthy trick.

STEPDAUGHTER A filthy trick? There it was in a pale blue envelope on the little mahogany table in the room behind the shop at Madame Pace's. You know Madame Pace, don't you? One of those Madames who sell "Robes et Manteaux" so that they can attract poor girls like me from decent families into their workroom.[9]

SON And she's bought the right to tyrannise over the whole lot of us with that money—with what he was going to pay her: and luckily—now listen carefully—he had no reason to pay it to her.

STEPDAUGHTER But it was close!

MOTHER [*Rising up angrily.*] Shame on you, daughter! Shame!

STEPDAUGHTER Shame? Not shame, revenge! I'm desperate, desperate to live that scene! The room . . . over here the showcase of coats, there the divan, there the mirror, and the screen, and over there in front of the window, that little mahogany table with the pale blue envelope and the money in it. I can see it all quite clearly. I could pick it up! But you should turn your faces away, gentlemen: because I'm nearly naked! I'm not blushing any longer—I leave that to him. [*Pointing at the* FATHER.] But I tell you he was very pale, very pale then. [*To the* PRODUCER.] Believe me.

PRODUCER I don't understand any more.

FATHER I'm not surprised when you're attacked like that! Why don't you put your foot down and let me have my say before you believe all these horrible slanders she's so viciously telling about me.

---

9. The implication is that Madame Pace (Italian for "peace") runs a call-girl operation under the guise of selling fashionable "dresses and coats."

STEPDAUGHTER   We don't want to hear any of your long winded fairy-stories.

FATHER   I'm not going to tell any fairy-stories! I want to explain things to him.

STEPDAUGHTER   I'm sure you do. Oh, yes! In your own special way.

[*The* PRODUCER *comes back up on stage to take control.*]

FATHER   But isn't that the cause of all the trouble? Words! We all have a world of things inside ourselves and each one of us has his own private world. How can we understand each other if the words I use have the sense and the value that I expect them to have, but whoever is listening to me inevitably thinks that those same words have a different sense and value, because of the private world he has inside himself too. We think we understand each other: but we never do. Look! All my pity, all my compassion for this woman [*Pointing to the* MOTHER.] she sees as ferocious cruelty.

MOTHER   But he turned me out of the house!

FATHER   There, do you hear? I turned her out! She really believed that I had turned her out.

MOTHER   You know how to talk. I don't . . . But believe me, sir, [*Turning to the* PRODUCER.] after he married me . . . I can't think why! I was a poor, simple woman.

FATHER   But that was the reason! I married you for your simplicity, that's what I loved in you, believing— [*He stops because she is making gestures of contradiction. Then, seeing the impossibility of making her understand, he throws his arms wide in a gesture of desperation and turns back to the* PRODUCER.] No, do you see? She says no! It's terrifying, sir, believe me, terrifying, her deafness, her mental deafness. [*He taps his forehead.*] Affection for her children, oh yes. But deaf, mentally deaf, deaf, sir, to the point of desperation.

STEPDAUGHTER   Yes, but make him tell you what good all his cleverness has brought us.

FATHER   If only we could see in advance all the harm that can come from the good we think we are doing.

[*The* LEADING ACTRESS, *who has been growing angry watching the* LEADING ACTOR *flirting with the* STEPDAUGHTER, *comes forward and snaps at the* PRODUCER.]

LEADING ACTRESS   Excuse me, are we going to go on with our rehearsal?

PRODUCER   Yes, of course. But I want to listen to this first.

YOUNG ACTOR   It's such a new idea.

YOUNG ACTRESS   It's fascinating.

LEADING ACTRESS   For those who are interested. [*She looks meaningfully at the* LEADING ACTOR.]

PRODUCER [*To the* FATHER.]   Look here, you must explain yourself more clearly. [*He sits down.*]

FATHER   Listen then. You see, there was a rather poor fellow working for me as my assistant and secretary, very loyal: he understood her in everything. [*Pointing to the* MOTHER.] But without a hint of deceit, you must believe that: he was good and simple, like her: neither of them was capable even of thinking anything wrong, let alone doing it.

STEPDAUGHTER   So instead he thought of it for them and did it too!

FATHER   It's not true! What I did was for their good—oh yes and mine too,

I admit it! The time had come when I couldn't say a word to either of them without there immediately flashing between them a sympathetic look: each one caught the other's eye for advice, about how to take what I had said, how not to make me angry. Well, that was enough, as I'm sure you'll understand, to put me in a bad temper all the time, in a state of intolerable exasperation.

PRODUCER   Then why didn't you sack this secretary of yours?

FATHER   Right! In the end I did sack him! But then I had to watch this poor woman wandering about in the house on her own, forlorn, like a stray animal you take in out of pity.

MOTHER   It's quite true.

FATHER [*Suddenly, turning to her, as if to stop her.*]   And what about the boy? Is that true as well?

MOTHER   But first he tore my son from me, sir.

FATHER   But not out of cruelty! It was so that he could grow up healthy and strong, in touch with the earth.

STEPDAUGHTER [*Pointing to the* SON *jeeringly.*]   And look at the result!

FATHER [*Quickly.*]   And is it my fault, too, that he's grown up like this? I took him to a nurse in the country, a peasant, because his mother didn't seem strong enough to me, although she is from a humble family herself. In fact that was what made me marry her. Perhaps it was superstitious of me; but what was I to do? I've always had this dreadful longing for a kind of sound moral healthiness.

[*The* STEPDAUGHTER *breaks out again into noisy laughter.*]

Make her stop that! It's unbearable.

PRODUCER   Stop it will you? Let me listen, for God's sake.

[*When the* PRODUCER *has spoken to her, she resumes her previous position . . . absorbed and distant, a half-smile on her lips. The* PRODUCER *comes down into the auditorium again to see how it looks from there.*]

FATHER   I couldn't bear the sight of this woman near me. [*Pointing to the* MOTHER.] Not so much because of the annoyance she caused me, you see, or even the feeling of being stifled, being suffocated that I got from her, as for the sorrow, the painful sorrow that I felt for her.

MOTHER   And he sent me away.

FATHER   With everything you needed, to the other man, to set her free from me.

MOTHER   And to set yourself free!

FATHER   Oh, yes, I admit it. And what terrible things came out of it. But I did it for the best, and more for her than for me: I swear it! [*Folds his arms: then turns suddenly to the* MOTHER.] I never lost sight of you did I? Until that fellow, without my knowing it, suddenly took you off to another town one day. He was idiotically suspicious of my interest in them, a genuine interest, I assure you, without any ulterior motive at all. I watched the new little family growing up round her with unbelievable tenderness, she'll confirm that. [*He points to the* STEPDAUGHTER.]

STEPDAUGHTER   Oh yes, I can indeed. I was a pretty little girl, you know, with plaits down to my shoulders and my little frilly knickers showing under my dress—so pretty—he used to watch me coming out of school. He came to see how I was maturing.

FATHER   That's shameful! It's monstrous.

STEPDAUGHTER   No it isn't! Why do you say it is?

FATHER   It's monstrous! Monstrous. [*He turns excitedly to the* PRODUCER *and goes on in explanation.*] After she'd gone away [*Pointing to the* MOTHER.] my house seemed empty. She'd been like a weight on my spirit but she'd filled the house with her presence. Alone in the empty rooms I wandered about like a lost soul. This boy here, [*Indicating the* SON.] growing up away from home—whenever he came back to the home—I don't know—but he didn't seem to be mine any more. We needed the mother between us, to link us together, and so he grew up by himself, apart, with no connection to me either through intellect or love. And then—it must seem odd, but it's true—first I was curious about and then strongly attracted to the little family that had come about because of what I'd done. And the thought of them began to fill all the emptiness that I felt around me. I needed, I really needed to believe that she was happy, wrapped up in the simple cares of her life, lucky because she was better off away from the complicated torments of a soul like mine. And to prove it, I used to watch that child coming out of school.

STEPDAUGHTER   Listen to him! He used to follow me along the street; he used to smile at me and when we came near the house he'd wave his hand—like this! I watched him, wide-eyed, puzzled. I didn't know who he was. I told my mother about him and she knew at once who it must be. [MOTHER *nods agreement.*] At first, she didn't let me go to school again, at any rate for a few days. But when I did go back, I saw him standing near the door again—looking ridiculous—with a brown paper bag in his hand. He came close and petted me: then he opened the bag and took out a beautiful straw hat with a hoop of rosebuds round it—for me!

PRODUCER   All this is off the point, you know.

SON [*Contemptuously.*]   Yes . . . literature, literature.

FATHER   What do you mean, literature? This is real life: real passions.

PRODUCER   That may be! But you can't put it on the stage just like that.

FATHER   That's right you can't. Because all this is only leading up to the main action. I'm not suggesting that this part should be put on the stage. In any case, you can see for yourself, [*Pointing at the* STEPDAUGHTER.] she isn't a pretty little girl any longer with plaits down to her shoulders.

STEPDAUGHTER   —and with frilly knickers showing under her frock.

FATHER   The drama begins now: and it's new and complex.

STEPDAUGHTER [*Coming forward, fierce and brooding.*]   As soon as my father died . . .

FATHER [*Quickly, not giving her time to speak.*]   They were so miserable. They came back here, but I didn't know about it because of the Mother's stubbornness. [*Pointing to the* MOTHER.] She can't really write you know; but she could have got her daughter to write, or the boy, or tell me that they needed help.

MOTHER   But tell me, sir, how could I have known how he felt?

FATHER   And hasn't that always been your fault? You've never known anything about how I felt.

MOTHER   After all the years away from him and after all that had happened.

FATHER   And was it my fault if that fellow took you so far away? [*Turning *back to the* PRODUCER.] Suddenly, overnight, I tell you, he'd found a job away from here without my knowing anything about it. I couldn't possibly trace them; and then, naturally I suppose, my interest in them grew less over the years. The drama broke out, unexpected and violent, when they came back: when I was driven in misery by the needs of my flesh, still alive with desire . . . and it is misery, you know, unspeakable misery for the man who lives alone and who detests sordid, casual affairs; not old enough to do without women, but not young enough to be able to go and look for one without shame! Misery? Is that what I called it. It's horrible, it's revolting, because there isn't a woman who will give her love to him any more. And when he realises this, he should do without . . . It's easy to say though. Each of us, face to face with other men, is clothed with some sort of dignity, but we know only too well all the unspeakable things that go on in the heart. We surrender, we give in to temptation: but afterwards we rise up out of it very quickly, in a desperate hurry to rebuild our dignity, whole and firm as if it were a gravestone that would cover every sign and memory of our shame, and hide it from even our own eyes. Everyone's like that, only some of us haven't the courage to talk about it.

STEPDAUGHTER   But they've all got the courage to do it!

FATHER   Yes! But only in secret! That's why it takes more courage to talk about it! Because if a man does talk about it—what happens then?—everybody says he's a cynic. And it's simply not true; he's just like everybody else; only better perhaps, because he's not afraid to use his intelligence to point out the blushing shame of human bestiality, that man, the beast, shuts his eyes to, trying to pretend it doesn't exist. And what about woman—what is she like? She looks at you invitingly, teasingly. You take her in your arms. But as soon as she feels your arms round her she closes her eyes. It's the sign of her mission, the sign by which she says to a man, "Blind yourself—I'm blind!"

STEPDAUGHTER   And when she doesn't close her eyes any more? What then? When she doesn't feel the need to hide from herself any more, to shut her eyes and hide her own shame. When she can see instead, dispassionately and dry-eyed this blushing shame of a man who has blinded himself, who is without love. What then? Oh, then what disgust, what utter disgust she feels for all these intellectual complications, for all this philosophy that points to the bestiality of man and then tries to defend him, to excuse him . . . I can't listen to him, sir. Because when a man says he needs to "simplify" life like this—reducing it to bestiality—and throws away every human scrap of innocent desire, genuine feeling, idealism, duty, modesty, shame, then there's nothing more contemptible and nauseating than his remorse—crocodile tears!

PRODUCER   Let's get to the point, let's get to the point. This is all chat.

FATHER   Right then! But a fact is like a sack—it won't stand up if it's empty. To make it stand up, first you have to put in it all the reasons and feelings that caused it in the first place. I couldn't possibly have known that when that fellow died they'd come back here, that they were desperately poor and that the Mother had gone out to work as a dressmaker, nor that she'd gone to work for Madame Pace, of all people.

STEPDAUGHTER   She's a very high-class dressmaker—you must understand that. She apparently has only high-class customers, but she has arranged things carefully so that these high-class customers in fact serve her—they give her a respectable front . . . without spoiling things for the other ladies at the shop who are not quite so high-class at all.

MOTHER Believe me, sir, the idea never entered my head that the old hag gave me work because she had an eye on my daughter . . .

STEPDAUGHTER Poor Mummy! Do you know what that woman would do when I took back the work that my mother had been doing? She would point out how the dress had been ruined by giving it to my mother to sew: she bargained, she grumbled. So, you see, I paid for it, while this poor woman here thought she was sacrificing herself for me and these two children, sewing dresses all night for Madame Pace.

[*The* ACTORS *make gestures and noises of disgust.*]

PRODUCER [*Quickly.*] And there one day, you met . . .

STEPDAUGHTER [*Pointing at the* FATHER.] Yes, him. Oh, he was an old customer of hers! What a scene that's going to be, superb!

FATHER With her, the mother, arriving—

STEPDAUGHTER [*Quickly, viciously.*] —Almost in time!

FATHER [*Crying out.*] —No, just in time, just in time! Because, luckily, I found out who she was in time. And I took them all back to my house, sir. Can you imagine the situation now, for the two of us living in the same house? She, just as you see her here: and I, not able to look her in the face.

STEPDAUGHTER It's so absurd! Do you think it's possible for me, sir, after what happened at Madame Pace's, to pretend that I'm a modest little miss, well brought up and virtuous just so that I can fit in with his damned pretensions to a "sound moral healthiness"?

FATHER This is the real drama for me; the belief that we all, you see, think of ourselves as one single person: but it's not true: each of us is several different people, and all these people live inside us. With one person we seem like this and with another we seem very different. But we always have the illusion of being the same person for everybody and of always being the same person in everything we do. But it's not true! It's not true! We find this out for ourselves very clearly when by some terrible chance we're suddenly stopped in the middle of doing something and we're left dangling there, suspended. We realise then, that every part of us was not involved in what we'd been doing and that it would be a dreadful injustice of other people to judge us only by this one action as we dangle there, hanging in chains, fixed for all eternity, as if the whole of one's personality were summed up in that single, interrupted action. Now do you understand this girl's treachery? She accidentally found me somewhere I shouldn't have been, doing something I shouldn't have been doing! She discovered a part of me that shouldn't have existed for her: and now she wants to fix on me a reality that I should never have had to assume for her: it came from a single brief and shameful moment in my life. This is what hurts me most of all. And you'll see that the play will make a tremendous impact from this idea of mine. But then, there's the position of the others. His . . . [*Pointing to the* SON.]

SON [*Shrugging his shoulders scornfully.*] Leave me out of it. I don't come into this.

FATHER   Why don't you come into this?

SON   I don't come into it and I don't want to come into it, because you know perfectly well that I wasn't intended to be mixed up with you lot.

STEPDAUGHTER   We're vulgar, common people, you see! He's a fine gentleman. But you've probably noticed that every now and then I look at him contemptuously, and when I do, he lowers his eyes—he knows the harm he's done me.

SON [*Not looking at her.*]   I have?

STEPDAUGHTER   Yes, you. It's your fault, dearie, that I went on the streets! Your fault! [*Movement of horror from the* ACTORS.] Did you or didn't you, with your attitude, deny us—I won't say the intimacy of your home— but that simple hospitality that makes guests feel comfortable? We were intruders who had come to invade the country of your "legitimacy"! [*Turning to the* PRODUCER.] I'd like you to have seen some of the little scenes that went on between him and me, sir. He says that I tyrannised over everyone. But don't you see? It was because of the way he treated us. He called it "vile" that I should insist on the right we had to move into his house with my mother—and she's his mother too. And I went into the house as its mistress.

SON [*Slowly coming forward.*]   They're really enjoying themselves, aren't they, sir? It's easy when they all gang up against me. But try to imagine what happened: one fine day, there is a son sitting quietly at home and he sees arrive as bold as brass, a young woman like this, who cheekily asks for his father, and heaven knows what business she has with him. Then he sees her come back with the same brazen look in her eye accompanied by that little girl there: and he sees her treat his father—without knowing why—in a most ambiguous and insolent way—asking him for money in a tone that leads one to suppose he really ought to give it, because he is obliged to do so.

FATHER   But I was obliged to do so: I owed it to your mother.

SON   And how was I to know that? When had I ever seen her before? When had I ever heard her mentioned? Then one day I see her come in with her, [*Pointing at the* STEPDAUGHTER.] that boy and that little girl: they say to me, "Oh, didn't you know? This is your mother, too." Little by little I began to understand, mostly from her attitude. [*Points to* STEPDAUGHTER.] Why they'd come to live in the house so suddenly. I can't and I won't say what I feel, and what I think. I wouldn't even like to confess it to myself. So I can't take any active part in this. Believe me, sir, I am a character who has not been fully developed dramatically, and I feel uncomfortable, most uncomfortable, in their company. So please leave me out of it.

FATHER   What! But it's precisely because you feel like this . . .

SON [*Violently exasperated.*]   How do you know what I feel?

FATHER   All right! I admit it! But isn't that a situation in itself? This withdrawing of yourself, it's cruel to me and to your mother: when she came back to the house, seeing you almost for the first time, not recognising you, but knowing that you're her own son . . . [*Turning to point out the* MOTHER *to the* PRODUCER.] There, look at her: she's weeping.

STEPDAUGHTER [*Angrily, stamping her foot.*]   Like the fool she is!

FATHER [*Quickly pointing at the* STEPDAUGHTER *to the* PRODUCER.]   She can't stand that young man, you know. [*Turning and referring to the* SON.] He says that he doesn't come into it, but he's really the pivot of the action! Look here at this little boy, who clings to his mother all the time, frightened, humiliated. And it's because of him over there! Perhaps this little boy's problem is the worst of all: he feels an outsider, more than the others do; he feels so mortified, so humiliated just being in the house,— because it's charity, you see. [*Quietly*.] He's like his father: timid; he doesn't say anything . . .

PRODUCER It's not a good idea at all, using him: you don't know what a nuisance children are on the stage.

FATHER He won't need to be on the stage for long. Nor will the little girl— she's the first to go.

PRODUCER That's good! Yes. I tell you all this interests me—it interests me very much. I'm sure we've the material here for a good play.

STEPDAUGHTER [*Trying to push herself in.*] With a character like me you have!

FATHER [*Driving her off, wanting to hear what the* PRODUCER *has decided.*] You stay out of it!

PRODUCER [*Going on, ignoring the interruption.*] It's new, yes.

FATHER Oh, it's absolutely new!

PRODUCER You've got a nerve, though, haven't you, coming here and throwing it at me like this?

FATHER I'm sure you understand. Born as we are for the *stage* . . .

PRODUCER Are you amateur actors?

FATHER No! I say we are born for the stage because . . .

PRODUCER Come on now! You're an old hand at this, at acting!

FATHER No I'm not. I only act, as everyone does, the part in life that he's chosen for himself, or that others have chosen for him. And you can see that sometimes my own passion gets a bit out of hand, a bit theatrical, as it does with all of us.

PRODUCER Maybe, maybe . . . But you do see, don't you, that without an author . . . I could give you someone's address . . .

FATHER Oh no! Look here! You do it.

PRODUCER Me? What are you talking about?

FATHER Yes, you. Why not?

PRODUCER Because I've never written anything!

FATHER Well, why not start now, if you don't mind my suggesting it? There's nothing to it. Everybody's doing it. And your job is even easier, because we're here, all of us, alive before you.

PRODUCER That's not enough.

FATHER Why isn't it enough? When you've seen us live our drama . . .

PRODUCER Perhaps so. But we'll still need someone to write it.

FATHER Only to write it down, perhaps, while it happens in front of him— live—scene by scene. It'll be enough to sketch it out simply first and then run through it.

PRODUCER [*Coming back up, tempted by the idea.*] Do you know I'm almost tempted . . . just for fun . . . it might work.

FATHER Of course it will. You'll see what wonderful scenes will come right out of it! I could tell you what they will be!

PRODUCER You tempt me . . . you tempt me! We'll give it a chance. Come with me to the office. [*Turning to the* ACTORS.] Take a break: but don't go far away. Be back in a quarter of an hour or twenty minutes. [*To the* FATHER.] Let's see, let's try it out. Something extraordinary might come out of this.

FATHER   Of course it will! Don't you think it'd be better if the others came too? [*Indicating the other* CHARACTERS.]

PRODUCER   Yes, come on, come on. [*Going, then turning to speak to the* ACTORS.] Don't forget: don't be late: back in a quarter of an hour.

[*The* PRODUCER *and the* SIX CHARACTERS *cross the stage and go. The* ACTORS *look at each other in astonishment.*]

LEADING ACTOR   Is he serious? What's he going to do?

YOUNG ACTOR   I think he's gone round the bend.

ANOTHER ACTOR   Does he expect to make up a play in five minutes?

YOUNG ACTOR   Yes, like the old actors in the commedia dell'arte![1]

LEADING ACTRESS   Well if he thinks I'm going to appear in that sort of nonsense . . .

YOUNG ACTOR   Nor me!

FOURTH ACTOR   I should like to know who they are.

THIRD ACTOR   Who do you think? They're probably escaped lunatics—or crooks.

YOUNG ACTOR   And is he taking them seriously?

YOUNG ACTRESS   It's vanity. The vanity of seeing himself as an author.

LEADING ACTOR   I've never heard of such a thing! If the theatre, ladies and gentlemen, is reduced to this . . .

FIFTH ACTOR   I'm enjoying it!

THIRD ACTOR   Really! We shall have to wait and see what happens next I suppose.

[*Talking, they leave the stage. Some go out through the back door, some to the dressing-rooms.*
The curtain stays up.
The interval lasts twenty minutes.]

Act Two

The theatre warning-bell sounds to call the audience back. From the dressing-rooms, the door at the back and even from the auditorium, the ACTORS, *the* STAGE MANAGER, *the* STAGE HANDS, *the* PROMPTER, *the* PROPERTY MAN *and the* PRODUCER, *accompanied by the* SIX CHARACTERS *all come back on to the stage.*
The house lights go out and the stage lights come on again.

PRODUCER   Come on, everybody! Are we all here? Quiet now! Listen! Let's get started! Stage manager?

STAGE MANAGER   Yes, I'm here.

PRODUCER   Give me that little parlour setting, will you? A couple of plain flats and a door flat will do. Hurry up with it!

[*The* STAGE MANAGER *runs off to order someone to do this immedi-*

---

1. A form of popular theater beginning in sixteenth-century Italy; the actors improvised dialogue according to basic comic or dramatic plots and in response to the audience's reaction.

ately and at the same time the PRODUCER *is making arrangements with the* PROPERTY MAN, *the* PROMPTER, *and the* ACTORS: *the two flats and the door flat are painted in pink and gold stripes.*]

PRODUCER [*To* PROPERTY MAN.]   Go see if we have a sofa in stock.

PROPERTY MAN   Yes, there's that green one.

STEPDAUGHTER   No, no, not a green one! It was yellow, yellow velvet with flowers on it: it was enormous! And so comfortable!

PROPERTY MAN   We haven't got one like that.

PRODUCER   It doesn't matter! Give me whatever there is.

STEPDAUGHTER   What do you mean, it doesn't matter? It was Mme. Pace's famous sofa.

PRODUCER   It's only for a rehearsal! Please, don't interfere. [*To the* STAGE MANAGER.] Oh, and see if there's a shop window, will you—preferably a long, low one.

STEPDAUGHTER   And a little table, a little mahogany table for the blue envelope.

STAGE MANAGER [*To the* PRODUCER.]   There's that little gold one.

PRODUCER   That'll do—bring it.

FATHER   A mirror!

STEPDAUGHTER   And a screen! A screen, please, or I won't be able to manage, will I?

STAGE MANAGER   All right. We've lots of big screens, don't you worry.

PRODUCER [*To* STEPDAUGHTER.]   Then don't you want some coat-hangers and some clothes racks?

STEPDAUGHTER   Yes, lots of them, lots of them.

PRODUCER [*To the* STAGE MANAGER.]   See how many there are and have them brought up.

STAGE MANAGER   Right, I'll see to it.

[*The* STAGE MANAGER *goes off to do it: and while the* PRODUCER *is talking to the* PROMPTER, *the* CHARACTERS *and the* ACTORS, *the* STAGE MANAGER *is telling the* SCENE SHIFTERS *where to set up the furniture they have brought.*]

PRODUCER [*To the* PROMPTER.]   Now you, go sit down, will you? Look, this is an outline of the play, act by act. [*He hands him several sheets of paper.*] But you'll need to be on your toes.

PROMPTER   Shorthand?

PRODUCER [*Pleasantly surprised.*]   Oh, good! You know shorthand?

PROMPTER   I don't know much about prompting, but I do know about shorthand.

PRODUCER   Thank God for that anyway! [*He turns to a* STAGE HAND.] Go fetch me some paper from my office—lots of it—as much as you can find!

[*The* STAGE HAND *goes running off and then comes back shortly with a bundle of paper that he gives to the* PROMPTER.]

PRODUCER [*Crossing to the* PROMPTER.]   Follow the scenes, one after another, as they are played and try to get the lines down . . . at least the most important ones. [*Then turning to the* ACTORS.] Get out of the way everybody! Here, go over to the prompt side [*Pointing to stage left.*] and pay attention.

LEADING ACTRESS   But, excuse me, we . . . .

PRODUCER [*Anticipating her.*]   You won't be expected to improvise, don't worry!

LEADING ACTOR   Then what are we expected to do?

PRODUCER   Nothing! Just go over there, listen and watch. You'll all be given your parts later written out. Right now we're going to rehearse, as well as we can. And they will be doing the rehearsal. [*He points to the* CHARACTERS.]

FATHER [*Rather bewildered, as if he had fallen from the clouds into the middle of the confusion on the stage.*]   We are? Excuse me, but what do you mean, a rehearsal?

PRODUCER   I mean a rehearsal—a rehearsal for the benefit of the actors. [*Pointing to the* ACTORS.]

FATHER   But if we are the characters . . .

PRODUCER   That's right, you're "the characters": but characters don't act here, my dear chap. It's actors who act here. The characters are there in the script—[*Pointing to the* PROMPTER.] that's when there is a script.

FATHER   That's the point! Since there isn't one and you have the luck to have the characters alive in front of you . . .

PRODUCER   Great! You want to do everything yourselves, do you? To act your own play, to produce your own play!

FATHER   Well yes, just as we are.

PRODUCER   That would be an experience for us, I can tell you!

LEADING ACTOR   And what about us? What would we be doing then?

PRODUCER   Don't tell me you think you know how to act! Don't make me laugh! [*The* ACTORS *in fact laugh.*] There you are, you see, you've made them laugh. [*Then remembering.*] But let's get back to the point! We need to cast the play. Well, that's easy: it almost casts itself. [*To the* SECOND ACTRESS.] You, the mother. [*To the* FATHER.] You'll need to give her a name.

FATHER   Amalia.

PRODUCER   But that's the real name of your wife isn't it? We can't use her real name.

FATHER   But why not? That is her name . . . But perhaps if this lady is to play the part . . . [*Indicating the* ACTRESS *vaguely with a wave of his hand.*] I don't know what to say . . . I'm already starting to . . . how can I explain it . . . to sound false, my own words sound like someone else's.

PRODUCER   Now don't worry yourself about it, don't worry about it at all. We'll work out the right tone of voice. As for the name, if you want it to be Amalia, then Amalia it shall be: or we can find another. For the moment we'll refer to the characters like this: [*To the* YOUNG ACTOR, *the juvenile lead.*] you are The Son. [*To the* LEADING ACTRESS.] You, of course, are The Stepdaughter.

STEPDAUGHTER [*Excitedly.*]   What did you say? That woman is me? [*Bursts into laughter.*]

PRODUCER [*Angrily.*]   What are you laughing at?

LEADING ACTRESS [*Indignantly.*]   Nobody has ever dared to laugh at me before! Either you treat me with respect or I'm walking out! [*Starting to go.*]

STEPDAUGHTER   I'm sorry. I wasn't really laughing at you.

PRODUCER [*To the* STEPDAUGHTER.]   You should feel proud to be played by . . .

LEADING ACTRESS [*Quickly, scornfully.*]   . . . that woman!

STEPDAUGHTER   But I wasn't thinking about her, honestly. I was thinking about me: I can't see myself in you at all . . . you're not a bit like me!

FATHER   Yes, that's right: you see, our meaning . . .

PRODUCER   What are you talking about, "our meaning"? Do you think you have exclusive rights to what you represent? Do you think it can only exist inside you? Not a bit of it!

FATHER   What? Don't we even have our own meaning?

PRODUCER   Not a bit of it! Whatever you mean is only material here, to which the actors give form and body, voice and gesture, and who, through their art, have given expression to much better material than what you have to offer: yours is really very trivial and if it stands up on the stage, the credit, believe me, will all be due to my actors.

FATHER   I don't dare to contradict you. But you for your part, must believe me—it doesn't seem trivial to us. We are suffering terribly now, with these bodies, these faces . . .

PRODUCER [*Interrupting impatiently.*]   Yes, well, the make-up will change that, make-up will change that, at least as far as the faces are concerned.

FATHER   Yes, but the voices, the gestures . . .

PRODUCER   That's enough! You can't come on the stage here as yourselves. It is our actors who will represent you here: and let that be the end of it!

FATHER   I understand that. But now I think I see why our author who saw us alive as we are here now, didn't want to put us on the stage. I don't want to offend your actors. God forbid that I should! But I think that if I saw myself represented . . . by I don't know whom . . .

LEADING ACTOR [*Rising majestically and coming forward, followed by a laughing group of* YOUNG ACTRESSES.]   By me, if you don't object.

FATHER [*Respectfully, smoothly.*]   I shall be honoured, sir. [*He bows.*] But I think, that no matter how hard this gentleman works with all his will and all his art to identify himself with me . . . [*He stops, confused.*]

LEADING ACTOR   Yes, go on.

FATHER   Well, I was saying the performance he will give, even if he is made up to look like me . . . I mean with the difference in our appearance . . . [*All the* ACTORS *laugh.*] it will be difficult for it to be a performance of me as I really am. It will be more like—well, not just because of his figure—it will be more an interpretation of what I am, what he believes me to be, and not how I know myself to be. And it seems to me that this should be taken into account by those who are going to comment on us.

PRODUCER   So you are already worrying about what the critics will say, are you? And I'm still waiting to get this thing started! The critics can say what they like: and we'll worry about putting on the play. If we can! [*Stepping out of the group and looking around.*] Come on, come on! Is the scene set for us yet? [*To the* ACTORS *and* CHARACTERS.] Out of the way! Let's have a look at it. [*Climbing down off the stage.*] Don't let's waste any more time. [*To the* STEPDAUGHTER.] Does it look all right to you?

SON   What! That? I don't recognise it at all.

PRODUCER   Good God! Did you expect us to reconstruct the room at the back of Mme. Pace's shop here on the stage? [*To the* FATHER.] Did you say the room had flowered wallpaper?

FATHER   White, yes.

PRODUCER   Well it's not white: it's striped. That sort of thing doesn't matter at all! As for the furniture, it looks to me as if we have nearly everything we need. Move that little table a bit further downstage. [*A* STAGE HAND *does it. To the* PROPERTY MAN.] Go and fetch an envelope, pale blue if you can find one, and give it to that gentleman there. [*Pointing to the* FATHER.]

STAGE HAND   An envelope for letters?

PRODUCER ⎱
FATHER ⎰   Yes, an envelope for letters!

STAGE HAND   Right. [*He goes off.*]

PRODUCER   Now then, come on! The first scene is the young lady's. [*The* LEADING ACTRESS *comes to the centre.*] No, no, not yet. I said the young lady's. [*He points to the* STEPDAUGHTER.] You stay there and watch.

STEPDAUGHTER [*Adding quickly.*]   . . . how I bring it to life.

LEADING ACTRESS [*Resenting this.*]   I shall know how to bring it to life, don't you worry, when I am allowed to.

PRODUCER [*His head in his hands.*]   Ladies, please, no more arguments! Now then. The first scene is between the young lady and Mme. Pace. Oh! [*Worried, turning round and looking out into the auditorium.*] Where is Mme. Pace?

FATHER   She isn't here with us.

PRODUCER   So what do we do now?

FATHER   But she is real. She's real too!

PRODUCER   All right. So where is she?

FATHER   May I deal with this? [*Turns to the* ACTRESSES.] Would each of you ladies be kind enough to lend me a hat, a coat, a scarf or something?

ACTRESSES [*Some are surprised or amused.*]   What? My scarf? A coat? What's he want my hat for? What are you wanting to do with them? [*All the* ACTRESSES *are laughing.*]

FATHER   Oh, nothing much, just hang them up here on the racks for a minute or two. Perhaps someone would be kind enough to lend me a coat?

ACTORS   Just a coat? Come on, more! The man must be mad.

AN ACTRESS   What for? Only my coat?

FATHER   Yes, to hang up here, just for a moment. I'm very grateful to you. Do you mind?

ACTRESSES [*Taking off various hats, coats, scarves, laughing and going to hang them on the racks.*]   Why not? Here you are. I really think it's crazy. Is it to dress the set?

FATHER   Yes, exactly. It's to dress the set.

PRODUCER   Would you mind telling me what you are doing?

FATHER   Yes, of course: perhaps, if we dress the set better, she will be drawn by the articles of her trade and, who knows, she may even come to join us . . . [*He invites them to watch the door at the back of the set.*] Look! Look!

   [*The door at the back opens and* MME. PACE *takes a few steps down-*

stage: she is a gross old harridan wearing a ludicrous carroty-coloured wig with a single red rose stuck in at one side, Spanish fashion: garishly made-up: in a vulgar but stylish red silk dress, holding an ostrich-feather fan in one hand and a cigarette between two fingers in the other. At the sight of this apparition, the ACTORS *and the* PRODUCER *immediately jump off the stage with cries of fear, leaping down into the auditorium and up the aisles. The* STEPDAUGHTER, *however, runs across to* MME. PACE, *and greets her respectfully, as if she were the mistress.*]

STEPDAUGHTER [*Running across to her.*]   Here she is! Here she is!

FATHER [*Smiling broadly.*]   It's her! What did I tell you? Here she is!

PRODUCER [*Recovering from his shock, indignantly.*]   What sort of trick is this?

LEADING ACTOR [*Almost at the same time as the others.*]   What the hell is happening?

JUVENILE LEAD   Where on earth did they get that extra from?

YOUNG ACTRESS   They were keeping her hidden!

LEADING ACTRESS   It's a game, a conjuring trick!

FATHER   Wait a minute! Why do you want to spoil a miracle by being factual? Can't you see this is a miracle of reality, that is born, brought to life, lured here, reproduced, just for the sake of this scene, with more right to be alive here than you have? Perhaps it has more truth than you have yourselves. Which actress can improve on Mme. Pace there? Well? That is the real Mme. Pace. You must admit that the actress who plays her will be less true than she is herself—and there she is in person! Look! My daughter recognised her straight away and went to meet her. Now watch—just watch this scene.

[*Hesitantly, the* PRODUCER *and the* ACTORS *move back to their original places on the stage.*

But the scene between the STEPDAUGHTER *and* MME. PACE *had already begun while the* ACTORS *were protesting and the* FATHER *explaining: it is being played under their breaths, very quietly, very naturally, in a way that is obviously impossible on stage. So when the* ACTORS' *attention is recalled by the* FATHER *they turn and see that* MME. PACE *has just put her hand under the* STEPDAUGHTER's *chin to make her lift her head up: they also hear her speak in a way that is unintelligible to them. They watch and listen hard for a few moments, then they start to make fun of them.*]

PRODUCER   Well?

LEADING ACTOR   What's she saying?

LEADING ACTRESS   Can't hear a thing!

JUVENILE LEAD   Louder! Speak up!

STEPDAUGHTER [*Leaving* MME. PACE *who has an astonishing smile on her face, and coming down to the* ACTORS.]   Louder? What do you mean, "Louder"? What we're talking about you can't talk about loudly. I could shout about it a moment ago to embarrass him [*Pointing to the* FATHER.] to shame him and to get my own back on him! But it's a different matter for Mme. Pace. It would mean prison for her.

PRODUCER   What the hell are you on about? Here in the theatre you have to make yourself heard! Don't you see that? We can't hear you even from here, and we're on the stage with you! Imagine what it would be like with an audience out front! You need to make the scene go! And after all, you would speak normally to each other when you're alone, and you will be, because we shan't be here anyway. I mean we're only here because it's a rehearsal. So just imagine that there you are in the room at the back of the shop, and there's no one to hear you.

[*The* STEPDAUGHTER, *with a knowing smile, wags her finger and her head rather elegantly, as if to say no.*]

PRODUCER   Why not?

STEPDAUGHTER [*Mysteriously, whispering loudly.*]   Because there is some-one who will hear if she speaks normally. [*Pointing to* MME. PACE.]

PRODUCER [*Anxiously.*]   You're not going to make someone else appear are you?

[*The* ACTORS *get ready to dive off the stage again.*]

FATHER   No, no. She means me. I ought to be over there, waiting behind the door: and Mme. Pace knows I'm there, so excuse me will you: I'll go there now so that I shall be ready for my entrance.

[*He goes towards the back of the stage.*]

PRODUCER [*Stopping him.*]   No, no wait a minute! You must remember the stage conventions! Before you can go on to that part . . .

STEPDAUGHTER [*Interrupts him.*]   Oh yes, let's get on with that part. Now! Now! I'm dying to do that scene. If he wants to go through it now, I'm ready!

PRODUCER [*Shouting.*]   But before that we must have, clearly stated, the scene between you and her. [*Pointing to* MME. PACE.] Do you see?

STEPDAUGHTER   Oh God! She's only told me what you already know, that my mother's needlework is badly done again, the dress is spoilt and that I shall have to be patient if I want her to go on helping us out of our mess.

MME. PACE [*Coming forward, with a great air of importance.*]   Ah, yes, sir, for that I do not wish to make a profit, to make advantage.

PRODUCER [*Half frightened.*]   What? Does she really speak like that?

[*All the* ACTORS *burst out laughing.*]

STEPDAUGHTER [*Laughing too.*]   Yes, she speaks like that, half in Spanish, in the silliest way imaginable!

MME. PACE   Ah it is not good manners that you laugh at me when I make myself to speak, as I can, English, señor.

PRODUCER   No, no, you're right! Speak like that, please speak like that, madam. It'll be marvelous. Couldn't be better! It'll add a little touch of comedy to a rather crude situation. Speak like that! It'll be great!

STEPDAUGHTER   Great! Why not? When you hear a proposition made in that sort of accent, it'll almost seem like a joke, won't it? Perhaps you'll want to laugh when you hear that there's an "old señor"² who wants to "amuse himself with me"—isn't that right, Madame?

MME. PACE   Not so old . . . but not quite young, no? But if he is not to your taste . . . he is, how you say, discreet!

[*The* MOTHER *leaps up, to the astonishment and dismay of the* ACTORS *who had not been paying any attention to her, so that when*

2. Old gentleman.

*she shouts out they are startled and then smilingly restrain her: how-
ever she has already snatched off* MME. PACE's *wig and flung it on
the floor.*]

MOTHER   You witch! Witch! Murderess! Oh, my daughter!

STEPDAUGHTER [*Running across and taking hold of the* MOTHER.]   No! No!
Mother! Please!

FATHER [*Running across to her as well.*]   Calm yourself, calm yourself!
Come and sit down.

MOTHER   Get her away from here!

STEPDAUGHTER [*To the* PRODUCER *who has also crossed to her.*]   My
mother can't bear to be in the same place with her.

FATHER [*Also speaking quietly to the* PRODUCER.]   They can't possibly be
in the same place! That's why she wasn't with us when we first came, do
you see! If they meet, everything's given away from the very beginning.

PRODUCER   It's not important, that's not important! This is only a first run-
through at the moment! It's all useful stuff, even if it is confused. I'll sort
it all out later. [*Turning to the* MOTHER *and taking her to sit down on her
chair.*]   Come on, my dear, take it easy; take it easy: come and sit down
again.

STEPDAUGHTER   Go on, Mme. Pace.

MME. PACE [*Offended.*]   Oh no, thank-you! I no longer do nothing here
with your mother present.

STEPDAUGHTER   Get on with it, bring in this "old señor" who wants to
"amuse himself with me"! [*Turning majestically to the others.*] You see,
this next scene has got to be played out—we must do it now. [*To* MME.
PACE.] Oh, you can go!

MME. PACE   Ah, I go, I go—I go! Most probably! I go!
   [*She leaves banging her wig back into place, glaring furiously at the
   ACTORS who applaud her exit, laughing loudly.*]

STEPDAUGHTER [*To the* FATHER.]   Now you come on! No, you don't need
to go off again! Come back! Pretend you've just come in! Look, I'm standing here with my eyes on the ground, modestly—well, come on, speak
up! Use that special sort of voice, like somebody who has just come in.
"Good afternoon, my dear."

PRODUCER [*Off the stage by now.*]   Look here, who's the director here, you
or me? [*To the* FATHER *who looks uncertain and bewildered.*] Go on, do
as she says: go upstage—no, no don't bother to make an entrance. Then
come down stage again.

   [*The* FATHER *does as he is told, half mesmerised. He is very pale but
   already involved in the reality of his re-created life, smiles as he draws
   near the back of the stage, almost as if he genuinely is not aware of
   the drama that is about to sweep over him. The* ACTORS *are immediately intent on the scene that is beginning now.*]

The Scene

FATHER [*Coming forward with a new note in his voice.*]   Good afternoon,
my dear.

STEPDAUGHTER [*Her head down trying to hide her fright.*]   Good afternoon.

FATHER [*Studying her a little under the brim of her hat which partly hides*

her face from him and seeing that she is very young, he exclaims to himself
a little complacently and a little guardedly because of the danger of being
compromised in a risky adventure.]   Ah . . . but . . . tell me, this won't be
the first time, will it? The first time you've been here?
STEPDAUGHTER   No, sir.
FATHER   You've been here before? [*And after the* STEPDAUGHTER *has nod-*
ded an answer.] More than once? [*He waits for her reply: tries again to*
look at her under the brim of her hat: smiles: then says.] Well then . . . it
shouldn't be too . . . May I take off your hat?
STEPDAUGHTER [*Quickly, to stop him, unable to conceal her shudder of fear*
and disgust.]   No, don't! I'll do it!
   [*She takes it off unsteadily.*
   The MOTHER *watches the scene intently with the* SON *and the two*
   smaller children who cling close to her all the time: they make a
   group on one side of the stage opposite the ACTORS: *She follows the*
   words and actions of the FATHER *and the* STEPDAUGHTER *in this*
   scene with a variety of expressions on her face—sadness, dismay,
   anxiety, horror: sometimes she turns her face away and sobs.]
MOTHER   Oh God! Oh God!
FATHER [*He stops as if turned to stone by the sobbing: then he goes on in the*
same tone of voice.]   Here, give it to me. I'll hang it up for you. [*He takes*
the hat in his hand.] But such a pretty, dear little head like yours should
have a much smarter hat than this! Would you like to help me choose
one, then, from these hats of Madame's hanging up here? Would you?
YOUNG ACTRESS [*Interrupting.*]   Be careful! Those are our hats!
PRODUCER [*Quickly and angrily.*]   For God's sake, shut up! Don't try to be
funny! We're rehearsing! [*Turns back to the* STEPDAUGHTER.] Please go
on, will you, from where you were interrupted.
STEPDAUGHTER [*Going on.*]   No, thank you, sir.
FATHER   Oh, don't say no to me please! Say you'll have one—to please me.
Isn't this a pretty one—look! And then it will please Madame too, you
know. She's put them out here on purpose, of course.
STEPDAUGHTER   No, look, I could never wear it.
FATHER   Are you thinking of what they would say at home when you went
in wearing a new hat? Goodness me! Don't you know what to do? Shall
I tell you what to say at home?
STEPDAUGHTER [*Furiously, nearly exploding.*]   That's not why! I couldn't
wear it because . . . as you can see: you should have noticed it before.
[*Indicating her black dress.*]
FATHER   You're in mourning! Oh, forgive me. You're right, I see that now.
Please forgive me. Believe me, I'm really very sorry.
STEPDAUGHTER [*Gathering all her strength and making herself overcome her*
contempt and revulsion.]   That's enough. Don't go on, that's enough. I
ought to be thanking you and not letting you blame yourself and get
upset. Don't think any more about what I told you, please. And I should
do the same. [*Forcing herself to smile and adding.*] I should try to forget
that I'm dressed like this.
PRODUCER [*Interrupting, turning to the* PROMPTER *in the box and jumping*
up on the stage again.]   Hold it, hold it! Don't put that last line down,
leave it out. [*Turning to the* FATHER *and the* STEPDAUGHTER.] It's going

well! It's going well! [*Then to the* FATHER *alone.*] Then we'll put in there
the bit that we talked about. [*To the* ACTORS.] That scene with the hats
is good, isn't it?

STEPDAUGHTER   But the best bit is coming now! Why can't we get on
with it?

PRODUCER   Just be patient, wait a minute. [*Turning and moving across to
the* ACTORS.] Of course, it'll all have to be made a lot more light-hearted.

LEADING ACTOR   We shall have to play it a lot quicker, I think.

LEADING ACTRESS   Of course: there's nothing particularly difficult in it.
[*To the* LEADING ACTOR.] Shall we run through it now?

LEADING ACTOR   Yes right . . . Shall we take it from my entrance? [*He goes
to his position behind the door upstage.*]

PRODUCER [*To the* LEADING ACTRESS.]   Now then, listen, imagine the
scene between you and Mme. Pace is finished. I'll write it up myself
properly later on. You ought to be over here I think—[*She goes the opposite way.*] Where are you going now?

LEADING ACTRESS   Just a minute, I want to get my hat—[*She crosses to
take her hat from the stand.*]

PRODUCER   Right, good, ready now? You are standing here with your head
down.

STEPDAUGHTER [*Very amused.*]   But she's not dressed in black!

LEADING ACTRESS   Oh, but I shall be, and I'll look a lot better than you
do, darling.

PRODUCER [*To the* STEPDAUGHTER.]   Shut up, will you! Go over there and
watch! You might learn something! [*Clapping his hands.*] Right! Come
on! Quiet please! Take it from his entrance.

   [*He climbs off stage so that he can see better. The door opens at the
   back of the set and the* LEADING ACTOR *enters with the lively, knowing air of an ageing roué.*[3] *The playing of the following scene by the*
   ACTORS *must seem from the very beginning to be something quite
   different from the earlier scene, but without having the faintest air
   of parody in it.*

      Naturally the STEPDAUGHTER *and the* FATHER *unable to see them-
   selves in the* LEADING ACTOR *and* LEADING ACTRESS, *hearing their
   words said by them, express their reactions in different ways, by gestures, or smiles or obvious protests so that we are aware of their
   suffering, their astonishment, their disbelief.*

      The PROMPTER's *voice is heard clearly between every line in the
   scene, telling the* ACTORS *what to say next.*]

LEADING ACTOR   Good afternoon, my dear.

FATHER [*Immediately, unable to restrain himself.*]   Oh, no!

   [*The* STEPDAUGHTER, *watching the* LEADING ACTOR *enter this way,
   bursts into laughter.*]

PRODUCER [*Furious.*]   Shut up, for God's sake! And don't you dare laugh
like that! We're never going to get anywhere at this rate.

STEPDAUGHTER [*Coming to the front.*]   I'm sorry, I can't help it! The lady
stands exactly where you told her to stand and she never moved. But if

---

3. Dissipated lover.

it were me and I heard someone say good afternoon to me in that way and with a voice like that I should burst out laughing—so I did.

FATHER [*Coming down a little too.*]   Yes, she's right, the whole manner, the voice . . .

PRODUCER   To hell with the manner and the voice! Get out of the way, will you, and let me watch the rehearsal!

LEADING ACTOR [*Coming down stage.*]   If I have to play an old man who has come to a knocking shop—

PRODUCER   Take no notice, ignore them. Go on please! It's going well, it's going well! [*He waits for the* ACTOR *to begin again.*] Right, again!

LEADING ACTOR   Good afternoon, my dear.

LEADING ACTRESS   Good afternoon.

LEADING ACTOR [*Copying the gestures of the* FATHER, *looking under the brim of the hat, but expressing distinctly the two emotions, first, complacent satisfaction and then anxiety.*]   Ah! But tell me . . . this won't be the first time I hope.

FATHER [*Instinctively correcting him.*]   Not "I hope"—"will it," "will it."

PRODUCER   Say "will it"—and it's a question.

LEADING ACTOR [*Glaring at the* PROMPTER.]   I distinctly heard him say "I hope."

PRODUCER   So what? It's all the same, "I hope" or "isn't it." It doesn't make any difference. Carry on, carry on. But perhaps it should still be a little bit lighter; I'll show you—watch me! [*He climbs up on the stage again, and going back to the entrance, he does it himself.*] Good afternoon, my dear.

LEADING ACTRESS   Good afternoon.

PRODUCER   Ah, tell me . . . [*He turns to the* LEADING ACTOR *to make sure that he has seen the way he has demonstrated of looking under the brim of the hat.*] You see—surprise . . . anxiety and self-satisfaction. [*Then, starting again, he turns to the* LEADING ACTRESS.] This won't be the first time, will it? The first time you've been here? [*Again turns to the* LEADING ACTOR *questioningly.*] Right? [*To the* LEADING ACTRESS.] And then she says, "No, sir." [*Again to* LEADING ACTOR.] See what I mean? More subtlety. [*And he climbs off the stage.*]

LEADING ACTRESS   No, sir.

LEADING ACTOR   You've been here before? More than once?

PRODUCER   No, no, no! Wait for it, wait for it. Let her answer first. "You've been here before?"

> [*The* LEADING ACTRESS *lifts her head a little, her eyes closed in pain and disgust, and when the* PRODUCER *says "Now" she nods her head twice.*]

STEPDAUGHTER [*Involuntarily.*]   Oh, my God! [*And she immediately claps her hand over her mouth to stifle her laughter.*]

PRODUCER   What now?

STEPDAUGHTER [*Quickly.*]   Nothing, nothing!

PRODUCER [*To* LEADING ACTOR.]   Come on, then, now it's you.

LEADING ACTOR   More than once? Well then, it shouldn't be too . . . May I take off your hat?

> [*The* LEADING ACTOR *says this last line in such a way and adds to it*

such a gesture that the STEPDAUGHTER, *even with her hand over her mouth trying to stop herself laughing, can't prevent a noisy burst of laughter.*

LEADING ACTRESS [*Indignantly turning.*] I'm not staying any longer to be laughed at by that woman!

LEADING ACTOR Nor am I! That's the end—no more!

PRODUCER [*To* STEPDAUGHTER, *shouting.*] Once and for all, will you shut up! Shut up!

STEPDAUGHTER Yes, I'm sorry . . . I'm sorry.

PRODUCER You're an ill-mannered little bitch! That's what you are! And you've gone too far this time!

FATHER [*Trying to interrupt.*] Yes, you're right, she went too far, but please forgive her . . .

PRODUCER [*Jumping on the stage.*] Why should I forgive her? Her behaviour is intolerable!

FATHER Yes, it is, but the scene made such a peculiar impact on us . . .

PRODUCER Peculiar? What do you mean peculiar? Why peculiar?

FATHER I'm full of admiration for your actors, for this gentleman [*To the* LEADING ACTOR.] and this lady. [*To the* LEADING ACTRESS.] But, you see, well . . . they're not us!

PRODUCER Right! They're not! They're actors!

FATHER That's just the point—they're actors. And they are acting our parts very well, both of them. But that's what's different. However much they want to be the same as us, they're not.

PRODUCER But why aren't they? What is it now?

FATHER It's something to do with . . . being themselves, I suppose, not being us.

PRODUCER Well we can't do anything about that! I've told you already. You can't play the parts yourselves.

FATHER Yes, I know, I know . . .

PRODUCER Right then. That's enough of that. [*Turning back to the* ACTORS.] We'll rehearse this later on our own, as we usually do. It's always a bad idea to have rehearsals with authors there! They're never satisfied. [*Turns back to the* FATHER *and the* STEPDAUGHTER.] Come on, let's get on with it; and let's see if it's possible to do it without laughing.

STEPDAUGHTER I won't laugh any more, I won't really. My best bit's coming up now, you wait and see!

PRODUCER Right: when you say "Don't think any more about what I told you, please. And I should do the same." [*Turning to the* FATHER.] Then you come in immediately with the line "I understand, ah yes, I understand" and then you ask . . .

STEPDAUGHTER [*Interrupting.*] Ask what? What does he ask?

PRODUCER Why you're in mourning.

STEPDAUGHTER No! No! That's not right! Look: when I said that I should try not to think abut the way I was dressed, do you know what he said? "Well then, let's take it off, we'll take it off at once, shall we, your little black dress."

PRODUCER That's great! That'll be wonderful! That'll bring the house down!

STEPDAUGHTER But it's the truth!

PRODUCER   The truth! Do me a favour will you? This is the theatre you know! Truth's all very well up to a point but . . .

STEPDAUGHTER   What do you want to do then?

PRODUCER   You'll see! You'll see! Leave it all to me.

STEPDAUGHTER   No. No I won't. I know what you want to do! Out of my feeling of revulsion, out of all the vile and sordid reasons why I am what I am, you want to make a sugary little sentimental romance. You want him to ask me why I'm in mourning and you want me to reply with the tears running down my face that it is only two months since my father died. No. No. I won't have it! He must say to me what he really did say. "Well then, let's take it off, we'll take it off at once, shall we, your little black dress." And I, with my heart still grieving for my father's death only two months before, I went behind there, do you see? Behind that screen and with my fingers trembling with shame and loathing I took off the dress, unfastened my bra . . .

PRODUCER [*His head in his hands.*]   For God's sake! What are you saying!

STEPDAUGHTER [*Shouting excitedly.*]   The truth! I'm telling you the truth!

PRODUCER   All right then, Now listen to me. I'm not denying it's the truth. Right. And believe me I understand your horror, but you must see that we can't really put a scene like that on the stage.

STEPDAUGHTER   You can't? Then thanks very much. I'm not stopping here.

PRODUCER   No, listen . . .

STEPDAUGHTER   No, I'm going. I'm not stopping. The pair of you have worked it all out together, haven't you, what to put in the scene. Well, thank you very much! I understand everything now! He wants to get to the scene where he can talk about his spiritual torments but I want to show you my drama! Mine!

PRODUCER [*Shaking with anger.*]   Now we're getting to the real truth of it, aren't we? Your drama—yours! But it's not only yours, you know. It's drama for the other people as well! For him [*Pointing to the* FATHER.] and for your mother! You can't have one character coming on like you're doing, trampling over the others, taking over the play. Everything needs to be balanced and in harmony so that we can show what has to be shown! I know perfectly well that we've all got a life inside us and that we all want to parade it in front of other people. But that's the difficulty, how to present only the bits that are necessary in relation to the other characters: and in the small amount we show, to hint at all the rest of the inner life of the character! I agree, it would be so much simpler, if each character, in a soliloquy or in a lecture could pour out to the audience what's bubbling away inside him. But that's not the way we work. [*In an indulgent, placating tone.*] You must restrain yourself, you see. And believe me, it's in your own interests: because you could so easily make a bad impression, with all this uncontrollable anger, this disgust and exasperation. That seems a bit odd, if you don't mind my saying so, when you've admitted that you'd been with other men at Mme. Pace's and more than once.

STEPDAUGHTER   I suppose that's true. But you know, all the other men were all him as far as I was concerned.

PRODUCER [*Not understanding.*]   Uum—? What? What are you talking about?

STEPDAUGHTER If someone falls into evil ways, isn't the responsibility for all the evil which follows to be laid at the door of the person who caused the first mistake? And in my case, it's him, from before I was even born. Look at him: see if it isn't true.

PRODUCER Right then! What about the weight of remorse he's carrying? Isn't that important? Then, give him the chance to show it to us.

STEPDAUGHTER But how? How on earth can he show all his long-suffering remorse, all his moral torments as he calls them, if you don't let him show his horror when he finds me in his arms one fine day, after he had asked me to take my dress off, a black dress for my father who had just died: and he finds that I'm the child he used to go and watch as she came out of school, me, a woman now, and a woman he could buy. [*She says these last words in a voice trembling with emotion.*]

[*The* MOTHER, *hearing her say this, is overcome and at first gives way to stifled sobs: but then she bursts out into uncontrollable crying. Everyone is deeply moved. There is a long pause.*]

STEPDAUGHTER [*As soon as the* MOTHER *has quietened herself she goes on, firmly and thoughtfully.*] At the moment we are here on our own and the public doesn't know about us. But tomorrow you will present us and our story in whatever way you choose, I suppose. But wouldn't you like to see the real drama? Wouldn't you like to see it explode into life, as it really did?

PRODUCER Of course, nothing I'd like better, then I can use as much of it as possible.

STEPDAUGHTER Then persuade my mother to leave.

MOTHER [*Rising and her quiet weeping changing to a loud cry.*] No! No! Don't let her! Don't let her do it!

PRODUCER But they're only doing it for me to watch—only for me, do you see?

MOTHER I can't bear it, I can't bear it!

PRODUCER But if it's already happened, I can't see what's the objection.

MOTHER No! It's happening now, as well: it's happening all the time. I'm not acting my suffering! Can't you understand that? I'm alive and here now but I can never forget that terrible moment of agony, that repeats itself endlessly and vividly in my mind. And these two little children here, you've never heard them speak have you? That's because they don't speak any more, not now. They just cling to me all the time: they help to keep my grief alive, but they don't really exist for themselves any more, not for themselves. And she [*Indicating the* STEPDAUGHTER.] . . . she has gone away, left me completely, she's lost to me, lost . . . you see her here for one reason only: to keep perpetually before me, always real, the anguish and the torment I've suffered on her account.

FATHER The eternal moment, as I told you, sir. She is here [*Indicating the* STEPDAUGHTER.] to keep me too in that moment, trapped for all eternity, chained and suspended in that one fleeting shameful moment of my life. She can't give up her role and you cannot rescue me from it.

PRODUCER But I'm not saying that we won't present that bit. Not at all! It will be the climax of the first act, when she [*He points to the* MOTHER.] surprises you.

FATHER That's right, because that is the moment when I am sentenced:

all our suffering should reach a climax in her cry. [*Again indicating the* MOTHER.]

STEPDAUGHTER   I can still hear it ringing in my ears! It was that cry that sent me mad! You can have me played just as you like: it doesn't matter! Dressed, too, if you want, so long as I can have at least an arm—only an arm—bare, because, you see, as I was standing like this [*She moves across to the* FATHER *and leans her head on his chest.*] with my head like this and my arms round his neck, I saw a vein, here in my arm, throbbing: and then it was almost as if that throbbing vein filled me with a shivering fear, and I shut my eyes tightly like this, like this and buried my head in his chest. [*Turning to the* MOTHER.] Scream, Mummy, scream. [*She buries her head in the* FATHER's *chest, and with her shoulders raised as if to try not to hear the scream, she speaks with a voice tense with suffering.*] Scream, as you screamed then!

MOTHER [*Coming forward to pull them apart.*]   No! She's my daughter! My daughter! [*Tearing her from him.*] You brute, you animal, she's my daughter! Can't you see she's my daughter?

PRODUCER [*Retreating as far as the footlights while the* ACTORS *are full of dismay.*]   Marvellous! Yes, that's great! And then curtain, curtain!

FATHER [*Running downstage to him, excitedly.*]   That's it, that's it! Because it really was like that!

PRODUCER [*Full of admiration and enthusiasm.*]   Yes, yes, that's got to be the curtain line! Curtain! Curtain!

> [*At the repeated calls of the* PRODUCER, *the* STAGE MANAGER *lowers the curtain, leaving on the apron in front, the* PRODUCER *and the* FATHER.]

PRODUCER [*Looking up to heaven with his arms raised.*]   The idiots! I didn't mean now! The bloody idiots—dropping it in on us like that! [*To the* FATHER, *and lifting up a corner of the curtain.*] That's marvellous! Really marvellous! A terrific effect! We'll end the act like that! It's the best tag line I've heard for ages. What a First Act ending! I couldn't have done better if I'd written it myself!

> [*They go through the curtain together.*]

Act Three

When the curtain goes up we see that the STAGE MANAGER *and* STAGE HANDS *have struck the first scene and have set another, a small garden fountain.*

From one side of the stage the ACTORS *come on and from the other the* CHARACTERS. *The* PRODUCER *is standing in the middle of the stage with his hand over his mouth, thinking.*

PRODUCER [*After a short pause, shrugging his shoulders.*]   Well, then: let's get on to the second act! Leave it all to me, and everything will work out properly.

STEPDAUGHTER   This is where we go to live at his house [*Pointing to the* FATHER.] In spite of the objections of him over there. [*Pointing to the* SON.]

PRODUCER [*Getting impatient.*]   All right, all right! But leave it all to me, will you?

STEPDAUGHTER   Provided that you make it clear that he objected!

MOTHER [*From the corner, shaking her head.*]   That doesn't matter. The worse it was for us, the more he suffered from remorse.

PRODUCER [*Impatiently.*]   I know, I know! I'll take it all into account. Don't worry!

MOTHER [*Pleading.*]   To set my mind at rest, sir, please do make sure it's clear that I tried all I could—

STEPDAUGHTER [*Interrupting her scornfully and going on.*]   —to pacify me, to persuade me that this despicable creature wasn't worth making trouble about! [*To the* PRODUCER.] Go on, set her mind at rest, because it's true, she tried very hard. I'm having a whale of a time now! You can see, can't you, that the meeker she was and the more she tried to worm her way into his heart, the more lofty and distant he became! How's that for a dramatic situation!

PRODUCER   Do you think that we can actually begin the Second Act?

STEPDAUGHTER   I won't say another word! But you'll see that it won't be possible to play everything in the garden, like you want to do.

PRODUCER   Why not?

STEPDAUGHTER [*Pointing to the* SON.]   Because to start with, he stays shut up in his room in the house all the time! And then all the scenes for this poor little devil of a boy happen in the house. I've told you once.

PRODUCER   Yes, I know that! But on the other hand we can't put up a notice to tell the audience where the scene is taking place, or change the set three or four times in each Act.

LEADING ACTOR   That's what they used to do in the good old days.

PRODUCER   Yes, when the audience was about as bright as that little girl over there!

LEADING ACTRESS   And it makes it easier to create an illusion.

FATHER [*Leaping up.*]   An illusion? For pity's sake don't talk about illusions! Don't use that word, it's especially hurtful to us!

PRODUCER [*Astonished.*]   And why, for God's sake?

FATHER   It's so hurtful, so cruel! You ought to have realised that!

PRODUCER   What else should we call it? That's what we do here—create an illusion for the audience . . .

LEADING ACTOR   With our performance . . .

PRODUCER   A perfect illusion of reality!

FATHER   Yes, I know that, I understand. But on the other hand, perhaps you don't understand us yet. I'm sorry! But you see, for you and for your actors what goes on here on the stage is, quite rightly, well, it's only a game.

LEADING ACTRESS [*Interrupting indignantly.*]   A game! How dare you! We're not children! What happens here is serious!

FATHER   I'm not saying that it isn't serious. And I mean, really, not just a game but an art, that tries, as you've just said, to create the perfect illusion of reality.

PRODUCER   That's right!

FATHER   Now try to imagine that we, as you see us here, [*He indicates himself and the other* CHARACTERS.] that we have no other reality outside this illusion.

PRODUCER [*Astonished and looking at the* ACTORS *with the same sense of bewilderment as they feel themselves.*] What the hell are you talking about now?

FATHER [*After a short pause as he looks at them, with a faint smile.*] Isn't it obvious? What other reality is there for us? What for you is an illusion you create, for us is our only reality. [*Brief pause. He moves towards the* PRODUCER *and goes on.*] But it's not only true for us, it's true for others as well, you know. Just think about it. [*He looks intently into the* PRODUCER's *eyes.*] Do you really know who you are? [*He stands pointing at the* PRODUCER.]

PRODUCER [*A little disturbed but with a half smile.*] What? Who I am? I am me!

FATHER What if I told you that that wasn't true: what if I told you that you were me?

PRODUCER I would tell you that you were mad!

[*The* ACTORS *laugh.*]

FATHER That's right, laugh! Because everything here is a game! [*To the* PRODUCER.] And yet you object when I say that it is only for a game that the gentleman there [*Pointing to the* LEADING ACTOR.] who is "himself" has to be "me," who, on the contrary, am "myself." You see, I've caught you in a trap.

[*The* ACTORS *start to laugh.*]

PRODUCER Not again! We've heard all about this a little while ago.

FATHER No, no. I didn't really want to talk about this. I'd like you to forget about your game. [*Looking at the* LEADING ACTRESS *as if to anticipate what she will say.*] I'm sorry—your artistry! Your art!—that you usually pursue here with your actors; and I am going to ask you again in all seriousness, who are you?

PRODUCER [*Turning with a mixture of amazement and annoyance, to the* ACTORS.] Of all the bloody nerve! A fellow who claims he is only a character comes and asks me who I am!

FATHER [*With dignity but without annoyance.*] A character, my dear sir, can always ask a man who he is, because a character really has a life of his own, a life full of his own specific qualities, and because of these he is always "someone." While a man—I'm not speaking about you personally, of course, but man in general—well, he can be an absolute "nobody."

PRODUCER All right, all right! Well, since you've asked me, I'm the Director, the Producer—I'm in charge! Do you understand?

FATHER [*Half smiling, but gently and politely.*] I'm only asking to try to find out if you really see yourself now in the same way that you saw yourself, for instance, once upon a time in the past, with all the illusions you had then, with everything inside and outside yourself as it seemed then—and not only seemed, but really was! Well then, look back on those illusions, those ideas that you don't have any more, on all those things that no longer seem the same to you. Don't you feel that not only this stage is falling away from under your feet but so is the earth itself, and that all these realities of today are going to seem tomorrow as if they had been an illusion?

PRODUCER So? What does that prove?

FATHER Oh, nothing much. I only want to make you see that if we [*Point-*

ing to himself and the other CHARACTERS.] have no other reality outside our own illusion, perhaps you ought to distrust your own sense of reality: because whatever is a reality today, whatever you touch and believe in and that seems real for you today, is going to be—like the reality of yesterday—an illusion tomorrow.

PRODUCER [*Deciding to make fun of him.*]   Very good! So now you're saying that you as well as this play you're going to show me here, are more real than I am?

FATHER [*Very seriously.*]   There's no doubt about that at all.

PRODUCER   Is that so?

FATHER   I thought you'd realised that from the beginning.

PRODUCER   More real than I am?

FATHER   If your reality can change between today and tomorrow—

PRODUCER   But everybody knows that it can change, don't they? It's always changing! Just like everybody else's!

FATHER [*Crying out.*]   But ours doesn't change! Do you see? That's the difference! Ours doesn't change, it can't change, it can never be different, never, because it is already determined, like this, for ever, that's what's so terrible! We are an eternal reality. That should make you shudder to come near us.

PRODUCER [*Jumping up, suddenly struck by an idea, and standing directly in front of the* FATHER.]   Then I should like to know when anyone saw a character step out of his part and make a speech like you've done, proposing things, explaining things. Tell me when, will you? I've never seen it before.

FATHER   You've never seen it because an author usually hides all the difficulties of creating. When the characters are alive, really alive and standing in front of their author, he has only to follow their words, the actions that they suggest to him: and he must want them to be what they want to be: and it's his bad luck if he doesn't do what they want! When a character is born he immediately assumes such an independence even of his own author that everyone can imagine him in scores of situations that his author hadn't even thought of putting him in, and he sometimes acquires a meaning that his author never dreamed of giving him.

PRODUCER   Of course I know all that.

FATHER   Well, then. Why are you surprised by us? Imagine what a disaster it is for a character to be born in the imagination of an author who then refuses to give him life in a written script. Tell me if a character, left like this, suspended, created but without a final life, isn't right to do what we are doing now, here in front of you. We spent such a long time, such a very long time, believe me, urging our author, persuading him, first me, then her, [*Pointing to the* STEPDAUGHTER.] then this poor Mother . . .

STEPDAUGHTER [*Coming down the stage as if in a dream.*]   It's true, I would go, would go and tempt him, time after time, in his gloomy study just as it was growing dark, when he was sitting quietly in an armchair not even bothering to switch a light on but leaving the shadows to fill the room: the shadows were swarming with us, we had come to tempt him. [*As if she could see herself there in the study and is annoyed by the presence of the* ACTORS.] Go away will you! Leave us alone! Mother there, with that son of hers—me with the little girl—that poor little kid always on his own—and then me with him [*Pointing to the* FATHER.] and then at last, just me, on my own, all on my own, in the shadows. [*She turns quickly as if she wants to cling on to the vision she has of herself, in the shadows.*] Ah, what scenes, what scenes we suggested to him! What a life I could have had! I tempted him more than the others!

FATHER   Oh yes, you did! And it was probably all your fault that he did nothing about it! You were so insistent, you made too many demands.

STEPDAUGHTER   But he wanted me to be like that! [*She comes closer to the* PRODUCER *to speak to him in confidence.*] I think it's more likely that he felt discouraged about the theatre and even despised it because the public only wants to see . . .

PRODUCER   Let's go on, for God's sake, let's go on. Come to the point will you?

STEPDAUGHTER   I'm sorry, but if you ask me, we've got too much happening already, just with our entry into his house. [*Pointing to the* FATHER.] You said that we couldn't put up a notice or change the set every five minutes.

PRODUCER   Right! Of course we can't! We must combine things, group them together in one continuous flowing action: not the way you've been wanting, first of all seeing your little brother come home from school and wander about the house like a lost soul, hiding behind the doors and brooding on some plan or other that would—what did you say it would do?

STEPDAUGHTER   Wither him . . . shrivel him up completely.

PRODUCER   That's good! That's a good expression. And then you "can see it there in his eyes, getting stronger all the time"—isn't that what you said?

STEPDAUGHTER   Yes, that's right. Look at him! [*Pointing to him as he stands next to his* MOTHER.]

PRODUCER   Yes, great! And then, at the same time, you want to show the little girl playing in the garden, all innocence. One in the house and the other in the garden—we can't do it, don't you see that?

STEPDAUGHTER   Yes, playing in the sun, so happy! It's the only pleasure I have left, her happiness, her delight in playing in the garden: away from the misery, the squalor of that sordid flat where all four of us slept and where she slept with me—with me! Just think of it! My vile, contaminated body close to hers, with her little arms wrapped tightly round my neck, so lovingly, so innocently. In the garden, wherever she saw me, she would run and take my hand. She never wanted to show me the big flowers, she would run about looking for the "little weeny" ones, so that she could show them to me; she was so happy, so thrilled! [*As she says this, tortured by the memory, she breaks out into a long desperate cry, dropping her head on her arms that rest on a little table. Everybody is very affected by her. The* PRODUCER *comes to her almost paternally and speaks to her in a soothing voice.*]

PRODUCER   We'll have the garden scene, we'll have it, don't worry: and you'll see, you'll be very pleased with what we do! We'll play all the scenes in the garden! [*He calls out to a* STAGE HAND *by name.*] Hey . . . , let down a few bits of tree, will you? A couple of cypresses will do, in front of the fountain. [*Someone drops in the two cypresses and a* STAGE HAND *secures them with a couple of braces and weights.*]

PRODUCER [*To the* STEPDAUGHTER.] That'll do for now, won't it? It'll just give us an idea. [*Calling out to a* STAGE HAND *by name again.*] Hey, . . . give me something for the sky will you?

STAGE HAND What's that?

PRODUCER Something for the sky! A small cloth to come in behind the fountain. [*A white cloth is dropped from the flies.*] Not white! I asked for a sky! Never mind: leave it! I'll do something with it. [*Calling out.*] Hey lights! Kill everything will you? Give me a bit of moonlight—the blues in the batten and a blue spot on the cloth . . . [*They do.*] That's it! That'll do! [*Now on the scene there is the light he asked for, a mysterious blue light that makes the* ACTORS *speak and move as if in the garden in the evening under a moon. To the* STEPDAUGHTER.] Look here now: the little boy can come out here in the garden and hide among the trees instead of hiding behind the doors in the house. But it's going to be difficult to find a little girl to play the scene with you where she shows you the flowers. [*Turning to the* LITTLE BOY.] Come on, come on, son, come across here. Let's see what it'll look like. [*But the* (LITTLE) BOY *doesn't move.*] Come on will you, come on. [*Then he pulls him forward and tries to make him hold his head up, but every time it falls down again on his chest.*] There's something very odd about this lad . . . What's wrong with him? My God, he'll have to say something sometime! [*He comes over to him again, puts his hand on his shoulder and pushes him between the trees.*] Come a bit nearer: let's have a look. Can you hide a bit more? That's it. Now pop your head out and look round. [*He moves away to look at the effect and as the* BOY *does what he has been told to do, the* ACTORS *watch impressed and a little disturbed.*] Ahh, that's good, very good . . . [*He turns to the* STEPDAUGHTER.] How about having the little girl, surprised to see him there, run across. Wouldn't that make him say something?

STEPDAUGHTER [*Getting up.*] It's no use hoping he'll speak, not as long as that creature's there. [*Pointing to the* SON.] You'll have to get him out of the way first.

SON [*Moving determinedly to one of the sets of steps leading off the stage.*] With pleasure! I'll go now! Nothing will please me better!

PRODUCER [*Stopping him immediately.*] Hey, no! Where are you going? Hang on!

[*The* MOTHER *gets up, anxious at the idea that he is really going and instinctively raising her arms as if to hold him back, but without moving from where she is.*]

SON [*At the footlights, to the* PRODUCER *who is restraining him there.*] There's no reason why I should be here! Let me go will you? Let me go!

PRODUCER What do you mean there's no reason for you to be here?

STEPDAUGHTER [*Calmly, ironically.*] Don't bother to stop him. He won't go!

FATHER You have to play that terrible scene in the garden with your mother.

SON [*Quickly, angry and determined.*] I'm not going to play anything! I've said that all along! [*To the* PRODUCER.] Let me go will you?

STEPDAUGHTER [*Crossing to the* PRODUCER.] It's all right. Let him go. [*She moves the* PRODUCER'*s hand from the* SON. *Then she turns to the* SON *and says.*] Well, go on then! Off you go!

[*The* SON *stays near the steps but as if pulled by some strange force he is quite unable to go down them: then to the astonishment and even the dismay of the* ACTORS, *he moves along the front of the stage towards the other set of steps down into the auditorium: but having got there, he again stays near and doesn't actually go down them. The* STEPDAUGHTER *who has watched him scornfully but very intently, bursts into laughter.*]

STEPDAUGHTER   He can't, you see? He can't! He's got to stay here! He must. He's chained to us for ever! No, I'm the one who goes, when what must happen does happen, and I run away, because I hate him, because I can't bear the sight of him any longer. Do you think it's possible for him to run away? He has to stay here with that wonderful father of his and his mother there. She doesn't think she has any other son but him. [*She turns to the* MOTHER.] Come on, come on, Mummy, come on! [*Turning back to the* PRODUCER *to point her out to him.*] Look, she's going to try to stop him . . . [*To the* MOTHER, *half compelling her, as if by some magic power.*] Come on, come on. [*Then to the* PRODUCER *again.*] Imagine how she must feel at showing her affection for him in front of your actors! But her longing to be near him is so strong that—look! She's going to go through that scene with him again! [*The* MOTHER *has now actually come close to the* SON *as the* STEPDAUGHTER *says the last line: she gestures to show that she agrees to go on.*]

SON [*Quickly.*]   But I'm not! I'm not! If I can't get away then I suppose I shall have to stay here; but I repeat that I will not have any part in it.

FATHER [*To the* PRODUCER, *excitedly.*]   You must make him!

SON   Nobody's going to make me do anything!

FATHER   I'll make you!

STEPDAUGHTER   Wait! Just a minute! Before that, the little girl has to go to the fountain. [*She turns to take the* LITTLE GIRL, *drops on her knees in front of her and takes her face between her hands.*] My poor little darling, those beautiful eyes, they look so bewildered. You're wondering where you are, aren't you? Well, we're on a stage, my darling! What's a stage? Well, it's a place where you pretend to be serious. They put on plays here. And now we're going to put on a play. Seriously! Oh, yes! Even you . . . [*She hugs her tightly and rocks her gently for a moment.*] Oh, my little one, my little darling, what a terrible play it is for you! What horrible things have been planned for you! The garden, the fountain . . . Oh, yes, it's only a pretend fountain, that's right. That's part of the game, my pretty darling: everything is pretends here. Perhaps you'll like a pretends fountain better than a real one: you can play here then. But it's only a game for the others; not for you, I'm afraid, it's real for you, my darling, and your game is in a real fountain, a big beautiful green fountain with bamboos casting shadows, looking at your own reflection, with lots of baby ducks paddling about, shattering the reflections. You want to stroke one! [*With a scream that electrifies and terrifies everybody.*] No, Rosetta, no! Your mummy isn't watching you, she's over there with that selfish bastard! Oh, God, I feel as if all the devils in hell were tearing me apart inside . . . And you . . . [*Leaving the* LITTLE GIRL *and turning to the* LITTLE BOY *in the usual way.*] What are you doing here, hanging about like a beggar? It'll be your fault too, if that little girl drowns; you're always like this, as if I wasn't paying the price for getting all of you into this house. [*Shaking his arm to make him take his hand out of his pocket.*] What have you got there? What are you hiding? Take it out, take your hand out! [*She drags his hand out of his pocket and to everyone's horror he is holding a revolver. She looks at him for a moment, almost with satisfaction: then she says, grimly.*] Where on earth did you get that? [*The* (LITTLE) BOY, *looking frightened, with his eyes wide and empty, doesn't answer.*] You idiot, if I'd been you, instead of killing myself, I'd have killed one of those two: either or both, the father and the son. [*She pushes him toward the cypress trees where he then stands watching: then she takes the* LITTLE GIRL *and helps her to climb in to the fountain, making her lie so that she is hidden: after that she kneels down and puts her head and arms on the rim of the fountain.*]

PRODUCER   That's good! It's good! [*Turning to the* STEPDAUGHTER.] And at the same time . . .

SON [*Scornfully.*]   What do you mean, at the same time? There was nothing at the same time! There wasn't any scene between her and me. [*Pointing to the* MOTHER.] She'll tell you the same thing herself, she'll tell you what happened.

> [*The* SECOND ACTRESS *and the* JUVENILE LEAD *have left the group of* ACTORS *and have come to stand nearer the* MOTHER *and the* SON *as if to study them so as to play their parts.*]

MOTHER   Yes, it's true. I'd gone to his room . . .

SON   Room, do you hear? Not the garden!

PRODUCER   It's not important! We've got to reorganize the events anyway. I've told you that already.

SON [*Glaring at the* JUVENILE LEAD *and the* SECOND ACTRESS.]   What do you want?

JUVENILE LEAD   Nothing. I'm just watching.

SON [*Turning to the* SECOND ACTRESS]   You as well! Getting ready to play her part are you? [*Pointing to the* MOTHER.]

PRODUCER   That's it. And I think you should be grateful—they're paying you a lot of attention.

SON   Oh, yes, thank you! But haven't you realised yet that you'll never be able to do this play? There's nothing of us inside you and you actors are only looking at us from the outside. Do you think we could go on living with a mirror held up in front of us that didn't only freeze our reflection for ever, but froze us in a reflection that laughed back at us with an expression that we didn't even recognise as our own?

FATHER   That's right! That's right!

PRODUCER [*To* JUVENILE LEAD *and* SECOND ACTRESS.]   Okay. Go back to the others.

SON   It's quite useless. I'm not prepared to do anything.

PRODUCER   Oh, shut up, will you, and let me listen to your mother. [*To the* MOTHER.] Well, you'd gone to his room, you said.

MOTHER   Yes, to his room. I couldn't bear it any longer. I wanted to empty my heart to him, tell him about all the agony that was crushing me. But as soon as he saw me come in . . .

SON   Nothing happened. I got away! I wasn't going to get involved. I never have been involved. Do you understand?

MOTHER   It's true! That's right!

PRODUCER   But we must make up the scene between you, then. It's vital!

MOTHER   I'm ready to do it! If only I had the chance to talk to him for a moment, to pour out all my troubles to him.

FATHER [*Going to the* SON *and speaking violently.*]   You'll do it! For your Mother! For your Mother!

SON [*More than ever determined.*]   I'm doing nothing!

FATHER [*Taking hold of his coat collar and shaking him.*]   For God's sake, do as I tell you! Do as I tell you! Do you hear what she's saying? Haven't you any feelings for her?

SON [*Taking hold of his* FATHER.]   No I haven't! I haven't! Let that be the end of it!

[*There is a general uproar. The* MOTHER *frightened out of her wits, tries to get between them and separate them.*]

MOTHER   Please stop it! Please!

FATHER [*Hanging on.*]   Do as I tell you! Do as I tell you!

SON [*Wrestling with him and finally throwing him to the ground near the steps. Everyone is horrified.*]   What's come over you? Why are you so frantic? Do you want to parade our disgrace in front of everybody? Well, I'm having nothing to do with it! Nothing! And I'm doing what our author wanted as well—he never wanted to put us on the stage.

PRODUCER   Then why the hell did you come here?

SON [*Pointing to the* FATHER.]   He wanted to, I didn't.

PRODUCER   But you're here now, aren't you?

SON   He was the one who wanted to come and he dragged all of us here with him and agreed with you in there about what to put in the play: and that meant not only what had really happened, as if that wasn't bad enough, but what hadn't happened as well.

PRODUCER   All right, then, you tell me what happened. You tell me! Did you rush out of your room without saying anything?

SON [*After a moment's hesitation.*]   Without saying anything. I didn't want to make a scene.

PRODUCER [*Needling him.*]   What then? What did you do then?

SON [*He is now the centre of everyone's agonised attention and he crosses the stage.*]   Nothing . . . I went across the garden . . . [*He breaks off gloomy and absorbed.*]

PRODUCER [*Urging him to say more, impressed by his reluctance to speak.*]   Well? What then? You crossed the garden?

SON [*Exasperated, putting his face into the crook of his arm.*]   Why do you want me to talk about it? It's horrible! [*The* MOTHER *is trembling with stifled sobs and looking towards the fountain.*]

PRODUCER [*Quietly, seeing where she is looking and turning to the* SON *with growing apprehension.*]   The little girl?

SON [*Looking straight in front, out to the audience.*]   There, in the fountain . . .

FATHER [*On the floor still, pointing with pity at the* MOTHER.]   She was trailing after him!

PRODUCER [*To the* SON, *anxiously.*]   What did you do then?

SON [*Still looking out front and speaking slowly.*]   I dashed across. I was going to jump in and pull her out . . . But something else caught my eye:

I saw something behind the tree that made my blood run cold: the little boy, he was standing there with a mad look in his eyes: he was standing looking into the fountain at his little sister, floating there, drowned.

> [*The* STEPDAUGHTER *is still bent at the fountain hiding the* LITTLE GIRL, *and she sobs pathetically, her sobs sounding like an echo. There is a pause.*]

SON [*Continued.*]   I made a move towards him: but then . . .

> [*From behind the trees where the* LITTLE BOY *is standing there is the sound of a shot.*]

MOTHER [*With a terrible cry she runs along with the* SON *and all the* ACTORS *in the midst of a great general confusion.*]   My son! My son! [*And then from out of the confusion and crying her voice comes out.*] Help! Help me!

PRODUCER [*Amidst the shouting he tries to clear a space whilst the* LITTLE BOY *is carried by his feet and shoulders behind the white skycloth.*]   Is he wounded? Really wounded?

> [*Everybody except the* PRODUCER *and the* FATHER *who is still on the floor by the steps, has gone behind the skycloth and stays there talking anxiously. Then independently the* ACTORS *start to come back into view.*]

LEADING ACTRESS [*Coming from the right, very upset.*]   He's dead! The poor boy! He's dead! What a terrible thing!

LEADING ACTOR [*Coming back from the left and smiling.*]   What do you mean, dead? It's all make-believe. It's a sham! He's not dead. Don't you believe it!

OTHER ACTORS FROM THE RIGHT   Make-believe? It's real! Real! He's dead!

OTHER ACTORS FROM THE LEFT   No, he isn't. He's pretending! It's all make-believe.

FATHER [*Running off and shouting at them as he goes.*]   What do you mean, make-believe? It's real! It's real, ladies and gentlemen! It's reality! [*And with desperation on his face he too goes behind the skycloth.*]

PRODUCER [*Not caring any more.*]   Make-believe?! Reality?! Oh, go to hell the lot of you! Lights! Lights! Lights!

> [*At once all the stage and auditorium is flooded with light. The PRODUCER heaves a sigh of relief as if he has been relieved of a terrible weight and they all look at each other in distress and with uncertainty.*]

PRODUCER   God! I've never known anything like this! And we've lost a whole day's work! [*He looks at the clock.*] Get off with you, all of you! We can't do anything now! It's too late to start a rehearsal. [*When the* ACTORS *have gone, he calls out.*] Hey, lights! Kill everything! [*As soon as he has said this, all the lights go out completely and leave him in the pitch dark.*] For God's sake!! You might have left the workers![4] I can't see where I'm going!

> [*Suddenly, behind the skycloth, as if because of a bad connection, a green light comes up to throw on the cloth a huge sharp shadow of the CHARACTERS, but without the LITTLE BOY and the LITTLE GIRL. The PRODUCER, seeing this, jumps off the stage, terrified. At the same time the flood of light on them is switched off and the stage is again*

---

4. Working lights.

bathed in the same blue light as before. Slowly the SON *comes on from the right, followed by the* MOTHER *with her arms raised towards him. Then from the left, the* FATHER *enters.*

They come together in the middle of the stage and stand there as if transfixed. Finally from the left the STEPDAUGHTER *comes on and moves towards the steps at the front: on the top step she pauses for a moment to look back at the other three and then bursts out in a raucous laugh, dashes down the steps and turns to look at the three figures still on the stage. Then she runs out of the auditorium and we can still hear her manic laughter out into the foyer and beyond.*

After a pause the curtain falls slowly.]

MARCEL PROUST
1871–1922

Proust's influence in twentieth-century letters is unequaled by that of any other writer. His massive novel sequence, *Remembrance of Things Past* (*À la recherche du temps perdu*), broke from nineteenth-century tradition to provide the example of a new kind of characterization and narrative line, a monumentally complex and precisely coordinated aesthetic structure, and a concept of the individual's cumulatively created profound identity—much of it buried in the experience of our senses—that has influenced writers everywhere modern Western literature is known. All of these innovations refer to an exploration of time in terms that parallel the influential work of Proust's contemporary, the philosopher Henri Bergson, with its emphasis on experience as duration, or *lived* time (rather than the artificial measurements of clock or calendar), and the importance of intuitive knowledge. Proust's plot refuses the immediate sense of direction given by traditional nineteenth-century novels: it acquires purpose gradually, through the relationship of different themes, and its collective intent appears only at the end, when Marcel's suddenly catalyzed memory grasps the relationship of all parts. Characters are not sketched in fully from the beginning but are revealed piece by piece, evolving inside the different perspectives of individual chapters; even the protagonist is not fully outlined before the end. Proust's novel is a monumental construction coordinated down to its smallest parts not by the development of traditional novel form but by a new structural vision; it suggested the availability of intuitive or nonrational elements as organizational principles in an example that continues to be a reference point for twentieth-century writers.

Marcel Proust was born on July 10, 1871, the older of two sons in a wealthy middle-class Parisian family. His father was a well-known doctor and professor of medicine, a Catholic from a small town outside Paris. His mother, a sensitive, scrupulous, and highly educated woman to whom Marcel was devoted, came from an urban Jewish family. Proust fell ill with severe asthma when he was nine and thereafter spent his childhood holidays at a seaside resort in Normandy that became the fictional model for Balbec. In spite of his illness, which limited what he could do, he graduated with honors from the Lycée Condorcet in Paris in 1889 and did a year's military service at Orléans (the fictional Doncières). As a student, Proust had met many young writers and composers, and he began to frequent the salons of the wealthy bourgeoisie and the aristocracy of the Faubourg Saint-Germain (an elegant area of Paris), from which he drew much of the material for his portraits of society. He wrote for Symbolist magazines such as *Le Banquet* and *La Revue blanche* and published a collection of essays, poems, and stories in an elegant book, *Pleasures and Days* (1896), with drawings by Madeleine Lemaire and music by Reynaldo Hahn. In 1899 (with his mother's help since he knew no English), he began to translate the English moralist and art critic John Ruskin.

Proust is known as the author of one work: the enormous, seven-volume exploration of time and consciousness called *Remembrance of Things Past*. As early as 1895, he had begun work on a shorter novel that traced the same themes and autobiographical awareness, but *Jean Santeuil* (published posthumously in 1952) never found a coherent structure for its numerous episodes and Proust abandoned it in 1899. Many episodes from the unfinished manuscript reflected Proust's interest in current events, especially the Dreyfus Affair (1894–1906) that was dividing France around issues of military honor, anti-Semitism, and national security. Themes, ideas, and some episodes from the earlier novel were absorbed into *Remembrance of Things Past,* and it is striking that the major difference (aside from length) between the two works is simply the extremely sophisticated and subtle structure that Proust devised for the later one.

Proust's health started seriously to decline in 1902, and to make matters worse, he lost both parents by 1905. The following year, his asthma worsening, he moved into a cork-lined, fumigated room at 102 Boulevard Haussmann in Paris, where he stayed until forced to move in 1919. From 1907 to 1914, he spent summers in the seacoast town of Cabourg (another source of material for the fictional Balbec), but when in Paris emerged rarely from his apartment and then only late at night for dinners with friends. In 1909 he conceived the structure of his novel as a whole and wrote its first and last chapters together. A first draft was finished by September 1912, but Proust had difficulty finding a publisher and finally published the first volume at his own expense in 1913. Though *Swann's Way* (*Du côté de chez Swann*) was a success, World War I delayed publication of subsequent volumes, and Proust began the painstaking revision and enlargement of the whole manuscript (from fifteen hundred to four thousand pages, and three to seven parts) that was to occupy him until his death on November 18, 1922. *Within a Budding Grove* (*À l'ombre des jeunes filles en fleurs,* or "In the shadow of young girls in flower") won the prestigious Goncourt Prize in 1919, and *The Guermantes Way* (*Le Côté de Guermantes*) followed in 1920–21. The last volume published in Proust's lifetime was *Cities of the Plain II* (*Sodome et Gomorrhe II,* or "Sodom and Gomorrah II," 1922), and the remaining volumes—*The Captive* (*La Prisonnière,* 1923), *The Fugitive* (*Albertine disparue,* or "Albertine disappeared," 1925), and *Time Regained* (*Le Temps retrouvé,* 1927)—were published posthumously from manuscripts on which he had been working. Written almost completely in the first person and based on events in the author's life (although by no means purely autobiographical), the novel is famous both for its evocation of the closed world of Parisian society at the turn of the century and as a meditation on time and human emotions.

When *Swann's Way* appeared in 1913, it was immediately seen as a new kind of fiction. Unlike nineteenth-century novels such as Flaubert's *Madame Bovary, Remembrance of Things Past* has no clear and continuous plot line building to a dénouement, nor (until the last volume, published in 1927) could the reader detect a consistent development of the central character, Marcel. Only at the end does the narrator recognize the meaning and value of what has preceded, and when he retells his story it is not from an omniscient, explanatory point of view but rather as a reliving and gradual assessment of Marcel's lifelong experience. Most of the novel sets forth a roughly chronological sequence of events, yet its opening pages swing through recollections of many times and places before settling on the narrator's childhood in Combray. The second section, *Swann in Love* (*Un Amour de Swann*), is a story told about another character and in the third person. Thus the novel proceeds by apparently discontinuous blocks of recollection, all bound together by the central consciousness of the narrator. This was always Proust's plan: he insisted that he had from the beginning a fixed structure and goal for the whole novel that reached down to the "solidity of the smallest parts," and his substantial revisions of the shorter first draft enriched an already existing structure without changing the sequence of scenes and events.

The overall theme of the novel is suggested by a literal translation of its title: "In Search of Lost Time." The narrator, a "Marcel" who suggests but is not identical with the author, is an old man weakened by a long illness who puzzles over the events of his past, trying to find in them a significant pattern. He begins with his childhood, ordered within the comfortable security of accepted manners and ideals in the family home at Combray. In succeeding volumes he goes out into the world, experiences love and disappointment, discovers the disparity between idealized images of places and their crude, sometimes banal reality, and is increasingly overcome by disillusionment with himself and society. Until the end of the novel, Marcel remains a *grand nerveux* (nervous or high-strung person), an extremely sensitive person impelled by the major experiences of his life—love, betrayal, art, separation, and death—to discard his earlier naive perspective and seek out a largely intuited meaning for life.

In the short ending chapter, things suddenly come into focus as Marcel reaches a new understanding of the role of time. Abruptly reliving a childhood experience when he sees a familiar book and recognizing the ravages of time in the aged and enfeebled figures of his old friends, Marcel faces the approach of death with a new sense of existential continuity and realizes that his vocation as an artist lies in giving form to this buried existence. Apparently lost, the past is still alive within us, a part of our being, and memory can recapture it to give coherence and depth to present identity. Marcel has not yet begun to write by the end of the last volume, *Time Regained*, but paradoxically the book that he plans to write is already there: Proust's *Remembrance of Things Past*.

The larger subject of the novel, penetrating its description of society and Marcel's experience, is "that invisible substance called time." Although neither ever claimed any direct connection (and Proust recognized more readily the influence of his philosophy professor, Darlu), Proust echoes the concerns of contemporary philosopher Bergson when he looks to intuition and a sense of lived experience for a way to represent reality. Bergson's opposition of intellect and intuition, his preference for *duration* (everyday lived time) as opposed to abstract or clock time as a means of knowledge, and his distinction between the interactive "social ego" and the individually "profound" or intuitive ego all correspond to themes in Proust. Marcel's awareness of his life in time is created through memory—not rational or "forced" but spontaneous or "involuntary" memory—the chance recollection that wells up from his subconscious mind when he repeats a previous action such as dipping cookies in lime-blossom tea, stumbling on a paving stone, hearing a spoon clatter, or glimpsing a familiar book. Involuntary memory is more powerful because it draws on a buried level of experience where the five senses are still linked. Life thus recalled comes to us in one piece, not separated into different categories for easier intellectual understanding. Sounds are connected with colors (the name *Brabant* with gold), and emotions with the settings in which they were experienced (sorrow with the smell of varnish on the stairway up to bed). Involuntary memory recreates a whole past world in all its concrete reality—and so does art. When Proust attributes such an absolute metaphysical value to art, making it a special means of knowledge and the focus of his book, he joins a special French tradition of "moralist" writers: those who, from Michel de Montaigne to Albert Camus, strive for clear vision and a sense of universal human values.

Proust's style has a unique "architectural" design that coordinates large blocks of material: themes, situations, places, and events recur and are transformed across time. His long sentences and mammoth paragraphs reflect the slow and careful progression of thought among the changing objects of its perception. The ending paragraph of the *Overture* is composed of two long sentences that encompass an enormous range of meditative detail as the narrator not only recalls his childhood world—the old gray house, garden, public square and country roads, Swann's park, the river, the villagers, and indeed the whole town of Combray—but simultaneously compares the suddenly arisen house to a stage set, and the unfolding village itself to the twists and turns of a Japanese flower taking on color and form inside a bowl of water: here, in the narrator's cup of lime-blossom tea. Characters are remembered in different settings and perspectives, creating a "multiple self" who is free to change and still remain the same. Thus Charles Swann appears first as the visitor who often delays the child Marcel's bedtime kiss from his mother, next as an anxious and disappointed lover, and finally as a tragic, dying man rejected by his friends, the Guermantes, in their haste to get to a ball. Marcel's grandmother appears throughout the scenes in Combray, later during a visit to the seaside resort of Balbec, still later in her death agonies when Marcel is unable truly to grieve, and finally as a sudden recollection when Marcel has trouble tying his shoelace in Balbec. Nor is it characters alone who undergo cumulative transformations. The little musical phrase that Marcel first hears as part of a sonata by the composer Vinteuil and that is associated with love in various settings recurs toward the end of the novel as part of a septet and becomes a revelation of the subtle constructions of art. Places overlap in the memory: the imagined and the real Balbec or Venice confront one another, and the church steeples of Vieuxvicq and Martinville are juxtaposed. On a linguistic level, Proust juxtaposes entire social roles and habits of mind through the interaction of different types of speech. When Charles and the Princesse de Guermantes meet in a bourgeois salon, their manner of speaking to each other creates a small "in-group" dialogue of the aristocracy and sets them off from everyone else. The flexibility of Proust's style, representing thought and habits of speech rather than following a superimposed common code, makes him an example of verbal and visionary innovation that is paralleled by other writers of the same period, such as James Joyce and Virginia Woolf, and is enormously influential on later writers of the "new novel" tradition.

The selection printed here, *Overture*, is the first chapter of *Swann's Way*, the first full volume of Proust's novel. "Swann's way" is one of the two directions in which Marcel's family used to take walks from their home in Combray, toward Tansonville, home of Charles Swann, and is associated with various scenes and anecdotes of love and private life. The longer walk toward the estate of the Guermantes (*The Guermantes Way*), a fictional family of the highest aristocracy appearing frequently in the novel, evokes an aura of high society and French history, a more public sphere. Fictional people and places mingle throughout with the real; names that are not annotated are Proust's inventions. The narrator of *Overture* is Marcel as an old man, and the French verb tense used in his recollections (here and throughout all but the final volume) is appropriately the imperfect, a tense of uncompleted action ("I used to . . . I would ask myself").

As the chapter title suggests, *Overture* introduces the work's themes and methods rather like the overture of an opera. All but one of the main characters appear or are mentioned, and the patterns of future encounters are set. Marcel, waiting anxiously for his beloved mother's response to a note sent down to her during dinner, suffers the same agony of separation as does Swann in his love for the promiscuous Odette, or the older Marcel himself for Albertine. The strange world of half-sleep, half-waking with which the novel begins prefigures later awakenings of memory. Long passages of intricate introspection, and sudden shifts of time and space, introduce us to the style and point of view of the rest of the book. The narrator shares the painful anxiety of little Marcel's desperate wait for his mother's bedtime kiss; for though his observations and judgments are tempered with mature wisdom, he is only at the beginning of his progress to full consciousness. The remembrance of things past is a key to further discovery but not an end in itself.

Overture ends with Proust's most famous image, summing up for many readers the world, the style, and the process of discovery of the Proustian vision. Nibbling at a madeleine (a small, rich cookielike pastry) that he has dipped in lime-blossom tea, Marcel suddenly has an overwhelming feeling of happiness. He soon associates this tantalizing, puzzling phenomenon with the memory of earlier times when he sipped tea with his Aunt Leonie. He realizes that there is something valuable about such passive, spontaneous, and sensuous memory, quite different from the abstract operations of reason. Although the Marcel of "Combray" does not yet know it, he will pursue the elusive significance of this moment of happiness until, in *Time Regained,* he can as a complete artist bring it to the surface and link past and present time in a fuller and richer identity.

Roger Shattuck, *Proust* (1974), is a general study including advice on "how to read" Proust; it is still useful although it predates the revised translation used here; George D. Painter, *Marcel Proust: A Biography* (rev. 1996), offers a comprehensive biography. An excellent general study is Germaine Brée, *Marcel Proust and Deliverance from Time* (1969), translated by R. J. Richards and A. D. Truitt. Terence Kilmartin, *A Reader's Guide to Remembrance of Things Past* (1984), is a handbook guide to Proust's characters, to persons referred to in the text, to places, and to themes, all keyed to the revised translation by the translator. Julia Kristeva, *Proust and the Sense of Time* (1993), trans. Stephen Bann, takes a broadly psychoanalytic approach. René Girard, *Proust: A Collection of Critical Essays* (1962); Harold Bloom, ed., *Marcel Proust's Remembrance of Things Past* (1987); and Barbara J. Bucknall, ed., *Critical Essays on Marcel Proust* (1987), are also recommended.

PRONOUNCING GLOSSARY

The following list uses common English syllables and stress accents to provide rough equivalents of selected words whose pronunciation may be unfamiliar to the general reader.

Bathilde: *bah-teeld'*

Charlus: *shar-lews'*

Chartres: *shar'-tr*

Combray: *cohm-bray'*

Corot: *core-oh'*

Duc: *dewk*

Faubourg Saint-Germain: *foh-boor'*
    sanh zhair–manh'

George Sand: *zhorzh sonh*

Maubant: *moh-bawnh'*

Maulévrier: *moh-lay'-vree-ay'*

Proust: *proost*

Quai d'Orleáns: *kay dor-lay-onh*

Saint-Cloud: *sanh–cloo'*

Saint-Loup: *sanh–loo'*

Sévigné: *say-veen-yay'*

Vinteuil: *van-teuh'-ee*

Remembrance of Things Past[1]

Swann's Way. Overture[2]

For a long time I used to go to bed early. Sometimes, when I had put out my candle, my eyes would close so quickly that I had not even time to say to myself: "I'm falling asleep." And half an hour later the thought that it was time to go to sleep would awaken me; I would make as if to put away the book which I imagined was still in my hands, and to blow out the light; I had gone on thinking, while I was asleep, about what I had just been reading, but these thoughts had taken a rather peculiar turn; it seemed to me that I

---

1. Translated by C. K. Scott Moncrieff and Terence Kilmartin.   2. The opening section of Combray, the first volume of *Swann's Way*.

1478 / Marcel Proust

myself was the immediate subject of my book: a church, a quartet, the rivalry between François I and Charles V.[3] This impression would persist for some moments after I awoke; it did not offend my reason, but lay like scales upon my eyes and prevented them from registering the fact that the candle was no longer burning. Then it would begin to seem unintelligible, as the thoughts of a former existence must be to a reincarnate spirit; the subject of my book would separate itself from me, leaving me free to apply myself to it or not; and at the same time my sight would return and I would be astonished to find myself in a state of darkness, pleasant and restful enough for my eyes, but even more, perhaps, for my mind, to which it appeared incomprehensible, without a cause, something dark indeed.

I would ask myself what time it could be; I could hear the whistling of trains, which, now nearer and now farther off, punctuating the distance like the note of a bird in a forest, showed me in perspective the deserted countryside through which a traveller is hurrying towards the nearby station; and the path he is taking will be engraved in his memory by the excitement induced by strange surroundings, by unaccustomed activities, by the conversation he has had and the farewells exchanged beneath an unfamiliar lamp, still echoing in his ears amid the silence of the night, by the imminent joy of going home.

I would lay my cheeks gently against the comfortable cheeks of my pillow, as plump and blooming as the cheeks of babyhood. I would strike a match to look at my watch. Nearly midnight. The hour when an invalid, who has been obliged to set out on a journey and to sleep in a strange hotel, awakened by a sudden spasm, sees with glad relief a streak of daylight showing under his door. Thank God, it is morning! The servants will be about in a minute: he can ring, and someone will come to look after him. The thought of being assuaged gives him strength to endure his pain. He is certain he heard footsteps: they come nearer, and then die away. The ray of light beneath his door is extinguished. It is midnight; someone has just turned down the gas; the last servant has gone to bed, and he must lie all night in agony with no one to bring him relief.

I would fall asleep again, and thereafter would reawaken for short snatches only, just long enough to hear the regular creaking of the wainscot,[4] or to open my eyes to stare at the shifting kaleidoscope of the darkness, to savour, in a momentary glimmer of consciousness, the sleep which lay heavy upon the furniture, the room, the whole of which I formed but an insignificant part and whose insensibility I should very soon return to share. Or else while sleeping I had drifted back to an earlier stage in my life, now for ever outgrown, and had come under the thrall of one of my childish terrors, such as that old terror of my great-uncle's pulling my curls which was effectually dispelled on the day—the dawn of a new era to me—when they were finally cropped from my head. I had forgotten that event during my sleep, but I remembered it again immediately I had succeeded in waking myself up to escape my great-uncle's fingers, and as a measure of precaution I would bury the whole of my head in the pillow before returning to the world of dreams.

Sometimes, too, as Eve was created from a rib of Adam, a woman would

3. Francis I (1496–1567), king of France, and Charles V (1500–1558), Holy Roman emperor and king of Spain, fought four wars over the empire's expansion in Europe.   4. The wooden paneling of the walls.

be born during my sleep from some strain in the position of my thighs. Conceived from the pleasure I was on the point of consummating, she it was, I imagined, who offered me that pleasure. My body, conscious that its own warmth was permeating hers, would strive to become one with her, and I would awake. The rest of humanity seemed very remote in comparison with this woman whose company I had left but a moment ago; my cheek was still warm from her kiss, my body ached beneath the weight of hers. If, as would sometimes happen, she had the features of some woman whom I had known in waking hours, I would abandon myself altogether to the sole quest of her, like people who set out on a journey to see with their eyes some city of their desire, and imagine that one can taste in reality what has charmed one's fancy. And then, gradually, the memory of her would dissolve and vanish, until I had forgotten the girl of my dream.

When a man is asleep, he has in a circle round him the chain of the hours, the sequence of the years, the order of the heavenly host. Instinctively, when he awakes, he looks to these, and in an instant reads off his own position on the earth's surface and the time that has elapsed during his slumbers; but this ordered procession is apt to grow confused, and to break its ranks. Suppose that, towards morning, after a night of insomnia, sleep descends upon him while he is reading, in quite a different position from that in which he normally goes to sleep, he has only to lift his arm to arrest the sun and turn it back in its course,[5] and, at the moment of waking, he will have no idea of the time, but will conclude that he has just gone to bed. Or suppose that he dozes off in some even more abnormal and divergent position, sitting in an armchair, for instance, after dinner: then the world will go hurtling out of orbit, the magic chair will carry him at full speed through time and space, and when he opens his eyes again he will imagine that he went to sleep months earlier in another place. But for me it was enough if, in my own bed, my sleep was so heavy as completely to relax my consciousness; for then I lost all sense of the place in which I had gone to sleep, and when I awoke in the middle of the night, not knowing where I was, I could not even be sure at first who I was; I had only the most rudimentary sense of existence, such as may lurk and flicker in the depths of an animal's consciousness; I was more destitute than the cave-dweller; but then the memory—not yet of the place in which I was, but of various other places where I had lived and might now very possibly be—would come like a rope let down from heaven to draw me up out of the abyss of not-being, from which I could never have escaped by myself: in a flash I would traverse centuries of civilisation, and out of a blurred glimpse of oil-lamps, then of shirts with turned-down collars, would gradually piece together the original components of my ego.

Perhaps the immobility of the things that surround us is forced upon them by our conviction that they are themselves and not anything else, by the immobility of our conception of them. For it always happened that when I awoke like this, and my mind struggled in an unsuccessful attempt to discover where I was, everything revolved around me through the darkness: things, places, years. My body, still too heavy with sleep to move, would endeavour to construe from the pattern of its tiredness the position of its various limbs, in order to deduce therefrom the direction of the wall, the

5. If his uplifted arm prevents him from seeing the sunlight, he will think it is still night.

location of the furniture, to piece together and give a name to the house in which it lay. Its memory, the composite memory of its ribs, its knees, its shoulder-blades, offered it a whole series of rooms in which it had at one time or another slept, while the unseen walls, shifting and adapting themselves to the shape of each successive room that it remembered, whirled round it in the dark. And even before my brain, lingering in cogitation over when things had happened and what they had looked like, had reassembled the circumstances sufficiently to identify the room, it, my body, would recall from each room in succession the style of the bed, the position of the doors, the angle at which the daylight came in at the windows, whether there was a passage outside, what I had had in my mind when I went to sleep and found there when I awoke. The stiffened side on which I lay would, for instance, in trying to fix its position, imagine itself to be lying face to the wall in a big bed with a canopy; and at once I would say to myself, "Why, I must have fallen asleep before Mamma came to say good night," for I was in the country at my grandfather's, who died years ago; and my body, the side upon which I was lying, faithful guardians of a past which my mind should never have forgotten, brought back before my eyes the glimmering flame of the night-light in its urn-shaped bowl of Bohemian glass that hung by chains from the ceiling, and the chimney-piece of Siena marble[6] in my bedroom at Combray, in my grandparents' house, in those far distant days which at this moment I imagined to be in the present without being able to picture them exactly, and which would become plainer in a little while when I was properly awake.

Then the memory of a new position would spring up, and the wall would slide away in another direction; I was in my room in Mme de Saint-Loup's[7] house in the country; good heavens, it must be ten o'clock, they will have finished dinner! I must have overslept myself in the little nap which I always take when I come in from my walk with Mme de Saint-Loup, before dressing for the evening. For many years have now elapsed since the Combray days when, coming in from the longest and latest walks, I would still be in time to see the reflection of the sunset glowing in the panes of my bedroom window. It is a very different kind of life that one leads at Tansonville, at Mme de Saint-Loup's, and a different kind of pleasure that I derive from taking walks only in the evenings, from visiting by moonlight the roads on which I used to play as a child in the sunshine; while the bedroom in which I shall presently fall asleep instead of dressing for dinner I can see from the distance as we return from our walk, with its lamp shining through the window, a solitary beacon in the night.

These shifting and confused gusts of memory never lasted for more than a few seconds; it often happened that, in my brief spell of uncertainty as to where I was, I did not distinguish the various suppositions of which it was composed any more than, when we watch a horse running, we isolate the successive positions of its body as they appear upon a bioscope.[8] But I had seen first one and then another of the rooms in which I had slept during my life, and in the end I would revisit them all in the long course of my waking

---

6. From central Italy, mottled and reddish in color. *Bohemian glass:* likely to have been ornately engraved. Bohemia (now part of the Czech Republic) was a major center of the glass industry. 7. Charles Swann's daughter, Gilberte, who has married Robert de Saint-Loup, a nephew of the Guermantes. 8. An early moving-picture machine that showed photographs in rapid succession.

dream: rooms in winter, where on going to bed I would at once bury my head in a nest woven out of the most diverse materials—the corner of my pillow, the top of my blankets, a piece of a shawl, the edge of my bed, and a copy of a children's paper—which I had contrived to cement together, bird-fashion, by dint of continuous pressure; rooms where, in freezing weather, I would enjoy the satisfaction of being shut in from the outer world (like the sea-swallow which builds at the end of a dark tunnel and is kept warm by the surrounding earth), and where, the fire keeping in all night, I would sleep wrapped up, as it were, in a great cloak of snug and smoky air, shot with the glow of the logs intermittently breaking out again in flame, a sort of alcove without walls, a cave of warmth dug out of the heart of the room itself, a zone of heat whose boundaries were constantly shifting and altering in temperature as gusts of air traversed them to strike freshly upon my face, from the corners of the room or from parts near the window or far from the fireplace which had therefore remained cold;—or rooms in summer, where I would delight to feel myself a part of the warm night, where the moonlight striking upon the half-opened shutters would throw down to the foot of my bed its enchanted ladder, where I would fall asleep, as it might be in the open air, like a titmouse which the breeze gently rocks at the tip of a sunbeam;—or sometimes the Louis XVI room,⁹ so cheerful that I never felt too miserable in it, even on my first night, and in which the slender columns that lightly supported its ceiling drew so gracefully apart to reveal and frame the site of the bed;—sometimes, again, the little room with the high ceiling, hollowed in the form of a pyramid out of two separate storeys, and partly walled with mahogany, in which from the first moment, mentally poisoned by the unfamiliar scent of vetiver,¹ I was convinced of the hostility of the violet curtains and of the insolent indifference of a clock that chattered on at the top of its voice as though I were not there; in which a strange and pitiless rectangular cheval-glass, standing across one corner of the room, carved out for itself a site I had not looked to find tenanted in the soft plenitude of my normal field of vision;² in which my mind, striving for hours on end to break away from its moorings, to stretch upwards so as to take on the exact shape of the room and to reach to the topmost height of its gigantic funnel, had endured many a painful night as I lay stretched out in bed, my eyes staring upwards, my ears straining, my nostrils flaring, my heart beating; until habit had changed the colour of the curtains, silenced the clock, brought an expression of pity to the cruel, slanting face of the glass, disguised or even completely dispelled the scent of vetiver, and appreciably reduced the apparent loftiness of the ceiling. Habit! that skilful but slow-moving arranger who begins by letting our minds suffer for weeks on end in temporary quarters, but whom our minds are none the less only too happy to discover at last, for without it, reduced to their own devices, they would be powerless to make any room seem habitable.

Certainly I was now well awake; my body had veered round for the last time and the good angel of certainty had made all the surrounding objects stand still, had set me down under my bedclothes, in my bedroom, and had

---

9. Furnished in late eighteenth-century style, named for the French monarch of the time and marked by great elegance. The room is that in which Marcel visits Robert de Saint-Loup in *Guermantes Way*. 1. The aromatic root of a tropical grass packaged as a moth repellent.   2. The narrator's room at the fictional seaside resort of Balbec, a setting in *Within a Budding Grove*.

fixed, approximately in their right places in the uncertain light, my chest of drawers, my writing-table, my fireplace, the window overlooking the street, and both the doors. But for all that I now knew that I was not in any of the houses of which the ignorance of the waking moment had, in a flash, if not presented me with a distinct picture, at least persuaded me of the possible presence, my memory had been set in motion; as a rule I did not attempt to go to sleep again at once, but used to spend the greater part of the night recalling our life in the old days at Combray with my great-aunt, at Balbec, Paris, Doncières, Venice, and the rest; remembering again all the places and people I had known, what I had actually seen of them, and what others had told me.

At Combray, as every afternoon ended, long before the time when I should have to go to bed and lie there, unsleeping, far from my mother and grand-mother, my bedroom became the fixed point on which my melancholy and anxious thoughts were centred. Someone had indeed had the happy idea of giving me, to distract me on evenings when I seemed abnormally wretched, a magic lantern,[3] which used to be set on top of my lamp while we waited for dinner-time to come; and, after the fashion of the master-builders and glass-painters of gothic days, it substituted for the opaqueness of my walls an impalpable iridescence, supernatural phenomena of many colours, in which legends were depicted as on a shifting and transitory window. But my sorrows were only increased thereby, because this mere change of lighting was enough to destroy the familiar impression I had of my room, thanks to which, save for the torture of going to bed, it had become quite endurable. Now I no longer recognised it, and felt uneasy in it, as in a room in some hotel or chalet, in a place where I had just arrived by train for the first time.

Riding at a jerky trot, Golo,[4] filled with an infamous design, issued from the little triangular forest which dyed dark-green the slope of a convenient hill, and advanced fitfully towards the castle of poor Geneviève de Brabant. This castle was cut off short by a curved line which was in fact the circum-ference of one of the transparent ovals in the slides which were pushed into position through a slot in the lantern. It was only the wing of a castle, and in front of it stretched a moor on which Geneviève stood lost in contempla-tion, wearing a blue girdle.[5] The castle and the moor were yellow, but I could tell their colour without waiting to see them, for before the slides made their appearance the old-gold sonorous name of Brabant had given me an unmis-takable clue. Golo stopped for a moment and listened sadly to the accom-panying patter read aloud by my great-aunt,[6] which he seemed perfectly to understand, for he modified his attitude with a docility not devoid of a degree of majesty, so as to conform to the indications given in the text; then he rode away at the same jerky trot. And nothing could arrest his slow progress. If the lantern were moved I could still distinguish Golo's horse advancing across the window-curtains, swelling out with their curves and diving into their folds. The body of Golo himself, being of the same supernatural sub-stance as his steed's, overcame every material obstacle—everything that

---

3. A kind of slide projector.   4. Villain of a fifth-century legend. He falsely accuses Geneviève de Brabant of adultery. Brabant was a principality in what is now Belgium.   5. Belt.   6. Marcel's great-aunt is reading the story to him as they wait for dinner.

seemed to bar his way—by taking it as an ossature[7] and embodying it in himself: even the door-handle, for instance, over which, adapting itself at once, would float irresistibly his red cloak or his pale face, which never lost its nobility or its melancholy, never betrayed the least concern at this transvertebration.

And, indeed, I found plenty of charm in these bright projections, which seemed to emanate from a Merovingian[8] past and shed around me the reflections of such ancient history. But I cannot express the discomfort I felt at this intrusion of mystery and beauty into a room which I had succeeded in filling with my own personality until I thought no more of it than of myself. The anaesthetic effect of habit being destroyed, I would begin to think—and to feel—such melancholy things. The door-handle of my room, which was different to me from all the other door-handles in the world, inasmuch as it seemed to open of its own accord and without my having to turn it, so unconscious had its manipulation become—lo and behold, it was now an astral body[9] for Golo. And as soon as the dinner-bell rang I would hurry down to the dining-room, where the big hanging lamp, ignorant of Golo and Bluebeard[1] but well acquainted with my family and the dish of stewed beef, shed the same light as on every other evening; and I would fall into the arms of my mother, whom the misfortunes of Geneviève de Brabant had made all the dearer to me, just as the crimes of Golo had driven me to a more than ordinarily scrupulous examination of my own conscience.

But after dinner, alas, I was soon obliged to leave Mamma, who stayed talking with the others, in the garden if it was fine, or in the little parlour where everyone took shelter when it was wet. Everyone except my grandmother, who held that "It's a pity to shut oneself indoors in the country," and used to have endless arguments with my father on the very wettest days, because he would send me up to my room with a book instead of letting me stay out of doors. "That is not the way to make him strong and active," she would say sadly, "especially this little man, who needs all the strength and will-power that he can get." My father would shrug his shoulders and study the barometer, for he took an interest in meteorology, while my mother, keeping very quiet so as not to disturb him, looked at him with tender respect, but not too hard, not wishing to penetrate the mysteries of his superior mind. But my grandmother, in all weathers, even when the rain was coming down in torrents and Françoise had rushed the precious wicker armchairs indoors so that they should not get soaked, was to be seen pacing the deserted rain-lashed garden, pushing back her disordered grey locks so that her forehead might be freer to absorb the health-giving draughts of wind and rain. She would say, "At last one can breathe!" and would trot up and down the sodden paths—too straight and symmetrical for her liking, owing to the want of any feeling for nature in the new gardener, whom my father had been asking all morning if the weather were going to improve—her keen, jerky little step regulated by the various effects wrought upon her soul by the intoxication of the storm, the power of hygiene, the stupidity of my upbringing and the symmetry of gardens, rather than by any anxiety (for that was quite unknown

7. Skeleton. 8. The first dynasty of French kings (500–751). 9. Spiritual counterpart of the physical body. According to the doctrine of Theosophy (a spiritualist movement originating in 1875), the astral body survives the death of the physical body. 1. The legendary wife murderer, presumably depicted on another set of slides.

to her) to save her plum-coloured skirt from the mudstains beneath which it would gradually disappear to a height that was the constant bane and despair of her maid.

When these walks of my grandmother's took place after dinner there was one thing which never failed to bring her back to the house: this was if (at one of those points when her circular itinerary brought her back, moth-like, in sight of the lamp in the little parlour where the liqueurs were set out on the card-table) my great-aunt called out to her: "Bathilde! Come in and stop your husband drinking brandy!" For, simply to tease her (she had brought so different a type of mind into my father's family that everyone made fun of her), my great-aunt used to make my grandfather, who was forbidden liqueurs, take just a few drops. My poor grandmother would come in and beg and implore her husband not to taste the brandy; and he would get angry and gulp it down all the same, and she would go out again sad and discouraged, but still smiling, for she was so humble of heart and so gentle that her tenderness for others and her disregard for herself and her own troubles blended in a smile which, unlike those seen on the majority of human faces, bore no trace of irony save for herself, while for all of us kisses seemed to spring from her eyes, which could not look upon those she loved without seeming to bestow upon them passionate caresses. This torture inflicted on her by my great-aunt, the sight of my grandmother's vain entreaties, of her feeble attempts, doomed in advance, to remove the liqueur-glass from my grandfather's hands—all these were things of the sort to which, in later years, one can grow so accustomed as to smile at them and to take the persecutor's side resolutely and cheerfully enough to persuade oneself that it is not really persecution; but in those days they filled me with such horror that I longed to strike my great-aunt. And yet, as soon as I heard her "Bathilde! Come in and stop your husband drinking brandy," in my cowardice I became at once a man, and did what all we grown men do when face to face with suffering and injustice: I preferred not to see them; I ran up to the top of the house to cry by myself in a little room beside the schoolroom and beneath the roof, which smelt of orris-root[2] and was scented also by a wild currant-bush which had climbed up between the stones of the outer wall and thrust a flowering branch in through the half-opened window. Intended for a more special and a baser use, this room, from which, in the daytime, I could see as far as the keep[3] of Roussainville-le-Pin, was for a long time my place of refuge, doubtless because it was the only room whose door I was allowed to lock, whenever my occupation was such as required an inviolable solitude: reading or daydreaming, secret tears or sensual gratification. Alas! I little knew that my own lack of will-power, my delicate health, and the consequent uncertainty as to my future, weighed far more heavily on my grandmother's mind than any little dietary indiscretion by her husband in the course of those endless perambulations, afternoon and evening, during which we used to see her handsome face passing to and fro, half raised towards the sky, its brown and wrinkled cheeks, which with age had acquired almost the purple hue of tilled fields in autumn, covered, if she were "going out," by a half-lifted veil, while upon them either the cold or some sad reflection invariably left the drying traces of an involuntary tear.

2. A powder then used as a deodorizer for rooms.   3. The best-fortified tower of a medieval castle. *Baser use*: as a toilet.

My sole consolation when I went upstairs for the night was that Mamma would come in and kiss me after I was in bed. But this good night lasted for so short a time, she went down again so soon, that the moment in which I heard her climb the stairs, and then caught the sound of her garden dress of blue muslin, from which hung little tassels of plaited straw, rustling along the double-doored corridor, was for me a moment of the utmost pain; for it heralded the moment which was bound to follow it, when she would have left me and gone downstairs again. So much so that I reached the point of hoping that this good night which I loved so much would come as late as possible, so as to prolong the time of respite during which Mamma would not yet have appeared. Sometimes when, after kissing me, she opened the door to go, I longed to call her back, to say to her "Kiss me just once more," but I knew that then she would at once look displeased, for the concession which she made to my wretchedness and agitation in coming up to give me this kiss of peace always annoyed my father, who thought such rituals absurd, and she would have liked to try to induce me to outgrow the need, the habit, of having her there at all, let alone get into the habit of asking her for an additional kiss when she was already crossing the threshold. And to see her look displeased destroyed all the calm and serenity she had brought me a moment before, when she had bent her loving face down over my bed, and held it out to me like a host[4] for an act of peace-giving communion in which my lips might imbibe her real presence and with it the power to sleep. But those evenings on which Mamma stayed so short a time in my room were sweet indeed compared to those on which we had guests to dinner, and therefore she did not come at all. Our "guests" were usually limited to M. Swann, who, apart from a few passing strangers, was almost the only person who ever came to the house at Combray, sometimes to a neighbourly dinner (but less frequently since his unfortunate marriage, as my family did not care to receive his wife) and sometimes after dinner, uninvited. On those evenings when, as we sat in front of the house round the iron table beneath the big chestnut-tree, we heard, from the far end of the garden, not the shrill and assertive alarm bell which assailed and deafened with its ferruginous,[5] interminable, frozen sound any member of the household who set it off on entering "without ringing," but the double tinkle, timid, oval, golden, of the visitors' bell, everyone would at once exclaim "A visitor! Who in the world can it be?" but they knew quite well that it could only be M. Swann. My great-aunt, speaking in a loud voice to set an example, in a tone which she endeavoured to make sound natural, would tell the others not to whisper so; that nothing could be more offensive to a stranger coming in, who would be led to think that people were saying things about him which he was not meant to hear; and then my grandmother, always happy to find an excuse for an additional turn in the garden, would be sent out to reconnoitre, and would take the opportunity to remove surreptitiously, as she passed, the stakes of a rose-tree or two, so as to make the roses look a little more natural, as a mother might run her hand through her boy's hair after the barber has smoothed it down, to make it look naturally wavy.

We would all wait there in suspense for the report which my grandmother would bring back from the enemy lines, as though there might be a choice between a large number of possible assailants, and then, soon after, my

4. Communion wafer.   5. Ironlike.

grandfather would say: "I can hear Swann's voice." And indeed one could tell him only by his voice, for it was difficult to make out his face with its arched nose and green eyes, under a high forehead fringed with fair, almost red hair, done in the Bressant style,[6] because in the garden we used as little light as possible, so as not to attract mosquitoes; and I would slip away unobtrusively to order the liqueurs to be brought out, for my grandmother made a great point, thinking it "nicer," of their not being allowed to seem anything out of the ordinary, which we kept for visitors only. Although a far younger man, M. Swann was very much attached to my grandfather, who had been an intimate friend of Swann's father, an excellent but eccentric man the ardour of whose feelings and the current of whose thoughts would often be checked or diverted by the most trifling thing. Several times in the course of a year I would hear my grandfather tell at table the story, which never varied, of the behaviour of M. Swann the elder upon the death of his wife, by whose bedside he had watched day and night. My grandfather, who had not seen him for a long time, hastened to join him at the Swanns' family property on the outskirts of Combray, and managed to entice him for a moment, weeping profusely, out of the death-chamber, so that he should not be present when the body was laid in its coffin. They took a turn or two in the park, where there was a little sunshine. Suddenly M. Swann seized my grandfather by the arm and cried, "Ah, my dear old friend, how fortunate we are to be walking here together on such a charming day! Don't you see how pretty they are, all these trees, my hawthorns, and my new pond, on which you have never congratulated me? You look as solemn as the grave. Don't you feel this little breeze? Ah! whatever you may say, it's good to be alive all the same, my dear Amédée!" And then, abruptly, the memory of his dead wife returned to him, and probably thinking it too complicated to inquire into how, at such a time, he could have allowed himself to be carried away by an impulse of happiness, he confined himself to a gesture which he habitually employed whenever any perplexing question came into his mind: that is, he passed his hand across his forehead, rubbed his eyes, and wiped his glasses. And yet he never got over the loss of his wife, but used to say to my grandfather, during the two years by which he survived her, "It's a funny thing, now; I very often think of my poor wife, but I cannot think of her for long at a time." "Often, but a little at a time, like poor old Swann," became one of my grandfather's favourite sayings, which he would apply to all manner of things. I should have assumed that this father of Swann's had been a monster if my grandfather, whom I regarded as a better judge than myself, and whose word was my law and often led me in the long run to pardon offences which I should have been inclined to condemn, had not gone on to exclaim, "But, after all, he had a heart of gold."

For many years, during the course of which—especially before his marriage—M. Swann the younger came often to see them at Combray, my great-aunt and my grandparents never suspected that he had entirely ceased to live in the society which his family had frequented, and that, under the sort of incognito which the name of Swann gave him among us, they were harbouring—with the complete innocence of a family of respectable innkeepers who have in their midst some celebrated highwayman without knowing it—

6. Close-cropped, like a crew cut; named after a French actor.

one of the most distinguished members of the Jockey Club, a particular friend of the Comte de Paris and of the Prince of Wales, and one of the men most sought after in the aristocratic world of the Faubourg Saint-Germain.[7]

Our utter ignorance of the brilliant social life which Swann led was, of course, due in part to his own reserve and discretion, but also to the fact that middle-class people in those days took what was almost a Hindu view of society, which they held to consist of sharply defined castes, so that everyone at his birth found himself called to that station in life which his parents already occupied, and from which nothing, save the accident of an exceptional career or of a "good" marriage, could extract you and translate you to a superior caste. M. Swann the elder had been a stockbroker; and so "young Swann" found himself immured for life in a caste whose members' fortunes, as in a category of tax-payers, varied between such and such limits of income. One knew the people with whom his father had associated, and so one knew his own associates, the people with whom he was "in a position to mix." If he knew other people besides, those were youthful acquaintances on whom the old friends of his family, like my relatives, shut their eyes all the more good-naturedly because Swann himself, after he was left an orphan, still came most faithfully to see us; but we would have been ready to wager that the people outside our acquaintance whom Swann knew were of the sort to whom he would not have dared to raise his hat if he had met them while he was walking with us. Had it been absolutely essential to apply to Swann a social coefficient peculiar to himself, as distinct from all the other sons of other stockbrokers in his father's position, his coefficient would have been rather lower than theirs, because, being very simple in his habits, and having always had a craze for "antiques" and pictures, he now lived and amassed his collections in an old house which my grandmother longed to visit but which was situated on the Quai d'Orléans,[8] a neighbourhood in which my great-aunt thought it most degrading to be quartered. "Are you really a connoisseur, now?" she would say to him: "I ask for your own sake, as you are likely to have fakes palmed off on you by the dealers," for she did not, in fact, endow him with any critical faculty, and had no great opinion of the intelligence of a man who, in conversation, would avoid serious topics and showed a very dull preciseness, not only when he gave us kitchen recipes, going into the most minute details, but even when my grandmother's sisters were talking to him about art. When challenged by them to give an opinion, or to express his admiration for some picture, he would remain almost offensively silent, and would then make amends by furnishing (if he could) some fact or other about the gallery in which the picture was hung, or the date at which it had been painted. But as a rule he would content himself with trying to amuse us by telling us about his latest adventure with someone whom we ourselves knew, such as the Combray chemist,[9] or our cook, or our coachman. These stories certainly used to make my great-aunt laugh, but she could never decide whether this was on account of the absurd rôle which Swann

7. A fashionable area of Paris on the left bank of the Seine; many of the French aristocracy lived there. *Jockey Club:* an exclusive men's club devoted not only to horseracing but to other diversions (such as the opera). The Comte de Paris (1838–1894) was heir apparent to the French throne, in the unlikely event that the monarchy were reinstated. The Prince of Wales became in 1901 King Edward VII of England. The implication is that Swann's social connections were not merely of the highest but of an idle and somewhat hedonistic sort. 8. A beautiful though less fashionable section in the heart of Paris, along the Seine. 9. Pharmacist.

invariably gave himself therein, or of the wit that he showed in telling them: "I must say you really are a regular character, M. Swann!"

As she was the only member of our family who could be described as a trifle "common," she would always take care to remark to strangers, when Swann was mentioned, that he could easily, had he so wished, have lived in the Boulevard Haussmann or the Avenue de l'Opéra, and that he was the son of old M. Swann who must have left four or five million francs,[1] but that it was a fad of his. A fad which, moreover, she thought was bound to amuse other people so much that in Paris, when M. Swann called on New Year's Day bringing her a little packet of *marrons glacés,* she never failed, if there were strangers in the room, to say to him: "Well, M. Swann, and do you still live next door to the bonded vaults,[2] so as to be sure of not missing your train when you go to Lyons?" and she would peep out of the corner of her eye, over her glasses, at the other visitors.

But if anyone had suggested to my great-aunt that this Swann, who, in his capacity as the son of old M. Swann, was "fully qualified" to be received by any of the "best people," by the most respected barristers and solicitors[3] of Paris (though he was perhaps a trifle inclined to let this hereditary privilege go by default), had another almost secret existence of a wholly different kind; that when he left our house in Paris, saying that he must go home to bed, he would no sooner have turned the corner than he would stop, retrace his steps, and be off to some salon on whose like no stockbroker or associate of stockbrokers had ever set eyes—that would have seemed to my aunt as extraordinary as, to a woman of wider reading, the thought of being herself on terms of intimacy with Aristaeus[4] and of learning that after having a chat with her he would plunge deep into the realms of Thetis, into an empire veiled from mortal eyes, in which Virgil depicts him as being received with open arms; or—to be content with an image more likely to have occurred to her, for she had seen it painted on the plates we used for biscuits at Combray—as the thought of having had to dinner Ali Baba,[5] who, as soon as he finds himself alone and unobserved, will make his way into the cave, resplendent with its unsuspected treasures.

One day when he had come to see us after dinner in Paris, apologising for being in evening clothes, Françoise told us after he had left that she had got it from his coachman that he had been dining "with a princess." "A nice sort of princess,"[6] retorted my aunt, shrugging her shoulders without raising her eyes from her knitting, serenely sarcastic.

Altogether, my great-aunt treated him with scant ceremony. Since she was of the opinion that he ought to feel flattered by our invitations, she thought it only right and proper that he should never come to see us in summer without a basket of peaches or raspberries from his garden, and that from each of his visits to Italy he should bring back some photographs of old masters for me.

1. Nearly a million dollars in the currency of the day; about two and a quarter million dollars by today's standards. *Boulevard Haussmann* and *Avenue de l'Opéra:* large modern avenues where the wealthy bourgeoisie (or middle class) liked to live. 2. A wine warehouse in southeastern Paris, close to the *Gare de Lyon,* the terminal from which trains depart for the industrial city of Lyon and other destinations in southeastern France. *Marrons glacés:* candied chestnuts, a traditional gift on New Year's Day, then a more common day for exchanging gifts than Christmas. 3. Trial lawyers and lawyers of other kinds. 4. Son of the Greek god Apollo. In Virgil's *Fourth Georgic,* Aristaeus seeks help from the sea nymph Thetis. 5. Hero of an *Arabian Nights* tale, a poor youth who discovers a robber's cave filled with treasure. 6. I.e., a "princess" of some shady level of society.

It seemed quite natural, therefore, to send for him whenever a recipe for some special sauce or for a pineapple salad was needed for one of our big dinner-parties, to which he himself would not be invited, being regarded as insufficiently important to be served up to new friends who might be in our house for the first time. If the conversation turned upon the princes of the House of France,[7] "gentlemen you and I will never know, will we, and don't want to, do we?" my great-aunt would say tartly to Swann, who had, perhaps, a letter from Twickenham[8] in his pocket; she would make him push the piano into place and turn over the music on evenings when my grandmother's sister sang, manipulating this person who was elsewhere so sought after with the rough simplicity of a child who will play with a collectors' piece with no more circumspection than if it were a cheap gewgaw. Doubtless the Swann who was a familiar figure in all the clubs of those days differed hugely from the Swann created by my great-aunt when, of an evening, in our little garden at Combray, after the two shy peals had sounded from the gate, she would inject and vitalise with everything she knew about the Swann family the obscure and shadowy figure who emerged, with my grandmother in his wake, from the dark background and who was identified by his voice. But then, even in the most insignificant details of our daily life, none of us can be said to constitute a material whole, which is identical for everyone, and need only be turned up like a page in an account-book or the record of a will; our social personality is a creation of the thoughts of other people. Even the simple act which we describe as "seeing someone we know" is to some extent an intellectual process. We pack the physical outline of the person we see with all the notions we have already formed about him, and in the total picture of him which we compose in our minds those notions have certainly the principal place. In the end they come to fill out so completely the curve of his cheeks, to follow so exactly the line of his nose, they blend so harmoniously in the sound of his voice as if it were no more than a transparent envelope, that each time we see the face or hear the voice it is these notions which we recognise and to which we listen. And so, no doubt, from the Swann they had constructed for themselves my family had left out, in their ignorance, a whole host of details of his life in the world of fashion, details which caused other people, when they met him, to see all the graces enthroned in his face and stopping at the line of his aquiline nose as at a natural frontier; but they had contrived also to put into this face divested of all glamour, vacant and roomy as an untenanted house, to plant in the depths of these undervalued eyes, a lingering residuum, vague but not unpleasing—half-memory and half-oblivion—of idle hours spent together after our weekly dinners, round the card-table or in the garden, during our companionable country life. Our friend's corporeal envelope had been so well lined with this residuum, as well as various earlier memories of his parents, that their own special Swann had become to my family a complete and living creature; so that even now I have the feeling of leaving someone I know for another quite different person when, going back in memory, I pass from the Swann whom I knew later and more intimately to this early Swann—this early Swann in whom I can distinguish the charming mistakes of my youth, and who in fact is less like his

7. The male members of the French royal family, such as the Comte de Paris. The spirit of the times was anti-Royalist, and in fact all claimants to the French throne and their heirs were banished from France by law in 1886.   8. Fashionable London suburb. The French royal family had a house there.

successor than he is like the other people I knew at that time, as though one's life were a picture gallery in which all the portraits of any one period had a marked family likeness, a similar tonality—this early Swann abounding in leisure, fragrant with the scent of the great chestnut-tree, of baskets of raspberries and of a sprig of tarragon.

And yet one day, when my grandmother had gone to ask some favour of a lady whom she had known at the Sacré Cœur[9] (and with whom, because of our notions of caste, she had not cared to keep up any degree of intimacy in spite of several common interests), the Marquise de Villeparisis, of the famous house of Bouillon, this lady had said to her:

"I believe you know M. Swann very well; he's a great friend of my nephews, the des Laumes."[1]

My grandmother had returned from the call full of praise for the house, which overlooked some gardens, and in which Mme de Villeparisis had advised her to rent a flat, and also for a repairing tailor and his daughter who kept a little shop in the courtyard, into which she had gone to ask them to put a stitch in her skirt, which she had torn on the staircase. My grandmother had found these people perfectly charming: the girl, she said, was a jewel, and the tailor the best and most distinguished man she had ever seen. For in her eyes distinction was a thing wholly independent of social position. She was in ecstasies over some answer the tailor had made to her, saying to Mamma:

"Sévigné[2] would not have put it better!" and, by way of contrast, of a nephew of Mme de Villeparisis whom she had met at the house:

"My dear, he is so common!"

Now, the effect of the remark about Swann had been, not to raise him in my great-aunt's estimation, but to lower Mme de Villeparisis. It appeared that the deference which, on my grandmother's authority, we owed to Mme de Villeparisis imposed on her the reciprocal obligation to do nothing that would render her less worthy of our regard, and that she had failed in this duty by becoming aware of Swann's existence and in allowing members of her family to associate with him. "What! She knows Swann? A person who, you always made out, was related to Marshal MacMahon!"[3] This view of Swann's social position which prevailed in my family seemed to be confirmed later on by his marriage with a woman of the worst type, almost a prostitute, whom, to do him justice, he never attempted to introduce to us—for he continued to come to our house alone, though more and more seldom—but from whom they felt they could establish, on the assumption that he had found her there, the circle, unknown to them, in which he ordinarily moved.

But on one occasion my grandfather read in a newspaper that M. Swann was one of the most regular attendants at the Sunday luncheons given by the Duc de X——, whose father and uncle had been among our most prominent statesmen in the reign of Louis-Philippe.[4] Now my grandfather was curious to learn all the smallest details which might help him to take a

9. A convent school in Paris, attended by daughters of the aristocracy and the wealthy bourgeoisie.   1. A fictional family. The Marquise de Villeparisis was a member of the Guermantes family. Proust enhances the apparent reality of the Guermantes by relating them to the historical house of Bouillon, a famous aristocratic family tracing its descent from the Middle Ages.   2. The Marquise de Sévigné (1626–1696), known for the lively style of her letters.   3. Marshal of France (1808–1893), elected president of the French Republic in 1873.   4. King of France from 1830 to 1848, father of the Comte de Paris.

mental share in the private lives of men like Molé, the Duc Pasquier, or the Duc de Broglie.[5] He was delighted to find that Swann associated with people who had known them. My great-aunt, on the other hand, interpreted this piece of news in a sense discreditable to Swann; for anyone who chose his associates outside the caste in which he had been born and bred, outside his "proper station," automatically lowered himself in her eyes. It seemed to her that such a one abdicated all claim to enjoy the fruits of the splendid connections with people of good position which prudent parents cultivate and store up for their children's benefit, and she had actually ceased to "see" the son of a lawyer of our acquaintance because he had married a "Highness" and had thereby stepped down—in her eyes—from the respectable position of a lawyer's son to that of those adventurers, upstart footmen or stable-boys mostly, to whom, we are told, queens have sometimes shown their favours. She objected, therefore, to my grandfather's plan of questioning Swann, when next he came to dine with us, about these people whose friendship with him we had discovered. At the same time my grandmother's two sisters, elderly spinsters who shared her nobility of character but lacked her intelligence, declared that they could not conceive what pleasure their brother-in-law could find in talking about such trifles. They were ladies of lofty aspirations, who for that reason were incapable of taking the least interest in what might be termed gossip, even if it had some historical import, or, generally speaking, in anything that was not directly associated with some aesthetic or virtuous object. So complete was their negation of interest in anything which seemed directly or indirectly connected with worldly matters that their sense of hearing—having finally come to realise its temporary futility when the tone of the conversation at the dinner-table became frivolous or merely mundane without the two old ladies' being able to guide it back to topics dear to themselves—would put its receptive organs into abeyance to the point of actually becoming atrophied. So that if my grandfather wished to attract the attention of the two sisters, he had to resort to some such physical stimuli as alienists adopt in dealing with their distracted patients: to wit, repeated taps on a glass with the blade of a knife, accompanied by a sharp word and a compelling glance, violent methods which these psychiatrists are apt to bring with them into their everyday life among the sane, either from force of professional habit or because they think the whole world a trifle mad.

Their interest grew, however, when, the day before Swann was to dine with us, and when he had made them a special present of a case of Asti, my great-aunt, who had in her hand a copy of the *Figaro* in which to the name of a picture then on view in a Corot exhibition were added the words, "from the collection of M. Charles Swann," asked: "Did you see that Swann is 'mentioned' in the *Figaro*?"[6]

"But I've always told you," said my grandmother, "that he had a great deal of taste."

5. Duc Achille Charles Leonce Victor de Broglie (1785–1870) had a busy public career that ended in 1851. Comte Louis Mathieu Molé (1781–1855) held various cabinet positions before becoming premier of France in 1836. Duc Etienne Denis de Pasquier (1767–1862) also held important public positions up to 1837. All were active during the reign of Louis-Philippe.   6. Leading Parisian newspaper. *Asti:* an Italian white wine. Jean Corot (1796–1875) was a French landscape painter, very popular at the time.

"You would, of course," retorted my great-aunt, "say anything just to seem different from *us*." For, knowing that my grandmother never agreed with her, and not being quite confident that it was her own opinion which the rest of us invariably endorsed, she wished to extort from us a wholesale condemnation of my grandmother's views, against which she hoped to force us into solidarity with her own. But we sat silent. My grandmother's sisters having expressed a desire to mention to Swann this reference to him in the *Figaro*, my great-aunt dissuaded them. Whenever she saw in others an advantage, however trivial, which she herself lacked, she would persuade herself that it was no advantage at all, but a drawback, and would pity so as not to have to envy them.

"I don't think that would please him at all; I know very well that I should hate to see my name printed like that, as large as life, in the paper, and I shouldn't feel at all flattered if anyone spoke to me about it."

She did not, however, put any very great pressure upon my grandmother's sisters, for they, in their horror of vulgarity, had brought to such a fine art the concealment of a personal allusion in a wealth of ingenious circumlocution, that it would often pass unnoticed even by the person to whom it was addressed. As for my mother, her only thought was of trying to induce my father to speak to Swann, not about his wife but about his daughter, whom he worshipped, and for whose sake it was understood that he had ultimately made his unfortunate marriage.

"You need only say a word; just ask him how she is. It must be so very hard for him."

My father, however, was annoyed: "No, no; you have the most absurd ideas. It would be utterly ridiculous."

But the only one of us in whom the prospect of Swann's arrival gave rise to an unhappy foreboding was myself. This was because on the evenings when there were visitors, or just M. Swann, in the house, Mamma did not come up to my room. I dined before the others, and afterwards came and sat at table until eight o'clock, when it was understood that I must go upstairs; that frail and precious kiss which Mamma used normally to bestow on me when I was in bed and just going to sleep had to be transported from the dining-room to my bedroom where I must keep it inviolate all the time that it took me to undress, without letting its sweet charm be broken, without letting its volatile essence diffuse itself and evaporate; and it was precisely on those very evenings when I needed to receive it with special care that I was obliged to take it, to snatch it brusquely and in public, without even having the time or the equanimity to bring to what I was doing the single-minded attention of lunatics who compel themselves to exclude all other thoughts from their minds while they are shutting a door, so that when the sickness of uncertainty sweeps over them again they can triumphantly oppose it with the recollection of the precise moment when they shut the door.

We were all in the garden when the double tinkle of the visitors' bell sounded shyly. Everyone knew that it must be Swann, and yet they looked at one another inquiringly and sent my grandmother to reconnoitre.

"See that you thank him intelligibly for the wine," my grandfather warned his two sisters-in-law. "You know how good it is, and the case is huge."

"Now, don't start whispering!" said my great-aunt. "How would you like to come into a house and find everyone muttering to themselves?"

"Ah! There's M. Swann," cried my father. "Let's ask him if he thinks it will be fine to-morrow."

My mother fancied that a word from her would wipe out all the distress which my family had contrived to cause Swann since his marriage. She found an opportunity to draw him aside for a moment. But I followed her: I could not bring myself to let her out of my sight while I felt that in a few minutes I should have to leave her in the dining-room and go up to my bed without the consoling thought, as on ordinary evenings, that she would come up later to kiss me.

"Now, M. Swann," she said, "do tell me about your daughter. I'm sure she already has a taste for beautiful things, like her papa."

"Come along and sit down here with us all on the verandah," said my grandfather, coming up to him. My mother had to abandon her quest, but managed to extract from the restriction itself a further delicate thought, like good poets whom the tyranny of rhyme forces into the discovery of their finest lines.

"We can talk about her again when we are by ourselves," she said, or rather whispered to Swann. "Only a mother is capable of understanding these things. I'm sure that hers would agree with me."

And so we all sat down round the iron table. I should have liked not to think of the hours of anguish which I should have to spend that evening alone in my room, without being able to go to sleep: I tried to convince myself that they were of no importance since I should have forgotten them next morning, and to fix my mind on thoughts of the future which would carry me, as on a bridge, across the terrifying abyss that yawned at my feet. But my mind, strained by this foreboding, distended like the look which I shot at my mother, would not allow any extraneous impression to enter. Thoughts did indeed enter it, but only on the condition that they left behind them every element of beauty, or even of humour, by which I might have been distracted or beguiled. As a surgical patient, thanks to a local anaesthetic, can look on fully conscious while an operation is being performed upon him and yet feel nothing, I could repeat to myself some favourite lines, or watch my grandfather's efforts to talk to Swann about the Duc d' Audiffret-Pasquier,[7] without being able to kindle any emotion from the one or amusement from the other. Hardly had my grandfather begun to question Swann about that orator when one of my grandmother's sisters, in whose ears the question echoed like a solemn but untimely silence which her natural politeness bade her interrupt, addressed the other with:

"Just fancy, Flora, I met a young Swedish governess today who told me some most interesting things about the co-operative movement in Scandinavia. We really must have her to dine here one evening."

"To be sure!" said her sister Flora, "but I haven't wasted my time either. I met such a clever old gentleman at M. Vinteuil's who knows Maubant[8] quite well, and Maubant has told him every little thing about how he gets up his

---

7. A fictitious nobleman.   8. Actor at the Comédie Française, the French national theater. M. Vinteuil is a fictitious composer and neighbor of the family.

parts. It's the most interesting thing I ever heard. He's a neighbour of M. Vinteuil's, and I never knew; and he is so nice besides."

"M. Vinteuil is not the only one who has nice neighbours," cried my aunt Céline in a voice that was loud because of shyness and forced because of premeditation, darting, as she spoke, what she called a "significant glance" at Swann. And my aunt Flora, who realised that this veiled utterance was Céline's way of thanking Swann for the Asti, looked at him also with a blend of congratulation and irony, either because she simply wished to underline her sister's little witticism, or because she envied Swann his having inspired it, or because she imagined that he was embarrassed, and could not help having a little fun at his expense.

"I think it would be worth while," Flora went on, "to have this old gentleman to dinner. When you get him going on Maubant or Mme Materna[9] he will talk for hours on end."

"That must be delightful," sighed my grandfather, in whose mind nature had unfortunately forgotten to include any capacity whatsoever for becoming passionately interested in the Swedish co-operative movement or in the methods employed by Maubant to get up his parts, just as it had forgotten to endow my grandmother's two sisters with a grain of that precious salt which one has oneself to "add to taste" in order to extract any savour from a narrative of the private life of Molé or of the Comte de Paris.

"By the way," said Swann to my grandfather, "what I was going to tell you has more to do than you might think with what you were asking me just now, for in some respects there has been very little change. I came across a passage in Saint-Simon[1] this morning which would have amused you. It's in the volume which covers his mission to Spain; not one of the best, little more in fact than a journal, but at least a wonderfully well written journal, which fairly distinguishes it from the tedious journals we feel bound to read morning and evening."

"I don't agree with you: there are some days when I find reading the papers very pleasant indeed," my aunt Flora broke in, to show Swann that she had read the note about his Corot in the *Figaro*.

"Yes," aunt Céline went one better, "when they write about things or people in whom we are interested."

"I don't deny it," answered Swann in some bewilderment. "The fault I find with our journalism is that it forces us to take an interest in some fresh triviality or other every day, whereas only three or four books in a lifetime give us anything that is of real importance. Suppose that, every morning, when we tore the wrapper off our paper with fevered hands, a transmutation were to take place, and we were to find inside it—oh! I don't know; shall we say Pascal's *Pensées*?"[2] He articulated the title with an ironic emphasis so as not to appear pedantic. "And then, in the gilt and tooled volumes which we open once in ten years," he went on, showing that contempt for worldly matters which some men of the world like to affect, "we should read that the Queen of the Hellenes had arrived at Cannes, or that the Princesse de

9. Austrian soprano, who took part in the premiere of Wagner's *Ring* cycle at Bayreuth in 1876.   1. The memoirs of the Duc de Saint-Simon (1675–1755) describe court life and intrigue during the reigns of Louis XIV and Louis XV. He was sent to Spain in 1721 to arrange the marriage of Louis XV and the daughter of the king of Spain.   2. The "Thoughts" of the French mathematician and religious philosopher Blaise Pascal (1623–1662) are comments on the human condition and one of the triumphant works of French classicism.

Léon had given a fancy dress ball. In that way we should arrive at a happy medium." But at once regretting that he had allowed himself to speak of serious matters even in jest, he added ironically: "What a fine conversation we're having! I can't think why we climb to these lofty heights," and then, turning to my grandfather: "Well, Saint-Simon tells how Maulévrier had had the audacity to try to shake hands with his sons.[3] You remember how he says of Maulévrier, 'Never did I find in that coarse bottle anything but ill-humour, boorishness, and folly.' "

"Coarse or not, I know bottles in which there is something very different," said Flora briskly, feeling bound to thank Swann as well as her sister, since the present of Asti had been addressed to them both. Céline laughed.

Swann was puzzled, but went on: " 'I cannot say whether it was ignorance or cozenage,' writes Saint-Simon. 'He tried to give his hand to my children. I noticed it in time to prevent him.' "

My grandfather was already in ecstasies over "ignorance or cozenage," but Mlle Céline—the name of Saint-Simon, a "man of letters," having arrested the complete paralysis of her auditory faculties—was indignant:

"What! You admire that? Well, that's a fine thing, I must say! But what's it supposed to mean? Isn't one man as good as the next? What difference can it make whether he's a duke or a groom so long as he's intelligent and kind? He had a fine way of bringing up his children, your Saint-Simon, if he didn't teach them to shake hands with all decent folk. Really and truly, it's abominable. And you dare to quote it!"

And my grandfather, utterly depressed, realising how futile it would be, against this opposition, to attempt to get Swann to tell him the stories which would have amused him, murmured to my mother: "Just tell me again that line of yours which always comforts me so much on these occasions. Oh, yes: 'What virtues, Lord, Thou makest us abhor!'[4] How good that is!"

I never took my eyes off my mother. I knew that when they were at table I should not be permitted to stay there for the whole of dinner-time, and that Mamma, for fear of annoying my father, would not allow me to kiss her several times in public, as I would have done in my room. And so I promised myself that in the dining-room, as they began to eat and drink and as I felt the hour approach, I would put beforehand into this kiss, which was bound to be so brief and furtive, everything that my own efforts could muster, would carefully choose in advance the exact spot on her cheek where I would imprint it, and would so prepare my thoughts as to be able, thanks to these mental preliminaries, to consecrate the whole of the minute Mamma would grant me to the sensation of her cheek against my lips, as a painter who can have his subject for short sittings only prepares his palette, and from what he remembers and from rough notes does in advance everything which he possibly can do in the sitter's absence. But to-night, before the dinner-bell had sounded, my grandfather said with unconscious cruelty: "The little man looks tired; he'd better go up to bed. Besides, we're dining late to-night."

And my father, who was less scrupulous than my grandmother or my mother in observing the letter of a treaty, went on: "Yes; run along; off to bed."

3. Maulévrier was the French ambassador to Spain. Saint-Simon considered him of inferior birth, and refused to let his own children shake Maulévrier's hand (*Memoirs*, vol. XXXIX). 4. From *Pompey's Death* (line 1072), a tragedy by the French dramatist Pierre Corneille (1606–1684).

I would have kissed Mamma then and there, but at that moment the dinner-bell rang.

"No, no, leave your mother alone. You've said good night to one another, that's enough. These exhibitions are absurd. Go on upstairs."

And so I must set forth without viaticum;[5] must climb each step of the staircase "against my heart," as the saying is, climbing in opposition to my heart's desire, which was to return to my mother, since she had not, by kissing me, given my heart leave to accompany me forth. That hateful staircase, up which I always went so sadly, gave out a smell of varnish which had, as it were, absorbed and crystallised the special quality of sorrow that I felt each evening, and made it perhaps even crueller to my sensibility because, when it assumed this olfactory guise, my intellect was powerless to resist it. When we have gone to sleep with a raging toothache and are conscious of it only as of a little girl whom we attempt, time after time, to pull out of the water, or a line of Molière[6] which we repeat incessantly to ourselves, it is a great relief to wake up, so that our intelligence can disentangle the idea of toothache from any artificial semblance of heroism or rhythmic cadence. It was the converse of this relief which I felt when my anguish at having to go up to my room invaded my consciousness in a manner infinitely more rapid, instantaneous almost, a manner at once insidious and brutal, through the inhalation—far more poisonous than moral penetration—of the smell of varnish peculiar to that staircase.

Once in my room I had to stop every loophole, to close the shutters, to dig my own grave as I turned down the bedclothes, to wrap myself in the shroud of my nightshirt. But before burying myself in the iron bed which had been placed there because, on summer nights, I was too hot among the rep curtains of the four-poster,[7] I was stirred to revolt, and attempted the desperate stratagem of a condemned prisoner. I wrote to my mother begging her to come upstairs for an important reason which I could not put in writing. My fear was that Françoise, my aunt's cook who used to be put in charge of me when I was at Combray, might refuse to take my note. I had a suspicion that, in her eyes, to carry a message to my mother when there was a guest would appear as flatly inconceivable as for the door-keeper of a theatre to hand a letter to an actor upon the stage. On the subject of things which might or might not be done she possessed a code at once imperious, abundant, subtle, and uncompromising on points themselves imperceptible or irrelevant, which gave it a resemblance to those ancient laws which combine such cruel ordinances as the massacre of infants at the breast with prohibitions of exaggerated refinement against "seething the kid in his mother's milk," or "eating of the sinew which is upon the hollow of the thigh."[8] This code, judging by the sudden obstinacy which she would put into her refusal to carry out certain of our instructions, seemed to have provided for social complexities and refinements of etiquette which nothing in Françoise's background or in her career as a servant in a village household could have put into her head; and we were obliged to assume that there was latent in her some past existence in the ancient history of France, noble and little under-

5. The communion wafer and wine given to the dying in Catholic rites.   6. French dramatist (1622–1673).   7. Bed with corner pillars to support a canopy and curtains. *Rep*: a heavy ribbed fabric.
8. Refers to the strict dietary laws of Deuteronomy 14.21 and Genesis 32.32, respectively.

stood, as in those manufacturing towns where old mansions still testify to their former courtly days, and chemical workers toil among delicately sculptured scenes from *Le Miracle de Théophile* or *Les quatre fils Aymon.*[9]

In this particular instance, the article of her code which made it highly improbable that—barring an outbreak of fire—Françoise would go down and disturb Mamma in the presence of M. Swann for so unimportant a person as myself was one embodying the respect she showed not only for the family (as for the dead, for the clergy, or for royalty), but also for the stranger within our gates; a respect which I should perhaps have found touching in a book, but which never failed to irritate me on her lips, because of the solemn and sentimental tones in which she would express it, and which irritated me more than usual this evening when the sacred character with which she invested the dinner-party might have the effect of making her decline to disturb its ceremonial. But to give myself a chance of success I had no hesitation in lying, telling her that it was not in the least myself who had wanted to write to Mamma, but Mamma who, on saying good night to me, had begged me not to forget to send her an answer about something she had asked me to look for, and that she would certainly be very angry if this note were not taken to her. I think that Françoise disbelieved me, for, like those primitive men whose senses were so much keener than our own, she could immediately detect, from signs imperceptible to the rest of us, the truth or falsehood of anything that we might wish to conceal from her. She studied the envelope for five minutes as though an examination of the paper itself and the look of my handwriting could enlighten her as to the nature of the contents, or tell her to which article of her code she ought to refer the matter. Then she went out with an air of resignation which seemed to imply: "It's hard lines on parents having a child like that."

A moment later she returned to say that they were still at the ice stage and that it was impossible for the butler to deliver the note at once, in front of everybody; but that when the finger-bowls were put round he would find a way of slipping it into Mamma's hand. At once my anxiety subsided; it was now no longer (as it had been a moment ago) until to-morrow that I had lost my mother, since my little note—though it would annoy her, no doubt, and doubly so because this stratagem would make me ridiculous in Swann's eyes—would at least admit me, invisible and enraptured, into the same room as herself, would whisper about me into her ear; since that forbidden and unfriendly dining-room, where but a moment ago the ice itself—with burned nuts in it—and the finger-bowls seemed to me to be concealing pleasures that were baleful and of a mortal sadness because Mamma was tasting of them while I was far away, had opened its doors to me and, like a ripe fruit which bursts through its skin, was going to pour out into my intoxicated heart the sweetness of Mamma's attention while she was reading what I had written. Now I was no longer separated from her; the barriers were down; an exquisite thread united us. Besides, that was not all: for surely Mamma would come.

As for the agony through which I had just passed, I imagined that Swann

---

9. The four sons of Aymon (French); heroic knights who together rode the magic horse Bayard. Théophile was saved from damnation by the Virgin Mary after having signed a pact with the Devil.

would have laughed heartily at it if he had read my letter and had guessed its purpose; whereas, on the contrary, as I was to learn in due course, a similar anguish[1] had been the bane of his life for many years, and no one perhaps could have understood my feelings at that moment so well as he; to him, the anguish that comes from knowing that the creature one adores is in some place of enjoyment where oneself is not and cannot follow—to him that anguish came through love, to which it is in a sense predestined, by which it will be seized upon and exploited; but when, as had befallen me, it possesses one's soul before love has yet entered into one's life, then it must drift, awaiting love's coming, vague and free, without precise attachment, at the disposal of one sentiment to-day, of another to-morrow, of filial piety or affection for a friend. And the joy with which I first bound myself apprentice, when Françoise returned to tell me that my letter would be delivered, Swann, too, had known well—that false joy which a friend or relative of the woman we love can give us, when, on his arrival at the house or theatre where she is to be found, for some ball or party or "first-night" at which he is to meet her, he sees us wandering outside, desperately awaiting some opportunity of communicating with her. He recognises us, greets us familiarly, and asks what we are doing there. And when we invent a story of having some urgent message to give to his relative or friend, he assures us that nothing could be simpler, takes us in at the door, and promises to send her down to us in five minutes. How we love him—as at that moment I loved Françoise—the good-natured intermediary who by a single word has made supportable, human, almost propitious the inconceivable, infernal scene of gaiety in the thick of which we had been imagining swarms of enemies, perverse and seductive, beguiling away from us, even making laugh at us, the woman we love! If we are to judge of them by him—this relative who has accosted us and who is himself an initiate in those cruel mysteries—then the other guests cannot be so very demoniacal. Those inaccessible and excruciating hours during which she was about to taste of unknown pleasures—suddenly, through an unexpected breach, we have broken into them; suddenly we can picture to ourselves, we possess, we intervene upon, we have almost created, one of the moments the succession of which would have composed those hours, a moment as real as all the rest, if not actually more important to us because our mistress is more intensely a part of it: namely, the moment in which he goes to tell her that we are waiting below. And doubtless the other moments of the party would not have been so very different from this one, would be no more exquisite, no more calculated to make us suffer, since this kind friend has assured us that "Of course, she will be delighted to come down! It will be far more amusing for her to talk to you than to be bored up there." Alas! Swann had learned by experience that the good intentions of a third party are powerless to influence a woman who is annoyed to find herself pursued even into a ballroom by a man she does not love. Too often, the kind friend comes down again alone.

My mother did not appear, but without the slightest consideration for my self-respect (which depended upon her keeping up the fiction that she had asked me to let her know the result of my search for something or other)

1. I.e., his unhappy love for Odette de Crécy, described in *Swann in Love*.

told Françoise to tell me, in so many words: "There is no answer"—words I have so often, since then, heard the hall-porters in grand hotels and the flunkeys in gambling-clubs and the like repeat to some poor girl who replies in bewilderment: "What! he said nothing? It's not possible. You did give him my letter, didn't you? Very well, I shall wait a little longer." And, just as she invariably protests that she does not need the extra gas which the porter offers to light for her, and sits on there, hearing nothing further except an occasional remark on the weather which the porter exchanges with a bell-hop whom he will send off suddenly, when he notices the time, to put some customer's wine on the ice, so, having declined Françoise's offer to make me some tea or to stay beside me, I let her go off again to the pantry, and lay down and shut my eyes, trying not to hear the voices of my family who were drinking their coffee in the garden.

But after a few seconds I realised that, by writing that note to Mamma, by approaching—at the risk of making her angry—so near to her that I felt I could reach out and grasp the moment in which I should see her again, I had cut myself off from the possibility of going to sleep until I actually had seen her, and my heart began to beat more and more painfully as I increased my agitation by ordering myself to keep calm and to acquiesce in my ill-fortune. Then, suddenly, my anxiety subsided, a feeling of intense happiness coursed through me, as when a strong medicine begins to take effect and one's pain vanishes: I had formed a resolution to abandon all attempts to go to sleep without seeing Mamma, had made up my mind to kiss her at all costs, even though this meant the certainty of being in disgrace with her for long afterwards—when she herself came up to bed. The calm which suc-ceeded my anguish filled me with an extraordinary exhilaration, no less than my sense of expectation, my thirst for and my fear of danger. Noiselessly I opened the window and sat down on the foot of my bed. I hardly dared to move in case they should hear me from below. Outside, things too seemed frozen, rapt in a mute intentness not to disturb the moonlight which, dupli-cating each of them and throwing it back by the extension in front of it of a shadow denser and more concrete than its substance, had made the whole landscape at once thinner and larger, like a map which, after being folded up, is spread out upon the ground. What had to move—a leaf of the chestnut-tree, for instance—moved. But its minute quivering, total, self-contained, finished down to its minutest gradation and its last delicate tremor, did not impinge upon the rest of the scene, did not merge with it, remained circum-scribed. Exposed upon this surface of silence which absorbed nothing of them, the most distant sounds, those which must have come from gardens at the far end of the town, could be distinguished with such exact "finish" that the impression they gave of coming from a distance seemed due only to their "pianissimo" execution, like those movements on muted strings so well performed by the orchestra of the Conservatoire[2] that, even though one does not miss a single note, one thinks nonetheless that they are being played somewhere outside, a long way from the concert hall, so that all the old subscribers—my grandmother's sisters too, when Swann had given them his seats—used to strain their ears as if they had caught the distant approach

2. The national music conservatory in Paris.

of an army on the march, which had not yet rounded the corner of the Rue de Trévise.[3]

I was well aware that I had placed myself in a position than which none could be counted upon to involve me in graver consequences at my parents' hands; consequences far graver, indeed, than a stranger would have imagined, and such as (he would have thought) could follow only some really shameful misdemeanour. But in the upbringing which they had given me faults were not classified in the same order as in that of other children, and I had been taught to place at the head of the list (doubtless because there was no other class of faults from which I needed to be more carefully protected) those in which I can now distinguish the common feature that one succumbs to them by yielding to a nervous impulse. But such a phrase had never been uttered in my hearing; no one had yet accounted for my temptations in a way which might have led me to believe that there was some excuse for my giving in to them, or that I was actually incapable of holding out against them. Yet I could easily recognise this class of transgressions by the anguish of mind which preceded as well as by the rigour of the punishment which followed them; and I knew that what I had just done was in the same category as certain other sins for which I had been severely punished, though infinitely more serious than they. When I went out to meet my mother on her way up to bed, and when she saw that I had stayed up in order to say good night to her again in the passage, I should not be allowed to stay in the house a day longer, I should be packed off to school[4] next morning; so much was certain. Very well: had I been obliged, the next moment, to hurl myself out of the window, I should still have preferred such a fate. For what I wanted now was Mamma, to say good night to her. I had gone too far along the road which led to the fulfilment of this desire to be able to retrace my steps.

I could hear my parents' footsteps as they accompanied Swann to the gate, and when the clanging of the bell assured me that he had really gone, I crept to the window. Mamma was asking my father if he had thought the lobster good, and whether M. Swann had had a second helping of the coffee-and-pistachio ice. "I thought it rather so-so," she was saying. "Next time we shall have to try another flavour."

"I can't tell you," said my great-aunt, "what a change I find in Swann. He is quite antiquated!" She had grown so accustomed to seeing Swann always in the same stage of adolescence that it was a shock to her to find him suddenly less young than the age she still attributed to him. And the others too were beginning to remark in Swann that abnormal, excessive, shameful and deserved senescence of bachelors, of all those for whom it seems that the great day which knows no morrow must be longer than for other men, since for them it is void of promise, and from its dawn the moments steadily accumulate without any subsequent partition[5] among offspring.

"I fancy he has a lot of trouble with that wretched wife of his, who lives with a certain Monsieur de Charlus,[6] as all Combray knows. It's the talk of the town."

My mother observed that, in spite of this, he had looked much less

3. A street in Combray.   4. I.e., boarding school.   5. Sharing, as under a will.   6. Brother of the duc de Guermantes.

unhappy of late. "And he doesn't nearly so often do that trick of his, so like his father, of wiping his eyes and drawing his hand across his forehead. I think myself that in his heart of hearts he no longer loves that woman."

"Why, of course he doesn't," answered my grandfather. "He wrote me a letter about it, ages ago, to which I took care to pay no attention, but it left no doubt as to his feelings, or at any rate his love, for his wife. Hullo! you two; you never thanked him for the Asti," he went on, turning to his sisters-in-law.

"What! we never thanked him? I think, between you and me, that I put it to him quite neatly," replied my aunt Flora.

"Yes, you managed it very well; I admired you for it," said my aunt Céline.

"But you did it very prettily, too."

"Yes; I was rather proud of my remark about 'nice neighbours.' "

"What! Do you call that thanking him?" shouted my grandfather. "I heard that all right, but devil take me if I guessed it was meant for Swann. You may be quite sure he never noticed it."

"Come, come; Swann isn't a fool. I'm sure he understood. You didn't expect me to tell him the number of bottles, or to guess what he paid for them."

My father and mother were left alone and sat down for a moment; then my father said: "Well, shall we go up to bed?"

"As you wish, dear, though I don't feel at all sleepy. I don't know why; it can't be the coffee-ice—it wasn't strong enough to keep me awake like this. But I see a light in the servants' hall: poor Françoise has been sitting up for me, so I'll get her to unhook me while you go and undress."

My mother opened the latticed door which led from the hall to the stair-case. Presently I heard her coming upstairs to close her window. I went quietly into the passage; my heart was beating so violently that I could hardly move, but at least it was throbbing no longer with anxiety, but with terror and joy. I saw in the well of the stair a light coming upwards, from Mamma's candle. Then I saw Mamma herself and I threw myself upon her. For an instant she looked at me in astonishment, not realising what could have happened. Then her face assumed an expression of anger. She said not a single word to me; and indeed I used to go for days on end without being spoken to, for far more venial offences than this. A single word from Mamma would have been an admission that further intercourse with me was within the bounds of possibility, and that might perhaps have appeared to me more terrible still, as indicating that, with such a punishment as was in store for me, mere silence and black looks would have been puerile. A word from her then would have implied the false calm with which one addresses a servant to whom one has just decided to give notice; the kiss one bestows on a son who is being packed off to enlist, which would have been denied him if it had merely been a matter of being angry with him for a few days. But she heard my father coming from the dressing-room, where he had gone to take off his clothes, and, to avoid the "scene" which he would make if he saw me, she said to me in a voice half-stifled with anger: "Off you go at once. Do you want your father to see you waiting there like an idiot?"

But I implored her again: "Come and say good night to me," terrified as I saw the light from my father's candle already creeping up the wall, but also making use of his approach as a means of blackmail, in the hope that my

mother, not wishing him to find me there, as find me he must if she continued to refuse me, would give in and say: "Go back to your room. I will come."

Too late: my father was upon us. Instinctively I murmured, though no one
heard me, "I'm done for!"

I was not, however. My father used constantly to refuse to let me do things
which were quite clearly allowed by the more liberal charters granted me by
my mother and grandmother, because he paid no heed to "principles," and
because for him there was no such thing as the "rule of law."[7] For some quite
irrelevant reason, or for no reason at all, he would at the last moment prevent
me from taking some particular walk, one so regular, so hallowed, that to
deprive me of it was a clear breach of faith; or again, as he had done this
evening, long before the appointed hour he would snap out: "Run along up
to bed now; no excuses!" But at the same time, because he was devoid of
principles (in my grandmother's sense), he could not, strictly speaking, be
called intransigent. He looked at me for a moment with an air of surprise
and annoyance, and then when Mamma had told him, not without some
embarrassment, what had happened, said to her: "Go along with him, then.
You said just now that you didn't feel very sleepy, so stay in his room for a
little. I don't need anything."

"But, my dear," my mother answered timidly, "whether or not I feel sleepy
is not the point; we mustn't let the child get into the habit . . ."

"There's no question of getting into a habit," said my father, with a shrug
of the shoulders; "you can see quite well that the child is unhappy. After all,
we aren't jailers. You'll end by making him ill, and a lot of good that will do.
There are two beds in his room; tell Françoise to make up the big one for
you, and stay with him for the rest of the night. Anyhow, I'm off to bed; I'm
not so nervy as you. Good night."

It was impossible for me to thank my father; he would have been exasperated by what he called mawkishness. I stood there, not daring to move; he
was still in front of us, a tall figure in his white nightshirt, crowned with the
pink and violet cashmere scarf which he used to wrap around his head since
he had begun to suffer from neuralgia, standing like Abraham in the engraving after Benozzo Gozzoli[8] which M. Swann had given me, telling Sarah that
she must tear herself away from Isaac. Many years have passed since that
night. The wall of the staircase up which I had watched the light of his candle
gradually climb was long ago demolished. And in myself, too, many things
have perished which I imagined would last for ever, and new ones have
arisen, giving birth to new sorrows and new joys which in those days I could
not have foreseen, just as now the old are hard to understand. It is a long
time, too, since my father has been able to say to Mamma: "Go along with
the child." Never again will such moments be possible for me. But of late I
have been increasingly able to catch, if I listen attentively, the sound of the
sobs which I had the strength to control in my father's presence, and which
broke out only when I found myself alone with Mamma. In reality their echo
has never ceased; and it is only because life is now growing more and more
quiet round about me that I hear them anew, like those convent bells which

7. Reference to the *ius gentium*, the "law of nations" or natural law supposed to govern international and
public relations. Marcel sees the relationship between himself and his mother and grandmother as a social
contract; his father is the unpredictable tyrant.   8. Florentine painter (1420–1497) whose frescoes at
Pisa contain scenes from the life of the biblical patriarch Abraham.

are so effectively drowned during the day by the noises of the street that one would suppose them to have stopped, until they ring out again through the silent evening air.

Mamma spent that night in my room: when I had just committed a sin so deadly that I expected to be banished from the household, my parents gave me a far greater concession than I could ever have won as the reward of a good deed. Even at the moment when it manifested itself in this crowning mercy, my father's behaviour towards me still retained that arbitrary and unwarranted quality which was so characteristic of him and which arose from the fact that his actions were generally dictated by chance expediencies rather than based on any formal plan. And perhaps even what I called his severity, when he sent me off to bed, deserved that title less than my mother's or my grandmother's attitude, for his nature, which in some respects differed more than theirs from my own, had probably prevented him from realising until then how wretched I was every evening, something which my mother and grandmother knew well; but they loved me enough to be unwilling to spare me that suffering, which they hoped to teach me to overcome, so as to reduce my nervous sensibility and to strengthen my will. Whereas my father, whose affection for me was of another kind, would not, I suspect, have had the same courage, for as soon as he had grasped the fact that I was unhappy he had said to my mother: "Go and comfort him."

Mamma stayed that night in my room, and it seemed that she did not wish to mar by recrimination those hours which were so different from anything that I had had a right to expect, for when Françoise (who guessed that something extraordinary must have happened when she saw Mamma sitting by my side, holding my hand and letting me cry unchided) said to her: "But, Madame, what is young master crying for?" she replied: "Why, Françoise, he doesn't know himself: it's his nerves. Make up the big bed for me quickly and then go off to your own." And thus for the first time my unhappiness was regarded no longer as a punishable offence but as an involuntary ailment which had been officially recognised, a nervous condition for which I was in no way responsible: I had the consolation of no longer having to mingle apprehensive scruples with the bitterness of my tears; I could weep henceforth without sin. I felt no small degree of pride, either, in Françoise's presence at this return to humane conditions which, not an hour after Mamma had refused to come up to my room and had sent the snubbing message that I was to go to sleep, raised me to the dignity of a grown-up person, brought me of a sudden to a sort of puberty of sorrow, a manumission of tears. I ought to have been happy; I was not. It struck me that my mother had just made a first concession which must have been painful to her, that it was a first abdication on her part from the ideal she had formed for me, and that for the first time she who was so brave had to confess herself beaten. It struck me that if I had just won a victory it was over her, that I had succeeded, as sickness or sorrow or age might have succeeded, in relaxing her will, in undermining her judgment; a black date in the calendar. And if I had dared now, I should have said to Mamma: "No, I don't want you to, you mustn't sleep here." But I was conscious of the practical wisdom, of what would nowadays be called the realism, with which she tempered the ardent idealism of my grandmother's nature, and I knew that now the mischief was done she would prefer to let me enjoy the soothing pleasure of her company, and not

to disturb my father again. Certainly my mother's beautiful face seemed to
shine again with youth that evening, as she sat gently holding my hands and
trying to check my tears; but this was just what I felt should not have been;
her anger would have saddened me less than this new gentleness, unknown
to my childhood experience; I felt that I had with an impious and secret
finger traced a first wrinkle upon her soul and brought out a first white hair
on her head. This thought redoubled my sobs, and then I saw that Mamma,
who had never allowed herself to indulge in any undue emotion with me,
was suddenly overcome by my tears and had to struggle to keep back her
own. When she realised that I had noticed this, she said to me with a smile:
"Why, my little buttercup, my little canary-boy, he's going to make Mamma
as silly as himself if this goes on. Look, since you can't sleep, and Mamma
can't either, we mustn't go on in this stupid way; we must do something; I'll
get one of your books." But I had none there. "Would you like me to get out
the books now that your grandmother is going to give you for your birthday?
Just think it over first, and don't be disappointed if there's nothing new for
you then."

I was only too delighted, and Mamma went to fetch a parcel of books of
which I could not distinguish, through the paper in which they were
wrapped, any more than their short, wide format but which, even at this first
glimpse, brief and obscure as it was, bade fair to eclipse already the paintbox
of New Year's Day and the silkworms of the year before. The books were *La
Mare au Diable, François le Champi, La Petite Fadette* and *Les Maîtres Son-
neurs*.[9] My grandmother, as I learned afterwards, had at first chosen Musset's
poems, a volume of Rousseau, and *Indiana*; for while she considered light
reading as unwholesome as sweets and cakes, she did not reflect that the
strong breath of genius might have upon the mind even of a child an influence at once more dangerous and less invigorating than that of fresh air and
sea breezes upon his body. But when my father had almost called her an
imbecile on learning the names of the books she proposed to give me,[1] she
had journeyed back by herself to Jouy-le-Vicomte to the bookseller's, so that
there should be no danger of my not having my present in time (it was a
boiling hot day, and she had come home so unwell that the doctor had
warned my mother not to allow her to tire herself so), and had fallen back
upon the four pastoral novels of George Sand.

"My dear," she had said to Mamma, "I could not bring myself to give the
child anything that was not well written."

The truth was that she could never permit herself to buy anything from
which no intellectual profit was to be derived, above all the profit which fine
things afford us by teaching us to seek our pleasures elsewhere than in the
barren satisfaction of worldly wealth. Even when she had to make someone
a present of the kind called "useful," when she had to give an armchair or
some table-silver or a walking-stick, she would choose "antiques," as though
their long desuetude had effaced from them any semblance of utility and

---

9. Novels of idealized country life by the French woman writer George Sand (1806–1876). The titles can
be translated as *The Devil's Pool, François the Foundling Discovered in the Fields, Little Fadette,* and *The
Master Bellringers.*   1. The works of Alfred de Musset (1810–1857) and Jean-Jacques Rousseau (1712–
1778), often romantic and sometimes confessional, and some works by Sand (*Indiana* was a novel of free
love), would be thought unsuitable reading for a young child.

fitted them rather to instruct us in the lives of the men of other days than to serve the common requirements of our own. She would have liked me to have in my room photographs of ancient buildings or of beautiful places. But at the moment of buying them, and for all that the subject of the picture had an aesthetic value, she would find that vulgarity and utility had too prominent a part in them, through the mechanical nature of their reproduction by photography. She attempted by a subterfuge, if not to eliminate altogether this commercial banality, at least to minimise it, to supplant it to a certain extent with what was art still, to introduce, as it were, several "thicknesses" of art: instead of photographs of Chartres Cathedral, of the Fountains of Saint-Cloud, or of Vesuvius, she would inquire of Swann whether some great painter had not depicted them, and preferred to give me photographs of "Chartres Cathedral" after Corot, of the "Fountains of Saint-Cloud" after Hubert Robert, and of "Vesuvius" after Turner,[2] which were a stage higher in the scale of art. But although the photographer had been prevented from reproducing directly these masterpieces or beauties of nature, and had there been replaced by a great artist, he resumed his odious position when it came to reproducing the artist's interpretation. Accordingly, having to reckon again with vulgarity, my grandmother would endeavour to postpone the moment of contact still further. She would ask Swann if the picture had not been engraved, preferring, when possible, old engravings with some interest of association apart from themselves, such, for example, as show us a masterpiece in a state in which we can no longer see it to-day (like Morghen's print of Leonardo's "Last Supper" before its defacement).[3] It must be admitted that the results of this method of interpreting the art of making presents were not always happy. The idea which I formed of Venice, from a drawing by Titian[4] which is supposed to have the lagoon in the background, was certainly far less accurate than what I should have derived from ordinary photographs. We could no longer keep count in the family (when my great-aunt wanted to draw up an indictment of my grandmother) of all the arm-chairs she had presented to married couples, young and old, which on a first attempt to sit down upon them had at once collapsed beneath the weight of their recipients. But my grandmother would have thought it sordid to concern herself too closely with the solidity of any piece of furniture in which could still be discerned a flourish, a smile, a brave conceit of the past. And even what in such pieces answered a material need, since it did so in a manner to which we are no longer accustomed, charmed her like those old forms of speech in which we can still see traces of a metaphor whose fine point has been worn away by the rough usage of our modern tongue. As it happened, the pastoral novels of George Sand which she was giving me for my birthday were regular lumber-rooms full of expressions that have fallen out of use and become quaint and picturesque, and are now only to be found in country dialects. And my grandmother had bought them in preference to other books, as she would more readily have taken a house with a gothic

2. The famous volcano near Naples, painted by J. M. W. Turner (1775–1851). The Cathedral of Chartres, painted in 1830 by Corot. The fountains in the old park at Saint-Cloud, outside Paris, painted by Hubert Robert (1733–1809). 3. Leonardo da Vinci's *Last Supper* was the subject of a famous engraving by Morghen, a late-eighteenth-century engraver. The paints in the original fresco had deteriorated rapidly, and a major restoration took place in the nineteenth century. 4. Venetian painter (1477–1576).

1506 / MARCEL PROUST

dovecot or some other such piece of antiquity as will exert a benign influence
on the mind by giving it a hankering for impossible journeys through the
realms of time.

Mamma sat down by my bed; she had chosen *François le Champi*, whose
reddish cover and incomprehensible title[5] gave it, for me, a distinct personality and a mysterious attraction. I had not then read any real novels. I had
heard it said that George Sand was a typical novelist. This predisposed me
to imagine that *François le Champi* contained something inexpressibly delicious. The narrative devices designed to arouse curiosity or melt to pity,
certain modes of expression which disturb or sadden the reader, and which,
with a little experience, he may recognise as common to a great many novels,
seemed to me—for whom a new book was not one of a number of similar
objects but, as it were, a unique person, absolutely self-contained—simply
an intoxicating distillation of the peculiar essence of *François le Champi*.
Beneath the everyday incidents, the ordinary objects and common words, I
sensed a strange and individual tone of voice. The plot began to unfold: to
me it seemed all the more obscure because in those days, when I read, I
used often to daydream about something quite different for page after page.
And the gaps which this habit left in my knowledge of the story were widened
by the fact that when it was Mamma who was reading to me aloud she left
all the love-scenes out. And so all the odd changes which take place in the
relations between the miller's wife and the boy, changes which only the
gradual dawning of love can explain, seemed to me steeped in a mystery
the key to which (I readily believed) lay in that strange and mellifluous name
of *Champi*, which invested the boy who bore it, I had no idea why, with its
own vivid, ruddy, charming colour. If my mother was not a faithful reader,
she was none the less an admirable one, when reading a work in which she
found the note of true feeling, in the respectful simplicity of her interpretation and the beauty and sweetness of her voice. Even in ordinary life, when
it was not works of art but men and women whom she was moved to pity or
admire, it was touching to observe with what deference she would banish
from her voice, her gestures, from her whole conversation, now the note of
gaiety which might have distressed some mother who had once lost a child,
now the recollection of an event or anniversary which might have reminded
some old gentleman of the burden of his years, now the household topic
which might have bored some young man of letters. And so, when she read
aloud the prose of George Sand, prose which is everywhere redolent of that
generosity and moral distinction which Mamma had learned from my grandmother to place above all other qualities in life, and which I was not to teach
her until much later to refrain from placing above all other qualities in literature too, taking pains to banish from her voice any pettiness or affectation
which might have choked that powerful stream of language, she supplied all
the natural tenderness, all the lavish sweetness which they demanded to
sentences which seemed to have been composed for her voice and which
were all, so to speak, within the compass of her sensibility. She found, to
tackle them in the required tone, the warmth of feeling which pre-existed
and dictated them, but which is not to be found in the words themselves,

5. *Champi* ("foundling") is an old French word the child Marcel would not have known.

and by this means she smoothed away, as she read, any harshness or discordance in the tenses of verbs, endowing the imperfect and the preterite[6] with all the sweetness to be found in generosity, all the melancholy to be found in love, guiding the sentence that was drawing to a close towards the one that was about to begin, now hastening, now slackening the pace of the syllables so as to bring them, despite their differences of quantity, into a uniform rhythm, and breathing into this quite ordinary prose a kind of emotional life and continuity.

My aching heart was soothed; I let myself be borne upon the current of this gentle night on which I had my mother by my side. I knew that such a night could not be repeated; that the strongest desire I had in the world, namely, to keep my mother in my room through the sad hours of darkness, ran too much counter to general requirements and to the wishes of others for such a concession as had been granted me this evening to be anything but a rare and artificial exception. To-morrow night my anguish would return and Mamma would not stay by my side. But when my anguish was assuaged, I could no longer understand it; besides, to-morrow was still a long way off; I told myself that I should still have time to take preventive action, although that time could bring me no access of power since these things were in no way dependent upon the exercise of my will, and seemed not quite inevitable only because they were still separated from me by this short interval.

And so it was that, for a long time afterwards, when I lay awake at night and revived old memories of Combray, I saw no more of it than this sort of luminous panel, sharply defined against a vague and shadowy background, like the panels which the glow of a Bengal light[7] or a searchlight beam will cut out and illuminate in a building the other parts of which remain plunged in darkness: broad enough at its base, the little parlour, the dining-room, the opening of the dark path from which M. Swann, the unwitting author of my sufferings, would emerge, the hall through which I would journey to the first step of that staircase, so painful to climb, which constituted, all by itself, the slender cone of this irregular pyramid; and, at the summit, my bedroom, with the little passage through whose glazed[8] door Mamma would enter; in a word, seen always at the same evening hour, isolated from all its possible surroundings, detached and solitary against the dark background, the bare minimum of scenery necessary (like the decor one sees prescribed on the title-page of an old play, for its performance in the provinces) to the drama of my undressing; as though all Combray had consisted of but two floors joined by a slender staircase, and as though there had been no time there but seven o'clock at night. I must own[9] that I could have assured any questioner that Combray did include other scenes and did exist at other hours than these. But since the facts which I should then have recalled would have been prompted only by voluntary memory, the memory of the intellect, and since the pictures which that kind of memory shows us preserve nothing of the past itself, I should never have had any wish to ponder over this residue of Combray. To me it was in reality all dead.

6. The imperfect is the tense of continued and incomplete action in the past, whereas the preterite describes a single completed action.   7. Fireworks.   8. I.e., with glass panes.   9. Admit.

Permanently dead? Very possibly.

There is a large element of chance in these matters, and a second chance occurrence, that of our own death, often prevents us from awaiting for any length of time the favours of the first.

I feel that there is much to be said for the Celtic belief that the souls of those whom we have lost are held captive in some inferior being, in an animal, in a plant, in some inanimate object, and thus effectively lost to us until the day (which to many never comes) when we happen to pass by the tree or to obtain possession of the object which forms their prison.[1] Then they start and tremble, they call us by our name, and as soon as we have recognised their voice the spell is broken. Delivered by us, they have overcome death and return to share our life.

And so it is with our own past. It is a labour in vain to attempt to recapture it: all the efforts of our intellect must prove futile. The past is hidden somewhere outside the realm, beyond the reach of intellect, in some material object (in the sensation which that material object will give us) of which we have no inkling. And it depends on chance whether or not we come upon this object before we ourselves must die.

Many years had elapsed during which nothing of Combray, save what was comprised in the theatre and the drama of my going to bed there, had any existence for me, when one day in winter, on my return home, my mother, seeing that I was cold, offered me some tea, a thing I did not ordinarily take. I declined at first, and then, for no particular reason, changed my mind. She sent for one of those squat, plump little cakes called "petites madeleines," which look as though they had been moulded in the fluted valve of a scallop shell. And soon, mechanically, dispirited after a dreary day with the prospect of a depressing morrow, I raised to my lips a spoonful of the tea in which I had soaked a morsel of the cake. No sooner had the warm liquid mixed with the crumbs touched my palate than a shudder ran through me and I stopped, intent upon the extraordinary thing that was happening to me. An exquisite pleasure had invaded my senses, something isolated, detached, with no suggestion of its origin. And at once the vicissitudes of life had become indifferent to me, its disasters innocuous, its brevity illusory—this new sensation having had on me the effect which love has of filling me with a precious essence; or rather this essence was not in me, it *was* me. I had ceased now to feel mediocre, contingent, mortal. Whence could it have come to me, this all-powerful joy? I sensed that it was connected with the taste of the tea and the cake, but that it infinitely transcended those savours, could not, indeed, be of the same nature. Whence did it come? What did it mean? How could I seize and apprehend it?

I drink a second mouthful, in which I find nothing more than in the first, then a third, which gives me rather less than the second. It is time to stop; the potion is losing its magic. It is plain that the truth I am seeking lies not in the cup but in myself. The drink has called it into being, but does not know it, and can only repeat indefinitely, with a progressive diminution of strength, the same message which I cannot interpret, though I hope at least to be able to call it forth again and to find it there presently, intact and at my disposal, for my final enlightenment. I put down the cup and examine

1. A belief attributed to Druids, the priests of the ancient Celtic peoples.

my own mind. It alone can discover the truth. But how? What an abyss of uncertainty, whenever the mind feels overtaken by itself; when it, the seeker, is at the same time the dark region through which it must go seeking and where all its equipment will avail it nothing. Seek? More than that: create. It is face to face with something which does not yet exist, to which it alone can give reality and substance, which it alone can bring into the light of day.

And I begin again to ask myself what it could have been, this unremembered state which brought with it no logical proof, but the indisputable evidence, of its felicity, its reality, and in whose presence other states of consciousness melted and vanished. I decide to attempt to make it reappear. I retrace my thoughts to the moment at which I drank the first spoonful of tea. I rediscover the same state, illuminated by no fresh light. I ask my mind to make one further effort, to bring back once more the fleeting sensation. And so that nothing may interrupt it in its course I shut out every obstacle, every extraneous idea, I stop my ears and inhibit all attention against the sounds from the next room. And then, feeling that my mind is tiring itself without having any success to report, I compel it for a change to enjoy the distraction which I have just denied it, to think of other things, to rest and refresh itself before making a final effort. And then for the second time I clear an empty space in front of it; I place in position before my mind's eye the still recent taste of that first mouthful, and I feel something start within me, something that leaves its resting-place and attempts to rise, something that has been embedded like an anchor at a great depth; I do not know yet what it is, but I can feel it mounting slowly; I can measure the resistance, I can hear the echo of great spaces traversed.

Undoubtedly what is thus palpitating in the depths of my being must be the image, the visual memory which, being linked to that taste, is trying to follow it into my conscious mind. But its struggles are too far off, too confused and chaotic; scarcely can I perceive the neutral glow into which the elusive whirling medley of stirred-up colours is fused, and I cannot distinguish its form, cannot invite it, as the one possible interpreter, to translate for me the evidence of its contemporary, its inseparable paramour, the taste, cannot ask it to inform me what special circumstance is in question, from what period in my past life.

Will it ultimately reach the clear surface of my consciousness, this memory, this old, dead moment which the magnetism of an identical moment has travelled so far to importune, to disturb, to raise up out of the very depths of my being? I cannot tell. Now I feel nothing; it has stopped, has perhaps sunk back into its darkness, from which who can say whether it will ever rise again? Ten times over I must essay the task, must lean down over the abyss. And each time the cowardice that deters us from every difficult task, every important enterprise, has urged me to leave the thing alone, to drink my tea and to think merely of the worries of to-day and my hopes for to-morrow, which can be brooded over painlessly.

And suddenly the memory revealed itself. The taste was that of the little piece of madeleine which on Sunday mornings at Combray (because on those mornings I did not go out before mass), when I went to say good morning to her in her bedroom, my aunt Léonie used to give me, dipping it first in her own cup of tea or tisane. The sight of the little madeleine had recalled nothing to my mind before I tasted it; perhaps because I had so often seen such things in the meantime, without tasting them, on the trays in pastry-cooks' windows, that their image had dissociated itself from those Combray days to take its place among others more recent; perhaps because of those memories, so long abandoned and put out of mind, nothing now survived, everything was scattered; the shapes of things, including that of the little scallop-shell of pastry, so richly sensual under its severe, religious folds, were either obliterated or had been so long dormant as to have lost the power of expansion which would have allowed them to resume their place in my consciousness. But when from a long-distant past nothing subsists, after the people are dead, after the things are broken and scattered, taste and smell alone, more fragile but more enduring, more unsubstantial, more persistent, more faithful, remain poised a long time, like souls, remembering, waiting, hoping, amid the ruins of all the rest; and bear unflinchingly, in the tiny and almost impalpable drop of their essence, the vast structure of recollection.

And as soon as I had recognised the taste of the piece of madeleine[2] soaked in her decoction of lime-blossom which my aunt used to give me (although I did not yet know and must long postpone the discovery of why this memory made me so happy) immediately the old grey house upon the street, where her room was, rose up like a stage set to attach itself to the little pavilion opening on to the garden which had been built out behind it for my parents (the isolated segment which until that moment had been all that I could see); and with the house the town, from morning to night and in all weathers, the Square where I used to be sent before lunch, the streets along which I used to run errands, the country roads we took when it was fine. And as in the game wherein the Japanese amuse themselves by filling a porcelain bowl with water and steeping in it little pieces of paper which until then are without character or form, but, the moment they become wet, stretch and twist and take on colour and distinctive shape, become flowers or houses or people, solid and recognisable, so in that moment all the flowers in our garden and in M. Swann's park, and the water-lilies on the Vivonne[3] and the good folk of the village and their little dwellings and the parish church and the whole of Combray and its surroundings, taking shape and solidity, sprang into being, town and gardens alike, from my cup of tea.

2. A small, rich cookielike pastry.   3. The local river.

THOMAS MANN
1875–1955

Thomas Mann's reputation as the great German novelist of the twentieth century represents only part of his stature; by the time of his death, he had become an international figure to whom people looked for statements on art, modern society, and the human condition. Continuing the great nineteenth-century tradition of psychological realism, Mann took as his subject the cultural and spiritual crises of Europe at the turn of the century. His career spanned a time of great change, including as it did the upheaval of two world wars and the visible disintegration of an entire society. Where other modern novelists, such as James Joyce, William Faulkner, and Virginia Woolf, stressed innovative language and style, Mann emphasized instead the society of his time and—inside that society—the universal human conflicts between art and life, sensuality and intellect, individual and social will.

Many of Mann's themes derive from the nineteenth-century German aesthetic tradition in which he grew up. The philosophers Schopenhauer and Nietzsche and the composer Wagner had the most influence on his work: Arthur Schopenhauer (1788–1860) for his vision of the artist's suffering and development; Friedrich Nietzsche (1844–1900) for his portrait of the diseased artist overcoming chaos and decay to produce, through discipline and will, artworks that justify existence; and Richard Wagner (1813–1883) for embodying the complete artist who controlled all aspects of his work: music, lyrics, the very staging of his operas. Mann's well-known use of the verbal *leitmotif* is also borrowed from Wagner, who would use in his operas a recurrent musical theme (the *leitmotif*) associated with a particular person, thing, action, or state of being. In Mann's literary adaptation, evocative phrases, repeated almost without change, link memories throughout the text and establish a cumulative emotional resonance. In the story *Tonio Kröger*, for example, Tonio's dual ancestry is repeatedly suggested by the contrasting phrases of the "dark, fiery mother, who played the piano and mandolin," and the father with his "thoughtful blue eyes" and "wild flower in the buttonhole." Inside the tradition of realistic narration, Mann created a highly organized literary structure with subtly interrelated themes and images that built up rich associations of ideas: in his own words, an "epic prose composition . . . understood by me as spiritual thematic pattern, as a musical complex of associations."

Mann was born in Lübeck, a historic seaport and commercial city in northern Germany, on June 6, 1875. His father was a grain merchant and head of the family firm; his mother came from a German-Brazilian family and was known for her beauty and musical talent. The contrast of Nordic and Latin that plays such a large part in Mann's work begins in his consciousness of his own heritage and is expanded to far-reaching symbolic levels. He disliked the scientific emphasis of his secondary education and left school in 1894 after repeating two years. Rejoining his family in Munich, where they had moved in 1891 after his father's death, he worked as an unpaid apprentice in a fire insurance business but found more interest in university lectures in history, political economy, and art. He decided against a business career after his first published story, *Fallen* (1896), received praise from the noted poet Richard Dehmel, and from 1896 to 1898 lived and wrote in Italy before returning to Munich for a two-year stint as manuscript reader for the satiric weekly *Simplicissimus*. In 1905, he married Katia Pringsheim, with whom he had six children. The short stories collected in *Little Herr Friedemann* (1899) were a success, and enabled Mann to find a publisher for his first major work, *Buddenbrooks* (1901).

Buddenbrooks describes the decline of a prosperous German family through four generations and is to some extent based on the history of the Mann family business. Nonetheless, the elements of autobiography are quickly absorbed into the more universal themes of the inner decay of the German burgher ("bourgeois," or middle-class) tradition and its growing isolation from other segments of society, a decline paralleled in the portrait of a developing artistic sensitivity and its relation to death. Children in the family of the self-confident, aggressive, and disciplined Consul Johann Buddenbrooks become increasingly introspective, hesitant, unhealthy, and artistic. The end of the family comes with young Hanno, a musical genius who is completely absorbed in his piano improvisations and thus prey to the fatal temptation of infinite beauty. In this novel, as in many later works, Mann's fictional world is governed by a tension or dualism between sensuous experience and intellect or will. A diseased and alienated imaginative soul is set against a healthy, gregarious, somewhat obtuse normal citizen; the erratic and poor artist against the disciplined and prosperous burgher; the dark, brown-eyed Latin against the blond, blue-eyed Nordic;

warm, unself-conscious feelings against icy intellect; freedom against authority; immorality and decadence against moral respectability; a longing for the eternal and infinite against active participation in everyday life.

There is no recommended resolution of these polarities, for if either overwhelms the other, tragedy must follow. In the seemingly autobiographical *Tonio Kröger*, the protagonist is portrayed as sensitive to the claims of both, and his growing awareness of their combined importance is a sign of maturity. Ideally, the artist must live both extremes at once, in constant lucidity and pain. In *Death in Venice* (1912), the author Gustave Aschenbach suffers and dies for having been unable to keep the balance; in the novel *Doctor Faustus* (1947), the composer Adrian Leverkühn sells his soul to experience both poles. In *Mario and the Magician* (1929), the sadistic hypnotist Cipolla is an artist in his fashion, exercising a fatally corrupt art in which all his psychological insight, cutting intellect, and iron will produce only torment for himself and others. Mann's letters and essays show that he felt deeply involved in the relations of the artist's life to the artwork, but his protagonists have their own identity and symbolize much more than Mann's own artistic career. As artist and craftsman, he always insisted on distinguishing the work of art from its raw material, the emotions and experiences of life. He cultivated objectivity, distance, and irony in his own works, and no character—including the narrator—is immune from the author's critical eye.

Throughout his writings up to and during World War I, Mann established himself as an important spokesman for modern Germany. His early conservatism and defense of an authoritarian nationalist government (*Reflections of a Non-Political Man*, 1918) gave way to an ardent defense of democracy and liberal humanism as the Nazis came to power. Mann's most famous novel, *The Magic Mountain* (1924), is a bildungsroman (a novel of the protagonist's education and development) that uses the isolation of a mountaintop tuberculosis sanitorium to gain perspective on the philosophic issues of twentieth-century Europe. The hero, Hans Castorp, has to decide how to live as he listens to the competing dogmas of the humanist Settembrini and the fanatic antirationalist Naphta, and undergoes a double temptation of oblivion through eroticism (Clavdia Chauchat) and death (symbolized by the isolated sanitorium). The novel ends with Castorp choosing active participation in a world at war; whether or not he survives the trenches is left unresolved, but he has taken charge of his own destiny. *The Magic Mountain* was immensely popular, and its author received the Nobel Prize in 1929. He was so much an international figure when he went into voluntary exile in Switzerland as Hitler came to power in 1933 that the Nazis, stung by his criticism, revoked his citizenship. Moving to America in 1938, he wrote and lectured against Nazism, and in 1944 he became an American citizen.

Mann's later works cover a range of themes. *Joseph, and His Brothers* (1933–45) is a tetralogy on the biblical tale of Joseph, who, abandoned for dead by his brothers, survives and comes to power in Egypt. *Doctor Faustus*, which Mann called "the novel of my epoch, dressed up in the story of a highly precarious and sinful artistic life," portrayed the composer Adrian Leverkühn as a modern Faust who personifies the temptation and corruption of contemporary Germany. Leverkühn makes a pact with the Devil to become aware of the extremes of his own personality, thus enriching his experience and his music. His pieces are rationally composed by using intellectual patterns derived from the twelve-tone row, an avant-garde theory of composition based on a sequence of twelve tones with no previous harmonic relations, instead of the traditional musical scale. His *Lamentation of Doctor Faustus* is a direct challenge in theme and technique to the scale-based tonality of that earlier German masterpiece, Beethoven's Ninth Symphony with its concluding *Ode to Joy*. A somber and compelling work, *Doctor Faustus* symbolizes the negation of life Mann found inherent in Hitler's attempt to reshape German culture. Well after the war, when Mann had moved to Zurich, he published a final, comic picture of the artist-figure as a confidence man who uses his skill and ironic insight to manipulate society (*The Confessions of Felix Krull*, 1954). Mann's last work before his death on August 12, 1955, the

Confessions recapitulates his familiar themes but in a lighthearted parody of traditional bildungsromans that is a far cry from the moral seriousness of earlier tales.

Mann's most famous novella, *Death in Venice,* was published in 1912, shortly after the writer's own vacation in Venice and two years before World War I. Its sense of impending doom involves the cultural disintegration of the "European soul" (soon to be expressed in the Great War) symbolized by the corruption and death of the writer Gustave Aschenbach during an epidemic. The story pictures a loss of psychological balance, a sickness of the artistic soul to match that of plague-ridden Venice masking its true condition before unsuspecting tourists. Erotic and artistic themes mingle as the respected Aschenbach, escaping a lifetime of laborious creation and self-discipline, allows himself to be swept away by the classical beauty of a young boy until he becomes a grotesque figure, dyeing his hair and rouging his cheeks in a vain attempt to appear young. The issue, however, is not Aschenbach's obsession with Tadzio but rather the way that this fatal love casts light on the artist's whole career.

Aschenbach has laboriously repressed emotions and spontaneity to achieve the disciplined, classical style of a master—and also to earn fame. Plagued by nervous exhaustion at the beginning of the story, he reacts to the sight of a foreign traveler with a "sudden, strange expansion of his inner space" and starts dreaming of exotic, dangerous landscapes. From the tropical swampland and tigers of the Ganges delta to the mountains of a later dream's Dionysiac revels, these visionary landscapes become a metaphor for all the subterranean impulses he has rejected in himself and for his art. Enigmatic figures guide Aschenbach's adventure of the emotions: the traveler, the grotesque old man on the boat, the gondolier, the street singer, and Tadzio himself interpreted as a godlike figure out of Greek myth or culture. Indeed, allusions to ancient myth and literature multiply rapidly as Aschenbach falls under Tadzio's spell and begins to rationalize his fascination as the artist's pursuit of divine beauty. Turning to Plato's *Phaedrus,* a dialogue that combines themes of love with the search for absolute beauty and truth, Aschenbach sketches his own "Platonic" argument as a meditation on the dual nature of the artist. It is the same dualism that was described by Nietzsche in *The Birth of Tragedy* (1872) as the complementary opposition of the Apollonian and Dionysian aspects of art. In serving Apollo, the god of clarity and light, Aschenbach has sacrificed an integral part of his artistic vision. He has developed an "official" note and been anthologized in textbooks, but he has lost spontaneity and joy; he lives with the tension of a clenched fist and suffers from repressed yearnings for freedom and mystic beauty. Aschenbach has betrayed the "dark god" Dionysus, who takes thorough and humiliating vengeance as the writer sinks into a passive, fatalistic acceptance of his feelings and remains to the end in the plague-stricken city. "Who can untangle the riddle of the artist's essence and character?" asks the narrator. *Death in Venice* is a crystallization of Mann's work at its best, displaying the penetrating detail of his social and psychological realism, the power of his tightly interwoven symbolic structure, and the cumulative impact of his artist-hero's fall.

Ignace Feuerlicht, *Thomas Mann* (1969), provides a general biographical introduction. Henry Hatfield, ed., *Thomas Mann: A Collection of Critical Essays* (1964), and Harold Bloom, ed., *Thomas Mann* (1986), present essays on different works and brief biographical information. Terence J. Reed, *Thomas Mann: The Uses of Tradition* (rev. 1996), is an excellent, well-written general study incorporating recent material. Richard Winston, *Thomas Mann: The Making of an Artist 1875–1911* (1981), the first volume of an unfinished study, is a detailed and authoritative presentation by the translator of Mann's diaries and letters.

PRONOUNCING GLOSSARY

The following list uses common English syllables and stress accents to provide rough equivalents of selected words whose pronunciation may be unfamiliar to the general reader.

Bildungsroman: *bil'-doongs-roh-mahn'*   Schwabing: *shva'-bing*

Föhringer Chaussée: *feuh-ring-er*   Wagner: *vahg'-ner*
     shoh-say'

Death in Venice[1]

CHAPTER 1

On a spring afternoon in 19—,[2] a year that for months glowered threateningly over our continent, Gustav Aschenbach—or von[3] Aschenbach, as he had been known officially since his fiftieth birthday—set off alone from his dwelling in Prinzregentenstrasse[4] in Munich on a rather long walk. He had been overstrained by the difficult and dangerous morning's work, which just now required particular discretion, caution, penetration, and precision of will: even after his midday meal the writer had not been able to halt the running on of the productive machinery within him, that "motus animi continuus" which Cicero[5] claims is the essence of eloquence, nor had he been able to obtain the relaxing slumber so necessary to him once a day to relieve the increasing demands on his resources. Thus, he sought the open air right after tea, hoping that fresh air and exercise would restore him and help him to have a profitable evening.

It was early May, and after weeks of cold, wet weather a premature summer had set in. The Englischer Garten,[6] although only beginning to come into leaf, was as muggy as in August and at the end near the city was full of vehicles and people out for a stroll. Increasingly quiet paths led Aschenbach toward Aumeister,[7] where he spent a moment surveying the lively crowd in the beer garden, next to which several hackneys and carriages were lingering; but then as the sun went down he took a route homeward outside the park over the open fields and, since he felt tired and thunder clouds now threatened over Föhring,[8] he waited at the North Cemetery stop for the tram that would take him directly back into the city.

As it happened he found the tram stop and the surrounding area deserted. Neither on the paved Ungererstrasse, whose streetcar-tracks stretched in glistening solitude toward Schwabing, nor on the Föhringer Chaussee[9] was there a vehicle to be seen, nothing stirred behind the fences of the stonemasons' shops, where the crosses, headstones, and monuments for sale formed a second, untenanted graveyard, and the Byzantine architecture of the mortuary chapel across the way lay silent in the glow of the departing

---

1. Translated by and some notes adapted from Clayton Koelb.   2. In 1911, when the story was written, the "Moroccan crisis" was precipitated when a German gunboat appeared off the coast of Agadir, prompting negotiations between France and Germany over their respective national interests. A series of similar diplomatic crises led to the outbreak of World War I in 1914.   3. From or of. *Von* appears in the names of only nobility. Aschenbach was made an honorary nobleman on his fiftieth birthday.   4. A street in Munich that forms the southern boundary of the Englischer Garten (English Garden). Mann lived in various apartments in this neighborhood.   5. Marcus Tullius Cicero (106–43 B.C.), Roman orator. *Motus animi continuus:* the continuous motion of the spirit (Latin, attributed to Cicero).   6. The English Garden, a nine-hundred-acre public park with diverse attractions that extended from the city to the water meadows of the Isar River.   7. A beer garden in the northern section.   8. A district in Munich.   9. A street. Ungererstrasse is a street that borders the North Cemetery. Schwabing is another district in Munich.

day. Its facade was decorated with Greek crosses and hieratic paintings in soft colors; in addition it displayed symmetrically arranged scriptural quotations in gold letters, such as, "They are entering the house of God," or, "May the eternal light shine upon them." Waiting, he found a few moments' solemn diversion in reading these formulations and letting his mind's eye bask in their radiant mysticism, when, returning from his reveries, he noticed a man in the portico, above the two apocalyptic beasts guarding the front steps. The man's not altogether ordinary appearance took his thoughts in a completely different direction.

It was not clear whether the man had emerged from the chapel through the bronze door or had climbed the steps up to the entry from the outside without being noticed. Aschenbach, without entering too deeply into the question, inclined to the first assumption. Moderately tall, thin, clean-shaven, and strikingly snub-nosed, the man belonged to the red-haired type and possessed a redhead's milky and freckled complexion. He was clearly not of Bavarian stock, and in any case the wide and straight-brimmed straw hat that covered his head lent him the appearance of a foreigner, of a traveler from afar. To be sure, he also wore the familiar native rucksack strapped to his shoulders and a yellowish Norfolk suit[1] apparently of loden cloth. He had a gray mackintosh over his left forearm, which he held supported against his side, and in his right hand he held a stick with an iron tip, which he propped obliquely against the ground, leaning his hip against its handle and crossing his ankles. With his head held up, so that his Adam's apple protruded nakedly from the thin neck that emerged from his loose sport shirt, he gazed intently into the distance with colorless, red-lashed eyes, between which stood two stark vertical furrows that went rather oddly with his short, turned-up nose. It may be that his elevated and elevating location had something to do with it, but his posture conveyed an impression of imperious surveillance, forti-tude, even wildness. His lips seemed insufficient, perhaps because he was squinting, blinded, toward the setting sun or maybe because he was afflicted by a facial deformity—in any case they were retracted to such an extent that his teeth, revealed as far as the gums, menacingly displayed their entire white length.

It is entirely possible that Aschenbach had been somewhat indiscreet in his half-distracted, half-inquisitive survey of the stranger, for he suddenly realized that his gaze was being returned, and indeed returned so belliger-ently, so directly eye to eye, with such a clear intent to bring matters to a head and force the other to avert his eyes, that Aschenbach, with an awkward sense of embarrassment, turned away and began to walk along the fence, intending for the time being to pay no more attention to the fellow. In a moment he had forgotten about him. But perhaps the man had the look of the traveler about him, or perhaps because he exercised some physical or spiritual influence, Aschenbach's imagination was set working. He felt a sud-den, strange expansion of his inner space, a rambling unrest, a youthful thirst for faraway places, a feeling so intense, so new—or rather so long unused and forgotten—that he stood rooted to the spot, his hands behind his back and his gaze to the ground, pondering the essence and direction of his emotion.

It was wanderlust and nothing more, but it was an overwhelming wander-

1. A belted suit.

lust that rose to a passion and even to a delusion. His desire acquired vision, and his imagination, not yet calmed down from the morning's work, created its own version of the manifold marvels and terrors of the earth, all of them at once now seeking to take shape within him. He saw, saw a landscape, a tropical swamp under a vaporous sky, moist, luxuriant, and monstrous, a sort of primitive wilderness of islands, morasses, and alluvial estuaries; saw hairy palm trunks rise up near and far out of rank fern brakes, out of thick, swollen, wildly blooming vegetation; saw wondrously formless trees sink their aerial roots into the earth through stagnant, green-shadowed pools, where exotic birds, their shoulders high and their bills shaped weirdly, stood motionless in the shallows looking askance amidst floating flowers that were white as milk and big as platters; saw the eyes of a lurking tiger sparkle between the gnarled stems of a bamboo thicket; and felt his heart pound with horror and mysterious desire. Then the vision faded, and with a shake of his head Aschenbach resumed his promenade along the fences bordering the head-stone-makers' yard.

He had regarded travel, at least since he had commanded the financial resources to enjoy the advantages of global transportation at will, as nothing more than a measure he had to take for his health, no matter how much it went against his inclination. Too much taken up with the tasks that his problematic self and the European soul posed for him, too burdened with the obligation of productivity, too averse to distraction to be a success as a lover of the world's motley show, he had quite contented himself with the view of the earth's surface anyone could get without stirring very far from home. He had never even been tempted to leave Europe. Especially now that his life was slowly waning, now that his artist's fear of never getting fin- ished—his concern that the sands might run out of the glass before he had done his utmost and given his all—could no longer be dismissed as pure fancy, his external existence had confined itself almost exclusively to the lovely city that had become his home and to the rustic country house he had built in the mountains where he spent the rainy summers.

Besides, even this impulse that had come over him so suddenly and so late in life was quickly moderated and set right by reason and a self-discipline practiced since early youth. He had intended to keep at the work to which he now devoted his life until he reached a certain point and then move out to the country. The thought of sauntering about the world, of thereby being seduced away from months of work, seemed all too frivolous, too contrary to plan, and ultimately impermissible. And yet he knew all too well why this temptation had assailed him so unexpectedly. He had to admit it to himself: it was the urge to escape that was behind this yearning for the far away and the new, this desire for release, freedom, and forgetfulness. It was the urge to get away from his work, from the daily scene of an inflexible, cold, and passionate service. Of course he loved this service and almost loved the ener- vating struggle, renewed each day, between his stubborn, proud, so-often- tested will and his growing lassitude, about which no one could be allowed to know and which the product of his toil could not be permitted to reveal in any way, by any sign of failure or of negligence. Yet it seemed reasonable not to overbend the bow and not to stifle obstinately the outbreak of such a vital need. He thought about his work, thought about the place where once again, today as yesterday, he had been forced to abandon it, a passage that would submit, it seemed, neither to patient care nor to surprise attack. He considered it again, sought once more to break through or untangle the logjam, then broke off the effort with a shudder of repugnance. The passage presented no extraordinary difficulty; what disabled him was the malaise of scrupulousness confronting him in the guise of an insatiable perfectionism. Even as a young man, to be sure, he had considered perfectionism the basis and most intimate essence of his talent, and for its sake he had curbed and cooled his emotions, because he knew that emotion inclines one to satisfaction with a comfortable approximation, a half of perfection. Was his enslaved sensitivity now avenging itself by leaving him, refusing to advance his project and give wings to his art, taking with it all his joy, all his delight in form and expression? It was not that he was producing bad work—that at least was the advantage of his advanced years; he felt every moment comfortably secure in his mastery. But, though the nation honored it, he himself was not pleased with his mastery, and indeed it seemed to him that his work lacked those earmarks of a fiery, playful fancy that, stemming from joy, gave more joy to his appreciative audience than did any inner content or weighty excellence. He was fearful of the summer in the country, all alone in the little house with the maid who prepared his meals and the servant who waited on him at table, fearful too of the familiar mountaintops and mountainsides that once more would surround him in his discontented, slow progress. And so what he needed was a respite, a kind of spur-of-the-moment existence, a way to waste some time, foreign air and an infusion of new blood, to make the summer bearable and productive. Travel it would be then—it was all right with him. Not too far, though, not quite all the way to the tigers. One night in a sleeping car and a siesta for three or maybe four weeks in some fashionable vacation spot in the charming south . . .

Such were his thoughts as the noise of the electric tram approached along the Ungererstrasse, and he decided as he got on to devote this evening to studying maps and time tables. Once aboard it occurred to him to look around for the man in the straw hat, his comrade in this excursion that had been, in spite of all, so consequential. But he could get no clear idea of the man's whereabouts; neither his previous location, nor the next stop, nor the tram car itself revealed any signs of his presence.

CHAPTER 2

Gustav Aschenbach, the author of the clear and vigorous prose epic on the life of Frederick the Great;[2] the patient artist who wove together with enduring diligence the novelistic tapestry *Maia*,[3] a work rich in characters and eminently successful in gathering together many human destinies under the shadow of a single idea; the creator of that powerful story bearing the title "A Man of Misery," which had earned the gratitude of an entire young generation by showing it the possibility for a moral resolution that passed through and beyond the deepest knowledge; the author, finally (and this

---

2. King Frederick II (1712–1786) started Prussia on its rise to domination of Germany and made his court a prominent European cultural center.   3. In Hindu religion, the illusory appearance of the world concealing a higher spiritual reality.

completes the short list of his mature works), of the passionate treatment of the topic "Art and Intellect,"[4] an essay whose power of organization and antithetical eloquence had prompted serious observers to rank it alongside Schiller's "On Naïve and Sentimental Poetry";[5] Gustav Aschenbach, then, was born the son of a career civil servant in the justice ministry in L., a district capital in the province of Silesia. His ancestors had been officers, judges, and government functionaries, men who had led upright lives of austere decency devoted to the service of king and country. A more ardent spirituality had expressed itself once among them in the person of a preacher; more impetuous and sensuous blood had entered the family line in the previous generation through the writer's mother, the daughter of a Bohemian music director. It was from her that he had in his features the traits of a foreign race. The marriage of sober conscientiousness devoted to service with darker, more fiery impulses engendered an artist and indeed this very special artist.

Since his entire being was bent on fame, he emerged early on as, perhaps not exactly precocious, but nonetheless, thanks to the decisiveness and peculiar terseness of his style, surprisingly mature and ready to go before the public. He was practically still in high school when he made a name for himself. Ten years later he learned how to keep up appearances, to manage his fame from his writing desk, to produce gracious and significant sentences for his necessarily brief letters (for many demands are made on such a successful and reliable man). By the age of forty, exhausted by the tortures and vicissitudes of his real work, he had to deal with a daily flood of mail bearing stamps from countries in every corner of the globe.

Tending neither to the banal nor to the eccentric, his talent was such as to win for his stories both the acceptance of the general public and an admiring, challenging interest from a more discerning audience. Thus he found himself even as a young man obliged in every way to achieve and indeed to achieve extraordinary things. He had therefore never known sloth, never known the carefree, laissez-faire attitude of youth. When he got sick in Vienna around the age of thirty-five, a canny observer remarked about him to friends, "You see, Aschenbach has always lived like this"—and the speaker closed the fingers of his left hand into a fist—"never like this"—and he let his open hand dangle comfortably from the arm of the chair. How right he was! And the morally courageous aspect of it was that, possessing anything but a naturally robust constitution, he was not so much born for constant exertion as he was called to it.

Medical concerns had prevented him from attending school as a child and compelled the employment of private instruction at home. He had grown up alone and without companions, and yet he must have realized early on that he belonged to a tribe in which talent was not so much a rarity as was the bodily frame talent needs to find its fulfillment, a tribe known for giving their best early in life but not for longevity. His watchword, however, was "Endure," and he saw in his novel about Frederick the Great precisely the apotheosis of this commandment, which seemed to him the essence of a selflessly active virtue. He harbored, moreover, a keen desire to live to a ripe

---

4. *Frederick, Maia, A Man of Misery,* and *Art and Intellect* are titles of projects Mann had worked on and abandoned.   5. An influential essay by the German Romantic writer Friedrich Schiller (1759–1805).

old age, for he had long believed that an artistic career could be called truly great, encompassing, indeed truly worthy of honor only if the artist were allotted sufficient years to be fruitful in his own way at all stages of human life.

Since he thus bore the burdens of his talent on slender shoulders and wished to carry those burdens far, he was in great need of discipline. Fortunately for him discipline was his heritage at birth from his paternal side. At forty, at fifty, even at an age when others squander and stray, content to put their great plans aside for the time being, he started his day at an early hour by dousing his chest and back with cold water. Then, placing two tall wax candles in silver candlesticks at the head of his manuscript, he would spend two or three fervently conscientious morning hours sacrificing on the altar of art the powers he had assembled during his sleep. It was forgivable—indeed it even indicated the victory of his moral force—that uninformed readers mistook the Maiaworld or the epic scroll on which unrolled Frederick's heroic life for the products of single sustained bursts of energy, whereas they actually grew into grandeur layer by layer, out of small daily doses of work and countless individual flashes of inspiration. These works were thoroughly excellent in every detail solely because their creator had endured for years under the pressure of a single project, bringing to bear a tenacity and perseverance similar to that which had conquered his home province,[6] and because he had devoted only his freshest and worthiest hours to actual composition.

If a work of the intellect is to have an immediate, broad, and deep effect, there must be a mysterious affinity, a correspondence between the personal fate of its originator and the more general fate of his contemporaries. People do not know why they accord fame to a particular work. Far from being experts, they suppose they see in it a hundred virtues that would justify their interest; but the real reason for their approval is something imponderable—it is sympathy. Aschenbach had actually stated forthrightly, though in a relatively inconspicuous passage, that nearly everything achieving greatness did so under the banner of "Despite"—despite grief and suffering, despite poverty, destitution, infirmity, affliction, passion, and a thousand obstacles. But this was more than an observation, it was the fruit of experience; no, it was the very formula for his life and his fame, the key to his work. Was it any wonder, then, that it was also the basis for the moral disposition and outward demeanor of his most original fictional characters?

Early on an observant critic had described the new type of hero that this writer preferred, a figure returning over and over again in manifold variation: it was based on the concept of "an intellectual and youthful manliness which grits its teeth in proud modesty and calmly endures the swords and spears as they pass through its body." It was a nice description, ingenious and precise, despite its seemingly excessive emphasis on passivity. For meeting one's fate with dignity, grace under pressure of pain, is not simply a matter of sufferance; it is an active achievement, a positive triumph, and the figure of St. Sebastian[7] is thus the most beautiful image, if not of art in general, then surely of the art under discussion here. Having looked at the characters in

6. As a result of the Seven Years' War (1759–63), Frederick the Great wrested Silesia from Austria. Today, most of Silesia has become a region in southwestern Poland.   7. A third-century Roman martyr whose arrow-pierced body was a popular subject for Renaissance painters.

Aschenbach's narrated world, having seen the elegant self-discipline that managed right up to the last moment to hide from the eyes of the world the undermining process, the biological decline, taking place within; having seen the yellow, physically handicapped ugliness that nonetheless managed to kindle its smoldering ardor into a pure flame, managed even to catapult itself to mastery in the realm of beauty; or having seen the pale impotence that pulls out of the glowing depths of the spirit enough power to force a whole frivolous people to fall at the feet of the cross, at the feet of that very impotence; or the lovable charm that survives even the empty and rigorous service of pure form; or the false, dangerous life of the born deceiver, with the quick enervation of its longing and with its artfulness—having seen all these human destinies and many more besides, it was easy enough to doubt that there could be any other sort of heroism than that of weakness. In any case, what kind of heroism was more appropriate to the times than this? Gustav Aschenbach was the poet of all those who work on the edge of exhaustion, of the overburdened, worn down moralists of achievement who nonetheless still stand tall, those who, stunted in growth and short of means, use ecstatic feats of will and clever management to extract from themselves at least for a period of time the effects of greatness. Their names are legion, and they are the heroes of the age. And all of them recognized themselves in his work; they saw themselves justified, exalted, their praises sung. And they were grateful; they heralded his name.

He had been once as young and rough as the times and, seduced by them, had made public blunders and mistakes, had made himself vulnerable, had committed errors against tact and good sense in word and deed. But he had won the dignity toward which, in his opinion, every great talent feels an inborn urge and spur. One could say in fact that his entire development had been a conscious and defiant rise to dignity, beyond any twinge of doubt and of irony that might have stood in his way.

Pleasing the great mass of middle-class readers depends mainly on offering vividly depicted, intellectually undemanding characterizations, but passionately uncompromising youth is smitten only with what is problematic; and Aschenbach had been as problematic and uncompromising as any young man can be. He had pandered to the intellect, exhausted the soil of knowledge, milled flour from his seed corn, revealed secrets, put talent under suspicion, betrayed art. Indeed, while his portrayals entertained, elevated, invigorated the blissfully credulous among his readers, as a youthful artist it was his cynical observations on the questionable nature of art and of the artist's calling that had kept the twenty-year-old element fascinated.

But it seems that nothing so quickly or so thoroughly blunts a high-minded and capable spirit as the sharp and bitter charm of knowledge; and it is certain that the melancholy, scrupulous thoroughness characteristic of the young seems shallow in comparison with the solemn decision of masterful maturity to disavow knowledge, to reject it, to move beyond it with head held high, to forestall the least possibility that it could cripple, dishearten, or dishonor his will, his capacity for action and feeling, or even his passion. How else could one interpret the famous story "A Man of Misery" save as an outbreak of disgust at the indecent psychologism then current? This disgust was embodied in the figure of that soft and foolish semi-villain who, out of weakness, viciousness, and moral impotence, buys a black-market destiny for himself by driving his wife into the arms of a beardless boy, who imagines profundity can justify committing the basest acts. The weight of the words with which the writer of that work reviled the vile announced a decisive turn away from all moral skepticism, from all sympathy with the abyss, a rejection of the laxity inherent in the supposedly compassionate maxim that to understand everything is to forgive everything. What was coming into play here—or rather, what was already in full swing—was that "miracle of ingenuousness reborn" about which there was explicit discussion, not without a certain mysterious emphasis, in one of the author's dialogues published only slightly later. Strange relationships! Was it an intellectual consequence of this "rebirth," of this new dignity and rigor, that just then readers began to notice an almost excessive increase in his sense of beauty, a noble purity, simplicity, and sense of proportion that henceforth gave his works such a palpable, one might say deliberately classical and masterful quality? But moral determination that goes beyond knowledge, beyond analytic and inhibiting perception—would that not also be a reduction, a moral simplification of the world and of the human soul and therefore also a growing potential for what is evil, forbidden, and morally unacceptable? And does form not have two faces? Is it not moral and amoral at the same time—moral insofar as form is the product and expression of discipline, but amoral and indeed immoral insofar as it harbors within itself by nature a certain moral indifference and indeed is essentially bent on forcing the moral realm to stoop under its proud and absolute scepter?

That is as may be. Since human development is human destiny, how could a life led in public, accompanied by the accolades and confidence of thousands, develop as does one led without the glory and the obligations of fame? Only those committed to eternal bohemianism would be bored and inclined to ridicule when a great talent emerges from its libertine chrysalis, accustoms itself to recognizing emphatically the dignity of the spirit, takes on the courtly airs of solitude, a solitude full of unassisted, defiantly independent suffering and struggle, and ultimately achieves power and honor in the public sphere. And how much playfulness, defiance, and indulgence there is in the way talent develops! A kind of official, educative element began in time to appear in Aschenbach's productions. His style in later years dispensed with the sheer audacity, the subtle and innovative shadings of his younger days, and moved toward the paradigmatic, the polished and traditional, the conservative and formal, even formulaic. Like Louis XIV[8]—as report would have it—the aging writer banished from his vocabulary every base expression. About this time it came to pass that the educational authorities began using selected passages from his works in their prescribed textbooks.[9] He seemed to sense the inner appropriateness of it, and he did not refuse when a German prince, newly ascended to the throne, bestowed on the author of *Frederick*, on his fiftieth birthday, a nonhereditary title.

Relatively early on, after a few years of moving about, a few tries at living here and there, he chose Munich as his permanent residence and lived there in bourgeois respectability such as comes to intellectuals sometimes, in exceptional cases. His marriage to a girl from a learned family, entered upon

---

8. King of France (1638–1715), the "great monarch" of the French classical period.   9. I.e., he received national recognition in the highly centralized German educational system.

when still a young man, was terminated after only a short term of happiness by her death. A daughter, already married, remained to him. He never had a son.

Gustav Aschenbach was a man of slightly less than middle height, dark-haired and clean shaven. His head seemed a little too big for a body that was almost dainty. His hair, combed back, receding at the top, still very full at the temples, though quite gray, framed a high, furrowed, and almost embossed-looking brow. The gold frame of his rimless glasses cut into the bridge of his full, nobly curved nose. His mouth was large, sometimes relaxed and full, sometimes thin and tense; his cheeks were lean and hollow, and his well-proportioned chin was marked by a slight cleft. Important destinies seemed to have played themselves out on this long-suffering face, which he often held tilted somewhat to one side. And yet it was art alone, not a difficult and troubled life, that had taken over the task of chiseling these features. Behind this brow was born the scintillating repartee between Voltaire and King Frederick on the subject of war; these eyes, looking tiredly but piercingly through the glasses, had seen the bloody inferno of the field hospitals during the Seven Years' War.[1] Indeed, even on the personal level art provides an intensified version of life. Art offers a deeper happiness, but it consumes one more quickly. It engraves upon the faces of its servants the traces of imaginary, mental adventures and over the long term, even given an external existence of cloistered quietude, engenders in them a nervous sensitivity, an over-refinement, a weariness and an inquisitiveness such as are scarcely ever produced by a life full of extravagant passions and pleasures.

CHAPTER 3

Several obligations of both a practical and a literary nature forced the eager traveler to remain in Munich for about two weeks after his walk in the park. Finally he gave instructions for his country house to be prepared for his moving in within a month's time and, on a day sometime between the middle and end of May, he took the night train to Trieste, where he remained only twenty-four hours and where he boarded the boat to Pola[2] on the morning of the next day.

What he sought was someplace foreign, someplace isolated, but someplace nonetheless easy to get to. He thus took up residence on an Adriatic island, a destination that had been highly spoken of in recent years and lay not far from the Istrian coast. It was populated by locals dressed in colorful rags who spoke in wildly exotic accents, and the landscape was graced by rugged cliffs on the coast facing the open sea. But the rain and oppressive air, the provincial, exclusively Austrian clientele at the hotel, and the lack of the peaceful, intimate relation with the sea that only a soft sandy beach can offer—these things irritated him, denied him a sense of having found the place he was looking for; he was troubled by a pressure within him pushing in a direction he could not quite grasp; he studied ship schedules, he sought about for something; and suddenly the surprising but obvious destination

---

1. A global war (1756–63) fought in Europe, North America, and India between European powers. François Marie Arouet de Voltaire (1694–1778), French writer and philosopher, was a guest at the court of Frederick the Great from 1750 until 1753, when he found it wise to leave after a disagreement. 2. Trieste (in Italy) and Pola (or Pula, in Croatia) are major ports at the head of the Adriatic Sea. Until 1919 they were Austrian possessions.

came to him. If you wanted to reach in a single night someplace incomparable, someplace as out of the ordinary as a fairy tale, where did you go? The answer was clear. What was he doing here? He had gone astray. It was over there that he had wanted to go all along. He did not hesitate a moment in remedying his error and gave notice of his departure. A week and a half after his arrival on the island a swift motorboat carried him and his baggage through the early morning mist across the water to the military port, where he landed only long enough to find the gangway leading him onto the damp deck of a ship that was already getting up steam for a trip to Venice.[3]

It was an aged vessel, long past its prime, sooty, and gloomy, sailing under the Italian flag. In a cavernous, artificially lit cabin in the ship's interior—to which Aschenbach had been conducted with smirking politeness by a hunchbacked, scruffy sailor the moment he embarked—sat a goateed man behind a desk. With his hat cocked over his brow and a cigarette butt hanging from the corner of his mouth, his facial features were reminiscent of an old time ringmaster. He took down the passengers' personal information and doled out tickets with the grimacing, easy demeanor of the professional. "To Venice!" He repeated Aschenbach's request, stretching his arm to dip his pen in the congealed remains at the bottom of his slightly tilted inkwell. "To Venice, first class! There, sir, you're all taken care of." He inscribed great letters like crane's feet on a piece of paper, poured blue sand out of a box onto them, poured it back into an earthenware bowl, folded the paper with his yellow, bony fingers, and resumed writing. "What a fine choice for your destination!" he babbled in the meantime. "Ah, Venice, a wonderful city! A city that is irresistible to cultured people both for its history and for its modern charm!" The smooth swiftness of his movements and the empty chatter with which he accompanied them had an anesthetic and diversionary effect, as if he were concerned that the traveler should change his mind about his decision to go to Venice. He hastily took the money and dropped the change on the stained cloth covering the table with the practiced swiftness of a croupier.[4] "Enjoy yourself, sir!" he said with a theatrical bow. "It is an honor to be of service to you. . . . Next, please!" he cried with his arm raised, acting as if he were still doing a brisk business, though in fact there was no one else there to do business with. Aschenbach returned above deck.

With one arm resting on the rail, he observed the passengers on board and the idle crowd loitering on the pier to watch the ship depart. The second-class passengers, both men and women, crouched on the forward deck using boxes and bundles as seats. A group of young people, apparently employees of businesses in Pola, who had banded together in great excitement for an excursion to Italy, formed the social set of the first upper deck. They made no little fuss over themselves and their plans, chattered, laughed, and took complacent enjoyment in their own continual gesturing. Leaning over the railing they called out in fluent and mocking phrases to various friends going about their business, briefcases under their arms, along the dockside street below, while the latter in turn made mock-threatening gestures with their walking sticks at the celebrants above. One of the merrymakers, wearing a bright yellow, overly fashionable summer suit, red tie, and a panama hat with

3. An ancient city whose network of bridges and canals links 118 islands in the Gulf of Venice. The Republic of Venice was headed by a doge (duke) and was a cultural, commercial, and political center in Europe from the fourteenth century.   4. Attendant at a gambling table who handles bets and money.

a cockily turned-up brim, outdid all the others in his screeching gaiety. But scarcely had Aschenbach gotten a closer look at him when he realized with something like horror that this youth was not genuine. He was old, no doubt about it. There were wrinkles around his eyes and mouth. The faint carmine of his cheeks was rouge; the brown hair beneath the colorfully banded hat was a wig; his neck was shrunken and sinewy; his clipped mustache and goatee were dyed; the full, yellowish set of teeth he exposed when he laughed was a cheap set of dentures; and his hands, bedecked with signet rings on both forefingers, were those of an old man. With a shudder Aschenbach watched him and his interaction with his friends. Did they not know, had they not noticed that he was old, that he had no right to wear their foppish and colorful clothes, had no right to pretend to be one of their own? They apparently tolerated him in their midst as a matter of course, out of habit, and treated him as an equal, answering in kind without reluctance when he teasingly poked one of them in the ribs. But how could this be? Aschenbach covered his brow with his hand and closed his eyes, which were feeling inflamed from not getting enough sleep. It seemed to him that things were starting to take a turn away from the ordinary, as if a dreamy estrangement, a bizarre distortion of the world were setting in and would spread if he did not put a stop to it by shading his eyes a bit and taking another look around him. Just at this moment he experienced a sensation of motion and, looking up with an unreasoning terror, realized that the heavy and gloomy hulk of the ship was slowly parting company with the stone pier. The engines ran alternately forward and reverse, and inch by inch the band of oily, iridescent water between the pier and the hull of the ship widened. After a set of cumbersome maneuvers the steamer managed to point its bowsprit toward the open sea. Aschenbach went over to the starboard side, where the hunchback had set up a deck chair for him and a steward dressed in a stained tailcoat offered him service.

The sky was gray and the wind was moist. The harbor and the island were left behind, and soon all sight of land vanished beyond the misty horizon. Flakes of coal soot saturated with moisture fell on the scrubbed, never drying deck. No more than an hour later a canvas canopy was put up, since it had started to rain.

Wrapped in his cloak, a book on his lap, the traveler rested, and the hours passed by unnoticed. It stopped raining; the linen canopy was removed. The horizon was unobstructed. Beneath the overcast dome of the sky the immense disk of the desolate sea stretched into the distance all around. But in empty, undivided space our sense of time fails us, and we lose ourselves in the immeasurable. Strange and shadowy figures—the old fop, the goatbeard from below deck—invaded Aschenbach's mind as he rested. They gestured obscurely and spoke the confused speech of dreams. He fell asleep.

At noon they called him to lunch down in the corridorlike dining hall onto which opened the doors of all the sleeping quarters and in which stood a long table. He dined at one end, while at the other the business employees from Pola, including the old fop, had been carousing since ten o'clock with the jolly captain. The meal was wretched and he soon got up. He felt an urgent need to get out, to look at the sky, to see if it might not be brightening over Venice.

It had never occurred to him that anything else could happen, for the city had always received him in shining glory. But the sky and the sea remained overcast and leaden. From time to time a misty rain fell, and he came to the realization that he would approach a very different Venice by sea than the one he had previously reached by land. He stood by the foremast, gazing into the distance, awaiting the sight of land. He remembered the melancholy, enthusiastic poet of long ago who had furnished his dreams with the domes and bell towers rising from these waters. He softly repeated to himself some of those verses in which the awe, joy, and sadness of a former time had taken stately shape[5] and, easily moved by sensations thus already formed, looked into his earnest and weary heart to see if some new enthusiasm or entanglement, some late adventure of feeling might be in store for him, the idle traveler.

Then the flat coastline emerged on the right; the sea became populated with fishing boats; the barrier island with its beach appeared. The steamer soon left the island behind to the left, slipping at reduced speed through the narrow harbor named after it.[6] They came to a full stop in the lagoon in view of rows of colorfully wretched dwellings and awaited the arrival of the launch belonging to the health service.

An hour passed before it appeared. One had arrived and yet had not arrived; there was no great hurry and yet one felt driven by impatience. The young people from Pola had come up on deck, apparently yielding to a patriotic attraction to the military trumpet calls resounding across the water from the public garden. Full of excitement and Asti, they shouted cheers at the *bersaglieri*[7] conducting drills over there. It was disgusting, however, to see the state into which the made-up old coot's false fellowship with the young people had brought him. His aged brain had not been able to put up the same resistance to the wine as the younger and more vigorous heads, and he was wretchedly drunk. His vision blurred; a cigarette dangled from his shaking fingers; he stood swaying tipsily in place, pulled to and fro by intoxication, barely able to maintain his balance. Since he would have fallen over at the first step, he dared not move from the spot. Yet he maintained a woeful bravado, buttonholing everyone who came near; he stammered, blinked, giggled, raised his beringed, wrinkled forefinger in fatuous banter, and ran the tip of his tongue around the corners of his mouth in an obscenely suggestive manner. Aschenbach watched him from under a darkened brow and was once again seized by a feeling of giddiness, as if the world were displaying a slight but uncontrollable tendency to distort, to take on a bizarre and sneering aspect. It was a feeling, to be sure, that conditions prevented him from indulging, for just then the engine began anew its pounding, and the ship, interrupted so close to its destination, resumed its course through the canal of San Marco.[8]

Once more, then, it lay before him, that most astounding of landing places, that dazzling grouping of fantastic buildings that the republic presented to the awed gaze of approaching mariners: the airy splendor of the palace and the Bridge of Sighs; the pillars on the water's edge bearing the lion and the

---

5. The lines are probably from *Sonnets on Venice* (1825) by the German classical poet August Graf Platen (1796–1835): "My eye left the high seas behind / as the temples of [the architect Andrea] Palladio rose from the waters."   6. Both the barrier island and the harbor are called Lido. The island is the site of a famous resort.   7. Elite Italian troops. *Asti:* or asti spumante, a sweet, sparkling Italian wine.   8. Saint Mark's Canal, named for the patron saint of Venice.

saint; the showy projecting flank of the fairy tale cathedral; the view toward
the gate and the great clock.[9] It occurred to him as he raised his eyes that
to arrive in Venice by land, at the railway station, was like entering a palace
by a back door; that one ought not to approach this most improbable of cities
save as he now did, by ship, over the high seas.

The engine stopped, gondolas swarmed about, the gangway was lowered,
customs officials boarded and haughtily went about their duties; disembar-
kation could begin. Aschenbach let it be known that he desired a gondola to
take him and his luggage over to the landing where he could get one of the
little steamboats that ran between the city and the Lido; for it was his intention to take up residence by the sea. His wishes met with acquiescence; a
call went down with his request to the water's surface where the gondoliers
were quarreling with each other in dialect. He was still prevented from dis-
embarking; his trunk presented problems; only with considerable difficulty
could it be pulled and tugged down the ladderlike gangway. He therefore
found himself unable for several moments to escape from the importunities
of the ghastly old impostor, who, driven by some dark drunken impulse, was
determined to bid elaborate farewell to the foreign traveler. "We wish you
the happiest of stays," he bleated, bowing and scraping. "Keeping a fond
memory of us! Au revoir, excusez, and bonjour,[1] your excellency!" He
drooled, he batted his eyes, he licked the corners of his mouth, and the dyed
goatee on his elderly chin bristled. "Our compliments," he babbled, two fingertips at his mouth, "our compliments to your beloved, your dearly beloved,
your lovely beloved . . ." And suddenly his uppers fell out of his jaw onto his
lower lip. Aschenbach took his chance to escape. "Your beloved, your sweet
beloved . . ." He heard the cooing, hollow, obstructed sounds behind his back
as he descended the gangway, clutching at the rope handrail as he went.

Who would not need to fight off a fleeting shiver, a secret aversion and
anxiety, at the prospect of boarding a Venetian gondola for the first time or
after a long absence? This strange conveyance, surviving unchanged since
legendary times and painted the particular sort of black[2] ordinarily reserved
for coffins, makes one think of silent, criminal adventures in a darkness full
of splashing sounds; makes one think even more of death itself, of biers and
gloomy funerals, and of that final, silent journey. And has anyone noticed
that the seat of one of these boats, this armchair painted coffin-black and
upholstered in dull black cloth, is one of the softest, most luxurious, most
sleep-inducing seats in the world? Aschenbach certainly realized this as he
sat down at the gondolier's feet, opposite his luggage lying in a copious pile
in the bow. The oarsmen were still quarreling in a rough, incomprehensible
language punctuated by threatening gestures. The peculiar quiet of this city
of water, however, seemed to soften their voices, to disembody them, to
disperse them over the sea. It was warm here in the harbor. Stroked by the
mild breath of the sirocco,[3] leaning back into the cushions as the yielding
element carried him, the traveler closed his eyes in the pleasure of indulging
in an indolence both unaccustomed and sweet. The trip will be short, he

9. A large clock tower built in the late fifteenth century. *Bridge of Sighs:* condemned prisoners would walk
over this bridge when proceeding to prison from the ducal palace. *Pillars:* one is surmounted by a statue
of St. Theodore stepping on a crocodile; the second, by a winged lion, emblem of St. Mark. *Cathedral:* the
Church of St. Mark.   1. Goodbye, excuse me, and good-day (French).   2. Legend explains the gondolas' traditional black through an ancient law forbidding ostentation.   3. A hot wind originating in the
Sahara, which becomes humid as it picks up moisture over the Mediterranean.

thought; if only it could last forever! The gondola rocked softly, and he felt himself slip away from the crowded ship and the clamoring voices.

How quiet, ever more quiet it grew around him! Nothing could be heard but the splashing of the oar, the hollow slap of the waves against the gondola's prow, rising rigid and black above the water with its halberdlike beak— and then a third thing, a voice, a whisper. It was the murmur of the gondolier, who was talking to himself through his clenched teeth in fits and starts, emitting sounds that were squeezed out of him by the labor of his arms. Aschenbach looked up and realized with some astonishment that the lagoon was widening about him and that he was traveling in the direction of the open sea. It seemed, then, that he ought not to rest quite so peacefully but instead make sure his wishes were carried out.

"I told you to take me to the steamer landing," he said with a half turn toward the stern. The murmur ceased. He received no answer.

"I told you to take me to the steamer landing!" he repeated, turning around completely and looking up into the face of the gondolier, whose figure, perched on the high deck and silhouetted against the dun sky, towered behind him. The man had a disagreeable, indeed brutal-looking appearance; he wore a blue sailor suit belted with a yellow sash, and a shapeless straw hat that was beginning to come unraveled and was tilted rakishly on his head. His facial features and the blond, curly mustache under his short, turned-up nose marked him as clearly not of Italian stock. Although rather slender of build, so that one would not have thought him particularly well suited to his profession, he plied his oar with great energy, putting his whole body into every stroke. Several times he pulled his lips back with the strain, baring his white teeth. His reddish eyebrows puckered, he looked out over his passenger's head and replied in a decisive, almost curt tone of voice: "You are going to the Lido."

Aschenbach responded, "Indeed. But I took the gondola only to get over to San Marco. I want to use the vaporetto."[4]

"You cannot use the vaporetto, sir."

"And why not?"

"Because the vaporetto does not accept luggage."

He was right about that; Aschenbach remembered. He said nothing. But the gruff, presumptuous manner of the man, so unlike the normal way of treating foreigners in this country, was not to be endured. He said, "That is my business. Perhaps I intend to put my luggage in storage. You will kindly turn back."

There was silence. The oar splashed, the waves slapped dully against the bow. And the murmuring and whispering began anew: the gondolier was talking to himself through his clenched teeth.

What to do? Alone at sea with this strangely insubordinate, uncannily resolute person, the traveler saw no way to enforce his wishes. And anyway, if he could just avoid getting angry, what a lovely rest he could have! Had he not wished the trip could last longer, could last forever? The smartest thing to do was to let matters take their course; more important, it was also the most pleasant thing to do. A magic circle of indolence seemed to surround the place where he sat, this low armchair upholstered in black, so gently

---

4. Little steamboat (Italian); used for public transport.

rocked by the rowing of the autocratic gondolier behind him. The idea that he might have fallen into the hands of a criminal rambled about dreamily in Aschenbach's mind, but it was incapable of rousing his thoughts to active resistance. More annoying was the possibility that all this was simply a device by which to extort money from him. A sense of duty or of pride, the memory, as it were, that one must prevent such things, induced him once more to pull himself together. He asked, "What do you want for the trip?"

And the gondolier, looking out over him, answered, "You will pay."

It was clear what reply was necessary here. Aschenbach said mechanically, "I will pay nothing, absolutely nothing, if you take me where I do not want to go."

"You want to go to the Lido."

"But not with you."

"I row you well."

True enough, thought Aschenbach, and relaxed. True enough, you row me well. Even if you are just after my money, even if you send me to the house of Aides[5] with a stroke of your oar from behind, you will have rowed me well.

But no such thing occurred. In fact, some company even happened by in the form of a boat filled with musicians, both men and women, who waylaid the gondola, sailing obtrusively right alongside. They sang to the accompaniment of guitars and mandolins and filled the quiet air over the lagoon with the strains of their mercenary tourist lyrics. Aschenbach threw some money in the hat they held out to him, whereupon they fell silent and sailed off. The murmur of the gondolier became perceptible once again as he talked to himself in fits and starts.

And so they arrived, bobbing in the wake of a steamer sailing back to the city. Two municipal officials walked up and down along the landing, their hands behind their backs and their faces turned to the lagoon. Aschenbach stepped from the gondola onto the dock assisted by one of those old men who seemed on hand, armed with a boathook, at every pier in Venice. Since he had no small coins with him, he crossed over to the hotel next to the steamer wharf to get change with which to pay the boatman an appropriate fee. His needs met in the lobby, he returned to find his baggage stowed on a cart on the dock. Gondola and gondolier had disappeared.

"He took off," said the old man with the boathook. "A bad man he was, sir, a man without a license. He's the only gondolier who doesn't have a license. The others telephoned over. He saw that we were on the lookout for him, so he took off."

Aschenbach shrugged his shoulders.

"You had a free ride, sir," the old man said, holding out his hat. Aschenbach threw some coins in it. He gave instructions that his luggage be taken to the Hotel des Bains[6] and then followed the cart along the boulevard of white blossoms, lined on both sides by taverns, shops, and boarding houses, that runs straight across the island to the beach.

He entered the spacious hotel from behind, from the garden terrace, and crossed the great lobby to reach the vestibule where the office was. Since he

5. A Greek spelling of *Hades,* the ruler of the world of the dead in Greek and Roman mythology. The newly dead entered the underworld by paying a coin to the boatman, Charon, who then ferried them across the river Styx. 6. Bathing hotel (French, literal trans.); a famous seaside hotel.

had a reservation, he was received with officious courtesy. A manager, a quiet, flatteringly polite little man with a black mustache and a French-style frock coat, accompanied him in the elevator to the third floor and showed him to his room. It was a pleasant place, furnished in cherry wood, decorated with highly fragrant flowers, and offering a view of the open sea through a set of tall windows. After the manager had withdrawn and while his luggage was being brought up and put in place in his room, he went up to one of the windows and looked out on the beach. It was nearly deserted in the afternoon lull, and the ocean, at high tide and bereft of sunshine, was sending long, low waves against the shore in a peaceful rhythm.

A lonely, quiet person has observations and experiences that are at once both more indistinct and more penetrating than those of one more gregarious; his thoughts are weightier, stranger, and never without a tinge of sadness. Images and perceptions that others might shrug off with a glance, a laugh, or a brief conversation occupy him unduly, become profound in his silence, become significant, become experience, adventure, emotion. Loneliness fosters that which is original, daringly and bewilderingly beautiful, poetic. But loneliness also fosters that which is perverse, incongruous, absurd, forbidden. Thus the events of the journey that brought him here— the ghastly old fop with his drivel about a beloved, the outlaw gondolier who was cheated of his reward—continued to trouble the traveler's mind. Though they did not appear contrary to reason, did not really give cause for second thoughts, the paradox was that they were nonetheless fundamentally and essentially odd, or so it seemed to him, and therefore troubling precisely because of this paradox. In the meantime his eyes greeted the sea, and he felt joy in knowing Venice to be in such comfortable proximity. He turned away at last, went to wash his face, gave some instructions to the maid with regard to completing arrangements to insure his comfort, and then put himself in the hands of the green-uniformed elevator operator, who took him down to the ground floor.

He took his tea on the terrace facing the sea, then went down to the shore and walked along the boardwalk for a good distance toward the Hotel Excelsior. When he got back it seemed about time to change for dinner. He did so slowly and precisely, the way he did everything, because he was used to working as he got dressed. Still, he found himself in the lobby a bit on the early side for dinner. There he found many of the hotel's guests gathered, unfamiliar with and affecting indifference to each other, sharing only the wait for the dinner bell. He picked up a newspaper from a table, sat down in a leather chair, and looked over the assembled company. It differed from that of his previous sojourn in a way that pleased him.

A broad horizon, tolerant and comprehensive, opened up before him. All the great languages of Europe melded together in subdued tones. Evening dress, the universal uniform of cultured society, provided a decorous external unity to the variety of humanity assembled here. There was the dry, long face of an American, a Russian extended family, English ladies, German children with French nannies. The Slavic component seemed to predominate. Polish was being spoken nearby.

It came from a group of adolescents and young adults gathered around a little wicker table under the supervision of a governess or companion. There were three young girls who looked to be fifteen to seventeen years old and a long-haired boy of maybe fourteen. Aschenbach noted with astonishment that the boy was perfectly beautiful. His face, pale and gracefully reserved, was framed by honey-colored curls. He had a straight nose and a lovely mouth and wore an expression of exquisite, divine solemnity. It was a face reminiscent of Greek statues from the noblest period of antiquity; it combined perfection of form with a unique personal charm that caused the onlooker to doubt ever having met with anything in nature or in art that could match its perfection. One could not help noticing, furthermore, that widely differing views on child-rearing had evidently directed the dress and general treatment of the siblings. The three girls, the eldest of whom was for all intents an adult, were got up in a way that was almost disfiguringly chaste and austere. Every grace of figure was suppressed and obscured by their uniformly habitlike half-length dresses, sober and slate-gray in color, tailored as if to be deliberately unflattering, relieved by no decoration save white, turned-down collars. Their smooth hair, combed tightly against their heads, made their faces appear nunnishly vacant and expressionless. It could only be a mother who was in charge here, one who never once considered applying to the boy the severity of upbringing that seemed required of her when it came to the girls. Softness and tenderness were the obvious conditions of the boy's existence. No one had yet been so bold as to take the scissors to his lovely hair, which curled about his brows, over his ears, and even further down the back of his neck—as it does on the statue of the "Boy Pulling a Thorn from his Foot."[7] His English sailor suit had puffy sleeves that narrowed at the cuff to embrace snugly the delicate wrists of his still childlike yet delicate hands. The suit made his slim figure seem somehow opulent and pampered with all its decoration, its bow, braidwork, and embroidery. He sat so that the observer saw him in profile. His feet were clad in black patent leather and arranged one in front of the other; one elbow was propped on the arm of his wicker chair with his cheek resting on his closed hand; his demeanor was one of careless refinement, quite without the almost submissive stiffness that seemed to be the norm for his sisters. Was he in poor health? Perhaps, for the skin of his face was white as ivory and stood out in sharp contrast to the darker gold of the surrounding curls. Or was he simply a coddled favorite, the object of a biased and capricious affection? Aschenbach was inclined to suppose the latter. There is inborn in every artistic disposition an indulgent and treacherous tendency to accept injustice when it produces beauty and to respond with complicity and even admiration when the aristocrats of this world get preferential treatment.

A waiter went about and announced in English that dinner was ready. Most of the company gradually disappeared through the glass door into the dining room. Latecomers passed by, arriving from the vestibule or from the elevators. Dinner was beginning to be served inside, but the young Poles still lingered by their wicker table. Aschenbach, comfortably seated in his deep armchair, his eyes captivated by the beautiful vision before him, waited with them.

The governess, a short, corpulent, rather unladylike woman with a red face, finally gave the sign to get up. With her brows raised she pushed back

---

7. A bronze Greco-Roman statue admired for the graceful pose and handsome appearance of the boy it depicts.

her chair and bowed as a tall lady, dressed in gray and white and richly bejeweled with pearls, entered the lobby. The demeanor of this woman was cool and measured; the arrangement of her lightly powdered hair and the cut of her clothes displayed the taste for simplicity favored by those who regard piety as an essential component of good breeding. She could have been the wife of a highly placed German official. Her jewelry was the only thing about her appearance that suggested fabulous luxury; it was priceless, consisting of earrings and a very long, triple strand of softly shimmering pearls, each as big as a cherry.

The boy and the girls had risen quickly. They bent to kiss their mother's hand while she, with a restrained smile on her well-preserved but slightly tired and rather pointy-nosed face, looked across the tops of their heads at the governess, to whom she directed a few words in French. Then she walked to the glass door. The young ones followed her, the girls in the order of their ages, behind them the governess, the boy last of all. For some reason he turned around before crossing the threshold. Since there was no one else left in the lobby, his strangely misty gray eyes met those of Aschenbach, who was sunk deep in contemplation of the departing group, his newspaper on his knees.

What he had seen was, to be sure, in none of its particulars remarkable. They did not go in to dinner before their mother; they had waited for her, greeted her respectfully when she came, and then observed perfectly normal manners going into the dining room. It was just that it had all happened so deliberately, with such a sense of discipline, responsibility, and self-respect, that Aschenbach felt strangely moved. He lingered a few moments more, then went along into the dining room himself. He was shown to his table, which, he noted with a brief twinge of regret, was very far away from that of the Polish family.

Tired but nonetheless mentally stimulated, he entertained himself during the tedious meal with abstract, even transcendent matters. He pondered the mysterious combination of regularity and individuality that is necessary to produce human beauty; proceeded then to the general problem of form and of art; and ultimately concluded that his thoughts and discoveries resembled those inspirations that come in dreams: they seem wonderful at the time, but in the sober light of day they show up as utterly shallow and useless. After dinner he spent some time smoking, sitting, and wandering about in the park, which was fragrant in the evening air. He went to bed early and passed the night in a sleep uninterruptedly deep but frequently enlivened by all sorts of dreams.

The next day the weather had gotten no better. There was a steady wind off the land. Under a pale overcast sky the sea lay in a dull calm, almost as if it had shriveled up, with a soberingly contracted horizon; it had receded so far from the beach that it uncovered several rows of long sandbars. When Aschenbach opened his window, he thought he could detect the stagnant smell of the lagoon.

He was beset by ill humor. He was already having thoughts of leaving. Once years ago, after several lovely weeks here in springtime, just such weather had been visited upon him and had made him feel so poorly that he had had to take flight from Venice like a fugitive. Was he not feeling once again the onset of the feverish listlessness he had felt then, the throbbing of his temples, the heaviness in his eyelids? To change his vacation spot yet again would be a nuisance; but if the wind did not shift soon, he simply could not remain here. He did not unpack everything, just in case. He ate at nine in the special breakfast room between the lobby and the dining room.

In this room prevailed the solemn stillness that great hotels aspire to. The waiters went about on tip-toe. The clink of the tea service and a half-whispered word were all one could hear. Aschenbach noticed the Polish girls and their governess at a table in the corner diagonally across from the door, two tables away. They sat very straight, their ash-blond hair newly smoothed down flat, their eyes red. They wore starched blue linen dresses with little white turned-down collars and cuffs, and they passed a jar of preserves to each other. They had almost finished their breakfast. The boy was not there.

Aschenbach smiled. Well, little Phaeacian, he thought. It seems you, and not they, have the privilege of sleeping to your heart's content. Suddenly cheered, he recited to himself the line:
"Changes of dress, warm baths, and downy beds."[8]

He ate his breakfast at a leisurely pace, received some mail that had been forwarded—delivered personally by the doorman, who entered the room with his braided hat in hand—and opened a few letters while he smoked a cigarette. Thus it happened that he was present for the entrance of the late sleeper they were waiting for over there in the corner.

He came through the glass door and traversed the silent room diagonally over to the table where his sisters sat. His carriage was extraordinarily graceful, not only in the way he held his torso but also in the way he moved his knees and set one white-shod foot in front of the other. He moved lightly, in a manner both gentle and proud, made more lovely still by the childlike bashfulness with which he twice lifted and lowered his eyelids as he went by, turning his face out toward the room. Smiling, he murmured a word in his soft, indistinct speech and took his place, showing his full profile to the observer. The latter was once more, and now especially, struck with amazement, indeed even alarm, at the truly godlike beauty possessed by this mortal child. Today the boy wore a lightweight sailor suit of blue and white striped cotton with a red silk bow on the chest, finished at the neck with a simple white upright collar. And above this collar, which did not even fit in very elegantly with the character of the costume, rose up that blossom, his face, a sight unforgettably charming. It was the face of Eros, with the yellowish glaze of Parian marble,[9] with delicate and serious brows, the temples and ears richly and rectangularly framed by soft, dusky curls.

Fine, very fine, thought Aschenbach with that professional, cool air of appraisal artists sometimes use to cover their delight, their enthusiasm when they encounter a masterpiece. He thought further: Really, if the sea and the sand were not waiting for me, I would stay here as long as you stay. With that, however, he departed, walking past the attentive employees through the lobby, down the terrace steps, and straight across the wooden walkway to the hotel's private beach. There he let a barefoot old man in linen pants, sailor shirt, and straw hat who managed affairs on the beach show him to his rented beach cabana and arrange a table and chair on its sandy, wooden

8. A reference to Homer's *Odyssey* 8.249. The Phaeacians were a peaceful, happy people who showed hospitality to the shipwrecked Odysseus.   9. White marble from the island of Paros was especially prized by sculptors in antiquity. Eros was the Greek god of love.

platform. Then he made himself comfortable in his beach chair, which he had pulled through the pale yellow sand closer to the sea.

The beach scene, this view of a carefree society engaged in purely sensual enjoyment on the edge of the watery element, entertained and cheered him as it always did. The gray, smooth ocean was already full of wading children, swimmers, and colorful figures lying on the sandbars with their arms crossed behind their heads. Others were rowing about in little flat-bottomed boats painted red and blue, capsizing to gales of laughter. People sat on the platforms of the cabanas, arranged in a long neat row along the beach, as if they were little verandas. In front of them people played games, lounged lazily, visited and chatted, some dressed in elegant morning clothes and others enjoying the nakedness sanctioned by the bold and easy freedom of the place. Down on the moist, hard sand there were a few individuals strolling about in white beach robes or in loose, brightly colored bathing dresses. To the right some children had built an elaborate sand castle and bedecked it with little flags in the colors of every country. Vendors of mussels, cakes, and fruit knelt and spread their wares before them. On the left, a Russian family was encamped in front of one of the cabanas that were set at a right angle between the others and the sea, thus closing that end of the beach. The family included men with beards and huge teeth; languid women past their prime; a young lady from a Baltic country, sitting at an easel and painting the ocean to the accompaniment of cries of frustration; two affable, ugly children; and an old maid in a babushka, displaying the affectionately servile demeanor of a slave. They resided there in grateful enjoyment, called out endlessly the names of their unruly, giddy children, exchanged pleasantries at surprising length in their few words of Italian with the jocular old man from whom they bought candy, kissed each other on the cheeks, and cared not a whit for anyone who might witness their scene of shared humanity.

Well, then, I will stay, thought Aschenbach. Where could things be better? His hands folded in his lap, he let his eyes roam the ocean's distances, let his gaze slip out of focus, grow hazy, blur in the uniform distances, mistiness of empty space. He loved the sea from the depth of his being: first of all because a hardworking artist needs his rest from the demanding variety of phenomena he works with and longs to take refuge in the bosom of simplicity and enormity; and, second, because he harbors an affinity for the undivided, the immeasurable, the eternal, the void. It was a forbidden affinity, directly contrary to his calling, and seductive precisely for that reason. To rest in the arms of perfection is what all those who struggle for excellence long to do; and is the void not a form of perfection? But while he was thus dreaming away toward the depths of emptiness, the horizontal line of the sea's edge was crossed by a human figure. When he had retrieved his gaze from the boundless realms and refocused his eyes, he saw it was the lovely boy who, coming from the left, was passing before him across the sand. He went barefoot, ready to go in wading, his slim legs bare from the knees down. He walked slowly but with a light, proud step, as if he were used to going about without shoes, and looked around at the row of cabanas that closed the end of the beach. The Russian family was still there, gratefully leading its harmonious existence, but no sooner had he laid eyes on them than a storm cloud of angry contempt crossed his face. His brow darkened, his lips began to curl, and from one side of his mouth emerged a bitter grimace that gouged a furrow in his cheek. He frowned so deeply that his eyes seemed pressed inward and sunken, seemed to speak dark and evil volumes of hatred from their depths. He looked down at the ground, cast one more threatening glance backward, and then, shrugging his shoulders as if to discard something and get away from it, he left his enemies behind.

A sort of delicacy or fright, something like a mixture of respect and shame, caused Aschenbach to turn away as if he had not seen anything; for it is repugnant to a chance witness, if he is a serious person, to make use of his observations, even to himself. But Aschenbach felt cheered and shaken at the same time—that is, happiness overwhelmed him. This childish fanaticism directed against the most harmless, good-natured target imaginable put into a human perspective something that otherwise seemed divinely indeterminate. It transformed a precious creation of nature that had before been no more than a feast for the eyes into a worthy object of deeper sympathy. It endowed the figure of the youngster, who had already shone with significance because of his beauty, with an aura that allowed him to be taken seriously beyond his years.

Still turned away, Aschenbach listened to the boy's voice, his clear, somewhat weak voice, by means of which he was trying to hail from afar his playmates at work on the sand castle. They answered him, calling again and again his name or an affectionate variation on his name. Aschenbach listened with a certain curiosity, unable to distinguish anything more than two melodious syllables—something like Adgio or more frequently Adgiu, with a drawn-out *u* at the end of the cry. The sound made him glad, it seemed to him that its harmony suited its object, and he repeated it softly to himself as he turned back with satisfaction to his letters and papers.

With his small traveling briefcase on his knees, he took his fountain pen and began to attend to various matters of correspondence. But after a mere quarter of an hour he was feeling regret that he should thus take leave in spirit and miss out on this, the most charming set of circumstances he knew of, for the sake of an activity he carried on with indifference. He cast his writing materials aside and turned his attention back to the sea; and not long after, distracted by the voices of the youngsters at the sand castle, he turned his head to the right and let it rest comfortably on the back of his chair, where he could once more observe the comings and goings of the exquisite Adgio.

His first glance found him; the red bow on his breast could not be missed. He was engaged with some others in setting up an old board as a bridge over the moat around the sand castle, calling out advice on proper procedure and nodding his head. There were about ten companions with him, boys and girls, most of an age with him but a few younger, chattering in a confusion of tongues—Polish, French, and even some Balkan languages. But it was his name that most often resounded through it all. He was evidently popular, sought after, admired. One companion, likewise a Pole, a sturdy boy called something like Yashu, who wore a belted linen suit and had black hair slicked down with pomade, seemed to be his closest friend and vassal. With the work on the sand castle finished for the time being, they went off together along the beach, arms about each other, and the one called Yashu gave his beautiful partner a kiss.

Aschenbach was tempted to shake his finger at him. "Let me give you a piece of advice, Kritobulos," he thought and smiled to himself. "Take a year's journey. You will need at least that much time for your recovery."[1] And then he breakfasted on large, fully ripe strawberries that he obtained from a peddler. It had gotten very warm, although the sun had not managed to pierce the layer of mist that covered the sky. Lassitude seized his spirit, while his senses enjoyed the enormous, lulling entertainment afforded by the quiet sea. The task of puzzling out what name it was that sounded like Adgio struck the serious man as a fitting, entirely satisfying occupation. With the help of a few Polish memories he determined that it was probably Tadzio he had heard, the nickname for Tadeusz. It was pronounced Tadziu in the form used for direct address.

Tadizo was taking a swim. Aschenbach, who had lost sight of him for a moment, spotted his head and then his arm, which rose as it stroked. He was very far out; the water apparently stayed shallow for a long way. But already his family seemed to be getting concerned about him, already women's voices were calling to him from the cabanas, shouting out once more this name that ruled over the beach almost like a watchword and that possessed something both sweet and wild in its soft consonants and drawn-out cry of *uuu* at the end. "Tadziu! Tadziu!" He turned back; he ran through the sea with his head thrown back, beating the resisting water into a foam with his legs. The sight of this lively adolescent figure, seductive and chaste, lovely as a tender young god, emerging from the depths of the sky and the sea with dripping locks and escaping the clutches of the elements—it all gave rise to mythic images. It was a sight belonging to poetic legends from the beginning of time that tell of the origins of form and of the birth of the gods. Aschenbach listened with his eyes closed to this mythic song reverberating within him, and once again he thought about how good it was here and how he wanted to stay.

Later on Tadzio lay on the sand, resting from his swim, wrapped in a white beach towel that was drawn up under his right shoulder, his head resting on his bare arm. Even when Aschenbach refrained from looking at him, instead reading a few pages in his book, he almost never forgot who was lying nearby or forgot that it would cost him only a slight turn of his head to the right to bring the adorable sight back into view. It almost seemed to him that he was sitting here with the express purpose of keeping watch over the resting boy. Busy as he might be with his own affairs, he maintained his vigilant care for the noble human figure not far away on his right. A paternal kindness, an emotional attachment filled and moved his heart, the attachment that someone who produces beauty at the cost of intellectual self-sacrifice feels toward someone who naturally possesses beauty.

After midday he left the beach, returned to the hotel, and took the elevator up to his room. There he spent a considerable length of time in front of the mirror looking at his gray hair and his severe, tired face. At the same time he thought about his fame and about the fact that many people recognized him on the street and looked at him with respect, all on account of those graceful, unerringly accurate words of his. He called the roll of the long list of successes his talent had brought him, as many as he could think of, and

---

1. Recalling Socrates' advice to Kritoboulos when the latter kissed Alcibiades' handsome son (Xenophon's *Memorabilia* 1.3).

even recalled his elevation to the nobility. He then retired to the dining room for lunch and ate at his little table. As he was entering the elevator when the meal was over, a throng of young people likewise coming from lunch crowded him to the back of the swaying little chamber. Tadzio was among them. He stood very close by, so close in fact that for the first time Aschenbach had the opportunity to view him not from a distance like a picture but minutely, scrutinizing every detail of his human form. Someone was talking to the boy, and while he was answering with his indescribably sweet smile they reached the second floor, where he got off, backing out, his eyes cast down. Beauty breeds modesty, Aschenbach thought and gave urgent consideration as to why. He had had occasion to notice, however, that Tadzio's teeth were not a very pleasing sight. They were rather jagged and pale and had no luster of health but rather a peculiar brittle transparency such as one sometimes sees in anemics. He is very sensitive, he is sickly, thought Aschenbach. He will probably not live long. And he refrained from trying to account for the feeling of satisfaction and reassurance that accompanied this thought.

He passed a couple of hours in his room and in the afternoon took the vaporetto across the stagnant-smelling lagoon to Venice. He got off at San Marco, took tea in the piazza,[2] and then, following his habitual routine in Venice, set off on a walk through the streets. It was this walk, however, that initiated a complete reversal of his mood and his plans.

The air in the little streets was odiously oppressive, so thick that the smells surging out of the dwellings, shops, and restaurants, a suffocating vapor of oil, perfume, and more, all hung about and failed to disperse. Cigarette smoke hovered in place and only slowly disappeared. The press of people in the small spaces annoyed rather than entertained him as he walked. The longer he went on, the more it became a torture. He was overwhelmed by that horrible condition produced by the sea air in combination with the sirocco, a state of both nervousness and debility at once. He began to sweat uncomfortably. His eyes ceased to function, his breathing was labored, he felt feverish, the blood pounded in his head. He fled from the crowded shop-lined streets across bridges into the poor quarter. There beggars molested him, and the evil emanations from the canals hindered his breathing. In a quiet piazza, one of those forgotten, seemingly enchanted little places in the interior of the city, he rested on the edge of a well, dried his forehead, and reached the conclusion that he would have to leave Venice.

For the second time, and this time definitively, it became clear that this city in this weather was particularly harmful to his health. To remain stubbornly in place obviously went against all reason, and the prospect of a change in the direction of the wind was highly uncertain. A quick decision had to be made. To return home this soon was out of the question. Neither his summer nor his winter quarters were prepared for his arrival. But this was not the only place with beaches on the ocean, and those other places did not have the noxious extra of the lagoon and its fever-inducing vapors. He recalled a little beach resort not far from Trieste that had been enthusiastically recommended to him. Why not go there and, indeed, without delay, so that yet another change of location would still be worthwhile? He declared himself resolved and stood up. At the next gondola stop he boarded

2. A famous public square in front of the church, lined by restaurants and cafés.

a boat to take him to San Marco through the dim labyrinth of canals, under graceful marble balconies flanked by stone lions, around corners of slippery masonry, past mournful palace facades affixed with business insignia[3] reflected in the garbage-strewn water. He had trouble getting to his destination, since the gondolier was in league with lace and glass factories and made constant efforts to induce him to stop at them to sightsee and buy; and so whenever the bizarre journey through Venice began to weave its magic, the mercenary lust for booty afflicting this sunken queen of cities[4] did what it could to bring the enchanted spirit back to unpleasant reality.

Upon returning to the hotel he did not even wait for dinner but went right to the office and declared that unforeseen circumstances compelled him to depart the next morning. With many expressions of regret the staff acknowledged the payment of his bill. He dined and then passed the mild evening reading magazines in a rocking chair on the rear terrace. Before going to bed he did all his packing for the morning's departure.

He did not sleep especially well, as the impending move made him restless. When he opened the windows the next morning the sky was still overcast, but the air seemed fresher and . . . he already started to have second thoughts. Had he been hasty or wrong to give notice thus? Was it a result of his sick and unreliable condition? If he had just put it off a bit, if he had just made an attempt to get used to the Venetian air or to hold out for an improvement in the weather instead of losing heart so quickly! Then, instead of this hustle and bustle, he would have a morning on the beach like the one yesterday to look forward to. Too late. Now he would have to go ahead with it, to wish today what he wished for yesterday. He got dressed and at eight o'clock took the elevator down to breakfast on the ground floor.

The breakfast room was still empty when he entered. A number of individual guests arrived while he sat waiting for his order. With his teacup at his lips he watched the Polish girls and their attendant come in. Severe and morning-fresh, eyes still red, they proceeded to their table in the corner by the window. Immediately thereafter the doorman approached him with hat in hand to tell him it was time to leave. The car was ready, he said, to take him and some other travelers to the Hotel Excelsior, and from there a motor boat would convey them through the company's private canal to the railroad station. Time was pressing, he said. Aschenbach found it not at all pressing. There was more than an hour until the departure of his train. He was annoyed at the habitual hotel practice of packing departing guests off earlier than necessary and informed the doorman that he wanted to finish his breakfast in peace. The man withdrew hesitatingly only to show up again five minutes later. The car simply could not wait longer, he said. Very well, let it go and take his trunks with it, Aschenbach replied with annoyance. As for himself, he preferred to take the public steamer at the proper time and asked that they let him take care of his own arrangements. The employee bowed. Aschenbach, happy to have fended off this nuisance, finished his meal without haste and even had the waiter bring him a newspaper. Time had become short indeed when at last he got up to leave. And it just so happened that at that very moment Tadzio came in through the glass door.

---

3. Once-stately Renaissance homes that now lodge businesses.   4. A major sea power by the fifteenth century, Venice was called Queen of the Seas.

He crossed the path of the departing traveler on his way to his family's table. He lowered his eyes modestly before the gray-haired, high-browed gentleman, only to raise them again immediately in his own charming way, displaying their soft fullness to him. Then he was past. Adieu, Tadzio, thought Aschenbach. I saw you for such a short time. And enunciating his thought as it occurred to him, contrary to his every habit, he added under his breath the words: "Blessings on you." He then made his departure, dispensed tips, received a parting greeting from the quiet little manager in the French frock coat, and left the hotel on foot, as he had arrived. Followed by a servant with his hand luggage, he traversed the island along the boulevard, white with flowers, that led to the steamer landing. He arrived, he took his seat—and what followed was a journey of pain and sorrow through the uttermost depths of regret.

It was the familiar trip across the lagoon, past San Marco, up the Grand Canal. Aschenbach sat on the curved bench in the bow, his arm resting on the railing, his hand shading his eyes. They left the public gardens behind them; the Piazzetta once more revealed its princely splendor, and soon it too was left behind. Then came the great line of palaces, and as the waterway turned there appeared the magnificent marble arch of the Rialto.[5] The traveler looked, and his heart was torn. He breathed the atmosphere of the city, this slightly stagnant smell of sea and of swamp from which he had felt so strongly compelled to flee, breathed it now deeply, in tenderly painful draughts. Was it possible that he had not known, had not considered how desperately he was attached to all this? What this morning had been a partial regret, a slight doubt as to the rightness of his decision, now became affliction, genuine pain, a suffering in his soul so bitter that it brought tears to his eyes more than once. He told himself he could not possibly have foreseen such a reaction. What was so hard to take, actually sometimes down-right impossible to endure, was the thought that he would never see Venice again, that this was a parting forever. Since it had become evident for the second time that the city made him sick, since for the second time he had been forced to run head over heels away, he would have to regard it henceforth as an impossible destination, forbidden to him, something he simply was not up to, something it would be pointless for him to try for again. Yes, he felt that, should he go away now, shame and spite would certainly prevent him from ever seeing the beloved city again, now that it had twice forced him to admit physical defeat. This conflict between the inclination of his soul and the capacity of his body seemed to the aging traveler suddenly so weighty and so important, his physical defeat so ignominious, so much to be resisted at all cost, that he could no longer grasp the ease with which he had reached the decision yesterday, without serious struggle, to acquiesce.

Meanwhile, the steamer was approaching the railway station, and his pain and helplessness were rising to the level of total disorientation. His tortured mind found the thought of departure impossible, the thought of return no less so. In such a state of acute inner strife he entered the station. It was already very late, he had not a moment to lose if he was to catch his train. He wanted to, and he did not want to. But time was pressing, it goaded him

5. A famous, highly arched bridge over the Grand Canal.

onward; he made haste to obtain his ticket and looked about in the bustle of the station for the hotel employee stationed here. This person appeared and announced that the large trunk was already checked and on its way. Already on its way? Yes indeed—to Como.⁶ To Como? After a frantic exchange, after angry questions and embarrassed answers, the fact emerged that the trunk had been put together with the baggage of other, unknown travelers in the luggage office at the Hotel Excelsior and sent off in precisely the wrong direction.

Aschenbach had difficulty maintaining the facial expression expected under such circumstances. An adventurous joy, an unbelievable cheerfulness seized his breast from within like a spasm. The hotel employee sped off to see if he could retrieve the trunk and returned, as one might have expected, with no success whatever. Only then did Aschenbach declare that he did not wish to travel without his luggage and that he had decided to return and await the recovery of the trunk at the Hotel des Bains. Was the company boat still here at the station? The man assured him it was waiting right at the door. With an impressive display of Italian cajolery he persuaded the agent to take back Aschenbach's ticket. He swore he would telegraph ahead, that no effort would be spared to get the trunk back with all due speed, and . . . thus came to pass something very odd indeed. The traveler, not twenty minutes after his arrival at the station, found himself once again on the Grand Canal on his way back to the Lido.

What a wondrous, incredible, embarrassing, odd and dreamlike adventure! Thanks to a sudden reversal of destiny, he was to see once again, within the very hour, places that he had thought in deepest melancholy he was leaving forever. The speedy little vessel shot toward its destination, foam flying before its bow, maneuvering with droll agility between gondolas and steamers, while its single passenger hid beneath a mask of annoyed resignation the anxious excitement of a boy playing hooky. Still from time to time his frame was shaken with laughter over this mischance, which he told himself could not have worked out better for the luckiest person in the world. Explanations would have to be made, amazed faces confronted, but then—so he told himself—all would be well again, a great disaster averted, a terrible error made right, and everything he thought he had left behind would be open to him once more, would be his to enjoy at his leisure. . . . And by the way, was it just the rapid movement of the boat, or could it really be that he felt a strong breeze off the ocean to complete his bliss?

The waves slapped against the concrete walls of the narrow canal that cut through the island to the Hotel Excelsior. A motor bus was waiting there for the returning traveler and conveyed him alongside the curling waves down the straight road to the Hotel des Bains. The little manager with the mustache and the cutaway frock coat came down the broad flight of steps to meet him.

With quiet cajolery the manager expressed his regret over the incident, declared it extremely embarrassing for himself personally and for the establishment, but expressed his emphatic approval of Aschenbach's decision to wait here for the return of his luggage. To be sure, his room was already taken, but another, by no means worse, stood ready. "Pas de chance, mon-sieur,"[7] said the elevator man with a smile as they glided upwards. And so the fugitive was billeted once again, and in a room that matched almost exactly his previous one in orientation and furnishings.

Tired, numb from the whirl of this strange morning, he distributed the contents of his small suitcase in his room and then sank down in an armchair by the open window. The sea had taken on a light green coloration, the air seemed thinner and purer, the beach with its cabanas and boats seemed more colorful, although the sky was still gray. Aschenbach looked out, his hands folded in his lap, content to be here once more, but shaking his head in reproach at his own fickle mood, his lack of knowledge of his own desires. He sat thus for perhaps an hour, resting and thoughtlessly dreaming. At noon he spied Tadzio, dressed in his striped linen suit with red bow, returning from the shore through the beach barrier and along the wooden walkway to the hotel. Aschenbach recognized him at once from his high vantage point even before he got a good look at him, and he was just about to form a thought something like: Look, Tadzio, you too have returned! But at that very moment he felt the casual greeting collapse and fall silent before the truth of his heart. He felt the excitement in his blood, the joy and pain in his soul, and recognized that it was because of Tadzio that his departure had been so difficult.

He sat quite still, quite unseen in his elevated location and looked into himself. His features were active; his brows rose; an alert, curious, witty smile crossed his lips. Then he raised his head and with both his arms, which were hanging limp over the arms of his chair, he made a slow circling and lifting movement that turned his palms forward, as if to signify an opening and extending of his embrace. It was a gesture of readiness, of welcome, and of relaxed acceptance.

CHAPTER 4

The god with fiery cheeks[8] now, naked, directed his horses, four-abreast, fire-breathing, day by day through the chambers of heaven, and his yellow curls fluttered along with the blast of the east wind. A silky-white sheen lay on the Pontos,[9] its broad stretches undulating languidly. The sands burned. Under the silvery shimmering blue of the ether there were rustcolored canvas awnings spread out in front of the beach cabanas, and one passed the morning hours in the sharply framed patch of shade they offered. But the evening was also delightful, when the plants in the park wafted balsamic perfumes, the stars above paced out their circuits, and the murmur of the night-shrouded sea, softly penetrating, cast a spell on the soul. Such an evening bore the joyful promise of another festive day of loosely ordered leisure, bejeweled with countless, thickly strewn possibilities of happy accidents.

The guest, whom accommodating mischance kept here, was far from disposed to see in the return of his belongings a reason to depart once more. He had been obliged to get along without a few things for a couple of days and to appear at meals in the great dining room wearing his traveling clothes.

7. No luck, sir (French). 8. Helios, Greek god of the sun (later equated with Apollo). 9. The sea (Greek, literal trans.); a figurative reference to the Adriatic Sea.

Then, when the errant baggage was finally set down once more in his room, he unpacked thoroughly and filled closets and drawers with his things, determined for the time being to stay indefinitely, happy to be able to pass the morning's hours on the beach in his silk suit and to present himself once more at his little table at dinner time wearing proper evening attire.

The benevolent regularity of this existence had at once drawn him into its power; the soft and splendid calm of this lifestyle had him quickly ensnared. What a fine place to stay, indeed, combining the charms of a refined southern beach resort with the cozy proximity of the wondrous, wonder-filled city! Aschenbach was no lover of pleasure. Whenever and wherever it seemed proper to celebrate, to take a rest, to take a few days off, he soon had to get back—it was especially so in his younger days—anxiously and reluctantly back to the affliction of his high calling, the sacred, sober service of his day-to-day life. This place alone enchanted him, relaxed his will, made him happy. Sometimes in the morning, under the canopy of his beach cabana, dreaming away across the blue of the southern sea, or sometimes as well on a balmy night, leaning back under the great starry sky on the cushions of a gondola taking him back home to the Lido from the Piazza San Marco, where he had tarried long—and the bright lights and the melting sounds of the serenade were left behind—he remembered his country home in the mountains, the site of his summertime struggles, where the clouds drifted through the garden, where in the evening fearful thunderstorms extinguished the lights in the house and the ravens he fed soared to the tops of the spruce trees. Then it might seem to him that he had been transported to the land of Elysium[1] at the far ends of the earth, where a life of ease is bestowed upon mortals, where there is no snow, no winter, no storms or streaming rain, but rather always the cooling breath rising from Okeanos,[2] where the days run out in blissful leisure, trouble-free, struggle-free, dedicated only to the sun and its revels.

Aschenbach saw the boy Tadzio often, indeed almost continually; limited space and a regular schedule common to all the guests made it inevitable that the lovely boy was in his vicinity nearly all day, with brief interruptions. He saw, he met him everywhere: in the hotel's public places, on the cooling boat trips to the city and back, in the ostentation of the piazza itself; and often too in the streets and byways a chance encounter would take place. Chiefly, however, it was the mornings on the beach that offered him with delightful regularity an extended opportunity to study and worship the charming apparition. Yes, it was this narrow and constrained happiness, this regularly recurring good fortune that filled him with contentment and joy in life, that made his stay all the more dear to him and caused one sunny day after another to fall so agreeably in line.

He got up early, as he otherwise did under the relentless pressure of work, and was one of the first on the beach when the sun was still mild and the sea lay white in the glare of morning dreams. He gave a friendly greeting to the guard at the beach barrier, said a familiar hello to the barefoot old man who got his place ready, spreading the brown awning and arranging the

---

1. Located at the western edge of the Earth, a pleasant otherworld for those heroes favored of the gods.   2. According to Greek mythology, a river encircling the world.

cabana furniture on the platform, and settled in. Three hours or four were then his in which, as the sun rose to its zenith and grew fearsome in strength and the sea turned a deeper and deeper blue, he could watch Tadzio.

He would see him coming from the left along the edge of the sea, would see him from the back as he appeared from between the cabanas, or sometimes would suddenly discover, not without a happy shudder, that he had missed his arrival and that he was already there, already in the blue and white bathing suit that was now his only article of attire on the beach, that he was already up to his usual doings in sand and sun—his charmingly trivial, lazily irregular life that was both recreation and rest, filled with lounging, wading, digging, catching, resting, and swimming, watched over by the women on the platform who called to him, making his name resound with their high voices: "Tadziu! Tadziu!" He would come running to them gesturing excitedly and telling them what he had done, showing them what he had found or caught: mussels and sea horses, jelly fish, crabs that ran off going sideways. Aschenbach understood not a single word he said, and though it may have been the most ordinary thing in the world it was all a vague harmony to his ear. Thus, foreignness raised the boy's speech to the level of music, a wanton sun poured unstinting splendor over him, and the sublime perspectives of the sea always formed the background and aura that set off his appearance.

Soon the observer knew every line and pose of this noble body that displayed itself so freely; he exulted in greeting anew every beauty, familiar though it had become, and his admiration, the discreet arousal of his senses, knew no end. They called the boy to pay his compliments to a guest who was attending the ladies at the cabana; he came running, still wet from the sea; he tossed his curls, and as he held out his hand he stood on one foot while holding the other up on tiptoe. His body was gracefully poised in the midst of a charming turning motion, while his face showed an embarrassed amiability, a desire to please that came from an aristocratic sense of duty. Sometimes he would lie stretched out with his beach towel wrapped about his chest, his delicately chiseled arm propped in the sand, his chin in the hollow of his hand. The one called Yashu sat crouching by him, playing up to him, and nothing could have been more enchanting than the smiling eyes and lips with which the object of this flattery looked upon his inferior, his vassal. Or he would stand at the edge of the sea, alone, separated from his friends, very near Aschenbach, erect, his hands clasped behind his neck, slowly rocking on the balls of his feet and dreaming off into the blue yonder, while little waves that rolled in bathed his toes. His honey-colored hair clung in circles to his temples and his neck; the sun made the down shine on his upper back; the subtle definition of the ribs and the symmetry of his chest stood out through the tight-fitting material covering his torso; his armpits were still as smooth as those of a statue, the hollows behind his knees shone likewise, and the blue veins showing through made his body seem to be made of translucent material. What discipline, what precision of thought was expressed in the stretch of this youthfully perfect body! But was not the rigorous and pure will that had been darkly active in bringing this divine form into the clear light of day entirely familiar to the artist in him? Was this same will not active in him, too, when he, full of sober passion, freed a slender form from the marble mass of language,[3] a form he had seen with his spiritual eye and that he presented to mortal men as image and mirror of spiritual beauty?

Image and mirror! His eyes embraced the noble figure there on the edge of the blue, and in a transport of delight he thought his gaze was grasping beauty itself, the pure form of divine thought, the universal and pure perfection that lives in the spirit and which here, graceful and lovely, presented itself for worship in the form of a human likeness and exemplar. Such was his intoxication; the aging artist welcomed the experience without reluctance, even greedily. His intellect was in labor, his educated mind set in motion. His memory dredged up ancient images passed on to him in the days of his youth, thoughts not until now touched by the spark of his personal involvement. Was it not written that the sun turns our attention from intellectual to sensuous matters?[4] It was said that the sun numbs and enchants our reason and memory to such an extent that the soul in its pleasure forgets its ordinary condition; its amazed admiration remains fixed on the loveliest of sun-drenched objects. Indeed, only with the help of a body can the soul rise to the contemplation of still higher things. Amor[5] truly did as mathematicians have always done by assisting slow-learning children with concrete pictures of pure forms: so, too, did the god like to make use of the figure and coloration of human youth in order to make the spiritual visible to us, furnishing it with the reflected glory of beauty and thus making of it a tool of memory, so that seeing it we might then be set aflame with pain and hope.

Those, at any rate, were the thoughts of the impassioned onlooker. He was capable of sustaining just such a high pitch of emotion. He spun himself a charming tapestry out of the roar of the sea and the glare of the sun. He saw the ancient plane tree not far from the walls of Athens,[6] that sacred, shadowy place filled with the scent of willow blossoms, decorated with holy images and votive offerings in honor of the nymphs and of Achelous.[7] The stream flowed in crystal clarity over smooth pebbles past the foot of the wide-branched tree. The crickets sang. Two figures reclined on the grass that gently sloped so that you could lie with your head held up; they were sheltered here from the heat of the day—an older man and a younger, one ugly and one handsome, wisdom at the side of charm. Amidst polite banter and wooing wit Socrates taught Phaedrus about longing and virtue. He spoke to him of the searing terror that the sensitive man experiences when his eye lights on an image of eternal beauty; spoke to him of the appetites of the impious, bad man who cannot conceive of beauty when he sees beauty's image and is incapable of reverence; spoke of the holy fear that overcomes a noble heart when a godlike face or a perfect body appears before him— how he then trembles and is beside himself and scarcely dares turn his eyes upon the sight and honors him who has beauty, indeed would even sacrifice to him as to a holy image, if he did not fear looking foolish in the eyes of

---

3. The Italian artist Michelangelo Buonarroti (1475–1564) explained that he created his statues by carving away the marble block until the figure within was set free.   **4.** In section 764E of the *Erotikos* (Dialogue on love) by the Greek essayist Plutarch (46–120).   **5.** The god of love (Latin).   **6.** A reference to the scene and some of the arguments in Plato's dialogue *Phaedrus*. Plato's school, or Academy, was located in a grove of plane trees outside Athens; in the dialogue, the young student Phaedrus tells Socrates of Lysias's speech on love, and Socrates responds with two speeches of his own.   **7.** A brook or small river in ancient Athens, here personified as a god.

others. For beauty, my dear Phaedrus, beauty alone is both worthy of love and visible at the same time; beauty, mark me well, is the only form of spirit that our senses can both grasp and endure. For what should become of us if divinity itself, or reason and virtue and truth were to appear directly to our senses? Would we not be overcome and consumed in the flames of love, as Semele[8] was at the sight of Zeus? Thus beauty is the sensitive man's way to the spirit—just the way, just the means, little Phaedrus. . . . And then he said the subtlest thing of all, crafty wooer that he was: he said that the lover was more divine than the beloved, because the god was in the former and not in the latter—perhaps the tenderest, most mocking thought that ever was thought, a thought alive with all the guile and the most secret bliss of love's longing.

A writer's chief joy is that thought can become all feeling, that feeling can become all thought. The lonely author possessed and commanded at this moment just such a vibrant thought, such a precise feeling: namely, that nature herself would shiver with delight were intellect to bow in homage before beauty. He suddenly wanted to write. They say, to be sure, that Eros loves idleness; the god was made to engage in no other activity. But at this moment of crisis the excitement of the love-struck traveler drove him to productivity, and the occasion was almost a matter of indifference. The intellectual world had been challenged to profess its views on a certain great and burning problem of culture and of taste, and the challenge had reached him. The problem was well known to him, was part of his experience; the desire to illuminate it with the splendor of his eloquence was suddenly irresistible. And what is more, he wanted to work here in the presence of Tadzio, to use the boy's physical frame as the model for his writing, to let his style follow the lines of that body that seemed to him divine, to carry his beauty into the realm of intellect as once the eagle carried the Trojan shepherd into the ethereal heavens.[9] Never had his pleasure in the word seemed sweeter to him, never had he known so surely that Eros dwelt in the word as now in the dangerous and delightful hours he spent at his rough table under the awning. There with his idol's image in full view, the music of his voice resounding in his ear, he formed his little essay after the image of Tadzio's beauty—composed that page-and-a-half of choice prose that soon would amaze many a reader with its purity, nobility, and surging depth of feeling. It is surely for the best that the world knows only the lovely work and not also its origins, not the conditions under which it came into being; for knowledge of the origins from which flowed the artist's inspiration would surely often confuse the world, repel it, and thus vitiate the effects of excellence. Strange hours! Strangely enervating effort! Strangely fertile intercourse between a mind and a body! When Aschenbach folded up his work and left the beach, he felt exhausted, even unhinged, as if his conscience were indicting him after a debauch.

The next morning as he was about to leave the hotel he chanced to notice from the steps that Tadzio was already on his way to the shore, alone; he was just approaching the beach barrier. He felt first a suggestion, then a com-

---

8. The mortal mother of Zeus's son Dionysus. She perished in flames when the king of the gods appeared (at her request) in his divine glory.   9. The young Trojan prince Ganymede was tending flocks when Zeus, in the form of an eagle, carried him off to Olympus where he became Zeus's lover and the cupbearer to the gods.

pulsion: the wish, the simple thought that he might make use of the opportunity to strike up a casual, cheerful acquaintanceship with this boy who
unwittingly had caused such a stir in his mind and heart, speak with him
and enjoy his answer and his gaze. The lovely lad sauntered along; he could
be easily caught up with; Aschenbach quickened his steps. He reached him
on the walkway behind the cabanas, was about to put his hand on his head
or on his shoulder, was about to let some word pass his lips, some friendly
French phrase. But then he felt his heart beating like a hammer, perhaps
only because of his rapid walk, so that he was short of breath and could only
have spoken in a trembling gasp. He hesitated, tried to master himself, then
suddenly feared he had been walking too long right behind the handsome
boy, feared he might notice, might turn around with an inquiring look. He
took one more run at him, but then he gave up, renounced his goal, and
hung his head as he went by.

Too late! he thought at that moment. Too late! But was it really too late?
This step he had failed to take might very possibly have led to something
good, to something easy and happy, to a salutary return to reality. But it may
have been that the aging traveler did not wish to return to reality, that he
was too much in love with his own intoxication. Who can untangle the riddle
of the artist's essence and character? Who can understand the deep instinctive fusion of discipline and a desire for licentiousness upon which that
character is based? For it is licentiousness to be unable to wish for a salutary
return to reality. Aschenbach was no longer inclined to self-criticism. The
taste, the intellectual constitution that came with his years, his self-esteem,
maturity, and the simplicity of age made him disinclined to analyze the
grounds for his behavior or to decide whether it was conscience or debauchery and weakness that caused him not to carry out his plan. He was confused;
he feared that someone, if only the custodian on the beach, might have
observed his accelerated gait and his defeat; he feared very much looking
foolish. And all the while he made fun of himself, of his comically solemn
anxiety. "We've been quite confounded," he thought, "and now we're as crestfallen as a gamecock that lets its wings droop during a fight.[1] It must surely
be the god himself who thus destroys our courage at the very sight of loveliness, who crushes our proud spirit so deeply in the dust. . . ." His thoughts
roamed playfully: he was far too arrogant to be fearful of a mere emotion.

He had already ceased to pay much attention to the extent of time he was
allowing himself for his holiday; the thought of returning home did not even
cross his mind. He had had an ample amount of money sent to him by mail.
His sole source of concern was the possible departure of the Polish family,
but he had privately obtained information, thanks to casual inquiries at the
hotel barber shop, that the Polish party had arrived only very shortly before
he did. The sun tanned his face and hands, the bracing salt air stimulated
his emotions. Just as he ordinarily used up all the resources he gathered from
sleep, nourishment, or nature on literary work, so now he expended each
contribution that sun, leisure, and sea air made to his daily increase in
strength in a generous, extravagant burst of enthusiasm and sentiment.

He slept fitfully; the exquisitely uniform days were separated by short
nights full of happy restlessness. To be sure he retired early, for at nine

1. From the Greek tragedian Phrynichus (512–476 B.C.) quoted in Plutarch's *Erotikos* (762E).

o'clock, when Tadzio had left the scene, the day was over as far as he was concerned. At the first glimmer of dawn, however, a softly penetrating pang of alarm awakened him, as his heart remembered its great adventure. No longer able to endure the pillow, he arose, wrapped himself in a light robe against the morning chill, and positioned himself at the open window to await the sunrise. This wonderful occurrence filled his sleep-blessed soul with reverence. Heaven, earth, and sea still lay in the ghostly, glassy pallor of dawn; a fading star still floated in the insubstantial distance. Then a breath of wind arose, a winged message from unapproachable abodes announcing that Eos was arising from the side of her spouse. There became visible on the furthest boundary between sea and sky that first sweet blush of red that reveals creation assuming perceptible form. The goddess was approaching, she who seduced young men, she who had stolen Kleitos and Kephalos and enjoyed the love of handsome Orion in defiance of all the envious Olympians.[2] A strewing of roses began there on the edge of the world, where all shone and blossomed in unspeakable purity. Childlike clouds, transfigured and luminous, hovered like attending Cupids in the rosy bluish fragrance. Purple light fell on the sea, then washed forward in waves. Golden spears shot up from below to the heights of the heavens, and the brilliance began to burn. Silently, with divine ascendancy, glow and heat and blazing flames spun upwards, as the brother-god's sacred chargers, hooves beating, mounted the heavens. The lonely, wakeful watcher sat bathed in the splendor of the god's rays; he closed his eyes and let the glory kiss his eyelids. With a confused, wondering smile on his lips he recognized feelings from long ago, early, exquisite afflictions of the heart that had withered in the severe service that his life had become and now returned so strangely transformed. He meditated, he dreamed. Slowly his lips formed a name, and still smiling, his face turned upward, his hands folded in his lap, he fell asleep once more in his armchair.

The whole day that had thus began in fiery celebration was strangely heightened and mythically transformed. Where did that breath of air come from, the one that suddenly played about his temples and ears so softly and significantly like a whisper from a higher realm? White feathery clouds stood in scattered flocks in the heavens like grazing herds that the gods tend. A stronger wind blew up; Poseidon's[3] steeds reared and ran, and the bulls obedient to the god with the blue-green locks lowered their horns and bellowed as they charged. But amid the boulders on the distant beach the waves hopped up like leaping goats. A magical world, sacred and animated by the spirit of Pan,[4] surrounded the beguiled traveler, and his heart dreamed tender fables. Often, as the sun set behind Venice, he would sit on a bench in the park to watch Tadzio, dressed in white with a colorful sash, delight in playing ball on the smooth, rolled gravel; and it was as if he were watching Hyacinthos, who had to die because two gods loved him.[5] Indeed he felt the

2. Eos, the Greek goddess of dawn, was known for seducing handsome young men, including Kleitos and Kephalos. When she took the hunter Orion for her lover, Artemis, the jealous goddess of the hunt, killed him with her arrows.   3. God of the sea and brother of Zeus in Greek mythology, associated with the horse and the bull.   4. A Greek demigod, half man and half goat, associated with fertility and sexuality.   5. Apollo and Zephyr, god of the west wind, both loved the youth Hyacinthos. When Apollo accidentally killed him in a discus game—Zephyr blew the discus off course—a flower marked with the Greek syllables "ai ai" ("alas!") sprang from the boy's blood. Apollo is an archer and musician as well as the god of the Delphic oracle.

painful envy Zephyros felt toward his rival in love, the god who abandoned his oracle, his bow, and his cithara to spend all his time playing with the beautiful boy. He saw the discus, directed by cruel jealousy, strike the lovely head; he too, turned pale as he received the stricken body; and the flower that sprang from that sweet blood bore the inscription of his unending lament. . . .

There is nothing stranger or more precarious than the relationship between people who know each other only by sight, who meet and watch each other every day, even every hour, yet are compelled by convention or their own whim to maintain the appearance of indifference and unfamiliarity, to avoid any word or greeting. There arises between them a certain restlessness and frustrated curiosity, the hysteria of an unsatisfied, unnaturally suppressed urge for acquaintanceship and mutual exchange, and in point of fact also a kind of tense respect. For people tend to love and honor other people so long as they are not in a position to pass judgment on them; and longing is the result of insufficient knowledge.

Some sort of relationship or acquaintance necessarily had to develop between Aschenbach and the young Tadzio, and with a pang of joy the older man was able to ascertain that his involvement and attentions were not altogether unrequited. For example, what impelled the lovely boy no longer to use the boardwalk behind the cabanas when he appeared on the beach in the morning but instead to saunter by toward his family's cabana on the front path, through the sand, past Aschenbach's customary spot, sometimes unnecessarily close by him, almost touching his table, his chair? Did Aschenbach's superior emotional energy exercise such an attraction, such a fascination on the tender, unreflecting object of those emotions? The writer waited daily for Tadzio's appearance; sometimes he would act as if he were busy when this event took place and let the lovely one pass by without seeming to notice. Sometimes, though, he would look up, and their eyes would meet. Both of them were gravely serious when it happened. In the refined and respectable bearing of the older man nothing betrayed his inner tumult; but in Tadzio's eyes there was the hint of an inquiry, of a thoughtful question. A hesitation became visible in his gait, he looked at the ground, he looked up again in his charming way, and when he was past there seemed to be something in his demeanor saying that only his good breeding prevented him from turning around.

One evening, however, something quite different happened. The Polish children and their governess were missing at the main meal in the large dining room. Aschenbach had taken note of it with alarm. Concerned about their absence, he was strolling in front of the hotel at the bottom of the terrace after dinner, dressed in his evening clothes and a straw hat, when he suddenly saw appear in the light of the arc lamps the nunlike sisters and their attendant, with Tadzio four steps behind. They were apparently returning from the steamer landing after having taken their meal for some reason in the city. It must have been cool on the water: Tadzio wore a dark blue sailor's coat with gold buttons and a sailor's hat to go with it. The sun and sea air had not browned him. His skin was the same marble-like yellow color it had been from the beginning. But today he seemed paler than usual, whether because of the cool temperature or because of the pallid moonglow cast by the lamps. His even brows showed in starker contrast, his eyes darkened to an even deeper tone. He was more beautiful than words could ever tell, and Aschenbach felt as he often had before the painful truth that words are capable only of praising physical beauty, not of rendering it visible.

He had not been expecting the exquisite apparition: it had come on unhoped for. He had not had time to fortify himself in a peaceful, respectable demeanor. Joy, surprise, and admiration might have been clearly displayed in the gaze that met that of the one he had so missed—and in that very second, it came to pass that Tadzio smiled. He smiled at Aschenbach, smiled eloquently, intimately, charmingly, and without disguise, with lips that began to open only as he smiled. It was the smile of Narcissus[6] leaning over the mirroring water, that deep, beguiled, unresisting smile that comes as he extends his arm toward the reflection of his own beauty—a very slightly distorted smile, distorted by the hopelessness of his desire to kiss the lovely lips of his shadow—a coquettish smile, curious and faintly pained, infatuated and infatuating.

He who had been the recipient of this smile rushed away with it as if it were a gift heavy with destiny. He was so thoroughly shaken that he was forced to flee the light of the terrace and the front garden and to seek with a hasty tread the darkness of the park in the rear. Strangely indignant and tender exhortations broke forth from him: "You must not smile so! Listen, no one is allowed to smile that way at anyone!" He threw himself on a bench; he breathed in the nocturnal fragrance of the plants, beside himself. Leaning back with his arms hanging at his sides, overpowered and shivering uncontrollably, he whispered the eternal formula of longing—impossible under these conditions, absurd, reviled, ridiculous, and yet holy and venerable even under these conditions—"I love you!"

CHAPTER 5

In the fourth week of his stay on the Lido Gustav Aschenbach made a number of disturbing discoveries regarding events in the outside world. In the first place it seemed to him that as the season progressed toward its height the number of guests at the hotel declined rather than increased. In particular it seemed that the German language ceased to be heard around him: lately his ear could detect only foreign sounds in the dining room and on the beach. He had taken to visiting the barbershop frequently, and in a conversation there one day he heard something that startled him. The barber had mentioned a German family that had just left after staying only a short time; then he added by way of flattering small talk, "But you're staying, sir, aren't you. You're not afraid of the disease." Aschenbach looked at him. "The disease?" he repeated. The man broke off his chatter, acted busy, ignored the question. When Aschenbach pressed the issue, he explained that he knew nothing and tried to change the subject with a stream of embarrassed eloquence.

That was at noon. In the afternoon Aschenbach sailed across to Venice in a dead calm and under a burning sun. He was driven by his mania to pursue the Polish children, whom he had seen making for the steamer landing along

6. A beautiful Greek youth who fell in love with his own image in a pool and drowned trying to reach it. "Tadzio's smile is Narcissus', who sees his own reflection—he sees it in the face of another / he sees his beauty in its effects. Coquettishness and tenderness are also in this smile" [Mann's note].

with their attendant. He did not find his idol at San Marco. But at tea, sitting at his round wrought-iron table on the shady side of the piazza, he suddenly smelled a peculiar aroma in the air, one that he now felt had been lurking at the edge of his consciousness for several days without his becoming fully aware of it. It was a medicinally sweet smell that put in mind thoughts of misery and wounds and ominous cleanliness. After a few moments' reflection he recognized it; then he finished his snack and left the piazza on the side opposite the cathedral. The odor became stronger in the narrow streets. At the street corners there were affixed printed posters in which the city fathers warned the population about certain illnesses of the gastric system that could be expected under these atmospheric conditions, advising that they should not eat oysters and mussels or use the water in the canals. The euphemistic nature of the announcement was obvious. Groups of local people stood together silently on the bridges and in the piazzas, and the foreign traveler stood among them, sniffing and musing.

There was a shopkeeper leaning in the doorway of his little vaulted quarters among coral necklaces and imitation amethyst trinkets, and Aschenbach asked him for some information about the ominous odor. The man took his measure with a heavy-lidded stare and then hastily put on a cheerful expression. "A precautionary measure, sir," he answered with many a gesture. "A police regulation that we must accept. The weather is oppressive, the sirocco is not conductive to good health. In short, you understand—perhaps they're being too careful. . . ." Aschenbach thanked him and went on. Even on the steamer that took him back to the Lido he could now detect the odor of disinfectant.

Once back at the hotel he went directly to the lobby to have a look at the newspapers. In the ones in foreign languages he found nothing. The German papers mentioned rumors, cited highly varying figures, quoted official denials, and offered doubts about their veracity. This explained the departure of the German and Austrian element. The citizens of other nations apparently knew nothing, suspected nothing, and were not yet concerned. "Best to keep quiet," thought Aschenbach anxiously, as he threw the papers back on the table. "Best to keep it under wraps." But at the same time his heart filled with a feeling of satisfaction over this adventure in which the outside world was becoming involved. For passion, like crime, does not sit well with the sure order and even course of everyday life; it welcomes every loosening of the social fabric, every confusion and affliction visited upon the world, for passion sees in such disorder a vague hope of finding an advantage for itself. Thus Aschenbach felt a dark satisfaction over the official cover-up of events in the dirty alleys of Venice. This heinous secret belonging to the city fused and became one with his own innermost secret, which he was likewise intent upon keeping. For the lovesick traveler had no concern other than that Tadzio might depart, and he recognized, not without a certain horror, that he would not know how to go on living were that to happen.

Recently he had not contented himself with allowing chance and the daily routine to determine his opportunities to see and be near the lovely lad; he pursued him, he lay in wait for him. On Sundays, for example, the Polish family never went to the beach. He guessed that they went to mass at San Marco. He followed speedily, entered the golden twilight of the sanctuary from the heat of the piazza, and found him, the one he had missed so, bent over a prie-dieu[7] taking part in the holy service. He stood in the background on the fissured mosaic floor, in the midst of a kneeling, murmuring crowd of people who kept crossing themselves, and felt the condensed grandeur of the oriental temple weigh voluptuously on his senses. Up in front the priest moved about, conducted his ritual, and chanted away, while incense billowed up and enshrouded the feeble flames of the altar candles. Mixed in with the sweet, heavy, ceremonial fragrance seemed to be another: the smell of the diseased city. But through all the haze and glitter Aschenbach saw how the lovely one up in front turned his head, looked for him, and found him.

When at last the crowd streamed out of the open portals into the shining piazza with its flocks of pigeons, the infatuated lover hid in the vestibule where he lay in wait, staking out his quarry. He saw the Polish family leave the church, saw the children take leave of their mother with great ceremony, saw her make for the Piazzetta on her way home. He ascertained that the lovely one, his cloisterly sisters, and the governess were on their way off to the right, through the clock tower gate, and into the Merceria,[8] and after giving them a reasonable head start he followed. He followed like a thief as they strolled through Venice. He had to stop when they lingered somewhere, had to flee into restaurants or courtyards to avoid them when they turned back. He lost them, got hot and tired as he searched for them over bridges and in dirty cul-de-sacs, and suffered long moments of mortal pain when he saw them coming toward him in a narrow passage where no escape was possible. And yet one cannot really say he suffered. He was intoxicated in head and heart, and his steps followed the instructions of the demon whose pleasure it is to crush under foot human reason and dignity.[9]

At some point or other Tadzio and his party would take a gondola, and Aschenbach, remaining hidden behind a portico or a fountain while they got in, did likewise shortly after they pulled away from the bank. He spoke quickly and in subdued tones to the gondolier, instructing him that a generous tip was in store for him if he would follow that gondola just now rounding the corner—but not too close, as unobtrusively as possible. Sweat trickled over his body as the gondolier, with the roguish willingness of a procurer, assured him in the same lowered tones that he would get service, that he would get conscientious service.

He leaned back in the soft black cushions and glided and rocked in pursuit of the other black, beak-prowed bark, to which his passion held him fastened as if by a chain. Sometimes he lost sight of it, and at those times he would feel worried and restless. But his boatman seemed entirely familiar with such assignments and always knew just how to bring the object of his desire back into view by means of clever maneuvers and quick passages and shortcuts. The air was still, and it smelled. The sun burned heavily through a haze that gave the sky the color of slate. Water gurgled against wood and stone. The cry of the gondolier, half warning and half greeting, received distant answer from out of the silent labyrinth as if by mysterious arrangement. Umbels of flowers hung down over crumbling walls from small gardens on higher ground. They were white and purple and smelled like almonds. Moorish window casings showed their forms in the haze. The marble steps of a church

7. Pray God (French, literal trans.); a low bench on which to kneel during prayers, with a raised shelf for elbows or book.   8. Commercial district north of the Piazza San Marco.   9. Dionysus, originally an Eastern fertility god, worshiped with wild dances in ecstatic rites.

descended into the waters; a beggar crouching there and asserting his misery held out his hat and showed the whites of his eyes as if he were blind; a dealer in antiques stood before his cavelike shop and with fawning gestures invited the passerby to stop, hoping for a chance to swindle him. That was Venice, that coquettish, dubious beauty of a city, half fairy tale and half tourist trap, in whose noisome air the fine arts once thrived luxuriantly and where musicians were inspired to create sounds that cradle the listener and seductively rock him to sleep. To the traveler in the midst of his adventure it seemed as if his eyes were drinking in just this luxury, as if his ears were wooed by just such melodies. He remembered, too, that the city was sick and was keeping its secret out of pure greed, and he cast an even more licentious leer toward the gondola floating in the distance before him.

Entangled and besotted as he was, he no longer wished for anything else than to pursue the beloved object that inflamed him, to dream about him when he was absent and to speak amorous phrases, after the manner of lovers, to his mere shadow. His solitary life, the foreign locale, and his late but deep transport of ecstasy encouraged and persuaded him to allow himself the most bewildering transgressions without timidity or embarrassment. That is how it happened that on his return from Venice late in the evening he had stopped on the second floor of the hotel in front of the lovely one's door, leaned his brow against the hinge in complete intoxication, unable for a protracted period to drag himself away, heedless of the danger of being caught in such an outrageous position.

Still, there were moments when he paused and half came to his senses. How has this come to pass? he wondered in alarm. How did I come to this? Like everyone who has achieved something thanks to his natural talents, he had an aristocratic interest in his family background. At times when his life brought him recognition and success he would think about his ancestors and try to reassure himself that they would approve, that they would be pleased, that they would have had to admire him. Even here and now he thought about them, entangled as he was in such an illicit experience, seized by such exotic emotional aberrations. He thought about their rigorous self-possession, their manly respectability, and he smiled a melancholy smile. What would they say? But then what would they have said about his whole life, a life that had so diverged, one might say degenerated, from theirs, a life under the spell of art that he himself had mocked in the precocity of his youth, this life that yet so fundamentally resembled theirs? He too had done his service, he too had practiced a strict discipline; he too had been a soldier and a man of war, like many of them. For art was a war, a grinding battle that one was just no longer up to fighting for very long these days. It was a life of self-control and a life lived in despite, a harsh, steadfast, abstemious existence that he had made the symbol of a tender and timely heroism. He had every right to call it manly, call it courageous, and he wondered if the love-god who had taken possession of him might be particularly inclined and partial somehow to those who lived such a life. Had not that very god enjoyed the highest respect among the bravest nations of the earth? Did they not say that it was because of their courage that he had flourished in their cities? Numerous war heroes of ages past had willingly borne the yoke imposed by the god, for a humiliation imposed by the god did not count. Acts that would have been denounced as signs of cowardice when done in other circumstances and for other ends—prostrations, oaths, urgent pleas, and fawning behavior—none redounded to the shame of the lover, but rather he more likely reaped praise for them.[1]

Such was the infatuated thinker's train of thought; thus he sought to offer himself support; thus he attempted to preserve his dignity. But at the same time he stubbornly kept on the track of the dirty doings in the city's interior, that adventure of the outside world that darkly joined together with his heart's adventure and nourished his passion with vague, lawless hopes. Obsessed with finding out the latest and most reliable news about the status and progress of the disease, he went to the city's coffee houses and leafed through the German newspapers, which had long since disappeared from the table in the hotel lobby. He read alternating assertions and denials. The number of illnesses and deaths might be as high as twenty, forty, even a hundred or more; but then in the next article or next issue any outbreak of the epidemic, if not categorically denied, would be reported as limited to a few isolated cases brought in by foreigners. There were periodic doubts, warnings, and protests against the dangerous game being played by the Italian authorities. Reliable information was simply not available.

The solitary guest was nonetheless conscious of having a special claim on his share in the secret. Though he was excluded, he took a bizarre pleasure in pressing knowledgeable people with insidious questions and forcing those who were part of the conspiracy of silence to utter explicit lies. At breakfast one day in the main dining room, for example, he engaged the manager in conversation. This unobtrusive little person in his French frock coat was going about between the tables greeting everyone and supervising the help. He made a brief stop at Aschenbach's table, too, for a casual chat. Now then why, the guest just happened to ask very casually, why in the world had they been disinfecting Venice for all this time? "It's a police matter," the toady answered, "a measure intended to stop in due and timely fashion any and all unwholesome conditions, any disturbance of the public health that might come about owing to the brooding heat of this exceptionally warm weather." "The police are to be commended," replied Aschenbach. After the exchange of a few more meteorological observations the manager took his leave.

On that very same day, in the evening after dinner, it happened that a little band of street singers from the city performed in the hotel's front garden. They stood, two men and two women, next to the iron lamppost of an arc light and raised their faces, shining in the white illumination, toward the great terrace, where the guests were enjoying this traditional popular entertainment while drinking coffee and cooling beverages. Hotel employees—elevator boys, waiters, and office personnel—stood by listening at the entrances to the lobby. The Russian family, zealous and precise in taking their pleasure, had wicker chairs moved down into the garden so as to be nearer the performers. There they sat in a semi-circle, in their characteristically grateful attitude. Behind the ladies and gentlemen stood the old slave woman in her turbanlike headdress.

The low-life virtuosos were extracting sounds from a mandolin, a guitar, a harmonica, and a squeaky violin. Interspersed among the instrumental

---

1. A reference to the Athenian code of love as described by Pausanias in Plato's *Symposium* sections 182d–e and 183b.

numbers were vocals in which the younger of the women blended her sharp, quavering voice with the sweet falsetto of the tenor in a love duet full of yearning. But the chief talent and real leader of the group was clearly the other man, the guitar player, who sang a kind of buffo[2] baritone while he played. Though his voice was weak, he was a gifted mime and projected remarkable comic energy. Often he would move away from the group, his great instrument under his arm, and advance toward the terrace with many a flourish. The audience rewarded his antics with rousing laughter. The Russians in particular, ensconced in their orchestra seats, displayed particular delight over all this southern vivacity and encouraged him with applause and cheers to ever bolder and more brazen behavior.

Aschenbach sat at the balustrade, cooling his lips from time to time with a mixture of pomegranate[3] juice and soda that sparkled ruby-red in his glass. His nerves greedily consumed the piping sounds, the vulgar, pining melodies; for passion numbs good taste and succumbs in all seriousness to enticements that a sober spirit would receive with humor or even reject scornfully. His features, reacting to the antics of the buffoon, had become fixed in a rigid and almost painful smile. He sat in an apparently relaxed attitude, and all the while he was internally tense and sharply attentive, for Tadzio stood no more than six paces away, leaning against the stone railing.

He stood there in the white belted suit that he sometimes wore to dinner, a figure of inevitable and innate grace, his left forearm on the railing, his ankles crossed, his right hand supported on his hip. He wore an expression that was not quite a smile but more an air of distant curiosity or polite receptivity as he looked down toward the street musicians. Sometimes he straightened up and, with a lovely movement of both arms that lifted his chest, he would pull his white blouse down through his leather belt. Occasionally, though—as the aging observer noted with triumph and even with horror, his reason staggering—Tadzio would turn his head to look across his left shoulder in the direction of the one who loved him, sometimes with deliberate hesitation, sometimes with sudden swiftness as if to catch him unawares. Their eyes never met, for an ignominious caution forced the errant lover to keep his gaze fearfully in check. The women guarding Tadzio were sitting in the back of the terrace, and things had reached the point that the smitten traveler had to take care lest his behavior should become noticeable and he fall under suspicion. Indeed his blood had nearly frozen on a number of occasions when he had been compelled to notice on the beach, in the hotel lobby, or in the Piazza San Marco that Tadzio was called away from his vicinity, that they were intent on keeping the boy away from him. He felt horribly insulted, and his pride flinched from unfamiliar tortures that his conscience prevented him from dismissing.

In the meantime the guitar player had begun singing a solo to his own accompaniment, a popular ditty in many verses that was quite the hit just then all over Italy. He was adept at performing it in a highly histrionic manner, and his band joined in the refrain each time, both with their voices and all their instruments. He was of a lean build, and even his face was thin to the point of emaciation. He stood there on the gravel in an attitude of imper-

---

2. Comic.   3. A tropical fruit with many seeds, associated both with Persephone, the queen of Hades, and with the world of the dead in Greek mythology.

tinent bravura, apart from his fellow performers, his shabby felt hat so far back on his head that a roll of red hair surged forth from beneath the brim, and as he thumped the guitar strings, he hurled his buffooneries toward the terrace above in an insistent recitative. The veins on his brow swelled in response to his exertions. He seemed not to be of Venetian stock, more likely a member of the race of Neapolitan comics, half pimp, half actor, brutal and daring, dangerous and entertaining. The lyrics of his song were as banal as could be, but in his mouth they acquired an ambiguous, vaguely offensive quality because of his facial expressions and his gestures, his suggestive winks and his manner of letting his tongue play lasciviously at the corner of his mouth. His strikingly large Adam's apple protruded nakedly from his scrawny neck, which emerged from the soft collar of a sport shirt worn in incongruous combination with more formal city clothes. His pale, snub-nosed face was beardless and did not permit an easy reckoning of his age; it seemed ravaged by grimaces and by vice. The two defiant, imperious, even wild-looking furrows that stood between his reddish eyebrows went rather oddly with the grin on his mobile lips. What particularly drew the attention of the lonely spectator, however, was his observation that this questionable figure seemed to carry with it its own questionable atmosphere. For every time the refrain began again the singer would commence a grotesque circular march, clowning and shaking the hands of his audience; every time his path would bring him directly underneath Aschenbach's spot, and every time that happened there wafted up to the terrace from his clothes and from his body a choking stench of carbolic acid.[4]

His song finished, he began collecting money. He started with the Russians, who produced a generous offering, and then ascended the steps. As bold as he had been during the performance, just so obsequious was he now. Bowing and scraping, he slithered about between the tables, a smile of crafty submissiveness laying bare his large teeth, and all the while the two furrows between his red eyebrows stood forth menacingly. The guests surveyed with curiosity and some revulsion this strange being who was gathering in his livelihood. They threw coins in his hat from a distance and were careful not to touch him. The elimination of the physical separation between the performer and his respectable audience always tends to produce a certain embarrassment, no matter how pleasurable the performance. The singer felt it and sought to excuse himself by acting servile. He came up to Aschenbach, and with him came the smell, though no one else in the vicinity seemed concerned about it.

"Listen," the lonely traveler said in lowered tones, almost mechanically. "They are disinfecting Venice. Why?" The jester answered hoarsely: "Because of the police. That, sir, is the procedure when it gets hot like this and when the sirocco comes. The sirocco is oppressive. It's not conducive to good health. . . ." He spoke as if he were amazed that anyone could ask such questions, and he demonstrated by pushing with his open palm just how oppressive the sirocco was. "So there is no disease in Venice?" Aschenbach asked very quietly through his closed teeth. The tense muscles in the comedian's face produced a grimace of comic perplexity. "A disease? What sort of disease? Is the sirocco a disease? Do you suppose our police force is a dis-

4. A chemical used as a disinfectant.

ease? You like to make fun, don't you? A disease! Why on earth? Some preventive measures, you understand. A police regulation to minimize the effects of the oppressive weather . . . ," he gesticulated. "Very well," Aschenbach said once again, briefly and quietly, and he dropped an indecently large coin into the hat. Then he indicated with a look that the man should go. He obeyed with a grin and a bow. But even before he reached the steps two hotel employees intercepted him and, putting their faces very close to his, cross-examined him in whispers. He shrugged, he protested, he swore that he had been circumspect. You could tell. Dismissed, he returned to the garden and, after making a few arrangements with his group by the light of the arc lamp, he stepped forward to offer one parting song.

It was a song the solitary traveler could not remember ever having heard before, an impudent Italian hit in an incomprehensible dialect embellished with a laughing refrain in which the whole group regularly joined, fortissimo. The refrain had neither words nor instrumental accompaniment; nothing was left but a certain rhythmically structured but still very natural-sounding laughter, which the soloist in particular was capable of producing with great talent and deceptive realism. Having reestablished a proper artistic distance between himself and his audience, he had regained all his former impudence. His artfully artificial laughter, directed impertinently up to the terrace, was the laughter of scorn. Even before the part of the song with actual lyrics had come to a close, one could see him begin to battle an irresistible itch. He would hiccup, his voice would catch, he would put his hand up to his mouth, he would twist his shoulders, and at the proper moment the unruly laughter would break forth, exploding in a hoot, but with such realism that it was infectious. It spread among the listeners so that even on the terrace an unfounded mirth set in, feeding on nothing but itself. This appeared only to double the singer's exuberance. He bent his knees, slapped his thighs, held his sides, fairly split with laughter; but he was no longer laughing, he was howling. He pointed his finger upwards, as if to say that there could be nothing funnier than the laughing audience up there, and soon everyone in the garden and on the veranda was laughing, including the waiters, elevator boys, and servants lingering in the doorways.

Aschenbach no longer reclined in his chair; he sat upright as if trying to defend himself or to flee. But the laughter, the rising smell of hospital sanitation, and the nearness of the lovely boy—all blended to cast a dreamy spell about him that held his mind and his senses in an unbreakable, inescapable embrace. In the general confusion of the moment he made so bold as to cast a glance at Tadzio, and when he did so he was granted the opportunity to see that the lovely lad answered his gaze with a seriousness equal to his own. It was as if the boy were regulating his behavior and attitude according to that of the man, as if the general mood of gaiety had no power over the boy so long as the man kept apart from it. This childlike and meaningful docility was so disarming, so overwhelming, that the gray-haired traveler could only with difficulty refrain from hiding his face in his hands. It had also seemed to him that Tadzio's habit of straightening up and taking a deep sighing breath suggested an obstruction in his breathing. "He is sickly; he will probably not live long," he thought once again with that sobriety that sometimes frees itself in some strange manner from intoxication and longing. Ingenuous solicitude mixed with a dissolute satisfaction filled his heart.

The Venetian singers had meanwhile finished their number and left, accompanied by applause. Their leader did not fail to adorn even his departure with jests. He bowed and scraped and blew kisses so that everyone laughed, which made him redouble his efforts. When his fellow performers were already gone, he pretended to back hard into a lamppost at full speed, then crept toward the gate bent over in mock pain. There at last he cast off the mask of the comic loser, unbent or rather snapped up straight, stuck his tongue out impudently at the guests on the terrace, and slipped into the darkness. The audience dispersed; Tadzio was already long gone from his place at the balustrade. But the lonely traveler remained sitting for a long time at his little table, nursing his pomegranate drink much to the annoyance of the waiters. The night progressed; time crumbled away. Many years ago in his parents' house there had been an hourglass. He suddenly could see the fragile and portentous little device once more, as though it were standing right in front of him. The rust-colored fine sand ran silently through the glass neck, and as it began to run out of the upper vessel a rapid little vortex formed.

In the afternoon of the very next day the obstinate visitor took a further step in his probing of the outside world, and this time he met with all possible success. What he did was to enter the English travel agency in the Piazza San Marco and, having changed some money at the cash register and having assumed the demeanor of a diffident foreigner, he directed his fateful question to the clerk who was taking care of him. The clerk was a wool-clad Briton, still young, his hair parted in the middle and eyes set close together, possessed of that steady, trustworthy bearing that stands out as so foreign and so remarkable among the roguishly nimble southerners. He began: "No cause for concern, sir. A measure of no serious importance. Such regulations are frequently imposed to ward off the ill effects of the heat and the sirocco. . . . " But when he raised his blue eyes he met the foreigner's gaze. It was a tired and rather sad gaze, and it was directed with an air of mild contempt toward his lips. The Englishman blushed. "That is," he continued in a low voice, somewhat discomfited, "the official explanation, which they see fit to stick to hereabouts. I can tell you, though, that there's a good deal more to it." And then, in his candid and comfortable language, he told the truth.

For some years now Asiatic cholera had shown an increasing tendency to spread and roam. The pestilence originated in the warm swamps of the Ganges delta,[5] rising on the foul-smelling air of that lushly uninhabitable primeval world, that wilderness of islands avoided by humankind where tigers lurk in bamboo thickets. It had raged persistently and with unusual ferocity throughout Hindustan; then it had spread eastwards to China and westwards to Afghanistan and Persia; and, following the great caravan routes, it had brought its horrors as far as Astrakhan and even Moscow. But while Europe was shaking in fear lest the specter should progress by land from Russia westward, it had emerged simultaneously in several Mediterranean port cities, having been carried in on Syrian merchant ships. It had raised its grisly head in Toulon and Malaga, shown its grim mask several times in Palermo and Naples, and seemed now firmly ensconced throughout Calabria and

5. In India.

Apulia.[6] The northern half of the peninsula had so far been spared. On a single day in mid-May of this year, however, the terrible vibrioid bacteria had been found on two emaciated, blackening corpses, that of a ship's hand and that of a woman who sold vegetables. These cases were hushed up. A week later, though, there were ten more, twenty more, thirty more, not localized but spread through various parts of the city. A man from the Austrian hinterlands who had come for a pleasant holiday of a few days in Venice died upon returning to his home town, exhibiting unmistakable symptoms. Thus it was that the first rumors of the affliction visited upon the city on the lagoon appeared in German newspapers. In response the Venetian authorities promulgated the assertion that matters of health had never been better in the city. They also immediately instituted the most urgent measures to counter the disease. But apparently the food supply—vegetables, meat, and milk—had been infected, for death, though denied and hushed up, devoured its way through the narrow streets. The early arrival of summer's heat made a lukewarm broth of the water in the canals and thus made conditions for the disease's spread particularly favorable. It almost seemed as though the pestilence had been reinvigorated, as if the tenacity and fecundity of its microscopic agitators had been redoubled. Cures were rare; out of a hundred infected eighty died, and in a particularly gruesome fashion, for the evil raged here with extreme ferocity. Often it took on its most dangerous form, commonly known as the "dry type." In such cases the body is unable to rid itself of the massive amounts of water secreted by the blood-vessels. In a few hours' time the patient dries up and suffocates, his blood as viscous as pitch, crying out hoarsely in his convulsions. It sometimes happened that a few lucky ones suffered only a mild discomfort followed by a loss of consciousness from which they would never again, or only rarely, awaken. At the beginning of June the quarantine wards of the Ospedale Civico quietly filled up, space became scarce in both of the orphanages, and a horrifyingly brisk traffic clogged the routes between the docks at the Fondamenta Nuove[7] and San Michele, the cemetery island. But the fear of adverse consequences to the city, concern for the newly opened exhibit of paintings in the public gardens, for the losses that the hotels, businesses, and the whole tourist industry would suffer in case of a panic or a boycott—these matters proved weightier in the city than the love of truth or respect for international agreements. They prompted the authorities stubbornly to maintain their policy of concealment and denial. The highest medical official in Venice, a man of considerable attainments, had angrily resigned his post and was surreptitiously replaced by a more pliable individual. The citizenry knew all about it, and the combination of corruption in high places with the prevailing uncertainty, the state of emergency in which the city was placed when death was striking all about, caused a certain demoralization of the lower levels of society. It encouraged those antisocial forces that shun the light, and they manifested themselves as immoderate, shameless, and increasingly criminal behavior. Contrary to the norm, one saw many drunks at evening time; people said that gangs of rogues made the streets unsafe at night; muggings and even murders multiplied. Already on two occasions it had come to light that alleged victims

6. Regions in southern Italy. Astrakhan, Toulon, Málaga, Palermo, and Naples are seaports in Russia, France, Spain, Sicily, and southern Italy, respectively.   7. New footings (Italian, literal trans.); the new piers. *Ospedale Civico*: city hospital.

of the plague had in fact been robbed of their lives by their own relatives who administered poison. Prostitution and lasciviousness took on brazen and extravagant forms never before seen here and thought to be at home only in the southern parts of the country and in the seraglios of the orient.

The Englishman explained the salient points of these developments. "You would do well," he concluded, "to depart today rather than tomorrow. The imposition of a quarantine cannot be more than a few days off." "Thank you," said Aschenbach and left the agency.

The piazza was sunless and sultry. Unsuspecting foreigners sat in the sidewalk cafes or stood in front of the cathedral completely covered with pigeons. They watched as the swarming birds beat their wings and jostled each other for their chance to pick at the kernels of corn offered to them in an open palm. In feverish excitement, triumphant in his possession of the truth, but with a taste of gall in his mouth and a fantastic horror in his heart, the lonely traveler paced back and forth over the flagstones of the magnificent plaza. He considered doing the decent thing, the thing that would cleanse him. Tonight after dinner he could go up to the lady with the pearls and speak to her. He planned exactly what he would say: "Permit me, Madame, stranger though I may be, to be of service to you with a piece of advice, a word of warning concerning a matter that has been withheld from you by self-serving people. Depart at once, taking Tadzio and your daughters with you. There is an epidemic in Venice." He could then lay his hand in farewell on the head of that instrument of a scornful deity, turn away, and flee this swamp. But at the same time he sensed that he was infinitely far from seriously wanting to take such a step. It would bring him back to his senses, would make him himself again; but when one is beside oneself there is nothing more abhorrent than returning to one's senses. He remembered a white building decorated with inscriptions that gleamed in the evening light, inscriptions in whose radiant mysticism his mind's eye had become lost. He remembered too that strange figure of the wanderer who had awakened in the aging man a young man's longing to roam in faraway and exotic places. The thought of returning home, of returning to prudence and sobriety, toil and mastery, was so repugnant to him that his face broke out in an expression of physical disgust. "Let them keep quiet," he whispered vehemently. And: "I will keep quiet!" The consciousness of his guilty complicity intoxicated him, just as small amounts of wine will intoxicate a weary brain. The image of the afflicted and ravaged city hovered chaotically in his imagination, incited in him inconceivable hopes, beyond all reason, monstrously sweet. How could that tender happiness he had dreamed of a moment earlier compare with these expectations? What value did art and virtue hold for him when he could have chaos? He held his peace and stayed.

That night he had a terrifying dream—if indeed one can call "dream" an experience that was both physical and mental, one that visited him in the depths of his sleep, in complete isolation as well as sensuous immediacy, but yet such that he did not see himself as physically and spatially present apart from its action. Instead, its setting was in his soul itself, and its events burst in upon him from outside, violently crushing his resistance, his deep, intellectual resistance, passing through easily and leaving his whole being, the culmination of a lifetime of effort, ravaged and annihilated.

It began with fear, fear and desire and a horrified curiosity about what was to come. Night ruled, and his senses were attentive; for from afar there approached a tumult, a turmoil, a mixture of noises: rattling, clarion calls and muffled thunder, shrill cheering on top of it all, and a certain howl with a drawn-out *uuu* sound at the end. All this was accompanied and drowned out by the gruesomely sweet tones of a flute playing a cooing, recklessly persistent tune that penetrated to the very bowels, where it cast a shameless enchantment. But there was a phrase, darkly familiar, that named what was coming: *"The stranger god!"*[8] A smoky glow welled up, and he recognized a mountain landscape like the one around his summer house. And in the fragmented light he could see people, animals, a swarm, a roaring mob, all rolling and plunging and whirling down from the forested heights, past tree-trunks and great moss-covered fragments of rock, overflowing the slope with their bodies, flames, tumult, and reeling circular dance. Women, stumbling over the fur skirts that hung too long from their belts, moaned, threw their heads back, shook their tambourines on high, brandished naked daggers and torches that threw off sparks, held serpents with flickering tongues by the middle of their bodies, or cried out, lifting their breasts in both hands. Men with horns on their brows, girdled with hides, their own skins shaggy, bent their necks and raised their arms and thighs, clashed brazen cymbals and beat furiously on drums, while smooth-skinned boys used garlanded staves to prod their goats, clinging to the horns so they could be dragged along, shouting with joy, when the goats sprang. And the ecstatic band howled the cry with soft consonants in the middle and a drawn-out *uuu* sound on the end, a cry that was sweet and wild at the same time, like none ever heard before: here it rang in the air like the bellowing of stags in rut; and there many voices echoed it back in anarchic triumph, using it to goad each other to dance and shake their limbs, never letting it fall silent. But it was all suffused and dominated by the deep, beckoning melody of the flute. Was it not also beckoning him, the resisting dreamer, with shameless persistence to the festival, to its excesses, and to its ultimate sacrifice? Great was his loathing, great his fear, sincere his resolve to defend his own against the foreign invader, the enemy of self-controlled and dignified intellect. But the noise and the howling, multiplied by the echoing mountainsides, grew, gained the upper hand, swelled to a madness that swept everything along with it. Fumes oppressed the senses: the acrid scent of the goats, the emanation of panting human bodies, a whiff as of stagnant water—and another smell perceptible through it all, a familiar reek of wounds and raging sickness. His heart pounded with the rhythm of the drum beats, his mind whirled, rage took hold of him and blinded him, he was overcome by a numbing lust, and his soul longed to join in the reeling dance of the god. Their obscene symbol,[9] gigantic, wooden, was uncovered and raised on high, and they howled out their watchword all the more licentiously. With foam on their lips they raved; they stimulated each other with lewd gestures and fondling hands; laughing and wheezing, they pierced each other's flesh with their pointed staves and then licked the bleeding limbs. Now among them, now a part of them, the dreamer belonged to the stranger god. Yes, they were he, and he was they, when they threw themselves on the animals, tearing

8. Dionysus (also Bacchus), whose cult was brought to Greece from Thrace and Phrygia. The dream describes the orgiastic rites of his worship. 9. The phallus.

and killing, devouring steaming gobbets of flesh, when on the trampled moss-covered ground there began an unfettered rite of copulation in sacrifice to the god. His soul tasted the lewdness and frenzy of surrender.

The afflicted dreamer awoke unnerved, shattered, a powerless victim of the demon. He no longer shunned the observant glances of people about him; he no longer cared if he was making himself a target of their suspicions. And in any case they were all departing, fleeing the sickness. Many cabanas now stood empty, the population of the dining room was seriously depleted, and in the city one only rarely saw a foreigner. The truth seemed to have leaked out, and in spite of the stubborn conniving of those with vested interests at stake, panic could no longer be averted. The lady with the pearls nonetheless remained with her family, perhaps because the rumors did not reach her or perhaps because she was too proud and fearless to succumb to them. Tadzio remained, and to Aschenbach, blind to all but his own concerns, it seemed at times that death and departure might very well remove all the distracting human life around them and leave him alone with the lovely one on this island. Indeed, in the mornings on the beach when his gaze would rest heavily, irresponsibly, fixedly on the object of his desire; or at the close of day when he would take up his shameful pursuit of the boy through narrow streets where loathsome death did its hushed-up business; then everything monstrous seemed to him to have a prosperous future, the moral law to have none.

He wished, like any other lover, to please his beloved and felt a bitter concern that it would not be possible. He added youthfully cheerful touches to his dress, took to using jewelry and perfume. Several times a day he took lengthy care getting dressed and then came down to the dining room all bedecked, excited and expectant. His aging body disgusted him when he looked at the sweet youth with whom he was smitten; the sight of his gray hair and his sharp facial features overwhelmed him with shame and hopelessness. He felt a need to restore and revive his body. He visited the barbershop more and more frequently.

Leaning back in the chair under the protective cloth, letting the manicured hands of the chattering barber care for him, he confronted the tortured gaze of his image in the mirror.

"Gray," he said with his mouth twisted.

"A bit," the man replied. "It's all because of a slight neglect, an indifference to externals—quite understandable in the case of important people, but still not altogether praiseworthy, all the less so since just such people ought not to harbor prejudices in matters of the natural and the artificial. If certain people were to extend the moral qualms they have about the cosmetic arts to their teeth, as logic compels, they would give no little offense. And anyway, we're only as old we feel in our hearts and minds. Gray hair can in certain circumstances give more of a false impression than the dye that some would scorn. In your case, sir, you have a right to your natural hair color. Will you allow me to give you back what is rightfully yours?"

"How?" Aschenbach inquired.

So the glib barber washed his customer's hair with two liquids, one clear and one dark, and it turned as black as it had been in youth. Then he rolled it with the curling iron into soft waves, stepped back and admired his handiwork.

"All that's left," he said, "is to freshen up the complexion a bit."

He went about, with ever renewed solicitude, moving from one task to another the way a person does who can never finish anything and is never satisfied. Aschenbach, resting comfortably, was in any case quite incapable of fending him off. Actually he was rather excited about what was happening, watching in the mirror as his brows took on a more decisive and symmetrical arch and his eyes grew in width and brilliance with the addition of a little shadow on the lids. A little further down he could see his skin, previously brown and leathery, perk up with a light application of delicate carmine rouge, his lips, pale and bloodless only a moment ago, swell like raspberries, the furrows in his cheeks and mouth, the wrinkles around his eyes give way to a dab of cream and the glow of youth. His heart pounded as he saw in the mirror a young man in full bloom. The cosmetic artist finally pronounced himself satisfied and thanked the object of his ministrations with fawning politeness, the way such people do. "A minor repair job," he said as he put a final touch to Aschenbach's appearance. "Now, sir, you can go and fall in love without second thoughts." The beguiled lover went out, happy as in a dream, yet confused and timid. His tie was red, and his broad-brimmed straw hat was encircled by a band of many colors.

A tepid breeze had come up; it rained only seldom and then not hard, but the air was humid, thick, and full of the stench of decay. Rustling, rushing, and flapping sounds filled his ears. He burned with fever beneath his makeup, and it seemed to him that the air was filled with vile, evil wind-spirits, impure winged sea creatures who raked over, gnawed over, and defiled with garbage the meals of their victim.[1] For the sultry weather ruined one's appetite, and one could not suppress the idea that all the food was poisoned with infection.

Trailing the lovely boy one afternoon, Aschenbach had penetrated deep into the maze in the heart of the diseased city. He had lost his sense of direction, for the little streets, canals, bridges, and piazzas in the labyrinth all looked alike. He could no longer even tell east from west, since his only concern had been not to lose sight of the figure he pursued so ardently. He was compelled to a disgraceful sort of discretion that involved clinging to walls and seeking protection behind the backs of passersby, and so he did not for some time become conscious of the fatigue, the exhaustion which a high pitch of emotion and continual tension had inflicted on his body and spirit. Tadzio walked behind the rest of his family. In these narrow streets he would generally let the governess and the nunlike sisters go first, while he sauntered along by himself, occasionally turning his head to assure himself with a quick glance of his extraordinary dawn-gray eyes over his shoulder that his lover was still following. He saw him, and he did not betray him. Intoxicated by this discovery, lured onward by those eyes, tied to the apron string of his own passion, the lovesick traveler stole forth in pursuit of his unseemly hope—but ultimately found himself disappointed. The Polish family had gone across a tightly arched bridge, and the height of the arch had hidden them from their pursuer. When he was at last able to cross, he could no longer find them. He searched for them in three directions—straight

1. "Harpies: hideously thin, they flew swiftly in, fell with insatiable greed on whatever food was there, ate without being satisfied, and *befouled* whatever they left with their filth" [Mann's note]. See Virgil's *Aeneid* 3.210–62.

ahead and to both sides along the narrow, dirty landing—but in vain. He finally had to give up, too debilitated and unnerved to go on.

His head was burning hot, his body was sticky with sweat, the scruff of his neck was tingling, an unbearable thirst assaulted him, and he looked about for immediate refreshment of any sort. In front of a small greengrocer's shop he bought some fruit, strawberries that were overripe and soft, and he ate them while he walked. A little piazza that was quite deserted and seemed enchanted opened out before him. He recognized it, for it was here that weeks ago he had made his thwarted plan to flee the city. He collapsed on the steps of the well in the very middle of the plaza and rested his head on the stone rim. It was quiet, grass grew between the paving stones, refuse lay strewn about. Among the weathered buildings of varying heights around the periphery was one that looked rather palatial. It had Gothic-arched windows, now gaping emptily, and little balconies decorated with lions. On the ground floor of another there was a pharmacy. Warm gusts of wind from time to time carried the smell of carbolic acid.

He sat there, the master, the artist who had attained to dignity, the author of the "Man of Misery," that exemplary work which had with clarity of form renounced bohemianism and the gloomy murky depths, had condemned sympathy for the abyss, reviled the vile. There he sat, the great success who had overcome knowledge and outgrown every sort of irony, who had accustomed himself to the obligations imposed by the confidence of his large audience. There he sat, the author whose greatness had been officially recognized and whose name bore the title of nobility, the author whose style children were encouraged to emulate—sat there with his eyes shut, though from time to time a mocking and embarrassed look would slip sidelong out from underneath his lids, only to conceal itself again swiftly; and his slack, cosmetically enhanced lips formed occasional words that emerged out of the strange dream-logic engendered in his half-dozing brain.[2]

"For beauty, Phaedrus—mark me well—only beauty is both divine and visible at the same time, and thus it is the way of the senses, the way of the artist, little Phaedrus, to the spirit. But do you suppose, my dear boy, that anyone could ever attain to wisdom and genuine manly honor by taking a path to the spirit that leads through the senses? Or do you rather suppose (I leave the decision entirely up to you) that this is a dangerously delightful path, really a path of error and sin that necessarily leads astray? For you must know that we poets cannot walk the path of beauty without Eros joining our company and even making himself our leader; indeed, heroes though we may be after our own fashion, disciplined warriors though we may be, still we are as women, for passion is our exaltation, and our longing must ever be for love. That is our bliss and our shame. Do you see, then, that we poets can be neither wise nor honorable, that we necessarily go astray, that we necessarily remain dissolute adventurers of emotion? The masterly demeanor of our style is a lie and a folly, our fame and our honor a sham, the confidence accorded us by our public utterly ridiculous, the education of the populace and of the young by means of art a risky enterprise that ought not to be allowed. For how can a person succeed in educating others who has an

2. Aschenbach adopts the role of Socrates in Plato's *Phaedrus* to examine the role of the artist. Although the Platonic dialogue briefly contrasts inspired art with mere technical perfection, it is chiefly concerned with moral choices and absolute beauty.

inborn, irremediable, and natural affinity for the abyss? We may well deny it and achieve a certain dignity, but wherever we may turn that affinity abides. Let us say we renounce analytical knowledge; for knowledge, Phaedrus, has neither dignity nor discipline; it is knowing, understanding, forgiving, formless and unrestrained; it has sympathy for the abyss; it *is* the abyss. Let us therefore resolutely reject it, and henceforth our efforts will be directed only toward beauty, that is to say toward simplicity, grandeur, and a new discipline, toward reborn ingenuousness and toward form. But form and ingenuousness, Phaedrus, lead to intoxication and to desire, might lead the noble soul to horrible emotional outrages that his own lovely discipline would reject as infamous, lead him to the abyss. Yes, they too lead to the abyss. They lead us poets there, I say, because we are capable not of resolution but only of dissolution. And now I shall depart, Phaedrus; but you stay here until you can no longer see me, and then you depart as well."

A few days afterwards Gustav von Aschenbach left the hotel at a later hour than usual, since he was feeling unwell. He was struggling with certain attacks of dizziness that were only partly physical and were accompanied by a powerfully escalating sense of anxiety and indecision, a feeling of having no prospects and no way out. He was not at all sure whether these feelings concerned the outside world or his own existence. He noticed in the lobby a great pile of luggage prepared for departure, and when he asked the doorman who was leaving, he received for an answer the aristocratic Polish name he had in his heart been expecting to hear all along. He took it in with no change in the expression on his ravaged face, briefly raising his head as people do to acknowledge casually the receipt of a piece of information they do not need, and asked, "When?" The answer came: "After lunch." He nodded and went to the beach.

It was dreary there. Rippling tremors crossed from near to far on the wide, flat stretch of water between the beach and the first extended sandbar. Where so recently there had been color, life, and joy, it was now almost deserted, and an autumnal mood prevailed, a feeling that the season was past its prime. The sand was no longer kept clean. A camera with no photographer to operate it stood on its tripod at the edge of the sea, a black cloth that covered it fluttering with a snapping noise in a wind that now blew colder.

Tadzio and three or four playmates that still remained were active in front of his family's cabana to Aschenbach's right; and, resting in his beach chair approximately halfway between the ocean and the row of cabanas, with a blanket over his legs, Aschenbach watched him once more. Their play was unsupervised, since the women must have been busy with preparations for their departure. The game seemed to have no rules and quickly degenerated. The sturdy boy with the belted suit and the black, slicked-down hair who was called Yashu, angered and blinded by sand thrown in his face, forced Tadzio into a wrestling match, which ended swiftly with the defeat of the weaker, lovely boy. It seemed as if in the last moments before leave-taking the subservient feelings of the underling turned to vindictive cruelty as he sought to take revenge for a long period of slavery. The winner would not release his defeated opponent but instead kneeled on his back and pushed his face in the sand, persisting for so long that Tadzio, already out of breath from the fight, seemed in danger of suffocating. He made spasmodic attempts to shake off his oppressor, lay still for whole moments, then tried again with no more than a twitch. Horrified, Aschenbach wanted to spring to the rescue, but then the bully finally released his victim. Tadzio was very pale; he got up halfway and sat motionless for several minutes supported on one arm, his hair disheveled and his eyes darkening. Then he rose to his feet and slowly walked away. They called to him, cheerfully at first but then with pleading timidity. He paid no attention. The black-haired boy, apparently instantly regretting his transgression, caught up with him and tried to make up. A jerk of a lovely shoulder put him off. Tadzio crossed diagonally down to the water. He was barefoot and wore his striped linen suit with the red bow.

He lingered at the edge of the sea with his head hung down, drawing figures in the wet sand with his toe. Then he went into the shallows, which at their deepest point did not wet his knees, strode through them, and progressed idly to the sandbar. Upon reaching it he stood for a moment, his face turned to the open sea, then began to walk slowly to the left along the narrow stretch of uncovered ground. Separated from the mainland by the broad expanse of water, separated from his mates by a proud mood, he strode forth, a highly remote and isolated apparition with wind-blown hair, wandering about out there in the sea, in the wind, on the edge of the misty boundlessness. Once more he stopped to gaze outward. Suddenly, as if prompted by a memory or an impulse, he rotated his upper body in a lovely turn out of its basic posture, his hand resting on his hip, and looked over his shoulder toward the shore. The observer sat there as he had sat once before, when for the first time he had met the gaze of those dawn-gray eyes cast back at him from that threshold. His head, resting on the back of the chair, had slowly followed the movements of the one who was striding about out there; now his head rose as if returning the gaze, then sank on his chest so that his eyes looked out from beneath. His face took on the slack, intimately absorbed expression of deep sleep. It seemed to him, though, as if the pale and charming psychagogue[3] out there were smiling at him, beckoning to him; as if, lifting his hand from his hip, he were pointing outwards, hovering before him in an immensity full of promise. And, as so often before, he arose to follow him.

Minutes passed before anyone rushed to the aid of the man who had collapsed to one side in his chair. They carried him to his room. And later that same day a respectfully shaken world received the news of his death.

3. Leader of souls to the underworld (Greek); a title of the god Hermes.

RAINER MARIA RILKE
1875–1926

Rainer Maria Rilke's search for the "great mysteries" of the universe combines his own intensely personal awareness with a range of broad questions that are ordinarily called religious. Whether his gaze is turned toward the objects and creatures of Earth, which he describes with extraordinary clarity and affection, or toward a higher intuited realm whose enigma remains to be deciphered, he seeks throughout a comprehensive vision of cosmic unity. Rilke absorbs what he sees around him—objects, people, gestures—until they become part of his consciousness and are ready to emerge in the words of a poem. "Looking is such a wonderful thing, about which we as yet know so little," he wrote his wife, Clara; "we are turned completely outward, but just when we are most outward, things seem to happen inside us." The poet's role, he says, is to observe with a fresh sensitivity "this fleeting world, which in some strange way / keeps calling to us," and to bear witness, through language, to the transfiguration of its materiality in human emotions. Rilke writes at a transitional moment in modern European letters: inheritor of the Symbolists in his allusive imagery and intuitions of cosmic order, and modernist in the "thing-centered" concreteness of individual descriptions, he also foreshadows existentialism as he struggles to comprehend the self's relation to the universe. The best-known and most influential German poet of the twentieth century, Rilke has been read and translated outside Europe in countries as far apart as the United States and Japan. He speaks to a variety of cultures and audiences even though he was perhaps the least socially oriented poet of his time.

Born in Prague on December 4, 1875, to German-speaking parents who separated when he was nine, Rilke had an unhappy childhood that included being dressed as a girl when he was young (thus his mother compensated for the earlier loss of a baby daughter) and being sent to military academies, where he was lonely and miserable, from 1886 to 1891. Illness caused his departure from the second academy; and after a year in business school, he worked in his uncle's law firm and studied at the University of Prague. Rilke hoped to persuade his family that he should devote himself to a literary career rather than business or law, and energetically wrote poetry (*Sacrifice to the Lares*, 1895, *Crowned by Dream*, 1896), plays, stories, and reviews. Moving to Munich in 1897, he met and fell in love with a fascinating and cultured older woman, Lou Andreas-Salomé, who would be a constant influence on him throughout his life. He accompanied Andreas-Salomé and her husband to Russia in 1899, where he met Leo Tolstoy and the painter Leonid Pasternak and—swayed by responding to Russian mysticism and the Russian landscape—wrote most of the poems later published as *The Book of Hours: The Book of Monastic Life* (1905) and a Romantic verse tale that became extremely popular, *The Tale of Love and Death of Cornet Christoph Rilke* (1906). After a second trip to Russia, Rilke spent some time at an artists' colony called Worpswede, where he met his future wife, the sculptor Clara Westhoff. They were married in March 1901 and settled in a cottage near the colony where Rilke wrote the second part of *The Book of Hours: The Book of Pilgrimage*. He and Clara separated in the following year, and Rilke moved to Paris where he embarked on a study of the French sculptor Auguste Rodin (1903).

Unhappy in Paris, where he felt lonely and isolated, he fled to Italy in 1903 to write the last section of *The Book of Hours: The Book of Poverty and Death*. Nonetheless, he had found in Paris a new kind of literary and artistic inspiration. He read French writers and especially Baudelaire, whose minutely realistic but strangely beautiful description of a rotting corpse (*A Carcass*) initiated, he felt, "the entire development toward objective expression, which we now recognize in Cézanne." In Rodin, too, he recognized a workmanlike dedication to the technical demands of his craft; an intense concentration on visible, tangible objects; and above all, a belief in art as an essentially religious activity. Although he wrote in distress to his friend Andreas-Salomé, complaining of nightmares and a sense of failure, it is at this time (and with her encouragement) that Rilke began his major work. The anguished, semiautobiographical spiritual confessions of *The Notebooks of Malte Laurids Brigge* (1910) date to this period, as do a series of *New Poems* (1907–08) in which he abandoned his earlier, impressionistic and Romantic style and developed a more intense Symbolic vision focused on objects. The *New Poems* emphasized physical reality, the absolute otherness and "thing-like" nature of what was observed—be it fountain, panther, flower, human being, or the "Archaic Torso of Apollo." "Thing-poems" (*Dinggedichte*), in fact, is a term often used to describe Rilke's writing at this time, with its open emphasis on material description. In a letter to Andreas-Salomé, he described the way that ancient art objects took on a peculiar luster once they were detached from history and seen as "things" in and for themselves: "No subject matter is attached to them, no irrelevant voice interrupts the silence of their concentrated reality . . . no history casts a shadow over their naked clarity—: they *are*. That is all . . . one day one of them reveals itself to you, and shines like a first star."

Such "things" are not dead or inanimate but supremely alive, filled with a strange vitality before the poet's glance: the charged sexuality of the marble torso, the metamorphosis of the Spanish dance in which the dancer's flamelike dress "becomes a furnace/ from which, like startled rattlesnakes, the long / naked arms uncoil, aroused and clicking" (*Spanish Dancer*), or the caged panther's circling "like a ritual dance around a center / in which a mighty will stands paralyzed" (*The Panther*). If things are not dead, neither is death unambiguous: when Rilke retells the ancient myth of Orpheus and his lost wife, Eurydice, the dead woman is seen as achieving a new and fuller existence in the underworld. "Deep within herself. Being dead / filled her beyond fulfillment. . . . She was already loosened like long hair, / poured out like fallen rain, / shared like a limitless supply. / She was already root." Themes of the interpenetration of life and death, the visible and invisible world, and creativity itself are taken up in Rilke's next major work, the sequence of ten elegies (mournful lyric poems, usually laments for loss, and generally of medium length) called the *Duino Elegies* (1923), which he was to begin in 1912 while spending the winter in Duino Castle near Trieste.

The composition of the *Duino Elegies* came in two bursts of inspiration separated by ten years. Despite Rilke's increasing reputation and the popularity of his earlier work, he felt frustrated and unhappy. It was not that he lacked friends or activity; back in Paris once more, he corresponded actively and traveled widely, visiting Italy, Flanders, Germany, Austria, Egypt, and Algeria. But social pressures and everyday anxieties kept him overly occupied, and when a patroness, Princess Marie von Thurn und Taxis-Hohenlohe, proposed that he stay by himself in her castle at Duino during the winter of 1911–12, he was delighted.

Completion did not come easily in the following years, however, with the beginning of World War I. After writing the third Duino elegy in Paris in 1913, Rilke left for Munich—never dreaming that his apartment and personal property would soon be confiscated as that of an enemy alien. In April 1915, everything was sold at public auction; that summer, Duino Castle was bombarded and reduced to ruins. Rilke wrote the somber fourth elegy in Munich on November 22 and 23, and the next day was called up for the draft. Three weeks later, at age forty, he was drafted and became a clerk in the War Archives Office in Vienna where he drew precise vertical and horizontal lines on paper until June 1916, when the intercession of friends released him from military service. Rilke composed little after this experience and feared that he would never be able to complete the Duino sequence. In 1922, however, a friend's purchase of the tiny Château de Muzot in Switzerland gave him a peaceful place to retire and write. He not only completed the *Duino Elegies* in Muzot but wrote in addition—as a memorial for the young daughter of a friend—a two-part sequence of fifty-five sonnets, the *Sonnets to Orpheus* (1923).

With the *Duino Elegies* and the *Sonnets to Orpheus*, Rilke's last great works were complete. The melancholy philosophic vision of the early elegies describes an angel of absolute reality, whose self-contained perfection is terrifyingly separate from mortal concerns. In the later elegies and the *Sonnets*, the idea of angelic perfection is balanced by a newly important human role for the human artist, who serves as a bridge between the worlds of Earth and of the angel. To the poet's initial sense of helplessness and alienation, the later poems respond that all creatures need the artist's transforming glance to reach full being. *Elegies* and the *Sonnets* together move toward a more positive celebration of simple Things. A sequence of symbolic figures suggests this development from uncertainty to affirmation, as the dominant angel of the *Elegies* gives way to the human poet Orpheus, who in turn retires into the background of the later *Sonnets* before Eurydice, the woman whose passing into the realm of the dead brings her fuller being. With this major affirmation of the essential unity of life and death, Rilke closed his two complementary sequences ("the little rust-colored sail of the Sonnets and the Elegies' gigantic white canvas") and wrote little—chiefly poems in French—over the next few years. Increasingly ill with leukemia, he died on December 29, 1926, as the result of a sudden infection after pricking himself on roses he cut for a friend in his garden.

The four selections from the *New Poems* printed here demonstrate Rilke's acutely visual imagination and the ambivalent objectivity of his "thing-poems." Whether a flamenco dancer, a caged panther, a swan entering the water, or the splendor of an ancient Greek statue, the subject is presented for itself—but it is also suffused with human emotions. These emotions are mixed and cannot be reduced to one meaning: for example, there is a combined sense of relief and yet obscurely terrifying mortality as the swan glides through the water, and the panther's numbed consciousness, contained force, and momentary tension clearly evoke some kind of response from the reader—pity? horror? fear of entrapment? awe?—but Rilke does not define it for us. Steel bars are the only world known by the caged panther, who has so far forgotten his natural habitat as to react only for a moment when an unexpected (and unspecified) image briefly penetrates his consciousness. The Spanish dancer moves with complete mastery through the traditional flamenco dance steps with all the brilliance and triumph of the flame to which she is compared (*flamenco* is derived from *flamear*, to flame). Both the swan's awkward progress on land and its majestic glide upon entering the water are compared in the poem to the passage from life to death. Concurrently, the detailed physical description makes it easy for readers to identify with the frustrations of the initial laborious advance—and the subsequent letting go and release into a new state of indifference and ease. The "archaic torso of Apollo" is not a living being, but a fifth-century B.C. Greek sculpture on display in the Louvre Museum in Paris. This headless marble torso is truly a "thing," a lifeless, even defaced chunk of stone. Yet such is the perfection of its luminous sensuality—descended, the speaker suggests, from the brilliant gaze of its missing head and "ripening" eyes—that it seems impossibly alive, and an inner radiance bursts starlike from the marble. The *human* vitality of this marble torso, a vitality achieved through artistic vision, challenges and puts to shame the observer's own puny existence. Nor is there any place to escape from the lesson, once it is recognized; instead, "You must change your life."

Ultimately, Rilke is celebrating the power of human creativity to refashion the world in its own image. The poet observes reality and creates from it a new form, a new being. For the poet, however, it is a process of making the visible angelically "invisible," and a bridge between two worlds; he "delivers" things by absorbing them into his imagination's inner dimension, asking, as at the end of the ninth *Elegy*, "Earth, isn't this what you want: to arise within us, / *invisible*?" Rilke's poetic journey, from the *New Poems* to the *Elegies* and the *Sonnets to Orpheus*, was an inward journey that created a bridge between two worlds, preserving the most intense moments of human experience by subjecting them to the transfiguring perspective of art.

J. F. Hendry, *The Sacred Threshold: A Life of Rainer Maria Rilke* (1983), and Patricia Pollock Brodsky, *Rainer Maria Rilke* (1988), are brief and readable biographies with numerous citations from Rilke's letters and work. Heinz F. Peters, *Rainer Maria Rilke: Masks and the Man* (1977), is a biographical and thematic study of Rilke's work and influence. Donald Prater, *A Ringing Glass: The Life of Rainer Maria Rilke* (1986), is an excellent account of the poet's life and the conditions in which his work developed and includes extensive quotations from many unpublished letters. William Rose and G. Craig Houston, eds., *Rainer Maria Rilke, Aspects of His Mind and Poetry* (1970), contains an excellent essay by C. M. Bowra on the *New Poems*.

PRONOUNCING GLOSSARY

The following list uses common English syllables and stress accents to provide rough equivalents of selected words whose pronunciation may be unfamiliar to the general reader.

Dinggedichte: *ding'-ge-dikh-tuh*   Muzot: *moo-zoh'*

FROM NEW POEMS[1]

Archaic Torso of Apollo[2]

We cannot know his legendary head[3]
with eyes like ripening fruit. And yet his torso
is still suffused with brilliance from inside,
like a lamp, in which his gaze, now turned to low,

gleams in all its power. Otherwise   5
the curved breast could not dazzle you so, nor could
a smile run through the placid hips and thighs
to that dark center where procreation flared.

Otherwise this stone would seem defaced
beneath the translucent cascade of the shoulders   10
and would not glisten like a wild beast's fur:

would not, from all the borders of itself,
burst like a star: for here there is no place
that does not see you. You must change your life.

Archaïscher Torso Apollos

Wir kannten nicht sein unerhörtes Haupt,
darin die Augenäpfel reiften. Aber
sein Torso glüht noch wie ein Kandelaber,
in dem sein Schauen, nur zurückgeschraubt,

sich hält und glänzt. Sonst könnte nicht der Bug   5
der Brust dich blenden, und im leisen Drehen

---

1. All selections translated by Stephen Mitchell.   2. The first poem in the second volume of Rilke's *New Poems* (1908), which were dedicated "to my good friend, Auguste Rodin" (the French sculptor, 1840–1917, whose secretary Rilke was for a brief period and on whom he wrote two monographs, in 1903 and 1907). The poem itself was inspired by an ancient Greek statue discovered at Miletus (a Greek colony on the coast of Asia Minor) that was called simply the *Torso of a Youth from Miletus*; since the god Apollo was an ideal of youthful male beauty, his name was often associated with such statues.   3. In a torso, the head and limbs are missing.

der Lenden könnte nicht ein Lächeln gehen
zu jener Mitte, die die Zeugung trug.

Sonst stünde dieser Stein entstellt und kurz
unter der Schultern durchsichtigem Sturz   10
und flimmerte nicht so wie Raubtierfelle;

und bräche nicht aus allen seinen Rändern
aus wie ein Stern: denn da ist keine Stelle,
die dich nicht sieht. Du mußt dein Leben ändern.

The Panther

In the Jardin des Plantes,[1] *Paris*

His vision, from the constantly passing bars,
has grown so weary that it cannot hold
anything else. It seems to him there are
a thousand bars; and behind the bars, no world.

As he paces in cramped circles, over and over,   5
the movement of his powerful soft strides
is like a ritual dance around a center
in which a mighty will stands paralyzed.

Only at times, the curtain of the pupils
lifts, quietly—. An image enters in,   10
rushes down through the tensed, arrested muscles,
plunges into the heart and is gone.

The Swan

This laboring through what is still undone,
as though, legs bound, we hobbled along the way,
is like the awkward walking of the swan.

And dying—to let go, no longer feel
the solid ground we stand on every day—   5
is like his anxious letting himself fall

into the water, which receives him gently
and which, as though with reverence and joy,
draws back past him in streams on either side;
while, infinitely silent and aware,   10
in his full majesty and ever more
indifferent, he condescends to glide.

---

1. A zoo in Paris. Rilke also admired, at Rodin's studio, the plaster cast of an ancient statue of a panther.

Spanish Dancer[1]

As on all its sides a kitchen-match darts white
flickering tongues before it bursts into flame:
with the audience around her, quickened, hot,
her dance begins to flicker in the dark room.

And all at once it is completely fire.   5

One upward glance and she ignites her hair
and, whirling faster and faster, fans her dress
into passionate flames, till it becomes a furnace
from which, like startled rattlesnakes, the long
naked arms uncoil, aroused and clicking.[2]   10

And then: as if the fire were too tight
around her body, she takes and flings it out
haughtily, with an imperious gesture,
and watches: it lies raging on the floor,
still blazing up, and the flames refuse to die—.   15
Till, moving with total confidence and a sweet
exultant smile, she looks up finally
and stamps it out with powerful small feet.

1. A traditional Spanish dance, the *flamenco* (from *flamear*, to flame).   2. The dancer accompanies herself with the rhythmic clicking of castanets (worn on the fingers).

WALLACE STEVENS
1879–1955

"A bucket of sand and a wishing lamp," Wallace Stevens once said, was all he needed to "create a world in half a second that would make this one look like a hunk of mud." His poetry invites us into an imaginative world that fuses poignantly sensuous images with the most abstract metaphysics. Stevens himself embodied contrasts: a Hartford insurance executive as well as a major American poet, he was never a part of the contemporary literary scene with its movements and isms. He was acquainted with current New York writers and artists, he collected modern art (which is often reflected in his poems), and later in his career he wrote and lectured about poetry; but it is not through these associations that he joins the mainstream of modern European and American letters. In his work Stevens combines two aspects of modernist tradition. His musical free verse and sensuous, significant imagery recall Symbolism, which he especially admired in the French poet Paul Verlaine. His stress on concrete, physical descriptions inside a philosophical framework is characteristic of "existential" writers such as Jean-Paul Sartre and Albert Camus. More than any other modern poet, Stevens inherited the Symbolists' desire to balance the intertwined concepts of concrete reality and human imagination. Like the Symbolists, too, he finds an ultimate human value in the artist's freedom to create the world anew in a "supreme fiction": *fiction*, because "true" reality can never be ascertained or re-created; *supreme*, because it is the highest aspiration of human creativity. This fiction is not yet the ungraspable "fictionality" of postmodernist writers such as Samuel Beckett and Alain Robbe-Grillet, for it does not dissolve into a series of competing perspectives. Instead, Stevens's modernist poetry holds up the ideal of a supreme artistic transformation whose creation bestows meaning on an otherwise meaningless universe.

Stevens was born in Reading, Pennsylvania, on October 2, 1879, the second of five children. His father was a schoolteacher and then attorney with diverse interests; his mother taught school. He enrolled at Harvard in 1897 as a nondegree student and while at college contributed poems, stories, and sketches to the Harvard *Advocate* (of which he became president) and the Harvard *Monthly*. He also came to know the philosopher and writer George Santayana, whose assertion of a common imaginative essence in religion and poetry appealed greatly to him.

Stevens left Harvard in 1900 to try journalism and then law school in New York; he received his degree and was admitted to the bar in 1904. After working as an attorney for several firms he finally entered the insurance business in 1908. In 1916 he joined a subsidiary of the Hartford Accident and Indemnity Company, becoming vice president of the parent company in 1934 and remaining there until his death in 1955. He dictated business correspondence and poems to the same secretary. In 1922 business affairs took him to Florida, and until 1940 he returned frequently to its warm and lush landscape, which contrasted in his poetry—both physically and emotionally—with the chillier climate of the north.

Stevens married Elsie V. Kachel in 1909, and in 1924 his daughter, Holly, was born; she later edited her father's letters. He published individual poems in little magazines (small avant-garde literary magazines) and was a friend of *Poetry* editor Harriet Monroe and of the poets William Carlos Williams and Marianne Moore. *Harmonium*, his first collection of poetry, appeared in 1923. In following years, Stevens's insurance career occupied most of his time, and he published little poetry until 1936, when *Ideas of Order* appeared. Later volumes included *The Man with the Blue Guitar* (1937), *Parts of a World* (1942), and a collection of prose essays, *The Necessary Angel* (1951). Stevens kept the two parts of his career quite separate but gradually became a well-known and influential poet, winning the Bollingen Prize for poetry in 1949 and the National Book Award in 1951 (for *The Auroras of Autumn*) and 1955 (for *The Collected Poems of Wallace Stevens*). He died of cancer on August 2, 1955.

Stevens's poetry expresses the dualism between reality and imagination, between things as they really are and as we perceive and then shape them. For we can never know reality directly; our five senses see, touch, taste, smell, and hear what is outside us, constructing an image of the world in which we live, but this world also exists separate from us and beyond our image of it. This paradox underlies all Stevens's poetry, which swings between the two poles of the shaping, creative imagination and the material world of which we are only partly aware. The names of real Connecticut towns or the state of Tennessee, an inventory of the trash in a dump, descriptions of coffee and oranges at breakfast, and marred old pieces of furniture inhabit his poems side by side with the most abstract speculations, transformations of everyday scenes, and visions of the edge of space. Poetic artifice—the playful and imaginative use of language—clothes the most mundane observations, as if to assert a relationship between verbal style and the real subject about which it tries to speak. Stevens once said that "it is pleasant to hear the milkman, and yet . . . the imaginative world is the only real world after all," and this balancing of dualities continues throughout his work.

Sunday Morning, one of Stevens's earlier poems, already reflects this dualism on several levels. The opening lines present a contrast between the comfortable self-indulgence of the Sunday morning breakfast table, warmly alive with sun and bright colors, and the traditional Christian dedication of the day to thoughts of human mortality redeemed by Christ's death. The contrast continues in a quasi-dialogue between the poet, who protests any attempt to transcend this world or death, and the woman, who speaks of paradise and some "imperishable bliss." Earth itself is sufficient paradise, says the poet, and "friendlier" than the untouchable sky or supernatural explanations of different religions; death is a necessary part of life's constant renewal and sharpens our awareness of love and beauty while they exist. The wholly natural beauty of the New England landscape at the poem's end, with its acceptance of death and change, suggests to the speaker a more real and human ideal than the unchanging perfection of eternal life.

The softer, more consolatory tone of *Sunday Morning* (which derives in part from Stevens's recollection of his mother's death in 1912), becomes bold and gaudier in *The Emperor of Ice-Cream,* which also deals—but more ironically—with the contrast of life and death. The scene is a wake: a dead woman lies covered with the same sheet on which she once embroidered fantail pigeons. Stevens, however, begins his poem in the kitchen with the festivities in which the survivors are taking part. For the day is devoted not only to the dead but to the living, in whose imperial court the ice cream server is emperor, and the women dressed in their best clothes are handmaidens. Words with erotic overtones (*concupiscent, wenches*) reinforce the scene's essential hedonism, in which the only reality that counts is the pleasure of the moment.

Yet there is another reality, that of the dead woman, who has now become a mere object much like her own furniture, and Stevens painstakingly registers its details. The dresser is made of pine wood and lacks three glass knobs; the dead woman's calloused feet protrude from the too-short embroidered sheet. Such close-up observation puts the woman in a new imaginative context, in a world of lifeless inanimate things whose stillness comments with grim finality on the first stanza's boisterous celebration. The empire of ice cream contains both life and death; people, flowers, and yesterday's newspapers all ultimately come down to the same level of bare physicality. Wisdom lies in accepting the common outcome of all earthly appearances— "Let be be finale of seem"—and in celebrating life while it remains.

Stevens's juxtaposition of reality and our imaginative perception of it is echoed throughout his writing by a dialectic of other oppositions, one idea being raised seemingly only to be challenged and tested by another. Thus the jar on a hill in Tennessee juxtaposes human intellect and aesthetic imagination against the unshaped wilderness of nature, and *Peter Quince at the Clavier* celebrates the immortal presence— in the memory—of a long-dead woman's physical beauty. Such balancing or counterpoint rejects a single perspective and opens up avenues for continued meditation.

Counterpoint is basically a musical term, and Stevens's work is filled with the imagery of musical performance: the harpsichord of *Peter Quince at the Clavier,* the singer in *The Idea of Order at Key West,* and the nightingale and even grackles of *The Man on the Dump.* Other poems speak of a blue guitar (the image taken from a painting by Pablo Picasso), an old horn, a lute, citherns, saxophones, not to mention the "tink and tank and tunk-a-tunk-tunk" of an unnamed instrument (perhaps a banjo). Musical images are used to describe events, such as the tambourinelike rhythm of Susanna's attendants arriving (with the additional musical end rhymes of *tambourines* and *Byzantines*), or emotions, like the erotic intensity of the elders' lustful glance ("The basses of their beings throb / In witching chords") and the comic counterpoint of their quivering nerves pulsing "pizzicati of Hosanna." Even the title of Stevens's book is the name of a musical instrument, *Harmonium,* and he had wanted to name his collected poems *The Whole of Harmonium.*

Music for Stevens was not, however, merely musical images in a poem, or the notion of harmonizing the sounds of words or holding contrasted ideas in counterpoint. It implied for him a supreme, intuited language, the "foreign song" of the gold-feathered bird on the edge of space in *Of Mere Being,* perhaps the same bird that sang to the emperor in Yeats's *Sailing to Byzantium.* The singer, bird or human, is the type of the poet, the "one of fictive music" who creates the world anew through the incantatory power of imagination.

The singer of *The Idea of Order at Key West* is such a poet, embodying imagination at its most ambitious: "She was the single artificer of the world / In which she sang." Nature itself cannot create such a world, for it lacks the igniting spark; while the sea may imitate human gestures and sounds, it cannot truly speak, and makes only "meaningless plungings of water and wind." Imagination is supreme; the singer has "the maker's rage to order words" (*poet* comes from a Greek word meaning "maker"), and her song creates for herself and for her listeners a world of imagination in which lights from the fishing boats seem to map out the night against which they shine.

The luminous beauty of the singer's world is only one of many possible poetic worlds, all of which take their place on the accumulated heap of poetry where the latest artificer sits as *The Man on the Dump*. The trash heap of history is the place to find outworn poetic images, from dewy clichés to the nightingale as traditional symbol for poetry (see Keats's *Ode to a Nightingale*, p. 605). In a poem filled with the debris of modern times, from old tires to dead cats, Stevens suggests that poetry's philosophical quest to name the "the" of existence cannot employ previous ages' images and ideas but must develop its own, even if they appear only the grating music of grackles or beatings on an old tin can. Yet all are engaged in the same enterprise, creating what he elsewhere called "supreme fictions" to give meaning to our lives.

Stevens's poetry celebrates the ability of the individual imagination to conceive its own world. Broader social or political themes are pushed to the background, even in texts (such as *The Man on the Dump* or *The Emperor of Ice-Cream*) that derive power from their realistic descriptions. Consequently, the politically minded critics of the 1930s accused the poet of being an escapist, content to be the "single artificer of his own world of mannerism." Stevens responded that to do otherwise was to misunderstand "the spiritual role of the poet," for this role was not to make political statements but to clarify basic issues by illuminating the relations between human subjectivity and a world of objects. Such an explanation may have seemed too philosophical to those seeking an openly committed literature, and Stevens's early work was largely unappreciated. The gaudy exuberance of its images made it seem less serious than the poetry of political commitment and visionary mysticism that Yeats was then writing, or Eliot's evocation in *The Waste Land* of a universal and profound despair. Only after World War II did Americans, and Europeans, realize that Stevens, too, was a master worthy to stand beside his greatest contemporaries.

A good general introduction is Robert Pack, *Wallace Stevens: An Approach to His Poetry* (1958). Robert Buttel, *Wallace Stevens: The Makings of Harmonium* (1967), discusses Stevens's early and middle work. Many views on Stevens are presented in Marie Borroff, ed., *Wallace Stevens: A Collection of Critical Essays* (1963). Michel Benamou, *Wallace Stevens and the Symbolist Imagination* (1972), is an interesting study of Stevens's themes and style compared with those of French Symbolist poets. Albert Gelpi, *Wallace Stevens: The Poetics of Modernism* (1985), presents seven essays situating Stevens's work in the context of twentieth-century modernism in English. Historical, philosophical, and artistic perspectives are discussed as well as Stevens's influence on contemporary poets. Janet McCann, *Wallace Stevens Revisited: "The Celestial Possible"* (1995), stresses metaphysical themes. John T. Newcomb, *Wallace Stevens and Literary Canons* (1992), examines the way Stevens's "canonical" reputation evolves in tandem with critical perspectives on American modernism. Glen MacLeod, *Wallace Stevens and Modern Art: From the Armory Show to Abstract Expression* (1993), traces the relations between Stevens's poetics and his understanding of issues in modern art.

Sunday Morning[1]

I

Complacencies of the peignoir, and late
Coffee and oranges in a sunny chair,
And the green freedom of a cockatoo
Upon a rug mingle to dissipate
The holy hush of ancient sacrifice.   5
She dreams a little, and she feels the dark
Encroachment of that old catastrophe,
As a calm darkens among water-lights.
The pungent oranges and bright, green wings
Seem things in some procession of the dead,   10
Winding across wide water, without sound.
The day is like wide water, without sound,
Stilled for the passing of her dreaming feet
Over the seas, to silent Palestine,
Dominion of the blood and sepulchre.[2]   15

II

Why should she give her bounty to the dead?
What is divinity if it can come
Only in silent shadows and in dreams?
Shall she not find in comforts of the sun,
In pungent fruit and bright, green wings, or else   20
In any balm or beauty of the earth,
Things to be cherished like the thought of heaven?[3]
Divinity must live within herself:
Passions of rain, or moods in falling snow;
Grievings in loneliness, or unsubdued   25
Elations when the forest blooms; gusty
Emotions on wet roads on autumn nights;
All pleasures and all pains, remembering
The bough of summer and the winter branch.
These are the measures destined for her soul.   30

III

Jove[4] in the clouds had his inhuman birth.
No mother suckled him, no sweet land gave
Large-mannered motions to his mythy mind
He moved among us, as a muttering king,
Magnificent, would move among his hinds,[5]   35
Until our blood, commingling, virginal,[6]
With heaven, brought such requital to desire

---

1. Although the central figure of the poem is clearly a woman sitting over late breakfast on Sunday morning instead of going to church, Stevens comments that "this is not essentially a woman's meditation on religion and the meaning of life. It is anybody's meditation" (Stevens's *Letters*, p. 250). 2. Throughout the stanza there are hints of Christ's Crucifixion and the celebration of the Mass. 3. "The poem is simply an expression of paganism" (Stevens's *Letters*, p. 250). 4. Ruler of the gods in Roman myth. Stevens softens the traditional story in which Jove's father, Cronus, swallows the infant shortly after birth. 5. Shepherds. 6. An allusion to the conception of Jesus in the womb of the Virgin Mary.

The very hinds discerned it, in a star.[7]
Shall our blood fail? Or shall it come to be
The blood of paradise? And shall the earth   40
Seem all of paradise that we shall know?
The sky will be much friendlier then than now,
A part of labor and a part of pain,
And next in glory to enduring love,
Not this dividing and indifferent blue.   45

IV

She says, "I am content when wakened birds,
Before they fly, test the reality
Of misty fields, by their sweet questionings;
But when the birds are gone, and their warm fields
Return no more, where, then, is paradise?"   50
There is not any haunt of prophecy,[8]
Nor any old chimera of the grave,
Neither the golden underground, nor isle
Melodious, where spirits gat them home,[9]
Nor visionary south, nor cloudy palm   55
Remote on heaven's hill, that has endured
As April's green endures; or will endure
Like her remembrance of awakened birds,
Or her desire for June and evening, tipped
By the consummation of the swallow's wings.   60

V

She says, "But in contentment I still feel
The need of some imperishable bliss."
Death is the mother of beauty; hence from her,
Alone, shall come fulfilment to our dreams
And our desires. Although she strews the leaves   65
Of sure obliteration on our paths,
The path sick sorrow took, the many paths
Where triumph rang its brassy phrase, or love
Whispered a little out of tenderness,
She makes the willow shiver in the sun   70
For maidens who were wont to sit and gaze
Upon the grass, relinquished to their feet.
She causes boys to pile new plums and pears
On disregarded plate.[1] The maidens taste
And stray impassioned in the littering leaves.   75

VI

Is there no change of death in paradise?
Does ripe fruit never fall? Or do the boughs
Hang always heavy in that perfect sky,

7. The star over Bethlehem that marked Jesus' birth.   8. E.g., like the oracle at Delphi.   9. The Elysian Fields, or Isles of the Blessed, where the heroes of Greek myth went after death.   1. "Plate is used
in the sense of so-called family plate. Disregarded refers to the disuse into which things fall that have been
possessed for a long time. I mean, therefore, that death releases and renews. What the old have come to
disregard, the young inherit and make use of" (Stevens's *Letters*, p. 183).

Unchanging, yet so like our perishing earth,
With rivers like our own that seek for seas   80
They never find, the same receding shores
That never touch with inarticulate pang?
Why set the pear upon those river-banks
Or spice the shores with odors of the plum?
Alas, that they should wear our colors there,   85
The silken weavings of our afternoons,
And pick the strings of our insipid lutes!
Death is the mother of beauty, mystical,
Within whose burning bosom we devise
Our earthly mothers waiting, sleeplessly.   90

VII

Supple and turbulent, a ring of men
Shall chant in orgy on a summer morn
Their boisterous devotion to the sun,
Not as a god, but as a god might be,
Naked among them, like a savage source.   95
Their chant shall be a chant of paradise,
Out of their blood, returning to the sky;
And in their chant shall enter, voice by voice,
The windy lake wherein their lord delights,
The trees, like serafin,² and echoing hills,   100
That choir among themselves long afterward.
They shall know well the heavenly fellowship
Of men that perish and of summer morn.
And whence they came and whither they shall go
The dew upon their feet shall manifest.³

                                                     105

VIII

She hears, upon that water without sound,
A voice that cries, "The tomb in Palestine
Is not the porch of spirits lingering.⁴
It is the grave of Jesus, where he lay."
We live in an old chaos of the sun,   110
Or old dependency of day and night,
Or island solitude, unsponsored, free,
Of that wide water, inescapable.
Deer walk upon our mountains, and the quail
Whistle about us their spontaneous cries;   115
Sweet berries ripen in the wilderness;
And, in the isolation of the sky,
At evening, casual flocks of pigeons make
Ambiguous undulations as they sink.
Downward to darkness, on extended wings.   120

---

2. Angels of the highest rank.   3. "Life is as fugitive as dew upon the feet of men dancing in dew. Men do not either come from any direction or disappear in any direction. Life is as meaningless as dew" (Stevens's *Letters*, p. 250).   4. I.e., remaining on Earth after the body is dead.

Peter Quince at the Clavier[1]

I

Just as my fingers on these keys
Make music, so the selfsame sounds
On my spirit make a music, too.

Music is feeling, then, not sound;
And thus it is that what I feel,   5
Here in this room, desiring you,

Thinking of your blue-shadowed silk,
Is music. It is like the strain
Waked in the elders by Susanna.[2]

Of a green evening, clear and warm,   10
She bathed in her still garden, while
The red-eyed elders watching, felt

The basses of their beings throb
In witching chords, and their thin blood
Pulse pizzicati of Hosanna.[3]   15

II

In the green water, clear and warm,
Susanna lay.
She searched
The touch of springs,
And found   20
Concealed imaginings.
She sighed,
For so much melody.

Upon the bank, she stood
In the cool   25
Of spent emotions.
She felt, among the leaves,
The dew
Of old devotions.

She walked upon the grass,   30
Still quavering.
The winds were like her maids,
On timid feet,

---

1. General term in the sixteenth century for a keyboard instrument, such as a harpsichord. In Shakespeare's *A Midsummer Night's Dream*, Peter Quince is the carpenter-playwright who directs his own play about the tragic lovers Pyramus and Thisbe. Both the play and the production amuse the noble audience. 2. In the biblical Apocrypha, a Babylonian woman falsely accused of adultery by lecherous elders who spied on her bathing. 3. A cry of praise to God. *Pizzicati:* notes sounded by plucking a string (as on a violin).

Fetching her woven scarves,
Yet wavering.   35

A breath upon her hand
Muted the night.
She turned—
A cymbal crashed,
And roaring horns.   40

III

Soon, with a noise like tambourines,
Came her attendant Byzantines.[4]

They wondered why Susanna cried
Against the elders by her side;

And as they whispered, the refrain   45
Was like a willow swept by rain.

Anon,[5] their lamps' uplifted flame
Revealed Susanna and her shame.

And then, the simpering Byzantines
Fled, with a noise like tambourines.   50

IV

Beauty is momentary in the mind—
The fitful tracing of a portal;
But in the flesh it is immortal.
The body dies; the body's beauty lives.
So evenings die, in their green going,   55
A wave, interminably flowing.
So gardens die, their meek breath scenting
The cowl of winter, done repenting.
So maidens die,[6] to the auroral
Celebration of a maiden's choral.[7]   60
Susanna's music touched the bawdy strings
Of those white elders; but, escaping,
Left only Death's ironic scraping.[8]
Now, in its immortality, it plays
On the clear viol[9] of her memory,   65
And makes a constant sacrament of praise.

---

4. Inhabitants of ancient Byzantium, a Christian empire of the Near East. "Somebody once called my attention to the fact that there were no Byzantines in Susanna's time. I hope that that bit of precious pedantry will seem as unimportant to you as it does to me" (Stevens's *Letters*, p. 250).   5. Soon.   6. As maidens, that is, become women.   7. Choral song.   8. Rasping fiddle music.   9. A stringed instrument of the sixteenth and seventeenth centuries, played with a bow; also a pun on *violation*.

Anecdote of the Jar

I placed a jar in Tennessee.
And round it was, upon a hill.
It made the slovenly wilderness
Surround that hill.

The wilderness rose up to it,   5
And sprawled around, no longer wild.
The jar was round upon the ground
And tall and of a port[1] in air.

It took dominion everywhere.
The jar was gray and bare.   10
It did not give of bird or bush,
Like nothing else in Tennessee.

The Emperor of Ice-Cream[1]

Call the roller of big cigars,
The muscular one, and bid him whip
In kitchen cups concupiscent[2] curds.
Let the wenches dawdle in such dress
As they are used to wear, and let the boys   5
Bring flowers in last month's newspapers.
Let be be finale of seem.[3]
The only emperor is the emperor of ice-cream.

Take from the dresser of deal,[4]
Lacking the three glass knobs, that sheet   10
On which she embroidered fantails[5] once
And spread it so as to cover her face.
If her horny feet protrude, they come
To show how cold she is, and dumb.
Let the lamp affix its beam.   15
The only emperor is the emperor of ice-cream.

---

1. Dignified bearing, manner.   **1.** "I think I should select from my poems as my favorite 'The Emperor of Ice-Cream.' This wears a deliberately commonplace costume, and yet seems to me to contain something of the essential gaudiness of poetry; that is the reason why I like it" (Stevens's *Letters*, p. 263).   **2.** Lusty, sensual. "The words 'concupiscent curds' . . . express the concupiscence of life, but, by contrast with the things in relation to them in the poem they express or accentuate life's destitution" (Stevens's *Letters*, p. 500).   **3.** "The true sense of 'Let be be the finale of seem' is let being become the conclusion or denouement of appearing to be: in short, icecream is an absolute good. The poem is obviously not about icecream, but about being as distinguished from seeming to be" (Stevens's *Letters*, p. 341).   **4.** Fir or pine wood.   **5.** Fantail pigeons.

The Idea of Order at Key West[1]

She sang beyond the genius of the sea.[2]
The water never formed to mind or voice,
Like a body wholly body, fluttering
Its empty sleeves; and yet its mimic motion
Made constant cry, caused constantly a cry,   5
That was not ours although we understood,
Inhuman, of the veritable ocean.

The sea was not a mask.[3] No more was she.
The song and water were not medleyed sound
Even if what she sang was what she heard.   10
Since what she sang was uttered word by word.
It may be that in all her phrases stirred
The grinding water and the gasping wind;
But it was she and not the sea we heard.

For she was the maker of the song she sang.   15
The ever-hooded, tragic-gestured sea
Was merely a place by which she walked to sing.
Whose spirit is this? we said, because we knew
It was the spirit that we sought and knew
That we should ask this often as she sang.   20

If it was only the dark voice of the sea
That rose, or even colored by many waves;
If it was only the outer voice of sky
And cloud, of the sunken coral water-walled,
However clear, it would have been deep air,   25
The heaving speech of air, a summer sound
Repeated in a summer without end
And sound alone. But it was more than that,
More even than her voice, and ours, among
The meaningless plungings of water and the wind,   30
Theatrical distances, bronze shadows heaped
On high horizons, mountainous atmospheres
Of sky and sea.
                    It was her voice that made
The sky acutest at its vanishing.   35
She measured to the hour its solitude.
She was the single artificer of the world
In which she sang. And when she sang, the sea,
Whatever self it had, became the self
That was her song, for she was the maker. Then we,   40

---

1. Published in *Ideas of Order* (1936). "In 'The Idea of Order at Key West' life has ceased to be a matter of chance. It may be that every man introduces his own order into the life about him. . . . But still there is order. . . . These are tentative ideas for the purposes of poetry" (Stevens's *Letters*, p. 293). Key West is the southernmost of the Florida keys, and Stevens spent midwinter vacations there for almost twenty years.   2. I.e., beyond the power of the sea to respond.   3. The movement of the waves, imitating fluttering sleeves, also emits an inhuman cry. The sea mimics the human body, but without a mind; it is not even as close as the mask worn by actors in ancient Greek drama.

As we beheld her striding there alone,
Knew that there never was a world for her
Except the one she sang and, singing, made.

Ramon Fernandez,[4] tell me, if you know,
Why, when the singing ended and we turned   45
Toward the town, tell why the glassy lights,
The lights in the fishing boats at anchor there,
As the night descended, tilting in the air,
Mastered the night and portioned out the sea,
Fixing emblazoned zones and fiery poles,[5]   50
Arranging, deepening, enchanting night.

Oh! Blessed rage for order, pale Ramon,
The maker's rage to order words of the sea,
Words of the fragrant portals, dimly-starred,
And of ourselves and of our origins,   55
In ghostlier demarcations, keener sounds.

The Man on the Dump

Day creeps down. The moon is creeping up.
The sun is a corbeil of flowers the moon Blanche[1]
Places there, a bouquet. Ho-ho . . . The dump is full
Of images. Days pass like papers[2] from a press.
The bouquets come here in the papers. So the sun,   5
And so the moon, both come, and the janitor's poems
Of every day, the wrapper on the can of pears,
The cat in the paper-bag, the corset, the box
From Esthonia:[3] the tiger chest, for tea.

The freshness of night has been fresh a long time.   10
The freshness of morning, the blowing of day, one says
That it puffs as Cornelius Nepos[4] reads, it puffs
More than, less than or it puffs like this or that.
The green smacks in the eye, the dew in the green
Smacks like fresh water in a can, like the sea   15

On a cocoanut—how many men have copied dew
For buttons, how many women have covered themselves
With dew, dew dresses, stones and chains of dew, heads
Of the floweriest flowers dewed with the dewiest dew.
One grows to hate these things except on the dump.   20

4. French critic (1894–1944) who described the way impressionistic techniques in literature impose a subjective order on reality. Stevens had read some of Fernandez's criticism, but denied that he intended any specific reference here.   5. As with the geographic zones and poles of the earth. *Emblazoned*: ornamented, usually with heraldic symbols.   1. A woman's name, etymologically signifying whiteness. *Corbeil*: basket.   2. Newspapers.   3. Or Estonia; a Baltic republic, once part of the Soviet Union.   4. Roman historian (first century B.C.), now little read, the author of brief anecdotal and highly moralized *Lives of Famous Men*.

Now, in the time of spring (azaleas, trilliams,
Myrtle, viburnums, daffodils, blue phlox),[5]
Between that disgust and this, between the things
That are on the dump (azaleas and so on)
And those that will be (azaleas and so on).   25
One feels the purifying change. One rejects
The trash.

        That's the moment when the moon creeps up
To the bubbling of bassoons. That's the time
One looks at the elephant-colorings of tires: 30
Everything is shed; and the moon comes up as the moon
(All its images are in the dump) and you see
As a man (not like an image of a man),
You see the moon rise in the empty sky.

One sits and beats an old tin can, lard pail.   35
One beats and beats for that which one believes.
That's what one wants to get near. Could it after all
Be merely oneself, as superior as the ear
To a crow's voice? Did the nightingale[6] torture the ear,
Pack the heart and scratch the mind? And does the ear   40
Solace itself in peevish birds? Is it peace,
Is it a philosopher's honeymoon,[7] one finds
On the dump? Is it to sit among mattresses of the dead,
Bottles, pots, shoes and grass and murmur *aptest eve*:
Is it to hear the blatter of grackles[8] and say   45
Invisible priest; is it to eject, to pull
The day to pieces and cry *stanza my stone?*[9]
Where was it one first heard of the Truth? The the.[1]

5. Spring flowers. **6.** Traditional image for lyric poetry; for example, in Keats's *Ode to a Nightingale*. **7.** Like a busman's holiday; that is, no respite at all. **8.** Noisy birds. **9.** Suggests a Romantic, mystical, "nightingale" poetry that turns its back on material reality. "Invisible priest" may recall Rilke's proposed artistic transformation of reality into an invisible higher reality (see *The Ninth Elegy*). **1.** "The truth" is an intangible absolute (like "*the* good"); what it specifies cannot be defined. The *the* itself however represents an urge to seek absolute meaning: to say *the*, not merely *a*.

JAMES JOYCE
1882–1941

Modernism is synonymous with James Joyce. An Irish writer who spent most of his life outside Ireland and became an international figure, Joyce created a narrative style that changed the way modern novelists were able to write about the world. Writers as widely separated as the American William Faulkner, the Irishman Samuel Beckett, the Colombian Gabriel García Márquez, and the French "new novelists" Alain Robbe-Grillet, Marguerite Duras, and Nathalie Sarraute have learned from his literary and linguistic innovations. From *Dubliners* to *Ulysses* and *Finnegans Wake*, Joyce found new ways to explore the daily lives and fragmentary dreams of characters (including his own youthful self) in the parochial Dublin society he had fled. Although he returned to Ireland as the starting point for all three works, he blamed Irish society for its narrowness and "moral paralysis" and repeatedly evoked the broader horizons of European culture and myth. Joyce's best-known contribution to modern literature is the stream of consciousness technique that attempts to reproduce the natural flow of thoughts and emotions. Stream of consciousness writing does not always seem logical, for thoughts tend to jump around in an arbitrary manner, but it can be very convincing since it gives the reader apparent access to the workings of a character's mind. The aim—and it is a characteristically modernist aim—is to obtain a fuller understanding of human experience by displaying subconscious associations along with conscious thoughts. Joyce's later work exploits these subterranean connections more and more, and his language becomes increasingly playful, as he strives to create a newly meaningful form of writing and to "forge in the smithy of my soul the uncreated conscience of my race."

Born in Dublin on February 2, 1882, to May Murray and John Stanislaus Joyce, he was given the impressive name of James Augustine Aloysius Joyce. His father held a well-paid and easy post in the civil service, and the family was comfortable until 1891, when his job was eliminated with a small pension and he declined to take up more demanding work elsewhere. The Joyce family (there were ten children) moved steadily down the social and economic scale, and life became difficult under the improvident guidance of a man whom Joyce later portrayed as "a drinker, a good fellow, a storyteller, somebody's secretary, something in a distillery, a tax-gatherer, a bankrupt, and at present a praiser of his own past." Joyce attended the well-known Catholic preparatory school of Clongowes Wood College from six to nine years of age, leaving when his family could no longer afford the tuition; two years later, he was admitted as a scholarship student to Belvedere College in Dublin. Both were Jesuit schools, and provided a rigorous Catholic training against which Joyce violently rebelled but which he was never able to forget. In Belvedere College, shaken by a dramatic hell-fire sermon shortly after his first experience with sex, he even thought of becoming a priest; the life of the senses and his vocation as an artist won out, however, and the sermon and his reaction to it became part of *A Portrait of the Artist as a Young Man*. After graduating from Belvedere in 1898, Joyce entered another Irish Catholic institution—University College, Dublin—where he consciously rebelled against Irish tradition and looked abroad for new values. Teaching himself Norwegian to read Henrik Ibsen in the original, he criticized the writers of the Irish Literary Renaissance as provincial and had no interest in joining their ranks. Like the hero of *Portrait*, Stephen Dedalus, he decided in 1902 to escape the stifling conventions of his native country and leave for the Continent.

This first trip did not last long. For six months, he supported himself in Paris by giving English lessons, but when his mother turned seriously ill he was called home. After her death, he taught school for a time in Dublin and then returned to the Continent with Nora Barnacle, a country woman from western Ireland with whom he had two children and whom he married in 1931. The young couple moved to Trieste, where Joyce taught English in a Berlitz school and where he started writing both the short stories collected as *Dubliners* (1914) and an early version (partially published as *Stephen Hero* in 1944) of *A Portrait of the Artist as a Young Man*. *Dubliners* sketches aspects of life in Dublin as Joyce knew it, which means that the parochiality, piety, and repressive conventions of Irish life are shown stifling artistic and psychological development. Whether it be the young boy who arrives too late at the fair in *Araby*, the poor-aunt laundress of *Clay*, or the frustrated writer Gabriel Conroy of *The Dead*, characters in *Dubliners* dream of a better life against a dismal and impoverishing background whose cumulative effect is one of despair. The style of *Dubliners* is more realistic than Joyce's later fiction, but he is already employing a structure of symbolic meanings and revelatory moments called "epiphanies." The all-blanketing white snow at the end of *The Dead* suggests the chill uniformity of death and Gabriel Conroy's alienation from (or, on another level, unity with) the rest of his world. It is Gabriel who observes the scene and whose suddenly expanded vision of the whole universe being swallowed up in oblivion constitutes an epiphany, a moment when everything fuses and makes sense in a larger spiritual perspective.

A *Portrait of the Artist as a Young Man* is based on Joyce's life until 1902, but the novel is clearly not a conventional autobiography and the reader recognizes in the first pages a radical experiment in fictional language. From the child's vocabulary and fragmented echoing of his parents' baby talk ("nicens little boy," "baby tuckoo") to the mature rhetoric of the end ("Old father, old artificer, stand me now and ever in good stead"), everything in *Portrait* is introduced sequentially and shaped to make the most powerful cumulative impact. Even Stephen's first naive thoughts prepare for themes developed later on: the importance of sense impressions, from the clammy bed to his mother's smell; the political symbolism of Dante's green and maroon hair-brushes; the bird imagery and threat of punishment on high in Dante's reproach; and the small boy's habit of thinking over things and rephrasing them in poetic language. Events that stand out in the young boy's mind, such as the humiliation of receiving an unfair spanking in school, are described with their full impact because they are not simply first-person (subjective) or third-person (objective) accounts but an imaginative combination of the two. An outside observer with access to all Stephen's feelings follows the course of events. *Portrait*, like *Dubliners*, is still in the tradition of naturalist narrative and specifically of the *Künstlerroman*, or artist-novel, which follows chronologically the career of its artist hero. Its sophisticated symbolism, use of epiphanies, and stress on dramatic dialogue, however, hint at the radical break with narrative tradition that Joyce was preparing in *Ulysses*.

Ulysses (1922) is one of the most celebrated instances of literary censorship. Its serial publication in the New York *Little Review* from 1918 to 1920 was stopped as obscene by the U.S. Post Office after a complaint from the New York Society for the Prevention of Vice. The novel was banned and all available copies were actually burned in England and America until a 1933 decision by Judge Woolsey in a U.S. district court lifted the ban in the United States. The problem was not new: Joyce's realistic descriptions of sensory experience from bedroom to bathroom, his playfully allusive use of language, and his antinationalist and antireligious attitudes had already offended many readers from *Dubliners* (which an Irish printer refused to print on the grounds that it was anti-Irish) to *Portrait* (which was refused as a "work of doubtful character even though it may be a classic"). While Joyce's descriptions have lost none of their pungency, it is hard to imagine a reader who would not be struck also by another side—by the "classical" density and enormous mythic scope of this complex, symbolic, and linguistically innovative novel. Openly referring to an ancient predecessor, the *Odyssey* of Homer ("Ulysses" is the Latin name for the hero Odysseus), *Ulysses* structures numerous episodes to suggest parallels with the Greek epic, and transforms the twenty-year Homeric journey home into the day-long wanderings through Dublin of an unheroic advertising man, Leopold Bloom, and a rebellious young teacher and writer from *Portrait*, Stephen Dedalus.

Bloom is in one sense a perfectly ordinary man, the "common man" of modern society. He comes to no great decisions (whereas Stephen decides to leave Ireland and dedicate himself to art), and his life will continue its uneventful and somewhat downtrodden way. Yet Bloom is the most fully developed character in the book, a man whose dimensions encompass the mythic overtones of the outcast (Ulysses or the Wandering Jew), the psychological tension of a father and husband cut off from family relationships, and (in bathroom, bedroom, and meat market) the most mundane domestic details. The ancient Ulysses was a man of many roles, and so is the modern Bloom. If the *Odyssey* has been described as one of the first voyages of Everyman, *Ulysses* shows Everyman in the twentieth century. According to T. S. Eliot, Joyce's paralleling of ancient myth and modern life is more than literary homage; it is "a way of controlling, of ordering, of giving a shape and significance to the immense panorama of futility and anarchy which is contemporary history."

There is no classical parallel, however, for the language of *Ulysses*, which has long been recognized as a paradigm of modernist style. Its quick shifts in points of view, changes of narrative voice, and blendings of the most exacting realism with hallucinatory scenes that combine memory and distorted current vision are the literary equivalent of cinematic montage. In addition, Joyce abandoned the regular syntax and logical sequences of traditional narrative for a style that tried to represent the flow of thought and emotion in a character's mind. A development of the "interior monologue," this stream of consciousness technique is far looser and freer in its fragmented, punning, freely associating representation of consciousness. Sometimes it is a sleepy jangle in which the relaxed mind lazily plays with sound associations: "Sinbad the Sailor and Tinbad the Tailor and Jinbad the Jailer and Whinbad the Whaler and Ninbad the Nailer and . . ." Sometimes it is more obscure, as in the introduction to a bar scene with its associative, fragmented vision and imitations of different sounds: "Bronze by gold heard the hoofirons, steelyringing Imperthnthn thnthnthn. Chips, picking chips off rocky thumbnail, chips. Horrid! And gold flushed more. A husky fife-note blew. Blew. Blue bloom in on the Gold pinnacled hair." In the famous ending to the novel, it combines passion and response in specific images called up from memory, as his wife, Molly, recalls her first yielding to Bloom: "O that awful deepdown torrent O and the sea the sea crimson sometimes like fire and the glorious sunsets and the figtrees in the Alameda gardens yes and all the queer little streets and pink and blue and yellow houses and the rosegardens and the jessamine and geraniums and cactuses . . . yes and then he asked me would I yes to say yes my mountain flower and first I put my arms around him yes and drew him down to me so he could feel my breasts all perfume yes and his heart was going like mad and yes I said yes I will Yes." The extraordinary thing about Joyce's stream of consciousness technique, as the perspicacious Judge Woolsey commented in his court decision, was that it represents the many layers of experience making up each individual's current consciousness: "Not only what is in the focus of each man's observation of the actual things about him, but also in a penumbral zone residua of past impressions, some recent and some drawn up by association from the domain of the subconscious." Taken to the extreme, it is so completely individualized that a reader who remains outside the personal code cannot break in; at its best, though, it can draw on echoes and clues already present in the text. The complicated inner reference in Ulysses provided a glimpse of unparalleled richness into human awareness and set a challenging example for narrative style after Joyce.

After the publication of Ulysses, Joyce spent the next seventeen years writing an even more complex work: Finnegans Wake (1939). Despite the title, which refers to a ballad in which the bricklayer Tim Finnegan is brought back to life at his wake when somebody spills whisky on him, the novel is the multivoiced, multidimensional dream of Humphrey Chimpden Earwicker: HCE, Here Comes Everybody, Haveth Childers Everywhere, Tristan, Humpty-Dumpty, and Allmen. HCE's dream includes his wife, Anna Earwicker, as Anna Livia Plurabelle, ALP, the voice of the river Liffey, or a suggestion of historical "holy wars," and together they constitute the originating pair of Adam and Eve. Finnegans Wake expands on the encyclopedic series of literary and cultural references underlying Ulysses and does so in language that has been even more radically broken apart and reassembled. Digressing exuberantly in all directions at once, with complex puns and hybrid words that mix languages, Finnegans Wake is—in spite of its cosmic symbolism—a game of language and reference by an artist "hoppy on akkant of his joyicity." It has not achieved the wide audience of Portrait or Ulysses, but when Joyce died in Zurich in 1941 he considered it the culmination of his career as a writer.

The Dead is the last and by far the fullest story in Dubliners, and it recapitulates many of the volume's themes. In 1906, Joyce had written to his publisher that the collection would be "a chapter of the moral history of my country," and he further explained that he had chosen Dublin because it was the "centre of paralysis" in Ireland. The city formed a background of blunted hopes and lost dreams: desperately poor, with large slums and many more people than jobs, it stagnated in political, religious, and cultural divisions that color the lives of characters in these stories. The book is arranged, Joyce explains, in an order that represents four aspects of life in the city: "childhood, adolescence, maturity and public life." Individual stories focus on one or a few characters, who may dream of a better life but are eventually frustrated by, or sink voluntarily back into, their shabby reality. Stories often end with a moment of special insight (an epiphany), visible to the reader but not always to the protagonist, that puts events in sharp and illuminating perspective.

Joyce's work draws heavily on real life, including his own; and several aspects of *The Dead* recall—and transmute—elements in his own life. As in other stories, the neighborhood setting is familiar from his youth. The real-life models for Miss Kate and Miss Julia were indeed music teachers (but they were married). Mr. Bartell d'Arcy evokes a contemporary tenor who performed under a similar name. The figure of Gabriel Conroy, who writes reviews for local journals, dislikes Irish nationalism, and prefers European culture, physically resembles photographs of Joyce—a lesser Joyce who might never have had the courage to leave home for Europe. The tale of Gretta's dead admirer, Michael Furey, echoes Nora Barnacle's similar experience. The sources of *Dubliners,* whether personal or social, are all inescapably real: so real, including coarse language and contemporary allusions, that publishers were unwilling to produce the volume for fear of libel or obscenity charges. An Irish publisher went so far as to print a censored version in 1909, but subsequently burned all the copies when he and Joyce had further disputes. In 1914, some nine years after its initial (later retracted) acceptance, *Dubliners* finally appeared.

The Dead is divided into three parts, chronicling the stages of the Misses Morkan's party and also stages by which Gabriel Conroy moves from the rather pompous, insecure, and externally oriented figure of the beginning to a man who has been forced to reassess himself and human relationships at the end. The party is an annual dinner dance that takes place after the New Year, probably on January 6, the Catholic Feast of the Epiphany (which many have connected with Gabriel's personal epiphany at the end of the story). A jovial occasion, it brings together friends and acquaintances for an evening of music, dancing, sumptuous food, and a formal after-dinner speech that Gabriel delivers. The undercurrents are not always harmonious, however, for small anxieties and personal frictions crop up that both create a realistic picture and suggest tensions in contemporary Irish society: nationalism, religion, poverty, and class differences. Gabriel has a position to maintain, and he is determined to live up to his responsibilities: he is at once cultured speaker and intellectual, carver and master of ceremonies, and the man whom the Misses Morkan expect to take care of occasional problems like alcoholic guests. He is a complex character, both a writer of real imagination (or we would not have the ending scene) and a narcissistic figure who is so used to focusing on himself that he has drawn apart from other people.

Three times in the course of the story Gabriel's self-image is challenged, each time by a woman. Lily, the maidservant in the beginning scene, rebuffs his patronizing questions with a bitter comment about men; immediately, Gabriel worries about his mistake and whether his speech will likewise take the wrong tone for its audience—that is, be above their heads. In the second episode, Miss Ivors's attack on his ignorance of Irish culture shakes him again, for he interprets it as an attempt to make him look ridiculous. Finally, just as Gabriel is thoroughly aroused by watching his wife's graceful figure and hopes to recapture a long-lost intimacy, he finds that she is thinking of a long-dead suitor, Michael Furey. Michael died because, ill, he made her a farewell visit; and Gabriel realizes that his own colorless self will never rival the memory of Furey's passionate devotion. The jovial evening has lost its sparkle; once again, Gabriel looks back in frustration and unhappiness, and this time recognizes signs of death and delusion everywhere. By the end of *The Dead*, he feels his identity "fading out into a grey impalpable world," approaching—in his artistic imagination—a state in which both living and dead are one community, blanketed by the snow that falls throughout the universe in his final vision.

Harry Levin, *James Joyce: A Critical Introduction* (1941), is an excellent and read-able general introduction. The standard and detailed biography, with illustrations, is Richard Ellmann, *James Joyce* (1982). Morris Beja, *James Joyce: A Literary Life* (1992), includes recent scholarship. Derek Attridge, ed., *The Cambridge Companion to James Joyce* (1990), and Mary T. Reynolds, ed., *James Joyce: A Collection of Critical Essays* (1993), treat various aspects of the work. Daniel R. Schwarz, ed., *The Dead* (1994), is a useful short book that includes the text and some contextual material, an account of *Dubliners'* history and criticism from the 1950s, and analyses by different authors using five modern critical perspectives. Diverse critical approaches are represented in Alan Roughley, *James Joyce and Critical Theory: An Introduction* (1991), and Su-zette A. Henke's feminist study *James Joyce and the Politics of Desire* (1990). John Wyse Jackson and Bernard McGinley, eds., *Joyce's Dubliners: An Illustrated Edition with Annotations* (1995), is a fascinating, copiously illustrated and documented edi-tion that includes allusions to other works and a capsule essay after each story. David Pierce, *James Joyce's Ireland* (1992), includes contemporary photographs by Dan Har-per and uses documents, photographs, and copious quotation to reconstruct Joyce's biography in historical context.

The Dead

Lily, the caretaker's daughter, was literally run off her feet. Hardly had she brought one gentleman into the little pantry behind the office on the ground floor and helped him off with his overcoat than the wheezy hall-door bell clanged again and she had to scamper along the bare hallway to let in another guest. It was well for her she had not to attend to the ladies also. But Miss Kate and Miss Julia had thought of that and had converted the bathroom upstairs into a ladies' dressing-room. Miss Kate and Miss Julia were there, gossiping and laughing and fussing, walking after each other to the head of the stairs, peering down over the banisters and calling down to Lily to ask her who had come.

It was always a great affair, the Misses Morkan's annual dance. Everybody who knew them came to it, members of the family, old friends of the family, the members of Julia's choir, any of Kate's pupils that were grown up enough and even some of Mary Jane's pupils too. Never once had it fallen flat. For years and years it had gone off in splendid style as long as anyone could remember; ever since Kate and Julia, after the death of their brother Pat, had left the house in Stoney Batter and taken Mary Jane, their only niece, to live with them in the dark gaunt house on Usher's Island,[1] the upper part of which they had rented from Mr. Fulham, the cornfactor on the ground floor. That was a good thirty years ago if it was a day. Mary Jane, who was then a little girl in short clothes, was now the main prop of the household for she had the organ[2] in Haddington Road. She had been through the Acad-emy[3] and gave a pupils' concert every year in the upper room of the Antient Concert Rooms. Many of her pupils belonged to better-class families on the Kingstown and Dalkey line.[4] Old as they were, her aunts also did their share. Julia, though she was quite grey, was still the leading soprano in Adam and

1. Not an island, but an area in western Dublin on the south bank of the river Liffey. Stoney Batter is a street of small shops and a few houses in Dublin.   2. I.e., earned money by playing the organ at church.   3. The Royal Academy of Music.   4. Railway to a fashionable section of Dublin.

Eve's, and Kate, being too feeble to go about much, gave music lessons to beginners on the old square[5] piano in the back room. Lily, the caretaker's daughter, did housemaid's work for them. Though their life was modest they believed in eating well; the best of everything: diamond-bone sirloins, three-shilling tea and the best bottled stout.[6] But Lily seldom made a mistake in the orders so that she got on well with her three mistresses. They were fussy, that was all. But the only thing they would not stand was back answers.

Of course they had good reason to be fussy on such a night. And then it was long after ten o'clock and yet there was no sign of Gabriel and his wife. Besides they were dreadfully afraid that Freddy Malins might turn up screwed.[7] They would not wish for worlds that any of Mary Jane's pupils should see him under the influence; and when he was like that it was some-times very hard to manage him. Freddy Malins always came late but they wondered what could be keeping Gabriel: and that was what brought them every two minutes to the banisters to ask Lily had Gabriel or Freddy come.

—O, Mr. Conroy, said Lily to Gabriel when she opened the door for him, Miss Kate and Miss Julia thought you were never coming. Good-night, Mrs. Conroy.

—I'll engage they did, said Gabriel, but they forgot that my wife here takes three mortal hours to dress herself.

He stood on the mat, scraping the snow from his goloshes, while Lily led his wife to the foot of the stairs and called out:

—Miss Kate, here's Mrs. Conroy.

Kate and Julia came toddling down the dark stairs at once. Both of them kissed Gabriel's wife, said she must be perished alive and asked was Gabriel with her.

—Here I am as right as the mail,[8] Aunt Kate! Go on up. I'll follow, called out Gabriel from the dark.

He continued scraping his feet vigorously while the three women went upstairs, laughing, to the ladies' dressing-room. A light fringe of snow lay like a cape on the shoulders of his overcoat and like toecaps on the toes of his goloshes; and, as the buttons of his overcoat slipped with a squeaking noise through the snow-stiffened frieze, a cold fragrant air from out-of-doors escaped from crevices and folds.

—Is it snowing again, Mr. Conroy? asked Lily.

She had preceded him into the pantry to help him off with his overcoat. Gabriel smiled at the three syllables she had given his surname and glanced at her. She was a slim, growing girl, pale in complexion and with hay-coloured hair. The gas in the pantry made her look still paler. Gabriel had known her when she was a child and used to sit on the lowest step nursing a rag doll.

—Yes, Lily, he answered, and I think we're in for a night of it.

He looked up at the pantry ceiling, which was shaking with the stamping and shuffling of feet on the floor above, listened for a moment to the piano and then glanced at the girl, who was folding his overcoat carefully at the end of a shelf.

—Tell me, Lily, he said in a friendly tone, do you still go to school?

—O no, sir, she answered. I'm done schooling this year and more.

---

5. I.e., upright. *Adam and Eve's*: popular name (taken from a nearby inn) for a Dublin Catholic church.   6. Strong beer.   7. Drunk.   8. Reliable as mail delivery.

—O, then, said Gabriel gaily, I suppose we'll be going to your wedding one of these fine days with your young man, eh?

The girl glanced back at him over her shoulder and said with great bitterness:

—The men that is now is only all palaver[9] and what they can get out of you.

Gabriel coloured as if he felt he had made a mistake and, without looking at her, kicked off his goloshes and flicked actively with his muffler at his patent-leather shoes.

He was a stout tallish young man. The high colour of his cheeks pushed upwards even to his forehead where it scattered itself in a few formless patches of pale red; and on his hairless face there scintillated restlessly the polished lenses and the bright gilt rims of the glasses which screened his delicate and restless eyes. His glossy black hair was parted in the middle and brushed in a long curve behind his ears where it curled slightly beneath the groove left by his hat.

When he had flicked lustre into his shoes he stood up and pulled his waistcoat down more tightly on his plump body. Then he took a coin rapidly from his pocket.

—O Lily, he said, thrusting it into her hands, it's Christmastime, isn't it? Just . . . here's a little. . . .

He walked rapidly towards the door.

—O no, sir! cried the girl, following him. Really, sir, I wouldn't take it.

—Christmas-time! Christmas-time! said Gabriel, almost trotting to the stairs and waving his hand to her in deprecation.

The girl, seeing that he had gained the stairs, called out after him:

—Well, thank you, sir.

He waited outside the drawing-room door until the waltz should finish, listening to the skirts that swept against it and to the shuffling of feet. He was still discomposed by the girl's bitter and sudden retort. It had cast a gloom over him which he tried to dispel by arranging his cuffs and the bows of his tie. Then he took from his waistcoat pocket a little paper and glanced at the headings he had made for his speech. He was undecided about the lines from Robert Browning[1] for he feared they would be above the heads of his hearers. Some quotation that they could recognise from Shakespeare or from the Melodies[2] would be better. The indelicate clacking of the men's heels and the shuffling of their soles reminded him that their grade of culture differed from his. He would only make himself ridiculous by quoting poetry to them which they could not understand. They would think that he was airing his superior education. He would fail with them just as he had failed with the girl in the pantry. He had taken up a wrong tone. His whole speech was a mistake from first to last, an utter failure.

Just then his aunts and his wife came out of the ladies' dressing-room. His aunts were two small plainly dressed old women. Aunt Julia was an inch or so the taller. Her hair, drawn low over the tops of her ears, was grey; and grey also, with darker shadows, was her large flaccid face. Though she was stout in build and stood erect her slow eyes and parted lips gave her the

9. Fancy talk.   1. English poet (1812–1889), who had a contemporary reputation for obscurity.   2. Thomas Moore's (1779–1852) immensely popular *Irish Melodies,* a collection of poems with many set to old Irish melodies.

appearance of a woman who did not know where she was or where she was going. Aunt Kate was more vivacious. Her face, healthier than her sister's, was all puckers and creases, like a shrivelled red apple, and her hair, braided in the same old-fashioned way, had not lost its ripe nut colour.

They both kissed Gabriel frankly. He was their favourite nephew, the son of their dead elder sister, Ellen, who had married T. J. Conroy of the Port and Docks.[3]

—Gretta tells me you're not going to take a cab back to Monkstown to-night, Gabriel, said Aunt Kate.

—No, said Gabriel, turning to his wife, we had quite enough of that last year, hadn't we? Don't you remember, Aunt Kate, what a cold Gretta got out of it? Cab windows rattling all the way, and the east wind blowing in after we passed Merrion.[4] Very jolly it was. Gretta caught a dreadful cold.

Aunt Kate frowned severely and nodded her head at every word.

—Quite right, Gabriel, quite right, she said. You can't be too careful.

—But as for Gretta there, said Gabriel, she'd walk home in the snow if she were let.

Mrs. Conroy laughed.

—Don't mind him, Aunt Kate, she said. He's really an awful bother, what with green shades for Tom's eyes at night and making him do the dumb-bells, and forcing Eva to eat the stirabout.[5] The poor child! And she simply hates the sight of it! . . . O, but you'll never guess what he makes me wear now!

She broke out into a peal of laughter and glanced at her husband, whose admiring and happy eyes had been wandering from her dress to her face and hair. The two aunts laughed heartily too, for Gabriel's solicitude was a standing joke with them.

—Goloshes! said Mrs. Conroy. That's the latest. Whenever it's wet underfoot I must put on my goloshes. To-night even he wanted me to put them on, but I wouldn't. The next thing he'll buy me will be a diving suit.

Gabriel laughed nervously and patted his tie reassuringly while Aunt Kate nearly doubled herself, so heartily did she enjoy the joke. The smile soon faded from Aunt Julia's face and her mirthless eyes were directed towards her nephew's face. After a pause she asked:

—And what are goloshes, Gabriel?

—Goloshes, Julia! exclaimed her sister. Goodness me, don't you know what goloshes are? You wear them over your . . . over your boots, Gretta, isn't it?

—Yes, said Mrs. Conroy. Guttapercha[6] things. We both have a pair now. Gabriel says everyone wears them on the continent.

—O, on the continent, murmured Aunt Julia, nodding her head slowly.

Gabriel knitted his brows and said, as if he were slightly angered:

—It's nothing very wonderful but Gretta thinks it very funny because she says the word reminds her of Christy Minstrels.[7]

—But tell me, Gabriel, said Aunt Kate, with brisk tact. Of course, you've seen about the room. Gretta was saying . . .

—O, the room is all right, replied Gabriel. I've taken one in the Gresham.

—To be sure, said Aunt Kate, by far the best thing to do. And the children, Gretta, you're not anxious about them?

---

3. The Dublin Port and Docks Board, which regulated customs and shipping. 4. A village on Dublin Bay. 5. Porridge. 6. A rubberlike substance. 7. *Goloshes* sounds like "golly shoes," which reminds Gretta of the Christy Minstrels, a popular blackface minstrel show.

—O, for one night, said Mrs. Conroy. Besides, Bessie will look after them.

—To be sure, said Aunt Kate again. What a comfort it is to have a girl like that, one you can depend on! There's that Lily, I'm sure I don't know what has come over her lately. She's not the girl she was at all.

Gabriel was about to ask his aunt some questions on this point but she broke off suddenly to gaze after her sister who had wandered down the stairs and was craning her neck over the banisters.

—Now, I ask you, she said, almost testily, where is Julia going? Julia! Julia! Where are you going?

Julia, who had gone halfway down one flight, came back and announced blandly:

—Here's Freddy.

At the same moment a clapping of hands and a final flourish of the pianist told that the waltz had ended. The drawing-room door was opened from within and some couples came out. Aunt Kate drew Gabriel aside hurriedly and whispered into his ear:

—Slip down, Gabriel, like a good fellow and see if he's all right, and don't let him up if he's screwed. I'm sure he's screwed. I'm sure he is.

Gabriel went to the stairs and listened over the banisters. He could hear two persons talking in the pantry. Then he recognised Freddy Malins' laugh. He went down the stairs noisily.

—It's such a relief, said Aunt Kate to Mrs. Conroy, that Gabriel is here. I always feel easier in my mind when he's here. . . . Julia, there's Miss Daly and Miss Power will take some refreshment. Thanks for your beautiful waltz, Miss Daly. It made lovely time.

A tall wizen-faced man, with a stiff grizzled moustache and swarthy skin, who was passing out with his partner said:

—And may we have some refreshment, too, Miss Morkan?

—Julia, said Aunt Kate summarily, and here's Mr. Browne and Miss Furlong. Take them in, Julia, with Miss Daly and Miss Power.

—I'm the man for the ladies, said Mr. Browne, pursing his lips until his moustache bristled and smiling in all his wrinkles. You know, Miss Morkan, the reason they are so fond of me is—

He did not finish his sentence, but, seeing that Aunt Kate was out of earshot, at once led the three young ladies into the back room. The middle of the room was occupied by two square tables placed end to end, and on these Aunt Julia and the caretaker were straightening and smoothing a large cloth. On the sideboard were arrayed dishes and plates, and glasses and bundles of knives and forks and spoons. The top of the closed square piano served also as a sideboard for viands and sweets. At a smaller sideboard in one corner two young men were standing, drinking hop-bitters.[8]

Mr. Browne led his charges thither and invited them all, in jest, to some ladies' punch, hot, strong and sweet. As they said they never took anything strong he opened three bottles of lemonade for them. Then he asked one of the young men to move aside, and, taking hold of the decanter, filled out for himself a goodly measure of whisky. The young men eyed him respectfully while he took a trial sip.

—God help me, he said, smiling, it's the doctor's orders.

His wizened face broke into a broader smile, and the three young ladies

8. Unfermented beer.

laughed in musical echo to his pleasantry, swaying their bodies to and fro, with nervous jerks of their shoulders. The boldest said:

—O, now, Mr. Browne, I'm sure the doctor never ordered anything of the kind.

Mr. Browne took another sip of his whiskey and said, with sidling mimicry:

—Well, you see, I'm like the famous Mrs. Cassidy, who is reported to have said: *Now, Mary Grimes, if I don't take it, make me take it, for I feel I want it.*

His hot face had leaned forward a little too confidentially and he had assumed a very low Dublin accent so that the young ladies, with one instinct, received his speech in silence. Miss Furlong, who was one of Mary Jane's pupils, asked Miss Daly what was the name of the pretty waltz she had played; and Mr. Browne, seeing that he was ignored, turned promptly to the two young men who were more appreciative.

A red-faced young woman, dressed in pansy,[9] came into the room, excitedly clapping her hands and crying:

—Quadrilles![1] Quadrilles!

Close on her heels came Aunt Kate, crying:

—Two gentlemen and three ladies, Mary Jane!

—O, here's Mr. Bergin and Mr. Kerrigan, said Mary Jane. Mr. Kerrigan, will you take Miss Power? Miss Furlong, may I get you a partner, Mr. Bergin. O, that'll just do now.

—Three ladies, Mary Jane, said Aunt Kate.

The two young gentlemen asked the ladies if they might have the pleasure, and Mary Jane turned to Miss Daly.

—O, Miss Daly, you're really awfully good, after playing for the last two dances, but really we're so short of ladies to-night.

—I don't mind in the least, Miss Morkan.

—But I've a nice partner for you, Mr. Bartell D'Arcy, the tenor. I'll get him to sing later on. All Dublin is raving about him.

—Lovely voice, lovely voice! said Aunt Kate.

As the piano had twice begun the prelude to the first figure Mary Jane led her recruits quickly from the room. They had hardly gone when Aunt Julia wandered slowly into the room, looking behind her at something.

—What is the matter, Julia? asked Aunt Kate anxiously. Who is it?

Julia, who was carrying in a column of table-napkins turned to her sister and said, simply, as if the question had surprised her:

—It's only Freddy, Kate, and Gabriel with him.

In fact right behind her Gabriel could be seen piloting Freddy Malins across the landing. The latter, a young man of forty, was of Gabriel's size and build, with very round shoulders. His face was fleshy and pallid, touched with colour only at the thick hanging lobes of his ears and at the wide wings of his nose. He had coarse features, a blunt nose, a convex and receding brow, tumid and protruded lips. His heavy-lidded eyes and the disorder of his scanty hair made him look sleepy. He was laughing heartily in a high key at a story which he had been telling Gabriel on the stairs and at the same time rubbing the knuckles of his left fist backwards and forwards into his left eye.

—Good-evening, Freddy, said Aunt Julia.

9. Violet. 1. An intricate square dance for four couples.

Freddy Malins bade the Misses Morkan good-evening in what seemed an offhand fashion by reason of the habitual catch in his voice and then, seeing that Mr. Browne was grinning at him from the sideboard, crossed the room on rather shaky legs and began to repeat in an undertone the story he had just told to Gabriel.

—He's not so bad, is he? said Aunt Kate to Gabriel.

Gabriel's brows were dark but he raised them quickly and answered:

—O no, hardly noticeable.

—Now, isn't he a terrible fellow! she said. And his poor mother made him take the pledge on New Year's Eve. But come on, Gabriel, into the drawing-room.

Before leaving the room with Gabriel she signalled to Mr. Browne by frowning and shaking her forefinger in warning to and fro. Mr. Browne nodded in answer and, when she had gone, said to Freddy Malins:

—Now, then, Teddy, I'm going to fill you out a good glass of lemonade just to buck you up.

Freddy Malins, who was nearing the climax of his story, waved the offer aside impatiently but Mr. Browne, having first called Freddy Malins' attention to a disarray in his dress,[2] filled out and handed him a full glass of lemonade. Freddy Malins' left hand accepted the glass mechanically, his right hand being engaged in the mechanical readjustment of his dress. Mr. Browne, whose face was once more wrinkling with mirth, poured out for himself a glass of whisky while Freddy Malins exploded, before he had well reached the climax of his story, in a kink of high-pitched bronchitic laughter and, setting down his untasted and overflowing glass, began to rub the knuckles of his left fist backwards and forwards into his left eye, repeating words of his last phrase as well as his fit of laughter would allow him.

Gabriel could not listen while Mary Jane was playing her Academy piece, full of runs and difficult passages, to the hushed drawing-room. He liked music but the piece she was playing had no melody for him and he doubted whether it had any melody for the other listeners, though they had begged Mary Jane to play something. Four young men, who had come from the refreshment-room to stand in the doorway at the sound of the piano, had gone away quietly in couples after a few minutes. The only persons who seemed to follow the music were Mary Jane herself, her hands racing along the key-board of lifted from it at the pauses like those of a priestess in momentary imprecation, and Aunt Kate standing at her elbow to turn the page.

Gabriel's eyes, irritated by the floor, which glittered with beeswax under the heavy chandelier, wandered to the wall above the piano. A picture of the balcony scene in *Romeo and Juliet* hung there and beside it was a picture of the two murdered princes[3] in the Tower which Aunt Julia had worked in red, blue and brown wools when she was a girl. Probably in the school they had gone to as girls that kind of work had been taught, for one year his mother had worked for him as a birthday present a waistcoat of purple tabinet,[4] with little foxes' heads upon it, lined with brown satin and having round mulberry buttons. It was strange that his mother had had no musical talent though

2. That his fly was open.   3. According to Shakespeare's *Richard III*, the young heirs to the British throne were murdered in the Tower of London by order of their uncle, the future Richard III. *Balcony scene*: Shakespeare's *Romeo and Juliet* 2.2.   4. A damasklike fabric.

Aunt Kate used to call her the brains carrier of the Morkan family. Both she and Julia had always seemed a little proud of their serious and matronly sister. Her photograph stood before the pierglass.[5] She held an open book on her knees and was pointing out something in it to Constantine who, dressed in a man-o'-war suit,[6] lay at her feet. It was she who had chosen the names for her sons for she was very sensible of the dignity of family life. Thanks to her, Constantine was now senior curate in Balbriggan and, thanks to her, Gabriel himself had taken his degree in the Royal University. A shadow passed over his face as he remembered her sullen opposition to his marriage. Some slighting phrases she had used still rankled in his memory; she had once spoken of Gretta as being country cute[7] and that was not true of Gretta at all. It was Gretta who had nursed her during all her last long illness in their house at Monkstown.

He knew that Mary Jane must be near the end of her piece for she was playing again the opening melody with runs of scales after every bar and while he waited for the end the resentment died down in his heart. The piece ended with a trill of octaves in the treble and a final deep octave in the bass. Great applause greeted Mary Jane as, blushing and rolling up her music nervously, she escaped from the room. The most vigorous clapping came from the four young men in the doorway who had gone away to the refreshment-room at the beginning of the piece but had come back when the piano had stopped.

Lancers were arranged. Gabriel found himself partnered with Miss Ivors. She was a frank-mannered talkative young lady, with a freckled face and prominent brown eyes. She did not wear a low-cut bodice and the large brooch which was fixed in the front of her collar bore on it an Irish device.

When they had taken their places she said abruptly:

—I have a crow to pluck[8] with you.

—With me? said Gabriel.

She nodded her head gravely.

—What is it? asked Gabriel, smiling at her solemn manner.

—Who is G. C.? answered Miss Ivors, turning her eyes upon him.

Gabriel coloured and was about to knit his brows, as if he did not understand, when she said bluntly:

—O, innocent Amy! I have found out that you write for *The Daily Express*.[9] Now, aren't you ashamed of yourself?

—Why should I be ashamed of myself? asked Gabriel, blinking his eyes and trying to smile.

—Well, I'm ashamed of you, said Miss Ivors frankly. To say you'd write for a rag like that. I didn't think you were a West Briton.[1]

A look of perplexity appeared on Gabriel's face. It was true that he wrote a literary column every Wednesday in *The Daily Express*, for which he was paid fifteen shillings. But that did not make him a West Briton surely. The books he received for review were almost more welcome than the paltry cheque. He loved to feel the covers and turn over the pages of newly printed books. Nearly every day when his teaching in the college was ended he used to wander down the quays to the second-hand booksellers, to Hickey's on Bachelor's Walk, to Webb's or Massey's on Aston's Quay, or to O'Clohissey's

5. A large mirror. 6. A sailor suit. 7. Unintelligent (not acute). 8. A bone to pick; an argument. 9. Conservative Dublin newspaper opposed to Irish independence. 1. An Irishman who supports union with Britain (an insult).

in the by-street. He did not know how to meet her charge. He wanted to say that literature was above politics. But they were friends of many years' standing and their careers had been parallel, first at the University and then as teachers: he could not risk a grandiose phrase with her. He continued blinking his eyes and trying to smile and murmured lamely that he saw nothing political in writing reviews of books.

When their turn to cross[2] had come he was still perplexed and inattentive. Miss Ivors promptly took his hand in a warm grasp and said in a soft friendly tone:

—Of course, I was only joking. Come, we cross now.

When they were together again she spoke of the University question,[3] and Gabriel felt more at ease. A friend of hers had shown her his review of Browning's poems. That was how she had found out the secret: but she liked the review immensely. Then she said suddenly:

—O, Mr. Conroy, will you come for an excursion to the Aran Isles[4] this summer? We're going to stay there a whole month. It will be splendid out in the Atlantic. You ought to come. Mr. Clancy is coming, and Mr. Kilkelly and Kathleen Kearney. It would be splendid for Gretta too if she'd come. She's from Connacht,[5] isn't she?

—Her people are, said Gabriel shortly.

—But you will come, won't you? said Miss Ivors, laying her warm hand eagerly on his arm.

—The fact is, said Gabriel, I have already arranged to go—

—Go where? asked Miss Ivors.

—Well, you know, every year I go for a cycling tour with some fellows and so—

—But where? asked Miss Ivors.

—Well, we usually go to France or Belgium or perhaps Germany, said Gabriel awkwardly.

—And why do you go to France and Belgium, said Miss Ivors, instead of visiting your own land?

—Well, said Gabriel, it's partly to keep in touch with the languages and partly for a change.

—And haven't you your own language to keep in touch with—Irish? asked Miss Ivors.

—Well, said Gabriel, if it comes to that, you know, Irish is not my language.

Their neighbours had turned to listen to the cross-examination. Gabriel glanced right and left nervously and tried to keep his good humour under the ordeal which was making a blush invade his forehead.

—And haven't you your own land to visit, continued Miss Ivors, that you know nothing of, your own people, and your own country?

—O, to tell you the truth, retorted Gabriel suddenly, I'm sick of my own country, sick of it!

—Why? asked Miss Ivors.

Gabriel did not answer for his retort had heated him.

---

2. A step in the square dance.   3. Controversy over the establishment of Irish Catholic universities to rival the dominant Protestant tradition of Oxford and Cambridge in England, and Trinity College in Dublin.   4. Off the west coast of Ireland, idealized by the nationalists as an example of unspoiled Irish culture and language.   5. The westernmost province of Ireland.

—Why? repeated Miss Ivors.

They had to go visiting together[6] and, as he had not answered her, Miss Ivors said warmly:

—Of course, you've no answer.

Gabriel tried to cover his agitation by taking part in the dance with great energy. He avoided her eyes for he had seen a sour expression on her face. But when they met in the long chain[7] he was surprised to feel his hand firmly pressed. She looked at him from under her brows for a moment quizzically until he smiled. Then, just as the chain was about to start again, she stood on tiptoe and whispered into his ear:

—West Briton!

When the lancers were over Gabriel went away to a remote corner of the room where Freddy Malins' mother was sitting. She was a stout feeble old woman with white hair. Her voice had a catch in it like her son's and she stuttered slightly. She had been told that Freddy had come and that he was nearly all right. Gabriel asked her whether she had had a good crossing. She lived with her married daughter in Glasgow and came to Dublin on a visit once a year. She answered placidly that she had had a beautiful crossing and that the captain had been most attentive to her. She spoke also of the beautiful house her daughter kept in Glasgow, and of all the nice friends they had there. While her tongue rambled on Gabriel tried to banish from his mind all memory of the unpleasant incident with Miss Ivors. Of course the girl or woman, or whatever she was, was an enthusiast but there was a time for all things. Perhaps he ought not to have answered her like that. But she had no right to call him a West Briton before people, even in joke. She had tried to make him ridiculous before people, heckling him and staring at him with her rabbit's eyes.

He saw his wife making her way towards him through the waltzing couples. When she reached him she said into his ear:

—Gabriel, Aunt Kate wants to know won't you carve the goose as usual. Miss Daly will carve the ham and I'll do the pudding.

—All right, said Gabriel.

—She's sending in the younger ones first as soon as this waltz is over so that we'll have the table to ourselves.

—Were you dancing? asked Gabriel.

—Of course I was. Didn't you see me? What words had you with Molly Ivors?

—No words. Why? Did she say so?

—Something like that. I'm trying to get that Mr. D'Arcy to sing. He's full of conceit, I think.

—There were no words, said Gabriel moodily, only she wanted me to go for a trip to the west of Ireland and I said I wouldn't.

His wife clasped her hands excitedly and gave a little jump.

—O, do go, Gabriel, she cried. I'd love to see Galway again.

—You can go if you like, said Gabriel coldly.

She looked at him for a moment, then turned to Mrs. Malins and said:

—There's a nice husband for you, Mrs. Malins.

While she was threading her way back across the room Mrs. Malins, with-

---

6. A square dance step. 7. Another square dance step.

out adverting to the interruption, went on to tell Gabriel what beautiful places there were in Scotland and beautiful scenery. Her son-in-law brought them every year to the lakes and they used to go fishing. Her son-in-law was a splendid fisher. One day he caught a fish, a beautiful big big fish, and the man in the hotel boiled it for their dinner.

Gabriel hardly heard what she said. Now that supper was coming near he began to think again about his speech and about the quotation. When he saw Freddy Malins coming across the room to visit his mother Gabriel left the chair free for him and retired into the embrasure of the window. The room had already cleared and from the back room came the clatter of plates and knives. Those who still remained in the drawing-room seemed tired of dancing and were conversing quietly in little groups. Gabriel's warm trembling fingers tapped the cold pane of the window. How cool it must be outside! How pleasant it would be to walk out alone, first along by the river and then through the park! The snow would be lying on the branches of the trees and forming a bright cap on the top of the Wellington Monument.[8] How much more pleasant it would be there than at the supper-table!

He ran over the headings of his speech: Irish hospitality, sad memories, the Three Graces, Paris,[9] the quotation from Browning. He repeated to himself a phrase he had written in his review: *One feels that one is listening to a thought-tormented music.* Miss Ivors had praised the review. Was she sincere? Had she really any life of her own behind all her propagandism? There had never been any ill-feeling between them until that night. It unnerved him to think that she would be at the supper-table, looking up at him while he spoke with her critical quizzing eyes. Perhaps she would not be sorry to see him fail in his speech. An idea came into his mind and gave him courage. He would say, alluding to Aunt Kate and Aunt Julia: *Ladies and Gentlemen, the generation which is now on the wane among us may have had its faults but for my part I think it had certain qualities of hospitality, of humour, of humanity, which the new and very serious and hypereducated generation that is growing up around us seems to me to lack.* Very good: that was one for Miss Ivors. What did he care that his aunts were only two ignorant old women?

A murmur in the room attracted his attention. Mr. Browne was advancing from the door, gallantly escorting Aunt Julia, who leaned upon his arm, smiling and hanging her head. An irregular musketry of applause escorted her also as far as the piano and then, as Mary Jane seated herself on the stool, and Aunt Julia, no longer smiling, half turned so as to pitch her voice fairly into the room, gradually ceased. Gabriel recognized the prelude. It was that of an old song of Aunt Julia's—*Arrayed for the Bridal.*[1] Her voice, strong and clear in tone, attacked with great spirit the runs which embellish the air and though she sang very rapidly she did not miss even the smallest of the grace notes. To follow the voice, without looking at the singer's face, was to feel and share the excitement of swift and secure flight. Gabriel applauded loudly with all the others at the close of the song and loud applause was borne in from the invisible supper-table. It sounded so genuine that a little colour struggled into Aunt Julia's face as she bent to replace in the music-

8. A tall obelisk in Phoenix Park, celebrating the duke of Wellington (1769–1852).   9. The Trojan prince of Homer's *Iliad*. *Three Graces:* daughters of Zeus and Eurynome in Greek mythology; they embodied (and bestowed) charm.   1. An English lyric by George Linley, drawn from the first act of Vincenzo Bellini's 1835 opera *I Puritani* (The puritans).

stand the old leather-bound song-book that had her initials on the cover. Freddy Malins, who had listened with his head perched sideways to hear her better, was still applauding when everyone else had ceased and talking animatedly to his mother who nodded her head gravely and slowly in acquiescence. At last, when he could clap no more, he stood up suddenly and hurried across the room to Aunt Julia whose hand he seized and held in both his hands, shaking it when words failed him or the catch in his voice proved too much for him.

—I was just telling my mother, he said, I never heard you sing so well, never. No, I never heard your voice so good as it is to-night. Now! Would you believe that now? That's the truth. Upon my word and honour that's the truth. I never heard your voice sound so fresh and so . . . so clear and fresh, never.

Aunt Julia smiled broadly and murmured something about compliments as she released her hand from his grasp. Mr. Browne extended his open hand towards her and said to those who were near him in the manner of a showman introducing a prodigy to an audience:

—Miss Julia Morkan, my latest discovery!

He was laughing very heartily at this himself when Freddy Malins turned to him and said:

—Well, Browne, if you're serious you might make a worse discovery. All I can say is I never heard her sing half so well as long as I am coming here. And that's the honest truth.

—Neither did I, said Mr. Browne. I think her voice has greatly improved.

Aunt Julia shrugged her shoulders and said with meek pride:

—Thirty years ago I hadn't a bad voice as voices go.

—I often told Julia, said Aunt Kate emphatically, that she was simply thrown away in that choir. But she never would be said by me.

She turned as if to appeal to the good sense of the others against a refractory child while Aunt Julia gazed in front of her, a vague smile of reminiscence playing on her face.

—No, continued Aunt Kate, she wouldn't be said or led by anyone, slaving there in that choir night and day, night and day. Six o'clock on Christmas morning! And all for what?

—Well, isn't it for the honour of God, Aunt Kate? asked Mary Jane, twisting round on the piano-stool and smiling.

Aunt Kate turned fiercely on her niece and said:

—I know all about the honour of God, Mary Jane, but I think it's not at all honourable for the pope to turn out the women out of the choirs that have slaved there all their lives and put little whipper-snappers of boys over their heads.[2] I suppose it is for the good of the Church if the pope does it. But it's not just, Mary Jane, and it's not right.

She had worked herself into a passion and would have continued in defence of her sister for it was a sore subject with her but Mary Jane, seeing that all the dancers had come back, intervened pacifically:

—Now, Aunt Kate, you're giving scandal to Mr. Browne who is of the other persuasion.

Aunt Kate turned to Mr. Browne, who was grinning at this allusion to his religion, and said hastily:

---

2. In 1903, Pope Pius X decreed that all church singers should be male.

—O, I don't question the pope's being right. I'm only a stupid old woman and I wouldn't presume to do such a thing. But there's such a thing as common everyday politeness and gratitude. And if I were in Julia's place I'd tell that Father Healy straight up to his face . . .

—And besides, Aunt Kate, said Mary Jane, we really are all hungry and when we are hungry we are all very quarrelsome.

—And when we are thirsty we are also quarrelsome, added Mr. Browne.

—So that we had better go to supper, said Mary Jane, and finish the discussion afterwards.

On the landing outside the drawing-room Gabriel found his wife and Mary Jane trying to persuade Miss Ivors to stay for supper. But Miss Ivors, who had put on her hat and was buttoning her cloak, would not stay. She did not feel in the least hungry and she had already overstayed her time.

—But only for ten minutes, Molly, said Mrs. Conroy. That won't delay you.

—To take a pick itself, said Mary Jane, after all your dancing.

—I really couldn't, said Miss Ivors.

—I am afraid you didn't enjoy yourself at all, said Mary Jane hopelessly.

—Ever so much, I assure you, said Miss Ivors, but you really must let me run off now.

—But how can you get home? asked Mrs. Conroy.

—O, it's only two steps up the quay.

Gabriel hesitated a moment and said:

—If you will allow me, Miss Ivors, I'll see you home if you really are obliged to go.

But Miss Ivors broke away from them.

—I won't hear of it, she cried. For goodness sake go in to your suppers and don't mind me. I'm quite well able to take care of myself.

—Well, you're the comical girl, Molly, said Mrs. Conroy frankly.

—*Beannacht libh*,[3] cried Miss Ivors, with a laugh, as she ran down the staircase.

Mary Jane gazed after her, a moody puzzled expression on her face, while Mrs. Conroy leaned over the banisters to listen for the hall-door. Gabriel asked himself was he the cause of her abrupt departure. But she did not seem to be in ill humour: she had gone away laughing. He stared blankly down the staircase.

At that moment Aunt Kate came toddling out of the supper-room, almost wringing her hands in despair.

—Where is Gabriel? she cried. Where on earth is Gabriel? There's everyone waiting in there, stage to let, and nobody to carve the goose!

—Here I am, Aunt Kate! cried Gabriel, with sudden animation, ready to carve a flock of geese, if necessary.

A fat brown goose lay at one end of the table and at the other end, on a bed of creased paper strewn with sprigs of parsley, lay a great ham, stripped of its outer skin and peppered over with crust crumbs, a neat paper frill round its shin and beside this was a round of spiced beef. Between these rival ends ran parallel lines of side-dishes: two little minsters[4] of jelly, red and yellow; a shallow dish full of blocks of blancmange and red jam, a large green leaf-shaped dish with a stalk-shaped handle, on which lay bunches of purple

---

3. Farewell; blessings on you (Irish).   4. Confectionaries shaped to look like cathedrals.

raisins and peeled almonds, a companion dish on which lay a solid rectangle of Smyrna figs, a dish of custard topped with grated nutmeg, a small bowl full of chocolates and sweets wrapped in gold and silver papers and a glass vase in which stood some tall celery stalks. In the center of the table there stood, as sentries to a fruit-stand which upheld a pyramid of oranges and American apples, two squat old-fashioned decanters of cut glass, one containing port and the other dark sherry. On the closed square piano a pudding in a huge yellow dish lay in waiting and behind it were three squads of bottles of stout and ale and minerals,[5] drawn up according to the colours of their uniforms, the first two black, with brown and red labels, the third and smallest squad white, with transverse green sashes.

Gabriel took his seat boldly at the head of the table and, having looked to the edge of the carver, plunged his fork firmly into the goose. He felt quite at ease now for he was an expert carver and liked nothing better than to find himself at the head of a well-laden table.

—Miss Furlong, what shall I send you? he asked. A wing or a slice of the breast?

—Just a small slice of the breast.

—Miss Higgins, what for you?

—O, anything at all, Mr. Conroy.

While Gabriel and Miss Daly exchanged plates of goose and plates of ham and spiced beef Lily went from guest to guest with a dish of hot floury potatoes wrapped in a white napkin. This was Mary Jane's idea and she had also suggested apple sauce for the goose but Aunt Kate had said that plain roast goose without apple sauce had always been good enough for her and she hoped she might never eat worse. Mary Jane waited on her pupils and saw that they got the best slices and Aunt Kate and Aunt Julia opened and carried across from the piano bottles of stout and ale for the gentlemen and bottles of minerals for the ladies. There was a great deal of confusion and laughter and noise, the noise of orders and counter-orders, of knives and forks, of corks and glassstoppers. Gabriel began to carve second helpings as soon as he had finished the first round without serving himself. Everyone protested loudly so that he compromised by taking a long draught of stout for he had found the carving hot work. Mary Jane settled down quietly to her supper but Aunt Kate and Aunt Julia were still toddling round the table, walking on each other's heels, getting in each other's way and giving each other unheeded orders. Mr. Browne begged of them to sit down and eat their suppers and so did Gabriel but they said there was time enough so that, at last, Freddy Malins stood up and, capturing Aunt Kate, plumped her down on her chair amid general laughter.

When everyone had been well served Gabriel said, smiling:

—Now, if anyone wants a little more of what vulgar people call stuffing let him or her speak.

A chorus of voices invited him to begin his own supper and Lily came forward with three potatoes which she had reserved for him.

—Very well, said Gabriel amiably, as he took another preparatory draught, kindly forget my existence, ladies and gentlemen, for a few minutes.

He sat to his supper and took no part in the conversation with which the table covered Lily's removal of the plates. The subject of talk was the opera company which was then at the Theatre Royal. Mr. Bartell D'Arcy, the tenor, a dark-complexioned young man with a smart moustache, praised very highly the leading contralto of the company but Miss Furlong thought she had a rather vulgar style of production. Freddy Malins said there was a negro chieftain[6] singing in the second part of the Gaiety pantomime who had one of the finest tenor voices he had ever heard.

—Have you heard him? he asked Mr. Bartell D'Arcy across the table.

—No, answered Mr. Bartell D'Arcy carelessly.

—Because, Freddy Malins explained, now I'd be curious to hear your opinion of him. I think he has a grand voice.

—It takes Teddy to find out the really good things, said Mr. Browne familiarly to the table.

—And why couldn't he have a voice too? asked Freddy Malins sharply. Is it because he's only a black?

Nobody answered this question and Mary Jane led the table back to the legitimate opera. One of her pupils had given her a pass for *Mignon*.[7] Of course it was very fine, she said, but it made her think of poor Georgina Burns. Mr. Browne could go back farther still, to the old Italian companies that used to come to Dublin—Tietjens, Ilma de Murzka, Campanini, the great Trebelli, Giuglini, Ravelli, Aramburo.[8] Those were the days, he said, when there was something like singing to be heard in Dublin. He told too of how the top gallery of the old Royal used to be packed night after night, of how one night an Italian tenor had sung five encores to *Let Me Like a Soldier Fall*,[9] introducing a high C every time, and of how the gallery boys would sometimes in their enthusiasm unyoke the horses from the carriage of some great *prima donna* and pull her themselves through the streets to her hotel. Why did they never play the grand old operas now, he asked, *Dinorah, Lucrezia Borgia*?[1] Because they could not get the voices to sing them: that was why.

—O, well, said Mr. Bartell D'Arcy, I presume there are as good singers today as there were then.

—Where are they? asked Mr. Browne defiantly.

—In London, Paris, Milan, said Mr. Bartell D'Arcy warmly. I suppose Caruso,[2] for example, is quite as good, if not better than any of the men you have mentioned.

—Maybe so, said Mr. Browne. But I may tell you I doubt it strongly.

—O, I'd give anything to hear Caruso sing, said Mary Jane.

—For me, said Aunt Kate, who had been picking a bone, there was only one tenor. To please me, I mean. But I suppose none of you ever heard of him.

—Who was he, Miss Morkan? asked Mr. Bartell D'Arcy politely.

—His name, said Aunt Kate, was Parkinson. I heard him when he was in his prime and I think he had then the purest tenor voice that was ever put into a man's throat.

—Strange, said Mr. Bartell D'Arcy. I never even heard of him.

—Yes, yes, Miss Morkan is right, said Mr. Browne. I remember hearing of old Parkinson but he's too far back for me.

—A beautiful pure sweet mellow English tenor, said Aunt Kate with enthusiasm.

Gabriel having finished, the huge pudding was transferred to the table.

6. Actually, a blackface performer.   7. Popular French opera (1866) by Ambroise Thomas.   8. Famous opera singers.   9. From William V. Wallace's romantic light opera *Maritana* (1845).   1. Operas by Giacomo Meyerbeer (1859) and Gaetani Donizetti (1833), respectively.   2. Enrico Caruso (1873–1921).

The clatter of forks and spoons began again. Gabriel's wife served out spoon-fuls of the pudding and passed the plates down the table. Midway down they were held up by Mary Jane, who replenished them with raspberry or orange jelly or with blancmange and jam. The pudding was of Aunt Julia's making and she received praises for it from all quarters. She herself said that it was not quite brown enough.

—Well, I hope, Miss Morkan, said Mr. Browne, that I'm brown enough for you because, you know, I'm all brown.

All the gentlemen, except Gabriel, ate some of the pudding out of com-pliment to Aunt Julia. As Gabriel never ate sweets the celery had been left for him. Freddy Malins also took a stalk of celery and ate it with his pudding. He had been told that celery was a capital thing for the blood and he was just then under doctor's care. Mrs. Malins, who had been silent all through the supper, said that her son was going down to Mount Melleray[3] in a week or so. The table then spoke of Mount Melleray, how bracing the air was down there, how hospitable the monks were and how they never asked for a penny-piece from their guests.

—And do you mean to say, asked Mr. Browne incredulously, that a chap can go down there and put up there as if it were a hotel and live on the fat of the land and then come away without paying a farthing?

—O, most people give some donation to the monastery when they leave, said Mary Jane.

—I wish we had an institution like that in our Church, said Mr. Browne candidly.

He was astonished to hear that the monks never spoke, got up at two in the morning and slept in their coffins.[4] He asked what they did it for.

—That's the rule of the order, said Aunt Kate firmly.

—Yes, but why? asked Mr. Browne.

Aunt Kate repeated that it was the rule, that was all. Mr. Browne still seemed not to understand. Freddy Malins explained to him, as best he could, that the monks were trying to make up for the sins committed by all the sinners in the outside world. The explanation was not very clear for Mr. Browne grinned and said:

—I like that idea very much but wouldn't a comfortable spring bed do them as well as a coffin?

—The coffin, said Mary Jane, is to remind them of their last end.

As the subject had grown lugubrious it was buried in a silence of the table during which Mrs. Malins could be heard saying to her neighbour in an indistinct undertone:

—They are very good men, the monks, very pious men.

The raisins and almonds and figs and apples and oranges and chocolates and sweets were now passed about the table and Aunt Julia invited all the guests to have either port or sherry. At first Mr. Bartell D'Arcy refused to take either but one of his neighbours nudged him and whispered something to him upon which he allowed his glass to be filled. Gradually as the last glasses were being filled the conversation ceased. A pause followed, broken only by the noise of the wine and by unsettlings of chairs. The Misses Mor-

---

3. A Trappist abbey whose hospitality included the treatment of wealthy alcoholics.   4. The coffin story is a popular fiction.

kan, all three, looked down at the tablecloth. Someone coughed once or twice and then a few gentlemen patted the table gently as a signal for silence. The silence came and Gabriel pushed back his chair and stood up.

The patting at once grew louder in encouragement and then ceased altogether. Gabriel leaned his ten trembling fingers on the tablecloth and smiled nervously at the company. Meeting a row of upturned faces he raised his eyes to the chandelier. The piano was playing a waltz tune and he could hear the skirts sweeping against the drawing-room door. People, perhaps, were standing in the snow on the quay outside, gazing up at the lighted windows and listening to the waltz music. The air was pure there. In the distance lay the park where the trees were weighted with snow. The Wellington Monument wore a gleaming cap of snow that flashed westward over the white field of Fifteen Acres.[5]

He began:

—Ladies and Gentlemen.

—It has fallen to my lot this evening, as in years past, to perform a very pleasing task but a task for which I am afraid my poor powers as a speaker are all too inadequate.

—No, no! said Mr. Browne.

—But, however that may be, I can only ask you to-night to take the will for the deed and to lend me your attention for a few moments while I endeavour to express to you in words what my feelings are on this occasion.

—Ladies and Gentlemen. It is not the first time that we have gathered together under this hospitable roof, around this hospitable board. It is not the first time that we have been the recipients—or perhaps, I had better say, the victims—of the hospitality of certain good ladies.

He made a circle in the air with his arm and paused. Everyone laughed or smiled at Aunt Kate and Aunt Julia and Mary Jane who all turned crimson with pleasure. Gabriel went on more boldly:

—I feel more strongly with every recurring year that our country has no tradition which does it so much honour and which it should guard so jealously as that of its hospitality. It is a tradition that is unique as far as my experience goes (and I have visited not a few places abroad) among the modern nations. Some would say, perhaps, that with us it is rather a failing than anything to be boasted of. But granted even that, it is, to my mind, a princely failing, and one that I trust will long be cultivated among us. Of one thing, at least, I am sure. As long as this one roof shelters the good ladies aforesaid—and I wish from my heart it may do so for many and many a long year to come—the tradition of genuine warm-hearted courteous Irish hospitality, which our forefathers have handed down to us and which we in turn must hand down to our descendants, is still alive among us.

A hearty murmur of assent ran around the table. It shot through Gabriel's mind that Miss Ivors was not there and that she had gone away discourteously: and he said with confidence in himself:

—Ladies and Gentlemen.

—A new generation is growing up in our midst, a generation actuated by new ideas and new principles. It is serious and enthusiastic for these new ideas and its enthusiasm, even when it is misdirected, is, I believe, in the

5. A section of Phoenix Park used for British military reviews.

main sincere. But we are living in a skeptical and, if I may use the phrase, a thought-tormented age: and sometimes I fear that this new generation, educated or hypereducated as it is, will lack those qualities of humanity, of hospitality, of kindly humour which belonged to an older day. Listening tonight to the names of all those great singers of the past it seemed to me, I must confess, that we were living in a less spacious age. Those days might, without exaggeration, be called spacious days: and if they are gone beyond recall let us hope, at least, that in gatherings such as this we shall still speak of them with pride and affection, still cherish in our hearts the memory of those dead and gone great ones whose fame the world will not willingly let die.

—Hear, hear! said Mr. Browne loudly.

—But yet, continued Gabriel, his voice falling into a softer inflection, there are always in gatherings such as this sadder thoughts that will recur to our minds: thoughts of the past, of youth, of changes, of absent faces that we miss here tonight. Our path through life is strewn with many such sad memories: and were we to brood upon them always we could not find the heart to go on bravely with our work among the living. We have all of us living duties and living affections which claim, and rightly claim, our strenuous endeavours.

—Therefore, I will not linger on the past. I will not let any gloomy moralising intrude upon us here to-night. Here we are gathered together for a brief moment from the bustle and rush of our everyday routine. We are met here as friends, in the spirit of good-fellowship, as colleagues, also to a certain extent, in the true spirit of *camaraderie*, and as the guests of—what shall I call them?—the Three Graces of the Dublin musical world.

The table burst into applause and laughter at this sally. Aunt Julia vainly asked each of her neighbours in turn to tell her what Gabriel had said.

—He says we are the Three Graces, Aunt Julia, said Mary Jane.

Aunt Julia did not understand but she looked up, smiling, at Gabriel, who continued in the same vein:

—Ladies and Gentlemen.

—I will not attempt to play to-night the part that Paris played on another occasion.[6] I will not attempt to choose between them. The task would be an invidious one and one beyond my poor powers. For when I view them in turn, whether it be our chief hostess herself, whose good heart, whose too good heart, has become a byword with all who know her, or her sister, who seems to be gifted with perennial youth and whose singing must have been a surprise and a revelation to us all to-night, or, last but not least, when I consider our youngest hostess, talented, cheerful, hard-working and the best of nieces, I confess, Ladies and Gentlemen, that I do not know to which of them I should award the prize.

Gabriel glanced down at his aunts and, seeing the large smile on Aunt Julia's face and the tears which had risen to Aunt Kate's eyes, hastened to his close. He raised his glass of port gallantly, while every member of the company fingered a glass expectantly, and said loudly:

—Let us toast them all three together. Let us drink to their health, wealth, long life, happiness and prosperity and may they long continue to hold the proud and self-won position which they hold in their profession and the position of honour and affection which they hold in our hearts.

6. Paris was required to judge a beauty contest between the Greek goddesses Hera, Athena, and Aphrodite; see n. 9, p. 1597.

All the guests stood up, glass in hand, and, turning towards the three seated ladies, sang in unison, with Mr. Browne as leader:

> *For they are jolly gay fellows,*
> *For they are jolly gay fellows,*
> *For they are jolly gay fellows,*
> *Which nobody can deny.*

Aunt Kate was making frank use of her handkerchief and even Aunt Julia seemed moved. Freddy Malins beat time with his pudding-fork and the singers turned towards one another, as if in melodious conference, while they sang, with emphasis:

> *Unless he tells a lie,*
> *Unless he tells a lie.*

Then, turning once more towards their hostesses, they sang:

> *For they are jolly gay fellows,*
> *For they are jolly gay fellows,*
> *For they are jolly gay fellows,*
> *Which nobody can deny.*

The acclamation which followed was taken up beyond the door of the supper-room by many of the other guests and renewed time after time, Freddy Malins acting as officer with his fork on high.

The piercing morning air came into the hall where they were standing so that Aunt Kate said:

—Close the door, somebody. Mrs. Malins will get her death of cold.

—Browne is out there, Aunt Kate, said Mary Jane.

—Browne is everywhere, said Aunt Kate, lowering her voice.

Mary Jane laughed at her tone.

—Really, she said archly, he is very attentive.

—He has been laid on here like the gas, said Aunt Kate in the same tone, all during the Christmas.

She laughed herself this time good-humouredly and then added quickly:

—But tell him to come in, Mary Jane, and close the door. I hope to goodness he didn't hear me.

At that moment the hall-door was opened and Mr. Browne came in from the doorstep, laughing as if his heart would break. He was dressed in a long green overcoat with mock astrakhan cuffs and collar and wore on his head an oval fur cap. He pointed down the snow-covered quay from where the sound of shrill prolonged whistling was borne in.

—Teddy will have all the cabs in Dublin out, he said.

Gabriel advanced from the little pantry behind the office, struggling into his overcoat and, looking round the hall, said:

—Gretta not down yet?

—She's getting on her things, Gabriel, said Aunt Kate.

—Who's playing up there? asked Gabriel.

—Nobody. They're all gone.

—O no, Aunt Kate, said Mary Jane. Bartell D'Arcy and Miss O'Callaghan aren't gone yet.

—Someone is strumming at the piano, anyhow, said Gabriel.

Mary Jane glanced at Gabriel and Mr. Browne and said with a shiver:

—It makes me feel cold to look at you two gentlemen muffled up like that. I wouldn't like to face your journey home at this hour.

—I'd like nothing better this minute, said Mr. Browne stoutly, than a rattling fine walk in the country or a fast drive with a good spanking goer between the shafts.

—We used to have a very good horse and trap at home, said Aunt Julia sadly.

—The never-to-be-forgotten Johnny, said Mary Jane, laughing.

Aunt Kate and Gabriel laughed too.

—Why, what was wonderful about Johnny? asked Mr. Browne.

—The late lamented Patrick Morkan, our grandfather, that is, explained Gabriel, commonly known in his later years as the old gentleman, was a glue-boiler.

—O, now, Gabriel, said Aunt Kate, laughing, he had a starch mill.

—Well, glue or starch, said Gabriel, the old gentleman had a horse by the name of Johnny. And Johnny used to work in the old gentleman's mill, walking round and round in order to drive the mill. That was all very well; but now comes the tragic part about Johnny. One fine day the old gentleman thought he'd like to drive out with the quality to a military review in the park.

—The Lord have mercy on his soul, said Aunt Kate compassionately.

—Amen, said Gabriel. So the old gentleman, as I said, harnessed Johnny and put on his very best tall hat and his very best stock collar and drove out in grand style from his ancestral mansion somewhere near Back Lane,[7] I think.

Everyone laughed, even Mrs. Malins, at Gabriel's manner and Aunt Kate said:

—O now, Gabriel, he didn't live in Back Lane, really. Only the mill was there.

—Out from the mansion of his forefathers, continued Gabriel, he drove with Johnny. And everything went on beautifully until Johnny came in sight of King Billy's[8] statue: and whether he fell in love with the horse King Billy sits on or whether he thought he was back again in the mill, anyhow he began to walk round the statue.

Gabriel paced in a circle round the hall in his goloshes amid the laughter of the others.

—Round and round he went, said Gabriel, and the old gentleman, who was a very pompous old gentleman, was highly indignant. *Go on, sir! What do you mean, sir? Johnny! Johnny! Most extraordinary conduct! Can't understand the horse!*

The peals of laughter which followed Gabriel's imitation of the incident were interrupted by a resounding knock at the hall-door. Mary Jane ran to open it and let in Freddy Malins. Freddy Malins, with his hat well back on his head and his shoulders humped with cold, was puffing and steaming after his exertions.

—I could only get one cab, he said.

—O, we'll find another along the quay, said Gabriel.

—Yes, said Aunt Kate. Better not keep Mrs. Malins standing in the draught.

---

7. A shabby street in a run-down area of Dublin.   8. William III, king of England from 1689 to 1702, defeated the Irish nationalists at the Battle of the Boyne.

Mrs. Malins was helped down the front steps by her son and Mr. Browne and, after many manœuvres, hoisted into the cab. Freddy Malins clambered in after her and spent a long time settling her on the seat, Mr. Browne helping him with advice. At last she was settled comfortably and Freddy Malins invited Mr. Browne into the cab. There was a good deal of confused talk, and then Mr. Browne got into the cab. The cabman settled his rug over his knees, and bent down for the address. The confusion grew greater and the cabman was directed differently by Freddy Malins and Mr. Browne, each of whom had his head out through a window of the cab. The difficulty was to know where to drop Mr. Browne along the route and Aunt Kate, Aunt Julia and Mary Jane helped the discussion from the doorstep with cross-directions and contradictions and abundance of laughter. As for Freddy Malins he was speechless with laughter. He popped his head in and out of the window every moment, to the great danger of his hat, and told his mother how the discussion was progressing till at last Mr. Browne shouted to the bewildered cabman above the din of everybody's laughter:

—Do you know Trinity College?

—Yes, sir, said the cabman.

—Well, drive bang up against Trinity College gates, said Mr. Browne, and then we'll tell you where to go. You understand now?

—Yes, sir, said the cabman.

—Make like a bird for Trinity College.

—Right, sir, cried the cabman.

The horse was whipped up and the cab rattled off along the quay amid a chorus of laughter and adieus.

Gabriel had not gone to the door with the others. He was in a dark part of the hall gazing up the staircase. A woman was standing near the top of the first flight, in the shadow also. He could not see her face but he could see the terracotta and salmonpink panels of her skirt which the shadow made appear black and white. It was his wife. She was leaning on the banisters, listening to something. Gabriel was surprised at her stillness and strained his ear to listen also. But he could hear little save the noise of laughter and dispute on the front steps, a few chords struck on the piano and a few notes of a man's voice singing.

He stood still in the gloom of the hall, trying to catch the air that the voice was singing and gazing up at his wife. There was grace and mystery in her attitude as if she were a symbol of something. He asked himself what is a woman standing on the stairs in the shadow, listening to distant music, a symbol of. If he were a painter he would paint her in that attitude. Her blue felt hat would show off the bronze of her hair against the darkness and the dark panels of her skirt would show off the light ones. *Distant Music* he would call the picture if he were a painter.

The hall-door was closed; and Aunt Kate, Aunt Julia and Mary Jane came down the hall, still laughing.

—Well, isn't Freddy terrible? said Mary Jane. He's really terrible.

Gabriel said nothing but pointed up the stairs towards where his wife was standing. Now that the hall-door was closed the voice and the piano could be heard more clearly. Gabriel held up his hand for them to be silent. The song seemed to be in the old Irish tonality[9] and the singer seemed uncertain

---

9. Based on five (and later seven) tones rather than the modern eight-tone scale.

both of his words and of his voice. The voice, made plaintive by distance and by the singer's hoarseness, faintly illuminated the cadence of the air with words expressing grief:

> O, the rain falls on my heavy locks
> And the dew wets my skin,
> My babe lies cold[1] . . .

—O, exclaimed Mary Jane. It's Bartell D'Arcy singing and he wouldn't sing all the night. O, I'll get him to sing a song before he goes.

—O do, Mary Jane, said Aunt Kate.

Mary Jane brushed past the others and ran to the staircase but before she reached it the singing stopped and the piano was closed abruptly.

—O, what a pity! she cried. Is he coming down, Gretta?

Gabriel heard his wife answer yes and saw her come down towards them. A few steps behind her were Mr. Bartell D'Arcy and Miss O'Callaghan.

—O, Mr. D'Arcy, cried Mary Jane, it's downright mean of you to break off like that when we were all in raptures listening to you.

—I have been at him all the evening, said Miss O'Callaghan, and Mrs. Conroy too and he told us he had a dreadful cold and couldn't sing.

—O, Mr. D'Arcy, said Aunt Kate, now that was a great fib to tell.

—Can't you see that I'm as hoarse as a crow? said Mr. D'Arcy roughly.

He went into the pantry hastily and put on his overcoat. The others, taken aback by his rude speech, could find nothing to say. Aunt Kate wrinkled her brows and made signs to the others to drop the subject. Mr. D'Arcy stood swathing his neck carefully and frowning.

—It's the weather, said Aunt Julia, after a pause.

—Yes, everybody has colds, said Aunt Kate readily, everybody.

—They say, said Mary Jane, we haven't had snow like it for thirty years; and I read this morning in the newspapers that the snow is general all over Ireland.

—I love the look of snow, said Aunt Julia sadly.

—So do I, said Miss O'Callaghan. I think Christmas is never really Christmas unless we have the snow on the ground.

—But poor Mr. D'Arcy doesn't like the snow, said Aunt Kate, smiling.

Mr. D'Arcy came from the pantry, fully swathed and buttoned, and in a repentant tone told them the history of his cold. Everyone gave him advice and said it was a great pity and urged him to be very careful of his throat in the night air. Gabriel watched his wife who did not join in the conversation. She was standing right under the dusty fanlight and the flame of the gas lit up the rich bronze of her hair which he had seen her drying at the fire a few days before. She was in the same attitude and seemed unaware of the talk about her. At last she turned towards them and Gabriel saw that there was colour on her cheeks and that her eyes were shining. A sudden tide of joy went leaping out of his heart.

—Mr. D'Arcy, she said, what is the name of that song you were singing?

—It's called *The Lass of Aughrim*, said Mr. D'Arcy, but I couldn't remember it properly. Why? Do you know it?

---

1. From "The Lass of Aughrim," a ballad about a peasant girl seduced by a lord; when she brings her baby to the castle door, the lord's mother imitates his voice and sends her away. Mother and child are drowned at sea, and the repentant lord curses his mother.

—*The Lass of Aughrim*, she repeated. I couldn't think of the name.

—It's a very nice air, said Mary Jane. I'm sorry you were not in voice to-night.

—Now, Mary Jane, said Aunt Kate, don't annoy Mr. D'Arcy. I won't have him annoyed.

Seeing that all were ready to start she shepherded them to the door where good-night was said:

—Well, good-night, Aunt Kate, and thanks for the pleasant evening.

—Good-night, Gabriel. Good-night, Gretta!

—Good-night, Aunt Kate, and thanks ever so much. Good-night, Aunt Julia.

—O, good-night, Gretta, I didn't see you.

—Good-night, Mr. D'Arcy. Good-night, Miss O'Callaghan.

—Good-night, Miss Morkan.

—Good-night, again.

—Good-night, all. Safe home.

—Good-night. Good-night.

The morning was still dark. A dull yellow light brooded over the houses and the river; and the sky seemed to be descending. It was slushy underfoot; and only streaks and patches of snow lay on the roofs, on the parapets of the quay and on the area railings. The lamps were still burning redly in the murky air and, across the river, the palace of the Four Courts[2] stood out menacingly against the heavy sky.

She was walking on before him with Mr. Bartell D'Arcy, her shoes in a brown parcel tucked under one arm and her hands holding her skirt up from the slush. She had no longer any grace of attitude but Gabriel's eyes were still bright with happiness. The blood went bounding along his veins; and the thoughts went rioting through his brain, proud, joyful, tender, valorous.

She was walking on before him so lightly and so erect that he longed to run after her noiselessly, catch her by the shoulders and say something foolish and affectionate into her ear. She seemed to him so frail that he longed to defend her against something and then to be alone with her. Moments of their secret life together burst like stars upon his memory. A heliotrope envelope was lying beside his breakfast-cup and he was caressing it with his hand. Birds were twittering in the ivy and the sunny web of the curtain was shimmering along the floor: he could not eat for happiness. They were standing on the crowded platform and he was placing a ticket inside the warm palm of her glove. He was standing with her in the cold, looking in through a grated window at a man making bottles in a roaring furnace. It was very cold. Her face, fragrant in the cold air, was quite close to his; and suddenly she called out to the man at the furnace:

—Is the fire hot, sir?

But the man could not hear her with the noise of the furnace. It was just as well. He might have answered rudely.

A wave of yet more tender joy escaped from his heart and went coursing in warm flood along his arteries. Like the tender fires of stars moments of their life together, that no one knew of or would ever know of, broke upon and illumined his memory. He longed to recall to her those moments, to

2. The Irish law courts building.

make her forget the years of their dull existence together and remember only their moments of ecstasy. For the years, he felt, had not quenched his soul or hers. Their children, his writing, her household cares had not quenched all their souls' tender fire. In one letter that he had written to her then he had said: *Why is it that words like these seem to me so dull and cold? Is it because there is no word tender enough to be your name?*

Like distant music these words that he had written years before were borne towards him from the past. He longed to be alone with her. When the others had gone away, when he and she were in their room in the hotel, then they would be alone together. He would call her softly:

—Gretta!

Perhaps she would not hear at once: she would be undressing. Then something in his voice would strike her. She would turn and look at him.

At the corner of Winetavern Street they met a cab. He was glad of its rattling noise as it saved him from conversation. She was looking out of the window and seemed tired. The others spoke only a few words, pointing out some building or street. The horse galloped along wearily under the murky morning sky, dragging his old rattling box after his heels, and Gabriel was again in a cab with her, galloping to catch the boat, galloping to their honeymoon.

As the cab drove across O'Connell Bridge Miss O'Callaghan said:

—They say you never cross O'Connell Bridge without seeing a white horse.

—I see a white man this time, said Gabriel.

—Where? asked Mr. Bartell D'Arcy.

Gabriel pointed to the statue,[3] on which lay patches of snow. Then he nodded familiarly to it and waved his hand.

—Good-night, Dan, he said gaily.

When the cab drew up before the hotel Gabriel jumped out and, in spite of Mr. Bartell D'Arcy's protest, paid the driver. He gave the man a shilling over his fare. The man saluted and said:

—A prosperous New Year to you, sir.

—The same to you, said Gabriel cordially.

She leaned for a moment on his arm in getting out of the cab and while standing at the curbstone, bidding the others good-night. She leaned lightly on his arm, as lightly as when she had danced with him a few hours before. He had felt proud and happy then, happy that she was his, proud of her grace and wifely carriage. But now, after the kindling again of so many memories, the first touch of her body, musical and strange and perfumed, sent through him a keen pang of lust. Under cover of her silence he pressed her arm closely to his side; and, as they stood at the hotel door, he felt that they had escaped from their lives and duties, escaped from home and friends and run away together with wild and radiant hearts to a new adventure.

An old man was dozing in a great hooded chair in the hall. He lit a candle in the office and went before them to the stairs. They followed him in silence, their feet falling in soft thuds on the thickly carpeted stairs. She mounted the stairs behind the porter, her head bowed in the ascent, her frail shoulders curved as with a burden, her skirt girt tightly about her. He could have flung his arms about her hips and held her still for his arms were trembling with

3. Of Daniel O'Connell (1775–1847), called "The Liberator" by the Irish independence movement.

desire to seize her and only the stress of his nails against the palms of his hands held the wild impulse of his body in check. The porter halted on the stairs to settle his guttering candle. They halted too on the steps below him. In the silence Gabriel could hear the falling of the molten wax into the tray and the thumping of his own heart against his ribs.

The porter led them along a corridor and opened a door. Then he set his unstable candle down on a toilet-table and asked at what hour they were to be called in the morning.

—Eight, said Gabriel.

The porter pointed to the tap of the electric-light and began a muttered apology but Gabriel cut him short.

—We don't want any light. We have light enough from the street. And I say, he added, pointing to the candle, you might remove that handsome article, like a good man.

The porter took up his candle again, but slowly for he was surprised by such a novel idea. Then he mumbled good-night and went out. Gabriel shot the lock to.

A ghostly light from the street lamp lay in a long shaft from one window to the door. Gabriel threw his overcoat and hat on a couch and crossed the room towards the window. He looked down into the street in order that his emotion might calm a little. Then he turned and leaned against a chest of drawers with his back to the light. She had taken off her hat and cloak and was standing before a large swinging mirror, unhooking her waist.[4] Gabriel paused for a few moments, watching her, and then said:

—Gretta!

She turned away from the mirror slowly and walked along the shaft of light towards him. Her face looked so serious and weary that the words would not pass Gabriel's lips. No, it was not the moment yet.

—You looked tired, he said.

—I am a little, she answered.

—You don't feel ill or weak?

—No, tired: that's all.

She went on to the window and stood there, looking out. Gabriel waited again and then, fearing that diffidence was about to conquer him, he said abruptly:

—By the way, Gretta!

—What is it?

—You know that poor fellow Malins? he said quickly.

—Yes. What about him?

—Well, poor fellow, he's a decent sort of chap after all, continued Gabriel in a false voice. He gave me back that sovereign I lent him and I didn't expect it really. It's a pity he wouldn't keep away from that Browne, because he's not a bad fellow at heart.

He was trembling now with annoyance. Why did she seem so abstracted? He did not know how he could begin. Was she annoyed, too, about something? If she would only turn to him or come to him of her own accord! To take her as she was would be brutal. No, he must see some ardour in her eyes first. He longed to be master of her strange mood.

4. I.e., loosening her waistband.

—When did you lend him the pound? she asked, after a pause.

Gabriel stove to restrain himself from breaking out into brutal language about the sottish Malins and his pound. He longed to cry to her from his soul, to crush her body against his, to overmaster her. But he said:

—O, at Christmas, when he opened that little Christmas-card shop in Henry Street.

He was in such a fever of rage and desire that he did not hear her come from the window. She stood before him for an instant, looking at him strangely. Then, suddenly raising herself on tiptoe and resting her hands lightly on his shoulders, she kissed him.

—You are a very generous person, Gabriel, she said.

Gabriel, trembling with delight at her sudden kiss and at the quaintness of her phrase, put his hands on her hair and began smoothing it back, scarcely touching it with his fingers. The washing had made it fine and brilliant. His heart was brimming over with happiness. Just when he was wishing for it she had come to him of her own accord. Perhaps her thoughts had been running with his. Perhaps she had felt the impetuous desire that was in him and then the yielding mood had come upon her. Now that she had fallen to him so easily he wondered why he had been so diffident.

He stood, holding her head between his hands. Then, slipping one arm swiftly about her body and drawing her towards him, he said softly:

—Gretta dear, what are you thinking about?

She did not answer nor yield wholly to his arm. He said again, softly:

—Tell me what it is, Gretta. I think I know what is the matter. Do I know?

She did not answer at once. Then she said in an outburst of tears:

—O, I am thinking about that song, *The Lass of Aughrim*.

She broke loose from him and ran to the bed and, throwing her arms across the bed-rail, hid her face. Gabriel stood stock-still for a moment in astonishment and then followed her. As he passed in the way of the cheval-glass he caught sight of himself in full length, his broad, well-filled shirt-front, the face whose expression always puzzled him when he saw it in a mirror and his glimmering gilt-rimmed eyeglasses. He halted a few paces from her and said:

—What about the song? Why does that make you cry?

She raised her head from her arms and dried her eyes with the back of her hand like a child. A kinder note than he had intended went into his voice.

—Why, Gretta? he asked.

—I am thinking about a person long ago who used to sing that song.

—And who was the person long ago? asked Gabriel, smiling.

—It was a person I used to know in Galway when I was living with my grandmother, she said.

The smile passed away from Gabriel's face. A dull anger began to gather again at the back of his mind and the dull fires of his lust began to glow angrily in his veins.

—Someone you were in love with? he asked ironically.

—It was a young boy I used to know, she answered, named Michael Furey. He used to sing that song, *The Lass of Aughrim*. He was very delicate.

Gabriel was silent. He did not wish her to think that he was interested in this delicate boy.

—I can see him so plainly, she said after a moment. Such eyes as he had: big dark eyes! And such an expression in them—an expression!

—O then, you were in love with him? said Gabriel.

—I used to go out walking with him,[5] she said, when I was in Galway. A thought flew across Gabriel's mind.

—Perhaps that was why you wanted to go to Galway with that Ivors girl? he said coldly.

She looked at him and asked in surprise:

—What for?

Her eyes made Gabriel feel awkward. He shrugged his shoulders and said:

—How do I know? To see him perhaps.

She looked away from him along the shaft of light towards the window in silence.

—He is dead, she said at length. He died when he was only seventeen. Isn't it a terrible thing to die so young as that?

—What was he? asked Gabriel, still ironically.

—He was in the gasworks,[6] she said.

Gabriel felt humiliated by the failure of his irony and by the evocation of this figure from the dead, a boy in the gasworks. While he had been full of memories of their secret life together, full of tenderness and joy and desire, she had been comparing him in her mind with another. A shameful consciousness of his own person assailed him. He saw himself as a ludicrous figure, acting as a pennyboy[7] for his aunts, a nervous well-meaning sentimentalist, orating to vulgarians and idealising his own clownish lusts, the pitiable fatuous fellow he had caught a glimpse of in the mirror. Instinctively he turned his back more to the light lest she might see the shame that burned upon his forehead.

He tried to keep up his tone of cold interrogation but his voice when he spoke was humble and indifferent.

—I suppose you were in love with this Michael Furey, Gretta, he said.

—I was great[8] with him at that time, she said.

Her voice was veiled and sad. Gabriel, feeling now how vain it would be to try to lead her whither he had purposed, caressed one of her hands and said, also sadly:

—And what did he die of so young, Gretta? Consumption, was it?

—I think he died for me, she answered.

A vague terror seized Gabriel at this answer as if, at that hour when he had hoped to triumph, some impalpable and vindictive being was coming against him, gathering forces against him in its vague world. But he shook himself free of it with an effort of reason and continued to caress her hand. He did not question her again for he felt that she would tell him of herself. Her hand was warm and moist: it did not respond to his touch but he continued to caress it just as he had caressed her first letter to him that spring morning.

—It was in the winter, she said, about the beginning of the winter when I was going to leave my grandmother's and come up here to the convent. And he was ill at the time in his lodgings in Galway and wouldn't be let out and his people in Oughterard[9] were written to. He was in decline, they said, or something like that. I never knew rightly.

She paused for a moment and sighed.

---

5. I.e., she dated him.   6. A utilities plant that manufactured coal gas. Working there was an unhealthy occupation.   7. Errand boy.   8. Close friends.   9. A small village in western Ireland.

—Poor fellow, she said. He was very fond of me and he was such a gentle boy. We used to go out together, walking, you know, Gabriel, like the way they do in the country. He was going to study singing only for his health. He had a very good voice, poor Michael Furey.

—Well; and then? asked Gabriel.

—And then when it came to the time for me to leave Galway and come up to the convent he was much worse and I wouldn't be let see him so I wrote a letter saying I was going up to Dublin and would be back in the summer and hoping he would be better then.

She paused for a moment to get her voice under control and then went on:

—Then the night before I left I was in my grandmother's house in Nun's Island,[1] packing up, and I heard gravel thrown up against the window. The window was so wet I couldn't see so I ran downstairs as I was and slipped out the back into the garden and there was the poor fellow at the end of the garden, shivering.

—And did you not tell him to go back? asked Gabriel.

—I implored of him to go home at once and told him he would get his death in the rain. But he said he did not want to live. I can see his eyes as well as well! He was standing at the end of the wall where there was a tree.

—And did he go home? asked Gabriel.

—Yes, he went home. And when I was only a week in the convent he died and he was buried in Oughterard where his people came from. O, the day I heard that, that he was dead!

She stopped, choking with sobs, and, overcome by emotion, flung herself face downward on the bed, sobbing in the quilt. Gabriel held her hand for a moment longer, irresolutely, and then, shy of intruding on her grief, let it fall gently and walked quietly to the window.

She was fast asleep.

Gabriel, leaning on his elbow, looked for a few moments unresentfully on her tangled hair and half-open mouth, listening to her deep-drawn breath. So she had had that romance in her life: a man had died for her sake. It hardly pained him now to think how poor a part he, her husband, had played in her life. He watched her while she slept as though he and she had never lived together as man and wife. His curious eyes rested long upon her face and on her hair: and, as he thought of what she must have been then, in that time of her first girlish beauty, a strange friendly pity for her entered his soul. He did not like to say even to himself that her face was no longer beautiful but he knew that it was no longer the face for which Michael Furey had braved death.

Perhaps she had not told him all the story. His eyes moved to the chair over which she had thrown some of her clothes. A petticoat string dangled to the floor. One boot stood upright, its limp upper fallen down: the fellow of it lay upon its side. He wondered at his riot of emotions of an hour before. From what had it proceeded? From his aunt's supper, from his own foolish speech, from the wine and dancing, the merrymaking when saying goodnight in the hall, the pleasure of the walk along the river in the snow. Poor

1. An island in the western city of Galway, on which is located the Convent of Poor Clares.

Aunt Julia! She, too, would soon be a shade with the shade of Patrick Morkan and his horse. He had caught that haggard look upon her face for a moment when she was singing *Arrayed for the Bridal*. Soon, perhaps, he would be sitting in that same drawing-room, dressed in black, his silk hat on his knees. The blinds would be drawn down and Aunt Kate would be sitting beside him, crying and blowing her nose and telling him how Julia had died. He would cast about in his mind for some words that might console her, and would find only lame and useless ones. Yes, yes: that would happen very soon.

The air of the room chilled his shoulders. He stretched himself cautiously along under the sheets and lay down beside his wife. One by one they were all becoming shades. Better pass boldly into that other world, in the full glory of some passion, than fade and wither dismally with age. He thought of how she who lay beside him had locked in her heart for so many years that image of her lover's eyes when he had told her that he did not wish to live.

Generous tears filled Gabriel's eyes. He had never felt like that himself towards any woman but he knew that such a feeling must be love. The tears gathered more thickly in his eyes and in the partial darkness he imagined he saw the form of a young man standing under a dripping tree. Other forms were near. His soul had approached that region where dwell the vast hosts of the dead. He was conscious of, but could not apprehend, their wayward and flickering existence. His own identity was fading out into a grey impalpable world: the solid world itself which these dead had one time reared and lived in was dissolving and dwindling.

A few light taps upon the pane made him turn to the window. It had begun to snow again. He watched sleepily the flakes, silver and dark, falling obliquely against the lamplight. The time had come for him to set out on his journey westward. Yes, the newspapers were right: snow was general all over Ireland. It was falling on every part of the dark central plain, on the treeless hills, falling softly upon the Bog of Allen and, farther westward, softly falling into the dark mutinous Shannon[2] waves. It was falling, too, upon every part of the lonely churchyard on the hill where Michael Furey lay buried. It lay thickly drifted on the crooked crosses and headstones, on the spears of the little gate, on the barren thorns. His soul swooned slowly as he heard the snow falling faintly through the universe and faintly falling, like the descent of their last end, upon all the living and the dead.

2. An estuary of the Shannon River, west-southwest of Dublin. The Bog of Allen is southwest of Dublin.

VIRGINIA WOOLF
1882–1941

Virginia Woolf did more than write innovative novels that stand on a par with those of Joyce and Proust; she also explained and exemplified a new kind of prose that she associated with feminine consciousness. Woolf is known for her precise evocations of states of mind—or of mind and body, since she refused to separate the two. She structures her novels according to her protagonists' moments of awareness, and in that way joins Proust and Joyce in their move away from the linear plots and objective descriptions of nineteenth-century realism. In novels like *Mrs. Dalloway* and *The Waves,* blocks of time are rearranged, different points of view juxtaposed, and incomplete perspectives set against each other to create a larger pattern. Alternating modes of narration prevent any single reference point and remind the reader that subjectivity is always at work, in literature and in everyday life. Woolf has an additional role in modernist literary history: she was an ardent feminist who explored—directly in her essays and indirectly in her novels and short stories—the situation of women in society, the construction of gender identity, and the predicament of the woman writer.

She was born Adeline Virginia Stephen on January 25, 1882, one of the four children of the eminent Victorian editor and historian Leslie Stephen and his wife, Julia. The family actively pursued intellectual and artistic interests, and Julia was admired and sketched by some of the most famous Pre-Raphaelite artists. Following the customs of the day, only the sons, Adrian and Thoby, were given formal and university education; Virginia and her sister, Vanessa (the painter Vanessa Bell), were instructed at home by their parents and depended for further education on their father's immense library. Virginia bitterly resented this unequal treatment and the systematic discouragement of women's intellectual development that it implied. Throughout her own work, themes of society's different attitudes toward men and women play a strong role, especially in *A Room of One's Own* (1929) and *Three Guineas* (1938). *A Room of One's Own* examines the history of literature written by women and contains also an impassioned plea that women writers be given conditions equal to those available for men: specifically, the privacy of a room in which to write and economic independence. (At the time Woolf wrote, it was unusual for women to have any money of their own or to be able to devote themselves to a career.) After her mother's death in 1895, Woolf was expected to take over the supervision of the family household, which she did until her father's death in 1904. Of fragile physical health after an attack of whooping cough when she was six, she suffered in addition a nervous breakdown after the death of each parent.

Woolf moved to central London with her sister and brother Adrian after their father's death, and took a house in the Bloomsbury district. They soon became the focus of what was later called the Bloomsbury Group, a gathering of writers, artists, and intellectuals impatient with conservative Edwardian society, who met regularly to discuss new ideas. It was an eclectic group and included the novelist E. M. Forster, the historian Lytton Strachey, the economist John Maynard Keynes, and the art critics Clive Bell (who married Vanessa) and Roger Fry (who introduced the group to postimpressionist painters such as Édouard Manet and Paul Cézanne). Woolf was not yet writing fiction, but contributed reviews to the *Times Literary Supplement,* taught literature and composition at Morley College (an institution with a volunteer faculty that provided educational opportunities for workers), and worked for the adult suffrage movement and a feminist group. In 1912 she married Leonard Woolf, who encouraged her to write and with whom she founded the Hogarth Press in 1917. The press became one of the most respected of the small literary presses and published works by such major authors as T. S. Eliot, Katherine Mansfield, Strachey, Forster, Maxim Gorky, and John Middleton Murry as well as Woolf's own novels and translations of Freud. Over the next two decades she produced her best-known work while coping with frequent bouts of physical and mental illness. Already depressed during World War II and exhausted after the completion of her last novel, *Between the Acts* (1941), she sensed the approach of a serious attack of insanity and the confinement it would entail: in such situations, she was obliged to "rest" and forbidden to read or write. In March 1941, she drowned herself in a river close to her Sussex home.

As a fiction writer, Woolf is best known for her poetic evocations of the way we think and feel. Like Proust and Joyce, she is superbly capable of evoking all the concrete, sensuous details of everyday experience; like them, she explores the structures of consciousness. Her rejection of nineteenth-century realism was not a criticism of the great realist novels like *Madame Bovary;* she turned her attention to more recent and derivative writers. What she really deplored was the microscopic, documentary realism that contemporaries like Arnold Bennett and John Galsworthy drew from the nineteenth-century masters. Their contemporary pretense of scientific objectivity was false, she felt: they claimed to stand outside the scene they described but refused to take into account the fact that there are no neutral observers. Worse, their goal of scientific objectivity often resulted in a mere chronological accumulation of details, the "appalling narrative business of . . . getting from lunch to dinner." Woolf had an explanation for this documentary style: she attributed it to a consciously masculine (or patriarchal) perspective that found security only in logic, order, and the accumulation of knowledge. She proposed, in contrast, a more subjective and, therefore, a more accurate account of experience. Her focus was not so much the object under observation as the way the observer perceived that object: "Let us record the atoms as they fall upon the mind in the order in which they fall, let us trace the pattern, however disconnected and incoherent in appearance, which each sight or incident scores upon the consciousness." Such writing, underwritten by a feminine creative consciousness, would open new avenues for modern literature.

Woolf's writing has been compared with postimpressionist art in the way that it emphasizes the abstract arrangement of perspectives to suggest additional networks of meaning. After two relatively traditional novels, she began to develop a more flexible approach that openly manipulated fictional structure. The continuously developing plot gave way to an organization by juxtaposed points of view; the experience of "real" or chronological time was displaced (although not completely) by a mind ranging ambiguously among its memories; and an intricate pattern of symbolic themes connected otherwise unrelated characters in the same story. All these techniques made new demands on the reader's ability to synthesize and re-create a whole picture. In *Jacob's Room* (1922), a picture of the hero must be assembled from a series of partial points of view. In *The Waves* (1931), the multiple perspective of different characters soliloquizing on their relationship to the dead Percival is broken by ten interludes that together construct an additional, interacting perspective when they describe the passage of a single day from dawn to dusk. Her novels may expand or telescope the sense of time: *Mrs. Dalloway* (1925) focuses apparently on Clarissa Dalloway's preparations for a party that evening but at the same time calls up—at different times, and according to different contexts—her whole life from childhood to her present age of fifty. Problems of identity are a constant concern in these shifting perspectives, and Woolf often portrays the search of unfulfilled personalities for whatever will complete them. Her work is studded with moments of heightened awareness (comparable to Joyce's epiphanies) in which a character suddenly *sees into* a person or situation. With Woolf, this moment is less a matter of mystical insight (as it is with Joyce) than a creation of the mind using all its faculties.

No one can read Woolf without being struck by the importance she gives to the creative imagination. Her major characters display a sensitivity beyond rational logic, and her narrative style celebrates the aesthetic impulse to coordinate many dimensions inside one harmoniously significant whole. Human beings are not complete, Woolf suggests, without exercising their intuitive and imaginative faculties. Like other modernist writers, she is fascinated by the creative process and often makes reference to it in her work. Whether describing the struggles of a painter in *To the Lighthouse* (1927) or of a writer in the story *An Unwritten Novel,* she illustrates the exploratory and the creative work of human imagination. Not all this work is visible in the finished painting or novel: observing, sifting, coordinating, projecting different interpretations and relationships, the mind performs an enormous labor of coordinating consciousness that cannot be captured entirely in any fixed form.

A Room of One's Own itself does not conform to any one fixed form. At once lecture and essay, autobiography and fiction, it originated in a pair of lectures on women and fiction given at Newnham and Girton Colleges (for women) at Cambridge University in 1928. Woolf warns her audience that, instead of defining either women or fiction, she will use "all the liberties and licenses of a novelist" to get at the matter obliquely, and leave her auditors to sort out the truth from the "lies [that] will flow from my lips." She will, she claims, retrace the days (that is, the narrator's days) preceding her visit, and lay bare the thought processes leading up to the lecture itself. The lecture, which is now identical with the thought processes leading up to it, is cast in the form of a meditative ramble through various parts of Oxbridge (a compound of Oxford and Cambridge Universities) and London. It includes the famous (and apparently true) anecdote in which she is warned off the university lawn and forbidden entrance to the library because she is a woman; a vivid contrast of the food and living quarters of women and men at Oxbridge; a literary history of English women writers and their socioeconomic situations; a concluding speculation on the androgynous nature of creativity with an exhortation to her young audience to write about the rich yet unrecorded experience of women; and, of course, the central chapters, printed here, that describe her research into definitions of women and offer the celebrated portrait of Judith Shakespeare.

In chapter 2, the narrator heads for the British Museum to locate a comprehensive definition of femininity. To her surprise and mounting anger, she discovers that the thousands of books on the subject written by fascinated men all define women as inferior animals, useful but somewhat alien in nature. Moreover, these same definitions have become prescriptions for generations of young women who learn to see themselves and their place in life accordingly. Raised in poverty and dependence, such women have neither the means nor the self-confidence to write seriously or to become anything other than the Victorian "Angel of the House." What they require, asserts the narrator, is the self-sufficiency brought by an annual income of five hundred pounds. (Woolf had recently inherited such an income.) Chapter 3 pursues similar themes, adding to the five hundred pounds the need for "a room of one's own" and the privacy necessary to follow out an idea. Moving to history, and focusing on the Elizabethan age after a discouraging inspection of Professor Trevelyan's *History of England*, it evokes the career of the "terribly gifted" Judith Shakespeare, William's imaginary sister. Judith has the same literary and dramatic ambitions as her brother, and she too finds her way to London, but she is blocked at each turn by her identity as a woman. Woolf does not belittle William Shakespeare with this contrast; instead, her narrator remarks meaningfully that his work reveals an "incandescent, unimpeded mind."

The bleak portrayals in these chapters are lightened by a great deal of satirical wit and humor, often conveyed by calculated fictional distortion. Woolf uses her novelist's license to subvert and criticize the patriarchal message she describes. The Reading Room of the British Museum, august repository of masculine knowledge about women, is seen as a (bald-headed) dome crowned with the names of famous men. The narrator's scholarly seeming list of feminine characteristics is not only amusingly biased but contradictory and incoherent; it implies that the "masculine" passion for lists and documentation is not the best way to learn about human nature. Professor von X.'s portrait is an open caricature linked to suggestions that his scientific disdain hides repressed fear and anger. *A Room of One's Own* is still famous for its vivid, scathing, and occasionally humorous portrayal of women as objects of male definition and disapproval. Its model of a feminine literary history, and its hypothesis of a separate feminine consciousness and manner of writing have had substantial influence on writers and literary theory in the latter half of the twentieth century.

Phyllis Rose, *Woman of Letters: A Life of Virginia Woolf* (1978), is a valuable biography; Edward Bishop, *Virginia Woolf* (1991), is a recent brief introduction. Two valuable collections of essays on Woolf's writing and her position in the modernist/postmodernist tradition are Patricia Clements and Isobel Grundy, eds., *Virginia Woolf: New Critical Essays* (1983), and Margaret Homans, ed., *Virginia Woolf: A*

Collection of Critical Essays (1993). Jane Marcus, *Virginia Woolf and the Language of Patriarchy* (1987), and Rachel Bowlby, *Feminist Destinations and Further Essays on Virginia Woolf* (1997), offer perceptive feminist analyses that include discussion of *A Room of One's Own*. Mark Hussey and Vara Neverow, eds., *Virginia Woolf: Emerging Perspectives* (1994), contains several essays on *A Room of One's Own*. S. P. Rosenbaum, ed., *Virginia Woolf: Women and Fiction* (1992), transcribes and edits two draft manuscripts that are the basis for *A Room of One's Own*. Gillian Beer, *Virginia Woolf: The Common Ground* (1996), offers four useful general essays and four discussions of specific novels. Patricia Ondek Laurence situates Woolf in *The Reading of Silence: Virginia Woolf in the English Tradition* (1991); comparative studies include Richard Pearce, *The Politics of Narration: James Joyce, William Faulkner, and Virginia Woolf* (1991).

From A Room of One's Own

CHAPTER TWO

The scene, if I may ask you to follow me, was now changed. The leaves were still falling, but in London now, not Oxbridge;[1] and I must ask you to imagine a room, like many thousands, with a window looking across people's hats and vans and motor-cars to other windows, and on the table inside the room a blank sheet of paper on which was written in large letters WOMEN AND FICTION, but no more. The inevitable sequel to lunching and dining at Oxbridge seemed, unfortunately, to be a visit to the British Museum. One must strain off what was personal and accidental in all these impressions and so reach the pure fluid, the essential oil of truth. For that visit to Oxbridge and the luncheon and the dinner had started a swarm of questions. Why did men drink wine and women water? Why was one sex so prosperous and the other so poor? What effect has poverty on fiction? What conditions are necessary for the creation of works of art?—a thousand questions at once suggested themselves. But one needed answers, not questions; and an answer was only to be had by consulting the learned and the unprejudiced, who have removed themselves above the strife of tongue and the confusion of body and issued the result of their reasoning and research in books which are to be found in the British Museum. If truth is not to be found on the shelves of the British Museum, where, I asked myself, picking up a notebook and a pencil, is truth?

Thus provided, thus confident and enquiring, I set out in the pursuit of truth. The day, though not actually wet, was dismal, and the streets in the neighborhood of the Museum were full of open coal-holes, down which sacks were showering; four-wheeled cabs were drawing up and depositing on the pavement corded boxes containing, presumably, the entire wardrobe of some Swiss or Italian family seeking fortune or refuge or some other desirable commodity which is to be found in the boarding-houses of Bloomsbury[2] in the winter. The usual hoarse-voiced men paraded the streets with plants on barrows. Some shouted; others sang. London was like a workshop. London was like a machine. We were all being shot backwards and forwards on this

---

1. A fictional university combining the names of Oxford and Cambridge Universities in England. It was at Cambridge University in October 1928 that Woolf delivered the talks titled "Women and Fiction" that later became *A Room of One's Own*.　　**2.** A residential and academic borough in London, site of the British Museum and various educational institutions.

plain foundation to make some pattern. The British Museum was another department of the factory. The swing-doors swung open; and there one stood under the vast dome, as if one were a thought in the huge bald forehead which is so splendidly encircled by a band of famous names.[3] One went to the counter; one took a slip of paper; one opened a volume of the catalogue, and . . . . . the five dots here indicate five separate minutes of stupefaction, wonder and bewilderment. Have you any notion how many books are written about women in the course of one year? Have you any notion how many are written by men? Are you aware that you are, perhaps, the most discussed animal in the universe? Here had I come with a notebook and a pencil proposing to spend a morning reading, supposing that at the end of the morning I should have transferred the truth to my notebook. But I should need to be a herd of elephants, I thought, and a wilderness of spiders, desperately referring to the animals that are reputed longest lived and most multitudinously eyed, to cope with all this. I should need claws of steel and beak of brass even to penetrate the husk. How shall I ever find the grains of truth embedded in all this mass of paper, I asked myself, and in despair began running my eye up and down the long list of titles. Even the names of the books gave me food for thought. Sex and its nature might well attract doctors and biologists; but what was surprising and difficult of explanation was the fact that sex—woman, that is to say—also attracts agreeable essayists, light-fingered novelists, young men who have taken the M.A. degree; men who have taken no degree; men who have no apparent qualification save that they are not women. Some of these books were, on the face of it, frivolous and facetious; but many, on the other hand, were serious and prophetic, moral and hortatory. Merely to read the titles suggested innumerable schoolmasters, innumerable clergymen mounting their platforms and pulpits and holding forth with a loquacity which far exceeded the hour usually allotted to such discourse on this one subject. It was a most strange phenomenon; and apparently—here I consulted the letter M—one confined to male sex. Women do not write books about men—a fact that I could not help welcoming with relief, for if I had first to read all that men have written about women, then all that women have written about men, the aloe that flowers once in a hundred years would flower twice before I could set pen to paper. So, making a perfectly arbitrary choice of a dozen volumes or so, I sent my slips of paper to lie in the wire tray, and waited in my stall, among the other seekers for the essential oil of truth.

What could be the reason, then, of this curious disparity, I wondered, drawing cart-wheels on the slips of paper provided by the British taxpayer for other purposes. Why are women, judging from this catalogue, so much more interesting to men than men are to women? A very curious fact it seemed, and my mind wandered to picture the lives of men who spend their time in writing books about women; whether they were old or young, married or unmarried, red-nosed or humpbacked—anyhow, it was flattering, vaguely, to feel oneself the object of such attention, provided that it was not entirely bestowed by the crippled and the infirm—so I pondered until all such frivolous thoughts were ended by an avalanche of books sliding down on to the desk in front of me. Now the trouble began. The student who has been

3. The names of famous men, including Chaucer, Spenser, Shakespeare, Milton, Pope, Wordsworth, Byron, Carlyle, and Tennyson, are painted in a circle around the dome of the Reading Room at the British Museum.

trained in research at Oxbridge has no doubt some method of shepherding his question past all distractions till it runs into its answer as a sheep runs into its pen. The student by my side, for instance, who was copying assiduously from a scientific manual was, I felt sure, extracting pure nuggets of the essential ore every ten minutes or so. His little grunts of satisfaction indicated so much. But if, unfortunately, one has had no training in a university, the question far from being shepherded to its pen flies like a frightened flock hither and thither, helter-skelter, pursued by a whole pack of hounds. Professors, schoolmasters, sociologists, clergymen, novelists, essayists, journalists, men who had no qualification save that they were not women, chased my simple and single question—Why are women poor?—until it became fifty questions; until the fifty questions leapt frantically into mid-stream and were carried away. Every page in my notebook was scribbled over with notes. To show the state of mind I was in, I will read you a few of them, explaining that the page was headed quite simply, WOMEN AND POVERTY, in block letters; but what followed was something like this:

Condition in Middle Ages of,
Habits in the Fiji Islands of,
Worshipped as goddesses by,
Weaker in moral sense than,
Idealism of,
Greater conscientiousness of,
South Sea Islanders, age of puberty among,
Attractiveness of,
Offered as sacrifice to,
Small size of brain of,
Profounder sub-consciousness of,
Less hair on the body of,
Mental, moral and physical inferiority of,
Love of children of,
Greater length of life of,
Weaker muscles of,
Strength of affections of,
Vanity of,
Higher education of,
Shakespeare's opinion of,
Lord Birkenhead's opinion of,
Dean Inge's opinion of,
La Bruyère's opinion of,
Dr. Johnson's opinion of,
Mr. Oscar Browning's[4] opinion of, . . .

Here I drew breath and added, indeed, in the margin, Why does Samuel Butler[5] say, "Wise men never say what they think of women"? Wise men never say anything else apparently. But, I continued, leaning back in my chair and looking at the vast dome in which I was a single but by now some-

4. A schoolmaster and later fellow of King's College, Cambridge (1837–1923); anecdotes about his strong opinions (see p. 1636) were published in a 1927 biography. The first earl of Birkenhead, F. E. Smith (1872–1930), a conservative politician who opposed women's suffrage and praised the domestic "true functions of womanhood." William Ralph Inge (1860–1954), dean of St. Paul's Cathedral in London and a religious writer. Jean de La Bruyère (1645–1696), French moralist and author of satirical *Characters* (1688), imitating the Greek writer Theophrastus. Samuel Johnson (1709–1784), author of moral essays and of the famous *A Dictionary of the English Language* (1747). 5. Satirical author (1835–1902) who wrote *Erewhon* (1872) and *The Way of All Flesh* (1903); his *Notebooks* are the source of this statement.

what harassed thought, what is so unfortunate is that wise men never think
the same thing about women. Here is Pope:[6]

Most women have no character at all.

And here is La Bruyère:

Les femmes sont extrêmes; elles sont meilleures ou pires que les hom-
mes—[7]

a direct contradiction by keen observers who were contemporary. Are they
capable of education or incapable? Napoleon thought them incapable.[8] Dr.
Johnson thought the opposite.[9] Have they souls or have they not souls? Some
savages say they have none. Others, on the contrary, maintain that women
are half divine and worship them on that account.[1] Some sages hold that
they are shallower in the brain; others that they are deeper in the consciousness. Goethe honoured them; Mussolini[2] despises them. Wherever one
looked men thought about women and thought differently. It was impossible
to make head or tail of it all, I decided, glancing with envy at the reader next
door who was making the neatest abstracts, headed often with an A or a B
or a C, while my own notebook rioted with the wildest scribble of contradictory jottings. It was distressing, it was bewildering, it was humiliating. Truth
had run through my fingers. Every drop had escaped.

I could not possibly go home, I reflected, and add as a serious contribution
to the study of women and fiction that women have less hair on their bodies
than men, or that the age of puberty among the South Sea Islanders[3] is
nine—or is it ninety?—even the handwriting had become in its distraction
indecipherable. It was disgraceful to have nothing more weighty or respectable to show after a whole morning's work. And if I could not grasp the truth
about W. (as for brevity's sake I had come to call her) in the past, why bother
about W. in the future? It seemed pure waste of time to consult all those
gentlemen who specialise in woman and her effect on whatever it may be—
politics, children, wages, morality—numerous and learned as they are. One
might as well leave their books unopened.

But while I pondered I had unconsciously, in my listlessness, in my desperation, been drawing a picture where I should, like my neighbour, have
been writing a conclusion. I had been drawing a face, a figure. It was the
face and the figure of Professor von X. engaged in writing his monumental
work entitled *The Mental, Moral, and Physical Inferiority of the Female*

6. Alexander Pope (1688–1744), translator of Homer and author of *An Essay on Man* (1733–34) and the
satirical *The Rape of the Lock* (1712–14).   7. Women are extreme; they are better or worse than men
(French).   8. Napoleon wrote: "What we ask of education is not that girls should think, but that they
should believe. The weakness of women's brains, the instability of their ideas, the place they will fill in
society, their need for perpetual resignation, and for an easy and generous type of charity—all this can only
be met by religion" (notes written on May 15, 1807, concerning the establishment of a girl's school at
Écouen).   9. " 'Men know that women are an overmatch for them, and therefore they choose the weakest
or the most ignorant. If they did not think so, they never could be afraid of women knowing as much as
themselves.' . . . In justice to the sex, I think it but candid to acknowledge that, in a subsequent conversation, he told me that he was serious in what he said."—BOSWELL, *The Journal of a Tour to the Hebrides*
[Woolf's note].   1. "The ancient Germans believed that there was something holy in women, and accordingly consulted them as oracles."—FRAZER, *Golden Bough* [Woolf's note].   2. Benito Mussolini (1883–
1945), Fascist dictator of Italy between 1922 and 1943. Johann Wolfgang von Goethe (1749–1832),
German author of *Faust*. "The eternal feminine draws us along" is the last line of *Faust*, Part 2.   3. The
native peoples of the islands in the south-central Pacific Ocean were the subject of several anthropological
studies in the early twentieth century, including Margaret Mead's widely read *Coming of Age in Samoa*
(1928).

Sex.[4] He was not in my picture a man attractive to women. He was heavily built; he had a great jowl; to balance that he had very small eyes; he was very red in the face. His expression suggested that he was labouring under some emotion that made him jab his pen on the paper as if he were killing some noxious insect as he wrote, but even when he had killed it that did not satisfy him; he must go on killing it; and even so, some cause for anger and irritation remained. Could it be his wife, I asked, looking at my picture. Was she in love with a cavalry officer? Was the cavalry officer slim and elegant and dressed in astrachan?[5] Had he been laughed at, to adopt the Freudian theory, in his cradle by a pretty girl? For even in his cradle the professor, I thought, could not have been an attractive child. Whatever the reason, the professor was made to look very angry and very ugly in my sketch, as he wrote his great book upon the mental, moral and physical inferiority of women. Drawing pictures was an idle way of finishing an unprofitable morning's work. Yet it is in our idleness, in our dreams, that the submerged truth sometimes comes to the top. A very elementary exercise in psychology, not to be dignified by the name of psycho-analysis, showed me, on looking at my notebook, that the sketch of the angry professor had been made in anger. Anger had snatched my pencil while I dreamt. But what was anger doing there? Interest, confusion, amusement, boredom—all these emotions I could trace and name as they succeeded each other throughout the morning. Had anger, the black snake, been lurking among them? Yes, said the sketch, anger had. It referred me unmistakably to the one book, to the one phrase, which had roused the demon; it was the professor's statement about the mental, moral and physical inferiority of women. My heart had leapt. My cheeks had burnt. I had flushed with anger. There was nothing specially remarkable, however foolish, in that. One does not like to be told that one is naturally the inferior of a little man— I looked at the student next me—who breathes hard, wears a ready-made tie, and has not shaved this fortnight. One has certain foolish vanities. It is only human nature, I reflected, and began drawing cart-wheels and circles over the angry professor's face till he looked like a burning bush or a flaming comet—anyhow, an apparition without human semblance or significance. The professor was nothing now but a faggot burning on the top of Hampstead Heath.[6] Soon my own anger was explained and done with; but curiosity remained. How explain the anger of the professors? Why were they angry? For when it came to analysing the impression left by these books there was always an element of heat. This heat took many forms; it showed itself in satire, in sentiment, in curiosity, in reprobation. But there was another element which was often present and could not immediately be identified. Anger, I called it. But it was anger that had gone underground and mixed itself with all kinds of other emotions. To judge from its odd effects, it was anger disguised and complex, not anger simple and open.

Whatever the reason, all these books,[7] I thought, surveying the pile on the

4. A fictional portrait, probably based on Otto Weininger's *Sex and Character* (1906), that distinguished between male (productive and moral) and female (negative and amoral) characteristics. 5. Curly lamb-skin. 6. A public open space in the village of Hampstead, in London. 7. E.g., *Fijian Society, or the Sociology and Psychology of the Fijians* (1921), by Reverend W. Deane, principal of a teachers' training college in Ndávuilévu, Fiji; and *The Hill Tribes of Fiji* (1922), by A. B. Brewster, a colonial functionary, mixed facts with interpretation. Reverend Deane remarks that "the amount of sexual immorality and pro-miscuous intercourse during the past forty years is appalling." Fiji is an island in the South Pacific (see n. 3, p. 1622).

desk, are worthless for my purposes. They were worthless scientifically, that is to say, though humanly they were full of instruction, interest, boredom, and very queer facts about the habits of the Fiji Islanders. They had been written in the red light of emotion and not in the white light of truth. Therefore they must be returned to the central desk and restored each to his own cell in the enormous honeycomb. All that I had retrieved from that morning's work had been the one fact of anger. The professors—I lumped them together thus—were angry. But why, I asked myself, having returned the books, why, I repeated, standing under the colonnade among the pigeons and the prehistoric canoes, why are they angry? And, asking myself this question, I strolled off to find a place for luncheon. What is the real nature of what I call for the moment their anger? I asked. Here was a puzzle that would last all the time that it takes to be served with food in a small restaurant somewhere near the British Museum. Some previous luncher had left the lunch edition of the evening paper on a chair, and, waiting to be served, I began idly reading the headlines. A ribbon of very large letters ran across the page. Somebody had made a big score in South Africa. Lesser ribbons announced that Sir Austen Chamberlain was at Geneva.[8] A meat axe with human hair on it had been found in a cellar. Mr. Justice —— commented in the Divorce Courts upon the Shamelessness of Women. Sprinkled about the paper were other pieces of news. A film actress had been lowered from a peak in California and hung suspended in mid-air. The weather was going to be foggy. The most transient visitor to this planet, I thought, who picked up this paper could not fail to be aware, even from this scattered testimony, that England is under the rule of a patriarchy. Nobody in their senses could fail to detect the dominance of the professor. His was the power and the money and the influence. He was the proprietor of the paper and its editor and sub-editor. He was the Foreign Secretary and the Judge. He was the cricketer; he owned the race-horses and the yachts. He was the director of the company that pays two hundred per cent to its shareholders. He left millions to charities and colleges that were ruled by himself. He suspended the film actress in mid-air. He will decide if the hair on the meat axe is human; he it is who will acquit or convict the murderer, and hang him, or let him go free. With the exception of the fog he seemed to control everything. Yet he was angry. I knew that he was angry by this token. When I read what he wrote about women I thought, not of what he was saying, but of himself. When an arguer argues dispassionately he thinks only of the argument; and the reader cannot help thinking of the argument too. If he had written dispassionately about women, had used indisputable proofs to establish his argument and had shown no trace of wishing that the result should be one thing rather than another, one would not have been angry either. One would have accepted the fact, as one accepts the fact that a pea is green or a canary yellow. So be it, I should have said. But I had been angry because he was angry. Yet it seemed absurd, I thought, turning over the evening paper, that a man with all this power should be angry. Or is anger, I wondered, somehow, the familiar, the attendant sprite on power? Rich people,

8. The site of the League of Nations. Chamberlain was the British Foreign Secretary between 1924 and 1929.

for example, are often angry because they suspect that the poor want to seize their wealth. The professors, or patriarchs, as it might be more accurate to call them, might be angry for that reason partly, but partly for one that lies a little less obviously on the surface. Possibly they were not "angry" at all; often, indeed, they were admiring, devoted, exemplary in the relations of private life. Possibly when the professor insisted a little too emphatically upon the inferiority of women, he was concerned not with their inferiority, but with his own superiority. That was what he was protecting rather hot-headedly and with too much emphasis, because it was a jewel to him of the rarest price. Life for both sexes—and I looked at them, shouldering their way along the pavement—is arduous, difficult, a perpetual struggle. It calls for gigantic courage and strength. More than anything, perhaps, creatures of illusion as we are, it calls for confidence in oneself. Without self-confidence we are as babes in the cradle. And how can we generate this imponderable quality, which is yet so invaluable, most quickly? By thinking that other people are inferior to oneself. By feeling that one has some innate superiority—it may be wealth, or rank, a straight nose, or the portrait of a grandfather by Romney[9]—for there is no end to the pathetic devices of the human imagination—over other people. Hence the enormous importance to a patriarch who has to conquer, who has to rule, of feeling that great numbers of people, half the human race indeed, are by nature inferior to himself. It must indeed be one of the chief sources of his power. But let me turn the light of this observation on to real life, I thought. Does it help to explain some of those psychological puzzles that one notes in the margin of daily life? Does it explain my astonishment the other day when Z, most humane, most modest of men, taking up some book by Rebecca West[1] and reading a passage in it, exclaimed, "The arrant feminist! She says that men are snobs!" The exclamation, to me so surprising—for why was Miss West an arrant feminist for making a possibly true if uncomplimentary statement about the other sex?—was not merely the cry of wounded vanity; it was a protest against some infringement of his power to believe in himself. Women have served all these centuries as looking-glasses possessing the magic and delicious power of reflecting the figure of man at twice its natural size. Without that power probably the earth would still be swamp and jungle. The glories of all our wars would be unknown. We should still be scratching the outlines of deer on the remains of mutton bones and bartering flints for sheepskins or whatever simple ornament took our unsophisticated taste. Supermen[2] and Fingers of Destiny would never have existed. The Czar and the Kaiser would never have worn their crowns or lost them. Whatever may be their use in civilized societies, mirrors are essential to all violent and heroic action. That is why Napoleon and Mussolini both insist so emphatically upon the inferiority of women, for if they were not inferior, they would cease to enlarge. That serves to explain in part the necessity that women so often are to men. And it serves to explain how restless they are under her criticism; how impos-

9. George Romney (1734–1802), portrait painter of eighteenth-century British society.   1. Pseudonym of Cicily Isabel Andrews (1892–1983), British novelist and journalist.   2. Fascist politicians, such as Adolf Hitler (1889–1945) in Germany and Mussolini in Italy, rationalized their aggressive policies by exploiting and distorting Friedrich Nietzsche's (1844–1900) concept of the *Übermensch*, or superior being (in *Thus Spake Zarathustra*, 1883–85).

sible it is for her to say to them this book is bad, this picture is feeble, or whatever it may be, without giving far more pain and rousing far more anger than a man would do who gave the same criticism. For if she begins to tell the truth, the figure in the looking-glass shrinks; his fitness for life is diminished. How is he to go on giving judgment, civilising natives, making laws, writing books, dressing up and speechifying at banquets, unless he can see himself at breakfast and at dinner at least twice the size he really is? So I reflected, crumbling my bread and stirring my coffee and now and again looking at the people in the street. The looking-glass vision is of supreme importance because it charges the vitality; it stimulates the nervous system. Take it away and man may die, like the drug fiend deprived of his cocaine. Under the spell of that illusion, I thought, looking out of the window, half the people on the pavement are striding to work. They put on their hats and coats in the morning under its agreeable rays. They start the day confident, braced, believing themselves desired at Miss Smith's tea party; they say to themselves as they go into the room, I am the superior of half the people here, and it is thus that they speak with that self-confidence, that self-assurance, which have had such profound consequences in public life and lead to such curious notes in the margin of the private mind.

But these contributions to the dangerous and fascinating subject of the psychology of the other sex—it is one, I hope, that you will investigate when you have five hundred a year of your own—were interrupted by the necessity of paying the bill. It came to five shillings and ninepence. I gave the waiter a ten-shilling note and he went to bring me change. There was another ten-shilling note in my purse; I noticed it, because it is a fact that still takes my breath away—the power of my purse to breed ten-shilling notes automatically. I open it and there they are. Society gives me chicken and coffee, bed and lodging, in return for a certain number of pieces of paper which were left me by an aunt, for no other reason than that I share her name.

My aunt, Mary Beton, I must tell you, died by a fall from her horse when she was riding out to take the air in Bombay. The news of my legacy reached me one night about the same time that the act was passed that gave votes to women.[3] A solicitor's letter fell into the post-box and when I opened it I found that she had left me five hundred pounds[4] a year for ever. Of the two—the vote and the money—the money, I own, seemed infinitely the more important. Before that I had made my living by cadging odd jobs from newspapers, by reporting a donkey show here or a wedding there; I had earned a few pounds by addressing envelopes, reading to old ladies, making artificial flowers, teaching the alphabet to small children in a kindergarten. Such were the chief occupations that were open to women before 1918. I need not, I am afraid, describe in any detail the hardness of the work, for you know perhaps women who have done it; nor the difficulty of living on the money when it was earned, for you may have tried. But what still remains with me as a worse infliction than either was the poison of fear and bitterness which those days bred in me. To begin with, always to be doing work that one did

---

3. Women were given the vote in 1918; the voting age was lowered from thirty to twenty-one in 1928.   4. Roughly nineteen thousand dollars today, calculating inflation and exchange rates between the pound and the dollar in 1928 and 1998. Such calculations are ultimately unreliable, however, since the relative cost of specific items (such as bread or rent) varies.

not wish to do, and to do it like a slave, flattering and fawning, not always necessarily perhaps, but it seemed necessary and the stakes were too great to run risks; and then the thought of that one gift which it was death to hide[5]—a small one but dear to the possessor—perishing and with it myself, my soul—all this became like a rust eating away the bloom of the spring, destroying the tree at its hearts. However, as I say, my aunt died; and whenever I change a ten-shilling note a little of that rust and corrosion is rubbed off; fear and bitterness go. Indeed, I thought, slipping the silver into my purse, it is remarkable, remembering the bitterness of those days, what a change of temper a fixed income will bring about. No force in the world can take from me my five hundred pounds. Food, house and clothing are mine for ever. Therefore not merely do effort and labour cease, but also hatred and bitterness. I need not hate any man; he cannot hurt me. I need not flatter any man; he has nothing to give me. So imperceptibly I found myself adopting a new attitude towards the other half of the human race. It was absurd to blame any class or any sex, as a whole. Great bodies of people are never responsible for what they do. They are driven by instincts which are not within their control. They too, the patriarchs, the professors, had endless difficulties, terrible drawbacks to contend with. Their education had been in some ways as faulty as my own. It had bred in them defects as great. True, they had money and power, but only at the cost of harbouring in their breasts an eagle, a vulture, for ever tearing the liver out and plucking at the lungs— the instinct for possession, the rage for acquisition which drives them to desire other people's fields and goods perpetually; to make frontiers and flags; battleships and poison gas; to offer up their own lives and their children's lives. Walk through the Admiralty Arch[6] (I had reached that monument), or any other avenue given up to trophies and cannon, and reflect upon the kind of glory celebrated there. Or watch in the spring sunshine the stockbroker and the great barrister going indoors to make money and more money and more money when it is a fact that five hundred pounds a year will keep one alive in the sunshine. These are unpleasant instincts to harbour, I reflected. They are bred of the conditions of life; of the lack of civilisation, I thought, looking at the statue of the Duke of Cambridge,[7] and in particular at the feathers in his cocked hat, with a fixity that they have scarcely ever received before. And, as I realised these drawbacks, by degrees fear and bitterness modified themselves into pity and toleration; and then in a year or two, pity and toleration went, and the greatest release of all came, which is freedom to think of things in themselves. That building, for example, do I like it or not? Is that picture beautiful or not? Is that in my opinion a good book or a bad? Indeed my aunt's legacy unveiled the sky to me, and substituted for the large and imposing figure of a gentleman, which Milton recommended for my perpetual adoration, a view of the open sky.

So thinking, so speculating, I found my way back to my house by the river. Lamps were being lit and an indescribable change had come over London since the morning hour. It was as if the great machine after labouring all day

5. From *When I Consider How My Light is Spent* by John Milton (1608–1673): "And that one talent which is death to hide, / Lodged with me useless."   6. A triple arch in Trafalgar Square (London) at the entrance to the Mall, erected in 1910.   7. An equestrian statue of the second duke of Cambridge (1819–1904), cousin of Queen Victoria, in the full dress uniform of a field marshal.

had made with our help a few yards of something very exciting and beautiful—a fiery fabric flashing with red eyes, a tawny monster roaring with hot breath. Even the wind seemed flung like a flag as it lashed the houses and rattled the hoardings.

In my little street, however, domesticity prevailed. The house painter was descending his ladder; the nursemaid was wheeling the perambulator carefully in and out back to nursery tea; the coal-heaver was folding his empty sacks on top of each other; the woman who keeps the green-grocer's shop was adding up the day's takings with her hands in red mittens. But so engrossed was I with the problem you have laid upon my shoulders that I could not see even these usual sights without referring them to one centre. I thought how much harder it is now than it must have been even a century ago to say which of these employments is the higher, the more necessary. Is it better to be a coal-heaver or a nursemaid; is the charwoman who has brought up eight children of less value to the world than the barrister who has made a hundred thousand pounds? It is useless to ask such questions; for nobody can answer them. Not only do the comparative values of charwoman and lawyers rise and fall from decade to decade, but we have no rods with which to measure them even as they are at the moment. I had been foolish to ask my professor to furnish me with "indisputable proofs" of this or that in his argument about women. Even if one could state the value of any one gift at the moment, those values will change; in a century's time very possibly they will have changed completely. Moreover, in a hundred years, I thought, reaching my own doorstep, women will have ceased to be the protected sex. Logically they will take part in all the activities and exertions that were once denied them. The nursemaid will heave coal. The shop-woman will drive an engine. All assumptions founded on the facts observed when women were the protected sex will have disappeared—as, for example (here a squad of soldiers marched down the street), that women and clergymen and gardeners live longer than other people. Remove that protection, expose them to the same exertions and activities, make them soldiers and sailors and engine-drivers and dock labourers, and will not women die off so much younger, so much quicker, than men that one will say, "I saw a woman today," as one used to say, "I saw an aeroplane." Anything may happen when womanhood has ceased to be a protected occupation, I thought, opening the door. But what bearing has all this upon the subject of my paper, Women and Fiction? I asked, going indoors.

CHAPTER THREE

It was disappointing not to have brought back in the evening some important statement, some authentic fact. Women are poorer than men because—this or that. Perhaps now it would be better to give up seeking for the truth, and receiving on one's head an avalanche of opinion hot as lava, discoloured as dish-water. It would be better to draw the curtains; to shut out distractions; to light the lamp; to narrow the enquiry and to ask the historian, who records not opinions but facts, to describe under what conditions women lived, not throughout the ages, but in England, say in the time of Elizabeth.[8]

8. Queen of England from 1558 to 1603.

For it is a perennial puzzle why no woman wrote a word of that extraordinary literature when every other man, it seemed, was capable of song or sonnet. What were the conditions in which women lived, I asked myself; for fiction, imaginative work that is, is not dropped like a pebble upon the ground, as science may be; fiction is like a spider's web, attached ever so lightly perhaps, but still attached to life at all four corners. Often the attachment is scarcely perceptible; Shakespeare's plays, for instance, seem to hang there complete by themselves. But when the web is pulled askew, hooked up at the edge, torn in the middle, one remembers that these webs are not spun in mid-air by incorporeal creatures, but are the work of suffering human beings, and are attached to grossly material things, like health and money and the houses we live in.

I went, therefore, to the shelf where the histories stand and took down one of the latest, Professor Trevelyan's *History of England*.[9] Once more I looked up Women, found "position of," and turned to the pages indicated. "Wife-beating," I read, "was a recognised right of man, and was practised without shame by high as well as low. . . . Similarly," the historian goes on, "the daughter who refused to marry the gentleman of her parents' choice was liable to be locked up, beaten and flung about the room, without any shock being inflicted on public opinion. Marriage was not an affair of personal affection, but of family avarice, particularly in the 'chivalrous' upper classes. . . . Betrothal often took place while one or both of the parties was in the cradle, and marriage when they were scarcely out of the nurses' charge." That was about 1470, soon after Chaucer's[1] time. The next reference to the position of women is some two hundred years later, in the time of the Stuarts.[2] "It was still the exception for women of the upper and middle class to choose their own husbands, and when the husband had been assigned, he was lord and master, so far at least as law and custom could make him. Yet even so," Professor Trevelyan concludes, "neither Shakespeare's women nor those of authentic seventeenth-century memoirs, like the Verneys and the Hutchinsons,[3] seem wanting in personality and character." Certainly, if we consider it, Cleopatra must have had a way with her; Lady Macbeth,[4] one would suppose, had a will of her own; Rosalind, one might conclude, was an attractive girl. Professor Trevelyan is speaking no more than the truth when he remarks that Shakespeare's women do not seem wanting in personality and character. Not being a historian, one might go even further and say that women have burnt like beacons in all the works of all the poets from the beginning of time—Clytemnestra, Antigone, Cleopatra, Lady Macbeth, Phèdre, Cressida, Rosalind, Desdemona, the Duchess of Malfi,[5] among the dramatists; then among the prose writers: Millamant, Clarissa, Becky Sharp, Anna Karenina, Emma Bovary, Madame de Guer-

9. Published in London in 1926. References are to pages 260–61 and, later, to pages 436–37. 1. Geoffrey Chaucer (1340?–1400), author of *The Canterbury Tales* (1390–1400). 2. The British royal house from 1603–1714 (except for the Commonwealth interregnum of 1649–60). 3. F. P. Verney compiled *The Memoirs of the Verney Family during the Seventeenth Century* (1892–99), and Lucy Hutchinson recounted her husband's life in *Memoirs of the Life of Colonel Hutchinson* (1806). 4. Heroine of Shakespeare's *Macbeth*. Cleopatra (69–30 B.C.), queen of Egypt and heroine of Shakespeare's *Antony and Cleopatra*. 5. Doomed heroine of John Webster's *The Duchess of Malfi* (ca. 1613). Clytemnestra is the heroine of Aeschylus's *Agamemnon* (458 B.C.). Antigone is the eponymous heroine of a 442 B.C. play by Sophocles. Phèdre is the heroine of Jean Racine's *Phèdre* (1677). Cressida, Rosalind, and Desdemona are heroines of Shakespeare's *Troilus and Cressida*, *As You Like It*, and *Othello*, respectively.

mantes[6]—the names flock to mind, nor do they recall women "lacking in personality and character." Indeed, if woman had no existence save in the fiction written by men, one would imagine her a person of the utmost importance; very various; heroic and mean; splendid and sordid; infinitely beautiful and hideous in the extreme; as great as a man, some think even greater.[7] But this is woman in fiction. In fact, as Professor Trevelyan points out, she was locked up, beaten and flung about the room.

A very queer, composite being thus emerges. Imaginatively she is of the highest importance; practically she is completely insignificant. She pervades poetry from cover to cover; she is all but absent from history. She dominates the lives of kings and conquerors in fiction; in fact she was the slave of any boy whose parents forced a ring upon her finger. Some of the most inspired words, some of the most profound thoughts in literature fall from her lips; in real life she could hardly read, could scarcely spell, and was the property of her husband.

It was certainly an odd monster that one made up by reading the historians first and the poets afterwards—a worm winged like an eagle; the spirit of life and beauty in a kitchen chopping up suet. But these monsters, however amusing to the imagination, have no existence in fact. What one must do to bring her to life was to think poetically and prosaically at one and the same moment, thus keeping in touch with fact—that she is Mrs. Martin, aged thirty-six, dressed in blue, wearing a black hat and brown shoes; but not losing sight of fiction either—that she is a vessel in which all sorts of spirits and forces are coursing and flashing perpetually. The moment, however, that one tries this method with the Elizabethan woman, one branch of illumination fails; one is held up by the scarcity of facts. One knows nothing detailed, nothing perfectly true and substantial about her. History scarcely mentions her. And I turned to Professor Trevelyan again to see what history meant to him. I found by looking at his chapter headings that it meant—

"The Manor Court and the Methods of Open-field Agriculture . . . The Cistercians and Sheep-farming . . . The Crusades . . . The University . . . The House of Commons . . . The Hundred Years' War . . . The Wars of the Roses . . . The Renaissance Scholars . . . The Dissolution of the Monasteries . . . Agrarian and Religious Strife . . . The Origin of English Sea-power . . . The Armada . . ." and so on. Occasionally an individual woman is mentioned, an Elizabeth, or a Mary; a queen or a great lady. But by no possible means could middle-class women with nothing but brains and character at their

---

6. A character in Marcel Proust's *Remembrance of Things Past* (*The Guermantes Way*; 1920–21). Millamant is the heroine of William Congreve's satirical comedy *The Way of the World* (1700). Clarissa is the eponymous heroine of Samuel Richardson's seven-volume epistolary novel (1747–48). Becky Sharp appears in William Thackeray's *Vanity Fair* (1847–48). Anna Karenina is the title character in a Leo Tolstoy novel (1875–77). Emma Bovary is the heroine of Gustave Flaubert's *Madame Bovary* (1856). 7. "It remains a strange and almost inexplicable fact that in Athena's city, where women were kept in almost Oriental suppression as odalisques or drudges, the stage should yet have produced figures like Clytemnestra and Cassandra, Atossa and Antigone, Phèdre and Medea, and all the other heroines who dominate play after play of the 'misogynist' Euripides. But the paradox of this world where in real life a respectable woman could hardly show her face alone in the street, and yet on the stage woman equals or surpasses man, has never been satisfactorily explained. In modern tragedy the same predominance exists. At all events, a very cursory survey of Shakespeare's work (similarly with Webster, though not with Marlowe or Jonson) suffices to reveal how this dominance, this initiative of women, persists from Rosalind to Lady Macbeth. So too in Racine; six of his tragedies bear their heroines' names; and what male characters of his shall we set against Hermione and Andromaque, Bérénice and Roxane, Phèdre and Athalie? So again with Ibsen; what men shall we match with Solveig and Nora, Hedda and Hilda Wangel and Rebecca West?"—F. L. LUCAS, *Tragedy*, pp. 114–15 [Woolf's note].

command have taken part in any one of the great movements which, brought together, constitute the historian's view of the past. Nor shall we find her in any collection of anecdotes. Aubrey[8] hardly mentions her. She never writes her own life and scarcely keeps a diary; there are only a handful of her letters in existence. She left no plays or poems by which we can judge her. What one wants, I thought—and why does not some brilliant student at Newnham or Girton[9] supply it?—is a mass of information; at what age did she marry; how many children had she as a rule; what was her house like; had she a room to herself; did she do the cooking; would she be likely to have a servant? All these facts lie somewhere, presumably, in parish registers and account books; the life of the average Elizabethan woman must be scattered about somewhere, could one collect it and make a book of it. It would be ambitious beyond my daring, I thought, looking about the shelves for books that were not there, to suggest to the students of those famous colleges that they should re-write history, though I own that it often seems a little queer as it is, unreal, lop-sided; but why should they not add a supplement to history? calling it, of course, by some inconspicuous name so that women might figure there without impropriety? For one often catches a glimpse of them in the lives of the great, whisking away into the background, concealing, I sometimes think, a wink, a laugh, perhaps a tear. And, after all, we have lives enough of Jane Austen; it scarcely seems necessary to consider again the influence of the tragedies of Joanna Baillie upon the poetry of Edgar Allan Poe; as for myself, I should not mind if the homes and haunts of Mary Russell Mitford[1] were closed to the public for a century at least. But what I find deplorable, I continued, looking about the bookshelves again, is that nothing is known about women before the eighteenth century. I have no model in my mind to turn about this way and that. Here am I asking why women did not write poetry in the Elizabethan age, and I am not sure how they were educated; whether they were taught to write; whether they had sitting-rooms to themselves; how many women had children before they were twenty-one; what, in short, they did from eight in the morning till eight at night. They had no money evidently; according to Professor Trevelyan they were married whether they liked it or not before they were out of the nursery, at fifteen or sixteen very likely. It would have been extremely odd, even upon this showing, had one of them suddenly written the plays of Shakespeare, I concluded, and I thought of that old gentleman, who is dead now, but was a bishop, I think, who declared that it was impossible for any woman, past, present, or to come, to have the genius of Shakespeare. He wrote to the papers about it. He also told a lady who applied to him for information that cats do not as a matter of fact go to heaven, though they have, he added, souls of a sort. How much thinking those old gentlemen used to save one! How the borders of ignorance shrank back at their approach! Cats do not go to heaven. Women cannot write the plays of Shakespeare.

Be that as it may, I could not help thinking, as I looked at the works of Shakespeare on the shelf, that the bishop was right at least in this; it would

---

8. John Aubrey (1626–1697), author of *Brief Lives*, which includes sketches of his famous contemporaries. 9. Woolf delivered her lectures at Newnham and Girton Colleges for women, part of Cambridge University in 1880 and 1873, respectively. 1. Dramatist, poet, and essayist (1787–1855), author of *Rienzi*, a tragedy in blank verse (1828), and *Our Village* (1832), sketches of country life. Austen (1775–1817), author of *Pride and Prejudice* (1813) and other novels. Baillie (1762–1851), poet and dramatist whose *Plays on the Passions* (1798–1812) were famous in her day.

have been impossible, completely and entirely, for any woman to have written the plays of Shakespeare in the age of Shakespeare. Let me imagine, since facts are so hard to come by, what would have happened had Shakespeare had a wonderfully gifted sister, called Judith,[2] let us say. Shakespeare himself went, very probably—his mother was an heiress—to the grammar school, where he may have learnt Latin—Ovid, Virgil and Horace[3]—and the elements of grammar and logic. He was, it is well known, a wild boy who poached rabbits, perhaps shot a deer, and had, rather sooner than he should have done, to marry a woman in the neighbourhood, who bore him a child rather quicker than was right. That escapade sent him to seek his fortune in London. He had, it seemed, a taste for the theatre; he began by holding horses at the stage door. Very soon he got work in the theatre, became a successful actor, and lived at the hub of the universe, meeting everybody, knowing everybody, practising his art on the boards, exercising his wits in the streets, and even getting access to the palace of the queen. Meanwhile his extraordinarily gifted sister, let us suppose, remained at home. She was as adventurous, as imaginative, as agog to see the world as he was. But she was not sent to school. She had no chance of learning grammar and logic, let alone of reading Horace and Virgil. She picked up a book now and then, one of her brother's perhaps, and read a few pages. But then her parents came in and told her to mend the stockings or mind the stew and not moon about with books and papers. They would have spoken sharply but kindly, for they were substantial people who knew the conditions of life for a woman and loved their daughter—indeed, more likely than not she was the apple of her father's eye. Perhaps she scribbled some pages up in an apple loft on the sly, but was careful to hide them or set fire to them. Soon, however, before she was out of her teens, she was to be betrothed to the son of a neighbouring wool-stapler. She cried out that marriage was hateful to her, and for that she was severely beaten by her father. Then he ceased to scold her. He begged her instead not to hurt him, not to shame him in this matter of her marriage. He would give her a chain of beads or a fine petticoat, he said; and there were tears in his eyes. How could she disobey him? How could she break his heart? The force of her own gift alone drove her to it. She made up a small parcel of her belongings, let herself down by a rope one summer's night and took the road to London. She was not seventeen. The birds that sang in the hedge were not more musical than she was. She had the quickest fancy, a gift like her brother's, for the tune of words. Like him, she had a taste for the theatre. She stood at the stage door; she wanted to act, she said. Men laughed in her face. The manager—a fat, loose-lipped man—guffawed. He bellowed something about poodles dancing and women acting—no woman, he said, could possibly be an actress. He hinted—you can imagine what. She could get no training in her craft. Could she even seek her dinner in a tavern or roam the streets at midnight? Yet her genius was for fiction and lusted to feed abundantly upon the lives of men and women and the study of their ways. At last—for she was very young, oddly like Shakespeare the poet in her face, with the same grey eyes and rounded brows—at last Nick Greene[4]

---

2. The name of Shakespeare's younger daughter.   3. Roman authors. Publius Ovidius Naso (43 B.C.–A.D. 17), author of the *Metamorphoses*. Publius Vergilius Maro (70–19 B.C.), author of the *Aeneid*. Quintus Horatius Flaccus (65–8 B.C.), author of *Odes* and satires.   4. A fictional character based on Shakespeare's contemporary Robert Greene (1558–1592) and appearing in Woolf's *Orlando*.

the actor-manager took pity on her; she found herself with child by that gentleman and so—who shall measure the heat and violence of the poet's heart when caught and tangled in a woman's body?—killed herself one winter's night and lies buried at some cross-roads where the omnibuses now stop outside the Elephant and Castle.[5]

That, more or less, is how the story would run, I think, if a woman in Shakespeare's day had had Shakespeare's genius. But for my part, I agree with the deceased bishop, if such he was—it is unthinkable that any woman in Shakespeare's day should have had Shakespeare's genius. For genius like Shakespeare's is not born among labouring, uneducated, servile people. It was not born in England among the Saxons and the Britons. It is not born today among the working classes. How, then, could it have been born among women whose work began, according to Professor Trevelyan, almost before they were out of the nursery, who were forced to it by their parents and held to it by all the power of law and custom? Yet genius of a sort must have existed among women as it must have existed among the working classes. Now and again an Emily Brontë or a Robert Burns[6] blazes out and proves its presence. But certainly it never got itself on to paper. When, however, one reads of a witch being ducked, of a woman possessed by devils, of a wise woman selling herbs, or even of a very remarkable man who had a mother, then I think we are on the track of a lost novelist, a suppressed poet, of some mute and inglorious[7] Jane Austen, some Emily Brontë who dashed her brains out on the moor or mopped and mowed about the highways crazed with the torture that her gift had put her to. Indeed, I would venture to guess that Anon, who wrote so many poems without signing them, was often a woman. It was a woman Edward Fitzgerald,[8] I think, suggested who made the ballads and the folk-songs, crooning them to her children, beguiling her spinning with them, or the length of the winter's night.

This may be true or it may be false—who can say?—but what is true in it, so it seemed to me, reviewing the story of Shakespeare's sister as I had made it, is that any woman born with a great gift in the sixteenth century would certainly have gone crazed, shot herself, or ended her days in some lonely cottage outside the village, half witch, half wizard, feared and mocked at. For it needs little skill in psychology to be sure that a highly gifted girl who had tried to use her gift for poetry would have been so thwarted and hindered by other people, so tortured and pulled asunder by her own contrary instincts, that she must have lost her health and sanity to a certainty. No girl could have walked to London and stood at a stage door and forced her way into the presence of actor-managers without doing herself a violence and suffering an anguish which may have been irrational—for chastity may be a fetish invented by certain societies for unknown reasons—but were none the less inevitable. Chastity had then, it has even now, a religious importance in a woman's life, and has so wrapped itself round with nerves and instincts that to cut it free and bring it to the light of day demands courage of the rarest. To have lived a free life in London in the sixteenth century would have meant for a woman who was poet and playwright a nervous stress and

5. A popular London pub.   6. Scottish poet (1759–1796). Brontë (1818–1848), author of *Wuthering Heights*.   7. A reference to Thomas Grey's line in *Elegy Written in a Country Churchyard* (1751): "Some mute inglorious Milton here may rest."   8. British author (1809–1883), known for his translation from the Persian of the *Rubáiyát of Omar Khayyám* (1859).

1634 / Virginia Woolf

dilemma which might well have killed her. Had she survived, whatever she had written would have been twisted and deformed, issuing from a strained and morbid imagination. And undoubtedly, I thought, looking at the shelf where there are no plays by women, her work would have gone unsigned. That refuge she would have sought certainly. It was the relic of the sense of chastity that dictated anonymity to women even so late as the nineteenth century. Currer Bell, George Eliot, George Sand,[9] all the victims of inner strife as their writings prove, sought ineffectively to veil themselves by using the name of a man. Thus they did homage to the convention, which if not implanted by the other sex was liberally encouraged by them (the chief glory of a woman is not to be talked of, said Pericles,[1] himself a much-talked-of man), that publicity in women is detestable. Anonymity runs in their blood. The desire to be veiled still possesses them. They are not even now as concerned about the health of their fame as men are, and, speaking generally, will pass a tombstone or a signpost without feeling an irresistible desire to cut their names on it, as Alf, Bert or Chas. must do in obedience to their instinct, which murmurs if it sees a fine woman go by, or even a dog, Ce chien est à moi.[2] And, of course, it may not be a dog, I thought, remembering Parliament Square, the Sièges Allée[3] and other avenues; it may be a piece of land or a man with curly black hair. It is one of the great advantages of being a woman that one can pass even a very fine negress without wishing to make an Englishwoman of her.

That woman, then, who was born with a gift of poetry in the sixteenth century, was an unhappy woman, a woman at strife against herself. All the conditions of her life, all her own instincts, were hostile to the state of mind which is needed to set free whatever is in the brain. But what is the state of mind that is most propitious to the act of creation, I asked. Can one come by any notion of the state that furthers and makes possible that strange activity? Here I opened the volume containing the Tragedies of Shakespeare. What was Shakespeare's state of mind, for instance, when he wrote Lear and Antony and Cleopatra? It was certainly the state of mind most favourable to poetry that there has ever existed. But Shakespeare himself said nothing about it. We only know casually and by chance that he "never blotted a line."[4] Nothing indeed was ever said by the artist himself about his state of mind until the eighteenth century perhaps. Rousseau[5] perhaps began it. At any rate, by the nineteenth century self-consciousness had developed so far that it was the habit for men of letters to describe their minds in confessions and autobiographies. Their lives also were written, and their letters were printed after their deaths. Thus, though we do not know what Shakespeare went through when he wrote Lear, we do know what Carlyle went through when he wrote the French Revolution; what Flaubert went through when he wrote Madame Bovary; what Keats[6] was going through when he tried to write poetry against the coming of death and the indifference of the world.

9. Pseudonyms of Emily Brontë; Mary Ann Evans (1819–1880), author of Middlemarch (1871–72); and Lucile-Aurore Dupin (1804–1876), author of Lélia (1833), respectively. 1. From the Greek leader Pericles' funeral oration (431 B.C.), as reported in Thucydides' history of the Peloponnesian War (2.35–46). 2. This dog is mine (French); from the philosopher Blaise Pascal's Thoughts (1657–58). He uses an anecdote about poor children to illustrate a universal impulse to assert property claims. 3. An avenue in Berlin containing statues of Hohenzollern rulers. Parliament Square is in London next to the Houses of Parliament and Westminster Abbey. 4. Ben Jonson's (1572–1637) description of Shakespeare. 5. Jean-Jacques Rousseau (1712–1778), French author of the Confessions (1781). 6. John Keats (1795–1821), British poet. Thomas Carlyle (1795–1881), essayist and historian, translator of Goethe and author of The French Revolution (1837).

And one gathers from this enormous modern literature of confession and self-analysis that to write a work of genius is almost always a feat of prodigious difficulty. Everything is against the likelihood that it will come from the writer's mind whole and entire. Generally material circumstances are against it. Dogs will bark; people will interrupt; money must be made; health will break down. Further, accentuating all these difficulties and making them harder to bear is the world's notorious indifference. It does not ask people to write poems and novels and histories; it does not need them. It does not care whether Flaubert finds the right word or whether Carlyle scrupulously verifies this or that fact. Naturally, it will not pay for what it does not want. And so the writer, Keats, Flaubert, Carlyle, suffers, especially in the creative years of youth, every form of distraction and discouragement. A curse, a cry of agony, rises from those books of analysis and confession. "Mighty poets in their misery dead"—that is the burden of their song. If anything comes through in spite of all this, it is a miracle, and probably no book is born entire and uncrippled as it was conceived.

But for women, I thought, looking at the empty shelves, these difficulties were infinitely more formidable. In the first place, to have a room of her own, let alone a quiet room or a sound-proof room, was out of the question, unless her parents were exceptionally rich or very noble, even up to the beginning of the nineteenth century. Since her pin money, which depended on the good will of her father, was only enough to keep her clothed, she was debarred from such alleviations as came even to Keats or Tennyson[7] or Carlyle, all poor men, from a walking tour, a little journey to France, from the separate lodging which, even if it were miserable enough, sheltered them from the claims and tyrannies of their families. Such material difficulties were formidable; but much worse were the immaterial. The indifference of the world which Keats and Flaubert and other men of genius have found so hard to bear was in her case not indifference but hostility. The world did not say to her as it said to them, Write if you choose; it makes no difference to me. The world said with a guffaw, Write? What's the good of your writing? Here the psychologists of Newnham and Girton might come to our help, I thought, looking again at the blank spaces on the shelves. For surely it is time that the effect of discouragement upon the mind of the artist should be measured, as I have seen a dairy company measure the effect of ordinary milk and Grade A milk upon the body of the rat. They set two rats in cages side by side, and of the two one was furtive, timid and small, and the other was glossy, bold and big. Now what food do we feed women as artists upon? I asked, remembering, I suppose, that dinner of prunes and custard. To answer that question I had only to open the evening paper and to read that Lord Birkenhead is of opinion—but really I am not going to trouble to copy out Lord Birkenhead's opinion upon the writing of women. What Dean Inge says I will leave in peace. The Harley Street specialist may be allowed to rouse the echoes of Harley Street with his vociferations without raising a hair on my head. I will quote, however, Mr. Oscar Browning, because Mr. Oscar Browning was a great figure in Cambridge at one time, and used to examine the students at Girton and Newnham. Mr. Oscar Browning was wont to declare "that the impression left on his mind, after looking over any set of examination papers, was that, irrespective of the marks he might give,

7. Alfred, Lord Tennyson (1809–1892), British poet.

the best woman was intellectually the inferior of the worst man." After saying that Mr. Browning went back to his rooms—and it is this sequel that endears him and makes him a human figure of some bulk and majesty—he went back to his rooms and found a stable-boy lying on the sofa—"a mere skeleton, his cheeks were cavernous and sallow, his teeth were black, and he did not appear to have the full use of his limbs. . . . 'That's Arthur' [said Mr. Browning]. 'He's a dear boy really and most high-minded.' " The two pictures always seem to me to complete each other. And happily in this age of biography the two pictures often do complete each other, so that we are able to interpret the opinions of great men not only by what they say, but by what they do.

But though this is possible now, such opinions coming from the lips of important people must have been formidable enough even fifty years ago. Let us suppose that a father from the highest motives did not wish his daughter to leave home and become writer, painter or scholar. "See what Mr. Oscar Browning says," he would say; and there was not only Mr. Oscar Browning; there was the *Saturday Review*; there was Mr. Greg[8]—the "essentials of a woman's being," said Mr. Greg emphatically, "are that *they are supported by, and they minister to, men*"—there was an enormous body of masculine opinion to the effect that nothing could be expected of women intellectually. Even if her father did not read out loud these opinions, any girl could read them for herself; and the reading, even in the nineteenth century, must have lowered her vitality, and told profoundly upon her work. There would always have been that assertion—you cannot do this, you are incapable of doing that—to protest against, to overcome. Probably for a novelist this germ is no longer of much effect; for there have been women novelists of merit. But for painters it must still have some sting in it; and for musicians, I imagine, is even now active and poisonous in the extreme. The woman composer stands where the actress stood in the time of Shakespeare. Nick Greene, I thought, remembering the story I had made about Shakespeare's sister, said that a woman acting put him in mind of a dog dancing. Johnson repeated the phrase two hundred years later of women preaching. And here, I said, opening a book about music, we have the very words used again in this year of grace, 1928, of women who try to write music. "Of Mlle. Germaine Tailleferre one can only repeat Dr. Johnson's dictum concerning a woman preacher, transposed into terms of music. 'Sir, a woman's composing is like a dog's walking on his hind legs. It is not done well, but you are surprised to find it done at all.' "[9] So accurately does history repeat itself.

Thus, I concluded, shutting Mr. Oscar Browning's life and pushing away the rest, it is fairly evident that even in the nineteenth century a woman was not encouraged to be an artist. On the contrary, she was snubbed, slapped, lectured and exhorted. Her mind must have been strained and her vitality lowered by the need of opposing this, of disproving that. For here again we come within range of that very interesting and obscure masculine complex which has had so much influence upon the woman's movement; that deep-seated desire, not so much that *she* shall be inferior as that *he* shall be superior, which plants him wherever one looks, not only in front of the arts, but barring the way to politics too, even when the risk to himself seems

---

8. William Rathbone Greg (1809–1891), cited from a *Saturday Review* essay titled *Why Are Women Redundant?* 9. *A Survey of Contemporary Music*, Cecil Gray, p. 246 [Woolf's note]. The statement is originally found in James Boswell's *Life of Johnson* (1791).

infinitesimal and the suppliant humble and devoted. Even Lady Bessborough,[1] I remembered, with all her passion for politics, must humbly bow herself and write to Lord Granville Leveson-Gower: " . . . notwithstanding all my violence in politics and talking so much on that subject, I perfectly agree with you that no woman has any business to meddle with that or any other serious business, farther than giving her opinion (if she is ask'd)." And so she goes on to spend her enthusiasm where it meets with no obstacle whatsoever upon that immensely important subject, Lord Granville's maiden speech in the House of Commons. The spectacle is certainly a strange one, I thought. The history of men's opposition to women's emancipation is more interesting perhaps than the story of that emancipation itself. An amusing book might be made of it if some young student at Girton or Newnham would collect examples and deduce a theory—but she would need thick gloves on her hands, and bars to protect her of solid gold.

But what is amusing now, I recollected, shutting Lady Bessborough, had to be taken in desperate earnest once. Opinions that one now pastes in a book labelled cock-a-doodle-dum and keeps for reading to select audiences on summer nights once drew tears, I can assure you. Among your grandmothers and great-grandmothers there were many that wept their eyes out. Florence Nightingale shrieked aloud in her agony.[2] Moreover, it is all very well for you, who have got yourselves to college and enjoy sitting-rooms—or is it only bed-sitting-rooms?—of your own to say that genius should disregard such opinions; that genius should be above caring what is said of it. Unfortunately, it is precisely the men or women of genius who mind most what is said of them. Remember Keats. Remember the words he had cut on his tombstone.[3] Think of Tennyson; think—but I need hardly multiply instances of the undeniable, if very, unfortunate, fact that it is the nature of the artist to mind excessively what is said about him. Literature is strewn with the wreckage of men who have minded beyond reason the opinions of others.

And this susceptibility of theirs is doubly unfortunate, I thought, returning again to my original enquiry into what state of mind is most propitious for creative work, because the mind of an artist, in order to achieve the prodigious effort of freeing whole and entire the work that is in him, must be incandescent, like Shakespeare's mind, I conjectured, looking at the book which lay open at *Antony and Cleopatra*. There must be no obstacle in it, no foreign matter unconsumed.

For though we say that we know nothing about Shakespeare's state of mind, even as we say that, we are saying something about Shakespeare's state of mind. The reason perhaps why we know so little of Shakespeare—compared with Donne or Ben Jonson or Milton—is that his grudges and spites and antipathies are hidden from us. We are not held up by some "revelation" which reminds us of the writer. All desire to protest, to preach, to proclaim an injury, to pay off a score, to make the world the witness of some hardship or grievance was fired out of him and consumed. Therefore his poetry flows from him free and unimpeded. If ever a human being got

---

1. Henrietta, Countess of Bessborough (1761–1821), who corresponded with Lord Granville George Leveson-Gower (1815–1891), British foreign secretary in William Gladstone's administrations and after him the leader of the Liberal Party.   2. See *Cassandra*, by Florence Nightingale, printed in *The Cause*, by R. Strachey [Woolf's note]. Nightingale (1820–1910), English nurse and founder of nursing as a profession for women.   3. "Here lies one whose name was writ in water."

his work expressed completely, it was Shakespeare. If ever a mind was incandescent, unimpeded, I thought, turning again to the bookcase, it was Shakespeare's mind.

FRANZ KAFKA
1883–1924

The predicament of Franz Kafka's writing is, for many, the predicament of modern civilization. Nowhere is the anxiety and alienation of twentieth-century society more visible than in his stories of individuals struggling to prevail against a vast, meaningless, and apparently hostile system. Identifying that system as bureaucracy, family, religion, language, or the invisible network of social habit is less important than recognizing the protagonists' bewilderment at being placed in impossible situations. Kafka's heroes are driven to find answers in an unresponsive world, and they are required to act according to incomprehensible rules administered by an inaccessible authority; small wonder that they fluctuate between fear, hope, anger, resignation, and despair. Kafka's fictional world has long fascinated contemporary writers, who find in it an extraordinary blend of prosaic realism and nightmarish, infinitely interpretable symbolism. Whether evoking the multilayered bureaucracy of the modern state, the sense of guilt felt by those facing the accusations of authority, or the vulnerability of characters who cannot make themselves understood, Kafka's descriptions are believable because of their scrupulous attention to detail: the flea on a fur collar, the dust under an unmade bed, the creases and yellowing of an old newspaper, or the helplessness of a beetle turned upside down. The sheer *ordinariness* of these details grounds the entire narrative, giving the reader a continuing expectation of reality even when events escape all logic and the situation is at its most hallucinatory. This paradoxical combination has appealed to a range of contemporary writers—each quite different from the other—who have read and absorbed Kafka's lesson: Samuel Beckett, Harold Pinter, Alain Robbe-Grillet, Gabriel García Márquez.

Kafka was born into cultural alienation: Jewish (though not truly part of the Jewish community) in Catholic Czechoslovakia, son of a German-speaking shopkeeper when German was the language of the imposed Austro-Hungarian government, and drawn to literature when his father—a domineering, self-made man—pushed him toward success in business. Nor was he happier at home. Resenting his father's overbearing nature and feeling deprived of maternal love, he nonetheless lived with his parents for most of his life and complained in long letters about his coldness and inability to love (despite numerous liaisons). Kafka took a degree in law to qualify himself for a position in a large accident-insurance corporation, where he worked until illness forced his retirement in 1922. By the time of his death from tuberculosis two years later, he had published a number of short stories and two novellas (*The Metamorphosis*, 1915; *In the Penal Colony*, 1919), but left behind him the manuscripts of three near-complete novels that—considering himself a failure—he asked to have burned. Instead, Kafka's executor, Max Brod, published the novels (*The Trial*, 1925; *The Castle*, 1926; *Amerika*, 1927) and a biography celebrating the genius of his tormented, guilt-ridden friend.

Despite the indubitable fact that Franz Kafka became a respected senior executive, handling claims, litigations, public relations, and his institute's annual reports, and was one of the few top German executives retained when Czechoslovakia finally gained independence in 1918, his image in the modern imagination is derived from the portraits of inner anguish given in his fiction, diaries, and letters. This "Kafka" is a tormented and sensitive soul, guiltily resentful of his job in a giant bureaucracy, unable to free himself from his family or to cope with the demands of love, physically feeble, and constantly beset by feelings of inferiority and doom in an existence whose laws he can never quite understand. "Before the Law," a parable published in Kafka's lifetime and included in *The Trial*, recounts the archetypal setting of the "Kafka" character: a countryman waits and waits throughout his lifetime for permission to enter a crucial Gate, where the doorkeeper (the first of many) repeatedly refuses him entrance. He tries everything from good behavior to bribes without success. Finally, as the now-aged countryman dies in frustration, he is told that the gate existed only for him, and that it is now being closed. For the countryman (as for Vladimir and Estragon in Beckett's *Waiting for Godot*, and indeed for much modern literature), there is no response. The Law that governs our existence is all-powerful but irrational; at least it is not to be understood by its human suppliants, a lesson that Kafka could have derived equally well from his readings in the Danish philosopher Søren Kierkegaard, in Friedrich Nietzsche, or in the Jewish Talmud.

The combination of down-to-earth, matter-of-fact setting and unreal or nightmarish events is the hallmark of Kafka's style. His characters speak prosaically and react in a commonsense way when such a response (given the situation) is utterly grotesque. A young businessman is changed overnight into a giant beetle (*The Metamorphosis*) or charged with undefined crimes and finally executed (*The Trial*); a would-be land surveyor is unable to communicate with the castle that employs him and that keeps sending incomprehensible messages (*The Castle*); a visitor to a penal colony observes a gigantic machine whose function is to execute condemned criminals by inscribing their sentence deeper and deeper into their flesh (*In the Penal Colony*). The term *surrealist* is often attached to this blend of everyday reality and dream configuration, with its implication of psychic undercurrents and cosmic significance stirring beneath the most ordinary-seeming existence. Kafka, however, had no connection with the Surrealists, whose vision of a miraculous level of existence hidden behind everyday life is the obverse of his heroes' vain attempts to maintain control over the impossible and the absurd.

Kafka's stories are not allegories, although many readers have been tempted to find in them an underlying message. A political reading sees them as indictments of faceless bureaucracy controlling individual lives in the modern totalitarian state. The sense of being found guilty by an entire society recalls the traditional theme of the Wandering Jew and predicts for many the Holocaust of World War II (in fact, Kafka's three sisters died in concentration camps). His heroes' self-conscious quest to fit into some meaningful structure, their ceaseless attempts to do the right thing when there is no rational way of knowing what that is, is the very picture of absurdity and alienation that existentialist philosophers and writers examined during and after World War II. The assumption that there is a Law, and the presence of protagonists who die in search for purity (*The Hunger Artist*) or in a humble admission of guilt (*The Trial*) allow the stories to be taken as religious metaphors. Kafka's desperately lucid analysis of the way his parents' influence shaped an impressionable child into an unhappy adult (*Letter to My Father*) articulates emotional tangles and parent-child rivalry with an openness and detail that recalls decades of psychoanalytical criticism following Freud. The picture of a sick society where individual rights and sensitivity no longer count and unreasoning torment is visited on the ignorant has been read as an indictment of disintegrating modern culture. Yet no one allegorical interpretation is finally possible, for all these potential meanings overlap as they expand toward social, familial, political, philosophical, and religious dimensions and constitute the richly allusive texture of separate tales by a master storyteller.

The Metamorphosis, Kafka's longest complete work published in his lifetime, is first of all a consummate narrative: the question "What happens next?" never disappears from the moment that Gregor Samsa wakes up to find himself transformed. "It was no dream," no nightmarish fantasy in which Gregor temporarily identified himself with other downtrodden vermin of society. Instead, this grotesque transformation is permanent, a single unshakable fact that renders almost comic his family's calculations and attempts to adjust. "The terror of art," said Kafka in a conversation about *The Metamorphosis,* is that "the dream reveals the reality." This artistic dream, become Gregor's reality, sheds light on the intolerable nature of his former daily existence. The other side of his job is its mechanical rigidity, personal rivalries, and threatening suspicion of any deviation from the norm. Gregor himself is part of this world, as he shows when he fawns on the manager and tries to manipulate him by criticizing their boss.

More disturbing is the transformation that takes place in Gregor's family, where the expected love and support turns into shamed acceptance and animal resentment now that Gregor has let the family down. Mother and sister are ineffectual, and their sympathy is slowly replaced by disgust. Gregor's father quickly reassumes his position of authority and beats the beetle back into his room: first with the businesslike newspaper and manager's cane, and later with a barrage of apples from the family table. Just before his death Gregor has become an "it" whose death is warmly wished by the whole family—and perhaps they are right, in one of Kafka's ironies. The beetle's death brings not remorse but a new lease on life to his family. Weak and passive when Gregor took care of them, they regain strength and vitality under the pressure of earning a living. Mother, father, and sister celebrate Gregor's death with a holiday trip out of town, into the sunshine and open air, where they make plans for the future.

Gregor Samsa may be a pathetic figure but he is not a tragic one. In his passiveness and unvoiced resentment, his willingness to exist at a surface level of adjustment to job and family, he has become an accomplice in his own fate. His descent into animal consciousness is not a true pilgrimage to inner awareness, even though it involves letting go the trappings of civilization. Rather, it is an obscuring of consciousness that is perfectly represented when he is swept out onto the dustheap at the end. From that point on, it is the family's story, continuing a career that has meant death for Gregor and joyous survival for his family, but in which both are reduced to existence on an animal level.

Anthony Thorlby, *Kafka: A Study* (1972), is a brief general introduction. Heinz Politzer, *Franz Kafka: Parable and Paradox* (1966), presents an interesting, readable study of symbolic relationships. Ernest Pawel, *The Nightmare of Reason: A Life of Franz Kafka* (1984), is an excellent contemporary biography with penetrating descriptions of his family and friends. Max Brod, *Franz Kafka: A Biography* (1960), is an early, admiring biography by a close friend and Kafka's executor. Ronald Gray, ed., *Kafka: A Collection of Critical Essays* (1962), is a useful early collection of essays on different works. Harold Bloom, ed., *Franz Kafka's The Metamorphosis* (1988), collects essays on spiritual, metaphorical, formal, social, and psychoanalytic aspects of *The Metamorphosis.* Jack Murray analyzes the sense of space in *The Landscapes of Alienation: Ideological Subversion in Kafka, Celine, and Onetti* (1991). Kurt Fickert, *End of a Mission: Kafka's Search for Truth in His Last Stories* (1993), interprets the stories as metaphors for an autobiographical quest to resolve personal problems.

The Metamorphosis[1]

I

One morning, upon awakening from agitated dreams, Gregor Samsa found himself, in his bed, transformed into a monstrous vermin. He lay on his hard,

---

1. Translated by Joachim Neugroschel.

armorlike back, and when lifting his head slightly, he could view his brown, vaulted belly partitioned by arching ridges, while on top of it, the blanket, about to slide off altogether, could barely hold. His many legs, wretchedly thin compared with his overall girth, danced helplessly before his eyes.

"What's happened to me?" he wondered. It was no dream. His room, a normal if somewhat tiny human room, lay quietly between the four familiar walls. Above the table, on which a line of fabric samples had been unpacked and spread out (Samsa was a traveling salesman), hung the picture that he had recently clipped from an illustrated magazine and inserted in a pretty gilt frame. The picture showed a lady sitting there upright, bedizened in a fur hat and fur boa, with her entire forearm vanishing inside a heavy fur muff that she held out toward the viewer.

Gregor's eyes then focused on the window, and the dismal weather—raindrops could be heard splattering on the metal ledge—made him feel quite melancholy.

"What if I slept a little more and forgot all about this nonsense," he thought. But his idea was impossible to carry out, for while he was accustomed to sleeping on his right side, his current state prevented him from getting into that position. No matter how forcefully he attempted to wrench himself over on his right side, he kept rocking back into his supine state. He must have tried it a hundred times, closing his eyes to avoid having to look at those wriggling legs, and he gave up only when he started feeling a mild, dull ache in his side such as he had never felt before.

"Oh, God," he thought, "what a strenuous profession I've picked! Day in, day out on the road. It's a lot more stressful than the work in the home office, and along with everything else I also have to put up with these agonies of traveling—worrying about making trains, having bad, irregular meals, meeting new people all the time, but never forming any lasting friendships that mellow into anything intimate. To hell with it all!"

Feeling a slight itch on his belly, he slowly squirmed along on his back toward the bedpost in order to raise his head more easily. Upon locating the itchy place, which was dotted with lots of tiny white specks that he could not fathom, he tried to touch the area with one of his legs, but promptly withdrew it, for the contact sent icy shudders through his body.

He slipped back into his former position.

"Getting up so early all the time," he thought, "makes you totally stupid. A man has to have his sleep. Other traveling salesmen live like harem women. For instance, whenever I return to the hotel during the morning to write up my orders, those men are still having breakfast. Just let me try that with my boss; I'd be kicked out on the spot. And anyway, who knows, that might be very good for me. If I weren't holding back because of my parents, I would have given notice long ago, I would have marched straight up to the boss and told him off from the bottom of my heart. He would have toppled from his desk! Besides, it's so peculiar the way he seats himself on it and talks down to the employees from his great height, and we also have to get right up close because he's so hard of hearing. Well, I haven't abandoned all hope; once I've saved enough to pay off my parents' debt to him—that should take another five or six years—I'll go through with it no matter what. I'll make a big, clean break! But for now, I've got to get up, my train is leaving at five A.M."

And he glanced at the alarm clock ticking on the wardrobe. "God

Almighty!" he thought. It was six-thirty, and the hands of the clock were calmly inching forward, it was even past the half hour, it was almost a quarter to. Could the alarm have failed to go off? From the bed, you could see that it was correctly set at four o'clock; it must have gone off. Yes, but was it possible to sleep peacefully through that furniture-quaking jangle? Well, fine, he had not slept peacefully, though probably all the more soundly. But what should he do now? The next train would be leaving at seven; and to catch it, he would have to rush like mad, and the samples weren't packed up yet, and he felt anything but fresh or sprightly. And even if he did catch the train, there would be no avoiding the boss's fulminations, for the errand boy must have waited at the five A.M. train and long since reported Gregor's failure to show up. The boy was the director's creature, spineless and mindless. Now what if Gregor reported sick? But that would be extremely embarrassing and suspect, for throughout his five years with the firm he had never been sick even once. The boss was bound to come over with the medical-plan doctor, upbraid the parents about their lazy son, and cut off all objections by referring to the doctor, for whom everybody in the world was in the best of health but work-shy. And besides, would the doctor be all that wrong in this case? Aside from his drowsiness, which was really superfluous after his long sleep, Gregor actually felt fine and was even ravenous.

As he speedily turned all these things over in his mind, but could not resolve to get out of bed—the alarm clock was just striking a quarter to seven—there was a cautious rap on the door near the top end of his bed.

"Gregor," a voice called—it was his mother—"it's a quarter to seven. Didn't you have a train to catch?"

The gentle voice! Gregor was shocked to hear his own response; it was unmistakably his earlier voice, but with a painful and insuppressible squeal blending in as if from below, virtually leaving words in their full clarity for just a moment, only to garble them in their resonance, so that you could not tell whether you had heard right. Gregor had meant to reply in detail and explain everything, but, under the circumstances, he limited himself to saying, "Yes, yes, thank you, Mother, I'm getting up."

Because of the wooden door, the change in Gregor's voice was probably not audible on the other side, for the mother was put at ease by his reassurance and she shuffled away. However, their brief exchange had made the rest of the family realize that Gregor, unexpectedly, was still at home, and the father was already at one side door, knocking weakly though with his fist: "Gregor, Gregor," he called, "what's wrong?" And after a short pause, he admonished him again, though in a deeper voice, "Gregor! Gregor!"

At the other side door, however, the sister plaintively murmured, "Gregor? Aren't you well? Do you need anything?"

Gregor replied to both sides, "I'm ready now," and by enunciating fastidiously with drawn-out pauses between words, he tried to eliminate anything abnormal from his voice. Indeed, the father returned to his breakfast; but the sister whispered, "Gregor, open up, I beg you." However, Gregor had absolutely no intention of opening up; instead, he praised the cautious habit he had developed during his travels of locking all doors at night, even in his home.

For now, he wanted to get up calmly and without being nagged, put on his clothes, above all have breakfast, and only then think about what to do next; for he realized he would come to no sensible conclusion by pondering in bed. He remembered that often, perhaps from lying awkwardly, he had felt a slight ache, which, upon his getting up, had turned out to be purely imaginary, and he looked forward to seeing today's fancies gradually fading away. He had no doubt whatsoever that the change in his voice was nothing but the harbinger of a severe cold, an occupational hazard of traveling salesmen.

Throwing off the blanket was quiet simple; all he had to do was puff himself up a little, and it dropped away by itself. Doing anything else, however, was difficult, especially since he was so uncommonly broad. He would have needed arms and hands to prop himself up, and all he had was the numerous tiny legs that kept perpetually moving every which way but without his managing to control them. If he tried to bend a leg, it first straightened out; and if he finally succeeded in taking charge of it, the other legs meanwhile all kept carrying on, as if emancipated, in extreme and painful agitation. "Just don't dawdle in bed," Gregor told himself.

To start with, he wanted to get out of bed with the lower part of his body; but this portion, which, incidentally, he had not yet seen and could not properly visualize, proved too cumbersome to move—it went so slowly. And when eventually, having grown almost frantic, he gathered all his strength and recklessly thrust forward, he chose the wrong direction and slammed violently into the lower bedpost, whereupon the burning pain he then felt made him realize that the lower part of his body might be precisely the most sensitive, at least for now.

He therefore first tried to get his upper portion out of the bed, and to do so he cautiously turned his head toward the side of the mattress. This actually proved easy; and eventually, despite its breadth and weight, his body bulk slowly followed the twisting of his head. But when his head was finally looming over the edge of the bed, in the free air, he was scared of advancing any further in this manner; for if he ultimately let himself plunge down like this, only an outright miracle would prevent injury to his head. And no matter what, he must not lose consciousness now of all times; he would be better off remaining in bed.

But when, sighing after repeating this exertion, he still lay there as before, watching his tiny legs battle each other perhaps even more fiercely and finding no way to bring peace and order to this idiosyncratic condition, he again mused that he could not possibly stay there. The most logical recourse would be to make any sacrifice whatsoever if there was even the slightest hope of his freeing himself from the bed. Yet at the same time, he did not neglect to keep reminding himself that a calm, indeed the calmest reflection was far superior to desperate resolves. In such moments, he fixed his eyes as sharply as he could on the window; but unfortunately, little comfort or encouragement could be drawn from the sight of the morning fog, which shrouded even the other side of the narrow street. "Already seven o'clock," he said to himself when the alarm clock struck again, "already seven o'clock and still such a thick fog." And for a short while, he lay quietly, breathing faintly, as if perhaps expecting the silence to restore real and normal circumstances.

But then he told himself, "I absolutely must be out of bed completely before the clock strikes seven-fifteen. Besides, by then someone from work will come to inquire about me, since the office opens before seven." And he now began seesawing the full length of his body at an altogether even rhythm in order to rock it from the bed. If he could get himself to tumble from the bed in this way, then he would no doubt prevent injury to his head by lifting it sharply while falling. His back seemed hard; nothing was likely to happen to it during the landing on the carpet. His greatest misgiving was about the loud crash that was sure to ensue, probably causing anxiety if not terror behind all the doors. Still, this risk had to be run.

By the time Gregor was already sticking halfway out of the bed (this new method was more of a game than a struggle, all he had to do was keep seesawing and wrenching himself along), it occurred to him how easy everything would be if someone lent him a hand. It would take only two strong people (he thought of his father and the maid); they would only have to slip their arms under his vaulted back, slide him out of the bed, crouch down with their burden, and then just wait patiently and cautiously as he flipped over to the floor, where he hoped his tiny legs would have some purpose. Now quite aside from the fact that the doors were locked, should he really call for assistance? Despite his misery, he could not help smiling at the very idea.

By now he was already seesawing so intensely that he barely managed to keep his balance, and so he would have to make up his mind very soon, for it was already ten after seven—when the doorbell rang. "It's someone from the office," he told himself, almost petrified, while his tiny legs only danced all the more hastily. For an instant, there was total hush. "They're not answering," Gregor said to himself, prey to some absurd hope. But then of course, the maid, as usual, strode firmly to the door and opened it. Gregor only had to hear the visitor's first word of greeting and he knew who it was— the office manager himself. Why oh why was Gregor condemned to working for a company where the slightest tardiness aroused the murkiest suspicions? Was every last employee a scoundrel, wasn't there a single loyal and dedicated person among them, a man who, if he failed to devote even a few morning hours to the firm, would go crazy with remorse, becoming absolutely incapable of leaving his bed? Wouldn't it suffice to send an office boy to inquire—if indeed this snooping were at all necessary? Did the office manager himself have to come, did the entire innocent family have to be shown that this was the only person who had enough brains to be entrusted with investigating this suspicious affair? And more because of these agitating reflections than because of any concrete decision, Gregor swung himself out of bed with all his might. There was a loud thud, but not really a crash. His fall was slightly cushioned by the carpet; and also, his back was more pliable than he had thought. Hence the dull thud was not so blatant. However, by not holding his head carefully enough, he had banged it; now he twisted it, rubbing it on the carpet in annoyance and pain.

"Something fell in there," said the office manager in the left-hand room. Gregor tried to imagine whether something similar to what had happened to him today might not someday happen to the office manager. After all, the possibility had to be granted. However, as if in brusque response to this question, the office manager now took a few resolute steps in the next room, causing his patent-leather boots to creak.

From the right-hand room, the sister informed Gregor in a whisper, "Gregor, the office manager is here."

"I know," said Gregor to himself, not daring to speak loudly enough for the sister to hear.

"Gregor," the father now said from the left-hand room, "the office manager has come to inquire why you didn't catch the early train. We have no idea what to tell him. Besides, he would like to speak to you personally. So please open the door. I'm sure he will be kind enough to overlook the disorder in the room."

"Good morning, Mr. Samsa," the office manager was calling amiably.

"He's not well," the mother said to the office manager while the father kept talking through the door, "he's not well, believe me, sir. Why else would Gregor miss a train! I mean, the boy thinks of nothing but his job. I'm almost annoyed that he never goes out in the evening; goodness, he's been back in town for a whole week now, but he's stayed in every single night. He just sits here at the table, quietly reading the newspaper or poring over timetables. The only fun he has is when he does some fretsawing. For instance, he spent two or three evenings carving out a small picture frame; you'd be amazed how pretty it is. It's hanging inside, in his room; you'll see it in a moment when Gregor opens the door. By the way, sir, I'm delighted that you're here; we could never have gotten Gregor to unlock the door by ourselves—he's so stubborn; and he must be under the weather, even though he denied it this morning."

"I'll be right there," said Gregor slowly and deliberately, but not stirring so as not to miss one word of the conversation.

"I can think of no other explanation either, Mrs. Samsa," said the manager, "I do hope it is nothing serious. Though still and all, I must say that for business reasons we businessmen—unfortunately or fortunately, as you will—very often must simply overcome a minor indisposition."

"Well, can the manager come into your room now?" asked the impatient father, knocking on the door again.

"No," said Gregor. In the left-hand room there was an embarrassed silence, in the right-hand room the sister began sobbing.

Why didn't she join the others? She had probably only just gotten out of bed and not yet started dressing. And what was she crying about? Because Gregor wouldn't get up and let the manager in, because he was in danger of losing his job, and because the boss would then go back to dunning Gregor's parents with his old claims? For the time being, those were most likely pointless worries. Gregor was still here and had no intention whatsoever of running out on his family. True, at this moment he was simply lying on the carpet, and no one aware of his condition would have seriously expected him to let in the manager. Indeed, Gregor could hardly be dismissed on the spot for this petty discourtesy, for which he would easily hit on an appropriate excuse later on. He felt it would make far more sense if they left him alone for now instead of pestering him with tears and coaxing. However, the others were in a state of suspense, which justified their behavior.

"Mr. Samsa," the manager now called out, raising his voice, "what is wrong? You are barricading yourself in your room, answering only 'yes' or 'no,' causing your parents serious and unnecessary anxieties, and—I only mention this in passing—neglecting your professional duties in a truly outrageous manner. I am speaking on behalf of your parents and the director of the firm and I am quite earnestly requesting an immediate and cogent explanation. I am dumbfounded, dumbfounded. I believed you to be a quiet, reasonable person, and now you suddenly seem intent on flaunting bizarre moods. This morning the director hinted at a possible explanation for your tardiness—it pertained to the cash collections that you were recently entrusted with—but in fact I practically gave him my word of honor that this explanation could not be valid. Now, however, I am witnessing your incomprehensible stubbornness, which makes me lose any and all desire to speak up for you in any way whatsoever. And your job is by no means rock solid. My original intention was to tell you all this in private, but since you are forcing me to waste my time here needlessly, I see no reason why your parents should not find out as well. Frankly, your recent work has been highly unsatisfactory. We do appreciate that this is not the season for doing a lot of business; still, there is no season whatsoever, there can be no season for doing no business at all, Mr. Samsa."

"But, sir," Gregor exclaimed, beside himself, forgetting everything else in his agitation, "I'll open the door immediately, this very instant. A slight indisposition, a dizzy spell have prevented me from getting up. I am still lying in bed. But now I am quite fresh again. I am getting out of bed this very second. Please be patient for another moment or two! It is not going as well as I expected. But I do feel fine. How suddenly it can overcome a person! Just last night I was quite well, my parents know I was—or rather, last night I did have a slight foreboding. It must have been obvious to anyone else. Just why didn't I report it at the office!? But one always thinks one can get over an illness without staying home. Sir! Please spare my parents! There are no grounds for any of the things you are accusing me of—in fact, no one has ever so much as breathed a word to me. Perhaps you have not seen the latest orders that I sent in. Anyhow, I *will* be catching the eight A.M. train, these several hours of rest have revitalized me. Do not waste any more of your time, sir; I'll be in the office myself instantly—please be kind enough to inform them of this and to give my best to the director!"

And while hastily blurting out all these things, barely knowing what he was saying, Gregor, most likely because of his practice in bed, had managed to get closer to the wardrobe and was now trying to pull himself up against it. He truly wanted to open the door, truly show himself and speak to the office manager; he was eager to learn what the others, who were so keen on his presence now, would say upon seeing him. If they were shocked, then Gregor would bear no further responsibility and could hold his peace. But if they accepted everything calmly, then he like-wise had no reason to get upset, and could, if he stepped on it, actually be in the station by eight. At first, he kept sliding down the smooth side of the wardrobe, but eventually he gave himself a final swing and stood there ignoring the burning pains in his abdomen, distressful as they were. Next he let himself keel over against the back of a nearby chair, his tiny legs clinging to the edges. In this way, he gained control of himself and he kept silent, for now he could listen to the office manager.

"Did you understand a single word of that?" the office manager asked the parents. "He's not trying to make fools of us, is he?!"

"For goodness' sake," the mother exclaimed, already weeping, "he may be seriously ill and we're torturing him. Grete! Grete!" she then shouted.

"Mother?" the sister called from the other side. They were communicating across Gregor's room. "You have to go to the doctor immediately. Gregor is sick. Hurry, get the doctor. Did you hear Gregor talking just now?"

"That was an animal's voice," said the manager, his tone noticeably soft compared with the mother's shouting.

"Anna! Anna!" the father called through the vestibule into the kitchen, clapping his hands, "Get a locksmith immediately!" And the two girls, their skirts rustling, were already dashing through the vestibule (how could the sister have dressed so quickly?) and tearing the apartment door open. No one heard it slamming; they must have left it open, as is common in homes that are struck by disaster.

Gregor, however, had grown much calmer. True, the others no longer understood what he said even though it sounded clear enough to him, clearer than before, perhaps because his ears had gotten used to it. But nevertheless, the others now believed there was something not quite right about him, and they were willing to help. His spirits were brightened by the aplomb and assurance with which their first few instructions had been carried out. He felt included once again in human society and, without really drawing a sharp distinction between the doctor and the locksmith, he expected magnificent and astonishing feats from both. Trying to make his voice as audible as he could for the crucial discussions about to take place, he coughed up a little, though taking pains to do so quite softly, since this noise too might sound different from human coughing, which he no longer felt capable of judging for himself. Meanwhile, the next room had become utterly hushed. Perhaps the parents and the office manager were sitting and whispering at the table, perhaps they were all leaning against the doors and eavesdropping.

Gregor slowly lumbered toward the door, shoving the chair along, let go of it upon arriving, tackled the door, held himself erect against it—the pads on his tiny feet were a bit sticky—and for a moment he rested from the strain. But then, using his mouth, he began twisting the key in the lock. Unfortunately he appeared to have no real teeth—now with what should he grasp the key?—but to make up for it his jaws were, of course, very powerful. They actually enabled him to get the key moving, whereby he ignored the likelihood of his harming himself in some way, for a brown liquid oozed from his mouth, flowing over the key and dripping to the floor.

"Listen," said the office manager in the next room, "he's turning the key." This was very encouraging for Gregor; but everyone should have cheered him on, including the father and the mother. "Attaboy, Gregor!" they should have shouted. "Don't let go, get that lock!" And imagining them all as suspensefully following his efforts, he obliviously bit into the key with all the strength he could muster. In tune with his progress in turning the key, he kept dancing around the lock, holding himself upright purely by his mouth and, as need be, either dangling from the key or pushing it down again with the full heft of his body. It was the sharper click of the lock finally snapping back that literally brought Gregor to. Sighing in relief, he told himself, "So I didn't need the locksmith after all," and he put his head on the handle in order to pull one wing of the double door all the way in.

Since he had to stay on the same side as the key, the door actually swung back quite far without his becoming visible. He had to twist slowly around the one wing, and very gingerly at that, to avoid plopping over on his back before entering the next room. He was still busy performing this tricky maneuver, with no time to heed anything else, when he heard the office manager blurt out a loud "Oh!"—it sounded like a whoosh of wind—and now he also saw him, the person nearest to the door, pressing his hand to his open mouth and slowly shrinking back as if he were being ousted by some unseeable but relentless force. The mother, who, despite the office manager's presence, stood there with her hair still undone and bristling, first gaped at the father, clasping her hands, then took two steps toward Gregor and collapsed, her petticoats flouncing out all around her and her face sinking quite undetectably into her breasts. The father clenched his fist, glaring at Gregor as if trying to shove him back into his room, then peered unsteadily around the parlor before covering his eyes with his hands and weeping so hard that his powerful chest began to quake.

Gregor did not step into the parlor after all; instead he leaned against his side of the firmly bolted second wing of the door, so that only half his body could be seen along with his head, which tilted sideways above it, peeping out at the others. Meanwhile the day had grown much lighter. Across the street, a portion of the endless, grayish black building (it was a hospital) stood out clearly with its regular windows harshly disrupting the façade. The rain was still falling, but only in large, visibly separate drops that were also literally hurled separately to the ground. The breakfast dishes still abundantly covered the table because breakfast was the most important meal of the day for Gregor's father; and he would draw it out for hours on end by reading various newspapers. The opposite wall sported a photograph of Gregor from his military days: it showed him as a lieutenant, hand on sword, with a carefree smile, demanding respect for his bearing and his uniform. The vestibule door was open, and since the apartment door was open too, one could see all the way out to the landing and the top of the descending stairs.

"Well," said Gregor, quite aware of being the only one who had kept calm, "I'll be dressed in a minute, pack up my samples, and catch my train. Would you all, would you all let me go on the road? Well, sir, you can see I am not stubborn and I enjoy working. Traveling is arduous, but I could not live without it. Why, where are you going, sir? To the office? Right? Will you report all this accurately? A man may be temporarily incapacitated, but that is precisely the proper time to remember his past achievements and to bear in mind that later on, once the obstacle is eliminated, he is sure to work all the harder and more intently. After all, I am so deeply obligated to the director, you know that very well. And then, I have to take care of my parents and my sister. I'm in a tight spot, but still I'll work my way out again. So please don't make things more difficult for me than they already are. Put in a good word for me at the office! People don't like a traveling salesman, I know. They think he makes barrels of money and has a wonderful life. They simply have no special reason to examine their prejudice. But you, sir, you have a better notion of what it's all about than the rest of the staff, why, than even—this is strictly between us—a better notion than even the director, who, as owner of the firm, is easily swayed against an employee. You also know very well that a traveling salesman, being away from the office most of the year, can so easily fall victim to gossip, coincidences, and unwarranted complaints, and he cannot possibly defend himself since he almost never finds out about them, except perhaps when he returns from a trip, exhausted, and personally suffers their awful consequences at home without fathoming their inscrutable causes. Sir, please do not leave without saying something to show that you agree with me at least to some small extent!"

But the office manager had already turned away at Gregor's very first words, and he only looked back at him over his twitching shoulder and with gaping lips. Indeed during Gregor's speech, the manager did not halt for even an instant. Rather, without losing sight of Gregor, he retreated toward the door, but only very gradually, as if there were some secret ban on leaving the room. He was already in the vestibule, and to judge by his abrupt movement when he finally pulled his leg out of the parlor, one might have thought he had just burned the sole of his foot. In the vestibule, however, he stretched out his right hand very far, toward the staircase, as if some unearthly redemption were awaiting him there.

Gregor realized he must on no account allow the office manager to leave in this frame of mind; if he did, Gregor's position at the office would be thoroughly compromised. The parents did not quite understand this. During these long years, they had become convinced that he was set up for life at this firm, and besides they were so preoccupied with their immediate problems as to have lost all sense of foresight. Gregor, however, did possess such foresight. The office manager had to be held back, calmed down, cajoled, and finally won over; Gregor's future and that of his family hinged on it! If only the sister had been here! She was intelligent; she had already started to cry when Gregor was still lying calmly on his back. And the office manager, that ladies' man, would certainly have let her take him in hand: she would have shut the apartment door, kept him in the vestibule, and talked him out of his terror. But the sister was not there, so Gregor had to act on his own. Forgetting that he was yet unacquainted with his current powers of movement and also that once again his words had possibly, indeed probably, not been understood, he left the wing of the door and lumbered through the opening. He intended to head toward the office manager, who was ludicrously clutching the banister on the landing with both hands. But Gregor, fumbling for support, yelped as he flopped down upon his many tiny legs. The instant this happened, he felt a physical ease and comfort for the first time that morning. His tiny legs had solid ground underneath, and he was delighted to note that they were utterly obedient—they even strove to carry him off to wherever he wished; and he already believed that the final recovery from all sufferings was at hand. He lay on the floor, wobbling because of his checked movement, not that far from his mother, who seemed altogether self-absorbed. But at that same moment, she unexpectedly leaped up, stretched her arms far apart, splayed her fingers, and cried, "Help! For God's sake, help!" Next she lowered her head as if to see Gregor more clearly, but then, in self-contradiction, she senselessly backed away, forgetting the covered table behind her, hurriedly sat down upon it without thinking, and apparently failed to notice that next to her the large coffeepot had been knocked over and was discharging a torrent of coffee full force upon the carpet.

"Mother, Mother," Gregor murmured, looking up at her. For an instant, the office manager had entirely slipped his mind; on the other hand, Gregor could not help snapping his jaws a few times at the sight of the flowing coffee. This prompted the mother to scream again, flee from the table, and collapse into the father's arms as he came dashing up to her. But Gregor had no time for his parents: the office manager was already on the stairs; with his chin on the banister, he took one final look back. Gregor broke into a run, doing his best to catch up with him. The office manager must have had an inkling of this, for he jumped down several steps at a time and disappeared. However, he did shout, "Ugh!" and his shout rang through the entire stairwell.

Unfortunately, the father, who so far had stayed relatively composed, seemed thoroughly bewildered by the office manager's flight. For, instead of rushing after him or at least not preventing Gregor from pursuing him, the father, with his right hand, grabbed the cane that the office manager, together with a hat and overcoat, had forgotten on a chair and, with his left hand, took a large newspaper from the table. Stamping his feet, he brandished the cane and the newspaper at Gregor in order to drive him back into his room. No pleading from Gregor helped, indeed no pleading was understood; no matter how humbly Gregor turned his head, the father merely stamped his feet all the more forcefully. Across the room, the mother had flung open a window despite the cool weather, and leaning way out, she buried her face in her hands. A strong draft arose between the street and the stairwell, the window curtains flew up, the newspapers rustled on the table, stray pages wafted across the floor. The father charged pitilessly, spewing hisses like a savage. Since Gregor as yet had no practice in moving backwards, it was really slow going. Had he only been permitted to wheel around, he would have been inside his room at once. But he was afraid it would take too long, trying the father's patience even more—and at any moment now the cane in the father's hand threatened to deal the lethal blow to Gregor's back or head. Ultimately, however, Gregor had no choice, for he realized with dismay that he did not even know how to stay the course when backing up. And so, while constantly darting fearful side glances at his father, he began rotating as swiftly as he could, though he was actually very slow. Perhaps the father sensed Gregor's good intention, for he did not interfere—instead, he occasionally even steered the pivoting motion from a distance with the tip of his cane. If only the father would stop that unbearable hissing! It made Gregor lose his head altogether. He had swung around almost fully when, constantly distracted by those hisses, he actually miscalculated and briefly shifted the wrong way. And then, as soon as he finally managed to get his head to the doorway, his body proved too broad to squeeze through all that readily. Naturally, in the father's present mood, it never even remotely crossed his mind to push back the other wing of the door and create a passage wide enough for Gregor. He was obsessed simply with forcing Gregor back into his room as fast as possible. Nor would he ever have stood for the intricate preparations that Gregor needed for hoisting himself on end and perhaps passing through the doorway in that posture. Instead, as if there were no hindrance, the father drove Gregor forward with a great uproar: behind Gregor the yelling no longer sounded like the voice of merely one father. Now it was do or die, and Gregor—come what might—jammed into the doorway. With one side of his body heaving up, he sprawled lopsided in the opening. His one flank was bruised raw, ugly splotches remained on the white door, and he was soon wedged in and unable to budge on his own. The tiny legs on his one side were dangling and trembling in midair and the tiny legs on his other side were painfully crushed against the floor. But now the father gave him a powerful shove from behind—a true deliverance. And

Gregor, bleeding heavily, flew far into his room. The door was slammed shut with the cane, and then the apartment was still at last.

II

It was almost dusk by the time Gregor emerged from his comatose sleep. He would certainly have awoken not much later even without being disturbed, for he felt sufficiently well rested; yet it seemed to him as if he had been aroused by fleeting steps and a cautious shutting of the vestibule door. The glow from the electric streetlamps produced pallid spots on the ceiling and the higher parts of the furniture, but down by Gregor it was dark. Slowly, still clumsily groping with his feelers, which he was just learning to appreciate, he lumbered toward the door to see what had been going on. His left side appeared to be one long, unpleasantly tightening scar, and he actually had to limp on his two rows of legs. One tiny leg, moreover, had been badly hurt during that morning's events (it was almost miraculous that only one had been hurt) and it dragged along lifelessly.

Only upon reaching the door did Gregor discover what had actually enticed him: it was the smell of something edible. For there stood a bowl full of fresh milk with tiny slices of white bread floating in it. He practically chortled for joy, being even hungrier now than in the morning, and he promptly dunked his head into the milk until it was nearly over his eyes. Soon, however, he withdrew his head in disappointment. Not only did the bruises on his left side make it difficult for him to eat—he could eat only if his entire wheezing body joined in—but he did not care for the milk, even though it had always been his favorite beverage, which was no doubt why his sister had placed it in his room. As a matter of fact, he turned away from the bowl almost with loathing and crawled back to the middle of the room.

In the parlor, as Gregor could see through the door crack, the gaslight was lit. But while at this time of day his father would usually take up his newspaper, an afternoon daily, and read it in a raised voice to the mother and sometimes also to the sister, not a sound was to be heard. Well, perhaps this practice of reading aloud, which the sister had always told Gregor about and written him about, had recently been discarded altogether. Yet while the entire apartment was hushed, it was anything but deserted.

"My, what a quiet life the family used to lead," Gregor thought to himself, and as he peered into the darkness, he felt a certain pride that he had managed to provide his parents and his sister with such a life in such a beautiful apartment. What if now all calm, all prosperity, all contentment should come to a horrifying end? Rather than lose himself in such ruminations, Gregor preferred to start moving, and so he crept up and down the room.

Once, during the long evening, one side door and then the other was opened a tiny crack and quickly shut again: somebody had apparently felt an urge to come in, but had then thought the better of it. Gregor halted right at the parlor door, determined to somehow bring in the hesitant visitor or at least find out who it was. But the door was not reopened, and Gregor waited in vain. That morning, when the doors had been locked, everybody had wanted to come in; but now that he had opened one door, and the rest had clearly been opened during the day, nobody came, and the keys were on the other side.

It was not until late at night that the light in the parlor was put out. Gregor could easily tell that the parents and the sister had stayed up this long, for, as he could clearly discern, all three of them were tiptoeing off. Since nobody would be visiting Gregor until morning, he had lots of time to reflect undisturbed and to figure out how to restructure his life. But the free, high-ceilinged room where he was forced to lie flat on the floor terrified him without his being able to pinpoint the cause; after all, it was his room and he had been living there for the last five years. Turning half involuntarily and not without a faint sense of embarrassment, he scurried under the settee, where, even though his back was a bit squashed and he could not lift his head, he instantly felt very cozy, regretting only that his body was too broad to squeeze in all the way.

There he remained for the rest of the night, either drowsing and repeatedly yanked awake by his hunger, or else fretting amid vague hopes, all of which, however, led to his concluding that for now he would have to lie low and, by being patient and utterly considerate, help the family endure the inconveniences that, as it happened, he was forced to cause them in his present state.

By early morning—it was still almost night—Gregor had a chance to test the strength of the resolutions he had just made, for the sister, almost fully dressed, opened the vestibule door and suspensefully peered in. She did not find him right away, but when she noticed him under the settee (goodness, he had to be somewhere, he couldn't just have flown away), she was so startled that unable to control herself she slammed the door from the outside. But, apparently regretting her behavior, she instantly reopened the door and tiptoed in as if visiting a very sick patient or even a stranger. Gregor, having pushed his head forward to the very edge of the settee, was watching her. Would she notice that he had barely touched the milk, though by no means for lack of hunger, and would she bring in some other kind of food more to his taste? If she did not do so on her own, he would rather starve to death than point it out to her, even while he felt a tremendous urge to scoot out from under the settee, throw himself at her feet, and beg her for some good food. But the sister, with some surprise, instantly noticed the full bowl, from which only a little milk had splattered all around. She promptly picked up the bowl, though not with her bare hands, but with a rag, and carried it away. Gregor was extremely curious as to what she would replace it with, and all sorts of conjectures ran through his mind. But he would never have hit on what the sister actually did in the goodness of her heart. Hoping to check his likes and dislikes, she brought him a whole array of food, all spread out on an old newspaper. There were old, half-rotten vegetables, some bones left over from supper and coated with a solidified white sauce, a few raisins and almonds, some cheese that Gregor had declared inedible two days ago, dry bread, bread and butter, and salted bread and butter. Furthermore, along with all those things, she brought some water in the bowl, which had probably been assigned to Gregor for good. And sensing that Gregor would not eat in front of her, she discreetly hurried away, even turning the key, just to show him that he could make himself as comfortable as he wished. Gregor's tiny legs whirred as he charged toward the food. His wounds, incidentally, must have healed up by now, he felt no handicap anymore, which was astonishing; for, as he recalled, after he had nicked his finger with a knife over a month ago, the injury had still been hurting the day before yesterday. "Am I less sensitive now?" he wondered, greedily sucking at the cheese, which had promptly exerted a more emphatic attraction on him than any of the other food. His eyes watered with contentment as he gulped down the cheese, the vegetables, and the sauce in rapid succession. By contrast, he did not relish the fresh foods, he could not even stand their smells, and he actually dragged the things he wanted to eat a short distance away. He was already done long since and was simply lazing in the same spot when the sister, to signal that he should withdraw, slowly turned the key. Startled, he jumped up though he was almost dozing, and scuttered back under the settee. However, it took a lot of self-control to remain there even during the few short moments that the sister spent in the room, for his body was slightly bloated from the ample food and he could scarcely breathe in that cramped space. Amid short fits of suffocation, he stared with somewhat bulging eyes while the unsuspecting sister, wielding a broom, swept up not only the leftovers but also the un- touched food, as if this too were now unusable; she then hastily dumped everything into a pail, shutting its wooden lid and carrying everything out. No sooner had she turned her back than he skulked out from under the settee and began stretching and puffing up.

That was how Gregor received his food every day: once in the morning, when the parents and the maid were still asleep, and the second time after the family lunch, for the parents would then take a brief nap while the sister would send the maid out on some errand. While the parents certainly did not want Gregor to starve either, they may not have endured knowing more about his eating than from hearsay, or the sister may have wished to spare them some—perhaps only slight—grief, for they were really suffering enough as it was.

Gregor could not find out what excuses they had come up with to get the doctor and the locksmith out of the apartment; for since he was not under- stood, no one, including the sister, assumed that he could understand them. And so, whenever she was in his room, he had to content himself with occa- sionally hearing her sighs and her appeals to the saints. It was only later, when she had gotten a bit accustomed to everything (naturally there could be no question of her ever becoming fully accustomed), Gregor sometimes caught a remark that was meant to be friendly or might be interpreted as such. "He certainly enjoyed it today," she would say when Gregor had pol- ished off a good portion of the food; while in the opposite event, which was gradually becoming more and more frequent, she would say almost sadly: "Now once again nothing's been touched."

But while Gregor could learn no news directly, he would eavesdrop, pick- ing up a few things from the adjacent rooms, and the instant he heard voices, he would promptly scuttle over to the appropriate door, squeezing his entire body against it. During the early period in particular, no conversation took place that was not somehow about him, even if only in secret. For two whole days, every single meal was filled with discussions about what they ought to do; but even between meals, they kept harping on the same theme, for there were always at least two family members in the apartment, since plainly nobody wished to stay home alone and they could by no means all go out at the same time. Furthermore, on the very first day, the maid—it was not quite clear how much she knew about what had occurred—had implored the mother on bended knees to dismiss her immediately. Then, saying goodbye a quarter hour later, she had tearfully thanked them for the dismissal as if it were the most benevolent deed that they had ever done for her; and without being asked, she had sworn a dreadful oath that she would never breathe a single word to anyone.

So now the sister, together with the mother, also had to do the cooking; but this was not much of a bother, for they ate next to nothing. Over and over, Gregor heard them urging one another to eat, though in vain, receiving no other answer than, "Thanks, I've had enough," or something similar. They may not have drunk anything either. The sister would often ask the father if he would like some beer and she warmly offered to go and get it herself; when he failed to respond, she anticipated any misgivings on his part by saying she could also send the janitor's wife. But then the father would finally utter an emphatic "No," and the subject was no longer broached.

In the course of the very first day, the father laid out their overall financial circumstances and prospects to both the mother and the sister. From time to time, he rose from the table to fetch some document or notebook from his small strongbox, which he had salvaged after the collapse of his business five years earlier. They heard him opening the complicated lock and then shutting it again after removing whatever he had been looking for. The father's explanations were to some extent the first pleasant news that Gregor got to hear since his imprisonment. He had been under the impression that the father had failed to rescue anything from his business—at least, the father had told him nothing to the contrary, nor, admittedly, had Gregor ever asked him. Gregor's sole concern at that time had been to do whatever he could to make the family forget as quickly as possible the business catastrophe that had plunged them all into utter despair. And so he had thrown himself into his job with tremendous fervor, working his way up, almost overnight, from minor clerk to traveling salesman, who, naturally, had an altogether different earning potential and whose professional triumphs were instantly translated, by way of commissions, into cash, which could be placed on the table at home for the astonished and delighted family. Those had been lovely times, and they had never recurred, at least not with that same luster, even though Gregor was eventually earning so much money that he was able to cover and indeed did cover all the expenditures of the family. They had simply grown accustomed to this, both the family and Gregor; they accepted the money gratefully, he was glad to hand it over, but no great warmth came of it. Only the sister had remained close to Gregor; and since she, unlike Gregor, loved music and could play the violin poignantly, he was secretly planning to send her to the conservatory next year regardless of the great expense that it was bound to entail and that would certainly be made up for in some other way. During Gregor's brief stays in the city, the conservatory was often mentioned in his talks with the sister, but only as a lovely dream that could never possibly be realized; nor did the parents care to hear these innocent references. But Gregor's ideas on the subject were very definite and he intended to make the solemn announcement on Christmas Eve.

Such were the thoughts, quite futile in his present condition, that ran through his mind as he clung upright to the door, eavesdropping. Sometimes he was so thoroughly exhausted that he could no longer listen. His head would then inadvertently bump against the door, but he promptly pulled it erect again; for even that slight tap had been heard in the next room, causing everyone to stop talking. "What's he up to now!?" the father would say after a while, obviously turning toward the door, and only then did the interrupted conversation gradually resume.

Gregor now learned precisely enough (for the father would often repeat his explanations, partly because he himself had not dealt with these matters in a long time and partly because the mother did not always understand everything right off) that despite the disaster, some assets, albeit a very tiny sum, had survived from the old days, growing bit by bit because of the untouched interest. Furthermore, since the money that Gregor had brought home every month (keeping only a little for himself) had never been fully spent, it had accumulated into a small principal. Gregor, behind his door, nodded eagerly, delighted at this unexpected thrift and prudence. Actually, he could have applied this surplus toward settling the father's debt to the director, thereby bringing the day when he could have been rid of that job a lot closer; but now, the way the father had arranged things was better, no doubt.

Of course this sum was by no means large enough for the family to live off the interest; it might suffice to keep them going for one, at most two years, and that was all. It was simply money that really should not be drawn on and that ought to be put aside for emergencies, while the money to live on had to be earned. But the father, though still healthy, was an old man, who had not done a lick of work in five years and in any case could not be expected to take on very much. During those five years, his first vacation in an arduous and yet unsuccessful life, he had grown very fat, becoming rather clumsy. And should perhaps the old mother go to work—she, who suffered from asthma, who found it strenuous just walking through the apartment, and who spent every other day on the sofa, gasping for air by the open window? Or should the sister go to work—she, who was still a child at seventeen and should certainly keep enjoying her lifestyle, which consisted of dressing nicely, sleeping late, lending a hand with the housekeeping, going out to a few modest amusements, and above all, playing the violin? At first, whenever the conversation turned to this need to earn money, Gregor would always let go of the door and throw himself on the cool leather sofa nearby, for he felt quite hot with shame and grief.

Often he would lie there all through the long night, not getting a wink of sleep and merely scrabbling on the leather for hours on end. Or else, undaunted by the great effort, he would shove a chair over to the window, clamber up to the sill, and, propped on the chair, lean against the panes, obviously indulging in some vague memory of the freedom he had once found by gazing out the window. For actually, from day to day, even the things that were rather close were growing hazier and hazier; he could no longer even make out the hospital across the street, the all-too-frequent sight of which he used to curse. And if he had not known for sure that he lived on Charlotte Street, a quiet but entirely urban thoroughfare, he might have believed that he was staring at a wasteland in which gray sky and gray earth blurred together indistinguishably. Only twice had the observant sister needed to see the chair standing by the window; now, whenever she tidied up the room she would push the chair back to the window—indeed, from then on she would even leave the inside casement ajar.

If only Gregor could have spoken to her and thanked her for everything she had to do for him, he would have endured her kind actions more readily; but instead they caused him great suffering. Of course, she tried to surmount the overall embarrassment as much as possible, and naturally, as time wore by, she succeeded more and more. However, Gregor too eventually gained a sharper sense of things. Her very entrance was already terrible for him. No sooner had she stepped in than, without even taking time to close the door— careful as she usually was to protect everyone else from seeing Gregor's room—she charged straight over to the window and, as if almost suffocating, yanked it open with hasty hands, lingering there briefly no matter how chilly the weather and inhaling deeply. This din and dashing terrified Gregor twice a day. Throughout her visits he would cower under the settee, fully realizing that she would certainly have preferred to spare him this disturbance if only she had been able to keep the window shut while staying in the same room with him.

Once—something like a month had passed since Gregor's metamorphosis, and there was truly no special reason why the sister should still be alarmed by his appearance—she turned up a bit earlier than usual and caught Gregor staring out the window, motionless and terrifyingly erect. He would not have been surprised if she had refused to come in since his position prevented her from opening the window immediately. But not only did she not come in, she actually recoiled and closed the door; an outsider might have honestly thought that Gregor had meant to ambush her and bite her. Naturally he hid under the settee at once, but then had to wait until noon for his sister to return, and she seemed far more upset than usual. It thus dawned on him that his looks were still unbearable to her and were bound to remain unbearable, which meant that it must have taken a lot of self-control for her not to run away upon glimpsing even the tiny scrap of his body that protruded from under the settee. So one day, hoping to spare her even this sight—the job took him four hours—he got the sheet on his back and lugged it over to the settee, arranging it in such a way that it concealed him entirely, thereby preventing the sister from seeing him even when she stooped down. After all, if she considered the sheet unnecessary, she could have removed it, for it was plain that Gregor could not possibly enjoy cutting himself off so thoroughly. But she left the sheet just as it was, and once, he even believed he caught a grateful glance when he cautiously lifted it a smidgen with his head to see how his sister was taking this innovation.

During the first two weeks, the parents could not get themselves to come into his room, and he often heard them expressing their great appreciation of the sister's efforts, whereas earlier they had often been cross with her for being, they felt, a somewhat useless girl. But now both the father and the mother would frequently wait outside Gregor's door while the sister tidied up inside, and upon reemerging, she promptly had to render a detailed account of what the room looked like, what Gregor had eaten, how he had behaved this time, and whether he was perhaps showing some slight improvement. The mother, incidentally, wanted to visit Gregor relatively soon. At first, the father and the sister tried to reason with her, and Gregor paid very close attention to their arguments, approving of them wholeheartedly. Later, however, the mother had to be held back forcibly, and when she then cried out, "Let me go to Gregor, he's my unhappy son! Don't you understand I have to go to him?" Gregor felt it might be a good idea if she did come in after all—not every day, naturally, but perhaps once a week: she was much better at everything than the sister, who, for all her courage, was still a child and might ultimately have taken on such a demanding task purely out of teenage capriciousness.

Gregor's wish to see his mother came true shortly. During the day, if only out of consideration for his parents, he did not want to appear at the window. On the other hand, he could not creep very far around the few square meters of the floor, he found it hard to lie still even at night, and eating soon gave him no pleasure whatsoever. So, for amusement, he got into the habit of prowling crisscross over the walls and ceiling. He particularly liked hanging from the ceiling. It was quite different from lying on the floor: he could breathe more freely and a faint tingle quivered through his body. In his almost blissful woolgathering up there, Gregor might, to his own surprise, let go and crash down on the floor. But since he naturally now controlled his body far more effectively than before, he was never harmed by that great plunge. The sister instantly noticed the new entertainment that Gregor had found for himself—after all, when creeping, he occasionally left traces of his sticky substance behind. And so, taking it into her head to enable Gregor to crawl over the widest possible area, she decided to remove the obstructive furniture—especially the wardrobe and the desk. However, there was no way she could manage this alone. She did not dare ask her father for help, and the maid would most certainly not have pitched in; for while this girl, who was about sixteen, had been valiantly sticking it out since the cook's departure, she had asked for the special favor of keeping the kitchen door locked all the time and opening it only when specifically called. As a result, the sister had no choice but to approach the mother one day during the father's absence. And indeed, with cries of joyful excitement, the mother came over, although falling silent at the door to Gregor's room. First, naturally, the sister checked inside to make sure everything was in order; only then did she let the mother enter. Gregor had hurriedly pulled the sheet lower and in tighter folds, truly making it look as if it had been tossed casually over the settee. This time, Gregor also refrained from peeping out from under the sheet: he would go without seeing the mother for now and was simply glad that she had come despite everything.

"Come on, he's out of sight," said the sister, evidently leading the mother by the hand. Gregor now heard the two delicate women pushing the very heavy old wardrobe from its place and the sister constantly insisting on doing the major share of the work, ignoring the warnings from the mother, who was afraid she would overexert herself. It took a very long time. After probably just a quarter hour of drudging, the mother said it would be better if they left the wardrobe here. For one thing, it was too heavy—they would not be done before the father's arrival; and if the wardrobe stood in the middle of the room, it would block Gregor's movements in all directions. Secondly, it was not at all certain that they were doing Gregor a favor by removing the furniture. She said that the opposite seemed to be the case, the sight of the bare wall literally made her heart bleed. And why wouldn't Gregor respond in the same way since he was long accustomed to the furniture and would therefore feel desolate in the empty room? "And isn't that," the mother concluded very softly (in fact, she persistently almost whispered, as if, not knowing Gregor's precise whereabouts, she wanted to keep him from hearing the very sound of her voice, convinced as she was that he did not understand the words), "and if we remove the furniture, isn't that like showing him that we've given up all hope of his improvement and that we're callously leaving him to his own devices? I believe it would be best if we tried to keep the room just as it was, so that when Gregor comes back to us he will find that nothing's been changed and it will be much easier for him to forget what happened."

Upon hearing the mother's words, Gregor realized that in the course of these two months the lack of having anyone to converse with, plus the monotonous life in the midst of the family, must have befuddled his mind, for there was no other way to account for how he could have seriously longed to have his room emptied out. Did he really want the warm room, so cozily appointed with heirlooms, transformed into a lair, where he might, of course, be able to creep, unimpeded, in any direction, though forgetting his human past swiftly and totally? By now, he was already on the verge of forgetting, and had been brought up sharply only by the mother's voice after not hearing it for a long time. Nothing should be removed, everything had to remain: he could not do without the positive effects of the furniture on his state of mind. And if the furniture interfered with his senselessly crawling about, then it was a great asset and no loss.

Unfortunately, the sister was of a different mind; in the discussions concerning Gregor, she had gotten into the habit—not without some justification, to be sure—of acting the great expert in front of the parents. So now the mother's advice was again reason enough for the sister to demand that they remove not only the wardrobe and the desk, in line with her original plan, but all the furniture except for the indispensable settee. Her resoluteness was, naturally, prompted not just by childish defiance and the unexpected self-confidence she had recently gained at such great cost. After all, she had observed that while he needed a lot of space to creep around in, Gregor, so far as could be seen, made no use whatsoever of the furniture. Perhaps, however, the enthusiasm of girls her age also played its part—an exuberance that they try to indulge every chance they get. It now inveigled Grete into making Gregor's situation even more terrifying, so she could do even more for him than previously. For most likely no one but Grete would ever dare venture into a room where Gregor ruled the bare walls all alone.

And so she dug in her heels, refusing to give in to the mother, who, apparently quite anxious and uncertain of herself in this room, soon held her tongue and, to the best of her ability, helped the sister push out the wardrobe. Well, Gregor could, if necessary, do without the wardrobe, but the desk had to remain. And no sooner had the squeezing, groaning women shoved the wardrobe through the doorway than Gregor poked his head out from under the settee to judge how he could intervene as cautiously and considerately as possible. But alas, it was precisely the mother who was the first to return while Grete was still in the next room, holding her arms around the wardrobe and rocking it back and forth by herself without, of course, getting it to budge from the spot. The mother, however, was not used to the sight of Gregor—it might sicken her. And so Gregor, terrified, scuttered backwards to the other end of the settee, but was unable to prevent the front of the sheet from stirring slightly. That was enough to catch the mother's eye. She halted, stood still for an instant, then went back to Grete.

Gregor kept telling himself that nothing out of the ordinary was happening, it was just some furniture being moved. But these comings and goings of the women, their soft calls to one another, the scraping of the furniture along the floor was, as he soon had to admit, like a huge rumpus pouring in on all sides. And no matter how snugly he pulled in his head and legs and pressed his body against the floor, he inevitably had to own up that he would not endure the hubbub much longer. They were clearing out his room, stripping him of everything he loved. They had already dragged away the wardrobe, which contained the fretsaw and other tools, and they were now unprying the solidly embedded desk, where he had done his assignments for business college, high school, why, even elementary school—and he really had no time to delve into the good intentions of the two women, whom, incidentally, he had almost forgotten about, for they were so exhausted that they were already laboring in silence, and all that could be heard was the heavy plodding of their feet.

And so, while the women were in the next room, leaning against the desk to catch their breath, he broke out, changing direction four times, for he was truly at a loss about what to rescue first—when he saw the picture of the woman clad in nothing but furs hanging blatantly on the otherwise empty wall. He quickly scrambled up to it and squeezed against the glass, which held him fast, soothing his hot belly. At least, with Gregor now covering it up, this picture would certainly not be carried off by anyone. He turned his head toward the parlor door, hoping to observe the women upon their return.

After granting themselves little rest, they were already coming back; Grete had put her arm around her mother, almost carrying her. "Well, what should we take next?" said Grete, looking around. At this point, her eyes met those of Gregor on the wall. It was no doubt only because of the mother's presence that she maintained her composure. Bending her face toward the mother to keep her from peering about, she said, although trembling and without thinking: "Come on, why don't we go back to the parlor for a moment?" It was obvious to Gregor that she wanted to get the mother to safety and then chase him down from the wall. Well, just let her try! He clung to his picture, refusing to surrender it. He would rather jump into Grete's face.

But Grete's words had truly unnerved the mother, who stepped aside, glimpsed the huge brown splotch on the flowered wallpaper, and cried out in a harsh, shrieking voice before actually realizing that this was Gregor, "Oh God, oh God!" With outspread arms as if giving up everything, she collapsed across the settee and remained motionless.

"Hey, Gregor!" the sister shouted with a raised fist and a penetrating glare. These were her first direct words to him since his metamorphosis. She ran into the next room to get some sort of essence for reviving the mother from her faint. Gregor also wanted to help (there was time enough to salvage the picture later), but he was stuck fast to the glass and had to wrench himself loose. He then also scurried into the next room as if he could give the sister some kind of advice as in earlier times, but then had to stand idly behind her while she rummaged through an array of vials. Upon spinning around, she was startled by the sight of him. A vial fell on the floor and shattered. A sliver of glass injured Gregor's face, and some corrosive medicine oozed from the sliver. Grete, without further delay, grabbed as many vials as she could hold and dashed over to the mother, slamming the door with her foot. Gregor was thus cut off from the mother, who might have been dying because of him; he had to refrain from opening the door lest he frighten away the sister, who had to remain with the mother. There was nothing he could do but wait, and so, tortured by self-rebukes and worries, he began to creep about—he crept over everything, walls, furniture, and ceiling, and finally, in his despair, when the entire room began whirling around him, he plunged down to the middle of the large table.

A short while passed, with Gregor lying there worn out. The entire apartment was still, which was possibly a good sign. Then the doorbell rang. The maid was, naturally, locked up in her kitchen, and so Grete had to go and answer the door. The father had come.

"What's happened?" were his first words; Grete's face must have revealed everything. She replied in a muffled voice, obviously pressing her face into his chest: "Mother fainted, but she's feeling better now. Gregor broke out."

"I expected it," said the father, "I kept telling you both, but you women refuse to listen."

It was clear to Gregor that the father had misinterpreted Grete's all-too-brief statement and leaped to the conclusion that Gregor had perpetrated some kind of violence. That was why he now had to try and placate the father, for he had neither the time nor the chance to enlighten him. He therefore fled to the door of his room, squeezing against it, so that the father, upon entering from the vestibule, could instantly see that Gregor had every intention of promptly returning to his room and that there was no need to force him back. All they had to do was open the door and he would vanish on the spot.

But the father was in no mood to catch such niceties. "Ah!" he roared upon entering, and his tone sounded both furious and elated. Gregor drew his head back from the door and raised it toward the father. He had really not pictured him as he was standing there now; naturally, because of his new habit of creeping around, Gregor had lately failed to concern himself with anything else going on in the apartment and he should actually have been prepared for some changes. And yet, and yet, was this still his father? The same man who used to lie buried in bed, exhausted, whenever Gregor started out on a business trip; who, whenever Gregor came home in the evening, would greet him, wearing a robe, in the armchair; who, being quite incapable of standing up, would only raise his arms as a sign of joy; and who, bundled up in his old overcoat, laboriously shuffled along during rare family strolls on a few Sundays during the year and on the highest holidays, always cautiously planting his cane, trudging a bit more slowly between Gregor and the mother (they were walking slowly as it was), and who, whenever he was about to say anything, nearly always halted and gathered the others around him? But now the father stood quite steady, in a snug blue uniform with gold buttons, such as attendants in banks wear; his heavy double chin unfurled over the high stiff collar of the jacket. From under his bushy eyebrows, the black eyes gazed fresh and alert; the once disheveled hair was now glossy, combed down, and meticulously parted. Removing his cap with its gold monogram, probably that of a bank, and pitching it in an arc the full length of the room over to the settee, he lunged toward Gregor, his face grim, his hands in his trouser pockets, the tails of his long uniform jacket swinging back. He himself most likely did not know what he had in mind; nevertheless he lifted his feet unusually high, and Gregor marveled at the gigantic size of his boot soles. But he did not dwell on this; after all, from the very first day of his new life, he had known that the father viewed only the utmost severity as appropriate for dealing with him. And so now Gregor scooted away, stopping only when the father halted, and skittering forward again the instant the father moved. In this way, they circled the room several times with nothing decisive happening; in fact, because of its slow tempo, the whole business did not even resemble a chase. That was why Gregor kept to the floor for now, especially since he feared that the father might view an escape to the walls or the ceiling as particularly wicked. Nevertheless, Gregor had to admit that he could not endure even this scurrying much longer, because for every step the father took, Gregor had to carry out an endless string of movements. He was already panting noticeably, just as his lungs had never been altogether reliable even in his earlier days. He was just barely staggering along, trying to focus all his strength on running, scarcely keeping his eyes open, feeling so numb that he could think of no other possible recourse than running, and almost forgetting that he was free to use the walls, which, however, were blocked here by intricately carved furniture bristling with sharp points and notches—when all at once a lightly tossed something flew down right next to him, barely missing him, and rolled on ahead of him. It was an apple. Instantly a second one flew after the first. Gregor halted, petrified. Any more running would be useless, for the father was dead set on bombarding him. He had filled his pockets with fruit from the bowl on the sideboard and, not taking sharp aim for the moment, was hurling apple after apple. Those small red apples ricocheted around the floor as if galvanized, colliding with one another. A weakly thrown apple grazed Gregor's back, sliding off harmlessly. Another one, however, promptly following it, actually dug right into his back. Gregor wanted to keep dragging himself along as though this startling and incredible pain would vanish with a change of location, yet he felt nailed to the spot and so he stretched out with all his senses in utter derangement. It was only with his final glance that he saw the door to his room burst open. The mother, wearing only a chemise (for the sister had undressed her to let her breathe more freely while unconscious), hurried out in front of the screaming sister and dashed toward the father. Stumbling over her unfastened petticoats as they glided to the floor one by one, she pressed against the father, flung her arms around his neck in total union with him—but now Gregor's eyesight failed entirely—and, with her hands clutching the back of the father's head, she begged him to spare Gregor's life.

III

Gregor's serious injury, from which he suffered for over a month (since no one had the nerve to remove the apple, it stayed lodged in his flesh as a visible memento), apparently reminded even the father that Gregor, despite his now dismal and disgusting shape, was a member of the family and could not be treated like an enemy. Instead, familial obligations dictated that they swallow their repulsion and endure, simply endure.

Now Gregor's injury may have cost him some mobility, no doubt for good, impelling him to take long, long minutes to shuffle across his room like an old war invalid (there was no question of his creeping up the walls). Still, this worsening of his condition was, to his mind, more than made up for by the fact that every evening the parlor door, which he would watch sharply for one or two hours in advance, was opened, so that he, lying in the darkness of his room and invisible from the parlor, was allowed to see the entire family at the illuminated table and, by general consent as it were, listen to their talks—rather, that is, than eavesdropping as before.

Of course, these were no longer the lively exchanges of earlier days, which Gregor had always somewhat wistfully mused about in the tiny hotel rooms whenever he had wearily collapsed into the damp bedding. Now, the evenings were usually very hushed. The father would doze off in his armchair shortly after supper; the mother and the sister would urge one another to keep still. The mother, hunched way over beneath the light, would be sewing fine lingerie for a fashion boutique; the sister, having found a job as salesgirl, was studying shorthand and French every evening in hopes of perhaps eventually obtaining a better position. Sometimes the father would wake up and, as if unaware that he had been sleeping, would say to the mother: "How long you've been sewing again today!" and doze off again while mother and sister smiled wearily at each other.

In a kind of obstinacy, the father refused to take off his attendant's uniform at home; and while his robe dangled uselessly on the clothes hook, he would slumber in his chair, fully dressed, as if always on duty and at his superior's beck and call even here. And so, despite all the painstaking efforts of mother and sister, the uniform, which had not been brand-new in the first place, grew less and less tidy, and Gregor would often spend entire evenings gazing at this soiled and spotted garment, which shone with its always polished gold buttons, while the old man slept a very uncomfortable and yet peaceful sleep.

The instant the clock struck ten, the mother, by speaking softly to the father, tried to awaken him and talk him into going to bed, for after all, this was no way to get proper sleep, which the father, who had to start work at six A.M., badly needed. But with the obstinacy that had gotten hold of him upon his becoming a bank attendant, he would always insist on remaining at the table a bit longer even though he invariably nodded out and, moreover, could then be coaxed only with the greatest difficulty to trade the chair for the bed. No matter how much the mother and the sister cajoled and gently admonished him, he would shake his head slowly for a quarter of an hour, keeping his eyes shut and refusing to stand up. The mother would tug at his sleeve, whispering honeyed words into his ear, and the sister would leave her homework to help the mother; but none of this had any effect on the father. He would merely sink deeper into his chair. It was only when the women lifted him under his armpits that he would open his eyes, glance to and fro between mother and sister, and say: "What a life. This is my rest in my old days." And supporting himself on the two women, he would ponderously struggle to his feet as if being the greatest burden on himself, let the two women steer him to the door, wave them off upon arriving and trudge on unaided, while the mother hastily discarded her sewing and the daughter her pen in order to run after him and continue being helpful.

Who in this overworked and exhausted family had time to look after Gregor any more than was absolutely necessary? The household was reduced further; the maid was now dismissed after all, and a gigantic bony charwoman with white hair fluttering around her head would come every morning and evening to do the heaviest chores. Everything else was taken care of by the mother along with her great amount of needlework. It even happened that various items of family jewelry, which mother and sister had once blissfully sported at celebrations and festivities, were now being sold off, as Gregor learned in the evenings from the general discussions of the prices they had obtained. Their greatest persistent complaint, though, was that since they could hit on no way of moving Gregor, they could not give up this apartment, which was much too large for their present circumstances. Gregor, however, realized it was not just their consideration for him that held them back, for they could have easily transported him in a suitable crate with a couple of air holes in it. The main obstacle to the family's relocation was their utter despair and their sense of being struck by a misfortune like no one else among their friends and relatives. Whatever the world demands of poor people, they carried out to an extreme: the father fetched breakfast for the minor bank tellers, the mother sacrificed herself to underwear for strangers, the sister, ordered around by customers, ran back and forth behind the counter. But those were the limits of the family's strength. And the injury in Gregor's back started hurting again whenever mother and sister, having returned from getting the father to bed, ignored their work as they huddled together cheek to cheek, and the mother, pointing toward Gregor's room, now said: "Close that door, Grete," so that Gregor was back in the dark, while the women in the next room mingled their tears or peered dry-eyed at the table.

Gregor spent his nights and days almost entirely without sleep. Occasionally he decided that the next time the door opened, he would take over the family's affairs as in the past. Now, after a long absence, the director and the office manager reappeared in his thoughts, the clerks and the trainees, the dim-witted errand boy, two or three friends from other companies, a chambermaid in a provincial hotel, a dear, fleeting memory, a milliner's cashier whom he had courted earnestly but too slowly—they all reappeared, mingling with strangers or forgotten people. Yet rather than helping him and his family, they were all unapproachable, and he was glad when they dwindled away. At other moments, he was in no mood to worry about his family—he was filled with sheer rage at being poorly looked after; and although unable to picture anything that might tempt his appetite, he did try to devise ways of getting into the pantry and, while not hungry, taking what was ultimately his due. No longer paying any heed to what might be a special treat for Gregor, the sister, before hurrying off to work in the morning and after lunch, would use her foot to shove some random food into Gregor's room. Then, in the evening, indifferent as to whether the food had been merely tasted or— most often the case—left entirely untouched, she would sweep it out with a swing of the broom. She would now tidy up the room in the evening, and she could not have done it any faster. Grimy streaks lined the walls, knots of dust and filth littered the floor. In the beginning, when the sister arrived, Gregor would station himself in such particularly offensive corners as if to chide her. But he could have waited there for weeks on end without her making any improvement; she certainly saw the dirt as clearly as he did, but she had simply made up her mind to leave it there. Nevertheless, with a touchiness that aside from being quite novel for her had actually seized hold of the entire family, she made sure that this tidying-up remained her bailiwick. Once, the mother had subjected Gregor's room to a major cleansing, which had required several buckets of water (the great dampness, of course, made Gregor ill, and afterwards he sprawled on the settee, embittered and immobile). But the mother's punishment was not long in coming. For that evening, the instant the sister noticed the change in Gregor's room, she ran, deeply offended, into the parlor, and even though the mother raised her hands beseechingly, the sister had a crying fit. The father was, naturally, startled out of his armchair, and both parents gaped, at first in helpless astonishment, until they too started in: the father upbraided the mother, on his right, for not leaving the cleaning to the sister and he yelled at the sister, on his left, warning her that she would never again be allowed to clean Gregor's room. The mother tried to drag the father, who was beside himself with rage, into the bedroom; the sister, quaking with sobs, kept hammering the table with her little fists; and Gregor hissed loudly in his fury because no one thought of closing his door to shield him from this spectacle and commotion.

But even if the sister, exhausted from her work at the shop, was fed up with looking after Gregor as before, by no means did the mother have to step in to keep Gregor from being neglected. For now the charwoman was here. This old widow, who, with the help of her strong bone structure, must have managed to overcome the worst things in her long life, felt no actual repugnance toward Gregor. While not really snooping, she had once happened to open the door to his room and, at the sight of Gregor, who, completely caught off guard, began scrambling every which way even though no one was chasing him, she had halted in astonishment with her hands folded on her abdomen. Since then, she had never failed to quickly open the door a crack every morning and evening and peep in on him. Initially, she would even summon him with phrases that she must have considered friendly, like "C'mon over, you old dung beetle!" or "Just look at the old dung beetle!" But Gregor refused to respond to such overtures; he stayed motionless in his place as though the door had not been opened. If only they had ordered this charwoman to clean his room daily instead of letting her gratuitously disturb him whenever the mood struck her! Early one morning, when a violent rain, perhaps a sign of the coming spring, was pelting against the windowpanes, the charwoman launched into her phrases again. Gregor felt so bitterly provoked that he charged toward her as if to attack, albeit slowly and feebly. But the charwoman, undaunted, merely heaved up a chair by the door and stood there with her mouth wide open, obviously intending to close it only when the chair in her hand smashed down into Gregor's back. "So that's as far as you're going?" she asked when he shifted away, and she calmly returned the chair to the corner.

Gregor was now eating next to nothing. It was only when he happened to pass the food left for him that he would playfully take a morsel into his mouth, keep it in for hours and hours, and then usually spit it out again. At first, he thought that his anguish about the condition of his room was what kept him from eating, but he very soon came to terms with those very changes. The family had gotten used to storing things here that could not be put anywhere else, and now there were many such items here, for they had rented out one room of the apartment to three boarders. These earnest gentlemen—all three had full beards, as Gregor once ascertained through the crack of the door—were sticklers for order, not only in their room, but also, since they were lodging here, throughout the apartment, especially the kitchen. They could not endure useless, much less dirty refuse. Moreover, they had largely brought in their own household goods. For this reason, many of the family's belongings had become superfluous; but while they had no prospects of selling them, they did not want to throw them out either. All these items wound up in Gregor's room—as did the ash bucket and the garbage can from the kitchen. If anything was unusable at the moment, the charwoman, who was always in a mad rush, would simply toss it into Gregor's room; luckily, he mostly saw only the object in question and the hand that held it. She may have intended to come for these things in her own good time or dump them all out in one fell swoop; but instead, they remained wherever they happened to land, unless Gregor twisted his way through the clutter, making it shift. At first, he had no choice, there being nowhere else for him to crawl; but later on it got to be more and more fun, even if, dead-tired and mournful after such treks, he would lie unstirring for hours on end.

Since the boarders sometimes also ate their supper at home in the common parlor, the door between that room and Gregor's would remain shut on those evenings. But Gregor easily did without the open door—after all, there had been evenings when he had not even taken advantage of it; instead, unnoticed by the family, he had crouched in the darkest nook of his room. Once, however, the charwoman had left the parlor door ajar, and it remained ajar even when the boarders came in that evening and the light was turned on. Settling down at the head of the table, where the father, the mother, and Gregor had eaten in earlier times, they unfolded their napkins and took hold of their knives and forks. Instantly the mother appeared in the kitchen doorway with a platter of meat and, right behind her, the sister with a heaping platter of potatoes. The steaming food gave off thick fumes. The platters were set down in front of the boarders, who bent over them as if to test the food before eating it; and indeed the man sitting in the middle, and apparently looked up to as an authority by the two others, cut up a piece of meat on the platter, clearly in order to determine whether it was tender enough or should perhaps be sent back to the kitchen. He was satisfied, and so mother and sister, who had been watching in suspense, began to smile with sighs of relief.

The family itself ate in the kitchen. Nevertheless, before heading there, the father would stop off in the parlor, bowing once, with his cap in his hand, and circle the table. The boarders would all rise and mumble something into their beards. Then, by themselves again, they would eat in almost total silence. It struck Gregor as bizarre that amid all the various and sundry noises of eating, he kept making out the noise of their chewing as if he were being shown that one needed teeth for eating and that one could accomplish nothing with even the most wonderful toothless jaws. "I do have an appetite," Gregor told himself, "but not for these foods. How well these boarders eat, and I'm starving to death!"

That very evening (Gregor could not recall hearing it all this time), the sound of the violin came from the kitchen. The boarders had already finished their supper. The middle one had pulled out a newspaper, giving the other two one page each; and now they were leaning back, reading and smoking.

When the violin began to play, the boarders pricked up their ears, got to their feet, and tiptoed over to the vestibule doorway, crowding into it and remaining there.

They must have been overheard from the kitchen, for the father called: "Do you gentlemen mind the violin? We can stop it immediately."

"Quite the contrary," said the middle gentleman, "would the young lady care to come and play in this room, which is far more convenient and comfortable?"

"Oh, thank you," called the father as if he were the violinist. The gentlemen came back into the parlor and waited. Soon the father arrived with the music stand, the mother with the sheet music, and the sister with the violin. The sister calmly prepared everything for the playing. The parents, having never rented out rooms before, which was why they were being so overly courteous to the boarders, did not dare sit in their own chairs. The father leaned against the door, slipping his right hand between two buttons of his buttoned-up uniform jacket; the mother, however, was offered a chair by one gentleman and, leaving it where he happened to place it, she sat off to the side, in a corner.

The sister began to play; the father and the mother, on either side, closely followed the motions of her hands. Gregor, drawn to the playing, had ventured a bit further out, so that his head was already sticking into the parlor. He was hardly aware of his recent lack of consideration toward the others, although earlier he had prided himself on being considerate. For now more than ever he had reason to hide, thoroughly coated as he was with the dust that shrouded everything in his room, flurrying about at the vaguest movement. Furthermore, threads, hairs, and scraps of leftover food were sticking to his back and his sides, for he had become much too apathetic to turn over and scour his back on the carpet as he used to do several times a day. And so, despite his present state, he had no qualms about advancing a bit across the spotless parlor floor.

Nor, to be sure, did anyone take any notice of him. The family was engrossed in the violin playing; the boarders, in contrast, their hands in their trouser pockets, had initially placed themselves much too close to the sister's music stand so they could all read the score, which was bound to fluster her. As a result, half muttering with lowered heads, they soon retreated to the window, where they remained, with the father eyeing them uneasily. It now truly seemed more than obvious that their hope of listening to a lovely or entertaining violin recital had been dashed, that they had had enough of the performance, and that it was only out of sheer courtesy that they were allowing themselves to be put upon in their leisure. It was especially the manner in which they all blew their cigar smoke aloft through their mouths and noses that hinted at how fidgety they were. And yet the sister was playing so beautifully. Her face was leaning to the side, her sad, probing eyes were following the lines of notes. Gregor crawled a bit farther out, keeping his head close to the floor, so that their eyes might possibly meet. Was he a beast to be so moved by music? He felt as if he were being shown the path to the unknown food he was yearning for. He was determined to creep all the way over to the sister, tug at her skirt to suggest that she take her violin and come into his room, for no one here would reward her playing as he intended to reward it. He wanted to keep her there and never let her out, at least not in his lifetime.

For once, his terrifying shape would be useful to him; he would be at all the doors of his room simultaneously, hissing at the attackers. His sister, however, should remain with him not by force, but of her own free will. She should sit next to him on the settee, leaning down to him and listening to him confide that he had been intent on sending her to the conservatory, and that if the misfortune had not interfered, he would have announced his plan to everyone last Christmas (Christmas was already past, wasn't it?), absolutely refusing to take "no" for an answer. After his declaration, the sister would burst into tears of emotion, and Gregor would lift himself all the way up to her shoulder and kiss her throat, which she had been keeping free of any ribbon or collar since she had first started working.

"Mr. Samsa!" the middle gentleman called to the father and, not wasting another word, pointed his index finger at Gregor, who was slowly edging forward. The violin broke off, the middle gentleman first smiled at his friends, shaking his head, and then looked back at Gregor. The father, instead of driving Gregor out, evidently considered it imperative first to calm the boarders, even though they were not the least bit upset and appeared to find Gregor more entertaining than the violin playing. The father hurried over to them and, with outspread arms, tried to push them into their room while simultaneously blocking their view of Gregor with his body. They now in fact began to grow a bit irate, though there was no telling whether it was due to the father's behavior or to their gradual realization that they had unknowingly had a neighbor like Gregor in the next room. They demanded explanations from the father, raised their arms like him, plucked at their beards, and only very slowly backed away toward their room. Meanwhile the sister had managed to overcome her bewilderment, caused by the abrupt end to her playing, and after a time of holding the violin and the bow in her slackly dangling hands and gazing at the score as if still playing, she suddenly pulled herself together, left the instrument in the mother's lap (she was still in her chair, her lungs heaving violently), and rushed into the next room, toward which the father was more and more forcefully herding the boarders. One could see the blankets and pillows in the beds flying aloft, then being neatly arranged under the sister's practiced hands. Before the gentlemen ever reached the room, she had finished making up the beds and slipped out. The father seemed once again so thoroughly overcome by his obstinacy that he neglected to pay the tenants the respect nevertheless due them. He merely kept shoving until the middle gentleman, who was already in the doorway of the room, brought him to a halt by thunderously stamping his foot. "I hereby declare," said the middle gentleman, raising his hand and looking around for the mother and the sister as well, "that in consideration of the repulsive conditions" (here he abruptly spit on the floor) "prevailing in this apartment and in this family, I am giving immediate notice in regard to my room. Naturally, I will not pay a single penny for the days I have resided here; on the other hand, I will give serious thought to the eventuality of pursuing some sort of claims against you, for which—believe me—excellent grounds can easily be shown." He paused and peered straight ahead as if expecting something. And indeed, his two friends promptly chimed in, saying, "We are giving immediate notice too." Thereupon he grabbed the doorknob and slammed the door with a crash.

The father, groping and staggering along, collapsed into his chair; he looked as if he were stretching out for his usual evening nap, but his head, dangling as if unsupported, revealed that he was anything but asleep. All this while, Gregor had been lying right where the boarders had first spotted him. His frustration at the failure of his plan, and perhaps also the feebleness caused by his persistent hunger, made it impossible for him to move. Dreading with some certainty that at any moment now he would have to bear the blame for the overall disaster, he waited. He was not even startled when the violin, sliding away from the mother's trembling fingers, plunged from her lap with a reverberating thud.

"My dear parents," said the sister, pounding her hand on the table by way of introduction, "things cannot go on like this. You may not realize it, but I do. I will not pronounce my brother's name in front of this monstrosity, and so all I will say is: We must try to get rid of it. We have done everything humanly possible to look after it and put up with it; I do not believe there is anything we can be reproached for."

"She couldn't be more right," said the father to himself. The mother, still struggling to catch her breath and with an insane look in her eyes, began to cough into her muffling hand.

The sister hurried over to the mother and held her forehead. The father, apparently steered to more concrete thoughts by the sister's words, sat bolt upright now, toying with his attendant's cap, which lay on the table, among the borders' leftover supper dishes. Every so often he glanced at Gregor, who kept silent.

"We've got to get rid of it," the sister now said exclusively to the father, for the mother heard nothing through her coughing, "it will kill the both of you, I can see it coming. People who have to work as hard as we do can't also endure this nonstop torture at home. I can't stand it anymore either." And she began sobbing so violently that her tears flowed down to the mother's face, from which she wiped them with mechanical gestures.

"But, child," said the father with compassion and marked understanding, "what should we do?"

The sister merely shrugged her shoulders to convey the perplexity that, in contrast with her earlier self-assurance, had overcome her as she wept.

"If he understood us," said the father, half wondering. The sister, in the thick of her weeping, wildly flapped her hand to signal that this was inconceivable.

"If he understood us," the father repeated, closing his eyes in order to take in the sister's conviction that this was impossible, "then perhaps we might come to some sort of terms with him. But as things are now—"

"It has to go," exclaimed the sister, "that's the only way, Father. You simply have to try and get rid of the idea that it is Gregor. Our real misfortune is that we believed it for such a long time. Just how can that possibly be Gregor? If that were Gregor, he would have realized long ago that human beings can't possibly live with such an animal and he would have left of his own accord. We might have no brother then, but we could go on living and honor his memory. Instead, this animal harries us, it drives out the boarders, it obviously wants to take over the whole apartment and make us sleep in the gutter. Look, Father," she suddenly screamed, "he's starting again!" And in a panic that Gregor could not for the life of him fathom, the sister actually deserted the mother. Literally thrusting away from her chair as if she would rather sacrifice her mother than remain near Gregor, she dashed behind the father, who, made frantic only by the sister's behavior, stood up, half raising his hands to shield her.

Yet Gregor never even dreamed of scaring anyone, least of all his sister. He had merely started wheeling around in order to lumber back to his room, although because of his sickly condition his movements did look peculiar, for he had to execute the intricate turns by repeatedly raising his head and banging it against the floor. He paused and looked around. His good intention seemed to have been recognized; the panic had only been momentary. Now they all gazed at him in dismal silence. The mother, stretching out her legs and pressing them together, sprawled in her chair, her eyes almost shut in exhaustion; the father and the sister sat side by side, she with her arm around his neck.

"Now maybe I can turn around," Gregor thought, resuming his labor. He could not help panting from the strain and he also had to rest intermittently. At least, no one was bullying him, and he was left to his own devices. Upon completing the turn, he headed straight back. Amazed that his room was far away, he could not understand how, given his feebleness, he had come this great distance almost unwittingly. But, absorbed in creeping rapidly, he scarcely noticed that no interfering word or outcry came from his family. It was only upon reaching the door that he turned his head—not all the way for he felt his neck stiffening; nevertheless, he did see that nothing had changed behind him, except that the sister had gotten to her feet. His final look grazed the mother, who was fast asleep by now.

No sooner was he inside his room than the door was hastily slammed, bolted, and locked. Gregor was so terrified by the sudden racket behind him that his tiny legs buckled. It was the sister who had been in such a rush. She had been standing there, waiting, and had then nimbly jumped forward, before Gregor had even heard her coming. "Finally!" she yelled to the parents while turning the key in the lock.

"What now?" Gregor wondered, peering around in the dark. He soon discovered that he could no longer budge at all. He was not surprised, it even struck him as unnatural that he had ever succeeded in moving on these skinny little legs. Otherwise he felt relatively comfortable. His entire body was aching, but it seemed to him as if the pains were gradually fading and would ultimately vanish altogether. He could barely feel the rotting apple in his back or the inflamed area around it, which were thoroughly cloaked with soft dust. He recalled his family with tenderness and love. His conviction that he would have to disappear was, if possible, even firmer than his sister's. He lingered in this state of blank and peaceful musing until the tower clock struck three in the morning. He held on long enough to glimpse the start of the overall brightening outside the window. Then his head involuntarily sank to the floor, and his final breath came feebly from his nostrils.

When the charwoman showed up early that morning (in her haste and sheer energy, and no matter how often she had been asked not to do it, she slammed all the doors so hard that once she walked in no peaceful sleep was possible anywhere in the apartment), and peeked in on Gregor as usual, she at first found nothing odd about him. Having credited him with goodness knows what brain power, she thought he was deliberately lying there so motionless, pretending to sulk. Since she happened to be clutching the long broom, she tried to tickle him from the doorway. This had no effect, and so she grew annoyed and began poking Gregor. It was only upon shoving him from his place but meeting no resistance that she became alert. When the true state of affairs now dawned on the charwoman, her eyes bulged in amazement and she whistled to herself. But instead of dawdling there, she yanked the bedroom door open and hollered into the darkness: "Go and look, it's croaked; it's lying there, absolutely croaked!"

Mr. and Mrs. Samsa sat upright in their matrimonial bed, trying to cope with the shock caused by the charwoman. When they managed to grasp what she meant, the two of them, one on either side, hastily clambered out of bed. Mr. Samsa threw the blanket over his shoulders, while Mrs. Samsa emerged in her nightgown; that was how they entered Gregor's room. Meanwhile, the door to the parlor, where Grete had been sleeping since the arrival of the boarders, had likewise opened; she was fully dressed and her face was pale as if she had not slept.

"Dead?" said Mrs. Samsa, quizzically eyeing the charwoman even though she could have gone to check everything for herself, or could have surmised it without checking.

"You bet," said the charwoman and by way of proof she thrust out the broom and pushed Gregor's corpse somewhat further to the side. Mrs. Samsa made as if to hold back the broom, but then let it be.

"Well," said Mr. Samsa, "now we can thank the Lord." He crossed himself and the three women imitated his example. Grete, her eyes glued to the corpse, said: "Just look how skinny he was. Well, he stopped eating such a long time ago. The food came back out exactly as it went in." And indeed, Gregor's body was utterly flat and dry; they realized this only now when it was no longer raised on its tiny legs and nothing else diverted their eyes.

"Grete, come into our room for a bit," said Mrs. Samsa, smiling wistfully, and Grete, not without looking back at the corpse, followed her parents into the bedroom. The charwoman closed the door to Gregor's room and opened the window all the way. Though it was still early morning, there was a touch of warmth in the fresh air. It was already late March, after all.

The three boarders stepped out of their room and, astonished, cast about for their breakfast; they had been forgotten. "Where is breakfast?" the middle gentleman peevishly asked the charwoman. But putting her finger on her lips, she hastily and silently beckoned for the gentlemen to come into Gregor's room. And come they did, and with their hands in the pockets of their somewhat threadbare jackets, they stood around Gregor's corpse in the now sunlit room.

Next, the bedroom door opened, and Mr. Samsa, in his livery, appeared with his wife on one arm and his daughter on the other. Their eyes were all slightly tearstained; now and then, Grete pressed her face into the father's arm.

"Leave my home at once!" Mr. Samsa told the three gentlemen, pointing at the door without releasing the women.

"What do you mean?" asked the middle gentleman, somewhat dismayed and with a sugary smile. The two other gentlemen held their hands behind their backs, incessantly rubbing them together as if gleefully looking forward to a grand argument that they were bound to win.

"I mean exactly what I said," replied Mr. Samsa, and with his two companions he made a beeline toward the tenant. The latter at first stood his ground, eyeing the floor as if his thoughts were being rearranged to form a new pattern in his head.

"Well, then we'll go," he said, looking up at Mr. Samsa as if, in a sudden burst of humility, he were requesting sanction even for this decision. Mr. Samsa, with bulging eyes, merely vouchsafed him a few brief nods. Thereupon the gentleman strode right into the vestibule. His two friends, who had been listening for a short while with utterly calm hands, now quite literally hopped after him as if fearing that Mr. Samsa might precede them into the vestibule and might thrust himself between them and their leader. Once in the vestibule, all three boarders pulled their hats from the coat rack, their canes from the umbrella stand, bowed wordlessly, and left the apartment. Impelled by a suspicion that proved to be thoroughly groundless, Mr. Samsa and the two women stepped out on the landing. As they leaned on the banister, they watched the three gentlemen marching down the long stairway slowly but steadily, vanishing on every floor in the regular twist of the staircase, and popping up again several moments later. The lower the gentlemen got, the more the Samsa family lost interest in them, and as a butcher's boy, proudly balancing a basket on his head, came toward the gentlemen and then mounted well beyond them, Mr. Samsa and the women left the banister, and as if relieved, they all returned to their apartment.

They decided to spend this day resting and strolling; not only had they earned this break from work, they absolutely needed it. And so they sat down at the table to write three letters of explanation: Mr. Samsa to his superiors, Mrs. Samsa to her customer, and Grete to her employer. As they were writing, the charwoman came in to tell them she was leaving, for her morning's work was done. The three letter writers at first merely nodded without glancing up; it was only when she kept hovering that they looked up in annoyance. "Well?" asked Mr. Samsa. The charwoman stood beaming in the doorway as if she were about to announce some great windfall for the family, but would do so only if they dragged it out of her. On her hat, the small, almost erect ostrich plume, which had annoyed Mr. Samsa throughout her service here, swayed lightly in all directions. "What can we do for you?" asked Mrs. Samsa, whom the charwoman respected the most.

"Well," the charwoman replied with such friendly chuckling that she had to break off, "listen, you don't have to worry about getting rid of that stuff in the next room. It's all been taken care of."

Mrs. Samsa and Grete huddled over their letters as if to keep writing; Mr. Samsa, aware that the charwoman was on the verge of launching into a blow-by-blow description, resolutely stretched out his arm to ward her off. Not being allowed to tell her story, she suddenly remembered that she was in an awful hurry, and clearly offended, she called out: "So long, everybody." She then vehemently whirled around and charged out of the apartment with a horrible slam of the door.

"She'll be dismissed tonight," said Mr. Samsa, receiving no answer from his wife or his daughter, for the charwoman had ruffled the peace and quiet that they had barely gained. Standing up, the two women went over to the window and remained there, clasped in each other's arms. Mr. Samsa looked back from his chair and silently watched them for a while. Then he exclaimed: "Come on, get over here. Forget about the past once and for all.

And show me a little consideration." The women, promptly obeying him, hurried over, caressed him, and swiftly finished their letters.

Then all three of them left the apartment together, which they had not done in months, and took the trolley out to the countryside beyond the town. The streetcar, where they were the only passengers, was flooded with warm sunshine. Leaning back comfortably in their seats, they discussed their future prospects and concluded that, upon closer perusal, these were anything but bad; for while they had never actually asked one another for any details, their jobs were all exceedingly advantageous and also promising. Naturally, the greatest immediate improvement in their situation could easily be brought about by their moving; they hoped to rent a smaller and cheaper apartment, but with a better location and altogether more practical than their current place, which had been found by Gregor. As they were conversing, both Mr. and Mrs. Samsa, upon seeing the daughter becoming more and more vivacious, realized almost in unison that lately, despite all the sorrows that had left her cheeks pale, she had blossomed into a lovely and shapely girl. Lapsing into silence and communicating almost unconsciously with their eyes, they reflected that it was high time they found a decent husband for her. And it was like a confirmation of their new dreams and good intentions that at the end of their ride the daughter was the first to get up, stretching her young body.

T. S. ELIOT
1888–1965

In poetry and in literary criticism, Thomas Stearns Eliot has a unique position as a writer who not only expressed but helped to define modernist taste and style. He rejected the narrative, moralizing, and frequently "noble" style of late Victorian poetry, employing instead precisely focused and often startling images and an elliptical, allusive, and ironic voice that had enormous influence on modern American poetry. His early essays on literature and literary history helped bring about not only a new appreciation of seventeenth-century "metaphysical" poetry but also a different understanding of the text, no longer seen as the inspired overflow of spontaneous emotion but as a carefully made aesthetic object. Yet much of Eliot's immediate impact was not merely formal but spiritual or philosophical. The search for meaning that pervades his work created a famous picture of the barrenness of modern culture in *The Waste Land* (1922), which juxtaposed images of past nobility and present decay, civilizations near and far, and biblical, mythical, and Buddhist allusions to evoke the dilemma of a composite, anxious, and infinitely vulnerable modern soul. Readers in different countries who know nothing of Eliot's other works are often familiar with *The Waste Land* as a literary-historical landmark representing the cultural crisis in European society after World War I. In many ways, Eliot's combination of spiritual insight and technical innovation carries on the tradition of the Symbolist poet who was both visionary artist and consummate craftsman.

Two countries, England and the United States, claim Eliot as part of their national literature. Born September 26, 1888, to a prosperous and educated family in St. Louis, Eliot went to Harvard University for his undergraduate and graduate education and moved to England only in 1915, where he became a British citizen in 1927.

While at Harvard, Eliot was influenced by the anti-Romantic humanist Irving Babbitt and the philosopher and aesthetician George Santayana. He later wrote a doctoral dissertation on the philosophy of F. H. Bradley, whose examination of private consciousness (*Appearance and Reality*) appears in Eliot's own later essays and poems. Eliot also found literary examples that would be important for him in future years: the poetry of Dante and John Donne, and the Elizabethan and Jacobean dramatists. In 1908 he read Arthur Symons's *The Symbolist Movement in Literature* and became acquainted with the French Symbolist poets, whose richly allusive images—as well as highly self-conscious, ironic, and craftsmanlike technique—he would adopt for his own. Eliot began writing poetry while in college and published his first major poem, *The Love Song of J. Alfred Prufrock,* in Chicago's *Poetry* magazine in 1915. When he moved to England, however, he began a many-sided career as poet, reviewer, essayist, editor, and later playwright. By the time he received the Nobel Prize for literature in 1948, Eliot was recognized as one of the most influential twentieth-century writers in English.

Eliot's first poems, in 1915, already displayed the evocative yet startling images, abrupt shifts in focus, and combination of human sympathy and ironic wit that would attract and puzzle his readers. The *Preludes* linked the "notion of some infinitely gentle / Infinitely suffering thing" with a harsh fatalism in which "The worlds revolve like ancient women / Gathering fuel in vacant lots." Prufrock's dramatic monologue openly tried to startle readers by asking them to imagine the evening spread out "like a patient etherised upon a table" and by changing focus abruptly between imaginary landscapes, metaphysical questions, drawing-room chatter, literary and biblical allusions, and tones of high seriousness set against the most banal and even sing-song speech. "I grow old . . . I grow old . . . / I shall wear the bottoms of my trousers rolled." The individual stanzas of *Prufrock* are individual scenes, each with its own coherence (for example, the third stanza's yellow fog as a cat). Together, they compose a symbolic landscape sketched in the narrator's mind as a combination of factual observation and subjective feelings: the delicately stated eroticism of the arm "downed with light brown hair," and the frustrated aggression in "I should have been a pair of ragged claws / Scuttling across the floors of silent seas." In its discontinuity, precise yet evocative imagery, mixture of romantic and everyday reference, formal and conversational speech, and in the complex and ironic self-consciousness of its most unheroic hero, *The Love Song of J. Alfred Prufrock* already displays many of the modernist traits typical of Eliot's entire work. Also typical is the theme of spiritual void and of a disoriented protagonist who—at least at this point—does not know how to cope with a crisis that is as much that of modern Western culture as it is his own personal tragedy.

Once established in London, Eliot married, taught briefly before taking a job in the foreign department of Lloyd's Bank (1917–25), and in 1925 joined the publishing firm of Faber & Faber. He wrote a number of essays and book reviews that were published in *The Sacred Wood* (1920) and *Homage to Dryden* (1924) and enjoyed a great deal of influence as assistant editor of the *Egoist* (1917–19) and founding editor of the quarterly *Criterion* from 1922 until it folded in 1939. Eliot helped shape changing literary tastes as much by his essays and literary criticism as by his poetry. Influenced himself by T. E. Hulme's proposal that the time had come for a classical literature of "hard, dry wit" after Romantic vagueness and religiosity and following Imagism's goal of clear, precise physical images phrased in everyday language, he outlined his own definitions of literature and literary history and contributed to a theoretical approach later known as the New Criticism. In his essay *Tradition and the Individual Talent* (1919), Eliot proclaimed that there existed a special level of great works—"masterpieces"—that formed among themselves an "ideal order" of quality even though, as individual works, they expressed the characteristic sensibility of their age. The best poets were aware of fitting into the cumulative "mind of Europe" (for Eliot, the humanistic tradition of Homer, Dante, and Shakespeare) and thus of being to some extent depersonalized in their works. Eliot's "impersonal theory of poetry" emphasizes the medium in which a writer works, rather than his or her inner state; craft and control rather than the Romantic ideal of a spontaneous overflow of private emotion. In a famous passage that compares the creative mind to the untouched catalyst of a chemistry experiment, he insists that the writer makes the art object out of language and the experience of any number of people. "The poet's mind is in fact a receptacle for seizing and storing up numberless feelings, phrases, images, which remain there until all the particles which can unite to form a new compound are present together." Poetry can and should express the whole being—intellectual and emotional, conscious and unconscious. In a review of Herbert Grierson's edition of the seventeenth-century Metaphysical poets (1921), Eliot praised the complex mixture of intellect and passion that characterized John Donne and the other Metaphysicals (and that characterized Eliot himself) and criticized the tendency of English literature after the seventeenth century to separate the language of analysis from that of feeling. His criticism of this "dissociation of sensibility" implied a change in literary tastes: from Milton to Donne, from Tennyson to Gerard Manley Hopkins, from Romanticism to classicism, from simplicity to complexity.

The great poetic example of this change came with *The Waste Land* in 1922. Eliot dedicated the poem to Ezra Pound, who had helped him revise the first draft, with a quotation from Dante praising the "better craftsman." Quotations from, or allusions to, a wide range of sources, including Shakespeare, Dante, Charles Baudelaire, Richard Wagner, Ovid, St. Augustine, Buddhist sermons, folk songs, and the anthropologists Jessie Weston and James Frazer, punctuate this lengthy poem, to which Eliot actually added explanatory notes when it was first published in book form. *The Waste Land* describes modern society in a time of cultural and spiritual crisis and sets off the fragmentation of modern experience against references (some in foreign languages) to a more stable cultural heritage. The ancient Greek prophet Tiresias is juxtaposed with the contemporary charlatan Madame Sosostris; celebrated lovers like Antony and Cleopatra with a house-agent's clerk who mechanically seduces an uninterested typist at the end of her day; the religious vision of St. Augustine and Buddhist sermons with a sterile world of rock and dry sand where "one can neither stand nor lie nor sit." The modern wasteland could be redeemed if it learned to answer (or perhaps, to ask) the right questions: a situation Eliot symbolized by oblique references to the legend of a knight passing an evening of trial in a Chapel Perilous, and healing a Fisher King by asking the right questions about the Holy Grail and its lance. The series of references (many from literary masterworks) that Eliot integrated into his poem were so many "fragments I have shored against my ruins," pieces of a puzzle whose resolution would bring "shantih," or the peace that passes understanding, but that is still out of reach as the poem's final lines in a foreign language suggest.

The most influential technical innovation in *The Waste Land* was the deliberate use of fragmentation and discontinuity. Eliot pointedly refused to supply any transitional passages or narrative thread and expected the reader to construct a pattern whose implications would make sense as a whole. This was a direct attack on linear habits of reading, which are here broken up with sudden introductions of a different scene or unexplained literary references, shifts in perspective, interpolation of a foreign language, changes from elegant description to barroom gossip, from Elizabethan to modern scenes, from formal to colloquial language. Eliot's rupture of traditional expectations served several functions. It contributed to the general picture of cultural disintegration that the poem expressed, it allowed him to exploit the Symbolist or allusive powers of language inasmuch as they now carried the burden of meaning, and finally—by drawing attention to its own technique—it exemplified modernist "self-reflexive" or self-conscious style. It is impossible to read a triple shift such as "I remember / Those are pearls that were his eyes. / 'Are you alive, or not? Is there nothing in your head?' "—moving from the narrator's meditative recall to a quotation from Shakespeare and the woman's blunt attack—without noticing the abrupt changes in style and tone. Eliot's "heap of broken images" and "fragments shored against my ruins" also took the shape of fragments of thought and speech, and as such embodied a new tradition of literary language.

The spiritual search of *Prufrock*, *Gerontion* (1919), and *The Waste Land* entered a new phase for Eliot in 1927, when he became a member of the Anglican Church. *Ash Wednesday* (1930) and a verse play on the death of the English St. Thomas à Becket (*Murder in the Cathedral*, 1935) display the same distress over the human condition but now within a framework of hope for those who have accepted religious discipline. Eliot began writing plays to reach a larger audience, of which the best known are *The Family Reunion* (1939), which recasts the Orestes story from Greek tragedy, and *The Cocktail Party* (1949), a drawing-room comedy that also explored its characters' search for salvation. He is still best known for his poetry, however, and his last major work in that genre is the *Four Quartets*, begun in 1934 and published in its entirety in 1943.

As their title suggests, the *Four Quartets* are divided into sections much like the movement of a musical quartet. Each has five sections, inside which themes are introduced, developed, and resolved, and each has the title of a place. *Little Gidding* is a village in Huntingdonshire, England, which was the home of a seventeenth-century Anglican Catholic religious community of which only a chapel (rebuilt after the English Civil Wars) remained. All the *Quartets* use varying forms of free verse, ranging from the most intense short lyrics to—for the first time—continuous narrative passages of the kind Eliot once disdained. Throughout, the poet ponders the relationship of historical change and eternal order.

Eliot's experiences in World War II as a watchman checking for fires during bombing raids enter into *Little Gidding*, and he uses the chapel in that village as the point of departure for a meditation on the meaning of strife and change in a universe that the mind strives to structure, always imperfectly, by the timeless truths of religion. The *Quartet* opens with a section that is itself divided into three separate movements, first establishing the season of "midwinter spring" with the sun blazing on ice, then the chapel as the goal of any season's journey, and finally the chapel as a place so consecrated by prayer that the dead may communicate with the living. The lyrics opening the second section mourn the place's present decay by all four elements of earth, air, fire, and water and pass on to an imaginary conversation between the poet, wandering after the last bomb and before the all-clear signal, and an anonymous "dead master." The mood is pessimistic, and the dead master (a "compound ghost" with elements of Eliot, the Virgil of Dante's *Divine Comedy*, and W. B. Yeats) prophesies a bitter old age full of remorse and impotent rage at human folly. Their conversation suggests a comparison between the air-raid scene and Dante's *Inferno*, for it echoes the triple-line stanzaic form of *The Divine Comedy* and recalls the Italian poet's own encounter with his former master Brunetto Latini, in Hell (*Inferno* 15.22–124). The rest of the poem, however, moves forward to a kind of resolution out of time. The third section's beginning rhetoric of logical persuasion ("There are three conditions") introduces the concept of memory expanding our perspectives and enabling us to transcend the narrow commitments of history and civil war. The intense lyrics of the short fourth section propose that the flames of the annunciatory dove (or bomb) may be purgation as well as destruction; and in the final section, as the afternoon draws to a close, the poet ends his meditation on past and present, time and eternity, by asserting his faith in a condition of mind and spirit that combines both *now* and *always*, a transcendental vision that is a "condition of complete simplicity" and "crowned knot of fire."

The poem's conclusion is thus a religious one, moving from the agony of history to an eternal, purifying flame that may recall a similar mystic vision of all-penetrating light at the end of Dante's *Paradiso*. It may seem paradoxical that the poet who is known for expressing the dilemma of modern consciousness and for developing a new poetic style appropriate to twentieth-century experience should resolve that experience in a metaphor of transcendence. From his earliest work, however, Eliot was preoccupied with the spiritual implications of the most mundane reality, and the yoking of concrete with transcendental vision defines at once the range and depth of his modernist style.

Bernard Bergonzi, *T. S. Eliot* (1972), and Tony Sharpe, *T. S. Eliot: A Literary Life* (1991), are brief and readable introductions to the life and works. Martin Scofield, *T. S. Eliot: The Poems* (1988), offers a concise, balanced discussion of the evolution of Eliot's poetry. *The Waste Land* is discussed in Jay Martin, ed., *Twentieth-Century Interpretations of The Waste Land* (1968); Lois A. Cuddy and David H. Hirsch, eds., *Critical Essays on T. S. Eliot's The Waste Land* (1991); and as part of John Mayer, *T. S. Eliot's Silent Voices* (1989), which analyzes themes of awareness and self-consciousness in the early poetry. *Little Gidding* is examined in Steve Ellis, *The English Eliot: Design, Language, and Landscape in Four Quartets* (1991), and Edward Lobb, ed., *Words in Time: New Essays on Eliot's Four Quartets* (1994). John Paul Riquelme, *Harmony of Dissonances: T. S. Eliot, Romanticism, and Imagination* (1991), links Eliot's response to Romanticism with postmodern views. Useful general collections are Linda Wagner, ed., *T. S. Eliot: A Collection of Criticism* (1974), and Ronald Bush, ed., *T. S. Eliot: The Modernist in History* (1991).

The Love Song of J. Alfred Prufrock

> *S'io credesse che mia risposta fosse*
> *A persona che mai tornasse al mondo,*
> *Questa fiamma staria senza piu scosse.*
> *Ma perciocche giammai di questo fondo*
> *Non torno vivo alcun, s'i'odo il vero,*
> *Senza tema d'infamia ti rispondo.*[1]

Let us go then, you and I,
When the evening is spread out against the sky
Like a patient etherised upon a table;
Let us go, through certain half-deserted streets,
The muttering retreats   5
Of restless nights in one-night cheap hotels
And sawdust restaurants with oyster-shells:
Streets that follow like a tedious argument
Of insidious intent
To lead you to an overwhelming question . . .   10
Oh, do not ask, "What is it?"
Let us go and make our visit.

In the room the women come and go
Talking of Michelangelo.[2]

The yellow fog that rubs its back upon the window-panes,   15
The yellow smoke that rubs its muzzle on the window-panes
Licked its tongue into the corners of the evening,

---

1. From Dante's *Inferno* 27.61–66, in which the false counselor Guido da Montefeltro, enveloped in flame, explains that he would never reveal his past if he thought the traveler could report it: "If I thought my reply were meant for one / who ever could return into the world, / this flame would stir no more; and yet, since none—/ if what I hear is true—ever returned / alive from this abyss, then without fear / of facing infamy, I answer you."   2. Michelangelo Buonarroti (1475–1564), famous Italian Renaissance sculptor, painter, architect, and poet; here, merely a topic of fashionable conversation.

Lingered upon the pools that stand in drains,
Let fall upon its back the soot that falls from chimneys,
Slipped by the terrace, made a sudden leap,   20
And seeing that it was a soft October night,
Curled once about the house, and fell asleep.

    And indeed there will be time[3]
For the yellow smoke that slides along the street,
Rubbing its back upon the window-panes;   25
There will be time, there will be time
To prepare a face to meet the faces that you meet;
There will be time to murder and create,
And time for all the works and days of hands[4]
That lift and drop a question on your plate;   30
Time for you and time for me,
And time yet for a hundred indecisions,
And for a hundred visions and revisions,
Before the taking of a toast and tea.

    In the room the women come and go   35
Talking of Michelangelo.

    And indeed there will be time
To wonder, "Do I dare?" and, "Do I dare?"
Time to turn back and descend the stair,
With a bald spot in the middle of my hair—   40
(They will say: "How his hair is growing thin!")
My morning coat, my collar mounting firmly to the chin,
My necktie rich and modest, but asserted by a simple pin—
(They will say: "But how his arms and legs are thin!")
Do I dare   45
Disturb the universe?
In a minute there is time
For decisions and revisions which a minute will reverse.

    For I have known them all already, known them all—
Have known the evenings, mornings, afternoons,   50
I have measured out my life with coffee spoons;
I know the voices dying with a dying fall[5]
Beneath the music from a farther room.
    So how should I presume?

    And I have known the eyes already, known them all—   55
The eyes that fix you in a formulated phrase,
And when I am formulated, sprawling on a pin,
When I am pinned and wriggling on the wall,
Then how should I begin

3. Echo of a love poem by Andrew Marvell (1621–1678), *To His Coy Mistress:* "Had we but world enough and time."   4. An implied contrast with the more productive agricultural labor of hands in the *Works and Days* of the Greek poet Hesiod (eighth century B.C.).   5. Recalls Duke Orsino's description of a musical phrase in Shakespeare's *Twelfth Night* (1.1.4): "It has a dying fall."

To spit out all the butt-ends of my days and ways? 60
  And how should I presume?

And I have known the arms already, known them all—
Arms that are braceleted and white and bare
(But in the lamplight, downed with light brown hair!)
Is it perfume from a dress 65
That makes me so digress?
Arms that lie along a table, or wrap about a shawl.
  And should I then presume?
  And how should I begin?

Shall I say, I have gone at dusk through narrow streets 70
And watched the smoke that rises from the pipes
Of lonely men in shirt-sleeves, leaning out of windows? . . .

  I should have been a pair of ragged claws
Scuttling across the floors of silent seas.

. . .

    And the afternoon, the evening, sleeps so peacefully! 75
Smoothed by long fingers,
Asleep . . . tired . . . or it malingers,
Stretched on the floor, here beside you and me.
Should I, after tea and cakes and ices,
Have the strength to force the moment to its crisis? 80
But though I have wept and fasted, wept and prayed,
Though I have seen my head (grown slightly bald) brought in upon a
      platter,
I am no prophet[6]—and here's no great matter;
I have seen the moment of my greatness flicker,
And I have seen the eternal Footman hold my coat, and snicker, 85
And in short, I was afraid.

  And would it have been worth it, after all,
After the cups, the marmalade, the tea,
Among the porcelain, among some talk of you and me,
Would it have been worth while, 90
To have bitten off the matter with a smile,
To have squeezed the universe into a ball
To roll it toward some overwhelming question,[7]
To say: "I am Lazarus, come from the dead,[8]
Come back to tell you all, I shall tell you all"— 95
If one, settling a pillow by her head,
  Should say: "That is not what I meant at all.
  That is not it, at all."

6. Salome obtained the head of the prophet John the Baptist on a platter as a reward for dancing before the tetrarch Herod (Matthew 14.3–11). 7. Another echo of *To His Coy Mistress*, when the lover suggests rolling "all our strength and all / our sweetness up into one ball" to send against the "iron gates of life." 8. The story of Lazarus, raised from the dead, is told in John 11.1–44.

And would it have been worth it, after all,
Would it have been worth while,   100
After the sunsets and the dooryards and the sprinkled streets,
After the novels, after the teacups, after the skirts that trail along
    the floor—
And this, and so much more?—
It is impossible to say just what I mean!
But as if a magic lantern⁹ threw the nerves in patterns on a screen: 105
Would it have been worth while
If one, settling a pillow or throwing off a shawl,
And turning toward the window, should say:
    "That is not it at all,
    That is not what I meant, at all."   110

. . .

    No! I am not Prince Hamlet, nor was meant to be;
Am an attendant lord, one that will do
To swell a progress,¹ start a scene or two,
Advise the prince; no doubt, an easy tool,
Deferential, glad to be of use,   115
Politic, cautious, and meticulous;
Full of high sentence, but a bit obtuse;
At times, indeed, almost ridiculous—
Almost, at times, the Fool.

    I grow old . . . I grow old . . .   120
I shall wear the bottoms of my trousers rolled.

    Shall I part my hair behind? Do I dare to eat a peach?
I shall wear white flannel trousers, and walk upon the beach.
I have heard the mermaids singing, each to each.

I do not think that they will sing to me.   125

    I have seen them riding seaward on the waves
Combing the white hair of the waves blown back
When the wind blows the water white and black.

    We have lingered in the chambers of the sea
By sea-girls wreathed with seaweed red and brown   130
Till human voices wake us, and we drown.

9. A slide projector.　　1. A procession of attendants accompanying a king or nobleman across the stage, as in Elizabethan drama.

The Waste Land[1]

"Nam Sibyllam quidem Cumis ego ipse oculis meis vidi in ampulla
pendere, et cum illi pueri dicerent: Σίβυλλα τί θέλεισ; respon-
debat illa: ἀποθανεῖν θέλω."[2]

For Ezra Pound
il miglior fabbro.[3]

I. The Burial of the Dead[4]

April is the cruellest month, breeding
Lilacs out of the dead land, mixing
Memory and desire, stirring
Dull roots with spring rain.
Winter kept us warm, covering   5
Earth in forgetful snow, feeding
A little life with dried tubers.
Summer surprised us, coming over the Starnbergersee[5]
With a shower of rain; we stopped in the colonnade,
And went on in sunlight, into the Hofgarten,[6]   10
And drank coffee, and talked for an hour.
Bin gar keine Russin, stamm' aus Litauen, echt deutsch.[7]
And when we were children, staying at the archduke's,
My cousin's, he took me out on a sled,
And I was frightened. He said, Marie,   15
Marie, hold on tight. And down we went.[8]
In the mountains, there you feel free.
I read, much of the night, and go south in the winter.

   What are the roots that clutch, what branches grow
Out of this stony rubbish? Son of man,[9]   20
You cannot say, or guess, for you know only
A heap of broken images, where the sun beats,
And the dead tree gives no shelter, the cricket no relief,[1]
And the dry stone no sound of water. Only
There is shadow under this red rock,   25
(Come in under the shadow of this red rock),
And I will show you something different from either
Your shadow at morning striding behind you

1. Eliot provided footnotes for *The Waste Land* when it was first published in book form; these notes are
included here. A general note at the beginning referred readers to the religious symbolism described in
Jessie L. Weston's study of the Grail legend, *From Ritual to Romance* (1920), and to fertility myths and
vegetation ceremonies (especially those involving Adonis, Attis, and Osiris) as described in the *The Golden
Bough* (1890–1918) by the anthropologist Sir James Frazer.   2. Lines from Petronius's *Satyricon* (ca.
A.D. 60) describing the Sibyl, a prophetess shriveled with age and suspended in a bottle. "For indeed I
myself have seen with my own eyes the Sibyl at Cumae, hanging in a bottle, and when those boys would
say to her: 'Sibyl, what do you want?' she would reply: 'I want to die.' "   3. The dedication to Pound,
who suggested cuts and changes in the first manuscript of *The Waste Land,* borrows words used by Guido
Guinizelli to describe his predecessor, the Provençal poet Arnaut Daniel, in Dante's *Purgatorio* (26.117):
he is "the better craftsman."   4. From the burial service of the Anglican Church.   5. A lake near
Munich.   6. A public park.   7. "I am certainly no Russian, I come from Lithuania and am pure
German." German settlers in Lithuania considered themselves superior to the Slavic natives.   8. Lines
8–16 recall *My Past,* the memoirs of Countess Marie Larisch.   9. "Cf. Ezekiel II,i" [Eliot's note]. The
passage reads "Son of man, stand upon thy feet, and I will speak unto thee."   1. "Cf. Ecclesiastes XII,
v" [Eliot's note]. "Also when they shall be afraid of that which is high, and fears shall be in the way, . . .
the grasshopper shall be a burden, and desire shall fail."

Or your shadow at evening rising to meet you;
I will show you fear in a handful of dust.   30

>   *Frisch weht der Wind*
>   *Der Heimat zu*
>   *Mein Irisch Kind,*
>   *Wo weilest du?*²

"You gave me hyacinths first a year ago;   35
"They called me the hyacinth girl."
—Yet when we came back, late, from the Hyacinth garden,
Your arms full, and your hair wet, I could not
Speak, and my eyes failed, I was neither
Living nor dead, and I knew nothing,   40
Looking into the heart of light, the silence.
*Oed' und leer das Meer.*³

   Madame Sosostris,⁴ famous clairvoyante,
Had a bad cold, nevertheless
Is known to be the wisest woman in Europe,   45
With a wicked pack of cards.⁵ Here, said she,
Is your card, the drowned Phoenician Sailor,
(Those are pearls that were his eyes.⁶ Look!)
Here is Belladonna, the Lady of the Rocks,
The lady of situations.   50
Here is the man with three staves, and here the Wheel,
And here is the one-eyed merchant, and this card,
Which is blank, is something he carries on his back,
Which I am forbidden to see. I do not find
The Hanged Man. Fear death by water.   55
I see crowds of people, walking round in a ring.
Thank you. If you see dear Mrs. Equitone,
Tell her I bring the horoscope myself:
One must be so careful these days.

   Unreal City,⁷   60
Under the brown fog of a winter dawn,

---

2. "V. *Tristan und Isolde*, I, verses 5–8" [Eliot's note]. A sailor in Richard Wagner's opera sings, "The wind blows fresh / Towards the homeland / My Irish child / Where are you waiting?" (German)   **3.** "Id. III, verse 24" [Eliot's note]. "Barren and empty is the sea" (German) is the erroneous report the dying Tristan hears as he waits for Isolde's ship in the third act of Wagner's opera.   **4.** A fortune-teller with an assumed Egyptian name, possibly suggested by a similar figure in a novel by Aldous Huxley (*Crome Yellow,* 1921).   **5.** "I am not familiar with the exact constitution of the Tarot pack of cards, from which I have obviously departed to suit my own convenience. The Hanged Man, a member of the traditional pack, fits my purpose in two ways: because he is associated in my mind with the Hanged God of Frazer, and because I associate him with the hooded figure in the passage of the disciples to Emmaus in Part V. The Phoenician Sailor and the Merchant appear later; also the 'crowds of people,' and Death by Water is executed in Part IV. The Man with Three Staves (an authentic member of the Tarot pack) I associate, quite arbitrarily, with the Fisher King himself" [Eliot's note]. Tarot cards are used for telling fortunes; the four suits (cup, lance, sword, and coin) are life symbols related to the Grail legend; and as Eliot suggests, various figures on the cards are associated with different characters and situations in *The Waste Land.* For example, the *drowned Phoenician Sailor* (line 47) recurs in the merchant from Smyrna (III) and Phlebas the Phoenician (IV). *Belladonna* (line 49)—a poison, hallucinogen, medicine, and cosmetic (in Italian, "beautiful lady"); also an echo of Leonardo da Vinci's painting of the Virgin, *Madonna of the Rocks*—heralds the neurotic society woman amid her jewels and perfumes (II). The *Wheel* (line 51) is the wheel of fortune. The Hanged Man (line 55) becomes the sacrificed fertility god whose death ensures resurrection and new life for his people.   **6.** A line from Ariel's song in Shakespeare's *The Tempest* (1.2.398), which describes the transformation of a drowned man.   **7.** "Cf. Baudelaire: 'Fourmillante cité, cité pleine de rêves, / Où le spectre en plein jour raccroche le passant' " [Eliot's note]. "Swarming city, city full of dreams, / Where the specter in broad daylight accosts the passerby"; a description of Paris from "The Seven Old Men" in *The Flowers of Evil* (1857).

A crowd flowed over London Bridge, so many,
I had not thought death had undone so many.[8]
Sighs, short and infrequent, were exhaled,[9]
And each man fixed his eyes before his feet.   65
Flowed up the hill and down King William Street,
To where Saint Mary Woolnoth kept the hours
With a dead sound on the final stroke of nine.[1]
There I saw one I knew, and stopped him, crying: "Stetson!
"You who were with me in the ships at Mylae![2]   70
"That corpse you planted last year in your garden,
"Has it begun to sprout? Will it bloom this year?
"Or has the sudden frost disturbed its bed?
"Oh keep the Dog far hence, that's friend to men,[3]
"Or with his nails he'll dig it up again!   75
"You! hypocrite lecteur!—mon semblable,—mon frère!"[4]

II. A Game of Chess[5]

The Chair she sat in, like a burnished throne,[6]
Glowed on the marble, where the glass
Held up by standards wrought with fruited vines
From which a golden Cupidon peeped out   80
(Another hid his eyes behind his wing)
Doubled the flames of sevenbranched candelabra
Reflecting light upon the table as
The glitter of her jewels rose to meet it,
From satin cases poured in rich profusion.   85
In vials of ivory and coloured glass
Unstoppered, lurked her strange synthetic perfumes,
Unguent, powdered, or liquid—troubled, confused
And drowned the sense in odours; stirred by the air
That freshened from the window, these ascended   90

8. "Cf. *Inferno* III, 55–57: 'si lunga tratta / di gente, ch'io non avrei mai creduto / che morte tanta n'avesse disfatta' " [Eliot's note]. "Behind that banner trailed so long a file / of people—I should never have believed / that death could have unmade so many souls"; not only is Dante amazed at the number of people who have died but he is also describing a crowd of people who were neither good nor bad—nonentities denied even the entrance to hell.   9. "Cf. *Inferno* IV, 25–27: 'Quivi, secondo che per ascoltare, / non avea pianto, / ma' che di sospiri, / che l'aura eterna facevan tremare' " [Eliot's note]. "Here, so far as I could tell by listening, there was no weeping but so many sighs that they caused the everlasting air to tremble"; the first circle of hell, or limbo, contained the souls of virtuous people who lived before Christ or had not been baptized.   1. "A phenomenon which I have often noticed" [Eliot's note]. The church is in the financial district of London, where King William Street is also located.   2. An "average" modern name (with business associations) linked to the ancient battle of Mylae (260 B.C.), where Rome was victorious over its commercial rival, Carthage.   3. "Cf. the Dirge in Webster's *White Devil*" [Eliot's note]. The dirge, or song of lamentation, sung by Cornelia in John Webster's play (1625), asks to "keep the wolf far thence, that's foe to men," so that the wolf's nails may not dig up the bodies of her murdered relatives. Eliot's reversal of dog for wolf, and friend for foe, domesticates the grotesque scene; it may also foreshadow rebirth since (according to Weston's book), the rise of the Dog Star, Sirius, announced the flooding of the Nile and the consequent return of fertility to Egyptian soil.   4. "V. Baudelaire, Preface to *Fleurs du Mal*" [Eliot's note]. Baudelaire's poem preface, titled "To the Reader," ended "Hypocritical reader!—my likeness!—my brother!" The poet challenges the reader to recognize that both are caught up in the worst sin of all—the moral wasteland of *ennui* ("boredom") as lack of will, the refusal to care one way or the other.   5. Reference to a play, *A Game of Chess* (1627) by Thomas Middleton (1580–1627); see n. 5, p. 1684. Part II juxtaposes two scenes of modern sterility: an initial setting of wealthy boredom, neurosis, and lack of communication, and a pub scene in which similar concerns of appearance, sexual attraction, and thwarted childbirth are brought out more visibly, and in more vulgar language.   6. "Cf. *Antony and Cleopatra*, II, ii, 1.190" [Eliot's note]. A paler version of Cleopatra's splendor as she met her future lover, Antony: "The barge she sat in, like a burnished throne, / Burned on the water."

In fattening the prolonged candle-flames,
Flung their smoke into the laquearia,[7]
Stirring the pattern on the coffered ceiling.
Huge sea-wood fed with copper
Burned green and orange, framed by the coloured stone,   95
In which sad light a carvèd dolphin swam.
Above the antique mantel was displayed
As though a window gave upon the sylvan scene[8]
The change of Philomel,[9] by the barbarous king
So rudely forced; yet there the nightingale[1]   100
Filled all the desert with inviolable voice
And still she cried, and still the world pursues,
"Jug Jug"[2] to dirty ears.
And other withered stumps of time
Were told upon the walls; staring forms   105
Leaned out, leaning, hushing the room enclosed.
Footsteps shuffled on the stair.
Under the firelight, under the brush, her hair
Spread out in fiery points
Glowed into words, then would be savagely still.   110

    "My nerves are bad to-night. Yes, bad. Stay with me.
Speak to me. Why do you never speak. Speak.
    What are you thinking of? What thinking? What?
I never know what you are thinking. Think."

    I think we are in rats' alley[3]   115
Where the dead men lost their bones.

    "What is that noise?"
                  The wind under the door.[4]
"What is that noise now? What is the wind doing?"
                  Nothing again nothing.   120
                          "Do
"You know nothing? Do you see nothing? Do you remember
"Nothing?"

    I remember
Those are pearls that were his eyes.   125
"Are you alive, or not? Is there nothing in your head?"
                         But

---

7. "Laquearia. V. *Aeneid*, I, 726: dependent lychni laquearibus aureis incensi, et noctem flammis funalia vincunt" [Eliot's note]. "Glowing lamps hang from the gold-paneled ceiling, and the torches conquer night with their flames"; the banquet setting of another classical love scene, in which Dido is inspired with a fatal passion for Aeneas.   8. "Sylvan scene. V. Milton, *Paradise Lost*, IV, 140" [Eliot's note]. Eden as first seen by Satan.   9. "V. Ovid, *Metamorphoses*, VI, Philomela" [Eliot's note]. Philomela was raped by her brother-in-law, King Tereus, who cut out her tongue so that she could not tell her sister, Procne. Later Procne is changed into a swallow and Philomela into a nightingale to save them from the king's rage after they have revenged themselves by killing his son.   1. "Cf. Part III, l.204" [Eliot's note].   2. Represents the nightingale's song in Elizabethan poetry.   3. "Cf. Part III, l.195" [Eliot's note].   4. "Cf. Webster: 'Is the wind in that door still?' " [Eliot's note]. From *The Devil's Law Case* (1623), 3.2.162, with the implied meaning "is there still breath in him?"

O O O O that Shakespeherian Rag—
It's so elegant
So intelligent 130
"What shall I do now? What shall I do?"
"I shall rush out as I am, and walk the street
"With my hair down, so. What shall we do to-morrow?
"What shall we ever do?"
                              The hot water at ten. 135
And if it rains, a closed car at four.
And we shall play a game of chess,[5]
Pressing lidless eyes and waiting for a knock upon the door.

    When Lil's husband got demobbed,[6] I said—
I didn't mince my words, I said to her myself, 140
HURRY UP PLEASE ITS TIME[7]
Now Albert's coming back, make yourself a bit smart.
He'll want to know what you done with that money he gave you
To get yourself some teeth. He did, I was there.
You have them all out, Lil, and get a nice set, 145
He said, I swear, I can't bear to look at you.
And no more can't I, I said, and think of poor Albert,
He's been in the army four years, he wants a good time,
And if you don't give it him, there's others will, I said.
Oh is there, she said. Something o' that, I said. 150
Then I'll know who to thank, she said, and give me a straight look.
HURRY UP PLEASE ITS TIME
If you don't like it you can get on with it, I said.
Others can pick and choose if you can't.
But if Albert makes off, it won't be for lack of telling. 155
You ought to be ashamed, I said, to look so antique.
(And her only thirty-one.)
I can't help it, she said, pulling a long face,
It's them pills I took, to bring it off, she said.
(She's had five already, and nearly died of young George.) 160
The chemist[8] said it would be all right, but I've never been the same.
You are a proper fool, I said.
Well, if Albert won't leave you alone, there it is, I said,
What you get married for if you don't want children?
HURRY UP PLEASE ITS TIME 165
Well, that Sunday Albert was home, they had a hot gammon,[9]
And they asked me in to dinner, to get the beauty of it hot—
HURRY UP PLEASE ITS TIME
HURRY UP PLEASE ITS TIME
Goonight Bill. Goonight Lou. Goonight May. Goonight. 170
Ta ta. Goonight. Goonight.
Good night, ladies, good night, sweet ladies, good night, good night.[1]

5. "Cf. the game of chess in Middleton's *Women Beware Women*" [Eliot's note]. In this scene, a woman is seduced in a series of strategic steps that parallel the moves of a chess game, which is occupying her mother-in-law at the same time.   6. Demobilized, discharged from the army.   7. The British bartender's warning that the pub is about to close.   8. The druggist, who gave her pills to cause a miscarriage.   9. Ham.   1. The popular song for a party's end ("Good Night, Ladies") shifts into Ophelia's last words in *Hamlet* (4.5.72) as she goes off to drown herself.

III. The Fire Sermon[2]

The river's tent is broken: the last fingers of leaf
Clutch and sink into the wet bank. The wind
Crosses the brown land, unheard. The nymphs are departed.   175
Sweet Thames, run softly, till I end my song.[3]
The river bears no empty bottles, sandwich papers,
Silk handkerchiefs, cardboard boxes, cigarette ends
Or other testimony of summer nights. The nymphs are departed.
And their friends, the loitering heirs of city directors;   180
Departed, have left no addresses.
By the waters of Leman I sat down and wept[4] . . .
Sweet Thames, run softly till I end my song,
Sweet Thames, run softly, for I speak not loud or long.
But at my back in a cold blast I hear[5]   185
The rattle of the bones, and chuckle spread from ear to ear.

A rat crept softly through the vegetation
Dragging its slimy belly on the bank
While I was fishing in the dull canal
On a winter evening round behind the gashouse   190
Musing upon the king my brother's wreck
And on the king my father's death before him.[6]
White bodies naked on the low damp ground
And bones cast in a little low dry garret,
Rattled by the rat's foot only, year to year.   195
But at my back from time to time I hear[7]
The sound of horns and motors, which shall bring[8]
Sweeney to Mrs. Porter in the spring.
O the moon shone bright on Mrs. Porter[9]
And on her daughter   200
They wash their feet in soda water
Et O ces voix d'enfants, chantant dans la coupole![1]

Twit twit twit
Jug jug jug jug jug jug

2. Reference to the Buddha's Fire Sermon (see n. 2, p. 1688), in which he denounced the fiery lusts and passions of earthly experience. "All things are on fire . . . with the fire of passion . . . of hatred . . . of infatuation." Part III describes the degeneration of even these passions in the sterile decadence of the modern Waste Land.   3. "V. Spenser, *Prothalamion*" [Eliot's note]. The line is the refrain of a marriage song by the Elizabethan poet Edmund Spenser (1552?–1599) and evokes a river of unpolluted pastoral beauty.   4. In Psalms 137.1, the exiled Hebrews sit by the rivers of Babylon and weep for their lost homeland. *Waters of Leman:* Lake Geneva (where Eliot wrote much of *The Waste Land*). A *leman* is a mistress or lover.   5. Distorted echo of Andrew Marvell's (1621–1678) poem *To His Coy Mistress:* "But at my back I always hear / Time's wingèd chariot hurrying near."   6. "Cf. *The Tempest* I.ii" [Eliot's note]. Ferdinand, the king's son, believing his father drowned and mourning his death, hears in the air a song containing the line that Eliot quotes earlier at lines 48 and 126.   7. "Cf. Marvell, 'To His Coy Mistress' " [Eliot's note].   8. "Cf. Day, *Parliament of Bees*: 'When of the sudden, listening, you shall hear, / A noise of horns and hunting, which shall bring / Actaeon to Diana in the spring, / Where all shall see her naked skin' " [Eliot's note]. The young hunter Actaeon was changed into a stag, hunted down, and killed when he came upon the goddess Diana bathing. Sweeney is in no such danger from his visit to Mrs. Porter.   9. "I do not know the origin of the ballad from which these lines are taken: it was reported to me from Sydney, Australia" [Eliot's note]. A song popular among Allied troops during World War I. One version continues lines 199–201 as follows: "And so they oughter / To keep them clean."   1. "V. Verlaine, *Parsifal*" [Eliot's note]. "And O these children's voices, singing in the dome!" (French); the last lines of a sonnet by Paul Verlaine (1844–1896), which ambiguously celebrates the Grail hero's chaste restraint. In Richard Wagner's opera, Parsifal's feet are washed to purify him before entering the presence of the Grail.

So rudely forc'd.   205
Tereu[2]

   Unreal City
Under the brown fog of a winter noon
Mr. Eugenides, the Smyrna merchant
Unshaven, with a pocket full of currants   210
C.i.f. London: documents at sight,[3]
Asked me in demotic French
To luncheon at the Cannon Street Hotel
Followed by a weekend at the Metropole.[4]

   At the violet hour, when the eyes and back   215
Turn upward from the desk, when the human engine waits
Like a taxi throbbing waiting,
I Tiresias,[5] though blind, throbbing between two lives,
Old man with wrinkled female breasts, can see
At the violet hour, the evening hour that strives   220
Homeward, and brings the sailor home from sea,[6]
The typist home at teatime, clears her breakfast, lights
Her stove, and lays out food in tins.
Out of the window perilously spread
Her drying combinations touched by the sun's last rays,   225
On the divan are piled (at night her bed)
Stockings, slippers, camisoles, and stays.
I Tiresias, old man with wrinkled dugs
Perceived the scene, and foretold the rest—
I too awaited the expected guest.   230
He, the young man carbuncular, arrives,
A small house agent's clerk, with one bold stare,
One of the low on whom assurance sits
As a silk hat on a Bradford[7] millionaire.
The time is now propitious, as he guesses,   235
The meal is ended, she is bored and tired,
Endeavours to engage her in caresses
Which still are unreproved, if undesired.
Flushed and decided, he assaults at once;
Exploring hands encounter no defence;   240
His vanity requires no response,

2. Tereus, who raped Philomela (see line 99); also the nightingale's song.   3. "The currants were quoted
at a price 'carriage and insurance free to London'; and the Bill of Lading etc. were to be handed to the
buyer upon payment of the sight draft" [Eliot's note].   4. Smyrna is an ancient Phoenician seaport, and
early Smyrna merchants spread the Eastern fertility cults. In contrast, their descendant Mr. Eugenides
("Well-born") invites the poet to lunch in a large commercial hotel and a weekend at a seaside resort in
Brighton.   5. "Tiresias, although a mere spectator and not indeed a 'character,' is yet the most important
personage in the poem, uniting all the rest. Just as the one-eyed merchant, seller of currants, melts into
the Phoenician Sailor, and the latter is not wholly distinct from Ferdinand Prince of Naples, so all the
women are one woman, and the two sexes meet in Tiresias. What Tiresias *sees*, in fact, is the substance of
the poem. The whole passage from Ovid is one of great anthropological interest" [Eliot's note]. The passage
then quoted from Ovid's *Metamorphoses* (3.320–38) describes how Tiresias spent seven years of his life as
a woman and thus experienced love from the point of view of both sexes. Blinded by Juno, he was recom-
pensed by Jove with the gift of prophecy.   6. "This may or may not appear as exact as Sappho's lines,
but I had in mind the 'longshore' or 'dory' fisherman, who returns at nightfall" [Eliot's note]. The Greek
poet Sappho's poem describes how the evening star brings home those whom dawn has sent abroad; there
is also an echo of Robert Louis Stevenson's (1850–1894) *Requiem* 1.221: "Home is the sailor, home from
the sea."   7. A manufacturing town in Yorkshire that prospered greatly during World War I.

And makes a welcome of indifference.
(And I Tiresias have foresuffered all
Enacted on this same divan or bed;
I who have sat by Thebes below the wall   245
And walked among the lowest of the dead.)[8]
Bestows one final patronising kiss,
And gropes his way, finding the stairs unlit . . .

　　She turns and looks a moment in the glass,
Hardly aware of her departed lover;   250
Her brain allows one half-formed thought to pass:
"Well now that's done: and I'm glad it's over."
When lovely woman stoops to folly and[9]
Paces about her room again, alone,
She smoothes her hair with automatic hand,   255
And puts a record on the gramophone.

　　"This music crept by me upon the waters"[1]
And along the Strand, up Queen Victoria Street.
O City city,[2] I can sometimes hear
Beside a public bar in Lower Thames Street,   260
The pleasant whining of a mandoline
And a clatter and a chatter from within
Where fishmen lounge at noon: where the walls
Of Magnus Martyr[3] hold
Inexplicable splendour of Ionian white and gold.   265

　　　　　　　The river sweats[4]
　　　　　　　Oil and tar
　　　　　　　The barges drift
　　　　　　　With the turning tide
　　　　　　　Red sails   270
　　　　　　　Wide
　　　　　　　To leeward, swing on the heavy spar.
　　　　　　　The barges wash
　　　　　　　Drifting logs
　　　　　　　Down Greenwich reach   275
　　　　　　　Past the Isle of Dogs.[5]
　　　　　　　　　Weialala leia
　　　　　　　　　Wallala leialala

8. Tiresias prophesied in the marketplace at Thebes for many years before dying and continuing to prophesy in Hades.　9. "V. Goldsmith, the song in *The Vicar of Wakefield*" [Eliot's note]. "When lovely woman stoops to folly / And finds too late that men betray / What charm can soothe her melancholy, / What art can wash her guilt away?" Oliver Goldsmith (ca. 1730–1774), *The Vicar of Wakefield* (1766).　1. "V. *The Tempest*, as above" [Eliot's note, referring to line 191]. Spoken by Ferdinand as he hears Ariel sing of his father's transformation by the sea, his eyes turning to pearls, his bones to coral, and everything else he formerly was into "something rich and strange."　2. A double invocation: the city of London and the City as London's central financial district (see lines 60 and 207). See also lines 375–76, the great cities of Western civilization.　3. "The interior of St. Magnus Martyr is to my mind one of the finest among Wren's interiors. See *The Proposed Demolition of Nineteen City Churches*: (P. S. King & Son, Ltd)" [Eliot's note]. The architect was Christopher Wren (1632–1723), and the church is located just below London Bridge on Lower Thames Street.　4. "The Song of the (three) Thames-daughters begins being here. From line 292 to 306 inclusive they speak in turn. V. *Götterdämmerung* III.i.: the Rhine-daughters" [Eliot's note]. In Wagner's opera *The Twilight of the Gods* (1876), the three Rhine-maidens mourn the loss of their gold, which gave the river its sparkling beauty; lines 177–78 here echo the Rhine-maidens' refrain.　5. A peninsula opposite Greenwich on the Thames.

Elizabeth and Leicester[6]
Beating oars   280
The stern was formed
A gilded shell
Red and gold
The brisk swell
Rippled both shores   285
Southwest wind
Carried down stream
The peal of bells
White towers
        Weialala leia   290
        Wallala leialala

"Trams and dusty trees.
Highbury bore me. Richmond and Kew
Undid me.[7] By Richmond I raised my knees
Supine on the floor of a narrow canoe."   295

"My feet are at Moorgate,[8] and my heart
Under my feet. After the event
He wept. He promised 'a new start.'
I made no comment. What should I resent?'

"On Margate Sands.[9]   300
I can connect
Nothing with nothing.
The broken fingernails of dirty hands.
My people humble people who expect
Nothing.'   305
        la la

To Carthage then I came[1]

Burning burning burning burning[2]
O Lord Thou pluckest me out[3]
O Lord Thou pluckest   310

burning

---

6. "V. Froude, *Elizabeth*, vol. I, ch. iv, letter of De Quadra to Philip of Spain: 'In the afternoon we were in a barge, watching the games on the river. (The queen) was alone with Lord Robert and myself on the poop, when they began to talk nonsense, and went so far that Lord Robert at last said, as I was on the spot there was no reason why they should not be married if the queen pleased" [Eliot's note]. Sir Robert Dudley (1532–1588), the earl of Leicester, was a favorite of Queen Elizabeth and at one point hoped to marry her.   7. "Cf. *Purgatorio*, V, 133: 'Ricorditi di me, che son la Pia; / Siena mi fe', disfecemi Maremma' " [Eliot's note]. La Pia, in Purgatory, recalls her seduction: "Remember me, who am La Pia. / Siena made me, Maremma undid me." Eliot's parody substitutes Highbury (a London suburb) and Richmond and Kew, popular excursion points on the Thames.   8. A London slum.   9. A seaside resort on the Thames.   1. "V. St. Augustine's *Confessions*: 'to Carthage then I came, where a cauldron of unholy loves sang all about mine ears' " [Eliot's note]. The youthful Augustine is described. Carthage is also the scene of Dido's faithful love for Aeneas, referred to in line 92.   2. "The complete text of the Buddha's Fire Sermon (which corresponds in importance to the Sermon on the Mount) from which these words are taken, will be found translated in the late Henry Clarke Warren's *Buddhism in Translation* (Harvard Oriental Studies). Mr. Warren was one of the great pioneers of Buddhist studies in the Occident" [Eliot's note]. The Sermon on the Mount is in Matthew 5–7.   3. "From St. Augustine's *Confessions* again. The collocation of these two representatives of eastern and western asceticism, as the culmination of this part of the poem is not an accident" [Eliot's note]. See also Zechariah 3.2, where the high priest Joshua is described as a "brand plucked out of the fire."

IV. Death by Water

Phlebas the Phoenician, a fortnight dead,
Forgot the cry of gulls, and the deep sea swell
And the profit and loss.
                          A current under sea   315
Picked his bones in whispers. As he rose and fell
He passed the stages of his age and youth
Entering the whirlpool.
                          Gentile or Jew
O you who turn the wheel and look to windward,   320
Consider Phlebas, who was once handsome and tall as you.

V. What the Thunder Said[4]

After the torchlight red on sweaty faces
After the frosty silence in the gardens
After the agony in stony places
The shouting and the crying   325
Prison and palace and reverberation
Of thunder of spring over distant mountains
He who was living is now dead[5]
We who were living are now dying
With a little patience   330

  Here is no water but only rock
Rock and no water and the sandy road
The road winding above among the mountains
Which are mountains of rock without water
If there were water we should stop and drink   335
Amongst the rock one cannot stop or think
Sweat is dry and feet are in the sand
If there were only water amongst the rock
Dead mountain mouth of carious teeth that cannot spit
Here one can neither stand nor lie nor sit   340
There is not even silence in the mountains
But dry sterile thunder without rain
There is not even solitude in the mountains
But red sullen faces sneer and snarl
From doors of mudcracked houses   345
                          If there were water
    And no rock
    If there were rock
    And also water
    And water   350
    A spring
    A pool among the rock

4. "In the first part of Part V three themes are employed: the journey to Emmaus, the approach to the Chapel Perilous (see Miss Weston's book) and the present decay of eastern Europe" [Eliot's note]. On their journey to Emmaus (Luke 24.13–34), Jesus' disciples were joined by a stranger who later revealed himself to be the crucified and resurrected Christ. The *thunder* of the title is a divine voice in the Hindu *Upanishads* (see n. 3, p. 1691).   5. Allusions to stages in Christ's Passion: the betrayal, prayer in the garden of Gethsemane, imprisonment, trial, crucifixion, and burial. Despair reigns, for this is death before the Resurrection.

If there were the sound of water only
Not the cicada[6]
And dry grass singing   355
But sound of water over a rock
Where the hermit-thrush[7] sings in the pine trees
Drip drop drip drop drop drop drop
But there is no water

Who is the third who walks always beside you?   360
When I count, there are only you and I together[8]
But when I look ahead up the white road
There is always another one walking beside you
Gliding wrapt in a brown mantle, hooded
I do not know whether a man or a woman   365
—But who is that on the other side of you?

What is that sound high in the air[9]
Murmur of maternal lamentation
Who are those hooded hordes swarming
Over endless plains, stumbling in cracked earth   370
Ringed by the flat horizon only
What is the city over the mountains
Cracks and reforms and bursts in the violet air
Falling towers
Jerusalem Athens Alexandria   375
Vienna London
Unreal

A woman drew her long black hair out tight
And fiddled whisper music on those strings
And bats with baby faces in the violet light   380
Whistled, and beat their wings
And crawled head downward down a blackened wall
And upside down in air were towers
Tolling reminiscent bells, that kept the hours
And voices singing out of empty cisterns and exhausted wells.   385

In this decayed hole among the mountains
In the faint moonlight, the grass is singing
Over the tumbled graves, about the chapel
There is the empty chapel, only the wind's home.
It has no windows, and the door swings,   390
Dry bones can harm no one.

---

6. Grasshopper or cricket; see line 23.   7. "The hermit-thrush which I have heard in Quebec Province.
. . . Its 'water-dripping song' is justly celebrated" [Eliot's note].   8. "The following lines were stimulated
by the account of one of the Antarctic expeditions (I forget which, but I think one of Shackleton's): it was
related that the party of explorers, at the extremity of their strength, had the constant delusion that there
was *one more member* than could actually be counted" [Eliot's note]. See also n. 4, p. 1689.   9. Eliot's
note to lines 367–77 refers to Hermann Hesse's *Blick ins Chaos* (Glimpse into chaos) and a passage that
reads, translated, "Already half of Europe, already at least half of Eastern Europe is on the way to Chaos,
drives drunk in holy madness on the edge of the abyss and sings at the same time, sings drunk and hymn-like,
as Dimitri Karamazov sang [in Dostoevsky's *The Brothers Karamazov*]. The offended bourgeois laughs at
the songs; the saint and the seer hear them with tears."

Only a cock stood on the rooftree
Co co rico co co rico[1]
In a flash of lightning. Then a damp gust
Bringing rain   395

    Ganga was sunken, and the limp leaves
Waited for rain, while the black clouds
Gathered far distant, over Himavant.[2]
The jungle crouched, humped in silence.
Then spoke the thunder   400
DA
Datta: what have we given?[3]
My friend, blood shaking my heart
The awful daring of a moment's surrender
Which an age of prudence can never retract   405
By this, and this only, we have existed
Which is not to be found in our obituaries
Or in memories draped by the beneficent spider[4]
Or under seals broken by the lean solicitor
In our empty rooms   410
DA
Dayadhvam:[5] I have heard the key
Turn in the door once and turn once only
We think of the key, each in his prison
Thinking of the key, each confirms a prison   415
Only at nightfall, aethereal rumours
Revive for a moment a broken Coriolanus[6]
DA
Damyata: The boat responded
Gaily, to the hand expert with sail and oar   420
The sea was calm, your heart would have responded
Gaily, when invited, beating obedient
To controlling hands
                        I sat upon the shore
Fishing,[7] with the arid plain behind me   425
Shall I at least set my lands in order?
London Bridge is falling down falling down falling down

1. European version of the cock's crow: *cock-a-doodle-doo*. The cock crowed in Matthew 26.34 and 74, after Peter had denied Jesus three times.　　2. A mountain in the Himalayas. *Ganga:* the river Ganges in India.　　3. " 'Datta, dayadhvam, damyata' (Give, sympathise, control). The fable of the meaning of the Thunder is found in the *Brihadaranyaka*—Upanishad 5,1" [Eliot's note]. In the fable, the word DA, spoken by the supreme being Prajapati, is interpreted as *Datta* ("to give alms"), *Dayadhvam* ("to sympathize or have compassion"), and *Damyata* ("to have self-control") by gods, human beings, and demons respectively. The conclusion is that when the thunder booms DA DA DA, Prajapati is commanding that all three virtues be practiced simultaneously.　　4. "Cf. Webster, *The White Devil*, V, vi: ' . . . they'll remarry / Ere the worm pierce your winding-sheet, ere the spider / Make a thin curtain for your epitaphs' " [Eliot's note].　　5. Eliot's note on the command "to sympathize" or reach outside the self, cites two descriptions of helpless isolation. The first comes from Dante's *Inferno* 33.46: as Ugolino, imprisoned in a tower with his children to die of starvation, says "And I heard below the door of the horrible tower being locked up"). The second is a modern description by the English philosopher F. H. Bradley (1846–1924) of the inevitably self-enclosed or private nature of consciousness: "My external sensations are no less private to myself than are my thoughts or my feelings. In either case my experience falls within my own circle, a circle closed on the outside; and, with all its elements alike, every sphere is opaque to the others which surround it. . . . In brief, regarded as an existence which appears in a soul, the whole world for each is peculiar and private to that soul" (*Appearance and Reality*).　　6. A proud Roman patrician who was exiled and led an army against his homeland. In Shakespeare's play, both his grandeur and his downfall come from a desire to be ruled only by himself.　　7. "V. Weston: *From Ritual to Romance*; chapter on the Fisher King" [Eliot's note].

Poi s'ascose nel foco che gli affina[8]
Quando fiam uti chelidon[9]—O swallow swallow
Le Prince d'Aquitaine à la tour abolie[1]   430
These fragments I have shored against my ruins
Why then Ile fit you. Hieronymo's mad againe.[2]
        Datta. Dayadhvam. Damyata.
               Shantih   shantih   shantih[3]

From Four Quartets

Little Gidding[1]

Midwinter spring is its own season
Sempiternal though sodden towards sundown,
Suspended in time, between pole and tropic.
When the short day is brightest, with frost and fire,
The brief sun flames the ice, on pond and ditches,   5
In windless cold that is the heart's heat,
Reflecting in a watery mirror
A glare that is blindness in the early afternoon.
And glow more intense than blaze of branch, or brazier,
Stirs the dumb spirit: no wind, but pentecostal fire[2]   10
In the dark time of the year. Between melting and freezing
The soul's sap quivers. There is no earth smell
Or smell of living thing. This is the spring time
But not in time's covenant. Now the hedgerow
Is blanched for an hour with transitory blossom   15
Of snow, a bloom more sudden
Than that of summer, neither budding nor fading,
Not in the scheme of generation.
Where is the summer, the unimaginable
Zero summer?   20
               If you came this way,
Taking the route you would be likely to take
From the place you would be likely to come from,
If you came this way in may time,[3] you would find the hedges
White again, in May, with voluptuary sweetness.   25

---

8. Eliot's note quotes a passage in the *Purgatorio* in which Arnaut Daniel (see n. 3, p. 1680) asks Dante to remember his pain. The line cited here, "then he hid himself in the fire which refines them" (*Purgatorio* 26.148), shows Daniel departing in fire which—in Purgatory—exists as a purifying rather than a destructive element.   9. "V. *Pervigilium Veneris*. Cf. Philomela in Parts II and III" [Eliot's note]. "When shall I be as a swallow?" A line from the *Vigil of Venus*, an anonymous late Latin poem, that asks for the gift of song; here associated with Philomela as a swallow, not the nightingale of lines 99–103 and 203–06.   1. "V. Gerard de Nerval, Sonnet *El Desdichado*" [Eliot's note]. The Spanish title means "The Disinherited One," and the sonnet is a monologue describing the speaker as a melancholy, ill-starred dreamer: "the Prince of Aquitaine in his ruined tower." Another line recalls the scene at the end of *Love Song of J. Alfred Prufrock* (p. 1676): "I dreamed in the grotto where sirens swim."   2. "V. Kyd's *Spanish Tragedy*" [Eliot's note]. Thomas Kyd's revenge play (1594) is subtitled "Hieronymo's Mad Againe." The protagonist "fits" his son's murderers into appropriate roles in a court entertainment so that they may all be killed.   3. "Shantih. Repeated as here, a formal ending to an Upanishad. 'The Peace which passeth understanding' is our equivalent to this word" [Eliot's note]. The *Upanishads* comment on the sacred Hindu scriptures, the *Vedas*.   1. A village in Huntingdonshire that housed a religious community in the seventeenth century. Eliot visited the (rebuilt) chapel on a midwinter day.   2. On the Pentecost day after Christ's resurrection, the apostles saw "cloven tongues like as of fire" (Acts 2.3) and were "filled with the Holy Ghost" (Acts 2.4).   3. When the May (Hawthorne) is in bloom.

It would be the same at the end of the journey,
If you came at night like a broken king,[4]
If you came by day not knowing what you came for,
It would be the same, when you leave the rough road
And turn behind the pig-sty to the dull façade   30
And the tombstone. And what you thought you came for
Is only a shell, a husk of meaning
From which the purpose breaks only when it is fulfilled
If at all. Either you had no purpose
Or the purpose is beyond the end you figured   35
And is altered in fulfilment. There are other places
Which also are the world's end, some at the sea jaws,
Or over a dark lake, in a desert or a city—
But this is the nearest, in place and time,
Now and in England.   40
               If you came this way,
Taking any route, starting from anywhere,
At any time or at any season,
It would always be the same: you would have to put off
Sense and notion. You are not here to verify,   45
Instruct yourself, or inform curiosity
Or carry report. You are here to kneel
Where prayer has been valid. And prayer is more
Than an order of words, the conscious occupation
Of the praying mind, or the sound of the voice praying.   50
And what the dead had no speech for, when living,
They can tell you, being dead: the communication
Of the dead is tongued with fire beyond the language of the living.
Here, the intersection of the timeless moment
Is England and nowhere. Never and always.   55

II

Ash on an old man's sleeve
Is all the ash the burnt roses leave.
Dust in the air suspended
Marks the place where a story ended.
Dust inbreathed was a house—   60
The wall, the wainscot and the mouse.
The death of hope and despair,
    This is the death of air.[5]

There are flood and drouth
Over the eyes and in the mouth,   65
Dead water and dead sand
Contending for the upper hand.
The parched eviscerate soil
Gapes at the vanity of toil,

4. Charles I, king of England (1600–1649), had visited the religious community several times and went there secretly after his final defeat in the English Civil War. 5. Allusion to "Fire lives in the death of air," a phrase from the pre-Socratic philosopher Heraclitus (535–475 B.C.) describing how one element (here, fire) lives at the expense of another (here, air).

Laughs without mirth.   70
    This is the death of earth.

Water and fire succeed
The town, the pasture and the weed.
Water and fire deride
The sacrifice that we denied.   75
Water and fire shall rot
The marred foundations we forgot,
Of sanctuary and choir.
    This is the death of water and fire.

In the uncertain hour before the morning[6]   80
    Near the ending of interminable night
    At the recurrent end of the unending
After the dark dove[7] with the flickering tongue
    Had passed below the horizon of his homing
    While the dead leaves still rattled on like tin   85
Over the asphalt where no other sound was
    Between three districts whence the smoke arose
    I met one walking, loitering and hurried
As if blown towards me like the metal leaves
    Before the urban dawn wind unresisting.   90
    And as I fixed upon the down-turned face
That pointed scrutiny with which we challenge
    The first-met stranger in the waning dusk
    I caught the sudden look of some dead master
Whom I had known, forgotten, half recalled   95
    Both one and many; in the brown baked features
    The eyes of a familiar compound ghost
Both intimate and unidentifiable.
    So I assumed a double part,[8] and cried
    And heard another's voice cry: "What! are *you* here?"   100
Although we were not. I was still the same,
    Knowing myself yet being someone other—
    And he a face still forming; yet the words sufficed
To compel the recognition they preceded.
    And so, compliant to the common wind,   105
    Too strange to each other for misunderstanding,
In concord at this intersection time
    Of meeting nowhere, no before and after,
    We trod the pavement in a dead patrol.
I said: "The wonder that I feel is easy,   110
    Yet ease is cause of wonder. Therefore speak:
    I may not comprehend, may not remember."

---

6. The narrative passage from here to the end of Part II is written in tercets, a form that recalls Dante's use of *terza rima* (triple rhyme) in *The Divine Comedy*. Eliot later commented that this section was "the nearest equivalent to a canto of the *Inferno* or *Purgatorio*" that he could create.   7. A play on the emblem of the Holy Spirit that descended to the apostles at Pentecost and on the then-current German slang for bomb, *Taube* ("dove").   8. The role of questioner of souls (after Dante in *The Divine Comedy*) and the role of one interrogating himself.

And he: "I am not eager to rehearse
  My thought and theory which you have forgotten.
  These things have served their purpose: let them be.   115
So with your own, and pray they be forgiven
  By others, as I pray you to forgive
  Both bad and good. Last season's fruit is eaten
And the fullfed beast shall kick the empty pail.
  For last year's words belong to last year's language   120
  And next year's words await another voice.
But, as the passage now presents no hindrance
  To the spirit unappeased and peregrine
  Between two worlds become much like each other,
So I find words I never thought to speak   125
  In streets I never thought I should revisit
  When I left my body on a distant shore.
Since our concern was speech, and speech impelled us
  To purify the dialect of the tribe[9]
  And urge the mind to aftersight and foresight,   130
Let me disclose the gifts reserved for age
  To set a crown upon your lifetime's effort.
  First, the cold friction of expiring sense
Without enchantment, offering no promise
  But bitter tastelessness of shadow fruit   135
  As body and soul begin to fall asunder.
Second, the conscious impotence of rage
  At human folly, and the laceration
  Of laughter at what ceases to amuse.
And last, the rending pain of re-enactment   140
  Of all that you have done, and been; the shame
  Of motives late revealed, and the awareness
Of things ill done and done to others' harm
  Which once you took for exercise of virtue.
  Then fools' approval stings, and honour stains.   145
From wrong to wrong the exasperated spirit
  Proceeds, unless restored by that refining fire
  Where you must move in measure, like a dancer."[1]
The day was breaking. In the disfigured street
  He left me, with a kind of valediction,   150
  And faded on the blowing of the horn.[2]

                              III

There are three conditions which often look alike
Yet differ completely, flourish in the same hedgerow:
Attachment to self and to things and to persons; detachment

9. In his epitaph-sonnet for Edgar Allan Poe, *The Tomb of Edgar Poe*, the French poet Stéphane Mallarmé (1842–1898) defines the poet's role as purifying speech by using ordinary language (*the dialect of the tribe*) in a more precise and yet complex way, creating a new structure of interlocking or multiple meanings (see lines 221–24.)   1. In Dante's *Purgatorio* (26.148), fire is seen as a purgative or refining element, and characters are enveloped in flames that move in accord with their bodies.   2. The horn that marks the all-clear signal after an air raid; also the disappearance of Hamlet's father's ghost (*Hamlet* 1.2.157): "It faded on the crowing of the cock."

From self and from things and from persons; and, growing between
    them, indifference 155
Which resembles the others as death resembles life,
Being between two lives—unflowering, between
The live and the dead nettle. This is the use of memory:
For liberation—not less of love but expanding
Of love beyond desire, and so liberation 160
From the future as well as the past. Thus, love of a country
Begins as attachment to our own field of action
And comes to find that action of little importance
Though never indifferent. History may be servitude,
History may be freedom. See, now they vanish, 165
The faces and places, with the self which, as it could, loved them,
To become renewed, transfigured, in another pattern.

Sin is Behovely,[3] but
All shall be well, and
All manner of thing shall be well. 170
If I think, again, of this place,
And of people, not wholly commendable,
Of no immediate kin or kindness,
But some of peculiar genius,
All touched by a common genius, 175
United in the strife which divided them;
If I think of a king at nightfall,
Of three men, and more, on the scaffold[4]
And a few who died forgotten
In other places, here and abroad, 180
And of one who died blind and quiet,[5]
Why should we celebrate
These dead men more than the dying?
It is not to ring the bell backward
Nor is it an incantation 185
To summon the spectre of a Rose.
We cannot revive old factions[6]
We cannot restore old policies
Or follow an antique drum.
These men, and those who opposed them 190
And those whom they opposed
Accept the constitution of silence
And are folded in a single party.
Whatever we inherit from the fortunate
We have taken from the defeated 195
What they had to leave us—a symbol:
A symbol perfected in death.

3. Inevitable. Lines 168–70 repeat the consoling words of Dame Juliana of Norwich, a fourteenth-century English mystic: "Sin is behovabil, but all shall be well and all manner of thing shall be well." 4. Charles I and his chief advisers were executed on the scaffold after the English Civil War. 5. The poet John Milton (1608–1674), who supported Parliament and the Commonwealth in the English Civil War. 6. Alluding to the factionalisms of history exemplified here in the Wars of the Roses (1555–85), when Yorkists, whose badge was the white rose, fought Lancastrians, whose badge was a red rose, for the English throne. The struggle ended in the strong centralized monarchy of the Tudors, whose Tudor Rose "in-folded" (cf. line 259) the other two. There is also allusion to the discovery, beyond history, of the vast rose of pure light seen by Dante in the *Paradiso* (30.112ff), evoked in line 261.

And all shall be well and
All manner of thing shall be well
By the purification of the motive   200
In the ground of our beseeching.

IV

The dove descending breaks the air
With flame of incandescent terror
Of which the tongues declare
The one discharge from sin and error.   205
The only hope, or else despair
　　Lies in the choice of pyre or pyre—
　　To be redeemed from fire by fire.

Who then devised the torment? Love.
Love is the unfamiliar Name   210
Behind the hands that wove
The intolerable shirt of flame[7]
Which human power cannot remove.
　　We only live, only suspire
　　Consumed by either fire or fire.   215

V

What we call the beginning is often the end
And to make an end is to make a beginning.
The end is where we start from. And every phrase
And sentence that is right (where every word is at home,
Taking its place to support the others,   220
The word neither diffident nor ostentatious,
An easy commerce of the old and the new,
The common word exact without vulgarity,
The formal word precise but not pedantic,
The complete consort[8] dancing together)   225
Every phrase and every sentence is an end and a beginning,
Every poem an epitaph. And any action
Is a step to the block, to the fire, down the sea's throat
Or to an illegible stone: and that is where we start.
We die with the dying: 230
See, they depart, and we go with them.
We are born with the dead:
See, they return, and bring us with them.
The moment of the rose and the moment of the yew-tree
Are of equal duration. A people without history   235
Is not redeemed from time, for history is a pattern
Of timeless moments. So, while the light fails
On a winter's afternoon, in a secluded chapel
History is now and England.

---

7. The shirt, poisoned with the blood of Nessus the centaur, that Deianeira (unknowingly) gave her husband, Hercules, to strengthen his love for her. Instead, the shirt so burned Hercules' flesh that he chose death on a funeral pyre to escape the agony.　　8. Both "harmony" and "company."

With the drawing of this Love and the voice of this Calling[9]   240
We shall not cease from exploration
And the end of all our exploring
Will be to arrive where we started
And know the place for the first time.
Through the unknown, remembered gate   245
When the last of earth left to discover
Is that which was the beginning;
At the source of the longest river
The voice of the hidden waterfall
And the children in the apple-tree   250
Not known, because not looked for
But heard, half-heard, in the stillness
Between two waves of the sea.
Quick now, here, now, always[1]—
A condition of complete simplicity   255
(Costing not less than everything)
And all shall be well and
All manner of thing shall be well
When the tongues of flame are in-folded
Into the crowned knot of fire   260
And the fire and the rose are one.

9. Line from *The Cloud of Unknowing*, a fourteenth-century book of Christian mysticism.   1. This same line occurs toward the end of *Burnt Norton*, the first of the *Four Quartets*, where it also follows voices of children hidden in foliage; there is a suggestion of sudden insight gained in a moment of passive openness to illumination.

ANNA AKHMATOVA
1889–1966

The voice of Anna Akhmatova is intensely personal, whether she speaks as lover, wife, and mother or as a national poet commemorating the mute agony of millions. From the subjective love lyrics of her earliest work to the communal mourning of *Requiem* and the many-layered drama of *Poem without a Hero,* she expresses universal themes in terms of individual experience, and historical events through the filter of basic emotions like fear, love, hope, and pain. Akhmatova is one of the great Russian poets of the twentieth century, but she retains a broad sense of European culture, both past and present, and fills her later works with references to Western music, literature, and art that give a startling breadth and scope to her very personalized poetry. Too cosmopolitan and too independent to be tolerated by the authorities, Akhmatova was viciously attacked and her books suppressed (1922–40) because they did not fit the government-approved model of literature: they were too "individualistic" and were not "socially useful." Although she was rehabilitated in the 1960s and achieved recognized status as national poet, Akhmatova was read in secret for a long time, chiefly for the perfection of her early love lyrics. After the death of Joseph Stalin in 1953, however, her collected poems—including poems of the war years and unknown texts written during the periods of enforced silence—brought the full range of her work to public attention.

She was born Anna Andreevna Gorenko on June 11, 1889, in a suburb of the Black

Sea port of Odessa and in a traditional society that she described as "Dostoevsky's Russia." Her father was a maritime engineer and her mother an independent woman of populist sympathies who belonged to an early revolutionary group called People's Will. The poet took the pen name of Akhmatova (accented on the second syllable) from her maternal great-grandmother, who was of Tatar descent. Her family soon moved to Tsarskoe Selo ("the Czar's Village"), a small town outside St. Petersburg that had been for centuries the summer palace of the czars, and also—perhaps more important for Akhmatova—a place where the great Romantic poet Alexandr Pushkin wrote his youthful works. She attended the local school at Tsarskoe Selo, but completed her degree in Kiev; in 1907, she briefly studied law at the Kiev College for Women before moving to St. Petersburg to study literature.

In Tsarskoe Selo, Akhmatova met Nikolai Gumilyov, whom she would marry in April 1910. After their marriage, the couple visited Paris during the spring of 1910 and 1911, meeting many writers and artists, including Amedeo Modigliani, who sketched Akhmatova several times and with whom she recalled wandering around Paris and reading aloud the poetry of Paul Verlaine. It was a time of change in the arts, and when the couple returned to St. Petersburg, Gumilyov helped organize a Poets' Guild that became the core of a new small literary movement, Acmeism, which rejected the romantic, quasi-religious aims of Russian Symbolism, and (like Imagism) valued clarity and concreteness, and a closeness to things of this Earth. The Symbolist–Acmeist debate went on inside a lively literary and social life, while the three main figures of Acmeism—Akhmatova, Gumilyov, and Osip Mandelstam—gained a reputation as important poets.

Akhmatova's first collection of poems, *Evening,* was published in the spring of 1912; it is an intensely personal collection of lyrics in which the poet describes evening as a time of awakening to love—and grief. There is a new clarity and directness to these traditionally romantic subjects, however, as for the first time in Russian poetry a woman in love expresses and analyzes her own emotions. In October of the same year, her son, Lev Gumilyov, was born; it was his arrest and imprisonment in 1935 that inspired the first poems of the cycle that would become *Requiem.* Lev was ultimately imprisoned for a total of fourteen years as the government sought a way to punish his mother, who would not or could not write according to the approved Socialist Realist style praising the government. Even after she had become a national poet known for her patriotic poetry during World War II, Akhmatova was still criticized by the Stalinist regime as a reactionary "half-harlot, half-nun" who wrote subjective love lyrics without social significance: the love poetry of *Evening, Rosary* (1914), and *The White Flock* (1917, published a month before the start of the Russian Revolution).

The White Flock was published during World War I, the destruction of which so shocked Akhmatova that she wrote, "This untimely death is so terrible / I cannot look at God's world." Yet more bloodshed was to follow in the civil war following the Revolution of 1917. Akhmatova refused to flee abroad, as many Russians were doing. Her marriage with Gumilyov was breaking up, and they divorced in 1918; she remarried an Assyriologist, Vladimir Shileiko, who did not approve of his wife's writing poetry and burned some of her poems (she divorced him in 1928). Akhmatova's political difficulties began in 1922. Although she and Gumilyov were divorced, his arrest and execution for counterrevolutionary activities in 1921 put her own status into question. After 1922 and the publication of *Anno Domini,* she was no longer allowed to publish, and was forced into the unwilling withdrawal from public activity that Russians call "internal emigration." Officially forgotten, she was not forgotten in fact; in the schools, her poems were copied out by hand and circulated among students who would never hear her name mentioned in a literature class.

Depending on a meager and irregular pension, Akhmatova prepared essays on the life and works of Pushkin, and wrote poems that would not appear until much later. Stalin's "Great Purge" of 1935–38 sent millions of people to prison camps, and made the 1930s a time of terror and uncertainty for everyone. It is this fear and misery that is expressed in *Requiem*, as the poet blends personal references to her own life with an awareness of the common plight. The art critic Nikolai Punin, with whom she lived from 1926 to 1940, was arrested briefly in 1935; Osip Mandelstam, her great friend, was exiled to Voronezh in May 1934, and then sent to a prison camp in 1938 and died there the same year; her son, Lev, was arrested briefly in 1935 and then again in 1938, remaining imprisoned until 1941, when he was allowed to enroll in military service. Composing *Requiem* itself was a risky act carried out over several years, and Akhmatova and her friend Lidia Chukovskaya memorized the stanzas to preserve the poem in the absence of written copy. Akhmatova wrote of Mandelstam (but perhaps of them all) that "in the room of the poet in disgrace / Fear and the Muse keep watch by turns / And the night comes on / That knows no dawn." A temporary lifting of the ban against her works in 1940 did not last; although she was allowed to publish a new collection, *From Six Books,* the edition was recalled by officials after six months.

It was in 1940 that Akhmatova became interested in larger musical forms and began thinking in terms of cycles of poems instead of her accustomed separate lyrics. She envisaged a larger framework for the core poems of *Requiem* in this year, and wrote the "Dedication" and two epilogues. She also began work on the *Poem without a Hero,* a long and complex verse narrative in three parts that sums up many of her earlier themes: love, death, creativity, the unity of European culture, and the suffering of her people. During World War II the poet was allowed a partial return to public life, addressing women on the radio during the siege of Leningrad (St. Petersburg) in 1941, and writing patriotic lyrics such as the famous *Courage* (published in *Pravda* in 1942) which rallied the Russian people to defend their homeland (and national language) from enslavement. Despite her patriotic activities, she was subject to vicious official attacks after the war. Stalin's Minister of Culture, Andrei Zhdanov, in a famous Report of 1946 proclaimed the doctrine of Socialist Realism as the official style, and attacked Akhmatova's "individualistic" writing as the "poetry of an over-wrought upper-class lady who frantically races back and forth between boudoir and chapel." Akhmatova was immediately expelled from the Writer's Union, which meant that she was not officially recognized as a professional writer (and hence could not earn her living in that career).

Unable once more to publish her work, she supported herself between 1946 and 1958 by translating poetry from a number of foreign languages. Her son had been arrested again in 1949, and hoping to obtain his release, she wrote the kind of adulatory poetry in praise of Stalin that the regime required. The attempt was unsuccessful, and her son remained in prison until 1956. The Stalinist cycle, *In Praise of Peace* (1950), contains such clumsy imitations of socialist-realist poetry that it has been considered a parody: "Where a tank rumbled, there is now a peaceful tractor." Akhmatova later directed that it be omitted from her collected works.

During the slow thaw that followed Stalin's death in 1953, Akhmatova was rehabilitated. Gradually her poems were allowed back into print; an edition of selected poems with added texts was published in 1958, and in the same year she was even elected to an honorary position on the executive council of the Writer's Union. In 1965 a larger collection appeared, *The Flight of Time,* which contained a new series called *The Seventh Book* as well as part of the still-unfinished *Poem without a Hero.* She took an interest in the young writers who flocked to her and supported those who—like Josif Brodsky—were accused by the new order of being a "parasite on the state." Akhmatova's work was already recognized internationally: Robert Frost visited her on his trip to the Soviet Union in 1962, *Requiem* was first published "without her consent" in Munich in 1963 (not until 1987 was the full text published in the Soviet Union), and in 1964 she traveled to Italy to receive the Taormina poetry prize. She was surrounded by admirers when she visited England in 1965 to receive an honorary degree from Oxford University. Her death in 1966 signaled the end of an era in modern Russian poetry, for she was the last of the famous "quartet" that also included Mandelstam, Tsvetaeva, and Pasternak.

Requiem is a lyrical cycle, a series of poems written on a common theme, but it is also a short epic narrative. The story it tells is acutely personal, even autobiographical, but like an epic it also transcends personal significance and describes (as in *The Song of Roland*) a moment in the history of a nation. Akhmatova, who had seen her husband and son arrested and her friends die in prison camps, was only one of millions who had suffered similar losses in the purges of the 1930s. The "Preface," "Dedication," and two epilogues to *Requiem* constitute a framework examining this image of a common fate, while the core of numbered poems develops a more subjective picture and the stages of an individual drama. In the inner poems, Akhmatova blends her separate personal losses—husband, son, and friends—to create a single focus, the figure of a mother grieving for her condemned son. In the frame, the poet identifies herself with the crowd of women with whom she waited for seventeen months outside the Leningrad prison—women who, in turn, represent bereaved women throughout the Soviet Union. The "I" of the speaker throughout remains anonymous, in spite of the fact that she describes her personal emotions in the central poems; her identity is that of a sorrowing mother, and she is distinguished from her fellow-sufferers only by the poetic gift that makes her the "exhausted mouth, / Through which a hundred million scream." *Requiem* is at once a public and a private poem, a picture of individual grief simultaneously linked to a national disaster, and a vision of community suffering that extends past even national disaster into medieval Russian history and Greek mythology. The martyrdom of the Soviet people is consistently pictured in religious terms, from the recurrent mention of crosses and crucifixion to the culminating image of maternal suffering in Mary, the mother of Christ.

The "Dedication" and "Prologue" establish the context for the poem as a whole: the mass arrests in the 1930s after the assassination on December 1, 1934, of Sergei Kirov, the top Communist Party official in Leningrad. The women waiting outside the Kresty ("Crosses") prison of Leningrad arrive at dawn in the coldest of weather, waiting for news of their loved ones, hoping to be allowed to pass them a parcel or a letter, and fearing the sentence of death or exile to the prison camps of frozen Siberia. Instead of living a natural life where "for someone the sunset luxuriates," these women and the prisoners are forced into a suspended existence of separation and uncertainty in which all values are inverted and the city itself has become only the setting for its prisons. It is a situation before which the great forces of nature bow in silent horror.

With the numbered poems, Akhmatova recounts the growing anguish of a bereaved mother as her son is arrested and sentenced to death. The speaker describes her husband's arrest at dawn, in the midst of the family. Her son was arrested later, and in the rest of the poem she relives her numbed incomprehension as she struggles against the increasing likelihood that he will be condemned to death. Recalling her own carefree adolescence in contrast to her current situation as she weeps outside the prison walls, or pleads with Stalin to relent, the mother has a premonition of his fate that pushes her into the temporary relief of insanity and forgetting, and to a desire for her own arrest and death. After sentence is passed, the traumatized mother can speak of his execution only in oblique terms that are at once universal and potentially consoling: by shifting the image of death onto the plane of the Crucifixion and God's will. It is a tragedy that cannot be comprehended or looked at directly just as, she suggests, at the Crucifixion "No one glanced and no one would have dared" to look at the grieving Mary. In the two epilogues, the grieving speaker returns from religious transcendence to Earth and current history. Here she takes on a newly composite identity, seeing herself not as an isolated sufferer but as reciprocally identified with the women whose fate she has shared. It is their memory she perpetuates by writing *Requiem* and it is in their memory that she herself lives on. No longer the victim of purely personal tragedy, she has become a bronze statue commemorating a community of suffering, a figure shaped by circumstances into a monument of public and private grief.

Sam Driver, *Anna Akhmatova* (1972), is an excellent introduction to Akhmatova's work and its historical context that stresses the years up to 1922, and Roberta Reeder, *Anna Akhmatova: Poet and Prophet* (1995), is a good recent biography. David Wells, *Anna Akhmatova: Her Poetry* (1996), is a readable, well-documented study that discusses works in chronological order. Amanda Haight, *Anna Akhmatova: A Poetic Pilgrimage* (1976), and Susan Amert, *In a Shattered Mirror: The Later Poetry of Anna Akhmatova* (1992), are perceptive book-length studies. Ronald Hingley, *Nightingale Fever: Russian Poets in Revolution* (1981), discusses Akhmatova, Pasternak, Tsvetaeva, and Mandelstam in the context of Russian literary history and Soviet politics up to the early years of World War II. Wendy Rosslyn, ed., *The Speech of Unknown Eyes: Akhmatova's Readers on Her Poetry* (1990), collects a range of different responses. Sharon Leiter, *Akhmatova's Petersburg* (1983), examines the image of St. Petersburg as a focus for spiritual and historical themes in Akhmatova's poetry. Anna Akhmatova, *My Half Century: Selected Prose,* ed. Ronald Meyer (1992), includes autobiographical material, correspondence, short pieces on other writers, and an essay on Akhmatova's prose.

Requiem[1]

1935–1940

No, not under the vault of alien skies,[2]
And not under the shelter of alien wings—
I was with my people then,
There, where my people, unfortunately, were.

1961

Instead of a Preface

In the terrible years of the Yezhov terror,[3] I spent seventeen months in the prison lines of Leningrad. Once, someone "recognized" me. Then a woman with bluish lips standing behind me, who, of course, had never heard me called by name before, woke up from the stupor to which every one had succumbed and whispered in my ear (everyone spoke in whispers there):

"Can you describe this?"

And I answered: "Yes, I can."

Then something that looked like a smile passed over what had once been her face.

April 1, 1957
Leningrad[4]

Dedication

Mountains bow down to this grief,
Mighty rivers cease to flow,

---

1. Translated by Judith Hemschemeyer.   2. A phrase borrowed from *Message to Siberia* by the Russian poet Pushkin (1799–1837).   3. In 1937–38, mass arrests were carried out by the secret police, headed by Nikolai Yezhov.   4. The prose preface was written after her son had been released from prison and it was possible to think of editing the poem for publication.

But the prison gates hold firm,
And behind them are the "prisoners' burrows"
And mortal woe.   5
For someone a fresh breeze blows,
For someone the sunset luxuriates—
We[5] wouldn't know, we are those who everywhere
Hear only the rasp of the hateful key
And the soldiers' heavy tread.   10
We rose as if for an early service,
Trudged through the savaged capital
And met there, more lifeless than the dead;
The sun is lower and the Neva[6] mistier,
But hope keeps singing from afar.   15
The verdict . . . And her tears gush forth,
Already she is cut off from the rest,
As if they painfully wrenched life from her heart,
As if they brutally knocked her flat,
But she goes on . . . Staggering . . . Alone . . .   20
Where now are my chance friends
Of those two diabolical years?
What do they imagine is in Siberia's storms,[7]
What appears to them dimly in the circle of the moon?
I am sending my farewell greeting to them.   25

March 1940

Prologue

That was when the ones who smiled
Were the dead, glad to be at rest.
And like a useless appendage, Leningrad
Swung from its prisons.
And when, senseless from torment,   5
Regiments of convicts marched,
And the short songs of farewell
Were sung by locomotive whistles.
The stars of death stood above us
And innocent Russia writhed   10
Under bloody boots
And under the tires of the Black Marias.[8]

I

They led you away at dawn,
I followed you, like a mourner,
In the dark front room the children were crying,[9]
By the icon shelf the candle was dying.

5. The women waiting in line before the prison gates.   6. The large river that flows through St. Petersburg.   7. Victims of the purges who were not executed were condemned to prison camps in Siberia.
Their wives were allowed to accompany them into exile, although they had to live in towns at a distance
from the camps.   8. Police cars for conveying those arrested.   9. Akhmatova's third husband, the art
historian Nikolai Punin, was arrested at dawn while the children (his daughter and her cousin) cried.

On your lips was the icon's chill.[1]   5
The deathly sweat on your brow . . . Unforgettable!—
I will be like the wives of the Streltsy,[2]
Howling under the Kremlin towers.

1935

II

Quietly flows the quiet Don,[3]
Yellow moon slips into a home.

He slips in with cap askew,
He sees a shadow, yellow moon.

This woman is ill,   5
This woman is alone,

Husband in the grave,[4] son in prison,
Say a prayer for me.

III

No, it is not I, it is somebody else who is suffering.
I would not have been able to bear what happened,
Let them shroud it in black,
And let them carry off the lanterns . . .
                                            Night.   5

1940

IV

You should have been shown, you mocker,
Minion of all your friends,
Gay little sinner of Tsarskoye Selo,[5]
What would happen in your life—
How three-hundredth in line, with a parcel,   5
You would stand by the Kresty prison,

Your tempestuous tears
Burning through the New Year's ice.
Over there the prison poplar bends,
And there's no sound—and over there how many   10
Innocent lives are ending now . . .

1. The icon—a small religious painting—was set on a shelf before which a candle was kept lit. Punin had kissed the icon before being taken away.   2. Elite troops organized by Ivan the Terrible around 1550. They rebelled and were executed by Peter the Great in 1698. Pleading in vain, their wives and mothers saw the men killed under the towers of the Kremlin.   3. The great Russian river, often celebrated in folk songs. This poem is modeled on a simple, rhythmic short folk song known as a *chastuska*.   4. Akhmatova's first husband, the poet Nikolai Gumilyov, was shot in 1921.   5. Akhmatova recalls her early, carefree, and privileged life in Tsarskoe Selo outside St. Petersburg.

V

For seventeen months I've been crying out,
Calling you home.
I flung myself at the hangman's[6] feet,
You are my son and my horror.
Everything is confused forever,   5
And it's not clear to me
Who is a beast now, who is a man,
And how long before the execution.
And there are only dusty flowers,
And the chinking of the censer, and tracks   10
From somewhere to nowhere.
And staring me straight in the eyes,
And threatening impending death,
Is an enormous star.[7]

1939

VI

The light weeks will take flight,
I won't comprehend what happened.
Just as the white nights[8]
Stared at you, dear son, in prison

So they are staring again,   5
With the burning eyes of a hawk,
Talking about your lofty cross,
And about death.

1939

VII

THE SENTENCE

And the stone word fell
On my still-living breast.
Never mind, I was ready.
I will manage somehow.

Today I have so much to do: 5
I must kill memory once and for all,
I must turn my soul to stone,
I must learn to live again—

Unless . . . Summer's ardent rustling
Is like a festival outside my window.   10

6. Stalin's. Akhmatova wrote a letter to him pleading for the release of her son.   7. The *star*, the *censer*, the foliage, and the confusion between beast and man recall apocalyptic passages in the Book of Revelation (8.5, 7, 10–11 and 9.7–10).   8. In St. Petersburg, because it is so far north, the nights around the summer solstice are never totally dark.

For a long time I've foreseen this
Brilliant day, deserted house.

June 22, 1939[9]
Fountain House

VIII

TO DEATH

You will come in any case—so why not now?
I am waiting for you—I can't stand much more.
I've put out the light and opened the door
For you, so simple and miraculous.
So come in any form you please,   5
Burst in as a gas shell
Or, like a gangster, steal in with a length of pipe,
Or poison me with typhus fumes.
Or be that fairy tale you've dreamed up,[1]
So sickeningly familiar to everyone—   10
In which I glimpse the top of a pale blue cap[2]
And the house attendant white with fear.
Now it doesn't matter anymore. The Yenisey[3] swirls,
The North Star shines.
And the final horror dims   15
The blue luster of beloved eyes.

August 19, 1939
Fountain House

IX

Now madness half shadows
My soul with its wing,
And makes it drunk with fiery wine
And beckons toward the black ravine.

And I've finally realized   5
That I must give in,
Overhearing myself
Raving as if it were somebody else.

And it does not allow me to take
Anything of mine with me   10
(No matter how I plead with it,
No matter how I supplicate):

Not the terrible eyes of my son—
Suffering turned to stone,

---

9. The date that her son was sentenced to labor camp.   1. A denunciation to the police for imaginary
crimes, common during the purges as people hastened to protect themselves by accusing their neighbors.   2. The NKVD (secret police) wore blue caps.   3. A river in Siberia along which there were
many prison camps.

Not the day of the terror, 15
Not the hour I met with him in prison,

Not the sweet coolness of his hands,
Not the trembling shadow of the lindens,
Not the far-off, fragile sound—
Of the final words of consolation. 20

May 4, 1940
Fountain House

X

CRUCIFIXION

"Do not weep for Me, Mother,
I am in the grave."

1

A choir of angels sang the praises of that momentous hour,
And the heavens dissolved in fire.
To his Father He said: "Why hast Thou forsaken me!"[4]
And to his Mother: "Oh, do not weep for Me . . ."[5]

1940
Fountain House

2

Mary Magdalene beat her breast and sobbed,
The beloved disciple[6] turned to stone,
But where the silent Mother stood, there
No one glanced and no one would have dared.

1943
Tashkent

Epilogue I

I learned how faces fall,
How terror darts from under eyelids,
How suffering traces lines
Of stiff cuneiform on cheeks,
How locks of ashen-blonde or black 5
Turn silver suddenly,
Smiles fade on submissive lips
And fear trembles in a dry laugh.
And I pray not for myself alone,
But for all those who stood there with me 10
In cruel cold, and in July's heat,
At that blind, red wall.

---

4. Jesus' last words from the Cross (Matthew 27.46).   **5.** These words and the epigraph refer to a line from the Russian Orthodox prayer sung at services on Easter Saturday: "Weep not for Me, Mother, when you look upon the grave." Jesus is comforting Mary with the promise of his resurrection.   **6.** The apostle John.

Epilogue II

Once more the day of remembrance[7] draws near.
I see, I hear, I feel you:

The one they almost had to drag at the end,
And the one who tramps her native land no more,

And the one who, tossing her beautiful head,   5
Said: "Coming here's like coming home."

I'd like to name them all by name,
But the list[8] has been confiscated and is nowhere to be found.

I have woven a wide mantle for them
From their meager, overheard words.   10

I will remember them always and everywhere,
I will never forget them no matter what comes.

And if they gag my exhausted mouth
Through which a hundred million scream,

Then may the people remember me   15
On the eve of my remembrance day.

And if ever in this country
They decide to erect a monument to me,

I consent to that honor
Under these conditions—that it stand   20

Neither by the sea, where I was born:
My last tie with the sea is broken,

Nor in the tsar's garden near the cherished pine stump,[9]
Where an inconsolable shade[1] looks for me,

But here, where I stood for three hundred hours,   25
And where they never unbolted the doors for me.

This, lest in blissful death
I forget the rumbling of the Black Marias,

Forget how that detested door slammed shut
And an old woman howled like a wounded animal.   30

---

7. In the Russian Orthodox Church, a memorial service is held on the anniversary of a death.   8. Of prisoners.   9. The gardens and park surrounding the summer palace in Tsarskoe Selo. Akhmatova writes elsewhere of the stump of a favorite tree in the gardens and of the poet Pushkin whom she describes as walking in the park.   1. A ghost; probably the restless spirit of Akhmatova's executed husband, Gumilyov, who courted her in Tsarskoe Selo.

And may the melting snow stream like tears
From my motionless lids of bronze,

And a prison dove coo in the distance,
And the ships of the Neva sail calmly on.

March 1940

DADA-SURREALIST POETRY: A SELECTION

Dada-Surrealist poetry was written for the intuitions. Not that it lacks structure, or its own inner logic, but it appeals directly to the impulsive, irrational, and unconscious layers of human experience. Part of a social and artistic revolution that began during World War I and flourished as a group movement until World War II, Dada-Surrealism exploded literary and artistic conventions to liberate the human imagination and catalyze, in each reader or spectator, an unending process of growth. Dada-Surrealist writers sought to present desire, not discipline; automatic writing, not rationality or grammar; dream worlds, not common sense; marvels (sur-realism), not realism; joyous pursuit of error, not predetermined routes to a goal; and art and poetry as living experience, not as products canonized or hung in museums. Their much-publicized attacks on audience expectations were intended to awaken minds that had been numbed by habit—by the day-to-day routine of work, respectability, and reverence for authority. Games (and they invented many) were perhaps the most authentic expression of Dada-Surrealist attitudes, for games required live participation by several people, an exchange of ideas, and successive moves that always opened new horizons.

It is thus paradoxical that Dada-Surrealism produced written works that became an influential part of literary history, reprinted and anthologized in their turn. This potential paradox was not lost on the group, and quarrels arose if anyone seemed too close to mainstream publication. Yet the major Dada-Surrealist writers were still artists who wished to create new forms, and they found in the movement a fresh vision and different concepts of poetic language. If their printed poetry had found its final shape, unlike a game, it was nonetheless written to launch a second game in the mind of the reader. By proposing startling combinations of images and ideas, and making these combinations attractive, Dada-Surrealist poets guided readers into trying new modes of thought. They created beautiful, unexpected combinations that were rationally impossible but made a strange, intuitive sense in terms of unconscious emotions or desires. In the earlier stages of the movement, they experimented with "automatic" writing: that is, they wrote without exerting conscious or rational control over the free flow of speech, to bring subterranean impulses to the surface. (The genuine automatism of Surrealist poetry is much debated, and some works printed as automatic poems were in fact edited for publication.) Some writers—like Tristan Tzara and Paul Eluard—eventually moved past Surrealism to other styles; others, like Kurt Schwitters and Aimé Césaire, were already working inside a larger framework. Only André Breton, the founding figure of Parisian Surrealism, remained true to its principles (which he usually defined) throughout his life. His own work strongly influenced Joyce Mansour, a younger writer whose macabre work is in many ways an ironic comment on the glorious visions of early Surrealism. Selections from the five writers presented here constitute a brief introduction to Dada-Surrealism but are only a small part of a movement whose influence has been felt worldwide in art and literature.

Tristan Tzara (born in Rumania as Samuel Rosenstock) is the best-known figure of Dadaism. This celebrity is in part owing to his own efforts, since Dadaism itself was a decentered movement, and early Dada groups existed in Berlin, Cologne, Hanover (Germany), Zürich, and New York, each with its distinguishing characteristics. In 1916, the German poet Hugo Ball had received permission to set up a literary cabaret in a Zürich bar; called the Cabaret Voltaire, it attracted a group of writers, artists, and performers who were fleeing the war and who were eager to attack conservative cultural institutions. The Cabaret Voltaire was the scene of raucous performances with masks, costumes, simultaneous readings, nonsense poetry, "sound" poetry, and chants with African drums—to mention only a few. (Modern "happenings" descend from Dadaist performance art.)

Tzara was part of the group, and when the Cabaret closed he became the most aggressive Dada publicist. His *First Dadaist Manifesto* of 1918 (he published seven, one of which is the *Proclamation without Pretention*) is a violent, nihilist, ironic attack on ready-made ideas ("I am against systems, the most acceptable system is the one of not having any system, on principle"). Throughout the manifesto, Tzara uses nonsense words and aggressive attacks to counteract conventional images of discipline and order: after "IDEAL IDEAL IDEAL" and "KNOWLEDGE KNOWLEDGE KNOWLEDGE" he shouts "BOOMBOOM BOOMBOOM BOOMBOOM." Yet there is both method and artistry in his madness, as can be seen in the concluding section of the *First Dadaist Manifesto, DADAIST DISGUST.* Tzara has just proclaimed "the opposition of all cosmic faculties" to the causes of this disgust, and he proceeds with a cumulative summary of such oppositions. Dada will abolish conventional ideas and social hierarchies; it will abolish the long view of chronological perspective, and live for the spontaneous joy of momentary madness; Dada unites contraries because definitions do not matter; and Dada reaches for freedom, which, in a burst of irrational images, turns out to be LIFE itself. It is "life" that is the goal and substance of Dadaist poetry, life that opposes any artificial and socially engineered restraints. Tzara's ironically titled *Proclamation without Pretention* contrasts Dadaist spontaneity and willingness to embrace living contradictions with academic "Art," which is concocted by an artistic "druggist" using formulas and logic. (Like Verlaine in his *Art of Poetry,* the Dadaist and Surrealist poets were suspicious of Art and Literature insofar as they evoked self-reproducing traditions: poetry, in its etymological sense as *creativity,* was far more important.) The wit and humor of this *Proclamation,* and its playful typography, make it far more than a manifesto.

Kurt Schwitters, who lived in Hanover, Germany, until the Nazis forced him to flee to England, is best known for his collages and "Merz" constructions. *Merz,* a nonsense word he extracted from a German bank sign, *Commerzbank,* became the artist's term for small and large artworks he constructed out of objects collected at random or obtained as personal mementos. His home in Hanover contained an enormous Merz column that grew outward and up through the ceiling over the years; it was destroyed during World War II. Schwitters's poetry includes, in addition to *Anna Blume,* the *Sonata in Vowels,* a startling and impressive sound poem in which a series of vowels is arranged in sonata form and performed by the artist as a piece of music. *Anna Blume* itself is a happily delirious love lyric that expresses the speaker's delight in both Anna's person and her first name (a palindrome: it can be read forward and backward). A conversational sequence of associations and contradictions, and the humorous parody of a logical syllogism, together create a gently sensual portrait.

When Tzara moved to Paris in 1920, he was welcomed enthusiastically by a group of young French poets that included Paul Eluard (born Eugène Grindel) and André Breton. Both are central figures in French Surrealism. Eluard reached a particularly wide audience with his love lyrics, magical evocations of transfigured landscapes that teach, in the poet's words, "how to see," and "to see otherwise, other things." Poems from *Capital of Pain* (1926) reshape familiar images into new subjective creations: the speaker is so close to his beloved that they seem to be somehow identical; elsewhere, she permeates the natural landscape and they are again indistinguishable.

Various images achieve the shock that the Surrealists prized for its ability to jolt readers out of their habitual ways of seeing: "She is standing on my eyelids," for example, may ultimately evoke the poet dreaming of his beloved but is first of all a startling image. Yet there is usually a kind of inner logic: the irrational (but imaginable) pictures of the second stanza are explained in the last lines, when the poet comments that her effect is to make him speak lyrical nonsense. Eluard's "seeing otherwise" is implicit in variously transfigured scenes that depict, on the one hand, the poet leaving everyday reality behind as he drifts into the rich inner life of dream and, on the other, a subjective moment that is constructed as a fleeting yet inexorable mirror. His visionary poetry, full of metamorphoses, points toward the "marvelous" state that was the Surrealists' poetic goal.

Breton, often called the Pope of Surrealism for his dedication to Surrealist principles and his insistence on doctrinal purity, outlined a series of core beliefs in the first Surrealist *Manifesto* (1924): absolute freedom of imagination, respect for madness as special inner vision, a belief in the revelatory power of dreams and the unconscious, a hatred of clichéd or predictable thinking (and a related fascination with chance), and the power of "mad love" to transcend rationality and project the lover to a sublime or marvelous state *beyond*. Breton is always alert for the moment when reality metamorphoses into Surrealist experience, and in *Vigilance* this alertness is rewarded: the dreaming poet sets his everyday surroundings on fire and observes a gradual change of state in which he himself finally participates. Another version of metamorphosis occurs in *Free Union*, a poem celebrating his wife in a cumulative series of associations that extend, finally, to the four basic elements: earth, air, fire, and water. *Free Union* means both free love and the free union or association of images: this series of apparently random associations with the woman (in imitation of the medieval *blason* or poem of extended comparison) is in fact organized by visual and sonorous associations, one sound or image suggesting another.

With Aimé Césaire and Joyce Mansour, Surrealist poetry takes on a new cast. Césaire is best known for his long poem *Notebook of a Return to the Native Land* (1939), several plays, and the *Discourse on Colonialism* (1950), and as a founder of Négritude. His Surrealist decade begins officially in 1941 when Breton, coming across Césaire's poetry in the journal *Tropiques,* arranges to meet him and becomes a fervent supporter. Césaire's *Miraculous Weapons* (1946) employs Surrealist verbal techniques in explosive scenes that emphasize processes of destruction, liberation, and new birth, all the while evoking the varied landscape of his native Martinique. These poems proceed by sequences of association and opposition, juxtaposing local and cosmic images. A chameleon, a child diving for coins, or a tropical tree appear simultaneously with the voice of thunderbolts, the mythic serpent sun, and a poet-prophet who is an organic part of the miracles he describes. Césaire was interested in liberating unconscious patterns of thought through the Surrealist tactic of automatic writing: *The Virgin Forest* is one such experiment, later separated into three shorter prose poems one of which, *Day and Night*, is printed here.

Joyce Mansour, an Egyptian who lived much of her adult life in Paris, was one of three contemporary poets praised by Breton in a 1960 interview, and she herself dedicated three books to Breton, recognizing his influence. Her work, however, reverses many of the traditional Surrealist themes and attitudes. Where the founding (male) Surrealist poets experience the marvelous through the mad love of a woman, Mansour develops the same visionary erotics in terms of men, and its horizons are not so celebratory. Her materialist, visceral, and predatory vision is focused in terms of this world and its images, not on an expanding, infinitely multiplied cosmos. Mansour's eyes may close, like Eluard's, in a dreamlike vision that contains impossible images, and she too may imagine identity with her partner, but the result is a self-conscious (and, therefore, faintly humorous) landscape of nightmare.

"Surrealism," says Breton, "is based on the belief in the superior reality of certain forms of previously neglected associations, in the omnipotence of dream, in the disinterested play of thought." The Dada-Surrealist attempt to uncover and reproduce such associations, and to use the free play of thought as model for literary creation, is still with us at the end of the twentieth century.

Valuable discussions of Dada include Alan Young, *Dada and After: Extremist Modernism and English Literature* (1981), and John D. Erickson, *Dada: Performance, Poetry, and Art* (1984). Studies of Surrealist poets include Mary Ann Caws, *The Poetry of Dada and Surrealism* (1970), and J. H. Matthews, *Surrealist Poetry in France* (1969), which has a chapter on Mansour. Maurice Nadeau, *History of Surrealism* (1954), trans. Richard Howard, is an early and authoritative history of Surrealism to 1939; it includes an extensive chronology and a selection of Surrealist documents. Herbert S. Gershman, *The Surrealist Revolution in France* (1974), is a good shorter account that also contains a chronology. William S. Rubin, *Dada, Surrealism and Their Heritage* (1968), gives a detailed history of Surrealist art with many superb illustrations; a shorter history is available in Dawn Ades, *Dada and Surrealism* (1974). Marcel Raymond, *From Baudelaire to Surrealism* (1950), trans. G. M., and *Anna Balakian, The Literary Origins of Surrealism* (1947), trace Surrealism's roots in European Romantic and Symbolist poetry. Discussions of Aimé Césaire include Gregson Davis, *Aimé Césaire* (1994), and A. James Arnold, *Modernism and Negritude* (1981).

TRISTAN TZARA
1896–1963

From Dada Manifesto 1918

DADAIST DISGUST[1]

Every product of disgust capable of becoming a negation of the family is *dada*; the whole being protesting in its destructive force with clenched fists: **DADA**; knowledge of all the means rejected up to this point by the timid sex of easy compromise and sociability: DADA; abolition of logic, dance of all those impotent to create: *DADA*; of all hierarchy and social equation installed for the preservation of values by our valets: DADA; each and every object, feelings and obscurities, apparitions and the precise shock of parallel lines, can be means for the combat: DADA; abolition of memory: **DADA**; abolition of archeology: *DADA*; abolition of the prophets: *DADA*; abolition of the future: DADA; an absolute indisputable belief in each god immediate product of spontaneity: **DADA**; elegant and unprejudicial leap from one harmony to the other sphere; trajectory of a word tossed like a sonorous cry of phonograph record; respecting all individualities in their momentary madness: serious, fearful, timid, ardent, vigorous, determined, enthusiastic; stripping its chapel of every useless awkward accessory; spitting out like a luminous waterfall any unpleasant or amorous thought, or coddling it—with the lively satisfaction of knowing that it doesn't matter—with the same intensity in the bush of his soul, free of insects for the aristocrats, and gilded with archangels' bodies. Freedom: ***DADA DADA DADA***, shrieking of contracted pains, intertwining of contraries and of all contradictions, grotesqueries, nonsequiturs: LIFE.

1. Both Tzara selections translated from the French by Mary Ann Caws. The last section of Tzara's *Dada Manifesto 1918.*

Proclamation without Pretention[2]

Art goes to sleep for the birth of a new world
"ART"—a *parrot word*—replaced by **DADA**
PLESIAUSAURUS,[3] or handkerchief
The talent WHICH YOU CAN LEARN *makes the poet a druggist*
TODAY *criticism balances no longer launches resemblances*   5
Hypertrophic painters hyperestheticized and hypnotized by the
hyacinths of muezzins of hypocritical appearance
CONSOLIDATE THE EXACT HARVEST OF CALCULATIONS
HYPERDROME[4] OF IMMORTAL GUARANTEES: *There is no importance there*
is no transparency or apparency   10
MUSICIANS BREAK YOUR BLIND INSTRUMENTS on the stage
The **SYRINGE** *is only for my understanding.* **I am writing because**
it is as natural as pissing as being sick
Art needs an operation
Art is a ***PRETENTION*** heated in the TIMIDITY of the urinary   15
basin, **Hysteria** born in the **Studio**

We are seeking **upright pure sober unique** strength we are
seeking **NOTHING** we affirm the **VITALITY** of each instant
the anti-philosophy of **Spontaneous** acrobatic
In this moment I hate the man who whispers before intermission—   20
eau de cologne—bitter theater. CHEERY WIND.
IF EVERYBODY SAYS THE OPPOSITE IT IS BECAUSE THEY ARE RIGHT.
Prepare the geyser actions of our blood—submarine formation
of transchromatic airplanes, cellular metals numbered in the
leap of images
                above the regulations of the   25
BEAUTIFUL and its control
It is not for the runts who are still worshipping
their navel

2. Published in 1918.   3. A large prehistoric marine reptile.   4. A play on *hyper* (above) and *hippo-*
drome (a racetrack for horses).

KURT SCHWITTERS
1887—1948

Anna Blume[1]

O beloved of my twenty-seven senses, I
love your!—you ye you your, I your, you my.
—We?
This belongs (by the way) elsewhere.
Who are you, uncounted female? You are   5
—are you? People say you are,—let

1. Translated from the German by David Britt. Published in 1919.

them say on, they don't know a hawk from a handsaw.[2]
You wear your hat upon your feet and walk round
on your hands, upon your hands you walk.
Halloo, your red dress, sawn up in white pleats.   10
Red I love Anna Blume, red I love your!—You
ye you your, I your, you my.—We?
This belongs (by the way) in icy fire.
Red bloom, red Anna Blume, what do people say?
Prize question: 1.) Anna Blume has a bird.   15
              2.) Anna Blume is red.
              3.) What colour is the bird?
Blue is the colour of your yellow hair.
Red is the cooing of your green bird.
You simple girl in a simple dress, you dear   20
green beast, I love your! You ye you your,
I your, you my.—We?
This belongs (by the way) in the chest of fires.
Anna Blume! Anna, a-n-n-a, I trickle your
name. Your name drips like softest tallow.   25
Do you know, Anna, do you know already?
You can also be read from behind, and you, you
the loveliest of all, are from behind, as you are from
before: "a-n-n-a".
Tallow trickles caressingly down my back.   30
Anna Blume, you trickle beast, I love your!

2. They don't know how the church tower stands (literally); i.e., they don't know the simplest things.

PAUL ELUARD
1895–1952

Woman in Love[1]

She is standing on my eyelids
And her hair is in mine,
She has the shape of my hands,
She has the color of my eyes,
She is engulfed in my shadow   5
Like a stone against the sky.

Her eyes are always open
She does not let me sleep.
Her dreams in broad daylight
Make suns evaporate,   10
Make me laugh, weep and laugh,
And speak without anything to say.

1. All Eluard selections translated from the French by Lloyd Alexander. The Eluard selections are taken from *Capital of Pain* (1926).

To Be Caught in One's Own Trap

It is a restaurant like the others. Must I believe I resemble no one? Next to me a great woman is beating eggs with her fingers. A passenger places his clothing on a table and avoids me. He is wrong, I don't know any mystery, I don't even know the meaning of the word. I have never looked for anything, never found anything, he is wrong to insist.

The storm that, off and on, leaves the fog turns my eyes and shoulders. Space then has doors and windows. The passenger announces to me I am not the same anymore. Not the same anymore! I gather the fragments of all my wonders. It is the great woman who told me that these are fragments of wonders, these fragments. I throw them in the healthy streams full of birds. The sea, the calm sea is between them like the sky in the light. Colors too, if someone talks to me of colors, I don't look anymore. Talk to me about shapes, I really need cause for concern.

Great woman, talk to me about shapes, or I fall asleep and I lead a rich life, my hands caught in my head and my head in my mouth, in my closed mouth, inward language.

[Nature Was Caught in the Nets of Your Life]

Nature was caught in the nets of your life.
The tree, your shadow, shows its naked flesh: the sky.
It has the voice of the sand and the gestures of the wind.
And everything you say moves behind you.

[She Is Always Unwilling to Understand]

She is always unwilling to understand, to listen,
She laughs to hide her fear of herself.
She has always walked beneath the arches of nights
And wherever she went
She left   5
The mark of broken things.

[Unknown, She Was My Favorite Shape]

Unknown, she was my favorite shape,
She who relieved me of the worry of being a man,
And I see her and I lose her and I suffer
My pain, like a little sunlight in cold water.

The Mirror of a Moment

It dissipates day,
It shows men the thin images of appearance,
It robs men of the possibility of amusement.
It is as hard as stone,
Formless stone,   5
The stone of movement and sight,
And its brilliance deforms all armor, all masks.
What the hand has taken does not deign to take the shape of the hand,
What has been understood no longer exists,
The bird was confused with the wind,   10
The sky with its truth,
Man with his reality.

ANDRÉ BRETON
1896–1966

Free Union[1]

Woman of mine with woodfire hair
With thoughts like flashes of heat lightning
With an hourglass waist
Woman of mine with an otterlike waist between the tiger's teeth
Woman of mine with a rosette mouth like a posy of stars of ultimate
    magnitude   5
With teeth like a white mouse's spoor on white earth
With a tongue of rubbed amber and glass
Woman of mine with a tongue like a stabbed communion host
With the tongue of a doll that opens and shuts its eyes
A tongue of incredible stone   10
Woman of mine with eyelashes like the strokes of a child's writing
With eyebrows like the rim of a swallow's nest
Woman of mine with temples of slate on a greenhouse roof
And mist on the window-panes
Woman of mine with champagne shoulders   15
Like a fountain of dolphin heads under ice
Woman of mine with matchstick wrists
Woman of mine with fingers of chance and the ace of hearts
With fingers of mown hay
Woman of mine with armpits of marten and beechnut[2]   20
And of Midsummer Night
Of privet and scalare[3] nests
With arms of sluice and sea foam
And of mingled wheat and mill

1. Both Breton selections translated from the French by Mary Ann Caws. Published in 1932.   2. The French word is suggested by the sound of *mown hay* in line 19.   3. A species of tropical fish that includes the angelfish.

Woman of mine with flare legs   25
With movements of clockwork[4] and despair
Woman of mine with calves of eldertree pith
Woman of mine with feet of initials[5]
With feet of keys on a ring with feet of Java sparrows[6] drinking
Woman of mine with a neck of impearled barley[7]   30
Woman of mine with the throat of a golden vale[8]
Of rendezvous in the very bed of the torrent
With breasts of night
Woman of mine with breasts of marine molehills
Woman of mine with breasts of rubied crucible   35
With breasts like the spectre of the rose[9] under the dew
Woman of mine with a belly unfolding like the fan of days
The belly of a giant claw
Woman of mine with the back of a bird in vertical flight
With a quicksilver back   40
A back of light
With a nape of rolled stone and moist chalk
And the drop of a glass just drained
Woman of mine with nacelle hips
With chandelier and arrow-feather hips   45
Like scapes of white peacock plumes
Of imperceptible sway
Woman of mine with buttocks of sandstone and amianthus
Woman of mine with swan's-back buttocks
Woman of mine with springtime buttocks   50
With the gladiolus sex
Woman of mine with the placer and platypus sex
Woman of mine with the sex of seaweed and oldtime sweets
Woman of mine with the mirror-like sex
Woman of mine with eyes full of tears   55
With violet-panoplied and magnetic-needle eyes
Woman of mine with savannah eyes
Woman of mine with eyes of water to be drunk in prison
Woman of mine with eyes of wood always under the axe
With water-level eyes the level of air earth and fire   60

Vigilance

In Paris the tower of Saint-Jacques[1] swaying
Like a sunflower
Sometimes runs its brow against the Seine and its shadow glides impercep-
    tibly among the tugs

---

4. Word play on a mechanical (*clockwork*) time fuse (*flare*).   **5.** Also a botanical term for fast-multiplying cells at the tips of roots and branches.   **6.** Birds of the finch family, often kept in cages. The French word's primary meaning is caulkers (of a boat's seams).   **7.** A play on pearl barley.   **8.** A reference to Val-d'or, a place in Saint-Cloud near Paris, or possibly a town in southwestern Quebec, Canada, where gold was discovered in 1909.   **9.** A poem by Théophile Gautier (1811–1872), which was the subject of a 1911 ballet by Sergey Diaghilev (1872–1929).   **1.** Only the tower remains of the Parisian church of Saint-Jacques-de-la-Boucherie, one of whose patrons was the medieval alchemist Nicolas Flamel (1330–1418). The tower was cherished by the Surrealists for its associations with alchemy.

At that moment on tiptoe in my sleep
I head for the room where I am lying   5
And set fire to it
So that nothing will remain of the consent wrung from me
The furniture then makes way for animals of the same size looking at me
    fraternally
Lions in whose manes the chairs are now burning out
Sharks whose white bellies absorb the last quivering of the sheets   10
At the hour of love and of blue eyelids
I see myself burning in turn I see that solemn hiding place of nothings
Which was once my body
Probed by the patient beaks of the fire-ibises
When all is finished I enter invisible into the ark   15
Taking no heed of the passersby of life whose shuffling steps are heard far
    off
I see the ridges of the sun
Through the hawthorn of the rain
I hear human linen tearing like a great leaf
Under the fingernails of absence and presence who are in collusion   20
All the looms are withering only a piece of perfumed lace remains of them
A shell of lace in the perfect shape of a breast
I touch nothing but the heart of things I hold the thread

AIMÉ CÉSAIRE

born 1913

Do Not Have Pity[1]

Smoke on, salt swamps

Rock-painted icons of the unknown
deflect towards me the muted nightfall
of their laughter

smoke on, salt marshes, sea-needle heart   5
dead stars coaxed by marvellous hands dart forth
from the pulp of my eyes
Smoke on smoke on
the thin penumbra of my voice cracks with
flaming red cities   10
and my pure hands irresistibly call forth
at a very far remove from the ancestral heritage
the invincible zeal of acid in the flesh of
life—sea swamps—

    like a viper sprung from the blond force of a blinding light.   15

---

1. All Césaire selections translated from the French by Gregson Davis. From *Miraculous Weapons* (1946).
The original title was "Do Not Have Pity for Me," a rebellious echo of the French poet Guillaume Apolli-
naire's (1880–1918) line "Have pity on me," which ends a description of the modern poet caught between
old and new orders (*The Pretty Redhead*).

Sun Serpent

Sun serpent: eye beguiling my eye
and the sea squalid with islands, finger joints cracking flame-throwing
roses, and my body lightning-blasted, unharmed,
the water hoists up carcasses of light lost in the gangway without ceremony
haloes of whirling ice encircle the smoking heart of crows   5
our hearts—
the voice of muffled thunderbolts rolling on their forked hinges
diffused by anolis lizards[2] through a landscape of broken glasses
vampire flowers relieving orchids of their spell
elixir of fire at the core   10
fire righteous fire, mango tree of night swaddled with bees
my desire: a contingent of tigers surprised amidst the sulphur
but at its arousal the tin is gilded with childhood layers
and my pebbled body gobbling fish gobbling doves gobbling slumbers . . .
the word Brazil is sugar in the depth of the swamp.   15

Day and Night

the sun the executioner the press of the masses the routine of dying and my
cry of wounded beast—and so it goes even unto the infinity of fevers, the
awesome floodgate of death bombarded by my very own aleutian eyes that
from wormy earth search amid earth and worms your eyes of flesh, of sun,
like the black urchin for the coin in the water where flows the never-failing
song of the virgin forest sprung from the silence of the earth, of my very own
aleutian eyes, and so it goes: the lewd leapfrog of hermaphrodite thoughts,
the calls of jaguars, of water-hole, of antelopes, of savannahs with their
branches plucked in the course of their first great adventure: the exquisite
cyathus subtending a beautiful nymph stripped of her leaves amid the milk
of manchineel[3] trees and the accolades of brotherhood leeches.

2. Antillean lizards related to iguanas.   3. Manzanilla.

JOYCE MANSOUR
1928–1987

[I Saw You through My Closed Eye]

I saw you through my closed eye[1]
Climbing the wall frightened of your dreams.
Your feet were losing their footing on the sleepy moss.
Your eyes were holding onto hanging nails.
While I screamed without opening my mouth   5
To open your head to the night.

1. All Mansour selections translated from the French by Serge Gavronsky. From *Screams* (1953).

[I Opened Your Head]

I opened your head
To read your thoughts.
I devoured your eyes
To taste your sight.
I drank your blood   5
To know your wants
And made of your shivering body
My nourishment.

[Men's Vices]

Men's vices
are my domain
Their wounds my sweet desserts
I love to chew on their vile thoughts
For their ugliness makes my beauty.   5

[Empty Black Haunted House]

Empty black haunted house
Our steps precede and follow us.
Rooms crowded with unfinished visions
Of objects beyond reach
Empty empty perverted house.   5
Your head walled in your eyes
That burn indecently blue
Haunt us call us
Fill our mouths.
Eternal inedible bread.   10

WILLIAM FAULKNER
1897–1962

William Faulkner's account of historical change in the American South far transcends
regional issues. He writes about the Old South becoming the New, about the clash
of generations and ways of life, about racial and family tragedies, and about the
opposition of good and evil in almost archetypal terms. His fantastic, sometimes allegorical depictions of events anticipate "magical realist" fiction. Yet Faulknerian style
is best known for innovative use of language and for brilliantly extended narrative
sentences. Adapting James Joyce's stream of consciousness technique, Faulkner pro-

vides insignts into his characters' minds that reveal and interpret the same stories they record. With Faulkner, the nineteenth-century Balzacian tradition of the human comedy—the novel as a panorama of society—acquires a new vocabulary and renewed historicity.

William Cuthbert Falkner was born on September 25, 1897, in New Albany, Mississippi, to a prosperous family with many ties to southern history. The eldest of four sons, Faulkner (he adopted this spelling in 1924 for his first book) was named for a great-grandfather who commanded a Confederate regiment in the Civil War, built railroads, and wrote novels. Faulkner's father worked for the family railroad until it was sold in 1902, afterwards moving his family to Oxford and eventually becoming business manager of the University of Mississippi. Faulkner's close acquaintance with southern customs and attitudes, his own experience as the descendant of a once-prosperous and influential family, and his attachment to the region of Lafayette County and the town of Oxford (Yoknapatawpha County and Jefferson in the novels) helped shape themes and setting in his fiction.

Young Faulkner did not like school, although he read widely in his grandfather's library and borrowed books from an older friend, Philip Stone. Leaving high school after two years to work as a bookkeeper in his grandfather's bank, he continued reading and discussing literature with Stone, who introduced him to the French writer Honoré de Balzac's novels and encouraged his writing. In the last six months of 1918 he trained in Canada as a fighter pilot—then a common way of getting more quickly into combat in World War I—but the war ended and he returned to Oxford to enroll at the university as a special student. While in school, Faulkner published poetry, prose, and drawings in *The Mississippian* and worked on the yearbook, but decided to leave the University in November 1920 to work in a New York bookstore. By December 1921 he had returned to Oxford, where he became postmaster at the university; three years later, he was dismissed for irresponsibility. During these years he wrote mainly poetry and seems to have been influenced by the French Symbolists: his first published poem, *L'Après-midi d'un faune*, takes its title from an earlier poem by Stéphane Mallarmé. With Stone's help, Faulkner published his first book, a collection of lyrics called *The Marble Faun* (also the title of a novel by Nathaniel Hawthorne) in 1924.

In 1925, Faulkner spent six months living in New Orleans, where he was attracted to a literary group associated with *The Double Dealer*, a magazine in which he himself published poems, essays, and prose sketches. The group's chief figure was the novelist Sherwood Anderson, author of a series of regional stories published as *Winesburg, Ohio*, who encouraged Faulkner to make fictional use of his southern background and who recommended his first novel (without having read it) to a publisher. After completing *Soldier's Pay* (published in 1926), Faulkner took a freighter to Europe, where he bicycled and hiked through Italy and France and lived for a short while in Paris. At the end of the year he returned to Mississippi, where he wrote his second novel, *Mosquitoes* (1927), a satire on the New Orleans group.

Taking up Anderson's earlier suggestion, Faulkner now embarked on the regional "Yoknapatawpha" (*yok-na-pa-taw'-pha*) series with *Sartoris* (1929), an account of the return home, marriage, and death of wounded veteran Bayard Sartoris. In Yoknapatawpha County, Faulkner created a whole fictional world with characters who reappear from novel to novel (a technique he would have encountered in Balzac's *Comédie humaine*). Here imaginary families such as the Sartorises, Compsons, Sutpens, McCaslins, and Snopeses rise to prosperity or fall into various kinds of weakness, degradation, and death. Individual characters work out destinies that are already half-shaped by family tradition and invisible community pressures. They are caught in close and often incestuous blood relationships and make their way in a world where the values, traditions, and privileges of an old plantation society are yielding to the values of a new mercantile class. A network of family dynasties illustrates this picture of a changing society: the decaying and impoverished Compson family (*The Sound and the Fury*, 1929); two generations of Sutpens rising to great wealth and dying in madness and isolation (*Absalom, Absalom!*, 1936); the McCaslin family with its history of incest, miscegenation, and guilt (*Go Down, Moses*, 1942); and the viciously grasping and ambitious "poor white" Snopes family (*The Hamlet*, 1940; *The Town*, 1957; *The Mansion*, 1959). These are violent works, and the murders, lynchings, and bestialities of all kinds that appear in them account for Faulkner's early American reputation as a lurid local writer. European critics, however—especially the French, who recognized his ability as early as 1931—were quick to recognize mythic overtones and classical and biblical prototypes in these tales of twisted family relationships.

After *Sartoris*, Faulkner experimented with a new style modeled on the stream of consciousness technique of Joyce's *Ulysses* for his next novel, *The Sound and the Fury*. Here, the Compson family's tragedy is told through several different points of view, the first of which is the disconnected and emotionally skewed world of the idiot Benjy. Both *Sartoris* and *The Sound and the Fury* were rejected several times before finally being published in 1929, and Faulkner supported himself during these years chiefly through odd jobs (working on a shrimp trawler, in a lumber mill, at a power plant, and as a carpenter, painter, and paper hanger), and then from his short stories, of which he sold thirty between 1930 and 1932. In 1929 he married Estelle Oldham Franklin, with whom he had one child, Jill, in 1933. Irritated at the difficulty of finding publishers for his serious or experimental works, Faulkner set out to write a best-seller—and succeeded. *Sanctuary*, a novel of the Deep South that described the rape and prostitution of a schoolgirl, murder, perjury, and the lynching of an innocent man, was made into a movie (*The Story of Temple Drake*) and brought its author invitations to work on movie scripts for a variety of Hollywood studios. From 1932 to 1955, the novelist added to his income by working as a film doctor, revising and collaborating on scripts for films such as *To Have and Have Not* and *The Big Sleep*. Although his works continued to receive critical praise, he did not have any commercial successes after *Sanctuary*; in 1945, when he was, according to the French writer and philosopher Jean-Paul Sartre, the idol of young French readers, almost all of his novels were out of print. It took an anthology, *The Portable Faulkner*, in 1946, to reintroduce Faulkner to a wide audience. In 1950 he won the Nobel Prize for Literature and used the prize money to establish the William Faulkner Foundation to assist Latin American writers and award educational scholarships to Mississippi blacks. Five years later he received the Pulitzer Prize and the National Book Award for *A Fable* (1954). Faulkner's last book was a comedy set in Yoknapatawpha County, *The Reivers* (1962). He died of a heart attack in Oxford, Mississippi, on July 6, 1962.

In Faulkner's world, men and women are measured by the breadth of their compassion or the quality of their endurance. Although there are villains, few wholly negative characters appear, and these are seen as grotesque distortions of humanity: the cruel and frustrated Jason Compson, or the impotent rapist Popeye of *Sanctuary*, who "had that vicious depthless quality of stamped tin." Heroes tend to be larger than life, casting their shadow even after death as does Addie Bundren in *As I Lay Dying* (1930), when Addie's dying wish obliges her family to accompany her coffin across Mississippi in a miniature epic journey through flood and fire. Heroes have the moral endurance of Bayard Sartoris II, who as a boy kills his grandmother's murderer and as a man faces down his father's killer—unarmed—to break the pattern of "honorable revenge"; or the physical endurance of the tall convict in *Old Man*, whose "whole purpose" was "to prove . . . just how much the human body could bear, stand, endure." Yet Faulkner's world is by no means unrelievedly somber. The everyday realism and earthy humor of his works have led to his being called a comic writer, in the broad sense that implies a universal vision encompassing the pettiness as well as the grandeur of human existence. Not all of his characters are heroes. Some are ordinary people whose perseverance and dedication to an idea, a person, or a way of life give them larger significance; some are thoughtful people driven by circumstances to question their own identity and values; some are idiots able only to feel a succession of emotions; some are simply confidence men. Faulkner generally describes such figures from the outside. We see them act, and we may even follow their thoughts in interior monologues, but we are receiving only traces of inner personalities that have already been decided and to which we have no real access.

The "truth" of the novels comes to us through a variety of perspectives and rhetorical strategies. Three different narrators in *Absalom, Absalom!* tell the story of Thomas Sutpen. The four points of view in *The Sound and the Fury* move from Benjy's childish imagined inner monologue to the adult monologues of his nervously suicidal and psychopathic brothers, and finally to a third-person narrative focusing on Dilsey, the black woman who has been in charge of family and household and who "endures." Fifty-nine sections of interior monologue in *As I Lay Dying* express the inner relationships of the Bundren family; and six pages of ledger-reading in *Go Down, Moses* explore those of the McCaslins. The convict in *Old Man* possesses a dogged, wilfully limited view of things modeled on simplistic cops-and-robbers stories and adventure tales. A narrative perspective may change tone, as happens at the end of the epic coffin journey in *As I Lay Dying* when the widowed Anse Bundren returns happily from town with a new set of false teeth, a new wife, and a phonograph. Chronology may be broken, as in the time changes represented by two typefaces in Benjy's section of *The Sound and the Fury*; details are exaggerated or distorted; dialect speech emphasizes the presence of the storyteller's art. Throughout, Faulkner's fluid style escapes rigid categories; it is a style of tensions and contradictions, of tragedy and humor, realism and mythic outreach, now short and laconic, now rambling.

One of the most widely read of Faulkner's works is *The Bear*, itself part of a larger volume called *Go Down, Moses*, which the writer called a novel although the first edition was published (apparently without his knowledge) as *Go Down, Moses and Other Stories*. *The Bear* is the fifth of seven chapters in *Go Down, Moses* and has been printed separately both as the well-known tale of the hunt (sections 1–3) and as the larger narrative (1–5), whose scope is chiefly defined by the extraordinary fourth section concerning Ike McCaslin after the hunt. Of this part, Faulkner wrote to his editor that there was "more meat in it than I thought, a section now that I am going to be proud of and which requires careful writing and rewriting to get it exactly right." The larger story broadens and extends the relationship with overall themes in *Go Down, Moses*: the legacy of slavery and incest, the expiation of guilt, and the moral status of owning property (whether land or people). Here Ike McCaslin, reading old family ledgers from the plantation, gradually deciphers his uncles' cryptic annotations to various expenses as well as the death of one Eunice, a slave. Eunice had a daughter, Tomasina, by the slave-owning grandfather, old Carothers McCaslin; when it became obvious that Tomasina was pregnant by the same Carothers McCaslin, her mother committed suicide. The next generation of McCaslins tries in various ways to make amends, but it is Ike who makes expiation the center of his existence. Tracking down Eunice's descendants—his cousins—to pay them their thousand-dollar legacies, he confronts the broader implications of the past: the theft and fragmentation of land that was once a wilderness owned in common and the contamination of this land by the institution of slavery. References to the Bible and moral responsibility fill the long dialogue in which he tries to explain things to his older cousin, McCaslin Edmonds. (The book's title, *Go Down, Moses*, alludes both to the biblical story of Moses rescuing the Israelites from slavery in Egypt and to a well-known Negro spiritual.) Ike decides finally (at twenty-one) to separate himself from the historical taint by renouncing his inheritance; for a while he makes a meager living as a carpenter and then, after a failed marriage, returns to the woods and a solitary life.

The first three sections of *The Bear,* and the concluding fifth section, introduce the themes of wilderness and lost harmony while describing a bear hunt during Ike's youth. Or rather, several bear hunts: although *The Bear* begins when Ike is sixteen, there are numerous flashbacks to earlier scenes as the youth is initiated into the wilderness. Guided by the part-Chickasaw Sam Fathers, "his spirit's father," he learns to strip himself of civilized defenses (gun, watch, and compass) and see Old Ben himself: "not even a mortal beast but an anachronism indomitable and invincible out of an old dead time . . . apotheosis of the old wild life which the little puny humans swarmed and hacked at in a fury of abhorrence and fear." Part of *The Bear's* appeal lies in these mythic overtones: the story presents at once a rite of passage for the youth, an archetypal image of the hunt, and a somber tribute to a disappearing natural world.

Stylistically, there is a notable difference between the sections describing the hunt and the more elaborate subjective narrative of section 4. The earlier sections are not as straightforward as the beginning seems to promise, however: "There was a man and a dog too this time." Almost immediately, sentences lengthen to include a range of memories and interpretations that emanate from the boy but are articulated in an expanded, omniscient perspective. Section 4 is heavily internalized, as the twenty-one-year-old Ike carries on a dialogue with his cousin McCaslin Edmonds in which punctuation is for the most part left out, and the two speakers are distinguished only by "and he" and "and McCaslin" at the end of paragraphs. One result of this style, an adaptation of the stream of consciousness technique, is that the reader seems to share Ike's memories and become part of the ongoing debate in his mind. Ike's distress, and the sequence of his reactions as he deciphers, questions, compares, interprets, and finally understands the family ledger, is famously expressed in the rush of a single unbroken sentence of more than eighteen hundred words (pp. 1763–66).

Ike's renunciation has been interpreted in various ways. To many, he is a sacrificial figure who atones for his family's guilt by renouncing an irretrievably tainted inheritance; symbolically, he rejects the exploitative materialism of industrial society and returns to a simpler life in harmony with nature. When an interviewer asked what Ike had gained by his renunciation, Faulkner responded "serenity . . . what would pass for wisdom." Others, however, have felt that Ike is ultimately a failure because he turns his back on life; that his passivity is mistaken and an abandonment of responsibility. Here, Faulkner commented to an overenthusiastic proponent of the first view: "I think a man ought to do more than just repudiate." Either reading vindicates Faulkner's role as a persuasive interpreter of cultural values and chronicler of historical change.

Suggested studies include Michael Millgate, *The Achievement of William Faulkner* (1963), a critical study of the novels and stories with a brief biography in the first chapter; Cleanth Brooks, *William Faulkner: The Yoknapatawpha Country* (1963), a basic literary analysis and study of Faulkner's mythical South in the Yoknapatawpha stories, with a list of Faulkner's fictional characters; and James B. Carothers, *William Faulkner's Short Stories* (1985), an examination of the short stories in the context of the novels. *William Faulkner, The Man and The Artist* (1987), is a vivid narrative biography written by historian Stephen B. Oates. Joseph Blotner is the author of *Faulkner: A Biography* (1974, 2 vols.), the authorized and immensely detailed biography. Doreen Fowler and Ann J. Abadie, eds., *Faulkner and the Craft of Fiction: Faulkner and Yoknapatawpha* (1989), collects useful essays on themes and narrative structures. Francis Lee Utley, Lynn Z. Bloom, and Arthur F. Kinney, eds., *Bear, Man, and God: Eight Approaches to William Faulkner's The Bear* (1971), contains valuable essays on various topics and includes excerpts from Faulkner interviews. *Go Down,*

Moses (1994), annotated by Nancy Dew Taylor, offers a detailed and informative series of annotations. James Early, *The Making of Go Down, Moses* (1972), describing earlier versions of *The Bear*, emphasizes themes, linguistic strategies, and conceptions of character. Linda Wagner-Martin, ed., *New Essays on Go Down, Moses* (1996), prints five essays that use modern critical perspectives to discuss tensions of race and gender.

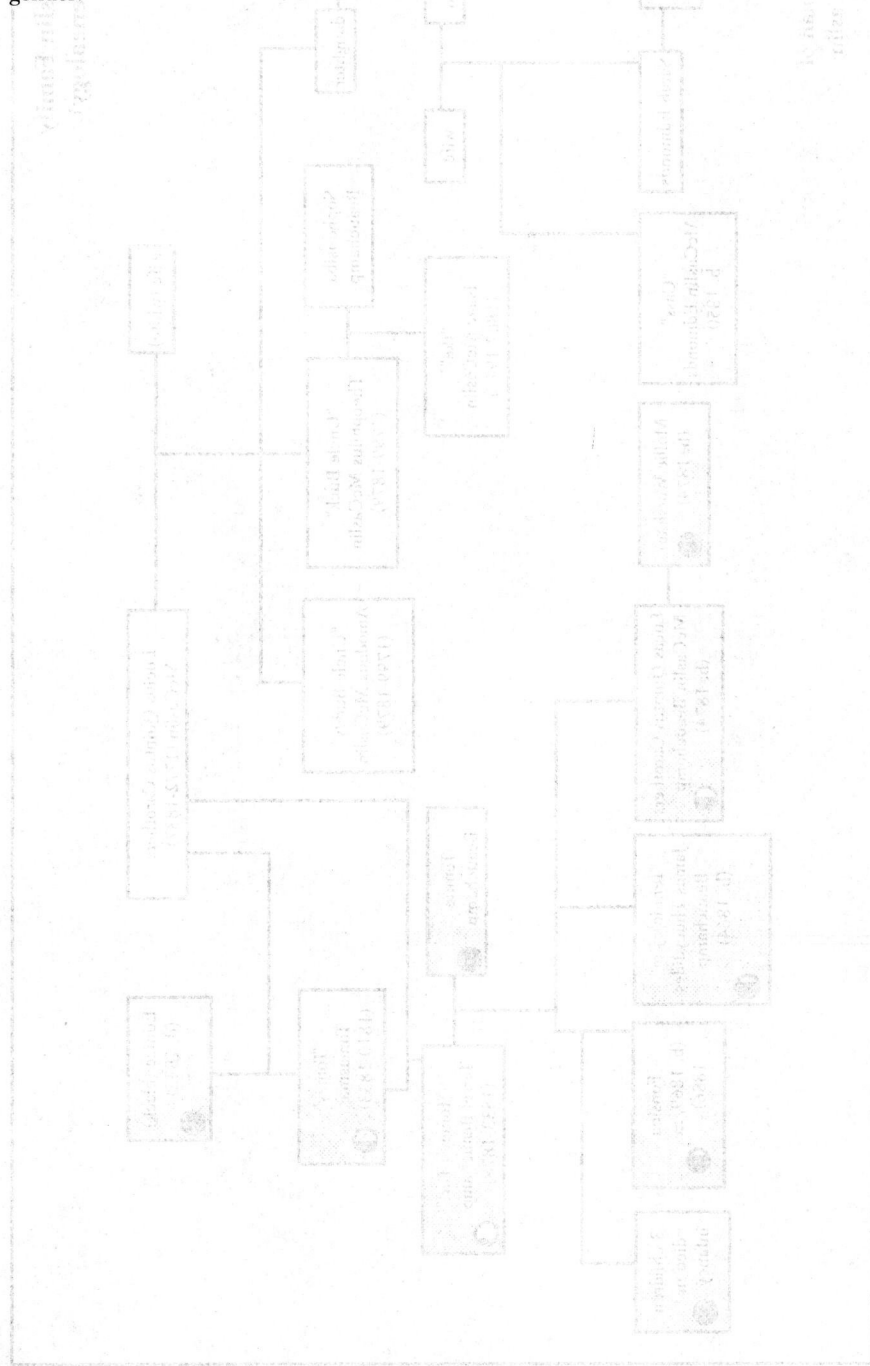

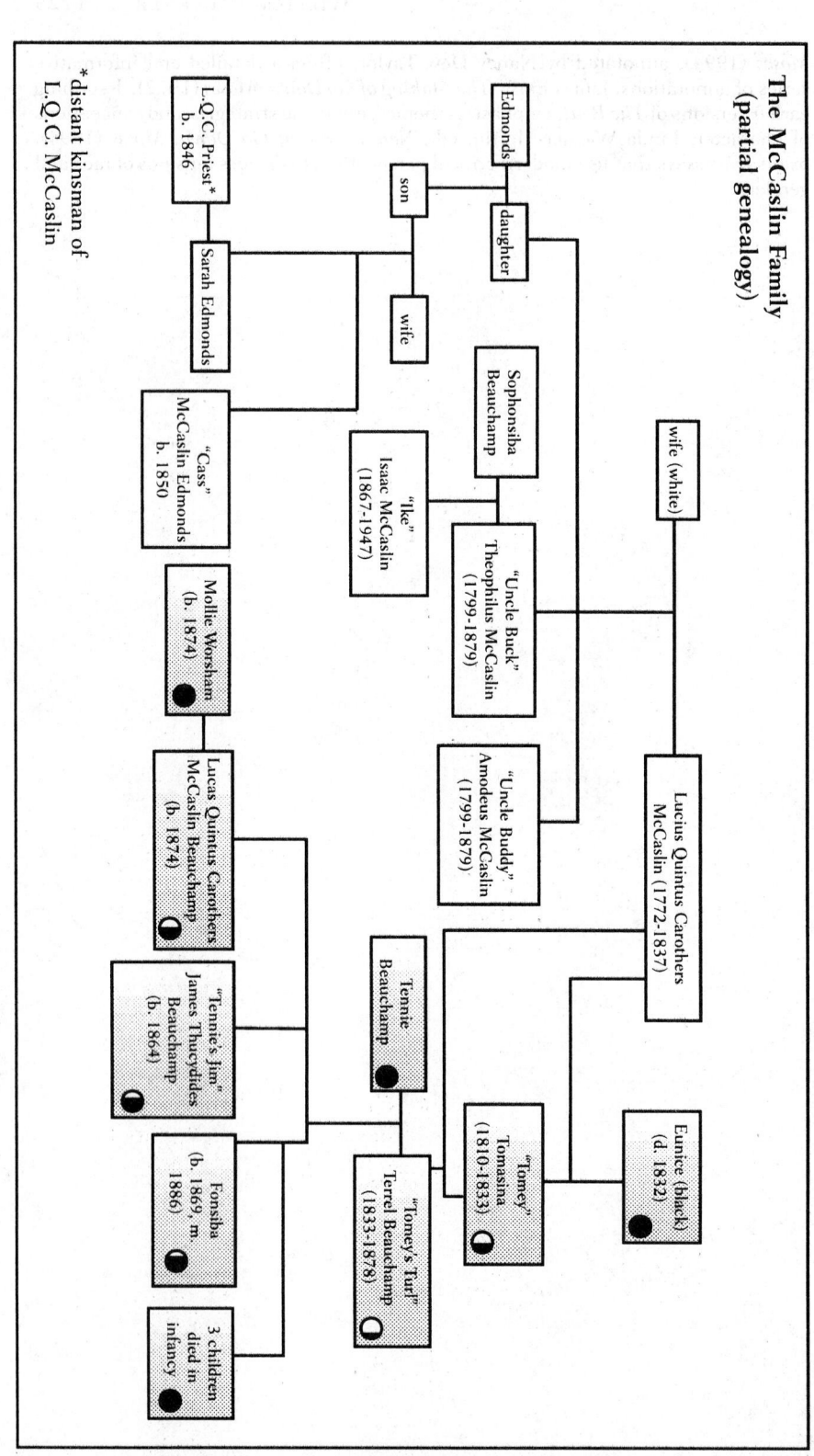

The McCaslin Family
(partial genealogy)

* distant kinsman of
L.Q.C. McCaslin

L.Q.C. Priest*
b. 1846

Edmonds

son

daughter

wife

Sarah Edmonds

"Cass"
McCaslin Edmonds
b. 1850

Sophonsiba
Beauchamp

"Ike"
Isaac McCaslin
(1867-1947)

"Uncle Buck"
Theophilus McCaslin
(1799-1879)

"Uncle Buddy"
Amodeus McCaslin
(1799-1879)

wife (white)

Lucius Quintus Carothers
McCaslin (1772-1837)

Mollie Worsham
(b. 1874)

Lucas Quintus Carothers
McCaslin Beauchamp
(b. 1874)

"Tennie's Jim"
James Thucydides
Beauchamp
(b. 1864)

Tennie
Beauchamp

Fonsiba
(b. 1869) m.
1886)

"Tomey's Turl"
Terrel Beauchamp
(1833-1878)

"Tomey"
Tomasina
(1810-1833)

Eunice (black)
(d. 1832)

3 children
died in
infancy

1726

From Go Down, Moses

The Bear

1

There was a man and a dog too this time. Two beasts, counting Old Ben, the bear, and two men, counting Boon Hogganbeck, in whom some of the same blood ran which ran in Sam Fathers, even though Boon's was a plebeian strain of it and only Sam and Old Ben and the mongrel Lion were taintless and incorruptible.

He was sixteen. For six years now he had been a man's hunter. For six years now he had heard the best of all talking. It was of the wilderness, the big woods, bigger and older than any recorded document:—of white man fatuous enough to believe he had bought any fragment of it, of Indian ruthless enough to pretend that any fragment of it had been his to convey; bigger than Major de Spain and the scrap he pretended to, knowing better; older than old Thomas Sutpen of whom Major de Spain had had it and who knew better; older even than old Ikkemotubbe, the Chickasaw[1] chief, of whom old Sutpen had had it and who knew better in his turn. It was of the men, not white nor black nor red but men, hunters, with the will and hardihood to endure and the humility and skill to survive, and the dogs and the bear and deer juxtaposed and reliefed[2] against it, ordered and compelled by and within the wilderness in the ancient and unremitting contest according to the ancient and immitigable rules which voided all regrets and brooked no quarter;—the best game of all, the best of all breathing and forever the best of all listening, the voices quiet and weighty and deliberate for retrospection and recollection and exactitude among the concrete trophies—the racked guns and the heads and skins—in the libraries of town houses or the offices of plantation houses or (and best of all) in the camps themselves where the intact and still-warm meat yet hung, the men who had slain it sitting before the burning logs on hearths when there were houses and hearths or about the smoky blazing of piled wood in front of stretched tarpaulins when there were not. There was always a bottle present, so that it would seem to him that those fine fierce instants of heart and brain and courage and wiliness and speed were concentrated and distilled into that brown liquor which not women, not boys and children, but only hunters drank, drinking not of the blood they spilled but some condensation of the wild immortal spirit, drinking it moderately, humbly even, not with the pagan's base and baseless hope of acquiring thereby the virtues of cunning and strength and speed but in salute to them. Thus it seemed to him on this December morning not only natural but actually fitting that this should have begun with whisky.

He realised later that it had begun long before that. It had already begun on that day when he first wrote his age in two ciphers and his cousin McCaslin brought him for the first time to the camp, the big woods, to earn for himself from the wilderness the name and state of hunter provided he in his turn were humble and enduring enough. He had already inherited then,

---

1. An American Indian tribe that originally inhabited what is now northern Mississippi and Alabama. Traditionally, all property was owned in common by the tribe.   2. Set off as if in sculptural *bas-relief*.

without ever having seen it, the big old bear with one trap-ruined foot that in an area almost a hundred miles square had earned for himself a name, a definite designation like a living man:—the long legend of corn-cribs broken down and rifled, of shoats and grown pigs and even calves carried bodily into the woods and devoured and traps and deadfalls[3] overthrown and dogs mangled and slain and shotgun and even rifle shots delivered at point-blank range yet with no more effect than so many peas blown through a tube by a child—a corridor of wreckage and destruction beginning back before the boy was born, through which sped, not fast but rather with the ruthless and irresistible deliberation of a locomotive, the shaggy tremendous shape. It ran in his knowledge before he ever saw it. It loomed and towered in his dreams before he even saw the unaxed woods where it left its crooked print, shaggy, tremendous, red-eyed, not malevolent but just big, too big for the dogs which tried to bay it, for the horses which tried to ride it down, for the men and the bullets they fired into it; too big for the very country which was its constricting scope. It was as if the boy had already divined what his senses and intellect had not encompassed yet: that doomed wilderness whose edges were being constantly and punily gnawed at by men with plows and axes who feared it because it was wilderness, men myriad and nameless even to one another in the land where the old bear had earned a name, and through which ran not even a mortal beast but an anachronism indomitable and invincible out of an old dead time, a phantom, epitome and apotheosis of the old wild life which the little puny humans swarmed and hacked at in a fury of abhorrence and fear like pygmies about the ankles of a drowsing elephant;—the old bear, solitary, indomitable, and alone; widowered childless and absolved of mortality—old Priam[4] reft of his old wife and outlived all his sons.

Still a child, with three years then two years then one year yet before he too could make one of them, each November he would watch the wagon containing the dogs and the bedding and food and guns and his cousin McCaslin and Tennie's Jim and Sam Fathers too until Sam moved to the camp to live, depart for the Big Bottom, the big woods. To him, they were going not to hunt bear and deer but to keep yearly rendezvous with the bear which they did not even intend to kill. Two weeks later they would return, with no trophy, no skin. He had not expected it. He had not even feared that it might be in the wagon this time with the other skins and heads. He did not even tell himself that in three years or two years or one year more he would be present and that it might even be his gun. He believed that only after he had served his apprenticeship in the woods which would prove him worthy to be a hunter, would he even be permitted to distinguish the crooked print, and that even then for two November weeks he would merely make another minor one, along with his cousin and Major de Spain and General Compson and Walter Ewell and Boon and the dogs which feared to bay it and the shotguns and rifles which failed even to bleed it, in the yearly pageant-rite of the old bear's furious immortality.

His day came at last. In the surrey with his cousin and Major de Spain

---

3. Hunters' traps in which a log falls on the animal when it takes the bait. *Shoats:* young pigs.   **4.** Ruler of Troy in Homer's *Iliad* who was killed by Achilles' son when the city fell.

and General Compson he saw the wilderness through a slow drizzle of November rain just above the ice point as it seemed to him later he always saw it or at least always remembered it—the tall and endless wall of dense November woods under the dissolving afternoon and the year's death, sombre, impenetrable (he could not even discern yet how, at what point they could possibly hope to enter it even though he knew that Sam Fathers was waiting there with the wagon), the surrey moving through the skeleton stalks of cotton and corn in the last of open country, the last trace of man's puny gnawing at the immemorial flank, until, dwarfed by that perspective into an almost ridiculous diminishment, the surrey itself seemed to have ceased to move (this too to be completed later, years later, after he had grown to a man and had seen the sea) as a solitary small boat hangs in lonely immobility, merely tossing up and down, in the infinite waste of the ocean while the water and then the apparently impenetrable land which it nears without appreciable progress, swings slowly and opens the widening inlet which is the anchorage. He entered it. Sam was waiting, wrapped in a quilt on the wagon seat behind the patient and steaming mules. He entered his novitiate to the true wilderness with Sam beside him as he had begun his apprenticeship in miniature to manhood after the rabbits and such with Sam beside him, the two of them wrapped in the damp, warm, negro-rank quilt while the wilderness closed behind his entrance as it had opened momentarily to accept him, opening before his advancement as it closed behind his progress, no fixed path the wagon followed but a channel nonexistent ten yards ahead of it and ceasing to exist ten yards after it had passed, the wagon progressing not by its own volition but by attrition of their intact yet fluid circumambience, drowsing, earless, almost lightless.

It seemed to him that at the age of ten he was witnessing his own birth. It was not even strange to him. He had experienced it all before, and not merely in dreams. He saw the camp—a paintless six-room bungalow set on piles above the spring high-water—and he knew already how it was going to look. He helped in the rapid orderly disorder of their establishment in it and even his motions were familiar to him, foreknown. Then for two weeks he ate the coarse rapid food—the shapeless sour bread, the wild strange meat, venison and bear and turkey and coon which he had never tasted before—which men ate, cooked by men who were hunters first and cooks afterward; he slept in harsh sheetless blankets as hunters slept. Each morning the gray of dawn found him and Sam Fathers on the stand, the crossing, which had been allotted him. It was the poorest one, the most barren. He had expected that; he had not dared yet to hope even to himself that he would even hear the running dogs this first time. But he did hear them. It was on the third morning—a murmur, sourceless, almost indistinguishable, yet he knew what it was although he had never before heard that many dogs running at once, the murmur swelling into separate and distinct voices until he could call the five dogs which his cousin owned from among the others. "Now," Sam said, "slant your gun up a little and draw back the hammers and then stand still."

But it was not for him, not yet. The humility was there; he had learned that. And he could learn the patience. He was only ten, only one week. The instant had passed. It seemed to him that he could actually see the deer, the buck, smoke-colored, elongated with speed, vanished, the woods, the gray solitude still ringing even when the voices of the dogs had died away; from far away across the sombre woods and the gray half-liquid morning there came two shots. "Now let your hammers down,"[5] Sam said.

He did so. "You knew it too," he said.

"Yes," Sam said. "I want you to learn how to do when you didn't shoot. It's after the chance for the bear or the deer has done already come and gone that men and dogs get killed."

"Anyway, it wasn't him," the boy said. "It wasn't even a bear. It was just a deer."

"Yes," Sam said, "it was just a deer."

Then one morning, it was in the second week, he heard the dogs again. This time before Sam even spoke he readied the too-long, too-heavy, man-size gun as Sam had taught him, even though this time he knew the dogs and the deer were coming less close than ever, hardly within hearing even. They didn't sound like any running dogs he had ever heard before even. Then he found that Sam, who had taught him first of all to cock the gun and take position where he could see best in all directions and then never to move again, had himself moved up beside him. "There," he said. "Listen." The boy listened, to no ringing chorus strong and fast on a free scent but a moiling yapping an octave too high and with something more than indecision and even abjectness in it which he could not yet recognise, reluctant, not even moving very fast, taking a long time to pass out of hearing, leaving even then in the air that echo of thin and almost human hysteria, abject, almost humanly grieving, with this time nothing ahead of it, no sense of a fleeing unseen smoke-colored shape. He could hear Sam breathing at his shoulder. He saw the arched curve of the old man's inhaling nostrils.

"It's Old Ben!" he cried, whispering.

Sam didn't move save for the slow gradual turning of his head as the voices faded on and the faint steady rapid arch and collapse of his nostrils. "Hah," he said. "Not even running. Walking."

"But up here!" the boy cried. "Way up here!"

"He do it every year," Sam said. "Once. Ash and Boon say he comes up here to run the other little bears away. Tell them to get to hell out of here and stay out until the hunters are gone. Maybe." The boy no longer heard anything at all, yet still Sam's head continued to turn gradually and steadily until the back of it was toward him. Then it turned back and looked down at him—the same face, grave, familiar, expressionless until it smiled, the same old man's eyes from which as he watched there faded slowly a quality darkly and fiercely lambent, passionate and proud. "He dont care no more for bears than he does for dogs or men neither. He come to see who's here, who's new in camp this year, whether he can shoot or not, can stay or not. Whether we got the dog yet that can bay and hold him until a man gets there with a gun. Because he's the head bear. He's the man." It faded, was gone; again they were the eyes as he had known them all his life. "He'll let them follow him to the river. Then he'll send them home. We might as well go too; see how they look when they get back to camp."

The dogs were there first, ten of them huddled back under the kitchen, himself and Sam squatting to peer back into the obscurity where they

<hr>

5. I.e., release them. Cocking the hammers prepares the double-barreled shotgun to fire.

crouched, quiet, the eyes rolling and luminous, vanishing, and no sound, only that effluvium which the boy could not quite place yet, of something more than dog, stronger than dog and not just animal, just beast even. Because there had been nothing in front of the abject and painful yapping except the solitude, the wilderness, so that when the eleventh hound got back about mid-afternoon and he and Tennie's Jim held the passive and still trembling bitch while Sam daubed her tattered ear and raked shoulder with turpentine and axle-grease, it was still no living creature but only the wilderness which, leaning for a moment, had patted lightly once her temerity. "Just like a man," Sam said. "Just like folks. Put off as long as she could having to be brave, knowing all the time that sooner or later she would have to be brave once so she could keep on calling herself a dog, and knowing beforehand what was going to happen when she done it."

He did not know just when Sam left. He only knew that he was gone. For the next three mornings he rose and ate breakfast and Sam was not waiting for him. He went to his stand alone; he found it without help now and stood on it as Sam had taught him. On the third morning he heard the dogs again, running strong and free on a true scent again, and he readied the gun as he had learned to do and heard the hunt sweep past on since he was not ready yet, had not deserved other yet in just one short period of two weeks as compared to all the long life which he had already dedicated to the wilderness with patience and humility; he heard the shot again, one shot, the single clapping report of Walter Ewell's rifle. By now he could not only find his stand and then return to camp without guidance, by using the compass his cousin had given him he reached Walter waiting beside the buck and the moiling of dogs over the cast entrails before any of the others except Major de Spain and Tennie's Jim on the horses, even before Uncle Ash arrived with the one-eyed wagon-mule which did not mind the smell of blood or even, so they said, of bear.

It was not Uncle Ash on the mule. It was Sam, returned. And Sam was waiting when he finished his dinner and, himself on the one-eyed mule and Sam on the other one of the wagon team, they rode for more than three hours through the rapid shortening sunless afternoon, following no path, no trail even that he could discern, into a section of country he had never seen before. Then he understood why Sam had made him ride the one-eyed mule which would not spook at the smell of blood, of wild animals. The other one, the sound one, stopped short and tried to whirl and bolt even as Sam got down, jerking and wrenching at the rein while Sam held it, coaxing it forward with his voice since he did not dare risk hitching it, drawing it forward while the boy dismounted from the marred one which would stand. Then, standing beside Sam in the thick great gloom of ancient woods and the winter's dying afternoon, he looked quietly down at the rotted log scored and gutted with claw-marks and, in the wet earth beside it, the print of the enormous warped two-toed foot. Now he knew what he had heard in the hounds' voices in the woods that morning and what he had smelled when he peered under the kitchen where they huddled. It was in him too, a little different because they were brute beasts and he was not, but only a little different—an eagerness, passive; an abjectness, a sense of his own fragility and impotence against the timeless woods, yet without doubt or dread; a flavor like brass in the sudden run of saliva in his mouth, a hard sharp constriction either in his brain or his stomach, he could not tell which and it did not matter; he knew only that for the first time he realised that the bear which had run in his listening and loomed in his dreams since before he could remember and which therefore must have existed in the listening and the dreams of his cousin and Major de Spain and even old General Compson before they began to remember in their turn, was a mortal animal and that they had departed for the camp each November with no actual intention of slaying it, not because it could not be slain but because so far they had no actual hope of being able to. "It will be tomorrow," he said.

"You mean we will try tomorrow," Sam said. "We aint got the dog yet."

"We've got eleven," he said. "They ran him Monday."

"And you heard them," Sam said. "Saw them too. We aint got the dog yet. It wont take but one. But he aint there. Maybe he aint nowhere. The only other way will be for him to run by accident over somebody that had a gun and knowed how to shoot it."

"That wouldn't be me," the boy said. "It would be Walter or Major or——"

"It might," Sam said. "You watch close tomorrow. Because he's smart. That's how come he has lived this long. If he gets hemmed up and has got to pick out somebody to run over, he will pick out you."

"How?" he said. "How will he know. . . ." He ceased. "You mean he already knows me, that I aint never been to the big bottom before, aint had time to find out yet whether I . . ." He ceased again, staring at Sam; he said humbly, not even amazed: "It was me he was watching. I dont reckon he did need to come but once."

"You watch tomorrow," Sam said. "I reckon we better start back. It'll be long after dark now before we get to camp."

The next morning they started three hours earlier than they had ever done. Even Uncle Ash went, the cook, who called himself by profession a camp cook and who did little else save cook for Major de Spain's hunting and camping parties, yet who had been marked by the wilderness from simple juxtaposition to it until he responded as they all did, even the boy who until two weeks ago had never even seen the wilderness, to a hound's ripped ear and shoulder and the print of a crooked foot in a patch of wet earth. They rode. It was too far to walk: the boy and Sam and Uncle Ash in the wagon with the dogs, his cousin and Major de Spain and General Compson and Boon and Walter and Tennie's Jim riding double on the horses; again the first gray light found him, as on that first morning two weeks ago, on the stand where Sam had placed and left him. With the gun which was too big for him, the breech-loader[6] which did not even belong to him but to Major de Spain and which he had fired only once, at a stump on the first day to learn the recoil and how to reload it with the paper shells, he stood against a big gum tree beside a little bayou whose black still water crept without motion out of a cane-brake, across a small clearing and into the cane again, where, invisible, a bird, the big woodpecker called Lord-to-God[7] by negroes, clattered at a dead trunk. It was a stand like any other stand, dissimilar only in incidentals to the one where he had stood each morning for two weeks; a territory new to him yet no less familiar than that other one which after two

6. A gun that is loaded behind the barrel (through the breech), as opposed to the earlier muzzle-loader style.   7. The impressively large pileated woodpecker.

weeks he had come to believe he knew a little—the same solitude, the same loneliness through which frail and timorous man had merely passed without altering it, leaving no mark nor scar, which looked exactly as it must have looked when the first ancestor of Sam Fathers' Chickasaw predecessors crept into it and looked about him, club or stone axe or bone arrow drawn and ready, different only because, squatting at the edge of the kitchen, he had smelled the dogs huddled and cringing beneath it and saw the raked ear and side of the bitch that, as Sam had said, had to be brave once in order to keep on calling herself a dog, and saw yesterday in the earth beside the gutted log, the print of the living foot. He heard no dogs at all. He never did certainly hear them. He only heard the drumming of the woodpecker stop short off, and knew that the bear was looking at him. He never saw it. He did not know whether it was facing him from the cane or behind him. He did not move, holding the useless gun which he knew now he would never fire at it, now or ever, tasting in his saliva that taint of brass which he had smelled in the huddled dogs when he peered under the kitchen.

Then it was gone. As abruptly as it had stopped, the woodpecker's dry hammering set up again, and after a while he believed he even heard the dogs—a murmur, scarce a sound even, which he had probably been hearing for a time, perhaps a minute or two, before he remarked it, drifting into hearing and then out again, dying away. They came nowhere near him. If it was dogs he heard, he could not have sworn to it; if it was a bear they ran, it was another bear. It was Sam himself who emerged from the cane and crossed the bayou, the injured bitch following at heel as a bird dog is taught to walk. She came and crouched against his leg, trembling. "I didn't see him," he said. "I didn't, Sam."

"I know it," Sam said. "He done the looking. You didn't hear him neither, did you?"

"No," the boy said. "I—"

"He's smart," Sam said. "Too smart." Again the boy saw in his eyes that quality of dark and brooding lambence as Sam looked down at the bitch trembling faintly and steadily against the boy's leg. From her raked shoulder a few drops of fresh blood clung like bright berries. "Too big. We aint got the dog yet. But maybe some day."

Because there would be a next time, after and after. He was only ten. It seemed to him that he could see them, the two of them, shadowy in the limbo from which time emerged and became time: the old bear absolved of mortality and himself who shared a little of it. Because he recognised now what he had smelled in the huddled dogs and tasted in his own saliva, recognised fear as a boy, a youth, recognises the existence of love and passion and experience which is his heritage but not yet his patrimony, from entering by chance the presence or perhaps even merely the bedroom of a woman who has loved and been loved by many men. *So I will have to see him*, he thought, without dread or even hope. *I will have to look at him.* So it was in June of the next summer. They were at the camp again, celebrating Major de Spain's and General Compson's birthdays. Although the one had been born in September and the other in the depth of winter and almost thirty years earlier, each June the two of them and McCaslin and Boon and Walter Ewell (and the boy too from now on) spent two weeks at the camp, fishing and shooting squirrels and turkey and running coons and wildcats with the dogs at night.

That is, Boon and the negroes (and the boy too now) fished and shot squirrels and ran the coons and cats, because the proven hunters, not only Major de Spain and old General Compson (who spent those two weeks sitting in a rocking chair before a tremendous iron pot of Brunswick stew, stirring and tasting, with Uncle Ash to quarrel with about how he was making it and Tennie's Jim to pour whisky into the tin dipper from which he drank it) but even McCaslin and Walter Ewell who were still young enough, scorned such other than shooting the wild gobblers with pistols for wagers or to test their marksmanship.

That is, his cousin McCaslin and the others thought he was hunting squirrels. Until the third evening he believed that Sam Fathers thought so too. Each morning he would leave the camp right after breakfast. He had his own gun now, a new breech-loader, a Christmas gift; he would own and shoot it for almost seventy years, through two new pairs of barrels and locks and one new stock, until all that remained of the original gun was the silver-inlaid trigger-guard with his and McCaslin's engraved names and the date in 1878. He found the tree beside the little bayou[8] where he had stood that morning. Using the compass he ranged from that point; he was teaching himself to be better than a fair woodsman without even knowing he was doing it. On the third day he even found the gutted log where he had first seen the print. It was almost completely crumbled now, healing with unbelievable speed, a passionate and almost visible relinquishment, back into the earth from which the tree had grown. He ranged the summer woods now, green with gloom, if anything actually dimmer than they had been in November's gray dissolution, where even at noon the sun fell only in windless dappling upon the earth which never completely dried and which crawled with snakes—moccasins and water-snakes and rattlers, themselves the color of the dappled gloom so that he would not always see them until they moved; returning to camp later and later and later, first day, second day, passing in the twilight of the third evening the little log pen enclosing the log barn where Sam was putting up the stock for the night. "You aint looked right yet," Sam said.

He stopped. For a moment he didn't answer. Then he said peacefully, in a peaceful rushing burst, as when a boy's miniature dam in a little brook gives way: "All right. Yes. But how? I went to the bayou. I even found that log again. I—"

"I reckon that was all right. Likely he's been watching you. You never saw his foot?"

"I . . ." the boy said. "I didn't . . . I never thought . . ."

"It's the gun," Sam said. He stood beside the fence, motionless, the old man, son of a negro slave and a Chickasaw chief, in the battered and faded overalls and the frayed five-cent straw hat which had been the badge of the negro's slavery and was now the regalia of his freedom. The camp—the clearing, the house, the barn and its tiny lot with which Major de Spain in his turn had scratched punily and evanescently at the wilderness—faded in the dusk, back into the immemorial darkness of the woods. *The gun,* the boy thought. *The gun.* "You will have to choose," Sam said.

He left the next morning before light, without breakfast, long before Uncle Ash would wake in his quilts on the kitchen floor and start the fire. He had

8. Creek or small river.

only the compass and a stick for the snakes. He could go almost a mile before he would need to see the compass. He sat on a log, the invisible compass in his hand, while the secret night-sounds which had ceased at his movements, scurried again and then fell still for good and the owls ceased and gave over to the waking day birds and there was light in the gray wet woods and he could see the compass. He went fast yet still quietly, becoming steadily better and better as a woodsman without yet having time to realise it; he jumped a doe and a fawn, walked them[9] out of the bed, close enough to see them— the crash of undergrowth, the white scut, the fawn scudding along behind her, faster than he had known it could have run. He was hunting right, upwind, as Sam had taught him, but that didn't matter now. He had left the gun; by his own will and relinquishment he had accepted not a gambit, not a choice, but a condition in which not only the bear's heretofore inviolable anonymity but all the ancient rules and balances of hunter and hunted had been abrogated. He would not even be afraid, not even in the moment when the fear would take him completely: blood, skin, bowels, bones, memory from the long time before it even became his memory—all save that thin clear quenchless lucidity which alone differed him from this bear and from all the other bears and bucks he would follow during almost seventy years, to which Sam had said: "Be scared. You cant help that. But dont be afraid. Aint nothing in the woods going to hurt you if you dont corner it or it dont smell that you are afraid. A bear or a deer has got to be scared of a coward the same as a brave man has got to be."

By noon he was far beyond the crossing on the little bayou, farther into the new and alien country than he had ever been, travelling now not only by the compass but by the old, heavy, biscuit-thick silver watch which had been his father's. He had left the camp nine hours ago; nine hours from now, dark would already have been an hour old. He stopped, for the first time since he had risen from the log when he could see the compass face at last, and looked about, mopping his sweating face on his sleeve. He had already relinquished, of his will, because of his need, in humility and peace and without regret, yet apparently that had not been enough, the leaving of the gun was not enough. He stood for a moment—a child, alien and lost in the green and soaring gloom of the markless wilderness. Then he relinquished completely to it. It was the watch and the compass. He was still tainted. He removed the linked chain of the one and the looped thong of the other from his overalls and hung them on a bush and leaned the stick beside them and entered it.

When he realised he was lost, he did as Sam had coached and drilled him: made a cast to cross his backtrack. He had not been going very fast for the last two or three hours, and he had gone even less fast since he left the compass and watch on the bush. So he went slower still now, since the tree could not be very far; in fact, he found it before he really expected to and turned and went to it. But there was no bush beneath it, no compass nor watch, so he did next as Sam had coached and drilled him: made this next circle in the opposite direction and much larger, so that the pattern of the two of them would bisect his track somewhere, but crossing no trace nor mark anywhere of his feet or any feet, and now he was going faster though

9. Sneaked up without frightening them.

still not panicked, his heart beating a little more rapidly but strong and steady enough, and this time it was not even the tree because there was a down log beside it which he had never seen before and beyond the log a little swamp, a seepage of moisture somewhere between earth and water, and he did what Sam had coached and drilled him as the next and the last, seeing as he sat down on the log the crooked print, the warped indentation in the wet ground which while he looked at it continued to fill with water until it was level full and the water began to overflow and the sides of the print began to dissolve away. Even as he looked up he saw the next one, and, moving, the one beyond it: moving, not hurrying, running, but merely keeping pace with them as they appeared before him as though they were being shaped out of thin air just one constant pace short of where he would lose them forever and be lost forever himself, tireless, eager, without doubt or dread, panting a little above the strong rapid little hammer of his heart, emerging suddenly into a little glade and the wilderness coalesced. It rushed, soundless, and solidified—the tree, the bush, the compass and the watch glinting where a ray of sunlight touched them. Then he saw the bear. It did not emerge, appear: it was just there, immobile, fixed in the green and windless noon's hot dappling, not as big as he had dreamed it but as big as he had expected, bigger, dimensionless against the dappled obscurity, looking at him. Then it moved. It crossed the glade without haste, walking for an instant into the sun's full glare and out of it, and stopped again and looked back at him across one shoulder. Then it was gone. It didn't walk into the woods. It faded, sank back into the wilderness without motion as he had watched a fish, a huge old bass, sink back into the dark depths of its pool and vanish without even any movement of its fins.

2

So he should have hated and feared Lion. He was thirteen then. He had killed his buck and Sam Fathers had marked his face with the hot blood, and in the next November he killed a bear. But before that accolade he had become as competent in the woods as many grown men with the same experience. By now he was a better woodsman than most grown men with more. There was no territory within twenty-five miles of the camp that he did not know—bayou, ridge, landmark trees and path; he could have led anyone direct to any spot in it and brought him back. He knew game trails that even Sam Fathers had never seen; in the third fall he found a buck's bedding-place by himself and unbeknown to his cousin he borrowed Walter Ewell's rifle and lay in wait for the buck at dawn and killed it when it walked back to the bed as Sam had told him how the old Chickasaw fathers did.

By now he knew the old bear's footprint better than he did his own, and not only the crooked one. He could see any one of the three sound prints and distinguish it at once from any other, and not only because of its size. There were other bears within that fifty miles which left tracks almost as large, or at least so near that the one would have appeared larger only by juxtaposition. It was more than that. If Sam Fathers had been his mentor and the backyard rabbits and squirrels his kindergarten, then the wilderness the old bear ran was his college and the old male bear itself, so long unwifed and childless as to have become its own ungendered progenitor, was his alma mater.[1]

He could find the crooked print now whenever he wished, ten miles or five miles or sometimes closer than that, to the camp. Twice while on stand during the next three years he heard the dogs strike its trail and once even jump it by chance, the voices high, abject, almost human in their hysteria. Once, still-hunting[2] with Walter Ewell's rifle, he saw it cross a long corridor of down timber where a tornado had passed. It rushed through rather than across the tangle of trunks and branches as a locomotive would, faster than he had ever believed it could have moved, almost as fast as a deer even because the deer would have spent most of that distance in the air; he realised then why it would take a dog not only of abnormal courage but size and speed too ever to bring it to bay. He had a little dog at home, a mongrel, of the sort called fyce by negroes, a ratter, itself not much bigger than a rat and possessing that sort of courage which had long since stopped being bravery and had become foolhardiness. He brought it with him one June and, timing them as if they were meeting an appointment with another human being, himself carrying the fyce with a sack over its head and Sam Fathers with a brace of the hounds on a rope leash, they lay downwind of the trail and actually ambushed the bear. They were so close that it turned at bay although he realised later this might have been from surprise and amazement at the shrill and frantic uproar of the fyce. It turned at bay against the trunk of a big cypress, on its hind feet; it seemed to the boy that it would never stop rising, taller and taller, and even the two hounds seemed to have taken a kind of desperate and despairing courage from the fyce. Then he realised that the fyce was actually not going to stop. He flung the gun down and ran. When he overtook and grasped the shrill, frantically pinwheeling little dog, it seemed to him that he was directly under the bear. He could smell it, strong and hot and rank. Sprawling, he looked up where it loomed and towered over him like a thunderclap. It was quite familiar, until he remembered: this was the way he had used to dream about it.

Then it was gone. He didn't see it go. He knelt, holding the frantic fyce with both hands, hearing the abased wailing of the two hounds drawing further and further away, until Sam came up, carrying the gun. He laid it quietly down beside the boy and stood looking down at him. "You've done seed him twice now, with a gun in your hands," he said. "This time you couldn't have missed him."

The boy rose. He still held the fyce. Even in his arms it continued to yap frantically, surging and straining toward the fading sound of the hounds like a collection of live-wire springs. The boy was panting a little. "Neither could you," he said. "You had the gun. Why didn't you shoot him?"

Sam didn't seem to have heard. He put out his hand and touched the little dog in the boy's arms which still yapped and strained even though the two hounds were out of hearing now. "He's done gone," Sam said. "You can slack off and rest now, until next time." He stroked the little dog until it began to grow quiet under his hand. "You's almost the one we wants," he said. "You

1. Cherished mother (Latin, literal trans.); one's former school or college. 2. The hunter alternately moves and stops, waiting for prey to pass by.

just aint big enough. We aint got that one yet. He will need to be just a little bigger than smart, and a little braver than either." He withdrew his hand from the fyce's head and stood looking into the woods where the bear and the hounds had vanished. "Somebody is going to, some day."

"I know it," the boy said. "That's why it must be one of us. So it wont be until the last day. When even he dont want it to last any longer."

So he should have hated and feared Lion. It was in the fourth summer, the fourth time he had made one in the celebration of Major de Spain's and General Compson's birthday. In the early spring Major de Spain's mare had foaled a horse colt. One evening when Sam brought the horses and mules up to stable them for the night, the colt was missing and it was all he could do to get the frantic mare into the lot. He had thought at first to let the mare lead him back to where she had become separated from the foal. But she would not do it. She would not even feint toward any particular part of the woods or even in any particular direction. She merely ran, as if she couldn't see, still frantic with terror. She whirled and ran at Sam once, as if to attack him in some ultimate desperation, as if she could not for the moment realise that he was a man and a long-familiar one. He got her into the lot at last. It was too dark by that time to back-track her, to unravel the erratic course she had doubtless pursued.

He came to the house and told Major de Spain. It was an animal, of course, a big one, and the colt was dead now, wherever it was. They all knew that. "It's a panther," General Compson said at once. "The same one. That doe and fawn last March." Sam had sent Major de Spain word of it when Boon Hogganbeck came to the camp on a routine visit to see how the stock had wintered—the doe's throat torn out, and the beast had run down the helpless fawn and killed it too.

"Sam never did say that was a panther," Major de Spain said. Sam said nothing now, standing behind Major de Spain where they sat at supper, inscrutable, as if he were just waiting for them to stop talking so he could go home. He didn't even seem to be looking at anything. "A panther might jump a doe, and he wouldn't have much trouble catching the fawn afterward. But no panther would have jumped that colt with the dam right there with it. It was Old Ben," Major de Spain said. "I'm disappointed in him. He has broken the rules. I didn't think he would have done that. He has killed mine and McCaslin's dogs, but that was all right. We gambled the dogs against him; we gave each other warning. But now he has come into my house and destroyed my property, out of season too. He broke the rules. It was Old Ben, Sam." Still Sam said nothing, standing there until Major de Spain should stop talking. "We'll back-track her tomorrow and see," Major de Spain said.

Sam departed. He would not live in the camp; he had built himself a little hut something like Joe Baker's, only stouter, tighter, on the bayou a quarter-mile away, and a stout log crib where he stored a little corn for the shoat he raised each year. The next morning he was waiting when they waked. He had already found the colt. They did not even wait for breakfast. It was not far, not five hundred yards from the stable—the three-months' colt lying on its side, its throat torn out and the entrails and one ham partly eaten. It lay not as if it had been dropped but as if it had been struck and hurled, and no cat-mark, no claw-mark where a panther would have gripped it while finding its throat. They read the tracks where the frantic mare had circled and at last rushed in with that same ultimate desperation with which she had whirled on Sam Fathers yesterday evening, and the long tracks of dead and terrified running and those of the beast which had not even rushed at her when she advanced but had merely walked three or four paces toward her until she broke, and General Compson said, "Good God, what a wolf!"

Still Sam said nothing. The boy watched him while the men knelt, measuring the tracks. There was something in Sam's face now. It was neither exultation nor joy nor hope. Later, a man, the boy realised what it had been, and that Sam had known all the time what had made the tracks and what had torn the throat out of the doe in the spring and killed the fawn. It had been foreknowledge in Sam's face that morning. *And he was glad*, he told himself. *He was old. He had no children, no people, none of his blood anywhere above earth that he would ever meet again. And even if he were to, he could not have touched it, spoken to it, because for seventy years now he had had to be a negro. It was almost over now and he was glad.*

They returned to camp and had breakfast and came back with guns and the hounds. Afterward the boy realised that they also should have known then what killed the colt as well as Sam Fathers did. But that was neither the first nor the last time he had seen men rationalise from and even act upon their misconceptions. After Boon, standing astride the colt, had whipped the dogs away from it with his belt, they snuffed at the tracks. One of them, a young dog hound without judgment yet, bayed once, and they ran for a few feet on what seemed to be a trail. Then they stopped, looking back at the men, eager enough, not baffled, merely questioning, as if they were asking "Now what?" Then they rushed back to the colt, where Boon, still astride it, slashed at them with the belt.

"I never knew a trail to get cold that quick," General Compson said.

"Maybe a single wolf big enough to kill a colt with the dam right there beside it dont leave scent," Major de Spain said.

"Maybe it was a hant," Walter Ewell said. He looked at Tennie's Jim. "Hah, Jim?"

Because the hounds would not run it, Major de Spain had Sam hunt out and find the tracks a hundred yards farther on and they put the dogs on it again and again the young one bayed and not one of them realised then that the hound was not baying like a dog striking game but was merely bellowing like a country dog whose yard has been invaded. General Compson spoke to the boy and Boon and Tennie's Jim: to the squirrel hunters. "You boys keep the dogs with you this morning. He's probably hanging around somewhere, waiting to get his breakfast off the colt. You might strike him."

But they did not. The boy remembered how Sam stood watching them as they went into the woods with the leashed hounds—the Indian face in which he had never seen anything until it smiled, except that faint arching of the nostrils on that first morning when the hounds had found Old Ben. They took the hounds with them on the next day, though when they reached the place where they hoped to strike a fresh trail, the carcass of the colt was gone. Then on the third morning Sam was waiting again, this time until they had finished breakfast. He said, "Come." He led them to his house, his little hut, to the corn-crib beyond it. He had removed the corn and had made a deadfall of the door, baiting it with the colt's carcass; peering between the logs, they saw an animal almost the color of a gun or pistol barrel, what little time they had to examine its color or shape. It was not crouched nor even standing. It was in motion, in the air, coming toward them—a heavy body crashing with tremendous force against the door so that the thick door jumped and clattered in its frame, the animal, whatever it was, hurling itself against the door again seemingly before it could have touched the floor and got a new purchase to spring from. "Come away," Sam said, "fore he break his neck." Even when they retreated the heavy and measured crashes continued, the stout door jumping and clattering each time, and still no sound from the beast itself—no snarl, no cry.

"What in hell's name is it?" Major de Spain said.

"It's a dog," Sam said, his nostrils arching and collapsing faintly and steadily and that faint, fierce milkiness in his eyes again as on that first morning when the hounds had struck the old bear. "It's the dog."

"*The* dog?" Major de Spain said.

"That's gonter hold Old Ben."

"Dog the devil," Major de Spain said. "I'd rather have Old Ben himself in my pack than that brute. Shoot him."

"No," Sam said.

"You'll never tame him. How do you ever expect to make an animal like that afraid of you?"

"I dont want him tame," Sam said; again the boy watched his nostrils and the fierce milky light in his eyes. "But I almost rather he be tame than scared, of me or any man or any thing. But he wont be neither, of nothing."

"Then what are you going to do with it?"

"You can watch," Sam said.

Each morning through the second week they would go to Sam's crib. He had removed a few shingles from the roof and had put a rope on the colt's carcass and had drawn it out when the trap fell. Each morning they would watch him lower a pail of water into the crib while the dog hurled itself tirelessly against the door and dropped back and leaped again. It never made any sound and there was nothing frenzied in the act but only a cold and grim indomitable determination. Toward the end of the week it stopped jumping at the door. Yet it had not weakened appreciably and it was not as if it had rationalised the fact that the door was not going to give. It was as if for that time it simply disdained to jump any longer. It was not down. None of them had ever seen it down. It stood, and they could see it now—part mastiff, something of Airedale and something of a dozen other strains probably, better than thirty inches at the shoulders and weighing as they guessed almost ninety pounds, with cold yellow eyes and a tremendous chest and over all that strange color like a blued gun-barrel.

Then the two weeks were up. They prepared to break camp. The boy begged to remain and his cousin let him. He moved into the little hut with Sam Fathers. Each morning he watched Sam lower the pail of water into the crib. By the end of that week the dog was down. It would rise and half stagger, half crawl to the water and drink and collapse again. One morning it could not even reach the water, could not raise its forequarters even from the floor. Sam took a short stick and prepared to enter the crib. "Wait," the boy said. "Let me get the gun—"

"No," Sam said. "He cant move now." Nor could it. It lay on its side while

Sam touched it, its head and the gaunted body, the dog lying motionless, the yellow eyes open. They were not fierce and there was nothing of petty malevolence in them, but a cold and almost impersonal malignance like some natural force. It was not even looking at Sam nor at the boy peering at it between the logs.

Sam began to feed it again. The first time he had to raise its head so it could lap the broth. That night he left a bowl of broth containing lumps of meat where the dog could reach it. The next morning the bowl was empty and the dog was lying on its belly, its head up, the cold yellow eyes watching the door as Sam entered, no change whatever in the cold yellow eyes and still no sound from it even when it sprang, its aim and co-ordination still bad from weakness so that Sam had time to strike it down with the stick and leap from the crib and slam the door as the dog, still without having had time to get its feet under it to jump again seemingly, hurled itself against the door as if the two weeks of starving had never been.

At noon that day someone came whooping through the woods from the direction of the camp. It was Boon. He came and looked for a while between the logs, at the tremendous dog lying again on its belly, its head up, the yellow eyes blinking sleepily at nothing: the indomitable and unbroken spirit. "What we better do," Boon said, "is to let that son of a bitch go and catch Old Ben and run him on the dog." He turned to the boy his weather-reddened and beetling face. "Get your traps together. Cass says for you to come on home. You been in here fooling with that horse-eating varmint long enough."

Boon had a borrowed mule at the camp; the buggy was waiting at the edge of the bottom. He was at home that night. He told McCaslin about it. "Sam's going to starve him again until he can go in and touch him. Then he will feed him again. Then he will starve him again, if he has to."

"But why?" McCaslin said. "What for? Even Sam will never tame that brute."

"We dont want him tame. We want him like he is. We just want him to find out at last that the only way he can get out of that crib and stay out of it is to do what Sam or somebody tells him to do. He's the dog that's going to stop Old Ben and hold him. We've already named him. His name is Lion."

Then November came at last. They returned to the camp. With General Compson and Major de Spain and his cousin and Walter and Boon he stood in the yard among the guns and bedding and boxes of food and watched Sam Fathers and Lion come up the lane from the lot—the Indian, the old man in battered overalls and rubber boots and a worn sheepskin coat and a hat which had belonged to the boy's father; the tremendous dog pacing gravely beside him. The hounds rushed out to meet them and stopped, except the young one which still had but little of judgment. It ran up to Lion, fawning. Lion didn't snap at it. He didn't even pause. He struck it rolling and yelping for five or six feet with a blow of one paw as a bear would have done and came on into the yard and stood, blinking sleepily at nothing, looking at no one, while Boon said, "Jesus. Jesus.—Will he let me touch him?"

"You can touch him," Sam said. "He dont care. He dont care about nothing or nobody."

The boy watched that too. He watched it for the next two years from that moment when Boon touched Lion's head and then knelt beside him, feeling the bones and muscles, the power. It was as if Lion were a woman—or perhaps Boon was the woman. That was more like it—the big, grave, sleepy-seeming dog which, as Sam Fathers said, cared about no man and no thing; and the violent, insensitive, hard-faced man with his touch of remote Indian blood and the mind almost of a child. He watched Boon take over Lion's feeding from Sam and Uncle Ash both. He would see Boon squatting in the cold rain beside the kitchen while Lion ate. Because Lion neither slept nor ate with the other dogs though none of them knew where he did sleep until in the second November, thinking until then that Lion slept in his kennel beside Sam Fathers' hut, when the boy's cousin McCaslin said something about it to Sam by sheer chance and Sam told him. And that night the boy and Major de Spain and McCaslin with a lamp entered the back room where Boon slept—the little, tight, airless room rank with the smell of Boon's unwashed body and his wet hunting-clothes—where Boon, snoring on his back, choked and waked and Lion raised his head beside him and looked back at them from his cold, slumbrous yellow eyes.

"Damn it, Boon," McCaslin said. "Get that dog out of here. He's got to run Old Ben tomorrow morning. How in hell do you expect him to smell anything fainter than a skunk after breathing you all night?"

"The way I smell aint hurt my nose none that I ever noticed," Boon said.

"It wouldn't matter if it had," Major de Spain said. "We're not depending on you to trail a bear. Put him outside. Put him under the house with the other dogs."

Boon began to get up. "He'll kill the first one that happens to yawn or sneeze in his face or touches him."

"I reckon not," Major de Spain said. "None of them are going to risk yawning in his face or touching him either, even asleep. Put him outside. I want his nose right tomorrow. Old Ben fooled him last year. I dont think he will do it again."

Boon put on his shoes without lacing them; in his long soiled underwear, his hair still tousled from sleep, he and Lion went out. The others returned to the front room and the poker game where McCaslin's and Major de Spain's hands waited for them on the table. After a while McCaslin said, "Do you want me to go back and look again?"

"No," Major de Spain said. "I call," he said to Walter Ewell. He spoke to McCaslin again. "If you do, dont tell me. I am beginning to see the first sign of my increasing age: I dont like to know that my orders have been disobeyed, even when I knew when I gave them that they would be.—A small pair," he said to Walter Ewell.

"How small?" Walter said.

"Very small," Major de Spain said.

And the boy, lying beneath his piled quilts and blankets waiting for sleep, knew likewise that Lion was already back in Boon's bed, for the rest of that night and the next one and during all the nights of the next November and the next one. He thought then: *I wonder what Sam thinks. He could have Lion with him, even if Boon is a white man. He could ask Major or McCaslin either. And more than that. It was Sam's hand that touched Lion first and Lion knows it.* Then he became a man and he knew that too. It had been all right. That was the way it should have been. Sam was the chief, the prince; Boon, the plebeian, was his huntsman. Boon should have nursed the dogs.

On the first morning that Lion led the pack after Old Ben, seven strangers appeared in the camp. They were swampers: gaunt, malaria-ridden men appearing from nowhere, who ran trap-lines for coons or perhaps farmed little patches of cotton and corn along the edge of the bottom, in clothes but little better than Sam Fathers' and nowhere near as good as Tennie's Jim's, with worn shotguns and rifles, already squatting patiently in the cold drizzle in the side yard when day broke. They had a spokesman; afterward Sam Fathers told Major de Spain how all during the past summer and fall they had drifted into the camp singly or in pairs and threes, to look quietly at Lion for a while and then go away: "Mawnin, Major. We heerd you was aimin to put that ere blue dawg on that old two-toed bear this mawnin. We figgered we'd come up and watch, if you dont mind. We wont do no shooting, lessen he runs over us."

"You are welcome," Major de Spain said. "You are welcome to shoot. He's more your bear than ours."

"I reckon that aint no lie. I done fed him enough cawn to have a sheer[3] in him. Not to mention a shoat three years ago."

"I reckon I got a sheer too," another said. "Only it aint in the bear." Major de Spain looked at him. He was chewing tobacco. He spat. "Hit was a heifer calf. Nice un too. Last year. When I finally found her, I reckon she looked about like that colt of yourn looked last June."

"Oh," Major de Spain said. "Be welcome. If you see game in front of my dogs, shoot it."

Nobody shot Old Ben that day. No man saw him. The dogs jumped him within a hundred yards of the glade where the boy had seen him that day in the summer of his eleventh year. The boy was less than a quarter-mile away. He heard the jump but he could distinguish no voice among the dogs that he did not know and therefore would be Lion's, and he thought, believed, that Lion was not among them. Even the fact that they were going much faster than he had ever heard them run behind Old Ben before and that the high thin note of hysteria was missing now from their voices was not enough to disabuse him. He didn't comprehend until that night, when Sam told him that Lion would never cry on a trail. "He gonter growl when he catches Old Ben's throat," Sam said. "But he aint gonter never holler, no more than he ever done when he was jumping at that two-inch door. It's that blue dog in him. What you call it?"

"Airedale," the boy said.

Lion was there; the jump was just too close to the river. When Boon returned with Lion about eleven that night, he swore that Lion had stopped Old Ben once but that the hounds would not go in and Old Ben broke away and took to the river and swam for miles down it and he and Lion went down one bank for about ten miles and crossed and came up the other but it had begun to get dark before they struck any trail where Old Ben had come up out of the water, unless he was still in the water when he passed the ford where they crossed. Then he fell to cursing the hounds and ate the supper Uncle Ash had saved for him and went off to bed and after a while the boy opened the door of the little stale room thunderous with snoring and the great grave dog raised its head from Boon's pillow and blinked at him for a moment and lowered its head again.

3. *Sheer*: share (dialect). *Cawn*: corn.

When the next November came and the last day, the day on which it was now becoming traditional to save for Old Ben, there were more than a dozen strangers waiting. They were not all swampers this time. Some of them were townsmen, from other county seats like Jefferson, who had heard about Lion and Old Ben and had come to watch the great blue dog keep his yearly rendezvous with the old two-toed bear. Some of them didn't even have guns and the hunting-clothes and boots they wore had been on a store shelf yesterday.

This time Lion jumped Old Ben more than five miles from the river and bayed and held him and this time the hounds went in, in a sort of desperate emulation. The boy heard them; he was that near. He heard Boon whooping; he heard the two shots when General Compson delivered both barrels, one containing five buckshot, the other a single ball, into the bear from as close as he could force his almost unmanageable horse. He heard the dogs when the bear broke free again. He was running now; panting, stumbling, his lungs bursting, he reached the place where General Compson had fired and where Old Ben had killed two of the hounds. He saw the blood from General Compson's shots, but he could go no further. He stopped, leaning against a tree for his breathing to ease and his heart to slow, hearing the sound of the dogs as it faded on and died away.

In camp that night—they had as guests five of the still terrified strangers in new hunting coats and boots who had been lost all day until Sam Fathers went out and got them—he heard the rest of it: how Lion had stopped and held the bear again but only the one-eyed mule which did not mind the smell of wild blood would approach and Boon was riding the mule and Boon had never been known to hit anything. He shot at the bear five times with his pump gun,[4] touching nothing, and Old Ben killed another hound and broke free once more and reached the river and was gone. Again Boon and Lion hunted as far down one bank as they dared. Too far; they crossed in the first of dusk and dark overtook them within a mile. And this time Lion found the broken trail, the blood perhaps, in the darkness where Old Ben had come up out of the water, but Boon had him on a rope, luckily, and he got down from the mule and fought Lion hand-to-hand until he got him back to camp. This time Boon didn't even curse. He stood in the door, muddy, spent, his huge gargoyle's face tragic and still amazed. "I missed him," he said. "I was in twenty-five feet of him and I missed him five times."

"But we have drawn blood," Major de Spain said. "General Compson drew blood. We have never done that before."

"But I missed him," Boon said. "I missed him five times. With Lion looking right at me."

"Never mind," Major de Spain said. "It was a damned fine race. And we drew blood. Next year we'll let General Compson or Walter ride Katie, and we'll get him."

Then McCaslin said, "Where is Lion, Boon?"

"I left him at Sam's," Boon said. He was already turning away. "I aint fit to sleep with him."

So he should have hated and feared Lion. Yet he did not. It seemed to him that there was a fatality in it. It seemed to him that something, he didn't

---

4. A repeating shotgun that fires only when a slide below the barrel is pushed in and out (i.e., pumped).

know what, was beginning; had already begun. It was like the last act on a set stage. It was the beginning of the end of something, he didn't know what except that he would not grieve. He would be humble and proud that he had been found worth to be a part of it too or even just to see it too.

3

It was December. It was the coldest December he had ever remembered. They had been in camp four days over two weeks, waiting for the weather to soften so that Lion and Old Ben could run their yearly race. Then they would break camp and go home. Because of these unforeseen additional days which they had had to pass waiting on the weather, with nothing to do but play poker, the whisky had given out and he and Boon were being sent to Memphis with a suitcase and a note from Major de Spain to Mr Semmes, the distiller, to get more. That is, Major de Spain and McCaslin were sending Boon to get the whisky and sending him to see that Boon got back with it or most of it or at least some of it.

Tennie's Jim waked him at three. He dressed rapidly, shivering, not so much from the cold because a fresh fire already boomed and roared on the hearth, but in that dead winter hour when the blood and the heart are slow and sleep is incomplete. He crossed the gap between house and kitchen, the gap of iron earth beneath the brilliant and rigid night where dawn would not begin for three hours yet, tasting, tongue palate and to the very bottom of his lungs the searing dark, and entered the kitchen, the lamp-lit warmth where the stove glowed, fogging the windows, and where Boon already sat at the table at breakfast, hunched over his plate, almost in his plate, his working jaws blue with stubble and his face innocent of water and his coarse, horse-mane hair innocent of comb—the quarter Indian, grandson of a Chickasaw squaw, who on occasion resented with his hard and furious fists the intimation of one single drop of alien blood and on others, usually after whisky, affirmed with the same fists and the same fury that his father had been the full-blood Chickasaw and even a chief and that even his mother had been only half white. He was four inches over six feet; he had the mind of a child, the heart of a horse, and little hard shoe-button eyes without depth or meanness or generosity or viciousness or gentleness or anything else, in the ugliest face the boy had ever seen. It looked like somebody had found a walnut a little larger than a football and with a machinist's hammer had shaped features into it and then painted it, mostly red; not Indian red but a fine bright ruddy color which whisky might have had something to do with but which was mostly just happy and violent out-of-doors, the wrinkles in it not the residue of the forty years it had survived but from squinting into the sun or into the gloom of cane-brakes where game had run, baked into it by the camp fires before which he had lain trying to sleep on the cold November or December ground while waiting for daylight so he could rise and hunt again, as though time were merely something he walked through as he did through air, aging him no more than air did. He was brave, faithful, improvident and unreliable; he had neither profession job nor trade and owned one vice and one virtue: whisky, and that absolute and unquestioning fidelity to Major de Spain and the boy's cousin McCaslin. "Sometimes I'd call them both virtues," Major de Spain said once. "Or both vices," McCaslin said.

He ate his breakfast, hearing the dogs under the kitchen, wakened by the smell of frying meat or perhaps by the feet overhead. He heard Lion once, short and peremptory, as the best hunter in any camp has only to speak once to all save the fools, and none other of Major de Spain's and McCaslin's dogs were Lion's equal in size and strength and perhaps even in courage, but they were not fools; Old Ben had killed the last fool among them last year.

Tennie's Jim came in as they finished. The wagon was outside. Ash decided he would drive them over to the log-line where they would flag the outbound log-train and let Tennie's Jim wash the dishes. The boy knew why. It would not be the first time he had listened to old Ash badgering Boon.

It was cold. The wagon wheels banged and clattered on the frozen ground; the sky was fixed and brilliant. He was not shivering, he was shaking, slow and steady and hard, the food he had just eaten still warm and solid inside him while his outside shook slow and steady around it as though his stomach floated loose. "They wont run this morning," he said. "No dog will have any nose today."

"Cep Lion," Ash said. "Lion dont need no nose. All he need is a bear." He had wrapped his feet in towsacks and he had a quilt from his pallet bed on the kitchen floor drawn over his head and wrapped around him until in the thin brilliant starlight he looked like nothing at all that the boy had ever seen before. "He run a bear through a thousand-acre ice-house. Catch him too. Them other dogs dont matter because they aint going to keep up with Lion nohow, long as he got a bear in front of him."

"What's wrong with the other dogs?" Boon said. "What the hell do you know about it anyway? This is the first time you've had your tail out of that kitchen since we got here except to chop a little wood."

"Aint nothing wrong with them," Ash said. "And long as it's left up to them, aint nothing going to be. I just wish I had knowed all my life how to take care of my health good as them hounds knows."

"Well, they aint going to run this morning," Boon said. His voice was harsh and positive. "Major promised they wouldn't until me and Ike get back."

"Weather gonter break today. Gonter soft up. Rain by night." Then Ash laughed, chuckled, somewhere inside the quilt which concealed even his face. "Hum up here, mules!" he said, jerking the reins so that the mules leaped forward and snatched the lurching and banging wagon for several feet before they slowed again into their quick, short-paced, rapid plodding. "Sides, I like to know why Major need to wait on you. It's Lion he aiming to use. I aint never heard tell of you bringing no bear nor no other kind of meat into this camp."

Now Boon's going to curse Ash or maybe even hit him, the boy thought. But Boon never did, never had; the boy knew he never would even though four years ago Boon had shot five times with a borrowed pistol at a negro on the street in Jefferson, with the same result as when he had shot five times at Old Ben last fall. "By God," Boon said, "he aint going to put Lion or no other dog on nothing until I get back tonight. Because he promised me. Whip up them mules and keep them whipped up. Do you want me to freeze to death?"

They reached the log-line and built a fire. After a while the log-train came up out of the woods under the paling east and Boon flagged it. Then in the warm caboose the boy slept again while Boon and the conductor and brakeman talked about Lion and Old Ben as people later would talk about Sullivan and Kilrain and, later still, about Dempsey and Tunney.[5] Dozing, swaying as the springless caboose lurched and clattered, he would hear them still talking, about the shoats and calves Old Ben had killed and the cribs he had rifled and the traps and deadfalls he had wrecked and the lead he probably carried under his hide—Old Ben, the two-toed bear in a land where bears with trap-ruined feet had been called Two-Toe or Three-Toe or Cripple-Foot for fifty years, only Old Ben was an extra bear (the head bear, General Compson called him) and so had earned a name such as a human man could have worn and not been sorry.

They reached Hoke's at sunup. They emerged from the warm caboose in their hunting clothes, the muddy boots and stained khaki and Boon's blue unshaven jowls. But that was all right. Hoke's was a sawmill and commissary and two stores and a loading-chute on a sidetrack from the main line, and all the men in it wore boots and khaki too. Presently the Memphis train came. Boon bought three packages of popcorn-and-molasses and a bottle of beer from the news butch[6] and the boy went to sleep again to the sound of his chewing.

But in Memphis it was not all right. It was as if the high buildings and the hard pavements, the fine carriages and the horse cars[7] and the men in starched collars and neckties made their boots and khaki look a little rougher and a little muddier and made Boon's beard look worse and more unshaven and his face look more and more like he should never have brought it out of the woods at all or at least out of reach of Major de Spain or McCaslin or someone who knew it and could have said, "Dont be afraid. He wont hurt you." He walked through the station, on the slick floor, his face moving as he worked the popcorn out of his teeth with his tongue, his legs spraddled and stiff in the hips as if he were walking on buttered glass, and that blue stubble on his face like the filings from a new gun-barrel. They passed the first saloon. Even through the closed doors the boy could seem to smell the sawdust and the reek of old drink. Boon began to cough. He coughed for something less than a minute. "Damn this cold," he said. "I'd sure like to know where I got it."

"Back there in the station," the boy said.

Boon had started to cough again. He stopped. He looked at the boy. "What?" he said.

"You never had it when we left camp nor on the train either." Boon looked at him, blinking. Then he stopped blinking. He didn't cough again. He said quietly:

"Lend me a dollar. Come on. You've got it. If you ever had one, you've still got it. I dont mean you are tight with your money because you aint. You just dont never seem to ever think of nothing you want. When I was sixteen a dollar bill melted off of me before I even had time to read the name of the bank that issued it."[8] He said quietly: "Let me have a dollar, Ike."

"You promised Major. You promised McCaslin. Not till we get back to camp."

5. Famous boxing matches. John L. Sullivan (1858–1918), heavyweight boxer who vanquished Jake Kilrain (1859–1937) in a seventy-five-round bare-knuckle championship fight held at a lumber camp in Richburg, Mississippi, on July 8, 1889. William H. ("Jack") Dempsey (1895–1983) tried unsuccessfully to regain his world championship from James J. ("Gene") Tunney (1898–1978) on September 22, 1927, before a large audience at Chicago's Soldier Field.   6. A vendor of newspapers and snacks on the train.   7. Horse-drawn streetcars.   8. Before 1865, various Mississippi banks and counties issued their own currency.

"All right," Boon said in that quiet and patient voice. "What can I do on just one dollar? You aint going to lend me another."

"You're damn right I aint," the boy said, his voice quiet too, cold with rage which was not at Boon, remembering: Boon snoring in a hard chair in the kitchen so he could watch the clock and wake him and McCaslin and drive them the seventeen miles in to Jefferson to catch the train to Memphis; the wild, never-bridled Texas paint pony which he had persuaded McCaslin to let him buy and which he and Boon had bought at auction for four dollars and seventy-five cents and fetched home wired between two gentle old mares with pieces of barbed wire and which had never even seen shelled corn before and didn't even know what it was unless the grains were bugs maybe and at last (he was ten and Boon had been ten all his life) Boon said the pony was gentled and with a towsack over its head and four negroes to hold it they backed it into an old two-wheeled cart and hooked up the gear and he and Boon got up and Boon said, "All right, boys. Let him go" and one of the negroes—it was Tennie's Jim—snatched the towsack off and leaped for his life and they lost the first wheel against a post of the open gate only at that moment Boon caught him by the scruff of the neck and flung him into the roadside ditch so he only saw the rest of it in fragments: the other wheel as it slammed through the side gate and crossed the back yard and leaped up onto the gallery and scraps of the cart here and there along the road and Boon vanishing rapidly on his stomach in the leaping and spurting dust and still holding the reins until they broke too and two days later they finally caught the pony seven miles away still wearing the hames[9] and the headstall of the bridle around its neck like a duchess with two necklaces at one time. He gave Boon the dollar.

"All right," Boon said. "Come on in out of the cold."

"I aint cold," he said.

"You can have some lemonade."

"I dont want any lemonade."

The door closed behind him. The sun was well up now. It was a brilliant day, though Ash had said it would rain before night. Already it was warmer; they could run tomorrow. He felt the old lift of the heart, as pristine as ever, as on the first day; he would never lose it, no matter how old in hunting and pursuit: the best, the best of all breathing, the humility and the pride. He must stop thinking about it. Already it seemed to him that he was running, back to the station, to the tracks themselves: the first train going south; he must stop thinking about it. The street was busy. He watched the big Norman draft horses, the Percherons;[1] the trim carriages from which the men in the fine overcoats and the ladies rosy in furs descended and entered the station. (They were still next door to it but one.) Twenty years ago his father had ridden into Memphis as a member of Colonel Sartoris' horse in Forrest's[2] command, up Main street and (the tale told) into the lobby of the Gayoso Hotel where the Yankee officers sat in the leather chairs spitting into the tall bright cuspidors and then out again, scot-free—

9. Curved harness pieces that fit around the neck of a horse.   1. Large, powerful farm horses used, like *Norman draft horses*, for heavy labor.   2. Confederate general Nathan Bedford Forrest (1821–1877). It was actually his brother, William, who rode into the Gayoso Hotel in an unsuccessful attempt to capture Union general Stephen Hurlbut. *Horse:* cavalry. In Faulkner's novels, Colonel Sartoris commanded a cavalry unit under General Forrest.

The door opened behind him. Boon was wiping his mouth on the back of his hand. "All right," he said. "Let's go tend to it and get the hell out of here."

They went and had the suitcase packed. He never knew where or when Boon got the other bottle. Doubtless Mr Semmes gave it to him. When they reached Hoke's again at sundown, it was empty. They could get a return train to Hoke's in two hours; they went straight back to the station as Major de Spain and then McCaslin had told Boon to do and then ordered him to do and had sent the boy along to see that he did. Boon took the first drink from his bottle in the wash room. A man in a uniform cap came to tell him he couldn't drink there and looked at Boon's face once and said nothing. The next time he was pouring into his water glass beneath the edge of a table in the restaurant when the manager (she was a woman) did tell him he couldn't drink there and he went back to the washroom. He had been telling the negro waiter and all the other people in the restaurant who couldn't help but hear him and who had never heard of Lion and didn't want to, about Lion and Old Ben. Then he happened to think of the zoo. He had found out that there was another train to Hoke's at three oclock and so they would spend the time at the zoo and take the three oclock train until he came back from the washroom for the third time. Then they would take the first train back to camp, get Lion and come back to the zoo where, he said, the bears were fed on ice cream and lady fingers and he would match Lion against them all.

So they missed the first train, the one they were supposed to take, but he got Boon onto the three oclock train and they were all right again, with Boon not even going to the washroom now but drinking in the aisle and talking about Lion and the men he buttonholed no more daring to tell Boon he couldn't drink there than the man in the station had dared.

When they reached Hoke's at sundown, Boon was asleep. The boy waked him at last and got him and the suitcase off the train and he even persuaded him to eat some supper at the sawmill commissary. So he was all right when they got in the caboose of the log-train to go back into the woods, with the sun going down red and the sky already overcast and the ground would not freeze tonight. It was the boy who slept now, sitting behind the ruby stove while the springless caboose jumped and clattered and Boon and the brake-man and the conductor talked about Lion and Old Ben because they knew what Boon was talking about because this was home. "Overcast and already thawing," Boon said. "Lion will get him tomorrow."

It would have to be Lion, or somebody. It would not be Boon. He had never hit anything bigger than a squirrel that anybody ever knew, except the negro woman that day when he was shooting at the negro man. He was a big negro and not ten feet away but Boon shot five times with the pistol he had borrowed from Major de Spain's negro coachman and the negro he was shooting at outed with a dollar-and-a-half mail-order pistol and would have burned Boon down with it only it never went off, it just went snicksnick-snicksnicksnick five times and Boon still blasting away and he broke a plate-glass window that cost McCaslin forty-five dollars and hit a negro woman who happened to be passing in the leg only Major de Spain paid for that; he and McCaslin cut cards, the plate-glass window against the negro woman's leg. And the first day on stand this year, the first morning in camp, the buck ran right over Boon; he heard Boon's old pump gun go whow. whow. whow.

whow. whow. and then his voice: "God damn, here he comes! Head him! Head him!" and when he got there the buck's tracks and the five exploded shells were not twenty paces apart.

There were five guests in camp that night, from Jefferson: Mr Bayard Sartoris and his son and General Compson's son and two others. And the next morning he looked out the window, into the gray thin drizzle of daybreak which Ash had predicted, and there they were, standing and squatting beneath the thin rain, almost two dozen of them who had fed Old Ben corn and shoats and even calves for ten years, in their worn hats and hunting coats and overalls which any town negro would have thrown away or burned and only the rubber boots strong and sound, and the worn and blueless guns,³ and some even without guns. While they ate breakfast a dozen more arrived, mounted and on foot: loggers from the camp thirteen miles below and saw-mill men from Hoke's and the only gun among them that one which the log-train conductor carried: so that when they went into the woods this morning Major de Spain led a party almost as strong, excepting that some of them were not armed, as some he had led in the last darkening days of '64 and '65.⁴ The little yard would not hold them. They overflowed it, into the lane where Major de Spain sat his mare while Ash in his dirty apron thrust the greasy cartridges into his carbine⁵ and passed it up to him and the great grave blue dog stood at his stirrup not as a dog stands but as a horse stands, blinking his sleepy topaz eyes at nothing, deaf even to the yelling of the hounds which Boon and Tennie's Jim held on leash.

"We'll put General Compson on Katie this morning," Major de Spain said. "He drew blood last year; if he'd had a mule then that would have stood, he would have—"

"No," General Compson said. "I'm too old to go helling through the woods on a mule or a horse or anything else any more. Besides, I had my chance last year and missed it. I'm going on a stand this morning. I'm going to let that boy ride Katie."

"No, wait," McCaslin said. "Ike's got the rest of his life to hunt bears in. Let somebody else—"

"No," General Compson said. "I want Ike to ride Katie. He's already a better woodsman than you or me either and in another ten years he'll be as good as Walter."

At first he couldn't believe it, not until Major de Spain spoke to him. Then he was up, on the one-eyed mule which would not spook at wild blood, looking down at the dog motionless at Major de Spain's stirrup, looking in the gray streaming light bigger than a calf, bigger than he knew it actually was—the big head, the chest almost as big as his own, the blue hide beneath which the muscles flinched or quivered to no touch since the heart which drove blood to them loved no man and no thing, standing as a horse stands yet different from a horse which infers only weight and speed while Lion inferred not only courage and all else that went to make up the will and desire to pursue and kill, but endurance, the will and desire to endure beyond all imaginable limits of flesh in order to overtake and slay. Then the dog looked at him. It moved its head and looked at him across the trivial uproar of the hounds, out of the yellow eyes as depthless as Boon's, as free as Boon's

---

3. Guns whose blued metal parts have lost their color.   4. Toward the end of the Civil War (1860–65).   5. A gun that is somewhat shorter than a rifle.

of meanness or generosity or gentleness or viciousness. They were just cold and sleepy. Then it blinked, and he knew it was not looking at him and never had been, without even bothering to turn its head away.

That morning he heard the first cry. Lion had already vanished while Sam and Tennie's Jim were putting saddles on the mule and horse which had drawn the wagon and he watched the hounds as they crossed and cast, snuffing and whimpering, until they too disappeared. Then he and Major de Spain and Sam and Tennie's Jim rode after them and heard the first cry out of the wet and thawing woods not two hundred yards ahead, high, with that abject, almost human quality he had come to know, and the other hounds joining in until the gloomed woods rang and clamored. They rode then. It seemed to him that he could actually see the big blue dog boring on, silent, and the bear too: the thick, locomotive-like shape which he had seen that day four years ago crossing the blow-down,[6] crashing on ahead of the dogs faster than he had believed it could have moved, drawing away even from the running mules. He heard a shotgun, once. The woods had opened, they were going fast, the clamor faint and fading on ahead; they passed the man who had fired—a swamper, a pointing arm, a gaunt face, the small black orifice of his yelling studded with rotten teeth.

He heard the changed note in the hounds' uproar and two hundred yards ahead he saw them. The bear had turned. He saw Lion drive in without pausing and saw the bear strike him aside and lunge into the yelling hounds and kill one of them almost in its tracks and whirl and run again. Then they were in a streaming tide of dogs. He heard Major de Spain and Tennie's Jim shouting and the pistol sound of Tennie's Jim's leather thong as he tried to turn them. Then he and Sam Fathers were riding alone. One of the hounds had kept on with Lion though. He recognised its voice. It was the young hound which even a year ago had had no judgment and which, by the lights of the other hounds anyway, still had none. *Maybe that's what courage is,* he thought. "Right," Sam said behind him. "Right. We got to turn him from the river if we can."

Now they were in cane: a brake.[7] He knew the path through it as well as Sam did. They came out of the undergrowth and struck the entrance almost exactly. It would traverse the brake and come out onto a high open ridge above the river. He heard the flat clap of Walter Ewell's rifle, then two more. "No," Sam said. "I can hear the hound. Go on."

They emerged from the narrow roofless tunnel of snapping and hissing cane, still galloping, onto the open ridge below which the thick yellow river, reflectionless in the gray and streaming light, seemed not to move. Now he could hear the hound too. It was not running. The cry was a high frantic yapping and Boon was running along the edge of the bluff, his old gun leaping and jouncing against his back on its sling made of a piece of cotton plowline. He whirled and ran up to them, wild-faced, and flung himself onto the mule behind the boy. "That damn boat!" he cried. "It's on the other side! He went straight across! Lion was too close to him! That little hound too! Lion was so close I couldn't shoot! Go on!" he cried, beating his heels into the mule's flanks. "Go on!"

They plunged down the bank, slipping and sliding in the thawed earth,

6. A tangle of trees and branches blown down by a cyclone or tornado.　　7. A cane brake is a twenty- to thirty-foot-high thicket of sugarcane, often used by bears as winter shelter.

crashing through the willows and into the water. He felt no shock, no cold, he on one side of the swimming mule, grasping the pommel with one hand and holding his gun above the water with the other, Boon opposite him. Sam was behind them somewhere, and then the river, the water about them, was full of dogs. They swam faster than the mules; they were scrabbling up the bank before the mules touched bottom. Major de Spain was whooping from the bank they had just left and, looking back, he saw Tennie's Jim and the horse as they went into the water.

Now the woods ahead of them and the rain-heavy air were one uproar. It rang and clamored; it echoed and broke against the bank behind them and reformed and clamored and rang until it seemed to the boy that all the hounds which had ever bayed game in this land were yelling down at him. He got his leg over the mule as it came up out of the water. Boon didn't try to mount again. He grasped one stirrup as they went up the bank and crashed through the undergrowth which fringed the bluff and saw the bear, on its hind feet, its back against a tree while the bellowing hounds swirled around it and once more Lion drove in, leaping clear of the ground.

This time the bear didn't strike him down. It caught the dog in both arms, almost loverlike, and they both went down. He was off the mule now. He drew back both hammers of the gun but he could see nothing but moiling spotted houndbodies until the bear surged up again. Boon was yelling something, he could not tell what; he could see Lion still clinging to the bear's throat and he saw the bear, half erect, strike one of the hounds with one paw and hurl it five or six feet and then, rising and rising as though it would never stop, stand erect again and begin to rake at Lion's belly with its forepaws. Then Boon was running. The boy saw the gleam of the blade in his hand and watched him leap among the hounds, hurdling them, kicking them aside as he ran, and fling himself astride the bear as he had hurled himself onto the mule, his legs locked around the bear's belly, his left arm under the bear's throat where Lion clung, and the glint of the knife as it rose and fell.

It fell just once. For an instant they almost resembled a piece of statuary: the clinging dog, the bear, the man stride its back, working and probing the buried blade. Then they went down, pulled over backward by Boon's weight, Boon underneath. It was the bear's back which reappeared first but at once Boon was astride it again. He had never released the knife and again the boy saw the almost infinitesimal movement of his arm and shoulder as he probed and sought; then the bear surged erect, raising with it the man and the dog too, and turned and still carrying the man and the dog it took two or three steps toward the woods on its hind feet as a man would have walked and crashed down. It didn't collapse, crumple. It fell all of a piece, as a tree falls, so that all three of them, man dog and bear, seemed to bounce once.

He and Tennie's Jim ran forward. Boon was kneeling at the bear's head. His left ear was shredded, his left coat sleeve was completely gone, his right boot had been ripped from knee to instep; the bright blood thinned in the thin rain down his leg and hand and arm and down the side of his face which was no longer wild but was quite calm. Together they prized Lion's jaws from the bear's throat. "Easy, goddamn it," Boon said. "Cant you see his guts are all out of him?" He began to remove his coat. He spoke to Tennie's Jim in that calm voice: "Bring the boat up. It's about a hundred yards down the bank there. I saw it." Tennie's Jim rose and went away. Then, and he could not remember if it had been a call or an exclamation from Tennie's Jim or if he had glanced up by chance, he saw Tennie's Jim stooping and saw Sam Fathers lying motionless on his face in the trampled mud.

The mule had not thrown him. He remembered that Sam was down too even before Boon began to run. There was no mark on him whatever and when he and Boon turned him over, his eyes were open and he said something in that tongue which he and Joe Baker had used to speak together. But he couldn't move. Tennie's Jim brought the skiff up; they could hear him shouting to Major de Spain across the river. Boon wrapped Lion in his hunting coat and carried him down to the skiff and they carried Sam down and returned and hitched the bear to the one-eyed mule's saddle-bow with Tennie's Jim's leash-thong and dragged him down to the skiff and got him into it and left Tennie's Jim to swim the horse and the two mules back across. Major de Spain caught the bow of the skiff as Boon jumped out and past him before it touched the bank. He looked at Old Ben and said quietly: "Well." Then he walked into the water and leaned down and touched Sam and Sam looked up at him and said something in that old tongue he and Joe Baker spoke. "You dont know what happened?" Major de Spain said.

"No, sir," the boy said. "It wasn't the mule. It wasn't anything. He was off the mule when Boon ran in on the bear. Then we looked up and he was lying on the ground." Boon was shouting at Tennie's Jim, still in the middle of the river.

"Come on, goddamn it!" he said. "Bring me that mule!"

"What do you want with a mule?" Major de Spain said.

Boon didn't even look at him. "I'm going to Hoke's to get the doctor," he said in that calm voice, his face quite calm beneath the steady thinning of the bright blood.

"You need a doctor yourself," Major de Spain said. "Tennie's Jim——"

"Damn that," Boon said. He turned on Major de Spain. His face was still calm, only his voice was a pitch higher. "Cant you see his goddamn guts are all out of him?"

"Boon!" Major de Spain said. They looked at one another. Boon was a good head taller than Major de Spain; even the boy was taller now than Major de Spain.

"I've got to get the doctor," Boon said. "His goddamn guts——"

"All right," Major de Spain said. Tennie's Jim came up out of the water. The horse and the sound mule had already scented Old Ben; they surged and plunged all the way up to the top of the bluff, dragging Tennie's Jim with them, before he could stop them and tie them and come back. Major de Spain unlooped the leather thong of his compass from his buttonhole and gave it to Tennie's Jim. "Go straight to Hoke's," he said. "Bring Doctor Crawford back with you. Tell him there are two men to be looked at. Take my mare. Can you find the road from here?"

"Yes, sir," Tennie's Jim said.

"All right," Major de Spain said. "Go on." He turned to the boy. "Take the mules and the horse and go back and get the wagon. We'll go on down the river in the boat to Coon bridge. Meet us there. Can you find it again?"

"Yes, sir," the boy said.

"All right. Get started."

He went back to the wagon. He realised then how far they had run. It was already afternoon when he put the mules into the traces and tied the horse's lead-rope to the tail-gate. He reached Coon bridge at dusk. The skiff was already there. Before he could see it and almost before he could see the water he had to leap from the tilting wagon, still holding the reins, and work around to where he could grasp the bit and then the ear of the plunging sound mule and dig his heels and hold it until Boon came up the bank. The rope of the led horse had already snapped and it had already disappeared up the road toward camp. They turned the wagon around and took the mules out and he led the sound mule a hundred yards up the road and tied it. Boon had already brought Lion up to the wagon and Sam was sitting up in the skiff now and when they raised him he tried to walk, up the bank and to the wagon and he tried to climb into the wagon but Boon did not wait; he picked Sam up bodily and set him on the seat. Then they hitched Old Ben to the one-eyed mule's saddle again and dragged him up the bank and set two skid-poles[8] into the open tail-gate and got him into the wagon and he went and got the sound mule[9] and Boon fought it into the traces, striking it across its hard hollow-sounding face until it came into position and stood trembling. Then the rain came down, as though it had held off all day waiting on them.

They returned to camp through it, through the streaming and sightless dark, hearing long before they saw any light the horn and the spaced shots to guide them. When they came to Sam's dark little hut he tried to stand up. He spoke again in the tongue of the old fathers; then he said clearly: "Let me out. Let me out."

"He hasn't got any fire," Major said. "Go on!" he said sharply.

But Sam was struggling now, trying to stand up. "Let me out, master," he said. "Let me go home."

So he stopped the wagon and Boon got down and lifted Sam out. He did not wait to let Sam try to walk this time. He carried him into the hut and Major de Spain got light on a paper spill from the buried embers on the hearth and lit the lamp and Boon put Sam on his bunk and drew off his boots and Major de Spain covered him and the boy was not there, he was holding the mules, the sound one which was trying again to bolt since when the wagon stopped Old Ben's scent drifted forward again along the streaming blackness of air, but Sam's eyes were probably open again on that profound look which saw further than them or the hut, further than the death of a bear and the dying of a dog. Then they went on, toward the long wailing of the horn and the shots which seemed each to linger intact somewhere in the thick streaming air until the next spaced report joined and blended with it, to the lighted house, the bright streaming windows, the quiet faces as Boon entered, bloody and quite calm, carrying the bundled coat. He laid Lion, blood coat and all, on his stale sheetless pallet bed which not even Ash, as deft in the house as a woman, could ever make smooth.

The sawmill doctor from Hoke's was already there. Boon would not let the doctor touch him until he had seen to Lion. He wouldn't risk giving Lion chloroform. He put the entrails back and sewed him up without it while Major de Spain held his head and Boon his feet. But he never tried to move. He lay there, the yellow eyes open upon nothing while the quiet men

---

8. They made a ramp of two poles set into the opened back of the wagon.   9. As opposed to the other, one-eyed mule.

in the new hunting clothes and in the old ones crowded into the little airless room rank with the smell of Boon's body and garments, and watched. Then the doctor cleaned and disinfected Boon's face and arm and leg and bandaged them and, the boy in front with a lantern and the doctor and McCaslin and Major de Spain and General Compson following, they went to Sam Fathers' hut. Tennie's Jim had built up the fire; he squatted before it, dozing. Sam had not moved since Boon had put him in the bunk and Major de Spain had covered him with the blankets, yet he opened his eyes and looked from one to another of the faces and when McCaslin touched his shoulder and said, "Sam. The doctor wants to look at you," he even drew his hands out of the blanket and began to fumble at his shirt buttons until McCaslin said, "Wait. We'll do it." They undressed him. He lay there—the copper-brown, almost hairless body, the old man's body, the old man, the wild man not even one generation from the woods, childless, kinless, people-less—motionless, his eyes open but no longer looking at any of them, while the doctor examined him and drew the blankets up and put the stethoscope back into his bag and snapped the bag and only the boy knew that Sam too was going to die.

"Exhaustion," the doctor said. "Shock maybe. A man his age swimming rivers in December. He'll be all right. Just make him stay in bed for a day or two. Will there be somebody here with him?"

"There will be somebody here," Major de Spain said.

They went back to the house, to the rank little room where Boon still sat on the pallet bed with Lion's head under his hand while the men, the ones who had hunted behind Lion and the ones who had never seen him before today, came quietly in to look at him and went away. Then it was dawn and they all went out into the yard to look at Old Ben, with his eyes open too and his lips snarled back from his worn teeth and his mutilated foot and the little hard lumps under his skin which were the old bullets (there were fifty-two of them, buckshot rifle and ball) and the single almost invisible slit under his left shoulder where Boon's blade had finally found his life. Then Ash began to beat on the bottom of the dishpan with a heavy spoon to call them to breakfast and it was the first time he could remember hearing no sound from the dogs under the kitchen while they were eating. It was as if the old bear, even dead there in the yard, was a more potent terror still than they could face without Lion between them.

The rain had stopped during the night. By midmorning the thin sun appeared, rapidly burning away mist and cloud, warming the air and the earth; it would be one of those windless Mississippi December days which are a sort of Indian summer's Indian summer. They moved Lion out to the front gallery, into the sun. It was Boon's idea. "Goddamn it," he said, "he never did want to stay in the house until I made him. You know that." He took a crowbar and loosened the floor boards under his pallet bed so it could be raised, mattress and all, without disturbing Lion's position, and they carried him out to the gallery and put him down facing the woods.

Then he and the doctor and McCaslin and Major de Spain went to Sam's hut. This time Sam didn't open his eyes and his breathing was so quiet, so peaceful that they could hardly see that he breathed. The doctor didn't even take out his stethoscope nor even touch him. "He's all right," the doctor said. "He didn't even catch cold. He just quit."

"Quit?" McCaslin said.

"Yes. Old people do that sometimes. Then they get a good night's sleep or maybe it's just a drink of whisky, and they change their minds."

They returned to the house. And then they began to arrive—the swamp-dwellers, the gaunt men who ran traplines and lived on quinine and coons and river water, the farmers of little corn-and-cotton-patches along the bottom's edge whose fields and cribs and pig-pens the old bear had rifled, the loggers from the camp and the sawmill men from Hoke's and the town men from further away than that, whose hounds the old bear had slain and traps and deadfalls he had wrecked and whose lead he carried. They came up mounted and on foot and in wagons, to enter the yard and look at him and then go on to the front where Lion lay, filling the little yard and overflowing it until there were almost a hundred of them squatting and standing in the warm and drowsing sunlight, talking quietly of hunting, of the game and the dogs which ran it, of hounds and bear and deer and men of yesterday vanished from the earth, while from time to time the great blue dog would open his eyes, not as if he were listening to them but as though to look at the woods for a moment before closing his eyes again, to remember the woods or to see that they were still there. He died at sundown.

Major de Spain broke camp that night. They carried Lion into the woods, or Boon carried him that is, wrapped in a quilt from his bed, just as he had refused to let anyone else touch Lion yesterday until the doctor got there; Boon carrying Lion, and the boy and General Compson and Walter and still almost fifty of them following with lanterns and lighted pine-knots—men from Hoke's and even further, who would have to ride out of the bottom in the dark, and swampers and trappers who would have to walk even, scattering toward the little hidden huts where they lived. And Boon would let nobody else dig the grave either and lay Lion in it and cover him and then General Compson stood at the head of it while the blaze and smoke of the pine-knots streamed away among the winter branches and spoke as he would have spoken over a man. Then they returned to camp. Major de Spain and McCaslin and Ash had rolled and tied all the bedding. The mules were hitched to the wagon and pointed out of the bottom and the wagon was already loaded and the stove in the kitchen was cold and the table was set with scraps of cold food and bread and only the coffee was hot when the boy ran into the kitchen where Major de Spain and McCaslin had already eaten. "What?" he cried. "What? I'm not going."

"Yes," McCaslin said, "we're going out tonight. Major wants to get on back home."

"No!" he said. "I'm going to stay."

"You've got to be back in school Monday. You've already missed a week more than I intended. It will take you from now until Monday to catch up. Sam's all right. You heard Doctor Crawford. I'm going to leave Boon and Tennie's Jim both to stay with him until he feels like getting up."

He was panting. The others had come in. He looked rapidly and almost frantically around at the other faces. Boon had a fresh bottle. He upended it and started the cork by striking the bottom of the bottle with the heel of his hand and drew the cork with his teeth and spat it out and drank. "You're damn right you're going back to school," Boon said. "Or I'll burn the tail off of you myself if Cass dont, whether you are sixteen or sixty. Where in hell do you expect to get without education? Where would Cass be? Where in hell would I be if I hadn't never went to school?"

He looked at McCaslin again. He could feel his breath coming shorter and shorter and shallower and shallower, as if there were not enough air in the kitchen for that many to breathe. "This is just Thursday. I'll come home Sunday night on one of the horses. I'll come home Sunday, then. I'll make up the time I lost studying Sunday night. McCaslin," he said, without even despair.

"No, I tell you," McCaslin said. "Sit down here and eat your supper. We're going out to—"

"Hold up, Cass," General Compson said. The boy did not know General Compson had moved until he put his hand on his shoulder. "What is it, bud?" he said.

"I've got to stay," he said. "I've got to."

"All right," General Compson said. "You can stay. If missing an extra week of school is going to throw you so far behind you'll have to sweat to find out what some hired pedagogue put between the covers of a book, you better quit altogether.—And you shut up, Cass," he said, though McCaslin had not spoken. "You've got one foot straddled into a farm and the other foot straddled into a bank; you aint even got a good hand-hold where this boy was already an old man long before you damned Sartorises and Edmondses invented farms and banks to keep yourselves from having to find out what this boy was born knowing and fearing too maybe but without being afraid, that could go ten miles on a compass because he wanted to look at a bear none of us had ever got near enough to put a bullet in and looked at the bear and came the ten miles back on the compass in the dark; maybe by God that's the why and the wherefore of farms and banks.—I reckon you still aint going to tell what it is?"

But still he could not. "I've got to stay," he said.

"All right," General Compson said. "There's plenty of grub left. And you'll come home Sunday, like you promised McCaslin? Not Sunday night: Sunday."

"Yes, sir," he said.

"All right," General Compson said. "Sit down and eat, boys," he said. "Let's get started. It's going to be cold before we get home."

They ate. The wagon was already loaded and ready to depart; all they had to do was to get into it. Boon would drive them out to the road, to the farmer's stable where the surrey had been left. He stood beside the wagon, in silhouette on the sky, turbaned like a Paythan[1] and taller than any there, the bottle tilted. Then he flung the bottle from his lips without even lowering it, spinning and glinting in the faint starlight, empty. "Them that's going," he said, "get in the goddamn wagon. Them that aint, get out of the goddamn way." The others got in. Boon mounted to the seat beside General Compson and the wagon moved, on into the obscurity until the boy could no longer see it, even the moving density of it amid the greater night. But he could still hear it, for a long while: the slow, deliberate banging of the wooden frame as it lurched from rut to rut. And he could hear Boon even when he could no longer hear the wagon. He was singing, harsh, tuneless, loud.

1. Or Pathan; member of an ethnic group living in parts of Afghanistan and northwest Pakistan.

That was Thursday. On Saturday morning Tennie's Jim left on McCaslin's woods-horse which had not been out of the bottom one time now in six years, and late that afternoon rode through the gate on the spent horse and on to the commissary where McCaslin was rationing[2] the tenants and the wage-hands for the coming week, and this time McCaslin forestalled any necessity or risk of having to wait while Major de Spain's surrey was being horsed and harnessed. He took their own, and with Tennie's Jim already asleep in the back seat he drove in to Jefferson and waited while Major de Spain changed to boots and put on his overcoat, and they drove the thirty miles in the dark of that night and at daybreak on Sunday morning they swapped to the waiting mare and mule and as the sun rose they rode out of the jungle and onto the low ridge where they had buried Lion: the low mound of unannealed earth where Boon's spade-marks still showed and beyond the grave the platform of freshly cut saplings bound between four posts and the blanket-wrapped bundle upon the platform[3] and Boon and the boy squatting between the platform and the grave until Boon, the bandage removed, ripped, from his head so that the long scoriations of Old Ben's claws resembled crusted tar in the sunlight, sprang up and threw down upon them with the old gun with which he had never been known to hit anything although McCaslin was already off the mule, kicked both feet free of the irons and vaulted down before the mule had stopped, walking toward Boon.

"Stand back," Boon said. "By God, you wont touch him. Stand back, McCaslin." Still McCaslin came on, fast yet without haste.

"Cass!" Major de Spain said. Then he said "Boon! You, Boon!" and he was down too and the boy rose too, quickly, and still McCaslin came on not fast but steady and walked up to the grave and reached his hand steadily out, quickly yet still not fast, and took hold the gun by the middle so that he and Boon faced one another across Lion's grave, both holding the gun, Boon's spent indomitable amazed and frantic face almost a head higher than McCaslin's beneath the black scoriations of beast's claws and then Boon's chest began to heave as though there were not enough air in all the woods, in all the wilderness, for all of them, for him and anyone else, even for him alone.

"Turn it loose, Boon," McCaslin said.

"You damn little spindling—" Boon said. "Dont you know I can take it away from you? Dont you know I can tie it around your neck like a damn cravat?"

"Yes," McCaslin said. "Turn it loose, Boon."

"This is the way he wanted it. He told us. He told us exactly how to do it. And by God you aint going to move him. So we did it like he said, and I been sitting here ever since to keep the damn wildcats and varmints away from him and by God—" Then McCaslin had the gun, down-slanted while he pumped the slide, the five shells snicking out of it so fast that the last one was almost out before the first one touched the ground and McCaslin dropped the gun behind him without once having taken his eyes from Boon's.

"Did you kill him, Boon?" he said. Then Boon moved. He turned, he moved like he was still drunk and then for a moment blind too, one hand out as he

2. Distributing food and materials.   3. Chickasaw burial customs held that the body of someone dying away from home should be placed on a platform to preserve it from wild animals.

blundered toward the big tree and seemed to stop walking before he reached the tree so that he plunged, fell toward it, flinging up both hands and catching himself against the tree and turning until his back was against it, backing with the tree's trunk his wild spent scoriated face and the tremendous heave and collapse of his chest, McCaslin following, facing him again, never once having moved his eyes from Boon's eyes. "Did you kill him, Boon?"

"No!" Boon said. "No!"

"Tell the truth," McCaslin said. "I would have done it if he had asked me to." Then the boy moved. He was between them, facing McCaslin; the water felt as if it had burst and sprung not from his eyes alone but from his whole face, like sweat.

"Leave him alone!" he cried. "Goddamn it! Leave him alone!"

4

then he was twenty-one. He could say it, himself and his cousin juxtaposed not against the wilderness but against the tamed land which was to have been his heritage,[4] the land which old Carothers McCaslin his grandfather had bought with white man's money from the wild men whose grandfathers without guns hunted it, and tamed and ordered or believed he had tamed and ordered it for the reason that the human beings he held in bondage and in the power of life and death had removed the forest from it and in their sweat scratched the surface of it to a depth of perhaps fourteen inches in order to grow something out of it which had not been there before and which could be translated back into the money he who believed he had bought it had had to pay to get it and hold it and a reasonable profit too: and for which reason old Carothers McCaslin, knowing better, could raise his children, his descendants and heirs, to believe the land was his to hold and bequeath since the strong and ruthless man has a cynical foreknowledge of his own vanity and pride and strength and a contempt for all his get: just as, knowing better, Major de Spain and his fragment of that wilderness which was bigger and older than any recorded deed: just as, knowing better, old Thomas Sutpen, from whom Major de Spain had had his fragment for money: just as Ikkemotubbe, the Chickasaw chief, from whom Thomas Sutpen had had the fragment for money or rum or whatever it was, knew in his turn that not even a fragment of it had been his to relinquish or sell

not against the wilderness but against the land, not in pursuit and lust but in relinquishment, and in the commissary as it should have been, not the heart perhaps but certainly the solar-plexus of the repudiated and relinquished: the square, galleried, wooden building squatting like a portent above the fields whose laborers it still held in thrall '65[5] or no and placarded over with advertisements for snuff and cures for chills and salves and potions manufactured and sold by white men to bleach the pigment and straighten the hair of negroes that they might resemble the very race which for two hundred years had held them in bondage and from which for another hundred years not even a bloody civil war would have set them completely free

himself and his cousin amid the old smells of cheese and salt meat and

4. Ike renounced his inherited property in favor of his first cousin once removed, McCaslin (Cass) Edmonds.   5. Even after the end of the Civil War in 1865, the freed slaves must depend on working in the fields.

kerosene and harness, the ranked shelves of tobacco and overalls and bottled medicine and thread and plow-bolts, the barrels and kegs of flour and meal and molasses and nails, the wall pegs dependant with plowlines and plow-collars and hames and trace-chains, and the desk and the shelf above it on which rested the ledgers in which McCaslin recorded the slow outward trickle of food and supplies and equipment which returned each fall as cotton made and ginned[6] and sold (two threads frail as truth and impalpable as equators yet cable-strong to bind for life them who made the cotton to the land their sweat fell on), and the older ledgers clumsy and archaic in size and shape, on the yellowed pages of which were recorded in the faded hand of his father Theophilus and his uncle Amodeus during the two decades before the Civil War, the manumission in title at least of Carothers Mc-Caslin's slaves:

'Relinquish,' McCaslin said. 'Relinquish. You, the direct male descendant of him who saw the opportunity and took it, bought the land, took the land, got the land no matter how, held it to bequeath, no matter how, out of the old grant, the first patent, when it was a wilderness of wild beasts and wilder men, and cleared it, translated it into something to bequeath to his children, worthy of bequeathment for his descendants' ease and security and pride and to perpetuate his name and accomplishments. Not only the male descendant but the only and last descendant in the male line and in the third generation, while I am not only four generations from old Carothers, I derived through a woman and the very McCaslin in my name is mine only by sufferance and courtesy and my grandmother's pride in what that man accomplished whose legacy and monument you think you can repudiate.' and he[7]

'I cant repudiate it. It was never mine to repudiate. It was never Father's and Uncle Buddy's to bequeath me to repudiate because it was never Grand-father's to bequeath them to bequeath me to repudiate because it was never old Ikkemotubbe's to sell to Grandfather for bequeathment and repudiation. Because it was never Ikkemotubbe's fathers' fathers' to bequeath Ikkemo-tubbe to sell to Grandfather or any man because on the instant when Ikke-motubbe discovered, realised, that he could sell it for money, on that instant it ceased ever to have been his forever, father to father to father, and the man who bought it bought nothing.'

'Bought nothing?' and he

'Bought nothing. Because He told in the Book how He created the earth, made it and looked at it and said it was all right, and then He made man.[8] He made the earth first and peopled it with dumb creatures, and then He created man to be His overseer on the earth and to hold suzerainty over the earth and the animals on it in His name, not to hold for himself and his descendants inviolable title forever, generation after generation, to the oblongs and squares of the earth, but to hold the earth mutual and intact in the communal anonymity of brotherhood, and all the fee He asked was pity and humility and sufferance and endurance and the sweat of his face for bread. And I know what you are going to say,' he said: 'That nevertheless Grandfather—' and McCaslin

---

6. I.e., cleaned of its seeds in a machine called the cotton gin.   7. Ike speaks. *And he* and *and McCaslin* indicate the alternation of speakers, an alternation that is held in abeyance from p. 1763 to p. 1766 while Isaac recalls reading and deciphering the family ledgers.   8. The first of a series of references to the biblical Book of Genesis.

'—did own it. And not the first. Not alone and not the first since, as your Authority states, man was dispossessed of Eden. Nor yet the second and still not alone, on down through the tedious and shabby chronicle of His chosen sprung from Abraham,[9] and of the sons of them who dispossessed Abraham, and of the five hundred years during which half the known world and all it contained was chattel to one city[1] as this plantation and all the life it contained was chattel and revokeless thrall to this commissary store and those ledgers yonder during your grandfather's life, and the next thousand years while men fought over the fragments of that collapse until at last even the fragments were exhausted and men snarled over the gnawed bones of the old world's worthless evening until an accidental egg[2] discovered to them a new hemisphere. So let me say it: That nevertheless and notwithstanding old Carothers did own it. Bought it, got it, no matter; kept it, held it, no matter; bequeathed it: else why do you stand here relinquishing and repudiating? Held it, kept it for fifty years until you could repudiate it, while He—this Arbiter, this Architect, this Umpire—condoned—or did He? looked down and saw—or did He? Or at least did nothing: saw, and could not, or did not see; saw, and would not, or perhaps He would not see—perverse, impotent, or blind: which?' and he

'Dispossessed.' and McCaslin

'What?' and he

'Dispossessed. Not impotent: He didn't condone; not blind, because He watched it. And let me say it. Dispossessed of Eden. Dispossessed of Canaan,[3] and those who dispossessed him dispossessed him dispossessed, and the five hundred years of absentee landlords in the Roman bagnios, and the thousand years[4] of wild men from the northern woods who dispossessed them and devoured their ravished substance ravished in turn again and then snarled in what you call the old world's worthless twilight over the old world's gnawed bones, blasphemous in His name until He used a simple egg to discover to them a new world where a nation of people could be founded in humility and pity and sufferance and pride of one to another. And Grandfather did own the land nevertheless and notwithstanding because He permitted it, not impotent and not condoning and not blind because He ordered and watched it. He saw the land already accursed even as Ikkemotubbe and Ikkemotubbe's father old Issetibbeha and old Issetibbeha's fathers too held it, already tainted even before any white man owned it by what Grandfather and his kind, his fathers, had brought into the new land which He had vouch-safed them out of pity and sufferance, on condition of pity and humility and sufferance and endurance, from that old world's corrupt and worthless twilight as though in the sailfuls of the old world's tainted wind which drove the ships—' and McCaslin

'Ah.'

'—and no hope for the land anywhere so long as Ikkemotubbe and Ikke-motubbe's descendants held it in unbroken succession. Maybe He saw that only by voiding the land for a time of Ikkemotubbe's blood and substituting

9. The Jews.   1. Rome at the height of its power (78 B.C.–A.D. 476).   2. An anecdote relates that Christopher Columbus, responding to those who belittled his achievement in discovering the New World, challenged his critics to make an egg stand on end. After they failed, he positioned the egg by first tapping one end to flatten it—showing that the difficult part is to be the first to find the solution.   3. The Bible's Promised Land, "flowing with milk and honey" (Exodus 3.8).   4. Beginning about A.D. 350, northern invaders (including Huns and Vikings) overran Europe and Asia. *Bagnios:* Roman public baths, meeting places, and sometimes brothels.

for it another blood, could He accomplish His purpose. Maybe He knew already what that other blood would be, maybe it was more than justice that only the white man's blood was available and capable to raise the white man's curse, more than vengeance when—' and McCaslin

'Ah.'

'—when He used the blood which had brought in the evil to destroy the evil as doctors use fever to burn up fever, poison to slay poison. Maybe He chose Grandfather out of all of them He might have picked. Maybe He knew that Grandfather himself would not serve His purpose because Grandfather was born too soon too, but that Grandfather would have descendants, the right descendants; maybe He had foreseen already the descendants Grand-father would have, maybe He saw already in Grandfather the seed progeni-tive of the three generations He saw it would take to set at least some of His lowly people free—' and McCaslin

'The sons of Ham!⁵ You who quote the Book: the sons of Ham.' and he

'There are some things He said in the Book, and some things reported of Him that He did not say. And I know what you will say now: That if truth is one thing to me and another thing to you, how will we choose which is truth? You dont need to choose. The heart already knows. He didn't have His Book written to be read by what must elect and choose, but by the heart, not by the wise of the earth because maybe they dont need it or maybe the wise no longer have any heart, but by the doomed and lowly of the earth who have nothing else to read with but the heart. Because the men who wrote his Book for Him were writing about truth and there is only one truth and it covers all things that touch the heart.' and McCaslin

'So these men who transcribed His Book for Him were sometime liars.' and he

'Yes. Because they were human men. They were trying to write down the heart's truth out of the heart's driving complexity, for all the complex and troubled hearts which would beat after them. What they were trying to tell, what He wanted said, was too simple. Those for whom they transcribed His words could not have believed them. It had to be expounded in the everyday terms which they were familiar with and could comprehend, not only those who listened but those who told it too, because if they who were that near to Him as to have been elected from among all who breathed and spoke language to transcribe and relay His words, could comprehend truth only through the complexity of passion and lust and hate and fear which drives the heart, what distance back to truth must they traverse whom truth could only reach by word-of-mouth?' and McCaslin

'I might answer that, since you have taken to proving your points and disproving mine by the same text, I dont know. But I dont say that, because you have answered yourself: No time at all if, as you say, the heart knows truth, the infallible and unerring heart. And perhaps you are right, since although you admitted three generations from old Carothers to you, there were not three. There were not even completely two. Uncle Buck and Uncle Buddy. And they not the first and not alone. A thousand other Bucks and

---

5. Noah's sons were Shem, Ham, and Japheth, described in the Old Testament as ancestors of the various human races. When Ham saw his father's nakedness, Noah cursed him and condemned Ham's son, Canaan, to be the perpetual servant of Shem and Japheth (Genesis 9.25–27). Since Ham represented the Canaanite (Mideastern) and African peoples, this passage was often used to justify the exploitation of blacks.

Buddies in less than two generations and sometimes less than one in this land which so you claim God created and man himself cursed and tainted. Not to mention 1865.' and he

'Yes. More men than Father and Uncle Buddy,' not even glancing toward the shelf above the desk, nor did McCaslin. They did not need to. To him it was as though the ledgers in their scarred cracked leather bindings were being lifted down one by one in their fading sequence and spread open on the desk or perhaps upon some apocryphal Bench or even Altar or perhaps before the Throne Itself for a last perusal and contemplation and refreshment of the Allknowledgeable before the yellowed pages and the brown thin ink in which was recorded the injustice and a little at least of its amelioration and restitution faded back forever into the anonymous communal original dust

the yellowed pages scrawled in fading ink by the hand first of his grandfather and then of his father and uncle, bachelors up to and past fifty and then sixty, the one who ran the plantation and the farming of it and the other who did the housework and the cooking and continued to do it even after his twin married and the boy himself was born

the two brothers who as soon as their father was buried moved out of the tremendously-conceived, the almost barn-like edifice which he had not even completed, into a one-room log cabin which the two of them built themselves and added other rooms to while they lived in it, refusing to allow any slave to touch any timber of it other than the actual raising into place the logs which two men alone could not handle, and domiciled all the slaves in the big house some of the windows of which were still merely boarded up with odds and ends of plank or with the skins of bear and deer nailed over the empty frames: each sundown the brother who superintended the farming would parade the negroes as a first sergeant dismisses a company, and herd them willynilly, man woman and child, without question protest or recourse, into the tremendous abortive edifice scarcely yet out of embryo, as if even old Carothers McCaslin had paused aghast at the concrete indication of his own vanity's boundless conceiving: he would call his mental roll and herd them in and with a hand-wrought nail as long as a flenching-knife[6] and suspended from a short deer-hide thong attached to the door-jamb for that purpose, he would nail to the door of that house which lacked half its windows and had no hinged back door at all, so that presently and for fifty years afterward, when the boy himself was big to hear and remember it, there was in the land a sort of folk-tale: of the countryside all night long full of skulking McCaslin slaves dodging the moonlit roads and the Patrol-riders[7] to visit other plantations, and of the unspoken gentlemen's agreement between the two white men and the two dozen black ones that, after the white man had counted them and driven the home-made nail into the front door at sundown, neither of the white men would go around behind the house and look at the back door, provided that all the negroes were behind the front one when the brother who drove it drew out the nail again at daybreak

the twins who were identical even in their handwriting, unless you had specimens side by side to compare, and even when both hands appeared on

6. Or flensing knife; a long flaying knife.   7. Groups of four men who rode the countryside to catch slaves who left their plantation without permission.

the same page (as often happened, as if, long since past any oral intercourse, they had used the diurnally advancing pages to conduct the unavoidable business of the compulsion which had traversed all the waste wilderness of North Mississippi in 1830 and '40[8] and singled them out to drive) they both looked as though they had been written by the same perfectly normal ten-year-old boy, even to the spelling, except that the spelling did not improve as one by one the slaves which Carothers McCaslin had inherited and pur-chased—Roscius and Phoebe and Thucydides and Eunice and their descen-dants, and Sam Fathers and his mother for both of whom he had swapped an underbred trotting gelding to old Ikkemotubbe, the Chickasaw chief from whom he had likewise bought the land, and Tennie Beauchamp whom the twin Amodeus had won from a neighbor in a poker-game, and the anomaly calling itself Percival Brownlee which the twin Theophilus had purchased, neither he nor his brother ever knew why apparently, from Bedford Forrest while he was still only a slave-dealer and not yet a general (It was a single page, not long and covering less than a year, not seven months in fact, begun in the hand which the boy had learned to distinguish as that of his father:

> Percavil Brownly 26yr Old. cleark @ Bookepper. bought from N. B. Forest at Cold Water[9] 3 Mar 1856 $265. dolars

and beneath that, in the same hand:

> 5 mar 1856 No bookepper any way Cant read. Can write his Name but I already put that down My self Says he can Plough but dont look like it to Me. sent to Feild to day Mar 5 1856

and the same hand:

> 6 Mar 1856 Cant plough either Says he aims to be a Precher so may be he can lead live stock to Crick to Drink

and this time it was the other, the hand which he now recognised as his uncle's when he could see them both on the same page:

> Mar 23th 1856 Cant do that either Except one at a Time Get shut of him

then the first again:

> 24 Mar 1856 Who in hell would buy him

then the second:

> 19th of Apr 1856 Nobody You put yourself out of Market at Cold Water two months ago I never said sell him Free him

the first:

> 22 Apr 1856 Ill get it out of him

the second:

> Jun 13th 1856 How $1 per yr 265$ 265 yrs Wholl sign his Free paper[1]

then the first again:

---

8. Chickasaw and Choctaw lands were sold cheaply to white settlers, starting a boom in land speculation that was known nationally as "Flush Times."   9. I.e., Coldwater, Mississippi.   1. A document attesting the free status of an ex-slave.

> 1 Oct 1856 Mule josephine Broke Leg @ shot Wrong stall wrong niger wrong everything $100. dolars

and the same:

> 2 Oct 1856 Freed Debit McCaslin @ McCaslin $265. dolars

then the second again:

> Oct 3th Debit Theophilus McCaslin Niger 265$ Mule 100$ 365$ He hasnt gone yet Father should be here

then the first:

> 3 Oct 1856 Son of a bitch wont leave What would father done

the second:

> 29th of Oct 1856 Renamed him

the first:

> 31 Oct 1856 Renamed him what

the second:

> Chrstms 1856 Spintrius[2]

) took substance and even a sort of shadowy life with their passions and complexities too as page followed page and year year; all there, not only the general and condoned injustice and its slow amortization but the specific tragedy which had not been condoned and could never be amortized, the new page and the new ledger, the hand which he could now recognise at first glance as his father's:

> Father dide Lucius Quintus Carothers McCaslin, Callina 1772 Missippy 1837. Dide and burid 27 June 1837
> Roskus. rased by Granfather in Callina Dont know how old. Freed 27 June 1837 Dont want to leave. Dide and Burid 12 Jan 1841
> Fibby Roskus Wife. bought by granfather in Callina says Fifty Freed 27 June 1837 Dont want to leave. Dide and burd 1 Aug 1849
> Thucydus Roskus @ Fibby Son born in Callina 1779. Refused 10acre peace fathers Will 28 Jun 1837 Refused Cash offer $200. dolars from A. @ T. McCaslin 28 Jun 1837 Wants to stay and work it out

and beneath this and covering the next five pages and almost that many years, the slow, day-by-day accrument of the wages allowed him and the food and clothing—the molasses and meat and meal, the cheap durable shirts and jeans and shoes and now and then a coat against rain and cold—charged against the slowly yet steadily mounting sum of balance (and it would seem to the boy that he could actually see the black man, the slave whom his white owner had forever manumitted by the very act from which the black man could never be free so long as memory lasted, entering the commissary, asking permission perhaps of the white man's son to see the ledger-page which he could not even read, not even asking for the white man's word,

---

2. From a Latin word meaning "male prostitute."

which he would have had to accept for the reason that there was absolutely no way under the sun for him to test it, as to how the account stood, how much longer before he could go and never return, even if only as far as Jefferson seventeen miles away) on to the double pen-stroke closing the final entry:

> 3 Nov 1841 By Cash to Thucydus McCaslin $200. dolars Set Up blaksmith in J. Dec 1841 Dide and burid in J. 17 feb 1854
> Eunice Bought by Father in New Orleans 1807 $650. dolars. Marrid to Thucydus 1809 Drownd in Crick Cristmas Day 1832

and then the other hand appeared, the first time he had seen it in the ledger to distinguish it as his uncle's, the cook and housekeeper whom even McCaslin, who had known him and the boy's father for sixteen years before the boy was born, remembered as sitting all day long in the rocking chair from which he cooked the food, before the kitchen fire on which he cooked it:

> June 21th 1833 Drownd herself

and the first:

> 23 Jun 1833 Who in hell ever heard of a niger drownding him self

and the second, unhurried, with a complete finality; the two identical entries might have been made with a rubber stamp save for the date:

> Aug 13th 1833 Drownd herself

and he thought *But why? But why?* He was sixteen then. It was neither the first time he had been alone in the commissary nor the first time he had taken down the old ledgers familiar on their shelf above the desk ever since he could remember. As a child and even after nine and ten and eleven, when he had learned to read, he would look up at the scarred and cracked backs and ends but with no particular desire to open them, and though he intended to examine them someday because he realised that they probably contained a chronological and much more comprehensive though doubtless tedious record than he would ever get from any other source, not alone of his own flesh and blood but of all his people, not only the whites but the black one too, who were as much a part of his ancestry as his white progenitors, and of the land which they had all held and used in common and fed from and on and would continue to use in common without regard to color or titular ownership, it would only be on some idle day when he was old and perhaps even bored a little since what the old books contained would be after all these years fixed immutably, finished, unalterable, harmless. Then he was sixteen. He knew what he was going to find before he found it. He got the commissary key from McCaslin's room after midnight while McCaslin was asleep and with the commissary door shut and locked behind him and the forgotten lantern stinking anew the rank dead icy air, he leaned above the yellowed page and thought not Why drowned herself, but thinking what he believed his father had thought when he found his brother's first comment: Why did Uncle Buddy think she had drowned herself? finding, beginning to find on the next succeeding page what he knew he would find, only this was still not it because he already knew this:

> *Tomasina called Tomy Daughter of Thucydus @ Eunice Born 1810 dide in Child bed June 1833 and Burd. Yr stars fell*[3]

nor the next:

> *Turl Son of Thucydus @ Eunice Tomy born Jun 1833 yr stars fell Fathers will*

and nothing more, no tedious recording filling this page of wages day by day and food and clothing charged against them, no entry of his death and burial because he had outlived his white half-brothers and the books which McCaslin kept did not include obituaries: just *Fathers will* and he had seen that too: old Carothers' bold cramped hand far less legible than his sons' even and not much better in spelling, who while capitalising almost every noun and verb, made no effort to punctuate or construct whatever, just as he made no effort either to explain or obfuscate the thousand-dollar legacy to the son of an unmarried slave-girl, to be paid only at the child's coming-of-age, bearing the consequence of the act of which there was still no definite incontrovertible proof that he acknowledged, not out of his own substance but penalising his sons with it, charging them a cash forfeit on the accident of their own paternity; not even a bribe for silence toward his own fame since his fame would suffer only after he was no longer present to defend it, flinging almost contemptuously, as he might a cast-off hat or pair of shoes, the thousand dollars which could have had no more reality to him under those conditions than it would have to the negro, the slave who would not even see it until he came of age, twenty-one years too late to begin to learn what money was. *So I reckon that was cheaper than saying My son to a nigger* he thought. *Even if My son wasn't but just two words. But there must have been love* he thought. *Some sort of love. Even what he would have called love: not just an afternoon's or a night's spittoon* There was the old man, old, within five years of his life's end, long a widower and, since his sons were not only bachelors but were approaching middleage, lonely in the house and doubt-less even bored since his plantation was established now and functioning and there was enough money now, too much of it probably for a man whose vices even apparently remained below his means; there was the girl, hus-bandless and young, only twenty-three when the child was born: perhaps he had sent for her at first out of loneliness, to have a young voice and movement in the house, summoned her, bade her mother send her each morning to sweep the floors and make the beds and the mother acquiescing since that was probably already understood, already planned: the only child of a couple who were not field hands and who held themselves something above the other slaves not alone for that reason but because the husband and his father and mother too had been inherited by the white man from his father, and the white man himself had travelled three hundred miles and better to New Orleans in a day when men travelled by horseback or steamboat, and bought the girl's mother as a wife for

3. The great meteor shower of November 12, 1833.

and that was all. The old frail pages seemed to turn of their own accord even while he thought *His own daughter His own daughter. No No Not even him* back to that one where the white man (not even a widower then) who never went anywhere any more than his sons in their time ever did and who did not need another slave, had gone all the way to New Orleans and bought one. And Tomey's Terrel was still alive when the boy was ten years old and he knew from his own observation and memory that there had already been some white in Tomey's Terrel's blood before his father gave him the rest of it; and looking down at the yellowed page spread beneath the yellow glow of the lantern smoking and stinking in that rank chill midnight room fifty years later, he seemed to see her actually walking into the icy creek on that Christmas day six months before her daughter's and her lover's (*Her first lover's* he thought. *Her first*) child was born, solitary, inflexible, griefless, ceremonial, in formal and succinct repudiation of grief and despair who had already had to repudiate belief and hope

that was all. He would never need look at the ledgers again nor did he; the yellowed pages in their fading and implacable succession were as much a part of his consciousness and would remain so forever, as the fact of his own nativity:

> *Tennie Beauchamp 21 yrs Won by Amodeus McCaslin from Hubert Beauchamp Esqre Possible Strait against three Treys in sigt Not called[4] 1859 Marrid to Tomys Turl 1859*

and no date of freedom because her freedom, as well as that of her first surviving child, derived not from Buck and Buddy McCaslin in the commissary but from a stranger in Washington[5] and no date of death and burial, not only because McCaslin kept no obituaries in his books, but because in this year 1883 she was still alive and would remain so to see a grandson by her last surviving child:

> *Amodeus McCaslin Beauchamp Son of tomys Turl @ Tennie Beauchamp 1859 dide 1859*

then his uncle's hand entire, because his father was now a member of the cavalry command of that man whose name as a slave-dealer he could not even spell: and not even a page and not even a full line:

> *Dauter Tomes Turl and tenny 1862*

and not even a line and not even a sex and no cause given though the boy could guess it because McCaslin was thirteen then and he remembered how there was not always enough to eat in more places than Vicksburg:

> *Child of tomes Turl and Tenny 1863*

and the same hand again and this one lived, as though Tennie's perseverance and the fading and diluted ghost of old Carothers' ruthlessness had at last conquered even starvation: and clearer, fuller, more carefully written and spelled than the boy had yet seen it, as if the old man, who should have been a woman to begin with, trying to run what was left of the plantation in his

---

4. Description of the poker hand with which Amodeus McCaslin won Tennie Beauchamp from Hubert Beauchamp (pronounced *bee'-chum*).   5. I.e., they were freed under President Abraham Lincoln's Emancipation Proclamation (1863).

brother's absence in the intervals of cooking and caring for himself and the fourteen-year-old orphan, had taken as an omen for renewed hope the fact that this nameless inheritor of slaves was at least remaining alive long enough to receive a name:

> James Thucydus Beauchamp[6] Son of Tomes Turl and Tenny Beauchamp Born 29th december 1864 and both Well Wanted to call him Theophilus but Tride Amodeus McCaslin and Callina McCaslin and both dide so Disswaded Them Born at Two clock A,m, both Well

but no more, nothing; it would be another two years yet before the boy, almost a man now, would return from the abortive trip into Tennessee with the still-intact third of old Carothers' legacy to his Negro son and his descendants, which as the three surviving children established at last one by one their apparent intention of surviving, their white half-uncles had increased to a thousand dollars each, conditions permitting, as they came of age, and completed the page himself as far as it would ever be completed when that day was long passed beyond which a man born in 1864 (or 1867 either, when he himself saw light) could have expected or himself hoped or even wanted to be still alive; his own hand now, queerly enough resembling neither his father's nor his uncle's nor even McCaslin's, but like that of his grandfather's save for the spelling:

> Vanished sometime on night of his twenty-first birthday Dec 29 1885. Traced by Isaac McCaslin to Jackson Tenn. and there lost. His third of legacy $1000.00 returned to McCaslin Edmonds Trustee this day Jan 12 1886

but not yet: that would be two years yet, and now his father's again, whose old commander was now quit of soldiering and slave-trading both; once more in the ledger and then not again and more illegible than ever, almost indecipherable at all from the rheumatism which now crippled him and almost completely innocent now even of any sort of spelling as well as punctuation, as if the four years during which he had followed the sword of the only man ever breathing who ever sold him a negro, let alone beat him in a trade, had convinced him not only of the vanity of faith and hope but of orthography too:

> Miss sophonsiba[7] b dtr t t @ t 1869

but not of belief and will because it was there, written, as McCaslin had told him, with the left hand, but there in the ledger one time more and then not again, for the boy himself was a year old, and when Lucas was born six years later, his father and uncle had been dead inside the same twelve-months almost five years; his own hand again, who was there and saw it, 1886, she was just seventeen, two years younger than himself, and he was in the commissary when McCaslin entered out of the first of dusk and said, 'He wants to marry Fonsiba,' like that: and he looked past McCaslin and saw the man, the stranger, taller than McCaslin and wearing better clothes than McCaslin and most of the other white men the boy knew habitually wore, who entered the room like a white man and stood in it like a white man, as though he

6. Tennie's Jim.   7. Also called Fonsiba; daughter of Tomey's Turl and Tennie.

had let McCaslin precede him into it not because McCaslin's skin was white but simply because McCaslin lived there and knew the way, and who talked like a white man too, looking at him past McCaslin's shoulder rapidly and keenly once and then no more, without further interest, as a mature and contained white man not impatient but just pressed for time might have looked. 'Marry Fonsiba?' he cried. 'Marry Fonsiba?' and then no more either, just watching and listening while McCaslin and the Negro talked:

'To live in Arkansas, I believe you said.'

'Yes. I have property there. A farm.'

'Property? A farm? You own it?'

'Yes.'

'You don't say Sir, do you?'

'To my elders, yes.'

'I see. You are from the North.'

'Yes. Since a child.'

'Then your father was a slave.'

'Yes. Once.'

'Then how do you own a farm in Arkansas?'

'I have a grant. It was my father's. From the United States. For military service.'

'I see,' McCaslin said. 'The Yankee army.'

'The United States army,' the stranger said; and then himself again, crying it at McCaslin's back:

'Call aunt Tennie! I'll go get her! I'll—' But McCaslin was not even including him; the stranger did not even glance back toward his voice, the two of them speaking to one another again as if he were not even there:

'Since you seem to have it all settled,' McCaslin said, 'why have you bothered to consult my authority at all?'

'I dont,' the stranger said. 'I acknowledge your authority only so far as you admit your responsibility toward her as a female member of the family of which you are the head. I dont ask your permission. I——'

'That will do!' McCaslin said. But the stranger did not falter. It was neither as if he were ignoring McCaslin nor as if he had failed to hear him. It was as though he were making, not at all an excuse and not exactly a justification, but simply a statement which the situation absolutely required and demanded should be made in McCaslin's hearing whether McCaslin listened to it or not. It was as if he were talking to himself, for himself to hear the words spoken aloud. They faced one another, not close yet at slightly less than foils' distance, erect, their voices not raised, not impactive, just succinct:

'—I inform you, notify you in advance as chief of her family. No man of honor could do less. Besides, you have, in your way, according to your lights and upbringing——'

'That's enough, I said,' McCaslin said. 'Be off this place by full dark. Go.' But for another moment the other did not move, contemplating McCaslin with that detached and heatless look, as if he were watching reflected in McCaslin's pupils the tiny image of the figure he was sustaining.

'Yes,' he said. 'After all, this is your house. And in your fashion you have. . . . But no matter. You are right. This is enough.' He turned back toward the door; he paused again but only for a second, already moving while he spoke: 'Be easy. I will be good to her.' Then he was gone.

'But how did she ever know him?' the boy cried. 'I never even heard of him before! And Fonsiba, that's never been off this place except to go to church since she was born——'

'Ha,' McCaslin said. 'Even their parents dont know until too late how seventeen-year-old girls ever met the men who marry them too, if they are lucky.' And the next morning they were both gone, Fonsiba too. McCaslin never saw her again, nor did he, because the woman he found at last five months later was no one he had ever known. He carried a third of the three-thousand-dollar fund in gold in a money-belt, as when he had vainly traced Tennie's Jim into Tennessee a year ago. They—the man—had left an address of some sort with Tennie, and three months later a letter came, written by the man although McCaslin's wife Alice had taught Fonsiba to read and write too a little. But it bore a different postmark from the address the man had left with Tennie, and he travelled by rail as far as he could and then by contracted stage and then by a hired livery rig and then by rail again for a distance: an experienced traveller by now and an experienced bloodhound too and a successful one this time because he would have to be; as the slow interminable empty muddy December miles crawled and crawled and night followed night in hotels, in roadside taverns of rough logs and containing little else but a bar, and in the cabins of strangers and the hay of lonely barns, in none of which he dared undress because of his secret golden girdle like that of a disguised one of the Magi[8] travelling incognito and not even hope to draw him but only determination and desperation, he would tell himself: *I will have to find her. I will have to. We have already lost one of them. I will have to find her this time.* He did. Hunched in the slow and icy rain, on a spent hired horse splashed to the chest and higher, he saw it—a single log edifice with a clay chimney which seemed in process of being flattened by the rain to a nameless and valueless rubble of dissolution in that roadless and even pathless waste of unfenced fallow and wilderness jungle— no barn, no stable, not so much as a hen-coop: just a log cabin built by hand and no clever hand either, a meagre pile of clumsily-cut firewood sufficient for about one day and not even a gaunt hound to come bellowing out from under the house when he rode up—a farm only in embryo, perhaps a good farm, maybe even a plantation someday, but not now, not for years yet and only then with labor, hard and enduring and unflagging work and sacrifice; he shoved open the crazy kitchen door in its awry frame and entered an icy gloom where not even a fire for cooking burned and after another moment saw, crouched into the wall's angle behind a crude table, the coffee-colored face which he had known all his life but knew no more, the body which had been born within a hundred yards of the room that he was born in and in which some of his own blood ran but which was now completely inheritor of generation after generation to whom an unannounced white man on a horse was a white man's hired Patroller wearing a pistol sometimes and a blacksnake whip always; he entered the next room, the only other room the cabin owned, and found, sitting in a rocking chair before the hearth, the man himself, reading—sitting there in the only chair in the house, before that miserable fire for which there was not wood sufficient to last twenty-four hours, in the same ministerial clothing in which he had entered the

---

8. A reference to the three wise kings of the Bible who traveled to Bethlehem bringing gifts for Jesus' birth (Matthew 2.1).

commissary five months ago and a pair of gold-framed spectacles which, when he looked up and then rose to his feet, the boy saw did not even contain lenses, reading a book in the midst of that desolation, that muddy waste fenceless and even pathless and without even a walled shed for stock to stand beneath: and over all, permeant, clinging to the man's very clothing and exuding from his skin itself, that rank stink of baseless and imbecile delusion, that boundless rapacity and folly, of the carpetbagger[9] followers of victorious armies.

'Dont you see?' he cried. 'Dont you see? This whole land, the whole South, is cursed, and all of us who derive from it, whom it ever suckled, white and black both, lie under the curse? Granted that my people brought the curse onto the land: maybe for that reason their descendants alone can—not resist it, not combat it—maybe just endure and outlast it until the curse is lifted. Then your peoples' turn will come because we have forfeited ours. But not now. Not yet. Dont you see?'

The other stood now, the unfrayed garments still ministerial even if not quite so fine, the book closed upon one finger to keep the place, the lenseless spectacles held like a music master's wand in the other workless hand while the owner of it spoke his measured and sonorous imbecility of the boundless folly and the baseless hope: 'You're wrong. The curse you whites brought into this land has been lifted. It has been voided and discharged. We are seeing a new era, an era dedicated, as our founders intended it, to freedom, liberty and equality for all, to which this country will be the new Canaan——'

'Freedom from what? From work? Canaan?' He jerked his arm, comprehensive, almost violent: whereupon it all seemed to stand there about them, intact and complete and visible in the drafty, damp, heatless, negro-stale negro-rank sorry room—the empty fields without plow or seed to work them, fenceless against the stock which did not exist within or without the walled stable which likewise was not there. 'What corner of Canaan is this?'

'You are seeing it at a bad time. This is winter. No man farms this time of year.'

'I see. And of course her need for food and clothing will stand still while the land lies fallow.'

'I have a pension,' the other said. He said it as a man might say *I have grace* or *I own a gold mine*. 'I have my father's pension too. It will arrive on the first of the month. What day is this?'

'The eleventh,' he said. 'Twenty days more. And until then?'

'I have a few groceries in the house from my credit account with the merchant in Midnight who banks my pension check for me. I have executed to him a power of attorney to handle it for me as a matter of mutual——'

'I see. And if the groceries dont last the twenty days?'

'I still have one more hog.'

'Where?'

'Outside,' the other said. 'It is customary in this country to allow stock to range free during the winter for food. It comes up from time to time. But no matter if it doesn't; I can probably trace its footprints when the need——'

'Yes!' he cried. 'Because no matter: you still have the pension check. And

9. Opportunist who packed his belongings in a satchel made of carpet material and came south to make a fortune off the ruin of the Confederacy.

the man in Midnight will cash it and pay himself out of it for what you have already eaten and if there is any left over, it is yours. And the hog will be eaten by then or you still cant catch it, and then what will you do?'

'It will be almost spring then,' the other said. 'I am planning in the spring——'

'It will be January,' he said. 'And then February. And then more than half of March—' and when he stopped again in the kitchen she had not moved, she did not even seem to breathe or to be alive except her eyes watching him; when he took a step toward her it was still not movement because she could have retreated no further: only the tremendous fathomless ink-colored eyes in the narrow, thin, too thin coffee-colored face watching him without alarm, without recognition, without hope. 'Fonsiba,' he said. 'Fonsiba. Are you all right?'

'I'm free,' she said. Midnight was a tavern, a livery stable, a big store (that would be where the pension check banked itself as a matter of mutual elimination of bother and fret, he thought) and a little one, a saloon and a blacksmith shop. But there was a bank there too. The president (the owner, for all practical purposes) of it was a translated Mississippian who had been one of Forrest's men too: and his body lightened of the golden belt for the first time since he left home eight days ago, with pencil and paper he multiplied three dollars by twelve months and divided it into one thousand dollars; it would stretch that way over almost twenty-eight years and for twenty-eight years at least she would not starve, the banker promising to send the three dollars himself by a trusty messenger on the fifteenth of each month and put it into her actual hand, and he returned home and that was all because in 1874 his father and his uncle were both dead and the old ledgers never again came down from the shelf above the desk to which his father had returned them for the last time that day in 1869. But he could have completed it:

Lucas Quintus Carothers McCaslin Beauchamp. Last surviving son and child of Tomey's Terrel and Tennie Beauchamp. March 17, 1874

except that there was no need: not *Lucius Quintus @c[1] @c @c*, but *Lucas Quintus*, not refusing to be called Lucius, because he simply eliminated that word from the name; not denying, declining the name itself, because he used three quarters of it; but simply taking the name and changing, altering it, making it no longer the white man's but his own, by himself composed, himself selfprogenitive and nominate, by himself ancestored, as, for all the old ledgers recorded to the contrary, old Carothers himself was

and that was all: 1874 the boy; 1888 the man, repudiated denied and free; 1895 and husband but no father, unwidowered but without a wife, and found long since that no man is ever free and probably could not bear it if he were; married then and living in Jefferson in the little new jerrybuilt bungalow which his wife's father had given them: and one morning Lucas stood suddenly in the doorway of the room where he was reading the Memphis paper and he looked at the paper's dateline and thought *It's his birthday. He's twenty-one today* and Lucas said: 'Whar's the rest of that money old Carothers left? I wants it. All of it.'

that was all: and McCaslin

1. Etc. (as Ike imagines the handwritten entry).

'More men than that one Buck and Buddy to fumble-heed that truth so mazed for them that spoke it and so confused for them that heard yet still there was 1865:' and he

'But not enough. Not enough of even Father and Uncle Buddy to fumble-heed in even three generations not even three generations fathered by Grandfather not even if there had been nowhere beneath His sight any but Grandfather and so He would not even have needed to elect and choose. But He tried and I know what you will say. That having Himself created them He could have known no more of hope than He could have pride and grief but He didn't hope He just waited because He had made them: not just because He had set them alive and in motion but because He had already worried with them so long: worried with them so long because He had seen how in individual cases they were capable of anything any height or depth remembered in mazed incomprehension out of heaven where hell was created too[2] and so He must admit them or else admit His equal somewhere and so be no longer God and therefore must accept responsibility for what He Himself had done in order to live with Himself in His lonely and paramount heaven. And He probably knew it was vain but He had created them and knew them capable of all things because He had shaped them out of the primal Absolute which contained all and had watched them since in their individual exaltation and baseness and they themselves not knowing why nor how nor even when: until at last He saw that they were all Grandfather all of them and that even from them the elected and chosen the best the very best He could expect (not hope mind; not hope) would be Bucks and Buddies and not even enough of them and in the third generation not even Bucks and Buddies but—' and McCaslin

'Ah:' and he

'Yes. If He could see Father and Uncle Buddy in Grandfather He must have seen me too.—an Isaac born into a later life than Abraham's and repudiating immolation: fatherless and therefore safe declining the altar because maybe this time the exasperated Hand might not supply the kid—' and McCaslin

'Escape:' and he

'All right. Escape.—Until one day He said what you told Fonsiba's husband that afternoon here in this room: *This will do. This is enough*: not in exasperation or rage or even just sick to death as you were sick that day: just *This is enough* and looked about for one last time, for one time more since He had created them, upon this land this South for which He had done so much with woods for game and streams for fish and deep rich soil for seed and lush springs to sprout it and long summers to mature it and serene falls to harvest it and short mild winters for men and animals and saw no hope anywhere and looked beyond it where hope should have been, where to East North and West lay illimitable that whole hopeful continent dedicated as a refuge and sanctuary of liberty and freedom from what you called the old world's worthless evening and saw the rich descendants of slavers, females of both sexes, to whom the black they shrieked of was another specimen another example like the Brazilian macaw brought home in a cage by a trav-

---

2. Because the rebellious angels were cast out of heaven into hell. (Cf. Victor Hugo's *Et nox facta est*, on p. 623.)

eller, passing resolutions about horror and outrage in warm and air-proof halls: and the thundering cannonade of politicians earning votes and the medicine-shows of pulpiteers earning Chatauqua fees,[3] to whom the outrage and the injustice were as much abstractions as Tariff or Silver[4] or Immortality and who employed the very shackles of its servitude and the sorry rags of its regalia as they did the other beer and banners and mottoes redfire and brimstone and sleight-of-hand and musical handsaws: and the whirling wheels which manufactured for a profit the pristine replacements of the shackles and shoddy garments as they wore out and spun the cotton and made the gins which ginned it and the cars and ships which hauled it, and the men who ran the wheels for that profit and established and collected the taxes it was taxed with and the rates for hauling it and the commissions for selling it: and He could have repudiated them since they were his creation now and forever more throughout all their generations until not only that old world from which He had rescued them but this new one too which He had revealed and led them to as a sanctuary and refuge were become the same worthless tideless rock cooling in the last crimson evening except that out of all that empty sound and bootless fury one silence, among that loud and moiling all of them just one simple enough to believe that horror and outrage were first and last simply horror and outrage and was crude enough to act upon that, illiterate and had no words for talking or perhaps was just busy and had no time to, one out of them all who did not bother Him with cajolery and adjuration then pleading then threat and had not even bothered to inform Him in advance what he was about so that a lesser than He might have even missed the simple act of lifting the long ancestral musket down from the deer-horns above the door, whereupon He said *My name is Brown*[5] too and the other *So is mine* and He *Then mine or yours cant be because I am against it* and the other *So am I* and He triumphantly *Then where are you going with that gun?* and the other told him in one sentence one word and He: amazed: Who knew neither hope nor pride nor grief *But your Association, your Committee, your Officers. Where are your Minutes, your Motions, your Parliamentary Procedures?* and the other *I aint against them. They are all right I reckon for them that have the time. I am just against the weak because they are niggers being held in bondage by the strong just because they are white.* So He turned once more to this land which He still intended to save because He had done so much for it—' and McCaslin

'What?' and he

'—to these people He was still committed to because they were his creations—' and McCaslin

'Turned back to us? His face to us?' and he

'—whose wives and daughters at least made soups and jellies for them when they were sick and carried the trays through the mud and the winter too into the stinking cabins and sat in the stinking cabins and kept fires going

3. Money from the Chautauqua Movement, a religiously based adult education program, begun in 1874, that expanded to include traveling programs, which later took on a carnival aspect.   4. In political debates over silver and gold as the basis of the U.S. currency, "sound-money" policies (chiefly northeastern business interests) feared inflation and supported gold, whereas the agricultural South and West supported the increased use of silver. The Bland-Allison Act of 1878 renewed the minting of silver dollars and mandated the increased purchase of silver bullion. *Tariff:* Republicans backed protective tariffs in the 1880 presidential campaign and accused Democrats of not supporting domestic industry.   5. John Brown (1800–1859), a militant abolitionist who was executed for leading an attack on the federal arsenal at Harpers Ferry, Virginia.

until crises came and passed but that was not enough: and when they were very sick had them carried into the big house itself into the company room itself maybe and nursed them there which the white man would have done too for any other of his cattle that was sick but at least the man who hired one from a livery wouldn't have and still that was not enough: so that He said and not in grief either Who had made them and so could know no more of grief than He could of pride or hope: *Apparently they can learn nothing save through suffering, remember nothing save when underlined in blood—'* and McCaslin

'Ashby on an afternoon's ride, to call on some remote maiden cousins of his mother or maybe just acquaintances of hers, comes by chance upon a minor engagement of outposts and dismounts and with his crimson-lined cloak for target leads a handful of troops he never saw before against an entrenched position of backwoods-trained riflemen. Lee's battle-order, wrapped maybe about a handful of cigars and doubtless thrown away when the last cigar was smoked, found by a Yankee Intelligence officer on the floor of a saloon behind the Yankee lines after Lee had already divided his forces before Sharpsburg.[6] Jackson on the Plank Road, already rolled up the flank which Hooker[7] believed could not be turned and, waiting only for night to pass to continue the brutal and incessant slogging which would fling that whole wing back into Hooker's lap where he sat on a front gallery in Chancellorsville[8] drinking rum toddies and telegraphing Lincoln that he had defeated Lee, is shot from among a whole covey of minor officers and in the blind night by one of his own patrols, leaving as next by seniority Stuart[9] that gallant man born apparently already horsed and sabred and already knowing all there was to know about war except the slogging and brutal stupidity of it: and that same Stuart off raiding Pennsylvania hen-roosts when Lee should have known of all of Meade just where Hancock was on Cemetery Ridge: and Longstreet too at Gettysburg[1] and that same Longstreet shot out of saddle by his own men in the dark by mistake just as Jackson was. His face to us? His face to us?' and he

'How else have made them fight? Who else but Jacksons and Stuarts and Ashbys and Morgans and Forrests?[2]—the farmers of the central and middle-west, holding land by the acre instead of the tens or maybe even the hundreds, farming it themselves and to no single crop of cotton or tobacco or cane, owning no slaves and needing and wanting none and already looking toward the Pacific coast, not always as long as two generations there and having stopped where they did stop only through the fortuitous mischance that an ox died or a wagon-axle broke. And the New England mechanics who didn't even own land and measured all things by the weight of water and the cost of turning wheels and the narrow fringe of traders and ship-owners still looking backward across the Atlantic and attached to the continent only by

6. The site of a Civil War battle. General Robert E. Lee (1807–1870) led the Confederate armies. A copy of Lee's orders for September 9, 1862, was used by a staff member to wrap cigars, which fell out of his pocket and were found by Union soldiers. 7. Joseph Hooker (1814–1879), general in the Union Army. Thomas J. ("Stonewall") Jackson (1824–1863), general in the Confederate Army. 8. Site of a major Confederate victory. 9. J. E. B. Stuart (1833–1864), Confederate general who was supposed to inform Lee of the Union Army's movements. 1. Site of the bloodiest battle of the Civil War and a significant Union victory. George Meade (1815–1872) and Winfield Hancock (1824–1886), Union generals whose forces occupied the high ground at Gettysburg (including Cemetery Ridge). James Longstreet (1821–1904), Confederate general. 2. Confederate generals.

their counting-houses. And those who should have had the alertness to see: the wildcat manipulators[3] of mythical wilderness town-sites; and the astuteness to rationalise: the bankers who held the mortgages on the land which the first were only waiting to abandon and on the railroads and steamboats to carry them still further west, and on the factories and the wheels and the rented tenements those who ran them lived in; and the leisure and scope to comprehend and fear in time and even anticipate: the Boston-bred (even when not born in Boston) spinster descendants[4] of long lines of similarly-bred and likewise spinster aunts and uncles whose hands knew no callus except that of the indicting pen, to whom the wilderness itself began at the top of tide and who looked, if at anything other than Beacon Hill, only toward heaven—not to mention all the loud rabble of the camp-followers of pioneers: the bellowing of politicians, the mellifluous choiring of self-styled men of God, the—' and McCaslin

'Here, here. Wait a minute:' and he

'Let me talk now. I'm trying to explain to the head of my family something which I have got to do which I dont quite understand myself, not in justification of it but to explain it if I can. I could say I dont know why I must do it but that I do know I have got to because I have got myself to have to live with for the rest of my life and all I want is peace to do it in. But you are the head of my family. More. I knew a long time ago that I would never have to miss my father, even if you are just finding out that you have missed your son.—the drawers of bills and the shavers of notes[5] and the schoolmasters and the self-ordained to teach and lead and all that horde of the semi-literate with a white shirt but no change for it, with one eye on themselves and watching each other with the other one. Who else could have made them fight: could have struck them so aghast with fear and dread as to turn shoulder to shoulder and face one way and even stop talking for a while and even after two years of it keep them still so wrung with terror that some among them would seriously propose moving their very capital into a foreign country lest it be ravaged and pillaged by a people whose entire white male population would have little more than filled any one of their larger cities: except Jackson in the Valley and three separate armies trying to catch him and none of them ever knowing whether they were just retreating from a battle or just running into one and Stuart riding his whole command entirely around the biggest single armed force this continent ever saw in order to see what it looked like from behind and Morgan[6] leading a cavalry charge against a stranded man-of-war. Who else could have declared a war against a power with ten times the area and a hundred times the men and a thousand times the resources, except men who could believe that all necessary to conduct a successful war was not acumen nor shrewdness nor politics nor diplomacy nor money nor even integrity and simple arithmetic but just love of land and courage——'

3. Speculators who bought, sold, and rented tracts of land in the Midwest that were originally given to homesteaders under the Homestead Act of 1862 or were acquired by purchasing land warrants given to ex-soldiers under an Act of Congress in 1847.   4. Many members of the activist Boston Female Antislavery Society were not born in Boston; Angelina and Sarah Grimké, for example, were born in Charleston, South Carolina. Despite Ike's claim, they were not all spinsters.   5. Bankers and moneylenders, respectively.   6. Morgan, leading a group of twelve men disguised as Union soldiers, burned the moored Federal steamboat *Minnetonka*. In 1862, by a forced march in Virginia's Shenandoah Valley, Jackson's small Confederate army eluded three Union armies sent to destroy them. Stuart, on a scouting mission, circled one hundred thousand Union troops commanded by General McClellan.

'And an unblemished and gallant ancestry and the ability to ride a horse,' McCaslin said. 'Dont leave that out.' It was evening now, the tranquil sunset of October[7] mazy with windless woodsmoke. The cotton was long since picked and ginned, and all day now the wagons loaded with gathered corn moved between field and crib, processional across the enduring land. 'Well, maybe that's what He wanted. At least, that's what He got.' This time there was no yellowed procession of fading and harmless ledger-pages. This was chronicled in a harsher book and McCaslin, fourteen and fifteen and sixteen, had seen it and the boy himself had inherited it as Noah's grandchildren had inherited the Flood although they had not been there to see the deluge: that dark corrupt and bloody time[8] while three separate peoples had tried to adjust not only to one another but to the new land which they had created and inherited too and must live in for the reason that those who had lost it were no less free to quit it than those who had gained it were:—those upon whom freedom and equality had been dumped overnight and without warning or preparation or any training in how to employ it or even just endure it and who misused it not as children would nor yet because they had been so long in bondage and then so suddenly freed, but misused it as human beings always misuse freedom, so that he thought *Apparently there is a wisdom beyond even that learned through suffering necessary for a man to distinguish between liberty and license;* those who had fought for four years and lost to preserve a condition under which that franchisement was anomaly and par-adox, not because they were opposed to freedom as freedom but for the old reasons for which man (not the generals and politicians but man) has always fought and died in wars: to preserve a status quo or to establish a better future one to endure for his children; and lastly, as if that were not enough for bitterness and hatred and fear, that third race even more alien to the people whom they resembled in pigment and in whom even the same blood ran, than to the people whom they did not,—that race threefold in one and alien even among themselves save for a single fierce will for rapine and pil-lage, composed of the sons of middle-aged Quartermaster lieutenants and Army sutlers[9] and contractors in military blankets and shoes and transport mules, who followed the battles they themselves had not fought and inher-ited the conquest they themselves had not helped to gain, sanctioned and protected even if not blessed, and left their bones and in another generation would be engaged in a fierce economic competition of small sloven farms with the black men they were supposed to have freed and the white descen-dants of fathers who had owned no slaves anyway whom they were supposed to have disinherited and in the third generation would be back once more in the little lost county seats as barbers and garage mechanics and deputy sher-iffs and mill- and gin-hands and power-plant firemen, leading, first in mufti then later in an actual formalised regalia of hooded sheets and passwords and fiery christian symbols, lynching mobs against the race their ancestors had come to save:[1] and of all that other nameless horde of speculators in human misery, manipulators of money and politics and land, who follow catastrophe and are their own protection as grasshoppers are and need no

7. October 1888.   8. The Reconstruction period (1865–77) following the Civil War.   9. Trades-people who sell provisions to soldiers.   1. Civilian, or regular dress (*mufti*), was soon replaced by the anonymity of hooded sheets worn by members of the Ku Klux Klan, an anti-black, anti-Catholic, anti-Semitic, and anti-immigrant organization.

blessing and sweat no plow or axe-helve and batten and vanish and leave no
bones, just as they derived apparently from no ancestry, no mortal flesh, no
act even of passion or even of lust: and the Jew who came without protection
too since after two thousand years he had got out of the habit of being or
needing it, and solitary, without even the solidarity of the locusts and in this
a sort of courage since he had come thinking not in terms of simple pillage
but in terms of his great-grandchildren, seeking yet some place to establish
them to endure even though forever alien: and unblessed: a pariah about the
face of the Western earth which twenty centuries later was still taking
revenge on him for the fairy tale with which he had conquered it. McCaslin
had actually seen it, and the boy even at almost eighty would never be able
to distinguish certainly between what he had seen and what had been told
him: a lightless and gutted and empty land where women crouched with the
huddled children behind locked doors and men armed in sheets and masks
rode the silent roads and the bodies of white and black both, victims not so
much of hate as of desperation and despair, swung from lonely limbs: and
men shot dead in polling-booths with the still wet pen in one hand and the
unblotted ballot in the other: and a United States marshal in Jefferson who
signed his official papers with a crude cross, an ex-slave called Sickymo, not
at all because his ex-owner was a doctor and apothecary but because, still a
slave, he would steal his master's grain alcohol and dilute it with water and
peddle it in pint bottles from a cache beneath the roots of a big sycamore
tree behind the drug store, who had attained his high office because his half-
white sister was the concubine of the Federal A.P.M.:[2] and this time Mc-
Caslin did not even say Look but merely lifted one hand, not even pointing,
not even specifically toward the shelf of ledgers but toward the desk, toward
the corner where it sat beside the scuffed patch on the floor where two
decades of heavy shoes had stood while the white man at the desk added
and multiplied and subtracted. And again he did not need to look because
he had seen this himself and, twenty-three years after the Surrender[3] and
twenty-four after the Proclamation, was still watching it: the ledgers, new
ones now and filled rapidly, succeeding one another rapidly and containing
more names than old Carothers or even his father and Uncle Buddy had ever
dreamed of; new names and new faces to go with them, among which the
old names and faces that even his father and uncle would have recognised,
were lost, vanished—Tomey's Terrel dead, and even the tragic and miscast
Percival Brownlee, who couldn't keep books and couldn't farm either, found
his true niche at last, reappeared in 1862 during the boy's father's absence
and had apparently been living on the plantation for at least a month before
his uncle found out about it, conducting impromptu revival meetings among
negroes, preaching and leading the singing also in his high sweet true
soprano voice and disappeared again on foot and at top speed, not behind
but ahead of a body of raiding Federal horse and reappeared for the third
and last time in the entourage of a travelling Army paymaster, the two of
them passing through Jefferson in a surrey at the exact moment when the
boy's father (it was 1866) also happened to be crossing the Square, the surrey
and its occupants traversing rapidly that quiet and bucolic scene and even

2. Assistant paymaster, not necessarily in the army.   3. The war ended on April 9, 1865, when Lee
surrendered to Union general Ulysses S. Grant.

in that fleeting moment and to others beside the boy's father giving an illusion of flight and illicit holiday like a man on an excursion during his wife's absence with his wife's personal maid, until Brownlee glanced up and saw his late co-master and gave him one defiant female glance and then broke[4] again, leaped from the surrey and disappeared this time for good and it was only by chance that McCaslin, twenty years later, heard of him again, an old man now and quite fat, as the well-to-do proprietor of a select New Orleans brothel; and Tennie's Jim gone, nobody knew where, and Fonsiba in Arkansas with her three dollars each month and the scholar-husband with his lenseless spectacles and frock coat and his plans for the spring; and only Lucas was left, the baby, the last save himself of old Carothers' doomed and fatal blood which in the male derivation seemed to destroy all it touched, and even he was repudiating and at least hoping to escape it;—Lucas, the boy of fourteen whose name would not even appear for six years yet among those rapid pages in the bindings new and dustless too since McCaslin lifted them down daily now to write into them the continuation of that record which two hundred years had not been enough to complete and another hundred would not be enough to discharge; that chronicle which was a whole land in miniature, which multiplied and compounded was the entire South, twenty-three years after surrender and twenty-four from emancipation—that slow trickle of molasses and meal and meat, of shoes and straw hats and overalls, of plow-lines and collars and heel-bolts and buckheads and clevises,[5] which returned each fall as cotton—the two threads frail as truth and impalpable as equators yet cable-strong to bind for life them who made the cotton to the land their sweat fell on: and he

'Yes. Binding them for a while yet, a little while yet. Through and beyond that life and maybe through and beyond the life of that life's sons and maybe even through and beyond that of the sons of those sons. But not always, because they will endure. They will outlast us because they are—' it was not a pause, barely a falter even, possibly appreciable only to himself, as if he couldn't speak even to McCaslin, even to explain his repudiation, that which to him too, even in the act of escaping (and maybe this was the reality and the truth of his need to escape) was heresy: so that even in escaping he was taking with him more of that evil and unregenerate old man who could summon, because she was his property, a human being because she was old enough and female, to his widower's house and get a child on her and then dismiss her because she was of an inferior race, and then bequeath a thousand dollars to the infant because he would be dead then and wouldn't have to pay it, than even he had feared. 'Yes. He didn't want to. He had to. Because they will endure. They are better than we are. Stronger than we are. Their vices are vices aped from white men or that white men and bondage have taught them: improvidence and intemperance and evasion—not laziness: evasion: of what white men had set them to, not for their aggrandisement or even comfort but his own—' and McCaslin

'All right. Go on: Promiscuity. Violence. Instability and lack of control. Inability to distinguish between mine and thine—' and he

'How distinguish, when for two hundred years mine did not even exist for them?' and McCaslin

'All right. Go on. And their virtues—' and he

4. I.e., broke cover, as hunted animals might do.   5. Metal parts used to join pieces of a plow.

'Yes. Their own. Endurance—' and McCaslin

'So have mules:' and he

'—and pity and tolerance and forbearance and fidelity and love of children—' and McCaslin

'So have dogs:' and he

'—whether their own or not or black or not. And more: what they got not only not from white people but not even despite white people because they had it already from the old free fathers a longer time free than us because we have never been free—' and it was in McCaslin's eyes too, he had only to look at McCaslin's eyes and it was there, that summer twilight seven years ago, almost a week after they had returned from the camp before he discovered that Sam Fathers had told McCaslin: an old bear, fierce and ruthless not just to stay alive but ruthless with the fierce pride of liberty and freedom, jealous and proud enough of liberty and freedom to see it threatened not with fear nor even alarm but almost with joy, seeming deliberately to put it into jeopardy in order to savor it and keep his old strong bones and flesh supple and quick to defend and preserve it; an old man, son of a Negro slave and an Indian king, inheritor on the one hand of the long chronicle of a people who had learned humility through suffering and learned pride through the endurance which survived the suffering, and on the other side the chronicle of a people even longer in the land than the first, yet who now existed there only in the solitary brotherhood of an old and childless Negro's alien blood and the wild and invincible spirit of an old bear; a boy who wished to learn humility and pride in order to become skillful and worthy in the woods but found himself becoming so skillful so fast that he feared he would never become worthy because he had not learned humility and pride though he had tried, until one day an old man who could not have defined either led him as though by the hand to where an old bear and a little mongrel dog showed him that, by possessing one thing other, he would possess them both; and a little dog, nameless and mongrel and many-fathered, grown yet weighing less than six pounds, who couldn't be dangerous because there was nothing anywhere much smaller, not fierce because that would have been called just noise, not humble because it was already too near the ground to genuflect, and not proud because it would not have been close enough for anyone to discern what was casting that shadow and which didn't even know it was not going to heaven since they had already decided it had no immortal soul, so that all it could be was brave even though they would probably call that too just noise. *'And you didn't shoot,'* McCaslin said. *'How close were you?'*

'I dont know,' he said. *'There was a big wood tick just inside his off hind leg. I saw that. But I didn't have the gun then.'*

'But you didn't shoot when you had the gun,' McCaslin said. *'Why?'* But McCaslin didn't wait, rising and crossing the room, across the pelt of the bear he had killed two years ago and the bigger one McCaslin had killed before he was born, to the bookcase beneath the mounted head of his first buck, and returned with the book and sat down again and opened it. *'Listen,'* he said. He read the five stanzas aloud and closed the book on his finger and looked up. *'All right,'* he said. *'Listen,'* and read again, but only one stanza this time and closed the book and laid it on the table. *'She cannot fade, though thou hast not thy bliss,'* McCaslin said: *'Forever wilt thou love, and she be fair.'*

'He's talking about a girl,' he said.

1782 / WILLIAM FAULKNER

'He had to talk about something,' McCaslin said. Then he said, 'He was talking about truth. Truth is one. It doesn't change. It covers all things which touch the heart—honor and pride and pity and justice and courage and love. Do you see now?' He didn't know. Somehow it had seemed simpler than that, simpler than somebody talking in a book about a young man and a girl he would never need to grieve over because he could never approach any nearer and would never have to get any further away. He had heard about an old bear and finally got big enough to hunt it and he hunted it four years and at last met it with a gun in his hands and he didn't shoot. Because a little dog—But he could have shot long before the fyce covered the twenty yards to where the bear waited, and Sam Fathers could have shot at any time during the interminable minute while Old Ben stood on his hind legs over them. . . . He ceased. McCaslin watched him, still speaking, the voice, the words as quiet as the twilight itself was: 'Courage and honor and pride, and pity and love of justice and of liberty. They all touch the heart, and what the heart holds to becomes truth, as far as we know truth. Do you see now?' and he could still hear them, intact in this twilight as in that one seven years ago, no louder still because they did not need to be because they would endure: and he had only to look at McCaslin's eyes beyond the thin and bitter smiling, the faint lip-lift which would have had to be called smiling;—his kinsman, his father almost, who had been born too late into the old time and too soon for the new, the two of them juxtaposed and alien now to each other against their ravaged patrimony, the dark and ravaged fatherland still prone and panting from its etherless operation:
    'Habet[6] then.—So this land is, indubitably, of and by itself cursed:' and he
    'Cursed:' and again McCaslin merely lifted one hand, not even speaking and not even toward the ledgers: so that, as the stereopticon condenses into one instantaneous field the myriad minutia of its scope, so did that slight and rapid gesture establish in the small cramped and cluttered twilit room not only the ledgers but the whole plantation in its mazed and intricate entirety—the land, the fields and what they represented in terms of cotton ginned and sold, the men and women whom they fed and clothed and even paid a little cash money at Christmas-time in return for the labor which planted and raised and picked and ginned the cotton, the machinery and mules and gear with which they raised it and their cost and upkeep and replacement—that whole edifice intricate and complex and founded upon injustice and erected by ruthless rapacity and carried on even yet with at times downright savagery not only to the human beings but the valuable animals too, yet solvent and efficient and, more than that: not only still intact but enlarged, increased; brought still intact by McCaslin, himself little more than a child then, through and out of the debacle and chaos of twenty years ago where hardly one in ten survived,[7] and enlarged and increased and would continue so, solvent and efficient and intact and still increasing so long as McCaslin and his McCaslin successors lasted, even though their surnames might not even be Edmonds then: and he: 'Habet too. Because that's it: not the land, but us. Not only the blood, but the name too; not only its color but

6. He has it (Latin, literal trans.); here he's had it. A phrase shouted at Roman gladiatorial bouts when one fighter landed a winning blow.   7. Few farms survived the Restoration intact.

its designation: Edmonds, white, but, a female line, could have no other but the name his father bore; Beauchamp, the elder line and the male one, but, black, could have had any name he liked and no man would have cared, except the name his father bore who had no name—' and McCaslin

'And since I know too what you know I will say now, once more let me say it: And one other, and in the third generation too, and the male, the eldest, the direct and sole and white and still McCaslin even, father to son to son—' and he

'I am free:' and this time McCaslin did not even gesture, no inference of fading pages, no postulation of the stereoptic whole, but the frail and iron thread strong as truth and impervious as evil and longer than life itself and reaching beyond record and patrimony both to join him with the lusts and passions, the hopes and dreams and griefs, of bones whose names while still fleshed and capable even old Carothers' grandfather had never heard: and he: 'And of that too:' and McCaslin

'Chosen, I suppose (I will concede it) out of all your time by Him as you say Buck and Buddy were from theirs. And it took Him a bear and an old man and four years just for you. And it took you fourteen years to reach that point and about that many, maybe more, for Old Ben, and more than seventy for Sam Fathers. And you are just one. How long then? How long?' and he

'It will be long. I have never said otherwise. But it will be all right because they will endure—' and McCaslin

'And anyway, you will be free.—No, not now nor ever, we from them nor they from us. So I repudiate too. I would deny even if I knew it were true. I would have to. Even you can see that I could do no else. I am what I am; I will be always what I was born and have always been. And more than me. More than me, just as there were more than Buck and Buddy in what you called His first plan which failed:' and he

'And more than me:' and McCaslin

'No. Not even you. Because mark. You said how on that instant when Ikkemotubbe realised that he could sell the land to Grandfather, it ceased forever to have been his. All right; go on: Then it belonged to Sam Fathers, old Ikkemotubbe's son. And who inherited from Sam Fathers, if not you? co-heir perhaps with Boon, if not of his life maybe, at least of his quitting it?' and he

'Yes. Sam Fathers set me free.' And Isaac McCaslin, not yet Uncle Ike, a long time yet before he would be uncle to half a county and still father to none, living in one small cramped fireless rented room in a Jefferson boarding-house where petit juries were domiciled during court terms and itinerant horse- and mule-traders stayed, with his kit of brand-new carpenter's tools and the shotgun McCaslin had given him with his name engraved in silver and old General Compson's compass (and, when the General died, his silver-mounted horn too) and the iron cot and mattress and the blankets which he would take each fall into the woods for more than sixty years and the bright tin coffee-pot

there had been a legacy, from his Uncle Hubert Beauchamp, his godfather, that bluff burly roaring childlike man from whom Uncle Buddy had won Tomey's Terrel's wife Tennie in the poker-game in 1859—'possible strait against three Treys in sigt Not called'—; no pale sentence or paragraph scrawled in cringing fear of death by a weak and trembling hand as a last desperate sop flung backward at retribution, but a Legacy, a Thing, possessing weight to the hand and bulk to the eye and even audible: a silver cup filled with gold pieces and wrapped in burlap and sealed with his godfather's ring in the hot wax, which (intact still) even before his Uncle Hubert's death and long before his own majority, when it would be his, had become not only a legend but one of the family lares. After his father's and his Uncle Hubert's sister's marriage they moved back into the big house, the tremendous cavern which old Carothers had started and never finished, cleared the remaining negroes out of it and with his mother's dowry completed it, at least the rest of the windows and doors and moved into it, all of them save Uncle Buddy who declined to leave the cabin he and his twin had built, the move being the bride's notion and more than just a notion and none ever to know if she really wanted to live in the big house or if she knew before hand that Uncle Buddy would refuse to move: and two weeks after his birth in 1867, the first time he and his mother came down stairs, one night and the silver cup sitting on the cleared dining-room table beneath the bright lamp and while his mother and his father and McCaslin and Tennie (his nurse: carrying him)— all of them again but Uncle Buddy—watched, his Uncle Hubert rang one by one into the cup the bright and glinting mintage and wrapped it into the burlap envelope and heated the wax and sealed it and carried it back home with him where he lived alone now without even his sister either to hold him down as McCaslin said or to try to raise him up as Uncle Buddy said, and (dark times then in Mississippi) Uncle Buddy said most of the niggers gone and the ones that didn't go even Hub Beauchamp could not have wanted: but the dogs remained and Uncle Buddy said Beauchamp fiddled while Nero fox-hunted[8]

   they would go and see it there; at last his mother would prevail and they would depart in the surrey, once more all save Uncle Buddy and McCaslin to keep Uncle Buddy company until one winter Uncle Buddy began to fail and from then on it was himself, beginning to remember now, and his mother and Tennie and Tomey's Terrel to drive: the twenty-two miles into the next county, the twin gateposts on one of which McCaslin could remember the half-grown boy blowing a fox-horn at breakfast dinner and supper-time and jumping down to open to any passer who happened to hear it but where there were no gates at all now, the shabby and overgrown entrance to what his mother still insisted that people call Warwick because her brother was if truth but triumphed and justice but prevailed the rightful earl of it, the paintless house which outwardly did not change but which on the inside seemed each time larger because he was too little to realise then that there was less and less in it of the fine furnishings, the rosewood and mahogany and walnut which for him had never existed anywhere anyway save in his mother's tearful lamentations and the occasional piece small enough to be roped somehow onto the rear or the top of the carriage on their return (And he remembered this, he had seen it: an instant, a flash, his mother's soprano 'Even my dress! Even my dress!' loud and outraged in the barren unswept hall; a face young and female and even lighter in color than Tomey's Terrel's for an instant in a closing door; a swirl, a glimpse of the silk gown and the flick and glint of an ear-ring: an apparition rapid and tawdry and illicit yet

8. A play on the old saying "Nero fiddled while Rome burned."

somehow even to the child, the infant still almost, breathless and exciting and evocative: as though, like two limpid and pellucid streams meeting, the child which he still was had made serene and absolute and perfect rapport and contact through that glimpsed nameless illicit hybrid female flesh with the boy which had existed at that stage of inviolable and immortal adolescence in his uncle for almost sixty years; the dress, the face, the ear-rings gone in that same aghast flash and his uncle's voice: 'She's my cook! She's my new cook! I had to have a cook, didn't I?' then the uncle himself, the face alarmed and aghast too yet still innocently and somehow even indomitably of a boy, they retreating in their turn now, back to the front gallery, and his uncle again, pained and still amazed, in a sort of desperate resurgence if not of courage at least of self-assertion: 'They're free now! They're folks too just like we are!' and his mother: 'That's why! That's why! My mother's house! Defiled! Defiled!' and his uncle: 'Damn it, Sibbey, at least give her time to pack her grip:' then over, finished, the loud uproar and all, himself and Tennie and he remembered Tennie's inscrutable face at the broken shutterless window of the bare room which had once been the parlor while they watched, hurrying down the lane at a stumbling trot, the routed compounder of his uncle's uxory: the back, the nameless face which he had seen only for a moment, the once-hooped dress ballooning and flapping below a man's overcoat, the worn heavy carpet-bag jouncing and banging against her knee, routed and in retreat true enough and in the empty lane solitary young-looking and forlorn yet withal still exciting and evocative and wearing still the silken banner captured inside the very citadel of respectability, and unforgettable.)

the cup, the sealed inscrutable burlap, sitting on the shelf in the locked closet, Uncle Hubert unlocking the door and lifting it down and passing it from hand to hand: his mother, his father, McCaslin and even Tennie, insisting that each take it in turn and heft it for weight and shake it again to prove the sound, Uncle Hubert himself standing spraddled before the cold unswept hearth in which the very bricks themselves were crumbling into a litter of soot and dust and mortar and the droppings of chimney-sweeps,[9] still roaring and still innocent and still indomitable: and for a long time he believed nobody but himself had noticed that his uncle now put the cup only into his hands, unlocked the door and lifted it down and put it into his hands and stood over him until he had shaken it obediently until it sounded then took it from him and locked it back into the closet before anyone else could have offered to touch it, and even later, when competent not only to remember but to rationalise, he could not say what it was or even if it had been anything because the parcel was still heavy and still rattled, not even when, Uncle Buddy dead and his father, at last and after almost seventy-five years in bed after the sun rose, said: 'Go get that damn cup. Bring that damn Hub Beauchamp too if you have to:' because it still rattled though his uncle no longer put it even into his hands now but carried it himself from one to the other, his mother, McCaslin, Tennie, shaking it before each in turn, saying: 'Hear it? Hear it?' his face still innocent, not quite baffled but only amazed and not very amazed and still indomitable: and, his father and Uncle Buddy both gone now, one day without reason or any warning the almost completely

---

9. Or chimney swifts, a sparrow-sized bird with long wings that nests in chimneys.

empty house in which his uncle and Tennie's ancient and quarrelsome great-grandfather (who claimed to have seen Lafayette[1] and McCaslin said in another ten years would be remembering God) lived, cooked and slept in one single room, burst into peaceful conflagration, a tranquil instantaneous sourceless unanimity of combustion, walls floors and roof: at sunup it stood where his uncle's father had built it sixty years ago, at sundown the four blackened and smokeless chimneys rose from a light white powder of ashes and a few charred ends of planks which did not even appear to have been very hot: and out of the last of evening, the last one of the twenty-two miles, on the old white mare which was the last of that stable which McCaslin remembered, the two old men riding double up to the sister's door, the one wearing his fox-horn on its braided deerhide thong and the other carrying the burlap parcel wrapped in a shirt, the tawny wax-daubed shapeless lump sitting again and on an almost identical shelf and his uncle holding the half-opened door now, his hand not only on the knob but one foot against it and the key waiting in the other hand, the face urgent and still not baffled but still and even indomitably not very amazed and himself standing in the half-opened door looking quietly up at the burlap shape become almost three times its original height and a good half less than its original thickness and turning away and he would remember not his mother's look this time nor yet Tennie's inscrutable expression but McCaslin's dark and aquiline face grave insufferable and bemused: then one night they waked him and fetched him still half-asleep into the lamp light, the smell of medicine which was familiar by now in that room and the smell of something else which he had not smelled before and knew at once and would never forget, the pillow, the worn and ravaged face from which looked out still the boy innocent and immortal and amazed and urgent, looking at him and trying to tell him until McCaslin moved and leaned over the bed and drew from the top of the night shirt the big iron key on the greasy cord which suspended it, the eyes saying Yes Yes Yes now, and cut the cord and unlocked the closet and brought the parcel to the bed, the eyes still trying to tell him even when he took the parcel so that was still not it, the hands still clinging to the parcel even while relinquishing it, the eyes more urgent than ever trying to tell him but they never did; and he was ten and his mother was dead too and McCaslin said, 'You are almost halfway now. You might as well open it:' and he: 'No. He said twenty-one:' and he was twenty-one and McCaslin shifted the bright lamp to the center of the cleared dining-room table and set the parcel beside it and laid his open knife beside the parcel and stood back with that expression of old grave intolerant and repudiating and he lifted it, the burlap lump which fifteen years ago had changed its shape completely overnight, which shaken gave forth a thin weightless not-quite-musical curiously muffled clatter, the bright knife-blade hunting amid the mazed intricacy of string, the knobby gouts of wax bearing his uncle's Beauchamp seal rattling onto the table's polished top and, standing amid the collapse of burlap folds, the unstained tin coffee-pot still brand new, the handful of copper coins and now he knew what had given them the muffled sound: a collection of minutely-folded scraps of paper sufficient almost for a rat's nest, of good linen bond,

---

1. The Marquis de Lafayette (1757–1834), who fought on the side of the colonists during the American Revolution, traveled through the South in 1825.

of the crude ruled paper such as negroes use, of raggedly-torn ledger-pages and the margins of newspapers and once the paper label from a new pair of overalls, all dated and all signed, beginning with the first one not six months after they had watched him seal the silver cup into the burlap on this same table in this same room by the light even of this same lamp almost twenty-one years ago:

> *I owe my Nephew Isaac Beauchamp McCaslin five (5) pieces Gold which I,O.U constitues My note of hand with Interest at 5 percent.*
> Hubert Fitz-Hubert Beauchamp
> *at Warwick 27 Nov 1867*

and he: 'Anyway he called it Warwick:' once at least, even if no more. But there was more:

> *Isaac 24 Dec 1867 I.O.U. 2 pieces Gold H.Fh.B. I.O.U. Isaac 1 piece Gold 1 Jan 1868 H.Fh.B.*

then five again then three then one then one then a long time and what dream, what dreamed splendid recoup, not of any injury or betrayal of trust because it had been merely a loan: nay, a partnership:

> *I.O.U. Beauchamp McCaslin or his heirs twenty-five (25) pieces Gold This & All preceeding constituting My notes of hand at twenty (20) percentum compounded annually. This date of 19th January 1873*
> Beauchamp

no location save that in time and signed by the single not name but word as the old proud earl himself might have scrawled Nevile:[2] and that made forty-three and he could not remember himself of course but the legend had it at fifty, which balanced: one: then one: then one: then one and then the last three and then the last chit, dated after he came to live in the house with them and written in the shaky hand not of a beaten old man because he had never been beaten to know it but of a tired old man maybe and even at that tired only on the outside and still indomitable, the simplicity of the last one the simplicity not of resignation but merely of amazement, like a simple comment or remark, and not very much of that:

> *One silver cup. Hubert Beauchamp*

and McCaslin: 'So you have plenty of coppers anyway. But they are still not old enough yet to be either rarities or heirlooms. So you will have to take the money:' except that he didn't hear McCaslin, standing quietly beside the table and looking peacefully at the coffee-pot and the pot sitting one night later on the mantel above what was not even a fireplace in the little cramped icelike room in Jefferson as McCaslin tossed the folded banknotes onto the bed and, still standing (there was nowhere to sit save on the bed) did not even remove his hat and overcoat: and he

'As a loan. From you. This one:' and McCaslin

'You cant. I have no money that I can lend to you. And you will have to

---

2. Hubert signs with the family name Beauchamp, as might the head of a noble family. His sister, Sophon-siba, liked to claim that he was the true earl of Warwick (England) inasmuch as the rights of a former countess of Warwick, Anne Beauchamp, were set aside upon the death of her husband, Richard Neville (1428–1471).

go to the bank and get it next month because I wont bring it to you:' and he could not hear McCaslin now either, looking peacefully at McCaslin, his kinsman, his father almost yet no kin now as, at the last, even fathers and sons are no kin: and he

'It's seventeen miles, horseback and in the cold. We could both sleep here:' and McCaslin

'Why should I sleep here in my house when you wont sleep yonder in yours?' and gone, and he looking at the bright rustless unstained tin and thinking and not for the first time how much it takes to compound a man (Isaac McCaslin for instance) and of the devious intricate choosing yet unerring path that man's (Isaac McCaslin's for instance) spirit takes among all that mass to make him at last what he is to be, not only to the astonishment of them (the ones who sired the McCaslin who sired his father and Uncle Buddy and their sister, and the ones who sired the Beauchamp who sired his Uncle Hubert and his Uncle Hubert's sister) who believed they had shaped him, but to Isaac McCaslin too

as a loan and used it though he would not have had to: Major de Spain offered him a room in his house as long as he wanted it and asked nor would ever ask any question, and old General Compson more than that, to take him into his own room, to sleep in half of his own bed and more than Major de Spain because he told him baldly why: 'You sleep with me and before this winter is out, I'll know the reason. You'll tell me. Because I don't believe you just quit. It looks like you just quit but I have watched you in the woods too much and I dont believe you just quit even if it does look damn like it:' using it as a loan, paid his board and rent for a month and bought the tools, not simply because he was good with his hands because he had intended to use his hands and it could have been with horses, and not in mere static and hopeful emulation of the Nazarene[3] as the young gambler buys a spotted shirt because the old gambler won in one yesterday, but (without the arrogance of false humility and without the false humbleness of pride, who intended to earn his bread, didn't especially want to earn it but had to earn it and for more than just bread) because if the Nazarene had found carpentering good for the life and ends He had assumed and elected to serve, it would be all right too for Isaac McCaslin even though Isaac McCaslin's ends, although simple enough in their apparent motivation, were and would be always incomprehensible to him, and his life, invincible enough in its needs, if he could have helped himself, not being the Nazarene, he would not have chosen it: and paid it back. He had forgotten the thirty dollars which McCaslin would put into the bank in his name each month, fetched it in to him and flung it onto the bed that first one time but no more; he had a partner now or rather he was the partner: a blasphemous profane clever old dipsomaniac who had built blockade-runners[4] in Charleston in '62 and '3 and had been a ship's carpenter since and appeared in Jefferson two years ago nobody knew from where nor why and spent a good part of his time since recovering from delirium tremens in the jail; they had put a new roof on the stable of the bank's president and (the old man in jail again still celebrating that job) he went to the bank to collect for it and the president said, 'I should

3. Jesus. 4. Ships that ran the blockade of Union ships outside the port of Charleston, South Carolina, during the Civil War.

borrow from you instead of paying you:' and it had been seven months now and he remembered for the first time, two-hundred-and-ten dollars, and this was the first job of any size and when he left the bank the account stood at two-twenty, two-forty to balance, only twenty dollars more to go, then it did balance though by then the total had increased to three hundred and thirty and he said, 'I will transfer it now:' and the president said, 'I cant do that. McCaslin told me not to. Haven't you got another initial you could use and open another account?' but that was all right, the coins the silver and the bills as they accumulated knotted into a handkerchief and the coffee-pot wrapped in an old shirt as when Tennie's great-grandfather had fetched it from Warwick eighteen years ago, in the bottom of the iron-bound trunk which old Carothers had brought from Carolina and his landlady said, 'Not even a lock! And you dont even lock your door, not even when you leave!' and himself looking at her as peacefully as he had looked at McCaslin that first night in this same room, no kin to him at all yet more than kin as those who serve you even for pay are your kin and those who injure you are more than brother or wife.

and had the wife now, got the old man out of jail and fetched him to the rented room and sobered him by superior strength, did not even remove his own shoes for twenty-four hours, got him up and got food into him and they built the barn this time from the ground up and he married her: an only child, a small girl yet curiously bigger than she seemed at first, solider perhaps, with dark eyes and a passionate heart-shaped face, who had time even on that farm[5] to watch most of the day while he sawed timbers to the old man's measurements: and she: 'Papa told me about you. That farm is really yours, isn't it?' and he

'And McCaslin's:' and she

'Was there a will leaving half of it to him?' and he

'There didn't need to be a will. His grandmother was my father's sister. We were the same as brothers:' and she

'You are the same as second cousins and that's all you ever will be. But I dont suppose it matters:' and they were married, they were married and it was the new country, his heritage too as it was the heritage of all, out of the earth, beyond the earth yet of the earth because his too was of the earth's long chronicle, his too because each must share with another in order to come into it and in the sharing they become one: for that while, one: for that little while at least, one: indivisible, that while at least irrevocable and unrecoverable, living in a rented room still but for just a little while and that room wall-less and topless and floorless in glory for him to leave each morning and return to at night; her father already owned the lot in town and furnished the material and he and his partner would build it, her dowry from one: her wedding-present from three, she not to know it until the bungalow was finished and ready to be moved into and he never knew who told her, not her father and not his partner and not even in drink though for a while he believed that, himself coming home from work and just time to wash and rest a moment before going down to supper, entering no rented cubicle since it would still partake of glory even after they would have grown old and lost it: and he saw her face then, just before she spoke: 'Sit down:' the two of

5. I.e., the farm where Ike is building a barn, not the McCaslin farm of the next question.

them sitting on the bed's edge, not even touching yet, her face strained and terrible, her voice a passionate and expiring whisper of immeasurable promise: 'I love you. You know I love you. When are we going to move?' and he

'I didn't—I didn't know—Who told you—' the hot fierce palm clapped over his mouth, crushing his lips into his teeth, the fierce curve of fingers digging into his cheek and only the palm slacked off enough for him to answer:

'The farm. Our farm. Your farm:' and he

'I—' then the hand again, finger and palm, the whole enveloping weight of her although she still was not touching him save the hand, the voice: 'No! No!' and the fingers themselves seeming to follow through the cheek the impulse to speech as it died in his mouth, then the whisper, the breath again, of love and of incredible promise, the palm slackening again to let him answer:

'When?' and he

'I—' then she was gone, the hand too, standing, her back to him and her head bent, the voice so calm now that for an instant it seemed no voice of hers that he ever remembered: 'Stand up and turn your back and shut your eyes:' and repeated before he understood and stood himself with his eyes shut and heard the bell ring for supper below stairs and the calm voice again: 'Lock the door:' and he did so and leaned his forehead against the cold wood, his eyes closed, hearing his heart and the sound he had begun to hear before he moved until it ceased and the bell rang again below stairs and he knew it was for them this time and he heard the bed and turned and he had never seen her naked before, he had asked her to once, and why: that he wanted to see her naked because he loved her and he wanted to see her looking at him naked because he loved her but after that he never mentioned it again, even turning his face when she put the nightgown on over her dress to undress at night and putting the dress on over the gown to remove it in the morning and she would not let him get into bed beside her until the lamp was out and even in the heat of summer she would draw the sheet up over them both before she would let him turn to her: and the landlady came up the stairs up the hall and rapped on the door and then called their names but she didn't move, lying still on the bed outside the covers, her face turned away on the pillow, listening to nothing, thinking of nothing, not of him anyway he thought then the landlady went away and she said, 'Take off your clothes:' her head still turned away, looking at nothing, thinking of nothing, waiting for nothing, not even him, her hand moving as though with volition and vision of its own, catching his wrist at the exact moment when he paused beside the bed so that he never paused but merely changed the direction of moving, downward now, the hand drawing him and she moved at last, shifted, a movement one single complete inherent not practiced and one time older than man, looking at him now, drawing him still downward with the one hand down and down and he neither saw nor felt it shift, palm flat against his chest now and holding him away with the same apparent lack of any effort or any need for strength, and not looking at him now, she didn't need to, the chaste woman, the wife, already looked upon all the men who ever rutted and now her whole body had changed, altered, he had never seen it but once and now it was not even the one he had seen but composite of all woman-flesh since man that ever of its own will reclined on its back and opened, and out of it somewhere, without any movement of lips even, the dying and invincible whisper: 'Promise:' and he

'Promise?'

'The farm.' He moved. He had moved, the hand shifting from his chest once more to his wrist, grasping it, the arm still lax and only the light increasing pressure of the fingers as though arm and hand were a piece of wire cable with one looped end, only the hand tightening as he pulled against it. 'No,' he said. 'No:' and she was not looking at him still but not like the other but still the hand: 'No, I tell you. I wont. I cant. Never:' and still the hand and he said, for the last time, he tried to speak clearly and he knew it was still gently and he thought, *She already knows more than I with all the man-listening in camps where there was nothing to read ever even heard of. They are born already bored with what a boy approaches only at fourteen and fifteen with blundering and aghast trembling:* 'I cant. Not ever. Remember:' and still the steady and invincible hand and he said Yes and he thought, *She is lost. She was born lost. We were all born lost* then he stopped thinking and even saying Yes, it was like nothing he had ever dreamed, let alone heard in mere man-talking until after a no-time he returned and lay spent on the insatiate immemorial beach and again with a movement one time more older than man she turned and freed herself and on their wedding night she had cried and he thought she was crying now at first, into the tossed and wadded pillow, the voice coming from somewhere between the pillow and the cachinnation: 'And that's all. That's all from me. If this dont get you that son you talk about, it wont be mine:' lying on her side, her back to the empty rented room, laughing and laughing

5

He went back to the camp one more time before the lumber company moved in and began to cut the timber. Major de Spain himself never saw it again. But he made them welcome to use the house and hunt the land whenever they liked, and in the winter following the last hunt when Sam Fathers and Lion died, General Compson and Walter Ewell invented a plan to corporate themselves, the old group, into a club and lease the camp and the hunting privileges of the woods—an invention doubtless of the somewhat childish old General but actually worthy of Boon Hogganbeck himself. Even the boy, listening, recognised it for the subterfuge it was: to change the leopard's spots when they could not alter the leopard, a baseless and illusory hope to which even McCaslin seemed to subscribe for a while, that once they had persuaded Major de Spain to return to the camp he might revoke himself, which even the boy knew he would not do. And he did not. The boy never knew what occurred when Major de Spain declined. He was not present when the subject was broached and McCaslin never told him. But when June came and the time for the double birthday celebration there was no mention of it and when November came no one spoke of using Major de Spain's house and he never knew whether or not Major de Spain knew they were going on the hunt though without doubt old Ash probably told him: he and McCaslin and General Compson (and that one was the General's last hunt too) and Walter and Boon and Tennie's Jim and old Ash loaded two wagons and drove two days and almost forty miles beyond any country the boy had ever seen before and lived in tents for the two weeks. And the next spring they heard (not from Major de Spain) that he had sold the timber-rights to a Memphis lumber company and in June the boy came to town with McCaslin one Saturday and went to Major de Spain's office—the big, airy, book-lined second-storey room with windows at one end opening upon the shabby hinder purlieus of stores and at the other a door giving onto the railed balcony above the Square, with its curtained alcove where sat a cedar water-bucket and a sugar-bowl and spoon and tumbler and a wicker-covered demijohn of whiskey, and the bamboo-and-paper punkah[6] swinging back and forth above the desk while old Ash in a tilted chair beside the entrance pulled the cord.

"Of course," Major de Spain said. "Ash will probably like to get off in the woods himself for a while, where he wont have to eat Daisy's cooking. Complain about it, anyway. Are you going to take anybody with you?"

"No sir," he said. "I thought that maybe Boon—" For six months now Boon had been town-marshal at Hoke's; Major de Spain had compounded with the lumber company—or perhaps compromised was closer, since it was the lumber company who had decided that Boon might be better as a town-marshal than head of a logging gang.

"Yes," Major de Spain said. "I'll wire him today. He can meet you at Hoke's. I'll send Ash on by the train and they can take some food in and all you will have to do will be to mount your horse and ride over."

"Yes sir," he said. "Thank you." And he heard his voice again. He didn't know he was going to say it yet he did know, he had known it all the time: "Maybe if you . . ." His voice died. It was stopped, he never knew how because Major de Spain did not speak and it was not until his voice ceased that Major de Spain moved, turned back to the desk and the papers spread on it and even that without moving because he was sitting at the desk with a paper in his hand when the boy entered, the boy standing there looking down at the short plumpish grey-haired man in sober fine broadcloth and an immaculate glazed shirt whom he was used to seeing in boots and muddy corduroy; unshaven, sitting the shaggy powerful long-hocked mare with the worn Winchester carbine across the saddle-bow and the great blue dog standing motionless as bronze at the stirrup, the two of them in that last year and to the boy anyway coming to resemble one another somehow as two people competent for love or for business who have been in love or in business together for a long time sometimes do. Major de Spain did not look up again.

"No. I will be too busy. But good luck to you. If you have it, you might bring me a young squirrel."

"Yes sir," he said. "I will."

He rode his mare, the three-year-old filly he had bred and raised and broken himself. He left home a little after midnight and six hours later, without even having sweated her, he rode into Hoke's, the tiny log-line junction which he had always thought of as Major de Spain's property too although Major de Spain had merely sold the company (and that many years ago) the land on which the sidetracks and loading-platforms and the commissary store stood, and looked about in shocked and grieved amazement even though he had had forewarning and had believed himself prepared: a new planing-mill already half completed which would cover two or three

6. A fan.

acres and what looked like miles and miles of stacked steel rails red with the light bright rust of newness and of piled crossties sharp with creosote, and wire corrals and feeding-troughs for two hundred mules at least and the tents for the men who drove them; so that he arranged for the care and stabling of his mare as rapidly as he could and did not look any more, mounted into the log-train caboose with his gun and climbed into the cupola and looked no more save toward the wall of wilderness ahead within which he would be able to hide himself from it once more anyway.

Then the little locomotive shrieked and began to move: a rapid churning of exhaust, a lethargic deliberate clashing of slack couplings traveling backward along the train, the exhaust changing to the deep slow clapping bites of power as the caboose too began to move and from the cupola he watched the train's head complete the first and only curve in the entire line's length and vanish into the wilderness, dragging its length of train behind it so that it resembled a small dingy harmless snake vanishing into weeds, drawing him with it too until soon it ran once more at its maximum clattering speed between the twin walls of unaxed wilderness as of old. It had been harmless once. Not five years ago Walter Ewell had shot a six-point buck from this same moving caboose, and there was the story of the half-grown bear: the train's first trip in to the cutting thirty miles away, the bear between the rails, its rear end elevated like that of a playing puppy while it dug to see what sort of ants or bugs they might contain or perhaps just to examine the curious symmetrical squared barkless logs which had appeared apparently from nowhere in one endless mathematical line overnight, still digging until the driver on the braked engine not fifty feet away blew the whistle at it, whereupon it broke frantically and took the first tree it came to: an ash sapling not much bigger than a man's thigh and climbed as high as it could and clung there, its head ducked between its arms as a man (a woman perhaps) might have done while the brakeman threw chunks of ballast at it, and when the engine returned three hours later with the first load of outbound logs the bear was halfway down the tree and once more scrambled back up as high as it could and clung again while the train passed and was still there when the engine went in again in the afternoon and still there when it came back out at dusk; and Boon had been in Hoke's with the wagon after a barrel of flour that noon when the train-crew told about it and Boon and Ash, both twenty years younger then, sat under the tree all that night to keep anybody from shooting it and the next morning Major de Spain had the log-train held at Hoke's and just before sundown on the second day, with not only Boon and Ash but Major de Spain and General Compson and Walter and Mc-Caslin, twelve then, watching, it came down the tree after almost thirty-six hours without even water and McCaslin told him how for a minute they thought it was going to stop right there at the barrow-pit where they were standing and drink, how it looked at the water and paused and looked at them and at the water again, but did not, gone, running, as bears run, the two sets of feet, front and back, tracking two separate though parallel courses.

It had been harmless then. They would hear the passing log-train sometimes from the camp; sometimes, because nobody bothered to listen for it or not. They would hear it going in, running light and fast, the light clatter of the trucks, the exhaust of the diminutive locomotive and its shrill peanut-parcher whistle[7] flung for one petty moment and absorbed by the brooding and inattentive wilderness without even an echo. They would hear it going out, loaded, not quite so fast now yet giving its frantic and toylike illusion of crawling speed, not whistling now to conserve steam, flinging its bitten laboring miniature puffing into the immemorial woodsface with frantic and bootless vainglory, empty and noisy and puerile, carrying to no destination or purpose sticks which left nowhere any scar or stump as the child's toy loads and transports and unloads its dead sand and rushes back for more, tireless and unceasing and rapid yet never quite so fast as the Hand which plays with it moves the toy burden back to load the toy again. But it was different now. It was the same train, engine cars and caboose, even the same enginemen brake-man and conductor to whom Boon, drunk then sober then drunk again then fairly sober once more all in the space of fourteen hours, had bragged that day two years ago about what they were going to do to Old Ben tomorrow, running with its same illusion of frantic rapidity between the same twin walls of impenetrable and impervious woods, passing the old landmarks, the old game crossings over which he had trailed bucks wounded and not wounded and more than once seen them, anything but wounded, bolt out of the woods and up and across the embankment which bore the rails and ties then down and into the woods again as the earth-bound supposedly move but crossing as arrows travel, groundless, elongated, three times its actual length and even paler, different in color, as if there were a point between immobility and absolute motion where even mass chemically altered, changing without pain or agony not only in bulk and shape but in color too, approaching the color of wind, yet this time it was as though the train (and not only the train but himself, not only his vision which had seen it and his memory which remembered it but his clothes too, as garments carry back into the clean edgeless blowing of air the lingering effluvium of a sick-room or of death) had brought with it into the doomed wilderness even before the actual axe the shadow and portent of the new mill not even finished yet and the rails and ties which were not even laid; and he knew now what he had known as soon as he saw Hoke's this morning but had not yet thought into words: why Major de Spain had not come back, and that after this time he himself, who had had to see it one time other, would return no more.

Now they were near. He knew it before the engine-driver whistled to warn him. Then he saw Ash and the wagon, the reins without doubt wrapped once more about the brake-lever as within the boy's own memory Major de Spain had been forbidding him for eight years to do, the train slowing, the slackened couplings jolting and clashing again from car to car, the caboose slowing past the wagon as he swung down with his gun, the conductor leaning out above him to signal the engine, the caboose still slowing, creeping, although the engine's exhaust was already slatting in mounting tempo against the unechoing wilderness, the crashing of draw-bars[8] once more travelling backward along the train, the caboose picking up speed at last. Then it was gone. It had not been. He could no longer hear it. The wilderness soared, musing, inattentive, myriad, eternal, green; older than any mill-shed, longer than any spurline. "Mr Boon here yet?" he said.

7. A steam whistle used by peanut vendors to attract business to their roasting machines.   8. Bars that attach railroad-car couplings.

"He beat me in," Ash said. "Had the wagon loaded and ready for me at Hoke's yistiddy when I got there and setting on the front steps at camp last night when I got in. He already been in the woods since fo daylight this morning. Said he gwine up to the Gum Tree and for you to hunt up that way and meet him." He knew where that was: a single big sweet-gum just outside the woods, in an old clearing; if you crept up to it very quietly this time of year and then ran suddenly into the clearing, sometimes you caught as many as a dozen squirrels in it, trapped, since there was no other tree near they could jump to. So he didn't get into the wagon at all.

"I will," he said.

"I figured you would," Ash said, "I fotch you a box of shells." He passed the shells down and began to unwrap the lines from the brake-pole.

"How many times up to now do you reckon Major has told you not to do that?" the boy said.

"Do which?" Ash said. Then he said: "And tell Boon Hogganbeck dinner gonter be on the table in a hour and if yawl want any to come on and eat it."

"In an hour?" he said. "It aint nine oclock yet." He drew out his watch and extended it face-toward Ash. "Look." Ash didn't even look at the watch.

"That's town time. You aint in town now. You in the woods."

"Look at the sun then."

"Nemmine the sun too," Ash said. "If you and Boon Hogganbeck want any dinner, you better come on in and get it when I tole you. I aim to get done in that kitchen because I got my wood to chop. And watch your feet. They're[9] crawling."

"I will," he said.

Then he was in the woods, not alone but solitary; the solitude closed about him, green with summer. They did not change, and, timeless, would not, anymore than would the green of summer and the fire and rain of fall and the iron cold and sometimes even snow

the day, the morning when he killed the buck and Sam marked his face with its hot blood, they returned to camp and he remembered old Ash's blinking and disgruntled and even outraged disbelief until at last McCaslin had had to affirm the fact that he had really killed it: and that night Ash sat snarling and unapproachable behind the stove so that Tennie's Jim had to serve the supper and waked them with breakfast already on the table the next morning and it was only half-past one oclock and at last out of Major de Spain's angry cursing and Ash's snarling and sullen rejoinders the fact emerged that Ash not only wanted to go into the woods and shoot a deer also but he intended to and Major de Spain said, 'By God, if we dont let him we will probably have to do the cooking from now on:' and Walter Ewell said, 'Or get up at midnight to eat what Ash cooks:' and since he had already killed his buck for this hunt and was not to shoot again unless they needed meat, he offered his gun to Ash until Major de Spain took command and allotted that gun to Boon for the day and gave Boon's unpredictable pump gun to Ash, with two buckshot shells but Ash said, 'I got shells:' and showed them, four: one buck, one of number three shot for rabbits, two of bird-shot and told one by one their history and their origin and he remembered not Ash's face alone but Major de Spain's and Walter's and General Compson's too, and Ash's voice: 'Shoot? In course they'll shoot! Genl

9. I.e., snakes are.

Cawmpson guv me this un'—the buckshot—'right outen the same gun he kilt that big buck with eight years ago. And this un'—it was the rabbit shell: triumphantly—'is oldern thisyer boy!' And that morning he loaded the gun himself, reversing the order: the bird-shot, the rabbit, then the buck so that the buckshot would feed first into the chamber, and himself without a gun, he and Ash walked beside Major de Spain's and Tennie's Jim's horses and the dogs (that was the snow) until they cast and struck, the sweet strong cries ringing away into the muffled falling air and gone almost immediately, as if the constant and unmurmuring flakes had already buried even the unformed echoes beneath their myriad and weightless falling, Major de Spain and Tennie's Jim gone too, whooping on into the woods; and then it was all right, he knew as plainly as if Ash had told him that Ash had now hunted his deer and that even his tender years had been forgiven for having killed one, and they turned back toward home through the falling snow—that is, Ash said, 'Now whut?' and he said, 'This way'—himself in front because, although they were less than a mile from camp, he knew that Ash, who had spent two weeks of his life in the camp each year for the last twenty, had no idea whatever where they were, until quite soon the manner in which Ash carried Boon's gun was making him a good deal more than just nervous and he made Ash walk in front, striding on, talking now, an old man's garrulous monologue beginning with where he was at the moment then of the woods and of camping in the woods and of eating in camps then of eating then of cooking it and of his wife's cooking then briefly of his old wife and almost at once and at length of a new light-colored woman who nursed next door to Major de Spain's and if she didn't watch out who she was switching her tail at he would show her how old was an old man or not if his wife just didn't watch him all the time, the two of them in a game trail through a dense brake of cane and brier which would bring them out within a quarter-mile of camp, approaching a big fallen tree-trunk lying athwart the path and just as Ash, still talking, was about to step over it the bear, the yearling, rose suddenly beyond the log, sitting up, its forearms against its chest and its wrists limply arrested as if it had been surprised in the act of covering its face to pray: and after a certain time Ash's gun yawed jerkily up and he said, 'You haven't got a shell in the barrel yet. Pump it:' but the gun already snicked and he said, 'Pump it. You haven't got a shell in the barrel yet:' and Ash pumped the action and in a certain time the gun steadied again and snicked and he said, 'Pump it:' and watched the buckshot shell jerk, spinning heavily, into the cane. This is the rabbit shot: he thought and the gun snicked and he thought: The next is bird-shot: and he didn't have to say Pump it; he cried, 'Dont shoot! Dont shoot!' but that was already too late too, the light dry vicious snick! before he could speak and the bear turned and dropped to all-fours and then was gone and there was only the log, the cane, the velvet and constant snow and Ash said, 'Now whut?' and he said, 'This way. Come on:' and began to back away down the path and Ash said, 'I got to find my shells:' and he said, 'Goddamn it, goddamn it, come on:' but Ash leaned the gun against the log and returned and stooped and fumbled among the cane roots until he came back and stooped and found the shells and they rose and at that moment the gun, untouched, leaning against the log six feet away and for that while even forgotten by both of them, roared, bellowed and flamed, and ceased: and he carried it now, pumped out the last mummified shell and gave that one also to Ash and, the action still open, himself carried the gun until he stood it in the corner behind Boon's bed at the camp

—; summer, and fall, and snow, and wet and saprife spring in their ordered immortal sequence, the deathless and immemorial phases of the mother who had shaped him if any had toward the man he almost was, mother and father both to the old man born of a Negro slave and a Chickasaw chief who had been his spirit's father if any had, whom he had revered and harkened to and loved and lost and grieved: and he would marry someday and they too would own for their brief while that brief unsubstanced glory which inherently of itself cannot last and hence why glory: and they would, might, carry even the remembrance of it into the time when flesh no longer talks to flesh because memory at least does last: but still the woods would be his mistress and his wife.

He was not going toward the Gum Tree. Actually he was getting farther from it. Time was and not so long ago either when he would not have been allowed here without someone with him, and a little later, when he had begun to learn how much he did not know, he would not have dared be here without someone with him, and later still, beginning to ascertain, even if only dimly, the limits of what he did not know, he could have attempted and carried it through with a compass, not because of any increased belief in himself but because McCaslin and Major de Spain and Walter and General Compson too had taught him at last to believe the compass regardless of what it seemed to state. Now he did not even use the compass but merely the sun and that only subconsciously, yet he could have taken a scaled map and plotted at any time to within a hundred feet of where he actually was; and sure enough, at almost the exact moment when he expected it, the earth began to rise faintly, he passed one of the four concrete markers set down by the lumber company's surveyor to establish the four corners of the plot which Major de Spain had reserved out of the sale, then he stood on the crest of the knoll itself, the four corner-markers all visible now, blanched still even beneath the winter's weathering, lifeless and shockingly alien in that place where dissolution itself was a seething turmoil of ejaculation tumescence conception and birth, and death did not even exist. After two winters' blanketings of leaves and the flood-waters of two springs, there was no trace of the two graves anymore at all. But those who would have come this far to find them would not need headstones but would have found them as Sam Fathers himself had taught him to find such: by bearings on trees: and did, almost the first thrust of the hunting knife finding (but only to see if it was still there) the round tin box manufactured for axle-grease and containing now Old Ben's dried mutilated paw, resting above Lion's bones.

He didn't disturb it. He didn't even look for the other grave where he and McCaslin and Major de Spain and Boon had laid Sam's body, along with his hunting horn and his knife and his tobacco-pipe, that Sunday morning two years ago; he didn't have to. He had stepped over it, perhaps on it. But that was all right. *He probably knew I was in the woods this morning long before I got here,* he thought, going on to the tree which had supported one end of the platform where Sam lay when McCaslin and Major de Spain found them—the tree, the other axle-grease tin nailed to the trunk, but weathered, rusted, alien too yet healed already into the wilderness' concordant generality, raising no tuneless note, and empty, long since empty of the food and tobacco he had put into it that day, as empty of that as it would presently be of this which he drew from his pocket—the twist of tobacco, the new bandanna handkerchief, the small paper sack of the peppermint candy which

Sam had used to love; that gone too, almost before he had turned his back, not vanished but merely translated into the myriad life which printed the dark mold of these secret and sunless places with delicate fairy tracks, which, breathing and biding and immobile, watched him from beyond every twig and leaf until he moved, moving again, walking on; he had not stopped, he had only paused, quitting the knoll which was no abode of the dead because there was no death, not Lion and not Sam: not held fast in earth but free in earth and not in earth but of earth, myriad yet undiffused of every myriad part, leaf and twig and particle, air and sun and rain and dew and night, acorn oak and leaf and acorn again, dark and dawn and dark and dawn again in their immutable progression and, being myriad, one: and Old Ben too, Old Ben too; they would give him his paw back even, certainly they would give him his paw back: then the long challenge and the long chase, no heart to be driven and outraged, no flesh to be mauled and bled—Even as he froze himself, he seemed to hear Ash's parting admonition. He could even hear the voice as he froze, immobile, one foot just taking his weight, the toe of the other just lifted behind him, not breathing, feeling again and as always the sharp shocking inrush from when Isaac McCaslin long yet was not, and so it was fear all right but not fright as he looked down at it. It had not coiled yet and the buzzer had not sounded either, only one thick rapid contraction, one loop cast sideways as though merely for purchase from which the raised head might start slightly backward, not in fright either, not in threat quite yet, more than six feet of it, the head raised higher than his knee and less than his knee's length away, and old, the once-bright markings of its youth dulled now to a monotone concordant too with the wilderness it crawled and lurked: the old one, the ancient and accursed about the earth, fatal and solitary and he could smell it now: the thin sick smell of rotting cucumbers and something else which had no name, evocative of all knowledge and an old weariness and of pariah-hood and of death. At last it moved. Not the head. The elevation of the head did not change as it began to glide away from him, moving erect yet off the perpendicular as if the head and that elevated third were complete and all: an entity walking on two feet and free of all laws of mass and balance and should have been because even now he could not quite believe that all that shift and flow of shadow behind that walking head could have been one snake: going and then gone; he put the other foot down at last and didn't know it, standing with one hand raised as Sam had stood that afternoon six years ago when Sam led him into the wilderness and showed him and he ceased to be a child, speaking the old tongue which Sam had spoken that day without premeditation either: "Chief," he said: "Grandfather."

He couldn't tell when he first began to hear the sound, because when he became aware of it, it seemed to him that he had been already hearing it for several seconds—a sound as though someone were hammering a gun-barrel against a piece of railroad iron, a sound loud and heavy and not rapid yet with something frenzied about it, as the hammerer were not only a strong man and an earnest one but a little hysterical too. Yet it couldn't be on the log-line because, although the track lay in that direction, it was at least two miles from him and this sound was not three hundred yards away. But even as he thought that, he realised where the sound must be coming from: who-ever the man was and whatever he was doing, he was somewhere near the edge of the clearing where the Gum Tree was and where he was to meet Boon. So far, he had been hunting as he advanced, moving slowly and quietly and watching the ground and the trees both. Now he went on, his gun unloaded and the barrel slanted up and back to facilitate its passage through brier and undergrowth, approaching as it grew louder and louder that steady savage somehow queerly hysterical beating of metal on metal, emerging from the woods, into the old clearing, with the solitary gum tree directly before him. At first glance the tree seemed to be alive with frantic squirrels. There appeared to be forty or fifty of them leaping and darting from branch to branch until the whole tree had become one green maelstrom of mad leaves, while from time to time, singly or in twos and threes, squirrels would dart down the trunk then whirl without stopping and rush back up again as though sucked violently back by the vacuum of their fellows' frenzied vortex. Then he saw Boon, sitting, his back against the trunk, his head bent, hammering furiously at something on his lap. What he hammered with was the barrel of his dismembered gun, what he hammered at was the breech of it. The rest of the gun lay scattered about him in a half-dozen pieces while he bent over the piece on his lap his scarlet and streaming walnut face, hammering the disjointed barrel against the gun-breech with the frantic abandon of a madman. He didn't even look up to see who it was. Still hammering, he merely shouted back at the boy in a hoarse strangled voice:

"Get out of here! Dont touch them! Dont touch a one of them! They're mine!"

BERTOLT BRECHT
1898–1956

Bertolt Brecht is a dominant figure in modern drama not only as the author of a half dozen plays that rank as modern classics but as the first master of a powerful new concept of theater. He was dissatisfied with the traditional notion, derived from Aristotle's *Poetics*, that drama should draw its spectators into identification with and sympathy for the characters, and with the realist aesthetic of naturalness and psychological credibility. Brecht saw only harm in such uncritical submission to illusions created on stage. Like Pirandello, he believed that the modern stage should break open the closed world established as a dramatic convention by writers such as Ibsen and Chekhov, whose audiences were to look at the action from a distance, as if it were a slice of real life going on behind an invisible "fourth wall." Unlike Pirandello, however, Brecht did not stress the anguish of individuals in society and the difficulty of knowing who we are; his focus was the community at large, and social responsibility. For Brecht, a political activist, the modern audience must not be allowed to indulge in passive emotional identification at a safe distance, or in the subjective whirlpool of existential identity crises. His characters are to be seen as members of society, and his audience must be educated and moved to action. The movement called "epic theater," which was born in the 1920s, suited his needs well, and through his plays, theoretical writings, and dramatic productions he developed its basic ideas into one of the most powerful theatrical styles of the century.

Eugen Berthold Brecht was born in the medieval town of Augsburg, Bavaria, on February 10, 1898. His father was a respected town citizen, director of a paper mill, and a Catholic. His mother, the daughter of a civil servant from the Black Forest, was a Protestant who raised young Berthold in her own faith. (The spelling *Bertolt* was adopted later.) Brecht attended local schools until 1917, when he enrolled in Munich University to study natural science and medicine. He continued his studies while acting as drama critic for an Augsburg newspaper and writing his own plays: *Drums in the Night* (1918) won the Kleist Prize in 1922. In 1918 Brecht was mobilized for a year as an orderly in a military hospital, and he pursued medical studies at Munich until 1921. In 1929 he married Helene Weigel, an actress who worked closely with him and for whom he wrote many leading roles. Together they would direct and make famous the theater group founded for them in 1949 in East Berlin: the Berliner Ensemble.

Moving to Berlin, Brecht worked briefly with the directors Max Reinhardt and Erwin Piscator but was chiefly interested in his own writing. In this pre-Marxist period he is especially concerned with the plight of the individual "common man," pushed around by social and economic forces beyond his control until he loses both identity and humanity. In *A Man's a Man* (1924–25), the timid dock worker Galy Gay is transformed by fright and persuasion into another person, the ferociously successful soldier Jeriah Jip. When Jip turns up at the end of the play, he is given Gay's former papers and forced to assume Gay's old identity. The play teaches that human personalities can be broken down and reassembled like a machine; the only weapon against such mindless manipulation is awareness, an awareness that enables people to understand and control their destiny.

Most of Brecht's plays are didactic, either openly or by implication. After he became a fervent Marxist in the mid-1920s, he considered it even more his moral and artistic duty to encourage the audience to remedy social ills. *The Threepenny Opera* (1928), a ballad opera written with composer Kurt Weill (1900–1950) and modeled on John Gay's *The Beggar's Opera* (1728), satirizes capitalist society from the point of view of outcasts and romantic thieves. Brecht also wrote a number of "lesson" plays intended to set forth Communist doctrine and to instruct the workers of Germany in the meaning of social revolution. The lesson was particularly harsh in *The Measures Taken* (1930), which describes the necessary execution of a young party member who has broken discipline and helped the local poor, thus postponing the revolution. Such drama, however doctrinally pure, was not likely to win adherents to the cause, and the lesson plays were condemned as unattractive and "intellectualist" by the Communist press in Berlin and Moscow.

Brecht's unorthodoxy, his pacifism, his enthusiasm for Marx, and his desire to create an activist popular theater that would embody a Marxist view of art all put him at odds with the rising power of Hitler's National Socialism. He fled Germany for Denmark in 1933, before the Nazis could include him in their purge of left-wing intellectuals; in 1935 he was deprived of his German citizenship. Brecht was to flee several more times as the Nazi invasions expanded throughout Europe: in 1939 he went to Sweden, in 1940 to Finland, and in 1941 to the United States, where he joined a colony of German expatriates in Santa Monica, California, working for the film industry. This was the period of some of his greatest plays: *The Life of Galileo* (1938–39), which attacks society for suppressing Galileo's discovery that the Earth revolves around the sun, but also condemns the scientist for not insisting openly on the truth; *Mother Courage and Her Children* (1939), which describes an avaricious peddler who doggedly pursues the profits to be made from war even though her own three children are victims of it; *The Good Woman of Setzuan* (1938–40), printed here, which shows how an instinctively good and generous person can survive in this world only by putting on a mask of hardness and calculation; and *The Caucasian Chalk Circle* (1944–45), which adapts the legendary choice of Solomon between two mothers who claim the same infant and decides in favor of the servant girl—who cared for the child—over the wealthy mother (the implied comparison is between those who do the work of society and those who merely profit from their possessions). In America, Brecht arranged for the translation of his work into English, and *Galileo*, with Charles Laughton in the title role, was produced in 1947. In the same year, Brecht was questioned by the House Un-American Activities Committee as part of a wide-ranging inquiry into possible Communist activity in the entertainment business. No charges were brought, but he left for Europe the day after being brought before the committee.

After leaving the United States, Brecht worked for a year in Zurich before going to Berlin with his wife, Helene Weigel, to stage *Mother Courage*. The East Berlin government offered the couple positions as directors of their own troupe, the Berliner Ensemble, and Brecht—who had just finished a theoretical work on the theater, *A Little Organon for the Theater* (1949)—turned his attention to the professional role of director. Although the East Berliners subsidized Brecht's work and advertised the artist's presence among them as a tribute to their own political system, they also obliged him to defend some of his plays against charges of political unorthodoxy and indeed to revise them. After 1934, the prevailing Communist Party view had upheld a style called "socialist realism," whose goal was to offer simple messages and to foster identification with revolutionary heroes. Brecht's mind was too keen and questioning, too attracted by irony and paradox, for him to provide the simplistic drama desired or to have a comfortable relation with authority, either of the right or of the left. After settling in East Berlin, he wrote no major new plays but only minor propaganda pieces and adaptations of classical works such as Molière's *Don Juan* and Shakespeare's *Coriolanus*. As an additional measure of protection, he took out Austrian citizenship through his wife's nationality. Brecht died in Berlin on August 14, 1956. Presumably, he would have taken ironic pleasure in the fact that, on February 10, 1998, the one hundredth anniversary of his birth was celebrated throughout Germany and included a presidential speech at the Berlin Academy of Arts.

The "epic theater" for which Brecht is known derives its name from a famous essay, *On Epic and Dramatic Poetry*, by Goethe and Schiller, who in 1797 described *dramatic* poetry as pulling the audience into emotional identification, in contrast to *epic* poetry, which by being distanced in the time, place, and nature of the action could be absorbed in calm contemplation. The idea of an epic theater is a paradox: how can a play engage an audience that is still held at a distance? Brecht's solution was to employ many "alienation effects" that were genuinely dramatic but that prevented total identification with the characters and forced spectators to think critically about what was taking place. In this, he echoed the work of the revolutionary Soviet director Vsevolod Meyerhold, whose antirealistic use of masks, pantomime, posters and film projections, song interludes, and direct address to the audience was well known to German audiences in the 1920s. These alienation effects have since become standard production techniques in the modern theater. In spite of Brecht's intentions and frequent revisions, however, the characters and situations of his plays remain emotionally engrossing, especially in his best-known works, such as *The Good Woman of Setzuan*.

Brecht's concept of an epic theater touches on all aspects of the form: dramatic structure, stage setting, music, and the actor's performance. The structure is to be open, episodic, and broken by dramatic or musical interludes. It is a "chronicle" that recounts events in an epic or distanced perspective. Episodes may also be performed independently as self-contained dramatic parables, instead of being organically tied to a centrally developing plot. Skits appear between scenes: in *A Man's a Man*, there is a fantastic interlude in which an elephant is accused of having murdered its mother. Songs break dramatic action and yet crystallize important themes: in *The Good Woman of Setzuan*, "The Song of Defenselessness" presents an outraged Shen Te masking herself and turning into Shui Ta; Yang Sun's lording it over his coworkers is satirized in "The Song of the Eighth Elephant." Sometimes a narrator comments on the action (as in *The Threepenny Opera* and *A Man's a Man*). The alienation effects are also heightened by setting most of the plays in far-away lands (China in *The Good*

Woman of Setzuan, India in *A Man's a Man*, England in *The Threepenny Opera*, the Soviet Union in *The Caucasian Chalk Circle*, Chicago in *Saint Joan of the Stockyards* and *The Resistible Rise of Arturo Ui*) or distant times (the seventeenth century in *Mother Courage*, Renaissance Italy in *Galileo*, or an imagined ghostly afterlife in *The Trial of Lucullus*).

Stagecraft and performance further support Brecht's concept of a critical, intellectualized theater. Events on stage may be announced beforehand by signs or accompanied by projected images during the action itself. Place-names printed on signs are suspended over the actors, and footlights and stage machinery are openly displayed. Masks are used for wicked people (for example, the Shui Ta personality in *The Good Woman of Setzuan*), or soldiers' faces are chalked white to suggest a stylized fear. Songs that interrupt the dramatic action are addressed directly to the audience, sometimes heralded by a sign Brecht called a "musical emblem." In addition, Brecht described a special kind of acting: actors should "demonstrate" their parts instead of being submerged in them. At rehearsals, Brecht often asked actors to speak their parts in the third person instead of the first. Such constant artificiality injected into all aspects of the performance makes it difficult for the audience to identify completely and unself-consciously with the characters on stage.

Audiences may react emotionally to Brecht's plays and characters, but their reactions are never simple. Brecht's characters are complex and inhabit complex situations. Galileo is both a dedicated scientist who sacrifices his reputation for honesty so as to complete his work, and a weak sensualist who fails to realize how his recantation will affect others' pursuit of scientific knowledge. In *The Good Woman of Setzuan*, the overgenerous Shen Te can survive only by periodically adopting the mask of a harshly practical "cousin," Shui Ta. Mother Courage is both a tragic mother figure and a small-time profiteer who loses her children as she battens on war. Brecht's work teems with such paradoxes at all levels. He is a cynic who deflates religious zeal, militant patriotism, and heroic example as delusions that lead the masses on to futile sacrifice; yet he is also a preacher who makes prominent use of traditional biblical language and imagery, and themes of individual sacrifice.

The Good Woman of Setzuan was written between 1938 and 1941, with the collaboration of Margarete Steffin and Ruth Berlau, and with music by Paul Dessau. Drafted painfully while Brecht, his family, Steffin, and Berlau sought refuge in Scandinavia from the Nazis' conquest of Europe, the play is stamped with bitter disillusionment at a world in which it is impossible to be good and survive. The "good woman," Shen Te, is forced to disguise herself as her male "cousin" and alter ego, the cruel Shui Ta, to save herself from a swarm of parasites and opportunists who will not leave her a roof over her head. Appearing alternately as the ruthless Shui Ta and the generous Shen Te, she embodies different ways of being, encounters different responses from the people around her, is gradually contaminated, and recognizes despairingly that she will always need to call on her wicked cousin to survive. The play's setting in China was probably suggested by a 1935 visit to Moscow, where Brecht was impressed by the highly stylized performances of the Chinese actor Mei Lan-fang, one of whose traditional roles was that of the woman warrior who must disguise herself as a man. Brecht had already written a short play and a story that described the way women were subordinated and exploited in traditional patriarchal society, a theme that returns strongly in *The Good Woman of Setzuan*. The opposition of men and women is not absolute, however, for the play contains both good and bad male and female characters. Indeed, the Woman of the English title may be misleading, even if Shen Te represents goodness, for the German title's *Mensch* means literally "person" or "human being" and embraces both genders. For Brecht, the problem of good and evil, and the need to reform a corrupt world, confronts both women and men. As the Epilogue tells the audience: "You write the happy ending to the play!"

Shen Te's story has a larger frame: the state of the universe or, more mundanely, the question of whether the world is so corrupt that affairs cannot be allowed to continue. Her situation arises from a good deed whose counterpart recurs in various world mythologies and also in the Bible: hospitality offered to disguised divine messengers, who reward the giver accordingly. Three Chinese gods visiting Earth in search of good people give Shen Te, a penniless prostitute, a thousand silver dollars in recompense for being the only person in Setzuan to give them lodging. Brecht borrows (as so often) from the Bible: specifically, from the Old Testament story of Sodom and Gomorrah, in which God sends angels down to find ten good people in the debauched city of Sodom so that it may be saved from destruction. Yet these modern gods are somewhat comic and certainly ineffectual. Wearing old-fashioned clothes and dusty shoes, they have been delegated as the result of a bureaucratic Resolution on high (whose terms they debate); they ignore inconvenient questions and merely repeat the conventional, inapplicable regulations; they are terrified of complications that would disturb the status quo and—in a verbal echo of Nazi slogans about proper order—they persuade themselves at the end that "everything is in order" and leave on a pink cloud despite Shen Te's despairing cries. These caricatured godlets represent the bureaucratic state more than anything else. Their refusal to be involved only reinforces Brecht's underlying thesis that "good" and "evil" are not divine but rather social issues and that the way to reform a corrupt world is for people to unite in common action focused on the common good.

The current translation, by Eric Bentley, Brecht's early translator and collaborator, is a performance-oriented version of the original text of 1941, undertaken with Brecht's approval.

Martin Esslin, *Brecht, The Man and His Work* (1974), John Fuegi, *Brecht and Company: Sex, Politics, and the Making of Modern Drama* (1994), and John Willett, *The Theatre of Bertolt Brecht: A Study from Eight Aspects* (1959), offer biographical and critical perspectives on the author and his work. John Willett, ed. and trans., *Brecht on Theatre: The Development of an Aesthetic* (1964), contains Brecht's own essays and lectures on his theater. Ronald Hayman, *Brecht: A Biography* (1983), offers a detailed view of Brecht's life. Eric Bentley, *The Brecht Commentaries 1943–1986* (1987), offers lively essays on the major plays, on Brecht's stagecraft, and on his place in modern culture by a friend and sometime colleague. The essays in Walter Benjamin, *Understanding Brecht* (1983), provide important insights into Brecht's work and modern thought by a close friend and major intellectual figure. *A Bertolt Brecht Reference Companion* (1997), edited by Siegfried Mews, offers seventeen diverse essays with an introduction and bibliography. *The Cambridge Companion to Brecht* (1994), edited by Peter Thompson and Glendry Sacks, contains an essay on *The Good Person of Szechwan*. Katherine Bliss Eaton, *The Theater of Meyerhold and Brecht* (1985), Anthony Tatlow, *The Mask of Evil: Brecht's Response to the Poetry, Theatre and Thought of China and Japan* (1977), and Renata Berg-Pan, *Bertolt Brecht and China* (1979), are valuable comparative studies.

PRONOUNCING GLOSSARY

The following list uses common English syllables and stress accents to provide rough equivalents of selected words whose pronunciation may be unfamiliar to the general reader.

Lin To: *lin taw*

Mi Tzu: *mee'-dz*

Setzuan: *sets-wan'*

Shen Te: *shun-teu*

Shu Fu: *shoo foo*

Shui Ta: *shway tah*

Yang Sun: *yahng sun*

Wong: *wahng*

The Good Woman of Setzuan[1]

CHARACTERS

WONG, *a water seller*

THREE GODS

SHEN TE, *a prostitute, later a shopkeeper*

MRS. SHIN, *former owner of Shen Te's shop*

A *family of eight* (HUSBAND, WIFE, BROTHER, SISTER–IN–LAW, GRANDFATHER, NEPHEW, NIECE, BOY)

An UNEMPLOYED MAN

A CARPENTER

MRS. MI TZU, *Shen Te's landlady*

Mr. SHUI TA

YANG SUN, *an unemployed pilot, later a factory manager*

An OLD WHORE

A POLICEMAN

An OLD MAN

An OLD WOMAN, *his wife*

Mr. SHU FU, *a barber*

MRS. YANG, *mother of Yang Sun*

GENTLEMEN, VOICES, PRIEST, WAITER, children (three), etc.

Prologue

At the gates of the half-Westernized city of Setzuan. Evening. WONG *the water seller[2] introduces himself to the audience.*

WONG I sell water here in the city of Setzuan. It isn't easy. When water is scarce, I have long distances to go in search of it, and when it is plentiful, I have no income. But in our part of the world there is nothing unusual about poverty. Many people think only the gods can save the situation. And I hear from a cattle merchant—who travels a lot—that some of the highest gods are on their way here at this very moment. Informed sources have it that heaven is quite disturbed at all the complaining.[3] I've been coming out here to the city gates for three days now to bid these gods welcome. I want to be the first to greet them. What about those fellows over there? No, no, they *work*. And that one there has ink on his fingers, he's no god, he must be a clerk from the cement factory. *Those* two are another story. They look as though they'd like to beat you. But gods don't need to beat you, do they? [THREE GODS *appear.*] What about those three? Old-fashioned clothes—dust on their feet— they *must* be gods! [*He throws himself at their feet.*] Do with me what you will, illustrious ones!

FIRST GOD [*With an ear trumpet.*] Ah! [*He is pleased.*] So we were expected?

WONG [*Giving them water.*] Oh, yes. And I *knew* you'd come.

FIRST GOD We need somewhere to stay the night. You know of a place?

WONG The whole town is at your service, illustrious ones! What sort of a place would you like?

1. Translated by Eric Bentley. Setzuan is a province in China; the play's setting is both the capital of Setzuan and, according to a later statement in the play, a generalized location: "wherever man is exploited by man." 2. Water peddlers were common in ancient China. 3. Heaven, in Chinese philosophy, was identical with absolute and transcendental order.

[*The* GODS *eye each other.*]

FIRST GOD   Just try the first house you come to, my son.

WONG   That would be Mr. Fo's place.

FIRST GOD   Mr. Fo.

WONG   One moment! [*He knocks at the first house.*]

VOICE FROM MR. FO'S.   No!

[WONG *returns a little nervously.*]

WONG   It's too bad. Mr. Fo isn't in. And his servants don't dare do a thing without his consent. He'll have a fit when he finds out who they turned away, won't he?

FIRST GOD [*Smiling.*]   He will, won't he?

WONG   One moment! The next house is Mr. Cheng's. Won't he be thrilled!

FIRST GOD   Mr. Cheng

[WONG *knocks.*]

VOICE FROM MR. CHENG'S   Keep your gods. We have our own troubles!

WONG [*Back with the* GODS.]   Mr. Cheng is very sorry, but he has a houseful of relations. I think some of them are a bad lot, and naturally, he wouldn't like you to see them.

THIRD GOD   Are we so terrible?

WONG   Well, only with bad people, of course. Everyone knows the province of Kwan is always having floods.

SECOND GOD   Really? How's that?

WONG   Why, because they're so irreligious.

SECOND GOD   Rubbish. It's because they neglected the dam.

FIRST GOD [*To* SECOND.]   Sh! [*To* WONG.] You're still in hopes, aren't you, my son?

WONG   Certainly. All Setzuan is competing for the honor! What happened up to now is pure coincidence. I'll be back. [*He walks away, but then stands undecided.*]

SECOND GOD   What did I tell you?

THIRD GOD   It *could* be pure coincidence.

SECOND GOD   The same coincidence in Shun, Kwan, and Setzuan? People just aren't religious any more, let's face the fact. Our mission has failed!

FIRST GOD   Oh come, we might run into a good person any minute.

THIRD GOD   How did the resolution read? [*Unrolling a scroll and reading from it.*] "The word can stay as it is if enough people are found [*At the word "found" he unrolls it a little more*] living lives worthy of human beings." Good people, that is. Well, what about this water seller himself? He's good, or I'm very much mistaken.

SECOND GOD   You're very much mistaken. When he gave us a drink, I had the impression there was something odd about the cup. Well, look! [*He shows the cup to the* FIRST GOD.]

FIRST GOD   A false bottom!

SECOND GOD   The man is a swindler.

FIRST GOD   Very well, count *him* out. That's one man among millions. And as a matter of fact, we only need one on *our* side. These atheists are saying, "The world must be changed because no one can *be* good and *stay* good." No one, eh? I say: let us find one—just one—and we have those fellows where we want them!

THIRD GOD [*To* WONG.]   Water seller, is it so hard to find a place to stay?

WONG   Nothing could be easier. It's just me. I don't go about it right.

THIRD GOD   Really?

> [*He returns to the others. A* GENTLEMAN *passes by.*]

WONG   Oh dear, they're catching on. [*He accosts the* GENTLEMAN.] Excuse the intrusion, dear sir, but three gods have just turned up. Three of the very highest. They need a place for the night. Seize this rare opportunity—to have real gods as your guests!

GENTLEMAN [*laughing*].   A new way of finding free rooms for a gang of crooks. [*Exit* GENTLEMAN.]

WONG [*shouting at him.*]   Godless rascal! Have you no religion, gentlemen of Setzuan? [*Pause*]. Patience, illustrious ones! [*Pause.*] There's only one person left. Shen Te, the prostitute. She *can't* say no. [*Calls up to a window.*] Shen Te!

> [SHEN TE *opens the shutters and looks out.*]

WONG   Shen Te, it's Wong. They're here, and nobody wants them. Will you take them?

SHEN TE   Oh, no, Wong, I'm expecting a gentleman.

WONG   Can't you forget about him for tonight?

SHEN TE   The rent has to be paid by tomorrow or I'll be out on the street.

WONG   This is no time for calculation, Shen Te.

SHEN TE   Stomachs rumble even on the Emperor's birthday, Wong.

WONG   Setzuan is one big dung hill!

SHEN TE   Oh, very well! I'll hide till my gentleman has come and gone. Then I'll take them. [*She disappears.*]

WONG   They mustn't see her gentleman or they'll know what she is.

FIRST GOD [*Who hasn't heard any of this.*]   I think it's hopeless.

> [*They approach* WONG.]

WONG [*Jumping, as he finds them behind him*].   A room has been found, illustrious ones! [*He wipes sweat off his brow.*]

SECOND GOD   Oh, good.

THIRD GOD   Let's see it.

WONG [*Nervously.*]   Just a minute. It has to be tidied up a bit.

THIRD GOD   Then we'll sit down here and wait.

WONG [*Still more nervous.*]   No, no! [*Holding himself back.*] Too much traffic, you know.

THIRD GOD [*With a smile.*]   Of course, if you *want* us to move.

> [*They retire a little. They sit on a doorstep.* WONG *sits on the ground.*]

WONG [*After a deep breath.*]   You'll be staying with a single girl—the finest human being in Setzuan!

THIRD GOD   That's nice.

WONG [*To the audience.*]   They gave me such a look when I picked up my cup just now.

THIRD GOD   You're worn out, Wong.

WONG   A little, maybe.

FIRST GOD   Do people here have a hard time of it?

WONG   The good ones do.

FIRST GOD   What about yourself!

WONG   You mean I'm not good. That's true. And I don't have an easy time either!

[*During this dialogue, a* GENTLEMAN *has turned up in front of Shen Te's House, and has whistled several times. Each time* WONG *has given a start.*]

THIRD GOD [*To* WONG, *softly.*] Psst! I think he's gone now.

WONG [*Confused and surprised.*] Ye-e-es.

[*The* GENTLEMAN *has left now, and* SHEN TE *has come down to the street.*]

SHEN TE [*softly.*] Wong!

[*Getting no answer, she goes off down the street.* WONG *arrives just too late, forgetting his carrying pole.*]

WONG [*Softly.*] Shen Te! Shen Te! [*To himself.*] So she's gone off to earn the rent. Oh dear, I can't go to the gods *again* with no room to offer them. Having failed in the service of the gods, I shall run to my den in the sewer pipe down by the river and hide from their sight!

[*He rushes off.* SHEN TE *returns, looking for him, but finding the* GODS. *She stops in confusion.*]

SHEN TE You are the illustrious ones? My name is Shen Te. It would please me very much if my simple room could be of use to you.

THIRD GOD Where is the water seller, Miss . . . Shen Te?

SHEN TE I missed him, somehow.

FIRST GOD Oh, he probably thought you weren't coming, and was afraid of telling us.

THIRD GOD [*Picking up the carrying pole.*] We'll leave this with you. He'll be needing it.

[*Led by* SHEN TE, *they go into the house. It grows dark, then light. Dawn. Again escorted by* SHEN TE, *who leads them through the half-light with a little lamp, the* GODS *take their leave.*]

FIRST GOD Thank you, thank you, dear Shen Te, for your elegant hospitality! We shall not forget! And give our thanks to the water seller—he showed us a good human being.

SHEN TE Oh, *I'm* not good. Let me tell you something: when Wong asked me to put you up, I hesitated.

FIRST GOD It's all right to hesitate if you then go ahead! And in giving us that room you did much more than you knew. You proved that good people still exist, a point that has been disputed of late—even in heaven. Farewell!

SECOND GOD Farewell!

THIRD GOD Farewell!

SHEN TE Stop, illustrious ones! I'm not sure you're right. I'd like to be good, it's true, but there's the rent to pay. And that's not all: I sell myself for a living. Even so I can't make ends meet, there's too much competition. I'd like to honor my father and mother and speak nothing but the truth and not covet my neighbor's house. I should love to stay with one man. But how? How is it done? Even breaking a few of your commandments,[4] I can hardly manage.

FIRST GOD [*Clearing his throat.*] These thoughts are but, um, the misgivings of an unusually good woman!

---

4. An allusion to the Decalogue of the Old Testament, and specifically to Commandments 4, 6, 8, 9, and 10 (Exodus 20).

THIRD GOD   Good-bye, Shen Te! Give our regards to the water seller!
SECOND GOD   And above all: be good! Farewell!
FIRST GOD   Farewell!
THIRD GOD   Farewell!
        [*They start to wave good-bye.*]
SHEN TE   But everything is so expensive, I don't feel sure I can do it!
SECOND GOD   That's not in our sphere. We never meddle with economics.
THIRD GOD   One moment. [*They stop.*] Isn't it true she might do better if
    she had more money?
SECOND GOD   Come, come! How could we ever account for it Up Above?
FIRST GOD   Oh, there are ways. [*They put their heads together and confer
    in dumb show. To* SHEN TE, *with embarrassment.*] As you say you can't
    pay your rent, well, um, we're not paupers, so of course we *insist* on
    paying for our room. [*Awkwardly thrusting money into her hands.*] There!
    [*Quickly.*] But don't tell anyone! The incident is open to misinter-
    pretation.
SECOND GOD   It certainly is!
FIRST GOD [*Defensively.*]   But there's no law against it! It was never
    decreed that a god mustn't pay hotel bills!
        [*The* GODS *leave.*]

1

*A small tobacco shop. The shop is not as yet completely furnished and hasn't
started doing business.*

SHEN TE [*To the audience.*]   It's three days now since the gods left. When
    they said they wanted to pay for the room, I looked down at my hand,
    and there was more than a thousand silver dollars![5] I bought a tobacco
    shop with the money, and moved in yesterday. I don't own the building,
    of course, but I can pay the rent, and I hope to do a lot of good here.
    Beginning with Mrs. Shin, who's just coming across the square with her
    pot. She had the shop before me, and yesterday she dropped in to ask
    for rice for her children. [*Enter* MRS. SHIN. *Both women bow.*] How do
    you do, Mrs. Shin.
MRS. SHIN   How do you do, Miss Shen Te. You like your new home?
SHEN TE   Indeed, yes. Did your children have a good night?
MRS. SHIN   In that hovel? The youngest is coughing already.
SHEN TE   Oh, dear!
MRS. SHIN   You're going to learn a thing or two in these slums.
SHEN TE   Slums? That's not what you said when you sold me the shop!
MRS. SHIN   Now don't start nagging! Robbing me and my innocent chil-
    dren of their home and then calling it a slum! That's the limit!
        [*She weeps.*]
SHEN TE [*Tactfully.*]   I'll get your rice.

5. Either official Chinese silver dollars (yuan) or coins from one of the foreign currencies in circula-
tion.

MRS. SHIN And a little cash while you're at it.

SHEN TE I'm afraid I haven't sold anything yet.

MRS. SHIN [*Screeching.*] I've got to have it. Strip the clothes from my back and then cut my throat, will you? I know what I'll do: I'll dump my children on your doorstep! [*She snatches the pot out of* SHEN TE's *hands.*]

SHEN TE Please don't be angry. You'll spill the rice.

[*Enter an elderly* HUSBAND *and* WIFE *with their shabbily dressed* NEPHEW.]

WIFE Shen Te, dear! You've come into money, they tell me. And we haven't a roof over our heads! A tobacco shop. We had one too. But it's gone. Could we spend the night here, do you think?

NEPHEW [*Appraising the shop.*] Not bad!

WIFE He's our nephew. We're inseparable!

MRS. SHIN And who are these . . . ladies and gentlemen?

SHEN TE They put me up when I first came in from the country. [*To the audience.*] Of course, when my small purse was empty, they put me out on the street, and they may be afraid I'll do the same to them [*To the newcomers, kindly.*] Come in, and welcome, though I've only one little room for you—it's behind the shop.

HUSBAND That'll do. Don't worry.

WIFE [*Bringing* SHEN TE *some tea.*] We'll stay over here, so we won't be in your way. Did you make it a tobacco shop in memory of your first real home? We can certainly give you a hint or two! That's one reason we came.

MRS SHIN [*To* SHEN TE.] Very nice! As long as you have a few customers too!

HUSBAND Sh! A customer!

[*Enter an* UNEMPLOYED MAN, *in rags.*]

UNEMPLOYED MAN Excuse me. I'm unemployed.

[MRS. SHIN *laughs.*]

SHEN TE Can I help you?

UNEMPLOYED MAN Have you any damaged cigarettes? I thought there might be some damage when you're unpacking.

WIFE What nerve, begging for tobacco! [*Rhetorically.*] Why don't they ask for bread?

UNEMPLOYED MAN Bread is expensive. One ciagarette butt and I'll be a new man.

SHEN TE [*Giving him cigarettes.*] That's very important—to be a new man. You'll be my first customer and bring me luck.

[*The* UNEMPLOYED MAN *quickly lights a cigarette, inhales, and goes off, coughing.*]

WIFE Was that right, Shen Te, dear?

MRS. SHIN If this is the opening of a shop, you can hold the closing at the end of the week.

HUSBAND I bet he had money on him.

SHEN TE Oh, no, he said he hadn't!

NEPHEW How d'you know he wasn't lying?

SHEN TE [*Angrily.*] How do you know he was?

WIFE [*Wagging her head.*] You're too good, Shen Te, dear. If you're going to keep this shop, you'll have to learn to say no.

HUSBAND   Tell them the place isn't yours to dispose of. Belongs to . . . some relative who insists on all accounts being strictly in order . . .

MRS. SHIN   That's right! What do you think you are—a philanthropist?

SHEN TE [*Laughing.*]   Very well, suppose I ask you for my rice back, Mrs. Shin?

WIFE [*Combatively, at* MRS. SHIN.]   So that's *her* rice?

    [*Enter the* CARPENTER, *a small man.*]

MRS. SHIN [*Who, at the sight of him, starts to hurry away.*]   See you tomorrow, Miss Shen Te! [*Exit* MRS. SHIN.]

CARPENTER   Mrs. Shin, it's you I want!

WIFE [*To* SHEN TE.]   Has she some claim on you?

SHEN TE   She hungry. That's a claim.

CARPENTER   Are you the new tenant? And filling up the shelves already? Well, they're not yours till they're paid for, ma'am. I'm the carpenter, so I should know.

SHEN TE   I took the shop "furnishings included."

CARPENTER   You're in league with that Mrs. Shin, of course. All right. I demand my hundred silver dollars.

SHEN TE   I'm afraid I haven't got a hundred silver dollars.

CARPENTER   Then you'll find it. Or I'll have you arrested.

WIFE [*Whispering to* SHEN TE.]   That relative: make it a cousin.

SHEN TE   Can't it wait till next month?

CARPENTER   No!

SHEN TE   Be a little patient, Mr. Carpenter, I can't settle all claims at once.

CARPENTER   Who's patient with me? [*He grabs a shelf from the wall.*] Pay up—or I take the shelves back!

WIFE   Shen Te! Dear! Why don't you let your . . . cousin settle this affair? [*To* CARPENTER.] Put your claim in writing. Shen Te's cousin will see you get paid.

CARPENTER [*Derisively.*]   Cousin, eh?

HUSBAND   Cousin, yes.

CARPENTER   I know these cousins!

NEPHEW   Don't be silly. He's a personal friend of mine.

HUSBAND   What a man! Sharp as a razor!

CARPENTER   All right. I'll put my claim in writing. [*Puts shelf on floor, sits on it, writes out bill.*]

WIFE [*To* SHEN TE.]   He'd tear the dress off your back to get his shelves. Never recognize a claim! That's my motto.

SHEN TE   He's done a job, and wants something in return. It's shameful that I can't give it to him. What will the gods say?

HUSBAND   You did your bit when you took *us* in.

    [*Enter the* BROTHER, *limping, and the* SISTER-IN-LAW, *pregnant.*]

BROTHER [*To* HUSBAND *and* WIFE.]   So this is where you're hiding out! There's family feeling for you! Leaving us on the corner!

WIFE [*Embarrassed, to* SHEN TE.]   It's my brother and his wife. [*To them.*] Now stop grumbling, and sit quietly in that corner. [*To* SHEN TE.] It can't be helped. She's in her fifth month.

SHEN TE   Oh yes. Welcome!

WIFE [*To the couple.*]   Say thank you. [*They mutter something.*] The cups are there. [*To* SHEN TE.] Lucky you bought this shop when you did!

SHEN TE [*Laughing and bringing tea.*]   Lucky indeed!

[*Enter* MRS. MI TZU, *the landlady.*]

MRS. MI TZU   Miss Shen Te? I am Mrs. Mi Tzu, your landlady. I hope our relationship will be a happy one. I like to think I give my tenants modern, personalized service. Here is your lease. [*To the others, as* SHEN TE *reads the lease.*] There's nothing like the opening of a little shop, is there? A moment of true beauty! [*She is looking around.*] Not very much on the shelves, of course. But everything in the gods' good time! Where are your references, Miss Shen Te?

SHEN TE   Do I *have* to have references?

MRS. MI TZU   After all, I haven't a notion who you are!

HUSBAND   Oh, *we'd* be glad to vouch for Miss Shen Te! We'd go through fire for her!

MRS. MI TZU   And who may *you* be?

HUSBAND [*Stammering.*]   Ma Fu, tobacco dealer.

MRS. MI TZU   Where is your shop, Mr. . . . Ma Fu?

HUSBAND   Well, um, I haven't got a shop—I've just sold it.

MRS. MI TZU   I see. [*To* SHEN TE.] Is there no one else that knows you?

WIFE [*Whispering to* SHEN TE.]   Your cousin! Your cousin!

MRS. MI TZU   This is a respectable house, Miss Shen Te. I never sign a lease without certain assurances.

SHEN TE [*Slowly, her eyes downcast.*]   I have . . . a cousin.

MRS. MI TZU   On the square? Let's go over and see him. What does he do?

SHEN TE [*As before.*]   He lives . . . in another city.

WIFE [*Prompting.*]   Didn't you say he was in Shung?

SHEN TE   That's right. Shung.

HUSBAND [*Prompting.*]   I had his name on the tip of my tongue, Mr. . . .

SHEN TE [*With an effort.*]   Mr. . . . Shui . . . Ta.

HUSBAND   That's it! Tall, skinny fellow!

SHEN TE   Shui Ta!

NEPHEW [*To* CARPENTER.]   *You* were in touch with him, weren't you? About the shelves?

CARPENTER [*Surlily.*]   Give him this bill. [*He hands it over.*] I'll be back in the morning. [*Exit* CARPENTER.]

NEPHEW [*Calling after him, but with his eyes on* MRS. MI TZU.]   Don't worry! Mr. Shui Ta pays on the nail!

MRS. MI TZU [*Looking closely at* SHEN TE.]   I'll be happy to make his acquaintance, Miss Shen Te. [*Exit* MRS. MI TZU.]
         [*Pause.*]

WIFE   By tomorrow morning she'll know more about you than you do yourself.

SISTER-IN-LAW [*To* NEPHEW.]   This thing isn't built to last.
         [*Enter* GRANDFATHER.]

WIFE   It's Grandfather! [*To* SHEN TE.] Such a good old soul!
         [*The* BOY *enters.*]

BOY [*Over his shoulder.*]   Here they are!

WIFE   And the boy, how he's grown! But he always could eat enough for ten.
         [*Enter the* NIECE.]

WIFE [*To* SHEN TE.]   Our little niece from the country. There are more of us now than in your time. The less we had, the more there were of us;

the more there were of us, the less we had. Give me the key. We must protect ourselves from unwanted guests. [*She takes the key and locks the door.*] Just make yourself at home. I'll light the little lamp.

NEPHEW [*A big joke.*]   I hope her cousin doesn't drop in tonight! The strict Mr. Shui Ta!

[SISTER-IN-LAW *laughs.*]

BROTHER [*Reaching for a cigarette.*]   One cigarette more or less . . .

HUSBAND   One cigarette more or less.

[*They pile into the cigarettes. The* BROTHER *hands a jug of wine round.*]

NEPHEW   Mr. Shui Ta'll pay for it!

GRANDFATHER [*Gravely, to* SHEN TE.]   How do you do?

[SHEN TE, *a little taken aback by the belatedness of the greeting, bows. She has the carpenter's bill in one hand, the landlady's lease in the other.*]

WIFE   How about a bit of a song? To keep Shen Te's spirits up?

NEPHEW   Good idea. Grandfather: you start!

SONG OF THE SMOKE

GRANDFATHER
    I used to think (before old age beset me)
      That brains could fill the pantry of the poor.
    But where did all my cerebration get me?
      I'm just as hungry as I was before.
        So what's the use?
          See the smoke float free
          Into ever colder coldness!
          It's the same with me[6]

HUSBAND   The straight and narrow path leads to disaster
      And so the crooked path I tried to tread.
    That got me to disaster even faster.
      (They say we shall be happy when we're dead.)
        So what's the use?
          See the smoke float free
          Into ever colder coldness!
          It's the same with me

NIECE   You older people, full of expectation,
      At any moment now you'll walk the plank!
    The future's for the younger generation!
      Yes, even if that future is a blank.
        So what's the use?
          See the smoke float free
          Into ever colder coldness!
          It's the same with me.

NEPHEW [*To the* BROTHER.]   Where'd you get that wine?

SISTER-IN-LAW [*Answering for the* BROTHER.]   He pawned the sack of tobacco.

---

6. The refrain in this song is taken from a poem Brecht wrote in the 1920s entitled *The Song of the Opium Den.*

HUSBAND [*Stepping in.*]   What? That tobacco was all we had to fall back on! You pig!

BROTHER   *You'd* call a man a pig because your wife was frigid! Did you refuse to drink it?

[*They fight. The shelves fall over.*]

SHEN TE [*Imploringly.*]   Oh don't! Don't break everything! Take it, take it all, but don't destroy a gift from the gods!

WIFE [*Disparagingly.*]   This shop isn't big enough. I should never have mentioned it to Uncle and the others. When *they* arrive, it's going to be disgustingly overcrowded.

SISTER-IN-LAW   And did you hear our gracious hostess? She cools off quick!

[*Voices outside. Knocking at the door.*]

UNCLE'S VOICE   Open the door!

WIFE   Uncle? Is that you, Uncle?

UNCLE'S VOICE   Certainly, it's me. Auntie says to tell you she'll have the children here in ten minutes.

WIFE [*To* SHEN TE.]   I'll have to let him in.

SHEN TE [*Who scarcely hears her.*]

> The little lifeboat is swiftly sent down
> Too many men too greedily
> Hold on to it as they drown.

1a

Wong's den in a sewer pipe.

WONG [*Crouching there.*]   All quiet! It's four days now since I left the city. The gods passed this way on the second day. I heard their steps on the bridge over there. They must be a long way off by this time, so I'm safe. [*Breathing a sigh of relief, he curls up and goes to sleep. In his dream the pipe becomes transparent, and the* GODS *appear. Raising an arm, as if in self-defense.*] I know, I know, illustrious ones! I found no one to give you a room—not in all Setzuan! There, it's out. Please continue on your way!

FIRST GOD [*Mildly.*]   But you did find someone. Someone who took us in for the night, watched over us in our sleep, and in the early morning lighted us down to the street with a lamp.

WONG   It was . . . Shen Te that took you in?

THIRD GOD   Who else?

WONG   And I ran away! "She isn't coming," I thought, "she just can't afford it."

GODS [*Singing.*]

> O you feeble, well-intentioned, and yet feeble chap
> Where there's need the fellow thinks there is no goodness!
> When there's danger he thinks courage starts to ebb away!
> Some people only see the seamy side!
> What hasty judgment! What premature desperation!

WONG   I'm *very* ashamed, illustrious ones.

FIRST GOD Do us a favor, water seller. Go back to Setzuan. Find Shen
Te, and give us a report on her. We hear that she's come into a little
money. Show interest in her goodness—for no one can be good for long
if goodness is not in demand. Meanwhile we shall continue the search,
and find other good people. After which, the idle chatter about the impossibility of goodness will stop!
[*The* GODS *vanish.*]

2

A knocking.

WIFE Shen Te! Someone at the door. Where is she anyway?
NEPHEW She must be getting the breakfast. Mr. Shui Ta will pay for it.
[*The* WIFE *laughs and shuffles to the door. Enter Mr.* SHUI TA *and
the* CARPENTER.]
WIFE Who is it?
SHUI TA I am Miss Shen Te's cousin.
WIFE What??
SHUI TA My name is Shui Ta.
WIFE Her cousin?
NEPHEW Her cousin?
NIECE But that was a joke. She hasn't got a cousin.
HUSBAND So early in the morning?
BROTHER What's all the noise?
SISTER-IN-LAW This fellow says he's her cousin.
BROTHER Tell him to prove it.
NEPHEW Right. If you're Shen Te's cousin, prove it by getting the
breakfast.
SHUI TA [*Whose regime begins as he puts out the lamp to save oil; loudly, to
all present, asleep or awake.*] Would you all please get dressed! Custom-
ers will be coming! I wish to open my shop!
HUSBAND *Your* shop? Doesn't it belong to our good friend Shen Te?
[SHUI TA *shakes his head.*]
SISTER-IN-LAW So we've been cheated. Where *is* the little liar?
SHUI TA Miss Shen Te has been delayed. She wishes me to tell you there
will be nothing she can do—now I am here.
WIFE [*Bowled over.*] I thought she was good!
NEPHEW Do you have to believe *him*?
HUSBAND I don't.
NEPHEW Then do something.
HUSBAND Certainly! I'll send out a search party at once. You, you, you,
and you, go out and look for Shen Te. [*As the* GRANDFATHER *rises and
makes for the door*] Not you, Grandfather, you and I will hold the fort.
SHUI TA You won't find Miss Shen Te. She has suspended her hospitable
activity for an unlimited period. There are too many of you. She asked
me to say: this is a tobacco shop, not a gold mine.

HUSBAND   Shen Te never said a thing like that. Boy, food! There's a bakery on the corner. Stuff your shirt full when they're not looking!

SISTER-IN-LAW   Don't overlook the raspberry tarts.

HUSBAND   And don't let the policeman see you.

[*The* BOY *leaves.*]

SHUI TA   Don't you depend on this shop now? Then why give it a bad name by stealing from the bakery?

NEPHEW   Don't listen to him. Let's find Shen Te. She'll give him a piece of her mind.

SISTER-IN-LAW   Don't forget to leave us some breakfast.

[BROTHER, SISTER-IN-LAW *and* NEPHEW *leave.*]

SHUI TA   [*To the* CARPENTER.]   You see, Mr. Carpenter, nothing has changed since the poet, eleven hundred years ago, penned these lines:

> A governor was asked what was needed
> To save the freezing people in the city.
> He replied:
> "A blanket ten thousand feet long
> To cover the city and all its suburbs."[7]

[*He starts to tidy up the shop.*]

CARPENTER   Your cousin owes me money. I've got witnesses. For the shelves.

SHUI TA   Yes, I have your bill. [*He takes it out of his pocket.*] Isn't a hundred silver dollars rather a lot?

CARPENTER   No deductions! I have a wife and children.

SHUI TA   How many children?

CARPENTER   Three.

SHUI TA   I'll make you an offer. Twenty silver dollars.

[*The* HUSBAND *laughs.*]

CARPENTER   You're crazy. Those shelves are real walnut.

SHUI TA   Very well, Take them away.

CARPENTER   What?

SHUI TA   They cost too much. Please take them away.

WIFE   Not bad! [*And she, too, is laughing.*]

CARPENTER   [*A little bewildered.*]   Call Shen Te, someone! [*To* SHUI TA.] She's good!

SHUI TA   Certainly. She's ruined.

CARPENTER   [*Provoked into taking some of the shelves.*]   All right, you can keep your tobacco on the floor.

SHUI TA   [*to the* HUSBAND.]   Help him with the shelves.

HUSBAND   [*Grins and carries one shelf over to the door where the* CARPENTER *now is.*]   Good-bye, shelves!

CARPENTER   [*To the* HUSBAND.]   You dog! You want my family to starve?

SHUI TA   I repeat my offer. I have no desire to keep my tobacco on the floor. Twenty silver dollars.

CARPENTER   [*With desperate aggressiveness.*]   One hundred!

[SHUI TA *shows indifference, looks through the window. The* HUSBAND *picks up several shelves.*]

---

7. Reference to a poem, *The Big Rug*, by the classical Chinese poet Po Chü-i (A.D. 772–846).

CARPENTER [*To* HUSBAND.]   You needn't smash them against the doorpost, you idiot! [*To* SHUI TA.] These shelves were made to measure. They're no use anywhere else!

SHUI TA   Precisely.

[*The* WIFE *squeals with pleasure.*]

CARPENTER [*Giving up, sullenly.*]   Take the shelves. Pay what you want to pay.

SHUI TA [*Smoothly.*]   Twenty silver dollars.

[*He places two large coins on the table. The* CARPENTER *picks them up.*]

HUSBAND [*Brings the shelves back in.*]   And quite enough too!

CARPENTER [*Slinking off.*]   Quite enough to get drunk on.

HUSBAND [*Happily.*]   Well, we got rid of *him*!

WIFE [*Weeping with fun, gives a rendition of the dialogue just spoken.*]   "Real walnut," says he. "Very well, take them away," says his lordship. "I have three children," says he. "Twenty silver dollars," says his lordship. "They're no use anywhere else," says he. "Pre-cisely," said his lordship! [*She dissolves into shrieks of merriment.*]

SHUI TA   And now: go!

HUSBAND   What's that?

SHUI TA   You're thieves, parasites. I'm giving you this chance. Go!

HUSBAND [*Summoning all his ancestral dignity.*]   That sort deserves no answer. Besides, one should never shout on an empty stomach.

WIFE   Where's that boy?

SHUI TA   Exactly. The boy. I want no stolen goods in this shop. [*Very loudly.*] I strongly advise you to leave! [*But they remain seated, noses in the air. Quietly.*] As you wish. [SHUI TA *goes to the door. A* POLICEMAN *appears.* SHUI TA *bows.*] I am addressing the officer in charge of this precinct?

POLICEMAN   That's right, Mr., um, what was the name, sir?

SHUI TA   Mr. Shui Ta.

POLICEMAN   Yes, of course, sir.

[*They exchange a smile.*]

SHUI TA   Nice weather we're having.

POLICEMAN   A little on the warm side, sir.

SHUI TA   Oh, a little on the warm side.

HUSBAND [*Whispering to the* WIFE.]   If he keeps it up till the boy's back, we're done for. [*Tries to signal* SHUI TA.]

SHUI TA [*Ignoring the signal.*]   Weather, of course, is one thing indoors, another out on the dusty street!

POLICEMAN   Oh, quite another, sir!

WIFE [*To the* HUSBAND.]   It's all right as long as he's standing in the doorway—the boy will see him.

SHUI TA   Step inside for a moment! It's quite cool indoors. My cousin and I have just opened the place. And we attach the greatest importance to being on good terms with the, um, authorities.

POLICEMAN [*Entering.*]   Thank you, Mr. Shui Ta. It *is* cool!

HUSBAND [*Whispering to the* WIFE.]   And now the boy *won't* see him.

SHUI TA [*Showing* HUSBAND *and* WIFE *to the* POLICEMAN.]   Visitors, I think my cousin knows them. They were just leaving.

HUSBAND [*Defeated.*]   Ye-e-es, we were . . . just leaving.

SHUI TA   I'll tell my cousin you couldn't wait.
  [*Noise from the street. Shouts of* "Stop, Thief!"]
POLICEMAN   What's that?
  [*The* BOY *is in the doorway with cakes and buns and rolls spilling out of his shirt. The* WIFE *signals desperately to him to leave. He gets the idea.*]
POLICEMAN   No, you don't. [*He grabs the* BOY *by the collar.*] Where's all this from?
BOY [*Vaguely pointing.*]   Down the street.
POLICEMAN [*Grimly.*]   So that's it. [*Prepares to arrest the* BOY.]
WIFE [*Stepping in.*]   And *we* knew nothing about it. [*To the* BOY.] Nasty little thief!
POLICEMAN [*Dryly.*]   Can you clarify the situation, Mr. Shui Ta?
  [SHUI TA *is silent.*]
POLICEMAN [*Who understands silence.*]   Aha. You're all coming with me—to the station.
SHUI TA   I can hardly say how sorry I am that *my* establishment . . .
WIFE   Oh, he saw the boy leave not ten minutes ago!
SHUI TA   And to conceal the theft asked a policeman in?
POLICEMAN   Don't listen to her, Mr. Shui Ta, I'll be happy to relieve you of their presence one and all! [*To all three.*] Out!
  [*He drives them before him.*]
GRANDFATHER [*Leaving last, gravely.*]   Good morning!
POLICEMAN   Good morning!
  [SHUI TA, *left alone, continues to tidy up.* MRS. MI TZU *breezes in.*]
MRS. MI TZU   *You're* her cousin, are you? Then have the goodness to explain what all this means—police dragging people from a respectable house! By what right does your Miss Shen Te turn my property into a house of assignation?—Well, as you see, I know all!
SHUI TA   Yes. My cousin has the worst possible reputation: that of being poor.
MRS. MI TZU   No sentimental rubbish, Mr. Shui Ta. Your cousin was a common . . .
SHUI TA   Pauper. Let's use the uglier word.
MRS. MI TZU   I'm speaking of her conduct, not her earnings. But there must have *been* earnings, or how did she buy all this? Several elderly gentlemen took care of it, I suppose. I repeat: this is a respectable house! I have tenants who prefer not to live under the same roof with such a person.
SHUI TA [*Quietly.*]   How much do you want?
MRS. MI TZU [*He is ahead of her now.*]   I beg your pardon.
SHUI TA   To reassure yourself. To reassure your tenants. How much will it cost?
MRS. MI TZU   You're a cool customer
SHUI TA [*Picking up the lease.*]   The rent is high. [*He reads on.*] I assume it's payable by the month?
MRS. MI TZU   Not in her case.
SHUI TA [*Looking up.*]   What?
MRS. MI TZU   Six months' rent payable in advance. Two hundred silver dollars.
SHUI TA   Six . . . ! Sheer usury! And where am I to find it?

MRS. MI TZU You should have thought of that before.

SHUI TA Have you no heart, Mrs. Mi Tzu? It's true Shen Te acted foolishly, being kind to all those people, but she'll improve with time. I'll see
to it she does. She'll work her fingers to the bone to pay her rent, and all
the time be as quiet as a mouse, as humble as a fly.

MRS. MI TZU Her social background . . .

SHUI TA Out of the depths! She came out of the depths! And before she'll
go back there, she'll work, sacrifice, shrink from nothing. . . . Such a
tenant is worth her weight in gold, Mrs. Mi Tzu.

MRS. MI TZU It's silver we were talking about, Mr. Shui Ta. Two hundred
silver dollars or . . .

  [Enter the POLICEMAN.]

POLICEMAN Am I intruding, Mr. Shui Ta?

MRS. MI TZU This tobacco shop is well known to the police, I see.

POLICEMAN Mr. Shui Ta has done us a service, Mrs. Mi Tzu. I am here
to present our official felicitations!

MRS. MI TZU That means less than nothing to me, sir. Mr. Shui Ta, all I
can say is: I hope your cousin will find my terms acceptable. Good day,
gentlemen. [Exit.]

SHUI TA Good day, ma'am.

  [Pause.]

POLICEMAN Mrs. Mi Tzu a bit of a stumbling block, sir?

SHUI TA She wants six months' rent in advance.

POLICEMAN And you haven't got it, eh? [SHUI TA is silent.] But surely you
can get it, sir? A man like you?

SHUI TA What about a woman like Shen Te?

POLICEMAN You're not staying, sir?

SHUI TA No, and I won't be back. Do you smoke?

POLICEMAN [Taking two cigars, and placing them both in his pocket.]
Thank you, sir—I see your point, Miss Shen Te—let's mince no words—
Miss Shen Te lived by selling herself. "What else could she have done?"
you ask. "How else was she to pay the rent?" True. But the fact remains,
Mr. Shui Ta, it is not respectable. Why not? A very deep question. But,
in the first place, love—love isn't bought and sold like cigars, Mr. Shui
Ta. In the second place, it isn't respectable to go waltzing off with someone that's paying his way, so to speak—it must be for love! Thirdly and
lastly, as the proverb has it: not for a handful of rice but for love! [Pause.
He is thinking hard.] "Well," you may say, "and what good is all this
wisdom if the milk's already spilt?" Miss Shen Te is what she is. Is where
she is. We have to face the fact that if she doesn't get hold of six months'
rent pronto, she'll be back on the streets. The question then as I see it—
everything in this world is a matter of opinion—the question as I see it
is: how is she to get hold of this rent? How? Mr. Shui Ta: I don't know.
[Pause.] I take that back, sir. It's just come to me. A husband. We must
find her a husband!

  [Enter a little OLD WOMAN.]

OLD WOMAN A good cheap cigar for my husband, we'll have been married
forty years tomorrow and we're having a little celebration.

SHUI TA Forty years? And you still want to celebrate?

OLD WOMAN As much as we can afford to. We have the carpet shop across
the square. We'll be good neighbors, I hope?

SHUI TA I hope so too.

POLICEMAN [*Who keeps making discoveries.*] Mr. Shui Ta, you know what we need? We need capital. And how do we acquire capital? We get married.

SHUI TA [*To* OLD WOMAN.] I'm afraid I've been pestering this gentleman with my personal worries.

POLICEMAN [*Lyrically.*] We can't pay six months' rent, so what do we do? We marry money.

SHUI TA That might not be easy.

POLICEMAN Oh, I don't know. She's a good match. Has a nice, growing business. [*To the* OLD WOMAN.] What do you think?

OLD WOMAN [*Undecided.*] Well—

POLICEMAN Should she put an ad in the paper?

OLD WOMAN [*Not eager to commit herself.*] Well, if *she* agrees—

POLICEMAN I'll write it for her. *You* lend us a hand, and *we* write an ad for you! [*He chuckles away to himself, takes out his notebook, wets the stump of a pencil between his lips, and writes away.*]

SHUI TA [*Slowly.*] Not a bad idea.

POLICEMAN "What . . . *respectable* . . . man . . . with small capital . . . widower . . . not excluded . . . desires . . . marriage . . . into flourishing . . . tobacco shop?" And now let's add: "Am . . . pretty . . . " No! . . . "Prepossessing appearance."

SHUI TA If you don't think that's an exaggeration?

OLD WOMAN Oh, not a bit. I've seen her.

> [*The* POLICEMAN *tears the page out of his notebook, and hands it over to* SHUI TA.]

SHUI TA [*With horror in his voice.*] How much luck we need to keep our heads above water! How many ideas! How many friends! [*To the* POLICEMAN.] Thank you, sir, I think I see my way clear.

3

Evening in the municipal park. Noise of a plane overhead. YANG SUN, *a young man in rags, is following the plane with his eyes: one can tell that the machine is describing a curve above the park.* YANG SUN *then takes a rope out of his pocket, looking anxiously about him as he does so. He moves toward a large willow. Enter two prostitutes, one old, the other the* NIECE *whom we have already met.*

NIECE Hello. Coming with me?

YANG SUN [*Taken aback.*] If you'd like to buy me a dinner.

OLD WHORE Buy you a dinner! [*To the* NIECE.] Oh, we know him—it's the unemployed pilot. Waste no time on him!

NIECE But he's the only man left in the park. And it's going to rain.

OLD WHORE Oh, how do you know?

> [*And they pass by.* YANG SUN *again looks about him, again takes his rope, and this time throws it round a branch of the willow tree. Again he is interrupted. It is the two prostitutes returning—and in such a hurry they don't notice him.*]

NIECE It's going to pour!

[*Enter* SHEN TE.]

OLD WHORE   There's that *gorgon* Shen Te! That *drove* your family out into the cold!

NIECE   It wasn't her. It was that cousin of hers. She offered to pay for the cakes. I've nothing against her.

OLD WHORE   I have, though. [*So that* SHEN TE *can hear.*] Now where could the little lady be off to? She may be rich now but that won't stop her snatching our young men, will it?

SHEN TE   I'm going to the tearoom by the pond.

NIECE   Is it true what they say? You're marrying a widower—with three children?

SHEN TE   Yes. I'm just going to see him.

YANG SUN [*His patience at breaking point.*]   Move on there! This is a park, not a whorehouse!

OLD WHORE   Shut your mouth!
   [*But the two prostitutes leave.*]

YANG SUN   Even in the farthest corner of the park, even when it's raining, you can't get rid of them! [*He spits.*]

SHEN TE [*Overhearing this.*]   And what right have you to scold them? [*But at this point she sees the rope.*] Oh!

YANG SUN   Well, what are you staring at?

SHEN TE   That rope. What is it for?

YANG SUN   Think! Think! I haven't a penny. Even if I had, I wouldn't spend it on you. I'd buy a drink of water.
   [*The rain starts.*]

SHEN TE [*Still looking at the rope.*]   What is the rope for? You mustn't!

YANG SUN   What's it to you? Clear out!

SHEN TE [*Irrelevantly.*]   It's raining.

YANG SUN   Well, don't try to come under this tree.

SHEN TE   Oh, no. [*She stays in the rain.*]

YANG SUN   Now go away. [*Pause.*] For one thing, I don't like your looks, you're bowlegged.

SHEN TE [*Indignantly.*]   That's not true!

YANG SUN   Well, don't show 'em to me. Look, it's raining. You better come under this tree.
   [*Slowly, she takes shelter under the tree.*]

SHEN TE   Why did you want to do it?

YANG SUN   You really want to know? [*Pause.*] To get rid of you! [*Pause.*] You know what a flyer is?

SHEN TE   Oh yes, I've met a lot of pilots. At the tearoom.

YANG SUN   You call *them* flyers? Think they know what a machine is? Just 'cause they have leather helmets? They gave the airfield director a bribe, that's the way *those* fellows got up in the air! Try one of them out sometime. "Go up to two thousand feet," tell him, "then let it fall, then pick it up again with a flick of the wrist at the last moment." Know what he'll say to that? "It's not in my contract." Then again, there's the landing problem. It's like landing on your own backside. It's no different, planes are human. Those fools don't understand. [*Pause.*] And I'm the biggest fool for reading the book on flying in the Peking school and skipping the page where it says: "We've got enough flyers and we don't need you." I'm a mail pilot with no mail. You understand that?

SHEN TE [*Shyly.*] Yes, I do.

YANG SUN No, you don't. You'd never understand that.

SHEN TE When we were little we had a crane with a broken wing. He made friends with us and was very good-natured about our jokes. He would strut along behind us and call out to stop us going too fast for him. But every spring and autumn when the cranes flew over the villages in great swarms, he got quite restless. [*Pause.*] I understand that.

[*She bursts out crying.*]

YANG SUN Don't!

SHEN TE [*Quieting down.*] No.

YANG SUN It's bad for the complexion.

SHEN TE [*Sniffing.*] I've stopped.

[*She dries her tears on her big sleeve. Leaning against the tree, but not looking at her, he reaches for her face.*]

YANG SUN You can't even wipe your own face. [*He is wiping it for her with his handkerchief. Pause.*]

SHEN TE [*Still sobbing.*] I don't know *anything!*

YANG SUN You interrupted me! What for?

SHEN TE It's such a rainy day. You only wanted to do . . . *that* because it's such a rainy day. [*To the audience.*]

> In our country
> The evenings should never be somber
> High bridges over rivers
> The gray hour between night and morning
> And the long, long winter:
> Such things are dangerous
> For, with all the misery,
> A very little is enough
> And men throw away an unbearable life.

[*Pause.*]

YANG SUN Talk about yourself for a change.

SHEN TE What about me? I have a shop.

YANG SUN [*Incredulous.*] You have a shop, have you? Never thought of walking the streets?

SHEN TE I did walk the streets. Now I have a shop.

YANG SUN [*Ironically.*] A gift of the gods, I suppose!

SHEN TE How did you know?

YANG SUN [*Even more ironical.*] One fine evening the gods turned up saying: here's some money!

SHEN TE [*Quickly.*] One fine morning.

YANG SUN [*Fed up.*] This isn't much of an entertainment.

[*Pause.*]

SHEN TE I can play the zither a little. [*Pause.*] And I can mimic men. [*Pause.*] I got the shop, so the first thing I did was to give my zither away. I can be as stupid as a fish now, I said to myself, and it won't matter.

> I'm rich now, I said
> I walk alone, I sleep alone
> For a whole year, I said
> I'll have nothing to do with a man.

YANG SUN And now you're marrying one! The one at the tearoom by the pond?

    [SHEN TE *is silent.*]

YANG SUN What do you know about love?

SHEN TE Everything.

YANG SUN Nothing. [*Pause.*] Or d'you just mean you enjoyed it?

SHEN TE No.

YANG SUN [*Again without turning to look at her, he strokes her cheek with his hand.*] You like that?

SHEN TE Yes.

YANG SUN [*Breaking off.*] You're easily satisfied, I must say. [*Pause.*] What a town!

SHEN TE You have no friends?

YANG SUN [*Defensively.*] Yes, I have! [*Change of tone.*] But they don't want to hear I'm still unemployed. "What?" they ask. "Is there still water in the sea?" You have friends?

SHEN TE [*Hesitating.*] Just a . . . cousin.

YANG SUN Watch him carefully.

SHEN TE He only came once. Then he went away. He won't be back. [YANG SUN *is looking away.*] But to be without hope, they say, is to be without goodness!

    [*Pause.*]

YANG SUN Go on talking. A voice is a voice.

SHEN TE Once, when I was a little girl, I fell, with a load of brushwood. An old man picked me up. He gave me a penny too. Isn't it funny how people who don't have very much like to give some of it away? They must like to show what they can do, and how could they show it better than by being kind? Being wicked is just like being clumsy. When we sing a song, or build a machine, or plant some rice, we're being kind. You're kind.

YANG SUN You make it sound easy.

SHEN TE Oh, no. [*Little pause.*] Oh! A drop of rain!

YANG SUN Where'd you feel it?

SHEN TE Between the eyes.

YANG SUN Near the right eye? Or the left?

SHEN TE Near the left eye.

YANG SUN Oh, good. [*He is getting sleepy.*] So you're through with men, eh?

SHEN TE [*With a smile.*] But I'm not bowlegged.

YANG SUN Perhaps not.

SHEN TE Definitely not.

    [*Pause.*]

YANG SUN [*Leaning wearily against the willow.*] I haven't had a drop to drink all day, I haven't eaten anything for *two* days. I couldn't love you if I tried.

    [*Pause.*]

SHEN TE   I like it in the rain.
    [*Enter* WONG *the water seller, singing.*]

        THE SONG OF THE WATER SELLER IN THE RAIN

        "Buy my water," I am yelling
        And my fury restraining
        For no water I'm selling
        'Cause it's raining, 'cause it's raining!
           I keep yelling: "Buy my water!"
           But no one's buying
           Athirst and dying
           And drinking and paying!
           Buy water!
           Buy water, you dogs!

        Nice to dream of lovely weather!
        Think of all the consternation
        Were there no precipitation
        Half a dozen years together!
           Can't you hear them shrieking: "Water!"
           Pretending they adore me?
           They all would go down on their knees before me!
           Down on your knees!
           Go down on your knees, you dogs!

        What are lawns and hedges thinking?
        What are fields and forests saying?
        "At the cloud's breast we are drinking!
        And we've no idea who's paying!"
           I keep yelling: "Buy my water!"
           But no one's buying
           Athirst and dying
           And drinking and paying!
           Buy water!
           Buy water, you dogs!

    [*The rain has stopped now.* SHEN TE *sees* WONG *and runs toward him.*]
SHEN TE   Wong! You're back! Your carrying pole's at the shop.
WONG   Oh, thank you, Shen Te. And how is life treating *you*?
SHEN TE   I've just met a brave and clever man. And I want to buy him a cup of your water.
WONG [*Bitterly.*]   Throw back your head and open your mouth and you'll have all the water you need—
SHEN TE [*Tenderly.*]

        I want *your* water, Wong
        The water that has tired you so
        The water that you carried all this way
        The water that is hard to sell because it's been raining.

I need it for the young man over there—he's a flyer!

> A flyer is a bold man:
> Braving the storms
> In company with the clouds
> He crosses the heavens
> And brings to friends in faraway lands
> The friendly mail!

[*She pays* WONG, *and runs over to* YANG SUN *with the cup. But* YANG
SUN *is fast asleep.*]

SHEN TE [*Calling to* SONG, *with a laugh.*]   He's fallen asleep! Despair and
rain and I have worn him out!

3a

Wong's den. The sewer pipe is transparent, and the GODS *again appear to* WONG
in a dream.

WONG [*Radiant*]   I've seen her, illustrious ones! And she hasn't changed!
FIRST GOD   That's good to hear.
WONG   She loves someone.
FIRST GOD   Let's hope the experience gives her the strength to stay good!
WONG   It does. She's doing good deeds all the time.
FIRST GOD   Ah? What sort? What sort of good deeds, Wong?
WONG   Well, she has a kind word for everybody.
FIRST GOD [*Eagerly.*]   And then?
WONG   Hardly anyone leaves her shop without tobacco in his pocket—
even if he can't pay for it.
FIRST GOD   Not bad at all. Next?
WONG   She's putting up a family of eight.
FIRST GOD [*Gleefully, to the* SECOND GOD.]   Eight! [*To* WONG.] And that's
not all, of course!
WONG   She bought a cup of water from me even thought it was raining.
FIRST GOD   Yes, yes, yes, all these smaller good deeds!
WONG   Even they run into money. A little tobacco shop doesn't make so
much.
FIRST GOD [*Sententiously.*]   A prudent gardener works miracles on the
smallest plot.
WONG   She hands out rice every morning. That eats up half her earnings.
FIRST GOD [*A little disappointed.*]   Well, as a beginning . . .
WONG   They call her the Angel of the Slums—whatever the carpenter may
say!
FIRST GOD   What's this? A carpenter speaks ill of her?
WONG   Oh, he only says her shelves weren't paid for in full.
SECOND GOD [*Who has a bad cold and can't pronounce his n's and
m's.*]   What's this? Not paying a carpenter? Why was that?
WONG   I suppose she didn't have the money.

SECOND GOD [*Severely.*] One pays what one owes, that's in our book of rules! First the letter of the law, then the spirit.

WONG But it wasn't Shen Te, illustrious ones, it was her cousin. She called *him* in to help.

SECOND GOD Then her cousin must never darken her threshold again!

WONG Very well, illustrious ones! But in fairness to Shen Te, let me say that her cousin is a businessman.

FIRST GOD Perhaps we should inquire what is customary? I find business quite unintelligible. But everybody's doing it. Business! Did the Seven Good Kings[8] do business? Did Kung the Just[8] sell fish?

SECOND GOD In any case, such a thing must not occur again!
[*The* GODS *start to leave.*]

THIRD GOD Forgive us for taking this tone with you, Wong, we haven't been getting enough sleep. The rich recommend us to the poor, and the poor tell us they haven't enough room.

SECOND GOD Feeble, feeble, the best of them!

FIRST GOD No great deeds! No heroic daring!

THIRD GOD On such a *small* scale!

SECOND GOD Sincere, yes, but what is actually *achieved*?
[*One can no longer hear them.*]

WONG [*Calling after them.*] I've thought of something, illustrious ones: Perhaps you shouldn't ask—too—much—all—at—once!

4

The square in front of Shen Te's tobacco shop. Besides Shen Te's place, two other shops are seen: the carpet shop and a barber's. Morning. Outside Shen Te's the GRANDFATHER, *the* SISTER-IN-LAW, *the* UNEMPLOYED MAN, *and* MRS. SHIN *stand waiting.*

SISTER-IN-LAW She's been out all night again.

MRS. SHIN No sooner did we get rid of that crazy cousin of hers than Shen Te herself starts carrying on! Maybe she does give us an ounce of rice now and then, but can you depend on her? Can you depend on her?
[*Loud voices from the barber's.*]

VOICE OF SHU FU What are you doing in my shop? Get out—at once!

VOICE OF WONG But sir. They all let me sell . . .
[WONG *comes staggering out of the barber's shop pursued by Mr.* SHU FU, *the barber, a fat man carrying a heavy curling iron.*]

SHU FU Get out, I said! Pestering my customers with your slimy old water! Get out! Take your cup!
[*He holds out the cup.* WONG *reaches out for it. Mr.* SHU FU *strikes his hand with the curling iron, which is hot.* WONG *howls.*]

SHU FU You had it coming my man!
[*Puffing, he returns to his shop. The* UNEMPLOYED MAN *picks up the cup and gives it to* WONG.]

8. The philosopher Confucius (551–479 B.C.). *Seven Good Kings*: legendary wise kings who personified the old order and traditional values.

UNEMPLOYED MAN You can report that to the police.

WONG My hand! It's smashed up!

UEMPLOYED MAN Any bones broken?

WONG I can't move my fingers.

UNEMPLOYED MAN Sit down. I'll put some water on it.

[WONG *sits.*]

MRS. SHIN The water won't cost you anything.

SISTER-IN-LAW You might have got a bandage from Miss Shen Te till she took to staying out all night. It's a scandal.

MRS. SHIN [*Despondently.*] If you ask me, she's forgotten we ever existed!

[*Enter* SHEN TE *down the street, with a dish of rice.*]

SHEN TE [*To the audience.*] How wonderful to see Setzuan in the early morning! I always used to stay in bed with my dirty blanket over my head afraid to wake up. This morning I saw the newspapers being delivered by little boys, the streets being washed by strong men, and fresh vegetables coming in from the country on ox carts. It's a long walk from where Yang Sun lives, but I feel lighter at every step. They say you walk on air when you're in love, but it's even better walking on the rough earth, on the hard cement. In the early morning, the old city looks like a great heap of rubbish! Nice, though, with all its little lights. And the sky, so pink, so transparent, before the dust comes and muddies it! What a lot you miss if you never see your city rising from its slumbers like an honest old craftsman pumping his lungs full of air and reaching for his tools, as the poet says! [*Cheerfully, to her waiting guests.*] Good morning, everyone, here's your rice! [*Distributing the rice, she comes upon* WONG.] Good morning, Wong, I'm quite lightheaded today. On my way over, I looked at myself in all the shop windows. I'd love to be beautiful.

[*She slips into the carpet shop. Mr.* SHU FU *has just emerged from his shop.*]

SHU FU [*To the audience.*] It surprises me how beautiful Miss Shen Te is looking today! I never gave her a passing thought before. But now I've been gazing upon her comely form for exactly three minutes! I begin to suspect I am in love with her. She is overpoweringly attractive! [*Crossly, to* WONG.] Be off with you rascal!

[*He returns to his shop.* SHEN TE *comes back out of the carpet shop with the* OLD MAN, *its proprietor, and his wife—whom we have already met—the* OLD WOMAN. SHEN TE *is wearing a shawl. The* OLD MAN *is holding up a looking glass for her.*]

OLD WOMAN Isn't it lovely? We'll give you a reduction because there's a little hole in it.

SHEN TE [*Looking at another shawl on the old woman's arm.*] The other one's nice too.

OLD WOMAN [*Smiling.*] Too bad there's no hole in that!

SHEN TE That's right. My shop doesn't make very much.

OLD WOMAN And your deeds eat it all up! Be more careful, my dear . . .

SHEN TE [*Trying on the shawl with the hole.*] Just now, I'm lightheaded! Does the color suit me?

OLD WOMAN You'd better ask a man.

SHEN TE [*To the* OLD MAN.] Does the color suit me?

OLD MAN You'd better ask your young friend.

SHEN TE   I'd like to have your opinion.

OLD MAN   It suits you very well. But wear it this way: the dull side out. [SHEN TE *pays up.*]

OLD WOMAN   If you decide you don't like it, you can exchange it. [*She pulls* SHEN TE *to one side.*]   Has he got money?

SHEN TE   [(*With a laugh*]   Yang Sun? Oh, no.

OLD WOMAN   Then how're you going to pay your rent?

SHEN TE   I'd forgotten about that.

OLD WOMAN   And next Monday is the first of the month! Miss Shen Te, I've got something to say to you. After we [*Indicating her husband.*] got to know you, we had our doubts about that marriage ad. We thought it would be better if you'd let *us* help you. Out of our savings. We reckon we could lend you two hundred silver dollars. We don't need anything in writing—you could pledge us your tobacco stock.

SHEN TE   You're prepared to lend money to a person like me?

OLD WOMAN   It's folks like you that need it. We'd think twice about lending anything to your cousin.

OLD MAN [*Coming up.*]   All settled, my dear?

SHEN TE   I wish the gods could have heard what your wife was just saying, Mr. Ma. They're looking for good people who're happy—and helping me makes you happy because you know it was love that got me into difficulties!

[*The old couple smile knowingly at each other.*]

OLD MAN   And here's the money, Miss Shen Te.

[*He hands her an envelope.* SHEN TE *takes it. She bows. They bow back. They return to their shop.*]

SHEN TE [*Holding up her envelope.*]   Look, Wong, here's six months' rent! Don't you believe in miracles now? And how do you like my new shawl?

WONG   For the young fellow I saw you with in the park?

[SHEN TE *nods.*]

MRS. SHIN   Never mind all that. It's time you took a look at this hand!

SHEN TE   Have you hurt your hand?

MRS. SHIN   That barber smashed it with his hot curling iron. Right in front of our eyes.

SHEN TE [*Shocked at herself.*]   And I never noticed! We must get you to a doctor this minute or who knows what will happen?

UNEMPLOYED MAN   It's not a doctor he should see, it's a judge. He can ask for compensation. The barber's filthy rich.

WONG   You think I have a chance?

MRS. SHIN [*With relish.*]   If it's really good and smashed. But is it?

WONG   I think so. It's very swollen. Could I get a pension?

MRS. SHIN   You'd need a witness.

WONG   Well, you all saw it. You could all testify.

[*He looks round. The* UNEMPLOYED MAN, *the* GRANDFATHER, *and the* SISTER-IN-LAW *are all sitting against the wall of the shop eating rice. Their concentration on eating is complete.*]

SHEN TE [*To* MRS. SHIN.]   You saw it yourself.

MRS. SHIN   I want nothing to do with the police. It's against my principles.

SHEN TE [*To* SISTER-IN-LAW.]   What about you?

SISTER-IN-LAW   Me? I wasn't looking.

SHEN TE [*To the* GRANDFATHER, *coaxingly.*]   Grandfather, *you'll* testify, won't you?

SISTER-IN-LAW   And a lot of good that will do. He's simple-minded.

SHEN TE [*To the* UNEMPLOYED MAN.]   You seem to be the only witness left.

UNEMPLOYED MAN   My testimony would only hurt him. I've been picked up twice for begging.

SHEN TE

Your brother is assaulted, and you shut your eyes?
He is hit, cries out in pain, and you are silent?
The beast prowls, chooses and seizes his victim, and you say:
"Because we showed no displeasure, he has spared us."

If no one present will be a witness, I will. I'll say *I* saw it.

MRS. SHIN [*Solemnly.*]   The name for that is perjury.

WONG   I don't know if I can accept that. Though maybe I'll have to. [*Looking at his hand.*] Is it swollen enough, do you think? The swelling's not going down.

UNEMPLOYED MAN   No, no, the swelling's holding up well.

WONG   Yes. It's *more* swollen if anything. Maybe my wrist is broken after all. I'd better see a judge at once.

[*Holding his hand very carefully, and fixing his eyes on it, he runs off.* MRS. SHIN *goes quickly into the barber's shop.*]

UNEMPLOYED MAN [*Seeing her.*]   She is getting on the right side of Mr. Shu Fu.

SISTER-IN-LAW   You and I can't change the world, Shen Te.

SHEN TE   Go away! Go away all of you! [*The* UNEMPLOYED MAN *, the* SISTER-IN-LAW *, and the* GRANDFATHER *stalk off, eating and sulking. To the audience.*]

They've stopped answering
They stay put
They do as they're told
They don't care
Nothing can make them look up
But the smell of food.

[*Enter* MRS. YANG, *Yang Sun's mother, out of breath.*]

MRS. YANG   Miss Shen Te. My son has told me everything. I am Mrs. Yang, Sun's mother. Just think. He's got an offer. Of a job as a pilot. A letter has just come. From the director of the airfield in Peking!

SHEN TE   So he can fly again! Isn't that wonderful!

MRS. YANG [*Less breathlessly all the time.*]   They won't give him the job for nothing. They want five hundred silver dollars.

SHEN TE   We can't let money stand in his way, Mrs. Yang!

MRS. YANG   If only you could help him out!

SHEN TE   I have the shop. I can try! [*She embraces* MRS. YANG.] I happen to have two hundred with me now. Take it. [*She gives her the old couple's money.*] It was a loan but they said I could repay it with my tobacco stock.

MRS. YANG   And they were calling Sun the Dead Pilot of Setzuan! A friend in need!

SHEN TE   We must find another three hundred.

MRS. YANG   How?

SHEN TE   Let me think. [*Slowly.*] I know someone who can help. I didn't
   want to call on his services again, he's hard and cunning. But a flyer must
   fly. And I'll make this the last time.
      [*Distant sound of a plane.*]
MRS. YANG   If the man you mentioned can do it . . . Oh, look, there's the
   morning mail plane, heading for Peking!
SHEN TE   The pilot can see us, let's wave!
      [*They wave. The noise of the engine is louder.*]
MRS. YANG   You know that pilot up there?
SHEN TE   Wave, Mrs. Yang! I know the pilot who will be up there. He gave
   up hope. But he'll do it now. One man to raise himself above the misery,
   above us all. [*To the audience.*]

> Yang Sun, my lover:
> Braving the storms
> In company with the clouds
> Crossing the heavens
> And bringing to friends in faraway lands
> The friendly mail!

4a

In front of the inner curtain. Enter SHEN TE *, carrying Shui Ta's mask. She sings.*

THE SONG OF DEFENSELESSNESS

> In our country
> A useful man needs luck
> Only if he finds strong backers
> Can he prove himself useful.
> The good can't defend themselves and
> Even the gods are defenseless.
>
> Oh, why don't the gods have their own ammunition
> And launch against badness their own expedition
> Enthroning the good and preventing sedition
> And bringing the world to a peaceful condition?
>
> Oh, why don't the gods do the buying and selling
> Injustice forbidding, starvation dispelling
> Give bread to each city and joy to each dwelling?
> Oh, why don't the gods do the buying and selling?

[*She puts on Shui Ta's mask and sings in his voice.*]

> You can only help one of your luckless brothers
> By trampling down a dozen others.
>
> Why is it the gods do not feel indignation
> And come down in fury to end exploitation
> Defeat all defeat and forbid desperation
> Refusing to tolerate such toleration?
>
> Why is it?

5

Shen Te's tobacco shop. Behind the counter, Mr. SHUI TA, *reading the paper.* MRS. SHIN *is cleaning up. She talks and he takes no notice.*

MRS. SHIN   And when certain rumors get about, what *happens* to a little place like this? It goes to pot. *I* know. So, if you want my advice, Mr. Shui Ta, find out just what has been going on between Miss Shen Te and that Yang Sun from Yellow Street. And remember: a certain interest in Miss Shen Te has been expressed by the barber next door, a man with twelve houses and only one wife,[9] who, for that matter, is likely to drop off at any time. A certain interest has been expressed. He was even inquiring about her means and, if *that* doesn't prove a man is getting serious, what would?
    [*Still getting no response, she leaves with her bucket.*]
YANG SUN'S VOICE   Is that Miss Shen Te's tobacco shop?
MRS. SHIN'S VOICE   Yes, it is, but it's Mr. Shui Ta who's here today.
    [SHUI TA *runs to the mirror with the short, light steps of* SHEN TE, *and is just about to start primping, when he realizes his mistake, and turns away, with a short laugh. Enter* YANG SUN. MRS. SHIN *enters behind him and slips into the back room to eavesdrop.*]
YANG SUN   I am Yang Sun. [SHUI TA *bows.*] Is Shen Te in?
SHUI TA   No.
YANG SUN   I guess you know our relationship? [*He is inspecting the stock.*] Quite a place! And I thought she was just talking big. I'll be flying again, all right. [*He takes a cigar, solicits and receives a light from* SHUI TA.] You think we can squeeze the other three hundred out of the tobacco stock?
SHUI TA   May I ask if it is your intention to sell at once?
YANG SUN   It was decent of her to come out with the two hundred but they aren't much use with the other three hundred still missing.
SHUI TA   Shen Te was overhasty promising so much. She might have to sell the shop itself to raise it. Haste, they say, is the wind that blows the house down.
YANG SUN   Oh, she isn't a girl to keep a man waiting. For one thing or the other, if you take my meaning.
SHUI TA   I take your meaning
YANG SUN [*Leering.*]   Uh, huh.
SHUI TA   Would you explain what the five hundred silver dollars are for?
YANG SUN   Want to sound me out? Very well. The director of the Peking airfield is a friend of mine from flying school. I give him five hundred: he gets me the job.
SHUI TA   The price is high.
YANG SUN   Not as these things go. He'll have to fire one of the present pilots—for negligence. Only the man he has in mind isn't negligent. Not easy, you understand. You needn't mention that part of it to Shen Te.
SHUI TA [*Looking intently at* YANG SUN.]   Mr. Yang Sun, you are asking my cousin to give up her possessions, leave her friends, and place her entire fate in your hands. I presume you intend to marry her?

9. Ancient Chinese law permitted a man to have more than one wife.

YANG SUN   I'd be prepared to.
  [*Slight pause.*]
SHUI TA   Those two hundred silver dollars would pay the rent here for six months. If you were Shen Te wouldn't you be tempted to continue in business?
YANG SUN   What? Can you imagine Yang Sun the flyer behind a counter? [*In an oily voice.*] "A strong cigar or a mild one, worthy sir?" Not in this century!
SHUI TA   My cousin wishes to follow the promptings of her heart, and, from her own point of view, she may even have what is called the right to love. Accordingly, she has commissioned me to help you to this post. There is nothing here that I am not empowered to turn immediately into cash. Mrs. Mi Tzu, the landlady, will advise me about the sale.
  [*Enter* MRS. MI TZU.]
MRS. MI TZU   Good morning, Mr. Shui Ta, you wish to see me about the rent? As you know it falls due the day after tomorrow.
SHUI TA   Circumstances have changed, Mrs. Mi Tzu: my cousin is getting married. Her future husband here, Mr. Yang Sun, will be taking her to Peking. I am interested in selling the tobacco stock.
MRS. MI TZU   How much are you asking, Mr. Shui Ta?
YANG SUN   Three hundred sil—
SHUI TA   Five hundred silver dollars.
MRS. MI TZU   How much did she pay for it, Mr. Shui Ta?
SHUI TA   A thousand. And very little has been sold.
MRS. MI TZU She was robbed. But I'll make you a special offer if you'll promise to be out by the day after tomorrow. Three hundred silver dollars.
YANG SUN [*Shrugging.*]   Take it, man, take it.
SHUI TA   It is not enough.
YANG SUN   Why not? Why not? Certainly, it's enough.
SHUI TA   Five hundred silver dollars.
YANG SUN   But why? We only need three!
SHUI TA [*To* MRS. MI TZU.]   Excuse me. [*Takes* YANG SUN *on one side.*] The tobacco stock is pledged to the old couple who gave my cousin the two hundred.
YANG SUN   Is it in writing?
SHUI TA   No.
YANG SUN [*To* MRS. MI TZU.]   Three hundred will do.
MRS. MI TZU   Of course, I need an assurance that Miss Shen Te is not in debt.
YANG SUN   Mr. Shui Ta?
SHUI TA   She is not in debt.
YANG SUN   When can you let us have the money?
MRS. MI TZU   The day after tomorrow. And remember: I'm doing this because I have a soft spot in my heart for young lovers! [*Exit.*]
YANG SUN [*Calling after her.*]   Boxes, jars and sacks—three hundred for the lot and the pain's over! [*To* SHUI TA.] Where else can we raise money by the day after tomorrow?
SHUI TA   Nowhere. Haven't you enough for the trip and the first few weeks?

YANG SUN   Oh, certainly.

SHUI TA   How much, exactly.

YANG SUN   Oh, I'll dig it up, even if I have to steal it.

SHUI TA   I see.

YANG SUN   Well, don't fall off the roof. I'll get to Peking somehow.

SHUI TA   Two people can't travel for nothing.

YANG SUN [*Not giving* SHUI TA *a chance to answer.*]   I'm leaving *her* behind. No millstones round *my* neck!

SHUI TA   Oh.

YANG SUN   Don't look at me like that!

SHUI TA   How precisely is my cousin to live?

YANG SUN   Oh, you'll think of something.

SHUI TA   A small request, Mr. Yang Sun. Leave the two hundred silver dollars here until you can show me two tickets for Peking.

YANG SUN   You learn to mind your own business, Mr. Shui Ta.

SHUI TA   I'm afraid Miss Shen Te may not wish to sell the shop when she discovers that . . .

YANG SUN   You don't know women. She'll want to. Even then.

SHUI TA [*A slight outburst.*]   She is a human being, sir! And not devoid of common sense!

YANG SUN   Shen Te is a woman: she *is* devoid of common sense. I only have to lay my hand on her shoulder, and church bells ring.

SHUI TA [*With difficulty.*]   Mr. Yang Sun!

YANG SUN   Mr. Shui Whatever-it-is!

SHUI TA   My cousin is devoted to you . . . because . . .

YANG SUN   Because I have my hands on her breasts. Give me a cigar. [*He takes one for himself, stuffs a few more in his pocket, then changes his mind and takes the whole box.*] Tell her I'll marry her, then bring me the three hundred. Or let her bring it. One or the other. [*Exit.*]

MRS. SHIN [*Sticking her head out of the back room.*]   Well, he has your cousin under his thumb, and doesn't care if all Yellow Street knows it!

SHUI TA [*Crying out.*]   I've lost my shop! And he doesn't love me! [*He runs berserk through the room, repeating these lines incoherently. Then stops suddenly, and addresses* MRS. SHIN.] Mrs. Shin, you grew up in the gutter, like me. Are we lacking in hardness? I doubt it. If you steal a penny from me, I'll take you by the throat till you spit it out! You'd do the same to me. The times are bad, this city is hell, but we're like ants, we keep coming, up and up the walls, however smooth! Till bad luck comes. Being in love, for instance. One weakness is enough, and love is the deadliest.

MRS. SHIN [*Emerging from the back room.*]   You should have a little talk with Mr. Shu Fu, the barber. He's a real gentleman and just the thing for your cousin. [*She runs off.*]

SHUI TA

> A caress becomes a stranglehold
> A sigh of love turns to a cry of fear
> Why are there vultures circling in the air?
> A girl is going to meet her lover.

[SHUI TA *sits down and Mr.* SHU FU *enters with* MRS. SHIN.]

SHUI TA   Mr. Shu Fu?

SHU FU Mr. Shui Ta.

> [*They both bow.*]

SHUI TA I am told that you have expressed a certain interest in my cousin Shen Te. Let me set aside all propriety and confess: she is at this moment in grave danger.

SHU FU Oh, dear!

SHUI TA She has lost her shop, Mr. Shu Fu.

SHU FU The charm of Miss Shen Te, Mr. Shui Ta, derives from the goodness, not of her shop, but of her heart. Men call her the Angel of the Slums.

SHUI TA Yet her goodness has cost her two hundred silver dollars in a single day: we must put a stop to it.

SHU FU Permit me to differ, Mr. Shui Ta. Let us, rather, open wide the gates to such goodness! Every morning, with pleasure tinged by affection, I watch her charitable ministrations. For they are hungry, and she giveth them to eat! Four of them, to be precise. Why only four? I ask. Why not four hundred?[1] I hear she has been seeking shelter for the homeless. What about my humble cabins behind the cattle run? They are at her disposal. And so forth. And so on. Mr. Shui Ta, do you think Miss Shen Te could be persuaded to listen to certain ideas of mine? Ideas like these?

SHUI TA Mr. Shu Fu, she would be honored.

> [*Enter* WONG *and the* POLICEMAN. *Mr.* SHU FU *turns abruptly away and studies the shelves.*]

WONG Is Miss Shen Te here?

SHUI TA No.

WONG I am Wong the water seller. You are Mr. Shui Ta?

SHUI TA I am.

WONG I am a friend of Shen Te's.

SHUI TA An intimate friend, I hear.

WONG [*To the* POLICEMAN.] You see? [*To* SHUI TA.] It's because of my hand.

POLICEMAN He hurt his hand, sir, that's a fact.

SHUI TA [*Quickly.*] You need a sling, I see. [*He takes a shawl from the back room, and throws it to* WONG.]

WONG But that's her new shawl!

SHUI TA She has no more use for it.

WONG But she bought it to please someone!

SHUI TA It happens to be no longer necessary.

WONG [*Making the sling.*] She is my only witness.

POLICEMAN Mr. Shui Ta, your cousin is supposed to have seen the barber hit the water seller with a curling iron.

SHUI TA I'm afraid my cousin was not present at the time

WONG But she was, sir! Just ask her! Isn't she in?

SHUI TA [*Gravely.*] Mr. Wong, my cousin has her own troubles. You wouldn't wish her to add to them by committing perjury?

WONG But it was she that told me to go to the judge!

SHUI TA Was the judge supposed to heal your hand?

---

1. An allusion to the biblical miracle of loaves and fishes, when Christ fed five thousand people (Matthew 14.13–21).

[*Mr.* SHU FU *turns quickly around.* SHUI TA *bows to* SHU FU, *and vice versa.*]

WONG [*Taking the sling off, and putting it back.*]   I see how it is.

POLICEMAN   Well, I'll be on my way. [*To* WONG.] And you be careful. If Mr. Shu Fu wasn't a man who tempers justice with mercy, as the saying is, you'd be in jail for libel. Be off with you!

[*Exit* WONG *followed by* POLICEMAN.]

SHUI TA   Profound apologies, Mr. Shu Fu.

SHU FU   Not at all, Mr. Shui Ta. [*Pointing to the shawl.*] The episode is over?

SHUI TA   It may take her time to recover. There are some fresh wounds.

SHUI TA   We shall be discreet. Delicate. A short vacation could be arranged . . .

SHUI TA   First of course, you and she would have to talk things over.

SHU FU   At a small supper in a small, but high-class, restaurant.

SHUI TA   I'll go and find her. [*Exit into back room.*]

MRS. SHIN [*Sticking her head in again.*]   Time for congratulations, Mr. Shu Fu?

SHU FU   Ah, Mrs. Shin! Please inform Miss Shen Te's guests they may take shelter in the cabins behind the cattle run!

[MRS. SHIN *nods, grinning.*]

SHU FU [*To the audience.*]   Well? What do you think of me, ladies and gentlemen? What could a man do more? Could he be less selfish? More farsighted? A small supper in a small but . . . Does that bring rather vulgar and clumsy thoughts into your mind? Ts, ts, ts. Nothing of the sort will occur. She won't even be touched. Not even accidentally while passing the salt. An exchange of ideas only. Over the flowers on the table—white chrysanthemums, by the way [*He writes down a note of this.*]—yes, over the white chrysanthemums, two young souls will . . . shall I say "find each other"? We shall NOT exploit the misfortune of others. Understanding? Yes. An offer of assistance? Certainly. But quietly. Almost inaudibly. Perhaps with a single glance. A glance that could also—mean more.

MRS. SHIN [*Coming forward.*]   Everything under control, Mr. Shu Fu?

SHU FU   Oh, Mrs. Shin, what do you know about this worthless rascal Yang Sun?

MRS. SHIN   Why, he's the most worthless rascal . . .

SHU FU   Is he really? You're sure? [*As she opens her mouth.*] From now on, he doesn't exist! Can't be found anywhere!

[*Enter* YANG SUN.]

YANG SUN   What's been going on here?

MRS. SHIN   Shall I call Mr. Shui Ta, Mr. Shu Fu? He wouldn't want strangers in here!

SHU FU   Mr. Shui Ta is in conference with Miss Shen Te. Not to be disturbed!

YANG SUN   Shen Te here? I didn't see her come in. What kind of conference?

SHU FU [*Not letting him enter the back room.*]   Patience, dear sir! And if by chance I have an inkling who you are, pray take note that Miss Shen Te and I are about to announce our engagement.

YANG SUN   What?

MRS. SHIN   You didn't expect that, did you?

[YANG SUN *is trying to push past the barber into the back room when* SHEN TE *comes out.*]

SHU FU My dear Shen Te, ten thousand apologies! Perhaps you . . .

YANG SUN What is it, Shen Te? Have you gone crazy?

SHEN TE [*Breathless.*] My cousin and Mr. Shu Fu have come to an under-standing. They wish to hear Mr. Shu Fu's plans for helping the poor.

YANG SUN Your cousin wants to part us.

SHEN TE Yes.

YANG SUN And you've agreed to it?

SHEN TE Yes.

YANG SUN They told you I was bad. [SHEN TE *is silent.*] And suppose I am. Does that make me need you less? I'm low, Shen Te, I have no money, I don't do the right thing but at least I put up a fight! [*He is near her now, and speaks in an undertone.*] Have you no eyes? Look at him. Have you forgotten already?

SHEN TE No.

YANG SUN How it was raining?

SHEN TE No.

YANG SUN How you cut me down from the willow tree? Bought me water? Promised me money to fly with?

SHEN TE [*Shakily.*] Yang Sun, what do you want?

YANG SUN I want you to come with me

SHEN TE [*In a small voice.*] Forgive me, Mr. Shu Fu, I want to go with Mr. Yang Sun.

YANG SUN We're lovers, you know. Give me the key to the shop. [SHEN TE *takes the key from around her neck.* YANG SUN *puts it on the counter. To* MRS. SHIN.] Leave it under the mat when you're through. Let's go, Shen Te.

SHU FU But this is rape! Mr. Shui Ta!!

YANG SUN [*To* SHEN TE.] Tell him not to shout.

SHEN TE Please don't shout for my cousin, Mr. Shu Fu. He doesn't agree with me, I know, but he's wrong. [*To the audience.*]

> I want to go with the man I love
> I don't want to count the cost
> I don't want to consider if it's wise
> I don't want to know if he loves me
> I want to go with the man I love.

YANG SUN That's the spirit.

[*And the couple leave.*]

5a

In front of the inner curtain. SHEN TE *in her wedding clothes, on the way to her wedding.*

SHEN TE Something terrible has happened. As I left the shop with Yang Sun, I found the old carpet dealer's wife waiting on the street, trembling all over. She told me her husband had taken to his bed—sick with all the worry and excitement over the two hundred silver dollars they lent me. She said it would be best if I gave it back now. Of course, I had to say I would. She said she couldn't quite trust my cousin Shui Ta or even my fiancé, Yang Sun. There were tears in her eyes. With my emotions in an uproar, I threw myself into Yang Sun's arms, I couldn't resist him. The things he'd said to Shui Ta had taught Shen Te nothing. Sinking into his arms, I said to myself:

> To let no one perish, not even oneself
> To fill everyone with happiness, even oneself
> Is so good

How could I have forgotten those two old people? Yang Sun swept me away like a small hurricane. But he's not a bad man, and he loves me. He'd rather work in the cement factory than owe his flying to a crime. Though, of course, flying *is* a great passion with Sun. Now, on the way to my wedding, I waver between fear and joy.

6

The "private dining room" on the upper floor of a cheap restaurant in a poor section of town. With SHEN TE: *the* GRANDFATHER, *the* SISTER-IN-LAW, THE NIECE, MRS. SHIN, *the* UNEMPLOYED MAN. *In a corner, alone, a* PRIEST.[2] *A* WAITER *pouring wine. Downstage,* YANG SUN *talking to his mother. He wears a diner jacket.*

YANG SUN   Bad news, Mamma. She came right out and told me she can't sell the shop for me. Some idiot is bringing a claim because he lent her the two hundred she gave you.
MRS. YANG   What did you say? Of course, you can't marry her now.
YANG SUN   It's no use saying anything to *her*. I've sent for her cousin, Mr. Shui Ta. He said there was nothing in writing.
MRS. YANG   Good idea. I'll go out and look for him. Keep an eye on things.
    [*Exit* MRS. YANG. SHEN TE *has been pouring wine.*]
SHEN TE [*To the audience, pitcher in hand.*]   I wasn't mistaken in him. He's bearing up well. Though it must have been an awful blow—giving up flying. I do love him so. [*Calling across the room to him.*] Sun, you haven't drunk a toast with the bride!
YANG SUN   What do we drink to?
SHEN TE   Why, to the future!
YANG SUN   When the bridegroom's dinner jacket won't be a hired one!
SHEN TE   But when the bride's dress will still get rained on sometimes!
YANG SUN   To everything we ever wished for!
SHEN TE   May all our dreams come true!
    [*They drink.*]
YANG SUN [*With loud conviviality.*]   And now, friends, before the wedding gets under way, I have to ask the bride a few questions. I've no idea what

kind of a wife she'll make, and it worries me. [*Wheeling on* SHEN TE.] For example. Can you make five cups of tea with three tea leaves?

SHEN TE   No.

YANG SUN   So I won't be getting very much tea. Can you sleep on a straw mattress the size of that book? [*He points to the large volume the* PRIEST *is reading.*]

SHEN TE   The two of us?

YANG SUN   The one of you.

SHEN TE   In that case, no.

YANG SUN   What a wife! I'm shocked!

[*While the audience is laughing, his mother returns. With a shrug of her shoulders, she tells* SUN *the expected guest hasn't arrived. The* PRIEST *shuts the book with a bang, and makes for the door.*]

MRS. YANG   Where are *you* off to? It's only a matter of minutes.

PRIEST [*Watch in hand.*]   Time goes on, Mrs. Yang, and I've another wedding to attend to. Also a funeral.

MRS. YANG [*Irately.*]   D'you think we planned it this way? I was hoping to manage with one pitcher of wine, and we've run through two already. [*Points to empty pitcher. Loudly.*] My dear Shen Te, I don't know where your cousin can be keeping himself!

SHEN TE   My cousin?!

MRS. YANG   Certainly. I'm old-fashioned enough to think such a close relative should attend the wedding.

SHEN TE   Oh, Sun, is it the three hundred silver dollars?

YANG SUN [*Not looking her in the eye.*]   Are you deaf? Mother says she's old-fashioned. And I say I'm considerate. We'll wait another fifteen minutes.

HUSBAND   Another fifteen minutes.

MRS. YANG [*Addressing the company.*]   Now you all know, don't you, that my son is getting a job as a mail pilot?

SISTER-IN-LAW   In Peking, too, isn't it?

MRS. YANG   In Peking, too! The two of us are moving to Peking!

SHEN TE   Sun, tell your mother Peking is out of the question now.

YANG SUN   Your cousin'll tell her. If he agrees. I don't agree.

SHEN TE [*Amazed, and dismayed.*]   Sun!

YANG SUN   I hate this godforsaken Setzuan. What people! Know what they look like when I half close my eyes? Horses! Whinnying, fretting, stamping, screwing their necks up! [*Loudly.*] And what is it the thunder says? They are su-per-flu-ous! [*He hammers out the syllables.*] They've run their last race! They can go trample themselves to death! [*Pause.*] I've got to get out of here.

SHEN TE   But I've promised the money to the old couple.

YANG SUN   And since you always do the wrong thing, it's lucky your cousin's coming. Have another drink.

SHEN TE [*Quietly.*]   My cousin can't be coming.

YANG SUN   How d'you mean?

SHEN TE   My cousin can't be where I am.

YANG SUN   Quite a conundrum!

SHEN TE [*Desperately.*]   Sun, I'm the one that loves you. Not my cousin. He was thinking of the job in Peking when he promised you the old couple's money—

YANG SUN   Right. And that's why he's bringing the three hundred silver
dollars. Here—to my wedding.

SHEN TE   He is not bringing the three hundred silver dollars.

YANG SUN   Huh? What makes you think that?

SHEN TE [*Looking into his eyes.*]   He says you only bought one ticket to
Peking.
        [*Short pause.*]

YANG SUN   That was yesterday. [*He pulls two tickets part way out of his
inside pocket, making her look under his coat.*] Two tickets. I don't want
Mother to know. She'll get left behind. I sold her furniture to buy these
tickets, so you see . . .

SHEN TE   But what's to become of the old couple?

YANG SUN   What's to become of me? Have another drink. Or do you
believe in moderation? If I drink, I fly again. And if you drink, you may
learn to understand me.

SHEN TE   You want to fly. But I can't help you.

YANG SUN   "Here's a plane, my darling—but it's only got one wing!"
        [*The* WAITER *enters.*]

WAITER   Mrs. Yang!

MRS. YANG   Yes?

WAITER   Another pitcher of wine, ma'am?

MRS. YANG   We have enough, thanks. Drinking makes me sweat.

WAITER   Would you mind paying, ma'am?

MRS. YANG [*To everyone.*]   Just be patient a few moments longer, everyone, Mr. Shui Ta is on his way over! [*To the* WAITER.] Don't be a
spoilsport.

WAITER   I can't let you leave till you've paid your bill, ma'am.

MRS. YANG   But they know me here!

WAITER   That's just it.

PRIEST [*Ponderously getting up.*]   I humbly take my leave. [*And he does.*]

MRS. YANG [*To the others, desperately.*]   Stay where you are, everybody!
The priest says he'll be back in two minutes!

YANG SUN   It's no good Mamma. Ladies and gentlemen, Mr. Shui Ta still
hasn't arrived and the priest has gone home. We won't detain you any
longer.
        [*They are leaving now*]

GRANDFATHER [*In the doorway, having forgotten to put his glass down.*]   To
the bride! [*He drinks, puts down the glass, and follows the others.*]
        [*Pause.*]

SHEN TE   Shall I go too?

YANG SUN   You? Aren't you the bride? Isn't this your wedding? [*He drags
her across the room, tearing her wedding dress.*] If we can wait, you can
wait. Mother calls me her falcon. She wants to see me in the clouds. But
I think it may be St. Nevercome's Day before she'll go to the door and
see my plane thunder by. [*Pause. He pretends the guests are still present.*]
Why such a lull in the conversation, ladies and gentlemen? Don't you
like it here? The ceremony is only slightly postponed—because an important guest is expected at any moment. Also because the bride doesn't
know what love is. While we're waiting, the bridegroom will sing a little
song. [*He does so.*]

THE SONG OF ST. NEVERCOME'S DAY

On a certain day, as is generally known,
    One and all will be shouting: Hooray, hooray!
For the beggar maid's son has a solid-gold throne
    And the day is St. Nevercome's Day
On St. Nevercome's, Nevercome's, Nevercome's Day
    He'll sit on his solid-gold throne

Oh, hooray, hooray! That day goodness will pay!
    That day badness will cost you your head!
And merit and money will smile and be funny
    While exchanging salt and bread
On St. Nevercome's, Nevercome's, Nevercome's Day
    While exchanging salt and bread

And the grass, oh, the grass will look down at the sky
    And the pebbles will roll up the stream
And all men will be good without batting an eye
    They will make of our earth a dream
On St. Nevercome's, Nevercome's, Nevercome's Day
    They will make of our earth a dream

And as for me, that's the day I shall be
    A flyer and one of the best
Unemployed man, you will have work to do
    Washerwoman, you'll get your rest
On St. Nevercome's, Nevercome's, Nevercome's Day
    Washerwoman, you'll get your rest

MRS. YANG   It looks like he's not coming.
    [*The three of them sit looking at the door.*]

6a

Wong's den. The sewer pipe is again transparent and again the GODS *appear to* WONG *in a dream.*

WONG   I'm so glad you've come, illustrious ones. It's Shen Te. She's in great trouble from following the rule about loving thy neighbor. Perhaps she's *too* good for this world!

FIRST GOD   Nonsense! You are eaten up by lice and doubts!

WONG   Forgive me, illustrious one, I only meant you might deign to intervene.

FIRST GOD   Out of the question! My colleague here intervened in some squabble or other only yesterday. [*He points to the* THIRD GOD, *who has a black eye.*] The results are before us!

WONG   She had to call on her cousin again. But not even he could help. I'm afraid the shop is done for.

THIRD GOD [*A little concerned.*]   Perhaps we should help after all?

FIRST GOD   The gods help those that help themselves.

WONG What if we *can't* help ourselves, illustrious ones?
      [*Slight pause.*]
SECOND GOD Try, anyway! Suffering ennobles!
FIRST GOD Our faith in Shen Te is unshaken!
THIRD GOD We certainly haven't found any *other* good people. You can
     see where we spend our nights from the straw on our clothes.
WONG You might help her find her way by—
FIRST GOD The good man finds his own way here below!
SECOND GOD The good woman too.
FIRST GOD The heavier the burden, the greater her strength!
THIRD GOD We're only onlookers, you know.
FIRST GOD And everything will be all right in the end, O ye of little faith!
      [*They are gradually disappearing through these last lines.*]

7

The yard behind Shen Te's shop. A few articles of furniture on a cart. SHEN TE
and MRS. SHIN *are taking the washing off the line.*

MRS. SHIN If you ask me, you should fight tooth and nail to keep the
     shop.
SHEN TE How can I? I have to sell the tobacco to pay back the two hun-
     dred silver dollars today.
MRS. SHIN No husband, no tobacco, no house and home! What are you
     going to live on?
SHEN TE I can work. I can sort tobacco.
MRS. SHIN Hey, look, Mr. Shui Ta's trousers! He must have left here stark
     naked!
SHEN TE Oh, he may have another pair, Mrs. Shin.
MRS. SHIN But if he's gone for good as you say, why has he left his pants
     behind?
SHEN TE Maybe he's thrown them away.
MRS. SHIN Can I take them?
SHEN TE Oh, no.
      [*Enter Mr.* SHU FU, *running.*]
SHU FU Not a word! Total silence! I know all. You have sacrificed your
     own love and happiness so as not to hurt a dear old couple who had put
     their trust in you! Not in vain does this district—for all its malevolent
     tongues—call you the Angel of the Slums! That young man couldn't rise
     to your level, so you left him. And now, when I see you closing up the
     little shop, that veritable haven of rest for the multitude, well, I cannot,
     I cannot let it pass. Morning after morning I have stood watching in the
     doorway not unmoved—while you graciously handed out rice to the
     wretched. Is that never to happen again? Is the good woman of Setzuan
     to disappear? If only you would allow *me* to assist you! Now don't say
     anything! No assurances, no exclamations of gratitude! [*He has taken out
     his checkbook.*] Here! A blank check. [*He places it on the cart.*] Just my
     signature. Fill it out as you wish. Any sum in the world. I herewith retire

from the scene, quietly, unobtrusively, making no claims, on tiptoe, full of veneration, absolutely selflessly . . . [*He has gone.*]

MRS. SHIN   Well! You're saved. There's always some idiot of a man. . . . Now hurry! Put down a thousand silver dollars and let me fly to the bank before he comes to his senses.

SHEN TE   I can pay you for the washing without any check.

MRS. SHIN   What? You're not going to cash it just because you might have to marry him? Are you crazy? Men like him *want* to be led by the nose! Are you still thinking of that flyer? All Yellow Street knows how he treated you!

SHEN TE

When I heard his cunning laugh, I was afraid
But when I saw the holes in his shoes, I loved him dearly.

MRS. SHIN   Defending that good-for-nothing after all that's happened!

SHEN TE [*Staggering as she holds some of the washing.*]   Oh!

MRS. SHIN [*Taking the washing from her, dryly.*]   So you feel dizzy when you stretch and bend? There couldn't be a little visitor on the way? If that's it, you can forget Mr. Shu Fu's blank check: it wasn't meant for a christening present!

[*She goes to the back with a basket. Shen Te's eyes follow* MRS. SHIN *for a moment. Then she looks down at her own body, feels her stomach, and a great joy comes into her eyes.*]

SHEN TE   O joy! A new human being is on the way. The world awaits him. In the cities the people say: he's got to be reckoned with, this new human being! [*She imagines a little boy to be present, and introduces him to the audience.*] This is my son, the well-known flyer!

Say: Welcome
To the conqueror of unknown mountains and unreachable regions
Who brings us our mail across the impassable deserts!

[*She leads him up and down by the hand.*]

Take a look at the world, my son. That's a tree. Tree, yes. Say: "Hello, tree!" And bow. Like this. [*She bows.*] Now you know each other. And, look, here comes the water seller. He's a friend, give him your hand. A cup of fresh water for my little son, please. Yes, it *is* a warm day. [*Handing the cup.*] Oh dear, a policeman, we'll have to make a circle round *him*. Perhaps we can pick a few cherries over there in the rich Mr. Pung's garden. But we mustn't be seen. You want cherries? Just like children with fathers. No, no, you can't go straight at them like that. Don't pull. We must learn to be reasonable. Well, have it your own way. [*She has let him make for the cherries.*] Can you reach? Where to put them? Your mouth is the best place. [*She tries one herself.*] Mmm, they're good. But the policeman, we must run! [*They run.*] Yes, back to the street. Calm now, so no one will notice us. [*Walking the street with her child, she sings.*]

Once a plum—'twas in Japan—
Made a conquest of a man
But the man's turn soon did come
For he gobbled up the plum

[*Enter* WONG, *with a child by the hand. He coughs.*]

SHEN TE   Wong!

WONG   It's about the carpenter, Shen Te. He's lost his shop, and he's been drinking. His children are on the streets. This is one. Can you help?

SHEN TE [*To the child.*]   Come here, little man. [*Takes him down to the footlights. To the audience.*]

>   You there! A man is asking you for shelter!
>   A man of tomorrow says: what about today?
>   His friend the conqueror, whom you know,
>   Is his advocate!

[*To* WONG.] He can live in Mr. Shu Fu's cabins. I may have to go there myself. I'm going to have a baby. That's a secret—don't tell Yang Sun—we'd only be in his way. Can you find the carpenter for me?

WONG   I knew you'd think of something. [*To the child.*] Good-bye, son, I'm going for your father.

SHEN TE   What about your hand, Wong? I wanted to help, but my cousin . . .

WONG   Oh, I can get along with one hand, don't worry. [*He shows how he can handle his pole with his left hand alone.*]

SHEN TE   But your right hand! Look, take this cart, sell everything that's on it, and go to the doctor with the money . . .

WONG   She's still good. But first I'll bring the carpenter. I'll pick up the cart when I get back [*Exit* WONG.]

SHEN TE [*To the child.*]   Sit down over here, son, till your father comes.
>   [*The child sits crosslegged on the ground. Enter the* HUSBAND *and* WIFE, *each dragging a large, full sack.*]

WIFE [*Furtively.*]   You're alone, Shen Te, dear?
>   [SHEN TE *nods. The* WIFE *beckons to the* NEPHEW *offstage. He comes on with another sack.*]

WIFE   Your cousin's away? [SHEN TE *nods.*] He's not coming back?

SHEN TE   No. I'm giving up the shop.

WIFE   That's why we're here. We want to know if we can leave these things in your new home. Will you do us this favor?

SHEN TE   Why, yes, I'd be glad to.

HUSBAND [*Cryptically.*]   And if anyone asks about them, say they're yours.

SHEN TE   Would anyone ask?

WIFE [*With a glance back at her husband.*]   Oh, someone might. The police, for instance. They don't seem to like us. Where can we put it?

SHEN TE   Well, I'd rather not get in any more trouble . . .

WIFE   Listen to her! The good woman of Setzuan!
>   [SHEN TE *is silent.*]

HUSBAND   There's enough tobacco in those sacks to give us a new start in life. We could have our own tobacco factory!

SHEN TE [*Slowly.*]   You'll have to put them in the back room
>   [*The sacks are taken offstage, while the child is alone. Shyly glancing about him, he goes to the garbage can, starts playing with the contents, and eating some of the scraps. The others return.*]

WIFE   We're counting on you, Shen Te!

SHEN TE   Yes. [*She sees the child and is shocked.*]

HUSBAND   We'll see you in Mr. Shu Fu's cabins.

NEPHEW   The day after tomorrow.

SHEN TE   Yes. Now, go. Go! I'm not feeling well.

[*Exeunt all three, virtually pushed off.*]

> He is eating the refuse in the garbage can!
> Only look at his little gray mouth!

[*Pause. Music.*]

> As this is the world *my* son will enter
> I will study to defend him.
> To be good to you, my son,
> I shall be a tigress to all others
> If I have to.
> And I shall have to.

[*She starts to go*]

> One more time, then. I hope really the last.

[*Exit* SHEN TE, *taking Shui Ta's trousers.* MRS. SHIN *enters and watches her with marked interest. Enter the* SISTER-IN-LAW *and the* GRANDFATHER.]

SISTER-IN-LAW   So it's true, the shop has closed down. And the furniture's in the back yard. It's the end of the road!

MRS. SHIN [*Pompously.*]   The fruit of high living, selfishness, and sensuality! Down the primrose path to Mr. Shu Fu's cabins—with you!

SISTER-IN-LAW   Cabins? Rat holes! He gave them to us because his soap supplies only went moldy there!

[*Enter the* UNEMPLOYED MAN.]

UNEMPLOYED MAN   Shen Te is moving?

SISTER-IN-LAW   Yes, She was sneaking away.

MRS. SHIN   She's ashamed of herself, and no wonder!

UNEMPLOYED MAN   Tell her to call Mr. Shui Ta or she's done for this time!

SISTER-IN-LAW   Tell her to call Mr. Shui Fa or *we're* done for this time!

[*Enter* WONG *and* CARPENTER, *the latter with a child on each hand.*]

CARPENTER   So we'll have a roof over our heads for a change!

MRS. SHIN   Roof? Whose roof?

CARPENTER   Mr. Shu Fu's cabins. And we have little Feng to thank for it. [*Feng, we find, is the name of the child already there; his father now takes him. To the other two.*] Bow to your little brother, you two!

[*The* CARPENTER *and the two new arrivals bow to Feng. Enter* SHUI TA.]

UNEMPLOYED MAN   Sst! Mr. Shui Ta!

[*Pause.*]

SHUI TA   And what is this crowd here for, may I ask?

WONG   How do you do, Mr. Shui Ta. This is the carpenter. Miss Shen Te promised him space in Mr. Shu Fu's cabins.

SHUI TA   That will not be possible.

CARPENTER   We can't go there after all?

SHUI TA   All the space is needed for other purposes.

SISTER-IN-LAW   You mean we have to get out? But we've got nowhere to go.

SHUI TA   Miss Shen Te finds it possible to provide employment. If the proposition interests you, you may stay in the cabins.

SISTER-IN-LAW [*With distaste.*]   You mean *work*? Work for Miss Shen Te?

SHUI TA   Making tobacco, yes. There are three bales here already. Would you like to get them?

SISTER-IN-LAW [*Trying to bluster.*]   We have our own tobacco! We were in the tobacco business before you were born!

SHUI TA [*To the* CARPENTER *and the* UNEMPLOYED MAN]   You *don't* have your own tobacco. What about you?

 [*The* CARPENTER *and the* UNEMPLOYED MAN *get the point, and go for the sacks. Enter* MRS. MI TZU.

MRS. MI TZU   Mr. Shui Ta? I've brought you your three hundred silver dollars.

SHUI TA   I'll sign your lease instead. I've decided not to sell.

MRS. MI TZU   What? You don't need the money for that flyer?

SHUI TA   No.

MRS. MI TZU   And you can pay six months' rent?

SHUI TA [*Takes the barber's blank check from the cart and fills it out.*]   Here is a check for ten thousand silver dollars. On Mr. Shu Fu's account. Look [*He shows her the signature on the check.*] Your six months' rent will be in your hands by seven this evening. And now, if you'll excuse me.

MRS. MI TZU   So it's Mr. Shu Fu now. The flyer has been given his walking papers. These modern girls! In my day they'd have said she was flighty. That poor, deserted Mr. Yang Sun!

 [*Exit* MRS. MI TZU. *The* CARPENTER *and the* UNEMPLOYED MAN *drag the three sacks back on the stage.*]

CARPENTER [*To* SHUI TA.]   I don't know why I'm doing this for you.

SHUI TA   Perhaps your children want to eat, Mr. Carpenter.

SISTER-IN-LAW [*Catching sight of the sacks.*]   Was my brother-in-law here?

MRS. SHIN   Yes, he was.

SISTER-IN-LAW   I thought as much. I know those sacks! That's our tobacco!

SHUI TA   Really? I thought it came from my back room! Shall we consult the police on the point?

SISTER-IN-LAW [*Defeated.*]   No.

SHUI TA   Perhaps you will show me the way to Mr. Shu Fu's cabins?

 [*Taking Feng by the hand,* SHUI TA *goes off, followed by the* CARPENTER *and his two older children, the* SISTER-IN-LAW, *the* GRANDFATHER, *and the* UNEMPLOYED MAN. *Each of the last three drags a sack. Enter* OLD MAN *and* OLD WOMAN.]

MRS. SHIN   A pair of pants—missing from the clothes line one minute—and next minute on the honorable backside of Mr. Shui Ta.

OLD WOMAN   We thought Miss Shen Te was here.

MRS. SHIN [*Preoccupied.*]   Well, she's not.

OLD MAN   There was something she was going to give us.

WONG   She was going to help me too. [*Looking at his hand.*]   It'll be too late soon. But she'll be back. This cousin has never stayed long.

MRS. SHIN [*Approaching a conclusion.*]   No, he hasn't, has he?

<hr />

7a

The Sewer Pipe: WONG *asleep. In his dream, he tells the* GODS *his fears. The* GODS *seem tired from all their travels. They stop for a moment and look over their shoulders at the water seller.*

WONG   Illustrious ones. I've been having a bad dream. Our beloved Shen
Te was in great distress in the rushes down by the river—the spot where
the bodies of suicides are washed up. She kept staggering and holding
her head down as if she was carrying something and it was dragging her
down into the mud. When I called out to her, she said she had to take
your Book of Rules[3] to the other side, and not get it wet, or the ink would
all come off. You had talked to her about the virtues, you know, the time
she gave you shelter in Setzuan.

THIRD GOD   Well, but what do you suggest, my dear Wong?

WONG   Maybe a little relaxation of the rules, Benevolent One, in view of
the bad times.

THIRD GOD   As for instance?

WONG   Well, um, good-will, for instance, might do instead of love?

THIRD GOD   I'm afraid that would create new problems.

WONG   Or, instead of justice, good sportsmanship?

THIRD GOD   That would only mean more work.

WONG   Instead of honor, outward propriety?

THIRD GOD   Still more work! No, no! The rules will have to stand, my dear
Wong!

[*Wearily shaking their heads, all three journey on.*]

8

*Shui Ta's tobacco factory in Shu Fu's cabins. Huddled together behind bars,
several families, mostly women and children. Among these people the* SISTER-IN-
LAW, *the* GRANDFATHER, *the* CARPENTER, *and his three children. Enter* MRS.
YANG *followed by* YANG SUN.

MRS. YANG [*To the audience.*]   There's something I just *have* to tell you:
strength and wisdom are wonderful things. The strong and wise Mr. Shui
Ta has transformed my son from a dissipated good-for-nothing into a
model citizen. As you may have heard, Mr. Shui Ta opened a small
tobacco factory near the cattle runs. It flourished. Three months ago—
I shall never forget it—I asked for an appointment, and Mr. Shui Ta
agree to see us—me and my son. I can see him now as he came through
the door to meet us. . . .

[*Enter* SHUI TA, *from a door.*]

SHUI TA   What can I do for you, Mrs. Yang?

MRS. YANG   This morning the police came to the house. We find you've
brought an action for breach of promise of marriage. In the name of
Shen Te. You also claim that Sun came by two hundred silver dollars by
improper means.

SHUI TA   That is correct.

MRS. YANG   Mr. Shui Ta, the money's all gone. When the Peking job didn't
materialize, he ran through it all in three days. I know he's a good-for-
nothing. He sold my furniture. He was moving to Peking without me.
Miss Shen Te thought highly of him at one time.

---

3. Reference to neo-Confucianist commentators' rigid and prescriptive interpretation of Confucius's *Ana-
lects*, especially regarding the role of women.

SHUI TA   What do *you* say, Mr. Yang Sun?

YANG SUN   The money's gone.

SHUI TA [*To* MRS. YANG.]   Mrs. Yang, in consideration of my cousin's incomprehensible weakness for your son, I am prepared to give him another chance. He can have a job—here. The two hundred silver dollars will be taken out of his wages.

YANG SUN   So it's the factory or jail?

SHUI TA   Take your choice.

YANG SUN   May I speak with Shen Te?

SHUI TA   You may not.

[*Pause.*]

YANG SUN [*Sullenly.*]   Show me where to go.

MRS. YANG   Mr. Shui Ta, you are kindness itself: the gods will reward you! [*To* YANG SUN.] And honest work will make a man of you, my boy. [YANG SUN *follows* SHUI TA *into the factory.* MRS. YANG *comes down again to the footlights.*] Actually, honest work didn't agree with him—at first. And he got no opportunity to distinguish himself till—in the third week—when the wages were being paid . . .

[SHUI TA *has a bag of money. Standing next to his foreman—the former* UNEMPLOYED MAN—*he counts out the wages. It is Yang Sun's turn.*]

UNEMPLOYED MAN [*Reading.*]   Carpenter, six silver dollars. Yang Sun, six silver dollars.

YANG SUN [*Quietly.*]   Excuse me, sir. I don't think it can be more than five. May I see? [*He takes the foreman's list.*] It says six working days. But that's a mistake, sir. I took a day off for court business. And I won't take what I haven't earned, however miserable the pay is!

UNEMPLOYED MAN   Yang Sun. Five silver dollars. [*To* SHUI TA.] A rare case, Mr. Shui Ta!

SHUI TA   How is it the book says six when it should say five?

UNEMPLOYED MAN   I must've made a mistake, Mr. Shui Ta. [*With a look at* YANG SUN.] It won't happen again.

SHUI TA [*Taking* YANG SUN *aside.*]   You don't hold back, do you? You give your all to the firm. You're even honest. Do the foreman's mistakes always favor the workers?

YANG SUN   He does have . . . friends.

SHUI TA   Thank you. May I offer you any little recompense?

YANG SUN   Give me a trial period of one week, and I'll prove my intelligence is worth more to you than my strength.

MRS. YANG [*Still down at the footlights.*]   Fighting words, fighting words! That evening, I said to Sun: "If you're a flyer, then fly, my falcon! Rise in the world!" And he got to be foreman. Yes, in Mr. Shui Ta's tobacco factory, he worked real miracles.

[*We see* YANG SUN *with his legs apart standing behind the workers, who are handing along a basket of raw tobacco above their heads.*]

YANG SUN   Faster! Faster! You, there, d'you think you can just stand around, now you're not foreman any more? It'll be your job to lead us in song. Sing!

[UNEMPLOYED MAN *starts singing. The others join in the refrain.*]

SONG OF THE EIGHTH ELEPHANT

Chang had seven elephants—all much the same—
  But then there was Little Brother
The seven, they were wild, Little Brother, he was tame
  And to guard them Chang chose Little Brother
    Run faster!
    Mr. Chang has a forest park
    Which must be cleared before tonight
    And already it's growing dark!

When the seven elephants cleared that forest park
  Mr. Chang rode high on Little Brother
While the seven toiled and moiled till dark
  On his big behind sat Little Brother
    Dig faster!
    Mr. Chang has a forest park
    Which must be cleared before tonight
    And already it's growing dark!

And the seven elephants worked many an hour
  Till none of them could work another
Old Chang, he looked sour, on the seven he did glower
  But gave a pound of rice to Little Brother
    What was that?
    Mr. Chang has a forest park
    Which must be cleared before tonight
    And already it's growing dark!

And the seven elephants hadn't any tusks
  The one that had the tusks was Little Brother
Seven are no match for one, if the one has a gun!
  How old Chang did laugh at Little Brother!
    Keep on digging!
    Mr. Chang has a forest park
    Which must be cleared before tonight
    And already it's growing dark!

[*Smoking a cigar,* SHUI TA *strolls by.* YANG SUN, *laughing, has joined in the refrain of the third stanza and speeded up the tempo of the last stanza by clapping his hands.*]

MRS. YANG And that's why I say: strength and wisdom are wonderful things. It took the strong and wise Mr. Shui Ta to bring out the best in Yang Sun. A real superior man is like a bell. If you ring it, it rings, and if you don't, it don't, as the saying is.[4]

---

4. A saying by the Chinese philosopher Mo-tzu (470–391 B.C.).

9

Shen Te's shop, now an office with club chairs and fine carpets. It is raining.
SHUI TA, *now fat, is just dismissing the* OLD MAN *and* OLD WOMAN. MRS. SHIN,
in obviously new clothes, looks on, smirking.

SHUI TA No! I canNOT tell you when we expect her back.

OLD WOMAN The two hundred silver dollars came today. In an envelope.
  There was no letter, but it must be from Shen Te. We want to write and
  thank her. May we have her address?

SHUI TA I'm afraid I haven't got it.

OLD MAN [*Pulling Old Woman's sleeve.*] Let's be going.

OLD WOMAN She's got to come back some time!
      [*They move off, uncertainly, worried.* SHUI TA *bows.*]

MRS. SHIN They lost the carpet shop because they couldn't pay their taxes.
  The money arrived too late.

SHUI TA They could have come to me.

MRS. SHIN People don't like coming to you.

SHUI TA [*Sits suddenly, one hand to his head.*] I'm dizzy.

MRS. SHIN After all, you *are* in your seventh month. But old Mrs. Shin
  will be there in your hour of trial! [*She cackles feebly.*]

SHUI TA [*In a stifled voice.*] Can I count on that?

MRS. SHIN We all have our price, and mine won't be too high for the great
  Mr. Shui Ta! [*She opens Shui Ta's collar.*]

SHUI TA It's for the child's sake. All of this.

MRS. SHIN "All for the child," of course.

SHUI TA I'm so fat. People must notice.

MRS. SHIN Oh no, they think it's 'cause you're rich.

SHIU TA [*More feelingly.*] What will happen to the child?

MRS. SHIN You ask that nine times a day. Why, it'll have the best that
  money can buy!

SHUI TA He must never see Shui Ta.

MRS. SHIN Oh, no. Always Shen Te.

SHUI TA What about the neighbors? There are rumors, aren't there?

MRS. SHIN As long as Mr. Shu Fu doesn't find out, there's nothing to
  worry about. Drink this.
      [*Enter* YANG SUN *in a smart business suit, and carrying a business-
      man's briefcase.* SHUI TA *is more or less in Mrs. Shin's arms.*]

YANG SUN [*Surprised.*] I guess I'm in the way.

SHUI TA [*Ignoring this, rises with an effort.*] Till tomorrow, Mrs. Shin.
      [MRS. SHIN *leaves with a smile, putting her new gloves.*]

YANG SUN Gloves now! She couldn't be fleecing you? And since when did
  you have a private life? [*Taking a paper from the briefcase.*] You haven't
  been at your best lately, and things are getting out of hand. The police
  want to close us down. They say that at the most they can only permit
  twice the lawful number of workers.

SHUI TA [*Evasively.*] The cabins are quite good enough.

YANG SUN For the workers maybe, not for the tobacco. They're too damp.
  We must take over some of Mrs. Mi Tzu's buildings.

SHUI TA Her price is double what I can pay.

YANG SUN   Not unconditionally. If she has me to stroke her knees she'll come down.

SHUI TA   I'll never agree to that.

YANG SUN   What's wrong? Is it the rain? You get so irritable whenever it rains.

SHUI TA   Never! I will never . . .

YANG SUN   Mrs. Mi Tzu'll be here in five minutes. *You* fix it. And Shu Fu will be with her. . . . What's all that noise?

    [*During the above dialogue,* WONG *is heard offstage, calling:* "The good Shen Te, where is she? Which of you has seen Shen Te, good people? Where is Shen Te?" *A knock. Enter* WONG.]

WONG   Mr. Shui Ta, I've come to ask when Miss Shen Te will be back, it's six months now. . . . There are rumors. People say something's happened to her.

SHUI TA   I'm busy. Come back next week.

WONG [*Excited.*]   In the morning there was always rice on her doorstep—for the needy. It's been there again lately!

SHUI TA   And what do people conclude from this?

WONG   That Shen Te is still in Setzuan! She's been . . . [*He breaks off.*]

SHUI TA   She's been what? Mr. Wong, if you're Shen Te's friend, talk a little less about her, that's my advice to you.

WONG   I don't want your advice! Before she disappeared, Miss Shen Te told me something very important—she's pregnant!

YANG SUN   What? What was that?

SHUI TA [*Quickly.*]   The man is lying.

WONG   A good woman isn't so easily forgotten, Mr. Shui Ta.

    [*He leaves.* SHUI TA *goes quickly into the back room.*]

YANG SUN [*To the audience.*]   Shen Te pregnant? So that's why. Her cousin sent her away, so I wouldn't get wind of it. I have a son, a Yang appears on the scene, and what happens? Mother and child vanish into thin air! That scoundrel, that unspeakable . . . [*The sound of sobbing is heard from the back room.*] What was that? Someone sobbing? Who was it? Mr. Shui Ta the Tobacco King doesn't weep his heart out. And where does the rice come from that's on the doorstep in the morning? [SHUI TA *returns. He goes to the door and looks out into the rain.*] Where is she?

SHUI TA   Sh! It's nine o'clock. But the rain's so heavy, you can't hear a thing.

YANG SUN   What do you want to hear?

SHUI TA   The mail plane.

YANG SUN   What?!

SHUI TA   I've been told *you* wanted to fly at one time. Is that all forgotten?

YANG SUN   Flying mail is night work. I prefer the daytime. And the firm is very dear to me—after all it belongs to my ex-fiancée, even if she's not around. And she's not, is she?

SHUI TA   What do you mean by that?

YANG SUN   Oh, well, let's say I haven't altogether—lost interest.

SHUI TA   My cousin might like to know that.

YANG SUN   I might not be indifferent—if I found she was being kept under lock and key.

SHUI TA   By whom?

YANG SUN   By you.

SHUI TA   What could you do about it?

YANG SUN   I could submit for discussion—my position in the firm.

SHUI TA   You are now my manager. In return for a more . . . appropriate position, you might agree to drop the inquiry into your ex-fiancée's whereabouts?

YANG SUN   I might.

SHUI TA   What position *would* be more appropriate?

YANG SUN   The one at the top.

SHUI TA   My own? [*Silence.*] And if I preferred to throw you out on your neck?

YANG SUN   I'd come back on my feet. With suitable escort.

SHUI TA   The police?

YANG SUN   The police.

SHUI TA   And when the police found no one?

YANG SUN   I might ask them not to overlook the back room. [*Ending the pretense.*] In short, Mr. Shui Ta, my interest in this young woman has not been officially terminated. I should like to see more of her. [*Into Shui Ta's face.*] Besides, she's pregnant and needs a friend. [*He moves to the door.*] I shall talk about it with the water seller.

[*Exit.* SHUI TA *is rigid for a moment, then he quickly goes into the back room. He returns with Shen Te's belongings: underwear, etc. He takes a long look at the shawl of the previous scene. He then wraps the things in a bundle, which, upon hearing a noise, he hides under the table. Enter* MRS. MI TZU *and Mr.* SHU FU. *They put away their umbrellas and galoshes.*]

MRS. MI TZU   I thought your manager was here, Mr. Shui Ta. He combines charm with business in a way that can only be to the advantage of all of us.

SHU FU   You sent for us, Mr. Shui Ta?

SHUI TA   The factory is in trouble.

SHU FU   It always is.

SHUI TA   The police are threatening to close us down unless I can show that the extension of our facilities is imminent.

SHU FU   Mr. Shui Ta, I'm sick and tired of your constantly expanding projects. I place cabins at your cousin's disposal; you make a factory of them. I hand your cousin a check; you present it. Your cousin disappears; you find the cabins too small and start talking of yet more—

SHUI TA   Mr. Shu Fu, I'm authorized to inform you that Miss Shen Te's return is now imminent.

SHU FU   Imminent? It's becoming his favorite word.

MRS. MI TZU   Yes, what does it mean?

SHUI TA   Mrs. Mi Tzu, I can pay you exactly half what you asked for your buildings. Are you ready to inform the police that I am taking them over?

MRS. MI TZU   Certainly, if I can take over your manager.

SHU FU   What?

MRS. MI TZU   He's so efficient.

SHUI TA   I'm afraid I need Mr. Yang Sun.

MRS. MI TZU   So do I.

SHUI TA   He will call on you tomorrow.

SHU FU   So much the better. With Shen Te likely to turn up at any moment, the presence of that young man is hardly in good taste.

SHUI TA So we have reached a settlement. In what was once the good Shen Te's little shop we are laying the foundations for the great Mr. Shui Ta's twelve magnificent super tobacco markets. You will bear in mind that though they call me the Tobacco King of Setzuan, it is my cousin's interests that have been served . . .

VOICES [*Off.*] The police, the police! Going to the tobacco shop! Something must have happened!

[*Enter* YANG SUN, WONG, *and the* POLICEMAN.]

POLICEMAN Quiet there, quiet, quiet! [*They quiet down.*] I'm sorry, Mr. Shui Ta, but there's a report that you've been depriving Miss Shen Te of her freedom. Not that I believe all I hear, but the whole city's in an uproar.

SHUI TA That's a lie.

POLICEMAN Mr. Yang Sun has testified that he heard someone sobbing in the back room.

SHU FU Mrs. Mi Tzu and myself will testify that no one here has been sobbing.

MRS. MI TZU We have been quietly smoking our cigars.

POLICEMAN Mr. Shui Ta, I'm afraid I shall have to take a look at that room. [*He does so. The room is empty.*] No one there, of course, sir.

YANG SUN But I heard sobbing. What's that?

[*He finds the clothes.*]

WONG Those are Shen Te's things. [*To crowd.*] Shen Te's clothes are here!

VOICES [*Off, in sequence.*] Shen Te's clothes!
—They've been found under the table!
—Body of murdered girl still missing!
—Tobacco King suspected!

POLICEMAN Mr. Shui Ta, unless you can tell us where the girl is, I'll have to ask you to come along.

SHUI TA I do not know.

POLICEMAN I can't say how sorry I am, Mr. Shui Ta. [*He shows him the door.*]

SHUI TA Everything will be cleared up in no time. There are still judges in Setzuan.

YANG SUN I heard sobbing!

9a

Wong's den. For the last time, the GODS *appear to the water seller in his dream. They have changed and show signs of a long journey, extreme fatigue, and plenty of mishaps. The* FIRST *no longer has a hat; the* THIRD *has lost a leg; all three are barefoot.*

WONG Illustrious ones, at last you're here. Shen Te's been gone for months and today her cousin's been arrested. They think he murdered her to get the shop. But I had a dream and in this dream Shen Te said her cousin was keeping her prisoner. You must find her for us, illustrious ones!

FIRST GOD We've found very few good people anywhere, and even they didn't keep it up. Shen Te is still the only one that stayed good.

SECOND GOD If she *has* stayed good.

WONG   Certainly she has. But she's vanished.

FIRST GOD   That's the last straw. All is lost!

SECOND GOD   A little moderation, dear colleague!

FIRST GOD [*Plaintively.*]   What's the good of moderation now? If she can't be found, we'll have to resign! The world is a terrible place! Nothing but misery, vulgarity, and waste! Even the countryside isn't what it used to be. The trees are getting their heads chopped off by telephone wires, and there's such a noise from all the gunfire, and I can't stand those heavy clouds of smoke, and—

THIRD GOD   The place is absolutely unlivable! Good intentions bring people to the brink of the abyss, and good deeds push them over the edge. I'm afraid our book of rules is destined for the scrap heap—

SECOND GOD   It's people! They're a worthless lot!

THIRD GOD   The world is too cold!

SECOND GOD   It's people! They're too weak!

FIRST GOD   Dignity, dear colleagues, dignity! Never despair! As for this world, didn't we agree that we only have to find one human being who can stand the place? Well, we found her. True, we lost her again. We must find her again, that's all! And at once!

[*They disappear.*]

10

Courtroom. Groups: SHU FU *and* MRS. MI TZU; YANG SUN *and* MRS. YANG; WONG, *the* CARPENTER, *the* GRANDFATHER, *the* NIECE, *the* OLD MAN, *the* OLD WOMAN; MRS. SHIN, *the* POLICEMAN; *the* UNEMPLOYED MAN, *the* SISTER-IN-LAW.

OLD MAN   So much power isn't good for one man.

UNEMPLOYED MAN   And he's going to open twelve super tobacco markets!

WIFE   One of the judges is a friend of Mr. Shu Fu's.

SISTER-IN-LAW   Another one accepted a present from Mr. Shui Ta only last night. A great fat goose.

OLD WOMAN [*To* WONG]   And Shen Te is nowhere to be found.

WONG   Only the gods will ever know the truth.

POLICEMAN   Order in the court! My lords the judges!

[*Enter the* THREE GODS *in judges' robes. We overhear their conversation as they pass along the footlights to their bench.*]

THIRD GOD   We'll never get away with it, our certificates were so badly forged.

SECOND GOD   My predecessor's "sudden indigestion" will certainly cause comment.

FIRST GOD   But he *had* just eaten a whole goose.

UNEMPLOYED MAN   Look at that! *New* judges.

WONG   New judges. And what good ones!

[*The* THIRD GOD *hears this, and turns to smile at* WONG. *The* GODS *sit. The* FIRST GOD *beats on the bench with his gavel. The* POLICEMAN *brings in* SHUI TA, *who walks with lordly steps. He is whistled[5] at.*]

5. Hissed.

POLICEMAN [*To* SHUI TA.]   Be prepared for a surprise. The judges have been changed.

[SHUI TA *turns quickly round, looks at them, and staggers.*]

NIECE   What's the matter now?

WIFE   The great Tobacco King nearly fainted.

HUSBAND   Yes, as soon as he saw the new judges.

WONG   Does *he* know who they are?

[SHUI TA *picks himself up, and the proceedings open.*]

FIRST GOD   Defendant Shui Ta, you are accused of doing away with your cousin Shen Te in order to take possession of her business. Do you plead guilty or not guilty?

SHUI TA   Not guilty, my lord.

FIRST GOD [*Thumbing through the documents of the case.*]   The first witness is the policeman. I shall ask him to tell us something of the respective reputations of Miss Shen Te and Mr. Shui Ta.

POLICEMAN   Miss Shen Te was a young lady who aimed to please, my lord. She liked to live and let live, as the saying goes. Mr. Shui Ta, on the other hand, is a man of principle. Though the generosity of Miss Shen Te forced him at times to abandon half measures, unlike the girl he was always on the side of the law, my lord. One time, he even unmasked a gang of thieves to whom his too trustful cousin had given shelter. The evidence, in short, my lord, proves that Mr. Shui Ta was *incapable* of the crime of which he stands accused!

FIRST GOD   I see. And are there others who could testify along, shall we say, the same lines?

[SHU FU *rises.*]

POLICEMAN [*Whispering to* GODS.]   Mr. Shu Fu—a very important person.

FIRST GOD [*Inviting him to speak.*]   Mr. Shu Fu!

SHU FU   Mr. Shui Ta is a businessman, my lord. Need I say more?

FIRST GOD   Yes.

SHU FU   Very well, I will. He is Vice President of the Council of Commerce and is about to be elected a Justice of the Peace. [*He returns to his seat.* MRS. MI TZU *rises.*]

WONG   Elected! *He* gave him the job!

[*With a gesture the* FIRST GOD *asks who* MRS. MI TZU *is.*]

POLICEMAN   Another very important person. Mrs. Mi Tzu.

FIRST GOD [*Inviting her to speak.*]   Mrs. Mi Tzu!

MRS. MI TZU   My lord, as Chairman of the Committee on Social Work, I wish to call attention to just a couple of eloquent facts: Mr. Shui Ta not only has erected a model factory with model housing in our city, he is a regular contributor to our home for the disabled. [*She returns to her seat.*]

POLICEMAN [*Whispering.*]   And she's a great friend of the judge that ate the goose!

FIRST GOD [*To the* POLICEMAN.]   Oh, thank you. What next? [*To the Court, genially.*]   Oh, yes. We should find out if any of the evidence is less favorable to the defendant.

[WONG, *the* CARPENTER, *the* OLD MAN, *the* OLD WOMAN, *the* UNEMPLOYED MAN, *the* SISTER-IN-LAW, *and the* NIECE *come forward.*]

POLICEMAN [*Whispering.*] Just the riffraff, my lord.

FIRST GOD [*Addressing the "riffraff."*] Well, um, riffraff—do you know anything of the defendant, Mr. Shui Ta?

WONG Too much, my lord.

UNEMPLOYED MAN What don't we know, my lord.

CARPENTER He ruined us.

SISTER-IN-LAW He's a cheat.

NIECE Liar.

WIFE Thief.

BOY Blackmailer.

BROTHER Murderer.

FIRST GOD Thank you. We should now let the defendant state his point of view.

SHUI TA I only came on the scene when Shen Te was in danger of losing what I had understood was a gift from the gods. Because I did the filthy jobs which someone had to do, they hate me. My activities were restricted to the minimum, my lord.

SISTER-IN-LAW He had us arrested!

SHUI TA Certainly. You stole from the bakery!

SISTER-IN-LAW Such concern for the bakery! You didn't want the shop for yourself, I suppose!

SHUI TA I didn't want the shop overrun with parasites.

SISTER-IN-LAW We had nowhere else to go.

SHUI TA There were too many of you.

WONG What about this old couple: Were *they* parasites?

OLD MAN We lost our shop because of you!

OLD WOMAN And we gave your cousin money!

SHUI TA My cousin's fiancé was a flyer. The money had to go to *him*.

WONG Did you care whether he flew or not? Did you care whether she married him or not? You wanted her to marry someone else! [*He points to* SHU FU.]

SHUI TA The flyer unexpectedly turned out to be a scoundrel.

YANG SUN [*Jumping up.*] Which was the reason you made him your manager?

SHUI TA Later on he improved.

WONG And when he improved, you sold him to her? [*He points out* MRS. MI TZU.]

SHUI TA She wouldn't let me have her premises unless she had him to stroke her knees!

MRS. MI TZU What? The man's a pathological liar. [*To him.*] Don't mention my property to me as long as you live! Murderer! [*She rustles off, in high dudgeon.*]

YANG SUN [*Pushing in.*] My lord, I wish to speak for the defendant.

SISTER-IN-LAW Naturally. He's your employer.

UNEMPLOYED MAN And the worst slave driver in the country.

MRS. YANG That's a lie! My lord, Mr. Shui Ta is a great man. He . . .

YANG SUN He's this and he's that, but he is not a murderer, my lord. Just fifteen minutes before his arrest I heard Shen Te's voice in his own back room.

FIRST GOD Oh? Tell us more!

YANG SUN I heard sobbing, my lord!

FIRST GOD   But lots of women sob, we've been finding.

YANG SUN   Could I fail to recognize her voice?

SHU FU   No, you made her sob so often yourself, young man!

YANG SUN   Yes. But I also made her happy. Till he [*Pointing at* SHUI TA.] decided to sell her to you!

SHUI TA   Because you didn't love her.

WONG   Oh, no: it was for the money, my lord!

SHUI TA   And what was the money for, my lord? For the poor! And for Shen Te so she could go on being good!

WONG   For the poor? That he sent to his sweatshops? And why didn't you let Shen Te be good when you signed the big check?

SHUI TA   For the child's sake, my lord.

CARPENTER   What about *my* children? What did he do about them?

[SHUI TA *is silent.*]

WONG   The shop was to be a fountain of goodness. That was the gods' idea. You came and spoiled it!

SHUI TA   If I hadn't, it would have run dry!

MRS. SHIN   There's a lot in that, my lord.

WONG   What have you done with the good Shen Te, bad man? She *was* good, my lords, she was, I swear it! [*He raises his hand in an oath.*]

THIRD GOD   What's happened to your hand, water seller?

WONG [*Pointing to* SHUI TA.]   It's all his fault, my lord, *she* was going to send me to a doctor— [*To* SHUI TA.] You were her worst enemy!

SHUI TA   I was her only friend!

WONG   Where is she then? Tell us where your good friend is!

[*The excitement of this exchange has run through the whole crowd.*]

ALL   Yes, where is she? Where is Shen Te? [*Etc.*]

SHUI TA   Shen Te . . . had to go.

WONG   Where? Where to?

SHUI TA   I cannot tell you! I cannot tell you!

ALL   Why? Why did she have to go away? [*Etc.*]

WONG [*Into the din with the first words, but talking on beyond the others.*]   Why not, why not? Why did she have to go away?

SHUI TA [*Shouting.*]   Because you'd all have torn her to shreds, that's why! My lords, I have a request. Clear the court! When only the judges remain, I will make a confession.

ALL [*Except* WONG, *who is silent, struck by the new turn of events.*]   So he's guilty? He's confessing! [*Etc.*]

FIRST GOD [*Using the gavel.*]   Clear the court!

POLICEMAN   Clear the court!

WONG   Mr. Shui Ta has met his match this time.

MRS. SHIN [*With a gesture toward the judges.*]   You're in for a little surprise.

[*The court is cleared. Silence.*]

SHUI TA   Illustrious ones!

[*The* GODS *look at each other, not quite believing their ears.*]

SHUI TA   Yes, I recognize you!

SECOND GOD [*Taking matters in hand, sternly.*]   What have you done with our good woman of Setzuan?

SHUI TA   I have a terrible confession to make: I am she! [*He takes off his mask, and tears away his clothes.* SHEN TE *stands there.*]

SECOND GOD   Shen Te!
SHEN TE   Shen Te, yes. Shui Ta *and* Shen Te. Both.

>   Your injunction
>   To be good and yet to live
>   Was a thunderbolt:
>   It has torn me in two
>   I can't tell how it was
>   But to be good to others
>   And myself at the same time
>   I could not do it
>   Your world is not an easy one, illustrious ones!
>   When we extend our hand to a beggar, he tears it off for us
>   When we help the lost, we are lost ourselves
>   And so
>   Since not to eat is to die
>   Who can long refuse to be bad?
>   As I lay prostrate beneath the weight of good intentions
>   Ruin stared me in the face
>   It was when I was unjust that I ate good meat
>   And hobnobbed with the mighty
>   Why?
>   Why are bad deeds rewarded?
>   Good ones punished?
>   I enjoyed giving
>   I truly wished to be the Angel of the Slums
>   But washed by a foster-mother in the water of the gutter
>   I developed a sharp eye
>   The time came when pity was a thorn in my side
>   And, later, when kind words turned to ashes in my mouth
>   And anger took over
>   I became a wolf
>   Find me guilty, then, illustrious ones,
>   But know:
>   All that I have done I did
>   To help my neighbor
>   To love my lover
>   And to keep my little one from want
>   For your great, godly deeds, I was too poor, too small.

[*Pause.*]

FIRST GOD [*Shocked.*]   Don't go on making yourself miserable, Shen Te!
   We're overjoyed to have found you!
SHEN TE   I'm telling you I'm the bad man who committed all those crimes!
FIRST GOD [*Using—or failing to use—his ear trumpet.*]   The good woman
   who did all those good deeds?
SHEN TE   Yes, but the bad man too!
FIRST GOD [*As if something had dawned.*]   Unfortunate coincidences!
   Heartless neighbors!
THIRD GOD [*Shouting in his ear.*]   But how is she to continue?
FIRST GOD   Continue? Well, she's a strong, healthy girl . . .
SECOND GOD   You didn't hear what she said!

FIRST GOD   I heard every word! She is confused, that's all! [*He begins to bluster.*] And what about this book of rules—we can't renounced our rules, can we? [*More quietly.*] Should the world be changed? How? By whom? The world should *not* be changed! [*At a sign from him, the lights turn pink, and music plays.*]

> And now the hour of parting is at hand.
> Dost thou behold, Shen Te, yon fleecy cloud?
> It is our chariot. At a sign from me
> 'Twill come and take us back from whence we came
> Above the azure vault and silver stars. . . .

SHEN TE   No! Don't go, illustrious ones!

FIRST GOD

> Our cloud has landed now in yonder field
> From which it will transport us back to heaven.
> Farewell, Shen Te, let not thy courage fail thee. . . .

[*Exeunt* GODS.]

SHEN TE   What about the old couple? They've lost their shop! What about the water seller and his hand? And I've got to defend myself against the barber, because I don't love him! And against Sun, because I do love him! How? How?

[*Shen Te's eyes follow the* GODS *as they are imagined to step into a cloud, which rises and moves forward over the orchestra and up beyond the balcony.*]

FIRST GOD [*From on high.*]   We have faith in you, Shen Te!

SHEN TE   There'll be a child. And he'll have to be fed. I can't stay here. Where shall I go?

FIRST GOD   Continue to be good, good woman of Setzuan!

SHEN TE   I need my bad cousin!

FIRST GOD   But not very often!

SHEN TE   Once a week at least!

FIRST GOD   Once a month will be quite enough!

SHEN TE [*Shrieking.*]   No, no! Help!

[*But the cloud continues to recede as the* GODS *sing.*]

VALEDICTORY HYMN

> What rapture, oh, it is to know
>   A good thing when you see it
> And having seen a good thing, oh,
>   What rapture 'tis to flee it
>
> Be good, sweet maid of Setzuan
>   Let Shui Ta be clever
> Departing, we forget the man
>   Remember your endeavor
>
> Because through all the length of days
>   Her goodness faileth never
> Sing hallelujah! Make Shen Te's
>   Good name live on forever!

SHEN TE Help!

Epilogue

You're thinking, aren't you, that this is no right
Conclusion to the play you've seen tonight?
After a tale, exotic, fabulous,
A nasty ending was slipped up on us.
We feel deflated too. We too are nettled
To see the curtain down and nothing settled.
How could a better ending be arranged?
Could one change people? Can the world be changed?
Would new gods do the trick? Will atheism?
Moral rearmament? Materialism?
It is for you to find a way, my friends,
To help good men arrive at happy ends.
You write the happy ending to the play!
There must, there must, there's got to be a way!

FEDERICO GARCÍA LORCA
1898–1936

Although he died young, the poet and playwright Federico García Lorca is the best-known writer of modern Spain, and perhaps the most famous Spanish writer since Cervantes. A member of the brilliant "Generation of 1927" (along with Jorgé Guillen, Vicente Aleixandre, Pedro Salinas, and Rafael Alberti), known for the striking imagery and lyric musicality of his work, Lorca is both classical and modern, traditional and innovative, difficult and popular, a voice combining regional and universal themes. The poetry and plays that began as (and always were) personal statements took on larger significance first as the expression of tragic conflicts in Spanish culture, and then as poignant laments for humanity—seen especially in the plight of those who are deprived, by society or simply by death, of the fulfillment that could have been theirs. When Lorca was dragged from a friend's house and executed by a Fascist squad on August 19, 1936, his murder outraged the whole European and American literary and artistic community and seemed to symbolize in addition the mindless destruction of humane and cultural values that loomed with the approach of World War II.

Lorca (despite the Spanish practice of using both paternal and maternal last names—correctly "García Lorca"—the author is generally called "Lorca") was born on June 5, 1898, in the small village of Fuentevaqueros, near the Andalusian city of Granada. His father was a prosperous farmer, and his mother, who had been a school-teacher, encouraged him to read widely and develop his musical talent. The composer Manuel de Falla befriended the young musician, who became an expert pianist and guitar player. Lorca began law studies at the University of Granada, where—after several years' absence—he received a degree in 1923. He published a book called *Impressions and Landscapes* (1918) after a trip through Spain, but left Granada in 1919 for Madrid, where he entered the Residencia de Estudiantes, a modern college established to provide a cosmopolitan education for Spanish youth. Madrid was not only the capital of Spain but also the center of intellectual and artistic ferment, and the Residencia attracted many of those who would be the most influential writers and artists of their generation (among the latter the artist Salvador Dalí and the film director Luis Buñuel). Lorca soon gained the reputation of a rising young poet from poetry, readings and the publication of a few poems in magazines, even before the appearance of his first collection of verse, the *Book of Poems* of 1921. Although he lived at the Residencia almost continuously until 1928, he never seriously pursued a degree but spent his time reading, writing, improvising music and poetry in company with his friends, and producing his first plays.

In these early years, before his departure for New York in 1929, Lorca concentrated on writing poetry, although he was clearly interested in the theater as well. *The Butterfly's Evil Spell* (1920), a fantasy about a cockroach who is hopelessly enchanted by the beauty of a butterfly, was staged in Barcelona; in 1923 Lorca wrote, designed sets for, and directed a puppet play on a theme from Andalusian folklore, *The Girl Who Waters the Sweet Basil Flower and the Inquisitive Prince,* for which De Falla himself arranged the music. Yet the major achievement of this period is the composition of several books of poetry, not all of which were published at the time: the *Book of Poems;* most of the *Songs* (1927); early versions of the poems in the *Poem of the Deep Song,* which was not published as a book until 1931, although several poems were recited at a 1922 Andalusian festival; and the *Gypsy Ballads* (1928), which was an immediate popular success.

The first collection, the *Book of Poems,* introduces themes that will be familiar in later works: death, an innocent or childlike point of view, a closeness to nature that takes the form of animal fables or symbolic meanings attached to images like the pomegranate ("the idea of blood enclosed / In a hard and bitter globe"), and overall a certain witty or ironic distance from the situations he describes. The playful tone never quite covers Lorca's constant preoccupation with death, however: death as the common fate that shadows our most vivid experiences. Speaking to a chorus of questioning children in *The Ballad of the Little Square,* the poet answers that he feels in his mouth only "the savor of the bones / of my great skull."

The *Poem of the Deep Song* marked a return to the gypsy themes and ballads of Lorca's home province of Andalusia, a region known for its mixture of Arab and Spanish culture and for a tradition of wandering gypsy singers who improvised, to guitar accompaniment, rhythmic laments on themes of love and death. The *cante jondo* ("deep song") was an ancient Andalusian ballad form that centered on repeated notes or phrases, and Lorca took full advantage (as he would in the *Lament for Ignacio Sánchez Mejías*) of the haunting quality that could be obtained through this obsessive refrain. The *Songs* written subsequently are noted for their lyricism and for the moments of experience they capture; however, many reach beyond the sensuously precise description of real objects to encompass abstract concepts, psychological states, and clusters of associations—as does the Symbolist poetry Lorca knew. Lorca describes how "the ear of grain keeps intact / its hard yellow laughter," how a little mute boy looks for his voice in a drop of water, and how Narcissus (both youth and flower) is mirrored in a double image in which "over your white eyes flicker / shadows and sleeping fish."

Lorca's next collection, the *Gypsy Ballads,* marks the beginning of his mature verse. Blending classical ballad form with scenes taken directly from contemporary life, the poet expresses, with images of violence and eroticism, the tragic struggle in which innocence, spontaneity, creativity, and freedom are repressed by society and by the inevitable limitations of human nature. In the famous *Ballad of the Spanish Civil Guard,* the militia with their "patent-leather souls" and heads filled with "a vague astronomy / of shapeless pistols" cut down the gypsies in their fantastic city with its banners and "cinnamon towers." The unsuspecting populace, caught in the midst of their festival, are helpless to prevent absolute destruction—the tile roofs become "furrows in the soil," and the burned city itself persists only in the sterile "play of moon and sand" on the poet's brow. A hostile, violent world is pictured here, in which even the wind pursues a young girl with lustful breath and "hot sword," and St. Eulalia's martyrdom and mutilation are described with a mixture of eroticism and horror. These themes are not restricted to poetry: they reoccur in a contemporary play, *Mariana Pineda* (1928), in which Lorca's heroine is executed for refusing to identify a group of revolutionaries (among them the lover who abandoned her).

Impelled by an emotional crisis, Lorca left Spain for New York in 1929, and there he wrote a series of poems later published as *Poet in New York* (1940). The collection does not focus exclusively on the city, however, and moves from the poet's youth in Europe to scenes of rural New York and northern Vermont as Lorca tries to come to terms with his own complex personality against a background of psychological, artistic, and social tensions. Blended with the familiar theme of doomed love and death is a tentative exploration of homosexuality, which Lorca could not admit inside traditional Spanish society, and which he expressed only with hesitation and anxiety in this and later works. A large part of the ten-section *Poet in New York,* however, focuses primarily on the city, which is seen as a frightening symbol of the modern industrial West. In a richly varied and densely metaphorical apocalyptic vision, Lorca juxtaposes two ways of life and creates a vision of contrast that, he said, "puts my poetic world in contact with the poetic world of New York." Beginning with a denunciation of the dehumanized commercial city-world of sterile concrete and glass, he moves on to celebrate the only area where the natural world survives: Harlem, with its "garnet violence deaf and dumb in the shadows," and its "great king a prisoner in a janitor's uniform." In the face of this universal despair there are foreshadowings of a coming upheaval when "the Stock Market will be a pyramid of moss" and the oppressed and deprived will unite to proclaim "the reign of the ear of corn." The book's ending sections mark an escape from New York to Havana and (in spite of a continued sense of alienation) to the dancelike harmony of a more primitive life.

From 1930 to his death in 1936, Lorca was extremely active in the theater both as writer and as director (after 1931) of a traveling theatrical group (La Barraca) subsidized by the Spanish Republic. After a series of farces that mixed romantically tragic and comic themes, he presented the tragedies for which he is best known: *Blood Wedding* (1933) and *Yerma* (1934). In 1936 he wrote the posthumously published *The House of Bernarda Alba* (1945). All Lorca's theater, from the early fantasy of *The Butterfly's Evil Spell* to the puppet plays, farces, and last tragedies, rejects the conventionally realistic nineteenth-century drama and employs an openly poetic form that suggests musical patterns, includes choruses, songs, and stylized movement, and may even (as in the fragmentary surrealist drama, *The Audience*) attack the audience itself. The tragic themes of Lorca's poetry emerge here in dramatic form, usually centering on the suffering of individual women whose instinctual fulfillment (through love or children) is denied by fate or social circumstance. In *Blood Wedding,* the Mother's last remaining son dies in a moonlit struggle with Leonardo, who has run away with his bride (Leonardo's former betrothed) on their wedding day. Leonardo (who also dies) is a member of the family that has killed the Mother's husband and other sons, and images of approaching death and sensual, frustrated love permeate the whole play. In *Yerma* (the title name also means desert or sterility), the heroine is caught between her own passionate, sensual nature, yearning to love and bear children, and the need—for honor's sake—to remain with a husband who cares only for a well-regulated house. When Yerma realizes the extent of Juan's spiritual as well as sexual sterility, she strangles him and (because she will not remarry) simultaneously kills her only chance to fulfill her natural instincts through bearing children. *The House of Bernarda Alba* (subtitled "A Drama About Women in the Villages of Spain") revolves around the same themes of sterility and frustrated love, as the repressed spinster daughters of the stern matriarch Bernarda Alba (and even the mad grandmother) reveal their common desire to marry a young man. Bernarda, however, upholds the proprieties that hedge in Spanish society; she refuses to let her daughters have visitors, ignores their rivalry over young Pepe el Romano (engaged to the wealthy oldest daughter, Angustias), recommends a painful death for an unwed mother being dragged through the streets, and—when the youngest daughter, Adela, commits suicide over Pepe, who has become her lover—seems chiefly concerned that Adela's body be dressed "as though she were a virgin." The conflict between social custom and individual need takes on mythic proportions in *The House of Bernarda Alba,* where only women appear on a stage that is strangely quarantined and painted white, and where the disturbing male principle represented by Pepe el Romano is reiterated by the noise of a stallion's hooves banging against stable walls.

In 1936, the year of his death, Lorca was revising a series of short lyric poems based on the Arabic forms of *casida* and the *gacela,* a collection eventually published in 1940 as *The Divan at Tamarit* (a "divan" is a poetic collection, and Lorca wrote the poems at a country house called after the ancient place-name of Tamarit). In the previous year, he had published a long elegiac poem on the death of his good friend, the famous bullfighter Ignacio Sánchez Mejías, who had been fatally gored by a bull on August 11, 1934, in Manzanares and died two days later in Madrid. Sánchez Mejías was a cultured man, well-known in literary circles and himself the author of a play, and Lorca's *Lament for Ignacio Sánchez Mejías* celebrates both his friend and the value of human grace and courage in a world where everything ends in death.

Lorca's *Lament* is not only cast as an elegy (a medium-length poem that mourns a death), but also recalls one of the most famous poems of Spanish literature: the *Verses on the Death of His Father* written by the medieval poet Jorge Manrique (1440–1479). Manrique's catalog of his father's noble qualities ("What a friend to his friends!"), and his description of individual lives as flowing into the sea of death, are echoed by passages in the modern elegy. Yet there is a fundamental difference between the two: while Manrique's elegy stresses religious themes and the prospect of eternal life, Lorca—in grim contrast—rejects such consolation and insists that his friend's death is permanent.

The four parts of the *Lament* incorporate a variety of forms and perspectives, all working together to suggest a progression from the report of death in the precise first line—"At five in the afternoon"—to the end where the dead man's nobility and elegance survive in "a sad breeze through the olive trees." The "deep song" technique of an insistent refrain coloring the whole organizes the first section, *Cogida* [the bull's toss] *and Death,* with its throbbing return to the moment of death. The scene in the arena wavers between an objective report—the boy with the shroud, the coffin on wheels—and the shared agony of the bull's bellowing and wounds burning like suns. Lorca moves in the next ballad section to a personal refusal of Sánchez Mejías's death ("I will not see it!"), and a request that images of whiteness cover up this spilled blood; instead, he imagines Ignacio climbing steps to seek dawn and a mystic meeting with his true self but encountering, bewildered, only his broken body. After a tribute to his princely friend, the poet finally admits what he cannot force himself to see: the finality of physical dissolution as moss and grass invade the buried bullfighter's skull.

In *The Laid Out Body,* a series of somber quatrains in regular meter recognizes the inevitability of death and dissolution (Ignacio's "pure shape which had nightingales" is now "filled with depthless holes"), and the fact that the bullfighter will be entombed in unyielding, lifeless stone. In this and the final section with its rhythmic free verse, Lorca accepts physical death ("even the sea dies!") but preserves, in his poetry, a vision of his noble countryman that surpasses such obliteration. For those who exist only on the unthinking, physical level (the bull, fig tree, household ants, the black satin of his funeral suit), Ignacio has indeed "died for ever." Yet human beings recognize other qualities beyond the physical and in fact shape their estimate of an individual according to these qualities. In life, Sánchez Mejías was known to his friends for "the signal maturity of your understanding . . . your appetite for death and the taste of its mouth." These qualities survive, for a while, in memory. Lorca, echoing the pride with which the Latin poet Horace claimed to perpetuate his subjects in a "monument of lasting bronze," sings of his friend "for posterity," and captures the life and death of Sánchez Mejías in his *Lament*.

Ian Gibson, *Federico García Lorca: A Life* (1989), is an extensive and detailed biography. Carl W. Cobb, *Federico García Lorca* (1967), is a good general biography. Candelas Newton, *Understanding Federico García Lorca* (1995), is a brief general discussion of the work; E. Honig, *García Lorca* (1980), provides a critical introduction in literary historical context; and C. B. Morris, *Son of Andalusia: The Lyrical Landscapes of Federico García Lorca* (1997), offers a more specialized view, with illustrations. Manuel Durán, ed., *Lorca: A Collection of Critical Essays* (1962), is a valuable collection of essays on the poet and his work (mainly the poetry). Manuel Durán and Francesca Colecchia, eds., *Lorca's Legacy* (1991), offer a range of essays and a recent bibliography.

Lament for Ignacio Sánchez Mejías[1]

1. Cogida[2] and Death

At five in the afternoon.
It was exactly five in the afternoon.
A boy brought the white sheet
at five in the afternoon.
A frail of lime[3] ready prepared   5
at five in the afternoon.
The rest was death, and death alone
at five in the afternoon.

The wind carried away the cottonwool[4]
at five in the afternoon.   10
And the oxide scattered crystal and nickel
at five in the afternoon.
Now the dove and the leopard[5] wrestle
at five in the afternoon.
And a thigh with a desolate horn   15
at five in the afternoon.
The bass-string struck up
at five in the afternoon.
Arsenic bells[6] and smoke
at five in the afternoon.   20
Groups of silence in the corners
at five in the afternoon.
And the bull alone with a high heart!
At five in the afternoon.
When the sweat of snow was coming   25
at five in the afternoon,
when the bull ring was covered in iodine
at five in the afternoon,
death laid eggs in the wound

1. Translated by Stephen Spender and J. L. Gili.   2. Harvesting (Spanish, literal trans.); the toss when the bull catches the bullfighter.   3. A disinfectant that was sprinkled on the body after death. *Frail*: a basket.   4. To stop the blood; the beginning of a series of medicinal, chemical, and inhuman images that emphasize the presence of death.   5. Traditional symbols for peace and violence; they wrestle with one another as the bullfighter's thigh struggles with the bull's horn.   6. Bells are rung to announce a death. The *bass-string* of the guitar strums a lament.

at five in the afternoon.   30
At five in the afternoon.
Exactly at five o'clock in the afternoon.

A coffin on wheels is his bed
at five in the afternoon.
Bones and flutes resound in his ears[7]   35
at five in the afternoon.
Now the bull was bellowing through his forehead
at five in the afternoon.
The room[8] was iridescent with agony
at five in the afternoon.   40
In the distance the gangrene now comes
at five in the afternoon.
Horn of the lily through green[9] groins
at five in the afternoon.
The wounds were burning like suns   45
at five in the afternoon,
and the crowd was breaking the windows[1]
at five in the afternoon.
At five in the afternoon.
Ah, that fatal five in the afternoon!   50
It was five by all the clocks!
It was five in the shade of the afternoon!

2. The Spilled Blood

I will not see it!

Tell the moon to come
for I do not want to see the blood   55
of Ignacio on the sand.
I will not see it!

The moon wide open.
Horse of still clouds,
and the grey bull ring of dreams   60
with willows in the barreras.[2]
I will not see it!

Let my memory kindle![3]
Warn the jasmines[4]
of such minute whiteness!   65
I will not see it!

The cow of the ancient world
passed her sad tongue

---

7. A suggestion of the medieval dance of death.   8. The room adjoining the arena where wounded bullfighters are taken for treatment.   9. Gangrene turns flesh a greenish color. *Lily:* the shape of the wound resembles this flower.   1. A Spanish idiom for the crowd's loud roar.   2. The barriers around the ring within which the fight takes place and over which a fighter may escape the bull's charge. *Willows:* symbols of mourning.   3. My memory burns within me (literal trans.).   4. The poet calls on (*warn* as "notify") the small white jasmine flowers to come and cover the blood.

over a snout of blood
spilled on the sand,   70
and the bulls of Guisando,[5]
partly death and partly stone,
bellowed like two centuries
sated with treading the earth.
No.   75
I do not want to see it!
I will not see it!

Ignacio goes up the tiers[6]
with all his death on his shoulders.
He sought for the dawn   80
but the dawn was no more.
He seeks for his confident profile
and the dream bewilders him.
He sought for his beautiful body
and encountered his opened blood.   85
Do not ask me to see it!
I do not want to hear it spurt
each time with less strength:
that spurt that illuminates
the tiers of seats, and spills   90
over the corduroy and the leather
of a thirsty multitude.
Who shouts that I should come near!
Do not ask me to see it!

His eyes did not close   95
when he saw the horns near,
but the terrible mothers
lifted their heads.[7]
And across the ranches,[8]
an air of secret voices rose,   100
shouting to celestial bulls,
herdsmen of pale mist.
There was no prince in Seville[9]
who could compare with him,
nor sword like his sword   105
nor heart so true.
Like a river of lions
was his marvellous strength,
and like a marble torso
his firm drawn moderation.   110
The air of Andalusian Rome
gilded his head[1]
where his smile was a spikenard[2]

5. Carved stone bulls from the Celtic past, a tourist attraction in the province of Madrid.   6. An imaginary scene in which the bullfighter mounts the stairs of the arena.   7. The three Fates traditionally raised their heads when the thread of life was cut.   8. Fighting bulls are raised on the ranches of Lorca's home province of Andalusia.   9. Leading city of Andalusia.   1. The image suggests a statue from Roman times, when Andalusia was part of the Roman Empire.   2. A small, white, fragrant flower common in Andalusia; by extension, the bullfighter's white teeth.

of wit and intelligence.
What a great torero[3] in the ring!   115
What a good peasant in the sierra![4]
How gentle with the sheaves!
How hard with the spurs!
How tender with the dew!
How dazzling in the fiesta!   120
How tremendous with the final
banderillas[5] of darkness!

But now he sleeps without end.
Now the moss and the grass
open with sure fingers   125
the flower of his skull.
And now his blood comes out singing;
singing along marshes and meadows,
sliding on frozen horns,
faltering soulless in the mist,   130
stumbling over a thousand hoofs
like a long, dark, sad tongue,
to form a pool of agony
close to the starry Guadalquivir.[6]
Oh, white wall of Spain!   135
Oh, black bull of sorrow!
Oh, hard blood of Ignacio!
Oh, nightingale of his veins!
No.
I will not see it!   140
No chalice can contain it,
no swallows[7] can drink it,
no frost of light can cool it,
nor song nor deluge of white lilies,
no glass can cover it with silver.   145
No.
I will not see it!

3. *The Laid Out Body*[8]

Stone is a forehead where dreams grieve
without curving waters and frozen cypresses.
Stone is a shoulder on which to bear Time   150
with trees formed of tears and ribbons and planets.[9]

I have seen grey showers move towards the waves
raising their tender riddled arms,

3. Bullfighter.   4. Mountainous country. Sánchez Mejías is seen as a good *serrano* or "man of the hills."   5. The multicolored short spears that are thrust in the bull's shoulders to provoke him to attack.   6. A great river that passes through all the major cities of Andalusia. The singing stream of the bullfighter's blood suggests both the river and a nightingale.   7. According to a Spanish legend of the Crucifixion, swallows—a symbol of innocence—drank the blood of Christ on the Cross. The poet is seeking ways of concealing the dead man's blood.   8. Present body (literal trans.); the Spanish expression for a funeral wake, when the body is laid out for public mourning. The title contrasts with that of the next section: *Absent Soul*.   9. Traditional funeral imagery carved on gravestones.

to avoid being caught by the lying stone
which loosens their limbs without soaking the blood.   155

For stone gathers seed and clouds,
skeleton larks and wolves of penumbra:
but yields not sounds nor crystals nor fire,
only bull rings and bull rings and more bull rings without walls.

Now Ignacio the well born lies on the stone.   160
All is finished. What is happening? Contemplate his face:
death has covered him with pale sulphur
and has placed on him the head of a dark minotaur.[1]

All is finished. The rain penetrates his mouth.
The air, as if mad, leaves his sunken chest,   165
and Love, soaked through with tears of snow,
warms itself on the peak of the herd.[2]

What are they saying? A stenching silence settles down.
We are here with a body laid out which fades away,
with a pure shape which had nightingales   170
and we see it being filled with depthless holes.

Who creases the shroud? What he says is not true![3]
Nobody sings here, nobody weeps in the corner,
nobody pricks the spurs, nor terrifies the serpent.
Here I want nothing else but the round eyes   175
to see this body without a chance of rest.

Here I want to see those men of hard voice.
Those that break horses and dominate rivers;
those men of sonorous skeleton who sing
with a mouth full of sun and flint.   180

Here I want to see them. Before the stone.
Before this body with broken reins.
I want to know from them the way out
for this captain strapped down by death.

I want them to show me a lament like a river   185
which will have sweet mists and deep shores,
to take the body of Ignacio where it loses itself
without hearing the double panting of the bulls.

Loses itself in the round bull ring of the moon
which feigns in its youth a sad quiet bull: 190
loses itself in the night without song of fishes
and in the white thicket of frozen smoke.

1. A monster from Greek myth: half man, half bull.   2. Of the ranch (literal trans.).   3. Lorca criticizes the conventional pieties voiced by someone standing close to the shrouded body; the poet prefers a
clear-eyed, realistic view of death.

I don't want them to cover his face with handkerchiefs
that he may get used to the death he carries.
Go, Ignacio; feel not the hot bellowing.   195
Sleep, fly, rest: even the sea dies!

4. Absent Soul

The bull does not know you, nor the fig tree,
nor the horses, nor the ants in your own house.
The child and the afternoon do not know you
because you have died for ever.   200

The back of the stone does not know you,
nor the black satin in which you crumble.
Your silent memory does not know you
because you have died for ever.

The autumn will come with small white snails,[4]   205
misty grapes and with clustered hills,
but no one will look into your eyes
because you have died for ever.

Because you have died for ever,
like all the death of the Earth,   210
like all the dead who are forgotten
in a heap of lifeless dogs.[5]

Nobody knows you. No. But I sing of you.
For posterity I sing of your profile and grace.
Of the signal maturity of your understanding.   215
Of your appetite for death and the taste of its mouth.
Of the sadness of your once valiant gaiety.

It will be a long time, if ever, before there is born
an Andalusian so true, so rich in adventure.
I sing of his elegance with words that groan,   220
and I remember a sad breeze through the olive trees.

From Llanto por Ignacio Sánchez Mejías

4. Alma Ausente

No te conoce el toro ni la higuera,
ni caballos ni hormigas de tu casa.
No te conoce el niño ni la tarde
porque te has muerto para siempre.

---

4. Actually, conch shell–shaped horns; the shepherds' horns that sound in the hills each fall as the sheep
are driven to new pastures.   5. Dogs as a (typically Continental) image for undignified, inferior creatures.

No te conoce el lomo de la piedra,   5
ni el raso negro donde te destrozas.
No te conoce tu recuerdo mudo
porque te has muerto para siempre.

El otoño vendrá con caracolas,
uva de niebla y montes agrupados,   10
pero nadie querrá mirar tus ojos
porque te has muerto para siempre.

Porque te has muerto para siempre,
como todos los muertos de la Tierra,
como todos los muertos que se olvidan   15
en un montón de perros apagados.

No te conoce nadie. No. Pero yo te canto.
Yo canto para luego tu perfil y tu gracia.
La madurez insigne de tu conocimiento.
Tu apetencia de muerte y el gusto de su boca.   20
La tristeza que tuvo tu valiente alegría.

Tardará mucho tiempo en nacer, si es que nace,
un andaluz tan claro, tan rico de aventura.
Yo canto su elegancia con palabras que gimen
y recuerdo una brisa triste por los olivos.   25

ALBERT CAMUS
1913–1960

Albert Camus is often linked with the contemporary philosopher Jean-Paul Sartre as
an "existentialist" writer, and indeed—as novelist, playwright, and essayist—he is
widely known for his analysis of two concerns basic to existentialism: its distinctive
assessment of the human condition and its search for authentic values. Yet Camus
rejected doctrinaire labels, and Sartre himself suggested that the author was better
placed in the tradition of French "moralist" writers such as Michel de Montaigne and
René Pascal, who analyzed human behavior inside an implied ethical context with its
own standards of good and evil. For Camus, liberty, justice, brotherhood, and happiness were some of these standards, along with the terms *revolt* and *absurd* that
described human nonacceptance of a world without meaning or value. From his
childhood among the very poor in Algiers to his later roles as journalist, Resistance
fighter, internationally famous literary figure, and winner of the Nobel Prize in 1957,
Camus never strayed from an intense awareness of the most basic levels of human
existence or from a sympathy with those—often poor and oppressed—who lived at
that level. "I can understand only in human terms. I understand the things I touch,
things that offer me resistance." He describes the raw experience of life as it is shared
by all human beings, and provides a bond between them. Camus's reaction to the
"absurd," the human condition stripped bare, is, therefore, quite different from Samuel Beckett's retreat into agonized subjectivity; where Beckett is haunted by the fictionality of experience, Camus asserts human consciousness and human solidarity as
the only values there are.

Camus was born on November 7, 1913, into a "world of poverty and light" in Mondavi, Algeria (then a colony of France). He was the second son in a poor family of mixed Alsatian-Spanish descent, and his father died in one of the first battles of World War I. The two boys lived together with their mother, uncle, and grandmother in a two-room apartment in the working-class section of the capital city, Algiers. Camus and his brother, Lucien, were raised by their strict grandmother while their mother worked as a cleaning woman to support the family. Images of the Mediterranean landscape, with its overwhelming, sensual closeness of sea and blazing sun, recur throughout his work, as does a profound compassion for those who—like his mother—labor unrecognized and in silence. (Camus's mother was illiterate and was left deaf and with a speech impediment by an untreated childhood illness.)

A passionate athlete as well as scholarship student, Camus completed his secondary education and enrolled as a philosophy student at the University of Algiers before contracting, at seventeen, the tuberculosis that undermined his health and shocked him with its demonstration of the human body's vulnerability to disease and death. Camus later finished his degree, but in the meantime he had gained from his illness a metaphor for everything that opposes and puts limits to human fulfillment and happiness: something he was later to term (after Antonin Artaud) the "plague" that infects bodies, minds, cities, and society. (*The Plague* is the title of his second novel.)

Camus lived and worked as a journalist in Algeria until 1940. He then moved to France when his political commentary (including a famous report on administrative mismanagement during a famine of Berber tribesmen) so embroiled him with the local government that his paper was suspended and he himself refused a work permit. Then as later, however, his work extended far beyond journalism. He published two collections of essays, *The Wrong Side and the Right Side* (1937) and *Nuptials* (1939), started a novel (*A Happy Death*), and founded a collective theater, Le Théâtre du Travail (The Labor Theater), for which he wrote and adapted a number of plays. The theater always fascinated Camus, possibly because it involved groups of people and live interaction between actors and audience. He not only continued to write plays after leaving Algeria (*Cross Purposes,* 1944; *The Just Assassins,* 1950) but was considering directing a new theater shortly before his death. The Labor Theater was a popular theater with performances on the docks in Algiers and was sponsored by the Communist Party, which Camus had joined in 1934. Like many intellectuals of his day, Camus found in the party a promising vehicle for social protest; he was unwilling to abandon either his independence or his convictions, however, and resigned in 1935 when the party line changed and he was asked to give up his support for Algerian nationalism. He left the Labor Theater in 1937 and, with a group of young Algerian intellectuals associated with the publishing house of Charlot, founded a similar but politically independent Team Theater (Théâtre de l'Equipe). During this decade, Camus also began work on his most famous novel, *The Stranger* (1942), the play *Caligula* (1944), and a lengthy essay defining his concept of the "absurd" hero, *The Myth of Sisyphus* (1942).

These three works established Camus's reputation as a philosopher of the absurd: the absurdly grotesque discrepancy between human beings' brief, material existence and their urge to believe in larger meanings—to "make sense" of a world that has no discernible sense. In *The Stranger,* Camus described a thirty-year-old clerk named Meursault who lives a series of "real" events: he attends his mother's funeral, makes love to his mistress, goes swimming, shoots an Arab on the beach, and is tried for murder. These events are described through Meursault's mind, and yet they appear without any connection, as if each one began a new world. They are simply a series of concrete, sensuous *facts* separated from each other and from any kind of human or social meaning. Meursault is finally condemned to death not for murder but for this alienation and for its failure to respond to society's expectations of proper behavior. Just before his execution, when he is infuriated by the prison chaplain's attempt to console him with thoughts of an afterlife, he rises to a new level of existential awareness and an ardent affirmation of life in the here-and-now, the only truly human field of action. Stylistically, much of *The Stranger*'s impact comes from the contrast between the immediacy of the physical experience described and the objective meaninglessness of that experience. On all levels, the novel reaffirms the importance of life lived moment by moment, in a total awareness that creates whatever meaning exists: the same awareness of his own activity that brings the mythological Sisyphus happiness when eternally pushing uphill the rock that will only roll down again, or the same search for an absolute honesty free of human pretenses that characterizes the mad emperor Caligula.

During World War II, Camus worked in Paris as a reader for the publishing firm of Gallimard, a post that he kept until his death in 1960. At the same time, he was part of the French Resistance and helped edit the underground journal *Combat*. His friendship with the existentialist philosopher Jean-Paul Sartre began in 1944, and after the war he and Sartre were internationally known as uncompromising analysts of the modern conscience. Camus's second novel, *The Plague* (1947), used a description of plague in a quarantined city, the Algerian Oran, to symbolize the spread of evil during World War II ("the feeling of suffocation from which we all suffered, and the atmosphere of threat and exile") and also to show the human struggle against physical and spiritual death in all its forms. Not content merely to symbolize his views in fiction, Camus also spoke out in philosophical essays and political statements, and his independent mind and refusal of doctrinaire positions brought him attacks from all sides. In the bitter struggle that brought independence to Algeria in 1962, Camus recognized the claims of both French and Arab Algerians to the land in which they were born. In the quest for social reform, he rejected any ideology that subordinated individual freedom and singled out Communism—the doctrine most reformist intellectuals saw as the only active hope—as a particular danger with its emphasis on the deindividualized and inevitable march of history. Camus's open anti-Communism led to a spectacular break with Sartre, whose review *Les Temps Modernes* (Modern times) condemned *The Rebel* (1951) in bitter personal attacks. The concept of revolt that Camus outlined in *The Rebel* was more ethical than political: he defined revolt as a basic nonacceptance of preestablished limits (whether by death or by oppression) that was shared by all human beings and, therefore, required a reciprocal acceptance and balancing of each person's rights. Such "revolt" was directly opposed to revolutionary nihilism in that it made the rebellious impulse a basis for social tolerance inside the individual's self-assertion; it had no patience for master plans that prescribed patterns of thought or action.

Five years after *The Rebel* was published, Camus produced a very different book in *The Fall* (1956). This novel is a rhetorical tour de force spoken by a fallen lawyer who uses all the tricks of language to confess his weaknesses and yet emerge triumphant, the omniscient judge of his fellow creatures. If Camus's *Notebooks* reveal in his early works a cycle of Sisyphus or the absurd, and his middle ones a Promethean cycle of revolt, *The Fall* inaugurates a third cycle, that of Nemesis, or judgment. It offers a complex, ironic picture that combines a yearning toward purity with a cynical debunking of all such attempts. The narrator, Clamence, is a composite personality including (among other things) satirized aspects of both Sartre and Camus, but it is impossible to get to the bottom of his character behind the layers of self-consciously manipulated language. The style itself challenges and disorients the reader, who is both included and excluded from a narration that presents Clamence's half of a dialogue in which "you," the reader, are presumed to be present as the other half.

Camus was a consummate artist as well as moralist, well aware of the opportunities as well as the illusions of his craft. When he received the Nobel Prize in 1957, his acceptance speech emphasized the artificial but necessary "human" order imposed by art on the chaos of immediate experience. The artist is important as *creator,* because he or she shapes a human perspective, allows understanding in human terms, and therefore provides a basis for action. By stressing the gap between art and reality,

Camus in effect provides a bridge between them as two poles of human understanding. His own works illustrate this act of bridging through their juxtaposition of realistic detail and almost mythic allegorization of human destiny. The symbolism of his titles, from *The Stranger* to the last collection of stories, *Exile and the Kingdom* (1957), repeatedly interprets human destiny in terms of a thematic opposition between the individual's sense of alienation and exile in the world, and simultaneous search for the true realm of human happiness and action.

With *The Guest,* taken from *Exile and the Kingdom,* Camus returns to the landscape of his native Algeria. The colonial context is crucial in this story, not only to explain the real threat of guerrilla reprisal at the end (Camus may be recalling the actual killing of rural schoolteachers in 1954) but to establish the dimensions of a political situation in which the government, police, educational system, and economic welfare of Algeria are all controlled by France. A similar colonial (or newly post-colonial) setting is used to indicate a charged political atmosphere in works by Nadine Gordimer, Naguib Mahfouz, Chinua Achebe, and Wole Soyinka. The beginning of Camus's story illustrates how French colonial education reproduces French, not local concerns: the schoolteacher's geography lesson outlines the four main rivers of France. The Arab is led along like an animal behind the gendarme Balducci, who rides a horse (here too, Camus may be recalling a humiliation reported two decades before and used to inspire Algerian nationalists). Within this political context, however, he concentrates on quite different issues: freedom, brotherhood, responsibility, and the ambiguity of actions along with the inevitability of choice.

The remote desert landscape establishes a total physical and moral isolation for events in the story. "No one, in this desert . . . mattered," and the schoolteacher and his guest must each decide on his own what to do. When Balducci invades Daru's monastic solitude and tells him that he must deliver the Arab to prison, Daru is outraged to be involved and, indeed, to have responsibility for another's fate. Cursing both the system that tries to force him into complicity and the Arab who has not had enough sense to get away, Daru tries in every way possible to avoid taking a stand. In the morning, however, when the Arab has not in fact run away, the schoolteacher makes up a package of food and money and passes on to the Arab his own freedom of choice. We cannot underestimate the quiet heroism of this act, by which Daru alienates himself from his own people and—unexpectedly—from the Arab's compatriots too; he is, he believes, conveying to a fellow human being the freedom of action, which all people require. This level of common humanity is strongly underlined throughout the whole story as a "sort of brotherhood" and "strange alliance" that comes from having shared food and drink, and slept as equals under the same roof. Such hospitality is also the nomadic "law of the desert" that establishes fellowship between guest and host (a law that Daru refers to when he points out the second road at the end). The host's humane hospitality has placed a new burden and reciprocal responsibility on his guest, one that may explain why the Arab chooses—in apparent freedom—the road to prison. Camus considered "Cain" and "The Law" as titles for this story before settling on *The Guest* (and the title word *l'hôte,* is identical for "guest" and "host" in French). Both guest and host are obliged to shoulder the ambiguous, and potentially fatal, burden of freedom.

Germaine Brée, *Albert Camus* (1964), is an excellent general study; see also *Camus: A Collection of Critical Essays* (1961). Phillip Rhein, *Albert Camus* (1969), is a brief introduction and biography. Herbert Lottman, *Albert Camus: A Biography* (1979), and Oliver Todd, *Albert Camus: A Life* (1997), are detailed biographies. English Showalter, *Exiles and Strangers: A Reading of Camus's Exile and the Kingdom* (1984), offers essays on the six stories of Camus's collection and separate comments on translations.

The Guest[1]

The schoolmaster was watching the two men climb toward him. One was on horseback, the other on foot. They had not yet tackled the abrupt rise leading to the schoolhouse built on the hillside. They were toiling onward, making slow progress in the snow, among the stones, on the vast expanse of the high, deserted plateau. From time to time the horse stumbled. Without hearing anything yet, he could see the breath issuing from the horse's nostrils. One of the men, at least, knew the region. They were following the trail although it had disappeared days ago under a layer of dirty white snow. The schoolmaster calculated that it would take them half an hour to get onto the hill. It was cold; he went back into the school to get a sweater.

He crossed the empty, frigid classroom. On the blackboard the four rivers of France,[2] drawn with four different colored chalks, had been flowing toward their estuaries for the past three days. Snow had suddenly fallen in mid-October after eight months of drought without the transition of rain, and the twenty pupils, more or less, who lived in the villages scattered over the plateau had stopped coming. With fair weather they would return. Daru now heated only the single room that was his lodging, adjoining the classroom and giving also onto the plateau to the east. Like the class windows, his window looked to the south too. On that side the school was a few kilometers from the point where the plateau began to slope toward the south. In clear weather could be seen the purple mass of the mountain range where the gap opened onto the desert.

Somewhat warmed, Daru returned to the window from which he had first seen the two men. They were no longer visible. Hence they must have tackled the rise. The sky was not so dark, for the snow had stopped falling during the night. The morning had opened with a dirty light which had scarcely become brighter as the ceiling of clouds lifted. At two in the afternoon it seemed as if the day were merely beginning. But still this was better than those three days when the thick snow was falling amidst unbroken darkness with little gusts of wind that rattled the double door of the classroom. Then Daru had spent long hours in his room, leaving it only to go to the shed and feed the chickens or get some coal. Fortunately the delivery truck from Tadjid, the nearest village to the north, had brought his supplies two days before the blizzard. It would return in forty-eight hours.

Besides, he had enough to resist a siege, for the little room was cluttered with bags of wheat that the administration left as a stock to distribute to those of his pupils whose families had suffered from the drought. Actually they had all been victims because they were all poor. Every day Daru would distribute a ration to the children. They had missed it, he knew, during these bad days. Possibly one of the fathers or big brothers would come this afternoon and he could supply them with grain. It was just a matter of carrying them over to the next harvest. Now shiploads of wheat were arriving from France and the worst was over. But it would be hard to forget that poverty, that army of ragged ghosts wandering in the sunlight, the plateaus burned

---

1. Translated by Justin O'Brien.   2. The Seine, Loire, Rhône, and Gironde rivers. French geography was taught in the French colonies.

to a cinder month after month, the earth shriveled up little by little, literally scorched, every stone bursting into dust under one's foot. The sheep had died then by thousands and even a few men, here and there, sometimes without anyone's knowing.

In contrast with such poverty, he who lived almost like a monk in his remote schoolhouse, nonetheless satisfied with the little he had and with the rough life, had felt like a lord with his whitewashed walls, his narrow couch, his unpainted shelves, his well, and his weekly provision of water and food. And suddenly this snow, without warning, without the foretaste of rain. This is the way the region was, cruel to live in, even without men—who didn't help matters either. But Daru had been born here. Everywhere else, he felt exiled.

He stepped out onto the terrace in front of the schoolhouse. The two men were now halfway up the slope. He recognized the horseman as Balducci, the old gendarme he had known for a long time. Balducci was holding on the end of a rope an Arab who was walking behind him with hands bound and head lowered. The gendarme waved a greeting to which Daru did not reply, lost as he was in contemplation of the Arab dressed in a faded blue jellaba, his feet in sandals but covered with socks of heavy raw wool, his head surmounted by a narrow, short *chèche*.[3] They were approaching. Balducci was holding back his horse in order not to hurt the Arab, and the group was advancing slowly.

Within earshot, Balducci shouted: "One hour to do the three kilometers from El Ameur!" Daru did not answer. Short and square in his thick sweater, he watched them climb. Not once had the Arab raised his head. "Hello," said Daru when they got up onto the terrace. "Come in and warm up." Balducci painfully got down from his horse without letting go the rope. From under his bristling mustache he smiled at the schoolmaster. His little dark eyes, deep-set under a tanned forehead, and his mouth surrounded with wrinkles made him look attentive and studious. Daru took the bridle, led the horse to the shed, and came back to the two men, who were now waiting for him in the school. He led them into his room. "I am going to heat up the classroom," he said. "We'll be more comfortable there." When he entered the room again, Balducci was on the couch. He had undone the rope tying him to the Arab, who had squatted near the stove. His hands still bound, the *chèche* pushed back on his head, he was looking toward the window. At first Daru noticed only his huge lips, fat, smooth, almost Negroid; yet his nose was straight, his eyes were dark and full of fever. The *chèche* revealed an obstinate forehead and, under the weathered skin now rather discolored by the cold, the whole face had a restless and rebellious look that struck Daru when the Arab, turning his face toward him, looked him straight in the eyes. "Go into the other room," said the schoolmaster, "and I'll make you some mint tea." "Thanks," Balducci said. "What a chore! How I long for retirement." And addressing his prisoner in Arabic: "Come on, you." The Arab got up and, slowly, holding his bound wrists in front of him, went into the classroom.

With the tea, Daru brought a chair. But Balducci was already enthroned on the nearest pupil's desk and the Arab had squatted against the teacher's

3. Scarf; here, wound as a turban around the head. *Jellaba*: a long hooded robe worn by Arabs in North Africa.

platform facing the stove, which stood between the desk and the window. When he held out the glass of tea to the prisoner, Daru hesitated at the sight of his bound hands. "He might perhaps be untied." "Sure," said Balducci. "That was for the trip." He started to get to his feet. But Daru, setting the glass on the floor, had knelt beside the Arab. Without saying anything, the Arab watched him with his feverish eyes. Once his hands were free, he rubbed his swollen wrists against each other, took the glass of tea, and sucked up the burning liquid in swift little sips.

"Good," said Daru. "And where are you headed?"

Balducci withdrew his mustache from the tea. "Here, son."

"Odd pupils! And you're spending the night?"

"No. I'm going back to El Ameur. And you will deliver this fellow to Tinguit. He is expected at police headquarters."

Balducci was looking at Daru with a friendly little smile.

"What's this story?" asked the schoolmaster. "Are you pulling my leg?"

"No, son. Those are the orders."

"The orders? I'm not . . ." Daru hesitated, not wanting to hurt the old Corsican.[4] "I mean, that's not my job."

"What! What's the meaning of that? In wartime people do all kinds of jobs."

"Then I'll wait for the declaration of war!"

Balducci nodded.

"O.K. But the orders exist and they concern you too. Things are brewing, it appears. There is talk of a forthcoming revolt. We are mobilized, in a way."

Daru still had his obstinate look.

"Listen, son," Balducci said. "I like you and you must understand. There's only a dozen of us at El Ameur to patrol throughout the whole territory of a small department[5] and I must get back in a hurry. I was told to hand this guy over to you and return without delay. He couldn't be kept there. His village was beginning to stir; they wanted to take him back. You must take him to Tinguit tomorrow before the day is over. Twenty kilometers shouldn't faze a husky fellow like you. After that, all will be over. You'll come back to your pupils and your comfortable life."

Behind the wall the horse could be heard snorting and pawing the earth. Daru was looking out the window. Decidedly, the weather was clearing and the light was increasing over the snowy plateau. When all the snow was melted, the sun would take over again and once more would burn the fields of stone. For days, still, the unchanging sky would shed its dry light on the solitary expanse where nothing had any connection with man.

"After all," he said, turning around toward Balducci, "what did he do?" And, before the gendarme had opened his mouth, he asked: "Does he speak French?"

"No, not a word. We had been looking for him for a month, but they were hiding him. He killed his cousin."

"Is he against us?"[6]

"I don't think so. But you can never be sure."

"Why did he kill?"

---

4. Balducci is a native of Corsica, a French island north of Sardinia. 5. French administrative and territorial division; like a country. 6. I.e., against the French colonial government.

"A family squabble, I think. One owed the other grain, it seems. It's not at all clear. In short, he killed his cousin with a billhook. You know, like a sheep, *kreezk!*"

Balducci made the gesture of drawing a blade across his throat and the Arab, his attention attracted, watched him with a sort of anxiety. Daru felt a sudden wrath against the man, against all men with their rotten spite, their tireless hates, their blood lust.

But the kettle was singing on the stove. He served Balducci more tea, hesitated, then served the Arab again, who, a second time, drank avidly. His raised arms made the jellaba fall open and the schoolmaster saw his thin, muscular chest.

"Thanks, kid," Balducci said. "And now, I'm off."

He got up and went toward the Arab, taking a small rope from his pocket.

"What are you doing?" Daru asked dryly.

Balducci, disconcerted, showed him the rope.

"Don't bother."

The old gendarme hesitated. "It's up to you. Of course, you are armed?"

"I have my shotgun."

"Where?"

"In the trunk."

"You ought to have it near your bed."

"Why? I have nothing to fear."

"You're crazy, son. If there's an uprising, no one is safe, we're all in the same boat."

"I'll defend myself. I'll have time to see them coming."

Balducci began to laugh, then suddenly the mustache covered the white teeth.

"You'll have time? O.K. That's just what I was saying. You have always been a little cracked. That's why I like you, my son was like that."

At the same time he took out his revolver and put it on the desk.

"Keep it; I don't need two weapons from here to El Ameur."

The revolver shone against the black paint of the table. When the gendarme turned toward him, the schoolmaster caught the smell of leather and horseflesh.

"Listen, Balducci," Daru said suddenly, "every bit of this disgusts me, and first of all your fellow here. But I won't hand him over. Fight, yes, if I have to. But not that."

The old gendarme stood in front of him and looked at him severely.

"You're being a fool," he said slowly. "I don't like it either. You don't get used to putting a rope on a man even after years of it, and you're even ashamed—yes, ashamed. But you can't let them have their way."

"I won't hand him over," Daru said again.

"It's an order, son, and I repeat it."

"That's right. Repeat to them what I've said to you: I won't hand him over."

Balducci made a visible effort to reflect. He looked at the Arab and at Daru. At last he decided.

"No, I won't tell them anything. If you want to drop us, go ahead; I'll not denounce you. I have an order to deliver the prisoner and I'm doing so. And now you'll just sign this paper for me."

"There's no need. I'll not deny that you left him with me."

"Don't be mean with me. I know you'll tell the truth. You're from hereabouts and you are a man. But you must sign, that's the rule."

Daru opened his drawer, took out a little square bottle of purple ink, the red wooden penholder with the "sergeant-major" pen he used for making models of penmanship, and signed. The gendarme carefully folded the paper and put it into his wallet. Then he moved toward the door.

"I'll see you off," Daru said.

"No," said Balducci. "There's no use being polite. You insulted me."

He looked at the Arab, motionless in the same spot, sniffed peevishly, and turned away toward the door. "Good-by, son," he said. The door shut behind him. Balducci appeared suddenly outside the window and then disappeared. His footsteps were muffled by the snow. The horse stirred on the other side of the wall and several chickens fluttered in fright. A moment later Balducci reappeared outside the window leading the horse by the bridle. He walked toward the little rise without turning around and disappeared from sight with the horse following him. A big stone could be heard bouncing down. Daru walked back toward the prisoner, who, without stirring, never took his eyes off him. "Wait," the schoolmaster said in Arabic and went toward the bedroom. As he was going through the door, he had a second thought, went to the desk, took the revolver, and stuck it in his pocket. Then, without looking back, he went into his room.

For some time he lay on his couch watching the sky gradually close over, listening to the silence. It was this silence that had seemed painful to him during the first days here, after the war. He had requested a post in the little town at the base of the foothills separating the upper plateaus from the desert. There, rocky walls, green and black to the north, pink and lavender to the south, marked the frontier of eternal summer. He had been named to a post farther north, on the plateau itself. In the beginning, the solitude and the silence had been hard for him on these wastelands peopled only by stones. Occasionally, furrows suggested cultivation, but they had been dug to uncover a certain kind of stone good for building. The only plowing here was to harvest rocks. Elsewhere a thin layer of soil accumulated in the hollows would be scraped out to enrich paltry village gardens. This is the way it was: bare rock covered three quarters of the region. Towns sprang up, flourished, then disappeared; men came by, loved one another or fought bitterly, then died. No one in this desert, neither he nor his guest, mattered. And yet, outside this desert neither of them, Daru knew, could have really lived.

When he got up, no noise came from the classroom. He was amazed at the unmixed joy he derived from the mere thought that the Arab might have fled and that he would be alone with no decision to make. But the prisoner was there. He had merely stretched out between the stove and the desk. With eyes open, he was staring at the ceiling. In that position, his thick lips were particularly noticeable, giving him a pouting look. "Come," said Daru. The Arab got up and followed him. In the bedroom, the schoolmaster pointed to a chair near the table under the window. The Arab sat down without taking his eyes off Daru.

"Are you hungry?"

"Yes," the prisoner said.

Daru set the table for two. He took flour and oil, shaped a cake in a frying-pan, and lighted the little stove that functioned on bottled gas. While the cake was cooking, he went out to the shed to get cheese, eggs, dates, and condensed milk. When the cake was done he set it on the window sill to cool, heated some condensed milk diluted with water, and beat up the eggs into an omelette. In one of his motions he knocked against the revolver stuck in his right pocket. He set the bowl down, went into the classroom, and put the revolver in his desk drawer. When he came back to the room, night was falling. He put on the light and served the Arab. "Eat," he said. The Arab took a piece of the cake, lifted it eagerly to his mouth, and stopped short.

"And you?" he asked.

"After you. I'll eat too."

The thick lips opened slightly. The Arab hesitated, then bit into the cake determinedly.

The meal over, the Arab looked at the schoolmaster. "Are you the judge?"

"No, I'm simply keeping you until tomorrow."

"Why do you eat with me?"

"I'm hungry."

The Arab fell silent. Daru got up and went out. He brought back a folding bed from the shed, set it up between the table and the stove, perpendicular to his own bed. From a large suitcase which, upright in a corner, served as a shelf for papers, he took two blankets and arranged them on the camp bed. Then he stopped, felt useless, and sat down on his bed. There was nothing more to do or to get ready. He had to look at this man. He looked at him, therefore, trying to imagine his face bursting with rage. He couldn't do so. He could see nothing but the dark yet shining eyes and the animal mouth.

"Why did you kill him?" he asked in a voice whose hostile tone surprised him.

The Arab looked away.

"He ran away. I ran after him."

He raised his eyes to Daru again and they were full of a sort of woeful interrogation. "Now what will they do to me?"

"Are you afraid?"

He stiffened, turning his eyes away.

"Are you sorry?"

The Arab stared at him openmouthed. Obviously he did not understand. Daru's annoyance was growing. At the same time he felt awkward and self-conscious with his big body wedged between the two beds.

"Lie down there," he said impatiently. "That's your bed."

The Arab didn't move. He called to Daru:

"Tell me!"

The schoolmaster looked at him.

"Is the gendarme coming back tomorrow?"

"I don't know."

"Are you coming with us?"

"I don't know. Why?"

The prisoner got up and stretched out on top of the blankets, his feet toward the window. The light from the electric bulb shone straight into his eyes and he closed them at once.

"Why?" Daru repeated, standing beside the bed.

The Arab opened his eyes under the blinding light and looked at him, trying not to blink.

"Come with us," he said.

In the middle of the night, Daru was still not asleep. He had gone to bed after undressing completely; he generally slept naked. But when he suddenly realized that he had nothing on, he hesitated. He felt vulnerable and the temptation came to him to put his clothes back on. Then he shrugged his shoulders; after all, he wasn't a child and, if need be, he could break his adversary in two. From his bed he could observe him, lying on his back, still motionless with his eyes closed under the harsh light. When Daru turned out the light, the darkness seemed to coagulate all of a sudden. Little by little, the night came back to life in the window where the starless sky was stirring gently. The schoolmaster soon made out the body lying at his feet. The Arab still did not move, but his eyes seemed open. A faint wind was prowling around the schoolhouse. Perhaps it would drive away the clouds and the sun would reappear.

During the night the wind increased. The hens fluttered a little and then were silent. The Arab turned over on his side with his back to Daru, who thought he heard him moan. Then he listened for his guest's breathing, become heavier and more regular. He listened to that breath so close to him and mused without being able to go to sleep. In this room where he had been sleeping alone for a year, this presence bothered him. But it bothered him also by imposing on him a sort of brotherhood he knew well but refused to accept in the present circumstances. Men who share the same rooms, soldiers or prisoners, develop a strange alliance as if, having cast off their armor with their clothing, they fraternized every evening, over and above their differences, in the ancient community of dream and fatigue. But Daru shook himself; he didn't like such musings, and it was essential to sleep.

A little later, however, when the Arab stirred slightly, the schoolmaster was still not asleep. When the prisoner made a second move, he stiffened, on the alert. The Arab was lifting himself slowly on his arms with almost the motion of a sleepwalker. Seated upright in bed, he waited motionless without turning his head toward Daru, as if he were listening attentively. Daru did not stir; it had just occurred to him that the revolver was still in the drawer of his desk. It was better to act at once. Yet he continued to observe the prisoner, who, with the same slithery motion, put his feet on the ground, waited again, then began to stand up slowly. Daru was about to call out to him when the Arab began to walk, in a quite natural but extraordinarily silent way. He was heading toward the door at the end of the room that opened into the shed. He lifted the latch with precaution and went out, pushing the door behind him but without shutting it. Daru had not stirred. "He is running away," he merely thought. "Good riddance!" Yet he listened attentively. The hens were not fluttering; the guest must be on the plateau. A faint sound of water reached him, and he didn't know what it was until the Arab again stood framed in the doorway, closed the door carefully, and came back to bed without a sound. Then Daru turned his back on him and fell asleep. Still later he seemed, from the depths of his sleep, to hear furtive steps around the schoolhouse. "I'm dreaming! I'm dreaming!" he repeated to himself. And he went on sleeping.

When he awoke, the sky was clear; the loose window let in a cold, pure air. The Arab was asleep, hunched up under the blankets now, his mouth open, utterly relaxed. But when Daru shook him, he started dreadfully, staring at Daru with wild eyes as if he had never seen him and such a frightened expression that the schoolmaster stepped back. "Don't be afraid. It's me. You must eat." The Arab nodded his head and said yes. Calm had returned to his face, but his expression was vacant and listless.

The coffee was ready. They drank it seated together on the folding bed as they munched their pieces of the cake. Then Daru led the Arab under the shed and showed him the faucet where he washed. He went back into the room, folded the blankets and the bed, made his own bed and put the room in order. Then he went through the classroom and out onto the terrace. The sun was already rising in the blue sky; a soft, bright light was bathing the deserted plateau. On the ridge the snow was melting in spots. The stones were about to reappear. Crouched on the edge of the plateau, the schoolmaster looked at the deserted expanse. He thought of Balducci. He had hurt him, for he had sent him off in a way as if he didn't want to be associated with him. He could still hear the gendarme's farewell and, without knowing why, he felt strangely empty and vulnerable. At that moment, from the other side of the schoolhouse, the prisoner coughed. Daru listened to him almost despite himself and then, furious, threw a pebble that whistled through the air before sinking into the snow. That man's stupid crime revolted him, but to hand him over was contrary to honor. Merely thinking of it made him smart with humiliation. And he cursed at one and the same time his own people who had sent him this Arab and the Arab too who had dared to kill and not managed to get away. Daru got up, walked in a circle on the terrace, waited motionless, and then went back into the schoolhouse.

The Arab, leaning over the cement floor of the shed, was washing his teeth with two fingers. Daru looked at him and said: "Come." He went back into the room ahead of the prisoner. He slipped a hunting-jacket on over his sweater and put on walking-shoes. Standing, he waited until the Arab had put on his *chèche* and sandals. They went into the classroom and the schoolmaster pointed to the exit, saying: "Go ahead." The fellow didn't budge. "I'm coming," said Daru. The Arab went out. Daru went back into the room and made a package of pieces of rusk, dates, and sugar. In the classroom, before going out, he hesitated a second in front of his desk, then crossed the threshold and locked the door. "That's the way," he said. He started toward the east, followed by the prisoner. But, a short distance from the schoolhouse, he thought he heard a slight sound behind them. He retraced his steps and examined the surroundings of the house, there was no one there. The Arab watched him without seeming to understand. "Come on," said Daru.

They walked for an hour and rested beside a sharp peak of limestone. The snow was melting faster and faster and the sun was drinking up the puddles at once, rapidly cleaning the plateau, which gradually dried and vibrated like the air itself. When they resumed walking, the ground rang under their feet. From time to time a bird rent the space in front of them with a joyful cry. Daru breathed in deeply the fresh morning light. He felt a sort of rapture before the vast familiar expanse, now almost entirely yellow under its dome of blue sky. They walked an hour more, descending toward the south. They reached a level height made up of crumbly rocks. From there on, the plateau sloped down, eastward, toward a low plain where there were a few spindly trees and, to the south, toward outcroppings of rock that gave the landscape a chaotic look.

Daru surveyed the two directions. There was nothing but the sky on the horizon. Not a man could be seen. He turned toward the Arab, who was looking at him blankly. Daru held out the package to him. "Take it," he said. "There are dates, bread, and sugar. You can hold out for two days. Here are a thousand francs too." The Arab took the package and the money but kept his full hands at chest level as if he didn't know what to do with what was being given him. "Now look," the schoolmaster said as he pointed in the direction of the east, "there's the way to Tinguit. You have a two-hour walk. At Tinguit you'll find the administration and the police. They are expecting you." The Arab looked toward the east, still holding the package and the money against his chest. Daru took his elbow and turned him rather roughly toward the south. At the foot of the height on which they stood could be seen a faint path. "That's the trail across the plateau. In a day's walk from here you'll find pasturelands and the first nomads. They'll take you in and shelter you according to their law." The Arab had now turned toward Daru and a sort of panic was visible in his expression. "Listen," he said. Daru shook his head: "No, be quiet. Now I'm leaving you." He turned his back on him, took two long steps in the direction of the school, looked hesitantly at the motionless Arab, and started off again. For a few minutes he heard nothing but his own step resounding on the cold ground and did not turn his head. A moment later, however, he turned around. The Arab was still there on the edge of the hill, his arms hanging now, and he was looking at the school-master. Daru felt something rise in his throat. But he swore with impatience, waved vaguely, and started off again. He had already gone some distance when he again stopped and looked. There was no longer anyone on the hill.

Daru hesitated. The sun was now rather high in the sky and was beginning to beat down on his head. The schoolmaster retraced his steps, at first some-what uncertainly, then with decision. When he reached the little hill, he was bathed in sweat. He climbed it as fast as he could and stopped, out of breath, at the top. The rock-fields to the south stood out sharply against the blue sky, but on the plain to the east a steamy heat was already rising. And in that slight haze, Daru, with heavy heart, made out the Arab walking slowly on the road to prison.

A little later, standing before the window of the classroom, the school-master was watching the clear light bathing the whole surface of the plateau, but he hardly saw it. Behind him on the blackboard, among the winding French rivers, sprawled the clumsily chalked-up words he had just read: "You handed over our brother. You will pay for this." Daru looked at the sky, the plateau, and, beyond, the invisible lands stretching all the way to the sea. In this vast landscape he had loved so much, he was alone.

FLANNERY O'CONNOR
1925–1964

A sense of grace, of mystery present in the smallest and most everyday details of life, penetrates the works of Flannery O'Connor. A religious writer whose fervent Catholicism was mixed with a fascination for the American South's fundamentalist intensity, a "grotesque" writer who believed in distortion as a way to call attention to the discrepancy between everyday and divine perspectives, a comic writer whose stories are laced with violence and death, O'Connor was also a regional writer, but only in the sense that the realistic portrait of her Georgia surroundings was a solid foundation for universal spiritual drama.

She was born Mary Flannery O'Connor in Savannah, Georgia, in 1925, to a devout Roman Catholic family. The family moved to Milledgeville, Georgia, in 1938, when her father was diagnosed with a terminal disease; he died in 1941. O'Connor was educated in parochial schools, attended Georgia State College for Women, and after graduating in 1945, enrolled in the creative writing program of the University of Iowa. While still in the program, she received the Rhinehart-Iowa Fiction award for a work in progress, *Wise Blood*; versions of four chapters were later published in the *Partisan Review, Sewanee Review,* and *New World Writing* before the novel appeared in 1952. During the two years following her graduation in 1947, O'Connor lived in New York and Connecticut; but in 1950, on a visit home, she fell ill with lupus erythematosus, the same disease that had killed her father. She and her mother moved to the family dairy farm near Milledgeville, where O'Connor wrote, raised peacocks, and endured with courage and humor the gradual progress of her disease. Over the next few years, she received a Kenyon fellowship and two O. Henry awards, but widespread recognition came with her first volume of short stories, *A Good Man Is Hard to Find* (1955), and she was thereafter in demand for lectures and interviews. On crutches after 1955, she remained chiefly in Georgia except for a trip with her mother in 1958 to the shrine at Lourdes, France, and to Rome, where she had an audience with the pope. When O'Connor died in August 1964, she was recognized as one of the most important writers of her time. Several volumes of letters, interviews, and occasional writings have been published posthumously, including a collection of essays and shorter pieces titled *Mystery and Manners* (1969), a passionate, lucid, and witty examination of writing, her own work, and the situation of the Catholic writer in the South. O'Connor's reputation continued to rise, and her posthumously published *Complete Stories* received a National Book Award in 1971.

Her first novel, *Wise Blood*, met an ambivalent reception in 1952. The cruelty, violence, and sordid opportunism of its twisted characters, of which one reviewer said "they seem not to belong to the human race at all," repelled readers who recognized its vivid satire of religious hypocrisy but looked in vain for a positive interpretation. The "wise blood" of the title, an inescapable inner tie to Christian mystery, proves a heavy burden for the protagonist, Hazel Motes, who spends his adult life trying unsuccessfully to escape the fundamentalist religion he learned from his grandfather, a fanatical preacher. Responding to criticism of the novel's negativity, O'Connor said later that, for her, Hazel Motes was an example of spiritual integrity in that he could not rid himself of the figure of Christ, "who moves from tree to tree in the back of his mind." A second novel, *The Violent Bear It Away* (1960), is permeated with the same Christian symbolism, as its protagonist, Francis Marion Tarwater, tries—also in violence, and also unsuccessfully—to escape the burden of prophecy laid on him by his grandfather.

O'Connor is best known for her short stories, collected in *A Good Man Is Hard to Find* (1955), *Everything That Rises Must Converge* (1965), and *The Complete Short Stories* (1971). *A Good Man Is Hard to Find* contains ten stories with a variety of plots and situations. A recurring theme is the sudden presence of a significant gesture, or moment of awareness, that focuses events up to that point in the larger perspective of religious mystery. Progress toward that mystery is stressed even more in *Everything That Rises Must Converge*, whose title refers to a concept of human spiritual evolution developed by the French Jesuit philosopher Teilhard de Chardin (1881–1955). Evolution itself, for Teilhard (who was also a paleontologist), was a gradual movement toward a supreme and universal consciousness, an "Omega point" synonymous with Christ's Second Coming. O'Connor admired Teilhard's writings, and characters in her second story collection are seen in relation to this implied transcendent point.

A *Good Man Is Hard to Find* attracted attention from the beginning for its mixture of comedy, harsh realism, and a religious vision that is associated with extreme or violent situations. O'Connor used violence to shock her audience into looking closely at the ordinary fabric of their lives, but also because she felt that human beings confront their inner natures only when forced away from everyday routines: "It is the extreme situation that best reveals what we are essentially." Small wonder that the stories were called "grotesque," when murder, dismemberment, and arson invade the most banal and commonplace scenes. A persuasive Bible salesman runs off with a woman's wooden leg after failing to seduce her; a deaf-mute bride is left at a diner by her new husband, a one-armed handyman with an urge to travel; and a family vacation becomes a bloodbath when the car runs into a ditch and attracts the attention of a psychopathic prison escapee. In each case, catastrophe occurs and lives take a new direction.

The cliché that provides the title for the first story—A good man is hard to find—is both tantalizingly familiar and ambiguous. O'Connor exploits the ambiguity to structure her narrative. In the first half, references to a "good man" are merely part of polite conversation. At Red Sammy's roadside restaurant, the grandmother tells Red Sam that he is a good man (because he let two mill hands charge gas), and he comments that nowadays, "a good man is hard to find" (because you used to be able to leave your door unlocked). Both are using the conventional language of social conversation, communicating through a code of manners that everyone, no matter how different, is expected to understand and accept. O'Connor explained elsewhere that "the South has survived in the past because its manners, however lopsided or inadequate they may have been, provided enough social discipline to hold us together and give us an identity." These manners include both behavior (where the grandchildren fall far short) and appearance. The grandmother dresses neatly with violets on her hat, and lace-trimmed collar and cuffs, so that (in one of O'Connor's macabre jokes) if she is found dead after a car accident, anyone seeing her will know that "she was a lady." Manners create a network of conventional points of view—political, racial, economic, and religious—that allow communication even among strangers. Yet they are no match for the extreme case, or for absolute definitions of good and evil, as the grandmother will discover when she tries the same soothing language on the Misfit.

The early scenes contain an almost cartoonlike grating comedy. John Wesley and June Star are model bratty children: they talk back to their grandmother, devour comic books, fight in the back seat of the car, insult everyone in sight, and whine to get their way. Their long-suffering parents are sketchily described: Bailey drives the car, wears a yellow sport shirt with bright blue parrots, and tries to keep order; his unnamed wife holds the baby and wears a green head-kerchief tied in two comic points. The constantly chattering, self-centered, and manipulative grandmother is the real focus of the first section, a role she will share with the Misfit later on.

The second half introduces one of the most disturbing figures in all O'Connor's stories: the Misfit, an escaped convict whose murderous alienation challenges all the certainties on which the grandmother's life is built. Even the landscape echoes this ominous turn of events; sparkling and beautiful outside Stone Mountain, it has become woods gaping like a dark open mouth or, after Bailey's murder, wind moving through the treetops like a "long satisfied insuck of breath." The multiple murder is inevitable as soon as the grandmother blurts out the Misfit's name; but dramatically, these murders move into the background while the grandmother and the Misfit pursue their carefully polite conversation. All the social strategies that she has counted on do not help the grandmother here, and in fact they serve only to point up the shallowness of her beliefs. Flattering the Misfit by calling him a good man, she elaborates: he has "good blood," he's "not common," he comes from "nice people." Yet the Misfit's retort is a powerful rejection of "good" as social standing, and he proceeds to reveal his own intense preoccupation with absolute good and evil. It is a complex portrait, a mixture of psychosis (the Oedipus complex the prison psychiatrist tried to explain to him) and a passionate spiritual curiosity that occurs in many of O'Connor's flawed prophets. The Misfit looks for ultimate answers, and he looks in terms of the Bible Belt society in which he has been raised. Since he can never know for sure if the biblical miracles actually happened, he has no rules to live by; and he revolts in rage and pain while asserting demonically, "No pleasure but meanness."

It is at this point that the grandmother's famous gesture occurs, and O'Connor raises the stakes from philosophical dialogue to religious encounter. Confused with grief and terror, unable to sustain the certainties that have served her until now, the grandmother registers only the Misfit's desperate face (and perhaps her son's shirt) and reaches out to him in pity. Stung by this invasion of his privacy, this assertion of a kinship that goes beyond "good blood" and touches on mystery, he shoots her and completes the tally of murders. Yet something more has happened: the grandmother herself, as the Misfit recognizes, has transcended her earlier shallowness and hypocrisy to become a "good woman" at the moment of death. The Misfit, in turn, may be pushed to his own extremity by that touch: he has lost his own guiding principle and declares, his eyes "pale and defenseless-looking," "It's no real pleasure in life." Both he and the grandmother exist on two levels: a banal, very physical, and sometimes comic realism and a coexisting spiritual dimension that intervenes in unpredictable moments of grace. Both elements are intertwined throughout O'Connor's work and have made her one of the most admired short-story writers of the twentieth century.

Margarey Earley Whitt, *Understanding Flannery O'Connor* (1995), is an excellent analytic overview of the complete work; it contains an annotated bibliography. Robert Brinkmeyer Jr., *The Art and Vision of Flannery O'Connor* (1989), is an illuminating study of characters and narrative strategy and of the relation between her Catholicism and Protestant fundamentalist images. Flannery O'Connor, *Mystery and Manners: Occasional Prose* (1969), ed. Sally Fitzgerald, contains many discussions of the contexts and implications of her work, including *A Good Man Is Hard to Find*. Robert Coles, *Flannery O'Connor's South* (1980), describes the social and historical setting of the work, including a chapter on "hard, hard religion." Suzanne M. Paulson, *Flannery O'Connor: A Study of the Short Fiction* (1988), reviews the fiction and presents a broad selection of passages from critics and O'Connor herself on her work.

A Good Man Is Hard to Find

The grandmother didn't want to go to Florida. She wanted to visit some of her connections in east Tennessee and she was seizing at every chance to change Bailey's mind. Bailey was the son she lived with, her only boy. He was sitting on the edge of his chair at the table, bent over the orange sports section of the *Journal*. "Now look here, Bailey," she said, "see here, read this," and she stood with one hand on her thin hip and the other rattling the newspaper at his bald head. "Here this fellow that calls himself The Misfit is aloose from the Federal Pen and headed toward Florida and you read here what it says he did to these people. Just you read it. I wouldn't take my children in any direction with a criminal like that aloose in it. I couldn't answer to my conscience if I did."

Bailey didn't look up from his reading so she wheeled around then and faced the children's mother, a young woman in slacks, whose face was as broad and innocent as a cabbage and was tied around with a green head-kerchief that had two points on the top like a rabbit's ears. She was sitting on the sofa, feeding the baby his apricots out of a jar. "The children have been to Florida before," the old lady said. "You all ought to take them some-where else for a change so they would see different parts of the world and be broad. They never have been to east Tennessee."

The children's mother didn't seem to hear her but the eight-year-old boy, John Wesley, a stocky child with glasses, said, "If you don't want to go to Florida, why dontcha stay at home?" He and the little girl, June Star, were reading the funny papers on the floor.

"She wouldn't stay at home to be queen for a day," June Star said without raising her yellow head.

"Yes and what would you do if this fellow, The Misfit, caught you?" the grandmother asked.

"I'd smack his face," John Wesley said.

"She wouldn't stay at home for a million bucks," June Star said. "Afraid she'd miss something. She has to go everywhere we go."

"All right, Miss," the grandmother said. "Just remember that the next time you want me to curl your hair."

June Star said her hair was naturally curly.

The next morning the grandmother was the first one in the car, ready to go. She had her big black valise that looked like the head of a hippopotamus in one corner, and underneath it she was hiding a basket with Pitty Sing, the cat, in it. She didn't intend for the cat to be left alone in the house for three days because he would miss her too much and she was afraid he might brush against one of the gas burners and accidentally asphyxiate himself. Her son, Bailey, didn't like to arrive at a motel with a cat.

She sat in the middle of the back seat with John Wesley and June Star on either side of her. Bailey and the children's mother and the baby sat in front and they left Atlanta at eight forty-five with the mileage on the car at 55890. The grandmother wrote this down because she thought it would be inter-esting to say how many miles they had been when they got back. It took them twenty minutes to reach the outskirts of the city.

The old lady settled herself comfortably, removing her white cotton gloves and putting them up with her purse on the shelf in front of the back window. The children's mother still had on slacks and still had her head tied up in a green kerchief, but the grandmother had on a navy blue straw sailor hat with a bunch of white violets on the brim and a navy blue dress with a small white dot in the print. Her collars and cuffs were white organdy trimmed with lace and at her neckline she had pinned a purple spray of cloth violets containing a sachet. In case of an accident, anyone seeing her dead on the highway would know at once that she was a lady.

She said she thought it was going to be a good day for driving, neither too hot nor too cold, and she cautioned Bailey that the speed limit was fifty-five miles an hour and that the patrolmen hid themselves behind billboards and small clumps of trees and sped out after you before you had a chance to slow down. She pointed out interesting details of the scenery: Stone Mountain;[1] the blue granite that in some places came up to both sides of the highway; the brilliant red clay banks slightly streaked with purple; and the various crops that made rows of green lace-work on the ground. The trees were full of silver-white sunlight and the meanest of them sparkled. The children were reading comic magazines and their mother had gone back to sleep.

"Let's go through Georgia fast so we won't have to look at it much," John Wesley said.

"If I were a little boy," said the grandmother, "I wouldn't talk about my native state that way. Tennessee has the mountains and Georgia has the hills."

"Tennessee is just a hillbilly dumping ground," John Wesley said, "and Georgia is a lousy state too."

"You said it," June Star said.

"In my time," said the grandmother, folding her thin veined fingers, "children were more respectful of their native states and their parents and everything else. People did right then. Oh look at the cute little pickaninny!"[2] she said and pointed to a Negro child standing in the door of a shack. "Wouldn't that make a picture, now?" she asked and they all turned and looked at the little Negro out of the back window. He waved.

"He didn't have any britches on," June Star said.

"He probably didn't have any," the grandmother explained. "Little niggers in the country don't have things like we do. If I could paint, I'd paint that picture," she said.

The children exchanged comic books.

The grandmother offered to hold the baby and the children's mother passed him over the front seat to her. She set him on her knee and bounced him and told him about the things they were passing. She rolled her eyes and screwed up her mouth and stuck her leathery thin face into his smooth bland one. Occasionally he gave her a faraway smile. They passed a large cotton field with five or six graves fenced in the middle of it, like a small island. "Look at the graveyard!" the grandmother said, pointing it out. "That was the old family burying ground. That belonged to the plantation."

"Where's the plantation?" John Wesley asked.

"Gone With the Wind,"[3] said the grandmother. "Ha. Ha."

When the children finished all the comic books they had brought, they opened the lunch and ate it. The grandmother ate a peanut butter sandwich and an olive and would not let the children throw the box and the paper napkins out the window. When there was nothing else to do they played a game by choosing a cloud and making the other two guess what shape it suggested. John Wesley took one the shape of a cow and June Star guessed a cow and John Wesley said, no, an automobile, and June Star said he didn't play fair, and they began to slap each other over the grandmother.

1. Tall granite mountain east of Atlanta, which has a large Confederate memorial carved on its northeast face.　2. Demeaning term for young black child.　3. Margaret Mitchell's immensely popular romantic novel (1936) about the South during the Civil War and Reconstruction.

The grandmother said she would tell them a story if they would keep quiet. When she told a story, she rolled her eyes and waved her head and was very dramatic. She said once when she was a maiden lady she had been courted by a Mr. Edgar Atkins Teagarden from Jasper, Georgia. She said he was a very good-looking man and a gentleman and that he brought her a water-melon every Saturday afternoon with his initials cut in it, E. A. T. Well, one Saturday, she said, Mr. Teagarden brought the watermelon and there was nobody at home and he left it on the front porch and returned in his buggy to Jasper, but she never got the watermelon, she said, because a nigger boy ate it when he saw the initials, E. A. T.! This story tickled John Wesley's funny bone and he giggled and giggled but June Star didn't think it was any good. She said she wouldn't marry a man that just brought her a watermelon on Saturday. The grandmother said she would have done well to marry Mr. Teagarden because he was a gentleman and had bought Coca-Cola stock when it first came out and that he had died only a few years ago, a very wealthy man.

They stopped at The Tower for barbecued sandwiches. The Tower was a part stucco and part wood filling station and dance hall set in a clearing outside of Timothy. A fat man named Red Sammy Butts ran it and there were signs stuck here and there on the building and for miles up and down the highway saying, TRY RED SAMMY'S FAMOUS BARBECUE. NONE LIKE FAMOUS RED SAMMY'S! RED SAM! THE FAT BOY WITH THE HAPPY LAUGH! A VETERAN! RED SAMMY'S YOUR MAN!

Red Sammy was lying on the bare ground outside The Tower with his head under a truck while a gray monkey about a foot high, chained to a small chinaberry tree,[4] chattered nearby. The monkey sprang back into the tree and got on the highest limb as soon as he saw the children jump out of the car and run toward him.

Inside, The Tower was a long dark room with a counter at one end and tables at the other and dancing space in the middle. They all sat down at a board table next to the nickelodeon[5] and Red Sam's wife, a tall burnt-brown woman with hair and eyes lighter than her skin, came and took their order. The children's mother put a dime in the machine and played "The Tennessee Waltz," and the grandmother said that tune always made her want to dance. She asked Bailey if he would like to dance but he only glared at her. He didn't have a naturally sunny disposition like she did and trips made him nervous. The grandmother's brown eyes were very bright. She swayed her head from side to side and pretended she was dancing in her chair. June Star said play something she could tap to so the children's mother put in another dime and played a fast number and June Star stepped out onto the dance floor and did her tap routine.

"Ain't she cute?" Red Sam's wife said, leaning over the counter. "Would you like to come be my little girl?"

"No I certainly wouldn't," June Star said. "I wouldn't live in a broken-down place like this for a million bucks!" and she ran back to the table.

"Ain't she cute?" the woman repeated, stretching her mouth politely.

"Aren't you ashamed?" hissed the grandmother.

Red Sam came in and told his wife to quit lounging on the counter and

4. Deciduous tree with intricately compound leaves, purple flowers, and yellow fruit.   5. Jukebox.

hurry up with these people's order. His khaki trousers reached just to his hip bones and his stomach hung over them like a sack of meal swaying under his shirt. He came over and sat down at a table nearby and let out a combination sigh and yodel. "You can't win," he said. "You can't win," and he wiped his sweating red face off with a gray handkerchief. "These days you don't know who to trust," he said. "Ain't that the truth?"

"People are certainly not nice like they used to be," said the grandmother.

"Two fellers come in here last week," Red Sammy said, "driving a Chrysler. It was a old beat-up car but it was a good one and these boys looked all right to me. Said they worked at the mill and you know I let them fellers charge the gas they bought? Now why did I do that?"

"Because you're a good man!" the grandmother said at once.

"Yes'm, I suppose so," Red Sam said as if he were struck with this answer.

His wife brought the orders, carrying the five plates all at once without a tray, two in each hand and one balanced on her arm. "It isn't a soul in this green world of God's that you can trust," she said. "And I don't count nobody out of that, not nobody," she repeated, looking at Red Sammy.

"Did you read about that criminal, The Misfit, that's escaped?" asked the grandmother.

"I wouldn't be a bit surprised if he didn't attack this place right here," said the woman. "If he hears about it being here, I wouldn't be none surprised to see him. If he hears it's two cent in the cash register, I wouldn't be a tall surprised if he . . ."

"That'll do," Red Sam said. "Go bring these people their Co'-Colas," and the woman went off to get the rest of the order.

"A good man is hard to find," Red Sammy said. "Everything is getting terrible. I remember the day you could go off and leave your screen door unlatched. Not no more."

He and the grandmother discussed better times. The old lady said that in her opinion Europe was entirely to blame for the way things were now. She said the way Europe acted you would think we were made of money and Red Sam said it was no use talking about it, she was exactly right. The children ran outside into the white sunlight and looked at the monkey in the lacy chinaberry tree. He was busy catching fleas on himself and biting each one carefully between his teeth as if it were a delicacy.

They drove off again into the hot afternoon. The grandmother took cat naps and woke up every few minutes with her own snoring. Outside of Toombsboro[6] she woke up and recalled an old plantation that she had visited in this neighborhood once when she was a young lady. She said the house had six white columns across the front and that there was an avenue of oaks leading up to it and two little wooden trellis arbors on either side in front where you sat down with your suitor after a stroll in the garden. She recalled exactly which road to turn off to get to it. She knew that Bailey would not be willing to lose any time looking at an old house, but the more she talked about it, the more she wanted to see it once again and find out if the little twin arbors were still standing. "There was a secret panel in this house," she said craftily, not telling the truth but wishing that she were, "and the story

6. A small town in central Georgia, thirty-two miles east of Macon.

went that all the family silver was hidden in it when Sherman[7] came through but it was never found . . ."

"Hey!" John Wesley said. "Let's go see it! We'll find it! We'll poke all the woodwork and find it! Who lives there? Where do you turn off at? Hey Pop, can't we turn off there?"

"We never have seen a house with a secret panel!" June Star shrieked. "Let's go to the house with the secret panel! Hey Pop, can't we go see the house with the secret panel!"

"It's not far from here, I know," the grandmother said. "It wouldn't take over twenty minutes."

Bailey was looking straight ahead. His jaw was as rigid as a horseshoe. "No," he said.

The children began to yell and scream that they wanted to see the house with the secret panel. John Wesley kicked the back of the front seat and June Star hung over her mother's shoulder and whined desperately into her ear that they never had any fun even on their vacation, that they could never do what THEY wanted to do. The baby began to scream and John Wesley kicked the back of the seat so hard that his father could feel the blows in his kidney.

"All right!" he shouted and drew the car to a stop at the side of the road. "Will you all shut up? Will you all just shut up for one second? If you don't shut up, we won't go anywhere."

"It would be very educational for them," the grandmother murmured.

"All right," Bailey said, "but get this: this is the only time we're going to stop for anything like this. This is the one and only time."

"The dirt road that you have to turn down is about a mile back," the grandmother directed. "I marked it when we passed."

"A dirt road," Bailey groaned.

After they had turned around and were headed toward the dirt road, the grandmother recalled other points about the house, the beautiful glass over the front doorway and the candle-lamp in the hall. John Wesley said that the secret panel was probably in the fireplace.

"You can't go inside this house," Bailey said. "You don't know who lives there."

"While you all talk to the people in front, I'll run around behind and get in a window," John Wesley suggested.

"We'll all stay in the car," his mother said.

They turned onto the dirt road and the car raced roughly along in a swirl of pink dust. The grandmother recalled the times when there were no paved roads and thirty miles was a day's journey. The dirt road was hilly and there were sudden washes[8] in it and sharp curves on dangerous embankments. All at once they would be on a hill, looking down over the blue tops of trees for miles around, then the next minute, they would be in a red depression with the dust-coated trees looking down on them.

"This place had better turn up in a minute," Bailey said, "or I'm going to turn around."

The road looked as if no one had traveled on it in months.

---

7. William Tecumseh Sherman (1820–1891), Union general famous for his army's destructive "march to the sea" during the Civil War. 8. Dips in the road where soil had washed away.

"It's not much farther," the grandmother said and just as she said it, a horrible thought came to her. The thought was so embarrassing that she turned red in the face and her eyes dilated and her feet jumped up, upsetting her valise in the corner. The instant the valise moved, the newspaper top she had over the basket under it rose with a snarl and Pitty Sing, the cat, sprang onto Bailey's shoulder.

The children were thrown to the floor and their mother, clutching the baby, was thrown out the door onto the ground; the old lady was thrown into the front seat. The car turned over once and landed right-side-up in a gulch off the side of the road. Bailey remained in the driver's seat with the cat—gray-striped with a broad white face and an orange nose—clinging to his neck like a caterpillar.

As soon as the children saw they could move their arms and legs, they scrambled out of the car, shouting, "We've had an ACCIDENT!" The grandmother was curled up under the dashboard, hoping she was injured so that Bailey's wrath would not come down on her all at once. The horrible thought she had had before the accident was that the house she had remembered so vividly was not in Georgia but in Tennessee.

Bailey removed the cat from his neck with both hands and flung it out the window against the side of a pine tree. Then he got out of the car and started looking for the children's mother. She was sitting against the side of the red gutted ditch, holding the screaming baby, but she only had a cut down her face and a broken shoulder. "We've had an ACCIDENT!" the children screamed in a frenzy of delight.

"But nobody's killed," June Star said with disappointment as the grandmother limped out of the car, her hat still pinned to her head but the broken front brim standing up at a jaunty angle and the violet spray hanging off the side. They all sat down in the ditch, except the children, to recover from the shock. They were all shaking.

"Maybe a car will come along," said the children's mother hoarsely.

"I believe I have injured an organ," said the grandmother, pressing her side, but no one answered her. Bailey's teeth were clattering. He had on a yellow sport shirt with bright blue parrots designed in it and his face was as yellow as the shirt. The grandmother decided that she would not mention that the house was in Tennessee.

The road was about ten feet above and they could see only the tops of the trees on the other side of it. Behind the ditch they were sitting in there were more woods, tall and dark and deep. In a few minutes they saw a car some distance away on top of a hill, coming slowly as if the occupants were watching them. The grandmother stood up and waved both arms dramatically to attract their attention. The car continued to come on slowly, disappeared around a bend and appeared again, moving even slower, on top of the hill they had gone over. It was a big black battered hearse-like automobile. There were three men in it.

It came to a stop just over them and for some minutes, the driver looked down with a steady expressionless gaze to where they were sitting, and didn't speak. Then he turned his head and muttered something to the other two and they got out. One was a fat boy in black trousers and a red sweat shirt with a silver stallion embossed on the front of it. He moved around on the right side of them and stood staring, his mouth partly open in a kind of loose grin. The other had on khaki pants and a blue striped coat and a gray hat pulled down very low, hiding most of his face. He came around slowly on the left side. Neither spoke.

The driver got out of the car and stood by the side of it, looking down at them. He was an older man than the other two. His hair was just beginning to gray and he wore silver-rimmed spectacles that gave him a scholarly look. He had a long creased face and didn't have on any shirt or undershirt. He had on blue jeans that were too tight for him and was holding a black hat and a gun. The two boys also had guns.

"We've had an ACCIDENT!" the children screamed.

The grandmother had the peculiar feeling that the bespectacled man was someone she knew. His face was as familiar to her as if she had known him all her life but she could not recall who he was. He moved away from the car and began to come down the embankment, placing his feet carefully so that he wouldn't slip. He had on tan and white shoes and no socks, and his ankles were red and thin. "Good afternoon," he said. "I see you all had you a little spill."

"We turned over twice!" said the grandmother.

"Oncet," he corrected. "We seen it happen. Try their car and see will it run, Hiram," he said quietly to the boy with the gray hat.

"What you got that gun for?" John Wesley asked. "Whatcha gonna do with that gun?"

"Lady," the man said to the children's mother, "would you mind calling them children to sit down by you? Children make me nervous. I want all you all to sit down right together there where you're at."

"What are you telling US what to do for?" June Star asked.

Behind them the line of woods gaped like a dark open mouth. "Come here," said their mother.

"Look here now," Bailey began suddenly, "we're in a predicament! We're in . . ."

The grandmother shrieked. She scrambled to her feet and stood staring. "You're the Misfit!" she said. "I recognized you at once!"

"Yes'm," the man said, smiling slightly as if he were pleased in spite of himself to be known, "but it would have been better for all of you, lady, if you hadn't of reckernized me."

Bailey turned his head sharply and said something to his mother that shocked even the children. The old lady began to cry and The Misfit reddened.

"Lady," he said, "don't you get upset. Sometimes a man says things he don't mean. I don't reckon he meant to talk to you thataway."

"You wouldn't shoot a lady, would you?" the grandmother said and removed a clean handkerchief from her cuff and began to slap at her eyes with it.

The Misfit pointed the toe of his shoe into the ground and made a little hole and then covered it up again. "I would hate to have to," he said.

"Listen," the grandmother almost screamed, "I know you're a good man. You don't look a bit like you have common blood. I know you must come from nice people!"

"Yes mam," he said, "finest people in the world." When he smiled he showed a row of strong white teeth. "God never made a finer woman than my mother and my daddy's heart was pure gold," he said. The boy with the red sweat shirt had come around behind them and was standing with his gun at his hip. The Misfit squatted down on the ground. "Watch them children, Bobby Lee," he said. "You know they make me nervous." He looked at the six of them huddled together in front of him and he seemed to be embarrassed as if he couldn't think of anything to say. "Ain't a cloud in the sky," he remarked, looking up at it. "Don't see no sun but don't see no cloud neither."

"Yes, it's a beautiful day," said the grandmother. "Listen," she said, "you shouldn't call yourself The Misfit because I know you're a good man at heart. I can just look at you and tell."

"Hush!" Bailey yelled. "Hush! Everybody shut up and let me handle this!" He was squatting in the position of a runner about to sprint forward but he didn't move.

"I pre-chate[9] that, lady," The Misfit said and drew a little circle in the ground with the butt of his gun.

"It'll take a half a hour to fix this here car," Hiram called, looking over the raised hood of it.

"Well, first you and Bobby Lee get him and that little boy to step over yonder with you," The Misfit said, pointing to Bailey and John Wesley. "The boys want to ast you something," he said to Bailey. "Would you mind stepping back in them woods there with them?"

"Listen," Bailey began, "we're in a terrible predicament! Nobody realizes what this is," and his voice cracked. His eyes were as blue and intense as the parrots in his shirt and he remained perfectly still.

The grandmother reached up to adjust her hat brim as if she were going to the woods with him but it came off in her hand. She stood staring at it and after a second she let it fall on the ground. Hiram pulled Bailey up by the arm as if he were assisting an old man. John Wesley caught hold of his father's hand and Bobby Lee followed. They went off toward the woods and just as they reached the dark edge, Bailey turned and supporting himself against a gray naked pine trunk, he shouted, "I'll be back in a minute, Mamma, wait on me!"

"Come back this instant!" his mother shrilled but they all disappeared into the woods.

"Bailey Boy!" the grandmother called in a tragic voice but she found she was looking at The Misfit squatting on the ground in front of her. "I just know you're a good man," she said desperately. "You're not a bit common!"

"Nome,[1] I ain't a good man," The Misfit said after a second as if he had considered her statement carefully, "but I ain't the worst in the world neither. My daddy said I was a different breed of dog from my brothers and sisters. 'You know,' Daddy said, 'it's some that can live their whole life out without asking about it and it's others has to know why it is, and this boy is one of the latters. He's going to be into everything!' " He put on his black hat and looked up suddenly and then away deep into the woods as if he were embarrassed again. "I'm sorry I don't have on a shirt before you ladies," he said,

9. Appreciate.   1. No, ma'am.

hunching his shoulders slightly. "We buried our clothes that we had on when we escaped and we're just making do until we can get better. We borrowed these from some folks we met," he explained.

"That's perfectly all right," the grandmother said. "Maybe Bailey has an extra shirt in his suitcase."

"I'll look and see terrectly,"[2] The Misfit said.

"Where are they taking him?" the children's mother screamed.

"Daddy was a card himself," The Misfit said. "You couldn't put anything over on him. He never got in trouble with the Authorities though. Just had the knack of handling them."

"You could be honest too if you'd only try," said the grandmother. "Think how wonderful it would be to settle down and live a comfortable life and not have to think about somebody chasing you all the time."

The Misfit kept scratching in the ground with the butt of his gun as if he were thinking about it. "Yes'm, somebody is always after you," he murmured.

The grandmother noticed how thin his shoulder blades were just behind his hat because she was standing up looking down on him. "Do you ever pray?" she asked.

He shook his head. All she saw was the black hat wiggle between his shoulder blades. "Nome," he said.

There was a pistol shot from the woods, followed closely by another. Then silence. The old lady's head jerked around. She could hear the wind move through the tree tops like a long satisfied insuck of breath. "Bailey Boy!" she called.

"I was a gospel singer for a while," The Misfit said. "I been most everything. Been in the arm service, both land and sea, at home and abroad, been twict married, been an undertaker, been with the railroads, plowed Mother Earth, been in a tornado, seen a man burnt alive oncet," and looked up at the children's mother and the little girl who were sitting close together, their faces white and their eyes glassy; "I even seen a woman flogged," he said.

"Pray, pray," the grandmother began, "pray, pray . . ."

"I never was a bad boy that I remember of," The Misfit said in an almost dreamy voice, "but somewheres along the line I done something wrong and got sent to the penitentiary. I was buried alive," and he looked up and held her attention to him by a steady stare.

"That's when you should have started to pray," she said. "What did you do to get sent to the penitentiary that first time?"

"Turn to the right, it was a wall," The Misfit said, looking up again at the cloudless sky. "Turn to the left, it was a wall. Look up it was a ceiling, look down it was a floor. I forget what I done, lady. I set there and set there, trying to remember what it was I done and I ain't recalled it to this day. Oncet in a while, I would think it was coming to me, but it never come."

"Maybe they put you in by mistake," the old lady said vaguely.

"Nome," he said. "It wasn't no mistake. They had the papers on me."

"You must have stolen something," she said.

The Misfit sneered slightly. "Nobody had nothing I wanted," he said. "It was a head-doctor at the penitentiary said what I had done was kill my daddy but I known that for a lie. My daddy died in nineteen ought nineteen of the

2. Directly; i.e., right away.

epidemic flu and I never had a thing to do with it. He was buried in the Mount Hopewell Baptist churchyard and you can go there and see for yourself."

"If you would pray," the old lady said, "Jesus would help you."

"That's right," The Misfit said.

"Well then, why don't you pray?" she asked trembling with delight suddenly.

"I don't want no hep," he said. "I'm doing all right by myself."

Bobby Lee and Hiram came ambling back from the woods. Bobby Lee was dragging a yellow shirt with bright blue parrots in it.

"Thow me that shirt, Bobby Lee," The Misfit said. The shirt came flying at him and landed on his shoulder and he put it on. The grandmother couldn't name what the shirt reminded her of. "No, lady," The Misfit said while he was buttoning it up, "I found out the crime don't matter. You can do one thing or you can do another, kill a man or take a tire off his car, because sooner or later you're going to forget what it was you done and just be punished for it."

The children's mother had begun to make heaving noises as if she couldn't get her breath. "Lady," he asked, "would you and that little girl like to step off yonder with Bobby Lee and Hiram and join your husband?"

"Yes, thank you," the mother said faintly. Her left arm dangled helplessly and she was holding the baby, who had gone to sleep, in the other. "Hep that lady up, Hiram," The Misfit said as she struggled to climb out of the ditch, "and Bobby Lee, you hold onto that little girl's hand."

"I don't want to hold hands with him," June Star said. "He reminds me of a pig."

The fat boy blushed and laughed and caught her by the arm and pulled her off into the woods after Hiram and her mother.

Alone with The Misfit, the grandmother found that she had lost her voice. There was not a cloud in the sky nor any sun. There was nothing around her but woods. She wanted to tell him that he must pray. She opened and closed her mouth several times before anything came out. Finally she found herself saying, "Jesus, Jesus," meaning, Jesus will help you, but the way she was saying it, it sounded as if she might be cursing.

"Yes'm," The Misfit said as if he agreed. "Jesus thown everything off balance. It was the same case with Him as with me except He hadn't committed any crime and they could prove I had committed one because they had the papers on me. Of course," he said, "they never shown me my papers. That's why I sign myself now. I said long ago, you get you a signature and sign everything you do and keep a copy of it. Then you'll know what you done and you can hold up the crime to the punishment and see do they match and in the end you'll have something to prove you ain't been treated right. I call myself The Misfit," he said, "because I can't make what all I done wrong fit what all I gone through in punishment."

There was a piercing scream from the woods, followed closely by a pistol report. "Does it seem right to you, lady, that one is punished a heap and another ain't punished at all?"

"Jesus!" the old lady cried. "You've got good blood! I know you wouldn't shoot a lady! I know you come from nice people! Pray! Jesus, you ought not to shoot a lady. I'll give you all the money I've got!"

"Lady," The Misfit said, looking beyond her far into the woods, "there never was a body that give the undertaker a tip."

There were two more pistol reports and the grandmother raised her head like a parched old turkey hen crying for water and called, "Bailey Boy, Bailey Boy!" as if her heart would break.

"Jesus was the only One that ever raised the dead." The Misfit continued, "and He shouldn't have done it. He thrown everything off balance. If He did what He said, then it's nothing for you to do but throw away everything and follow Him, and if He didn't, then it's nothing for you to do but enjoy the few minutes you got left the best way you can—by killing somebody or burning down his house or doing some other meanness to him. No pleasure but meanness," he said and his voice had become almost a snarl.

"Maybe He didn't raise the dead," the old lady mumbled, not knowing what she was saying and feeling so dizzy that she sank down in the ditch with her legs twisted under her.

"I wasn't there so I can't say He didn't," The Misfit said. "I wisht I had of been there," he said, hitting the ground with his fist. "It ain't right I wasn't there because if I had of been there I would of known. Listen lady," he said in a high voice, "if I had of been there I would of known and I wouldn't be like I am now." His voice seemed about to crack and the grandmother's head cleared for an instant. She saw the man's face twisted close to her own as if he were going to cry and she murmured, "Why you're one of my babies. You're one of my own children!" She reached out and touched him on the shoulder. The Misfit sprang back as if a snake had bitten him and shot her three times through the chest. Then he put his gun down on the ground and took off his glasses and began to clean them.

Hiram and Bobby Lee returned from the woods and stood over the ditch, looking down at the grandmother who half sat and half lay in a puddle of blood with her legs crossed under her like a child's and her face smiling up at the cloudless sky.

Without his glasses, The Misfit's eyes were red-rimmed and pale and defenseless-looking. "Take her off and throw her where you thrown the others," he said, picking up the cat that was rubbing itself against his leg.

"She was a talker, wasn't she?" Bobby Lee said, sliding down the ditch with a yodel.

"She would of been a good woman," The Misfit said, "if it had been somebody there to shoot her every minute of her life."

"Some fun!" Bobby Lee said.

"Shut up, Bobby Lee," The Misfit said. "It's no real pleasure in life."

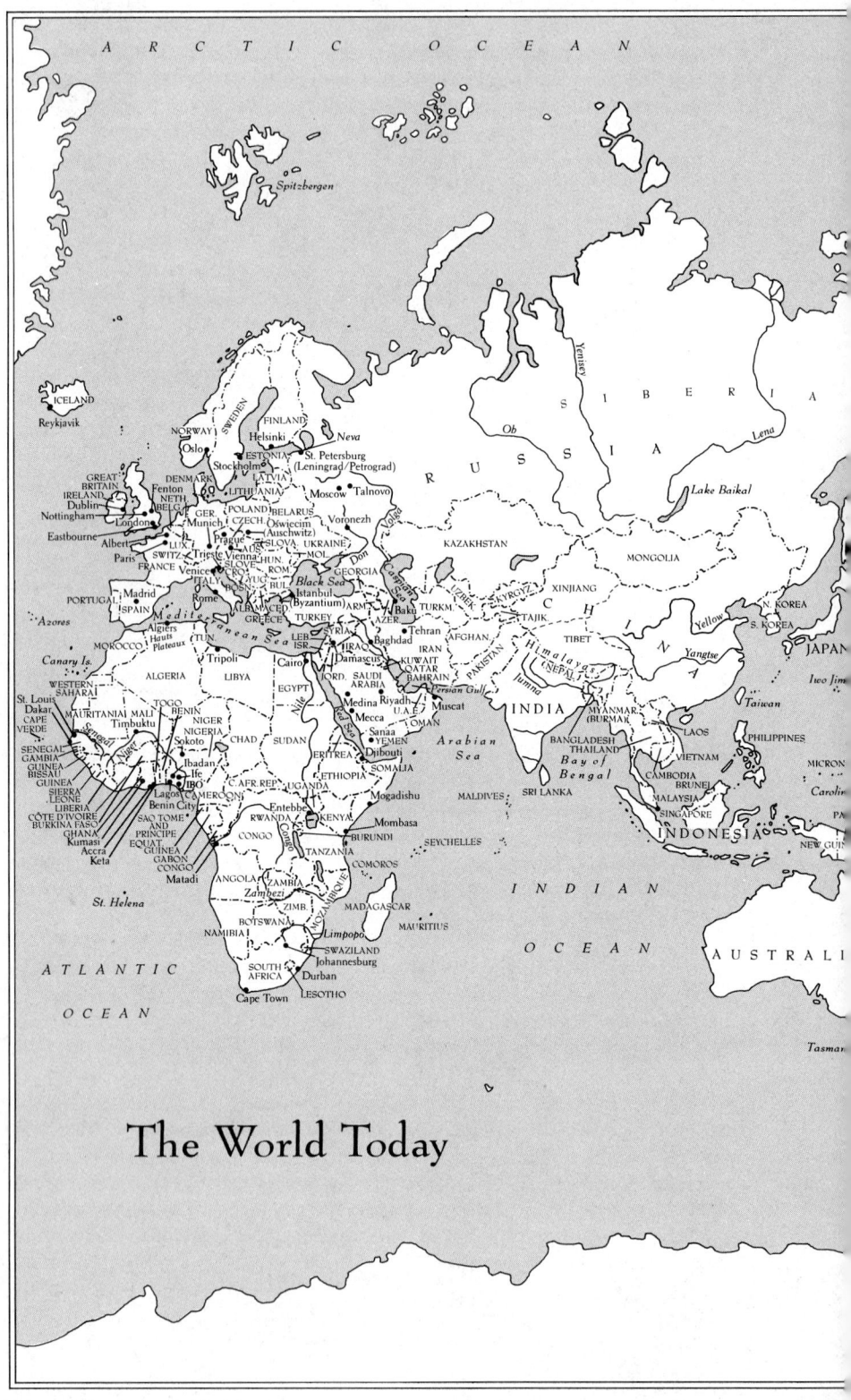

The World Today

GREENLAND

ALASKA

Nuuk

Labrador
Sea

C A N A D A

Bering Sea

Hudson
Bay

Aleutian Islands

NORTH

PACIFIC

OCEAN

Vancouver

Montreal
Ottawa
Toronto
Wingham

Missouri

UNITED

Colorado

San Francisco

STATES

Chicago
Ohio

New York
Washington, D.C.

ATLANTIC

NAVAJO Taos
ZUNI
LAGUNA

Los Angeles

Rio Grande

Mississippi

OCEAN

HAWAII
Honolulu

MEXICO

Key West

DOMINICAN
REPUBLIC

Mexico City

Havana
CUBA
BELIZE
JAMAICA

HAITI PUERTO RICO

Guadeloupe
Martinique
St. Lucia
Bridgetown
Barbados

MARSHALL
ISLANDS

GUATEMALA
EL SALVADOR
HONDURAS
NICARAGUA
COSTA RICA
PANAMA

Caribbean Sea

Caracas
VENEZUELA

GUYANA
SURINAME
FR. GUIANA

NAURU

KIRIBATI

Bogotá
COLOMBIA

TUVALU

Quito
ECUADOR

Galapagos Is.

Amazon

SOLOMON
ISLANDS

B R A Z I L

Recife

VANUATU

WESTERN
SAMOA

Samoa Is.

French Polynesia

PERU

Lima

La Paz
BOLIVIA

BORORO

Brasília

FIJI

TONGA

Tahiti

CHILE

Asunción

Paraná

Rio de
Janeiro
São Paulo
PARAGUAY
URUGUAY

New Caledonia

SOUTH

PACIFIC

Santiago

Buenos Aires
ARGENTINA

Montevideo

NEW
ZEALAND

OCEAN

Falkland Is.

Antarctic
Peninsula

Chazaud

Masterpieces of the
Twentieth Century:
Contemporary Explorations

Modernism became something wholly different after the midcentury, separating into a profusion of styles and perspectives that express the range and diversity of contemporary cultural experience. Writers in the latter half of the century see their newly canonized predecessors—Joyce, Proust, Eliot, Woolf, Mann, and Stevens, for example—as part of a "high modernism" that champions formal innovation but preserves its roots in mainstream thought. In this view, the high modernist quest for more-profound insight and inclusive vision does not so much break with the past as it continues an idealist Western tradition that reaches back to Homer and the Bible. In seeking to uncover what is essentially human, the argument runs, this idealism fails to take into account the stubborn diversity of human backgrounds and points of view. Yet the late-twentieth-century writer cannot afford to ignore such diversity, which is increasingly visible when events in Asia, Africa, Europe, and the Americas are in the daily news, the United Nations has 185 member nations, and over six thousand languages are spoken around the world. The advances of science and social theory, moreover, suggest that basic concepts need to be rephrased to explain that any description of reality is only approximate (Heisenberg's uncertainty principle), that any logical system is incomplete because it cannot see itself from an exterior perspective (Gödel), and that we construct our image of reality on the basis of shifting patterns of perception (Freud). Contemporary writers do not necessarily hunt for a central motivating principle, therefore, but give difference its due; instead of revealing profundity, they present the tantalizing play of surfaces, hinting at a human reality that is not easily organized into coherent systems but remains basically "jagged" (Ezra Pound's term).

It would be a mistake, nonetheless, to assume a complete rupture in style and vision. First of all, there are writers such as Solzhenitsyn, who celebrates the past as a means to counteract contemporary decadence. Moreover, if the modernist revolution retained connections with its past, the same may be said for its successors. Contemporary writers have not forgotten Joyce's playful language and his emphasis on the textures of local experience, Proust's interrogation of the way memory reshapes our picture of the world, Eliot's tantalizing juxtaposition of fragments of reality, Stevens's provoking contrasts of concrete and ideal, Mann's strong sense of living in a particular moment in history, or Woolf's analysis of socially created images of identity (especially for women). Instead, they profit from modernist innovations in language and perspective at the same time that they find different ways to articulate the world of *their* experience. The diversity and multiple perspectives that characterize twentieth-century geopolitics and science also shape artistic tradition and even the way we go about reading literary works. In the latter part of the twentieth century, no single view of reality is universally accepted, and no one model of artistic excellence. We are already involved in "contemporary explorations."

What, then, of masterpieces? When there are so many different perspectives, is it still possible to single out certain works as models for appreciation? In many instances, the word *masterpiece* has simply become a bland term of praise. Book reviewers enthusiastically inform their readers that they are in the presence of a "contemporary masterpiece," even if most of these works will not be read fifty years later. This is not a new problem, for each age has its own disagreements about what is worth preserving and why. Many works currently accepted as masterpieces—including selections presented earlier in this anthology—were shocking or under-valued when they were written. Their authors were attacked, brought to trial, or simply ignored because they violated social conventions or flouted academic rules. If these works have been preserved when their best-selling competitors are forgotten, the reason is that they have proven more interesting in the long run: they can bear reading and rereading. They have survived what has been called the test of time, providing stimulus and satisfaction for generations of readers in different situations and cultural contexts.

The authors presented in this section, from Jorge Luis Borges to Chinua Achebe and Leslie Marmon Silko, are contemporary writers whose impact over recent decades indicates that they, too, will be read by succeeding generations. They represent a great range of style and subject matter. Some experiment with games of language and perspective, demonstrating how language shapes our grasp of reality. Others prefer a traditionally realist style, depicting major issues that have marked twentieth-century culture. Still others blend realistic discourse with religious or visionary dimensions, hinting at a further truth that surpasses physical description.

One of the best-known movements in late-twentieth-century Western literature carries experiments with language to an extreme. Often called postmodernism or poststructuralism, it is a style that plays with allusions, interruptions, contradictions, and blurred reference, as if to disorient a reader who seeks to reduce human events to one demonstrated meaning. Where high modernism wished to reveal a core of profound experience through innovative form, these rhetorical writers are suspicious of profundity: calling something "profound," after all, implies that it is specially true and valuable, and reflects the speaker's own value judgment. Modern authors who wish to avoid such judgments will forego images of depth and profundity and limit themselves to inconclusive surface images. Thus Alain Robbe-Grillet resists drawing conclusions when he gives conflicting versions of a single scene in *The Secret Room:* the only conclusions will belong to his readers, tantalized by inconsistency and forced to "write" their own solutions. Interruptions and hesitant allusions create a significant pattern in *The Barking,* as Ingeborg Bachmann uses the broken rhythms of conver-sation between a mother and daughter-in-law to show how both have been unable to articulate the dominant truth of their lives, namely the sadistic cruelty of the son and husband, Leo. Again, the reader must piece things together and spell out relation-ships. Samuel Beckett is often taken as the arch-example of this writerly style and its philosophy. In *Endgame,* he uses spare dialogue and a nearly barren stage to invite readers and playgoers to fill in the blanks of meaning. Such arbitrary constructions of meaning are a recurrent theme in *Endgame,* which therefore assumes the status of a text reflecting on its own nature—a prize theme of postmodernists.

Readers will find that certain easily identified strategies are at work in much of this literature, strategies whose general aim is to avoid creating any sense of completeness or any central reference point. In fiction, the implied authorial personality (the co-ordinating core, for example, of Proust's great novel) is replaced with an anonymous and even self-contradictory narrative viewpoint (the "unnameable" narrator in Beck-ett's novel of that name, or the impersonal and contradictory narrative perspective in Robbe-Grillet's *The Secret Room*). Just as there is no unified authorial perspective, so individual characters do not develop a consistent psychological identity. Instead, they must be read moment by moment, in terms of the specific situations in which they appear. Like Hamm and Clov in Beckett's *Endgame,* such characters interact in a meaningless void, acting and reacting inside a permanent present, located in an ambiguously allusive situation that cannot be defined in external terms. Even the time in which they appear does not seem to have any solid chronological basis. It leads nowhere: in *Endgame*, we are not sure whether the action of the play concludes or is simply part of a repetitive pattern. Time is similarly evasive in other works: in *The Secret Room,* it moves backward; in Jorge Luis Borges's *The Garden of Forking Paths,* it is a labyrinth of parallel universes. All three authors choose to create a new reality through words, rather than reproducing realistic circumstances. In doing so, they suggest that there is really no difference: we always use words to describe (and, therefore, shape) reality. The line is not always easy to draw: Luigi Pirandello, Marcel Proust, Bertolt Brecht, and particularly Franz Kafka and James Joyce are experimental modernist writers who have also been called precursors of postmodernism.

Many of the writers in this section—those as far apart as Richard Wright, Alexander Solzhenitsyn, Doris Lessing, Tadeusz Borowski, Chinua Achebe, and Alice Munro—choose to work in a more realistic tradition. Writing in Russia, Rhodesia (Zimbabwe), Poland, Nigeria, Canada, and the southern United States, they give their fictions the appearance of documentary reality, whether it be life in a small town, scenes of racial and cultural conflict, or descriptions of the concentration camp experience during the World War II Holocaust. Their work does not call attention to its own textuality but links pictures of everyday life with social and psychological issues. Wright's depiction of Dave Saunders in *The Man Who Was Almost a Man* uses a poverty-stricken black community in the South as the setting for an adolescent crisis that involves gun ownership and the measure of manhood. Solzhenitsyn describes Matryona's life and death in an obscure Russian village, dramatizing in the process ethical tensions within modern Russian society. Protagonists in Lessing and Achebe are firmly rooted in their different African environments, and their personal evolution is intertwined with the history of colonialism and racial conflict. Munro evokes small-town life in Ontario but also a young girl's startled recognition that the most ordinary relationships are made of impenetrable layers of experience. Tadeusz Borowski, giving a bleak and unremittingly factual account of life in the Auschwitz-Birkenau concentration camp, describes competing struggles for physical and spiritual survival and raises fundamental questions about human nature.

Sometimes the most concrete and quasi-documentary descriptions suddenly take on a different life, however, expanding into new, mysterious, and even magical realms. Such is the work of Gabriel García Márquez, the Colombian "magical realist" whose portrayal of a fatally ill political campaigner blurs the frontiers between appearance and reality, with paper birds and butterflies that fly out to sea or perch on a wall and a traveling facade that pictures a prosperous village in the voter's future. A religious dimension mysteriously presents itself in Mahfouz's *Zaabalawi,* in which the protagonist's search throughout modern, Westernized Cairo is also a metaphorical quest to rediscover God. Lodged in another tradition, Silko's *Yellow Woman* uses its setting in the American Southwest as a point of departure for a (possibly) mystical meeting based on Laguna Indian legend.

Whether contemporary writers experiment with form or probe local experience, they all have something to say about cultural identity. Even Borges's insular work draws on an encyclopedic awareness of different periods and civilizations. Perspectives multiply as it appears that we will discover human nature—if at all—only by juxtaposing many diverse and fluid images. Chinua Achebe describes this impulse to see life from different angles in terms of an old Igbo belief: "Wherever Something stands, Something Else will stand beside it. Nothing is absolute." Without diminishing the description of social reality in earlier-twentieth-century literature, it is possible to say that Western literature in the latter half of the twentieth century has given unprecedented recognition to different ethnic, sexual, and cultural identities, both depicted as subject matter and embodied in narrative perspective. In many ways, the pluralism of literary styles and the willingness to blur the boundaries of previous generic and descriptive conventions correspond to the diversity of a new geopolitical age and the increasing sophistication of scientific theory. As a result, the canonical core of the Western tradition is seen in a richer perspective, and the tradition itself evolves and expands. What was once a simplified model of the Western heritage has turned out, on examination, to be much more heterogeneous and much more interesting.

FURTHER READING

Daniel R. Schwarz, *Reconfiguring Modernism: Explorations in the Relationships between Modern Art and Modern Literature* (1997), is a comparative study. Ihab and Sally Hassan, eds., *Essays in Innovation/Renovation: New Perspectives on the Humanities* (1983), explores change in contemporary Western culture. Marjorie Perloff, *The Poetics of Indeterminacy* (1981), has significance beyond its primary focus on contemporary English and American poetry stemming from the French tradition. See also Perloff, ed., *Postmodern Genres* (1989), for a collection of essays on postmodernism in art and literature.Susan Rubin Suleiman, *Subversive Intent: Gender, Politics, and the Avant garde* (1990), analyzes the cultural implications of avant-garde artistic practices. Jean-Michel Rabate, *The Ghosts of Modernity* (1996), uses poststructural methods to reread the history of modernity; it includes references to Symbolist writers. Nancy K. Miller, ed., *The Poetics of Gender* (1986), presents essays on various aspects of feminist criticism. Elise Boulding, *The Underside of History: A View of Women through Time* (1992), complements traditional histories by drawing attention to the position and contributions of women. Sarah Lawall, ed., *Reading World Literature: Theory, History, Practice* (1994), includes a theoretical introduction to the subject of world literature and twelve essays on specific topics.

CONTEMPORARY EXPLORATIONS

TEXTS	CONTEXTS
1944 Jorge Luis Borges, *The Garden of Forking Paths*	
	1945 World War II ends with dropping of atomic bombs on Hiroshima and Nagasaki • United Nations, Arab League founded
	1946 Churchill's "Iron Curtain" speech marks beginning of Cold War • Pan-African Federation formed
	1947 Religious massacres accompany partition of India and Pakistan into independent states • Transistor invented
1948 Ezra Pound, *Pisan Cantos* • Tadeusz Borowski, *Ladies and Gentlemen, to the Gas Chamber*	**1948** Creation of Jewish state in Palestine
	1949 Communist People's Republic of China established • Apartheid instituted in South Africa
	1950–1953 Korean War involves North and South Korea, the United Nations, and China
1952 Ralph Ellison, *Invisible Man*	**1952** Revolution in Egypt, which becomes a republic in 1953 • First hydrogen bomb
	1953 Discovery of DNA structure launches modern genetic science
1955 Alain Robbe-Grillet, *The Voyeur*	
	1956 First Congress of Black Writers meets in Paris
1957 Samuel Beckett, *Endgame*	
1958 Chinua Achebe, *Things Fall Apart*	**1958** European Common Market established • Algerian War of Independence (1958–1962)
1960 Marguerite Duras, *Hiroshima mon amour*	**1960–1962** Independence for Belgian Congo, Uganda, Tanganyika, Nigeria
	1961 Soviet astronaut orbits Earth
1962 Doris Lessing, *The Golden Notebook* • Alain Robbe-Grillet, *Snapshots*, which includes *The Secret Room*	**1962–1973** United States engaged in Vietnam War
1963 Anna Akhmatova, *Requiem* • Naguib Mahfouz, *God's World*, which includes *Zaabalawi* • Alexander Solzhenitsyn, *Matryona's Home*	
	1966 First Dakar Arts Festival provides showcase for African culture
1967 Gabriel García Márquez, *One Hundred Years of Solitude*	

Boldface titles indicate works in the anthology.

CONTEMPORARY EXPLORATIONS

TEXTS	CONTEXTS
1968 Alice Munro, *Dance of the Happy Shades,* which includes **Walker Brothers Cowboy**	
	1969 American astronaut is first man on moon
1970 Gabriel García Márquez, **Death Constant Beyond Love**	
1972 Ingeborg Bachmann, *Three Paths to the Lake,* which includes **The Barking**	
	1973 Arab oil producers cut off shipments to nations supporting Israel; ensuing energy crisis reshapes global economy
1980 Salman Rushdie, *Midnight's Children*	
1981 Leslie Marmon Silko, *Ceremony* and *Storyteller,* which includes **Yellow Woman**	1981 AIDS virus identified and named; kills six million worldwide by 1996
	1986 Nuclear disaster in Chernobyl spreads radiation contamination throughout Europe
	1987 World stock market crash
	1989 Mikhail Gorbachev restructures the Soviet state • Berlin Wall demolished
	1990 East and West Germany united
	1991 United States and USSR agree to arms reduction • Economic chaos and nationalist unrest bring end of Soviet Union
	1992 Rio Earth Summit: 178 nations discuss global environmental damage and disagree on economic responsibility • Fighting between Christian Serbs and Muslim Croats marks beginning of ethnic wars in the former Yugoslavia; UN troops intervene and effect temporary peace
	1993 European Community, the West's largest trading unit, formed; talks begin on a common currency
	1994 Nelson Mandela becomes president of South Africa after first multiracial elections • Israel and PLO sign peace agreement and begin negotiating its conditions
	1997 Scientists in Scotland create Dolly, the clone of an adult sheep

JORGE LUIS BORGES
1899–1986

Although other modernist writers are known for their formal innovations, it is the Argentinian Jorge Luis Borges who represents, above all, the gamelike or playful aspect of literary creation. The "real world" is only one of the possible realities in Borges's multiple universe, which treats history, fantasy, and science fiction as having equal claim on our attention: since they all can be imagined, they all are perhaps equally real. His is a world of pure thought, in which abstract fictional games are played out when an initial situation or concept is pushed to its elegantly logical extreme. If everything is possible, there is no need for the artificial constraints imposed by conventional artistic attempts to represent reality: no need for psychological consistency, for a realistic setting, or for a story that unfolds in ordinary time and space. The voice telling the story becomes lost inside the setting it creates, just as a drawing by Saul Steinberg or Maurits Escher depicts a pen drawing the rest of the landscape in which it appears. Not unexpectedly, this thorough immersion in the play of subjective imagination appealed to writers like the French "new novelists," who were experimenting with shifting perspectives and a refusal of objective reality. For a long time, Borges's European reputation outstripped his prestige in his native land.

Borges was born in Buenos Aires, Argentina, on August 24, 1899, to a prosperous family whose ancestors were distinguished in Argentinian history. The family moved early to a large house whose library and garden were to form an essential part of his literary imagination. His paternal grandmother being English, the young Borges knew English as soon as Spanish and was educated by an English tutor until he was nine. Traveling in Europe, the family was caught in Geneva at the outbreak of World War I; Borges attended secondary school in Switzerland and throughout the war, at which time he learned French and German. After the war they moved to Spain, where he associated with a group of young experimental poets known as the Ultraists. When Borges returned home in 1921, he founded his own group of Argentinian Ultraists (their mural-review, *Prisma,* was printed on sign paper and plastered on walls); became close friends with the philosopher Macedonio Fernandez, whose dedication to pure thought and linguistic intricacies greatly influenced his own attitudes; and contributed regularly to the avant-garde review *Martin Fierro,* at that time associated with an apolitical art for art's sake attitude quite at odds with that of the Boedo group of politically committed writers. Although devoted to pure art, Borges consistently opposed the military dictatorship of Juan Perón and made his political views plain in speeches and nonliterary writings even if they were not included in his fiction. His attitude did not go unnoticed: in 1946, the Perón regime removed him from the librarian's post that he had held since 1938 and offered him a job as a chicken inspector.

During the 1930s, Borges turned to short narrative pieces and in 1935 published a collection of sketches titled *Universal History of Infamy.* His more mature stories—brief, metaphysical fictions whose density and elegance at times approach poetry—came as an experiment after a head injury and operation in 1938. *The Garden of Forking Paths* (1941), his first major collection, introduced him to a wider public as an intellectual and idealist writer, whose short stories subordinated familiar techniques of character, scene, plot, and narrative voice to a central idea, which was often a philosophical concept. This concept was used not as a lesson or dogma but as the starting point of fantastic elaborations to entertain readers within the game of literature.

Borges's imaginative world is an immense labyrinth, a "garden of forking paths" in which images of mazes and infinite mirroring, cyclical repetition and recall, illustrate the effort of an elusive narrative voice to understand its own significance and that of the world. In *Borges and I,* he comments on the parallel existence of two Borgeses:

the one who exists in his work (the one his readers know) and the living, fleshly identity felt by the man who sets pen to paper. "Little by little, I am giving over everything to him . . . I do not know which one of us has written this page." Borges has written on the idea (derived from the British philosophers David Hume and George Berkeley) of the individual self as a cluster of different perceptions, and he further elaborates this notion in his fictional proliferation of identities and alternate realities. Disdaining the "psychological fakery" of realistic novels (the "draggy novel of characters"), he prefers writing that is openly artful, concerned with technique for its own sake, and invents its own multidimensional reality.

Stories in *The Garden of Forking Paths*, *Fictions* (1944), and *The Aleph* (1949) develop these themes in a variety of styles. Borges is fond of detective stories (and has written a number of them) in which the search for an elusive explanation, given carefully planted clues, matters more than how recognizable the characters may be. In *Death and the Compass*, a mysterious murderer leaves tantalizing traces that refer to points of the compass and lead the detective into a fatal trap that closes on him at a fourth compass point, symbolized by the architectural lozenges of the house in which he dies. The author composes an art of puzzles and discovery, a grand code that treats our universe as a giant library where meaning is locked away in endless hexagonal galleries (*The Library of Babel*), as an enormous lottery whose results are all the events of our lives (*The Lottery in Babylon*), as a series of dreams within dreams (*The Circular Ruins*), or as a small iridescent sphere containing all of the points in space (*The Aleph*). In *Pierre Menard, Author of the "Quixote,"* the narrator is a scholarly reviewer of a certain fictitious Menard, whose masterwork has been to rewrite *Don Quixote* as if it were created today: not revise it, or yet transcribe it, but actually *reinvent* it word for word. He has succeeded; the two texts are "verbally identical" although Menard's modern version is "more ambiguous" than Cervantes's and thus "infinitely richer."

The imaginary universe of *Tlön, Uqbar, Orbis Tertius* exemplifies the mixture of fact and fiction with which Borges invites us to speculate on the solidity of our own world. The narrator is engaged in tracking down mysterious references to a country called Tlön, whose language, science, and literature are exactly opposite (and perhaps related to) our own. For example, the Tlönians use verbs or adjectives instead of nouns, since they have no concept of objects in space, and their science consists of an association of ideas in which the most astounding theory becomes the truth. In a postscript, the narrator reveals that the encyclopedia has turned out to be an immense scholarly hoax, yet also mentions that strange and unearthly objects—recognizably from Tlön—have recently been found.

The intricate, riddling, mazelike ambiguity of Borges's stories earned him international reputation and influence, to the point that a "style like Borges" has become a recognized term. In Argentina, he was given the prestigious post of Director of the National Library after the fall of Perón in 1955, and in 1961 he shared the International Publishers' Prize with Samuel Beckett. Always nearsighted, he grew increasingly blind in the mid-1950s and was forced to dictate his work. Nonetheless, he continued to travel, teach, and lecture in the company of his wife, Else Astete Milan, whom he married in 1967. Borges lived until his death in his beloved Buenos Aires, the city he celebrated in his first volume of poetry.

The Garden of Forking Paths begins as a simple spy story purporting to reveal the hidden truth about a German bombing raid during World War I. Borges alludes to documented facts: the geographic setting of the town of Albert and the Ancre River; a famous Chinese novel as Ts'ui Pên's proposed model; the *History of the World War (1914–1918)* published by B. H. Liddell Hart in 1934. Official history is undermined on the first page, however, both by the newly discovered confession of Dr. Yu Tsun and by his editor's suspiciously defensive footnote. Ultimately, Yu Tsun will learn from his ancestor's novel that history is a labyrinth of alternate possibilities (much like the "alternate worlds" of science fiction).

Borges executes his detective story with the traditional carefully planted clues. We know from the beginning that Yu Tsun—even though arrested—has successfully out-witted his rival, Captain Richard Madden; that his problem was to convey the name of a bombing target to his chief in Berlin; that he went to the telephone book to locate someone capable of transmitting his message; and that he had one bullet in his revolver. The cut-off phone call, the chase at the railroad station, and Madden's hasty arrival at Dr. Albert's house provide the excitement and pressure expected in a straightforward detective plot. Quite different spatial and temporal horizons open up halfway through, however. Coincidences—those chance relationships that might well have happened differently—introduce the idea of forking paths or alternate possible routes for history. Both Yu Tsun and Richard Madden are aliens trying to prove their worth inside their respective bureaucracies; the road to Stephen Albert's house turns mazelike always to the left; the only suitable name in the phone book—the man Yu Tsun must kill—is a Sinologist who has reconstructed the labyrinthine text written long ago by Yu Tsun's ancestor. This text, Ts'ui Pên's *The Garden of Forking Paths*, describes the universe as an infinite series of alternate versions of experience. In different versions of the story (taking place at different times), Albert and Yu Tsun are enemies—or friends—or not even there. The war and Richard Madden appear diminished (although no less real) in such a kaleidoscopic perspective, for they exist in only one of many possible dimensions. Yet Madden hurries up the walk, and cur-rent reality returns to demand Albert's death. It may seem as though the vision of other worlds in which Albert continues to exist (or is Yu Tsun's enemy) would soften the murderer's remorse for his deed. Instead, it makes more poignant the narrator's realization that in this dimension no other way could be found.

Useful biographies are James Woodall, *The Man in the Mirror of the Book: A Life of Jorge Luis Borges* (1996), and James Woodall, *Borges: A Life* (1996). Martin S. Stabb, *Borges Revisited* (1991), is a general introduction to the man and his work. Jaime Alazraki, ed., *Critical Essays on Jorge Luis Borges* (1987), assembles articles and reviews (including the 1970 *Autobiographical Essay*), four comparative essays, and a general introduction that offer valuable perspectives on Borges's writing as well as his impact on American writers and critics. Linda S. Maier, *Borges and the European Avant-garde* (1996), focuses on the European scene. Edna Aizenberg, ed., *Borges and His Successors: the Borgesian Impact on Literature and the Arts* (1990), is a wide-ranging collection of essays describing Borges as the precursor of postmodern fiction and criticism. Anna Maria Barrenechea, *Borges The Labyrinth Maker* (1965), dis-cusses Borges's intricate style, while Daniel Balderston, *Out of Context: Historical Reference and the Representation of Reality in Borges* (1993), focuses on the texts' manipulation of fictional and historical reality. Fernando Sorrentino, *Seven Conver-sations with Jorge Luis Borges* (1981), is a series of informal, widely ranging interviews from 1972, with a prefaced list of the topics of each conversation.

PRONOUNCING GLOSSARY

The following list uses common English syllables and stress accents to provide rough equiv-alents of selected words whose pronunciation may be unfamiliar to the general reader.

Borges: *bore'-kess*

Hsi P'êng: *shee pung*

Hung Lu Meng: *hoong low mung*

Ts'ui Pên: *tsoo-ay pun*

Yu Tsun: *yew tsoo-en*

The Garden of Forking Paths[1]

On page 22 of Liddell Hart's *History of World War I* you will read that an attack against the Serre-Montauban line by thirteen British divisions (supported by 1,400 artillery pieces), planned for the 24th of July, 1916, had to be postponed until the morning of the 29th. The torrential rains, Captain Liddell Hart comments, caused this delay, an insignificant one, to be sure.

The following statement, dictated, reread and signed by Dr. Yu Tsun, former professor of English at the *Hochschule* at Tsingtao,[2] throws an unsuspected light over the whole affair. The first two pages of the document are missing.

" . . . and I hung up the receiver. Immediately afterwards, I recognized the voice that had answered in German. It was that of Captain Richard Madden. Madden's presence in Viktor Runeberg's apartment meant the end of our anxieties and—but this seemed, *or should have seemed*, very secondary to me—also the end of our lives. It meant that Runeberg had been arrested or murdered.[3] Before the sun set on that day, I would encounter the same fate. Madden was implacable. Or rather, he was obliged to be so. An Irishman at the service of England, a man accused of laxity and perhaps of treason, how could he fail to seize and be thankful for such a miraculous opportunity: the discovery, capture, maybe even the death of two agents of the German Reich?[4] I went up to my room; absurdly I locked the door and threw myself on my back on the narrow iron cot. Through the window I saw the familiar roofs and the cloud-shaded six o'clock sun. It seemed incredible to me that that day without premonitions or symbols should be the one of my inexorable death. In spite of my dead father, in spite of having been a child in a symmetrical garden of Hai Feng, was I—now—going to die? Then I reflected that everything happens to a man precisely, precisely *now*. Centuries of centuries and only in the present do things happen; countless men in the air, on the face of the earth and the sea, and all that really is happening is happening to me . . . The almost intolerable recollection of Madden's horselike face banished these wanderings. In the midst of my hatred and terror (it means nothing to me now to speak of terror, now that I have mocked Richard Madden, now that my throat yearns for the noose) it occurred to me that that tumultuous and doubtless happy warrior did not suspect that I possessed the Secret. The name of the exact location of the new British artillery park on the River Ancre. A bird streaked across the gray sky and blindly I translated it into an airplane and that airplane into many (against the French sky) annihilating the artillery station with vertical bombs. If only my mouth, before a bullet shattered it, could cry out that secret name so it could be heard in Germany . . . My human voice was very weak. How might I make it carry to the ear of the Chief? To the ear of that sick and hateful man who knew nothing of Runeberg and me save that we were in Stafford

1. Translated by Donald A. Yates. 2. Or Ch'ing-tao; a major port in east China, part of territory leased to (and developed by) Germany in 1898. *Hochschule*: university (German). 3. "A hypothesis both hateful and odd. The Prussian spy Hans Rabener, alias Viktor Runeberg, attacked with drawn automatic the bearer of the warrant for his arrest, Captain Richard Madden. The latter, in self-defense, inflicted the wound which brought about Runeberg's death [Editor's note]." This entire note is by Borges as "Editor." 4. Empire (German).

shire[5] and who was waiting in vain for our report in his arid office in Berlin, endlessly examining newspapers . . . I said out loud: *I must flee.* I sat up noiselessly, in a useless perfection of silence, as if Madden were already lying in wait for me. Something—perhaps the mere vain ostentation of proving my resources were nil—made me look through my pockets. I found what I knew I would find. The American watch, the nickel chain and the square coin, the key ring with the incriminating useless keys to Runeberg's apartment, the notebook, a letter which I resolved to destroy immediately (and which I did not destroy), a crown, two shillings and a few pence, the red and blue pencil, the handkerchief, the revolver with one bullet. Absurdly, I took it in my hand and weighed it in order to inspire courage within myself. Vaguely I thought that a pistol report can be heard at a great distance. In ten minutes my plan was perfected. The telephone book listed the name of the only person capable of transmitting the message; he lived in a suburb of Fenton,[6] less than a half hour's train ride away.

I am a cowardly man. I say it now, now that I have carried to its end a plan whose perilous nature no one can deny. I know its execution was terrible. I didn't do it for Germany, no. I care nothing for a barbarous country which imposed upon me the abjection of being a spy. Besides, I know of a man from England—a modest man—who for me is no less great than Goethe.[7] I talked with him for scarcely an hour, but during that hour he was Goethe . . . I did it because I sensed that the Chief somehow feared people of my race—for the innumerable ancestors who merge within me. I wanted to prove to him that a yellow man could save his armies. Besides, I had to flee from Captain Madden. His hands and his voice could call at my door at any moment. I dressed silently, bade farewell to myself in the mirror, went downstairs, scrutinized the peaceful street and went out. The station was not far from my home, but I judged it wise to take a cab. I argued that in this way I ran less risk of being recognized; the fact is that in the deserted street I felt myself visible and vulnerable, infinitely so. I remember that I told the cab driver to stop a short distance before the main entrance. I got out with voluntary, almost painful slowness; I was going to the village of Ashgrove but I bought a ticket for a more distant station. The train left within a very few minutes, at eight-fifty. I hurried; the next one would leave at nine-thirty. There was hardly a soul on the platform. I went through the coaches; I remember a few farmers, a woman dressed in mourning, a young boy who was reading with fervor the *Annals* of Tacitus,[8] a wounded and happy soldier. The coaches jerked forward at last. A man whom I recognized ran in vain to the end of the platform. It was Captain Richard Madden. Shattered, trembling, I shrank into the far corner of the seat, away from the dreaded window.

From this broken state I passed into an almost abject felicity. I told myself that the duel had already begun and that I had won the first encounter by frustrating, even if for forty minutes, even if by a stroke of fate, the attack of my adversary. I argued that this slightest of victories foreshadowed a total victory. I argued (no less fallaciously) that my cowardly felicity proved that

5. County in west-central England.   6. In Lincolnshire, a county in east England.   7. Johann Wolfgang von Goethe (1749–1832), German poet, novelist, and dramatist; author of *Faust*; often taken as representing the peak of German cultural achievement.   8. Cornelius Tacitus (55–117), Roman historian whose *Annals* give a vivid picture of the decadence and corruption of the Roman Empire under Tiberius, Claudius, and Nero.

I was a man capable of carrying out the adventure successfully. From this weakness I took strength that did not abandon me. I foresee that man will resign himself each day to more atrocious undertakings; soon there will be no one but warriors and brigands; I give them this counsel: *The author of an atrocious undertaking ought to imagine that he has already accomplished it, ought to impose upon himself a future as irrevocable as the past.* Thus I proceeded as my eyes of a man already dead registered the elapsing of that day, which was perhaps the last, and the diffusion of the night. The train ran gently along, amid ash trees. It stopped, almost in the middle of the fields. No one announced the name of the station. "Ashgrove?" I asked a few lads on the platform. "Ashgrove," they replied. I got off.

A lamp enlightened the platform but the faces of the boys were in shadow. One questioned me, "Are you going to Dr. Stephen Albert's house?" Without waiting for my answer, another said, "The house is a long way from here, but you won't get lost if you take this road to the left and at every crossroads turn again to your left." I tossed them a coin (my last), descended a few stone steps and started down the solitary road. It went downhill, slowly. It was of elemental earth; overhead the branches were tangled; the low, full moon seemed to accompany me.

For an instant, I thought that Richard Madden in some way had penetrated my desperate plan. Very quickly, I understood that that was impossible. The instructions to turn always to the left reminded me that such was the common procedure for discovering the central point of certain labyrinths. I have some understanding of labyrinths: not for nothing am I the great grandson of that Ts'ui Pên who was governor of Yunnan and who renounced worldly power in order to write a novel that might be even more populous than the *Hung Lu Meng*[9] and to construct a labyrinth in which all men would become lost. Thirteen years he dedicated to these heterogeneous tasks, but the hand of a stranger murdered him—and his novel was incoherent and no one found the labyrinth. Beneath English trees I meditated on that lost maze: I imagined it inviolate and perfect at the secret crest of a mountain; I imagined it erased by rice fields or beneath the water; I imagined it infinite, no longer composed of octagonal kiosks and returning paths, but of rivers and provinces and kingdoms . . . I thought of a labyrinth of labyrinths, of one sinuous spreading labyrinth that would encompass the past and the future and in some way involve the stars. Absorbed in these illusory images, I forgot my destiny of one pursued. I felt myself to be, for an unknown period of time, an abstract perceiver of the world. The vague, living countryside, the moon, the remains of the day worked on me, as well as the slope of the road which eliminated any possibility of weariness. The afternoon was intimate, infinite. The road descended and forked among the now confused meadows. A high-pitched, almost syllabic music approached and receded in the shifting of the wind, dimmed by leaves and distance. I thought that a man can be an enemy of other men, of the moments of other men, but not of a country: not of fireflies, words, gardens, streams of water, sunsets. Thus I arrived before a tall, rusty gate. Between the iron bars I made out a poplar grove and a pavilion. I understood suddenly two things, the first trivial, the second almost

9. *The Dream of the Red Chamber* (1791) by Ts'ao Hsüeh-ch'in; the most famous Chinese novel, a love story and panorama of Chinese family life involving more than 430 characters. (Also called *The Story of the Stone*.)

unbelievable: the music came from the pavilion, and the music was Chinese. For precisely that reason I had openly accepted it without paying it any heed. I do not remember whether there was a bell or whether I knocked with my hand. The sparkling of the music continued.

From the rear of the house within a lantern approached: a lantern that the trees sometimes striped and sometimes eclipsed, a paper lantern that had the form of a drum and the color of the moon. A tall man bore it. I didn't see his face for the light blinded me. He opened the door and said slowly, in my own language: "I see that the pious Hsi P'êng persists in correcting my solitude. You no doubt wish to see the garden?"

I recognized the name of one of our consuls and I replied, disconcerted, "The garden?"

"The garden of forking paths."

Something stirred in my memory and I uttered with incomprehensible certainty, "The garden of my ancestor Ts'ui Pên."

"Your ancestor? Your illustrious ancestor? Come in."

The damp path zigzagged like those of my childhood. We came to a library of Eastern and Western books. I recognized bound in yellow silk several volumes of the Lost Encyclopedia, edited by the Third Emperor of the Luminous Dynasty but never printed.[1] The record on the phonograph revolved next to a bronze phoenix. I also recall a *famille rose*[2] vase and another, many centuries older, of that shade of blue which our craftsmen copied from the potters of Persia . . .

Stephen Albert observed me with a smile. He was, as I have said, very tall, sharp-featured, with gray eyes and a gray beard. He told me that he had been a missionary in Tientsin "before aspiring to become a Sinologist."

We sat down—I on a long, low divan, he with his back to the window and a tall circular clock. I calculated that my pursuer, Richard Madden, could not arrive for at least an hour. My irrevocable determination could wait.

"An astounding fate, that of Ts'ui Pên," Stephen Albert said. "Governor of his native province, learned in astronomy, in astrology and in the tireless interpretation of the canonical books, chess player, famous poet and calligrapher—he abandoned all this in order to compose a book and a maze. He renounced the pleasures of both tyranny and justice, of his populous couch, of his banquets and even of erudition—all to close himself up for thirteen years in the Pavilion of the Limpid Solitude. When he died, his heirs found nothing save chaotic manuscripts. His family, as you may be aware, wished to condemn them to the fire; but his executor—a Taoist or Buddhist monk—insisted on their publication."

"We descendants of Ts'ui Pên," I replied, "continue to curse that monk. Their publication was senseless. The book is an indeterminate heap of contradictory drafts. I examined it once: in the third chapter the hero dies, in the fourth he is alive. As for the other undertaking of Ts'ui Pên, his labyrinth . . ."

"Here is Ts'ui Pên's labyrinth," he said, indicating a tall lacquered desk.

---

1. The Yung-lo emperor of the Ming ("bright") Dynasty commissioned a massive encyclopedia between 1403 and 1408. A single copy of the 11,095 manuscript volumes was made in the mid-1500s; the original was later destroyed, and only 370 volumes of the copy remain today.   2. Pink family (French); refers to a Chinese decorative enamel ranging in color from an opaque pink to purplish rose. *Famille rose* pottery was at its best during the reign of Yung Chên (1723–1735).

"An ivory labyrinth!" I exclaimed. "A minimum labyrinth."

"A labyrinth of symbols," he corrected. "An invisible labyrinth of time. To me, a barbarous Englishman, has been entrusted the revelation of this diaphanous mystery. After more than a hundred years, the details are irretrievable; but it is not hard to conjecture what happened. Ts'ui Pên must have said once: *I am withdrawing to write a book.* And another time: *I am withdrawing to construct a labyrinth.* Every one imagined two works; to no one did it occur that the book and the maze were one and the same thing. The Pavilion of the Limpid Solitude stood in the center of a garden that was perhaps intricate; that circumstance could have suggested to the heirs a physical labyrinth. Ts'ui Pên died; no one in the vast territories that were his came upon the labyrinth; the confusion of the novel suggested to me that *it* was the maze. Two circumstances gave me the correct solution of the problem. One: the curious legend that Ts'ui Pên had planned to create a labyrinth which would be strictly infinite. The other: a fragment of a letter I discovered."

Albert rose. He turned his back on me for a moment; he opened a drawer of the black and gold desk. He faced me and in his hands he held a sheet of paper that had once been crimson, but was now pink and tenuous and cross-sectioned. The fame of Ts'ui Pên as a calligrapher had been justly won. I read, uncomprehendingly and with fervor, these words written with a minute brush by a man of my blood: *I leave to the various futures (not to all) my garden of forking paths.* Wordlessly, I returned the sheet. Albert continued:

"Before unearthing this letter, I had questioned myself about the ways in which a book can be infinite. I could think of nothing other than a cyclic volume, a circular one. A book whose last page was identical with the first, a book which had the possibility of continuing indefinitely. I remembered too that night which is at the middle of the Thousand and One Nights when Scheherazade[3] (through a magical oversight of the copyist) begins to relate word for word the story of the Thousand and One Nights, establishing the risk of coming once again to the night when she must repeat it, and thus on to infinity. I imagined as well a Platonic, hereditary work, transmitted from father to son, in which each new individual adds a chapter or corrects with pious care the pages of his elders. These conjectures diverted me; but none seemed to correspond, not even remotely, to the contradictory chapters of Ts'ui Pên. In the midst of this perplexity, I received from Oxford the manuscript you have examined. I lingered, naturally, on the sentence: *I leave to the various futures (not to all) my garden of forking paths.* Almost instantly, I understood: 'The garden of forking paths' was the chaotic novel; the phrase 'the various futures (not to all)' suggested to me the forking in time, not in space. A broad rereading of the work confirmed the theory. In all fictional works, each time a man is confronted with several alternatives, he chooses one and eliminates the others; in the fiction of Ts'ui Pên, he chooses—simultaneously—all of them. *He creates,* in this way, diverse futures, diverse times which themselves also proliferate and fork. Here, then, is the explanation of the novel's contradictions. Fang, let us say, has a secret; a stranger calls at his door; Fang resolves to kill him. Naturally, there are several possible outcomes: Fang can kill the intruder, the intruder can kill Fang, they

---

3. The narrator of the collection also known as the *Arabian Nights*, a thousand and one tales supposedly told by Scheherazade to her husband, Shahrayar, king of Samarkand, to postpone her execution.

both can escape, they both can die, and so forth. In the work of Ts'ui Pên, all possible outcomes occur; each one is the point of departure for other forkings. Sometimes, the paths of this labyrinth converge: for example, you arrive at this house, but in one of the possible pasts you are my enemy, in another, my friend. If you will resign yourself to my incurable pronunciation, we shall read a few pages."

His face, within the vivid circle of the lamplight, was unquestionably that of an old man, but with something unalterable about it, even immortal. He read with slow precision two versions of the same epic chapter. In the first, an army marches to a battle across a lonely mountain; the horror of the rocks and shadows makes the men undervalue their lives and they gain an easy victory. In the second, the same army traverses a palace where a great festival is taking place; the resplendent battle seems to them a continuation of the celebration and they win the victory. I listened with proper veneration to these ancient narratives, perhaps less admirable in themselves than the fact that they had been created by my blood and were being restored to me by a man of a remote empire, in the course of a desperate adventure, on a Western isle. I remember the last words, repeated in each version like a secret commandment: *Thus fought the heroes, tranquil their admirable hearts, violent their swords, resigned to kill and to die.*

From that moment on, I felt about me and within my dark body an invisible, intangible swarming. Not the swarming of the divergent, parallel and finally coalescent armies, but a more inaccessible, more intimate agitation that they in some manner prefigured. Stephen Albert continued:

"I don't believe that your illustrious ancestor played idly with these variations. I don't consider it credible that he would sacrifice thirteen years to the infinite execution of a rhetorical experiment. In your country, the novel is a subsidiary form of literature; in Ts'ui Pên's time it was a despicable form. Ts'ui Pên was a brilliant novelist, but he was also a man of letters who doubtless did not consider himself a mere novelist. The testimony of his contemporaries proclaims—and his life fully confirms—his metaphysical and mystical interests. Philosophic controversy usurps a good part of the novel. I know that of all problems, none disturbed him so greatly nor worked upon him so much as the abysmal problem of time. Now then, the latter is the only problem that does not figure in the pages of the *Garden*. He does not even use the word that signifies *time*. How do you explain this voluntary omission?"

I proposed several solutions—all unsatisfactory. We discussed them. Finally, Stephen Albert said to me:

"In a riddle whose answer is chess, what is the only prohibited word?"

I thought a moment and replied, "The word *chess*."

"Precisely," said Albert. "*The Garden of Forking Paths* is an enormous riddle, or parable, whose theme is time; this recondite cause prohibits its mention. To omit a word always, to resort to inept metaphors and obvious periphrases, is perhaps the most emphatic way of stressing it. That is the tortuous method preferred, in each of the meanderings of his indefatigable novel, by the oblique Ts'ui Pên. I have compared hundreds of manuscripts, I have corrected the errors that the negligence of the copyists has introduced, I have guessed the plan of this chaos, I have re-established—I believe I have re-established—the primordial organization, I have translated the entire work: it is clear to me that not once does he employ the word 'time.' The explanation is obvious: *The Garden of Forking Paths* is an incomplete, but not false, image of the universe as Ts'ui Pên conceived it. In contrast to Newton and Schopenhauer,[4] your ancestor did not believe in a uniform, absolute time. He believed in an infinite series of times, in a growing, dizzying net of divergent, convergent and parallel times. This network of times which approached one another, forked, broke off, or were unaware of one another for centuries, embraces *all* possibilities of time. We do not exist in the majority of these times; in some you exist, and not I; in others I, and not you; in others, both of us. In the present one, which a favorable fate has granted me, you have arrived at my house; in another, while crossing the garden, you found me dead; in still another, I utter these same words, but I am a mistake, a ghost."

"In every one," I pronounced, not without a tremble to my voice, "I am grateful to you and revere you for your re-creation of the garden of Ts'ui Pên."

"Not in all," he murmured with a smile. "Time forks perpetually toward innumerable futures. In one of them I am your enemy."

Once again I felt the swarming sensation of which I have spoken. It seemed to me that the humid garden that surrounded the house was infinitely saturated with invisible persons. Those persons were Albert and I, secret, busy and multiform in other dimensions of time. I raised my eyes and the tenuous nightmare dissolved. In the yellow and black garden there was only one man; but this man was as strong as a statue . . . this man was approaching along the path and he was Captain Richard Madden.

"The future already exists," I replied, "but I am your friend. Could I see the letter again?"

Albert rose. Standing tall, he opened the drawer of the tall desk; for the moment his back was to me. I had readied the revolver. I fired with extreme caution. Albert fell uncomplainingly, immediately. I swear his death was instantaneous—a lightning stroke.

The rest is unreal, insignificant. Madden broke in, arrested me. I have been condemned to the gallows. I have won out abominably; I have communicated to Berlin the secret name of the city they must attack. They bombed it yesterday; I read it in the same papers that offered to England the mystery of the learned Sinologist Stephen Albert who was murdered by a stranger, one Yu Tsun. The Chief had deciphered this mystery. He knew my problem was to indicate (through the uproar of the war) the city called Albert, and that I had found no other means to do so than to kill a man of that name. He does not know (no one can know) my innumerable contrition and weariness.

For Victoria Ocampo

---

4. German philosopher (1788–1860), whose concept of will proceeded from a concept of the self as enduring through time. In *Seven Conversations with Jorge Luis Borges*, Borges also comments on Schopenhauer's interest in the "oneiric [dreamlike] essence of life." Newton (1642–1727), English mathematician and philosopher best known for his formulation of laws of gravitation and motion.

SAMUEL BECKETT
1906–1989

The sparest, starkest representation of the human condition in all its "absurd" emptiness fills Samuel Beckett's novels and plays. Not that other authors do not concern themselves with the problem of representing reality, but where Pirandello plays with allusions to an elusive identity, Joyce with the stream of consciousness, and Proust with layers of the self reconstituted through affective memory, Beckett's world is haunted—like that of Kafka—by an absence of meaning at the core. Whether expressed by the protagonist's ramblings in the novels *Molloy* (1951), *Malone Dies* (1951), or *The Unnamable* (1953), by the stripped-down dialogue of the plays *Waiting for Godot* (1952) and *Endgame* (1957), or by the telegraphic style of a late novel, *How It Is* (1961), Beckett's characters engage in a desperate attempt to find or to create meaning for themselves. Born into a world without reason, they live out their lives waiting for an explanation that never comes and whose existence may be only a figment of their imagination. In the meantime, human relationships are reduced to the most elemental tensions of cruelty, hope, frustration, and disillusionment around themes of birth, death, human emotions, material obstacles, and unending consciousness. Beckett's comedy of errors is a bitter one and, even in its puns and parodies, draws heavily on what the author has described as "the power of the text to claw."

Like Joyce and Yeats, Beckett was born in Ireland; like Joyce, he chose to live abroad for most of his life. Born near Dublin on April 13, 1906, he was educated in Ireland and received a B.A. from Trinity College in 1927. From 1928 to 1930, he taught English at the École Normale Supérieure in Paris, where he met James Joyce and was for a while influenced by the older novelist's exuberant and punning use of language. Beckett wrote an essay on the early stages of Joyce's *Finnegans Wake* and later helped in the French translation of part of the book. In 1930 he entered a competition for a poem on the subject of time and won first prize with a ninety-eight-line (and seventeen-footnote) monologue, *Whoroscope*, spoken by the seventeenth-century French physicist and philosopher René Descartes. Beckett returned to Trinity College where he took an M.A. in 1931, published an essay on Proust, and stayed on the following year to teach French. It was a brief academic career, for he gave up teaching in 1932 and, after living in England, France, and Germany, made Paris his permanent home in 1937. Although two early novels, *Murphy* (1938) and *Watt* (1953), were written in English, Beckett was already turning to French as his preferred language for original composition; in the years after World War II, he wrote almost exclusively in French and only later translated (often with substantial changes) the same texts into English. He said that he wrote in French because it was easier to write "without style"—without the native speaker's temptation to elegance and virtuoso display. Although no generalization holds true for all cases, comparing the French and English versions of the same work often suggests just such a contrast, with the French text closer to basic grammatical forms and, therefore, possessing a harsher, less nuanced focus.

Whether comic or despairing (often both), Beckett's characters ring changes on the Cartesian image of the Rational Man that has been at the base of Western cultural attitudes ever since the philosopher René Descartes moved from specific questions about the physical sciences to the larger question of human existence. Descartes, like Beckett, went back to zero in order not to be led astray by any preconceived assumptions or doctrines. He doubted everything—except that he doubted, which in itself indicated that he was thinking and that if "I think, therefore I am" (*Cogito, ergo sum*). Upon that certainty Descartes erected a logical system for exploring the natural universe and explaining the human condition. Beckett is not so sure that logic allows us to know what we are looking at, or in fact to match up our terminology with reality at all. In *Watt*, the protagonist is caught in a peculiar hesitation inasmuch as things, "if they consented to be named, did so as it were with reluctance." He looks at a pot, but "it was not a pot, the more he looked, the more he reflected, the more he felt sure of that, that it was not a pot at all. It resembled a pot, it was almost a pot, but it was not a pot of which one could say, Pot, pot and be comforted." The gentle bewilderment that Watt feels turns bitter and more dangerous in later novels such as the famous trilogy (*Molloy, Malone Dies,* and *The Unnamable*), or in *How It Is,* which refuses to present any image of rational control as it murmurs, free of punctuation, the monologue of an unstructured consciousness inside an accompanying "quaqua [bzzz bzzz] on all sides."

The narrative perspective in the trilogy moves from a series of related monologue stories, in which narrators come more and more to resemble one another, to the ramblings of an "unnamable" speaker who seems to represent them all at the end. In *Molloy,* there are two interlocking points of view, as first Molloy tells of setting out on a bicycle to visit his bedridden mother, a search that takes him months and leads him all over (with many echoes of Homer's *Odyssey*). The last we hear of Molloy is that he is crippled and has lost his bicycle but is determined still to proceed if only by rolling; Moran takes over at that point and describes a corresponding search for Molloy in the course of which he loses his bicycle, is crippled, and ends up frustrated back home. The next novel, *Malone Dies,* is similarly divided between protagonists, even if in the mind of a single narrator: a dying and bedridden Malone writes the diary of his last days and also composes the story of Macmann, who is to die at the same moment as Malone and apparently does so as the novel ends. The last in the trilogy, *The Unnamable,* has no fixed authorial perspective or claim to responsibility. "I'm in words, made of words." Someone (unnamed and—by now—clearly unnamable) is seated in an undefined gray space and time, writing a series of stories that may be the tales of Malone, Malloy, and Moran, or of a new Mahood who also becomes Worm, who may in turn be the narrator writing stories about himself; or it may simply evoke the act of storytelling as it creates fictions of life to establish some mode of reality. In 1949, when the trilogy was just complete, Beckett published a dialogue on modern art that described the artist's disgust with traditional art's "puny exploits . . . doing a little better the same old thing" and his preference for "the expression that there is nothing to express, nothing with which to express, nothing from which to express, no power to express, no desire to express, together with the obligation to express." The disintegration of narrative perspective in Beckett's fiction is one means of denying that there is a knowable "something to express," or an authoritative point of view from which to express "nothing."

How can one possibly make a convincing stage play out of "nothing"? The popularity of Beckett's first performed play, *Waiting for Godot* (French version presented 1953; English, 1955), showed that absurdist theater—with its empty, repetitive dialogue, its grotesquely bare yet apparently symbolic settings, and its refusal to build to a dramatic climax—had meaning even for audiences used to theatrical realism and logically developing plots. These audiences found two clownlike tramps, Vladimir and Estragon (Didi and Gogo), talking, quarreling, falling down, contemplating suicide, and generally filling up time with conversation that ranges from vaudeville patter to metaphysical speculation as they wait under a tree for a Godot who never comes. Instead, the two are joined in the middle of each act by another grotesque pair: the rich Pozzo and his brutally abused servant Lucky, whom he leads around by a rope tied to his neck. The popular interpretation of "Godot" as a diminutive for "God," and of the play as a statement of existential anguish at the inexplicable human condition, is scarcely defused by Beckett's caution that "If by Godot I had meant God, I would have said God." Yet identifying Godot is less important than identifying the ignominious plight on stage as symbolically our own and identifying *with* the characters as they express the anxious, often repugnant but also comic picture of human relationships in an absurd universe.

After the popular success of *Waiting for Godot,* Beckett wrote *Endgame* (French version performed 1957; English, 1958) and a series of stage plays and brief pieces for the radio. The stage plays have the same bare yet striking settings: *Krapp's Last Tape* (1958) presents an old man sitting at a table with his tape recorder, recalling a love affair thirty years past; and *Happy Days* (1961) portrays a married couple in which Winnie, the wife, chatters ceaselessly about her possessions although she is buried up to her waist in the first act and to her neck in the second. When Beckett received the Nobel Prize for Literature in 1969, he was recognized as the purest exponent of the twentieth century's chief philosophical dilemma: the notion of the "absurd," or the grotesque contradiction between human attempts to discover meaning in life and the simultaneous conviction that there is no "meaning" available that we have not created ourselves. *Endgame,* often called Beckett's major achievement, is a prime example of this dilemma.

When the curtain rises on *Endgame,* it is as though the world were awaking from sleep. The sheets draping the furniture and central character are taken off, and Hamm sets himself in motion like an actor or chess pawn: "Me . . . to play." Yet we are also near the end for, as the title implies, nothing new will happen; an "endgame" is the final phase of a chess game, the stage at which the end is predictably in sight although the play must still be completed. Throughout, the theme of "end," "finish," "no more" is sounded, even while Hamm notes the passage of time: "Something is taking its course." But time does not lead anywhere; it is either past or present, and always barren. The past exists as Nagg's and Nell's memories, as Hamm's story, which may or may not describe Clov's entry into the home, and as a period in which Clov once loved Hamm. The present shows four characters dwindling away, alone in a dead world, caught between visions of dusty hell and dreams of life reborn. In one of the biblical echoes that permeate the play, Hamm and Clov repeatedly evoke the last words of the crucified Jesus in the Gospel according to St. John: "It is finished." But this is not a biblical morality play, and *Endgame* describes a world not of divine but of self-creation. Hamm may be composing and directing the entire performance: a storyteller and playwright with "asides" and "last soliloquy" whose "dialogue" keeps Clov on stage against his will, a mad artist who (when looking out the window onto a flourishing world) can see only dust and ashes, or a magician presiding over an imaginary kingdom who concludes an inner story and unavailing prayer with Prospero's line from Shakespeare's *The Tempest* (4.1.148): "Our revels now are ended." Or he may simply be aware of their lives *as* a performance without any other meaning: Shakespeare's passage continues later: "We are such stuff / As dreams are made on, and our little life / Is rounded with a sleep." The situation at the end of the play is little changed—only barer, as Hamm discards his stick, whistle, and dog, "reckoning closed and story ended." Yet Clov is still waiting to leave as Hamm covers his face, and it is not impossible that the play will resume in precisely the same terms tomorrow.

Endgame, like *Waiting for Godot* (and like Kafka's stories), has been given a number of symbolic interpretations. Some refer to Beckett's love of wordplay: Hamm as Hamm-actor, Hammlet, Hammer, and Nag and Nell as shortened forms of *Nägel* and *nello,* German and Italian words for "nail," which are invoked as crucifixion themes suggesting the martyrdom of humanity. The setting of a boxlike room with two windows is seen as a skull, the seat of consciousness, or (emphasizing the bloody handkerchief and the reference to fontanelles—the soft spot in the skull of a newborn child) as a womb. The characters' isolation in a dead world after an unnamed catastrophe (which may be Hamm's fault) suggests the world after atomic holocaust; or, for those who recall Beckett's fascination with the apathetic figure of Belacqua waiting, in the Purgatory of Dante's *Divine Comedy,* for his punishment to begin, it evokes an image of pre-Purgatorial consciousness. The ashcans in which Hamm has "bottled" his parents, and the general cruelty between characters, are to represent the dustbin of modern Western civilized values. Hamm and Clov represent the uneasy adjustment of soul and body, the class struggle of rich and poor, or the master-slave relationship in all senses (including the slave's acceptance of his victimization). Clearly Beckett has created a structure that accommodates all these readings while authorizing none.

He himself said to director Alan Schneider that he was less interested in symbolism than in describing a "local situation," an interaction of four characters in a given set of circumstances, and that the audience's interpretation was its own responsibility.

Beckett both authorized and denied these interpretations. He pruned down an earlier, more anecdotal two-act play to achieve *Endgame*'s skeletal plot and almost anonymous characters, and in doing so created a structure that immediately elicits the reader's instinct to "fill in the blanks." His puns and allusions openly point to a further meaning that *may* be contained in the implied reference, but may also be part of an infinite regress of meaning—expressing the "absurd" itself. Working against too heavy an insistence on symbolic meanings is the fact that the play is also funny—especially when performed on stage. The characters popping out of ashcans, the jerky, repetitive motions with which Clov carries out his master's commands, and the often obscene vaudeville patter accompanied by appropriate gestures, all provide a comic perspective that keeps *Endgame* from sinking into tragic despair. The intellectual distance offered by comedy is entirely in keeping with the more somber side of the play, which rejects pathos and constantly drags its characters' escapist fancies down to the minimal facts of survival: food, shelter, sleep, painkiller. Thus it is possible to say that *Endgame* describes—but only among many other things—what it is like to be alive, declining toward death in a world without meaning.

Samuel Beckett, *Endgame: with a Revised Text* (1992), ed. S. E. Gontarski, is a revised text based on productions directed or supervised by Beckett; the attached theatrical notebooks often clarify situations and settings. Arthur N. Athanason, *Endgame: The Ashbin Play* (1993), is a brief introduction; and Alexander Astro, *Understanding Samuel Beckett* (1990), discusses the complete work with interpretations emphasizing cultural and linguistic aspects. Andrew Kennedy, *Samuel Beckett* (1989), provides a compact, comprehensive overview of Beckett's work with separate chapters on the major plays and novels. Richard Begam, *Samuel Beckett and the End of Modernity* (1996), discusses Beckett in the context of postmodernism. Useful biographies are Deirdre Bair, *Samuel Beckett: A Biography* (1993); Anthony Cronin, *Samuel Beckett: The Last Modernist* (1996); Lois G. Gordon, *The World of Samuel Beckett, 1906–1946* (1996); and James Knowlson, *Damned to Fame: The Life of Samuel Beckett* (1996). Hugh Kenner, *Samuel Beckett: A Critical Study* (1974), is an earlier but still valuable discussion of Beckett's work, and Steven Connor, ed., *Waiting for Godot and Endgame—Samuel Beckett* (1992), includes eleven essays, of which seven are wholly or partially on *Endgame*.

Endgame[1]

For Roger Blin

CHARACTERS

NAGG
NELL
HAMM
CLOV

Bare interior.
Gray light.
Left and right back, high up, two small windows, curtains drawn.
Front right, a door. Hanging near door, its face to wall, a picture.

1. Translated by the author.

Front left, touching each other, covered with an old sheet, two ashbins.
Center, in an armchair on castors, covered with an old sheet, HAMM.
Motionless by the door, his eyes fixed on HAMM, CLOV. *Very red face.*
Brief tableau.

[CLOV *goes and stands under window left. Stiff, staggering walk. He looks up at window left. He turns and looks at window right. He goes and stands under window right. He looks up at window right. He turns and looks at window left. He goes out, comes back immediately with a small step-ladder, carries it over and sets it down under window left, gets up on it, draws back curtain. He gets down, takes six steps (for example) towards window right, goes back for ladder, carries it over and sets it down under window right, gets up on it, draws back curtain. He gets down, takes three steps towards window left, goes back for ladder, carries it over and sets it down under window left, gets up on it, looks out of window. Brief laugh. He gets down, takes one step towards window right, goes back for ladder, carries it over and sets it down under window right, gets up on it, looks out of window. Brief laugh. He gets down, goes with ladder towards ashbins, halts, turns, carries back ladder and sets it down under window right, goes to ashbins, removes sheet covering them, folds it over his arm. He raises one lid, stoops and looks into bin. Brief laugh. He closes lid. Same with other bin. He goes to* HAMM, *removes sheet covering him, folds it over his arm. In a dressing-gown, a stiff toque*[2] *on his head, a large blood-stained handkerchief over his face, a whistle hanging from his neck, a rug over his knees, thick socks on his feet,* HAMM *seems to be asleep.* CLOV *looks him over. Brief laugh. He goes to door, halts, turns towards auditorium.*]

CLOV [*Fixed gaze, tonelessly.*]   Finished, it's finished, nearly finished, it must be nearly finished. [*Pause.*] Grain upon grain, one by one, and one day, suddenly, there's a heap, a little heap, the impossible heap. [*Pause.*] I can't be punished any more. [*Pause.*] I'll go now to my kitchen, ten feet by ten feet by ten feet, and wait for him to whistle me. [*Pause.*] Nice dimensions, nice proportions, I'll lean on the table, and look at the wall, and wait for him to whistle me.

[*He remains a moment motionless, then goes out. He comes back immediately, goes to window right, takes up the ladder and carries it out. Pause.* HAMM *stirs. He yawns under the handkerchief. He removes the handkerchief from his face. Very red face. Black glasses.*]

HAMM   Me— [*He yawns.*]—to play.[3] [*He holds the handkerchief spread out before him.*] Old Stancher![4] [*He takes off his glasses, wipes his eyes, his face, the glasses, puts them on again, folds the handkerchief and puts it back neatly in the breast-pocket of his dressing-gown. He clears his throat, joins the tips of his fingers.*] Can there be misery— [*He yawns.*]—loftier than mine? No doubt. Formerly. But now? [*Pause.*] My father? [*Pause.*] My mother? [*Pause.*] My . . . dog? [*Pause.*] Oh I am willing to believe they suffer as much as such creatures can suffer. But does that mean their sufferings equal mine? No doubt. [*Pause.*] No, all is a— [*He yawns.*]—bsolute, [*Proudly.*] the bigger a man is the fuller he is. [*Pause. Gloomily.*] And the emptier. [*He sniffs.*] Clov! [*Pause.*] No, alone. [*Pause.*] What dreams! Those forests! [*Pause.*] Enough, it's time it ended, in the

2. A fitted cloth hat with little or no brim, sometimes indicating official status as with a judge's toque.   3. Hamm announces that it is his move at the beginning of *Endgame:* the comparison is with a game of chess, of which the "endgame" is the final stage.   4. The handkerchief that stanches his blood.

shelter too. [*Pause.*] And yet I hesitate, I hesitate to . . . to end. Yes, there it is, it's time it ended and yet I hesitate to— [*He yawns.*]—to end. [*Yawns.*] God, I'm tired, I'd be better off in bed. [*He whistles. Enter* CLOV *immediately. He halts beside the chair.*] You pollute the air! [*Pause.*] Get me ready, I'm going to bed.

CLOV   I've just got you up.

HAMM   And what of it?

CLOV   I can't be getting you up and putting you to bed every five minutes, I have things to do. [*Pause.*]

HAMM   Did you ever see my eyes?

CLOV   No.

HAMM   Did you never have the curiosity, while I was sleeping, to take off my glasses and look at my eyes?

CLOV   Pulling back the lids? [*Pause.*] No.

HAMM   One of these days I'll show them to you. [*Pause.*] It seems they've gone all white. [*Pause.*] What time is it?

CLOV   The same as usual.

HAMM   [*Gesture towards window right.*]   Have you looked?

CLOV   Yes.

HAMM   Well?

CLOV   Zero.

HAMM   It'd need to rain.

CLOV   It won't rain. [*Pause.*]

HAMM   Apart from that, how do you feel?

CLOV   I don't complain.

HAMM   You feel normal?

CLOV   [*Irritably.*]   I tell you I don't complain.

HAMM   I feel a little queer. [*Pause.*] Clov!

CLOV   Yes.

HAMM   Have you not had enough?

CLOV   Yes! [*Pause.*] Of what?

HAMM   Of this . . . this . . . thing.

CLOV   I always had. [*Pause.*] Not you?

HAMM   [*Gloomily.*]   Then there's no reason for it to change.

CLOV   It may end. [*Pause.*] All life long the same questions, the same answers.

HAMM   Get me ready. [CLOV *does not move.*] Go and get the sheet. [CLOV *does not move.*] Clov!

CLOV   Yes.

HAMM   I'll give you nothing more to eat.

CLOV   Then we'll die.

HAMM   I'll give you just enough to keep you from dying. You'll be hungry all the time.

CLOV   Then we won't die. [*Pause.*] I'll go and get the sheet. [*He goes towards the door.*]

HAMM   No! [CLOV *halts.*] I'll give you one biscuit per day. [*Pause.*] One and a half. [*Pause.*] Why do you stay with me?

CLOV   Why do you keep me?

HAMM   There's no one else.

CLOV   There's nowhere else. [*Pause.*]

HAMM You're leaving me all the same.

CLOV I'm trying.

HAMM You don't love me.

CLOV No.

HAMM You loved me once.

CLOV Once!

HAMM I've made you suffer too much. [*Pause.*] Haven't I?

CLOV It's not that.

HAMM [*Shocked.*] I haven't made you suffer too much?

CLOV Yes!

HAMM [*Relieved.*] Ah you gave me a fright! [*Pause. Coldly.*] Forgive me. [*Pause. Louder.*] I said, Forgive me.

CLOV I heard you. [*Pause.*] Have you bled?

HAMM Less. [*Pause.*] Is it not time for my pain-killer?

CLOV No. [*Pause.*]

HAMM How are your eyes?

CLOV Bad.

HAMM How are your legs?

CLOV BAD.

HAMM But you can move.

CLOV Yes.

HAMM [*Violently.*] Then move! [CLOV *goes to back wall, leans against it with his forehead and hands.*] Where are you?

CLOV Here.

HAMM Come back! [CLOV *returns to his place beside the chair.*] Where are you?

CLOV Here.

HAMM Why don't you kill me?

CLOV I don't know the combination of the cupboard. [*Pause.*]

HAMM Go and get two bicycle-wheels.

CLOV There are no more bicycle-wheels.

HAMM What have you done with your bicycle?

CLOV I never had a bicycle.

HAMM The thing is impossible.

CLOV When there were still bicycles I wept to have one. I crawled at your feet. You told me to go to hell. Now there are none.

HAMM And your rounds? When you inspected my paupers. Always on foot?

CLOV Sometimes on horse. [*The lid of one of the bins lifts and the hands of* NAGG *appear, gripping the rim. Then his head emerges. Nightcap. Very white face.* NAGG *yawns, then listens.*] I'll leave you, I have things to do.

HAMM In your kitchen?

CLOV Yes.

HAMM Outside of here it's death. [*Pause.*] All right, be off. [*Exit* CLOV. *Pause.*] We're getting on.

NAGG Me pap![5]

HAMM Accursed progenitor!

NAGG Me pap!

5. Food, mush.

HAMM   The old folks at home! No decency left! Guzzle, guzzle, that's all
they think of. [*He whistles. Enter* CLOV. *He halts beside the chair.*] Well!
I thought you were leaving me.
CLOV   Oh not just yet, not just yet.
NAGG   Me pap!
HAMM   Give him his pap.
CLOV   There's no more pap.
HAMM   [*To* NAGG.]   Do you hear that? There's no more pap. You'll never
get any more pap.
NAGG   I want me pap!
HAMM   Give him a biscuit. [*Exit* CLOV.] Accursed fornicator! How are your
stumps?
NAGG   Never mind me stumps.
          [*Enter* CLOV *with biscuit.*]
CLOV   I'm back again, with the biscuit. [*He gives biscuit to* NAGG *who fin-
gers it, sniffs it.*]
NAGG [*Plaintively.*]   What is it?
CLOV   Spratt's medium.⁶
NAGG [*As before.*]   It's hard! I can't!
HAMM   Bottle him!
          [CLOV *pushes* NAGG *back into the bin, closes the lid.*]
CLOV [*Returning to his place beside the chair.*]   If age but knew!
HAMM   Sit on him!
CLOV   I can't sit.
HAMM   True. And I can't stand.
CLOV   So it is.
HAMM   Every man his speciality. [*Pause.*] No phone calls? [*Pause.*] Don't
we laugh?
CLOV [*After reflection.*]   I don't feel like it.
HAMM [*After reflection.*]   Nor I. [*Pause.*] Clov!
CLOV   Yes.
HAMM   Nature has forgotten us.
CLOV   There's no more nature.
HAMM   No more nature! You exaggerate.
CLOV   In the vicinity.
HAMM   But we breathe, we change! We lose our hair, our teeth! Our
bloom! Our ideals!
CLOV   Then she hasn't forgotten us.
HAMM   But you say there is none.
CLOV [*Sadly.*]   No one that ever lived ever thought so crooked as we.
HAMM   We do what we can.
CLOV   We shouldn't. [*Pause.*]
HAMM   You're a bit of all right, aren't you?⁷
CLOV   A smithereen.⁸ [*Pause.*]
HAMM   This is slow work. [*Pause.*] Is it not time for my pain-killer?
CLOV   No. [*Pause.*] I'll leave you, I have things to do.
HAMM   In your kitchen?
CLOV   Yes.

---

6. A common plain cookie.   7. You're pretty good, aren't you? (British slang).   8. A tiny bit.

HAMM   What, I'd like to know.

CLOV   I look at the wall.

HAMM   The wall! And what do you see on your wall? Mene, mene?[9] Naked
    bodies?

CLOV   I see my light dying.

HAMM   Your light dying! Listen to that! Well, it can die just as well here,
    your light. Take a look at me and then come back and tell me what you
    think of *your* light. [*Pause.*]

CLOV   You shouldn't speak to me like that. [*Pause.*]

HAMM [*Coldly.*]   Forgive me. [*Pause. Louder.*] I said, Forgive me.

CLOV   I heard you.
    [*The lid of* NAGG's *bin lifts. His hands appear, gripping the rim.
    Then his head emerges. In his mouth the biscuit. He listens.*]

HAMM   Did your seeds come up?

CLOV   No.

HAMM   Did you scratch round them to see if they had sprouted?

CLOV   They haven't sprouted.

HAMM   Perhaps it's still too early.

CLOV   If they were going to sprout they would have sprouted. [*Violently.*]
    They'll never sprout!
    [*Pause.* NAGG *takes biscuit in his hand.*]

HAMM   This is not much fun. [*Pause.*] But that's always the way at the end
    of the day, isn't it, Clov?

CLOV   Always.

HAMM   It's the end of the day like any other day, isn't it, Clov?

CLOV   Looks like it. [*Pause.*]

HAMM [*Anguished.*]   What's happening, what's happening?

CLOV   Something is taking its course. [*Pause.*]

HAMM   All right, be off. [*He leans back in his chair, remains motionless.*
    CLOV *does not move, heaves a great groaning sigh.* HAMM *sits up.*] I thought
    I told you to be off.

CLOV   I'm trying. [*He goes to door, halts.*] Ever since I was whelped.
    [*Exit* CLOV.]

HAMM   We're getting on.
    [*He leans back in his chair, remains motionless.* NAGG *knocks on
    the lid of the other bin. Pause. He knocks harder. The lid lifts and
    the hands of* NELL *appear, gripping the rim. Then her head emerges.
    Lace cap. Very white face.*]

NELL   What is it, my pet? [*Pause.*] Time for love?

NAGG   Were you asleep?

NELL   Oh no!

NAGG   Kiss me.

NELL   We can't.

NAGG   Try.
    [*Their heads strain towards each other, fail to meet, fall apart again.*]

NELL   Why this farce, day after day? [*Pause.*]

NAGG   I've lost me tooth.

---

9. From Daniel 5.25: "Mene, mene, tekel, upharsin"; words written by a divine hand on the wall during
the feast of Belshazzar, king of Babylon. They predict doom and tell the king "Thou art weighed in the
balances, and art found wanting" (Daniel 5.27).

NELL When?

NAGG I had it yesterday.

NELL [*Elegiac.*] Ah yesterday!
      [*They turn painfully towards each other.*]

NAGG Can you see me?

NELL Hardly. And you?

NAGG What?

NELL Can you see me?

NAGG Hardly.

NELL So much the better, so much the better.

NAGG Don't say that. [*Pause.*] Our sight has failed.

NELL Yes.
      [*Pause. They turn away from each other.*]

NAGG Can you hear me?

NELL Yes. And you?

NAGG Yes. [*Pause.*] Our hearing hasn't failed.

NELL Our what?

NAGG Our hearing.

NELL No. [*Pause.*] Have you anything else to say to me?

NAGG Do you remember—

NELL No.

NAGG When we crashed on our tandem[1] and lost our shanks.
      [*They laugh heartily.*]

NELL It was in the Ardennes.
      [*They laugh less heartily.*]

NAGG On the road to Sedan.[2] [*They laugh still less heartily.*] Are you
      cold?

NELL Yes, perished. And you?

NAGG [*Pause.*] I'm freezing. [*Pause.*] Do you want to go in?

NELL Yes.

NAGG Then go in. [NELL *does not move.*] Why don't you go in?

NELL I don't know. [*Pause.*]

NAGG Has he changed your sawdust?

NELL It isn't sawdust. [*Pause. Wearily.*] Can you not be a little accurate,
      Nagg?

NAGG Your sand then. It's not important.

NELL It is important. [*Pause.*]

NAGG It was sawdust once.

NELL Once!

NAGG And now it's sand. [*Pause.*] From the shore. [*Pause. Impatiently.*]
      Now it's sand he fetches from the shore.

NELL Now it's sand.

NAGG Has he changed yours?

NELL No.

NAGG Nor mine. [*Pause.*] I won't have it! [*Pause. Holding up the biscuit.*]
      Do you want a bit?

NELL No. [*Pause.*] Of what?

NAGG Biscuit. I've kept you half. [*He looks at the biscuit. Proudly.*] Three

---

1. A bicycle built for two. 2. Town in northern France where the French were defeated in the Franco-
Prussian War (1870). Ardennes is a forest in northern France, the scene of bitter fighting in both world
wars.

quarters. For you. Here. [*He proffers the biscuit.*] No? [*Pause.*] Do you not feel well?

HAMM [*Wearily.*]   Quiet, quiet, you're keeping me awake. [*Pause.*] Talk softer. [*Pause.*] If I could sleep I might make love. I'd go into the woods. My eyes would see . . . the sky, the earth. I'd run, run, they wouldn't catch me. [*Pause.*] Nature! [*Pause.*] There's something dripping in my head. [*Pause.*] A heart, a heart in my head. [*Pause.*]

NAGG [*Soft.*]   Do you hear him? A heart in his head! [*He chuckles cautiously.*]

NELL   One mustn't laugh at those things, Nagg. Why must you always laugh at them?

NAGG   Not so loud!

NELL [*Without lowering her voice.*]   Nothing is funnier than unhappiness, I grant you that. But—

NAGG [*Shocked.*]   Oh!

NELL   Yes, yes, it's the most comical thing in the world. And we laugh, we laugh, with a will, in the beginning. But it's always the same thing. Yes, it's like the funny story we have heard too often, we still find it funny, but we don't laugh any more. [*Pause.*] Have you anything else to say to me?

NAGG   No.

NELL   Are you quite sure? [*Pause.*] Then I'll leave you.

NAGG   Do you not want your biscuit? [*Pause.*] I'll keep it for you. [*Pause.*] I thought you were going to leave me.

NELL   I am going to leave you.

NAGG   Could you give me a scratch before you go?

NELL   No. [*Pause.*] Where?

NAGG   In the back.

NELL   No. [*Pause.*] Rub yourself against the rim.

NAGG   It's lower down. In the hollow.

NELL   What hollow?

NAGG   The hollow! [*Pause.*] Could you not? [*Pause.*] Yesterday you scratched me there.

NELL [*Elegiac.*]   Ah yesterday!

NAGG   Could you not? [*Pause.*] Would you like me to scratch you? [*Pause.*] Are you crying again?

NELL   I was trying. [*Pause.*]

HAMM   Perhaps it's a little vein. [*Pause.*]

NAGG   What was that he said?

NELL   Perhaps it's a little vein.

NAGG   What does that mean? [*Pause.*] That means nothing. [*Pause.*] Will I tell you the story of the tailor?

NELL   No. [*Pause.*] What for?

NAGG   To cheer you up.

NELL   It's not funny.

NAGG   It always made you laugh. [*Pause.*] The first time I thought you'd die.

NELL   It was on Lake Como.[3] [*Pause.*] One April afternoon. [*Pause.*] Can you believe it?

---

3. A large lake and tourist resort in northern Italy, near the Swiss border.

NAGG What?

NELL That we once went out rowing on Lake Como. [*Pause.*] One April afternoon.

NAGG We had got engaged the day before.

NELL Engaged!

NAGG You were in such fits that we capsized. By rights we should have been drowned.

NELL It was because I felt happy.

NAGG [*Indignant.*] It was not, it was not, it was my story and nothing else. Happy! Don't you laugh at it still? Every time I tell it. Happy!

NELL It was deep, deep. And you could see down to the bottom. So white. So clean.

NAGG Let me tell it again. [*Raconteur's voice.*] An Englishman, needing a pair of striped trousers in a hurry for the New Year festivities, goes to his tailor who takes his measurements. [*Tailor's voice.*] "That's the lot, come back in four days, I'll have it ready." Good. Four days later. [*Tailor's voice.*] "So sorry, come back in a week, I've made a mess of the seat." Good, that's all right, a neat seat can be very ticklish. A week later. [*Tailor's voice.*] "Frightfully sorry, come back in ten days. I've made a hash of the crotch." Good, can't be helped, a snug crotch is always a teaser. Ten days later. [*Tailor's voice.*] "Dreadfully sorry, come back in a fortnight, I've made a balls of the fly." Good, at a pinch, a smart fly is a stiff proposition. [*Pause. Normal voice.*] I never told it worse. [*Pause. Gloomy.*] I tell this story worse and worse. [*Pause. Raconteur's voice.*] Well, to make it short, the bluebells are blowing and he ballockses[4] the buttonholes. [*Customer's voice.*] "God damn you to hell, Sir, no, it's indecent, there are limits! In six days, do you hear me, six days, God made the world. Yes Sir, no less Sir, the WORLD! And you are not bloody well capable of making me a pair of trousers in three months!" [*Tailor's voice, scandalized.*] "But my dear Sir, my dear Sir, look— [*Disdainful gesture, disgustedly.*]—at the world— [*Pause.*] and look— [*Loving gesture, proudly.*]—at my TROUSERS!"

> [*Pause. He looks at* NELL *who has remained impassive, her eyes unseeing, breaks into a high forced laugh, cuts it short, pokes his head towards* NELL, *launches his laugh again.*]

HAMM Silence!

> [NAGG *starts, cuts short his laugh.*]

NELL You could see down to the bottom.

HAMM [*Exasperated.*] Have you not finished? Will you never finish? [*With sudden fury.*] Will this never finish? [NAGG *disappears into his bin, closes the lid behind him.* NELL *does not move. Frenziedly.*] My kingdom for a nightman![5] [*He whistles. Enter* CLOV.] Clear away this muck! Chuck it in the sea!

> [CLOV *goes to bins, halts.*]

NELL So white.

HAMM What? What's she blathering about?

> [CLOV *stoops, takes* NELL's *hand, feels her pulse.*]

---

4. "Bollixes," botches. 5. Parody of Shakespeare's *Richard III*, where the defeated king seeks a horse to escape from the battlefield: "A horse! a horse! My kingdom for a horse!" (5.4.7).

NELL [*To* CLOV.]   Desert!

   [CLOV *lets go her hand, pushes her back in the bin, closes the lid.*]

CLOV [*Returning to his place beside the chair.*]   She has no pulse.

HAMM   What was she drivelling about?

CLOV   She told me to go away, into the desert.

HAMM   Damn busybody! Is that all?

CLOV   No.

HAMM   What else?

CLOV   I didn't understand.

HAMM   Have you bottled her?

CLOV   Yes.

HAMM   Are they both bottled?

CLOV   Yes.

HAMM   Screw down the lids. [CLOV *goes towards door.*] Time enough. [CLOV *halts.*] My anger subsides, I'd like to pee.

CLOV [*With alacrity.*]   I'll go and get the catheter. [*He goes towards door.*]

HAMM   Time enough. [CLOV *halts.*] Give me my pain-killer.

CLOV   It's too soon. [*Pause.*] It's too soon on top of your tonic, it wouldn't act.

HAMM   In the morning they brace you up and in the evening they calm you down. Unless it's the other way round. [*Pause.*] That old doctor, he's dead naturally?

CLOV   He wasn't old.

HAMM   But he's dead?

CLOV   Naturally. [*Pause.*] *You* ask *me* that? [*Pause.*]

HAMM   Take me for a little turn. [CLOV *goes behind the chair and pushes it forward.*] Not too fast! [CLOV *pushes chair.*] Right round the world! [CLOV *pushes chair.*] Hug the walls, then back to the center again. [CLOV *pushes chair.*] I was right in the center, wasn't I?

CLOV [*Pushing.*]   Yes.

HAMM   We'd need a proper wheel-chair. With big wheels. Bicycle wheels! [*Pause.*] Are you hugging?

CLOV [*Pushing.*]   Yes.

HAMM [*Groping for wall.*]   It's a lie! Why do you lie to me?

CLOV [*Bearing closer to wall.*]   There! There!

HAMM   Stop! [CLOV *stops chair close to back wall.* HAMM *lays his hand against wall.*] Old wall! [*Pause.*] Beyond is the . . . other hell. [*Pause. Violently.*] Closer! Closer! Up against!

CLOV   Take away your hand. [HAMM *withdraws his hand.* CLOV *rams chair against wall.*] There!

   [HAMM *leans towards wall, applies his ear to it.*]

HAMM   Do you hear? [*He strikes the wall with his knuckles.*] Do you hear? Hollow bricks! [*He strikes again.*] All that's hollow! [*Pause. He straightens up. Violently.*] That's enough. Back!

CLOV   We haven't done the round.

HAMM   Back to my place! [CLOV *pushes chair back to center.*] Is that my place?

CLOV   Yes, that's your place.

HAMM   Am I right in the center?

CLOV   I'll measure it.

HAMM   More or less! More or less!

CLOV [*Moving chair slightly.*]   There!

HAMM   I'm more or less in the center?

CLOV   I'd say so.

HAMM   You'd say so! Put me right in the center!

CLOV   I'll go and get the tape.

HAMM   Roughly! Roughly! [CLOV *moves chair slightly.*] Bang in the center!

CLOV   There! [*Pause.*]

HAMM   I feel a little too far to the left. [CLOV *moves chair slightly.*] Now I feel a little too far to the right. [CLOV *moves chair slightly.*] I feel a little too far forward. [CLOV *moves chair slightly.*] Now I feel a little too far back. [CLOV *moves chair slightly.*] Don't stay there, [*i.e., behind the chair*] you give me the shivers.

[CLOV *returns to his place beside the chair.*]

CLOV   If I could kill him I'd die happy. [*Pause.*]

HAMM   What's the weather like?

CLOV   As usual.

HAMM   Look at the earth.

CLOV   I've looked.

HAMM   With the glass?

CLOV   No need of the glass.

HAMM   Look at it with the glass.

CLOV   I'll go and get the glass.

[*Exit* CLOV.]

HAMM   No need of the glass!

[*Enter* CLOV *with telescope.*]

CLOV   I'm back again, with the glass. [*He goes to window right, looks up at it.*] I need the steps.

HAMM   Why? Have you shrunk? [*Exit* CLOV *with telescope.*] I don't like that, I don't like that.

[*Enter* CLOV *with ladder, but without telescope.*]

CLOV   I'm back again, with the steps. [*He sets down ladder under window right, gets up on it, realizes he has not the telescope, gets down.*] I need the glass. [*He goes towards door.*]

HAMM [*Violently.*]   But you have the glass!

CLOV [*Halting, violently.*]   No, I haven't the glass!

[*Exit* CLOV.]

HAMM   This is deadly.

[*Enter* CLOV *with telescope. He goes towards ladder.*]

CLOV   Things are livening up. [*He gets up on ladder, raises the telescope, lets it fall.*] I did it on purpose. [*He gets down, picks up the telescope, turns it on auditorium.*] I see . . . a multitude . . . in transports . . . of joy.[6] [*Pause.*] That's what I call a magnifier. [*He lowers the telescope, turns towards* HAMM.] Well? Don't we laugh?

HAMM [*After reflection.*]   I don't.

CLOV [*After reflection.*]   Nor I. [*He gets up on ladder, turns the telescope on the without.*] Let's see. [*He looks, moving the telescope.*] Zero . . . [*he looks*] . . . zero . . . [*he looks*] . . . and zero.

6. Echo of Revelation 7.9–10: "After this I beheld, and, lo, a great multitude, which . . . cried with a loud voice, saying, Salvation."

HAMM   Nothing stirs. All is—

CLOV   Zer—

HAMM   [*Violently.*]   Wait till you're spoke to! [*Normal voice.*] All is . . . all is . . . all is what? [*Violently.*] All is what?

CLOV   What all is? In a word? Is that what you want to know? Just a moment. [*He turns the telescope on the without, looks, lowers the telescope, turns towards* HAMM.] Corpsed. [*Pause.*] Well? Content?

HAMM   Look at the sea.

CLOV   It's the same.

HAMM   Look at the ocean!

    [CLOV *gets down, takes a few steps towards window left, goes back for ladder, carries it over and sets it down under window left, gets up on it, turns the telescope on the without, looks at length. He starts, lowers the telescope, examines it, turns it again on the without.*]

CLOV   Never seen anything like that!

HAMM   [*Anxious.*]   What? A sail? A fin? Smoke?

CLOV   [*Looking.*]   The light is sunk.

HAMM   [*Relieved.*]   Pah! We all knew that.

CLOV   [*Looking.*]   There was a bit left.

HAMM   The base.

CLOV   [*Looking.*]   Yes.

HAMM   And now?

CLOV   [*Looking.*]   All gone.

HAMM   No gulls?

CLOV   [*Looking.*]   Gulls!

HAMM   And the horizon? Nothing on the horizon?

CLOV   [*Lowering the telescope, turning towards* HAMM, *exasperated.*]   What in God's name could there be on the horizon? [*Pause.*]

HAMM   The waves, how are the waves?

CLOV   The waves? [*He turns the telescope on the waves.*] Lead.

HAMM   And the sun?

CLOV   [*Looking.*]   Zero.

HAMM   But it should be sinking. Look again.

CLOV   [*Looking.*]   Damn the sun.

HAMM   Is it night already then?

CLOV   [*Looking.*]   No.

HAMM   Then what is it?

CLOV   [*Looking.*]   Gray. [*Lowering the telescope, turning towards* HAMM, *louder.*] Gray! [*Pause. Still louder.*] GRRAY! [*Pause. He gets down, approaches* HAMM *from behind, whispers in his ear.*]

HAMM   [*Starting.*]   Gray! Did I hear you say gray?

CLOV   Light black. From pole to pole.

HAMM   You exaggerate. [*Pause.*] Don't stay there, you give me the shivers. [CLOV *returns to his place beside the chair.*]

CLOV   Why this farce, day after day?

HAMM   Routine. One never knows. [*Pause.*] Last night I saw inside my breast. There was a big sore.

CLOV   Pah! You saw your heart.

HAMM   No, it was living. [*Pause. Anguished.*] Clov!

CLOV   Yes.

HAMM   What's happening?

CLOV   Something is taking its course. [*Pause.*]

HAMM   Clov!

CLOV [*Impatiently.*]   What is it?

HAMM   We're not beginning to . . . to . . . mean something?

CLOV   Mean something! You and I, mean something! [*Brief laugh.*] Ah that's a good one!

HAMM   I wonder. [*Pause.*] Imagine if a rational being came back to earth, wouldn't he be liable to get ideas into his head if he observed us long enough. [*Voice of rational being.*] Ah, good, now I see what it is, yes, now I understand what they're at! [CLOV *starts, drops the telescope and begins to scratch his belly with both hands. Normal voice.*] And without going so far as that, we ourselves . . . [*With emotion.*] . . . we ourselves . . . at certain moments . . . [*Vehemently.*] To think perhaps it won't all have been for nothing!

CLOV [*Anguished, scratching himself.*]   I have a flea!

HAMM   A flea! Are there still fleas?

CLOV   On me there's one. [*Scratching.*] Unless it's a crablouse.

HAMM [*Very perturbed.*]   But humanity might start from there all over again! Catch him, for the love of God!

CLOV   I'll go and get the powder.
        [*Exit* CLOV.]

HAMM   A flea! This is awful! What a day!
        [*Enter* CLOV *with a sprinkling-tin.*]

CLOV   I'm back again, with the insecticide.

HAMM   Let him have it!
        [CLOV *loosens the top of his trousers, pulls it forward and shakes powder into the aperture. He stoops, looks, waits, starts, frenziedly shakes more powder, stoops, looks, waits.*]

CLOV   The bastard!

HAMM   Did you get him?

CLOV   Looks like it. [*He drops the tin and adjusts his trousers.*] Unless he's laying doggo.

HAMM   Laying! Lying you mean. Unless he's *lying* doggo.

CLOV   Ah? One says lying? One doesn't say laying?

HAMM   Use your head, can't you. If he was laying we'd be bitched.

CLOV   Ah. [*Pause.*] What about that pee?

HAMM   I'm having it.

CLOV   Ah that's the spirit, that's the spirit! [*Pause.*]

HAMM [*With ardour.*]   Let's go from here, the two of us! South! You can make a raft and the currents will carry us away, far away, to other . . . mammals!

CLOV   God forbid!

HAMM   Alone, I'll embark alone! Get working on that raft immediately. Tomorrow I'll be gone for ever.

CLOV [*Hastening towards door.*]   I'll start straight away.

HAMM   Wait! [CLOV *halts.*] Will there be sharks, do you think?

CLOV   Sharks? I don't know. If there are there will be. [*He goes towards door.*]

HAMM   Wait! [CLOV *halts.*] Is it not yet time for my pain-killer?

CLOV [*Violently.*]   No! [*He goes towards door.*]

HAMM   Wait! [CLOV *halts.*] How are your eyes?

CLOV   Bad.

HAMM   But you can see.

CLOV   All I want.

HAMM   How are your legs?

CLOV   Bad.

HAMM   But you can walk.

CLOV   I come . . . and go.

HAMM   In my house. [*Pause. With prophetic relish.*] One day you'll be blind, like me. You'll be sitting there, a speck in the void, in the dark, for ever, like me. [*Pause.*] One day you'll say to yourself, I'm tired, I'll sit down, and you'll go and sit down. Then you'll say, I'm hungry, I'll get up and get something to eat. But you won't get up. You'll say, I shouldn't have sat down, but since I have I'll sit on a little longer, then I'll get up and get something to eat. But you won't get up and you won't get anything to eat. [*Pause.*] You'll look at the wall awhile, then you'll say, I'll close my eyes, perhaps have a little sleep, after that I'll feel better, and you'll close them. And when you open them again there'll be no wall any more. [*Pause.*] Infinite emptiness will be all around you, all the resurrected dead of all the ages wouldn't fill it, and there you'll be like a little bit of grit in the middle of the steppe. [*Pause.*] Yes, one day you'll know what it is, you'll be like me, except that you won't have anyone with you, because you won't have had pity on anyone and because there won't be anyone left to have pity on. [*Pause.*]

CLOV   It's not certain. [*Pause.*] And there's one thing you forget.

HAMM   Ah?

CLOV   I can't sit down.

HAMM   [*Impatiently.*]   Well you'll lie down then, what the hell! Or you'll come to a standstill, simply stop and stand still, the way you are now. One day you'll say, I'm tired, I'll stop. What does the attitude matter? [*Pause.*]

CLOV   So you all want me to leave you.

HAMM   Naturally.

CLOV   Then I'll leave you.

HAMM   You can't leave us.

CLOV   Then I won't leave you. [*Pause.*]

HAMM   Why don't you finish us? [*Pause.*] I'll tell you the combination of the cupboard if you promise to finish me.

CLOV   I couldn't finish you.

HAMM   Then you won't finish me. [*Pause.*]

CLOV   I'll leave you, I have things to do.

HAMM   Do you remember when you came here?

CLOV   No. Too small, you told me.

HAMM   Do you remember your father?

CLOV   [*Wearily.*]   Same answer. [*Pause.*] You've asked me these questions millions of times.

HAMM   I love the old questions. [*With fervor.*] Ah the old questions, the old answers, there's nothing like them! [*Pause.*] It was I was a father to you.

CLOV   Yes. [*He looks at* HAMM *fixedly.*] You were that to me.

HAMM   My house a home for you.

CLOV   Yes. [*He looks about him.*] This was that for me.

HAMM [*Proudly.*]   But for me, [*Gesture towards himself.*] no father. But for Hamm, [*Gesture towards surroundings.*] no home. [*Pause.*]

CLOV   I'll leave you.

HAMM   Did you ever think of one thing?

CLOV   Never.

HAMM   That here we're down in a hole. [*Pause.*] But beyond the hills? Eh? Perhaps it's still green. Eh? [*Pause.*] Flora! Pomona! [*Ecstatically.*] Ceres![7] [*Pause.*] Perhaps you won't need to go very far.

CLOV   I can't go very far. [*Pause.*] I'll leave you.

HAMM   Is my dog ready?

CLOV   He lacks a leg.

HAMM   Is he silky?

CLOV   He's a kind of Pomeranian.

HAMM   Go and get him.

CLOV   He lacks a leg.

HAMM   Go and get him! [*Exit* CLOV.] We're getting on.
   [*Enter* CLOV *holding by one of its three legs a black toy dog.*]

CLOV   Your dogs are here. [*He hands the dog to* HAMM *who feels it, fondles it.*]

HAMM   He's white, isn't he?

CLOV   Nearly.

HAMM   What do you mean, nearly? Is he white or isn't he?

CLOV   He isn't. [*Pause.*]

HAMM   You've forgotten the sex.

CLOV [*Vexed.*]   But he isn't finished. The sex goes on at the end. [*Pause.*]

HAMM   You haven't put on his ribbon.

CLOV [*Angrily.*]   But he isn't finished, I tell you! First you finish your dog and then you put on his ribbon! [*Pause.*]

HAMM   Can he stand?

CLOV   I don't know.

HAMM   Try. [*He hands the dog to* CLOV *who places it on the ground.*] Well?

CLOV   Wait! [*He squats down and tries to get the dog to stand on its three legs, fails, lets it go. The dog falls on its side.*]

HAMM [*Impatiently.*]   Well?

CLOV   He's standing.

HAMM [*Groping for the dog.*]   Where? Where is he?
   [CLOV *holds up the dog in a standing position.*]

CLOV   There. [*He takes* HAMM's *hand and guides it towards the dog's head.*]

HAMM [*His hand on the dog's head.*]   Is he gazing at me?

CLOV   Yes.

HAMM [*Proudly.*]   As if he were asking me to take him for a walk?

CLOV   If you like.

HAMM [*As before.*]   Or as if he were begging me for a bone. [*He withdraws his hand.*] Leave him like that, standing there imploring me.
   [CLOV *straightens up. The dog falls on its side.*]

CLOV   I'll leave you.

---

7. In Roman mythology, the goddesses of flowers, fruits, and fertility.

HAMM   Have you had your visions?

CLOV   Less.

HAMM   Is Mother Pegg's light on?

CLOV   Light! How could anyone's light be on?

HAMM   Extinguished!

CLOV   Naturally it's extinguished. If it's not on it's extinguished.

HAMM   No, I mean Mother Pegg.

CLOV   But naturally she's extinguished! [*Pause.*] What's the matter with you today?

HAMM   I'm taking my course. [*Pause.*] Is she buried?

CLOV   Buried! Who would have buried her?

HAMM   You.

CLOV   Me! Haven't I enough to do without burying people?

HAMM   But you'll bury me.

CLOV   No I won't bury you. [*Pause.*]

HAMM   She was bonny once, like a flower of the field. [*With reminiscent leer.*] And a great one for the men!

CLOV   We too were bonny—once. It's a rare thing not to have been bonny—once. [*Pause.*]

HAMM   Go and get the gaff.

[CLOV *goes to door, halts.*]

CLOV   Do this, do that, and I do it. I never refuse. Why?

HAMM   You're not able to.

CLOV   Soon I won't do it any more.

HAMM   You won't be able to any more. [*Exit* CLOV.] Ah the creatures, the creatures, everything has to be explained to them.

[*Enter* CLOV *with gaff.*]

CLOV   Here's your gaff. Stick it up. [*He gives the gaff to* HAMM *who, wielding it like a puntpole, tries to move his chair.*]

HAMM   Did I move?

CLOV   No.

[HAMM *throws down the gaff.*]

HAMM   Go and get the oilcan.

CLOV   What for?

HAMM   To oil the castors.

CLOV   I oiled them yesterday.

HAMM   Yesterday! What does that mean? Yesterday!

CLOV [*Violently.*]   That means that bloody awful day, long ago, before this bloody awful day. I use the words you taught me. If they don't mean anything any more, teach me others. Or let me be silent. [*Pause.*]

HAMM   I once knew a madman who thought the end of the world had come. He was a painter—and engraver. I had a great fondness for him. I used to go and see him, in the asylum. I'd take him by the hand and drag him to the window. Look! There! All that rising corn! And there! Look! The sails of the herring fleet! All that loveliness! [*Pause.*] He'd snatch away his hand and go back into his corner. Appalled. All he had seen was ashes. [*Pause.*] He alone had been spared. [*Pause.*] Forgotten. [*Pause.*] It appears the case is . . . was not so . . . so unusual.

CLOV   A madman! When was that?

HAMM   Oh way back, way back, you weren't in the land of the living.

CLOV   God be with the days!
       [*Pause.* HAMM *raises his toque.*]
HAMM   I had a great fondness for him. [*Pause. He puts on his toque again.*]
       He was a painter—and engraver.
CLOV   There are so many terrible things.
HAMM   No, no, there are not so many now. [*Pause.*] Clov!
CLOV   Yes.
HAMM   Do you not think this has gone on long enough?
CLOV   Yes! [*Pause.*] What?
HAMM   This . . . this . . . thing.
CLOV   I've always thought so. [*Pause.*] You not?
HAMM   [*Gloomily.*]   Then it's a day like any other day.
CLOV   As long as it lasts. [*Pause.*] All life long the same inanities.
HAMM   I can't leave you.
CLOV   I know. And you can't follow me. [*Pause.*]
HAMM   If you leave me how shall I know?
CLOV   [*Briskly.*]   Well you simply whistle me and if I don't come running
       it means I've left you. [*Pause.*]
HAMM   You won't come and kiss me goodbye?
CLOV   Oh I shouldn't think so. [*Pause.*]
HAMM   But you might be merely dead in your kitchen.
CLOV   The result would be the same.
HAMM   Yes, but how would I know, if you were merely dead in your
       kitchen?
CLOV   Well . . . sooner or later I'd start to stink.
HAMM   You stink already. The whole place stinks of corpses.
CLOV   The whole universe.
HAMM   [*Angrily.*]   To hell with the universe. [*Pause.*] Think of something.
CLOV   What?
HAMM   An idea, have an idea. [*Angrily.*] A bright idea!
CLOV   Ah good. [*He starts pacing to and fro, his eyes fixed on the ground,
       his hands behind his back. He halts.*] The pains in my legs! It's unbeliev-
       able! Soon I won't be able to think any more.
HAMM   You won't be able to leave me. [CLOV *resumes his pacing.*] What
       are you doing?
CLOV   Having an idea. [*He paces.*] Ah! [*He halts.*]
HAMM   What a brain! [*Pause.*] Well?
CLOV   Wait! [*He meditates. Not very convinced.*] Yes . . . [*Pause. More con-
       vinced.*] Yes! [*He raises his head.*] I have it! I set the alarm. [*Pause.*]
HAMM   This is perhaps not one of my bright days, but frankly—
CLOV   You whistle me. I don't come. The alarm rings. I'm gone. It doesn't
       ring. I'm dead. [*Pause.*]
HAMM   Is it working? [*Pause. Impatiently.*] The alarm, is it working?
CLOV   Why wouldn't it be working?
HAMM   Because it's worked too much.
CLOV   But it's hardly worked at all.
HAMM   [*Angrily.*]   Then because it's worked too little!
CLOV   I'll go and see. [*Exit* CLOV. *Brief ring of alarm off. Enter* CLOV *with
       alarm-clock. He holds it against* HAMM's *ear and releases alarm. They listen
       to it ringing to the end. Pause.*] Fit to wake the dead! Did you hear it?

HAMM Vaguely.
CLOV The end is terrific!
HAMM I prefer the middle. [*Pause.*] Is it not time for my pain-killer?
CLOV No! [*He goes to door, turns.*] I'll leave you.
HAMM It's time for my story. Do you want to listen to my story.
CLOV No.
HAMM Ask my father if he wants to listen to my story.
    [CLOV *goes to bins, raises the lid of* NAGG's, *stoops, looks into it. Pause. He straightens up.*]
CLOV He's asleep.
HAMM Wake him.
    [CLOV *stoops, wakes* NAGG *with the alarm. Unintelligible words.* CLOV *straightens up.*]
CLOV He doesn't want to listen to your story.
HAMM I'll give him a bon-bon.
    [CLOV *stoops. As before.*]
CLOV He wants a sugar-plum.
HAMM He'll get a sugar-plum.
    [CLOV *stoops. As before.*]
CLOV It's a deal. [*He goes towards door.* NAGG's *hands appear, gripping the rim. Then the head emerges.* CLOV *reaches door, turns.*] Do you believe in the life to come?
HAMM Mine was always that. [*Exit* CLOV.] Got him that time!
NAGG I'm listening.
HAMM Scoundrel! Why did you engender me?
NAGG I didn't know.
HAMM What? What didn't you know?
NAGG That it'd be you. [*Pause.*] You'll give me a sugar-plum?
HAMM After the audition.
NAGG You swear?
HAMM Yes.
NAGG On what?
HAMM My honor.
    [*Pause. They laugh heartily.*]
NAGG Two.
HAMM One.
NAGG One for me and one for—
HAMM One! Silence! [*Pause.*] Where was I? [*Pause. Gloomily.*] It's finished, we're finished. [*Pause.*] Nearly finished. [*Pause.*] There'll be no more speech. [*Pause.*] Something dripping in my head, ever since the fontanelles. [*Stifled hilarity of* NAGG.] Splash, splash, always on the same spot. [*Pause.*] Perhaps it's a little vein. [*Pause.*] A little artery. [*Pause. More animated.*] Enough of that, it's story time, where was I? [*Pause. Narrative tone.*] The man came crawling towards me, on his belly. Pale, wonderfully pale and thin, he seemed on the point of— [*Pause. Normal tone.*] No, I've done that bit. [*Pause. Narrative tone.*] I calmly filled my pipe—the meerschaum, lit it with . . . let us say a vesta, drew a few puffs. Aah! [*Pause.*] Well, what is it *you* want? [*Pause.*] It was an extraordinarily bitter day, I remember, zero by the thermometer. But considering it was Christmas Eve there was nothing . . . extra-ordinary about that. Season-

able weather, for once in a way. [*Pause.*] Well, what ill wind blows you my way? He raised his face to me, black with mingled dirt and tears. [*Pause. Normal tone.*] That should do it. [*Narrative tone.*] No, no, don't look at me, don't look at me. He dropped his eyes and mumbled something, apologies I presume. [*Pause.*] I'm a busy man, you know, the final touches, before the festivities, you know what it is. [*Pause. Forcibly.*] Come on now, what is the object of this invasion? [*Pause.*] It was a glorious bright day, I remember, fifty by the heliometer,[8] but already the sun was sinking down into the . . . down among the dead. [*Normal tone.*] Nicely put, that. [*Narrative tone.*] Come on now, come on, present your petition and let me resume my labors. [*Pause. Normal tone.*] There's English for you. Ah well . . . [*Narrative tone.*] It was then he took the plunge. It's my little one, he said. Tsstss, a little one, that's bad. My little boy, he said, as if the sex mattered. Where did he come from? He named the hole. A good half-day, on horse. What are you insinuating? That the place is still inhabited? No no, not a soul, except himself and the child— assuming he existed. Good. I enquired about the situation at Kov, beyond the gulf. Not a sinner. Good. And you expect me to believe you have left your little one back there, all alone, and alive into the bargain? Come now! [*Pause.*] It was a howling wild day, I remember, a hundred by the anemometer.[9] The wind was tearing up the dead pines and sweeping them . . . away. [*Pause. Normal tone.*] A bit feeble, that. [*Narrative tone.*] Come on, man, speak up, what is you want from me, I have to put up my holly. [*Pause.*] Well to make it short it finally transpired that what he wanted from me was . . . bread for his brat? Bread? But I have no bread, it doesn't agree with me. Good. Then perhaps a little corn? [*Pause. Normal tone.*] That should do it. [*Narrative tone.*] Corn, yes, I have corn, it's true, in my granaries. But use your head. I give you some corn, a pound, a pound and a half, you bring it back to your child and you make him—if he's still alive—a nice pot of porridge, [NAGG *reacts.*] a nice pot and a half of porridge, full of nourishment. Good. The colors come back into his little cheeks—perhaps. And then? [*Pause.*] I lost patience. [*Violently.*] Use your head, can't you, use your head, you're on earth, there's no cure for that! [*Pause.*] It was an exceedingly dry day, I remember, zero by the hygrometer.[1] Ideal weather, for my lumbago. [*Pause. Violently.*] But what in God's name do you imagine? That the earth will awake in spring? That the rivers and seas will run with fish again? That there's manna in heaven still for imbeciles like you? [*Pause.*] Gradually I cooled down, sufficiently at least to ask him how long he had taken on the way. Three whole days. Good. In what condition he had left the child. Deep in sleep. [*Forcibly.*] But deep in what sleep, deep in what sleep already? [*Pause.*] Well to make it short I finally offered to take him into my service. He had touched a chord. And then I imagined already that I wasn't much longer for this world. [*He laughs. Pause.*] Well? [*Pause.*] Well? Here if you were careful you might die a nice natural death, in peace and comfort. [*Pause.*] Well? [*Pause.*] In the end he asked me would I consent to take in the child as well—if he were still alive. [*Pause.*] It was the moment I was waiting for.

8. Literally, a "sun meter." Ordinarily, a telescope used to measure distances between celestial bodies.   9. A wind meter.   1. A moisture meter.

[*Pause.*] Would I consent to take in the child . . . [*Pause.*] I can see him still, down on his knees, his hands flat on the ground, glaring at me with his mad eyes, in defiance of my wishes. [*Pause. Normal tone.*] I'll soon have finished with this story. [*Pause.*] Unless I bring in other characters. [*Pause.*] But where would I find them? [*Pause.*] Where would I look for them? [*Pause. He whistles. Enter* CLOV.] Let us pray to God.

NAGG   Me sugar-plum!

CLOV   There's a rat in the kitchen!

HAMM   A rat! Are there still rats?

CLOV   In the kitchen there's one.

HAMM   And you haven't exterminated him?

CLOV   Half. You disturbed us.

HAMM   He can't get away?

CLOV   No.

HAMM   You'll finish him later. Let us pray to God.

CLOV   Again!

NAGG   Me sugar-plum!

HAMM   God first! [*Pause.*] Are you right?

CLOV [*Resigned.*]   Off we go.

HAMM [*To* NAGG.]   And you?

NAGG [*Clasping his hands, closing his eyes, in a gabble.*]   Our Father which art—

HAMM   Silence! In silence! Where are your manners? [*Pause.*] Off we go. [*Attitudes of prayer. Silence. Abandoning his attitude, discouraged.*] Well?

CLOV [*Abandoning his attitude.*]   What a hope! And you?

HAMM   Sweet damn all! [*To* NAGG.] And you?

NAGG   Wait! [*Pause. Abandoning his attitude.*] Nothing doing!

HAMM   The bastard! He doesn't exist!

CLOV   Not yet.

NAGG   Me sugar-plum!

HAMM   There are no more sugar-plums! [*Pause.*]

NAGG   It's natural. After all I'm your father. It's true if it hadn't been me it would have been someone else. But that's no excuse. [*Pause.*] Turkish Delight,[2] for example, which no longer exists, we all know that, there is nothing in the world I love more. And one day I'll ask you for some, in return for a kindness, and you'll promise it to me. One must live with the times. [*Pause.*] Whom did you call when you were a tiny boy, and were frightened, in the dark? Your mother? No. Me. We let you cry. Then we moved you out of earshot, so that we might sleep in peace. [*Pause.*] I was asleep, as happy as a king, and you woke me up to have me listen to you. It wasn't indispensable, you didn't really need to have me listen to you. [*Pause.*] I hope the day will come when you'll really need to have me listen to you, and need to hear my voice, any voice. [*Pause.*] Yes, I hope I'll live till then, to hear you calling me like when you were a tiny boy, and were frightened, in the dark, and I was your only hope. [*Pause.* NAGG *knocks on lid of* NELL's *bin. Pause.*] Nell! [*Pause. He knocks louder. Pause. Louder.*] Nell! [*Pause.* NAGG *sinks back into his bin, closes the lid behind him. Pause.*]

2. A sticky sweet candy.

HAMM   Our revels now are ended.[3] [*He gropes for the dog.*] The dog's gone.

CLOV   He's not a real dog, he can't go.

HAMM [*Groping.*]   He's not there.

CLOV   He's lain down.

HAMM   Give him up to me. [CLOV *picks up the dog and gives it to* HAMM. HAMM *holds it in his arms. Pause.* HAMM *throws away the dog.*] Dirty brute! [CLOV *begins to pick up the objects lying on the ground.*] What are you doing?

CLOV   Putting things in order. [*He straightens up. Fervently.*] I'm going to clear everything away! [*He starts picking up again.*]

HAMM   Order!

CLOV [*Straightening up.*]   I love order. It's my dream. A world where all would be silent and still and each thing in its last place, under the last dust. [*He starts picking up again.*]

HAMM [*Exasperated.*]   What in God's name do you think you are doing?

CLOV [*Straightening up.*]   I'm doing my best to create a little order.

HAMM   Drop it!
       [CLOV *drops the objects he has picked up.*]

CLOV   After all, there or elsewhere. [*He goes towards door.*]

HAMM [*Irritably.*]   What's wrong with your feet?

CLOV   My feet?

HAMM   Tramp! Tramp!

CLOV   I must have put on my boots.

HAMM   Your slippers were hurting you? [*Pause.*]

CLOV   I'll leave you.

HAMM   No!

CLOV   What is there to keep me here?

HAMM   The dialogue. [*Pause.*] I've got on with my story. [*Pause.*] I've got on with it well. [*Pause. Irritably.*] Ask me where I've got to.

CLOV   Oh, by the way, your story?

HAMM [*Surprised.*]   What story?

CLOV   The one you've been telling yourself all your days.

HAMM   Ah you mean my chronicle?

CLOV   That's the one. [*Pause.*]

HAMM [*Angrily.*]   Keep going, can't you, keep going!

CLOV   You've got on with it, I hope.

HAMM [*Modestly.*]   Oh not very far, not very far. [*He sighs.*] There are days like that, one isn't inspired. [*Pause.*] Nothing you can do about it, just wait for it to come. [*Pause.*] No forcing, no forcing, it's fatal. [*Pause.*] I've got on with it a little all the same. [*Pause.*] Technique, you know. [*Pause. Irritably.*] I say I've got on with it a little all the same.

CLOV [*Admiringly.*]   Well I never! In spite of everything you were able to get on with it!

HAMM [*Modestly.*]   Oh not very far, you know, not very far, but nevertheless, better than nothing.

CLOV   Better than nothing! Is it possible?

HAMM   I'll tell you how it goes. He comes crawling on his belly—

CLOV   Who?

---

3. Lines spoken by Prospero in Shakespeare's *The Tempest* 4.1.148.

HAMM   What?

CLOV   Who do you mean, he?

HAMM   Who do I mean! Yet another.

CLOV   Ah him! I wasn't sure.

HAMM   Crawling on his belly, whining for bread for his brat. He's offered a job as gardener. Before— [CLOV *bursts out laughing.*] What is there so funny about that?

CLOV   A job as gardener!

HAMM   Is that what tickles you?

CLOV   It must be that.

HAMM   It wouldn't be the bread?

CLOV   Or the brat. [*Pause.*]

HAMM   The whole thing is comical, I grant you that. What about having a good guffaw the two of us together?

CLOV   [*After reflection.*]   I couldn't guffaw again today.

HAMM   [*After reflection.*]   Nor I. [*Pause.*] I continue then. Before accepting with gratitude he asks if he may have his little boy with him.

CLOV   What age?

HAMM   Oh tiny.

CLOV   He would have climbed the trees.

HAMM   All the little odd jobs.

CLOV   And then he would have grown up.

HAMM   Very likely. [*Pause.*]

CLOV   Keep going, can't you, keep going!

HAMM   That's all. I stopped there. [*Pause.*]

CLOV   Do you see how it goes on.

HAMM   More or less.

CLOV   Will it not soon be the end?

HAMM   I'm afraid it will.

CLOV   Pah! You'll make up another.

HAMM   I don't know. [*Pause.*] I feel rather drained. [*Pause.*] The prolonged creative effort. [*Pause.*] If I could drag myself down to the sea! I'd make a pillow of sand for my head and the tide would come.

CLOV   There's no more tide. [*Pause.*]

HAMM   Go and see is she dead.
    [CLOV *goes to bins, raises the lid of* NELL'*s, stoops, looks into it. Pause.*]

CLOV   Looks like it.
    [*He closes the lid, straightens up.* HAMM *raises his toque. Pause. He puts it on again.*]

HAMM   [*With his hand to his toque.*]   And Nagg?
    [CLOV *raises lid of* NAGG'*s bin, stoops, looks into it. Pause.*]

CLOV   Doesn't look like it. [*He closes the lid, straightens up.*]

HAMM   [*Letting go his toque.*]   What's he doing? [CLOV *raises lid of* NAGG'*s bin, stoops, looks into it. Pause.*]

CLOV   He's crying. [*He closes lid, straightens up.*]

HAMM   Then he's living. [*Pause.*] Did you ever have an instant of happiness?

CLOV   Not to my knowledge. [*Pause.*]

HAMM   Bring me under the window. [CLOV *goes towards chair.*] I want to feel the light on my face. [CLOV *pushes chair.*] Do you remember, in the beginning, when you took me for a turn? You used to hold the chair too high. At every step you nearly tipped me out. [*With senile quaver.*] Ah great fun, we had, the two of us, great fun. [*Gloomily.*] And then we got into the way of it. [CLOV *stops the chair under window right.*] There already? [*Pause. He tilts back his head.*] Is it light?

CLOV   It isn't dark.

HAMM [*Angrily.*]   I'm asking you is it light.

CLOV   Yes. [*Pause.*]

HAMM   The curtain isn't closed?

CLOV   No.

HAMM   What window is it?

CLOV   The earth.

HAMM   I knew it! [*Angrily.*] But there's no light there! The other! [CLOV *stops the chair under window left.* HAMM *tilts back his head.*] That's what I call light! [*Pause.*] Feels like a ray of sunshine. [*Pause.*] No?

CLOV   No.

HAMM   It isn't a ray of sunshine I feel on my face?

CLOV   No. [*Pause.*]

HAMM   Am I very white? [*Pause. Angrily.*] I'm asking you am I very white!

CLOV   Not more so than usual. [*Pause.*]

HAMM   Open the window.

CLOV   What for?

HAMM   I want to hear the sea.

CLOV   You wouldn't hear it.

HAMM   Even if you opened the window?

CLOV   No.

HAMM   Then it's not worth while opening it?

CLOV   No.

HAMM [*Violently.*]   Then open it! [CLOV *gets up on the ladder, opens the window. Pause.*] Have you opened it?

CLOV   Yes. [*Pause.*]

HAMM   You swear you've opened it?

CLOV   Yes. [*Pause.*]

HAMM   Well . . . ! [*Pause.*] It must be very calm. [*Pause. Violently.*] I'm asking you is it very calm!

CLOV   Yes.

HAMM   It's because there are no more navigators. [*Pause.*] You haven't much conversation all of a sudden. Do you not feel well?

CLOV   I'm cold.

HAMM   What month are we? [*Pause.*] Close the window, we're going back. [CLOV *closes the window, gets down, pushes the chair back to its place, remains standing behind it, head bowed.*] Don't stay there, you give me the shivers! [CLOV *returns to his place beside the chair.*] Father! [*Pause. Louder.*] Father! [*Pause.*] Go and see did he hear me.

[CLOV *goes to* NAGG's *bin, raises the lid, stoops. Unintelligible words.* CLOV *straightens up.*]

CLOV   Yes.

HAMM   Both times?

[CLOV *stoops. As before.*]

CLOV Once only.

HAMM The first time or the second?
    [CLOV *stoops. As before.*]

CLOV He doesn't know.

HAMM It must have been the second.

CLOV We'll never know. [*He closes lid.*]

HAMM Is he still crying?

CLOV No.

HAMM The dead go fast. [*Pause.*] What's he doing?

CLOV Sucking his biscuit.

HAMM Life goes on. [CLOV *returns to his place beside the chair.*] Give me a rug. I'm freezing.

CLOV There are no more rugs. [*Pause.*]

HAMM Kiss me. [*Pause.*] Will you not kiss me?

CLOV No.

HAMM On the forehead.

CLOV I won't kiss you anywhere. [*Pause.*]

HAMM [*Holding out his hand.*] Give me your hand at least. [*Pause.*] Will you not give me your hand?

CLOV I won't touch you. [*Pause.*]

HAMM Give me the dog. [CLOV *looks round for the dog.*] No!

CLOV Do you not want your dog?

HAMM No.

CLOV Then I'll leave you.

HAMM [*Head bowed, absently.*] That's right.
    [CLOV *goes to door, turns.*]

CLOV If I don't kill that rat he'll die.

HAMM [*As before.*] That's right. [*Exit* CLOV. *Pause.*] Me to play. [*He takes out his handkerchief, unfolds it, holds it spread out before him.*] We're getting on. [*Pause.*] You weep, and weep, for nothing, so as not to laugh, and little by little . . . you begin to grieve. [*He folds the handkerchief, puts it back in his pocket, raises his head.*] All those I might have helped. [*Pause.*] Helped! [*Pause.*] Saved. [*Pause.*] Saved! [*Pause.*] The place was crawling with them! [*Pause. Violently.*] Use your head, can't you, use your head, you're on earth, there's no cure for that! [*Pause.*] Get out of here and love one another! Lick your neighbor as yourself![4] [*Pause. Calmer.*] When it wasn't bread they wanted it was crumpets. [*Pause. Violently.*] Out of my sight and back to your petting parties! [*Pause.*] All that, all that! [*Pause.*] Not even a real dog! [*Calmer.*] The end is in the beginning and yet you go on. [*Pause.*] Perhaps I could go on with my story, end it and begin another. [*Pause.*] Perhaps I could throw myself out on the floor. [*He pushes himself painfully off his seat, falls back again.*] Dig my nails into the cracks and drag myself forward with my fingers. [*Pause.*] It will be the end and there I'll be, wondering what can have brought it on and wondering what can have . . . [*He hesitates.*] . . . why it was so long coming. [*Pause.*] There I'll be, in the old shelter, alone against the silence and . . . [*He hesitates.*] . . . the stillness. If I can hold my peace, and sit quiet, it will be all over with sound, and motion, all

---

4. Parody of Jesus' words in the Bible: "Thou shalt love thy neighbor as thyself" (Matthew 19.19).

over and done with. [*Pause.*] I'll have called my father and I'll have called my . . . [*He hesitates.*] . . . my son. And even twice, or three times, in case they shouldn't have heard me, the first time, or the second. [*Pause.*] I'll say to myself, He'll come back. [*Pause.*] And then? [*Pause.*] And then? [*Pause.*] He couldn't, he has gone too far. [*Pause.*] And then? [*Pause. Very agitated.*] All kinds of fantasies! That I'm being watched! A rat! Steps! Breath held and then . . . [*He breathes out.*] Then babble, babble, words, like the solitary child who turns himself into children, two, three, so as to be together, and whisper together, in the dark. [*Pause.*] Moment upon moment, pattering down, like the millet grains of . . . [*He hesitates.*] . . . that old Greek,[5] and all life long you wait for that to mount up to a life. [*Pause. He opens his mouth to continue, renounces.*] Ah let's get it over! [*He whistles. Enter* CLOV *with alarm-clock. He halts beside the chair.*] What? Neither gone nor dead?

CLOV   In spirit only.

HAMM   Which?

CLOV   Both.

HAMM   Gone from me you'd be dead.

CLOV   And vice versa.

HAMM   Outside of here it's death! [*Pause.*] And the rat?

CLOV   He's got away.

HAMM   He can't go far. [*Pause. Anxious.*] Eh?

CLOV   He doesn't need to go far. [*Pause.*]

HAMM   Is it not time for my pain-killer?

CLOV   Yes.

HAMM   Ah! At last! Give it to me! Quick! [*Pause.*]

CLOV   There's no more pain-killer. [*Pause.*]

HAMM [*Appalled.*]   Good . . . ! [*Pause.*] No more pain-killer!

CLOV   No more pain-killer. You'll never get any more pain-killer. [*Pause.*]

HAMM   But the little round box. It was full!

CLOV   Yes. But now it's empty.

> [*Pause.* CLOV *starts to move about the room. He is looking for a place to put down the alarm-clock.*]

HAMM [*Soft.*]   What'll I do? [*Pause. In a scream.*] What'll I do? [CLOV *sees the picture, takes it down, stands it on the floor with its face to the wall, hangs up the alarm-clock in its place.*] What are you doing?

CLOV   Winding up.

HAMM   Look at the earth.

CLOV   Again!

HAMM   Since it's calling to you.

CLOV   Is your throat sore? [*Pause.*] Would you like a lozenge? [*Pause.*] No. [*Pause.*] Pity. [*He goes, humming, towards window right, halts before it, looks up at it.*]

HAMM   Don't sing.

CLOV [*Turning towards* HAMM.]   One hasn't the right to sing any more?

5. Zeno of Elea, a Greek philosopher active around 450 B.C., known for logical paradoxes that reduce to absurdity various attempts to define *Being*. Aristotle reports that Zeno's paradox on sound questioned: If a grain of millet falling makes no sound, how can a bushel of grains make any sound? (Aristotle's *Physics* 5.250a.19).

HAMM   No.

CLOV   Then how can it end?

HAMM   You want it to end?

CLOV   I want to sing.

HAMM   I can't prevent you.

[*Pause.* CLOV *turns towards window right.*]

CLOV   What did I do with that steps? [*He looks around for ladder.*] You didn't see that steps? [*He sees it.*] Ah, about time. [*He goes towards window left.*] Sometimes I wonder if I'm in my right mind. Then it passes over and I'm as lucid as before. [*He gets up on ladder, looks out of window.*] Christ, she's under water! [*He looks.*] How can that be? [*He pokes forward his head, his hand above his eyes.*] It hasn't rained. [*He wipes the pane, looks. Pause.*] Ah what a fool I am! I'm on the wrong side! [*He gets down, takes a few steps towards window right.*] Under water! [*He goes back for ladder.*] What a fool I am! [*He carries ladder towards window right.*] Sometimes I wonder if I'm in my right senses. Then it passes off and I'm as intelligent as ever. [*He sets down ladder under window right, gets up on it, looks out of window. He turns towards* HAMM.] Any particular sector you fancy? Or merely the whole thing?

HAMM   Whole thing.

CLOV   The general effect? Just a moment. [*He looks out of window. Pause.*]

HAMM   Clov.

CLOV [*Absorbed.*]   Mmm.

HAMM   Do you know what it is?

CLOV [*As before.*]   Mmm.

HAMM   I was never there. [*Pause.*] Clov!

CLOV [*Turning towards* HAMM, *exasperated.*]   What is it?

HAMM   I was never there.

CLOV   Lucky for you. [*He looks out of window.*]

HAMM   Absent, always. It all happened without me. I don't know what's happened. [*Pause.*] Do you know what's happened? [*Pause.*] Clov!

CLOV [*Turning towards* HAMM, *exasperated.*]   Do you want me to look at this muckheap, yes or no?

HAMM   Answer me first.

CLOV   What?

HAMM   Do you know what's happened?

CLOV   When? Where?

HAMM [*Violently.*]   When! What's happened? Use your head, can't you! What has happened?

CLOV   What for Christ's sake does it matter? [*He looks out of window.*]

HAMM   I don't know.

[*Pause.* CLOV *turns towards* HAMM.]

CLOV [*Harshly.*]   When old Mother Pegg asked you for oil for her lamp and you told her to get out to hell, you knew what was happening then, no? [*Pause.*] You know what she died of, Mother Pegg? Of darkness.

HAMM [*Feebly.*]   I hadn't any.

CLOV [*As before.*]   Yes, you had. [*Pause.*]

HAMM   Have you the glass?

CLOV   No, it's clear enough as it is.

HAMM   Go and get it.
  [*Pause.* CLOV *casts up his eyes, brandishes his fists. He loses balance, clutches on to the ladder. He starts to get down, halts.*]
CLOV   There's one thing I'll never understand. [*He gets down.*] Why I always obey you. Can you explain that to me?
HAMM   No. . . . Perhaps it's compassion. [*Pause.*] A kind of great compassion. [*Pause.*] Oh you won't find it easy, you won't find it easy.
  [*Pause.* CLOV *begins to move about the room in search of the telescope.*]
CLOV   I'm tired of our goings on, very tired. [*He searches.*] You're not sitting on it? [*He moves the chair, looks at the place where it stood, resumes his search.*]
HAMM [*Anguished.*]   Don't leave me there! [*Angrily* CLOV *restores the chair to its place.*] Am I right in the center?
CLOV   You'd need a microscope to find this— [*He sees the telescope.*] Ah, about time. [*He picks up the telescope, gets up on the ladder, turns the telescope on the without.*]
HAMM   Give me the dog.
CLOV [*Looking.*]   Quiet!
HAMM [*Angrily.*]   Give me the dog!
  [CLOV *drops the telescope, clasps his hands to his head. Pause. He gets down precipitately, looks for the dog, sees it, picks it up, hastens towards* HAMM *and strikes him violently on the head with the dog.*]
CLOV   There's your dog for you!
  [*The dog falls to the ground. Pause.*]
HAMM   He hit me!
CLOV   You drive me mad, I'm mad!
HAMM   If you must hit me, hit me with the axe. [*Pause.*] Or with the gaff, hit me with the gaff. Not with the dog. With the gaff. Or with the axe.
  [CLOV *picks up the dog and gives it to* HAMM *who takes it in his arms.*]
CLOV [*Imploringly.*]   Let's stop playing!
HAMM   Never! [*Pause.*] Put me in my coffin.
CLOV   There are no more coffins.
HAMM   Then let it end! [CLOV *goes towards ladder.*] With a bang! [CLOV *gets up on ladder, gets down again, looks for telescope, sees it, picks it up, gets up ladder, raises telescope.*] Of darkness! And me? Did anyone ever have pity on me?
CLOV [*Lowering the telescope, turning towards* HAMM.]   What? [*Pause.*] Is it me you're referring to?
HAMM [*Angrily.*]   An aside, ape! Did you never hear an aside before? [*Pause.*] I'm warming up for my last soliloquy.
CLOV   I warn you. I'm going to look at this filth since it's an order. But it's the last time. [*He turns the telescope on the without.*] Let's see. [*He moves the telescope.*] Nothing . . . nothing . . . good . . . good . . . nothing . . . goo— [*He starts, lowers the telescope, examines it, turns it again on the without. Pause.*] Bad luck to it!
HAMM   More complications! [CLOV *gets down.*] Not an underplot, I trust.
  [CLOV *moves ladder nearer window, gets up on it, turns telescope on the without.*]

CLOV [*Dismayed.*]   Looks like a small boy!

HAMM [*Sarcastic.*]   A small . . . boy!

CLOV   I'll go and see. [*He gets down, drops the telescope, goes towards door, turns.*] I'll take the gaff. [*He looks for the gaff, sees it, picks it up, hastens towards door.*]

HAMM   No! [CLOV *halts.*]

CLOV   No? A potential procreator?

HAMM   If he exists he'll die there or he'll come here. And if he doesn't . . . [*Pause.*]

CLOV   You don't believe me? You think I'm inventing? [*Pause.*]

HAMM   It's the end, Clov, we've come to the end. I don't need you any more. [*Pause.*]

CLOV   Lucky for you. [*He goes towards door.*]

HAMM   Leave me the gaff.
[CLOV *gives him the gaff, goes towards door, halts, looks at alarm-clock, takes it down, looks round for a better place to put it, goes to bins, puts it on lid of* NAGG's *bin. Pause.*]

CLOV   I'll leave you. [*He goes towards door.*]

HAMM   Before you go . . . [CLOV *halts near door.*] . . . say something.

CLOV   There is nothing to say.

HAMM   A few words . . . to ponder . . . in my heart.

CLOV   Your heart!

HAMM   Yes. [*Pause. Forcibly.*] Yes! [*Pause.*] With the rest, in the end, the shadows, the murmurs, all the trouble, to end up with. [*Pause.*] Clov. . . . He never spoke to me. Then, in the end, before he went, without my having asked him, he spoke to me. He said . . .

CLOV [*Despairingly.*]   Ah . . . !

HAMM   Something . . . from your heart.

CLOV   My heart!

HAMM   A few words . . . from your heart. [*Pause.*]

CLOV [*Fixed gaze, tonelessly, towards auditorium.*]   They said to me, That's love, yes, yes, not a doubt, now you see how—

HAMM   Articulate!

CLOV [*As before.*]   How easy it is. They said to me, That's friendship, yes, yes, no question, you've found it. They said to me, Here's the place, stop, raise your head and look at all that beauty. That order! They said to me. Come now, you're not a brute beast, think upon these things and you'll see how all becomes clear. And simple! They said to me, What skilled attention they get, all these dying of their wounds.

HAMM   Enough!

CLOV [*As before.*]   I say to myself—sometimes, Clov, you must learn to suffer better than that if you want them to weary of punishing you—one day. I say to myself—sometimes, Clov, you must be there better than that if you want them to let you go—one day. But I feel too old, and too far, to form new habits. Good, it'll never end, I'll never go. [*Pause.*] Then one day, suddenly, it ends, it changes, I don't understand, it dies, or it's me, I don't understand, that either. I ask the words that remain—sleeping, waking, morning, evening. They have nothing to say. [*Pause.*] I open the door of the cell and go. I am so bowed I only see my feet, if I open my eyes, and between my legs a little trail of black dust. I say to myself that the earth is extinguished, though I never saw it lit. [*Pause.*] It's easy going. [*Pause.*] When I fall I'll weep for happiness. [*Pause. He goes towards door.*]

HAMM   Clov! [CLOV *halts, without turning.*] Nothing. [CLOV *moves on.*] Clov!

    [CLOV *halts, without turning.*]

CLOV   This is what we call making an exit.

HAMM   I'm obliged to you, Clov. For your services.

CLOV [*Turning, sharply.*]   Ah pardon, it's I am obliged to you.

HAMM   It's we are obliged to each other. [*Pause.* CLOV *goes towards door.*] One thing more. [CLOV *halts.*] A last favor. [*Exit* CLOV.] Cover me with the sheet. [*Long pause.*] No? Good. [*Pause.*] Me to play. [*Pause. Wearily.*] Old endgame lost of old, play and lose and have done with losing. [*Pause. More animated.*] Let me see. [*Pause.*] Ah yes! [*He tries to move the chair, using the gaff as before. Enter* CLOV, *dressed for the road. Panama hat, tweed coat, raincoat over his arm, umbrella, bag. He halts by the door and stands there, impassive and motionless, his eyes fixed on* HAMM, *till the end.* HAMM *gives up.*] Good. [*Pause.*] Discard. [*He throws away the gaff, makes to throw away the dog, thinks better of it.*] Take it easy. [*Pause.*] And now? [*Pause.*] Raise hat. [*He raises his toque.*] Peace to our . . . arses. [*Pause.*] And put on again. [*He puts on his toque.*] Deuce. [*Pause. He takes off his glasses.*] Wipe. [*He takes out his handkerchief and, without unfolding it, wipes his glasses.*] And put on again. [*He puts on his glasses, puts back the handkerchief in his pocket.*] We're coming. A few more squirms like that and I'll call. [*Pause.*] A little poetry. [*Pause.*] You prayed— [*Pause. He corrects himself.*] You CRIED for night; it comes— [*Pause. He corrects himself.*] It FALLS: now cry in darkness. [*He repeats, chanting.*] You cried for night; it falls: now cry in darkness.[6] [*Pause.*] Nicely put, that. [*Pause.*] And now? [*Pause.*] Moments for nothing, now as always, time was never and time is over, reckoning closed and story ended. [*Pause. Narrative tone.*] If he could have his child with him. . . . [*Pause.*] It was the moment I was waiting for. [*Pause.*] You don't want to abandon him? You want him to bloom while you are withering? Be there to solace your last million last moments? [*Pause.*] He doesn't realize, all he knows is hunger, and cold, and death to crown it all. But you! You ought to know what the earth is like, nowadays. Oh I put him before his responsibilities! [*Pause. Normal tone.*] Well, there we are, there I am, that's enough. [*He raises the whistle to his lips, hesitates, drops it. Pause.*] Yes, truly! [*He whistles. Pause. Louder. Pause.*] Good. [*Pause.*] Father! [*Pause. Louder.*] Father! [*Pause.*] Good. [*Pause.*] We're coming. [*Pause.*] And to end up with? [*Pause.*] Discard. [*He throws away the dog. He tears the whistle from his neck.*] With my compliments. [*He throws whistle towards auditorium. Pause. He sniffs. Soft.*] Clov! [*Long pause.*] No? Good. [*He takes out the handkerchief.*] Since that's the way we're playing it . . . [*He unfolds handkerchief.*] . . . let's play it that way . . . [*He unfolds.*] . . . and speak no more about it . . . [*He finishes unfolding.*] . . .

6. Parody of a line from the poem *Meditation*, by Baudelaire: "You were calling for evening; it falls; here it is."

speak no more. [*He holds handkerchief spread out before him.*] Old
stancher! [*Pause.*] You . . . remain.
> [*Pause. He covers his face with handkerchief, lowers his arms to
> armrests, remains motionless.*]
> [*Brief tableau.*]

Curtain

RICHARD WRIGHT
1908–1960

Richard Wright is known internationally for powerful naturalist fiction that describes
alienated protagonists trapped in a materialistic and repressive society. He is equally
well known for another reason: his novels, short stories, autobiography, and essays
made him the twentieth-century's most forceful exponent of African-American consciousness. From his explosive first novel, *Native Son* (1940), to the political essays
of his later years, Wright explored the phenomenon of racism in modern society.
Concurrently, he pursued questions of existential identity, wrote about economic
inequities, and maintained that his characters' struggle transcended any purely racial
or gender definition. Realistic settings, an often hallucinatory narrative, and the violent protest embedded in his works opened new horizons for contemporary readers
and new possibilities for young African-American writers. Wright himself left the
United States during the anti-Communist witch-hunts of the late forties, and spent
the last fifteen years of his life in Paris. There he was welcomed by writers and
intellectuals like the existentialist philosopher Jean-Paul Sartre, the modernist writer
Gertrude Stein, and the Swedish sociologist Gunnar Myrdal. He continued to write
fiction but devoted much of his time to political and cultural issues, giving lectures
and writing polemic essays based on travels in Africa, Asia, and Spain.

Wright was born in 1908 on a farm near Natchez, Mississippi. His father was a
poor and illiterate sharecropper, and his mother taught in black country schools.
When Wright was five years old, his father deserted the family, and the family moved
several times to be with relatives while Wright's mother worked. A brief period of
prosperity in Arkansas ended when they had to flee town after the saloon-keeper uncle
with whom they were living was shot by envious whites. After Wright's mother suffered a paralytic stroke in 1919, the family was forced to move to her parents' house
in Jackson, Mississippi. Wright's education was irregular, and in many ways he was
self-taught: attending segregated black public schools and a Seventh Day Adventist
school until ninth grade, he was frequently absent because of family illness or inability
to buy books and clothes. The future novelist learned about the larger world from
library books that he not only had to acquire by subterfuge but also had to conceal.
His grandmother and aunt, strict Seventh Day Adventists, believed fiction immoral
and burned any novels or magazines he brought home. The privations and violence
of those early years, his rebellion against a fanatically strict religious upbringing, and
his long puzzlement over racism—his grandmother appeared white, and as a child he
did not feel a part of racial divisions—are described in *Uncle Tom's Children* (1938)
and in the autobiographical *Black Boy* (1945).

After graduating from junior high school in 1925, Wright worked two years for an
optical company in Memphis. He read widely, exploring many of the European
authors praised by contemporary editor and satirist H. L. Mencken, whose scathing

critique of American culture astonished and impressed him. Like other black writers of his generation, Wright found in the naturalist tradition of Europe and America a style congenial to what he had to say. He was particularly struck by the direct, factual, and seemingly objective manner of the American novelists Theodore Dreiser and Sinclair Lewis: "All my life had shaped me for the realism, the naturalism of the modern novel." His first-written, posthumously published novel, *Lawd Today* (1963), contains pages of dialogue that read like transcriptions of overheard speech. Later works go beyond this documentary style, as Wright finds affinities with the prose styles of Marcel Proust and the expatriate writer Gertrude Stein, and as he comes into contact with other American writers who show him diverse literary techniques adaptable to his own vision.

In 1927, eager to escape the South, Wright moved to Chicago, one of the northern cities that Southern blacks saw as havens of opportunity and acceptance. Life was not easy in Chicago: he supported himself as a porter, dishwasher, and postal clerk; and when he lost his job in the Depression, he went on relief sweeping streets. Soon he found work with the WPA Federal Writers' project, one of many federal projects created to help jobless people through the Depression. He wrote guidebooks for the WPA and poems, fiction, and essays on his own; in addition, he read authors like Dostoevsky, Gogol, Baudelaire, Mann, Proust, and T. S. Eliot and works in psychology and sociology. A friend introduced him to the John Reed Club, a Communist literary group, and he became a member of the Party in 1933. He withdrew from the Party in 1942, however, after becoming disillusioned with its emphasis on international political objectives and concurrent disregard for Wright's chief concerns: individualism, black civil rights, and artistic freedom.

Wright's first short-story collection, *Uncle Tom's Children* (1938), is set in the South, and all four stories are concerned with racism. (A new edition in 1940 included a fifth story and an autobiographical essay, *The Ethics of Living Jim Crow*.) The stories are tense with terror, beatings, and murder, and only one (*Fire and Cloud*) gives any sense of even momentary triumph. *Big Boy Leaves Home*, the often-reprinted first story, describes a teenager's flight after three of his friends are killed—one in a horrific scene of tarring, feathering, and burning alive. *Uncle Tom's Children* won first prize in a Federal Writers' Project competition sponsored by *Story* magazine and was named one of the ten best books of the year. Still Wright was dissatisfied. He felt that something was lacking: "I found that I had written a book which even bankers' daughters could read and weep over and feel good about. I swore that if I ever wrote another book, no one would weep over it; that it would be so hard and deep that they would face it without the consolation of tears." Perhaps he had in mind the philosophical and political dimension of his later novels, starting with *Native Son*; perhaps, like Bertolt Brecht, he felt he could not teach his audience unless he prevented them from identifying too closely with his characters.

With *Native Son*, the account of a black chauffeur in Chicago who kills two women (one white and the other his black girlfriend) and is brought to trial after a lengthy manhunt, Wright finds the "hard and deep" tone he sought. The novel is, on one level, a lurid drama of murder, futile attempts to hide evidence, and eventual discovery; but it is also a dramatic account of poverty in the black ghetto and a psychological portrait of the hatred, fear, and confusion that characterize its violent protagonist, Bigger Thomas. In the lengthy third section, Wright presents a sociological analysis in the words of Bigger's Communist defense lawyer, who almost abandons any effective defense of his client for a lengthy denunciation of the society that made him a criminal. The ending of the novel shows a condemned Bigger surrounded by people who have their own interpretations of his condition, and Bigger himself just beginning to attain a sense of his own identity: "what I wanted, what I am." The novel appeared in 1940 as a Book-of-the-Month Club selection (with some deletions required by the publisher); it quickly broke sales records, and the novelist became a national figure.

Wright's style combines naturalism—that is, realistic description governed by "scientific" principles of environmental influence—and a poetic or symbolic style. Obsessive themes and color associations imply extended networks of meaning: the color white, for example, is always vaguely threatening and recurs in nightmares. The famous opening scene of *Native Son,* in which Bigger kills a monstrous rat invading his family kitchen, establishes a violent, doom-laden atmosphere that prefigures Bigger's own destiny to be hunted like an animal and killed. Realistic narrative often shifts into obsessed imaginings and fantastic dreams that suggest the action of larger psychological or cultural forces.

After his move to Paris in the mid-forties, Wright's work developed more global and universal themes. Now openly anti-Communist, he continued to push for revolutionary reform in *Black Power* (1954, an essay on Ghana), *Pagan Spain* (1956), and the lectures of *White Man, Listen!* (1957). His model for reform, however, was Western and industrial, a perspective that did not appeal to many African writers of the négritude (black identity) movement. The new novels became more philosophical and even didactic. *Savage Holiday* (1954), using Freudian symbolism (and white characters); *The Outsider* (1957), dramatizing existential themes in a collapsing society; and *The Long Dream* (1958), the first volume of a projected trilogy on black experience, move beyond racial questions to explore the human condition. Some critics have argued that Wright's exile in Europe cut him off from his roots and that the later novels are comparatively weak. Yet all share Wright's great theme in which a protagonist passes through violent crises that force a coming to terms with his or her identity and role in society. This subject, he asserted, is "the main burden of all serious fiction . . . character-destiny and the items, social, political, and personal, of that character-destiny." When Wright died of a heart attack on November 28, 1960, he was in the midst of many unfinished projects, including a book of haiku poetry.

The Man Who Was Almost a Man is drawn from the posthumously published *Eight Men* (1961), a collection of five stories, two radio plays, and an autobiographical essay that were written at different periods. An early version of the story, *Almos' a Man,* was published in 1941, and itself stems from a projected novel about a black boxer, *Tarbaby's Dawn.* Like much of Wright's fiction, *The Man Who Was Almost a Man* derives its setting and themes from the author's experience even though events are altered to fit the requirements of the story. Here racial issues are only hinted at as part of the background, while emphasis is put on the difficult passage from adolescence to maturity and on the vulnerability of fragile personalities to being defined from outside.

Seventeen-year-old Dave Saunders is desperate to be considered a man: his family, coworkers, employer, and the store owner all call him "boy" and remind him that he is only a child. He comes from a strict family that guides his every step. Treated like a child, he responds by seeing adulthood as a matter of power: and power, to Dave, means a gun. With a gun, people would have to respect him; he could "kill anybody, black or white." When Dave's attempts at gun practice turn sour, his adolescent vulnerability is badly hurt as he is ridiculed by his coworkers, betrayed—as he sees it—by his mother, promised a beating by his father, and required to pay for the dead mule with his wages for the next two years. Humiliation tips the balance between accepting responsibility for his actions and running away. It is not as a man that he flees, however, but as an adolescent whose whole sense of identity is now locked up with the gun. Like the railroad tracks stretching ahead, "away to somewhere, somewhere where he could be a man," Dave's escape is presented not as a solution but as a continuation of the same problem.

The Man Who Was Almost a Man is a good example of Wright's ability to combine realistic description with modernist techniques expressing a state of mind. His skillful use of dialect and his knowledgeable description of local scenes and attitudes place the story firmly in its sociohistorical setting. A more poetic approach is used to convey Dave's emotional turmoil: sensual images suggest his quasi-erotic response to the revolver, and an internalized point of view reproduces his startled pain when he shoots the gun and his horror when he realizes that he has just shot Jenny. Time slows down while Dave ineffectually plugs the mule's wounds with earth and watches her die; time slows again, and faces blur, when he is the humiliated focus of the crowd's attention. This blend of narrative realism and modernist manipulation of language typifies Wright's best work and makes *The Man Who Was Almost a Man* one of his most popular stories.

Michel Fabre, *The Unfinished Quest of Richard Wright* (rev. ed. 1992), trans. Isabel Barzun, is an excellent and readable biography. Useful essay collections that reprint reviews of Wright's work are Robert J. Butler, ed., *The Critical Response to Richard Wright* (1995), and Henry Louis Gates Jr. and K. A. Appiah, eds., *Richard Wright: Critical Perspectives Past and Present* (1993), which contains an essay specifically on the short stories. In addition are Harold Bloom, ed., *Richard Wright* (1987); Arnold Rampersad, ed., with Bruce Simon and Jeffrey Tucker, *Richard Wright: A Collection of Critical Essays* (1995); and Richard Macksey and Frank E. Moorer, eds., *Richard Wright, A Collection of Critical Essays* (1984).

The Man Who Was Almost a Man

Dave struck out across the fields, looking homeward through paling light. Whut's the use talkin wid em niggers in the field? Anyhow, his mother was putting supper on the table. Them niggers can't understan nothing. One of these days he was going to get a gun and practice shooting, then they couldn't talk to him as though he were a little boy. He slowed, looking at the ground. Shucks, Ah ain scareda them even ef they are biggern me! Aw, Ah know whut Ahma do. Ahm going by ol Joe's sto n git that Sears Roebuck catlog n look at them guns. Mebbe Ma will lemme buy one when she gits mah pay from ol man Hawkins. Ahma beg her t gimme some money. Ahm ol ernough to hava gun. Ahm seventeen. Almost a man. He strode, feeling his long loose-jointed limbs. Shucks, a man oughta hava little gun aftah he done worked hard all day.

He came in sight of Joe's store. A yellow lantern glowed on the front porch. He mounted steps and went through the screen door, hearing it bang behind him. There was a strong smell of coal oil and mackerel fish. He felt very confident until he saw fat Joe walk in through the rear door, then his courage began to ooze.

"Howdy, Dave! Whutcha want?"

"How yuh, Mistah Joe? Aw, Ah don wanna buy nothing. Ah jus wanted t see ef yuhd lemme look at tha catlog erwhile."

"Sure! You wanna see it here?"

"Nawsuh. Ah wans t take it home wid me. Ah'll bring it back termorrow when Ah come in from the fiels."

"You plannin on buying something?"

"Yessuh."

"Your ma lettin you have your own money now?"

"Shucks. Mistah Joe, Ahm gittin t be a man like anybody else!"

Joe laughed and wiped his greasy white face with a red bandanna.

"Whut you plannin on buyin?"

Dave looked at the floor, scratched his head, scratched his thigh, and smiled. Then he looked up shyly.

"Ah'll tell yuh, Mistah Joe, ef yuh promise yuh won't tell."

"I promise."

"Waal, Ahma buy a gun."

"A gun? Whut you want with a gun?"

"Ah wanna keep it."

"You ain't nothing but a boy. You don't need a gun."

"Aw, lemme have the catlog, Mistah Joe. Ah'll bring it back."

Joe walked through the rear door. Dave was elated. He looked around at barrels of sugar and flour. He heard Joe coming back. He craned his neck to see if he were bringing the book. Yeah, he's got it. Gawddog, he's got it!

"Here, but be sure you bring it back. It's the only one I got."

"Sho, Mistah Joe."

"Say, if you wanna buy a gun, why don't you buy one from me? I gotta gun to sell."

"Will it shoot?"

"Sure it'll shoot."

"Whut kind is it?"

"Oh, it's kinda old . . . a left-hand Wheeler.[1] A pistol. A big one."

"Is it got bullets in it?"

"It's loaded."

"Kin Ah see it?"

"Where's your money?"

"Whut yuh wan fer it?"

"I'll let you have it for two dollars."

"Just two dollahs? Shucks, Ah could buy tha when Ah git mah pay."

"I'll have it here when you want it."

"Awright, suh. Ah be in fer it."

He went through the door, hearing it slam again behind him. Ahma git some money from Ma n buy me a gun! Only two dollahs! He tucked the thick catalogue under his arm and hurried.

"Where yuh been, boy?" His mother held a steaming dish of black-eyed peas.

"Aw, Ma, Ah jus stopped down the road t talk wid the boys."

"Yuh know bettah t keep suppah waitin."

He sat down, resting the catalogue on the edge of the table.

"Yuh git up from there and git to the well n wash yosef! Ah ain feedin no hogs in mah house!"

She grabbed his shoulder and pushed him. He stumbled out of the room, then came back to get the catalogue.

"Whut this?"

"Aw, Ma, it's jusa catlog."

"Who yuh git it from?"

"From Joe, down at the sto."

"Waal, thas good. We kin use it in the outhouse."

"Naw, Ma." He grabbed for it. "Gimme ma catlog, Ma."

She held onto it and glared at him.

"Quit hollerin at me! Whut's wrong wid yuh? Yuh crazy?"

---

1. The first revolving pistol, patented by Captain Artemus Wheeler in 1818; it was superseded by the Colt revolver after 1830.

"But Ma, please. It ain mine! It's Joe's! He tol me t bring it back t im termorrow."

She gave up the book. He stumbled down the back steps, hugging the thick book under his arm. When he had splashed water on his face and hands, he groped back to the kitchen and fumbled in a corner for the towel. He bumped into a chair; it clattered to the floor. The catalogue sprawled at his feet. When he had dried his eyes he snatched up the book and held it again under his arm. His mother stood watching him.

"Now, ef yuh gonna act a fool over that ol book, Ah'll take it n burn it up."

"Naw, Ma, please."

"Waal, set down n be still!"

He sat down and drew the oil lamp close. He thumbed page after page, unaware of the food his mother set on the table. His father came in. Then his small brother.

"Whutcha got there, Dave?" his father asked.

"Jusa catlog," he answered, not looking up.

"Yeah, here they is!" His eyes glowed at blue-and-black revolvers. He glanced up, feeling sudden guilt. His father was watching him. He eased the book under the table and rested it on his knees. After the blessing was asked, he ate. He scooped up peas and swallowed fat meat without chewing. Buttermilk helped to wash it down. He did not want to mention money before his father. He would do much better by cornering his mother when she was alone. He looked at his father uneasily out of the edge of his eye.

"Boy, how come yuh don quit foolin wid tha book n eat yo suppah?"

"Yessuh."

"How you n ol man Hawkins gitten erlong?"

"Suh?"

"Can't yuh hear? Why don yuh lissen? Ah ast yu how wuz yuh n ol man Hawkins gittin erlong?"

"Oh, swell, Pa. Ah plows mo lan than anybody over there."

"Waal, yuh oughta keep yo mind on whut yuh doin."

"Yessuh."

He poured his plate full of molasses and sopped it up slowly with a chunk of cornbread. When his father and brother had left the kitchen, he still sat and looked again at the guns in the catalogue, longing to muster courage enough to present his case to his mother. Lawd, ef Ah only had tha pretty one! He could almost feel the slickness of the weapon with his fingers. If he had a gun like that he would polish it and keep it shining so it would never rust. N Ah'd keep it loaded, by Gawd!

"Ma?" His voice was hesitant.

"Hunh?"

"Ol man Hawkins give yuh mah money yit?"

"Yeah, but ain no usa yuh thinking bout throwin nona it erway. Ahm keepin tha money sos yuh kin have cloes t go to school this winter."

He rose and went to her side with the open catalogue in his palms. She was washing dishes, her head bent low over a pan. Shyly he raised the book. When he spoke, his voice was husky, faint.

"Ma, Gawd knows Ah wans one of these."

"One of whut?" she asked, not raising her eyes.

"One of these," he said again, not daring even to point. She glanced up at the page, then at him with wide eyes.

"Nigger, is yuh gone plumb crazy?"

"Aw, Ma—"

"Git outta here! Don yuh talk t me bout no gun! Yuh a fool!"

"Ma, Ah kin buy one fer two dollahs."

"Not ef Ah knows it, yuh ain!"

"But yuh promised me one—"

"Ah don care whut Ah promised! Yuh ain nothing but a boy yit!"

"Ma, ef yuh lemme buy one Ah'll *never* ast yuh fer nothing no mo."

"Ah tol yuh t git outta here! Yuh ain gonna toucha penny of tha money fer no gun! Thas how come Ah has Mistah Hawkins t pay yo wages t me, cause Ah knows yuh ain got no sense."

"But, Ma, we needa gun. Pa ain got no gun. We needa gun in the house. Yuh kin never tell whut might happen."

"Now don yuh try to maka fool outta me, boy! Ef we did hava gun, yuh wouldn't have it!"

He laid the catalogue down and slipped his arm around her waist.

"Aw, Ma, Ah done worked hard alla summer n ain ast yuh fer nothin, is Ah, now?"

"Thas whut yuh spose t do!"

"But Ma, Ah wans a gun. Yuh kin lemme have two dollahs outta mah money. Please, Ma. I kin give it to Pa . . . Please, Ma! Ah loves yuh, Ma."

When she spoke her voice came soft and low.

"Whut yu wan wida gun, Dave? Yuh don need no gun. Yuh'll git in trouble. N ef yo pa jus thought Ah let yuh have money t buy a gun he'd hava fit."

"Ah'll hide it, Ma. It ain but two dollahs."

"Lawd, chil, whut's wrong wid yuh?"

"Ain nothin wrong, Ma. Ahm almos a man now. Ah wans a gun."

"Who gonna sell yuh a gun?"

"Ol Joe at the sto."

"N it don cos but two dollahs?"

"Thas all, Ma. Jus two dollahs. Please, Ma."

She was stacking the plates away; her hands moved slowly, reflectively. Dave kept an anxious silence. Finally, she turned to him.

"Ah'll let yuh git tha gun ef yuh promise me one thing."

"Whut's tha, Ma?"

"Yuh bring it straight back t me, yuh hear? It be fer Pa."

"Yessum! Lemme go now, Ma."

She stooped, turned slightly to one side, raised the hem of her dress, rolled down the top of her stocking, and came up with a slender wad of bills.

"Here," she said. "Lawd knows yuh don need no gun. But yer pa does. Yuh bring it right back t me, yuh hear? Ahma put it up. Now ef yuh don, Ahma have yuh pa lick yuh so hard yuh won fergit it."

"Yessum."

He took the money, ran down the steps, and across the yard.

"Dave! Yuuuuuh Daaaaave!"

He heard, but he was not going to stop now. "Naw, Lawd!"

The first movement he made the following morning was to reach under his pillow for the gun. In the gray light of dawn he held it loosely, feeling a sense of power. Could kill a man with a gun like this. Kill anybody, black or white. And if he were holding his gun in his hand, nobody could run over him; they would have to respect him. It was a big gun, with a long barrel and a heavy handle. He raised and lowered it in his hand, marveling at its weight.

He had not come straight home with it as his mother had asked; instead he had stayed out in the fields, holding the weapon in his hand, aiming it now and then at some imaginary foe. But he had not fired it; he had been afraid that his father might hear. Also he was not sure he knew how to fire it.

To avoid surrendering the pistol he had not come into the house until he knew that they were all asleep. When his mother had tiptoed to his bedside late that night and demanded the gun, he had first played possum; then he had told her that the gun was hidden outdoors, that he would bring it to her in the morning. Now he lay turning it slowly in his hands. He broke it, took out the cartridges, felt them, and then put them back.

He slid out of bed, got a long strip of old flannel from a trunk, wrapped the gun in it, and tied it to his naked thigh while it was still loaded. He did not go in to breakfast. Even though it was not yet daylight, he started for Jim Hawkins' plantation. Just as the sun was rising he reached the barns where the mules and plows were kept.

"Hey! That you, Dave?"

He turned. Jim Hawkins stood eying him suspiciously.

"What're yuh doing here so early?"

"Ah didn't know Ah wuz gittin up so early, Mistah Hawkins. Ah wuz fixin t hitch up ol Jenny n take her t the fiels."

"Good. Since you're so early, how about plowing that stretch down by the woods?"

"Suits me, Mistah Hawkins."

"O.K. Go to it!"

He hitched Jenny to a plow and started across the fields. Hot dog! This was just what he wanted. If he could get down by the woods, he could shoot his gun and nobody would hear. He walked behind the plow, hearing the traces creaking, feeling the gun tied tight to his thigh.

When he reached the woods, he plowed two whole rows before he decided to take out the gun. Finally, he stopped, looked in all directions, then untied the gun and held it in his hand. He turned to the mule and smiled.

"Know whut this is, Jenny? Naw, yuh wouldn know! Yuhs jusa ol mule! Anyhow, this is a gun, n it kin shoot, by Gawd!"

He held the gun at arm's length. Whut t hell, Ahma shoot this thing! He looked at Jenny again.

"Lissen here, Jenny! When Ah pull this ol trigger, Ah don wan yuh t run n acka fool now!"

Jenny stood with head down, her short ears pricked straight. Dave walked off about twenty feet, held the gun far out from him at arm's length, and turned his head. Hell, he told himself, Ah ain afraid. The gun felt loose in his fingers; he waved it wildly for a moment. Then he shut his eyes and tightened his forefinger. Bloom! A report half deafened him and he thought his right hand was torn from his arm. He heard Jenny whinnying and galloping over the field, and he found himself on his knees, squeezing his fingers hard between his legs. His hand was numb; he jammed it into his mouth, trying to warm it, trying to stop the pain. The gun lay at his feet. He did not quite know what had happened. He stood up and stared at the gun as though it were a living thing. He gritted his teeth and kicked the gun. Yuh almos broke mah arm! He turned to look for Jenny; she was far over the fields, tossing her head and kicking wildly.

"Hol on there, ol mule!"

When he caught up with her she stood trembling, walling her big white eyes at him. The plow was far away; the traces had broken. Then Dave stopped short, looking, not believing. Jenny was bleeding. Her left side was red and wet with blood. He went closer. Lawd, have mercy! Wondah did Ah shoot this mule? He grabbed for Jenny's mane. She flinched, snorted, whirled, tossing her head.

"Hol on now! Hol on."

Then he saw the hole in Jenny's side, right between the ribs. It was round, wet, red. A crimson stream streaked down the front leg, flowing fast. Good Gawd! Ah wuzn't shootin at tha mule. He felt panic. He knew he had to stop that blood, or Jenny would bleed to death. He had never seen so much blood in all his life. He chased the mule for half a mile, trying to catch her. Finally she stopped, breathing hard, stumpy tail half arched. He caught her mane and led her back to where the plow and gun lay. Then he stooped and grabbed handfuls of damp black earth and tried to plug the bullet hole. Jenny shuddered, whinnied, and broke from him.

"Hol on! Hol on now!"

He tried to plug it again, but blood came anyhow. His fingers were hot and sticky. He rubbed dirt into his palms, trying to dry them. Then again he attempted to plug the bullet hole, but Jenny shied away, kicking her heels high. He stood helpless. He had to do something. He ran at Jenny; she dodged him. He watched a red stream of blood flow down Jenny's leg and form a bright pool at her feet.

"Jenny . . . Jenny," he called weakly.

His lips trembled. She's bleeding t death! He looked in the direction of home, wanting to go back, wanting to get help. But he saw the pistol lying in the damp black clay. He had a queer feeling that if he only did something, this would not be; Jenny would not be there bleeding to death.

When he went to her this time, she did not move. She stood with sleepy, dreamy eyes; and when he touched her she gave a low-pitched whinny and knelt to the ground, her front knees slopping in blood.

"Jenny . . . Jenny . . ." he whispered.

For a long time she held her neck erect; then her head sank, slowly. Her ribs swelled with a mighty heave and she went over.

Dave's stomach felt empty, very empty. He picked up the gun and held it gingerly between his thumb and forefinger. He buried it at the foot of a tree. He took a stick and tried to cover the pool of blood with dirt—but what was the use? There was Jenny lying with her mouth open and her eyes walled and glassy. He could not tell Jim Hawkins he had shot his mule. But he had to tell something. Yeah, Ah'll tell em Jenny started gittin wil n fell on the joint of the plow. . . . But that would hardly happen to a mule. He walked across the field slowly, head down.

It was sunset. Two of Jim Hawkins' men were over near the edge of the woods digging a hole in which to bury Jenny. Dave was surrounded by a knot of people, all of whom were looking down at the dead mule.

"I don't see how in the world it happened," said Jim Hawkins for the tenth time.

The crowd parted and Dave's mother, father, and small brother pushed into the center.

"Where Dave?" his mother called.

"There he is," said Jim Hawkins.

His mother grabbed him.

"Whut happened, Dave? Whut yuh done?"

"Nothin."

"C mon, boy, talk," his father said.

Dave took a deep breath and told the story he knew nobody believed.

"Waal," he drawled. "Ah brung ol Jenny down here sos Ah could do mah plowin. Ah plowed bout two rows, just like yuh see." He stopped and pointed at the long rows of upturned earth. "Then somethin musta been wrong wid ol Jenny. She wouldn ack right a-tall. She started snortin n kickin her heels. Ah tried t hol her, but she pulled erway, rearin n goin in. Then when the point of the plow was stickin up in the air, she swung erroun n twisted herself back on it . . . She stuck herself n started t bleed. N fo Ah could do anything, she wuz dead."

"Did you ever hear of anything like that in all your life?" asked Jim Hawkins.

There were white and black standing in the crowd. They murmured. Dave's mother came close to him and looked hard into his face. "Tell the truth, Dave," she said.

"Looks like a bullet hole to me," said one man.

"Dave, whut yuh do wid the gun?" his mother asked.

The crowd surged in, looking at him. He jammed his hands into his pockets, shook his head slowly from left to right, and backed away. His eyes were wide and painful.

"Did he hava gun?" asked Jim Hawkins.

"By Gawd, Ah tol yuh tha wuz a gun wound," said a man, slapping his thigh.

His father caught his shoulders and shook him till his teeth rattled.

"Tell whut happened, yuh rascal! Tell whut . . ."

Dave looked at Jenny's stiff legs and began to cry.

"Whut yuh do wid tha gun?" his mother asked.

"Whut wuz he doin wida gun?" his father asked.

"Come on and tell the truth," said Hawkins. "Ain't nobody going to hurt you . . ."

His mother crowded close to him.

"Did yuh shoot tha mule, Dave?"

Dave cried, seeing blurred white and black faces.

"Ahh ddinn gggo tt sshooot hher . . . Ah ssswear ffo Gawd Ahh ddin . . . Ah wuz a-tryin t sssee ef the old gggun would sshoot—"

"Where yuh git the gun from?" his father asked.

"Ah got it from Joe, at the sto."

"Where yuh git the money?"

"Ma give it t me."

"He kept worryin me, Bob. Ah had t. Ah tol im t bring the gun right back t me . . . It was fer yuh, the gun."

"But how yuh happen to shoot that mule?" asked Jim Hawkins.

"Ah wuzn shootin at the mule, Mistah Hawkins. The gun jumped when Ah pulled the trigger . . . N fo Ah knowed anythin Jenny was there a-bleedin."

Somebody in the crowd laughed. Jim Hawkins walked close to Dave and looked into his face.

"Well, looks like you have bought you a mule, Dave."

"Ah swear fo Gawd, Ah didn go t kill the mule, Mistah Hawkins!"

"But you killed her!"

All the crowd was laughing now. They stood on tiptoe and poked heads over one another's shoulders.

"Well, boy, looks like yuh done bought a dead mule! Hahaha!"

"Ain tha ershame."

"Hohohohoho."

Dave stood, head down, twisting his feet in the dirt.

"Well, you needn't worry about it, Bob," said Jim Hawkins to Dave's father. "Just let the boy keep on working and pay me two dollars a month."

"Whut yuh wan fer yo mule, Mistah Hawkins?"

Jim Hawkins screwed up his eyes.

"Fifty dollars."

"Whut yuh do wid tha gun?" Dave's father demanded.

Dave said nothing.

"Yuh wan me t take a tree n beat yuh till yuh talk!"

"Nawsuh!"

"Whut yuh do wid it?"

"Ah throwed it erway."

"Where?"

"Ah . . . Ah throwed it in the creek."

"Waal, c mon home. N firs thing in the mawnin git to tha creek n fin tha gun."

"Yessuh."

"Whut yuh pay fer it?"

"Two dollahs."

"Take tha gun n git yo money back n carry it t Mistah Hawkins, yuh hear? N don fergit Ahma lam you black bottom good fer this! Now march yosef on home, suh!"

Dave turned and walked slowly. He heard people laughing. Dave glared, his eyes welling with tears. Hot anger bubbled in him. Then he swallowed and stumbled on.

That night Dave did not sleep. He was glad that he had gotten out of killing the mule so easily, but he was hurt. Something hot seemed to turn over inside him each time he remembered how they had laughed. He tossed on his bed, feeling his hard pillow. N Pa says he's gonna beat me . . . He remembered other beatings, and his back quivered. Naw, naw, Ah sho don wan im t beat me tha way no mo. Dam em all! Nobody ever gave him anything. All he did was work. They treat me like a mule, n then they beat me. He gritted his teeth. N Ma had t tell on me.

Well, if he had to, he would take old man Hawkins that two dollars. But that meant selling the gun. And he wanted to keep that gun. Fifty dollars for a dead mule.

He turned over, thinking how he had fired the gun. He had an itch to fire it again. Ef other men kin shoota gun, by Gawd, Ah kin! He was still, listening. Mebbe they all sleepin now. The house was still. He heard the soft breathing of his brother. Yes, now! He would go down and get that gun and see if he could fire it! He eased out of bed and slipped into overalls.

The moon was bright. He ran almost all the way to the edge of the woods. He stumbled over the ground, looking for the spot where he had buried the gun. Yeah, here it is. Like a hungry dog scratching for a bone, he pawed it up. He puffed his black cheeks and blew dirt from the trigger and barrel. He broke it and found four cartridges unshot. He looked around; the fields were filled with silence and moonlight. He clutched the gun stiff and hard in his fingers. But, as soon as he wanted to pull the trigger, he shut his eyes and turned his head. Naw, Ah can't shoot wid mah eyes closed n mah head turned. With effort he held his eyes open; then he squeezed. *Blooooom!* He was stiff, not breathing. The gun was still in his hands. Dammit, he'd done it! He fired again. *Blooooom!* He smiled. *Blooooom! Blooooom! Click, click.* There! It was empty. If anybody could shoot a gun, he could. He put the gun into his hip pocket and started across the fields.

When he reached the top of a ridge he stood straight and proud in the moonlight, looking at Jim Hawkins' big white house, feeling the gun sagging in his pocket. Lawd, ef Ah had just one mo bullet Ah'd taka shot at tha house. Ah'd like t scare ol man Hawkins jusa little . . . Jusa enough t let im know Dave Saunders is a man.

To his left the road curved, running to the tracks of the Illinois Central. He jerked his head, listening. From far off came a faint *hoooof-hoooof; hoooof-hoooof; hoooof-hoooof.* . . . He stood rigid. Two dollahs a mont. Les see now . . . Tha means it'll take bout two years. Shucks! Ah'll be dam!

He started down the road, toward the tracks. Yeah, here she comes! He stood beside the track and held himself stiffly. Here she comes, erroun the ben . . . C mon, yuh slow poke! C mon! He had his hand on his gun; something quivered in his stomach. Then the train thundered past, the gray and brown box cars rumbling and clinking. He gripped the gun tightly; then he jerked his hand out of his pocket. Ah betcha Bill wouldn't do it! Ah betcha . . . The cars slid past, steel grinding upon steel. Ahm ridin yuh ternight, so hep me Gawd! He was hot all over. He hesitated just a moment; then he grabbed, pulled atop of a car, and lay flat. He felt his pocket; the gun was still there. Ahead the long rails were glinting in the moonlight, stretching away, away to somewhere, somewhere where he could be a man . . .

NAGUIB MAHFOUZ
born 1911

The foremost novelist writing in Arabic traces his roots to the civilization of the ancient Egyptians, over five thousand years ago. Past and present combine for Naguib Mahfouz as he interrogates the destiny of his people and their often-traumatic adjustment to modern industrial society. Without Mahfouz, it is said, the turbulent history of twentieth-century Egypt would never be known. His fictional families and frustrated middle-class clerks have documented the successive stages of Egyptian social and political life from the time the country cast off foreign rule and became a "post-colonial" society. Time, in fact, is the real protagonist of his novels: the time in which individuals live and die, governments come and go, and social values are transformed—time, ultimately, as the conqueror that reduces human endeavor to nothing and forces attention on spiritual truth. Mahfouz's novels and short stories have millions of readers throughout the Arab world, and a growing audience in the West, because they deal with basic human issues in a realistic social context. Generations of Arabs have read his works or seen them adapted to film and television, and his characters have become household words. Mahfouz the craftsman has also wrought a change in Arabic prose, synthesizing traditional literary style and modern speech to create a new literary language understood by Arabs everywhere.

Readers of his best-known works, however, will find many similarities with the nineteenth-century realist novel in Europe. Mahfouz has been called the "Balzac of Egypt"—a comparison to the great French novelist and panoramic chronicler of society Honoré de Balzac (1799–1850)—and he is well acquainted with the works of Gustave Flaubert, Leo Tolstoy, and other nineteenth-century novelists. Traditional Arabic literature has many forms of narrative, but the novel is not one of them; and contemporary writers like Mahfouz have adapted the Western form to their own needs. Their readers will find familiar nineteenth-century strategies such as a chronological plot, unified characters, the inclusion of documentary information and realistic details, a panoramic view of society including a strong moral and humanistic perspective, and—typically if not necessarily—a picture of urban middle-class life. Among twentieth-century authors Mahfouz might be compared with Alexander Solzhenitsyn for his realist style and analysis of national identity. The Egyptian author employs allegory much more than do traditionally realist authors, however, and his most recent work has made use of fragmented and absurdist techniques as well as a variety of classical Arabic forms. He continues to be preoccupied with individual experience inside what he calls the "tragedies of society," although his focus is not restricted to the individualized existentialism of Jean-Paul Sartre or Albert Camus and embraces a complex of social relationships. Like the nineteenth-century novelists he follows, Mahfouz believes in the social function of art and the concomitant responsibility of the writer. His books have been censored and banned in many Arab countries, and he was blacklisted for several years for supporting Egypt's 1979 peace treaty with Israel.

Naguib Mahfouz was born in Cairo on December 11, 1911, the youngest of seven children in the family of a civil servant. The family moved from their home in the old Jamaliya district to the suburbs of Cairo when the boy was young. He attended government schools and entered the University of Cairo in 1930, graduating in 1934 with a degree in philosophy. These were not quiet years: Egypt, officially under Turkish rule, had been occupied by the British since 1883 and was declared a British protectorate at the start of World War I in 1914. Mahfouz grew up in the midst of an ongoing struggle for national independence that culminated in a violent uprising against the British in 1919 and the negotiation of a constitutional monarchy in 1923. The consistent focus on Egyptian cultural identity that permeates his work may well have its roots in this early turbulent period. The difficulty of disentangling cultural traditions, however, is indicated by the fact that Mahfouz's first published book was a 1932 translation of an English work on ancient Egypt.

While at the university, Mahfouz made friends with the socialist and Darwinian thinker Salama Musa and began to write articles for Musa's journal *Al-Majalla al-Jadida* (The modern magazine). In 1938, he published his first collection of stories, *Whispers of Madness*, and in 1939 the first of three historical novels set in ancient Egypt. He planned at that time to write a set of forty books on the model of the historical romance written by the British novelist Sir Walter Scott (1771–1832).

These first novels already included modern references, and few missed the criticism of King Farouk in *Radubis* (1943) or the analogy in *The Struggle for Thebes* (1944) between the ancient Egyptian battle to expel Hyksos usurpers and twentieth-century rebellions against foreign rule. In 1945 Mahfouz shifted decisively to the realistic novel and a portrayal of modern society. He focused on the social and spiritual dilemmas of the middle class in Cairo, documenting in vivid detail the life of an urban society that represented modern Egypt.

The major work of this period, and Mahfouz's masterwork in many eyes, is *The Cairo Trilogy* (1956–57), three volumes depicting the experience of three generations of a Cairo family between 1918 and 1944. Into this story, whose main protagonist Mahfouz has called Time, is woven a social history of Egypt after World War I. Mahfouz's achievement was recognized in the State Prize for literature in 1956, but he himself temporarily ceased to write after finishing the *Trilogy* in 1952. In that year, an officers' coup headed by Gamal Abdel Nasser overthrew the monarchy and instituted a republic that promised democratic reforms, and there was a change in the panorama of Egyptian society that Mahfouz described. Although the author was at first optimistic about the new order, he soon recognized that not much had changed for the general populace. When he started publishing again in 1959, his works included much open criticism of the Nasser regime.

Although he had become the best-known writer in the Arab world, his works read by millions, Mahfouz like other Arab authors could not make a living from his books. Copyright protection was minimal, and without copyright protection even best-selling authors received only small sums for their books. Until he began writing for motion pictures in the 1960s, he supported himself and his family through various positions in governmental ministries and as a contributing editor for the leading newspaper, *Al-Ahram*. Attached to the Ministry of Culture in 1954, he adapted novels for film and television and later became director-general of the governmental Cinema Organization. (Cinema, radio, and television are nationalized industries in Egypt.) After his retirement from the civil service in 1971, Mahfouz continued to publish articles and short stories in *Al-Ahram*, where most of his novels have appeared in serialized form before being issued as paperbacks. When he received the Nobel Prize in 1988, at the age of seventy-seven, he was still publishing a weekly column, "Point of View," in *Al-Ahram*.

Three years after *The Cairo Trilogy* brought him international praise, Mahfouz shocked many readers with a new book, *Children of Gebelawi*. Serialized in *Al-Ahram*, *Children of Gebelawi* is on the surface another description of a patriarchal family evolving in modern times. The story of the patriarch Gebelawi and his disobedient or ambitious children, however, is also an allegory of religious history. Its personification of God, Adam, and the prophets—among whom science is included as the youngest and most destructive son—and its simultaneous portrayal of the prophets as primarily social reformers rather than religious figures, scandalized orthodox believers. The book was banned throughout the Arab world except in Lebanon, and the Jordan League of Writers attacked Mahfouz as a "delinquent man" whose novels were "plagued with sex and drugs." *Children of Gebelawi* remains unpublished in Egypt to this day.

Mahfouz took up writing short stories again in the early 1960s after concentrating on novels for two decades. His second collection, *God's World* (1963), combined social realism and metaphysical speculation. He also began to move away from an "objective," realistic style toward one that emphasized subjective and mystic awareness, drawing on an Islamic mystical tradition whose comprehensive tolerance is far from (and often opposed by) the rigid beliefs of contemporary Muslim fundamentalists. The perceptions of individual characters govern works such as *The Thief and the Dogs* (1962), the story of a released prisoner who—seeking revenge on his unfaithful wife and the man who betrayed him—is trapped by police dogs and shot; and *Miramar* (1967), in which different points of view describe the disappointed love of a young servant girl, her determination to shape her own career, and the death of a lodger. Mahfouz did not abandon social commentary in his new mode. Individual characters represent particular classes or even (with *Miramar*'s servant girl) Egypt itself, and the film made from *Miramar* attracted large audiences for its sharp criticism of the dominant political party, the Arab Socialist Union. In *Mirrors* (1972), brief accounts of fifty-four different characters "mirror" various aspects of contemporary Egyptian society.

Mahfouz's approach changed again in the late 1960s; social commentary in the novels became even more direct, while individual stories grew more fragmented and even absurdist in style. Egypt's defeat by Israel in the June 1967 war had a shattering effect on the nation's self-confidence, and Mahfouz responded to what he saw as the country's spiritual dilemma. Stories written between October and December 1967 and collected in *Under the Bus Shelter* repeatedly show contradictory and incomprehensible events happening to perplexed and frustrated people. An almost cinematic style emerged, emphasizing dialogue over interpretation; some pieces in later collections resemble one-act plays. In the title story of *Under the Bus Shelter,* people waiting for a bus observe beatings, a car crash with several deaths, a couple making love on a corpse, dancing, the rapid construction of a monumental grave in which both corpses and lovers are buried, inaudible speeches, a man who may possibly be the director of the film (if it *is* a film) but may also be a thug, a decapitation, and finally "a group of official-looking men wandering around" whose appearance frightens off the others— until the puzzled observers are shot by a previously apathetic policeman when they ask questions. Several novels in the 1970s and 1980s reveal a similar bleak perspective in a more didactic style; *There Only Remains One Hour* (1982), for example, portrays current events as a sequence of failed efforts to achieve peace and prosperity.

Mahfouz's style continues to evolve in new directions. His most recent work has adapted classical Arabic narrative forms such as the *maqama* (elaborate rhymed trickster tales) or folk narratives like the *Arabian Nights* into imaginative sequences such as *The Nights of "The Thousand and One Nights"* or *The Epic of the Riff-Raff.* While these latest works have disconcerted adherents of his earlier, realistic style, they are an integral part of the Egyptian writer's attempt to find new ways to express Arabic culture and to comment from a broader, often prophetic perspective on the contemporary scene. That Mahfouz is impelled by a sense of moral purpose is evident throughout his works, and perhaps no more so than in his Nobel Prize acceptance speech in 1988. Speaking first for Arabic letters but also as a representative of the Third World, he addressed the leaders of a Western civilization that has allowed science and technology to outweigh basic human values. "The developed world and the third world are but one family. Each human being bears responsibility towards it by the degree of what he has obtained of knowledge, wisdom, and civilization. . . . In the name of the third world: Be not spectators to our miseries." The "able ones, the civilized ones," he added, perhaps ironically, must be guided by the collective needs of humanity. He continues to defend humanitarian values in Egypt as well. After Islamic fundamentalists pressured the Ministry of Culture into establishing precensorship for books in 1994, Mahfouz attacked this "intellectual terrorism" against the arts; he was later stabbed in the neck and lost the use of his writing hand.

Zaabalawi, a story included in *God's World,* contains many of Mahfouz's predominant themes. Written two years after *Children of Gebelawi,* it echoes the earlier work's religious symbolism in the mysterious character of Zaabalawi himself. It is also a social document: the narrator's quest for Zaabalawi brings him before various representatives of modern Egyptian society inside a realistically described Cairo. *Zaabalawi,* therefore, takes on the character of a social and metaphysical allegory. Its terminally ill narrator seeks to be cured in a quest that implies not only physical healing but also religious salvation. He has already exhausted the resources of medical science and, in desperation, he decides to seek out a holy man whose name he recalls from childhood tales.

In the initial stage of his search, the protagonist is coldly received by a lawyer and a district officer, former acquaintances of Zaabalawi who have become worldly, materialistic, and highly successful. Moreover, these bureaucrats who depend on reason, technology, and businesslike efficiency can do no more than send him to old addresses or draw him city maps. Zaabalawi is still alive, they say, but he is unpredictable and hard to find now that he no longer inhabits his old home—a now-dilapidated mansion in front of which an old bookseller sells used books on mysticism and theology. In contrast, the calligrapher and composer to whom the narrator next turns welcome him as a person. Indeed, the composer reproves him for thinking only of his errand and overlooking the value of getting to know another human being. The relationship among art, human sympathy, and spiritual values is made clear, for Zaabalawi is close to both artists and has provided inspiration for their best works. In the last scene, at the Negma Bar, Mahfouz fuses the realistic description of a hardened drinker with a dream-vision of another, peaceful world. At this stage of the quest, the narrator is not even allowed to state his errand but must place himself on a level with his drunken host before being allowed to speak. When he does sink into oblivion (in stages that suggest a mystic stripping-away of rational faculties), he is rewarded in his dreams by a glimpse of paradise and wakes to find that Zaabalawi has been beside him as he slept. *Zaabalawi* ends as it began—"I have to find Zaabalawi"—but the seeker is now more confident, and the route more clearly marked.

Roger M. A. Allen, *The Arabic Novel: An Historical and Critical Introduction* (1982), is an authoritative introduction that situates Mahfouz in the context of modern Arabic literature and includes a bibliography of works in Arabic and Western languages. The author's own perspective is given in Najib Mahfuz, *Echoes of an Autobiography* (1997), trans. Denys Johnson-Davies. Sasson Somekh, "Za'balawi"—Author, Theme and Technique" in *Journal of Arabic Literature* (1970), examines the story as a "double-layered" structure governed by references to Sufi mysticism. Michael Beard and Adnan Haydar, eds., *Naguib Mahfouz: From Regional Fame to Global Recognition* (1993), assembles eleven original essays on themes, individual works, and cultural contexts in Mahfouz's work. Trevor le Gassick, ed., *Critical Perspectives on Naguib Mahfouz* (1991), reprints articles on Mahfouz's work up to the 1970s. Rasheed El-Enany, ed., *Naguib Mahfouz: The Pursuit of Meaning* (1993), is an excellent study that includes biography, analyses of novels, short stories, and plays and a guide for further reading. Comparative studies include Mona Mikhail, *Studies in the Short Fiction of Mahfouz and Idris* (1992), an introductory work juxtaposing themes in Hemingway, Idris, Mahfouz, and Camus; and Samia Mehrez, *Egyptian Writers between History and Fiction: Essays on Naguib Mahfouz, Sonallah Ibrahim, and Gamal al-Ghitani* (1994).

PRONOUNCING GLOSSARY

The following list uses common English syllables and stress accents to provide rough equivalents of selected words whose pronunciation may be unfamiliar to the general reader.

Hassanein: *hassan-ayn'*

Naguib Mahfouz: *nah-geeb' mah-fooz'*

Qamar: *qa-mar'*

Umm al-Ghulam: *oum al–ghol-am'*

Wanas al-Damanhouri: *wan'-nas ad–dam-an-oo'-ree*

Zaabalawi: *zah-bah-lah'-wee*

Zaabalawi[1]

Finally I became convinced that I had to find Sheikh[2] Zaabalawi.

The first time I had heard of his name had been in a song:

> Oh what's become of the world, Zaabalawi?
> They've turned it upside down and taken away its taste.

It had been a popular song in my childhood, and one day it had occurred to me to demand of my father, in the way children have of asking endless questions:

"Who is Zaabalawi?"

He had looked at me hesitantly as though doubting my ability to understand the answer. However, he had replied, "May his blessing descend upon you, he's a true saint of God, a remover of worries and troubles. Were it not for him I would have died miserably—"

In the years that followed, I heard my father many a time sing the praises of this good saint and speak of the miracles he performed. The days passed and brought with them many illnesses, for each one of which I was able, without too much trouble and at a cost I could afford, to find a cure, until I became afflicted with that illness for which no one possesses a remedy. When I had tried everything in vain and was overcome by despair, I remembered by chance what I had heard in my childhood: Why, I asked myself, should I not seek out Sheikh Zaabalawi? I recollected my father saying that he had made his acquaintance in Khan Gaafar[3] at the house of Sheikh Qamar, one of those sheikhs who practiced law in the religious courts, and so I took myself off to his house. Wishing to make sure that he was still living there, I made inquiries of a vendor of beans whom I found in the lower part of the house.

"Sheikh Qamar!" he said, looking at me in amazement. "He left the quarter ages ago. They say he's now living in Garden City and has his office in al-Azhar Square."[4]

I looked up the office address in the telephone book and immediately set off to the Chamber of Commerce Building, where it was located. On asking to see Sheikh Qamar, I was ushered into a room just as a beautiful woman with a most intoxicating perfume was leaving it. The man received me with a smile and motioned me toward a fine leather-upholstered chair. Despite the thick soles of my shoes, my feet were conscious of the lushness of the costly carpet. The man wore a lounge suit and was smoking a cigar; his manner of sitting was that of someone well satisfied both with himself and with his worldly possessions. The look of warm welcome he gave me left no doubt in my mind that he thought me a prospective client, and I felt acutely embarrassed at encroaching upon his valuable time.

"Welcome!" he said, prompting me to speak.

"I am the son of your old friend Sheikh Ali al-Tatawi," I answered so as to put an end to my equivocal position.

---

1. Translated by Denys Johnson-Davies.   2. A title of respect (originally "old man"), often indicating rulership.   3. Gaafar Market, an area of shops.   4. An area of Cairo close to the famous mosque and university of al-Azhar.

A certain languor was apparent in the glance he cast at me; the languor was not total in that he had not as yet lost all hope in me.

"God rest his soul," he said. "He was a fine man."

The very pain that had driven me to go there now prevailed upon me to stay.

"He told me," I continued, "of a devout saint named Zaabalawi whom he met at Your Honor's. I am in need of him, sir, if he be still in the land of the living."

The languor became firmly entrenched in his eyes, and it would have come as no surprise if he had shown the door to both me and my father's memory.

"That," he said in the tone of one who has made up his mind to terminate the conversation, "was a very long time ago and I scarcely recall him now."

Rising to my feet so as to put his mind at rest regarding my intention of going, I asked, "Was he really a saint?"

"We used to regard him as a man of miracles."

"And where could I find him today?" I asked, making another move toward the door.

"To the best of my knowledge he was living in the Birgawi Residence in al-Azhar," and he applied himself to some papers on his desk with a resolute movement that indicated he would not open his mouth again. I bowed my head in thanks, apologized several times for disturbing him, and left the office, my head so buzzing with embarrassment that I was oblivious to all sounds around me.

I went to the Birgawi Residence, which was situated in a thickly populated quarter. I found that time had so eaten at the building that nothing was left of it save an antiquated façade and a courtyard that, despite being supposedly in the charge of a caretaker, was being used as a rubbish dump. A small, insignificant fellow, a mere prologue to a man, was using the covered entrance as a place for the sale of old books on theology and mysticism.

When I asked him about Zaabalawi, he peered at me through narrow, inflamed eyes and said in amazement, "Zaabalawi! Good heavens, what a time ago that was! Certainly he used to live in this house when it was habitable. Many were the times he would sit with me talking of bygone days, and I would be blessed by his holy presence. Where, though, is Zaabalawi today?"

He shrugged his shoulders sorrowfully and soon left me, to attend to an approaching customer. I proceeded to make inquiries of many shopkeepers in the district. While I found that a large number of them had never even heard of Zaabalawi, some, though recalling nostalgically the pleasant times they had spent with him, were ignorant of his present whereabouts, while others openly made fun of him, labeled him a charlatan, and advised me to put myself in the hands of a doctor—as though I had not already done so. I therefore had no alternative but to return disconsolately home.

With the passing of days like motes in the air, my pains grew so severe that I was sure I would not be able to hold out much longer. Once again I fell to wondering about Zaabalawi and clutching at the hope his venerable name stirred within me. Then it occurred to me to seek the help of the local sheikh of the district; in fact, I was surprised I had not thought of this to begin with. His office was in the nature of a small shop, except that it contained a desk and a telephone, and I found him sitting at his desk, wearing a jacket over his striped galabeya.[5] As he did not interrupt his conversation with a man sitting beside him, I stood waiting till the man had gone. The sheikh then looked up at me coldly. I told myself that I should win him over by the usual methods, and it was not long before I had him cheerfully inviting me to sit down.

"I'm in need of Sheikh Zaabalawi," I answered his inquiry as to the purpose of my visit.

He gazed at me with the same astonishment as that shown by those I had previously encountered.

"At least," he said, giving me a smile that revealed his gold teeth, "he is still alive. The devil of it is, though, he has no fixed abode. You might well bump into him as you go out of here, on the other hand you might spend days and months in fruitless searching."

"Even you can't find him!"

"Even I! He's a baffling man, but I thank the Lord that he's still alive!"

He gazed at me intently, and murmured, "It seems your condition is serious."

"Very."

"May God come to your aid! But why don't you go about it systematically?" He spread out a sheet of paper on the desk and drew on it with unexpected speed and skill until he had made a full plan of the district, showing all the various quarters, lanes, alleyways, and squares. He looked at it admiringly and said, "These are dwelling-houses, here is the Quarter of the Perfumers, here the Quarter of the Coppersmiths, the Mouski,[6] the police and fire stations. The drawing is your best guide. Look carefully in the cafés, the places where the dervishes perform their rites, the mosques and prayer-rooms, and the Green Gate,[7] for he may well be concealed among the beggars and be indistinguishable from them. Actually, I myself haven't seen him for years, having been somewhat preoccupied with the cares of the world, and was only brought back by your inquiry to those most exquisite times of my youth."

I gazed at the map in bewilderment. The telephone rang, and he took up the receiver.

"Take it," he told me, generously. "We're at your service."

Folding up the map, I left and wandered off through the quarter, from square to street to alleyway, making inquiries of everyone I felt was familiar with the place. At last the owner of a small establishment for ironing clothes told me, "Go to the calligrapher[8] Hassanein in Umm al-Ghulam—they were friends."

I went to Umm al-Ghulam,[9] where I found old Hassanein working in a deep, narrow shop full of signboards and jars of color. A strange smell, a mixture of glue and perfume, permeated its every corner. Old Hassanein was squatting on a sheepskin rug in front of a board propped against the wall; in the middle of it he had inscribed the word "Allah"[1] in silver lettering. He was engrossed in embellishing the letters with prodigious care. I stood behind

5. The traditional Arabic robe, over which this modernized district officer wears a European jacket.
6. The central bazaar.   7. A medieval gate in Cairo.   8. One who practices the art of decorative lettering (literally "beautiful writing"), which is respected as a fine art in Arabic and Asian cultures.   9. A street in Cairo.   1. God (Arabic).

him, fearful of disturbing him or breaking the inspiration that flowed to his masterly hand. When my concern at not interrupting him had lasted some time, he suddenly inquired with unaffected gentleness, "Yes?"

Realizing that he was aware of my presence, I introduced myself. "I've been told that Sheikh Zaabalawi is your friend; I'm looking for him," I said.

His hand came to a stop. He scrutinized me in astonishment. "Zaabalawi! God be praised!" he said with a sigh.

"He *is* a friend of yours, isn't he?" I asked eagerly.

"He was, once upon a time. A real man of mystery: he'd visit you so often that people would imagine he was your nearest and dearest, then would disappear as though he'd never existed. Yet saints are not to be blamed."

The spark of hope went out with the suddenness of a lamp snuffed by a power-cut.

"He was so constantly with me," said the man, "that I felt him to be a part of everything I drew. But where is he today?"

"Perhaps he is still alive?"

"He's alive, without a doubt. . . . He had impeccable taste, and it was due to him that I made my most beautiful drawings."

"God knows," I said, in a voice almost stifled by the dead ashes of hope, "how dire my need for him is, and no one knows better than you[2] of the ailments in respect of which he is sought."

"Yes, yes. May God restore you to health. He is, in truth, as is said of him, a man, and more. . . ."

Smiling broadly, he added, "And his face possesses an unforgettable beauty. But where is he?"

Reluctantly I rose to my feet, shook hands, and left. I continued wandering eastward and westward through the quarter, inquiring about Zaabalawi from everyone who, by reason of age or experience, I felt might be likely to help me. Eventually I was informed by a vendor of lupine[3] that he had met him a short while ago at the house of Sheikh Gad, the well-known composer. I went to the musician's house in Tabakshiyya,[4] where I found him in a room tastefully furnished in the old style, its walls redolent with history. He was seated on a divan, his famous lute beside him, concealing within itself the most beautiful melodies of our age, while somewhere from within the house came the sound of pestle and mortar and the clamor of children. I immediately greeted him and introduced myself, and was put at my ease by the unaffected way in which he received me. He did not ask, either in words or gesture, what had brought me, and I did not feel that he even harbored any such curiosity. Amazed at his understanding and kindness, which boded well, I said, "O Sheikh Gad, I am an admirer of yours, having long been enchanted by the renderings of your songs."

"Thank you," he said with a smile.

"Please excuse my disturbing you," I continued timidly, "but I was told that Zaabalawi was your friend, and I am in urgent need of him."

"Zaabalawi!" he said, frowning in concentration. "You need him? God be with you, for who knows, O Zaabalawi, where you are."

"Doesn't he visit you?" I asked eagerly.

2. One of the calligrapher's major tasks is to write religious documents and prayers to Allah.
3. Beans.   4. A quarter named for the straw trays made and sold there.

"He visited me some time ago. He might well come right now; on the other hand I mightn't see him till death!"

I gave an audible sigh and asked, "What made him like that?"

The musician took up his lute. "Such are saints or they would not be saints," he said, laughing.

"Do those who need him suffer as I do?"

"Such suffering is part of the cure!"

He took up the plectrum and began plucking soft strains from the strings. Lost in thought, I followed his movements. Then, as though addressing myself, I said, "So my visit has been in vain."

He smiled, laying his cheek against the side of the lute. "God forgive you," he said, "for saying such a thing of a visit that has caused me to know you and you me!"

I was much embarrassed and said apologetically, "Please forgive me; my feelings of defeat made me forget my manners."

"Do not give in to defeat. This extraordinary man brings fatigue to all who seek him. It was easy enough with him in the old days when his place of abode was known. Today, though, the world has changed, and after having enjoyed a position attained only by potentates, he is now pursued by the police on a charge of false pretenses. It is therefore no longer an easy matter to reach him, but have patience and be sure that you will do so."

He raised his head from the lute and skillfully fingered the opening bars of a melody. Then he sang:

I make lavish mention, even though I blame myself, of those I love,
For the stories of the beloved are my wine.[5]

With a heart that was weary and listless, I followed the beauty of the melody and the singing.

"I composed the music to this poem in a single night," he told me when he had finished. "I remember that it was the eve of the Lesser Bairam.[6] Zaabalawi was my guest for the whole of that night, and the poem was of his choosing. He would sit for a while just where you are, then would get up and play with my children as though he were one of them. Whenever I was overcome by weariness or my inspiration failed me, he would punch me playfully in the chest and joke with me, and I would bubble over with melodies, and thus I continued working till I finished the most beautiful piece I have ever composed."

"Does he know anything about music?"

"He is the epitome of things musical. He has an extremely beautiful speaking voice, and you have only to hear him to want to burst into song and to be inspired to creativity. . . ."

"How was it that he cured those diseases before which men are powerless?"

"That is his secret. Maybe you will learn it when you meet him."

But when would that meeting occur? We relapsed into silence, and the hubbub of children once more filled the room.

Again the sheikh began to sing. He went on repeating the words "and I have a memory of her" in different and beautiful variations until the very

5. From a poem by the medieval mystic poet Ibn al-Farid, who represents spiritual ecstasy as a kind of drunkenness.   6. A major Islamic holiday, celebrated for three days to end the month's fasting during Ramadan.

walls danced in ecstasy. I expressed my wholehearted admiration, and he gave me a smile of thanks. I then got up and asked permission to leave, and he accompanied me to the front door. As I shook him by the hand, he said, "I hear that nowadays he frequents the house of Hagg Wanas al-Damanhouri. Do you know him?"

I shook my head, though a modicum of renewed hope crept into my heart.

"He is a man of private means," the sheikh told me, "who from time to time visits Cairo, putting up at some hotel or other. Every evening, though, he spends at the Negma Bar in Alfi Street."

I waited for nightfall and went to the Negma Bar. I asked a waiter about Hagg Wanas, and he pointed to a corner that was semisecluded because of its position behind a large pillar with mirrors on all four sides. There I saw a man seated alone at a table with two bottles in front of him, one empty, the other two-thirds empty. There were no snacks or food to be seen, and I was sure that I was in the presence of a hardened drinker. He was wearing a loosely flowing silk galabeya and a carefully wound turban; his legs were stretched out toward the base of the pillar, and as he gazed into the mirror in rapt contentment, the sides of his face, rounded and handsome despite the fact that he was approaching old age, were flushed with wine. I approached quietly till I stood but a few feet away from him. He did not turn toward me or give any indication that he was aware of my presence.

"Good evening, Mr. Wanas," I greeted him cordially.

He turned toward me abruptly, as though my voice had roused him from slumber, and glared at me in disapproval. I was about to explain what had brought me to him when he interrupted in an almost imperative tone of voice that was none the less not devoid of an extraordinary gentleness, "First, please sit down, and, second, please get drunk!"

I opened my mouth to make my excuses but, stopping up his ears with his fingers, he said, "Not a word till you do what I say."

I realized I was in the presence of a capricious drunkard and told myself that I should at least humor him a bit. "Would you permit me to ask one question?" I said with a smile, sitting down.

Without removing his hands from his ears he indicated the bottle. "When engaged in a drinking bout like this, I do not allow any conversation between myself and another unless, like me, he is drunk, otherwise all propriety is lost and mutual comprehension is rendered impossible."

I made a sign indicating that I did not drink.

"That's your lookout," he said offhandedly. "And that's my condition!"

He filled me a glass, which I meekly took and drank. No sooner had the wine settled in my stomach than it seemed to ignite. I waited patiently till I had grown used to its ferocity, and said, "It's very strong, and I think the time has come for me to ask you about—"

Once again, however, he put his fingers in his ears. "I shan't listen to you until you're drunk!"

He filled up my glass for the second time. I glanced at it in trepidation; then, overcoming my inherent objection, I drank it down at a gulp. No sooner had the wine come to rest inside me than I lost all willpower. With the third glass, I lost my memory, and with the fourth the future vanished. The world turned round about me and I forgot why I had gone there. The man leaned toward me attentively, but I saw him—saw everything—as a mere meaningless series of colored planes. I don't know how long it was before my head sank down onto the arm of the chair and I plunged into deep sleep. During it, I had a beautiful dream the like of which I had never experienced. I dreamed that I was in an immense garden surrounded on all sides by luxuriant trees, and the sky was nothing but stars seen between the entwined branches, all enfolded in an atmosphere like that of sunset or a sky overcast with cloud. I was lying on a small hummock of jasmine petals, more of which fell upon me like rain, while the lucent spray of a fountain unceasingly sprinkled the crown of my head and my temples. I was in a state of deep contentedness, of ecstatic serenity. An orchestra of warbling and cooing played in my ear. There was an extraordinary sense of harmony between me and my inner self, and between the two of us and the world, everything being in its rightful place, without discord or distortion. In the whole world there was no single reason for speech or movement, for the universe moved in a rapture of ecstasy. This lasted but a short while. When I opened my eyes, consciousness struck at me like a policeman's fist and I saw Wanas al-Damanhouri regarding me with concern. Only a few drowsy customers were left in the bar.

"You have slept deeply," said my companion. "You were obviously hungry for sleep."

I rested my heavy head in the palms of my hands. When I took them away in astonishment and looked down at them, I found that they glistened with drops of water.

"My head's wet," I protested.

"Yes, my friend tried to rouse you," he answered quietly.

"Somebody saw me in this state?"

"Don't worry, he is a good man. Have you not heard of Sheikh Zaabalawi?"

"Zaabalawi!" I exclaimed, jumping to my feet.

"Yes," he answered in surprise. "What's wrong?"

"Where is he?"

"I don't know where he is now. He was here and then he left."

I was about to run off in pursuit but found I was more exhausted than I had imagined. Collapsed over the table, I cried out in despair, "My sole reason for coming to you was to meet him! Help me to catch up with him or send someone after him."

The man called a vendor of prawns and asked him to seek out the sheikh and bring him back. Then he turned to me. "I didn't realize you were afflicted. I'm very sorry. . . ."

"You wouldn't let me speak," I said irritably.

"What a pity! He was sitting on this chair beside you the whole time. He was playing with a string of jasmine petals he had around his neck, a gift from one of his admirers, then, taking pity on you, he began to sprinkle some water on your head to bring you around."

"Does he meet you here every night?" I asked, my eyes not leaving the doorway through which the vendor of prawns had left.

"He was with me tonight, last night and the night before that, but before that I hadn't seen him for a month."

"Perhaps he will come tomorrow," I answered with a sigh.

"Perhaps."

"I am willing to give him any money he wants."

Wanas answered sympathetically, "The strange thing is that he is not open to such temptations, yet he will cure you if you meet him."

"Without charge?"

"Merely on sensing that you love him."

The vendor of prawns returned, having failed in his mission.

I recovered some of my energy and left the bar, albeit unsteadily. At every street corner I called out "Zaabalawi!" in the vague hope that I would be rewarded with an answering shout. The street boys turned contemptuous eyes on me till I sought refuge in the first available taxi.

The following evening I stayed up with Wanas al-Damanhouri till dawn, but the sheikh did not put in an appearance. Wanas informed me that he would be going away to the country and would not be returning to Cairo until he had sold the cotton crop.

I must wait, I told myself; I must train myself to be patient. Let me content myself with having made certain of the existence of Zaabalawi, and even of his affection for me, which encourages me to think that he will be prepared to cure me if a meeting takes place between us.

Sometimes, however, the long delay wearied me. I would become beset by despair and would try to persuade myself to dismiss him from my mind completely. How many weary people in this life know him not or regard him as a mere myth! Why, then, should I torture myself about him in this way?

No sooner, however, did my pains force themselves upon me than I would again begin to think about him, asking myself when I would be fortunate enough to meet him. The fact that I ceased to have any news of Wanas and was told he had gone to live abroad did not deflect me from my purpose; the truth of the matter was that I had become fully convinced that I had to find Zaabalawi.

Yes, I have to find Zaabalawi.

ALEXANDER SOLZHENITSYN
born 1918

The reputation of Russian novelist Alexander Solzhenitsyn is divided almost equally between two complementary aspects: he continues the tradition of the realistic nineteenth-century novel (following the example of his compatriots Tolstoy and Dostoevsky), and he has assumed the role of moral conscience in a modern society where both East and West are fatally flawed. Expelled from the Soviet Union in 1974 and stripped of his citizenship until a new regime restored it in 1990, Solzhenitsyn proclaims the virtues of an older, religious way of life as the only salvation for a civilization that has been dehumanized by political oppression and materialist greed. Art and literature, he feels, are "endowed with the miraculous power to communicate" and thus make it possible for people to experience situations that they have not lived. This basis of common communication erases divisions and allows us to have "a single system of evaluation for evil deeds and for good ones." Solzhenitsyn tries to encompass both the historian's and the moralist's aims when he writes about the history of his own country in the twentieth century and paints a picture of human suffering and moral endurance under oppression. Like Thomas Mann, he includes a range of characters and diverse social types in novels that allude to larger social issues; unlike Mann, his tone is overtly moral and even didactic, especially in his later works. Solzhenitsyn is impelled to testify for all those who cannot speak: for the woman in *Cancer Ward* (1968), for example, who says "Where can I read about us? Will that be only in a hundred years?" His testimony ranges from the more personal account of a day in concentration camp (*One Day in the Life of Ivan Denisovich*, 1963) to broad historical panoramas such as *August 1914* (1971), which focuses on the defeat of the Russian Second Army in East Prussia during World War I, and *Gulag Archipelago* (1973–75), a description of the Soviet concentration camp system. Clearly he finds the form of the realistic novel—expanded, in *August 1914,* with documents and imitation film scripts—the most appropriate method for representing the truth of history. Solzhenitsyn has little patience with avant-garde literature, which, he says, "has been thought up by empty-headed people." Instead, he tries to render the essence of history by blending documented fact and narrative fiction in his creative works and, in recent years, by editing and publishing (in Russian) historical documents from pre-Revolutionary Russia.

He was born Alexander Isayevich Solzhenitsyn on December 11, 1918, in Kislovodsk, in the northern Caucasus. His father had died six months earlier, and his mother supported them in Rostov-on-Don by working as a typist. The family was extremely poor, and—although Solzhenitsyn would have preferred studying literature in Moscow—he was obliged upon graduation from high school to enroll in the local Department of Mathematics at Rostov University. The choice, he says, was a lucky one, for his double degree in mathematics and physics allowed him to spend four years of his prison camp sentence in a relatively privileged *sharashka*, or research institute, instead of at hard manual labor. During 1939–41 he also took correspondence courses from the Institute of History, Philosophy, and Literature in Moscow. When Solzhenitsyn graduated in 1941, in the middle of World War II, he was immediately inducted into the army, where he drove horse-drawn transport vehicles until he was sent to artillery school in 1942. That November he was put in charge of an artillery reconnaissance battery at the front, a position he held until his sudden arrest in February 1945.

The military censor had found passages in his letters to a friend that were—even under a pseudonym—visibly disrespectful of Stalin, and Solzhenitsyn was sentenced in July to eight years in the prison camps. From 1946 to 1950 he worked as a mathematician in research institutes staffed by prisoners (such as that described in *The First Circle*) but in 1950 was taken to a new kind of camp for political prisoners only, where he worked as a manual laborer. After his sentence was ostensibly over, an administrative order sent him into perpetual exile in southern Kazakhstan. Solzhenitsyn spent the years of exile teaching physics and mathematics in a rural school and wrote prose in secret. The tumor that had developed in his first labor camp grew worse, and in 1954 the author received treatment in a clinic in Tashkent (recalled in the novel *Cancer Ward*). He returned to exile in 1955 (the year he wrote *The First Circle*) and was not released until June 1956. Official rehabilitation came in 1957, and the author moved to Ryazan in European Soviet Union where he continued to teach physics and mathematics, while secretly writing fiction, until 1962. *Matryona's Home* and *One Day in the Life of Ivan Denisovich* were written during this period.

At the age of forty-two, Solzhenitsyn had written a great deal but published nothing. In 1961, however, it looked as though the climate of political censorship might change. Nikita Khrushchev had just publicly attacked the "cult of personality" and hero worship that had surrounded Stalin, and the poet and editor Alexander Tvardovsky called on writers to portray "truth," not the artificial picture of perfect Soviet society that Stalin preferred. Solzhenitsyn was encouraged to submit *One Day in the Life of Ivan Denisovich,* which appeared (with Khrushchev's approval) in the November 1962 issue of Tvardovsky's journal *Novy Mir.* In January 1963 Tvardovsky published the stories *Matryona's Home* and *Incident at Krechetovka Station* but—with the exception of two short stories and an article on style—Solzhenitsyn would not be allowed to publish anything more in his native land. Even the highly praised *One Day in the Life of Ivan Denisovich* was removed from candidacy for the Lenin Prize in 1963. Khrushchev himself was forced into retirement in October 1964, and the temporary loosening of censorship came to an end. The novel *The First Circle* (already accepted by *Novy Mir*) and two plays (*The Lovegirl and the Innocent*, written 1954; *Candle in the Wind*, written 1960) were prohibited during 1964–65, and *Cancer Ward*, after the type was already partially set, was refused publication permission by the Writers' Union in 1966. Solzhenitsyn protested both the censorship and the fact that the Writers' Union did not defend its members before official attacks, but instead he himself was expelled from the Writers' Union in 1969, after *The First Circle* and *Cancer Ward* had appeared in the West. The only means of publishing officially unacceptable works was to convey them abroad to a Western publishing house or to circulate them in *samizdat* ("self-publishing") form by circulating copies of typewritten manuscripts. Solzhenitsyn made arrangements to have his works published in the West, and continued work on the larger historical novels: *The Gulag Archipelago*, which he had begun earlier, and *August 1914*, which he wrote in 1969–70. In 1970 he was awarded the Nobel Prize for Literature, which he accepted in absentia because he was afraid that he would not be permitted to re-enter the Soviet Union once he left. After the publication abroad of the first volume of *The Gulag Archipelago*, however, he was arrested in February 1974 and expelled from the country. From 1974 to 1976 Solzhenitsyn lived in Zurich, and in 1976 he moved to the United States, where he lived in seclusion on a farm in Vermont. The expulsion remained in effect until the new president of the Soviet Union, Mikhail S. Gorbachev, offered in 1990 to restore Solzhenitsyn's citizenship as part of an attempt to rehabilitate artists and writers disgraced during previous regimes. Solzhenitsyn did not accept the offer, and later in the year he refused a prize awarded him by the Russian Republic for *The Gulag Archipelago*, noting that the book was not widely available in the Soviet Union and that the "phenomenon of the Gulag" had not been overcome. In September 1991, however, the old charge of treason was officially dropped, and the writer returned to Russia in May 1994 to widespread public acclaim. The novelist expected, and was expected, to be a prominent voice in contemporary Russian society—for a while, he even had a television program. His moral strictures and nostalgia for a simpler past, however, proved alien to a post-Soviet society intent on prosperity. Still a respected moral authority, Solzhenitsyn seems nowadays fated to speak from the margin.

Solzhenitsyn's first three novels have in common the themes of imprisonment, of personal suffering, and of the moral purity to be gained by those who endure and learn from their suffering. *One Day in the Life of Ivan Denisovich* is the story, told at a very basic level of hunger, cold, and brutally demanding work, of one fairly good day in the life of a prison camp inmate, the peasant Ivan Denisovich Shukhov. When the book appeared, it was the first public recognition of Stalin's prison camp system, and Solzhenitsyn's matter-of-fact narration of the prisoners' day-to-day struggle to survive and retain their humanity shocked readers in Russia and in the West. Shukhov is not a heroic figure, or even portrayed as particularly intelligent, but in his deprivation he has found a core of inner spiritual strength that might well be envied, Solzhenitsyn suggests, by those outside prison who compromise their principles, and accede to injustices, for fear of losing what they have.

The worlds of *Cancer Ward* and *The First Circle* are more privileged than that of *One Day in the Life of Ivan Denisovich*, but each retains the atmosphere of imprisonment and imminent death, and each composes a picture of society by juxtaposing characters with different backgrounds and different points of view. Solzhenitsyn calls this technique of juxtaposition "polyphonic" or many-voiced: he writes a "polyphonic novel with concrete details specifying the time and place of action. A novel without a central hero. . . . Each character becomes central when the action reverts to him." In *Cancer Ward*, thirteen patients representing different social and political classes are brought together in a ward at the cancer clinic in Tashkent; this micro-cosm of Soviet society is faced with sickness, suffering, death, and an authoritarian medical system that administers treatment without explaining it (or its side effects) to the patient. The ward becomes a metaphor for Soviet society, a metaphor given further dimensions when the inmates articulate their different values in response to a story by Tolstoy: "What Men Live By." The ultimate question is not collective but individual, says Kostoglotov: a man may be a member of a collective, "but only while he's alive. . . . He has to die alone."

The same emphasis on the testing of individual values occurs in *The First Circle*, a novel whose title refers to the least painful circle of Hell in Dante's *Inferno* and indicates here the *sharashka* or prisoner-staffed research section of the Mavrino Institute. The prisoners working in the *sharashka* are under pressure from their supe-riors (who are under pressure from Stalin) to produce spying devices, including a method for identifying voices on taped telephone calls, and an impregnable tele-phone coding system for Stalin. If they do not produce satisfactory work, they are sent back to almost-certain death in the labor camps (the lower circles of this Hell); if they do, they become part of the police state. No one is free, not even the dictator who is imprisoned by his own suspicions. The whole society of *The First Circle* is an Inferno, and only by sacrificing everything can one hope to retain spiritual freedom.

Solzhenitsyn turned next to a larger panoramic scope, where the authorial voice would dominate and interpret a mass of historical information. *August 1914* is the first volume of a planned trilogy inquiring into the course of modern Russian history: later volumes (of which a few chapters have appeared in journals and in the fictional portrait, *Lenin in Zurich*) are titled after revolutionary dates, *October 1916* and *March 1917*. *August 1914* describes the defeat of the Second Russian Army in East Prussia during World War I and—in a consciously fragmented style that moves from scene to scene, includes extracts of documents, newspapers, proverbs, and songs, and provides sections marked "Screen" that imitate film scripts—attempts to depict a broad social panorama with characters from all classes, thus recording a moment in history from an epic point of view.

The second broad panorama is *The Gulag Archipelago*, a three-volume, seven-section account of Stalin's widespread prison camp system. (*Gulag* stands for "Chief Administration of Corrective Labor Camps," camps that were scattered across the Soviet Union like islands in a sea [the archipelago].) Solzhenitsyn describes the hor-ror of these camps in quasi-anecdotal form, using personal experience, oral testi-mony, excerpts of documents, written eyewitness reports, and altogether a massive collection of evidence accumulated inside *An Attempt at Artistic Investigation* (the subtitle). In this book, perhaps even more than in *August 1914,* there is a tension between the bare facts that Solzhenitsyn transmits and the spiritual interpretation of history into which they fit. The author is overtly present, commenting, guessing intuititively from context when particular facts are missing, and stressing in his own voice the theme that has pervaded all his work: the purification of the soul through suffering. The title of the fourth section, "The Soul and Barbed Wire," symbolizes the recurrent opposition of soul and imprisoning society that has become familiar to his readers.

Since Solzhenitsyn is such a dedicated anti-Communist and anti-Marxist, many Westerners have jumped to the conclusion that he is in favor of the Western demo-cratic system. Such is not the case. He looks back to an earlier, more nationalist and spiritual authoritarianism represented for him by the image of Holy Russia: "For a thousand years Russia lived with an authoritarian order . . . that authoritarian order possessed a strong moral foundation . . . Christian Orthodoxy." In a speech given at Harvard in 1978, *A World Split Apart,* he criticized Western democracy's "herd instinct" and "need to accommodate mass standards," its emphasis on "well-being" and "constant desire to have still more things," its "spiritual exhaustion" in which "mediocrity triumphs under the guise of democratic restraints." Once again, he returns to the theme of purification by suffering that permeates his fiction: "We have been through a spiritual training far in advance of Western experience. The complex and deadly crush of life has produced stronger, deeper, and more interesting personalities than those generated by standardized Western well-being."

One of those strong and deep personalities is surely Matryona in *Matryona's Home*. Solzhenitsyn's story, which is probably modeled on the old Russian literary form of the saint's life, is a testimony to Matryona's absolute simplicity, her refusal to possess anything more than the basic necessities (she will not raise a pig to kill for food), her willingness to help others without promise of reward, and finally to let her greedy in-laws tear down part of her own home and cart it off. The narrator of the story, like Solzhenitsyn an ex-convict and mathematics teacher, has buried himself deep in the country to avoid signs of modern Soviet society and to find—if it still exists—an image of the Old Russia. The town of Talnovo itself is tainted, not just by the *kolkhoz* (collective farm) system, which ceases to consider Matryona part of the collective as soon as she becomes ill, but also by the laziness, selfishness, and predatory greed of its inhabitants. Yet there remains Matryona. Her life has been filled with disappointment and deprivation, and she remains an outsider in a materialist society that despises her lack of acquisitive instinct, but she seems to live in a dimension of spiritual contentment and love that is unknown to those around her. Only the narrator, who has learned to value essential qualities from his own experience in the concentration camps, is able finally to recognize her as "the righteous one," one of those whose spiritual merit seems alien to modern society, yet is needed to save society from divine retribution (Genesis 18.23–33).

Andrej Kodjak, *Alexander Solzhenitsyn* (1978), provides a biographical and critical introduction to Solzhenitsyn up to his deportation from the Soviet Union in 1974; it includes a discussion of Russian terms. Michael Scammell's detailed *Solzhenitsyn: A Biography* (1984) is complemented by D. M. Thomas, *Alexander Solzhenitsyn: A Century in His Life* (1998), which adds new information and a discussion of the writer's work after his return to Russia. Kathryn B. Feuer, ed., *Solzhenitsyn: A Collection of Critical Essays* (1976), contains a range of essays on aspects and particular works, including *Matryona's Home*. John B. Dunlop, Richard S. Haugh, and Michael Nicholson, eds., *Solzhenitsyn in Exile: Critical Essays and Documentary Material* (1985), offer critical essays and discussions of Solzhenitsyn's reception in different countries. John Dunlop, Richard Haugh, Alexis Klimoff, eds., *Aleksandr Solzhenitsyn: Critical Essays and Documentary Materials* (1973), is a useful collection with a wide range of essays and reprinted texts, including a short autobiography by Solzhenitsyn and his Nobel Prize lecture.

PRONOUNCING GLOSSARY

The following list uses common English syllables and stress accents to provide rough equivalents of selected words whose pronunciation may be unfamiliar to the general reader.

Matryona Vasilyevna: *mah-tryaw'-nuh*   Vysokoye Polye: *vi-saw'-kuh-yuh pawl'-*

vah-seel'-yev-nuh   *yuh*

Matryona's Home[1]

1

A hundred and fifteen miles from Moscow trains were still slowing down to a crawl a good six months after it happened. Passengers stood glued to the windows or went out to stand by the doors. Was the line under repair, or what? Would the train be late?

---

1. Translated by H. T. Willetts.

It was all right. Past the crossing the train picked up speed again and the passengers went back to their seats.

Only the engine drivers knew what it was all about.

The engine drivers and I.

In the summer of 1953 I was coming back from the hot and dusty desert, just following my nose—so long as it led me back to European Russia. Nobody waited or wanted me at my particular place, because I was a little matter of ten years overdue. I just wanted to get to the central belt, away from the great heats, close to the leafy muttering of forests. I wanted to efface myself, to lose myself in deepest Russia . . . if it was still anywhere to be found.

A year earlier I should have been lucky to get a job carrying a hod this side of the Urals.[2] They wouldn't have taken me as an electrician on a decent construction job. And I had an itch to teach. Those who knew told me that it was a waste of money buying a ticket, that I should have a journey for nothing.

But things were beginning to move.[3] When I went up the stairs of the N—— Regional Education Department and asked for the Personnel Section, I was surprised to find Personnel sitting behind a glass partition, like in a chemist's shop, instead of the usual black leather-padded door. I went timidly up to the window, bowed, and asked, "Please, do you need any mathematicians somewhere where the trains don't run? I should like to settle there for good."

They passed every dot and comma in my documents through a fine comb, went from one room to another, made telephone calls. It was something out of the ordinary for them too—people always wanted the towns, the bigger the better. And lo and behold, they found just the place for me—Vysokoe Polye. The very sound of it gladdened my heart.

Vysokoe Polye[4] did not belie its name. It stood on rising ground, with gentle hollows and other little hills around it. It was enclosed by an unbroken ring of forest. There was a pool behind a weir. Just the place where I wouldn't mind living and dying. I spent a long time sitting on a stump in a coppice and wishing with all my heart that I didn't need breakfast and dinner every day but could just stay here and listen to the branches brushing against the roof in the night, with not a wireless anywhere to be heard and the whole world silent.

Alas, nobody baked bread in Vysokoe Polye. There was nothing edible on sale. The whole village lugged its victuals in sacks from the big town.

I went back to the Personnel Section and raised my voice in prayer at the little window. At first they wouldn't even talk to me. But then they started going from one room to another, made a telephone call, scratched with their pens, and stamped on my orders the word "Torfoprodukt."

Torfoprodukt? Turgenev[5] never knew that you can put words like that together in Russian.

2. Mountain chain separating European Russia from (Asiatic) Siberia.   3. Stalin's death, on March 5, 1953, brought a gradual relaxation of the Soviet state's repressive policies.   4. High meadow.   5. A master of Russian prose style (1818–1883), best known for the novel *Fathers and Sons* (1861) and for a series of sympathetic sketches of peasant life published as *A Sportsman's Sketches* (1882). *Torfoprodukt*: peat product; a new word made by combining two words of Germanic origin: *torf* ("peat") and *produckt*.

On the station building at Torfoprodukt, an antiquated temporary hut of gray wood, hung a stern notice, BOARD TRAINS ONLY FROM THE PASSENGERS' HALL. A further message had been scratched on the boards with a nail, *And Without Tickets*. And by the booking office, with the same melancholy wit, somebody had carved for all time the words, *No Tickets*. It was only later that I fully appreciated the meaning of these addenda. Getting to Torfoprodukt was easy. But not getting away.

Here too, deep and trackless forests had once stood and were still standing after the Revolution. Then they were chopped down by the peat cutters and the neighboring kolkhoz.[6] Its chairman, Shashkov, had razed quite a few hectares of timber and sold it at a good profit down in the Odessa region.

The workers' settlement sprawled untidily among the peat bogs—monotonous shacks from the thirties, and little houses with carved façades and glass verandas, put up in the fifties. But inside these houses I could see no partitions reaching up to the ceilings, so there was no hope of renting a room with four real walls.

Over the settlement hung smoke from the factory chimney. Little locomotives ran this way and that along narrow-gauge railway lines, giving out more thick smoke and piercing whistles, pulling loads of dirty brown peat in slabs and briquettes. I could safely assume that in the evening a loudspeaker would be crying its heart out over the door of the club and there would be drunks roaming the streets and, sooner or later, sticking knives in each other.

This was what my dream about a quiet corner of Russia had brought me to—when I could have stayed where I was and lived in an adobe hut looking out on the desert, with a fresh breeze at night and only the starry dome of the sky overhead.

I couldn't sleep on the station bench, and as soon as it started getting light I went for another stroll round the settlement. This time I saw a tiny marketplace. Only one woman stood there at that early hour, selling milk, and I took a bottle and started drinking it on the spot.

I was struck by the way she talked. Instead of a normal speaking voice, she used an ingratiating singsong, and her words were the ones I was longing to hear when I left Asia for this place.

"Drink, and God bless you. You must be a stranger round here?"

"And where are you from?" I asked, feeling more cheerful.

I learnt that the peat workings weren't the only thing, that over the railway lines there was a hill, and over the hill a village, that this village was Talnovo, and it had been there ages ago, when the "gipsy woman" lived in the big house and the wild woods stood all round. And farther on there was a whole countryside full of villages—Chaslitsy, Ovintsy, Spudni, Shevertni, Shestimirovo, deeper and deeper into the woods, farther and farther from the railway, up towards the lakes.

The names were like a soothing breeze to me. They held a promise of backwoods Russia. I asked my new acquaintance to take me to Talnovo after the market was over and find a house for me to lodge in.

It appeared that I was a lodger worth having: in addition to my rent, the school offered a truckload of peat for the winter to whoever took me. The woman's ingratiating smile gave way to a thoughtful frown. She had no room

6. Collective farm.

herself, because she and her husband were "keeping" her aged mother, so she took me first to one lot of relatives then to another. But there wasn't a separate room to be had and both places were crowded and noisy.

We had come to a dammed-up stream that was short of water and had a little bridge over it. No other place in all the village took my fancy as this did: there were two or three willows, a lopsided house, ducks swimming on the pond, geese shaking themselves as they stepped out of the water.

"Well, perhaps we might just call on Matryona," said my guide, who was getting tired of me by now. "Only it isn't so neat and cozy-like in her house, neglects things she does. She's unwell."

Matryona's house stood quite near by. Its row of four windows looked out on the cold backs, the two slopes of the roof were covered with shingles, and a little attic window was decorated in the old Russian style. But the shingles were rotting, the beam ends of the house and the once mighty gates had turned gray with age, and there were gaps in the little shelter over the gate.

The small gate was fastened, but instead of knocking my companion just put her hand under and turned the catch, a simple device to prevent animals from straying. The yard was not covered, but there was a lot under the roof of the house. As you went through the outer door a short flight of steps rose to a roomy landing, which was open, to the roof high overhead. To the left, other steps led up to the top room, which was a separate structure with no stove, and yet another flight led down to the basement. To the right lay the house proper, with its attic and its cellar.

It had been built a long time ago, built sturdily, to house a big family, and now one lonely woman of nearly sixty lived in it.

When I went into the cottage she was lying on the Russian stove[7] under a heap of those indeterminate dingy rags which are so precious to a working man or woman.

The spacious room, and especially the big part near the windows, was full of rubber plants in pots and tubs standing on stools and benches. They peopled the householder's loneliness like a speechless but living crowd. They had been allowed to run wild, and they took up all the scanty light on the north side. In what was left of the light, and half-hidden by the stovepipe, the mistress of the house looked yellow and weak. You could see from her clouded eyes that illness had drained all the strength out of her.

While we talked she lay on the stove face downward, without a pillow, her head toward the door, and I stood looking up at her. She showed no pleasure at getting a lodger, just complained about the wicked disease she had. She was just getting over an attack; it didn't come upon her every month, but when it did, "It hangs on two or three days so as I shan't manage to get up and wait on you. I've room and to spare, you can live here if you like."

Then she went over the list of other housewives with whom I should be quieter and cozier and wanted me to make the round of them. But I had already seen that I was destined to settle in this dimly lit house with the tarnished mirror, in which you couldn't see yourself, and the two garish posters (one advertising books, the other about the harvest), bought for a ruble each to brighten up the walls.

---

7. A large stove built of masonry, used for both heating and cooking.

Matryona Vasilyevna made me go off round the village again, and when I called on her the second time she kept trying to put me off, "We're not clever, we can't cook, I don't know how we shall suit. . . ." But this time she was on her feet when I got there, and I thought I saw a glimmer of pleasure in her eyes to see me back. We reached an agreement about the rent and the load of peat which the school would deliver.

Later on I found out that, year in year out, it was a long time since Matryona Vasilyevna had earned a single ruble. She didn't get a pension. Her relatives gave her very little help. In the kolkhoz she had worked not for money but for credits; the marks recording her labor days in her well-thumbed workbook.

So I moved in with Matryona Vasilyevna. We didn't divide the room. Her bed was in the corner between the door and the stove, and I unfolded my camp bed by one window and pushed Matryona's beloved rubber plants out of the light to make room for a little table by another. The village had electric light, laid on back in the twenties, from Shatury. The newspapers were writing about "Ilyich's little lamps," but the peasants talked wide-eyed about "Tsar Light."[8]

Some of the better-off people in the village might not have thought Matryona's house much of a home, but it kept us snug enough that autumn and winter. The roof still held the rain out, and the freezing winds could not blow the warmth of the stove away all at once, though it was cold by morning, especially when the wind blew on the shabby side.

In addition to Matryona and myself, a cat, some mice, and some cockroaches lived in the house.

The cat was no longer young, and was gammy-legged as well. Matryona had taken her in out of pity, and she had stayed. She walked on all four feet but with a heavy limp: one of her feet was sore and she favored it. When she jumped from the stove she didn't land with the soft sound a cat usually makes, but with a heavy thud as three of her feet struck the floor at once— such a heavy thud that until I got used to it, it gave me a start. This was because she stuck three feet out together to save the fourth.

It wasn't because the cat couldn't deal with them that there were mice in the cottage: she would pounce into the corner like lightning and come back with a mouse between her teeth. But the mice were usually out of reach because somebody, back in the good old days, had stuck embossed wallpaper of a greenish color on Matryona's walls, and not just one layer of it but five. The layers held together all right, but in many places the whole lot had come away from the wall, giving the room a sort of inner skin. Between the timber of the walls and the skin of wallpaper the mice had made themselves runs where they impudently scampered about, running at times right up to the ceiling. The cat followed their scamperings with angry eyes, but couldn't get at them.

Sometimes the cat ate cockroaches as well, but they made her sick. The only thing the cockroaches respected was the partition which screened the mouth of the Russian stove and the kitchen from the best part of the room.

8. The newspapers reflect the new order. *Ilyich:* i.e., Vladimir Ilyich Lenin (1870–1924), leader of the 1917 Russian Revolution and first head of the new state. The peasants still think in terms of the emperor (*Tsar*, or czar).

They did not creep into the best room. But the kitchen at night swarmed with them, and if I went in late in the evening for a drink of water and switched on the light the whole floor, the big bench, and even the wall would be one rustling brown mass. From time to time I brought home some borax from the school laboratory and we mixed it with dough to poison them. There would be fewer cockroaches for a while, but Matryona was afraid that we might poison the cat as well. We stopped putting down poison and the cockroaches multiplied anew.

At night, when Matryona was already asleep and I was working at my table, the occasional rapid scamper of mice behind the wallpaper would be drowned in the sustained and ceaseless rustling of cockroaches behind the screen, like the sound of the sea in the distance. But I got used to it because there was nothing evil in it, nothing dishonest. Rustling was life to them.

I even got used to the crude beauty on the poster, forever reaching out from the wall to offer me Belinsky, Panferov,[9] and a pile of other books—but never saying a word. I got used to everything in Matryona's cottage.

Matryona got up at four or five o'clock in the morning. Her wall clock was twenty-seven years old and had been bought in the village shop. It was always fast, but Matryona didn't worry about that—just as long as it didn't lose and make her late in the morning. She switched on the light behind the kitchen screen and moving quietly, considerately, doing her best not to make a noise, she lit the stove, went to milk the goat (all the livestock she had was this one dirty-white goat with twisted horns), fetched water and boiled it in three iron pots: one for me, one for herself, and one for the goat. She fetched potatoes from the cellar, picking out the littlest for the goat, little ones for herself and egg-sized ones for me. There were no big ones, because her garden was sandy, had not been manured since the war, and she always planted with potatoes, potatoes, and potatoes again, so that it wouldn't grow big ones.

I scarcely heard her about her morning tasks. I slept late, woke up in the wintry daylight, stretched a bit, and stuck my head out from under my blanket and my sheepskin. These, together with the prisoner's jerkin round my legs and a sack stuffed with straw underneath me, kept me warm in bed even on nights when the cold wind rattled our wobbly windows from the north. When I heard the discreet noises on the other side of the screen I spoke to her, slowly and deliberately:

"Good morning, Matryona Vasilyevna!"

And every time the same good-natured words came to me from behind the screen. They began with a warm, throaty gurgle, the sort of sound grandmothers make in fairy tales.

"M-m-m . . . same to you too!"

And after a little while, "Your breakfast's ready for you now."

She didn't announce what was for breakfast, but it was easy to guess: taters in their jackets or tatty soup (as everybody in the village called it), or barley gruel (no other grain could be bought in Torfoprodukt that year, and even the barley you had to fight for, because it was the cheapest and people bought

9. Fedor Ivanovich Panferov (1896–1960), socialist-realist writer popular in the 1920s, best known for his novel *The Iron Flood*. Vissarion Grigoryevich Belinsky (1811–1848), Russian literary critic who emphasized social and political ideas.

it up by the sack to fatten their pigs on it). It wasn't always salted as it should be, it was often slightly burnt, it furred the palate and the gums, and it gave me heartburn.

But Matryona wasn't to blame: there was no butter in Torfoprodukt either, margarine was desperately short, and only mixed cooking fat was plentiful, and when I got to know it, I saw that the Russian stove was not convenient for cooking: the cook cannot see the pots and they are not heated evenly all round. I suppose the stove came down to our ancestors from the Stone Age, because you can stoke it up once before daylight, and food and water, mash and swill will keep warm in it all day long. And it keeps you warm while you sleep.

I ate everything that was cooked for me without demur, patiently putting aside anything uncalled-for that I came across: a hair, a bit of peat, a cockroach's leg. I hadn't the heart to find fault with Matryona. After all, she had warned me herself.

"We aren't clever, we can't cook—I don't know how we shall suit. . . ."

"Thank you," I said quite sincerely.

"What for? For what is your own?" she answered, disarming me with a radiant smile. And, with a guileless look of her faded blue eyes, she would ask, "And what shall I cook you for just now?"

For just now meant for supper. I ate twice a day, like at the front. What could I order for just now? It would have to be one of the same old things, taters or tater soup.

I resigned myself to it, because I had learned by now not to look for the meaning of life in food. More important to me was the smile on her roundish face, which I tried in vain to catch when at last I had earned enough to buy a camera. As soon as she saw the cold eye of the lens upon her, Matryona assumed a strained or else an exaggeratedly severe expression.

Just once I did manage to get a snap of her looking through the window into the street and smiling at something.

Matryona had a lot of worries that winter. Her neighbors put it into her head to try and get a pension. She was all alone in the world, and when she began to be seriously ill she had been dismissed from the kolkhoz as well. Injustices had piled up, one on top of another. She was ill, but was not regarded as a disabled person. She had worked for a quarter of a century in the kolkhoz, but it was a kolkhoz and not a factory, so she was not entitled to a pension for herself. She could only try and get one for her husband, for the loss of her breadwinner. But she had had no husband for twelve years now, not since the beginning of the war, and it wasn't easy to obtain all the particulars from different places about his length of service and how much he had earned. What a bother it was getting those forms through! Getting somebody to certify that he'd earned, say, three hundred rubles a month; that she lived alone and nobody helped her; what year she was born in. Then all this had to be taken to the Pension Office. And taken somewhere else to get all the mistakes corrected. And taken back again. Then you had to find out whether they would give you a pension.

To make it all more difficult the Pension Office was twelve miles east of Talnovo, the Rural Council Offices six miles to the west, the Factory District Council an hour's walk to the north. They made her run around from office to office for two months on end, to get an *i* dotted or a *t* crossed. Every trip took a day. She goes down to the Rural District Council—and the secretary isn't there today. Secretaries of rural councils often aren't here today. So come again tomorrow. Tomorrow the secretary is in, but he hasn't got his rubber stamp. So come again the next day. And the day after that back she goes yet again, because all her papers are pinned together and some cockeyed clerk has signed the wrong one.

"They shove me around, Ignatich," she used to complain to me after these fruitless excursions. "Worn out with it I am."

But she soon brightened up. I found that she had a sure means of putting herself in a good humor. She worked. She would grab a shovel and go off to pull potatoes. Or she would tuck a sack under her arm and go after peat. Or take a wicker basket and look for berries deep in the woods. When she'd been bending her back to bushes instead of office desks for a while, and her shoulders were aching from a heavy load, Matryona would come back cheerful, at peace with the world and smiling her nice smile.

"I'm on to a good thing now, Ignatich. I know where to go for it (peat she meant), a lovely place it is."

"But surely my peat is enough, Matryona Vasilyevna? There's a whole truckload of it."

"Pooh! Your peat! As much again, and then as much again, that might be enough. When the winter gets really stiff and the wind's battling at the windows, it blows the heat out of the house faster than you can make the stove up. Last year we got heaps and heaps of it. I'd have had three loads in by now. But they're out to catch us. They've summoned one woman from our village already."

That's how it was. The frightening breath of winter was already in the air. There were forests all round, and no fuel to be had anywhere. Excavators roared away in the bogs, but there was no peat on sale to the villagers. It was delivered, free, to the bosses and to the people round the bosses, and teachers, doctors, and workers got a load each. The people of Talnovo were not supposed to get any peat, and they weren't supposed to ask about it. The chairman of the kolkhoz walked about the village looking people in the eye while he gave his orders or stood chatting and talked about anything you liked except fuel. He was stocked up. Who said anything about winter coming?

So just as in the old days they used to steal the squire's wood, now they pinched peat from the trust. The women went in parties of five or ten so that they would be less frightened. They went in the daytime. The peat cut during the summer had been stacked up all over the place to dry. That's the good thing about peat, it can't be carted off as soon as it's cut. It lies around drying till autumn, or, if the roads are bad, till the snow starts falling. This was when the women used to come and take it. They could get six peats in a sack if it was damp, or ten if it was dry. A sackful weighed about half a hundredweight and it sometimes had to be carried over two miles. This was enough to make the stove up once. There were two hundred days in the winter. The Russian stove had to be lit in the mornings, and the "Dutch"[1] stove in the evenings.

"Why beat about the bush?" said Matryona angrily to someone invisible.

---

1. Not a real tiled Dutch stove, but a cheap small stove (probably made from an oil barrel) that provided heat with less fuel than a big Russian stove.

"Since there've been no more horses, what you can't have around yourself you haven't got. My back never heals up. Winter you're pulling sledges, summer it's bundles on your back, it's God's truth I'm telling you."

The women went more than once in a day. On good days Matryona brought six sacks home. She piled my peat up where it could be seen and hid her own under the passageway, boarding up the hole every night.

"If they don't just happen to think of it, the devils will never find it in their born days," said Matryona smiling and wiping the sweat from her brow.

What could the peat trust do? Its establishment didn't run to a watchman for every bog. I suppose they had to show a rich haul in their returns, and then write off so much for crumbling, so much washed away by the rain. Sometimes they would take it into their heads to put out patrols and try to catch the women as they came into the village. The women would drop their sacks and scatter. Or somebody would inform and there would be a house-to-house search. They would draw up a report on the stolen peat and threaten a court action. The women would stop fetching it for a while, but the approach of winter drove them out with sledges in the middle of the night.

When I had seen a little more of Matryona I noticed that, apart from cooking and looking after the house, she had quite a lot of other jobs to do every day. She kept all her jobs, and the proper times for them, in her head and always knew when she woke up in the morning how her day would be occupied. Apart from fetching peat and stumps which the tractors unearthed in the bogs, apart from the cranberries which she put to soak in big jars for the winter ("Give your teeth an edge, Ignatich," she used to say when she offered me some), apart from digging potatoes and all the coming and going to do with her pension, she had to get hay from somewhere for her one and only dirty-white goat.

"Why don't you keep a cow, Matryona?"

Matryona stood there in her grubby apron, by the opening in the kitchen screen, facing my table, and explained to me.

"Oh, Ignatich, there's enough milk from the goat for me. And if I started keeping a cow she'd eat me out of house and home in no time. You can't cut the grass by the railway track, because it belongs to the railway, and you can't cut any in the woods, because it belongs to the foresters, and they won't let me have any at the kolkhoz because I'm not a member any more, they reckon. And those who are members have to work there every day till the white flies swarm and make their own hay when there's snow on the ground—what's the good of grass like that? In the old days they used to be sweating to get the hay in at midsummer, between the end of June and the end of July, while the grass was sweet and juicy."

So it meant a lot of work for Matryona to gather enough hay for one skinny little goat. She took her sickle and a sack and went off early in the morning to places where she knew there was grass growing—round the edges of fields, on the roadside, on hummocks in the bog. When she had stuffed her sack with heavy fresh grass she dragged it home and spread it out in her yard to dry. From a sackful of grass she got one forkload of dry hay.

The farm had a new chairman, sent down from the town not long ago, and the first thing he did was to cut down the garden plots for those who were not fit to work. He left Matryona a third of an acre of sand—when there was over a thousand square yards just lying idle on the other side of the fence. Yet when they were short of working hands, when the women dug in their heels and wouldn't budge, the chairman's wife would come to see Matryona. She was from the town as well, a determined woman whose short gray coat and intimidating glare gave her a somewhat military appearance. She walked into the house without so much as a good morning and looked sternly at Matryona. Matryona was uneasy.

"Well now, Comrade Vasilyevna," said the chairman's wife, drawing out her words. "You will have to help the kolkhoz! You will have to go and help cart manure out tomorrow!"

A little smile of forgiveness wrinkled Matryona's face—as though she understood the embarrassment which the chairman's wife must feel at not being able to pay her for her work.

"Well—er," she droned. "I'm not well, of course, and I'm not attached to you any more . . . ," then she hurried to correct herself, "What time should I come then?"

"And bring your own fork!" the chairman's wife instructed her. Her stiff skirt crackled as she walked away.

"Think of that!" grumbled Matryona as the door closed. "Bring your own fork! They've got neither forks nor shovels at the kolkhoz. And I don't have a man who'll put a handle on for me!"

She went on thinking about it out loud all evening.

"What's the good of talking, Ignatich. I must help, of course. Only the way they work it's all a waste of time—don't know whether they're coming or going. The women stand propped up on their shovels and waiting for the factory whistle to blow twelve o'clock. Or else they get on to adding up who's earned what and who's turned up for work and who hasn't. Now what I call work, there isn't a sound out of anybody, only—oh dear, dear—dinner time's soon rolled round—what, getting dark already."

In the morning she went off with her fork.

But it wasn't just the kolkhoz—any distant relative, or just a neighbor, could come to Matryona of an evening and say, "Come and give me a hand tomorrow, Matryona. We'll finish pulling the potatoes."

Matryona couldn't say no. She gave up what she should be doing next and went to help her neighbor, and when she came back she would say without a trace of envy, "Ah, you should see the size of her potatoes, Ignatich! It was a joy to dig them up. I didn't want to leave the allotment, God's truth I didn't."

Needless to say, not a garden could be plowed without Matryona's help. The women of Talnovo had got it neatly worked out that it was a longer and harder job for one woman to dig her garden with a spade than for six of them to put themselves in harness and plow six gardens. So they sent for Matryona to help them.

"Well—did you pay her?" I asked sometimes.

"She won't take money. You have to try and hide it on her when she's not looking."

Matryona had yet another troublesome chore when her turn came to feed the herdsmen. One of them was a hefty deaf mute, the other a boy who was never without a cigaret in his drooling mouth. Matryona's turn came round only every six weeks, but it put her to great expense. She went to the shop to buy canned fish and was lavish with sugar and butter, things she never ate herself. It seems that the housewives showed off in this way, trying to outdo one another in feeding the herdsmen.

"You've got to be careful with tailors and herdsmen," Matryona explained. "They'll spread your name all round the village if something doesn't suit them."

And every now and then attacks of serious illness broke in on this life that was already crammed with troubles. Matryona would be off her feet for a day or two, lying flat out on the stove. She didn't complain and didn't groan, but she hardly stirred either. On these days Masha, Matryona's closest friend from her earliest years, would come to look after the goat and light the stove. Matryona herself ate nothing, drank nothing, asked for nothing. To call in the doctor from the clinic at the settlement would have seemed strange in Talnovo and would have given the neighbors something to talk about—what does she think she is, a lady? They did call her in once, and she arrived in a real temper and told Matryona to come down to the clinic when she was on her feet again. Matryona went, although she didn't really want to; they took specimens and sent them off to the district hospital—and that's the last anybody heard about it. Matryona was partly to blame herself.

But there was work waiting to be done, and Matryona soon started getting up again, moving slowly at first and then as briskly as ever.

"You never saw me in the old days, Ignatich. I'd lift any sack you liked, I didn't think a hundredweight was too heavy. My father-in-law used to say, 'Matryona, you'll break your back.' And my brother-in-law didn't have to come and help me lift on the cart. Our horse was a warhorse, a big strong one."

"What do you mean, a warhorse?"

"They took ours for the war and gave us this one instead—he'd been wounded. But he turned out a bit spirited. Once he bolted with the sledge right into the lake, the men folk hopped out of the way, but I grabbed the bridle, as true as I'm here, and stopped him. Full of oats that horse was. They liked to feed their horses well in our village. If a horse feels his oats he doesn't know what heavy means."

But Matryona was a long way from being fearless. She was afraid of fire, afraid of "the lightning," and most of all she was for some reason afraid of trains.

"When I had to go to Cherusti,[2] the train came up from Nechaevka way with its great big eyes popping out and the rails humming away—put me in a regular fever. My knees started knocking. God's truth I'm telling you!" Matryona raised her shoulders as though she surprised herself.

"Maybe it's because they won't give people tickets, Matryona Vasilyevna?"

"At the window? They try to shove only first-class tickets on to you. And the train was starting to move. We dashed about all over the place, 'Give us tickets for pity's sake.' "

"The men folk had climbed on top of the carriages. Then we found a door

---

2. About 100 miles east of Moscow and some 250 miles northwest of Nechaevka.

that wasn't locked and shoved straight in without tickets—and all the carriages were empty, they were all empty, you could stretch out on the seat if you wanted to. Why they wouldn't give us tickets, the hardhearted parasites, I don't know. . . ."

Still, before winter came, Matryona's affairs were in a better state than ever before. They started paying her at last a pension of eighty rubles. Besides this she got just over one hundred from the school and me.

Some of her neighbors began to be envious.

"Hm! Matryona can live forever now! If she had any more money, she wouldn't know what to do with it at her age."

Matryona had some new felt boots made. She bought a new jerkin. And she had an overcoat made out of the worn-out railwayman's greatcoat given to her by the engine driver from Cherusti who had married Kira, her foster daughter. The hump-backed village tailor put a padded lining under the cloth and it made a marvelous coat, such as Matryona had never worn before in all her sixty years.

In the middle of winter Matryona sewed two hundred rubles into the lining of this coat for her funeral. This made her quite cheerful.

"Now my mind's a bit easier, Ignatich."

December went by, January went by—and in those two months Matryona's illness held off. She started going over to Masha's house more often in the evening, to sit chewing sunflower seeds with her. She herself didn't invite guests in the evening out of consideration for my work. Once, on the feast of the Epiphany, I came back from school and found a party going on and was introduced to Matryona's three sisters, who called her "nan-nan" or "nanny" because she was the oldest. Until then not much had been heard of the sisters in our cottage—perhaps they were afraid that Matryona might ask them for help.

But one ominous event cast a shadow on the holiday for Matryona. She went to the church three miles away for the blessing of the water and put her pot down among the others. When the blessing was over, the women went rushing and jostling to get their pots back again. There were a lot of women in front of Matryona and when she got there her pot was missing, and no other vessel had been left behind. The pot had vanished as though the devil had run off with it.

Matryona went round the worshipers asking them, "Have any of you girls accidentally mistook somebody else's holy water? In a pot?"

Nobody owned up. There had been some boys there, and boys got up to mischief sometimes. Matryona came home sad.

No one could say that Matryona was a devout believer. If anything, she was a heathen, and her strongest beliefs were superstitious: you mustn't go into the garden on the fast of St. John or there would be no harvest next year. A blizzard meant that somebody had hanged himself. If you pinched your foot in the door, you could expect a guest. All the time I lived with her I didn't once see her say her prayers or even cross herself. But, whatever job she was doing, she began with a "God bless us," and she never failed to say "God bless you," when I set out for school. Perhaps she did say her prayers, but on the quiet, either because she was shy or because she didn't want to embarrass me. There were icons[3] on the walls. Ordinary days they were left in darkness, but for the vigil of a great feast, or on the morning of a holiday, Matryona would light the little lamp.

She had fewer sins on her conscience than her gammy-legged cat. The cat did kill mice.

Now that her life was running more smoothly, Matryona started listening more carefully to my radio. (I had, of course, installed a speaker, or as Matryona called it, a peeker.)[4]

When they announced on the radio that some new machine had been invented, I heard Matryona grumbling out in the kitchen, "New ones all the time, nothing but new ones. People don't want to work with the old ones any more, where are we going to store them all?"

There was a program about the seeding of clouds from airplanes. Matryona, listening up on the stove, shook her head, "Oh, dear, dear, dear, they'll do away with one of the two—summer or winter."

Once Shalyapin[5] was singing Russian folk songs. Matryona stood listening for a long time before she gave her emphatic verdict, "Queer singing, not our sort of singing."

"You can't mean that, Matryona Vasilyevna—just listen to him."

She listened a bit longer and pursed her lips, "No, it's wrong. It isn't our sort of tune, and he's tricky with his voice."

She made up for this another time. They were broadcasting some of Glinka's[6] songs. After half a dozen of these drawing-room ballads, Matryona suddenly came from behind the screen clutching her apron, with a flush on her face and a film of tears over her dim eyes.

"That's our sort of singing," she said in a whisper.

2

So Matryona and I got used to each other and took each other for granted. She never pestered me with questions about myself. I don't know whether she was lacking in normal female curiosity or just tactful, but she never once asked if I had been married. All the Talnovo women kept at her to find out about me. Her answer was, "You want to know—you ask him. All I know is he's from distant parts."

And when I got round to telling her that I had spent a lot of time in prison, she said nothing but just nodded, as though she had already suspected it.

And I thought of Matryona only as the helpless old woman she was now and didn't try to rake up her past, didn't even suspect that there was anything to be found there.

I knew that Matryona had got married before the Revolution and had come to live in the house I now shared with her, and she had gone "to the stove" immediately. (She had no mother-in-law and no older sister-in-law, so it was

---

3. Religious images or portraits, usually painted on wood. A small lamp was set in front of the icons to illuminate them.   4. The translator is imitating Solzhenitsyn's wordplay. In the original, the narrator calls the speaker *razvedka* ("scout," literal trans; a military term); Matryona calls it *rozetka* (an electric plug).   5. Feodor Ivanovich Shalyapin (or Chaliapin, 1873–1938), Russian operatic bass with an international reputation as a great singer and actor; he included popular Russian music in his song recitals.   6. Mikhail Ivanovich Glinka (1804–1857), Russian composer who was instrumental in developing a "Russian" style of music, including the two operas *A Life for the Czar* and *Ruslan and Ludmila.*

her job to put the pots in the oven on the very first morning of her married life.) I knew that she had had six children and that they had all died very young, so that there were never two of them alive at once. Then there was a sort of foster daughter, Kira. Matryona's husband had not come back from the last war. She received no notification of his death. Men from the village who had served in the same company said that he might have been taken prisoner, or he might have been killed and his body not found. In the eight years that had gone by since the war Matryona had decided that he was not alive. It was a good thing that she thought so. If he was still alive he was probably in Brazil or Australia and married again. The village of Talnovo and the Russian language would be fading from his memory.

One day when I got back from school, I found a guest in the house. A tall, dark man, with his hat on his lap, was sitting on a chair which Matryona had moved up to the Dutch stove in the middle of the room. His face was completely surrounded by bushy black hair with hardly a trace of gray in it. His thick black moustache ran into his full black beard, so that his mouth could hardly be seen. Black side-whiskers merged with the black locks which hung down from his crown, leaving only the tips of his ears visible; his broad black eyebrows met in a wide double span. But the front of his head as far as the crown was a spacious bald dome. His whole appearance made an impression of wisdom and dignity. He sat squarely on his chair, with his hands folded on his stick, and his stick resting vertically on the floor, in an attitude of patient expectation, and he obviously hadn't much to say to Matryona, who was busy behind the screen.

When I came in, he eased his majestic head round toward me and suddenly addressed me, "Schoolmaster, I can't see you very well. My son goes to your school. Grigoryev, Antoshka."

There was no need for him to say any more. However strongly inclined I felt to help this worthy old man, I knew and dismissed in advance all the pointless things he was going to say. Antoshka Grigoryev was a plump, red-faced lad in 8-D who looked like a cat that's swallowed the cream. He seemed to think that he came to school for a rest and sat at his desk with a lazy smile on his face. Needless to say, he never did his homework. But the worst of it was that he had been put up into the next class from year to year because our district, and indeed the whole region and the neighboring region were famous for the high percentage of passes they obtained; the school had to make an effort to keep its record up. So Antoshka had got it clear in his mind that however much the teachers threatened him they would promote him in the end, and there was no need for him to learn anything. He just laughed at us. There he sat in the eighth class, and he hadn't even mastered his decimals and didn't know one triangle from another. In the first two terms of the school year I had kept him firmly below the passing line and the same treatment awaited him in the third.

But now this half-blind old man, who should have been Antoshka's grandfather rather than his father, had come to humble himself before me—how could I tell him that the school had been deceiving him for years, and that I couldn't go on deceiving him, because I didn't want to ruin the whole class, to become a liar and a fake, to start despising my work and my profession.

For the time being I patiently explained that his son had been very slack, that he told lies at school and at home, that his record book must be checked frequently, and that we must both take him severely in hand.

"Severe as you like, Schoolmaster," he assured me, "I beat him every week now. And I've got a heavy hand."

While we were talking I remembered that Matryona had once interceded for Antoshka Grigoryev, but I hadn't asked what relation of hers he was and I had refused to do what she wanted. Matryona was standing in the kitchen doorway like a mute suppliant on this occasion too. When Faddey Miron-ovich left, saying that he would call on me to see how things were going, I asked her, "I can't make out what relation this Antoshka is to you, Matryona Vasilyevna."

"My brother-in-law's son," said Matryona shortly, and went out to milk the goat.

When I'd worked it out, I realized that this determined old man with the black hair was the brother of the missing husband.

The long evening went by, and Matryona didn't bring up the subject again. But late at night, when I had stopped thinking about the old man and was working in a silence broken only by the rustling of the cockroaches and the heavy tick of the wall-clock, Matryona suddenly spoke from her dark corner, "You know, Ignatich, I nearly married him once."

I had forgotten that Matryona was in the room. I hadn't heard a sound from her—and suddenly her voice came out of the darkness, as agitated as if the old man were still trying to win her.

I could see that Matryona had been thinking about nothing else all evening.

She got up from her wretched rag bed and walked slowly toward me, as though she were following her own words. I sat back in my chair and caught my first glimpse of a quite different Matryona.

There was no overhead light in our big room with its forest of rubber plants. The table lamp cast a ring of light round my exercise books, and when I tore my eyes from it the rest of the room seemed to be half-dark and faintly tinged with pink. I thought I could see the same pinkish glow in her usually sallow cheeks.

"He was the first one who came courting me, before Efim did—he was his brother—the older one—I was nineteen and Faddey was twenty-three. They lived in this very same house. Their house it was. Their father built it."

I looked round the room automatically. Instead of the old gray house rot-ting under the faded green skin of wallpaper where the mice had their play-ground, I suddenly saw new timbers, freshly trimmed, not yet discolored, and caught the cheerful smell of pine tar.

"Well, and what happened then?"

"That summer we went to sit in the woods together," she whispered. "There used to be a woods where the stable yard is now. They chopped it down. I was just going to marry him, Ignatich. Then the German war started. They took Faddey into the army."

She let fall these few words—and suddenly the blue and white and yellow July of the year 1914 burst into flower before my eyes: the sky still peaceful, the floating clouds, the people sweating to get the ripe corn in. I imagined them side by side, the black-haired Hercules with a scythe over his shoulder, and the red-faced girl clasping a sheaf. And there was singing out under the open sky, such songs as nobody can sing nowadays, with all the machines in the fields.

"He went to the war—and vanished. For three years I kept to myself and waited. Never a sign of life did he give."

Matryona's round face looked out at me from an elderly threadbare head-scarf. As she stood there in the gentle reflected light from my lamp, her face seemed to lose its slovenly workday wrinkles, and she was a scared young girl again with a frightening decision to make.

Yes . . . I could see it. The trees shed their leaves, the snow fell and melted. They plowed and sowed and reaped again. Again the trees shed their leaves, and the snow fell. There was a revolution. Then another revolution. And the whole world was turned upside down.

"Their mother died and Efim came to court me. 'You wanted to come to our house,' he says, 'so come.' He was a year younger than me, Efim was. It's a saying with us—sensible girls get married after Michaelmas, and silly ones at midsummer. They were shorthanded. I got married. . . . The wedding was on St. Peter's day, and then about St. Nicholas' day[7] in the winter he came back—Faddey, I mean, from being a prisoner in Hungary."

Matryona covered her eyes.

I said nothing.

She turned toward the door as though somebody were standing there. "He stood there at the door. What a scream I let out! I wanted to throw myself at his feet! . . . but I couldn't. 'If it wasn't my own brother,' he says, 'I'd take my ax to the both of you.' "

I shuddered. Matryona's despair, or her terror, conjured up a vivid picture of him standing in the dark doorway and raising his ax to her.

But she quieted down and went on with her story in a sing-song voice, leaning on a chairback, "Oh dear, dear me, the poor dear man! There were so many girls in the village—but he wouldn't marry. I'll look for one with the same name as you, a second Matryona, he said. And that's what he did—fetched himself a Matryona from Lipovka. They built themselves a house of their own and they're still living in it. You pass their place every day on your way to school."

So that was it. I realized that I had seen the other Matryona quite often. I didn't like her. She was always coming to my Matryona to complain about her husband—he beat her, he was stingy, he was working her to death. She would weep and weep, and her voice always had a tearful note in it. As it turned out, my Matryona had nothing to regret, with Faddey beating his Matryona every day of his life and being so tightfisted.

"Mine never beat me once," said Matryona of Efim. "He'd pitch into another man in the street, but me he never hit once. Well, there was one time—I quarreled with my sister-in-law and he cracked me on the forehead with a spoon. I jumped up from the table and shouted at them, 'Hope it sticks in your gullets, you idle lot of beggars, hope you choke!' I said. And off I went into the woods. He never touched me any more."

Faddey didn't seem to have any cause for regret either. The other Matryona

7. December 19 (December 6, old style). *Michaelmas:* October 12 (September 29, old style). *St. Peter's Day:* probably July 12 (June 29, old style), Sts. Peter and Paul's Day.

had borne him six children (my Antoshka was one of them, the littlest, the runt) and they had all lived, whereas the children of Matryona and Efim had died, every one of them, before they reached the age of three months, without any illness.

"One daughter, Elena, was born and was alive when they washed her, and then she died right after. . . . My wedding was on St. Peter's day, and it was St. Peter's day I buried my sixth, Alexander."

The whole village decided that there was a curse on Matryona.

Matryona still nodded emphatic belief when she talked about it. "There was a *course*[8] on me. They took me to a woman who used to be a nun to get cured, she set me off coughing and waited for the *course* to jump out of me like a frog. Only nothing jumped out."

And the years had run by like running water. In 1941 they didn't take Faddey into the army because of his poor sight, but they took Efim. And what had happened to the elder brother in the First World War happened to the younger in the Second—he vanished without a trace. Only he never came back at all. The once noisy cottage was deserted, it grew old and rotten, and Matryona, all alone in the world, grew old in it.

So she begged from the other Matryona, the cruelly beaten Matryona, a child of her womb (or was it a drop of Faddey's blood?), the youngest daughter, Kira.

For ten years she brought the girl up in her own house, in place of the children who had not lived. Then, not long before I arrived, she had married her off to a young engine driver from Cherusti. The only help she got from anywhere came in dribs and drabs from Cherusti: a bit of sugar from time to time, or some of the fat when they killed a pig.

Sick and suffering, and feeling that death was not far off, Matryona had made known her will: the top room, which was a separate frame joined by tie beams to the rest of the house, should go to Kira when she died.[9] She said nothing about the house itself. Her three sisters had their eyes on it too.

That evening Matryona opened her heart to me. And, as often happens, no sooner were the hidden springs of her life revealed to me than I saw them in motion.

Kira arrived from Cherusti. Old Faddey was very worried. To get and keep a plot of land in Cherusti the young couple had to put up some sort of building. Matryona's top room would do very well. There was nothing else they could put up, because there was no timber to be had anywhere. It wasn't Kira herself so much, and it wasn't her husband, but old Faddey who was consumed with eagerness for them to get their hands on the plot at Cherusti.

He became a frequent visitor, laying down the law to Matryona and insisting that she should hand over the top room right away, before she died. On these occasions I saw a different Faddey. He was no longer an old man propped up by a stick, whom a push or a harsh word would bowl over. Although he was slightly bent by backache, he was still a fine figure; in his sixties he had kept the vigorous black hair of a young man; he was hot and urgent.

Matryona had not slept for two nights. It wasn't easy for her to make up

---

8. *Curse/course* reflects wordplay in the Russian original, where a similar misuse of language indicates Matryona's lack of formal education.   9. Lumber was scarce and valuable, and old houses were well built. Moving houses or sections of houses is still common in the country.

her mind. She didn't grudge them the top room, which was standing there idle, any more than she ever grudged her labor or her belongings. And the top room was willed to Kira in any case. But the thought of breaking up the roof she had lived under for forty years was torture to her. Even I, a mere lodger, found it painful to think of them stripping away boards and wrenching out beams. For Matryona it was the end of everything.

But the people who were so insistent knew that she would let them break up her house before she died.

So Faddey and his sons and sons-in-law came along one February morning, the blows of five axes were heard and boards creaked and cracked as they were wrenched out. Faddey's eyes twinkled busily. Although his back wasn't quite straight yet, he scrambled nimbly up under the rafters and bustled about down below, shouting at his assistants. He and his father had built this house when he was a lad, a long time ago. The top room had been put up for him, the oldest son, to move into with his bride. And now he was furiously taking it apart, board by board, to carry it out of somebody else's yard.

After numbering the beam ends and the ceiling boards, they dismantled the top room and the storeroom underneath it. The living room and what was left of the landing they boarded up with a thin wall of deal. They did nothing about the cracks in the wall. It was plain to see that they were wreckers, not builders, and that they did not expect Matryona to be living there very long.

While the men were busy wrecking, the women were getting the drink ready for moving day—vodka would cost too much. Kira brought forty pounds of sugar from the Moscow region, and Matryona carried the sugar and some bottles to the distiller under cover of night.

The timbers were carried out and stacked in front of the gates, and the engine-driver son-in-law went off to Cherusti for the tractor.

But the very same day a blizzard, or "a blower," as Matryona once called it, began. It howled and whirled for two days and nights and buried the road under enormous drifts. Then, no sooner had they made the road passable and a couple of trucks had gone by, than it got suddenly warmer. Within a day everything was thawing out, damp mist hung in the air and rivulets gurgled as they burrowed into the snow, and you could get stuck up to the top of your jackboots.

Two weeks passed before the tractor could get at the dismantled top room. All this time Matryona went around like someone lost. What particularly upset her was that her three sisters came, with one voice called her a fool for giving the top room away, said they didn't want to see her any more, and went off. At about the same time the lame cat strayed and was seen no more. It was just one thing after another. This was another blow to Matryona.

At last the frost got a grip on the slushy road. A sunny day came along, and everybody felt more cheerful. Matryona had had a lucky dream the night before. In the morning she heard that I wanted to take a photograph of somebody at an old-fashioned handloom. (There were looms still standing in two cottages in the village; they wove coarse rugs on them.) She smiled shyly and said, "You just wait a day or two, Ignatich, I'll just send off the top room there and I'll put my loom up, I've still got it, you know, and then you can snap me. Honest to God!"

She was obviously attracted by the idea of posing in an old-fashioned setting. The red frosty sun tinged the window of the curtailed passageway with a faint pink, and this reflected light warmed Matryona's face. People who are at ease with their consciences always have nice faces.

Coming back from school before dusk I saw some movement near our house. A big new tractor-drawn sledge was already fully loaded, and there was no room for a lot of the timbers, so old Faddey's family and the helpers they had called in had nearly finished knocking together another homemade sledge. They were all working like madmen, in the frenzy that comes upon people when there is a smell of good money in the air or when they are looking forward to some treat. They were shouting at one another and arguing.

They could not agree on whether the sledges should be hauled separately or both together. One of Faddey's sons (the lame one) and the engine-driver son-in-law reasoned that the sledges couldn't both be taken at once because the tractor wouldn't be able to pull them. The man in charge of the tractor, a hefty fat-faced fellow who was very sure of himself, said hoarsely that he knew best, he was the driver, and he would take both at once. His motives were obvious: according to the agreement, the engine driver was paying him for the removal of the upper room, not for the number of trips he had to make. He could never have made two trips in a night—twenty-five kilometers each way, and one return journey. And by morning he had to get the tractor back in the garage from which he had sneaked it out for this job on the side.

Old Faddey was impatient to get the top room moved that day, and at a nod from him his lads gave in. To the stout sledge in front they hitched the one they had knocked together in such a hurry.

Matryona was running about among the men, fussing and helping them to heave the beams on the sledge. Suddenly I noticed that she was wearing my jacket and had dirtied the sleeves on the frozen mud round the beams. I was annoyed and told her so. That jacket held memories for me: it had kept me warm in the bad years.

This was the first time that I was ever angry with Matryona Vasilyevna.

Matryona was taken aback. "Oh dear, dear me," she said. "My poor head. I picked it up in a rush, you see, and never thought about it being yours. I'm sorry, Ignatich."

And she took it off and hung it up to dry.

The loading was finished, and all the men who had been working, about ten of them, clattered past my table and dived under the curtain into the kitchen. I could hear the muffled rattle of glasses and, from time to time, the clink of a bottle, the voices got louder and louder, the boasting more reckless. The biggest braggart was the tractor driver. The stink of hooch floated in to me. But they didn't go on drinking long. It was getting dark and they had to hurry. They began to leave. The tractor driver came out first, looking pleased with himself and fierce. The engine-driver son-in-law, Faddey's lame son, and one of his nephews were going to Cherusti. The others went off home. Faddey was flourishing his stick, trying to overtake somebody and put him right about something. The lame son paused at my table to light up and suddenly started telling me how he loved Aunt Matryona, and that he had got married not long ago, and his wife had just had a son. Then they shouted for him and he went out. The tractor set up a roar outside.

After all the others had gone, Matryona dashed out from behind the screen. She looked after them, anxiously shaking her head. She had put on her jacket and her headscarf. As she was going through the door, she said to me, "Why ever couldn't they hire two? If one tractor had cracked up, the other would have pulled them. What'll happen now, God only knows!"

She ran out after the others.

After the boozing and the arguments and all the coming and going, it was quieter than ever in the deserted cottage, and very chilly because the door had been opened so many times. I got into my jacket and sat down to mark exercise books. The noise of the tractor died away in the distance.

An hour went by. And another. And a third. Matryona still hadn't come back, but I wasn't surprised. When she had seen the sledge off, she must have gone round to her friend Masha.

Another hour went by. And yet another. Darkness, and with it a deep silence had descended on the village. I couldn't understand at the time why it was so quiet. Later, I found out that it was because all evening not a single train had gone along the line five hundred yards from the house. No sound was coming from my radio, and I noticed that the mice were wilder than ever. Their scampering and scratching and squeaking behind the wallpaper was getting noisier and more defiant all the time.

I woke up. It was one o'clock in the morning, and Matryona still hadn't come home.

Suddenly I heard several people talking loudly. They were still a long way off, but something told me that they were coming to our house. And sure enough, I heard soon afterward a heavy knock at the gate. A commanding voice, strange to me, yelled out an order to open up. I went out into the pitch darkness with a torch. The whole village was asleep, there was no light in the windows, and the snow had started melting in the last week so that it gave no reflected light. I turned the catch and let them in. Four men in greatcoats went on toward the house. It's a very unpleasant thing to be visited at night by noisy people in greatcoats.

When we got into the light though, I saw that two of them were wearing railway uniforms. The older of the two, a fat man with the same sort of face as the tractor driver, asked, "Where's the woman of the house?"

"I don't know."

"This is the place the tractor with a sledge came from?"

"This is it."

"Had they been drinking before they left?"

All four of them were looking around, screwing up their eyes in the dim light from the table lamp. I realized that they had either made an arrest or wanted to make one.

"What's happened then?"

"Answer the question!"

"But . . ."

"Were they drunk when they went?"

"Were they drinking here?"

Had there been a murder? Or hadn't they been able to move the top room? The men in greatcoats had me off balance. But one thing was certain: Matryona could do time for making hooch.

I stepped back to stand between them and the kitchen door. "I honestly didn't notice. I didn't see anything." (I really hadn't seen anything—only heard.) I made what was supposed to be a helpless gesture, drawing attention to the state of the cottage: a table lamp shining peacefully on books and exercises, a crowd of frightened rubber plants, the austere couch of a recluse, not a sign of debauchery.

They had already seen for themselves, to their annoyance, that there had been no drinking in that room. They turned to leave, telling each other this wasn't where the drinking had been then, but it would be a good thing to put in that it was. I saw them out and tried to discover what had happened. It was only at the gate that one of them growled. "They've all been cut to bits. Can't find all the pieces."

"That's a detail. The nine o'clock express nearly went off the rails. That would have been something." And they walked briskly away.

I went back to the hut in a daze. Who were "they"? What did "all of them" mean? And where was Matryona?

I moved the curtain aside and went into the kitchen. The stink of hooch rose and hit me. It was a deserted battlefield: a huddle of stools and benches, empty bottles lying around, one bottle half-full, glasses, the remains of pickled herring, onion, and sliced fat pork.

Everything was deathly still. Just cockroaches creeping unperturbed about the field of battle.

They had said something about the nine o'clock express. Why? Perhaps I should have shown them all this? I began to wonder whether I had done right. But what a damnable way to behave—keeping their explanations for official persons only.

Suddenly the small gate creaked. I hurried out on to the landing. "Matryona Vasilyevna?"

The yard door opened, and Matryona's friend Masha came in, swaying and wringing her hands. "Matryona—our Matryona, Ignatich—"

I sat her down, and through her tears she told me the story.

The approach to the crossing was a steep rise. There was no barrier. The tractor and the first sledge went over, but the towrope broke and the second sledge, the homemade one, got stuck on the crossing and started falling apart—the wood Faddey had given them to make the second sledge was no good. They towed the first sledge out of the way and went back for the second. They were fixing the towrope—the tractor driver and Faddey's lame son, and Matryona (heaven knows what brought her there) were with them, between the tractor and the sledge. What help did she think she could be to the men? She was forever meddling in men's work. Hadn't a bolting horse nearly tipped her into the lake once, through a hole in the ice? Why did she have to go to the damned crossing? She had handed over the top room and owed nothing to anybody. The engine driver kept a lookout in case the train from Cherusti rushed up on them. Its headlamps would be visible a long way off. But two engines coupled together came from the other direction, from our station, backing without lights. Why they were without lights nobody knows. When an engine is backing, coal dust blows into the driver's eyes from the tender and he can't see very well. The two engines flew into them and crushed the three people between the tractor and the sledge to pulp. The tractor was wrecked, the sledge was matchwood, the rails were buckled, and both engines turned over.

"But how was it they didn't hear the engines coming?"

"The tractor engine was making such a din."

"What about the bodies?"

"They won't let anybody in. They've roped them off."

"What was that somebody was telling me about the express?"

"The nine o'clock express goes through our station at a good clip and on to the crossing. But the two drivers weren't hurt when their engines crashed, they jumped out and ran back along the line waving their hands, and they managed to stop the train. The nephew was hurt by a beam as well. He's hiding at Klavka's now so that they won't know he was at the crossing. If they find out they'll drag him in as a witness. . . . 'Don't know lies up, and do know gets tied up.' Kira's husband didn't get a scratch. He tried to hang himself, they had to cut him down. It's all because of me, he says, my aunty's killed and my brother. Now he's gone and given himself up. But the mad-house is where he'll be going, not prison. Oh, Matryona, my dearest Matryona. . . ."

Matryona was gone. Someone close to me had been killed. And on her last day I had scolded her for wearing my jacket.

The lovingly drawn red and yellow woman in the book advertisement smiled happily on.

Old Masha sat there weeping a little longer. Then she got up to go. And suddenly she asked me, "Ignatich, you remember, Matryona had a gray shawl. She meant it to go to my Tanya when she died, didn't she?"

She looked at me hopefully in the half-darkness—surely I hadn't forgotten?

No, I remembered. "She said so, yes."

"Well, listen, maybe you could let me take it with me now. The family will be swarming in tomorrow and I'll never get it then." And she gave me another hopeful, imploring look. She had been Matryona's friend for half a century, the only one in the village who truly loved her.

No doubt she was right.

"Of course—take it."

She opened the chest, took out the shawl, tucked it under her coat, and went out.

The mice had gone mad. They were running furiously up and down the walls, and you could almost see the green wallpaper rippling and rolling over their backs.

In the morning I had to go to school. The time was three o'clock. The only thing to do was to lock up and go to bed.

Lock up, because Matryona would not be coming.

I lay down, leaving the light on. The mice were squeaking, almost moaning, racing and running. My mind was weary and wandering, and I couldn't rid myself of an uneasy feeling that an invisible Matryona was flitting about and saying good-bye to her home.

And suddenly I imagined Faddey standing there, young and black-haired, in the dark patch by the door, with his ax uplifted. "If it wasn't my own brother, I'd chop the both of you to bits."

The threat had lain around for forty years, like an old broad sword in a corner, and in the end it had struck its blow.

3

When it was light the women went to the crossing and brought back all that was left of Matryona on a hand sledge with a dirty sack over it. They threw off the sack to wash her. There was just a mess . . . no feet, only half a body, no left hand. One woman said, "The Lord has left her her right hand. She'll be able to say her prayers where she's going."

Then the whole crowd of rubber plants were carried out of the cottage—these plants that Matryona had loved so much that once when smoke woke her up in the night she didn't rush to save her house but to tip the plants onto the floor in case they were suffocated. The women swept the floor clean. They hung a wide towel of old homespun over Matryona's dim mirror. They took down the jolly posters. They moved my table out of the way. Under the icons, near the windows, they stood a rough unadorned coffin on a row of stools.

In the coffin lay Matryona. Her body, mangled and lifeless, was covered with a clean sheet. Her head was swathed in a white kerchief. Her face was almost undamaged, peaceful, more alive than dead.

The villagers came to pay their last respects. The women even brought their small children to take a look at the dead. And if anyone raised a lament, all the women, even those who had looked in out of idle curiosity, always joined in, wailing where they stood by the door or the wall, as though they were providing a choral accompaniment. The men stood stiff and silent with their caps off.

The formal lamentation had to be performed by the women of Matryona's family. I observed that the lament followed a coldly calculated, age-old ritual. The more distant relatives went up to the coffin for a short while and made low wailing noises over it. Those who considered themselves closer kin to the dead woman began their lament in the doorway and when they got as far as the coffin, bowed down and roared out their grief right in the face of the departed. Every lamenter made up her own melody. And expressed her own thoughts and feelings.

I realized that a lament for the dead is not just a lament, but a kind of politics. Matryona's three sisters swooped, took possession of the cottage, the goat, and the stove, locked up the chest, ripped the two hundred rubles for the funeral out of the coat lining, and drummed it into everybody who came that only they were near relatives. Their lament over the coffin went like this, "*Oh, nanny, nanny! Oh nan-nan!* All we had in the world was you! You could have lived in peace and quiet, you could. And we should always have been kind and loving to you. Now your top room's been the death of you. Finished you off, it has, the cursed thing! Oh, why did you have to take it down? Why didn't you listen to us?"

Thus the sisters' laments were indictments of Matryona's husband's family: they shouldn't have made her take the top room down. (There was an underlying meaning, too: you've taken the top room, all right, but we won't let you have the house itself!)

Matryona's husband's family, her sisters-in-law, Efim and Faddey's sisters, and the various nieces lamented like this, "*Oh poor auntie, poor auntie!* Why didn't you take better care of yourself! Now they're angry with us for sure. Our own dear Matryona you were, and it's your own fault! The top room is nothing to do with it. Oh why did you go where death was waiting for you? Nobody asked you to go there. And what a way to die! Oh why didn't you listen to us?" (Their answer to the others showed through these laments: we are not to blame for her death, and the house we'll talk about later.)

But the "second" Matryona, a coarse, broad-faced woman, the substitute Matryona whom Faddey had married so long ago for the sake of her name, got out of step with family policy, wailing and sobbing over the coffin in her simplicity, *"Oh my poor dear sister!* You won't be angry with me, will you now? Oh-oh-oh! How we used to talk and talk, you and me! Forgive a poor miserable woman! You've gone to be with your dear mother, and you'll come for me some day, for sure! Oh-oh-oh-oh! . . ."

At every "oh-oh-oh" it was as though she were giving up the ghost. She writhed and gasped, with her breast against the side of the coffin. When her lament went beyond the ritual prescription, the women, as though acknowledging its success, all started saying, "Come away now, come away."

Matryona came away, but back she went again, sobbing with even greater abandon. Then an ancient woman came out of a corner, put her hand on Matryona's shoulder, and said, "There are two riddles in this world: how I was born, I don't remember, how I shall die, I don't know."

And Matryona fell silent at once, and all the others were silent, so that there was an unbroken hush.

But the old woman herself, who was much older than all the other old women there and didn't seem to belong to Matryona at all, after a while started wailing, "Oh, my poor sick Matryona! Oh my poor Vasilyevna! Oh what a weary thing it is to be seeing you into your grave!"

There was one who didn't follow the ritual, but wept straight-forwardly, in the fashion of our age, which has had plenty of practice at it. This was Matryona's unfortunate foster daughter, Kira, from Cherusti, for whom the top room had been taken down and moved. Her ringlets were pitifully out of curl. Her eyes looked red and bloodshot. She didn't notice that her headscarf was slipping off out in the frosty air and that her arm hadn't found the sleeve of her coat. She walked in a stupor from her foster mother's coffin in one house to her brother's in another. They were afraid she would lose her mind, because her husband had to go on trial as well.

It looked as if her husband was doubly at fault: not only had he been moving the top room, but as an engine driver, he knew the regulations about unprotected crossings and should have gone down to the station to warn them about the tractor. There were a thousand people on the Urals express that night, peacefully sleeping in the upper and lower berths of their dimly lit carriages, and all those lives were nearly cut short. All because of a few greedy people, wanting to get their hands on a plot of land, or not wanting to make a second trip with a tractor.

All because of the top room, which had been under a curse ever since Faddey's hands had started itching to take it down.

The tractor driver was already beyond human justice. And the railway authorities were also at fault, both because a busy crossing was unguarded and because the coupled engines were traveling without lights. That was why they had tried at first to blame it all on the drink, and then to keep the case out of court.

The rails and the track were so twisted and torn that for three days, while the coffins were still in the house, no trains ran—they were diverted onto another line. All Friday, Saturday, and Sunday, from the end of the investigation until the funeral, the work of repairing the line went on day and night. The repair gang was frozen, and they made fires to warm themselves and to light their work at night, using the boards and beams from the second sledge, which were there for the taking, scattered around the crossing.

The first sledge just stood there, undamaged and still loaded, a little way beyond the crossing.

One sledge, tantalizingly ready to be towed away, and the other perhaps still to be plucked from the flames—that was what harrowed the soul of black-bearded Faddey all day Friday and all day Saturday. His daughter was going out of her mind, his son-in-law had a criminal charge hanging over him, in his own house lay the son he had killed, and along the street the woman he had killed and whom he had once loved. But Faddey stood by the coffins, clutching his beard, only for a short time, and went away again. His high forehead was clouded by painful thoughts, but what he was thinking about was how to save the timbers of the top room from the flames and from Matryona's scheming sisters.

Going over the people of Talnovo in my mind, I realized that Faddey was not the only one like that.

Property, the people's property, or my property, is strangely called our "goods." If you lose your goods, people think you disgrace yourself and make yourself look foolish.

Faddey dashed about, never stopping to sit down, from the settlement to the station, from one official to another, there he stood with his bent back, leaning heavily on his stick, and begged them all to take pity on an old man and give him permission to recover the top room.

Somebody gave permission. And Faddey gathered together his surviving sons, sons-in-law, and nephews, got horses from the kolkhoz and from the other side of the wrecked crossing, by a roundabout way that led through three villages, brought the remnants of the top room home to his yard. He finished the job in the early hours of Sunday morning.

On Sunday afternoon they were buried. The two coffins met in the middle of the village, and the relatives argued about which of them should go first. Then they put them side by side on an open sledge, the aunt and the nephew, and carried the dead over the damp snow, with a gloomy February sky above, to the churchyard two villages away. There was an unkind wind, so the priest and the deacon waited inside the church and didn't come out to Talnovo to meet them.

A crowd of people walked slowly behind the coffins, singing in chorus. Outside the village they fell back.

When Sunday came the women were still fussing around the house. An old woman mumbled psalms by the coffin, Matryona's sisters flitted about, popping things into the oven, and the air round the mouth of the stove trembled with the heat of red-hot peats, those Matryona had carried in a sack from a distant bog. They were making unappetizing pies with poor flour.

When the funeral was over and it was already getting on toward evening, they gathered for the wake. Tables were put together to make a long one, which hid the place where the coffin had stood in the morning. To start with, they all stood round the table, and an old man, the husband of a sister-in-law, said the Lord's Prayer. Then they poured everybody a little honey and warm water,[1] just enough to cover the bottom of the bowl. We spooned it up without bread or anything, in memory of the dead. Then we ate something and drank vodka and the conversation became more animated. Before the jelly they all stood up and sang "Eternal remembrance" (they explained to me that it had to be sung before the jelly). There was more drinking. By now they were talking louder than ever, and not about Matryona at all. The sister-in-law's husband started boasting, "Did you notice, brother Christians, that they took the funeral service slowly today? That's because Father Mikhail noticed me. He knows I know the service. Other times, it's saints defend us, homeward wend us, and that's all."

At last the supper was over. They all rose again. They sang "Worthy Is She." Then again, with a triple repetition of "Eternal Remembrance."[2] But the voices were hoarse and out of tune, their faces drunken, and nobody put any feeling into this "eternal memory."

Then most of the guests went away, and only the near relatives were left. They pulled out their cigarets and lit up, there were jokes and laughter. There was some mention of Matryona's husband and his disappearance. The sister-in-law's husband, striking himself on the chest, assured me and the cobbler who was married to one of Matryona's sisters, "He was dead, Efim was dead! What could stop him coming back if he wasn't? If I knew they were going to hang me when I got to the old place, I'd come back just the same!"

The cobbler nodded in agreement. He was a deserter and had never left the old place. All through the war he was hiding in his mother's cellar.

The stern and silent old woman who was more ancient than all the ancients was staying the night and sat high up on the stove. She looked down in mute disapproval on the indecently animated youngsters of fifty and sixty.

But the unhappy foster daughter, who had grown up within these walls, went away behind the kitchen screen to cry.

Faddey didn't come to Matryona's wake—perhaps because he was holding a wake for his son. But twice in the next few days he walked angrily into the house for discussions with Matryona's sisters and the deserting cobbler.

The argument was about the house. Should it go to one of the sisters or to the foster daughter? They were on the verge of taking it to court, but they made peace because they realized that the court would hand over the house to neither side, but to the Rural District Council. A bargain was struck. One sister took the goat, the cobbler and his wife got the house, and to make up Faddey's share, since he had "nursed every bit of timber here in his arms," in addition to the top room which had already been carried away, they let him have the shed which had housed the goat and the whole of the inner fence between the yard and the garden.

Once again the insatiable old man got the better of sickness and pain and became young and active. Once again he gathered together his surviving sons

---

1. Traditionally Russians have *kutiia*, a wheat pudding with honey and almonds, at funerals and memorial gatherings; the villagers are too poor to have the main ingredients and their honey and water are symbolic of the *kutiia*. 2. Dirges, religious hymns sung to honor the dead. The village still follows religious rituals in time of crisis and does not use the civil ceremony proposed by the Soviet government.

and sons-in-law, they dismantled the shed and the fence, he hauled the timbers himself, sledge by sledge, and only toward the end did he have Antoshka of 8-D, who didn't slack this time, to help him.

They boarded Matryona's house up till the spring, and I moved in with one of her sisters-in-law, not far away. This sister-in-law on several occasions came out with some recollection of Matryona and made me see the dead woman in a new light. "Efim didn't love her. He used to say, 'I like to dress in an educated way, but she dresses any old way, like they do in the country.' Well then, he thinks, if she doesn't want anything, he might as well drink whatever's to spare. One time I went with him to the town to work, and he got himself a madam there and never wanted to come back to Matryona."

Everything she said about Matryona was disapproving. She was slovenly, she made no effort to get a few things about her. She wasn't the saving kind. She didn't even keep a pig, because she didn't like fattening them up for some reason. And the silly woman helped other people without pay. (What brought Matryona to mind this time was that the garden needed plowing, and she couldn't find enough helpers to pull the plow.)

Matryona's sister-in-law admitted that she was warmhearted and straightforward, but pitied and despised her for it.

It was only then, after these disapproving comments from her sister-in-law, that a true likeness of Matryona formed before my eyes, and I understood her as I never had when I lived side by side with her.

Of course! Every house in the village kept a pig. But she didn't. What can be easier than fattening a greedy piglet that cares for nothing in the world but food! You warm his swill three times a day, you live for him—then you cut his throat and you have some fat.

But she had none.

She made no effort to get things round her. She didn't struggle and strain to buy things and then care for them more than life itself.

She didn't go all out after fine clothes. Clothes, that beautify what is ugly and evil.

She was misunderstood and abandoned even by her husband. She had lost six children, but not her sociable ways. She was a stranger to her sisters and sisters-in-law, a ridiculous creature who stupidly worked for others without pay. She didn't accumulate property against the day she died. A dirty-white goat, a gammy-legged cat, some rubber plants. . . .

We had all lived side by side with her and had never understood that she was the righteous one without whom, as the proverb says, no village can stand.[3]

Nor any city.

Nor our whole land.

---

3. See Genesis 18.23–33, the story of Sodom.

DORIS LESSING
born 1919

The clash between cultures, between attitudes within cultures, and between elements of one's own personality, as well as the attempt to integrate opposing elements into a higher level of consciousness, are all fundamental to Doris Lessing's work and are explored in a style that ranges from the detailed realism of her earliest stories to the fantasies and "inner-space fiction" of her novels of the 1970s. Lessing herself has lived in the midst of such conflicts: brought up in the British colony of Rhodesia, she has written harsh indictments of colonial society and its cruel blindness to black culture and rights; living in London, she has described political and social issues and the way they determine interpersonal relationships; as a woman pursuing independence and the right to shape her own identity, she has investigated the psychology of the self in both sexual and intellectual terms and pondered the relations of the individual to the community. Lessing's social realism, her description of the frustrated and incomplete relationships between human beings, and her yearning (especially evident in the later novels) for a higher plane of awareness in which there is perfect understanding recall D. H. Lawrence's criticism of society and his vision of perfect harmony in tune with nature. Yet there are important differences, including Lessing's refusal to accept the archetypal roles of the sexes that Lawrence found the key to natural harmony. Her own experience could not be content with such answers, and her stories and novels have never ceased to explore the layers of consciousness that make up individual identity and social interaction.

She was born Doris May Tayler in Persia (now Iran), on October 22, 1919. Her parents were British—her mother a nurse and her father a clerk in the Imperial Bank of Persia who had been crippled in World War I and whose horror-filled memories of the "war to end war" punctuate her recollections of childhood. In 1925 her father decided to start a new life in British Africa, where the colonial government of Rhodesia (now Zimbabwe) was offering economic incentives to encourage the immigration of white settlers. For ten shillings an acre, he bought three thousand acres of farming land in Mashonaland, a section of Southern Rhodesia that was the homeland of the Matabele tribe but from which the government had evicted most of the population. The farm never prospered. Lessing attended a convent school in the capital city of Salisbury (now Harare) until fourteen, but considers herself largely self-educated from her avid reading of classics of European and American literature. She especially loved the nineteenth-century novel, and Tolstoy, Dostoevsky, Stendhal, and the other great realists impressed her with their "climate of ethical judgement" in which she felt "the warmth, the compassion, the humanity, the love of people" that are so important in her own works. Gradually she became aware of the problems of racial injustice in her new home and of the fact that she was one of a privileged class of white immigrants who had displaced the previous owners of the land. As she later noted, she was "a member of the white minority, pitted against a black majority that was abominably treated and still is." Themes of this early awakening, which combines a strong attachment to the land itself with horror at racial inequities and the sterility of white civilization in Rhodesia, run through much of her work: in particular, her first novel *The Grass Is Singing* (1949) and the collected *African Stories* (1964). To Lessing, "literature should be committed" in the face of all forms of tyranny. She herself was politically active in Rhodesia and a member of the British Communist Party from 1952 until 1956, the year of the intervention in Hungary. Much of her writing describes the painful clash of two ideals—individual conscience and collective good—as they were embodied for Lessing in her experience of communism. Her political activism and descriptions of racial injustice made their mark, and in 1956 she was declared a prohibited alien in both Southern Rhodesia and South Africa.

While still in Rhodesia, Lessing worked in several office jobs in Salisbury and made two unsuccessful marriages (Lessing is the surname of her second husband). In 1949 she moved to England with the son of her second marriage and published *The Grass Is Singing*. It was an immediate success, and she was henceforth able to make her living as a writer. She began the five-volume series *Children of Violence* (1952–69), which follows the life of a symbolically named heroine, Martha Quest, whose career in many instances parallels Lessing's own. *Children of Violence* is the portrait of an age and two cultures, and it explores with Lessing's characteristic energy a series of moral and intellectual issues for the time: the (female) protagonist's pursuit of individual freedom and the right to achieve her own identity, parent-child relationships, race relations, the hopes and frustrations of political idealism, reason versus irrationality, the shaping influence of culture and historical events. It follows the form of the nineteenth-century *Bildungsroman,* or "education novel": Martha Quest moves toward greater understanding of the cultural forces acting on her, but it cannot be said that she controls the process of her development as consciously as will Lessing's later protagonists.

The Golden Notebook (1962), Lessing's most famous novel, makes a sharp break with the linear style of narrative found in *Children of Violence* and in the bildungsroman tradition. Once again, a protagonist (Anna Wulf) is struggling to build a unified identity from the multiple selves that constitute her fragmented personality. Linear narrative, however, cannot do justice to these many dimensions, or to the exploratory process by which Anna finally creates a free, integrated personality. "The point of that book was the relation of its parts to each other," said Lessing, and this relation (although framed by a conventional short novel called *Free Women*) is essentially that of an overlapping series of differently colored notebooks that contain Anna's different versions of her experience: black for Africa, red for politics, yellow for a fictionalized version with herself as a character named Ella, and blue for a factual diary. By analyzing her life from these different perspectives, Anna is able to understand and synthesize their interaction: to write, ultimately, the "Golden Notebook," which is "all of me in one book." A chronological account of the events would start with Anna's breakdown and inability to write and end with her regained equilibrium after a tangled love affair with a similarly split character, Saul Green. Such an account would miss the core of the book, however, or the process by which it all happens: Lessing's detailed description of a mind healing itself by recalling and assessing its relationships with other people, adjusting earlier views according to new insights, weighing (and sometimes rejecting) the explanations of psychoanalysis, comparing different ways of interpreting experience, and measuring the constantly changing whole against the test of each new encounter.

Although *The Golden Notebook* is now taken as one of the major novels of the twentieth century, it was seen at the time chiefly as a feminist manifesto—a one-sided appraisal that infuriated the author. To accusations of being "unfeminine" and a "man-hater" for putting into print emotions of female aggression, hostility, and resentment, she responded dryly, "apparently what many women were thinking, feeling, experiencing came as a great surprise." Yet, she notes, when at the same time novels and plays caustically attacked women as underminers and betrayers, "these attitudes in male writers were taken for granted, accepted as sound philosophical bases, as quite normal, certainly not as woman-hating, aggressive, or neurotic." Lessing's feminism is often a matter of establishing balances and an insistence on honesty of emotions and critical self-awareness in all her protagonists, whether male (*The Temptation of Jack Orkney*, 1963) or female (Anna Wulf).

The newly integrated "all of me" at the end of *The Golden Notebook* has broken beyond intellectualized understanding and reached "beyond the region where words could be made to have sense." In the "inner-space fiction" written during the 1970s and early 1980s, Lessing took up these themes of quasi-mystical insight: first with a schizophrenic hero whose cosmic imaginings are closer to psychic wholeness than his normal life (*Briefing for a Descent into Hell*, 1971), later in the dream-exploration of other "bizarre" dimensions beyond the "ordinary" living-room wall (*Memoirs of a Survivor,* 1974), and most recently in a science-fiction series, *Canopus in Argos: Archives* (1979–83), which describes the different protagonists' consciousness evolving under pressure to a higher plane of existence. These later books, as Lessing states, are influenced by Sufi mysticism with its insistence on detached perception and the evolution of consciousness and on learning as a process of discovering the right questions. The wordless moment of understanding that comes when the right question is asked may seem a long way from Lessing's first novels about race relations in Southern Rhodesia, or Martha Quest's awakening to emotional, intellectual, and political maturity. In each case, however, a process of listening to experience is required. The focus has not changed when she writes in the "Afterword" to the fourth Canopus novel: "It seems to me that we do not know nearly enough about ourselves." The attempt to know about ourselves, to grow through such knowledge, and to achieve harmony in this world or "in worlds or dimensions elsewhere" pervades her entire work.

Annoyed at criticism of her shift to science fiction, Lessing published two realistic novels under the name of Jane Somers: *The Diary of a Good Neighbor* (1983), a novel that gave graphic descriptions of the difficulties of aging and illness, and its sequel *If the Old Could . . .* (1984). Sales were respectable but not outstanding; and when both were reprinted in 1984 as *The Diaries of Jane Somers,* Lessing announced that she had published them under a pseudonym to test whether the critics who had disliked her new style would recognize the "realistic" Lessing under another name. They did not. Since then, she has produced realistic stories with a satirical or symbolic twist: *The Good Terrorist* (1985), a satire of naive British terrorists who arrange a homey atmosphere in a London squat while carrying out bombing raids, and *The Fifth Child* (1988), which recounts the gradual destruction of a London family by their "alien" and uncontrollably savage fifth child. Lectures reprinted in *Prisons We Choose to Live Inside* (1987) reject the savagery that has dominated human history and that persists in wars such as the Afghan resistance, which Lessing documents in *The Wind Blows Away Our Words* (1987). The writer's role, she asserts, is to be both committed and detached, clarifying issues and suggesting remedies for those who are caught up in "mass emotions and social conditions." As both novelist and non-fiction writer, Lessing upholds the concept of the writer as a moral figure, whether the "moralist" of the French tradition who awakens our conscience to ethical issues (Albert Camus), or the polemic voice sounded in novels and essays by Alexander Solzhenitsyn.

The Old Chief Mshlanga is one of Lessing's earliest African stories, written during the period from 1950 to 1958 when she wrote most of her African fiction and published in *This Was the Old Chief's Country* (1951). This collection, together with five novellas set in Africa in *Five* (1953) and her best-selling novel *The Grass Is Singing* (1949), established Lessing as an important interpreter of modern Africa—or rather, of the colonial experience in Africa. She herself draws the distinction between the African experience as it can be understood by African whites and as it is felt by the black Africans whose heritage has been forcibly displaced. Lessing writes in the preface to her 1973 *Collected African Stories:*

> It can be said of all white-dominated Africa that it was—and indeed still is—the Old Chief's Country. So all the stories I write of a certain kind, I think of as belonging under that heading: tales about white people, sometimes about black people, living in a landscape that not so very long ago was settled by black tribes, living in complex societies that the white people are only just beginning to study, let alone understand. . . .
>
> I am not able to write about what has been lost, which was and still is recorded orally. As a writer that is my biggest regret, as it is of all the white writers from Africa I have known. The tribal life that was broken seems now to have had more real dignity, more responsibility for what is important in people—their self-

respect, more tolerance of individuality, than our way of living has. The breakup of that society, the time of chaos that followed it, is as dramatic a story as any; but if you are a white writer, it is a story that you are told by others.

The dispossession that underlies the plot of *The Old Chief Mshlanga* began with the economic infiltration of the country by white colonizers, soon formalized in Chartered Company policies that divided land into categories of "alienated" (owned by white settlers) and "unalienated" (occupied by natives, including the Reserves whose inhabitants paid a head tax). The official Land Apportionment Act of 1930 confirmed this arrangement by separating the territory into areas called Native and European. The figure of the Old Chief bridges past and present, a proud era fifty years earlier when his people owned the entire country and the diminished present in which they can be forcibly relocated on a Reserve after disagreeing with a white settler. Yet it is not the Old Chief who is the protagonist; significantly, his situation is pushed into the background until the middle of the story, when it intrudes on the consciousness of a young white settler girl. Only gradually does the "vein of richness" that he and his people represent come to light. By the end of the story the tribe has disappeared. The girl visits their village to find it disintegrating into the riotously fertile landscape, and the richness of their existence is preserved mainly as an obscure recognition in her mind.

Yet in spite of her comment that "there was nothing there," the girl's close description of the lush scene shows that her eyes have been opened to an African presence that initially she could not see. The gain, however, is one-sided: even now it cannot bring her closer to the experience of the tribespeople but is restricted to a feeling for the landscape. There is no advantage for the Old Chief: he and his people have disappeared into a symbolic essence, buried in a "richness" that inheres in the land even when it is turned over to a new settler—as it will be. Lessing's observant young girl has been changed by the encounter with the Old Chief, but hers is a bleak awakening that includes a sense of loss and indirect responsibility. Perhaps, one day, she will write about it.

Ruth Whittaker, *Doris Lessing* (1988), is a concise, informative discussion of Lessing's fiction to 1985; it includes biographical contexts and selective bibliography. Two volumes of Lessing's autobiography are published as *Under My Skin* (1995) and *Walking in the Shade: Volume Two of My Autobiography, 1949–1962* (1997). Michael Thorpe, *Doris Lessing's Africa* (1978), is a valuable historical and critical commentary on Lessing's writings about Africa. Claire Sprague and Virginia Tiger, *Critical Essays on Doris Lessing* (1986), offers diverse perspectives on the range of Lessing's work; numerous interviews on a range of subjects are collected in Doris May Lessing, *Putting Questions Differently: Interviews with Doris Lessing, 1964–1994* (1994). A good critical study of the novels is Roberta Rubenstein, *The Novelistic Vision of Doris Lessing* (1979). Perspectives on women and literature are the focus of Gayle Greene, *Doris Lessing: The Poetics of Change* (1994).

The Old Chief Mshlanga

They were good, the years of ranging the bush over her father's farm which, like every white farm, was largely unused, broken only occasionally by small patches of cultivation. In between, nothing but trees, the long sparse grass, thorn and cactus and gully, grass and outcrop and thorn. And a jutting piece of rock which had been thrust up from the warm soil of Africa unimaginable eras of time ago, washed into hollows and whorls by sun and wind that had travelled so many thousands of miles of space and bush, would hold the

weight of a small girl whose eyes were sightless for anything but a pale wil-
lowed river, a pale gleaming castle—a small girl singing: "Out flew the web
and floated wide, the mirror cracked from side to side . . ."[1]

Pushing her way through the green aisles of the mealie[2] stalks, the leaves
arching like cathedrals veined with sunlight far overhead, with the packed
red earth underfoot, a fine lace of red starred witchweed would summon up
a black bent figure croaking premonitions: the Northern witch, bred of cold
Northern forests, would stand before her among the mealie fields, and it was
the mealie fields that faded and fled, leaving her among the gnarled roots of
an oak, snow falling thick and soft and white, the woodcutter's fire glowing
red welcome through crowding tree trunks.

A white child, opening its eyes curiously on a sun-suffused landscape, a
gaunt and violent landscape, might be supposed to accept it as her own, to
make the msasa trees and the thorn trees as familiars, to feel her blood
running free and responsive to the swing of the seasons.

This child could not see a msasa tree,[3] or the thorn, for what they were.
Her books held tales of alien fairies, her rivers ran slow and peaceful, and
she knew the shape of the leaves of an ash or an oak, the names of the little
creatures that lived in English streams, when the words "the veld"[4] meant
strangeness, though she could remember nothing else.

Because of this, for many years, it was the veld that seemed unreal; the
sun was a foreign sun, and the wind spoke a strange language.

The black people on the farm were as remote as the trees and the rocks.
They were an amorphous black mass, mingling and thinning and massing
like tadpoles, faceless, who existed merely to serve, to say "Yes, Baas,"[5] take
their money and go. They changed season by season, moving from one farm
to the next, according to their outlandish needs, which one did not have to
understand, coming from perhaps hundreds of miles north or east, passing
on after a few months—where? Perhaps even as far away as the fabled gold
mines of Johannesburg,[6] where the pay was so much better than the few
shillings a month and the double handful of mealie meal twice a day which
they earned in that part of Africa.

The child was taught to take them for granted: the servants in the house
would come running a hundred yards to pick up a book if she dropped it.
She was called "Nkosikaas"—Chieftainess, even by the black children her
own age.

Later, when the farm grew too small to hold her curiosity, she carried a
gun in the crook of her arm and wandered miles a day, from vlei to vlei, from
kopje[7] to kopje, accompanied by two dogs: the dogs and the gun were an
armour against fear. Because of them she never felt fear.

If a native came into sight along the kaffir[8] paths half a mile away, the
dogs would flush him up a tree as if he were a bird. If he expostulated (in
his uncouth language which was by itself ridiculous) that was cheek. If one
was in a good mood, it could be a matter for laughter. Otherwise one passed
on, hardly glancing at the angry man in the tree.

1. The child is reciting lines 114–15 from Tennyson's *The Lady of Shalott*. 2. Maize; corn. 3. A
large tree of central Africa, notable for the vivid colorings (pink through copper) of its spring foliage and
for the fragrance of its white flowers. 4. Unenclosed country, open grassland. 5. Boss. 6. The
largest city in the Union (now Republic) of South Africa. 7. A small hill (Afrikaans). *Vlei:* a shallow
pool or swamp (Afrikaans). 8. A black African; usually used disparagingly.

On the rare occasions when white children met together they could amuse themselves by hailing a passing native in order to make a buffoon of him; they could set the dogs on him and watch him run; they could tease a small black child as if he were a puppy—save that they would not throw stones and sticks at a dog without a sense of guilt.

Later still, certain questions presented themselves in the child's mind; and because the answers were not easy to accept, they were silenced by an even greater arrogance of manner.

It was even impossible to think of the black people who worked about the house as friends, for if she talked to one of them, her mother would come running anxiously: "Come away; you mustn't talk to natives."

It was this instilled consciousness of danger, of something unpleasant, that made it easy to laugh out loud, crudely, if a servant made a mistake in his English or if he failed to understand an order—there is a certain kind of laughter that is fear, afraid of itself.

One evening, when I was about fourteen, I was walking down the side of a mealie field that had been newly ploughed, so that the great red clods showed fresh and tumbling to the vlei beyond, like a choppy red sea; it was that hushed and listening hour, when the birds send long sad calls from tree to tree, and all the colours of earth and sky and leaf are deep and golden. I had my rifle in the curve of my arm, and the dogs were at my heels.

In front of me, perhaps a couple of hundred yards away, a group of three Africans came into sight around the side of a big antheap. I whistled the dogs close in to my skirts and let the gun swing in my hand, and advanced, waiting for them to move aside, off the path, in respect for my passing. But they came on steadily, and the dogs looked up at me for the command to chase. I was angry. It was "cheek"[9] for a native not to stand off a path, the moment he caught sight of you.

In front walked an old man, stooping his weight on to a stick, his hair grizzled white, a dark red blanket slung over his shoulders like a cloak. Behind him came two young men, carrying bundles of pots, assegais,[1] hatchets.

The group was not a usual one. They were not natives seeking work. These had an air of dignity, of quietly following their own purpose. It was the dignity that checked my tongue. I walked quietly on, talking softly to the growling dogs, till I was ten paces away. Then the old man stopped, drawing his blanket close.

"Morning, Nkosikaas," he said, using the customary greeting for any time of the day.

"Good morning," I said. "Where are you going?" My voice was a little truculent.

The old man spoke in his own language, then one of the young men stepped forward politely and said in careful English: "My Chief travels to see his brothers beyond the river."

A Chief! I thought, understanding the pride that made the old man stand before me like an equal—more than an equal, for he showed courtesy, and I showed none.

The old man spoke again, wearing dignity like an inherited garment, still

9. Impudence.　1. Spears.

standing ten paces off, flanked by his entourage, not looking at me (that would have been rude) but directing his eyes somewhere over my head at the trees.

"You are the little Nkosikaas from the farm of Baas Jordan?"

"That's right," I said.

"Perhaps your father does not remember," said the interpreter for the old man, "but there was an affair with some goats. I remember seeing you when you were . . ." The young man held his hand at knee level and smiled.

We all smiled.

"What is your name?" I asked.

"This is Chief Mshlanga," said the young man.

"I will tell my father that I met you," I said.

The old man said: "My greetings to your father, little Nkosikaas."

"Good morning," I said politely, finding the politeness difficult, from lack of use.

"Morning, little Nkosikaas," said the old man, and stood aside to let me pass.

I went by, my gun hanging awkwardly, the dogs sniffing and growling, cheated of their favourite game of chasing natives like animals.

Not long afterwards I read in an old explorer's book the phrase: "Chief Mshlanga's country." It went like this: "Our destination was Chief Mshlanga's country, to the north of the river; and it was our desire to ask his permission to prospect for gold in his territory."

The phrase "ask his permission" was so extraordinary to a white child, brought up to consider all natives as things to use, that it revived those questions, which could not be suppressed: they fermented slowly in my mind.

On another occasion one of those old prospectors who still move over Africa looking for neglected reefs, with their hammers and tents, and pans for sifting gold from crushed rock, came to the farm and, in talking of the old days, used that phrase again: "This was the Old Chief's country," he said. "It stretched from those mountains over there way back to the river, hundreds of miles of country." That was his name for our district: "The Old Chief's Country"; he did not use our name for it—a new phrase which held no implication of usurped ownership.

As I read more books about the time when this part of Africa was opened up, not much more than fifty years before, I found Old Chief Mshlanga had been a famous man, known to all the explorers and prospectors. But then he had been young; or maybe it was his father or uncle they spoke of—I never found out.

During that year I met him several times in the part of the farm that was traversed by natives moving over the country. I learned that the path up the side of the big red field where the birds sang was the recognized highway for migrants. Perhaps I even haunted it in the hope of meeting him: being greeted by him, the exchange of courtesies, seemed to answer the questions that troubled me.

Soon I carried a gun in a different spirit; I used it for shooting food and not to give me confidence. And now the dogs learned better manners. When I saw a native approaching, we offered and took greetings; and slowly that other landscape in my mind faded, and my feet struck directly on the African soil, and I saw the shapes of tree and hill clearly, and the black people moved back, as it were, out of my life: it was as if I stood aside to watch a slow intimate dance of landscape and men, a very old dance, whose steps I could not learn.

But I thought: this is my heritage, too; I was bred here; it is my country as well as the black man's country; and there is plenty of room for all of us, without elbowing each other off the pavements and roads.

It seemed it was only necessary to let free that respect I felt when I was talking with old Chief Mshlanga, to let both black and white people meet gently, with tolerance for each other's differences: it seemed quite easy.

Then, one day, something new happened. Working in our house as servants were always three natives: cook, houseboy, garden boy. They used to change as the farm natives changed: staying for a few months, then moving on to a new job, or back home to their kraals.[2] They were thought of as "good" or "bad" natives; which meant: how did they behave as servants? Were they lazy, efficient, obedient, or disrespectful? If the family felt good-humoured, the phrase was: "What can you expect from raw black savages?" If we were angry, we said: "These damned niggers, we would be much better off without them."

One day, a white policeman was on his rounds of the district, and he said laughingly: "Did you know you have an important man in your kitchen?"

"What!" exclaimed my mother sharply. "What do you mean?"

"A Chief's son." The policeman seemed amused. "He'll boss the tribe when the old man dies."

"He'd better not put on a Chief's son act with me," said my mother.

When the policeman left, we looked with different eyes at our cook: he was a good worker, but he drank too much at week-ends—that was how we knew him.

He was a tall youth, with very black skin, like black polished metal, his tightly growing black hair parted white man's fashion at one side, with a metal comb from the store stuck into it; very polite, very distant, very quick to obey an order. Now that it had been pointed out, we said: "Of course, you can see. Blood always tells."

My mother became strict with him now she knew about his birth and prospects. Sometimes, when she lost her temper, she would say: "You aren't the Chief yet, you know." And he would answer her very quietly, his eyes on the ground: "Yes, Nkosikaas."

One afternoon he asked for a whole day off, instead of the customary half-day, to go home next Sunday.

"How can you go home in one day?"

"It will take me half an hour on my bicycle," he explained.

I watched the direction he took; and the next day I went off to look for this kraal; I understood he must be Chief Mshlanga's successor: there was no other kraal near enough our farm.

Beyond our boundaries on that side the country was new to me. I followed unfamiliar paths past *kopjes* that till now had been part of the jagged horizon, hazed with distance. This was Government land, which had never been cultivated by white men; at first I could not understand why it was that it appeared, in merely crossing the boundary, I had entered a completely fresh

---

2. Native villages; collections of huts surrounding a central space.

type of landscape. It was a wide green valley, where a small river sparkled, and vivid water-birds darted over the rushes. The grass was thick and soft to my calves, the trees stood tall and shapely.

I was used to our farm, whose hundreds of acres of harsh eroded soil bore trees that had been cut for the mine furnaces and had grown thin and twisted, where the cattle had dragged the grass flat, leaving innumerable criss-crossing trails that deepened each season into gullies, under the force of the rains.

This country had been left untouched, save for prospectors whose picks had struck a few sparks from the surface of the rocks as they wandered by; and for migrant natives whose passing had left, perhaps, a charred patch on the trunk of a tree where their evening fire had nestled.

It was very silent: a hot morning with pigeons cooing throatily, the midday shadows lying dense and thick with clear yellow spaces of sunlight between and in all that wide green park-like valley, not a human soul but myself.

I was listening to the quick regular tapping of a woodpecker when slowly a chill feeling seemed to grow up from the small of my back to my shoulders, in a constricting spasm like a shudder, and at the roots of my hair a tingling sensation began and ran down over the surface of my flesh, leaving me goose-fleshed and cold, though I was damp with sweat. Fever? I thought; then uneasily, turned to look over my shoulder; and realized suddenly that this was fear. It was extraordinary, even humiliating. It was a new fear. For all the years I had walked by myself over this country I had never known a moment's uneasiness; in the beginning because I had been supported by a gun and the dogs, then because I had learnt an easy friendliness for the Africans I might encounter.

I had read of this feeling, how the bigness and silence of Africa, under the ancient sun, grows dense and takes shape in the mind, till even the birds seem to call menacingly, and a deadly spirit comes out of the trees and the rocks. You move warily, as if your very passing disturbs something old and evil, something dark and big and angry that might suddenly rear and strike from behind. You look at groves of entwined trees, and picture the animals that might be lurking there; you look at the river running slowly, dropping from level to level through the vlei, spreading into pools where at night the bucks come to drink, and the crocodiles rise and drag them by their soft noses into underwater caves. Fear possessed me. I found I was turning round and round, because of that shapeless menace behind me that might reach out and take me; I kept glancing at the files of *kopjes* which, seen from a different angle, seemed to change with every step so that even known land-marks, like a big mountain that had sentinelled my world since I first became conscious of it, showed an unfamiliar sunlit valley among its foothills. I did not know where I was. I was lost. Panic seized me. I found I was spinning round and round, staring anxiously at this tree and that, peering up at the sun which appeared to have moved into an eastern slant, shedding the sad yellow light of sunset. Hours must have passed! I looked at my watch and found that this state of meaningless terror had lasted perhaps ten minutes.

The point was that it was meaningless. I was not ten miles from home: I had only to take my way back along the valley to find myself at the fence; away among the foothills of the *kopjes* gleamed the roof of a neighbour's house, and a couple of hours' walking would reach it. This was the sort of fear that contracts the flesh of a dog at night and sets him howling at the full moon. It had nothing to do with what I thought or felt; and I was more disturbed by the fact that I could become its victim than of the physical sensation itself: I walked steadily on, quietened, in a divided mind, watching my own pricking nerves and apprehensive glances from side to side with a disgusted amusement. Deliberately I set myself to think of this village I was seeking, and what I should do when I entered it—if I could find it, which was doubtful, since I was walking aimlessly and it might be anywhere in the hundreds of thousands of acres of bush that stretched about me. With my mind on that village, I realized that a new sensation was added to the fear: loneliness. Now such a terror of isolation invaded me that I could hardly walk; and if it were not that I came over the crest of a small rise and saw a village below me, I should have turned and gone home. It was a cluster of thatched huts in a clearing among trees. There were neat patches of mealies and pumpkins and millet, and cattle grazed under some trees at a distance. Fowls scratched among the huts, dogs lay sleeping on the grass, and goats friezed a *kopje* that jutted up beyond a tributary of the river lying like an enclosing arm around the village.

As I came close I saw the huts were lovingly decorated with patterns of yellow and red and ochre mud on the walls; and the thatch was tied in place with plaits of straw.

This was not at all like our farm compound, a dirty and neglected place, a temporary home for migrants who had no roots in it.

And now I did not know what to do next. I called a small black boy, who was sitting on a lot playing a stringed gourd, quite naked except for the strings of blue beads round his neck, and said: "Tell the Chief I am here." The child stuck his thumb in his mouth and stared shyly back at me.

For minutes I shifted my feet on the edge of what seemed a deserted village, till at last the child scuttled off, and then some women came. They were draped in bright cloths, with brass glinting in their ears and on their arms. They also stared, silently; then turned to chatter among themselves.

I said again: "Can I see Chief Mshlanga?" I saw they caught the name; they did not understand what I wanted. I did not understand myself.

At last I walked through them and came past the huts and saw a clearing under a big shady tree, where a dozen old men sat crosslegged on the ground, talking. Chief Mshlanga was leaning back against the tree, holding a gourd in his hand, from which he had been drinking. When he saw me, not a muscle of his face moved, and I could see he was not pleased: perhaps he was afflicted with my own shyness, due to being unable to find the right forms of courtesy for the occasion. To meet me, on our own farm, was one thing; but I should not have come here. What had I expected? I could not join them socially: the thing was unheard of. Bad enough that I, a white girl, should be walking the veld alone as a white man might: and in this part of the bush where only Government officials had the right to move.

Again I stood, smiling foolishly, while behind me stood the groups of brightly clad, chattering women, their faces alert with curiosity and interest, and in front of me sat the old men, with old lined faces, their eyes guarded, aloof. It was a village of ancients and children and women. Even the two young men who kneeled beside the Chief were not those I had seen with him previously: the young men were all away working on the white men's farms and mines, and the Chief must depend on relatives who were temporarily on holiday for his attendants.

"The small white Nkosikaas is far from home," remarked the old man at last.

"Yes," I agreed, "it is far." I wanted to say: "I have come to pay you a friendly visit, Chief Mshlanga." I could not say it. I might now be feeling an urgent helpless desire to get to know these men and women as people, to be accepted by them as a friend, but the truth was I had set out in a spirit of curiosity: I had wanted to see the village that one day our cook, the reserved and obedient young man who got drunk on Sundays, would one day rule over.

"The child of Nkosi Jordan is welcome," said Chief Mshlanga.

"Thank you," I said, and could think of nothing more to say. There was a silence, while the flies rose and began to buzz around my head; and the wind shook a little in the thick green tree that spread its branches over the old men.

"Good morning," I said at last. "I have to return now to my home."

"Morning, little Nkosikaas," said Chief Mshlanga.

I walked away from the indifferent village, over the rise past the staring amber-eyed goats, down through the tall stately trees into the great rich green valley where the river meandered and the pigeons cooed tales of plenty and the woodpecker tapped softly.

The fear had gone; the loneliness had set into stiff-necked stoicism; there was now a queer hostility in the landscape, a cold, hard, sullen indomitability that walked with me, as strong as a wall, as intangible as smoke; it seemed to say to me: you walk here as a destroyer. I went slowly homewards, with an empty heart: I had learned that if one cannot call a country to heel like a dog, neither can one dismiss the past with a smile in an easy gush of feeling, saying: I could not help it, I am also a victim.

I only saw Chief Mshlanga once again.

One night my father's big red land was trampled down by small sharp hooves, and it was discovered that the culprits were goats from Chief Mshlanga's kraal. This had happened once before, years ago.

My father confiscated all the goats. Then he sent a message to the old Chief that if he wanted them he would have to pay for the damage.

He arrived at our house at the time of sunset one evening, looking very old and bent now, walking stiffly under his regally-draped blanket, leaning on a big stick. My father sat himself down in his big chair below the steps of the house; the old man squatted carefully on the ground before him, flanked by his two young men.

The palaver was long and painful, because of the bad English of the young man who interpreted, and because my father could not speak dialect, but only kitchen kaffir.

From my father's point of view, at least two hundred pounds' worth of damage had been done to the crop. He knew he could not get the money from the old man. He felt he was entitled to keep the goats. As for the old Chief, he kept repeating angrily: "Twenty goats! My people cannot lose twenty goats! We are not rich, like the Nkosi Jordan, to lose twenty goats at once."

My father did not think of himself as rich, but rather as very poor. He spoke quickly and angrily in return, saying that the damage done meant a great deal to him, and that he was entitled to the goats.

At last it grew so heated that the cook, the Chief's son, was called from the kitchen to be interpreter, and now my father spoke fluently in English, and our cook translated rapidly so that the old man could understand how very angry my father was. The young man spoke without emotion, in a mechanical way, his eyes lowered, but showing how he felt his position by a hostile uncomfortable set of the shoulders.

It was now in the late sunset, the sky a welter of colours, the birds singing their last songs, and the cattle, lowing peacefully, moving past us towards their sheds for the night. It was the hour when Africa is most beautiful; and here was this pathetic, ugly scene, doing no one any good.

At last my father stated finally: "I'm not going to argue about it. I am keeping the goats."

The old Chief flashed back in his own language: "That means that my people will go hungry when the dry season comes."

"Go to the police, then," said my father, and looked triumphant.

There was, of course, no more to be said.

The old man sat silent, his head bent, his hands dangling helplessly over his withered knees. Then he rose, the young men helping him, and he stood facing my father. He spoke once again, very stiffly; and turned away and went home to his village.

"What did he say?" asked my father of the young man, who laughed uncomfortably and would not meet his eyes.

"What did he say?" insisted my father.

Our cook stood straight and silent, his brows knotted together. Then he spoke. "My father says: All this land, this land you call yours, is his land, and belongs to our people."

Having made this statement, he walked off into the bush after his father, and we did not see him again.

Our next cook was a migrant from Nyasaland, with no expectations of greatness.

Next time the policeman came on his rounds he was told this story. He remarked: "That kraal has no right to be there; it should have been moved long ago. I don't know why no one has done anything about it. I'll have a chat with the Native Commissioner next week. I'm going over for tennis on Sunday, anyway."

Some time later we heard that Chief Mshlanga and his people had been moved two hundred miles east, to a proper Native Reserve; the Government land was going to be opened up for white settlement soon.

I went to see the village again, about a year afterwards. There was nothing there. Mounds of red mud, where the huts had been, had long swathes of rotting thatch over them, veined with the red galleries of the white ants. The pumpkin vines rioted everywhere, over the bushes, up the lower branches of trees so that the great golden balls rolled underfoot and dangled overhead: it was a festival of pumpkins. The bushes were crowding up, the new grass sprang vivid green.

The settler lucky enough to be allotted the lush warm valley (if he chose to cultivate this particular section) would find, suddenly, in the middle of a mealie field, the plants were growing fifteen feet tall, the weight of the cobs dragging at the stalks, and wonder what unsuspected vein of richness he had struck.

TADEUSZ BOROWSKI
1922–1951

Incarcerated in the extermination camps of Auschwitz-Birkenau and Dachau between the ages of twenty and twenty-two, a tormented suicide by gas at twenty-nine, Tadeusz Borowski wrote stories of life in the camps that have made him the foremost writer of the "literature of atrocity." The stories' brutal realism and matter-of-fact tone convey, as passionate declamations could never do, the mind-numbing horror of a situation in which systematic slaughter was the background for everyday life. The narrator of these stories, modeled on Borowski but also a composite figure, has become part of the concentration camp system, to survive. He assists the Kapos, or senior prisoners who organize the camp; has a job in the system; and carries a burden of guilt that cannot quite be suppressed by his adopted impersonal attitude. Borowski's stories shocked their postwar audience by their uncompromising honesty: here were no saintly victims and demoniacally evil executioners, but human beings going about the business of extermination or, reduced to near-animal level, cooperating in their own and others' destruction. Any belief in civilization, in common humanity, or in divine Providence is sorely tested; Borowski's bleak picture questions everything and does not pretend to offer encouragement. His fiction is still read for its powerful evocation of the death camps, for its analysis of human relationships under pressure, and for an agonizing portrayal of individuals forced to choose between physical or spiritual survival.

Tadeusz Borowski was born on November 12, 1922, in the Polish city of Żytomierz, part of the then-Soviet Ukraine. When he was three years old, his father was sent to a labor camp in Siberia as a suspected dissident; four years later, his mother was deported as well, and Tadeusz and his twelve-year-old brother were separated. He was raised by an aunt and educated in a Soviet school until a prisoner exchange in 1932 brought his father home and his mother's release in 1934 reunited the family. Money was scarce, however, and the young boy was sent away to a Franciscan boarding school where he could be educated inexpensively. Much later, he commented that he had never had a family life: "either my father was sitting in Murmansk or my mother was in Siberia, or I was in a boarding school, on my own or in a camp." World War II began when he was still sixteen, and—since the Nazis did not permit higher education for Poles—Borowski continued his studies at Warsaw University via illegal underground classes. Unlike his fellow students, he refused to join political groups and did not become involved in the resistance; he wanted merely to write poetry, continue his literary studies, and write a master's thesis on the poetry of Leopold Staff. Polish publications were illegal, however, and his first poetry collection, *Wherever the Earth* (1942)—run off in 165 copies on a clandestine mimeograph machine—was enough to condemn him. *Wherever the Earth* prefigures the bleak perspective of the concentration camp stories: prophesying the end of the human race, it sees the world as a gigantic labor camp and the sky as a "low, steel lid" or "a factory ceiling" (an oppressive image he may have adapted from Baudelaire's *Spleen LXXXI*, see p. 1152). Borowski and his fiancée, Maria Rundo, were arrested in late February 1943 and sent to Auschwitz two months later. In the meantime, he was able to see from his cell window both the Jewish uprising in the Warsaw ghetto and the ghetto's fiery destruction by Nazi soldiers.

Borowski's camp experiences are reproduced in the 1948 story collection *Farewell to Maria*, from which *Ladies and Gentlemen, to the Gas Chamber* is taken. Arriving in Auschwitz, he was put to hard labor with the other prisoners; but after a bout with pneumonia, he learned to survive by taking a position as an orderly in the Auschwitz hospital—which was not just a clinic but a place where prisoners were used as experimental subjects. Maria had been sent to the women's barracks at the same camp, and he wrote her daily letters that were smuggled in. The story *Auschwitz, Our Home* contains a series of such letters and conveys, in addition to reassurances of his love, the writer's succeeding moods of hope, anger, cynicism, and despair ("We remain as numb as trees when they are being cut down"). Love lyrics written to Maria in 1942, published by his friends in 1944, display the sensuous softness of dream and contrast sharply with the camp stories' harsh illumination.

> I'm dreamy today. Noise from the street,
> the sky-curtain's rustlings, every
> sound comes in like the horizon's smoke
> through a mist.
> . . . It's how at night
> I take your hair in my hand, let its
> waves flow through my palm and
> stay quiet, full of you,
> as sleep is quiet now in me.
> (trans. Addison Bross)

The narrator's dispassionate tone in the stories, as he describes senseless cruelty and mass murder, individual scenes of desperation, or the eccentric emotions of people about to die, continue to shock many readers. Borowski is certainly describing a world of antiheroes, those who survive by accommodating themselves to things as they are and avoiding acts of heroism. His second collection of stories, *World of Stone* (1948), uses the same tone to describe life in the repatriation camps (he spent two years in such camps before being sent home) and the writer's disgust at the false normalcy of postwar society. Yet his impersonality is chiefly a shield; vulnerable, he finds a way to cope with overwhelming events by holding them at a distance. Borowski is recording events for future testimony, and he writes to his fiancée, "I do not know whether we shall survive, but I like to think that one day we shall have the courage to tell the world the whole truth and call it by its proper name." At the end of *The World of Stone*, his ambition is "to grasp the true significance of the events, things, and people I have seen. For I intend to write."

Upon his return to Poland after the war, Borowski's searing talent was recognized; the stories *Ladies and Gentlemen, to the Gas Chamber* and *A Day at Harmensee* (a subcamp of Auschwitz) had been published, and he became a prominent writer. He married Maria and was courted by Poland's Stalinist government. At the government's urging, he wrote journalism and weekly stories that followed political lines and employed a newly strident tone. The Cold War had begun, and Borowski was persuaded that he had joined a popular revolution that would prevent any more horrors like Auschwitz. He went so far as to do intelligence work in Berlin for the Polish secret police in 1949. The revelation of Soviet prison camps, however, and political purges in Poland, gradually disillusioned him: once more, he was part of a concentration camp system and complicit with the oppressors. He committed suicide by gas on July 3, 1951.

Ladies and Gentlemen, to the Gas Chamber was written in Munich, at a repatriation camp where Borowski was sent after his release from Dachau (many Birkenau prisoners were transferred as the Allied Armies moved farther into Germany). Narrated in an impersonal tone by one of the prisoners, the story describes the extermination camp of Birkenau, the second and largest of three concentration camps at Auschwitz (Polish: Oświęcim), an enclosed world of hierarchical authority and desperate struggles to survive. Food, shoes, shirts, underwear: this vital currency of the camp is obtained when new prisoners are stripped of their belongings as they arrive in railway cattle cars. The story could equally well have been titled *A Day with Canada*, for it follows the narrator's first trip to the railroad station with the labor battalion "Canada." The trip will salvage goods from a train bringing fifteen thousand Polish Jews, former inhabitants of the cities Sosnowiec and Będzin. By the end of the day, most of the travelers will be burning in the crematorium, and the camp will live for a few more days on the loot from "a good, rich transport."

Borowski suggests the systematic dehumanization of the camps from the beginning: people are equated with lice, and they mill around by naked thousands in blocked-off sections. Lice and people are poisoned with the same gas, sealed tightly into the camp or expelled from a section by the delousing process. People will later be equated with sick horses (the converted stables retain their old signs), lumber and concrete trucked in from the railroad station, and insects whose jaws work away on moldy pieces of bread. Constantly supervised, subject to arbitrary rules and punishment, malnourished and pushed to exhaustion, their identities reduced to numbers tattooed on the arm, the prisoners live in the shadow of a hierarchical authority that is to be feared and placated. Paradoxically, their common vulnerability leads to alienation and rage at their fellow victims rather than at the executioners. The Nazis have foreseen everything, explains his friend Henri, including the fact that helplessness needs to vent itself on someone weaker. The only way to cope is to distance oneself from what is happening, to become a cog in the machine so that one does not really experience what is happening—to suspend, for the moment, one's humanity.

Borowski emphasizes the range of cultures and languages brought together in Birkenau, and that variety is contrasted with the rigid narrowness of their jailers. French, Russian, and German phrases appear in this Polish-language story, as well as the camp "Esperanto" spoken by the Greeks. Separate scenes focus on the suffering of individual men, women, and children; and the narrator mentions the chaotic, multi-colored appearance of the crowds in their rags and variously striped uniforms. Over and against this cultural multiplicity is set the narrowly homogeneous model of the Nazi authorities: a lock-step "one mass, one will," bred from "Aryan" genes and trained in obedience to the Führer. The soldier with his blond hair and blue eyes, or the blond woman commandant who wears her hair in a "Nordic" knot, offer images of the proposed master race. The SS officers are sleek, clean-shaven, and well-fed; they dress in identical uniforms with silver insignia, shiny boots, whips and revolvers, and briefcases to keep records in order. It is a picture of prosperity and efficient organization, all the more chilling in its pretense of normalcy and civilized behavior. The same officer who urges prisoners ("Gentlemen") to be orderly and show goodwill suddenly whips a woman stooping to pick up a handbag. Sharp contrasts emphasize the hollowness of their civilized image: a group of officers shake hands and share news from home and family pictures while the train of deportees rolls into the station; an officer fumbles with a balky cigarette lighter as he orders the labor detail to remove infants' corpses from the cattle car; another officer superciliously refers to a desperate woman who tries to escape being condemned with her child as an "unnatural mother."

It is the narrator's first experience with the Canada salvage team, and he expects that his carefully cultivated impersonality will work as well here as it has in the camp. This day will test his defenses, however, and his ability to survive through willful alienation. For a while, he registers events intellectually, noting the dimensions of the camp and crematoria. Soon, however, unforeseen emotional challenges arise and his control becomes shaky.

Words of sympathy from a condemned woman strike home: his vision blurs, and he asks Henri, "Are we good people?" It is only the first in a series of shocks, however, culminating when an apparently dead body grasps his hand. Vomiting from the cumulative horror, the narrator finds that the two dimensions he has tried to keep apart have temporarily fused—and he retreats once more to a dream of alienation. The narrator's utter defeat and despair are underlined when the returning labor battalion moves aside for an SS detachment singing lustily about conquering the world. Borowski's story was written after the Nazi downfall, but for the moment the picture is one of a spiritual desolation that not only illustrates a shameful moment in modern history but raises questions about what it means to be civilized, or even "human."

Brief discussions of Borowski are found in Czeslaw Milosz, *The History of Polish Literature* (1969); and from a different perspective, Sidra DeKoven Ezrahi, *By Words Alone: The Holocaust in Literature* (1980). Jan Kott, "Introduction" to *This Way for the Gas, Ladies and Gentlemen* (1967), and Jan Walc, "When the Earth Is No Longer a Dream and Cannot Be Dreamed through to the End," *Polish Review* (1987), combine biography and literary analysis. Selections from the poetry are available in *Selected Poems* (1990), trans. Tadeusz Pióro with Larry Rafferty, and "Five Poems by Tadeusz Borowski," *Polish Review* (1983), trans. Addison Bross. Also pertinent are the *Historical Atlas of the Holocaust* (1996) and psychiatrist Bruno Bettelheim's analysis of different responses to genocide in *Surviving the Holocaust* (1986).

PRONOUNCING GLOSSARY

The following list uses common English syllables and stress accents to provide rough equivalents of selected words whose pronunciation may be unfamiliar to the general reader.

Auschwitz: *ow'-shvits*

Birkenau: *beer'-ken-ow*

Katowice: *kah-toh-veet'-seh*

Sosnowiec-Będzin: *sos-navv'-yets ben-een*

Tadeusz Borowski: *tah-day'-oosh baw-raw-skee*

Ladies and Gentlemen, to the Gas Chamber[1]

The whole camp[2] went about naked. True, we had already passed through the delousing process and received our clothing back from the tanks filled with a dilution of cyclone[3] in water which so excellently poisoned lice in clothing and people in gas chambers—and only the blocks separated from us by trestles had not yet been issued clothing, nonetheless both the former and the latter went about naked: the heat was terrific. The camp was sealed up tight. Not a prisoner, not a louse could venture beyond its gates. The work of the commandos[4] had stopped. Thousands of naked people milled about all day on the roads and roll-call grounds; they siestaed under walls and on the roofs. People slept on bare boards, for the straw mattresses and blankets were being disinfected. The FKL[5] could be seen from the last blocks; delousing was going on there, too. Twenty-eight thousand women had been stripped and turned out of the blocks; they could be seen right now scrambling on the meadows, roads and roll-call grounds.

The morning is spent in waiting for dinner, contents of food parcels are being eaten, friends visited. The hours pass slowly as they do in extreme heat. Even the usual recreation is lacking: the wide roads to the crematoria

---

1. Translated by Jadwiga Zwolska.   2. Auschwitz II, or Birkenau, the largest of the Nazi extermination camps, established in October 1941 near the town of Birkenau, Poland. Its death toll is usually estimated between 1 million and 2.5 million people.   3. Cyclone-B, the extermination gas.   4. Labor battalions. 5. Frauen Konzentration Lager: Women's concentration camp (German).

are empty. There have been no transports for some days. Part of "Canada"[6] has been liquidated and assigned to a commando. Being well-fed and rested they chanced on the hardest one: the Harmensee.[7] For envious justice rules in the camp: when a mighty one falls, his friends make every effort that he may fall as low as possible. Canada, our Canada, is not like Fiedler's,[8] fragrant with resin, only with French perfume, but fewer tall pines probably grow there than the number of diamonds and coins—collected from all Europe—cached here.

Several of us are sitting right now on a top bunk swinging our legs in a carefree manner. We take out white, extravagantly baked bread: crumbly, falling to pieces, a little provoking in taste, but, for all that, bread that had not been moulding for weeks. Bread sent from Warsaw.[9] Barely a week ago, my mother had it in her hands. Good God . . .

We get out bacon and onions, open a tin of condensed milk. Huge, dripping with sweat, Henri yearns aloud for French wine brought by the transports from Strasbourg, from the vicinities of Paris, from Marseilles[1] . . .

"Listen, *mon ami*,[2] when we go on the loading platform again, I'll bring you real champagne. You've never drunk it, have you?"

"No. But you won't be able to smuggle it across the gate, so don't string me along. You'd better 'organize' a pair of shoes—you know, perforated leather, with a double sole.[3] And I'm not mentioning a sports shirt, you've promised me one long ago."

"Patience, patience. When the transports come I'll bring you everything. We'll go on the loading platform again."

"What if there won't be any more transports for the smokestack?"[4] I threw in maliciously. "You see how things eased up in the camp: unlimited food parcels, flogging not allowed. You've written home, haven't you? . . . People say all sorts of things about the regulations, you yourself do a lot of gabbing. Anyhow, damn it, they'll run out of people."

"Don't talk nonsense," says the plump Marseillaise, his face spiritual like a Cosway[5] miniature (he's my friend, and yet I don't know his name). His mouth filled with a sardine sandwich, he repeated, "don't talk nonsense," swallowing with difficulty ('it went down, damn it,') "don't talk nonsense, they can't run out of people or we'd all be finished in the camp. We all live on what they bring."

"Well, not all. We have food parcels . . ."

"You have, and a pal of yours has, and tens of your pals have them. You Poles have them, and not all of you at that. But we, the Jews, the Russkis? and what then? If we, the transport 'organization,' had nothing to eat, would you be eating these food parcels of yours so calmly? We wouldn't let you."

"You'd let us, or you'd die of starvation like the Greeks. Whoever in the camp has food, has power."

"You've got them and we've got them, so why quarrel?"

6. The name given to the camp stores (as well as prisoners working there) where valuables and clothing taken from prisoners were sorted for dispatch to Germany. Like the nation of Canada, the store symbolized wealth and prosperity to the camp inmates.   7. One of the subcamps outside Birkenau itself.   8. Arkady Fiedler, Polish writer of travel books, one of which was about Canada.   9. Capital of Poland; most of its Jewish residents were executed by the Nazis.   1. A large French port on the Mediterranean Sea. Strasbourg is a city in northeast France.   2. My friend (French).   3. A Hungarian style.   4. The crematorium.   5. Richard Cosway (1740–1821), an English miniaturist, or painter of miniature portraits that could be kept in a locket.

That is true, no use quarreling. You have them and I have them, we eat together, sleep in one bunk. Henri cuts the bread, makes a tomato salad. It has a marvellous taste with the mustard from the camp canteen.

Under us, in the block, naked, sweating people mill about. They move here and there in the passages between the bunks, alongside the huge, ingeniously built stove, amidst the improvements which change the stables (there is still a sign on the door saying that *verseuchte Pferde*[6]—infected horses, should be sent to such and such a place) into a cozy home for more than half a thousand men. They nest on the lower bunks by eights and nines: stinking of sweat and excrement, their cheeks emaciated, they lie naked and bony. Under me, on the very bottom bunk—a rabbi; he has covered his head[7] with a bit of rag torn from the blanket and is reading a Hebrew prayer book (there's plenty of that kind of reading here . . .) in a loud and monotonous lament.

"Maybe we could shut him up? He yells as though he had caught God by the feet."

"I don't feel like getting down from the bunk. Let him yell; he'll go all the quicker to the smokestack."

"Religion is the opium of the people.[8] I like to smoke opium," the Marseillaise to my left, who is a communist and a *rentier*,[9] adds sententiously.

"If they did not believe in God and in a life beyond they'd have wrecked the crematorium long ago."

"And why don't you do it?"

The sense of the question is metaphoric, however, the Marseillaise replies, "Idiot," stuffs his mouth with a tomato and gestures as though he would say something, but he munches and keeps silent. We just finished stuffing ourselves when a bigger hubbub started near the door of the block: the Mussulmen[1] jumped back and scurried off among the bunks. A messenger ran into the block leader's cubbyhole. After a moment the block leader emerged[2] majestically.

"Canada! Fall in! Snappy now! A transport's coming!"

"Good God," shouted Henri, leaping down from the bunk.

The Marseillaise choked on the tomato, grabbed his coat, shouted *"raus"*[3] to those who sat below him, and in a moment they were already in the doorway. Everything seethed on the other bunks. Canada was going to the loading platform.

"Henri, shoes!" I shouted as a farewell. *"Keine Angst,"*[4] he shouted back, already outside.

I packed up the food and tied the satchel with string. In it, cheek by jowl with Portuguese sardines, lay onions and tomatoes from my father's garden in Warsaw, and the bacon from the "Bacutil" in Lublin (from my brother) mingled with genuine candied fruit from Salonika.[5] I tied it all up, pulled my trousers on and climbed down from the bunk.

6. Infected horses (German).   7. Jews are expected to keep their heads covered while at prayer.   8. A quotation from the German political philosopher Karl Marx (1818–1883).   9. Someone with unearned income, a stockholder (French).   1. Or Muslim; people who had given up, considered the camp pariahs.   2. A Kapo, or senior prisoner in charge of a group of prisoners.   3. Outside (German). 4. Don't panic (German).   5. Major port city in northeast Greece. Lublin is a city in eastern Poland. *Bacutil*: A meat-products company with branches in many Polish cities.

"*Platz!*"[6] I shouted, shouldering my way through the Greeks. They drew aside. In the door I came upon Henri.

"*Allez, allez, vite, vite!*"

"*Was ist los?*"[7]

"Do you want to go to the loading platform with us?"

"Can do."

"Then hurry, take your coat. They're a few men short, I spoke to the kapo," and he pushed me out of the block.

We lined up, someone wrote down our numbers, someone at the head shouted: "march, march" and we ran up to the gates accompanied by the babel of the multitude already being driven back to the block with thongs. It was not everyone that could go to the loading platform . . . Good-byes said, we are already at the gate.

"*Links, zwei, drei, vier! Mützen ab!*"[8] Straightened up, with arms held stiffy at hips, we pass through the gate with a brisk, springy step—almost gracefully. Holding a huge tablet in his hand, a sleepy SS[9]-man counts drowsily, separating with his finger in the air every five men.

"*Hundert!*"[1] he shouted when the last five had passed him.

"*Stimmt!*"[2] a hoarse voice calls back from the head.

We march rapidly, almost at a run. Many outposts: youngsters with automatics. We pass all the sectors of Camp II B: the untenanted *Lager*[3] C, Czech and quarantine, and plunge deep among the apple and pear trees of the military hospital; amidst the exotic verdure, as though out of the moon, strangely exuberant these few sunny days, we pass in an arc some sort of wooden sheds, pass the big *Postenkette* lines and in a run reach the highway—we are there. A few score metres more, and among the trees—the loading platform.

It was an idyllic platform, as is usual with rural stations lost in remote areas. A square, bordered with the green of tall trees, was strewn with gravel. A tiny wooden shack squatted down at one side of the road, uglier and more jerry-built than the ugliest and flimsiest station shack. Farther away lay great stacks of rails, railway sleepers, piles of deal boards, parts of wooden sheds, bricks, stones and concrete well-rings. It is here that goods are unloaded for Birkenau: material for the expansion of the camp and people for the gas chambers. An ordinary work day: trucks drive up, take lumber, cement, people . . .

Guards take their places on the rails, on the lumber, under the green shade of the Silesian[4] chestnuts, they surround the loading platform with a tight circle. They wipe perspiration from their foreheads and drink from their canteens. The heat is terrific, the sun stands motionless in the zenith. "Fall out!" We sit in patches of shade under the stacked rails. The hungry Greeks (a few of them have managed, the devil knows how, to slip out with us) ferret

---

6. Make room (German).　7. What's the matter? (German). *Allez, allez, vite, vite!*: Come on, come on, quickly, quickly! (French).　8. Left, two, three, four! Caps off! (German).　9. Abbreviation for *Schutzstaffel* (Protective echelon, German), the Nazi police system that began as Hitler's private guard and grew, by 1939, to a powerful 250,000-member military and political organization that administered all state security functions. The SS was divided into many bureaucratic units, one of which, the Death's Head Battalions, managed the concentration camps. Selected for physical perfection and (Aryan) racial purity, SS members wore black or gray-green uniforms decorated with silver insignia.　1. A hundred! (German).　2. Right! (German).　3. Camp (German).　4. Probably local chestnuts. Silesia, in central Europe, was partitioned between Poland, Czechoslovakia, and Germany after World War I; Germany occupied Polish Silesia in 1939.

among the rails; someone finds a tin of food, mouldy buns, an unfinished tin of sardines. They eat.

"*Schweinedreck*,"[5] a tall, young guard with abundant blond hair and dreamy blue eyes, spits at them. "After all, you'll have so much grub in a moment that you won't be able to gobble it all. You'll have your fill for a long time." He adjusts his automatic and wipes his face with a handkerchief.

"Swine," we confirm in unison.

"Hey you, fatty," the guard's shoe touches lightly the back of Henri's neck. "*Pass mal auf*,[6] want a drink?"

"I'm thirsty, but I've no marks," the Frenchman replies in a business-like manner.

"Too bad."

"But, *Herr*[7] Guard, doesn't my word mean anything any more? Hasn't *Herr* Guard done business with me? How much?"

"A hundred. A deal?"

"A deal."

We drink the insipid and tasteless water on tick against the money and people not yet here.

"Look here, you," the Frenchman says throwing away the empty bottle which crashes somewhere away on the rails, "take no money, for there may be a search. And, anyway, what the hell d'you need money for, you've got enough to eat. Don't take a suit either, for that's suspicious, and might look like a get-away. Take a shirt, but only a silk one and with a collar. Underneath, a gym vest. And if you find anything to drink, don't call me. I can take care of myself. And look out you don't get walloped."

"Do they whip you?"

"That's normal. One has to have eyes in the back. *Arschaugen*."[8]

All around us sit the Greeks; like huge, inhuman insects they move their jaws greedily and voraciously devour mouldy chunks of bread. They are uneasy because they do not know what they're going to do. They are alarmed by the lumber and the rails. They don't like lifting heavy loads.

"*Was wir arbeiten?*"[9] they ask.

"*Nix. Transport kommen, alles Krematorium, compris?*"[1]

"*Alles verstehen*," they reply in the crematorium Esperanto.[2] They calm down; they won't have to load the rails on trucks or carry the lumber.

In the meantime the loading platform has become more and more noisy and crowded. The foremen are dividing up the groups, assigning some to opening and unloading the railway cars that are to arrive; others they assign to the wooden steps and explain to them how to work properly. These were wide, portable steps like those to mount a rostrum. Roaring motorcycles arrived bringing non-commissioned SS officers, hefty, well fed men in glossy top-boots, with bespangled silver insignia, their faces churly and shiny. Some arrived with brief cases, others had flexible reed canes. This gave them an official and efficient air. They entered the canteen—for that miserable shack

---

5. Dirty pigs (German).   6. See here (German).   7. Mister (German).   8. Eyes in your ass (German, literal trans.).   9. What are we working on? (German).   1. Nothing. Transport coming, everything crematorium, understood? (German; *compris* is French).   2. An artificial language created in 1887 by L. L. Zamenhof to simplify communication between different nationalities. *Alles verstehen*: Everything understood.

was their canteen where in summer they drank mineral water, *Sudeten-quelle*,[3] and in winter warmed themselves with hot wine.

They greeted one another in stately fashion: the arm stretched out in the Roman manner[4] and then, cordially shaking hands, they smiled warmly at one another, talked about letters, news from home, their children; they showed one another photographs. Some of them promenaded in the square with dignity, the gravel crunched, the boots crunched, the silver distinctions gleamed on the collars and the bamboo canes swished impatiently.

The throng in vari-coloured camp stripes lay in the narrow strips of shade under the rails, breathed heavily and unevenly, chattered in their own tongue, gazed lazily and indifferently at the majestic people in the green uniforms, at the green of the trees—near and unattainable, at the spires of a distant church from which a belated Angelus[5] was just being rung.

"The transport's coming," said someone, and all of them rose expectantly. The freight cars were coming around the bend, the locomotive driving from behind. The brakeman standing on the tender, leaned out, waved his arm and whistled. The locomotive whistled screechingly in reply, panted, and the train chugged slowly along the station. In the small, barred windows could be seen human faces, pale and crumpled, dishevelled as though they had not had enough sleep; terrified women, and men who, strange to say, had hair. They passed slowly and looked at the station in silence. And then, inside the cars there began a seething and a pounding on the wooden walls.

"Water! Air!" rose dull, despairing shrieks.

Human faces leaned out of windows, mouths desperately gasped for air. Having drawn a few gulps of air the people left the windows and others stormed their places and then also disappeared. The screams and the rattling grew louder and louder.

A man in a green uniform more bespangled with silver than that of the others, frowned with disgust. He puffed on his cigarette, then threw it away with a sudden motion, transferred his brief case from his right to his left hand and beckoned to a guard. The latter slowly removed his automatic from his shoulder, took aim and fired a round at the railway cars. Silence fell. In the meantime trucks backed up to the train, stools were placed at the back of each, and the camp workers took positions expertly at the cars. The giant with the brief case made a sign with his hand.

"Whoever takes gold or anything else but food will be shot as a thief of *Reich*property. Understood? *Verstanden?*"

"*Jawohl!*"[6] came the shout, discordant but expressing good will.

"*Also loos!*[7] To work!"

The bolts clattered, the freight cars were opened. A wave of fresh air rushed inside, stunning people as though with monoxide gas. Packed to the limit, overwhelmed by a fantastic amount of luggage: suitcases, satchels, gladstone bags, rucksacks and bundles of every description (for they were

---

3. Water from the Sudetenland or Sudeten Mountains; a narrow strip of land on the northern and western borders of the Czech Republic. The Sudeten was annexed by Hitler in 1938. 4. The official "Heil Hitler!" (Hail Hitler!) salute, with the straight right arm abruptly raised in imitation of ancient Roman military salutes. Adolf Hitler was chancellor of Germany under Nazism (1933–45). 5. A call to prayer, rung three times a day in the Catholic Church. *Green uniforms:* i.e., the regular gray-green army uniforms. 6. Yes! (German). *Verstanden:* understand? (German). 7. Then get going!

bringing everything that had constituted their former life and was to start their future) they were squeezed into terribly cramped quarters, fainting from the heat, being suffocated and smothering others. Now they had clustered around the open door, panting like fish thrown on sand.

"Attention! Get down with your luggage. Take everything. Place all your duds in a pile near the car. Hand over your coats. It's summer. March to the left. Understand?"

"Sir, what's going to happen to us?"—uneasy, nerves quivering, they are already jumping down onto the gravel.

"Where are you from?"

"Sosnowiec, Będzin.[8] Sir, what'll happen?" They stubbornly repeat the questions, gazing fervently into strange, tired eyes.

"I don't know, I don't understand Polish."

There is the law of the camp that people going to their death must be deceived to the last moment. It is the only permissible form of pity. The heat is sweltering. The sun has reached its zenith, the burnished sky trembles, the air shimmers; the wind, which blows through us intermittently, is merely hot, moist air. Lips are already cracked, the mouth savours the salty taste of blood. The body is weak and stiff from lying long in the sun. To drink, oh, to drink!

Like a stupefied, blind river that seeks a new bed, the motley throng, heavily laden, pours out of the car. But before they regain consciousness after being stunned by the fresh air and the smell of verdure, their baggage is torn from their hands, coats pulled off them, handbags snatched from the women's hands, sunshades taken away.

"But, mister, that's my sunshade, I can't . . ."

"*Verboten*,"[9] a guard barks through his teeth, hissing loud. In the back stands an SS-man: calm, self-possessed, expert.

"*Meine Herrschaften*,[1] don't throw your things about like that. You must show a little good will." He speaks kindly, and the thin cane bends with the nervous movement of his hands.

"Yes, sir, yes, sir," they reply in unison passing by, and walk at a brisker pace alongside the train cars. A woman bends down and quickly picks up a handbag. The cane swished, the woman cried out, stumbled and fell under the feet of the crowd. A child running behind her squeaked: "*Mamele!*"— just a tousled little girl . . .

The heap of things grows: suitcases, bundles, rucksaks, travel rugs, clothes, and handbags which open in falling and spill rainbow-coloured banknotes, gold, watches; in front of the car doors there rise piles of bread, collections of jars with multi-coloured jams and marmalades; pyramids of hams and sausages swell out, sugar spills on the gravel. Trucks packed with people drive away with an infernal racket amidst the lamentations and the shrieks of women wailing for their children separated from them, while the men, in stupefied silence, suddenly remain alone. They are the ones who went to the right: the young and healthy, they will go to the camp. They will not escape gassing, but first they will be put to work.

The trucks drive away and return continuously like some monstrous

8. Two cities in Katowice province (southern Poland). Będzin was also the site of a concentration camp, and more than ten thousand of its inhabitants were exterminated. 9. Forbidden (German).
1. Gentlemen (German).

assembly line. The Red-Cross[2] ambulance goes back and forth ceaselessly. The huge, blood-red cross on the radiator cover melts in the sun. The Red-Cross ambulance travels tirelessly: it is precisely this car that carries that gas, the gas which will poison these people.

Those from "Canada" who are near the steps have not a moment's rest: they separate the people for gassing from those who go to the camp; they push the former on to the steps and pack them in the trucks: sixty, more or less, to a truck.

A young, clean-shaven gentleman, an SS-man, stands at the side with a notebook in his hand; each truck means a check mark—when sixteen trucks pass, it means a thousand, more or less. The gentleman is poised and accurate. No truck will leave without his knowledge and his check mark. *Ordnung muss sein.*[3] The check marks swell into thousands, the thousands swell into whole transports of which brief mention is made: "From Salonika," "from Strasbourg," "from Rotterdam."[4] Today's transport will be referred to as "from Będzin." But it will receive the permanent name of "Będzin–Sosnowiec." Those who will go to the work camp from this transport will receive numbers 131–132. Thousands, of course, but abbreviated they will be referred to just like that: 131–132.

The transports grow with the passing of weeks, months, years. When the war is over, the cremated will be counted. There will be four and a half million of them. The bloodiest battle of the war, the greatest victory of Germany united in solidarity. *Ein Reich, ein Volk, ein Führer*[5] and—four crematoria. But in Oświęcim there will be sixteen crematoria capable of incinerating fifty thousand bodies daily. The camp is being expanded until its electrified wire fence will reach the Vistula;[6] it will be inhabited by 300,000 people in camp stripes, it will be called *Verbrecher-Stadt*—the City of Criminals. No, they will not run short of people. Jews will be cremated, Poles will be cremated, Russians will be cremated; people will come from the West and from the South, from the continent and from islands. People in prison stripes will come, they will rebuild ruined German towns, plough the fallow soil and when they weaken from pitiless toil, from an eternal *Bewegung!*[7] *Bewegung!* the doors of the gas chambers will open. The chambers will be improved, more economical, more cleverly camouflaged. They will be like those in Dresden about which legends were already rife.

The cars are already empty. A thin, pock-marked SS-man calmly glances inside, nods his head with disgust, encompasses us with his glance and points inside:

"*Rein.*[8] Clean it out!"

We jump inside. Babies, naked monsters with huge heads and bloated bellies, lie scattered about in corners amidst human excrement and lost watches. They are carried out like chickens: a few of them making a handful.

"Don't take them to the truck. Let the women have them," says the SS-man lighting a cigarette. His lighter has stuck, he is extremely busy with it.

"For God's sake, take these babies," I burst out, for the women run away from me in terror, drawing in their heads between lifted shoulders.

2. Ordinary trucks were painted with Red Cross insignia to quiet incoming prisoners by suggesting that they would receive humane treatment and medical care. 3. Order in everything (German). 4. Large port city in the Netherlands. 5. One State, One People, One Leader! (the slogan of Nazi Germany). 6. A river running through central Poland. 7. Hurry up! (German). 8. Clean it (German).

The name of God is strangely unnecessary, for the women with the children go to the trucks, all of them—there is no exception. We all know what that means and look at one another with hate and horror.

"What's that, you don't want them?" The pock-marked SS-man asked as though surprised and reproachful, and starts to ready his revolver.

"No need to shoot, I'll take them."

A grey-haired, tall lady took the infants from me and for a while looked straight into my eyes.

"You poor child," she whispered smiling. Stumbling on the gravel she walked away.

I leaned on the side of a railway car. I was extremely tired. Someone is tugging my arm.

"*En avant,*⁹ under the rails, come on!"

I gaze: the face flickers before my eyes, it melts—it huge and transparent—it becomes confused with the trees, immobile and strangely black, with the pouring throngs . . . I blink my eyes sharply: Henri.

"Look here, Henri, are we good people?"

"Why ask stupid questions?"

"You see, my friend, an unreasonable rage at these people wells up in me that I must be here on their account. I am not in the least sorry for them, that they're going to the gas chambers. May the ground open under them all. I'd throw myself on them with my fists. This must be pathological, I can't understand it."

"Oh, no, quite the contrary, it's normal, foreseen and taken into account. You are tired with this unloading business, you're rebellious, and rage can best be vented on someone weaker. It's even desirable that you should vent it. That's common sense, *compris?*" says the Frenchman somewhat ironically, placing himself comfortably under the rails. "Look at the Greeks, they know how to make the best of it. They gobble up everything they lay their hands on; I saw one of them finish a whole jar of jam."

"Cattle. Half of them will die tomorrow of the trots."

"Cattle? You, too, were hungry."

"Cattle," I repeat obstinately. I close my eyes, hear the shrieks, feel the trembling of the ground and the humid air on my lips. My throat is completely dry.

The flow of people is endless, the trucks growl like enraged dogs. Corpses are brought out of the cars before my eyes; trampled children, cripples laid out with the corpses, and crowds, crowds . . . Railway cars are brought alongside the loading platform, the piles of rags, suitcases and rucksacks grow, people get out, look at the sun, breathe, beg for water, enter the trucks, drive away. Again cars are rolled up, again people . . . I feel the pictures become confused within me, I don't know if all this is really happening, or if I'm dreaming. I suddenly see the green of trees rocking with an entire street, with a motley crowd: but yes, it's the Avenue!¹ My head is whirring. I feel that in a moment I will vomit.

Henri tugs at my arm.

"Don't sleep, we're going to load the stuff."

There are no more people. Stirring up huge clouds of dust, the last trucks

9. Forward (French).   1. A famous boulevard in the center of Warsaw that used to be the Polish king's route from the current Old Town to outside the city.

move along the highway in the distance, the train has left, the SS-men walk stiff-necked on the emptied loading platform, the silver on their collars sparkling. Their boots gleam, their bloated red faces shine. There is a woman among them. Only now do I realize that she been here all the time, this dried-up, bosomless, bony woman. Sparse, colourless hair combed smoothly back and tied in a "Nordic"[2] knot, her hands in the pockets of her wide trouser-skirt. She strides from one end of the loading platform to the other, a rat-like, rancorous smile on her dry lips. She hates feminine beauty with the hatred of a repulsive woman aware of her repulsiveness. Yes, I have seen her many times and well remember her; she's the commandant of the FKL; she has come to look over her acquisitions, for some of the women have been stood aside and will walk to the camp. Our boys, hairdressers from Zaune,[3] will shave their heads completely and will have no end of fun at the sight of their humiliation, so alien to camp life.

So we load the stuff. We drag the heavy valises, spacious, well stocked, and with an effort throw them on the truck. There they are stacked, rammed down, crammed; anything that can be cut is carved up with a knife for the pleasure of it and in search of alcohol and perfume; the latter is poured right over oneself. One of the valises opens up: clothing, shirts, books tumble out . . . I grab a bundle, it is heavy, I open it: gold, two good handfuls—watch cases, bracelets, rings, necklaces, diamonds . . .

"*Gib her*,"[4]—an SS-man says calmly, holding up an open brief case full of gold and coloured foreign banknotes. He closes it, gives it to an officer, takes another empty one and stands on guard at another truck. The gold will go to the *Reich*.[5]

Heat, sweltering heat. The air stands like an immobile, white-hot column. Throats are parched, every spoken word causes pain. Oh, for a drink! We work feverishly: faster and faster, if only to get into shade, if only to rest. We finish loading, the last trucks leave; we pick up every bit of paper lying on the railway track, dig out of the fine gravel the alien rubbish of the transport, "so that no trace of that filth is left," and at the moment when the last truck disappears beyond the trees and we finally go towards the rails to rest and drink (maybe the Frenchman will again buy it from the guard?), the whistle of the railway man is heard from beyond the bend. Slowly, extremely slowly cars roll up, the locomotive whistles back screechingly, from the windows human faces look out, pale and crumpled and flattened like paper cut-outs, their eyes huge and feverish. The trucks are here already, and the calm gentleman with his notebook; the SS-men with brief cases for the gold and money come out of the canteen. We open the cars.

No, self-control is no longer possible. Valises are brutally jerked out of people's hands, overcoats torn off. "Go on, go on, move on!" They go, they pass on. Men, women, children. Some of them know . . .

Here is a woman walking quickly, hurrying imperceptibly but feverishly. A small child only a few years old, with the rosy, chubby face of a cherub, runs after her; it cannot catch up with her and holds out its little arms crying: "Mummy, mummy!"

"You, woman, pick up the child!"

"It isn't mine, sir, it isn't mine!" the woman shouts hysterically and, cov-

---

2. A northern (especially Scandinavian) style, encouraged by the Nazis to establish an image of Teutonic racial purity. 3. The "sauna" barracks, in front of Canada, where prisoners were bathed, shaved, and deloused. 4. Give it to me (German). 5. The German state.

ering her face with her hands, runs away. She wants to hide, she wants to catch up with the other women who will not go by truck, who will walk, who will live. She is young, healthy and pretty, she wants to live.

But the child follows her, complaining loudly:

"Mummy, mummy, don't run away!"

"It isn't mine, no, it isn't!"

Finally, Andrei, a sailor from Sevastopol,[6] caught up with her. His eyes were bleary from vodka and the heat. He caught up with her, knocked her off her feet with one wide swing of his arm, grabbed her by the hair when she was falling and put her on her feet her again. His face is livid with rage.

"Oh, you, *yebi tvoyu mat' blad' jevreyskaya!*[7] So you'd run away from your child! I'll fix you, you whore!" He caught her round her waist, choked down her shriek with a huge paw and with a swing threw her like a heavy sack of grain on the truck.

"That's for you! Take it, you bitch!" and threw the child at her feet.

"*Gut gemacht,* that's how unnatural mothers should be punished," said the SS-man who stood at the truck. "*Gut, gut Russki.*"[8]

"Shut up!" Andrei growled through his teeth and walked up to the railway cars. He drew out a canteen hidden under a pile of rags, unscrewed it, put it to his mouth and then to mine. Raw alcohol. It burns the throat. A roar in the head, my legs wobble under me, my gorge rises.

Suddenly, from this tide of humanity which, like a river driven by an invisible force, blindly pushes on toward the trucks, a girl emerged, jumped lightly from the car onto the gravel, and looked about her with a searching glance like one surprised at something.

Thick blond hair has spilled in a soft wave on her shoulders; she tossed it back impatiently. She instinctively passed her hands over her blouse, furtively adjusted her skirt. She stood like that for a moment. Finally, she tore her eyes away from the crowd and her gaze moved over our faces as though searching for someone. Unconsciously I sought to catch her glance, until our eyes met.

"Listen, tell me, where are they taking us?"

I looked at her. Here, before me, stood a girl with beautiful blond hair, wonderful breasts in an organdy summer blouse, her look wise and mature. Here she stood looking straight into my face and waited. Here, the gas chamber: mass death, loathsome and revolting. Here, the camp: a shaved head, quilted Soviet trousers in all that heat, the obnoxious, sickly odour of dirty, overheated feminine body; the animal hunger, inhuman toil, and the same gas chamber, only the death still more disgusting, more revolting, more horrible. Whoever has once entered here will never again pass the sentry post, not even as a handful of ashes, will never return to his former life.

"Why did she ever bring it here, they'll take it away from her," I thought automatically, seeing on her wrist a wonderful watch on a fine, gold bracelet. Tuśka had one like it, but hers was on a narrow, black ribbon.

"Listen, answer me."

I remained silent. She set her mouth.

"I already know," she said with a shade of haughty contempt in her voice, throwing her head back; boldly she walked up to the trucks. Someone wanted to stop her, but she boldly moved him aside and ran up the steps into the nearly filled truck. In the distance I saw only the thick, blond hair tousled by the speed.

I went into cars, carried out the infants, threw out the luggage. I touched corpses but could not overcome the wild terror welling up within me. I ran away from them but they lay everywhere: placed side by side on the gravel, on the edge of the concrete platform, in the cars. Babies, repulsive, naked women, men twisted by convulsions. I ran away as far as I could. Someone caned me across the back, out of the corner of my eye I notice a cursing SS-man, I slip away from him and mix with the stripe-clad "Canada." Finally, I again crawl under the rails. The sun has gone down over the horizon and bathes the loading platform with its bloody, waning light. The shadows of the trees grow monstrously long; in the silence that settles on nature with the coming of evening, human cries soar skywards ever louder, ever more insistently.

It was only from here, from under the rails, that the entire inferno seething on the platform can be seen. Here is a couple fallen on the ground, locked in a desperate embrace. He has dug his fingers convulsively into her flesh and caught her dress in his teeth. She is shrieking hysterically, swearing, blaspheming until, trampled down by a boot, she gurgles and is still. Torn apart like pieces of wood, they are driven like animals into a truck. Here, four men from "Canada" strain under the weight of a corpse: a huge, swollen old woman: they swear and sweat with the effort, kick out of the way stray children who get underfoot all over the platform and howl horribly like dogs. They catch the children by the neck, by the head and arms and throw them in a pile on the trucks. Those four cannot manage to lift the woman to the truck, they call others and with a collective heave push the mountain of flesh on the floor of the truck. Huge, bloated, swollen corpses are carried from the whole ramp. Thrown among these are cripples, paralyzed, smothered and unconscious people. The mountain of corpses seethes, whines and howls. The driver starts the motor and drives away.

"*Halt, halt!*" the SS-man shrieks from a distance. "Stop, stop, damn you!"

They are dragging an old man in a full dress suit with an armband on his sleeve. His head is knocked about on the gravel and the stones, he groans and laments incessantly and monotonously: "*Ich will mit dem Herrn Kommendanten sprechen,*[9] I want to speak to the commandant." He repeats this with senile doggedness all the way. Thrown into the truck, trampled down by someone's foot, smothered, he continues to rattle: "*Ich will mit dem. . .*"

"Calm down, man!" calls out a young SS-man to him, laughing boisterously, "in half an hour you will speak to the supreme commandant! Only don't forget to say '*Heil Hitler*' to him."

Others carry a little girl who has only one leg, they hold her by the arms and that leg. Tears stream down her cheeks, and she whimpers pitifully: "Gentlemen, it hurts, it hurts . . ." They throw her on the truck with the corpses. She will be cremated alive with them.

Night falls, cool and starlit. We lie on the rails. It is immensely quiet. On tall posts anemic lamps throw out circles of light into the impenetrable dark-

9. I want to speak with the commandant (German).

ness. A step into it and a man disappears irretrievably. But the eyes of the guards watch carefully. The automatics are ready to fire.

"Have you changed your shoes?" Henri asks me.

"No."

"Why not?"

"Man, I've had enough, completely enough."

"So soon, after the first transport? Just think, I . . . since Christmas, probably a million people have passed through my hands. The transports from around Paris are the worst ones, a man always comes upon acquaintances."

"And what do you tell them?"

"That they're going to have a bath and then we'll meet in the camp, And what would you say?"

I remain silent. We drink coffee spiked with alcohol; someone opens a tin of cocoa, mixes it with sugar. This is ladled up with the hand; the cocoa pastes up the mouth. Again coffee, again alcohol.

"What are we waiting for, Henri?"

"There'll be another transport. But no one knows."

"If there's another, I'm not going to unload it. I can't do it."

"It's got hold of you, yes? A fine 'Canada!'" Henri smiles benevolently and disappears in the dark. He returns shortly.

"Very well. But be careful that the SS-man doesn't catch you. You'll stay here all the time. And I'll fix you up with a pair of shoes."

"Don't bother me with the shoes."

I am sleepy. It is deep night.

Again *antreten,* again a transport. Cars emerge from the dark, pass the strip of light and again disappear in the gloom. The loading platform is small but the circle of light is still smaller. We will unload the cars as they come, one by one. Trucks growl somewhere, they back up to the steps, spectrally black, their reflectors light up the trees. *Wasser! Luft!*[1] The same all over again, a late showing of the same film: they discharge a volley from their automatics; the railway cars calm down. Only a little girl has leaned down to her waist from the little window of the car and losing her balance fell to the gravel. For a while she lay stunned, finally got up and started walking around in a circle, faster and faster, waving her arms stiffly as if at calisthenics, drawing her breath in noisily, and monotonously and howling shrilly. Suffocating—she has gone mad. She set the nerves on edge, so an SS-man ran up to her and kicked her with a hobbled boot in the small of the back; she fell. He pressed her down with his foot, took his revolver out and fired once and then again; she lay, kicking the ground with her feet until she stiffened. The cars begin to be opened.

I was again at the cars. A warm, sweetish odour gushed out. The car is filled to half its height with a mound of humanity: immobile, horribly tangled up but still steaming.

"*Ausladen!*"[2] sounded the voice of the SS-man who emerged out of the dark. On his breast hung a portable reflector. He lighted up the inside of the car.

"Why are you standing so stupidly? Unload!" and he swished his cane across my back. I grabbed the arm of a corpse, his hand closed convulsively around mine. I jerked away with a shriek and ran off. My heart pounded, my

1. Water! Air! (German). 2. Unload! (German).

gorge rose. Nausea suddenly doubled me up. Crouching under the car I vomited. Staggering, I stole away under the stack of rails.

I lay on the kind, cool iron and dreamed of returning to the camp, about my bunk on which there is no straw mattress, about a bit of sleep among comrades who will not go to the gas chambers in the night. All at once the camp seemed like some haven of quiet; others are constantly dying and somehow one is still alive, has something to eat, strength to work, has a fatherland, a home, a girl . . .

The lights twinkle spectrally, the wave of humanity flows endlessly—turbid, feverish, stupefied. It seems to these people that they are beginning a new life in the camp and they prepare themselves psychologically for a hard struggle for existence. They do not know that they will immediately die and that the gold, the money, the diamonds which they providently conceal in the folds and seams of their clothing, in the heels of their shoes, in recesses of their bodies, will no longer be needed by them. Efficient, business-like people will rummage in their intestines, pull gold from under the tongue, diamonds from the placenta and the rectum. They will pull out their gold teeth and send them in tightly nailed-up cases to Berlin.[3]

The black figures of the SS-men walk about calm and proficient. The gentleman with the notebook in hand puts down the last check marks, adds up the figures; fifteen thousand.

Many, many trucks have driven off to the crematorium.

They are finishing up. The corpses spread on the ramp will be taken by the last truck, the luggage is all loaded. "Canada," loaded with bread, jams, sugar, smelling of perfume and clean underwear, lines up to march away. The "kapo" finishes packing the tea cauldron with gold, silk, and coffee. That's for the guards at the gates, they will let the commando pass without a search. For a few days the camp will live off that transport: eat its hams and its sausages, its preserved and fresh fruit, drink its brandies and liqueurs, wear its underwear, trade in its gold and luggage. Much will be taken out of the camp by civilians to Silesia, to Cracow and points beyond. They will bring cigarettes, eggs, vodka and letters from home.

For a few days the camp will speak about the "Sosnowiec-Będzin" transport. It was a good, rich transport.

When we return to the camp, the stars begin to pale, the sky becomes more and more transparent, rises higher up above us: the night clears. It foretells a fine, hot day.

Mighty columns of smoke rise up from the crematoria and merge into a huge, black river which rolls very slowly across the sky over Birkenau and disappears beyond the forests in the direction of Trzebinia.[4] The Sosnowiec transport is already being cremated.

We pass an SS detachment marching with machine guns to change the guard. They walk in step, shoulder to shoulder, one mass, one will.

"*Und morgen die ganze Welt . . .*"[5] they sing lustily.

"*Rechts ran!*[6] To the right march!" comes the order from up front. We move out of their way.

---

3. The capital of Germany.   4. A town west of Auschwitz, near Krakow.   5. And tomorrow the whole world (German); the last line of the Nazi song "The Rotten Bones Are Shaking," written by Hans Baumann. The previous line reads "for today Germany belongs to us."   6. To the right, get going! (German).

ALAIN ROBBE-GRILLET
born 1922

More than anyone else, Alain Robbe-Grillet represents in his novels, *ciné-romans* (film-novels), and theoretical statements the rejection of the nineteenth-century realistic tradition and the exploration of a new "mental realism." Terms such as *antinovel* and *new novel,* early applied to his works, reflect both the turning away from older models (like Balzac and Flaubert) and the notion that a new experiment with form is under way. Not that it is completely new; clearly there are links to other twentieth-century works in the modernist tradition. Robbe-Grillet himself mentions the influence of Kafka, Camus, and Faulkner (as well as *Alice in Wonderland*), and other readers will note parallel experimentation in Pirandello, Woolf, Beckett, and Joyce. Moreover, Robbe-Grillet calls on some of the same sources of fascination as his nineteenth-century predecessors. He may not use a linear plot, but he writes ambiguous, circular detective stories where erotic and violent crimes *seem* to have been committed. He may refuse to portray a consistently developing character, but his minute descriptions of objects and gestures impel the reader to imagine an underlying psychology and to speculate on the meaning of the observer's repetition and distortion of details.

Nonetheless, with Robbe-Grillet, we move to a particular phenomenon of mid-twentieth-century literature and a prime example of what has been called the post-modernist tradition. To the breakdown of conventional storytelling models familiar from literary modernism, he adds an insistence on the artificiality of all writing and representation. Reader are faced with cumulative uncertainty: with a self-contained "text" in which there is no stable narrative voice or "authorized" explanation. Here is not the abstractly intellectual puzzle of Borges but an often terrifying evocation of a sensuous reality that will not stay in place. This literature has become a "game" (as it is for Borges), but it is a deadly game. Playing with erotic and murderous images, with the treacherous undercurrents of an apparently familiar reality, Robbe-Grillet fascinates and sometimes repels his readers. At the same time that he reminds us that we cannot know what we see and that we share the world with a host of objects different from ourselves, he entices us to figure out the meaning of events—only to reestablish, at every turn, the absolute subjectivity of our most "objective" perceptions. We cannot be disengaged from Robbe-Grillet's descriptions, because they make a direct appeal to our senses; they manipulate our awareness of physical experience. Throughout his career, Robbe-Grillet has explored the limits of representation with a collagelike technique that remains more true to life, he feels, than the planned coherence of a conventionally "realistic" novel.

Robbe-Grillet was born in Brittany, in northwestern France, to a family of scientists and engineers. His early training was not at all literary: in 1939 and 1941 the future writer took baccalaureate degrees in mathematics and natural science, and in 1946 (his career interrupted by forced labor in a German factory) a further degree from the National Agronomy Institute. He began work with the National Institute of Statistics and published an article on livestock possibilities before deciding to work part-time in his sister's biology laboratory and write a novel. This novel, *A Regicide,* was completed in 1949 but not published until 1978, well after Robbe-Grillet had become a successful novelist. In the meantime he took a position with an agricultural institute that sent him to Martinique, in the West Indies, to supervise banana plantations. Falling ill in 1951, Robbe-Grillet took advantage of the leisure time in the hospital and on the voyage home to write his second novel, *The Erasers,* which was immediately accepted and appeared in 1953.

The Erasers is a puzzling detective story involving confused identities, an abortive assassination carried out exactly twenty-four hours later by the muddled detective sent to investigate the original attempt, repeated allusions to the Oedipus myth, changing perspectives, and an overwhelming copiousness of detail about the most mundane natural objects. The novel became famous for its meticulous description of a tomato wedge cataloged with such scientific precision that it took on an objective existence of its own and implicitly challenged the human-centered orientation of a perspective that would see it only as part of a salad. "The flesh on the periphery, compact and uniform, of a fine chemical red, is evenly thick between a strip of shiny skin and the compartment where the seeds are lined up, yellow, well sized, held in place by a thin layer of greenish jelly alongside a swelling of the heart. This latter, of a faded and slightly grainy pink, begins, on the side of the depression below, in a cluster of white veins, one of which extends up to the seeds—in, perhaps, a somewhat uncertain manner." While minutely detailed descriptions are not new in literature, this catalog of physical properties had additional significance for its readers because it correlated so well with the notion, in contemporary phenomenological or existential philosophy, that we should recognize that things have their own existence separate from ourselves, their own "being-in-the-world."

The Erasers received the Fénéon Prize in 1954, but was not widely known; it was not until the scandal caused by The Voyeur (1955) that Robbe-Grillet reached a wide audience. Although The Voyeur was awarded the Critics' Prize in 1955, the jury was split between those who believed that it was not a "novel" at all (and was immoral and insane to boot) and those who admired its formal innovations. Mathias, the "voyeur" of the title, is a traveling watch salesman who may or may not have murdered a young girl during a sales trip on an island. The reader must piece together a version of what happened from a fragmented time span during which Mathias neglects to describe certain crucial hours, from actions and anxieties that suggest a guilty conscience, from a schizophrenic crisis when the crime is described in a café, and from obsessive erotic imaginings that may be just that—imaginings—or may be traces of the crime.

With the controversy over The Voyeur, Robbe-Grillet and his new mode of writing became the focus of critical debate in France. In Objective Literature, the influential critic Roland Barthes proposed that Robbe-Grillet had discovered a truer "neutral" writing by focusing on objects instead of repeating traditional socially inspired interpretations of reality. In 1955 Robbe-Grillet began a series of articles on modern literature, which he collected in 1963 as For a New Novel. The term new novel became popular; and although not all those described as "new novelists" wrote in the same way, they all rejected the traditional novel's assumption of a core of meaning—with a logically developing plot and psychologically consistent characters—that claimed to reflect a similar core of meaning in society. His next two novels, Jealousy (1957) and In the Labyrinth(1959), as well as the separate short pieces collected in Snapshots (1962), exploit the ideas developed in these articles, seeking patterns of potential meaning behind extended, objective description. In 1959 he temporarily abandoned novels to experiment with films, writing the script for Last Year at Marienbad (1961, filmed by Alain Resnais) and writing and directing The Immortal One (1963). Films, like novels, allowed Robbe-Grillet to manipulate visions of reality as he insistently focused on surfaces and shapes, presented different versions of the same scene, composed a sound track that contradicted or commented on photographed action and—in recent works—challenged his own imagination by including unexpected incidents that occurred on location. Robbe-Grillet published the scenarios of Last Year at Marienbad and The Immortal One, and a more documentary account of The Progressing Slippages of Pleasure (1974) as ciné-romans, which represent his pluralistic, decentered view of reality in audiovisual as well as verbal form.

Novels up to and including In the Labyrinth could still be interpreted as the subterranean story of a single protagonist. Later novels eliminated that anchoring center to display the presence of many centers—each a competing version of reality. Here emphasis is on the writer's freedom to create different and even mutually contradictory worlds and on the readers' freedom to choose and arrange their own version of events. Some passages do not really fit into any of the story lines; the action progresses according to the suggestions of wordplay or verbal echoes; the same narrative persona may appear grammatically as "he" or "she"; or books are composed in collage fashion. Robbe-Grillet has been taught in the classroom for many years as a master of formal experimentation and only recently challenged on the quarantined atmosphere and obsessive sadism of his work. Women, for example, are repeatedly victimized, and terror and death are constant themes. Uncomfortable, perhaps, at this change in critical perspective, he has justified sadistic fantasies in his work partly as reflecting popular themes in a correspondingly sadistic and dehumanized world and partly as the therapeutic expression of his own obsessions (therapeutic for Robbe-Grillet because they are brought to a conscious level and thereby subject to change).

Therapeutic or not, there is no mistaking the basic images of Robbe-Grillet's world or the disturbing angles from which they are presented. *The Secret Room,* reprinted here from *Snapshots,* arranges in an artistic homage to the Symbolist painter Gustave Moreau (1826–98) many of Robbe-Grillet's most obsessive images: the spreading bloodstain; the young woman stretched out erotically in chains and stabbed under the left breast; the ascending staircase; the different points of view directed down on the victim; the mysterious, anonymous criminal; and even the figure eight of smoke coiling upward from the incense burner. The scene is bound to shock for its overt sadism, for the artistic savoring of human sacrifice, and for the erotic pleasure it suggests in female victimization. It would not be appropriate to ignore or repress this response, for the subject matter is not neutral or intended as such. Robbe-Grillet has presented an additional challenge, however, by insisting on the stylized *unreality* of the scene and by displacing the reader's attention to the technical triumph in which verbal art emulates a painterly style. The text imitates the Oriental luxury and morbid eroticism of a famous painter so convincingly that one could almost name the artist even without the dedication. Yet this verbal art goes beyond its painterly model when Robbe-Grillet adds to it the passage of time, thus bringing a strange life to the subject seen paradoxically both as a finished canvas and as recreated stages of the same murderous event. It is a bizarre and disturbing scene, made to unsettle readers who try to reconcile its various aspects: its manipulation of stereotypes of the victimized woman, the horror of the helpless sacrifice, and an alienated perspective that is attributed to art but at the same time suggests sadistic impersonality.

Ilona Leki, *Alain Robbe-Grillet* (1983), is a good biography and survey of Robbe-Grillet's work in historical context, discussing each work, with a last chapter on the films. Introductory essays to Alain Robbe-Grillet, *Two Novels* (1993, 1965), discuss the author's descriptive strategies. Bruce Morrissette, *The Novels of Robbe-Grillet* (1975), provides a valuable critical study that takes the works and films in chronological order. Morrissette, *Novel and Film: Essays in Two Genres* (1985), makes Robbe-Grillet the chief example in a discussion of modern cinematic vision. Ben Stoltzfus, *Alain Robbe-Grillet and the New French Novel* (1964), is an earlier introduction to Robbe-Grillet in the context of the emerging new novel form. Raylene L. Ramsay, *Robbe-Grillet and Modernity: Science, Sexuality, and Subversion* (1992), interrogates contemporary culture and the thematics of sexual violence.

PRONOUNCING GLOSSARY

The following list uses common English syllables and stress accents to provide rough equivalents of selected words whose pronunciation may be unfamiliar to the general reader.

Alain Robbe-Grillet: *ah-lanh' rob–gree-yay'*   Gustave Moreau: *gyew-stahv' mor-oh'*

The Secret Room[1]

To Gustave Moreau[2]

The first thing to be seen is a red stain, of a deep, dark, shiny red, with almost black shadows. It is in the form of an irregular rosette, sharply outlined, extending in several directions in wide outflows of unequal length, dividing and dwindling afterward into single sinuous streaks. The whole stands out against a smooth, pale surface, round in shape, at once dull and pearly, a hemisphere joined by gentle curves to an expanse of the same pale color— white darkened by the shadowy quality of the place: a dungeon, a sunken room, or a cathedral—glowing with a diffused brilliance in the semidarkness.

Farther back, the space is filled with the cylindrical trunks of columns, repeated with progressive vagueness in their retreat toward the beginning of a vast stone stairway, turning slightly as it rises, growing narrower and narrower as it approaches the high vaults where it disappears.

The whole setting is empty, stairway and colonnades. Alone, in the foreground, the stretched-out body gleams feebly, marked with the red stain—a white body whose full, supple flesh can be sensed, fragile, no doubt, and vulnerable. Alongside the bloody hemisphere another identical round form, this one intact, is seen at almost the same angle of view; but the haloed point at its summit, of darker tint, is in this case quite recognizable, whereas the other one is entirely destroyed, or at least covered by the wound.

In the background, near the top of the stairway, a black silhouette is seen fleeing, a man wrapped in a long, floating cape, ascending the last steps without turning around, his deed accomplished. A thin smoke rises in twisting scrolls from a sort of incense burner placed on a high stand of ironwork with a silvery glint. Nearby lies the milkwhite body, with wide streaks of blood running from the left breast, along the flank and on the hip.

It is a fully rounded woman's body, but not heavy, completely nude, lying on its back, the bust raised up somewhat by thick cushions thrown down on the floor, which is covered with Oriental rugs. The waist is very narrow, the neck long and thin, curved to one side, the head thrown back into a darker area where, even so, the facial features may be discerned, the partly opened mouth, the wide-staring eyes, shining with a fixed brilliance, and the mass of long, black hair spread out in a complicated wavy disorder over a heavily folded cloth, of velvet perhaps, on which also rest the arm and shoulder.

It is a uniformly colored velvet of dark purple, or which seems so in this lighting. But purple, brown, blue also seem to dominate in the colors of the cushions—only a small portion of which is hidden beneath the velvet cloth, and which protrude noticeably, lower down, beneath the bust and waist— as well as in the Oriental patterns of the rugs on the floor. Farther on, these same colors are picked up again in the stone of the paving and the columns, and vaulted archways, the stairs, and the less discernible surfaces that disappear into the farthest reaches of the room.

The dimensions of this room are difficult to determine exactly; the body of the young sacrificial victim seems at first glance to occupy a substantial

---

1. Translated by Bruce Morrissette.   2. French Symbolist painter (1826–1898), known for exotic, luminous scenes with subtly erotic and morbid overtones, such as *The Death of Darius* and *Dance of Salome*.

portion of it, but the vast size of the stairway leading down to it would imply rather that this is not the whole room, whose considerable space must in reality extend all around, right and left, as it does toward the faraway browns and blues among the columns standing in line, in every direction, perhaps toward other sofas, thick carpets, piles of cushions and fabrics, other tortured bodies, other incense burners.

It is also difficult to say where the light comes from. No clue, on the columns or on the floor, suggests the direction of the rays. Nor is any window or torch visible. The milkwhite body itself seems to light the scene, with its full breasts, the curve of its thighs, the rounded belly, the full buttocks, the stretched-out legs, widely spread, and the black tuft of the exposed sex, provocative, proffered, useless now.

The man has already moved several steps back. He is now on the first steps of the stairs, ready to go up. The bottom steps are wide and deep, like the steps leading up to some great building, a temple or theater; they grow smaller as they ascend, and at the same time describe a wide, helical curve, so gradually that the stairway has not yet made a half-turn by the time it disappears near the top of the vaults, reduced then to a steep, narrow flight of steps without handrail, vaguely outlined, moreover, in the thickening darkness beyond.

But the man does not look in this direction, where his movement nonetheless carries him; his left foot on the second step and his right foot already touching the third, with his knee bent, he has turned around to look at the spectacle for one last time. The long, floating cape thrown hastily over his shoulders, clasped in one hand at his waist, has been whirled around by the rapid circular motion that has just caused his head and chest to turn in the opposite direction, and a corner of the cloth remains suspended in the air as if blown by a gust of wind; this corner, twisting around upon itself in the form of a loose S, reveals the red silk lining with its gold embroidery.

The man's features are impassive, but tense, as if in expectation—or perhaps fear—of some sudden event, or surveying with one last glance the total immobility of the scene. Though he is looking backward, his whole body is turned slightly forward, as if he were continuing up the stairs. His right arm—not the one holding the edge of the cape—is bent sharply toward the left, toward a point in space where the balustrade should be, if this stairway had one, an interrupted gesture, almost incomprehensible, unless it arose from an instinctive movement to grasp the absent support.

As to the direction of his glance, it is certainly aimed at the body of the victim lying on the cushions, its extended members stretched out in the form of a cross, its bust raised up, its head thrown back. But the face is perhaps hidden from the man's eyes by one of the columns, standing at the foot of the stairs. The young woman's right hand touches the floor just at the foot of this column. The fragile wrist is encircled by an iron bracelet. The arm is almost in darkness, only the hand receiving enough light to make the thin, outspread fingers clearly visible against the circular protrusion at the base of the stone column. A black metal chain running around the column passes through a ring affixed to the bracelet, binding the wrist tightly to the column.

At the top of the arm a rounded shoulder, raised up by the cushions, also stands out well lighted, as well as the neck, the throat, and the other shoulder, the armpit with its soft hair, the left arm likewise pulled back with its wrist bound in the same manner to the base of another column, in the extreme foreground; here the iron bracelet and the chain are fully displayed, represented with perfect clarity down to the slightest details.

The same is true, still in the foreground but at the other side, for a similar chain, but not quite as thick, wound directly around the ankle, running twice around the column and terminating in a heavy iron embedded in the floor. About a yard farther back, or perhaps slightly farther, the right foot is identically chained. But it is the left foot, and its chain, that are the most minutely depicted.

The foot is small, delicate, finely modeled. In several places the chain has broken the skin, causing noticeable if not extensive depressions in the flesh. The chain links are oval, thick, the size of an eye. The ring in the floor resembles those used to attach horses; it lies almost touching the stone pavement to which it is riveted by a massive iron peg. A few inches away is the edge of a rug; it is grossly wrinkled at this point, doubtless as a result of the convulsive, but necessarily very restricted, movements of the victim attempting to struggle.

The man is still standing about a yard away, half leaning over her. He looks at her face, seen upside down, her dark eyes made larger by their surrounding eyeshadow, her mouth wide open as if screaming. The man's posture allows his face to be seen only in a vague profile, but one senses in it a violent exaltation, despite the rigid attitude, the silence, the immobility. His back is slightly arched. His left hand, the only one visible, holds up at some distance from the body a piece of cloth, some dark-colored piece of clothing, which drags on the carpet, and which must be the long cape with its gold-embroidered lining.

This immense silhouette hides most of the bare flesh over which the red stain, spreading from the globe of the breast, runs in long rivulets that branch out, growing narrower, upon the pale background of the bust and the flank. One thread has reached the armpit and runs in an almost straight, thin line along the arm; others have run down toward the waist and traced out, along one side of the belly, the hip, the top of the thigh, a more random network already starting to congeal. Three or four tiny veins have reached the hollow between the legs, meeting in a sinuous line, touching the point of the V formed by the outspread legs, and disappearing into the black tuft.

Look, now the flesh is still intact: the black tuft and the white belly, the soft curve of the hips, the narrow waist, and, higher up, the pearly breasts rising and falling in time with the rapid breathing, whose rhythm grows more accelerated. The man, close to her, one knee on the floor, leans farther over. The head, with its long, curly hair, which alone is free to move somewhat, turns from side to side, struggling; finally the woman's mouth twists open, while the flesh is torn open, the blood spurts out over the tender skin, stretched tight, the carefully shadowed eyes grow abnormally large, the mouth opens wider, the head twists violently, one last time, from right to left, then more gently, to fall back finally and become still, amid the mass of black hair spread out on the velvet.

Afterward, the whole setting is empty, the enormous room with its purple shadows and its stone columns proliferating in all directions, the monumental staircase with no handrail that twists upward, growing narrower and vaguer as it rises into the darkness, toward the top of the vaults where it disappears.

Near the body, whose wound has stiffened, whose brilliance is already growing dim, the thin smoke from the incense burner traces complicated scrolls in the still air: first a coil turned horizontally to the left, which then straightens out and rises slightly, then returns to the axis of its point of origin, which it crosses as it moves to the right, then turns back in the first direction, only to wind back again, thus forming an irregular sinusoidal[3] curve, more and more flattened out, and rising, vertically, toward the top of the canvas.

3. S-shaped.

INGEBORG BACHMANN
1926–1973

Ingeborg Bachmann's reputation as one of the most significant postwar writers in the German language is almost overshadowed by her image as an interpreter of women's experience and a critic of fascism. Winning early fame as a brilliant young poet whose vivid yet philosophical lyrics brought her prize after prize, she abandoned poetry in mid-career to write fiction that would say what "needed to be said" and speak for those who could not speak for themselves. Women in particular became the protagonists of her later work. Bachmann described the complex and frequently unrecognized forces that shape women's social experience and constitute "ways of death" as often as ways of life. Her powerful intellect and gift for precise description fused with a lyric tendency and strong ethical concerns to create a remarkable body of work that has been translated into twenty-two languages and continues to influence contemporary writers.

Bachmann was born on June 25, 1926, in Klagenfurt, a city in southern Austria close to the Italian and Yugoslavian borders. She was the oldest of three children; her father was a teacher and later a school principal, and her mother's family operated a knitwear firm. Although she lived outside Austria for most of her adult life, moving permanently to Rome in 1963, much of her work is dominated by the image of a spiritual "Austria" whose fluctuating borders and multiethnic heritage create a unique view of the world. Several languages are spoken in her home province of Carinthia, and the valley in which she lived had two names, German and Slovene. Austria itself, although politically powerless, was the former center of the multinational Hapsburg Empire and still participated in many cultures. The notion of physical and psychological boundaries permeates all levels of her writing, along with glimpses of an ideal freedom to move beyond artificial frontiers. Bachmann's own experience of political borders was sharpened when the Nazis marched into Klagenfurt in 1938. She was twelve years old, and that moment, she said, marked the end of her childhood. Attending schools in Klagenfurt throughout the war, she graduated in 1944 and studied briefly in Innsbruck and Graz before entering the University of Vienna in 1946.

Bachmann's first story, *The Ferryboat*, was published in 1946; other stories and her first poems appeared over the next few years. While earning recognition as a creative writer, she also pursued a degree in philosophy with minors in psychology and German literature. She prized the analytical philosophy of the Vienna School (proscribed under Hitler) and rejected the "German irrationalism" represented by existential philosopher Martin Heidegger (1889–1976). Her doctoral dissertation (1950) was openly critical in analyzing the reception of Heidegger's philosophy. Three years later she published a major appreciative essay on the Viennese linguistic philosopher Ludwig Wittgenstein (1889–1951). What fascinated her about Wittgenstein was *"his despairing attempt to chart the limits of linguistic expression"* (emphasis in original), an attempt that is paralleled in her own poetry and fiction.

In the years following her doctorate, Bachmann traveled to Paris and London; gave poetry readings; held a series of jobs, ranging from scriptwriter to newspaper correspondent; and began to write in different genres. She worked briefly in the office of the American occupation authorities in Vienna and was a member of the broadcasting group Red/White/Red between 1951 and 1953. For Red/White/Red she wrote a number of radio plays, including adaptations of works by Thomas Wolfe and Louis Mac-Neice. Her translation of MacNeice's radio script *The Dark Tower* was produced with music by British composer Benjamin Britten, and Bachmann's interest in mixed genres continued after she left Red/White/Red. Her second radio play, *The Cicadas*, was produced in 1954 with music by composer Hans Werner Henze, who later set several of her poems to music. Bachmann collaborated with Henze on other occasions and wrote the libretti for two of his operas as well as a ballet scenario. During the 1950s, she also wrote a novel, *City without a Name*, only to have it rejected by five publishers. Her early reputation was clearly based on the poetry, and recognition came quickly for her extraordinary combination of striking natural images and abstract argument. Addressing the constellation Ursa Major, she began "Great Bear, come down, shaggy night, / cloud-coated beast with the old eyes, star eyes. / Through the thickets your paws break / shimmering with their claws, / star claws." Her first volume, *Mortgaged Time*, appeared in 1953, and in the same year she received the prestigious annual prize awarded by Group 47 (a group of Austrian writers who banded together in 1947 in an effort to establish new directions for German literature). A second collection, *Invocation of the Great Bear*, was published in 1956, by which time she had moved to Rome, published poems in the international poetry journal *Botteghe oscure*, received a second prize, and been the subject of a cover story in the popular German magazine *Der Spiegel*.

Bachmann's work took a sharp turn in the 1960s, so that critics have often spoken of the "two Bachmanns," the first a more hermetic writer aiming at formal beauty, and the second a socially engaged writer of prose who once proclaimed: "I no longer try to make each sentence a work of art. The only thing that matters is what needs to be said." While there is a visible change in emphasis from poetry to prose (her last poem, *No More Delicacies*, was written in 1964 as she began the novel sequence *Ways of Death*), Bachmann's later fiction makes great use of lyrical elements. Unlike Alexander Solzhenitsyn or Naguib Mahfouz, she never attempted to emulate the linear style of the nineteenth-century realist novel. The prose writers who interest her are those who take a modernist perspective on problems of identity, communication, and narrative discourse: Marcel Proust, Italo Svevo (1861–1928), James Joyce, Franz Kafka, Robert Musil (1880–1942), William Faulkner, and Samuel Beckett, all of whom she discussed at length in her 1959–60 lectures *Questions of Contemporary Poetry* at the University of Frankfurt. She related their exploratory style to the problem of the self in modern society, a focus that she adapted to her own circumstances in later work.

Even during the 1950s Bachmann had been concerned with political issues. As "R. K." in Rome, she wrote political articles for a West German newspaper from 1954 to 1955, and she later joined a committee that opposed equipping the German army with atomic weapons. In the 1960s, she wrote a public letter to Simon Wiesenthal that protested reducing the statute of limitations for Nazi war crimes, and she later marched and signed declarations against the Vietnam War. She used her influence with a major publisher to block a translation of Anna Akhmatova's poems by a former leader of the Hitler Youth (she had met Akhmatova in Rome). The change in her writing was not a sudden affirmation of social responsibility, therefore, but a new way of understanding how her writing could be an instrument of social change. Stories such as *Youth in an Austrian Town* and *Among Murderers and Madmen*, from her prize-winning collection, *The Thirtieth Year* (1961), already depicted the historical context of German fascism. Their style, however, is relatively picturesque, their conflicts inner and individual, and their situations symbolic or extraordinary. One story in the collection is narrated by a water nymph; in another, a trial judge breaks down when attempting to ascertain the truth about a defendant who has the same name.

Shifting to broader social themes, Bachmann concentrated on women's experience. Instead of choosing unusual situations, she lingered over the implications of everyday scenes, describing the daily life of Austrian women who were, individually and collectively, victims of a patriarchal society. Readers accustomed to Bachmann's elegantly precise poetry were disconcerted by the presence, in the story collection *Three Paths to the Lake* (1972), of a prosaic "women's literature" that presented not only mundane topics but also rambling narrators and a diffuse awareness. Yet Bachmann's skill was still evident in the way she orchestrated inner references into a structure of cumulative significance, or employed an apparently undisciplined stream of consciousness to reveal repressed thoughts and thought patterns in women who had never been allowed to develop their own voice and identity.

There is a strong link between the writer's earlier preoccupation with fascism and her later studies of women. Fascism must begin somewhere, she said, before it becomes a political movement and an agent of mass destruction. She located the principles of fascism—the oppression of the weak and a sadistic desire for dominance and control—uncomfortably close to home, in the subordination of women by men. "Fascism is the first thing in the relationship between a man and a woman," she declared in an interview. Such repression permeates society in many forms. Bachmann's character Franziska Jordan (the victimized wife of her unfinished novel, *The Franza Case*) compares her situation to that of aborigines or preindustrial cultures in modern society: "I am a Papuan woman." In this view, the social structures of a patriarchal society gather all control into a central point dominated by white men, who in turn reinforce their power by pushing to the margins any other cultural or psychological identity. These newly marginalized figures, moreover, are kept in their place by being defined as childlike and primitive. Discouraged from developing a voice of their own, unable to put their experience into words, they lose control of their identity. Like modern philosophers of language and psychoanalysts, Bachmann realized that language is crucial to a sense of self. Experience that cannot be expressed is unrecognizable and soon *unspeakable*. The moral task of a writer, she felt, was to find the right words for that experience. By bringing the unspeakable into the light of consciousness, Bachmann hoped to operate a change in social consciousness itself.

She envisaged a novel cycle, *Ways of Death*, that would illuminate women's experience through the linked stories of individual figures appearing and reappearing in major or minor roles. Two projected novels, *The Franza Case* and *Requiem for Fanny Goldmann*, remained unfinished and have been published only as posthumous fragments. In 1966, however, Bachmann gave readings from a novel that would be published as *Malina* (1971), a challenging modernist work that includes a variety of forms and techniques: fairy tale, letters, dream sequences, dramatic dialogue, and finally the inexplicable disappearance of the narrator from a story that previously depended on her. The violent dreams in the second chapter, including a vision of Malina's father as a Nazi murderer, and a "cemetery of murdered daughters," give symbolic expression to Bachmann's horror of fascism as a consistent pattern of violence directed first against individual women and leading to mass destruction.

The Franza Case presents similar themes even more directly. Franziska Jordan (who also appears in *The Barking*) is married to the respected Viennese psychiatrist Leo Jordan, a man with sadistic tendencies and a fascination with Nazism. Franziska ("Franza") is his third wife, and he is systematically driving her mad as he did the others. He destroys her sanity by leaving notes on her "case" around the house for her to find, and in a desperate attempt to save herself she flees the clinic in which she had been placed and travels to Egypt with her brother. In the purity of a desert setting remote from the Viennese society where Dr. Jordan rules, she hopes to understand "who I am, where I come from, what is wrong with me, and what I am looking for in this waste"—in short, to reconstruct her violated identity. She never has a chance to recover from the damage inflicted by Dr. Jordan's psychological torture, for violence catches up with her again when she is attacked and raped. After Franziska's death, her brother Martin returns home alive but unable to explain what has happened. The cumulative effect is of a series of little murders, different in scale from the genocide of World War II but remarkably similar in the exercise of power to control, to suppress, and to kill.

Bachmann was still working on *Ways of Death* when she herself died in Rome on October 17, 1973, three weeks after the night her apartment caught fire and she was badly burned. Her second collection of stories, *Three Paths to the Lake*, had appeared the previous year, with characters and themes growing directly out of *Ways of Death*. In the spring of 1973 she had traveled to Poland to give a series of readings, during which time she also visited the concentration camps at Auschwitz and Birkenau. The camps were a reminder of the destructive arrogance of power and of a fascist mentality whose presence and cost she made it her task to describe.

The Barking, taken from *Three Paths to the Lake*, chronicles another aspect of *The Franza Case*. The major figure is Leo Jordan's mother, now old and in failing health, who is befriended by her daughter-in-law Franziska. In a series of conversations, the topic of which is invariably the brilliant Leo, the two women inadvertently bring to light his real selfishness and cruelty. Old Frau Jordan is unable to admit her fear and dislike of Leo and has lived a devoted lie all her life. Rather than recognize the truth emerging from these conversations, she escapes into hallucinations of barking dogs. The barking that barricades her from her son and removes "the fear of an entire lifetime" merely suggests rebellion, and yet it does recall the resentment voiced earlier by her pet dog, Nuri, who was given away because he barked at Dr. Jordan.

Franziska, in contrast, becomes more critical of Leo's behavior even though she also cannot bring herself to blame him openly. Her relationship with Leo disintegrates during the course of the story, although we are never told exactly why. There is no indication here of the systematic attempt to drive Franziska mad that governs *The Franza Case*, but certainly the picture of a homophobic, control-obsessed psychiatrist who belittles human relationships and specializes in concentration camp psychoses implies, for Bachmann, an essentially Nazi mentality. Much of the story's strength lies in its subtly *indirect* depiction of this mentality and its simultaneous analysis of the roots of power. Leo Jordan is described obliquely, through the eyes of his dependent mother and wife. He instills fear in them and controls their lives, but this control also depends on their willingness to obliterate their own personalities to appease him. Bachmann leaves open the possibility of other modes of being: Frau Jordan's truly maternal relationship with another child, Kiki; Franziska's care for her mother-in-law; and Franziska's brother's generosity in paying the taxi bills his dead sister had incurred for Frau Jordan. The fate of the story's two main characters, however, bleakly illustrates Bachmann's conviction that the oppressive power relationships of fascism begin at an insidiously personal level, in the relationships of men and women, and in a systematic disrespect for human individuality.

Karen Achberger, *Understanding Ingeborg Bachmann* (1995), is a good overview of Bachmann's work; it includes a short biography and bibliographic references. Introductions by Mark Anderson to Bachmann's *In the Storm of Roses: Selected Poems* (1986) and *Three Paths to the Lake: Stories* (1989) provide an excellent short overview of the writer's poetry and prose. Gudrun Brokoph-Mauch, *Thunder Rumbling at My Heels: Tracing Ingeborg Bachmann* (1997), may also be consulted. Juliet Wigmore, "Ingeborg Bachmann" in Keith Bullivant, ed., *The Modern German Novel* (1987), discusses *Malina* and the *Ways of Death* cycle. Inta Ezergailis, *Women Writers—The Divided Self* (1982), has chapters on Bachmann and Doris Lessing, among others. A special issue of *Modern Austrian Literature* (1979) devoted to Austrian women writers contains several essays on Bachmann.

PRONOUNCING GLOSSARY

The following list uses common English syllables and stress accents to provide rough equivalents of selected words whose pronunciation may be unfamiliar to the general reader.

Bachmann: *bakh'-mahn*

Franziska: *frahn-tsis'-kah*

Frau: *frow*

Johannes: *yoh-hah'-nes*

The Barking[1]

Old Frau[2] Jordan had been called "old Frau Jordan" for the past three decades because there had been first one and now another young Frau Jordan, and although she did live in Hietzing,[3] she had only a one-room apartment in a dilapidated villa, with a tiny kitchen and no more than half a tub in the bathroom. From her distinguished son Leo, the professor, she received 1,000 schillings[4] per month, and somehow she managed to make do, although those 1,000 schillings had depreciated so much over the last twenty years that she was just barely able to pay an older woman, a certain Frau Agnes, who "looked in" on her twice a week, to tidy up a little, just "the bare minimum." She even saved some of the money for birthday and Christmas presents for her son and grandson from her son's first marriage, whom the first young wife sent over punctually every Christmas to pick up his present. Leo on the other hand was too busy to notice, and since he had become famous and his local prestige had blossomed into international renown, he was busier than ever. Things only changed when the latest young Frau Jordan began to visit the old woman as often as she could, a really nice, likable girl, as the old woman soon admitted to herself, but at each visit she said only: But Franziska, it's not right, you shouldn't come so often, it's such a waste. You two surely have enough expenses as it is, but Leo is just such a good son!

Franziska always brought something with her, delicacies and sherry, some pastries, because she had guessed that the old woman liked to take a sip now and then and, moreover, attached great importance to having something in the house "for the company." After all, Leo might drop by, and he mustn't notice how much she was missing and that all day long she wondered how to allocate her money and how much she could put aside for presents. Her apartment was meticulously clean, but gave off a faint "old-woman" smell which she was not aware of and which put Leo Jordan to flight, apart from the fact that he had no time to lose and no idea what to talk about with his eighty-five-year-old mother. Sometimes, seldom, he had been amused—that much Franziska knew—namely, when he was having a relationship with a married woman, because then old Frau Jordan had gone without sleep and made strange, convoluted allusions, trembling for his safety: she believed that the married men whose wives Leo Jordan was living with were dangerous and jealous and bloodthirsty, and she wasn't able to calm down until he married Franziska, who did not have a jealous husband lurking in the bushes but was young and cheerful, an orphan, admittedly not from an educated family, but at least with a brother who had gone to college. Families of the

1. Translated by Mary Fran Gilbert.   2. Mrs. (German).   3. A suburb west of Vienna, Austria.
4. The basic Austrian unit of currency.

educated classes and educated men in general carried great weight with Frau Jordan, although she didn't do much socializing; she only heard about things. But her son had the right to marry into an educated family. The old woman and Franziska talked almost exclusively about Leo, because he was the only productive topic the two of them had, and Franziska was shown the photo album over and over again, Leo in a stroller, Leo at the beach, and Leo through the years, taking hikes, pasting stamps in his collection, and so on until his military service.

The Leo she came to know through the old woman was a completely different Leo from the man she had married, and when the two women sat drinking their sherry the old woman would say: He was a complicated child, a strange boy, actually you could tell all along that he was destined for great things.

For a while Franziska was happy to hear these assertions, that Leo was so good to his mother and had always done everything conceivable to help her, but then she noticed that something was wrong, and with dismay she realized—the old woman was afraid of her son. It began with the old woman saying, sometimes hastily and parenthetically (she believed it to be a clever tactic that Franziska would never see through because she was blinded by admiration for her husband): But please don't mention a word of it to Leo, you know how concerned he is, it might upset him, whatever you do, please don't tell him that something is wrong with my knee, it's such a little thing, he might get upset about it.

Although Franziska had since learned that Leo never got upset at all, certainly not because of his mother, and only listened to her reports with half an ear, she suppressed this first realization. Unfortunately she had already told him about the knee but swore to the old woman she wouldn't say a word. Leo had reacted with annoyance and then, to placate her, had explained that he really couldn't drive out to Hietzing because of such a trifle. Just tell her— he rattled off some medical terminology—she should buy this and that and do and walk as little as possible. Franziska bought the medication without further comment and claimed in Hietzing that she had secretly spoken with one of her husband's assistants without mentioning any names and that he had given her this advice, although she was at a loss as to how to keep the old woman in bed without the help of a nurse. But she no longer had enough courage to approach Leo about it, because a nurse cost money, and now she was caught in the middle. On the one hand Frau Jordan didn't want anything to do with it, and on the other Leo Jordan—albeit for completely different reasons—simply didn't want to hear about it. When Frau Jordan's knee was swollen, Franziska lied to her husband several times; she drove quickly to Hietzing, allegedly to the hairdresser's, and straightened up the little apartment, bringing all sorts of things with her. She purchased a radio but was uneasy afterward: Leo was bound to notice the expenditure, so she quickly transferred the money back and broke into the meager savings she had set aside for some sort of emergency which would hopefully never arise and could only be a minor emergency at any rate. She and her brother had divided what little remained after the death of their entire family, with the exception of a cottage in southern Carinthia[5] which was slowly falling into disrepair. In the end she called a general practitioner in the neighborhood and asked

---

5. A southwestern province of Austria.

him to treat the old woman for a while, paying him out of her own savings. More importantly, she didn't dare reveal to the doctor who she was and who the old woman was, because that would only have hurt Leo's reputation, and protecting Leo's reputation was also in Franziska's best interest. But the old woman thought much more selflessly: there was no way she could ask her famous son to go so far as to come and take a look at her knee. She had used a cane before on occasion, but after this knee problem she really needed it, so Franziska sometimes drove her to town. Shopping with the old woman was a somewhat laborious undertaking: once she had only needed a comb, but there were no combs like the ones "in her day," and although the old woman was polite, standing in the store with erect dignity, she annoyed the little saleswoman by eyeing the price tags suspiciously, unable to refrain from telling Franziska in a clearly audible whisper that the prices here were outrageous, they'd better go somewhere else. The saleswoman, who was in no position to judge how important buying this comb was to the old woman, replied rudely that they wouldn't find this comb cheaper anywhere in town. Franziska launched into embarrassed negotiations with the mother, took the comb the old woman wanted but looked on as costing a fortune and quickly paid for it, saying: Just consider it a Christmas present from us, a present in advance. Prices have really gone up horrendously everywhere. The old woman didn't say a word, she sensed her defeat, but still, if prices really were so outrageous—a comb like this used to cost two schillings and nowadays it cost sixty—well then there wasn't much left for her to understand in this world.

After a while the topic "the good son" had been exhausted and Franziska repeatedly steered the conversation to the old woman herself, because the only thing she knew was that Leo's father had died young of a heart attack or stroke, quite suddenly, on a staircase, and that must have been a long time ago, because if you stopped to figure it out this woman had been a widow for almost half a century. First she had worked for years to raise her only child, and then she was suddenly an old woman nobody cared about anymore. She never spoke about her marriage, only in connection with Leo who had had a very difficult life, without a father, and she was so preoccupied with Leo that she failed to see the parallel to Franziska, who had lost both her parents when she was young. Her son was the only one who could have had a difficult time, and then it turned out that it hadn't been so bad after all, because a distant cousin had paid for his education, a certain Johannes about whom Franziska had heard very little, merely a few derogatory, critical references to some eternal—now aging—loafer who was swimming in money and supposedly led a life of idleness with all its ridiculous affectations. He dabbled a little in art, collected Chinese lacquerware, and was just another one of those freeloaders found in every family. Franziska knew also that he was homosexual, but she was really amazed how someone like Leo, whose very profession obliged him to uphold a neutral and scientific attitude toward homosexuality and phenomena of a quite different magnitude, could go on and on about this cousin as though he had somehow, through his own negligence, fallen prey to works of art, homosexuality, and an inheritance to boot, but at that time Franziska still admired her husband too much to be more than irritated and hurt. With relief she heard from the old woman, in discussing those hard times, that Leo was infinitely grateful and had been a big help to this Johannes, who was then in the throes of a number of personal crises—which were better left untold. The old woman hesitated and then added, because she was, after all, sitting opposite the wife of a psychiatrist: I think you should know that Johannes is sexual.

Franziska controlled herself and suppressed a laugh, it was surely the most daring revelation the old woman had roused herself to in years, but with Franziska she was opening up more and more. She told her how Leo had often given Johannes advice, naturally free of charge, but Johannes was a hopeless case, and if a person didn't have the willpower to change it was understandable that he would be at his wits' end, and from what she heard, Johannes just kept on with it, the same as always. Franziska carefully translated this naive story into reality and understood even less why Leo talked about this cousin in such a disparaging and malicious way. At that time the obvious reason escaped her, namely, that Leo was reluctant to be reminded of his mother and his former wives and lovers who were nothing to him but a conspiracy of creditors from whom he could escape only by belittling them to himself and others. His tirades about his first wife were similar: she had been the epitome of everything diabolical, unappreciative and spiteful, traits that had not been revealed in depth until the divorce when her aristocratic father had hired a lawyer for her to secure some of the money for the child, money she'd given him when he was a young doctor and hard times had struck again. It was an alarmingly large sum to Franziska but, as she was told, one could expect nothing less from the "baroness," as Leo ironically called her, because the family had always treated him like an upstart, without having the slighest idea who was dwelling in their midst. It amused him to note that the "baroness" had never remarried and lived in total seclusion. After him she hadn't been able to find another fool—young and gullible and poor, as he had been—who would have married such a deserving Fräulein. She had understood nothing about his work, absolutely nothing, and although she behaved fairly in respect to the agreement about their son, sending him for regular visits and teaching him to respect his father, she obviously did it for no other reason than to prove to the world how generous she was.

The brilliant doctor's rise to fame along the thorny path of suffering had already become Franziska's religion at that time, and again and again she reproached herself with the image of him making his way, against indescribable odds and despite the obstacle that dreadful marriage posed, all the way to the top. And the cross he was forced to bear because of his mother, the financial and moral burden, was no light one for him, but that at least Franziska could take off his shoulders. Although it otherwise might not have occurred to her to spend her free hours with an old woman the time became something special when she thought of Leo: a helping hand, evidence of her love for him, allowing him to devote his undivided attention to his work.

Leo was just too good to her, he told her that she was overdoing it, the way she took care of his mother, a telephone call now and again would have sufficed. For the past few years the old woman had had a telephone which she feared more than loved: she didn't like to talk on the phone and always shouted into the mouthpiece and couldn't hear what the other party said, and besides that, the phone was too expensive, but of course Franziska wasn't to mention that to Leo. Once the old woman—prompted by Franziska and a second glass of sherry—did in fact begin to talk about the old days, the very old days, and it turned out that she wasn't from an educated family, her father had knit gloves and socks in a small factory in Lower Austria and she had been the oldest of eight children, but then she'd had a wonderful time when she took up employment with a Greek family, immensely rich people with a little boy, the most beautiful child she had ever laid eyes on, and she was his nursemaid. Being a nursemaid was a really good job, nothing degrading about it, and the Greek's young wife had had servants aplenty, oh yes, she'd had a real stroke of luck, such a good position had been hard to find back then. The child's name was Kiki, at least everyone had called him Kiki. When the old woman began talking about Kiki more and more frequently, remembering every detail—what Kiki had said, how cute and affectionate he was, the walks they'd taken together—her eyes lit up as they never did when she spoke of her own child. Kiki had simply been a little angel, never naughty, she stressed, never naughty at all, and the separation must have been terrible, they hadn't told Kiki that the Fräulein was leaving, and she had cried all night long, and once, years later, she had tried to find out what had become of the family. First she'd heard that they were traveling, then that they were back in Greece, and now she had no idea whatsoever what had happened to Kiki, who must be over sixty by now, yes, over sixty she said pensively, and she had been forced to leave because the Greek family had planned their first major trip and couldn't take her along, and when they left the young wife had given her a wonderful present. The old woman stood up and rummaged in a jewelry box, then showed her the brooch from Kiki's mother, it was the real thing, with diamonds, but she still asked herself today if they hadn't let her go because the wife had noticed that Kiki was more attached to her than to his own mother, she could understand that all right, but it had been the hardest blow of all, and she had never completely recovered from it. Franziska regarded the brooch thoughtfully; perhaps it really was quite valuable, she didn't know much about jewelry, but she was beginning to realize something else: this Kiki must have meant more to the old woman than Leo. She often hesitated to talk about Leo's childhood, or she began only to break off in fright saying abruptly: It was just childish nonsense, you know boys are so hard to raise, he didn't do it on purpose, he was just having such a bad time and it was all I could do to make ends meet. But you get everything back a hundredfold when a child has grown up and made his own way and become so famous, he takes after his father more than me, you know.

Franziska carefully handed back the brooch, and once again the old woman started in fear. Please Franziska, don't mention a word of this to Leo, it could annoy him. I have my plans, you know, if I get sick I could sell it so that I won't become even more of a burden to him. Franziska embraced the old woman with a hug that was both timid and fierce. Don't ever do that, promise me you'll never sell this brooch. You're not a burden to us at all!

On the way home she made one detour after the other, in a state of inner turmoil, this poor woman shouldn't sell her brooch while she and Leo spent money freely, went on trips, entertained. She kept debating what she should say to Leo, but a first, faint alarm sounded inside her, because even though the old woman had her quirks and exaggerated things, she must be right about something, and so in the end she didn't say a word about it at home and only reported cheerfully that his mother was doing very well. But before they left for a conference in London she arranged a contract with a garage which ran a private taxi service, made a downpayment, and said to the old woman: An idea has occurred to us, because you shouldn't walk too far by yourself. Just call a taxi when you want to go out, it hardly costs a thing, it's just a favor from an old patient, but don't say anything about it, especially not to Leo, you know how he is, he doesn't like it when you thank him and everything, and you just ride to town when you need something, and have the taxi wait, but always have Herr Pineider take you, the young one. He doesn't know that his father was one of Leo's patients though, that comes under professional secrecy, you know, I was, just there and talked to him, and you have to promise me, for Leo's sake, that you'll take the taxi, it would ease our minds. In the beginning, the old woman made little use of the taxi, and Franziska scolded her for it when she returned from England; her leg had worsened and the old woman had naturally done all her shopping on foot, once even going so far as to take the streetcar into town because one could hardly get anything in Hietzing, and Franziska said firmly, as if to a stubborn child: This is definitely not to happen again.

They exhausted one topic after another: Kiki, the life of a young nursemaid in Vienna before the First World War and before her marriage, and sometimes it was only Franziska who talked, especially when she had just returned from a trip with Leo, a brilliant talk he'd delivered at the conference, and that he had given her this offprint for his mother. The old woman labored through the title with an effort: "The Significance of Endogenous and Exogenous Factors in Connection with the Occurrence of Paranoid and Depressive Psychoses in Former Concentration Camp Inmates and Refugees." Franziska assured her it was merely the groundwork for a much larger study he was working on, and he was even letting her help him with it. It would probably become the most significant and the first really important book in the field. A work of incalculable impact.

The old woman was strangely mute, surely she didn't understand the implications of these studies, maybe nothing at all of what her son was doing. Then she said, surprisingly: I hope he won't make too many enemies with it, here in Vienna, and then there's that other thing . . .

Franziska grew agitated: But that's exactly the point, that would be a very good thing, it's a provocation, too, and Leo isn't afraid of anyone, for him it's the only thing that counts, that has a purpose far beyond its scientific significance.

Yes, of course, the old woman said quickly, and he knows how to defend himself, and if you're famous you always have enemies. I was just thinking about Johannes, but that's so long ago now. Did you know that he was in a concentration camp for a year and a half before the war ended? Franziska was surprised, she hadn't known, but she failed to see the connection. The old woman didn't want to say any more but then continued: It meant a certain amount of danger for Leo, having a relative who, well, you know what I mean. Yes, of course, said Franziska, still somewhat confused; sometimes the old woman had such a roundabout way of saying things without really saying them, and she couldn't make head or tail of it, although suddenly she was bursting with pride that a member of Leo's family had been through something so terrible and that Leo, in his tactful, modest way, had never said anything about it to her, not even about the danger he must have faced as a young doctor. That afternoon the old woman didn't want to go on talking; she merely asked disjointedly: Do you hear it, too?

What?

The dogs, the old woman said. There were never so many dogs in Hietzing, I've heard them barking again, and they bark at night, too. Frau Schönthal next door has a poodle now. It doesn't bark much though, it's such a nice dog, I see her almost every day when I go shopping, but we only say hello, her husband doesn't have much of an education.

Franziska drove home as quickly as she could; this time she wanted to ask Leo if there was anything to the fact that his mother had suddenly begun talking about dogs, if it was an alarming symptom, maybe it had something to do with her age. She had also noticed that the old woman had been upset once about ten schillings which had been lying on the table and then disappeared when Frau Agnes left, all this excitement about ten missing schillings, certainly she had only imagined it anyway, weren't those all signs of the process of aging? It couldn't possibly have been the cleaning woman, she was what people in certain circles—that is, in better circles—called a "God-fearing" woman who came more out of pity than for the money, which she didn't need anyway—she did it as a favor and nothing more. And old Frau Jordan's pitiful presents—an ancient, threadbare purse or some other useless paraphernalia—would hardly have induced Frau Agnes to come; she had realized long ago that she had nothing to expect from the old woman or from her son, and she knew nothing of Franziska's enthusiastic plans for improving the situation; Franziska had chided the old woman as though she were a child, because she didn't want to lose this valuable help over a bout of senile obstinacy and an unfounded suspicion.

More and more often she found the old woman at the window when she arrived, and they no longer sat together when Franziska came to drink sherry and nibble on pastries. The business with the dogs continued, although at the same time her hearing problem grew worse, and Franziska was at a loss. Something had to be done, and Leo, whom she bothered with none of this, was not going to avoid devoting some attention to his mother one of these days. Only then things started becoming complicated between Leo and herself, and she discovered that he had so intimidated her that she was afraid of him. But at least once, in a fit of her old courage, she overcame her inexplicable fear and suggested at dinner: Why don't we invite your mother to come and stay with us, we have enough room, and then our Rosi could always be with her and you would never have to worry, besides, she's so quiet and undemanding, she would never disturb you, and certainly not me, I'm suggesting it for your sake because I know how much you worry. Leo was in a good mood that evening and secretly happy about something. She didn't realize what it was but had decided to make use of the opportunity, and he answered, laughing: What an idea, you have no feel for the situation, my dear, you can't uproot an elderly person after a while, it would only depress her and she needs her freedom, she's a strong woman who has lived alone for decades. You don't know her the way I do, she would die of fright here, just from the kind of people who come over. She'd probably debate for hours on end whether to use the bathroom, out of fear that one of us just might want to use it. Come on, my little Franziska, please don't make such a face, I think your impulse is touching and admirable, but that wonderful idea of yours would be the death of her. Believe me, it's just that I happen to know more about these things.

But this business with the dogs . . . ? Franziska began to stutter, she hadn't wanted to talk about it and would gladly have immediately taken back what she'd said. She was no longer capable of putting her apprehension into words.

What, her husband asked in a completely different tone of voice, she doesn't still want a mutt, does she? I don't understand, Franziska answered. Why should she—you don't mean she wants to have a dog, do you?

Of course I do, and I'm more than glad that this childish interlude has blown over so quickly, at her age she just couldn't handle a dog, she should take care of herself, that's more important to me, a dog is such a nuisance, she has no idea what they would mean, with her advancing senility. She never said anything about it, Franziska replied half-heartedly, I don't think she wants a dog. I wanted to say something entirely different, but it's not important, sorry. Would you like a cognac, are you going to work later, should I type anything for you?

At her next visit Franziska didn't know how to persuade the old woman, who was always on the alert, to give her answers she needed to know. She approached the subject in a roundabout way, remarking casually: Incidentally, I saw Frau Schönthal's dog today, really a cute dog, I like poodles a lot, actually all animals, because I grew up in the country, you know, we always had dogs, I mean my grandparents and everyone in the village, and cats, too, of course. Wouldn't it be good for you to have a dog or a cat, now that you have trouble reading. I mean, certainly that kind of thing passes, but I for one would absolutely love to have a dog. But you know, in the city it's just a bother and not really fair to the dog, but here in Hietzing, where it can frisk around in the yard and you can go for walks . . .

The old woman exclaimed in agitation: A dog, no, no, I don't want a dog! Franziska realized she had done something wrong, but felt at the same time that she hadn't offended the old woman as she might have had she suggested a parrot or canaries: it must have been something else entirely that had put her in such a state of agitation. After a while the old woman said very quietly: Nuri was a really nice dog, and I got along well with him, that was, let me think, it must have been five years ago, but then I had to give him away, to a home or a place where they resell them. Leo doesn't like dogs. No, what am I saying, it was different, there was something in that dog I can't really understand, he couldn't stand Leo, he always jumped at him and barked madly whenever Leo made the slightest move toward the door, and then once he almost bit him, and Leo was so indignant, of course that's understandable, when a dog is that wild, but he was never like that otherwise, not even with strangers, and then naturally I gave him away. I couldn't let Leo be barked at and bitten by Nuri, no, that would have been too much, Leo should be able to feel at home when he visits me and not have to get angry about some poorly trained dog.

Franziska thought that, although there was no longer a dog who jumped at him and disliked him, Leo came seldom enough as it was, and even less often since Franziska came instead. How long had it been anyway since his last visit? Once the three of them had gone for a short ride along the Weinstrasse and into the Helenenthal and lunched at an inn with his mother; otherwise Franziska always came alone.

Be sure not to say anything to Leo, though, that business with Nuri really hurt his feelings, he's very sensitive, you know, and to this day I can't forgive myself for being so selfish as to want to have Nuri, but old people are very selfish, dear Franziska, you can't understand that yet, you're still so young and good, but when you're very old you get all these selfish desires, and you can't just let yourself give in to them. What would have become of me if Leo hadn't taken care of me, his father died all of a sudden like that and there was no time to make any arrangements, and there wasn't any money, either, my husband was a little careless, no, not a spendthrift, but he had a hard time of it and didn't have much of a knack with money, Leo doesn't take after him in that respect. In those days I could still work, the boy was a reason to keep going, and I was still young, but what would I do nowadays? My one fear has always been having to go to an old people's home, but Leo would never stand for that, and if I didn't have this apartment I'd have to go to some home, and I guess a dog isn't worth all that. Franziska listened to her, clenched up inside, and she said to herself: So that's it, that's it, she gave her dog away for his sake. And she asked herself: What kind of people are we?—because she was incapable of thinking: What kind of a man is my husband!—we're just so cruel, and she thinks she's selfish, and all the time we have everything we want! In order to hide her tears she quickly unpacked a small package from Meinl, little things, and acted as though she hadn't understood. Oh, by the way, I'm so scatterbrained today, I've only brought you the tea and coffee and a little smoked salmon and Russian salad. Actually it doesn't go together all that well, but I was really flustered at the store because Leo is leaving and one of the manuscripts isn't finished yet. But he'll give you a call tonight, and he'll be back in a week anyway.

He needs a break, the old woman said, see to it that he gets one if you can, you two haven't had any vacation at all yet this year. Franziska said brightly: That's a good idea, I'll convince him some way or another, I just need to think of a strategy, but thanks a lot, that's really a good piece of advice, he's constantly overworked, you know, and at some point I have to make him slow down.

What Franziska did not know was that this was her last visit to the old woman and she no longer needed the strategy, because other things came to pass, events of such hurricane force that she almost forgot the old woman and a great many other things as well.

In her fear, the old woman didn't ask her son on the phone why Franziska had stopped coming. She was worried, but her son sounded cheerful and unconcerned, and once he even came over and stayed for twenty minutes. He didn't touch the pastries, he didn't finish the sherry and he didn't talk about Franziska, but he did talk quite a bit about himself, and that made her ecstatic because it had been such a long time since he had spoken about himself. So he was leaving on vacation now, he needed a break, but the word "Mexico" gave the old woman a mild shock, wasn't that the place where they had scorpions and revolutions and savages and earthquakes, but he laughed reassuringly, kissed her and promised to write. He sent a few postcards, which she read religiously. Franziska hadn't added her regards. Once Franziska called her from Carinthia. Really, the money these young people throw out the window! Franziska had only called to ask if everything was okay. Then they talked about Leo, but the old woman kept shouting at the most inappropriate times: It's getting too expensive, child, but Franziska kept talking, yes, she had finally succeeded, he was finally taking a break, and she had had to go to her brother's, there was something to settle here, that was why she hadn't been able to accompany Leo. Family matters in Carinthia. Because of the house. Then the old woman received a strange envelope with a few lines from Franziska. She didn't say anything, just sent her regards and wrote that she would like her to have this photo she had taken herself, the photograph was of Leo, apparently on the Semmering Pass,[6] laughing in a snowy landscape in front of a large hotel. The old woman decided not to say anything to Leo; he wouldn't have asked her anyway. She hid the photograph under the brooch in her jewelry box.

She could no longer read books and was bored by the radio; newspapers were all she wanted, and Frau Agnes got them for her. It took her hours to decipher them, she read the obituaries and always felt a certain satisfaction when someone younger than herself had passed away. Well, look at that, Professor Haderer too, he could hardly have been more than seventy. Frau Schönthal's mother had died, too, of cancer, she wasn't even sixty-five. The old woman stiffly offered her condolences in the grocery store and didn't even look at the poodle, and then she went home and stood at the window. She slept more than old people are said to sleep, but she often awoke, only to hear the dogs again. She was startled whenever the cleaning woman came: since Franziska's visits had ended, it bothered her when anyone came over, and she had the impression that she was changing. Now she actually was frightened of suddenly collapsing in the street or losing control of herself when she had to go to town for something, and so she obediently called young Herr Pineider, who drove her around. And she became accustomed to this small precaution for her own safety. She completely lost her sense of time, and when Leo once came by to see her, deeply tanned, she no longer knew if he was returning from Mexico or when he had been there at all. But she was careful not to ask, and gathered from something he said that he had just arrived from Ischia,[7] back from a trip to Italy. Confused, she said: Good, good. That was good for you. And while he was telling her something the dogs began to bark, several of them, all at once, very near, and she was so completely encircled by the barking and a very gentle, gentle terror that she was no longer afraid of her son. The fear of an entire lifetime suddenly left her.

When he said on his way out: Next time I'll bring Elfi over, you have to meet her one of these days! she had no idea what he was talking about. Wasn't he married to Franziska anymore, how long had it been, how many wives was that now anyway, she could no longer remember how long he had lived with Franziska and when, and she said: Go ahead and bring her over. Fine. Whatever is best for you. The barking was so close now that for an instant she was certain that Nuri was with her again and would jump at him and bark. She wished he would finally leave, she wanted to be alone. She thanked him out of habit, just in case, and he asked in astonishment: Whatever for? Now I really did go and forget to bring you my book after all. A phenomenal success. I'll have it sent.

Well then, thank you so much my child. Send it over, but unfortunately

6. In the Alps in southern Austria, known as a tourist resort and center for winter sports. 7. An island vacation spot north of the Bay of Naples.

your dumb old mother can hardly read anymore and doesn't understand much anyway.

She let him embrace her and found herself alone again surrounded by the barking. It came from every garden and house in Hietzing, an invasion of the beasts had begun, the dogs came closer, barking to her, and she stood erect, as always, no longer dreaming of the time with Kiki and the Greeks, no longer thinking of the day when the last ten schillings had disappeared and Leo had lied to her. Instead she redoubled her efforts to hide things better, wishing she could throw them away, especially the brooch and the photograph, so that Leo wouldn't find anything after she died. But she couldn't think of a good hiding place, maybe the bucket with the scraps, but she trusted Frau Agnes less and less, too, because she would have had to give her the rubbish, and she suspected that the woman would rummage through it and find the brooch. Once she said, a little too harshly: At least you could give the bones and the leftovers to the dogs.

The cleaning woman looked at her in amazement and asked: What dogs? To the dogs, of course, insisted the old woman in an imperious tone, I want the dogs to have them!

She was a suspicious looking creature, a thief. She probably took the bones home with her.

To the dogs, I said. Can't you understand me, are you deaf or something? No wonder, at your age.

Then the barking diminished, and she thought: someone has chased the dogs off or given them away, because now it was no longer that same powerful, recurrent, barking. The fainter the barking, the more adamant she became: she was only biding her time until the louder barking resumed. One had to be able to wait, and she could wait. All at once it was no longer a barking sound, although there was no doubt it came from the dogs in the neighborhood. It wasn't a growling either, just now and again the great, wild, triumphant howling of a single dog, then a whimpering, the faint barking of all the others fading into the distance.

One day nearly two years after the death of his sister Franziska, Dr. Martin Ranner received a bill from a company by the name of Pineider for taxi services listed separately by date, for which Frau Franziska Jordan had made a downpayment and signed a contract. But because only very few trips had been made while Franziska was alive and the majority after her death he called the company for an explanation of this mysterious bill. Although the explanation actually explained very little, he had no desire to call his former brother-in-law or ever see him again, so he paid the fares, in installments, for a woman he had never known and never had anything to do with. He came to the conclusion that the old Frau Jordan must have passed away some time ago; the company had let several months go by since her last trip, perhaps out of reverence, before asserting its claims.

GABRIEL GARCÍA MÁRQUEZ
born 1928

One of the great novelists and prose stylists of the twentieth century, Gabriel García Márquez possesses both the technical virtuosity of the French "new novelists" and the breadth and historical scope of the traditional realistic writer. His most famous work, *One Hundred Years of Solitude* (1967), is also the best-known novel from the amazing literary explosion of the 1960s and 1970s called the Latin American "Boom," and embodies the mixture of fantasy and realism called "magical realism." In this novel and related stories, he follows the rise and fall of the Buendía family fortunes in a mythical town called Macondo, and sketches at the same time an echoing, intricate pattern of social, cultural, and psychological themes that become a symbolic picture of Latin American society. Not all of García Márquez's works are about Macondo, but the same themes and images reappear throughout: the contrast of dreamlike and everyday reality and the "magical" aspect of fictional creation, mythic overtones often rooted in local folklore, the representation of broader social and psychological conflicts through regional tales, the essential solitude of individuals facing love and death in a society of which they never quite seem a part. García Márquez is a political novelist in that many of his fictional situations are openly drawn from conditions in Latin American history, so that local readers will recognize current history in the change from prosperity to misery in Macondo that accompanies the presence and withdrawal of the banana company, the massacre of striking banana workers by government forces in 1928, the extreme separation of rich and poor, and the grotesquely oppressive power of political dictators pictured most recently in *The Autumn of the Patriarch* (1975). Yet his fiction achieves its impact not because of its base in real events but because these events are transformed and interpreted inside an artistic vision that—experimenting with many forms—creates a fictional universe all its own.

García Márquez was born in the small town of Aracataca in the "banana zone" of Colombia on March 6, 1928, to Gabriel Eligio García and Maria Márquez Iguarán. The first of twelve children, he was raised by his maternal grandparents until his grandfather died in 1936. He attributes his love of fantasy to his grandmother, who would tell him fantastic tales whenever she did not want to answer his questions. The recurring image of an old military man battered by circumstances (the grandfather of *Leaf Storm,* 1955; the protagonist of *No One Writes to the Colonel,* 1958; and in his younger days, Colonel Aureliano Buendía of *One Hundred Years of Solitude*) likewise recalls his grandfather, a retired colonel who had served on the Liberal side of a civil war at the beginning of the century. A scholarship student at the National Colegio in Zipaquirá, García Márquez received his bachelor's degree in 1946 and studied law at universities in Bogotá and Cartagena from 1947 to 1950. In 1947 he published his first story, *The Third Resignation,* a Kafkaesque tale of a man who continued to grow and retain consciousness in his coffin for seventeen years after his death. García Márquez had worked as a journalist while studying law, and in 1950 he abandoned his legal studies for journalism in order to have more time as a writer. His first novel, *Leaf Storm,* was published in 1955 and—in its use of interior monologue and juxtaposition of different perspectives—shows the strong influence of Faulkner. He would soon abandon the more subjective Faulknerian style for an objective manner derived both from his experience in journalism and from Ernest Hemingway. In *Leaf Storm,* we may perceive reality through the mind of a ten-year-old boy: "The heat won't let you breathe in the closed room. You can hear the sun buzzing in the streets, but that's all. The air is stagnant, like concrete; you get the feeling that it could get all twisted like a sheet of steel." In his next novel, *No One Writes to the Colonel,* an impersonal narrator catalogues the actions of the colonel about to make coffee: "He removed the pot from the fire, poured half the water onto the earthen floor, and scraped the inside of the can with a knife until the last scrapings of the ground coffee, mixed with bits of rust, fell into the pot."

In 1954 García Márquez had joined the newspaper *El Espectador* (The spectator) in Bogotá; a report he wrote in 1955 that indirectly revealed corruption in the navy irritated the Rojas Pinilla dictatorship, and the paper was shut down. Working in Paris as *El Espectador*'s foreign correspondent when he learned that his job had been abolished, he lived in extreme poverty for the next year while beginning *The Evil Hour* (1962) and *No One Writes to the Colonel*. In 1957, after traveling in Eastern Europe, he returned to Latin America. Here he worked for several different newspapers in Venezuela, and later for the international press agency, Prensa Latina, in Cuba and New York, and for the Mexican periodicals *La Familia* and *Sucesos* (a sensationalist magazine) before beginning to write film scripts in 1963. A collection of short stories, *Big Mama's Funeral*, was published in 1962, along with the first edition of *The Evil Hour*, which, printed in Spain, was later repudiated by the author because of tampering by proofreaders. In 1965 the various themes and characters he had been developing throughout his earlier novels and short stories came together as the fully developed concept of a new book, and García Márquez shut himself up in his study for a year and a half to write *One Hundred Years of Solitude*. Published in 1967, the novel was a best-seller, immediately translated into numerous (now twenty-five) languages; it received prizes in Italy and France in 1969, and—when published in English in 1970—was chosen by American critics as one of the dozen best books of the year.

Layers of meaning accumulate around a core story in *One Hundred Years*, as the history of the doomed Buendía family takes on different and intertwined shades of significance. The family is cursed from the moment that its founder, José Arcadio Buendía, kills a friend who had insulted him and consummates an incestuous marriage; he then sets out in search of the sea and stops to settle in Macondo. Throughout a hundred years of family history in the nineteenth and twentieth centuries, the Buendías are soldiers, scholars, merchants, explorers, revolutionaries, inventors, lovers, ascetics, labor organizers, and above all stubborn individuals. Yet these individuals are caught up in, and defined by, a larger family history of which they sometimes appear only interrelated, component parts: names echo one another, and parallel situations evoke a feeling of half-recognition inside a mirrorlike pattern of structural oppositions. The Buendía story is set in history but also exists on a mythic level: Remedios the Beauty is lifted up into heaven clutching her sheets when she dies, and when José Arcadio is killed, blood runs from his ear down the street all the way to his mother in her kitchen. The last Buendía is born with the sign of the curse—a pig's tail—and dies eaten by ants at the end. Yet this is not really the end, for in the very last pages, after his son's death and as a whirlwind gathers to destroy Macondo, Aureliano Babilonia reads the manuscript left by the dead magician Melquíades. At last able to decipher a text that could not be read until one hundred years had passed, Aureliano Babilonia finds that this text is the story of his own family; thus he is learning about his own existence, predicted and described a century ago. "It was the history of the family, written by Melquíades, down to the most trivial details, one hundred years ahead of time. He had written it in Sanskrit, which was his mother tongue, and he had encoded the even lines in the private cipher of the Emperor Augustus and the odd ones in a Lacedemonian military code." Behind García Márquez there is yet another author—Melquíades—who has written *One Hundred Years of Solitude*, a novel whose complexity and self-contained referentiality recall the circular fictions of Borges.

The magical realism of *One Hundred Years of Solitude* depends on the juxtaposition of real and fantastic worlds, and it elicits a series of interpretations whose variety can be emulated only by interpretations of Kafka. For some readers, the novel is an allegory of the human condition and its fall from innocence; for others, it recounts the destructive, alienating influence on Latin American society of the aggressive individualism in Western culture; for others, it depicts essential human loneliness and the failure to communicate—even in love; for still others, it is a "total fiction" peculiarly valid for intricate repetitive patterns that refer to folklore and real life but finally create only a fictional universe. Each interpretation draws on the novel's blurring of real and unreal worlds, so that historical facts become the basis for fiction and fictional manipulation liberates our perspective on reality—a typically modernist method of using the imagination to encourage historical change.

After *One Hundred Years of Solitude,* García Márquez found new ways to combine magical-realist techniques and social commentary. In 1972, he published a collection of seven stories, *The Incredible and Sad Story of Innocent Eréndira and Her Heartless Grandmother,* which contains the story printed here, *Death Constant Beyond Love.* From the title story, in which Eréndira's monstrously fat, tattooed, green-blooded grandmother is finally murdered after prostituting her grandchild to the entire countryside to repay a debt, to symbolic fantasies such as *A Very Old Man with Enormous Wings* (in which a castaway angel is exhibited in a chicken coop until his feathers grow back and he can fly away), the author presents tales in which the substance is incredible but the details themselves are highly realistic. The winged man smells bad and his wings are infested with parasites; the farm truck in which Eréndira tries to escape with her lover has an old motor and cannot outrun the military patrol summoned by her grandmother. The mixture of fantasy and realism is not easily interpretable in a single symbolic sense: Eréndira's prostitution may be political and cultural as well as personal, and larger social relationships may be symbolized in the town's attitude toward the angel. Throughout, the narrative line can easily be followed but also interpreted in several ways.

Increasingly preoccupied with contemporary political events, he next published *The Autumn of the Patriarch,* an intricate study of the idea of dictatorship embodied in reactions to a first, false death of the patriarch (his double was assassinated instead), and a second, apparently real death, on which new authorities are already gathering to divide up the power. García Márquez is aiming at more than a specific political situation: he points to a habit of mind, a social lethargy in which there is no apparent connection between the passive acceptance of life as it always has been and the manipulation of society by a succession of dictators. In his next novel, *Chronicle of a Death Foretold* (1981), he describes the same inertia in a small town where everyday life continues its ordinary gossipy routine around two life-shattering events: the rejection of Angela Vicario by her new husband when he finds she is not a virgin, and her brothers' murder of the local dandy whom she names (probably falsely) as her seducer. Against the background of a whole society's passive complicity in a murder that everyone knows will happen, it is death and love that are the two overriding realities.

In recent years—questioning the effectiveness of literature to remedy the social ills he so often describes—García Márquez has been more and more active politically, speaking out for revolutionary governments in Latin America and organizing assistance for political prisoners. Living in Mexico City, he continues to write, including a number of stories that are still unpublished and an account of Cuba under the U.S. blockade. He received the Nobel Prize for literature in 1982.

The story printed here, *Death Constant Beyond Love* (1970), also has a political background although its protagonist, Senator Onésimo Sánchez, is seen chiefly as he struggles with his elemental problem of death. He is no hero: in *Innocent Eréndira* he writes a letter vouching for the grandmother's morality, and in this story he is clearly a corrupt politician who accepts bribes and stays in power by helping the local property owners avoid reform. His electoral train is a traveling circus with carnival wagons, fireworks, a readymade audience of hired Indians, and a cardboard village with imitation brick houses and a painted ocean liner to offer the illusion of future prosperity; he uses carefully placed gifts to encourage support and a feeling of dependence.

Yet the background of poverty and corruption, the entertaining spectacle of the

2054 / GABRIEL GARCÍA MÁRQUEZ

senator's "fictional world," and the political campaign itself fade into insignificance before broader themes of life and death. Forty-two, happily married, in full control of his own and others' lives as a successful politician in midcareer, he is made to feel suddenly helpless, vulnerable, and alone when told that all this will stop and he will be dead "forever" by next Christmas. Theoretically, he knows that death is inevitable and nature cannot be defeated. He has read the Stoic philosopher Marcus Aurelius (A.D. 121–180) and even refers to the *Meditations*, which recommends the cheerful acceptance of natural order (including death and oblivion), criticizes the delusions of those "who have tenaciously stuck to life," and stresses both the tranquil "ordering of the mind" and the idea that human beings are all "fellow-citizens" of a shared "political community." The example of the philosopher is not mere chance: Marcus Aurelius was also a political figure, a Roman emperor who wrote his *Meditations* as personal guidelines in a time of plague and political unrest.

The senator does gain some Stoic insight into the illusions of his career: he notices how similar are the dusty village and the worn cardboard facade that represents its hopes, and he is fed up with what he recognizes to be background maneuverings that keep him in power by prolonging the exploitation of the poor. But he also loses sympathy for the barefoot Indians standing in the square, and his newly alienated perspective is not accompanied by the Stoic injunction to maintain a just and ordered mind and to accept everything that happens as necessary and good. In this crisis, the senator is reduced to a basic and instinctual existence, expressed in García Márquez's recurrent themes of solitude, love, and death. The beautiful Laura provides an opportunity for him to sublimate his fear of death in erotic passion (inextricably intertwined, according to Freud). His choice means scandal and the destruction of his political career, but by now Onésimo Sánchez has felt the emptiness of his earlier activities and is engaged in a struggle to cheat death.

He does not succeed, of course, and dies weeping with rage that death separates him from Laura Farina. *Death Constant Beyond Love* has reversed the ambitious claim of a famous sonnet by the Spanish Golden Age writer Quevedo (1580–1645), according to which there is "Love Constant Beyond Death." Such love is an illusion, for it is death that awaits us beyond everything else. García Márquez repeatedly plays on these oppositions and inversions when he describes the real village and the cardboard version created by false political promises, the paper birds that magically take on life and fly out to sea, the paper butterfly that seems to fly and lands on the wall, the bribery money that flaps around like butterflies, the grotesquely padlocked chastity belt that Laura Farina wears, and even the initial opposition between the senator's living rose (symbol of womanhood and love) and the roseless town (named "The Viceroy's Rosebush") where he encounters his destiny. His destiny is to be liberated from some illusions but not all: his final delusion is to try to hide from death in erotic love. The senator's defeat at the end, which is clearly emphasized as a defeat, suggests that his response was a futile retreat, and—at the same time that it evokes pity for his loneliness, terror, and rage—puts in question what that response should be.

Regina Janes, *Gabriel García Márquez, Revolutions in Wonderland* (1981), is an excellent general study on García Márquez in a Latin American context. Other useful introductions to the writer and his work are George P. McMurray, *Gabriel García Márquez* (1977), and Robin W. Fiddian, *García Márquez* (1995). The summer 1972 issue of *Books Abroad* is dedicated to García Márquez. Harley D. Oberhelman, ed., *Gabriel Garcia Márquez: A Study of the Short Fiction* (1991), includes a bibliography.

Death Constant Beyond Love[1]

Senator Onésimo Sánchez had six months and eleven days to go before his death when he found the woman of his life. He met her in Rosal del Virrey,[2] an illusory village which by night was the furtive wharf for smugglers' ships, and on the other hand, in broad daylight looked like the most useless inlet on the desert, facing a sea that was arid and without direction and so far from everything no one would have suspected that someone capable of changing the destiny of anyone lived there. Even its name was a kind of joke, because the only rose in that village was being worn by Senator Onésimo Sánchez himself on the same afternoon when he met Laura Farina.

It was an unavoidable stop in the electoral campaign he made every four years. The carnival wagons had arrived in the morning. Then came the trucks with the rented Indians[3] who were carried into the towns in order to enlarge the crowds at public ceremonies. A short time before eleven o'clock, along with the music and rockets and jeeps of the retinue, the ministerial automobile, the color of strawberry soda, arrived. Senator Onésimo Sánchez was placid and weatherless inside the air-conditioned car, but as soon as he opened the door he was shaken by a gust of fire and his shirt of pure silk was soaked in a kind of light-colored soup and he felt many years older and more alone than ever. In real life he had just turned forty-two, had been graduated from Göttingen[4] with honors as a metallurgical engineer, and was an avid reader, although without much reward, of badly translated Latin classics. He was married to a radiant German woman who had given him five children and they were all happy in their home, he the happiest of all until they told him, three months before, that he would be dead forever by next Christmas.

While the preparations for the public rally were being completed, the senator managed to have an hour alone in the house they had set aside for him to rest in. Before he lay down he put in a glass of drinking water the rose he had kept alive all across the desert, lunched on the diet cereals that he took with him so as to avoid the repeated portions of fried goat that were waiting for him during the rest of the day, and he took several analgesic pills before the time prescribed so that he would have the remedy ahead of the pain. Then he put the electric fan close to the hammock and stretched out naked for fifteen minutes in the shadow of the rose, making a great effort at mental distraction so as not to think about death while he dozed. Except for the doctors, no one knew that he had been sentenced to a fixed term, for he had decided to endure his secret all alone, with no change in his life, not because of pride but out of shame.[5]

He felt in full control of his will when he appeared in public again at three in the afternoon, rested and clean, wearing a pair of coarse linen slacks and a floral shirt, and with his soul sustained by the anti-pain pills. Nevertheless, the erosion of death was much more pernicious than he had supposed, for as he went up onto the platform he felt a strange disdain for those who were

1. Translated by Gregory Rabassa.   2. The Rosebush of the Viceroy (governor).   3. People descended from the original inhabitants of the continent; generally poorer and less privileged than those descended from Spanish or Portuguese colonists.   4. A well-known German university.   5. "Death is such as generation is, a mystery of nature . . . altogether not a thing of which any man should be ashamed" (Marcus Aurelius, *Meditations* 4.5).

fighting for the good luck to shake his hand, and he didn't feel sorry as he had at other times for the groups of barefoot Indians who could scarcely bear the hot saltpeter coals of the sterile little square. He silenced the applause with a wave of his hand, almost with rage, and he began to speak without gestures, his eyes fixed on the sea, which was sighing with heat. His measured, deep voice had the quality of calm water, but the speech that had been memorized and ground out so many times had not occurred to him in the nature of telling the truth, but, rather, as the opposite of a fatalistic pronouncement by Marcus Aurelius in the fourth book of his *Meditations*.

"We are here for the purpose of defeating nature," he began, against all his convictions. "We will no longer be foundlings in our own country, orphans of God in a realm of thirst and bad climate, exiles in our own land. We will be different people, ladies and gentlemen, we will be a great and happy people."

There was a pattern to his circus. As he spoke his aides threw clusters of paper birds into the air and the artificial creatures took on life, flew about the platform of planks, and went out to sea. At the same time, other men took some prop trees with felt leaves out of the wagons and planted them in the saltpeter soil behind the crowd. They finished by setting up a cardboard façade with make-believe houses of red brick that had glass windows, and with it they covered the miserable real-life shacks.

The senator prolonged his speech with two quotations in Latin in order to give the farce more time. He promised rainmaking machines, portable breeders for table animals, the oils of happiness which would make vegetables grow in the saltpeter and clumps of pansies in the window boxes. When he saw that his fictional world was all set up, he pointed to it. "That's the way it will be for us, ladies and gentlemen," he shouted. "Look! That's the way it will be for us."

The audience turned around. An ocean liner made of painted paper was passing behind the houses and it was taller than the tallest houses in the artificial city. Only the senator himself noticed that since it had been set up and taken down and carried from one place to another the superimposed cardboard town had been eaten away by the terrible climate and that it was almost as poor and dusty as Rosal del Virrey.

For the first time in twelve years, Nelson Farina didn't go to greet the senator. He listened to the speech from his hammock amidst the remains of his siesta, under the cool bower of a house of unplaned boards which he had built with the same pharmacist's hands with which he had drawn and quartered his first wife. He had escaped from Devil's Island[6] and appeared in Rosal del Virrey on a ship loaded with innocent macaws, with a beautiful and blasphemous black woman he had found in Paramaribo[7] and by whom he had a daughter. The woman died of natural causes a short while later and she didn't suffer the fate of the other, whose pieces had fertilized her own cauliflower patch, but was buried whole and with her Dutch name in the local cemetery. The daughter had inherited her color and her figure along with her father's yellow and astonished eyes, and he had good reason to imagine that he was rearing the most beautiful woman in the world.

6. A former French penal colony off the coast of French Guiana in northern South America.   7. Capital of Suriname (formerly Dutch Guiana) and a large port.

Ever since he had met Senator Onésimo Sánchez during his first electoral campaign, Nelson Farina had begged for his help in getting a false identity card which would place him beyond the reach of the law. The senator, in a friendly but firm way, had refused. Nelson Farina never gave up, and for several years, every time he found the chance, he would repeat his request with a different recourse. But this time he stayed in his hammock, condemned to rot alive in that burning den of buccaneers. When he heard the final applause, he lifted his head, and looking over the boards of the fence, he saw the back side of the farce: the props for the buildings, the framework of the trees, the hidden illusionists who were pushing the ocean liner along. He spat without rancor.

"*Merde*," he said. "*C'est le Blacamán de la politique.*"[8]

After the speech, as was customary, the senator took a walk through the streets of the town in the midst of the music and the rockets and was besieged by the townspeople, who told him their troubles. The senator listened to them good-naturedly and he always found some way to console everybody without having to do them any difficult favors. A woman up on the roof of a house with her six youngest children managed to make herself heard over the uproar and the fireworks.

"I'm not asking for much, Senator," she said. "Just a donkey to haul water from Hanged Man's Well."

The senator noticed the six thin children. "What became of your husband?" he asked.

"He went to find his fortune on the island of Aruba,"[9] the woman answered good-humoredly, "and what he found was a foreign woman, the kind that put diamonds on their teeth."

The answer brought on a roar of laughter.

"All right," the senator decided, "you'll get your donkey."

A short while later an aide of his brought a good pack donkey to the woman's house and on the rump it had a campaign slogan written in indelible paint so that no one would ever forget that it was a gift from the senator.

Along the short stretch of street he made other, smaller gestures, and he even gave a spoonful of medicine to a sick man who had had his bed brought to the door of his house so he could see him pass. At the last corner, through the boards of the fence, he saw Nelson Farina in his hammock, looking ashen and gloomy, but nonetheless the senator greeted him, with no show of affection.

"Hello, how are you?"

Nelson Farina turned in his hammock and soaked him in the sad amber of his look.

"*Moi, vous savez,*"[1] he said.

His daughter came out into the yard when she heard the greeting. She was wearing a cheap, faded Guajiro Indian[2] robe, her head was decorated with colored bows, and her face was painted as protection against the sun, but even in that state of disrepair it was possible to imagine that there had

8. Shit. He's the Blacamán of politics (French). Blacamán is a charlatan and huckster who appears in several stories, including *Blacamán the Good, Vendor of Miracles*.   9. Off the coast of Venezuela, famous as a tourist resort.   1. Oh well, as for me, you know (French).   2. Inhabitant of the rural Guajira Peninsula of northern Colombia. The figure of Laura Farina is thus connected with the rustic poor, with earthy reality (*farina* means "flour"), and with erotic inspiration. (*Laura* was the beloved celebrated by the Italian Renaissance poet Francis Petrarch, 1304–1374.)

never been another so beautiful in the whole world. The senator was left breathless. "I'll be damned!" he breathed in surprise. "The Lord does the craziest things!"

That night Nelson Farina dressed his daughter up in her best clothes and sent her to the senator. Two guards armed with rifles who were nodding from the heat in the borrowed house ordered her to wait on the only chair in the vestibule.

The senator was in the next room meeting with the important people of Rosal del Virrey, whom he had gathered together in order to sing for them the truths he had left out of his speeches. They looked so much like all the ones he always met in all the towns in the desert that even the senator himself was sick and tired of that perpetual nightly session. His shirt was soaked with sweat and he was trying to dry it on his body with the hot breeze from an electric fan that was buzzing like a horse fly in the heavy heat of the room.

"We, of course, can't eat paper birds," he said. "You and I know that the day there are trees and flowers in this heap of goat dung, the day there are shad instead of worms in the water holes, that day neither you nor I will have anything to do here, do I make myself clear?"

No one answered. While he was speaking, the senator had torn a sheet off the calendar and fashioned a paper butterfly out of it with his hands. He tossed it with no particular aim into the air current coming from the fan and the butterfly flew about the room and then went out through the half-open door. The senator went on speaking with a control aided by the complicity of death.

"Therefore," he said, "I don't have to repeat to you what you already know too well: that my reelection is a better piece of business for you than it is for me, because I'm fed up with stagnant water and Indian sweat, while you people, on the other hand, make your living from it."

Laura Farina saw the paper butterfly come out. Only she saw it because the guards in the vestibule had fallen asleep on the steps, hugging their rifles. After a few turns, the large lithographed butterfly unfolded completely, flattened against the wall, and remained stuck there. Laura Farina tried to pull it off with her nails. One of the guards, who woke up with the applause from the next room, noticed her vain attempt.

"It won't come off," he said sleepily. "It's painted on the wall."

Laura Farina sat down again when the men began to come out of the meeting. The senator stood in the doorway of the room with his hand on the latch, and he only noticed Laura Farina when the vestibule was empty.

"What are you doing here?"

"C'est de la part de mon père,"[3] she said.

The senator understood. He scrutinized the sleeping guards, then he scrutinized Laura Farina, whose unusual beauty was even more demanding than his pain, and he resolved then that death had made his decision for him.

"Come in," he told her.

Laura Farina was struck dumb standing in the doorway to the room: thousands of bank notes were floating in the air, flapping like the butterfly. But the senator turned off the fan and the bills were left without air and alighted on the objects in the room.

3. My father sent me (French).

"You see," he said, smiling, "even shit can fly."

Laura Farina sat down on a schoolboy's stool. Her skin was smooth and firm, with the same color and the same solar density as crude oil, her hair was the mane of a young mare, and her huge eyes were brighter than the light. The senator followed the thread of her look and finally found the rose, which had been tarnished by the saltpeter.

"It's a rose," he said.

"Yes," she said with a trace of perplexity. "I learned what they were in Riohacha."[4]

The senator sat down on an army cot, talking about roses as he unbuttoned his shirt. On the side where he imagined his heart to be inside his chest he had a corsair's tattoo of a heart pierced by an arrow. He threw the soaked shirt to the floor and asked Laura Farina to help him off with his boots.

She knelt down facing the cot. The senator continued to scrutinize her, thoughtfully, and while he was untying the laces he wondered which one of them would end up with the bad luck of that encounter.

"You're just a child," he said.

"Don't you believe it," she said. "I'll be nineteen in April."

The senator became interested.

"What day?"

"The eleventh," she said.

The senator felt better. "We're both Aries,"[5] he said. And smiling, he added:

"It's the sign of solitude."

Laura Farina wasn't paying attention because she didn't know what to do with the boots. The senator, for his part, didn't know what to do with Laura Farina, because he wasn't used to sudden love affairs and, besides, he knew that the one at hand had its origins in indignity. Just to have some time to think, he held Laura Farina tightly between his knees, embraced her about the waist, and lay down on his back on the cot. Then he realized that she was naked under her dress, for her body gave off the dark fragrance of an animal of the woods, but her heart was frightened and her skin disturbed by a glacial sweat.

"No one loves us," he sighed.

Laura Farina tried to say something, but there was only enough air for her to breathe. He laid her down beside him to help her, he put out the light and the room was in the shadow of the rose. She abandoned herself to the mercies of her fate. The senator caressed her slowly, seeking her with his hand, barely touching her, but where he expected to find her, he came across something iron that was in the way.

"What have you got there?"

"A padlock,"[6] she said.

"What in hell!" the senator said furiously and asked what he knew only too well. "Where's the key?"

Laura Farina gave a breath of relief.

"My papa has it," she answered. "He told me to tell you to send one of

---

4. A port on the Guajira Peninsula.   5. The first sign in the zodiac; people born between March 21 and April 19 are said to be under the sign of Aries.   6. She is wearing a chastity belt, a medieval device worn by women to prevent sexual intercourse.

your people to get it and to send along with him a written promise that you'll straighten out his situation."

The senator grew tense. "Frog[7] bastard," he murmured indignantly. Then he closed his eyes in order to relax and he met himself in the darkness. *Remember*, he remembered, *that whether it's you or someone else, it won't be long before you'll be dead and it won't be long before your name won't even be left.*[8]

He waited for the shudder to pass.

"Tell me one thing," he asked then. "What have you heard about me?"

"Do you want the honest-to-God truth?"

"The honest-to-God truth."

"Well," Laura Farina ventured, "they say you're worse than the rest because you're different."

The senator didn't get upset. He remained silent for a long time with his eyes closed, and when he opened them again he seemed to have returned from his most hidden instincts.

"Oh, what the hell," he decided. "Tell your son of a bitch of a father that I'll straighten out his situation."

"If you want, I can go get the key myself," Laura Farina said.

The senator held her back.

"Forget about the key," he said, "and sleep awhile with me. It's good to be with someone when you're so alone."

Then she laid his head on her shoulder with her eyes fixed on the rose. The senator held her about the waist, sank his face into woods-animal armpit, and gave in to terror. Six months and eleven days later he would die in that same position, debased and repudiated because of the public scandal with Laura Farina and weeping with rage at dying without her.

---

7. Epithet for "French."   8. A direct translation of a sentence from Marcus Aurelius's *Meditations* (4.6).

CHINUA ACHEBE
born 1930

The best-known African writer today is the Nigerian Chinua Achebe, whose first novel, *Things Fall Apart*, exploded the colonialist image of Africans as childlike people living in a primitive society. Achebe's novels, stories, poetry, and essays have made him a respected and prophetic figure in Africa. In Western countries, where he has traveled, taught, and lectured widely, he is admired as a major writer who has given an entirely new direction to the English-language novel. Achebe has created not only the African postcolonial novel with its new themes and characters but also a complex narrative point of view that questions cultural images—including its own—with a subtle irony and compassion born from bicultural experience. His vantage point is different from that of Doris Lessing or Albert Camus, two authors whose work is also concerned with African experience: Achebe writes, as he says, "from the inside." For him as for many other writers in this volume, literature is important because it liberates the human imagination; it "begins as an adventure in self-discovery and ends in wisdom and human conscience."

Chinua Achebe was born in the town of Ogidi, an Igbo-speaking town of Eastern Nigeria, on November 16, 1930. He was the fifth of six children in the family of Isaiah Okafor Achebe, a teacher for the Church Missionary Society, and his wife, Janet. Achebe's parents christened him Albert after Prince Albert, husband of Queen Victoria. When he entered the university the author rejected his British name in favor of his indigenous name Chinua, which abbreviates Chinualumogu, or "My spirit come fight for me." Achebe's novels offer a picture of Igbo society with its fierce egalitarianism and "town meeting" debates. Two cultures coexisted in Ogidi: on the one hand, African social customs and traditional religion, and on the other, British colonial authority and Christianity. Instead of being torn between the two, Achebe found himself curious about both ways of life and fascinated with the dual perspective that came from living "at the crossroads of cultures."

He attended Church schools in Ogidi where instruction was carried out in English after the first two years. Achebe read the various books in his father's library, most of them primers or Church related, but he also listened eagerly to his mother and sister when they told traditional Igbo stories. Entering a prestigious government college (secondary school) in Umuahia, he immediately took advantage of its well-stocked library. Achebe later commented on the crucial importance of books in creating writers and committed readers, noting that private secondary schools had few if any books and that almost all the first generation of Nigerian writers—including himself and Wole Soyinka (born 1934)—had gone to a government college.

After graduating in 1948, Achebe entered University College, Ibadan, on a scholarship to study medicine. In the following year he changed to a program in liberal arts that combined English, history, and religious studies. Research in the last two fields deepened his knowledge of Nigerian history and culture; the assigned literary texts, however, brought into sharp focus the distorted image of African culture offered by British colonial literature. Reading Joyce Cary's *Mister Johnson* (1939), a novel recommended for its depiction of life in Nigeria, he was shocked to find Nigerians described as violent savages with passionate instincts and simple minds: "and so I thought if this was famous, then perhaps someone ought to try and look at this from the inside." He began writing while at the university, contributing articles and sketches to several campus papers and publishing four stories in the *University Herald,* a magazine whose editor he became in his third year.

Upon receiving his B.A. in 1953, Achebe joined the Nigerian Broadcasting Service, working in the Talks Section and traveling to London in 1956 to attend the British Broadcasting Corporation Staff School. Promotions came quickly; he was named head of the Talks Section in 1957, controller of the Eastern Region Stations in 1959, and in 1961 director of External Services in charge of the Voice of Nigeria. The radio position was more than a merely administrative post, for Achebe and his colleagues were working to create a sense of shared national identity through broadcasting national news and information about Nigerian culture. Ever since the end of World War II, Nigeria had been torn by intellectual and political rivalries that overlaid the common struggle for independence (achieved in 1960). The three major ethnolinguistic groups—Yoruba, Hausa-Fulani, and Igbo (once spelled Ibo)—were increasingly locked in economic and political rivalry at the same time they were fighting to erase the vestiges of British colonial rule. These problems eventually boiled over in the Nigerian Civil War (1967–70). The persistence of political corruption is depicted in *A Man of the People* (1966) and *Anthills of the Savannah* (1987).

Achebe is convinced of the writer's social responsibility, and he draws frequent contrasts between the European "art for art's sake" tradition and an African belief in the indivisibility of art and society. His favorite example is the Owerri Igbo custom of *mbari,* a communal art project in which villagers selected by the priest of the earth goddess Ala live in a forest clearing for a year or more, working under the direction of master artists to prepare a temple of images in the goddess's honor. This creative communal enterprise and its culminating festival are diametrically opposed, he says, to the European custom of secluding art objects in museums or private collections. Instead, *mbari* celebrates art as a cultural process, affirming that "art belongs to all and is a 'function' of society." Achebe's own practice as novelist, poet, essayist, founder and editor of two journals, lecturer, and active representative of African letters exemplifies this commitment to the community.

His first novel, *Things Fall Apart* (1958), was a conscious attempt to counteract the distortions of Cary's *Mister Johnson* by describing the richness and complexity of traditional African society before the colonial and missionary invasion. It was important, Achebe said, to "teach my readers that their past—with all its imperfections— was not one long night of savagery from which the first Europeans acting on God's behalf delivered them." The novel was recognized immediately as an extraordinary work of literature in English. It also became the first classic work of modern African fiction, translated into nine languages, and Achebe became for many readers and writers the teacher of a whole generation. In 1959 he received the Margaret Wrong Memorial Prize, and in 1960—after the publication of a sequel, *No Longer at Ease*— he received the Nigerian National Trophy for literature. His later novels continue to examine the individual and cultural dilemmas of Nigerian society, although their background varies from the traditional religious society of *Arrow of God* (1964) to thinly disguised accounts of contemporary political strife.

Achebe's reputation as the "father of the African novel in English" does not depend solely on his accounts of Nigerian society. In contrast with writers such as Ngugi wa Thiong'o (b. 1938), who insist that the contemporary African writer has a moral obligation to write in one of the tribal languages, Achebe maintains his right to compose in the English he has used since his school days. His literary language is an English skillfully blended with Igbo vocabulary, proverbs, images, and speech patterns to create a new voice embodying the linguistic pluralism of modern African experience. By including standard English, Igbo, and pidgin in different contexts, Achebe demonstrates the existence of a diverse society that is otherwise concealed behind language barriers—a culture, he suggests, that escaped colonial officials who wrote about African character without ever understanding the language. He also thereby acknowledges that his primary African audience is composed of younger, schooled readers who are relatively fluent in English.

It is hard to overestimate the influence of Nigerian politics on Achebe's life after 1966. In January, a military coup d'état led by young Igbo officers overthrew the government; six months later, a second coup led by non-Igbo officers took power. Ethnic rivalries intensified: thousands of Igbos were killed and driven out of the north. Achebe and his family fled the capital of Lagos when soldiers were sent to find him, and the novelist became a senior research fellow at the University of Nigeria, Nsukka (in Eastern Nigeria). In May 1967 the eastern region, mainly populated by Igbo-speakers, seceded as the new nation of Biafra. From then on until the defeat of Biafra in January 1970, a bloody civil war was waged with high civilian casualties and widespread starvation. Achebe traveled in Europe, North America, and Africa to win support for Biafra, proclaiming that "no government, black or white, has the right to stigmatize and destroy groups of its own citizens without undermining the basis of its own existence." A group of his poems about the war won the Commonwealth Poetry Prize in 1972, the same year that he published a volume of short stories, *Girls at War*, and left Nigeria to take up a three-year position at the University of Massachusetts at Amherst. Returning to Nsukka as professor of literature in 1976, Achebe continued to participate in his country's political life. He published an attack on the corrupt leadership in *The Trouble with Nigeria* (1983) and—drawing on circumstances surrounding a fifth military coup in 1985—produced his fifth novel, *Anthills of the Savannah*, in 1987. Although it reiterates Achebe's familiar indictment of ruthless politicians, alienated intellectuals, and those who accept dictatorship as a route to reform, this novel offers hope for the future through a return to the people and a symbolic child born at the end: a girl child with a boy's name, "May the Path Never

Close." Badly hurt in a car accident the year after *Anthills* was published, Achebe slowly recovered and returned to his writing. He currently teaches at Bard College.

A predominant theme in Achebe's novels and essays is the notion of balance or interdependence: balance between earth and sky, individual and community, man and woman, or different perspectives on the same situation. Igbo thought is fundamentally dualistic, the novelist explains: "Wherever Something stands, Something Else will stand beside it. Nothing is absolute." Extremes carry the seeds of destruction. Indeed, destruction follows in Achebe's novels whenever balance is disturbed: when Okonkwo in *Things Fall Apart* represses any signs of "female" softness; when the priest Ezeulu in *Arrow of God* is imprisoned and refuses to authorize the feast of the New Yam, without which his people cannot plant their crops; and when, in later books, the lust for power and possessions blinds Nigerian leaders to the needs of the people.

The fundamental image of this balance is contained in the Igbo concept of *chi*, which recurs throughout Achebe's work. *Chi* is a personal deity, a fragment of the supreme being unique for each individual. A person's *chi*, says Achebe, may be visualized "as his other identity in spirit-land—his *spirit being* complementing his terrestrial *human being*." It is both all-powerful and subject to persuasion: "When a man says yes his *chi* says yes also," but at the same time "a man does not challenge his *chi* to a wrestling match." *Chi* is simultaneously destiny and an internal commitment that cannot be denied, a religious concept and also a picture of psychic harmony. Both aspects are linked throughout Achebe's novels, beginning with *Things Fall Apart*. In killing Ikemefuna, whom he loves and who calls him father, Okonkwo sins not only against the earth goddess, protector of family relations, but also against his inmost feelings and thus against his *chi*. If Okonkwo's destiny (*chi*) is marked by bad luck, one reason may be that—driven by fear of resembling his father—he struggles to repress part of his personality (*chi*), with predictably ill results. In the final assessment, no one can fully explain *chi*: it is mysteriously uncertain, the element of fate over which we have no real control.

Things Fall Apart is both Okonkwo's tragedy and that of his society. The title (taken from William Butler Yeats's *The Second Coming*) introduces a narrative in which a complex and dignified traditional society disintegrates before foreign invaders who assault its political, economic, and religious institutions. The setting is eastern Nigeria around the turn of the century in the clan of Umuofia, which is composed of nine interrelated villages. One of these villages, Iguedo, is the home of the protagonist Okonkwo, an ambitious and powerful man who is driven by the memory of his father's failure and weakness.

During the first two-thirds of the book, Achebe paints the picture of a rich and coherent society, establishing an image of traditional African culture into which the final chapters' missionaries, court messengers, and district commissioner intrude as alien and disruptive elements. In sharp contrast to the simplified vision of African life given by European novelists Joyce Cary, Joseph Conrad, or Graham Greene, he explores the complex feelings and interpersonal relationships of diverse villagers seen as men, women, parents, children, friends, neighbors, or priests of the local deities. The intricate patterns of Umuofia's economic and social customs also emerge, belying European images of African "primitive" simplicity. No one who has read about Obierika's intricate marriage negotiations, the etiquette of *kola* hospitality, the religious "week of peace," Ezeudu's elaborate funeral rites, the domestic arbitration conducted by the *egwugwu* court, the female kinship customs linking families and villages, or indeed Umuofia's entire set of taboos and punishments will find this a simple society. The title system itself, which plays such a large part in the novel, is an ingenious social strategy for redistributing wealth throughout the community. The four honorific *ozo* titles (*Ozo, Idemili, Omalo*, and *Erulu*), through which a man enters the spiritual community of his ancestors and achieves increasing levels of prestige, are acquired in festivities during which the candidate divests himself of excess material wealth. There is a dignity and purpose to this society despite inner tensions that—as Achebe shows—create pain as well as vulnerability to attack from outside. The moderate Obierika disapproves of killing Ikemefuna and begins to question the practice of throwing away twins; one of the first converts to Christianity is a woman who gave birth to several sets of twins, all of whom were exposed (left in the wild) at birth. The general subordination of women is another source of tensions that have taken longer to surface. Whatever its cultural differences from European society, however, this is a highly organized and complex society that offers a great deal of continuity and coherence to its members.

Igbo names, like names throughout black Africa, consist of whole phrases or sentences. Some names are dictated by circumstance (referring to the day of birth, for example) and some (the "given" name selected by the child's father, for example) reflect the family situation or a child's expected destiny. Adults may earn additional titles of honor. Achebe uses the connotations of personal names to reinforce important themes in *Things Fall Apart*. Okonkwo's father's character as a lazy, artistic, and improvident man is suggested by the name Unoka, signifying "the home is supreme." Okonkwo's son Nwoye, who has inherited his grandfather's peace-loving nature and artistic qualities, is named after the second day of the Igbo week (*Oye*); unlike Okonkwo, Nwoye lacks a prefix specifying adulthood or even gender, for *Nwa* means "child." Ikemefuna, who is condemned to death by the Oracle and will be killed by his adoptive father, is named "My strength should not be dissipated." Although all names have significance, only those with some relevance to the story will be annotated in this edition.

Okonkwo's character and career suggest epic dimensions. He is on the one hand a hero of enormous energy and determination, "one of the greatest men in Umuofia" as his friend Obierika says, but his particular mode of greatness also causes his downfall. Like Achilles in Homer's *Iliad*, Okonkwo clings to traditionally respected values of pride and warlike aggression, and he will die to preserve those values. His unwillingness to change sets him apart from the community and eventually isolates him from the clan with its emphasis on group decisions. Okonkwo is a passionate man who counts on physical strength, hard work, and courage to make his way. Humiliated by his father's laziness, shameful death, and lack of title, compelled early to support the entire family, he struggles desperately to root out any sign of inherited "feminine" weakness in himself or his son Nwoye. By cultivating strength and valor, he finds a way to surpass his father and become one of the village leaders. Okonkwo is not without tender feelings: he loves his wife Ekwefi; his daughter, Ezinma; and the youth Ikemefuna who is given to him to foster. When he cuts down Ikemefuna so as not to appear weak, he is shattered for days thereafter. Nonetheless, his obsession with fierce masculinity and his open disrespect for "womanly" qualities of gentleness, compassion, and peace separate him not only from other members of his clan such as the more balanced Obierika but also from the earth goddess herself. This imbalance leads to disaster.

A recent and full biography is Ezenwa Ohaeto, *Chinua Achebe: A Biography* (1997). C. L. Innes, *Chinua Achebe* (1990), is a comprehensive study of Achebe's work through 1988 that emphasizes his literary techniques and Africanization of the novel. Simon Gikandi, *Reading Chinua Achebe: Language and Ideology in Fiction* (1991), is also recommended. Robert M. Wren, *Achebe's World: The Historical and Cultural Context of the Novels of Chinua Achebe* (1980), provides historical background and cultural context for Achebe's novels and includes glossary and bibliography. Studies of *Things Fall Apart* include Kate Turkington, *Chinua Achebe: Things Fall Apart* (1977), a concise introductory study; and the nine essays in Solomon Ogbede Iyasere, ed., *Understanding Things Fall Apart: Selected Essays and Criticism* (1998). C. L. Innes and Bernth Lindfors, eds., *Critical Perspectives on Chinua Achebe*, (1978), collect twenty-one essays on Achebe's work (almost exclusively the novels) through 1973. G. D. Killam, *The Writings of Chinua Achebe* (1977), is a commentary on

Achebe's work through the mid-1970s, concentrating on the first four novels. Also of interest is Chinua Achebe, *Conversations with Chinua Achebe* (1997), ed. Bernth Lindfors.

PRONOUNCING GLOSSARY

The following list uses common English syllables and stress accents to provide rough equivalents of selected words whose pronunciation may be unfamiliar to the general reader. Most of the names in *Things Fall Apart* are pronounced basically as they would be in English (for example, Okonkwo as *oh-kon'-kwo*), except that Igbo (like other African languages and Chinese) is a tonal language and also uses high or low tones for individual syllables.

Chielo: *chee'-ay-loh*

Chinua Achebe: *chin'-oo-ah ah-chay'-bay*

egwugwu: *eg-woog'-woo*

Erulu: *air-oo'-loo*

Ezeani: *ez-ah'-nee*

Ezeugo: *e'-zoo-goh*

Idemili: *ee-day-mee'lee*

Igbo: *ee'-boh*

Ikemefuna: *ee-kay-may'-foo-na*

mbari: *mbah'-ree*

Ndulue: *in'-doo-loo'-eh*

Nwakibie: *nwa'-kee-ee'-bee-yay*

Nwayieke: *nwah'-ee-eh'-kay*

Umuofia: *oo'-moo-off'-yah*

Things Fall Apart

Turning and turning in the widening gyre
The falcon cannot hear the falconer;
Things fall apart; the centre cannot hold;
Mere anarchy is loosed upon the world . . .
—W. B. Yeats, "The Second Coming"

Part One

1

Okonkwo[1] was well known throughout the nine villages and even beyond. His fame rested on solid personal achievements. As a young man of eighteen he had brought honor to his village by throwing Amalinze the Cat. Amalinze was the great wrestler who for seven years was unbeaten, from Umuofia to Mbaino.[2] He was called the Cat because his back would never touch the earth. It was this man that Okonkwo threw in a fight which the old men agreed was one of the fiercest since the founder of their town engaged a spirit of the wild for seven days and seven nights.

The drums beat and the flutes sang and the spectators held their breath. Amalinze was a wily craftsman, but Okonkwo was as slippery as a fish in water. Every nerve and every muscle stood out on their arms, on their backs and their thighs, and one almost heard them stretching to breaking point. In the end Okonkwo threw the Cat.

---

1. Man [*oko*] born on Nkwo Day; the name also suggests stubborn male pride.   2. Four settlements. Umuofia means children of the forest (literal trans.); but *ofia* ("forest") also means "bush" or land untouched by European influence.

That was many years ago, twenty years or more, and during this time Okonkwo's fame had grown like a bush-fire in the harmattan.[3] He was tall and huge, and his bushy eyebrows and wide nose gave him a very severe look. He breathed heavily, and it was said that, when he slept, his wives and children in their houses could hear him breathe. When he walked, his heels hardly touched the ground and he seemed to walk on springs, as if he was going to pounce on somebody. And he did pounce on people quite often. He had a slight stammer and whenever he was angry and could not get his words out quickly enough, he would use his fists. He had no patience with unsuccessful men. He had had no patience with his father.

Unoka,[4] for that was his father's name, had died ten years ago. In his day he was lazy and improvident and was quite incapable of thinking about tomorrow. If any money came his way, and it seldom did, he immediately bought gourds of palm-wine, called round his neighbors and made merry. He always said that whenever he saw a dead man's mouth he saw the folly of not eating what one had in one's lifetime. Unoka was, of course, a debtor, and he owed every neighbor some money, from a few cowries[5] to quite substantial amounts.

He was tall but very thin and had a slight stoop. He wore a haggard and mournful look except when he was drinking or playing on his flute. He was very good on his flute, and his happiest moments were the two or three moons after the harvest when the village musicians brought down their instruments, hung above the fireplace. Unoka would play with them, his face beaming with blessedness and peace. Sometimes another village would ask Unoka's band and their dancing egwugwu[6] to come and stay with them and teach them their tunes. They would go to such hosts for as long as three or four markets,[7] making music and feasting. Unoka loved the good fare and the good fellowship, and he loved this season of the year, when the rains had stopped and the sun rose every morning with dazzling beauty. And it was not too hot either, because the cold and dry harmattan wind was blowing down from the north. Some years the harmattan was very severe and a dense haze hung on the atmosphere. Old men and children would then sit round log fires, warming their bodies. Unoka loved it all, and he loved the first kites[8] that returned with the dry season, and the children who sang songs of welcome to them. He would remember his own childhood, how he had often wandered around looking for a kite sailing leisurely against the blue sky. As soon as he found one he would sing with his whole being, welcoming it back from its long, long journey, and asking it if it had brought home any lengths of cloth.

That was years ago, when he was young. Unoka, the grown-up, was a failure. He was poor and his wife and children had barely enough to eat. People laughed at him because he was a loafer, and they swore never to lend him any more money because he never paid back. But Unoka was such a man that he always succeeded in borrowing more, and piling up his debts.

3. A dusty wind from the Sahara.   4. Home is supreme.   5. Glossy half-inch-long tan-and-white shells, collected in strings and used as money. A bag of twenty-four thousand cowries weighed about sixty pounds and, at the time of the story, was worth approximately one British pound.   6. Here, masked performers as part of musical entertainment.   7. Counting one important market day a week, roughly two English weeks. The Igbo week has four days: Eke, Oye, Afo, and Nkwo. Eke is a rest day and the main market day; Afo, a half day on the farm; and Oye and Nkwo, full work days.   8. A kind of hawk.

One day a neighbor called Okoye[9] came in to see him. He was reclining on a mud bed in his hut playing on the flute. He immediately rose and shook hands with Okoye, who then unrolled the goatskin which he carried under his arm, and sat down. Unoka went into an inner room and soon returned with a small wooden disc containing a kola nut, some alligator pepper and a lump of white chalk.[1]

"I have kola," he announced when he sat down, and passed the disc over to his guest.

"Thank you. He who brings kola brings life. But I think you ought to break it," replied Okoye, passing back the disc.

"No, it is for you, I think," and they argued like this for a few moments before Unoka accepted the honor of breaking the kola. Okoye, meanwhile, took the lump of chalk, drew some lines on the floor, and then painted his big toe.[2]

As he broke the kola, Unoka prayed to their ancestors for life and health, and for protection against their enemies. When they had eaten they talked about many things: about the heavy rains which were drowning the yams, about the next ancestral feast and about the impending war with the village of Mbaino. Unoka was never happy when it came to wars. He was in fact a coward and could not bear the sight of blood. And so he changed the subject and talked about music, and his face beamed. He could hear in his mind's ear the blood-stirring and intricate rhythms of the *ekwe* and the *udu* and the *ogene*,[3] and he could hear his own flute weaving in and out of them, decorating them with a colorful and plaintive tune. The total effect was gay and brisk, but if one picked out the flute as it went up and down and then broke up into short snatches, one saw that there was sorrow and grief there.

Okoye was also a musician. He played on the *ogene*. But he was not a failure like Unoka. He had a large barn full of yams and he had three wives. And now he was going to take the Idemili title,[4] the third highest in the land. It was a very expensive ceremony and he was gathering all his resources together. That was in fact the reason why he had come to see Unoka. He cleared his throat and began:

"Thank you for the kola. You may have heard of the title I intend to take shortly."

Having spoken plainly so far, Okoye said the next half a dozen sentences in proverbs. Among the Ibo the art of conversation is regarded very highly, and proverbs are the palm-oil with which words are eaten. Okoye was a great talker and he spoke for a long time, skirting round the subject and then hitting it finally. In short, he was asking Unoka to return the two hundred cowries he had borrowed from him more than two years before. As soon as Unoka understood what his friend was driving at, he burst out laughing. He

---

9. Man born on Oye Day; a generic "Everyman" name.   1. Signifies coolness and peace and is offered in rituals of hospitality so that the guest may draw his personal emblem on the floor. *Kola nut:* a bitter, caffeine-rich nut that is broken and eaten ceremonially; it indicates life or vitality. *Alligator pepper:* black pepper, known as the "pepper for kola" to distinguish it from cooking pepper, or chilies.   2. If the guest has taken the first title, he marks his big toe. Higher titles require different facial markings.   3. A bell-shaped gong made from two pieces of sheet iron. *Ekwe:* a wooden drum, about three feet long, that produces high and low tones (as does the Igbo language). *Udu:* a clay pot with a hole to one side of the neck opening; various resonant tones are produced when the hole is struck with one hand while the other hand covers or uncovers the top.   4. A title of honor named after the river god Idemili, to whom the python is sacred. *Barn:* not a building, but a walled enclosure for the yam stacks (frames on which individual yams are tied, shaded with palm leaves, and exposed to circulating air).

laughed loud and long and his voice rang out clear as the *ogene,* and tears stood in his eyes. His visitor was amazed, and sat speechless. At the end, Unoka was able to give an answer between fresh outbursts of mirth.

"Look at that wall," he said, pointing at the far wall of his hut, which was rubbed with red earth so that it shone. "Look at those lines of chalk;" and Okoye saw groups of short perpendicular lines drawn in chalk. There were five groups, and the smallest group had ten lines. Unoka had a sense of the dramatic and so he allowed a pause, in which he took a pinch of snuff and sneezed noisily, and then he continued: "Each group there represents a debt to someone, and each stroke is one hundred cowries. You see, I owe that man a thousand cowries. But he has not come to wake me up in the morning for it. I shall pay you, but not today. Our elders say that the sun will shine on those who stand before it shines on those who kneel under them. I shall pay my big debts first." And he took another pinch of snuff, as if that was paying the big debts first. Okoye rolled his goatskin and departed.

When Unoka died he had taken no title at all and he was heavily in debt. Any wonder then that his son Okonkwo was ashamed of him? Fortunately, among these people a man was judged according to his worth and not according to the worth of his father. Okonkwo was clearly cut out for great things. He was still young but he had won fame as the greatest wrestler in the nine villages. He was a wealthy farmer and had two barns full of yams, and had just married his third wife. To crown it all he had taken two titles and had shown incredible prowess in two inter-tribal wars. And so although Okonkwo was still young, he was already one of the greatest men of his time. Age was respected among his people, but achievement was revered. As the elders said, if a child washed his hands he could eat with kings. Okonkwo had clearly washed his hands and so he ate with kings and elders. And that was how he came to look after the doomed lad who was sacrificed to the village of Umuofia by their neighbors to avoid war and bloodshed. The ill-fated lad was called Ikemefuna.[5]

2

Okonkwo had just blown out the palm-oil lamp and stretched himself on his bamboo bed when he heard the *ogene* of the town crier piercing the still night air. *Gome, gome, gome, gome,* boomed the hollow metal. Then the crier gave his message, and at the end of it beat his instrument again. And this was the message. Every man of Umuofia was asked to gather at the market place tomorrow morning. Okonkwo wondered what was amiss, for he knew certainly that something was amiss. He had discerned a clear overtone of tragedy in the crier's voice, and even now he could still hear it as it grew dimmer and dimmer in the distance.

The night was very quiet. It was always quiet except on moonlight nights. Darkness held a vague terror for these people, even the bravest among them. Children were warned not to whistle at night for fear of evil spirits. Dangerous animals became even more sinister and uncanny in the dark. A snake was never called by its name at night, because it would hear. It was called a string. And so on this particular night as the crier's voice was gradually swal-

---

5. My strength should not be dissipated.

lowed up in the distance, silence returned to the world, a vibrant silence made more intense by the universal trill of a million million forest insects.

On a moonlight night it would be different. The happy voices of children playing in open fields would then be heard. And perhaps those not so young would be playing in pairs in less open places, and old men and women would remember their youth. As the Ibo say: "When the moon is shining the cripple becomes hungry for a walk."

But this particular night was dark and silent. And in all the nine villages of Umuofia a town crier with his *ogene* asked every man to be present tomorrow morning. Okonkwo on his bamboo bed tried to figure out the nature of the emergency—war with a neighboring clan? That seemed the most likely reason, and he was not afraid of war. He was a man of action, a man of war. Unlike his father he could stand the look of blood. In Umuofia's latest war he was the first to bring home a human head. That was his fifth head; and he was not an old man yet. On great occasions such as the funeral of a village celebrity he drank his palm-wine from his first human head.

In the morning the market place was full. There must have been about ten thousand men there, all talking in low voices. At last Ogbuefi Ezeugo stood up in the midst of them and bellowed four times, *"Umuofia kwenu,"*[6] and on each occasion he faced a different direction and seemed to push the air with a clenched fist. And ten thousand men answered *"Yaa!"* each time. Then there was perfect silence. Ogbuefi Ezeugo was a powerful orator and was always chosen to speak on such occasions. He moved his hand over his white head and stroked his white beard. He then adjusted his cloth, which was passed under his right armpit and tied above his left shoulder.

"Umuofia kwenu," he bellowed a fifth time, and the crowd yelled in answer. And then suddenly like one possessed he shot out his left hand and pointed in the direction of Mbaino, and said through gleaming white teeth firmly clenched: "Those sons of wild animals have dared to murder a daughter of Umuofia." He threw his head down and gnashed his teeth, and allowed a murmur of suppressed anger to sweep the crowd. When he began again, the anger on his face was gone and in its place a sort of smile hovered, more terrible and more sinister than the anger. And in a clear unemotional voice he told Umuofia how their daughter had gone to market at Mbaino and had been killed. That woman, said Ezeugo, was the wife of Ogbuefi Udo,[7] and he pointed to a man who sat near him with a bowed head. The crowd then shouted with anger and thirst for blood.

Many others spoke, and at the end it was decided to follow the normal course of action. An ultimatum was immediately dispatched to Mbaino asking them to choose between war on the one hand, and on the other the offer of a young man and a virgin as compensation.

Umuofia was feared by all its neighbors. It was powerful in war and in magic, and its priests and medicine men were feared in all the surrounding country. Its most potent war-medicine was as old as the clan itself. Nobody knew how old. But on one point there was general agreement—the active principle in that medicine had been an old woman with one leg. In fact, the

---

6. United Umuofia! An orator's call on the audience to respond as a group. *Ogbuefi*: cow killer (literal trans.); indicates someone who has taken a high title (e.g., the Idemili title) for which the celebration ceremony requires the slaughter of a cow. *Ezeugo*: a name denoting a priest or high initiate, someone who wears the eagle feather.　　7. Peace.

medicine itself was called *agadi-nwayi*, or old woman. It had its shrine in the center of Umuofia, in a cleared spot. And if anybody was so foolhardy as to pass by the shrine after dusk he was sure to see the old woman hopping about.

And so the neighboring clans who naturally knew of these things feared Umuofia, and would not go to war against it without first trying a peaceful settlement. And in fairness to Umuofia it should be recorded that it never went to war unless its case was clear and just and was accepted as such by its Oracle—the Oracle of the Hills and the Caves. And there were indeed occasions when the Oracle had forbidden Umuofia to wage a war. If the clan had disobeyed the Oracle they would surely have been beaten, because their dreaded *agadi-nwayi* would never fight what the Ibo call *a fight of blame*.

But the war that now threatened was a just war. Even the enemy clan knew that. And so when Okonkwo of Umuofia arrived at Mbaino as the proud and imperious emissary of war, he was treated with great honor and respect, and two days later he returned home with a lad of fifteen and a young virgin. The lad's name was Ikemefuna, whose sad story is still told in Umuofia unto this day.

The elders, or *ndichie*, met to hear a report of Okonkwo's mission. At the end they decided, as everybody knew they would, that the girl should go to Ogbuefi Udo to replace his murdered wife. As for the boy, he belonged to the clan as a whole, and there was no hurry to decide his fate. Okonkwo was, therefore, asked on behalf of the clan to look after him in the interim. And so for three years Ikemefuna lived in Okonkwo's household.

Okonkwo ruled his household with a heavy hand. His wives, especially the youngest, lived in perpetual fear of his fiery temper, and so did his little children. Perhaps down in his heart Okonkwo was not a cruel man. But his whole life was dominated by fear, the fear of failure and of weakness. It was deeper and more intimate than the fear of evil and capricious gods and of magic, the fear of the forest, and of the forces of nature, malevolent, red in tooth and claw. Okonkwo's fear was greater than these. It was not external but lay deep within himself. It was the fear of himself, lest he should be found to resemble his father. Even as a little boy he had resented his father's failure and weakness, and even now he still remembered how he had suffered when a playmate had told him that his father was *agbala*. That was how Okonkwo first came to know that *agbala* was not only another name for a woman, it could also mean a man who had taken no title. And so Okonkwo was ruled by one passion—to hate everything that his father Unoka had loved. One of those things was gentleness and another was idleness.

During the planting season Okonkwo worked daily on his farms from cock-crow until the chickens went to roost. He was a very strong man and rarely felt fatigue. But his wives and young children were not as strong, and so they suffered. But they dared not complain openly. Okonkwo's first son, Nwoye,[8] was then twelve years old but was already causing his father great anxiety for his incipient laziness. At any rate, that was how it looked to his father, and he sought to correct him by constant nagging and beating. And so Nwoye was developing into a sad-faced youth.

8. Child born on Oye Day.

Okonkwo's prosperity was visible in his household. He had a large compound enclosed by a thick wall of red earth. His own hut, or *obi*, stood immediately behind the only gate in the red walls. Each of his three wives had her own hut, which together formed a half moon behind the *obi*. The barn was built against one end of the red walls, and long stacks of yam stood out prosperously in it. At the opposite end of the compound was a shed for the goats, and each wife built a small attachment to her hut for the hens. Near the barn was a small house, the "medicine house" or shrine where Okonkwo kept the wooden symbols of his personal god and of his ancestral spirits. He worshiped them with sacrifices of kola nut, food and palm-wine, and offered prayers to them on behalf of himself, his three wives and eight children.

So when the daughter of Umuofia was killed in Mbaino, Ikemefuna came into Okonkwo's household. When Okonkwo brought him home that day he called his most senior wife and handed him over to her.

"He belongs to the clan," he told her. "So look after him."

"Is he staying long with us?" she asked.

"Do what you are told, woman," Okonkwo thundered, and stammered. "When did you become one of the *ndichie* of Umuofia?"

And so Nwoye's mother took Ikemefuna to her hut and asked no more questions.

As for the boy himself, he was terribly afraid. He could not understand what was happening to him or what he had done. How could he know that his father had taken a hand in killing a daughter of Umuofia? All he knew was that a few men had arrived at their house, conversing with his father in low tones, and at the end he had been taken out and handed over to a stranger. His mother had wept bitterly, but he had been too surprised to weep. And so the stranger had brought him, and a girl, a long, long way from home, through lonely forest paths. He did not know who the girl was, and he never saw her again.

3

Okonkwo did not have the start in life which many young men usually had. He did not inherit a barn from his father. There was no barn to inherit. The story was told in Umuofia, of how his father, Unoka, had gone to consult the Oracle of the Hills and the Caves to find out why he always had a miserable harvest.

The Oracle was called Agbala,[9] and people came from far and near to consult it. They came when misfortune dogged their steps or when they had a dispute with their neighbors. They came to discover what the future held for them or to consult the spirits of their departed fathers.

The way into the shrine was a round hole at the side of a hill, just a little bigger than the round opening into a henhouse. Worshipers and those who came to seek knowledge from the god crawled on their belly through the hole and found themselves in a dark, endless space in the presence of Agbala. No one had ever beheld Agbala, except his priestess. But no one who had

9. The Oracle is masculine, but his priestess, or Voice, is feminine.

ever crawled into his awful shrine had come out without the fear of his power. His priestess stood by the sacred fire which she built in the heart of the cave and proclaimed the will of the god. The fire did not burn with a flame. The glowing logs only served to light up vaguely the dark figure of the priestess.

Sometimes a man came to consult the spirit of his dead father or relative. It was said that when such a spirit appeared, the man saw it vaguely in the darkness, but never heard its voice. Some people even said that they had heard the spirits flying and flapping their wings against the roof of the cave.

Many years ago when Okonkwo was still a boy his father, Unoka, had gone to consult Agbala. The priestess in those days was a woman called Chika.[1] She was full of the power of her god, and she was greatly feared. Unoka stood before her and began his story.

"Every year," he said sadly, "before I put any crop in the earth, I sacrifice a cock to Ani, the owner of all land. It is the law of our fathers. I also kill a cock at the shrine of Ifejioku, the god of yams. I clear the bush and set fire to it when it is dry. I sow the yams when the first rain has fallen, and stake them when the young tendrils appear. I weed—"

"Hold your peace!" screamed the priestess, her voice terrible as it echoed through the dark void. "You have offended neither the gods nor your fathers. And when a man is at peace with his gods and his ancestors, his harvest will be good or bad according to the strength of his arm. You, Unoka, are known in all the clan for the weakness of your machete and your hoe. When your neighbors go out with their ax to cut down virgin forests, you sow your yams on exhausted farms that take no labor to clear. They cross seven rivers to make their farms; you stay at home and offer sacrifices to a reluctant soil. Go home and work like a man."

Unoka was an ill-fated man. He had a bad *chi* or personal god, and evil fortune followed him to the grave, or rather to his death, for he had no grave. He died of the swelling which was an abomination to the earth goddess. When a man was afflicted with swelling in the stomach and the limbs he was not allowed to die in the house. He was carried to the Evil Forest and left there to die. There was the story of a very stubborn man who staggered back to his house and had to be carried again to the forest and tied to a tree. The sickness was an abomination to the earth, and so the victim could not be buried in her bowels. He died and rotted away above the earth, and was not given the first or the second burial. Such was Unoka's fate. When they carried him away, he took with him his flute.

With a father like Unoka, Okonkwo did not have the start in life which many young men had. He neither inherited a barn nor a title, nor even a young wife. But in spite of these disadvantages, he had begun even in his father's lifetime to lay the foundations of a prosperous future. It was slow and painful. But he threw himself into it like one possessed. And indeed he was possessed by the fear of his father's contemptible life and shameful death.

There was a wealthy man in Okonkwo's village who had three huge barns, nine wives and thirty children. His name was Nwakibie[2] and he had taken

---

1. Sky is supreme.   2. The child surpasses his neighbors.

the highest but one title which a man could take in the clan. It was for this man that Okonkwo worked to earn his first seed yams.

He took a pot of palm-wine and a cock to Nwakibie. Two elderly neighbors were sent for, and Nwakibie's two grown-up sons were also present in his *obi*. He presented a kola nut and an alligator pepper, which were passed round for all to see and then returned to him. He broke the nut saying: "We shall all live. We pray for life, children, a good harvest and happiness. You will have what is good for you and I will have what is good for me. Let the kite perch and let the eagle perch too. If one says no to the other, let his wing break."

After the kola nut had been eaten Okonkwo brought his palm-wine from the corner of the hut where it had been placed and stood it in the center of the group. He addressed Nwakibie, calling him "Our father."

"*Nna ayi*," he said. "I have brought you this little kola. As our people say, a man who pays respect to the great paves the way for his own greatness. I have come to pay you my respects and also to ask a favor. But let us drink the wine first."

Everybody thanked Okonkwo and the neighbors brought out their drinking horns from the goatskin bags they carried. Nwakibie brought down his own horn, which was fastened to the rafters. The younger of his sons, who was also the youngest man in the group, moved to the center, raised the pot on his left knee and began to pour out the wine. The first cup went to Okonkwo, who must taste his wine before anyone else.[3] Then the group drank, beginning with the eldest man. When everyone had drunk two or three horns, Nwakibie sent for his wives. Some of them were not at home and only four came in.

"Is Anasi not in?" he asked them. They said she was coming. Anasi was the first[4] wife and the others could not drink before her, and so they stood waiting.

Anasi was a middle-aged woman, tall and strongly built. There was authority in her bearing and she looked every inch the ruler of the womenfolk in a large and prosperous family. She wore the anklet of her husband's titles, which the first wife alone could wear.

She walked up to her husband and accepted the horn from him. She then went down on one knee, drank a little and handed back the horn. She rose, called him by his name and went back to her hut. The other wives drank in the same way, in their proper order, and went away.

The men then continued their drinking and talking. Ogbuefi Idigo was talking about the palm-wine tapper, Obiako, who suddenly gave up his trade.

"There must be something behind it," he said, wiping the foam of wine from his mustache with the back of his left hand. "There must be a reason for it. A toad does not run in the daytime for nothing."

"Some people say the Oracle warned him that he would fall off a palm tree and kill himself," said Akukalia.

"Obiako has always been a strange one," said Nwakibie. "I have heard that many years ago, when his father had not been dead very long, he had gone to consult the Oracle. The Oracle said to him, 'Your dead father wants you

---

3. A ceremonial gesture; one who gives wine tastes it first to show that it is not poisoned. 4. First or favorite wife—not always the same.

to sacrifice a goat to him.' Do you know what he told the Oracle? He said, 'Ask my dead father if he ever had a fowl when he was alive.'" Everybody laughed heartily except Okonkwo, who laughed uneasily because, as the saying goes, an old woman is always uneasy when dry bones are mentioned in a proverb. Okonkwo remembered his own father.

At last the young man who was pouring out the wine held up half a horn of the thick, white dregs and said, "What we are eating is finished." "We have seen it," the others replied. "Who will drink the dregs?" he asked. "Whoever has a job in hand," said Idigo, looking at Nwakibie's elder son Igwelo with a malicious twinkle in his eye.

Everyone agreed that Igwelo should drink the dregs. He accepted the half-full horn from his brother and drank it. As Idigo had said, Igwelo had a job in hand because he had married his first wife a month or two before. The thick dregs of palm-wine were supposed to be good for men who were going in to their wives.

After the wine had been drunk Okonkwo laid his difficulties before Nwakibie.

"I have come to you for help," he said. "Perhaps you can already guess what it is. I have cleared a farm but have no yams to sow. I know what it is to ask a man to trust another with his yams, especially these days when young men are afraid of hard work. I am not afraid of work. The lizard that jumped from the high iroko tree to the ground said he would praise himself if no one else did. I began to fend for myself at an age when most people still suck at their mothers' breasts. If you give me some yam seeds I shall not fail you."

Nwakibie cleared his throat. "It pleases me to see a young man like you these days when our youth has gone so soft. Many young men have come to me to ask for yams but I have refused because I knew they would just dump them in the earth and leave them to be choked by weeds. When I say no to them they think I am hard-hearted. But it is not so. Eneke the bird[5] says that since men have learned to shoot without missing, he has learned to fly without perching. I have learned to be stingy with my yams. But I can trust you. I know it as I look at you. As our fathers said, you can tell a ripe corn by its look. I shall give you twice four hundred yams. Go ahead and prepare your farm."

Okonkwo thanked him again and again and went home feeling happy. He knew that Nwakibie would not refuse him, but he had not expected he would be so generous. He had not hoped to get more than four hundred seeds. He would now have to make a bigger farm. He hoped to get another four hundred yams from one of his father's friends at Isiuzo.[6]

Sharecropping was a very slow way of building up a barn of one's own. After all the toil one only got a third of the harvest. But for a young man whose father had no yams, there was no other way. And what made it worse in Okonkwo's case was that he had to support his mother and two sisters from his meager harvest. And supporting his mother also meant supporting his father. She could not be expected to cook and eat while her husband starved. And so at a very early age when he was striving desperately to build a barn through sharecropping Okonkwo was also fending for his father's house. It was like pouring grains of corn into a bag full of holes. His mother

---

5. Proverbial.   6. Head of the road; a small town.

and sisters worked hard enough, but they grew women's crops, like coco-yams, beans and cassava. Yam, the king of crops, was a man's crop.[7]

The year that Okonkwo took eight hundred seed-yams from Nwakibie was the worst year in living memory. Nothing happened at its proper time; it was either too early or too late. It seemed as if the world had gone mad. The first rains were late, and, when they came, lasted only a brief moment. The blazing sun returned, more fierce than it had ever been known, and scorched all the green that had appeared with the rains. The earth burned like hot coals and roasted all the yams that had been sown. Like all good farmers, Okonkwo had begun to sow with the first rains. He had sown four hundred seeds when the rains dried up and the heat returned. He watched the sky all day for signs of rain clouds and lay awake all night. In the morning he went back to his farm and saw the withering tendrils. He had tried to protect them from the smoldering earth by making rings of thick sisal leaves around them. But by the end of the day the sisal rings were burned dry and gray. He changed them every day, and prayed that the rain might fall in the night. But the drought continued for eight market weeks and the yams were killed.

Some farmers had not planted their yams yet. They were the lazy easygoing ones who always put off clearing their farms as long as they could. This year they were the wise ones. They sympathized with their neighbors with much shaking of the head, but inwardly they were happy for what they took to be their own foresight.

Okonkwo planted what was left of his seed-yams when the rains finally returned. He had one consolation. The yams he had sown before the drought were his own, the harvest of the previous year. He still had the eight hundred from Nwakibie and the four hundred from his father's friend. So he would make a fresh start.

But the year had gone mad. Rain fell as it had never fallen before. For days and nights together it poured down in violent torrents, and washed away the yam heaps. Trees were uprooted and deep gorges appeared everywhere. Then the rain became less violent. But it went from day to day without a pause. The spell of sunshine which always came in the middle of the wet season did not appear. The yams put on luxuriant green leaves, but every farmer knew that without sunshine the tubers would not grow.

That year the harvest was sad, like a funeral, and many farmers wept as they dug up the miserable and rotting yams. One man tied his cloth to a tree branch and hanged himself.

Okonkwo remembered that tragic year with a cold shiver throughout the rest of his life. It always surprised him when he thought of it later that he did not sink under the load of despair. He knew that he was a fierce fighter, but that year had been enough to break the heart of a lion.

"Since I survived that year," he always said, "I shall survive anything." He put it down to his inflexible will.

His father, Unoka, who was then an ailing man, had said to him during that terrible harvest month: "Do not despair. I know you will not despair.

7. Yams, a staple food in Western Africa, were a sacred crop generally cultivated only by men and eaten either roasted or boiled. *Coco-yams* (a brown root also called taro) and *cassava* (or manioc, which is refined in various ways to remove natural cyanide) were low-status root vegetables, prepared for eating by boiling and pounding.

You have a manly and a proud heart. A proud heart can survive a general failure because such a failure does not prick its pride. It is more difficult and more bitter when a man fails *alone.*"

Unoka was like that in his last days. His love of talk had grown with age and sickness. It tried Okonkwo's patience beyond words.

4

"Looking at a king's mouth," said an old man, "one would think he never sucked at his mother's breast." He was talking about Okonkwo, who had risen so suddenly from great poverty and misfortune to be one of the lords of the clan. The old man bore no ill will towards Okonkwo. Indeed he respected him for his industry and success. But he was struck, as most people were, by Okonkwo's brusqueness in dealing with less successful men. Only a week ago a man had contradicted him at a kindred meeting which they held to discuss the next ancestral feast. Without looking at the man Okonkwo had said: "This meeting is for men." The man who had contradicted him had no titles. That was why he had called him a woman. Okonkwo knew how to kill a man's spirit.

Everybody at the kindred meeting took sides with Osugo[8] when Okonkwo called him a woman. The oldest man present said sternly that those whose palm-kernels were cracked for them by a benevolent spirit should not forget to be humble. Okonkwo said he was sorry for what he had said, and the meeting continued.

But it was really not true that Okonkwo's palm-kernels had been cracked for him by a benevolent spirit. He had cracked them himself. Anyone who knew his grim struggle against poverty and misfortune could not say he had been lucky. If ever a man deserved his success, that man was Okonkwo. An an early age he had achieved fame as the greatest wrestler in all the land. That was not luck. At the most one could say that his *chi* or personal god was good. But the Ibo people have a proverb that when a man says yes his *chi* says yes also. Okonkwo said yes very strongly; so his *chi* agreed. And not only his *chi* but his clan too, because it judged a man by the work of his hands. That was why Okonkwo had been chosen by the nine villages to carry a message of war to their enemies unless they agreed to give up a young man and a virgin to atone for the murder of Udo's wife. And such was the deep fear that their enemies had for Umuofia that they treated Okonkwo like a king and brought him a virgin who was given to Udo as wife, and the lad Ikemefuna.

The elders of the clan had decided that Ikemefuna should be in Okonkwo's care for a while. But no one thought it would be as long as three years. They seemed to forget all about him as soon as they had taken the decision.

At first Ikemefuna was very much afraid. Once or twice he tried to run away, but he did not know where to begin. He thought of his mother and his three-year-old sister and wept bitterly. Nwoye's mother was very kind to him and treated him as one of her own children. But all he said was: "When shall I go home?" When Okonkwo heard that he would not eat any food he came into the hut with a big stick in his hand and stood over him while he

---

8. Low-status [*osu*] person.

swallowed his yams, trembling. A few moments later he went behind the hut and began to vomit painfully. Nwoye's mother went to him and placed her hands on his chest and on his back. He was ill for three market weeks, and when he recovered he seemed to have overcome his great fear and sadness.

He was by nature a very lively boy and he gradually became popular in Okonkwo's household, especially with the children. Okonkwo's son, Nwoye, who was two years younger, became quite inseparable from him because he seemed to know everything. He could fashion out flutes from bamboo stems and even from the elephant grass. He knew the names of all the birds and could set clever traps for the little bush rodents. And he knew which trees made the strongest bows.

Even Okonkwo himself became very fond of the boy—inwardly of course. Okonkwo never showed any emotion openly, unless it be the emotion of anger. To show affection was a sign of weakness; the only thing worth demonstrating was strength. He therefore treated Ikemefuna as he treated everybody else—with a heavy hand. But there was no doubt that he liked the boy. Sometimes when he went to big village meetings or communal ancestral feasts he allowed Ikemefuna to accompany him, like a son, carrying his stool and his goatskin bag. And, indeed, Ikemefuna called him father.

Ikemefuna came to Umuofia at the end of the carefree season between harvest and planting. In fact he recovered from his illness only a few days before the Week of Peace began. And that was also the year Okonkwo broke the peace, and was punished, as was the custom, by Ezeani, the priest of the earth goddess.

Okonkwo was provoked to justifiable anger by his youngest wife, who went to plait her hair at her friend's house and did not return early enough to cook the afternoon meal. Okonkwo did not know at first that she was not at home. After waiting in vain for her dish he went to her hut to see what she was doing. There was nobody in the hut and the fireplace was cold.

"Where is Ojiugo?" he asked his second wife, who came out of her hut to draw water from a gigantic pot in the shade of a small tree in the middle of the compound.

"She has gone to plait her hair."

Okonkwo bit his lips as anger welled up within him.

"Where are her children? Did she take them?" he asked with unusual coolness and restraint.

"They are here," answered his first wife, Nwoye's mother. Okonkwo bent down and looked into her hut. Ojiugo's children were eating with the children of his first wife.

"Did she ask you to feed them before she went?"

"Yes," lied Nwoye's mother, trying to minimize Ojiugo's thoughtlessness.

Okonkwo knew she was not speaking the truth. He walked back to his *obi* to await Ojiugo's return. And when she returned he beat her very heavily. In his anger he had forgotten that it was the Week of Peace. His first two wives ran out in great alarm pleading with him that it was the sacred week. But Okonkwo was not the man to stop beating somebody half-way through, not even for fear of a goddess.

Okonkwo's neighbors heard his wife crying and sent their voices over the compound walls to ask what was the matter. Some of them came over to see for themselves. It was unheard of to beat somebody during the sacred week.

Before it was dusk Ezeani, who was the priest of the earth goddess, Ani, called on Okonkwo in his *obi*. Okonkwo brought out kola nut and placed it before the priest.

"Take away your kola nut. I shall not eat in the house of a man who has no respect for our gods and ancestors."

Okonkwo tried to explain to him what his wife had done, but Ezeani seemed to pay no attention. He held a short staff in his hand which he brought down on the floor to emphasize his points.

"Listen to me," he said when Okonkwo had spoken. "You are not a stranger in Umuofia. You know as well as I do that our forefathers ordained that before we plant any crops in the earth we should observe a week in which a man does not say a harsh word to his neighbor. We live in peace with our fellows to honor our great goddess of the earth without whose blessing our crops will not grow. You have committed a great evil." He brought down his staff heavily on the floor. "Your wife was at fault, but even if you came into your *obi* and found her lover on top of her, you would still have committed a great evil to beat her." His staff came down again. "The evil you have done can ruin the whole clan. The earth goddess whom you have insulted may refuse to give us her increase, and we shall all perish." His tone now changed from anger to command. "You will bring to the shrine of Ani tomorrow one she-goat, one hen, a length of cloth and a hundred cowries." He rose and left the hut.

Okonkwo did as the priest said. He also took with him a pot of palm-wine. Inwardly, he was repentant. But he was not the man to go about telling his neighbors that he was in error. And so people said he had no respect for the gods of the clan. His enemies said his good fortune had gone to his head. They called him the little bird *nza*[9] who so far forgot himself after a heavy meal that he challenged his *chi*.

No work was done during the Week of Peace. People called on their neighbors and drank palm-wine. This year they talked of nothing else but the *nso-ani*[1] which Okonkwo had committed. It was the first time for many years that a man had broken the sacred peace. Even the oldest men could only remember one or two other occasions somewhere in the dim past.

Ogbuefi Ezeudu, who was the oldest man in the village, was telling two other men who came to visit him that the punishment for breaking the Peace of Ani had become very mild in their clan.

"It has not always been so," he said. "My father told me that he had been told that in the past a man who broke the peace was dragged on the ground through the village until he died. But after a while this custom was stopped because it spoiled the peace which it was meant to preserve."

"Somebody told me yesterday," said one of the younger men, "that in some clans it is an abomination for a man to die during the Week of Peace."

"It is indeed true," said Ogbuefi Ezeudu. "They have that custom in Obo-doani.[2] If a man dies at this time he is not buried but cast into the Evil Forest. It is a bad custom which these people observe because they lack understanding. They throw away large numbers of men and women without

9. The one that talks back (literal trans.); a small aggressive bird. In the story, it is easily defeated (alternatively, caught by a hawk) when it becomes enough to challenge its personal god.   1. Sin, abomination against the Earth goddess Ani.   2. The town of the land (literal trans); i.e., Anytown, Nigeria.

burial. And what is the result? Their clan is full of the evil spirits of these unburied dead, hungry to do harm to the living."

After the Week of Peace every man and his family began to clear the bush to make new farms. The cut bush was left to dry and fire was then set to it. As the smoke rose into the sky kites appeared from different directions and hovered over the burning field in silent valediction. The rainy season was approaching when they would go away until the dry season returned.

Okonkwo spent the next few days preparing his seed-yams. He looked at each yam carefully to see whether it was good for sowing. Sometimes he decided that a yam was too big to be sown as one seed and he split it deftly along its length with his sharp knife. His eldest son, Nwoye, and Ikemefuna helped him by fetching the yams in long baskets from the barn and in counting the prepared seeds in groups of four hundred. Sometimes Okonkwo gave them a few yams each to prepare. But he always found fault with their effort, and he said so with much threatening.

"Do you think you are cutting up yams for cooking?" he asked Nwoye. "If you split another yam of this size, I shall break your jaw. You think you are still a child. I began to own a farm at your age. And you," he said to Ikemefuna, "do you not grow yams where you come from?"

Inwardly Okonkwo knew that the boys were still too young to understand fully the difficult art of preparing seed-yams. But he thought that one could not begin too early. Yam stood for manliness, and he who could feed his family on yams from one harvest to another was a very great man indeed. Okonkwo wanted his son to be a great farmer and a great man. He would stamp out the disquieting signs of laziness which he thought he already saw in him.

"I will not have a son who cannot hold up his head in the gathering of the clan. I would sooner strangle him with my own hands. And if you stand staring at me like that," he swore, "Amadiora[3] will break your head for you!"

Some days later, when the land had been moistened by two or three heavy rains, Okonkwo and his family went to the farm with baskets of seed-yams, their hoes and machetes, and the planting began. They made single mounds of earth in straight lines all over the field and sowed the yams in them.

Yam, the king of crops, was a very exacting king. For three or four moons it demanded hard work and constant attention from cock-crow till the chickens went back to roost. The young tendrils were protected from earth-heat with rings of sisal leaves. As the rains became heavier the women planted maize, melons and beans between the yam mounds. The yams were then staked, first with little sticks and later with tall and big tree branches. The women weeded the farm three times at definite periods in the life of the yams, neither early nor late.

And now the rains had really come, so heavy and persistent that even the village rain-maker no longer claimed to be able to intervene. He could not stop the rain now, just as he would not attempt to start it in the heart of the dry season, without serious danger to his own health. The personal dynamism required to counter the forces of these extremes of weather would be far too great for the human frame.

And so nature was not interfered with in the middle of the rainy season.

3. God of thunder and lightning.

Sometimes it poured down in such thick sheets of water that earth and sky seemed merged in one gray wetness. It was then uncertain whether the low rumbling of Amadiora's thunder came from above or below. At such times, in each of the countless thatched huts of Umuofia, children sat around their mother's cooking fire telling stories, or with their father in his *obi* warming themselves from a log fire, roasting and eating maize. It was a brief resting period between the exacting and arduous planting season and the equally exacting but light-hearted month of harvests.

Ikemefuna had begun to feel like a member of Okonkwo's family. He still thought about his mother and his three-year-old sister, and he had moments of sadness and depression. But he and Nwoye had become so deeply attached to each other that such moments became less frequent and less poignant. Ikemefuna had an endless stock of folk tales. Even those which Nwoye knew already were told with a new freshness and the local flavor of a different clan. Nwoye remembered this period very vividly till the end of his life. He even remembered how he had laughed when Ikemefuna told him that the proper name for a corn cob with only a few scattered grains was *eze-agadi-nwayi*, or the teeth of an old woman. Nwoye's mind had gone immediately to Nwayieke, who lived near the udala tree.[4] She had about three teeth and was always smoking her pipe.

Gradually the rains became lighter and less frequent, and earth and sky once again became separate. The rain fell in thin, slanting showers through sunshine and quiet breeze. Children no longer stayed indoors but ran about singing:

> The rain is falling, the sun is shining,
> Alone Nnadi[5] is cooking and eating.

Nwoye always wondered who Nnadi was and why he should live all by himself, cooking and eating. In the end he decided that Nnadi must live in that land of Ikemefuna's favorite story where the ant holds his court in splendor and the sands dance forever.

5

The Feast of the New Yam was approaching and Umuofia was in a festival mood. It was an occasion for giving thanks to Ani, the earth goddess and the source of all fertility. Ani played a greater part in the life of the people than any other deity. She was the ultimate judge of morality and conduct. And what was more, she was in close communion with the departed fathers of the clan whose bodies had been committed to earth.

The Feast of the New Yam was held every year before the harvest began, to honor the earth goddess and the ancestral spirits of the clan. New yams could not be eaten until some had first been offered to these powers. Men and women, young and old, looked forward to the New Yam Festival because it began the season of plenty—the new year. On the last night before the festival, yams of the old year were all disposed of by those who still had them. The new year must begin with tasty, fresh yams and not the shriveled and fibrous crops of the previous year. All cooking pots, calabashes and wooden

---

4. African star apple tree. *Nwayieke*: Woman born on Eke Day.   5. Father is there or Father exists.

bowls were thoroughly washed, especially the wooden mortar in which yam was pounded. Yam foo-foo[6] and vegetable soup was the chief food in the celebration. So much of it was cooked that, no matter how heavily the family ate or how many friends and relatives they invited from neighboring villages, there was always a large quantity of food left over at the end of the day. The story was always told of a wealthy man who set before his guests a mound of foo-foo so high that those who sat on one side could not see what was happening on the other, and it was not until late in the evening that one of them saw for the first time his in-law who had arrived during the course of the meal and had fallen to on the opposite side. It was only then that they exchanged greetings and shook hands over what was left of the food.

The New Yam Festival was thus an occasion for joy throughout Umuofia. And every man whose arm was strong, as the Ibo people say, was expected to invite large numbers of guests from far and wide. Okonkwo always asked his wives' relations, and since he now had three wives his guests would make a fairly big crowd.

But somehow Okonkwo could never become as enthusiastic over feasts as most people. He was a good eater and he could drink one or two fairly big gourds of palm-wine. But he was always uncomfortable sitting around for days waiting for a feast or getting over it. He would be very much happier working on his farm.

The festival was now only three days away. Okonkwo's wives had scrubbed the walls and the huts with red earth until they reflected light. They had then drawn patterns on them in white, yellow and dark green. They then set about painting themselves with cam wood and drawing beautiful black patterns on their stomachs and on their backs. The children were also decorated, especially their hair, which was shaved in beautiful patterns. The three women talked excitedly about the relations who had been invited, and the children reveled in the thought of being spoiled by these visitors from the motherland. Ikemefuna was equally excited. The New Yam Festival seemed to him to be a much bigger event here than in his own village, a place which was already becoming remote and vague in his imagination.

And then the storm burst. Okonkwo, who had been walking about aimlessly in his compound in suppressed anger, suddenly found an outlet.

"Who killed this banana tree?" he asked.

A hush fell on the compound immediately.

"Who killed this tree? Or are you all deaf and dumb?"

As a matter of fact the tree was very much alive. Okonkwo's second wife had merely cut a few leaves off it to wrap some food, and she said so. Without further argument Okonkwo gave her a sound beating and left her and her only daughter weeping. Neither of the other wives dared to interfere beyond an occasional and tentative, "It is enough, Okonkwo," pleaded from a reasonable distance.

His anger thus satisfied, Okonkwo decided to go out hunting. He had an old rusty gun made by a clever blacksmith who had come to live in Umuofia long ago. But although Okonkwo was a great man whose prowess was universally acknowledged, he was not a hunter. In fact he had not killed a rat

---

6. A mashed, edible base that is shaped into balls with the fingers and then indented for cupping and eating soup.

with his gun. And so when he called Ikemefuna to fetch his gun, the wife who had just been beaten murmured something about guns that never shot. Unfortunately for her, Okonkwo heard it and ran madly into his room for the loaded gun, ran out again and aimed at her as she clambered over the dwarf wall of the barn. He pressed the trigger and there was a loud report accompanied by the wail of his wives and children. He threw down the gun and jumped into the barn, and there lay the woman, very much shaken and frightened but quite unhurt. He heaved a heavy sigh and went away with the gun.

In spite of this incident the New Yam Festival was celebrated with great joy in Okonkwo's household. Early that morning as he offered a sacrifice of new yam and palm-oil to his ancestors he asked them to protect him, his children and their mothers in the new year.

As the day wore on his in-laws arrived from three surrounding villages, and each party brought with them a huge pot of palm-wine. And there was eating and drinking till night, when Okonkwo's in-laws began to leave for their homes.

The second day of the new year was the day of the great wrestling match between Okonkwo's village and their neighbors. It was difficult to say which the people enjoyed more—the feasting and fellowship of the first day or the wrestling contest of the second. But there was one woman who had no doubt whatever in her mind. She was Okonkwo's second wife, Ekwefi, whom he nearly shot. There was no festival in all the seasons of the year which gave her as much pleasure as the wrestling match. Many years ago when she was the village beauty Okonkwo had won her heart by throwing the Cat in the greatest contest within living memory. She did not marry him then because he was too poor to pay her bride-price. But a few years later she ran away from her husband and came to live with Okonkwo. All this happened many years ago. Now Ekwefi[7] was a woman of forty-five who had suffered a great deal in her time. But her love of wrestling contests was still as strong as it was thirty years ago.

It was not yet noon on the second day of the New Yam Festival. Ekwefi and her only daughter, Ezinma,[8] sat near the fireplace waiting for the water in the pot to boil. The fowl Ekwefi had just killed was in the wooden mortar. The water began to boil, and in one deft movement she lifted the pot from the fire and poured the boiling water over the fowl. She put back the empty pot on the circular pad in the corner, and looked at her palms, which were black with soot. Ezinma was always surprised that her mother could lift a pot from the fire with her bare hands.

"Ekwefi," she said, "is it true that when people are grown up, fire does not burn them?" Ezinma, unlike most children, called her mother by her name.

"Yes," replied Ekwefi, too busy to argue. Her daughter was only ten years old but she was wiser than her years.

"But Nwoye's mother dropped her pot of hot soup the other day and it broke on the floor."

Ekwefi turned the hen over in the mortar and began to pluck the feathers.

"Ekwefi," said Ezinma, who had joined in plucking the feathers, "my eyelid is twitching."

7. An abbreviation of "Do you have a cow?"; the cow being a symbol of wealth. Okonkwo would presumably have repaid Ekwefi's bride-price to her first husband.   8. True beauty (literal trans.), or goodness.

"It means you are going to cry," said her mother.

"No," Ezinma said, "it is this eyelid, the top one."

"That means you will see something."

"What will I see?" she asked.

"How can I know?" Ekwefi wanted her to work it out herself.

"Oho," said Ezinma at last. "I know what it is—the wrestling match."

At last the hen was plucked clean. Ekwefi tried to pull out the horny beak but it was too hard. She turned round on her low stool and put the beak in the fire for a few moments. She pulled again and it came off.

"Ekwefi!" a voice called from one of the other huts. It was Nwoye's mother, Okonkwo's first wife.

"Is that me?" Ekwefi called back. That was the way people answered calls from outside. They never answered yes for fear it might be an evil spirit calling.

"Will you give Ezinma some fire to bring to me?" Her own children and Ikemefuna had gone to the stream.

Ekwefi put a few live coals into a piece of broken pot and Ezinma carried it across the clean swept compound to Nwoye's mother.

"Thank you, Nma," she said. She was peeling new yams, and in a basket beside her were green vegetables and beans.

"Let me make the fire for you," Ezinma offered.

"Thank you, Ezigbo," she said. She often called her Ezigbo, which means "the good one."

Ezinma went outside and brought some sticks from a huge bundle of firewood. She broke them into little pieces across the sole of her foot and began to build a fire, blowing it with her breath.

"You will blow your eyes out," said Nwoye's mother, looking up from the yams she was peeling. "Use the fan." She stood up and pulled out the fan which was fastened into one of the rafters. As soon as she got up, the troublesome nanny goat, which had been dutifully eating yam peelings, dug her teeth into the real thing, scooped out two mouthfuls and fled from the hut to chew the cud in the goats' shed. Nwoye's mother swore at her and settled down again to her peeling. Ezinma's fire was now sending up thick clouds of smoke. She went on fanning it until it burst into flames. Nwoye's mother thanked her and she went back to her mother's hut.

Just then the distant beating of drums began to reach them. It came from the direction of the *ilo*, the village playground. Every village had its own *ilo* which was as old as the village itself and where all the great ceremonies and dances took place. The drums beat the unmistakable wrestling dance— quick, light and gay, and it came floating on the wind.

Okonkwo cleared his throat and moved his feet to the beat of the drums. It filled him with fire as it had always done from his youth. He trembled with the desire to conquer and subdue. It was like the desire for a woman.

"We shall be late for the wrestling," said Ezinma to her mother.

"They will not begin until the sun goes down."

"But they are beating the drums."

"Yes. The drums begin at noon but the wrestling waits until the sun begins to sink. Go and see if your father has brought out yams for the afternoon."

"He has. Nwoye's mother is already cooking."

"Go and bring our own, then. We must cook quickly or we shall be late for the wrestling."

Ezinma ran in the direction of the barn and brought back two yams from the dwarf wall.

Ekwefi peeled the yams quickly. The troublesome nanny goat sniffed about, eating the peelings. She cut the yams into small pieces and began to prepare a pottage, using some of the chicken.

At that moment they heard someone crying just outside their compound. It was very much like Obiageli,[9] Nwoye's sister.

"Is that not Obiageli weeping?" Ekwefi called across the yard to Nwoye's mother.

"Yes," she replied. "She must have broken her waterpot."

The weeping was now quite close and soon the children filed in, carrying on their heads various sizes of pots suitable to their years. Ikemefuna came first with the biggest pot, closely followed by Nwoye and his two younger brothers. Obiageli brought up the rear, her face streaming with tears. In her hand was the cloth pad on which the pot should have rested on her head.

"What happened?" her mother asked, and Obiageli told her mournful story. Her mother consoled her and promised to buy her another pot.

Nwoye's younger brothers were about to tell their mother the true story of the accident when Ikemefuna looked at them sternly and they held their peace. The fact was that Obiageli had been making *inyanga*[1] with her pot. She had balanced it on her head, folded her arms in front of her and began to sway her waist like a grown-up young lady. When the pot fell down and broke she burst out laughing. She only began to weep when they got near the iroko tree outside their compound.

The drums were still beating, persistent and unchanging. Their sound was no longer a separate thing from the living village. It was like the pulsation of its heart. It throbbed in the air, in the sunshine, and even in the trees, and filled the village with excitement.

Ekwefi ladled her husband's share of the pottage into a bowl and covered it. Ezinma took it to him in his *obi*.

Okonkwo was sitting on a goatskin already eating his first wife's meal. Obiageli, who had brought it from her mother's hut, sat on the floor waiting for him to finish. Ezinma placed her mother's dish before him and sat with Obiageli.

"Sit like a woman!" Okonkwo shouted at her. Ezinma brought her two legs together and stretched them in front of her.

"Father, will you go to see the wrestling?" Ezinma asked after a suitable interval.

"Yes," he answered. "Will you go?"

"Yes." And after a pause she said: "Can I bring your chair for you?"

"No, that is a boy's job." Okonkwo was specially fond of Ezinma. She looked very much like her mother, who was once the village beauty. But his fondness only showed on very rare occasions.

"Obiageli broke her pot today," Ezinma said.

"Yes, she has told me about it," Okonkwo said between mouthfuls.

"Father," said Obiageli, "people should not talk when they are eating or pepper may go down the wrong way."

"That is very true. Do you hear that, Ezinma? You are older than Obiageli but she has more sense."

9. Born to eat (born into prosperity).　　1. Showing off.

He uncovered his second wife's dish and began to eat from it. Obiageli took the first dish and returned to her mother's hut. And then Nkechi came in, bringing the third dish. Nkechi was the daughter of Okonkwo's third wife.

In the distance the drums continued to beat.

6

The whole village turned out on the *ilo*, men, women and children. They stood round in a huge circle leaving the center of the playground free. The elders and grandees of the village sat on their own stools brought there by their young sons or slaves. Okonkwo was among them. All others stood except those who came early enough to secure places on the few stands which had been built by placing smooth logs on forked pillars.

The wrestlers were not there yet and the drummers held the field. They too sat just in front of the huge circle of spectators, facing the elders. Behind them was the big and ancient silk-cotton tree which was sacred. Spirits of good children lived in that tree waiting to be born. On ordinary days young women who desired children came to sit under its shade.

There were seven drums and they were arranged according to their sizes in a long wooden basket. Three men beat them with sticks, working feverishly from one drum to another. They were possessed by the spirit of the drums.

The young men who kept order on these occasions dashed about, consulting among themselves and with the leaders of the two wrestling teams, who were still outside the circle, behind the crowd. Once in a while two young men carrying palm fronds ran round the circle and kept the crowd back by beating the ground in front of them or, if they were stubborn, their legs and feet.

At last the two teams danced into the circle and the crowd roared and clapped. The drums rose to a frenzy. The people surged forward. The young men who kept order flew around, waving their palm fronds. Old men nodded to the beat of the drums and remembered the days when they wrestled to its intoxicating rhythm.

The contest began with boys of fifteen or sixteen. There were only three such boys in each team. They were not the real wrestlers; they merely set the scene. Within a short time the first two bouts were over. But the third created a big sensation even among the elders who did not usually show their excitement so openly. It was as quick as the other two, perhaps even quicker. But very few people had ever seen that kind of wrestling before. As soon as the two boys closed in, one of them did something which no one could describe because it had been as quick as a flash. And the other boy was flat on his back. The crowd roared and clapped and for a while drowned the frenzied drums. Okonkwo sprang to his feet and quickly sat down again. Three young men from the victorious boy's team ran forward, carried him shoulder high and danced through the cheering crowd. Everybody soon knew who the boy was. His name was Maduka, the son of Obierika.[2]

The drummers stopped for a brief rest before the real matches. Their bodies shone with sweat, and they took up fans and began to fan themselves. They also drank water from small pots and ate kola nuts. They became ordi-

2. The heart eats [enjoys] more.

2086 / CHINUA ACHEBE

nary human beings again, talking and laughing among themselves and with others who stood near them. The air, which had been stretched taut with excitement, relaxed again. It was as if water had been poured on the tightened skin of a drum. Many people looked around, perhaps for the first time, and saw those who stood or sat next to them.

"I did not know it was you," Ekwefi said to the woman who had stood shoulder to shoulder with her since the beginning of the matches.

"I do not blame you," said the woman. "I have never seen such a large crowd of people. Is it true that Okonkwo nearly killed you with his gun?"

"It is true indeed, my dear friend. I cannot yet find a mouth with which to tell the story."

"Your *chi* is very much awake, my friend. And how is my daughter, Ezinma?"

"She has been very well for some time now. Perhaps she has come to stay."

"I think she has. How old is she now?"

"She is about ten years old."

"I think she will stay. They usually stay if they do not die before the age of six."

"I pray she stays," said Ekwefi with a heavy sigh.

The woman with whom she talked was called Chielo.[3] She was the priestess of Agbala, the Oracle of the Hills and the Caves. In ordinary life Chielo was a widow with two children. She was very friendly with Ekwefi and they shared a common shed in the market. She was particularly fond of Ekwefi's only daughter, Ezinma, whom she called "my daughter." Quite often she bought beancakes and gave Ekwefi some to take home to Ezinma. Anyone seeing Chielo in ordinary life would hardly believe she was the same person who prophesied when the spirit of Agbala was upon her. The drummers took up their sticks and the air shivered and grew tense like a tightened bow.

The two teams were ranged facing each other across the clear space. A young man from one team danced across the center to the other side and pointed at whomever he wanted to fight. They danced back to the center together and then closed in.

There were twelve men on each side and the challenge went from one side to the other. Two judges walked around the wrestlers and when they thought they were equally matched, stopped them. Five matches ended in this way. But the really exciting moments were when a man was thrown. The huge voice of the crowd then rose to the sky and in every direction. It was even heard in the surrounding villages.

The last match was between the leaders of the teams. They were among the best wrestlers in all the nine villages. The crowd wondered who would throw the other this year. Some said Okafo was the better man; others said he was not the equal of Ikezue.[4] Last year neither of them had thrown the other even though the judges had allowed the contest to go on longer than was the custom. They had the same style and one saw the other's plans beforehand. It might happen again this year.

Dusk was already approaching when their contest began. The drums went

---

3. Chi who plants.   4. Strength is complete (a boastful name).

mad and the crowds also. They surged forward as the two young men danced into the circle. The palm fronds were helpless in keeping them back.

Ikezue held out his right hand. Okafo seized it, and they closed in. It was a fierce contest. Ikezue strove to dig in his right heel behind Okafo so as to pitch him backwards in the clever *ege* style. But the one knew what the other was thinking. The crowd had surrounded and swallowed up the drummers, whose frantic rhythm was no longer a mere disembodied sound but the very heartbeat of the people.

The wrestlers were now almost still in each other's grip. The muscles on their arms and their thighs and on their backs stood out and twitched. It looked like an equal match. The two judges were already moving forward to separate them when Ikezue, now desperate, went down quickly on one knee in an attempt to fling his man backwards over his head. It was a sad miscalculation. Quick as the lightning of Amadiora, Okafo raised his right leg and swung it over his rival's head. The crowd burst into a thunderous roar. Okafo was swept off his feet by his supporters and carried home shoulder high. They sang his praise and the young women clapped their hands:

> Who will wrestle for our village?
>   Okafo will wrestle for our village.
> Has he thrown a hundred men?
>   He has thrown four hundred men.
> Has he thrown a hundred Cats?
>   He has thrown four hundred Cats.
> Then send him word to fight for us.

7

For three years Ikemefuna lived in Okonkwo's household and the elders of Umuofia seemed to have forgotten about him. He grew rapidly like a yam tendril in the rainy season, and was full of the sap of life. He had become wholly absorbed into his new family. He was like an elder brother to Nwoye, and from the very first seemed to have kindled a new fire in the younger boy. He made him feel grown-up; and they no longer spent the evenings in mother's hut while she cooked, but now sat with Okonkwo in his *obi*, or watched him as he tapped his palm tree for the evening wine. Nothing pleased Nwoye now more than to be sent for by his mother or another of his father's wives to do one of those difficult and masculine tasks in the home, like splitting wood, or pounding food. On receiving such a message through a younger brother or sister, Nwoye would feign annoyance and grumble aloud about women and their troubles.

Okonkwo was inwardly pleased at his son's development, and he knew it was due to Ikemefuna. He wanted Nwoye to grow into a tough young man capable of ruling his father's household when he was dead and gone to join the ancestors. He wanted him to be a prosperous man, having enough in his barn to feed the ancestors with regular sacrifices. And so he was always happy when he heard him grumbling about women. That showed that in time he would be able to control his women-folk. No matter how prosperous a man was, if he was unable to rule his women and his children (and especially his women) he was not really a man. He was like the man in the song who had ten and one wives and not enough soup for his foo-foo.

So Okonkwo encouraged the boys to sit with him in his *obi*, and he told them stories of the land—masculine stories of violence and bloodshed. Nwoye knew that it was right to be masculine and to be violent, but somehow he still preferred the stories that his mother used to tell, and which she no doubt still told to her younger children—stories of the tortoise and his wily ways, and of the bird *eneke-nti-oba*[5] who challenged the whole world to a wrestling contest and was finally thrown by the cat. He remembered the story she often told of the quarrel between Earth and Sky long ago, and how Sky withheld rain for seven years, until crops withered and the dead could not be buried because the hoes broke on the stony Earth. At last Vulture was sent to plead with Sky, and to soften his heart with a song of the suffering of the sons of men. Whenever Nwoye's mother sang this song he felt carried away to the distant scene in the sky where Vulture, Earth's emissary, sang for mercy. At last Sky was moved to pity, and he gave to Vulture rain wrapped in leaves of coco-yam. But as he flew home his long talon pierced the leaves and the rain fell as it had never fallen before. And so heavily did it rain on Vulture that he did not return to deliver his message but flew to a distant land, from where he had espied a fire. And when he got there he found it was a man making a sacrifice. He warmed himself in the fire and ate the entrails.

That was the kind of story that Nwoye loved. But he now knew that they were for foolish women and children, and he knew that his father wanted him to be a man. And so he feigned that he no longer cared for women's stories. And when he did this he saw that his father was pleased, and no longer rebuked him or beat him. So Nwoye and Ikemefuna would listen to Okonkwo's stories about tribal wars, or how, years ago, he had stalked his victim, overpowered him and obtained his first human head. And as he told them of the past they sat in darkness or the dim glow of logs, waiting for the women to finish their cooking. When they finished, each brought her bowl of foo-foo and bowl of soup to her husband. An oil lamp was lit and Okonkwo tasted from each bowl, and then passed two shares to Nwoye and Ikemefuna.

In this way the moons and the seasons passed. And then the locusts came. It had not happened for many a long year. The elders said locusts came once in a generation, reappeared every year for seven years and then disappeared for another lifetime. They went back to their caves in a distant land, where they were guarded by a race of stunted men. And then after another lifetime these men opened the caves again and the locusts came to Umuofia.

They came in the cold harmattan season after the harvests had been gathered, and ate up all the wild grass in the fields.

Okonkwo and the two boys were working on the red outer walls of the compound. This was one of the lighter tasks of the after-harvest season. A new cover of thick palm branches and palm leaves was set on the walls to protect them from the next rainy season. Okonkwo worked on the outside of the wall and the boys worked from within. There were little holes from one side to the other in the upper levels of the wall, and through these Okonkwo passed the rope, or *tie-tie,*[6] to the boys and they passed it round the wooden stays and then back to him; and in this way the cover was strengthened on the wall.

---

5. The swallow with the ear of a crocodile [who is deaf] (literal trans.); a bird who proverbially flies without perching.   6. A creeper used as a rope to lash sections in building (pidgin English from "to tie").

The women had gone to the bush to collect firewood, and the little children to visit their playmates in the neighboring compounds. The harmattan was in the air and seemed to distill a hazy feeling of sleep on the world. Okonkwo and the boys worked in complete silence, which was only broken when a new palm frond was lifted on to the wall or when a busy hen moved dry leaves about in her ceaseless search for food.

And then quite suddenly a shadow fell on the world, and the sun seemed hidden behind a thick cloud. Okonkwo looked up from his work and wondered if it was going to rain at such an unlikely time of the year. But almost immediately a shout of joy broke out in all directions, and Umuofia, which had dozed in the noon-day haze, broke into life and activity.

"Locusts are descending," was joyfully chanted everywhere, and men, women and children left their work or their play and ran into the open to see the unfamiliar sight. The locusts had not come for many, many years, and only the old people had seen them before.

At first, a fairly small swarm came. They were the harbingers sent to survey the land. And then appeared on the horizon a slowly moving mass like a boundless sheet of black cloud drifting towards Umuofia. Soon it covered half the sky, and the solid mass was now broken by tiny eyes of light like shining star dust. It was a tremendous sight, full of power and beauty.

Everyone was now about, talking excitedly and praying that the locusts should camp in Umuofia for the night. For although locusts had not visited Umuofia for many years, everybody knew by instinct that they were very good to eat. And at last the locusts did descend. They settled on every tree and on every blade of grass; they settled on the roofs and covered the bare ground. Mighty tree branches broke away under them, and the whole country became the brown-earth color of the vast, hungry swarm.

Many people went out with baskets trying to catch them, but the elders counseled patience till nightfall. And they were right. The locusts settled in the bushes for the night and their wings became wet with dew. Then all Umuofia turned out in spite of the cold harmattan, and everyone filled his bags and pots with locusts. The next morning they were roasted in clay pots and then spread in the sun until they became dry and brittle. And for many days this rare food was eaten with solid palm-oil.

Okonkwo sat in his *obi* crunching happily with Ikemefuna and Nwoye, and drinking palm-wine copiously, when Ogbuefi Ezeudu came in. Ezeudu was the oldest man in this quarter of Umuofia. He had been a great and fearless warrior in his time, and was now accorded great respect in all the clan. He refused to join in the meal, and asked Okonkwo to have a word with him outside. And so they walked out together, the old man supporting himself with his stick. When they were out of earshot, he said to Okonkwo:

"That boy calls you father. Do not bear a hand in his death." Okonkwo was surprised, and was about to say something when the old man continued:

"Yes, Umuofia has decided to kill him. The Oracle of the Hills and the Caves has pronounced it. They will take him outside Umuofia as is the custom, and kill him there. But I want you to have nothing to do with it. He calls you his father."

The next day a group of elders from all the nine villages of Umuofia came to Okonkwo's house early in the morning, and before they began to speak in low tones Nwoye and Ikemefuna were sent out. They did not stay very long, but when they went away Okonkwo sat still for a very long time supporting his chin in his palms. Later in the day he called Ikemefuna and told him that he was to be taken home the next day. Nwoye overheard it and burst into tears, whereupon his father beat him heavily. As for Ikemefuna, he was at a loss. His own home had gradually become very faint and distant. He still missed his mother and his sister and would be very glad to see them. But somehow he knew he was not going to see them. He remembered once when men had talked in low tones with his father; and it seemed now as if it was happening all over again.

Later, Nwoye went to his mother's hut and told her that Ikemefuna was going home. She immediately dropped her pestle with which she was grinding pepper, folded her arms across her breast and sighed, "Poor child."

The next day, the men returned with a pot of wine. They were all fully dressed as if they were going to a big clan meeting or to pay a visit to a neighboring village. They passed their cloths under the right arm-pit, and hung their goatskin bags and sheathed machetes over their left shoulders. Okonkwo got ready quickly and the party set out with Ikemefuna carrying the pot of wine. A deathly silence descended on Okonkwo's compound. Even the very little children seemed to know. Throughout that day Nwoye sat in his mother's hut and tears stood in his eyes.

At the beginning of their journey the men of Umuofia talked and laughed about the locusts, about their women, and about some effeminate men who had refused to come with them. But as they drew near to the outskirts of Umuofia silence fell upon them too.

The sun rose slowly to the center of the sky, and the dry, sandy footway began to throw up the heat that lay buried in it. Some birds chirruped in the forests around. The men trod dry leaves on the sand. All else was silent. Then from the distance came the faint beating of the *ekwe*. It rose and faded with the wind—a peaceful dance from a distant clan.

"It is an *ozo* dance,"[7] the men said among themselves. But no one was sure where it was coming from. Some said Ezimili, others Abame or Aninta. They argued for a short while and fell into silence again, and the elusive dance rose and fell with the wind. Somewhere a man was taking one of the titles of his clan, with music and dancing and a great feast.

The footway had now become a narrow line in the heart of the forest. The short trees and sparse undergrowth which surrounded the men's village began to give way to giant trees and climbers which perhaps had stood from the beginning of things, untouched by the ax and the bush-fire. The sun breaking through their leaves and branches threw a pattern of light and shade on the sandy footway.

Ikemefuna heard a whisper close behind him and turned round sharply. The man who had whispered now called out aloud, urging the others to hurry up.

"We still have a long way to go," he said. Then he and another man went before Ikemefuna and set a faster pace.

Thus the men of Umuofia pursued their way, armed with sheathed machetes, and Ikemefuna, carrying a pot of palm-wine on his head, walked in their midst. Although he had felt uneasy at first, he was not afraid now. Okonkwo walked behind him. He could hardly imagine that Okonkwo was

---

7. Part of the *ozo* rituals, the spiritual ceremonies that accompanied the taking of titles.

not his real father. He had never been fond of his real father, and at the end of three years he had become very distant indeed. But his mother and his three-year-old sister . . . of course she would not be three now, but six. Would he recognize her now? She must have grown quite big. How his mother would weep for joy, and thank Okonkwo for having looked after him so well and for bringing him back. She would want to hear everything that had happened to him in all these years. Could he remember them all? He would tell her about Nwoye and his mother, and about the locusts. . . . Then quite suddenly a thought came upon him. His mother might be dead. He tried in vain to force the thought out of his mind. Then he tried to settle the matter the way he used to settle such matters when he was a little boy. He still remembered the song:

> Eze elina, elina!
> Sala
> Eze ilikwa ya
> Ikwaba akwa oligholi
> Ebe Danda nechi eze
> Ebe Uzuzu nete egwu
> Sala[8]

He sang it in his mind, and walked to its beat. If the song ended on his right foot, his mother was alive. If it ended on his left, she was dead. No, not dead, but ill. It ended on the right. She was alive and well. He sang the song again, and it ended on the left. But the second time did not count. The first voice gets to Chukwu, or God's house. That was a favorite saying of children. Ikemefuna felt like a child once more. It must be the thought of going home to his mother.

One of the men behind him cleared his throat. Ikemefuna looked back, and the man growled at him to go on and not stand looking back. The way he said it sent cold fear down Ikemefuna's back. His hands trembled vaguely on the black pot he carried. Why had Okonkwo withdrawn to the rear? Ikemefuna felt his legs melting under him. And he was afraid to look back.

As the man who had cleared his throat drew up and raised his machete, Okonkwo looked away. He heard the blow. The pot fell and broke in the sand. He heard Ikemefuna cry, "My father, they have killed me!" as he ran towards him. Dazed with fear, Okonkwo drew his machete and cut him down. He was afraid of being thought weak.

As soon as his father walked in, that night, Nwoye knew that Ikemefuna had been killed, and something seemed to give way inside him, like the snapping of a tightened bow. He did not cry. He just hung limp. He had had the same kind of feeling not long ago, during the last harvest season. Every child loved the harvest season. Those who were big enough to carry even a few yams in a tiny basket went with grown-ups to the farm. And if they could not help in digging up the yams, they could gather firewood together for roasting the ones that would be eaten there on the farm. This roasted yam soaked in red palm-oil and eaten in the open farm was sweeter than any meal

8. King don't eat, don't eat / Sala / King if you eat it / You will weep for the abomination / Where Danda installs a king / Where Uzuzu dances / Sala. *Sala*: meaningless refrain. *Danda*: the ant. *Uzuzu*: sand. Ikemefuna reassures himself by singing his favorite song about the country where the "sands dance forever" (see p. 2080).

at home. It was after such a day at the farm during the last harvest that Nwoye had felt for the first time a snapping inside him like the one he now felt. They were returning home with baskets of yams from a distant farm across the stream when they heard the voice of an infant crying in the thick forest. A sudden hush had fallen on the women, who had been talking, and they had quickened their steps. Nwoye had heard that twins were put in earthenware pots and thrown away in the forest, but he had never yet come across them. A vague chill had descended on him and his head had seemed to swell, like a solitary walker at night who passes an evil spirit on the way. Then something had given way inside him. It descended on him again, this feeling, when his father walked in, that night after killing Ikemefuna.

8

Okonkwo did not taste any food for two days after the death of Ikemefuna. He drank palm-wine from morning till night, and his eyes were red and fierce like the eyes of a rat when it was caught by the tail and dashed against the floor. He called his son, Nwoye, to sit with him in his *obi*. But the boy was afraid of him and slipped out of the hut as soon as he noticed him dozing.

He did not sleep at night. He tried not to think about Ikemefuna, but the more he tried the more he thought about him. Once he got up from bed and walked about his compound. But he was so weak that his legs could hardly carry him. He felt like a drunken giant walking with the limbs of a mosquito. Now and then a cold shiver descended on his head and spread down his body.

On the third day he asked his second wife, Ekwefi, to roast plantains for him. She prepared it the way he liked—with slices of oil-bean and fish.

"You have not eaten for two days," said his daughter Ezinma when she brought the food to him. "So you must finish this." She sat down and stretched her legs in front of her. Okonkwo ate the food absent-mindedly. 'She should have been a boy,' he thought as he looked at his ten-year-old daughter. He passed her a piece of fish.

"Go and bring me some cold water," he said. Ezinma rushed out of the hut, chewing the fish, and soon returned with a bowl of cool water from the earthen pot in her mother's hut.

Okonkwo took the bowl from her and gulped the water down. He ate a few more pieces of plantain and pushed the dish aside.

"Bring me my bag," he asked, and Ezinma brought his goatskin bag from the far end of the hut. He searched in it for his snuff-bottle. It was a deep bag and took almost the whole length of his arm. It contained other things apart from his snuff-bottle. There was a drinking horn in it, and also a drinking gourd, and they knocked against each other as he searched. When he brought out the snuff-bottle he tapped it a few times against his knee-cap before taking out some snuff on the palm of his left hand. Then he remembered that he had not taken out his snuff-spoon. He searched his bag again and brought out a small, flat, ivory spoon, with which he carried the brown snuff to his nostrils.

Ezinma took the dish in one hand and the empty water bowl in the other and went back to her mother's hut. "She should have been a boy," Okonkwo said to himself again. His mind went back to Ikemefuna and he shivered. If only he could find some work to do he would be able to forget. But it was the season of rest between the harvest and the next planting season. The only work that men did at this time was covering the walls of their compound with new palm fronds. And Okonkwo had already done that. He had finished it on the very day the locusts came, when he had worked on one side of the wall and Ikemefuna and Nwoye on the other.

"When did you become a shivering old woman," Okonkwo asked himself, "you, who are known in all the nine villages for your valor in war? How can a man who has killed five men in battle fall to pieces because he has added a boy to their number? Okonkwo, you have become a woman indeed."

He sprang to his feet, hung his goatskin bag on his shoulder and went to visit his friend, Obierika.

Obierika was sitting outside under the shade of an orange tree making thatches from leaves of the raffia-palm. He exchanged greetings with Okonkwo and led the way into his *obi*.

"I was coming over to see you as soon as I finished that thatch," he said, rubbing off the grains of sand that clung to his thighs.

"Is it well?" Okonkwo asked.

"Yes," replied Obierika. "My daughter's suitor is coming today and I hope we will clinch the matter of the bride-price. I want you to be there."

Just then Obierika's son, Maduka, came into the *obi* from outside, greeted Okonkwo and turned towards the compound.

"Come and shake hands with me," Okonkwo said to the lad. "Your wrestling the other day gave me much happiness." The boy smiled, shook hands with Okonkwo and went into the compound.

"He will do great things," Okonkwo said. "If I had a son like him I should be happy. I am worried about Nwoye. A bowl of pounded yams can throw him in a wrestling match. His two younger brothers are more promising. But I can tell you, Obierika, that my children do not resemble me. Where are the young suckers that will grow when the old banana tree dies? If Ezinma had been a boy I would have been happier. She has the right spirit."

"You worry yourself for nothing," said Obierika. "The children are still very young."

"Nwoye is old enough to impregnate a woman. At his age I was already fending for myself. No, my friend, he is not too young. A chick that will grow into a cock can be spotted the very day it hatches. I have done my best to make Nwoye grow into a man, but there is too much of his mother in him."

"Too much of his grandfather," Obierika thought, but he did not say it. The same thought also came to Okonkwo's mind. But he had long learned how to lay that ghost. Whenever the thought of his father's weakness and failure troubled him he expelled it by thinking about his own strength and success. And so he did now. His mind went to his latest show of manliness.

"I cannot understand why you refused to come with us to kill that boy," he asked Obierika.

"Because I did not want to," Obierika replied sharply. "I had something better to do."

"You sound as if you question the authority and the decision of the Oracle, who said he should die."

"I do not. Why should I? But the Oracle did not ask me to carry out its decision."

"But someone had to do it. If we were all afraid of blood, it would not be done. And what do you think the Oracle would do then?"

"You know very well, Okonkwo, that I am not afraid of blood; and if anyone tells you that I am, he is telling a lie. And let me tell you one thing, my friend. If I were you I would have stayed at home. What you have done will not please the Earth. It is the kind of action for which the goddess wipes out whole families."

"The Earth cannot punish me for obeying her messenger," Okonkwo said. "A child's fingers are not scalded by a piece of hot yam which its mother puts into its palm."

"That is true," Obierika agreed. "But if the Oracle said that my son should be killed I would neither dispute it nor be the one to do it."

They would have gone on arguing had Ofoedu[9] not come in just then. It was clear from his twinkling eyes that he had important news. But it would be impolite to rush him. Obierika offered him a lobe of the kola nut he had broken with Okonkwo. Ofoedu ate slowly and talked about the locusts. When he finished his kola nut he said:

"The things that happen these days are very strange."

"What has happened?" asked Okonkwo.

"Do you know Ogbuefi Ndulue?"[1] Ofoedu asked.

"Ogbuefi Ndulue of Ire village," Okonkwo and Obierika said together.

"He died this morning," said Ofoedu.

"That is not strange. He was the oldest man in Ire," said Obierika.

"You are right," Ofoedu agreed. "But you ought to ask why the drum has not beaten to tell Umuofia of his death."

"Why?" asked Obierika and Okonkwo together.

"That is the strange part of it. You know his first wife who walks with a stick?"

"Yes. She is called Ozoemena."[2]

"That is so," said Ofoedu. "Ozoemena was, as you know, too old to attend Ndulue during his illness. His younger wives did that. When he died this morning, one of these women went to Ozoemena's hut and told her. She rose from her mat, took her stick and walked over to the *obi*. She knelt on her knees and hands at the threshold and called her husband, who was laid on a mat. 'Ogbuefi Ndulue,' she called, three times, and went back to her hut. When the youngest wife went to call her again to be present at the washing of the body, she found her lying on the mat, dead."

"That is very strange, indeed," said Okonkwo. "They will put off Ndulue's funeral until his wife has been buried."[3]

"That is why the drum has not been beaten to tell Umuofia."

"It was always said that Ndulue and Ozoemena had one mind," said Obierika. "I remember when I was a young boy there was a song about them. He could not do anything without telling her."

"I did not know that," said Okonkwo. "I thought he was a strong man in his youth."

"He was indeed," said Ofoedu.

9. The ancestors are our guide.　1. Life has arrived.　2. Another bad thing will not happen.　3. A wife dying shortly after her husband was sometimes considered guilty of his death, so the village preserves appearances by burying Ozoemena before announcing Ogbuefi Ndulue's death.

Okonkwo shook his head doubtfully.

"He led Umuofia to war in those days," said Obierika.

Okonkwo was beginning to feel like his old self again. All that he required was something to occupy his mind. If he had killed Ikemefuna during the busy planting season or harvesting it would not have been so bad; his mind would have been centered on his work. Okonkwo was not a man of thought but of action. But in absence of work, talking was the next best.

Soon after Ofoedu left, Okonkwo took up his goatskin bag to go.

"I must go home to tap my palm trees for the afternoon," he said.

"Who taps your tall trees for you?" asked Obierika.

"Umezulike," replied Okonkwo.

"Sometimes I wish I had not taken the ozo title," said Obierika. "It wounds my heart to see these young men killing palm trees in the name of tapping."

"It is so indeed," Okonkwo agreed. "But the law of the land must be obeyed."

"I don't know how we got that law," said Obierika. "In many other clans a man of title is not forbidden to climb the palm tree. Here we say he cannot climb the tall tree but he can tap the short ones standing on the ground. It is like Dimaragana, who would not lend his knife for cutting up dogmeat because the dog was taboo to him, but offered to use his teeth."

"I think it is good that our clan holds the ozo title in high esteem," said Okonkwo. "In those other clans you speak of, ozo is so low that every beggar takes it."

"I was only speaking in jest," said Obierika. "In Abame and Aninta the title is worth less than two cowries. Every man wears the thread of title on his ankle, and does not lose it even if he steals."

"They have indeed soiled the name of ozo," said Okonkwo as he rose to go.

"It will not be very long now before my in-laws come," said Obierika.

"I shall return very soon," said Okonkwo, looking at the position of the sun.

There were seven men in Obierika's hut when Okonkwo returned. The suitor was a young man of about twenty-five, and with him were his father and uncle. On Obierika's side were his two elder brothers and Maduka, his sixteen-year-old son.

"Ask Akueke's mother to send us some kola nuts," said Obierika to his son. Maduka vanished into the compound like lightning. The conversation at once centered on him, and everybody agreed that he was as sharp as a razor.

"I sometimes think he is too sharp," said Obierika, somewhat indulgently. "He hardly ever walks. He is always in a hurry. If you are sending him on an errand he flies away before he has heard half of the message."

"You were very much like that yourself," said his eldest brother. "As our people say, 'When mother-cow is chewing grass its young ones watch its mouth.' Maduka has been watching your mouth."

As he was speaking the boy returned, followed by Akueke,[4] his half-sister,

---

4. Wealth of Eke (a divinity). Similar names built on ako ("wealth") connote riches and are associated with the idea of women as a form of exchangeable material wealth.

carrying a wooden dish with three kola nuts and alligator pepper. She gave the dish to her father's eldest brother and then shook hands, very shyly, with her suitor and his relatives. She was about sixteen and just ripe for marriage. Her suitor and his relatives surveyed her young body with expert eyes as if to assure themselves that she was beautiful and ripe.

She wore a coiffure which was done up into a crest in the middle of the head. Cam wood was rubbed lightly into her skin, and all over her body were black patterns drawn with *uli*.[5] She wore a black necklace which hung down in three coils just above her full, succulent breasts. On her arms were red and yellow bangles, and on her waist four or five rows of *jigida*, or waist beads.

When she had shaken hands, or rather held out her hand to be shaken, she returned to her mother's hut to help with the cooking.

"Remove your *jigida* first," her mother warned as she moved near the fireplace to bring the pestle resting against the wall. "Every day I tell you that *jigida* and fire are not friends. But you will never hear. You grew your ears for decoration, not for hearing. One of these days your *jigida* will catch fire on your waist, and then you will know."

Akueke moved to the other end of the hut and began to remove the waistbeads. It had to be done slowly and carefully, taking each string separately, else it would break and the thousand tiny rings would have to be strung together again. She rubbed each string downwards with her palms until it passed the buttocks and slipped down to the floor around her feet.

The men in the *obi* had already begun to drink the palm-wine which Akueke's suitor had brought. It was a very good wine and powerful, for in spite of the palm fruit hung across the mouth of the pot to restrain the lively liquor, white foam rose and spilled over.

"That wine is the work of a good tapper," said Okonkwo.

The young suitor, whose name was Ibe, smiled broadly and said to his father: "Do you hear that?" He then said to the others: "He will never admit that I am a good tapper."

"He tapped three of my best palm trees to death," said his father, Ukegbu.

"That was about five years ago," said Ibe, who had begun to pour out the wine, "before I learned how to tap." He filled the first horn and gave to his father. Then he poured out for the others. Okonkwo brought out his big horn from the goatskin bag, blew into it to remove any dust that might be there, and gave it to Ibe to fill.

As the men drank, they talked about everything except the thing for which they had gathered. It was only after the pot had been emptied that the suitor's father cleared his voice and announced the object of their visit.

Obierika then presented to him a small bundle of short broomsticks. Ukegbu counted them.

"They are thirty?" he asked.

Obierika nodded in agreement.

"We are at last getting somewhere," Ukegbu said, and then turning to his brother and his son he said: "Let us go out and whisper together." The three rose and went outside. When they returned Ukegbu handed the bundle of

---

5. A liquid made from crushed seeds, which caused the skin to pucker temporarily. It was used to create black tattoolike decorations. *Cam wood*: a shrub. The powdered red heartwood of the shrub was used as a cosmetic dye.

sticks back to Obierika. He counted them; instead of thirty there were now only fifteen. He passed them over to his eldest brother, Machi, who also counted them and said:

"We had not thought to go below thirty. But as the dog said, 'If I fall down for you and you fall down for me, it is play.' Marriage should be a play and not a fight; so we are falling down again." He then added ten sticks to the fifteen and gave the bundle to Ukegbu.

In this way Akuke's bride-price was finally settled at twenty bags of cowries. It was already dusk when the two parties came to this agreement.

"Go and tell Akueke's mother that we have finished," Obierika said to his son, Maduka. Almost immediately the women came in with a big bowl of foo-foo. Obierika's second wife followed with a pot of soup, and Maduka brought in a pot of palm-wine.

As the men ate and drank palm-wine they talked about the customs of their neighbors.

"It was only this morning," said Obierika, "that Okonkwo and I were talking about Abame and Aninta, where titled men climb trees and pound foo-foo for their wives."

"All their customs are upside-down. They do not decide bride-price as we do, with sticks. They haggle and bargain as if they were buying a goat or a cow in the market."

"That is very bad," said Obierika's eldest brother. "But what is good in one place is bad in another place. In Umunso they do not bargain at all, not even with broomsticks. The suitor just goes on bringing bags of cowries until his in-laws tell him to stop. It is a bad custom because it always leads to a quarrel."

"The world is large," said Okonkwo. "I have even heard that in some tribes a man's children belong to his wife and her family."

"That cannot be," said Machi. "You might as well say that the woman lies on top of the man when they are making the children."

"It is like the story of white men who, they say, are white like this piece of chalk," said Obierika. He held up a piece of chalk, which every man kept in his *obi* and with which his guests drew lines on the floor before they ate kola nuts. "And these white men, they say, have no toes."[6]

"And have you never seen them?" asked Machi.

"Have you?" asked Obierika.

"One of them passes here frequently," said Machi. "His name is Amadi."

Those who knew Amadi laughed. He was a leper, and the polite name for leprosy was "the white skin."

9

For the first time in three nights, Okonkwo slept. He woke up once in the middle of the night and his mind went back to the past three days without making him feel uneasy. He began to wonder why he had felt uneasy at all. It was like a man wondering in broad daylight why a dream had appeared so terrible to him at night. He stretched himself and scratched his thigh where a mosquito had bitten him as he slept. Another one was wailing near his

6. They wear shoes.

right ear. He slapped the ear and hoped he had killed it. Why do they always go for one's ears? When he was a child his mother had told him a story about it. But it was as silly as all women's stories. Mosquito, she had said, had asked Ear to marry him, whereupon Ear fell on the floor in uncontrollable laughter. "How much longer do you think you will live?" she asked. "You are already a skeleton." Mosquito went away humiliated, and any time he passed her way he told Ear that he was still alive.

Okonkwo turned on his side and went back to sleep. He was roused in the morning by someone banging on his door.

"Who is that?" he growled. He knew it must be Ekwefi. Of his three wives Ekwefi was the only one who would have the audacity to bang on his door.

"Ezinma is dying," came her voice, and all the tragedy and sorrow of her life were packed in those words.

Okonkwo sprang from his bed, pushed back the bolt on his door and ran into Ekwefi's hut.

Ezinma lay shivering on a mat beside a huge fire that her mother had kept burning all night.

"It is *iba*,"[7] said Okonkwo as he took his machete and went into the bush to collect the leaves and grasses and barks of trees that went into making the medicine for *iba*.

Ekwefi knelt beside the sick child, occasionally feeling with her palm the wet, burning forehead.

Ezinma was an only child and the center of her mother's world. Very often it was Ezinma who decided what food her mother should prepare. Ekwefi even gave her such delicacies as eggs, which children were rarely allowed to eat because such food tempted them to steal. One day as Ezinma was eating an egg Okonkwo had come in unexpectedly from his hut. He was greatly shocked and swore to beat Ekwefi if she dared to give the child eggs again. But it was impossible to refuse Ezinma anything. After her father's rebuke she developed an even keener appetite for eggs. And she enjoyed above all the secrecy in which she now ate them. Her mother always took her into their bedroom and shut the door.

Ezinma did not call her mother *Nne* like all children. She called her by her name, Ekwefi, as her father and other grown-up people did. The relationship between them was not only that of mother and child. There was something in it like the companionship of equals, which was strengthened by such little conspiracies as eating eggs in the bedroom.

Ekwefi had suffered a good deal in her life. She had borne ten children and nine of them had died in infancy, usually before the age of three. As she buried one child after another her sorrow gave way to despair and then to grim resignation. The birth of her children, which should be a woman's crowning glory, became for Ekwefi mere physical agony devoid of promise. The naming ceremony after seven market weeks became an empty ritual. Her deepening despair found expression in the names she gave her children. One of them was a pathetic cry, Onwumbiko—"Death, I implore you." But Death took no notice; Onwumbiko died in his fifteenth month. The next child was a girl, Ozoemena—"May it not happen again." She died in her eleventh month, and two others after her. Ekwefi then became defiant and called her next child Onwuma—"Death may please himself." And he did.

---

7. A fever accompanied by jaundice, probably caused by malaria.

After the death of Ekwefi's second child, Okonkwo had gone to a medicine man, who was also a diviner of the Afa Oracle,[8] to inquire what was amiss. This man told him that the child was an *ogbanje*, one of those wicked children who, when they died, entered their mothers' wombs to be born again.

"When your wife becomes pregnant again," he said, "let her not sleep in her hut. Let her go and stay with her people. In that way she will elude her wicked tormentor and break its evil cycle of birth and death."

Ekwefi did as she was asked. As soon as she became pregnant she went to live with her old mother in another village. It was there that her third child was born and circumcised on the eighth day. She did not return to Okonkwo's compound until three days before the naming ceremony. The child was called Onwumbiko.

Onwumbiko was not given proper burial when he died. Okonkwo had called on another medicine man who was famous in the clan for his great knowledge about *ogbanje* children. His name was Okagbue Uyanwa. Okagbue was a very striking figure, tall, with a full beard and a bald head. He was light in complexion and his eyes were red and fiery. He always gnashed his teeth as he listened to those who came to consult him. He asked Okonkwo a few questions about the dead child. All the neighbors and relations who had come to mourn gathered round them.

"On what market-day was it born?" he asked.

"*Oye*," replied Okonkwo.

"And it died this morning?"

Okonkwo said yes, and only then realized for the first time that the child had died on the same market-day as it had been born. The neighbors and relations also saw the coincidence and said among themselves that it was very significant.

"Where do you sleep with your wife, in your *obi* or in her own hut?" asked the medicine man.

"In her hut."

"In future call her into your *obi*."

The medicine man then ordered that there should be no mourning for the dead child. He brought out a sharp razor from the goatskin bag slung from his left shoulder and began to mutilate the child. Then he took it away to bury in the Evil Forest, holding it by the ankle and dragging it on the ground behind him. After such treatment it would think twice before coming again, unless it was one of the stubborn ones who returned, carrying the stamp of their mutilation—a missing finger or perhaps a dark line where the medicine man's razor had cut them.

By the time Onwumbiko died Ekwefi had become a very bitter woman. Her husband's first wife had already had three sons, all strong and healthy. When she had borne her third son in succession, Okonkwo had gathered a goat for her, as was the custom. Ekwefi had nothing but good wishes for her. But she had grown so bitter about her own *chi* that she could not rejoice with others over their good fortune. And so, on the day that Nwoye's mother celebrated the birth of her three sons with feasting and music, Ekwefi was the only person in the happy company who went about with a cloud on her brow. Her husband's wife took this for malevolence, as husbands' wives were

8. One who communicates with the clients' ancestors by reading patterns made by objects (e.g., seeds, teeth, shells) thrown on a flat surface.

wont to. How could she know that Ekwefi's bitterness did not flow outwards to others but inwards into her own soul; that she did not blame others for their good fortune but her own evil *chi* who denied her any?

At last Ezinma was born, and although ailing she seemed determined to live. At first Ekwefi accepted her, as she had accepted others—with listless resignation. But when she lived on to her fourth, fifth and sixth years, love returned once more to her mother, and, with love, anxiety. She determined to nurse her child to health, and she put all her being into it. She was rewarded by occasional spells of health during which Ezinma bubbled with energy like fresh palm-wine. At such times she seemed beyond danger. But all of a sudden she would go down again. Everybody knew she was an *ogbanje*. These sudden bouts of sickness and health were typical of her kind. But she had lived so long that perhaps she had decided to stay. Some of them did become tired of their evil rounds of birth and death, or took pity on their mothers, and stayed. Ekwefi believed deep inside her that Ezinma had come to stay. She believed because it was that faith alone that gave her own life any kind of meaning. And this faith had been strengthened when a year or so ago a medicine man had dug up Ezinma's *iyi-uwa*. Everyone knew then that she would live because her bond with the world of *ogbanje* had been broken. Ekwefi was reassured. But such was her anxiety for her daughter that she could not rid herself completely of her fear. And although she believed that the *iyi-uwa* which had been dug up was genuine, she could not ignore the fact that some really evil children sometimes misled people into digging up a specious one.

But Ezinma's *iyi-uwa* had looked real enough. It was a smooth pebble wrapped in a dirty rag. The man who dug it up was the same Okagbue who was famous in all the clan for his knowledge in these matters. Ezinma had not wanted to cooperate with him at first. But that was only to be expected. No *ogbanje* would yield her secrets easily, and most of them never did because they died too young—before they could be asked questions.

"Where did you bury your *iyi-uwa*?" Okagbue had asked Ezinma. She was nine then and was just recovering from a serious illness.

"What is *iyi-uwa*?" she asked in return.

"You know what it is. You buried it in the ground somewhere so that you can die and return again to torment your mother."

Ezinma looked at her mother, whose eyes, sad and pleading, were fixed on her.

"Answer the question at once," roared Okonkwo, who stood beside her. All the family were there and some of the neighbors too.

"Leave her to me," the medicine man told Okonkwo in a cool, confident voice. He turned again to Ezinma. "Where did you bury your *iyi-uwa*?"

"Where they bury children," she replied, and the quiet spectators murmured to themselves.

"Come along then and show me the spot," said the medicine man.

The crowd set out with Ezinma leading the way and Okagbue following closely behind her. Okonkwo came next and Ekwefi followed him. When she came to the main road, Ezinma turned left as if she was going to the stream.

"But you said it was where they bury children?" asked the medicine man.

"No," said Ezinma, whose feeling of importance was manifest in her sprightly walk. She sometimes broke into a run and stopped again suddenly.

The crowd followed her silently. Women and children returning from the stream with pots of water on their heads wondered what was happening until they saw Okagbue and guessed that it must be something to do with *ogbanje*. And they all knew Ekwefi and her daughter very well.

When she got to the big udala tree Ezinma turned left into the bush, and the crowd followed her. Because of her size she made her way through trees and creepers more quickly then her followers. The bush was alive with the tread of feet on dry leaves and sticks and the moving aside of tree branches. Ezinma went deeper and deeper and the crowd went with her. Then she suddenly turned round and began to walk back to the road. Everybody stood to let her pass and then filed after her.

"If you bring us all this way for nothing I shall beat sense into you," Okonkwo threatened.

"I have told you to let her alone. I know how to deal with them," said Okagbue.

Ezinma led the way back to the road, looked left and right and turned right. And so they arrived home again.

"Where did you bury your *iyi-uwa?*" asked Okagbue when Ezinma finally stopped outside her father's *obi*. Okagbue's voice was unchanged. It was quiet and confident.

"It is near that orange tree," Ezinma said.

"And why did you not say so, you wicked daughter of Akalogoli?" Okonkwo swore furiously. The medicine man ignored him.

"Come and show me the exact spot," he said quietly to Ezinma.

"It is here," she said when they got to the tree.

"Point at the spot with your finger," said Okagbue.

"It is here," said Ezinma touching the ground with her finger. Okonkwo stood by, rumbling like thunder in the rainy season.

"Bring me a hoe," said Okagbue.

When Ekwefi brought the hoe, he had already put aside his goatskin bag and his big cloth and was in his underwear, a long and thin strip of cloth wound round the waist like a belt and then passed between the legs to be fastened to the belt behind. He immediately set to work digging a pit where Ezinma had indicated. The neighbors sat around watching the pit becoming deeper and deeper. The dark top soil soon gave way to the bright red earth with which women scrubbed the floors and walls of huts. Okagbue worked tirelessly and in silence, his back shining with perspiration. Okonkwo stood by the pit. He asked Okagbue to come up and rest while he took a hand. But Okagbue said he was not tired yet.

Ekwefi went into her hut to cook yams. Her husband had brought out more yams than usual because the medicine man had to be fed. Ezinma went with her and helped in preparing the vegetables.

"There is too much green vegetable," she said.

"Don't you see the pot is full of yams?" Ekwefi asked. "And you know how leaves become smaller after cooking."

"Yes," said Ezinma, "that was why the snake-lizard killed his mother."

"Very true," said Ekwefi.

"He gave his mother seven baskets of vegetables to cook and in the end there were only three. And so he killed her," said Ezinma.

"That is not the end of the story."

"Oho," said Ezinma. "I remember now. He brought another seven baskets and cooked them himself. And there were again only three. So he killed himself too."

Outside the *obi* Okagbue and Okonkwo were digging the pit to find where Ezinma had buried her *iyi-uwa*. Neighbors sat around, watching. The pit was now so deep that they no longer saw the digger. They only saw the red earth he threw up mounting higher and higher. Okonkwo's son, Nwoye, stood near the edge of the pit because he wanted to take in all that happened.

Okagbue had again taken over the digging from Okonkwo. He worked, as usual, in silence. The neighbors and Okonkwo's wives were now talking. The children had lost interest and were playing.

Suddenly Okagbue sprang to the surface with the agility of a leopard.

"It is very near now," he said. "I have felt it."

There was immediate excitement and those who were sitting jumped to their feet.

"Call your wife and child," he said to Okonkwo. But Ekwefi and Ezinma had heard the noise and run out to see what it was.

Okagbue went back into the pit, which was now surrounded by spectators. After a few more hoe-fuls of earth he struck the *iyi-uwa*. He raised it carefully with the hoe and threw it to the surface. Some women ran away in fear when it was thrown. But they soon returned and everyone was gazing at the rag from a reasonable distance. Okagbue emerged and without saying a word or even looking at the spectators he went to his goatskin bag, took out two leaves and began to chew them. When he had swallowed them, he took up the rag with his left hand and began to untie it. And then the smooth, shiny pebble fell out. He picked it up.

"Is this yours?" he asked Ezinma.

"Yes," she replied. All the women shouted with joy because Ekwefi's troubles were at last ended.

All this had happened more than a year ago and Ezinma had not been ill since. And then suddenly she had begun to shiver in the night. Ekwefi brought her to the fireplace, spread her mat on the floor and built a fire. But she had got worse and worse. As she knelt by her, feeling with her palm the wet, burning forehead, she prayed a thousand times. Although her husband's wives were saying that it was nothing more than *iba*, she did not hear them.

Okonkwo returned from the bush carrying on his left shoulder a large bundle of grasses and leaves, roots and barks of medicinal trees and shrubs. He went into Ekwefi's hut, put down his load and sat down.

"Get me a pot," he said, "and leave the child alone."

Ekwefi went to bring the pot and Okonkwo selected the best from his bundle, in their due proportions, and cut them up. He put them in the pot and Ekwefi poured in some water.

"Is that enough?" she asked when she had poured in about half of the water in the bowl.

"A little more . . . I said a *little*. Are you deaf?" Okonkwo roared at her.

She set the pot on the fire and Okonkwo took up his machete to return to his *obi*.

"You must watch the pot carefully," he said as he went, "and don't allow it to boil over. If it does its power will be gone." He went away to his hut and

Ekwefi began to tend the medicine pot almost as if it was itself a sick child. Her eyes went constantly from Ezinma to the boiling pot and back to Ezinma.

Okonkwo returned when he felt the medicine had cooked long enough. He looked it over and said it was done.

"Bring me a low stool for Ezinma," he said, "and a thick mat."

He took down the pot from the fire and placed it in front of the stool. He then roused Ezinma and placed her on the stool, astride the steaming pot. The thick mat was thrown over both. Ezinma struggled to escape from the choking and overpowering steam, but she was held down. She started to cry.

When the mat was at last removed she was drenched in perspiration. Ekwefi mopped her with a piece of cloth and she lay down on a dry mat and was soon asleep.

10

Large crowds began to gather on the village *ilo* as soon as the edge had worn off the sun's heat and it was no longer painful on the body. Most communal ceremonies took place at that time of the day, so that even when it was said that a ceremony would begin "after the midday meal" everyone understood that it would begin a long time later, when the sun's heat had softened.

It was clear from the way the crowd stood or sat that the ceremony was for men. There were many women, but they looked on from the fringe like outsiders. The titled men and elders sat on their stools waiting for the trials to begin. In front of them was a row of stools on which nobody sat. There were nine of them. Two little groups of people stood at a respectable distance beyond the stools. They faced the elders. There were three men in one group and three men and one woman in the other. The woman was Mgbafo and the three men with her were her brothers. In the other group were her husband, Uzowulu, and his relatives. Mgbafo and her brothers were as still as statues into whose faces the artist has molded defiance. Uzowulu and his relatives, on the other hand, were whispering together. It looked like whispering, but they were really talking at the top of their voices. Everybody in the crowd was talking. It was like the market. From a distance the noise was a deep rumble carried by the wind.

An iron gong sounded, setting up a wave of expectation in the crowd. Everyone looked in the direction of the *egwugwu*[9] house. *Gome, gome, gome* went the gong, and a powerful flute blew a high-pitched blast. Then came the voices of the *egwugwu*, guttural and awesome. The wave struck the women and children and there was a backward stampede. But it was momentary. They were already far enough where they stood and there was room for running away if any of the *egwugwu* should go towards them.

The drum sounded again and the flute blew. The *egwugwu* house was now a pandemonium of quavering voices: *Aru oyim de de de dei!*[1] filled the air as the spirits of the ancestors, just emerged from the earth, greeted themselves in their esoteric language. The *egwugwu* house into which they emerged faced the forest, away from the crowd, who saw only its back with the many-

9. Here the term refers to the village's highest spiritual and judicial authority, prominent men who, after putting on elaborate ceremonial costumes, embody the village's ancestral spirits.   1. Body of my friend, greetings!

colored patterns and drawings done by specially chosen women at regular intervals. These women never saw the inside of the hut. No woman ever did. They scrubbed and painted the outside walls under the supervision of men. If they imagined what was inside, they kept their imagination to themselves. No woman ever asked questions about the most powerful and the most secret cult in the clan.

Aru oyim de de de dei! flew around the dark, closed hut like tongues of fire. The ancestral spirits of the clan were abroad. The metal gong beat continuously now and the flute, shrill and powerful, floated on the chaos.

And then the *egwugwu* appeared. The women and children sent up a great shout and took to their heels. It was instinctive. A woman fled as soon as an *egwugwu* came in sight. And when, as on that day, nine of the greatest masked spirits in the clan came out together it was a terrifying spectacle. Even Mgbafo took to her heels and had to be restrained by her brothers.

Each of the nine *egwugwu* represented a village of the clan. Their leader was called Evil Forest. Smoke poured out of his head.

The nine villages of Umuofia had grown out of the nine sons of the first father of the clan. Evil Forest represented the village of Umueru, or the children of Eru, who was the eldest of the nine sons.

"*Umuofia kwenu!*" shouted the leading *egwugwu,* pushing the air with his raffia arms. The elders of the clan replied, "*Yaa!*"

"*Umuofia kwenu!*"

"*Yaa!*"

"*Umuofia kwenu!*"

"*Yaa!*"

Evil Forest then thrust the pointed end of his rattling staff into the earth. And it began to shake and rattle, like something agitating with a metallic life. He took the first of the empty stools and the eight other *egwugwu* began to sit in order of seniority after him.

Okonkwo's wives, and perhaps other women as well, might have noticed that the second *egwugwu* had the springy walk of Okonkwo. And they might also have noticed that Okonkwo was not among the titled men and elders who sat behind the row of *egwugwu.* But if they thought these things they kept them within themselves. The *egwugwu* with the springy walk was one of the dead fathers of the clan. He looked terrible with the smoked raffia body, a huge wooden face painted white except for the round hollow eyes and the charred teeth that were as big as a man's fingers. On his head were two powerful horns.

When all the *egwugwu* had sat down and the sound of the many tiny bells and rattles on their bodies had subsided, Evil Forest addressed the two groups of people facing them.

"Uzowulu's body, I salute you," he said. Spirits always addressed humans as "bodies." Uzowulu bent down and touched the earth with his right hand as a sign of submission.

"Our father, my hand has touched the ground," he said.

"Uzowulu's body, do you know me?" asked the spirit.

"How can I know you, father? You are beyond our knowledge."

Evil Forest then turned to the other group and addressed the eldest of the three brothers.

"The body of Odukwe, I greet you," he said, and Odukwe bent down and touched the earth. The hearing then began.

Uzowulu stepped forward and presented his case.

"That woman standing there is my wife, Mgbafo. I married her with my money and my yams. I do not owe my in-laws anything. I owe them no yams. I owe them no coco-yams. One morning three of them came to my house, beat me up and took my wife and children away. This happened in the rainy season. I have waited in vain for my wife to return. At last I went to my in-laws and said to them, 'You have taken back your sister. I did not send her away. You yourselves took her. The law of the clan is that you should return her bride-price.' But my wife's brothers said they had nothing to tell me. So I have brought the matter to the fathers of the clan. My case is finished. I salute you."

"Your words are good," said the leader of the *egwugwu*. "Let us hear Odukwe. His words may also be good."

Odukwe was short and thickset. He stepped forward, saluted the spirits and began his story.

"My in-law has told you that we went to his house, beat him up and took our sister and her children away. All that is true. He told you that he came to take back her bride-price and we refused to give it him. That also is true. My in-law, Uzowulu, is a beast. My sister lived with him for nine years. During those years no single day passed in the sky without his beating the woman. We have tried to settle their quarrels time without number and on each occasion Uzowulu was guilty—"

"It is a lie!" Uzowulu shouted.

"Two years ago," continued Odukwe, "when she was pregnant, he beat her until she miscarried."

"It is a lie. She miscarried after she had gone to sleep with her lover."

"Uzowulu's body, I salute you," said Evil Forest, silencing him. "What kind of lover sleeps with a pregnant woman?" There was a loud murmur of approbation from the crowd. Odukwe continued:

"Last year when my sister was recovering from an illness, he beat her again so that if the neighbors had not gone in to save her she would have been killed. We heard of it, and did as you have been told. The law of Umuofia is that if a woman runs away from her husband her bride-price is returned. But in this case she ran away to save her life. Her two children belong to Uzowulu. We do not dispute it, but they are too young to leave their mother. If, in the other hand, Uzowulu should recover from his madness and come in the proper way to beg his wife to return she will do so on the understanding that if he ever beats her again we shall cut off his genitals for him."

The crowd roared with laughter. Evil Forest rose to his feet and order was immediately restored. A steady cloud of smoke rose from his head. He sat down again and called two witnesses. They were both Uzowulu's neighbors, and they agreed about the beating. Evil Forest then stood up, pulled out his staff and thrust it into the earth again. He ran a few steps in the direction of the women; they all fled in terror, only to return to their places almost immediately. The nine *egwugwu* then went away to consult together in their house. They were silent for a long time. Then the metal gong sounded and the flute was blown. The *egwugwu* had emerged once again from their underground home. They saluted one another and then reappeared on the *ilo*.

"*Umuofia kwenu!*" roared Evil Forest, facing the elders and grandees of the clan.

"*Yaa!*" replied the thunderous crowd; then silence descended from the sky and swallowed the noise.

Evil Forest began to speak and all the while he spoke everyone was silent. The eight other *egwugwu* were as still as statues.

"We have heard both sides of the case," said Evil Forest. "Our duty is not to blame this man or to praise that, but to settle the dispute." He turned to Uzowulu's group and allowed a short pause.

"Uzowulu's body, I salute you," he said.

"Our father, my hand has touched the ground," replied Uzowulu, touching the earth.

"Uzowulu's body, do you know me?"

"How can I know you, father? You are beyond our knowledge," Uzowulu replied.

"I am Evil Forest. I kill a man on the day that his life is sweetest to him."

"That is true," replied Uzowulu.

"Go to your in-laws with a pot of wine and beg your wife to return to you. It is not bravery when a man fights with a woman." He turned to Odukwe, and allowed a brief pause.

"Odukwe's body, I greet you," he said.

"My hand is on the ground," replied Odukwe.

"Do you know me?"

"No man can know you," replied Odukwe.

"I am Evil Forest, I am Dry-meat-that-fills-the-mouth, I am Fire-that-burns-without-faggots. If your in-law brings wine to you, let your sister go with him. I salute you." He pulled his staff from the hard earth and thrust it back.

"*Umuofia kwenu!*" he roared, and the crowd answered.

"I don't know why such a trifle should come before the *egwugwu*," said one elder to another.

"Don't you know what kind of man Uzowulu is? He will not listen to any other decision," replied the other.

As they spoke two other groups of people had replaced the first before the *egwugwu*, and a great land case began.

11

The night was impenetrably dark. The moon had been rising later and later every night until now it was seen only at dawn. And whenever the moon forsook evening and rose at cock-crow the nights were as black as charcoal.

Ezinma and her mother sat on a mat on the floor after their supper of yam foo-foo and bitter-leaf soup. A palm-oil lamp gave out yellowish light. Without it, it would have been impossible to eat; one could not have known where one's mouth was in the darkness of that night. There was an oil lamp in all the four huts on Okonkwo's compound, and each hut seen from the others looked like a soft eye of yellow half-light set in the solid massiveness of night.

The world was silent except for the shrill cry of insects, which was part of the night, and the sound of wooden mortar and pestle as Nwayieke pounded her foo-foo. Nwayieke lived four compounds away, and she was notorious for her late cooking. Every woman in the neighborhood knew the sound of Nwayieke's mortar and pestle. It was also part of the night.

Okonkwo had eaten from his wives' dishes and was now reclining with his back against the wall. He searched his bag and brought out his snuff-bottle. He turned it on to his left palm, but nothing came out. He hit the bottle against his knee to shake up the tobacco. That was always the trouble with Okeke's snuff. It very quickly went damp, and there was too much saltpeter in it. Okonkwo had not bought snuff from him for a long time. Idigo was the man who knew how to grind good snuff. But he had recently fallen ill.

Low voices, broken now and again by singing, reached Okonkwo from his wives' huts as each woman and her children told folk stories. Ekwefi and her daughter, Ezinma, sat on a mat on the floor. It was Ekwefi's turn to tell a story.

"Once upon a time," she began, "all the birds were invited to a feast in the sky. They were very happy and began to prepare themselves for the great day. They painted their bodies with red cam wood and drew beautiful patterns on them with *uli*.

"Tortoise saw all these preparations and soon discovered what it all meant. Nothing that happened in the world of the animals ever escaped his notice; he was full of cunning. As soon as he heard of the great feast in the sky his throat began to itch at the very thought. There was a famine in those days and Tortoise had not eaten a good meal for two moons. His body rattled like a piece of dry stick in his empty shell. So he began to plan how he would go to the sky."

"But he had no wings," said Ezinma.

"Be patient," replied her mother. "That is the story. Tortoise had no wings, but he went to the birds and asked to be allowed to go with them.

" 'We know you too well,' said the birds when they had heard him. 'You are full of cunning and you are ungrateful. If we allow you to come with us you will soon begin your mischief.'

" 'You do not know me,' said Tortoise. 'I am a changed man. I have learned that a man who makes trouble for others is also making it for himself.'

"Tortoise had a sweet tongue, and within a short time all the birds agreed that he was a changed man, and they each gave him a feather, with which he made two wings.

"At last the great day came and Tortoise was the first to arrive at the meeting place. When all the birds had gathered together, they set off in a body. Tortoise was very happy and voluble as he flew among the birds, and he was soon chosen as the man to speak for the party because he was a great orator.

" 'There is one important thing which we must not forget,' he said as they flew on their way. 'When people are invited to a great feast like this, they take new names for the occasion. Our hosts in the sky will expect us to honor this age-old custom.'

"None of the birds had heard of this custom but they knew that Tortoise, in spite of his failings in other directions, was a widely traveled man who knew the customs of different peoples. And so they each took a new name. When they had all taken, Tortoise also took one. He was to be called *All of you.*

"At last the party arrived in the sky and their hosts were very happy to see them. Tortoise stood up in his many-colored plumage and thanked them for their invitation. His speech was so eloquent that all the birds were glad they had brought him, and nodded their heads in approval of all he said. Their hosts took him as the king of the birds, especially as he looked somewhat different from the others.

"After kola nuts had been presented and eaten, the people of the sky set before their guests the most delectable dishes Tortoise had ever seen or dreamed of. The soup was brought out hot from the fire and in the very pot in which it had been cooked. It was full of meat and fish. Tortoise began to sniff aloud. There was pounded yam and also yam pottage cooked with palm-oil and fresh fish. There were also pots of palm-wine. When everything had been set before the guests, one of the people of the sky came forward and tasted a little from each pot. He then invited the birds to eat. But Tortoise jumped to his feet and asked: 'For whom have you prepared this feast?'

" 'For all of you,' replied the man.

"Tortoise turned to the birds and said: 'You remember that my name is *All of you*. The custom here is to serve the spokesman first and the others later. They will serve you when I have eaten.'

"He began to eat and the birds grumbled angrily. The people of the sky thought it must be their custom to leave all the food for their king. And so Tortoise ate the best part of the food and then drank two pots of palm-wine, so that he was full of food and drink and his body filled out in his shell.

"The birds gathered round to eat what was left and to peck at the bones he had thrown all about the floor. Some of them were too angry to eat. They chose to fly home on an empty stomach. But before they left each took back the feather he had lent to Tortoise. And there he stood in his hard shell full of food and wine but without any wings to fly home. He asked the birds to take a message for his wife, but they all refused. In the end Parrot, who had felt more angry than the others, suddenly changed his mind and agreed to take the message.

" 'Tell my wife,' said Tortoise, 'to bring out all the soft things in my house and cover the compound with them so that I can jump down from the sky without very great danger.'

"Parrot promised to deliver the message, and then flew away. But when he reached Tortoise's house he told his wife to bring out all the hard things in the house. And so she brought out her husband's hoes, machetes, spears, guns and even his cannon. Tortoise looked down from the sky and saw his wife bringing things out, but it was too far to see what they were. When all seemed ready he let himself go. He fell and fell and fell until he began to fear that he would never stop falling. And then like the sound of his cannon he crashed on the compound."

"Did he die?" asked Ezinma.

"No," replied Ekwefi. "His shell broke into pieces. But there was a great medicine man in the neighborhood. Tortoise's wife sent for him and he gathered all the bits of shell and stuck them together. That is why Tortoise's shell is not smooth."

"There is no song in the story," Ezinma pointed out.

"No," said Ekwefi. "I shall think of another one with a song. But it is your turn now."

"Once upon a time," Ezinma began, "Tortoise and Cat went to wrestle against Yams—no, that is not the beginning. Once upon a time there was a great famine in the land of animals. Everybody was lean except Cat, who was fat and whose body shone as if oil was rubbed on it . . ."

She broke off because at that very moment a loud and high-pitched voice broke the outer silence of the night. It was Chielo, the priestess of Agbala, prophesying. There was nothing new in that. Once in a while Chielo was possessed by the spirit of her god and she began to prophesy. But tonight she was addressing her prophecy and greetings to Okonkwo, and so everyone in his family listened. The folk stories stopped.

"*Agbala do-o-o-o! Agbala ekeneo-o-o-o,*"[2] came the voice like a sharp knife cutting through the night. "*Okonkwo! Agbala ekene gio-o-o-o! Agbala cholu ifu ada ya Ezinmao-o-o-o!*"[3]

At the mention of Ezinma's name Ekwefi jerked her head sharply like an animal that had sniffed death in the air. Her heart jumped painfully within her.

The priestess had now reached Okonkwo's compound and was talking with him outside his hut. She was saying again and again that Agbala wanted to see his daughter, Ezinma. Okonkwo pleaded with her to come back in the morning because Ezinma was now asleep. But Chielo ignored what he was trying to say and went on shouting that Agbala wanted to see his daughter. Her voice was as clear as metal, and Okonkwo's women and children heard from their huts all that she said. Okonkwo was still pleading that the girl had been ill of late and was asleep. Ekwefi quickly took her to their bedroom and placed her on their high bamboo bed.

The priestess screamed. "Beware, Okonkwo!" she warned. "Beware of exchanging words with Agbala. Does a man speak when a god speaks? Beware!"

She walked through Okonkwo's hut into the circular compound and went straight toward Ekwefi's hut. Okonkwo came after her.

"Ekwefi," she called, "Agbala greets you. Where is my daughter, Ezinma? Agbala wants to see her."

Ekwefi came out from her hut carrying her oil lamp in her left hand. There was a light wind blowing, so she cupped her right hand to shelter the flame. Nwoye's mother, also carrying an oil lamp, emerged from her hut. The children stood in the darkness outside their hut watching the strange event. Okonkwo's youngest wife also came out and joined the others.

"Where does Agbala want to see her?" Ekwefi asked.

"Where else but in his house in the hills and the caves?" replied the priestess.

"I will come with you, too," Ekwefi said firmly.

"*Tufia-a!*"[4] the priestess cursed, her voice cracking like the angry bark of thunder in the dry season. "How dare you, woman, to go before the mighty Agbala of your own accord? Beware, woman, lest he strike you in his anger. Bring me my daughter."

Ekwefi went into her hut and came out again with Ezinma.

"Come, my daughter," said the priestess. "I shall carry you on my back. A baby on its mother's back does not know that the way is long."

---

2. Agbala wants something! Agbala greets.　3. Agbala greets you! Agbala wants to see his daughter Ezinma!　4. A curse in words meaning "spitting" or "clearing out," often accompanied by spitting.

Ezinma began to cry. She was used to Chielo calling her "my daughter." But it was a different Chielo she now saw in the yellow half-light.

"Don't cry, my daughter," said the priestess, "lest Agbala be angry with you."

"Don't cry," said Ekwefi, "she will bring you back very soon. I shall give you some fish to eat." She went into the hut again and brought down the smoke-black basket in which she kept her dried fish and other ingredients for cooking soup. She broke a piece in two and gave it to Ezinma, who clung to her.

"Don't be afraid," said Ekwefi, stroking her head, which was shaved in places, leaving a regular pattern of hair. They went outside again. The priestess bent down on one knee and Ezinma climbed on her back, her left palm closed on her fish and her eyes gleaming with tears.

"Agbala do-o-o-o! Agbala ekeneo-o-o-o! . . ." Chielo began once again to chant greetings to her god. She turned round sharply and walked through Okonkwo's hut, bending very low at the eaves. Ezinma was crying loudly now, calling on her mother. The two voices disappeared into the thick darkness.

A strange and sudden weakness descended on Ekwefi as she stood gazing in the direction of the voices like a hen whose only chick has been carried away by a kite. Ezinma's voice soon faded away and only Chielo was heard moving farther and farther into the distance.

"Why do you stand there as though she had been kidnapped?" asked Okonkwo as he went back to his hut.

"She will bring her back soon," Nwoye's mother said.

But Ekwefi did not hear these consolations. She stood for a while, and then, all of a sudden, made up her mind. She hurried through Okonkwo's hut and went outside. "Where are you going?" he asked.

"I am following Chielo," she replied and disappeared in the darkness. Okonkwo cleared his throat, and brought out his snuff-bottle from the goat-skin bag by his side.

The priestess's voice was already growing faint in the distance. Ekwefi hurried to the main footpath and turned left in the direction of the voice. Her eyes were useless to her in the darkness. But she picked her way easily on the sandy footpath hedged on either side by branches and damp leaves. She began to run, holding her breasts with her hands to stop them flapping noisily against her body. She hit her left foot against an outcropped root, and terror seized her. It was an ill omen. She ran faster. But Chielo's voice was still a long way away. Had she been running too? How could she go so fast with Ezinma on her back? Although the night was cool, Ekwefi was beginning to feel hot from her running. She continually ran into the luxuriant weeds and creepers that walled in the path. Once she tripped up and fell. Only then did she realize, with a start, that Chielo had stopped her chanting. Her heart beat violently and she stood still. Then Chielo's renewed outburst came from only a few paces ahead. But Ekwefi could not see her. She shut her eyes for a while and opened them again in an effort to see. But it was useless. She could not see beyond her nose.

There were no stars in the sky because there was a rain-cloud. Fireflies went about with their tiny green lamps, which only made the darkness more profound. Between Chielo's outbursts the night was alive with the shrill tremor of forest insects woven into the darkness.

"*Agbala do-o-o-o!* . . . *Agbala ekeneo-o-o-o!* . . ." Ekwefi trudged behind, neither getting too near nor keeping too far back. She thought they must be going towards the sacred cave. Now that she walked slowly she had time to think. What would she do when they got to the cave? She would not dare to enter. She would wait at the mouth, all alone in that fearful place. She thought of all the terrors of the night. She remembered that night, long ago, when she had seen *Ogbu-agali-odu*, one of those evil essences loosed upon the world by the potent "medicines" which the tribe had made in the distant past against its enemies but had now forgotten how to control. Ekwefi had been returning from the stream with her mother on a dark night like this when they saw its glow as it flew in their direction. They had thrown down their water-pots and lain by the roadside expecting the sinister light to descend on them and kill them. That was the only time Ekwefi ever saw *Ogbu-agali-odu*. But although it had happened so long ago, her blood still ran cold whenever she remembered that night.

The priestess's voice came at longer intervals now, but its vigor was undiminished. The air was cool and damp with dew. Ezinma sneezed. Ekwefi muttered, "Life to you." At the same time the priestess also said, "Life to you, my daughter." Ezinma's voice from the darkness warmed her mother's heart. She trudged slowly along.

And then the priestess screamed. "Somebody is walking behind me!" she said. "Whether you are spirit or man, may Agbala shave your head with a blunt razor! May he twist your neck until you see your heels!"

Ekwefi stood rooted to the spot. One mind said to her: "Woman, go home before Agbala does you harm." But she could not. She stood until Chielo had increased the distance between them and she began to follow again. She had already walked so long that she began to feel a slight numbness in the limbs and in the head. Then it occurred to her that they could not have been heading for the cave. They must have by-passed it long ago; they must be going towards Umuachi, the farthest village in the clan. Chielo's voice now came after long intervals.

It seemed to Ekwefi that the night had become a little lighter. The cloud had lifted and a few stars were out. The moon must be preparing to rise, its sullenness over. When the moon rose late in the night, people said it was refusing food, as a sullen husband refuses his wife's food when they have quarrelled.

"*Agbala do-o-o-o! Umuachi! Agbala ekene unuo-o-o!*" It was just as Ekwefi had thought. The priestess was now saluting the village of Umuachi. It was unbelievable, the distance they had covered. As they emerged into the open village from the narrow forest track the darkness was softened and it became possible to see the vague shape of trees. Ekwefi screwed her eyes up in an effort to see her daughter and the priestess, but whenever she thought she saw their shape it immediately dissolved like a melting lump of darkness. She walked numbly along.

Chielo's voice was now rising continuously, as when she first set out. Ekwefi had a feeling of spacious openness, and she guessed they must be on the village *ilo*, or playground. And she realized too with something like a jerk that Chielo was no longer moving forward. She was, in fact, returning.

Ekwefi quickly moved away from her line of retreat. Chielo passed by, and they began to go back the way they had come.

It was a long and weary journey and Ekwefi felt like a sleepwalker most of the way. The moon was definitely rising, and although it had not yet appeared on the sky its light had already melted down the darkness. Ekwefi could now discern the figure of the priestess and her burden. She slowed down her pace so as to increase the distance between them. She was afraid of what might happen if Chielo suddenly turned round and saw her.

She had prayed for the moon to rise. But now she found the half-light of the incipient moon more terrifying than darkness. The world was now peopled with vague, fantastic figures that dissolved under her steady gaze and then formed again in new shapes. At one stage Ekwefi was so afraid that she nearly called out to Chielo for companionship and human sympathy. What she had seen was the shape of a man climbing a palm tree, his head pointing to the earth and his legs skywards. But at that very moment Chielo's voice rose again in her possessed chanting, and Ekwefi recoiled, because there was no humanity there. It was not the same Chielo who sat with her in the market and sometimes bought bean-cakes for Ezinma, whom she called her daughter. It was a different woman—the priestess of Agbala, the Oracle of the Hills and Caves. Ekwefi trudged along between two fears. The sound of her benumbed steps seemed to come from some other person walking behind her. Her arms were folded across her bare breasts. Dew fell heavily and the air was cold. She could no longer think, not even about the terrors of night. She just jogged along in a half-sleep, only waking to full life when Chielo sang.

At last they took a turning and began to head for the caves. From then on, Chielo never ceased in her chanting. She greeted her god in a multitude of names—the owner of the future, the messenger of earth, the god who cut a man down when his life was sweetest to him. Ekwefi was also awakened and her benumbed fears revived.

The moon was now up and she could see Chielo and Ezinma clearly. How a woman could carry a child of that size so easily and for so long was a miracle. But Ekwefi was not thinking about that. Chielo was not a woman that night.

"*Agbala do-o-o-o! Agbala ekeneo-o-o-o! Chi negbu madu ubosi ndu ya nato ya uto daluo-o-o!* . . ."[5]

Ekwefi could already see the hills looming in the moonlight. They formed a circular ring with a break at one point through which the foot-track led to the center of the circle.

As soon as the priestess stepped into this ring of hills her voice was not only doubled in strength but was thrown back on all sides. It was indeed the shrine of a great god. Ekwefi picked her way carefully and quietly. She was already beginning to doubt the wisdom of her coming. Nothing would happen to Ezinma, she thought. And if anything happened to her could she stop it? She would not dare to enter the underground caves. Her coming was quite useless, she thought.

As these things went through her mind she did not realize how close they

---

5. Agbala wants something! Agbala greets . . . God who kills a man on the day his life is so pleasant he give thanks!

were to the cave mouth. And so when the priestess with Ezinma on her back disappeared through a hole hardly big enough to pass a hen, Ekwefi broke into a run as though to stop them. As she stood gazing at the circular darkness which had swallowed them, tears gushed from her eyes, and she swore within her that if she heard Ezinma cry she would rush into the cave to defend her against all the gods in the world. She would die with her.

Having sworn that oath, she sat down on a stony ledge and waited. Her fear had vanished. She could hear the priestess's voice, all its metal taken out of it by the vast emptiness of the cave. She buried her face in her lap and waited.

She did not know how long she waited. It must have been a very long time. Her back was turned on the footpath that led out of the hills. She must have heard a noise behind her and turned round sharply. A man stood there with a machete in his hand. Ekwefi uttered a scream and sprang to her feet.

"Don't be foolish," said Okonkwo's voice. "I thought you were going into the shrine with Chielo," he mocked.

Ekwefi did not answer. Tears of gratitude filled her eyes. She knew her daughter was safe.

"Go home and sleep," said Okonkwo. "I shall wait here."

"I shall wait too. It is almost dawn. The first cock has crowed."

As they stood there together, Ekwefi's mind went back to the days when they were young. She had married Anene because Okonkwo was too poor then to marry. Two years after her marriage to Anene she could bear it no longer and she ran away to Okonkwo. It had been early in the morning. The moon was shining. She was going to the stream to fetch water. Okonkwo's house was on the way to the stream. She went in and knocked at his door and he came out. Even in those days he was not a man of many words. He just carried her into his bed and in the darkness began to feel around her waist for the loose end of her cloth.

12

On the following morning the entire neighborhood wore a festive air because Okonkwo's friend, Obierika, was celebrating his daughter's *uri*. It was the day on which her suitor (having already paid the greater part of her bride-price) would bring palm-wine not only to her parents and immediate relatives but to the wide and extensive group of kinsmen called *umunna*. Everybody had been invited—men, women and children. But it was really a woman's ceremony and the central figures were the bride and her mother.

As soon as day broke, breakfast was hastily eaten and women and children began to gather at Obierika's compound to help the bride's mother in her difficult but happy task of cooking for a whole village.

Okonkwo's family was astir like any other family in the neighborhood. Nwoye's mother and Okonkwo's youngest wife were ready to set out for Obierika's compound with all their children. Nwoye's mother carried a basket of coco-yams, a cake of salt and smoked fish which she would present to Obierika's wife. Okonkwo's youngest wife, Ojiugo, also had a basket of plantains and coco-yams and a small pot of palm-oil. Their children carried pots of water.

Ekwefi was tired and sleepy from the exhausting experiences of the previous night. It was not very long since they had returned. The priestess, with Ezinma sleeping on her back, had crawled out of the shrine on her belly like a snake. She had not as much as looked at Okonkwo and Ekwefi or shown any surprise at finding them at the mouth of the cave. She looked straight ahead of her and walked back to the village. Okonkwo and his wife followed at a respectful distance. They thought the priestess might be going to her house, but she went to Okonkwo's compound, passed through his *obi* and into Ekwefi's hut and walked into her bedroom. She placed Ezinma carefully on the bed and went away without saying a word to anybody.

Ezinma was still sleeping when everyone else was astir, and Ekwefi asked Nwoye's mother and Ojiugo to explain to Obierika's wife that she would be late. She had got ready her basket of coco-yams and fish, but she must wait for Ezinma to wake.

"You need some sleep yourself," said Nwoye's mother. "You look very tired."

As they spoke Ezinma emerged from the hut, rubbing her eyes and stretching her spare frame. She saw the other children with their water-pots and remembered that they were going to fetch water for Obierika's wife. She went back to the hut and brought her pot.

"Have you slept enough?" asked her mother.

"Yes," she replied, "Let us go."

"Not before you have had your breakfast," said Ekwefi. And she went into her hut to warm the vegetable soup she had cooked last night.

"We shall be going," said Nwoye's mother. "I will tell Obierika's wife that you are coming later." And so they all went to help Obierika's wife—Nwoye's mother with her four children and Ojiugo with her two.

As they trooped through Okonkwo's *obi* he asked: "Who will prepare my afternoon meal?"

"I shall return to do it," said Ojiugo.

Okonkwo was also feeling tired, and sleepy, for although nobody else knew it, he had not slept at all last night. He had felt very anxious but did not show it. When Ekwefi had followed the priestess, he had allowed what he regarded as a reasonable and manly interval to pass and then gone with his machete to the shrine, where he thought they must be. It was only when he had got there that it had occurred to him that the priestess might have chosen to go round the villages first. Okonkwo had returned home and sat waiting. When he thought he had waited long enough he again returned to the shrine. But the Hills and the Caves were as silent as death. It was only on his fourth trip that he had found Ekwefi, and by then he had become gravely worried.

Obierika's compound was as busy as an anthill. Temporary cooking tripods were erected on every available space by bringing together three blocks of sun-dried earth and making a fire in their midst. Cooking pots went up and down the tripods, and foo-foo was pounded in a hundred wooden mortars. Some of the women cooked the yams and the cassava, and others prepared vegetable soup. Young men pounded the foo-foo or split firewood. The children made endless trips to the stream.

Three young men helped Obierika to slaughter the two goats with which the soup was made. They were very fat goats, but the fattest of all was tethered to a peg near the wall of the compound. It was as big as a small cow.

Obierika had sent one of his relatives all the way to Umuike to buy that goat. It was the one he would present alive to his in-laws.

"The market of Umuike is a wonderful place," said the young man who had been sent by Obierika to buy the giant goat. "There are so many people on it that if you threw up a grain of sand it would not find a way to fall to earth again."

"It is the result of a great medicine," said Obierika. "The people of Umuike wanted their market to grow and swallow up the markets of their neighbors. So they made a powerful medicine. Every market day, before the first cock-crow, this medicine stands on the market ground in the shape of an old woman with a fan. With this magic fan she beckons to the market all the neighboring clans. She beckons in front of her and behind her, to her right and to her left."

"And so everybody comes," said another man, "honest men and thieves. They can steal your cloth from off your waist in that market."

"Yes," said Obierika. "I warned Nwankwo to keep a sharp eye and a sharp ear. There was once a man who went to sell a goat. He led it on a thick rope which he tied round his wrist. But as he walked through the market he realized that people were pointing at him as they do to a madman. He could not understand it until he looked back and saw that what he led at the end of the tether was not a goat but a heavy log of wood."

"Do you think a thief can do that kind of thing single-handed?" asked Nwankwo.

"No," said Obierika. "They use medicine."

When they had cut the goats' throats and collected the blood in a bowl, they held them over an open fire to burn off the hair, and the smell of burning hair blended with the smell of cooking. Then they washed them and cut them up for the women who prepared the soup.

All this anthill activity was going smoothly when a sudden interruption came. It was a cry in the distance: *Oji odu achu ijiji-o-o!* (*The one that uses its tail to drive flies away!*) Every woman immediately abandoned whatever she was doing and rushed out in the direction of the cry.

"We cannot all rush out like that, leaving what we are cooking to burn in the fire," shouted Chielo, the priestess. "Three or four of us should stay behind."

"It is true," said another woman. "We will allow three or four women to stay behind."

Five women stayed behind to look after the cooking-pots, and all the rest rushed away to see the cow that had been let loose. When they saw it they drove it back to its owner, who at once paid the heavy fine which the village imposed on anyone whose cow was let loose on his neighbors' crops. When the women had exacted the penalty they checked among themselves to see if any woman had failed to come out when the cry had been raised.

"Where is Mgbogo?" asked one of them.

"She is ill in bed," said Mgbogo's next-door neighbor. "She has *iba*."

"The only other person is Udenkwo," said another woman, "and her child is not twenty-eight days yet."

Those women whom Obierika's wife had not asked to help her with the cooking returned to their homes, and the rest went back, in a body, to Obierika's compound.

"Whose cow was it?" asked the women who had been allowed to stay behind.

"It was my husband's," said Ezelagbo. "One of the young children had opened the gate of the cowshed."

Early in the afternoon the first two pots of palm-wine arrived from Obierika's in-laws. They were duly presented to the women, who drank a cup or two each, to help them in their cooking. Some of it also went to the bride and her attendant maidens, who were putting the last delicate touches of razor to her coiffure and cam wood on her smooth skin.

When the heat of the sun began to soften, Obierika's son, Maduka, took a long broom and swept the ground in front of his father's *obi*. And as if they had been waiting for that, Obierika's relatives and friends began to arrive, every man with his goatskin bag hung on one shoulder and a rolled goatskin mat under his arm. Some of them were accompanied by their sons bearing carved wooden stools. Okonkwo was one of them. They sat in a half-circle and began to talk of many things. It would not be long before the suitors came.

Okonkwo brought out his snuff-bottle and offered it to Ogbuefi Ezenwa, who sat next to him. Ezenwa[6] took it, tapped it on his kneecap, rubbed his left palm on his body to dry it before tipping a little snuff into it. His actions were deliberate, and he spoke as he performed them:

"I hope our in-laws will bring many pots of wine. Although they come from a village that is known for being closefisted, they ought to know that Akueke is the bride for a king."

"They dare not bring fewer than thirty pots," said Okonkwo. "I shall tell them my mind if they do."

At that moment Obierika's son, Maduka, led out the giant goat from the inner compound, for his father's relatives to see. They all admired it and said that that was the way things should be done. The goat was then led back to the inner compound.

Very soon after, the in-laws began to arrive. Young men and boys in single file, each carrying a pot of wine, came first. Obierika's relatives counted the pots as they came. Twenty, twenty-five. There was a long break, and the hosts looked at each other as if to say, "I told you." Then more pots came. Thirty, thirty-five, forty, forty-five. The hosts nodded in approval and seemed to say, "Now they are behaving like men." Altogether there were fifty pots of wine. After the pot-bearers came Ibe, the suitor, and the elders of his family. They sat in a half-moon, thus completing a circle with their hosts. The pots of wine stood in their midst. Then the bride, her mother and a half a dozen other women and girls emerged from the inner compound, and went round the circle shaking hands with all. The bride's mother led the way, followed by the bride and the other women. The married women wore their best cloths and the girls wore red and black waist-beads and anklets of brass.

When the women retired, Obierika presented kola nuts to his in-laws. His eldest brother broke the first one. "Life to all of us," he said as he broke it. "And let there be friendship between your family and ours."

The crowd answered: "*Ee-e-e!*"

6. King from childhood (strong praise).

"We are giving you our daughter today. She will be a good wife to you. She will bear you nine sons like the mother of our town."

"Ee-e-e!"

The oldest man in the camp of the visitors replied: "It will be good for you and it will be good for us."

"Ee-e-e!"

"This is not the first time my people have come to marry your daughter. My mother was one of you."

"Ee-e-e!"

"And this will not be the last, because you understand us and we understand you. You are a great family."

"Ee-e-e!"

"Prosperous men and great warriors." He looked in the direction of Okonkwo. "Your daughter will bear us sons like you."

"Ee-e-e!"

The kola was eaten and the drinking of palm-wine began. Groups of four or five men sat round with a pot in their midst. As the evening wore on, food was presented to the guests. There were huge bowls of foo-foo and steaming pots of soup. There were also pots of yam pottage. It was a great feast.

As night fell, burning torches were set on wooden tripods and the young men raised a song. The elders sat in a big circle and the singers went round singing each man's praise as they came before him. They had something to say for every man. Some were great farmers, some were orators who spoke for the clan; Okonkwo was the greatest wrestler and warrior alive. When they had gone round the circle they settled down in the center, and girls came from the inner compound to dance. At first the bride was not among them. But when she finally appeared holding a cock in her right hand, a loud cheer rose from the crowd. All the other dancers made way for her. She presented the cock to the musicians and began to dance. Her brass anklets rattled as she danced and her body gleamed with cam wood in the soft yellow light. The musicians with their wood, clay and metal instruments went from song to song. And they were all gay. They sang the latest song in the village:

> If I hold her hand
> She says, "Don't touch!"
> If I hold her foot
> She says, "Don't touch!"
> But when I hold her waist-beads
> She pretends not to know.

The night was already far spent when the guests rose to go, taking their bride home to spend seven market weeks with her suitor's family. They sang songs as they went, and on their way they paid short courtesy visits to prominent men like Okonkwo, before they finally left for their village. Okonkwo made a present of two cocks to them.

13

Go-di-di-go-go-di-go. Di-go-go-di-go. It was the *ekwe* talking to the clan. One of the things every man learned was the language of the hollowed-out wooden instrument. Diim! Diim! Diim! boomed the cannon at intervals.

The first cock had not crowed, and Umuofia was still swallowed up in sleep and silence when the *ekwe* began to talk, and the cannon shattered the silence. Men stirred on their bamboo beds and listened anxiously. Somebody was dead. The cannon seemed to rend the sky. Di-go-go-di-go-di-di-go-go floated in the message-laden night air. The faint and distant wailing of women settled like a sediment of sorrow on the earth. Now and again a full-chested lamentation rose above the wailing whenever a man came into the place of death. He raised his voice once or twice in manly sorrow and then sat down with the other men listening to the endless wailing of the women and the esoteric language of the *ekwe*. Now and again the cannon boomed. The wailing of the women would not be heard beyond the village, but the *ekwe* carried the news to all the nine villages and even beyond. It began by naming the clan: *Umuofia obodo dike*, "the land of the brave." *Umuofia obodo dike! Umuofia obodo dike!* It said this over and over again, and as it dwelt on it, anxiety mounted in every heart that heaved on a bamboo bed that night. Then it went nearer and named the village: *Iguedo*[7] of the yellow grinding-stone!" It was Okonkwo's village. Again and again Iguedo was called and men waited breathlessly in all the nine villages. At last the man was named and people sighed "E-u-u, Ezeudu is dead." A cold shiver ran down Okonkwo's back as he remembered the last time the old man had visited him. "That boy calls you father," he had said. "Bear no hand in his death."

Ezeudu was a great man, and so all the clan was at his funeral. The ancient drums of death beat, guns and cannon were fired, and men dashed about in frenzy, cutting down every tree or animal they saw, jumping over walls and dancing on the roof. It was a warrior's funeral, and from morning till night warriors came and went in their age groups. They all wore smoked raffia skirts and their bodies were painted with chalk and charcoal. Now and again an ancestral spirit or *egwugwu* appeared from the underworld, speaking in a tremulous, unearthly voice and completely covered in raffia. Some of them were very violent, and there had been a mad rush for shelter earlier in the day when one appeared with a sharp machete and was only prevented from doing serious harm by two men who restrained him with the help of a strong rope tied round his waist. Sometimes he turned round and chased those men, and they ran for their lives. But they always returned to the long rope he trailed behind. He sang, in a terrifying voice, that Ekwensu, or Evil Spirit, had entered his eye.

But the most dreaded of all was yet to come. He was always alone and was shaped like a coffin. A sickly odor hung in the air wherever he went, and flies went with him. Even the greatest medicine men took shelter when he was near. Many years ago another *egwugwu* had dared to stand his ground before him and had been transfixed to the spot for two days. This one had only one hand and it carried a basket full of water.

But some of the *egwugwu* were quite harmless. One of them was so old and infirm that he leaned heavily on a stick. He walked unsteadily to the place where the corpse was laid, gazed at it a while and went away again—to the underworld.

The land of the living was not far removed from the domain of the ances-

---

7. The yellow grindstone.

tors. There was coming and going between them, especially at festivals and also when an old man died, because an old man was very close to the ancestors. A man's life from birth to death was a series of transition rites which brought him nearer and nearer to his ancestors.

Ezeudu had been the oldest man in his village, and at his death there were only three men in the whole clan who were older, and four or five others in his own age group. Whenever one of these ancient men appeared in the crowd to dance unsteadily the funeral steps of the tribe, younger men gave way and the tumult subsided.

It was a great funeral, such as befitted a noble warrior. As the evening drew near, the shouting and the firing of guns, the beating of drums and the brandishing and clanging of machetes increased.

Ezeudu had taken three titles in his life. It was a rare achievement. There were only four titles in the clan, and only one or two men in any generation ever achieved the fourth and highest. When they did, they became the lords of the land. Because he had taken titles, Ezeudu was to be buried after dark with only a glowing brand to light the sacred ceremony.

But before this quiet and final rite, the tumult increased tenfold. Drums beat violently and men leaped up and down in frenzy. Guns were fired on all sides and sparks flew out as machetes clanged together in warriors' salutes. The air was full of dust and the smell of gunpowder. It was then that the one-handed spirit came, carrying a basket full of water. People made way for him on all sides and the noise subsided. Even the smell of gunpowder was swallowed in the sickly smell that now filled the air. He danced a few steps to the funeral drums and then went to see the corpse.

"Ezeudu!" he called in his guttural voice. "If you had been poor in your last life I would have asked you to be rich when you come again. But you were rich. If you had been a coward, I would have asked you to bring courage. But you were a fearless warrior. If you had died young, I would have asked you to get life. But you lived long. So I shall ask you to come again the way you came before. If your death was the death of nature, go in peace. But if a man caused it, do not allow him a moment's rest." He danced a few more steps and went away.

The drums and the dancing began again and reached fever-heat. Darkness was around the corner, and the burial was near. Guns fired the last salute and the cannon rent the sky. And then from the center of the delirious fury came a cry of agony and shouts of horror. It was as if a spell had been cast. All was silent. In the center of the crowd a boy lay in a pool of blood. It was the dead man's sixteen-year-old son, who with his brothers and half-brothers had been dancing the traditional farewell to their father. Okonkwo's gun had exploded and a piece of iron had pierced the boy's heart.

The confusion that followed was without parallel in the tradition of Umuofia. Violent deaths were frequent, but nothing like this had ever happened.

The only course open to Okonkwo was to flee from the clan. It was a crime against the earth goddess to kill a clansman, and a man who committed it must flee from the land. The crime was of two kinds, male and female. Okonkwo had committed the female, because it had been inadvertent. He could return to the clan after seven years.

That night he collected his most valuable belongings into head-loads. His wives wept bitterly and their children wept with them without knowing why. Obierika and half a dozen other friends came to help and to console him. They each made nine or ten trips carrying Okonkwo's yams to store in Obierika's barn. And before the cock crowed Okonkwo and his family were fleeing to his motherland. It was a little village called Mbanta,[8] just beyond the borders of Mbaino.

As soon as the day broke, a large crowd of men from Ezeudu's quarter stormed Okonkwo's compound, dressed in garbs of war. They set fire to his houses, demolished his red walls, killed his animals and destroyed his barn. It was the justice of the earth goddess, and they were merely her messengers. They had no hatred in their hearts against Okonkwo. His greatest friend, Obierika, was among them. They were merely cleansing the land which Okonkwo had polluted with the blood of a clansman.

Obierika was a man who thought about things. When the will of the goddess had been done, he sat down in his *obi* and mourned his friend's calamity. Why should a man suffer so grievously for an offense he had committed inadvertently? But although he thought for a long time he found no answer. He was merely led into greater complexities. He remembered his wife's twin children, whom he had thrown away. What crime had they committed? The Earth had decreed that they were an offense on the land and must be destroyed. And if the clan did not exact punishment for an offense against the great goddess, her wrath was loosed on all the land and not just on the offender. As the elders said, if one finger brought oil it soiled the others.

Part Two

14

Okonkwo was well received by his mother's kinsmen in Mbanta. The old man who received him was his mother's younger brother, who was now the eldest surviving member of that family. His name was Uchendu,[9] and it was he who had received Okonkwo's mother twenty and ten years before when she had been brought home from Umuofia to be buried with her people. Okonkwo was only a boy then and Uchendu still remembered him crying the traditional farewell: "Mother, mother, mother is going."

That was many years ago. Today Okonkwo was not bringing his mother home to be buried with her people. He was taking his family of three wives and their children to seek refuge in his motherland. As soon as Uchendu saw him with his sad and weary company he guessed what had happened, and asked no questions. It was not until the following day that Okonkwo told him the full story. The old man listened silently to the end and then said with some relief: "It is a female *ochu*."[1] And he arranged the requisite rites and sacrifices.

Okonkwo was given a plot of ground on which to build his compound, and two or three pieces of land on which to farm during the coming planting season. With the help of his mother's kinsmen he built himself an *obi* and three huts for his wives. He then installed his personal god and the symbols of his departed fathers. Each of Uchendu's five sons contributed three hun-

8. Small town.　9. The thought created by life.　1. Murder, manslaughter.

dred seed-yams to enable their cousin to plant a farm, for as soon as the first rain came farming would begin.

At last the rain came. It was sudden and tremendous. For two or three moons the sun had been gathering strength till it seemed to breathe a breath of fire on the earth. All the grass had long been scorched brown, and the sands felt like live coals to the feet. Evergreen trees wore a dusty coat of brown. The birds were silenced in the forests, and the world lay panting under the live, vibrating heat. And then came the clap of thunder. It was an angry, metallic and thirsty clap, unlike the deep and liquid rumbling of the rainy season. A mighty wind arose and filled the air with dust. Palm trees swayed as the wind combed their leaves into flying crests like strange and fantastic coiffure.

When the rain finally came, it was in large, solid drops of frozen water which the people called "the nuts of the water of heaven." They were hard and painful on the body as they fell, yet young people ran about happily picking up the cold nuts and throwing them into their mouths to melt.

The earth quickly came to life and the birds in the forests fluttered around and chirped merrily. A vague scent of life and green vegetation was diffused in the air. As the rain began to fall more soberly and in smaller liquid drops, children sought for shelter, and all were happy, refreshed and thankful.

Okonkwo and his family worked very hard to plant a new farm. But it was like beginning life anew without the vigor and enthusiasm of youth, like learning to become left-handed in old age. Work no longer had for him the pleasure it used to have, and when there was no work to do he sat in a silent half-sleep.

His life had been ruled by a great passion—to become one of the lords of the clan. That had been his life-spring. And he had all but achieved it. Then everything had been broken. He had been cast out of his clan like a fish onto a dry, sandy beach, panting. Clearly his personal god or *chi* was not made for great things. A man could not rise beyond the destiny of his *chi*. The saying of the elders was not true—that if a man said yea his *chi* also affirmed. Here was a man whose *chi* said nay despite his own affirmation.

The old man, Uchendu, saw clearly that Okonkwo had yielded to despair and he was greatly troubled. He would speak to him after the *isa-ifi*[2] ceremony.

The youngest of Uchendu's five sons, Amikwu, was marrying a new wife. The bride-price had been paid and all but the last ceremony had been performed. Amikwu and his people had taken palm-wine to the bride's kinsmen about two moons before Okonkwo's arrival in Mbanta. And so it was time for the final ceremony of confession.

The daughters of the family were all there, some of them having come a long way from their homes in distant villages. Uchendu's eldest daughter had come from Obodo, nearly half a day's journey away. The daughters of Uchendu's brothers were also there. It was a full gathering of *umuada*,[3] in the same way as they would meet if a death occurred in the family. There were twenty-two of them.

They sat in a big circle on the ground and the bride sat in the center with

---

2. A ceremony to ascertain that a wife (here, a promised bride) had been faithful to her husband during a separation.   3. The daughters, who, according to Igbo custom, married outside the clan, perform a special initiation upon returning home for important gatherings.

a hen in her right hand. Uchendu sat by her, holding the ancestral staff of the family. All the other men stood outside the circle, watching. Their wives watched also. It was evening and the sun was setting.

Uchendu's eldest daughter, Njide, asked the questions.

"Remember that if you do not answer truthfully you will suffer or even die at childbirth," she began. "How many men have lain with you since my brother first expressed the desire to marry you?"

"None," she answered simply.

"Answer truthfully," urged the other women.

"None?" asked Njide.

"None," she answered.

"Swear on this staff of my fathers," said Uchendu.

"I swear," said the bride.

Uchendu took the hen from her, slit its throat with a sharp knife and allowed some of the blood to fall on his ancestral staff.

From that day Amikwu took the young bride to his hut and she became his wife. The daughters of the family did not return to their homes immediately but spent two or three days with their kinsmen.

On the second day Uchendu called together his sons and daughters and his nephew, Okonkwo. The men brought their goatskin mats, with which they sat on the floor, and the women sat on a sisal mat spread on a raised bank of earth. Uchendu pulled gently at his gray beard and gnashed his teeth. Then he began to speak, quietly and deliberately, picking his words with great care:

"It is Okonkwo that I primarily wish to speak to," he began. "But I want all of you to note what I am going to say. I am an old man and you are all children. I know more about the world than any of you. If there is any one among you who thinks he knows more let him speak up." He paused, but no one spoke.

"Why is Okonkwo with us today? This is not his clan. We are only his mother's kinsmen. He does not belong here. He is an exile, condemned for seven years to live in a strange land. And so he is bowed with grief. But there is just one question I would like to ask him. Can you tell me, Okonkwo, why it is that one of the commonest names we give our children is Nneka, or "Mother is Supreme?" We all know that a man is the head of the family and his wives do his bidding. A child belongs to its father and his family and not to its mother and her family. A man belongs to his fatherland and not to his motherland. And yet we say Nneka—'Mother is Supreme.' Why is that?"

There was silence. "I want Okonkwo to answer me," said Uchendu.

"I do not know the answer," Okonkwo replied.

"You do not know the answer? So you see that you are a child. You have many wives and many children—more children than I have. You are a great man in your clan. But you are still a child, *my* child. Listen to me and I shall tell you. But there is one more question I shall ask you. Why is it that when a woman dies she is taken home to be buried with her own kinsmen? She is not buried with her husband's kinsmen. Why is that? Your mother was brought home to me and buried with my people. Why was that?"

Okonkwo shook his head.

"He does not know that either," said Uchendu, "and yet he is full of sorrow because he has come to live in his motherland for a few years." He laughed a mirthless laughter, and turned to his sons and daughters. "What about you? Can you answer my question?"

They all shook their heads.

"Then listen to me," he said and cleared his throat. "It's true that a child belongs to its father. But when a father beats his child, it seeks sympathy in its mother's hut. A man belongs to his fatherland when things are good and life is sweet. But when there is sorrow and bitterness he finds refuge in his motherland. Your mother is there to protect you. She is buried there. And that is why we say that mother is supreme. Is it right that you, Okonkwo, should bring to your mother a heavy face and refuse to be comforted? Be careful or you may displease the dead. Your duty is to comfort your wives and children and take them back to your fatherland after seven years. But if you allow sorrow to weigh you down and kill you, they will all die in exile." He paused for a long while. "These are now your kinsmen." He waved at his sons and daughters. "You think you are the greatest sufferer in the world? Do you know that men are sometimes banished for life? Do you know that men sometimes lose all their yams and even their children? I had six wives once. I have none now except that young girl who knows not her right from her left. Do you know how many children I have buried—children I begot in my youth and strength? Twenty-two. I did not hang myself, and I am still alive. If you think you are the greatest sufferer in the world ask my daughter, Akueni, how many twins she has borne and thrown away. Have you not heard the song they sing when a woman dies?

> For whom is it well, for whom is it well?
> There is no one for whom it is well.

"I have no more to say to you."

15

It was in the second year of Okonkwo's exile that his friend, Obierika, came to visit him. He brought with him two young men, each of them carrying a heavy bag on his head. Okonkwo helped them put down their loads. It was clear that the bags were full of cowries.

Okonkwo was very happy to receive his friend. His wives and children were very happy too, and so were his cousins and their wives when he sent for them and told them who his guest was.

"You must take him to salute our father," said one of the cousins.

"Yes," replied Okonkwo. "We are going directly." But before they went he whispered something to his first wife. She nodded, and soon the children were chasing one of their cocks.

Uchendu had been told by one of his grandchildren that three strangers had come to Okonkwo's house. He was therefore waiting to receive them. He held out his hands to them when they came into his *obi*, and after they had shaken hands he asked Okonkwo who they were.

"This is Obierika, my great friend. I have already spoken to you about him."

"Yes," said the old man, turning to Obierika. "My son has told me about you, and I am happy you have come to see us. I knew your father, Iweka. He was a great man. He had many friends here and came to see them quite often. Those were good days when a man had friends in distant clans. Your generation does not know that. You stay at home, afraid of your next-door neighbor. Even a man's motherland is strange to him nowadays." He looked at Okonkwo. "I am an old man and I like to talk. That is all I am good for now." He got up painfully, went into an inner room and came back with a kola nut.

"Who are the young men with you?" he asked as he sat down again on his goatskin. Okonkwo told him.

"Ah," he said. "Welcome, my sons." He presented the kola nut to them, and when they had seen it and thanked him, he broke it and they ate.

"Go into that room," he said to Okonkwo, pointing with his finger. "You will find a pot of wine there."

Okonkwo brought the wine and they began to drink. It was a day old, and very strong.

"Yes," said Uchendu after a long silence. "People traveled more in those days. There is not a single clan in these parts that I do not know very well. Aninta, Umuazu, Ikeocha, Elumelu, Abame—I know them all."

"Have you heard," asked Obierika, "that Abame is no more?"

"How is that?" asked Uchendu and Okonkwo together.

"Abame has been wiped out," said Obierika. "It is a strange and terrible story. If I had not seen the few survivors with my own eyes and heard their story with my own ears, I would not have believed. Was it not on an Eke day that they fled into Umuofia?" he asked his two companions, and they nodded their heads.

"Three moons ago," said Obierika, "on an Eke market day a little band of fugitives came into our town. Most of them were sons of our land whose mothers had been buried with us. But there were some too who came because they had friends in our town, and others who could think of nowhere else open to escape. And so they fled into Umuofia with a woeful story." He drank his palm-wine, and Okonkwo filled his horn again. He continued:

"During the last planting season a white man had appeared in their clan."

"An albino," suggested Okonkwo.

"He was not an albino. He was quite different." He sipped his wine. "And he was riding an iron horse.[4] The first people who saw him ran away, but he stood beckoning to them. In the end the fearless ones went near and even touched him. The elders consulted their Oracle and it told them that the strange man would break their clan and spread destruction among them." Obierika again drank a little of his wine. "And so they killed the white man and tied his iron horse to their sacred tree because it looked as if it would run away to call the man's friends. I forgot to tell you another thing which the Oracle said. It said that other white men were on their way. They were locusts, it said, and that first man was their harbinger sent to explore the terrain. And so they killed him."

"What did the white man say before they killed him?" asked Uchendu.

"He said nothing," answered one of Obierika's companions.

"He said something, only they did not understand him," said Obierika. "He seemed to speak through his nose."

"One of the men told me," said Obierika's other companion, "that he

4. Bicycle.

repeated over and over again a word that resembled Mbaino. Perhaps he had been going to Mbaino and had lost his way."

"Anyway," resumed Obierika, "they killed him and tied up his iron horse. This was before the planting season began. For a long time nothing happened. The rains had come and yams had been sown. The iron horse was still tied to the sacred silk-cotton tree. And then one morning three white men led by a band of ordinary men like us came to the clan. They saw the iron horse and went away again. Most of the men and women of Abame had gone to their farms. Only a few of them saw these white men and their followers. For many market weeks nothing else happened. They have a big market in Abame on every other Afo day and, as you know, the whole clan gathers there. That was the day it happened. The three white men and a very large number of other men surrounded the market. They must have used a powerful medicine to make themselves invisible until the market was full. And they began to shoot. Everybody was killed, except the old and the sick who were at home and a handful of men and women whose *chi* were wide awake and brought them out of that market."[5] He paused.

"Their clan is now completely empty. Even the sacred fish in their mysterious lake have fled and the lake has turned the color of blood. A great evil has come upon their land as the Oracle had warned."

There was a long silence. Uchendu ground his teeth together audibly. Then he burst out:

"Never kill a man who says nothing. Those men of Abame were fools. What did they know about the man?" He ground his teeth again and told a story to illustrate his point. "Mother Kite once sent her daughter to bring food. She went, and brought back a duckling. 'You have done very well,' said Mother Kite to her daughter, 'but tell me, what did the mother of this duckling say when you swooped and carried its child away?' 'It said nothing,' replied the young kite. It just walked away.' 'You must return the duckling,' said Mother Kite. 'There is something ominous behind the silence.' And so Daughter Kite returned the duckling and took a chick instead. 'What did the mother of this chick do?' asked the old kite. 'It cried and raved and cursed me,' said the young kite. 'Then we can eat the chick,' said her mother. 'There is nothing to fear from someone who shouts.' Those men of Abame were fools."

"They were fools," said Okonkwo after a pause. "They had been warned that danger was ahead. They should have armed themselves with their guns and their machetes even when they went to market."

"They have paid for their foolishness," said Obierika. "But I am greatly afraid. We have heard stories about white men who made the powerful guns and the strong drinks and took slaves away across the seas, but no one thought the stories were true."

"There is no story that is not true," said Uchendu. "The world has no end, and what is good among one people is an abomination with others. We have albinos among us. Do you not think that they came to our clan by mistake, that they have strayed from their way to a land where everybody is like them?"

---

5. Achebe bases his account on a similar incident in 1905 when British troops massacred the town of Ahiara in reprisal for the death of a missionary.

Okonkwo's first wife soon finished her cooking and set before their guests a big meal of pounded yams and bitter-leaf soup. Okonkwo's son, Nwoye, brought in a pot of sweet wine tapped from the raffia palm.

"You are a big man now," Obierika said to Nwoye. "Your friend Anene asked me to greet you."

"Is he well?" asked Nwoye.

"We are all well," said Obierika.

Ezinma brought them a bowl of water with which to wash their hands. After that they began to eat and to drink the wine.

"When did you set out from home?" asked Okonkwo.

"We had meant to set out from my house before cock-crow," said Obierika. "But Nweke did not appear until it was quite light. Never make an early morning appointment with a man who has just married a new wife." They all laughed.

"Has Nweke married a wife?" asked Okonkwo.

"He has married Okadigbo's second daughter," said Obierika.

"That is very good," said Okonkwo. "I do not blame you for not hearing the cock crow."

When they had eaten, Obierika pointed at the two heavy bags.

"That is the money from your yams," he said. "I sold the big ones as soon as you left. Later on I sold some of the seed-yams and gave out others to sharecroppers. I shall do that every year until you return. But I thought you would need the money now and so I brought it. Who knows what may happen tomorrow? Perhaps green men will come to our clan and shoot us."

"God will not permit it," said Okonkwo. "I do not know how to thank you."

"I can tell you," said Obierika. "Kill one of your sons for me."

"That will not be enough," said Okonkwo.

"Then kill yourself," said Obierika.

"Forgive me," said Okonkwo, smiling. "I shall not talk about thanking you any more."

16

When nearly two years later Obierika paid another visit to his friend in exile the circumstances were less happy. The missionaries had come to Umuofia. They had built their church there, won a handful of converts and were already sending evangelists to the surrounding towns and villages. That was a source of great sorrow to the leaders of the clan; but many of them believed that the strange faith and the white man's god would not last. None of his converts was a man whose word was heeded in the assembly of the people. None of them was a man of title. They were mostly the kind of people that were called *efulefu*, worthless, empty men. The imagery of an *efulefu* in the language of the clan was a man who sold his machete and wore the sheath to battle. Chielo, the priestess of Agbala, called the converts the excrement of the clan, and the new faith was a mad dog that had come to eat it up.

What moved Obierika to visit Okonkwo was the sudden appearance of the latter's son, Nwoye, among the missionaries in Umuofia.

"What are you doing here?" Obierika had asked when after many difficulties the missionaries had allowed him to speak to the boy.

"I am one of them," replied Nwoye.

"How is your father?" Obierika asked, not knowing what else to say.

"I don't know. He is not my father," said Nwoye, unhappily.

And so Obierika went to Mbanta to see his friend. And he found that Okonkwo did not wish to speak about Nwoye. It was only from Nwoye's mother that he heard scraps of the story.

The arrival of the missionaries had caused a considerable stir in the village of Mbanta. There were six of them and one was a white man. Every man and woman came out to see the white man. Stories about these strange men had grown since one of them had been killed in Abame and his iron horse tied to the sacred silk-cotton tree. And so everybody came to see the white man. It was the time of the year when everybody was at home. The harvest was over.

When they had all gathered, the white man began to speak to them. He spoke through an interpreter who was an Ibo man, though his dialect was different and harsh to the ears of Mbanta. Many people laughed at his dialect and the way he used words strangely. Instead of saying "myself" he always said "my buttocks."[6] But he was a man of commanding presence and the clansmen listened to him. He said he was one of them, as they could see from his color and his language. The other four black men were also their brothers, although one of them did not speak Ibo. The white man was also their brother because they were all sons of God. And he told them about this new God, the Creator of all the world and all the men and women. He told them that they worshipped false gods, gods of wood and stone. A deep murmur went through the crowd when he said this. He told them that the true God lived on high and that all men when they died went before Him for judgment. Evil men and all the heathen who in their blindness bowed to wood and stone were thrown into a fire that burned like palm-oil. But good men who worshipped the true God lived forever in His happy kingdom. "We have been sent by this great God to ask you to leave your wicked ways and false gods and turn to Him so that you may be saved when you die," he said.

"Your buttocks understand our language," said someone light-heartedly and the crowd laughed.

"What did he say?" the white man asked his interpreter. But before he could answer, another man asked a question: "Where is the white man's horse?" he asked. The Ibo evangelists consulted among themselves and decided that the man probably meant bicycle. They told the white man and he smiled benevolently.

"Tell them," he said, "that I shall bring many iron horses when we have settled down among them. Some of them will even ride the iron horse themselves." This was interpreted to them but very few of them heard. They were talking excitedly among themselves because the white man had said he was going to live among them. They had not thought about that.

At this point an old man said he had a question. "Which is this god of yours," he asked, "the goddess of the earth, the god of the sky, Amadiora of the thunderbolt, or what?"

The interpreter spoke to the white man and he immediately gave his

6. The Igbo language has high and low tones so that the same word may have different meanings according to its pronunciation. Here, Achebe is probably referring to a famous pair of near-homonyms: íké ("strength") and íkè ("buttocks").

2128 / Chinua Achebe

answer. "All the gods you have named are not gods at all. They are gods of deceit who tell you to kill your fellows and destroy innocent children. There is only one true God and He has the earth, the sky, you and me and all of us."

"If we leave our gods and follow your god," asked another man, "who will protect us from the anger of our neglected gods and ancestors?"

"Your gods are not alive and cannot do you any harm," replied the white man. "They are pieces of wood and stone."

When this was interpreted to the men of Mbanta they broke into derisive laughter. These men must be mad, they said to themselves. How else could they say that Ani and Amadiora were harmless? And Idemili and Ogwugwu too? And some of them began to go away.

Then the missionaries burst into song. It was one of those gay and rollicking tunes of evangelism which had the power of plucking at silent and dusty chords in the heart of an Ibo man. The interpreter explained each verse to the audience, some of whom now stood enthralled. It was a story of brothers who lived in darkness and in fear, ignorant of the love of God. It told of one sheep out on the hills, away from the gates of God and from the tender shepherd's care.

After the singing the interpreter spoke about the Son of God whose name was Jesu Kristi. Okonkwo, who only stayed in the hope that it might come to chasing the men out of the village or whipping them, now said:

"You told us with your own mouth that there was only one god. Now you talk about his son. He must have a wife, then." The crowd agreed.

"I did not say He had a wife," said the interpreter, somewhat lamely.

"Your buttocks said he had a son," said the joker. "So he must have a wife and all of them must have buttocks."

The missionary ignored him and went on to talk about the Holy Trinity. At the end of it Okonkwo was fully convinced that the man was mad. He shrugged his shoulders and went away to tap his afternoon palm-wine.

But there was a young lad who had been captivated. His name was Nwoye, Okonkwo's first son. It was not the mad logic of the Trinity that captivated him. He did not understand it. It was the poetry of the new religion, something felt in the marrow. The hymn about brothers who sat in darkness and in fear seemed to answer a vague and persistent question that haunted his young soul—the question of the twins crying in the bush and the question of Ikemefuna who was killed. He felt a relief within as the hymn poured into his parched soul. The words of the hymn were like the drops of frozen rain melting on the dry palate of the panting earth. Nwoye's callow mind was greatly puzzled.

17

The missionaries spent their first four or five nights in the marketplace, and went into the village in the morning to preach the gospel. They asked who the king of the village was, but the villagers told them that there was no king. "We have men of high title and the chief priests and the elders," they said.

It was not very easy getting the men of high title and the elders together after the excitement of the first day. But the missionaries persevered, and in the end they were received by the rulers of Mbanta. They asked for a plot of land to build their church.

Every clan and village had its "evil forest." In it were buried all those who died of the really evil diseases, like leprosy and smallpox. It was also the dumping ground for the potent fetishes of great medicine men when they died. An "evil forest" was, therefore, alive with sinister forces and powers of darkness. It was such a forest that the rulers of Mbanta gave to the missionaries. They did not really want them in their clan, and so they made them that offer which nobody in his right senses would accept.

"They want a piece of land to build their shrine," said Uchendu to his peers when they consulted among themselves. "We shall give them a piece of land." He paused, and there was a murmur of surprise and disagreement. "Let us give them a portion of the Evil Forest. They boast about victory over death. Let us give them a real battlefield in which to show their victory." They laughed and agreed, and sent for the missionaries, whom they had asked to leave them for a while so that they might "whisper together." They offered them as much of the Evil Forest as they cared to take. And to their greatest amazement the missionaries thanked them and burst into song.

"They do not understand," said some of the elders. "But they will understand when they go to their plot of land tomorrow morning." And they dispersed.

The next morning the crazy men actually began to clear a part of the forest and to build their house. The inhabitants of Mbanta expected them all to be dead within four days. The first day passed and the second and third and fourth, and none of them died. Everyone was puzzled. And then it became known that the white man's fetish had unbelievable power. It was said that he wore glasses on his eyes so that he could see and talk to evil spirits. Not long after, he won his first three converts.

Although Nwoye had been attracted to the new faith from the very first day, he kept it secret. He dared not go too near the missionaries for fear of his father. But whenever they came to preach in the open marketplace or the village playground, Nwoye was there. And he was already beginning to know some of the simple stories they told.

"We have now built a church," said Mr. Kiaga, the interpreter, who was now in charge of the infant congregation. The white man had gone back to Umuofia, where he built his headquarters and from where he paid regular visits to Mr. Kiaga's congregation at Mbanta.

"We have now built a church," said Mr. Kiaga, "and we want you all to come in every seventh day to worship the true God."

On the following Sunday, Nwoye passed and repassed the little red-earth and thatch building without summoning enough courage to enter. He heard the voice of singing and although it came from a handful of men it was loud and confident. Their church stood on a circular clearing that looked like the open mouth of the Evil Forest. Was it waiting to snap its teeth together? After passing and repassing by the church, Nwoye returned home.

It was well known among the people of Mbanta that their gods and ancestors were sometimes long-suffering and would deliberately allow a man to go on defying them. But even in such cases they set their limit at seven market weeks or twenty-eight days. Beyond that limit no man was suffered to go. And so excitement mounted in the village as the seventh week approached since the impudent missionaries built their church in the Evil Forest. The villagers were so certain about the doom that awaited these men that one or two converts thought it wise to suspend their allegiance to the new faith.

At last the day came by which all the missionaries should have died. But they were still alive, building a new red-earth and thatch house for their teacher, Mr. Kiaga. That week they won a handful more converts. And for the first time they had a woman. Her name was Nneka, the wife of Amadi, who was a prosperous farmer. She was very heavy with child.

Nneka had had four previous pregnancies and childbirths. But each time she had borne twins, and they had been immediately thrown away. Her husband and his family were already becoming highly critical of such a woman and were not unduly perturbed when they found she had fled to join the Christians. It was a good riddance.

One morning Okonkwo's cousin, Amikwu, was passing by the church on his way from the neighboring village, when he saw Nwoye among the Christians. He was greatly surprised, and when he got home he went straight to Okonkwo's hut and told him what he had seen. The women began to talk excitedly, but Okonkwo sat unmoved.

It was late afternoon before Nwoye returned. He went into the *obi* and saluted his father, but he did not answer. Nwoye turned round to walk into the inner compound when his father, suddenly overcome with fury, sprang to his feet and gripped him by the neck.

"Where have you been?" he stammered.

Nwoye struggled to free himself from the choking grip.

"Answer me," roared Okonkwo, "before I kill you!" He seized a heavy stick that lay on the dwarf wall and hit him two or three savage blows.

"Answer me!" he roared again. Nwoye stood looking at him and did not say a word. The women were screaming outside, afraid to go in.

"Leave that boy at once!" said a voice in the outer compound. It was Okonkwo's uncle, Uchendu. "Are you mad?"

Okonkwo did not answer. But he left hold of Nwoye, who walked away and never returned.

He went back to the church and told Mr. Kiaga that he had decided to go to Umuofia where the white missionary had set up a school to teach young Christians to read and write.

Mr. Kiaga's joy was very great. "Blessed is he who forsakes his father and his mother for my sake," he intoned. "Those that hear my words are my father and my mother."

Nwoye did not fully understand. But he was happy to leave his father. He would return later to his mother and his brothers and sisters and convert them to the new faith.

As Okonkwo sat in his hut that night, gazing into a log fire, he thought over the matter. A sudden fury rose within him and he felt a strong desire to take up his machete, go to the church and wipe out the entire vile and miscreant gang. But on further thought he told himself that Nwoye was not worth fighting for. Why, he cried in his heart, should he, Okonkwo, of all people, be cursed with such a son? He saw clearly in it the finger of his personal god or *chi*. For how else could he explain his great misfortune and exile and now his despicable son's behavior? Now that he had time to think of it, his son's crime stood out in its stark enormity. To abandon the gods of one's father and go about with a lot of effeminate men clucking like old hens was the very depth of abomination. Suppose when he died all his male children decided to follow Nwoye's steps and abandon their ancestors? Okonkwo felt a cold shudder run through him at the terrible prospects, like the prospect of annihilation. He saw himself and his fathers crowding round their ancestral shrine waiting in vain for worship and sacrifice and finding nothing but ashes of bygone days, and his children the while praying to the white man's god. If such a thing were ever to happen, he, Okonkwo, would wipe them off the face of the earth.

Okonkwo was popularly called the "Roaring Flame." As he looked into the log fire he recalled the name. He was a flaming fire. How then could he have begotten a son like Nwoye, degenerate and effeminate? Perhaps he was not his son. No! he could not be. His wife had played him false. He would teach her! But Nwoye resembled his grandfather, Unoka, who was Okonkwo's father. He pushed the thought out of his mind. He, Okonkwo, was called a flaming fire. How could he have begotten a woman for a son? At Nwoye's age Okonkwo had already become famous throughout Umuofia for his wrestling and his fearlessness.

He sighed heavily, and as if in sympathy the smoldering log also sighed. And immediately Okonkwo's eyes were opened and he saw the whole matter clearly. Living fire begets cold, impotent ash. He sighed again, deeply.

18

The young church in Mbanta had a few crises early in its life. At first the clan had assumed that it would not survive. But it had gone on living and gradually becoming stronger. The clan was worried, but not overmuch. If a gang of *efulefu* decided to live in the Evil Forest it was their own affair. When one came to think of it, the Evil Forest was a fit home for such undesirable people. It was true they were rescuing twins from the bush, but they never brought them into the village. As far as the villagers were concerned, the twins still remained where they had been thrown away. Surely the earth goddess would not visit the sins of the missionaries on the innocent villagers?

But on one occasion the missionaries had tried to overstep the bounds. Three converts had gone into the village and boasted openly that all the gods were dead and impotent and that they were prepared to defy them by burning all their shrines.

"Go and burn your mothers' genitals," said one of the priests. The men were seized and beaten until they streamed with blood. After that nothing happened for a long time between the church and the clan.

But stories were already gaining ground that the white man had not only brought a religion but also a government. It was said that they had built a place of judgment in Umuofia to protect the followers of their religion. It was even said that they had hanged one man who killed a missionary.

Although such stories were now often told they looked like fairy-tales in Mbanta and did not as yet affect the relationship between the new church and the clan. There was no question of killing a missionary here, for Mr. Kiaga, despite his madness, was quite harmless. As for his converts, no one could kill them without having to flee from the clan, for in spite of their worthlessness they still belonged to the clan. And so nobody gave serious thought to the stories about the white man's government or the consequences of killing the Christians. If they became more troublesome than they already were they would simply be driven out of the clan.

And the little church was at that moment too deeply absorbed in its own troubles to annoy the clan. It all began over the question of admitting outcasts.

These outcasts, or *osu*, seeing that the new religion welcomed twins and such abominations, thought that it was possible that they would also be received. And so one Sunday two of them went into the church. There was an immediate stir; but so great was the work the new religion had done among the converts that they did not immediately leave the church when the outcasts came in. Those who found themselves nearest to them merely moved to another seat. It was a miracle. But it only lasted till the end of the service. The whole church raised a protest and was about to drive these people out, when Mr. Kiaga stopped them and began to explain.

"Before God," he said, "there is no slave or free. We are all children of God and we must receive these our brothers."

"You do not understand," said one of the converts. "What will the heathen say of us when they hear that we receive *osu* into our midst? They will laugh."

"Let them laugh," said Mr. Kiaga. "God will laugh at them on the judgment day. Why do the nations rage and the peoples imagine a vain thing? He that sitteth in the heavens shall laugh. The Lord shall have them in derision."

"You do not understand," the convert maintained. "You are our teacher, and you can teach us the things of the new faith. But this is a matter which we know." And he told him what an *osu* was.

He was a person dedicated to a god, a thing set apart—a taboo for ever, and his children after him. He could neither marry nor be married by the free-born. He was in fact an outcast, living in a special area of the village, close to the Great Shrine. Wherever he went he carried with him the mark of his forbidden caste—long, tangled and dirty hair. A razor was taboo to him. An *osu* could not attend an assembly of the free-born, and they, in turn, could not shelter under his roof. He could not take any of the four titles of the clan, and when he died he was buried by his kind in the Evil Forest. How could such a man be a follower of Christ?

"He needs Christ more than you and I," said Mr. Kiaga.

"Then I shall go back to the clan," said the convert. And he went. Mr. Kiaga stood firm, and it was his firmness that saved the young church. The wavering converts drew inspiration and confidence from his unshakable faith. He ordered the outcasts to shave off their long, tangled hair. At first they were afraid they might die.

"Unless you shave off the mark of your heathen belief I will not admit you into the church," said Mr. Kiaga. "You fear that you will die. Why should that be? How are you different from other men who shave their hair? The same God created you and them. But they have cast you out like lepers. It is against the will of God, who has promised everlasting life to all who believe in His holy name. The heathen say you will die if you do this or that, and you are afraid. They also said I would die if I built my church on this ground. Am I dead? They said I would die if I took care of twins. I am still alive. The heathen speak nothing but falsehood. Only the word of our God is true."

The two outcasts shaved off their hair, and soon they were the strongest adherents of the new faith. And what was more, nearly all the *osu* in Mbanta followed their example. It was in fact one of them who in his zeal brought the church into serious conflict with the clan a year later by killing the sacred python, the emanation of the god of water.

The royal python was the most revered animal in Mbanta and all the surrounding clans. It was addressed as "Our Father," and was allowed to go wherever it chose, even into people's beds. It ate rats in the house and sometimes swallowed hens' eggs. If a clansman killed a royal python accidentally, he made sacrifices of atonement and performed an expensive burial ceremony such as was done for a great man. No punishment was prescribed for a man who killed the python knowingly. Nobody thought that such a thing could ever happen.

Perhaps it never did happen. That was the way the clan at first looked at it. No one had actually seen the man do it. The story had arisen among the Christians themselves.

But, all the same, the rulers and elders of Mbanta assembled to decide on their action. Many of them spoke at great length and in fury. The spirit of wars was upon them. Okonkwo, who had begun to play a part in the affairs of his motherland, said that until the abominable gang was chased out of the village with whips there would be no peace.

But there were many others who saw the situation differently, and it was their counsel that prevailed in the end.

"It is not our custom to fight for our gods," said one of them. "Let us not presume to do so now. If a man kills the sacred python in the secrecy of his hut, the matter lies between him and the god. We did not see it. If we put ourselves between the god and his victim we may receive blows intended for the offender. When a man blasphemes, what do we do? Do we go and stop his mouth? No. We put our fingers into our ears to stop us hearing. That is a wise action."

"Let us not reason like cowards," said Okonkwo. "If a man comes into my hut and defecates on the floor, what do I do? Do I shut my eyes? No! I take a stick and break his head. That is what a man does. These people are daily pouring filth over us, and Okeke says we should pretend not to see." Okonkwo made a sound full of disgust. This was a womanly clan, he thought. Such a thing could never happen in his fatherland, Umuofia.

"Okonkwo has spoken the truth," said another man. "We should do something. But let us ostracize these men. We would then not be held accountable for their abominations."

Everybody in the assembly spoke, and in the end it was decided to ostracize the Christians. Okonkwo ground his teeth in disgust.

That night a bell-man went through the length and breadth of Mbanta proclaiming that the adherents of the new faith were thenceforth excluded from the life and privileges of the clan.

The Christians had grown in number and were now a small community of men, women and children, self-assured and confident. Mr. Brown, the white missionary, paid regular visits to them. "When I think that it is only eighteen months since the Seed was first sown among you," he said, "I marvel at what the Lord hath wrought."

It was Wednesday in Holy Week and Mr. Kiaga had asked the women to bring red earth and white chalk and water to scrub the church for Easter; and the women had formed themselves into three groups for this purpose. They set out early that morning, some of them with their water-pots to the stream, another group with hoes and baskets to the village red-earth pit, and the others to the chalk quarry.

Mr. Kiaga was praying in the church when he heard the women talking excitedly. He rounded off his prayer and went to see what it was all about. The women had come to the church with empty water-pots. They said that some young men had chased them away from the stream with whips. Soon after, the women who had gone for red earth returned with empty baskets. Some of them had been heavily whipped. The chalk women also returned to tell a similar story.

"What does it all mean?" asked Mr. Kiaga, who was greatly perplexed.

"The village has outlawed us," said one of the women. "The bell-man announced it last night. But it is not our custom to debar anyone from the stream or the quarry."

Another woman said, "They want to ruin us. They will not allow us into the markets. They have said so."

Mr. Kiaga was going to send into the village for his men-converts when he saw them coming on their own. Of course they had all heard the bellman, but they had never in all their lives heard of women being debarred from the stream.

"Come along," they said to the women. "We will go with you to meet those cowards." Some of them had big sticks and some even machetes.

But Mr. Kiaga restrained them. He wanted first to know why they had been outlawed.

"They say that Okoli killed the sacred python," said one man.

"It is false," said another. "Okoli told me himself that it was false."

Okoli was not there to answer. He had fallen ill on the previous night. Before the day was over he was dead. His death showed that the gods were still able to fight their own battles. The clan saw no reason then for molesting the Christians.

19

The last big rains of the year were falling. It was the time for treading red earth with which to build walls. It was not done earlier because the rains were too heavy and would have washed away the heap of trodden earth; and it could not be done later because harvesting would soon set in, and after that the dry season.

It was going to be Okonkwo's last harvest in Mbanta. The seven wasted and weary years were at last dragging to a close. Although he had prospered in his motherland Okonkwo knew that he would have prospered even more in Umuofia, in the land of his fathers where men were bold and warlike. In these seven years he would have climbed to the utmost heights. And so he regretted every day of his exile. His mother's kinsmen had been very kind to him, and he was grateful. But that did not alter the facts. He had called the first child born to him in exile Nneka—"Mother is Supreme"—out of politeness to his mother's kinsmen. But two years later when a son was born he called him Nwofia—"Begotten in the Wilderness."

As soon as he entered his last year in exile Okonkwo sent money to Obierika to build him two huts in his old compound where he and his family would live until he built more huts and the outside wall of his compound. He could not ask another man to build his own *obi* for him, nor the walls of his compound. Those things a man built for himself or inherited from his father.

As the last heavy rains of the year began to fall, Obierika sent word that the two huts had been built and Okonkwo began to prepare for his return, after the rains. He would have liked to return earlier and build his compound that year before the rains stopped, but in doing so he would have taken something from the full penalty of seven years. And that could not be. So he waited impatiently for the dry season to come.

It came slowly. The rain became lighter and lighter until it fell in slanting showers. Sometimes the sun shone through the rain and a light breeze blew. It was a gay and airy kind of rain. The rainbow began to appear, and sometimes two rainbows, like a mother and her daughter, the one young and beautiful, and the other an old and faint shadow. The rainbow was called the python of the sky.

Okonkwo called his three wives and told them to get things together for a great feast. "I must thank my mother's kinsmen before I go," he said.

Ekwefi still had some cassava left on her farm from the previous year. Neither of the other wives had. It was not that they had been lazy, but that they had many children to feed. It was therefore understood that Ekwefi would provide cassava for the feast. Nwoye's mother and Ojiugo would provide the other things like smoked fish, palm-oil and pepper for the soup. Okonkwo would take care of meat and yams.

Ekwefi rose early on the following morning and went to her farm with her daughter, Ezinma, and Ojiugo's daughter, Obiageli, to harvest cassava tubers. Each of them carried a long cane basket, a machete for cutting down the soft cassava stem, and a little hoe for digging out the tuber. Fortunately, a light rain had fallen during the night and the soil would not be very hard. "It will not take us long to harvest as much as we like," said Ekwefi.

"But the leaves will be wet," said Ezinma. Her basket was balanced on her head, and her arms folded across her breasts. She felt cold. "I dislike cold water dropping on my back. We should have waited for the sun to rise and dry the leaves."

Obiageli called her "Salt" because she said that she disliked water. "Are you afraid you may dissolve?"

The harvesting was easy, as Ekwefi had said. Ezinma shook every tree violently with a long stick before she bent down to cut the stem and dig out the tuber. Sometimes it was not necessary to dig. They just pulled the stump, and earth rose, roots snapped below, and the tuber was pulled out.

When they had harvested a sizable heap they carried it down in two trips to the stream, where every woman had a shallow well for fermenting her cassava.

"It should be ready in four days or even three," said Obiageli. "They are young tubers."

"They are not all that young," said Ekwefi. "I planted the farm nearly two years ago. It is a poor soil and that is why the tubers are so small."

Okonkwo never did things by halves. When his wife Ekwefi protested that two goats were sufficient for the feast he told her that it was not her affair.

"I am calling a feast because I have the wherewithal. I cannot live on the bank of a river and wash my hands with spittle. My mother's people have been good to me and I must show my gratitude."

And so three goats were slaughtered and a number of fowls. It was like a wedding feast. There was foo-foo and yam pottage, egusi[7] soup and bitter-leaf soup and pots and pots of palm-wine.

All the *umunna*[8] were invited to the feast, all the descendants of Okolo, who had lived about two hundred years before. The oldest member of this extensive family was Okonkwo's uncle, Uchendu. The kola nut was given him to break, and he prayed to the ancestors. He asked them for health and children. "We do not ask for wealth because he that has health and children will also have wealth. We do not pray to have more money but to have more kinsmen. We are better than animals because we have kinsmen. An animal rubs its itching flank against a tree, a man asks his kinsman to scratch him." He prayed especially for Okonkwo and his family. He then broke the kola nut and threw one of the lobes on the ground for the ancestors.

As the broken kola nuts were passed round, Okonkwo's wives and children and those who came to help them with the cooking began to bring out the food. His sons brought out the pots of palm-wine. There was so much food and drink that many kinsmen whistled in surprise. When all was laid out, Okonkwo rose to speak.

"I beg you to accept this little kola," he said. "It is not to pay you back for all you did for me in these seven years. A child cannot pay for its mother's milk. I have only called you together because it is good for kinsmen to meet."

Yam pottage was served first because it was lighter than foo-foo and because yam always came first. Then the foo-foo was served. Some kinsmen ate it with egusi soup and others with bitter-leaf soup. The meat was then shared so that every member of the *umunna* had a portion. Every man rose in order of years and took a share. Even the few kinsmen who had not been able to come had their shares taken out for them in due term.

As the palm-wine was drunk one of the oldest members of the *umunna* rose to thank Okonkwo:

"If I say that we did not expect such a big feast I will be suggesting that we did not know how open-handed our son, Okonkwo, is. We all know him, and we expected a big feast. But it turned out to be even bigger than we expected. Thank you. May all you took out return again tenfold. It is good in these days when the younger generation consider themselves wiser than their sires to see a man doing things in the grand, old way. A man who calls his kinsmen to a feast does not do so to save them from starving. They all have food in their own homes. When we gather together in the moonlit village ground it is not because of the moon. Every man can see it in his own compound. We come together because it is good for kinsmen to do so. You may ask why I am saying all this. I say it because I fear for the younger generation, for you people." He waved his arm where most of the young men sat. "As for me, I have only a short while to live, and so have Uchendu and Unachukwu and Emefo. But I fear for you young people because you do not understand how strong is the bond of kinship. You do not know what it is to

7. Melon seed, which is roasted, ground, and cooked in soup.   8. Children of the father (literal trans.); the clan (male).

speak with one voice. And what is the result? An abominable religion has settled among you. A man can now leave his father and his brothers. He can curse the gods of his fathers and his ancestors, like a hunter's dog that suddenly goes mad and turns on his master. I fear for you; I fear for the clan." He turned again to Okonkwo and said, "Thank you for calling us together."

Part Three

20

Seven years was a long time to be away from one's clan. A man's place was not always there, waiting for him. As soon as he left, someone else rose and filled it. The clan was like a lizard; if it lost its tail it soon grew another.

Okonkwo knew these things. He knew that he had lost his place among the nine masked spirits who administered justice in the clan. He had lost the chance to lead his warlike clan against the new religion, which, he was told, had gained ground. He had lost the years in which he might have taken the highest titles in the clan. But some of these losses were not irreparable. He was determined that his return should be marked by his people. He would return with a flourish, and regain the seven wasted years.

Even in his first year in exile he had begun to plan for his return. The first thing he would do would be to rebuild his compound on a more magnificent scale. He would build a bigger barn than he had had before and he would build huts for two new wives. Then he would show his wealth by initiating his sons into the *ozo* society. Only the really great men in the clan were able to do this. Okonkwo saw clearly the high esteem in which he would be held, and he saw himself taking the highest title in the land.

As the years of exile passed one by one it seemed to him that his *chi* might now be making amends for the past disaster. His yams grew abundantly, not only in his motherland but also in Umuofia, where his friend gave them out year by year to sharecroppers.

Then the tragedy of his first son had occurred. At first it appeared as if it might prove too great for his spirit. But it was a resilient spirit, and in the end Okonkwo overcame his sorrow. He had five other sons and he would bring them up in the way of the clan.

He sent for the five sons and they came and sat in his *obi*. The youngest of them was four years old.

"You have all seen the great abomination of your brother. Now he is no longer my son or your brother. I will only have a son who is a man, who will hold his head up among my people. If any one of you prefers to be a woman, let him follow Nwoye now while I am alive so that I can curse him. If you turn against me when I am dead I will visit you and break your neck."

Okonkwo was very lucky in his daughters. He never stopped regretting that Ezinma was a girl. Of all his children she alone understood his every mood. A bond of sympathy had grown between them as the years had passed.

Ezinma grew up in her father's exile and became one of the most beautiful girls in Mbanta. She was called Crystal of Beauty, as her mother had been called in her youth. The young ailing girl who had caused her mother so much heartache had been transformed, almost overnight, into a healthy, buoyant maiden. She had, it was true, her moments of depression when she would snap at everybody like an angry dog. These moods descended on her suddenly and for no apparent reason. But they were very rare and short-lived. As long as they lasted, she could bear no other person but her father.

Many young men and prosperous middle-aged men of Mbanta came to marry her. But she refused them all, because her father had called her one evening and said to her: "There are many good and prosperous people here, but I shall be happy if you marry in Umuofia when we return home."

That was all he had said. But Ezinma had seen clearly all the thought and hidden meaning behind the few words. And she had agreed.

"Your half-sister, Obiageli, will not understand me," Okonkwo said. "But you can explain to her."

Although they were almost the same age, Ezinma wielded a strong influence over her half-sister. She explained to her why they should not marry yet, and she agreed also. And so the two of them refused every offer of marriage in Mbanta.

"I wish she were a boy," Okonkwo thought within himself. She understood things so perfectly. Who else among his children could have read his thoughts so well? With two beautiful grown-up daughters his return to Umuofia would attract considerable attention. His future sons-in-law would be men of authority in the clan. The poor and unknown would not dare to come forth.

Umuofia had indeed changed during the seven years Okonkwo had been in exile. The church had come and led many astray. Not only the low-born and the outcast but sometimes a worthy man had joined it. Such a man was Ogbuefi Ugonna,[9] who had taken two titles, and who like a madman had cut the anklet of his titles and cast it away to join the Christians. The white missionary was very proud of him and he was one of the first men in Umuofia to receive the sacrament of Holy Communion, or Holy Feast as it was called in Ibo. Ogbuefi Ugonna had thought of the Feast in terms of eating and drinking, only more holy than the village variety. He had therefore put his drinking-horn into his goatskin bag for the occasion.

But apart from the church, the white men had also brought a government. They had built a court where the District Commissioner judged cases in ignorance. He had court messengers who brought men to him for trial. Many of these messengers came from Umuru on the bank of the Great River, where the white men first came many years before and where they had built the center of their religion and trade and government. These court messengers were greatly hated in Umuofia because they were foreigners and also arrogant and high-handed. They were called kotma,[1] and because of their ash-colored shorts they earned the additional name of Ashy-Buttocks. They guarded the prison, which was full of men who had offended against the white man's law. Some of these prisoners had thrown away their twins and some had molested the Christians. They were beaten in the prison by the kotma and made to work every morning clearing the government compound and fetching wood for the white Commissioner and the court messengers. Some of these prisoners were men of title who should be above such mean

9. Father's honor (with the eagle feather). 1. Court messenger (pidgin English).

occupation. They were grieved by the indignity and mourned for their neglected farms. As they cut grass in the morning the younger men sang in time with the strokes of their machetes:

> *Kotma* of the ash buttocks,
> He is fit to be a slave.
> The white man has no sense,
> He is fit to be a slave.

The court messengers did not like to be called Ashy-Buttocks, and they beat the men. But the song spread in Umuofia.

Okonkwo's head was bowed in sadness as Obierika told him these things.

"Perhaps I have been away too long," Okonkwo said, almost to himself. "But I cannot understand these things you tell me. What is it that has happened to our people? Why have they lost the power to fight?"

"Have you not heard how the white man wiped out Abame?" asked Obierika.

"I have heard," said Okonkwo. "But I have also heard that Abame people were weak and foolish. Why did they not fight back? Had they no guns and machetes? We would be cowards to compare ourselves with the men of Abame. Their fathers had never dared to stand before our ancestors. We must fight these men and drive them from the land."

"It is already too late," said Obierika sadly. "Our own men and our sons have joined the ranks of the stranger. They have joined his religion and they help to uphold his government. If we should try to drive out the white men in Umuofia we should find it easy. There are only two of them. But what of our own people who are following their way and have been given power? They would go to Umuru and bring the soldiers, and we would be like Abame." He paused for a long time and then said: "I told you on my last visit to Mbanta how they hanged Aneto."

"What has happened to that piece of land in dispute?" asked Okonkwo.

"The white man's court has decided that it should belong to Nnama's family, who had given much money to the white man's messengers and interpreter."

"Does the white man understand our custom about land?"

"How can he when he does not even speak our tongue? But he says that our customs are bad; and our own brothers who have taken up his religion also say that our customs are bad. How do you think we can fight when our own brothers have turned against us? The white man is very clever. He came quietly and peaceably with his religion. We were amused at his foolishness and allowed him to stay. Now he has won our brothers, and our clan can no longer act like one. He has put a knife on the things that held us together and we have fallen apart."

"How did they get hold of Aneto to hang him?" asked Okonkwo.

"When he killed Oduche in the fight over the land, he fled to Aninta to escape the wrath of the earth. This was about eight days after the fight, because Oduche had not died immediately from his wounds. It was on the seventh day that he died. But everybody knew that he was going to die and Aneto got his belongings together in readiness to flee. But the Christians had told the white man about the accident, and he sent his *kotma* to catch Aneto. He was imprisoned with all the leaders of his family. In the end

Oduche died and Aneto was taken to Umuru and hanged. The other people were released, but even now they have not found the mouth with which to tell of their suffering."

The two men sat in silence for a long while afterwards.

21

There were many men and women in Umuofia who did not feel as strongly as Okonkwo about the new dispensation. The white man had indeed brought a lunatic religion, but he had also built a trading store and for the first time palm-oil and kernel[2] became things of great price, and much money flowed into Umuofia.

And even in the matter of religion there was a growing feeling that there might be something in it after all, something vaguely akin to method in the overwhelming madness.

This growing feeling was due to Mr. Brown, the white missionary, who was very firm in restraining his flock from provoking the wrath of the clan. One member in particular was very difficult to restrain. His name was Enoch and his father was the priest of the snake cult. The story went around that Enoch had killed and eaten the sacred python, and that his father had cursed him.

Mr. Brown preached against such excess of zeal. Everything was possible, he told his energetic flock, but everything was not expedient. And so Mr. Brown came to be respected even by the clan, because he trod softly on its faith. He made friends with some of the great men of the clan and on one of his frequent visits to the neighboring villages he had been presented with a carved elephant tusk, which was a sign of dignity and rank. One of the great men in that village was called Akunna[3] and he had given one of his sons to be taught the white man's knowledge in Mr. Brown's school.

Whenever Mr. Brown went to that village he spent long hours with Akunna in his *obi* talking through an interpreter about religion. Neither of them succeeded in converting the other but they learned more about their different beliefs.

"You say that there is one supreme God who made heaven and earth," said Akunna on one of Mr. Brown's visits. "We also believe in Him and call Him Chukwu. He made all the world and the other gods."

"There are no other gods," said Mr. Brown. "Chukwu is the only God and all others are false. You carve a piece of wood—like that one" (he pointed at the rafters from which Akunna's carved *Ikenga*[4] hung), "and you call it a god. But it is still a piece of wood."

"Yes," said Akunna. "It is indeed a piece of wood. The tree from which it came was made by Chukwu, as indeed all minor gods were. But He made them for His messengers so that we could approach Him through them. It is like yourself. You are the head of your church."

"No," protested Mr. Brown. "The head of my church is God Himself."

---

2. The red fleshy husk of the palm nut is crushed manually to produce cooking oil, leaving a fibrous residue along with hard kernels. The Europeans bought both the red oil and the kernels, from which they could extract a very fine oil by using machines.   3. Father's wealth.   4. A carved wooden figure with the horns of a ram that symbolized the strength of a man's right hand. Every adult male kept an *Ikenga* in his personal shrine.

"I know," said Akunna, "but there must be a head in this world among men. Somebody like yourself must be the head here."

"The head of my church in that sense is in England."

"That is exactly what I am saying. The head of your church is in your country. He has sent you here as his messenger. And you have also appointed your own messengers and servants. Or let me take another example, the District Commissioner. He is sent by your king."

"They have a queen," said the interpreter on his own account.

"Your queen sends her messenger, the District Commissioner. He finds that he cannot do the work alone and so he appoints kotma to help him. It is the same with God, or Chukwu. He appoints the smaller gods to help Him because His work is too great for one person."

"You should not think of Him as a person," said Mr. Brown. "It is because you do so that you imagine He must need helpers. And the worst thing about it is that you give all the worship to the false gods you have created."

"That is not so. We make sacrifices to the little gods, but when they fail and there is no one else to turn to we go to Chukwu. It is right to do so. We approach a great man through his servants. But when his servants fail to help us, then we go to the last source of hope. We appear to pay greater attention to the little gods but that is not so. We worry them more because we are afraid to worry their Master. Our fathers knew that Chukwu was the Overlord and that is why many of them gave their children the name Chuk-wuka—"Chukwu is Supreme.""

"You said one interesting thing," said Mr. Brown. "You are afraid of Chukwu. In my religion Chukwu is a loving Father and need not be feared by those who do His will."

"But we must fear Him when we are not doing His will," said Akunna. "And who is to tell His will? It is too great to be known."

In this way Mr. Brown learned a good deal about the religion of the clan and he came to the conclusion that a frontal attack on it would not succeed. And so he built a school and a little hospital in Umuofia. He went from family to family begging people to send their children to his school. But at first they only sent their slaves or sometimes their lazy children. Mr. Brown begged and argued and prophesied. He said that the leaders of the land in the future would be men and women who had learned to read and write. If Umuofia failed to send her children to the school, strangers would come from other places to rule them. They could already see that happening in the Native Court, where the D.C. was surrounded by strangers who spoke his tongue. Most of these strangers came from the distant town of Umuru on the bank of the Great River where the white man first went.

In the end Mr. Brown's arguments began to have an effect. More people came to learn in his school, and he encouraged them with gifts of singlets[5] and towels. They were not all young, these people who came to learn. Some of them were thirty years old or more. They worked on their farms in the morning and went to school in the afternoon. And it was not long before the people began to say that the white man's medicine was quick in working. Mr. Brown's school produced quick results. A few months in it were enough

5. Undershirts, T-shirts.

2142 / CHINUA ACHEBE
2142 / CHINUA ACHEBE

to make one a court messenger or even a court clerk. Those who stayed longer became teachers; and from Umuofia laborers went forth into the Lord's vineyard. New churches were established in the surrounding villages and a few schools with them. From the very beginning religion and education went hand in hand.

Mr. Brown's mission grew from strength to strength, and because of its link with the new administration it earned a new social prestige. But Mr. Brown himself was breaking down in health. At first he ignored the warning signs. But in the end he had to leave his flock, sad and broken.

It was in the first rainy season after Okonkwo's return to Umuofia that Mr. Brown left for home. As soon as he had learned of Okonkwo's return five months earlier, the missionary had immediately paid him a visit. He had just sent Okonkwo's son, Nwoye, who was now called Isaac,[6] to the new training college for teachers in Umuru. And he had hoped that Okonkwo would be happy to hear of it. But Okonkwo had driven him away with the threat that if he came into his compound again, he would be carried out of it.

Okonkwo's return to his native land was not as memorable as he had wished. It was true his two beautiful daughters aroused great interest among suitors and marriage negotiations were soon in progress, but, beyond that, Umuofia did not appear to have taken any special notice of the warrior's return. The clan had undergone such profound change during his exile that it was barely recognizable. The new religion and government and the trading stores were very much in the people's eyes and minds. There were still many who saw these new institutions as evil, but even they talked and thought about little else, and certainly not about Okonkwo's return.

And it was the wrong year too. If Okonkwo had immediately initiated his two sons into the *ozo* society as he had planned he would have caused a stir. But the initiation rite was performed once in three years in Umuofia, and he had to wait for nearly two years for the next round of ceremonies.

Okonkwo was deeply grieved. And it was not just a personal grief. He mourned for the clan, which he saw breaking up and falling apart, and he mourned for the warlike men of Umuofia, who had so unaccountably become soft like women.

22

Mr. Brown's successor was the Reverend James Smith, and he was a different kind of man. He condemned openly Mr. Brown's policy of compromise and accommodation. He saw things as black and white. And black was evil. He saw the world as a battlefield in which the children of light were locked in mortal conflict with the sons of darkness. He spoke in his sermons about sheep and goats and about wheat and tares. He believed in slaying the prophets of Baal.

Mr. Smith was greatly distressed by the ignorance which many of his flock showed even in such things as the Trinity and the Sacraments. It only showed that they were seeds sown on a rocky soil. Mr. Brown had thought of nothing but numbers. He should have known that the kingdom of God did not depend

6. Son of Abraham, offered to God as a sacrifice (Genesis 22).

on large crowds. Our Lord Himself stressed the importance of fewness. Narrow is the way and few the number. To fill the Lord's holy temple with an idolatrous crowd clamoring for signs was a folly of everlasting consequence. Our Lord used the whip only once in His life—to drive the crowd away from His church.

Within a few weeks of his arrival in Umuofia Mr. Smith suspended a young woman from the church for pouring new wine into old bottles. This woman had allowed her heathen husband to mutilate her dead child. The child had been declared an *ogbanje,* plaguing its mother by dying and entering her womb to be born again. Four times this child had run its evil round. And so it was mutilated to discourage it from returning.

Mr. Smith was filled with wrath when he heard of this. He disbelieved the story which even some of the most faithful confirmed, the story of really evil children who were not deterred by mutilation, but came back with all the scars. He replied that such stories were spread in the world by the Devil to lead men astray. Those who believed such stories were unworthy of the Lord's table.

There was a saying in Umuofia that as a man danced so the drums were beaten for him. Mr. Smith danced a furious step and so the drums went mad. The over-zealous converts who had smarted under Mr. Brown's restraining hand now flourished in full favor. One of them was Enoch, the son of the snake-priest who was believed to have killed and eaten the sacred python. Enoch's devotion to the new faith had seemed so much greater than Mr. Brown's that the villagers called him the outsider who wept louder than the bereaved.

Enoch was short and slight of build, and always seemed in great haste. His feet were short and broad, and when he stood or walked his heels came together and his feet opened outwards as if they had quarreled and meant to go in different directions. Such was the excessive energy bottled up in Enoch's small body that it was always erupting in quarrels and fights. On Sundays he always imagined that the sermon was preached for the benefit of his enemies. And if he happened to sit near one of them he would occasionally turn to give him a meaningful look, as if to say, "I told you so." It was Enoch who touched off the great conflict between church and clan in Umuofia which had been gathering since Mr. Brown left.

It happened during the annual ceremony which was held in honor of the earth deity. At such times the ancestors of the clan who had been committed to Mother Earth at their death emerged again as *egwugwu* through tiny antholes.

One of the greatest crimes a man could commit was to unmask an *egwugwu* in public, or to say or do anything which might reduce its immortal prestige in the eyes of the uninitiated. And this was what Enoch did.

The annual worship of the earth goddess fell on a Sunday, and the masked spirits were abroad. The Christian women who had been to church could not therefore go home. Some of their men had gone out to beg the *egwugwu* to retire for a short while for the women to pass. They agreed and were already retiring, when Enoch boasted aloud that they would not dare to touch a Christian. Whereupon they all came back and one of them gave Enoch a good stroke of the cane, which was always carried. Enoch fell on him and tore off his mask. The other *egwugwu* immediately surrounded their desecrated companion, to shield him from the profane gaze of women and children, and led him away. Enoch had killed an ancestral spirit, and Umuofia was thrown into confusion.

That night the Mother of the Spirits walked the length and breadth of the clan, weeping for her murdered son. It was a terrible night. Not even the oldest man in Umuofia had ever heard such a strange and fearful sound, and it was never to be heard again. It seemed as if the very soul of the tribe wept for a great evil that was coming—its own death.

On the next day all the masked *egwugwu* of Umuofia assembled in the marketplace. They came from all the quarters of the clan and even from the neighboring villages. The dreaded Otakagu came from Imo, and Ekwensu, dangling a white cock, arrived from Uli. It was a terrible gathering. The eerie voices of countless spirits, the bells that clattered behind some of them, and the clash of machetes as they ran forwards and backwards and saluted one another, sent tremors of fear into every heart. For the first time in living memory the sacred bull-roarer was heard in broad daylight.

From the marketplace the furious band made for Enoch's compound. Some of the elders of the clan went with them, wearing heavy protections of charms and amulets. These were men whose arms were strong in *ogwu*, or medicine. As for the ordinary men and women, they listened from the safety of their huts.

The leaders of the Christians had met together at Mr. Smith's parsonage on the previous night. As they deliberated they could hear the Mother of Spirits wailing for her son. The chilling sound affected Mr. Smith, and for the first time he seemed to be afraid.

"What are they planning to do?" he asked. No one knew, because such a thing had never happened before. Mr. Smith would have sent for the District Commissioner and his court messengers, but they had gone on tour on the previous day.

"One thing is clear," said Mr. Smith. "We cannot offer physical resistance to them. Our strength lies in the Lord." They knelt down together and prayed to God for delivery.

"O Lord, save Thy people," cried Mr. Smith.

"And bless Thine inheritance," replied the men.

They decided that Enoch should be hidden in the parsonage for a day or two. Enoch himself was greatly disappointed when he heard this, for he had hoped that a holy war was imminent; and there were a few other Christians who thought like him. But wisdom prevailed in the camp of the faithful and many lives were thus saved.

The band of *egwugwu* moved like a furious whirlwind to Enoch's compound and with machete and fire reduced it to a desolate heap. And from there they made for the church, intoxicated with destruction.

Mr. Smith was in his church when he heard the masked spirits coming. He walked quietly to the door which commanded the approach to the church compound, and stood there. But when the first three or four *egwugwu* appeared on the church compound he nearly bolted. He overcame this impulse and instead of running away he went down the two steps that led up to the church and walked towards the approaching spirits.

They surged forward, and a long stretch of the bamboo fence with which the church compound was surrounded gave way before them. Discordant bells clanged, machetes clashed and the air was full of dust and weird sounds. Mr. Smith heard a sound of footsteps behind him. He turned round and saw Okeke, his interpreter. Okeke had not been on the best of terms with his master since he had strongly condemned Enoch's behavior at the meeting of the leaders of the church during the night. Okeke had gone as far as to say that Enoch should not be hidden in the parsonage, because he would only draw the wrath of the clan on the pastor. Mr. Smith had rebuked him in very strong language, and had not sought his advice that morning. But now, as he came up and stood by him confronting the angry spirits, Mr. Smith looked at him and smiled. It was a wan smile, but there was deep gratitude there.

For a brief moment the onrush of the *egwugwu* was checked by the unexpected composure of the two men. But it was only a momentary check, like the tense silence between blasts of thunder. The second onrush was greater than the first. It swallowed up the two men. Then an unmistakable voice rose above the tumult and there was immediate silence. Space was made around the two men, and Ajofia began to speak.

Ajofia was the leading *egwugwu* of Umuofia. He was the head and spokesman of the nine ancestors who administered justice in the clan. His voice was unmistakable and so he was able to bring immediate peace to the agitated spirits. He then addressed Mr. Smith, and as he spoke clouds of smoke rose from his head.

"The body of the white man, I salute you," he said, using the language in which immortals spoke to men.

"The body of the white man, do you know me?" he asked.

Mr. Smith looked at his interpreter, but Okeke, who was a native of distant Umuru, was also at a loss.

Ajofia laughed in his guttural voice. It was like the laugh of rusty metal. "They are strangers," he said, "and they are ignorant. But let that pass." He turned round to his comrades and saluted them, calling them the fathers of Umuofia. He dug his rattling spear into the ground and it shook with metallic life. Then he turned once more to the missionary and his interpreter.

"Tell the white man that we will not do him any harm," he said to the interpreter. "Tell him to go back to his house and leave us alone. We liked his brother who was with us before. He was foolish, but we liked him, and for his sake we shall not harm his brother. But this shrine which he built must be destroyed. We shall no longer allow it in our midst. It has bred untold abominations and we have come to put an end to it." He turned to his comrades. "Fathers of Umuofia, I salute you"; and they replied with one guttural voice. He turned again to the missionary. "You can stay with us if you like our ways. You can worship your own god. It is good that a man should worship the gods and the spirits of his fathers. Go back to your house so that you may not be hurt. Our anger is great but we have held it down so that we can talk to you."

Mr. Smith said to his interpreter: "Tell them to go away from here. This is the house of God and I will not live to see it desecrated."

Okeke interpreted wisely to the spirits and leaders of Umuofia: "The white man says he is happy you have come to him with your grievances, like friends. He will be happy if you leave the matter in his hands."

"We cannot leave the matter in his hands because he does not understand our customs, just as we do not understand his. We say he is foolish because he does not know our ways, and perhaps he says we are foolish because we do not know his. Let him go away."

Mr. Smith stood his ground. But he could not save his church. When the *egwugwu* went away the red-earth church which Mr. Brown had built was a pile of earth and ashes. And for the moment the spirit of the clan was pacified.

23

For the first time in many years Okonkwo had a feeling that was akin to happiness. The times which had altered so unaccountably during his exile seemed to be coming round again. The clan which had turned false on him appeared to be making amends.

He had spoken violently to his clansmen when they had met in the market-place to decide on their action. And they had listened to him with respect. It was like the good old days again, when a warrior was a warrior. Although they had not agreed to kill the missionary or drive away the Christians, they had agreed to do something substantial. And they had done it. Okonkwo was almost happy again.

For two days after the destruction of the church, nothing happened. Every man in Umuofia went about armed with a gun or a machete. They would not be caught unawares, like the men of Abame.

Then the District Commissioner returned from his tour. Mr. Smith went immediately to him and they had a long discussion. The men of Umuofia did not take any notice of this, and if they did, they thought it was not important. The missionary often went to see his brother white man. There was nothing strange in that.

Three days later the District Commissioner sent his sweet-tongued messenger to the leaders of Umuofia asking them to meet him in his headquarters. That also was not strange. He often asked them to hold such palavers, as he called them. Okonkwo was among the six leaders he invited.

Okonkwo warned the others to be fully armed. "An Umuofia man does not refuse a call," he said. "He may refuse to do what he is asked; he does not refuse to be asked. But the times have changed, and we must be fully prepared."

And so the six men went to see the District Commissioner, armed with their machetes. They did not carry guns, for that would be unseemly. They were led into the courthouse where the District Commissioner sat. He received them politely. They unslung their goatskin bags and their sheathed machetes, put them on the floor, and sat down.

"I have asked you to come," began the Commissioner, "because of what happened during my absence. I have been told a few things but I cannot believe them until I have heard your own side. Let us talk about it like friends and find a way of ensuring that it does not happen again."

Ogbuefi Ekwueme[7] rose to his feet and began to tell the story.

"Wait a minute," said the Commissioner. "I want to bring in my men so that they too can hear your grievances and take warning. Many of them come

---

7. A person who does what he says (a praise name).

from distant places and although they speak your tongue they are ignorant of your customs. James! Go and bring in the men." His interpreter left the courtroom and soon returned with twelve men. They sat together with the men of Umuofia, and Ogbuefi Ekwueme began to tell the story of how Enoch murdered an *egwugwu*.

It happened so quickly that the six men did not see it coming. There was only a brief scuffle, too brief even to allow the drawing of a sheathed machete. The six men were handcuffed and led into the guardroom.

"We shall not do you any harm," said the District Commissioner to them later, "if only you agree to cooperate with us. We have brought a peaceful administration to you and your people so that you may be happy. If any man ill-treats you we shall come to your rescue. But we will not allow you to ill-treat others. We have a court of law where we judge cases and administer justice just as it is done in my own country under a great queen. I have brought you here because you joined together to molest others, to burn people's houses and their place of worship. That must not happen in the dominion of our queen, the most powerful ruler in the world. I have decided that you will pay a fine of two hundred bags of cowries. You will be released as soon as you agree to this and undertake to collect that fine from your people. What do you say to that?"

The six men remained sullen and silent and the Commissioner left them for a while. He told the court messengers, when he left the guardroom, to treat the men with respect because they were the leaders of Umuofia. They said, "Yes, sir," and saluted.

As soon as the District Commissioner left, the head messenger, who was also the prisoners' barber, took down his razor and shaved off all the hair on the men's heads. They were still handcuffed, and they just sat and moped.

"Who is the chief among you?" the court messengers asked in jest. "We see that every pauper wears the anklet of title in Umuofia. Does it cost as much as ten cowries?"

The six men ate nothing throughout that day and the next. They were not even given any water to drink, and they could not go out to urinate or go into the bush when they were pressed. At night the messengers came in to taunt them and to knock their shaven heads together.

Even when the men were left alone they found no words to speak to one another. It was only on the third day, when they could no longer bear the hunger and the insults, that they began to talk about giving in.

"We should have killed the white man if you had listened to me," Okonkwo snarled.

"We could have been in Umuru now waiting to be hanged," someone said to him.

"Who wants to kill the white man?" asked a messenger who had just rushed in. Nobody spoke.

"You are not satisfied with your crime, but you must kill the white man on top of it." He carried a strong stick, and he hit each man a few blows on the head and back. Okonkwo was choked with hate.

As soon as the six men were locked up, court messengers went into Umuofia to tell the people that their leaders would not be released unless they paid a fine of two hundred and fifty bags of cowries.

"Unless you pay the fine immediately," said their head-man, "we will take your leaders to Umuru before the big white man, and hang them."

This story spread quickly through the villages, and was added to as it went. Some said that the men had already been taken to Umuru and would be hanged on the following day. Some said that their families would also be hanged. Others said that soldiers were already on their way to shoot the people of Umuofia as they had done in Abame.

It was the time of the full moon. But that night the voice of children was not heard. The village *ilo* where they always gathered for a moon-play was empty. The women of Iguedo did not meet in their secret enclosure to learn a new dance to be displayed later to the village. Young men who were always abroad in the moonlight kept to their huts that night. Their manly voices were not heard on the village paths as they went to visit their friends and lovers. Umuofia was like a startled animal with ears erect, sniffing the silent, ominous air and not knowing which way to run.

The silence was broken by the village crier beating his sonorous *ogene*. He called every man in Umuofia, from the Akakanma age group upwards, to a meeting in the marketplace after the morning meal. He went from one end of the village to the other and walked all its breadth. He did not leave out any of the main footpaths.

Okonkwo's compound was like a deserted homestead. It was as if cold water had been poured on it. His family was all there, but everyone spoke in whispers. His daughter Ezinma had broken her twenty-eight-day visit to the family of her future husband, and returned home when she heard that her father had been imprisoned, and was going to be hanged. As soon as she got home she went to Obierika to ask what the men of Umuofia were going to do about it. But Obierika had not been home since morning. His wives thought he had gone to a secret meeting. Ezinma was satisfied that something was being done.

On the morning after the village crier's appeal the men of Umuofia met in the marketplace and decided to collect without delay two hundred and fifty bags of cowries to appease the white man. They did not know that fifty bags would go to the court messengers, who had increased the fine for that purpose.

24

Okonkwo and his fellow prisoners were set free as soon as the fine was paid. The District Commissioner spoke to them again about the great queen, and about peace and good government. But the men did not listen. They just sat and looked at him and at his interpreter. In the end they were given back their bags and sheathed machetes and told to go home. They rose and left the courthouse. They neither spoke to anyone nor among themselves.

The courthouse, like the church, was built a little way outside the village. The footpath that linked them was a very busy one because it also led to the stream, beyond the court. It was open and sandy. Footpaths were open and sandy in the dry season. But when the rains came the bush grew thick on either side and closed in on the path. It was now dry season.

As they made their way to the village the six men met women and children going to the stream with their waterpots. But the men wore such heavy and fearsome looks that the women and children did not say "*nno*" or "welcome" to them, but edged out of the way to let them pass. In the village little groups of men joined them until they became a sizable company. They walked silently. As each of the six men got to his compound, he turned in, taking some of the crowd with him. The village was astir in a silent, suppressed way.

Ezinma had prepared some food for her father as soon as news spread that the six men would be released. She took it to him in his *obi*. He ate absent-mindedly. He had no appetite; he only ate to please her. His male relations and friends had gathered in his *obi*, and Obierika was urging him to eat. Nobody else spoke, but they noticed the long stripes on Okonkwo's back where the warder's whip had cut into his flesh.

The village crier was abroad again in the night. He beat his iron gong and announced that another meeting would be held in the morning. Everyone knew that Umuofia was at last going to speak its mind about the things that were happening.

Okonkwo slept very little that night. The bitterness in his heart was now mixed with a kind of childlike excitement. Before he had gone to bed he had brought down his war dress, which he had not touched since his return from exile. He had shaken out his smoked raffia skirt and examined his tall feather head-gear and his shield. They were all satisfactory, he had thought.

As he lay on his bamboo bed he thought about the treatment he had received in the white man's court, and he swore vengeance. If Umuofia decided on war, all would be well. But if they chose to be cowards he would go out and avenge himself. He thought about wars in the past. The noblest, he thought, was the war against Isike. In those days Okudo[8] was still alive. Okudo sang a war song in a way that no other man could. He was not a fighter, but his voice turned every man into a lion.

"Worthy men are no more," Okonkwo sighed as he remembered those days. "Isike will never forget how we slaughtered them in that war. We killed twelve of their men and they killed only two of ours. Before the end of the fourth market week they were suing for peace. Those were days when men were men."

As he thought of these things he heard the sound of the iron gong in the distance. He listened carefully, and could just hear the crier's voice. But it was very faint. He turned on his bed and his back hurt him. He ground his teeth. The crier was drawing nearer and nearer until he passed by Okonkwo's compound.

"The greatest obstacle in Umuofia," Okonkwo thought bitterly, "is that coward, Egonwanne.[9] His sweet tongue can change fire into cold ash. When he speaks he moves our men to impotence. If they had ignored his womanish wisdom five years ago, we would not have come to this." He ground his teeth. "Tomorrow he will tell them that our fathers never fought a 'war of blame.' If they listen to him I shall leave them and plan my own revenge."

The crier's voice had once more become faint, and the distance had taken the harsh edge off his iron gong. Okonkwo turned from one side to the other and derived a kind of pleasure from the pain his back gave him. "Let Egon-

8. Great eagle feather (a praise name). 9. Wealth of a sibling.

wanne talk about a 'war of blame' tomorrow and I shall show him my back and head." He ground his teeth.

The marketplace began to fill as soon as the sun rose. Obierika was waiting in his *obi* when Okonkwo came along and called him. He hung his goatskin bag and his sheathed machete on his shoulder and went out to join him. Obierika's hut was close to the road and he saw every man who passed to the marketplace. He had exchanged greetings with many who had already passed that morning.

When Okonkwo and Obierika got to the meeting place there were already so many people that if one threw up a grain of sand it would not find its way to the earth again. And many more people were coming from every quarter of the nine villages. It warmed Okonkwo's heart to see such strength of numbers. But he was looking for one man in particular, the man whose tongue he dreaded and despised so much.

"Can you see him?" he asked Obierika.

"Who?"

"Egonwanne," he said, his eyes roving from one corner of the huge market-place to the other. Most of the men sat on wooden stools they had brought with them.

"No," said Obierika, casting his eyes over the crowd. "Yes, there he is, under the silk-cotton tree. Are you afraid he would convince us not to fight?"

"Afraid? I do not care what he does to *you.* I despise him and those who listen to him. I shall fight alone if I choose."

They spoke at the top of their voices because everybody was talking, and it was like the sound of a great market.

"I shall wait till he has spoken," Okonkwo thought. "Then I shall speak."

"But how do you know he will speak against war?" Obierika asked after a while.

"Because I know he is a coward," said Okonkwo. Obierika did not hear the rest of what he said because at that moment somebody touched his shoulder from behind and he turned round to shake hands and exchange greetings with five or six friends. Okonkwo did not turn round even though he knew the voices. He was in no mood to exchange greetings. But one of the men touched him and asked about the people of his compound.

"They are well," he replied without interest.

The first man to speak to Umuofia that morning was Okika, one of the six who had been imprisoned. Okika was a great man and an orator. But he did not have the booming voice which a first speaker must use to establish silence in the assembly of the clan. Onyeka[1] had such a voice; and so he was asked to salute Umuofia before Okika began to speak.

"*Umuofia kwenu!*" he bellowed, raising his left arm and pushing the air with his open hand.

"*Yaa!*" roared Umuofia.

"*Umuofia kwenu!*" he bellowed again, and again and again, facing a new direction each time. And the crowd answered, "*Yaa!*"

There was immediate silence as though cold water had been poured on a roaring flame.

1. "Who surpasses [God]?" (a rhetorical question).

Okika sprang to his feet and also saluted his clansmen four times. Then he began to speak:

"You all know why we are here, when we ought to be building our barns or mending our huts, when we should be putting our compounds in order. My father used to say to me: 'Whenever you see a toad jumping in broad daylight, then know that something is after its life.' When I saw you all pouring into this meeting from all the quarters of our clan so early in the morning, I knew that something was after our life." He paused for a brief moment and then began again:

"All our gods are weeping. Idemili is weeping, Ogwugwu is weeping, Agbala is weeping, and all the others. Our dead fathers are weeping because of the shameful sacrilege they are suffering and the abomination we have all seen with our eyes." He stopped again to steady his trembling voice.

"This is a great gathering. No clan can boast of greater numbers or greater valor. But are we all here? I ask you: Are all the sons of Umuofia with us here?" A deep murmur swept through the crowd.

"They are not," he said. "They have broken the clan and gone their several ways. We who are here this morning have remained true to our fathers, but our brothers have deserted us and joined a stranger to soil their fatherland. If we fight the stranger we shall hit our brothers and perhaps shed the blood of a clansman. But we must do it. Our fathers never dreamed of such a thing, they never killed their brothers. But a white man never came to them. So we must do what our fathers would never have done. Eneke the bird was asked why he was always on the wing and he replied: 'Men have learned to shoot without missing their mark and I have learned to fly without perching on a twig.' We must root out this evil. And if our brothers take the side of evil we must root them out too. And we must do it *now*. We must bail this water now that it is only ankle-deep. . . ."

At this point there was a sudden stir in the crowd and every eye was turned in one direction. There was a sharp bend in the road that led from the marketplace to the white man's court, and to the stream beyond it. And so no one had seen the approach of the five court messengers until they had come round the bend, a few paces from the edge of the crowd. Okonkwo was sitting at the edge.

He sprang to his feet as soon as he saw who it was. He confronted the head messenger, trembling with hate, unable to utter a word. The man was fearless and stood his ground, his four men lined up behind him.

In that brief moment the world seemed to stand still, waiting. There was utter silence. The men of Umuofia were merged into the mute backcloth of trees and giant creepers, waiting.

The spell was broken by the head messenger. "Let me pass!" he ordered.

"What do you want here?"

"The white man whose power you know too well has ordered this meeting to stop."

In a flash Okonkwo drew his machete. The messenger crouched to avoid the blow. It was useless. Okonkwo's machete descended twice and the man's head lay beside his uniformed body.

The waiting backcloth jumped into tumultuous life and the meeting was stopped. Okonkwo stood looking at the dead man. He knew that Umuofia would not go to war. He knew because they had let the other messengers escape. They had broken into tumult instead of action. He discerned fright in that tumult. He heard voices asking: "Why did he do it?"

He wiped his machete on the sand and went away.

25

When the District Commissioner arrived at Okonkwo's compound at the head of an armed band of soldiers and court messengers he found a small crowd of men sitting wearily in the *obi*. He commanded them to come outside, and they obeyed without a murmur.

"Which among you is called Okonkwo?" he asked through his interpreter.

"He is not here," replied Obierika.

"Where is he?"

"He is not here!"

The Commissioner became angry and red in the face. He warned the men that unless they produced Okonkwo forthwith he would lock them all up. The men murmured among themselves, and Obierika spoke again.

"We can take you where he is, and perhaps your men will help us."

The Commissioner did not understand what Obierika meant when he said, "Perhaps your men will help us." One of the most infuriating habits of these people was their love of superfluous words, he thought.

Obierika with five or six others led the way. The Commissioner and his men followed, their firearms held at the ready. He had warned Obierika that if he and his men played any monkey tricks they would be shot. And so they went.

There was a small bush behind Okonkwo's compound. The only opening into this bush from the compound was a little round hole in the red-earth wall through which fowls went in and out in their endless search for food. The hole would not let a man through. It was to this bush that Obierika led the Commissioner and his men. They skirted round the compound, keeping close to the wall. The only sound they made was with their feet as they crushed dry leaves.

Then they came to the tree from which Okonkwo's body was dangling, and they stopped dead.

"Perhaps your men can help us bring him down and bury him," said Obierika. "We have sent for strangers from another village to do it for us, but they may be a long time coming."

The District Commissioner changed instantaneously. The resolute administrator in him gave way to the student of primitive customs.

"Why can't you take him down yourselves?" he asked.

"It is against our custom," said one of the men. "It is an abomination for a man to take his own life. It is an offense against the Earth, and a man who commits it will not be buried by his clansmen. His body is evil, and only strangers may touch it. That is why we ask your people to bring him down, because you are strangers."

"Will you bury him like any other man?" asked the Commissioner.

"We cannot bury him. Only strangers can. We shall pay your men to do it. When he has been buried we will then do our duty by him. We shall make sacrifices to cleanse the desecrated land."

Obierika, who had been gazing steadily at his friend's dangling body, turned suddenly to the District Commissioner and said ferociously: "That man was one of the greatest men in Umuofia. You drove him to kill himself; and now he will be buried like a dog. . . ." He could not say any more. His voice trembled and choked his words.

"Shut up!" shouted one of the messengers, quite unnecessarily.

"Take down the body," the Commissioner ordered his chief messenger, "and bring it and all these people to the court."

"Yes, sah," the messenger said, saluting.

The Commissioner went away, taking three or four of the soldiers with him. In the many years in which he had toiled to bring civilization to different parts of Africa he had learned a number of things. One of them was that a District Commissioner must never attend to such undignified details as cutting a hanged man from the tree. Such attention would give the natives a poor opinion of him. In the book which he planned to write he would stress that point. As he walked back to the court he thought about that book. Every day brought him some new material. The story of this man who had killed a messenger and hanged himself would make interesting reading. One could almost write a whole chapter on him. Perhaps not a whole chapter but a reasonable paragraph, at any rate. There was so much else to include, and one must be firm in cutting out details. He had already chosen the title of the book, after much thought: *The Pacification of the Primitive Tribes of the Lower Niger.*

ALICE MUNRO
born 1931

"I don't take up a story and follow it as if it were a road, taking me somewhere, with views and neat diversions along the way," writes Alice Munro in her essay *What Is Real?* "I go into it and move back and forth and settle here and there, and stay in it for a while." This description of Munro the reader applies equally to Munro the writer. Munro's stories join the familiar to the enigmatic in a style that, like Virginia Woolf's, savors the nuances and subtleties of human relationships. Combining this writerly style with a keen attention to physical and psychological detail that places her in the realist tradition of Tolstoy and Chekhov, Munro's short fiction is marked by compassion and the awareness of multiple points of view. Whether focused on fox farming, high school dances, chance sexual encounters, marriage and divorce, or discovery and self-discovery, Munro's vision frequently centers on the lives of girls and women and on their introspective responses to the world around them. This writing is less concerned with "getting somewhere" than with settling here and there to reveal the mystery and complexity of seemingly simple day-to-day realities.

Born Alice Anne Laidlaw in the Scots-Irish community of Wingham, Ontario, Munro began writing stories in her teens—tales of romance and adventure far removed from her rural Canadian home. Her parents, Robert Eric Laidlaw and Ann Chamney Laidlaw, struggled throughout their marriage to make ends meet—fox farming during the Depression, selling wares door to door, raising turkeys—but no venture was successful enough to lift the family out of poverty. In 1949, Munro enrolled at the University of Western Ontario, leaving school in 1951 to marry James Munro and moving with him to Vancouver, British Columbia. While raising three daughters and managing a bookshop there during the 1950s and 1960s, Munro honed her story-telling skills. When, in 1968, *Dance of the Happy Shades* (from which the story printed here is taken) introduced her to the reading public, the response was overwhelming. Praised by critics, recipient also of the prestigious Governor General's Award for fiction (the first of three), she had found a place for herself in the world of professional writers. In 1972 she published *Lives of Girls and Women*, a novel composed of a series of linked stories, all recounting the emergence of the character Del Jordan from her confined childhood to a career and an adult identity far transcending the borders of her hometown of Jubilee. This was followed in 1974 by a third book of stories: *Something I've Been Meaning to Tell You*. Munro's first marriage ended in divorce in 1976, after which she remarried and moved to the central Canadian town of Clinton, Ontario. Since then, she has published five other collections of short fiction: *Who Do You Think You Are?: Stories* (1978; published outside Canada as *The Beggar Maid*, 1979), *The Moons of Jupiter* (1982), *The Progress of Love* (1986), *Friend of My Youth* (1990), and *Open Secrets* (1994). She continues to receive prizes and awards.

The vagaries of life in rural Canada figure prominently in Munro's writing, and because of this, some critics have labeled her a "regionalist." Her characters often inhabit small fictional towns similar to the Wingham of her youth, and the area of *Walker Brothers Cowboy* recalls just such a region in southwestern Ontario. Yet the worlds of human relationships that they create for themselves are more expansive and universal than the term *regionalist* implies. In this, she resembles James Joyce in *Dubliners*, William Faulkner writing about his mythic Yoknapatawpha County, and writers of the modern American South for whom she feels a marked affinity: Flannery O'Connor, Eudora Welty, Carson McCullers, and Walker Percy. Munro too focuses on interconnected lives in small communities and on the puzzles and discoveries of growing up. Her most memorable characters—Del Jordan of *Lives of Girls and Women*, and Rose of the story cycle *The Beggar Maid*—though distinct in their circumstances and personalities, share a breadth of vision and an openness to life's inconstancies that makes them seem larger and more significant than their surroundings. Through their eyes, we see a world not of heroic resolutions and tragic ends or of a linear progression from "here" to "there" but rather of moments and of details; of disappointments and small victories; and above all, of the inevitable swoop and sway between intimacy and alienation. What we see most powerfully is the masks we all wear, "the faces we put on to meet the faces that we meet" (to paraphrase T. S. Eliot). Munro's characters disguise themselves from themselves and from others, but seek at the same time to be unmasked, discovered, and more fully human. Describing her fondness for the short-story form, Munro says: "I like looking at people's lives over a number of years, without continuity. Like catching them in snapshots. And I like the way people relate, or don't relate, to the people they were earlier." Like Munro's later work, *Walker Brothers Cowboy* catches a snapshot of the relationship between a character's present and past lives. The same story also illustrates the way the writer manipulates the boundaries between autobiography and fiction, basing her stories in personal experience but also radically changing historical facts. Thus there actually was a Nora who loved dancing and clothes with flowered prints; and Nora did give a dance lesson to the nine-year-old Alice Laidlaw, whose father was a traveling salesman; and Alice was impressed by Nora's vitality and joy. The romantic nostalgia that is so crucial to *Walker Brothers Cowboy*, however, is complete fiction; according to Munro, Nora would have been fifteen when her father married at twenty-five. Using memory, introspection, and a supreme gift for adapting reality to her ends, Munro the storyteller creates characters who struggle to understand and accept the vicissitudes of human relationships and, correspondingly, of life itself.

One of Munro's best-known stories, *Walker Brothers Cowboy* is the first story of her first collection, *Dance of the Happy Shades* (1968), and it already reveals the mixture of realistic observation and overtones of mystery that permeate her work. The small towns with their cracking sidewalks, the isolated farmhouses, the pricks of sunlight that come through a straw hat: such details not only confirm the solid reality of these scenes but also establish an atmosphere of awareness and discovery that will be important later on. Here, two children accompany their father, a door-to-door salesman, on a sales trip around the back country roads of southwest Ontario. The narrator, a solitary young girl, reports the day's events in a matter-of-fact tone, sketching in the process a picture of the family and its everyday existence. Their disappointed, plaintive, somewhat snobbish mother strives to maintain appearances and cannot resign herself to having come down in the world; their father copes cheerfully, telling the children stories as they walk by the lake or making up funny songs as they drive from place to place; the narrator and her younger brother, usually required to stay in their yard, find the sales trip a chance for adventure. It is a settled existence, with small frictions and disappointments but no surprises. An unscheduled trip to Nora's home, however, opens up other dimensions by hinting at an unforgotten romance in their father's past. The contrasts between the cheerless mother and Nora—full of warmth and vitality—are quietly implied, and the father's unaccustomed silence as they drive back home suggests emotional undercurrents that were previously invisible. The narrator's life—once so familiar and ordinary—has been changed into a different kind of landscape: "into something you will never know, with all kinds of weathers, and distances you cannot imagine."

Catherine S. Ross, *Alice Munro: A Double Life* (1991), is a compact, readable biography that highlights the sources of Munro's writing; it includes a bibliography, photographs, maps, and interview comments about Nora. E. D. Blodgett, *Alice Munro* (1988), introduces the writer and her work. J. R. Struthers, "Alice Munro and the American South" in John Moss, ed., *The Canadian Novel: Here and Now* (1983), is also recommended. Louis MacKendrick, ed., *Probable Fictions: Alice Munro's Narrative Acts* (1983), is an excellent survey of critical essays and of interviews with the author herself. For more on Munro's approach to gender issues and male/female relationships, see Beverly Rasporich, *Dance of the Sexes: Art and Gender in the Fiction of Alice Munro* (1990).

Walker Brothers Cowboy[1]

After supper my father says, "Want to go down and see if the Lake's still there?" We leave my mother sewing under the dining-room light, making clothes for me against the opening of school. She has ripped up for this purpose an old suit and an old plaid wool dress of hers, and she has to cut and match very cleverly and also make me stand and turn for endless fittings, sweaty, itching from the hot wool, ungrateful. We leave my brother in bed in the little screened porch at the end of the front veranda, and sometimes he kneels on his bed and presses his face against the screen and calls mournfully, "Bring me an ice-cream cone!" but I call back, "You will be asleep," and do not even turn my head.

Then my father and I walk gradually down a long, shabby sort of street, with Silverwoods Ice Cream signs standing on the sidewalk, outside tiny, lighted stores. This is in Tuppertown, an old town on Lake Huron,[2] an old

1. A traveling salesman for a Canadian door-to-door sales company that is probably modeled on the still-operating Watkins Products firm.   2. One of the Great Lakes, bordering on Ontario (Canada) and eastern Michigan. Place names are both real and invented. Real places mentioned in the story include Sunshine, a small town close to Munro's childhood home in Wingham; Dungannon, a small town close to Goderich; Fort William, which merged with Port Arthur in 1970 to become the city of Thunder Bay; and Brantford, a city in southeastern Ontario. Other place names, like Tuppertown, Turnaround, and Boylesbridge, are adapted or fictitious.

grain port. The street is shaded, in some places, by maple trees whose roots have cracked and heaved the sidewalk and spread out like crocodiles into the bare yards. People are sitting out, men in shirtsleeves and undershirts and women in aprons—not people we know but if anybody looks ready to nod and say, "Warm night," my father will nod too and say something the same. Children are still playing. I don't know them either because my mother keeps my brother and me in our own yard, saying he is too young to leave it and I have to mind him. I am not so sad to watch their evening games because the games themselves are ragged, dissolving. Children, of their own will, draw apart, separate into islands of two or one under the heavy trees, occupying themselves in such solitary ways as I do all day, planting pebbles in the dirt or writing in it with a stick.

Presently we leave these yards and houses behind; we pass a factory with boarded-up windows, a lumberyard whose high wooden gates are locked for the night. Then the town falls away in a defeated jumble of sheds and small junkyards, the sidewalk gives up and we are walking on a sandy path with burdocks, plantains, humble nameless weeds all around. We enter a vacant lot, a kind of park really, for it is kept clear of junk and there is one bench with a slat missing on the back, a place to sit and look at the water. Which is generally gray in the evening, under a lightly overcast sky, no sunsets, the horizon dim. A very quiet, washing noise on the stones of the beach. Further along, towards the main part of town, there is a stretch of sand, a water slide, floats bobbing around the safe swimming area, a lifeguard's rickety throne. Also a long dark-green building, like a roofed veranda, called the Pavilion, full of farmers and their wives, in stiff good clothes, on Sundays. That is the part of the town we used to know when we lived at Dungannon and came here three or four times a summer, to the Lake. That, and the docks where we would go and look at the grain boats, ancient, rusty, wallowing, making us wonder how they got past the breakwater let alone to Fort William.

Tramps hang around the docks and occasionally on these evenings wander up the dwindling beach and climb the shifting, precarious path boys have made, hanging on to dry bushes, and say something to my father which, being frightened of tramps, I am too alarmed to catch. My father says he is a bit hard up himself. "I'll roll you a cigarette if it's any use to you," he says, and he shakes tobacco out carefully on one of the thin butterfly papers, flicks it with his tongue, seals it and hands it to the tramp, who takes it and walks away. My father also rolls and lights and smokes one cigarette of his own.

He tells me how the Great Lakes came to be. All where Lake Huron is now, he says, used to be flat land, a wide flat plain. Then came the ice, creeping down from the North, pushing deep into the low places. Like *that*—and he shows me his hand with his spread fingers pressing the rock-hard ground where we are sitting. His fingers make hardly any impression at all and he says, "Well, the old ice cap had a lot more power behind it than this hand has." And then the ice went back, shrank back towards the North Pole where it came from, and left its fingers of ice in the deep places it had gouged, and ice turned to lakes and there they were today. They were *new*, as time went. I try to see that plain before me, dinosaurs walking on it, but I am not able even to imagine the shore of the Lake when the Indians were there, before Tuppertown. The tiny share we have of time appalls me, though my father seems to regard it with tranquillity. Even my father, who sometimes seems to me to have been at home in the world as long as it has lasted, has really lived on this earth only a little longer than I have, in terms of all the time there has been to live in. He has not known a time, any more than I, when automobiles and electric lights did not at least exist. He was not alive when this century started. I will be barely alive—old, old—when it ends. I do not like to think of it. I wish the Lake to be always just a lake, with the safe-swimming floats marking it, and the breakwater and the lights of Tuppertown.

My father has a job, selling for Walker Brothers. This is a firm that sells almost entirely in the country, the back country. Sunshine, Boylesbridge, Turnaround—that is all his territory. Not Dungannon where we used to live, Dungannon is too near town and my mother is grateful for that. He sells cough medicine, iron tonic, corn plasters, laxatives, pills for female disorders, mouthwash, shampoo, liniment, salves, lemon and orange and raspberry concentrate for making refreshing drinks, vanilla, food coloring, black and green tea, ginger, cloves, and other spices, rat poison. He has a song about it, with these two lines:

> And have all liniments and oils,
> For everything from corns to boils. . . .

Not a very funny song, in my mother's opinion. A peddler's song, and that is what he is, a peddler knocking at backwoods kitchens. Up until last winter we had our own business, a fox farm. My father raised silver foxes and sold their pelts to the people who make them into capes and coats and muffs. Prices fell, my father hung on hoping they would get better next year, and they fell again, and he hung on one more year and one more and finally it was not possible to hang on anymore, we owed everything to the feed company. I have heard my mother explain this, several times, to Mrs. Oliphant, who is the only neighbor she talks to. (Mrs. Oliphant also has come down in the world, being a schoolteacher who married the janitor.) We poured all we had into it, my mother says, and we came out with nothing. Many people could say the same thing, these days, but my mother has no time for the national calamity, only ours. Fate has flung us onto a street of poor people (it does not matter that we were poor before; that was a different sort of poverty), and the only way to take this, as she sees it, is with dignity, with bitterness, with no reconciliation. No bathroom with a claw-footed tub and a flush toilet is going to comfort her, nor water on tap and sidewalks past the house and milk in bottles, not even the two movie theatres and the Venus Restaurant and Woolworths so marvellous it has live birds singing in its fan-cooled corners and fish as tiny as fingernails, as bright as moons, swimming in its green tanks. My mother does not care.

In the afternoons she often walks to Simon's Grocery and takes me with her to help carry things. She wears a good dress, navy blue with little flowers, sheer, worn over a navy-blue slip. Also a summer hat of white straw, pushed down on the side of the head, and white shoes I have just whitened on a newspaper on the back steps. I have my hair freshly done in long damp curls which the dry air will fortunately soon loosen, a stiff large hair ribbon on top of my head. This is entirely different from going out after supper with my father. We have not walked past two houses before I feel we have become objects of universal ridicule. Even the dirty words chalked on the sidewalk are laughing at us. My mother does not seem to notice. She walks serenely like a lady shopping, like a *lady* shopping, past the housewives in loose belt-less dresses torn under the arms. With me her creation, wretched curls and flaunting hair bow, scrubbed knees and white socks—all I do not want to be. I loathe even my name when she says it in public, in a voice so high, proud, and ringing, deliberately different from the voice of any other mother on the street.

My mother will sometimes carry home, for a treat, a brick of ice cream—pale Neapolitan; and because we have no refrigerator in our house we wake my brother and eat it at once in the dining room, always darkened by the wall of the house next door. I spoon it up tenderly, leaving the chocolate till last, hoping to have some still to eat when my brother's dish is empty. My mother tries then to imitate the conversations we used to have at Dungannon, going back to our earliest, most leisurely days before my brother was born, when she would give me a little tea and a lot of milk in a cup like hers and we would sit out on the step facing the pump, the lilac tree, the fox pens beyond. She is not able to keep from mentioning those days. "Do you remember when we put you in your sled and Major pulled you?" (Major our dog, that we had to leave with neighbors when we moved.) "Do you remember your sandbox outside the kitchen window?" I pretend to remember far less than I do, wary of being trapped into sympathy or any unwanted emotion.

My mother has headaches. She often has to lie down. She lies on my brother's narrow bed in the little screened porch, shaded by heavy branches. "I look up at that tree and I think I am at home," she says.

"What you need," my father tells her, "is some fresh air and a drive in the country." He means for her to go with him, on his Walker Brothers route.

That is not my mother's idea of a drive in the country.

"Can I come?"

"Your mother might want you for trying on clothes."

"I'm beyond sewing this afternoon," my mother says.

"I'll take her then. Take both of them, give you a rest."

What is there about us that people need to be given a rest from? Never mind. I am glad enough to find my brother and make him go to the toilet and get us both into the car, our knees unscrubbed, my hair unringleted. My father brings from the house his two heavy brown suitcases, full of bottles, and sets them on the back seat. He wears a white shirt, brilliant in the sunlight, a tie, light trousers belonging to his summer suit (his other suit is black, for funerals, and belonged to my uncle before he died), and a creamy straw hat. His salesman's outfit, with pencils clipped in the shirt pocket. He goes back once again, probably to say goodbye to my mother, to ask her if she is sure she doesn't want to come, and hear her say, "No. No thanks, I'm better just to lie here with my eyes closed." Then we are backing out of the driveway with the rising hope of adventure, just the little hope that takes you over the bump into the street, the hot air starting to move, turning into a breeze, the houses growing less and less familiar as we follow the shortcut my father knows, the quick way out of town. Yet what is there waiting for us all afternoon but hot hours in stricken farmyards, perhaps a stop at a country

store and three ice-cream cones or bottles of pop, and my father singing?
The one he made up about himself has a title—"The Walker Brothers Cowboy"—and it starts out like this:

> Old Ned Fields, he now is dead,
> So I am ridin' the route instead. . . .

Who is Ned Fields? The man he has replaced, surely, and if so he really
is dead; yet my father's voice is mournful-jolly, making his death some kind
of nonsense, a comic calamity. "Wisht I was back on the Rio Grande,[3] plun-
gin' through the dusky sand." My father sings most of the time while driving
the car. Even now, heading out of town, crossing the bridge and taking the
sharp turn onto the highway, he is humming something, mumbling a bit of
a song to himself, just tuning up, really, getting ready to improvise, for out
along the highway we pass the Baptist Camp, the Vacation Bible Camp, and
he lets loose:

> Where are the Baptists, where are the Bapists,
> where are all the Baptists today?
> They're down in the water, in Lake Huron water,
> with their sins all a-gittin' washed away."

My brother takes this for straight truth and gets up on his knees trying to
see down to the Lake. "I don't see any Baptists," he says accusingly. "Neither
do I, son," says my father. "I told you, they're down in the Lake."

No roads paved when we left the highway. We have to roll up the windows
because of dust. The land is flat, scorched, empty. Bush lots at the back of the
farms hold shade, black pine-shade like pools nobody can ever get to. We
bump up a long lane and at the end of it what could look more unwelcoming,
more deserted than the tall unpainted farmhouse with grass growing uncut
right up to the front door, green blinds down, and a door upstairs opening on
nothing but air? Many houses have this door, and I have never yet been able
to find out why. I ask my father and he says they are for walking in your sleep.
What? Well, if you happen to be walking in your sleep and you want to step
outside. I am offended, seeing too late that he is joking, as usual, but my
brother says sturdily, "If they did that they would break their necks."

The 1930s. How much this kind of farmhouse, this kind of afternoon seem
to me to belong to that one decade in time, just as my father's hat does, his
bright flared tie, our car with its wide running board (an Essex, and long past
its prime). Cars somewhat like it, many older, none dustier, sit in the farmyards. Some are past running and have their doors pulled off, their seats
removed for use on porches. No living things to be seen, chickens or cattle.
Except dogs. There are dogs lying in any kind of shade they can find, dreaming, their lean sides rising and sinking rapidly. They get up when my father
opens the car door, he has to speak to them. "Nice boy, there's a boy, nice
old boy." They quiet down, go back to their shade. He should know how to
quiet animals, he has held desperate foxes with tongs around their necks.
One gentling voice for the dogs and another, rousing, cheerful, for calling
at doors. "Hello there, missus, it's the Walker Brothers man and what are

---

3. A large river that begins in Colorado and flows south, becoming the border between Mexico and the
United States.

you out of today?" A door opens, he disappears. Forbidden to follow, forbidden even to leave the car, we can just wait and wonder what he says. Sometimes trying to make my mother laugh, he pretends to be himself in a farm kitchen, spreading out his sample case. "Now then, missus, are you troubled with parasitic life? Your children's scalps, I mean. All those crawly little things we're too polite to mention that show up on the heads of the best of families? Soap alone is useless, kerosene is not too nice a perfume, but I have here—" Or else, "Believe me, sitting and driving all day the way I do I *know* the value of these fine pills. Natural relief. A problem common to old folks too, once their days of activity are over—How about you, Grandma?" He would wave the imaginary box of pills under my mother's nose and she would laugh finally, unwillingly. "He doesn't say that really, does he?" I said, and she said no of course not, he was too much of a gentleman.

One yard after another, then, the old cars, the pumps, dogs, views of gray barns and falling-down sheds and unturning windmills. The men, if they are working in the fields, are not in any fields that we can see. The children are far away, following dry creek beds or looking for blackberries, or else they are hidden in the house, spying at us through cracks in the blinds. The car seat has grown slick with our sweat. I dare my brother to sound the horn, wanting to do it myself but not wanting to get the blame. He knows better. We play I Spy, but it is hard to find many colors. Gray for the barns and sheds and toilets and houses, brown for the yard and fields, black or brown for the dogs. The rusting cars show rainbow patches, in which I strain to pick out purple or green; likewise I peer at doors for shreds of old peeling paint, maroon or yellow. We can't play with letters, which would be better, because my brother is too young to spell. The game disintegrates anyway. He claims my colors are not fair, and wants extra turns.

In one house no door opens, though the car is in the yard. My father knocks and whistles, calls, "Hullo there ! Walker Brothers man!" but there is not a stir of reply anywhere. This house has no porch, just a bare, slanting slab of cement on which my father stands. He turns around, searching the barnyard, the barn whose mow must be empty because you can see the sky through it, and finally he bends to pick up his suitcases. Just then a window is opened upstairs, a white pot appears on the sill, is tilted over and its contents splash down the outside wall. The window is not directly above my father's head, so only a stray splash would catch him. He picks up his suitcases with no particular hurry and walks, no longer whistling, to the car. "Do you know what that was?" I say to my brother. "*Pee*." He laughs and laughs.

My father rolls and lights a cigarette before he starts the car. The window has been slammed down, the blind drawn, we never did see a hand or face. "Pee, pee," sings my brother ecstatically. "Somebody dumped down pee!" "Just don't tell your mother that," my father says. "She isn't liable to see the joke." "Is it in your song?" my brother wants to know. My father says no but he will see what he can do to work it in.

I notice in a little while that we are not turning in any more lanes, though it does not seem to me that we are headed home. "Is this the way to Sunshine?" I ask my father, and he answers, "No, ma'am, it's not." "Are we still in your territory?" He shakes his head. "We're going *fast*," my brother says approvingly, and in fact we are bouncing along through dry puddle-holes so that all the bottles in the suitcases clink together and gurgle promisingly.

Another lane, a house, also unpainted, dried to silver in the sun.

"I thought we were out of your territory."

"We are."

"Then what are we going in here for?"

"You'll see."

In front of the house a short, sturdy woman is picking up washing, which had been spread on the grass to bleach and dry. When the car stops she stares at it hard for a moment, bends to pick up a couple more towels to add to the bundle under her arm, comes across to us and says in a flat voice, neither welcoming nor unfriendly, "Have you lost your way?"

My father takes his time getting out of the car. "I don't think so," he says. "I'm the Walker Brothers man."

"George Golley is our Walker Brothers man," the woman says, "and he was out here no more than a week ago. Oh, my Lord God," she says harshly, "it's you."

"It was, the last time I looked in the mirror," my father says.

The woman gathers all the towels in front of her and holds on to them tightly, pushing them against her stomach as if it hurt. "Of all the people I never thought to see. And telling me you were the Walker Brothers man."

"I'm sorry if you were looking forward to George Golley," my father says humbly.

"And look at me, I was prepared to clean the henhouse. You'll think that's just an excuse but it's true. I don't go round looking like this every day." She is wearing a farmer's straw hat, through which pricks of sunlight penetrate and float on her face, a loose, dirty print smock, and canvas shoes. "Who are those in the car, Ben? They're not yours?"

"Well, I hope and believe they are," my father says, and tells our names and ages. "Come on, you can get out. This is Nora, Miss Cronin. Nora, you better tell me, is it still Miss, or have you got a husband hiding in the woodshed?"

"If I had a husband that's not where I'd keep him, Ben," she says, and they both laugh, her laugh abrupt and somewhat angry. "You'll think I got no manners, as well as being dressed like a tramp," she says. "Come on in out of the sun. It's cool in the house."

We go across the yard ("Excuse me taking you in this way but I don't think the front door has been opened since Papa's funeral, I'm afraid the hinges might drop off"), up the porch steps, into the kitchen, which really is cool, high-ceilinged, the blinds of course down, a simple, clean, threadbare room with waxed worn linoleum, potted geraniums, drinking-pail and dipper, a round table with scrubbed oilcloth. In spite of the cleanness, the wiped and swept surfaces, there is a faint sour smell—maybe of the dishrag or the tin dipper or the oilcloth, or the old lady, because there is one, sitting in an easy chair under the clock shelf. She turns her head slightly in our direction and says, "Nora? Is that company?"

"Blind," says Nora in a quick explaining voice to my father. Then, "You won't guess who it is, Momma. Hear his voice."

My father goes to the front of her chair and bends and says hopefully, "Afternoon, Mrs. Cronin."

"Ben Jordan," says the old lady with no surprise. "You haven't been to see us in the longest time. Have you been out of the country?"

My father and Nora look at each other.

"He's married, Momma," says Nora cheerfully and aggressively. "Married and got two children and here they are." She pulls us forward, makes each of us touch the old lady's dry, cool hand while she says our names in turn. Blind! This is the first blind person I have ever seen close up. Her eyes are closed, the eyelids sunk away down, showing no shape of the eyeball, just hollows. From one hollow comes a drop of silver liquid, a medicine, or a miraculous tear.

"Let me get into a decent dress," Nora says. "Talk to Momma. It's a treat for her. We hardly ever see company, do we, Momma?"

"Not many makes it out this road," says the old lady placidly. "And the ones that used to be around here, our old neighbors, some of them have pulled out."

"True everywhere," my father says.

"Where's your wife then?"

"Home. She's not too fond of the hot weather, makes her feel poorly."

"Well." This is a habit of country people, old people, to say "well," meaning, "Is that so?" with a little extra politeness and concern.

Nora's dress, when she appears again—stepping heavily on Cuban heels down the stairs in the hall—is flowered more lavishly than anything my mother owns, green and yellow on brown, some sort of floating sheer crêpe, leaving her arms bare. Her arms are heavy, and every bit of her skin you can see is covered with little dark freckles like measles. Her hair is short, black, coarse and curly, her teeth very white and strong. "It's the first time I knew there was such a thing as green poppies," my father says, looking at her dress.

"You would be surprised all the things you never knew," says Nora, sending a smell of cologne far and wide when she moves and displaying a change of voice to go with the dress, something more sociable and youthful. "They're not poppies anyway, they're just flowers. You go and pump me some good cold water and I'll make these children a drink." She gets down from the cupboard a bottle of Walker Brothers Orange syrup.

"You telling me you were the Walker Brothers man!"

"It's the truth, Nora. You go and look at my sample cases in the car if you don't believe me. I got the territory directly south of here."

"Walker Brothers? Is that a fact? You selling for Walker Brothers?"

"Yes, ma'am."

"We always heard you were raising foxes over Dungannon way."

"That's what I was doing, but I kind of run out of luck in that business."

"So where're you living? How long've you been out selling?"

"We moved into Tuppertown. I been at it, oh, two, three months. It keeps the wolf from the door. Keeps him as far away as the back fence."

Nora laughs. "Well, I guess you count yourself lucky to have the work. Isabel's husband in Brantford, he was out of work the longest time. I thought if he didn't find something soon I was going to have them all land in here to feed, and I tell you I was hardly looking forward to it. It's all I can manage with me and Momma."

"Isabel married," my father says. "Muriel married too?"

"No, she's teaching school out West. She hasn't been home for five years. I guess she finds something better to do with her holidays. I would if I was her." She gets some snapshots out of the table drawer and starts showing him. "That's Isabel's oldest boy, starting school. That's the baby sitting in her carriage. Isabel and her husband. Muriel. That's her roommate with her. That's a fellow she used to go around with, and his car. He was working in a bank out there. That's her school, it has eight rooms. She teaches Grade Five." My father shakes his head. "I can't think of her any way but when she was going to school, so shy I used to pick her up on the road—I'd be on my way to see you—and she would not say one word, not even to agree it was a nice day."

"She's got over that."

"Who are you talking about?" says the old lady.

"Muriel. I said she's got over being shy."

"She was here last summer."

"No, Momma, that was Isabel. Isabel and her family were here last summer. Muriel's out West."

"I meant Isabel."

Shortly after this the old lady falls asleep, her head on the side, her mouth open. "Excuse her manners," Nora says. "It's old age." She fixes an afghan over her mother and says we can all go into the front room where our talking won't disturb her.

"You two," my father says. "Do you want to go outside and amuse yourselves?"

Amuse ourselves how? Anyway, I want to stay. The front room is more interesting than the kitchen, though barer. There is a gramophone and a pump organ and a picture on the wall of Mary, Jesus' mother—I know that much—in shades of bright blue and pink with a spiked band of light around her head. I know that such pictures are found only in the homes of Roman Catholics and so Nora must be one. We have never known any Roman Catholics at all well, never well enough to visit in their houses. I think of what my grandmother and my Aunt Tena, over in Dungannon, used to always say to indicate that somebody was a Catholic. *So-and-so digs with the wrong foot,* they would say. *She digs with the wrong foot.* That was what they would say about Nora.[4]

Nora takes a bottle, half full, out of the top of the organ and pours some of what is in it into the two glasses that she and my father have emptied of the orange drink.

"Keep it in case of sickness?" my father says.

"Not on your life," says Nora. "I'm never sick. I just keep it because I keep it. One bottle does me a fair time, though, because I don't care for drinking alone. Here's luck!" She and my father drink and I know what it is. Whisky. One of the things my mother has told me in our talks together is that my father never drinks whisky. But I see he does. He drinks whisky and he talks of people whose names I have never heard before. But after a while he turns to a familiar incident. He tells about the chamberpot that was emptied out the window. "Picture me there," he says, "hollering my heartiest. *Oh, lady, it's your Walker Brothers man, anybody home?*" He does himself hollering, grinning absurdly, waiting, looking up in pleased expectation, and then—oh, ducking, covering his head with his arms, looking as if he begged for mercy (when he never did anything like that, I was watching), and Nora laughs, almost as hard as my brother did at the time.

"That isn't true! That's not a word true!"

4. Protestant–Catholic feuds were transplanted to southern Ontario by Irish settlers.

"Oh, indeed it is, ma'am. We have our heroes in the ranks of Walker Brothers. I'm glad you think it's funny," he says sombrely.

I ask him shyly, "Sing the song."

"What song? Have you turned into a singer on top of everything else?"

Embarrassed, my father says, "Oh, just this song I made up while I was driving around, it gives me something to do, making up rhymes."

But after some urging he does sing it, looking at Nora with a droll, apologetic expression, and she laughs so much that in places he has to stop and wait for her to get over laughing so he can go on, because she makes him laugh too. Then he does various parts of his salesman's spiel. Nora when she laughs squeezes her large bosom under her folded arms. "You're crazy," she says. "That's all you are." She sees my brother peering into the gramophone and she jumps up and goes over to him. "Here's us sitting enjoying ourselves and not giving you a thought, isn't it terrible?" she says. "You want me to put a record on, don't you? You want to hear a nice record? Can you dance? I bet your sister can, can't she?"

I say no. "A big girl like you and so good-looking and can't dance!" says Nora. "It's high time you learned. I bet you'd make a lovely dancer. Here, I'm going to put on a piece I used to dance to and even your daddy did, in his dancing days. You didn't know your daddy was a dancer, did you? Well, he is a talented man, your daddy!"

She puts down the lid and takes hold of me unexpectedly around the waist, picks up my other hand, and starts making me go backwards. "This is the way, now, this is how they dance. Follow me. This foot, see. One and one-two. One and one-two. That's fine, that's lovely, don't look at your feet! Follow me, that's right, see how easy? You're going to be a lovely dancer! One and one-two. One and one-two. Ben, see your daughter dancing!" *Whispering while you cuddle near me, Whispering so no one can hear me . . .* [5]

Round and round the linoleum, me proud, intent, Nora laughing and moving with great buoyancy, wrapping me in her strange gaiety, her smell of whisky, cologne, and sweat. Under the arms her dress is damp, and little drops form along her upper lip, hang in the soft black hairs at the corners of her mouth. She whirls me around in front of my father—causing me to stumble, for I am by no means so swift a pupil as she pretends—and lets me go, breathless.

"Dance with me, Ben."

"I'm the world's worst dancer, Nora, and you know it."

"I certainly never thought so."

"You would now."

She stands in front of him, arms hanging loose and hopeful, her breasts, which a moment ago embarrassed me with their warmth and bulk, rising and falling under her loose flowered dress, her face shining with the exercise, and delight.

"Ben."

My father drops his head and says quietly, "Not me, Nora."

So she can only go and take the record off. "I can drink alone but I can't dance alone," she says. "Unless I am a whole lot crazier than I think I am."

---

5. From the popular song "Whispering," words and music by John Schonberger, Vincent Rose, and Richard Coburn. The original 1920 recording by Paul Whiteman's band was one of the first records to sell a million copies.

"Nora," says my father, smiling. "You're not crazy."

"Stay for supper."

"Oh, no. We couldn't put you to the trouble."

"It's no trouble. I'd be glad of it."

"And their mother would worry. She'd think I'd turned us over in a ditch."

"Oh, well. Yes."

"We've taken a lot of your time now."

"Time," says Nora bitterly. "Will you come by ever again?"

"I will if I can," says my father.

"Bring the children. Bring your wife."

"Yes, I will," says my father. "I will if I can."

When she follows us to the car he says, "You come to see us too, Nora. We're right on Grove Street, left-hand side going in, that's north, and two doors this side—east—of Baker Street."

Nora does not repeat these directions. She stands close to the car in her soft, brilliant dress. She touches the fender, making an unintelligible mark in the dust there.

On the way home my father does not buy any ice cream or pop, but he does go into a country store and get a package of licorice, which he shares with us. She digs with the wrong foot, I think, and the words seem sad to me as never before, dark, perverse. My father does not say anything to me about not mentioning things at home, but I know, just from the thoughtfulness, the pause when he passes the licorice, that there are things not to be mentioned. The whisky, maybe the dancing. No worry about my brother, he does not notice enough. At most he might remember the blind lady, the picture of Mary.

"Sing," my brother commands my father, but my father says gravely, "I don't know, I seem to be fresh out of songs. You watch the road and let me know if you see any rabbits."

So my father drives and my brother watches the road for rabbits and I feel my father's life flowing back from our car in the last of the afternoon, darkening and turning strange, like a landscape that has an enchantment on it, making it kindly, ordinary and familiar while you are looking at it, but changing it, once your back is turned, into something you will never know, with all kinds of weathers, and distances you cannot imagine.

When we get closer to Tuppertown the sky becomes gently overcast, as always, nearly always, on summer evenings by the Lake.

LESLIE MARMON SILKO
born 1948

Novelist, poet, memoirist, and writer of short fiction, Leslie Marmon Silko, within the confines of a single work, can comfortably alternate between prose and poetry in a manner reminiscent of the traditional Native American narrators from whom she descends. Among her primary concerns as an artist are the continuity of native tradition and the power of ancient forces to govern modern life. The people of whom she writes draw vitality from the mysterious personifications that represent the land; and reciprocally, the land maintains, or regains, its freshness through prescribed contact with its human tenants. Conflict, illness, and despair are traced to a disharmony between people and nature, sometimes recognizable in the form of witchcraft. Such trouble is as old as time itself and perhaps ineradicable. For healing to take place, at least temporarily, the disharmony and its perpetrators must be removed. It follows that modern evils are neither caused nor cured by Western civilization. The West simply does not have that power. Control, then, rests in the hands of those who harness the energies of native thought. The techniques involve ritual and, especially, storytelling. Since the latter implies a mixture of humor and detachment, it is understandable that Silko's work, for all its seriousness and its lyricism, is marked by a touch of irreverence. She is well acquainted with the proverbial trickster, Coyote, and has demonstrated that she herself is an accomplished live teller of Coyote tales. But storytelling holds more than amusement. "I will tell you something about stories," protests an unnamed voice in one of her novels. "They aren't just entertainment. Don't be fooled."

Storytelling has deep roots. But if a story is to be viable it must be constantly reshaped; and Silko is an unabashed reshaper. Her view of tradition as an ever-shifting body of knowledge, responsive to new influences even if deeply planted, is objectively correct, yet it may also be said to emerge from her personal background. She has written:

> My family are the Marmons at Old Laguna on the Laguna Pueblo Reservation where I grew up. We are mixed bloods—Laguna, Mexican, white—but the way we live is like Marmons, and if you are from Laguna Pueblo you will understand what I mean. All those languages, all those ways of living are combined, and we live somewhere on the fringes of all three. But I don't apologize for this any more—not to whites, not to full bloods—our origin is unlike any other. My poetry, my storytelling rise out this source.

She has also written: "I grew up at Laguna Pueblo. I am of mixed-breed ancestry, but what I know is Laguna. This place I am from is everything I am as a writer and human being."

Situated on a knoll above the San José River, forty miles west of the Rio Grande, Laguna Pueblo, like its near neighbor Acoma, is one of the Keresan-speaking communities of northern New Mexico. In existence at its present site since the 1400s, it has absorbed migrants from other Keresan towns and from among the Zuni, Hopi, and Navajo. In the 1860s and 1870s, two surveyors from Ohio, first Walter Marmon and, a little later, his brother, Robert, both government employees, settled in Laguna and married Laguna women. The Marmons wrote a constitution for Laguna, modeled after the U.S. Constitution, and each served a term as governor of the pueblo, an office never before held by a nonnative. The second of the two Marmons to arrive in Laguna, Robert Gunn Marmon, was the great-grandfather of Leslie Marmon Silko.

Born in Albuquerque on March 5, 1948, Silko spent her early years at Laguna, attending Laguna Day School until fifth grade, when she was transferred to Manzano Day School, a small private school in Albuquerque. Between 1964 and 1969 she attended the University of New Mexico (where she earned a B.A. in English), married, and gave birth to the first of her two sons, Cazimir Silko. During these years she published her first story, *Tony's Story*, a provocative tale of witchery and renewal that foreshadowed her masterwork, *Ceremony*, which would not appear for another decade.

Following graduation, she stayed on at the university and taught courses in creative writing and oral literature. After giving birth to her second son, Robert William Chapman, she studied for three semesters in the university's American Indian Law Program, with the intention of filing native land claims. In 1971 a National Endowment for the Arts Discovery Grant changed her mind about law school, and she quit to devote herself to writing. Seven of her stories, including *Yellow Woman,* were published in 1974 in a collection edited by Kenneth Rosen—*The Man to Send Rain Clouds: Contemporary Stories by American Indians.* It was from this that her reputation began to build.

The novel *Ceremony,* her first large-scale work, appeared in 1977. Widely hailed, it propelled her into the front rank of a growing legion of indigenous writers in the United States whose combined activity would now be recognized as a Native American renaissance. This group's success in winning critical attention and a broad audience would be comparable to the earlier "boom" in Latin American letters that had brought acclaim to such writers as Jorge Luis Borges and Gabriel García Márquez. The Kiowa novelist N. Scott Momaday, whose *House Made of Dawn* had won the Pulitzer Prize in 1969, was already being viewed as the father of the new movement; and the prolific, talented Louise Erdrich, of Chippewa descent, would eventually be accorded its greatest commercial success. But it was Silko—and *Ceremony*—that enabled the movement to come of age.

Though of average length, *Ceremony* is an extremely complex novel; it has two casts of characters, one predominantly male and human, the other female-dominated and intimately connected to the landscape. It is a story of illness and healing, witchery and exorcism, drought and revivification, with political overtones that acknowledge the influence of nonnative society without permitting this to overwhelm or even direct the inner core of native experience. *Ceremony* is a love story but of a special Native American kind that connects the human and nonhuman worlds, transferring power from nature to culture. With a sure grasp of its material, the novel rolls to its conclusion, sweeping up smaller, parablelike stories along the way, creating a many-chambered vehicle that energizes subplots as well as the larger story.

On the strength of *Ceremony,* Silko in 1981 was awarded a MacArthur Fellowship. That same year she brought out a second large work, *Storyteller,* combining previously published poems and short stories (including *Yellow Woman*) with new material in an arrangement one critic has called an autobiography. It is at least partly that, partly a tribute to Laguna, and partly a showcase in which her earlier work, contextualized, takes on a deeper significance.

Another result of *Ceremony* had been the opportunity to teach at the University of Arizona in Tucson. But with the MacArthur grant Silko was able to withdraw from teaching and (while continuing to live in Tucson) concentrate on an ambitious new writing project. Virtually silent for ten years, as rumors of a major new novel kept building, Silko in due course brought forth *The Almanac of the Dead* (1991). An ocean of story, spreading far beyond Laguna Pueblo to embrace all of North America, including Mexico, Silko's largest work documents the imagined history of an American apocalypse. Inspired by prophetic texts ranging from the Maya Books of Chilam Balam to the songs of the Plains Ghost Dance, native people in league with the spirits of their ancestors conspire to heal the American land and rid it of alien influence. As the various stories converge and the millennium draws near, an irresistible army led by twin heroes, newly emerged from ancient Native American tradition, marches northward out of Mexico to reclaim the continent. In the words of one critic the novel is a "wild, jarring, graphic, mordant, prodigious book" with "genius in the sheer, tireless variousness of its interconnecting tales."

Over the years, as Silko's work has expanded and deepened, one of her shortest and earliest pieces, *Yellow Woman,* has continued to grow in esteem. Often reprinted, it became the subject of a volume of critical essays published in 1993. In traditional Laguna lore Yellow Woman is either the heroine or a minor character in a wide range of tales. Occasionally Yellow Woman is mentioned together with her three sisters, Blue Woman, Red Woman, and White Woman, thus completing the four colors of corn. But although she may originally have been a corn spirit, she eventually became a kind of Everywoman. In fact, a traditional Laguna prayer-song, recited at the naming ceremony for a newborn daughter, begins, "Yellow Woman is born, Yellow Woman is born." In narrative lore, however, Yellow Woman most frequently appears in tales of abduction, where she is said to have been captured by a strange man at a stream while she is fetching water. Her captor, who carries her off to another world, is sometimes a kachina, or ancestral spirit; and when at last she returns to her home she is imbued with new power that proves of value for her people. In Silko's version, these traditional elements are constantly in the foreground. Or are they merely in the background? The story's ambiguity, frequently commented on by critics, is the source of its fascination.

Gregory Salyer, *Leslie Marmon Silko* (1997), is a brief introduction to the author and her work; Helen Jaskoski, *Leslie Marmon Silko: A Study of the Short Fiction* (1998), focuses on the stories. Leslie Silko, *Sacred Water: Narratives and Pictures* (1994), is an autobiographical narrative. Melody Graulich, ed., *"Yellow Woman": Leslie Marmon Silko* (1993), is a collection of pertinent critical essays. The story itself is profitably read, or reread, in Silko's *Storyteller* (1981), where it appears in context with several of her other short pieces on the Yellow Woman theme. For traditional texts on Yellow Woman and other figures in Laguna mythology, the best source is Franz Boas, *Keresan Texts* (1928); the stories in Boas's volume were obtained in 1919–21 from several Laguna informants, including Leslie Silko's great-grandfather, Robert Marmon.

PRONOUNCING GLOSSARY

The following list uses common English syllables and stress accents to provide rough equivalents of selected words whose pronunciation may be unfamiliar to the general reader.

kachina: *kuh-chee'-nuh*   Keres: *kay'-ruhs*

ka'tsina: *kuht-see'-nuh*

Yellow Woman

My thigh clung to his with dampness, and I watched the sun rising up through the tamaracks and willows. The small brown water birds came to the river and hopped across the mud, leaving brown scratches in the alkali-white crust. They bathed in the river silently. I could hear the water, almost at our feet where the narrow fast channel bubbled and washed green ragged moss and fern leaves. I looked at him beside me, rolled in the red blanket on the white river sand. I cleaned the sand out of the cracks between my toes, squinting because the sun was above the willow trees. I looked at him for the last time, sleeping on the white river sand.

I felt hungry and followed the river south the way we had come the afternoon before, following our footprints that were already blurred by lizard tracks and bug trails. The horses were still lying down, and the black one whinnied when he saw me but he did not get up—maybe it was because the corral was made out of thick cedar branches and the horses had not yet felt the sun like I had. I tried to look beyond the pale red mesas to the pueblo. I knew it was there, even if I could not see it, on the sandrock hill above the river, the same river that moved past me now and had reflected the moon last night.

The horse felt warm underneath me. He shook his head and pawed the sand. The bay whinnied and leaned against the gate trying to follow, and I remembered him asleep in the red blanket beside the river. I slid off the horse and tied him close to the other horse, I walked north with the river again, and the white sand broke loose in footprints over footprints.

"Wake up."

He moved in the blanket and turned his face to me with his eyes still closed. I knelt down to touch him.

"I'm leaving."

He smiled now, eyes still closed. "You are coming with me, remember?" He sat up now with his bare dark chest and belly in the sun.

"Where?"

"To my place."

"And will I come back?"

He pulled his pants on. I walked away from him, feeling him behind me and smelling the willows.

"Yellow Woman," he said.

I turned to face him. "Who are you?" I asked.

He laughed and knelt on the low, sandy bank, washing his face in the river. "Last night you guessed my name, and you knew why I had come."

I stared past him at the shallow moving water and tried to remember the night, but I could only see the moon in the water and remember his warmth around me.

"But I only said that you were him and that I was Yellow Woman—I'm not really her—I have my own name and I come from the pueblo on the other side of the mesa. Your name is Silva and you are a stranger I met by the river yesterday afternoon."

He laughed softly. "What happened yesterday has nothing to do with what you will do today, Yellow Woman."

"I know—that's what I'm saying—the old stories about the ka'tsina[1] spirit and Yellow Woman can't mean us."

My old grandpa liked to tell those stories best. There is one about Badger and Coyote who went hunting and were gone all day, and when the sun was going down they found a house. There was a girl living there alone, and she had light hair and eyes and she told them that they could sleep with her. Coyote wanted to be with her all night so he sent Badger into a prairie-dog hole, telling him he thought he saw something in it. As soon as Badger crawled in, Coyote blocked up the entrance with rocks and hurried back to Yellow Woman.

"Come here," he said gently.

He touched my neck and I moved close to him to feel his breathing and to hear his heart. I was wondering if Yellow Woman had known who she was—if she knew that she would become part of the stories. Maybe she'd had another name that her husband and relatives called her so that only the ka'tsina from the north and the storytellers would know her as Yellow Woman. But I didn't go on; I felt him all around me, pushing me down into the white river sand.

Yellow Woman went away with the spirit from the north and lived with him and his relatives. She was gone for a long time, but then one day she came back and she brought twin boys.

"Do you know the story?"

1. Kachina, an ancestral spirit.

"What story?" He smiled and pulled me close to him as he said this. I was afraid lying there on the red blanket. All I could know was the way he felt, warm, damp, his body beside me. This is the way it happens in the stories, I was thinking, with no thought beyond the moment she meets the ka'tsina spirit and they go.

"I don't have to go. What they tell in stories was real only then, back in time immemorial, like they say."

He stood up and pointed at my clothes tangled in the blanket. "Let's go," he said.

I walked beside him, breathing hard because he walked fast, his hand around my wrist. I had stopped trying to pull away from him, because his hand felt cool and the sun was high, drying the river bed into alkali. I will see someone, eventually I will see someone, and then I will be certain that he is only a man—some man from nearby—and I will be sure that I am not Yellow Woman. Because she is from out of time past and I live now and I've been to school and there are highways and pickup trucks that Yellow Woman never saw.

It was an easy ride north on horseback. I watched the change from the cottonwood trees along the river to the junipers that brushed past us in the foothills, and finally there were only piñons, and when I looked up at the rim of the mountain plateau I could see pine trees growing on the edge. Once I stopped to look down, but the pale sandstone had disappeared and the river was gone and the dark lava hills were all around. He touched my hand, not speaking, but always singing softly a mountain song and looking into my eyes.

I felt hungry and wondered what they were doing at home now—my mother, my grandmother, my husband, and the baby. Cooking breakfast, saying, "Where did she go?—maybe kidnapped." And Al going to the tribal police with the details: "She went walking along the river."

The house was made with black lava rock and red mud. It was high above the spreading miles of arroyos and long mesas. I smelled a mountain smell of pitch and buck brush. I stood there beside the black horse, looking down on the small, dim country we had passed, and I shivered.

"Yellow Woman, come inside where it's warm."

He lit a fire in the stove. It was an old stove with a round belly and an enamel coffeepot on top. There was only the stove, some faded Navajo blankets, and a bedroll and cardboard box. The floor was made of smooth adobe plaster, and there was one small window facing east. He pointed at the box.

"There's some potatoes and the frying pan." He sat on the floor with his arms around his knees pulling them close to his chest and he watched me fry the potatoes. I didn't mind him watching me because he was always watching me—he had been watching me since I came upon him sitting on the river bank trimming leaves from a willow twig with his knife. We ate from the pan and he wiped the grease from his fingers on his Levi's.

"Have you brought women here before?" He smiled and kept chewing, so I said, "Do you always use the same tricks?"

"What tricks?" He looked at me like he didn't understand.

"The story about being a ka'tsina from the mountains. The story about Yellow Woman."

Silva was silent; his face was calm.

"I don't believe it. Those stories couldn't happen now," I said.

He shook his head and said softly, "But someday they will talk about us, and they will say, 'Those two lived long ago when things like that happened.'"

He stood up and went out. I ate the rest of the potatoes and thought about things—about the noise the stove was making and the sound of the mountain wind outside. I remembered yesterday and the day before, and then I went outside.

I walked past the corral to the edge where the narrow trail cut through the black rim rock. I was standing in the sky with nothing around me but the wind that came down from the blue mountain peak behind me. I could see faint mountain images in the distance miles across the vast spread of mesas and valleys and plains. I wondered who was over there to feel the mountain wind on those sheer blue edges—who walks on the pine needles in those blue mountains.

"Can you see the pueblo?" Silva was standing behind me.

I shook my head. "We're too far away."

"From here I can see the world." He stepped out on the edge. "The Navajo reservation begins over there." He pointed to the east. "The Pueblo boundaries are over here." He looked below us to the south, where the narrow trail seemed to come from. "The Texans have their ranches over there, starting with that valley, the Concho Valley. The Mexicans run some cattle over there too."

"Do you ever work for them?"

"I steal from them," Silva answered. The sun was dropping behind us and the shadows were filling the land below. I turned away from the edge that dropped forever into the valleys below.

"I'm cold," I said, "I'm going inside." I started wondering about this man who could speak the Pueblo language so well but who lived on a mountain and rustled cattle. I decided that this man Silva must be Navajo, because Pueblo men didn't do things like that.

"You must be a Navajo."

Silva shook his head gently. "Little Yellow Woman," he said, "you never give up, do you? I have told you who I am. The Navajo people know me, too." He knelt down and unrolled the bedroll and spread the extra blankets out on a piece of canvas. The sun was down, and the only light in the house came from outside—the dim orange light from sundown.

I stood there and waited for him to crawl under the blankets.

"What are you waiting for?" he said, and I lay down beside him. He undressed me slowly like the night before beside the river—kissing my face gently and running his hands up and down my belly and legs. He took off my pants and then he laughed.

"Why are you laughing?"

"You are breathing so hard."

I pulled away from him and turned my back to him.

He pulled me around and pinned me down with his arms and chest. "You don't understand, do you, little Yellow Woman? You will do what I want."

And again he was all around me with his skin slippery against mine, and I was afraid because I understood that his strength could hurt me. I lay underneath him and I knew that he could destroy me. But later, while he slept beside me, I touched his face and I had a feeling—the kind of feeling for him that overcame me that morning along the river. I kissed him on the forehead and he reached out for me.

When I woke up in the morning he was gone. It gave me a strange feeling because for a long time I sat there on the blankets and looked around the little house for some object of his—some proof that he had been there or maybe that he was coming back. Only the blankets and the cardboard box remained. The .30-30 that had been leaning in the corner was gone, and so was the knife I had used the night before. He was gone, and I had my chance to go now. But first I had to eat, because I knew it would be a long walk home.

I found some dried apricots in the cardboard box, and I sat down on a rock at the edge of the plateau rim. There was no wind and the sun warmed me. I was surrounded by silence. I drowsed with apricots in my mouth, and I didn't believe that there were highways or railroads or cattle to steal.

When I woke up, I stared down at my feet in the black mountain dirt. Little black ants were swarming over the pine needles around my foot. They must have smelled the apricots. I thought about my family far below me. They would be wondering about me, because this had never happened to me before. The tribal police would file a report. But if old Grandpa weren't dead he would tell them what happened—he would laugh and say, "Stolen by a ka'tsina, a mountain spirit. She'll come home—they usually do." There are enough of them to handle things. My mother and grandmother will raise the baby like they raised me. Al will find someone else, and they will go on like before, except that there will be a story about the day I disappeared while I was walking along the river. Silva had come for me; he said he had. I did not decide to go. I just went. Moonflowers blossom in the sand hills before dawn, just as I followed him. That's what I was thinking as I wandered along the trail through the pine trees.

It was noon when I got back. When I saw the stone house I remembered that I had meant to go home. But that didn't seem important any more, maybe because there were little blue flowers growing in the meadow behind the stone house and the gray squirrels were playing in the pines next to the house. The horses were standing in the corral, and there was a beef carcass hanging on the shady side of a big pine in front of the house. Flies buzzed around the clotted blood that hung from the carcass. Silva was washing his hands in a bucket full of water. He must have heard me coming because he spoke to me without turning to face me.

"I've been waiting for you."

"I went walking in the big pine trees."

I looked into the bucket full of bloody water with brown-and-white animal hairs floating in it. Silva stood there letting his hand drip, examining me intently.

"Are you coming with me?"

"Where?" I asked him.

"To sell the meat in Marquez."

"If you're sure it's O.K."

"I wouldn't ask you if it wasn't," he answered.

He sloshed the water around in the bucket before he dumped it out and set the bucket upside down near the door. I followed him to the corral and watched him saddle the horses. Even beside the horses he looked tall, and I asked him again if he wasn't Navajo. He didn't say anything; he just shook his head and kept cinching up the saddle.

"But Navajos are tall."

"Get on the horse," he said, "and let's go."

The last thing he did before we started down the steep trail was to grab the .30-30 from the corner. He slid the rifle into the scabbard that hung from his saddle.

"Do they ever try to catch you?" I asked.

"They don't know who I am."

"Then why did you bring the rifle?"

"Because we are going to Marquez where the Mexicans live."

The trail leveled out on a narrow ridge that was steep on both sides like an animal spine. On one side I could see where the trail went around the rocky gray hills and disappeared into the southeast where the pale sandrock mesas stood in the distance near my home. On the other side was a trail that went west, and as I looked far into the distance I thought I saw the little town. But Silva said no, that I was looking in the wrong place, that I just thought I saw houses. After that I quit looking off into the distance; it was hot and the wildflowers were closing up their deep-yellow petals. Only the waxy cactus flowers bloomed in the bright sun, and I saw every color that a cactus blossom can be; the white ones and the red ones were still buds, but the purple and the yellow were blossoms, open full and the most beautiful of all.

Silva saw him before I did. The white man was riding a big gray horse, coming up the trail towards us. He was traveling fast and the gray horse's feet sent rocks rolling off the trail into the dry tumbleweeds. Silva motioned for me to stop and we watched the white man. He didn't see us right away, but finally his horse whinnied at our horses and he stopped. He looked at us briefly before he lapped the gray horse across the three hundred yards that separated us. He stopped his horse in front of Silva, and his young fat face was shadowed by the brim of his hat. He didn't look mad, but his small, pale eyes moved from the blood-soaked gunny sacks hanging from my saddle to Silva's face and then back to my face.

"Where did you get the fresh meat?" the white man asked.

"I've been hunting," Silva said, and when he shifted his weight in the saddle the leather creaked.

"The hell you have, Indian. You've been rustling cattle. We've been looking for the thief for a long time."

The rancher was fat, and sweat began to soak through his white cowboy shirt and the wet cloth stuck to the thick rolls of belly fat. He almost seemed to be panting from the exertion of talking, and he smelled rancid, maybe because Silva scared him.

Silva turned to me and smiled. "Go back up the mountain, Yellow Woman."

The white man got angry when he heard Silva speak in a language he couldn't understand. "Don't try anything, Indian. Just keep riding to Marquez. We'll call the state police from there."

The rancher must have been unarmed because he was very frightened and if he had a gun he would have pulled it out then. I turned my horse around and the rancher yelled, "Stop!" I looked at Silva for an instant and there was something ancient and dark—something I could feel in my stomach—in his eyes, and when I glanced at his hand I saw his finger on the trigger of the .30-30 that was still in the saddle scabbard. I slapped my horse across the flank and the sacks of raw meat swung against my knees as the horse leaped up the trail. It was hard to keep my balance, and once I thought I felt the saddle slipping backward; it was because of this that I could not look back.

I didn't stop until I reached the ridge where the trail forked. The horse was breathing deep gasps and there was a dark film of sweat on its neck. I looked down in the direction I had come from, but I couldn't see the place. I waited. The wind came up and pushed warm air past me. I looked up at the sky, pale blue and full of thin clouds and fading vapor trails left by jets.

I think four shots were fired—I remember hearing four hollow explosions that reminded me of deer hunting. There could have been more shots after that, but I couldn't have heard them because my horse was running again and the loose rocks were making too much noise as they scattered around his feet.

Horses have a hard time running downhill, but I went that way instead of uphill to the mountain because I thought it was safer. I felt better with the horse running southeast past the round gray hills that were covered with cedar trees and black lava rock. When I got to the plain in the distance I could see the dark green patches of tamaracks that grew along the river; and beyond the river I could see the beginning of the pale sandrock mesas. I stopped the horse and looked back to see if anyone was coming; then I got off the horse and turned the horse around, wondering if it would go back to its corral under the pines on the mountain. It looked back at me for a moment and then plucked a mouthful of green tumbleweeds before it trotted back up the trail with its ears pointed forward, carrying its head daintily to one side to avoid stepping on the dragging reins. When the horse disappeared over the last hill, the gunny sacks full of meat were still swinging and bouncing.

I walked toward the river on a wood-hauler's road that I knew would eventually lead to the paved road. I was thinking about waiting beside the road for someone to drive by, but by the time I got to the pavement I had decided it wasn't very far to walk if I followed the river back the way Silva and I had come.

The river water tasted good, and I sat in the shade under a cluster of silvery willows. I thought about Silva, and I felt sad at leaving him; still, there was something strange about him, and I tried to figure it out all the way back home.

I came back to the place on the river bank where he had been sitting the first time I saw him. The green willow leaves that he had trimmed from the branch were still lying there, wilted in the sand. I saw the leaves and I wanted to go back to him—to kiss him and to touch him—but the mountains were too far away now. And I told myself, because I believe it, he will come back sometime and be waiting again by the river.

I followed the path up from the river into the village. The sun was getting low, and I could smell supper cooking when I got to the screen door of my house. I could hear their voices inside—my mother was telling my grandmother how to fix the Jell-O and my husband, Al, was playing with the baby. I decided to tell them that some Navajo had kidnaped me, but I was sorry that old Grandpa wasn't alive to hear my story because it was the Yellow Woman stories he liked to tell best.

A Note on Translation

Reading literature in translation is a pleasure on which it is fruitless to frown. The purist may insist that we ought always read in the original languages, and we know ideally that this is true. But it is a counsel of perfection, quite impractical even for the purist, since no one in a lifetime can master all the languages whose literatures it would be a joy to explore. Master languages as fast as we may, we shall always have to read to some extent in translation, and this means we must be alert to what we are about: if in reading a work of literature in translation we are not reading the "original," what precisely are we reading? This is a question of great complexity, to which justice cannot be done in a brief note, but the following sketch of some of the considerations may be helpful.

One of the memorable scenes of ancient literature is the meeting of Hector and Andromache in book 6 of Homer's *Iliad*. Hector, leader and mainstay of the armies defending Troy, is implored by his wife, Andromache, to withdraw within the city walls and carry on the defense from there, where his life will not be constantly at hazard. In Homer's text her opening words to him are these: δαιμόνιε, φθίσει σε τὸ σὸν μένος (daimonie, phthisei se to son menos). How should they be translated into English?

Here is how they have actually been translated into English by capable translators, at various periods, in verse and prose:

1. George Chapman, 1598:

> O noblest in desire,
> Thy mind, inflamed with others' good, will set thy self on fire.

2. John Dryden, 1693:

> Thy dauntless heart (which I foresee too late),
> Too daring man, will urge thee to thy fate.

3. Alexander Pope, 1715:

> Too daring Prince! . . .
> For sure such courage length of life denies,
> And thou must fall, thy virtue's sacrifice.

4. William Cowper, 1791:

> Thy own great courage will cut short thy days,
> My noble Hector . . .

5. Lang, Leaf, and Myers, 1883 (prose):

> Dear my lord, this thy hardihood will undo thee. . . .

6. A. T. Murray, 1924 (prose):

> Ah, my husband, this prowess of thine will be thy doom. . . .

7. E. V. Rieu, 1950 (prose):

> "Hector," she said, "you are possessed. This bravery of yours will be your end."

8. I. A. Richards, 1950 (prose):

"Strange man," she said, "your courage will be your destruction."

9. Richmond Lattimore, 1951:

Dearest,
Your own great strength will be your death. . . .

10. Robert Fitzgerald, 1979:

O my wild one, your bravery will be
Your own undoing!

11. Robert Fagles, 1990:

reckless one,
Your own fiery courage will destroy you!

From these strikingly different renderings of the same six words, certain facts about the nature of translation begin to emerge. We notice, for one thing, that Homer's word μένος (menos) is diversified by the translators into "mind," "dauntless heart," "such courage," "great courage," "hardihood," "prowess," "bravery," "courage," "great strength," "bravery," and "fiery courage." The word has in fact all these possibilities. Used of things, it normally means "force"; of animals, "fierceness" or "brute strength" or (in the case of horses) "mettle"; of men and women, "passion" or "spirit" or even "purpose." Homer's application of it in the present case points our attention equally—whatever particular sense we may imagine Andromache to have uppermost—to Hector's force, strength, fierceness in battle, spirited heart and mind. But since English has no matching term of like inclusiveness, the passage as the translators give it to us reflects this lack and we find one attribute singled out to the exclusion of the rest.

Here then is the first and most crucial fact about any work of literature read in translation. It cannot escape the linguistic characteristics of the language into which it is turned: the grammatical, syntactical, lexical, and phonetic boundaries that constitute collectively the individuality or "genius" of that language. A Greek play or a Russian novel in English will be governed first of all by the resources of the English language, resources that are certain to be in every instance very different, as the efforts with μένος show, from those of the original.

Turning from μένος to δαιμόνιε (daimonie) in Homer's clause, we encounter a second crucial fact about translations. Nobody knows exactly what shade of meaning δαιμόνιε had for Homer. In later writers the word normally suggests divinity, something miraculous, wondrous; but in Homer it appears as a vocative of address for both chieftain and commoner, man and wife. The coloring one gives it must, therefore, be determined either by the way one thinks a Greek wife of Homer's era might actually address her husband (a subject on which we have no information whatever) or in the way one thinks it suitable for a hero's wife to address her husband in an epic poem, that is to say, a highly stylized and formal work. In general, the translators of our century have abandoned formality to stress the intimacy; the wifeliness; and, especially in Lattimore's case, a certain chiding tenderness, in Andromache's appeal: (6) "Ah, my husband," (7) "Hector" (with perhaps a hint, in "you are possessed," of the alarmed distaste with which wives have so often viewed their husbands' bellicose moods), (8) "Strange man," (9) "Dearest," (10) "O my wild one" (mixing an almost motherly admiration with reproach and concern), and (11) "reckless one." On the other hand, the older translators have obviously removed Andromache to an epic or heroic distance from her beloved, whence she sees and kindles to his selfless courage, acknowledging, even in the moment of pleading with him to be otherwise, his moral grandeur and the tragic destiny this too certainly implies: (1) "O noblest in desire, . . . inflamed by others' good"; (2) "Thy dauntless heart (which I foresee too late), / Too daring man"; (3) "Too daring Prince! . . . / And thou must fall, thy virtue's sacrifice"; (4) "My noble Hector." Even the less specific "Dear my lord" of Lang, Leaf, and Myers looks in the same direction because of its echo of the speech of countless Shakespearean men and women who have shared this powerful moral sense: "Dear my lord, make me acquainted with your cause of grief"; "Perseverance, dear my lord, keeps honor bright"; etc.

The fact about translation that emerges from all this is that just as the translated work reflects the individuality of the language it is turned into, so it reflects the individuality of the age in which it is made, and the age will permeate it everywhere like yeast in dough. We think of one kind of permeation when we think of the governing verse forms and attitudes toward verse at a given epoch. In Chapman's time, experiments seeking an "heroic" verse form for English were widespread, and accordingly he tries a "fourteener" couplet (two rhymed lines of seven stresses each) in his *Iliad* and a pentameter couplet in his *Odyssey*. When Dryden and Pope wrote, a closed pentameter couplet had become established as the heroic form par excellence. By Cowper's day, thanks largely to the prestige of *Paradise Lost,* the couplet had gone out of fashion for narrative poetry in favor of blank verse. Our age, inclining to prose and in verse to proselike informalities and relaxations, has, predictably, produced half a dozen excellent prose translations of the *Iliad* but only three in verse (by Fagles, Lattimore, and Fitzgerald), all relying on rhythms that are much of the time closer to the verse of William Carlos Williams and some of the prose of novelists like Faulkner than to the swift firm tread of Homer's Greek. For if it is true that what we translate from a given work is what, wearing the spectacles of our time, we see in it, it is also true that we see in it what we have the power to translate.

Of course, there are other effects of the translator's epoch on a translation besides those exercised by contemporary taste in verse and verse forms. Chapman writes in a great age of poetic metaphor and, therefore, almost instinctively translates his understanding of Homer's verb φθίσει (phthisei, "to cause to wane, consume, waste, pine") into metaphorical terms of flame, presenting his Hector to us as a man of burning generosity who will be consumed by his very ardor. This is a conception rooted in large part in the psychology of the Elizabethans, who had the habit of speaking of the soul as "fire," of one of the four temperaments as "fiery," of even the more material bodily processes, like digestion, as if they were carried on by the heat of fire ("concoction," "decoction"). It is rooted too in that characteristic Renaissance élan so unforgettably expressed in characters such as Tamburlaine and Dr. Faustus, the former of whom exclaims to the stars above:

> . . . I, the chiefest lamp of all the earth,
> First rising in the East with mild aspect,
> But fixèd now in the meridian line,
> Will send up fire to your turning spheres,
> And cause the sun to borrow light of you. . . .

Pope and Dryden, by contrast, write to audiences for whom strong metaphor has become suspect. They, therefore, reject the fire image (which we must recall is not present in the Greek) in favor of a form of speech more congenial to their age, the *sententia* or aphorism, and give it extra vitality by making it the scene of a miniature drama: in Dryden's case, the hero's dauntless heart "urges" him (in the double sense of physical as well as moral pressure) to his fate; in Pope's, the hero's courage, like a judge, "denies" continuance of life, with the consequence that he "falls"—and here Pope's second line suggests analogy to the sacrificial animal—the victim of his own essential nature, of what he is.

To pose even more graphically the pressures that a translator's period brings, consider the following lines from Hector's reply to Andromache's appeal that he withdraw, first in Chapman's Elizabethan version, then in Lattimore's twentieth-century one:

Chapman, 1598:

> The spirit I did first breathe
> Did never teach me that—much less since the contempt of death
> Was settled in me, and my mind knew what a Worthy was,
> Whose office is to lead in fight and give no danger pass
> Without improvement. In this fire must Hector's trial shine.
> Here must his country, father, friends be in him made divine.

Lattimore, 1951:

> and the spirit will not let me, since I have learned to be valiant
> and to fight always among the foremost ranks of the Trojans,
> winning for my own self great glory, and for my father.

If one may exaggerate to make a necessary point, the world of Henry V and Othello suddenly gives way here to our own, a world whose discomfort with any form of heroic self-assertion is remarkably mirrored in the burial of Homer's key terms (*spirit, valiant, fight, foremost, glory*)—five out of twenty-two words in the original, five out of thirty-six in the translation—in a cushioning huddle of harmless sounds.

Besides the two factors so far mentioned (language and period) as affecting the character of a translation, there is inevitably a third—the translator, with a particular degree of talent; a personal way of regarding the work to be translated; a special hierarchy of values, moral, aesthetic, metaphysical (which may or may not be summed up in a "worldview"); and a unique style or lack of it. But this influence all readers are likely to bear in mind, and it needs no laboring here. That, for example, two translators of Hamlet, one a Freudian, the other a Jungian, will produce impressively different translations is obvious from the fact that when Freudian and Jungian argue about the play in English they often seem to have different plays in mind.

We can now return to the question from which we started. After all allowances have been made for language, age, and individual translator, is anything of the original left? What, in short, does the reader of translations read? Let it be said at once that in utility prose—prose whose function is mainly referential—the reader who reads a translation reads everything that matters. "Nicht Rauchen," "Défense de Fumer," and "No Smoking," posted in a railway car, make their point, and the differences between them in sound and form have no significance for us in that context. Since the prose of a treatise and of most fiction is preponderantly referential, we rightly feel, when we have paid close attention to Cervantes or Montaigne or Machiavelli or Tolstoy in a good English translation, that we have had roughly the same experience as a native Spaniard, Frenchman, Italian, or Russian. But *roughly* is the correct word; for good prose points iconically *to* itself as well as referentially beyond itself, and everything that it points to in itself in the original (rhythms, sounds, idioms, wordplay, etc.) must alter radically in being translated. The best analogy is to imagine a Van Gogh painting reproduced in the medium of tempera, etching, or engraving: the "picture" remains, but the intricate interanimation of volumes with colorings with brushstrokes has disappeared.

When we move on to poetry, even in its longer narrative and dramatic forms— plays like Oedipus, poems like the *Iliad* or *The Divine Comedy*—our situation as English readers worsens appreciably, as the many unlike versions of Andromache's appeal to Hector make very clear. But, again, only appreciably. True, this is the point at which the fact that a translation is *always* an interpretation explodes irresistibly on our attention; but if it is the best translation of its time, like Robert Fagles's translation of the *Iliad* for our time, the result will be not only a sensitive interpretation but also a work with intrinsic interest in its own right—at very best, a true work of art, a new poem. In these longer works, moreover, even if the translation is uninspired, many distinctive structural features—plot, setting, characters, meetings, partings, confrontations, and specific episodes generally—survive virtually unchanged. It is only when the shorter, primarily lyrical forms of poetry are presented that the reader of translations faces insuperable disadvantage. In these forms, the referential aspect of language has a tendency to disappear into, or, more often, draw its real meaning and accreditation from, the iconic aspect. Let us look for just a moment at a brief poem by Federico García Lorca and its English translation (by Stephen Spender and J. L. Gili):

> ¡Alto pinar!
> Cuatro palomas por el aire van.
>
> Cuatro palomas
> vuelan y tornan.
> Llevan heridas
> sus cuatro sombras.
>
> ¡Bajo pinar!
> Cuatro palomas en la tierra están.

> the pine trees:
> Four pigeons go through the air.
>
> Four pigeons
> fly and turn round.
> They carry wounded
> their four shadows.
>
> Below the pine trees:
> Four pigeons lie on the earth.

In this translation the referential sense of the English words follows with remarkable exactness the referential sense of the Spanish words they replace. But the life of Lorca's poem does not lie in that sense. It lies in such matters as the abruptness, like an intake of breath at a sudden revelation, of the two exclamatory lines (1 and 7), which then exhale musically in images of flight and death; or as the echoings of *palomas* in *heridas* and *sombras,* bringing together (as in fact the hunter's gun has done) these unrelated nouns and the unrelated experiences they stand for in a sequence that seems, momentarily, to have all the logic of a tragic action, in which *doves* become *wounds* become *shadows,* or as the external and internal rhyming among the five verbs, as though all motion must (as in fact it must) end with *están.*

Since none of this can be brought over into another tongue (least of all Lorca's rhythms), the translator must decide between leaving a reader to wonder why Lorca is a poet to be bothered about at all and making a new but true poem, whose merit will almost certainly be in inverse ratio to its likeness to the original. Samuel Johnson made such a poem in translating Horace's famous *Diffugere nives,* and so did A. E. Housman. If we juxtapose the last two stanzas of each translation, and the corresponding Latin, we can see at a glance that each has the consistency and inner life of a genuine poem and that neither of them (even if we consider only what is obvious to the eye, the line-lengths) is very close to Horace:

> Cum semel occideris, et de te splendida Minos
>   fecerit arbitria,
> non, Torquate, genus, non te facundia, non te
>   restituet pietas.

Infernis neque enim tenebris Diana pudicum
  liberat Hippolytum
nec Lethaea valet Theseus abrumpere caro
  vincula Pirithoo.

Johnson:

Not you, Torquatus, boast of Rome,
When Minos once has fixed your doom,
Or eloquence, or splendid birth,
Or virtue, shall restore to earth.
Hippolytus, unjustly slain,
Diana calls to life in vain;
Nor can the might of Theseus rend
The chains of hell that hold his friend.

Housman:

When thou descendest once the shades among,
  The stern assize and equal judgment o'er,
Not thy long lineage nor thy golden tongue,
  No, nor thy righteousness, shall friend thee more.

Night holds Hippolytus the pure of stain,
  Diana steads him nothing, he must stay;
And Theseus leaves Pirithous in the chain
  The love of comrades cannot take away.

    The truth of the matter is that when the translator of short poems chooses to be literal, most or all of the poetry is lost; and when the translator succeeds in forging a new poetry, most or all of the original author is lost.

    The best practical advice for those of us who must read poems in English translations is to focus intently on the images and dramatic scenes these poems evoke and ask ourselves what there is in them or in their effect on each other that produces each poem's particular electricity. To that extent, we can compensate for a part of our losses, learn something positive about the immense explosive powers of imagery, and rest easy in the secure knowledge that translation even in the mode of the short poem brings us (despite losses) closer to the work itself than not reading it at all. "To a thousand cavils," said Samuel Johnson, "one answer is sufficient; the purpose of a writer is to be read, and the criticism which would destroy the power of pleasing must be blown aside." Johnson was defending Pope's Homer for those marks of its own time and place that make it the great interpretation it is, but Johnson's exhilarating common sense applies equally to the problem we are considering here. Literature is to be read, and the criticism that would destroy the reader's power to make some form of contact with much of the world's great writing must indeed be blown aside.

MAYNARD MACK

("Jour et nuit") from LES ARMES MIRACULEUSES by Aimé Césaire. Copyright of original text © Editions Gallimard, 1946. Translation copyright © 1998 by Gregson Davis. Reprinted by permission of Gallimard and the translator. *Serpent Sun* ("Soleil Serpent") in "Les armes miraculeuses" from LA POÉSIE by Aimé Césaire. Copyright © Editions du Seuil, 1994. Translation copyright © 1998 by Gregson Davis. Reprinted by permission of Editions du Seuil and the translator.

Anton Chekhov: *The Lady with the Dog* from A. P. Chekhov, SHORT STORIES AND NOVELS. Translated by Ivy Litvinov. Reprinted by permission of the Ivy Litvinov Estate. *The Cherry Orchard* by Anton Chekhov from THE PORTABLE CHEKHOV, by Anton Chekhov, edited by Avrahm Yarmolinsky. Copyright © 1947, 1968 by Viking Penguin, Inc. Renewed © 1975 by Avrahm Yarmolinsky. Used by permission of Viking Penguin, a division of Penguin Books USA, Inc.

Sor Juana Inés de la Cruz: *Reply to Sor Filotea de la Cruz* from A WOMAN OF GENIUS, translated by Margaret Sayers Peden. Copyright © 1982 by Lime Rock Press, Inc., Salisbury, CT 06086. Reprinted by permission of Lime Rock Press, Inc. No part may be reprinted without express permission of the original publisher.

Emily Dickinson: Poems 216, 258, 303, 328, 435, 449, 465, 585, 632, 712, 1084, 1129, 1207, and 1593 from THE POEMS OF EMILY DICKINSON, Thomas H. Johnson, ed., Cambridge, Mass: The Belknap Press of Harvard University Press. Copyright © 1951, 1955, 1979, 1983 by the President and Fellows of Harvard College. Reprinted by permission of the publishers and Trustees of Amherst College. Poems 341, 519, 657 and 754 from THE COMPLETE POEMS OF EMILY DICKINSON, edited by Thomas H. Johnson. Copyright © 1929 by Martha Dickinson Bianchi; copyright © renewed 1957, 1963 by Mary L. Hampson. Reprinted by permission of Little, Brown & Company and the publishers and Trustees of Amherst College.

Fyodor Dostoevsky: from NOTES FROM UNDERGROUND, A NORTON CRITICAL EDITION by Fyodor Dostoevsky, translated by Michael R. Katz. Translation copyright © 1989 by W. W. Norton & Company, Inc. Reprinted by permission of W. W. Norton & Company, Inc.

T. S. Eliot: *The Waste Land* and *The Love Song of J. Alfred Prufrock* from COLLECTED POEMS 1909–1962. Reprinted by permission of Faber & Faber, Ltd. *Little Gidding* from FOUR QUARTETS. Copyright ©1943 by T. S. Eliot and renewed 1971 by Esme Valerie Eliot. Reprinted by permission of Harcourt Brace & Company and Faber & Faber, Ltd.

Paul Eluard: *Woman in Love* by Paul Eluard, translated by Lloyd Alexander, from UNINTERRUPTED POETRY. Copyright © 1975 by New Directions Publishing Corp. Reprinted by permission of New Directions Publishing Corp. *To Be Caught in One's Own Trap*, [*Nature Was Caught in the Nets of Your Life* (VII)], [*She Is Always Unwilling to Understand* (VIII)], [*Unknown, She Was My Favorite Shape* (X)], and *The Mirror of a Moment*, from CAPITAL OF PAIN, translated by R. M. Weisman, published in Japan by Mushinsha Ltd., 1973. Reprinted by permission of the publisher.

William Faulkner: *The Bear* from THE COLLECTED SHORT STORIES OF WILLIAM FAULKNER. Copyright © 1950 by Random House, Inc. Copyright renewed 1977 by Jill Faulkner Summers. Reprinted by permission.

Gustave Flaubert: from MADAME BOVARY translated by Francis Steegmuller. Copyright © 1957 by Francis Steegmuller. Reprinted by permission of Random House, Inc.

Sigmund Freud: *Dora: Fragment of an Analysis of a Case of Hysteria* from THE COLLECTED PAPERS, VOLUME III by Sigmund Freud. Authorized translation under the supervision of Alix and James Strachey. Published by Basic Books, Inc., by arrangement with the Hogarth Press, Ltd., and The Institute of Psycho-Analysis, London. Reprinted by permission of Basic Books, a subsidiary of Perseus Books Group, LLC.

Federico García Lorca: *Lament for Ignacio Sánchez Mejías*, translated by Stephen Spender & J. L. Gili from THE SELECTED POEMS OF FEDERICO GARCÍA LORCA. Copyright © 1955 by New Directions Publishing Corp. Reprinted by permission of New Directions Publishing Corp.

Gabriel García Márquez: *Death Constant beyond Love* from INNOCENT ERENDIRA AND OTHER STORIES by Gabriel García Márquez. English translation copyright © 1978 by Harper & Row, Publishers, Inc. Reprinted by permission of HarperCollins Publishers, Inc.

Johann Wolfgang von Goethe: from FAUST by Johann Wolfgang von Goethe, translated by Walter Kaufmann. Translation copyright © 1961 by Walter Kaufmann. Used by permission of Doubleday, a division of Bantam Doubleday Dell Publishing Group, Inc.

Alice Munro: *Walker Brothers Cowboy* from DANCE OF THE HAPPY SHADES by Alice Munro. Copyright © 1968 by Alice Munro. Originally published by McGraw-Hill Ryerson. Reprinted by permission of the Virginia Barber Literary Agency, Inc. and McGraw-Hill Ryerson. All rights reserved.

Novalis (Friedrich von Hardenberg): *Yearning for Death* from HYMNS TO THE NIGHT AND OTHER WRITINGS translated by Charles E. Passage. Copyright © 1960 by the Liberal Arts Press, Inc.

Flannery O'Connor: *A Good Man Is Hard to Find* from A GOOD MAN IS HARD TO FIND AND OTHER STORIES. Copyright © 1953 by Flannery O'Connor and renewed 1981 by Regina O'Connor. Reprinted by permission of Harcourt Brace & Company.

Alexander Pope: *The Rape of the Lock* from THE RAPE OF THE LOCK with notes by Samuel Holt Monk. Copyright © 1962, 1968 by W. W. Norton & Company, Inc. Copyright renewed 1990. Reprinted by permission of W. W. Norton & Company, Inc.

Marcel Proust: *Swann's Way: Overture* from REMEMBRANCE OF THINGS PAST, translated by C. K. Scott Moncrieff and Terence Kilmartin. Translation copyright © 1981 by Random House, Inc., and Chatto & Windus. Reprinted by permission of Random House, Inc.

Alexander Sergeyevich Pushkin: *The Queen of Spades* from THE COMPLETE PROSE TALES OF ALEXANDR SERGEYEVICH PUSHKIN, by Gillon R. Aitken, translator. Copyright © 1966 by Barrie and Rockcliff (Barrie Books Ltd). Reprinted by permission of W. W. Norton & Company, Inc., and the translator.

Jean Racine: PHAEDRA, A TRAGEDY IN FIVE ACTS (1677) by Jean Racine, Introduction and English translation copyright © 1986 by Richard Wilbur, reprinted by permission of Harcourt Brace & Company. CAUTION: Professionals and amateurs are hereby warned that this translation, being fully protected under the copyright laws of the United States of America, the British Empire, including the Dominion of Canada, and all other countries which are signatories to the Universal Copyright Convention and the International Copyright Union, is subject to royalty. All rights, including professional, amateur, motion picture, recitation, lecturing, public reading, radio broadcasting and television, are strictly reserved. Particular emphasis is laid on the question of readings, permission for which must be secured from the author's agent in writing. Inquiries on professional rights (except for amateur rights) should be addressed to Mr. Gilbert Parker, Curtis Brown, Ltd., 10 Astor Place, New York, NY 10003; inquiries on translation should be addressed to Harcourt Brace & Company, Publishers, Orlando, FL 32887.

Rainer Maria Rilke: poems from THE SELECTED POETRY OF RAINER MARIA RILKE, edited and translated by Stephen Mitchell. Copyright © 1982 by Stephen Mitchell. Reprinted by permission of Random House, Inc.

Arthur Rimbaud: *The Drunken Boat*, translated by Stephen Stepanchev. Reprinted by permission of the translator. All other poems from A SEASON IN HELL: THE ILLUMINATIONS by Arthur Rimbaud, translated by Enid Rhodes Peschel. Translation copyright © 1973 by Oxford University Press, Inc. Used by permission of Oxford University Press, Inc.

Alain Robbe-Grillet: *The Secret Room* from SNAPSHOTS by Alain Robbe-Grillet (New York: Grove Press, Inc., 1968). Originally published as INSTANTANÉS, copyright © 1962 by Les Éditions de Minuit. Reprinted by permission of Georges Borchardt, Inc.

Kurt Schwitters: *Anna Blume* translated by David Britt from DADA ART AND ANTI-ART, edited by Hans Richter. Copyright © 1965. Reprinted by permission of Thames & Hudson Ltd.

Leslie Marmon Silko: *Yellow Woman* from STORYTELLER. Copyright © 1981 by Leslie Marmon Silko. Published by Seaver Books, NY, NY. Reprinted by permission of the publisher.

Alexander Solzhenitsyn: *Matyrona's Home*, translated by H. T. Willets. First published in May 1963 issue of *Encounter*.

Wallace Stevens: *Anecdote of the Jar, The Emperor of Ice Cream, Peter Quince at the Clavier*, and *Sunday Morning*, copyright © 1923, copyright renewed 1951 by Wallace Stevens. *The Idea of Order at Key West*, copyright © 1936 by Wallace Stevens, copyright renewed 1964 by Holly Stevens. *The Man on the Dump*, copyright © 1942 by Wallace Stevens, copyright renewed 1970 by Holly Stevens. All from THE COLLECTED POEMS OF WALLACE STEVENS. Reprinted by permission of Alfred A. Knopf, Inc.

Jonathan Swift: *A Modest Proposal* from IRISH TRACTS 1727–1733, edited by Herbert Davis. Copyright © 1955. Reprinted by permission of Basil Blackwell.

Tristan Tzara: excerpt from *Dada Manifesto 1918* and *Proclamation without Pretention* reprinted by permission of the translator, Mary Ann Caws.

Paul Verlaine: poems from PAUL VERLAINE: SELECTED POEMS, translated/edited by C. F. MacIntyre. Copyright © 1948 by The Regents of the University of California. Reprinted by permission of the University of California Press.

François-Marie Arouet de Voltaire: *Candide* from CANDIDE, OR OPTIMISM: A NORTON CRITICAL EDITION, SECOND EDITION by Voltaire, translated by Robert M. Adams. Translation copyright © 1991, 1966 by W. W. Norton & Company, Inc. Reprinted by permission of W. W. Norton & Company, Inc.

Virginia Woolf: chapters 2 and 3 from A ROOM OF ONE'S OWN by Virginia Woolf. Copyright © 1929 by Harcourt Brace & Company and renewed 1957 by Leonard Woolf. Reprinted by permission of the publisher and The Society of Authors as the Literary Representative of the Estate of Virginia Woolf.

Dorothy Wordsworth: excerpt from THE GRASMERE JOURNALS, edited by Pamela Woof. Copyright © 1991. Reprinted by permission of Oxford University Press.

Richard Wright: *The Man Who Was Almost a Man* from EIGHT MEN: SHORT STORIES by Richard Wright. Copyright © 1940, 1961 by Richard Wright. Copyright renewed 1989 by Ellen Wright. Published by HarperCollins. Reprinted by permission of HarperCollins Publishers, Inc.

William Butler Yeats: *Easter 1916* and *The Second Coming*, copyright © 1924 by Macmillan Publishing Company, copyright renewed 1952 by Bertha Georgie Yeats. *Leda and the Swan, Sailing to Byzantium*, and *Among School Children*, copyright © 1928 by Macmillan Publishing Company, copyright renewed 1956 by Bertha Georgie Yeats. *Byzantium*, copyright © 1933 by Macmillan Publishing Company, copyright renewed 1961 by Bertha Georgie Yeats. *Lapis Lazuli* and *The Circus Animals' Desertion*, copyright 1940 by Bertha Georgie Yeats, copyright renewed 1968 by Bertha Georgie Yeats, Michael Butler Yeats, and Anne Yeats. All selections from THE COLLECTED WORKS OF W. B. YEATS, VOLUME I: THE POEMS edited by Richard J. Finneran. Reprinted by permission of Scribner, a Division of Simon & Schuster and A. P. Watt Ltd on behalf of Michael Yeats.

Every effort has been made to contact the copyright holders of each of the selections. Rights holders of any selections not credited should contact W. W. Norton & Company, Inc., 500 Fifth Avenue, New York, NY 10110, in order for a correction to be made in the next reprinting of our work.

Index

The Norton Anthology
of World Masterpieces

THE WESTERN TRADITION

Seventh Edition

VOLUME 2

The Norton Anthology
of World Masterpieces

THE WESTERN TRADITION

Seventh Edition

Sarah Lawall, *General Editor*

PROFESSOR OF COMPARATIVE LITERATURE
AND ADJUNCT PROFESSOR OF FRENCH,
UNIVERSITY OF MASSACHUSETTS, AMHERST

Maynard Mack, *General Editor Emeritus*

STERLING PROFESSOR OF ENGLISH EMERITUS,
YALE UNIVERSITY

VOLUME 2
Literature of Western Culture Since the Renaissance

W • W • NORTON & COMPANY • *New York* • *London*

Editor: Peter Simon
Production Manager: Diane O'Connor
Project Editors: Kurt Wildermuth, Kathryn M. Talalay, Kate Lovelady
Manuscript Editors: Kurt Wildermuth, Candace Levy
Permissions: Kristin Sheerin
Editorial Assistant: Benjamin Reynolds
Cover and Text Design: Antonina Krass
Art Research: Neil Ryder Hoos

Since this page cannot legibly accommodate
all of the copyright notices, pp. 2183–87
constitute an extension of the copyright page.

The text of this book is composed in Fairfield Medium
with the display set in Bernhard Modern.
Composition by Binghamton Valley Composition.
Manufacturing by R. R. Donnelley & Sons.

Cover illustration: Gustave Caillebotte. *Paris Street; Rainy Day* (detail). 1876/77. Oil on
canvas, 212.2 x 276.2 cm. The Art Institute of Chicago. Charles H. and Mary F. S.
Worcester Collection, 1964.336. Photograph © 1998 The Art Institute of Chicago.

Library of Congress Cataloging-in-Publication Data

The Norton anthology of world masterpieces : the Western tradition /
    Sarah Lawall, general editor ; Maynard Mack, general editor
    emeritus. — 7th ed.
        p.   cm.
    Includes bibliographical references and index.
    Contents: v. 1. Literature of Western culture through the
Renaissance — v. 2. Literature of Western culture since the
Renaissance.

    ISBN 0-393-97289-5 (pbk.: v. 1). — ISBN 0-393-97300-X (pbk.: v. 2)

    1. Literature—Collections.   I. Lawall, Sarah N.   II. Mack,
Maynard, 1909–   .
PN6014.N66   1998
808.8—dc21   98-35047
                                                                        CIP

W. W. Norton & Company, Inc., 500 Fifth Avenue, New York, N.Y. 10110
www.wwnorton.com

W. W. Norton & Company Ltd., 10 Coptic Street, London WC1A 1PU

6 7 8 9 0